ART HISTORY

REVISED EDITION

ART HISTORY

Marilyn Stokstad

The University of Kansas

REVISED EDITION

in collaboration with Bradford R. Collins
University of South Carolina, Columbia

with chapters by Stephen Addiss, Chu-tsing Li
Marylin M. Rhie, and Christopher D. Roy

Harry N. Abrams, Inc., and Prentice Hall, Inc., Publishers

DEDICATED TO MY SISTER, KAREN L.S. LEIDER, AND MY NIECE, ANNA J. LEIDER

Publishers: *Paul Gottlieb, Bud Therien*
Project management and editorial direction: *Julia Moore*
Project consultation: *Jean Smith*
Developmental editing, Prentice Hall: *David Chodoff*
Developmental editing, Abrams: *Ellyn Childs Allison, Sabra Maya Feldman, Mark Getlein, James Leggio,
    Sheila Franklin Lieber, Jean Smith, Elaine Banks Stainton*
Design, art direction, and production: *Lydia Gershey, with Yonah Schurink of Communigraph*
Photo editing, rights and reproduction: *Lauren Boucher, Jennifer Bright, Helen Lee, Catherine Ruello,
    Janice Ackerman, Diana Gongora Pilar*
Marketing strategy, Prentice Hall: *Sheryl Adams*
New media: *Alison Pendergast*
Market research, Prentice Hall: *Seth Reichlin*
Maps and timelines: *York Production Services*
Illustration: *John McKenna*
Editorial assistance, Prentice Hall: *Marion Gottlieb*
Project assistance, Prentice Hall: *Mary Amoon*
Project editing: *Jungha Oh*
Indexing: *Peter and Erica Rooney*

Library of Congress Cataloging-in-Publication Data

Stokstad, Marilyn, 1929–
        Art history / Marilyn Stokstad: in collaboration with Bradford R. Collins: with chapters by Stephen
Addiss . . . [et al.]. – Rev. ed.
            p.   cm.
        Includes bibliographical references and index.
        ISBN 0–8109–1991–5 (Abrams hardcover set). —ISBN 0–13–082583–2 (Prentice Hall hardcover).
        ISBN 0–13–082581–6 (paperback, Vol. 1). —ISBN 0–13–082582–4 (paperback, Vol. 2).

    1. Art—History.   I. Collins, Bradford R., 1942–   .   II. Addiss, Stephen, 1935–   .   III. Title.
N5300.S923   1999
709—dc21   98–25873
                                                                                CIP

Prentice Hall, Inc.
Simon & Schuster/A Viacom Company

Send inquiries to:
        Marketing Manager
        Humanities and Social Sciences, Prentice Hall, Inc.
        One Lake Street
        Upper Saddle River, N.J. 07458
        http://www.prenhall.com

Printed and bound in Japan

On the cover and pages 2–3: Flower Still Life, by Rachel Ruysch. After 1700. Oil on canvas. The Toledo Museum
of Art, Ohio (detail of fig. 19-58)

On the chapter-opening pages: 34–35, Stonehenge (detail of fig. 1-21); 60–61, gold crown from Kalhu (detail of
fig. 2-25); 90–91, Great Pyramids, Giza (detail of fig. 3-10):126–127, *Landscape*, Thera (detail of fig. 4-18);
150–151, *Marshals and Young Women*, from the Parthenon (detail of fig. 5-48); 220–221, *The Unswept Floor*,
mosaic (detail of fig. 6-70); 286–287, *Anastasis*, fresco, Istanbul (detail of fig. 7-52); 336–337, *muqarnas* dome,
the Alhambra (detail of fig. 8-12); 364–365, Cave Temple of Shiva, Elephanta (detail of fig. 9-20); 394–395,
Admonition of the Imperial Instuctress (detail of fig. 10-10); 420–421, Scene from *The Tale of Genji* (detail of fig.
11-13); 442–443. Maya vessel (detail of fig. 12-12); 464–465, *The Herders' Village*, wall painting, Algeria (detail
of fig. 13-1); 478–479, Purse cover, from Sutton Hoo burial ship (detail of fig. 14-7); 506–507, *Dream of Henry I,
Worcester Chronicle* (detail of fig. 15-28); 544–545, *Shrine of the Three Kings* (detail of fig. 16-56); 610–611, Laurana, Courtyard of the Ducal Palace, Urbino (detail of fig. 17-63); 678–679, Brueghel the Elder, *Carrying of the
Cross* (detail of fig. 18-58); 748–749, Peeters, *Still Life with Flowers, Goblet, Dried Fruit, and Pretzels* (detail of fig.
19-40); 820–821, page from *Hamza-nama*, a Mughal manuscript from North India (detail of fig. 20-5); 834–835,
Shitao, *Landscape*, from a Qing dynasty album (detail of fig. 21-12); 852–853, contemporary Japanese ceramic
vessels (detail of fig. 22-16); 872–873, Machu Picchu, Peru (detail of fig. 23-7); 892–893, feather cloak, from
Hawaii (detail of fig. 24-11); 908–909, Ashanti *kente* cloth, from Ghana (detail of fig. 25-11); 926–927, Turner,
The Fighting "Téméraire" (detail of fig. 26-29); 978–979, Renoir. *Moulin de la Galette* (detail of fig. 27-51);
1022–1023, Robert Delaunay, *Homage to Blériot* (detail of fig. 28-46); 1106–1107, Paik, *Electronic Superhighway*
(detail of illustration on page 1157)

Brief Contents

Preface to the First Edition

I have been privileged to teach art history for nearly four decades. Over that time I have become persuaded that our purpose in the introductory course should not be to groom scholars-to-be but rather to nurture an educated, enthusiastic public for the arts. I have also come to believe that we are not well-enough served by the major introductory textbooks presently available, all of which originated two or more generations ago. What is needed is a new text for a new generation of teachers and students, a text that balances formalist traditions with the newer interests of contextual art history and also meets the needs of a diverse and fast-changing student population. In support of that philosophy I offer *Art History*.

I firmly believe students should *enjoy* their art history survey. Only then will they learn to appreciate art as the most tangible creation of the human imagination. To this end we have sought in many ways to make *Art History* a sensitive, accessible, engaging textbook.

We have made *Art History* contextual, in the best sense of the term. Throughout the text we treat the visual arts not in a vacuum but within the essential contexts of history, geography, politics, religion, and culture; and we carefully define the parameters—social, religious, political, and cultural—that either constrained or liberated individual artists.

Art History **is both comprehensive and inclusive.** Our goal has been to reach beyond the West to include a critical examination of the arts of other regions and cultures, presenting a global view of art through the centuries. We cover not only the world's most significant paintings and works of sculpture and architecture but also drawings, photographs, works in metal and ceramics, textiles, and jewelry. We have paid due respect to the canon of great monuments of the history of art, but we also have treated artists and artworks not previously acknowledged. We have drawn throughout on the best and most recent scholarship, including new discoveries (the prehistoric cave paintings in the Ardèche gorge in southern France, for example) and new interpretations of well-known works. And, bearing in mind the needs of undergraduate readers, we have sought wherever feasible to discuss works on view in many different museums and collections around the United States, including college and university museums.

No effort has been spared to make this book a joy to read and use—in fact, to make it a work of art in itself. Chapter introductions set the scene for the material to come, frequently making use of contemporary references to which readers can easily relate. While the text carries the central narrative of *Art History*, set-off boxes present interesting and instructive material that enriches the text. A number of thought-provoking boxes focus on such critical issues as "the myth of 'primitive' art" and the way the titles given to works of art may affect our perception of them. Other boxes provide insights into contextual influences, such as women as art patrons, the lives of major religious leaders, and

significant literary movements. **Elements of Architecture** boxes explicate basic architectural forms and terminology. **Technique** boxes explore how artworks have been made, from prehistoric cave paintings to Renaissance frescoes to how photography works. **Maps and timelines** visually place artworks in time and space, and time scales on each page let readers know where they are within the period each chapter covers. A **Parallels** feature in every chapter presents comparative information in tabular form that puts the major events and artworks discussed in that chapter in a global context. Finally, *Art History* includes **an unprecedented illustration program** of some 1,350 photographs—more than half in full color and some not published before—as well as hundreds of original line drawings (including architectural plans and cutaways) that have been created specifically for this book.

Art History **represents the joint effort of a distinguished team of scholars and educators.** Single authorship of a work such as this is no longer a viable proposition: our world has become too complex, the research on and interpretation of art too sophisticated, for that to work. An individual view of art may be very persuasive—even elegant—but it remains personal; we no longer look for a single "truth," nor do we hold to a canon of artworks to the extent we once did. An effort such as this requires a team of scholar-teachers, all with independent views and the capability of treating the art they write about in its own terms and its own cultural context. The overarching viewpoint—the controlling imagination—is mine, but the book would not have been complete without the work of the following distinguished contributing authors:

Stephen Addiss, Tucker Boatwright Professor in the Humanities at the University of Richmond, Virginia

Bradford R. Collins, Associate Professor in the Art Department, University of South Carolina, Columbia

Chu-tsing Li, Professor Emeritus at the University of Kansas, Lawrence

Marylin M. Rhie, Jessie Wells Post Professor of Art and Professor of East Asian Studies at Smith College

Christopher D. Roy, Professor of Art History at the University of Iowa in Iowa City

Finally, the book would not have been possible without the substantial efforts of Marion Spears Grayson, an independent scholar with a Ph.D. from Columbia University who previously taught at Tufts University and Rice University. Her refinements and original contributions greatly enhanced the overall presentation. The book has also benefited greatly from the invaluable assistance and advice of scores of other scholars and teachers who have generously answered my questions, given their recommendations on organization and priorities, and provided specialized critiques.

Preface to the Revised Edition

I want to thank my many friends and colleagues for welcoming *Art History* into their lives and their classrooms. I knew I wanted a new textbook for my students, but I had no idea how widespread that same desire was. In the three years since Abrams and Prentice Hall introduced *Art History*, it has exceeded all our hopes for its acceptance.

In light of the success of the original edition, you may ask why we have brought out a revision so soon. One of the reasons, in fact, is that the original edition has proved more than strong enough to make practicable this revision in a relatively short time. The changes are of two kinds: small **improvements of content and expression,** and **substantive changes to chapters on three periods of Western art: Renaissance, Baroque and Rococo,** and **Modernism.** To be exact, **Chapters 1 through Chapter 16 contain eighty-six changes,** and all but a few of these are in chapters on the Western tradition.

Of the thirteen chapters between Chapters 17 and 29, seven have been rethought and reorganized. We addressed the only consistent criticism of the original edition—that Giotto was confined to the Gothic chapter—by treating him in this edition within the context of both Italian Gothic art (in Chapter 16) and as the early Renaissance giant he was (in Chapter 17). To rework chapters on the modern period, my excellent collaborator, Bradford R. Collins, contributed the entire story by beginning with Neoclassicism and Romanticism (Chapter 26) and revisiting and rewriting the chapters he had written for the original edition: Chapters 27, 28, and 29. In the process, more than fifty works of art were changed and as many more were moved around in order to make the narrative of the nineteenth and twentieth centuries more coherent than ever.

Our old friend **"popular demand" brought in a few canonical works.** I too found it impossible to teach twentieth-century art without Picasso's *Guernica* and Wright's *Fallingwater*. And I apologize to all the saints and sinners of the sixteenth century for my original treatment of Titian: *The Pesaro Madonna* is here now (and *Isabella d'Este* stays).

I hope you all will enjoy this edition and, as you have done so generously and graciously over the last three years, will continue to share your comments and suggestions with me.

Acknowledgments to the First Edition

Writing and producing this book has been a far more challenging undertaking than any of us originally thought it would be. Were it not for the editorial and organizational expertise of Julia Moore, we never would have pulled it off. She inspired, orchestrated, and guided the team of editors, researchers, photo editors, designers, and illustrators who contributed their talents to the volume you now hold. Paul Gottlieb and Bud Therien convinced me to undertake the project, and with Phil Miller were unfailingly supportive throughout its complex gestation. A team of developmental editors led by David Chodoff at Prentice Hall and Jean Smith at Abrams refined the final manuscript to make it clear and accessible to students. Special thanks are due to Ellyn Childs Allison, Sheila Franklin Lieber, and Steve Rigolosi for their careful developmental work during the crucial early stages; to Mark Getlein for his extraordinary care in developing the chapters on Asian and African art; and to Gerald Lombardi for his work on the chapters on Western art since the Renaissance. Photo researchers Lauren Boucher, Jennifer Bright, Helen Lee, and Catherine Ruello performed miracles in finding the illustrations we needed—and, because of their zeal in finding the best pictures, sometimes helped us see what we wanted. John McKenna's drawings have brought exactly the right mix of information, clarity, and human presence to the illustration program. Special thanks also to Nancy Corwin, who was an essential resource on the history of craft, and to Jill Leslie Furst for her assistance on the chapters on the art of Pacific cultures and the art of the Americas. Designer Lydia Gershey and associate Yonah Schurink have broken new ground with their clear and inviting design and layout. Alison Pendergast, marketing manager, contributed many helpful insights as the book neared completion. My research assistants at the University of Kansas, Katherine Giele, Richard Watters, and Michael Willis, have truly earned my everlasting gratitude.

Every chapter has been read by one or more specialists: Barbara Abou-El-Haj, SUNY Binghamton; Jane Aiken, Virginia Polytechnic; Vicki Artimovich, Bellevue Community College; Elizabeth Atherton, El Camino College; Ulku Bates, Columbia University; Joseph P. Becherer, Grand Rapids Community College; Janet Catherine Berlo, University of Missouri, St. Louis; Roberta Bernstein, SUNY Albany; Edward Bleiberg, University of Memphis; Daniel Breslauer, University of Kansas; Ronald Buksbaum, Capital Community Technical College; Petra ten-Doesschate Chu, Seton Hall University; John Clarke, University of Texas, Austin; Robert Cohon, The Nelson-Atkins Museum of Art; Frances Colpitt, University of Texas, San Antonio; Lorelei H. Corcoran, University of Memphis; Ann G. Crowe, Virginia Commonwealth University; Pamela Decoteau, Southern Illinois University; Susan J. Delaney, Mira Costa College; Walter B. Denny, University of Massachusetts, Amherst; Richard DePuma, University of Iowa; Brian Dursam, University of Miami; Ross Edman, University of Illinois, Chicago; Gerald Eknoian, DeAnza State College; Mary S. Ellett, Randolph-Macon College; James D. Farmer, Virginia Commonwealth University; Craig Felton, Smith College; Mary F. Francey, University of Utah; Joanna Frueh, University of Nevada, Reno; Mark Fullerton, Ohio State University; Anna Gonosova, University of California, Irvine; Robert Grigg; Glenn Harcourt, University of Southern California; Sharon Hill, Virginia Commonwealth University; Mary Tavener Holmes, New York City; Paul E. Ivey, University of Arizona; Carol S. Ivory, Washington State University; Nina Kasanof, Sage Junior College of Albany; John F. Kenfield, Rutgers University; Ruth Kolarik, Colorado College; Jeffrey Lang, University of Kansas; William A. Lozano, Johnson County Community College; Franklin Ludden, Ohio State University; Lisa F. Lynes, North Idaho College; Joseph Alexander MacGillivray, Columbia University; Janice Mann, Wayne State University; Michelle Marcus, The Metropolitan

Museum of Art; Virginia Marquardt, University of Virginia; Peggy McDowell, University of New Orleans; Sheila McNally, University of Minnesota; Victor H. Miesel, University of Michigan; Vernon Minor, University of Colorado, Boulder; Anta Montet-White, University of Kansas; Anne E. Morganstern, Ohio State University; William J. Murnane, University of Memphis; Lawrence Nees, University of Delaware; Sara Orel, Northeast Missouri State University; John G. Pedley, University of Michigan; Elizabeth Pilliod, Oregon State University; Nancy H. Ramage, Ithaca College; Ida K. Rigby, San Diego State University; Howard Risatti, Virginia Commonwealth University; Ann M. Roberts, University of Iowa; Stanley T. Rolfe, University of Kansas; Wendy W. Roworth, University of Rhode Island; James H. Rubin, SUNY Stony Brook; John Russell, Columbia University; Patricia Sands, Pratt Institute; Thomas Sarrantonio, SUNY New Paltz; Diane G. Scillia, Kent State University; Linda Seidel, University of Chicago; Nancy Sevcenko, Cambridge, Massachusetts; Tom Shaw, Kean College; Jan Sheridan, Erie Community College; Anne R. Stanton, University of Missouri, Columbia; Thomas Sullivan, OSB, Benedictine College (Conception Abbey); Janis Tomlinson, Columbia University; the late Eleanor Tufts; Dorothy Verkerk, University of North Carolina, Chapel Hill; Roger Ward, The Nelson-Atkins Museum of Art; Mark Weil, Washington University, St. Louis; Alison West, New York City; Randall White, New York University; and David Wilkins, University of Pittsburgh.

Others who have tried to keep me from errors of fact and interpretation—who have shared ideas and course syllabi, read chapters or sections of chapters, and offered suggestions and criticism—include: Janet Rebold Benton, Pace University; Elizabeth Gibson Broun, National Museum of America Art; Robert G. Calkins, Cornell University; William W. Clark, Queens College, CUNY; Jaqueline Clipsham; Alessandra Comini, Southern Methodist University; Susan Craig, University of Kansas; Charles Cuttler; University of Iowa; Ralph T. Coe, Santa Fe; Nancy Corwin, University of Kansas; Patricia Darish, University of Kansas; Lois Drewer, Index of Christian Art; Charles Eldredge, University of Kansas; James Enyeart, Eastman House, Rochester; Ann Friedman, J. Paul Getty Museum; Mary D. Garrard, American University; Walter S. Gibson, Case Western Reserve University; Stephen Goddard, University of Kansas; Paula Gerson; Dorothy Glass, SUNY Buffalo; the late Jane Hayward, The Cloisters, The Metropolitan Museum of Art; Robert Hoffmann, The Smithsonian Institution; Luke Jordan, University of Kansas; Charles Little, The Metropolitan Museum of Art; Karen Mack, University of Kansas; Richard Mann, San Francisco State University; Bob Martin, Haskel Indian Nations University; Amy McNair, University of Kansas; Sara Jane Pearman, The Cleveland Museum of Art; Michael Plante, H. Sophie Newcomb Memorial College; John Pultz, University of Kansas; Virginia Raguin, College of the Holy Cross; Pamela Sheingorn, Baruch College, CUNY; James Seaver, University of Kansas; Caryle K. Smith, University of Akron; Walter Smith, University of Akron; Lauren Soth, Carleton College; Linda Stone-Ferrier, University of Kansas; Michael Stoughton, University of Minnesota; Elizabeth Valdez del Alamo, Montclair State College; and Ann S. Zielinski, SUNY Plattsburgh.

Finally, the book was class tested with students under the direction of these teachers: Fred C. Albertson, University of Memphis; Betty J. Crouther, University of Mississippi; Linda M. Gigante, University of Louisville; Jennifer Haley, University of Nebraska, Lincoln; Cynthia Hahn, Florida State University; Lawrence R. Hoey, University of Wisconsin, Milwaukee; Delane O. Karalow, Virginia Commonwealth University; Charles R. Mack, University of South Carolina, Columbia; Brian Madigan, Wayne State University; Merideth Palumbo, Kent State University; Sharon Pruitt, East Carolina State University; J. Michael Taylor, James Madison University; Marcilene K. Wittmer, University of Miami; and Marilyn Wyman, San Jose State University.

A Final Word

As each of us develops a genuine appreciation of the arts, we come to see them as the ultimate expression of human faith and integrity as well as creativity. I have tried here to capture that creativity, courage, and vision in such a way as to engage and enrich even those encountering art history for the very first time. If I have done that, I will feel richly rewarded.

Marilyn Stokstad
Spring 1995

Acknowledgments to the Revised Edition

Many people reviewed the original edition of *Art History* and helped with the changes and revisions to the Revised Edition. By period, they are Jean Middleton James, the entire text; Judith Oliver (Colgate University), the European Middle Ages; Edward Olszewski (Case Western Reserve University) and Edward Eglinski (The University of Kansas), Renaissance and Baroque; David Cateforis (The University of Kansas) and Grace Flam (Salt Lake City Community College), modern art and architecture; and Marta Braun (Ryerson Polytechnic University), photography.

Others whose comments were especially helpful include James Adams (Manchester College), Anthony Alofsin (University of Texas at Austin), Sara Blick (Kenyon College), Larry Beck, Nancy Corwin (Tulane University), Stephen Goddard (The University of Kansas), Wendy Kindred (University of Maine at Fort Kent), Aileen Laing (Sweet Briar College), and Amy Ogata (Cleveland Institute of Art).

Many of those acknowledged in the original edition assisted with the Revised Edition, especially Robert Calkins, Robert Cohon, Susan Craig, Charles Cuttler, Charles Eldredge, Eileen Fry, Walter Gibson, Dorothy Glass, Charles Little, Bob Martin, Amy McNair, Anta Montet-White, Sara Orel, Sarajane Pearman, John Pultz, Pamela Sheingorn, James Seaver, Linda Stone-Ferrier, Elizabeth Valdez del Alamo, Roger Ward, and Ann Zielinski.

Again, thanks to my wonderful editor at Abrams, Julia Moore, and to those who worked with her so competently, Jean Smith and Jungha Oh. Photo researchers Diana Pilar Gongora and Janice Ackerman have my gratitude, and so do Lydia Gershey and Yonah Schurink, designers extraordinary.

Marilyn Stokstad
Lawrence, Kansas
June 1998

Contents

Introduction

1. Wall painting with four horses, Vallon-Pont-d'Arc, Ardèche gorge, France. c. 28,000 BCE. Paint on limestone

I stood in front of that exquisite panel with the four horses' heads and . . . I was so overcome that I cried. It was like going into an attic and finding a da Vinci [painting]. Except that this great [artist] was unknown." With these words Jean Clottes, an eminent French authority on prehistoric cave art, described viewing one of the 300 breathtakingly beautiful paintings just discovered in a huge limestone cavern near the Ardèche River in southern France (Marlise Simons, "In a French Cave, Wildlife Scenes from a Long-Gone World," *The New York Times*, January 24, 1995, page C10).

These remarkable animal images, fixed in time and preserved undisturbed in their remote cavern, were created some 30,000 years ago (fig. 1). That such representations were made at all is evidence of a uniquely human trait. And what animals are painted here? When were they painted, and how have they been preserved? Why were the paintings made, and what do they tell us about the people who made them? All these questions—what is depicted, how, when, why—are subjects of art history. And, because *these* magnificent images come from a time before there were written records, they provide the best information available not just about early humans' art but also about their reality.

ART AND REALITY

What is art? And what is reality? Especially today, why should one draw or paint, carve or model, when an image can be captured with a camera? In a nineteenth-century painting, *Interior with Portraits* (fig. 2), by the American artist Thomas LeClear, two children stand painfully still while a photographer prepares to take their picture. The paintings and sculpture that fill the studio have been shoved aside to make way for a new kind of art—the photograph. As the photographer adjusts the lens of his camera, we see his baggy pants but not his head. Is LeClear suggesting that the painter's head (brain and eye) is being replaced by the lens (a kind of mechanical brain and eye) of the camera? Or even that the artist and the camera have become a single recording eye? Or is this painting a witty commentary on the nature of reality? Art history leads us to ask such questions.

LeClear's painting resembles a snapshot in its record of studio clutter, but LeClear made subtle changes in what he saw. Using the formal elements of painting—the arrangement of shapes and colors—he focused attention on the children rather than on the interesting and distracting objects that surround them. Light falls on the girl and boy and intensifies the brilliant coral and green of the cloth on the floor. Softer coral shades in the curtain and the upholstered chair

2. Thomas LeClear. *Interior with Portraits*. c. 1865. Oil on canvas, 25⅞ x 40½" (65.7 x 102.9 cm). National Museum of American Art, Smithsonian Institution, Washington, D.C. Museum purchase made possible by the Pauline Edwards Bequest

frame the image, and the repeated colors balance each other. LeClear also reminds us that art is an illusion: the photograph will show the children in a vast landscape with a rug and animal skin, but the painting reveals that the landscape is just a two-dimensional painted backdrop and the rug and animal skin just slightly worn, painted cloth. These observations make us realize that the painting is more than a portrait; it is also a commentary on the artist as a creator of illusions.

Certainly there is more to this painting—and to most paintings—than one first sees. We can simply enjoy *Interior with Portraits* as a record of nineteenth-century America, but we can also study the history of the painting to probe deeper into its significance. Who are the children? Why was their portrait painted? Who owned the painting? The answers to these questions lead us to further doubts about the reality of this seemingly "realistic" work.

Thomas LeClear worked in Buffalo, New York, from 1847 to 1863. The painting, which is now in the National Museum of American Art in Washington, D.C., once belonged to the Sidway family of Buffalo. Family records show that the girl in the painting, Parnell Sidway, died in 1849; the boy, her younger brother James Sidway, died in 1865 while working as a volunteer fire fighter. Evidence suggests that the painting was not made until the 1860s, well after Parnell's death and when James was a grown man—or possibly after his death, too. LeClear moved to New York City in 1863, and the studio seen in the painting may be one he borrowed from his son-in-law there. Another clue to the painting's date is the camera, which is a type that was not used before 1860. The Sidway children, then, could never have posed for this painting. It must, instead, be a memorial portrait, perhaps painted by LeClear from a photograph. In short, this image of "reality" cannot be "real." Art historical research reveals a story entirely different from what observation of the painting alone suggests.

This new knowledge leads us to further speculations on the nature of art. The memorial portrait, with its re-creation of vanished childhood, is a reflection on life and death. In

3. Margaret Bourke-White. *Fort Peck Dam, Montana.* 1936

4. First cover, *Life* magazine, November 23, 1936

this context, the ambiguities we noticed before—the contrast between the reality of the studio and the unreal landscape on the cloth in the background, the juxtaposition between the new medium of photography and the old-fashioned, painted portrait on an easel—take on deeper significance. LeClear seems to be commenting on the tension between nature and art, on art and reality, and on the role of the artist as a recording eye and controlling imagination.

But what about the reality of photographs? Today the camera has become a universal tool for picture making. Even though we know that film can be manipulated and photographs made to "lie," we generally accept that the camera tells the truth. We forget that in a photograph a vibrant, moving, three-dimensional world has been immobilized, reduced to two dimensions, and sometimes recorded in black and white.

Photographs can be powerful works of art. In the 1930s and 1940s people waited as eagerly for the weekly arrival of *Life* magazine, with its photojournalism and photo essays, as people do today for their favorite television program. An extraordinary photographer of that time was Margaret Bourke-White, whose photograph of Peck Dam (fig. 3), used on the cover of the first issue of *Life* in 1936 (fig. 4), made a dramatic social-political statement about the role of government. In the depths of the economic depression of the 1930s, public works like the dam in the picture, which controlled floods and provided electric power, gave people hope for a better life. Bourke-White's photograph is a symbol of the power of technology and engineering over nature. It seems to equate the monumental grandeur of the dam with the architectural marvels of the past—Egyptian pyramids, the Roman Colosseum, medieval European castles. The arrangement of elements in the image reflects techniques that had been perfected by artists over the centuries: the repetition of simple forms, a steady recession into space, and a dramatic contrast of light and dark. Two red bands with bold white lettering turn the photograph into a handsome piece of **graphic design**, that is, a work in which art and design, typography, and printing are brought together to communicate a message.

Bourke-White's skillful capturing of the powerful dam reminds us that the camera is merely a mechanical tool for making records until an artist puts it to use. Anyone who has ever taken a snapshot of a friend only to find that the finished picture includes unnoticed rubbish and telephone wires will recognize the importance of the human brain's ability to filter and select. But an artist's vision can turn the everyday world into a superior reality—perhaps simply more focused or intense, certainly more imaginative.

We can easily understand a photograph of a dam, the imagery in a painting of a nineteenth-century artist's studio is not too strange to us, and even prehistoric animal paintings in a cave have a haunting familiarity. Other works, however, present a few more challenges. The fifteenth-century painting *The Annunciation,* by Jan van Eyck (fig. 5), is an excellent example of how some artists try to paint more than the eye can see and more than the mind can grasp. We can enjoy the painting for its visual characteristics—the drawing, colors, and arrangement of shapes—but we need the help of art history and information about the painting's cultural context if we want to understand it fully. Jan van Eyck (1390–1441) lived in the wealthy city of Bruges, in what is now Belgium, in the first half of the fifteenth century. The painting seems to be set in Jan van Eyck's own time in a church with stone walls and arches, tile floor, wooden roof, stained-glass windows, and wall paintings. The artist has so carefully recreated the colors and textures of every surface that he convinces us of the truth of his vision. Clearly something strange and wonderful is happening. We see a richly robed youth with splendid multicolored wings interrupting a kneeling young woman's reading. The two figures gesture gracefully upward toward a dove flying down streaks of gold. Golden letters float from their lips, forming the Latin words that mean "Hail, full of grace" and "Behold the handmaiden of the Lord." But only if we know something about the symbols, or **iconography**, of Christian art does the subject of the painting become clear. The scene is the Annunciation, the moment when the angel Gabriel tells the Virgin Mary that she will bear the Son of God, Jesus Christ (recounted in the New Testament of the Christian Bible, Luke l:26–38). All the details have a meaning. The dove symbolizes the Holy Spirit. The white lilies are symbols of Mary. The one stained-glass window of God (flanked by wall paintings of Moses) is

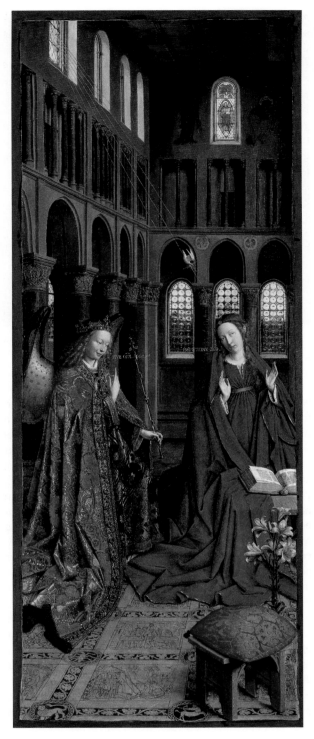

5. Jan van Eyck. *The Annunciation.* c. 1434–36. Oil on canvas, transferred from panel, painted surface 35³⁄₈ x 13⁷⁄₈" (90.2 x 34.1 cm). National Gallery of Art, Washington, D.C. Andrew W. Mellon Collection 1937.1.39

juxtaposed with the three windows enclosing Mary (representing the Trinity of Father, Son, and Holy Spirit), and this contrast suggests that a new era is about to begin. The signs of the zodiac in the floor tiles indicate the traditional date of the Annunciation, March 25. The placement of the figures in a much later architectural setting is quite unreal, however.

Art historians explain that Jan van Eyck not only is representing a miracle but also is illustrating the idea that Mary is the new Christian Church.

Art historians learn all they can about the lives of artists and those close to them. Seeking information about Jan van Eyck, for example, they have investigated his brother Hubert, Jan's wife, Margaret, and his chief patron, the duke of Burgundy. They are also fascinated by painting techniques—in this case the preparation of the wood panel, the original drawing, and the building of the images in transparent oil layers. The history of the painting (its **provenance**) is important too—its transfer from wood panel to canvas, its cleaning and restoration, and its trail of ownership. The painting, given by American financier Andrew W. Mellon to the National Gallery of Art in Washington, D.C., was once owned by Tsar Nicholas I of Russia.

In this book we study the history of art around the world from earliest times to the present. Although we treat Western art in the most detail, we also look extensively at the art of other regions. The qualities of a work of art, the artist who made it, the patron who paid for it, the audiences who have viewed it, and the places in which it has been displayed—all are considered in our study of art's history.

ART AND THE IDEA OF BEAUTY

For thousands of years people have sought to create objects of beauty and significance—objects we call art—that did more than simply help them survive. The concept of beauty, however, has found expression in a variety of **styles**, or manners of representation. The figure from Galgenburg, Austria, made more than 33,000 years ago, illustrates an **abstract** style (fig. 6). Its maker simplified shapes, eliminated all but the essentials, and emphasized the underlying human forms. An equally abstract vision of woman can be seen in Kitagawa Utamaro's *Woman at the Height of Her Beauty* (fig. 7). This late-eighteenth-century Japanese work, printed in color from a **woodblock**, or image carved out of a block of wood, is the creation of a complex society regulated by convention and ritual. The woman's dress and hairstyle defy the laws of nature. Rich textiles turn her body into a pattern, and pins hold her hair in elaborate shapes. Utamaro renders the patterned silks and carved pins meticulously, but he depicts the woman's face with a few sweeping lines. The elaboration of surface detail to create ornamental effects combined with an effort to capture the essence of form is characteristic of abstract art.

Two of the other works we have looked at so far—LeClear's *Interior with Portraits* and Jan van Eyck's *Annunciation*—exemplify a contrasting style known as **realism**. Realistic art, even if it represents an imagined or supernatural subject, has a surface reality; the artists appear, with greater or lesser accuracy, to be recording exactly what they see. Realistic art, as we have noted, can carry complex messages and be open to individual interpretation.

Realism and abstraction represent opposite approaches to the representation of beauty. In a third style, called **idealism**, artists aim to represent things not as they are but as they ought to be. In ancient Greece and Rome artists made intense observations of the world around them and then subjected

6. Human figure, found at Galgenburg, Austria. c. 31,000 BCE. Stone, height 3" (7.4 cm). Naturhistorisches Museum, Vienna

7. Kitagawa Utamaro. *Woman at the Height of Her Beauty*. Mid-1790s. Color woodblock print, 15 1/8 x 10" (38.5 x 25.5 cm). Spencer Museum of Art, University of Kansas, Lawrence
William Bridges Thayer Memorial

8. Attributed to Aulos, son of Alexas. Gem with Apollo and Cassandra. 40–20 BCE. Gold with engraved carnelian, ring 1³/₈ x 1" (3.4 x 2.5 cm), gem ¹³/₁₆ x ³/₄" (1.9 x 2.1 cm). The Nelson-Atkins Museum of Art, Kansas City, Missouri

Purchase: Acquired through the generosity of Mr. and Mrs. Robert S. Everitt (F93-22)

Apollo fell in love with Cassandra, and although she rejected him he gave her a potent gift—the ability to foretell the future, symbolized by the raven. To show his disappointment, the frustrated Apollo added a spiteful twist to his gift—no one would believe Cassandra's prophetic warnings. Today, doom-sayers are still called Cassandras, and ravens are associated with prophecy.

their observations to mathematical analysis to define what they considered to be perfect forms. Emphasizing human rationality, they eliminated accidents of nature and sought balance and harmony in their work. Their sculpture and painting established ideals that have inspired Western art ever since. The term *Classical,* which refers to the period in ancient Greek history when this type of idealism emerged, has come to be used broadly (and with a lowercase *c*) as a synonym for the peak of perfection in any period.

Classical idealism can pervade even the smallest works of art. About 2,000 years ago a Roman gem cutter known as Aulos added the opulence of imperial Rome to the ideals of Classical Greece when he engraved a deep-red, precious stone with the figures of the tragic princess Cassandra and the Greek god Apollo (fig. 8). Cassandra sleeps by rocky cliffs and a twisting laurel tree that suggest the dramatic natural setting of Delphi, Greece, a site sacred to Apollo. The god leans on the laurel tree, also sacred to him, with his cloak draped loosely and gracefully behind him. Apollo and Cassandra have the strong athletic bodies and regular facial features that charac-

terize Classical art, and their graceful poses and elegant drapery seem at the same time ideally perfect and perfectly natural. These beautiful figures and their story of frustrated love were not meant to be seen in a museum (a *museum* literally is the home of Apollo's Muses, the goddesses of learning and the arts). The carved gem was set in a gold finger ring and would have been constantly before its wearer's eyes. This sculpture reminds us that exceptional art can come in any size and material and can be intended for daily personal use as well as for special, occasional contemplation.

The flawless perfection of Classical idealism could be dramatically modified by artists more concerned with emotions than pure form. The calm of Cassandra and Apollo contrasts with the melodramatic representation of a story from the ancient Greek legend of the Trojan War. The priest Laocoön (fig. 9), who attempted to warn the Trojans against the Greeks, was strangled along with his two sons by serpents. Heroic and tragic, Laocoön represents a good man destroyed by forces beyond his control. His features twist in agony, and the muscles of his superhuman torso and arms extend and knot as he struggles. This sculpture, then at least sixteen centuries old, was rediscovered in Rome in the 1500s, and it inspired artists such as Michelangelo to develop a heroic style. Through the centuries people have returned again and again to the ideals of Classical art. In the United States official sculpture and architecture often copy Classical forms, and even the National Museum of American Art is housed in a Greek-style building.

How different from this ideal of physical beauty the perception and representation of spiritual beauty can be. A fifteenth-century bronze sculpture from India represents Punitavati, a beautiful and generous woman who was deeply devoted to the Hindu god Shiva (fig. 10). Abandoned by her greedy husband because she gave food to beggars, Punitavati offered her beauty to Shiva. Shiva accepted her offering, turning her into an emaciated, fanged hag. According to legend, Punitavati, with clanging cymbals, provides the music for Shiva as he dances the cosmic dance of destruction and creation that keeps the universe in motion. To the followers of Shiva, Punitavati became a saint called Karaikkalammaiyar. The bronze sculpture, although it depicts the saint's hideous appearance, is nevertheless beautiful both in its formal qualities and in its message of generosity and sacrifice.

Some works of art defy simple categories, and artists may go to extraordinary lengths to represent their visions. The art critic Robert Hughes called James Hampton's (1909–1964) *Throne of the Third Heaven of the Nations' Millennium General Assembly* (fig. 11) "the finest piece of visionary art produced by an American." Yet this fabulous creation is composed of discarded furniture, flashbulbs, and all sorts of trash tacked together and wrapped in aluminum and gold foil and purple paper. The primacy of painting, especially oil painting, is gone. Hampton's inspiration, whether divine or not, knows no bounds. He worked as a janitor to support himself while, in a rented garage, he built his monument to Jesus. In rising tiers, thrones and altars are prepared for Jesus and Moses, the New Testament at the right, the Old Testament at the left. Everything is labeled and described, but Hampton invented his own language and writing system to express his vision. Although his language is still not fully

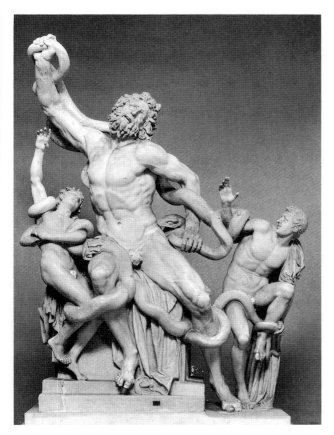

9. Hagesandros, Polydoros, and Athanadoros of Rhodes. *Laocoön and His Sons*, perhaps the original of the 2nd or 1st century BCE or a Roman copy of the 1st century CE. Marble, height 8' (2.44 m). Musei Vaticani, Museo Pio Clementino, Cortile Ottagono, Rome

10. *Punitavati* (*Karaikkalammaiyar*), Shiva saint, from Karaikkal, India. 15th century. Bronze, height 16¼" (41.3 cm). The Nelson-Atkins Museum of Art, Kansas City, Missouri
Purchase: Nelson Trust (33-533)

understood, its major source is the Bible, especially the Book of Revelation. On one of many placards he wrote his artist's credo: "Where there is no vision, the people perish" (Proverbs 29:18).

These different ideas of art and beauty remind us that as viewers we enter into an agreement with artists, who, in turn, make special demands on us. We re-create works of art for ourselves as we bring to them our own experiences. Without our participation they are only hunks of stone or metal or pieces of paper or canvas covered with ink or colored paints. Artistic styles change with time and place. From extreme realism at one end of the spectrum to entirely non-representational art at the other, artists have worked with varying degrees of realism, idealism, and abstraction. The challenge for the student of art history is to discover not only how but why these changes have occurred and ultimately what of significance can be learned from them, what meaning they carry.

ARTISTS

We have focused so far on works of art. What of the artists who make the art? Biologists have pointed out that human beings are mammals with very large brains and that these large brains demand stimulation. Curious, active, inventive humans constantly look, taste, smell, and listen. They invent fine arts, fine food, fine perfume, and fine music. They play games, invent rituals,

11. James Hampton. *Throne of the Third Heaven of the Nations' Millennium General Assembly*. c. 1950–64. Gold and silver aluminum foil, colored Kraft paper, and plastic sheets over wood, paperboard, and glass, 10'6" x 27' x 14'6" (3.2 x 8.23 x 4.42 m). National Museum of American Art, Smithsonian Institution, Washington, D.C.

and speculate on the nature of things, on the nature of life. They constantly communicate with each other, and some of them even try to communicate with the past and future.

We have seen that some artists try to record the world as they see it, and they attempt to educate or convince their viewers with straightforward stories or elaborate symbols.

Others create works of art inspired by an inner vision. Like the twentieth-century American Georgia O'Keeffe (fig. 12) they attempt to express in images what cannot be expressed in words. An organized religion such as Christianity or Buddhism may motivate them, but the artists may also divorce themselves from any social group and attempt to record personal visions or intense mystical experiences. These inner visions may spring from entirely secular insights, and the artist's motivation or intention may be quite different from the public perception of her or his art.

Originally, artists were considered artisans, or craftspeople. The master (and sometimes the mistress) of a workshop was the controlling intellect, the organizer, and the inspiration for others. Utamaro's color woodblock prints, for example, were the product of a team effort. In the workshop Utamaro drew and painted pictures for his assistants to transfer to individual blocks of wood. They carved the lines and color areas, covered the surface with ink or colors, then transferred the image to paper. Since ancient times artists have worked in teams to produce great buildings, paintings, and stained glass. The same spirit is evident today in the complex glassworks of American Dale Chihuly. His team of artist-craftspeople is skilled in the ancient art of glassmaking, but Chihuly remains the controlling mind and imagination. Once created, his pieces are transformed whenever they are assembled. Thus each work takes on a new life in accordance with the mind, eye, and hand of each owner-patron. Made in the 1990s, *Violet Persian Set with Red Lip Wraps* (fig. 13) has twenty separate pieces whose relationship to each other is determined by the imagination of the assembler. Like a fragile sea creature of the endangered coral reefs, the glass is vulnerable to thoughtless depredation, yet it is timeless in its reminder of primeval life. The purple captures light, color, and movement for a weary second. Artists, artisans, and patrons unite in an ever-changing individual yet communal act of creation.

About 600 years ago, artists in western Europe, especially in Italy, began to think of themselves as divinely inspired creative geniuses rather than as team workers. Painters like Guercino (Giovanni Francesco Barbieri, 1591–1666) took the evangelist Luke as their model, guide, and protector—their patron saint. People believed that Saint Luke had painted a portrait of the Virgin Mary holding the Christ Child. In Guercino's painting *Saint Luke Displaying a Painting of the Virgin* (fig. 14), the saint still holds his palette and brushes while an angel holds the painting on the easel. A book, a quill pen, and an inkpot decorated with a statue of an ox (a symbol for Luke) rest on a table behind the saint, reminders that he wrote one of the Gospels of the New Testament. The message Guercino conveys is that Saint Luke is a divinely inspired and endowed artist and that all artists share in this inspiration through their association with their patron saint.

Even the most inspired artists had to learn their trade through study or years of **apprenticeship** to a master. In his painting *The Drawing Lesson* (fig. 15), Dutch artist Jan Steen (1626–1679) takes us into an artist's studio where an apprentice watches his master teaching a young woman. The woman has been drawing from a sculpture because women then were not permitted to work from live nude models.

12. Georgia O'Keeffe. *Portrait of a Day, First Day.* 1924. Oil on canvas, 35 x 18" (89 x 45.8 cm). Spencer Museum of Art, University of Kansas, Lawrence
Gift of the Georgia O'Keeffe Foundation

The year before she painted *Portrait of a Day, First Day,* O'Keeffe wrote, "One day seven years ago [I] found myself saying to myself—I can't live where I want to—I can't go where I want to—I can't even say what I want to— School and things that painters have taught me even keep me from painting as I want to. I decided I was a very stupid fool not to at least paint as I wanted to and say what I wanted to when I painted as that seemed to be the only thing I could do that didn't concern anybody but myself—that was nobody's business but my own. . . I found that I could say things with color and shapes that I couldn't say in any other way—things that I had no words for. Some of the wise men say it is not painting, some of them say it is" (cited in *Alfred Stieglitz Presents One Hundred Pictures: Oils, Watercolors, Pastels, Drawings by Georgia O'Keeffe, American*, The Anderson Galleries, New York, exhibition brochure, January 29–February 10, 1923).

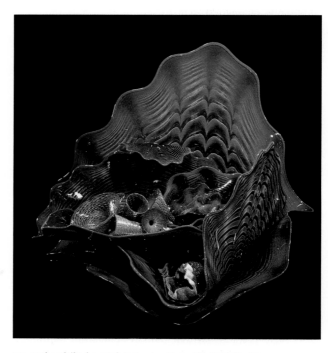

13. Dale Chihuly. *Violet Persian Set with Red Lip Wraps.* 1990. Glass, 26 x 30 x 25" (66 x 76.2 x 63.5 cm). Spencer Museum of Art, University of Kansas, Lawrence
Peter T. Bohan Acquisition Fund

14. Guercino. *Saint Luke Displaying a Painting of the Virgin.* 1652–53. Oil on canvas, 7'3" x 5'11" (2.21 x 1.81 m). The Nelson-Atkins Museum of Art, Kansas City, Missouri Purchase (F83-55)

15. Jan Steen. *The Drawing Lesson.* 1665. Oil on wood, 19 3/8 x 16 1/4" (49.3 x 41 cm). The J. Paul Getty Museum, Malibu, California

Plaster reproductions hang on the wall and stand on the shelf, and a carved boy-angel has been suspended from the ceiling in front of a large tapestry. The painter holds his own palette, and we see his painting set on an easel in the background. Like Thomas LeClear's painting of the photographer's studio, *The Drawing Lesson* is a valuable record of an artist's equipment and workplace, including such things as the musical instruments, furniture, glass, ceramics, and basketry used in the seventeenth century.

The painting is more than a realistic **genre painting** (scene from daily life) or **still life** (an arrangement of objects). *The Drawing Lesson* is also an **allegory**, or symbolic representation of the arts. The objects in the studio symbolize painting, sculpture, and music. The sculpture of the ox on the shelf is more than a bookend; as we have already seen, it symbolizes Saint Luke, the painters' patron saint. The basket in the foreground holds not only the woman's fur muff but also a laurel wreath, a symbol of Apollo and the classical tribute for excellence.

ARTISTS AND ART HISTORY

Artists draw on their predecessors in ways that make each work a very personal history of art. They build on the works of the past, either inspired by or reacting against them, but always challenging them with their new creations. The influence of Jan Steen's genre painting, for example, can be seen in Thomas LeClear's *Interior with Portraits,* and Guercino's Saint Luke is based on an earlier **icon**—or miraculous image—he had seen in his local church. In his 1980–1990 *Vaquero* (Cowboy), Luis Jimenez revitalizes a sculptural form with roots in antiquity, the equestrian monument, or statue of a horse and rider (fig. 16).

16. Luis Jimenez. *Vaquero.* Modeled 1980, cast 1990. Cast fiberglass and epoxy, height 16'6" (5.03 m). National Museum of American Art, Smithsonian Institution, Washington, D.C.

This white-hatted, gun-slinging bronco buster whoops it up in front of the stately, classical colonnade of the Old Patent Building (now the National Museum of American Art, the National Portrait Gallery, and the Archives of American Art). The Old Patent Office was designed in 1836 and finished in 1867. One of the finest Neoclassical buildings in the United States and the site of Abraham Lincoln's second inaugural ball, it was supposed to be destroyed for a parking lot when it was acquired by the Smithsonian in 1958.

Vaquero also reflects Jimenez's Mexican and Texan heritage and his place in a tradition of Hispanic American art that draws on many sources, including the art of the Maya, Aztec, and other great Native American civilizations, the African culture of the Caribbean Islands, and the transplanted art of Spain and Portugal.

Equestrian statues have traditionally been stately symbols of power and authority, with the rider's command over the animal emblematic of human control over lesser beings, nature, and the passions. Jimenez's bucking bronco turns this tradition, or at least the horse, on its head. Rather than a stately symbol of human control, he gives us a horse and cowboy united in a single exuberant and dynamic force. Located in front of the National Museum of American Art, the work can be seen as a witty satire on Washington, D.C.'s bronze monuments to soldiers. At the same time, it reminds us that real *vaqueros* included hard-working African Americans and Hispanic Americans who had little in common with the cowboys of popular fiction.

In his work, Jimenez has abandoned traditional bronze and marble for fiberglass. He first models a sculpture in a plastic paste called plasticine on a steel armature; then he makes a fiberglass mold, from which he casts the final sculpture, also in fiberglass. The materials and processes are the same as those used to make many automobile bodies, and as with automobiles, the process allows an artist to make several "originals." After a sculpture is assembled and polished, it is sprayed with the kind of acrylic urethane used to coat the outside of jet airplanes. Jimenez applies colors with an airbrush and coats the finished sculpture with three more layers of acrylic urethane to protect the color and emphasize its distinctive, sleek, gleaming surface. *Vaquero* is true public, popular art. It appeals to every kind of audience from the rancher to the connoisseur.

When artists appropriate and transform images from the past the way Jimenez appropriated the equestrian form, they enrich the **aesthetic** vocabulary of the arts in general. *Vaquero* resonates through the ages with associations to cultures distant in time and place that give it added meaning. This kind of aesthetic free-for-all encourages artistic diversity and discourages the imposition of a single correct or canonical (approved) approach or point of view. In the jargon of our time, no medium is *privileged*, and no group of artists is *marginalized*.

ART AND SOCIETY

The visual arts are among the most sophisticated forms of human communication, at once shaping and shaped by the social context in which they find expression. Artists are often interpreters of their times. They can also be enlisted to serve social ends in forms that range from heavy-handed propaganda to the more subtle persuasiveness of Margaret Bourke-White's photographs for *Life* magazine. From the priests and priestesses in ancient Egypt to the representatives of various faiths today, religious leaders have understood the value of the visual arts in educating people about doctrine and in reinforcing their faith. Especially beginning in the eleventh century in western Europe, architecture and sculpture provided settings for elaborate rites and inspiring and instructive art. At the Cathedral of Santiago de Compostela in north-

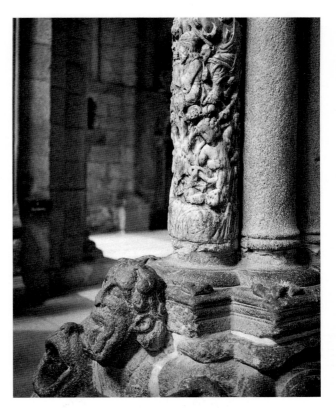

17. *Pórtico de la Gloria*. Photograph by Joan Myers. 1988

Tradition required that pilgrims to the Cathedral of Santiago de Compostela place their fingers in the tendrils of the carved Tree of Jesse as they asked Saint James's blessing on arrival in the church. Millions of fingers have worn away the carving, leaving a rich patina of age. The twelfth-century sculpture still inspires twentieth-century artists such as photographer Joan Myers.

western Spain, which shelters the tomb of Saint James, the marble of the central portal has been polished and the twelfth-century sculpture have been worn down by the touch of pilgrims' fingers (fig. 17).

Marxist art historians once saw art as an expression of great social forces rather than of individual genius, but most people now agree that neither history and economics nor philosophy and religion alone can account for the art of a Rembrandt or Michelangelo. The same applies to extraordinary "ordinary" people, too, who have created powerful art to satisfy their own inner need to communicate ideas. In Lucas, Kansas, in 1905, Samuel Perry Dinsmoor, a visionary populist, began building his Garden of Eden (fig. 18). By 1927 he had surrounded his home with twenty-nine concrete trees ranging from 8 to 40 feet high. He filled the branches with figures that told the biblical story of the Creation and the Expulsion from the Garden of Eden under the ever-present—and electrified—Eye of God. Adam and Eve succumb to the serpent; Cain strikes down Abel. Evil and death enter the world as creatures attack each other. In Dinsmoor's modern world, people defend themselves through their right to vote. Under the protection of the Goddess of Liberty draped in an American flag, a man and woman literally cut down big business with a saw labeled "ballot." Dinsmoor communicated his ideas forcefully and directly through haunting imagery. At dusk his electric

18. Samuel Perry Dinsmoor. *Goddess of Liberty and the Destruction of the Trusts by the Ballot*. Garden of Eden, Lucas, Kansas. 1905–32. Painted concrete and cement, over-lifesize

19. Roger Shimomura. *Diary* (Minidoka Series #3) 1978. Acrylic on canvas, 4'11⅞" x 6'1/16" (1.52 x 1.83 m). Spencer Museum of Art, University of Kansas, Lawrence

20. *Christine Presenting Her Book to the Queen of France*. 1410–15. Tempera and gold on vellum, image approx. 5½ x 6¾" (14 x 17 cm). The British Library, London MS. Harley 4431, folio 3

light bulbs—his repeated "Ever-Seeing Eye of God"—illuminate the concrete and cement figures with an unearthly glow.

Not all art with social impact is public on the scale of a pilgrimage church or a half-acre concrete Garden of Eden. Artists like Roger Shimomura turn painting and prints into powerful statements. American citizens of Japanese ancestry were forcibly confined in internment camps during World War II. Shimomura based his 1978 painting *Diary* (fig. 19) on his grandmother's record of the family's experience in an internment camp in Idaho. Shimomura painted his grandmother writing while he (the toddler) and his mother stand by an open door—a door that opens on a barbed-wire-enclosed compound. In his painting Shimomura has combined two formal traditions, the Japanese art of color woodblock prints (see fig. 7) and American Pop Art to create a personal style that expresses his own dual culture as it makes a powerful political statement.

ARTISTS AND PATRONS

Rare, valuable, beautiful, and strange things appeal to human curiosity. People who are not artists "use" art, too. They have collected special objects since prehistoric times when people buried the dead with necklaces of fox teeth. Collections of "curiosities" were passed along from one generation to the next, gaining luster or mysterious power with age. Art enhanced the owners' prestige, created an aura of power and importance, and impressed others. Many collectors truly love works of art. When collectors study diligently, they become scholars; when their expertise turns to questions of refined evaluation, they become what we call **connoisseurs**.

The patrons of art constitute a very special kind of audience for the artist. Patrons provide economic support for art and vicariously participate in its creation. In earlier periods artists depended on the patronage of individuals and the institutions they represented. An early-fifteenth-century painting shows the French writer Christine de Pisan presenting her work to the queen of France (fig. 20). Christine was a patron, too, for she hired painters and scribes to copy, illustrate, and decorate her books. She especially admired the painting of a woman artist named Anastaise, considering her work unsurpassed in the city of Paris, which she believed had the world's best painters of miniatures.

When a free market developed for art works, artists became entrepreneurs. In a painting by the seventeenth-

21. Gillis van Tilborch. *Cabinet d'Amateur with a Painter.*
c. 1660–70. Oil on canvas, 38¼ x 51" (97.15 x 129.54 cm).
Spencer Museum of Art, University of Kansas, Lawrence

22. James McNeill Whistler. *Harmony in Blue and Gold.* The
Peacock Room, northeast corner, from a house owned by
Frederick Leyland, London. 1876–77. Oil paint and metal
leaf on canvas, leather, and wood, 13'11⅞" x 33'2" x
19'11½" (4.26 x 10.11 x 6.83 m). Freer Gallery, Smithsonian Institution, Washington, D.C. (04.61)

century Flemish painter Gillis van Tilborch, an artist and an art dealer display their wares to patrons, who examine the treasures brought before them (fig. 21). Paintings cover the walls, and sculpture and precious objects stand on the table and floor. The painting provides a fascinating catalog of the fine arts of the seventeenth century and the taste of seventeenth-century connoisseurs.

Relations between artists and patrons are not always so congenial as Tilborch portrayed them. Patrons can change their minds about a commission or purchase or fail to pay their bills. Such conflicts can have simple beginnings and unexpected results. In the late nineteenth century the Liverpool shipping magnate Frederick Leyland asked James McNeill Whistler, an American painter living in London, what color to paint the shutters in the dining room where he planned to hang Whistler's painting *The Princess from the Land of Porcelain.* The room had been decorated with expensive embossed and gilded leather and finely crafted shelves to show off Leyland's Asian porcelain collection. Whistler was inspired by the Japanese theme of his own painting as well as the porcelain, and he was also caught up in the wave of enthusiasm for Japanese art sweeping Europe. He painted the window shutters with splendid turquoise, blue, and gold peacocks. Then, while Leyland was away, he painted the entire room (fig. 22), replacing the gilded leather on the walls with turquoise peacock feathers. Leyland was shocked and angry when he saw the results. Whistler, however, memorialized the confrontation with a painting of a pair of fighting peacocks on one wall of the room. One of the peacocks represents the outraged artist, and the other, standing on a pile of coins, represents the incensed patron. The Peacock Room, which Whistler called *Harmony in Blue and Gold,* is an extraordinary example of total design, and Leyland did not change it. The American collector Henry Freer, who sought to unite the aesthetics of East and West, later acquired the room and donated it on his death to a museum in the Smithsonian Institution in Washington, D.C., where it can now be appreciated by all. Today museums are the primary collectors and preservers of art.

THE KEEPERS OF ART: MUSEUMS

From time immemorial people have gathered together objects that they considered to be precious, objects that were made of valuable material or that conveyed the idea of power and prestige. The curators, or keepers of such collections, assisted patrons in obtaining the best pieces. The idea of what is best and what is worth collecting and preserving varies from one generation to another. Yesterday's popular magazine (see fig. 4) is today's example of fine photography and graphic design.

An art museum can be thought of in two ways: as a scholarly research institute where curators care for and study their collections and teach new scholar-curators, and as a public institution dedicated to exhibiting and explaining the collections. The first university art museum in the United States was established in 1832 at Yale University. Today museums with important research and educational functions are to be found in many universities and colleges, and museums with good collections are widespread. One does not have to live in a major population center to experience wonderful art. Of the twenty-six works illustrated in this chapter, eleven are located near the author in Kansas and Missouri, and four of these are in a single university museum. No one would assert that Kansas is the art capital of the world; the point is that encounters with the real objects are not out of most people's range. And no matter how faithful the quality of reproductions in a book or a slide or a monitor showing an image from a CD-ROM, there is no substitute for a "live interview" with an actual work of art or architecture.

The display of art is a major challenge for curators. Art must be put on public view in a way that ensures its safety

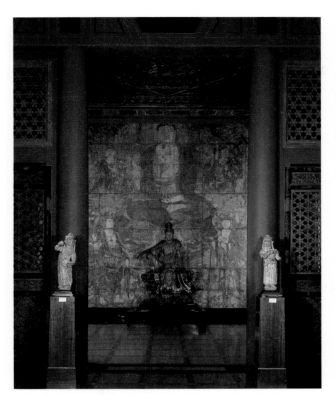

23. *The Water and Moon Kuan-yin Bodhisattva*. Northern
Sung or Liao dynasty, 11th–12th century. Wood with
paint, height 7'11" (2.41 m). Mural painting, 14th century;
wooden screens, 17th century. The Nelson-Atkins
Museum of Art, Kansas City, Missouri
Purchase: Nelson Trust (34.10)

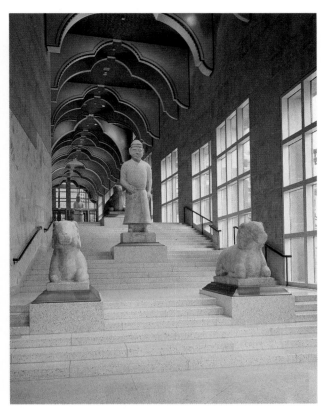

24. Robert Venturi and Denise Scott-Brown. Stair Hall with
Ming dynasty tomb figures, Seattle Art Museum. 1986–91

and also enhances its qualities and clarifies its significance.
The installation of Chinese sculpture at the Nelson-Atkins
Museum of Art in Kansas City (fig. 23) and at the Seattle Art
Museum (fig. 24) illustrate two imaginative approaches to
this challenge.

A polychromed and gilded wooden bodhisattva, or
enlightened being, in the Nelson-Atkins Museum of Art sits
majestically in front of a mural painting of the Buddha. The
sculpture and painting are exceptional in their own right,
and together they form a magnificent ensemble, placed in a
re-created temple setting with screens from the seventeenth
century. The curators successfully established an environment that recalls the religious context of the art, subtly
emphasizes its importance, and provides it with a measure
of security.

The Seattle Art Museum had different problems to solve.
Their carved-stone Chinese tomb figures had stood outdoors
in a park for years. Weather-beaten and moss-covered, they
had been almost ignored. The new Seattle Art Museum,
designed by Robert Venturi and Denise Scott-Brown and finished in 1991, had a monumental stairwell that united the
museum interior with the steep city street outside. The figures were cleaned, restored, and placed on the stairs like
welcoming guardians for the galleries above. Set under colorful festive arches, they provide a monumental and semi-

serious contrast to the witty, theatrical, and "irreverent"
architecture—the museum coffee shop interrupts their stately
procession—and serve as an appropriate symbol for a city
that prides itself as a link between East and West.

"I KNOW WHAT I LIKE"

Our involvement with art may be casual
or intense, naive or sophisticated. At
first we may simply react instinctively
to a painting or building or photograph,
but this level of "feeling" about art—"I
know what I like"—can never be fully satisfying.

Opinions as to what constitutes a work of art change
over time. Impressionist paintings of the late nineteenth century, now among the most avidly sought and widely collected,
were laughed at when first displayed. They seemed rough
and unfinished—merely "impressions"—rather than the careful depictions of nature people then expected to see. Impressionist painters like Claude Monet in his *Boulevard des
Capucines, Paris* (fig. 25) tried to capture in paint on canvas
the reflected light that registers as color in human eyes.
Rather than carefully drawing forms he knew to exist—the
branches and leaves of trees, dark-clothed figures—he recorded immediate visual sensations with flecks of color. The
rough texture provides a two-dimensional interest that is
quite independent of the painting's subject. The mind's eye

25. Claude Monet. *Boulevard des Capucines, Paris*. 1873–74. Oil on canvas, 31¼ x 23¼" (79.4 x 59.1 cm). The Nelson-Atkins Museum of Art, Kansas City, Missouri
Purchase: the Kenneth A. and Helen F. Spencer Foundation Acquisition Fund (F72-35)

26. Vincent van Gogh. *Sunflowers*. 1888. Oil on canvas, 36¼ x 28¾" (92.1 x 73 cm). The National Gallery, London

interprets the array of colors as the solid forms of nature, suddenly perceiving the coral daubs in the lower right, for example, as a balloon man. When the critic Louis Leroy reviewed this painting the first time it was exhibited, he sneered: "Only, be so good as to tell me what those innumerable black tongue-lickings in the lower part of the picture represent?" (*Le Charivari*, April 25, 1874). Today we easily see a street in early spring filled with horse-drawn cabs and strolling men and women. In this magical moment the long-dead artist and the live viewers join to re-create nineteenth-century Paris.

Art history, in contrast to art criticism, combines the formal analysis of works of art—concentrating mainly on the visual elements in the work of art—with the study of the works' broad historical context. Art historians draw on biography to learn about artists' lives, social history to understand the economic and political forces shaping artists, their patrons, and their public, and the history of ideas to gain an understanding of the intellectual currents influencing artists' work. They also study the history of other arts—including music, drama, literature—to gain a richer sense of the context of the visual arts. Every sculpture or painting presents a challenge. Even a glowing painting like Vincent van Gogh's *Sunflowers* (fig. 26), of 1888, to which we may react with spontaneous enthusiasm, forces us to think about art, as well as feel and admire it.

Our first reaction is that *Sunflowers* is a joyous, colorful

painting of a simple subject. But this is far more than a bunch of flowers in a simple pot in a sunlit room. Art history makes us search for more. The surface of the painting is richly built up—van Gogh laid on the thick oil paint with careful calculation. The brilliant yellow ground that looks flat in a reproduction in fact resembles a tightly woven basket or textile, so deliberately and carefully placed are the small brushstrokes. The space is suggested simply—by two horizontal stripes, two bands of gold different in intensity and separated by just the slightest blue line, the color of maximum contrast. Here, in fact, there is no space, no setting; we imagine a table, a sun-filled room. But did van Gogh see a pot of flowers on a windowsill, against the blazing, shimmering heat and light of the true sun? Van Gogh had a troubled life, and that knowledge makes us reflect on the possible meaning of the painting to him—for the painting, despite its brightness, reflects something ominous, a foreboding of the artist's loneliness and despair to come.

As viewers we participate in the re-creation of a work of art, and its meaning changes from individual to individual, from era to era. Once we welcome the arts into our life, we have a ready source of sustenance and challenge that grows, changes, mellows, and enriches our daily experience. No matter how much we study or read about art and artists, eventually we return to the contemplation of the work itself, for art is the tangible evidence of the ever-questing human spirit.

Starter Kit

This is a very basic primer of concepts and working assumptions used in the study of art history—a quick reference guide for this entire book and for encounters with art in general.

What Art Is

A work of art may be described in basic, nonphilosophical terms as having two components: FORM and CONTENT. It is also distinguished by STYLE, MEDIUM, and PERIOD.

FORM. Referring to purely visual aspects of art and architecture, form includes LINE, COLOR, TEXTURE, SPATIAL QUALITIES, and COMPOSITION. These various attributes are often referred to as FORMAL ELEMENTS.

Line is an element—usually drawn or painted—that defines SHAPE with a more-or-less continuous mark. The movement of the viewer's eyes over the surface of the work of art may follow a path determined by the artist and so create imaginary lines, or LINES OF FORCE.

Color has several attributes. These include HUE, VALUE, and INTENSITY.

> HUE is what we think of when we hear the word *color*. Red, yellow, and blue are the PRIMARY COLORS because other colors (SECONDARY COLORS of orange, green, and purple) can be created by mixing (combining) them. Red, orange, and yellow are known as warm colors; and green, blue, and purple as cool colors.
>
> VALUE is the relative degree of lightness or darkness in the range from white to black and is created by the amount of light reflected from an object's surface. A dark green has a deeper value than a light green, for example, and light gray has a lighter value than dark gray.
>
> INTENSITY is the degree of brightness or dullness of color. For this reason, the word *saturation* is synonymous with *intensity*.

Texture is the tactile quality of a surface. It is perceived and described with words like *smooth*, *polished*, *satiny*, *rough*, *coarse*, or *oily*. Texture takes two forms: the texture of the actual surface of the work of art and the implied (imaginary) surface of the object the artist is representing.

Spatial qualities include MASS, VOLUME, and SPACE.
> MASS and VOLUME are properties of three-dimensional objects. They take up space.
>
> SPACE may be three-dimensional and actual, as with sculpture and architecture, or may be represented in two dimensions. Unfilled space is referred to as NEGATIVE SPACE; solids are referred to as POSITIVE SPACE.

Composition is the organization, or arrangement, of form in a work of art.
> PICTORIAL DEPTH (SPATIAL RECESSION) is a specialized aspect of composition in which the three-dimensional world is

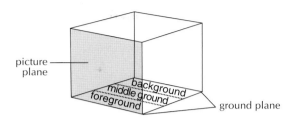

27. Diagram of picture space

represented in two dimensions in paintings and drawings. Artists have used many methods to depict objects as seeming to recede from the two-dimensional surface, called the PICTURE PLANE. The area "behind" the picture plane is called the PICTURE SPACE and conventionally contains three "zones": FOREGROUND, MIDDLE GROUND, and BACKGROUND (fig. 27). Perpendicular to the picture plane, forming the "floor" of the space, is the GROUND PLANE.

Various techniques for conveying a sense of pictorial depth have been preferred by artists in different cultures and at different times (fig. 28).

CONTENT. Content is a less specific aspect of a work of art than is form. There is also less agreement as to what content is. Content includes SUBJECT MATTER, which quite simply is what is represented, even when that consists strictly of lines and formal elements—lines and color without recognizable subject matter, for example. Content includes the IDEAS contained in a work. When used inclusively, the term *content* can embrace the social, political, and economic contexts in which a work was created, the intention of the artist, the reception of the beholder (the AUDIENCE) to the work, and ultimately the meaning in the work of art.

The study of the "what" of subject matter is ICONOGRAPHY. ICONOLOGY has come to mean the study of the "why" of subject matter.

STYLE. Understandably, specialized terminology is used to describe style in art history. Expressed very broadly, style is the combination of form and content characteristics that make a work distinctive.

Representational and **nonrepresentational style** (also called NONOBJECTIVE) refer to whether the subject matter is or is not recognizable.

Linear describes the style in which an artist uses line as the primary means of definition. When shadows and shading or modeling and highlights dominate, the style may be called PAINTERLY. Architecture and sculpture may be linear or painterly.

Realistic, naturalistic, and **idealized** are often-found descriptions of style. REALISM is the attempt to depict objects as they are in actual, visible reality. NATURALISM is a style of depiction in which the physical appearance of the rendered image in nature is the primary inspiration. A work in a naturalistic style resembles the original but not with the same exactitude

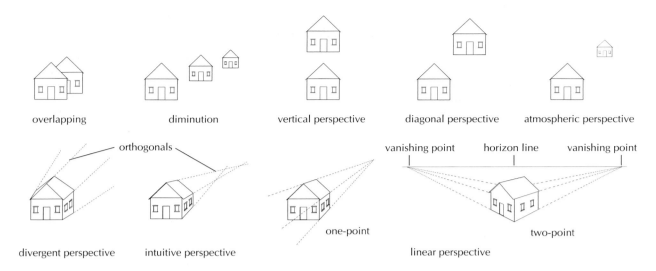

overlapping   diminution   vertical perspective   diagonal perspective   atmospheric perspective

orthogonals

vanishing point   horizon line   vanishing point

one-point

two-point

divergent perspective   intuitive perspective   linear perspective

28. Pictorial devices for depicting recession in space

Among the simpler devices are OVERLAPPING, in which partially covered elements are meant to be seen as located behind those covering them, and DIMINUTION, in which smaller elements are meant to be perceived as being farther away than larger ones. In VERTICAL and DIAGONAL PERSPECTIVE, elements are stacked vertically or diagonally, with the higher elements meant to be perceived as deeper in space. Another way of suggesting depth is through ATMOSPHERIC PERSPECTIVE, which depicts objects in the far distance with less clarity than nearer objects, often in bluish gray hues, and treats the sky as paler near the horizon. For many centuries DIVERGENT PERSPECTIVE, in which forms widen slightly and lines diverge as they recede in space, was used by East Asian artists. INTUITIVE PERSPECTIVE, such as that in some late medieval European art, uses the opposite: forms become more narrow and lines converge the farther away they are from the viewer, approximating the optical experience of spatial recession. LINEAR PERSPECTIVE, also called SCIENTIFIC, MATHEMATICAL, ONE-POINT, or Renaissance perspective, is an elaboration and standardization of intuitive perspective and was developed in fifteenth-century Italy. It uses mathematical formulas to construct illusionistic images in which all elements are shaped by imaginary lines called ORTHOGONALS that converge in one or more VANISHING POINTS on a HORIZON LINE. Linear perspective is the system that most people in Euro-American cultures think of as perspective. Because it is the visual code they are accustomed to reading, they accept as "truth" the distortions it imposes, including FORESHORTENING, in which, for instance, the soles of the feet in the foreground are the largest element of a figure lying on the ground.

and literalness as a work in a realistic style. IDEALIZATION strives for perfection that is grounded in prevailing values of a culture. Classical Greek sculpture is an example of art that is both naturalistic and idealized. ABSTRACTION is the stylistic opposite of the last three styles, because the artist makes forms that do not depict observable objects—often with the intention of extracting the essence of an object or idea. Much prehistoric art is abstract in this way. EXPRESSIONISTIC style appeals to the subjective responses of the beholder, often through exaggeration of form and expression.

MEDIUM. What is meant by medium (here we have used the plural *mediums*, to distinguish the word from the press *media*) is the material from which a given object is made. Even broader than medium is the distinction between two-dimensional, three-dimensional, mixed-medium, and ephemeral arts.

Two-dimensional arts include painting, drawing, the graphic arts, and photography.

Three-dimensional arts are sculpture, architecture, and many ornamental and practical arts.

Mixed medium includes categories such as collage and assemblage, in which the two-dimensional surface is built up from elements that are not painted, such as pieces of paper or metal or garments.

Ephemeral arts include such chiefly modern categories as performance art, earthworks, cinema, video art, and computer art, all of which have a central temporal aspect in that the artwork is viewable for a finite period of time and then disappears forever, is in a constant state of change, or must be replayed to be experienced.

Painting includes wall painting and fresco, illumination (decoration of books with paintings), panel painting (paintings on wood panels), miniature painting, handscroll and hanging scroll painting, and easel painting.

Drawings may be sketches (quick visual notes for larger drawings or paintings); studies (more carefully drawn analyses of details or entire compositions); drawings as complete artworks in themselves; and cartoons (full-scale drawings made in preparation for work in another medium, such as fresco).

Graphic arts are the printed arts—images that are reproducible and that traditionally include woodcut, engraving, etching, drypoint, and lithography.

Still photographs are a two-dimensional art.

Sculpture is a three-dimensional work of art that is carved, modeled, or assembled. Carved sculpture is reductive in the sense that the image is created by taking material away.

TECHNIQUE

Lost-Wax Casting

The lost-wax casting process (also called *cire perdue*, the French term) has been used for many centuries. It probably started in Egypt. By 200 BCE the technique was known in China and ancient Mesopotamia and was soon after used by the Benin peoples in Africa. It spread to ancient Greece sometime in the sixth century BCE and was widespread in Europe until the eighteenth century, when a piece-mold process came to predominate. The usual metal is bronze, an alloy of copper and tin, or sometimes brass, an alloy of copper and zinc.

The progression of drawings here shows the steps used by Benin sculptors. A heat-resistant "core" of clay—approximating the shape of the sculpture-to-be (and eventually becoming the hollow inside the sculpture)—was covered by a layer of wax about the thickness of the final sculpture. The sculptor carved the details in the wax. Rods and a pouring cup made of wax were attached to the model. A thin layer of fine, damp sand was pressed very firmly into the surface of the wax model, and then model, rods, and cup were encased in thick layers of clay. When the clay was completely dry, the mold was heated to melt out the wax. The mold was then turned upside down to receive the molten metal, which for the Benin was brass, heated to the point of liquification. The cast was placed in the ground. When the metal was completely cool, the outside clay cast and the inside core were broken up and removed, leaving the cast brass sculpture. Details were polished to finish the piece of sculpture, which could not be duplicated because the mold had been destroyed in the process.

Wood and stone sculpture, large and small, is carved sculpture because the material is not malleable. Modeled sculpture is considered additive, meaning that the object is built up from a material such as clay that is soft enough to be molded and shaped. Metal sculpture is usually cast (see "Lost-Wax Casting," above) or is assembled by welding or similar means of joining.

Sculpture is either FREESTANDING (sculpture in the round) or in RELIEF, which means projecting from the surface of which it is a part. Relief may be HIGH RELIEF, with parts of the sculpture projecting far off the background, or LOW RELIEF, in which the projections are only slightly raised. SUNKEN RELIEF, found mainly in Egyptian sculpture, is imagery carved into the surface, with the highest part of the relief being the flat surface.

Architecture is three-dimensional and highly spatial, and it is closely bound up with developments in technology and materials. An example of the relationship among technology, materials, and function is how space is spanned (see "Elements of Architecture," page 32).

Buildings are represented by a number of two-dimensional schematic drawings, including plans, elevations, sections, and cutaways (fig. 29). PLANS are imaginary slices through a building at approximately waist height. Everything below the slice is drawn as if looking straight down from above. ELEVATIONS are exterior sides of a building as if seen from a moderate distance but without any perspective dis-

29. Diagrammatic drawings of buildings

tortion. SECTIONS are imaginary vertical slices from top to bottom through a building that reveal elements "cut" by the slice. CUTAWAY DRAWINGS show both inside and outside elements from an oblique angle.

Other mediums. Besides painting, drawing, graphic arts, photography, sculpture, and architecture, works of art are made in the mediums of ceramic and glass, textile and stitchery, metalwork and enamel, and many other materials. Today anything—even "junk," the discards of society—can be turned into a work of art.

PERIOD. A word often found in art historical writing, *period* means the historical era from which a work of art comes. It is good practice not to use the words *style* and *period* interchangeably. Style is the sum of many influences and characteristics, including the period of its creation. An example of good usage is: "an American house from the Colonial period built in the Georgian style."

ELEMENTS OF ARCHITECTURE

Space-Spanning Construction Devices

Gravity pulls on everything, presenting great challenges to the need to cover spaces. The purpose of the spanning element is to transfer weight to the ground. The simplest space-spanning device is post-and-lintel construction, in which uprights are spanned by a horizontal element. However, if not flexible, a horizontal element over a wide span breaks under the pressure of its own weight and the weight it carries.

Corbeling, the building up of overlapping stones, is another simple method for transferring weight to the ground. Arches, round or pointed, span space. Vaults, which are essentially extended arches, move weight out from the center of the covered space and down through the corners. The cantilever is a variant of post-and-lintel construction. When concrete is reinforced with steel or iron rods, the inherent brittleness of cement and stone is then overcome because of metal's flexible qualities. The concrete can then span much more space and bear heavier loads. Suspension works to counter the effect of gravity by lifting the spanning element upward. Trusses of wood or metal are relatively lightweight spanners but cannot bear heavy loads. Large-scale modern construction is chiefly steel frame and relies on steel's properties of strength and flexibility to bear great loads. The balloon frame, an American innovation, is based in post-and-lintel principles and exploits the lightweight, flexible properties of wood.

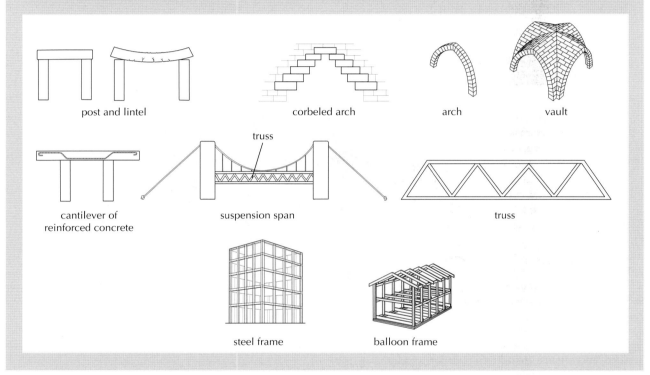

post and lintel

corbeled arch

arch

vault

cantilever of reinforced concrete

truss

suspension span

truss

steel frame

balloon frame

What Art History Is

Art history is a humanistic field of inquiry that studies visual culture. Increasingly, art history seeks to understand the role of visual culture in societies around the world and to learn more about the people and cultures who created the individual artworks through close yet multidimensional study of the art itself. Art history embraces many different approaches to visual culture. CONTEXTUAL ART HISTORY seeks to place and understand art as one expression of complex social, economic, political, and religious influences on the culture and the individuals within it. FORMALISM, or FORMAL ANALYSIS, examines and analyzes the formal elements of works of art, in and of themselves. The most traditional approach is CONNOISSEURSHIP, the almost intimate appreciation and evaluation of works of art for their intrinsic attributes, including genuineness and quality. Connoisseurship necessarily involves AESTHETICS, a branch of philosophy concerned with the nature of beauty and taste. This book combines contextual art history and formal analysis, while acknowledging other approaches.

Museums

When you visit a museum, you need no special preparation, but planning can enhance your enjoyment. Several museum resources can help you as you study the works of art there. Publications such as exhibition catalogs and museum handbooks have entries on the artworks. Postcards are an inexpensive way to take an image home.

Museum behavior is simple common sense: don't do anything that endangers the art or interferes with other people's enjoyment of it. In the galleries take a quick look around to get a sense of what is there before going back to look more carefully at individual works that attract you. You can be systematic or selective. When you approach a work of art, look at it and think about it before you read the label. You may not see the same works of art that you have studied in this book, but you will see pieces that relate to both the ideas and the artworks presented in *Art History*. Reading about art—whether in books, in catalogs, or on museum labels—should supplement, not substitute for, looking at works of art.

Use Notes

The various features of this book reinforce each other, helping the reader to become comfortable with terminology and concepts specific to art history.

Introduction and Starter Kit   The Introduction is an invitation to the pleasures of art history. The Starter Kit that follows the Introduction is a highly concise primer of basic concepts and tools. The outside margins of the Starter Kit pages are tinted to make them easy to find.

Captions   There are two kinds of captions in this book: short and long. Short captions identify information specific to the work of art or architecture illustrated:

> artist (when known)
> title or descriptive name of work
> date
> original location (if moved to a museum or other site)
> material or materials a work is made of
> size (height before width) in feet and inches, with
>   centimeters and meters in parentheses
> present location

The order of these elements varies, depending on the type of work illustrated. Dimensions are not given for architecture, for most wall painting, or for architectural sculpture. Some captions have one or more lines of small print below the identification section of the caption that gives museum or collection information. This is rarely required reading.

Long captions contain information of many kinds that complements the main text.

Definitions of Terms   You will encounter the basic terms of art history in three places:

IN THE TEXT, where words appearing in **boldface** type are defined, or glossed, at the first use; some terms are explained more than once, especially those that experience shows are hard to remember.

IN BOXED FEATURES on technique and other subjects and in Elements of Architecture boxes, where labeled drawings and diagrams visually reinforce the use of terms.

IN THE GLOSSARY at the end of the volume, which contains all the words in **boldface** type in the text and boxes. The Glossary begins on page G1, and the outside margins are tinted to make the Glossary easy to find.

Maps, Timelines, Parallels, and Time Scales   At the beginning of each chapter is a map with all the places mentioned in the chapter. Above the map, a timeline runs from the earliest through the latest years covered in that chapter. Small drawings of major artworks in the chapter are sited on the map at the places from which they come and are placed on the timelines at the times of their creation. In this way these major works are visually linked in time and place.

Parallels, a table near the beginning of every chapter, uses the main chapter sections to organize artistic and other events "at home and abroad." The Parallels offer a selection of simultaneous events for comparison without suggesting that there are direct connections between them.

Time scales appear in the upper corners of pages, providing a fast check on progress through the period.

Boxes   Special material that complements, enhances, explains, or extends the text is set off in three types of tinted boxes. Elements of Architecture boxes clarify specifically architectural features, such as "Space-Spanning Construction Devices" in the Starter Kit (page 32). Technique boxes (see "Lost-Wax Casting," page 31) amplify the methodology by which a type of artwork is created. Other boxes treat special-interest material related to the text.

Bibliography   The Bibliography, at the end of this book beginning on page B1, contains books in English, organized by general works and by chapter, that are basic to the study of art history today, as well as works cited in the text.

Dates, Abbreviations, and Other Conventions   This book uses the designations BCE and CE, abbreviations for "before the Common Era" and "Common Era," instead of BC ("before Christ") and AD ("Anno Domini," "the year of our Lord"). The first century BCE is the period from 99 BCE to 1 BCE; the first century CE is from the year 1 CE to 99 CE. Similarly, the second century BCE is the period from 199 BCE to 100 BCE; the second century CE extends from 100 CE to 199 CE.

100s	99–1	1–99	100s
second	first	first	second
century BCE	century BCE	century CE	century CE

Circa ("about" or "approximately") is used with dates, spelled out in the text and abbreviated to "c." in the captions, when an exact date is not yet verified.

An illustration is called a "figure," or "fig." Figure 6-70 is the seventieth numbered illustration in Chapter 6. Figures 1 through 29 are in the Introduction and the Starter Kit. There are two types of figures: photographs of artworks or of models, and line drawings. The latter are used when a work cannot be photographed or when a diagram or simple drawing is the clearest way to illustrate an object or a place.

When introducing artists, we use the words *active* and *documented* with dates—in addition to "b." (for "born") and "d." (for "died"). "Active" means that an artist worked during the years given. "Documented" means that documents link the person to the date.

Accents are used for words in Spanish, Italian, French, and German only.

With few exceptions, names of museums and other cultural bodies in Western European countries are given in the form used in that country.

Titles of Works of Art   Most paintings and sculpture created in Europe and the United States in the last 500 years have been given formal titles, either by the artist or by critics and art historians. Such formal titles are printed in italics. In other traditions and cultures, a single title is not important or even recognized. In this book we use formal titles of artworks in cases where they are established and descriptive titles of artworks where titles are not established. If a work is best known by its non-English title, such as Manet's *Dejeuner sur l'Herbe* (*Luncheon on the Grass*), the original language precedes the translation.

CHAPTER 1

Prehistory and Prehistoric Art in Europe

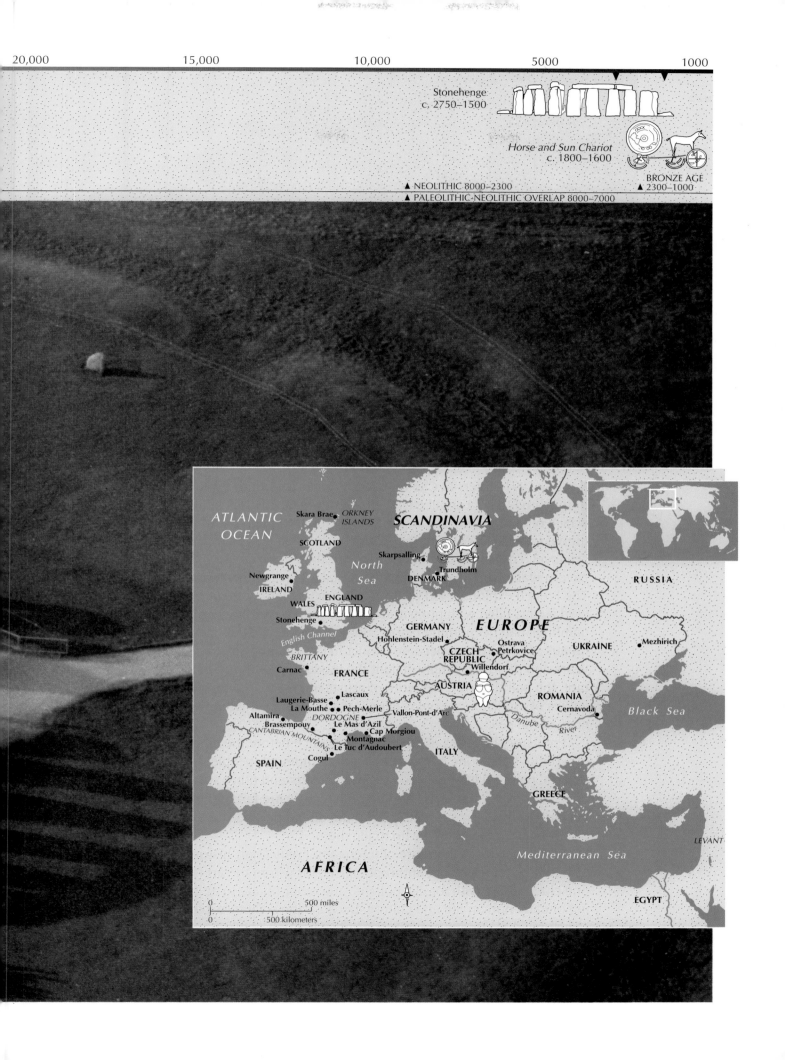

Stonehenge
c. 2750–1500

Horse and Sun Chariot
c. 1800–1600

BRONZE AGE
2300–1000

▲ NEOLITHIC 8000–2300
▲ PALEOLITHIC-NEOLITHIC OVERLAP 8000–7000

ATLANTIC
OCEAN

Skara Brae • ORKNEY ISLANDS

SCANDINAVIA

SCOTLAND

Skarpsalling •

North Sea

Trundholm •

Newgrange •

DENMARK

IRELAND

RUSSIA

WALES   ENGLAND

Stonehenge •

GERMANY   EUROPE

English Channel

Hohlenstein-Stadel •

UKRAINE   • Mezhirich

BRITTANY

Ostrava
• Petrkovice

CZECH
REPUBLIC

Carnac •   FRANCE

• Willendorf

AUSTRIA

ROMANIA

Lascaux •

Danube River

Black Sea

Laugerie-Basse •

La Mouthe •   • Pech-Merle

• Cernavoda

Altamira •   DORDOGNE

Vallon-Pont-d'Arc

Brassempouy •   • Le Mas d'Azil

CANTABRIAN MOUNTAINS   • Cap Morgiou

Montagnac •

Le Tuc d'Audoubert

ITALY

SPAIN   Cogul •

GREECE

Mediterranean Sea

AFRICA

LEVANT

EGYPT

0 _____ 500 miles
0 _____ 500 kilometers

1-1. *Auk,* Cosquer cave, Cap Morgiou, France. c. 16,500 BCE. Charcoal and manganese dioxide on limestone

In July 1991, divers at Cap Morgiou, France, set out to explore what appeared to be a small cave with an entrance 121 feet below the surface of the Mediterranean. After swimming through a narrow, rising tunnel for nearly 600 feet, they suddenly bobbed up into a cavern above sea level. Looking around, they found to their amazement that the cavern walls were decorated with animal images and human handprints. The French explorers, led by diving instructor Henri Cosquer, had discovered a cave filled with prehistoric paintings in a region where no such paintings had been found before. Some of them, like the image of a playful auk, a seabird that became extinct in the Mediterranean about 150 years ago (fig. 1-1), simply delight the modern viewer. But more important, the paintings are the work of artists who recorded the interests and values of prehistoric peoples living on a hillside near what was then the edge of the sea.

Prehistory includes all of human existence before the emergence of writing. Long, long before that defining moment, people were carving objects, painting images, and creating shelters and other structures. These works of prehistoric art and architecture are fascinating in part because they are so supremely beautiful and in part because of what they disclose about the people who made them.

Prehistoric art is therefore of interest not only to art historians, but also to archeologists and anthropologists, for whom the art is only one clue—along with fossils, pollens, and other finds—to an understanding of early human life and culture. Because the sculpture, paintings, and structures that survive are only the tiniest fraction of what was created over such a long span of time, conclusions and interpretations drawn from them have to be quite theoretical, making prehistoric art one of the most speculative areas of art history.

THE PALEOLITHIC PERIOD

Archeological evidence indicates that the earliest upright human species came into being 4.4 million years ago in Africa. How and when modern humans evolved is the subject of lively debate, but anthropologists now agree that the hominids called *Homo sapiens* ("wise humans") appeared about 200,000 years ago and that the species to which we belong, *Homo sapiens sapiens*, evolved about 120,000 to 100,000 years ago. Modern humans spread across Asia, into Europe, and finally to Australia and the Americas. The results of the most recently developed dating techniques suggest that this vast movement of people took place much earlier than anthropologists had thought possible, mainly between 100,000 and 20,000 years ago. Not only did these early modern humans have the ability to travel great distances, but as the introduction to the galleries of the National Museum of Natural History in Washington, D.C., notes, they had "aesthetic spirit and questing intellect." This book presents the tangible record of that uniquely human "aesthetic spirit."

Systematic study of ancient remains began only about 200 years ago. Struck by the wealth of stone tools, weapons, and figures found at ancient living sites, those first scholars named the whole period of early human development the "Stone Age." Today's researchers divide the Stone Age into three major periods: the Paleolithic (from the Greek *paleo-*, "old," and *lithos*, "stone"), the Meso-lithic (Greek *meso-*, "middle"), and the Neolithic (Greek *neo-*, "new"). The Paleolithic period is itself divided into three phases, Lower, Middle, and Upper, reflecting their relative position in excavated strata, or layers. The Upper Paleolithic period in Europe began between 42,000 and 37,000 years ago and lasted until the end of the Ice Age, about 9000–8000 BCE. Much of northern Europe was covered by glaciers in the transitional period between the Upper Paleolithic and Neolithic and therefore presents few human traces from the period, which corresponds to the Mesolithic in other parts of the world. With the gradual retreat of the ice, people from the Near East migrated onto the continent between about 11,000 and 8,000 years ago, bringing the beginnings of Neolithic culture with them. Although the precise dates for these periods vary from place to place, the divisions are useful as we examine developments in the arts. This chapter presents the prehistoric art of Europe; later chapters consider the prehistoric art of other continents and cultures.

In the Upper Paleolithic period, very long before the development of writing, our early ancestors created another form of communication: the visual arts. Many examples of sculpture, painting, architecture, and other arts have survived the long passage of time to move us, challenge us, and provide us with insights into the lives and beliefs of their makers. Nevertheless, it is nearly impossible to determine what "art" communicated to the people who experienced it in such early times, or what values its creators attached to it.

36,000 BCE 1000 BCE

PARALLELS

Years	Period	Prehistoric Europe	World
c. 40,000–8000 BCE	Upper Paleolithic	*Lion-Human*; *Woman from Willendorf*; mammoth-bone shelters; cave paintings	**70,000–8000 BCE** Ice Age
			11,500–10,000 BCE Wooden buildings in South America (Chile); first pottery vessels (Japan); dogs domesticated; bow and arrow
c. 8000–7000 BCE	Paleolithic-Neolithic overlap		
c. 8000–2300 BCE	Neolithic	End of Ice Age; plants domesticated; Skara Brae settled; megalithic tombs; unfired clay vessels; Stonehenge; megalithic figures	**8000–1000 BCE** Plants domesticated, animal husbandry (Near East, Southeast Asia, the Americas); potter's wheel (Egypt); development of metallurgy (Near East); earliest pictographs (Sumer); development of writing (China, India); Great Pyramids at Giza (Egypt); *Stela of Hammurabi* (Babylonia)
c. 2300–1000 BCE	Bronze Age	*Horse and Sun Chariot*	

1-2. Reconstruction drawing of mammoth-bone house from
     Ukraine. c. 16,000–10,000 BCE

The Beginning of Architecture

People have always found ingenious ways of providing
themselves with shelter. It was always possible to
occupy the mouth of a cave or to fashion a hut or tent
next to a protective cliff. Traditionally, *architecture* has
been a term applied to the enclosure of spaces with at
least some aesthetic intent, and some would object to
its use in connection with such improvisations. But
building even the simplest of shelters requires a degree
of imagination and planning deserving of the name
"architecture."

In the Upper Paleolithic period, people in some regions were building shelters that were far from simple.
Circular or oval huts of light branches and hides might
measure as much as 15 to 20 feet in diameter. (Modern
tents to accommodate six people vary from 10-by-11-
foot ovals to 14-by-7-foot rooms.) Some peoples colored
their floors with powdered ocher, a naturally occurring
iron ore ranging in color from yellow to red to brown.
Most activities were centered on the inside fire pit, or
hearth; it was there that food was prepared and tools and
utensils were fashioned. Larger dwellings might have
had more than one hearth and other spaces set aside for
different uses—working stone, making clothing, sleeping, and dumping refuse.

Well-preserved examples of Upper Paleolithic dwellings in Russia and Ukraine reveal the great ingenuity of
peoples living in those less-hospitable northern regions.
To meet the need for solid, weatherproof shelter in the
treeless grasslands, these builders created settlements of
up to ten houses using the bones of the woolly mammoth, a kind of elephant now extinct (fig. 1-2). One of the
best-preserved mammoth-bone villages, discovered in
Mezhirich, Ukraine, dates from 16,000–10,000 BCE. Most
of its houses were from 13 to 26 feet in diameter, and the
largest one measured 24 by 33 feet and was cleverly
constructed of dozens of mammoth skulls, shoulder
blades, pelvis bones, jawbones, and tusks. The long,
curving tusks made excellent roof supports and effective
arched door openings. The bone framework was probably covered with animal hides and turf. Inside the
dwelling, archeologists found fifteen small hearths that
still contained ashes and charred bones left by its final
occupants.

1-3. *Lion-Human*, from Hohlenstein-Stadel, Germany.
     c. 30,000–26,000 BCE. Mammoth ivory, height 11⅝"
     (29.6 cm). Ulmer Museum, Ulm, Germany

Small Sculpture

The earliest known works of sculpture are small figures,
or figurines, of people and animals and date from about
32,000 BCE. Thousands of such figures in bone, ivory,
stone, and clay have been found across Europe and Asia.

A human figure carved from a piece of mammoth
ivory nearly a foot tall—much larger than most early
figurines—was found broken into numerous fragments
at Hohlenstein-Stadel, Germany (fig. 1-3). At first it appeared that its head had been lost, but when one of
the excavators placed the head from what was thought
to be another figurine atop the reassembled body, it was
found to be a perfect fit. Astonishingly, the head in question represented some species of cat. Was this lively,
powerful figure intended to represent a person wearing

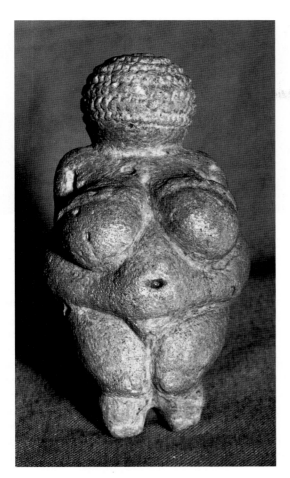

1-4. *Woman from Willendorf*, Austria. c. 22,000–21,000 BCE. Limestone, height 4³/₈" (11 cm). Naturhistorisches Museum, Vienna

1-5. *Woman from Ostrava Petrkovice*, Czech Republic. c. 23,000 BCE. Hematite, height 1³/₄" (4.6 cm). Archeological Institute, Brno

a lion mask and taking part in some ritual? Or is this a portrayal of some imagined creature, half human and half beast? The inability to identify and interpret the figures portrayed in the art of this early period is frustrating. Some conclusions about the material existence of prehistoric people can be drawn from the available evidence—their physical appearance, their diet, tools, and types of dwellings. It is even possible to guess something of their social organization and attitudes toward each other. But it is much more difficult to form any notion of their intellectual and spiritual life. One of the few things that can be said conclusively about the *Lion-Human* is that it took sophisticated thinking to create such a creature never seen in nature. With considerable technical skill, a gifted artist from as long as 30,000 years ago managed to produce a work that still inspires wonder.

Animals and unclothed women are the subjects of most of the small sculpture from the Upper Paleolithic period. The most famous female figure from the period was discovered near Willendorf, Austria. The *Woman from Willendorf* (fig. 1-4) dates from about 22,000–21,000 BCE and is a mere 4³/₈ inches tall. Carved from limestone and originally colored with red ocher, the figure is composed of rounded shapes that convey stability, dignity, and permanence—and incidentally make the work seem

much larger than it actually is. The sculptor has carved the stone in such a way as to convey the body's fleshiness, exaggerating its female attributes by giving it pendulous breasts, a big belly with deep navel, wide hips, and solid thighs. The gender-neutral parts of the body—the face, the arms, the legs—have been reduced to mere vestiges.

Another carved figure found in what is now the Czech Republic, the *Woman from Ostrava Petrkovice*, presents an entirely different perception of the female form (fig. 1-5). It is less than 2 inches tall and dates from about 23,000 BCE. Archeologists excavating an oval house stockpiled with flintstone and rough chunks of hematite, the iron oxide ore powdered to make ocher pigment, discovered the figure next to the hearth. Someone at the house had apparently picked up one of the pieces of hematite and shaped it into the figure of a youthful, athletic woman in an animated pose, with one hip slightly raised and a knee bent as if she were walking.

The hematite woman is so beautiful that one longs to be able to see her face. Perhaps it resembled the one preserved on a fragment from another female figure found in France. This is a tiny head in ivory known as the *Woman from Brassempouy* (fig. 1-6), which dates from about 22,000 BCE. The person who carved it was

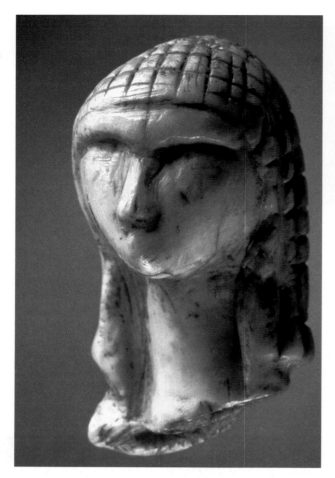

1-6. *Woman from Brassempouy*, Grotte du Pape, Brassempouy, Landes, France. c. 22,000 BCE. Ivory, height 1¼" (3 cm). Musée des Antiquités Nationales, St.-Germain-en-Laye

1-7. *Pregnant Woman and Deer* (?), from Laugerie-Basse, France. c. 14,000–10,000 BCE. Engraved reindeer antler, 2½ x 4" (6.7 x 10.5 cm). Musée des Antiquités Nationales, St.-Germain-en-Laye

concerned solely with those contours necessary to identify the piece as a human head—an egg shape atop a graceful neck, a wide nose, and a strongly defined browline suggesting deep-set eyes. The cap of shoulder-length hair is decorated with a grid pattern perhaps representing curls or braiding. This is an example of **abstraction**: the reduction of shapes and appearances to basic forms that do not faithfully reproduce those of the thing represented.

Instead of copying a specific person's face detail by detail, the artist provided only those features common to all of us. This is what is known as a memory image, one that relies on the generic shapes and relationships that readily spring to mind at the mention of a specific object—in this case the human head. Although it is impossible to know what motivated the artist to carve them in just this way, the simplified planes of the tiny face from Brassempouy appeal to our twentieth-century taste for abstraction. Intentionally or not, with this figure some prehistoric artist managed to communicate something essentially human. Even isolated from any cultural context, its human presence shines across the millennia.

Because so many of the surviving human figures from the period are female, some scholars have speculated that prehistoric societies were matriarchal, or dominated by women. Others believe that these female

figures, many of them visibly pregnant, are a reflection of the religious notions of these early people. They suggest that early religion was chiefly concerned with perpetuating the familiar cycles of nature, thereby ensuring the continuing life of people, animals, and vegetation, and that these female figurines were created as fertility symbols. Quite likely, the *Woman from Willendorf,* the *Woman from Brassempouy,* and other Upper Paleolithic figures like them did have such a function (see "The Power of Naming," opposite). But they can also be interpreted as representations of actual women, as expressions of ideal beauty, as erotic images, as ancestor figures, or even as dolls meant to help young girls learn women's roles. Given the diversity of ages and physical types represented, it is possible that they were any or all of these.

Such self-contained, three-dimensional pieces are examples of **sculpture in the round**. Prehistoric carvers also produced **relief sculpture** in stone, bone, and ivory. In relief sculpture the surrounding material is carved away to a certain depth, forming a background that sets off the figure. A fine example of portable relief carving from the Upper Paleolithic is a 4-inch fragment of reindeer antler, dating from about 14,000–10,000 BCE, that reveals a new complexity in both subject matter and technique (fig. 1-7). On the side shown, a large deer or bison stands over a reclining woman who is unmistakably pregnant. The carver observed and rendered the slender woman's enlarged abdomen quite accurately. To emphasize the figures' contours, which are carved in very **low relief**, the artist used both **U-** and **V-**shaped gouges along with a technique called **beveling**—cutting at an angle—to create more-pronounced shadows. Also, by interrupting the lines of the woman's legs to make way for those of the deer, the artist created the illusion of space, with one figure realistically positioned behind the other. The woman wears bracelets on her raised left arm and also possibly a necklace, reflecting the delight human beings have taken in adorning themselves since very early times. As early as 35,000 years ago, they made ornamental beads from shells, teeth, bone, ivory, and stone, and at least 23,000 years ago they buried their dead with bits of finery like headbands and necklaces.

THE POWER OF NAMING

Words are only symbols for ideas. But the very words we invent—or our ancestors invented—reveal a certain view of the world and can shape our thinking. Early people recognized quite clearly the power of words and names. In the Old Testament, God gave Adam dominion over the animals (Genesis 1:28) and allowed him to name them: ". . . whatever the man called each of them, that would be its name. The man gave names to all the cattle, all the birds of the air, and all the wild animals" (Genesis 2:19–20). Today, we still exert the power of naming when we select a name for a baby, call a friend by a complimentary nickname, or use demeaning words to dehumanize those we dislike.

Our ideas about a work of art can also be affected by names, even the ones used in a caption in a book. Before the twentieth century, many works of art had no "names." Names were eventually supplied by the works' owners or by scholars writing about them. The names thus attached to works may express the cultural prejudices of those responsible for them or of the times generally.

An excellent example of such distorting prejudice is provided by the names early scholars gave to the hundreds of small prehistoric statues of women they found. The first of these to be discovered (see fig. 1-4) was promptly dubbed the "Venus of Willendorf" after the place where it had been found. Venus was the Roman goddess of love and beauty, and the use of her name for the newly discovered figure sent a message that this figure was associated with religious belief, that it represented an ideal of womanhood, and that it was one of a long line of images of "classical" feminine beauty. In no time, the majority of such sculptures from the Upper Paleolithic came to be known as "Venus figures." The name was repeated so often that even scholars began to assume that these had to be fertility figures and mother goddesses. In fact, they probably were, although there is no absolute proof that the sculptures had religious significance or were imputed to have supernatural powers. What if these simply represent obese women?

Our ability to understand and interpret works of art creatively is easily compromised by distracting labels. Even knowing that the figure was once labeled the "Venus of Willendorf" influences the way we look at it. The tradition of a name, no matter how wrongheaded, makes it extremely difficult to challenge accepted belief. Calling a prehistoric figure a "woman" instead of "Venus" frees us to think about it in new and different ways.

Cave Art

About 30,000 years ago, art in Europe entered a rich and sophisticated phase. Many of the images painted on the walls of caves in southern France and northern Spain were painted between circa 28,000 and 10,000 BCE. The earliest known site of prehistoric cave paintings in Europe was discovered in December 1994 near Vallon-Pont-d'Arc in southern France—a tantalizing trove of hundreds of animal and bird paintings (see fig. 1). The caves in question must have had a special meaning, because people returned to them time after time over many generations, in some cases over thousands of years. These subterranean galleries were not used as living quarters, but the evidence of artifacts and footprints suggests that they were gathering places where the social bond was somehow reaffirmed and strengthened. It may be that people congregated in them to celebrate initiation rites or the sealing of social alliances—just as we gather today for baptisms, bar mitzvahs, weddings, funerals, or town meetings.

The most dramatic of these cave images are paintings of grazing, running, or resting animals. Among the animals represented are the wild horse, the bison, the mammoth, the bear, the panther, the owl, deer, aurochs (extinct ancestors of oxen), the woolly-haired rhino, and the wild goat, or ibex. Also included are occasional people, both male and female, many handprints, and hundreds of geometric markings such as grids, circles, and dots. The paintings of animals in the Cosquer cave at Cap Morgiou (see fig. 1-1) were created about 16,500 BCE, but the first of the handprints found there date from long before, as early as 25,000 BCE. In other caves, painters

1-8. *Spotted Horses and Human Hands*, Pech-Merle cave, Dordogne, France. c. 16,000 BCE. Paint on limestone, length approx. 11'2" (3.4 m)

worked not only in large caverns but also far back in the smallest chambers and recesses, many of which are almost inaccessible today. Small stone lamps found in such caves (see fig. 1-15) indicate that they worked in the dim flicker of light from burning animal fat. Occasional small holes have been found carved into a cave's rock walls. These may have been used to anchor the scaffolding needed for painting the cave's high ceilings and walls.

A cave site at Pech-Merle, in France, appears to have been used and abandoned several times over a period of 5,000 years. Images of animals, handprints, and nearly

600 geometric symbols have been found in thirty different parts of the underground complex. The earliest artists to work in the cave, some 18,000 years ago, specialized in painting horses (fig. 1-8). All of their horses have small, finely detailed heads, heavy bodies, massive extended necks, and legs tapering to almost nothing at the hooves. The horses were then overlaid with bright red circles. Some interpreters see these circles as ordinary spots on the animals' coats, but others see them as magic rock weapons hurled at the painted horses in a ritual meant to assure success in the hunt.

The handprints on the walls at Pech-Merle and other cave sites were almost certainly not idle graffiti or accidental smudges but were intended to communicate something. Some are positive images made by simply coating the hand with color pigment and pressing it against the wall. Others are negative images: the surrounding space rather than the hand shape itself is painted. Negative images were made by placing the hand with fingers spread apart against the wall, then spitting or spraying paint around it with a reed blowpipe—an artist's tool found in such caves. Most of the handprints are small enough to be those of women or even children, yet footprints preserved in the mud floors at other caves show that they were visited by people of all sizes. A series of giant aurochs at Pech-Merle, painted in simple outlines without color, has been dated to a later period, about 15,000 BCE. Sometime afterward, other figures were created near the mouth of the cave by **incising**, or scratching lines into the walls' surface. Thanks to rapid advances in laboratory analysis techniques, it is only a matter of time until all prehistoric wall paintings can be dated more precisely.

The first cave paintings attributed to the Upper Paleolithic period were those discovered at Altamira, near Santander in the Cantabrian Mountains of northern

TECHNIQUE

PREHISTORIC WALL PAINTING

In a dark cave in France, working by the light of a flickering lamp fueled with animal fat, an artist places charcoal in his mouth, chews it, diluting it with saliva and water, then spews it out against the wall, using his hand as a stencil. The artist is Michel Lorblanchet, a cave archeologist. He is showing us how the original artists at Pech-Merle created their magnificent paintings. Other archeologists use sophisticated scientific techniques to analyze the color pigments they used to date their works, but Lorblanchet, inspired by his research on the cave painting of Australian aboriginals, seeks to re-create the actual experience of those early painters.

Having successfully reproduced a smaller painting of animals in 1979, Lorblanchet turned to the best-known and most complex of the Pech-Merle paintings, the one of the spotted horses. He first made a light sketch in charcoal, then painted the horses' outlines using the spitting technique described above. By turning himself into a human spray can, he can produce clear lines on the rough stone surface much more easily than he could with a brush. To create the line of a horse's back, with its clean upper edge and blurry lower one, he simply blew pigment below his hand; to capture its angular rump, he placed his hand vertically against the wall, holding it slightly curved; to produce the sharpest lines, such as those of the upper hind leg and tail, he placed his hands side by side and blew between them. The forelegs and the hair on the horses' bellies he executed with finger painting, and to create a stencil for the dense, round spots he punched a hole in a piece of leather. In some places he chose to blow a thicker pigment through a reed, in others he applied it with a brush made by chewing the end of a twig.

Lorblanchet had painted his first panel in less than two hours; thirty-two hours were needed to reproduce the spotted horses. The fact that he could execute such a work in a relatively short time tends to confirm that a single artist—perhaps with the help of an assistant to mix pigments and tend the lamp—created the original. It has also been noted that all of the handprints are the same size. The main pigments used in the original were ochers for the reds and manganese dioxide for the blacks. Since manganese dioxide is poisonous if swallowed, Lorblanchet worked with charcoal. Jean Clottes, who has studied the composition of pigments used in cave painting in France and contributed a great deal toward their accurate dating, has determined that pigments used in a given region remained fairly consistent but that the "recipe" for the medium—the precise mix of saliva, water, and other liquids used to bind them—varied over time and from place to place.

Scientists are now very close to pinning down exactly when a given cave painting was executed, and imaginative archeologists like Lorblanchet are showing us how they were done. Although we may never know just what these paintings meant to the artists who produced them, the very process of creating them must have been rich with significance. Lorblanchet puts it quite eloquently: "Human breath, the most profound expression of a human being, literally breathes life onto a cave wall" (*Archeology*, November–December 1991, page 30).

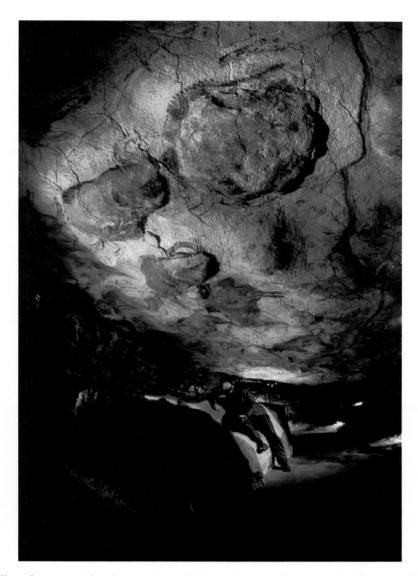

1-9. *Bison*, on the ceiling of a cave at Altamira, Spain. c. 12,000 BCE. Paint on limestone, length approx. 8'3" (2.5 m)

No one knew of the existence of prehistoric cave painting until one day in 1879, when a young girl exploring with her father on the family estate in Altamira crawled through a small opening in the ground and found herself in a cave chamber whose ceiling was covered with painted animals. Her father searched the rest of the cave, then told authorities about the remarkable find. Few people believed that these amazing works could have been done by "primitive" people, and the scientific community declared the paintings a hoax. They were accepted as authentic only in 1902, after many other cave paintings, drawings, and engravings had been discovered at other spots in northern Spain and in France.

Spain. They were recently determined to have been created about 12,000 BCE. The Altamira artists painted the bodies of their animals over and around natural irregularities in the cave's walls and ceilings to create sculptural effects. To produce the herd of bison on the ceiling of the main cavern (fig. 1-9), they used rich red and brown ochers to paint the large areas of the animals' shoulders, backs, and flanks, then added the details of the legs, tails, heads, and horns in black and brown. They must have observed the bison herd with great care in order to capture the distinctive appearance of the beasts.

The best-known cave paintings are those found in 1940 at Lascaux, in the Dordogne region of southern France. These have been dated to about 15,000–13,000

BCE (fig. 1-10). The Lascaux artists also used the contours of the rock as part of their compositions (fig. 1-11). They painted cows, bulls, horses, and deer along natural ledges, where the smooth, white limestone of the ceiling and upper wall meets a rougher surface below. The animals appear singly, in rows, face to face, tail to tail, and even painted on top of one other. As in other caves, their most characteristic features have been emphasized. Horns, eyes, and hooves are shown as seen from the front, yet heads and bodies are rendered in profile. Even when their poses are exaggerated or distorted, the animals are full of life and energy, and the accuracy in the drawing of their silhouettes, or outlines, still astonishes us.

36,000 BCE   1000 BCE

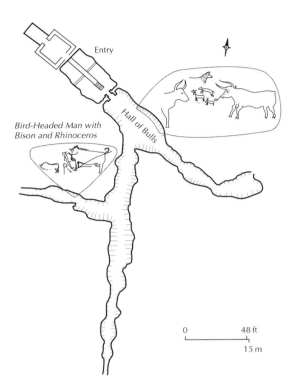

Entry

Bird-Headed Man with Bison and Rhinoceros

Hall of Bulls

0   48 ft

15 m

1-10. Plan of Lascaux caves, Dordogne, France

One scene at Lascaux is unusual not only because it includes a human figure but also because it is the only painting in the cave complex that seems to tell a story (fig. 1-12). It was discovered on a wall at the bottom of a 16-foot shaft containing spears and a stone lamp. A figure who could be a hunter, highly stylized but recognizably male and wearing a bird's-head mask, appears to be lying on the ground. A great bison looms above him. Below him lie a staff, or baton, and a spear thrower—a device that allowed hunters to throw farther and with greater force—the outer end of which has been carved in the shape of a bird. The long, diagonal line slanting across the bison's hindquarters is a spear. The bison has been disemboweled and will soon die. To the left of the cleft in the wall is a woolly rhinoceros—possibly the bison's slayer.

What is this scene really telling us? Why did the artist portray the man as only a sticklike figure when the bison was rendered with such accurate detail? It may be that the painting illustrates a myth or legend regarding the death of a hero. Perhaps it illustrates an actual event. Or it might depict the vision of a shaman. Shamans were—and still are—people thought to have special powers, an ability to foretell events and assist their people through contact with spirits. They typically make use of trance

1-11. Hall of Bulls, Lascaux caves. c. 15,000–13,000 BCE. Paint on limestone

Discovered in 1940 and opened to the public after World War II, the prehistoric "museum" at Lascaux soon became one of the most popular tourist sites in France. Too popular, for the many visitors sowed the seeds of the paintings' destruction in the form of heat, humidity, exhaled carbon dioxide, and other insidious contaminants from the outside world. The cave was closed to the public in 1963, so that conservators might battle with an aggressive fungus that had attacked the paintings. Eventually they won, but instead of reopening the site, the authorities created a facsimile of it. Visitors at what is called Lascaux II may now view copies of the painted scenes without harming the precious originals.

44   PREHISTORY AND PREHISTORIC ART IN EUROPE

1-12. *Bird-Headed Man with Bison and Rhinoceros*, Lascaux caves. Paint on limestone, length approx. 9' (2.75 m)

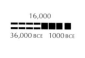

states, in which they claim to receive communications from their spirit guides. The images they use to record their visions tend to be abstract, incorporating geometric figures and combinations of human and animal forms such as the bird-headed man in this scene from Lascaux or the lion-headed figure discussed above (see fig. 1-3). Some scholars have interpreted the horses with red dots on them at Pech-Merle as a shamanistic combination of natural and geometric forms. Shamans have claimed that the dots make the spirits' images permanent.

Caves were sometimes adorned with relief sculpture as well as paintings. In some instances, an artist simply heightened the resemblance of a natural projecting rock to a familiar animal form. Other reliefs were created by **modeling**, or shaping, the damp clay of the cave's floor. An excellent example of such work in clay from about 13,000 BCE is preserved at Le Tuc d'Audoubert, in the Dordogne region of France. Working with the clay underfoot, some early sculptor created two bison leaning against a ridge of rock (fig. 1-13). A third, smaller bison lies on the

1-13. *Bison*, Le Tuc d'Audoubert, Ariège, France. c. 13,000 BCE. Unbaked clay, length 25" (63.5 cm) and 24" (60.9 cm)

16,000

36,000 BCE   1000 BCE

cave floor. Although these beasts are modeled in very **high relief**, they display the same conventions as earlier painted ones, with emphasis on the broad masses of the meat-bearing flanks and shoulders. To make the animals even more lifelike, their creator engraved short parallel lines below their necks to represent their shaggy coats. Numerous small footprints found in the clay floor of this cave must have been left by young people, suggesting that initiation rites may well have been performed here.

The prehistoric artists who worked in caves must have felt that their art would be of some specific benefit to their communities. Perhaps Upper Paleolithic cave art was the product of rituals intended to gain the favor of supernatural forces. If so, its significance may have had less to do with the finished painting than with the very act of creating it.

THE MEANING OF PREHISTORIC CAVE PAINTINGS

What motivated people 30,000 or even 15,000 years ago to paint thousands of images of humans and animals on the walls of caves? During the last hundred years, anthropologists and art historians have devised countless theories to explain prehistoric art, but these often tell us as much about the theorizers and their times as they do about the art itself. For all their useful insights, scholars still have not fully explained the meaning of these images.

The idea that human beings have an inherent desire to decorate themselves and their surroundings—that an "aesthetic sense" is somehow innate to the human species—found ready acceptance in the nineteenth century. That was the century in which some artists promoted the idea of "art for art's sake," and many believed that people created works of art for the sheer love of beauty. Scientists agree that human beings have an aesthetic impulse and take pleasure in pursuing nonpractical activities, but the effort and organization required to accomplish the great paintings of Lascaux indicate that their creators were motivated by more than simple pleasure.

Early in the twentieth century, scholars rejected the idea of art for art's sake as a romantic notion. Led by Salomon Reinach, who believed that art fulfills a social function and that aesthetics are culturally relative, they proposed that prehistoric cave paintings might be products both of totemistic ceremonies, rites performed to strengthen the bonds within specific clans, and of increase ceremonies, or attempts to enhance the fertility of the animals on which people depended for food. In 1903 Reinach proposed that cave paintings were expressions of "sympa-thetic magic." Encountered in many societies to this day, sympathetic magic relies on two principal assumptions: first, that things that look the same can have a physical influence on each other, and second, that things once in contact continue to act upon each other even at great distances. In the case of cave paintings, it may have been thought that producing a picture of a bison lying down would make sure that hunters found their prey asleep, or that ritual killing of the picture of a bison would ensure the hunters' triumph over the beast itself.

In the early 1920s, Abbé Henri Breuil took these ideas somewhat further and concluded that cave paintings were early forms of religious expression. Convinced that caves were used as places of worship and the settings for initiation rites, he interpreted them as aids in rituals and in instruction.

In the second half of the twentieth century, scholars have tended to base their interpretations on rigorous scientific method and current social theory. Leading French scholars such as André Leroi-Gourhan and Annette Laming-Emperaire dismissed the "hunting magic" theory, noting that analysis of debris from human settlements revealed that the animals used most frequently for food were not the ones traditionally portrayed in cave art. Influenced by structuralist theories, these same scholars discovered that cave images were often systematically organized, with different animals predominating in different areas of the cave.

Although they disagreed on details, Leroi-Gourhan and Laming-Emperaire concluded that the cave images are definitely meaningful pictures. As Laming-Emperaire put it, the paintings "might be mythical representations . . . they might be the concrete expression of a very ancient metaphysical system . . . they might be religious, depicting supernatural beings. They might be all these at one and the same time . . ." (Annette Laming-Emperaire, *La signification de l'art rupestre paléolithique*, 1962, pages 236–237). She felt certain that horses, bison, and women suggested "calm, peace, harmony," and were "concerned with love and life."

Ongoing research continues to discover new cave images and correct earlier errors of fact or interpretation. A restudy of the Altamira cave in the 1980s led Leslie G. Freeman to conclude that there artists had faithfully represented a herd of bison during the mating season, with females occupying the center space and males standing at the outside to defend the herd. Instead of being dead, asleep, or disabled—as earlier observers had supposed—the bison on the ground are simply "dust wallowing," common behavior during the breeding season. All in all, Freeman concluded that the great ceiling mural is simply a depiction of what hunters actually might have seen in late summer.

The recent discovery of paintings in the cave at Cap Morgiou reminds us how great a role chance plays in our endeavors. Meanwhile, rigorous scientific experimentation and the development of new dating techniques have enhanced our ability to place prehistoric artifacts in time with greater accuracy (see "How Early Art Is Dated," page 49). Anthropological studies have extended our knowledge of the cultures out of which cave art emerged. The study of cave painting is a rapidly changing field. It is altogether appropriate that curators at the National Museum of Natural History in Washington, D.C., chose to place over their ever-changing exhibit illustrating early human culture a prominent label reading "What's New."

Portable Art

An aesthetic sense and the ability to pose and solve problems are among the characteristics unique to human beings. That these characteristics were richly developed in very early times is evident from Paleolithic artifacts of all kinds. The most common tools and utensils of the period are not only functional but also portable works of art.

A spear thrower from Le Mas d'Azil in southwestern France (fig. 1-14) is a splendid example. It is about a foot long and made of antler. Geometric patterns decorate its shaft. The functional hook at the end takes the form of a young ibex in the process of giving birth.

Driven by the ever-present need to assure an adequate supply of food, early hunters devised an ingenious way to increase the range of their spears. All that was required was a stick with a notch or socket on one end. Balancing a spear atop the stick with the end of the shaft seated in the stick's socket, they could then swing their arm in a great arc, giving the spear much greater momentum before setting it in flight. They often carved the notched ends of such spear throwers into images of animals. We do not know whether these animals represented some sort of personal or family emblem serving to identify the thrower's owner or were intended to assure the hunter's triumph over the prey. The young ibex on this spear thrower could simply reflect the hunter's hope of finding the animal standing still. It may be that the carver of this hunting implement was honoring the forces of regeneration that are so powerfully manifest at the moment a new life enters the world. In any case, the carver's sharp observation of nature and skillful rendering of the birthing doe created a practical object that we readily appreciate today—in an age no longer in need of spear throwers—as an elegant work of art.

Prehistoric lamps provide another example of objects that were both functional and aesthetically pleasing. Some are carved in simple abstract shapes admirably designed to hold oil and wicks and to be easily portable. Others were adorned with engraved images, like one found at La Mouthe, France (fig. 1-15). The creator of this lamp decorated its bowl with the image of an ibex. The animal's distinctive head is shown in profile, its sweeping horns reflecting the curved outline of the lamp itself.

Objects like the ibex lamp were made by people whose survival, up until about 10,000 years ago, depended upon their skill at hunting animals and gathering wild grains and other edible plants. But a change was already under way that would alter human existence forever.

1-14. Ibex-headed spear thrower, from Le Mas d'Azil, Ariège, France. 16,000–9000 BCE. Carved antler, length 11⅝" (30 cm). Musée de la Préhistoire, Le Mas d'Azil

1-15. Lamp with ibex design, from La Mouthe cave, Dordogne, France. 15,000–13,000 BCE. Engraved stone, 6¾ x 4¾" (17.2 x 12 cm). Musée des Antiquités Nationales, St.-Germain-en-Laye

THE NEOLITHIC PERIOD

In modern times, advances in medicine, transportation, weapons, and communication have abruptly changed human life over the span of just a few generations. Many thousands of years ago, change came much more slowly. The warming of the climate that brought an end to the Ice Age was so gradual that the people of the time could not have known it was occurring, yet it altered life as dramatically as any changes that have come since. The retreating glaciers exposed large temperate regions, and rising ocean levels changed the shorelines of continents, in some places making islands of major land masses. It was in this period, for example, about 6000 BCE, that the land bridge connecting England with the rest of Europe disappeared beneath the waters of what are now known as the North Sea and the English Channel. Europe became covered with grassy plains supporting new edible plants and forests that lured great herds of animals, such as deer, farther and farther northward. At the same time, the people in these more-hospitable regions were finding ways to enhance their chances of survival. The bow and arrow was invented and became the weapon of choice for hunters. Bows were easier to carry and much more accurate at longer range than spears and spear throwers. Dugout boats came into use, opening up new areas for fishing and hunting. With each such advance the overall standard of living improved.

The changing environment led to a new way of life. Although still essentially hunters and gatherers, people began domesticating animals and working the land to cultivate plants. As they gained greater control over their food supply, they no longer had to move around as before but could establish settled communities. None of these changes occurred overnight. Between 10,000 and 5,000 years ago, peoples in the Levant—the lands along the eastern shore of the Mediterranean—began domesticating wild grasses, developing them into more-productive grains such as wheat. In this same period, the people of Southeast Asia learned to grow millet and rice and those in the Americas began to cultivate the bottle gourd and eventually corn. Dogs probably first joined with human hunters more than 11,000 years ago, and cattle, goats, and other animals were later domesticated along with plants. Large numbers of people became farmers, living in villages and producing more than enough food to support themselves—thus freeing some people in the village to attend to other communal needs. Over time these early societies became increasingly complex. Although the majority may still have been involved in the production of food, others specialized in political and military affairs, still others in matters of religion. The new farming culture gradually spread across Europe, reaching Spain and France by 5000 BCE. Farmers in the Paris region were using plows by 4000 BCE.

These fundamental changes in the prehistoric way of life mark the beginning of the Neolithic period. These shifts occurred in some regions sooner than others. To determine the onset of the Neolithic in a specific region, archeologists look for the evidence of three conditions: an organized, ongoing system of agriculture; animal husbandry, or the maintenance of herds of domesticated animals; and permanent, year-round settlements. By the end of the period, villages had increased in size, trading had been developed between distant regions, and advanced building technology had led to the construction of some of the world's most awe-inspiring architectural monuments.

Rock-Shelter Art

The period of transition between Paleolithic and Neolithic culture saw the rise of a distinctive art combining schematic images—simplified, diagrammatic renderings—and geometric forms with depictions of people and animals engaged in everyday activities. Artists of the time preferred to paint and engrave such works on easily accessible, shallow rock shelters. In style, technique, and subject matter, these rock-shelter images are quite different from those found in Upper Paleolithic cave art. The style is abstract, and the technique is often simple line drawing, with no addition of color. Paintings from this period portray striking new themes: people are depicted in energetic poses, whether engaged in battle, hunting, or possibly dancing. They are found in many places near the Mediterranean coast but are especially numerous, beginning about 6000 BCE, in a region located in northeastern Spain.

At Cogul, near Lérida in Catalonia, the large surfaces of a rock shelter are decorated with elaborate narrative scenes involving dozens of relatively small figures—men, women, children, animals, even insects (fig. 1-16). These date from between 4000 and 2000 BCE (see "How Early Art Is Dated," opposite). No specific landscape features are indicated, but occasional painted patterns of animal tracks give the sense of a rocky terrain, like that of the surrounding barren hillsides. In the detail shown here, a number of women are seen gracefully strolling or standing about, some in pairs holding hands. The women's small waists are emphasized by large, pendulous breasts. They wear skirts with scalloped hemlines revealing large calves and sturdy ankles, and all of them appear to have shoulder-length hair. The women stand near several long-horned cattle. These animals are larger than others appearing above, as though the artist wished to suggest a recession of the landscape into the distance, where other cattle, the Spanish ibex, red deer, and a pig can be seen grazing.

The manner in which this representation of distance has been created is a significant change in Upper Paleolithic painting. A pair of ibexes visible just above the cattle as well as a dog in the foreground are shown leaping forward with legs fully extended. This pose, called a flying gallop, has been used to indicate speed in a running animal from prehistory to the present.

In other paintings at the site, not shown here, some women seem to be looking after children while others carry baskets, gather food, and work the earth with digging sticks. It is easy to imagine that these paintings served solely as a record of daily life. They must have had some greater significance, however, for like other earlier cave paintings they were repainted many times over the centuries.

Because rock shelters were so accessible, people no doubt continued to visit these art sites long after their original purpose had been forgotten. At Cogul, in fact, there are inscriptions in Latin and an early form of Spanish left by Roman-era visitors—2,000-year-old graffiti intermingled with the much more ancient paintings.

1-16. *Women and Animals*, facsimile of detail of rock-shelter painting in Cogul, Lérida, Spain.
c. 4000–2000 BCE. Museo Arqueológico, Barcelona

HOW EARLY ART IS DATED When the first Upper Paleolithic cave paintings were discovered at Altamira, Spain, in 1879, they were promptly rejected as forgeries by the Lisbon Congress on Prehistoric Archeology. Seven years later, it was shown that similar paintings discovered in France were indeed thousands of years old because a layer of mineral deposits had built up on top of them. Since those first discoveries, archeologists have developed increasingly sophisticated ways of dating such finds. During the twentieth century, archeologists have primarily used two approaches to determine an artifact's age. **Relative dating** relies on the chronological relationships among objects in either a single excavation or several sites. If archeologists have determined, for example, that pottery types A, B, and C follow each other chronologically at one site, they can apply that knowledge to another site; even if "type B" is the only pottery present, it can be assigned a relative date. **Absolute dating** aims to determine a precise span of calendar years in which an artifact was created. Arriving at even approximate absolute dates for prehistoric sculpture, painting, and architecture is extremely difficult.

Dating a work of art is easiest if the site at which it is discovered has not been disturbed. Archeologists have developed painstaking methods by which they can record each find at a given "dig" by its area, the layer (or stratum) in which it was found, and its relationship to other artifacts and preset markers.

Radiometric dating measures the degree to which radioactive materials have disintegrated and is the most accurate of several methods of absolute dating. One of the earliest radiometric methods developed is still used for dating organic (plant or animal) materials—including some of the pigments used in cave paintings. It measures a carbon isotope called radiocarbon, or carbon-14. Another measures potassium-argon ratios. The carbon-14 content in a living organism is constantly being replenished. When the organism dies, it stops absorbing carbon-14 and starts to lose its store of it. Experiments over the years have determined the rates at which most types of dead organic matter lose their radiocarbon. Under the right circumstances, the amount of carbon-14 remaining in an artifact made of an organic material can tell us how long ago the organism died. This method has serious drawbacks for dating works of art, however. Using carbon-14 dating on a carved antler or wood sculpture shows only when the animal died or the tree was cut down, not when the artist created the work, which could have been centuries later. Also, some part of the object must be destroyed to conduct this kind of test—something rarely desirable in a work of art. For this reason, researchers frequently test organic materials found in the same context as the work of art rather than the work itself.

Radiocarbon dating is most accurate for materials no more than 30,000 to 40,000 years old. Potassium-argon dating, which measures the decay of a radioactive potassium isotope into a stable isotope of argon, an inert gas, is most reliable with materials more than a million years old. For the long span of time for which neither method is very reliable, two newer techniques have been used in reports since the mid-1980s. Thermoluminescence dating measures the irradiation of the crystal structure of a material such as flint or pottery and the soil in which it is found, determined by the luminescence produced when a sample is heated. Electron spin resonance techniques involve a magnetic field and microwave irradiation to date a material such as tooth enamel and its surrounding soil.

Recent experiments have helped to date cave paintings with increasing precision. Twelve different radiocarbon-analysis series have determined that the animal images in the Cosquer cave are definitely 18,500 years old, the handprints 27,000 years old. Jean Clottes's analysis of pigments used in other caves in France has shown that different generations of painters used different "recipes" when mixing their paints, a finding that further improves attempts to date particular cave paintings.

1-17. Plan, village of Skara Brae, Orkney Islands, Scotland. c. 3100–2600 BCE

Architecture

As people adopted a settled, agricultural way of life, they began to build large structures to serve as dwellings, storage spaces, and shelters for their animals. In Europe, timber had become abundant after the disappearance of the glaciers, and Neolithic people, like their Paleolithic predecessors, continued to construct buildings out of wood and other plant materials. People clustered their dwellings in villages and eventually larger towns, and outside their settlements, they built tombs and ritual centers so huge that they still have the power to fill us with awe.

Dwellings and Villages. A northern European village frequently consisted of only three or four long timber buildings, each of them housing forty-five to fifty people. These houses might be up to 150 feet long, and they included large granaries, or storage space for the harvest, a necessity in agricultural communities. The structures were rectangular, with a row of posts down the center supporting a ridgepole, a long horizontal beam against which the slanting roof poles were braced. Their walls were probably made of what is known as wattle and daub, branches woven in a basketlike pattern, then covered with mud or clay. They were most likely roofed with thatch, some plant material such as reeds or straw tied over a framework of poles. Similar structures can still be seen today in some regions, serving as animal shelters or even dwellings.

Around 4000 BCE, Neolithic settlers began to locate their communities at sites most easily defended, near rivers, on plateaus, or in swamps. For additional protection, they also frequently surrounded them with wooden walls, earth embankments, and ditches.

A Neolithic settlement has been excellently preserved at Skara Brae, in the Orkney Islands off the northern coast of Scotland (fig. 1-17). This one happens to have been constructed of stone, an abundant building material in this austere, treeless landscape. A huge prehistoric storm buried this seaside village under a layer of sand. Another freak storm brought it to light again in 1850. The ruins thus exposed to view present a vivid picture of Neolithic life in the far north. Among the utensils found in these Orkney structures are stone cooking pots, a whalebone basin, a stone mortar for grinding, and pottery with incised decoration. Comparison of these artifacts with objects from sites farther south and laboratory analysis of the village's organic refuse date the settlement at Skara Brae to about 3100–2600 BCE, indicating that it lay buried for well over 4,000 years.

The village consists of a compact cluster of dwellings linked together by covered passageways. Each of the houses is in the shape of a square with rounded corners. The largest one measures 20 by 21 feet, the smallest 13 by 14 feet. Their walls were formed of layers of flat stones, with each layer, or **course**, projecting slightly inward over the one below. This type of construction is called **corbeling**. In some structures such inward-sloping walls come together at the top in what is known as a **corbel vault**, but at Skara Brae they stopped short of meeting, and the remaining open space was covered with hides or turf. There are smaller corbel-vaulted rooms within the main walls of some of the houses that may have been used for storage. One room, possibly a latrine, has a drain leading out under its wall.

The houses of Skara Brae were well equipped with space-saving built-in furniture. In the room shown (fig. 1-18), a large rectangular hearth with a stone seat at one end occupies the center of the space. Rectangular stone beds, some of them engraved with simple ornaments, stand against the walls on each side of the hearth. These boxlike beds would probably have been filled with heather "mattresses" and covered with warm furs. In the left corner is a sizable storage niche built into the thick outside wall. Smaller storage niches were provided over

1-18. House interior, Skara Brae (house 7 in fig. 1-17)

each of the beds. Stone tanks lined with clay to make them watertight are partly sunk into the floor. These were probably used as containers for live bait, for it is clear that the people at Skara Brae were skilled fisherfolk.

On the back wall is a two-shelf cabinet that is a splendid example of what is known as **post-and-lintel construction**. In this structural system, two or more vertical elements (posts) are used to support a bridging horizontal one (lintel). The principle has been used throughout history, not only for structures as simple as these shelves but also in huge stone monuments like Stonehenge (see fig. 1-23) and the temples of Egypt (Chapter 3) and Greece (Chapter 5).

Ceremonial and Tomb Architecture. In western and northern Europe, Neolithic people commonly erected ceremonial structures and tombs using huge stones. In some cases they had to transport these great stones over long distances. The monuments thus created are examples of what is known as megalithic architecture, the descriptive term derived from the Greek word roots for large *(mega-)* and stone *(lithos)*. Architecture formed of such massive elements testifies to a more complex, stratified society than any encountered before. Only

strong leaders could have assembled and maintained the required labor force. Skilled engineers were needed to devise methods for shaping, transporting, and aligning the stones. Finally, powerful religious figures must have been involved, identifying the society's need for such structures and dictating their design. The accomplishments of the builders of these monuments are all the more impressive considering the short life expectancy of the time. It was uncommon for anyone to survive past the age of thirty. As one anthropologist has noted, these imposing structures were the work of teenagers.

Elaborate megalithic tombs first appeared in the Neolithic period. Some were built for single burials, others as mausoleums consisting of multiple burial chambers. The simplest type of megalithic tomb was the **dolmen**, built on the post-and-lintel principle. The tomb chamber was formed of huge upright stones supporting one or more tablelike rocks, or **capstones**. The structure was then mounded over with smaller rocks and dirt to form what is called a **cairn**. A more imposing structure was the **passage grave**, which was entered by one or more narrow, stone-lined passageways into a large room at the cairn's center (see "Elements of Architecture," page 53).

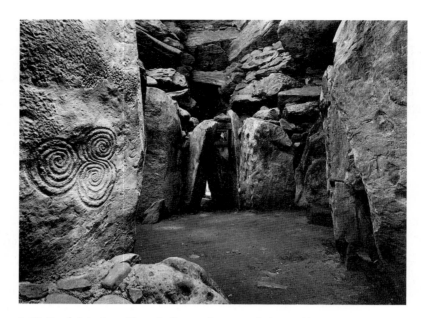

1-19. Tomb interior with corbeling and engraved stones, Newgrange,
Ireland. c. 3000–2500 BCE

1-20. Menhir alignments at Ménec, Carnac, France. c. 4250–3750 BCE

One legend of Celtic Brittany explains the origin of the Carnac menhirs quite graphically. It relates that a defeated army retreating toward the sea found no ships waiting to carry it to safety. When the desperate warriors turned around and took up their battle stations in preparation for a fight to the death, they were miraculously transformed into stone. Another legend claims that the stones were invading Roman soldiers who were "petrified" in their tracks by a local saint named Cornely.

ELEMENTS OF ARCHITECTURE

Dolmen and Passage Grave

The **dolmen** was made up of a **post-and-lintel** frame of large, stone slabs "roofed" with one or more **capstones**, then mounded over with dirt and smaller stones called a **cairn**. This construction created a small, fully enclosed burial chamber.

Today, most dolmens are exposed, giving the erroneous impression that they were built as open-air graves.

The **passage grave** was a burial chamber, also covered over by an earth-and-pebble cairn, that was entered through a long, slab-lined passageway or passageways. The central space was sometimes segmented into several chambers and usually held multiple burials.

dolmen

passage grave

At Newgrange, in Ireland, an elaborate passage grave (fig. 1-19) was discovered in a cairn that originally stood some 44 feet tall and measured about 280 feet in diameter. The mound was built of sod and river pebbles and was set off by a circle of decorated standing stones around its perimeter. Its passageway, 62 feet long and lined with standing stones, leads into a three-part chamber with a corbeled vault rising to a height of 19 feet. The stones at the entrance and along the passageway are engraved with linear designs, mainly rings, spirals, and diamond shapes. These patterns must have been marked out using strings or compasses, then carved by pecking at the rock surface with tools made of antlers. Such large and richly decorated structures did more than honor the distinguished dead; they were truly public architecture that fostered communal pride and a group identity. As is the case with the elaborate mausoleums and funerary monuments being built today, their function was both practical and symbolic.

Many megalithic structures were not tombs at all but ritual centers that must have attracted the people of an entire region. In the Carnac district on the south coast of Brittany, in France, thousands of **menhirs**, or single vertical megaliths, were set up sometime between 4250 and 3750 BCE. Over 3,000 of them still stand in a two-mile stretch near Ménec (fig. 1-20). Each of these squared-off stones weighs several tons. They were placed in either circular patterns known as **cromlechs** or straight rows known as **alignments**. There are thirteen rows of alignments, their stones graduated in height from about 3 feet on the eastern end to upward of 13 feet toward the west. The east-west orientation of the alignments suggests some connection to the movement of the sun. Neolithic farming peoples, whose well-being depended on a recurring cycle of sowing, growing, harvesting, and fallow

seasons, would have had every reason to worship the sun and do all they could to assure its regular motion through the year. The menhirs at Carnac may well have marked off an established procession route for large groups of people celebrating public rites. It is also possible that they were points of reference for careful observation of the sun, moon, and stars.

Of all the megalithic monuments in Europe, the one that has stirred the imagination of the public most strongly is Stonehenge, on Salisbury Plain in southern England (figs. 1-21, 1-22, 1-23). A **henge** is a circle of stones or posts, often surrounded by a ditch with built-up embankments. Laying out such circles with accuracy would have posed no particular problem. Their architects likely relied on the human compass, a simple but effective surveying method that persisted well into modern times. All that is required is a length of cord either cut or knotted to mark the desired radius of the circle. A person holding one end of the cord is stationed in the center; a co-worker, holding the other end and keeping the cord taut, steps off the circle's circumference.

Stonehenge is not the largest such circle from the Neolithic period, but because it was repeatedly reworked to incorporate new elements, it is one of the most complicated megalithic sites. It must have had, or developed, an extraordinary importance in its region. It is the product of at least four major building phases between about 2750 and 1500 BCE. In the earliest stage, its builders dug a deep, circular ditch, placing the excavated material on the inside rim to form an embankment more than 6 feet high. Digging through the turf, they exposed the chalk substratum characteristic of this part of England, thus creating a brilliant white circle about 330 feet in diameter. An "avenue" from the henge toward the northeast led well outside the embankment to a pointed sarsen megalith—sarsen is a

1-21. Stonehenge, Salisbury Plain, Wiltshire, England. c. 2750–1500 BCE

gray sandstone—brought from a quarry 23 miles away. Today, this so-called heel stone, tapered toward the top and weighing about 35 tons, stands about 16 feet high. The ditches and embankments bordering the approach avenue were constructed somewhat later, at the same time as the huge megalithic monument we see today.

By about 2100 BCE, Stonehenge included all of the internal elements reflected in the drawing shown here (fig. 1-22). Dominating the center was a horseshoe-shaped arrangement of five sandstone trilithons, or pairs of upright stones topped by lintels. The one at the middle stood considerably taller than the rest, rising to a height of 24 feet, and its lintel was more than 15 feet long and 3 feet thick. This group was surrounded by the so-called sarsen circle, a ring of sandstone uprights weighing up to 50 tons each and standing 20 feet tall. This circle, 106 feet in diameter, was capped by a continuous lintel. The uprights were tapered slightly toward the top, and the gently curved lintel sections were secured by mortise and tenon joints, a conical projection from one piece fitting into a hole in the next. Just inside the sarsen circle was once a ring of bluestones—worked blocks of a bluish dolerite found only in the mountains of southern Wales, 150 miles away. Why the builders of Stonehenge felt it necessary to use specifically this type of stone is one of

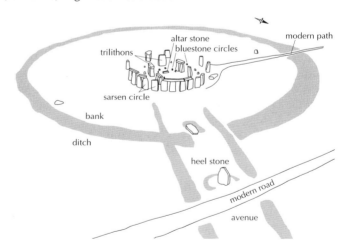

1-22. Diagram of Stonehenge, showing elements discussed here

the many mysteries of Stonehenge. Clearly the stones were highly prized, for centuries later, about 1500 BCE, they were reused to form a smaller horseshoe inside the trilithons that encloses the so-called altar stone.

Whoever stood at the exact center of Stonehenge on the morning of the summer solstice 4,000 years ago would have seen the sun rise directly over the heel stone (fig. 1-23). The observer could then warn people that the

1-23. *Within Circle, Looking Toward Heel Stone, Stonehenge, 1967.* Photograph by Paul Caponigro

Caponigro, a great enthusiast of megalithic architecture, spent twenty years photographing prehistoric structures all over Europe. He admirably captures the harmonious grace and simplicity of Stonehenge by positioning his camera directly above the large "altar stone" at the heart of the complex and aiming it toward the heel stone outside the monument's perimeter. It is from this spot that a dawn visitor to the site at the time of the summer solstice can see the sun rise directly over that distant marker.

sun's strength would shortly begin to wane, that the days would grow shorter and the nights cooler until the country was once more gripped by winter.

Through the ages, many theories have been advanced to explain Stonehenge. (Most of these explanations say more about the times in which they were put forward than about Stonehenge.) In the Middle Ages, it was thought that the monument had been built by Merlin, the magician of the King Arthur legend. Later, the site was incorrectly associated with the religious practices of the Druids. It continues to challenge the ingenuity of scholars even today. Because its orientation is clearly related to the movement of the sun, some think it may have been a kind of observatory, with the help of which prehistoric astronomers could track any number of cosmic events. Anthropologists suspect that the structure was an important site for major public ceremonies, possibly planting or harvest rituals. Whatever its original function may have been, Stonehenge continues to fascinate the public. Crowds of people still gather there at midsummer to thrill to its mystery. Why such megalithic structures were built may never be discovered, but the technology developed for building them was a major advance, one that made possible, among other things, a new kind of sculpture.

Sculpture and Ceramics

Having learned how to cut and transport massive blocks of stone, Neolithic sculptors were capable of carving large, freestanding stone figures. Their menhir statues, dating from between 3500 and 2000 BCE, stood 3 to 4 feet high, and all were carved in a similar way. Elements of the human figure reduced to near-geometric forms were incised on all four sides of a single upright block. Faces were usually suggested by a vertical ridge for the nose and a horizontal one for the browline. Rarely is there any indication of a mouth. Incised linear patterns on the sides and backs of such figures have been interpreted as ribs and backbones, but it is possible that they were meant to represent elements of ritual costume or body painting. A typical menhir statue is the one of a woman found in Montagnac, in southern France (fig. 1-24). The face is composed of a straight nose, a heavy, continuous brow, and protruding eyes. Above the browline is something resembling a headband. What first appears to be a square jaw and wide, rectangular mouth is actually the outline of a piece of jewelry, probably a necklace with a single bead at the center. The woman's hands are raised to cover her breasts, so that each of her arms has the shape of the letter **U**. A belt encircles her waist. Some

1-24. Menhir statue of a woman, from Montagnac, France. c. 2000 BCE. Limestone, height approx. 33" (85 cm). Muséum d'Histoire Naturelle et Préhistoire, Nîmes

figures of women have no arms or hands—only breasts and a necklace. Men often carry weapons.

In southern France, solitary menhir statues have been discovered on wooded hills and sometimes near tombs or villages. Set on hilly sites, they may have served as "guardians" and signposts for travelers making their way to sacred places. Those in the vicinity of tombs may have been "guardians of the dead." Some female figures found near dwellings are thought to have been household protectors.

Besides working in stone, Neolithic artists also commonly used clay. Their ceramics, whether figures of people and animals or vessels, display a high degree of technical skill and aesthetic imagination. This art required a different kind of conceptual leap. In the sculpture previously discussed, artists created their work out of an existing substance, such as stone, bone, or wood. To produce ceramic works, artists had to combine certain substances with clay—bone ash was a common addition— then subject the objects formed of that mixture to high heat for a period of time, thus creating an entirely new material. Among the ceramic figures discovered at a pottery-production center in the Danube River valley at Cernavoda, Romania, are a seated man and woman who form a most engaging pair (fig. 1-25).

1-25. Figures of a man and a woman, from Cernavoda, Romania. c. 4000–3500 BCE. Ceramic, height 4¹/₂" (11.5 cm). National Museum of Antiquities, Bucharest

TECHNIQUE

POTTERY AND CERAMICS

The terms *pottery* and *ceramics* may be used interchangeably—and often are, which causes some confusion. The word *ceramics* came into use only in the nineteenth century. Because it covers all baked-clay wares, *ceramics* is technically a more inclusive term than *pottery*.

Pottery is all baked-clay **ware** except porcelain, which is at the "high end" of ceramic technology. Raw clay becomes a porous pottery when heated to at least 500° centigrade. It then holds its shape permanently and will not disintegrate in water. Fired at 800° centigrade, pottery is technically known as earthenware. When subjected to temperatures between 1200° and 1400°, certain stone elements in the clay vitrify, or become glassy, and the result is a stronger type of ceramics called stoneware.

Pottery vessels can be formed in several ways. It is possible, though difficult, to raise up the sides from a ball of raw clay. Another method is to coil long rolls of soft, raw clay, stack them on top of each other to form a container, and then smooth them by hand. A third possibility is to simply press the clay over an existing form, a dried gourd for example. By about 4000 BCE, Egyptian potters had developed the potter's wheel, a round, spinning platform on which it is relatively simple to produce a uniformly shaped vessel in a very short time.

The potter's wheel appeared in the ancient Near East about 3250 BCE and in China about 3000 BCE. After a pot is formed, it is allowed to dry completely before it is fired. For proper firing, the temperature must be maintained at a relatively uniform level. Low-fired prehistoric pottery is art made at the hearth, but special ovens for firing pottery, called **kilns**, have been discovered at prehistoric sites in Europe dating from as early as 32,000 BCE.

Fragments of low-fired ceramics are the most common artifacts found in excavations of prehistoric settlements. Pottery is relatively fragile, and new vessels are constantly in demand to replace broken ones. Moreover, pottery disintegrates very, very slowly. Pottery fragments, or **potsherds**, serve as a major key in dating lost cultures and reconstructing their living and trading patterns. One of the first ways of decorating pottery was simple incising—scratching lines into the surface of the clay before it was left to dry. By the dawn of the Bronze Age, about 2300 BCE, vessels were produced in a wide variety of specialized forms and decorated with great finesse.

The artist who made them shaped their bodies out of simple cylinders of clay but managed to pose them in ways that make them seem very true to life. The woman, spread-hipped and big-bellied, sits directly on the ground, her hands placed on her raised knee. The man hunkers on a low perch, holding his head in his hands and seemingly lost in contemplation—or at least trying to think, for he looks perplexed. It is easy to imagine the pair next to their hearth, the worker and the worrier. No aura of sacred purpose surrounds these two, despite the fact that they had accompanied their owner to the grave.

One of the unresolved puzzles of prehistory is why people in Europe did not produce pottery vessels much earlier. They understood how to make clay figures as hard as stone by firing them in an oven at high temperatures as early as 32,000 BCE. Yet it was not until about 7000 BCE that they began making vessels using the same technique—some 3,000 years after the first appearance of such vessels in Japan, for instance. Some anthropologists argue that clay is a medium of last resort for vessels. Compared to hollow gourds, wooden bowls, or woven baskets, clay vessels are heavy and quite fragile, and firing them requires a very high level of expertise.

Excellence in ceramics depends upon the degree to which a given vessel combines domestic utility, visual beauty, and fine execution (see "Pottery and Ceramics," above). Much of the surviving Neolithic pottery is so exemplary in this regard that it has been difficult to select only one or two examples for inclusion here. A group of bowls from Denmark, made in the third millennium BCE, provides only a hint of the extraordinary achievements of Neolithic artists working in clay (fig. 1-26). Taking their

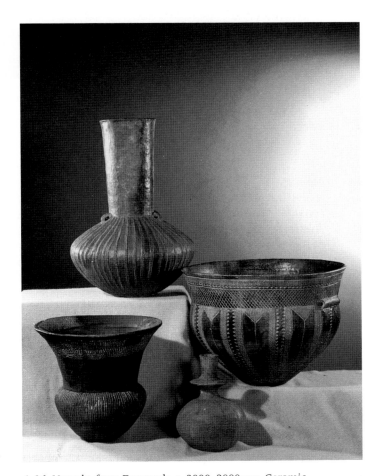

1-26. Vessels, from Denmark. c. 3000–2000 BCE. Ceramic, heights range from 5³/4" to 12¹/4" (14.5 to 31 cm). National Museum, Copenhagen

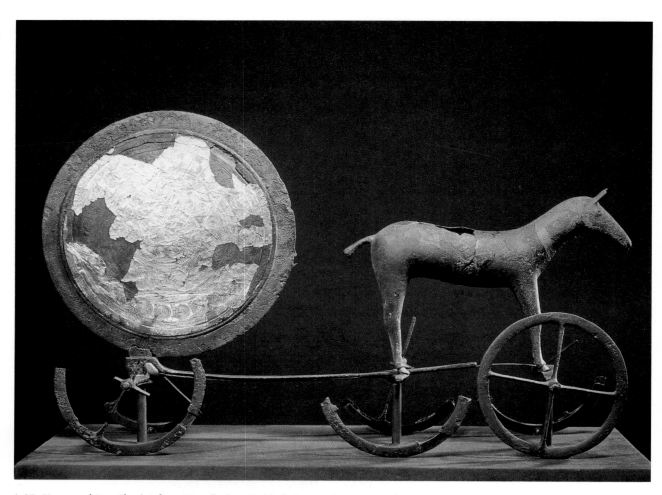

1-27. *Horse and Sun Chariot*, from Trundholm, Zealand, Denmark. c. 1800–1600 BCE. Bronze, length 23¼" (59.2 cm). National Museum, Copenhagen

forms from baskets and bags, the earliest pots were round and pouchlike and had built-in loops so that they could be suspended on cords. The earliest pieces in the illustration are the globular bottle with a collar around its neck (bottom center), a form perhaps inspired by eggs or gourd containers, and the flask with loops (top). Even when potters began making pots with flat bottoms that could stand without tipping, they often added hanging loops as part of the design. Some of the ornamentation of these pots, including hatched engraving and stitchlike patterns, seems to reproduce the texture of the baskets and bags that preceded ceramics as containers. It was also possible to decorate clay vessels by impressing stamps into their surface or scratching it with sticks, shells, or toothed implements. Many of these techniques appear to have been used to decorate the flat-bottomed vase with the wide, flaring top (bottom left), a popular type of container that came to be known as a funnel beaker.

The large engraved bowl (center right), found at Skarpsalling, is considered to be the finest piece of northern Neolithic pottery yet discovered. The potter lightly incised its sides with delicate linear patterns, then rubbed white chalk into them so that they would stand out against the dark body of the bowl—a technique similar to the one called **niello**, used to enhance linear designs incised in metal. Much of the finest art to survive from the Neolithic period is the work of potters; it is an art of the oven and the hearth.

THE BRONZE AGE

Neolithic culture persisted in northern Europe until about 2000 BCE. Metals made their appearance in the region about 2300. In southern Europe and the Aegean, copper, gold, and tin had been mined, worked, and traded even earlier (Chapter 4). Exquisite objects made of bronze—an alloy, or mixture, of tin and copper—are frequently found in the settlements and graves of early northern farming communities, especially in Britain and Scandinavia, where major mining and smelting centers developed. The period that follows the introduction of metalworking is commonly called the Bronze Age.

1-28. Schematic drawing of incised designs on unseen side of the *Horse and Sun Chariot* from Trundholm

A remarkable sculpture from the Bronze Age in Scandinavia depicts a wheeled horse pulling a cart laden with a large, upright disk commonly thought to represent the sun (fig. 1-27). The work dates from between 1800 and 1600 BCE and was discovered at what is now Trundholm, in Denmark. Horses had been domesticated in Ukraine by about 4000 BCE, but the first evidence of wheeled chariots and wagons designed to exploit the animals' strength dates from about 2000 BCE. Rock engravings in northern Europe show the sun being drawn through the sky by either an animal or a bird. These may be an indication that there was a widespread sun cult in the region, with special ritual practices. The Trundholm horse and sun cart could have been rolled from place to place in a ritual reenactment of the sun's passage across the sky.

The valuable materials from which the sculpture was made and the great attention devoted to its details attest to its importance. The horse, cart, and sun disk were cast in bronze. After two faults in the casting had been repaired, the horse was given its surface finish, and its head and neck were incised with ornamentation (fig. 1-28). Light striking its eyes turned them into tiny suns. Elaborate and very delicate designs were engraved on its collar and harness. The bronze sun disk, cast in two pieces, was engraved with concentric rings filled with zigzags, circles, spirals, and loops. A thin sheet of beaten gold was then applied to one of the bronze disks and pressed into the incised patterns. Finally, the disks were sealed together by means of an encircling metal band. The patterns on the horse tend to be geometric and rectilinear, but those of the sun disk are continuous and curvilinear, suggestive of the movement of the sun itself.

Much of what we know about prehistoric peoples is based on the art they produced—from the smallest carvings to menhir statues, from cave paintings to household wares. Progress continues to be made toward an understanding of when and how these works were created. We may never know *why* some of them were made. But the remote eras into which they afford us glimpses seem strangely familiar. The sheer artistry and immediacy of the images left by these very early ancestors connect us to them as surely as the earliest written records link us to those who came later.

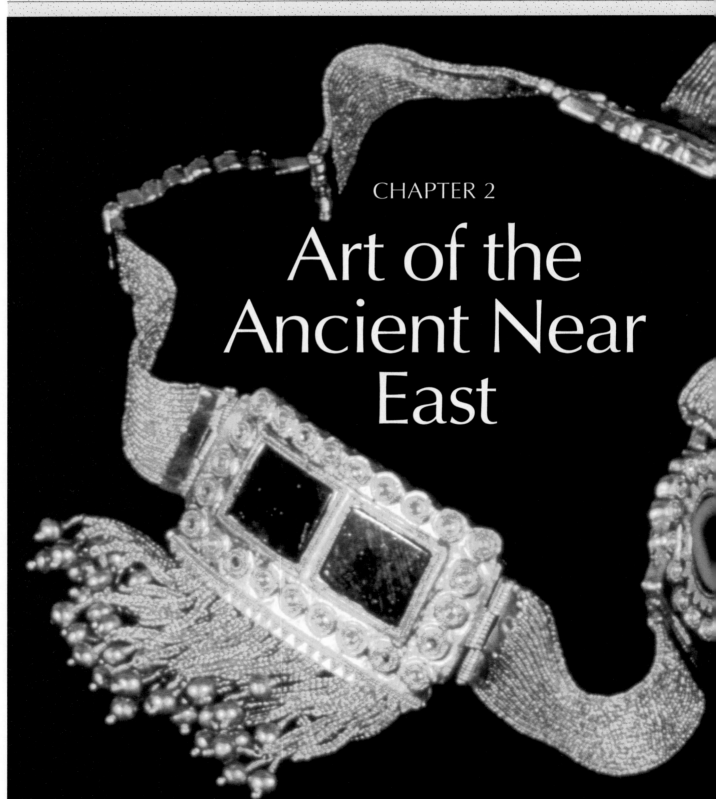

CHAPTER 2

Art of the Ancient Near East

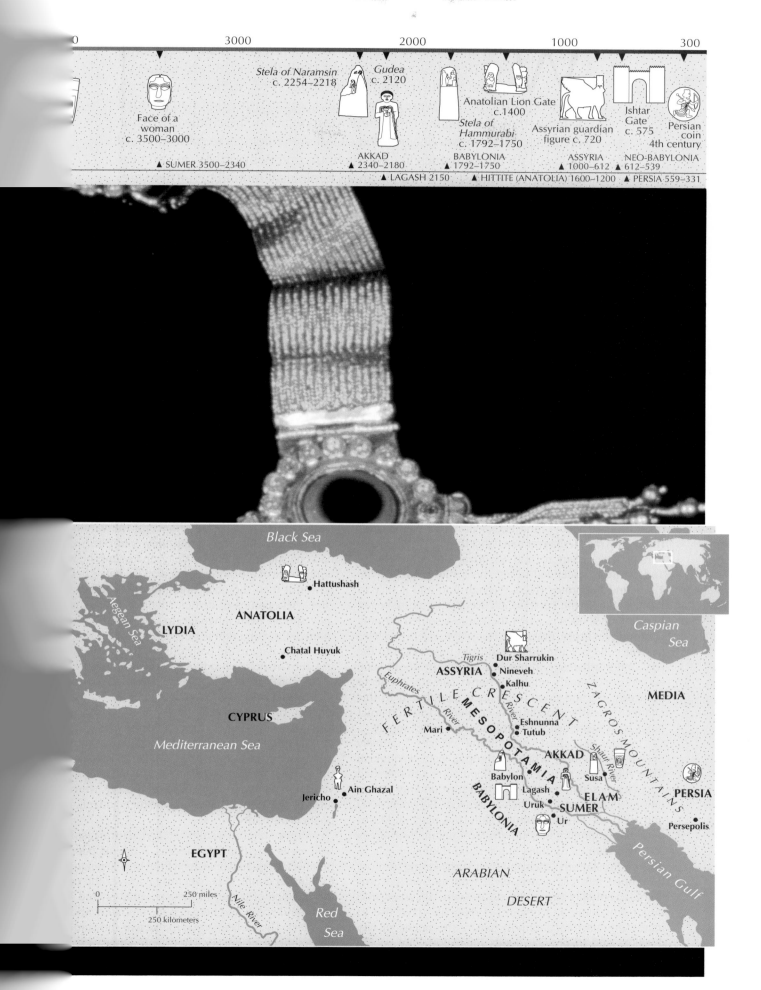

| 0 | 3000 | 2000 | 1000 | 300 |

Face of a woman c. 3500–3000

Stela of Naramsin c. 2254–2218

Gudea c. 2120

Stela of Hammurabi c. 1792–1750

Anatolian Lion Gate c.1400

Assyrian guardian figure c. 720

Ishtar Gate c. 575

Persian coin 4th century

▲ SUMER 3500–2340 ▲ AKKAD 2340–2180 ▲ BABYLONIA 1792–1750 ▲ ASSYRIA 1000–612 ▲ NEO-BABYLONIA 612–539

▲ LAGASH 2150 ▲ HITTITE (ANATOLIA) 1600–1200 ▲ PERSIA 559–331

Black Sea

Hattushash

ANATOLIA

LYDIA

Aegean Sea

Chatal Huyuk

CYPRUS

Mediterranean Sea

Caspian Sea

Tigris

Dur Sharrukin

ASSYRIA

Nineveh

Kalhu

MEDIA

Euphrates

FERTILE CRESCENT

MESOPOTAMIA

ZAGROS MOUNTAINS

Eshnunna

Mari

Tutub

Shaur River

Jericho

Ain Ghazal

BABYLONIA

Babylon

AKKAD

Susa

PERSIA

Lagash

ELAM

Uruk

SUMER

Ur

Persepolis

EGYPT

Nile River

ARABIAN

DESERT

Persian Gulf

Red Sea

0   250 miles

250 kilometers

W hen allied forces in the Persian Gulf region launched Operation Desert Storm in January 1991, their air attack on Iraq provoked an outcry from archeologists and art historians around the world. The bombs were not just falling on an army that had invaded Kuwait; they were falling on ancient Mesopotamia, the cradle of Western civilization, the most concentrated site of archeological remains on earth, places with fabled names like Nineveh, Ur, and Babylon. As one archeologist noted, "Almost all of Iraq is an archeological mound . . . . There are half a million archeological sites from all periods. About 40,000 or 50,000 of them are considered quite important. Between 100 and 200 of them were ancient capital cities" (William H. Honan, "Attacks on Iraq Worry and Divide Archeologists," *The New York Times,* February 9, 1991). Some of the most important of these ancient sites have not yet been located; others have been found but not excavated. Ironically, the great "archeological mound" is formed of accumulated layers of vanquished and vanished cultures, for people have been fighting over this area almost since the first settlements formed there.

THE FERTILE CRESCENT

Well before settled farming communities arose in Europe and Egypt, agriculture emerged in the ancient Near East in an area long referred to as the Fertile Crescent. Geographically, the ancient Near East encompasses Anatolia (roughly modern Turkey), Mesopotamia (Iraq today), and Persia (Iran). The "crescent" rose along the Mediterranean coast through modern Jordan, Israel, Lebanon, and Syria, arched into central Turkey, and descended along the fertile plains of the Tigris and Euphrates rivers through Iraq and a slice of western Iran to the Persian Gulf. Neolithic culture began here about 9000 BCE, when the earliest settled farming communities arose, first in the hills above rivers and later in river valleys. Farming spread from this region to the east and northwest and reached Europe by about 5000 BCE. Mesopotamia's relatively harsh climate, prone to both drought and flood, may have contributed to this change, as early agriculturists cooperated to construct large-scale systems for controlling their water supply.

In the Near East, agricultural villages gradually evolved into cities, which anthropologists distinguish from villages as having a large population and a settled area clearly separated from its rural surroundings. Trade among distant communities increased. Between 4000 and 3000 BCE, a major cultural shift took place in Mesopotamia. Beginning in southern Mesopotamia, complex societies with hierarchies of priests and kings began to appear. Prosperous cities and their surrounding territory developed into city-states, each with its own government. Eventually these city-states were absorbed into larger kingdoms and empires. Urban life gave rise to increasing specialization. To satisfy the needs of city dwellers and to provide goods for export, city people began to develop skills besides those for farming. Workshops for milling flour and making bricks, pottery, cloth, carpets, and metalware sprang up, and the construction of temples and palaces kept builders and artists busy.

The peoples of the ancient Near East were polytheistic; they worshiped numerous gods and goddesses, attributing to them power over human activities and the forces of nature. The importance of the various deities depended on the area of life they controlled. Each city had one special protective deity, and people believed the dominance of the city depended on its deity's being more powerful than the gods and goddesses of surrounding cities. The names of deities changed over time and as they spread from language to language. For example, Inanna, the Sumerian goddess of fertility, love, and war, was equivalent to the Babylonians' Ishtar, the Egyptians' Isis, the Greeks' Aphrodite, and the Romans' Venus.

A class of religious specialists emerged to control rituals and sacred sites. Large **temple complexes**—clusters of religious, administrative, and service buildings—developed in each city as centers of worship and also as thriving businesses. The religious establishment administered substantial property, received a portion of the harvest, and engaged in various other commercial ventures. Religious and political power were closely interrelated, and both women and men had religious and political authority.

Mesopotamia's wealth and agricultural resources, as well as its few natural defenses, made its peoples vulnerable to repeated invasions from hostile neighbors and to internal conflicts between rivals. Over the centuries, the balance of power in Mesopotamia shifted between north and south and between local powers and outside invaders. The earliest group to rise was the Sumerians in the southern region. For a brief period they were eclipsed by the Akkadians, their neighbors to the north. When

2-1. Reconstruction drawings of houses at Ain Ghazal, Jordan. c. 7200–5000 BCE

The top drawing shows one anthropologist's view of what the village looked like; below are four stages of construction.

invaders from farther north in turn conquered the Akkadians, the Sumerians regained power locally. The Babylonians were the next to ascend to dominance in the south. Later, the center of power shifted to the Assyrians in the north, then back again to Babylonia, called Neo-Babylonia. Throughout this time, important cultural centers arose outside the margins of Mesopotamia as well, such as the Hittite kingdom in Anatolia, Elam on the plain between the Tigris River and the Zagros Mountains to the east, and Persia, east of Elam. Beginning in the sixth century BCE, the Achaemenid Persians, a nomadic people from the mountains of modern-day Iran, forged an empire that included not only Mesopotamia but the entire Near East and beyond.

The art produced in the ancient Near East was undoubtedly influenced by these broad political events. Interior and exterior trade relations, which determined the exchange of styles, techniques, and materials, had a greater impact on it, however, as did the dictates and needs of religion. The evolution of political and religious powers, specialization of roles, and cultural blending through trade and conquest that culminated in the mighty Persian Empire had begun thousands of years earlier, when people had begun to come together in the first Neolithic cities.

EARLY NEOLITHIC CITIES

Jericho, one of the earliest cities in the Near East, is located in the West Bank territory at the site of a natural spring where humans have lived for nearly 12,000 years. Here, as throughout the ancient Near East, where wood and stone were scarce, people turned to the earth beneath their feet for construction materials. From the ninth millennium BCE on, they molded bricks out of clay, then hardened them in the sun. These "mud bricks" were quite durable in the dry climate and provided sturdy, well-insulated shelter. Sometime between 8000 and 7000 BCE, Jericho was home to about 2,000 people living in mud-brick houses protected by a stone wall 5 feet thick and 12 to 17 feet high. The site covered 6 acres, an enormous size for its time.

An even larger Neolithic city was discovered accidentally during road construction just outside Amman, Jordan, in 1981. Ain Ghazal ("spring of the gazelles"), dated from about 7200 to 5000 BCE, occupied 30 acres on a slope that was laboriously shaped into terraces stabilized by stone retaining walls. Its houses had double stone walls with a core of dirt and pebbles, probably sealed with a layer of mud (fig. 2-1). On the interior, regularly spaced wood posts supported roof beams, which are believed to have been

PARALLELS

Dominant Culture	Years	Near East	World
Early Neolithic	c. 9000 BCE	Jericho; Ain Ghazal; Chatal Huyuk	
Elam	c. 7000–600 BCE		
			4000–3000 BCE Potter's wheel (Egypt)
Sumer	c. 3500–2340 BCE	Earliest pictographs; wheeled carts; potter's wheel; White	
	c. 2150–2030 BCE	Temple ziggurat; bronze tools and weapons; *Gilgamesh* epic	**3000–2000 BCE** World population about 100 million; hieroglyphic writing (Egypt); potter's wheel (China); first pottery in Americas (Ecuador); Stonehenge (England); Pyramids at Giza (Egypt)
Akkad	c. 2340–2180 BCE		
Lagash	c. 2150 BCE		
			2000–1000 BCE
Babylonia	c. 1792–1750 BCE	*Stela of Hammurabi*	Shang dynasty (China); Olmec civilization (Mesoamerica)
Hittite (Anatolia)	c. 1600–1200 BCE	Iron tools and weapons	
Assyria	c. 1000–612 BCE		**1000–336 BCE**
Neo-Babylonia	c. 612–539 BCE	Ishtar Gate	First Olympian Games (Greece); birth of Siddhartha Gautama, founder of Buddhism (Nepal); Parthenon (Greece);
Persia	c. 559–331 BCE	Persepolis built; Alexander the Great conquers Persia	Alexander the Great becomes king of Macedonia

covered by thickly woven branches and grasses sealed with mud. The lower walls, support posts, and floors were covered with plaster, a mixture of burned limestone ash and sand that dried quickly into a hard, water-resistant surface. These houses must have resembled the adobe pueblos that native peoples of the American Southwest began to build more than 7,000 years later.

Rather than expand the city beyond the safety and convenience of the original terraces, the people of Ain Ghazal met their growing need for space by reworking existing houses—dividing large rooms into smaller ones, adding storage pits, and enlarging hearths. As in other Neolithic settlements, the family dead were buried in graves below the floors around the hearths. Evidence from these graves suggests that infant mortality was high but that about a fifth of the population lived to be older than fifty.

Among the objects recovered from Ain Ghazal are plaster containers and painted plaster figures up to 3 feet tall (fig. 2-2). Sculptors molded the figures by applying wet plaster to frames of twigs and grasses bound together in the shape of the human form. Inset cowrie shells formed the eyes, and small dots of the black, tarlike substance bitumen—which Near Eastern artists used frequently—formed the pupils. These statues may have been related to ancestor worship, possibly practiced at this and other nearby early Neolithic sites. Because the figures show individual characteristics, they seem to memorialize particular people. The feet of one figure, for example, have six toes, more likely a deliberate representation of a rare genetic trait than a slipup by the sculptor.

Although agriculture appears to have been the economic mainstay of these new permanent communities, other specialized activities, such as manufacturing and trade, were also important. Chatal Huyuk, a sizable city in Anatolia occupied from about 6500 to 5500 BCE, developed a thriving trade in obsidian, a rare, black volcanic glass that was used from Paleolithic into modern times for making sharp blades.

The inhabitants of Chatal Huyuk lived in densely clustered single-story buildings grouped around shared courtyards, which were used as garbage dumps. The cities were easy to defend because they had no streets or open plazas and were protected with continuous, unbroken exterior walls. People moved around by crossing from rooftop to rooftop, entering houses through openings in their roofs. Many of the interior spaces were elaborately decorated and are assumed to be shrines. Walls

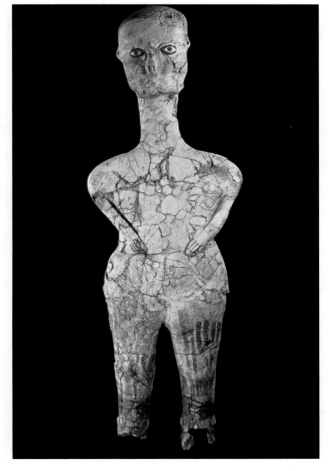

2-2. Figure, from Ain Ghazal, Jordan. c. 7000–6000 BCE.
Clay plaster with cowrie shell, bitumen, and paint,
height approx. 35" (90 cm). National Museum, Amman,
Jordan

2-3. Composite reconstruction drawing of a shrine room at
Chatal Huyuk, Turkey. c. 6500–5500 BCE

Many ancient Near Eastern cities still lie undiscovered.
In most cases an archeological site in a region is signaled by a large mound—known locally as a *tell*, *tepe*,
or *huyuk*—that represents the accumulated debris of
generations of human habitation. When properly excavated, such mounds yield concrete evidence about the
people who inhabited them. Valuable scientific information is lost when treasure hunters, who have no interest in the context in which they find things, loot sites
for artifacts to sell on the international art market. To
them, an object from an unknown context is just an
object. Even scientific excavation destroys context, and
subsequent investigators are forced to rely on the excavators' detailed records. This is especially true at Chatal
Huyuk, which was reburied after it was excavated in
the 1950s.

had bold geometric designs, painted animal scenes,
actual animal skulls and horns, and three-dimensional
shapes resembling breasts and horned animals. On
some walls, women were shown giving birth to bulls. In
one chamber, a leopard-headed woman—portrayed in a
high-arched wall area above three large, projecting bulls'
heads—braces herself as she gives birth to a ram
(fig. 2-3). Although this dramatic image suggests worship
of a fertility goddess, any such interpretation is risky
because so little is known about the culture.

Like other early Near Eastern settlements, Chatal
Huyuk seems to have been abandoned suddenly, for
unknown reasons, and never reoccupied. The concentration of people and resources in such communities
nevertheless represented a step toward the larger and
more complex city-states that were to emerge in Mesopotamia and become usual in the ancient Near East.

SUMER First cities, then city-states, developed between about 3500 and 2800 BCE along the
rivers of southern Mesopotamia, and the cities in this
region are known collectively as Sumer. The inhabitants
of this region had migrated from the north, but their origins are otherwise obscure.

The Sumerians have been credited with many "firsts":
inventing the wagon wheel and the plow, casting objects
in copper and bronze, and—perhaps the Sumerians'
greatest contribution to later civilizations—inventing a
system of writing between 3300 and 3000 BCE. This
method used a **cuneiform** ("wedge-shaped") script impressed into clay tablets with a **stylus** (writing instrument) and was developed by wealthy temples to keep
business records (see "Cuneiform Writing," page 66).
Thousands of Sumerian tablets painstakingly translated
by modern scholars document the gradual evolution of
not only writing but also arithmetic, another tool necessary for commerce. They also show the emergence of an
organized system of justice with written law codes and
the world's first written literature (see "Sumerian Literature," page 67).

The Sumerians' most notable contribution to architecture was the **ziggurat**, a stepped pyramidal structure
with a temple or shrine on top. The first such structures
were the result of repeated rebuilding at a sacred site,
with rubble from one structure serving as the foundation
for the next. Elevating religious sites on platforms originally may have been a way to protect shrines from
flooding. Whatever their origin, these sacred structures

CUNEIFORM WRITING

The Sumerians developed the earliest known system of writing in the late third millennium BCE, apparently for the purpose of keeping agricultural records. The earliest preserved tablets date to around 3300 BCE and represent an accounting system for food and other products traded at Uruk. The symbols on these thin clay slabs are **pictographs**, simple pictures that represent a thing or a concept. The head of a bull, for example, represents "bull." These pictographs were incised in the moist clay with a pointed tool. Between 2900 and 2400 BCE, the symbols evolved from simple pictures into phonograms—representations of the sounds of syllables in the Sumerian language—thus becoming a true writing system. During the same centuries, scribes adopted a **stylus** with one triangular, wedge end and one pointed end that could be pressed rapidly and repeatedly into a wet clay tablet to create the symbols, or characters, now increasingly abstract. Early modern scholars termed the ancient writing of Mesopotamia **cuneiform**, from the Latin words for "wedge-shaped," after the wedge-shaped marks made by the stylus.

The illustration here shows several examples of the shift from pictograph to cuneiform writing. The drawing of a bowl, which means "bread" and "food" and dates from about 3100 BCE, had been reduced by about 2400 BCE to a four-stroke sign, and by about 700 BCE to a highly abstract vertical arrangement of strokes. Combined with the pictograph and, later, cuneiform sign for head, the composite sign came to mean "to eat."

Cuneiform writing was a difficult skill, and few people in ancient Mesopotamia mastered it. Selected

stylus

children attended schools where they learned to read and write by copying their teachers' lessons. Clay exercise tablets have been excavated with a teacher's sample on one side and a student's efforts on the other. Only boys attended schools, but a small number of girls did learn to read and write, probably by being tutored at home. One of the fascinating things these ancient tablets reveal is that some 4,000 years ago there were textile businesses—concerned with both weaving and export—organized and operated by women entrepreneurs.

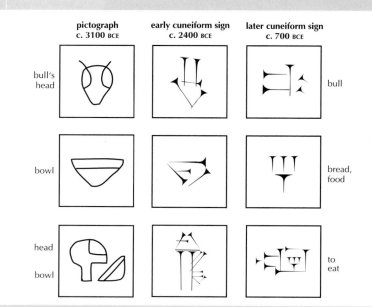

pictograph c. 3100 BCE	early cuneiform sign c. 2400 BCE	later cuneiform sign c. 700 BCE	
bull's head			bull
bowl			bread, food
head / bowl			to eat

---

towering above the flat plain proclaimed the wealth, prestige, and stability of a city's rulers and glorified its protective gods. Ziggurats functioned symbolically, too, as lofty bridges between the earth and the heavens—a meeting place for humans and their gods. They were given names such as "House of the Mountain" and "Bond between Heaven and Earth," and temples were known as "waiting rooms" because the priests and priestesses waited there for the gods and goddesses to reveal themselves. Ziggurats were impressive not because of size alone but also because their exterior surfaces were decorated with elaborate patterns of colored clay mosaics and reliefs. The gods would have been pleased with all this handiwork, it was said, because they abhorred laziness in their people.

There were two large temple complexes at Uruk (modern Warka, Iraq), the first independent Sumerian city-state. One complex was dedicated to Inanna, the goddess of fertility, and the other probably to the sky god Anu, another major deity. The Anu Ziggurat was built up in stages over the centuries until it ultimately rose to a height of about 40 feet. Around 3100 BCE, a temple was

erected on top that modern archeologists refer to as the White Temple because it was made of white-washed brick (fig. 2-4). This now-ruined structure was laid out as a simple rectangle oriented to the points of the compass. An off-center doorway on one of the long sides led into a large chamber containing a raised platform and altar; smaller spaces opened off this main chamber.

Many courtyards and interior walls in both the Inanna and the Anu compounds were decorated in a technique apparently invented at Uruk, the so-called **cone mosaic** (see "Cone Mosaic," page 68). Thousands of colored cones—shaped stone or baked clay—were pressed like thumbtacks into the wet plaster walls, their flat "heads" creating shimmering, multicolored designs. The technique was extremely labor intensive, but cone mosaics were exceptionally beautiful and durable.

About a thousand years after the completion of the White Temple, the people of Ur (modern Muqaiyir), a city along the Euphrates south of Uruk, built a ziggurat dedicated to the moon god Nanna, also called Sin, that illustrates the mature ziggurat form (fig. 2-5). Although

SUMERIAN LITERATURE

Among the tens of thousands of cuneiform tablets excavated thus far in Sumer, only a small number—fewer than 6,000, containing about 30,000 lines of text—record religious myths, heroic tales, legendary histories, hymns, songs of mourning, and so-called wisdom texts, consisting of essays, debates, proverbs, and fables. These make up the world's oldest written literature, and they tell us much about Sumerian beliefs. Most are written as poetry, and some may have been performed with music.

One group of stories and hymns concerns the goddess Inanna. In one of these, Inanna, a young, untried upstart from Uruk, decides to go to Eridu, a city to the south of Uruk, to visit Enki, the god of wisdom.

> Enki and Inanna drank beer
> together.
> They drank more beer together.
> They drank more and more beer
> together.
> With their bronze vessels filled
> to overflowing,
> With the vessels of Urash,
> Mother of the Earth,
> They toasted each other; they
> challenged each other.
>
> Enki, swaying with drink,
> toasted Inanna:
> "In the name of my power!
> In the name of my holy
> shrine!
> To my daughter Inanna I shall
> give
> The high priesthood!
> Godship!
> The noble, enduring crown!
> The throne of kingship!"
>
> Inanna replied:
> "I take them!"

Enki toasts Inanna another thirteen times, each time bestowing upon her more of his special powers, and each time she accepts his gifts. Only after Inanna has gathered all eighty of his powers into her boat and sailed away does the drink-crazed old god realize what he has done. Desperate, he sends a series of supernatural forces after the retreating boat, but each time Inanna's servant fights them off. Inanna eventually enters Uruk's city gate amid much rejoicing and triumphantly presents her new divine powers, one by one, to her people. Enki and the city of Eridu are forced to acknowledge the glory of Inanna's Uruk, and all proceed to enjoy peace and prosperity. (Text and summary adapted from Wolkstein and Kramer, pages 12–27.)

The best-known literary work of ancient Mesopotamia is the *Epic of Gilgamesh*. Its origins are Sumerian, but only fragments of the Sumerian version survive. The fullest version, written in Akkadian, was found in the library of the Assyrian king Assurbanipal (ruled 669–c. 627 BCE) in Nineveh (modern Kuyunjik, Iraq). It recounts the adventures of Gilgamesh, a legendary Sumerian king of Uruk, and his companion Enkidu. When Enkidu dies, a despondent Gilgamesh sets out to find the secret of eternal life from Utnapishtim and his wife, the only survivors of a great flood sent by the gods to destroy the world, and the only people to whom the gods ever granted eternal life. Gilgamesh ultimately learns to accept his mortality.

2-4. Reconstruction drawing of the Anu Ziggurat and White Temple, Uruk (modern Warka, Iraq). c. 3100 BCE

2-5. Nanna Ziggurat, Ur (modern Muqaiyir, Iraq). c. 2100–2050 BCE

2-6. Face of a woman, from Uruk (modern Warka, Iraq). c. 3500–3000 BCE. Marble, height approx. 8" (20.3 cm). Iraq Museum, Baghdad

TECHNIQUE
CONE MOSAIC

To decorate wall surfaces and other architectural elements, Sumerians at Uruk devised the **cone mosaic**. The technique used small, cone-shaped cylinders of colored stone or baked clay that were pushed into a thick layer of wet plaster. The cones were closely spaced in rows to form bands of angular, decorative patterns such as zigzag, diamond, herringbone, and flame. Clay cones have been excavated in other sites throughout Mesopotamia, which suggests that other peoples adopted the Sumerian technique.

located on the site of an earlier temple, this imposing mud-brick structure was elevated by design, not as the result of successive rebuildings. Its base is a rectangle 190 by 130 feet with three sets of stairs converging at an imposing entrance gate atop the first platform. Each platform is angled outward from top to base, probably to prevent rainwater from forming puddles and eroding the mud-brick pavement. The first two levels of the ziggurat and their retaining walls have been reconstructed in recent times. Little remains of the upper level and the temple.

Sculpture of this period was associated with religion, and large statues were commonly placed in temples as objects of devotion. A striking marble face from Uruk may once have been part of such an image (fig. 2-6). Beardless, it may represent a goddess. With its compelling empty-eyed stare and sensitively rendered features, this lifesize face demonstrates the skill attained by Sumerian sculptors at roughly the time the White Temple was being built. The marble face would have been attached to a wooden head on a full-size wooden body. Now stripped of the plaited gold hair or flowing wig with which it was originally adorned, and lacking the **inlay**, that is, set-in decoration for the brows and eyes—probably shell for the whites and deep blue lapis lazuli for the pupils—and the paint on the lips and skin, the face is reduced to a stark, white mask.

A tall, carved, alabaster vase found near the ruins of a temple at Uruk almost certainly served some religious

2-7. Carved vase (both sides), from Uruk (modern Warka, Iraq). c. 3500–3000 BCE. Alabaster, height 36" (91 cm). Iraq Museum, Baghdad

2-8. *Inanna Receiving an Offering*, detail of the upper register of the carved vase from Uruk (fig. 2-7)

purpose (fig. 2-7). It is decorated with bands, or **registers**, in **low relief**, a technique in which figures are carved to project only slightly from a flat background. Its lower registers show the natural world, including plants and animals. In the lowest register, over a wavy line signifying water, barley and date palms grow; above them, on a solid **groundline**, rams and ewes alternate, facing right. In the middle register, facing in the opposite direction, a line of unclothed priests strides forward, carrying baskets heaped with food that may have been temple offerings or wedding gifts. Size was associated with importance in Mesopotamian art, and the sturdy priests are shown simultaneously in side or profile view (heads and legs) and in three-quarter view (torsos), which makes both shoulders visible and increases their breadth.

The repetition of figures found in the first two bands disappears in the top register, where the imagery is more complex. Inanna, in her role as fertility goddess, stands in front of her shrine, indicated by two reed door poles draped with curtains (fig. 2-8). She wears a long robe and the horned headdress of a deity. Her right hand is raised in a gesture of greeting or blessing, and she faces a naked priest, who presents a sort of cornucopia. Behind him are other offering bearers; the last one holds a tasseled belt for the figure ahead, who may be a ruler. Through the doorway to her shrine, her wealth is displayed: animals, containers of fruit, large vases like this one, and what appears to be a temple model with a man and woman inside. The scene is usually interpreted as the ritual mar-

riage between the divine female and a human male during the annual spring New Year's festival, which was meant to assure fertility for the city's crops, livestock, and people during the coming year.

The sculptors of the vase told their story with great economy and clarity through the use of symbolic detail. They organized the picture space into registers that show the symbolic ascent from plants and animals to the goddess and that mirror the physical ascent of a ziggurat from level to level. They also condensed and focused the narrative, much as modern comic-strip artists do. For the next 2,500 years this use of registers was the preferred Near Eastern method for relating events in visual terms.

Marble statues dated to about 2900–2600 BCE from ruins of a temple at Eshnunna (modern Tell Asmar, Iraq) reveal a somewhat humbler aspect of Mesopotamian religious art (fig. 2-9). These **votive figures**—statues made as an act of worship to the gods—depict individuals. They represent an early example of an ancient Near Eastern religious practice—the setting up of simple, small statues of individual worshipers in a shrine before the larger, more elaborate image of a god. The early figurines from Ain Ghazal may have served this function, and the face of a woman from Uruk may have been part of such a figure, although there is no proof of it. Apparently anyone who could afford to might commission a self-portrait and dedicate it to a shrine. A simple inscription might identify the figure just as "One who offers prayers." Longer inscriptions might recount in detail all

2-9.   Votive statues, from the Square Temple, Eshnunna (modern Tell Asmar, Iraq). c. 2900–2600 BCE. Limestone, alabaster, and gypsum, height of largest figure approx. 30" (76.3 cm). The Oriental Institute of the University of Chicago; Iraq Museum, Baghdad

the things accomplished in the god's honor. Cuneiform texts reveal the importance of fixing on a god with an attentive gaze, hence the wide-open eyes. These stand-ins are at perpetual attention, making eye contact and chanting their donors' praises through eternity.

The sculptors of the Eshnunna statues reduced the face, hair, body, and clothing to simple geometric shapes. The figures stand solemnly, hands clasped in respect. Like the face of a woman from Uruk, arched brows inlaid with dark shell, stone, or bitumen once emphasized their huge, staring eyes. The male figures, bare-chested and dressed in sheepskin skirts, are stocky and muscular, with heavy legs and large feet, big shoulders, and cylindrical bodies. The two female figures (the tall, regal woman near the center and the smaller woman at the far left) have somewhat slighter figures but are just as square-shouldered as the men.

The earliest pottery in the Near East dates to about 7000 BCE. Decorated vessels excavated in large numbers from grave sites provide some sense of the development of pottery styles in various regions. One popular type of Sumerian painted ceramic was Scarlet Ware, produced

from around 3000 to 2350 BCE (fig. 2-10). Designs on these vessels, predominantly in red with touches of black, were painted with colored mixtures of clay and water. Circles, herringbones, zigzags, diamonds, and other geometric patterns, as well as animal images, were common motifs. The vase pictured here is about a foot tall and includes human figures, which is unusual.

From about 3000 BCE on, Sumerian artisans worked in various metals, including the hard metal alloy bronze (hence the name "Bronze Age" for the period that followed the Neolithic). Many of their metal creations were decorated with—or were in the shape of—animals or composite animal-human-bird creatures. They did extraordinary work in precious metals, often combining them with other materials. A superb example of their skill is a lyre—a kind of harp—from the tomb of Queen Puabi of Ur (c. 2685 BCE), which combines wood, gold, lapis lazuli, and shell (fig. 2-11). From one end of the lyre, the three-dimensional head of a bearded bull glares. The head is intensely lifelike despite the fantastic, decoratively patterned blue beard and the simplified nose.

On the panel below the head, four horizontal regis-

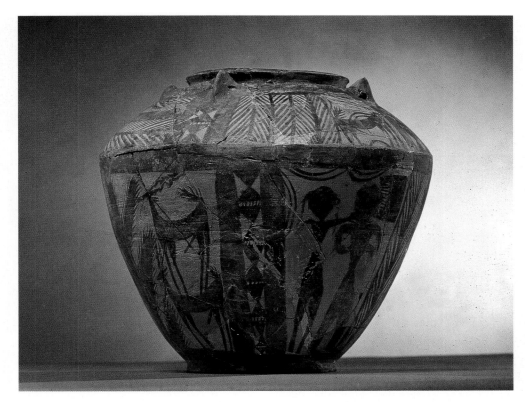

2-10. Scarlet Ware vase, from Tutub (modern Tell Khafajeh, Iraq). c. 3000–2350 BCE. Ceramic, height 11¾" (30 cm). Iraq Museum, Baghdad

The archeologist's best friend is the potsherd, or piece of broken pottery. Ceramic vessels are easily broken, yet the fragments are almost indestructible. Their earliest appearance at a site marks the time when people in the region began producing ceramics. Pottery styles, like automobile designs and fashions in clothing, change over time. Archeologists are able to determine the chronological order of such changes. By matching the potsherds excavated at a site with the types in this sequence, they can determine the relative date of the site (see "How Early Art Is Dated," page 49).

ters present scenes executed in inlaid shell (fig. 2-12). In the bottom register a man in scorpion dress holds what are probably ritual objects in his upraised hands. He is attended by a goat standing on its hind legs and holding out two tall cups, perhaps filled from the large container from which a ladle protrudes. The scene above this one depicts a pair of animal musicians. A seated donkey plucks the strings of a bull lyre—showing how such instruments were played—while a standing bear braces the instrument's frame and a seated jackal plays a small percussion instrument, perhaps a rattle. The next register shows animal attendants, also walking erect, bringing food and drink for a feast. On the left a wolf with a knife in its belt carries a table piled high with pork and mutton. A lion follows with a large wine jug and drinking bowl. In the top panel, facing forward, is an athletic man with long hair and a full beard, naked except for a wide belt. He is clasping two rearing human-headed bulls.

These scenes have puzzled scholars, but a new interpretation sheds light on their meaning. Because the lyre and others like it were found in graves and were used in funeral rites, their imagery probably depicts the fantastic realm of the dead. The animals are the traditional guardians at the gateway through which the newly dead must pass. Cuneiform tablets preserve songs of mourning from Sumer, which may have been chanted by priests to lyre music at funerals.

At roughly the same time written records first appeared, Sumerian temple staff and merchants developed stamps and seals for identifying documents and establishing property ownership. At first, Sumerians used simple clay stamps with designs **incised** (cut) into one surface to sign documents and to mark clay seals on container lids and storage-room doorways. Pressed against a damp clay surface, the seal left a mirror image of its distinctive design that could not be easily altered once dry. Around 3400 BCE, temple record keepers redesigned the stamp seal in the form of a cylinder. Sumerian **cylinder seals**, usually less than 2 inches high, were made of a hard stone, such as marble, so that the tiny but often elaborate scenes carved into them would not wear away. The scene on the fine example in figure 2-13 includes, on the right, a spoils-of-the-hunt depiction. The lone human

2-11. Bull lyre, from the tomb of Queen Puabi, Ur (modern Muqaiyir, Iraq). c. 2685 BCE. Wood with gold, lapis lazuli, and shell, reassembled in modern wood support. University Museum, University of Pennsylvania, Philadelphia

2-12. Mythological figures, detail of the sound box of the bull lyre from Ur (fig. 2-11). Wood with shell inlay, 12¼ x 4½" (31.1 x 11 cm)

2-13. Cylinder seal from Sumer and its impression. c. 2500 BCE. Marble, height approx. 1¾" (4.5 cm). The Metropolitan Museum of Art, New York
Gift of Walter Hauser, 1955 (55.65.4)

The distinctive design on the stone cylinder seal on the left "belonged" to its owner, like a coat of arms in the European Middle Ages or a modern cattle-rancher's brand. When rolled across soft clay applied to the closure to be sealed—a jar lid, the knot securing a bundle, or the door to a room—the cylinder left a raised image, or band of repeated raised images, of the design. Sealing discouraged unauthorized people from secretly gaining access to goods or information.

is flanked by his kill, and he looks over his shoulder at the dead female deer hanging by its heels. On the left, two pairs of rearing, mane-draped beasts, one with a human face, appear to be sparring for dominance. As later Assyrian reliefs will show, it was an enduring tradition in Near Eastern art to depict leaders protecting their people from both human and animal enemies as well as exerting control over the natural world. Often the human enemies turned out to be warlike invaders, drawn by Sumer's natural resources and prosperity.

AKKAD During the period of Sumerian power, the fertile Mesopotamian plain attracted a people known as the Akkadians, who settled the area near modern Baghdad to the north of Uruk and adopted Sumerian culture. Unlike the Sumerians, the Akkadians spoke a Semitic language (a language in the same family as Arabic and Hebrew). Under the powerful military and political figure Sargon I (ruled c. 2332–2279 BCE), they conquered the Sumerian cities and brought most of Mesopotamia under their control. For more than half a century, Sargon ruled this empire from his capital at Akkad, the actual site of which is yet to be discovered. As "King of the Four Quarters of the World," he assumed broad earthly powers. He also sought to elevate himself to the status of a god, setting a precedent followed by later Akkadian rulers.

Enheduanna, the daughter of Sargon I, was a major public figure who combined the roles of princess, priestess, politician, poet, and prophet and wielded exceptional power. During her lifetime, she was considered the embodiment of the goddess Ningal, the wife of the moon god Nanna, and after her death she herself may have been elevated to the status of goddess. She was apparently the only person to hold the office of high priestess for both the ziggurat of Nanna, the moon god of Ur, and the ziggurat of Anu, the sky god of Uruk, Sumer's two most prestigious gods. She began the tradition of

2-14. *Disk of Enheduanna*, from Ur (modern Muqaiyir, Iraq). c. 2300 BCE. Alabaster, diameter approx. 10" (25.4 cm). University Museum, University of Pennsylvania, Philadelphia

An inscription on the back of the disk reads: "Enheduanna, priestess of the moon god, [wife] of the moon god, child of Sargon the king of the universe, in Ishtar's temple of Ur she built [an altar] and named it . . . Offering Table of Heaven" (adapted from William W. Hallo, "Enheduanna," *Harvard Magazine*, May–June 1994, page 48).

princesses serving as high priestesses, and she complemented her father's political consolidation of his empire by uniting religious authority within it. Her hymns in praise of Sargon and Inanna are among the earliest literary works whose author's name is known. She is memorialized on several cylinder seals, as well as on an inscribed alabaster disk that bears her picture (fig. 2-14).

2-15. Head of a man, from Nineveh (modern Kuyunjik, Iraq). c. 2300–2200 BCE. Bronze, height 14³⁄₈" (36.5 cm). Iraq Museum, Baghdad

The figures carved in **high relief** in a band across the middle of this disk are participating in a ritual at the base of a ziggurat, seen at the far left. A nude priest pours ceremonial liquid from a pitcher onto an offering stand. The tall figure behind him, wearing a flounced robe and priestess's headdress, is presumed to be Enheduanna. She and the two figures to her right, probably priests with shaven heads, raise one hand in a gesture of reverent greeting. The disk shape of this work is unique and may have to do with its dedication to the moon god.

Enheduanna's well-documented career is an exception to the otherwise sparse information available about the Akkadians. Few artifacts can be traced to the courts of Akkad, making a lifesize bronze head dating from about 2300–2200 BCE especially precious (fig. 2-15). Its facial features and hairstyle probably reflect a generalized male ideal rather than the appearance of a specific individual. Also, it is possible that the head was symbolically mutilated to destroy its power, for the ears appear to have been deliberately removed, as have the inlays that would have filled the eye sockets.

The concept of imperial authority was literally carved in stone in another Akkadian work, the *Stela of Naramsin* (fig. 2-16). This 6½-foot-high **stela**, or upright stone slab, commemorates a military victory of Naramsin, Sargon's grandson and successor, and is an early example of a work of art created to celebrate the achievements of an individual ruler. In a sharp break with visual tradition, the sculptors replaced the horizontal registers with wavy ground lines. The images stand on their own, with no explanatory inscription. Watched over by three solar deities, symbolized by the rayed suns in the sky, Naramsin ascends a mountain

2-16. *Stela of Naramsin*. c. 2254–2218 BCE. Limestone, height 6'6" (1.98 m). Musée du Louvre, Paris

This stela probably came originally from Sippar, an Akkadian city on the Euphrates River, in what is now Iraq. It was not discovered at Sippar, however, but at the Elamite city of Susa (modern Shush, Iran), some 300 miles to the southeast. Raiders from Elam presumably took it there as booty in the twelfth century BCE.

wearing the horned crown used to identify gods. His soldiers follow at rhythmic intervals, passing conquered enemy forces sprawled in death or begging for mercy. Both the king and his warriors hold their weapons upright. The godlike king is immediately recognizable. He stands at the dramatic center of the scene, closest to the mountaintop, silhouetted against the sky. As in most art from the Near East, his greater size in relationship to his soldiers is an indication of his greater importance. Although this stela depicts Akkadians in triumph, they managed to dominate the region for only about another half century.

LAGASH In about 2180 BCE, the Akkadian Empire fell under attack by the Guti, a mountain people from the northeast. The Guti controlled most of the Mesopotamian plain for a brief time, then the Sumerians regained control of their own region and

2-17. Votive statue of Gudea, from Lagash (modern Telloh, Iraq). c. 2120 BCE. Diorite, height 29" (73.7 cm).
    Musée du Louvre, Paris

Akkad. One large Sumerian city-state remained independent during the period of Guti control. This was Lagash, on the Tigris River in the southeast, under the ruler Gudea. Gudea built and restored many temples, in which he placed votive statues representing both himself as governor and the ideal of good rule that he embodied. The statues are made of diorite, a very hard stone that was difficult to work, prompting the sculptors to use compact, simplified forms for the portraits that are unusually durable. Twenty of them survive, all looking much alike, making Gudea's face a familiar one in ancient Near Eastern art.

Whether the ruler was shown sitting or standing, the smooth fall of his robe provided ample space for long cuneiform inscriptions. The text of the one shown here (fig. 2-17) relates that Gudea dedicated himself, the sculpture, and the temple in which the sculpture resided to the goddess Geshtinanna, the divine poet and interpreter of dreams. Imposing and impressive, this statue seems **monumental**, although it is only 2½ feet tall. Here Gudea holds a vessel from which life-giving water flows in two streams filled with leaping fish. (At least one statue has been found of a goddess holding a vessel engineered to spout real water, which would have poured down her robe.) The full face below the cuffed sheepskin hat appears youthful and serene, and the smoothly muscled body is clothed in a long garment similar to that worn by the female votive figures from Eshnunna. The oversized, wide-open eyes—better to return the gaze of the deity—and broad, bunched-up shoulders express intense concentration. The sculptor's top-heavy treatment of the human body, as in other Mesopotamian figures, emphasizes its power centers: the eyes, head, chest, and arms. Images of Gudea present him as a strong, peaceful, pious ruler worthy of divine favor.

BABYLON AND MARI

For the next 300 years, periods of political turmoil alternated with periods of stable government in Mesopotamia. The Amorites, a Semitic-speaking people from the Arabian desert to the west, moved into the region and eventually reunited Sumer under Hammurabi (ruled 1792–1750 BCE). The capital city was Babylon, and the residents are called Babylonians. Among Hammurabi's achievements was a written legal code that listed the laws of his realm and the penalties for breaking them.

Hammurabi's code occupies most of the *Stela of Hammurabi*, a finely carved stone about 7 feet tall, but the relief sculpture at the top shows the king standing before the supreme judge, the sun god Shamash (fig. 2-18). The figures were executed in smooth, rounded forms with a minimum of linear surface detail. Shamash wears the four-tiered, horned headdress that marks him as a god and a robe that bares one shoulder and ends in a stiff, flounced skirt. Rays of the sun rise from behind his shoulders, and in his right hand he holds a measuring rod and a rope ring, symbols of justice and power. Hammurabi faces Shamash confidently, his hand raised in a gesture of greeting. Any suggestion of familiarity in the lack of

2-18. *Stela of Hammurabi*, from Susa (modern Shush, Iran). c. 1792–1750 BCE. Basalt, height of stela approx. 7' (2.13 m), height of relief 28" (71.1 cm). Musée du Louvre, Paris

In the introductory section of the stela's long cuneiform inscription, Hammurabi declared that with this code of law he intended "to cause justice to prevail in the land and to destroy the wicked and the evil, that the strong might not oppress the weak nor the weak the strong." Most of the 300 or so entries that follow deal with commercial and property matters. Only sixty-eight relate to domestic problems, and a mere twenty deal with physical assault. Punishments depended on the gender and social standing of the offender. Like the *Stela of Naramsin*, this stela was removed to Susa by Elamite invaders.

distance between the two is offset by the formality of his pose. The smaller, earthly law enforcer remains standing in the presence of the much larger divine judge, seated on his ziggurat throne. The Babylonian sculptor of this stela, like the Akkadian sculptor of the *Stela of Naramsin* (see fig. 2-16), indicated the relative importance of the

2-19. *Investiture of Zimrilim*, facsimile of a wall painting on mud plaster from the palace at Mari (modern Tell Hariri, Iraq), Court 106. c. 1750 BCE. Height 5'5" (1.7 m). Musée du Louvre, Paris

figures by size. The temple-form throne represented their mountain meeting site.

As kingship and empire became increasingly important, palace architecture overshadowed temple architecture. The great palace of another Amorite king, Hammurabi's contemporary Zimrilim (ruled 1779–1757 BCE), reflects this trend. Zimrilim's capital city of Mari was strategically located on the Euphrates River about 250 miles northwest of Babylon. It prospered from commercial traffic on the river and was notable for its well-built houses, sophisticated sanitation system, and bronze-working industry. The palace boasted an enormous courtyard paved in alabaster, several temples and shrines, hundreds of other rooms and courtyards, and a notable art collection. Zimrilim and Hammurabi had once been allies, but in 1757 BCE Hammurabi marched against Mari and destroyed Zimrilim's palace. A few murals from the palace have survived and provide rare examples of this fragile ancient Near Eastern art form.

The subjects of the murals range from geometric patterns in the royal family's quarters to military and religious scenes in the administrative areas. One, in the palace's main courtyard, shows Zimrilim receiving his authority from Ishtar, the Babylonian goddess of war, fertility, and love (fig. 2-19). The central panels, devoted to the investiture ceremony, are organized in the formal, symmetrical style familiar in earlier Sumerian art. In the framed upper register, the goddess, holding weapons and resting her foot on a lion—all emblems of power—extends to the king emblems of rule, the rod and the ring. Other deities look on, affirming the king's assumption of office. Below, a pair of goddesses face each other, holding tall plants in red vases. They are surrounded by streams of water that flow from the vases—a theme familiar from the Gudea statue (see fig. 2-17)—and merge in the center to form a canopy. Flanking these two

2-20. *Blue Bird*, detail of the wall painting from Mari (fig. 2-19)

panels are first a pair of towering aloelike plants with fan-shaped, **stylized** foliage. The **stylization** is especially evident in the patterned forms of the fronds, which exaggerate the spiny leaf shapes. Then there are three tiers of mythical animals—bulls, winged lions, and crowned, human-headed winged creatures—all facing inward. Beyond these are date palms being climbed by two fruit pickers. An enormous blue bird, of a species still found in the Mari region, spreads its wings in the right-hand tree (fig. 2-20). At the edges of the picture two

2-21. *Assurnasirpal II Killing Lions*, from the palace complex of Assurnasirpal II, Kalhu (modern Nimrud, Iraq). c. 850 BCE. Alabaster, height approx. 39" (99.1 cm). The British Museum, London

2-22. Reconstruction drawing of the citadel and palace complex of Sargon II, Dur Sharrukin (modern Khorsabad, Iraq). c. 721–706 BCE

gigantic goddesses, hands raised, bestow their approval. Eye-catching checked and striped patterning throughout the mural makes its surface sparkle. The colors have darkened considerably, but they probably included blue, orange, red, brown, and white. The way in which paint was used here reveals what Mesopotamian art looked like when it was new.

ASSYRIA

After the centuries of power struggles among Sumer, Akkad, Lagash, and Mari in southern Mesopotamia, a people called the Assyrians began to rise to dominance in northern Mesopotamia. They had become very powerful by about 1400 BCE, and after about 1000 BCE they began to conquer neighboring regions. By the end of the ninth century BCE, they controlled most of Mesopotamia, and by the early seventh century BCE they had extended their influence as far west as Egypt. Soon afterward they succumbed to internal weakness and external enemies, and by 600 BCE their empire had collapsed.

Various cities served at one time or another as the Assyrians' capital, and Assyrian architectural monuments include fine palaces set atop high platforms inside these fortified cities. The palaces were decorated with scenes of victorious battles, presentations of tribute to the king, combat between men and beasts, and religious imagery.

During his reign (883–859 BCE), Assurnasirpal II moved the capital to Kalhu (modern Nimrud) on the east bank of the Tigris River and undertook an ambitious building program. His architects fortified the city with mud-brick walls 5 miles long, 120 feet thick, and 42 feet high, and his engineers constructed a canal that irrigated fields and provided water for the expanded population of the city. According to an inscription commemorating the event, Assurnasirpal gave a party for 69,574 people to celebrate the dedication of the new capital in 879 BCE. Most of the buildings in Kalhu were made from mud bricks, but alabaster—a more impressive and durable material—was used for architectural decorations such as panels with scenes carved in low relief that depict the king participating in religious rituals, events from his war campaigns, and hunting expeditions.

In a vivid lion-hunting scene (fig. 2-21), Assurnasirpal II stands in a chariot pulled by galloping horses and draws his bow against an attacking lion that already has four arrows protruding from its body. Another beast, pierced by arrows, lies dead or dying on the ground. This was probably a ceremonial hunt, in which the king, protected by men with swords and shields, rode back and forth killing captured animals as they were released one by one into an enclosed area. The immediacy of this image marks a shift in Mesopotamian art away from a sense of timelessness and toward visual narrative. As in many earlier works, *Assurnasirpal II Killing Lions* shows a man confronting wild beasts. Unlike earlier works, however, the man is not part of nature, standing among animals as their equal, but has assumed dominion over nature. There is no question in this scene who will prevail.

Sargon II (ruled 721–705 BCE) built a new Assyrian capital at Dur Sharrukin (modern Khorsabad). An inscription says the grand project consumed the king day and night, but it was abandoned after his death. Excavations have enabled archeologists to reconstruct the city's appearance (fig. 2-22). A walled **citadel**, or fortress, containing 200 rooms and 30 courtyards lay at the northwest side of the city and straddled the city wall. The **palace complex**, centered at the back of the citadel on a raised, fortified platform about 52 feet high, is a monumental example of the use of art as propaganda to support political power. Guarded by two towers, it was accessible only by a wide ramp leading up from an open square, around which the residences of important government and religious officials were clustered. Beyond the ramp was the main courtyard, with service buildings on the right and

2-23. Guardian figure, from the entrance to the throne room, palace of Sargon II. c. 720 BCE. Limestone, height 16' (4.86 m). The Oriental Institute of the University of Chicago

Gates and doorways in Assyrian royal complexes were commonly protected by images of winged bulls with human heads. They were believed to guard against evil influences. As here, they were rendered with very realistic details—note the veins in the legs and the plumage of the wings—and their bodies were articulated in a lifelike way. At times, however, they were provided with a most unrealistic fifth leg, so that when viewed from the front they appeared to stand still, but when viewed from the side they seemed to be in motion.

temples on the left. The heart of the palace, protected by a reinforced wall with only two small, off-center doors, lay past the main courtyard. Within the inner compound was a second courtyard, lined with narrative relief panels showing tribute bearers, that functioned as an audience hall. Visitors would have entered the king's throne room from this courtyard through a stone gate sculpted in high relief with colossal guardian figures, such as the human-headed bull illustrated here (fig. 2-23). These hybrid creatures also flank the gates of the citadel. Ranging from 13 to 16 feet tall and weighing about 40 tons, they would have been formidable stone guardians for a royal audience.

The ziggurat at Dur Sharrukin was set off in an open space between the temple complex and the palace. It towered over the city, declaring the might of Assyria's kings and symbolizing their claim to empire. It probably had seven levels, each about 18 feet high and painted a different color. The four levels still remaining were once white, black, blue, and red. Instead of separate flights of stairs between the levels, a single, squared-off spiral ramp rose continuously from the base, becoming smaller in circumference as it went up.

1000
7000 BCE   1 CE

2-24. *Assurbanipal and His Queen in the Garden,* from the palace at Nineveh (modern Kuyunjik, Iraq). c. 647 BCE. Alabaster, height approx. 21" (53.3 cm). The British Museum, London

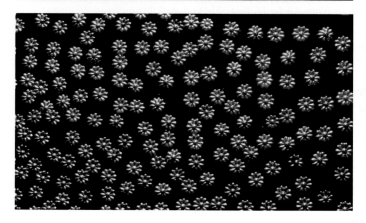

Assurbanipal (ruled 669–c. 627 BCE), king of the Assyrians three generations after Sargon II, had his capital at Nineveh (modern Kuyunjik). His palace was decorated with alabaster panels carved with pictorial narratives in low relief. Most show the king and his subjects in battle and hunting, but there are occasional scenes of palace life. One panel shows the king and queen in a pleasure garden (fig. 2-24). The king reclines on a couch, and the queen sits in a chair at his feet. Some servants arrive with trays of food, while others wave whisks to protect the royal couple from insects. A large, Egyptian-looking necklace hangs from the end of the couch at the right—perhaps the king has taken it off while he relaxes, or perhaps it is displayed here as a symbolic reference to Assurbanipal's conquest of Egypt in 663 BCE. This apparently tranquil domestic scene is actually a victory celebration. The king's weapons (sword, bow, and quiver of arrows) are on the table behind him, and the upside-down severed head of his vanquished enemy hangs from a tree at the far left. It was common during this period to display the heads and corpses of enemies as a form of psychological warfare, and Assurbanipal's generals would have sent him the head as a trophy.

Although much Assyrian art is relief carving, other arts were developing. One of the most spectacular archeological finds in the Near East was the discovery, beginning in 1988, of more than a thousand pieces of gold jewelry weighing more than 125 pounds in three Assyrian royal tombs at Kalhu dated from the ninth and eighth centuries BCE (fig. 2-25). The refinement and superb artistry of the crowns, necklaces, bracelets, armbands, ankle bracelets, and other ornaments recovered from these tombs—almost entirely Assyrian made—could never be discerned from depictions of jewelry in stone sculpture.

2-25. Earrings, crown, and rosettes, from the tomb of Queen Yabay, Kalhu (modern Nimrud, Iraq). Late 8th century BCE. Gold. Iraq Museum, Baghdad

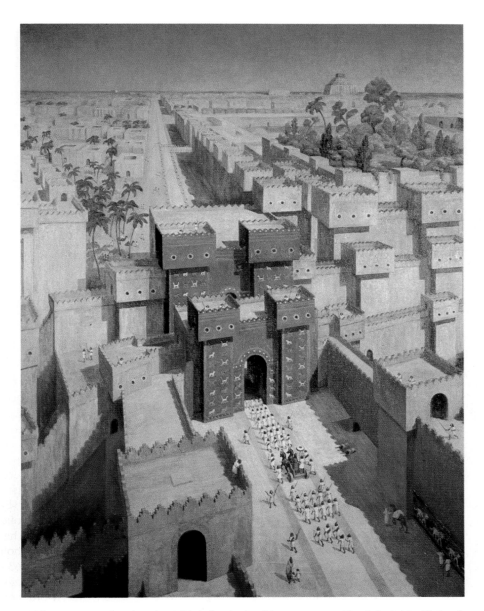

2-26. Reconstruction drawing of Babylon in the 6th century BCE. The Oriental Institute of the University of Chicago

In this view, the palace of Nebuchadnezzar II, with its famous Hanging Gardens, can be seen just behind and to the right of the Ishtar Gate, to the west of the Processional Way. The Marduk Ziggurat looms up in the far distance on the east bank of the Euphrates. This structure was at times believed to be the biblical Tower of Babel—Bab-il was an early form of the city's name.

NEO-BABYLONIA

At the end of the seventh century BCE, the Medes from western Iran and the Scythians from the frigid regions of modern Russia and Ukraine invaded the northern and eastern parts of Assyria. Meanwhile, under a new royal dynasty, the Babylonians reasserted themselves. This Neo-Babylonian kingdom began attacking Assyrian cities in 615 BCE and formed a treaty with the Medes. In 612 BCE, an allied army of Medes and Neo-Babylonians captured Nineveh. When the dust settled, Assyria was no more. The Medes controlled a swath of land below the Black and Caspian seas, and the Neo-Babylonians controlled a region that stretched from modern Turkey to northern Arabia and from Mesopotamia to the Mediterranean Sea.

The most famous Neo-Babylonian ruler was Nebuchadnezzar II (ruled 604–562 BCE). A great patron of architecture, he built temples dedicated to the Babylonian gods throughout his realm and transformed Babylon—the cultural, political, and economic hub of his empire—into one of the most splendid cities of its day. Babylon straddled the Euphrates River, its two sections joined by a bridge. The older eastern sector was traversed by a broad avenue named "May the Enemy Not Have Victory," also called the Processional Way because it was the route taken by religious processions honoring the city's patron god, Marduk (fig. 2-26). This street, laid with large stone slabs set in a bed of bitumen, was up to 66 feet wide at some points. It ran east from the Euphrates bridge past the temple district, then turned

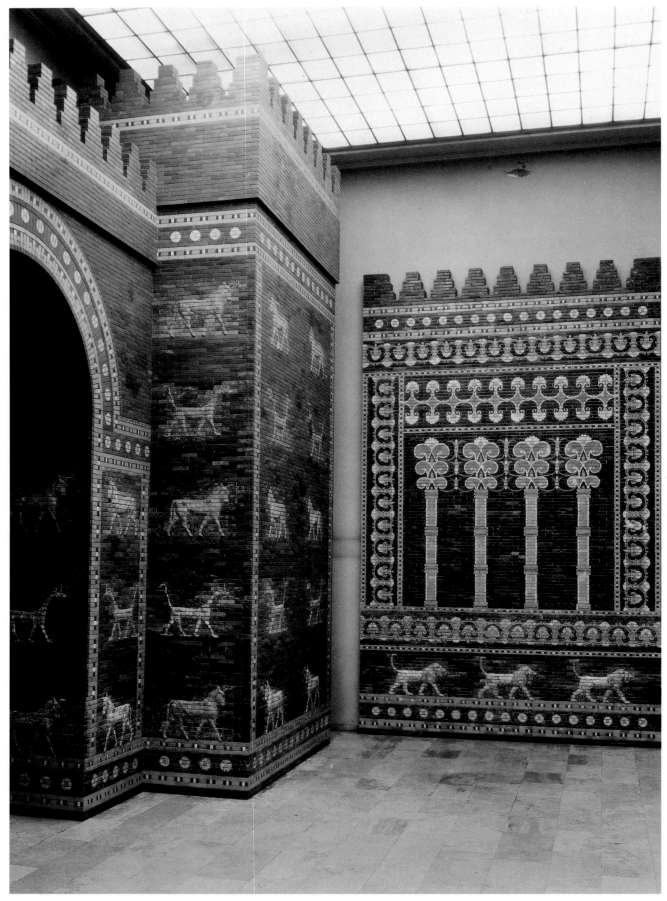

2-27. Ishtar Gate and throne room wall, from Babylon (Iraq). c. 575 BCE. Glazed brick. Staatliche Museen zu Berlin, Preussischer Kulturbesitz, Vorderasiatisches Museum

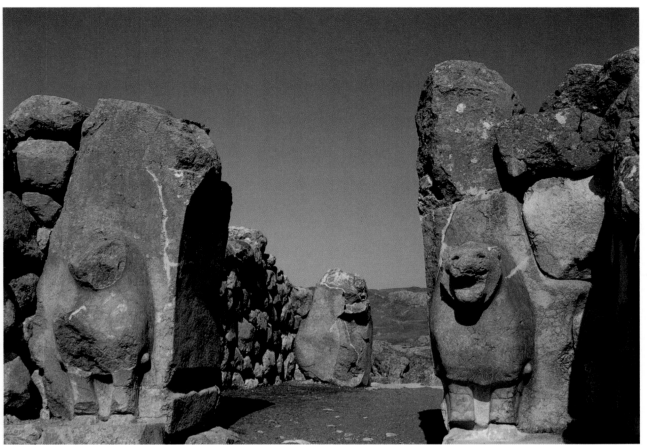

2-28. Lion Gate, Hattushash (near modern Boghazkeui, Turkey). c. 1400 BCE. Limestone

northward to end at the Ishtar Gate, one of the main entrances to the city. Along the way, the walls on both sides were faced with turquoise bricks that were **glazed** (painted and fired) and topped with notches, or **crenellation**. Among the brilliant turquoise bricks, specially molded, gold-colored bricks form images of lions striding along in honor of the goddess Ishtar.

The double-arched Ishtar Gate, a symbol of Babylonian power, was guarded by four crenellated towers. It is decorated with tiers of the dragons sacred to Marduk and the bulls with blue horns and tails associated with a number of other deities. Now reconstructed inside one of the Berlin State Museums, the Ishtar Gate is installed next to a panel from the outer wall of the throne room in Nebuchadnezzar's nearby palace (fig. 2-27). In this fragment, lions walk in a zone beneath stylized palm trees reminiscent of those in the mural from Mari (see fig. 2-19). Among Babylon's other marvels, none of which survive, were the city's walls, its fabled Hanging Gardens (see "The Seven Wonders of the World," page 102), and the Marduk Ziggurat. All that remains of this ziggurat, which ancient documents describe as painted white, black, crimson, blue, orange, silver, and gold, is the outline of its base and traces of the lower stairs.

Outside of Mesopotamia, other cultures—those of Anatolia, Elam, and Persia—were developing simultaneously and would have an impact on Mesopotamia before one of them, Persia, eventually overwhelmed it.

ANATOLIA

Anatolia, before the rise of the Assyrians, had been home to several independent cultures that resisted Mesopotamian domination. The most powerful was the Hittite civilization, whose founders had moved into the mountains and plateaus of central Anatolia from the east and established their capital at Hattushash (near modern Boghazkeui, Turkey) about 1600 BCE. Through trade and conquest, they created an empire that stretched along the coast of the Mediterranean Sea in the area of modern Syria and Lebanon, bringing them into conflict with the Egyptian Empire, which was expanding into the same region from the south (Chapter 3). The Hittites also made incursions into Mesopotamia. They were apparently the first people to work in iron, which they used for fittings for war chariots, weapons, sickles and plowshares for farmers, and chisels and hammers for sculptors and masons. They are noted for the artistry of their fine metalwork and for their imposing palace citadels with double walls and fortified gateways.

The foundations and base walls of the Hittite stronghold at Hattushash, which date to around 1400 BCE, were constructed with stone supplied from local quarries, but the upper walls, stairways, and walkways were finished in brick. The blocks of stone used to frame doorways were decorated in high relief with a variety of guardian figures, some 7-foot-tall, half-human–half-animal creatures, others naturalistically rendered animals like the lions shown here (fig. 2-28). These sculpted figures were

Some of the most bitter resentments spawned by war—whether in Mesopotamia in the twelfth century BCE or in our own time—have involved the "liberation" or "protection" of art objects and other artifacts of great value and meaning to the people from whom they were taken. Museums around the world have been enhanced, if not outright stocked, with paintings, sculpture, and other works either snatched by invading armies or acquired as a result of conquest, prolonged occupation, or economic domination. Two historically priceless objects unearthed in the excavations of Elamite Susa, for example—the Akkadian *Stela of Naramsin* (see fig. 2-16) and the Babylonian *Stela of Hammurabi* (see fig. 2-18)—were not Elamite at all, but Mesopotamian.

Both had been brought there as military trophies by an Elamite king, who added an inscription to the *Stela of Naramsin* explaining that he had merely "protected" it.

The same rationale has been used in modern times to justify the removal of countless works of art from their cultural contexts. The Rosetta Stone, the key to the modern decipherment of Egyptian hieroglyphics, was discovered in Egypt by French troops in 1799, fell into British hands when they forced the French from Egypt, and ultimately ended up in the British Museum in London. In the early nineteenth century, a British nobleman, Lord Elgin, removed many renowned Classical Greek reliefs from the Parthenon on the Acropolis in Athens with the blessing of the Ottoman authorities who governed Greece at the time. Although

his actions may indeed have protected the reliefs from neglect and the ravages of the Greek war of independence, they have remained installed, like the Rosetta Stone, in the British Museum, despite continuing protests from Greece. The Ishtar Gate from Babylon (see fig. 2-27) is now in a museum in Germany. Many works in German collections were similarly "protected" at the end of World War II and are surfacing now. In the United States, Native Americans are increasingly vocal in their demands that artifacts and human remains collected by anthropologists and archeologists and lodged in the country's museums be returned to them. "To the victor," it is said, "belong the spoils." It continues to be a matter of passionate debate whether or not this notion is appropriate in the case of revered cultural artifacts.

part of the architecture itself, not added to it separately. The boulders-becoming-creatures on the so-called Lion Gate harmonize with the colossal scale of this construction. Despite extreme weathering, the lions have endured over the millennia and still convey a sense of vigor and permanence.

ELAM

The strip of fertile plain known as Elam, between the Tigris River and the Zagros Mountains to the east (in present-day Iran), had become a flourishing farming region by 7000 BCE. About this time the city of Susa, later the capital of an Elamite kingdom, was established on the Shaur River. Elam had close cultural ties to Mesopotamia, but the two regions were often in conflict. In the twelfth century BCE, Elamite invaders looted art treasures from Mesopotamia and carried them back to Susa (see "Protection or Theft?," above).

In about 4000 BCE, Susa was a center of pottery production. Twentieth-century excavations there have uncovered nearly 8,000 finely formed and painted vessels (beakers, bowls, and jars), as well as coarse domestic **wares**. The fine wares have thin, fragile shells that suggest they were not meant for everyday use. Decorations painted in brown glaze on the pale yellow clay are sometimes purely geometric but are more often a graceful combination of geometric designs and stylized natural forms, mainly from the animal world, expertly balanced between repetition and variation of forms.

One handleless cup, or beaker, nearly a foot tall and weighing about 8 pounds, presents a pair of ibexes (only one of which is visible) that have been reduced to pure geometric form (fig. 2-29). On each side, the great sweep of the animals' horns encloses a small circular motif, or **roundel**, containing what might be a leaf pattern or a line of birds in flight. A narrow band above the ibexes shows

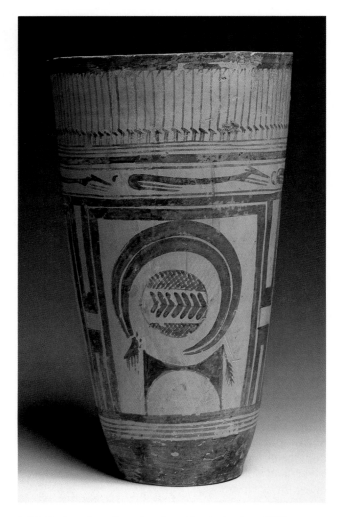

2-29. Beaker, from Susa (modern Shush, Iran). c. 4000 BCE. Ceramic, painted in brown glaze, height 11¼" (28.6 cm). Musée du Louvre, Paris

2-30. *Woman Spinning*, from Susa (modern Shush, Iran). c. 8th–7th century BCE. Bitumen compound, 3⁵/₈ x 5¹/₈" (9.2 x 13 cm). Musée du Louvre, Paris

short-haired, long-nosed dogs at rest. In the wide top band, stately wading birds stand motionless.

Susa's ingenious artisans produced a gray bitumen-based compound that could be molded while soft and carved when hard. From this compound, which still defies laboratory analysis, they made a variety of practical and decorative objects. An especially fine example, a 3⁵/₈-inch-high fragment from a larger relief, dates from the eighth to the seventh century BCE (fig. 2-30). It shows an important-looking woman adorned with many ornaments. Her hair is elegantly styled, and her garment has a patterned border. She sits barefoot and cross-legged on a lion-footed stool covered with sheepskin, spinning thread onto a large spindle. A fish lies on an offering stand in front of her, together with six round objects (perhaps fruit). A young servant, probably female, stands behind the woman, fanning her. At the lower right-hand corner of the fragment is what appears to be a portion of a long, flounced garment such as deities are frequently shown wearing, which might indicate the presence of a god or goddess to whom the offering is being made. Interpretation of this scene is difficult; it might be a banquet scene, perhaps in connection with a religious rite.

PERSIA

In the sixth century BCE, the Persians, a formerly nomadic, Indo-European-speaking people related to the Medes, began to seize power. From the region of Parsa, or Persis (modern Fars), southeast of Susa, they eventually overwhelmed Mesopotamia and the rest of the ancient Near East and established a vast empire. The rulers of this new empire traced their ancestry to a semilegendary Iranian king named Achaemenes and are known as the Achaemenids. Their dramatic expansion began in 559 BCE with the ascension of a remarkable leader, Cyrus II (called the Great, ruled 559–530 BCE). By the time of his death the Persian Empire included Babylonia; the land of the Medes, which stretched across northern Iran through Anatolia; and some of the Aegean islands far to the west. Cyrus's son Cambyses II (ruled 529–522 BCE) added Egypt and Cyprus. When Darius I (ruled 521–486 BCE), the son of a government official, took the throne, he proclaimed: "I am Darius, great King, King of Kings, King of countries, King of this earth." Darius and his successors went on to rule for nearly two centuries, expanding the Achaemenid Empire to both east and west.

Darius, like many powerful rulers, created monuments to serve as visible symbols of his authority. He made Susa his first capital and commissioned a 32-acre administrative compound to be built there. In about 518 BCE, he began construction of Parsa, a new capital in the Persian homeland in the Zagros highlands. Today this city, known as Persepolis, the name the Greeks gave it, is one of the best-preserved ancient sites in the Near East (fig. 2-31). Darius imported materials, workers, and artists from all over his empire for his building projects. He even ordered work to be executed in Egypt and transported to his capital. The result was a new style of art that combined many different cultural traditions, including Persian, Mede, Mesopotamian, Egyptian, and Greek. This artistic integration was simply a side effect of Darius's political strategy.

In Assyrian fashion, the imperial complex at Persepolis was set on a raised platform and laid out on a rectangular **grid,** or system of crossed lines. The platform was 40 feet high and measured 1,500 by 900 feet. It was accessible only from a single ramp made of wide, shallow steps to allow equestrians to ride up rather than dismount and climb on foot. Construction was spread out over nearly sixty years, and Darius lived to see the erection of only a treasury, the Apadana (audience hall), and a very small palace for himself. The Apadana, set above the rest of the complex on a second terrace (fig. 2-32),

2-31. Plan of the ceremonial complex, Persepolis, Iran. 518–c. 460 BCE

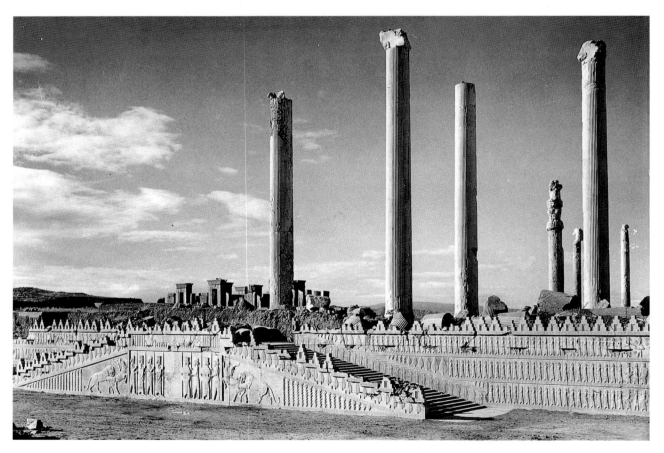

2-32. Apadana (audience hall) of Darius and Xerxes, ceremonial complex, Persepolis, Iran. 518–c. 460 BCE

The ancient historian Cleiarchus of Alexandria relates that Alexander the Great and his troops accidentally torched the royal compound at Persepolis during a wild banquet in celebration of their victory over the Persians. It is more probable that Alexander had it destroyed deliberately. The site was never rebuilt, and its ruins were never buried. Scholars have been measuring, mapping, and studying what remains of the complex for the past 200 years. Various pieces of architectural ornament have been stripped from Persepolis for display in museums around the world.

2-33. Partially reconstructed column with complete capital, from the ceremonial complex, Persepolis, Iran. Iranbastan Museum, Teheran

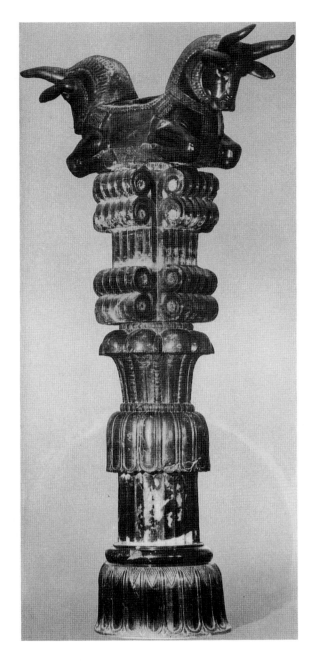

had open porches on three sides and a square hall large enough to hold several thousand people. Darius's son Xerxes I (ruled 485–465 BCE) added a sprawling palace complex for himself, enlarged the treasury building, and began a vast new public reception space, the Hall of 100 Columns, with its own guard gate. Most of the remaining work was done under Xerxes' heir, Artaxerxes I (ruled 464–425 BCE).

The multicultural composition of imperial Persia is evident in the varied appearance of the many hundreds of **columns** found in Persepolis (see "Elements of Architecture," page 101). Although they were all executed with a distinctly Persian flavor, the columns reflect design ideas from Mede, Egyptian, and possibly Greek sources. They stood atop bell-shaped **bases** (foundations) decorated with leaves. Their **shafts**, or vertical supports, were carved with evenly spaced vertical channels called **fluting**, which exaggerated their height and gave them a feeling of delicate refinement. The **capitals**, the top section of the columns on which ceiling beams rested, were lavishly decorated with a combination of palm fronds, papyrus flowers, other plant forms, double vertical scrolls, and the heads and forequarters of kneeling creatures placed back to back (fig. 2-33). Traces of pigment reveal that the Persepolis structures were originally richly painted in red, green, yellow, and blue. Large relief panels from Persepolis also show influences from Mesopotamian, Egyptian, and Greek cultures. In those panels, the garments that reveal the body beneath and have fine, knife-edged pleats especially reflect Greek sources and may indeed have been done by Greek sculptors.

Like some Assyrian palace reliefs, those at Persepolis were concerned with displays of allegiance and economic prosperity rather than with heroic exploits. In one relief Darius holds an audience while his son and heir, Xerxes, listens from behind the throne (fig. 2-34). Such

2-34. *Darius and Xerxes Receiving Tribute*, detail of a relief from the stairway leading to the Apadana, ceremonial complex, Persepolis, Iran. 491–486 BCE. Limestone, height 8'4" (2.54 m). Iranbastan Museum, Teheran

TECHNIQUE

PERSIAN METAL-WORKING

The intricate lion's-head **terminals** of the gold **torque** seen in figure 2-35 were probably made using the **lost-wax casting** process, a technique for fabricating fine metal objects developed at a very early date. A shape was carved out of wax exactly as the finished object was to look. This wax "sculpture" was then enclosed in a heat-resistant material such as clay or plaster. (If the piece was to be hollow, the wax was formed around a heat-resistant core.) Once the clay or plaster mold had dried, it was heated and the melted wax ran out through a vent. Molten metal was then poured into the mold. After the casting had cooled and the mold was removed, the metalsmith could decorate and finish the piece.

On this torque, tiny **inlays** made of lapis lazuli, turquoise, and mother-of-pearl are part of the design. First, the worker chiseled little wells in the surface of the face and lower part of the neck, then filled the holes with inlays of the same size and shape. Most of these inlays have been lost, but one piece can still be seen on the side of the head and two more at the top of the body. A different technique was used to create the intricate inlay work on the lion's neck. Here, pieces of fine gold wire, known as **filigree**, were arranged in a pattern on the neck and subjected to just enough heat to fuse them to it. Diamond-shaped inlays were then inserted into the spaces outlined by the filigree.

empty well inlay inlay filigree wire inlay empty wells empty wells

2-35. Torque with lion's-head terminals, from Susa (modern Shush, Iran). 4th century BCE. Gold with lapis lazuli, turquoise, and mother-of-pearl, diameter 8" (20.2 cm). Musée du Louvre, Paris

panels would have looked quite different when they were freshly painted in rich tones of deep blue, scarlet, green, purple, and turquoise, with metal objects such as Darius's crown and necklace covered in **gold leaf**, or sheets of hammered gold.

The Persians' decorative arts—including ornamented weapons, domestic wares, horse trappings, and jewelry—demonstrate high levels of technical and artistic sophistication. The imaginative use of animals in these arts can be seen in a late Achaemenid gold **torque**, or

neckpiece, found in a Persian tomb at Susa and dated to the fourth century BCE (fig. 2-35). The tiny lion heads that form the ends, or **terminals**, of this piece are represented naturalistically, but the intricate inlays of lapis lazuli, turquoise, and mother-of-pearl transform them into pure ornament. In the Roman mosaic copy of a famous fourth-century BCE Greek painting (see fig. 5-70), Darius III of Persia (ruled 335–330 BCE) wears an identical torque.

The Persians learned to mint standard coinage from the Lydians of western Anatolia after Cyrus the Great defeated Lydia's fabulously wealthy King Croesus in 546 BCE (see "Coining Money," opposite). Croesus's wealth—the source of the lasting expression "rich as Croesus"—had made Lydia an attractive target for an aggressive empire builder like Cyrus. One type of Persian coin, the gold daric, named for Darius and first minted during his regime (fig. 2-36), is among the most valuable coins in the world today. Commonly called an "archer," it shows the well-armed emperor wearing his crown and carrying a lance in his right hand; he lunges forward as if he had just let fly an arrow from his bow.

At its height, the Persian Empire extended from Africa to India. Only mainland Greeks successfully resisted the armies of the Achaemenids, preventing them from advancing into Europe (Chapter 5). And it was a Greek who ultimately put an end to their empire. In 334 BCE, Alexander the Great of Macedonia crossed into Anatolia and swept through Mesopotamia, defeating Darius III and nearly laying waste the magnificent Persepolis in 331 BCE. Although the Persian Empire was at an end, the art style unified there during the Achaemenid period clearly shows its links with Greece as well as with Egypt, which may have been heavily influenced by Mesopotamian culture.

2-36. Daric, a coin first minted under Darius I of Persia. 4th century BCE. Gold. Heberden Coin Room, Ashmolean Museum, Oxford

TECHNIQUE
COINING MONEY

Long before the invention of coins, the people of the ancient world had used gold, silver, bronze, and copper in either raw lumps or bricks as a medium of exchange for trade. But each piece had to be weighed every time it was used to establish its exact value. The Lydians of western Anatolia began the practice of producing metal coins in standard weights in the seventh century BCE, adapting the concept of the seal—a Sumerian invention—to designate their value. Until about 525 BCE, coins bore an image on one side only. One of the most beautiful of these earliest coins is illustrated here, a coin first minted during the reign of the Lydian king Croesus (ruled 560–546 BCE). It is stamped with the heads and forelegs of a bull and lion, who face each other. The back side has only a squarish depression left by the punch used to force the metal into the mold.

To make two-faced coins, the ancients used a punch and anvil, each of which held a die, or mold, incised with the design to be impressed in the coin. A metal blank weighed out to the exact amount of the denomination was placed over the anvil die, the one containing the design for the obverse ("head") of the coin. The punch, with the die of the reverse ("tail") design, was then placed on top of the metal blank and struck with a mallet. After Cyrus the Great of Persia conquered Anatolia, he and his successors minted coins using the Lydian weight system. Beginning in the reign of Darius I, kings' portraits appear on coins, proclaiming the ruler's sovereignty and his control of the coin of the realm. This custom is still very much alive throughout the world. Because we often know at least approximately when a given ancient monarch ruled, the discovery in an archeological excavation of coins bearing that ruler's portrait helps to date the objects around them.

obverse   reverse

mallet

punch

die for reverse

metal coin blank

die for obverse

anvil

Front and back of a gold coin first minted under Croesus, king of Lydia. 560–546 BCE. Heberden Coin Room, Ashmolean Museum, Oxford

1 CE
7000 BCE   1 CE

BCE 4000   3500   3000   2500

Hierakonpolis jar
c. 3500–3400

Palette of
Narmer
c. 3150–3125

Pyramids at
c. 2601–25

▲ PREDYNASTIC PRE-3150   ▲ EARLY DYNASTIC 3150–2700   ▲ OLD KINGDOM 2700–2190

CHAPTER 3

Art of Ancient Egypt

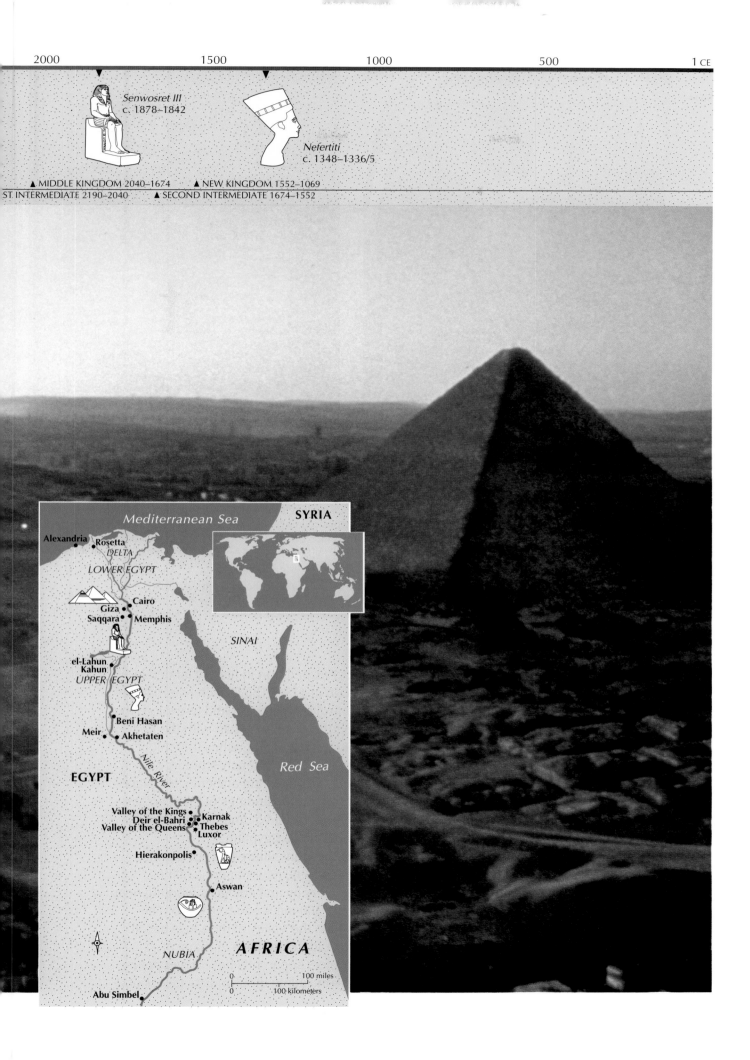

Senwosret III
c. 1878–1842

Nefertiti
c. 1348–1336/5

▲ MIDDLE KINGDOM 2040–1674   ▲ NEW KINGDOM 1552–1069

ST. INTERMEDIATE 2190–2040   ▲ SECOND INTERMEDIATE 1674–1552

Mediterranean Sea   **SYRIA**

Alexandria   Rosetta
DELTA

LOWER EGYPT

Cairo
Giza
Saqqara   Memphis

SINAI

el-Lahun
Kahun

UPPER EGYPT

Beni Hasan

Meir   Akhetaten

Nile River

Red Sea

EGYPT

Valley of the Kings
Deir el-Bahri   Karnak
Valley of the Queens   Thebes
Luxor

Hierakonpolis

Aswan

NUBIA   *A F R I C A*

0   100 miles
0   100 kilometers

Abu Simbel

3-1. Funerary mask of Tutankhamun (ruled 1336/5–1327 BCE), from the tomb of Tutankhamun, Valley of the Kings, Deir el-Bahri, photographed the day it was discovered—October 28, 1925

A collar of dried flowers and beads covered the chest portion of the mask, and a linen scarf was draped around the head. The mask had been placed over the upper part of the young king's mummified body, which was enclosed in three coffins nested like a set of Russian dolls. These coffins were placed in a quartzite "box" that was itself encased within three gilt wooden shrines, each larger than the last. The innermost coffin, made of solid gold, is illustrated in figure 3-41. Tutankhamun's burial chamber was not the only royal tomb to survive unpillaged to the twentieth century, but it is by far the richest find.

3-2. Funerary mask of Tutankhamun. Gold inlaid with glass and semiprecious stones. Height 21¼" (54.5 cm). Egyptian Museum, Cairo

The first large-scale "archeological" expedition in history landed in Egypt with the armies of Napoleon in 1798. The French commander went there intending to take control of the region and to explore the possibility of digging a canal to connect the Mediterranean with the Red Sea. Clearly, he also sensed that Egypt sheltered great riches that might be won for France, for he took with him some 200 French scholars and charged them with mapping, excavating, and studying ancient sites. Napoleon's military adventure ended in failure, but the findings of his scholars, eventually published in thirty-six richly illustrated volumes, unleashed among his contemporaries a craze for all things Egyptian.

Popular fascination with this ancient African culture has not dimmed since Napoleon's time. As recently as May 1995, newspaper headlines around the world heralded a major discovery by archeologists working near Thebes, an ancient Egyptian capital some 300 miles south of Cairo. The huge, unusual burial complex they found in the Valley of the Kings has at least sixty-seven chambers, believed to hold the remains of many of Ramesses II's fifty-two sons. Because looters apparently have never penetrated the back chambers, the contents—including thousands of pieces of pottery, statue fragments, beads, and jewelry—provide extraordinary documentation of a period in the thirteenth-century BCE when Ramesses II was expanding the Egyptian empire and building some of the monumental architecture for which Egypt is known.

Looters, ancient and modern, have been attracted to tombs by simple greed, archeologists and historians by scholarly interest. Ironically, one reason that *this* burial complex had not been discovered by either group was that its entrance was obscured by debris from a nearby excavation in the 1920s: the remarkable tomb of Tutankhamun (King Tut). When the "Treasures of Tutankhamun" exhibit was mounted in the late 1970s, some 7 million visitors flocked to six of the world's major museums to marvel at a selection of artifacts placed in the tomb of an Egyptian ruler more than 3,000 years ago (figs. 3-1, 3-2, 3-41).

Much of what we know about life in ancient Egypt we owe to that culture's preoccupation with death. Many of Egypt's written records were lost in the accidental burning in Roman times of the great library at Alexandria—a fire that destroyed more than 700,000 ancient documents—and we must deduce what we can about Egypt from the decoration and outfitting of tombs like Tutankhamun's. The rulers of Egypt, even in earliest times, sought to immortalize themselves through the art and architecture they commissioned for their final resting places, and in a sense they succeeded richly. They are well remembered.

NEOLITHIC AND PREDYNASTIC EGYPT

The Greek traveler and historian Herodotus, writing in the fifth century BCE, remarked that "Egypt is the gift of the Nile." This great river—the longest in the world—has two major tributaries: the Blue Nile, which originates in the mountains of Ethiopia, and the White Nile, fed by a number of smaller rivers rising deep in equatorial Africa. The two tributary Niles merge at the city of Khartoum, in Sudan. From there, the Nile proper winds northward into Egypt, then flows through it in a relatively straight line to the Mediterranean, where it forms a broad delta before emptying into the sea. Before it was dammed in the twentieth century at Aswan, the lower river, swollen with the runoff of heavy seasonal rains in the south, overflowed its banks for several months each year. Every time the floodwaters receded, they left behind a new layer of rich silt, which made the valley and delta uncommonly fertile, an attractive habitat for prehistoric hunters and gatherers.

By about 8000 BCE, the valley's inhabitants had become relatively sedentary, living off its abundance of fish, game, and wild plants. It was not until about 5500 BCE that they adopted the agricultural, village way of life associated with Neolithic culture (Chapter 1). At that time the climate of North Africa was growing increasingly dry. To secure an adequate supply of water for their crops and their own domestic use, the early agriculturalists along the Nile—much as had those in Mesopotamia—cooperated to control the river's flow, constructing dams and irrigation canals. It was apparently this common need that led many smaller riverside settlements to form alliances with their neighbors. Over time, these primitive federations expanded further by conquering and absorbing weaker communities. By about 3500 BCE there were several larger states, or chiefdoms, in the lower Nile Valley.

The Predynastic period, roughly 4350 to 3150 BCE, was a time of social and political transition preceding the unification of Egypt under a single ruler and the formation of the dynasties, in which members of the same family inherited Egypt's throne. During this period, a new type of leadership emerged in which political control was bolstered by the rulers' claims to have divine powers. Their subjects, in turn, expected such leaders to protect them not only from outside aggression but also from natural catastrophes such as droughts and insect plagues. If a ruler failed to do this, he was removed from power and a more promising leader installed. A royal ritual practiced in the Dynastic period suggests that early rulers may even have been killed when their supposed supernatural powers failed to work. In this later ritual, called the *sed* festival, the king in the thirtieth year of his reign was symbolically buried and resurrected as a means of renewing his "divine" powers. Preceding this, he ran a race on a specially built track in order to prove his physical fitness.

The surviving art of the Predynastic period consists chiefly of ceramic figurines, decorated pottery, and reliefs carved on stone plaques and pieces of ivory. A few examples of Predynastic wall painting—lively scenes filled with small figures of people and animals—were found in

3-3. *Jar with River Scene*, from Hierakonpolis. Predynastic, c. 3500–3400 BCE. Painted clay, 7 x 8¼" (17.5 x 20.9 cm). The Brooklyn Museum

Excavations of H. deMorgan 1907–8 (09.889.400)

though the forms they represent are reduced to the barest means. Two figures of nearly equal size, a man and woman, stand on the roof of the cabin on the left. The woman arches her long arms over her head in a gesture that may be an expression of mourning, while the man beside her and a smaller figure atop the other cabin reach out toward her. These three people possess a quality of expressiveness: the power of what they *feel* is evident.

what was either a temple or a tomb at Hierakonpolis, in Upper Egypt. This Predynastic town of mud-brick houses distributed over about 100 acres was once home to as many as 10,000 people.

Among the artifacts found at Hierakonpolis is a pottery jar, dating from about 3500–3400 BCE. It is made of buff-colored clay and decorated with a river scene in a dark reddish brown (fig. 3-3). Zigzag lines around the mouth of the jar symbolize the waters of the Nile, upon which floats a boomerang-shaped boat. According to one interpretation, the boat is laden with coffins, and the scene symbolizes the human journey on the "river of Life and Death." Palm fronds affixed to a pole on the prow bend in the wind, indicating the direction of the vessel's movement. The boat has two cabins on its deck, and a row of vertical strokes along the bottom of its hull represents oars. These lines and strokes are a kind of **abstract** visual shorthand. We recognize what they stand for even

EARLY DYNASTIC EGYPT

About 3150 BCE Egypt became a consolidated state. According to Egyptian legend, the country had previously evolved into two major kingdoms—the Two Lands—Upper Egypt in the south and Lower Egypt in the north. Some powerful ruler from Upper Egypt, referred to in an ancient document as "Menes king–Menes god," finally conquered Lower Egypt and merged the Two Lands into a single kingdom. Modern Egyptologists, experts on the history and culture of ancient Egypt, suspect that the unification process was more gradual than the legend would have us believe.

In the third century BCE, an Egyptian priest and historian named Manetho compiled a chronological listing of Egypt's rulers since the most ancient times that was based on temple records and inscriptions on temple walls. He grouped them into dynasties, or families, and included the length of each king's reign. Although the list has been much modified since Manetho's time and scholars do not fully agree about many of its dates, this dynastic chronology is still the accepted guide to ancient Egypt's long history. Manetho listed thirty dynasties that ruled the country between about 3150 and 332 BCE, when it was conquered by the Greeks. Egyptologists have grouped these dynasties into larger periods reflecting broad historical developments. This chapter covers the Predynastic period through the New Kingdom (1069 BCE), and the dating system used throughout is based on the work of French Egyptologist Nicolas Grimal.

EGYPTIAN SYMBOLS

Symbolic of kingship, the crowned figure is everywhere in Egyptian art. The false beard of a dead king is long, braided, and ends in a knob. A living king is portrayed with a shorter, squared-off beard (see fig. 3-15). The cobra, "she who rears up," was equated with the sun, the king, and some deities.

The god Horus, king of the earth and a force for good, is represented most characteristically as a falcon. Horus's eyes (*wedjat*) were regarded as symbolic of the sun and moon. The *wedjat* here is the solar eye. The ankh is symbolic of everlasting life. The scarab was associated with the creator god Atum and the rising sun.

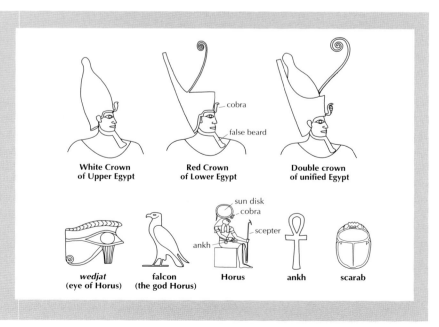

White Crown of Upper Egypt

Red Crown of Lower Egypt — cobra, false beard

Double crown of unified Egypt

wedjat (eye of Horus)

falcon (the god Horus)

Horus — sun disk, cobra, scepter, ankh

ankh

scarab

Years	Period	Egypt	World
Before 3150 BCE	Predynastic	Painted clay pottery	c. 3500–3000 BCE Earliest pictographs (Sumer); pictographs evolve into ideograms and phonograms (China, India); Skara Brae settled (Scotland)
c. 3150–2700 BCE	Early Dynastic (or Archaic) Dynasties 1–2	Egypt united under "Menes"; *Palette of Narmer*; development of hieroglyphic writing; manufacture and export of papyrus scrolls	
c. 2700–2190 BCE	Old Kingdom Dynasties 3–6	Djoser's stepped pyramid; Great Pyramids at Giza	
c. 2190–2040 BCE	First Intermediate Dynasties 7–10		c. 2000 BCE *Gilgamesh* epic (Sumer); widespread use of bronze tools (Thailand, China, northern Europe); earliest Minoan palace at Knossos (Crete); first city-state in Anatolia
c. 2040–1674 BCE	Middle Kingdom Dynasties 11–14	Rock-cut tombs; faience *Hippopotamus*	
c. 1674–1552 BCE	Second Intermediate Dynasties 15–17	Hyksos, from eastern Mediterranean, occupy Nile Delta	c. 1600–1500 BCE Pacific islands colonized; Shang dynasty (China); citadel at Mycenae (Greece)
c. 1552–1069 BCE	New Kingdom Dynasties 18–20	Great Temple of Amun, Karnak; *Nefertiti*	c. 1450–1200 BCE Minoan palaces destroyed (Crete); spread of phonetic alphabet devised by Canaanites (eastern Mediterranean); Israelites led out of Egypt by Moses (Canaan); Olmec civilization (Mesoamerica)

Religious Beliefs

Herodotus thought the Egyptians the most religious people he had ever encountered. It is certainly true that religious beliefs permeate Egyptian art of all periods, and some knowledge of them is needed to understand the art.

At the time of the Early Dynastic period, Egypt's rulers were worshiped as gods after their deaths; thus, ordinary Egyptians considered their kings to be their link to the invisible gods of the universe. To please the gods and ensure their continuing goodwill toward the state, Egypt's kings built them splendid temples and provided for priests to maintain them. The priests were responsible for seeing to it that statues of the gods, placed deep in the innermost rooms of their temples, were never without fresh food and clothing. The many gods and goddesses were depicted in various forms, some as human beings, others as animals, and still others as creatures half human, half animal.

Osiris, for example, the god of the dead, regularly appears in human form, as does his wife, Isis. The sky god Horus, however, was most often depicted as having a human body but the head of a hawk. The sun god Ra appears at some times as a cobra, at other times as a scarab beetle (see "Egyptian Symbols," opposite).

Certain gods took on different forms over the course of time, and a given god might be worshiped in different parts of the country under different names. In the New Kingdom at Thebes, the great creation god Amun and the sun god Ra came to be venerated as the single deity Amun-Ra. Everywhere else in Egypt in this period the two continued to be thought of as separate gods. At the heart of Egyptian religion are stories that explain how the world, the gods, and human beings came into being (see "Egyptian Myths of Creation," page 96).

Egyptian religious beliefs reflect the sense of an ordered cosmos. The movements of the heavenly bodies,

EGYPTIAN MYTHS OF CREATION

Herodotus's contention that the Egyptians were the most obsessively religious people he knew is amply supported by the large number of gods encountered in ancient Egyptian documents. At one time even the Nile itself was revered as a god. Early Egyptian creation myths provide a convenient introduction to many of the earliest and most important deities in Egypt's confusing and sometimes contradictory pantheon. One myth, focusing on the origins of the gods themselves, relates that the sun god Ra—or Ra-Atum—formed himself out of the waters of chaos, or unformed matter, emerging from them seated atop a mound of sand hardened by his own rays. By spitting—or ejaculating—he then created the gods of wetness and dryness, Tefnut and Shu, who in turn begat the male Geb (earth) and the female Nut (sky). Geb and Nut produced two sons, Osiris and Seth—the gods of goodness and evil, respectively—and two daughters, Isis and Nephthys (Isis can be seen in figure 3-43).

Taking Isis as his wife, Osiris became king of Egypt. His envious brother Seth promptly killed Osiris and hacked his body to pieces, snatching the throne for himself. Isis and her sister, Nephthys, gathered up the scattered remains and, with the help of the god Anubis, patched Osiris back together. Despite her husband's mutilated condition, Isis somehow managed to conceive a son—Horus. Once Horus was on the scene (another power for good capable of guarding the interests of Egypt), he defeated Seth and became king of the earth, while Osiris retired to the underworld as overseer of the realm of the dead (see fig. 3-44).

As for the creation of human beings, it is said in one story that Ra once lost an eye. Unperturbed, he replaced it with a new one. When the old eye was found and brought back to him, it began to cry, angered that it was no longer of any use. Human beings were born from its tears. In a variation on this myth, the people of Memphis insisted that it was their local god Ptah who created humankind, having formed us on his potter's wheel.

Some rulers of Akkad in the ancient Near East were held to be gods, and by the time of the Early Dynastic period, Egypt's kings were revered as gods in human form. A New Kingdom practice helps to explain the Egyptian belief of that period regarding the origin of rulers. Each year as part of the *opet* festival, the celebration of the flooding of the Nile, the statue of the god Amun from the temple at Karnak was carried in rich procession, along with statues of his wife and son, Mut and Khonsu, to their alternate temple at Luxor, to the south. Inscriptions in the processional colonnade record that while at Luxor the all-powerful god miraculously conceives a future ruler of Egypt.

---

the workings of the gods, and the humblest of human activities were all thought to be part of a grand design of balance and harmony. Death was to be feared only by those who lived in such a way as to disrupt that harmony; upright souls could be confident that their spirits would live on eternally.

The *Palette of Narmer*

The legendary king-god Menes may have been an actual king named Narmer (Dynasty 1, ruled c. 3150–3125 BCE), known from a famous stone plaque, the *Palette of Narmer* (fig. 3-4), found at Hierakonpolis. The palette is a slate slab carved in low relief on both sides with scenes and identifying inscriptions. The ruler's name appears on both sides in **pictographs**, or picture writing, in a small square at the top: a horizontal fish *(nar)* above a vertical chisel *(mer)*. The cow heads on each side of his name symbolize the protective goddess Hathor.

Palettes, flat stones with a circular depression on one side, were common utensils of the time. They were used for mixing eye paint. Men and women both painted their eyelids to help prevent infections in the eyes and perhaps to reduce the glare of the sun, much as football players today blacken their cheekbones before a game. The *Palette of Narmer* has the same form as these common objects but is much larger. It and other large palettes decorated with animals, birds, and occasionally human figures probably had a ceremonial function.

King Narmer appears as the main character in the various scenes on the palette. They may commemorate a specific battle, or they may simply make use of established images of conquest to proclaim Narmer the great unifier, protector, and leader of the Egyptian people. As in the *Stela of Naramsin* (see fig. 2-16), the ruler is shown larger than the other human figures on the palette to indicate his divine status. Interestingly, the kneeling man that Narmer holds by the hair and prepares to strike with his heavy mace would be very close to the king's height if he were standing (fig. 3-4, left). His size suggests that he may represent Narmer's counterpart, the conquered ruler of Lower Egypt. Narmer himself wears the White Crown of Upper Egypt, and from his waistband hangs a ceremonial bull's tail signifying strength. He is barefoot, suggesting that this is not an illustration of an actual military encounter but rather a symbolic representation of a hero's preordained victory. An attendant standing behind Narmer holds his sandals. Above Narmer's kneeling foe, the god Horus, in the form of a hawk with a human hand, holds a rope tied around the neck of a man's head next to a few stylized stalks of **papyrus**, a plant that grew in profusion along the lower Nile. This combination of symbols again makes it clear that Lower Egypt has been tamed. In the bottom **register**, below Narmer's feet, two of his enemies appear to be running away, or perhaps they are sprawled on the ground just as they fell when they were killed.

On the other side of the palette (fig. 3-4, right), Narmer is shown in the top register wearing the Red Crown of Lower Egypt, making it clear that he now rules both lands. Here his name—the fish and chisel—appears not only in the rectangle at the top but also next to his

3-4. *Palette of Narmer*, from Hierakonpolis. Dynasty 1, c. 3150–3125 BCE. Slate, height 25" (63.5 cm). Egyptian Museum, Cairo

head. With his sandal bearer again in attendance, he marches behind his minister of state and four men carrying standards that may symbolize different regions of the country. Before them, under the watchful eye of the hawk Horus, is a gory depiction of the enemy dead. The decapitated bodies of Lower Egyptian warriors have been placed in two neat rows, their heads between their feet.

In the center register, the elongated necks of two monstrous creatures with feline heads, each held on a leash by an attendant, curve gracefully around the rim of the cup of the palette. The intertwining of their necks is possibly another reference to the union of the Two Lands. In the bottom register, a bull menaces a fallen foe outside the walls of a fortress. The bull, an animal known for its great strength and virility, is probably meant to symbolize the king.

The images carved on the palette are strong and direct, and although scholars disagree about some of their specific meanings, their overall message is simple and clear: a king named Narmer rules over the unified land of Egypt with a strong hand. Narmer's palette is particularly important because of the way it uses pictographs and symbols, showing much about the development of writing in Egypt. Moreover, it provides very early examples of the quite unusual way Egyptian artists solved the problem of depicting the human form in two-dimensional art such as relief sculpture or painting.

Representation of the Human Figure

Forceful and easy to comprehend, the images on the Narmer palette present a king's exploits as he wished them to be remembered. For the next several thousand years, much of Egyptian art was created to meet the demand of royal patrons for similarly graphic, indestructible testimonies to their glory.

Many of the figures on the palette are shown in poses that would be impossible to assume in real life. By Narmer's time, Egyptian artists, using the "memory image" (see Chapter 1), had arrived at a unique way of drawing the human figure. The Egyptians' aim was to represent each part of the body from the most characteristic angle. Heads are shown in profile, to best capture the subject's identifying features. Eyes, however, are most expressive when seen from the front, so artists rendered the eyes in these profile heads in frontal view. As for the rest of the body, they treated the shoulders as though from the front, but at the waist they twisted the figure drastically to be able to show hips, legs, and feet in profile. If both hands were required in front of a figure, artists routinely lengthened the arm reaching across the body rather than turn the body sideways. Unless the degree of action demanded otherwise, they placed one foot in front of the other on the **groundline**, showing both from the inside, with high-arched insteps and a single big toe. This artistic

3-5. *Sculptors at Work*, relief from Saqqara. Dynasty 5, c. 2510–2460 BCE. Painted stone. Egyptian Museum, Cairo

tradition, or convention, was followed especially in the depiction of royalty and other dignitaries, and it was considered so successful that it persisted until the fourth century BCE. Persons of lesser social rank engaged in more active tasks tended to be represented more naturally (compare the figure of Narmer with those of his standard bearers in figure 3-4, right). Similarly, long-standing conventions governed the depiction of animals, insects, inanimate objects, landscape, and architecture. Flies, for example, are always shown from above, bees from the side.

In three-dimensional sculpture, figures could be constructed as they are in life. A painted relief from the funerary complex at Saqqara, created at least 600 years later than the *Palette of Narmer*, shows that artists working in two dimensions were perfectly capable of drawing "normal" figures as well (fig. 3-5). It shows a pair of sculptors putting the finishing touches on a statue. The "living" sculptors are portrayed in the conventional twisted pose, while the statue itself appears in full profile, as it would in reality.

Just as Egyptian artists adhered to artificial convention in the posing of figures, they also proportioned their figures in accordance with an ideal image of the human form, following an established **canon of proportions**. The ratios between a figure's height and all of its component parts were clearly prescribed. They were calculated as multiples of a specific unit of measure such as the width of the closed fist. It is likely that the ideal was in fact dictated to schools of artists by their royal patrons. Egypt's royalty in a given period may or may not have been of a different racial makeup than the general populace. In any case, they considered themselves a superior breed and

3-6. Diagram of a hypothetical grid for canon of proportions in use during the Old Kingdom

This canon set the height of the human body from heel to hairline at eighteen times the width of the fist. (There are eighteen squares between the heel of the king's left foot and the top of his headdress.) The hypothetical grid shown here is overlaid on a simple drawing of the statue of *Menkaure and His Wife, Queen Khamerernebty* (fig. 3-15). The proportions are for the figure on the left. Because the queen had to be smaller than the king, she was carved according to another, slightly smaller canon.

wished to have their own specific physical attributes held up to the masses as those befitting majesty.

The specific measure employed and the proportions derived from it varied slightly over time, but the underlying concept and the means by which it was implemented did not. Having determined the size of a desired figure, the artist first covered the area the figure was to occupy with a grid made up of a fixed number of squares (fig. 3-6). The figure could then be sketched quite mechanically. If the width of the fist was the canon's basic unit of measure, the artist saw to it that each hand was one square wide. Knowing that the knee should fall a prescribed number of squares above the groundline, the waist *x* number of squares above the knee, and so on made the process quite formulaic. The grid itself was either removed or covered up as the work progressed.

THE OLD KINGDOM

The Old Kingdom (2700–2190 BCE) was a time of social cohesion and political stability, despite changes in Egypt's climate that made droughts and plagues of insects increasingly common and the need of the country's rulers to mount occasional military excursions to defend its borders. The increasing wealth of the ruling families of the period is reflected in the size and complexity of the tomb structures they commissioned for themselves. Court sculptors were regularly called upon to create lifesize, even colossal royal portraits in stone. Kings were not the only patrons of the arts, however. Numerous government officials and administrators also could afford to have their tombs decorated with elaborate carvings.

Funerary Architecture

Central to ancient Egyptian religious belief was the notion that an essential part of every human personality was its life force, or spirit. This spirit, called the **ka**, lived on after the death of the body, forever engaged in the activities it had enjoyed in its former existence. The ka needed a body to live in, but in the absence of one of flesh and blood, a sculpted likeness of the deceased was adequate. It was especially important to provide a comfortable home for the ka of a departed king, so that even in the afterlife it would continue to ensure the well-being of the Egyptian state.

The need to fulfill the requirements of the ka led the Egyptians to develop elaborate funerary rites and structures. They preserved the bodies of the dead with care and placed them in burial chambers filled with all of the supplies and furnishings the ka might require throughout eternity (see "Preserving the Dead," page 121). The quantity and value of these grave goods were so great that tombs were routinely plundered by looters even in ancient times.

In the Early Dynastic period, the most common type of tomb structure in Egypt was the **mastaba**, a flat-topped, one-story building with slanted walls erected above an underground burial chamber (see "Elements of Architecture," page 103). Mastabas were customarily

constructed of mud brick, but toward the end of Dynasty 3 more and more incorporated cut stone, at least as an exterior facing, or **veneer**. In its simplest form, the mastaba contained a **serdab**, a small, sealed room housing the ka statue of the deceased, and a chapel designed to receive mourning relatives with their offerings. A vertical shaft led from the top of the mastaba down to the actual burial chamber, where the remains of the deceased reposed in a **sarcophagus**, or stone coffin, surrounded by the appropriate grave goods. This chamber was sealed off once interment was completed. Mastaba burial remained the standard for Egyptian royalty for centuries. Many such structures were enlarged with numerous underground chambers to accommodate whole families.

The kings of Dynasties 3 and 4 were the first to devote huge sums to the design, construction, and decoration of more extensive aboveground funerary complexes. These structures tended to be grouped together in a **necropolis**—literally, a city of the dead—at the edge of the desert on the west bank of the Nile, for the land of the dead was held to be in the direction of the setting sun. Two of the most extensive of these early necropolises are those at Saqqara and Giza, just outside modern Cairo.

Djoser's Funerary Complex at Saqqara. For his tomb complex at Saqqara, King Djoser (Dynasty 3, ruled c. 2681–2662 BCE) commissioned the earliest known monumental architecture in Egypt (fig. 3-7). The designer of the complex was a man called Imhotep. His name appears inscribed on the pedestal of Djoser's ka statue in the serdab of the funerary temple to the north of the tomb. He is thus the first architect in history known by name. Born into a prominent family, Imhotep was highly educated and served as one of Djoser's chief advisers on affairs of state. It appears that he first planned Djoser's tomb as a single-story mastaba, then later decided to enlarge upon the concept. In the end, what he produced was a stepped pyramid (fig. 3-8) consisting of six mastabalike elements of decreasing size placed on top of each other (see "Elements of Architecture," page 103). Although his final structure resembles the **ziggurats** of Mesopotamia, it differs in both its planned concept and its purpose of protecting a tomb. Djoser's imposing structure was originally faced with a veneer of limestone. From its top a 92-foot shaft descended to a granite-lined burial vault.

The adjacent funerary temple, where priests performed their final rituals before placing the king's mummified body in its tomb, was also used for continuing worship of the dead king. In the form of his ka statue, Djoser was able to observe these devotions through two peepholes bored through the wall between the serdab and the funerary chapel. To the east of the pyramid were sham buildings—simple masonry shells filled with debris—representing chapels, palaces with courtyards, and other structures. They were provided so that the dead king could continue to observe the *sed* rituals that had ensured his long reign. His spirit could await the start of the ceremonies in a pavilion near the entrance to the

3-7. Plan of Djoser's funerary complex, Saqqara. c. 2681–2662 BCE (Dynasty 3)

Situated on a level terrace, this huge commemorative complex—some 1,800 feet long by 900 feet wide—was designed as a sort of miniature replica of the king's earthly realm. Its enclosing wall, fitted out with fourteen gates, only one of which was actually functional, represented the realm's boundaries. Inside rose the tomb structure proper, a funerary temple, and other buildings and courtyards for the king's use in the hereafter.

3-8. Stepped pyramid of Djoser, Saqqara. Limestone, height 204' (62 m)

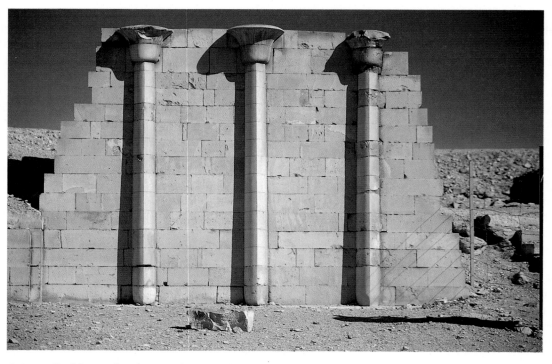

3-9. Wall of the North Palace, with engaged columns in the form of papyrus blossoms. Funerary complex of Djoser, Saqqara

ELEMENTS OF ARCHITECTURE
Column and Colonnade

A **column** is a cylindrical, upright **pillar** that has three sections: a **base**, a **shaft**, and a top, called a **capital**. Most columns are **freestanding** and are used to support weight, usually a roof. When used decoratively and attached to a wall, a column is referred to as an **engaged column** or **attached column** (see fig. 3-9).

A **colonnade** is a row of columns supporting a horizontal member. Egyptians used columns, with and without bases, in their **temple complexes**, in forms that are based on river plants. Persian columns use the same elements very differently.

lotus bud   **lotus flower**   **fluted**

Egyptian columns   **Persian column**

colonnade

complex in its southeast corner. The running trials of the *sed* festival took place in a long outdoor courtyard within the complex. After proving himself, the king's spirit proceeded first to the South Palace then to the North Palace, to be symbolically crowned once again as king of Egypt's Two Lands.

Imhotep's architecture employs the most elemental structural techniques and the purest of geometric forms.

Although most of the stone wall surfaces were left plain, in some places he made effective use of **columns**. Some of these are plain except for fluting, others take the form of stylized plants. The **engaged columns** spaced along the exterior walls of the North Palace, for example (fig. 3-9), resemble stalks of papyrus. Stylized papyrus blossoms serve as their capitals. These columns may have been patterned after the bundled papyrus stalks early

3-10. Great Pyramids, Giza. Dynasty 4, c. 2601–2515 BCE. Erected by (from left) Menkaure, Khafre, and Khufu. Granite and lime-stone, height of pyramid of Khufu 450' (137 m)

For many centuries it was not known that the pyramids were the tombs of early Egyptian rulers. One theory was that they were gigantic silos for storing grain during periods of drought and famine. This notion was fostered in part by the discovery that the pyramids' accessible interior spaces were empty. The designers of the pyramids tried to ensure that the king and the tomb "home" would never be disturbed. Khufu's builders placed his tomb chamber in the very heart of the mountain of masonry, at the end of a long, narrow, steeply rising passageway, sealed off after the king's burial by a 50-ton stone block. Three false passageways, either deliberately meant to mislead or the result of changes in plan as construction progressed, obscured the location of the tomb. Despite such precautions, early looters managed to penetrate to the tomb chamber and make off with Khufu's funeral treasure.

Egyptian builders used to reinforce mud walls and symbolized Lower Egypt. By contrast, the architectural decorations of the South Palace featured plants symbolic of Upper Egypt, the flowering sedge and the lotus (see "Elements of Architecture," page 101).

The Pyramids at Giza. The architectural form most closely identified with Egypt is the true pyramid with a square base and four sloping triangular faces. The first such structures were erected in Dynasty 4 (see "Ele-

ments of Architecture," opposite). The angled sides of the pyramids may have been meant to represent the slanting rays of the sun, for inscriptions on the walls of pyramid tombs built in Dynasties 5 and 6 tell of deceased kings climbing up the rays to join the sun god Ra.

Egypt's most famous funerary structures are the three great pyramid tombs at Giza (fig. 3-10). These were built by the Dynasty 4 kings Khufu (ruled c. 2601–2578 BCE), Khafre (ruled c. 2570–2544 BCE), and Menkaure (ruled c. 2533–2515 BCE). The Greeks were so impressed

THE SEVEN WONDERS OF THE WORLD Lists for travelers of marvelous sights not to miss are known from many ancient civilizations. Such lists—more or less consistent—make their appearance in the writings of various Greek authors as early as 200–100 BCE, their attractions heralded as the Seven Wonders of the World. Not surprisingly, the majority of the sites included were examples of the Greeks' own engineering and architectural skill. The oldest of these "wonders," and the only one still reasonably intact today, is the trio of pyramids at Giza (see fig. 3-10), built between 2601 and 2515 BCE. The next oldest, the so-called Hanging Gardens built for Nebuchadnezzar II in Babylon in the sixth century BCE (see fig. 2-26), had disappeared long before it made the list, although sections of what are believed to be its foundations have been excavated. The Greek entries, none of which survive, must be imagined from written descriptions, sculptural fragments, and archeological reconstructions. They include the temple of the goddess Artemis at Ephesos, from the sixth century BCE; the statue of the god Zeus at Olympia by Pheidias, about 430 BCE; the Mausoleum at Halikarnassos, fourth century BCE (figure 5-61 shows a conjectural reconstruction of it); the Colossus of Rhodes, a bronze statue of the sun god Helios the height of a ten-story building, completed in 282 BCE (our own word *colossal* comes from this Greek term for an outsize human statue); and the lighthouse that guarded the port at Alexandria, in Egypt, built about 290 BCE and more than four times as tall as the Colossus. It is intriguing that people at this point in history chose to list the world's wonders. It is particularly telling that all of these wonders were the work of human hands.

3-11. Plan of the funerary complex, Giza

by these huge, shining monuments—"pyramid" is a Greek term—that they numbered them among the world's architectural marvels (see "The Seven Wonders of the World," opposite). The early Egyptians referred to the Giza tombs as "Horizon of Khufu," "Great Is Khafre," and "Divine Is Menkaure," thus acknowledging the desire of these rulers to commemorate themselves as divine beings. The oldest and largest of the Giza pyramids is that of Khufu, which covers 13 acres at its base and rises to a height of about 450 feet in its deteriorated state. It was originally finished with a sheath of polished limestone that lifted its apex some 30 feet above the present summit, to roughly the height of a 48-story modern skyscraper. The pyramid of Khafre, the only one of the three that still has a remnant of its veneer at the top, is slightly smaller than Khufu's. Menkaure's is considerably smaller than the other two.

Next to each of the pyramids was a funerary temple connected by causeway, or elevated road, to a valley temple on the bank of the Nile (fig. 3-11). When a king died, his body was ferried across the Nile from the royal palace to his valley temple, where it was received with

ELEMENTS OF ARCHITECTURE

Mastaba to Pyramid

As the gateway to the afterlife for Egyptian kings and members of the royal court, the Egyptian burial structure began as a low rectangular **mastaba** with an internal serdab and chapel, then a mastaba with attached chapel and serdab (not shown). Later, mastaba forms of decreasing size were stacked over an underground burial chamber to form the stepped pyramid. The culmination of the Egyptian burial chamber is the pyramid, in which the actual burial site may be within the pyramid—not below ground—with false chambers, false doors, and confusing passageways to foil potential tomb robbers.

mastaba

stepped pyramid

pyramid

3-12. Valley temple of Khafre, Giza. Dynasty 4, c. 2570–2544 BCE. Granite posts and lintels, alabaster floor

elaborate ceremonies. It was then carried up the causeway to his funerary temple and placed in its chapel. There family members presented it with offerings of food and drink, and priests performed the rite known as the "opening of the mouth," in which the deceased's spirit consumed a meal. Then the body was entombed in a well-hidden vault inside the pyramid (see "Elements of Architecture," page 103). Khafre's funerary complex is the best preserved today. His valley temple was constructed of massive blocks of red granite. The corridor shown in figure 3-12 led to a chamber that once held a ka statue of the king (see fig. 3-13).

Constructing a pyramid was a formidable undertaking. A huge labor force had to be assembled, housed, and fed. Most of the cut stone blocks used in building the Giza complex—each weighing an average of two and a half tons—were quarried either on the site or nearby. Teams of workers transported them by sheer muscle power, at times employing small logs as rollers or pouring water on sand to create a slippery surface over which they could drag the blocks on sleds.

Scholars and engineers have advanced various theories about the method used in raising the pyramids. Some have been tested in computerized projections and a few in actual building attempts on a small but representative scale. The most efficient means of getting the stones into position might have been to build a temporary, gently sloping ramp around the body of the pyramid as it grew higher. The ramp might then be dismantled as the slabs of the stone veneer were laid from the top down. Clearly the architects who oversaw the building of such massive structures were capable of the most sophisticated mathematical calculations, for there was no room for trial and error. They had to make certain that the huge foundation layer was absolutely level and that the angle of each of the slanting sides remained constant so that the stones would meet precisely in the center at the top. They carefully oriented the pyramids to the points of the compass and may have incorporated other symbolic astronomical calculations as well. These im-

mense monuments reflect not only the desire of a trio of kings to attain immortality but also the strength of the Egyptians' belief that a deceased ruler continued to affect the well-being of the state and his people from beyond the grave.

Sculpture

As was the custom, Khafre commissioned various stone portraits of himself to perpetuate his memory for all time. In his roughly lifesize ka statue, discovered inside his valley temple, he was portrayed as an enthroned king (fig. 3-13). The Great Sphinx, a colossal monument some 65 feet tall standing just behind the valley temple, combines his head with the long body of a crouching lion (fig. 3-14). Both images have the same compactness, symmetry of form, and simple, blocklike shape. Carved from a large rock formation left intact after stone had been quarried around it, Khafre's Great Sphinx was not the first such portrayal of a king, and there are many later ones. But in size it has no equal.

In his ka statue, Khafre sits erect on a simple but elegant throne. Horus perches on the back of the throne, protectively enfolding the king's head with his wings. Lions—symbols of regal authority—form the throne's sides, and the intertwined lotus and papyrus plants beneath the seat symbolize the king's power over Upper and Lower Egypt. Khafre wears the traditional royal costume: a short kilt, a linen headdress with *uraeus*, the cobra symbol of Ra, and a false beard symbolic of royalty. Viewed from the front (fig. 3-13, left), the vertical lines of the legs, torso, and upper arms convey a strong sense of dignity, calm, and above all permanence. The statue was carved in diorite, a stone chosen for its great durability, and the figure's compactness—the arms pressed tight to the body, and the body firmly anchored in the block—ensured that the image would provide an alternative home for the king's ka for eternity.

When carving such a statue, Egyptian sculptors approached each face of the block as though they were simply carving a relief. In one the figure would be seen straight on from the front, in the others from the side or the back. Carving deeper and deeper, they finally ended up with a three-dimensional figure, and all that remained was to refine its forms and work up its surface details.

Dignity, calm, and permanence also characterize the double portrait of King Menkaure and Queen Khamerernebty, Khafre's son and daughter-in-law (fig. 3-15). But the sculptor's handling of the composition of this work, discovered in Menkaure's valley temple, makes it far less austere than Khafre's ka statue. The couple's separate figures, close in size, form a single unit, tied together by the stone out of which they emerge. They are further united by the queen's symbolic gesture of embrace. Her right hand emerges from behind to lie gently against his ribs, and her left hand rests on his upper arm. The king, depicted in accordance with the Egyptian ideal as an athletic, youthful figure nude to the waist, stands in a very Egyptian balanced pose with one foot in front of the other, his arms straight at his sides and his fists tightly

3-13. *Khafre*, from Giza. Dynasty 4, c. 2570–2544 BCE. Diorite, height 5'6⅛" (1.68 m). Egyptian Museum, Cairo

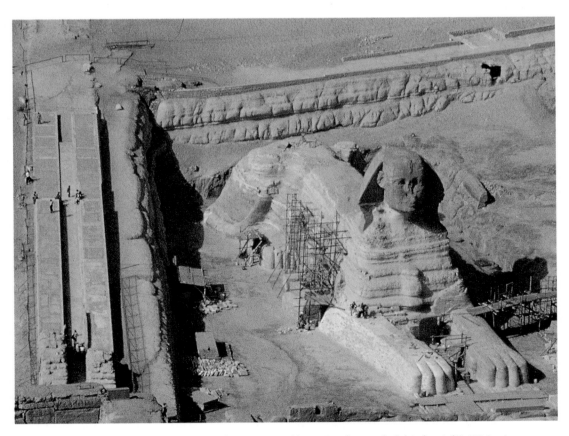

3-14. Great Sphinx, Giza. Dynasty 4, c. 2570–2544 BCE. Sandstone, height about 65' (19.8 m)

3-15. *Menkaure and His Wife, Queen Khamerernebty*, from Giza. Dynasty 4, c. 2515 BCE. Slate, height 54¹/₂" (142.3 cm). Museum of Fine Arts, Boston

Harvard University–MFA Expedition

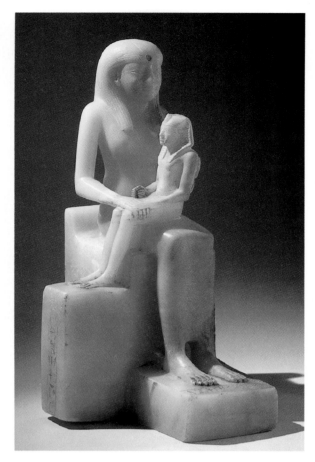

3-16. *Pepy II and His Mother, Queen Merye-ankhnes*. Dynasty 6, c. 2383–2289? BCE. Calcite, height 15¹/₄" (39.2 cm). The Brooklyn Museum

Charles Edwin Wilbour Fund (39.119)

clenched. His equally youthful queen mimics his striding pose but with a smaller step forward. The sculptor exercised remarkable skill in rendering her sheer, close-fitting garment, which clearly reveals the curves of her body. The time-consuming task of polishing this double statue was never completed, indicating that the work may have been undertaken only a few years before Menkaure's death in about 2515 BCE.

An example of a type of royal portraiture that made its appearance in Dynasty 6 (2460–2200 BCE) is presented in figure 3-16. In this statue the figure of Pepy II (ruled c. 2383–2289? BCE), wearing the royal kilt and headdress but reduced to the size of a child, is seated on his mother's lap. The work thus pays homage to Queen Merye-ankhnes, who wears a vulture-skin headdress linking her to the goddess Nekhbet and proclaiming her of royal blood. If Pepy II inherited the throne at the age of six, as Manetho claimed, then the queen may have acted as regent until he was old enough to rule alone. The sculptor placed the figure of the king at a right angle to that of his mother, thus providing two "frontal" views—the queen facing forward, the king to the side. In another break with convention, he freed the queen's arms and legs from the stone block of the throne, giving her figure greater independence.

Old Kingdom sculptors were commissioned to produce portraits not only of kings and nobles but also of many figures of lesser prominence. As can be seen from the *Seated Scribe* (fig. 3-17), a painted limestone statue from Dynasty 5, these works tend to be livelier and less formal than royal portraits. The scribe's sedentary occupation has taken its toll on his physique, leaving him soft and flabby. His face, however, reveals an alert intelligence. He sits holding a papyrus scroll partially unrolled on his lap, his right hand clasping a now-lost reed pen. The modern viewer is likely to think this portrait realistic, but in fact it is a quite conventional Old Kingdom depiction of a man of lower class—however respected his position. Many other such statues of the period exhibit the same round head and face, large wide-open eyes, genial expression, and cap of hair cut close to the skull.

Tomb Decoration

In order to provide the ka with the most pleasant possible living quarters for eternity, wealthy families often had the interior walls and ceilings of their tombs decorated with paintings and reliefs. Much of this decoration was symbolic or religious, especially in royal tombs, but it could also include a wide variety of everyday scenes

3-17. *Seated Scribe*. Dynasty 5, c. 2510–2460 BCE. Painted limestone, height 21"
(53 cm). Musée du Louvre, Paris

Egyptian scribes began training in childhood. Theirs was a strenuously
guarded profession, its skills generally passed down from father to son.
Some girls learned to read and write, and although careers as scribes seem
generally to have been closed to them, there is a Middle Kingdom word for
female scribe. Would-be scribes were required to learn not only reading and
writing but also arithmetic, algebra, religion, and law. The studies were
demanding, but the rewards were great. An observation found in an exercise tablet, probably copied from a book of instruction, offers encouragement: "Become a scribe so that your limbs remain smooth and your hands
soft, and you can wear white and walk like a man of standing whom [even]
courtiers will greet" (cited in Strouhal, page 216). A high-ranking scribe
with a reputation as a great scholar could hope to be appointed to one of
several "houses of life," where lay and priestly scribes copied, compiled,
studied, and repaired valuable sacred and scientific texts. Completed texts
were placed in related institutions called "houses of books," some of the
earliest known libraries.

recounting momentous events in the life of the deceased
or showing them engaged in routine activities. Tombs
therefore provide a wealth of information about ancient
Egyptian culture.

A scene in the large mastaba of a Dynasty 5 government official named Ti—a commoner who had
achieved great power at court and amassed sufficient
wealth to build an elaborate home for his immortal
spirit—shows him watching a hippopotamus hunt (fig.
3-18). The artists who created this painted limestone

relief employed a number of established conventions.
They depicted the river as if seen from above, rendering it
as a band of parallel wavy lines below the boats. The
creatures in the river, however—fish, a crocodile, and
hippopotamuses—are shown in profile for easy identification. The shallow boats carrying Ti and his men skim
along the surface of the water unhampered by the
papyrus stalks, shown as parallel vertical lines, that choke
the marshy edges of the river. At the top of the panel,
where Egyptian convention often placed background

3-18. *Ti Watching a Hippopotamus Hunt.* Tomb of Ti, Saqqara. Dynasty 5, c. 2510–2460 BCE. Painted limestone relief, height approx. 45" (114.3 cm)

This relief forms part of the decoration of a mastaba tomb discovered by the French archeologist Auguste Mariette in 1865. Among Mariette's many other famous finds was the ka statue of Khafre (see fig. 3-13). A pioneer Egyptologist, Mariette was a man of great heart, intellect, and diverse talents. It was he who provided the composer Giuseppe Verdi with the scenario for the opera *Aida,* set in ancient Egypt. He pressed the Egyptians to establish the National Antiquities Service to protect, preserve, and study the country's art monuments. In gratitude, they later placed a statue of him in the new Egyptian Museum in Cairo. At his death, his remains were brought back to his beloved Egypt for burial.

scenes, several animals are seen stalking birds among the papyrus leaves and flowers. The erect figure of Ti, rendered in the traditional twisted pose, looms over this teeming Nile environment. The actual hunters, being of lesser rank and engaged in more-strenuous activities, are rendered more realistically.

In Egyptian art, as in that of the ancient Near East, scenes showing a ruler hunting wild animals served to illustrate the power to maintain order and balance. By dynastic times, hunting had become primarily a showy pastime for the nobility. The hippopotamus hunt, however, was more than simple sport. Hippos tended to wander off into fields, inflicting untold damage on crops. Killing them was an official duty of members of the court. Furthermore, it was believed that the companions of Seth, the god of darkness, disguised themselves as hippopotamuses. Tomb depictions of such hunts therefore illustrated not only the valor of the deceased but also the triumph of good over evil.

THE MIDDLE KINGDOM

The collapse of the Old Kingdom, with its long succession of kings ruling the whole of Egypt, was followed by roughly 150 years of political turmoil traditionally referred to as the First Intermediate period. In about 2040 BCE a prince Mentuhotep II, from Thebes, finally managed to reunite the country. He and his successors reasserted royal power, but beginning with the next dynasty, political authority became less centralized. Provincial governors claimed increasing powers for themselves, effectively limiting the king's responsibility to national concerns such as the defense of Egypt's frontiers. It was in the Middle Kingdom that Egypt's kings began maintaining standing armies to patrol the country's borders, especially its southern reaches in Lower Nubia, south of modern Aswan.

Another royal responsibility was the planning and construction of large-scale water management projects. Although farmers had long diverted the waters of the Nile to irrigate their crops, specific terms having to do with such projects—"canal" and "levee," for example—make their first appearance in Middle Kingdom documents and inscriptions. The first mention of ingenious methods of raising water from the level of the river to higher ground also dates from this period. Regional administrators and the farmers themselves were left to supervise irrigation locally. In this period Egypt's farmers enjoyed relatively liberal rights and freedoms, even though they were required to turn over most of what they produced to the nobles or priests who owned the land they worked. Those who failed to meet prescribed annual yields were subject to harsh punishments.

Architecture and Town Planning

The remains of Kahun, a town built by Senwosret II (Dynasty 12, ruled c. 1895–1878 BCE) near his pyramid tomb complex at el-Lahun, offer a unique view of the Middle Kingdom's social structure. Although the Egyptians used more-durable materials in the construction of tombs, they built their own dwellings with simple mud bricks. The bricks have either disintegrated over time or been carried away by farmers for their value as fertilizer, leaving only the foundations. From them, archeologists have developed a map of the site showing straight streets and avenues laid out in a mainly east-west orientation (fig. 3-19). The resulting rectangular blocks were divided into lots for homes and other buildings.

Kahun was built to provide housing for the king and the many officials, priests, and workers required in the service of his court. The town's design reflects three distinct economic and social levels. Appropriately, Senwosret's own semifortified residence occupied the highest ground and fronted on a large, open square. The district to the east of his palace, connected to the square by a

3-19. Plan of the northern section of Kahun, built during the reign of Senwosret II near modern el-Lahun. Dynasty 12, c. 1895–1878 BCE

wide avenue, was occupied by priests, court officials, and their families. Their houses were large and comfortable, with private living quarters and public rooms grouped around central courtyards. Some had as many as seventy rooms spread out over half an acre. The workers were housed in the western district, set off from the rest of the town by a solid wall. Their families made do with small, five-room row houses built back to back along straight, narrow streets.

Tomb Art and Tomb Construction

Tomb art reveals much about domestic life in the Middle Kingdom. Wall paintings, reliefs, and even small models of houses and farm buildings complete with figurines of workers and animals reproduce everyday scenes on the estates of the deceased. Many of these models survive because they were made of inexpensive materials of no interest to early grave robbers. One from Thebes, made of wood, plaster, and copper in about 2009–1997 BCE, reproduces a portion of a house (fig. 3-20). The flat-roofed structure opens into a walled garden through a **portico**, or columned porch, having papyrus columns with stylized lotus capitals. The garden has a central pool flanked by sycamore trees. Although water was precious and only the wealthy could afford their own backyard source, some pools, lined with masonry and stocked with water lilies and fish, were so large that a small boat might be kept at the edge for fishing.

3-20. Model of a house and garden, from Thebes. Dynasty 11, c. 2009–1997 BCE. Painted and plastered wood and copper, length 33" (83.8 cm). The Metropolitan Museum of Art, New York

Purchase, Rogers Fund and Edward S. Harkness Gift, 1920 (20.3.13)

3-21. Rock-cut tombs, Beni Hasan. Dynasty 12, c. 1991–1785 BCE. At the left is the entrance to the tomb of the provincial governor and commander-in-chief Amen-emhet.

3-22. Plan and elevation of a typical rock-cut tomb at Beni Hasan

During Dynasties 11 and 12, members of the nobility and high-level officials frequently commissioned **rock-cut tombs**—burial places hollowed out of the faces of cliffs—such as those in the necropolis at Beni Hasan on the east bank of the Nile. The various chambers of such tombs and their ornamental columns, lintels, false doors, and niches were all carved out of solid rock (fig. 3-21). Each one was therefore like a single, complex piece of sculpture, attesting to the great skill of their designers and carvers. A typical Beni Hasan tomb included an

TECHNIQUE

EGYPTIAN PAINTING AND RELIEF SCULPTURE

Painting relies for its effect on color and line. **Relief sculpture** usually depends on the play of light and shadow alone, but in Egypt, relief sculpture was also painted. The walls and closely spaced columns of Egyptian tombs and temples provided large surfaces for decoration, and in fact nearly every square inch of them was adorned with colorful figural scenes and hieroglyphic texts. Up until Dynasty 18 (New Kingdom), the only colors used were black, white, red, yellow, blue, and green. They were never mixed. **Modeling** might be indicated by overpainted lines in a contrasting color, but never by shading of the basic color pigment. In time, more colors were added to the palette, but the primacy of line was never challenged. In terms of composition, with comparatively few exceptions, figures, scenes, and texts were presented in bands, or registers. Usually the base line at the bottom of each register represented the ground. Determining the sequence in which a set of images is to be read can be problematic because it may run either horizontally or vertically.

The preliminary steps in the creation of paintings and relief carvings were virtually identical. Surfaces to be painted had to be smooth, so in some cases a coat of plaster was applied. The next step was to lay out the registers with painted lines and draw the appropriate grid (see fig. 3-6). In the remarkable photograph of a wall section in the unfinished Dynasty 19 tomb of Horemheb in the Valley of the Kings, the red base lines and horizontals of the grid are clearly visible. The general shapes of the hieroglyphs have also been sketched in red. The actual preparatory drawings from which the carver or carvers were to work are in black. Egyptian artists worked in teams, each member of which had developed a particular skill. The sculptor who executed the carving on the right was following someone else's drawing. Had there been time to finish the tomb, other hands would have smoothed the surface of this limestone relief, and still others would have made fresh drawings to guide the artists assigned to paint it.

3-23. *Harvest Scene*, tempera facsimile by Nina de Garis Davies of a wall painting in the tomb of Khnumhotep, Beni Hasan. Dynasty 12, c. 1928–1895 BCE

3-24. *Senwosret III*. Dynasty 12, c. 1878–1842 BCE. Black granite, height 21½" (54.8 cm). The Brooklyn Museum Charles Edwin Wilbour Fund (52.1)

entrance portico, a main hall, and a small burial chamber set back in its farthest recesses (fig. 3-22). The hall might be quite large, with slightly vaulted ceilings and rows of freestanding papyrus-style columns. Rock-cut tombs at other spots along the Nile exhibit variations on this simple plan, with different types of entrances and different interior layouts.

The walls of rock-cut tombs were commonly ornamented with painted scenes. Relief decorations were rare. Among the best-preserved paintings at Beni Hasan are those in the Dynasty 12 tomb of the local lord Khnumhotep, some of which present spirited depictions of life on his farms. In one scene, two men picking figs are forced to compete for the fruit with three friendly baboons seated in the trees (fig. 3-23). The baskets heaped high with neatly arranged figs indicate that the harvest is plentiful despite the animals' thievery. Like the hunters in the Old Kingdom painted relief of Ti on a hippopotamus hunt (see fig. 3-18), these active farmworkers are shown in almost full profile, not in the twisted pose prescribed for royalty.

Sculpture

Royal portraits from the Middle Kingdom do not always exhibit the idealized rigidity of earlier examples. Emulating a trend in nonofficial portrait sculpture, artists of the preceding First Intermediate period had already begun to move away from the conventional portrayal of kings as vigorous but placid young men. A number of Middle Kingdom sculptors continued in this direction, expressing a special awareness of the hardship and fragility of human existence. A statue of Senwosret III (Dynasty 12, ruled c. 1878–1842 BCE) serves as an example of this new sensibility (fig. 3-24). Senwosret was a dynamic king and successful general who led four military expeditions into Nubia, overhauled the central administration at home, and did much toward regaining control over the country's increasingly independent nobles. His portrait statue seems to reflect not only his achievements but also

There is little indication of how ancient Egyptians viewed the artists who created portraits of kings and nobles and recorded so many details of contemporary life, but they must have been admired and respected. Some certainly had a high opinion of themselves, as we learn from an inscription on the tombstone of a Middle Kingdom sculptor: "I am an artist who excels in my art, a man above the common herd in knowledge. I know the proper attitude for a statue [of a man]; I know how a woman holds herself, [and how] a spearman lifts his arm. . . . There is no man famous for this knowledge other than I myself and my eldest son" (cited in Montet, page 159).

something of his personality and his inner thoughts. He appears to be a man wise in the ways of the world but lonely, saddened, and burdened by the weight of his responsibilities.

The statue shows the king in the conventional block-like pose, seated, immobile, frontal, and erect. Despite its size—it is less than 2 feet tall—it conveys the sense of monumentality already noted in the much larger ka statue of the Old Kingdom ruler Khafre (see fig. 3-13). There are nevertheless significant differences between the two. Khafre gazes into eternity confident and serene, whereas Senwosret III appears preoccupied and emotionally drained. Deep creases line his sagging cheeks, his eyes are sunken, his eyelids droop, and his jaw is sternly set.

Intended or not, his image betrays a pessimistic view of life, a degree of distrust similar to that reflected in the advice given by Amenemhet I, this Senwosret's great-great-grandfather and the founder of his dynasty, to his son Senwosret I (cited in Breasted, page 231):

Fill not thy heart with a brother,
Know not a friend,
Nor make for thyself intimates, . . .
When thou sleepest, guard for thyself thine
    own heart;
For a man has no people [supporters],
In the day of evil.

Small Objects Found in Tombs

Middle Kingdom art of all kinds and in all mediums, from official portrait statues such as that of Senwosret III to the least-imposing symbolic objects and delicate bits of jewelry, exhibits the desire of the period's artists for well-observed, accurate detail. A hippopotamus figurine discovered in the Dynasty 12 tomb of a governor named Senbi, for example, has all the characteristics of the beast itself: the rotund body on stubby legs, the massive head with protruding eyes, the tiny ears and distinctive nostrils (fig. 3-25). The figurine is an example of Egyptian **faience**, with its distinctive lustrous glaze (see "Glassmaking and Egyptian Faience," below). The artist chose to make the hippo the watery blue of its river habitat, then painted lotus blossoms on its flanks, jaws, and head, giving the impression that the creature is standing in a tangle of aquatic plants. Such figures were often placed in tombs so that the deceased might engage in an eternal hippopotamus hunt, enjoying the sense of moral triumph that entailed (see the discussion of *Ti Watching a Hippopotamus Hunt*, fig. 3-18).

The simple beauty of this faience hippopotamus contrasts sharply with the intricate splendor of a pectoral, or chest ornament, found at el-Lahun (fig. 3-26). Executed in gold and inlaid with semiprecious stones, it was

3-25. *Hippopotamus*, from the tomb of Senbi (Tomb B.3), Meir. Dynasty 12, c. 1962–1895 BCE. Faience, length 7⅞" (20 cm). The Metropolitan Museum of Art, New York
Gift of Edward S. Harkness, 1917 (17.9.1)

3-26. Pectoral of Senwosret II, from the tomb of Princess Sithathoryunet, el-Lahun. Dynasty 12, c. 1895–1878 BCE. Gold and semiprecious stones, length 3¼" (8.2 cm). The Metropolitan Museum of Art, New York
Purchase, Rogers Fund and Henry Walters Gift, 1916 (16.1.3)

TECHNIQUE

GLASSMAKING AND EGYPTIAN FAIENCE

Glass is produced by subjecting a mixture of sand, lime, and sodium carbonate or sodium sulphate to a very high temperature. It can be made to be transparent, translucent, or opaque and, with the addition of certain substances, can be created in a vast range of colors. No one knows precisely when or where the technique of glassmaking was first developed. By the Predynastic period, the Egyptians were already experimenting with a substance called glass paste, or Egyptian **faience**. When fired, this mixture produced a smooth and shiny opaque finish. At first it was used to form small objects, mainly beads, charms, and color **inlays**. It was later employed as an ornamental colored glaze for pottery wares and clay figurines (see fig. 3-25).

The first evidence of all-glass vessels and other hollow objects dates from the early New Kingdom. At that time glassmaking was restricted to royal workshops, and only the aristocracy and priestly class could commission work from them. The first objects to be made entirely of glass in Egypt were produced by the technique known as core glass. A lump of sandy clay molded into the desired shape of the finished vessel was wrapped in strips of cloth, then skewered on a fireproof rod. It was then briefly dipped into a pot of molten glass. Once the resulting coating of glass had cooled, the clay core was removed through the opening left by the skewer. To decorate the vessel thus created, glassmakers frequently heated thin rods of glass of different colors to the melting point and fused them to its surface in elegant wavy patterns, zigzags, and swirls (see fig. 3-39).

HIERO-GLYPHIC, HIERATIC, AND DEMOTIC WRITING

Ancient Egypt developed three types of writing, all of which are known today by the names the Greeks gave them. The earliest system employed a large number of symbols called **hieroglyphs** (from the Greek *hieros*, "sacred," and *glyphein*, "to carve"). As their name suggests, the Greeks believed they were filled with religious significance. Some of these symbols were simple pictures of creatures or objects, or **pictographs**, similar to those used by the Sumerians. Others were phonograms, or signs representing spoken sounds.

For record-keeping, correspondence, and manuscripts of all sorts, the earliest scribes must also have used this system of signs. In time, however, they evolved a kind of shorthand version of hieroglyphs—simplified forms that could be written more quickly in lines of script on papyrus scrolls. This type of writing is called **hieratic**, another term derived from the Greek word for "sacred." Even after this script was perfected, inscriptions in reliefs or paintings and on ceremonial objects continued to be written in hieroglyphics.

The third type of writing came into use only in the eighth century BCE, as written communication ceased to be restricted exclusively to priests and scribes. It was less formal and was easier to master, and the Greeks referred to it as **demotic** writing (from *demos*, "the people"). From this time on, all three systems were in use, each for its own specific purpose: religious documents were written in hieratic, inscriptions on monuments in hieroglyphics, and all other texts in demotic.

The Egyptian language gradually died out as the result of centuries of foreign rule, beginning with the arrival of the Greeks in 332 BCE. The last documents written in it date from the fourteenth century CE, by which time the great majority of Egypt's inhabitants spoke Arabic. Modern scholars were therefore faced with the task of deciphering these various types of writing in a long-forgotten language. The key appeared in the form of the Rosetta Stone, named after the Delta town

B 3.6
68%
FPO

The Rosetta Stone with its three tiers of writing, from top to bottom: hieroglyphic, demotic, and Greek. The stone itself is nearly black. It is shown here with the script reversed to appear black.

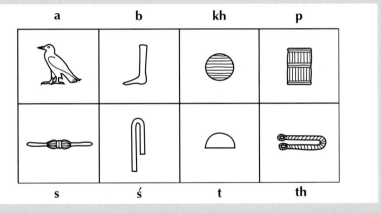

Eight hieroglyphs with the sounds they represent. Used in combinations, such phonogramic hieroglyphs were especially useful in rendering foreign names.

near the spot where one of Napoleon's officers discovered it in 1799. This irregular-shaped fragment of a stone stela dated from 196 BCE. On it, a decree issued by the priests at Memphis honoring the ruler Ptolemy V had been carved in hieroglyphics, hieratic, and demotic Greek. Even with the Greek translation, the two Egyptian texts proved to be incomprehensible until Thomas Young, an English physician interested in ancient Egypt, linked some of the hieroglyphs to specific names in the Greek version in 1818. A short time later, the brilliant Frenchman Jean-François Champollion (1790–1832) located the names Ptolemy and Cleopatra in both of the Egyptian scripts. Having thereby determined the phonetic symbols for P, O, L, and T in demotic, he was able to slowly build up an "alphabet" of hieroglyphs, and by 1822 he had deciphered the two Egyptian texts. Thanks to him, today's Egyptologists are able to read each new inscription or document from ancient Egypt that comes to light.

discovered in the funerary complex of Senwosret II, in the tomb of the king's daughter Sithathoryunet. The pectoral's design incorporates the name of Senwosret II and a number of familiar symbols. Two Horus falcons perch on its base, and above their heads are a pair of coiled cobras, symbols of Ra, wearing the ankh, the symbol of life. Between the two cobras, a **cartouche**—an oval formed by a loop of rope—contains the **hieroglyphs** (symbols) of the king's name. The sun disk of Ra appears at the top, and a scarab beetle, another symbol of Ra suggestive of rebirth, at the bottom. Below the cartouche, a kneeling male figure helps the falcons support a double arch of notched palm ribs, a hieroglyphic symbol meaning "millions of years." Decoded, the pectoral's combination of images yields the message: "May the sun god give eternal life to Senwosret II."

THE NEW KINGDOM

During the Second Intermediate period—another turbulent interruption in the succession of dynasties ruling a unified country—an eastern Mediterranean people called the Hyksos invaded Egypt's northernmost regions. It was only under the early rulers of Dynasty 18 (established in 1552 BCE) that the country regained its political and economic strength. The first kings of what is known as the New Kingdom managed to regain control of the entire Nile region from Nubia in the south to the Mediterranean in the north. Roughly a century later, one of the same dynasty's most dynamic kings, Tuthmose III (ruled 1479–1425 BCE), even succeeded in extending Egypt's influence along the eastern Mediterranean coast as far as the region of modern Syria. His accomplishment was the result of some fifteen or more military campaigns and his own skill at diplomacy. Tuthmose III was the first ruler to refer to himself as "pharaoh," a term that simply meant "great house." Egyptians used it in the same way that people in the United States commonly speak of "the White House" when they really mean the current president. The successors of Tuthmose III continued to use the term, and it ultimately found its way into the Hebrew Bible—and modern usage—as the name for the kings of Egypt.

By the beginning of the fourteenth century BCE, the most powerful Near Eastern kings acknowledged the rulers of Egypt as their equals. Marriages contracted between Egypt's ruling families and Near Eastern royalty helped to forge a generally cooperative network of kingdoms in the region. Among the benefits of such cooperation were stimulated trade and the promise of mutual aid at times of natural disaster and outside threats to established borders. Over time, however, Egyptian influence beyond the Nile diminished, and the power of Egypt's kings began to wane even within the country itself.

Great Temple Complexes

At the height of the New Kingdom, rulers undertook extensive building programs along the entire length of the Nile. Their palaces, forts, and administrative centers

3-27. Map of the Thebes district

disappeared long ago, but remnants of temples and tombs of this great age have endured. Even in their ruined state, they grandly attest to the expanded powers and political triumphs of their builders. Early in this period the priests of the god Amun in Thebes, Egypt's capital city through most of the New Kingdom, had gained such dominance that worship of the Theban triad of deities—Amun, his wife Mut, and their son Khonsu—had spread throughout the country. Temples to these and other gods were a major focus of royal art patronage, as were tombs and temples erected to glorify the kings themselves.

Temples to the Gods at Karnak and Luxor. Two temple districts consecrated primarily to the worship of Amun, Mut, and Khonsu arose near Thebes, one at Karnak to the north and the other at Luxor to the south (fig. 3-27). Little of the earliest construction at Karnak survives, but the remains of New Kingdom additions to the Great Temple of Amun still dominate the landscape (fig. 3-28). Access to the heart of the temple, a sanctuary containing the statue of Amun, was through a principal courtyard, a **hypostyle hall**—a vast hall filled with columns—and a number of smaller halls and courts. Massive gateways, called **pylons**, set off each of these separate elements. The greater part of Pylons II through VI and the areas behind them were renovated or newly built and embellished with colorful wall reliefs between the reigns of Tuthmose I (Dynasty 18, ruled c. 1506–1493 BCE) and Ramesses II (Dynasty 19, ruled c. 1279–1212 BCE). A sacred lake to the south of the temple, where the king and priests might undergo ritual purification before entering the temple, was also added in this period. Behind the sanctuary of Amun, Tuthmose III erected a court and festival temple to his own glory. Amenhotep III (Dynasty 18, ruled 1390–1352 BCE) later placed a large stone statue of Khepri, the scarab beetle symbolic of the rising sun and everlasting life, next to the sacred lake.

Religious worship in ancient Egypt was not a matter of daily or weekly rituals performed in the presence of a congregation of laypeople. Only kings and priests were allowed to enter the sanctuary of Amun for the required devotions, including washing the god's statue every

avenue of
human-headed
sphinxes

PRECINCT
OF MONTU

← to Nile

Great Temple of Amun

avenue of
ram-headed
sphinxes

hypostyle standing
hall   obelisk   sanctuary   court

court

to the Temple of
Amenhotep IV →

festival
temple of
Tuthmose III

scarab

PRECINCT
OF AMUN

court
VII

court
VIII

sacred lake

Temple
of Khonsu

court

IX

court

X

sed festival
temple of
Amenhotep III

avenue
of rams

avenue of
ram-headed
sphinxes

*Note: Pylons are numbered
I through X*

to Luxor
and Thebes
↓

PRECINCT
OF MUT
↓

1600

4000 BCE   1 CE

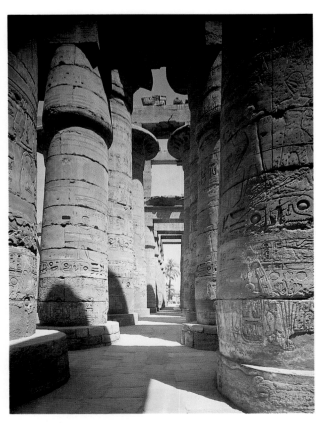

3-30. Hypostyle hall, Great Temple of Amun, Karnak

**3-28. Plan of the Great Temple of Amun, Karnak.
New Kingdom**

The Karnak site had been an active religious center
for more than 2,000 years before these structures were
erected on it. Over the nearly 500 years of the New
Kingdom, successive kings busily renovated and expanded the Amun temple. Later rulers added pylons,
courtyards, hypostyle halls, statues, and temples or
shrines to other deities to the east, west, and south of
the main temple until the complex covered about 60
acres, an area as large as a dozen football fields. In this
ongoing process, it was common to demolish older
structures and use their materials in new construction.

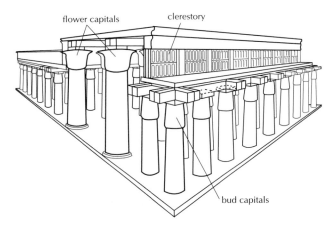

flower capitals   clerestory

bud capitals

3-29. Reconstruction drawing of the hypostyle hall, Great
Temple of Amun, Karnak. Dynasty 19, c. 1294–1212 BCE

morning and clothing it in a new garment, as well as providing it with tempting meals twice a day. The god was
thought to derive nourishment from the spirit of the food,
which the priests then removed and ate themselves.
Ordinary people were rarely permitted beyond the fore-
courts of the hypostyle halls, where they found themselves surrounded by inscriptions and images of kings
and the god on columns and walls. During religious festivals, however, they lined the routes along which the
statues of the gods were carried in ceremonial boats. At
such times they were permitted to submit petitions to the
priests for requests and favors they wished the gods to
answer.

Between Pylons II and III at Karnak stands the enormous hypostyle hall erected in the reigns of the Dynasty
19 rulers Sety I (ruled 1294–1279 BCE) and his son
Ramesses II (ruled c. 1279–1212 BCE). Called the "Temple
of the Spirit of Sety, Beloved of Ptah in the House of
Amun," it was perhaps used for royal coronation ceremonies. Ramesses II referred to it in more mundane
terms as "the place where the common people extol the
name of his majesty." The hall was 340 feet wide and 170
feet long. Its 134 closely spaced columns supported a
stepped, flat stone roof, the center section of which rose
some 30 feet higher than the rest (figs. 3-29, 3-30). The
columns supporting this higher part of the roof are 66 feet
tall and 12 feet in diameter, with massive lotus flower
capitals. The smaller columns on each side have lotus
bud capitals that must have seemed to march off forever
into the darkness.

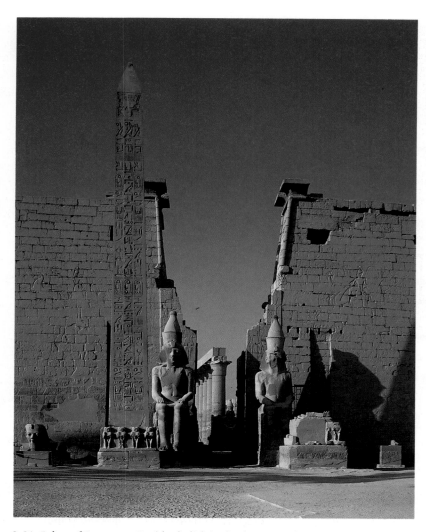

3-31. Pylon of Ramesses II with obelisk in the foreground, Temple of Amun, Mut, and Khonsu, Luxor. Dynasty 19, c. 1279–1212 BCE

In each of the side walls of the higher center section there was a long row of window openings, creating what is known as a **clerestory**. These openings were filled with stone grillwork, so they cannot have provided much light, but they did permit a cooling flow of air through the hall. Despite the dimness of the interior, artists were required to cover nearly every inch of the columns, walls, and cross-beams with reliefs.

The sacred district at Luxor was already the site of a splendid temple complex by the thirteenth century BCE. Ramesses II further enlarged the complex with the addition of a pylon and a **peristyle court**, or open courtyard ringed with columns and covered walkways (fig. 3-31). In front of his pylon stood two colossal statues of the king and a pair of **obelisks**—slender, slightly tapered square shafts of stone capped by a pyramidal shape called a **pyramidion**. The faces of the pylon are ornamented with reliefs detailing the king's military exploits. The walls of the courtyard present additional reliefs of Ramesses, shown together with various deities, his wife, seventeen of his sons, and other royal children, some hundred of whom he had by eight official wives and numerous concubines during his sixty-seven-year reign.

The Funerary Temple of Hatshepsut. The dynamic female ruler Hatshepsut (Dynasty 18, ruled c. 1478–1458 BCE) is a notable figure in a period otherwise dominated by male warrior-kings. Besides Hatshepsut, three other queens ruled Egypt—the little-known Sobekneferu and Twosret, and the notoriously famous Cleopatra, much later. The daughter of Tuthmose I, Hatshepsut married her half brother, who then reigned for fourteen years as Tuthmose II. When he died, she became regent for his underage son—Tuthmose III—born to one of his concubines. Hatshepsut had herself declared king by the priests of Amun, a maneuver that prevented Tuthmose III from assuming the throne for twenty years. In art she was represented in all the ways a male ruler would have been, even as a human-headed sphinx (fig. 3-32), and she was called "His Majesty." Sculpted portraits show her in the traditional royal trappings: kilt, linen headcloth, broad beaded collar, false beard, and bull's tail hanging from her waist.

Hatshepsut's closest adviser, a courtier named Senenmut, was instrumental in carrying out her ambitious building program. Her most innovative undertaking was her own funerary temple at Deir el-Bahri (fig. 3-33).

The structure was not intended to be her tomb; Hatshepsut was to be buried, like other New Kingdom rulers, in a necropolis known as the Valley of the Kings, about half a mile to the northwest (see fig. 3-27). Her funerary temple was magnificently positioned against high cliffs and oriented toward the Great Temple of Amun at Karnak, some miles away on the east bank of the Nile. The complex follows an **axial** plan—that is, all of its separate elements are symmetrically arranged along a dominant center line (fig. 3-34). An elevated causeway lined with sphinxes once ran from a valley temple on the Nile, since destroyed, to the first level of the complex, a huge open space before a long row of columns, or **colonnade** (see "Elements of Architecture," page 101). From there, the visitor ascended a long, straight ramp flanked by pools of water to the second level. At the ends of the columned porticos on this level were shrines to Anubis and Hathor.

3-32. *Hatshepsut as Sphinx*, from Deir el-Bahri. Dynasty 18, c. 1478–1458 BCE. Red granite, height 5'4" (164 cm). The Metropolitan Museum of Art, New York

Rogers Fund, 1931 (31.3.166)

Of the Egyptian queens who went down in history as "living gods" themselves and not merely "wives of gods," Hatshepsut may well have been the most commanding. Among the reliefs in her funerary temple at Deir el-Bahri (see fig. 3-33), she placed—just as a male king might have—a depiction of her divine birth. There she is portrayed as the daughter of her earthly mother, Queen Ahmose, and the god Amun. She also honored her real father, Tuthmose I, by dedicating a chapel to him in her temple.

3-34. Plan of the funerary temple of Hatshepsut, Deir el-Bahri. Dynasty 18, c. 1478–1458 BCE

3-33. Funerary temple of Hatshepsut, Deir el-Bahri. At the far left, ramp and base of the funerary temple of Mentuhotep II. Dynasty 11, c. 2009–1997 BCE

3-35. Temples of Ramesses II (left) and Nefertari (right), Abu Simbel, Nubia. Dynasty 19, c. 1279–1212 BCE

These two temples are no longer in their original location. That site was inundated as the result of the construction of the Aswan High Dam in the 1960s. An international campaign to salvage these monuments raised large sums of money, and astute engineers found a way to move the temples to a spot some 215 feet higher and 690 feet farther back from the river. The facade sculpture and the inner temple walls were cut into blocks and reassembled against artificial cliffs.

Relief scenes and inscriptions in the south portico relate that Hatshepsut sent a fleet of ships to Punt, an exotic, half-legendary kingdom probably located on the Red Sea or the Gulf of Aden, to bring back rare myrrh trees for the temple's terraces. The uppermost level consisted of another colonnade fronted by colossal royal statues, and behind this a large hypostyle hall with chapels to Hatshepsut, her father, and the gods Amun and Ra-Horakhty—the power of the sun at dawn and dusk. Centered in the hall's back wall was the entrance to the temple's innermost sanctuary. This small chamber was cut deep into the cliff in the manner of Middle Kingdom rock-cut tombs.

Hatshepsut's funerary temple, with its lively alternating of open spaces and grandiose architectural forms, projects an imposing image of authority. In its day, its remarkable union of nature and architecture, with many different levels and contrasting textures—water, stone columns, trees, and cliffs—made it far more impressive than the bleak expanse of stone ruins and sand that confronts the visitor today.

The Temple of Ramesses II at Abu Simbel. At the time of Ramesses II (ruled c. 1279–1212 BCE), whom some believe to be the "pharaoh" of the biblical story of Moses and the Exodus, Egypt was a mighty empire. Ramesses was a bold military commander and an effective political strategist. In about 1263 BCE he secured a peace agree-

ment with the Hittites, a rival power centered in Anatolia (Chapter 2) that had tried to expand its borders to the west and south at the Egyptians' expense. He reaffirmed that agreement a little over a decade later by marrying a Hittite princess.

In the course of his long and prosperous reign, Ramesses II initiated building projects on a scale rivaling the Old Kingdom pyramids at Giza. The most awe-inspiring of his many architectural monuments is found at Abu Simbel in Nubia, Egypt's southernmost region. There Ramesses ordered the construction of two temples, a large one to himself and a smaller one to his chief wife, Nefertari.

Like Hatshepsut's funerary temple at Deir el-Bahri, the monumental grandeur of the king's temple communicates to the viewer a sense of unlimited majesty. It was carved out of the face of a cliff in the manner of a rock-cut tomb but far surpasses earlier temples created in this way. Its dominant feature is a row of four colossal seated statues of the king, each more than 65 feet tall (fig. 3-35). Large figures of Nefertari and other family members stand next to his feet, but they seem mere dolls by comparison, since they do not even reach the height of the king's giant stone knees. The interior of the temple stretches back some 160 feet and was oriented in such a way that on the most important day of the Egyptian calendar the first rays of the rising sun shot through its entire depth to illuminate a row of four statues—the king

3-36. *Akhenaten and His Family*, from Akhetaten (modern Tell el-Amarna). Dynasty 18, 1348–1336/5 BCE. Painted limestone relief, 12¼ x 15¼" (31.1 x 38.7 cm). Staatliche Museen zu Berlin, Preussischer Kulturbesitz, Ägyptisches Museum

Egyptian relief sculptors often employed the technique seen here, called sunken relief. In ordinary reliefs, the background is carved away so that the figures project out from the finished surface. In this technique, the original flat surface of the stone is the background, and the outlines of the figures are deeply incised, permitting the development of three-dimensional forms within them. If an ordinary relief became badly worn, a sculptor might restore it by recarving it as a sunken relief.

and the gods Amun, Ptah, and Ra-Horakhty—placed against the back wall. The front of the smaller nearby temple to Nefertari is adorned with six statues 33 feet tall, two of the queen wearing the headdress of Hathor, and four of her husband.

Akhenaten and the Art of the Amarna Period

The most unusual ruler in the history of ancient Egypt was Amenhotep IV, who came to the throne in 1352 BCE (Dynasty 18). In his seventeen-year reign, he radically transformed the political, spiritual, and cultural life of the country. He founded a new religion honoring a single supreme god, the life-giving sun disk Aten, and accordingly changed his own name in 1348 BCE to Akhenaten ("One Who Is Effective on Behalf of Aten"). Abandoning Thebes, the capital of Egypt since the beginning of his dynasty and a city firmly in the grip of the priests of Amun, Akhenaten built a new capital much farther north, calling it Akhetaten ("Horizon of the Aten"). Borrowing from the modern name for this site, Tell el-Amarna, historians refer to his reign as the Amarna period.

The king saw himself as Aten's son, and at his new capital he presided over the worship of Aten as a divine priest. His chief queen, Nefertiti, served as a divine priest-ess. Temples to Aten were open courtyards, where altars could be bathed in the direct rays of the sun. In art Aten is depicted as a round sun sending down long thin rays ending in human hands, some of which hold the ankh, or symbol of life.

Akhenaten stressed the philosophical principle of *maat*, or divine truth, and one of his kingly titles was "Living in Maat." Such concern for truth found expression in new artistic conventions. In portraits of the king artists emphasized his unusual physical characteristics—long, thin arms and legs, a protruding stomach, swelling thighs, a thin neck supporting an elongated skull. Unlike his predecessors, and in keeping with his penchant for candor, Akhenaten urged his artists to portray the royal family in informal situations. Even private houses in the capital city were adorned with reliefs of the king and his family, an indication that he managed to substitute veneration of the royal household for the traditional worship of families of gods, such as that of Amun, Mut, and Khonsu.

A painted relief of Akhenaten, Queen Nefertiti, and three of their daughters exemplifies the new openness and a new figural style (fig. 3-36). In this **sunken relief**—the outlines of the figures have been carved into the surface of the stone, making it unnecessary to cut away the background—the king and queen sit on cushioned thrones playing with their children. The base of the queen's

3-37. *Queen Tiy*, from Kom Medinet Ghurab (near el-Lahun). Dynasty 18, c. 1390–1352 BCE. Boxwood, ebony, glass, gold, lapis lazuli, cloth, clay, and wax, height 3¾" (9.4 cm). Staatliche Museen zu Berlin, Preussischer Kulturbesitz, Ägyptisches Museum

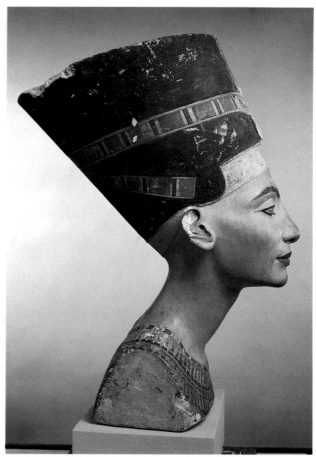

3-38. *Nefertiti*, from Akhetaten (modern Tell el-Amarna). Dynasty 18, c. 1348–1336/5 BCE. Limestone, height 20" (51 cm). Staatliche Museen zu Berlin, Preussischer Kulturbesitz, Ägyptisches Museum

This famous head was discovered along with various drawings and other items relating to commissions for the royal family in the studio of the sculptor Tuthmose at Akhetaten, the capital city during the Amarna period. Bust portraits, consisting solely of the head and shoulders, were rare in New Kingdom art. Scholars believe that Tuthmose may have made this one as a finished model to follow in sculpting or painting other images of his patron. From depictions of sculptors at work, we know that some statues were made in parts and then assembled, but there is no indication that this head was meant to be attached to a body.

throne is adorned with the stylized symbol of a unified Egypt, which has led some historians to conclude that Nefertiti acted as co-ruler with her husband. The royal couple is receiving the blessings of Aten, whose ray-hands penetrate the open pavilion and hold ankhs to their nostrils, giving them the "breath of life." Other ray-hands caress the hieroglyphic inscriptions in the center. The king holds one child and lovingly pats her head. The youngest of the three perches on Nefertiti's arm and tries to attract her attention by stroking her cheek. The oldest sits on the queen's lap, tugging at her mother's hand and pointing to her father. The children are nude, and the younger two have shaved heads, a custom of the time. The oldest wears the sidelock of youth, a patch of hair left to grow and hang at one side of the head in a braid. The artist has conveyed the engaging behavior of the children and the loving concern of their parents in a way not even hinted at in earlier royal portraiture in Egypt.

Akhenaten's goals were actively supported not only by Nefertiti but also by his mother, Queen Tiy. She had been the chief wife of the king's father, Amenhotep III (Dynasty 18, ruled 1390–1352 BCE), and played a significant role in affairs of state during his reign. Queen Tiy's personality emerges from a miniature portrait head that reveals the exquisite bone structure of her powerful face, with its arched brows, uptilted eyes, and expressive mouth (fig. 3-37). This portrait contrasts sharply with a head of Nefertiti, in which her comparatively expressionless face—the heavy-lidded eyes and half smile—divulges almost nothing about her personal qualities (fig. 3-38). Part of the beauty of this portrait head is the result of the artist's dramatic use of color. The hues of the blue head-dress and its colorful band are repeated in the rich red, blue, green, and gold of the jewelry. The queen's brows, eyelids, cheeks, and lips are heightened with color, as they no doubt were with cosmetics in real life. Whether or not Nefertiti's beauty is exaggerated, phrases used by her subjects when referring to her—"Fair of Face," "Mistress of Happiness," "Great of Love," "Endowed with Favors"—tend to support the artist's rendering.

The art of glassmaking flourished in the Amarna period. The craft could only be practiced by artists working for the king, and Akhenaten's new capital had its own glassmaking workshops. A fish-shaped bottle produced there was meant to hold scented oil (fig. 3-39). It is an example of what is known as **core glass**, named to indi-

3-39. Fish-shaped vase, from Akhetaten (modern Tell el-Amarna). Dynasty 18, c. 1348–1336/5 BCE. Core glass, length 5⅛" (13 cm). The British Museum, London

cate the early technique used in its manufacture (see "Glassmaking and Egyptian Faience," page 112). Its body was created first from glass tinted with cobalt, a dark blue metallic oxide. The surface was then decorated with swags resembling fish scales by heating small rods of white and orange glass to the point that they fused to the body and could be manipulated with a pointed tool. The fish that lent its shape to the bottle has been identified as a *bolti*, a species that carried its eggs in its mouth and spit out its offspring when they hatched. It was therefore a common symbol for birth and regeneration, especially the sort of self-generation that Akhenaten attributed to the sun disk Aten.

Domestic objects routinely placed in tombs as grave goods often had similar symbolic significance. One such item is a hand mirror, less than 10 inches tall, discovered in a Dynasty 18 tomb (fig. 3-40). Its handle is formed by

3-40. Hand mirror. Dynasty 18, c. 1552–1314/1295 BCE. Bronze, height 9¾" (24.6 cm). The Brooklyn Museum
Charles Edwin Wilbour Fund (37.365E)

PRESERVING THE DEAD The world's fascination with Egyptian mummies has a long history. In the Middle Ages and even up into the eighteenth century, Europeans prized pulverized mummy remains and swallowed them in various solutions, believing them to be of great medicinal value. One of the first concerns of the Egyptian National Antiquities Service after its founding in the second half of the nineteenth century was how to prevent people from stealing and destroying ancient human remains, as well as mummies of hundreds of thousands of cats and millions of ibises.

No actual ancient recipes for preserving the dead have been found, but the basic process seems clear enough from images found in tombs, the descriptions of later Greek writers such as Herodotus and Plutarch, scientific analysis of mummies, and modern experiments. By the time of the New Kingdom, the routine was

roughly as follows. The dead body was taken to a mortuary, a special structure used exclusively for embalming. Under the supervision of a priest, workers removed the brains, generally through the nose, and emptied the body cavity through an incision in the left side. They then placed the body, together with its major internal organs, in a vat of natron, a naturally occurring salt. It was left to steep in this solution for a period of a month or more. This caused the skin to blacken, so once the workers had retrieved a body from the vat and carefully dried it, they often dyed it to restore something of its color, using red ocher for a man, yellow ocher for a woman. They then packed the body cavity with clean linen, provided by the family of the deceased and soaked in various herbs and ointments. They wrapped the major organs in separate packets, either putting them in special containers to be placed in the tomb chamber or

stuffing them back into the body.

The tedious ritual of wrapping the body could now begin. They first wound the trunk and each of the limbs separately with cloth strips, then wrapped the whole body in a shroud. They then wound it in additional strips of cloth, layer after layer, to produce the familiar mummy shape. The linen winders often inserted good luck charms and other smaller objects among the wrappings. If the family happened to have furnished a Book of the Dead (see fig. 3-44), a selection of magic spells meant to help the deceased survive a "last judgment" and win everlasting life, it was tucked in between the mummy's legs.

Egyptians developed these techniques to ensure that the ka, or life force, could live on in the body in the afterlife. Whenever possible, a portrait statue was provided as an alternative home for the ka in the event that the mummy disintegrated.

the figure of a slender young woman, probably a dancer, balancing a giant lotus blossom on her head. Her arms reach out to support the flower's elongated sepals, forming with them a highly decorative shape. The mirror itself is a metal disk polished to a high gloss to create a reflecting surface. On one level, the young woman can be thought of as an attendant obediently holding the mirror for the person wishing to gaze in it. But she might also be interpreted as a fertility goddess supporting the sun disk. This elegant luxury item could have been placed in the tomb to symbolize the blessings of Aten and the hope that the deceased would live eternally in peace.

The Sarcophagus of Tutankhamun

Akhenaten's new religion and revolutionary ideas regarding the conduct appropriate for royalty outlived him by only a few years. His successors—it is not clear how they were related to him—had brief and troubled reigns, and the priesthood of Amun quickly regained its former power. The young king Tutankhaten (ruled 1336/35–1327 BCE) returned to traditional religious beliefs, changing his name to Tutankhamun. He also turned his back on Akhenaten's new city and moved his court to Memphis. He died quite young and was buried in the Valley of the Kings. Remarkably, although early looters did rob the tomb complex, his sealed inner tomb chamber was never plundered, and when it was opened in the 1920s its incredible riches were discovered just as they had been left. His body lay inside three nested coffins that identified him with Osiris, the god of the dead. The innermost coffin in the shape of a mummy is the richest of the three, for it is made of several hundred pounds of solid gold, with a "scrap value" of about $1.5 million (fig. 3-41). Its surface is decorated with colored enamelwork and semiprecious gemstones, as well as very finely incised linear designs and hieroglyphic inscriptions. The king holds a crook and a flail—an implement used in threshing grain. Both symbols were closely associated with Osiris and were a traditional part of the royal regalia at the time. The king's features as reproduced on the coffin are those of a very young man. Even though they may not reflect Tutankhamun's actual appearance, the unusually full lips and thin-bridged nose hint at the continued influence of the Amarna period style and its dedication to actual appearances.

Tomb Decoration

Living along the Nile was like living next to a major highway. Travel by boat was commonplace, an aspect of everyday life that is amply illustrated in tomb decorations. Paintings depict actual trips taken by the deceased, the ferrying upriver or down of their bodies in the course of funeral rites, and the symbolic journey into the afterlife, providing a great deal of information about Egyptian boats of this period. An especially beautiful, finely drawn example of such illustration dates from about 1348–1327 BCE (fig. 3-42). It comes from the tomb of the viceroy Amenhotep Huy at Qurnet Murai, across the Nile from

3-41. Inner coffin of Tutankhamun's sarcophagus, from the tomb of Tutankhamun, Valley of the Kings. Dynasty 18, 1336/5–1327 BCE. Gold inlaid with glass and semiprecious stones, height 6'7/8" (1.85 m). Egyptian Museum, Cairo

The English archeologist Howard Carter had worked in Egypt for more than twenty years before he undertook a last expedition, sponsored by the wealthy British amateur Egyptologist Lord Carnarvon, after World War I. In November 1922 Carter discovered the entrance to the tomb of King Tutankhamun, the only Dynasty 18 royal burial place still unidentified. By November his workers had cleared their way down to its antechamber, which was found to contain unbelievable treasures: jewelry, textiles, gold-covered furniture, a carved and inlaid throne, four gold chariots, and other precious objects. In February 1923, they pierced through the wall separating the anteroom from the actual burial chamber, and in early January of the following year—having taken great care to catalog all the intervening riches and prepare for their safe removal—they finally reached the king's astonishing sarcophagus. Figure 3-1 shows Tutankhamun's funerary mask as it was first seen in October 1925.

3-42. *State Ship*, detail of a tempera facsimile by Charles K. Wilkinson of a wall painting in the tomb of Governor Amenhotep
    Huy, Qurnet Murai. Dynasty 18, c. 1348–1327 BCE. The Metropolitan Museum of Art, New York
    Rogers Fund, 1930 (30.4.19)

Thanks to the prevailing northerly winds, ships could easily sail southward up the Nile. When traveling downriver they
were obliged to rely on oar power. Accordingly, the hieroglyph depicting a ship with a billowing sail came to mean "to
travel south"—whether by water or on land—whereas the one showing a boat without a sail meant "to travel north." The
earliest Egyptian boats were made of papyrus stalks tied tightly together to make them watertight. Wood was in short
supply, and the materials required for building large wooden vessels such as the one shown here had to be imported.
Because the banks of the Nile were often choked with reeds, Egyptian boats tended to have shallow hulls without a keel.
They were steered by means of a rudder in the stern. A large vessel required a captain, a pilot, and a large crew to tend
the oars and sails.

Thebes. Huy served as governor of Nubia, and here his
official sailing ship is shown ready to set off in a souther-
ly direction, perhaps to take him to Nubia. His horses are
in their stalls, the rowers are in place, and the crew
stands ready to trim the sails as soon as the navigator has
tested the depth of the water and the captain has given
the signal to depart.

The artists responsible for decorating the private
tomb of Nefertari, the wife of Ramesses II, in the Valley
of the Queens near Deir el-Bahri worked in a new style
diverging very subtly but distinctively from earlier conventions. In one of the tomb's many beautiful, large-fig-
ured scenes, Nefertari offers jars of perfumed ointment to
the goddess Isis (fig. 3-43). The queen wears the vulture-
skin headdress of royalty, a royal collar, and a long,
transparent white gown. Isis, seated on her throne
behind a table heaped with offerings, holds a long
scepter in her left hand, the ankh in her right. She too
wears the vulture headdress, but hers is surmounted by
the horns of Hathor framing a sun disk, clear indications
of her divinity. The outline drawing and use of clear

3-43. *Queen Nefertari Making an Offering to Isis*, wall painting
    in the tomb of Nefertari, Valley of the Queens, near Deir
    el-Bahri. Dynasty 19, c. 1279–1212 BCE

RESTORING THE TOMB OF NEFERTARI

The tomb of Queen Nefertari, wife of Ramesses II, was discovered in the Valley of the Queens, near Deir el-Bahri, in 1904. Although it had been looted of everything that could be carried away, it still contained splendid large-figure wall paintings of the deceased queen in the company of the gods (see fig. 3-43).

Thanks to Egypt's dry climate and the care with which most tombs were sealed, many such paintings remained in excellent condition for thousands of years. Strangely, the ones in Nefertari's tomb had begun to deteriorate soon after they were completed. Conservators have theorized that the walls were left quite damp when priests sealed the tomb, so that salts from the plaster leached to the surface. Over time, this tended to loosen the layer of pigment, causing it to flake. The dampness also allowed various funguses to attack the paint. The process of disintegration accelerated dramatically when the tomb was opened to the public. Its many visitors raised the humidity level and introduced dirt and bacteria from outside. The resulting damage was so great by 1940 that the tomb was closed to the public.

In 1968 the Egyptian National Antiquities Service and the Getty Conservation Institute in Santa Monica, California, undertook a multi-million-dollar conservation project to save the tomb's decorations. The painting restorers Paolo and Laura Mora were commissioned to supervise the work, which was carried out by a team of Italian and Egyptian conservators. Their first priority was to stop the paint from flaking and the plaster from crumbling any further. Over the course of a year, their crew applied over 10,000 "bandages" made of Japanese mulberry-pulp paper to the tomb's interior surfaces.

Once the paint and plaster had been stabilized, the restorers could begin their real work. Their goal was to salvage every flake of paint they could from these works created more than 3,000 years earlier. They carefully cleaned the paintings with cotton swabs dipped in distilled water. Using hypodermic needles and a special resin glue, they were able to reattach small spots of loose plaster or pigment. Larger detached areas were removed whole, cleaned, then glued back in place. In the past, it was common practice for conservators to re-create sections that had been wholly lost with conjectural painting of their own, but according to current thinking within the profession it is preferable to simply make such gaps less obvious by shading

Getty Conservation Institute conservator S. Rickerby at work in Chamber K, Tomb of Nefertari, Valley of the Queens, near Deir el-Bahri

them in tones matched to adjacent work. This was the procedure in Nefertari's tomb.

Thanks to the extremely painstaking labor of professional restorers like these, many such ancient treasures have been rescued for the instruction and delight of future generations.

---

colors reflect traditional practices, but quite new is the slight modeling of the body forms by small changes of hue to increase their appearance of solidity. The skin color of these women is much darker than that conventionally used for females in earlier periods, and lightly brushed-in shading makes their eyes and lips stand out more than before (see "Restoring the Tomb of Nefertari," above). The tomb's artists used particular care in placing the hieroglyphic inscriptions around these figures, creating an unusually harmonious overall design.

Books of the Dead

By the time of the New Kingdom, the Egyptians had come to believe that only a person free from sin could enjoy an afterlife. The dead were thought to undergo a "last judgment" consisting of two tests presided over by Osiris and supervised by Anubis, the overseer of funerals and cemeteries, represented as a man with a jackal's head. The deceased were first questioned by a delegation of deities about their behavior in life. Then their hearts, which the Egyptians believed to be the seat of the soul, were weighed on a scale against an ostrich feather, the symbol of Maat, goddess of truth.

These beliefs gave rise to one specific funerary practice especially popular among the nonroyal classes. Family members would commission papyrus scrolls containing magical texts or spells to help the dead survive the tests, and they had the embalmers place the scrolls among the wrappings of their loved ones' mummified bodies. Early collectors of Egyptian artifacts referred to such scrolls, often beautifully illustrated, as Books of the Dead. They varied considerably in content. A scene from a Dynasty 19 example, created for a man named Hunefer, shows him at three successive stages in his induction into the afterlife (fig. 3-44). At the left, Anubis leads him by the hand to the spot where he will weigh his heart, contained in a tiny jar, against the "feather of Truth." Maat herself appears atop the balancing arm of the scales wearing the feather as a headdress. A monster—part crocodile, part lion, and part hippopotamus—watches eagerly for a sign from the ibis-headed

3-44. *Judgment before Osiris*, illustration from a Book of the Dead. Dynasty 19, c. 1285 BCE. Painted papyrus, height 15⅝"
(39.8 cm). The British Museum, London

Osiris, the god of the underworld, appears on the right, enthroned in a richly ornamented pavilion, or chapel, in the "Hall
of the Two Truths." Here the souls of the deceased were thought to be subjected to a "last judgment" to determine
whether they were worthy of eternal life. Osiris was traditionally depicted as a mummified man wrapped in a white linen
shroud. His other trappings are those of an Egyptian king. He wears the double crown, incorporating those of both
Upper and Lower Egypt, a false beard, and a wide beaded collar, and he brandishes the symbolic crook and flail in front
of his chest. The figure in the center combining a man's body with the head of an ibis, a wading bird related to the
heron, is the god Thoth. He here functions as a sort of court stenographer—appropriately, for he was revered as the
inventor of hieroglyphic writing.

god Thoth, who prepares to record the result of the
weighing. This creature is Ammit, the dreaded "Eater of
the Dead."

But the "Eater" is left to go hungry. Hunefer passes
the test, and on the right Horus presents him to Osiris.
The god of the underworld sits on a throne floating on a
lake of natron, the substance used to preserve the flesh
of the deceased from decay (see "Preserving the Dead,"
page 121). The four sons of Horus, each of whom was
entrusted with the care of one of the deceased's vital
organs, stand atop a huge lotus blossom rising up out of
the lake. The goddesses Nephthys and Isis stand behind
the throne, supporting the god's left arm with a tender
gesture similar to the one seen in the Old Kingdom sculpture of Menkaure and his queen (see fig. 3-15). In the top
register, Hunefer makes his appearance in the afterlife,
kneeling before the nine gods of Heliopolis—the sacred
city of the sun god Ra—and five personifications of life-
sustaining principles.

Life was short in ancient times. Few people could
expect to live beyond their twenties. All hoped to escape

the "Eater" and live on eternally in the company of the
gods. But they also doubtless heeded the advice given in
"The Harper's Song," a poem inscribed on a wall in the
tomb of the Dynasty 14 king Inyotef VII at Dra Abu el-
Naga (cited in Strouhal, page 266):

None comes from there
To tell of their state
To calm our hearts
Until we go where they have gone.
Hence rejoice in your heart . . .
Make holiday, do not weary of it.

No one *has* come from there to tell us how the
ancient Egyptians fared after death, but the art they produced has assured them of immortality. Their continuing
creativity over many long centuries was acknowledged
and admired by contemporary peoples—as it was by
their eventual conquerors.

CHAPTER 4

Aegean Art

0

1500

1000

Bull Jumper
c. 1700–1550

Funerary mask
c. 1550–1500

▲ MYCENAEAN 1400–1100

100 miles

100 kilometers

Ionian Sea

Aegean Sea

Troy

ANATOLIA

Athens

ATTICA

Mycenae

Tiryns

PELOPONNESE

CYCLADES

Syros

Paros

Naxos

Keros

Sparta

Pylos

Vapheio

Melos

Thera

Akrotiri

RHODES

Mediterranean Sea

CRETE

Knossos

Chryssolakkos

Mallia

Palaikastro

Hagia Triada

Gournia

Zakro

Phaistos

Down through the ages, philosophers and visionaries from Plato to the Beatles have dreamed of utopian kingdoms under the sea where untold wealth could be found. The undersea realm the Beatles explored in *Yellow Submarine* was clearly fictional, but the "lost island of Atlantis" described by Plato in his *Timaeus* and *Critias* may have had some basis in fact. There is evidence that it may have been the island of Thera, also known as Santorini, in the Cyclades. Until it erupted in the seventeenth century BCE, the nearly 5,000-foot-tall volcano that dominated the island must have looked much like Japan's Mount Fuji, a majestic presence whose lower slopes were home to many people. When the volcano came to life, people had time to escape with what they could carry, but then the entire peak blew apart and the greater part of the island, like the fabled Atlantis, disappeared into the sea. All that remained was a crescent of jagged cliffs, fragments of what had been the mountain's base, some 13 miles in diameter. Extensive excavations of the ancient site at Akrotiri, on Thera, have been carried out since 1967, and treasures have indeed been found. Under a layer of ash as much as 15 feet deep, well-preserved wall paintings and artifacts have been discovered that open a window on ancient Aegean culture during one of its richest periods.

THE AEGEAN WORLD

From about 5,000 to 3,000 years ago, the early European civilizations known as Aegean flourished on mainland Greece and on the islands offshore in the Aegean Sea, including the large southern island of Crete and a cluster of smaller ones called the Cyclades. Scholars of these cultures have long studied their ruined palaces, fortresses, and tombs. In recent years the collaboration of archeologists and art historians, working with researchers in such fields as the history of trade and climate change, is providing a much clearer picture of Aegean society in which to place Aegean architecture, sculpture, metalwork, ceramics, and wall paintings.

Although the Aegean peoples were primarily farmers and herders, their lives were greatly influenced by their proximity to the sea. The sea provided their dry, rocky homelands with a defense against invaders, but because they were skillful seafarers, it also provided them a convenient link between the mainland and the islands, as well as the world beyond. Their contacts with Egypt and the civilizations of the Near East were especially important.

From about 3000 to 1000 BCE, one of the hallmarks of Aegean society was the use of bronze, an alloy that was superior to pure copper for making weapons and tools. Using metal ores from Europe, Arabia, and Anatolia, Aegean peoples created metalwares that became prized exports. The sudden technological shift to bronze, presumably as a result of contact with other cultures, occurred at the end of the Aegean Neolithic period and spurred a new consolidation of political and economic power in the Aegean Bronze Age.

Beginning in the third millennium BCE, **palace complexes**, perhaps patterned after Near Eastern and Egyptian administrative centers, began to play a key role in the development of Aegean civilization. They appear to have functioned as religious, political, and economic hubs for Aegean society. A number of palace sites have been excavated, providing a wealth of art and information. However, a great many questions about that society remain unanswered, partly because only one of the three main Aegean writing systems has been deciphered.

What little is known about Aegean civilization from studying its art suggests that religion was probably epiphanic—meaning that during rituals gods and goddesses were believed to appear to their worshipers, often in the form of human stand-ins. The chief deities seem to have been goddesses who controlled various aspects of the natural world and therefore had much in common with goddesses in other early cultures. These Aegean deities may also have been the ancestors of the later Greek goddesses Demeter, Artemis, and Athena. Female images are the most common form of religious art found in Aegean graves, hilltop sacred sites, and palace shrines and may represent goddesses, priestesses, or female worshipers.

Probably the thorniest problem in Aegean archeology is that of dating (see "The Date Debate," opposite). Archeologists have developed a chronological system for the Aegean Bronze Age, but dating specific sites and objects continues to be difficult and controversial. You may therefore encounter dates different from those given here and should expect dating to change in the future.

Our study of Aegean art focuses on three cultures: early Cycladic (on the islands of the Cyclades), Minoan (on Crete), and Mycenaean (in mainland Greece). It begins about 3000 BCE and ends about 1100 BCE.

THE DATE DEBATE Considerable controversy has arisen over the dating of Aegean objects almost since they were first excavated. New evidence is challenging established ideas of *what* happened *when* in the Aegean. It is too soon to tell if the debate is truly over, but scholars using a combination of methods are very close to pinning down the key dates.

Because of the absence of written records, archeologists have used changes in pottery styles to construct a **relative chronology** for the Aegean Bronze Age. A relative chronology indicates how old objects are in relation to each other but cannot assign them absolute dates. Influenced by the division of Egyptian history into Old, Middle, and New Kingdoms, Sir Arthur Evans used ceramic finds from different excavation levels at Knossos to devise a similar chronological framework for Crete, dividing Minoan culture into three periods: Early Minoan, Middle Minoan, and Late Minoan. Later archeologists extended this system to the Cyclades and the mainland (the divisions of the Helladic period, Greece's Bronze Age, correspond more or less to those of the Minoan) and refined it over the years. Still, it remains inexact.

Fortunately, historical records have survived from the Near East and Egypt going back to the third millennium. By the careful cross-cultural referencing of lucky finds—datable foreign trade goods at undated Aegean sites or undated Aegean trade goods in datable foreign contexts—scholars are now beginning to be able to assign dates to the relative chronology's periods, with a view toward arriving at an **absolute chronology**. Radiocarbon, or carbon-14, dating is increasingly useful as a method for dating Aegean organic material, though some dates can only be determined within a span of two or three centuries.

After decades of painstaking work establishing relative and absolute chronologies for the Aegean, archeologists generally agreed that a huge volcanic explosion on the Cycladic island of Thera had thoroughly devastated Minoan civilization on Crete, only 60 miles to the south, about 1450 BCE.

New evidence—namely, stunted growth in tree rings from Ireland and California and traces of volcanic ash in ice cores from Greenland—puts the date of the Thera eruption in the 1620s. This finding leaves Minoan and Mycenaean dating in serious disarray, and the debate over how to realign the chronologies for Aegean civilizations and their trading partners, particularly Egypt, is just beginning.

How has this affected the dating of Minoan and Mycenaean artworks illustrated in this chapter? Specific dates cannot be assigned until the results of the debate are in. While experts ponder the evidence, the rest of us must fall back on the relative chronology system of dating established long ago for the Aegean region. Although this system also lost its chronological underpinnings when the date of the Thera eruption was called into question, many of the interrelationships and stylistic categories on which it is based must still be valid. For that reason, best-guess beginning and ending dates have here been assigned for the Middle and Late Minoan stylistic periods and for Helladic art, then the artworks have been placed within this framework in their familiar positions. Thus the dates given indicate only how old objects may be relative to each other between the more-or-less absolute cut-off dates of 2000 and 1100. Artworks from the island of Thera therefore have simply been dated "before 1630–1500 BCE."

THE CYCLADIC ISLANDS IN THE BRONZE AGE

A thriving late Neolithic and early Bronze Age culture existed on the Cycladic Islands, where people engaged in agriculture, herding, manufacturing, and trade. They used local stone to build fortified towns and hillside burial chambers. Because they left no written records and their origins remain obscure, their art is one of our main sources of information about them, as is the case with other Neolithic cultures. From about 6000 BCE on, Cycladic artists had used a coarse, poor-quality local clay to make a variety of objects. Some 3,000 years later, they continued to produce relatively crude but often engaging ceramic figurines of humans and animals, as well as domestic and ceremonial **wares**.

Among the more unusual products of Cycladic potters were vessels resembling large frying pans made of **terra-cotta**, an orange-brown, low-fired clay. They ornamented these "frying pans" with **stylized** designs, either painted or **incised** before firing. The vessels seem to have been used as display objects as well as containers. The elaborate decoration on one side of a pan from Syros, dated 2500–2200 BCE, indicates that it was never intended to be blackened by a cooking fire (fig. 4-1). A

4-1. "Frying pan," from Syros, Cyclades. c. 2500– 2200 BCE. Terra-cotta, diameter 11" (28 cm), depth 2³⁄₈" (6 cm). National Archeological Museum, Athens

PARALLELS

Years	Culture	Aegean	World
c. 3000–1600 BCE	Cycladic	"Frying pans"; marble figures; landscape painting; destruction of Thera	c. 3000–2000 BCE Potter's wheel (China); Great Pyramids at Giza (Egypt); ziggurats (Sumer); Stonehenge (England)
c. 3000–1400 BCE	Minoan	Bronze tools and weapons; written scripts; Knossos and other palace complexes; *Woman or Goddess with Snakes*; *Bull Jumper*; gold jewelry; potter's wheel; Kamares Ware	c. 2000–1100 BCE *Gilgamesh* epic (Sumer); widespread use of bronze tools (Thailand, China, northern Europe); Shang dynasty (China); *Stela of Hammurabi* (Babylonia); Lion Gate (Turkey); Olmec civilization (Mesoamerica)
c. 1400–1100 BCE	Mycenaean	Citadel at Mycenae; beehive tombs; "Treasury of Atreus"; shaft-grave treasures; *Warrior Vase*	

wide, geometric border encircles a scene showing a boat on a sea of waves depicted as linked spirals. With its curved hull and long banks of oars, the boat resembles those seen in Neolithic Egyptian art from Hierakonpolis (see fig. 3-3). The large fish to the left is probably a carved prow ornament. In the small area set off in the "handle," the artist incised a triangular symbol for the female pubic area, perhaps an indication that these objects were symbolic representations of the uterus and female genitalia. The pans may therefore have had some magical association with pregnancy and childbirth, as well as death, for they are most often found at gravesites.

The Cyclades, especially the islands of Naxos and Paros, had ample supplies of a fine and durable white marble that became the medium of choice for sculptors. Out of it they created a unique type of nude figure ranging in size from a few inches to about 5 feet tall. To shape the stone, these sculptors used scrapers and chisels made of obsidian from the island of Melos and polishing stones of emery, or corundum, from Naxos. The introduction of metal tools may have made it possible for them to carve on a larger scale, but since the stone fractured easily, they continued to limit themselves to simplified sculptural forms.

A few male figurines have been found, including depictions of musicians and acrobats, but they are greatly outnumbered by representations of women. The earliest female figures had simple, violinlike shapes. From these, a more familiar type evolved that has become the best-known type of Cycladic art (fig. 4-2).

4-2. Two figures of women, from the Cyclades. c. 2500–2200 BCE. Marble, heights 13" (33 cm) and 25" (63.4 cm). Museum of Cycladic Art, Athens
Courtesy of the N. P. Goulandris Foundation

4-3. *Harp Player*, from Keros, Cyclades. c. 2500–2200 BCE. Marble, height 8½" (21.6 cm). National Archeological Museum, Athens

The smaller Cycladic figures have been found mainly in and around graves. Although their specific use and meaning are unclear, one interpretation is that they were used by some of the population for worship in the home and then buried with their owners, often after being symbolically broken as part of the funeral ritual. According to this theory, the larger statues were not grave goods but were set up for communal worship, whether as representations of the supernatural or as **votive figures**. The contents of Aegean burial sites could point to a belief in an afterlife. From the evidence, however, it seems that Aegean culture, unlike that of Egypt, was primarily concerned with life in the present.

CRETE AND THE MINOAN CIVILIZATION

Around 3000 BCE, a distinctive culture now called Minoan came into being on the island of Crete. Its name comes from a much later legend that told of Minos, a king who ruled from the palace at Knossos (see "The Legend of the Minotaur," page 132). Crete is the largest of the Aegean islands, 150 miles long and 36 miles wide. It was economically self-sufficient, producing its own grains, olives and other fruits, and cattle and sheep. Because it lacked the ores necessary for bronze production, it was forced to look outward. Crete took advantage of its strategic location and many safe harbors to become a wealthy sea power, trading with mainland Greece, Egypt, the Near East, Anatolia, and perhaps beyond.

Minoan civilization reached its peak about 1600 BCE and remained powerful until about 1450 BCE. Although a number of written records from the period are preserved, very little is known about Minoan daily life. The two earliest forms of Cretan writing, called hieroglyphic and Linear A, continue to defy translation, and the surviving documents in a later script, Linear B—a very early form of Greek imported from the mainland—have proven to be only administrative records and temple inventories, offering no information about many aspects of Minoan culture.

The dominant architectural structures on Crete from roughly 1900 to 1300 BCE were great palace complexes, which were simultaneously administrative, commercial, and religious centers. Scattered across the island, these complexes were long thought to have been unfortified, but it is now known that they were safeguarded by formidable watchtowers and stone walls extending into the countryside. Little is known about the role kings might have played in palace society. Recent scholars have placed greater emphasis on the priestesses who seem to have overseen the all-important goddess worship in these centers. It has been speculated that the palace complexes, kingship, and priestess-run goddess cults are distinctively Minoan adaptations of Near Eastern or Egyptian institutions, but the evidence is contradictory. The Near Eastern palace of Zimrilim at Mari (see Chapter 2, especially fig. 2-19) provides an instructive comparison. It has many similarities to Cretan palaces, such as scale and layout and the depiction of goddesses or

Compared with Egyptian statues from the same time (see fig. 3-13), Cycladic marbles from roughly 2500 BCE appear to many modern eyes like pared-down, elegant renderings of the figure's essence. With their simple contours, the female statuettes shown here seem not far removed from the marble slabs out of which they were carved. Their tilted-back heads, folded arms, and down-pointed toes indicate that the figures were intended to lie on their backs, as if asleep or dead. Anatomical detail has been kept to a minimum; the body's natural articulation lines at the hips, knees, and ankles are indicated, and the pubic area is marked with a lightly incised triangle. These statues are now paintless, but they originally had painted facial features, hair, and ornaments in black, red, and blue.

The *Harp Player* from Keros is fully developed **sculpture in the round** (fig. 4-3), yet its body shape is just as simplified as that of the female figurines. The sculptor gave equal attention to the negative, or empty, spaces and the solid forms, which balance each other. The figure has been reduced to its geometric essentials, yet with careful attention to those elements that best characterize an actual musician. The harpist sits on a high-backed chair with a splayed base, head tilted back as if singing, knees and feet apart for stability, and arms raised, bracing the instrument with one hand while plucking its strings with the other. So expressive is the pose that we can almost hear the song.

4-4. Bird's-eye reconstruction drawing of the palace complex, Knossos, Crete. c. 1700–1300 BCE

Key: 1. west porch; 2. main corridor; 3. main stairs; 4. north-south corridor; 5. warehouse storage; 6. central courtyard; 7. so-called Throne Room (actually a ritual space); 8. west staircase and stepped porch; 9. main shrine; 10. grand staircase; 11. light well; 12. Hall of the Double Axes (main reception hall); 13. so-called Queen's Quarters; 14. outdoor performance area

priestesses in wall paintings. However, Minoan architecture is less massive and more open, and its palace art does not celebrate kings.

The walls of early Minoan palaces were made of rubble and mud bricks faced with cut and finished limestone. This was the first use of **dressed stone** as a building material in the Aegean. Columns and other interior elements were made of wood. In both the palaces and their surrounding towns, timber appears to have been used for framing and bracing walls so that its strength and flexibility would minimize damage from earthquakes. Nevertheless, a major earthquake in about 1750 BCE damaged

THE LEGEND OF THE MINOTAUR According to Greek legend, the Minotaur was a monster, half man and half bull. He was the son of Pasiphae, the wife of King Minos of Crete, and a bull belonging to the sea god Poseidon. The monster lived in the so-called Labyrinth, a maze constructed by the king's court artist and architect, Daedalus. To satisfy the Minotaur's appetite for human flesh and to keep him tranquil, King Minos ordered the city of Athens, which he ruled, to pay him a yearly tribute tax of fourteen young men and women. Theseus, the son of King Aegeus of Athens, vowed to free his people from this grisly burden by slaying the monster.

He set out for Crete with the doomed young Athenians, promising his father that on his return voyage he would replace his ship's black sails with white ones as a signal of victory. In the manner of ancient heroes, Theseus won the heart of the Cretan princess Ariadne, who gave him a sword with which to kill the Minotaur and a spindle of thread to mark the path he took into the Labyrinth. Theseus defeated the Minotaur, followed his trail of thread back out of the maze, and sailed off to Athens with Ariadne and the relieved Athenians. Along the way, his ship put into port on the island of Naxos, where Theseus had a change of heart and left Ariadne behind as she lay sleeping. In his haste to return home, he "forgot" to raise the white sails.

When Aegeus saw the black-sailed ship approaching, he drowned himself in the sea that now bears his name. Theseus thus became king of Athens.

Such psychologically complex myths have long inspired European artists. In William Shakespeare's *A Midsummer Night's Dream*, the play-within-the-play celebrates the marriage of Theseus to the Amazon queen Hippolyta. The plight of Theseus's abandoned lover Ariadne—who finds comfort in the arms of the Greek god Dionysos—is the subplot of an opera by Richard Strauss. In our own time, Pablo Picasso used the Minotaur as a symbol of the Spanish dictator Francisco Franco and the horrors of the Spanish Civil War.

4-5. Palace complex, Knossos, Crete

The town at the foot of the palace had paved streets, comfortable houses, and an advanced water supply and drainage system. "Mansions" dotted the Cretan countryside outside such towns.

several palaces, including the best known of them at Knossos and Phaistos. The structures were then repaired and enlarged. The resulting "new palaces"—multistoried, flat-roofed, and with many columns—shared a number of features. They were designed to maximize light, air, and adaptability, as well as to define access and circulation patterns. Daylight and fresh air entered through staggered levels, open stairwells, and strategically placed air shafts and light wells.

The focus of the complex was inward, toward a spacious rectangular courtyard from which a maze of corridors and staircases led to other courtyards, private rooms and apartments, administrative and ritual areas, storerooms, and baths. Walls were generally coated with plaster, and some of them were painted with murals. Floors were either of plaster, plaster mixed with pebbles, stone, wood, or beaten earth. The palaces' residential quarters had many attractions: sunlit courtyards, richly colored murals, and extraordinarily sophisticated plumbing systems: at Knossos, a network of terra-cotta pipes was laid beneath the palace. Clusters of workshops in and around the complexes suggest that artistic production was officially controlled. Palaces were clearly commercial centers, for their storeroom walls were lined with enormous clay jars for oil and wine, and stone-lined pits in their floors were designed for the storage of grain. The huge scale of their centralized management of foodstuffs became apparent when excavators at Knossos found in a single storeroom enough ceramic jars to hold 20,000 gallons of olive oil.

The Palace Complex at Knossos

Minoan civilization remained very much a mystery until Sir Arthur Evans discovered the buried ruins of the extraordinary palace complex at Knossos, on Crete's north coast, in 1900 CE. Evans spent the rest of his life excavating and reconstructing the buildings he had found (see "Pioneers of Aegean Archeology," page 143). The site had been occupied in the Neolithic period, then built over with a succession of Bronze Age palaces. The last of these "old palaces," erected about 1900 BCE, formed the core of an elaborate new one built after an earthquake in about 1700 BCE. In its heyday, the palace complex covered six acres (figs. 4-4, 4-5). In later Greek legend the Knossos palace was called the Labyrinth, meaning the House of the Double Axes (Greek *labrys*, "double ax"), because double-ax motifs were used in it as architectural decoration (see fig. 4-12 for a three-dimensional example). Because the layout of the complex was so dauntingly complicated, the word *labyrinth* came to mean a maze.

In typical Cretan fashion, the religious, residential, manufacturing, and warehouse spaces of the new palace were organized around a large central courtyard. There were entrances at the four corners, but the main ceremonial approach seems to have been from the southwest. The route to the center of the complex from any of these entrances involved a number of turns. From the central courtyard, a few steps led down into the (misnamed) Throne Room to the west, and a grand staircase on the east side descended to the Hall of the Double

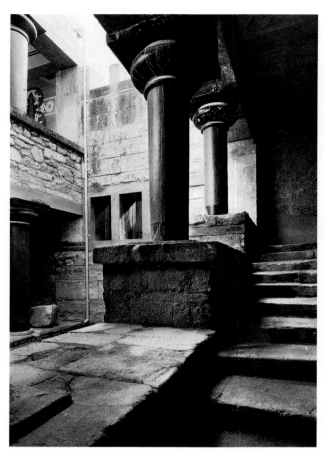

4-6. Court with staircase reconstructed by Sir Arthur Evans, leading to the southeast residential quarter, palace complex, Knossos, Crete

The hundreds of tapered, cushion-capitaled columns of the palace were made of wood, most painted a bright red, and only fragments of them survive. Sir Arthur Evans's restorers installed concrete replicas of columns, capitals, and lintels based on ceramic house models and paintings from the Minoan period. Today's archeologists might not attempt such wholesale reconstruction without absolutely authentic documentation, and they would make certain that reconstructed elements could never be mistaken for the originals.

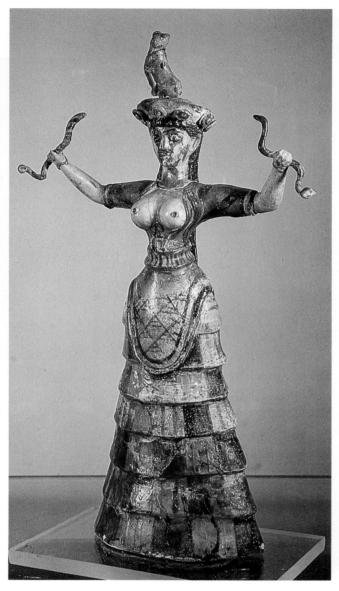

4-7. *Woman or Goddess with Snakes,* from the palace complex, Knossos, Crete. c. 1700–1550 BCE. Faience, height 11 5/8" (29.5 cm). Archeological Museum, Iraklion, Crete

Axes, an unusually grand example of a Minoan hall. This hall and others were supported by the uniquely Minoan type of wood columns that became standard in Aegean palace architecture. The tree trunks from which they were made were inverted so that they tapered toward the bottom. Thus, the top, supporting massive roof beams, was wider than the bottom (fig. 4-6). There is some evidence to suggest that Minoan builders were eventually unable to replace columns damaged by earthquakes or burned by invaders because they had already stripped the island of large trees, and this deforestation may have been one of the reasons why the palace-complex structure was finally abandoned.

Sculpture

Surviving Minoan sculpture consists mainly of small, finely executed works, largely on religious subjects, in wood, ivory, precious metals, stone, and **faience**. The *Woman or Goddess with Snakes* from the palace at Knossos is intriguing both as a ritual object and as a work of art (fig. 4-7). Female figurines incorporating serpents were fashioned on Crete as far back as 6000 BCE and may have been associated—as they were elsewhere—with water, regenerative power, and protection of the home. Some early Minoan Bronze Age examples have tall, flaring headdresses with circles on the front and a writhing mass of intertwining snakes on the back.

The nearly foot-tall faience figurine from Knossos was found with other ceremonial objects in a pit in one of the palace's temple storerooms. Bare-breasted, arms extended, and brandishing a snake in each hand, the woman is a commanding presence. A wild cat is perched on her crown, which is ornamented with circles resembling those on the headdresses of earlier such statues. This shapely figure is dressed in a fitted, open bodice with

4-8. *Bull Jumper* (?), from the palace complex, Knossos, Crete. c. 1700–1550 BCE. Ivory with gilt bronze wire, length 11⁵/₈" (29.5 cm). Archeological Museum, Iraklion, Crete

an apron over a typically Minoan long tiered skirt. A wide belt cinches the waist. The red, blue, and green geometric patterning on her clothing looks rather like snakeskin. In other pieces of this type, snakes sometimes wind around the woman's waist and arms.

Realistic elements and formal, stylized ones are so skillfully combined in this figure and others of its kind that they have both liveliness and power. In part because of this blending of elements, there is disagreement over whether these statues represent deities or their human attendants. These figures share certain stylistic and thematic features with Near Eastern sculpture, but both the style and the subject can be traced back to older Cretan examples as well.

A number of early cultures associated their gods and god-rulers with powerful animals, especially the lion and the bull. Depictions of bulls appear quite often in Minoan art, rendered with an intensity not seen since the prehis-

toric cave paintings at Altamira and Lascaux (Chapter 1), yet neither their images nor later myths offer any proof that the Minoans worshiped a bull god. According to later Greek legend, King Minos kept the bull-man called the Minotaur captive in his palace, but the creature was not an object of religious veneration (see "The Legend of the Minotaur," page 132). In addition to serving as livestock, bulls were apparently sacrificed by the Minoans on outdoor altars and figured in a rite called bull jumping. Paintings and sculpture show that both women and men, perhaps trained acrobats, took part in this dangerous contest, but its significance remains a mystery.

An ivory figurine of a nude leaping youth (fig. 4-8) was probably originally suspended above one of the ceramic bulls found with it in the palace at Knossos. Despite its deteriorated state, this lithe figure captures the energy of athleticism as it vaults through space. Later Greek culture glorified its athletes, and figures like this

4-9. *Harvester Vase*, from Hagia Triada, Crete. c. 1650–1450 BCE. Steatite, diameter 4¹/₂" (11.3 cm). Archeological Museum, Iraklion, Crete

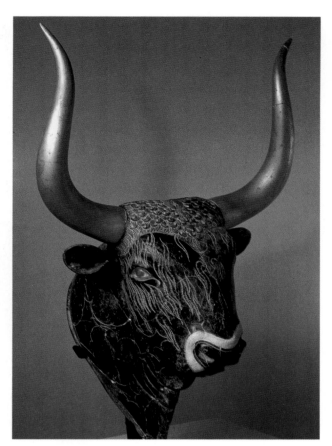

4-10. Bull's-head rhyton, from the palace complex, Knossos, Crete. c. 1550–1450 BCE. Steatite with shell, rock crystal, and red jasper, the gilt-wood horns restored, height 12" (30.5 cm). Archeological Museum, Iraklion, Crete

one may mark the beginning of the practice. The artistry of the ivory figurine is remarkable: its tiny fingernails, the raised veins on the backs of its hands, and its wavy hair are all painstakingly rendered—the latter with gilt, or gold-covered, wire.

Minoan sculptors also excelled in working in hard stone. One of the treasures of Cretan art is the *Harvester Vase*, an egg-shaped **rhyton**—a vessel used for pouring liquids during sacred ceremonies—barely 4¹/₂ inches in diameter (fig. 4-9). Made of steatite, or soapstone, it was probably originally covered with **gold leaf**, or sheets of hammered gold (see "Aegean Metalwork," opposite). A rowdy procession of twenty-seven men has been crowded onto its curving surface. The piece is exceptional for the freedom with which the figures occupy three-dimensional space, overlapping and jostling one another instead of marching in orderly single file across the surface in the manner of Near Eastern or Egyptian art. Also new is the exuberance of this scene, especially the emotions shown on the harvesters' faces. The merrymakers march and chant to the beat of a sistrum—a rattlelike percussion instrument—played by a man who sings at the top of his voice. The uneven arrangement of elements reinforces the boisterousness of the scene. The men have large, coarse features and sinewy bodies so thin that their ribs stick out. Perhaps they have suffered a lean time, which gives them all the more reason to celebrate a good harvest.

Rhytons were often given the form of a bull's head. The sculptor of one of this type found in a residence near the palace at Knossos used a block of greenish black steatite to create an image that approaches animal portraiture in its decorative detailing (fig. 4-10). Lightly engraved lines, filled with white powder to make them stand out, show the animal's coat: short, curly hair on top of the head, longer shaggy strands on the sides, and circular patterns to suggest its dappled coloring. White bands of shell outline the nostrils, and painted rock crystal and red jasper form the eyes. The horns, now restored, were made of wood covered with gold leaf. Bull's-head rhytons were used for pouring ritual fluids—water, wine, or perhaps even blood. They were not actual containers; liquid was poured into a hole in the neck and flowed out from the mouth.

Metalwork

By about 1700 BCE, Aegean metalworkers were producing decorative objects rivaling those of Near Eastern jewelers, whose techniques they seem to have borrowed. A necklace pendant in gold found at Chryssolakkos (fig. 4-11) employs several of these techniques (see "Aegean Metalwork," opposite). The artist arched a pair of bees or wasps around a honeycomb, providing their sleek bodies with a single pair of outspread wings—a visual "two in one." The pendant hangs from a spiderlike form, with

TECHNIQUE

Aegean artists imported gold to create exquisite luxury goods. Their techniques, some probably learned from Near Eastern metalsmiths, included **lost-wax casting**, **inlay**, **filigree**, **repoussé** (embossing), **granulation**, **niello**, and **gilding**. The *Vapheio Cup* (fig. 4-13) and the funerary mask (fig. 4-27) are examples of repoussé, in which the artist gently hammered out relief forms from the back of a thin sheet of gold. Experienced goldsmiths may have done simple designs freehand or used standard wood forms or punches. For more elaborate decorations they would first have sculpted the entire relief design in wood or clay and then used this form as a mold over which to shape the gold sheet.

Cretan jewelers were especially skilled at decorating their goldwork with minute granules, or balls, of gold fused to the surfaces, as seen on the bees/wasps pendant (fig. 4-11). The secret of this technique, called granulation, was only recently rediscovered after being lost for nearly a thousand years. The major mystery was how the granules were attached, since all modern solders—heated metal alloys used as adhesives—melted and overwhelmed the tiny, gold globules. The ancient smiths are now believed to have used a complex copper-based solder that fused strongly but nearly invisibly.

The artists who created the Mycenaean dagger blades (fig. 4-28) employed a special technique called niello, which has continued as a common method of metal decoration up to the present time. Powdered nigellum—a black alloy of lead, silver, and copper with sulfur—was rubbed into very fine engraved lines in the object being decorated, then fused to the surrounding metal with heat. Niello work was used for contrasting detail on both **relief** figures and backgrounds.

Gilding, the application of a gold finish to an object made of some other material, was a technically demanding process by which paper-thin sheets of hammered gold called **gold leaf** were meticulously affixed to the surface to be gilded. This was done with amazing delicacy for the individual bronze wire "hairs" of the Minoan ivory *Bull Jumper* (fig. 4-8) as well as for the now-bare stone surface of the *Harvester Vase* (fig. 4-9). The wooden horns of the bull's-head rhyton, too, were gilded (fig. 4-10).

4-11. Pendant in the form of two bees or wasps, from Chryssolakkos, near Mallia, Crete. c. 1700–1550 BCE. Gold, height approx. 1¹³/₁₆" (4.6 cm). Archeological Museum, Iraklion, Crete

This pendant has been interpreted by some as two bees embracing a drop of honey, by others as two wasps fighting. Mallia's goldsmiths may have been influenced by Egyptian artists, who often depicted bees in this way.

what appear to be long legs encircling a tiny, gold ball. Small disks dangle from the ends of the wings and the point where the insects' bodies meet. The simplified geometric patterns and shapes manage to convey close observation of the insects' actual appearance.

Another object notable for its symmetry is the double ax, a motif familiar from the palace at Knossos. The double ax was both a tool and a prominent Minoan cult object associated with blood sacrifice. Since it some- times appears painted above a bull's head on Minoan pottery, it would seem that bulls may have been sacri- ficed, and the Minotaur legend raises the possibility that human beings were as well. The double ax was associ- ated with several deities, and its image appears in almost every Minoan art form, especially at religious sites. Both functional bronze axes and miniature gold replicas have been discovered. A large and richly decorated double ax made from a thick sheet of bronze was found in the cen- tral shrine treasury at Zakro, a palace complex on the eastern tip of Crete (fig. 4-12). The entire surface of its butterfly-shaped blades with perforated rims is incised with a design of lilylike flowers.

The skills of Minoan artists, particularly metalsmiths, made them highly sought after, especially in mainland Greece. Two magnificent gold cups found in a large tomb at Vapheio, on the mainland south of Sparta, were made about 1650–1450 BCE, either by Minoan artists or by local ones trained in Minoan style and techniques. One of them is shown here (fig. 4-13). Their relief designs were executed in **repoussé**—the technique of hammering from the inside. Their handles were attached with rivets, and they were then lined with sheet gold. In the scenes that circle the cups, men are depicted trying to capture bulls in various ways. On this one, a half-nude man has roped a bull's hind leg. The figures dominate the land- scape, which literally bulges with a muscular vitality that belies the cups' small size—they are only 3½ inches tall. The indication of olive trees could mean that the scene is a sacred grove and that these might be illustrations of exploits in some long-lost heroic tale rather than com- monplace hunting scenes.

4-12. Drawing of a bronze double ax with double blades, from Zakro, Crete. c. 1650–1500 BCE

Double-bladed axes were associated with ritual use. This ax may have adorned the wooden column of a palace or been set atop a wooden pole, as double axes are shown to be on some sarcophagi.

4-13. *Vapheio Cup*, found near Sparta, Greece. c. 1650–1450 BCE. Gold, height 3½" (8.9 cm). National Archeological Museum, Athens

1500 3000 BCE 1000 BCE

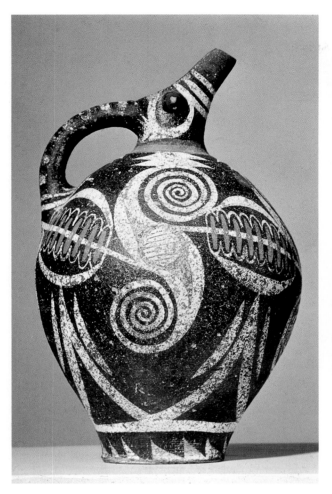

4-14. Kamares Ware jug, from Phaistos, Crete. c. 2000–1900 BCE. Ceramic, height 10⅝" (27 cm). Archeological Museum, Iraklion, Crete

4-15. *Octopus Flask*, from Palaikastro, Crete. c. 1500–1450 BCE. Marine Style ceramic, height 11" (28 cm). Archeological Museum, Iraklion, Crete

Ceramics

The development of new types of clay wares was probably a result of the emergence of palace complexes in the early second millennium BCE, when the potter's wheel was introduced and large-scale production was centralized in palace workshops. One of these new types is called Kamares Ware, after the cave overlooking the palace complex at Phaistos, in southern Crete, where it was first discovered. The hallmarks of this select ware—exported as far away as Egypt and Syria—were its delicacy, its use of color, and its energetically stylized, painted decoration. An example from about 2000–1900 BCE has a globular body and a "beaked" pouring spout (fig. 4-14). Decorated with black, brown, red, and creamy white pigments, the jug's rounded contours are complemented by bold, curving forms derived from plants and animals.

Another striking vessel from the eastern site of Palaikastro, a stoppered bottle known as the *Octopus Flask*, was made about 1500–1450 BCE (fig. 4-15). This is one of a group of pieces decorated in the so-called Marine Style, which probably celebrates Cretan sea power, then at its height. Like microscopic life teeming in a drop of pond water, sea creatures float across the sphere between an octopus's tangled tentacles. The decoration on the Kamares Ware jug reinforces the solidity of its surface, but here the pottery skin seems to dissolve. The painter captured the grace and energy of natural forms while presenting them as a stylized design in harmony with the vessel's shape.

Wall Painting

Minoan painters also worked on a larger scale, covering palace rooms with geometric borders, views of nature, and scenes of human activity. Murals can be painted either on a still-wet plaster surface or on a dry one. In the wet technique, pigments bind well to the wall, but the painter is forced to work very quickly. In the dry one, the painter does not need to hurry, but the pigments tend to flake off in time. There is some controversy over which technique was used by the artists at Knossos. They may have employed both techniques in different paintings, or even a combination of the two. Their standard colors were red, yellow, black, white, green, and blue. Like the Egyptian tomb painters, the Minoan palace artists filled in the outlines of their figures and objects with unshaded areas of pure color. Minoan wall painting, however, especially of landscapes, is quite different in feeling from Egyptian painting.

Almost all of the wall paintings in the Knossos palace complex date from the "new palace" period, after about 1700 BCE. By reconstructing them, archeologists

4-16. *Bull Jumping*, wall painting with areas of modern reconstruction, from the palace complex, Knossos, Crete. c. 1550–1450 BCE. Height approx. 24½" (62.3 cm). Archeological Museum, Iraklion, Crete

Careful sifting during excavation preserved many fragments of the paintings that once covered the palace walls. The pieces were painstakingly sorted and cleaned by restorers and reassembled into puzzle pictures that still had more pieces missing than found. The next step was to fill in the gaps with colors similar to the original ones, but lighter and grayer in tone. It is therefore obvious which are the restored portions, but the eye can still read and enjoy the image.

are learning more about the functions of some of the architectural spaces the paintings enhanced. For example, the small chamber in the west wing that Sir Arthur Evans called the Throne Room has now been identified as an epiphanic ritual space, in part on the basis of the imagery employed in its murals. Lilies, associated with

goddess-priestess celebrations, are among their prominent motifs. Taken together, the wall paintings at Knossos may have referred to some seasonal festival or series of festivals in honor of a goddess.

One of the best-preserved scenes is *Bull Jumping*, part of a group of paintings with bulls as subjects from a

THE WRECK AT ULU BURUN Shipwrecks can provide vast amounts of information about the material culture of societies whose contact with the rest of the world was by sea. The wreck of a trading vessel was discovered in the vicinity of Ulu Burun, off the south coast of modern Turkey between Rhodes and Cyprus. Thought to have sunk between 1400 and 1350 BCE, during the late Helladic period, the boat carried a cargo of metals, especially copper and tin ingots for making bronze, as well as a number of bronze weapons and tools. There was also a ton of terebinth on board, an aromatic resin used in making incense and perfume, as well as a variety of fruits, nuts, and spices. There were jewelry and beads, logs of African ebony for making fine furniture, ivory tusks for carving, ostrich eggs, and raw blocks of blue glass for use in faience and glassmaking workshops. Among the many gold objects was a scarab associated with Nefertiti, the wife of the Egyptian pharaoh Akhenaten (Chapter 3). The ship also carried more mundane items, including fishhooks, sinkers for fish lines and nets, sets of weights for use on scales, and ceramic wares made by potters from the Near East, mainland Greece, as well as Cyprus.

Its varied cargo suggests that this trading vessel cruised from port to port, loading and unloading goods as it went. Which direction it was headed when it sank and where its home port might have been are still unknown, but the boat had clearly made a large circuit encompassing the coasts of Egypt, the Middle East, the Near East, Anatolia, and mainland Greece. It may even have navigated in and out of the Black Sea and as far west as Sardinia. It is tempting to see this trading vessel as evidence of Aegean entrepreneurship—there were merchant-traders in the Near East by this time—but some scholars believe that Aegean foreign trade, like that in Egypt, was conducted exclusively as exchange between courts by palace administrators.

4-17. *Priestess* (?), detail of a wall painting from Akrotiri, Thera, Cyclades. Before 1630–1500 BCE. National Archeological Museum, Athens. (For an explanation of the date used here and for figure 4-18, see "The Date Debate," page 129.)

room in the palace's east wing (fig. 4-16). The work may represent an initiation or fertility ritual. Three scantily clad, youthful figures arc around a dappled, charging bull. The pale-skinned person at the right—probably a woman—is either beginning or finishing her vault, the dark-skinned man is in the midst of his, and the pale-skinned woman at the left grasps the bull by its horns. The bull's thundering power and sinuous grace are masterfully rendered. Variegated overlapping ovals set within striped bands frame the action.

The art of wall painting seems to have spread along with other Minoan cultural influences to both the Cyclades and mainland Greece. The Cycladic island Thera (today also called Santorini) was so heavily under Cretan influence at this time that it was virtually an outpost of Minoan culture. When the island literally blew apart in the 1620s BCE, vivid murals were preserved under layers of volcanic ash in residences at Akrotiri. These paintings provide clues about life on the island before the inhabitants fled. Some of the subjects also occur in Cretan art, but others are new. One fragment, for example, may show a young priestess of the snake goddess, a familiar Cretan subject, making a ceremonial offering (fig. 4-17). The beautifully drawn figure stands with her torso in three-quarter view and her head in profile. Her frontal eye suggests Egyptian conventions. Her features bear a striking resemblance to many modern Greek faces. The woman wears an elegant robe with patterned sleeves and ornamental bands, bracelets, a necklace, and large earrings. Such figures customarily have long, flowing hair, but this one appears to wear a fitted cap crowned by a snake. If the artists on Thera followed the Knossos practice of matching mural subject to room function, then this painting would have adorned a ritual space.

Another mural is an astonishing landscape unlike anything previously encountered in ancient art (fig. 4-18). A viewer standing in the center of the room is surrounded by orange-and-blue-striped rocky hillocks sprouting oversize deep red lilies. Swallows, represented by a few deft lines, swoop above and around the flowers. The artist's vision unifies the rhythmic flow of the undulating landscape, the stylized patterning imposed on the natural forms, and the decorative use of bright colors alternating with neutral tones, which were perhaps meant to represent areas of shadow. The impression is one of organic life and growth, a celebration of the natural world symbolized by the lilies.

For reasons not entirely clear, Minoan civilization declined after about 1500 BCE, and between about 1450 and 1375 BCE the Cretan palace complexes succumbed to conquest by mainland Greeks. Knossos was burned, but

4-18. *Landscape*, wall painting with areas of modern reconstruction from Akrotiri, Thera, Cyclades. Before 1630–1500 BCE. National Archeological Museum, Athens

the invaders appear to have continued using the site for many years. By 1400 BCE the center of political and cultural power in the Aegean had shifted to mainland Greece, which at that time was home to wealthy warrior-kings.

MAINLAND GREECE AND THE MYCENAEAN CIVILIZATION

Archeologists have used the term *Helladic* (from *Hellas*, the Greek word for Greece) to designate the Bronze Age in Greece. The Helladic period extends from about 3000 to 1000 BCE, overlapping with the Minoan chronology of Crete. In the early part of this period, Greek-speaking peoples invaded the mainland. They brought advanced metalworking, ceramic, and architectural techniques and displaced the indigenous Neolithic culture. When Minoan culture declined after about 1500 BCE, a Late Helladic mainland culture known as Mycenaean, after the city of Mycenae, rose to dominance in the Aegean region.

Mycenaean culture was influenced by Minoan culture, but there was a marked difference in their social, political, and geographic circumstances. Life in Mycenaean strongholds such as Mycenae, Tiryns, and Pylos probably contrasted sharply with life in the open palace complexes on Crete 92 miles away. The communities centered around these strongholds were controlled by local princes or kings, and evidence from tombs dating to between 1600 and 1500 BCE suggests that at that time they were growing both increasingly wealthy and increasingly stratified.

PIONEERS OF AEGEAN ARCHEOLOGY

The pioneering figure in the modern study of Aegean civilization was the German Heinrich Schliemann (1822–1890), who was inspired by Homer's epic tales, the *Iliad* and the *Odyssey*. The son of an impoverished minister, from whom he inherited a love of literature and languages, Schliemann was forced by economic circumstances to follow a "commercial" rather than a classical course of study and enter the business world. He worked hard, grew rich, and retired in 1863 to pursue his lifelong dream of becoming an archeologist. Between 1865 and 1868, he studied archeology and Greek in Paris, then in 1869–1870 he began conducting field work in Greece and Turkey.

Scholars of that time considered Homer's stories pure fiction, but by studying the descriptions of geography in the *Iliad*, Schliemann located the multilayered site at Hissarlik, in modern Turkey, the sixth level of which is generally accepted as being Homer's Troy. Although he had agreed to give the Turkish government half of all valuable finds in exchange for permission to dig, Schliemann kept for himself a copper pot containing objects in gold and silver that he discovered in May 1873. After having been sued by the Turks, he set up a fund to establish a national museum in Turkey, but he never returned the treasure, which was hidden for years. It came to light again only in the mid-1990s in Russia, where the Red Army had taken it, along with other art treasures, at the end of World War II.

After his success at Hissarlik, Schliemann pursued his hunch that the grave sites of Homer's Greek royal family would be found inside the citadel at Mycenae. He did indeed find opulent burials in shaft graves uncovered near the Lion(ess) Gate, but accumulated scientific data later proved the graves to be too early to contain the bodies of Atreus, Agamemnon, and their relatives—if these legendary figures ever existed. Today's scholars, however, do accept the possibility that some Homeric legends are based on actual events.

In 1887 Schliemann tried unsuccessfully to buy a site on the island of Crete, where he hoped to find the palace of the legendary King Minos. That discovery fell to a British archeologist, Sir Arthur Evans (1851–1941), who led the excavation of the palace at Knossos between 1900 and 1905. It was Evans who gave the name "Minoan"—after King Minos—to Cretan civilization from the Bronze Age. The chief focus in his study was on examples of early Minoan writing. He also made a first attempt to establish an absolute chronology for Minoan art, basing his conjectures on datable Egyptian artifacts found in the Cretan ruins and on Cretan finds in Egypt. Later scholars have revised and refined his datings.

Men were not the only energetic researchers in the field in those days. Sophia Schliemann contributed much to her husband's work, and an American woman, Harriet Boyd—assisted by Edith Hall—was responsible for the excavation of Gournia, which is one of the best-preserved Bronze Age towns in Crete. She published her findings in 1908.

View of Schliemann's excavation site of Troy from a 19th-century publication

Architecture

The Citadel at Mycenae. Later Greek writers recalled Mycenae, located near the east coast of the Peloponnese in southern Greece, as the home of the conquerors of the great city of Troy (fig. 4-19). Even today, the monumental gateway to the **citadel** at Mycenae (fig. 4-20) is an impressive reminder of the city's warlike past. The gate itself dates from about 1300–1200 BCE, perhaps a century later than the first of the citadel's **ring walls**, or surrounding walls. Because of its size, proportions, and construction techniques, the gate conveys the same impression of military strength as does the Lion Gate of the ancient Hittite citadel near modern Boghazkeui,

Turkey (see fig. 2-28). Although formed of megaliths, this gate is very different in purpose and style from other megalithic structures of the time—Stonehenge, for example (Chapter 1). The basic architecture of this gate is **post-and-lintel construction** with a **relieving arch** above. The **corbel** arch "relieved" the lintel of the weight of the wall that rose above it to a height of about 50 feet. As in Near Eastern citadels, the gate was provided with guardian figures. The Mycenaean sculptors placed a pair of lions or lionesses nearly 9½ feet tall in the arch opening. Their missing heads were sculpted separately—of bronze or gold—then fastened into holes in the stone. The two animals, one on each side of a Minoan-style column, stand facing each other, their forepaws resting on

4-19. Mycenae, Greece. c. 1600–1200 BCE

The citadel's hilltop position and fortified ring wall are clearly visible. The Lioness Gate (fig. 4-20) is at the lower left, approached by a dirt path.

stone altars. From this gate, a long, stone passageway led into the citadel proper, at the center of which stood the king's palace.

Tombs assumed much greater prominence for Helladic period cultures of the mainland than for the Minoans, and ultimately they became the most architecturally sophisticated monuments of the entire Aegean period. By about 1600 BCE, the region's kings and princes had begun building large aboveground burial places commonly referred to as **beehive tombs** because of their rounded, conical shape. In their round plan, beehive tombs are somewhat similar to the prehistoric European megalithic tombs called **passage graves**, such as the one at Newgrange, Ireland (Chapter 1). In stone-lined pits off the center chambers of these structures, Helladic ruling families laid out their dead in opulent costumes and jewelry and surrounded them with ceremonial weapons, gold and silver wares, and other articles indicative of their high status, wealth, and power.

More than a hundred such tombs have been found on mainland Greece, nine of them in the vicinity of Mycenae. Possibly the most impressive is the so-called Treasury of Atreus (fig. 4-21), which dates from about 1300 to 1200 BCE. The structure is an example of **cyclopean construction**, so called because it was believed that only the

4-20. Lioness Gate, Mycenae. c. 1300–1200 BCE. Limestone relief, height of sculpture approx. 9'6" (2.9 m)

4-21. Cutaway drawing of the beehive tomb called the Treasury of Atreus, Mycenae, Greece. c. 1300–1200 BCE

race of giants known as the Cyclopes could have moved such massive stones. A walled passageway through the earthern mound covering the tomb, about 120 feet long and 20 feet wide and open to the sky, led to the tomb's entrance **facade**. The original entrance was 34 feet high and the door was 18 feet high, faced with bronze plaques and flanked by engaged, Minoan-type columns of green marble. The section above the lintel had smaller engaged columns on each side, and the relieving triangle was disguised behind a marble panel. The stone surfaces were incised with geometric bands and **chevrons**—inverted **V**s—filled with **running spirals**, a favored Aegean motif seen in earlier Cycladic and Minoan art (see figs. 4-1, 4-12). The main tomb chamber (fig. 4-22) is a circular room 47 1/2 feet in diameter and 43 feet high. It is roofed with a **corbeled vault** built up in regular **courses**, or layers, of **ashlar**—squared stones—smoothly leaning inward and carefully calculated to meet in a single **capstone** at the peak, a remarkable engineering feat.

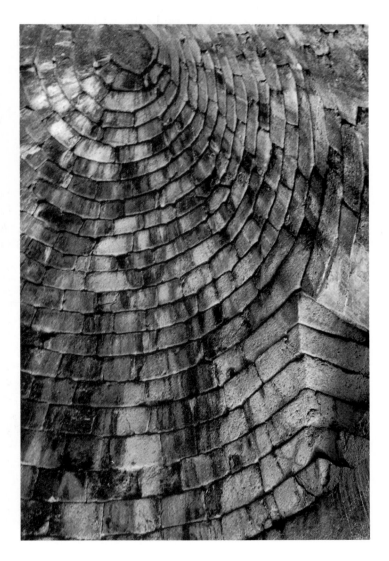

4-22. Corbeled vault, interior of the Treasury of Atreus. Stone, height of vault approx. 43' (13 m), diameter 47'6" (14.48 m)

This great beehive tomb, which remained half buried until it was excavated by Christos Stamatakis in 1878, is neither a storage space for treasures nor likely to be connected to Atreus, the father of King Menelaus and Agamemnon, who led the campaign against Troy in Homer's *Iliad*. For over a thousand years, this Mycenaean tomb remained the largest uninterrupted interior space built in Europe. The first European structure to exceed it in size was the Pantheon in Rome (Chapter 6), built in the first century BCE.

4-23. Plan of the citadel at Tiryns, Greece. c. 1300–1200 BCE

The Citadel at Tiryns. The builders of the citadel at Tiryns (fig. 4-23), about ten miles from Mycenae, made up for the site's lack of natural defenses by drawing heavily on their knowledge of military strategy. Homer referred to the resulting fortress as "Tiryns of the Great Walls." Its ring wall was about 20 feet thick, and the inner palace walls were similarly massive. The main entrance gate was approached along a narrow ramp that rose clockwise along the ring wall, forcing attacking soldiers to climb with their right sides exposed to the defenders on top of the wall and awkwardly try to cover themselves with shields held on their left arms. If they were lucky enough to reach the entrance, they still had to fight their way through a series of inner fortified gates. Corbel-vaulted casemates, or enclosures within the thickness of the ring walls, provided spaces for storing armaments and emergency shelter for soldiers or even for townspeople seeking safety within the citadel (fig. 4-24). In the unlikely event that the citadel gate was breached, the people inside could escape through openings from which they could combat attackers without opening the main gate.

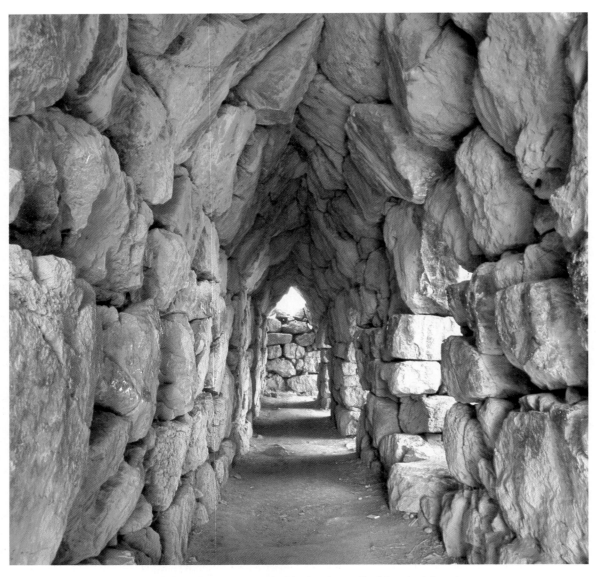

4-24. Corbel-vaulted casemate inside the ring wall of the citadel at Tiryns

4-25. Reconstruction drawing of the megaron in the palace at Pylos, Greece. c. 1300–1200 BCE. Drawing in Antonopouleion Archeological Museum, Pylos

The palace area at Tiryns featured a large audience hall called a **megaron**, or "great room," accessible to the main courtyard through a porch and a vestibule—a much more direct approach than the winding path imposed on visitors in a Minoan palace. In the typical megaron plan, four large columns around a central hearth supported the ceiling. The roof section above the hearth was either raised or open to admit light and air and permit smoke to escape. Architectural historians surmise that the megaron eventually came to be specifically associated with royalty. The later Greeks therefore adapted its form when building temples, which they saw as earthly palaces for their gods.

The Palace at Pylos. Tiryns required heavy defense works because of its location. The people of Pylos, in the extreme southwest of the Peloponnese, perhaps felt that their more remote location made military attack there less likely. The palace at Pylos, built about 1300–1200 BCE, followed the megaron plan and was built on a raised site without walls. Set behind a porch and vestibule facing the courtyard, the Pylos megaron was a

magnificent display of architectural and decorative prowess. The reconstructed view provided here (fig. 4-25) shows how the combined throne room and audience hall, with fluted Minoan-type columns supporting heavy ceiling beams, might have looked when new. Every inch was painted—the floors, ceilings, beams, and door frames with brightly colored abstract designs, and the walls with large mythical animals and highly stylized plant and landscape forms.

Linear B clay tablets found in the ruins of the palace include an inventory of the palace furnishings that indicates they were as elegant as the architecture. The listing on one tablet reads: "One ebony chair with golden back decorated with birds; and a footstool decorated with ivory pomegranates. One ebony chair with ivory back carved with a pair of finials and with a man's figure and heifers; one footstool, ebony inlaid with ivory and pomegranates." It may be that the people of Pylos should have taken greater care to protect themselves. Within a century of its construction, the palace was destroyed by fires, apparently set during the violent upheavals that brought about the collapse of Mycenaean Greek dominance.

4-26. *Two Women with a Child*, found in the palace at Mycenae, Greece. c. 1400–1200 BCE. Ivory, height 2¾" (7.5 cm). National Archeological Museum, Athens

Sculpture

Mainland artists were exposed to Minoan art through trading and even perhaps by working side by side with Minoan artists brought back by the Greek conquerors of the island. A carved ivory group of two women and a child (fig. 4-26), less than 3 inches high and found in the palace shrine at Mycenae, appears to be a product of Minoan-Mycenaean artistic exchange. Dating from about 1400–1200 BCE, the miniature exhibits carefully observed natural forms, an intricately interlocked composition, and finely detailed rendering. Because there are no clues to the identity or the significance of the group, we might easily interpret it as generational—with grandmother, mother, and child—but the figures could just as well represent two nymphs or devotees attending a child-god. In either case, the mood of affection and tenderness among the three is unmistakable, and, tiny as it is, the sculpture counters the militaristic vein of so much Mycenaean art.

Metalwork

The beehive tombs at Mycenae had been looted long before Heinrich Schliemann arrived to search for Homeric Greece, but the contents of the **shaft graves** he excavated in the 1870s reflect mainland culture at an even earlier date (see "Pioneers of Aegean Archeology," page 143). Shaft graves were vertical pits 20 to 25 feet deep, and those entombing rulers and their families were enclosed in a circle of standing stone slabs. Magnificent metal treasures in the form of swords, daggers, scepters,

4-27. Funerary mask, from the royal tombs at Mycenae, Greece. c. 1550–1500 BCE. Gold, height approx. 12" (35 cm). National Archeological Museum, Athens

When Heinrich Schliemann excavated the royal shaft graves just inside the Lion(ess) Gate at Mycenae in 1876, he believed that he had discovered the bodies of the legendary family of Atreus, including his son Agamemnon. Schliemann dubbed this gold mask from one of the graves the "Mask of Agamemnon"—a name it still carries in many books. Schliemann's discoveries at Mycenae and Troy have led scholars to conclude that the Homeric tales may have been rooted in historical fact, but Schliemann himself was unaware that the graves at Mycenae predate the possible siege of Troy by about three centuries, so that the funeral mask could not have been Agamemnon's, even if he was an actual person.

jewelry, and drinking cups were often buried with members of the elite. As in the tombs of Egyptian royalty, some of the men were found wearing masks of gold or a silver-gold alloy called electrum, as if to preserve their heroic features forever. The realistic features embossed on the gold funerary mask often mistakenly called the "Mask of Agamemnon" (fig. 4-27), dated about 1550–1500 BCE, seem uncannily like those of a death mask cast from the actual face of the deceased—broad cheekbones, strong chin, thin, pointed nose, full beard and moustache, closed, bulging eyes, and narrow eyebrows.

Also found in one of the shaft graves at Mycenae were three bronze dagger blades decorated with inlaid scenes (fig. 4-28). The Mycenaean artist cut shapes out of different-colored metals—copper, silver, and gold—then set them into the bronze blades. Silver and gold inlays had to be first backed with copper. The fine details

4-28. Dagger blades,
from shaft graves
at Mycenae,
Greece. c. 1550–
1500 BCE. Bronze
inlaid with
gold, silver, and
copper, lengths
6³⁄₈" (16.3 cm),
8⁷⁄₁₆"(21.4 cm), and
9³⁄₈" (23.8 cm).
National Archeo-
logical Museum,
Athens

were added in **niello** (see "Aegean Metalwork," page 137). In the *Iliad*, Homer's epic poem about the Trojan War written before 700 BCE, Agamemnon's armor and Achilles's shield are described as having similar decorations. The decorations of the two larger blades—depicting men with shields battling three lions, and three lions racing across a rocky landscape—are typically Aegean in the animated and naturalistic treatment of the figures. Interestingly, the scene on the shortest blade, showing a leopard attacking ducks in a papyrus swamp, clearly reflects Egyptian influence.

Ceramics

In the final phase of the Helladic period, Mycenaean potters created highly refined ceramics in uniform sizes and shapes. Although their vessels were superior in terms of technique, the decorations applied to them were generally less innovative, more conventional than those of earlier wares. A narrative scene ornaments the Mycenaean *Warrior Vase*, dating from about 1300–1100 BCE (fig. 4-29). On the side shown here, a woman at the far left bids farewell to a group of helmeted men with beribboned lances and large shields marching off to the right. There is none of the vibrant energy of the *Harvester Vase* or the *Vapheio Cup* in this scene. The only indication of the woman's emotions is the symbolic gesture of an arm raised to her head, and the figures of the men are seemingly interchangeable parts in a rigidly disciplined war machine.

4-29. *Warrior Vase*, from Mycenae, Greece. c. 1300–1100 BCE. Ceramic, height 16" (41 cm). National Archeological Museum, Athens

Mycenaean civilization did not have a long history. By 1200 BCE, aggressive invaders were crossing into mainland Greece, and within a century they had taken control of the major cities and citadels. The period between about 1100 and 900 BCE was a kind of "dark age" in the Aegean, marked by political, economic, and artistic instability and upheaval. But a new culture was forming, one that looked back to the exploits of the Helladic warrior-princes as the glories of a heroic age and at the same time formed the basis of a new Greek civilization.

BCE 1000   800   600

Centaur
late 10th century

Dipylon
vase
c. 750

Corinthian
pitcher
c. 600

Kouros
c. 600

▲ PROTO-GEOMETRIC 1000–900 ▲ GEOMETRIC 900–700   ▲ ORIENTALIZING 700–600   ▲ ARCHAIC 600–480

CHAPTER 5

Art of Ancient Greece

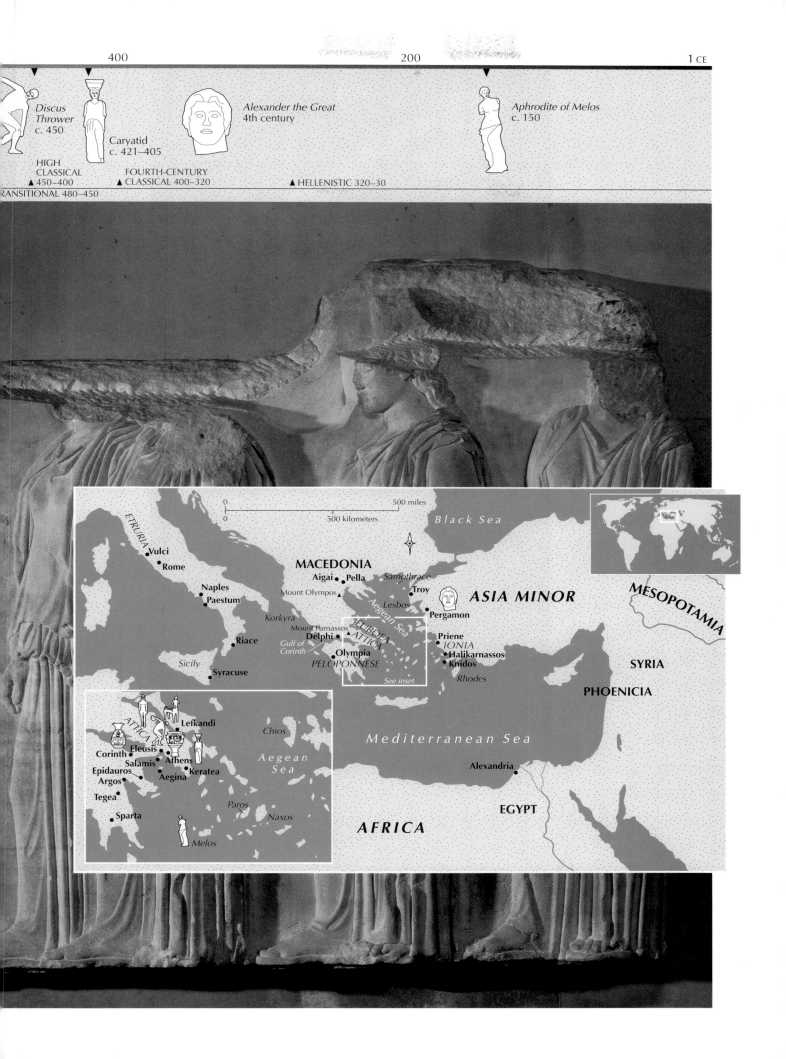

Discus
Thrower
c. 450

Caryatid
c. 421–405

Alexander the Great
4th century

Aphrodite of Melos
c. 150

HIGH
CLASSICAL
▲ 450–400

FOURTH-CENTURY
▲ CLASSICAL 400–320

▲ HELLENISTIC 320–30

RANSITIONAL 480–450

ETRURIA

Vulci

Rome

Naples

Paestum

Korkyra

Riace

Sicily

Syracuse

MACEDONIA

Aigai • Pella

Mount Olympos ▲

Samothrace

Troy

Lesbos

Pergamon

Aegean Sea

Mount Parnassos ▲

Delphi ● ATTICA

EUBOEA

Gulf of
Corinth

Olympia

PELOPONNESE

See inset

ASIA MINOR

Priene ●

IONIA

● Halikarnassos

Knidos

Rhodes

MESOPOTAMIA

SYRIA

PHOENICIA

Black Sea

Mediterranean Sea

Alexandria

0   500 miles
0   500 kilometers

ATTICA

Lefkandi

Corinth

Eleusis

Salamis

Athens

Keratea

Epidauros

Aegina

Argos

Tegea

Sparta

Chios

Aegean
Sea

Paros

Naxos

Melos

EGYPT

AFRICA

5-1.   Myron. *Discus Thrower* (*Diskobolos*), Roman copy after the original bronze
of c. 450 BCE. Marble, height 5'1" (1.54 m). Museo Nazionale Romano,
Rome

A sense of awe fills the stadium when the athletes recognized as the fastest runners in the world enter for the second day of competition. With the opening ceremonies behind them, each runner has only one goal: to win—to earn recognition as the best, to receive the award, the praise, and the financial rewards that accompany victory. The runners have come from near and far, as will the wrestlers and riders, the discus throwers and long jumpers, the boxers and javelin hurlers who will compete within sight of the Olympic flame. The year is 776 BCE.

At first, the scene seems comfortably familiar. Every four years, then as now, the best athletes came together. Attention shifted from political confrontation to physical competition, to individual human beings who seemed able to surpass even their own abilities in the glory of an ideal. And indeed these are common elements. Yet at those first Olympian Games, the athletes gathered on sacred ground, the Sanctuary of Hera and Zeus, near Olympia, Greece, to pay tribute to the supreme god and his consort. The first day's ceremonies were sacrifices, and the awards given at the Temple of Hera were crowns of wild olives. The winners' deeds were celebrated by poets long after their victories, and the greatest of the athletes might well live the rest of their lives at public expense. They were idealized for centuries in extraordinary Greek sculpture, such as the *Discus Thrower* created in bronze by Myron in about 450 BCE (fig. 5-1). The Olympian Games were so significant that many Greeks date the beginning of their history as a nation to those first games. (The Roman emperor Theodosius banned the games in 394 CE, and they were not resumed until 1896.) In recognition of the original games, the modern Olympics begin with the lighting of a flame from a torch ignited by the sun at Olympia, Greece, and carried by relay to that year's site. For many people, this image is an appropriate symbol for the way the light of inspiration was carried from ancient Greece throughout the Western world.

THE EMERGENCE OF GREEK CIVILIZATION

More than 2,000 years have passed since the artists and architects of ancient Greece worked, yet their achievements continue to have a profound influence. The early Greeks' concepts of human beauty and of strength and dignity in architectural design no longer set the standards for Western art, but their genius and high aspirations are still awe-inspiring. Their legacy is especially remarkable given their relatively small numbers, the almost constant warfare that beset them, and the often harsh economic conditions of the time.

Greek artists sought a level of perfection that led them continually to improve upon their past accomplishments through changes in style and approach. For this reason, the history of Greek art contrasts dramatically with that of Egyptian art, where the desire for permanence and continuity induced artists to maintain many artistic conventions for nearly 3,000 years. In the relatively short span from around 900 BCE to about 100 BCE, Greek artists explored a succession of new ideas to produce a body of work in every medium—from pottery and painting to sculpture and architecture—that exhibits clear stylistic and technical progression. The periods into which ancient Greek art is traditionally divided reflect the definable stages in this stylistic progression rather than political developments. Nevertheless, knowledge of the politics, religion, and culture of ancient Greece is vital to understanding its art.

Following the collapse of Mycenaean dominance about 1100 BCE, the Aegean region experienced a period of disorganization during which most prior cultural developments, including writing, were destroyed or forgotten. The mainland, the Aegean islands, and the coastal areas of Asia Minor were left open to new waves of migrating peoples. Although nothing is known of their origins or the dates of their arrivals, some of these immigrants may have been responsible for bringing Iron Age technology to these regions.

No archeological evidence exists to support it, but later Greek legendary history claimed that people called Dorians had invaded the mainland from the north and displaced the earlier settlers, called Aeolians and Ionians, forcing their migration to the Aegean islands and western Asia Minor. The Spartans of Peloponnesos claimed to have descended from the god-hero Herakles through the Dorians, who established themselves in west central Greece. The Athenians claimed descent from the Ionians who had supposedly occupied the Attic peninsula (Athens and environs) in early times, and they maintained close political ties with the Ionian culture of western Asia Minor.

By about 900 BCE, the inhabitants of the Aegean region, living in self-sufficient, close-knit communities and all speaking some form of the same language, were again beginning to flourish. It was these people, a fusion of the new migrants and earlier inhabitants, who came to be called Greeks. The early Greeks developed a distinctive form of city-state in the ninth and eighth centuries BCE called the polis (plural poleis). These centers provided a

PARALLELS

Years	Period	Greece	World
c. 900–700 BCE	Geometric	Dipylon vase; Homer's *Iliad* and *Odyssey*; first Olympian Games; alphabet adopted	**c. 900–700 BCE** Upanishads (India); Olmec pyramids (Mesoamerica); Etruscans settle central Italy; legendary founding of Rome (Italy); fall of Zhou dynasty (China); first goldwork in South America
c. 700–600 BCE	Orientalizing	Black-figure and white-ground vase painting	**c. 700–600 BCE** Demotic script (Egypt); Assyrian empire falls; growth of permanent villages in North America
c. 600–480 BCE	Archaic	Doric and Ionic orders; Temple of Hera (Argos); Temple of Artemis (Korkyra); red-figure vase painting; *Calf Bearer*; *François Vase*; Temple of Hera I (Paestum, Italy); Sanctuary of Apollo, Siphnian Treasury (Delphi); Temple of Aphaia (Aegina); *Aesop's Fables*; *Kroisos*; Sappho	**c. 600–400 BCE** Hanging Gardens (Babylon); birth of Laozi, founder of Daoism, (China); Cyrus the Great (Persia) defeats Babylon; birth of Siddartha Gautama, founder of Buddhism (Nepal); Confucius (China); first fixed-value coins (Lydia); iron introduced in China; last Old Testament book written
c. 480–450 BCE	Transitional (Early Classical)	*Kritios Boy*; *Charioteer*; *Riace Warriors*; Myron's *Discus Thrower*; the Pan Painter's *Artemis Slaying Actaeon*; First Peloponnesian War; Sophocles; Aeschylus	
c. 450–400 BCE	High Classical	*The Canon* of Polykleitos; Polykleitos's *Spear Bearer*; *Little Girl with Birds*; Corinthian order; Perikles' rule; Kallikrates and Iktinos's Parthenon (Athens); Mnesikles' Propylaia and Erechtheion (Athens); Kallikrates' Temple of Athena Nike (Athens); Socrates; Herodotus; Euripides; Second Peloponnesian War	
c. 400–320 BCE	Fourth-Century (Late Classical)	Sanctuary of Athena Pronaia (Delphi); Mausoleum (Halikarnassos); Praxiteles' *Aphrodite of Knidos* and *Hermes and the Infant Dionysos*; Lysippos's *The Scraper*; rule of Alexander the Great; *Abduction of Persephone*; Plato; Aristotle	**c. 400–30 BCE** London founded (England); mound-building cultures (North America); lighthouse of Alexandria (Egypt); Rome subjugates Italy; Great Wall (China); Han dynasty (China); Rosetta Stone (Egypt); Great Stupa at Sanchi (India); Julius Caesar invades Gaul and Britain; sundial invented (China)
c. 320–30 BCE	Hellenistic	Theater at Epidauros; Cossutius's Temple of Olympian Zeus (Athens); Altar of Zeus (Pergamon); Colossos of Rhodes; Hagesandros, Polydoros, and Athanodoros's *Laocoön*; *Nike of Samothrace*; *Aphrodite of Melos*	

political identity for their residents, and they stimulated and nourished the emerging Greek civilization. Each was independent, deciding its own form of government, securing its own economic support, and managing its own domestic and foreign affairs.

The Greek mainland and the Aegean islands had little farmland, forcing the new communities, like their Bronze Age predecessors, to depend on trade with other regions to meet the needs of their growing populations. During the eighth century BCE, the Greeks, stimulated through such contacts, developed a new writing system, which was probably adopted from the Phoenicians, a Near Eastern people who dominated Mediterranean trade after the collapse of Mycenaean civilization. Many city-states developed sizable merchant fleets that ranged from the Black Sea to Africa, exchanging Aegean products—olive oil, pottery, and metal wares—for grain, textiles, precious metals, wood for shipbuilding, and other goods. To facilitate trade, the city-states established outlying colonies, some of which became wealthy, influential commercial centers in their own right while maintaining close cultural and economic ties to their cities of origin. Colonists from Corinth on mainland Greece, for example, founded the famed city of Syracuse on the eastern coast of Sicily.

The Greek city-states were at first ruled by aristocratic councils. Then, beginning about 700 BCE and extending into the sixth century BCE, self-appointed leaders called "tyrants" imposed a dictatorial form of rule, often with popular support, in many city-states. These tyrants were not always tyrannical in the modern sense, and many cities prospered and expanded under their rule. At their best, they fostered urban development at home and sought economic rather than military influence abroad. Among the emerging city-states, Corinth, located on major land and sea trade routes, was for a time the most powerful. By the sixth century BCE, Athens, located in Attica on the east coast of the mainland, began to assume both commercial and cultural preeminence.

Athens and the Concept of Democratic Rule

The Greeks contributed more to posterity than their art. Their customs, institutions, and ideas have also had an enduring influence in many parts of the world. Countries that highly esteem athletic prowess reflect an ancient Greek ideal. Systems of higher education in the United States and Europe also owe much to ancient Greek models. Perhaps most significant, representative governments throughout the world today owe a debt to ancient Greek experiments in democracy.

The idea that all citizens should share in the rights and responsibilities of government began to emerge in Athens in the sixth century BCE, although only a few privileged males were citizens. In 594 BCE the leaders of Athens, facing an economic crisis and popular discontent, appointed the poet-statesman Solon to institute reforms and revise the city's constitution, extending citizenship to males of many classes. In 560 BCE an aristo-

crat named Peisistratos seized control of Athens and ruled as tyrant until 527 BCE. A shrewd planner and visionary, Peisistratos generated considerable wealth for the city and enhanced it culturally by holding great festivals, building many temples and fountains, and having the official texts of Homer's works recorded. After Peisistratos's second son and successor was ousted in 510 BCE, the development of democratic institutions resumed. Following a period of factional sparring, a leader named Kleisthenes, with the support of the people, gained control of the city. Kleisthenes, often called the "father of democracy," instituted reforms that broadened the representative base of Athenian government, effectively reducing the dominance of the old aristocratic families. He made the deme, a territorial unit equivalent to a precinct, into the basic political unit that sent 50 representatives to a new 500-member council, called the boule. This council carried out routine administrative functions and prepared legislation for consideration by the assembly of all citizens. Although this form of government was democratic in principle, it was open only to adult male citizens. Women took no official part in government, nor did slaves or men born outside Athens.

Religious Beliefs and Sacred Places

The creation of the world, according to ancient Greek legend, involved a battle between the earth gods, called Titans or Giants, and the sky gods. The victors were the sky gods, whose home was believed to be atop Mount Olympos in the northeast corner of the Greek mainland. The Greeks saw their gods as immortal and endowed with supernatural powers, but, more than peoples of the ancient Near East and the Egyptians had, they visualized them in human form and attributed to them human weaknesses and emotions. Among the most important Olympian deities were the ruling gods Zeus and Hera; Apollo, god of the sun; Poseidon, god of the sea; Ares, god of war; Aphrodite, goddess of love; Artemis, goddess of hunting and the moon; and Athena, a powerful goddess who governed several important aspects of human life (see "Greek and Roman Deities and Heroes," page 156).

In addition to Mount Olympos, many sites throughout Greece, called **sanctuaries**, were sacred to one or more of the gods. The Greeks believed that the gods themselves selected these sites to show favor toward their human worshipers. Local people then enclosed the sanctuaries with walls and designated them as sacred ground. The earliest sanctuaries had one or more outdoor altars or shrines and a sacred natural element such as a tree, a rock, or a spring. As additional buildings were added over time, a sanctuary might become a palatial home for the gods, called a **temenos**, with one or more temples, several **treasuries** for storing valuable offerings, various monuments and statues, housing for priests and visitors, an outdoor dance floor or permanent theater for ritual performances and literary competitions, and a **stadium** for athletic events. The Sanctuary of Hera and Zeus near Olympia, in the western Peloponnese, housed an extensive athletic facility with training rooms and arenas

GREEK AND ROMAN DEITIES AND HEROES

The ancient Greeks had many deities, and myths about them varied over time. Many deities had several forms, or manifestations. Athena, for example, was revered as a goddess of wisdom, a warrior goddess, a goddess of victory, and a goddess of purity and maidenhood, among others. The Romans later adopted the Greek deities but sometimes attributed to them slightly different characteristics. What follows is a simplified list of the major Greek deities and heroes, with their Roman names in parentheses when they exist. The list includes some of the most important characteristics of each deity or hero, which often identify them in art.

According to the most widespread legend, twelve major sky gods and goddesses established themselves in palatial splendor on Mount Olympos in northeastern Greece after defeating the earth deities, called Giants or Titans, for control of the earth and sky. The first five deities are the children of Earth and Sky.

ZEUS (Jupiter), supreme deity. Mature, bearded man; holds scepter or lightning bolt; eagle and oak tree are sacred to him.

HERA (Juno), goddess of marriage. Sister/wife of Zeus. Mature; cow and peacock are sacred to her.

HESTIA (Vesta), goddess of the hearth. Sister of Zeus. Her sacred flame burned in communal hearths.

POSEIDON (Neptune), god of the sea. Holds a three-pronged spear; horse is sacred to him.

HADES (Pluto), god of the underworld, the dead, and wealth. His helmet makes the wearer invisible.

The remaining seven sky gods, the offspring of the first five, are:

ARES (Mars), god of war. Son of Zeus and Hera. Wears armor; vulture and dog are sacred to him.

HEPHAISTOS (Vulcan), god of the forge, fire, and metal handicrafts. Son of Hera (in some myths, also of Zeus); husband of Aphrodite. Lame, sometimes ugly; wears blacksmith's apron, carries hammer.

APOLLO (Phoebus), god of the sun, light, truth, music, archery, and healing. Sometimes identified with Helios (the Sun), who rides a chariot across the daytime sky. Son of Zeus and Leto (a descendant of Earth); brother of Artemis. Carries bow and arrows or sometimes lyre; dolphin and laurel are sacred to him.

ARTEMIS (Diana), goddess of the hunt, wild animals, and the moon. Sometimes identified with Selene (the Moon), who rides a chariot or oxcart across the night sky. Daughter of Zeus and Leto; sister of Apollo. Carries bow and arrows, is accompanied by hunting dogs; deer and cypress are sacred to her.

ATHENA (Minerva), goddess of wisdom, war, victory, the city, and civilization. Daughter of Zeus, sprang fully grown from his head. Wears helmet and carries shield and spear; owl and olive trees are sacred to her.

APHRODITE (Venus), goddess of love. Daughter of Zeus and Dione; alternatively, daughter of Poseidon, born of his sperm mixed with sea foam; wife of Hephaistos. Myrtle, dove, sparrow, and swan are sacred to her.

HERMES (Mercury), messenger of the gods, god of fertility and luck, guide of the dead to the underworld, and god of thieves, commerce, and the marketplace. Son of Zeus and Maia, the daughter of Atlas, a Giant who supports the sky on his shoulders. Wears winged sandals and hat; carries caduceus, a wand with two snakes entwined around it.

Other important deities include:

DEMETER (Ceres), goddess of grain and agriculture.

PERSEPHONE (Proserpina), goddess of fertility and queen of the underworld. Wife of Hades; daughter of Demeter.

DIONYSOS (Bacchus), god of wine, the grape harvest, and inspiration. Shown surrounded by grape vines and grape clusters; carries a wine cup. His female followers are called **maenads** (Bacchantes).

EROS (Cupid), god of love. In some myths, the son of Aphrodite.

Shown as an infant or young boy, sometimes winged; carries bow and arrows.

EOS (Aurora), goddess of dawn.

GE, goddess of the earth; mother of the Titans.

ASKLEPIOS (Aesculapius), god of healing.

AMPHITRITE, goddess of the sea. Wife of Poseidon.

PAN, protector of shepherds, god of the wilderness and of music. Half man, half goat, he carries panpipes.

NIKE, goddess of victory. Often shown winged and flying.

Some specifically Roman gods not worshiped by the Greeks include:

FORTUNA, goddess of fate (fortune).

PRIAPUS, god of fertility.

SATURN, god of harvests.

JANUS, god of beginnings and endings. Has two faces, enabling him to look forward and backward.

POMONA, goddess of gardens and orchards.

TERMINUS, god of boundaries.

Important human heroes include:

HERAKLES (Hercules). A man of great and diverse strengths; granted immortality for his achievements, including the Twelve Labors.

PERSEUS. Killed Medusa, the snake-haired monster.

THESEUS. Killed the Minotaur, a bull-monster that killed and ate young men and maidens in a labyrinth in the palace of King Minos of Crete (see "The Legend of the Minotaur," page 132).

Heroes of the Trojan War include:

ODYSSEUS (Ulysses), Achilles, Patroclus, and Ajax among the Greeks; Paris, Hector, Priam, Sarpedon, and Aeneas (progenitor of the Romans) among the Trojans.

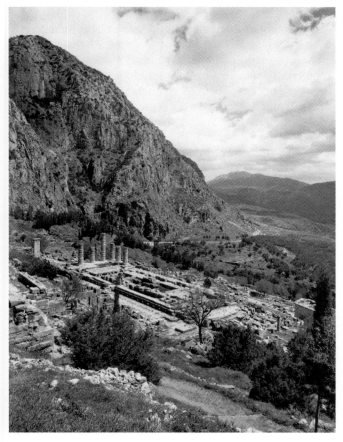

5-2. Sanctuary of Apollo, Delphi. 4th century BCE

A feature of this sacred home of the Greek god Apollo, built on the site of a sixth-century temple destroyed in an earthquake, was a natural site in the area believed to be an oracle, a place where the god communicated with humans. At this oracle, Apollo communicated through a woman medium called the Pythia. To prepare herself to receive his messages, she chewed sacred laurel leaves and drank water from the sacred Kassotis Spring, both of which are thought to have induced hallucinations. She then sat over the crevice on a three-legged stool, or tripod. When she had received the god's message, which might be a response to a petitioner's question, she conveyed it in often cryptic and ambiguous language. The Greeks attributed many twists of fate to misinterpretations of the Pythia's statements. King Croesus of Lydia in Asia Minor, for example, came to Delphi in the mid-sixth century BCE to consult Apollo about his military plans. The message he received was that he would cross a river and destroy a great kingdom. He took this to mean the Halys River, beyond which lay the Persian Empire, and he ordered his generals to launch an assault against the Persians. Ironically, the kingdom he destroyed was his own, when his troops crossed the Halys and were wiped out by the Persians.

for track and field events. It was here, beginning in 776 BCE, that the ancient prototypes of today's Olympic Games were held.

The Sanctuary of Apollo at Delphi is located in a rugged landscape near the Gulf of Corinth on a high plateau in the shadow of Mount Parnassos (fig. 5-2). Here, according to Greek myth, the sky was attached to

5-3. Reconstruction drawing of the Sanctuary of Apollo, Delphi. c. 400 BCE

the omphalos (navel) of the earth by an umbilical cord. Here too, it was said, Apollo fought and killed the Python, the serpent son of the earth goddess Ge, who stood guard over his mother's shrine in the gorge below the site. This myth has been interpreted as a metaphorical account of the conquest of the Early Bronze Age people of Greece, whose religion centered on female earth deities, by a wave of new settlers who believed in a supreme male sky god.

From very early times, the sanctuary at Delphi was renowned as an **oracle**, a place where a god was believed to communicate to humans by means of cryptic messages delivered to human intermediaries, or mediums. The Greeks and their leaders routinely sought advice at such places, relying on temple priests for help in interpreting the messages. Even foreign rulers sought help at Delphi, where the god Apollo spoke through a woman medium called the Pythia. Delphi was also the site of the Pythian Games, a festival that, like the Olympian Games, attracted participants from all over Greece. The principal events were not the athletic contests that took place, but rather the dance and poetry competitions in honor of Apollo. The sanctuary grounds were filled with hundreds of statues dedicated to the victors of the competitions, a kind of Pythian Games hall of fame (see fig. 5-37).

A reconstruction drawing of the Sanctuary of Apollo as it looked about 400 BCE (fig. 5-3) shows that the main temple, performance and athletic areas, and other buildings and monuments cleverly made full use of limited space while providing easy access. After visitors climbed the steep path up the lower slopes of Parnassos, they entered the sanctuary by a ceremonial gate in the southeast corner. From there they zigzagged up the Sacred Way, so named because it was the route of religious processions during festivals. Moving past the numerous treasuries and memorials built by Greece's various city-states (see fig. 5-16), they soon arrived at the long **colonnade** of the Temple of Apollo. This structure, built about 530 BCE on the ruins of an earlier temple, remained standing until it was destroyed by an earthquake in 373 BCE. Below the temple was a **stoa**, a columned pavilion open on three sides, built by the people of Athens. There visitors rested, talked, or watched ceremonial dancing on an outdoor pavement called a *halos.* At the back of the sanctuary on a higher level of the rocky plateau was a stadium area for athletic games.

Greek sanctuaries are quite different from the religious complexes of the ancient Egyptians (see, for example, the funerary complex of Hatshepsut, figs. 3-33, 3-34). Egyptian builders dramatized the power of gods or god-rulers by placing their temples at the ends of long, straight, processional ways. The Greeks, in contrast, treated each building and monument within a temenos as an independent element in an arrangement of structures to be integrated with the natural features of the site. It is tempting to draw a parallel between this manner of organizing space and the way Greeks organized themselves politically: every structure, like every Greek citizen, was a unique entity meant to be encountered separately within its own environment while being closely allied with other entities in a larger scheme of common purpose.

Historical Divisions of Greek Art

The names by which the major periods of Greek art are known have remained standard despite changing interpretations that have led some to question their appropriateness. The primary source of information about Greek art before the seventh century BCE is pottery, and the Geometric period owes its name to the geometric, or rectilinear, forms with which artists of the time decorated ceramic vessels. The Orientalizing period is named for the apparent influence of Egyptian and Near Eastern art on Greek pottery of that time, spread through trading contacts and also through the travels and migrations of artists themselves. The name of the third period, Archaic, meaning "old" or "old-fashioned," stresses a presumed contrast between the art of that time and the art of the following Classical period, which was thought to be the most admirable and highly developed—a view that no longer prevails among contemporary art historians.

The Classical period has been subdivided into three phases: the Transitional or Early Classical, from about 480 to 450 BCE; the High Classical, from about 450 to the end of the fifth century BCE; and the Late Classical, from about 400 to about 320 BCE. "Transitional" is particularly appropriate for the Early Classical period in sculpture because it bridges the change from the relatively stiff Archaic human figures to the more realistically active Classical figures, but it was also a time of change for architecture and painting. Art historians still use these subdivisions as convenient chronological markers, but they no longer see them as chapters in a story detailing the "rise and decline" of the Classical style. For this reason, the neutral term Fourth Century has largely replaced the term Late Classical, with its implication of decline.

The name of the final period of Greek art, Hellenistic, means "Greek-like." This period dates from the last decades of the fourth century, when Philip II of Macedon and his son Alexander conquered Greece and the Persian Empire. Hellenistic art was produced throughout this vast region as its non-Greek inhabitants gradually became imbued with Greek culture under Alexander and his successors. The history and art of ancient Greece end with the fall of Egypt, the last bastion of Hellenistic rule, to the Romans in 31–30 BCE.

THE GEOMETRIC PERIOD

The first appearance of a specifically Greek style of vase painting, as opposed to Minoan or Mycenaean, dates to about 1050 BCE. This style—known as Proto-geometric because it preceded and anticipated the Geometric style—was characterized by linear motifs, such as spirals, diamonds, and

5-4. *Centaur,* from Lefkandi, Euboea. Late 10th century BCE. Terra-cotta, height 14⅛" (36 cm). Archeological Museum, Eretria

5-5. Vase, from the Dipylon Cemetery, Athens. c. 750 BCE. Terra-cotta, height 42⅝"
(108 cm). The Metropolitan Museum of Art, New York
Rogers Fund, 1914 (14.130.14)

crosshatching, rather than the stylized plants, birds, and sea creatures characteristic of Minoan vase painting. The Geometric style proper, an extremely complex form of decoration, became widespread after about 900 BCE in all types of art and endured until about 700 BCE.

Ceramic Decoration

A striking ceramic figure of a half-horse, half-human creature called a centaur dates to the end of the tenth century BCE (fig. 5-4). This figure exemplifies two aspects of the Protogeometric style: the use of geometric forms in painted decoration, and the reduction of human and animal body parts in sculptural works to simple geometric solids such as cubes, pyramids, cylinders, and spheres. It is unusual, however, because of its size (more than a foot tall) and because its hollow body was formed like a vase on a potter's wheel. The artist added solid legs, arms, and a tail (now missing) to this body, and when these were dry, painted on the bold, abstract designs with a clay **slip**. The slip fired to dark brown, standing out against the lighter color of the unslipped portions of the figure. Centaurs, prominent in Greek mythology, had both a good and a bad side and may have symbolized the similar dual nature of humans. This centaur, discovered in a cemetery, had been deliberately broken into two pieces that were buried in adjacent graves. Clearly, the object had special significance for the people buried in the graves, their mourners, or both.

5-6. Detail of the Dipylon Cemetery vase (fig. 5-5)

Some vases discovered in the ancient cemetery of Athens just outside the Dipylon Gate, once the main western entrance into the city, exemplify the complex decoration typical of the Geometric style proper. Here human beings are depicted as part of a narrative, in a sharp departure from vase painting of earlier periods. The large funerary vase illustrated here, a grave marker meant to hold offerings, dated to about 750 BCE, provides a detailed record of the funerary rituals for an obviously important person (figs. 5-5, 5-6). The body of the deceased is placed on its side on a high platform at the center of the top **register** of the vase. Male and female figures stand on each side of the body, their arms raised and both hands placed on top of their heads in a gesture interpreted as expressing anguish—it suggests that the mourners are literally tearing their hair with grief. In the bottom register, horse-drawn chariots and foot soldiers, who look like walking shields with tiny antlike heads and muscular legs, form a well-ordered procession.

The **abstract** forms used to represent human figures on this vase—triangles for torsos, more triangles for the heads in profile, round dots for eyes, long, thin rectangles for arms, tiny waists, and long legs with bulging thigh and calf muscles—are typical of the Geometric style. Figures are shown in either full-frontal or full-profile views that emphasize flat patterns and outline shapes. No attempt has been made to create the illusion of three-dimensional forms occupying real space. The artist has nevertheless a deep sense of human loss by exploiting the rigidity, solemnity, and strong rhythmic accents of the carefully arranged elements.

Egyptian funerary art reflected the belief that the dead, in the afterworld, could continue to engage in activities they enjoyed while alive. Greek funerary art, in contrast, focused on the emotional reactions of the survivors, not the fate of the dead. The scene of human mourning and veneration on this vase contains no supernatural beings, nor any identifiable reference to an afterlife that might have provided solace for the bereaved. According to the Greeks, the deceased entered a place of mystery and obscurity that humans could not define precisely.

Metal Sculpture

Greek artists of the Geometric period produced many figurines of wood, ivory, clay, and especially cast bronze. These small statues of humans and animals are similar to those painted on the vases. A tiny bronze of this type, *Man and Centaur*, dates to about 750 BCE and is less than 4½ inches tall (fig. 5-7). The sculptor reduced the body parts of the figures to simple geometric shapes, arranging them in a composition of solid forms and open, or **negative, spaces** that makes the piece pleasing from every view. Because the two figures confront each other in a seemingly peaceful way, they have been interpreted to be Achilles and Chiron, his teacher, but they could also be Herakles and the vengeful Nessos, who plotted his death, or an entirely different pair of mythical figures. Most such works have been found in sanctuaries, suggesting that they may have been votive offerings to the gods or perhaps trophies given to the winners of the various competitions regularly held at those sites.

The First Greek Temples

Few ancient Greek temples remain standing today. Their history has been pieced together largely from the debris of fallen columns, broken lintels, and fragments of sculptural decoration recovered from archeological excavations and somewhat from surviving ceramic models. The earliest remains of identifiably Greek temples date from

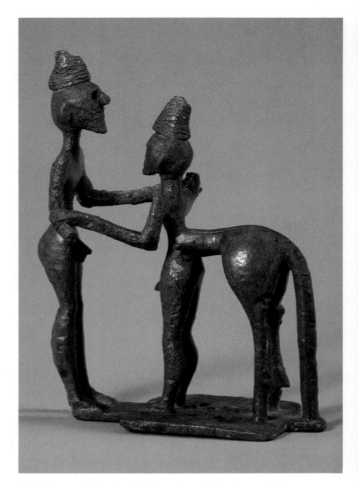

5-7. *Man and Centaur*, perhaps from Olympia. c. 750 BCE. Bronze, height 4⁵/₁₆" (11.1 cm). The Metropolitan Museum of Art, New York
Gift of J. Pierpont Morgan, 1917 (17.190.2072)

the Geometric period. They consist of stone foundations that define buildings laid out in a simple rectangle or in a rectangular form with one or both ends rounded, and they were built presumably to shelter a statue of the god to whom the temple was dedicated. Nothing is left of their walls and roofs, which were constructed of mud brick and wood.

Small ceramic models, such as one from the eighth century BCE found in the Sanctuary of Hera near Argos, give some idea how Geometric period temples might have looked (fig. 5-8). The rectangular structure has a door at one end sheltered by a projecting **porch** supported on two sturdy columns. The steeply pitched roof forms a triangular area, or **gable**, in the **facade**, or front wall, that is pierced by an opening directly above the door. The abstract designs painted on the roof and side walls are similar to those used on other Geometric period ceramics; whether they reflect the way temples were actually decorated is not known.

Temple interiors followed an enduring basic plan adapted from the Mycenaean palace **megaron** (compare fig. 4-23 with plan (a) in "Elements of Architecture," page 164). The large audience hall of the megaron became the

5-8. Model of a temple, found in the Sanctuary of Hera, Argos. Mid-8th century BCE. Terra-cotta, length 14½" (36.8 cm). National Archeological Museum, Athens

main room of the temple, called the **cella** or **naos**. In the center of this room, where the hearth would have been in the megaron, stood a statue of the god to whom the temple was dedicated. The small reception room that preceded the audience hall in the megaron became the temple's vestibule, called the **pronaos**.

THE ORIENTALIZING PERIOD

By the seventh century BCE, vase painters in major pottery centers in Greece had moved away from the dense decoration of the Geometric style to create more open compositions built around large motifs that included real and imaginary animals, abstract plant forms, and human figures. The source of these motifs can be traced to the arts of the Near East, Asia Minor, and Egypt. Greek painters did not simply copy the work of Eastern artists, however. Instead, they drew on work in a variety of mediums—including sculpture, metalwork, and textiles—to invent an entirely new approach to vase painting.

Among the first artists to make Orientalizing changes in pottery decoration were those of Corinth, a port city where luxury wares from eastern cultures were imported. A Corinthian **olpe**, or wide-mouthed pitcher, dating to about 600 BCE shows the Orientalizing style in the large mythical creatures silhouetted against a plain background dotted with stylized flower forms called **rosettes** (fig. 5-9). This vase also displays a new Corinthian technique for using background and foreground colors extending from black through browns and reds to pure white. The type shown here, called **black-figure**, features dark shapes silhouetted against a background of

5-9. Pitcher (olpe), from Corinth. c. 600 BCE. Ceramic with black-figure decoration, height 11½" (30 cm). The British Museum, London

very pale buff, the natural color of the Corinthian clay. Sometimes the background of a pot was painted as well, using a very fine, pure clay slip that turned almost white in the firing (see "Greek Painted Vases," page 162). The artist incised fine details inside the silhouetted shapes with a sharp tool and added touches of white and reddish purple **gloss**, or clay slip mixed with metallic color pigments, to enhance the design.

The new Corinthian techniques were soon picked up by rival centers of pottery production. An **oinochoe**, or wine pitcher, from the island of Rhodes, for example, which dates to about 650–625 BCE, was decorated with the black-figure and white-slip techniques (fig. 5-10). Against a plain background scattered with strong, simple geometric motifs, the artist arranged a two-register parade of ibexes, geese, songbirds, and a griffin, a mythical animal with a lion's body and an eagle's head and wings. The ibex was such a popular design element with the Rhodes painters that some art historians refer to their vase decoration as the "Wild Goat Style." The abstract

The three main types of Greek painted vase decoration are called **black-figure**, **red-figure**, and **white-ground**. The artists who produced them had to be both skilled painters and highly trained and experienced ceramic technicians. They did not simply paint designs on a finished clay vessel. To create their works they had to master a complex procedure involving the use of specially prepared **slips** (mixtures of clay and water), the application of the slips to different areas in varying thicknesses, and the careful manipulation of the firing process in a kiln, or closed oven, to control the amount of oxygen reaching the vessel. If all went as planned (and sometimes it didn't), the designs painted in slip, which could barely be seen on the clay pot before firing, emerged afterward in the desired range of colors.

The firing process for both black-figure and red-figure painting involved three stages. In the first, a large amount of oxygen was allowed into the kiln, which "fixed" the whole vase in one overall color that depended on the composition of the clay used. In the second, or "reduction," stage, the oxygen in the **kiln** was reduced to a minimum, turning the whole vessel black, and the temperature raised to the point at which the slip partially vitrified (became glasslike). In the third phase, oxygen was allowed back into the kiln, turning the unslipped areas red. The partially vitrified slipped areas, sealed against the oxygen, remained black.

In black-figure painting, artists painted designs—figures, objects, or abstract motifs—in silhouette on the clay vessel. Then, using a sharp tool called a **stylus**, they cut through the slip to the body of the vessel to incise linear details within the silhouettes. In red-figure painting, the approach was reversed, and the background around the designs was painted with the slip. The linear details inside the shapes were also painted with the same slip, instead of being incised. In both techniques, artists often enhanced their work with touches of white and reddish purple **gloss**, metallic pigments mixed with slip.

White-ground vases became very popular in the High Classical period, especially for funerary use. The white ground, used since Archaic times, was created by painting the vessel with a highly refined, purified clay slip that turned white during the firing. The design elements were added to the white ground with either the black- or red-figure technique. After firing, the artists frequently enhanced their compositions by painting on details and areas of bright and pastel hues using **tempera**, a paint made from egg yolks, water, and pigments. Because the tempera paints were fragile, these colors flaked off easily, and few perfect examples have survived.

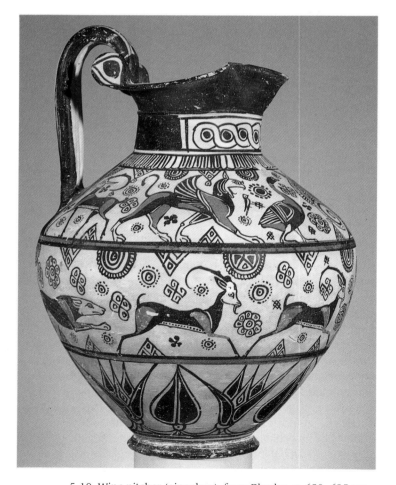

5-10. Wine pitcher (oinochoe), from Rhodes. c. 650–625 BCE. Ceramic with black-figure decoration on light ground, height 12¼" (31 cm). Museum of Fine Arts, Boston
Gift of Mrs. S. T. Morse

bud or leaf patterns in the bottom register are similar to the lotus-bud motifs found in Egyptian art.

THE ARCHAIC PERIOD

The Archaic period, from about 600 to 480 BCE, was one of cultural energy and achievement during which the Greek city-states on the mainland, on the Aegean islands, and in far-flung colonies grew and flourished. Athens, which had lagged behind the other city-states in population and economic development, began moving artistically, commercially, and politically to the forefront.

All Greek arts developed rapidly during the Archaic period. The poet Sappho on the island of Lesbos was writing poetry that would inspire the geographer Strabo, near the end of the millennium, to write: "Never within human memory has there been a woman to compare with her as a poet." On another island, the semilegendary slave Aesop was relating animal fables that became lasting elements in Western culture. Artists shared in the growing prosperity of the city-states by competing for lucrative commissions from city councils and wealthy individuals, who sponsored the creation of temples, shrines, government buildings, **monumental** sculpture, and fine ceramic wares. During this period, potters and vase painters first began to sign their works.

Temple Architecture

As Greek temples grew steadily in size and complexity over the centuries, stone and marble replaced the earlier mud-brick and wood construction. Temple builders evolved a number of standardized plans, ranging from simple one- and two-room structures with columned

5-11. Temple of Hera I, Paestum, Italy. c. 550 BCE

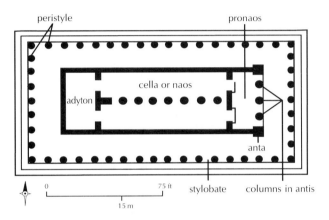

5-12. Plan of the Temple of Hera I, Paestum

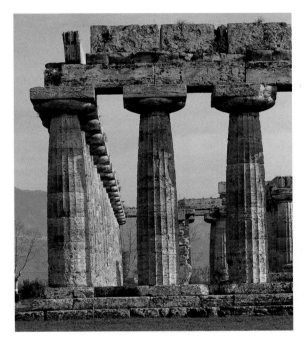

5-13. Corner view of the Temple of Hera I, Paestum

porches to multiroomed structures with double porches surrounded by columns (see "Elements of Architecture," page 164). They also experimented with the design of temple **elevations**—the arrangement, proportions, and appearance of the temple foundation, the columns, and the lintels. Two standardized elevation designs, the **Doric order** and the **Ionic order**, emerged during the Archaic period. The **Corinthian order**, a variant of the Ionic order, became so popular later that it too is treated today as a standard Greek order (see "Elements of Architecture," page 165).

The site of Paestum, a Greek colony established in the seventh century BCE about fifty miles south of the modern city of Naples, Italy, contains some rare examples of early Greek temples. Although these temples reflect contemporary architectural developments on mainland Greece, they also bear the stamp of their particular colonial setting and are not typical of all Archaic Greek temples. The earliest standing temple there, built about 550 BCE, was dedicated to Hera, the queen of the gods (fig. 5-11). It is known today as Hera I to distinguish it from a second temple to Hera built adjacent to it about a century later.

Hera I is a large, rectangular, stone **post-and-lintel** structure with a stepped foundation supporting a **peristyle**, a row of columns that surrounds all four sides (fig. 5-12). This single peristyle defines Hera I as a **peripteral** temple; a double peristyle (two rows of columns) defines

a **dipteral** temple. The columns stand on the top surface of the **stylobate**. The peristyle of Hera I originally supported a tall lintel area called the **entablature**. A peaked roof rested on the **cornice**, the slightly projecting topmost element of the entablature. At each end, the horizontal cornice of the entablature and the **raking** (slanted) **cornices** of the roof defined a triangular gable called the **pediment**.

The elevation design of Hera I was a local variation on the earliest major Greek order, the Doric. The standard form of the Doric order—incomplete on Hera I because of the damage it has suffered—includes fluted columns without bases resting directly on the stylobate; plain column capitals made up of two distinct parts, the round **echinus** and the square **abacus**; and a three-part entablature consisting of a plain, flat band, called the **architrave**, topped by a decorated band, called the **frieze**, and capped with a cornice of continuous carved stone bands called **moldings**. In the Doric frieze, flat

ELEMENTS OF ARCHITECTURE
Greek Temple Plans

The simplest early temples consist of a single room, the **cella** or **naos**, with side walls incorporating **pillars** projecting forward to frame two columns **in antis** (literally, "between the pillars") (a). In a **prostyle** temple (b) the columns form a **portico**, or walkway, only across the building's front. An **amphiprostyle** temple (c) has a row of columns (**colonnade**) at both the front and back ends of the structure, not on the sides. If the colonnade runs around all four sides of the building, forming a **peristyle**, the temple is **peripteral** (d); if the surrounding colonnade is two columns deep, the temple is **dipteral** (e).

(a) in antis
Siphnian Treasury
Delphi, c. 530–525 BCE

(b) prostyle
Temple B, Selinus
Sicily, 6th century BCE

(c) amphiprostyle
Temple of Athena Nike
Athens, c. 425 BCE

Plans are not to scale

(d) peripteral
Parthenon, Athens, 447–438 BCE

(e) dipteral
Temple of Apollo, Didyma, Turkey, begun 313 BCE

areas called **metopes** alternate with **triglyphs**, projecting blocks with three vertical grooves. The metopes were usually decorated with figures, either painted on or sculpted in relief and then painted.

Fragments of terra-cotta tiles painted in bright colors have been found in the rubble of Hera I, suggesting that they adorned parts of the temple, possibly the metopes. No sculptural fragments have survived. The Hera I builders created an especially robust column, only about four times as high as its maximum diameter, topped with a widely flaring capital (fig. 5-13). This design creates an impression of great stability and permanence. As the column shafts rise, they swell in the middle and contract again toward the top, a common attribute of Greek columns known as **entasis**. This subtle adjustment gives a sense of energy and upward lift. In a local innovation not part of the standard Doric order, Hera I has an uneven number of columns—nine—across the short ends of the peristyle, placing a column instead of a space at the center of the ends. The entrance to the pronaos also has a central column, and a row of columns runs down the center of the wide cella to help support the ceiling. The statue of Hera may have been housed in the **adyton**, the small auxiliary space at the end of the cella proper. The unusual two-aisle arrangement suggests that the temple may have housed a second god statue, possibly of Zeus.

ELEMENTS OF ARCHITECTURE

The Greek Architectural Orders

The three classical Greek architectural orders are the Doric, the Ionic, and the Corinthian. The Doric and Ionic orders were well developed by about 600 BCE. The Doric order is the oldest and plainest of the three orders. The Ionic order is named after Ionia, a region occupied by Greeks on the west coast of Anatolia and the islands off the coast. The Corinthian order, a variation of the Ionic, began to appear around 450 BCE and was initially used by the Greeks in interiors. Later, the Romans appropriated the Corinthian order and elaborated it, as we shall see in Chapter 6.

The basic components of the Greek orders are the **column** and the **entablature**, which function as post and lintel. All types of columns have a **shaft** and a **capital**; some also have a **base**. Columns are formed of round sections, or **drums**, which are joined inside by metal pegs. In Greek temple architecture, columns stand on the **stylobate**, the "floor" of the temple; the levels below the stylobate form the **stereobate**.

The **Doric order** shaft rises directly from the stylobate, without a base. The shaft is **fluted** but not as deeply as in the other orders. At the top of the shaft is the **necking**, which provides a transition to the capital. The Doric capital itself has two parts, the rounded **echinus** and the tabletlike **abacus**. As in the other orders, the entablature includes the **architrave**, the **frieze**, and the **cornice**, the topmost, projecting horizontal element.

The **Ionic order** has more elegant proportions than the Doric, its height being about nine times the diameter of the column at its base, as opposed to the Doric column's five-and-a-half-to-one ratio. The flutes on the columns are deeper and closer together and are separated by flat surfaces, fillets. The hallmark of the Ionic capital, which has a thin, cushionlike abacus, is the distinctive scrolled **volute**.

The **Corinthian order** was originally developed by the Greeks for use in interiors but came to be used on temple exteriors as well. Its elaborate capitals are sheathed with stylized **acanthus** leaves, and sometimes **rosettes**, and they often have scrolled elements at the corners and a **boss**, or projecting ornament, at the top center of each "side."

Doric order

Ionic order

Corinthian order

5-14. Reconstruction of the west pediment of the Temple of Artemis, Korkyra (Corfu), after G. Rodenwaldt. c. 600–580 BCE

Architectural Sculpture

As Greek temples grew larger and more complex, sculptural decoration took on increased importance. The Greeks may have looked to the civilizations south and east of them for ideas on combining sculpture with architecture, but the results were far from Egyptian or Near Eastern in appearance.

Among the earliest surviving examples of Greek pedimental sculpture are fragments of the ruined Doric order Temple of Artemis on the island of Korkyra (Corfu) off the northwest coast of the mainland, which date to about 580 BCE (fig. 5-14). The figures in this sculpture were carved on separate slabs, then installed in the pediment space. They stand in such **high relief** from the background plane that they seem to burst out of their architectural frame, which was more than 9 feet tall at the peak. At the center is the rampaging snake-haired Medusa (fig. 5-15), one of three winged female monsters called Gorgons. Medusa had the power to turn humans to stone if they looked upon her face, and in this sculpture she fixes viewers with huge glaring eyes as if to work her dreadful magic on them. Flanking Medusa are the flying horse Pegasus on the left (only part of his rump and tail remain) and the giant Chrysaor on the right. These were Medusa's posthumous children, born from the blood that gushed from her neck after she was beheaded by the legendary hero Perseus. The crouching felines next to them literally bump their heads against the raking cornices of the roof. Dying human warriors lie on the ends of the pediment, their heads tucked into its corners and their knees rising with its sloping sides.

An especially noteworthy collaboration between builder and sculptor can still be imagined from the remains—housed today in the museum at Delphi—of the small but luxurious Siphnian Treasury, built in the Sanctuary of Apollo at Delphi between about 530 and 525 BCE. An old reconstruction of the facade of this building, now dismantled, shows a pronaos with two **caryatids**—

5-15. *Medusa*, fragment of sculpture from the west pediment of the Temple of Artemis, Korkyra. c. 580 BCE. Limestone, height of pediment at the center 9'2" (2.79 m). Archeological Museum, Korkyra

Ancient Greeks would have seen the image of Medusa at the center of this pediment as both menacing and protective. According to legend, countless people tried to kill this monster, only to die themselves merely because they looked at her face. The clever Greek hero Perseus succeeded because he beheaded her while looking only at her reflection in his polished shield. Thus the Medusa head became a popular decoration for Greek armor. See, for example, the shield of Ajax in figure 5-29.

columns carved in the form of draped women—set flush with the ends of the side walls, which were reinforced by square pillars, or **antae** (fig. 5-16). (This type of temple plan is called **in antis**, meaning "between the pillars"; see "Elements of Architecture," page 164.) The stately caryatids, with their finely pleated, flowing garments, are raised on **pedestals** and balance elaborately carved capitals on their heads. The capitals support a tall entablature conforming to the Ionic order, which features a plain, slightly extended architrave and a continuous

5-16. Reconstruction of the Siphnian Treasury, using fragments found in the Sanctuary of Apollo, Delphi. c. 530–525 BCE. Marble. Fragments: Archeological Museum, Delphi

This old reconstruction—probably from the east and west facades, using real sculptural remains filled out with reproductions—has been dismantled. The museum now exhibits separately the actual fragments of the treasury. The photograph is useful, however, in providing a general idea of how elegant and richly ornamented the eight small treasury buildings at Delphi were in their original state, perched near one another on the hillside. The figural sculpture and decorative moldings were probably once painted in strong colors, mainly dark blue, bright red, and white, with touches of yellow to resemble gold. The people who commissioned this treasury were from Siphnos, an island in the Aegean Sea just southwest of the Cyclades.

5-17. *Battle between the Gods and the Giants,* fragments of the north frieze of the Siphnian Treasury, from the Sanctuary of Apollo, Delphi. c. 530–525 BCE. Marble, height 26" (66 cm). Archeological Museum, Delphi

frieze, one uninterrupted by projecting elements. The frieze usually held a continuous band of figures carved in relief that was often set off by bands of richly carved moldings. The standard Ionic order column is slender and fluted, with a base of plain moldings and a distinctive **volute** capital, consisting of a square echinus with two opposing "rolled" sides topped by a thin abacus that may be decorated with carving (see "Elements of Architecture," page 165). As in this case, caryatids sometimes

substitute for the standard columns in the Ionic order.

Both the continuous frieze and the pediments of the Siphnian Treasury were originally filled with relief sculpture. A surviving section of the frieze from the building's north side, which shows a scene from the legendary battle between the sky gods and the earth gods, is one of the earliest known examples of a trend in Greek relief sculpture toward a more natural representation of space (fig. 5-17). To give a sense of three dimensions, the sculptor

5-18. Reconstruction drawing of the east pediment of the Temple of Aphaia, Aegina. c. 480 BCE

5-19. *Dying Warrior*, fragment of sculpture from the east pediment of the Temple of Aphaia, Aegina. c. 480 BCE. Marble, length 6' (1.83 m). Staatliche Antikensammlungen und Glyptothek, Munich

placed some figures behind others, overlapping as many as three of them and varying the depth of the relief from high on the foreground figures to lower and lowest on the figures behind. But countering any sense of deep recession, all the figures were made the same height with their feet on the same **groundline**.

The long pediments of Greek temples provided a perfect stage for storytelling, but the triangular pediment created a problem in composition. The sculptor of the east pediment of the Doric Temple of Aphaia at Aegina (fig. 5-18), dated to about 480 BCE, provided a creative solution that became a design standard, appearing with variations throughout the fifth century BCE. The subject of the Aphaia pediment, rendered in fully three-dimension-

al figures, is most likely a Trojan War battle scene. Fallen warriors fill the angles at both ends of the pediment base, while others crouch, lunge, and reel, rising in height toward an image of Athena as warrior goddess under the peak of the roof. The erect goddess, larger than the other figures and flanked by two defenders facing approaching opponents, dominates the center of the scene and stabilizes the entire composition.

Among the best-preserved fragments from this pedimental scene is the *Dying Warrior* from the far left corner, a tragic but noble figure struggling to rise while dying (fig. 5-19). This figure originally would have been painted and fitted with authentic bronze accessories, heightening the sense of reality it conveys. Fully exploiting the difficult framework of the pediment corner, the sculptor portrayed the soldier's uptilted, twisted form turning in space, capturing his agony and vulnerability. The subtle modeling of the body conveys the softness of human flesh, which is contrasted with the hard, metallic geometry of the shield and helmet.

Freestanding Sculpture

In addition to decorating temple architecture, sculptors of the Archaic period created a new type of large, free-standing statue. A few surviving examples are made of wood or terra-cotta, but most are made of white marble, which is readily available in Greece, particularly on the islands of Paros and Naxos. Usually lifesize or larger, these male and female figures were depicted in reclining, seated, standing, and occasionally moving poses. They were painted in bright, lifelike colors and sometimes bore inscriptions indicating that they had been commissioned by individual men or women for some commemorative purpose. Many have been found marking graves, but the majority have been discovered in sanctuaries to the gods, where they were placed on pedestals lining the sacred way from the entrance to the main temple.

Traditionally, a female statue of this type is called a **kore** (plural korai), Greek for "young woman," and a male statue is called a **kouros** (plural kouroi), Greek for "young man." The Archaic korai were always clothed and are thought to have represented deities, priestesses, and nymphs, the young female immortals who served as attendants to the gods. The kouroi, nearly always nude, have been variously identified as gods, warriors, and victorious athletes. Because the Greeks associated young, athletic males with fertility and family continuity, the figures may have been symbolic ancestor figures. Pliny the Elder, a Roman naturalist and historian of the first century CE, believed that some of them portrayed famous athletes. He wrote:

> It was not customary to make effigies [portraits] of men unless, through some illustrious cause, they were worthy of having their memory perpetuated; the first example was a victory in the sacred contest, especially at Olympia, where it was the custom to dedicate statues of all who had been victorious; and in the case of those who had been winners there three times they moulded [sculpted] a likeness from the actual features of the person, which they call "icons" (*Naturalis Historia* 34.16-17, cited in Pollitt, page 30).

A kouros figure dating to about 600 BCE (fig. 5-20) is reminiscent of standing males in Egyptian sculpture, such as the statue of Menkaure with his queen (see fig. 3-15). Like Egyptian figures, this young Greek is shown

5-20. Kouros. c. 600 BCE. Marble, height 6'4" (1.93 m). The Metropolitan Museum of Art, New York Fletcher Fund, 1932 (32.11.1)

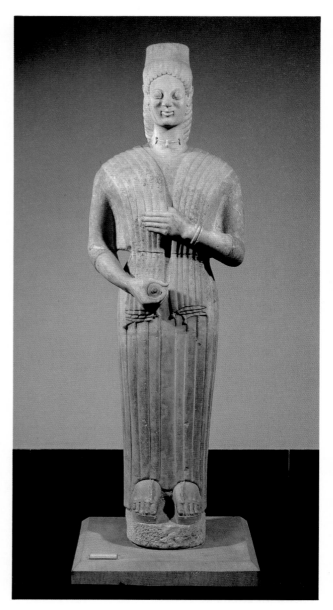

5-21. *Kroisos*(?), from a cemetery at Anavysos, near Athens. c. 525 BCE. Marble with remnants of paint, height 6'4" (1.93 m). National Archeological Museum, Athens

5-22. Kore, from a cemetery at Keratea, near Athens. 570–560 BCE. Marble with remnants of red paint, height 6'3" (1.9 m). Staatliche Museen zu Berlin, Preussischer Kulturbesitz, Antikensammlung

frontally, arms rigidly at his sides, fists clenched, and one leg slightly in front of the other. However, Greek artists of the Archaic period did not share the Egyptian obsession with permanence; they cut away all stone from around the body and introduced variations in appearance from figure to figure. Greek statues may be suggestive of the marble block from which they were carved, but they have a notable athletic quality quite unlike Egyptian statues. Here the artist delineated the figure's anatomy with ridges and grooves that form geometric patterns. The head is an ovoid shape with heavy features and schematized hair evenly knotted into tufts and tied back with a narrow ribbon. The eyes are relatively large and wide open, and the mouth forms a characteristic closed-lip smile known as the **Archaic smile**, apparently used to enliven the expressions of figures. In Egyptian sculpture, male figures were always at least partially clothed, wear-

ing articles associated with their status, such as the headdresses, beaded pectorals, and kilts that identified kings. The total nudity of the Greek kouroi, in contrast, removes them from a specific time, place, or social class.

A kouros dated about seventy-five years later than figure 5-20 clearly shows in its swelling, rounded body forms the increasing interest of artists and their patrons in a more lifelike rendering of the human figure (fig. 5-21). The pose, wiglike hair, and Archaic smile echo the earlier style of kouros, but the torso and limbs were rendered with greater anatomical accuracy and may have been done from a specific human model. The statue, a grave monument to a fallen war hero, often called *Kroisos*, may portray a particular individual of that name. The inscription reads: "Stop and grieve at the tomb of the dead Kroisos, slain by wild Ares [god of war] in the front rank of battle."

The first Archaic korai appear to date somewhat later than the earliest kouroi. An early kore found in a cemetery at Keratea, for example, dates to about 570–560 BCE (fig. 5-22). The erect, immobile pose, full-bodied figure, and 6-foot height—accentuated by a crown and thick-soled clogs—seem appropriate to a goddess, although the statue may represent a priestess or a nymph attendant. The thick robe falls in regularly spaced, parallel folds like the fluting on a Greek column, further emphasizing its stately appearance. Traces of pigment indicate that the robe was once red, a color often used as a base for the application of thin sheets of gold. The figure holds a pomegranate in her right hand, an **attribute** (identifying symbol) of Persephone, the goddess of the underworld and the harvest. A popular subject with artists was the myth in which young Persephone, the daughter of the earth goddess Demeter, was abducted by Hades, the god of the underworld. While she was mourning her separation from her mother, she became hungry and ate a pomegranate from Hades' garden, unaware that this act would destine her to become Hades' queen and live eternally in the underworld. Through her mother's intercession with Zeus, however, she was allowed to live aboveground for six months out of every year, from spring to autumn. Thus Persephone and the pomegranate—which has many seeds—symbolized fertility and the seasonal cycles of rebirth (spring and summer) and death (autumn and winter) associated with the cultivation of crops.

The *Peplos Kore* (fig. 5-23), which dates to about 530 BCE, was recovered from debris on the **Acropolis** of Athens, a flat-topped hill that was the original site of the city and later served as a fortress and religious sanctuary (*acro* means "high" and *polis* means "city"). Many votive and commemorative statues like the *Peplos Kore* were placed in the sanctuary over the centuries, but few have survived. In 480 BCE the desperate Athenians, anticipating an attack by Persian forces, fled to the Acropolis and apparently used some of the statues there to build barricades. When the Persians later sacked the city, these works suffered further destruction, and they finally were used as fill in the reconstruction of the Acropolis after the Persian invasion.

The *Peplos Kore* is named for its distinctive garment, called a **peplos**—a draped rectangle of cloth, usually wool, folded over the top and belted to give a bloused effect. The *Peplos Kore* has the same motionless, vertical pose of the earlier kore but a more rounded, feminine figure. Its bare arms and head convey a greater sense of soft flesh covering a real bone structure, and its smile and hair are somewhat more individualized and less conventionalized. The figure once wore a metal crown and earrings and has traces of **encaustic** painting, a mixture of **pigments** and hot wax that left a shiny, hard surface when it congealed.

Another kore (fig. 5-24), dating to about 520 BCE, may have been made by a sculptor from Chios, an island off the coast of Asia Minor. Although the arms and legs of this figure have been lost and its face has been damaged, it is impressive for its sculpted costuming and the large

5-23. *Peplos Kore*, from the Acropolis, Athens. c. 530 BCE. Marble, height 48" (123 cm). Acropolis Museum, Athens

amount of paint that still adheres to it. Like the *Kroisos* (see fig. 5-21) and the *Peplos Kore,* it reflects a trend toward an increasingly lifelike depiction of anatomical forms that would peak in the fifth century BCE. The kore wears a garment called a **chiton**, a relatively lightweight, basic article of clothing that originated in Ionia on the coast of Asia Minor but became popular throughout Greece. Over it, a cloak called a **himation** is draped diagonally and fastened on one shoulder. The fine pleating and gathering of the chiton indicate that it was made of a lighter fabric than the peplos, probably linen. The elaborate hairstyle and abundance of jewelry add to the opulent effect. A close look at what remains of the figure's legs reveals a rounded thigh showing clearly through the thin fabric of the chiton.

5-24. Kore, from Chios (?). c. 520 BCE. Marble, height 21⁷/₈"
(56.6 cm). Acropolis Museum, Athens

5-25. *Calf Bearer* (*Moschophoros*), from the Acropolis, Athens.
c. 560 BCE. Marble, height 5'5" (1.65 m). Acropolis
Museum, Athens

Not all Archaic statues followed the conventional kouros or kore models for standing figures. A different type is a large statue fragment called the *Calf Bearer* (*Moschophoros*) (fig. 5-25). This statue, dated about 560 BCE, was also found in the rubble of the Acropolis, in the Sanctuary of Athena. It probably represents a priest or worshiper carrying an animal intended for sacrifice on the altar of a deity. The figure's smile, tufted hairdo, and wide-open eyes with large irises and semicircular eyebrows all reflect the Archaic style. Its short-cropped

beard is similar to that of other statues of the period depicting men in active poses, but the gauze-thin robe is unusual. The sculptor has rendered the calf with acute detail, capturing its almost dazed look and the twisted position in which its captor holds its forelegs.

Vase Painting

Greek vases, no matter how richly decorated, were created in only a few forms, which combined beauty with amphora   neck amphora   Panathenaic amphora   hydria   hydria (calpis)   oinochoe   olpe

lip
neck
shoulder
body
foot

volute krater   bell krater   calyx krater   kylix   kantharos   lekythos   pyxis

5-26. Standard Greek vase shapes

specific utilitarian functions (fig. 5-26). The artists who painted them had to accommodate their work to these fixed shapes. During the Archaic period, Athens became the dominant center for pottery manufacture and trade in Greece. Athenian painters adopted many Corinthian techniques, especially black-figure painting, which became the principal mode of decoration throughout Greece in the sixth century BCE. Unlike the Corinthians, who painted large, mythical beasts against floral backgrounds, Athenian painters retained a format that was characteristic of the Geometric period, with narrow bands of decoration and relatively small figures. Compared with the Athenian Geometric period vases found in the Dipylon Cemetery (see fig. 5-5), there are fewer bands and the geometric patterning around the figures is reduced.

An important transitional work, the *François Vase*, illustrates these changes (fig. 5-27). This vase, which dates to about 570 BCE, is a **volute krater**. A **krater** is a large vessel used for mixing the traditional Greek drink of wine and water, and a volute krater is one with scroll-shaped, or volute, handles. The *François Vase* was discovered by an archeologist named François in an Etruscan cemetery; it had been brought to central Italy by a people especially fond of Greek vases. It is one of the earliest known vessels signed by both the potter who made it (Ergotimos) and the painter who decorated it (Kleitias). Kleitias's subjects were episodes from religious myth and legendary history, which he identified with inscriptions, providing an important pictorial record of the Greek pantheon. In all, the vase contains about 200 human and animal figures.

The main narrative scene, which occupies the third band down from the top and encircles the whole vase, is the marriage of Peleus and Thetis, the parents of Achilles. Thetis was a sea nymph and Peleus the king of Thessaly, and their wedding was attended by the Olympian gods. In the segment seen in figure 5-27, Peleus stands in front

5-27. Ergotimos and Kleitias. *François Vase*, black-figure decoration on a volute krater. c. 570 BCE. Ceramic, height 26" (66 cm). Museo Archeològico Nazionale, Florence

This large mixing bowl was made and decorated by Athenian artists but discovered in modern times in an Etruscan tomb. The Etruscans, who were living in Etruria in central Italy at the time the early Roman civilization emerged, were great admirers and collectors of Greek pottery. Not only did they import vases, but they also brought in Greek artists to teach their techniques and styles to local artists. Because so much Greek and Greek-style pottery was discovered in Etruria, collectors in the nineteenth and early twentieth centuries called all ancient Greek vases "Etruscan."

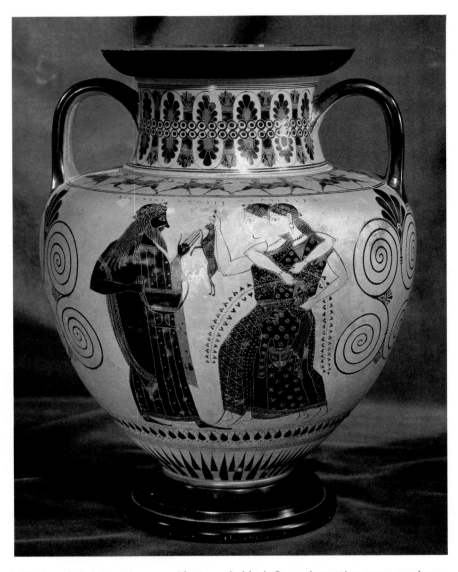

5-28. Amasis Painter. *Dionysos with Maenads,* black-figure decoration on an amphora.
c. 540 BCE. Ceramic, height of amphora 13" (33.3 cm). Bibliothèque Nationale, Paris

of his palace, on the right, greeting the deities, who are arriving in a grand procession of chariots. The scenes on the neck of the vessel show, from the top down: the hunt for the dangerous Kalydonian Boar, led by the hero Meleager, and the funeral games in honor of Patroclus, Achilles' close friend who died in the Trojan War. On the body of the krater, below Peleus and Thetis, is a depiction of the ambush of the Trojan prince Troilus by Achilles. The Orientalizing style (see figs. 5-9, 5-10) is still evident on this Archaic period vase in the next band down, decorated with deer, griffins, and plant forms. On the foot of the vessel, very small warriors do battle with long-necked cranes, illustrating a story dating back to Homer's day that became a popular theme with vase painters. There are only three bands of pure geometric design—one of elongated triangles radiating up from the foot of the vessel and two narrow bands of looped decoration on the foot.

Over time, Athenian vase painters continued to decrease the number of bands and increase the size of figures until a single scene, usually one per side, filled the whole body of a vessel. A mid-sixth-century BCE **amphora**—a large, all-purpose storage jar—illustrates this development (fig. 5-28). The decoration on this vessel, a depiction of the wine god Dionysos with **maenads**, his female worshipers, has been attributed to an anonymous artist called the Amasis Painter, because work of this distinctive style was first recognized on vessels signed by a prolific potter named Amasis. Most of the Amasis Painter's work is found on small vessels, but this handsome amphora is an exception.

In the scene shown here, two maenads, arms around each other's shoulders, skip forward to present their offerings—a long-eared rabbit and a small deer—to Dionysos. The maenad holding the deer wears the skin of a spotted panther (or leopard), its head still attached, draped over her shoulders and secured with a belt at her waist. The god, an imposing, richly dressed figure, clasps a large **kantharos** (wine cup). A band of grape leaves, an attribute of Dionysos, forms the groundline on which the

5-29. Exekias. *The Suicide of Ajax*, black-figure decoration on an amphora. c. 540 BCE. Ceramic, height of amphora 27" (69 cm). Château-Musée, Boulogne-sur-Mer, France

figures stand, and the maenads each carry a piece of grapevine. This encounter between humans and a god appears to be a joyful, celebratory occasion rather than one of reverence or fear. The Amasis Painter favored strong shapes and patterns, generally disregarding conventions for making figures appear to occupy real space, and emphasized fine details, such as the large, delicate petal and spiral designs below each handle, the figures' meticulously arranged hair, and the bold patterns on their clothing.

Another Athenian artist of the mid-sixth century BCE, Exekias, signed his vessels as both potter and painter. Exekias took his subjects from Greek legend, matching painted composition to vessel shape with great sensitivity. A scene on an amphora, *The Suicide of Ajax,* recounts an episode from the legends of the Trojan War (fig. 5-29). Ajax was a fearless Greek warrior, second only to Achilles in bravery. After the death of Achilles, however, the Greeks bestowed his magic armor on Odysseus rather than Ajax. Distraught by this humiliation—com-

5-30. "A.D." Painter. *Women at a Fountain House,* black-figure decoration on a hydria. 520–510 BCE. Ceramic, height of hydria 20⅞" (53 cm). Museum of Fine Arts, Boston
William Francis Warden Fund

water, and the trip to the communal well, or fountain house, would have been an important daily event. The scene on the hydria shows five women gathered at such a place. In the shade of the columned porch, three of the women patiently fill hydrias like the one on which they are painted. A fourth balances her empty jug on her head as she waits, while a fifth woman, without a jug, appears to be waving in greeting to someone. The women's skin is painted white, a convention for female figures found also in Egyptian and Minoan art. Incising and touches of reddish purple paint were used to create fine details in the architecture and in the figures' clothing and hair.

The composition of this vase painting is a fine balance of vertical, horizontal, rectangular, and rounded elements. The columns, the decorative vertical borders, and even the streams of water flowing from the animal-head spigots echo the upright figures of the women. The wide black band forming the groundline, the architrave above the colonnade, and the left-to-right movement of the horse-drawn chariots across the shoulder area of the hydria emphasize the horizontal, friezelike arrangement of the women across the width of the vase. This geometric framework is softened by the rounded contours of the female bodies, the globular water vessels, the circular **palmettes** (fan-shaped petal designs) framing the main scene, and the arching bodies of the galloping horses on the shoulder.

In the last third of the sixth century BCE, while "A.D." and others were still creating handsome black-figure wares, some pottery painters turned away from this meticulous process to a variation called **red-figure** decoration (see "Greek Painted Vases," page 162). This new method, as its name suggests, resulted in vessels with red figures against a black background, the opposite of black-figure painting. In the earlier method, artists painted figures on a vessel in a slip that turned black in the firing process, leaving the unpainted body of the vessel as the reddish background. Linear details on the figures were incised through the slip. In red-figure wares, the same dark slip was painted on as background around the outlined figures, which were left unpainted. Linear details were applied on the figures with a fine brush dipped in the slip. The result was a lustrous dark vessel with light-colored figures with dark-painted details. The greater freedom and flexibility of this more direct approach led artists to adopt it widely in a relatively short time.

One of the best-known artists specializing in the red-figure technique was the Athenian Euphronios, who was praised especially for his study of human anatomy. His rendering of the *Death of Sarpedon,* which dates to about 515 BCE, is painted on a **calyx krater,** so called because its handles curve up like a flower calyx (fig. 5-31). According to Homer's *Iliad,* Sarpedon, a Trojan warrior, was killed by the Greek warrior Patroclus, who had borrowed the magic armor of his comrade Achilles. Euphronios shows the winged figures of Hypnos (Sleep) and Thanatos (Death) carrying the dead Trojan warrior from the battlefield. Watching over the scene is Hermes, the messenger of the gods, identified by his winged hat and

pounded by his family ties to Achilles, who was his cousin—Ajax killed himself. Other artists showed the great warrior either dying or already dead, but Exekias has captured the story's most poignant moment, showing Ajax preparing to die. He has set aside his helmet, shield, and spear and crouches beneath a tree, planting his sword upright in a mound of dirt so that he can fall upon it. The painting exemplifies the quiet beauty and perfect equilibrium for which Exekias's works are so admired today. Two upright elements—the tree on the left and the shield on the right—frame and balance the figure of Ajax, their in-curving lines echoing the swelling shape of the amphora and the rounding of the hero's powerful back as he bends forward. The whole composition focuses the viewer's attention on the head of Ajax and its dangerous proximity to the point of his sword.

Not all subjects used for vase painting involved gods and heroes. A handsome example of black-figure decoration, painted about 510 BCE on an Athenian **hydria,** or water jug, by an artist who signed the work with the initials "A.D.," gives an interesting insight into everyday Greek city life (fig. 5-30). The majority of women in ancient Greece were restricted to their homes and occupied with household tasks. Few houses had running

5-31. Euphronios. *Death of Sarpedon,* red-figure decoration on a calyx krater. c. 515 BCE. Ceramic, height of krater 18" (45.7 cm). The Metropolitan Museum of Art, New York

5-32. Foundry Painter. *A Bronze Foundry,* red-figure decoration on a kylix from Vulci, Italy. 490–480 BCE. Ceramic, diameter of kylix 12" (31 cm). Staatliche Museen zu Berlin, Preussischer Kulturbesitz, Antikensammlung

caduceus, a staff with coiled snakes. Hermes is there in another important role, as the guide who leads the dead to the netherworld.

Euphronios, like the painter "A.D.," created a perfectly balanced composition of verticals and horizontals that take the shape of the vessel into account. The bands of decoration above and below the scene echo the long horizontal of the dead fighter's body, which seems to levitate in the gentle grasp of its bearers, and the inward-curving lines of the handles mirror the arching backs of Hypnos and Thanatos. The upright figures of the lance bearers on each side and Hermes in the center counterbalance the horizontal elements of the composition. The

painter, while conveying a sense of the mass and energy of the subjects, also portrayed amazingly fine details of their clothing, musculature, and facial features with the fine tip of a brush. Euphronios created the impression of real space around the figures by **foreshortening** body forms and limbs—Sarpedon's left leg, for example—so that they appear to be coming toward or receding from the viewer.

A red-figure **kylix,** or drinking cup, from Vulci, Italy, provides another example of the adaptation of scenic composition to vessel shape (fig. 5-32). The artist used the entire circular underside of this piece, which dates to about 490–480 BCE, to illustrate the workings of a contemporary foundry for casting lifesize and monumental bronze figures. The artist, known as the Foundry Painter, successfully organized this continuous scene within the flaring space that extends upward from the foot of the vessel. The small circle that marks the attachment of the foot to the vessel serves as the groundline for all the figures. The wedges of background space between the figures are cleverly presented as the walls of the workshop, filled with hanging tools and other foundry paraphernalia: hammers, an ax and saw, molds of a human foot and hand, and several sketches. These sketches include one of a horse, some of human busts, and three of human figures, one in an active pose, one in a standing pose, and one seated.

On the section shown here, a worker wearing what looks like a modern-day construction helmet squats to tend the furnace on the left. The man in the center, perhaps the supervisor, leans on a staff, while a third worker, on the right, assembles the already-cast parts of a leaping figure that are braced against a molded support. The unattached head lies between his feet. The scene continues past the handles, where more workers are shown putting the finishing touches on a larger-than-lifesize striding warrior figure. This painting provides clear evidence that the Greeks were creating large **hollow-cast** bronze statues in active poses—in marked contrast to the static pose of the Archaic kouroi—as early as the first decades of the fifth century BCE. Unfortunately, no examples of these early bronze figures have yet been found.

THE TRANSITIONAL OR EARLY CLASSICAL PERIOD

In the early decades of the fifth century BCE, the Greek city-states, which for several centuries had developed relatively unimpeded by external powers, faced a formidable threat to their independence from the expanding Persian Empire. Cyrus the Great had incorporated the Greek cities of Ionia in Asia Minor into his empire in 546 BCE. After several failed invasions, in 480 BCE the Persians came with a large force and destroyed many Greek cities, including Athens. In a series of encounters—at Thermopylae and Plataea on land and in the straits of Salamis at sea—an alliance of Greek city-states led by Athens and Sparta, the dominant power on the Peloponnese, first blunted, then

5-33. Reconstruction drawing of the west pediment of the Temple of Zeus, Olympia. c. 470–456 BCE

repulsed the invasion. By 479 BCE the stalwart armies and the small but formidable navies of the Greeks had triumphed over their enemies, and the victors turned to the task of rebuilding their devastated cities.

Some scholars have argued that the Greeks' success against the Persians imbued them with a self-confidence that accelerated the development of Greek art, inspiring artists to seek new and more effective ways to express their cities' accomplishments. In any case, the period that followed the Persian Wars, extending from about 480 to about 450 BCE, was a time of marked transition. Artists built on ideas that had emerged in earlier periods and at the same time initiated entirely new stylistic experiments. With the enthusiastic support of their patrons, they sought more **realistic** ways to portray the human figure in painting and sculpture and to place figures in more **naturalistic** settings (see "Realism and Naturalism," below).

Architectural Sculpture

Just a few years after the Persians had been routed, the citizens of Olympia began a new Doric temple to Zeus in the Sanctuary of Hera and Zeus. The temple was completed between 470 and 456 BCE. Today the massive temple base and columns, fallen capitals, and almost all the pediments remain, monumental even in ruins. Appropriately for its Olympian setting, the temple was decorated with works of sculpture celebrating legendary Greek victories, all of which are presented as due to the direct intervention of the gods Zeus, Apollo, and Athena.

The sculptural scene that once adorned the west pediment shows Apollo helping the Lapiths in their battle with the centaurs (fig. 5-33). This legendary battle erupted after the centaurs drank too much wine at the wedding feast of the Lapith king and tried to carry off some Lapith women. Apollo stands implacable at the center of the scene, quelling the disturbance supernaturally simply by raising his arm (fig. 5-34). Although some figures were restored later and may not exactly reflect their original appearance, the rising, falling, triangular composition attests to the skill of the artist. The contrast of angular forms with turning, twisting action poses dramatizes the physical struggle, which may have been symbolic of the triumph of reason over passion and civilization over barbarism.

The metope reliefs of the temple illustrated the mythological Twelve Labors imposed by King Eurystheus of Tiryns on Herakles. The hero, with the aid of the gods and his own phenomenal strength, accomplished these seemingly impossible tasks, thereby earning immortality. One of the labors was to steal gold apples from the garden of the Hesperides, the nymphs who guarded the trees that produced them. To do this, Herakles enlisted the aid of the giant Atlas, whose job was to hold up the heavens. Herakles offered to take on this job himself while Atlas fetched the apples for him. In the episode shown here (fig. 5-35), Herakles is at the center with the heavens on his shoulders. Atlas, on the right, holds out the gold apples to him. As we can see, and Atlas cannot, the human Herakles is backed, literally, by the goddess Athena, who effortlessly supports the sky with one hand.

REALISM AND NATURALISM Is it redundant to say that artists "sought more **realistic** ways to portray the human figure in painting and sculpture and to place figures in more **naturalistic** settings"? Are *realistic* and *naturalistic* interchangeable here, or is there a subtle difference in the way the two words are used?

Both realism and naturalism are defined as the attempt to depict observable things accurately and objectively, even imitatively. Thus, in the passage cited above, it may seem that the two words mean exactly the same thing and that the author was simply avoiding repetition. But as with many terms used in art historical writing, these words have a subtle shading that may not be apparent in their dictionary definitions.

In the visual arts, *realism* is most often used to describe the representation of people and other living creatures in an accurate, "warts and all" fashion. Detailed portraits of people, as well as pictures of animals or imaginary figures, are often described as "realistic." *Naturalism*, on the other hand, has a "softer" meaning, generally referring to the true-to-life depiction of the natural world, especially landscape and background elements. Although both terms involve realistic representation, they can carry a slightly different meaning depending on the context in which they are used—as demonstrated in the sentence above.

Many such words appear in the literature of art history. Those that are used in this book are explained in the text and are defined in the Glossary.

5-34. *Apollo with Battling Lapiths and Centaurs,* fragments of relief sculpture from the west pediment of the Temple of Zeus, Olympia. c. 470–456 BCE. Marble, height of *Apollo* 10'2" (3.1 m). Archeological Museum, Olympia

The artist has balanced the erect, frontal view of the heavily clothed Athena with profile views of the two nude male figures. Sculpted in high relief, the figures reflect a strong interest in realism. Even the rather severe columnlike figure of the goddess suggests the flesh of her body pressing through the graceful fall of heavy drapery.

5-35. *Athena, Herakles, and Atlas,* metope relief from the frieze of the Temple of Zeus, Olympia. Marble, height 5'3" (1.59 m). Archeological Museum, Olympia

The Greeks believed Herakles was the founder of the Olympian Games, held every four years at Olympia beginning in 776 BCE. Supposedly, Herakles drew up the rules for the games and decided that the stadium should be 600 feet long. The contests had a strong religious aspect, and the victors were rewarded with olive branches from the Sacred Grove of the gods instead of gold, silver, or bronze medals. The Olympian Games came to be so highly regarded that the city-states suspended all political activities while the games were in progress. The games ended in 394 CE, when they were banned by the Christian emperor Theodosius. The discovery and excavation of the site of the sanctuary at Olympia in the late nineteenth century stimulated great interest in the games, inspiring the French baron Pierre de Coubertin to revive them on an international scale. The first modern Olympic Games were held in Athens in 1896.

Freestanding Sculpture

In the remarkably short time of only a few generations, Greek sculptors moved far from the rigid, frontal presentation of the human figure embodied in the Archaic

5-36. *Kritios Boy.* c. 480 BCE. Marble, height 46" (116 cm). Acropolis Museum, Athens

kouroi. One of the earliest and finest extant freestanding marble figures to exhibit more natural, lifelike qualities is the *Kritios Boy* of about 480 BCE (fig. 5-36). The damaged figure, excavated from the debris on the Athenian Acropolis, was thought by its finders to be by the Greek sculptor Kritios, whose work was known only from Roman copies. Unlike most Archaic kouroi, which represent young men and are usually large, the *Kritios Boy* appears adolescent, and the complete figure would have been only a little over 3 feet tall. Despite his age, the *Kritios Boy* looks like an accomplished athlete. The solid, rounded body forms, large facial features, and thoughtful expression—which lacks even a trace of the Archaic smile—give the figure an air of extraordinary solemnity. The easy pose contrasts markedly with the rigid, evenly balanced, straight-shouldered, forward-stepping pose of Archaic kouroi. The boy's weight rests on his left leg, making it the engaged leg, and his unengaged right leg bends slightly at the knee. A noticeable curve in his spine counters the slight shifting of his hips and a subtle drop of one of his shoulders.

A major problem for anyone trying to create a freestanding sculpture is to assure that it won't fall over. Solving this problem requires a familiarity with the statics of sculptural materials—their ability to maintain equilibrium under various conditions. At the end of the Archaic period a new technique for **hollow-casting** of bronze was developed. This technique created a far more flexible medium than solid marble or other stone and became the medium of choice for Greek sculptors. Although it is possible to create freestanding figures with outstretched arms and legs far apart in stone, hollow-cast bronze more easily permits vigorous and even off-balance action poses. After the introduction of the new technique, the figure in action became a popular subject among the ancient Greeks. Sculptors sought to find poses that seemed to capture a natural feeling of continuing movement rather than an arbitrary moment frozen in time.

Unfortunately, foundries began almost immediately to recycle metal from old statues into new works, so few original Greek bronzes have survived. A spectacular lifesize bronze, the *Charioteer* (fig. 5-37), cast about 470 BCE, was saved from the metal scavengers only because it was buried during a major earthquake in 373 BCE. Archeologists found it in its original location in the Sanctuary of Apollo, along with fragments of a bronze chariot and horses. According to its inscription, it commemorates a victory by a driver sponsored by King Polyzalos of Gela (Sicily) in the Pythian Games of 478 or 474 BCE. The erect, flat-footed pose of the *Charioteer* and the long, columnar fluting of the robe are reminiscent of the Archaic style, but other characteristics place this work closer to the more lifelike *Kritios Boy*, recalling Pliny the Elder's claim that three-time winners in Greek competitions had their features memorialized in statues.

Unlike the Archaic *Kroisos*, for example (see fig. 5-21), the charioteer's head turns to one side, slightly away from the viewer. The rather intimidating expression is relieved by the use of glittering, colored-glass eyes and fine silver eyelashes. Although the smoothed-out facial features suggest an idealized conception of youthful male good looks, they are distinctive enough to be those of a particular individual. The feet, with their closely observed toes, toenails, and swelled veins over the instep, are so realistic that they seem to have been cast from molds made from the feet of a living person. The folds of the robe fall in a natural way, varying in width and depth, and the whole garment seems capable of swaying and rippling should the charioteer move slightly or encounter a sudden breeze.

In the early 1970s CE, divers recovered a pair of bigger-than-lifesize bronze figures from the seabed off the southern coast of Italy. Known as the *Riace Warriors*,

5-37. *Charioteer*, from the Sanctuary of Apollo, Delphi. c. 470 BCE. Bronze, height 5'11" (1.8 m). Archeological Museum, Delphi

The setting of a work of art affects the impression it makes. Today, this stunning figure is exhibited on a low base in the peaceful surroundings of a museum, isolated from other works and spotlighted for close examination. Its effect would have been very different in its original outdoor location, standing in a horse-drawn chariot atop a tall monument. Viewers in ancient times, exhausted from the steep climb to the sanctuary, possibly jostled by crowds of fellow pilgrims, could have absorbed only its overall effect, not the fine details of the face, robe, and body visible to today's viewers.

THE DISCOVERY AND CONSERVATION OF THE *RIACE WARRIORS*

In 1972 a vacationer who was scuba diving in the Ionian Sea off the south coast of Italy near the beach resort of Riace found what appeared to be a human elbow and upper arm protruding from the sand in about 25 feet of water. Taking a closer look, he discovered that the arm was made of metal, not flesh, and when he pushed away the sand he realized that it was part of a large statue. Investigating further, he soon uncovered a second statue nearby. He marked the location with a diver's buoy and reported his discovery to the director of the local museum, who also happened to be the Superintendent of Antiquities for the region. An experienced team of underwater salvagers then raised the statues, which turned out to be bronze warriors more than 6 feet tall. They were complete in every respect, except for their swords, their shields, and one helmet.

Where did the *Warriors* come from? In ancient times, there had been a Greek colony at the tip of Italy. The statues had probably been on a ship bound from or to that colony. But there was no evidence of a shipwreck in the vicinity of the find, leading to the conclusion that they must have accidentally slipped off the deck in rough seas or been deliberately jettisoned. After centuries underwater, the *Warriors* were entirely corroded and covered with lime accretions on their exterior surfaces, as the illustration shows. The clay cores used in the casting process were still inside the statues, adding to the deterioration by absorbing lime and sea salts.

To restore the *Warriors,* conservators first removed all the exterior corrosion and lime encrustations using surgeon's scalpels, pneumatic drills with 3-millimeter heads, and high-technology equipment such as sonar (sound-wave) probes and micro-sanders. Then they painstakingly removed the clay core through existing holes in the heads and feet using hooks, scoops, jets of distilled water, and concentrated solutions of peroxide. Finally, they cleaned the figures thoroughly by soaking them in solvent solutions and sealed them with a fixative specially designed for use on metals (see fig. 5-38 left).

The *Warriors* were put on view in 1980. Since then, additional steps have been taken to assure their preservation for future generations. In 1993 conservators used a sonar probe mounted with two miniature video cameras to remove any remaining clay from inside the statues. With the cameras, they were able to find bits of clay, which they then blasted with sound waves from the probe. The statues were then flushed out with water.

Back of the *Young Warrior* from Riace prior to conservation. Museo Archeològico Nazionale, Reggio Calabria, Italy

these original Greek statues date to about 460–450 BCE. Just what mishap sent them to the bottom is not known. They were not found with a wreck, so they may have fallen off a ship accidentally or perhaps been thrown from a ship in distress. The meticulous work of conservators has restored them to their original glory (see "The Discovery and Conservation of the *Riace Warriors,*" above). A look at one of them, the so-called *Young Warrior,* reveals a striking balance between idealized anatomical forms and naturalistic details (fig. 5-38). The supple athletic musculature suggests a youthfulness belied by the maturity of the almost haggard facial features. Sharp cheekbones protrude through the figure's thin flesh, deep lines run from the nose to the corners of the mouth, and unmistakable bags sag beneath the eyes. Other minutely detailed touches—the navel, the swelling veins in the backs of the hands, and the strand-by-strand rendering of the hair—are also in marked contrast to the idealized, youthful smoothness of the rest of the body. The sculptor heightened these lifelike effects by inserting eyeballs of bone and colored glass into the eye sockets, applying eyelashes and eyebrows of separately cast, fine strands

5-38. *Young Warrior*, found in the sea off Riace, Italy. c. 460–450 BCE. Bronze with bone and glass eyes, silver teeth, and copper lips and nipples, height 6'8" (2.03 m). Museo Archeològico Nazionale, Reggio Calabria, Italy

of bronze, insetting the lips and nipples with pinkish copper, and plating the teeth that show between the parted lips with silver.

The *Discus Thrower* (*Diskobolos*), reproduced at the beginning of this chapter, was created in bronze by the sculptor Myron probably about 450 BCE (see fig. 5-1). It is known today only from Roman copies in marble, but in its original form it must have been as lifelike in its details as the *Young Warrior* from Riace. Like a sports photographer, Myron caught the athlete at a critical moment, the breathless instant before the concentrated energy of his body will unwind to propel the discus into space. His muscular torso is coiled tightly into a forward arch, and his powerful throwing arm is poised at the top of his backswing. Myron earned the adulation of his contem-

poraries, and it is interesting that he was as warmly admired for a sculpture that has not survived—a bronze cow—as for the *Discus Thrower*.

Vase Painting

Vase painters continued to work with the red-figure technique throughout the fifth century BCE, refining their styles and experimenting with new compositions. Among the outstanding vase painters of the Transitional period was the prolific Pan Painter, who was inspired by the less-heroic myths of the gods to create an admirable body of red-figure works. The artist's name comes from a work involving the god Pan on one side of a bell-shaped krater that dates to about 470 BCE. The other side

5-39. Pan Painter. *Artemis Slaying Actaeon,* red-figure decoration on a bell krater. c. 470 BCE. Ceramic, height of krater 14 5/8"
(37 cm). Museum of Fine Arts, Boston
James Fund and by Special Contribution

of this krater shows *Artemis Slaying Actaeon* (fig. 5-39).
The most common version of this story is that Actaeon,
while out hunting, happened upon Artemis, the goddess
of the hunt, at her bath. The enraged goddess caused
Actaeon's own dogs to mistake him for a stag, and they
turned on him and killed him. The Pan Painter shows
Artemis herself about to finish off the unlucky hunter
with an arrow from her bow. The angry goddess and the
fallen Actaeon each form roughly triangular shapes that
conform to the flaring shape of the vessel. They are
linked by the inverted triangular space between them.
The scene is so dramatically rendered that one does not
immediately notice the slender, graceful lines of the figures and the delicately detailed draperies that are the
hallmarks of the Pan Painter's style.

THE HIGH CLASSICAL PERIOD

The High Classical period of Greek
art, from about 450 to 400 BCE, corresponds roughly to an extended
period of conflict between Sparta
and Athens, which had emerged as
the leading city-states in the Greek world in the wake of
the Persian Wars. Sparta dominated the Peloponnese and
much of the rest of mainland Greece. Athens dominated
the Aegean and became the wealthy and influential center of a maritime empire. In a series of conflicts known
as the First Peloponnesian War (461–445 BCE), the Athenians were ultimately foiled in their attempts to expand into
mainland Greece. After a brief interlude of peace, war
erupted once again. This new struggle, which was known
as the Second Peloponnesian War (431–404 BCE), came

5-40. Plan of the Agora (marketplace), Athens, c. 400 BCE

to an end with the eventual defeat of Athens.

With the exception of a few brief interludes, a dynamic, charismatic leader named Perikles dominated Athenian politics and culture from 462 BCE until his death in 429 BCE. Although the comedy writers of the time sometimes mocked him, calling him "Zeus" and "the Olympian" because of his haughty, reserved personality, Athens achieved its greatest wealth and influence under his direction. He led Athens through the First Peloponnesian War and negotiated the peace that ended it. He instituted political reforms that greatly increased the scope of Athenian democracy. And he was a great patron of the arts, encouraging the use of Athenian wealth for the adornment of the city and utilizing the talents of the city's artists to promote a public image of peace, prosperity, and power. He brought new splendor to the sanctuaries of the gods who protected Athens and rebuilt much of the Acropolis, which had been laid waste by the Persians in 480 BCE. Perikles once said of his city and its accomplishments, "future generations will marvel at us, as the present age marvels at us now." It was a prophecy he himself helped fulfill.

Classical Greece is today strongly identified with Athens, and the study of Classical art has long focused on the abundance of architectural monuments that have graced that city. Athens originated as a Neolithic site on the Acropolis. As the city grew, the Acropolis was used primarily for religious rites and ceremonies, devoted mainly to the worship of the goddess Athena, the city's namesake and protector. The lower town, enclosed by a protective **ring wall**, became the residential and business center. In Athens, as in most cities of ancient Greece, commercial, civic, and social life revolved around the marketplace, or **agora**.

The Athens Agora

The Athens Agora, which has been extensively excavated and studied, was situated at the foot of the Acropolis (fig. 5-40). It began as an unadorned open square where farmers and artisans displayed their wares. Over time, various public and private structures were erected around and within its perimeter on both sides of the Panathenaic Way, a ceremonial road used during an important festival in honor of Athena. A stone drainage system was installed to prevent flooding, and a large fountain house was built to provide water for surrounding homes, administrative buildings, and shops. By 400 BCE, as figure 5-40 shows, the Agora contained several religious and administrative structures and even a small racetrack. Among the religious structures were a good-sized temple to Hephaistos, the god of the forge; an altar to the Twelve Gods (local deities not to be confused with the great gods of Mount Olympos); and a shrine that may have honored the Eponymous Heroes, the legendary ancestors of the Athenians. The Agora was home to the Athens city mint, its military headquarters, and two buildings devoted to court business. One of these was a large hall where the dikasts, who acted as both judges and jury, tried major cases. The other was a lesser court where the heliaia, a group of citizens selected by the drawing of lots, decided civil and criminal cases. Thanks to a reform by Perikles, the heliaia were paid for their services like modern jurors.

Several large stoas offered protection from the sun and rain, providing a place for strolling and talking business, politics, or philosophy. The stoa, a distinctively Greek structure found nearly everywhere people gathered, could range in appearance from a simple roof held up by columns to a substantial, sometimes architecturally impressive, building with two stories and shops along one side. The Painted Stoa, built on the north side of the Athens Agora about 460 BCE, was so called because it was decorated with paintings by the most famous artists of the time, including Polygnotos of Thasos (active c. 475–450 BCE). Nothing survives of Polygnotos's work, but his contemporaries praised him for his ability to create the illusion of spatial recession in landscapes, his ability to render female figures clothed in transparent draperies, and his skill at rendering facial expressions conveying the full range of human emotions.

While city business could be, and often was, conducted in the stoas, agora districts also came to include buildings with specific administrative functions. In the Athens Agora, the 500-member boule, or council, met in a building called the bouleuterion. This structure, built before 450 BCE, was laid out on a simple rectangular megaron plan with a vestibule and large meeting room. Near the end of the fifth century BCE, a new bouleuterion was constructed to the west of the old one. This too had a rectangular plan. The interior, however, may have had permanent tiered seating arranged in an ascending semicircle around a ground-level **podium**, or raised platform, as in the outdoor theaters of the time. Nearby was a small, round building with six columns supporting a conical roof, a type of structure known as a **tholos**. Built about 465 BCE, this tholos was the meeting place of the 50-member executive committee of the boule. The committee members dined there at the city's expense, and, rotating the responsibility among themselves, a few of them always spent the night there to be available for any pressing business that might arise.

Some private houses could also be found in the Agora at this time. Compared with the often grand public buildings, houses in Classical Athens were rarely more than simple rectangular structures of **stucco**-faced mud brick with wooden posts and lintels supporting roofs of terra-cotta tiles. Rooms were small and few, consisting mainly of a kitchen, a dayroom in which women could sew, weave, and do other chores, a dining room with couches for reclining around a small table, a bedroom or two, and occasionally an indoor bathroom. Where space was not at a premium, houses sometimes opened onto small courtyards or porches.

The Acropolis

After Persian troops destroyed the Acropolis in 480 BCE, the Athenians initially vowed to keep it in ruins as a memorial. Perikles convinced them otherwise and set about rebuilding it to a new magnificence. One reason for this project was to honor the gods, especially Athena, who had helped the Greeks defeat the Persians. But Perikles also hoped to create a visual expression of Athenian values and civic pride that would glorify his city and bolster its status as the capital of the empire he was instrumental in building. He placed his close friend Pheidias, a renowned sculptor, in charge of the rebuilding and assembled under him the most talented artists and artisans in Athens and its surrounding countryside.

The cost and labor involved in this undertaking were staggering. Quantities of gold, ivory, and exotic woods had to be imported. Some 22,000 tons of marble had to be transported 10 miles from mountain quarries to city workshops. Perikles was severely criticized by his political opponents for this extravagance, but it never cost him popular support. In fact, many working-class Athenians—laborers, carpenters, masons, sculptors, and the merchants and carters who kept them supplied and fed—benefited from his expenditures.

Work on the Acropolis continued after Perikles' death and was completed by the end of the fifth century BCE (fig. 5-41). Visitors to the Acropolis in 400 BCE would have climbed a steep ramp on the west side of the hill to the sanctuary entrance, perhaps pausing to admire the small, marble temple dedicated to Athena Nike (Athena as the goddess of victory in war), poised on a projection of rock above the ramp. Turning left, they would have passed through the center of an impressive porticoed gatehouse called the Propylaia. (The Greeks called the gate to a religious precinct a **propylon**, meaning "outer gateway"; for gateways and vestibules opening to large enclosed spaces, they used the plural, propylaia.) Upon emerging from the gatehouse, they would have confronted a huge bronze figure of Athena Promachos (the Defender). This statue, designed and executed by Pheidias between about 465 and 455 BCE, showed the goddess in a helmet and bearing a spear. So tall was it that sailors entering Athens's port of Piraeus, about 10 miles away, could see the sun reflected off the helmet and spear tip. Behind this statue was a walled precinct that enclosed the Erechtheion, a temple dedicated to several deities. Visitors would have been able to see the upper part of this temple above the precinct wall.

To the left they would have seen several other small religious structures. Immediately to their right was a large stoa with projecting wings dedicated to Artemis Brauronia (the protector of wild animals). Beyond this stoa on the right stood the largest building on the Acropolis, looming above the precinct wall that enclosed it. This was the Parthenon, a temple dedicated to Athena Parthenos (the Virgin Athena). Walking along the main path, visitors would have come to the propylon to the Parthenon precinct. Passing through, they would have viewed the temple from its northwest corner. Ahead of

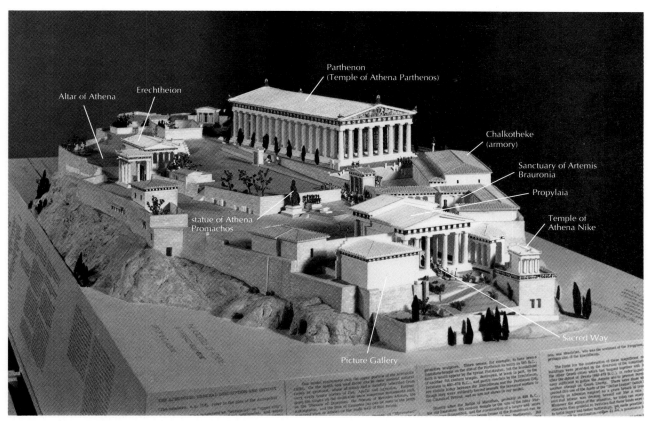

5-41. Model of the Acropolis, Athens, c. 400 BCE. Royal Ontario Museum, Toronto

them, to the right of the Parthenon, was the Chalkotheke, or armory. The cella of the Parthenon faced east. To reach it, the visitors would have had to walk along the north side of the temple past an outdoor altar to Athena, where priests and worshipers made offerings to the goddess. With permission from the priests, they would have climbed the east steps of the Parthenon to look into the cella and see a colossal gold and ivory statue of Athena, created by Pheidias and installed in the temple in 432 BCE.

Although a few small structures were added in the Hellenistic and Roman periods, the Acropolis changed little after 400 BCE. In the third century CE, it fell into disuse and disrepair. Later, the Erechtheion became first a Christian church, then a Turkish harem. The Parthenon, once the sacred home of Athena, also became a Christian church and later served as a mosque. In 1687 it was used by Ottoman soldiers to store gunpowder during a war between the Ottoman Empire and the Venetian Republic. A shell struck it and the gunpowder exploded, destroying the cella and the roof and toppling many columns. The Acropolis then lay in ruins until restoration projects were undertaken there in the nineteenth and twentieth centuries. Thanks to these restorations, modern visitors can again experience some of the splendor of the Athenian sanctuary to the gods and appreciate the great pride the people of ancient Athens took in it. Unfortunately, a dramatic rise in air pollution since the 1960s presents a new threat to the monuments and a new challenge to the conservators who are dedicated to preserving them.

The Parthenon. Sometime around 490 BCE the Athenians began work on a new temple to Athena Parthenos that was still unfinished when the Persians sacked the Acropolis a decade later. Kimon of Athens then hired the architect Kallikrates to begin rebuilding on the old site. Work was halted briefly and resumed by Perikles, who then commissioned the architect Iktinos to redesign a larger temple utilizing the existing foundation and stone elements already in place. No expense was spared on this elegant new palace for Athena. The finest white marble was used throughout, even on the roof, in place of the more usual terra-cotta tiles.

The planning and execution of the Parthenon required extraordinary mathematical and mechanical skills and would have been impossible without a large contingent of distinguished architects and builders, as well as talented sculptors and painters. The result is thus as much a testament to the administrative skills as to the artistic vision of Pheidias, who supervised the entire project. The building was completed in 438 BCE, and its sculptural decoration, designed by Pheidias and executed by himself and other sculptors in his workshop, was completed in 432 BCE (fig. 5-42).

The exterior form of the Parthenon is that of a typical Doric order peripteral temple on a three-step platform. The peristyle consists of forty-six columns, eight as viewed from each end and seventeen as viewed from the sides. The Parthenon's architects made many subtle adjustments in the lines of the structure and the placement of columns to refine the design and possibly to counter-

5-42. Kallikrates and Iktinos. Parthenon, Acropolis, Athens. 447–438 BCE. View from the northwest

act the effects of various optical illusions that would otherwise seem to distort its appearance when it was viewed from a distance. Long horizontal lines, for example, usually appear to sag in the center, but they do not here because the architects made both the base of the temple and the entablature curve upward slightly toward the center. In other refinements, the columns have a subtle swelling, or entasis, and tilt inward slightly from bottom to top, and the space between columns is less at the corners than elsewhere. These gentle curves and shifts in the arrangement of elements give the Parthenon a buoyant, organic appearance and prevent it from looking like a heavy, lifeless stone box. It is, in effect, a gigantic marble sculpture.

The extensive decoration of the Parthenon strongly reflects Pheidias's unifying vision despite being the product of many individuals. A coherent, stylistic whole, the sculptural decoration conveys a number of political and ideological themes: the triumph of the democratic Greek city-states over Persia's imperial forces, the preeminence of Athens thanks to the favor of Athena, and the triumph of an enlightened Greek civilization over despotism and barbarism.

Like the pediments of most temples, including the Temple of Aphaia at Aegina (see fig. 5-18), those of the Parthenon were filled with **sculpture in the round** set on the deep shelves of the cornice and secured to the wall with metal pins. Unfortunately, much of the Parthenon's pedimental sculpture has been damaged or lost over the

centuries. Using the locations of the pinholes, scholars nevertheless have been able to determine the placement of surviving statues and infer the poses of missing ones. The west pediment sculpture, facing the entrance to the Acropolis, illustrated the contest that Athena won over the sea god Poseidon for rule over the Athenians. The east pediment figures, above the entrance to the cella, illustrated the birth of Athena, fully grown and clad in armor, from the brow of her father, Zeus. The missing central element was probably Zeus seated on a throne with the just-born adult Athena standing at his side.

The statues from the east pediment are the best preserved of the two groups (fig. 5-43). Flanking the central figures were groups of three goddesses followed by single reclining male figures. In the left corner was the sun god Apollo in his chariot and in the right corner was the moon goddess Selene in hers. The reclining male nude on the left has been variously identified as Herakles, Ares, or Dionysos. His easy pose conforms to the slope of the pediment without a hint of awkwardness. The standing female figure just to the left of center is Iris, messenger of the gods, already spreading the news of Athena's birth. The three female figures on the right side (fig. 5-44), two sitting upright and one reclining, were once thought to be the Three Fates, whom the Greeks believed appeared at the birth of a child and determined its destiny. Most art historians now think that they are goddesses, perhaps Hestia (a sister of Zeus and the goddess of the hearth), Aphrodite, and her mother, Dione

pollo and horses   Dionysos   Persephone Demeter   Iris
f his chariot team

Hestia (?)   Dione   Aphrodite

Selene and one horse
of her chariot team

5-43. Photographic mock-up of the east pediment of the Parthenon (using photographs of the extant marble sculpture
c. 438–432 BCE). The missing sculpture in the center equals in amount what is seen here.

At the beginning of the nineteenth century, Thomas Bruce, the British earl of Elgin and ambassador to Constantinople, acquired much of the surviving sculpture from the Parthenon, which was being used for military purposes. He shipped it back to London in 1801 to decorate a lavish mansion for himself and his wife. By the time he returned to England a few years later, his wife had left him and the ancient treasures were at the center of a financial dispute. Finally, he sold the sculpture for a very low price. Referred to as the *Elgin Marbles,* most of the sculpture is now in the British Museum, including all the elements seen here except the torso of *Selene,* which is in the Acropolis Museum, Athens. The Greek government has tried unsuccessfully in recent times to have the *Elgin Marbles* returned.

(one of Zeus's many consorts). These monumental interlocked figures seem to be awakening from a deep sleep, slowly rousing from languor to mental alertness. The sculptor, whether Pheidias or someone working in the Pheidian style, expertly rendered the female form beneath the fall of draperies. The clinging fabric both covers and reveals, creating circular patterns rippling with a life of their own over torsos, breasts, and knees and uniting the three figures into a single mass.

The Doric frieze on the exterior of the Parthenon was decorated with ninety-two metope reliefs, fourteen on each end and thirty-two along each side. These reliefs, which took only six years to complete, depicted legendary battles, symbolized by combat between two representative figures: a Lapith against a centaur; a god against a Giant; a Greek against a Trojan; or a Greek against an Amazon, a member of the mythical tribe of female warriors sometimes said to be the daughters of the war god Ares.

Among the best-preserved metope reliefs are those from the south side, including several depicting the battle between the Lapiths and the centaurs. The small panel shown here (fig. 5-45)—with its choice of a perfect moment of pause within a fluid action, its reduction of forms to their most characteristic essentials, and its choice of a single, timeless image to stand for an entire historical episode—captures the essence of High Classical art. So dramatic is the **X**-shaped composition that we easily accept its visual contradictions. Like the *Discus Thrower* (see fig. 5-1), the Lapith is caught at an instant of total equilibrium. What should be a grueling tug-of-war between a man and a man-beast appears instead as an athletic ballet choreographed to show off the Lapith warrior's muscles and graceful movements against the implausible backdrop of his carefully draped cloak. As noted earlier (see fig. 5-34), the legend of the Lapiths and centaurs may have symbolized the triumph of reason over animal passion.

Enclosed within the Parthenon's Doric order peristyle, the body of the temple consists of a cella, opening to the east, and an unconnected auxiliary space opening

5-44. *Three Seated Goddesses* (possibly Hestia, Dione, and Aphrodite), from the east pediment of the Parthenon. Marble, over-lifesize. The British Museum, London

5-45. *Lapith Fighting a Centaur,* metope relief from the Doric frieze on the south side of the Parthenon. c. 440 BCE. Marble, height 56" (1.42 m). The British Museum, London

5-46. View of the outer Doric and inner Ionic friezes at the west end of the Parthenon

to the west. Short colonnades in front of each entrance support an entablature with an Ionic order frieze in relief that extends along both sides of the temples, for a total frieze length of 525 feet (fig. 5-46). The subject of this frieze is a procession almost certainly celebrating the festival of the Great Panathenaia, which took place in Athens every four years. In this ceremony, the women of the city carried a new wool peplos to the Acropolis sanctuary to clothe an ancient wooden cult statue of Athena housed there. Although the shrine housing the statue was partly ruined by the Persians in 480 BCE, the statue apparently remained there until it was moved to a new shrine to Athena in the Erechtheion about 405 BCE. The Panathenaic procession began just outside the city walls in the Kerameikos quarter, where the pottery-makers' workshops were located. People assembled there in a cemetery among the grave monuments of their ancestors. They then marched into the city through the Dipylon Gate, across the busy Agora along the Panathenaic Way, and up the ramp to the Acropolis. From the Propylaia, they moved onto the Sacred Way and completed their journey at Athena's altar.

The figures in Pheidias's portrayal of this major ceremony—skilled riders managing powerful steeds, for example (fig. 5-47), or graceful but physically sturdy young walkers (fig. 5-48)—seem to be representative types, ideal inhabitants of a successful city-state. The underlying message of the frieze as a whole is that the Athenians are a healthy, vigorous people, enjoying individual rights but united in a democratic civic body looked upon with favor by the gods. The people were inseparable from and symbolic of the city itself. Despite its patriotic intent, the frieze probably drew wrath from Athenians who felt that it was disrespectful of the gods to decorate a religious building with scenes of contemporary human activity rather than mythological figures. Pheidias was supposedly accused of even depicting himself and Perikles among the figures in the procession, but no one in modern times has been able to identify what might be their portraits.

As with the metope relief of the *Lapith Fighting a Centaur* (see fig. 5-45) viewers of the processional frieze easily accept its disproportions, spatial incongruities, and such implausible compositional features as all the animal and human figures standing on the same groundline, and upright men and women being as tall as rearing horses. Carefully planned rhythmic variations—changes in the speed of the participants in the procession as it winds around the walls—contribute to the effectiveness of the frieze: horses plunge ahead at full gallop; women proceed with a slow, stately step, parade marshals pause to look back at the progress of those behind them; and human-looking deities rest on conveniently placed benches as they await the arrival of the marchers. In executing the frieze, the sculptors took into account the spectators' low viewpoint and the dim lighting inside the peristyle. They carved the top of the frieze band in higher relief than the lower part, thus tilting the figures out to catch the reflected light from the pavement and permit a clearer reading of the action. The subtleties in the sculpture may not have been as evident to Athenians in the fifth century BCE as they are now, because the frieze, seen at the top of a high wall and between columns, was originally completely painted. The background was dark blue and the figures were in contrasting red and ocher, accented with glittering gold and real metal details such as bronze bridles and bits on the horses.

5-47. *Horsemen,* detail of the *Procession,* from the Ionic frieze on the north side of the Parthenon. c. 438–432 BCE. Marble, height 41¾" (106 cm). The British Museum, London

5-48. *Marshals and Young Women,* detail of the *Procession,* from the Ionic frieze on the east side of the Parthenon. c. 438–432 BCE. Marble, height 43" (109 cm). Musée du Louvre, Paris

The Propylaia and the Erechtheion. Upon completion of the Parthenon, Perikles commissioned an architect named Mnesikles to design the Propylaia (fig. 5-49). Work began on it in 437 and stopped in 432 BCE, with the structure still incomplete. Visitors approaching the gateway from either the city or the sanctuary side saw a Doric facade. Inside the central passageway, they walked along a ramp between rows of tall, slender, Ionic columns. These columns, which supported a raised roof, were placed far enough apart to allow wheeled vehicles to pass between them. The Propylaia had no sculptural decoration, but its north wing was the earliest known museum, a gallery built specifically to house a collection of paintings for public view. The unfinished right wing became a passageway to the Temple of Athena Nike.

The Erechtheion, also designed by Mnesikles, was the second-largest structure erected on the Acropolis under Perikles' building program (fig. 5-50). Work began on it in the 430s and ended in 405 BCE, just before the fall of Athens to Sparta. Its asymmetrical plan and several levels reflect its multiple functions in housing many different shrines, as well as the sharply sloping terrain on which it was located. The mythical contest between the sea god Poseidon and Athena for patronage over Athens was said to have occurred within the Erechtheion precinct. During this contest, Poseidon struck a rock with his trident (three-pronged harpoon), bringing forth a spout of water. This sacred rock, believed to bear the marks of the trident, was enclosed in the Erechtheion's

5-49. Mnesikles. Propylaia, Acropolis, Athens. 437–432 BCE. View from the southeast, facing the Picture Gallery

north porch. Another shrine housed a sacred spring dedicated to Erechtheus, a legendary king of Athens, during whose reign the goddess Demeter was said to have instructed the Athenians in the agricultural arts. The Erechtheion also contained a memorial to the legendary founder of Athens, Kekrops, half man and half serpent, who acted as the judge in the contest between Athena and Poseidon. And it housed a new shrine for the wooden cult statue of Athena that was the center of the Panathenaic festival.

5-50. Mnesikles. Erechtheion, Acropolis, Athens. 430s–405 BCE. View from the east

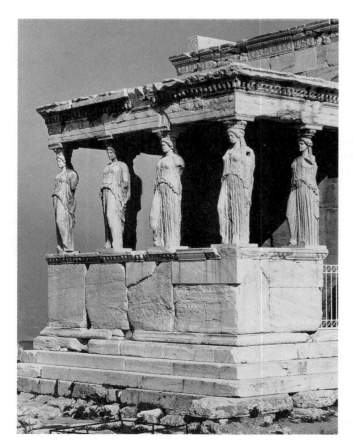

5-51. Porch of the Maidens (Caryatid Porch), Erechtheion, Acropolis, Athens. 421–405 BCE

The Erechtheion was entered from porches on the north, east, and south sides. The most famous of these is the Porch of the Maidens (fig. 5-51), on the south side facing the Parthenon. Raised on a high base, its six stately caryatids with simple Doric capitals support an Ionic entablature made up of bands of carved molding. In a pose characteristic of Classical figures, each caryatid's weight is supported on one engaged leg, while the free leg, bent at the knee, rests on the ball of the foot. Viewed from straight on, the three caryatids on the left have their right legs engaged, and the three on the right have their left legs engaged, creating a sense of symmetry and rhythm. The vertical fall of the drapery on the engaged side resembles the fluting of a column shaft and provides a sense of stability, whereas the bent leg gives an impression of relaxed grace and effortless support. The hair of each caryatid falls in a loose but massive knot around its neck, a device that strengthens the weakest point in the sculpture while appearing entirely natural.

The Temple of Athena Nike. The Temple of Athena Nike (Athena as the goddess of victory in war), located south of the Propylaia (fig. 5-52), was designed and built about 425 BCE, probably by Kallikrates. It is an Ionic order temple built on an **amphiprostyle** plan, that is, with a porch at each end (see "Elements of Architecture," page 164). The porch facing out over the city is **blind**, with no entrance to the cella. Reduced to rubble during the Turkish occupation of Greece in the seventeenth century, the

5-52. Kallikrates. Temple of Athena Nike, Acropolis, Athens. c. 425 BCE

temple has since been rebuilt. Its diminutive size, about 27 by 19 feet, and refined Ionic decoration are in marked contrast to the massive Doric Propylaia adjacent to it. Between 410 and 407 BCE, the temple was surrounded by a parapet, or low wall, faced with narrative relief panels depicting Athena presiding over her winged attendants, called Victories, as they prepared for a victory celebration. The parapet no longer exists, but some of the panels from it have survived. One of the most admired is of *Nike (Victory) Adjusting Her Sandal* (fig. 5-53). The figure bends forward gracefully, causing her ample chiton to slip off one shoulder. Her large wings, one open and one closed, effectively balance this unstable pose. Unlike the decorative swirls of heavy fabric covering the Parthenon goddesses or the weighty pleats of the robes of the Erechtheion caryatids, the textile covering this *Nike* appears delicate and light, clinging to her body like wet silk.

Sculpture and *The Canon* of Polykleitos

Just as Greek architects defined and followed a set of standards for ideal temple design, Greek sculptors sought an ideal of human beauty. Studying human appearances closely, the sculptors of the High Classical period selected those attributes they considered the most desirable, such as regular facial features, smooth skin, and particular body proportions, and combined them into a single ideal of physical perfection. This quest for the ideal can be seen also in the philosophy of Socrates (c. 470–399 BCE) and his disciple Plato (c. 429–347 BCE), both of whom argued that all objects in the physical world were reflections of ideal forms that could be discovered through reason.

The best-known art theorist of the Classical period was the sculptor Polykleitos of Argos. About 450 BCE he developed a set of rules for constructing the ideal human figure, which he set down in a treatise called *The Canon* (*kanon* is Greek for "measure," "rule," or "law"). To illustrate his theory, Polykleitos created a larger-than-lifesize bronze statue, the *Spear Bearer* (*Doryphoros*). Neither the treatise nor the original statue has survived, but both were widely discussed in the writings of his contemporaries, and later Roman artists made copies in stone of the *Spear Bearer*. By studying the most exact of these copies, or **replicas**, scholars have tried to determine the set of measurements that defined the ideal of human proportions in Polykleitos's canon, which must have

5-53. *Nike (Victory) Adjusting Her Sandal,* fragment of relief decoration from the parapet (now destroyed), Temple of Athena Nike, Acropolis, Athens. 410–407 BCE. Marble, height 42" (107 cm). Acropolis Museum, Athens nition of the beautiful as it applied to the human figure, making it possible to replicate human perfection in the tangible form of sculpture.

The marble replica of the *Spear Bearer* illustrated here (fig. 5-54) shows a male athlete, perfectly balanced with the whole weight of the upper body supported over the straight (engaged) right leg. The left leg is bent at the knee, with the left foot poised on the ball with the heel raised high—an unnatural pose for anyone to try to maintain. The pattern of tension and relaxation is reversed in the arrangement of the arms, with the right relaxed on the engaged side and the left bent to support the weight of the (missing) spear. This dynamically balanced body pose—characteristic of High Classical standing figure sculpture—differs to some degree from that of the *Kritios Boy* (see fig. 5-36) of a generation earlier. The tilt of the hipline in the *Spear Bearer* is a little more pronounced to accommodate the raising of the left foot onto its ball, and the head is turned toward the same side as the engaged leg. A comparison of the *Spear Bearer* to the *Young Warrior* from Riace (see fig. 5-38) is also informative. The treatment of the torso and groin is quite similar in both, and their poses are nearly identical, except for the slightly different positions of the unengaged left legs and the fact that the heel of the *Spear Bearer* is raised. The *Young Warrior* seems to stand still in alert relaxation. The *Spear Bearer* appears to have paused for a moment in perfect equilibrium, ready to step forward instantly.

Stela Sculpture

Individual panels, or **stelae**, decorated in relief were extremely popular among the Greeks for memorials, votive offerings, and tomb monuments. Stela sculpture was affected by the same general trends as figural sculpture, but it also frequently showed more compositional variety and freedom. A relief panel depicting *Demeter, Persephone, and Triptolemos,* dating about 440 BCE, was found in the ruins of the Sanctuary of Demeter and Persephone at Eleusis, near Athens (fig. 5-55). The sanctuary was said to be located on the very spot where Persephone was picking flowers when Hades kidnapped her and took her to the underworld. The king of Eleusis extended his hospitality to Persephone's grieving mother, Demeter, the goddess of grain, as she searched for her lost daughter. In return for this kindness, Demeter gave his people the gift of grain and instructed them in farming.

The stela shows Demeter on the left and Persephone on the right. Triptolemos, the husky youth standing between them, is sometimes identified as Demeter's son but more often as a pupil chosen by the goddesses to help spread the knowledge of agriculture among the Greeks. The subject of the relief seems to be the initiation of the boy by Demeter, who holds up a sheaf of grain and presents him with what appears to be a bag of seeds while Persephone places her hand over his head in blessing. The robust, heavily draped bodies of the women bear a resemblance to the Pheidian treatment of women on the Parthenon, whereas their young initiate brings to mind the earlier *Kritios Boy* (see fig. 5-36). The sculptor

5-54. Polykleitos. *Spear Bearer* (*Doryphoros*), Roman copy after the original bronze of c. 450–440 BCE. Marble, height 6'6" (2 m); tree trunk and brace strut are Roman additions. Museo Archeològico Nazionale, Naples, Italy

been based on the ratios between some basic unit to the length of various body parts. Some studies suggest that his basic unit may have been the length of the figure's index finger or the width of its hand across the knuckles; others suggest that it was the height of the head from chin to hairline. To Polykleitos, the beautiful was synonymous with the good. He sought a mathematical defi-

5-55. *Demeter, Persephone, and Triptolemos,* stela from
Eleusis. c. 440 BCE. Marble, height 7'2³⁄₈" (2.19 m).
National Archeological Museum, Athens

An extremely influential and mysterious cult developed
around Demeter and Persephone, comparable to that of
Isis and Osiris in Egypt. Unlike most sanctuaries, the
Sanctuary of Demeter and Persephone at Eleusis was
under the private control of two aristocratic families
and closed to all but initiated worshipers. Cult members were forbidden on pain of death to describe what
happened inside the walls, and any outsider found trying to enter illegally would have been killed. None of
the cult's activities—the Mysteries of Eleusis—was ever
revealed, but they probably involved a ritual reenactment of Persephone's abduction and descent into the
underworld and her return to earth.

5-56. *Little Girl with Birds,* grave stela from Paros. c. 450–440
BCE. Marble, height 31¹⁄₂" (80 cm). The Metropolitan
Museum of Art, New York
Fletcher Fund (1927.27.45)

has rendered the figures freely and naturally, rather than
according to a strict canon, conveying not only the narrative elements of this symbolic event but also a sense of
the warm maternal relationships among mother, daughter, and son-protégé.

The Greeks used stelae decorated with reliefs and
inscriptions to mark graves, much as tombstones are
used today. Although such markers were banned in
Athenian cemeteries from about 510 to 430 BCE, no such
restriction applied in other regions, where they remained
popular. Children, as well as adults, were memorialized
on these stones. Intimate, personalized scenes like that
of the *Little Girl with Birds* were typical of High Classical
grave stela decoration (fig. 5-56). Dating about 450–440
BCE, this stela was found on the Aegean island of Paros

and is made of fine white Parian marble. Its top is missing, but it probably once had a decorative **finial,** or
crowning ornament.

The realistic treatment of the child's body and her
idealized facial features suggest that the sculptor was
familiar with stylistic developments in Athens, but the
simple, dignified treatment of drapery, the stylized hairdo, and the subtle yet simple way in which the "story" or
meaning of the relief is conveyed bring it closer in
approach and feeling to the metope reliefs on the Temple of Zeus at Olympia (see fig. 5-35). The little girl is
dressed as a miniature adult in the same type of peplos
that her mother would have worn, and her hair is carefully arranged in waves and curls with a knot at the back
of her head. Her chubby arms and the way she kisses one

of her pet doves are purely childlike, however, and like a child, she seems unconcerned for her clothing. The peplos, a bit too long for her, pulls down at the center as though she were standing on its hem, and the claws of the doves have caught and pulled up the top. Traces of pigment indicate that the work was enhanced with some painted details.

Vase Painting

Although red-figure vase painting continued throughout the Classical period, a new style of **white-ground** decoration grew in popularity. White backgrounds had been applied on black-figure vases as early as the seventh century BCE (see fig. 5-9), but the white-ground techniques of the High Classical period were far more complex than those earlier efforts (see "Greek Painted Vases," page 162). Artists used either a black-figure or a red-figure technique to register basic design elements on a white background. They also began to enhance the fired vessel with a full range of colors using **tempera** paint, an opaque, water-based medium mixed with glue or egg white. This fragile decoration deteriorated easily but can still be seen on many vases. White-figure painting must have echoed the style of contemporary paintings on walls and panels, but no examples of those have survived for comparison.

White-ground vases were used in particular as devotional or commemorative pieces in the fifth century BCE. The tall, slender, one-handled **lekythos**, used to pour liquids during religious rituals, was the most common choice for these works. Funerary lekythoi have been found both in and on tombs. Some convey grief and loss with a scene of a departing figure bidding farewell, others with a picture of a grave stela draped with garlands. More common are scenes of the dead person in the prime of life, engaged in a seemingly everyday activity that on close scrutiny is imbued with signs of separation and loss.

A white-ground lekythos decorated about 450–440 BCE in the style of the Achilles Painter (an anonymous artist whose style is known from another vase depicting the hero Achilles) shows a young servant girl offering a small chest of valuables to a well-dressed woman of regal bearing, the dead person whom the vessel memorializes (fig. 5-57). The scene contains no overt signs of grief, but a quiet sadness pervades it. The two figures are separated by the white, central void of the vessel, and their glances just fail to meet. The woman does not actively reach to accept her jewels. Instead, she barely extends her arm, and the palm of her hand turns toward her body.

CLASSICAL ART OF THE FOURTH CENTURY

After the Spartans defeated Athens in 404 BCE, they set up a pro-Spartan government led by the tyrant Kritias. This government was so oppressive that within a year the Athenians rebelled against it, killed Kritias, and restored democracy. Athens recovered its independence and its economy

5-57. Style of Achilles Painter. *Woman and Maid*, white-ground and black-figure decoration on a lekythos, with additional painting in tempera. c. 450–440 BCE. Ceramic, height 15⅛" (38.4 cm). Museum of Fine Arts, Boston
Francis Bartlett Fund

revived, but it never regained its dominant political and military status. Sparta failed to establish a lasting pre-eminence over the rest of Greece, and the city-states again began to struggle among themselves. Although Athens had lost its empire, it retained its reputation as a center of artistic and intellectual accomplishment. In 387 BCE the great philosopher-teacher Plato founded a school just outside Athens, as did Plato's student Aristotle later.

Among Aristotle's students was young Alexander of Macedon, whose father, Philip II, established Macedonian dominance over the Greek city-states in 338 BCE. When Philip was assassinated two years later, his throne and empire passed to Alexander, known to history as Alexander the Great. This able young leader, just entering his twenties, quelled the still-rebellious Greek city-states, then rallied them behind him for a war of revenge and conquest that carried him to Egypt, where the priests of Amun greeted him as a god, and as far east as India, where his weary troops finally balked at further campaigning. His dreams of endless conquest frustrated, Alexander began retracing his path homeward but died of a fever in Babylon in 323 BCE, at the age of thirty-three. Art historians mark the end of the Classical period in Greek art with his death and the subsequent breakup of his vast new empire.

The work of Greek artists during the fourth century BCE exhibits a high level of creativity and technical accomplishment. Changing political conditions never seriously dampened the Greek creative spirit. Indeed, the artists of the second half of the century in particular experimented widely with new subjects and styles. Although they observed the basic Classical approach to composition and form, they no longer adhered rigidly to its conventions. Their innovations were supported by a sophisticated and diverse new group of patrons, including the Macedonian courts of Philip and Alexander, wealthy aristocrats in Asia Minor, and foreign rulers anxious to import Greek wares and sometimes Greek artists.

Architecture and Architectural Sculpture

Despite the instability of the fourth century BCE, Greek cities undertook innovative architectural projects. Architects developed variations on the Classical ideal in urban planning, temple design, and the design of two increasingly popular structures, the tholos and the monumental tomb. In contrast to the previous century, much of this activity took place outside of Athens and even in areas outside of mainland Greece, notably in Asia Minor.

The Orthogonal City Plan. In older Greek cities such as Athens, which grew up on the site of an ancient **citadel**, buildings and streets developed irregularly according to the needs of their inhabitants and the requirements of the terrain. As early as the eighth century BCE, however, builders in some western Greek settlements began to implement a rigid, mathematical concept of urban development based on the **orthogonal** (right-angled) **plan**. New cities or razed sections in old cities

5-58. Plan and detail of the city of Priene, western Turkey. 4th century BCE

were laid out on straight, evenly spaced parallel streets that intersected at right angles to create rectangular blocks. These blocks, or plats, were then subdivided into identical building plots. The orthogonal plan probably originated in Egypt, where it was used early in the second millennium BCE at such sites as el-Lahun, a city built by Senwosret II in Upper Egypt about 1895–1878 BCE (see fig. 3-19).

During the High Classical period, Greek architects promoted the orthogonal system as an ideal for city planning. Hippodamos of Miletos, a major urban planner of the fifth century BCE, had views on the city philosophically akin to those of Socrates and aesthetically akin to those of Polykleitos; all three believed that humans could arrive at a model of perfection through reason. According to Hippodamos, who seems to have been more concerned with abstract principles of order than with the human individual, the ideal city should be divided into three zones—sacred, public, and private—and limited to 10,000 citizens divided into three classes—artists, farmers, and soldiers. The basic Hippodamian plat was a square 600 feet on each side, divided into quarters. Each quarter was subdivided into six rectangular building plots measuring 100 by 150 feet on a side, a scheme widely used in Western cities and suburbs today.

Many Greek cities with orthogonal plans were laid out on relatively flat land that posed few obstacles to regularity. Miletos, in Asia Minor, for example, was redesigned by Hippodamos after its partial destruction by the Persians. Later the orthogonal plan was applied on less-hospitable terrain, such as that of Priene, which lies across the plain from Miletos on a rugged hillside. Priene, which originated about 1000 BCE, was rebuilt on a variation of the Hippodamian plan in the mid-fourth century BCE (fig. 5-58). The terrain of the city sloped steeply toward a rocky acropolis. As a result, the broad avenues crossing the slope were on a fairly level grade, but the narrower intersecting streets had to be stepped like stairs in places to make them passable and maintain the orthogonal pattern. Public buildings lay near the

5-59. Tholos, Sanctuary of Athena Pronaia, Delphi. c. 400 BCE

Often the term following the name "Athena" is an epithet, or title, identifying one of the goddess's many roles in ancient Greek belief. For example, as patron of craftspeople, she was referred to as Athena Ergane (Athena of the Worker). As guardian of the city-states, she was Athena Polias. The term "Pronaia" in this sanctuary name simply means "in front of the temples," referring to the sanctuary's location preceding several temples higher up along the mountain path.

5-60. Plan and section of the tholos, Sanctuary of Athena Pronaia, Delphi

intersection of the central axes, surrounded by private housing blocks measuring roughly 120 by 160 feet subdivided into building plots of about 30 by 80 feet. The agora, stadium, temple precincts, and other large structures occupied rectangular plots but interrupted the grid because of their size. The city's wall, unlike the city itself, followed the contours of the land, utilizing the defensive advantages offered by the site. The city's planners made no attempt to accommodate their grid to this irregular perimeter, leaving irregular plots wherever whole ones could not be imposed.

The Tholos. Buildings with a circular plan had a long history in Greece going back to Mycenaean beehive tombs (see fig. 4-21). In later times a variety of tholoi, or circular-plan buildings, were erected. Some were shrines or monuments and some, like the fifth-century BCE tholos in the Athens Agora (see fig. 5-40), were administrative buildings, but the function of many, such as a tholos built shortly after 400 BCE in the Sanctuary of Athena Pronaia at Delphi, is unknown (figs. 5-59, 5-60). Theodoros, the presumed architect, was from Phokaia in Asia Minor. The exterior was of the Doric order, as seen from

400

1000 BCE   1 CE

5-61. Reconstruction drawing of the Mausoleum (tomb of Mausolos), Halikarnassos (modern Bodrum, Turkey). c. 353 BCE

the three columns and a piece of the entablature that have been restored. Other remnants suggest that the interior featured a ring of columns with capitals carved to resemble the curling leaves of the acanthus plant. This type of capital came to be called "Corinthian" in Roman times (see "Elements of Architecture," page 165). It had been used on roof-supporting columns in temple interiors since the mid-fifth century BCE, but it was not used on building exteriors until the Hellenistic period.

The Monumental Tomb. Monumental tombs were designed as large, showy memorials to their wealthy owners. One such tomb was built for Mausolos, prince of Karia, at Halikarnassos in Asia Minor, where Herodotus, the "father of history," had been born more than a century earlier. This monument (fig. 5-61) was so spectacular that later writers glorified it as one of the Seven Wonders of the World. Mausolos, whose name has given us the term **mausoleum** (a large burial structure), was the Persian governor of the region. He admired Greek culture and brought to his court Greek writers, entertainers, and artists, as well as the greatest sculptors to decorate his tomb. The structure was completed after his death in 353 BCE under the direction of his wife, Artemisia, who was rumored to have drunk her dead husband's ashes mixed with wine.

Except for traces of the foundation, a few scattered stones, and many fragments of sculpture and moldings that are now in various museums, Mausolos's tomb vanished in the Middle Ages. Although early descriptions are

5-62. *Mausolos*(?), from the Mausoleum (tomb of Mausolos), Halikarnassos. Marble, height 9'10" (3 m). The British Museum, London

often ambiguous, the structure probably stood about 150 feet high and rose from a base measuring 126 by 105 feet. The elevation consisted of three main sections: a plain-surfaced podium, a colonnaded section in the Ionic order, and a stepped roof. The roof section measured about 24½ feet high and was topped with marble statues of a four-horse chariot and driver. The exterior decoration consisted of Ionic friezes and an estimated 250 freestanding statues, lifesize or larger, including more

200   ART OF ANCIENT GREECE

than 50 lions around the roofline. The friezes were sculpted in relief with battle scenes of Lapiths against centaurs and Greeks against Amazons. As reconstructed in figure 5-61, statues of Mausolos's relatives and ancestors stood between the columns in the colonnade; statues of hunters killing lions, boars, and deer encircled the next level down; below them was a circle of unidentified standing figures; and around the base was a battle between Greeks and Persians. Originally, all the sculptural elements of the tomb were painted.

A preserved male statue from the tomb was long believed to be of Mausolos himself (fig. 5-62). The man's broad face, long, thick hair, short beard and moustache, and stocky body could represent the features of a particular individual, but it is more likely that the statue represents a new heroic ideal—a glorification of experience, maturity, and intellect over youthful physical beauty and athletic vigor. The heavy swathing of drapery drawn into a thick mass around the waist reveals the underlying body forms while providing the necessary bulk to make the figure impressive to a viewer at the bottom of the monument.

Sculpture

Throughout the fifth century BCE, sculptors carefully maintained the equilibrium between simplicity and ornament that is fundamental to Greek Classical art. Standards established by Pheidias and Polykleitos in the mid-fifth century BCE for the ideal proportions and idealized forms of the human figure had generally been accepted by the next generation of artists. Fourth-century artists, on the other hand, challenged and modified those standards. The artists of mainland Greece, in particular, developed a new canon of proportions for male figures—some 8 or more "heads" tall rather than the 6½- or 7-head height of earlier works. The calm, noble detachment characteristic of earlier figures gave way to more sensitively rendered images of men and women with expressions of wistful introspection, dreaminess, or even fleeting anxiety. Patrons lost some of their interest in images of mighty Olympian gods and legendary heroes and acquired a taste for depictions of minor deities in lighthearted moments. This period also saw the earliest depictions of fully nude women in major works of art.

The fourth century BCE was dominated by three sculptors—Praxiteles, Skopas, and Lysippos. Praxiteles was active in Athens from about 370 to 335 BCE or later. According to the Greek traveler Pausanias, writing in the second century CE, one of Praxiteles' most popular works was a statue of the messenger god Hermes teasing the baby Dionysos with a bunch of grapes, which he finds irresistible. Just such a sculpture in marble, *Hermes and the Infant Dionysos,* was discovered in the ruins of the ancient Temple of Hera in the Sanctuary of Hera and Zeus at Olympia (fig. 5-63). It was accepted as an authentic work by Praxiteles until recent studies indicated that it is probably a very good Hellenistic or Roman copy of an original of about 300–250 BCE made by the followers of Praxiteles.

5-63. Followers of Praxiteles. *Hermes and the Infant Dionysos,* probably a Roman copy after an original of c. 300–250 BCE. Marble, with remnants of red paint on the lips and hair, height 7'1" (2.16 m). Archeological Museum, Olympia

Discovered in the rubble of the ruined Temple of Hera at Olympia in 1875, this statue is now widely accepted as a very good Roman copy. Support for this conclusion comes from certain elements typical of Roman sculpture: Hermes' sandals, which recent studies suggest are not accurate for a fourth-century BCE date; the supporting element of crumpled fabric covering a tree stump; and the use of a reinforcing strut, or brace, between Hermes' hip and the tree stump.

If it is a faithful copy, it reflects a number of differences between Praxiteles' style and that of the late fifth century. His Hermes has a smaller head and a more youthful body than Polykleitos's *Spear Bearer,* and its off-balance, **S**-curve pose contrasts clearly with that of the earlier work (see fig. 5-54). This sculptor also created a sensuous play of light over the figure's surface. The gleam of the smoothly finished flesh contrasts with the textured quality of the crumpled draperies and the rough locks of hair, even on the baby's head. Surely owed to Praxiteles is the humanized treatment of the subject—

two gods, one a loving adult and the other a playful child, caught in a moment of absorbed companionship. The interaction of the two across real space through gestures and glances creates an overall effect far different from that of the noble, austere deities of the fifth century BCE on the pediments and metopes of the Temple of Zeus (see figs. 5-34, 5-35), near where the work was found.

Around 350 BCE Praxiteles created a statue of Aphrodite that was purchased by the city of Knidos in Asia Minor. Although artists of the fifth century BCE had begun to hint boldly at the naked female body beneath tissue-thin drapery, as in *Nike Adjusting Her Sandal* (see fig. 5-53), and a few earlier works by lesser-known artists showed female nudity, this *Aphrodite* was apparently the first statue by a well-known Greek sculptor to depict a fully nude woman, and it set a new standard (fig. 5-64). Although nudity among athletic young men was admired in Greek society, among women it had been considered a sign of low character, which may explain the reticence to depict it. The eventual wide acceptance of female nudes in large statuary may be related to the gradual merging of the Greeks' concept of their goddess Aphrodite with some of the characteristics of the Phoenician goddess Astarte (the Babylonian Ishtar), who was nearly always shown nude in Near Eastern art.

In the version of the statue seen here, actually a composite of two Roman copies, the goddess is preparing to take a bath, with a water jug and her discarded clothing at her side. Her right arm and hand extend in what appears at first glance to be a gesture of modesty, which in fact seems only to emphasize her nakedness. The bracelet on her left arm has a similar effect. Her well-toned body, with its square shoulders, thick waist, and slim hips, conveys a sense of athletic strength. She leans forward slightly with one knee in front of the other in a seductive pose that emphasizes the swelling forms of her thighs and abdomen.

Writers of the time relate that Praxiteles' original statue was of such enchanting beauty that it served as a public model of high moral value. According to an old legend, the sculpture was so realistic that Aphrodite herself made a journey to Knidos to see it and cried out in shock, "Where did Praxiteles see me naked?" The Knidians were so proud of their *Aphrodite* that they placed it in an open shrine where people could view it from every side. Hellenistic and Roman copies probably numbered in the hundreds, and nearly fifty survive in various collections today.

Skopas, another artist who was greatly admired in ancient times, had a brilliant career as both sculptor and architect that took him around the Greek world. Unfortunately, little survives, either originals or copies, that can be reliably attributed to him, even though early writers credited him with one whole side of the sculptural decoration of Mausolos's tomb. If the literary accounts are accurate, Skopas introduced a new style of sculpture admired in its time and influential in the following Hellenistic period. In relief compositions, he favored very active, dramatic poses over balanced, harmonious ones, and he was especially noted for the expression of emo-

5-64. Praxiteles. *Aphrodite of Knidos,* composite of two similar Roman copies after the original marble of c. 350 BCE. Marble, height 6'8" (2.03 m). Musei Vaticani, Museo Pio Clementino, Gabinetto delle Maschere, Rome

In this composite of two Roman copies, the head is from one copy and the body from another. Seventeenth- and eighteenth-century restorers added the nose, the neck, the right forearm and hand, most of the left arm, and the feet and parts of the legs. This kind of restoration would rarely be undertaken today, but it was frequently done and considered quite acceptable in the past, when archeologists were trying to put together a body of work documenting the appearances of lost Greek statues. It was also done to create a piece suitable for sale to a private individual or for display in a museum.

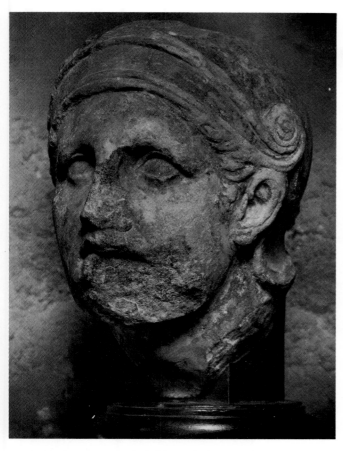

5-65. Skopas, or made in his workshop. Head from a pedimental figure, Temple of Athena Alea, Tegea. c. 340 BCE. Marble, height 11¾" (30 cm). National Archeological Museum, Athens

tion in the facial features and body gestures of his figures.

One of the most likely, though limited, sources of knowledge for his sculptural style is a group of fragments from the Temple of Athena Alea (Athena as goddess of good and bad fortune) at Tegea in southern Greece. Skopas supervised the construction of this temple, and if he did not actually create the statues, they must have been designed and executed according to his specifications, just as the sculptural decoration of the Parthenon was designed by Pheidias and executed by others under his close direction. Among the fragments is a head from a figure originally in one of the pediments (fig. 5-65). Even in its damaged condition, the head conveys intensity with its deep-set eyes, heavy brow, slightly parted lips, and a gaze that seems to look far into the future.

The sculptor Lysippos is unique in that many details of his life are known. He claimed to be entirely self-taught and asserted that "nature" was his only model, but he must have received training in the technical aspects of his profession in the vicinity of his home in Sikyon, near Corinth. Although he expressed great admiration for Polykleitos, his own figures reflect a different set of proportions than those of the fifth-century BCE master, with small heads and slender bodies like those of Prax-iteles. For his famous work *The Scraper (Apoxyomenos)*,

known today only from Roman copies, he chose a typi-cal Classical subject, a nude male athlete, but treated it in an unusual way (fig. 5-66). Instead of a figure actively engaged in a sport or standing in the Classical shallow **S** curve, Lysippos depicted a young man methodically removing oil and dirt from his body with a scraping tool called a *strigil*. Judging from the athlete's expression, his thoughts are far from his mundane task. His deep-set eyes, dreamy stare, heavy forehead, and tousled hair may reflect the influence of Skopas.

The Scraper, tall and slender with a relatively small head, makes a telling comparison with Polykleitos's *Spear Bearer* (see fig. 5-54). Not only does it reflect a dif-ferent canon of proportions, but the figure's weight is also more evenly distributed between the engaged leg and the free one, with the free foot almost flat on the ground. The legs are also in a wider stance to counterbalance the out-stretched arms. The *Spear Bearer* is contained within fair-ly simple, compact contours and oriented to a frontal view. In contrast, the arms of *The Scraper* break free into the surrounding space, requiring the viewer to move around the statue to absorb its full aspect. Roman authors, who may have been describing the bronze orig-inal rather than a copy, remarked on the subtle modeling of *The Scraper*'s elongated body and the spatial extension of its pose.

Lysippos was widely known and admired for his monumental statues of Zeus, which may be why he was summoned to do a portrait of Alexander the Great. Lysip-pos portrayed Alexander as a full-length standing figure with an upraised arm holding a scepter, just as he is believed to have posed Zeus, though none of these stat-ues still exists.

A head found at Pergamon that was once part of a standing figure is believed to be from one of several copies of Lysippos's original of Alexander (fig. 5-67). It depicts a ruggedly handsome, heavy-featured young man with a large Adam's apple and short, tousled hair. The treatment of the hair may be a visual reference to the mythical hero Herakles, who killed the Nemean Lion as his First Labor and is often portrayed wearing its head and pelt as a hooded cloak. Alexander would have felt great kinship with Herakles, whose acts of bravery and strength earned him immortality. The Pergamon head was not meant to be entirely true to life. The artist ren-dered certain features in an idealized manner to convey a specific message about the subject. The deep-set eyes are unfocused and meditative, and the low forehead is heavily lined, as though the figure were contemplating decisions of great consequence and waiting to receive divine advice.

According to the Roman-era historian Plutarch, Lysippos depicted Alexander in a characteristic medita-tive pose, "with his face turned upward toward the sky, just as Alexander himself was accustomed to gaze, turn-ing his neck gently to one side" (cited in Pollitt, page 20). Because this description fits the marble head from Pergamon and others like it so well, the heads have been thought to be copies of the Alexander statue. On the other hand, the heads could also be viewed as

5-66. Lysippos. *The Scraper* (*Apoxyomenos*), Roman copy after the original bronze of c. 330 BCE. Marble, height 6'9" (2.06 m).
Musei Vaticani, Museo Pio Clementino, Gabinetto dell'Apoxyomenos, Rome

5-67. *Alexander the Great,* head from a Hellenistic copy (c. 200 BCE) of a statue, possibly after a 4th-century BCE original by Lysippos. Marble fragment, height 16⅛" (41 cm). Archeological Museum, Istanbul, Turkey

5-69. *Abduction of Persephone,* detail of a wall painting in Tomb I (Small Tomb), Vergina, Macedonia. c. 366 BCE. Height approx. 39½" (100.3 cm)

5-68. *Alexander the Great,* 4-drachma coin issued by Lysimachos of Thrace. 306–281 BCE. Silver, diameter 1⅛" (30 mm). The British Museum, London

conventional, idealized "types" rather than identifiable portraits of Alexander. A reasonably reliable image of Alexander is found on a coin issued by Lysimachos, king of Thrace, in the late fourth and early third centuries BCE (fig. 5-68). It shows Alexander in profile wearing the curled ram's-horn headdress that identifies him as the Greek-Egyptian god Zeus-Amun. It is interesting to compare the low forehead, high-bridged nose, large lips, and thick neck to the Pergamon head.

Wall Painting and Mosaics

Greek painting has so far been discussed only in terms of pottery decoration because little remains of paintings in other mediums. Some excavations in the 1970s have enriched our knowledge of fourth-century BCE painting. At Vergina, the ancient Macedonian capital of Aigai, two previously undiscovered tombs were found in a large mound called the Great Tumulus, in a cemetery complex. Dated from **potsherds** to around the middle of the fourth century BCE, both tombs were decorated with wall paintings. The larger of the tombs (Tomb II), which contained a rich casket, armor, and golden wreaths, may be that of Alexander's father, Philip II.

A mural in the smaller of the tombs (Tomb I) depicts the kidnapping of Persephone by Hades (fig. 5-69). Even in its deteriorated state, the *Abduction of Persephone* is clearly the work of an outstanding artist. This mural, with its vigorous drawing style, complex foreshortening, and dynamic brushwork, proves claims by early observers such as Pliny the Elder that Greek painters were skilled in capturing the appearance of the real world. It also contradicts the view often held before its discovery that dramatic, dynamic figural representation in Greek art was confined to Hellenistic sculpture of the third to first century BCE. Hades has just snatched Persephone and is carrying her off in his chariot. The convincing twists of the figures, the foreshortened view of the huge wheels on the chariot, and the swirl of draperies capture the story's

5-70. *Alexander the Great Confronts Darius III at the Battle of Issos,* Roman mosaic copy after a Greek painting of
c. 310 BCE, perhaps by Philoxenos or Helen of Egypt. Museo Archeològico Nazionale, Naples

action, conveying the intensity of the struggle and the violent emotions it has provoked. Hades, with his determined expression, contrasts strikingly with the young Persephone, who evokes pity with her helpless gestures. The subject, certainly appropriate for a tomb painting, may be a metaphor for rebirth, the changing seasons, the cycle of life and death.

Later, Roman patrons greatly admired Greek murals and commissioned copies, as either wall paintings or mosaics, to decorate their homes. These copies provide another source of evidence about fourth-century BCE Greek painting. Together with evidence from red-figure vase painting, they indicate a growing taste for dramatic narrative subjects. A second-century BCE mosaic, *Alexander the Great Confronts Darius III at the Battle of Issos* (fig. 5-70), was based on an original wall painting of about 310 BCE. Pliny the Elder attributed the original to Philoxenos of Eretria; a recent theory claimed it was by a well-known woman painter, Helen of Egypt (see "Women Artists in Ancient Greece," opposite). Like the *Abduction*

5-71. Gnosis. *Stag Hunt,* detail of mosaic floor decoration
from Pella, Macedonia. 300 BCE. Pebbles, height 10'2"
(3.1 m). Archeological Museum, Pella. Signed at top:
"Gnosis made it"

WOMEN ARTISTS IN ANCIENT GREECE

Although their numbers must have been relatively few, women artists probably worked in many mediums in ancient Greece. Several of them are mentioned by ancient writers. Pliny the Elder, for example, listed Aristarete, Eirene, Iaia, Kalypso, Olympias, and Timarete. Helen, a painter from Egypt who had been trained by her father, is known to have worked in the fourth century BCE and may have been responsible for the original wall painting of Alexander the Great at the Battle of Issos (see fig. 5-70).

From pictorial evidence, we know that women worked in pottery-making workshops. The hydria illustrated here, dating from about 450 BCE, shows a woman artist in such a workshop, but it is somewhat ambiguous as to her status. The composition focuses on the male painters, who are being approached by Nikes bearing victory wreaths, symbolizing victory in an artistic competition. The woman, well-dressed, sits on a raised dais painting the largest vase in the workshop. She is isolated from the other artists and left out of the awards ceremony. Perhaps women were simply excluded from participating in public artistic competitions, as they were, for the most part, in athletics.

Another interpretation, however, is that the woman is the head of this workshop. Secure in her own status, perhaps she has encouraged her young assistants to enter contests so that they may further their own careers and bring glory to the workshop as a whole.

A Vase Painter and Assistants Crowned by Athena and Victories, composite photograph of the red-figure decoration on a hydria from Athens. c. 450 BCE. Private collection

of Persephone, this scene is one of violent action, gestures, and radical foreshortening, all devised to elicit the viewer's response to a dramatic situation. Astride a horse at the left, his hair blowing free and his neck bare, Alexander challenges the helmeted and armored Persian leader, who stretches out his arm in a gesture of defeat and apprehension as his charioteer whisks him back toward safety in the Persian ranks. Presumably in close imitation of the original painting, the mosaicist created the illusion of solid figures through modeling, mimicking the play of light on three-dimensional surfaces by touching protrusions with highlights and shading undercut areas and areas in shadow. The same techniques were used in the *Abduction of Persephone,* but its condition makes them difficult to see in a photographic reproduction.

The great interest of fourth-century BCE artists in creating a believable illusion of the real world was the subject of anecdotes repeated by later writers. One popular legend involved a floral designer named Glykera—widely praised for the artistry with which she wove blossoms and greenery into stunning wreaths, swags, and garlands for religious processions and festivals—and Pausias, the foremost painter of the day. Pausias challenged Glykera to a contest, claiming that he could paint a picture of one of her complex works that would appear as lifelike to the spectator as her real one. According to the legend, he succeeded. It is thus not surprising, although perhaps unfair, that the opulent floral borders so popular in later Greek painting and mosaics are described as "Pausanian" rather than "Glykeran."

A mosaic floor from a palace at Pella in Macedonia provides an example of a Pausanian design. Dated about 300 BCE, the floor features a series of framed hunting scenes, such as the *Stag Hunt* (fig. 5-71), prominently signed by an artist named Gnosis. Blossoms, leaves, spiraling tendrils, and twisting, undulating stems frame this scene, echoing the linear patterns formed by the hunters, the dog, and the struggling stag. The over-lifesize human and animal figures are accurately drawn and modeled in light and shade. The dog's front legs are expertly foreshortened to create the illusion that the animal is turning at a sharp angle into the picture. The work is all the more impressive because it was not made with uniformly cut marble in different colors but with a carefully selected assortment of natural pebbles. The background was formed of dark stones, and the figures and floral designs were made of light-colored stones. The smallest pebbles were used to "paint" in the delicate shading and to create subtle details.

The Art of the Goldsmith

The work of Greek goldsmiths, which gained international popularity in the Classical period, followed the same stylistic trends and achieved the same high standards of technique and execution found in the other art mediums. Goldsmiths' work was especially admired by the Scythians, a once-nomadic people from northern Asia who themselves had an ancient tradition of outstanding goldwork. An elaborate example of Greek artistry, a large, gold pectoral dating from the fourth century BCE, was found in a Scythian chief's tomb in the Caucasus Mountains (fig. 5-72). A series of four gold **torques** of increasing diameter separates each of the sections. The upper and lower bands have figures, and the center one contains a stylized floral design that strongly resembles the floral border on the Pella floor (see fig. 5-71). In the pectoral's top band, the artist re-created a typical scene of Scythian daily life. At the center, two men are making a cloth shirt, while at the right another man milks a goat. Around them are cows and horses with their nursing calves and foals, all portrayed with great naturalistic detail. In contrast, the bottom band is devoted to a Near Eastern theme of animal combat, with griffinlike beasts attacking a group of horses. Is there a lesson here—that the domestication of animals is justified because it offers them protection from the dangers of the wild?

5-72. Pectoral, from the tomb of a Scythian at Ordzhonikidze, Russia. 4th century BCE. Gold, diameter 12" (30.6 cm). Historical Museum, Kiev

The jewelry designs popular with Greek women of the period were romantic ones. An embossed gold diadem dating from the late fourth century BCE, to be worn in the hair like a small crown (fig. 5-73), depicts a pair of mythological lovers, Ariadne—a Cretan princess abandoned by her lover, Theseus, on the island of Naxos—and the wine god Dionysos, who found and married her. The two recline back to back, listening to a concert played by women musicians seated between giant spiraling forms like those on both sides of the listening couple. The harpist at the near right in pose and instrument recalls

5-73. Diadem, reputed to have been found in a tomb near the Hellespont. Late 4th century BCE. Gold, 14½" (36.8 cm). The Metropolitan Musem of Art, New York
Rogers Fund, 1906 (06.1217.1)

5-74. Earrings. c. 330–300 BCE. Hollow-cast gold, height
2³⁄₈" (6 cm). The Metropolitan Musem of Art, New York
Harris Brisbane Dick Fund, 1937 (37.11.9–10)

the Cycladic *Harp Player* (see fig. 4-3). The tumbling leafy
spirals somewhat resemble the floral elements of the
Scythian pectoral.

A specialty of Greek goldsmiths was the design of
earrings in the form of tiny works of sculpture. These
were often placed on the ears of marble statues of goddesses, but they adorned real ears as well. An earring
designed as the youth Ganymede in the grasp of an eagle
(Zeus) (fig. 5-74), dated about 330–300 BCE, is both a
charming decoration and a technical tour de force.
Slightly more than 2 inches high, it was hollow-cast
using the **lost-wax** process, no doubt to make it light on
the ear. Despite its small size, the earring conveys all the
drama of its subject. Action subjects like this, with the
depiction of swift movement through space, were to
become a hallmark of Hellenistic art.

THE HELLENISTIC PERIOD

When Alexander died in 323
BCE, he left a vast empire with
no administrative structure and
no accepted successor. Almost
at once his generals turned
against one another, local leaders tried to regain their
lost autonomy, and the empire began to break apart. The
Greek city-states formed a new mutual-protection
league but never again achieved significant power.
Democracy survived in form but not substance in governments dominated by local rulers.

By the early third century BCE, three major powers
had emerged out of the chaos, ruled by three of Alexander's generals and their heirs: Antigonus, Ptolemy, and
Seleucus. The Antigonids controlled Macedonia and

mainland Greece; the Ptolemies ruled Egypt; and the
Seleucids controlled Asia Minor, Mesopotamia, and Persia. Over the course of the second and first centuries BCE
these kingdoms succumbed to the growing empire centered in Rome. Ptolemaic Egypt endured the longest,
almost two and one-half centuries. The death in 30 BCE of
its last ruler, the remarkable Cleopatra, marks the end of
the Hellenistic period.

Alexander's most lasting legacy was the spread of
Greek culture far beyond its original borders. The Ptolemaic capital, Alexandria in Egypt, a prosperous seaport
known for its lighthouse (another of the Seven Wonders
of the World, according to ancient writers), emerged as a
great Hellenistic center of learning and the arts. Its
library, estimated to have contained 700,000 papyrus and
parchment scrolls, was rivaled only by the library at Pergamon in Asia Minor.

Artists of the Hellenistic period had a vision noticeably different from that of their predecessors. Where earlier artists sought the ideal and the general, Hellenistic
artists sought the individual and the specific. They turned
increasingly away from the heroic and to the everyday,
from gods to mortals, from aloof serenity to individual
emotion, and from drama to melodramatic pathos. A
trend introduced in the fourth century BCE—the appeal to
the senses through lustrous or glittering surface treatments and to the emotions with dramatic subjects and
poses—became more pronounced. Even the architecture
of the Hellenistic period largely reflected the contemporary taste for high drama.

Theaters

In ancient Greece, the theater was more than mere entertainment; it was a vehicle for the communal expression
of religious belief through music, poetry, and dance. In
very early times, theater performances took place on the
hard-packed dirt or stone-surfaced pavement of an outdoor threshing floor (*halos*)—the same type of floor later
incorporated into religious sanctuaries. Whenever feasible, dramas were also presented facing a steep hill that
served as a kind of natural theater. Eventually such sites
were made into permanent open-air auditoriums. At
first, tiers of seats were simply cut into the side of the hill.
Later, builders improved them with stone.

During the fifth century BCE, the plays primarily were
tragedies in verse based on popular myths and were performed at a festival dedicated to Dionysos. At this time,
the three great Greek tragedians—Aeschylus, Sophocles,
and Euripides—were creating the works that would
define tragedy for centuries. Many theaters were built in
the fourth century BCE, including those on the side of the
Athenian Acropolis and in the sanctuary at Delphi, also
for the performance of music and dance during the festival of Dionysos. Because theaters were used continuously and frequently modified over many centuries, no
early theaters have survived in their original form.

The largely intact theater at Epidauros, however,
which dates from the early third century BCE, presents
good examples of the characteristics of early theaters

5-75. Theater, Epidauros. Early 3rd century BCE and later

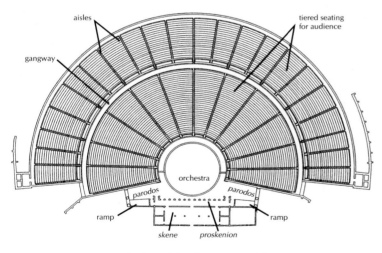

5-76. Plan of the theater at Epidauros

(figs. 5-75, 5-76). A semicircle of tiered seats built into the hillside overlooked the circular performance area, called the orchestra, at the center of which was an altar to Dionysos. Rising behind the orchestra was a two-tiered stage structure made up of the vertical *skene* (scene)—an architectural backdrop for performances and a screen for the backstage area—and the *proskenion* (**proscenium**), a raised platform in front of the *skene* that was increasingly used over time as an extension of the orchestra. Ramps connecting the *proskenion* with lateral passageways (*parodoi*; singular *parodos*) provided access to the stage for performers. Steps gave the audience access to the fifty-five rows of seats and divided the seating area into uni-

form wedge-shaped sections. The tiers of seats above the wide corridor, or gangway, were added at a much later date. This design provided uninterrupted sight lines and good acoustics and allowed for efficient crowd control of the 12,000 spectators. It has not been greatly improved upon since.

The Corinthian Order in Architecture

During the Hellenistic period there was increasing innovation in public architecture. A variant of the Ionic order featuring a tall, slender column with a Corinthian capital, for example, began to challenge the dominance of the Doric and Ionic orders on building exteriors. Invented in the late fifth century BCE, this highly decorative carved capital had previously been used only indoors, as in the tholos at Delphi (see fig. 5-60). Today, the Corinthian variant is routinely treated as a third Greek order (see "Elements of Architecture," page 165). In the Corinthian column the echinus becomes an unfluted extension of the column shaft set off by a collar molding called an **astragal**. From the astragal sprout curly acanthus leaves and coiled flower spikes reminiscent of the coiled volutes of the Ionic capital. The slightly flaring abacus has concave sides with a center relief element called a **boss**. The Corinthian entablature features a stepped-out architrave and bands of carved moldings, often including a line of vertical toothlike elements called **dentils**, just above the continuous frieze. The Corinthian design became a lasting symbol of elegance and refinement that is still used on banks, churches, and office buildings.

The Corinthian order Temple of the Olympian Zeus, located in the lower city of Athens at the foot of the Acropolis, was commissioned by the Seleucid ruler Antiochus IV and was designed by the Roman architect Cossutius in the second century BCE (fig. 5-77). The temple's unusually large foundation, measuring 135 by 354 feet, is that of an earlier temple dating to the mid-sixth century BCE. Work halted in 164 BCE and was not completed until three centuries later under Roman rule. The temple's great Corinthian columns may be the second-century BCE originals or Roman replicas of them. The peristyle soars 57 feet above the stylobate. Viewed through its columns the Parthenon seems modest in comparison. But for all its height and luxurious decoration, the design of the new temple followed long-established norms. It stood on a three-stepped base, it had an enclosed room or series of rooms enclosed within a screen of columns, and its proportions and details followed traditional standards. Quite simply, it is a Greek temple grown very large.

5-77. Temple of the Olympian Zeus, Athens. Building and rebuilding phases: foundation mid-6th century BCE; temple designed by Cossutius, begun 175 BCE, left unfinished 164 BCE, completed 132 CE using Cossutius's design

Sculpture

Hellenistic sculptors produced an enormous variety of work in a wide range of materials, techniques, and styles. The period was marked by two broad and conflicting trends. One (sometimes called anti-Classical) led away from Classical models and toward experimentation with new forms and subjects; the other led back to Classical models, with artists selecting aspects of certain favored works by fourth-century sculptors and incorporating them into new styles.

The Pergamene Style. The kingdom of Pergamon, a breakaway state within the Seleucid realm, established itself in the early third century BCE on the site of an ancient city in western Asia Minor. It quickly became a leading center of arts patronage and the hub of a new sculptural style that had far-reaching influence throughout the Hellenistic period. This new style is illustrated by a group of sculpture from a monument commemorating the victory in 230 BCE of Attalos I (ruled 241–197 BCE) over the Gauls, a Celtic people who invaded from the north. These figures, originally in bronze but known today only from Roman copies in marble, were mounted on a large pedestal. They depict the murder-suicide of the Gallic chieftain and his wife (fig. 5-78) and the slow demise of a wounded soldier-trumpeter (fig. 5-79), extolling their dignity and heroism in defeat. Their wiry, unkempt hair and the trumpeter's twisted neck ring, or torque (the only item of dress the Celts wore in battle), identify them as "barbarians." The artist has sought to arouse the viewer's admiration and pity for his subjects. The chieftain, for example, still supports his dead wife as he plunges the sword into his own breast. The trumpeter, fatally injured, struggles to stay up, but the slight bowing of his supporting right arm and his unseeing downcast gaze indicate that he is on the point of death. This kind of deliberate attempt to elicit a specific emotional response in the viewer is known as **expressionism**, and it was to become a characteristic of Hellenistic art.

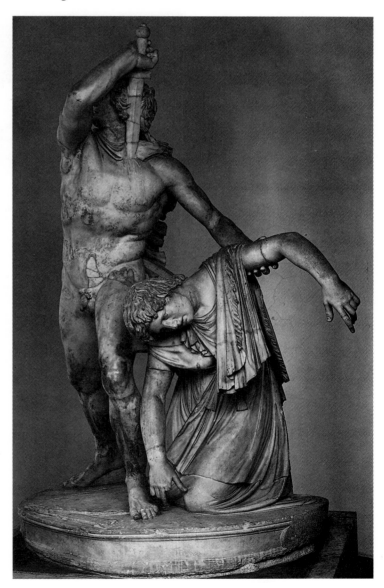

5-78. *Gallic Chieftain Killing His Wife and Himself*, Roman copy after the original bronze of c. 220 BCE. Marble, height 6'11" (2.1 m). Museo Nazionale Romano, Rome

5-79. Epigonos(?). *Dying Gallic Trumpeter*, Roman copy after the original bronze of c. 220 BCE. Marble, lifesize. Museo Capitolino, Rome

The marble copies of these works are now separated, and no one knows exactly how the originals were positioned. Probably they formed part of an interlocked, multifigured pyramidal group that could have been viewed and appreciated from nearly every angle. Pliny the Elder described a work like the *Dying Gallic Trumpeter*, attributing it to an artist named Epigonos. Recent research indicates that Epigonos probably knew the early-fifth-century BCE sculpture of the Temple of Aphaia at Aegina, which included the *Dying Warrior* (see fig. 5-19), and could have had it in mind when he created his own works.

The style and approach of the works in the monument to the defeated Gauls became more pronounced and dramatic in later works, culminating in the decorative frieze on the base of the great altar at Pergamon (fig. 5-80). The wings and staircase to the entrance of the altar have been reconstructed inside a Berlin museum from fragments from the site. The original altar was a single-story structure with an Ionic colonnade raised on a high podium and entrances on each side. The main entrance, as shown here, was reached by a monumental staircase 68 feet wide and nearly 30 feet deep. The running frieze decoration, probably executed during the

reign of Eumenes II (197–159 BCE), depicts the battle between the Gods and the Giants, a mythical struggle that the Greeks are thought to have used as a metaphor for contemporary conflict—in this case, Pergamon's victory over the Gauls.

The panels are about 7 1/2 feet high on the ends and taper to a few inches at the top of the steps. They show the Greek gods fighting not only human-looking Giants, but also grotesque hybrids emerging from the bowels of the earth. In a detail of the frieze (fig. 5-81), the goddess Athena at the left has grabbed the hair of a winged, serpent-tailed male monster and forced him to his knees. Inscriptions along the base of the sculpture identify him as Alkyoneos, a son of the earth goddess Ge, who rises from the ground on the right in maternal wrath as she reaches toward Athena. At the far right, a winged Nike rushes to Athena's assistance.

The figures in the Pergamon frieze not only fill up the sculptural space, they break out of their architectural boundaries and invade the space in front of it. They crawl out of the frieze onto the steps, where visitors had to pass them on their way up to the shrine. Many consider this theatrical and complex interaction of space and form to be a benchmark of the Hellenistic style, just as they con-

5-80. Reconstructed west front of the altar from Pergamon, Turkey. C. 166–156 BCE. Marble. Staatliche Museen zu Berlin, Preussischer Kulturbesitz, Pergamonmuseum

5-81. *Athena Attacking the Giants,* detail of the frieze from the east front of the altar from Pergamon. Marble, frieze height 7'6" (2.3 m). Staatliche Museen zu Berlin, Preussischer Kulturbesitz, Pergamon-museum

sider the balanced restraint of the Parthenon sculpture to be the benchmark of the High Classical style. Where fifth-century BCE artists sought horizontal and vertical equilibrium and control, the Pergamene artists sought to balance opposing forces in three-dimensional space along diagonal lines. The High Classical preference for smooth, sculpted surfaces reflecting a clear, even light has been replaced by a preference for dramatic contrasts of light and shade playing over complex forms sculpted in high relief with deep undercutting. The composure and stability admired in the Classical style have given way to extreme expressions of pain, stress, wild anger, fear, and despair. In the High Classical style, figures stood remote in their own space. In the Fourth-Century style they reached out into their immediate environment. In the Hellenistic style, they impose themselves, often forcefully, on the spectator. Whereas the High Classical artist asked only for an intellectual commitment, the Hellenistic artist demanded that the viewer respond both physically and emotionally.

5-82. *Nike (Victory) of Samothrace,* from the Sanctuary of the Great Gods, Samothrace. c. 190 BCE (?). Marble, height 8' (2.44 m). Musée du Louvre, Paris

The wind-whipped costume and raised wings of this victory goddess indicate that she has just alighted on the prow of the stone ship that formed the original base of the statue. The work probably memorialized an important naval victory, perhaps the Rhodian triumph over the Seleucid king Antiochus III in 190 BCE. Lacking its head and arms, the Nike and a fragment of its ship base were discovered in the ruins of the Sanctuary of the Great Gods by a French explorer in 1863. Soon after, it entered the collection of the Louvre Museum in Paris. Poised high on the landing of the grand staircase, this famous Hellenistic sculpture continues to catch the eye and the imagination of thousands of museum visitors.

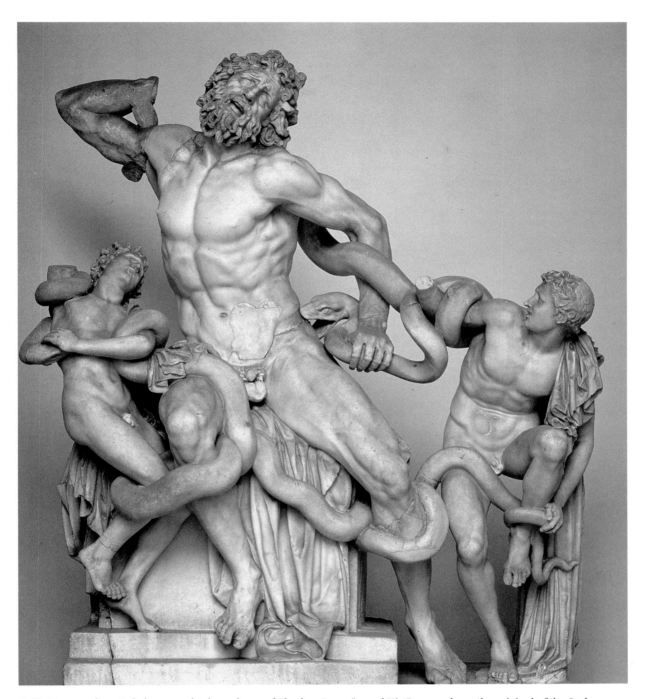

5-83. Hagesandros, Polydoros, and Athanadoros of Rhodes. *Laocoön and His Sons,* perhaps the original of the 2nd or 1st century BCE or a Roman copy of the 1st century CE. Marble, height 8' (2.44 m). Musei Vaticani, Museo Pio Clementino, Cortile Ottagono, Rome

The *Nike (Victory) of Samothrace* (fig. 5-82) is more theatrical still. In its original setting—in a hillside niche high above the city of Samothrace and perhaps drenched with spray from a fountain—this 8-foot-high goddess of victory must have reminded the Samothracians of the god-character in Greek plays who descends from heaven to determine the outcome of the drama. The fact that victory in real life does often seem miraculous makes this image of a goddess alighting suddenly on a ship breathtakingly appropriate for a war memorial. The forward momentum of the *Nike*'s heavy body is balanced by the powerful backward thrust of its enormous wings. The large, open movements of the figure, the strong contrasts of light and dark on the deeply sculpted forms, and the contrasting textures of feathers, fabric, and skin are reminiscent of the sculptures on the Altar of Zeus at Pergamon, though it is not known which work is earlier.

Pergamene artists very likely inspired the work of Hagesandros, Polydoros, and Athanadoros, three sculptors on the island of Rhodes named by Pliny the Elder as the creators of the famed *Laocoön and His Sons* (fig. 5-83). This work, in the collection of the Vatican since its

THE TROJAN WAR

The legend of the Trojan War and its aftermath held a central place in the imagination of the ancient Greeks, inspiring the great epics of Homer—the *Iliad* and the *Odyssey*—and providing the poets and artists of the Classical period and beyond with a rich source of subject matter. According to the legend, the cause of the war was a woman's infidelity. While on a visit to the city of Sparta in southern Greece, young Paris, the son of King Priam of Troy, fell in love with Helen, a human daughter of Zeus who was the wife of the Spartan king Menelaus. With the help of Aphrodite, the goddess of love, she and Paris fled to Troy, a rich city in northwestern Asia Minor. The angry Greeks dispatched ships and a huge army to bring Helen back. Led by Agamemnon, king of Mycenae and the brother of Menelaus, the Greek forces laid siege to Troy. The two sides were deadlocked for ten years, until a ruse devised by the warrior Odysseus allowed the Greeks to win: the Greeks pretended to give up the siege and built a huge wooden horse to leave behind as a parting gift to the goddess Athena, or so they led the Trojans to believe.

In fact, Greek warriors were hidden inside the wooden horse. After the Trojans pulled the horse inside the gates of Troy, the Greeks slipped out and opened the gates to their comrades, who slaughtered the Trojans and burned the city.

The source of this legend is thought to have been a real attack on a coastal city of Asia Minor by mainland Greeks during the Late Bronze Age. The assault more likely resulted from a struggle for control over trade in and out of the Black Sea than from the abduction of a Helladic ruler's wife. Tales of the conflict, modified over the centuries, endured in a tradition of oral poetry into the eighth or seventh century BCE, when the epics that are attributed to Homer were written down.

Homer's *Iliad* recounts an incident that took place during the long siege of Troy. Achilles, offended by Agamemnon, refuses to fight, and in his absence the Greeks suffer reverses. His friend Patroclus borrows his magical armor and kills many Trojans (including the warrior Sarpedon, see fig. 5-31) before he is killed by the Trojan hero Hector (another son of Priam). Achilles, to avenge his friend's death, returns to the battle and slays Hector. Homer's *Odyssey* recounts the trials and triumphs of Odysseus, who was doomed to years of wandering after the war before he could return to his faithful wife, Penelope. Among the many other stories of the Trojan War that found their way into art and literature were the death of Agamemnon, slain by his wife Clytemnestra when he arrived home, and the suicide of Ajax (see fig. 5-29).

The Romans, too, found inspiration in the legendary struggle at Troy.

Seeking heroic origins for themselves, they claimed descent from Aeneas, a Trojan warrior. As recounted in the *Aeneid*, an epic by the Roman poet Vergil (70–19 BCE), Aeneas and his followers escaped from Troy and found their way to Italy.

As early as the seventeenth century CE, adventurers began searching for Troy. In the early nineteenth century, the Englishman Charles MacLaren and the American Frank Calvert both concluded that the remains of the legendary city might be found at the Hissarlik Mound in northwestern Turkey. When this relatively small mound—less than 700 feet across—was excavated, first by the German archeologist Heinrich Schliemann from 1872 to 1890 (see "Pioneers of Aegean Archeology," page 143) and later by an American team under Carl Blegen in the 1930s, it was found to contain the remains of at least nine successive cities, the earliest of which dated to at least 3000 BCE. The seventh of these shows evidence of a terrible fire, which led early researchers to identify it as the Troy of legend. A more recent hypothesis, however, is that the so-called Troy 7 was destroyed by a fire of natural causes and that Homer's city is more likely to have been the earlier Troy 6. This city flourished for at least 500 years, between about 1800 and 1300 BCE. At its height, its fortifications were substantially reinforced, suggesting that it was threatened by a powerful enemy.

excavation in Rome in 1506, has been assumed by many art historians to be the original version, although others argue that it is a brilliant copy commissioned by an admiring Roman patron. The date of the original work is also uncertain—either second or first century BCE. The complex sculptural composition illustrates an episode from the Trojan War (see "The Trojan War," above). The Trojans' priest Laocoön warned them not to take the wooden horse (filled with Greeks) inside their walls. The gods who supported the Greeks in the war retaliated by sending serpents into Troy to destroy Laocoön and his sons. The struggling figures, anguished faces, intricate diagonal movements, and skillful unification of diverse forces in a complex composition all suggest a strong relationship between Rhodian and Pergamene sculptors. Unlike the monument to the conquered Gauls, the *Laocoön* was composed to be seen from the front,

within a short distance. As a result, although sculpted in the round, the three figures appear as very high relief and are more like the relief sculpture on the Altar of Zeus.

Small-Scale Statues. Although "huge," "enormous," and "larger-than-life" are terms correctly applied to much Hellenistic sculpture, artists of the time also created fine works on a small scale. The grace, dignity, and energy of the 8-foot-tall *Nike of Samothrace* can also be found in a bronze only 8½ inches tall (fig. 5-84). This figure of a heavily veiled and masked dancing woman twists sensually under the gauzy, layered fabric in a complex spiral movement. The dancer clearly represents an artful professional performer who would have been equally in demand for religious celebrations and secular court entertainments. Private patrons must have delighted in such intimate works, which were made in large

5-84. *Veiled and Masked Dancer.* Late 3rd or 2nd century BCE. Bronze, height 8⅛" (20.7 cm). The Metropolitan Museum of Art, New York
Bequest of Walter C. Baker, 1971 (1972.118.95)

5-85. *Market Woman.* 2nd century BCE. Marble, height 49½" (125.7 cm). The Metropolitan Museum of Art, New York
Rogers Fund, 1909 (09.39)

numbers and featured a wide variety of subjects and treatments. This bronze would have been costly, but many such graceful figurines were produced in inexpensive terra-cotta from preshaped molds and would have been accessible to a very broad market.

The appeal to the emotions in the sculpture at Pergamon signals a social change between the Classical and Hellenistic periods. In contrast to the Classical world, which was characterized by relative cultural unity and social homogeneity, the Hellenistic world was varied and multicultural. In this environment, artists turned from **idealism**, the quest for perfect form, to realism, the attempt to portray the world as it is. Portraiture, for example, became popular during the Hellenistic period, as did the representation of people from every level of

society. Patrons were fascinated by depictions of unusual physical types as well as of ordinary individuals.

A marble statue a little over 4 feet tall, which has long been called *Market Woman* (fig. 5-85), may represent a peasant woman on her way to the agora with three chickens and a basket of vegetables. Despite the bunched and untidy way the figure's dress hangs, it appears to be of an elegant design and made of fine fabric. The hair too bears some semblance of a once-careful arrangement. These characteristics, along with the woman's sagging lower jaw, unfocused stare, and lack of concern for her exposed breasts, have led some to speculate that she may represent an aging, dissolute follower of the wine god Dionysos on her way to make an offering. Whether an aging peasant or a Dionysian

5-86. *Aphrodite of Melos* (also called *Venus de Milo*). c. 150 BCE. Marble, height 6'10"
(2.1 m). Musée du Louvre, Paris

The original appearance of this famous statue's missing arms has been much
debated. When it was dug up in a field in 1820, some broken pieces found with
it (now lost) indicated that the figure was holding out an apple in its right hand.
Many judged these fragments to be part of a later restoration, not part of the
original statue. The image of Aphrodite admiring herself in the highly polished
shield of the war god Ares was popular in the second century BCE, so this figure
could have been holding a shield. If so, it would have been off to one side, tilted
at an angle, and probably resting on the goddess's left thigh. This theoretical
"restoration" seems to offer an explanation for the pronounced **S**-curve of the
pose and the otherwise unnatural forward projection of the knee.

celebrant, the subject of this work is the antithesis of the *Nike of Samothrace*. Yet, in formal terms, both sculpted figures are **expressionistic**. Both stretch out assertively into the space around them, both demand an emotional response from the viewer, and both display technical virtuosity in the rendering of forms and textures. They are closer to each other stylistically than either is to the *Nike Adjusting Her Sandal* or the *Aphrodite of Knidos* (see figs. 5-53, 5-64).

The Classical Alternative. Not all Hellenistic artists followed the trend toward realism and expressionism that characterized the artists of Pergamon and Rhodes. Some turned to the past, creating an eclectic style by reexamining and borrowing elements from earlier Classical styles and combining them with new elements. Certain popular sculptors, no doubt encouraged by patrons nostalgic for the past, looked back especially to Praxiteles and Lysippos for their models. This renewed interest in the style of the fourth century BCE is exemplified by the *Aphrodite of Melos* (fig. 5-86), found on the island of Melos by French excavators in the early nineteenth century. The sculpture was intended by its maker to recall the *Aphrodite* of Praxiteles (see fig. 5-64), and indeed the head with its dreamy gaze is very Praxitelean. The figure has the heavier proportions of High Classical sculpture, but the twisting stance and the strong projection of the knee are typical of Hellenistic art of the third century BCE and later. The drapery around the lower part of the body also has the rich, three-dimensional quality associated with the Hellenistic sculpture of Rhodes and Pergamon. The sensuous juxtaposition of nude flesh with the texture of draperies, which seem about to slip off the figure, adds a strong, insistent note of erotic tension that can only be Hellenistic in concept and intent.

Also illustrative of this eclectic trend, but using other sources, is the larger-than-lifesize *Hellenistic Ruler* (fig. 5-87), which may reflect the heroic figure types favored for official and religious sculpture by Lysippos in the lost statues of Zeus and Alexander the Great. Certainly the elongated body proportions and small head recall Lysippos's *Scraper* (see fig. 5-66). Yet the impression of Hellenistic realism overrides the lingering suggestions of Classical heroism and idealism. Hellenistic rulers often fancied themselves divine, and the overdeveloped musculature of this figure, the individualized features of the jowly face, and the arrogant pose suggest the unbridled power of an earthly ruler elevated to the status of a demigod.

By the late first century BCE, the influence of Greek painting, sculpture, and architecture was paramount in the artistic communities of the emerging Roman civilization. Roman patrons and artists maintained their enthusiasm for Greek art into early Christian times. Indeed, so strong was the urge to emulate the great Greek artists

5-87. *Hellenistic Ruler.* c. 150–140 BCE. Bronze, height 7'9" (2.37 m). Museo Nazionale Romano, Rome

that, as we have seen throughout this chapter, much of our knowledge of Greek achievements comes primarily through Roman replicas of Greek artworks and descriptions of Greek art by Roman-era writers.

Apollo
from Veii
c. 500

She-Wolf
c. 500–480

▲ ETRUSCAN SUPREMACY 700–509 ▲ REPUBLICAN PERIOD 509–27

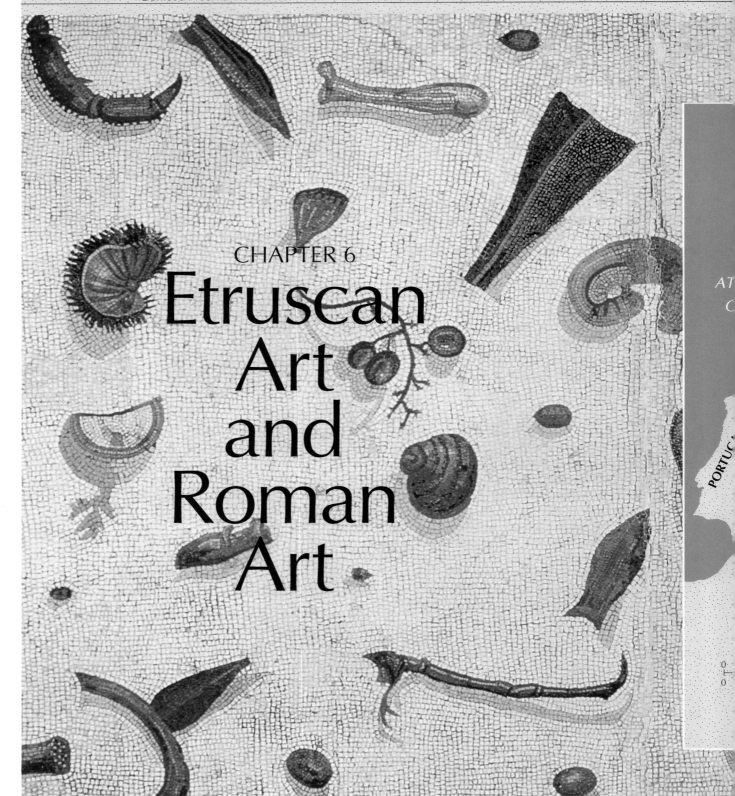

CHAPTER 6

Etruscan Art and Roman Art

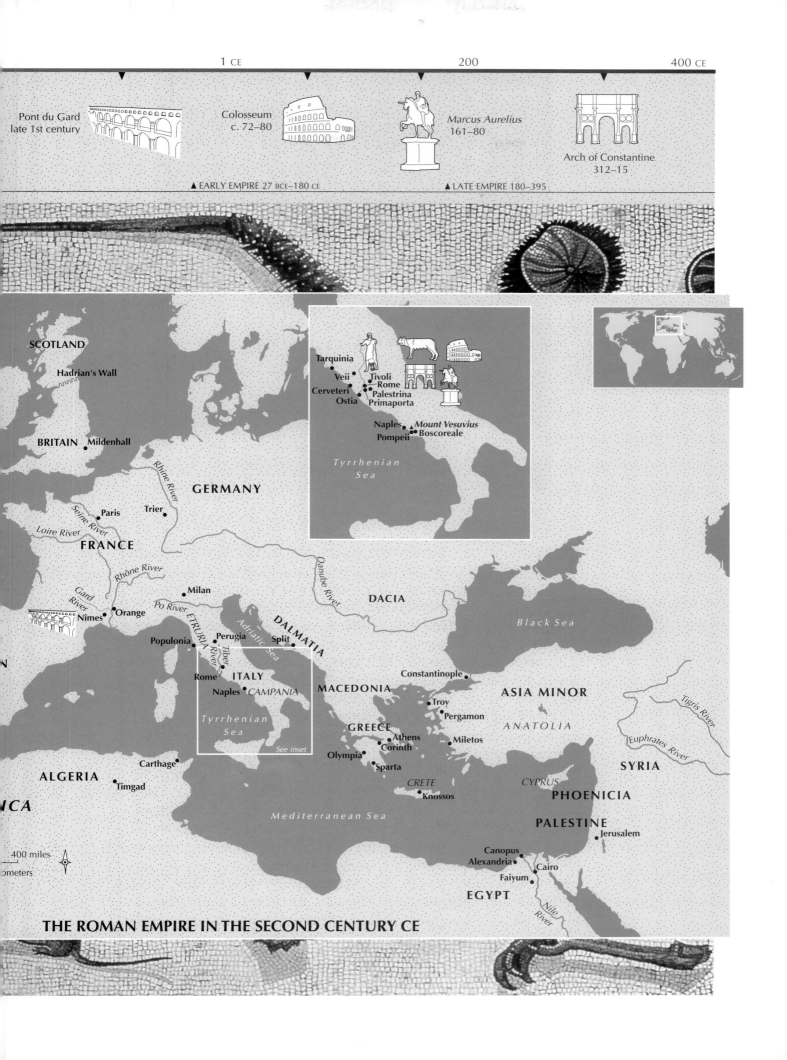

Timeline

1 CE	200	400 CE

Pont du Gard late 1st century

Colosseum c. 72–80

Marcus Aurelius 161–80

Arch of Constantine 312–15

▲ EARLY EMPIRE 27 BCE–180 CE   ▲ LATE EMPIRE 180–395

Map

SCOTLAND

Hadrian's Wall

BRITAIN   Mildenhall

GERMANY

Rhine River

Paris   Trier

Seine River

Loire River

FRANCE

Rhône River

Gard River

Nîmes   Orange

Milan

Po River

ETRURIA

Populonia

Perugia

Tiber River

Rome

ITALY

Naples   CAMPANIA

Tyrrhenian Sea

See inset

Carthage

ALGERIA

Timgad

NCA

400 miles

ometers

Danube River

DACIA

Adriatic Sea

DALMATIA

Split

MACEDONIA

Black Sea

Constantinople

ASIA MINOR

Troy

Pergamon

ANATOLIA

GREECE

Athens

Corinth

Miletos

Olympia

Sparta

CRETE

CYPRUS

Knossos

Tigris River

Euphrates River

SYRIA

PHOENICIA

PALESTINE

Jerusalem

Mediterranean Sea

Canopus

Alexandria   Cairo

Faiyum

EGYPT

Nile River

Inset

Tarquinia

Veii   Tivoli

Cerveteri   Rome

Ostia   Palestrina   Primaporta

Naples   Mount Vesuvius   Boscoreale

Pompeii

Tyrrhenian Sea

THE ROMAN EMPIRE IN THE SECOND CENTURY CE

6-1. *Cityscape*, detail of a Second Style wall painting from a bedroom in the House of Publius Fannius Synistor, Boscoreale. Late 1st century CE. The Metropolitan Museum of Art, New York

Rogers Fund, 1903 (03.14.13)

There must have been warning signs, that steamy August dawn in 79 CE, before the top of Mount Vesuvius exploded, spewing tiny fragments of volcanic rock, clouds of fine ash, and deadly gases over surrounding towns and farms and burying every trace of their existence. Those who fled took with them everything of value that could be carried. Those who stayed were quickly and completely entombed—the gladiator straining against his chains, the woman trying to shelter her child. In Pompeii, a popular resort for Roman patricians, some 2,000 people died. Among the eruption's victims was Pliny the Elder (23–79 CE), author of *Naturalis Historia* (*Natural History*), an encyclopedia of natural science, geography, and art. He was commander of the Roman fleet in the Tyrrhenian Sea and died from toxic gases while trying in vain to help those on shore. His nephew, Pliny the Younger, was also in the area but lived to describe the horror: "The sea appeared to have shrunk, . . . the shore had widened, and many sea creatures were beached on the sand. In the other direction loomed a horrible black cloud ripped by sudden bursts of fire, writhing snakelike and revealing sudden flashes larger than lightning. . . . And now came the ashes . . . " (*Letters to Tacitus* 6.16, 20).

Rain falling with the ashes created a "cement" that formed an airproof seal. Absolutely everything—people, plants, foods, houses and their contents, public buildings—was encased. The eruption was so powerful and the volcanic material so voluminous that the course of nearby rivers changed, and sea beaches were built up so much that the original site of Pompeii ended up farther from the sea, obscuring its original location for seventeen centuries. When the first excavators began to work, they found that even things that had disintegrated over time, such as flesh and wood, left perfect molds of their original shapes and textures in the solidified mass of volcanic material. Excavators devised methods for injecting plaster into such cavities and digging carefully around it to see what would be revealed—perhaps a man clutching his treasure, a hapless pet, or simply the root systems of garden plants and trees.

About three-fourths of Pompeii has now been excavated, and what has been revealed is a record of the material culture of first-century Roman civilization more detailed than any available for other early peoples. The fine examples of Republican buildings during a time of transition are especially remarkable. Most dramatic are the paintings on the walls of private dwellings. Some open "windows" onto bizarre urban landscapes that resemble stage sets (fig. 6-1), while others depict exotic rituals and dreamlike, sacred landscapes.

Pompeii's history—from its founding about 600 BCE by invaders who would later be overrun, to its becoming a Roman colony, to the disastrous moment it was frozen in time—mirrors that of the land from which it rose.

ETRUSCAN CIVILIZATION

The boot-shaped Italian peninsula, shielded to the north by the Alps, juts into the Mediterranean Sea, exposing its inhabitants in ancient times to the influence of Near Eastern, Egyptian, and Greek civilizations. Beginning about 750 BCE, Greek colonists dominated Italy's southern coastal regions. Between the seventh and sixth centuries BCE a people known as the Etruscans gained control of northern and much of central Italy. Central Italy was also home to a variety of peoples who spoke a closely related set of languages called Italic. Among these were the Latin-speaking inhabitants of Rome, a town on the Tiber River, who were, for a time, ruled by kings of Etruscan lineage. By the end of the first millennium BCE, the Romans had curtailed Etruscan power, unified Italy, and established an empire that encompassed the entire Mediterranean region.

Etruscan society emerged in the seventh century BCE in Etruria (modern Tuscany). No surviving examples of the Etruscans' literature have been found, but numerous inscriptions on tombs show that although their alphabet resembles the Greek alphabet, their language was apparently unrelated to any other European language. This linguistic distinctiveness for a long time made the Etruscans' origins a puzzle, but recent research suggests that they were the descendants of a people called the Villanovans, who had occupied the northern and western regions of Italy since the Bronze Age. Herodotus claimed that they had originally come from Lydia, in Asia Minor, in the twelfth century BCE.

Etruscan wealth was based on Etruria's fertile soil and abundance of metal ore. The Etruscans, who were noted as both metalworkers and sailors, exploited these resources in the close trading relations they maintained with the Greeks and with the Phoenicians, on the eastern coast of the Mediterranean Sea (in what is modern Lebanon). Organized into a loose federation of a dozen cities, including the major port of Populonia on the west coast of Italy, the Etruscans reached the height of their power in the sixth century BCE when they expanded into the Po River valley to the north and the Campania region to the south. Their power was in decline by the fifth century BCE, and by the third century BCE they had come within Rome's expanding dominion.

The Etruscans were deeply influenced by Greek culture except with respect to the role of women, who were better educated and more conspicuous in Etruscan than in Greek society, perhaps because of the prominence of female deities in Etruscan religion. Although Etruscan artists patronized Greek artists and drew inspiration from Greek and Near Eastern sources, they never slavishly copied what they admired. Instead, they assimilated these influences, combining them with their own traditions to create distinctive styles of architecture, sculpture, and wall painting. The Romans, too, borrowed heavily from the Greeks, and they also absorbed Etruscan culture, spreading Etruscan innovations in architecture and urban planning throughout their vast empire.

The Etruscan City

The Etruscan city was laid out on a grid plan around two main streets—one usually running north-south and the other east-west—that divided it into four sections, or quadrangles. The intersection of these streets was the town's business center, and residential areas spread out from it in all directions. Most cities were surrounded by walls with protective gates and towers. As a city's population grew, its boundaries expanded and building lots were added as needed, so that its overall plan was rarely

PARALLELS

Years	Period	Etruria/Rome	World
c. 800–700 BCE	Pre-Etruscan	Legendary founding of Rome; Greek colonies in southern Italy	**c. 800–700 BCE** Homer's *Iliad* and *Odyssey* (Greece); first Olympian Games (Greece); Greek alphabet adopted; Upanishads (India); fall of Zhou dynasty (China)
c. 700–509 BCE	Etruscan supremacy	Etruscan supremacy in central Italy; *Apollo* from Veii	**c. 700–500 BCE** Black-figure and red-figure vase painting (Greece); Byzantium founded; Sappho; Hanging Gardens (Babylon); birth of Laozi, founder of Daoism (China); Cyrus the Great (Persia) defeats Babylon; birth of Siddhartha Gautama, founder of Buddhism (Nepal); *Aesop's Fables* (Greece)
c. 509–27 BCE	Republican	Roman unification of Italy; Punic Wars (North Africa); invention of concrete; Sanctuary of Fortuna; Pont du Gard (Gaul); Cicero; Vergil	**c. 500–1 BCE** Greek orders; Confucius (China); Sophocles, Aeschylus, Euripides, Herodotus (Greece); last Old Testament book written; Polykleitos, Praxiteles, Lysippos (Greece); Parthenon (Greece); London founded (England); Alexander the Great (Greece) conquers Persia; Colossos of Rhodes; Han dynasty (China); unification of China; *Nike of Samothrace* (Greece); Great Wall (China); mound-building cultures (North America); *Ramayana* epic (India); *Aphrodite of Melos* (Greece)
c. 27 BCE–180 CE	Early Empire	Emperor Augustus; Ara Pacis; Horace; Julio-Claudian dynasties; Pliny the Elder; Colosseum; eruption of Vesuvius; Emperor Trajan; Emperor Hadrian; Pantheon; Tetrarchs; *Marcus Aurelius*; empire at greatest extent	**c. 1–400 CE** Crucifixion of Jesus (Jerusalem); Yayoi and Kofun eras (Japan); Maya civilization (Mesoamerica); first Gupta dynasty (India)
c. 180–395 CE	Late Empire	Severan emperors; Baths of Caracalla; Emperor Diocletian; Emperor Constantine; Constantinople established; Christianity becomes official religion of empire; empire permanently divided	

6-2. Porta Augusta, Perugia. 2nd century BCE

6-3. Reconstruction of an Etruscan temple, based on descriptions by Vitruvius. University of Rome, Istituto di Etruscologia e Antichità Italiche

the originally symmetrical walled quadrangles. Because the Etruscans created house-shaped funerary urns and decorated the interiors of tombs to resemble houses, we know that their houses were rectangular mud-brick structures built either around a central courtyard or around an **atrium**, a room with a shallow indoor pool for drinking, cooking, and bathing fed by rainwater through a large opening in the roof.

The second-century BCE city gate of Perugia, called the Porta Augusta, is one of the few surviving examples of Etruscan architecture (fig. 6-2). A tunnel-like passageway between two huge towers, this gate is significant for two features that anticipate developments in Roman architecture. One is the monumental **round arch**, which is extended into a semicircular ceiling, called a **barrel vault**, over the passageway. The other is the decorative **post-and-lintel** design superimposed on the plain face of the gate.

The round arch was not an Etruscan or Roman invention—ancient Near Eastern, Egyptian, and Greek builders had been familiar with it—but the Romans, apparently following Etruscan example, were the first to make widespread use of it (see "Elements of Architecture," page 226). Unlike the **corbeled** arch, formed when overhanging **courses** of masonry meet at the top, the round arch rises from **jambs**, or vertical stone supports, that border an opening. Precisely cut, wedge-shaped stone blocks called **voussoirs**, supported during construction by a temporary wooden frame, curve up and inward from the tops of the jambs and are locked into place by the insertion of the final voussoir, called the **keystone**, at the top center. The arch of the Porta Augusta, which consists of a double row of voussoirs, is set off by a square frame surmounted by a horizontal decorative element resembling an **entablature**. This is lined with a row of circular panels, or **roundels**, alternating with rectangular, columnlike uprights called **pilasters**. The effect is vaguely reminiscent of the **triglyphs** and **metopes** of a Greek Doric **frieze**. Above this entablaturelike element is a second, smaller arch opening, now filled in, that is flanked by tall pilasters.

6-4. Plan of an Etruscan temple, based on descriptions by Vitruvius

Temples and Their Decoration

From early on, the Etruscans incorporated Greek deities and heroic figures into their pantheon. They also may have adapted from ancient Mesopotamia the practice of using divination to predict, and possibly alter, future events. Beyond this, little is known about their religious beliefs and practices. All that remains of Etruscan temples is a few foundations. Knowledge of their appearance comes from ceramic **votive** models and from the writings of the Roman architect Vitruvius, who sometime between 46 and 39 BCE compiled descriptions of the Etruscan and Roman architecture of his day. His account indicates that Etruscan temples (fig. 6-3) were generally similar to Greek **prostyle** temples (see "Elements of Architecture," page 164). They were raised on a platform called a **podium** and had a single flight of steps leading up to a front porch. Columns and an entablature supported the section of roof that projected over the porch. The ground plan (fig. 6-4) was almost square

ELEMENTS OF ARCHITECTURE

Arch, Vault, and Dome

The basic arch used in Western architecture is the round arch, and the most elemental type of vaulting is the extension of the round arch, called a barrel vault. The round arch and barrel vault were known and were put to limited use by Mesopotamians and Egyptians long before the Etruscans began their experiments with building elements. But it was the Romans who realized the potential strength and versatility of these architectural features and exploited them to the fullest degree.

The **round arch** displaces most of the weight, or downward thrust (see arrows on diagrams), of the masonry above it to its curving sides and transmits that weight to the supporting uprights (door or window **jambs**, **columns**, or **piers**), and from there to the ground. Arches may require added support, called **buttressing**, from adjacent masonry elements. Brick or cut-stone arches are formed by fitting together wedge-shaped pieces, called **voussoirs**, until they meet and are locked together at the top center by the final piece, called the **keystone**. Until the mortar dries, an arch is held in place by wooden scaffolding, called **centering**. The inside surface of the arch is called the **intrados**, the outside curve of the arch the **extrados**. The points from which the curves of the arch rise, called **springings**, are often reinforced by masonry **imposts**. The wall areas adjacent to the curves of the arch are **spandrels**. In a succession of arches, called an **arcade**, the space encompassed by each arch and its supports is called a **bay**.

The **barrel vault** is constructed in the same manner as the round arch. The outside pressure exerted by the curving sides of the barrel vault usually requires buttressing within or outside the supporting walls. When two barrel-vaulted spaces intersect each other on the perpendicular, the result is a **groin vault**, or **cross vault**. The Romans used the groin vault to construct some of their grandest interior spaces, and they made the round arch the basis for their great freestanding triumphal arches.

A third type of vaulted ceiling brought to technical perfection by the Romans is the hemispheric **dome**. The rim of the dome is supported on a circular wall, as in the Pantheon (figs. 6-55, 6-56). This wall is called a **drum** when it is raised on top of a main structure. Often a circular opening, called an **oculus**, is left at the top.

round arch

barrel vault

groin vault

and divided equally between porch and interior space. Often, as in figure 6-4, the interior space was divided into three rooms that probably housed cult statues. The building was entered directly from a courtyard or open city square.

The basic construction material of an Etruscan temple was mud brick. The columns and entablatures were made of wood or a quarried volcanic rock called tufa, which hardens upon exposure to the air. The bases,

shafts (sometimes fluted), and capitals of the columns could resemble those of either the Greek Doric or the Greek Ionic orders, and the entablature had a frieze resembling that of the Doric order. Vitruvius used the term *Tuscan order* for the variation that resembled the Doric order, with an unfluted shaft and a simplified base, capital, and entablature (see "Elements of Architecture," below). Although Etruscan temples were stark and geometrically simple in form, they were embellished with

ELEMENTS OF ARCHITECTURE
Roman Architectural Orders

Both Greek and Roman orders—columns with their entablatures—are known as classical orders. Each order is made up of a system of interdependent parts whose proportions are based on mathematical ratios. In Greek and Roman architecture, no element of an order could be changed without producing a corresponding change in the other elements.

The Etruscans and Romans adapted Greek architectural orders to their own tastes and uses. For example, the Etruscans modified the Greek Doric order by adding a base to the column. The Romans created the **Composite order** by incorporating the **volute** motif of the Greek Ionic capital with other forms from the Greek Corinthian order. The sturdy, unfluted **Tuscan order**, also a Roman development, derived from the Greek Doric order by way of Etruscan models. In this diagram, the two Roman orders are shown on **pedestals**, which consist of a **plinth**, a **dado**, and a **cornice**.

Doric order   Ionic order   Corinthian order   Composite order   Tuscan order

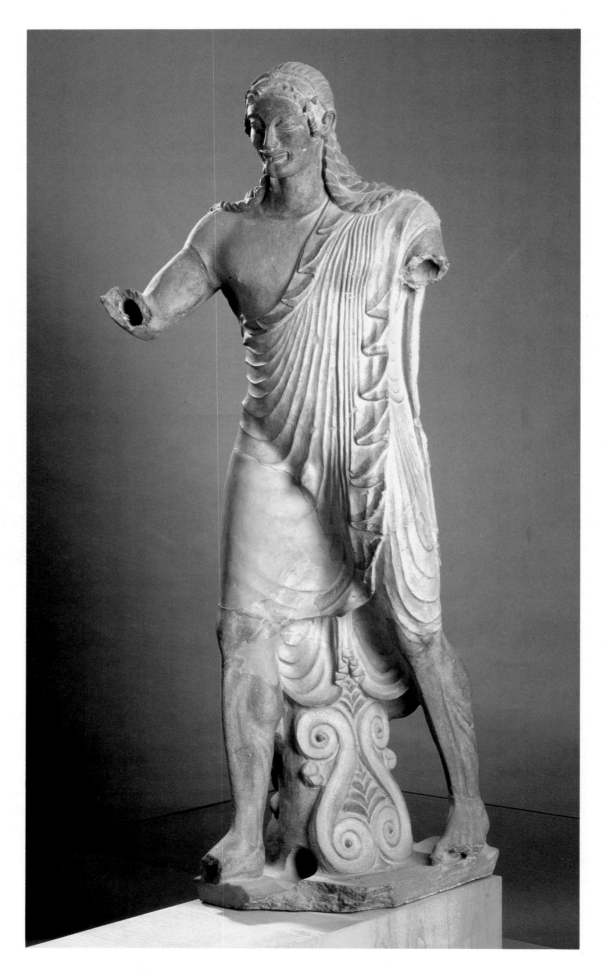

dazzling displays of terra-cotta sculpture. In an innovative feature, the temple roof served as a base for large statue groups.

Etruscan artists excelled at making monumental terra-cotta sculpture, a task of great technical and physical difficulty. A splendid example is a lifesize figure of Apollo. Dating from about 500 BCE and originally part of a four-figure scene depicting one of the labors of Hercules, the figure has survived from the temple at Veii (fig. 6-5). This scene showed Apollo and Hercules fighting for possession of a deer sacred to Diana while she and Mercury looked on (see "Roman Counterparts of Greek Gods," page 234). Apollo is shown in an active pose, looking as if he had just stepped over the decorative scrolled element that helps support the sculpture. This group of figures must have lent great vitality to the otherwise static appearance of the temple they graced.

The well-developed body form and the **Archaic smile** of the *Apollo* from Veii clearly demonstrate that Etruscan sculptors were familiar with the Greek Archaic period kouroi. A comparison of the *Apollo* and the nearly contemporary Greek *Kroisos* (see fig. 5-21) reveals differences as well as obvious similarities. Unlike the Greek figure, the body of the Etruscan *Apollo* is partially concealed by a robe with knife-edge pleats that cascades to his knees. The forward-moving pose of the Etruscan statue also has a vigor that is only implied in the balanced, tense stance of the Greek figure. This quality of energy expressed in purposeful movement is characteristic of Etruscan sculpture and, especially, tomb painting.

Tombs

Etruscan beliefs about the afterlife may have been somewhat similar to those of the Egyptians. Unlike the Egyptians, with their elaborate embalming techniques, the Etruscans favored cremation, but they nevertheless clearly thought of tombs as homes for the deceased. The Etruscan cemetery of La Banditaccia at Cerveteri (fig. 6-6) was laid out like a small town, with "streets" running between the grave mounds. The tomb chambers were partially or entirely excavated below the ground, and some were hewn out of bedrock. They were roofed over,

6-5. (opposite) *Apollo*, from Veii. c. 500 BCE. Painted terra-cotta, height 5'10" (1.8 m). Museo Nazionale di Villa Giulia, Rome

This lifesize figure is made of terra-cotta ("baked clay"), the same material used for pottery containers. Making and firing a large clay sculpture such as this one requires great technical skill. The artist must know how to construct the figures so that they do not collapse under their own weight while the clay is still wet and must know how to fire them, a process that requires precisely regulating the temperature in a large kiln for a long period of time. Etruscan terra-cotta artists must have been well known, for some of their names have come down to us, including that of a sculptor from Veii called Vulca, in whose workshop this *Apollo* may have been created.

6-6. Etruscan cemetery of La Banditaccia, Cerveteri. 7th–4th century BCE

6-7. Burial chamber, Tomb of the Reliefs, Cerveteri. 3rd century BCE

sometimes with corbeled vaulting, and covered with dirt and stones.

Some tombs were carved out of the rock to resemble rooms in a house. The Tomb of the Reliefs, for example, has a flat ceiling supported by square, stone posts (fig. 6-7). Its walls were plastered and painted, and it was provided with a full range of furnishings, some real, others simulated in **stucco**, a slow-drying type of plaster that can be easily modeled or molded. Pots, jugs, robes, axes, and other items were carved into the posts to look like real objects hanging on hooks. Rendered in **low relief** at the bottom of the center post is the family dog. As these details suggest, the Etruscans made every effort to provide earthly comforts for their dead, but tomb decorations also sometimes included frightening creatures from Etruscan mythology. On the back wall of the Tomb of the Reliefs is another kind of dog—a beast with many heads—that probably represents Cerberus, the guardian of the gates of the underworld, an appropriate funerary image.

6-8. Sarcophagus, from Cerveteri. c. 520 BCE. Terra-cotta, length 6'7" (2.06 m). Museo Nazionale di Villa Giulia, Rome

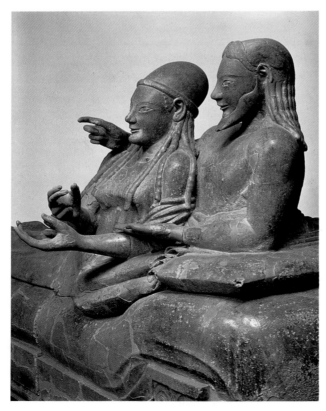

6-9. Detail of sarcophagus from Cerveteri

Sarcophagi, or coffins, also sometimes provided a domestic touch. In an example from Cerveteri of about 520 BCE, made entirely of terra-cotta (fig. 6-8), a husband and wife are shown reclining comfortably, as if they were on a couch. Rather than a cold, somber memorial to the dead, we see two lively, happy individuals rendered in sufficient detail to convey current hair and clothing styles (fig. 6-9). These genial hosts, with their smooth, conventionalized body forms and faces, their uptilted, almond-shaped eyes, and their benign smiles, make curious signs with their fingers, as if to communicate something important to the living viewer—perhaps an invitation to dine with them for eternity. Portrait coffins like this evolved from earlier terra-cotta cinerary jars with sculpted heads of the dead person whose ashes they held.

Brightly colored paintings of convivial scenes of feasting, dancing, musical performances, athletic contests, hunting, fishing, and other pleasures sometimes decorate tomb walls. Many of these murals are faded and flaking, but those on the tombs at Tarquinia are well preserved. In a detail of a painted frieze in the Tomb of the Lionesses, from about 480–470 BCE, a young man and woman engage in an energetic dance to the music of a double flute (fig. 6-10). These and other figures are grouped around the walls within a carefully arranged setting of stylized trees, birds, fish, animals, and architectural elements. Unlike in Greek tomb paintings,

6-10. *Musicians and Dancers*, detail of a wall painting, Tomb of the Lionesses, Tarquinia. C. 480–470 BCE

The Etruscan method of painting decorations on walls has often been called fresco, but there are continuing doubts as to whether that designation is correct. Fresco is essentially painting with water-based pigments on a still-damp layer of fresh plaster applied in sections over a finished wall surface. The pigment soaks in and becomes an integral part of the plaster coating. Laboratory analyses to determine whether or not Etruscan wall paintings are true frescoes have been inconclusive. Some investigators think they are frescoes, while others claim that sections that appear to be fresco resulted from the artist accidentally painting on a wall before the plaster had dried.

women are active participants. The Etruscan painters had a remarkable ability to suggest that their subjects inhabit a bright, tangible world just beyond the tomb walls. The dancers and musicians seem to be here with us now, performing exuberantly, not enacting the formal rituals of a remote, long-dead civilization.

Bronze Work

The skill of Etruscan artists who worked in bronze was widely acknowledged in ancient times. Especially im-pressive are the few examples of large-scale **sculpture in the round** that have survived the wholesale recycling of bronze objects over the centuries. One of these bronzes, which dates to about 500 BCE, portrays a she-wolf (fig. 6-11). This creature, with her open, snarling mouth, lean, tense body, thin flanks, protruding ribs, and heavy, milk-filled teats—evidence that she has recently given birth—appears at the same time ferocious and an object of sympathy. The naturalistic rendering of these details contrasts with the decorative, stylized rendering of the tightly curled ruff of fur around the animal's neck,

6-11. *She-Wolf.* c. 500–480 BCE. Bronze, height 33½" (85 cm). Museo Capitolino, Rome

Although this sculpture was almost certainly the work of an Etruscan artist, it has long been associated with Rome. According to an ancient Roman legend, twin infants named Romulus and Remus, who had been abandoned on the banks of the Tiber River by a wicked uncle and left there to die, were suckled by a she-wolf that had come to the river to drink. The twins were raised by a shepherd, and when they grew up, they decided to build a city near the spot where they had been rescued by the wolf. They quarreled, however, about its exact location. Romulus killed Remus and then established a small settlement that would become the great city of Rome, an event that, according to tradition, occurred in 753 BCE. Romulus ruled the city for forty years as its first king. Long after the Roman Empire had fallen, the people living in Rome, who remembered the legend, installed the *She-Wolf* on the Capitoline Hill. During the Renaissance, castings of Romulus and Remus as suckling infants were added to this original statue, which remains on the Capitoline Hill to this day in a museum—a symbol of the city's 2,000-year history. Sometimes it is referred to as the *Capitoline Wolf* or the *Wolf of Rome.*

which was incised with a sharp cutting tool. The eyes, made of glass paste, were inserted after the figure was cast and incised.

After Etruria had fallen within Rome's orbit, Etruscan artists continued in high regard and gained the support of Roman patrons. A head that was once part of a bronze statue of a man may be an example of an important Roman commission (fig. 6-12). Often alleged to be a portrait of Lucius Junius Brutus, the founder and first consul of the Roman Republic (in 509 BCE), the head traditionally has been dated about 300 BCE, long after Brutus's death. Although it may represent an unknown Roman dignitary of the third century BCE, it could also be an imaginary portrait of an ancient hero (perhaps Brutus), a type of sculpture that gained great popularity in the first century BCE. The rendering of the strong, broad face with

its heavy brows, firmly set lips, and wide-open eyes (made of painted ivory) is scrupulously detailed. The sculptor seems also to have sought to convey the psychological complexity of the subject, showing him as a somewhat world-weary man who nevertheless projects strong character and great strength of purpose. We saw a similar approach to portraiture in the statue of the Egyptian ruler Senwosret III (see fig. 3-24) made some fifteen centuries earlier.

Etruscan bronze workers also created small items for either funerary or domestic use, such as a bronze mirror that dates from about 350 BCE (fig. 6-13). The subject of the decoration engraved on the back is a winged man, identified by the inscription as the Greek priest Calchas, who accompanied the legendary army of Greek heroes under Agamemnon to Troy (see "The Trojan War," page

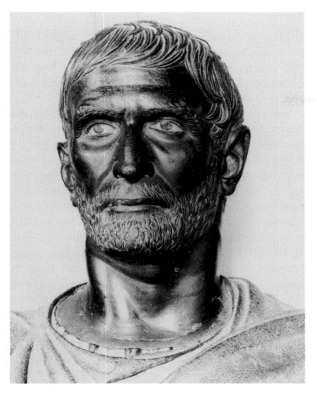

6-12. Head of a man. c. 300 BCE. Bronze, height 12½"
(31.8 cm). Palazzo dei Conservatori, Rome

6-13. Mirror. c. 350 BCE. Engraved bronze, diameter 6"
(15.3 cm). Musei Vaticani, Museo Gregoriano Etrusco,
Rome

One of the methods the Etruscans used to attempt to predict the future involved interpreting the signs found in the entrails and organs, especially the liver, of sacrificial animals. That is the unusual subject engraved on the back of this sumptuous bronze mirror. Etruscan diviners (fortune tellers) would not only determine the meaning of what they saw in the animal entrails, they would also suggest a course of action to take according to whether the omens were good or bad.

216). According to Homer, the Greeks often consulted Calchas when they were uncertain about the gods' will or how to secure their favor in the war. Greeks, Etruscans, and Romans all believed the appearance of animal entrails could reveal the future. Here Calchas is shown bending over a table, intently studying the liver of a sacrificed animal, possibly a reference to an incident in the legend of the Trojan War in which Calchas, called upon to determine why the Greek fleet had been left becalmed on its way to Troy, told Agamemnon that he had to sacrifice his daughter Iphigenia. In another legend, Calchas retired after the war to his vineyards, where he died an ironic death, laughing at a prophecy that he would not live to drink his own wine. Perhaps alluding to this story, the artist has shown Calchas surrounded by grapevines and with a jug at his feet. The complex pose, the naturalistic suggestions of a rocky setting, and the pull and twist of drapery that emphasize the figure's three-dimensionality convey a sense of realism. About the time that this mirror was created, southern Etruria fell under the dominance of Rome, whose march to total control of the Italian peninsula was well under way.

ROMAN CIVILIZATION

At its greatest extent in the early second century CE, the Roman Empire reached from the Euphrates River to North Africa to Scotland. The vast territory ringed the Mediterranean Sea—*mare nostrum*, or "our sea," the Romans called it. As the Romans absorbed the peoples they conquered, they imposed on them a legal, administrative, and cultural structure that endured for some five centuries—in the eastern Mediterranean until the fifteenth century—leaving a lasting mark on the civilizations that emerged in Europe and elsewhere in their wake.

The people responsible for these accomplishments not surprisingly saw themselves in heroic terms and attributed heroic origins to themselves. According to one popular legend, rendered in epic verse by the poet Vergil (70–19 BCE) in his *Aeneid*, the Roman people were the offspring of a Trojan survivor of the Trojan War. This hero, Aeneas, was the mortal son of the goddess Venus. Thanks to his mother's intervention with Jupiter, the king of the gods, he and some compatriots escaped from the burning Troy and made their way to Italy. There they gave life to the race that, in fulfillment of a promise by Jupiter to Venus, was destined to rule the world. Another popular legend tells the story of Rome's founding by Romulus and Remus, the twin sons of Mars, the god of war, by a mortal princess from the central Italian city of Alba Longa (see caption, fig. 6-11).

Archeologists and historians have developed a more mundane picture of Rome's origins. In Neolithic times, groups of people who spoke a common language—Latin—and lived primarily by raising and tending sheep settled in permanent villages across the plains of Latium, south of the Tiber River, as well as on the seven hills that would eventually become Rome (the Palatine, Aventine, Caelian, Capitoline, Esquiline, Quirinal, and Viminal). These first settlements were little more than

200 BCE
800 BCE   400 CE

REIGNS OF SIGNIFICANT ROMAN EMPERORS

	Augustus	27 BCE–14 CE
Julio-Claudian	Tiberius	14–37 CE
	Caligula	37–41
	Claudius	41–54
	Nero	54–68
Flavian	Vespasian	69–79
	Titus	79–81
	Domitian	81–96
	Nerva	96–98
	Trajan	98–117
	Hadrian	117–138
Antonine	Antoninus Pius	138–161
	Marcus Aurelius	161–180
	Commodus	180–192
Severan	Septimius Severus	193–211
	Caracalla	211–217
	Severus Alexander	222–235
	Diocletian	284–305
	Constantine I	306–337

ROMAN COUNTERPARTS OF GREEK GODS

Roman Name	Greek God
Jupiter	Zeus, king of the gods
Juno	Hera, Zeus's wife and sister, queen of the gods
Minerva	Athena, goddess of wisdom
Mars	Ares, god of war
Apollo; also Phoebus	Apollo, god of the sun and reason
Venus	Aphrodite, goddess of love
Diana	Artemis, goddess of the moon and hunting
Mercury	Hermes, messenger of the gods
Pluto	Hades, god of the underworld
Bacchus	Dionysos, god of wine
Vulcan	Hephaistos, god of fire
Vesta	Hestia, goddess of hearth and family
Ceres	Demeter, goddess of agriculture
Neptune	Poseidon, god of the sea
Cupid or Amor	Eros, god of love
Hercules	Herakles

Although sometimes worshiped as a god, strictly speaking Hercules is a hero known for his physical strength.

More information about Greek gods and their attributes appears on page 156, "Greek and Roman Deities and Heroes."

clusters of small, round huts, but by the sixth century BCE Rome, located at an important crossing of the Tiber, had developed into a major transportation hub and trading center. By the Republican period nearly a million people lived there.

Early Rome was governed by a series of kings and an advisory body of leading citizens called the Senate. The population was divided into two classes, a wealthy and powerful upper class, the patricians, and a lower class, the plebeians. The last kings of Rome were members of an Etruscan family, the Tarquins. Legend has it that the last ruler in this line, Tarquinius Superbus, was a despot whose behavior led to his overthrow in 509 BCE, marking the beginning of what is known as the Republican period. The Senate, dominated by patrician families, gained in prestige and authority, and the early history of the Republic was marked by a struggle by plebeians against patricians for political and economic equality.

During the fifth century BCE, by a process of alliance and conquest, Rome began to incorporate neighboring territories in Italy. By 275 BCE Rome controlled the entire Italian peninsula. This expansion led to a confrontation with the powerful empire of Carthage, the Phoenician city on the north coast of Africa, which controlled Spain, Sicily, and the western North African coast. In a series of conflicts known as the Punic Wars (264–146 BCE), the Romans ultimately subdued the Carthaginians, destroyed Carthage, and gained control of the western Mediterranean. By the mid-second century BCE they had subdued Macedonia and Greece, and by 44 BCE had conquered most of Gaul (modern France) and the eastern Mediterranean.

During this period of overseas expansion, Rome changed from an essentially agricultural society to a commercial and political power. The warfare and expansion strained Rome's political system, weakening the authority of the Senate and leading ultimately to a series of civil wars among powerful generals whose authority derived from the support of their troops. In 46 BCE Julius Caesar emerged victorious over his rivals, had himself declared dictator, assumed autocratic powers, and ruled Rome until his assassination in 44 BCE. The renewed fighting that followed Caesar's death ended with the unquestioned supremacy of his grandnephew and heir, Octavian, over Rome and all its possessions.

Although Octavian maintained the forms of Republican government, he retained real authority for himself, and his ascension marks the end of the Republic. In 27 BCE he was granted the religious title *Augustus*, which came to mean "supreme ruler," and he is known to history by that name as the first emperor of Rome (see "Reigns of Significant Roman Emperors," above). Assisted by his astute and pragmatic second wife, Livia, Augustus proved to be an incomparable administrator. He brought opposing factions under his control and established efficient rule throughout the empire. In 12 CE he was given the title *Pontifex Maximus*, or High Priest, and thus also became the empire's highest religious official. After his death in 14 CE, the Senate ordered him to be venerated as a state god. This powerful man laid the foundation for an extended period of stability, internal peace, and economic prosperity known as the *Pax Romana*—the Roman Peace—which lasted about 200 years.

Conquering and maintaining a vast empire required not only inspired leadership and tactics but also careful planning, massive logistical support, and great administrative skill. Some of Rome's most enduring contributions to Western civilization—its system of law, its governmental and administrative structures, and its enormous construction of civil architecture—reflect these qualities.

To facilitate the development and administration of the empire, as well as to make city life comfortable and attractive to its citizens, the Roman government undertook building programs of unprecedented scale and complexity, mandating the construction of central administrative centers (**basilicas**), racetracks (**circuses** and **stadiums**), theaters, public baths, roads, bridges, **aqueducts**, middle-class housing, and even whole new towns. To accomplish these tasks without sacrificing beauty, efficiency, and human well-being, Roman builders and architects developed rational planning, durable materials, and highly sophisticated engineering methods.

To move their armies about efficiently, speed communications between Rome and the farthest reaches of the empire, and promote commerce, the Romans built a vast and sophisticated network of roads. Many modern European highways still follow the lines laid down by Roman engineers, and Roman-era foundations underlie the streets of more than a few cities. Roman bridges are still in use, and remnants of Roman aqueducts need only repairs and connecting links to make them function once again to carry fresh water over long distances.

Despite their power, the Romans liked to portray themselves as simple country folk who had never lost their love of nature. Even though they were essentially city dwellers, the wealthy maintained country estates and the middle classes enjoyed their town-home gardens. Similar to United States presidents like George Washington and Thomas Jefferson, who returned regularly to their estates, many Roman emperors were attached to country villas, which served them both as functioning farms and as places of recreation. Wealthy Romans even brought nature indoors by commissioning artists to paint landscapes on the interior walls of their homes. As these wealthy Romans developed an ever more luxurious life, however, the cost of the expanding empire became an increasing burden on the less fortunate, which eventually led to the occurrence of intermittent internal conflict.

Like the Etruscans, the Romans greatly admired Greek and Hellenistic culture and borrowed heavily from it. Historians have even suggested that although Rome conquered the Hellenistic world, Greek culture conquered Roman culture. The Romans used Greek orders to decorate their architecture, imported Greek art, and employed Greek artists. In 146 BCE they stripped the Greek city of Corinth of its art treasures and shipped them back to Rome.

Ironically, this love of Greek art was not accompanied by universal admiration for artists. As Plutarch, a Greek commentator of the first century CE, wrote: "No gifted young man, upon seeing the Zeus of Pheidias at Olympia, ever wanted to be Pheidias nor, upon seeing the Hera at Argos, ever wanted to be Polykleitos. . . . For it does not necessarily follow that, if a work is delightful because of its gracefulness, the man who made it is worthy of our serious regard." Although there must have been significant exceptions, professional artists were generally considered little more than skilled laborers.

Again like the Etruscans, the Romans adopted the Greek gods and heroes as their own. (This chapter uses the Roman names of these figures; see "Roman Counterparts of Greek Gods," opposite.) The Romans assimilated Greek religious beliefs and practices into a form of state religion. When, after Augustus, the emperors were deified—in part to attract and focus the allegiance of the culturally diverse populations that had come under Roman rule—the state religion took on a highly political cast. Worship of ancient gods was mingled with homage to past rulers and oaths of allegiance to the living one, and the official religion became increasingly ritualized, perfunctory, and distant from the everyday life of the average person. As a result, many Romans adopted the more personal, mystical religious beliefs of the peoples they had conquered. The cult of Isis and Osiris was introduced from Egypt; from Anatolia came the cult of the Great Mother; and belief in the all-powerful God of Judaism and Christianity spread from Palestine. In the third century CE, an exclusively male cult of a Persian hero-god called Mithras also became popular, especially with the soldier-emperors and their troops. All these so-called mystery religions flourished alongside the state religion with its Olympian deities and deified emperors, despite occasional government efforts to suppress them.

ART OF THE REPUBLICAN PERIOD AND THE BEGINNING OF THE EMPIRE

During the Republic, the first great period of Roman architecture, sculpture, and painting initially reflected Etruscan influences. As the empire expanded, exposure to the art of Greece and of other cultures began to be reflected in increasingly eclectic styles. Although Roman architects built religious buildings, palaces, and tombs for the rich and powerful, they were also concerned with satisfying the needs of ordinary people in the large and varied population of their empire. To meet those needs as efficiently and inexpensively as possible, they created new building forms, discovered new structural principles, and developed new materials.

Architecture in Roman Italy

Roman architects relied heavily on the round arch and barrel vaulting. Beginning in the second century BCE, they also relied increasingly on a new building material, cast **concrete** (see "Elements of Architecture," page 236). In

6-14. Sanctuary of Fortuna, Palestrina. Begun c. 100 BCE

ELEMENTS OF ARCHITECTURE

Roman Construction

The Romans were pragmatic, and their pragmatism extended from recognizing and exploiting undeveloped potential in construction methods and physical materials to organizing large-scale building works. Their exploitation of the arch and the vault is typical of their adapt-and-improve approach. Their "invention" and use of **concrete**, beginning in the first century BCE, was a technological breakthrough of the greatest importance.

In the earliest concrete wall construction, workers filled a framework of rough stones with concrete: stone rubble soaked in a binder made from volcanic sand and clay. This stone-wall construction method, called *opus incertum*, was followed by *opus reticulatum*, in which the framework is a diagonal web of smallish, pyramidal con-

crete bricks set in a cross pattern. By the first century CE, Roman builders were setting concrete bricks in level courses, pointed ends inward, in a technique called *opus testaceum*.

The composite-material bricks were homely and were generally covered, or **veneered**, with better-looking materials, such as marble, stone, mosaic, and tile. Thus, an essential difference between Greek and Roman architecture is that Greek buildings reveal the building material itself, whereas Roman buildings show only the applied surface.

Concrete-based construction freed the Romans from the limits of right-angle forms and comparatively short spans. With this freedom, Roman builders pushed the established limits of architecture, creating some very large and highly original spaces, many based on the curve.

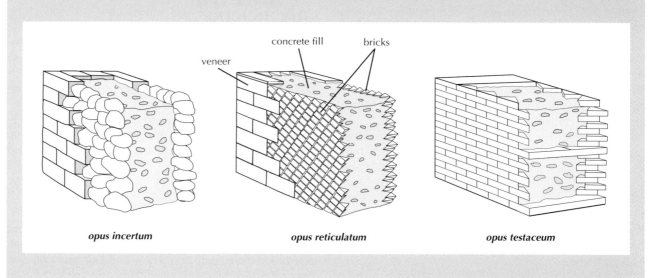

opus incertum   *opus reticulatum*   *opus testaceum*

6-15. Axonometric reconstruction drawing of the Sanctuary of Fortuna, showing the seven terraces

contrast to stone—which was expensive, time-consuming to quarry, and difficult to transport, cut to size, and set in place—the components of concrete were cheap, light, and easily transported. Stone structures required skilled workers, whereas concrete structures could be built by a large, semiskilled work force directed by one or two trained and experienced supervisors.

Roman concrete consisted of powdered lime, sand (in particular a volcanic sand called pozzolana found in abundance near Pompeii), and various types of rubble, such as small rocks and broken pottery. These were mixed with water, causing a chemical reaction that hardened them into a strong, solid mass. At first concrete was used mainly for poured foundations, but with technical advances it became indispensable for the construction of walls, arches, and vaults for ever larger buildings. Its one weakness was that it absorbed moisture, so builders covered exposed concrete surfaces with a veneer of brick or cut stone; then they often added an overlay of plaster for good measure.

After World War II, teams clearing the rubble from bombings of Palestrina, about 16 miles southeast of Rome, discovered the remains of the Sanctuary of Fortuna, an example of Roman Republican architectural planning and concrete construction at its most creative (figs. 6-14, 6-15). The sanctuary, dedicated to the goddess of fate and chance, was begun about 100 BCE and was grander than any building in Rome in its time. Its design and size show the clear influence of Hellenistic architecture, such as the long colonnade and the co-

lossal scale of the great altar from Pergamon (see fig. 5-80). Built of concrete covered with a veneer of stucco and finely cut limestone, it consists of a series of open, partially open, and closed spaces on seven vaulted platforms or terraces that rise up a steep hillside. Worshipers ascended long ramps to the second level, then steep staircases to successively higher levels.

In a departure from Hellenistic style, the Romans incorporated several rounded elements that relieved the structure's strict regularity and created a new kind of architectural rhythm: symmetrically placed **exedrae** (half-circle niches) on the fourth level, rows of round-arch openings on the fifth and sixth levels, and finally, on the seventh level, a huge, theaterlike, semicircular colonnaded pavilion reached by a broad semicircular staircase from a large, open terrace. Behind this pavilion was a small **tholos** temple to Fortuna, hiding the ancient rock-cut cave where important acts of divination, predicting future events, had taken place from early times. The overall **axial** plan—the way it directs movement from the large, open terrace up the semicircular staircase, through the portico, to the tiny tholos temple, to the cave—brings to mind the great Egyptian temples, such as that of Hatshepsut at Deir el-Bahri (see fig. 3-33).

More typical of Roman religious architecture than isolated, walled sanctuaries like those favored by the Greeks were small urban temples built, in the Etruscan manner, in the midst of congested commercial centers. An early example in Rome, nearly contemporary with the Sanctuary of Fortuna, is a small, rectangular temple

6-16. Temple perhaps dedicated to Portunus, Forum Boarium (cattle market), Rome. Late 2nd century BCE

6-17. Plan of the temple perhaps dedicated to Portunus

perhaps dedicated to Portunus, the god of harbors and ports, that stands beside the Tiber River (figs. 6-16, 6-17). With a rectangular **cella** and a porch at one end reached by a single flight of steps, this temple, built in the late second century BCE, echoes the Greek prostyle plan. Almost like a piece of sculpture, it stands on a raised platform, or podium. The Ionic columns are freestanding on the porch and **engaged** around the cella. The entablature above the columns on the porch continues around the cella as a decorative frieze. The plan of this structure resembles that of a **peripteral** temple, but because the columns around the cella are engaged even though they appear to be freestanding, it is called **pseudo-peripteral**. This design, with variations in the orders used with it, was to become standard for Roman temples.

City Life and Domestic Architecture

Pompeii was a thriving center of about 20,000 inhabitants on the day Mount Vesuvius erupted. An ancient village that had grown and spread over many centuries, it lacked the gridlike regularity of newer Roman cities, but its layout was typical for its time. Temples and government buildings surrounded a main square, or **forum**; paved streets were lined with shops and houses; and enclosing all was a protective wall with fortified gates (fig. 6-18). The forum was the center of civic life in Roman towns and cities, as the **agora** was in Greek cities. Business was conducted in its basilicas and pavilions, religious duties performed in its temples, and

6-18. Plan of the city of Pompeii in 79 CE

6-19. Reconstruction drawing and plan of the House of Pansa, Pompeii. 2nd century BCE

speeches presented in its open square. For recreation, people went to the nearby baths or the events in the amphitheater.

The people of Pompeii lived in houses behind or above a row of shops, or in two- or three-story apartment buildings, or in gracious private residences with one or more gardens. Even upper-class homes often had street-level shops. If there was no shop, the wall facing the street was usually solid except for the door, an indication of the emphasis on interior rather than exterior design. In a sense, the inner orientation of domestic architecture reflects the central and sacred place of hearth and home in Roman religion.

A Roman house usually consisted of small rooms laid out on a straight, generally symmetrical plan, as illustrated in the reconstruction drawing of the House of Pansa in Pompeii (fig. 6-19). From the entrance, a corridor led to the atrium, a large space with a shallow pool for catching rainwater through an opening in the roof. The organization of the front part of the house—the centrally located atrium surrounded by small rooms—originated with the Etruscans. Figure 6-20 shows the atrium

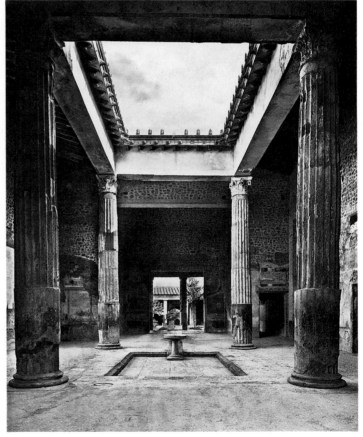

6-20. Atrium, House of the Silver Wedding, Pompeii. Early 1st century CE

Ancient Roman houses excavated at Pompeii and elsewhere are usually named after the families or individuals who once lived in them. In many cases, the owner is unknown. This house received its unusual name as a commemorative gesture. It was excavated in 1893, the year of the silver wedding anniversary of Italy's King Humbert and his wife, Margaret of Savoy, who had supported archeological fieldwork at Pompeii.

THE URBAN GARDEN

The remains of urban gardens preserved in the volcanic fallout at Pompeii have been the focus of a decades-long study by archeologist Wilhelmina Jashemski. Her work has revealed much about the layout of ancient Roman gardens and the plants cultivated in them. Early archeologists, searching for more tangible remains, usually destroyed evidence about gardens, but in 1973 Jashemski and her colleagues had the opportunity to work on the previously undisturbed **peristyle** garden—a planted interior court enclosed by columns—of the House of G. Polybius in Pompeii. Workers first removed layers of debris and volcanic material to expose the level of the soil as it was before the eruption in 79 CE. They then collected samples of pollen, seeds, and other organic material and carefully injected plaster into underground root cavities to make casts for later study. These materials enabled botanists to identify the types of plants and trees cultivated in the garden, to estimate their size, and to determine where they had been planted. Some houses had both peristyle gardens and separate vegetable gardens.

The evidence from this and other excavations indicates that most urban gardens served a practical function. They were planted with fruit- and nut-bearing trees and occasionally with olive trees. Only the great luxury gardens were rigidly landscaped. Most gardens were randomly planted or, at best, arranged in irregular rows.

The garden in the house of Polybius was surrounded on three sides by a portico, which protected a large cistern on one side that supplied the house and garden with water. Young lemon trees in pots lined the fourth side of the garden, and nail holes in the wall above the pots indicated that the trees had been espaliered—pruned and trained—a practice still in use today. Fig, cherry, and pear trees filled the garden space, and traces of a fruit-picking ladder, wide at the bottom and narrow at the top to fit among the branches, was found on the site. This evidence suggests

Wall niche, from a garden in Pompeii. Mid-1st century CE. Mosaic, 43¾ x 31½" (111 x 80 cm). Fitzwilliam Museum, University of Cambridge, England

that the garden was a densely planted orchard similar to the one painted on the dining-room walls of the villa of the empress Livia in Primaporta (see fig. 6-36).

An aqueduct built during the reign of the emperor Augustus gave Pompeii's residents access to a reliable and plentiful supply of water, replacing their dependence on wells and rainwater basins. This new source allowed them to add pools, fountains, and flowering plants that needed large amounts of water to their gardens. In contrast to the earlier, unordered plantings, formal gardens with low, clipped borders and plantings of ivy, ornamental box-

wood, laurel, myrtle, acanthus, and rosemary—all mentioned by writers of the time—became fashionable. There is also evidence of topiary work, the clipping of shrubs and hedges into fanciful shapes. Sculpture and purely decorative fountains became popular. The peristyle garden of the House of the Vettii, for example, had more than a dozen fountain statues jetting water into marble basins (fig. 6-21). In the most elegant peristyles, mosaic decorations covered the floors, walls, and even the fountains. Some of the earliest wall mosaics, such as the one illustrated here, were created as backdrops for fountains.

in the well-preserved House of the Silver Wedding in Pompeii. Beyond the atrium, in a reception room called the tablinum, portrait busts of the family's ancestors might be displayed, and the head of the household conferred with clients. In later houses the tablinum often opened onto a central peristyle court, surrounded by a colonnaded walkway, or portico. The more private areas—such as the dining room, the family sitting room, bedrooms, the kitchen, and servants' quarters—usually were entered through the peristyle court.

Roman houses reflect architectural ideals seen also in monumental and public construction. The Romans, with their love of nature, softened the abstract regularity of their homes with beautifully planted gardens in the peristyle court (see "The Urban Garden," opposite). Larger residences also had a separate kitchen garden. In Pompeii, where the mild southern climate would have permitted gardens to flourish year-round, the peristyle court was often turned into an outdoor living room with wall murals, fountains, and sculpture on pedestals, as in the House of the Vettii (fig. 6-21), which dates from the mid-first century CE.

6-21. Peristyle garden, House of the Vettii, Pompeii. Mid-1st century CE

Architecture in the Provinces

In many areas of Europe and the Mediterranean, impressive examples of Roman engineering still stand, powerful reminders of Rome's rapid spread and enduring impact. The Pont du Gard near Nîmes in southern France has a 900-foot span and rises 180 feet above the Gard River (fig. 6-22). Still in use in the twentieth century as a bridge for pedestrians and carts, it was originally an aqueduct, part of a system that brought water to Nîmes from the springs of Uzès 30 miles to the north. This feat of hydraulic engineering, impressive even by modern standards, is thought to have been executed under the direction of Augustus's son-in-law Agrippa about 20 BCE. At the time it was built, the aqueduct could provide 100 gallons of water a day for every person in Nîmes.

6-22. Pont du Gard, Nîmes, France. Late 1st century BCE

6-23. Maison
Carrée,
Nîmes,
France.
c. 20 BCE

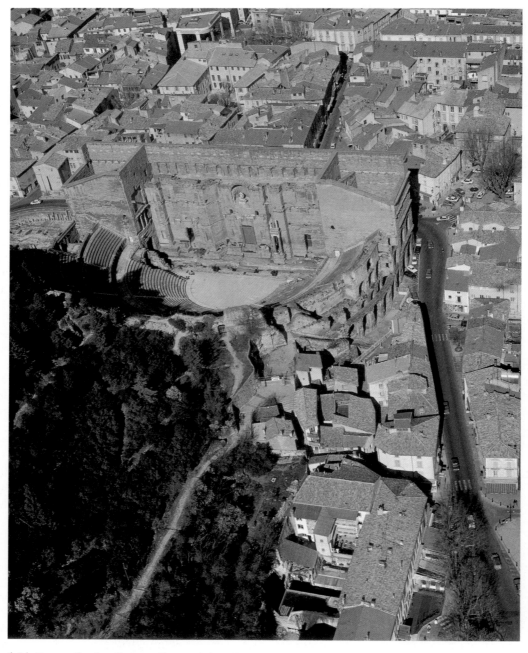

6-24. Roman theater, Orange, France. 1st century BCE

Because of renovations, plays can still be staged at this theater, one of the rare Roman theaters still being used for its original purpose.

ROMAN FUNERARY PRACTICES Like the Etruscans, the early Romans generally cremated their dead and placed the ashes in special cinerary urns or vases. Unlike the Etruscans, however, they made no effort to provide an earthly domestic setting for the deceased. Instead, they frequently kept the ash containers, together with busts and casts from death masks of their ancestors and family documents, on view in their homes, often in a room called the tablinum at one end of the atrium.

In Rome related individuals or members of social clubs and other organizations established private group cemeteries. When a group's members had used up the ground-level space in their cemetery, they tunneled underground to create a **hypogeum**, or **catacomb**. The tunnels extended from one edge of the cemetery property to the other, descending to another level as space filled up. They were lined with niches for urns and busts of the dead and opened into small side chambers called **cubicula**.

The Romans memorialized their dead in elaborate funeral celebrations and left small offerings at their grave sites every February. They revered their ancestors and kept death masks as a way of remembering them. Pliny the Elder, writing in the first century CE, describes this practice: "Wax impressions of the face were set out on separate chests [at home], so that they might serve as the portraits which were carried in family funeral processions, and thus, when anyone died, the entire roll of his ancestors, all who ever existed, was present" (*Naturalis Historia* 35.6–7). The wax death masks were sometimes cast in plaster, and sculptors might be commissioned to create bust portraits of the dead. Sculptors might also be asked to create imaginary portraits of illustrious, long-dead ancestors to be displayed in the tablinum and carried in funeral processions.

An oration in honor of the deceased, delivered by the family's most eminent member, was an important part of a Roman funeral. For much of the Republican period, only men were honored by such orations, but in 102 BCE the consul Catulus set a new precedent by giving an oration for his mother, Popilia. One of Julius Caesar's famed speeches was an oration for his aunt Julia. In it he traced her lineage to Rome's kings on her mother's side and to the gods on her father's side.

The Pont du Gard was constructed of beautifully sized and precisely cut stones from a nearby quarry. It consists of three **arcades** (walls with a series of regularly spaced arched openings) stacked one on the other and exemplifies the simplest use of the arch as a structural element. The arches of the thick base arcade spring from huge stone piers (square or rectangular support posts) and support a roadbed approximately 20 feet wide. The arches of the second arcade span the same distance as those of the base, but it is much narrower than the first and set on one side of the roadbed. The third arcade, the narrowest and shortest of the three, supports the water trough. It has three arches for every one of the second arcade. A purely utilitarian structure, the aqueduct was left undecorated, and the projecting blocks inserted to support scaffolding during construction were left to provide easy access for repairs. It nevertheless conveys a sense of balance, proportion, rhythmic harmony, and integration into its natural setting.

The city of Nîmes is located in what was once one of the richest provinces of the empire and contains several other well-preserved Roman structures. One of these, a temple known as the Maison Carrée, or Square House, is similar to the temple dedicated to Portunus in Rome but is larger and much more richly decorated (fig. 6-23). Built in the forum at Nîmes about 20 BCE and later dedicated to Gaius and Lucius Caesar, the grandsons of Augustus, the Maison Carrée differs from its prototype only in its size and its use of the more opulent Corinthian order. Both the aqueduct and the temple seem to summarize Roman architecture: technologically advanced but conservative in design. It is perhaps these qualities that appealed to the American president and amateur architect Thomas Jefferson, who visited Nîmes and was said to have found inspiration in the Maison Carrée for his own designs.

The Romans carried on the Greek and Hellenistic tradition of building large outdoor theaters, using suitable hillsides for the purpose of creating freestanding structures on level terrain. A well-preserved example of the hillside type can be found at Orange, also in southern France but north of Nîmes, on the east side of the Rhône (fig. 6-24). As in Greek theaters, the seating is arranged in a semicircular cone shape. The orchestra, which in Greek theaters is circular and is part of the performance area, has here been reduced to a semicircle and made part of the seating area. A raised stage with an elaborate enclosing wall faces the audience. Built during the reign of Augustus in the first century BCE, the theater held as many as 7,000 spectators. In its heyday, the plain masonry of the wall, 335 feet long and 123 1/2 feet high, was disguised with columns and **pediments** and presided over by a statue of the emperor in a central niche. Unlike Greek-style theaters, in which the surrounding environment is part of the performance setting, this theater isolated audience and actors alike in an entirely architectural environment.

Republican Sculpture

Sculptors of the Republican period sought to create believable images based on careful observations of their surroundings. The convention of rendering accurate and faithful portraits of individuals, called **verism**, may be derived from Roman ancestor veneration and the practice of making death masks of deceased relatives (see "Roman Funerary Practices," above). In any case, patrons of the Republican period clearly admired veristic por-

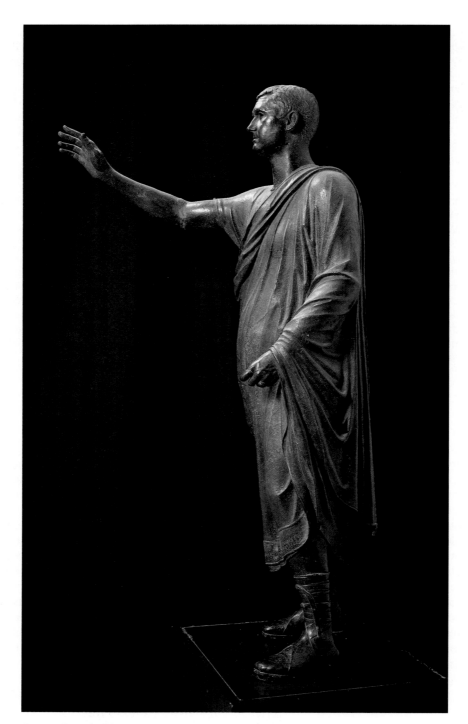

6-25. *Aulus Metellus*, found in the vicinity of Lake Trasimeno. Late 2nd or early
1st century BCE. Bronze, height 5'11" (1.8 m). Museo Archeològico Nazionale,
Florence

6-26. *Taking of the Roman Census*, frieze from a large base for statuary, possibly from the Temple of Neptune, Rome. c. 70 BCE.
Marble, height 32" (81.3 cm). Musée du Louvre, Paris

6-27. Ara Pacis. 13–9 BCE. Marble, approx. 34'5" (10.5 m) x 38' (11.6 m). Rome

The Ara Pacis—a war monument as famous in its day as the Vietnam Veterans' Memorial is in ours—has been reconstructed and is kept well preserved in a modern pavilion built at the time of the centennial of Italian unification in 1970. The pavilion is located beside the Tiber River near the tomb of Augustus, who commissioned the Ara Pacis as a memorial to his military conquests. The reign of Augustus marks the beginning of the *Pax Romana*, or Roman Peace, a period of stability in the empire that lasted nearly two centuries.

traits, and it is not surprising that they often turned to skilled Etruscan artists to execute them. The large bronze portrait statue of Aulus Metellus (fig. 6-25), the work of an Etruscan artist, dates to the late second or early first century BCE. The name of the subject, a Roman official, is inscribed on the hem of the toga in Etruscan letters. The statue, known from early times as "The Orator," depicts him addressing a gathering, his arm outstretched and slightly raised, a pose so expressive of authority and persuasiveness that it gained favor among later patrons. The orator wears sturdy laced leather boots and a folded and draped garment called a toga, both characteristic of a Roman official. According to Pliny the Elder, large statues like this were often placed atop columns as memorials to the individuals portrayed.

Historical events in ancient Rome were often preserved in the durable medium of relief sculpture. Perhaps the earliest historical reliefs discovered in Rome are two long marble panels dating from the early first century BCE, one of which depicts the *Taking of the Roman Census* (fig. 6-26). This panel and another now housed in a Munich museum may have been part of a base for a group of statues in one of Rome's temples, perhaps the Temple of Neptune. The left half of the panel shows the official registration of citizens; the right half shows a lustrum, a ritual that involved the sacrificial killing of animals, in this case a bull, a sheep, and a large pig being led in a procession to the altar at the center. The identity

of the censor (official census taker) commemorated in this panel is not certain, making it impossible to date precisely. Some scholars have suggested that he is Marcus Antonius, an orator who was elected censor of Rome in 97 BCE. The sculptor's desire to convey in detail specific contemporary events, which required depicting the subjects with complete clarity, overrode concerns for an artistically balanced composition.

Augustan Sculpture

Drawing inspiration from Etruscan and Greek art as well as Republican traditions, Roman artists of the imperial period made their own distinctive contribution to the history of sculpture. They enriched and developed the art of portraiture, creating both official images and representations of private individuals; they recorded contemporary historical events on commemorative arches, columns, and mausoleums erected in public places; and they contributed unabashedly to Roman imperial propaganda.

The Ara Pacis, the Altar of Augustan Peace, was erected in Rome by Augustus between 13 and 9 BCE to commemorate his triumphal return to the city following the end of civil war and the establishment of firm Roman rule in Spain and France (fig. 6-27). In form, the rectangular structure is a Roman adaptation of earlier Greek and Hellenistic altars. Its decoration is a thoughtful union of portraiture and allegory, religion and politics, the

6-28. *Imperial Procession*, detail of a relief on the Ara Pacis. Height 5'2" (1.6 m)

> The middle-aged man with the shrouded head at the far left is Marcus Agrippa, who would have been Augustus's successor had he not died in 12 CE, the year after the Ara Pacis was dedicated. The bored but well-behaved youngster pulling at Agrippa's robe—and being restrained gently by the hand of the man behind him—is probably Agrippa's son, Gaius Caesar. The heavily swathed woman next to Agrippa on the right is probably Augustus's wife, Livia, followed by the elder of her two sons, Tiberius, who would become the next emperor. Behind Tiberius is Antonia, the niece of Augustus, looking back at her husband, Drusus, Livia's younger son. She grasps the hand of Germanicus, one of her younger children. Behind their uncle Drusus are Gnaeus and Domitia, children of Antonia's older sister, who can be seen standing quietly beside them. The depiction of children in an official relief was new to the Augustan period and reflects Augustus's desire to promote private family life.

private and the public. The interior re-creates in marble the temporary altar—surrounded by garlands of flowers suspended in **swags**, or loops, from bucrania (ox skulls)—that would have been set up for the triumphal celebration. The ox skulls symbolize sacrificial offerings, and the garlands, which include flowering plants from every season, signify continuous peace.

Roman realism reached a new level of specificity in the sculpted panels along the exterior of the north and south sides of the Ara Pacis, which depict long double lines of mostly senators and imperial family members. These people appear to be waiting, after a just-completed procession, for other ceremonies to begin. At the head of the line on the south side of the altar is the badly damaged figure of Augustus. Surrounded by priests and other officials, he is probably performing a religious ritual. A detail shows many members of his family waiting at some distance behind him (fig. 6-28). Unlike the Greek sculptors who created the procession on the frieze of the Parthenon (see fig. 5-48), the Roman sculptors of the Ara Pacis depicted actual individuals. They also attempted to suggest spatial depth by carving the closest elements in high relief and those farther back in increasingly lower relief. In a device reminiscent of the Altar of Zeus at Pergamon (see fig. 5-81), they have drawn us, as spectators, visually into the event by making the feet of the nearest figures project from the architectural **groundline** into our space. Like the Parthenon sculptors, the Roman sculp-

6-29. *Allegory*, relief on the Ara Pacis. Height 5'2" (1.6 m)

6-30. *Augustus of Primaporta*. Early 1st century CE (perhaps a copy of a bronze statue of c. 20 BCE). Marble, height 6'8" (2.03 m). Musei Vaticani, Braccio Nuovo, Rome

tors have provided no background setting for the figures.

Moving from this procession, with its immediacy and naturalness, to the east and west ends of the enclosure walls, we find panels of a quite different character. The best-preserved of these is a balanced and composed scene, an allegorical representation of the peace and prosperity that Augustus has presumably brought to the empire (fig. 6-29). Scholars disagree on the identity of the figures. The woman in the center may be Tellus Mater, or Mother Earth, symbolically nurturing the Roman people, represented by the two chubby babies in her arms. She may also be a maternal form of Venus, or Ceres, the goddess of grain, or simply a personification (symbol in human form) of peace. She is accompanied by two young women with billowing veils, one seated on the back of a flying swan, the other reclining on a sea monster or dragon. They are personifications of the sea wind and the land wind. The sea wind, symbolized by the sea dragon and waves, would have reminded Augustus's contemporaries of Rome's dominion over the Mediterranean; the land wind, symbolized by the swan, the jug of fresh water, and the wetlands vegetation, would have suggested the fertility of Roman lands. The underlying alle-

gorical theme—the Abundant Earth—is reinforced by the flowers and foliage in the background and the domesticated animals in the foreground.

Although the inclusion in this panel of features of the natural world—sky, water, rocks, and foliage—represents something new in monumental sculpture, the idealized figures themselves are clearly drawn from Greek sources (see, for example, fig. 5-53). The artists have conveyed a sense of three-dimensionality and volume by turning the figures in space and wrapping them in revealing swaths of cloth. The scene is set into a frame of architectural elements carved in low relief. Corinthian order pilasters support a simple entablature. A wide **molding** with a Greek key pattern (**meander**) joins the pilasters and divides the wall into two horizontal segments. The lower panels are covered with stylized vine and flower forms. Similar forms, in a more rigid vertical pattern, overlay the pilasters, culminating in the **acanthus** capitals. The delicacy and minute detail with which these spiraling vegetal forms are rendered are characteristic of Roman architectural decoration.

The *Augustus of Primaporta* (fig. 6-30), so named because it was discovered in the country villa belonging

800 BCE   400 CE

6-31. *Livia*. c. 20 BCE. Marble, height approx. 15" (38.5 cm). Antiquarium, Pompeii

to Augustus's wife, Livia, at Primaporta, demonstrates the creative assimilation of earlier sculptural traditions into a new context. It also illustrates the use of imperial portraiture for political propaganda, a practice among Romans that began with Augustus. The sculptor of this bigger-than-life marble statue eloquently adapted the orator's gesture of the *Aulus Metellus* (see fig. 6-25), combining it with the pose and body proportions prescribed by the Greek Polykleitos and exemplified in his *Spear Bearer* (see fig. 5-54). (Roman artists made many copies of this famous sculpture, and many Roman statues reflect its influence.) The god Cupid, son of the goddess Venus, rides a dolphin next to the emperor's right calf, probably a reference to the claim of the emperor's family, the Julians, to descent from the goddess Venus through her human son Aeneas. Although Augustus wears a cuirass (torso armor) and holds a commander's baton, his feet are bare, suggesting to some scholars that the work was made after his death and commemo-

rates his **apotheosis**, or elevation to divine status. Augustus was in his late seventies when he died, but the features of this statue are those of a vigorous, young ruler. If it is a posthumous work, it might have been copied from a now-lost bronze statue. Since the decorations on the cuirass allude to Augustus's victory over the Parthians in 20 BCE, the original statue may have commemorated that event.

Taken as a whole, this imposing statue creates a recognizable image of Augustus, but one that is far removed from the kind of intensely individualized portrait that was popular during the Republican period. Its purpose was to encourage the Roman people to identify the beneficence of the state with the emperor's person. Whether it is seen as a general praising his troops or a peacetime leader speaking words of encouragement to his people, it projects an image of the emperor as a benign ruler, touched by the gods, governing by reason and persuasion, not autocratic power.

248   ETRUSCAN ART AND ROMAN ART

6-32. *Gemma Augustea*. Early 1st century CE. Onyx, 7½ x 9" (19 x 23 cm). Kunsthistorisches Museum, Vienna

Augustus's wife, Livia, was a strong and resourceful woman who remained by his side for more than fifty years. For both, this was a second marriage. Augustus had married his first wife for political reasons and divorced her after the birth of what would be his only child, Julia. Livia had two children, Tiberius (the future second emperor of Rome) and Drusus, by her first husband, Tiberius Claudius Nero, who divorced her so that she could marry Augustus. A portrait bust of her, dated about 20 BCE, when she was in her mid-thirties, reveals a striking woman with strong features and a serene expression (fig. 6-31). Although her marriage to Augustus was childless, she was an influential promoter of social legislation aimed at increasing the Roman birth rate. She supported laws that favored marriage and family, provided increased legal protection to married women, and penalized bachelors, unmarried women, and childless wives or widows. These laws made family life not only a desirable state but a patriotic duty.

The apotheosis of Augustus after his death in 14 CE is apparently the subject of a large onyx **cameo** (a gemstone carved in low relief) known as the *Gemma Augustea* (fig. 6-32). The emperor, being crowned with a victor's wreath, sits at the center right of the top panel. He has assumed the identity of Jupiter, the king of the gods, and an eagle, sacred to Jupiter, stands at his feet. Sitting next to him may be Livia, portrayed as a goddess personification of Rome. The sea-goat in the roundel between them may represent Capricorn, one of the constellations in the zodiac, indicating the time of year. The shield that serves as Augustus-Jupiter's footstool refers to the alleged descent of the Julian family from the war god Mars through his human children Romulus and Remus. Tiberius, the adopted son of Augustus, is shown holding a lance and stepping out of a chariot at the left. Returning victorious from the German front, he is ready to assume the imperial throne as the designated heir of Augustus. Below the transcendent realm of the godly

rulers is the earthly one, where Roman soldiers are raising a **trophy**—a post or standard on which armor captured from the defeated enemy is displayed. Like prisoners who were paraded out during a celebration of Tiberius's victory over the Germans in 12 CE, the cowering, shackled barbarians on the bottom right wait to be tied to this trophy.

The sculptor of this exquisite low relief created it by carving the relief elements out of the white layer and leaving the lower layer of blue as a background. The execution was so skillful that it nearly overshadows the equally fine design and conception. The *Gemma Augustea* brilliantly combines idealized, heroic figures of a kind characteristic of Classical Greek art, the dramatic action of Hellenistic art, and a purely Roman approach to the depiction of historical events. Even though it is unusually large and its subject matter and treatment highly propagandistic, this cameo was probably commissioned by Augustus's widow for commemorative use.

Wall Painting

The study of the development of Roman wall painting after the second century BCE is greatly indebted to the recovery of many examples preserved relatively fresh and intact within the volcanic debris that descended over the communities surrounding Vesuvius during its eruption. The interior walls of Roman houses were plain, smooth plaster surfaces without any architectural features. On these invitingly flat, empty surfaces, artists painted decorations that varied greatly in appearance and subject matter. Their technique involved mixing pigment in a solution of lime and soap with a little wax added, applying the images, polishing with a special metal, glass, or stone burnisher, then buffing with a cloth. At Pompeii these decorations can be grouped into four types, or styles, that succeeded each other with some overlap. The first two began during the Republican period, and the last two are associated with the Roman Empire. Although the Pompeiian styles are no longer used to assign dates to architecture, they are a convenient way to examine wall painting in the Roman world.

In the First Style (c. 200–80 BCE), artists created the illusion that the walls were actually covered with thin slabs of colored marble set off by real architectural details such as molded plaster columns. In the Second Style (c. 80–15 BCE) they extended the space of a room visually with painted scenes of figures on a shallow "stage" or with a landscape or cityscape seen close up. Architectural details such as columns were painted rather than molded plaster. In the Third Style (c. 15 BCE–45 CE) they emphasized the wall surface again by painting it a solid color, decorated with slender, whimsical architectural details, within which small, delicate vignettes appear. The Fourth Style (beginning c. 45 CE) was a complex combination of the features found in the other three styles, bringing together the more realistic architectural details of the First and Second styles with even greater fantasy than in the Third Style. The Third and Fourth styles are treated beginning on page 256.

6-33. *Initiation Rites of the Cult of Bacchus* (?), detail of a Second Style wall painting in the Villa of the Mysteries, Pompeii. c. 50 BCE

One of the most famous painted rooms in Roman art is in the so-called Villa of the Mysteries at Pompeii (fig. 6-33). The room must have been a shrine or meeting place for a religious cult, probably that of Bacchus, the god of vegetation, fertility, wine, and the arts, who was one of the most important deities in Pompeii, along with Hercules and Venus. The Second Style murals depict what has been interpreted as the initiation rites of a new member of the cult, which was for a long time limited exclusively to women. The artists first painted an architectural setting consisting of a marble **dado**, a decoration on the lower part of a wall, and an elegant **frieze** supported by pilasters around the top of the wall. The action takes place along the top of the dado in a raised, shallow stage space with a backdrop painted a brilliant, deep red (now known as Pompeiian red) very popular with Roman painters. The stage runs around the entire room and the scenes on it depict a succession of events that culminate in the acceptance of the initiate into the cult.

The visual space of the paintings includes the viewer, who feels like a participant in the action. In the portion of the room seen in the illustration, a priestess (on the left) prepares to reveal draped cult objects, a

6-34. Reconstructed bedroom, from the House of Publius Fannius Synistor, Boscoreale, near Pompeii. Late 1st century CE, with some later furnishings. The Metropolitan Museum of Art, New York
Rogers Fund, 1903 (03.14.13)

Although the elements in the room are from a variety of places and dates, they give a sense of how the original furnished room might have looked. The floor mosaic, found near Rome, dates to the second century CE. At its center is an image of a priest offering a basket with a snake to a cult image of Isis. The couch and footstool, which are inlaid with bone and glass, date from the first century CE. The wall paintings, original to the Boscoreale villa, may have been inspired by theater scene painting.

winged figure whips a female initiate lying across the lap of another woman, and a devotee dances with cymbals, perhaps to drown out the cries from the whipping. According to another interpretation, the dancing figure is the initiate herself, who has risen to dance with joy at the conclusion of her trials. The whole may be showing a purification ritual meant to bring enlightenment and blissful union with the god.

The walls of a room from a villa at Boscoreale, a suburb of Pompeii, have been restored as a bedroom in the Metropolitan Museum of Art in New York and furnished with items roughly contemporary with the original villa. The Second Style paintings on the walls use the same type of shallow "stage" as the illusions in the Villa of the Mysteries, but in this case a fantastic urban panorama surrounds the room and provides a closed-off view of a Roman city (fig. 6-34). The wall surfaces dissolve into columns and cornices, swinging garlands, and niches. There is no sense of space beyond these forms into which the viewer might move. Were we able to walk through one of the painted doors we would find ourselves lost in an incomprehensible maze of floating forms. This scene is made for viewing only, like backdrops for a theatrical set, which may have been the inspiration for this type of home decoration. Other details in the room reinforce this theatrical association. On the rear wall, next to the window, for example, is a painting of a grotto with a fountain surmounted by a grape arbor, a visual reference to Bacchus, the traditional setting for a kind of drama known as a satyr play. On the side walls, theatrical masks hang from the center of each bay.

The splendid portal in the painting at the far left end of the left wall of the room is flanked by potted plants and a statue of a goddess. Beyond this portal is a complex jumble of buildings with balconies, windows, arcades, and roofs at different levels that end in a magnificent colonnade (fig. 6-35). The vine-wrapped column that seems to sit on the ledge painted at the bottom of the wall and to support an entablature near the top of it enhances the illusion that we are looking into space. The mask hanging in the center of this framing element is a reminder that the composition has more to do with

6-35. *Cityscape*, detail of a Second Style wall painting from a bedroom in the House of Publius Fannius Synistor, Boscoreale. Late 1st century CE. The Metropolitan Museum of Art, New York
Rogers Fund, 1903 (03.14.13)

theatrical design than with reality. Nevertheless, the artist has used **intuitive perspective** to create a general impression of real space. The architectural details follow diagonal lines that the eye interprets as parallel lines receding into the distance, and figures and objects that we are meant to understand as far away from the surface plane of the wall are shown smaller than those meant to appear near to it.

The Second Style decoration of the dining-room walls of the Villa of Livia at Primaporta exemplifies yet another approach to creating a sense of slightly expanded space (fig. 6-36). Instead of rendering a stage set or a

6-36. *Garden Scene*, detail of a Second Style wall painting from the Villa of Livia at Primaporta, near Rome. Late 1st century BCE. Museo Nazionale Romano, Rome

cityscape, the artist literally painted away the wall surfaces to create the illusion of being on a porch or pavilion looking out over a low, paneled wall toward an orchard of heavily laden fruit trees. These and the flowering shrubs are filled with a variety of wonderfully observed birds. When the Republican period drew to a close, the styles of painting, especially the Third Style, continued to dominate, but other art forms—most particularly architecture—would be put to new purposes.

THE EARLY EMPIRE: THE JULIO-CLAUDIAN AND FLAVIAN DYNASTIES

Augustus's successor was his stepson Tiberius, and in acknowledgment of the lineage of both, the dynasty—the succession of related rulers—that begins with Tiberius is known as the Julio-Claudian (14–69 CE). Although this dynasty produced some capable administrators, it was also marked by suspicion, intrigue, and terror in Rome. It ended with the reign of the despotic and capricious Nero. A brief period of civil war followed Nero's death in 68 CE, during which it became clear that the power to elevate emperors rested with the army and not with the Senate and other assemblies in Rome. Eventually, a powerful general, Vespasian, seized control of the government. The dynasty he founded, the Flavian, ruled from 69 to 96 CE. The emperors in this dynasty, Vespasian (ruled 69–79 CE), Titus (ruled 79–81 CE), and Domitian (ruled 81–96 CE), restored imperial finances and stabilized the empire's frontiers. Domitian's autocratic reign saw a return of intrigue and terror to the capital.

Architecture

The Colosseum, one of Rome's greatest monuments, was built during the reign of Vespasian (fig. 6-37). Construction on it began in 72 CE, and it was dedicated by Titus in 80 CE, after Vespasian's death. In this enormous entertainment center (it measures 615 by 510 feet and is 159 feet high) Roman audiences watched a variety of athletic events and spectacles, including animal hunts, fights to the death between gladiators or between gladiators and wild animals, performances of trained animals and acrobats, and even mock sea battles, for which the arena was flooded by a built-in mechanism. The Flavians erected it to bolster their popularity in Rome, and its name then was the Flavian Amphitheater. The name "Colosseum," by which it came to be known, derived from the Colossus, a bigger-than-life statue of Nero that had been left standing next to it. The opening performances in 80 CE lasted 100 days, during which time, it was claimed, 9,000 wild animals and 2,000 gladiators were killed.

The floor of the Colosseum was laid over a foundation of service rooms and tunnels that provided a backstage area for the athletes, performers, animals, and equipment. (This floor was covered in sand, or *arena* in Latin, hence the English term "arena.") Some 50,000 spectators could easily move through the seventy-six

6-37. Colosseum, Rome. 72–80 CE

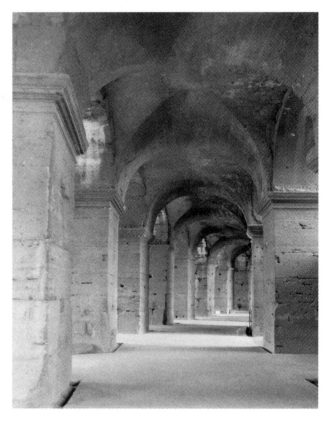

6-38. Colosseum. View of a radial passage with barrel and groin vaulting

entrance doors to the three sections of seats and the standing area at the top. Each had an uninterrupted view of the spectacle below. Like many stadiums today, the Colosseum was oval with a surrounding exterior wall and ascending tiers of seats laid over barrel-vaulted corridors that provided access to them (fig. 6-38). Entrance tunnels connected the ring corridors to the inside ramps and seats on each level. The intersection of the entrance tunnels and the ring corridors, both barrel-vaulted, created what is called a **groin vault** (see "Elements of Architecture," page 226). The walls on the top level of the

6-39. Colosseum

arena supported an awning system that could shade the seating areas. Former seamen who had experience in handling ropes, pulleys, and large expanses of canvas were employed to work the apparatus.

The curving, outer wall of the Colosseum consists of three levels of arcade surmounted by a wall-like **attic** (top) **story**. Each arch in the arcades is framed by engaged columns, which support entablaturelike bands marking the divisions between levels (fig. 6-39). Each level also uses a different architectural order: the plain Tuscan order on the ground level, the Ionic on the second level, the Corinthian on the third, and flat pilasters on the fourth. The attic story is broken only by small, square windows, which originally alternated with gilded-bronze shield-shaped ornaments called **cartouches**. These were supported on **corbels** (brackets) that are still in place and can be seen in the illustration. Engaged Corinthian pilasters above the Corinthian columns of the third level support another row of corbels beneath the projecting cornice. All of these elements are purely decorative and serve no structural function. As we saw with

the Porta Augusta (see fig. 6-2), the addition of post-and-lintel decoration to arched structures was an Etruscan innovation. The systematic use of the orders in a logical succession from sturdy Tuscan to lighter Ionic to decorative Corinthian follows a tradition inherited from Hellenistic architecture (see "Elements of Architecture," page 227). This orderly, dignified, and visually satisfying way of articulating (organizing) the facades of large buildings is still popular. Unfortunately, much of the facade and the rest of the Colosseum were dismantled as a source of marble, metal fittings, and materials for later buildings.

The Arch of Titus

When Domitian assumed the throne in 81 CE, he immediately commissioned a **triumphal arch** to honor his brother and deified predecessor, Titus (fig. 6-40). During a triumph—a formal victory celebration granted to a general or emperor on his return to Rome after a significant campaign—the victorious leader paraded with his

6-40. Arch of Titus, Rome. c. 81 CE. Concrete and white marble, height 50' (15 m)

The dedication inscribed across the tall attic story above the arch opening reads: "The Senate and the Roman People to the Deified Titus Flavius Vespasianus Augustus, son of the Deified Vespasian." The Romans typically recorded historic occasions and identified monuments with solemn prose and beautiful inscriptions in stone. The use by the sculptors of elegant Roman capital letters—perfectly sized and spaced to be read from a distance and cut with sharp terminals (serifs) to catch the light—established a standard that calligraphers and alphabet designers still follow.

6-41. *Spoils from the Temple of Solomon, Jerusalem*, relief in the passageway of the Arch of Titus. Marble, height 6'8" (2.03 m)

troops, captives, and booty through the city. A triumphal arch was a freestanding stone arch erected to commemorate the occasion. The Arch of Titus memorializes his capture of Jerusalem in August 70 CE.

The arch, constructed of concrete and faced with marble, is essentially a freestanding gateway pierced by a passageway covered by a barrel vault. Originally the whole arch served as a giant base, 50 feet tall, for a statue of a four-horse chariot and driver, a typical triumphal symbol. Applied to the faces of the arch are columns in the **Composite order**—capitals are formed by superimposing Ionic **volutes** on a Corinthian capital—supporting an entablature. The inscription on the attic story declares that the Senate and the Roman people erected the monument to honor Titus.

Titus's capture of Jerusalem ended a fierce campaign to crush a revolt of the Jews in Palestine. His troops sacked and destroyed the Second Temple of Jerusalem and carted off its sacred treasures. These spoils were displayed in Rome during Titus's triumphal procession, impressing the Jewish eyewitness and historian Flavius Josephus (*The Jewish War*):

> The most interesting of all were the spoils seized from the Temple of Jerusalem: a gold table weighing many talents, and a lampstand, also made of gold, which was made in a form different from that which we usually employ. For there was a central shaft fastened to the base; then spandrels [branches] extended from this in an arrangement which rather resembled the shape of a trident, and on the end of each of these spandrels a lamp was forged. There were seven of these, emphasizing the honor accorded the number seven among the Jews. The law of the Jews [Ark of the Covenant] was borne along after these as the last of the spoils. . . . Vespasian drove along behind [it] . . . and Titus followed him; Domitian rode beside them, dressed in a dazzling fashion and riding a horse which was worth seeing.

The reliefs on the inside walls of the arch, capturing the drama of the occasion, depict Titus's soldiers flaunting this booty as they carry it through the streets of Rome (fig. 6-41). Viewing them, the observer can feel that boisterous, disorderly crowd and might expect at any moment to hear the shouts and chanting of the participants.

The mood of the procession depicted in these reliefs contrasts with the relaxed but formal solemnity of the procession depicted on the Ara Pacis (see fig. 6-28). Like the sculptors of the Ara Pacis, the sculptors of the Arch of Titus showed the spatial relationships among figures by rendering close elements in higher relief than those more distant. A **menorah**, or seven-branched candleholder, from the Temple of Jerusalem dominates the scene. Reflecting their concern for representing objects as well as people in a believable manner, the sculptors rendered this menorah as if seen from the low point of view of a spectator at the event, and they have positioned the arch on the right through which the procession is about to pass on a diagonal from the background. Using a technique also encountered on the Ara Pacis, the sculptors have **undercut** the foreground figures and have used low relief for the figures in the background. The panel on the other side of the arch interior shows Titus riding in his chariot as a participant in the ceremonies. On the vaulted ceiling, which shows his apotheosis, an eagle carries him to a heavenly meeting with the gods.

Plebeian Relief Sculpture

Like Rome's rulers, eminent individuals who could afford to do so also sought to memorialize themselves in art. Most of the private commissions by the plebeians were related to funerary situations. The most popular decorations of funerary reliefs were portraits of the deceased, garlands, and narrative themes, sometimes of mythological figures, sometimes of biographical scenes associated with the deceased. A fine example of such sculpture is a relief on the mausoleum of the plebeian Haterius family (fig. 6-42). The relief memorializes the construction of the mausoleum itself, an occurrence that has led some scholars to believe that it was perhaps created for the tomb of an architect or a builder. The sculptor of the relief, like the sculptor of the *Taking of the Roman Census* (see fig. 6-26), sacrificed clear organization and composition in order to convey as much information as possible—far more than can be readily absorbed. The viewer should approach the image as a "tourist," ready to wander about studying this and that area, and examining with fascination the giant, human-powered crane at the left being maneuvered into place over the still-unfinished mausoleum. For the student of architecture, the image of the mausoleum is an encyclopedia of decorative motifs—**egg-and-dart** moldings, garlands looped in swags, busts in shell-shaped niches, and vegetal reliefs that are symmetrical and upright. The robust Corinthian columns are heavily carved with spiraling garlands. Viewed as a whole, the jumbled structural elements and perspectives make the mausoleum look as if it is about to tumble to the ground.

Unlike the sculptors who worked on the Ara Pacis, the artists who created reliefs of the type found on the tomb of the Haterius family were relatively unfamiliar with the techniques and intentions of the Classical Greek sculptors. Their patrons were probably relatively unsophisticated, though quite clear about what they wanted. The sculptural style that emerged from such commissions was characterized by crowded compositions and deeply undercut forms, with stocky figures and a detailed but visually unrealistic way of presenting its subject matter or "story." This style, however, would become more and more prevalent, ultimately displacing the patrician style in both public and private art throughout the empire.

Portrait Sculpture

Two approaches to portrait sculpture were popular during the reign of the Flavians. A bust of a young woman, whose identity is not known, exemplifies one of

6-42. *Mausoleum under Construction*, relief from the tomb of the Haterius family, Via Labicana, Rome. Late 1st century CE. Marble, height 41" (104 cm). Musei Vaticani, Museo Gregoriano Profano, ex Lateranense, Rome

these (fig. 6-43). This bust is an idealized portrait in the manner of the *Augustus of Primaporta* (see fig. 6-30). It includes well-observed, recognizable features—a strong nose and jaw, heavy brows, deep-set eyes, and a long neck—but the smoothly rendered flesh and soft, full lips impart an idealized, youthful glow. The hair is piled high in a mass of ringlets in the latest court fashion. Executing it required skillful chiseling and **drillwork**. With a drill, a sculptor can rapidly cut deep grooves with straight sides that look like dark lines at a distance. In this case the drill created the holes in the center of the subject's curls. The overall effect, from a distance, is very lifelike. The play of natural light over the more subtly sculpted surfaces gives the illusion of being reflected off real skin and hair.

The second approach, exemplified by a bust of an older woman (fig. 6-44), reflects a revival of the verist style popular in the Republican period. The comic writers of the Flavian era liked to satirize older women who vainly sought to preserve their youthful looks, but the subject of this portrait, though she too wore her hair in the latest style, was apparently not at all proud about her looks. The work she commissioned shows her exactly as she appeared in her own mirror, with all the signs of her age—well earned and magnificent in their own way—recorded on her face for future generations to admire.

6-43. *Young Flavian Woman*. c. 90 CE. Marble, height 25" (65.5 cm). Museo Capitolino, Rome

The typical Flavian hairstyle seen on this woman and the older woman in figure 6-44 required a patient hairdresser handy with a curling iron and with a special knack for turning the back of the head into an intricate basketweave of braids. Male writers loved to scoff at the results. Martial described the style precisely as "a globe of hair." Statius spoke of "the glory of woman's lofty front, her storied hair." And Juvenal waxed comically poetic: "See her from the front; she is Andromache [an epic heroine]. From behind she looks half the size—a different woman you would think" (cited in Balsdon, page 256).

6-44. *Middle-Aged Flavian Woman*. Late 1st century CE. Marble, height 9½" (24.1 cm). Musei Vaticani, Museo Gregoriano Profano, ex Lateranense, Rome

Wall Painting

From the time of Augustus through about 45 CE, the third of the four styles identified at Pompeii predominated in Roman wall painting. In this Third Style, walls were treated mostly as solid, planar surfaces adorned with decorative details and "framed" paintings. The Third Style painting on a wall in the House of M. Lucretius Fronto in Pompeii dates to the mid-first century CE. As we see in a detail (fig. 6-45), the artist painted the wall in panels of black and red that emphasize its flatness. An echo of Second Style architecture can be seen in the borders between the panels and the suggestion of an upper level, but these elements show no logical layout and lack any significant illusion of depth. The rectangular pictures seem to be mounted on the black and red panels or placed in front of them, but they are actually painted on the wall. The scene with figures in the center is flanked by two small simulated window openings protected by grilles. The two pictures of country houses appear to be mounted on **filigree**.

The paintings that adorned Third and Fourth Style walls had every kind of subject, including historical and mythological scenes, landscapes and city views, portraits, and exquisitely rendered **still lifes**, or representations of inanimate objects. A still-life panel from a Fourth Style wall painting in the House of Julia Felix in Pompeii (fig. 6-46) depicts everyday domestic wares and the

6-45. Detail of a Third Style wall painting in the House of M. Lucretius Fronto, Pompeii. Mid-1st century CE

6-46. *Still Life*, detail of a wall painting from the House of Julia Felix, Pompeii. Late 1st century CE. Museo Archeològico Nazionale, Naples

6-47. *Sacred Landscape*, detail of a wall painting, from Pompeii. 62–79 CE. Museo Archeològico Nazionale, Naples

6-48. *Young Woman Writing*, detail of a wall painting, from Pompeii. Late 1st century CE. Diameter 14⅝" (37 cm). Museo Archeològico Nazionale, Naples

The fashionable young woman seems to be pondering what she will write about with her stylus on the beribboned writing tablet that she holds in her other hand. Romans used pointed styluses to engrave letters on thin, wax-coated ivory or wood tablets in much the way we might use a small chalkboard; errors could be easily smoothed over. When a text or letter was considered ready, it was copied onto expensive papyrus or parchment. Tablets like these were also used by schoolchildren for their homework.

makings of a meal—eggs and recently caught game birds. The items have been carefully grouped for clarity and balance in a near-symmetrical arrangement. The focus of the composition is the round plate filled with eggs and the household containers that flank it. The towel on a hook on the right of the painting and the subtle suggestion of triangularity in the bottle tilted against the end of the shelf echo the pyramidal shape of the brace of dead birds above the plate. A strong, clear light floods the picture from the left, casting shadows and enhancing the illusion of real objects in real space. Other paintings in this house show graphically the role of women at the time and how, so unlike their Greek contemporaries, they had an active life outside the home.

During the first century CE, landscape painting became especially accomplished in Pompeii. Its appeal was captured by Pliny the Elder, who described it in *Naturalis Historia* (35.116–117) as "that most delightful technique of painting walls with representations of villas, porticoes and landscape gardens, woods, groves, hills, pools, channels, rivers, coastlines—in fact, every sort of thing which one might want, and also various representations of people within them walking or sailing . . . and also fishing, fowling, or hunting or even harvesting the wine-grapes."

An example from Pompeii of a Third Style sacred landscape—a special type of landscape painting that usually includes shrines, statues, trees, water, rocks, figures, and animals—dates from the decade and a half between an earthquake in 62 CE and the final destruction of the city in 79 CE, the period in which Pliny wrote (fig. 6-47). In this scene, a brook runs through a meadow surrounded by rocky hills and trees. Altars and small temples are scattered about, and an open pavilion encloses a sacred tree. A shepherd crosses the bridge, followed by a goat. Watching over the scene is Terminus, the god of boundaries, in the form of a **herm** statue—a head and torso that merges at hip level into a plain plinth, or base. Two conventions

create the illusion of space: distant objects are rendered proportionally smaller than near objects, and the colors become slightly grayer near the horizon, an effect called **atmospheric perspective** that reproduces the tendency of distant objects to appear hazy.

Roman artists sought to capture a sense of peaceful, unspoiled nature in their landscapes, and the overall effect of this painting is one of wonder-invoking nature. It depicts the *locus amoenus*, the "lovely place" extolled by poets, where people lived effortlessly in union with the land. Such an idealized view of the world, rendered with free, fluid brushwork and delicate color, did not appear again in Western art until the latter part of the nineteenth century with the painting of the French Impressionists.

Portraits, perhaps imaginary ones, were popular for wall paintings. A late-first-century CE **tondo** (circular panel) from a house in Pompeii contains a portrait of a *Young Woman Writing* (fig. 6-48). The sitter has regular features and curly hair caught in a golden net. As in a modern studio portrait photograph, with its careful lighting and retouching, she is portrayed in an idealized fashion. In a convention popular among women patrons, she

ROMAN WOMEN AND THE ARTS

If we were to judge from the conflicting accounts of Roman writers, Roman women were either shockingly wicked and willful, totally preoccupied with clothes, hairstyles, and social events, or well-educated, talented, and active members of family and society. In ancient Rome, as in the contemporary world, sin sold better than saintliness, and for that reason written attacks on women by their male contemporaries must be viewed with some reservation. In fact, careful study has shown that Roman women were far freer and more engaged in society than their Greek counterparts. Many women received a formal education, and a well-educated woman was admired as much as a well-educated man. The upper classes hired tutors for their daughters and less-affluent families sent both sons and daughters to school until they were twelve years old. In school, under a male teacher, boys and girls studied the same subjects. Although many middle-class women became physicians, shopkeepers, and even overseers in such male-dominated businesses as shipbuilding, education was valued not so much for any practical training it might provide as for the desirable status it imparted.

Ovid (43 BCE–c. 17 CE) advised all young women to read both the Greek classics and contemporary Roman literature, including his own, of course. Women conversant with political and cultural affairs and with a reputation for good conversation enjoyed the praise and admiration of some male writers. A few women even took up literature themselves. A woman named Julia Balbilla was well respected for her poetry. Another, Sulpicia, a writer of elegies, was accepted into male literary circles. Her works were recommended by the author Martial to men and women alike. The younger Agrippina, sister of the emperor Caligula and mother of Nero, wrote a history of her illustrious family.

Women were also encouraged to become accomplished singers, instrumentalists, and even dancers, so long as they did not perform publicly. During the imperial period, actors—both male and female—were considered among the most disreputable members of society, no matter how much their talents were admired, and men were forbidden by law to marry actresses. One courageous (and very wealthy) woman managed despite such restrictions to found and run her own dance company. Almost nothing appears in literature about women in the visual arts, no doubt because artists were not highly regarded. But the tomb relief illustrated here is clear proof that women did become professional painters. The tomb's occupant is shown in her studio with paint pots, palette, and brushes and a young nude model waiting for her to turn and begin work.

Painter in Her Studio, tomb relief. 2nd century CE. Villa Albani, Rome

is shown nibbling on the tip of a writing stylus. Her sweet mien and clear-eyed but unfocused and contemplative gaze suggest that she is composing a piece of writing. Perhaps, like many Roman women, she was a professional writer (see "Roman Women and the Arts," above) who wanted to be admired for her intellectual attainments. The paintings in Pompeii reveal much about the lives of women during this period. Some, like Julia Felix, were the owners of houses where paintings were found. Others were the subjects of the painters, and they are shown as rich and poor, young and old, employed as business managers and domestic workers. They participated in all aspects of daily life fully and apparently comparably to men.

THE EARLY EMPIRE: THE "GOOD EMPERORS"

Five very competent rulers— Nerva (ruled 96–98 CE), Trajan (ruled 98–117 CE), Hadrian (ruled 117–138 CE), Antoninus Pius (ruled 138–161 CE), and Marcus Aurelius (ruled 161–180 CE)— succeeded the Flavians. Until Marcus Aurelius, none of them had natural sons, and they adopted able members of the Senate to be their successors. Known as the "Five Good Emperors," they oversaw a long period of stability and prosperity. Italy and the provinces flourished equally, and official and private patronage of the arts vastly increased. Under Trajan the empire reached its greatest extent. He annexed Dacia (roughly modern Romania) in

6-49. Model of the Imperial Forums, Rome. c. 46 BCE–117 CE

106 CE and expanded the empire's boundaries in the Middle East. His successor, Hadrian, consolidated the empire's borders and imposed far-reaching social, administrative, and military reforms. Hadrian was well educated and widely traveled, and his admiration for Greek culture spurred new building programs throughout the empire. By the reign of Marcus Aurelius, the empire was facing increasing strains and external threats.

Architecture in Rome and Environs

The Romans believed that their rule extended to the ends of the Western world, but Rome remained the heart and nerve center of the empire. During his long and peaceful reign, Augustus paved the city's old Republican Forum, restoring its temples and basilicas, and built the first

Imperial Forum. These projects marked the beginning of a continuing effort to transform the capital itself into a magnificent monument to imperial rule. Modern Rome has almost obliterated the ancient city, so we can only imagine its appearance from drawings, plans, and models. These models show major monuments such as the Colosseum, the Arch of Titus, the Circus Maximus (a track for chariot races), the Imperial Forums, the round, domed temple called the Pantheon, and the aqueducts among the densely packed temples, monuments, baths, warehouses, and homes that choked the city center.

The largest and most elaborate of the Imperial Forums (fig. 6-49) was that of Trajan, which he had constructed on a large piece of property next to the earlier forums of Augustus and Julius Caesar. For this major undertaking, Trajan chose a Greek architect, Apollo-

6-50. Reconstruction drawing of the central hall, Basilica Ulpia, Rome. 113 CE

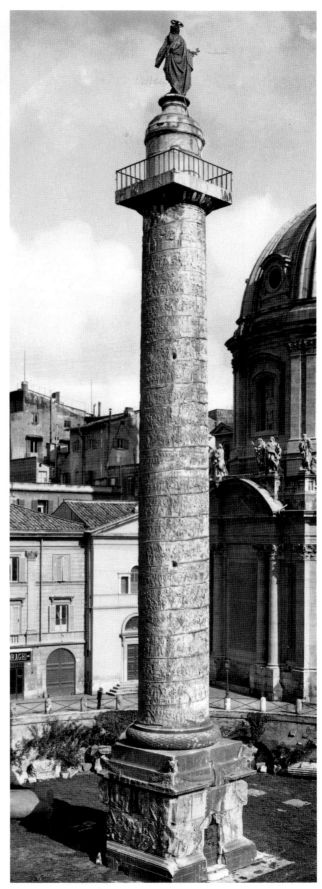

6-51. Column of Trajan, Rome. 106–13 CE. Marble, overall height with base 125' (38 m), column alone, 97'8" (29.77 m)

dorus of Damascus, who designed the forum around a straight, central axis that leads from the Forum of Augustus through a triple-arched gate surmounted by a bronze chariot group into a large, colonnaded courtyard with a statue of Trajan on horseback at its center. Perpendicular to the courtyard and closing it off at the north end was the main building in the forum, the Basilica Ulpia, dedicated in 113 CE and named for the family to which Trajan belonged. A basilica was a large, rectangular building with a rounded extension, called an **apse**, at each end. A general-purpose administrative structure, it could be adapted to many uses. The Basilica Ulpia was a court of law. Others served as imperial audience chambers, army drill halls, and schools. An important feature of the basilica design was that it provided easy access in and out. Its capacious and adaptable interior later made it attractive to Christians, who appropriated it for their churches.

The Basilica Ulpia had several doors on the long sides. The interior space was partitioned into a large, central area bordered by two colonnaded aisles that were surmounted by open galleries (fig. 6-50). The central space was taller than the surrounding gallery, creating a **clerestory** with windows, as in the Egyptian **hypostyle hall** (see fig. 3-29), that brought light to the interior of the building. The apse spaces at each end of the building provided imposing settings for judges when the court was in session.

Just behind the Basilica Ulpia were twin libraries built to house the emperors' large collections of Latin and Greek manuscripts. These buildings flanked an open court in which Trajan erected a large column to commemorate his victory over the Dacians (fig. 6-51). The column was built between 106 and 113 CE and was both a monument to him and his tomb. The Temple of the Divine Trajan stands opposite the Basilica Ulpia, defining the fourth side of the court and closing off the end of the forum. It was built by the emperor Hadrian after his predecessor's death and apotheosis in 117.

The relief decoration on the Column of Trajan spirals upward in a band that would stretch about 656 feet if unfurled. Like a giant scroll, it contains a continuous pictorial narrative of the entire history of the Dacian

6-52. *Romans Crossing the Danube and Building a Fort*, detail of the lowest part of the Column of Trajan. Height of the spiral band approx. 36" (91 cm)

campaign. This remarkable sculptural feat involved creating more than 2,500 individual figures—including soldiers, animals, and hangers-on—linked by landscape, architecture, and the recurring figure of Trajan. The artist took care to make all of the scroll legible. The narrative band slowly expands from about 3 feet in height at the bottom, near the viewer, to 4 feet at the top, where it is far from the viewer, and the natural and architectural frames for the scenes have been kept small relative to the important figures in them.

The scene at the bottom of the column (fig. 6-52) shows the army crossing the Danube River on a pontoon (floating) bridge as the campaign gets under way. A giant river god, providing supernatural support, looks on. In the scene above, soldiers have begun constructing a battlefield headquarters in Dacia from which the men on the frontiers will receive orders, food, and weapons. Throughout the narrative, which is, after all, a spectacular piece of imperial propaganda, Trajan is portrayed as a strong, stable, and efficient commander of a well-run army, whereas his barbarian enemies are shown as pathetically disorganized and desperate. The hardships of war—death, destruction, and the suffering of innocent people—are ignored, and, of course, the Romans never lose a battle.

During the site preparation for the forum, much of the commercial district on the Quirinal Hill had to be razed and excavated. To make up for the loss, Trajan ordered the construction of a handsome public market in the shadow of the forum's wall (fig. 6-53). The complete ex-

6-53. Axonometric drawing of the Markets of Trajan, Rome. 100–12 CE

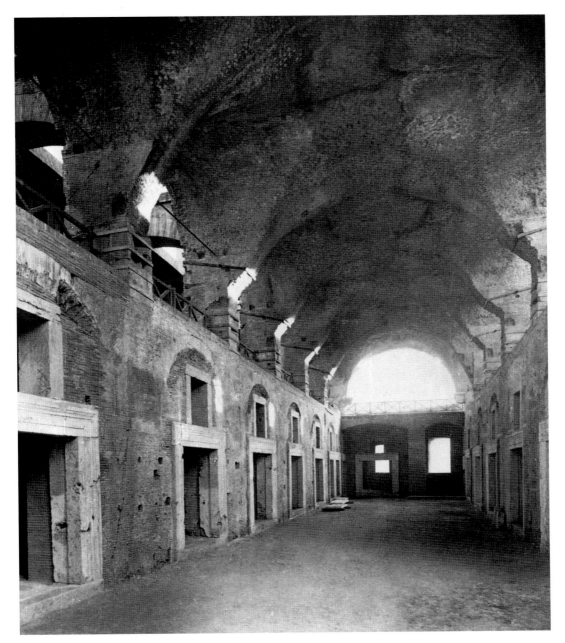

6-54. Main hall, Markets of Trajan

tent of this much-damaged structure, which would have compared favorably with any modern indoor shopping mall, is unknown. The remaining building is a semicircular structure that follows the shape of the huge exedra in the east wall of the Forum of Trajan. The market had more than 150 individual shop spaces on several levels and included a large groin-vaulted main hall (fig. 6-54). In compliance with a building code that was put into effect after a disastrous fire in 64 CE, it was made of brick-faced concrete, with only some detailing in stone and wood.

One of the most remarkable ancient buildings surviving in Rome is a temple to the Olympian gods called the Pantheon ("all the gods"). It was built under the patronage of Emperor Hadrian between 125 and 128 CE on the site of a temple erected by Agrippa in 27–25 BCE but

later destroyed. The approach to the temple gives little suggestion of what it must have looked like when it stood separate from any surrounding structures. Nor is there any hint of what lies beyond the entrance porch, which was raised originally on a podium (now covered by centuries of dirt and street construction) and made to resemble the facade of a typical Roman temple (fig. 6-55). Behind this porch is a giant **rotunda** (a circular building) with 20-foot-thick walls that rise nearly 75 feet. Supported on these is a huge, round, bowl-shaped dome, 143 feet in diameter and 143 feet from the floor at its summit (fig. 6-56). Standing at the center of this nearly spherical temple, the visitor feels isolated from the real world and intensely aware of the shape and tangibility of the space itself rather than the solid surfaces of the architecture

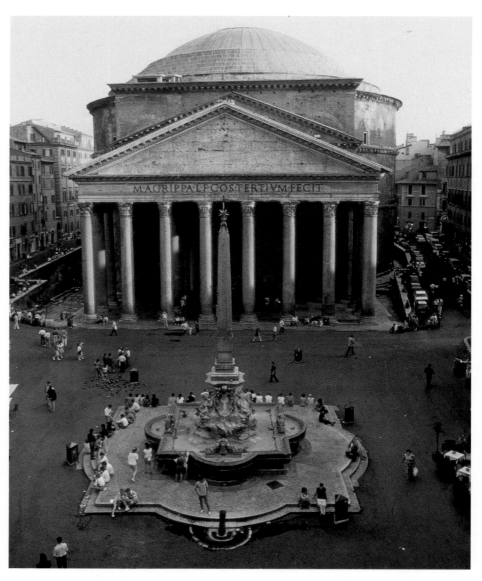

6-55. Pantheon, Rome. 125–28 CE

Although this magnificent monument was designed and constructed entirely during the reign of the emperor Hadrian, the long inscription on the architrave clearly states that it was built by "Marcus Agrippa, son of Lucius, who was consul three times." Agrippa, the son-in-law and valued adviser of Emperor Augustus, died in 12 BCE, but he was responsible for the building of a previous temple on this site in 27–25 BCE, which the Pantheon replaced. In essence Hadrian simply made a grand gesture to the memory of the illustrious Agrippa, rather than using the new building to memorialize himself.

enclosing it. The eye is drawn upward over the circle patterns made by the sunken panels, or **coffers**, in the dome's ceiling to the light entering the 29-foot-wide **oculus**, or central opening. Clouds can be seen through this opening on clear days; rain falls through it on wet ones, then drains off as planned by the original engineer; and occasionally a bird flies through it. But the empty, luminous space also imparts a sense of apotheosis, a feeling that one could rise buoyantly upward to escape the spherical hollow of the building and commune with the gods.

The simple shape of the Pantheon's dome belies its sophisticated design and engineering. Its surface of marble veneer disguises the internal brick arches and concrete that support it. The walls, which form the structural **drum** that holds up and buttresses the dome, are disguised by a wealth of architectural detail—columns, exedrae, pilasters, and entablatures—in two tiers. Seven niches, rectangular alternating with semicircular, originally held statues of the gods. This simple repetition of square against circle, which was established on a large scale by the juxtaposition of the rectilinear portico against the rotunda, is found throughout the building. The square, boxlike coffers inside the dome, which help lighten the weight of the masonry, may once have contained gilded bronze **rosettes** or stars suggesting the heavens.

oculus

coffered ceiling

stepped dome

drum

portico

rotunda

6-56. Reconstruction drawing of the Pantheon

It is not clear what the early Romans themselves thought of this architectural monument, so well known to travelers and students today, because it was rarely mentioned by any contemporary writers. An exception was Ammianus Marcellinus, who described it in 357 CE with restrained praise as being "rounded like the boundary of the horizon, and vaulted with a beautiful loftiness." Although the Pantheon has inspired hundreds—perhaps thousands—of faithful copies, inventive variants, and eclectic borrowings over the centuries, only recently have the true complexity and the innovative engineering of its construction been fully understood.

Hadrian was a great builder whose undertakings extended beyond public architecture to private dwellings. For his splendid villa at Tivoli outside Rome (fig. 6-57), he instructed his architects to re-create his favorite places throughout the empire: the Grove of Academe outside Athens in which Plato had founded his academy; the Painted Stoa in the Agora of Athens; and various buildings in and near the Ptolemaic capital of Alexandria, Egypt. Hadrian's Villa was not a single building but an architectural complex of many buildings, lakes, and gardens spread over half a square mile. Each section had its own inner logic, and each took advantage of natural land formations and attractive views. The individual buildings were not large, but they were extremely complex, providing ingenious examples of Roman planning and engineering. The villa's architects exploited to the fullest the flexibility offered by concrete construction. They surfaced structures with veneers of marble and travertine and with exquisite mosaics resembling paintings (see fig. 6-69). And they landscaped with pools, fountains, and plants, turning the villa into a place of sensuous and sumptuous delight. An area with a long reflecting pool, called the Canopus after a site Hadrian had seen at that city on the Nile near Alexandria, was framed by a fanciful colonnade with alternating semicircular and straight entablatures (fig. 6-58). The spaces between the

replica of Grove
of Academe

Canopus

Piazza d'Oro

baths

stadium

replica of
Painted Stoa

maritime
theater

6-57. Model of Hadrian's Villa, Tivoli. c. 135 CE

6-58. Canopus, Hadrian's Villa

columns were filled with copies of Greek statues. So great was Hadrian's love of Greek sculpture that he even had the **caryatids** of the Erechtheion (see fig. 5-51) replicated for his pleasure palace.

Architecture in the Provinces

During his reign, Trajan founded and built a new town at Timgad in the Algerian desert that was once home to 15,000 people (figs. 6-59, 6-60). This abandoned and ruined city has revealed almost as much about the culture of the empire as the cities buried by Vesuvius. The Roman architects who designed such new towns, cities,

and forts or who expanded and rebuilt existing ones were masters of urban planning. Adopting the grid plan of the Etruscan and later Greek cities, they divided towns into four quarters defined by intersecting north-south and east-west arteries, called, respectively, the *cardo* and the *decumanus* by modern archeologists. A town forum was usually located at this intersection. Terrain and climate had little effect on this simple, efficient plan, imposing in its symmetry, which remained much the same throughout the empire.

Timgad was a community where soldiers and their families, especially those who had served in the region, went when they retired. As such, it reflects the depen-

6-59. Plan of Timgad, Algeria. Begun c. 100 CE

dence of emperors on the support of their troops, for retiring soldiers received a pension in money or land. As land became scarce in Italy, the emperors established provincial communities like Timgad. As initially laid out, it was a square of about 30 acres with four equal districts set off by the main streets. The forum and a theater straddled the *cardo* just south of the intersection with the *decumanus* at the town center. Other amenities included a library and several public baths. Elaborate triumphal arches marked the main entrances to the town, and its streets, paved with precisely cut and fitted ashlar blocks, were once colonnaded (fig. 6-61).

Another of Trajan's projects was a grand market on the south side of Miletos in Asia Minor. Markets were an essential part of city life, and improving them, often with

6-60. Ruins of Timgad

6-61. *Decumanus* (main east-west thoroughfare), Timgad

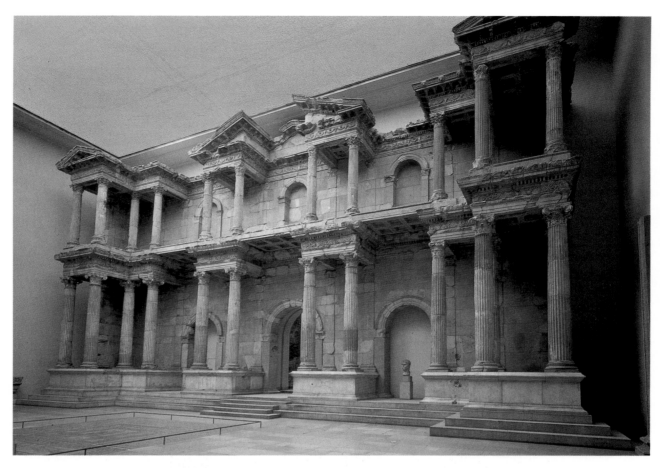

6-62. Market Gate, from Miletos (Turkey). c. 120 CE. Staatliche Museen zu Berlin, Preussischer Kulturbesitz, Antikensammlung

splendid architectural settings, was a way for wealthy families as well as emperors to curry popular favor. Only the core of Trajan's market buildings survives. The gate added in 120 CE, however, exemplifies the grandeur of some of these provincial projects (fig. 6-62). The two-story structure, now inside a museum in Berlin, is about 54 feet wide and resembles somewhat the backdrop of a Roman theater. It also brings to mind the fanciful illusionistic architecture seen in Pompeiian wall paintings. In its original setting, it functioned as a porchlike entrance to the market square. The facade, with its projecting ends, has three arched openings, and the whole is screened by a series of paired columns. The columns on the lower level are of the Composite order. These support short sections of entablature with carved friezes that in turn support the cornice of the second level. The shorter Corinthian columns and entablatures on the second level repeat the design of the lower level, except that the two center pairings support a **broken pediment**, which consists of the ends of a typical triangular pediment without a middle. The overall effect of structures like the gate at Miletos, with their design and structural innovations, was to evoke a sense of awe in the everyday passerby.

Hadrian's Wall, in northern Britain, was at the opposite end of the empire (fig. 6-63). Unlike the market gate, with its commercial, civilian setting, the wall and the forts that protected it were strictly military structures. This stone barrier snakes from coast to coast across a narrow (80-mile-wide) part of Britain. Some 4 to 5 feet thick and originally 15 feet high, it created a symbolic as well as a physical boundary between Roman territory and that of the barbarian Picts and Scots to the north. Towers were located at every mile mark. Seventeen larger camps, located at regular intervals, housed auxiliary forces ready to respond to any trouble the sentries might spot. These camps—like towns modeled on them—were laid out in a grid, with main streets dividing them into blocks (fig. 6-64). In the center were the praetorium (the commander's house and administrative headquarters), granaries, and the hospital, and surrounding these were barracks. These facilities and the wall itself are impressive reminders of the Roman occupation of northern Europe.

Relief Sculpture

The port of Ostia near Rome had grown so busy by the early empire that it was expanded with a new artificial harbor a short distance from the sea and connected to it by a canal. This harbor came to be known as Trajan's Harbor after he expanded it further. A relief panel created about 200 CE and discovered near the harbor marvelously combines a depiction of bustling seaport life

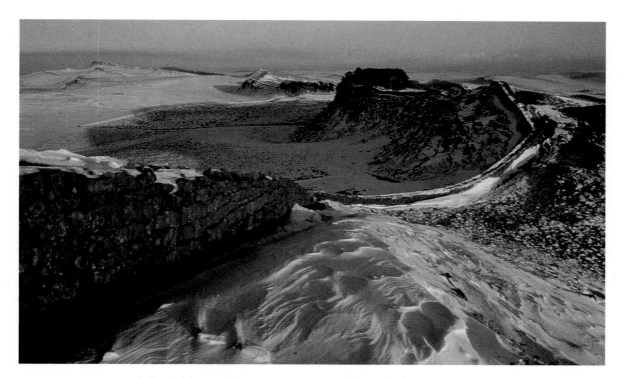

6-63. Hadrian's Wall, seen near Housesteads, England. 2nd century CE

6-64. Plan of the former Roman fort near Housesteads, England. 2nd century CE

6-65. *Allegorical Harbor Scene*, relief found near Trajan's Harbor, Ostia. c. 200 CE. Marble. Museo Torlonia, Rome

with an allegorical representation of Rome's maritime power (fig. 6-65). Like earlier plebeian sculpture, this panel conveys a great deal of specific information. Minutely detailed figures of sailors, dockworkers, and harbor supervisors are shown hard at work, ship passengers settle themselves under sails, and large figures of the gods in Classical Greek poses overlook the activities. At the top right is Bacchus, leaning on his staff and pouring wine from a jug into the sea. At the center stands the sea god Neptune holding his trident. The well-outfitted ship that appears to be entering the harbor bears the symbol of Rome on its sail—a she-wolf nursing the twins Romulus and Remus. Flying above the ship is an eagle, and on each side of it are two figures—a personification of the Senate on the right and of the Roman people on the left—extending wreaths of triumph. In the background is the harbor's lighthouse with its perpetual flame, and on the right, behind the ship with furled sails, can be seen the attic story of a triumphal arch, atop which is a statue of a rider and a chariot pulled by four elephants.

6-66. *Hadrian Hunting Boar and Sacrificing to Apollo*, roundels made for a monument to Hadrian and reused on the Arch of Constantine. 130–38 CE. Marble, roundel diameter 40" (102 cm)

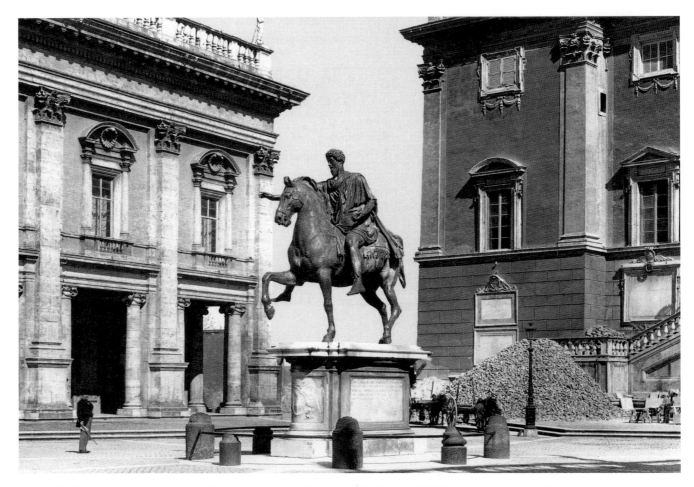

6-67. *Marcus Aurelius*. 161–80 CE. Bronze, originally gilded; height of statue 11'6" (3.5 m). Formerly in the Piazza del Campidoglio, Rome

This statue stood for centuries in the piazza fronting on the palace and church of Saint John Lateran in Rome. In January 1538 Pope Paul III had it moved to the Capitoline Hill, where it became the focus of a renovation and building program that created the Piazza del Campidoglio as it looks today. The statue is shown here in its original location, in the center of the piazza with the Palazzo Senatorio behind it and the Palazzo Nuovo (New Palace, today the Capitoline Museum) at the left. After being removed from its base for cleaning and restoration work some years ago, it was taken inside the Capitoline Museum to preserve it from the continued effects of Rome's polluted air.

the sculptor of these roundels has included elements of a natural landscape setting but kept them relatively small, using them to frame the proportionally larger figures. The idealized heads, form-enhancing drapery, and graceful yet energetic movement of the figures owe a distant debt to the works of Praxiteles and Lysippos (Chapter 5), but the well-observed details of the features and the bits of landscape are characteristically Roman. Much of the sculpture of the mid-second century CE shows the influence of Hadrian's love of Greek art, and for a time Roman artists achieved a level of idealized figural depiction close to that of Classical Greece. In the fourth century CE, Emperor Constantine had the roundels from the Hadrian monument placed on his own triumphal arch (see fig. 6-84) and had Hadrian's head in each scene recarved with his own features or those of his father, Constantius Chlorus.

Portrait Sculpture

Marcus Aurelius, like Hadrian, was a successful military commander, but he was equally proud of his intellectual attainments. In a lucky error—or twist of fortune—a once-gilded bronze equestrian statue of the emperor (fig. 6-67) came early but mistakenly to be revered as a statue of Constantine, the first Christian emperor, and escaped the fate of being melted down, which befell all other bronze equestrian statues from antiquity. The emperor is dressed in the tunic and short, heavy cloak of a commander. The raised foreleg of his horse is poised to trample a figure of a crouching barbarian (lost). His head, with its thick, curly hair and full beard (a style that was begun by Hadrian to enhance his image and then became popular among Roman men), resembles the traditional "philosopher" portraits of the Republican period. The emperor wears no armor and carries no weapons; like the Egyptian kings, he conquers effortlessly by the will of the gods. And like his illustrious predecessor Augustus, he reaches out to the people in a persuasive, beneficent gesture.

It is difficult to balance the composition of an equestrian portrait so that the rider stands out as the dominant figure without making the horse look too small. The sculptor of this equestrian statue of Marcus Aurelius found a balance acceptable to viewers of the time and, in doing so, created a model for later artists. The horse's high-arched neck, massive head, and short body suggest that it is from a Spanish breed of strong, compact, agile, and relatively small animals prized as war steeds.

Marcus Aurelius was succeeded by his son Commodus, a man without political skill, administrative competence, or intellectual distinction. During his unfortunate reign (180–192 CE) he devoted himself to luxury and frivolous pursuits. He did, however, attract some of the finest artists of the day for his commissions. A marble bust of Commodus dressed as Hercules reflects his character (fig. 6-68). The sculptor's sensitive modeling and expert drillwork exploit the play of light and shadow on the figure and bring out the textures of the hair, beard, facial features, and drapery. The portrait conveys the

6-68. *Commodus as Hercules*. c. 190 CE. Marble, height 46½" (118 cm). Palazzo dei Conservatori, Rome

The emperor Commodus, son of Marcus Aurelius, was not just decadent, he was probably insane. He claimed at various times to be the reincarnation of Hercules and the incarnation of the god Jupiter, and he even appeared in public as a gladiator. He ordered the months of the Roman year to be renamed after him and changed the name of Rome to Colonia Commodiana. When he proposed to assume the consulship dressed and armed as a gladiator, his associates, including his mistress, arranged to have him strangled in his bath by a wrestling partner. In this portrait, the emperor is shown in the guise of Hercules, adorned with references to the hero's legendary labors: his club, the skin and head of the Nemean Lion, and the golden apples from the garden of the Hesperides.

An example of official imperial sculpture offers an enlightening contrast to the *Allegorical Harbor Scene*. Like his predecessors, Hadrian used monumental sculpture to promote himself and his accomplishments. Several large, circular reliefs or roundels—originally part of a monument that no longer exists—contain images designed to affirm his imperial stature and right to rule (fig. 6-66). In the scene on the left, he demonstrates his courage and physical prowess in a boar hunt. Other roundels, not included here, show him confronting a bear and a lion. At the right, in a show of piety and appreciation to the gods for their support of his endeavors, Hadrian makes a sacrificial offering to Apollo at an outdoor altar. As did the sculptor of the Column of Trajan,

TECHNIQUE

ROMAN MOSAICS

Mosaics were used widely in Hellenistic times and became enormously popular for decorating homes in the Roman period. **Mosaic** designs are created with pebbles or with small, regularly shaped pieces of hard stone, marble, or manufactured colored glass, called **tesserae**. Today the stones are usually glued onto a firm backing, but in ancient times they were pressed into a kind of soft cement called grout. When the stones were firmly set, the spaces between them were also filled with cement. After the surface dried, it was cleaned and polished. At first, mosaics were used mainly as durable, water-resistant coverings on floors and pavements. They were done in a narrow range of colors depending on the natural color of the stone—often earth tones or simply black or some other dark color on a light background. When they began to appear on walls at outdoor fountains, a wide range of colors was used (see "The

Urban Garden," page 240). So accomplished were some mosaicists that they could create works that looked like paintings. In fact, at the request of patrons, they often copied well-known paintings employing a technique in which very small tesserae, in all the needed colors, were laid down in irregular, curving lines that very effectively mimicked painted brushstrokes.

Mosaic production was made more efficient by the development of emblemata (the plural of **emblema**, "central design"). These small, mosaic compositions were created in the artist's workshop in square or rectangular trays of marble or terra-cotta. They could be made in advance, carried to a work site, and inserted into a floor or wall otherwise decorated with a simple background mosaic in a plain or geometric pattern. Emblemata were often salvaged from older floors and reused in new ones much later.

illusion of life and movement, but it also captures its subject's foolishness. The weakness of the man comes through the grand pretensions of his costume.

Mosaics

Pictorial mosaics covered the floors of fine houses, villas, and public buildings throughout the empire. Working with very small tesserae (pieces of glass or stone) and a wide range of colors, mosaicists achieved remarkable illusionistic effects (see "Roman Mosaics," above). A floor mosaic from Hadrian's Villa at Tivoli illustrates extraordinary artistry (fig. 6-69). It may be a copy of a work by the Greek artist Zeuxis, of the late fifth century BCE, who was said to have done a much-admired painting of a fight between centaurs and wild animals. In a

6-69. *Battle of Centaurs and Wild Beasts*, from Hadrian's Villa, Tivoli. c. 118–28 CE. Mosaic, 23 x 36" (58.4 x 91.4 cm). Staatliche Museen zu Berlin, Preussischer Kulturbesitz, Antikensammlung

6-70. Heracleitus. *The Unswept Floor*, mosaic variant of a 2nd-century BCE painting by Sosos of Pergamon. 2nd century CE. Musei Vaticani, Museo Gregoriano Profano, ex Lateranense, Rome

rocky landscape with only a few bits of green, an enraged male centaur raises a large boulder over his head to crush a tiger that has attacked and severely wounded another centaur. Two other felines apparently took part in the attack—the white leopard on the rocks to the left and the dead lion at the feet of the male centaur. The mosaicist rendered the figures with three-dimensional shading, **foreshortening**, and a great sensitivity to a range of figure types, including human torsos and powerful animals, living and dead, in a variety of poses.

The skill of Hellenistic painters like Pausias (Chapter 5) in creating images of flowers and fruit that fooled the beholder into thinking they were real seems to have inspired a long-lasting tradition of realistic still-life illustration. These works fascinated and amused both artists and patrons of the Roman period. In the second century BCE, in Pergamon, an artist named Sosos created a large painting that included a **trompe l'oeil** ("fool the eye") representation of a floor littered with refuse. Three centuries later, the Roman mosaicist Heracleitus adapted this design in a work called *The Unswept Floor* (fig. 6-70). It shows a mouse among table scraps—meat bones, shellfish, fruit, and nuts—seemingly tossed aside for the family pets. The objects are all intensely observed and re-created in meticulous detail, even to the shadows they cast on the floor, which seem to be the result of a single light source—perhaps an open door—raking across from the right.

THE LATE EMPIRE: FROM THE SEVERAN DYNASTY TO THE TETRARCHS

The reign of Commodus marked the beginning of a period of political and economic decline. Barbarian groups pressed on Rome's frontiers, and many settled within them, disrupting provincial government. As strains spread throughout the empire, imperial rule became increasingly military. Soon the army controlled the government, and the Imperial Guards set up and deposed rulers almost at will, often selecting candidates from among poorly educated, power-hungry provincial leaders in their own ranks.

Under the Severan emperors (193–235 CE) who succeeded Commodus, the arts continued to flourish. Septimius Severus (ruled 193–211 CE) and his Syrian wife, Julia Domna, restored public buildings, commissioned official portraits, and made some splendid additions to the old Republican Forum, including the transformation of the House of the Vestal Virgins, who served the Temple of Vesta, into a large, luxurious residence. Septimius's sons, Caracalla and Geta, succeeded him as co-emperors in 211 CE, but in 212 CE, Caracalla murdered Geta and ruled alone until he in turn was murdered by his successor in 217 CE.

The death of Severus Alexander (ruled 222–235 CE), the last in the Severan line, began a half-century of

6-71. Baths of Caracalla, Rome. c. 211–17 CE

Although the well-to-do usually had private baths in their homes, women and men enjoyed the pleasures of socializing at the public baths. They did not do so together, however. In some cities, women and men had separate bathhouses, but it was also common for them to share one facility at different times of the day. Everyone—from nobles to working people—was allowed to use the public baths, no matter how grand. Men had access to the full range of facilities, including hot, tepid, and cold baths, moist- and dry-heat chambers (like saunas), pools for swimming, and outdoor areas for sunbathing or exercising in the nude. Women generally refrained from using very hot baths, dry-heat chambers, and the outdoor areas.

anarchy that ended with the rise to power of Emperor Diocletian (ruled 284–305 CE). This brilliant politician and general reversed the empire's declining fortunes, but he also initiated an increasingly autocratic form of rule, and toward the end of his reign he unleashed the persecution of Christians. He and his successors imposed ever more burdensome taxes on their subjects, and under them the social structure of the empire became increasingly rigid.

To distribute the task of defending and administering the empire and to assure an orderly succession, Diocletian devised a form of government called the Tetrarchy, or rule by four. Diocletian divided the empire in two; with the title of Augustus he would rule in the East, while another Augustus, Maximian, would rule in the West. Each Augustus designated a subordinate and heir, who held the title of Caesar. Each of the two regions was thus administered by one of these two co-rulers and his second-in-command. Although Diocletian intended that on the death or retirement of an Augustus, his Caesar would replace him and name a new Caesar, the plan failed when Diocletian tried to implement it.

Architecture

The year before his death in 211, Septimius Severus began a popular public-works project, the construction of magnificent new public baths on the southeast side of Rome (fig. 6-71). The baths were inaugurated in 216–217 CE by his son and successor, Caracalla. For the Romans,

6-72. Plan of the Baths of Caracalla

baths were recreational and educational centers, not simply places to clean themselves, and the emperors built large bathing complexes to gain public favor. The marble, brick, and concrete Baths of Caracalla, as they are now called, were laid out on a strictly symmetrical plan. The bathing facilities were located together in the center of the main building to make efficient use of the below-ground furnaces that heated them and to allow bathers to move comfortably from hot to cold pools and finish with a swim (fig. 6-72). Many other facilities—exercise rooms, shops, latrines, and dressing rooms—were housed on each side of the bathing block. The baths alone covered 5 acres. The entire complex, which included gardens, a

6-73. Model of Palace of Diocletian, Split, Serbian Croatia. c. 300 CE. Museo della Civiltà Romana, Rome

6-74. Peristyle court, Palace of Diocletian

stadium, libraries, a painting gallery, auditoriums, and huge water reservoirs, covered an area of 50 acres.

The great palaces such as Hadrian's Villa were often as extensive and semipublic as the Minoan palace at Knossos. Diocletian broke this tradition by building a huge and well-fortified imperial residence at Split, on the Dalmatian coast, after he retired from active rule (fig. 6-73). Revolutionary in design, the building recalls the compact, regular plan of a Roman army camp rather than the irregular, sprawling design of Hadrian's Villa. The palace was surrounded by a wall, a reflection of the unstable conditions of the time. It consisted of a rectangu-lar enclosure 650 by 550 feet crossed by two colonnaded streets that divided it into quarters, each with a specific function. The emperor's residential complex, which included the reception hall on the main, north-south axis of the palace, faced the sea. Ships bearing supplies or providing transport for the emperor tied up at the narrow landing stage. The support staff lived and worked in buildings near the main gate. A colonnaded avenue extended from this entrance, leading to a peristyle court that ended in a grand facade with an enormous arched doorway through which the emperor made his cere-monial appearances (fig. 6-74). Like the Canopus at

6-75. *Caracalla*. Early 3rd century CE. Marble, height 14½" (36.2 cm). The Metropolitan Museum of Art, New York

Samuel D. Lee Fund, 1940 (40.11.1A)

The emperor Caracalla (ruled 211–217 CE) was consistently represented with a malignant, scowling expression, a convention meant to convey a particular message to the viewer: the emperor was not a god, not an effete intellectual, not a soft patrician, but a hard-as-nails, battle-toughened military man, a lethal opponent ready to defend himself and his empire.

Hadrian's Villa, the columns of the peristyle court supported arches rather than entablatures (see fig. 6-58). On one side of the court, the arcade opened onto Diocletian's mausoleum; on the other side, it opened onto the Temple of Jupiter.

Portrait Sculpture

Emperor Caracalla emerges from his portraits as a man of chilling and calculating ruthlessness. In the example shown here (fig. 6-75) the sculptor has enhanced the intensity of the emperor's expression by producing strong contrasts of light and dark with sensitive drill and chisel work. Even the marble eyes have been drilled and engraved to catch the light in a way that makes them glitter. It is hard to believe that Caracalla could have favored a portrait that showed him in such unflattering terms, yet he clearly did. Unable to charm his subjects, he apparently preferred to terrify them. The contrast between this style and that of the portraits of Augustus is a telling reflection of the changing character of imperial rule. Augustus presented himself as the first among equals, ruling by persuasion; Caracalla presented himself as a no-nonsense ruler of iron-fisted determination.

The successors of the Severan emperors—the more than two dozen so-called soldier-emperors who attempted to rule the empire before the rise of Diocletian—continued to favor the style of Caracalla's portraits. A bust of Philip the Arab (ruled 244–249 CE), however, does not convey the same malevolence as

6-76. *Philip the Arab*. 244–49 CE. Marble, height 26" (71.1 cm).
Musei Vaticani, Braccia Nuovo, Rome

6-77. *The Tetrarchs*. c. 305 CE. Porphyry, height of figures 51"
(129 cm). Installed in the Middle Ages at the corner of
the facade of the Church of San Marco, Venice

Caracalla's portraits (fig. 6-76). Philip's expression is more tense and worried, suggesting a troubled man in troubled times. Philip had been the head of the Imperial Guard but had plotted to murder and replace his predecessor, Emperor Gordian III (ruled 238–244 CE), whom he was pledged to defend. Philip's own short reign also ended in assassination.

Philip is shown wearing a new style of toga that is typical of late imperial dress. Made of heavy material, it hangs in a few stiff folds and drapes across the chest in a broad, flat band. The sculptor first modeled the broad structure of the emperor's head, then used both chisel and drill to deepen shadows and heighten the effects of light in the furrows of his face and in his drapery. Unlike the portraits of Marcus Aurelius and Commodus, in which hair and beard were carved to show individual locks, in this portrait tiny flicks of the chisel suggest the texture of hair. Around the mouth, these small scratches sometimes give the impression of tension as they catch the light playing over the surface. The overall impact of the work depends on the effects of light and the imagination of the spectator as much as on the carved stone itself. What comes through from Philip's twisted brow, sidelong upward glance, quizzical lips, and tightened jaw muscles is a sense of guile, deceit, and fear.

During the turmoil of the third century, Roman artists lost interest in representing the natural world, emphasizing instead the symbolic or general qualities of their subjects and expressing them in increasingly simplified, geometric forms. By the mid-third century, portraits had begun to convey the anxious state of mind of the emperors and the people they ruled. A further turn toward abstraction and symbolic representation can be seen in *The Tetrarchs*, a depiction of Diocletian and his three co-rulers from the early fourth century CE (fig. 6-77). Hardly a realistic portrait of Diocletian, his co-ruler Maximian, and their Caesars, it reads instead like a symbolic representation of four-man rule. The four figures—two with beards, probably the senior Augusti, and two clean shaven, probably the Caesars, their adopted sons—are nearly identical. Dressed in military garb and clasping swords at their sides, they embrace each other in a show of imperial unity, proclaiming a kind of peace through concerted strength and vigilance. As a piece of propaganda and a summary of the state of affairs at the time, it is unsurpassed. The sculpture is made of porphyry, a purple stone from Egypt reserved for imperial use. The hardness of the stone, which makes it difficult to carve, and perhaps the sculptor's familiarity with Egyptian artistic conventions, may have contributed to the extremely

6-78. *Battle between the Romans and the Barbarians*, detail of the *Ludovisi Battle Sarcophagus*, found near Rome. c. 250 CE. Marble, height approx. 5' (1.52 m). Museo Nazionale Romano, Rome

abstract style of the work. The most striking features of *The Tetrarchs*—the simplification of natural forms to geometric shapes, the disregard for normal human proportions, and the emphasis on a message or idea—can nevertheless be seen in most Roman art by the end of the third century.

Sarcophagus Reliefs

Although portraits and narrative reliefs were the major forms of public sculpture during the second and third centuries CE, changing funerary practices—a shift from cremation to burial—led to a growing demand for funerary sculpture. A wealthy Roman might commission an elegant stone or marble sarcophagus to be placed in a mausoleum. Workshops throughout the empire produced thousands of these sarcophagi, which were carved with reliefs that ranged in complexity from simple geometric or floral ornaments to scenes involving large numbers of figures. The subjects of the more elaborate reliefs varied widely. Some included events from the life of the deceased and some showed dramatic scenes from Greek mythology and drama, such as the tragedies of Agamemnon's family, the events of the Trojan War, or the Labors of Hercules. Scenes of Bacchus and his followers were extremely popular, no doubt because this cult offered its worshipers an afterlife of perpetual ecstasy in union with the god.

A famous carved stone coffin known as the *Ludovisi Battle Sarcophagus* (after a seventeenth-century owner) dates to about 250 CE (fig. 6-78). It shows a battle be-

tween Romans and barbarians in a style that has roots in the sculptural traditions of Hellenistic Pergamon. The Romans at the top of the panel are efficiently dispatching the barbarians—clearly identifiable by their heavy, twisted locks and scraggly beards—who lie fallen, dying, or beaten at the bottom of the panel. The artist has made no attempt to create a realistic spatial environment. The bare-headed young Roman commander, addressing his troops with an outstretched arm from the back of his valiant steed, is shown in the midst of the battle in a formal equestrian pose like that of the equestrian statue of Marcus Aurelius (see fig. 6-67).

Painting

A portrait of the family of Septimius Severus provides a remarkable insight into the history of the Severan dynasty in addition to revealing something about early-third-century CE painting (fig. 6-79). The work is in the highly formal style of a region in northwestern Egypt called Faiyum, and it is probably a souvenir of an imperial visit to Egypt. The emperor, clearly identified by his distinctive divided beard and curled moustache, wears an enormous crown. Next to him is his wife, Julia Domna, portrayed with similarly recognizable features— full face, large nose, and masses of waving hair. She looks out at the viewer in a defiant manner. Their two sons, Geta and Caracalla, stand in front of them, but Geta's features have been defaced. Perhaps because we know that he grew up to be a ruthless dictator, little Caracalla looks in this portrait like a disagreeable child. Soon

6-79. *Septimius Severus, Julia Domna, and Their Children, Caracalla and Geta*, from Faiyum, Egypt. c. 200 CE. Painted wood, diameter 14" (35.6 cm). Staatliche Museen zu Berlin, Preussischer Kulturbesitz, Antikensammlung

after Septimius's death, Caracalla murdered Geta, perhaps with Julia Domna's help, and in a decree called *damnatio memoriae* declared that Geta's memory be abolished. Clearly the owners of this painting complied with the decree. The work emphasizes the trappings of imperial wealth and power—crowns, jewels, and direct, forceful expressions—rather than attempting a deep, psychological study. The rather hard drawing style, with its broadly brushed-in draperies, contrasts markedly with that of earlier portraits, such as the *Young Woman Writing* (see fig. 6-48).

Despite the trend toward abstraction, the earlier tradition of slightly idealized but realistic portraiture was slow to die out, probably because it showed patrons as they wanted to be remembered. In the *Family of Vunnerius Keramus* (fig. 6-80), the subjects are rendered as individuals, although the artist has emphasized their great almond-shaped eyes. The work seems to reflect the advice of Philostratus, who, writing in the late third century CE, commented: "The person who would properly master this art [of painting] must also be a keen observer of human nature and must be capable of discerning the signs of people's characters even though they are silent; he should be able to discern what is revealed in the expression of the eyes, what is found in the character of

6-80. *Family of Vunnerius Keramus*. c. 250 CE. Gold leaf sealed between glass, diameter 2³⁄₈" (6 cm). Museo Civico dell'Età Cristiana, Brescia

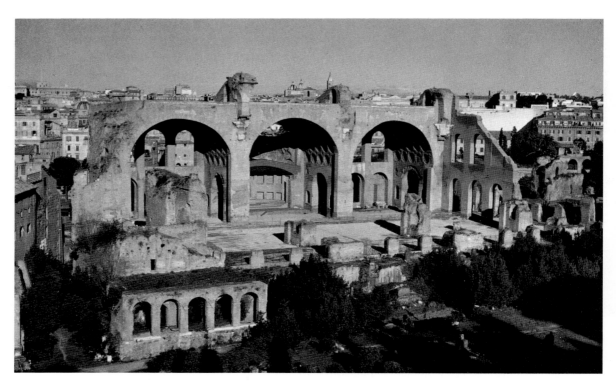

6-81. Basilica of Maxentius and Constantine, Rome. 306–13 CE

the brows, and, to state the point briefly, whatever indicates the condition of the mind."

The *Family of Vunnerius Keramus* was engraved and painted on sheets of **gold leaf**, then cut out and sealed between two layers of glass. This fragile, delicate medium, most often used for the bottoms of glass bowls or cups—many of which survive—seems appropriate for an age of material insecurity and emotional intensity. Curiously, this particular piece was inserted by a later Christian owner as the central jewel in a decorated seventh-century cross.

THE LATE EMPIRE: CONSTANTINE THE GREAT AND HIS LEGACY

In 305 CE Diocletian abdicated and forced his fellow Augustus, Maximian, to do likewise. The orderly succession he had hoped for failed to occur, and Augusti and Caesars began almost immediately to jockey with each other for position and advantage. Two main contenders emerged in the western part of the empire: Maximian's son Maxentius (ruled 306–312 CE), and Constantine I, known as The Great (ruled 306–337 CE), son of the Augustus Constantius. Constantine emerged victorious in 312 after defeating Maxentius at the Battle of the Milvian Bridge, at the entrance to Rome. According to a legend popular for centuries, Constantine had a vision the night before the battle in which he saw a flaming cross in the sky and heard these words: "In this sign you shall conquer." The next morning he ordered that his army's shields and standards be inscribed with the monogram ☧ (formed of the Greek letters *chi* and *rho*, standing for *Christos*). The legend says that the victorious Constantine then showed his gratitude by ending persecution of Christians and recognizing Christianity as a lawful religion. (In fact *chi* and *rho* used together had long been an abbreviation of the Greek word *chrestos*, meaning "auspicious," and this was probably the reason Constantine used the monogram.) Whatever the impulse, in 313 CE, together with Licinius, who was Augustus in the East, Constantine issued the Edict of Milan, a model of religious toleration: "With sound and most upright reasoning. . . we resolved that authority be refused to no one to follow and choose the observance or form of worship that Christians use, and that authority be granted to each one to give his mind to that form of worship which he deems suitable to himself, to the intent that the Divinity . . . may in all things afford us his wonted care and generosity" (Eusebius, *Ecclesiastical History* 10.5.5). The Edict of Milan granted freedom to all religious groups, not just Christians. Constantine remained the *Pontifex Maximus*, or High Priest, of Rome's state religion and also reaffirmed his devotion during his reign to the military's favorite god, Mithras, and to the Invincible Sun, *Sol Invictus*, a manifestation of Helios Apollo, the sun god.

In 324 Constantine defeated Licinius, his last rival, and would rule as sole emperor until his death in 337. He made the port city of Byzantium his new capital, renaming it Constantinople. This new capital (modern Istanbul, in Turkey) was dedicated in 330, and thereafter Rome, which had already ceased to be the seat of government in the West, declined in importance.

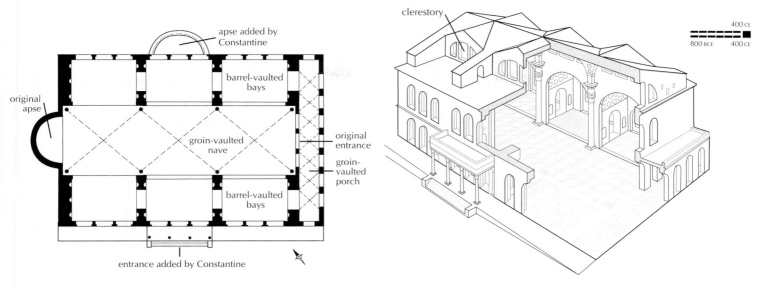

6-82. Plan and isometric reconstruction of the Basilica of Maxentius and Constantine

The original plan for the basilica called for a single entrance on the southeast side, facing a single apse on the north-west. After building had begun, Constantine's architects added another entrance on the southwest, probably to accommodate crowds, and another apse across the hall. The effect was to dilute the focus on the original apse, with its gigantic statue of the emperor (see fig. 6-86).

Architecture

Maxentius, who controlled Rome throughout his short reign, ordered the repair of many buildings there and had others built. His most impressive undertaking was a huge new basilica just southeast of the Imperial Forums called the Basilica Nova, or New Basilica (fig. 6-81). Now known as the Basilica of Maxentius and Constantine, this was the last important imperial government building erected in Rome itself. It functioned, like all basilicas, as an administrative center and provided a magnificent setting for the emperor when he appeared as supreme judge. Earlier basilicas, such as Trajan's Basilica Ulpia (see fig. 6-50), had been columnar halls, but Maxentius ordered his engineers to create the kind of large, unbroken, vaulted space found in public baths. The central hall was covered with groined vaults, and the side aisles were covered with lower barrel vaults that acted as **buttresses**, or projecting supports, for the central groin vault and allowed generous window openings in the clerestory areas over the side walls. Three of these brick-and-concrete barrel vaults still loom beside the streets of modern Rome. The basilica originally measured 300 by 215 feet and the vaults of the central **nave** rose to a height of 114 feet. A groin-vaulted porch extended across the short side (on the southeast) and sheltered a triple entrance to the central hall. At the opposite end of the long axis of the hall was an apse of the same width, which acted as a focal point for the building (fig. 6-82).

Constantine undertook a building campaign that became empirewide by the later years of his reign (Chapter 7). Among his achievements was a new palace and a basilica, built about 310 CE, at Trier, the capital of the northern Germanic territories. The exterior of this build-

6-83. Basilica, Trier, Germany. Early 4th century CE

ing still looks much as it did in the early fourth century, with a few exceptions (fig. 6-83). Over the centuries, the ground level has risen and covered a high podium beneath the structure, and decorative exterior elements on walls and around windows have disappeared. Unlike the Basilica Ulpia, the building is entered through one end and has a single apse opposite the entrance, on which all attention is focused. Inside, it carries further the preference for large, unbroken spaces seen in the Basilica of Maxentius and Constantine. It has no side aisles, has a flat wooden-truss ceiling, and is lit by two rows of windows in the long walls and around the apse. The directional focus along a central axis from entrance to apse was adopted by Christians for use in churches.

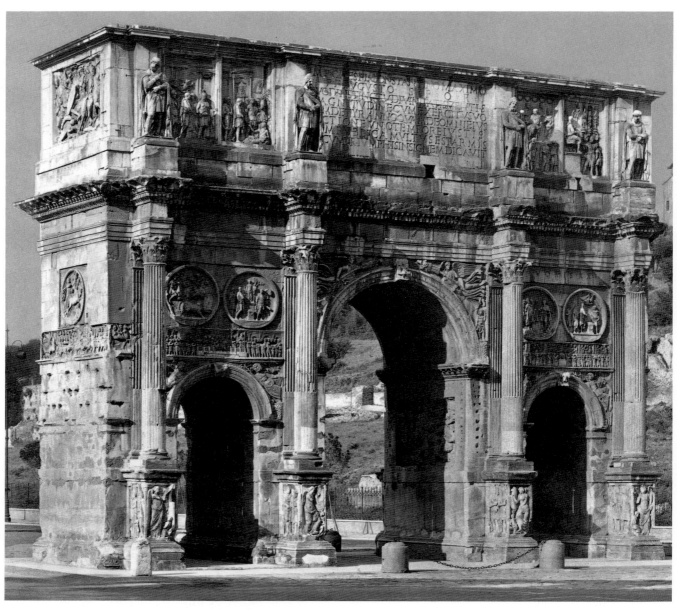

6-84. Arch of Constantine, Rome. 312–15 CE (dedicated July 25, 315)

This massive, triple-arched monument to Emperor Constantine's victory over Maxentius in 312 CE is a wonder of recycled sculpture. On the attic story, flanking the inscription over the central arch, are relief panels taken from a monument celebrating the victory of Marcus Aurelius over the Germans in 174 CE. On the attached piers framing these panels are large statues of prisoners made to celebrate Trajan's victory over the Dacians in the early second century CE. On the inner walls of the central arch (not seen here) are reliefs also commemorating Trajan's conquest of Dacia. Over each of the side arches are pairs of giant roundels taken from a monument to Hadrian (see fig. 6-66). The rest of the decoration is contemporary with the arch.

6-85. *Constantine Speaking to the People*, relief panel from the Arch of Constantine. Marble

The Arch of Constantine

In Rome, next to the Colosseum, the Senate erected a memorial to Constantine's victory over Maxentius (fig. 6-84), a huge, triple arch that dwarfs the nearby Arch of Titus (see fig. 6-40). Its three barrel-vaulted passageways are flanked by columns on high pedestals and surmounted by a large attic story with elaborate sculptural decoration and a traditional laudatory inscription: "To the Emperor Constantine from the Senate and the Roman People. Since through divine inspiration and great wisdom he has delivered the state from the tyrant and his party by his army and noble arms, [we] dedicate this arch, decorated with triumphal insignia." The "triumphal insignia" were in part looted from earlier monuments made for Constantine's illustrious predecessors, the "good emperors" Trajan, Hadrian, and Marcus Aurelius. The reused items in effect transferred the old Roman virtues of strength, courage, and piety associated with these earlier emperors to Constantine. New reliefs made for the arch recount the story of his victory and symbolize his power and generosity. A panel in one of the **lintels**, for example, depicts Constantine, in the center, making his first public speech after the triumph over Maxentius (fig. 6-85). The emperor (his head is missing) is seated in the Republican Forum on a temporary speaker's platform in front of a monument to the Tetrarchs (the columns with the statues on top of them) and flanked by images of Marcus Aurelius and Hadrian. The Basilica Julia and the Arch of Tiberius are to the left and the Arch of Septimius Severus is to the right.

Although these new reliefs reflect the long-standing Roman affection for depicting important events with realistic detail, they nevertheless represent a significant change in style, approach, and subject matter that distinguishes them from the reused elements in the arch. The stocky, mostly frontal, look-alike figures—reminiscent of figures in plebeian-style works—are compressed by the miniature buildings of the forum into the foreground plane. The arrangement and appearance of the uniform and undifferentiated participants below the enthroned Constantine clearly isolate the new Augustus and connect him visually with the illustrious predecessors on each side of him. This two-dimensional, hierarchical approach and stiff style is far removed from the realism of earlier imperial reliefs. With its emphasis on authority, ritual, and symbolic meaning rather than outward form, this style was adopted by the emerging Christian Church. Constantinian art is thus a bridge between the art of the imperial past and the art of the European Middle Ages (roughly 476 to 1453 CE).

Portrait Sculpture

Constantine, seeking to impress the people of Rome with visible symbols of his authority, put his own stamp on projects Maxentius had started. To the Basilica Nova he added an imposing new entrance in the center of the long side and a giant apse facing it across the three aisles. After he had begun to construct his new capital in

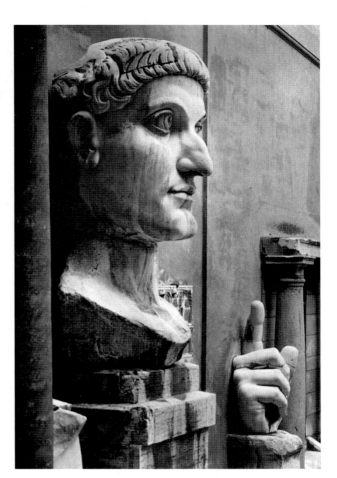

6-86. *Constantine the Great*, from the Basilica of Maxentius and Constantine, Rome. 325–26 CE. Marble, height of head 8'6" (2.6 m). Palazzo dei Conservatori, Rome

This fragment came from a statue of the seated emperor. The original sculpture combined marble, wood, and bricks. Only a few marble fragments survive—the head, a hand, a knee, an elbow, and a foot. The body might have been made of colored stone or of wood and bricks sheathed in bronze. This statue, although made of less-expensive materials, must have been as awe-inspiring as the gigantic ivory and gold-clad statues of Zeus at Olympia and Athena on the Acropolis in Athens, made in the fifth century BCE by Pheidias, the favorite sculptor of Perikles. Constantine was a master at the use of portrait statues to spread imperial propaganda. Heads like this, made according to official specifications, were shipped throughout the provinces to be attached to bodies that were locally sculpted.

the East, he commissioned a colossal, 30-foot portrait statue of himself and had it placed in the original apse (fig. 6-86). This statue was, in effect, a permanent stand-in for the emperor in Rome, representing him whenever the conduct of business legally required his presence. The sculpture combines features of traditional Roman portraiture with the abstract qualities evident in *The Tetrarchs* (see fig. 6-77). The defining characteristics of Constantine's face—his heavy jaw, hooked nose, and jutting chin—have been incorporated into a rigid, symmetrical pattern in which other features, such as his eyes, eyebrows, and hair, have been simplified into repeated

6-87. *Helen, Mother of Constantine.* c. 320 CE. Marble. Museo Capitolino, Rome

6-88. *Julian the Apostate,* coin issued 361–63 CE. Gold. The British Museum, London

geometric arcs. The result is a work that projects imperial power and dignity with no hint of human frailty or imperfection.

Constantine's mother, Helen, a devout Christian, played an important part in her son's career. Credited by legend with the discovery of Christ's cross, she was later made a saint and represented in Christian art. In one monumental portrait (fig. 6-87), she was depicted in the manner of a Classical Greek reclining goddess.

THE LATE EMPIRE: ROMAN TRADITIONALISM IN ART AFTER CONSTANTINE

Constantine was baptized formally into the Christian religion on his deathbed in 337 CE. After his death there was a period of civil war, the reuniting of the empire under his son, Constantius II, then the brief reign (361–363 CE) of Julian, bringing with it religious tumult. Julian the Apostate, as Christian writers called him (apostate means "religious defector"), rejected Christianity and sought to reinstate the worship of Rome's ancestral gods. Himself a follower of Mithras, Julian officially forbade Christian scholars from teaching pre-Christian Greek and Roman literature and wrote treatises attacking the ideas of contemporary Christian writers. He did not ban Christianity but tried to undermine it by adapting some of its liturgical devices and charitable practices for the worship of the traditional gods. He had himself portrayed on coins as a bearded scholar-philosopher (fig. 6-88), an ancient portrait convention also favored by his illustrious predecessor Marcus Aurelius.

Julian died in battle and was succeeded by a series of Christian emperors. By the end of the fourth century, Christianity had become the official religion of the empire, and non-Christians had become the targets of persecution. Many people resisted this shift and tried to revive classical culture. Among them were the Roman patricians Quintus Aurelius Symmachus, a strong opponent of Christianity, and Virius Nicomachus Flavianus, a champion of paganism. A famous ivory **diptych**—a pair of panels attached with hinges—attests to the close relationship between their families. One family's name is inscribed at the top of each joined panel of the diptych, which may commemorate a marriage between the families. On the panel inscribed "*Symmachorum*" (fig. 6-89), a stately, elegantly attired priestess makes a ritual offering, apparently to Bacchus, at a beautifully decorated altar. She is assisted by a small child, and the event takes place out of doors under the oak tree sacred to Jupiter. The Roman ivory carvers of the fourth century were extremely skillful, and their wares were widely admired and commissioned by pagans and Christians alike. For conservative patrons like the Nichomachus and Symmachus families, they were able to imitate Augustan style effortlessly. The exquisite rendering of the drapery and foliage is reminiscent of the reliefs on the Ara Pacis (see fig. 6-28).

Classical subject matter remained attractive to artists and patrons, and imperial repression could not immediately extinguish it. Even such great Christian thinkers as bishop and saint Gregory of Nazianzus spoke out in support of the right of the people to appreciate and enjoy their classical heritage, so long as they were not seduced by it to return to pagan practices. As a result, stories of the ancient gods and heroes entered the secular realm as lively, visually delightful, and even erotic decorative elements. As a large silver platter dating from the mid-fourth century CE shows, themes involving Bacchus, the god of grapevines and fertility, continued to

6-89. *Priestess of Bacchus*(?), right panel of a diptych.
c. 390–401 CE. Ivory, 11³/₄ x 5¹/₂" (29.9 x 14 cm).
Victoria and Albert Museum, London

6-90. Dish, from Mildenhall, England. Mid-4th century CE.
    Silver, diameter approx. 24" (61 cm). The British
    Museum, London

provide artists with the opportunity to create elaborate figural compositions displaying the nude or lightly draped human body in complex, dynamic poses (fig. 6-90). The Bacchic revelers whirl, leap, and sway in a dance to the piping of satyrs (half men, half goats) around a circular central design. In the center, the head of the sea god Oceanus is ringed by nude females frolicking in the waves with fantastic sea creatures. In the outer circle, Bacchus is the one stable element. Wine jug on his shoulder and one foot on the haunches of his panther, he listens to a male follower begging for another drink. Only a few figures away, the pitifully drunken hero Hercules has lost his lion-skin mantle and collapsed in a stupor into the supporting arms of two satyrs. The detail, clarity, and liveliness of this platter reflect the work of a skillful artist. Deeply engraved lines emphasize the contours of the subtly modeled bodies, echoing the technique of undercutting used to add depth to figures in stone and marble reliefs and suggesting a connection between silver working and relief sculpture.

Found in a cache of both pagan and Christian treasures near Mildenhall, England, the platter may have been made elsewhere and imported into Britain. It suggests the wealth to be found in the outlying provinces of the Roman Empire. Such opulent items were often hidden away or buried to protect them from theft and looting, a sign of the breakdown of the long Roman peace. The plate's style and subject matter reflect a society in transition. Even as Roman authority gave way to local rule by powerful barbarian tribes in much of the West, many people continued to appreciate classical learning and to treasure Greek and Roman art. In the East, classical traditions and styles endured to become an important element of Byzantine art.

100 CE   300   500   700

Orant figure,
Priscilla catacomb
3rd century

Old Saint Peter's
c. 320–27

Mausoleum of Galla
Placidia c. 425–26

Hagia Sophia
532–37

▲ EARLY CHRISTIAN c. 100–6TH CENTURY   ▲ IMPERIAL CHRISTIAN 313–c. 6TH CENTURY   ▲ EARLY BYZANTINE 527–867

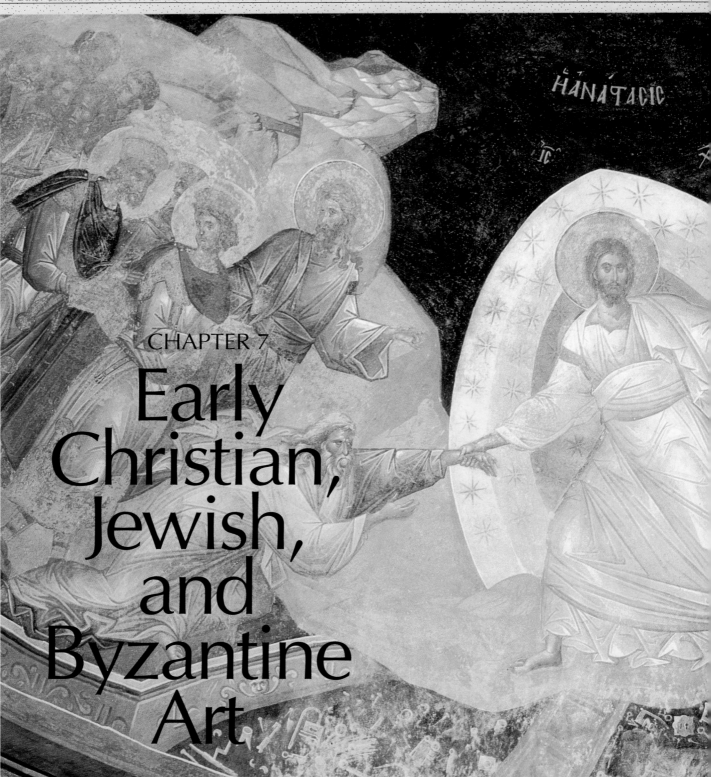

CHAPTER 7

Early Christian, Jewish, and Byzantine Art

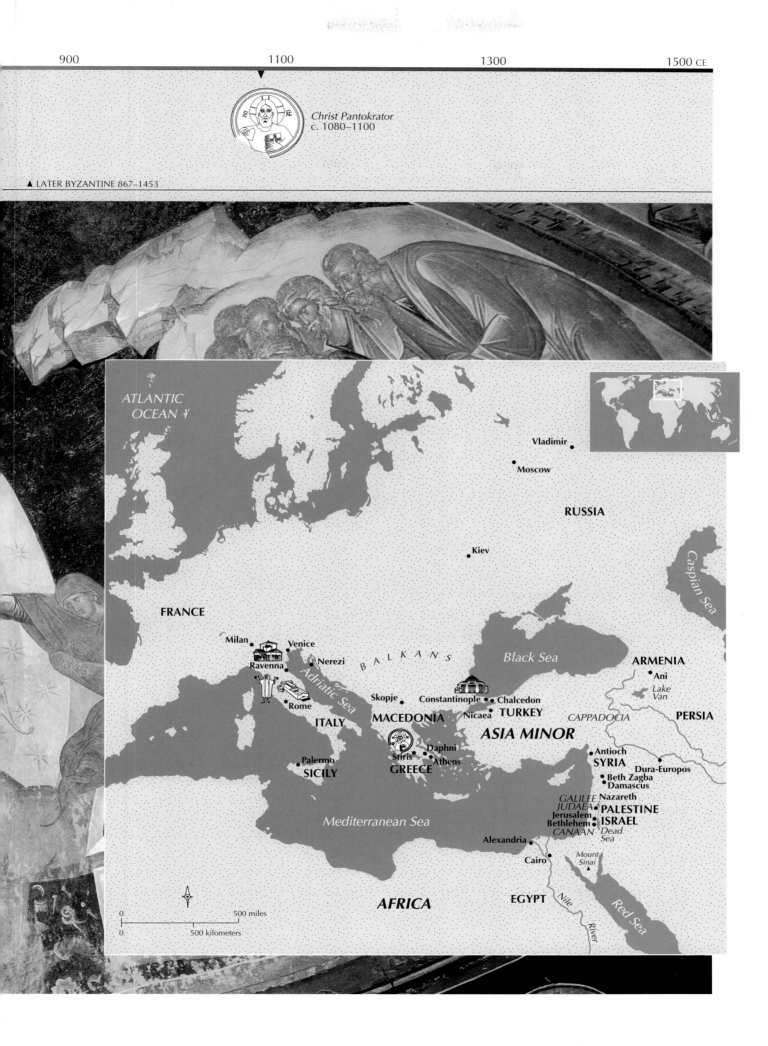

Christ Pantokrator.
c. 1080–1100

ATLANTIC
OCEAN

Vladimir

Moscow

RUSSIA

Kiev

FRANCE

Milan
Venice
Nerezi
Ravenna

B A L K A N S

Black Sea

ARMENIA
Ani
Lake
Van

Adriatic Sea

Skopje

Rome

MACEDONIA

Constantinople   Chalcedon
Nicaea   TURKEY

CAPPADOCIA

PERSIA

ITALY

ASIA MINOR

Palermo

Stiris
GREECE

Daphni
Athens

SICILY

Antioch
SYRIA
Dura-Europos
Beth Zagba
Damascus

Mediterranean Sea

GALILEE Nazareth
JUDAEA
Jerusalem
Bethlehem
CANAAN Dead
Sea

PALESTINE
ISRAEL

Alexandria

Cairo

Mount
Sinai

AFRICA

EGYPT

Nile

Red Sea

River

Caspian Sea

0   500 miles
0   500 kilometers

7-1. *Emperor Justinian and His Attendants*, mosaic on north wall of the apse, Church of San Vitale, Ravenna, Italy. c. 547. 8'8" x 12' (2.64 x 3.65 m)

In a large mosaic on the wall of a church on the northeast coast of Italy, the sixth-century Roman emperor known as Justinian the Great stands firmly between representatives of church and state (fig. 7-1). He dominates the scene just as he dominated his times, which are often referred to as the Golden Age of Justinian. As head of state, Justinian wears a huge jeweled crown and a purple cloak; as head of church, he carries a large golden paten to hold the Host, the symbolic body of Jesus Christ. The Church officials at his left hold a jeweled cross and a gospel book symbolizing Christ and his church. Justinian's soldiers stand behind the chi rho monogram, Greek letters, the initials of Christ. On the opposite wall Empress Theodora, also dressed in royal purple, offers a golden chalice, for the liturgical wine (see fig. 7-32).

Ironically, neither Justinian nor Theodora probably ever set foot in the Church of San Vitale in Ravenna, whose dedication these mosaics commemorate. Nevertheless, the mosaics are shimmering examples of a major art form of the time that dramatically illustrate the close relationship between secular and religious power in Justinian's world.

JEWS AND CHRISTIANS IN THE ROMAN EMPIRE

Three religions that arose in the Near East dominate the spiritual life of the Western world: Judaism, Christianity, and Islam. All three religions are monotheistic; followers hold that only one god created and rules the universe. Traditional Jews believe that God made a covenant, or pact, with their ancestors, the Hebrews, and that they are God's chosen people. They await the coming of a savior, the Messiah, "the anointed one." Traditional Christians believe that Jesus of Nazareth was that Messiah (the title *Christ* is derived from the Greek term meaning "Messiah"). They believe that God took human form, preached among men and women and suffered execution, then rose from the dead and ascended to heaven after establishing the Christian Church under the leadership of the apostles (his closest disciples). Muslims, while accepting the Hebrew prophets and Jesus as divinely inspired, believe Muhammad to be God's (Allah's) last and greatest prophet, the Messenger of God through whom Islam was revealed some six centuries after Jesus' lifetime. All three are "religions of the book" that have written records of their God's will and words: the Hebrew Scriptures of the Jews; the Christian Bible, which includes the Hebrew Scriptures as its Old Testament as well as the Christian New Testament; and the Muslim Koran, believed to be the Word of God revealed in Arabic directly to Muhammad through the angel Gabriel. Jewish and Early Christian art and Byzantine art, including some of the later art of the Eastern Orthodox Church, are considered in this chapter. Islamic art is discussed in Chapter 8, and Christian art of the European Middle Ages in Chapters 14, 15, and 16.

Early Judaism

The Jewish people trace their origin to the patriarchs Abraham, Isaac, and Jacob. According to the Hebrew Scriptures, Jacob's twelve sons founded the twelve tribes of Israel, who migrated to Egypt, where they lived for several hundred years until harshly oppressed by one of the pharaohs. In the thirteenth century BCE the prophet Moses led them out of slavery in Egypt and back to the promised land of Canaan between the Mediterranean Sea and the Jordan River in what was later called Palestine. The Hebrew Scriptures relate how, on their journey, God (YHWH, or Yahweh) reaffirmed his special relationship with the Israelites and gave Moses the Ten Commandments, the Tablets of the Law, on Mount Sinai.

The Tablets of the Law were housed in the profoundly sacred Ark of the Covenant, a gold-covered wooden box whose construction was prescribed in the Hebrew Scriptures (Exodus 25:10–21), topped by two **cherubim**, or attendant angels. The Israelites carried the ark with them on their desert wanderings until they finally conquered Canaan and built a permanent temple in Jerusalem in the tenth century BCE under King Solomon. The Babylonians destroyed the First Temple in 586 BCE, and about seventy years later, a second, smaller temple was built. Herod the Great, king of the region (ruled 37 BCE–4 CE), began the rebuilding and enlarging of the Second Temple. It was the rebuilt Second Temple of Jerusalem whose destruction and looting by the Romans in 70 CE were so vividly described by the Jewish chronicler Josephus (Chapter 6). The sacred treasures carried off to Rome in triumph included ritual articles and the great golden **menorah**, the seven-arm lamp illustrated on the Arch of Titus (see fig. 6–41).

The Jews had the Temple in Jerusalem, but they also had buildings where they gathered, later known as synagogues. Specialized architecture was less central in Judaism than in many religions, and a synagogue could be any large room. Synagogues' role as places of study expanded, and they began to serve as places for prayer for the dispersed community following the destruction of Jerusalem. They were also the sites where Torah scrolls, containing the Pentateuch, the first five books of the Hebrew Scriptures (Genesis, Exodus, Leviticus, Numbers, and Deuteronomy), were read publicly and kept in curtained shrines. Judaism's rich ceremonial affirmation of Jewish history and belief inspired the creation of scrolls, books, and ritual objects. Important rituals included commemorative meals, among them the Passover seder marking the Israelites' perilous journey out of Egypt. Early Jewish spiritual life emphasized religious learning and an individual's direct relationship with God. After the destruction of the Second Temple, there no longer was an organized priesthood.

Early Christianity

Christians believe in one God manifest in three Persons: the Trinity of Father (God), Son (Jesus Christ), and Holy Spirit. According to Christian belief, Jesus was the son of God by a human mother, the Virgin Mary (the Incarnation). His ministry on earth ended when he was executed by being nailed to a cross (the Crucifixion). He rose from the dead (the Resurrection) and ascended into heaven (the Ascension). Christian belief, especially about the divinity of Jesus, was formalized at the first all-Church Council, called by Constantine I at Nicaea (modern Iznik, Turkey) in 325.

The life and teachings of Jesus of Nazareth, who was born sometime between 8 and 4 BCE and was crucified at the age of thirty-three, were recorded between about 70 and 100 CE in the New Testament as books attributed to the Four Evangelists, Matthew, Mark, Luke, and John. These books are known as the Gospels (from an Old English translation of a Latin word derived from the Greek *euangelion*, "good news"). In addition to the Gospels, the New Testament includes an account of the Acts of the Apostles (one book) and the Epistles, twenty-one letters of advice and encouragement to Christian communities in cities and towns in Greece, Asia Minor, and other parts of the Roman Empire. Thirteen of these letters are attributed to a Jewish convert, Saul, who took the Christian name of Paul. The twenty-seventh and final book is the Revelation (the Apocalypse), a series of enigmatic visions and prophecies concerning the eventual triumph of

ROME, CONSTANTINOPLE, AND CHRISTIANITY

The relationship of church and state in the Roman-Byzantine world between the fourth and twelfth centuries was complex. This is a simplified account of the intertwined histories of the Roman and Byzantine Empires and the Eastern and Western Churches.

At its height in the second century CE, the Roman Empire extended from the Euphrates River to Scotland, an immense territory that was nearly impossible to defend and administer. Emperor Diocletian (ruled 284–305 CE) attempted a solution by dividing rule among four imperial tetrarchs (including himself) to oversee the Eastern and Western holdings of the empire in 286. Diocletian's experiment failed, leaving political chaos in its wake (Chapter 6). After Constantine I (ruled 306–337) defeated his rivals and became sole emperor in 324, he instituted numerous reforms. These in-cluded moving the empire's capital in 330 from Rome to Byzantium, located at the intersection of Europe and Asia. The site offered great advantages in military defense and trade, as well as escape from deteriorating conditions in Rome. The new capital, renamed Constantinople, was the sole seat of the Roman Empire until 395, when the empire split permanently in two, becoming the Western (Roman) Empire and the Eastern (Byzantine) Empire. What remained of the greatly weakened Roman Empire in the West collapsed in 476.

Constantinople inherited Rome's role as the center of power and culture. At its greatest extent, in the sixth century, the Eastern Empire included most of the area around the Mediterranean, including northern Africa, the Levant, Anatolia, and all of Greece, much of Italy, and a small part of Spain. The Byzantines always called themselves Romans and their empire the Eastern Roman Empire, despite the cultural division that had existed between the two parts of the Roman Empire: the Latin-speaking West, where urban society was the product of comparatively recent imperial conquest, and the Greek-speaking East, heir to much older civilizations. The Byzantine Empire lasted until 1453, when Constantinople became an Islamic capital under the Ottoman Turks.

When the empire divided in the late fourth century, the Christian Church developed two branches, Eastern and Western; although in disagreement for centuries over doctrine and jurisdiction, the Church did not officially split until 1054. Since then, there has been the Western, or Catholic, Church and the Eastern, or Orthodox, Church. Through all this, Rome has continued as the seat of the Western Church, led by the pope. The patriarch of Constantinople has headed the Eastern Church, which, over time, has developed along regional lines, with several national patriarchs as semiautonomous leaders.

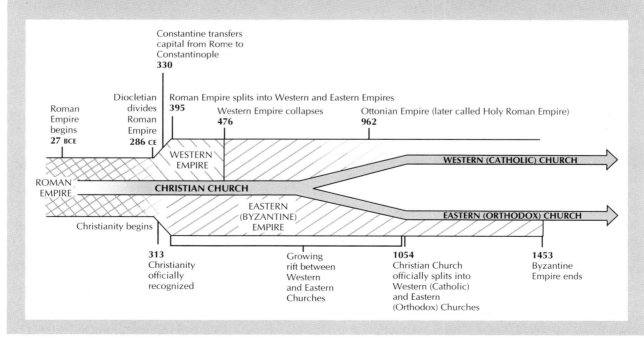

God at the end of the world, written about 95 CE.

Jesus was born during the reign of Emperor Augustus (ruled 27 BCE–14 CE), when Herod the Great ruled as a Roman protectorate the Jewish kingdom of Judaea and much of the rest of Palestine, as well as parts of what are now Lebanon, Syria, and Jordan. Following Herod's death in 4 BCE, Judaea came under direct Roman rule, leading to widespread political and social unrest. Among the movements opposing Roman oppression were Jewish religious cults centered on prophetic figures such as Jesus. This religious dissent was documented in the famous Dead Sea Scrolls found in caves near the Dead Sea in the 1940s and 1950s. Tiberius (ruled 14–37 CE) was emperor during the three-year period in which Jesus is thought to have preached. Jesus' arrest and crucifixion probably occurred not long after Pontius Pilate was appointed administrator of Judaea in 26 CE.

The Gospels' sometimes conflicting accounts relate that Jesus was a descendant of the Jewish royal house of King David and that he was born in Bethlehem in Judaea, where his mother, Mary, and her husband, Joseph, had gone to be registered in the Roman census. He grew up in Nazareth in Galilee (in what is now northern Israel), where Joseph was a carpenter. At the age of thirty, Jesus gathered about him a group of disciples, male and female, preaching love and charity, a personal relationship with God, the forgiveness of sins, and the promise of life after death.

Jesus limited his ministry primarily to Jews; Paul and the apostles, as well as later followers, took Jesus' teachings to non-Jews. Despite sporadic persecutions, Christianity persisted and spread throughout the Roman Empire. The faith had great appeal for the poor and powerless. Yet many early converts were women and people from the privileged classes. As more well-educated, upper-class Romans joined the Church during its first century of rapid growth, they gradually instituted a more elaborate organizational structure coupled with increasingly sophisticated doctrine, both of which evolved over the next centuries. The New Testament underwent significant editing, and the early Church tended to merge biblical stories, changes reflected in later Christian ritual and art. Saint Augustine (354–430) and Saint Gregory of Nazianzus (c. 330–c. 389) incorporated elements of Greek and Roman philosophy into the texts.

Christian communities were organized by geographical units, along the lines of Roman provincial governments. Senior Church officials called bishops served as governors of dioceses made up of smaller units, parishes, headed by priests. Bishops' headquarters—known as sees, or seats—were often in former provincial capitals. (A bishop's church is a cathedral, a word derived from the Latin word *cathedra*, which meant "chair," but took on the meaning "bishop's throne.") More powerful bishops came to be called archbishops, among whom the archbishops of Jerusalem, Rome, Constantinople, Alexandria, and Antioch (in southern Turkey) were the most important. The bishop of Rome eventually became head of the Western Church, holding the titles patriarch and pope. The patriarch of Constantinople became the head of the

Eastern Church. In spite of tensions between East and West, the Church remained united until 1054, when the Western pope and Eastern patriarch declared one another to be in error, and the Church split in two. Since this schism, the pope has been the supreme authority in the Western, Catholic Church, and the patriarch with his metropolitans (equivalent to archbishops) has governed the Eastern, Orthodox Church. (See "Rome, Constantinople, and Christianity," opposite.)

JEWISH ART AND EARLY CHRISTIAN ART

Jews were forbidden to make images that might be worshiped as idols, but this prohibition against representational art was applied primarily to sculpture in the round in early Judaism. Jewish art during the Roman Empire combined both Near Eastern and classical Greek and Roman elements to depict Jewish subject matter, both symbolic and narrative. Since Christianity claimed to have arisen out of Judaism, its art incorporated many symbols and narrative representations from the Hebrew Scriptures and other Jewish sources. Christian rites prompted the development of special buildings—churches and baptistries—as well as specialized equipment, and Christians began to use the visual arts to instruct the laity as well as to glorify God. Almost no examples of specifically Christian art exist before the early third century, and even then it drew its styles and imagery from Jewish and classical traditions. In this process, known as **syncretism**, artists assimilate images from other traditions, giving them new meanings; such borrowings can be unconscious or quite deliberate. **Orant** figures—worshipers with arms outstretched—for example, can be pagan, Jewish, or Christian, depending on the context in which they occur.

Perhaps the most important of these syncretic images is the **Good Shepherd**. In pagan art, he was Hermes the shepherd or Orpheus among the animals, but Jews and Christians saw him as the Good Shepherd of the Twenty-third Psalm: "The Lord is my shepherd; there is nothing I lack" (Psalms 23:1).

Painting and Sculpture

A late-second- or early-third-century mural in the Catacomb of Priscilla, one of the underground burial chambers outside Rome (see "Roman Funerary Practices," page 243), shows a group of men and women dressed in white and arranged around a semicircular table with platters and a large drinking cup (fig. 7-2). This *Banquet Scene*, painted in the crescent-shaped upper part of the wall called a **lunette**, may depict a Passover seder. Alternatively, it could represent either a pagan or a Christian banquet, because the pictorial theme is common to all three religions.

Although the subject of the *Banquet Scene* is difficult to be sure of, Jewish catacombs usually display certain symbolic objects specific to Judaism. A lunette mural in a Jewish catacomb in the Villa Torlonia in Rome, for

7-2. *Banquet Scene*, wall painting in the Catacomb of Priscilla, Rome. Late 2nd or early 3rd century

7-3. *Menorahs and Ark of the Covenant*, wall painting in a Jewish catacomb, Villa Torlonia, Rome. 3rd century. 3'11" x 5'9" (1.19 x 1.8 m)

example (fig. 7-3), shows the Ark of the Covenant flanked by two seven-branch menorahs that resemble the one carved on the Arch of Titus (see fig. 6-41). The original menorah had been constructed to light the portable sanctuary, or tabernacle, which had housed the ark during the early years of the Israelite kingdom (Exodus 25:31–40). After the First Temple had been built in Jerusalem, the menorah and ark were placed in it. The menorah form was probably derived from the ancient Near Eastern Tree of Life, symbolizing both the end of exile and the paradise to come. The painting includes two symbols of the Jewish autumn harvest festival of Sukkoth, which also commemorates the Israelites' period of wandering in the desert: a palm branch on the right and an etrog (citron fruit) on the left.

Christians used catacombs for burials and funeral services before their religion was granted official recognition. In the Christian Catacomb of the Jordani, dating from the third century, long rectangular niches in the walls, called **loculi**, each held two or three bodies (fig. 7-4). More affluent families created small rooms, or **cubicula**, off the main passages to house **sarcophagi**. The cubicula were hewn out of the soft tufa, a volcanic rock, then plastered and painted with imagery related to their owners' religious beliefs. The painters used the rapid brushwork, brilliant colors, and shaded forms of contemporary Roman painting. The finest Early Christian catacomb paintings imitated murals in houses such as those preserved at Pompeii and Primaporta (see figs. 6-33, 6-36). Each scene was composed simply and clearly to convey its religious message.

Communal Christian worship focused on the central "mystery," or miracle, of the Incarnation and the promise of salvation. At its core was the ritual consumption of bread and wine, identified as the body and blood of Christ, which Jesus had instructed his followers to eat and drink in remembrance of him. Around these acts an elaborate religious ceremony, or liturgy, called the Eucharist (also known as Holy Communion or Mass) developed. The grapevine and grape cluster of the

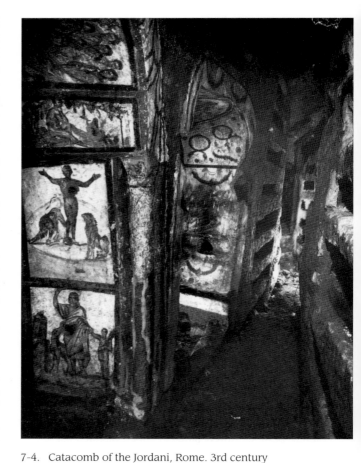

7-4. Catacomb of the Jordani, Rome. 3rd century

The narrow underground passage is lined with rectangular burial niches, once sealed with tile or stone slabs. On the left, arched doorways lead to small burial chambers that held sarcophagi and more wall niches. Typical subjects for Christian tomb paintings are Old Testament redemption stories, symbolizing God's power to save his people from death. At the center of the upper square panel on the left is Daniel in a den of lions that, miraculously, did not eat him (Daniel 6:16–23). The panel below shows Abraham, whom God tested by commanding him to sacrifice his son Isaac (Genesis 22:1–14).

Years	Period	Roman/Byzantine Empires	World
c. 100–6th century CE	Early Christian	New Testament completed; catacomb paintings; persecution of Christians; Constantinople established; Christians granted freedom to worship in empire	**c. 100–300** Yayoi and Kofun eras (Japan); Maya civilization (Mesoamerica); Goths invade Asia Minor; Three Kingdoms period (China); Buddhism spreads in China
313–c. 6th century	Imperial Christian	Old Saint Peter's; Santa Costanza; Christianity is official religion of empire; empire permanently divided; Vulgate Bible; Mausoleum of Galla Placidia; Italy falls to Ostrogoths	**c. 300–500** First Gupta dynasty (India); Arabic script developed; library at Alexandria burns (Egypt); Attila the Hun; earliest surviving Hindu temples (India)
527–867	Early Byzantine	Hagia Sophia; San Vitale; Sant'Apollinare; Emperor Justinian reconquers Italy; Second Council of Nicaea refutes Iconoclasm	**c. 500–900** Birth of Muhammad, founder of Islam (Arabia); Buddhism in Japan; plague kills half the population of Europe; Koran; Muslim conquests; first block-printed text (China); first permanent Japanese capital at Nara; Charlemagne is made emperor of the West; bronze casting in South America; *Diamond Sutra* (China)
867–1453	Later Byzantine	Hosios Loukas; separation of Eastern and Western Christian Churches; San Marco; Crusaders sack Constantinople; Dante's *Divine Comedy*; Boccaccio's *Decameron*; beginning of the Renaissance in Europe; Muslim Turks conquer Constantinople	**c. 900–1450** First Viking colony in Greenland; Lady Murasaki's *Tale of Genji* (Japan); the Crusades; Jenghiz Khan rules Mongols; Magna Carta (England); Hundred Years' War (England, France); Black Death in Europe; Chaucer's *Canterbury Tales* (England); Joan of Arc (France)

Roman god Bacchus were borrowed to symbolize the wine of the Eucharist and the blood of Christ (see "Christian Symbols," page 294). Feast scenes such as that in the Catacomb of Priscilla (see fig. 7-2) were appropriated to represent the Last Supper, in which Jesus inaugurated the Eucharist at a Passover meal with his disciples.

In a lunette painting in another cubiculum of the Catacomb of Priscilla, a veiled female orant—hands raised in prayer—dominates the room (fig. 7-5). The woman is flanked by images of a teacher-philosopher with pupils on the left and a woman holding a child on her lap on the right. Although its context indicates that this is a Christian site, its imagery derives from traditional classical

7-5. *Teacher and Pupils, Orant, and Woman and Child*, wall painting in a lunette, Crypt of the Veiled Lady, Catacomb of Priscilla, Rome. 3rd century

CHRISTIAN SYMBOLS

Symbols have always played an important part in Christian art. Some were devised just for Christianity, but most were borrowed from pagan and Jewish traditions and adapted for Christian use.

Dove

The Old Testament dove is a symbol of purity, representing peace when it is shown bearing an olive branch. In Christian art a white dove is the symbolic embodiment of the Holy Spirit and is often shown descending from heaven, sometimes haloed and radiating celestial light.

Fish

The fish was one of the earliest symbols for Jesus Christ. Because of its association with baptism in water, it came to stand for all Christians. Fish are sometimes depicted with bread and wine to represent the Eucharist.

Lamb (Sheep)

The lamb, an ancient sacrificial animal, symbolizes Jesus' sacrifice on the cross as the Lamb of God, its pouring blood redeeming the sins of the world. The Lamb of God (*Agnus*

Dei in Latin) may appear holding a cross-shaped scepter and/or a victory banner with a cross (signifying Christ's resurrection). The lamb sometimes stands on a cosmic rainbow or a mountaintop. A flock of sheep represents the apostles—or all Christians—cared for by their Good Shepherd, Jesus Christ. John the Baptist points to the Lamb of God, that is, Christ.

Matthew   Mark

Luke   John

Four Evangelists

The evangelists who wrote the New Testament Gospels are traditionally associated with the following creatures: Saint Matthew, a man (or angel); Saint Mark, a lion; Saint Luke, an ox; and Saint John, an eagle. These emblems derive from visionary biblical texts and may be depicted either as the saints' **attributes** (identifying accessories) or their embodiments (stand-ins for the saints themselves).

alpha   omega

alpha and omega
I and X

chi rho

Monograms

Alpha (the first letter of the Greek alphabet) and omega (the last) signify

God as the beginning and end of all things. This symbolic device was popular from Early Christian times through the Middle Ages. Alpha and omega often flank the abbreviation *IX* or *XP*. The initials *I* and *X* are the first letters of *Jesus* and *Christ* in Greek. The initials *XP*, known as the chi rho, were the first two letters of the word *Christos*. These emblems are sometimes enclosed by a circle.

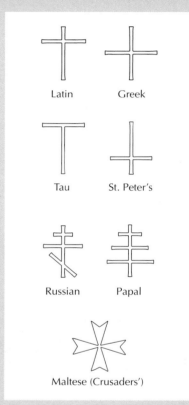

Latin   Greek

Tau   St. Peter's

Russian   Papal

Maltese (Crusaders')

Cross

The primary Christian emblem, the cross, symbolizes the suffering and triumph of Jesus' crucifixion and resurrection as Christ. It also stands for Jesus Christ himself, as well as the Christian religion as a whole. Crosses have taken various forms at different times and places, the two most common in Christian art being the Latin and Greek.

---

themes: philosopher, mother and child, and praying supplicant. In a Christian interpretation, the philosopher can be seen as Jesus teaching and the woman as the Virgin Mary with the Christ Child, both important in later Christian art.

A fourth-century Roman catacomb contained bones, or relics, of Saints Pietro and Marcellino. Pietro and Marcellino were two third-century Roman stalwarts executed—

martyred—for their Christian faith. Catacombs with niches for the bones of martyrs and saints were sought-after burial places. Here the domed ceiling of a cubiculum is partitioned by five medallions linked by the arms of a cross (fig. 7-6). At the center is a Good Shepherd, whose pose has roots in Greek sculpture. In its new context, the image was a reminder of Jesus' promise: "I am the good shepherd. A good shepherd lays down his

7-6. *Good Shepherd, Orants, and Story of Jonah,* painted ceiling of the Catacomb of Pietro and Marcellino, Rome. 4th century

life for the sheep" (John 10:11). The semicircular compartments at the ends of the arms of the cross tell the Old Testament story of Jonah and the sea monster (Jonah 1–2), in which God caused Jonah to be thrown overboard in a storm, swallowed by a monster, and released, repentant and unscathed, three days later. This story was reinterpreted by Christians as a parable of Christ's death and resurrection—and hence of the everlasting life awaiting true believers—and was a popular subject in Christian catacombs. On the left, Jonah is thrown from the boat; on the right, the monster spews him up; and at the center, Jonah reclines in the shade of a gourd vine, a symbol of paradise. Orants praying for the souls of the departed stand between the medallions.

Sculpture that is clearly Christian is even rarer than painting from before the time of Constantine I. What there is consists mainly of small statues and reliefs, many of them Good Shepherd images. A remarkable set of marble figurines, probably made in the third century in Asia Minor, also depicts the Jonah story (fig. 7-7); their function is unknown. Carved of a fine alabasterlike marble, they illustrate the biblical story with the same literalness and enthusiasm as the paintings on the catacomb ceiling.

Dura-Europos

The variety of religious buildings found in modern Syria at the abandoned Roman outpost of Dura-Europos, a Hellenistic fortress taken over by the Romans in 165 CE, illustrates the cosmopolitan character of frontier Roman society in the second and third centuries. Although Dura-Europos was destroyed in 256 CE by Persian forces, important parts of the stronghold have been excavated, including a Jewish **house-synagogue**, a Christian **house-church**, shrines to the Persian gods Mithras and Zoroaster, and temples to Roman ancestral gods. The Jewish and Christian structures were preserved because they had been built against the inside wall of the southwest rampart. When the desperate citizens attempted to

7-7. *Jonah Swallowed* and *Jonah Cast Up,* two statuettes of a group from the eastern Mediterranean, probably Asia Minor. 3rd century. Marble, heights 20 5/16" (51.6 cm) and 16" (40.6 cm). The Cleveland Museum of Art
John L. Severance Fund, 65.237, 65.238

7-8.   Wall with Torah niche, from a house-synagogue, Dura-Europos, Syria. 244–45. Tempera on plaster, section approx. 40' long. Reconstructed in the National Museum, Damascus, Syria

strengthen this fortification in futile preparation for the final attack, they buried these buildings. The entire site was abandoned and rediscovered only in 1920 by a French army officer.

In the house-synagogue, the congregational area was sealed off from the rest of the building. Its main room had only two special architectural features, a bench along its walls and a niche for the Torah scrolls (fig. 7-8). Women were seated in an alcove, separated from men.

Jewish representational art flourished in the third century, as seen in the murals that covered this synagogue's interior. Narrative and symbolic scenes depicting events from Jewish history unfold in three registers of framed panels. The work of more than one artist, they are done in a style in which statically posed, almost two-dimensional figures float against a neutral background. In *Finding of the Baby Moses* (fig. 7-9), Moses' mother sets him afloat in a reed basket in the shallows of the Nile in an attempt to save him from the pharaoh's decree that all Jewish male infants be put to death (Exodus 1:8–2:10). He is found by the pharaoh's daughter, who acknowledges him as her own child. The painting shows these events unfolding in a continuous narrative set in a narrow fore-ground space. At the right, the princess sees the child hidden in the bulrushes; at the center, she wades nude into the water to save him; and at the left, she hands him to a nurse (actually his own mother). The frontal poses, strong outlines, and flat colors are distinctive pictorial devices; they are, in fact, features of later Byzantine art, perhaps derived from works such as this.

The Christian house-church, which was about 300 yards from the house-synagogue, had been a Roman-

7-9.   *Finding of the Baby Moses*, detail of a wall painting from a house-synagogue, Dura-Europos, Syria. Second half of 3rd century. Copy in tempera on plaster. Yale University Art Gallery, New Haven, Connecticut
Dura-Europus Collection

style dwelling built around a peristyle court. A red cross painted above the main entrance designated it as a gathering place for Christians. The congregation seems to have grown so much that by about 231 the space devoted to the church included a large meeting or dining hall, a room with a raised platform at one end for the leaders, and a small chamber that served perhaps for teaching initiates or as a place for storing liturgical equipment. Opening off this large hall was a **baptistry**, or place for

7-10. Small-scale model of walls and baptismal font, from the baptistry of a Christian house-church, Dura-Europos, Syria. c. 240. Yale University Art Gallery, New Haven, Connecticut
Dura-Europos Collection

7-11. Reconstruction drawing of Old Saint Peter's basilica, Rome. c. 320–27; atrium added in later 4th century

baptism, built into a niche and equipped with a water basin, above which were images of the Good Shepherd and of Adam and Eve (fig. 7-10). These murals reminded new Christians that humanity had been deprived of immortality by Original Sin, when the first man and woman disobeyed God and ate fruit from the forbidden tree of the knowledge of good and bad offered them by an evil serpent. But the Good Shepherd (Jesus Christ) came to earth to carry his sheep (Christians) to salvation and eternal life. Baptism washed away sin, leaving the initiate reborn as a member of the community of the faithful.

IMPERIAL CHRISTIAN ARCHITECTURE AND ART

In 313 the Edict of Milan granted all people in the Roman Empire freedom to worship whatever god they wished. This religious toleration, combined with Constantine's active support of Christianity, allowed Christianity to enter a new phase, developing a sophisticated philosophical and ethical system that incorporated many ideas from Greek and Roman philosophy. Church scholars edited and commented on the Bible, and Saint Jerome (c. 347–c. 420), the papal secretary, undertook a new translation from Hebrew, Greek, and Latin versions into Latin, the language of the Western Church. Completed about 400, this so-called Vulgate became the official version of the Bible. (The term *Vulgate* derives from the same Latin word as *vulgar*, meaning "common" or "popular.") Christians also gained political influence in this period. The Christian writer Lactantius (c. 240–320), for example, tutored Constantine I's son Crispus; and Eusebius (c. 260–c. 339), bishop of Caesarea, was a trusted imperial adviser from about 315 to 339. These transformations in the philosophical and political arenas coincided with a dramatic increase in imperial architecture.

Architecture and Its Decoration

As soon as he had consolidated imperial power, around 324, Constantine I began a vast building program that included many religious structures (Chapter 6). Among these was a grand palace complex for the city's bishop, the highest-ranking Church official in the Roman Empire. The emperor ordered a monumental **basilica** constructed at the place where Christians believed Saint Peter to be buried. Also, after Constantine's mother, Helena, visited Palestine about 325, she convinced him to build a number of churches and shrines in Jerusalem; shrines were constructed as personal acts of devotion, sometimes commemorating a person or event in the patron's life.

Basilica-Plan Churches. In the early second century Christians in Rome had placed a monument over what they believed to be the burial place of the apostle Peter. According to tradition, Saint Peter (died c. 64 CE), the first bishop of Rome, was crucified upside down at his own request so that his martyrdom would be seen as lesser than Jesus' crucifixion. Perhaps as early as 320, Constantine decided to construct a grand new basilica on the site of Peter's tomb to protect it and make it accessible to the faithful, glorifying the memory of the martyred apostle. As the pope's church, it came to signify as well the superior power of the bishop of Rome over all other bishops in Christendom.

Our knowledge of Old Saint Peter's (so called because it was completely replaced by a new building in the sixteenth century) is based on written descriptions, drawings made before and while it was being dismantled, the study of other churches inspired by it, and modern archeological excavations at the site (fig. 7-11). Its builders leveled the hillside cemetery on which it was to be located, destroying many tombs; then atop a large, concrete foundation they erected a building complex arranged on

ELEMENTS OF ARCHITECTURE

Basilica-Plan and Central-Plan Churches

The forms of early Christian buildings were based on two classical prototypes: rectangular Roman basilicas (see figs. 6-49, 6-50) and round-domed structures—rotundas—such as the Pantheon (see figs. 6-55, 6-56). As in Old Saint Peter's in Rome (fig. 7-11), **basilica-plan** churches are characterized by a forecourt, the **atrium**, leading to a porch, the **narthex**, spanning one of the building's short ends. Doorways—known collectively as the church's **portal**—lead from the narthex into a long central area called a **nave**. The high-ceiling nave is separated from aisles on either side by rows of columns. The nave is lit by windows along its upper story—called a **clerestory**—that rises above the side aisles' roofs. At the opposite end of the nave from the narthex is a semicircular projection, the **apse**. The apse functions as the building's symbolic core where the altar, raised on a platform, is located. Sometimes there is also a **transept**, a horizontal wing that crosses the nave in front of the apse, making the building T-shaped; this is known as a Tau plan. When additional space (a choir) separates the transept and the apse, the plan is called a **Latin cross**.

Central-plan structures were first used by Christians as tombs, baptism centers (**baptistries**), and shrines to martyrs (**martyria**). (The **Greek-cross plan**, in which two similarly sized "arms" intersect at their centers, is a type of central plan.) Instead of the longitudinal axis of basilican churches, which draws worshipers forward toward the apse, central-plan churches such as Ravenna's San Vitale (see figs. 7-29, 7-30) have a more vertical axis. This makes the **dome**, a symbolic "vault of heaven," a natural focus over the main worship area. Like basilicas, central-plan churches generally have an atrium, a narthex, and an apse. The **naos** is the space containing the central dome, sanctuary, and apse.

basilicia-plan church

central-plan church

a central axis similar to the old Forum of Trajan (see fig. 6-49). Worshipers climbed a flight of steps to a large gatehouse and crossed a colonnaded atrium with a central fountain to reach the church's entrance.

Old Saint Peter's included architectural elements arranged in a way that has characterized Christian basilica-plan churches ever since (see "Elements of Architecture," above). A narthex, or porch, across the width of the building protected five doorways—a large, central portal into the nave and two portals on each side opening directly to double side aisles. The nave rose one story higher than these aisles to provide for an upper-level

clerestory, the windows of which lit the interior. Nave and aisles had open, timberwork ceilings. The nave was lined with columns supporting an entablature, whereas the columns of the side aisles supported a series of round arches. At the end of the nave and aisles was a transept, which crossed them at right angles and projected at each end, a **T** form that anticipated the later Latin-cross church plan. This area served as common ground for rituals in which both congregation and clergy participated.

Saint Peter's bones supposedly lie below, marked in the nave by a permanent, pavilionlike structure supported on four columns called a **ciborium**. Catacombs lay

7-12. Nave, Church of Saint Paul's Outside the Walls, Rome. Begun 385; rebuilt after a fire in 1823

proportions, simple geometric forms, and a dramatic contrast between exterior simplicity and interior luxury. A view of the nave of the Church of Saint Paul's Outside the Walls, begun in 385, gives some sense of what the interior of Old Saint Peter's might have been like (fig. 7-12). The long nave ends, like Old Saint Peter's, in a triumphal arch that springs from columns topped with short sections of entablature. Unlike Saint Peter's, arcades of tall Corinthian columns supporting arches define both nave and side aisles. After a fire in the early nineteenth century, the original open-rafter ceiling was replaced by a **coffered** one with recessed panels.

The combination of architectural grandeur, adaptability, and practicality in fourth-century basilica-plan churches proved so valuable that Roman architects almost a century later looked to them for inspiration when designing the Church of Santa Maria Maggiore (Saint Mary the Great, fig. 7-13). As in Old Saint Peter's, columns supporting an entablature line the two-story nave, which ends in a triumphal arch leading to the sanctuary, where the altar is located. Santa Maria Maggiore was the first church in Rome dedicated to the Virgin Mary after the Church Council of Ephesus (431) declared her to be Theotokos, bearer of God. In the mosaics of this church, the humble earthly mother of Jesus was first given the regal appearance often seen in Western art. (The Virgin remains a humble mother in Eastern representations.) On the triumphal arch's left **spandrel**—the surface between the exterior curves of adjoining arches or walls—she is shown enthroned, flanked by attending angels and crowned as an empress.

beneath the church, and over time a large **crypt**, or underground vault, was used for the burial of popes. Sarcophagi and tomb monuments eventually also lined the side aisles. Old Saint Peter's thus served a variety of functions. It was a congregational church, a pilgrimage shrine commemorating a place of martyrdom and containing the relics of a holy person, and a funeral hall–burial place. Old Saint Peter's could hold at least 14,000 worshipers, and it remained the largest of all Christian churches until the eleventh century.

Like many later churches, Old Saint Peter's depended for its aesthetic effect on sheer size, harmonious

7-13. Nave, Church of Santa Maria Maggiore, Rome. 432–40

7-14. *Parting of Lot and Abraham*, mosaic in the nave arcade, Church of Santa Maria Maggiore. Panel approx. 4'11" x 6'8" (1.2 x 2 m)

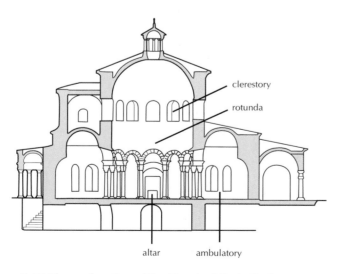

7-15. Plan and section of the Church of Santa Costanza, Rome. c. 338–50

The mosaics of the Church of Santa Maria Maggiore reflect a renewed interest in the earlier classicizing style of Roman art that arose during the reign of Pope Sixtus III (432–440). The mosaics along the nave walls, in framed panels high above the worshipers, illustrate Old Testament stories of the Jewish patriarchs and heroes— Abraham, Jacob, Moses, and Joshua—whom Christians believe foretold the coming of Christ and his activities on earth. Twenty-seven of the original forty-two **triforium** mosaics remain. These panels were not only didactic— that is, they were not simply intended to instruct the congregation. Instead, like most of the decorations in great Christian churches from this time forward, they were meant to praise God through their splendor, to make churches symbolic embodiments of the Heavenly Jerusalem that awaited believers, and to tell a history.

Some of the most effective compositions are those in which a few large figures dominate the foreground space, as in the *Parting of Lot and Abraham* (fig. 7-14), a story told in the first book of the Hebrew Scriptures (Genesis 13:1–12). The people of Abraham and his nephew Lot, dwelling together, had grown too numerous, so the two agreed to separate and lead their followers in different directions. On the right, Lot and his daughters turn toward the land of Jordan, while Abraham and his wife stay in the land of Canaan. This parting is highly significant to both Jews and Christians since Abraham was the founder of the Israelite nation from which Jesus descended.

In the mosaic, the toga-clad men share a parting look as they gather their robes about them and turn decisively away from each other. The space between them in the center of the composition emphasizes their irreversible decision to part. Clusters of heads in the background represent Abraham's and Lot's followers, a contemporary artistic convention used effectively here. References to the earlier Roman **illusionistic** style can be seen in the solid three-dimensional rendering of foreground figures, the hint of perspective in the building, and the landscape setting, with its bit of foliage and touches of blue sky. The mosaic was created with thousands of marble and glass **tesserae** set closely together. The use of graduated colors creates shading from light to dark, producing three-dimensional effects that are offset by strong outlines. These outlines, coupled with the sheen of the gold tesserae, tend to flatten the forms.

Central-Plan Churches. A second type of ancient building—the **tholos**, or tomb with central plan and vertical axis—also served Christian builders for tombs, martyrs' churches, and baptistries (see "Elements of Architecture," page 298). One of the earliest surviving central-plan Christian buildings is the **mausoleum** of Constantina, the daughter of Constantine, which was built outside the walls of Rome just before 350 (fig. 7-15). The mausoleum was consecrated as a church in 1256 and is now dedicated to Santa Costanza (the Italian form of the Christian princess's name). The building consists of a tall rotunda with an encircling **barrel-vaulted** passageway called an **ambulatory** (fig. 7-16). A double ring of paired columns with Composite capitals and richly

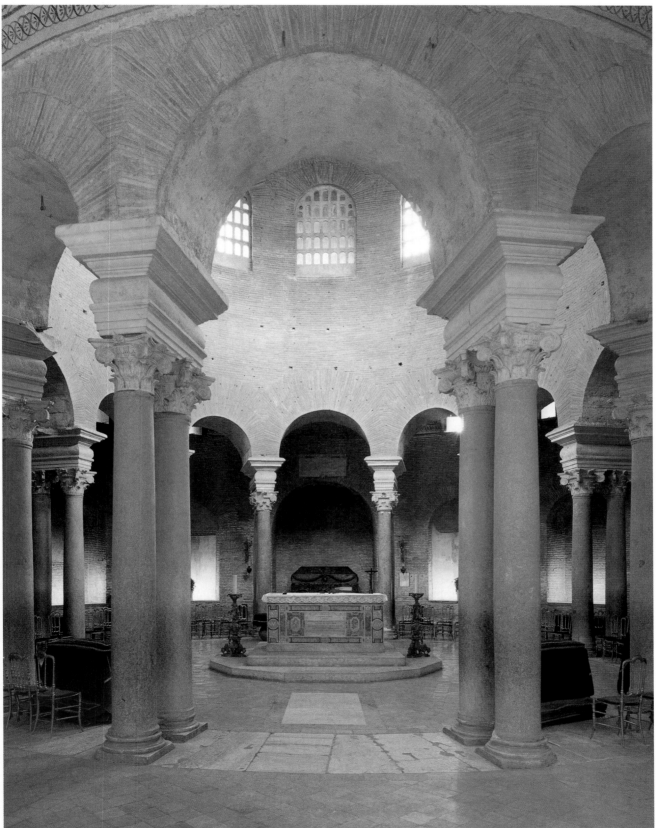

7-16. Church of Santa Costanza. View through ambulatory into central space

7-17. *Harvesting of Grapes*, mosaic in the the ambulatory vault, Church of Santa Costanza

7-18. Mausoleum of Galla Placidia, Ravenna, Italy. c. 425–26

molded entablature blocks supports the arcade and dome. The building's interior was entirely sheathed in mosaics and fine marble.

Mosaics in the ambulatory vault recall the catacombs' syncretic images. One section, for example, is covered with a tangle of grapevines filled with **putti**—naked male child-angels, or cherubs, derived from classical art—who vie with the birds to harvest the grapes (fig. 7-17). Along the bottom edges on each side, putti drive wagonloads of grapes toward pavilions covering large vats in which more putti trample the grapes into juice. The technique, subject, and style are Roman, but the meaning has been altered. The scene would have been familiar to the pagan followers of Bacchus, but in a Christian context the wine could suggest the wine of the Eucharist. For Constantina the scene probably evoked only one, Christian, interpretation; her pagan husband, however, may have recognized the double allusion.

As Rome lost its political importance, major buildings were erected in the new Italian capitals of Milan and Ravenna, to the north. In 395 Emperor Theodosius I split the Roman Empire into Eastern and Western divisions, each ruled by one of his sons. Arcadius (ruled 383–408), who had already ruled the Eastern part of the empire from Constantinople jointly with his father, assumed complete control of the Eastern Empire. The younger Honorius (ruled 395–423) established himself first at the new Western Roman Empire capital of Milan in northern Italy. When Germanic settlers laid siege to Milan in 402,

Honorius moved his capital to the east coast of Italy at Ravenna, whose naval base, Classis, had been important since the early days of the empire. In addition to military security, Ravenna offered direct access by sea to Constantinople. Ravenna flourished under Roman rule, and when Italy fell to the Ostrogoths in 476, the city became one of their headquarters. It still contains a remarkable group of well-preserved fifth- and sixth-century monuments.

One of the earliest surviving Christian structures in Ravenna is a funerary chapel attached to the church of the imperial palace (now Santa Croce, meaning "Holy Cross"). Built about 425–426, the chapel was constructed when Honorius's half sister, Galla Placidia, was acting as regent (ruled 425–c. 440) in the West for her son. The chapel came to be called the Mausoleum of Galla Placidia because she and her family were once believed to be buried there (fig. 7-18). This small building is **cruciform**, or cross-shaped; each of its arms is covered with a barrel vault, and the space at the intersection of the arms is covered with a **pendentive dome,** a dome continuous with its **pendentives**. The plain exterior is decorated with **blind arcading**—a series of ornamental arches applied to a solid wall—tall slit windows, and a simple **cornice** that surrounds and unifies the four arms. The vaults covering the arms of the cross have been hidden from view on the outside by sloping, tile-covered roofs.

The interior of the chapel contrasts remarkably with the exterior, a transition designed to simulate the passage from the real world into a supernatural one (fig. 7-19). The worshiper looking from the western entrance across to the eastern bay of the chapel sees a brilliant, abstract pattern of mosaic filling the barrel vault, suggesting a starry sky. Panels of veined marble sheath the walls below. Bands of luxuriant foliage and floral designs derived from funerary garlands cover the four central arches, and the walls above them are filled with the figures of standing apostles gesturing like orators. Birds

7-19. Mausoleum of Galla Placidia, eastern bays with sarcophagus niches in the arms and lunette mosaic of the *Martyrdom of Saint Lawrence*

flanking a small fountain between the apostles symbolize eternal life in heaven. In the lunette, a mosaic symbolically depicts the third-century martyrdom of Saint Lawrence, to whom the building was probably dedicated. The saint holds a cross and gestures under the window toward the metal gridiron, or grill, on which he was literally roasted. At the left stands a tall cabinet containing the Gospels, signifying the faith for which he died.

Opposite Saint Lawrence, in a lunette over the entrance portal, is the *Good Shepherd* (fig. 7-20). A comparison of this version with a fourth-century depiction of the same subject (see fig. 7-6) reveals significant changes in content and design. The Ravenna mosaic contains many familiar classical elements, such as illusionistic shading and shadows to suggest a single light source acting on solid forms, a suggestion of landscape, and traditional animal poses. The image of Jesus, however, has changed. In the fourth-century painting he was a simple shepherd boy carrying an animal on his shoulders; in the mosaic he is a young adult wearing imperial robes of gold and purple and holding a long, golden staff that ends in a cross instead of a shepherd's crook. There is a large, golden halo behind his head, a device artists used to distinguish rulers from ordinary people. (Later, halos were reserved for holy personages—God, Jesus Christ, the Virgin Mary, angels, or saints.) The stylized elements of a natural landscape are there but are arranged more rigidly than before. Individual plants have been placed at regular intervals to fill the spaces between animals, and the

7-20. *Good Shepherd*, mosaic in the lunette over the west entrance, Mausoleum of Galla Placidia

rocks are stepped back into a shallow space that rises from the foreground plane and ends in foliage fronds. The rocky band at the bottom of the lunette scene, resembling a cliff face riddled with clefts, separates the divine image from worshipers.

Just as the political role of Ravenna changed in the fourth and fifth centuries, so did the religious belief of its leaders. The early Christian Church faced many

7-21. Clerestory and dome, Baptistry of the Orthodox, Ravenna, Italy. Early 5th century; dome remodeled c. 450–60

philosophical and doctrinal controversies, some of which resulted in serious splits, called schisms, within the Church. When this happened, its leaders gathered in church councils to decide on the orthodox, or official, position and denounce others as heretical. Two early forms of Christianity that were rejected were Arianism and Monophysitism.

Arianism was named after Arius (c. 250–336), a leader in the church of Alexandria. He and his followers believed that Jesus was coeternal with God but not fully divine, having been made by God. The first Church Council, called by Constantine at Nicaea in 325, declared the doctrine of the Trinity to be orthodox and denounced Arianism as heretical.

Monophysites took the opposite viewpoint from Arians. They believed that Jesus was an entirely divine being even while on earth. Attempting to address this belief, the Council of Chalcedon, near Constantinople, in 451 declared Jesus to be of two natures—human and divine—united in one. This declaration did not put an end to Monophysitism, which remained strong in Egypt, Syria, Palestine, and Armenia in Asia Minor.

In Ravenna two baptistries still stand as witness to these disputes: the Baptistry of the Orthodox and the Baptistry of the Arians. The Baptistry of the Orthodox was constructed next to the Cathedral of Ravenna in the early fourth century. Bishop Neon had it renovated and refurbished between 450 and 460, replacing the wooden

ceiling with a dome and adding splendid interior decoration in marble, stucco, and mosaic (fig. 7-21). On the clerestory level, an arcade springing from columns with large **impost** blocks repeats blind arcading below. Each main arch contains three arches framing a window. Flanking the windows are figures of Old Testament prophets in relief surmounted by pediments containing shell motifs. The pediment above the figure to the left of each window is round, whereas that on the right is pointed. The main arcading acts visually to turn the domed ceiling into a huge canopy tethered to the imposts of the columns.

In the dome itself, concentric rings of decoration draw the eye upward to a central image that reflects the structure's function: the baptism of Jesus by Saint John the Baptist, Jesus' older cousin, a desert hermit whom Christians regard as the last of the Old Testament prophets and the first of the New Testament saints, the forerunner of Jesus. The lowest ring consists of **trompe l'oeil**—a French term applied to highly illusionistic painting that "fools the eye." Among these deceptive "architectural elements" are eight circular niches, four of them containing altars holding gospel books. The four niches alternating with them hold empty thrones under ciboria. The empty thrones symbolize the throne that awaits Christ's Second Coming (Matthew 25:31–36), when he will return to earth and prepare his people for Judgment Day. In the next ring, toga-clad apostles stand holding

7-22. *Resurrection and Angel with Two Marys at the Tomb,*
panel of a diptych, found in Rome. c. 400. Ivory,
14½ x 5⅜" (37 x 13.5 cm). Castello Sforzesco, Milan

their crowns of martyrdom, stylized golden plant forms dividing the deep blue ground between them. Although the figures cast dark shadows on the pale green grass, their cloudlike robes, shot through with golden rays, give them an otherworldly presence. The landscape setting of the Baptism of Jesus in the central **tondo**—a circular image—exhibits classical roots, and the representation of the Jordan River in human form recalls pagan imagery. The background, however, is not the blue of the earthly sky but the gold of paradise. Already in the mid-fifth century, artists working for the Christian Church had begun to reinterpret and transform Roman naturalism into an abstract style better suited to the spiritual goals of their patrons.

7-23. *Sarcophagus of Junius Bassus.* c. 359. Marble, 4' x 8'
(1.2 x 2.4 m). Grottoes of Saint Peter, Vatican, Rome.

Sculpture

In sculpture, as in architecture, Christians adapted Roman forms for their own needs. Commemorative ivory **diptychs**—two carved panels hinged together—originated with Roman politicians elected to the post of consul, who sent to friends and colleagues notices of that event, and, later, other events, inscribed in wax on the inner sides of a pair of carved ivory panels (see fig. 6-89). Christians adapted the practice for religious use at least by the fifth century, inscribing a diptych with the names of people to be remembered with prayers during Mass. An ivory panel found in Rome and dating to about 400 may have been an early example of this practice (fig. 7-22). The top register shows the moment of Christ's resurrection in both symbolic and narrative terms. While the soldiers guarding his tomb sleep, the evangelists Luke (represented by the ox in the upper left) and Matthew (represented by the man in the upper right) acknowledge the event from the clouds. The bottom register shows the moment when Mary mother of James and Mary Magdalen learn from a young man whose "appearance was like lightning and . . . clothing was white as snow" (Matthew 28:1–6) that the tomb is empty. The top panels of the carved doors of the tomb show the Raising of Lazarus, the Gospel story in which Jesus brings a man back to life to prove his divine power. In the top right door panel the shrouded Lazarus emerges from his tomb, symbolizing the Christian promise of life after death. The varied natural poses of the figures, the solid modeling of the bodies beneath their drapery, the architectural details of the tomb, and the decorative framing patterns all indicate the classical roots of this work, which in its theme is completely Christian.

Monumental stone sculpture can be studied in sarcophagi, such as the elaborately carved *Sarcophagus of Junius Bassus* (fig. 7-23). Bassus was a Roman official who, as an inscription here tells us, died on August 25,

ICONOGRAPHY OF THE LIFE OF JESUS

Iconography is the study of subject matter in art. It involves identifying both what a work of art represents—its literal meaning—and the deeper significance of what is represented—its symbolic meaning. Stories about the life of Jesus, grouped in "cycles," form the basis of Christian iconography. What follows is an outline of those cycles and the main events of each.

THE INCARNATION CYCLE AND THE CHILDHOOD OF JESUS

This cycle contains events surrounding the conception and birth of Jesus.

The Annunciation: The archangel Gabriel informs the Virgin Mary that God has chosen her to bear his son. A dove represents the Incarnation, her miraculous conception of Jesus through the Holy Spirit.

The Visitation: Mary visits her older cousin Elizabeth, pregnant with the future Saint John the Baptist. Elizabeth is the first to acknowledge the divinity of the child Mary is carrying. The two women rejoice.

The Nativity: Jesus is born to Mary in Bethlehem. The Holy Family—Jesus, Mary, and her husband, Joseph—is shown in a house, a stable, or, in Byzantine art, in a cave.

The Annunciation to the Shepherds and **The Adoration of the Shepherds**: An angel announces Jesus' birth to humble shepherds. They hasten to Bethlehem to honor him.

The Adoration of the Magi: The Magi—wise men from the East—follow a bright star to Bethlehem to honor Jesus as King of the Jews, presenting him with precious gifts: gold (symbolizing kingship), frankincense (divinity), and myrrh (death). In the European Middle Ages the Magi were identified as three kings.

The Massacre of the Innocents and **The Flight into Egypt**: An angel warns Joseph that King Herod—to eliminate the threat of a newborn rival king—plans to murder all the babies in Bethlehem. The Holy Family flees to Egypt.

The Presentation in the Temple: Mary and Joseph bring the infant Jesus to the Temple in Jerusalem, where he is presented to the high priest. It is prophesied that Jesus will redeem humankind but that Mary will suffer great sorrow.

Jesus among the Doctors: In Jerusalem for the celebration of Passover, Joseph and Mary find the twelve-year-old Jesus in serious discussion with Temple scholars. This is seen as a sign of his coming ministry.

THE PUBLIC MINISTRY CYCLE

In this cycle Jesus preaches his message.

The Baptism: At age thirty Jesus is baptized by John the Baptist in the Jordan River. He sees the Holy Spirit and hears a heavenly voice proclaiming him God's son. This marks the beginning of his ministry.

The Calling of Matthew: Passing by the customhouse, Jesus sees Matthew, a tax collector, to whom he says, "Follow me." Matthew complies, becoming one of the apostles.

Jesus and the Samaritan Woman at the Well: On his way from Judaea to Galilee, Jesus rests by a spring called Jacob's Well. Contrary to Jewish custom, he asks a local Samaritan woman drawing water for a drink. The apostles are surprised to find them conversing.

Jesus Walking on the Water: The apostles, in a storm-tossed boat, see Jesus walking toward them on the water. Peter tries to go out to meet Jesus, but begins to sink, and Jesus saves him. When Jesus reaches the boat, the storm stops.

The Raising of Lazarus: Jesus brings his friend Lazarus back to life four days after he has died. Lazarus emerges from the tomb wrapped in his shroud.

The Delivery of the Keys to Peter: Jesus designates Peter as his successor, symbolically turning over to him the keys to the kingdom of heaven.

The Transfiguration: Jesus is transformed into a dazzling vision on Mount Tabor in Galilee as his closest disciples—Peter, James, and John the Evangelist—look on. A cloud overshadows them, and a heavenly voice proclaims Jesus to be God's son.

The Cleansing of the Temple: Jesus, in anger, drives money changers and animal traders from the Temple.

THE PASSION CYCLE

This cycle contains events surrounding Jesus' death and resurrection. (*Passio* is Latin for "suffering.")

The Entry into Jerusalem: Jesus, riding a donkey, and his disciples enter Jerusalem in triumph. Crowds honor them, spreading clothes and palm fronds in their path.

The Last Supper: During the Passover seder, Jesus reveals his impending death to his disciples. Instructing them to drink wine (his blood) and eat bread (his body) in remembrance of him, he lays the foundation for the Christian Eucharist (Mass).

Jesus Washing the Apostles' Feet: After the Last Supper, Jesus humbly washes the apostles' feet to set an example of humility. Peter, embarrassed, protests.

The Agony in the Garden: In the Garden of Gethsemane on the Mount of Olives, Jesus struggles between his

359, at the age of forty-two. The front panel has two registers divided by columns into shallow stage spaces of equal width. On the top level, the columns are surmounted by an entablature incised with the inscription in Roman capital letters. On the bottom register, they support alternating triangular and arched roof gables resembling little houses. Each stage, with the exception of one in the lower register containing the nude figures of Adam and Eve, is filled by toga-clad figures with short legs, long bodies, and large heads. Fragments of architecture, various types of seating, and occasional trees suggest the material setting for each scene.

human fear of pain and death and his divine strength to overcome them (*agon* is Greek for "contest"). An angelic messenger bolsters his courage. The apostles sleep nearby, oblivious.

The Betrayal (The Arrest): Judas Iscariot, one of the apostles, accepts a bribe to point Jesus out to his enemies. Judas brings an armed crowd to Gethsemane. He kisses Jesus, a prearranged signal. Peter makes a futile attempt to defend Jesus from the Roman soldiers who seize him.

The Denial of Peter: Jesus is brought to the palace of the Jewish high priest, Caiaphas, to be interrogated for claiming to be the Messiah. Peter follows, and there he three times denies knowing Jesus, as Jesus predicted he would.

Jesus before Pilate: Jesus is taken to Pontius Pilate, the Roman governor of Judaea, and charged with treason for calling himself King of the Jews. He is sent to Herod Antipas, ruler of Galilee, who scorns him. Pilate proposes freeing Jesus but is shouted down by the mob, which demands that he be crucified. Pilate washes his hands before the crowd to signify that Jesus' blood is on its hands, not his.

The Flagellation (The Scourging): Jesus is whipped by his Roman captors.

Jesus Crowned with Thorns (The Mocking of Jesus): Pilate's soldiers torment Jesus. They dress him in royal robes, crown him with thorns, and kneel before him, hailing him as King of the Jews.

The Bearing of the Cross (The Road to Calvary): Jesus bears the cross from Pilate's house to Golgotha, where he is executed. Medieval artists depicted this event and its accompanying incidents in fourteen images known as the Stations of the Cross: (1) Jesus is condemned to death; (2) Jesus picks up the cross; (3) Jesus falls for the first time; (4) Jesus meets his grieving mother; (5) Simon of Cyrene is forced to help Jesus carry the cross; (6) Veronica wipes Jesus' face with her veil; (7) Jesus falls again; (8) Jesus admonishes the women of Jerusalem; (9) Jesus falls a third time; (10) Jesus is stripped; (11) Jesus is nailed to the cross; (12) Jesus dies on the cross; (13) Jesus is taken down from the cross; (14) Jesus is entombed.

The Crucifixion: The earliest representations of the Crucifixion are abstract, showing either a cross alone or a cross and a lamb. Later depictions include some or all of the following narrative details: two criminals (one penitent, the other not), are crucified on either side of Jesus; the Virgin Mary, John the Evangelist, Mary Magdalen, and other followers mourn at the foot of the cross; Roman soldiers torment Jesus—one extends a sponge on a pole with vinegar instead of water for him to drink, another stabs him in the side with a spear, and others gamble for his clothes; a skull identifies the execution ground as Golgotha, "the place of the skull," where Adam was buried. The association symbolizes the promise of redemption: the blood flowing from Jesus' wounds will wash away Adam's Original Sin.

The Descent from the Cross (The Deposition): Jesus' followers take his body down from the cross. Joseph of Arimathea and Nicodemus wrap it in linen with myrrh and aloe. Also present are the grief-stricken Virgin, John the Evangelist, and sometimes Mary Magdalen, other disciples, and angels.

The Lamentation (Pietà or *Vesperbild*): Jesus' sorrowful followers gather around his body. An image of the Virgin mourning alone with Jesus across her lap is known as a pietà (from the Latin *pietas*, "pity") or, in German, a *Vesperbild*.

The Entombment: Jesus' mother and friends place his body in a nearby sarcophagus, or rock tomb. This is done hastily because of the approaching Jewish Sabbath.

The Descent into Limbo (The Harrowing of Hell): No longer in mortal form, Jesus, now called Christ, descends into limbo, or hell, to free deserving souls, among them Adam, Eve, and Moses.

The Resurrection (The Anastasis): Three days after his death, Christ leaves his tomb while the soldiers guarding it sleep.

The Marys at the Tomb (The Holy Women at the Sepulchre): Christ's female followers—usually including Mary Magdalen and the mother of the apostle James, also named Mary—discover his empty tomb. An angel announces Christ's resurrection. The soldiers guarding the tomb sleep.

Noli Me Tangere **("Do Not Touch Me"), The Supper at Emmaus**, and **The Incredulity of Thomas**: Christ makes a series of appearances to his followers in the forty days between his resurrection and his ascension. He first appears to Mary Magdalen, who thinks he is a gardener. She reaches out to him, but he warns her not to touch him. In the Supper at Emmaus, he shares a meal with his apostles. In the Incredulity of Thomas, Christ invites the doubting apostle to touch the wound in his side to convince Thomas of his resurrection.

The Ascension: Christ ascends to heaven from the Mount of Olives, disappearing in a cloud. His disciples, often accompanied by the Virgin, watch.

The scenes illustrate events in both the Old and New Testaments arranged in symbolic rather than narrative order. On the top left, Abraham, the first Hebrew patriarch, learns that he has passed the test of faith and need not sacrifice his son Isaac. Christians saw in this story a prophetic sign of Christ's sacrifice on the cross. In the next frame to the right, the apostle Peter has just been arrested for preaching after the death of Jesus. Jesus himself appears in the center frame as a teacher-philosopher flanked by Saints Peter and Paul. In a reference to the pagan past, Christ in this scene rests his feet on the head of Aeolus, the god of the winds in classical mythology,

7-24. *Good Shepherd Sarcophagus*, from the Catacomb of Praetextatus, Rome. Late 4th century. Marble. Monumenti, Musei e Gallerie Pontificie, Vatican, Rome

shown with a veil billowing behind him. To Christians he personified the skies, so that Christ is meant to be seen as seated above, in heaven, where he is giving the Christian Law to his disciples, imitating the Hebrew Scriptures' account of God dispensing the Law to Moses. Next are two scenes from Christ's Passion (see "Iconography of the Life of Jesus," page 307), his arrest (second from right) and his appearance before Pontius Pilate (far right). The frame on the bottom left shows the Old Testament story of Job, whose trials provided a model for the sufferings of Christian martyrs. Next on the right is the Fall of Adam and Eve. Lured by the serpent, they have eaten the forbidden fruit and, becoming conscious of their nakedness, are trying to hide their genitals with leaves. At the bottom center, Jesus makes his triumphal entry into Jerusalem. The next frame to the right shows Daniel in the lions' den, and the frame on the bottom right shows Saint Paul being led to his martyrdom. These exemplars of Old and New Testament faith and acceptance of divine will merge here with the theme of salvation through Jesus Christ.

Another sarcophagus found in Rome, known as the *Good Shepherd Sarcophagus*, dates to the end of the fourth century (fig. 7-24). It combines an image of the Good Shepherd with a pattern of putti harvesting grapes like that found on the ceiling of the Church of Santa Costanza (see fig. 7-17). The sculptors clearly intended the shepherds to be seen as statues raised on bases, and the large sheep arching over their shoulders set off their heads like halos. The busy putti climb through the vines to pluck grapes, which they trample in the winepress between the statue bases on the right. On the left, one milks a ewe while his companion holds the lamb that would otherwise be nursing from its mother. The shallow relief was made to seem higher through deep undercutting around the figures and the use of **drillwork**. The imagery of the catacomb paintings here finds enduring three-dimensional form.

EARLY BYZANTINE ART

During the fifth and sixth centuries, while people living in the Italian peninsula experienced invasions and religious controversy, the Eastern Empire flourished. Its capital, Constantinople, remained secure behind massive walls defended by the imperial army and navy. Its control of land and sea routes between Europe and Asia made many of its people wealthy. Their patronage, as well as that of the imperial family, made the city an artistic center, and Greek scholarship and philosophy continued to be taught in its schools. Influences from the regions under the empire's control—Syria, Palestine, Egypt, Persia, and Greece—gradually combined to create a distinctive Byzantine culture.

In the sixth century, Byzantine political power, wealth, and culture reached its height under Emperor Justinian I (ruled 527–565), ably seconded by Empress Theodora (c. 500–548). With the leadership of General Belisarius, imperial forces recovered northern Africa, Sicily, much of Italy, and part of Spain. Ravenna became the administrative capital of Byzantine Italy. The pope, although officially subject to Ravenna, remained head of the Western Church. However, the Byzantine policy of caesaropapism, whereby the emperor was head of both church and state, became a growing source of friction between the two halves of Christendom (see "Rome, Constantinople, and Christianity," page 290). As Slavs and Bulgars moved into the Balkan peninsula in southeastern Europe, they, too, came under the sway of the empire. Only on the frontier with the Persian Empire to the east did Byzantine armies falter, and there Justinian bought peace with tribute. To centralize his government and impose a uniform legal system, Justinian began a thorough compilation of Roman law known as the Justinian Code. Written in Latin, this code was later to serve as the foundation for the legal systems of Europe.

The Church and Its Decoration

Constantinople. Justinian focused his building and renovation campaign on the capital of the Eastern Empire, Constantinople, but little remains of his architectural projects or of the old imperial city itself. A magnificent exception is the Church of Hagia Sophia (Holy Wisdom, fig. 7-25). This church replaced a fourth-century building erected during the reign of Constantine's son and successor in the East, Constantius II, after the old church was destroyed during riots in 532. Spurred by Justinian's religious and political foes, the excitable crowds at a racetrack close to the imperial palace took to the streets. They set fire to the church, and soon half the city was destroyed. The empress Theodora, a brilliant, politically shrewd woman, is said to have spurred Justinian to resist the rioters, saying, "Purple makes a fine shroud"—meaning that she would rather die an empress (purple was the royal color) than flee for her life. Taking up her words as a battle cry, imperial forces under Belisarius crushed the rebels. As soon as order was restored, Justinian and Theodora embarked on a building campaign that overshadowed any in the city since the reign of Constantine two centuries earlier.

Justinian chose two scholar-theoreticians, Anthemius of Tralles and Isidorus of Miletus, to rebuild Hagia Sophia as an embodiment of imperial power and Christian glory. Anthemius was a specialist in geometry and optics, and Isidorus a specialist in physics who had also studied vaulting. They developed a daring and magnificent design. The dome of the church provided a vast, golden, light-filled canopy high above a processional space for the many priests and members of the imperial court who assembled there to celebrate the Eucharist.

The new Hagia Sophia was not constructed by the miraculous intervention of angels, as was rumored, but by mortal builders in only five years (532–537). The architects, engineers, and masons who built it benefited from the accumulated experience of a long tradition of great architecture. Procopius of Caesarea, who chronicled Justinian's reign, claimed poetically that Hagia Sophia's gigantic dome seemed to hang suspended on a "golden chain from Heaven." Legend has it that Justinian himself, aware that architecture can be a potent symbol of earthly power, compared his accomplishment with that of the legendary builder of the First Temple in Jerusalem, saying, "Solomon, I have outdone you."

Hagia Sophia was based on a central plan with a dome inscribed in a square (fig. 7-26). To form a longitudinal nave, **conches**—semidomes—expand outward from the central dome to connect with the narthex on one end and the conch of the sanctuary apse on the other. This central core, called the **naos** in Byzantine architecture, is flanked by side aisles; **galleries**, or stories open to and overlooking the naos, are located above the aisles.

The main dome of Hagia Sophia is supported on pendentives, triangular curving wall sections built between the four huge arches that spring from piers at the corners of the dome's square base (see "Elements of Architec-

7-25. Anthemius of Tralles and Isidorus of Miletus. Church of Hagia Sophia, Istanbul, Turkey. 532–37. View from the southwest

The body of the original church is now surrounded by later additions, including the minarets built after 1453 under the Ottoman Turks.

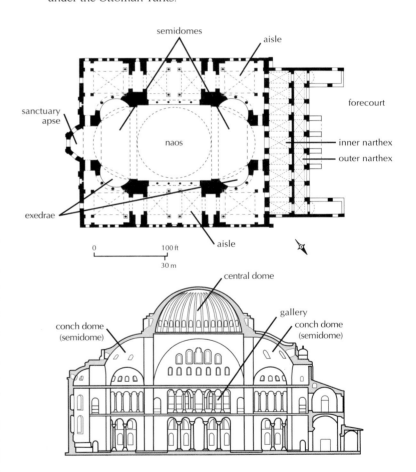

7-26. Plan and section of the Church of Hagia Sophia

ture," page 310). The origin of the dome on pendentives, which became the preferred method for supporting domes in Byzantine architecture, is obscure, but Hagia Sophia represents its earliest use in a major building. Here two semidomes flanking the main dome rise above **exedrae** with their own conch domes at the four corners

ELEMENTS OF ARCHITECTURE

Pendentives and Squinches

Pendentives and squinches are two methods of supporting a round dome or its drum over a square or rectangular space. Pendentives are structural elements between arches that form a circular opening on which the dome sits. Squinches are bracketlike constructions or **corbels**, fitted into the walls' upper corners beneath the dome. Because squinches create an octagon, which is close in shape to a circle, they provide a solid base on which a dome may rest. Byzantine builders experimented with both pendentives (as at Hagia Sophia, fig. 7-27) and squinches. Elaborate squinch-supported domes became a hallmark of Islamic interiors (as at Córdoba's Great Mosque, see fig. 8-7).

dome on pendentives

dome on squinches

of the nave. Unlike the Pantheon's dome, which is solid with an **oculus** at the top (see fig. 6-56), Hagia Sophia's dome has a band of forty windows around its base. This daring concept challenged architectural logic by weakening the integrity of the masonry but created the all-important circle of light that makes the dome appear to float (fig. 7-27). In fact, when the first dome fell in 558, it did so because a pier and pendentive shifted and the dome was too shallow, not because of the windows. Confident of their revised technical methods and undeterred, the architects designed a steeper dome that put the summit 20 feet higher above the floor. Exterior **buttressing** was added, and although repairs had to be made in 869, 989, and 1346, the church has since withstood the shock of earthquakes.

As in a basilica-plan church, worshipers entered Hagia Sophia through a forecourt and outer and inner narthexes on a central axis. Once through the portals, though, their gaze was drawn upward into the dome and then forward by the succession of domed spaces to the distant sanctuary. With this inspired design Anthemius and Isidorus had reconciled an inherent conflict in

church architecture between the desire for a symbolically soaring space and the need to focus attention on the altar and the liturgy. The domed design came to be favored by the Eastern Church.

The liturgy used in Hagia Sophia in the sixth century has been lost, but it presumably resembled the later rites of the Eastern Orthodox Church. Assuming that was the case, the celebration of the Mass took place behind a screen—at Hagia Sophia an embroidered curtain, in later churches an **iconostasis**, or wall hung with devotional paintings called **icons** ("images" in Greek). The emperor was the only layperson permitted to enter the sanctuary. Others stood in the aisles (men) or galleries (women). Processions of clergy moved in a circular path from the sanctuary into the nave and back five or six times during the ritual. The focus of the congregation was on the screen of images and up into the dome rather than ahead to the altar and apse. The upward focus reflects the interest of Byzantine philosophers in Neoplatonic theories that viewed meditation as a way to rise from the material world into a spiritual state. Worshipers standing on the church floor must have felt such a spiritual uplift as

7-27. Church of Hagia Sophia

Hypatius of Ephesus, writing in the mid-sixth century, justified decorating churches in a luxurious manner as a means to inspire piety in the congregation. He wrote: "We, too, permit material adornment in the sanctuaries, not because God considers gold and silver, silken vestments and vessels encrusted with gems to be precious and holy, but because we allow every order of the faithful to be guided in a suitable manner and to be led up to the Godhead, inasmuch as some men are guided even by such things towards the intelligible beauty, and from the abundant light of the sanctuaries to the intelligible and immaterial light" (cited in Mango, page 117).

7-28. *Transfiguration of Christ*, mosaic in the apse, Church of the Virgin, Monastery of Saint Catherine, Mount Sinai, Egypt. c. 548–65

they gazed at the mosaics of saints, angels, and, in the golden central dome, heaven itself.

The churches of Constantinople were once filled with the products of imperial patronage: mosaics, rich furniture, and objects of gold, silver, and silk. Mosaics now in the Monastery of Saint Catherine on Mount Sinai in Egypt were one such donation. The apse mosaic of the monastery's church depicts the Transfiguration on Mount Tabor (see "Iconography of the Life of Jesus," page 306) in a simple, direct manner (fig. 7-28). Dated between 548 and 565, this imposing work shows the transfigured Christ in a triple blue **mandorla**, an almond-shaped halo that surrounds Christ's whole figure, against a golden sky that fills the apse conch. The visionary figure of Christ emits rays of light, and the standing Old Testament prophets Moses and Elijah descend to affirm his divinity. The astonished apostles on the ground are identified as

Saint Peter below, Saint John at the left, and Saint James at the right. A supernatural wind seems to catch the ends of their robes, whipping them into curiously jagged shapes. The apostles fall to the ground in fear and amazement, while Christ stands calmly in the relaxed pose of a Greek-Roman athlete or orator. Mount Tabor is suggested only by a narrow strip at the bottom, half green and half reflecting the golden light. This abstract rendering contrasts with the continuing classical influence seen in the figures' substantial bodies, revealed by their tightly wrapped drapery.

The formal character of the *Transfiguration of Christ* mosaic reflects an evolving approach to representation that began several centuries earlier. As was discussed in Chapter 6, the character of imperial rule began to change in the fourth century in ways that were reflected in works of art like *The Tetrarchs* (see fig. 6-77) and the relief pan-narthex

exedrae

stairs to gallery

central dome area

ambulatory

sanctuary

apse

apsidal chapels

gallery

central dome area

apse

abstraction of figures, use of reverse perspective, and standardized conventions to portray individuals and events.

Ravenna. Ravenna was conquered by the Byzantine Empire from the Ostrogoths in 540 and served as a base for the further conquest of Italy, completed by Justinian I in 553. Much of our knowledge of the art of this turbulent period—from the time of Honorius (emperor of the Western Roman Empire) through Arian Ostrogothic control to the triumphant victory of the Byzantine Empire—comes from the well-preserved monuments at Ravenna.

In 526 Ecclesius, bishop of Ravenna from 521 to 532, commissioned two new churches, one for the city and one for its port, Classis. With funding from a wealthy local banker, construction began on a central-plan church in Ravenna dedicated to the fourth-century Roman martyr Saint Vitalis and a basilica-plan church in the port dedicated to Saint Apollinaris, the first bishop of Ravenna. Neither was completed until after Justinian had conquered Ravenna and established it as the Byzantine administrative capital of Italy. The Church of San Vitale was dedicated in 547, followed by the Church of Sant' Apollinare in Classe two years later.

The design of San Vitale is basically an octagon extended by exedralike semicircular bays, ambulatory, and gallery that are covered by a round dome (fig. 7-29). The strict symmetry of the design is broken by the extension of one bay into a rectangular sanctuary and apse that projects through one of the octagonal sides of the shell. Circular chapels with rectangular altar spaces flank this apse projection. A separate but long-gone narthex in the form of a long, oval vestibule set off-axis led to a palace complex. Triangular bays led to cylindrical stair towers that gave access to the second-floor gallery. This sophisticated design has distant roots in Roman buildings such as Santa Costanza (see fig. 7-15).

The floor plan of San Vitale only begins to convey the effect of the complex, interpenetrating interior spaces of the church, an effect that was enhanced by the offset narthex with its double sets of doors leading into the nave. People entering from the right saw only arched openings, whereas those entering from the left approached on axis with the sanctuary, which they saw straight ahead of them. The round dome, hidden on the exterior by an octagonal shell and a tile-covered roof, is a light, strong structure ingeniously created out of interlocking ceramic tubes and mortar. The whole rests on eight large piers that frame the exedrae and the sanctuary. These two-story exedrae open through arches into the outer aisles on the ground floor and into galleries on the second floor. They expand the circular central space physically and also create an airy, floating sensation, reinforced by the liberal use of gold tesserae in the surface decoration.

els on the Arch of Constantine (see fig. 6-85). The emperor became an increasingly remote figure surrounded by pomp and ceremony; orators often used terms like *Sacred*, *Majestic*, or *Eternalness* to address him. In the official art of the period, a conventionalized style somewhat similar to that seen in Egyptian and Near Eastern works displaced the naturalism of Greek and Roman classicism. In Christian art, especially, an early interest in capturing the visual appearance of the material world gave way to a new **hieratic**—formally abstract or priestly—style that sought to express essential religious meaning rather than exact external appearance. Attempting to create tangible images that would stand for intangible Christian concepts, artists rejected the space, light, color, and physicality of the real world in favor of a timeless supernatural world. The new style was characterized by geometric simplification of forms, an expressionistic

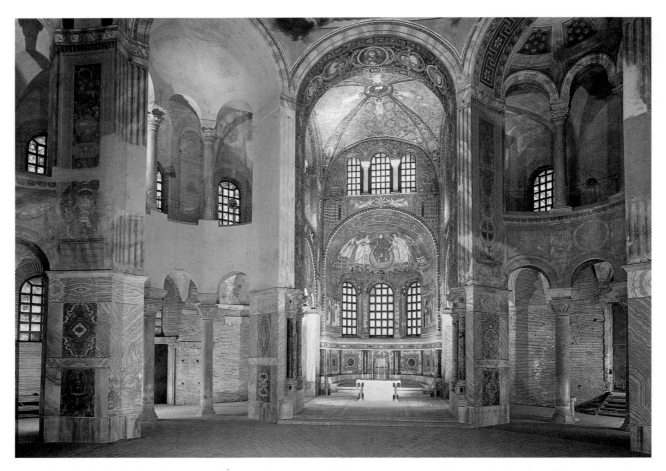

7-30. Church of San Vitale. View across the central space toward the sanctuary apse with mosaic showing Christ enthroned and flanked by Saint Vitalis and Bishop Ecclesius

In the conch of the sanctuary apse, an image of Christ enthroned is flanked by Saint Vitalis and Bishop Ecclesius, who presents a model of the church to Christ (fig. 7-30). The other sanctuary images relate to its use for the celebration of the Eucharist. Pairs of lambs flanking a cross decorate impost blocks above the intricately interlaced carving of the marble column capitals. The lunette on the south wall shows an altar table set with a chalice for wine and two patens, liturgical plates, to which the high priest Melchizedek on the right brings an offering of bread, and Abel, on the left, carries a sacrificial lamb (fig. 7-31). Their identities are known from the inscriptions above their heads.

The prophets Isaiah (right) and Moses (left) appear in the spandrels. Moses, while tending his sheep, heard the voice of an angel of God coming from a bush that was burning with a fire that did not destroy it. Moses is shown reaching down to remove his shoes, a symbolic gesture of respect in the presence of God or on holy ground. In the gallery zone of the sanctuary the Four Evangelists are depicted, two on each wall, and in the vault the Lamb of God supported by four angels appears in a field of vine scrolls.

Justinian and Theodora did not attend the dedication ceremonies for the Church of San Vitale conducted by Archbishop Maximianus in 547—they may never have set foot in Ravenna—but two large mosaic panels that face each other across its apse make their presence known. Justinian (see fig. 7-1), on the north wall, carries a large golden paten for the Host and stands next to Maximianus, who holds a golden, jewel-encrusted cross. The priestly celebrants at the right carry the Gospels, encased in a gold-and-jewel book cover, symbolizing the coming of the Word, and a censer containing burning incense to purify the altar prior to the Mass.

Theodora, singled out by a gold halolike disk and a fluted shell canopy, carries a huge golden chalice studded with jewels (fig. 7-32). She presents this both as an offering for the Mass and as a gift of great value for Christ. With it she emulates the Magi (see "Iconography of the Life of Jesus," page 306), depicted at the bottom of her purple robe, who brought valuable gifts of gold, frankincense (fragrant wood), and myrrh (expensive, perfumed oil) to the infant Jesus. A courtyard fountain stands to the left of the panel and patterned draperies adorn the openings at left and right. The huge jeweled and pearl-hung crown nearly dwarfs her delicate features, yet the empress dominates these worldly trappings by the intensity of her gaze.

The mosaic decoration in the Church of San Vitale presents a unique mixture of imperial ritual, Old Testament narrative, and Christian liturgical symbolism that dissolves its architecture into shimmering light and color. The setting around Theodora—the conch, the

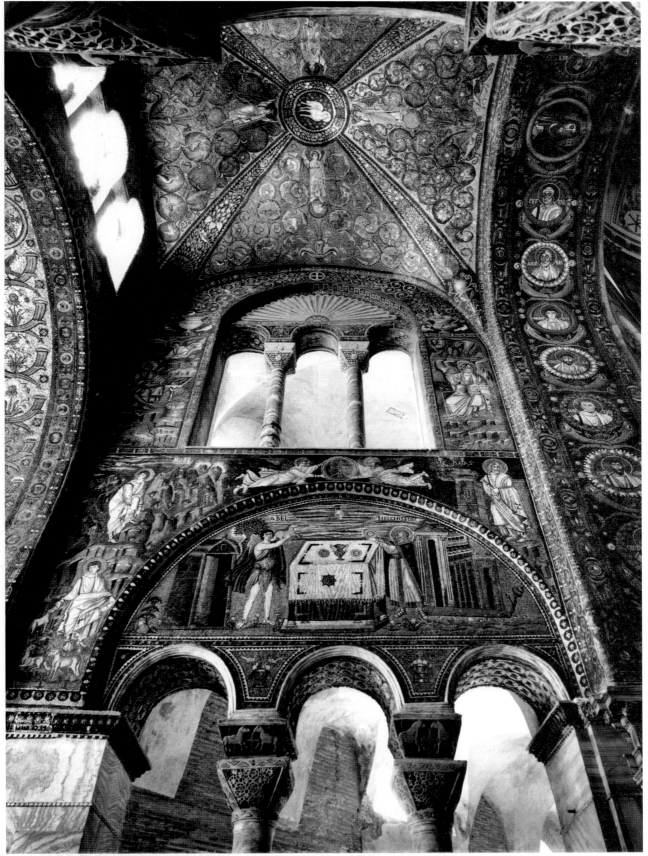

7-31. Church of San Vitale, south wall of the sanctuary, with Abel and Melchizedek in the lunette, Moses and Isaiah in the spandrels, portraits of the evangelists in the gallery zone, and the Lamb of God in the vault

7-32. *Empress Theodora and Her Attendants,* mosaic on south wall of the apse, Church of San Vitale. c. 547.
8'8" x 12' (2.64 x 3.65 m)

Just like royalty today, Theodora was the subject of much comment and conjecture in her time. Described in a "secret history" by a contemporary, the historian Procopius, as a small-boned woman with sparkling eyes and a will of iron, she was said to have been an actress, considered a risqué profession. Her father was an animal trainer for the circus, where the young heir to the imperial throne, Justinian, met her. Although Theodora's background was unacceptable in high circles, Justinian remained devoted to her. He named a new province, Theodorias, for her and treated her almost as if she were co-emperor. Theodora died in 548, not long after this mosaic portrait was completed.

fluted pedestal, the open door, and the swagged draperies—are classical illusionistic devices, yet the mosaicists deliberately avoid making them space-creating elements. Byzantine artists accepted the idea that objects exist in space, but they no longer conceived pictorial space the way Roman artists had, as a view of the natural world seen through a "window," the picture plane, and extending back from it toward a distant horizon. In Byzantine aesthetic theory, eye and image were joined by invisible rays of sight so that pictorial space extended forward from the picture plane to the eye of the beholder and included the real space between them. Parallel lines appear to diverge as they get farther away and objects seem to tip up in a representational system known as **reverse perspective**.

Bishop Maximianus consecrated the Church of Sant'Apollinare in Classe in 549 (fig. 7-33). The atrium has disappeared, but the simple geometry of the brick exterior clearly reflects the basilica's interior spaces. A narthex entrance spans the full width of the ground floor; a long, tall nave with a clerestory ends in a semicircular apse; and side aisles flank the nave.

On the interior, nothing interferes visually with the movement forward from the entrance to the raised sanctuary (fig. 7-34), which extends directly from a triumphal-arch opening into the semicircular apse. The conch mosaic depicts an array of human and animal figures in

7-33. Church of Sant'Apollinare in Classe, the former port of Ravenna (Classis), Italy. 533–49

a stylized landscape and has many levels of meaning. A jeweled cross with the face of Christ at its center symbolizes the Transfiguration—Jesus' revelation of his divinity. The Hand of God reaches down from glowing clouds. The Old Testament figures Moses and Elijah emerge from clouds at each side, symbolically legitimizing the newer religion and attesting to the divine event. The apostles Peter, James, and John—represented here by the three sheep with raised heads—likewise witness

7-34. *The Transfiguration of Christ with Saint Apollinaris, First Bishop of Ravenna,* mosaic in the apse, Church of Sant'Apollinare in Classe

7-35. *Archangel Michael,* panel of a diptych, probably from the court workshop at Constantinople. Early 6th century. Ivory, 17 x 5½" (43.3 x 14 cm). The British Museum, London

The other half of this devotional piece, now lost, would have completed the Greek inscription across the top, which begins: "Receive these gifts, and having learned the cause. . . ." Perhaps the other panel contained the portrait of the emperor or another high official who was presenting the panels as a gift to an important colleague, acquaintance, or family member.

7-36. Page with *Wild Blackberry,* from *De Materia Medica,* by Pedanius Dioscorides (1st century), copy made and illustrated in Constantinople for Princess Anicia Juliana. c. 512. Tempera on vellum, 15 x 13" (38.1 x 33 cm). Österreichische Nationalbibliothek, Vienna

the event. At the center below the cross, Saint Apollinaris, in bishop's robes, is shown as an orant. The twelve lambs flanking him represent the apostles. Stalks of blooming lilies, along with tiny trees and other plants, birds, and oddly shaped rocks, fill the green mountain landscape. Unlike the landscape in the *Good Shepherd* lunette of the Mausoleum of Galla Placidia (see fig. 7-20), these highly stylized forms bear little resemblance to nature. The artists eliminated any suggestion of spatial recession by making the trees and lambs at the top of the golden sky larger than those at the bottom. The pictorial abstraction of the gigantic cross bearing the face of Christ dominates the conch.

In the mosaics on the wall above the apse, which were added in the seventh and ninth centuries, Christ, now portrayed with a cross inscribed in his halo and flanked by symbols representing the evangelists, blesses and holds the Gospels. Sheep (the apostles) emerge from triumphal gateways and climb golden rocks toward their leader and teacher.

Ivories, Manuscripts, and Panel Paintings. Ivory reliefs were a popular product of the court workshops of Constantinople in the early sixth century. A treasured example of this form is a panel depicting an archangel, a high-ranking angel, probably Michael (fig. 7-35). The artist has rendered the figure in a classical style but has otherwise created an image meant entirely to convey certain abstract concepts. In his beauty, physical presence, and elegant setting, the archangel is comparable to the priestess of Bacchus in the Symmachus panel (see fig. 6-89). His

EARLY FORMS OF THE BOOK

Since people began to write some 5,000 years ago, they have kept records on a variety of materials, including clay or wax tablets, pieces of broken pottery, papyrus, animal skins, and finally paper. The extended works that we call books have taken two forms: **rotulus** and **codex**. A rotulus is a continuous rolled strip, or scroll. A codex (plural codices), like the modern book, is made up of sheets bound together on one side. Egyptian scribes made scrolls from sheets of papyrus glued together. Scrolls were also made from thin sheets of cleaned, scraped, and trimmed sheep- or calfskin, a material known as **parchment** or, when softer and lighter, **vellum**. Scrolls were written to be read either horizontally or vertically. Each end was attached to a rod; the reader slowly unfurled the scroll from one rod to the other.

At the end of the first century CE, the codex replaced the scroll as the predominant book form in the West. A basic unit of the early codex was the eight-leaf quire, made by folding a large sheet of parchment three times, cutting it, and then sewing it on one side, or by folding two sheets and sewing the two stacked sheets together.

Until the invention of printing, all books were **manuscripts**, that is, written by hand. From early on, manuscripts often included illustrations, but techniques for combining pic-

tures and text varied. The simplest solution was to place illustrations above or below the text, but they might also be placed within the text or set off with frames. Illustrations in books came to be called **miniatures**, from *minium*, the Latin word for a reddish lead pigment. Manuscripts decorated with gold and colors were said to be **illuminated**. Manuscript illumination became increasingly specialized during the European Middle Ages, with some experts doing only borders, others decorating initials, others painting pictures, and still others applying gold leaf.

Heavy covers in the form of wooden boards covered with leather functioned as a press to keep the sheets of a codex flat. Very rich manuscripts sometimes had covers decorated with precious metals, jewels, ivory, and enamels. The thickness and weight of parchment and vellum made it impractical to produce a very large manuscript, such as an entire Bible, in a single volume. As a result, individual sections were made into separate books. The Gospels, the Psalms, and the first five books of the Old Testament (the Pentateuch), for example, were often bound individually. These weighty tomes were stored flat on shelves in cabinets like the one holding the Gospels shown here and visible in the mosaic of Saint Lawrence in the Mausoleum of Galla Placidia.

Bookstand with Gospels codices, detail of a mosaic in the eastern lunette, Mausoleum of Galla Placidia, Ravenna, Italy. c. 425–26 (see fig. 7-19)

spatial relation to the architectural frame around him, however, is not realistic. His heels rest on the top step of a stair that clearly lies behind the columns and pedestals, but the rest of his body projects in front of them in a way that would cause a human to teeter and fall forward. The image suggests both the joyful promise of life in the hereafter and its sobering counterpart, the torments of hell for those found wanting in the eyes of God. The angel is shown here as a divine messenger, holding a staff of authority in his left hand and a sphere symbolizing worldly power in his right, a message reinforced by repetition: within the arch is a cross-topped orb, framed by a wreath, against the background of a scalloped-shell canopy.

Manuscripts, or handwritten books, were also commissioned by the Byzantine court. Among these was a botanical encyclopedia known by its Latin title, *De Mate-*

ria Medica, listing the appearance, properties, and medicinal uses of plants. The encyclopedia was compiled in the first century CE by a Greek physician named Pedanius Dioscorides (c. 40–c. 90), who probably traveled as a physician with the Roman army. His work was the first systematic treatment of such material and, in its time, was a highly regarded scientific treatise. Generations of scribes—professional document writers—copied it. The earliest known surviving copy, from Constantinople and dated to about 512, was given to Princess Anicia Juliana, whose father had been emperor in the West for a few months in 472. It is in codex form, consisting of individual sheets bound together on one side (see "Early Forms of the Book," above). The illustrators transformed what was a practical reference book in Greek into an exquisitely illustrated work suitable for the imperial library (fig. 7-36).

7-37. Page with *Rebecca at the Well*, from *Book of Genesis*, probably made in Syria or Palestine. Early 6th century. Tempera, gold, and silver paint on purple-dyed vellum, 13¼ x 9⅞" (33.7 x 25 cm). Österreichische National-bibliothek, Vienna

Although Dioscorides' work is secular and pagan, Christians found religious as well as medical significance in the plants it catalogs. For example, the wild blackberry bramble illustrated here came by tradition to represent the burning bush of Moses and the purity of the Virgin Mary.

Byzantine manuscripts often used very costly materials. Although plain sheets of **vellum** (a fine writing surface made from calfskin) and natural pigments were used in this copy of *De Materia Medica*, purple-dyed vellum and inks of gold and silver were used in a *Book of Genesis* (fig. 7-37). The book was probably made in Syria or Palestine, and the purple vellum indicates that it may have been for an imperial patron (costly purple dye, made from the shells of murex mollusks, often was restricted to imperial use). The Genesis book, like the *De Materia Medica*, is in codex form and written in Greek. Illustrations appear below the text at the bottom of the pages. The illustration of the story of Rebecca at the Well (Genesis 24) shown here appears to be a single scene, but it actually mimics the continuous narrative of a scroll. Events that take place at different times in the story follow in succession. Rebecca, the heroine of the story, appears at the left walking away from the walled city of Nahor with a large jug on her shoulder to fetch water. She walks along a miniature colonnaded road toward a spring personified by a reclining pagan water nymph with a flowing jar. In the foreground, Rebecca, her jug now full, encounters a thirsty camel driver and offers him

water to drink. Unknown to her, he is Abraham's servant Eliezer in search of a bride for Abraham's son Isaac. Her generosity leads to marriage with Isaac. Although the realistic poses and rounded, full-bodied figures in this painting reflect an earlier Roman painting tradition, the unnatural purple of the background and the glittering silver ink of the text act to remove the scene from the mundane world.

An illustrated Gospels, signed by a monk named Rabbula and completed in February 586 at the Monastery of Saint John the Evangelist in Beth Zagba, Syria, provides a near-contemporary example of a quite different approach to religious manuscript decoration. Its illustrations may have been inspired by church paintings and mosaics. They are intended not only to depict biblical events but also to present the Christian story through a complex, multileveled symbolism. Besides full-page illustrations like those of the Crucifixion and the Ascension shown here, there are also lively smaller scenes, or **vignettes**, in the margins.

The Crucifixion in the *Rabbula Gospels* presents a detailed picture of Christ's death and resurrection (fig. 7-38). He appears twice, on the cross in the center of the upper register and with the two Marys—the mother of James and Mary Magdalen—at the right in the lower register. The Byzantine Christ is a living king who triumphs over death. He is shown as a mature, bearded figure, not the youthful shepherd depicted in the catacombs. Even on the cross he is dressed in a long, purple robe, called a colobium, that signifies his royal status. (In many Byzantine images he also wears a jeweled crown.) At his sides are the repentant and unrepentant criminals who were supposedly crucified with him. Beside the thief at the left stand the Virgin and Saint John the Evangelist; beside the thief at the right are the holy women. Soldiers beneath the cross throw dice for Jesus' clothes. A centurion stands on either side of the cross. One of them, Longinus, pierces Jesus' side with a lance; the other, Stephaton, gives him vinegar instead of water to drink from a sponge. The small disks in the heavens represent the sun and moon. In the lower register, directly under Jesus on the cross, stands the tomb, with its open door and stunned or sleeping guards. This scene represents the Resurrection. The angel reassures the holy women at the left, and Christ himself appears to them at the right. All these events (described in Matthew 28) take place in an otherworldly setting indicated by the glowing bands of color in the sky. The austere mountains behind the crosses give way to the lush foliage of the garden around the tomb. This very complete representation of the orthodox view of the Crucifixion may have been intended to counter the claim of the Monophysites that Christ was entirely divine.

The ascension of Christ into heaven (fig. 7-39) is described in the New Testament: "[A]s they [his apostles] were looking on, he was lifted up, and a cloud took him from their sight" (Acts of the Apostles 1:9). The cloud has been transformed into a **mandorla** supported by two angels. Two other angels follow, holding victory crowns in fringed cloths. The image directly under the mandorla

7-38. Page with *The Crucifixion,* from the *Rabbula Gospels,* from Beth Zagba, Syria. 586. 13¼ x 10½" (33.7 x 26.7 cm). Biblioteca Medicea Lauren-ziana, Florence

7-39. Page with *The Ascension,* from the *Rabbula Gospels*

ICONOCLASM Christianity, like Judaism and Islam, has always been uneasy with the power of religious images. The early Church feared that the faithful would worship the works of art themselves instead of what they represented. This discomfort grew into a major controversy in the Eastern Church as images increasingly replaced holy relics as objects of devotion from the late sixth century on. Many **icons** were believed to have been created miraculously, and all were thought to have magical protective and healing powers. Prayer rituals came to include prostration before images surrounded by candles, practices that seemed to some dangerously close to idol worship.

In 726 Emperor Leo III launched a campaign of **iconoclasm** ("image breaking"), decreeing that all religious images were idols and should be destroyed. In the decades that followed, Iconoclasts undertook widespread destruction of devotional pictures of Jesus Christ, the Virgin Mary, and the saints. Those who defended devotional images (Iconodules) were persecuted. The veneration of images was briefly restored under Empress Irene following the Second Council of Nicaea in 787, but the Iconoclasts regained power in 814. In 843 Empress Theodora, widow of Theophilus, the last of the iconoclastic emperors, reversed her husband's policy.

While the Iconoclasts held power, they enhanced imperial authority at the expense of the Church by undermining the untaxed wealth and prestige of monasteries, whose great collections of devotional art drew thousands of worshipers. They also increased tensions between the Eastern Church and the papacy, which defended the veneration of images and refused to acknowledge the emperor's authority to ban it. The Iconoclasts claimed that representations of Jesus Christ, because they portrayed him as human, promoted heresy by separating his divine from his human nature or by misrepresenting the two natures as one. Iconodules countered that upon assuming human form as Jesus, God took on all human characteristics, including visibility. According to this view, images of Christ, testifying to that visibility, demonstrate faith in his dual nature and not, as the Iconoclasts claimed, denial of it: "How, indeed, can the Son of God be acknowledged to have been a man like us . . . if he cannot, like us, be depicted?" (Saint Theodore the Studite, cited in Snyder, page 128).

Those who defended images made a distinction between veneration—a respect for icons as representations of sacred personages—and worship of icons as embodiments of divinity, or idols. Moreover, they saw image making not only as an effective teaching tool but also as a humble parallel to the divine act of creation, when "God created man in his image" (Genesis 1:27).

combines fiery wheels and the four beasts of the Hebrew prophet Ezekiel's vision (Ezekiel 1). The four beasts also appear in the New Testament's Revelation and are associated with the Four Evangelists: Matthew, an angel; Mark, a lion; Luke, an ox; and John, an eagle. Christians interpreted this vision as a precursor of the vision of Judgment Day described in Revelation.

Below the vision, the Virgin Mary stands calmly in the pose of an orant, while angels at her side confront the astonished apostles. One angel gestures at the departing Christ and the other appears to be offering an explanation of the event to attentive listeners (Acts of the Apostles 1:10–11). The prominence accorded Mary here can be interpreted as a result of her status of Theotokos, or Godbearer. She may also represent the Christian community on earth, that is, the Church. As we noted earlier, the Christian world at this time was filled with debate over the exact natures of Christ, the Trinity, and the Virgin Mary. Taken as a whole, the *Rabbula Gospels* would provide evidence of the owner's adherence to orthodoxy.

Eastern Christians prayed to Christ, Mary, and the saints while looking at images of them on icons. The first such image was believed to have been a portrait of Jesus that appeared miraculously on the scarf with which Saint Veronica wiped his face along the road to the execution ground. Church doctrine toward the veneration of icons was ambivalent. Key figures of the Eastern Church, such as Saint Basil the Great of Cappadocia (c. 329–379) and Saint John of Damascus (c. 675–749), distinguished between idolatry—the worship of images—and the veneration of an idea or holy person depicted in a work of art. The Eastern Church thus prohibited the worship of icons but accepted them as aids to meditation and prayer. The images were thought to act as intermediaries between worshipers and the holy personages they depicted.

Most early icons were destroyed in the eighth century in a reaction to the veneration of images known as iconoclasm (see "Iconoclasm," above), making those that have survived especially precious. A few very beautiful examples were preserved in the Monastery of Saint Catherine on Mount Sinai, among them the *Virgin and Child with Saints and Angels* (fig. 7-40). As Theotokos, Mary was viewed as the powerful, ever-forgiving intercessor, or go-between, appealing to her Divine Son for mercy on behalf of repentant worshipers. She was also called the Seat of Wisdom, and many images of the Virgin and Child, like this one, show her holding Jesus on her lap in a way that suggests that she represents the throne of Solomon. The Christian warrior-saints Theodore (left) and George (right)—both legendary figures said to have slain dragons, representing the triumph of the Church over the "evil serpent" of paganism—stand at each side, while angels behind them look heavenward. The artist who painted the Christ Child, the Virgin, and the angels worked in a Roman-derived, illusionistic technique and created almost realistic figures. The male saints are much more stylized; this artist barely hints at real bodies beneath the richly patterned textiles of their cloaks.

7-40. *Virgin and Child with Saints and Angels*, icon, Monastery of Saint Catherine, Mount Sinai, Egypt. Second half of 6th century. Encaustic on wood, 27 x 18⅞" (69 x 48 cm)

LATER BYZANTINE ART

Byzantine Christian art enjoyed three major productive phases. The first golden age began with the reign of Justinian I in the sixth century and centered on Constantinople, ending in the eighth century, when the Iconoclasts rose to power in the Eastern Church. A second golden age began in 867 under the Macedonian dynasty and lasted until Christian Crusaders from the West occupied Constantinople in 1204 (Chapter 15). Byzantine culture flourished again in the fourteenth and early fifteenth centuries until Constantinople was conquered by Muslim Ottoman Turks in 1453. Because Byzantine art was the art of the Eastern Orthodox Church, it spread with Christianity through eastern Europe and became the source for national styles that still exist today. The Byzantine artistic tradition was, in the words of one scholar, "monumental, kaleidoscopic, constantly open to fashion, energizing and far-reaching" (Beckwith, page 344).

Architecture and Its Decoration

When Constantinople became a Muslim city in 1453, many of its churches were destroyed or extensively rebuilt, but enough remain to give us an idea of what the city's Christian architecture looked like during the preceding centuries. Many central-plan domed churches, so favored by Byzantine architects, also survived in outlying regions. These structures exhibit the builders' taste for a multiplicity of geometric forms, verticality, and rich, decorative effects both inside and out. Some of the earliest surviving examples, abandoned and partially ruined today, are in ancient Armenia, a land fought over for much of its history by the various empires surrounding it. Christianity arrived very early in this region and became so entrenched that foreign traders traveling the east-west Silk Road in the seventh century called its capital, Ani, the "city of a thousand and one churches." The Armenian Orthodox Church was separate from the Eastern Orthodox

7-41. Church of the Holy Cross, Isle of Aght'amar, Lake Van, Armenia (modern Turkey). 915–21

7-42. Churches of the Monastery of Hosios Loukas, near Stiris, Greece. Katholikon (left), early 11th century; Church of the Virgin Theotokos (right), 10th century

Church, and the two architectural styles, while sharing certain features, sometimes diverged markedly.

One of the most exceptional Armenian central-plan domed churches is the Church of the Holy Cross, built between 915 and 921 on the Isle of Aght'amar in Lake Van in eastern Asia Minor (fig. 7-41). Originally part of a luxurious royal complex, the church was the product of the unusual and sophisticated taste of King Gagik of Vaspurakan (ruled 900/904–937). To build it, the king brought artisans "who came from every land" (cited in Thierry, page 173). A profusion of exterior stone sculpture is carved directly into the building blocks. Included are stylized figures in low, almost flat, relief; frieze bands in higher relief with deep undercutting; and fully three-dimensional projecting animal heads. King Gagik is shown at the bottom, to the left of the center window, holding a nearly three-dimensional model of the church. Interestingly, Gagik is taller and more impressive in his wreathlike halo and patterned robes than Christ on the right. Various saints and archangels surround the bottom of the building, and two frieze bands, one above the arched openings and the other running under the eaves, show animals amid grapevines, a reminder of the heavenly paradise.

The two Churches of the Monastery of Hosios Loukas, built a few miles from the village of Stiris, Greece, in the tenth and eleventh centuries, provide excellent examples of the architecture of the second Byzantine golden age (figs. 7-42, 7-43). The Church of the Virgin Theotokos, on the right in the illustration, is joined to the Katholikon, on the left. Both churches are essentially compact, central-plan structures. Their exterior decoration is striking—light-colored stone and red brick arranged in decorative patterns. This style of decoration is known as cloisonné because the courses of brick outline the stone blocks and set them off like the fine-line

7-43. Plan of the Churches of the Monastery of Hosios Loukas

partitions (cloisons) in enamelwork. The dome of the Theotokos rises on pendentives over a square core; that of the Katholikon rises on squinches and an octagonal core. (Squinches, like pendentives, are devices for supporting a dome on a square base; see "Elements of Architecture," page 310.) The domes are enriched by high vaults covering interior bays. Narthexes and tall sanctuary apses with flanking rooms further complicate the space.

The high central space in the interior of the Katholikon carries the eye of the worshiper upward into the main dome, which soars above a ring of tall arched windows (fig. 7-44). Unlike Hagia Sophia, with its clear, sweeping geometric forms, the two churches of Hosios Loukas have a complex variety of forms, including domes, groin vaults, barrel vaults, pendentives, and

7-44. Central dome and apse, Katholikon, Monastery of Hosios Loukas. Early 11th century and later

7-45. Plan of the Cathedral of San Marco, Venice. Begun 1063

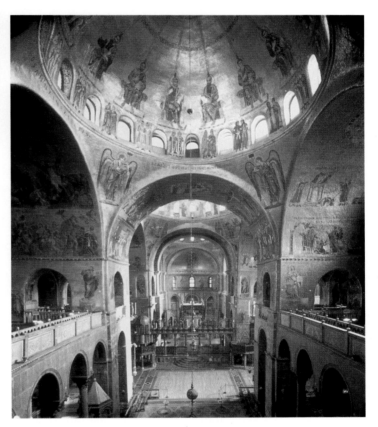

7-46. Cathedral of San Marco. View looking toward apse

The church is the third one built on the site. It is both the palace chapel and the martyrium where the bones of the patron of Venice, Saint Mark, are preserved. This great multidomed structure, consecrated as the Venice Cathedral in 1807, has been reworked continually, right to the present day.

squinches. (The squinches in the Katholikon are the small, fan-shaped niches above the corners of the lower walls.) Single, double, and triple windows create intricate and unusual patterns of light, illuminating a painting (originally a mosaic) of Christ Pantokrator, Ruler of the Universe, in the center of the main dome. The secondary, sanctuary dome of the Katholikon is decorated with a mosaic of the Lamb of God surrounded by the Twelve Apostles, and the apse conch has a mosaic of the Virgin and Child. Scenes from the Old and New Testaments and figures of saints fill the interior with brilliant color and dramatic images.

At the end of the tenth century, Constantinople granted the northeastern Italian city of Venice, already a dominant sea power in the Adriatic, a special trade status that allowed its merchants to control much of the commercial interchange between the East and the West. Venetian architects looked to the Byzantine domed church for inspiration when the city's ruler, the doge, commissioned a much larger church to replace the palace chapel in 1063. This chapel had served since the ninth century as a **martyrium**, holding the relics of the martyr Saint Mark the Apostle, which were brought to Venice from Alexandria in the ninth century. The Cathedral of San Marco has a Greek-cross plan, each square unit of which is covered by a dome (fig. 7-45). There are five great domes in all, separated by barrel vaults and supported by pendentives. Unlike Hagia Sophia, with its flow of space from the narthex through the nave to the apse (see fig. 7-27), San Marco's domed compartments—covered with golden mosaics—produce a complex space with five vertical axes (fig. 7-46).

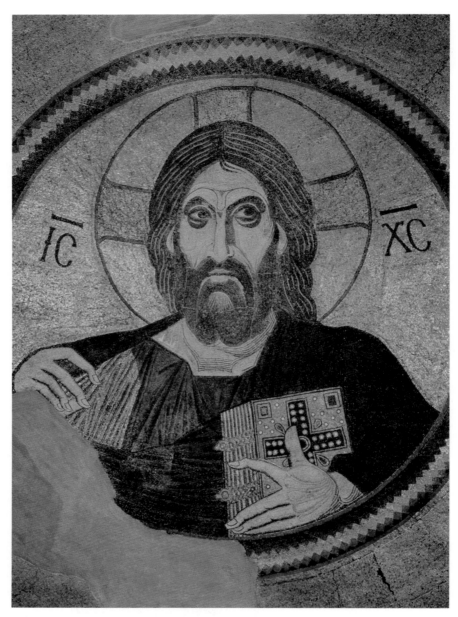

7-47. *Christ Pantokrator*, mosaic in the central dome, Church of the Dormition, Daphni, Greece. Central dome, c. 1080–1100

Eleventh-century mosaicists looked with renewed interest at models from the past, studying both classical art and the art of the Justinian era. They conceived their compositions in terms of an intellectual rather than a physical ideal. While representing the human figure and narrative subjects, some artists eliminated all unnecessary details, focusing on the essential elements of a scene to convey its mood and message. Other artists seemed absorbed in depicting anecdotal details, so that well-proportioned figures clothed in form-defining garments might also have draperies with patterns of geometric folds and jagged, flying ends bearing no relation to gravity. Instead of modeling forms with subtle tonal gradations, artists often relied on strong juxtapositions of light and dark areas.

The decoration of the Church of the Dormition at Daphni, Greece, provides an excellent eleventh-century example of these developments. (The term *dormition*—which comes from the Latin word for "sleep," which, in turn, derives from the Greek word for "sleep"—refers to the ascension to heaven of the Virgin Mary at the moment of her death.) The *Christ Pantokrator*, a bust-length mosaic portrayal, fills the central dome of the church (fig. 7-47). This awe-inspiring image, hovering in golden glory, is more than a picture of the Christian Savior; it is a powerful evocation of his promised judgment, with its reward for the faithful and punishment for sinners.

On a wall in the north arm of the church is an image of Christ crucified (fig. 7-48). Jesus is shown with bowed head and sagging body, his eyes closed in death. Gone is the royal robe; a nearly nude figure hangs on the cross. Unlike the Crucifixion scene in the sixth-century *Rabbula Gospels*, which depicts many people, some anguished

7-48. *Crucifixion*, mosaic in the north arm of the east wall, Church of the Dormition

and others indifferent or hostile (see fig. 7-38), the artist of this image shows just two other figures, Mary and the young apostle John, to whom Jesus had entrusted the care of his mother after his death. John cannot hide his grief, but Mary, gesturing toward Christ, seems briefly to have overcome hers. The arc of blood and water springing from Jesus' side refers to the Eucharist. The simplification of contours and reduction of forms to essentials give the image great emotional power. It conveys a sense of timelessness and otherworldly space, a golden universe anchored to the material world by a few flowers, which suggest the promise of new life. The mound of rocks and the skull at the bottom of the cross represent Golgotha, the "place of the skull," a hill outside ancient Jerusalem where Adam was thought to be buried and the Crucifixion was said to have taken place. To the faithful, Jesus Christ was the new Adam sent by God to save

humanity through his own sacrifice. As Paul wrote in his First Letter to the Corinthians: "For just as in Adam all die, so too in Christ shall all be brought to life" (I Corinthians 15:22). The timelessness and simplicity of the image aid the Christian worshiper seeking to achieve a mystical union with the divine through prayer and meditation.

Other notable mosaics were created on the island of Sicily, a crossroads of Byzantine, Muslim, and European influence. Sicily was ruled by Muslims from 827 to the end of the eleventh century, when it fell to the Normans, descendants of the Viking settlers of northern France. The Norman Roger II (ruled 1105–1154) was crowned king in Palermo in 1130, and the pope, who assumed ecclesiastical jurisdiction over Sicily for "God and Saint Peter," endorsed Norman rule. In the first half of the twelfth century, Sicily became one of the richest and most enlightened kingdoms in Europe. Roger II extended

EARLY CHRISTIAN, JEWISH, AND BYZANTINE ART   *327*

7-49. *Nativity*, wall mosaic in the Palatine Chapel, Palermo, Sicily. c. 1140–89

7-50. *Lamentation*, fresco in the Church of Saint Panteleimon, Nerezi, near Skopje, Republic of Macedonia. c. 1164

An Islamic-style timber ceiling, inlaid marble floor and lower walls, and mosaic upper walls dramatically combine classical, Islamic, and Byzantine elements into an exotic whole.

Of special interest are the mosaic decorations completed between about 1140 and 1189 using the Byzantine style and technique but showing a Western preference for narrative over iconic images (fig. 7-49). In a wall mosaic, the Nativity story's events have been transformed into an exciting multipart drama, with each scene isolated by the rhythmic contours of hillocks and caves. At the center is the cave that, in the Eastern tradition, was the birthplace of Jesus. Mary lies on a mattress and supports the newborn Jesus on a solid, altarlike manger, where he is adored by the ox and the ass, symbols for Jews and Christians. At the lower right, the two midwives who had assisted at the birth are preparing a basin of water to bathe the baby. At the upper left, three angels seem to urge the Magi forward while pointing at the Star of Bethlehem, from which a single ray descends to the infant Jesus. The angel at the upper right has just announced the birth to three shepherds who appear in an extension of the mosaic on a neighboring wall, not shown here, at a right angle to this one. Two of the Magi appear a second time at the right presenting their gifts (the third is on the wall with the shepherds). Only Joseph at the lower left sits alone, lost in quiet contemplation of the miraculous events.

When money was no object, mosaic was the medium of choice for Byzantine wall decorations, but the less expensive and less durable medium of wall painting was also used effectively in many places. Paintings cover the walls of the small domed church dedicated to Saint Panteleimon on a mountainside near the Macedonian city of Skopje. Built in about 1164 under a distant relative of Emperor Alexios I, the church may have been decorated by painters from a major center working with local artists. Among the finest paintings is the *Lamentation*, a scene showing the body of the crucified Jesus mourned by his mother, John, Peter, and perhaps Joseph of Arimathea, the wealthy man who offered his nearby mausoleum to house the body (fig. 7-50). The tension and quietude of this scene, which evoke the repressed feelings of the mourners for the untimely loss of a son, a friend, and a leader, contrast with the joyful bustle surrounding the Palermo *Nativity*. The horizontal composition emphasizes the prostrate form of the dead Jesus, and the repetition of rounded backs and rounded hills seems to make visible the waves of emotion sweeping over the living participants. The tender gestures of Mary pressing her cheek to her dead son's and John kissing his limp hand also convey the intensity of the moment. Because it evokes a powerful emotional rather than an intellectual response, the work is said to be **expressionistic**.

The third golden age of Byzantine art began after Western Crusaders, who had occupied Constantinople in 1204, were expelled from the city in 1261. The patronage of emperors, wealthy courtiers, and the Church stimulated renewed church building. In this new work, the physical requirements of the clergy and the liturgy took

religious toleration to the kingdom's diverse population, which included Latins, Greeks, Arabs, and Jews. He involved all factions in his government, permitted everyone to participate equally in the kingdom's economy, and issued official documents in Latin, Greek, and Arabic.

Roger's court in his capital city of Palermo was a brilliant and exotic mixture of Norman, Muslim, and Byzantine cultures. The Palatine (palace) Chapel there reflects this diversity. The Western-style basilica-plan church has a Byzantine dome on squinches over the crossing.

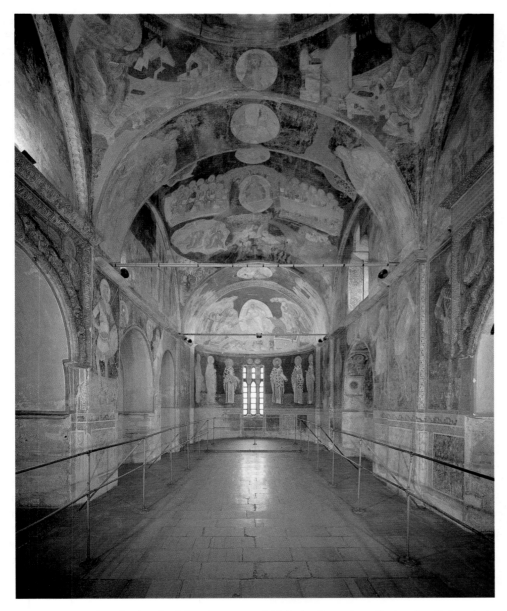

7-51. Funerary chapel, Church of the Monastery of Christ in Chora (now Kariye djami), Istanbul, Turkey. c. 1315–21

precedence over costly interior decorations. The buildings, nevertheless, often reflect excellent construction skills and elegant and refined design.

New ambulatory aisles, narthexes, and side chapels were added to many small, existing churches. Among these is the former Church of the Monastery of Christ in Chora, Constantinople, now a mosque known as Kariye djami. The expansion of this church was one of several projects that Theodore Metochites, the administrator of the Imperial Treasury at Constantinople, sponsored between 1315 and 1321. A humanist, poet, and scientist, Metochites became a monk in this monastery sometime after 1330. He added a two-story annex to its church on the north side, two narthexes on the west side, and a funerary chapel on the south side. These structures con-

tain the most impressive interior decorations remaining in Constantinople from the late Byzantine period.

The funerary chapel is entirely painted (fig. 7-51). The resurrection of Christ, depicted in the apse conch, and the Last Judgment, painted on the ceiling vault, are themes appropriate to a funerary chapel. Large figures of the church fathers (a group of especially revered early Christian writers of the history and teachings of the Church), saints, and martyrs line the walls below. Sarcophagi, surmounted by portraits of the deceased, once stood in the side niches. Trompe l'oeil ("fool the eye") painting imitates marble panels in the surrounding **dado**. The painters bound their pigments with oil or egg and applied them directly over fresh wet plaster. This frescolike technique allowed rapid work and produced rich colors.

7-52. *Anastasis*, painting in the apse of the funerary chapel, Church of the Monastery of Christ in Chora

7-53. *The First Steps of Mary*, mosaic in the inner narthex, Church of the Monastery of Christ in Chora

A painting of the Resurrection known as the *Anastasis* fills the funerary chapel's apse vault (fig. 7-52). Artists in the West usually depicted the Resurrection as the Triumphant Christ (*Christus Triumphans*) emerging from his tomb in glory. The *Anastasis*, instead, depicts Christ's Harrowing of Hell to rescue Adam and Eve and other devout people from Satan. Christ appears as a savior in white,

moving with such force that even his star-studded mandorla has been set awry. He has trampled down the doors of hell; tied Satan into a helpless bundle; and shattered locks, chains, and bolts, which lie scattered over the ground. He drags the elderly Adam and Eve from their open sarcophagi with such force that their bodies seem airborne. Behind him are Old Testament prophets and kings, as well as his cousin John the Baptist.

In the inner narthex of the church, mosaics depicting scenes from the life of the Virgin Mary, a popular medieval cycle that included many subjects taken from popular tradition rather than from the Bible, fill the upper walls and vaults. Among them is a touching portrayal of Mary as an infant just learning to walk (fig. 7-53). The child, who appears as a tiny adult swathed in the dark draperies she will be shown wearing in later life, totters away from her nurse toward the encouraging arms of her mother, Anna (Saint Anne). The gestures and movement of the figures, although drawn with the exaggerated, elongated proportions and angular drapery of the late Byzantine style, create a mood of amused tenderness. The swinging draperies reinforce the curving arcs of the women's bodies, which along with the architectural elements form a protective, enfolding screen around the insecure toddler.

Constantinople had close ties with Russia, and Christianity was introduced there in the late tenth century. Orthodox churches in Russia followed the traditional Byzantine plan of a dome over a Greek cross. Over the centuries the Russian preference for complexity and height led to a spectacular architectural style epitomized by the Cathedral of Saint Basil the Blessed in Moscow (fig. 7-54). Originally dedicated to the Intercession of the Virgin Mary, it was rededicated to Saint Basil the Blessed. The first Russian czar, Ivan IV, known as the Terrible (1530–1584), commissioned the church, and the architects Barna and Postnik designed it. Construction took place between 1555 and 1561. One of its most striking features is its combination of a Byzantine domed church with the steeply pitched Russian tent roof form called a *shater*, which kept dangerously large accumulations of snow from forming. The large, central *shater* seems to have spawned a brood of lesser domes of varying sizes. The multiplication of shapes and sizes and the layering of the surfaces with geometric relief elements all work to distract us from the underlying central plan—a central building surrounded by four arms ending in domed octagons and four domed cubical areas (fig. 7-55). Such an arrangement, a square with four corner units plus a center unit, is called a **quincunx**. Each of the exterior units has its own tall drum and a dome that seems to grow budlike from a tall, slender stalk. This spectacular church shows the evolution of Byzantine art into a distinctly national style found in later Russian Orthodox churches elsewhere, including the United States.

Ivories and Metalwork

During the second Byzantine golden age, from 867 to the Crusaders' occupation of Constantinople in 1204, artists

7-54. Barna and Postnik. Cathedral of Saint Basil the Blessed, Moscow. 1555–61

Like most mid-sixteenth-century Russian churches, the entire exterior of Saint Basil's was originally painted white, and the domes were gilded. The bright colors we see today were added by later generations. The name of the church has also changed. It was originally dedicated to the Intercession of the Virgin Mary, a reflection of the veneration of Mary in the Eastern Church.

7-55. Plan of the Cathedral of Saint Basil the Blessed

7-56. *Harbaville Triptych*. Late 10th century. Ivory, 11 x 9½" closed (28 x 24.1 cm). Musée du Louvre, Paris

of impeccable ability and high aesthetic sensibility produced small luxury items of a personal nature for members of the court as well as for the Church. Many of these items were commissioned by rulers and high secular and church functionaries as official gifts for one another. As such they had to be portable, sturdy, and exquisitely refined. In style these works tended to combine classical elements with iconic compositions, successfully joining simple beauty and religious meaning. Such a piece is the *Harbaville Triptych*, dating from the late tenth century (fig. 7-56). This small ivory devotional piece represents Christ flanked by Mary and Saint John the Baptist, a group known as **Deesis**. The saints act as intercessors on behalf of worshipers. The figures exist in a neutral space given definition only by the small bases under the feet of the saints and by Christ's throne. Although conceived as essentially frontal and rigid, the figures have rounded shoulders, thighs, and knees that suggest physical substance beneath a linear, decorative drapery.

The refined taste and skillful work that characterize the arts of the eleventh and twelfth centuries were also expressed in precious materials such as silver and gold. One of the prizes the Crusaders took back to Venice in 1204, after their sack of Constantinople, was a silver-gilt and enamel icon of the archangel Michael. The icon was presumably made in the tenth century in a court workshop (fig. 7-57). The angel's head and hands, executed in relief, are surrounded by intricate relief and enamel decoration. Halo, wings, and liturgical garments are in delicate **cloisonné** and the framing borders are inset with enamel **roundels** (see "Byzantine Metalworking," page 333). The colorful brilliance of the patterned setting removes the image from the physical world, although the archangel appears here in essentially the same frontal pose and with the same idealized and timeless youthfulness with which he was portrayed in a sixth-century ivory panel (see fig. 7-35). The sheer artistry of this icon

7-57. *Archangel Michael*, icon. 10th century. Silver gilt and enamel, 19 x 14" (48 x 36 cm). Treasury of the Cathedral of San Marco, Venice

TECHNIQUE

BYZANTINE METAL-WORKING

Byzantine metalworkers and enamelers had an international reputation for their high-quality work. They were particularly skilled in the use of **cloisonné** enamel, which is produced by soldering a network of fine copper, gold, or silver wires in a desired pattern to a panel made of similar metal and then filling up the cells (**cloisons**) with powdered colored glass. When the object is heated, the glass powder melts and fuses onto the surface of the metal to create small, jewellike sections.

The icon of Archangel Michael (fig. 7-57) is an especially elaborate example of Byzantine metalwork. Using the **repoussé** technique, the artists pounded out the central image of the archangel from the back of a thin plate of silver. The silver was then gilded. Colorful cloisonné creates the effect of silk garments with jewels, and small cloisonné portrait medallions decorate the border. Such medallions are often found detached from their original context and incorporated into new works.

7-58. Page with *David the Psalmist*, from the *Paris Psalter*. Mid-10th century. Paint on vellum, sheet size 14 x 10¼" (35.6 x 26 cm). Bibliothèque Nationale, Paris

About a third of the Old Testament was written in poetry, and among its most famous poems are those in the Book of Psalms. According to ancient tradition, the author of the Psalms was King David himself, the young shepherd and musician who killed the Philistine giant Goliath and later became king of Israel. In Christian times, the Psalms were also copied into a book called a Psalter, used for private reading and meditation. *Psalm* and *Psalter* come from a word meaning the sound or action of playing a stringed instrument (the psaltery).

seems to lift the image to a lofty plane where light and color supplant form and material substance becomes pure spirit, an effect valued by the Neoplatonic Church philosophers of the time.

Manuscripts

Several luxuriously illustrated manuscripts have survived from the second golden age. As was true of the artists who decorated church interiors, the illustrators of these manuscripts combined intense religious expression, aristocratic elegance, and a heightened appreciation for rich decorative forms. The *Paris Psalter* from the mid-tenth century is one example (fig. 7-58). Like the earlier *Rabbula Gospels* (see figs. 7-38, 7-39), the Psalter (a version of the Psalms) includes scenes set off in frames on pages without text. Fourteen full-page paintings illustrate the *Paris Psalter*, the first of which is devoted to

7-59. Page with *Joshua Leading the Israelites,* from the *Joshua Roll,* made in Constantinople. 10th century. Vellum rotulus with brown ink and colored washes, height of scroll 12¾" (32.4 cm). Biblioteca Apostolica Vaticana, Rome

David, the Israelite king, traditionally the author of the Old Testament's Book of Psalms. The illuminators turned to earlier classical illustrations as source material. The idealized, massive, three-dimensional figures reside in a receding space with lush foliage and a meandering stream that seem directly transported from a Roman "sacred landscape" (see fig. 6-47). The architecture of the city and the ribbon-tied memorial column also derive from conventions in Greek and Roman funerary art, and in the ancient manner, the illustrator has personified abstract ideas and landscape features, an artistic technique known as **allegory**. Melody, a female figure, leans casually on David's shoulder, while another woman, perhaps the wood nymph Echo, peeks out from behind the column. The reclining youth in the lower foreground is a personification of Mount Bethlehem, as we learn from his inscription. The dog watching over the sheep and goats while his master strums the harp suggests the classical subject of Orpheus's charming the wild animals with music. The subtle modeling of forms, the integration of the figures into a three-dimensional space, and the use of **atmospheric perspective** all enhance the classical flavor of the painting.

The *Joshua Roll* (fig. 7-59), a tenth-century manuscript in scroll form also believed to have been created in a Constantinople **scriptorium** (writing room for scribes), reflects an approach different from that of the *Paris Psalter*. The illustrators worked on plain vellum, using ink and colored washes to convey the exploits of Moses' suc-

7-60. *Virgin of Vladimir,* icon, probably from Constantinople. Faces only, 12th century; the rest has been retouched. Tempera on panel, height approx. 31" (78 cm). Tretyakov Gallery, Moscow cessor, Joshua, the Old Testament hero of the Battle of Jericho (Joshua 6:1–20), who conquered the promised land and whom Christians considered a precursor of Christ. In the section shown here, the events described in the text are depicted in a continuous landscape that recedes from the large foreground figures to distant cities and landforms. Strategically placed labels within the pictures identify the figures. The main character, Joshua, is at the far right. Crowned with a halo, unhelmeted but wearing upper-body armor, he leads his soldiers toward the Jordan River. Despite its stylization, this painting, too, serves as a reminder of the classical roots of Byzantine culture.

Painted Icons

The distinction drawn in Church doctrine between the worship of images, which was forbidden as idolatry, and the veneration of the idea or person they represented was frequently lost on the laity, many of whom attributed miraculous powers to icons. A new way of portraying the Virgin and Child in Byzantine art that emerged in the eleventh and twelfth centuries reflects a growing desire for a more immediate and personal religion. (A similar trend was seen in the art of western Europe about the same time.) Paintings of this type, known as the Virgin of Compassion, show Mary and the Christ Child pressing their cheeks together and gazing tenderly at each other. The source for this humanized portrayal was widely thought to be a portrait painted by the evangelist Luke following a vision he had of the Nativity. An icon of this type known as the *Virgin of Vladimir* remains to this day perhaps the most revered holy image in Russia (fig. 7-60). Some worshipers believed it to be the very painting done by Luke. Almost from its creation (probably in Constantinople) the panel was thought to protect the people of the city where it resided. It arrived in Kiev sometime between 1131 and 1136 and was moved to the city of Suzdal and then to Vladimir in 1155. In 1480 it was moved permanently to Moscow, where it graced the Cathedral of the Dormition in the Kremlin.

Another remarkable icon, this one from the third period in Byzantine art, is *The Old Testament Trinity (Three Angels Visiting Abraham)*, a large panel created between 1410 and 1420 by the famed artist-monk Andrey Rublyov (fig. 7-61). It was commissioned in honor of the abbot Sergius of the Trinity-Sergius Monastery, near Moscow. This icon clearly illustrates how late Byzantine artists relied on time-honored mathematical conventions to create ideal figures, as did the ancient Greeks, thus giving their work remarkable consistency. Unlike the Greeks, who based their formulas on close observation of nature, Byzantine artists invented an ideal geometry and depicted human forms and features according to it. Here the circle forms the underlying geometric figure, emphasized by

7-61. Andrey Rublyov. *The Old Testament Trinity (Three Angels Visiting Abraham)*, icon. c. 1410–20. Tempera on panel, 55½ x 44½" (141 x 113 cm). Tretyakov Gallery, Moscow

Representing the dogma of the Trinity—one God in three Persons—was a great challenge to artists. One solution, used here and in other late-medieval work, was to show God as three identical individuals and to use an event in the Old Testament, the story of the Hebrew patriarch Abraham and his wife, Sarah, who entertained three strangers who were in fact divine beings.

the form of the haloed heads. Although this formulaic approach imposed a basic uniformity, talented artists like Rublyov managed, nevertheless, to create a personal style of expression within it. To capture the sense of the spiritual in his work, Rublyov relied on typical conventions—simple contours, elongation of the body, and a focus on a limited number of characters—such as those in the mosaics at Daphni (see figs. 7-47, 7-48). Yet a sweet, poetic ambience distinguishes Rublyov's work.

In this artist's hands, the Byzantine style took on new life just as western European artists were beginning a classically inspired revivalist movement called the Renaissance. During the same period in the East, Constantinople was overrun by the forces of the Ottoman sultan Muhammad II, and the Eastern Empire became part of the Islamic world, with its own very rich aesthetic heritage.

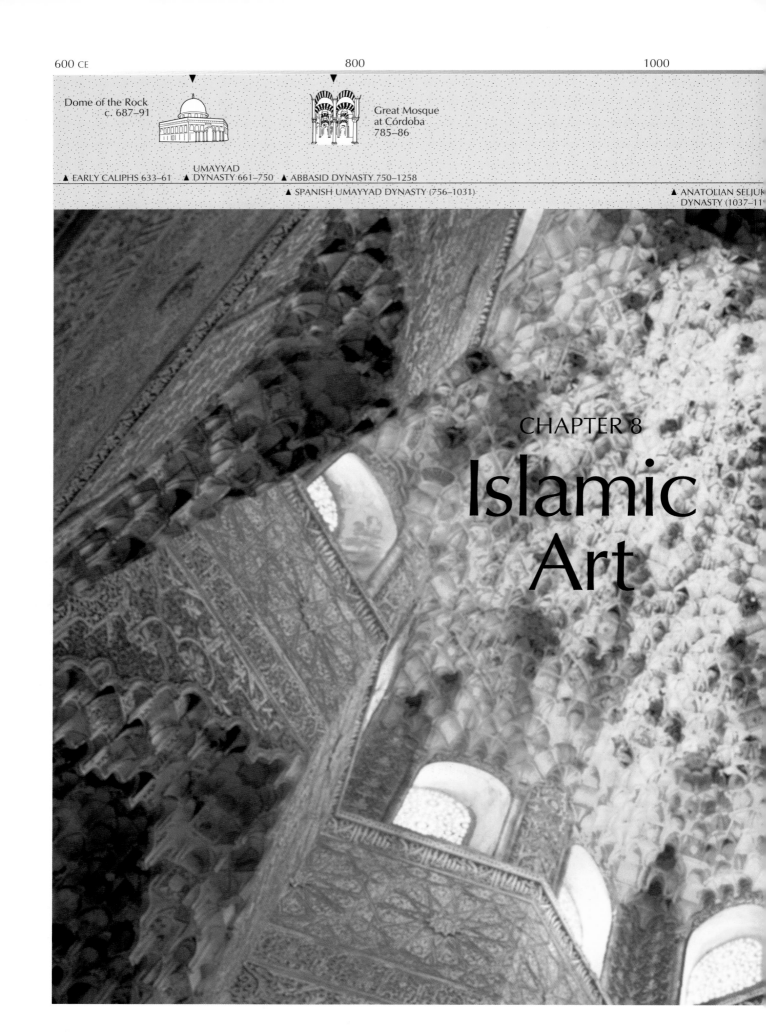

600 CE   800   1000

Dome of the Rock
c. 687–91

Great Mosque
at Córdoba
785–86

▲ EARLY CALIPHS 633–61   ▲ UMAYYAD DYNASTY 661–750   ▲ ABBASID DYNASTY 750–1258

▲ SPANISH UMAYYAD DYNASTY (756–1031)

▲ ANATOLIAN SELJUK
DYNASTY (1037–11

CHAPTER 8

Islamic Art

1200
1400
1600 CE

Seljuk pitcher
early 13th century

Tugra
c. 1555–60

▲ OTTOMAN EMPIRE 1290–1918
▲ EGYPTIAN MAMLUK DYNASTY (1252–1517)
▲ SPANISH NASRID DYNASTY (1232–1492)   ▲ TURKIC TIMURID DYNASTY (1370–1507)

ATLANTIC
OCEAN
FRANCE
Vienna
Pisa
SPAIN
Córdoba   Granada
ITALY
Edirne
Black Sea
Istanbul
ANATOLIA
MOROCCO
Mediterranean Sea
SYRIA
PALESTINE
Damascus
Amman
Jerusalem
Mshatta
Cairo
JORDAN
IRAQ
Baghdad
Samarra
Tigris River
Euphrates River
Tabriz
Caspian Sea
Aral Sea
Samarkand
UZBEKISTAN
KHURASAN
Herat
AFGHANISTAN
PERSIA
Isfahan
Indus River
INDIA
Persian Gulf
EGYPT
Nile River
Medina
Mecca
ARABIA
Red Sea
Arabian
Sea
SUDAN

0   1000 miles
0   1000 kilometers

8-1. Page from Koran (surah 47:36) in kufic script, from Syria. 9th century. Ink, pigments, and gold on vellum, 9³⁄₈ x 13¹⁄₈" (23.8 x 33.3 cm). The Metropolitan Museum of Art, New York
Rogers Fund, 1937 (37.99.2)

During the holy month of Ramadan in 610 CE, a merchant named al-Amin ("the Trusted One") sought solitude in a cave on Mount Hira, a few miles north of Mecca, in Arabia. On that night, "The Night of Power and Excellence," the angel Gabriel is believed to have appeared to him and commanded him to recite revelations from God. In that moment this merchant became Muhammad, the Messenger of God. The revelations dictated by Gabriel at Mecca formed the basis of a religion called Islam ("submission to God's will"), whose adherents are referred to as Muslims ("those who have submitted to God"). Today, nearly a billion Muslims turn five times a day toward Mecca to pray.

The Word of God was recorded in a book known as the Koran ("recitation"), which is a compilation of Muhammad's revelations. To transcribe these revelations, Arabic was adopted as the uniform script wherever Islam spread, and the very act of transcribing the Koran became sacred.

To accomplish this holy task, which is summarized in the ancient Arabic expression "Purity of writing is purity of the soul," scribes developed **calligraphy**, the art of writing, to an extraordinary degree (fig. 8-1). A prohibition against depicting representational images in religious art, as well as the naturally decorative nature of Arabic script, led to the use of calligraphic decoration on religious architecture, carpets, and handwritten documents. Perhaps the foremost characteristic of Islamic religious art, wherever it is found in the world and among every race, is the presence of Koranic Arabic, used for reading and prayer, and for decoration.

ISLAM AND EARLY ISLAMIC SOCIETY

Islam spread rapidly after its founding, encompassing much of Africa, Europe, and Asia. The art of this vast region draws its distinctive character both from Islam itself and from the diverse cultural traditions of the world's Muslims. Because Islam discouraged the use of figurative images, particularly in religious contexts—unlike Christian art of the same period—Islamic artists developed a rich vocabulary of **aniconic**, or nonfigural, ornament that is a hallmark of Islamic work. This vocabulary includes complex geometric patterns and the scrolling vines known outside the Islamic world as arabesques. Figural representation, to the extent it was permitted (which varied from time to time and place to place), first developed most prominently in regions with strong pre-Islamic figural traditions, such as those that had been under the control of the Byzantine and Roman empires. Stylized forms for representing animals and plants developed in the regions that had been under the control of the Sassanian dynasty of Persia (modern Iran), the heirs of the artistic traditions of the ancient Near East, who ruled from 226 to 641. Because the Arabian birthplace of Islam was not noted for its art, these Persian and Roman-Byzantine influences shaped Islamic art in its formative centuries.

Much of Islamic art can be seen as an interplay between pure abstraction and organic form. For Muslims, abstraction helps free the mind from the contemplation of material form, opening it to the enormity of the divine presence. Islamic artists excelled in surface decoration, using repeated and expanding patterns to suggest timelessness and infinite extension. Shimmering surfaces created by dense, highly controlled patterning are characteristic of much later Islamic art, including architecture, carpet making, calligraphy, and book illustration.

Muslims date the beginning of their history to the flight of the Prophet Muhammad from Mecca to Medina—an exodus called in Arabic the *hijra*—in 622 (see "The Life of the Prophet Muhammad," pages 340, 341). Over the next decade Muhammad succeeded in uniting the warring clans of Arabia under the banner of Islam.

Following the Prophet's death in 632, four of his closest associates assumed the title of caliph, or successor: Abu Bakr (ruled 633–634), Umar (ruled 634–644), Uthman (ruled 644–656), and finally Ali (ruled 656–661). According to tradition, during the time of Uthman, the Koran assumed its final form.

The accession of Ali provoked a power struggle that led to his assassination. Muawiya (ruled 661–680), Ali's rival and a close relative of Uthman, then became caliph, founding the Umayyad dynasty (661–750). This struggle resulted in enduring divisions within Islam. Followers of Ali, known as Shiites, regard him as the Prophet's rightful successor and the first three caliphs as illegitimate. Sunni Muslims, in contrast, recognize all of the first four caliphs as "rightly guided." Today about 10 percent of the world's Muslims are Shiites and about 85 percent Sunni.

Beginning in the seventh century, Islam expanded dramatically. In just two decades, seemingly unstoppable Muslim armies conquered the Sassanian Persian Empire, Egypt, and the Byzantine provinces of Syria and Palestine. By the early eighth century, under the Umayyads, they had reached India, conquered all of North Africa and Spain, and penetrated France to within 100 miles of Paris before being turned back. The circumstances in Islamic lands of Christians and Jews who did not convert to Islam was neither uniform nor consistent. In general, as "People of the Book"—non-Muslim followers of a monotheistic religion based on a revealed scripture—they enjoyed a protected status. However, they were also subject to a special tax and restrictions on dress and employment.

Islam has proven a remarkably adaptable faith. Part of that adaptability is due to its emphasis on the believer's direct, personal relationship with God through prayer and a corresponding lack of ceremonial paraphernalia. Every Muslim must observe the Five Pillars, or duties, of faith. The most important of these is the statement of faith: "There is no god but God and Muhammad is his messenger." Next come ritual prayer five times a day, charity to the poor, fasting during the month of Ramadan, and a pilgrimage to Mecca—Muhammad's birthplace and the site of the Kaaba, Islam's holiest structure—once in a lifetime for those able to undertake it.

THE LIFE OF THE PROPHET MUHAMMAD

Muhammad, the prophet of Islam, was born about 570 in Mecca, a major pilgrimage center in west-central Arabia, to a prominent family that traced its ancestry to Ishmael, son of the biblical patriarch Abraham. Orphaned as a small child, Muhammad spent his early years among the Beduin, desert nomads. When he returned to Mecca, he became a trader's agent, accompanying caravans across the desert. At the age of twenty-five he married his employer, Khadija, a well-to-do, forty-year-old widow, and they had six children.

After Muhammad received the revelations from God in 610, the first to accept him as Prophet was his wife. Other early converts included members of his clan and a few friends, among them the first four successors, or caliphs, who led the faithful after Muhammad's death. As the number of converts grew, Muhammad encountered increasing opposition from Mecca's ruling clans, including some leaders of his own clan. They objected to both his religious teachings and the threat they posed to the trade that accompanied Mecca's status as a pilgrimage site. In 622 Muhammad and his companions fled Mecca and settled in the oasis town of Yathrib, which the Muslims renamed Medina, the Prophet's City. It is to this event, called the *hijra* ("emigration"), that Muslims date the beginning of their history. After years of fighting, Muhammad and his followers won control of Mecca in 630 with an army of 10,000, and its inhabitants converted to Islam. The Kaaba—a cube-shaped stone structure draped with black cloth that had once been the focus of idol worship—became the sacred center of Islam, toward which Muslims around the globe still turn to pray. Shortly thereafter, Islam spread throughout Arabia.

Muhammad married eleven times. (Muslim law allows men four coequal wives at once, although the Prophet was permitted more.) Some of these marriages were political and others were to provide for women in need—a social duty in a society in which clan feuds killed many men. Within the framework of Islam, women gained rights where there had been none before. Their degree of freedom depended greatly on the time and the place, but some became monarchs of countries such as Yemen and Indonesia, and many were significant sponsors of architecture programs.

Muhammad is reputed to have been a vigorous, good-looking man for whom the world was a fragrant paradise. One of his wives, Aisha, provided much of the information available about his personal life. "People used to ask [Aisha] how the Prophet lived at home. Like an ordinary man, she answered. He would sweep the house, stitch his own clothes, mend his own sandals, water the camels, milk the goats, help the servants at their work, and eat his meals with them; and he would go fetch a thing we needed from the market" (cited in Glassé, page 281).

After making a farewell pilgrimage to Mecca, Muhammad died in Medina in 632. According to his wishes, he was buried in his house, in Aisha's room, where he breathed his last. His tomb is a major pilgrimage site. A generation after his death his revelations, which he continued to receive throughout his life, were assembled in 114 chapters, called surahs, organized from longest to shortest, each surah divided into verses. This is the sacred scripture of Islam, called the Koran ("recitation"), which is the core of the faith. Another body of work, the Hadith ("account"), compiled over the centuries, contains sayings of the Prophet, anecdotes about him, and additional revelations. The Koran and the Hadith are the foundation of Islamic law, guiding the lives of nearly a billion Muslims around the world.

Muslims consider Muhammad to be the last in a succession of prophets, or messengers of God, that includes Adam, Abraham, Ishmael, Moses, and Jesus. Like Judaism and Christianity but unlike the other religions prevalent in Arabia at the time, Islam is monotheistic, recognizing only a single, all-powerful deity. Muhammad's teaching emphasized the all-pervading immateriality of God and banned idol worship.

This painting shows Muhammad traveling by camel to a desert market fair to seek the support of his

Muslims are expected to participate in congregational worship at a **mosque** (*masjid* in Arabic) on Friday. When not at a mosque, the faithful simply kneel wherever they are to pray, facing the Kaaba in Mecca. The Prophet Muhammad himself lived simply and advised his companions not to waste their resources on elaborate architecture. Instead, he instructed and led them in prayer in a mud-brick structure, now known as the Mosque of the Prophet, adjacent to his home in Medina. This was a square enclosure with verandas supported by palm-tree trunks that framed a large courtyard. Muhammad spoke from a low platform on the south veranda. This simple arrangement—a walled courtyard with a separate space on one side housing a **minbar** (pulpit) for the imam (prayer leader)—became the model for the design of later mosques.

ART DURING THE EARLY CALIPHATES

The caliphs of the aggressively expansionist Umayyad dynasty ruled from their capital at Damascus (in modern Syria). They were essentially desert chieftains who had scant interest in fostering the arts except for poetry, which had been held in high esteem among Arabs since pre-Islamic times, and architecture. The building of shrines and mosques throughout the empire in this period represented both the authority of the new rulers and the growing acceptance of Islam. The caliphs of the Abbasid dynasty, who replaced the Umayyads in 750 and ruled until 1258, governed in the grand manner of ancient Persian emperors from their capitals at Baghdad and Samarra (in modern Iraq). Their long and cosmopolitan reign saw achievements in med-powerful uncle for his religious movement as well as to make converts among the fairgoers. He is accompanied by two close associates, the merchant Abu Bakr and the young warrior Ali. Abu Bakr, the first caliph, was the father of Muhammad's wife Aisha. Ali, husband of Muhammad's daughter Fatima, was the fourth caliph. The power struggle that ended in his death led to the rise of the Shiite sect. Although the faces of Abu Bakr and Ali are shown, that of Muhammad, in keeping with the Islamic injunction against idolatry and the making of idols, is not. The degree of representation permitted in Islamic art varied from place to place and from period to period depending in part on the strictness with which the injunction against idol making was interpreted and the purpose a work of art was to serve. This example suggests what was acceptable for an illustration of its type at the Ottoman court at the end of the sixteenth century.

The Prophet Muhammad and His Companions Traveling to the Fair, from a later copy of the *Siyar-i Nabi* (Life of the Prophet) of al-Zarir (14th century), Istanbul, Turkey. 1594. Pigments and gold on paper, 10⅝ x 15" (27 x 38 cm). New York Public Library, New York. Spencer Collection

icine, mathematics, the natural sciences, philosophy, literature, music, and art. They were generally tolerant of the ethnically diverse populations in the territories they subjugated and admired the cultural traditions of Byzantium, Persia, India, and China. (The early art of India is discussed in Chapter 9 and that of China in Chapter 10.)

Architecture

As Islam spread, architects adapted freely from Roman, Christian, and Persian models, which include the basilica, the martyrium, the peristyle house, and the palace audience hall. The Dome of the Rock in Jerusalem, built about 687–691, is the oldest surviving Islamic sanctuary and is today the holiest site in Islam after Mecca and Medina (fig. 8-2). It stands on the summit of the Temple Mount (Mount Moriah) and encloses a rock outcropping (fig. 8-3) that has long been sacred to the Jews, who identify it as the site on which Abraham prepared to sacrifice his son Isaac. Jews, Christians, and Muslims associate the site with the creation of Adam and the Temple of Solomon. Muslims also identify it as the site from which Muhammad, led by the angel Gabriel, ascended to heaven in the Night Journey, passing through the spheres of heaven to the presence of God.

The Dome of the Rock was built by Syrian artisans trained in the Byzantine tradition, and its centralized plan—octagons within octagons—derived from both Byzantine and early Christian architecture. Unlike its Byzantine models, however, with their plain exteriors, the Dome of the Rock, crowned with a golden dome that dominates the Jerusalem skyline, is opulently decorated

PARALLELS

Years	Period	Early Islam	World
633–661	Early caliphs	Conquest of Arabia, Sassanian Persia, Egypt, Syria, Palestine	**c. 600–800** *Beowulf* (England); first Japanese capital at Nara; first block-print text (China)
661–750	Umayyad dynasty	Conquest of India, North Africa, southern France; capital at Damascus; Dome of the Rock; Mshatta palace	
750–1258	Abbasid dynasty	Umayyad dynasty in Spain; Great Mosque at Córdoba; capital at Baghdad, then Samarra (836); Great Mosque at Samarra; Samarkand ware; Seljuk dynasty in Anatolia; Masjid-i Jami at Isfahan; Mamluk dynasty in Egypt	**c. 800–1000** Charlemagne is made emperor of the West; bronze casting in South America; *Diamond Sutra* (China); first Viking colony in Greenland **c. 1000–1200** Lady Murasaki's *Tale of Genji* (Japan); separation of Eastern and Western Christian Churches; William the Conqueror (England); the Crusades
1290–1918	Ottoman Empire	Alhambra at Granada; Ottomans take Constantinople; Selimiye Cami (Edirne)	**c. 1200–1500** Jenghiz Khan rules Mongols; Magna Carta (England); Kublai Khan rules Mongols; Dante's *Divine Comedy* (Italy); beginning of Renaissance in Europe; Hundred Years' War (England/France); Black Death in Europe; Great Schism of Roman Church; Chaucer's *Canterbury Tales* (England); Joan of Arc (France); Gutenberg first prints Bible (Germany); Columbus's voyages (Spain); Spanish Inquisition

both outside and inside. The central space is covered by a dome on a tall **drum** supported by an arcade. Concentric aisles enclose the rock. As at San Vitale in Ravenna (see fig. 7-30), interior surfaces were originally decorated with marble **dadoes** at ground level and glass mosaics above. Remains of the mosaics show Byzantine-style foliage combined in a new style with jewel-like Sassanian Persian insignia. This imagery consists of a double-winged motif often associated with Sassanian royalty. The more than 700 feet of Arabic inscriptions on the structure are a distinctly Islamic feature. Written in one script on the interior and another on the exterior, these inscriptions include the references to Jesus Christ in the Koran. Later Islamic architects built similar domed octagonal sanctuaries and saints' tombs from Morocco to China.

The Umayyad caliphs, disregarding the Prophet's advice about architectural austerity, built for themselves palatial hunting retreats on the edge of the desert. With profuse interior decoration depicting exotic human and animal subjects in stucco, mosaic, and paint, some had swimming pools, baths, and domed, private rooms. One of the later desert palaces was begun in the 740s at Mshatta (near present-day Amman, Jordan). Although never completed, this square, stone-walled complex is nevertheless impressively monumental (fig. 8-4). It measured about 470 feet on each side, and its outer walls and gates were guarded by towers and bastions reminiscent of a Roman fort. The space was divided roughly into thirds, with the center section containing a huge courtyard. The main spaces were a mosque and a domed, basilica-plan audience hall that was flanked by four

8-2. Dome of the Rock, Jerusalem, Israel. c. 687–91

8-3. Cutaway
drawing of
the Dome
of the Rock

8-4. Plan and facade of the palace, Mshatta, Jordan. c. 750

8-5. Frieze, detail of facade, palace, Mshatta. Stone. Staatliche Museen zu Berlin, Preussischer Kulturbesitz, Museum für Islamische Kunst

private apartments, or *bayts*. *Bayts* grouped around small courtyards, for the use of the caliph's relatives and guests, occupied the remainder of the building.

Unique among the surviving palaces, Mshatta was decorated with a **frieze** that extended in a band about 16 feet high across the base of its facade. This frieze was divided by a zigzag molding into triangular compartments, each punctuated by a large **rosette** carved in high relief (fig. 8-5). The compartments were filled with intricate carvings in low relief that included interlacing scrolls inhabited by birds and other animals (there were no animals on the mosque side of the building), urns, and candlesticks. Similar designs in both sculpture and mosaic adorned the interiors of Roman and Byzantine buildings but were never on exterior surfaces, and the designs were not so densely interwoven. Beneath one of the rosettes, two facing lions drink from an urn from which grows the Tree of Life, an ancient Persian motif.

With the development of mosque architecture during the early Umayyad period, the characteristic elements of this place of communal worship began to emerge (see "Elements of Architecture," opposite). There were facilities for ritual cleansing before entering the consecrated space, a *sahn*, or courtyard, and a large covered space to accommodate Friday prayers. Worshipers prayed facing the **qibla** wall, which was oriented toward Mecca. A niche called a **mihrab** differentiated the qibla wall from the others. The imam delivered a sermon from the minbar, near the qibla wall. Some mosques included an enclosure called a *maqsura* near the mihrab for dignitaries. Muezzins, or criers, called the faithful to prayer from one or more towers, or **minarets** (literally "lighthouses"), on the exterior. Some early mosques were housed in modified pre-Islamic buildings.

When the Abbasids overthrew the Umayyads in 750, a survivor of the Umayyad dynasty, Abd ar-Rahman I (ruled 756–788), fled across North Africa into southern Spain (known as "al-Andalus" in Arabic), where, with the support of Syrian Muslim settlers, he established himself as the provincial ruler, or amir. The Umayyads continued to rule in Spain from their capital in Córdoba for the next three centuries (756–1031) and were noted patrons of the arts. Thus one of the finest surviving examples of Umayyad architecture, the Great Mosque of Córdoba, is in Spain.

This sprawling structure was begun on the site of a church in 785. Repeatedly enlarged until the fifteenth century, when it returned to Christian use, it combines

ELEMENTS OF ARCHITECTURE

Mosque Plans

The earliest mosques were pillared **hypostyle halls** such as the Great Mosque at Córdoba (see fig. 8-6). Approached through an open courtyard, the *sahn*, their interiors are divided by rows of columns leading, at the far end, to the mihrab niche of a qibla wall, which is oriented toward Mecca.

A second type, the **four-iwan mosque**, was originally associated with **madrasas** (schools for advanced study). The iwans—monumental barrel-vaulted halls with wide-open, arched entrances—faced each other across a central *sahn*; related structures spread out behind and around the iwans. Four-iwan mosques were most developed in Persia, in buildings like Isfahan's Masjid-i Jami (see fig. 8-13).

Central-plan mosques, such as the Selimiye Cami at Edirne (see fig. 8-17), were derived from Istanbul's Hagia Sophia (see fig. 7-27) and are typical of Ottoman Turkish architecture. Central-plan interiors are dominated by a large domed space uninterrupted by structural supports. Worship is directed, as in other mosques, toward a qibla wall and its mihrab opposite the entrance.

hypostyle mosque
Great Mosque, Córdoba

four-iwan mosque
Masjid-i Jami, Isfahan

Plans are not to scale

central-plan mosque
Selimiye Cami, Edirne

Umayyad, Abbasid, and pre-Islamic influences into a distinctive Western Islamic style. The marble columns and capitals in the **hypostyle** prayer hall were recycled from the ruins of classical buildings in the region, which had been a wealthy Roman province (fig. 8-6). Two tiers of arches, one over the other, surmount these columns; the upper tier springs from rectangular posts that rise from the columns. This double-tiered design, which was widely imitated, effectively increases the height of the interior space and provides ample light and air within it. The distinctively shaped **horseshoe arches**—a form known from Roman times and favored by the Visigoths, Spain's pre-Islamic rulers—came to be closely associated with Islamic architecture in the West (see "Elements of Architecture," page 347). Another distinctive feature of these arches, also adopted from Roman and Byzantine precedents, is the alternation of pale stone and red brick **voussoirs** forming the curved arch. In the view of one art historian, the overall effect of these features transforms the hall into "a wild three-dimensional maze, a hall of mirrors in which the constant echo of arches and the unruly staccato of colors confuse the viewer, presenting a challenge to unravel the [mosque's] complexities" (Dodds, pages 12–13).

In the final century of Umayyad rule, Córdoba emerged as a major commercial and intellectual hub and a flourishing center for the arts. It surpassed Christian Europe economically and in science, literature, and philosophy. Beginning with Abd ar-Rahman III (ruled 912–961), the Umayyads boldly claimed the title of caliph. Al-Hakam II (ruled 961–976) made the Great Mosque a focus of royal patronage, commissioning costly and luxurious renovations that disturbed many of his subjects. The caliph attempted to answer their objections to paying for such ostentation with an inscription giving thanks to God, who "helped him in the building of this eternal place, with the goal of making this mosque more spacious for his subjects, something which both he and they greatly wanted" (cited in Dodds, page 23). Among al-Hakam's renovations was a new mihrab with three bays

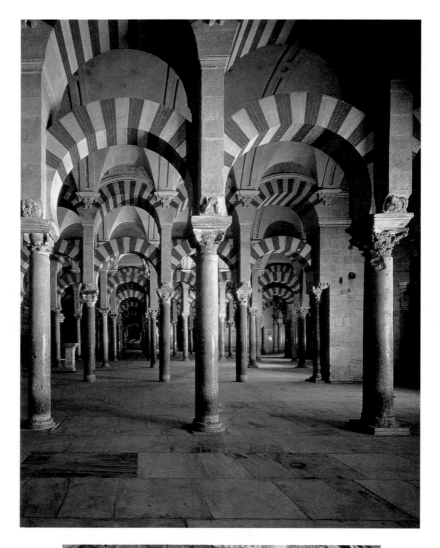

8-6. Prayer hall, Great Mosque, Córdoba, Spain. Begun 785–86

8-7. Dome in front of the mihrab, Great Mosque. 965

ELEMENTS OF ARCHITECTURE

Arches and Muqarnas

Islamic builders used a number of innovative structural devices. Among these were two arch forms, the **horseshoe arch** (see fig. 8-6) and the **ogival**, or pointed, **arch** (see fig. 8-14). There are many variations of each, some of which disguise their structural function beneath complex decoration.

Technically, a **_muqarnas_** is a **corbeled squinch** (see "Elements of Architecture," page 310). _Muqarnas_ may be used singly or in multiples (see fig. 8-12). Originally they served a structural purpose as interlocking, load-bearing, niche-shaped vaulting units. Over time they became increasingly ornamental, intricately faceted surfaces. They are frequently used to line mihrabs and, on a larger scale, to support domes.

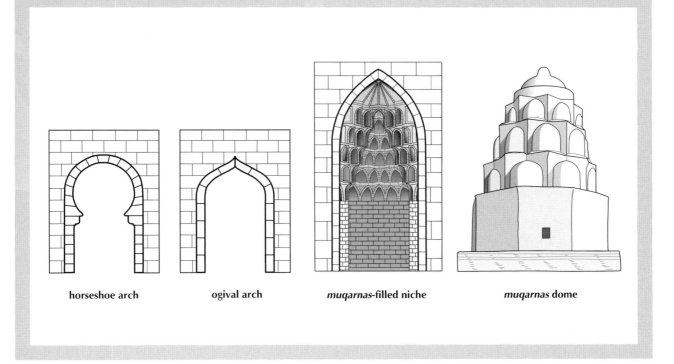

horseshoe arch   ogival arch   _muqarnas_-filled niche   _muqarnas_ dome

8-8. Great Mosque of al-Mutawakkil, Samarra, Iraq. 847–52

Minarets, the most readily identifiable feature of Islamic religious architecture, began as rectangular, stepped towers. They were first erected in western Asia, probably as commemorative victory monuments. Visible from many miles away, they may also have functioned as signposts on desert caravan routes. The classic tall, cylindrical minaret evolved in Persia in roughly the mid-tenth century.

in front of it. The melon-shaped, ribbed dome seems to float over a web of intersecting arches that emerge from their supporting piers (fig. 8-7). Lushly patterned mosaics with inscriptions, geometric motifs, and stylized vegetation clothe the domes in brilliant color and gold.

In the eastern Islamic world, the caliphs of the Abbasid dynasty ruled from Baghdad for more than a century after they seized power from the Umayyads. In 836, however, Caliph al-Mutasim (ruled 833–842) established a heavily fortified new capital at Samarra, about 60 miles north of Baghdad. In the mid-ninth century, Caliph al-Mutawakkil (ruled 847–861) began construction of the Great Mosque of Samarra (fig. 8-8). In ruins today, it was for a long time the largest mosque in the Islamic world. It featured a hypostyle prayer hall 525 feet wide at the qibla wall and 25 perpendicular aisles. The fortresslike wall enclosing the complex was more than 8 feet thick and about 33 feet high, with curved buttressing and round corner towers. The facade may originally have had mosaic decoration. An unusual spiral-ramp minaret, perhaps inspired by the **ziggurats** of the ancient Near East, rises more than 160 feet next to the mosque wall.

Calligraphy

The Arabic language and script have held a unique position in Islamic society and art from the beginning. As the language of the Koran and Muslim liturgy, Arabic has been a powerful unifying force within Islam. Reverence for the Koran as the word of God extended by association to the act of writing, and generations of extraordinary scribes made Arabic calligraphy one of the glories of Islam. Arabic script is written from right to left, and each of its letters takes one of three forms depending on its position in a word. With its rhythmic interplay between verticals and horizontals, this system lends itself to myriad variations.

Writing pervaded Islamic art. In addition to manuscripts, it featured prominently in architecture and on smaller-scale objects made of metal, glass, cloth, ceramic, and wood. The earliest scripts, called kufic (from the city of Kufa in modern Iraq), were angular and evolved from inscriptions on stone monuments. Kufic scripts were especially suitable for carved or woven inscriptions, as well as those on coins and other metalware; they are still used for Koran chapter headings. Most early Korans had only three to five lines per page and customarily had large letters because two readers shared one book (although they would have known the text by heart). A page from a ninth-century Syrian Koran exemplifies a style common from the eighth to the tenth century (see fig. 8-1). Red diacritical marks (pronunciation guides) accent the dark brown ink. Horizontals are elongated and fat-bodied letters are also emphasized. The chapter heading is set against an ornate gold band that contrasts with the simplicity of the letters.

Because calligraphy was a holy occupation, calligraphers enjoyed the highest status of all artists in Islamic society. Included in their numbers were a few princes and women. Their training was long and arduous, and their work usually anonymous. Not until the later Islamic centuries did it become common for calligraphers to sign their work, and even then only the most accomplished were allowed this privilege. Apprentice scribes had to learn secret formulas for inks and paints, become skilled in the proper ways to sit, breathe, and manipulate their tools, and develop their individual specialties. They also had to absorb the complex literary traditions and numerical symbolism that had developed around Arabic letters over the centuries.

The Koran was usually written on **vellum**, which, like parchment, was made from animal skin. Paper, a Chinese invention, was first imported into the Islamic realm in the mid-eighth century. Muslims subsequently learned how to make high-quality, rag-based paper and established their own paper mills. By about 1000, paper had largely replaced vellum and parchment, encouraging the proliferation of increasingly elaborate and decorative cursive scripts, which generally superseded kufic by the thirteenth century. Among the most influential calligraphers in this process was a woman named Shuhda. By the tenth century, more than twenty cursive scripts had come into use. They were standardized by Ibn Muqla

8-9. Bowl with kufic border, Samarkand, Uzbekistan. 9th–10th century. Earthenware with slip, pigment, and glaze, diameter 14½" (37 cm). Musée du Louvre, Paris

The white ground of this piece imitated prized Chinese porcelains made of fine white kaolin clay. Both Samarkand and Khurasan were connected to the Silk Road (Chapter 10), the great caravan route to China, and were influenced by Chinese culture.

(d. 940), an Abbasid minister, who fixed the proportions of the letters in each and devised a method for teaching calligraphy that is still in use. The great calligrapher Yaqut al-Mustasim (d. 1299), the Turkish secretary of the last Abbasid caliph, codified six basic calligraphic styles, including thuluth (see fig. 8-20), naskhi (see the illustration in "The Life of the Prophet Muhammad," page 341), and *muhaqqaq* (see fig. 8-14). Al-Mustasim reputedly made more than 1,000 copies of the Koran.

Ceramic and Textile Arts

Kufic-style letters were used effectively as the only decoration on a type of white pottery made in the ninth and tenth centuries in and around Nishapur (a region also known as Khurasan, in modern northeastern Iran) and Samarkand (in modern Uzbekistan in Central Asia). Now known as Samarkand ware, it was the ancestor of a ware produced until fairly recently by Central Asian peasants. In the example here, a bowl of medium quality, clear lead glaze was applied over a black inscription on a white slip-painted ground (fig. 8-9). The letters have been elongated to fill the bowl's rim, stressing their vertical elements. The inscription translates: "Knowledge, the beginning of it is bitter to taste, but the end is sweeter than honey," an apt choice for tableware. Inscriptions on Samarkand ware provide a storehouse of such popular sayings.

8-10. Textile with elephants and camels, from Khurasan, Persia (Iran). c. 960. Dyed silk, compound weave, largest fragment 37 x 20½" (94 x 52 cm). Musée du Louvre, Paris

Silk textiles were both sought-after luxury items and a medium of economic exchange. Government-controlled factories, known as *tiraz*, produced cloth for the court as well as for official gifts and payments. A number of fine Islamic fabrics have been preserved in the treasuries of medieval European churches, where they were used for priests' ceremonial robes, altar cloths, and covers for Christian saints' relics.

A different kufic inscription appears on a roughly contemporary fragment of silk from Khurasan (fig. 8-10): "Glory and happiness to the Commander Abu Mansur Bukhtakin, may God prolong his prosperity." Such formulaic inscriptions were extremely common in Islamic art, appearing as generic blessings on ordinary goods sold in the marketplace or, as here, personalized on "special orders." They can sometimes help determine where and when a work was made, but they can also be frustratingly uninformative when not much is known about the patron named in an object's inscription. Stylistic comparisons—in this case with other textiles, with the way similar subjects appear in other mediums, and with other kufic inscriptions—can reveal more about it than the inscription alone.

This fragment shows two elephants with rich ornamental coverings facing each other on a dark red ground, each with a mythical griffin between its hooves. A caravan of two-humped, Bactrian camels linked with rope moves up the left side, part of the elaborately patterned borders. The inscription at the bottom is upside-down, suggesting that the missing portion of the textile was the mirror image of the surviving fragment, with another pair of elephants joined back-to-back to this pair. The piece was created using an enormously complicated and expensive-to-operate drawloom weaving system that was best suited for this kind of repetitive pattern. The technique and design derive from the sumptuous pattern-woven silks of Sassanian Persia. The Persian weavers had, in turn, adapted Chinese silk technology to the Sassanian taste for paired heraldic beasts and other Near Eastern imagery. This tradition, with modifications—the depiction of animals, for example, became less naturalistic—continued after the Islamic conquest of Persia.

LATER ISLAMIC ART The Abbasid caliphate began to disintegrate in the ninth century, and thereafter power in the Islamic world became fragmented among the more or less independent regional rulers. The eleventh century saw the rise of the Seljuks, a Turkic people who had served as soldiers for the Abbasid caliphs and converted to Islam in the tenth century. Seljuk rulers united Persia and most of Mesopotamia, establishing a dynasty that endured from 1037 to 1194. A branch of the dynasty ruled much of Anatolia (Turkey) from the late eleventh to the beginning of the fourteenth century. Among the Seljuks of Anatolia, a number of queens and princesses were avid patrons of the arts and sponsored the building of mosques, mausoleums, schools, and baths. In the early thirteenth century, the Mongols—non-Muslims led by Jenghiz Khan (ruled 1206–1227) and his successors—swept out of Central Asia, encountering weak resistance as far as Egypt, where the young Mamluk dynasty (1252–1517), founded by descendants of slave soldiers (*mamluk* means "slave"), held them off. In the West,

8-11. Court of the Lions, Palace of the Lions (Palacio de los Leones), Alhambra, Granada, Spain. Completed c. 1380

Granada, with its ample water supply, had long been known as a city of gardens. The twelve stone lions in the fountain in the center of this court were salvaged from the ruins of an earlier palatial complex on the Alhambra hill. The earlier structure was begun in the late eleventh century by a high Granadan official of Jewish heritage named Samuel ibn Naghralla and completed by his son Yusuf in the early twelfth century. Commentators of the time praised this complex, with its pools, fountains, and gardens. No doubt it was a source of inspiration for the builders of the later palaces.

Islamic control of Spain gradually succumbed to expanding Christian forces, ending altogether in 1492.

With the breakdown of Seljuk power in Anatolia in the early fourteenth century, another group of Muslim Turks seized power in the northwestern part of that region, having migrated there from their homeland in Central Asia. Known as the Ottomans, after an early leader named Osman, they pushed their territorial boundaries westward and, in spite of setbacks inflicted by the Mongols, ultimately created an empire that extended over Anatolia, western Persia, Iraq, Syria, Palestine, western Arabia (including Mecca and Medina), India, Southeast Asia, North Africa (including Egypt and the Sudan), and much of eastern Europe. In 1453 they captured Constantinople (renaming it Istanbul) and brought the Byzantine Empire to an end. The Ottoman Empire lasted until the end of World War I in 1918. Another dynasty, the Safavids, established a Shiite state in Persia in the early years of the sixteenth century.

Although Islam remained a dominant and unifying force throughout these developments, the later history of Islamic society and art is a largely regional phenomenon. The following discussion focuses on architecture, port-

able arts, manuscript illumination, and calligraphy from Spain, North Africa, and western Asia.

Architecture

The best-preserved later Islamic monument left standing after the Christian reconquest of Spain in 1492 is the Alhambra. This fortified hilltop palace complex was the seat of the Nasrids (1232–1492), the last Spanish Muslim dynasty, whose territory had shrunk to the region around Granada in southeastern Spain. The Alhambra remained fairly intact in part because it represented the defeat of Islam to the victorious Christian monarchs, who restored, maintained, and occupied it as much for its commemorative value as for its beauty.

The Alhambra, which emerged from the distinctive local traditions established by the Córdoba Umayyads, exemplifies the growing regionalism in Islamic art. The complex was begun in 1238 on the site of a pre-Islamic fortress by the founder of the Nasrid dynasty. Successive rulers expanded it, and it took its present form in the fourteenth century. Literally a small town extending for about half a mile along the crest of a high hill overlook-

8-12. *Muqarnas* dome, Hall of the Abencerrajes, Palace of the Lions

ing Granada, it included government buildings, royal residences, gates, mosques, baths, servants' quarters, barracks, stables, a mint, workshops, and gardens.

Although it offered views to the landscape below, the architectural focus of the Alhambra was largely inward toward its lush courtyard gardens. They embodied the Muslim vision of paradise as a well-watered, walled garden (the English word *paradise* comes from the Persian term for an enclosed park, *faradis*). The so-called Palace of the Lions was a private retreat built by Muhammad V (ruled 1362–1391) in the late fourteenth century. At its heart is the Court of the Lions, a rectangular courtyard named for a marble fountain surrounded by stone lions (fig. 8-11). Although sanded today, the Court of the Lions was originally a garden, probably planted with aromatic

shrubs, flowers, and small citrus trees between the water channels that radiate from the fountain. Second-floor balconies overlook the courtyard. On the outside wall of a pavilion on the north side of the court (not visible in the illustration), a second-floor **mirador**—a projection with windows on three sides—looked out onto a large, lower garden and the plain below.

Four pavilions used for dining and performances of music, poetry, and dance open onto the Court of the Lions. One of these, the two-storied Hall of the Abencerrajes on the south side, may have been used year-round as a music room. Like the other pavilions (all of which had good acoustics), it is covered by a domed ceiling (fig. 8-12). The star-shaped dome rests on clustered **squinches** called ***muqarnas*** (see "Elements of Architecture,"

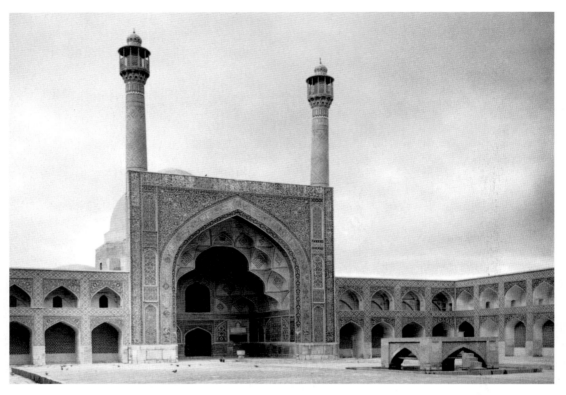

8-13. Courtyard, Masjid-i Jami (Great Mosque), Isfahan, Persia (Iran). 11th–18th century. View from the northeast

page 347). A honeycomb of *muqarnas* likewise covers the apex of the dome. The effect is of architectural lace, material form made immaterial.

The Alhambra was a sophisticated pleasure palace, an attempt to create paradise on earth. Imagining it as it once was—glittering with carved and painted stucco ornament, stained glass, glazed tiles, and lush carpets, its pavilions and gardens filled with courtiers dressed in glowing silks, jewelry, and cloth-of-gold—one can understand why it was legendary in its own time.

In the eastern Islamic world, the Seljuk rulers proved themselves enlightened patrons of the arts. One far-reaching development during their reign was the introduction of the four-iwan mosque. In this plan, **iwans**, which are large, rectangular, barrel-vaulted halls with monumental arched openings, face each other across a courtyard. Reflecting the influence of Sufism, a literary and philosophical movement that arose in the late tenth and early eleventh centuries, iwans may represent symbolic gateways between outside and inside, open and closed, the material and the spiritual.

Iwans first appeared in **madrasas**, schools for advanced study that were the precursors of the modern uni-

8-14. Mosaic mihrab, from the Madrasa Imami, Isfahan, Persia (Iran). c. 1354 (restored). Glazed and painted ceramic on plaster, 11'3" x 7'6" (3.43 x 2.89 m). The Metropolitan Museum of Art, New York
Harris Brisbane Dick Fund (39.20)

One of the three Koranic inscriptions on this mihrab dates it to approximately 1354. Note the combination of decorated kufic and cursive *muhaqqaq* scripts.

8-15. Qibla wall, main iwan (mosque), in a madrasa, Sultan Hasan complex, Cairo, Egypt. 1356–63

versity. Beginning in the eleventh century, hundreds of these institutions were founded and many are still in existence. Rulers and wealthy individuals endowed them as a form of pious charity. The four-iwan mosque may have evolved from the need to provide separate quarters for four schools of thought within madrasas.

The Masjid-i Jami (Great Mosque) in the center of the Seljuk capital of Isfahan (in modern Iran) was originally a hypostyle mosque. In the late eleventh century it was refurbished with two great brick domes, and in the twelfth century with four iwans and a monumental gate flanked by paired minarets (fig. 8-13). Construction continued sporadically on this mosque into the eighteenth century, but it retained its basic four-iwan layout, which became standard in Persia. The massive qibla iwan, on the south, is a twelfth-century structure with fourteenth-century *muqarnas* and seventeenth-century exterior tilework and minarets. The brick masonry on the interior of the iwans is unadorned; the facades, however, are sheathed in brilliant blue architectural tilework—an Islamic trademark for which this monument is justly famous.

A fourteenth-century mosaic mihrab originally from a madrasa in Isfahan but now in the Metropolitan Museum of Art in New York is one of the finest examples of early architectural ceramic decoration in Islamic art (fig. 8-14). More than 11 feet tall, it was made with a painstaking process that involved cutting each piece of tile individually, including the pieces making up the letters on the curving surface of the niche. The color scheme—white against turquoise and cobalt blue with accents of dark yellow and green—was typical of this type of decoration, as was the harmonious but contrasting use of dense organic and geometric patterns.

A madrasa-mausoleum-mosque complex built in the mid-fourteenth century by the Mamluk sultan Hasan in Cairo, Egypt, shows Seljuk influence (fig. 8-15). The iwans in this structure functioned as classrooms, and students were housed in neighboring rooms. Hasan's domed tomb lies beyond the qibla wall of the largest of the four iwans, which served as the mosque for the entire complex. The walls and vaulting inside this main iwan are undecorated except for a wide stucco frieze band. Originally painted, this band combines calligraphy and

8-16. Sinan. Selimiye Cami (Mosque of Selim), Edirne, Turkey. 1570–74

The minarets that pierce the sky around the prayer hall of this mosque, their sleek, fluted walls and needle-nosed spires soaring to more than 295 feet, are only 12½ feet in diameter at the base, an impressive feat of engineering. Only royal mosques were permitted multiple minarets, and more than two was highly unusual.

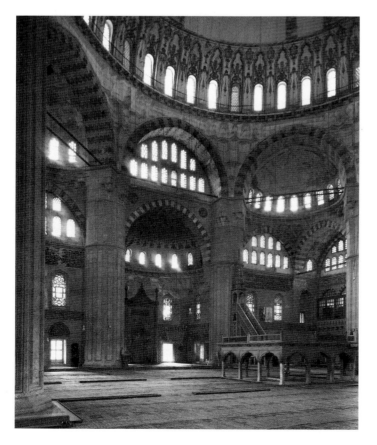

intricate carved scrollwork. The mihrab features marble panels, a double recess, and slender columns supporting **ogival arches**, a pointed form characteristic of Seljuk architecture (see "Elements of Architecture," page 347). Marble inlays create blue, red, and white stripes on the voussoirs, echoing the brick and stone bands of Umayyad architecture (see figs. 8-4, 8-6). Except for its elaborately carved door, the thronelike minbar at the right is made of carved stone instead of the usual wood.

After conquering Constantinople, the rulers of the Ottoman Empire converted the church of Hagia Sophia into a mosque, framing it with graceful Turkish-style minarets and adding calligraphic decorations to the interior (see figs. 7-25, 7-27). Inspired by this great Byzantine structure, Ottoman architects developed a domed, **central-plan** mosque. The finest example of this new form was the work of the architect Sinan (c. 1490–1588). Sinan began his career in the army and was chief engineer during the Ottoman siege of Vienna (1526–1529). He rose through the ranks to become chief architect for Suleyman (known as "the Lawgiver" and "the Magnificent"), the tenth Ottoman sultan (ruled 1520–1566). Suleyman, whose reign marked the height of Ottoman power, sponsored a building program on a scale not seen since the glory days of the Roman Empire. Sinan is credited with

8-17. Selimiye Cami

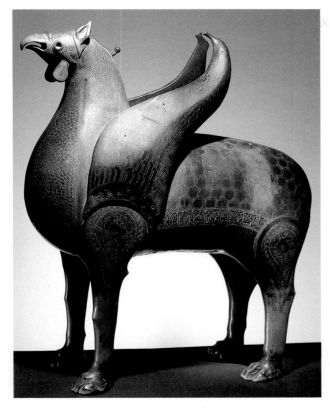

8-18. Griffin, from the Islamic Mediterranean. 11th century. Bronze, height 42⅛" (107 cm). Museo dell'Opera del Duomo, Pisa

8-19. Shazi. Pen box, from Persia (Iran) or Afghanistan. 1210–11. Brass with silver and copper; height 2", length 12⅝", width 2½" (5 x 31.4 x 6.4 cm). Freer Gallery of Art, Smithsonian Institution, Washington, D.C. (36.7)

The inscriptions on this box include some twenty honorific phrases extolling its owner, al-Mulk. The inscription in naskhi script on the lid calls him the "luminous star of Islam." The largest inscription, written in animated naskhi (an animated script is one with human or animal forms in it), asked twenty-four blessings for him from God. Shazi, the designer of the box, signed and dated it in animated kufic on the side of the lid, making it one of the earliest examples of a signed work in Islamic art. Al-Mulk enjoyed his box for only ten years; he was killed in the Mongol sack of Merv in 1221.

more than 300 imperial commissions, including palaces, madrasas and Koran schools, burial chapels, public kitchens and hospitals, caravansaries—way stations for caravans—treasure houses, baths, bridges, viaducts, and 124 large and small mosques.

Sinan's crowning accomplishment, completed when he was at least eighty, was a mosque he designed at the provincial capital of Edirne for Suleyman's son, Selim II (ruled 1566–1574), in the third quarter of the sixteenth century (fig. 8-16). The gigantic spherical dome that tops this structure is more than 102 feet in diameter, larger than the dome of Hagia Sophia. It covers a building of great geometric complexity on the exterior and complete coherence on the interior, a space at once soaring and serene. In addition to the mosque, the complex housed a madrasa and other educational buildings, a burial ground, a hospital, and charity kitchens, as well as an income-producing covered market and baths. Framed by the vertical lines of four minarets, the mosque shifts from square to octagon to circle as it moves upward and inward. Raised on a base at the city's edge, it dominates the skyline.

The interior seems superficially very much like Hagia Sophia's: an open expanse under a vast dome floating on a ring of light (fig. 8-17). The mosque, however, is a true central-plan structure and lacks Hagia Sophia's longitudinal pull from entrance to sanctuary. A small fountain covered by a muezzin platform emphasizes this centralization. The arches supporting the dome spring from eight enormous piers topped with *muqarnas*. Smaller half-domes between the piers define the corners of a square. Windows at every level flood the interior's cream-colored stone, restrained tile decoration, and softly glowing carpets with light.

Portable Arts

Islamic society was cosmopolitan, fostering the circulation of goods and the movement of people through trade and pilgrimage. In this context, portable objects such as textiles and books assumed greater cultural importance than buildings, and decorative objects were valued as much for the status they bestowed as for their usefulness.

Metal. Islamic metalworkers inherited the techniques of their Roman, Byzantine, and Sassanian predecessors, applying them to new forms, such as incense burners and water pitchers in the shape of fanciful animals and birds. One example of their work, an unusually large and stylized griffin, may originally have been a fountain spout (fig. 8-18). Its place of origin is unknown—suggestions range from Persia to Spain—but it found its way somehow, through trade or pillage, to Italy, where it was displayed atop the cathedral in Pisa from about 1100 to 1828. Made of cast bronze, it is decorated with incised feathers, scales, and silk trappings. The trappings on the creature's thighs include animals in medallions; the bands of cloth across its chest and back are decorated with kufic lettering and scale and circle patterns.

The Islamic world was administered by educated leaders who often commissioned personalized containers—emblems of their class—for their pens, ink, and blotting sand. One such container, an inlaid brass box, was the possession of Majd al-Mulk al-Muzaffar, the grand vizier, or chief minister, of Khurasan in the early thirteenth century (fig. 8-19). The work of an artist

8-20. Bottle, from Syria. Mid-14th century. Blown glass with enamels and gilding, 19½ x 9¾" (49.7 x 24.8 cm). Freer Gallery of Art, Smithsonian Institution, Washington, D.C. (34.20)

named Shazi, it was cast, engraved, embossed, and inlaid with consummate skill. Scrolls, interlacing designs, and human and animal figures enliven its calligraphic inscriptions. All these elements, animate as well as inanimate, seem to be engaged in lively conversation. That a work of such quality was made of brass rather than a costlier metal may seem odd. A severe silver shortage in the mid-twelfth century had prompted the development of inlaid brass pieces like this one that used the more precious metal sparingly. Humbler brassware would have been available in the marketplace to those of more modest means than the vizier.

Glass. Glass, according to the twelfth-century poet al-Hariri, is "congealed of air, condensed of sunbeam motes, molded of the light of the open plain, or peeled from a white pearl" (cited in Jenkins, page 3). Made with the most ordinary of ingredients—sand and ash—glass is the most ethereal of materials. It first appeared roughly 4,000 years ago, and the tools and techniques for making it have changed little in the past 2,000 years. Like their counterparts working in metal, Islamic glassmakers generally adapted earlier practices to new forms. They were particularly innovative in the application of enameled decoration in gold and various colors. A tall, elegant enameled bottle from the mid-fourteenth century exemplifies their skill (fig. 8-20). One of several objects either given by Mamluk rulers to the Rasulid rulers of Yemen (southern Arabia) or ordered by the Rasulids from Mamluk workshops in Syria, it bears a large inscription nam-

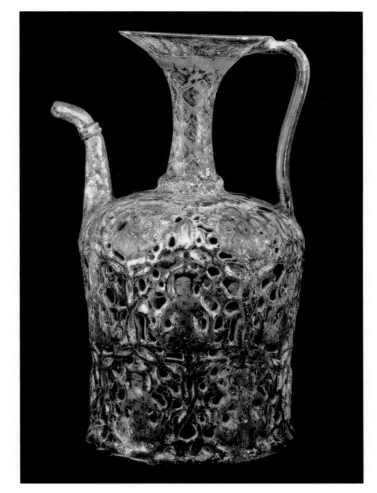

8-21. Pitcher, from Kashan, Persia (Iran). Early 13th century. Glazed and painted fritware, height 11¹³⁄₁₆" (30 cm). The al-Sabah Collection, Kuwait

Fritware was used to make beads in ancient Egypt and may have been rediscovered there by Islamic potters searching for a substitute for Chinese porcelain. Composed of one part white clay, ten parts quartz, and one part quartz fused with soda, it produced a brittle, white ware when fired. The colors on this double-walled pitcher and others like it were produced by applying mineral glazes over black painted detailing. The deep blue comes from cobalt and the turquoise from copper. Lusterware, a thin, transparent glaze with a metallic sheen, was applied over the colored glazes. Lusterware was to become a trademark of later Islamic ceramics.

ing and honoring a Rasulid sultan in thuluth—a popular Mamluk cursive script—and the Rasulid insignia, a five-petaled red rosette.

Ceramics. Seljuk potters produced tableware in a range of styles and techniques. Unusual among them was a double-walled form found on a group of early-thirteenth-century pitchers that may have derived from a similar form used by Roman glassmakers. The Seljuk pitchers, with their carved openwork shells and solid inner bodies, were difficult to execute. The form was probably intended more to be decorative than to serve a practical function like insulation. The shell of one of them (fig. 8-21) is a forest of twining vines in which perch cross-legged figures. Textilelike patterning covers its neck and an inscription encircles its rim. The pitchers are made of **fritware**—a mixture of white clay, quartz, and soda that fires into a brittle, white material—and are coated with a thin, transparent glaze that is known as **lusterware.**

Textiles. The tradition of silk weaving that passed from Sassanian Persia to Islamic artisans in the early Islamic period (see fig. 8-10) was kept alive in Muslim Spain, where it was both economically and culturally important. Spanish designs, with their emphasis on architecture-like forms beginning in the thirteenth century, reflect a different aesthetic than those found in the earlier works. The pattern in the central section of a magnificent silk and gold banner (fig. 8-22) resembles the plan of a

8-22. Banner of Las Navas de Tolosa, from southern Spain. First half of 13th century. Silk tapestry-weave with gilt parchment, 10'9⅞" x 7'2⅝" (3.3 x 2.2 m). Museo de Telas Medievales, Monasterio de Santa Maria la Real de Las Huelgas, Burgos, Spain. Patrimonio Nacional

TECHNIQUE

CARPET MAKING

Because textiles, especially floor coverings, are destroyed through use, very few rugs from before the sixteenth century have survived. There are two basic types of carpets: flat-weaves and pile, or knotted. Both can be made on either vertical or horizontal frames. The best-known flat-weaves today are Turkish kilims, which are typically woven in wool with bold, geometric patterns and sometimes with embroidered details. Kilim weaving is done in the **tapestry** technique, which allows free placement of each area of color (a).

Knotted carpets are an ancient invention. The oldest known example, excavated in Siberia and dating to the fourth or fifth century BCE, has designs evocative of Achaemenid Persian art, suggesting that the technique may have originated in ancient Persia. In knotted rugs the pile—the plush, thickly tufted surface—is made by tying colored strands of yarn, usually wool but occasion-

square inch, each one tied separately by hand.

Although royal workshops produced the most luxurious carpets (see fig. 8-23), most knotted rugs have traditionally been made in tents and homes (see fig. 8-24). Carpets were woven by either women or men, depending on local custom. The photograph in this box shows two women, sisters in Ganakkale province in Turkey, weaving a large carpet in a typical Turkish pattern. The woman in the foreground pushes a row of knots tightly against the row below it with a wood comb called a beater. The other woman pulls a dark red weft yarn against the warp threads before tying a knot. Working between September and May, these women may weave five carpets, tying up to 5,000 knots a day. Generally, an older woman works with a young girl, who learns the art of carpet weaving at the loom and eventually passes it on to the next generation.

a. Kilim weaving pattern used in flat-weaving

b. Turkish knots, used typically in Anatolia (Turkey) to make pile, or knotted, carpets

ally silk for deluxe carpets, onto the vertical elements (**warp**) of a yarn grid (b or c). These knotted loops are later sheared, cut, and trimmed to form the plush surface of the carpet. Rows of knots alternate with flat-woven rows (**weft**) that hold the carpet together. The weft is usually in undyed yarn and is eventually hidden by the colored knots. Two common tying techniques are the symmetrical "Turkish" knot, which works well for straight-line designs (b), and the asymmetrical "Persian" knot, used for rendering curvilinear patterns (c). The greater the number of knots, the denser and more durable the pile. The finest carpets have a hundred knots per

c. Persian knots, favored by Persian carpet makers

8-23. Garden carpet, from central Persia (Iran). Second half of 17th century. Woolen pile, cotton warps, cotton and wool wefts, 17'5" x 14'2" (5.31 x 4.32 m). The Burrell Collection, Glasgow Museums, Scotland

Spanish courtyard garden (see fig. 8-11), and the Koranic inscriptions that surround it include a reference to the Garden of Eden as a refuge from earthly suffering. The banner was captured in battle by Christian forces not long after it was made.

Since the late Middle Ages, the Islamic art form best known in the non-Islamic West has probably been the carpet. Knotted rugs (see "Carpet Making," page 359) from Persia and Turkey were so highly prized among Westerners that they were often displayed on tables rather than floors. Persian taste favored intricate, elegant designs that evoked the gardens of paradise. Written accounts indicate that such designs appeared on Persian carpets as early as the seventh century. In one fabled royal carpet, garden paths were rendered in real gold, leaves were modeled with emeralds, and highlights on flowers, fruits, and birds were created from pearls and other jewels.

A special kind of garden carpet, possibly derived from drawings by town planners and mapmakers, shows a bird's-eye view of an enclosed park. One such carpet from the second half of the seventeenth century depicts a walled hunting preserve irrigated by an H-shaped system of channels. In the middle is a basin filled with floating plants, fish, and birds (fig. 8-23). All kinds of animals and birds, some resting and others hunting, inhabit the

dense forests of leafy trees and blooming shrubs in the rectangular sections. The very finest carpets, like this, woven of cotton and wool or silk and wool in royal workshops, were as much status symbols *within* the Islamic world as they were *beyond* it.

Rugs and mats have long been used for Muslim prayer, which involves repeated kneeling and touching of the forehead to the floor. Prayer rugs came to be distinguished, particularly in Turkey, by mihrab-shaped frames or arches. The worshiper oriented the arch toward Mecca and stood within it. Portable, individual-size carpets could be unrolled as needed for the five daily prayers, either at a mosque or elsewhere. (This is still done today.) Like garden carpets, these were emblems of social prestige and were considered lucky, even magical. Many mosques were literally "carpeted" with wool pile rugs received as pious donations; wealthy patrons gave large, multiple-arched prayer rugs (note, for example, the rugs on the floor of the Selimiye Cami in figure 8-17).

An eighteenth-century carpet from western or central Turkey contains a representation of the Kaaba surrounded by its barricade and framed by a calligraphylike enclosure wall in the shape of a mihrab arch (fig. 8-24). Minarets in the enclosure wall flank the Kaaba barricade, and a minbar, banner flying, stands in front of it flanked by more minarets. Medallions dot the lower portion of

8-24. Prayer carpet with the Kaaba, from western or central Turkey. 18th century. Wool, 57½ x 43¾" (146 x 111 cm). Museum of Turkish and Islamic Arts, Istanbul

8-25. Koran frontispiece (right half of two-page spread), Cairo, Egypt. c. 1368. Ink, pigments, and gold on paper, 24 x 18" (61 x 45.7 cm). National Library, Cairo. Ms. 7

The Koran to which this page belonged was donated in 1369 by Sultan Shaban to the madrasa established by his mother. Throughout the manuscript, as here, there is evidence of close collaboration between illuminator and scribe.

the carpet. The elongated six-sided shapes at the bottom may be foot marks.

Manuscript Illumination and Calligraphy

The art of book production flourished in the later Islamic centuries. Muslim societies enjoyed a high level of literacy among both women and men thanks to Islam's emphasis on the study of the Koran. Books on a wide range of secular as well as religious subjects were available, although even modest books copied on paper were fairly costly. Libraries, often associated with madrasas, were endowed by members of the educated elite. Books made for royal patrons had luxurious bindings and highly embellished pages, the result of workshop collaboration between noted calligraphers and illustrators. New scripts were developed for new literary forms.

The **illuminators**, or manuscript illustrators, of Mamluk Egypt executed superlative nonfigural designs for Korans. Geometric and botanical ornamentation reached unprecedented heights of sumptuousness and mathematical complexity in their work. As in contemporary architectural decoration, strict underlying geometric organization was combined with luxurious allover patterning. In an impressive frontispiece page originally paired with its mirror image on the facing left page, energy radi-

ates from a sixteen-pointed starburst, filling the central square (fig. 8-25). The surrounding ovals and medallions are filled with interlacing foliage and stylized flowers that provide a backdrop for Koranic quotations. The page's resemblance to court carpets was not coincidental: designers worked in more than one medium, leaving the execution of their efforts to specialized artisans.

In addition to religious works, scribes also copied and recopied famous secular texts, especially scientific treatises, manuals of all kinds, fiction, and poetry. Painters supplied illustrations for these books and created individual small-scale paintings—**miniatures**—that were collected by the wealthy and placed in albums. Miniature painting was highly regarded because of its connection with books, whereas mural painting (associated with the far less exalted craft of architecture) was not. One of the great royal centers of miniature painting was at Herat in Khurasan (in modern Iran). An academy of painting and calligraphy was founded there in the early fifteenth century under the cultured patronage of the Turkic Timurid dynasty (1370–1507).

The most famous artist of this school was Kamal al-Din Bihzad (c. 1440–1514). He headed the academy from about 1469 until the Safavids supplanted the Timurids and established their capital at Tabriz (in northwestern Persia) in 1506. Following this upheaval, Bihzad moved

8-26. Kamal al-Din Bihzad. *The Caliph Harun al-Rashid Visits the Turkish Bath*, from a later copy of the *Khamsa* (Five Poems) of Nizami (12th century), Herat, Khurasan (Iran). c. 1494. Ink and pigments on paper, approx. 7 x 6" (17.8 x 15.3 cm). The British Library, London.

Oriental and India Office Collections (Ms. Or. 6810, fol. 27v)

Despite early warnings against it as a place for the dangerous indulgence of the pleasures of the flesh, the bathhouse *(hammam)*, adapted from Roman and Hellenistic predecessors, became an important social center in much of the Islamic world. The remains of an eighth-century *hammam* are still standing in Jordan, and a twelfth-century *hammam* is still in use in Damascus. *Hammams* had a small entrance to keep in the heat, which was supplied by ducts running under the floors. The main room had pipes in the wall with steam vents. Unlike the Romans, who bathed and swam in pools of water, Muslims preferred to splash themselves from basins, and floors were slanted for drainage. A *hammam* was frequently located near a mosque, part of the commercial complex provided by the patron to generate income for the mosque's upkeep.

to Tabriz and briefly resumed his career there. The Herat academy, and Bihzad himself, executed commissions for both royal and nonroyal patrons. Under his leadership, top painters for the first time were permitted to sign their work. Unsigned miniatures by the more talented of his numerous students are often confused with his. Bihzad is remembered for having injected a vivid new naturalism and an interest in the psychological drama of everyday subjects into the super-refined, glittering dreamworld of the academy style. His influence on the next generations of painters was enormous.

Among Bihzad's authentic works are paintings done around 1494 to illustrate the *Khamsa* (Five Poems) by the twelfth-century mystic poet Nizami. These paintings demonstrate Bihzad's ability to render human activity convincingly. He set his scenes within complex, stagelike architectural spaces that are stylized according to Timurid conventions, creating a visual balance between activity and architecture. In *The Caliph Harun al-Rashid Visits the Turkish Bath* (fig. 8-26), the bathhouse, its tiled entrance leading to a high-ceilinged dressing room with brick walls, provides the structuring element. Attendants wash long, decorative towels and hang them to dry on overhead clotheslines. A worker reaches for one of the towels with a long pole, and a client prepares to wrap himself discreetly in a towel before removing his outer garments. The blue door on the left leads to a room where the caliph is being groomed by his barber while

8-27. Illuminated *tugra* of Sultan Suleyman, from Istanbul, Turkey. c. 1555–60. Ink, paint, and gold on paper, removed from a firman and trimmed to 20½ x 25⅜" (52 x 64.5 cm). The Metropolitan Museum of Art, New York
Rogers Fund, 1938 (38.149.1)

attendants bring buckets of water for his bath. The balanced placement of colors and architectural ornaments within each section ties the scene together in a unified whole.

A half century later at the Ottoman court of Sultan Suleyman in Constantinople, the imperial workshops also produced remarkable illuminated manuscripts. In addition, following a practice begun by the Seljuks and Mamluks, the Ottomans put calligraphy to another, political use, developing the design of imperial emblems—***tugras***—into a specialized art form. Ottoman *tugras* combined the ruler's name with the title khan ("lord"), his father's name, and the motto "Eternally Victorious" into an unvarying monogram. *Tugras* symbolized the authority of the sultan and of those select officials who were also granted an emblem. They appeared on seals, coins, and buildings, as well as on official documents called firmans, imperial edicts supplementing Muslim law, or sharia.

Suleyman issued hundreds of firmans. A high court official was entrusted with the important responsibility of affixing Suleyman's *tugra* at the top of official scrolls. For documents like imperial grants to charitable projects that required particularly fancy *tugras*, specialist calligraphers and illuminators were employed. The *tugra* shown here (fig. 8-27) is from a document endowing an institution in Jerusalem that had been established by Suleyman's wife, Sultana Hurrem.

Tugras on paper were always outlined in black or blue with three long, vertical strokes (*tug* means "horsetail") to the right of two horizontal teardrops, one inside the other. Early *tugras* were purely calligraphic, but decorative fill patterns became fashionable in the sixteenth century. This fill decoration had become more naturalistic by the 1550s and in later centuries spilled outside the emblems' boundary lines.

Figure 8-27 shows a rare, oversized *tugra* that required more than the usual skill to execute. The sweeping, fluid line had to be drawn with perfect control according to set proportions, and a mistake meant starting over. The color scheme of the delicate floral interlace enclosed in the body of the *tugra* was inspired by Chinese blue-and-white ceramics; similar designs appear on Ottoman ceramics and textiles.

The Ottoman *tugra* is a sophisticated merging of abstraction with naturalism, boldness with delicacy, political power with informed patronage, and function—both utilitarian and symbolic—with adornment. As such, it is a fitting conclusion for this brief survey of Islamic art.

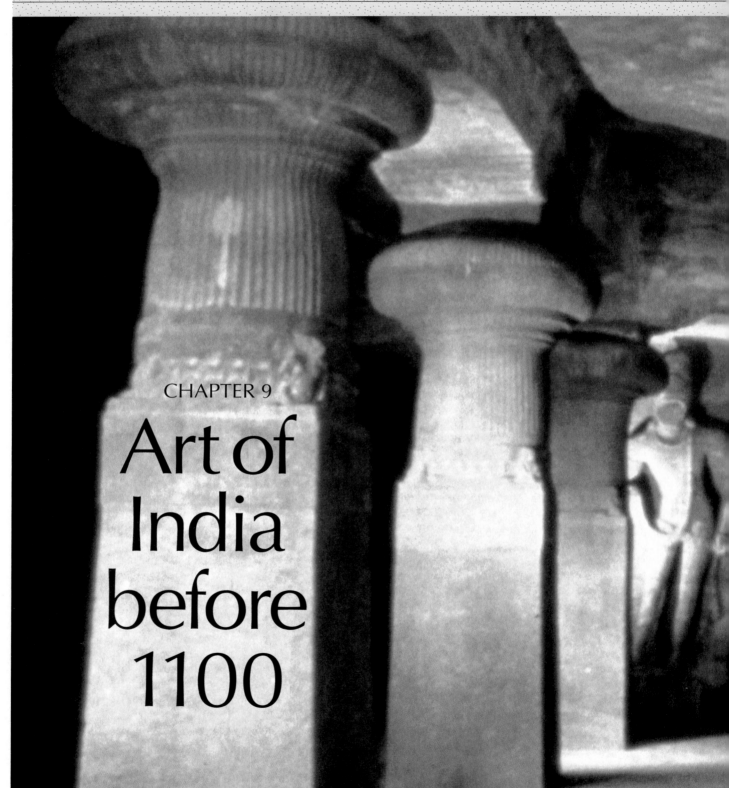

CHAPTER 9

Art of India before 1100

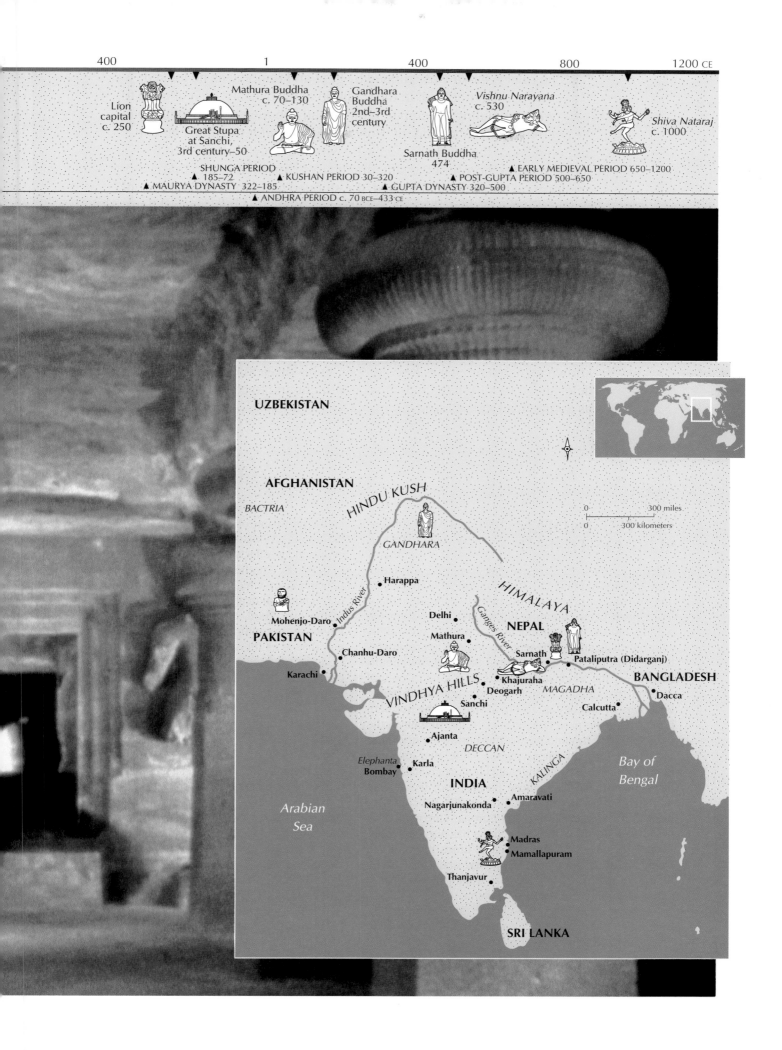

400   1   400   800   1200 CE

Lion capital c. 250

Great Stupa at Sanchi, 3rd century–50

Mathura Buddha c. 70–130

Gandhara Buddha 2nd–3rd century

Sarnath Buddha 474

Vishnu Narayana c. 530

Shiva Nataraj c. 1000

SHUNGA PERIOD 185–72

▲ EARLY MEDIEVAL PERIOD 650–1200

▲ MAURYA DYNASTY 322–185

▲ KUSHAN PERIOD 30–320

▲ POST-GUPTA PERIOD 500–650

▲ GUPTA DYNASTY 320–500

▲ ANDHRA PERIOD c. 70 BCE–433 CE

UZBEKISTAN

AFGHANISTAN

BACTRIA

HINDU KUSH

GANDHARA

Harappa

Mohenjo-Daro

PAKISTAN

Chanhu-Daro

Karachi

Indus River

Delhi

Mathura

HIMALAYA

Ganges River

NEPAL

Sarnath

Pataliputra (Didarganj)

BANGLADESH

Dacca

Khajuraha

Deogarh

MAGADHA

Calcutta

VINDHYA HILLS

Sanchi

Ajanta

DECCAN

Elephanta
Bombay

Karla

KALINGA

Bay of Bengal

INDIA

Arabian Sea

Nagarjunakonda

Amaravati

Madras

Mamallapuram

Thanjavur

SRI LANKA

0   300 miles
0   300 kilometers

The ruler Ashoka was stunned by grief and remorse as he looked across the battlefield. In the tradition of his dynasty, he had gone to war, expanding his empire until he had conquered many of the peoples of the Indian subcontinent. Now, in 261 BCE, after the final battle in his conquest of the northern states, he was suddenly—unexpectedly—shocked by the horror of the suffering he had caused. It is said that only one form on the battlefield moved, the stooped figure of a Buddhist monk slowly making his way through the carnage. Watching this spectral figure, Ashoka abruptly turned the moment of triumph into one of renunciation. Decrying violence and warfare, he gave his royal support to Buddhism to help establish it as a major official religion of his realm. From that moment on, he set a noble example by living his belief in nonviolence and kindness to all beings.

In his impassioned propagation of Buddhism, Ashoka stimulated an intensely rich period of art. He erected monuments to the Buddha throughout his empire—shrines, monasteries, sculpture, and the columns known as Ashokan pillars (see fig. 9-6). In his missionary ardor, he sent delegates throughout the Indian subcontinent and to countries as distant as Syria, Egypt, and Greece.

THE INDIAN SUBCONTINENT

The South Asian subcontinent, or Indian subcontinent, as it is commonly called, includes the present-day countries of India, southeastern Afghanistan, Pakistan, Nepal, Bangladesh, and Sri Lanka. Throughout the history of the area, these lands have been culturally linked and are among the world's oldest, most productive, and most profoundly spiritual civilizations. Present-day India is approximately one-third the size of the United States. A low mountain range, the Vindhya Hills, acts as a kind of natural division that demarcates North India and South India, which are of approximately equal size. On the northern border rises the protective barrier of the Himalaya, the world's tallest mountains. To the northwest are other mountains through whose passes came invasions and immigrations that profoundly affected the civilization of the subcontinent. Over these passes, too, wound the major trade routes that linked the Indian subcontinent by land to the rest of Asia and Europe. Surrounded on the remaining sides by oceans, India has also been connected to the world since ancient times by maritime trade, and during much of the period under discussion here it formed part of a coastal trading network that extended from eastern Africa to China.

Differences in language, climate, and terrain within India have fostered distinct regional and cultural characteristics and artistic traditions. However, despite such regional diversity, several overarching traits tend to unite Indian art. Most immediately evident is a distinctive sense of beauty. Indian artists delight in full forms and a profusion of ornament, texture, and color. This extraordinary visual generosity is considered auspicious, and it reflects a belief in the abundance and favor of the gods. Another characteristic is the pervasive role of symbolism, which imbues Indian art with intellectual and emotional depths far beyond its immediate appeal to the eye. Third, and perhaps most important, is an emphasis on capturing the vibrant, pulsating quality of a world seen as infused with the dynamics of the divine. Gods and humans, ideas and abstractions come forth clothed in tactile, sensuous forms, radiant with inner spirit.

INDUS VALLEY CIVILIZATION

The earliest civilization of South Asia was nurtured in the lower reaches of the Indus River (in present-day Pakistan and in northwestern India). Known as the Indus Valley or Harappan civilization (after Harappa, the first-discovered site), it flourished from approximately 2700 to 1500 BCE, or during roughly the same time as the Old Kingdom period of Egypt, the Minoan civilization of the Aegean, and the dynasties of Ur and Babylon in Mesopotamia. Indeed, it is considered along with Egypt and Mesopotamia as one of the world's earliest urban, river-valley civilizations.

It was the chance discovery in the late nineteenth century of some small seals like those in figure 9-1 that provided the first clue that an ancient civilization had existed in this region. The seals appeared to be related to, but not the same as, seals known from ancient Mesopotamia (see fig. 2-13). Excavations begun in the 1920s

9-1. Seal impressions, from the Indus Valley civilization: a., d. horned animal;
b. buffalo; c. sacrificial rite to a goddess (?); e. yogi; f. three-headed animal.
c. 2500–1500 BCE. Seals: steatite, each approx. 1¼ x 1¼" (3.2 x 3.2 cm)

More than 2,000 small seals and impressions have been found, offering an
intriguing window on the Indus Valley civilization. Usually carved from
steatite stone, the seals were coated with alkali and then fired to produce a
lustrous, white surface. A perforated knob on the back of each may have
been for suspending them. The most popular subjects are animals, the most
common being a one-horned bovine standing before an altarlike object (a,
c). Animals on Indus Valley seals are often portrayed with remarkable naturalism, their taut, well-modeled surfaces implying their underlying skeletal
structures. The function of the seals, beyond sealing packets, remains
enigmatic, and the pictographic script that appears so prominently in the
impressions has yet to be deciphered.

and continuing into the present have subsequently uncovered a number of major urban areas at points along
the lower Indus River, including Harappa, Mohenjo-
Daro, and Chanhu-Daro.

The ancient cities of the Indus Valley resemble each
other in design and construction, suggesting a unified
and coherent culture. At Mohenjo-Daro, the best preserved of the sites, archeologists discovered an elevated
"citadel" area, presumably containing important government structures, surrounded by a wall about 50 feet

high. Among these buildings is the so-called Great Bath,
a large, watertight pool that may have been used for ritual purposes. Stretching out below this elevated area
was the city, arranged in a gridlike plan with wide
avenues and narrower side streets. Its houses, often two
stories high, were generally built around a central courtyard. Like other Indus Valley cities, Mohenjo-Daro was
constructed of fired brick, in contrast to the less-durable
sun-dried brick used in other cultures of the time. The
city included a network of covered drainage systems that

PARALLELS

Years	Dynasty/Period	Indian Subcontinent	World
c. 2700–1500 BCE	**Indus Valley civilization**	Mohenjo-Daro "citadel"; seals; Harappa torso	**c. 2700–1500 BCE** Great Pyramids at Giza (Egypt); Stonehenge (England); Minoan culture (Crete); citadel at Mycenae (Greece)
c. 1500–322 BCE	**Vedic period**	Aryan invasions; Veda; Upanishads; birth of Siddhartha Gautama, founder of Buddhism; birth of Mahavira, founder of Jainism; *Mahabharata*; *Ramayana*	**c. 1500–1000 BCE** *Stela of Hammurabi* (Babylonia); Israelites led out of Egypt by Moses (Canaan); Olmec civilization (Mesoamerica) **c. 1000–500 BCE** Legendary founding of Rome (Italy); first Olympian Games (Greece); black-figure and red-figure vase painting (Greece); Hanging Gardens (Babylon); Sappho (Greece); birth of Laozi, founder of Daoism (China); Cyrus the Great (Persia) defeats Babylon; *Aesop's Fables* (Greece)
c. 322–185 BCE	**Maurya dynasty**	"Conversion" of Ashoka; Ashokan pillars	**c. 500 BCE–100 CE** Confucius (China); Sophocles, Aeschylus, Euripides, Herodotus (Greece); *The Canon* of Polykleitos (Greece); Parthenon (Greece); Alexander the Great (Greece) conquers Persia; Colossos of Rhodes; Han dynasty (China); *Nike of Samothrace, Aphrodite of Melos* (Greece); crucifixion of Jesus (Jerusalem); Emperor Augustus (Italy); Colosseum (Italy)
c. 185 BCE–30 CE	**Shunga/early Andhra period**	Shunga dynasty (central India); Andhra dynasty (southern India); Great Stupa at Sanchi; rock-cut halls	
c. 30–433 CE	**Kushan/later Andhra period**	Kushan dynasty (northern India and Central Asia); Andhra dynasty (southern India); rule of Kanishka; first images of the Buddha; Gandhara, Mathura, and Amaravati schools	**c. 100–500 CE** Pantheon (Italy); Yayoi and Kofun eras (Japan); Buddhism in China; Maya civilization (Mesoamerica); Emperor Constantine (Italy)
c. 320–500 CE	**Gupta dynasty**	Mathura and Sarnath Gupta schools	
c. 500–650 CE	**Post-Gupta period**	Pallava dynasty (southern India); rise of Hinduism; Dharmaraja Ratha (temple)	**c. 500–800 CE** Hagia Sophia (Turkey); Buddhism in Japan; birth of Muhammad, founder of Islam (Arabia); plague kills half of European population; Tang dynasty (China); Koran (Arabia); Muslim conquests of Arabia, Persia, Syria, Iraq, Egypt, Carthage; Charlemagne is made emperor of the West
c. 650–1100 CE	**Early Medieval period**	Pallava dynasty (southern India); Chola dynasty (southern India); Pala dynasty (northeastern India); Chandella dynasty (northern India); *Dancing Shiva*; conquest by Islam	**c. 800–1100 CE** First Viking colony in Greenland; Lady Murasaki's *Tale of Genji* (Japan); separation of Eastern and Western Christian Churches; the Crusades

9-2. Bust of a man, from Mohenjo-Daro, Indus Valley civilization. c. 2000 BCE. Limestone, height 6⅞" (17.5 cm). National Museum of Pakistan, Karachi

9-3. Torso, from Harappa, Indus Valley civilization. c. 2000 BCE. Red sandstone, height 3¾" (9.5 cm). National Museum, New Delhi

channeled away waste and rainwater. Clearly the technical and engineering skills of this civilization were highly advanced. At its peak, about 2500 to 2000 BCE, Mohenjo-Daro was approximately 6 to 7 square miles in size and had a population of about 20,000 to 50,000.

Although little is known about the Indus Valley civilization, a majority of motifs on the seals as well as the few artworks that have been discovered strongly suggest continuities with later South Asian culture. Seal (f) in figure 9-1, for example, depicts a man in the meditative posture associated in Indian culture with a yogi, one who seeks mental and physical purification and self-control, usually for spiritual purposes. In seal (d), persons with elaborate headgear in a row or procession observe a figure standing in a tree—possibly a goddess—and a kneeling worshiper. This scene may offer some insight into the religious or ritual customs of Indus Valley peoples, whose deities may have been ancient prototypes of later Indian gods and goddesses.

Numerous **terra-cotta** figurines and a few small stone and bronze statuettes have been found. They reveal an astonishing maturity of artistic conception and technique. Two main styles appear: one is related to Mesopotamian art in its motifs and rather abstract rendering, while the other foreshadows the later Indian artistic tradition in its sensuous naturalism.

The bust of a man in figure 9-2 is an example of the Mesopotamian style. The man's garment is patterned with a **trefoil**, or three-lobed, motif found in Mesopotamian art as well. Although the striated beard and the smooth, planar surfaces of the face reflect Mesopotamian treatment of the head, distinctive physical traits emerge, including a narrow forehead, a broad nose, thick lips, and large, wide eyes. These traits may well record something of the appearance of the Indus Valley peoples. The depressions of the trefoil pattern were originally filled with red paste and the eyes **inlaid** with shell. The narrow band encircling the head falls in back into two long strands and may be an indication of rank. Certainly with its formal pose and simplified, geometric form the statue conveys a human presence of great dignity.

A nude male torso found at Harappa is an example of the contrasting naturalistic style (fig. 9-3). Less than 4 inches tall, it is one of the most extraordinary portrayals of the human form to survive from any early civilization. In contrast to the more athletic male ideal developed in ancient Greece, this sculpture emphasizes the soft texture of the human body and the subtle nuances of muscular form. The abdomen is relaxed in the manner of a yogi able to control his breath. With these characteristics the Harappa torso forecasts the essential aesthetic attributes of later Indian sculpture.

9-4. *Large Painted Jar with Border Containing Birds*, from Chanhu-Daro, Indus Valley civilization. c. 2400–2000 BCE. Reddish buff clay, height 9⅞" (25 cm). Museum of Fine Arts, Boston

Joint Expedition of the American School of Indic and Iranian Studies and the Museum of Fine Arts, Boston

No paintings from the Indus Valley civilization have yet been found, but there are remains of handsome painted ceramic vessels (fig. 9-4). Formed on a potter's wheel and fired at high temperatures, the vessels are quite large and generally have a rounded bottom. They are typically decorated with several zones of bold, linear designs painted in black **slip.** Flower, leaf, bird, and fish motifs predominate. The elegant vessel here, for example, is decorated with peacocks poised gracefully among leafy branches in the upper zone and rows of leaves formed by a series of intersecting circles in the lower zone. Such geometric patterning is typical of Indus Valley decoration.

The reasons for the demise of this flourishing civilization are not yet understood. All we know is that apparently around 1500 BCE—possibly because of climate changes, a series of natural disasters, or invasions—the cities of the Indus Valley civilization declined, and over the next thousand years predominantly rural societies evolved.

THE VEDIC PERIOD

The centuries between the demise of the Indus Valley civilization and the rise of the first unified empire in the late fourth century BCE are generally referred to as the Vedic period. Named for the Vedas, a body of sacred writings that took shape over these centuries, the Vedic period witnessed profound changes in social structure and the formation of three of the four major enduring religions of India—Hinduism, Buddhism, and Jainism.

The period is marked by the dominance of Indo-European Aryans, a pastoral, seminomadic warrior people believed to have entered India sometime around 1500 BCE from the northwest. Gradually they supplanted the indigenous populations that had created the Indus Valley urban centers. The Aryans brought a language called Sanskrit, a hierarchical social order, and religious practices that centered on the propitiation of gods through fire sacrifice. The oldest layers of the Vedas, dating from the first centuries of Aryan presence, consist of hymns to such Aryan gods as the divine king Indra—the Vedic counterpart of the later Greek god Zeus. The importance of the fire sacrifice and the concept of religiously sanctioned social classes persisted through the Vedic period. At some point, the class structure became hereditary, with lasting consequences for Indian society.

During the latter part of this period, from about 800 BCE, the Upanishads were composed. These metaphysical texts examine the meanings of the earlier, more cryptic Vedic hymns. They focus on the relationship between the individual soul, or atman, and the universal soul, or Brahman, as well as on other concepts central to subsequent Indian philosophy. One is the assertion that the material world is illusory and that only Brahman is real

HINDUISM

Hinduism is not one integral religion but many related sects, each taking its particular deity as supreme. In Vaishnavism the supreme deity is Vishnu, in Shaivism it is Shiva, and in Shaktism it is the Goddess, Devi—a deity worshiped under many different names and in various forms. Each deity is revealed and depicted in multiple ways. Vishnu, for example, has ten major incarnations in which he manifests himself in the world. Shiva has numerous, complex "aspects" that reveal his nature, which is full of apparent contradictions and extremes. Devi has forms indicative of beauty, wealth, and auspiciousness, but also forms of wrath, pestilence, and power. Indeed, she can be more powerful than the male gods.

Though these three major Hindu sects differ from one another, they all draw upon the texts of the Vedas, which are believed to be sacred revelation. Of critical importance to all Hindu practice is ritual sacrifice, which harks back to ancient times—possibly as early as the Indus Valley period—when offerings were placed into fire in the belief that it would carry prayers to the gods. Purity is essential if the sacrifice is to be effective. If any element of the sacrificial rite becomes polluted, Hindus believe that the deity will be displeased and the sacrifice rejected. As Brahmins, a social category dating back to Vedic times, priests are highly trained ritual specialists and are considered more pure than others. They perform ceremonies on behalf of other Hindus.

Hindu sacrifice is performed for a purpose, which is generally to obtain the favor of a deity in the hope that this will lead to moksha, or liberation from samsara, the endless cycle of birth, death, and rebirth. Hindu belief also holds that all action is performed for a purpose and that every action has its consequences. Desire for the fruits of our actions keeps us trapped in samsara. But there is hope. If we can consider our actions as sacrificial offerings to god, then we will no longer be attached to their fruits, for these now properly belong also to the deity. With this in mind, we will act for the god's sake, not out of desire for ourselves. Pleased with our devotion, he or she will grant us moksha, an eternal state of sat, cit, and ananda—pure being, pure consciousness, and pure bliss. The most compelling and influential expression of these beliefs occurs in the Bhagavad Gita, a section of the Mahabharata, where Krishna, an incarnation of Vishnu, reveals them as truths to the warrior Arjuna on the battlefield.

Philosophically, Hindu deities are believed to arise from a state of being called Brahman or Formless One—a state of pure sat, cit, and ananda—into a Subtle Body stage. From the Subtle Body emanates our world of space-time and all that it contains. Into this world the deity then manifests itself in Gross Body form in order to help living beings. These three stages of a deity's emanation from One to the Many—Formless One, Subtle Body, and Gross Body—underlie much Hindu art and architecture.

---

and eternal. Another holds that our existence is cyclical and that beings are caught in samsara, a relentless cycle of birth, life, death, and rebirth. The goal of religious life is to attain liberation from samsara and to unite our individual atman with the eternal universal Brahman.

The latter portion of the Vedic period also saw the flowering of India's epic literature, written in the melodious and complex Sanskrit language. By around 400 BCE, the eighteen-volume *Mahabharata*, the longest epic in world literature, and the *Ramayana*, the most popular and enduring religious epic in India and Southeast Asia, were taking shape. These texts, the cornerstones of Indian literature, relate histories of gods and humans that bring the philosophical ideas of the Vedas to a more accessible and popular level.

In this stimulating religious, philosophical, and literary climate numerous religious communities arose. The most influential teachers of these times were Shakyamuni Buddha and Mahavira. The Buddha, or "enlightened one," lived and taught in India around 500 BCE; his teachings form the basis of the Buddhist religion (see "Buddhism"). Mahavira (599–527 BCE), regarded as the last of twenty-four highly purified super-beings called "pathfinders" (tirthankaras), was the founder of the Jain religion. Both Shakyamuni Buddha and Mahavira espoused some basic Upanishadic tenets, such as the cyclical nature of existence and the need for liberation from the material world. However, they rejected the authority of the Vedas, and with it the legitimacy of the fire sacrifice and the hereditary class structure of Vedic society, with its powerful, exclusive priesthood. In contrast, Buddhism and Jainism were open to all, regardless of social position.

Buddhism became a vigorous force in South Asia and provided the impetus for much of the major art created between the third century BCE and the fifth century CE. The Vedic tradition, meanwhile, continued to evolve, emerging later as Hinduism, a loose term that encompasses the many religious forms that resulted from the mingling of Vedic culture with indigenous, local beliefs (see "Hinduism").

THE MAURYA PERIOD

After about 700 BCE, cities again began to appear on the subcontinent, especially in the north, where numerous kingdoms arose. For most of its subsequent history, India remained a constantly shifting mosaic of regional dynastic kingdoms. From time to time, however, a particularly powerful dynasty formed an empire. The first of these was the Maurya dynasty (c. 322–185 BCE), which extended its rule over all but the southernmost portion of the subcontinent.

The art of the Maurya period reflects an age of heroes and the rise to prominence of Buddhism, which became

BUDDHISM The Buddhist religion developed from the teachings of Shakyamuni Buddha, who lived from about 563 to 483 BCE in the present-day regions of Nepal and central India. He was born Prince Siddhartha Gautama, the child of the ruler of the small kingdom of the Shakya clan. At his birth, it is believed, it was foretold that he would become either a chakravartin—a "world-conquering" ruler—or a buddha—a "fully enlightened" being. Hoping for a ruler rather than a holy man, Siddhartha's father tried to surround his son with pleasure and shield him from pain. Yet the prince was eventually exposed to the sufferings of old age, sickness, and death—the inevitable fate of all mortal beings. Deeply troubled by what he perceived to be the desperate human condition, Siddhartha left the palace, his family, and his inheritance to live as an ascetic in the wilderness. He was twenty-nine years old. After six years of meditation, he attained complete enlightenment while sitting under a pipal tree at Bodh Gaya.

Following his enlightenment, Shakyamuni, meaning "sage of the Shakyas," gave his first teaching in the Deer Park at Sarnath. Here he expounded the Four Noble Truths, which are the foundation of Buddhism: (1) life is suffering; (2) this suffering has a cause, which is ignorance; (3) this ignorance can be overcome and extinguished; (4) the way to overcome this ignorance is by fol-lowing the eightfold path of right view, right resolve, right speech, right action, right livelihood, right effort, right mindfulness, and right concentration. The Buddha continued to teach until his death at the age of eighty. After he died, his many disciples developed his teachings and established the world's oldest monastic institutions.

A buddha is not a god but rather one who sees the ultimate nature of the world and is therefore no longer subject to samsara, the cycle of birth, death, and rebirth that otherwise holds us in its grip, no matter whether we are born into the worlds of the various gods, humans, animals, tortured spirits, or hell beings.

The early form of Buddhism, known as Theravada or Hinayana, stresses self-cultivation for the purpose of attaining nirvana, which is the extinction of samsara for oneself. Around the turn of the millennium, however, major developments took place in Buddhism that greatly enlarged its scope. Its philosophical basis was clarified and its literature expanded. The goal was no longer nirvana for oneself, but buddhahood for every being throughout the universe. Compassion for all beings became the primary motivating force. The attainment of buddhahood, viewed as a higher state than nirvana, was the ultimate means by which one could fulfill the compassionate vow of saving all beings. This form of Buddhism, known as Mahayana, became popular mainly in northern India and eventually also took root and flourished in China, Korea, and Japan. Theravada Buddhism, in contrast, continued mainly in southern India, Sri Lanka, and Southeast Asia.

Mahayana Buddhism recognizes not only Shakyamuni Buddha but also numerous other buddhas from the past, present, and future. Some of these buddhas became as popular as Shakyamuni. One such is Maitreya, the next buddha to appear on earth. Another is Amitabha Buddha, the Buddha of Infinite Light and Infinite Life (that is, incorporating all space and time), who dwells in a paradise known as the Western Pure Land. Amitabha Buddha became particularly popular in East Asia. Mahayana Buddhism also developed the category of **bodhisattvas**, meaning "those whose essence is wisdom." Bodhisattvas are saintly, great beings who are on the brink of achieving buddhahood but have vowed to help others achieve buddhahood before crossing over themselves.

In art, bodhisattvas and buddhas are most clearly distinguished by their clothing and adornments: bodhisattvas wear the princely garb of India, while buddhas wear a monk's robe. In Hinduism a deity may dwell in its image, but in Buddhism portrayals of buddhas and bodhisattvas are recognized as purely symbolic, and no spirit is believed to reside within.

---

the official state religion under the greatest king of the dynasty, Ashoka (ruled c. 273–232 BCE). The belief of the time fostered the ideal of upholding dharma, the divinely ordained moral law believed to keep the universe from falling into chaos. The authority of dharma seems fully embodied in a lifesize statue found at Didarganj, near the Maurya capital of Pataliputra (fig. 9-5). The statue probably represents a **yakshi**, a spirit associated in popular belief with the productive forces of nature. With its large breasts and pelvis, the figure embodies the Indian association of female beauty with procreative abundance, bounty, and auspiciousness—qualities that in turn reflect the generosity of the gods and the workings of dharma in the world.

Sculpted from fine-grained sandstone, the statue conveys the yakshi's authority through the frontal rigor of her pose, the massive volumes of her form, and the strong, linear patterning of her ornaments and dress. Alleviating and counterbalancing this hierarchical formality are her soft, youthful face, the precise definition of prominent features such as the stomach muscles, and the polished sheen of her exposed flesh. This lustrous polish, the technique of which is a lost secret, is a special feature of Mauryan sculpture.

In addition to depictions of popular deities like the yakshis and their male counterparts, **yakshas**, the Maurya period is known for art associated with the imperial sponsorship of Buddhism. Emperor Ashoka, grandson of the dynasty's founder, is considered one of India's greatest rulers. After viewing the carnage on the bloody battlefield described at the beginning of this chapter, he vowed to become a chakravartin, or "world-conquering" ruler, not through the force of arms but through spreading the teachings of the Buddha. Among the monuments

9-6. Lion capital, from an Ashokan pillar at Sarnath, Uttar Pradesh, India. Maurya period, c. 250 BCE. Polished sandstone, height 7' (2.13 m). Archaeological Museum, Sarnath

9-5. *Yakshi Holding a Fly Whisk*, from Didarganj, Patna, Bihar, India. Maurya period, c. 250 BCE. Polished sandstone, height 5'4¼" (1.63 m). Patna Museum, Patna

Discovered near the ancient Maurya capital of Pataliputra, this sculpture has become one of the most famous works of Indian art. Holding a fly whisk in her raised right hand, the yakshi wears only a long shawl and a skirtlike cloth. The cloth rests low on her hips, held in place by a girdle. Subtly sculpted parallel creases indicate that it is gathered closely about her legs. The ends, drawn back up over the girdle, cascade down to her feet in a broad, central loop of flowing folds ending in a zigzag of hems. Draped low over her back, the shawl passes through the crook of her arm and then flows to the ground. (The missing left side of the shawl probably mirrored this motion.) The yakshi's jewelry is prominent. A double strand of pearls hangs between her breasts, its shape echoing and emphasizing the voluptuous curves of her body. Another strand of pearls encircles her neck. She wears a simple tiara, plug earrings, and rows of bangles. The nubbled tubes about her ankles probably represent anklets made of beaten gold. Her hair is bound in a large bun in back, and a small bun sits on her forehead. This hairstyle appears again in Indian sculptures of the later Kushan period (c. second century CE).

he erected to Buddhism throughout his empire were monolithic **pillars** set up primarily at sites related to events in the Buddha's life.

Pillars had been used as flag-bearing standards in India since earliest times. The creators of the Ashokan pillars seem to have adapted this already-ancient form to the symbolism of Indian creation myths and the new religion of Buddhism. The fully developed Ashokan pillar, a slightly tapered sandstone **shaft**, usually rested on a stone foundation slab sunk more than 10 feet into the ground and rose to a height of around 50 feet. On it were carved inscriptions referring to Buddhist teachings or exhorting the Buddhist community to unity. At the top, carved from a separate block of sandstone, an elaborate **capital** bore animal sculpture. Both shaft and capital were given the characteristic Maurya polish. Scholars believe that the pillars symbolized the *axis mundi*, or "axis of the world," joining earth with the cosmos. It represented the vital link between the human and celestial realms, and through it the cosmic order was impressed onto the terrestrial world.

The capital in figure 9-6 originally crowned the pillar erected at Sarnath in northeast India, the site of the

9-7. Great Stupa, Sanchi, Madhya Pradesh, India. Founded 3rd century BCE, enlarged c. 150–50 BCE

Buddha's first teaching. The lowest portion represents the down-turned petals of a lotus blossom. Because the lotus flower emerges from murky waters without any mud sticking to its petals, it symbolizes the presence of divine purity in the imperfect world. Above the lotus is an **"abacus"** embellished with **low-relief** carvings of wheels, called chakras, alternating with four different animals: lion, horse, bull, and elephant. The animals may symbolize the four great rivers of the world, which are spoken of in the same Indian creation myth that express-es the important *axis mundi* concept. Standing on this abacus are four back-to-back lions. Facing the four cardinal directions, the lions may be emblematic of the universal nature of Buddhism. Their roar might be com-pared to the speech of the Buddha that spreads far and wide. The lions may also refer to the Buddha himself, who is known as "the lion of the Shakya clan" (the clan into which the Buddha was born as crown prince). The lions originally supported a great copper wheel, now lost. A universal Buddhist symbol, the wheel refers to Buddhist teaching, for with his sermon at Sarnath the Buddha "set the wheel of the doctrine in motion."

Their formal, heraldic pose imbues the lions with something of the monumental quality evident in the stat-ue of the yakshi earlier. We also find the same delight in the strong patterning of realistic elements: veins and ten-dons stand out on the legs; the claws are large and pow-erful; the mane is richly textured; and the jaws have a loose and fluttering edge.

THE PERIOD OF THE SHUNGAS AND EARLY ANDHRAS

With the demise of the Maurya Empire, India returned to local rule by regional dynasties. Be-tween the second century BCE and the early first century CE, the most important of these dynasties were the Shungas in central India and the early Andhras in South India. Dur-ing this period, Buddhism continued as the main inspira-tion for art, and some of the most important and magnificent early Buddhist structures were created.

Stupas

Probably no early Buddhist structure is more famous than the Great Stupa at Sanchi in central India (fig. 9-7). Originally built by King Ashoka in the Maurya period, the Great Stupa was part of a large monastery complex crowning the top of a hill. During the mid-second centu-ry BCE the stupa was enlarged to its present size, and the surrounding stone railing was constructed. About 100 years later, elaborately carved stone gateways were added to the railing.

Stupas are fundamentally important in the Buddhist world (see "Elements of Architecture," opposite). The first Buddhist stupas were constructed to house the Bud-dha's relics—the remains after his cremation. At that time (c. 483 BCE) the relics were divided into eight por-tions and placed in eight **reliquaries**. Each reliquary was

ELEMENTS OF ARCHITECTURE

Stupas and Temples

Buddhist architecture in South Asia consists mainly of stupas and temples, often at monastic complexes containing **viharas** (monks' cells and common areas). All of these may be either structural—built up from the ground—or rock-cut—hewn out of a mountainside. **Stupas** derive from burial mounds and contain relics beneath a solid, dome-shaped core. A major stupa is surrounded by a railing that creates a sacred path for ritual circumambulation at ground level. This railing is punctuated by gateways called **toranas**, aligned with the cardinal points; access is through the eastern torana. The stupa sits on a round or square **plinth**; stairs lead to an upper circumambulatory path around the platform's edge. On top of the stupa's dome a railing defines a square, from the center of which rises a mast supporting tiers of disk-shaped "umbrellas."

Hindu architecture in South Asia consists mainly of temples, either structural or rock-cut, executed in a num-ber of styles and dedicated to a vast range of deities. The two general Hindu temple types are the northern and southern styles—corresponding to North India and South India, respectively. Within these broad categories there is great stylistic diversity. Hindu temples are raised on plinths and are dominated by their superstructures, towers called **shikharas** in the North and **vimanas** in the South. Shikharas are crowned by **amalakas**, vimanas by large **capstones**. On the interior, a series of **mandapas** (halls) leads to an inner sanctuary, the *garbhagriha*, which contains a sacred image. An *axis mundi* runs vertically up from the cosmic waters below the earth, through the *garbhagriha*'s image, and out through the top of the tower. Unlike a Buddhist stupa's *axis mundi*, however, that of a Hindu temple is implied rather than actual.

Jain architecture consists mainly of structural and rock-cut monasteries and temples. Jain halls and temples have much in common with their Buddhist and Hindu counterparts. Buddhist, Hindu, and Jain temples may share a site.

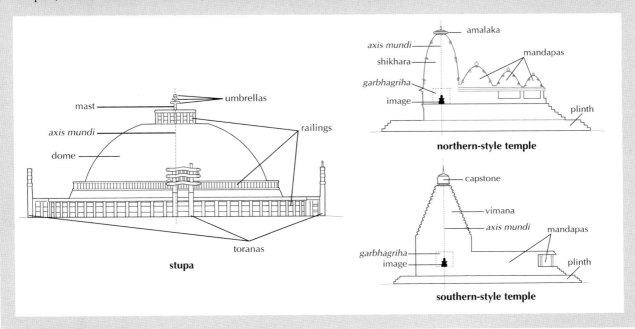

stupa

northern-style temple

southern-style temple

then encased in its own burial mound, called a stupa. In the mid-third century BCE King Ashoka opened these original eight stupas and divided their relics among many more stupas, probably including the one at Sanchi. Since the early stupas held actual remains of the Buddha, they were venerated as his body and, by extension, his enlightenment and attainment of nirvana—liberation from rebirth. The method of veneration was, and still is, to circumambulate, or walk around, the stupa in a clock-wise direction, following the sun's path across the sky. Anyone was free to venerate the stupa, for in the Bud-dhist tradition a monastery and its stupa are open to all.

A stupa may be small and plain or large and elabo-rate. Its form may vary from region to region, but its symbolic meaning remains virtually the same. The Great Stupa at Sanchi is a representative of the early central Indian type. Its solid, hemispherical **dome** was built up from rubble and dirt, faced with **dressed stone**, then covered with a shining white plaster made from lime and powdered seashells. The dome—echoing the arc of the sky—sits on a raised base. Around its perimeter is an upper circumambulatory walkway enclosed by a railing and approached by a pair of staircases. As is often true in religious architecture, the railing provides a physical and symbolic boundary between an inner, sacred area and the outer, profane world. On top of the dome, another stone railing, square in shape, defines the abode of the gods atop the cosmic mountain. It encloses the top of a mast bearing three stone disks, or "umbrellas," of decreasing size. These disks have been interpreted in various ways. They may refer to the Buddhist concept of the three realms of existence—desire, form, and form-lessness. The mast itself is an *axis mundi*, connecting the cosmic waters below the earth with the celestial realm above it and anchoring everything in its proper place. The stupa's plan is a carefully calculated **mandala**, or

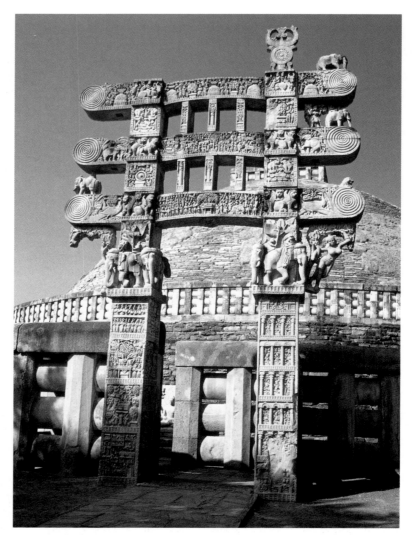

9-8. North torana of the Great Stupa at Sanchi. Early Andhra period, mid-1st century BCE. Stone, height 35' (10.66 m)

cosmic diagram, in the form of an ancient solar symbol called a svastika.

An 11-foot-tall stone railing rings the entire stupa, enclosing another, wider, circumambulatory path at ground level. Carved with octagonal uprights and lens-shaped crossbars, it probably simulates the wooden railings of the time. This design became a pervasive motif in early Indian art, appearing time and again both in relief sculpture and as architectural ornament. Four stone gateways, or **toranas**, punctuate the railing (fig. 9-8). Set at the four cardinal directions, the toranas symbolize the Buddhist cosmos. According to an inscription, they were sculpted by ivory carvers from the nearby town of Vidisha. The only elements of the Great Stupa at Sanchi to be ornamented with sculpture, the toranas rise to a height of 35 feet. Their square posts are carved with symbols and scenes drawn mostly from the Buddha's life and his past lives. Vines, lotuses, geese, and mythical animals decorate the sides, while guardians sculpted on the lowest panel of each inner side protect the entrance. The "capitals" above consist of four back-to-back elephants

on the north and east gates, dwarfs on the south gate, and lions on the west gate. The capitals in turn support a three-tiered superstructure whose posts and crossbars are elaborately carved with still more symbols and scenes and studded with freestanding sculpture depicting such subjects as yakshis and yakshas, riders on real and mythical animals, and the Buddhist wheel. As in all known early Buddhist art, the Buddha himself is not shown in human form. Instead, he is represented by symbols such as his footprints, an empty "enlightenment" seat, or a stupa.

Forming a bracket between each capital and the lowest crossbar is a sculpture of a yakshi (fig. 9-9). These yakshis are some of the finest female figures in Indian art, and they make an instructive comparison with the yakshi of the Maurya period (see fig. 9-5). The earlier figure was distinguished by a formal, somewhat rigid pose, an emphasis on realistic details, and a clear distinction between clothed and nude parts of the body. In contrast, the Sanchi yakshi leans daringly into space with casual abandon, supported by one leg as the other charmingly crosses

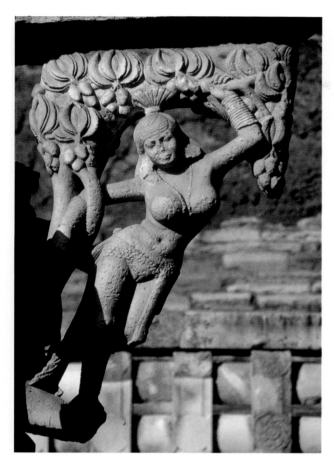

9-9. Yakshi bracket figure, on the east torana of the Great Stupa at Sanchi. Stone, height approx. 60" (152.4 cm)

9-10. Section of the chaitya hall at Karla, Maharashtra, India. Early Andhra period, second half of 1st century BCE

9-11. Chaitya hall at Karla

behind. Her thin, diaphanous garment is noticeable only by its hems, and so she appears almost nude, which emphasizes the unity of her form. The band pulling gently at her abdomen accentuates the suppleness of her flesh. The swelling forms of her body with their lovely arching curves seem to bring this deity's procreative and bountiful essence to life. As anthropomorphic symbol of the waters, she is the source of life. Here she personifies the sap of the tree, which flowers at her touch.

The profusion of designs, symbols, scenes, and figures carved on all sides of the gateways to the Great Stupa not only relate the history and lore of Buddhism but also represent the teeming life of the world and the gods. Arrayed as protectors of the stupa, these forms, by their auspicious presence, indicate the wondrous nature of the site and augur the happiness of those who come to it.

Buddhist Rock-Cut Halls

From ancient times caves have been considered hallowed places in India, for they were frequently the abode of holy ones and ascetics. Around the second century BCE, Buddhist monks began to hew caves for their own use out of the stone plateaus in the western region of India known as the Deccan. The exteriors and interiors were carved from top to bottom like great pieces of sculpture, with all details completely finished in stone.

To enter one of these remarkable halls is to feel immediately removed to an otherworldly, sacred space. The energy of the living rock, the mysterious atmosphere created by the dark recess, the echo that magnifies the smallest sound—all combine to promote a state of intensely heightened awareness.

The monastic community made two types of rock-cut halls. One was the **vihara**, used for the living quarters of the monks, and the other was the **chaitya**, meaning "sacred," which usually enshrined a stupa. A chaitya hall at Karla, dating from around the latter half of the first century BCE, is the largest and most fully developed example of these early Buddhist works (figs. 9-10, 9-11). At the entrance, a series of columns once supported a balcony, in front of which a pair of Ashokan-type pillars stood. The walls of the vestibule area are carved in relief with rows of small balcony railings and arched windows, simulating the facade of a great multistoried palace. At the base of the side walls, enormous statues of elephants seem to be supporting the entire structure on their backs. Filling almost the entire upper portion of the main facade is a large horseshoe-shaped opening called a "sun window" or "chaitya window," which provides the main source of light for the hall's interior. The window was originally fitted with a carved wood screen, some of which still remains, that softened and filtered the light within.

Three entrances in the main facade lead to the interior. The two side entrances are each approached through a shallow pool of water, which symbolically purifies visitors as it washes their dusty feet. Flanking the entrances are sculpted panels of **mithuna** couples, amorous male and female figures that evoke the harmony and fertility of life. The interior hall, 123 feet long, has a 46-foot-high ceiling carved in the form of a **barrel vault** ornamented with arching wooden ribs. A wide central aisle and two narrower side aisles lead to the stupa situated in the rounded **apse** at the far end.

The closely spaced columns that separate the side aisles from the main aisle are unlike any known in the West, and they are important examples in the long and complex evolution of the many Indian styles. The base resembles a large pot set on a stepped pyramid of planks. From this potlike form rises a massive octagonal shaft. Crowning the shaft, a bell-shaped lotus capital supports an inverted pyramid of planks, which serves in turn as a platform for sculpture. The statues facing the main aisle depict pairs of kneeling elephants, each bearing a *mithuna* couple; those facing the side aisles depict pairs of horses also bearing couples. These figures, the only sculpture within this austere hall, represent the nobility coming to pay homage at the temple. The pillars around the apse are plain, and the stupa is simply portrayed. A railing motif ornaments the base; the dome was once crowned with wooden "umbrella" disks, only one of which remains. The symbolism of this stupa is the same as that of the stupa at Sanchi, although it, like nearly everything in the cave, is carved from the living rock. Both exterior and interior were once brightly painted.

THE KUSHAN AND LATER ANDHRA PERIOD Around the first century CE the regions of present-day Afghanistan, Pakistan, and North India came under the control of the Kushans, a nomadic people from Central Asia. The impact of the Kushan dynasty on Indian culture was significant, but their history is clouded by lack of clear dates. The beginning of the long reign of their most illustrious king, Kanishka, is variously dated from 78 to 143 CE. A patron of Buddhism, Kanishka caused many stupas and monasteries to be built, thus giving a renewed impetus to the religion.

Buddhism during this period was undergoing the profound developments that resulted in the form known as Mahayana, or Great Vehicle (see "Buddhism," page 371). This vital new movement, which was to sweep most of northern India and eastern Asia, probably inspired the first depictions of the Buddha himself in art. (Previously, as in the Great Stupa at Sanchi, the Buddha had been indicated solely by symbols.) It is not known where the first Buddha image appeared. However, the

9-12. *Standing Buddha*, from Gandhara (Pakistan). Kushan period, c. 2nd–3rd century CE. Schist, height 7'6" (2.28 m). Lahore Museum, Lahore

two earliest schools of representation arose in the Gandhara region in the northwest (present-day Pakistan and Afghanistan) and in the famous religious center of Mathura in central India. Both of these areas were ruled by the Kushans. Slightly later, a third school, known as the Amaravati school after its most famous site, developed to the south in the region ruled by the Andhras.

While all three schools cultivated distinct styles, they shared a basic **iconography** in which the Buddha is readily recognized by certain characteristics. He wears a monk's robe called a *sanghati*, a long length of cloth draped over the left shoulder and around the body. The Buddha is said to have had thirty-two major distinguishing marks, called *lakshana*, some of which also passed into the iconography of his image (see "Buddhist Symbols," page 427). These include a golden-colored body,

9-13. *Buddha and Attendants*, from Katra Keshavdev, Mathura, Madhya Pradesh, India. Kushan period, c. late 1st–early 2nd century BCE. Red sandstone, height 27¼" (69.2 cm). Government Museum, Mathura

long arms that reached to his knees, the impression of a wheel (chakra) on the palms of his hands and the soles of his feet, and the **urna**—a tuft of white hair between his eyebrows. Because he had been a prince in his youth and had worn the customary heavy earrings, his earlobes are usually shown elongated. The top of his head is said to have had a protuberance called an **ushnisha**, which in images often resembles a bun or topknot and is symbolic of his enlightenment.

The Gandhara School

A typical image from the Gandhara school portrays the Buddha as a superhuman figure, more powerful and heroic than an ordinary human (fig. 9-12). This over-lifesize Buddha dates to the fully developed stage of the Gandhara style around the third century CE. It is carved from schist, a fine-grained dark stone. The Buddha's body, revealed through the folds of the garment, is broad and massive, with heavy shoulders and limbs and a well-defined torso. His left knee bends gently, suggesting a slightly relaxed posture.

The treatment of the *sanghati* is especially characteristic of the Gandhara manner. Tight, riblike folds alternate with delicate creases, setting up a clear, rhythmic pattern of heavy and shallow lines. On the upper part of the figure the folds break asymmetrically along the left arm; on the lower part they drape in a symmetric **U** shape. The strong tension of the folds suggests life and power within the image. This complex fold pattern resembles the treatment of togas on certain Roman statues (see fig. 6-25), and it exerted a strong influence on portrayals of the Buddha in Central and East Asia. The Gandhara region's history of relations with the Hellenistic world may have prepared the ground for this strongly Western style in its art. Pockets of Hellenistic culture had thrived in neighboring Bactria (present-day northern Afghanistan and southern Uzbekistan) since the fourth century BCE, when the Greeks under Alexander the Great reached the borders of India. Also, Gandhara's position near the East-West trade routes appears to have stimulated contact with Roman culture in the Near East during the early centuries of the first millennium CE.

The Mathura School

The second major school of Buddhist art in the Kushan period, that at Mathura, was not allied with the Hellenistic-Roman tradition. Instead, its style evolved from representations of yakshas, the indigenous male nature deities. Images produced at Mathura during the early days of the school may well be the first representations of the Buddha to appear in art.

The **stela** in figure 9-13 is one of the finest of the

MUDRAS

Mudras (meaning "signs" in Sanskrit) are ancient symbolic hand gestures seen primarily in Buddhist art, where they function iconographically. Mudras are regarded as physical expressions of different states of being and are used during meditation to release these energies. Following are the most common mudras in Asian art.

Dharmachakra mudra

The gesture of teaching, setting the chakra (wheel) of the dharma (law, or doctrine) in motion. Hands are at chest level.

Dhyana mudra

A gesture of meditation and balance, symbolizing the path toward enlightenment. Hands are in the lap, the lower representing maya, the physical world of illusion, the upper representing nirvana, enlightenment and release from the world.

Vitarka mudra

This variant of *dharmachakra* mudra stands for intellectual debate. The right hand is at shoulder level, pointing downward, while the left is at hip level pointing upward.

Abhaya mudra

The gesture of reassurance, blessing, and protection, this mudra means "do not fear." The right hand is at shoulder level, palm outward.

Bhumisparsha mudra

This gesture calls the earth to witness Shakyamuni Buddha's enlightenment at Bodh Gaya. A seated figure's right hand reaches toward the ground, palm inward.

Varada mudra

The gesture of charity, symbolizing the fulfillment of all wishes. Alone, this mudra is made with the right hand; when combined with *abhaya* mudra in standing buddha figures, the left hand is shown in *varada* mudra.

early Mathura images. Carved in **high relief** from a block of red sandstone, it depicts a seated Buddha with two attendants. The Buddha sits in a yogic posture on a pedestal supported by lions. His right hand is raised in a symbolic gesture meaning "have no fear." Images of the Buddha rely on a repertoire of such symbolic gestures, called **mudras**, to communicate certain ideas, such as teaching, meditation, or the attaining of enlightenment (see "Mudras"). The Buddha's urna, his *ushnisha*, and the impressions of wheels on the palms and soles of his feet are all clearly visible in this figure. Behind his head is a large, circular halo; the scallop points of its border represent radiating light. Behind the halo are branches of the pipal tree, the tree under which the Buddha was seated when he achieved enlightenment. Two celestial beings hover above.

As in the Gandhara school, a powerful impression of the Buddha is emphasized. Yet the Mathura Buddha's riveting outward gaze and alert posture impart a more intense, concentrated energy to the image. The robe is pulled tightly over the body, allowing the fleshy form to be seen as almost nude. Where the pleats of the *sanghati* appear, such as over the left arm and fanning out between the legs, they are depicted abstractly through compact parallel formations of ridges with an **incised** line in the center of each ridge. This characteristic Mathura tendency to abstraction also appears in the face, whose features take on geometric shapes, as in the rounded forms of the widely opened eyes. Nevertheless, the heavy torso with its subtle and soft modeling is strongly naturalistic.

The Amaravati School

Events from the Buddha's life were popular subjects in the reliefs decorating Buddhist stupas and temples. One example from Nagarjunakonda, a site of the third major school of this period, the southern or Amaravati school, depicts a scene from the Buddha's life when he was a prince called Siddhartha, before his renunciation and subsequent quest for enlightenment (fig. 9-14). Carved in low relief, the panel reveals a scene of pleasure around a pool of water. Gathered around Siddhartha, the largest figure and the only male, are some of the palace women. One holds his foot, entreating him to come into the water; another sits with legs drawn up on the nearby rock; others lean over his shoulder or fix their hair; one comes into the scene with a box of jewels on her head. The panel is framed by decorated columns, crouching lions, and amorous *mithuna* couples. (One of these couples is visible at the right of the illustration.) The scene is skillfully orchestrated to revolve around the prince as the main focus of all eyes. Typical of the southern school, the figures are slighter than those of the Gandhara and Mathura schools. They are sinuous and mobile, even while at rest. The rhythmic nuances of the limbs and varied postures not only create interest in the activity of each individual but also engender a light and joyous effect.

During the first to third century CE, each of these three major schools of Buddhist art developed its own distinct

9-14. *Siddhartha in the Palace*, detail of a relief from Nagarjunakonda, Andhra Pradesh, India. Later Andhra period, c. 3rd century CE. Limestone. National Museum, New Delhi

In his *Buddhacharita*, a long poem about the life of the Buddha, the great Indian poet Ashvagosha (c. 100 CE) describes Prince Siddhartha's life in the palace: "The monarch [Siddhartha's father], reflecting that the prince must see nothing untoward that might agitate his mind, assigned him a dwelling in the upper storeys of the palace and did not allow him access to the ground. Then in the pavilions, white as the clouds of autumn, with apartments suited to each season and resembling heavenly mansions come down to earth, he passed the time with the noble music of singing-women." Later, during an outing, a series of unexpected encounters confront Siddhartha with the nature of mortality. Deeply shaken, he cannot bring himself to respond to the perfumed entreaties of the women who greet him on his return: "For what rational being would stand or sit or lie at ease, still less laugh, when he knows of old age, disease and death?" In this relief, the prince, though surrounded by women in the pleasure garden, seems already to bear the sobering demeanor of these thoughts, which were to change his life profoundly and affect the world.

(Translated by E. H. Johnston)

9-15. *Standing Buddha*, from Sarnath, Uttar Pradesh, India. Gupta period, 474 CE. Chunar sandstone, height 6'4" (1.93 m). Archaeological Museum, Sarnath

idiom for expressing the complex imagery of Buddhism and depicting the image of the Buddha. The Gandhara and Amaravati schools declined over the ensuing centuries, mainly due to the demise of the major dynasties that had supported their Buddhist establishments. However, the schools of central India, including the school of Mathura, continued to develop, and from them came the next major development in Indian Buddhist art.

THE GUPTA PERIOD

The Guptas, the founders of a dynasty in the eastern region of central India known as Magadha, expanded their territories during the course of the fourth century to form an empire that encompassed northern and much of southern India. Though the peak of Gupta power lasted only about 130 years (c. 320–450 CE), the influence of Gupta culture was felt for centuries.

The Gupta period, extending from around 320 to 500 CE, is renowned for its high artistic and literary culture. Buddhism reached its greatest influence, and Hinduism,

sponsored by Gupta monarchs, began the ascendancy that led to its eventual domination of Indian religious life. Art flourished, and the Gupta legacy includes some of India's most widely admired masterpieces of sculpture and painting.

Buddhist Sculpture

Two schools of Buddhist sculpture dominated in northern India: the Mathura, one of the major schools of the earlier Kushan period, and the school at Sarnath. Both reached their artistic peak during the second half of the fifth century.

The standing Buddha in figure 9-15 embodies the fully developed Sarnath Gupta style. Carved from fine-grained sandstone, the figure stands in a mildly relaxed

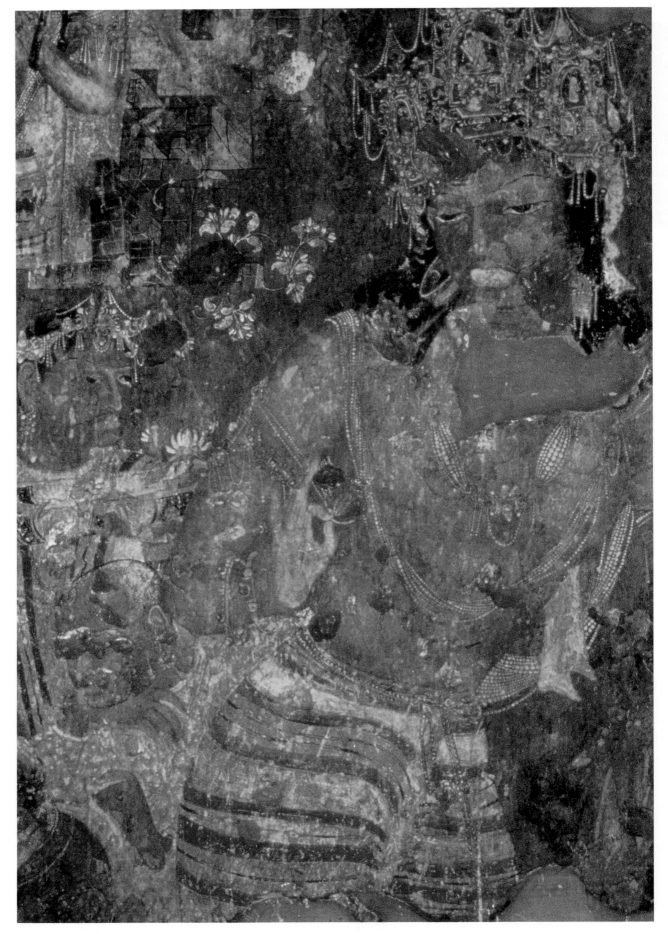

9-16. *Bodhisattva*, detail of a wall painting in Cave I, Ajanta, Maharashtra, India. Gupta period, c. 475 CE pose, the body clearly visible through a clinging robe. This plain *sanghati*, portrayed with none of the creases and folds so prominent in the Kushan period images, is distinctive of the Sarnath school. Its effect is to concentrate attention on the perfected form of the body, which emerges in high relief. The body is graceful and slight, with broad shoulders and a well-proportioned torso. Only a few lines of the garment at the neck, waist, and hems interrupt the purity of its subtly shaped surfaces. Even the face, smooth and ovoid, shows this refined elegance. The downcast eyes suggest otherworldly introspection, yet the gentle, open posture maintains a human link. Behind the head are the remains of a large, circular halo. Carved in concentric circles of pearls and foliage, it would have contrasted dramatically with the plain surfaces of the figure.

The Sarnath Gupta style reveals the Buddha in perfection and equilibrium. He is not interpreted as a powerful, superhuman presence but as a being whose spiritual purity is evidenced by, and in some way fused with, his physical purity. The nature of the fully enlightened seems completely synonymous with the nature of the fully human—an expression fitting the true nature of a buddha.

Painting

The Gupta aesthetic also found expression in painting. Some of the finest surviving works are murals from the Buddhist rock-cut halls of Ajanta in the Deccan area of western India. Under a local dynasty, many caves were carved around 475 CE, including Cave I, a large vihara hall with monks' chambers around the sides and a Buddha shrine chamber in the back. The walls of the central court were covered with murals painted in **fresco** technique with mineral pigments on a prepared plaster surface. Some of these paintings depict episodes from the Buddha's past lives. Flanking the entrance to the shrine are two large bodhisattvas, one of which is seen in figure 9-16.

Bodhisattvas are beings who are in the process of becoming buddhas and have reached a high level of spiritual attainment already. They are distinguished from buddhas in art by their princely garments (like those worn by Shakyamuni as a prince) rather than the monk's *sanghati*. The bodhisattva here is lavishly adorned with delicate ornaments. He wears a complicated crown with many tiny pearl festoons, large earrings, long necklaces of twisted pearl strands, armbands, and bracelets. A striped cloth covers his lower body. The graceful bending posture imparts his sympathetic attitude as he gazes serenely outward toward the viewer. His spiritual power is suggested by his large size in comparison with the surrounding figures.

The naturalism of the style balances outline and softly graded color tones. The outline drawing, always a major ingredient of Indian painting, creates clearly defined shapes; the tonal gradations impart the illusion of three-dimensional form, with lighter tones used for protruding parts such as the nose, brows, shoulders, and chest muscles. Together with the details of the jewels,

these highlighted areas resonate against the subdued tonality of the figure and the somber, flower-strewn background. Interest in sophisticated, realistic detail is balanced, in typical Gupta fashion, by the magnetic beauty of the languorous human form. In no other known examples of Indian painting do bodhisattvas appear so magnanimous and graciously divine yet at the same time so palpably human. This particular synthesis, evident also in the Sarnath statue, is the glory of Gupta artistic achievement.

THE POST-GUPTA PERIOD

As Buddhism flourished in India during the fifth century, Hinduism, supported by the Gupta monarchs, began to rise in popularity. Hindu temples and sculptures of the Hindu gods, though known earlier, appeared with increasing frequency during the Gupta period and its aftermath in the post-Gupta era of the sixth to mid-seventh century.

The Early Northern Temple

The Hindu temple developed many different forms throughout India, but it can be classified broadly into two types, northern and southern. The northern type is chiefly distinguished by a superstructure called a **shikhara** (see "Elements of Architecture," page 375). The shikhara rises as a solid mass above the flat stone ceiling and windowless walls of the sanctum, or **garbhagriha**, which houses an image of the temple's deity. As it rises, it curves inward in a mathematically determined ratio. (In mathematical terms, the shikhara is a paraboloid.) Crowning the top is a circular, cushionlike element called an **amalaka**, which means "sunburst." From the amalaka a **finial** takes the eye to a point where the earthly world is thought to join the cosmic world. An imaginary *axis mundi* penetrates the entire temple, running from the point of the finial, through the exact center of the amalaka and shikhara, down through the center of the *garbhagriha* and its image, finally passing through the base of the temple and into the earth below. In this way the temple becomes a conduit between the celestial realms and the earth. This theme, familiar from Ashokan pillars and Buddhist stupas, is carried out with elaborate exactitude in Hindu temples, and it is one of the most important elements in the rationale behind their form and function (see "Meaning and Ritual in Hindu Temples and Images," page 385).

One of the earliest northern-style temples is the temple of Vishnu at Deogarh in central India, which dates from around 530 CE (fig. 9-17). Much of the shikhara has crumbled away, and so we cannot determine its original shape with precision. Nevertheless, it was clearly a massive, solid structure built of large cut stones. It would have given the impression of a mountain, which is one of several metaphoric meanings of a Hindu temple. This early temple has only one chamber, the *garbhagriha*, which corresponds to the center of a sacred diagram called a mandala on which the entire temple site is patterned. As the deity's residence, the *garbhagriha* is likened to a sacred cavern within the "cosmic mountain" of the temple.

9-17. Vishnu Temple at Deogarh, Uttar Pradesh, India. c. 530 CE

The entrance to a Hindu temple is elaborate and meaningful. The doorway at Deogarh is well preserved and an excellent example (fig. 9-18). Because the entrance takes a worshiper from the mundane world into the sacred, stepping over a threshold is considered a purifying act. Two river goddesses, one on each upper corner of the **lintel**, symbolize the purifying waters flowing down over the entrance. These imaginary waters also provide symbolic nourishment for the vines and flowers decorating some of the vertical **jambs**. The innermost vines sprout from the navel of a dwarf, one of the popular motifs in Indian art. *Mithuna* couples and small replicas of the temple line other jambs. At the bottom, male and female guardians flank the doorway. Above the door, in the center, is a small image of the god Vishnu, to whom the temple is dedicated.

Large panels sculpted in relief with images of Vishnu appear as "windows" on the temple's exterior. These elaborately framed panels are not windows in the ordinary sense. They do not function literally to let light *into* the temple; they function symbolically to let the light of the deity *out* of the temple so it may be seen by those outside. The panels thus symbolize the third phase of Vishnu's threefold emanation from Brahman, the Formless One, into our physical world. (For a discussion of the emanation of Hindu deities, see "Hinduism," page 372.)

One panel depicts Vishnu lying on the Cosmic Waters at the beginning of creation (fig. 9-19). This vision

9-18. Doorway of the Vishnu Temple at Deogarh

9-19. *Vishnu Narayana on the Cosmic Waters*, relief panel in the Vishnu Temple at Deogarh. Stone

MEANING AND RITUAL IN HINDU TEMPLES AND IMAGES

The Hindu temple is one of the most complex and meaningful architectural forms in Asian art. Age-old symbols and ritual functions are embedded not only in a structure's many parts but also in the process of construction itself. Patron, priest, and architect worked as a team to ensure the sacred nature of the structure from start to finish. No artist or artisan was more highly revered in Indian society than the architect, who could oversee the construction of an abode in which a deity would dwell.

For a god to take up residence, however, everything had to be done properly. By the sixth century CE, the necessary procedures and explanations had been recorded in exacting detail in a group of texts called the *Silpa Shastra*. First, a site was chosen that was auspicious—promised to bode well. A site near water was especially favored, for water makes the earth fruitful. Next, the ground was prepared, an elaborate process that took several years. Various spirits who were already inhabiting the site were "invited" to leave so that the temple might be raised on pure ground. The ground was then plowed and planted, and the resulting crop was harvested through two seasons. After that, cows—sacred beasts since the Indus Valley civilization—were pastured there. Through their stomping, breathing, and feeding on the site, they lent it their potency. When construction began, each phase was accompanied by ritual to ensure its purity and sanctity.

All Hindu temples are built on a mystical plan known as a **mandala**, a schematic design of a sacred realm or space. Specifically, Hindu temples are based on the Vastupurusha mandala, the mandala of the Cosmic Man, the primordial progenitor of the human species. His body, fallen on earth, is imagined as superimposed on the mandala design; together, they form the base on which the temple rises.

Although the Vastupurusha mandala can be drawn in any number of different ways, it always takes the form of a square subdivided into a number of equal squares (usually sixty-four) surrounding a central square. The central square represents Brahman, the primordial, unmanifest Formless One. This square corresponds to the temple's sanctum, the windowless *garbhagriha*, or "womb chamber." The nature of Brahman is clear, pure light; that we perceive the *garbhagriha* as dark is a testament to our deluded nature. The surrounding squares belong to lesser deities, while the outermost compartments hold protector gods. These compartments are usually represented by the enclosing wall of a temple compound.

The *garbhagriha* houses the temple's main image—most commonly one of the forms of Vishnu, Shiva, or Devi. Usually this image is a sculpture made of stone, bronze, or wood. The image is made with the understanding that the god will inhabit it. To ensure perfection, its proportions follow a set canon, and rituals surround its making. When the image is completed, a priest recites mantras, or mystic syllables, that bring the deity into the image. The belief that a deity is literally present is not taken lightly. Even in India today, any image "under worship"—whether it be in a temple or a field, an ancient work or a modern piece—will be respected and not taken from the people who worship it.

A Hindu temple is a place for individual devotion, not congregational worship. It is the place where a devotee can make offerings to one or more deities and be in the presence of the god who is embodied in the image in the *garbhagriha*. Worship generally consists of prayers and offerings such as food and flowers or water and oil for the image, but it can also be much more elaborate, including dancing and ritual sacrifices.

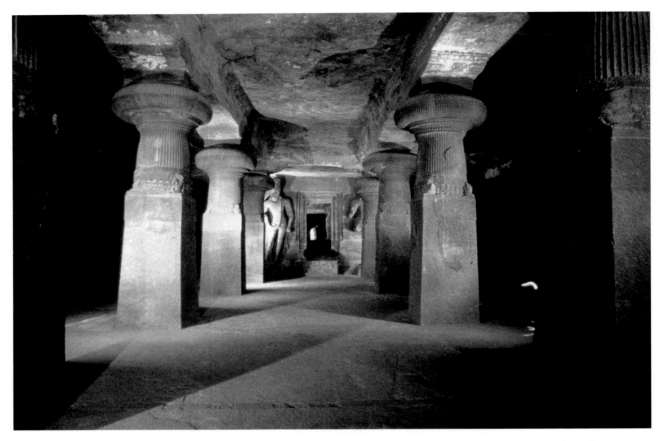

9-20. Cave-Temple of Shiva at Elephanta, Maharashtra, India. Mid-6th century CE. View along the east-west axis to the lingam shrine

represents the Subtle Body, or second, stage of the deity's emanation. Vishnu sleeps on the serpent of infinity, Ananta, whose body coils endlessly into space. Stirred by his female aspect (shakti, or female energy), personified here by the goddess Lakshmi, seen holding his foot, Vishnu dreams the universe into existence. From his navel springs a lotus (shown in this relief behind Vishnu), and the unfolding of space-time begins. The first being to be created is Brahma (not to be confused with Brahman), who appears here as the central, four-headed figure in the row of gods portrayed above the reclining Vishnu. Brahma turns himself into the universe of space and time by thinking, "May I become Many."

The sculptor has depicted Vishnu as a large, resplendent figure with four arms. His size and his many arms connote his omniscient powers. He is lightly garbed but richly ornamented. The ideal of the Gupta style persists in the smooth, perfected shape of the body and in the delight in details of jewelry, including Vishnu's characteristic cylindrical crown. The four rightmost figures in the frieze below personify Vishnu's powers. They stand ready to fight the appearance of evil, represented at the left of the frieze by two demons who threaten to kill Brahma and jeopardize all creation.

The birth of the universe and the appearance of evil are thus portrayed here in three clearly organized **registers**. Typical of Indian religious and artistic expression,

these momentous events are set before our eyes not in terms of abstract symbols but as a drama acted out by gods in superhuman form. The birth of the universe is imagined not as a "big bang" of infinitesimal particles from a supercondensed black hole but as a lotus unfolding from the navel of Vishnu.

Monumental Narrative Reliefs

Another major Hindu god, Shiva, was known in Vedic times as Rudra, "the howler." He was "the wild red hunter" who protected beasts and inhabited the forests. As Shiva, which means "benign," this god exhibits a wide range of aspects or forms, both gentle and wild: he is the Great Yogi who dwells for vast periods of time in meditation in the Himalaya; he is also the Husband par excellence who makes love to the goddess Parvati for eons at a time; he is the Slayer of Demons; and he is the Cosmic Dancer who dances the destruction and re-creation of the world. Shiva takes such seemingly contradictory natures purposefully, in order to make us question reality.

Many of these forms of Shiva appear in the monumental relief panels adorning the Cave-Temple of Shiva carved in the mid-sixth century on the island of Elephanta off the coast of Bombay in western India. The cave-temple is complex in layout and conception, perhaps to reflect the nature of Shiva. While most temples

9-21. *Eternal Shiva*, rock-cut relief in the Cave-Temple of Shiva at Elephanta. Mid-6th century CE. Height approx. 11' (3.4 m)

have one entrance, this temple offers three—one facing north, one east, and one west. The interior, impressive in its size and grandeur, is designed along two main axes, one running north-south, the other east-west. The three entrances provide the only source of light, and the resulting cross- and back-lighting effects add to the sense of the cave as a place of mysterious, almost confusing complexity. A worshiper seems to be in a world where the usual expectations are absent and is thrown off-balance—fit preparation for a meeting with Shiva, the most unpredictable of the Hindu gods.

Along the east-west axis, large pillars cut from the living rock appear to support the low ceiling and its beams although, as with all architectural elements in a cave-temple, they are not structural (fig. 9-20). The pillars form orderly rows, but the rows are hard to discern within the framework of the cave shape, which is neither square nor longitudinal, but a combination of overlapping mandalas that create a symmetric yet irregular space. The pillars are an important aesthetic component of the cave. An unadorned, square base rises to nearly half the total height. Above is a circular column, which has a pleasingly curved contour and a billowing "cushion" capital. Both column and capital are delicately **fluted**, adding a surprising refinement to these otherwise sturdy forms. The main focus of the east-west axis is a square **lingam shrine**, shown here at the

center of the illustration. Each of its four entrances is flanked by a pair of colossal standing guardian figures. In the center of the shrine is the lingam, the phallic symbol of Shiva. The lingam represents the presence of Shiva as the unmanifest Formless One, or Brahman. It symbolizes both his erotic nature and his aspect as the Great Yogi who controls his seed. The lingam is synonymous with Shiva and is seen in nearly every Shiva temple and shrine.

The main focus of the north-south axis, in contrast, is a relief on the south wall depicting Shiva in his Subtle Body, the second stage of the threefold emanation. A huge bust of the deity represents his Sadashiva, or Eternal Shiva, aspect (fig. 9-21). Three heads are shown resting upon the broad shoulders of the upper body, but five heads are implied: the fourth in back and the fifth, never depicted, on top. The heads summarize Shiva's fivefold nature as creator (back), protector (left shoulder), destroyer (right shoulder), obscurer (front), and releaser (top). The head in the front depicts Shiva deep in introspection. The massiveness of the broad head, the large eyes barely delineated, and the mouth with its heavy lower lip suggest the serious depths of the god. Lordly and majestic, he easily supports his huge crown, intricately carved with designs and jewels, and the matted, piled-up hair of a yogi. On his left shoulder, his protector nature is depicted as female, with curled hair and a pearl-festooned crown. On his right shoulder, his wrathful, destroyer nature wears a fierce expression, and snakes encircle his neck.

Like the relief panels at the temple to Vishnu in Deogarh (see fig. 9-19), the reliefs at Elephanta are early examples of the Hindu monumental narrative tradition. Measuring 11 feet in height, they are set in recessed niches, one on either side of each of the three entrances and three on the south wall. The panels portray the range of Shiva's powers and some of his different aspects, presented in the context of narratives that help devotees understand his nature. Taken as a whole, the reliefs represent the third stage of emanation, the Gross Body manifestation of Shiva in our world. Indian artists often convey the many aspects or essential nature of a deity through multiple heads or arms. Their gift is to portray these additions with such convincing naturalism that we readily accept their visions. Here, for example, the artist has united three heads onto a single body so skillfully that we still relate to the statue as an essentially human presence.

The third great Hindu deity is Devi, a designation covering many deities who embody the feminine. In general, Devi represents the brilliant power of shakti, a divine energy understood as feminine. Shakti is needed to overcome the demons of our afflictions, such as ignorance and pride. Among the most widely worshiped goddesses are Lakshmi, goddess of wealth and beauty, and Durga, the warrior goddess.

Durga is the essence of the splendid conquering powers of the gods. A large relief at Mamallapuram, near Madras, in southeastern India, depicts Durga in her popular form as the slayer of Mahishasura, the buffalo

9-22. *Durga Mahishasura-mardini (Durga as Slayer of the Buffalo Demon),* rock-cut relief, Mamallapuram, Tamil Nadu, India. Pallava period, c. mid-7th century CE. Granite, height approx. 9' (2.7 m)

demon (fig. 9-22). Triumphantly riding her lion, a symbol of her shakti, the eight-armed Durga battles the demon. His huge figure with its human body and buffalo head is shown lunging to the right, fleeing from her onslaught. His warriors are falling to the ground. Accompanied by energetic, dwarfish warriors, victorious Durga, though smaller in size, sits erect and alert, flashing her weapons. Thus the moods of victory and defeat are clearly distinguished between the left and right sides of the panel. The artist clarifies the drama by focusing our attention on the two principal actors. Surrounding figures play secondary roles that support the main action, adding visual interest and variety.

Stylistically, this and other panels at Mamallapuram represent the final flowering of the Indian monumental relief tradition. Here, as elsewhere, the reliefs portray stories of the gods and goddesses, whose heroic deeds unfold before our eyes. Executed under the dynasty of the Pallavas, which flourished in southern India from the seventh to ninth century CE, this panel also illustrates the gentle, simplified figure style characteristic of Pallava sculpture. Figures tend to be slim and elegant with little ornament, and the rhythms of line and form have a graceful, unifying, and humanizing charm.

9-23. Dharmaraja Ratha, Mamallapuram, Tamil Nadu, India. Pallava period, c. mid-7th century CE

9-24. Kandariya Mahadeva temple, Khajuraho, Madhya Pradesh, India. Chandella dynasty, Early Medieval period, c. 1000 CE

The Early Southern Temple

The coastal city of Mamallapuram was also a major temple site under the Pallavas. Along the shore are many large granite boulders and cliffs, and from these the Pallava stone cutters carved reliefs, halls, and temples. Among the most interesting Pallava creations is a group of temples known as the Five Rathas, which preserve a sequence of early architectural styles. As with other rock-cut temples, the Five Rathas were probably carved in the style of contemporary wood or brick structures that have long since disappeared.

One of this group, the Dharmaraja Ratha, epitomizes the early southern-style temple (fig. 9-23). Though strikingly different in appearance from the northern style, it uses the same symbolism and it, too, is based on a mandala. The temple, square in plan, remains unfinished, and the *garbhagriha* usually found inside was never hollowed out. On the lower portion, only the columns and exterior niches have been carved. The use of a single deity in each niche forecasts the main trend in temple sculpture in the centuries ahead. As the tradition of narrative reliefs began dying out, the stories they told became concentrated in statues of individual deities, which alone suffice to conjure up entire mythological episodes through characteristic poses and a few symbolic objects.

Southern and northern temples are most clearly distinguished by their respective superstructures. The Dharmaraja Ratha does not culminate in the paraboloid of the northern shikhara but in a pyramidal tower called a **vimana**. Each story of the vimana is articulated by a **cornice** and carries a row of miniature shrines. Both shrines and cornices are decorated with a window motif from

which faces peer. The shrines not only serve to demarcate each story but also provide a measure of the loftiness of this palace for a god. Crowning the vimana is a dome-shaped octagonal **capstone** quite different from the amalaka of the northern style.

During the centuries that followed, both northern- and southern-style temples developed into complex, monumental forms, but their basic structure and symbolism remained the same as those we have seen in these simple, early examples at Deogarh and Mamallapuram.

THE EARLY MEDIEVAL PERIOD

During the Early Medieval period, which extends roughly from the mid-seventh to the eleventh century, many small kingdoms and dynasties flourished. Some were relatively long-lived, such as the Pallavas and Cholas in the south and the Palas in the northeast. Though Buddhism remained strong in a few areas—notably under the Palas—it generally declined. On the other hand, the Hindu gods Vishnu, Shiva, and the Goddess (mainly Durga) grew increasingly popular. Local kings rivaled each other in the building of temples to their favored deity, and many complicated and subtle variations of the Hindu temple emerged with astounding rapidity in different regions. By around 1000 CE the Hindu temple had reached unparalleled heights of grandeur and engineering.

The Monumental Northern Temple

The Kandariya Mahadeva, a temple dedicated to Shiva at Khajuraho in central India, was probably built by a ruler of the Chandella dynasty in the late tenth or early

9-25. Rajarajeshvara Temple to Shiva, Thanjavur, Tamil Nadu, India. Chola dynasty, Early Medieval period, 1003–1010 CE

eleventh century (fig. 9-24). Khajuraho was the capital and main temple site for the Chandellas, who constructed more than eighty temples there, about twenty-five of which are well preserved. The Kandariya Mahadeva temple is in the northern style, with a shikhara rising over its *garbhagriha*. Larger, more extensively ornamented, and expanded through the addition of halls on the front and porches to the sides and back, the temple seems at first glance to have little in common with its precursor at Deogarh (see fig. 9-17). Actually, however, the basic elements and their symbolism remain unchanged.

As at Deogarh, the temple rests on a stone terrace that sets off a sacred space from the mundane world. A steep flight of stairs at the front (to the right in the illustration) leads to a series of three halls (distinguished on the outside by three pyramidal roofs) preceding the *garbhagriha*. Called **mandapas**, the halls symbolically represent the Subtle Body stage of the threefold emanation. They serve as spaces for ritual, such as dances performed for the deity, and for the presentation of offerings. The temple is built of stone blocks using only **post-and-lintel construction**. The vault and arch are not used, and thus the interior spaces are not large.

The exterior has a strong sculptural presence, and the total effect is of a massive mountain (again, the "cosmic mountain") composed of ornately carved stone. Rising over the *garbhagriha*, the shikhara is the tallest element of the temple, reaching to a little over 100 feet. The top is crowned by an amalaka, which is rather small on this particular temple.

The shikhara is bolstered by the addition of many smaller shikhara motifs bundled around it. This decorative scheme adds a complex richness to the surface, but it also somewhat obscures the shape of the main shikhara. As a whole the shikhara is rather slender and its upward movement quite swift and impetuous. The roofs of the mandapas contribute to the impression of rapid ascent by growing progressively taller as they near the shikhara.

Despite its apparent complexity, the temple has a clear structure and forms a unified composition. The towers of the superstructure are separated from the lower portion by strong horizontal **moldings** and by the open spaces over the mandapas and porches. The moldings and rows of sculpture adorning the lower part of the temple create a horizontal emphasis that stabilizes the vertical thrust of the superstructure. Three rows of sculpture—some 600 figures—are integrated into the exterior walls. Approximately 3 feet tall and carved in high relief, the sculptures depict gods and goddesses, some in erotic postures. They are thought to express Shiva's divine bliss, the manifestation of his presence within, and the transformation of one to many.

In addition to its horizontal emphasis, the lower portion of the temple is characterized by vertical convex/concave movements created by protruding and receding elements. These impart an impression similar to **engaged columns** and **buttressing** segments, and they account for much of the rich texture of the exterior. The porches, two on each side and one in the back, contribute to the impression of complexity by adding outward expansions to the ground plan, yet their curved bases also reinforce the sweeping vertical movements that unify the entire structure.

The Monumental Southern Temple

The Cholas, who superseded the Pallavas in the mid-ninth century, founded a dynasty that governed most of the far south well into the late thirteenth century. The Chola dynasty reached its peak during the reign of Rajaraja I (ruled 985–1014 CE). As an expression of gratitude for his many victories in battle, Rajaraja built the Rajarajeshvara Temple to Shiva in his capital, Thanjavur (Tanjore). Known alternatively as the Brihadeshvara, this temple is the supreme achievement of the southern style of Hindu architecture (fig. 9-25). The temple stands within a huge, walled compound near the banks of the Kaveri River. Though some smaller shrines dot the compound, the Rajarajeshvara dominates the area.

Clarity of structure combined with a formal balance of parts and refined decor create a majestically powerful structure in the Rajarajeshvara. Rising to an astonishing height of 216 feet, this temple was probably the tallest structure in India in its time. Like the Kandariya Mahadeva temple at Khajuraho, the Rajarajeshvara has a longitudinal axis and greatly expanded dimensions, especially with regard to its superstructure. Typical of the southern style, the mandapa halls at the front of the Rajarajeshvara have flat roofs, as opposed to the pyramidal roofs of the northern style.

The base of the vimana, which houses the *garbhagriha*, rises for two stories, with each story emphatically articulated by a large cornice. The exterior walls are ornamented with niches, each of which holds a single statue, usually depicting a form of Shiva. The clear, regular, and wide spacing of the niches imparts a calm balance and formality to the lower portion of the temple, in marked contrast to the irregular, sloping, concave-convex rhythms of the northern style.

The vimana of the Rajarajeshvara is a towering, four-sided, hollow pyramid that rises for thirteen stories. Each story is decorated with miniature shrines, window motifs, and robust dwarf figures who seem to be holding up the next story. Because these sculptural elements are not large in the overall scale of the vimana, they appear well integrated into the surface and do not obscure the powerful shape. This is quite different from the effect of the

smaller shikhara motifs on the shikhara of the Kandariya Mahadeva temple. Notice also that in the earlier southern style as embodied in the Dharmaraja Ratha (see fig. 9-23), the shrines on the vimana were much larger in proportion to the whole and thus appeared individually nearly as prominent as the vimana's overall shape.

Because the Rajarajeshvara vimana is not obscured by its decorative motifs, its skyward ascent becomes more forceful and aggressive. At the top is an octagonal dome-shaped capstone similar to the one that crowned the earlier southern-style temple. This huge capstone is exactly above, and the same size as, the *garbhagriha* housed thirteen stories below. It thus evokes the presence of the shrine a final time before the point separating the worldly from the cosmic sphere above.

The Bhakti Movement in Art

Throughout the Early Medieval period two major religious movements were taking place that affected Hindu practice and its art: the tantric, or esoteric, and the bhakti, or devotional. Although both movements evolved throughout India, the influence of tantric sects appeared during this period primarily in the art of the north, while the bhakti movements found artistic expression mostly in the south.

The bhakti devotional movement was based on ideas expressed in ancient texts, especially the *Bhagavad Gita*. Bhakti revolves around the ideal relationship between humans and deities. According to bhakti, it is the gods who create maya, or illusion, in which we are all trapped. They also reveal truth to those who truly love them and whose minds are open to them. Rather than focusing on ritual and the performance of dharma according to the Vedas, bhakti stresses an intimate, personal, and loving relation with god, and the complete devotion and giving up of oneself to god. Inspired and influenced by bhakti, southern artists produced some of India's greatest and most humanistic works, as revealed in the few remaining paintings and in the famous bronze works of sculpture.

Rajaraja's building of the Rajarajeshvara was in part a reflection of the fervent movement of Shiva bhakti that had already reached its peak by that time. The corridors of the circumambulatory passages around its *garbhagriha* were originally adorned with frescoes. Overpainted in later times, they were only recently rediscovered. One painting apparently depicts the ruler Rajaraja himself, not as a warrior or majestic king on his throne, but as a simple mendicant humbly standing behind his religious teacher (fig. 9-26). With his white beard and dark skin, the aged teacher contrasts with the youthful, bronze-skinned king. The position of the two suggests that the saintly teacher, who in the devotee's or bhakta's view is equated with god, is both closely and yet respectfully treated by the king. Both figures openly allude to their devotion to Shiva by holding a small flower as an offering, and both emulate Shiva in their appearance by wearing their hair in the "ascetic locks" of Shiva in his Great Yogi aspect.

9-26. *Rajaraja I and His Teacher*, detail of a wall painting in the Rajarajeshvara Temple to Shiva. Chola dynasty, Early Medieval period,
c. 1010 CE

The portrayal does not represent individuals so much as a contrast of types: the old and the youthful, the teacher and the devotee, the saint and the king—the highest religious and worldly models, respectively—united as followers of Shiva. Line is the essence of the painting. With strength and grace, the even, skillfully executed line defines the boldly simple forms and features. There is no excessive detail, very little shading, and no highlighting such as we saw in the Gupta paintings at Ajanta (see fig. 9-16). A cool, sedate calm infuses the monumental figures, but the power of line also invigorates them with a sense of strength and inner life.

Perhaps no sculpture is more representative of Chola bronzes than the famous statue of Shiva Nataraja, or Dancing Shiva (fig. 9-27). The dance of Shiva is a dance of cosmic proportions, signifying the cycle of death and rebirth of the universe; it is also a dance for each individual, signifying the liberation of the believer through

Shiva's compassion. In the iconography of the Nataraja, perfected over the centuries, this sculpture shows Shiva with four arms dancing on the prostrate body of Apas-maru, a dwarf figure who symbolizes "becoming" and whom Shiva controls. Shiva's extended left hand holds a ball of fire; a circle of fire, now lost, formerly ringed the god as well. The fire is emblematic of the destruction of samsara and the physical universe as well as the destruction of maya and our ego-centered concepts. Shiva's back right hand holds a drum; its beat represents the irrevocable rhythms of creation and destruction, birth and death. His front right arm gestures the "have no fear" mudra (see "Mudras," page 380). The front left arm, gracefully stretched across his body with the hand pointing to his raised foot, signifies the promise of liberation.

The artist has rendered the complex pose with great clarity. The central axis of the figure, which aligns with the nose, navel, and insole of the weight-bearing foot,

9-27. *Nataraja: Siva as King of Dance*. South India, Chola dynasty, 11th century. Bronze, H. 43⁷/₈" (111.5 cm). The Cleveland Museum of Art
© The Cleveland Museum of Art, 1998, Purchase from the J. H. Wade Fund, 1930.331

The fervent religious devotion of the bhakti movement was fueled in no small part by the sublime writings of a series of poet-saints who lived in the south of India. One of these poet-saints, Appar, who lived from the late sixth to mid-seventh century, wrote this tender, personal vision of the Shiva Nataraja. The ash the poem refers to is one of many symbols associated with the deity. In penance for having lopped off one of the five heads of Brahma, the first created being, Shiva smeared his body with ashes and went about as a beggar.

> If you could see
> the arch of his brow,
> the budding smile
> on lips red as the kovvai fruit,
> cool matted hair,
> the milk-white ash on coral skin,
> and the sweet golden foot
> raised up in dance,
> then even human birth on this wide earth
> would become a thing worth having.

(Translated by Indira Vishvanathan Peterson)

maintains the center of balance and equilibrium while the remaining limbs extend asymmetrically far to each side. Shiva wears a short loincloth, a ribbon tied above his waist, and delicately tooled ornaments. The scant clothing reveals the beauty of his perfected form with its broad shoulders tapering to a supple waist. The jewelry is restrained and the detail does not detract from the unity of the body.

The deity does not appear self-absorbed and introspective as he did in the Eternal Shiva relief at Elephanta (see fig. 9-21). Instead, he turns to face the viewer while openly extending his body to the sides. He appears lordly and aloof, yet fully aware of his benevolent role as he generously displays himself for the devotee. Like the Sarnath Gupta Buddha (see fig. 9-15), the Chola Nataraja presents a characteristically Indian synthesis of the godly and the human, this time expressing the bhakti belief in the importance of an intimate and personal rela-

tionship with a lordly god through whose compassion one is saved. The earlier Hindu emphasis on ritual and the depiction of the heroic feats of the gods, though not denied, is subsumed into the all-encompassing, humanizing factor of grace.

The bhakti movement spread during the ensuing Late Medieval period into North India. This period, however, also witnessed the incursion of a new religious culture into the subcontinent, Islam. From the tenth century on, the passes at the northwest again brought invaders, this time in the form of various Turkic, Persian, and Afghan Islamic factions. Islam brought with it a rich artistic tradition of its own. Yet just as new religious forms eventually evolved from Islam's long and complex interaction with the peoples of the subcontinent, so too did uniquely Indian forms of Islamic art arise, adding yet another dimension to India's artistic heritage.

Deity image from a *cong*
before 3000 BCE

▲ NEOLITHIC c. 5000–2000 BCE

CHAPTER 10

Chinese Art before 1280

1000   1 CE   1000   1300 CE

Fang ding
c. 12th century

Soldiers from Qin
mausoleum
c. 210 BCE

Model of Han house
1st century CE

Rock-cut Buddha,
Shanxi c. 460

Ceramic camel
c. 750

Guan Ware
vase
13th century

BRONZE AGE c. 1700–221

QIN c. 221–206 BCE

HAN c. 206 BCE–220 CE

SIX DYNASTIES
c. 220–579

SUI DYNASTY
c. 589–617

TANG DYNASTY c. 618–907

SONG DYNASTY
c. 960–1279

MONGOLIA

XINJIANG

SILK ROAD

SILK ROAD   Dunhuang

MANCHURIA

GOBI DESERT   GREAT WALL

INNER MONGOLIA

GREAT WALL

Beijing

Yungang   Datong   Mancheng
Wutaishan
(Mount Wutai)   HEBEI

Yellow River   SHANXI   SHANDONG

Houjiazhuang   KOREA

CHINA   Anyang   *Yellow
Sea*

GANSU   Kaifeng   Jiaxiang

Jiangzhai   Lintong   JAPAN

Banpo   Xi'an   HENAN

SHAANXI

QINLING
MOUNTAINS

TIBET   Suixian   Shanghai   *Hangzhou
Bay*

Yangzi River   Hangzhou   Yuyao

HIMALAYA MOUNTAINS   ZHEJIANG

Changsha   Fanshan

MYANMAR   Mawangdui

HUNAN   Taipei

TAIWAN

Xi River   Canton

VIETNAM   Hong Kong

*South China
Sea*

LAOS

0   500 miles
0   500 kilometers

10-1.   Soldiers, from the mausoleum of the first emperor of Qin, Lintong, Shaanxi. Qin dynasty, c. 210 BCE. Earthenware, lifesize

As long as anyone could remember, the huge mound in China's Shaanxi province had been part of the landscape. No one dreamed that an astonishing treasure lay beneath the surface until one day in 1974 when peasants digging a well accidentally brought to light the first hint of the riches. When archeologists began to excavate the mound, they were stunned by what they found: a vast underground army of more than 7,000 lifesize clay soldiers and horses standing in military formation, facing east, ready for battle (fig. 10-1). Originally painted in vivid colors, they emerged from the earth a ghostly gray. For more than 2,000 years, while the tumultuous history of China unfolded overhead, they had guarded the tomb of Emperor Shihuangdi, the ruthless ruler who first united the states of China into an empire.

In 1990 a road-building crew in central China accidentally uncovered an even richer vault, containing perhaps tens of thousands of terra-cotta figures. Although excavations there are barely under way, the artifacts so far uncovered are exceptional both in artistic quality and in what they tell us about life—and death—during the Han dynasty, about 100 years later than the Qin find.

Archeology is a relatively young discipline in China. Only since the 1920s have scholars methodically dug into the layers of history that lie buried at thousands of sites across the country. Yet in that short period so much has been unearthed that ancient Chinese history has been rewritten many times.

THE MIDDLE KINGDOM

Among the cultures of the world, China is distinguished by its long, uninterrupted development, now traced back some 8,000 years. From Qin, pronounced "chin," comes our name for the country the Chinese call the Middle Kingdom, the country in the center of the world. Modern China occupies a large landmass in the center of Asia, covering an area slightly larger than the continental United States. Within its borders lives one-fifth of the human race.

The historical and cultural heart of China—sometimes called Inner China—is the land watered by its three great rivers, the Yellow, the Yangzi, and the Xi. The Qinling Mountains divide Inner China into north and south, regions with strikingly different climates, cultures, and historical fates. In the south the Yangzi River flows through lush green hills to the fertile plains of the delta. Along the southern coastline, rich with natural harbors, arose China's port cities, the focus of a vast maritime trading network. The Yellow River, nicknamed "China's Sorrow" because of its disastrous floods, winds through the north. The north country is a dry land of steppe and desert, hot in the summer and lashed by cold winds in the winter. Over its vast and vulnerable frontier have come the nomadic invaders that are a recurring theme in Chinese history, as well as caravans and emissaries from Central Asia, India, Persia, and, eventually, Europe.

NEOLITHIC CULTURES

Early archeological evidence led scholars to believe that agriculture, the cornerstone technology of the Neolithic period, made its way to China from the ancient Near East. More recent findings, however, have shown that agriculture based on rice and millet arose independently in East Asia before 5000 BCE and that knowledge of Near Eastern grains followed some 2,000 years later. One of the clearest signs of Neolithic culture in China is the vigorous emergence of towns and cities. At Jiangzhai, near modern Xi'an, for example, the foundations of more than 100 dwellings have been discovered surrounding the remains of a community center, a cemetery, and a kiln. Dated to about 4000 BCE, the ruins point to the existence of a highly developed early society. Elsewhere, the foundations of the earliest known palace have been uncovered and dated to about 2000 BCE.

PARALLELS

Years	Period	China	World
c. 5000–2000 BCE	Neolithic	Beginning of agriculture; Painted Pottery cultures	c. 5000–2000 BCE Beginning of agriculture in North Africa; potter's wheel (Egypt); Great Pyramids at Giza (Egypt); Indus Valley civilization (India)
c. 1700–221 BCE	Bronze Age	Legendary (?) Xia dynasty; Shang dynasty; development of writing; bronze casting; Zhou dynasty; birth of Confucius, Laozi, Mozi; iron tools and weapons	c. 2000–1000 BCE Minoan and Mycenaean cultures (Aegean); *Stela of Hammurabi* (Babylonia); development of metallurgy (Near East); Olmec civilization (Mesoamerica)
c. 221–206 BCE	Qin dynasty	Unification of China; centralized bureaucracy; standardized coinage; standardized written language; clay figures; Great Wall	c. 1000 BCE–500 CE First Olympian Games (Greece); black-figure and red-figure vase painting (Greece); birth of Siddhartha Gautama, founder of Buddhism (Nepal); Parthenon (Greece); Great Stupa at Sanchi (India); crucifixion of Jesus (Jerusalem); Colosseum (Italy); first Gupta dynasty (India); first Hindu temples (India)
c. 206 BCE–220 CE	Han dynasty	Silk Road; Daoism; Confucianism made state philosophy; Buddhism introduced	
c. 220–579 CE	Six Dynasties	Nomad invasions; growth of Buddhism; rock-cut caves; monumental buddhas	c. 500–1300 CE Birth of Muhammad, founder of Islam (Arabia); Muslim conquests; Hagia Sophia (Turkey); separation of Eastern and Western Christian Churches; the Crusades; Spanish Inquisition
c. 589–617 CE	Sui dynasty	Reunification of China; Pure Land Buddhism grows; Daoism ascendant	
c. 618–907 CE	Tang dynasty	Repression of Buddhism; figure painting; Nanchan Temple	
c. 960–1279 CE	Song dynasty	Neo-Confucianism; landscape painting; Guan Ware; invasion by Kublai Khan's Mongols	

Painted Pottery

In China as elsewhere distinctive forms of Neolithic pottery identify different cultures. One of the most interesting objects thus far recovered is a shallow red bowl with a turned-out rim (fig. 10-2). Found in the village of Banpo near present-day Xi'an, it was crafted sometime between 5000 and 3000 BCE. The bowl is an artifact of the Yangshao culture, one of the most important of the so-called Painted Pottery cultures of Neolithic China. Although the potter's wheel had not yet been developed, the bowl is perfectly round and its surfaces are highly polished, bearing witness to a distinctly advanced technology. The decorations are especially intriguing. The marks on the rim may be among the earliest evidence of the beginnings of writing in China, which had been fully developed by the time the first definitive examples appeared in the later Bronze Age.

Inside the bowl, a pair of stylized fish suggest that fishing and hunting were important activities for the villagers. The image between the fish represents a human face with four more fish, one on each side. Although there is no certain interpretation of the image, it probably served some magical purpose. Perhaps it is a depic-

10-2. Bowl, from Banpo, near Xi'an, Shaanxi. Neolithic period, Yangshao culture, 5000–3000 BCE. Painted pottery, height 7" (17.8 cm). Banpo Museum

Schematic drawing of a *cong*

tion of an ancestral figure who could assure an abundant catch, for worship of ancestors and nature spirits was a fundamental element of later Chinese beliefs.

Beyond the Yellow River Valley

Banpo lies near the great bend in the Yellow River, in the area traditionally regarded as the cradle of Chinese civilization—though archeological finds have revealed that Neolithic cultures arose over a far broader area. Recent excavations in sites near the Hangzhou Bay, in the southeastern coastal region, have turned up half-human, half-animal images more than 5,000 years old (fig. 10-3). Large, round eyes linked by a bar like the frames of eyeglasses, a flat nose, and a rectangular mouth protrude slightly from the background pattern of wirelike lines. Above the forehead, a second, smaller face grimaces from under a huge headdress. The image is one of eight carved in **low relief** on the outside of a large jade *cong*, an object resembling a cylindrical tube encased in a rectangular block. This *cong* must have been an object of great importance, for it was found near the head of a person buried in a large tomb at the top of a mound that served as an altar. Hundreds of jade objects have been recovered from this mound, which measures about 66 feet square and rises in three levels.

The intricacy of the carving shows the technical sophistication of this jade-working culture, named the Liangzhu, which seems to have emerged around 4000 BCE. Jade, cherished by the Chinese throughout their history, is extremely hard and is difficult to carve. Liangzhu artists must have used sand as an abrasive to slowly grind the stone down, but we can only wonder at how they produced such fine work.

The meaning of the masklike image is open to interpretation. Its combination of human and animal features seems to show how the ancient Chinese imagined supernatural beings, either deities or dead ancestors. Strikingly similar masks later formed the primary deco-

10-3. Image of a deity, detail from a *cong* recovered from Tomb 12, Fanshan, Yuyao, Zhejiang. Neolithic period, Liangzhu culture, before 3000 BCE. Jade, 3 1/2 x 6 7/8" (8.8 x 17.5 cm). Zhejiang Provincial Museum, Hangzhou

The *cong* is one of the most prevalent and mysterious of early Chinese jade shapes. Originating in the Neolithic era, it continued to play a prominent role in burials through the Shang and Zhou dynasties. Many scholars believe that the *cong* was connected with shamanism, the practice of contacting the spirit world. They suggest that the circle symbolized heaven; the square, earth; and the hollow, the axis connecting these two realms. The animals found carved on many *cong* may have portrayed the shaman's helpers or alter egos.

rative motif of Bronze Age ritual objects. Still later, Chinese historians began referring to the ancient motif as **taotie**, but its original meaning had already been lost. The jade carving here seems to be a forerunner of this most central and mysterious image. It suggests that eventually the various Neolithic cultures of China merged to form a single culture despite their separate origins thousands of miles apart.

BRONZE AGE CHINA

China entered its Bronze Age in the second millennium BCE. As with agriculture, scholars at first theorized that the technology had been imported from the Near East. It is now clear, however, that bronze

1400 BCE

5000 BCE   1300 CE

TECHNIQUE

PIECE-MOLD CASTING

The early **piece-mold technique** for bronze casting is more complex than the **lost-wax** process developed in the ancient Mediterranean and Near East. Although we do not know the exact steps ancient Chinese artists followed, we can deduce the general procedure for casting a simple vessel.

First, a model of the bronze-to-be was made of clay and dried. To create the mold, damp clay was pressed onto the model; after the clay dried, it was cut away in pieces, which were keyed for later reassembly and then fired. The model itself was shaved down to serve as the core for the mold. The pieces of the mold were reassembled around the core and held in place by bronze spacers, which locked the core in position and ensured an even casting space. The reassembled mold was then covered with another layer of clay, and a spue, or pouring duct, was cut into the clay to receive the molten metal. A riser duct may also have been cut to allow the hot gases to escape. Molten bronze was then poured into the mold. When the metal had cooled, the mold was broken apart with a hammer. Finally, the vessel could be burnished—a long process that involved scouring the surface with increasingly fine abrasives.

casting using the **piece-mold casting** technique arose independently in China, where it was brought to an unparalleled level of excellence.

Shang Dynasty

Traditional Chinese histories tell of three Bronze Age dynasties: the Xia, the Shang, and the Zhou. Modern scholars had tended to dismiss the Xia and Shang as legendary, but recent archeological discoveries have now fully established the historical existence of the Shang (c. 1700–1100 BCE) and point strongly to the historical existence of the Xia as well.

Shang kings ruled from a succession of capitals in the Yellow River Valley, where archeologists have found walled cities, palaces, and vast royal tombs. Their state was surrounded by numerous other states—some rivals, others clients—and their culture spread widely. Society seems to have been highly stratified, with a ruling group that had the bronze technology needed to make weapons. They maintained their authority in part by claiming power as shamans, intermediaries between the supernatural and human realms. The chief Shang deity, Shangdi, may have been a sort of Great Ancestor. Nature and fertility spirits were also honored, and regular sacrifices were believed necessary to keep the spirits of dead ancestors alive so that they might help the living.

Shang shamans communicated with the supernatural world through **oracle** bones. An animal bone or piece of tortoiseshell was inscribed with a question and heated until it cracked. Then a shaman interpreted the crack as an answer. Oracle bones, many of which have been recovered and deciphered, contain the earliest known form of Chinese writing, a script fully recognizable as the ancestor of the system still in use today (see "Chinese Characters," below).

CHINESE CHARACTERS

Each word in Chinese is represented by its own unique picture, called a character or **calligraph**. Some characters originated as **pictographs**, images that mean what they depict. Writing reforms over the centuries have often disguised the resemblance, but if we place modern characters next to their oracle-bone ancestors, the picture comes back into focus:

	water	horse	moon	child	tree	mountain
ancient	𝍖	𝍖	𝍖	𝍖	𝍖	𝍖
modern	水	馬	月	子	木	山

Other characters are **ideographs**, pictures that represent abstract concepts or ideas:

sun + moon = bright

日 月 明

woman + child = good

女 子 好

Most characters were formed by combining a radical, which gives the field of meaning, with a phonetic, which originally hinted at pronunciation. For example, words that have to do with water have the character for "water" 水 abbreviated to three strokes 氵 as their radical. Thus "to bathe" 沐, pronounced *mu*, consists of the water radical and the phonetic 木, which by itself means "tree" and is also pronounced *mu*. Here are other "water" characters. Notice that the connection to water is not always literal.

river sea weep pure, clear extinguish, destroy

河 海 泣 清 滅

These phonetic borrowings took place centuries ago. Many words have shifted in pronunciation, and for this and other reasons there is no way to tell how a character is pronounced or what it means just by looking at it. While at first this may seem like a disadvantage, in the case of Chinese it is actually a strength. Spoken Chinese has many dialects. Some are so far apart in sound as to be virtually different languages. But while speakers of different dialects cannot understand each other, they can still communicate through writing, for no matter how they say a word, they write it with the same character. Writing has thus played an important role in maintaining the unity of Chinese civilization through the centuries.

10-4. *Fang ding*, from Tomb 1004, Houjiazhuang, Anyang, Henan. Shang dynasty, Anyang period, c. 12th century BCE. Bronze, height 24½" (62.2 cm). Academia Sinica, Taipei, Taiwan

Ritual Bronzes. Shang tombs reveal a warrior culture of great splendor and violence. Many humans and animals were sacrificed to accompany the deceased. In one tomb, for example, chariots were found with the skeletons of their horses and drivers; in another, dozens of human skeletons lined the approaches to the central burial chamber. Above all, the tombs contain thousands of jade, ivory, and lacquer objects, gold and silver ornaments, and bronze vessels. The enormous scale of Shang burials illustrates the great wealth of the civilization and the power of a ruling class able to consign such great quantities of treasure to the earth, as well as reverence for the dead in this culture.

Bronze vessels are the most admired and studied of Shang artifacts. Like oracle bones and jade objects, they were connected with shamanistic practices, serving as containers for ritual offerings of food and wine. A basic repertoire of about thirty shapes evolved. Some shapes clearly derive from earlier pottery forms, others seem to reproduce wooden containers, while still others are purely sculptural and take the form of fantastic composite animals.

The illustrated bronze *fang ding*, a square vessel with four legs, is one of hundreds of vessels recovered from the royal tombs near the last of the Shang capitals, Yin, present-day Anyang (fig. 10-4). Weighing more than 240 pounds, it is one of the largest Shang bronzes ever recovered. In typical Shang style its surface is decorated with a complex array of images based on animal forms. The taotie, usually so prominent, does not appear. Instead, a large deer's head adorns the center of each side, and images of deer are repeated on all four legs. The rest of the surface is filled with images resembling birds, dragons, and other fantastic creatures. Such images seem to be related to the hunting life of the Shang,

but their deeper significance is unknown. Sometimes strange, sometimes fearsome, Shang creatures seem always to have a sense of mystery, evoking the Shang attitude toward the supernatural world.

Zhou Dynasty

Around 1100 BCE, the Shang were conquered by the Zhou, from western China. During the Zhou dynasty (1100–221 BCE), a feudal society developed, with nobles related to the king ruling over numerous small states. (Zhou nobility are customarily ranked in English by such titles as duke and marquis.) The supreme deity became known as Tian, or Heaven, and the king ruled as the Son of Heaven. Heaven remained the personal cult of China's sovereigns until the end of imperial rule in the early twentieth century.

The first 300 years of this longest Chinese dynasty were generally stable and peaceful. In 771 BCE, however, the Zhou suffered defeat at the hands of a nomadic tribe in the west. Although they quickly established a new capital to the east, their authority had been crippled, and the later Eastern Zhou period was a troubled one. States grew increasingly independent, giving the Zhou kings merely nominal allegiance. Smaller states were swallowed up by their larger neighbors. During the time historians call the Spring and Autumn period (770–476 BCE), ten or twelve states, later reduced to seven, emerged as powers. During the ensuing Warring States period (402–221 BCE), intrigue, treachery, and increasingly ruthless warfare became routine.

Against this background of constant social unrest, China's great philosophers arose, such thinkers as Confucius, Laozi, and Mozi. Traditional histories speak of China's "one hundred schools" of philosophy, indicating a shift of focus from the supernatural to the human

10-5.   Set of sixty-five bells, from the tomb of Marquis Yi of Zeng, Suixian, Hubei. Zhou dynasty,
433 BCE. Bronze, with bronze and timber frame; frame height 9' (2.74 m), length 25' (7.62 m).
Hubei Provincial Museum, Wuhan

world. Nevertheless, elaborate burials on an even larger scale reflected the continuation of traditional beliefs.

Ritual bronze objects continued to play an important role during the Zhou dynasty, and new forms developed. One of the most spectacular recent discoveries is a carillon of sixty-five bronze bells arranged in a formation 25 feet long (fig. 10-5), found in the tomb of Marquis Yi of the state of Zeng. Each bell is precisely calibrated to sound two tones—one when struck at the center, another when struck nearer the rim. The bells are arranged in scale patterns in a variety of registers, and several musicians would have moved around the carillon, striking the bells in the appointed order.

Music may well have played a part in rituals for communicating with the supernatural, for the taotie typically appears on the front and back of each bell. The image is now much more intricate and stylized, partly in response to the refinement available with the lost-wax process, which had replaced the older piece-mold technique. On the coffin of the marquis are painted guardian warriors with half-human, half-animal attributes. The marquis, who died in 433 BCE, must have been a great lover of music, for among the more than 15,000 objects recovered from his tomb were many musical instruments. Zeng was one of the smallest and shortest-lived states of the Eastern Zhou, but the contents of this tomb, in quantity and quality, attest to the high level of its culture.

THE CHINESE EMPIRE: QIN DYNASTY

Toward the middle of the third century BCE, the state of Qin launched military campaigns that led to its triumph over the other states by 221 BCE. For the first time in its history, China was united under a single ruler. This first emperor of Qin, Shihuangdi, a man of exceptional ability, power, and ruthlessness, was fearful of both assassination and rebellion. Throughout his life, he sought ways to attain immortality. Even before uniting China, he began his own **mausoleum** at Lintong, in Shaanxi province. This project continued throughout his life and after his death, until rebellion abruptly ended the dynasty in 206 BCE. Since that time, the mound over the mausoleum has always been visible, but not until its accidental discovery in 1974 was the army of clay soldiers and horses even imagined (see fig. 10-1). Modeled from clay and then fired, the figures claim a prominent place in the great tradition of Chinese ceramic art. Individualized faces and meticulously rendered uniforms and armor demonstrate the sculptors' skill. Literary sources suggest that the tomb itself, which has not yet been opened, reproduces the world as it was known to the Qin, with stars overhead and rivers and mountains below. Thus did the tomb's architects try literally to ensure that the underworld—the world of souls and spirits—would be as good as the human world.

Qin rule was harsh and repressive. Laws were based on a totalitarian philosophy called legalism, and all other philosophies were banned, their scholars executed, and their books burned. Yet the Qin also established the mechanisms of centralized bureaucracy that molded China both politically and culturally into a single entity. Under the Qin, the country was divided into provinces and prefectures, the writing system and coinage were standardized, highways were built to link different parts of the country with the capital, and battlements on the northern frontier were connected to form the Great Wall. China's rulers to the present day have followed the administrative framework first laid down by the Qin.

HAN DYNASTY

The commander who overthrew the Qin became the next emperor and founded the Han dynasty (206 BCE–220 CE). During this period the Chinese enjoyed a peaceful, prosperous, and stable life. Borders were extended and secured, and Chinese control over strategic stretches of Central Asia led to the opening of the Silk Road, a land route that linked China by trade all the way to Rome (see "The Silk Road," opposite).

The early Han dynasty marks the twilight of China's so-called mythocentric age, when people believed in a close relationship between the human and supernatural worlds, reflected in all the art we have looked at so far. From this time comes one of the most valuable works in Chinese art, a **T**-shaped silk banner that summarizes this early worldview (fig. 10-6). Found in the tomb of a noblewoman on the outskirts of present-day Changsha, the

THE SILK ROAD

At its height, in the second century CE, the Silk Road was the longest road in the world, a 5,000-mile network of caravan routes from the Han capital of Luoyang on the Yellow River to Rome. The Western market for Chinese luxury goods such as silk and lacquer seemed limitless. For these goods, Westerners paid in gold and silver, for the West produced nothing that China desired in trade.

The journey began at the Jade Gate (Yumen), at the westernmost end of the Great Wall, where Chinese merchants turned their goods over to Central Asian traders. Goods would change hands many more times before reaching the Mediterranean. Caravans headed first for the desert oasis of Dunhuang. Here northern and southern routes diverged to skirt the vast Taklamakan Desert. At Khotan, travelers on the southern route could turn off toward a mountain pass into Kashmir, in northern India. Or they could continue on, meeting up with the northern route at Kashgar, on the western border of the Taklamakan, before proceeding over the Pamir Mountains into present-day Afghanistan. There, travelers could turn off into the Kushan Empire that stretched down into India, or they could continue on west through present-day Uzbekistan, Iran, and Iraq, arriving finally at Antioch, in Syria, on the coast of the Mediterranean. From there, land and sea routes led on to Rome.

Sections of the Silk Road were used throughout history by traders, travelers, conquerors, emissaries, pilgrims, missionaries, explorers, and adventurers. But only twice was the entire length of it open, with relatively safe passage likely from end to end. The first time was during the days of the Han dynasty and the Roman Empire. The second was during the thirteenth and fourteenth centuries, when the route lay within the borders of the vast Mongol Empire.

10-6. Painted banner, from the tomb of the wife of the Marquis of Dai, Mawangdui, Changsha, Hunan. Han dynasty, c. 160 BCE. Colors on silk, height 6'8½" (2.05 m). Hunan Provincial Museum, Changsha

DAOISM

Daoism is a kind of nature mysticism that brings together many ancient Chinese ideas regarding humankind and the universe. One of its first philosophers is said to have been a contemporary of Confucius (551–479 BCE) named Laozi, who is credited with writing a slim volume called the *Daodejing*, or *The Way and Its Power*. Later, a philosopher name Zhuangzi (369–286 BCE) took up many of the same ideas in a book that is known simply by his name, *Zhuangzi*. Together the two texts formed a body of ideas that crystallized into a school of thought during the Han period.

A *dao* is a way or path. The *Dao* is the Ultimate Way, the Way of the universe. The Way cannot be named or described, but it can be hinted at. It is like water. Nothing is more flexible and yielding, yet water can wear down the hardest stone. Water flows downward, seeking the lowest ground. Similarly, a Daoist sage seeks a quiet life, humble and hidden, unconcerned with worldly success. The Way is great precisely because it is small. In fact, it is nothing, yet nothing turns out to be essential (cited in Cleary, page 14):

> When the potter's wheel makes a pot
> the use of the pot
> is precisely where there is nothing.

To recover the Way, we must unlearn. We must return to a state of nature. To follow the Way, we must practice *wu wei*, or nondoing. "Strive for non-striving," advises the *Daodejing*.

All our attempts at asserting our egos, at making things happen, are like swimming against a current and thus ultimately futile, even harmful. If we let the current carry us, however, we will travel far. Similarly, a life that follows the Way will be a life of pure effectiveness, accomplishing much with little effort.

It is often said that the Chinese are Confucians in public and Daoists in private, and the two approaches do seem to balance each other. Confucianism is a rational political philosophy that emphasizes morality, conformity, duty, and self-discipline. Daoism is an intuitive philosophy that emphasizes individualism, nonconformity, and a return to nature. If a Confucian education molded scholars outwardly into responsible, ethical officials, Daoism provided some breathing room for the artist and poet inside.

banner dates from the second century BCE and is painted with scenes representing the three levels of the universe: heaven, earth, and the underworld.

The heavenly realm is shown at the top, in the crossbar of the **T**. In the upper right corner is the sun, inhabited by a mythical crow; in the upper left, a mythical toad stands on a crescent moon. Between them is a primordial deity shown as a man with a long serpent's tail—a Han imagining of the Great Ancestor. Dragons and other celestial creatures swarm below.

A gate, indicated by two upside-down **T**s and guarded by two seated figures, stands where the horizontal of heaven meets the banner's long, vertical stem. Two intertwined dragons loop through a circular jade piece known as a *bi*, itself usually a symbol of heaven, dividing this vertical segment into two areas. The portion above the *bi* represents the earthly realm. Here, the deceased woman and her three attendants stand on a platform while two kneeling figures offer gifts. The lower portion represents the underworld. Silk draperies and a stone chime hanging from the *bi* form a canopy for the platform below. Like the bronze bells we saw earlier, stone chimes were ceremonial instruments dating from Zhou times. On the platform, ritual bronze vessels contain food and wine for the deceased, just as they did in Shang tombs. The squat, muscular man holding up the platform stands in turn on a pair of fish whose bodies form another *bi*. The fish and the other strange creatures in this section are inhabitants of the underworld.

Daoism and Confucianism

The Han dynasty marked not only the end of the mythocentric age but also the beginning of a new age. During this dynasty, Daoism and Confucianism, two of the many philosophies formulated during the troubled times of the Eastern Zhou, became central in Chinese thought. Their influence since then has been continuous and fundamental.

Daoism emphasizes the close relationship between humans and nature. It is concerned with bringing the individual life into harmony with the *Dao*, or Way, of the universe (see "Daoism," above). For some a secular, philosophical path, Daoism on a popular level developed into an organized religion, absorbing many traditional folk practices such as shamanism and the search for immortality.

Immortality was as intriguing to Han rulers as it had been to the first emperor of Qin. Daoist adepts experimented endlessly with diet, physical exercise, and other techniques in the belief that immortal life could be achieved on earth. A popular Daoist legend told of the Isles of the Immortals in the Eastern Sea, depicted on a bronze incense burner from the tomb of Prince Liu Sheng, who died in 113 BCE (fig. 10-7). Around the bowl, gold **inlay** outlines the stylized waves of the sea. Above them rises the mountainous island, busy with birds, animals, and people who had discovered the secret of immortality. Technically, this exquisite piece represents the ultimate development of the long tradition of bronze casting in China.

Confucianism and the State

In contrast to the metaphysical focus of Daoism, Confucianism is concerned with the human world, and its goal is the attainment of peace. To this end, it proposes an ethical system based on correct relationships among people. Beginning with self-discipline in the individual, Confucianism goes on to achieve correct relationships with the family, including ancestors, then, in ever-widening circles, with friends and others all the way up to the emperor (see "Confucius and Confucianism," opposite).

10-7. Incense burner, from the tomb of Prince Liu Sheng, Mancheng, Hebei. Han dynasty, 113 BCE. Bronze with gold inlay, height 10¼" (26 cm). Hebei Provincial Museum, Shijiazhuang

CONFUCIUS AND CONFUCIANISM

Confucius was born in 551 BCE in the state of Lu, roughly present-day Shandong province, into a declining aristocratic family. While still in his teens he set his heart on becoming a scholar; by his early twenties he had begun to teach.

By Confucius's lifetime, warfare for supremacy among the various states of China had begun, and the traditional social fabric seemed to be breaking down. Looking back to the early Zhou dynasty as a sort of golden age, Confucius thought about how a just and harmonious society could again emerge. For many years he sought a ruler who would put his ideas into effect, but to no avail. Frustrated, he spent his final years teaching. After his death in 479 BCE, his sayings were collected by his disciples and their followers into a book known in English as the *Analects*, which is the only record of his words.

At the heart of Confucian thought is the concept of *ren*, or human-heartedness. *Ren* emphasizes morality and empathy as the basic standards for all human interaction. The virtue of *ren* is most fully realized in the Confucian ideal of the *junzi*, or gentleman. Originally indicating noble birth, the term was redirected to mean one who through education and self-cultivation had become a superior person, right-thinking and right-acting in all situations. A *junzi* is the opposite of a petty or small-minded person. His characteristics include moderation, inner integrity, self-control, loyalty, reciprocity, and altruism. His primary concern is justice.

Together with human-heartedness and justice, Confucius emphasized *li*, or etiquette. *Li* includes scrupulous everyday manners as well as ritual, ceremony, protocol—all of the formalities of social interaction. Such forms, Confucius felt, choreographed life so that an entire society moved in harmony. *Ren* and *li* operate in the realm of the Five Constant Relationships that define Confucian society: parent and child, husband and wife, elder sibling and younger sibling, elder friend and younger friend, ruler and subject. Deference to age is clearly built into this view, as is the deference to authority that made Confucianism popular with emperors. Yet responsibilities flow the other way as well: the duty of a ruler is to earn the loyalty of subjects, of a husband to earn the respect of his wife, of age to guide youth wisely.

10-8. Detail from a rubbing of a relief in the Wu family shrine (Wuliangci), Jiaxiang, Shandong. Han dynasty, 151 CE. Stone, 27½ x 66½" (70 x 169 cm)

Emphasis on social order and respect for authority made Confucianism especially attractive to Han rulers, who were eager to distance themselves from the disastrous legalism of the Qin. The Han emperor Wu (ruled 141–87 BCE) made Confucianism the official imperial philosophy, and it remained the state ideology of China for more than 2,000 years, until the end of imperial rule in the twentieth century. Once institutionalized, Confucianism took on so many rituals that it too eventually assumed the form and force of a religion. Han philosophers contributed to this process by infusing Confucianism with traditional Chinese cosmology. They emphasized the Zhou idea, taken up by Confucius, that the emperor ruled by the mandate of heaven. Heaven itself was reconceived more abstractly as the moral force underlying the universe. Thus the moral system of Confucian society became a reflection of the universal order.

Confucian subjects turn up frequently in Han art. Among the most famous examples are the reliefs from the Wu family shrines built in 151 CE in Jiaxiang. Carved and engraved in low relief on stone slabs, the scenes were meant to teach such basic Confucian themes as respect for the emperor, filial piety, and wifely devotion. Daoist motifs also appear, as do figures from traditional myths and legends. Such mixed **iconography** is characteristic of Han art.

One relief shows a two-story building, with women in the upper floor and men in the lower (fig. 10-8). The central figures in both floors are receiving visitors, some of whom bear gifts. The scene seems to depict homage to the first emperor of the Han dynasty, indicated by his larger size. The birds and small figures on the roof may represent mythical creatures and immortals, while to the

left the legendary archer Yi shoots at one of the suncrows. (Myths tell how Yi shot all but one of the ten crows of the ten suns so that the earth would not dry out.) Across the lower register, a procession brings more dignitaries to the reception.

When compared to the Han dynasty banner (see fig. 10-6), this late Han relief clearly shows the change that has taken place in the Chinese worldview. The banner places equal emphasis on heaven, earth, and the underworld; human beings are dwarfed by a great swarming of supernatural creatures and divine beings. In the Wu shrine, the focus is clearly on the human realm. The composition conveys the importance of the emperor as the holder of the mandate of heaven and illustrates the fundamental Confucian themes of social order and decorum.

Architecture

Contemporary literary sources are eloquent on the wonders of the Han capital. Unfortunately, nothing of Han architecture remains except ceramic models. One model of a house found in a tomb, where it was provided for the dead to use in the afterlife, represents a typical Han dwelling (fig. 10-9). Its four stories are crowned with a watchtower and face a small walled courtyard. Pigs and oxen probably occupied the ground floor, while the family lived in the upper stories.

Aside from the multilevel construction, the most interesting feature of the house is the bracketing system supporting the rather broad eaves of its tiled roofs. **Bracketing** became a standard element of East Asian architecture, not only in private homes but more typically in palaces and temples. Another interesting aspect of

10-9. Tomb model of a house. Eastern Han dynasty, 1st century CE. Painted earthenware, 52 x 33½ x 27" (132.1 x 85.1 x 68.6 cm). The Nelson-Atkins Museum of Art, Kansas City, Missouri

Purchase, Nelson Trust (33–521)

the model is the elaborate painting on the exterior walls. Much of the painting is purely decorative, though some of it illustrates structural features such as posts and lintels. Still other images evoke the world outdoors: notice the trees flanking the gateway with crows perched in their branches. Literary sources describe the walls of Han palaces as decorated with paint and lacquer but also inlaid with precious metals and stones.

SIX DYNASTIES With the fall of the Han dynasty in 220 CE, China splintered into three warring kingdoms. In 280 CE the empire was briefly reunited, but invasions by nomadic peoples from Central Asia, a source of trouble throughout Chinese history, soon forced the court to flee south. For the next 250 years, northern and southern China developed separately. In the north, sixteen kingdoms carved out by invaders rose and fell before giving way to a succession of largely foreign dynasties. Warfare was commonplace. Tens of thousands of Chinese fled south, where six short-lived Dynasties succeeded each other in a period of almost constant turmoil broadly known as Six Dynasties or Southern and Northern Dynasties (220–579 CE).

In such chaos, the Confucian system lost much influence. In the south especially, many intellectuals—the creators and custodians of China's high culture—turned to Daoism, which contained a strong escapist element. Educated to serve the government, they increasingly withdrew from public life. They wandered the landscape, drank, wrote poems, practiced calligraphy, and expressed their disdain for the world through willfully eccentric behavior.

The rarefied intellectual escape route of Daoism was available only to the educated elite. Far more people sought answers in the magic and superstitions of Daoism in its religious form. Though weak and disorganized, the southern courts continued to patronize traditional Chinese culture, and Confucianism remained the official doctrine. Yet ultimately it was a new influence, Buddhism, that brought the greatest comfort to the troubled China of the Six Dynasties.

Painting

Although few paintings survive from the Six Dynasties, abundant descriptions in literary sources make it clear that the period was an important one. Landscape, later a major theme of Chinese art, first appeared as a subject during this era. For Daoists, wandering through China's countryside was a source of spiritual refreshment. Painters and scholars of the Six Dynasties found that wandering in the mind's eye through a painted landscape could serve the same purpose. This new emphasis on the spiritual value of painting contrasted with the Confucian view, which had emphasized art's moral and didactic uses.

Reflections on the tradition of painting also inspired the first works on theory and aesthetics. One of the earliest and most succinct formulations of the ideals of Chinese painting are the six principles set out by the scholar Xie He (c. 500–c. 535 CE). The first two principles in particular offer valuable insight to anyone seeking to understand the spirit in which China's painters worked.

The first principle announces that "spirit consonance" imbues a painting with "life's movement." This "spirit" is the Daoist *qi*, the breath that animates all creation, the energy that flows through all things. When a painting has *qi*, it will be alive with inner essence, not merely outward resemblance. Artists must cultivate their own spirit so that this universal energy flows through them and infuses their work. The second principle recognizes that brushstrokes are the "bones" of a picture, its primary structural element. The Chinese judge a painting above all by the quality of its brushwork. Each brushstroke is a vehicle of expression; it is through the vitality of a painter's brushwork that "spirit consonance" makes itself felt. We can sense this attitude already in the rapid, confident brushstrokes that outline the figures of the Han banner and again in the more controlled, rhythmical lines of one of the most important of the very few works surviving from this period, a painted scroll known as *Admonitions of the Imperial Instructress to Court Ladies.* Attributed to the painter Gu Kaizhi (c. 344–406 CE), it alternates illustrations and text to relate seven Confucian stories of wifely virtue from Chinese history.

10-10. Attributed to Gu Kaizhi. Detail of *Admonitions of the Imperial Instructress to Court Ladies*. Six Dynasties period, c. 344–406 CE. Handscroll, ink and colors on silk, 9³/₄" x 11' 6" (24.8 cm x 3.5 m). The British Museum, London

The first illustration depicts the courage of Lady Feng (fig. 10-10). An escaped circus bear rushes toward her husband, a Han emperor, who is filled with fear. Behind his throne, two female servants have turned to run away. Before him, two male attendants, themselves on the verge of panic, try to fend off the bear with spears. Only Lady Feng is calm as she rushes forward to place herself between the beast and the emperor.

The style of the painting is typical of the fourth century. The figures are drawn with a brush in a thin, even-width line, and a few outlined areas are filled with color. Facial features, especially those of the men, are quite well depicted. Movement and emotion are shown through conventions such as the bands flowing from Lady Feng's dress, indicating that she is rushing forward, and the upturned strings on both sides of the emperor's head, suggesting his fear. There is no hint of a setting; instead, the artist relies on careful placement of the figures to create a sense of depth.

The painting is on silk, a Chinese material with origins in the remote past. Silk was typically woven in bands about 12 inches wide and up to 20 or 30 feet long. Early Chinese painters thus developed the format used here, the handscroll—a long, narrow, horizontal composition, compact enough to be held in the hands when rolled up. **Handscrolls** are intimate works, meant to be viewed by only two or three people at a time. They were not displayed completely unrolled as we commonly see them today in museums. Rather, viewers would open a scroll and savor it slowly from right to left, displaying only a foot or two at a time.

Calligraphy

The emphasis on the expressive quality and structural importance of brushstrokes finds its purest embodiment in **calligraphy**. The same brushes are used for both painting and calligraphy, and a relationship between them was recognized as early as Han times. In his teachings Confucius had extolled the importance of the pursuit of knowl-

10-11. Wang Xizhi. Portion of a letter from the *Feng Ju* album. Six Dynasties period, mid-4th century CE. Ink on paper, 9³/₄ x 18¹/₂" (24.7 x 46.8 cm). National Palace Museum, Taipei, Taiwan

The stamped calligraphs that appear on Chinese artworks are seals—personal emblems. The use of seals dates from the Zhou dynasty, and to this day seals traditionally employ the archaic characters, known appropriately as "seal script," of the Zhou or Qin. Cut in stone, a seal may state a formal, given name, or it may state any of the numerous personal names that China's painters and writers adopted throughout their lives. A treasured work of art often bears not only the seal of its maker but also those of collectors and admirers through the centuries. In the Chinese view, these do not disfigure the work but add another layer of interest. This sample of Wang Xizhi's calligraphy, for example, bears the seals of two Song dynasty emperors, a Song official, a famous collector of the sixteenth century, and two emperors of the Qing dynasty of the eighteenth and nineteenth centuries.

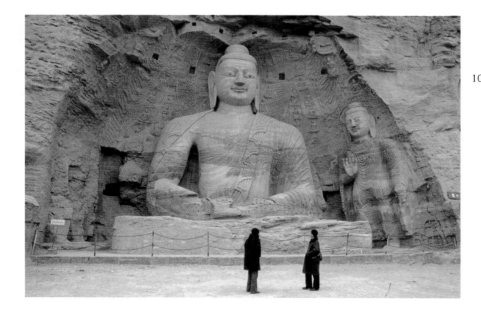

10-12. Seated Buddha, Cave 20, Yungang, Datong, Shanxi. Northern Wei dynasty, c. 460 CE. Stone, height 45' (13.7 m)

edge and the arts. Among the visual arts, painting was felt to reflect moral concerns, while calligraphy was believed to reveal the style and character of the writer.

Calligraphy is regarded as one of the highest forms of expression in China. For more than 2,000 years, China's literati ("educated"), all of them Confucian scholars, have enjoyed being connoisseurs and practitioners of this abstract art. During the fourth century, calligraphy came to full maturity. The most important practitioner of the day was Wang Xizhi (c. 303–361 CE), whose works have served as models of excellence for all subsequent generations. The example here comes from a letter, now somewhat damaged and mounted as part of an album, known as *Feng Ju* (fig. 10-11).

Feng Ju is an example of "walking" style, which is neither too formal nor too free but is done in a relaxed, easygoing manner. Brushstrokes vary in width and length, creating rhythmic vitality. Individual characters remain distinct, yet within each character the strokes are run together and simplified as the brush moves from one to the other without lifting off the page. The effect is fluid and graceful, yet still strong and dynamic. It was Wang Xizhi who first made this an officially accepted style, to be learned along with other styles.

Buddhism

Buddhism originated in India during the fifth century BCE (Chapter 9), then gradually spread north into Central Asia. With the opening of the Silk Road during the Han dynasty, its influence reached China. To the Chinese of the Six Dynasties, beset by constant warfare and social devastation, Buddhism offered consolation in life and the promise of salvation after death. The faith spread throughout the country to all social levels, first in the north, where many of the invaders promoted it as the official religion, then slightly later in the south, where it found its first great patron in the emperor Liang Wudi (ruled 502–549 CE). Thousands of temples and monasteries were built, and many people became monks and nuns.

Almost nothing remains in China of the Buddhist architecture of the Six Dynasties, but we can see what it must have looked like in the Japanese temple Horyu-ji (see fig. 11-5), which was based on Chinese models of this period. The slender forms and linear grace of Horyu-ji have much in common with the figures in Gu Kaizhi's handscroll, and they indicate the delicate, almost weightless style cultivated in southern China.

The most impressive works of Buddhist art surviving from the Six Dynasties are the hundreds of northern rock-cut caves that line the Silk Road between Xinjiang in Central Asia and the Yellow River Valley. Both the caves and the sculpture that fill them were carved from the solid rock of the cliffs. Small caves high above the ground were retreats for monks and pilgrims, while larger caves at the base of the cliffs were wayside shrines and temples.

The caves at Yungang, in Shanxi province, contain many examples of the earliest phase of Buddhist sculpture in China, including the monumental seated Buddha in Cave 20 (fig. 10-12). The figure was carved in the latter part of the fifth century by imperial decree of a ruler of the Northern Wei dynasty (386–535 CE), the longest-lived and most stable of the northern kingdoms. Most Wei rulers were avid patrons of Buddhism, and under their rule the religion made its greatest advances in the north.

The front part of the cave has crumbled away, and the 45-foot statue is now exposed to the open air, clearly visible from a distance. The elongated ears, protuberance on the head (*ushnisha*), and monk's robe (*sanghati*) are traditional attributes of the Buddha. The masklike face, full torso, massive shoulders, and shallow, stylized drapery indicate strong Central Asian influence. The overall effect is remote and even slightly severe, a far cry from the more sensuous expression of the early traditions in India. The image of Buddha became increasingly formal and unearthly as it traveled east from its origins, reflecting a fundamental difference in the way the Chinese and the Indians visualize their deities.

10-13. Altar to Amitabha Buddha. Sui dynasty, 593 CE. Bronze, height 30⅛"
(76.5 cm). Museum of Fine Arts, Boston

Gift of Mrs. W. Scott Fitz (22.407) and Gift of Edward Holmes Jackson in memory of
his mother, Mrs. W. Scott Fitz (47.1407–1412)

SUI AND TANG DYNASTIES

In 589 CE a general from the last of the northern dynasties replaced a child emperor and established a dynasty of his own, the Sui. Defeating all opposition, he molded China into a centralized empire as it had been in Han times. The new emperor was a devout Buddhist, and his reunification of China coincided with a fusion of the several styles of Buddhist sculpture that had developed. This new style is seen in a bronze altar to Amitabha Buddha (fig. 10-13), one of the many buddhas espoused by Mahayana Buddhism. Amitabha dwelled in the Western Pure Land, a paradise into which his faithful followers were promised rebirth. With its comparatively simple message of salvation, the Pure Land sect eventually became the most popular form of Buddhism in China.

The altar depicts Amitabha in his paradise, seated on a lotus throne beneath a canopy of trees. Each leaf cluster is set with jewels. Seven celestial nymphs sit on the topmost clusters, and ropes of pearls hang from the tree trunks. Behind Amitabha's head is a halo of flames. To his left, the **bodhisattva** Guanyin holds a pomegranate; to his right, another bodhisattva clasps his hands in prayer. Behind are four disciples who first preached the teachings of the Buddha. On the lower level, an incense burner is flanked by seated dogs and two smaller bodhisattvas. Focusing on Amitabha's benign expression and filled with objects symbolizing his power, the altar combines the sensuality of Indian styles, the schematic abstraction of Central Asian art, and the Chinese emphasis on linear grace and rhythm into a harmonious new style.

The short-lived Sui dynasty fell in 617 CE, but in reunifying the empire it paved the way for one of the greatest dynasties in Chinese history, the Tang (618–907 CE). Even today many Chinese living abroad still call themselves "Tang people." To them, Tang implies that part of

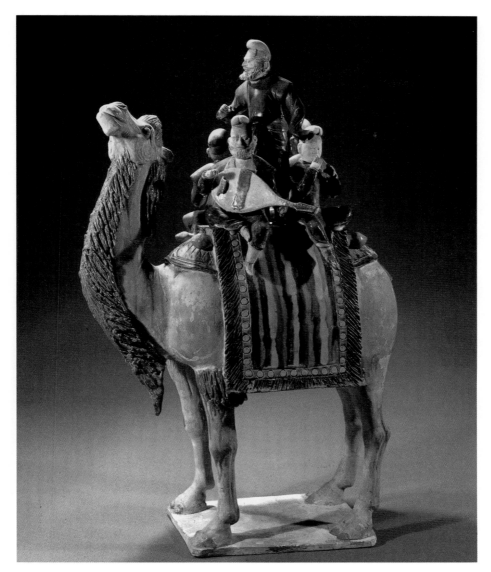

10-14. *Camel Carrying a Group of Musicians*, from a tomb near Xi'an, Shanxi. Tang dynasty, c. mid-8th century CE. Earthenware with three-color glaze, height 26⅛" (66.5 cm). Museum of Chinese History, Beijing

the Chinese character that is strong and vigorous (especially in military power), noble and idealistic, but also realistic and pragmatic.

Under a series of ambitious and forceful emperors, Chinese control again reached over Central Asia. As in Han times, goods, ideas, and influence flowed across the Silk Road. In the South China Sea, Arab and Persian ships carried on a lively trade with coastal cities. Chinese cultural influence in East Asia was so important that Japan and Korea sent thousands of students to study Chinese civilization.

Cosmopolitan and tolerant, Tang China was confident in itself and curious about the world. Many foreigners came to the splendid new capital, Chang'an (present-day Xi'an), and they are often depicted in the art of the period. A ceramic statue of a camel carrying a troupe of musicians reflects the Tang fascination with the "exotic" Turkic cultures of Central Asia (fig. 10-14). The

three bearded musicians (one with his back to us) are Central Asian, while the two smooth-shaven ones are Han Chinese. Two-humped Bactrian camels, themselves exotic Central Asian "visitors," were beasts of burden in the caravans that crisscrossed the Silk Road. The motif of musicians on camelback seems to have been popular in the Tang dynasty, for it also appears in some paintings.

Stylistically, the statue reveals a new interest in **naturalism**, an important trend in both painting and sculpture. Compared to the rigid, staring ceramic soldiers of the first emperor of Qin, the Tang group is alive with gesture and expression. The majestic camel throws its head back; the musicians are vividly captured in mid-performance. Ceramic figurines such as this, produced by the thousands for Tang tombs, offer a glimpse into the gorgeous variety of Tang life. The statue's three-color **glaze** technique was a specialty of Tang ceramicists. The glazes—usually chosen from a restricted palette of

10-15. *The Western Paradise of Amitabha Buddha*, detail of a wall painting in Cave 217, Dunhuang, Gansu. Tang dynasty, c. 750 CE. 10'2" x 16' (3.1 x 4.86 m)

amber, yellow, green, and white—were splashed freely and allowed to run over the surface during firing to convey a feeling of spontaneity. The technique seems symbolic of Tang culture itself in its robust, colorful, and cosmopolitan expressiveness.

Buddhist Art and Architecture

Buddhism reached its greatest development in China during the Tang dynasty. From emperors and empresses to common peasants, virtually the entire country adopted the Buddhist faith. A Tang vision of the most popular sect, Pure Land, was expressed in a wall painting from a cave in Dunhuang (fig. 10-15). A major stop along the Silk Road, Dunhuang has some 500 caves carved out of its sandy cliffs, all filled with painted clay sculpture and decorated with wall paintings from floor to ceiling. The site was worked on continuously from the fifth to the fourteenth century, a period of almost a thousand years. Rarely in art's history do we have the opportunity to study such an extended period of stylistic and iconographic evolution in one place.

Amitabha Buddha is seated in the center, surrounded by four bodhisattvas who serve as his messengers to the world. Two other groups of bodhisattvas are clus-

tered at the right and left. In the foreground, musicians and dancers create a heavenly atmosphere. In the background, great halls and towers rise: the artist has imagined the Western Paradise in terms of the grandeur of Tang palaces. Indeed, the lavish entertainment could just as easily be taking place at the imperial court. This worldly vision of paradise contrasts tellingly with the simple portrayal in the earlier Sui altarpiece (see fig. 10-13), and it gives us our best visualization of the splendor of Tang civilization at a time when Chang'an was probably the greatest city in the world.

The early Tang emperors proclaimed a policy of religious tolerance, but during the ninth century a conservative reaction set in. Confucianism was reasserted and Buddhism was briefly persecuted as a "foreign" religion. Thousands of temples, shrines, and monasteries were destroyed and innumerable bronze statues melted down. Nevertheless, several Buddhist structures survive from the Tang dynasty, one of which, the Nanchan Temple, is the first important example of Chinese architecture.

Nanchan Temple. Of the few structures earlier than 1400 to have survived, the Nanchan Temple is the most significant, for it shows characteristics of both temples

10-16. Nanchan Temple, Wutaishan, Shanxi. Tang dynasty, 782 CE

and palaces of the Tang dynasty (fig. 10-16). Located on Mount Wutai in the eastern part of Shanxi province, this small hall was constructed in 782 CE. The tiled roof, first seen in the Han tomb model (see fig. 10-9), has taken on a curved silhouette. Quite subtle here, this curve became increasingly pronounced in later centuries. The very broad overhanging eaves are supported by a correspondingly elaborate bracketing system.

Also typical is the **bay** system of construction, in which a cubic unit of space, a bay, is formed by four posts and their lintels. The bay functioned in Chinese architecture as a sort of module, a basic unit of construction. To create larger structures, an architect multiplied the number of bays. Thus the Nanchan Temple—modest in scope with three bays—gives an idea of the vast, multistoried palaces of the Tang depicted in such paintings as the one from Dunhuang.

Great Wild Goose Pagoda. Another important monument of Tang architecture is the Great Wild Goose Pagoda at the Ci'en Temple in Xi'an, the Tang capital (fig. 10-17). The temple was constructed in 645 CE for the famous monk Xuanzang on his return from a sixteen-year pilgrimage to India. At Ci'en Temple, Xuanzang taught and translated the materials he had brought back with him.

The **pagoda**, a typical East Asian Buddhist structure, originated in the Indian Buddhist **stupa**, the elaborated burial mound that housed relics of the Buddha (see "Elements of Architecture," page 414). In India the stupa had developed a multistoried form in the Gandharan region under the Kushan dynasty (c. 50–250 CE). In China this idea blended with a traditional Han watchtower to produce the pagoda. Built entirely in masonry, the Great Wild Goose Pagoda nevertheless imitates the wooden architecture of the time. The walls are decorated in low relief to resemble bays, and bracket systems are reproduced

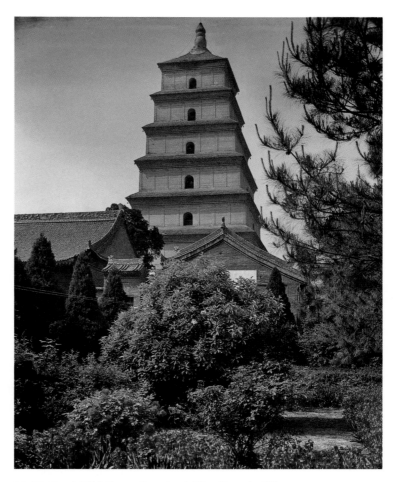

10-17. Great Wild Goose Pagoda at Ci'en Temple, Xi'an, Shanxi. Tang dynasty, first erected 645 CE; rebuilt mid-8th century CE

under the projecting roofs of each story. Although modified and repaired in later times (its seven stories were originally five), the pagoda still preserves the essence of Tang architecture in its simplicity, symmetry, proportions, and grace.

ELEMENTS OF ARCHITECTURE
Pagodas

Pagodas are the most characteristic of East Asian architectural forms. Originally associated with Buddhism, pagodas developed from Indian stupas as Buddhism spread northeastward along the Silk Road. Stupas merged with the watchtowers of Han dynasty China in multistoried stone structures with projecting tiled roofs. This transformation culminated in wooden pagodas with upward-curving roofs supported by elaborate bracketing in China, Korea, and Japan. Buddhist pagodas retain the *axis mundi* masts of stupas. Like their South Asian prototypes, early East Asian pagodas were solid, with small devotional spaces hollowed out; later examples often provided access to the ground floor and sometimes to upper levels. The layout and construction of pagodas, as well as the number and curve of their roofs, vary depending on the time and place.

Drawings are not to scale

early stupa
India, 2nd century BCE

later stupa
Central Asia, 5th–6th
century CE

watchtower
China, Han dynasty,
c. 206 BCE–220 CE

stone pagoda
northwestern China,
c. 5th century CE

wooden pagoda
Japan, 7th century CE

Figure Painting

Later artists looking back on their heritage recognized the Tang dynasty as China's great age of figure painting. Unfortunately, very few scroll paintings that can be definitely identified as Tang still exist. We can get some idea of the character of Tang figure painting from the wall paintings of Dunhuang (see fig. 10-15). Another way to savor the particular flavor of Tang painting is to look at copies made by later Song dynasty artists, which are far better preserved. An outstanding example of this practice is *Ladies Preparing Newly Woven Silk*, attributed to Huizong (ruled 1101–1125 CE), the last emperor of the Northern Song dynasty (fig. 10-18). A long handscroll in several sections, it depicts the activities of court women as they weave and iron silk. An inscription on the scroll informs us that the painting is a copy of a famous work by Zhang Xuan, an eighth-century painter known for his depictions of women at the Tang court. The original no longer exists, so we cannot know how faithful the copy is. Still, its refined lines and bright colors seem to share not only the grace and simplicity of Tang sculpture and architecture but also the quiet beauty characteristic of Tang painting.

1300 CE
5000 BCE   1300 CE

10-18. Attributed to Emperor Huizong. Detail of *Ladies Preparing Newly Woven Silk,* copy after a lost painting by Zhang Xuan. Northern Song dynasty, early 12th century. Handscroll, ink and colors on silk, 14 1/2 x 57 1/4" (36.8 x 145.5 cm). Museum of Fine Arts, Boston
Chinese and Japanese Special Fund

Confucius said of himself, "I merely transmit, I do not create; I love and revere the ancients." In this spirit, Chinese painters regularly copied paintings of earlier masters. Painters made copies both to absorb the lessons of their great predecessors and to perpetuate the achievements of the past. In later centuries, painters took up the practice of regularly executing a work "in the manner of" some particularly revered ancient master. This was at once an act of homage, a declaration of artistic allegiance, and a way of reinforcing a personal connection with the past.

SONG DYNASTY

A brief period of disintegration followed the fall of the Tang dynasty before China was again united, this time under the Song dynasty (960–1279 CE), which established a new capital at Bienjing (present-day Kaifeng), near the Yellow River. In contrast to the outgoing confidence of the Tang, the mood during the Song was more introspective, a reflection of China's weakened military situation. In 1126 the Jurchen tribes of Manchuria invaded China, sacked the capital, and took possession of much of the northern part of the country. Song forces withdrew south and established a new capital at Hangzhou. From this point on, the dynasty is known as Southern Song (1127–1279), with the first portion in retrospect called Northern Song (960–1126).

Although China's territory had diminished, its wealth had increased because of advances in agriculture, commerce, and technology begun under the Tang. Patronage was plentiful, and the arts flourished. Song culture is noted for its highly refined taste and intellectual grandeur. Where the Tang had reveled in exoticism, eagerly absorbing influences from Persia, India, and Central Asia, Song culture was more self-consciously Chinese. Philosophy experienced its most creative era since the "one hundred schools" of the Zhou. Song scholarship was brilliant, especially in history, and its poetry is noted for its depth. But the finest expressions of the Song are in art, especially painting and ceramics.

Neo-Confucianism

Song philosophers continued the process, begun during the Tang, of restoring Confucianism to dominance. In strengthening Confucian thought, philosophers drew on Daoism and especially Buddhism, even as they openly rejected Buddhism itself as foreign. These innovations provided Confucianism with a metaphysical aspect it had previously lacked, allowing it to propose a more satisfying, all-embracing explanation of the universe. This new synthesis of China's three main paths of thought is called Neo-Confucianism.

Neo-Confucianism teaches that the universe consists of two interacting forces known as *li* (principle or idea) and *qi* (matter). All pine trees, for example, consist of an underlying *li* we might call "Pine Tree Idea" brought into the material world through *qi*. All the *li* of the universe, including humans, are but aspects of an eternal first principle known as the Great Ultimate, which is completely present in every object. Our task as human beings is to rid our *qi* of impurities through education and self-cultivation so that our *li* may realize its oneness with the Great Ultimate. This lifelong process resembles the

CHINESE ART BEFORE 1280   *415*

striking to attain buddhahood, and if we persist in our attempts, one day we will be enlightened—the term itself comes directly from Buddhism.

Landscape Painting

The Neo-Confucian ideas found visual expression in art, especially in landscape, which became the most highly esteemed subject for painting. Northern Song artists studied nature closely to master its many appearances— the way each species of tree grew, the distinctive character of each rock formation, the changes of the seasons, the myriad birds, blossoms, and insects. This passion for realistic detail was the artist's form of self-cultivation: mastering outward forms showed an understanding of the principles behind them.

Yet despite the convincing accumulation of detail, the paintings do not record a specific site. The artist's goal was to paint the eternal essence of mountain-ness, for example, not to reproduce the appearance of a particular mountain. Painting a landscape required an artist to orchestrate his cumulative understanding of *li* in all its aspects—mountains and rocks, streams and waterfalls, trees and grasses, clouds and mist. A landscape painting thus expressed the desire for the spiritual communion with nature that was the key to enlightenment. As the tradition progressed, landscape also became a vehicle for conveying human emotions, even for speaking indirectly of one's own deepest feelings.

In the earliest times, art reflected the mythocentric worldview of the ancient Chinese. During the period when the three religions dominated people's lives, there was a major shift in which religious images and human actions became the most important subjects. The choice of landscape as the chief means of expression, reflecting the general Chinese desire to avoid direct depiction of the human condition and to show things instead in a symbolic manner, was the second great shift in the focus of Chinese art. The major form of Chinese artistic expression thus moved from the mythical, through the religious and ethical, and finally to the philosophical and aesthetic.

One of the first great masters of Song landscape was the eleventh-century painter Fan Kuan (active c. 990–1030), whose surviving major work, *Travelers among Mountains and Streams*, is generally regarded as one of the greatest monuments in the history of Chinese art (fig. 10-19). The work is physically large—almost 7 feet high—but the sense of monumentality also radiates from the composition itself, which makes its impression even when much reduced.

The composition unfolds in three stages, comparable to the three acts of a drama. At the bottom a large, low-lying group of rocks, taking up about one-eighth of the picture surface, establishes the extreme foreground. The rest of the landscape pushes back from this point. In anticipating the shape and substance of the mountains to come, the rocks introduce the main theme of the work, much as the first act of a drama introduces the principal characters. In the middle ground, travelers and their

10-19. Fan Kuan. *Travelers among Mountains and Streams*. Northern Song dynasty, early 11th century. Hanging scroll, ink and colors on silk, height 6'9 1/4" (2.06 m). National Palace Museum, Taipei, Taiwan

mules are coming from the right. They are somewhat shocking, for we suddenly realize our human scale— how small we are, how vast nature is! This middle ground takes up twice as much picture surface as the foreground, and, like the second act of a play, shows variation and development. Instead of a solid mass, the rocks here are separated into two groups by a waterfall spanned by a bridge. In the hills to the right, the rooftops of a temple stand out above the trees.

Mist veils the transition to the background, with the result that the mountain looms suddenly. This background area, almost twice as large as the foreground and middle ground combined, is the climactic third act of the drama. As our eyes begin their ascent, the mountain solidifies. Its ponderous weight increases as it billows upward, finally bursting into the sprays of energetic brushstrokes that describe the scrubby growth on top. To

10-20. Xu Daoning. Detail of *Fishing in a Mountain Stream*. Northern Song dynasty, mid-11th century. Handscroll, ink on silk, 19" x 6'10" (48.9 cm x 2.09 m). The Nelson-Atkins Museum of Art, Kansas City, Missouri

Purchase, Nelson Trust (33–1559)

the right, a slender waterfall plummets, not to balance the powerful upward thrust of the mountain but simply to enhance it by contrast. The whole painting, then, conveys the feeling of climbing a high mountain, leaving the human world behind to come face to face with the Great Ultimate in a spiritual communion.

All the elements are depicted with precise detail and in proper scale. Jagged brushstrokes describe the contours of rocks and trees and express their rugged character. Layers of short, staccato strokes (called "raindrop texture" in Chinese) accurately mimic the texture of the rock surface. Spatial recession from foreground through middle ground to background is logically and convincingly handled, if not yet quite continuous.

Although it contains realistic details, the landscape represents no specific place. In its forms, the artist expresses the ideal forms behind appearances; in the rational, ordered composition, he expresses the intelligence of the universe. The arrangement of the mountains, with the central peak flanked by lesser peaks on each side, seems to reflect both the ancient Confucian notion of social hierarchy, with the emperor flanked by his ministers, and the Buddhist motif of the Buddha with bodhisattvas at his side. The landscape, a view of nature uncorrupted by human habitation, expresses a kind of Daoist ideal. Thus we find the three strains of Chinese thought united, much as they are in Neo-Confucianism itself.

The ability of Chinese landscape painters to take us out of ourselves and to let us wander freely through their sites is closely linked to the avoidance of **perspective** as it is understood in the West. Fifteenth-century European painters, searching for fidelity to appearances, developed a "scientific" system for recording exactly the view that could be seen from a single, fixed vantage point. The goal of Chinese painting is precisely to get away from such limits and show a totality beyond what we are normally given to see. If we can imagine the ideal for centuries of Western painters as a photograph, which shows only what can be seen from a fixed viewpoint, we can imagine the ideal for Chinese artists as a film camera aloft in a balloon: distant, all-seeing, and mobile.

The sense of shifting perspective is clearest in the handscroll, where our vantage point changes constantly as we move through the painting. One of the finest handscrolls to survive from the Northern Song is *Fishing in a Mountain Stream* (fig. 10-20), a 7-foot-long painting

executed in the middle of the eleventh century by Xu Daoning (c. 970–c. 1052). Starting from a thatched hut in the right foreground, we follow a path that leads to a broad, open view of a deep vista dissolving into distant mists and mountain peaks. (Remember that viewers observed only a small section of the scroll at a time. To mimic the effect, use two pieces of paper to frame a small viewing area, then move them slowly leftward.) Crossing over a small footbridge, we are brought back to the foreground with the beginning of a central group of high mountains that show extraordinary shapes. Again our path winds back along the bank, and we have a spectacular view of the highest peaks from another small footbridge the artist has placed for us. At the far side of the bridge, we find ourselves looking up into a deep valley, where a stream lures our eyes far into the distance. We can imagine ourselves resting for a moment in the small pavilion the artist offers us halfway up the valley on the right. Or perhaps we may spend some time with the fishers in their boats as the valley gives way to a second, smaller group of mountains, serving both as an echo of the spectacular central group and as a transition to the painting's finale, a broad, open vista. As we cross the bridge here, we meet travelers coming toward us, who will have our experience in reverse. Gazing out into the distance and reflecting on our journey, we again feel that sense of communion with nature that is the goal of Chinese artistic expression.

Such handscrolls have no counterpart in the Western visual arts and are often compared instead to the tradition of Western music, especially symphonic compositions. Both are generated from opening motifs that are developed and varied, both are revealed over time, and in both our sense of the overall structure relies on memory, for we do not see the scroll or hear the composition all at once.

The Northern Song fascination with exactitude extended beyond landscape. The emperor Huizong, whose copy of *Ladies Preparing Newly Woven Silk* was seen in figure 10-18, gathered around himself a group of court painters who shared his passion for quiet, exquisitely detailed, delicately colored paintings of birds and flowers. Other painters specialized in domestic and wild animals, still others in palaces and buildings. One of the most spectacular products of this passion for observation is *Spring Festival on the River*, a long handscroll painted in the first quarter of the twelfth century by Zhang

10-21. Zhang Zeduan. Detail of *Spring Festival on the River*. Northern Song dynasty, early 12th century. Handscroll, ink and colors on silk, 9³/₄" x 7'4" (24.8 cm x 2.28 m). The Palace Museum, Beijing

10-22. Xia Gui. Detail of *Twelve Views from a Thatched Hut*. Southern Song dynasty, early 13th century. Handscroll, ink on silk, height 11" (28 cm), length of extant portion 7'7 ¹/₄" (2.31 m). The Nelson-Atkins Museum of Art, Kansas City, Missouri Purchase, Nelson Trust (32-159/2)

Zeduan, an artist connected to the court (fig. 10-21). Beyond its considerable visual delights, the painting is also an invaluable record of daily life in the Song capital.

The painting is set on the day of a festival, when local inhabitants and visitors from the countryside thronged the streets. One high point is the scene reproduced here, which takes place at the Rainbow Bridge. The large boat to the right is probably bringing goods from the southern part of China up the Grand Canal that ran through the city at that time. The sailors are preparing to pass beneath the bridge by lowering the sail and taking down the mast. Excited figures on ship and shore gesture wildly, shouting orders and advice, while a noisy crowd gathers at the bridge railing to watch. Stalls on the bridge are selling food and other merchandise; wine shops and eating places line the banks of the canal. Everyone is on the move. Some people are busy carrying goods, some are shopping, some are simply enjoying themselves. Each figure is splendidly animated and full of purpose; the buildings and boats are perfect in every detail—the artist's knowledge of this bustling world was indeed encyclopedic.

Little is known about the painter Zhang Zeduan other than that he was a member of the scholar-official class, the highly educated elite of imperial China. Interestingly, some of Zhang Zeduan's peers were already beginning to cultivate quite a different attitude toward painting as a form of artistic expression, one that placed overt skill at the lowest end of the scale of values. This emerging scholarly aesthetic later came to dominate Chi-

nese thinking about art, with the result that only in the twentieth century has *Spring Festival* again found an audience willing to hold it in the highest esteem.

Southern Song

Landscape painting took a very different course after the fall of the north and the removal of the court to its new capital in the south, Hangzhou. This new sensibility is reflected in the extant portion of *Twelve Views from a Thatched Hut* (fig. 10-22) by Xia Gui (c. 1180–1230), a member of the newly established Academy of Painters. In general, academy members continued to favor such subjects as birds and flowers in the highly refined, elegantly colored court style patronized by Huizong. Xia Gui, however, was interested in landscape and cultivated his own style. Only the last four of the twelve views that originally made up this long handscroll have survived, but they are enough to illustrate the unique quality of his approach.

In sharp contrast to the majestic, austere landscapes of the Northern Song painters, Xia Gui presents an intimate and lyrical view of nature. Subtly modulated, perfectly controlled ink washes evoke a landscape veiled in mist, while a few deft brushstrokes suffice to indicate the details showing through—the grasses growing by the bank, the fishers at their work, the trees laden with moisture, the two bent-backed figures carrying their heavy load along the path that skirts the hill. Simplified forms, stark contrasts of light and dark, asymmetrical composition, and great expanses of blank space suggest a fleeting world that can be captured only in glimpses. The intangible is somehow more real than the tangible. By limiting himself to a few essential details, the painter evokes a far deeper feeling for what lies beyond.

This development in Song painting from the rational and intellectual to the emotional and intuitive, from the tangible to the intangible, had a parallel in philosophy. During the late twelfth century a new school of Neo-Confucianism called "School of the Mind" insisted that self-cultivation could be achieved through contemplation, which might lead to sudden enlightenment. The idea of

osity and freely intuitive insights of Xia Gui's landscape.

In 1279 the Southern Song dynasty fell to the conquering forces of the Mongol leader Kublai Khan. China was subsumed into the vast Mongol empire, the largest empire the world has ever seen. Mongol rulers founded the Yuan dynasty (1279–1368), setting up their capital in the northeast, in what is now Beijing. Yet the cultural center of China remained in the south, in the cities that rose to prominence during the Song. This separation of political and cultural centers, coupled with a lasting resentment of "barbarian" rule, created the climate for later developments in the arts.

sudden enlightenment may have come from Chan Buddhism, better known in the West by its Japanese name, Zen. Chan Buddhists rejected such formal paths to enlightenment as scripture, knowledge, and ritual in favor of meditation and techniques designed to "short-circuit" the rational mind. Xia Gui's painting seems also to follow this intuitive approach.

The subtle and sophisticated paintings of the Song were created for a highly cultivated audience equally discerning in other arts such as ceramics. Building on the considerable accomplishments of the Tang, Song potters achieved a technical and aesthetic perfection that has made their wares models of excellence throughout the world. Like their painter contemporaries, Song potters turned away from the exuberance of Tang styles to create more quietly beautiful pieces.

The most highly prized of the many types of Song ceramics is Guan Ware, made mainly for imperial use (fig. 10-23). The everted lip, high neck, and rounded body of this simple vase show a strong sense of harmony. Aided by a lustrous white glaze, the form flows without break from base to lip. The piece has an introspective quality as eloquent as the blank spaces in Xia Gui's painting. The aesthetic of the Song is most evident in the crackle pattern that spreads over the surface. The crackle technique was probably discovered accidentally, but it came to be used deliberately in some of the finest Song wares. In the play of irregular, spontaneous crackles over a perfectly regular, perfectly planned form we can sense the same spirit that hovers behind the self-effacing virtu-

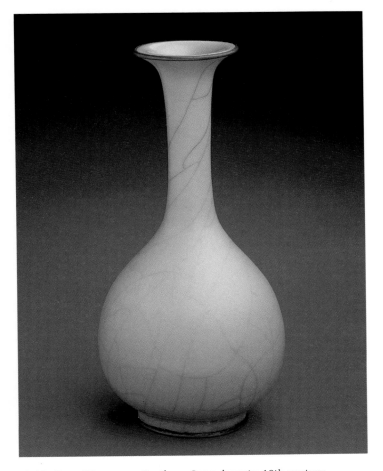

10-23. Guan Ware vase. Southern Song dynasty, 13th century. Porcelaneous stoneware with crackled glaze, height 6⅝" (16.8 cm). Percival David Foundation of Chinese Art, London

Jomon figure
c. 2000 BCE

JOMON c. 12,000–300 BCE

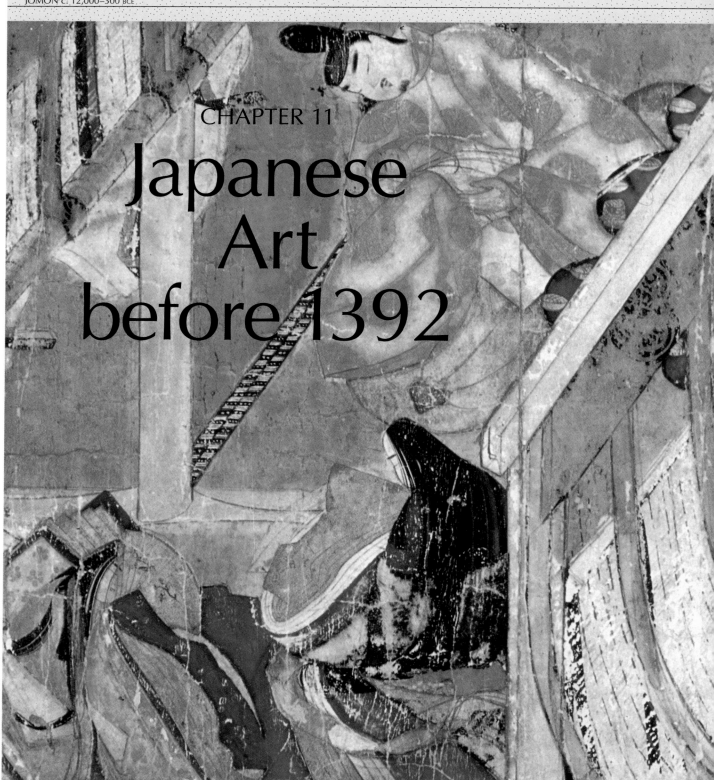

CHAPTER 11

Japanese Art before 1392

Timeline

1 CE	500	1000	1400 CE

Haniwa
c. 6th century CE

Shaka Triad
c. 623 CE

*Amida
Buddha*
c. 700 CE

Byodo-in
c. 1053 CE

Kuya Preaching
c. 1185–1207 CE

▲ YAYOI c. 300 BCE–300 CE

KOFUN
▲ c. 300–552 CE

ASUKA
▲ 552–646

▲ HEIAN 794–1185

KAMAKURA
▲ 1185–1392

▲ NARA 646–794

Map

CHINA

Hokkaido

Sea of
Japan

JAPAN

Honshu

KOREA

Asahi
Mound

Tokyo

Kurokoma
Kamakura

Kyoto   Uji
Nara   Ise
Asuka

Shikoku

Kyushu

PACIFIC
OCEAN

| 0 | 200 miles |
| 0 | 200 kilometers |

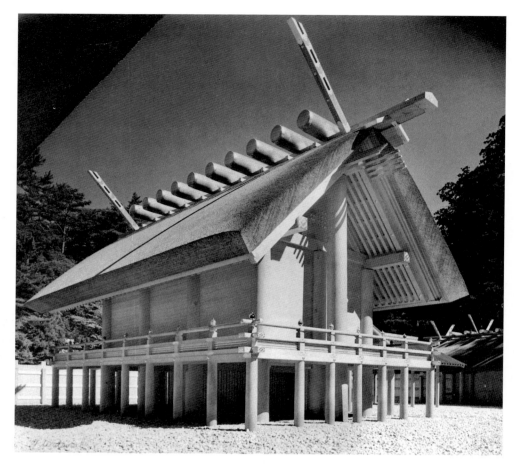

11-1. Inner shrine, Ise, Mie Prefecture. Early 1st century CE; rebuilt 1993

The shrine at Ise, on the coast southwest of Tokyo, is rebuilt every twenty years in exactly the same ancient Japanese style by expert carpenters who have been trained in this task since childhood. One of the most popular pilgrimage sites in Japan, visited by millions each year, this exquisitely proportioned shrine has been ritually rebuilt at intervals for nearly 2,000 years, most recently in 1993 (fig. 11-1). In this way, the temple—like Japanese culture itself—is both ancient and endlessly new.

The shrine, dedicated to the sun goddess, the legendary progenitor of Japan's imperial family, reflects several of the recurring features in Japanese art. Over a period of many centuries and in works of art in many mediums, these characteristic features appear, seem to vanish, then reappear in different guises in different epochs. The first of these characteristics is a respect for and delight in natural materials. Wooden architecture, for example, is often left unpainted—as is the bare cypress wood at Ise—and ceramics frequently display all or some of their clay bodies.

Another feature is a taste for asymmetry. Instead of the evenly balanced compositions frequently seen in Chinese and European art, the Japanese enjoy paintings and prints that seem off-balance but are actually adroitly composed. This affection for asymmetry is also evident in Japanese poetry, typically three or five lines long rather than the even number of lines in the verse of most other cultures.

Japanese art is also marked by a sense of humor and playfulness that can appear in the most unexpected contexts, including religious art of great power and depth. In many Japanese works of art, strong contrasts create a sense of drama that heightens this spirit of fun.

Finally, the Japanese have been able over the centuries to tolerate, even welcome, paradoxes and illogic in their lives and art. They have produced at the same time works that are simple and profound as well as works that are ornate and decorative. They have strongly preserved their own cultural heritage while welcoming and creatively transforming foreign influences—first from China and Korea and more recently from the West. As the shrine at Ise so eloquently illustrates, they also have maintained a sense of history while always being up-to-date.

PREHISTORIC JAPAN

The earliest traces of human habitation in Japan are at least 30,000 years old. At that time the islands were still linked to the East Asian landmass, forming a ring from Siberia to Korea around the present-day Sea of Japan, which was then a lake. With the end of the last Ice Age there, some 15,000 years ago, melting glaciers caused the sea level to rise, gradually submerging the lowland links and creating the islands as we know them today. Sometime after, Paleolithic peoples gave way to Neolithic hunter-gatherers, who crafted stone tools and gradually developed the ability to make and use ceramics. Recent scientific dating methods have shown some works of Japanese pottery to date earlier than 10,000 BCE, making them the oldest now known.

11-2. Vessel, from the Asahi Mound, Toyama Prefecture. Jomon period, c. 2000 BCE. Low-fired ceramic, height 14¾" (37.4 cm). Collection of Tokyo University

Jomon Period

The Jomon period (c. 12,000–300 BCE) is named for the cord-marked patterns found on much of the pottery produced during this time. Jomon people were able to develop an unusually sophisticated hunting-gathering culture in part because they were protected from large-scale invasions by their island setting and also because of their abundant food supply. Around 5000 BCE, agriculture emerged with the planting and harvesting of beans and gourds. Some 4,000 years later rice began to be cultivated, but still the Jomon remained primarily a hunting-gathering society using stone tools and weapons. Its people lived in small communities; in the early Jomon period there were seldom more than ten or twelve dwellings together. All in all, the Jomon people seem to have enjoyed a peaceful life, giving them the opportunity to develop their artistry for even such practical endeavors as ceramics.

Jomon ceramics may have begun in imitation of reed baskets, as many early examples suggest. Other early Jomon pots have pointed bottoms. Judging from the burn marks along the sides, they must have been planted firmly into soft earth or sand, then used for cooking. Applying fire to the sides rather than the bottom allowed the vessels to heat more fully and evenly. Still other early vessels were crafted with straight sides and flat bottoms, a shape that was useful for storage as well as cooking and eventually became the norm. Often the vessels were decorated with patterns made by pressing cord onto the damp clay (jomon means "cord markings"). Jomon usually crafted their vessels by building them up with coils of clay, then firing them in bonfires at relatively low temperatures. It is thought that Jomon pottery was made by women, as was the practice in most early societies, especially before the use of the potter's wheel.

During the middle Jomon period (2500–1500 BCE), pottery reached a high degree of creativity. By this time communities were somewhat larger, and each family may have wanted its ceramic vessels to have a unique design. The basic form remained the straight-sided cooking or storage jar, but the rim now took on spectacular, flamboyant shapes, as seen in one example from the Asahi Mound (fig. 11-2). Middle Jomon potters made full

PARALLELS

Years	Period	Japan	World
c. 12,000–300 BCE	Jomon	Hunting and gathering; beginning of agriculture; decorated ceramic vessels; *dogu* figures	c. 12,000–300 BCE End of Ice Age in Europe; plants and animals domesticated (Near East, Southeast Asia, the Americas); development of metallurgy (Near East); development of writing (China, India); Great Pyramids at Giza (Egypt); Shang dynasty (China); Olmec civilization (Mesoamerica); birth of Siddhartha Gautama, founder of Buddhism (Nepal); Parthenon (Greece); Alexander the Great (Greece) conquers Persia
c. 300 BCE–300 CE	Yayoi	Class structure; bronze tools and weapons; ironworking	c. 300 BCE–300 CE Roman unification of Italy; Han dynasty (China); Great Wall (China); crucifixion of Jesus (Jerusalem); Emperor Augustus (Italy); Buddhism in China; *Ramayana* epic (India); Maya civilization (Mesoamerica)
c. 300–552 CE	Kofun	Centralization of government; *haniwa* figures; Shintoism	c. 300–800 CE First Gupta dynasty (India); Christianity becomes official religion of Roman Empire; Attila the Hun (Mongolia); first Hindu temples (India); birth of Muhammad, founder of Islam (Arabia); Hagia Sophia (Turkey); Muslim conquests; Tang dynasty (China); Koran (Arabia); *Beowulf* (England); first block-print text (China); Charlemagne made emperor of the West
c. 552–646 CE	Asuka	Buddhism; influx of writing and other culture from China and Korea; Horyu-ji	
c. 646–794 CE	Nara	First permanent capital at Nara; Todai-ji; first histories and poetry collections; golden age of Buddhist painting; capital moved to Kyoto	
c. 794–1185 CE	Heian	Lady Murasaki's *Tale of Genji*; Esoteric Buddhism and Pure Land Buddhism arise; Byodo-in; development of Japanese writing system	c. 800–1400 CE Bronze casting in South America; *Diamond Sutra* (China); first Viking colony in Greenland; the Crusades; Jenghiz Khan rules Mongols; Renaissance begins in Europe; Black Death in Europe; Chaucer's *Canterbury Tales* (England)
c. 1185–1392 CE	Kamakura	Rise of Minamoto and Taira clans; Pure Land Buddhism dominates; *raigo*; Zen Buddhism arises	

use of the tactile quality of clay, bending and twisting it as well as **incising** and applying designs. They favored asymmetrical shapes, although certain elements in the geometric patterns are repeated. Some designs may have had specific meanings, but the lavishly creative vessels also display a playful artistic spirit. Rather than working toward practical goals (such as better firing techniques or more useful shapes), the Jomon potters seem to have been simply enjoying to the full their imaginative vision.

The people of the middle and late Jomon period also used clay to fashion small human figures. These figures were never fully realistic but rather were distorted into fascinating shapes. Called *dogu*, they tend to have large faces, small arms and hands, and compact bodies. Some of the later *dogu* seem to be wearing round goggles over their eyes. Others have heart-shaped faces. One of the finest, from Kurokoma, has a face remarkably like a cat's (fig. 11-3). The slit eyes and mouth have a haunting quality, as does the gesture of one hand touching the chest. The marks on the face, neck, and shoulders suggest tattooing and were probably incised with a bamboo stick. The raised area behind the face may indicate a Jomon hairstyle.

11-3. *Dogu*, from Kurokoma, Yamanashi Prefecture. Jomon period, c. 2000 BCE. Low-fired earthenware, height 10" (25.2 cm). Tokyo National Museum

The purpose of Jomon *dogu* remains unknown, but most scholars believe that they were effigies, figures representing the owner or someone else, and that they manifested a kind of sympathetic magic. Jomon people may have believed, for example, that they could transfer an illness or other unhappy experience to a *dogu*, then break it to destroy the misfortune. So many of these figures were deliberately broken and discarded that this theory has gained acceptance, but *dogu* may have had different functions at different times. Regardless of their purpose, the images still retain a powerful sense of magic thousands of years after they were created.

Yayoi and Kofun Periods

During the Yayoi (300 BCE–300 CE) and Kofun (300–552 CE) eras, several features of Japanese culture became firmly established. Most important of these was the transformation of Japan into an agricultural nation, with rice cultivation becoming widespread. This momentous change was stimulated by the arrival of immigrants from Korea, who brought with them more complex forms of society and government.

As it did elsewhere in the world, the shift from hunting and gathering to agriculture brought profound social changes, including larger permanent settlements, the division of labor into agricultural and nonagricultural tasks, more hierarchical forms of social organization, and a more centralized government. The emergence of a class structure can be dated to the Yayoi period, as can the development of metal technology. Bronze was used to create weapons as well as ceremonial objects such as

bells. Iron knives were developed later in this period, eventually replacing stone tools in everyday life.

Yayoi people lived in thatched houses with sunken floors and stored their food in raised granaries. The granary architecture, with its use of natural wood and thatched roofs, reveals the Japanese appreciation of natural materials, and the style of these raised granaries persisted in the architectural designs of shrines in later centuries (see fig. 11-1).

The trend toward centralization of government became more pronounced during the ensuing Kofun, or "old tombs," period, named for the large royal tombs that were built then. With the emergence of a more complex social order, the veneration of leaders grew into the beginnings of an imperial system. Still in existence today in Japan, this system eventually equated the emperor (or, very rarely, empress) with deities such as the sun goddess. When an emperor died, chamber tombs were constructed following Korean examples. Various grave goods were placed inside the tomb chambers, including large amounts of pottery, presumably to pacify the spirits of the dead and to serve them in their next life. Many Korean potters came to Japan in the fifth century, bringing their knowledge of finishing techniques and improved kilns. Their new form of gray-green pottery was first used for ceremonial purposes in Japan and later entered daily life.

The Japanese government has never allowed the major sacred tombs to be excavated, but much is known about the mortuary practices of Kofun era Japan. Some of the huge tombs of the fifth and sixth centuries were constructed in a shape resembling a large keyhole and surrounded by **moats** dug to preserve the sacred land from commoners. Tomb sites might extend over more than 400 acres, with artificial hills built over the tombs themselves. On the top of the hills ceramic sculptures called **haniwa** were placed.

The first *haniwa* were simple cylinders that may have held jars with ceremonial offerings. Gradually these cylinders came to be made in the shapes of ceremonial objects, houses, and boats. Still later, living creatures were added to the repertoire of *haniwa* subjects, including birds, deer, dogs, monkeys, cows, and horses. Finally, *haniwa* in human shapes were crafted, including males and females of all types, professions, and classes (fig. 11-4).

Haniwa illustrate several enduring characteristics of Japanese aesthetic taste. Unlike Chinese tomb ceramics, which were often beautifully glazed, *haniwa* were left unglazed to reveal their clay bodies. *Haniwa* do not show the interest in technical skill seen in Chinese ceramics. Instead, their makers explored the expressive potentials of simple and bold form. *Haniwa* shapes are never perfectly symmetrical; the slightly off-center placement of the eye slits, the irregular cylindrical bodies, and the unequal arms give them great life and individuality. No one knows what purpose *haniwa* served. The popular theory that they were intended as tomb guardians is weakened by their origin as cylinders and by the mundane subjects they portray. Indeed, they seem to

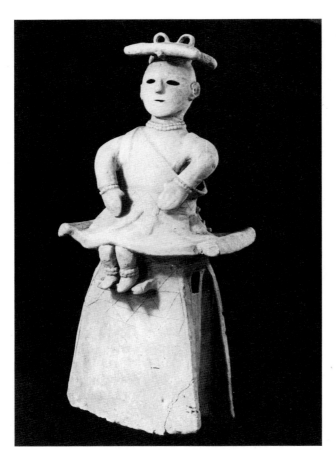

11-4. *Haniwa,* from Kyoto. Kofun period, 6th century CE. Earthenware, height 27" (68.5 cm). Tokyo National Museum

There have been many theories as to the function of *haniwa.* The figures seem to have served as some kind of link between the world of the dead, over which they were placed, and the world of the living, from which they could be viewed. This figure has been identified as a seated female shaman, wearing a robe, belt, and necklace and carrying a mirror at her waist. In early Japan, shamans acted as agents between the natural and the supernatural worlds, just as *haniwa* figures were links between the living and the dead.

represent every aspect of Kofun period society. They may also reflect some of the beliefs of Shinto.

Shinto is often described as the indigenous religion of Japan, but whether it was originally a religion in the usual sense of the word is debatable. Perhaps Shinto is most accurately characterized as a loose confederation of beliefs in deities (kami). These kami were thought to inhabit many different aspects of nature, including particularly hoary and magnificent trees, rocks, waterfalls, and living creatures such as deer. Shinto also represents the ancient beliefs of the Japanese in purification through ritual use of water. Later, in response to the arrival of Buddhism in the sixth century CE, Shinto became somewhat more systematized, with shrines, a hierarchy of deities, and more strictly regulated ceremonies. Nevertheless, even today in many parts of Japan a **torii**, or wooden gateway, is the only sign that a place is sacred. Nature itself, not the gateway, is venerated.

One of the great Shinto monuments is the shrine at Ise (see fig. 11-1). Features typical of Shinto architecture include wooden piles raising the building off the ground, a thatched roof held in place by horizontal logs, the use of unpainted cypress wood, and the overall feeling of natural simplicity rather than overwhelming size or elaborate decoration. Only members of the imperial family and a few Shinto priests are allowed inside the fourfold enclosure housing the sacred shrine. The shrine in turn houses the three sacred symbols of Shinto—a sword, a mirror, and a jewel. This structure, which still preserves some features of Yayoi era granaries, is the one rebuilt every twenty years.

ASUKA PERIOD

Japan has experienced several periods of intense cultural transformation. Perhaps the greatest time of change was the beginning of the Asuka period (552–646 CE). During a single century, new forms of philosophy, medicine, music, foods, clothing, agricultural methods, city planning, and arts and architecture were introduced into Japan from Korea and China. The three most significant introductions, however, were Buddhism, a centralized governmental structure, and a system of writing. Each was adopted and gradually modified to suit Japanese conditions, and each has been an enduring heritage.

Buddhism reached Japan in Mahayana form, with its many buddhas and **bodhisattvas** (see "Buddhism," page 371). After being accepted by the imperial family, it was soon adopted as a state religion. Buddhism represented not only different gods but an entirely new concept of religion itself. Where Shinto had found deities in beautiful and imposing natural areas, Buddhist worship was focused in temples. At first this change must have seemed strange, for the Chinese-influenced architecture and elaborate **iconography** introduced by Buddhism (see "Buddhist Symbols," opposite) contrasted sharply with the simple and natural aesthetics of earlier Japan. Yet Buddhism offered a rich cosmology with profound teachings of meditation and enlightenment. Moreover, the new religion was accompanied by many highly developed aspects of continental culture, including new methods of painting and sculpture.

The most significant surviving early Japanese temple is Horyu-ji, located on Japan's central plains not far from Nara. The temple was founded in 607 CE by Prince Shotoku (574–622 CE), who ruled Japan as a regent and became the most influential early proponent of Buddhism. Rebuilt after a fire in 670, Horyu-ji is the oldest wooden temple in the world. It is so famous that visitors are often surprised at its modest size. Yet its just proportions and human scale, together with the artistic treasures it contains, make Horyu-ji an enduringly beautiful monument to the early Buddhist faith of Japan.

The main compound of Horyu-ji consists of a rectangular courtyard surrounded by covered corridors, one of which contains a gateway. Within the compound are only two buildings, the **kondo**, or golden hall, and a five-story **pagoda**. The simple layout of the compound is

BUDDHIST SYMBOLS A few of the most important Buddhist symbols, which have myriad variations, are described here in their most generalized forms.

Lotus flower

Usually shown as a white water lily, the lotus (Sanskrit, *padma*) symbolizes spiritual purity, the wholeness of creation, and cosmic harmony. The flower's stem is an *axis mundi*.

Lotus throne

Buddhas are frequently shown seated on an open lotus, either single or double, a representation of nirvana.

Chakra

An ancient sun symbol, the wheel (chakra) symbolizes both the various states of existence (the Wheel of Life) and the Buddhist doctrine (the Wheel of the Law). A chakra's exact meaning depends on how many spokes it has.

Marks of a buddha

A buddha is distinguished by thirty-two physical attributes (*lakshanas*). Among them are a bulge on top of the head (*ushnisha*), a tuft of hair between the eyebrows (*urna*), elongated earlobes, and thousand-spoked chakras on the soles of the feet.

Mandala

Mandalas are diagrams of cosmic realms, representing order and meaning within the spiritual universe. They may be simple or complex, three- or two-dimensional—as in an Indian stupa (see fig. 9-7) or a hanging scroll—and they assume a wide array of forms. The Womb World mandala, an early Japanese type used for meditation, depicts and symbolizes different aspects of "buddha nature." One is shown in figure 11-9

lotus flower

single lotus throne

double lotus throne

marks of a buddha

chakra

mandala

Womb World mandala

11-5.   Main compound, Horyu-ji, Nara Prefecture. Asuka period, 7th century CE

asymmetrical, yet the large *kondo* is perfectly balanced by the tall, slender pagoda (fig. 11-5). The *kondo* is filled with Buddhist images and is used for worship and ceremonies. The pagoda serves as a reliquary and is not entered. Other monastery buildings lie outside the main compound, including an outer gate, a lecture hall, a repository for sacred texts, a belfry, and dormitories for monks.

Among the many treasures still preserved in Horyu-ji is a miniature shrine decorated with paintings in lacquer. It is known as the Tamamushi Shrine after the tamamushi beetle, whose iridescent wings were originally affixed to the shrine to make it glitter, much like mother-of-pearl. There has been some debate whether the·shrine was made in Korea, in Japan, or perhaps by Korean artisans in Japan. The question of whether it is, in fact, a "Japanese" work of art misses the point that Buddhism was so international at that time that matters of nationality were irrelevant.

The Tamamushi Shrine is a replica of an even more ancient palace-form building, and its architectural details preserve a tradition predating Horyu-ji itself. Its paintings are among the few two-dimensional works of art to survive from the Asuka period. Most celebrated among them are two that illustrate jataka tales, stories about former lives of the Buddha. One depicts the future Buddha nobly sacrificing his life in order to feed his body ·to a starving tigress and her cubs (fig. 11-6). The tigers are at first too weak to eat him, so he must jump off a cliff to break open his flesh. The anonymous artist has

11-6.   *Hungry Tigress Jataka*, panel of the Tamamushi Shrine, Horyu-ji. Asuka period, c. 650 CE. Lacquer on wood, height of shrine 7'7¾" (2.33 m). Horyu-ji Treasure House

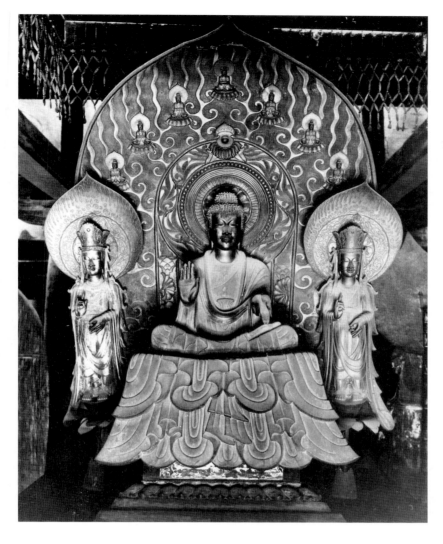

11-7. Tori Busshi. *Shaka Triad*, in the *kondo*, Horyu-ji. Asuka period, c. 623 CE. Gilt bronze, height of seated figure 34¹/₂" (87.5 cm)

created a full narrative within a single frame. The graceful form of the Buddha appears three times, harmonized by the curves of the rocky cliff and tall sprigs of bamboo. First, he hangs his shirt on a tree, then he dives downward onto the rocks, and finally he is devoured by the starving animals. The elegantly slender renditions of the figure and the somewhat abstract treatment of the cliff, trees, and bamboo represent an international Buddhist style largely shared during this time by China, Korea, and Japan. These illustrations for the jataka tales helped spread Buddhism in Japan.

Another example of the international style of early Buddhist art at Horyu-ji is the sculpture called the *Shaka Triad*, by Tori Busshi (fig. 11-7). (Shaka is the Japanese name for Shakyamuni, the historical Buddha.) Tori Busshi was a third-generation Japanese, whose grandfather had emigrated to Japan from China as part of an influx of craftspeople and artists. The *Shaka Triad* reflects the strong influence of Chinese art of the Northern Wei dynasty (see fig. 10-12). The frontal pose, the outsized face and hands, and the linear treatment of the drapery all suggest that Tori Busshi was well aware of earlier continental models, while the fine bronze casting of the figures shows his advanced technical skill. The *Shaka Triad* and the Tamamushi Shrine reveal how

quickly Buddhist art became an important feature of Japanese culture. During an age when Japan was being unified under an imperial system, Buddhism introduced a form of compassionate idealism that is clearly expressed in its art.

NARA PERIOD The Nara period (646–794) is named for Japan's first permanent imperial capital. Previously, when an emperor died, his capital was considered tainted, and for reasons of purification (and perhaps also of politics) his successor usually selected a new site. With the emergence of a complex, Chinese-style government, however, this custom was no longer practical. By establishing a permanent capital in Nara, the Japanese were able to enter a new era of growth and consolidation. Nara swelled to a population of perhaps 200,000 people. During this period the imperial system finally established an effective government that could no longer be threatened by the powerful aristocratic families that had traditionally dominated the political world.

One positive result of strong central authority was the construction in Nara of magnificent Buddhist temples and monasteries that dwarfed those built previously. Even today a large area of Nara is a park where numerous temples preserve magnificent Nara period art and architecture. The grandest of these temples, Todai-ji, is so large that the area surrounding only one of its pagodas could accommodate the entire main compound of Horyu-ji. When it was built, and for a thousand years thereafter, Todai-ji was the largest wooden structure in the world. The park area of Nara also contains a number of other splendid temples, but not all the monuments of Nara are Buddhist. There are several Shinto shrines, and deer wander freely, reflecting Japan's Shinto heritage.

Buddhism and Shinto have coexisted quite comfortably in Japan over the ages. One seeks enlightenment, the other purification, and since these ideals did not clash, neither did the two forms of religion. Although there were occasional attempts to promote one over the other, more often they were seen as complementary, and to this day most Japanese see nothing inconsistent about having Shinto weddings and Buddhist funerals.

While Shinto became more formalized during the Nara period, Buddhism advanced to become the single most significant element in Japanese culture. One important method for transmitting Buddhism in Japan was through the copying of Buddhist sacred texts, the sutras. They were believed to be so beneficial and magical that occasionally a single word would be cut out from a sutra and worn as an amulet. Someone with hearing problems, for example, might use the word for "ear."

Copying the words of the Buddha was considered an effective act of worship by the nobility; it also enabled Japanese courtiers as well as clerics to become familiar with the Chinese system of writing—with both secular and religious results. During this period, the first histories of Japan were written, strongly modeled upon Chinese precedents, and the first collection of Japanese poetry, the *Manyoshu*, was compiled. The *Manyoshu* includes Buddhist verse, but the majority of the poems are secular, including many love songs in the five-line tanka form such as this example by the late-seventh-century courtier Hitomaro (all translations from Japanese are by Stephen Addiss unless otherwise noted):

> Did those
> who lived in past ages
> lie sleepless
> as I do tonight
> longing for my beloved?

Unlike the poetry, most other art of the Nara period is sacred, with a robust splendor that testifies to the fervent belief and great energy of early Japanese Buddhists. Some of the finest Buddhist paintings of the late seventh century were preserved in Japan on the walls of the golden hall of Horyu-ji until a fire in 1949 defaced and partially destroyed them. Fortunately, they had been thoroughly documented before the fire in a series of color photographs. These murals represent what many scholars believe to be the golden age of Buddhist painting, an era that embraces the Tang dynasty in China (618–907 CE), the United Silla period in Korea (668–935 CE), and the Nara period in Japan.

11-8. *Amida Buddha*, fresco in the *kondo*, Horyu-ji. Nara period, c. 700 CE. Ink and colors (now severely damaged), 10'3" x 8'6" (3.13 x 2.6 m)

One of the finest of the Horyu-ji murals is thought to represent Amida (Amitabha in Chinese and Sanskrit), the Buddha of the Western Paradise (fig. 11-8). Delineated in the thin, even brushstrokes known as iron-wire lines, Amida's body is rounded, his face is fully fleshed and serene, and his hands form the "revealing the Buddhist law" **mudra** (see "Mudras," page 380). Instead of the somewhat abstract style of the Asuka period, there is now a greater emphasis on realistic detail and body weight in the figure. The parallel folds of drapery show the enduring influence of the Gandharan style current in India 500 years earlier (see fig. 9-12), but the face is fully East Asian in contour and spirit.

The Nara period was an age of great belief, and Buddhism permeated the upper levels of society. Indeed, one of the few empresses in Japanese history wanted to cede her throne to a Buddhist monk. Her advisers and other influential courtiers became extremely worried, and they finally decided to move the capital away from Nara, where they felt Buddhist influence had become overpowering. The move of the capital to Kyoto marked the end of the Nara period.

HEIAN PERIOD The influences from China and Korea were fully absorbed and transformed by the Japanese during the Heian period (794–1185). Generally peaceful conditions contributed to a new air of self-reliance on the part of the Japanese. Ties to China were severed in the mid-ninth century, and the imperial government was sustained by support from aristocratic families. An efficient method of writing the Japanese language was developed, and the rise of vernacular literature generated such masterpieces as the

11-9. Womb World mandala, To-ji, Kyoto. Heian period, late 9th century CE. Hanging scroll, colors on silk, 6' x 5'1½" (1.83 x 1.54 m)

Mandalas are used not only in teaching but also as vehicles for practice. A monk, initiated into secret teachings, may gradually work out from the center, meditating upon and assuming the gestures of each deity in turn so that he absorbs some of the deity's powers. The monk may also recite magical phrases called mantras as an aid to meditation. The goal is to achieve enlightenment through the powers of the different forms of the Buddha. Mandalas are created in sculptural and architectural forms as well as in paintings. Their integration of the two most basic shapes, the circle and the square, is an expression of the principles of ancient geomancy (divining by means of lines and figures) as well as Buddhist cosmology.

world's first novel, Lady Murasaki's *Tale of Genji*. During these four centuries of splendor and refinement, two major forms of religion emerged: first Esoteric, tantric Buddhism and later Pure Land Buddhism.

Esoteric Buddhism

With the removal of the capital to Kyoto, the older Nara temples lost their influence. Soon two new Esoteric sects of Buddhism, named Tendai and Shingon, grew to dominate Japanese religious life. Strongly influenced by polytheistic religions such as Hinduism, Esoteric Buddhism included a daunting number of deities, each with magical powers. The historical Buddha was no longer very important. Instead, the universal Buddha (called Dainichi, "Great Sun," in Japanese) was believed to preside over the universe. He was accompanied by buddhas and bodhisattvas, as well as guardian deities who formed fierce counterparts to the more benign gods.

Esoteric Buddhism is hierarchical, and its deities have complex relationships to each other. Learning all the different gods and their interrelationships was assisted greatly by works of art, especially **mandalas**, cosmic diagrams of the universe that portray the deities in schematic order. The Womb World mandala from To-ji, for example, is entirely filled with depictions of gods. Dainichi is at the center, surrounded by buddhas of the four directions (fig. 11-9). Other deities, including some

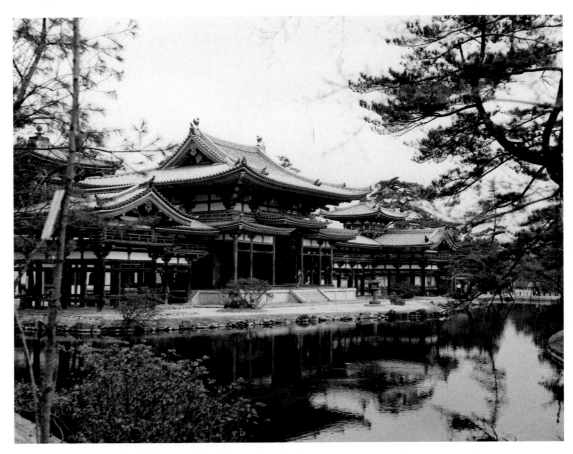

11-10. Byodo-in, Uji, Kyoto Prefecture. Heian period, c. 1053

with multiple heads and limbs, branch out in diagrammatical order, each with a specific symbol of power. To believers the mandala represents an ultimate reality beyond their visible world.

Perhaps the most striking attribute of many Esoteric Buddhist images is their sense of spiritual force and potency, especially in depictions of the wrathful deities, which are often surrounded by flames. Esoteric Buddhism, with its intricate theology and complex doctrines, was a religion for the educated aristocracy, not for the masses. Its network of deities, hierarchy, and ritual found a parallel in the elaborate social divisions of the Heian court.

Pure Land Buddhism

During the latter half of the Heian period, a rising military class threatened the peace and tranquillity of court life. The beginning of the eleventh century was also the time for which the decline of Buddhism had been prophesied. In these uncertain years, many Japanese were ready for another form of Buddhism that would offer a more direct means of salvation than the elaborate rituals of the Esoteric sects.

Pure Land Buddhism, although it had existed in Japan earlier, now came to prominence. It taught that the Western Paradise (the Pure Land) of the Amida Buddha could be reached through nothing more than faith. In its

ultimate form, Pure Land Buddhism held that the mere chanting of a mantra—the phrase *Namu Amida Butsu* ("Hail to Amida Buddha")—would lead to rebirth in Amida's paradise. This doctrine soon swept throughout Japan. Spread by traveling monks who took the chant to all parts of the country, it appealed to people of all levels of education and sophistication. Pure Land Buddhism has remained the most popular form of Buddhism in Japan ever since.

One of the most beautiful temples of Pure Land Buddhism is the Byodo-in, located in the Uji Mountains not far from Kyoto (fig. 11-10). The temple itself was originally a secular palace created to suggest the palace of Amida in the Western Paradise. It was built for a member of the powerful Fujiwara family who served as the leading counselor to the emperor. After the counselor's death in the year 1052 the palace was converted into a temple. The Byodo-in is often called Phoenix Hall, not only for the pair of phoenix images on its roof but also because the shape of the building itself suggests the mythical bird. The lightness of its thin columns gives the Byodo-in a sense of airiness, as though the entire temple could easily rise up through the sky to the Western Paradise of Amida. The hall rests gently in front of an artificial pond created in the shape of the Sanskrit letter *A*, the sacred symbol for Amida.

The Byodo-in's central image of Amida, carved by the master sculptor Jocho (d. 1057), exemplifies the trayals of buddhas and bodhisattvas for the many temples constructed and dedicated to the Pure Land faith. It also reaffirmed the Japanese love of wood, which during the Heian period became the major medium for sculpture.

Surrounding the Amida on the walls of the Byodo-in are smaller wooden figures of bodhisattvas and angels, some playing musical instruments. Everything about the Byodo-in was designed to suggest the paradise that awaits the fervent believer after death. Its remarkable state of preservation after more than 900 years allows visitors to experience the late Heian period religious ideal at its most splendid.

Poetry and Calligraphy

While Buddhism pervaded the Heian era, a refined secular culture also arose at court that has never been equaled in Japan. Gradually over the course of four centuries, the influence from China waned. Although court nobles continued to write many poems in Chinese, both men and women wrote in the new kana script of their native language (see "Writing, Language, and Culture," page 434). With its simple, flowing symbols interspersed with more complex Chinese characters, the new writing system allowed Japanese poets to create an asymmetrical **calligraphy** quite unlike that of China.

Refinement was greatly valued among the Heian period aristocracy. A woman would be admired merely for the way she arranged the twelve layers of her robes by color, or a man for knowing which kind of incense was being burned. Much of court culture was centered upon the sophisticated expression of human love through the five-line tanka. A courtier leaving his beloved at dawn would send her a poem wrapped around a single flower still wet with dew. If his words or his calligraphy were less than stylish, however, he would not be welcome to visit her again. In turn, if she could not reply with equal elegance, he might not wish to repeat their amorous interlude. Society was ruled by taste, and pity any man or woman at court who was not accomplished in several forms of art.

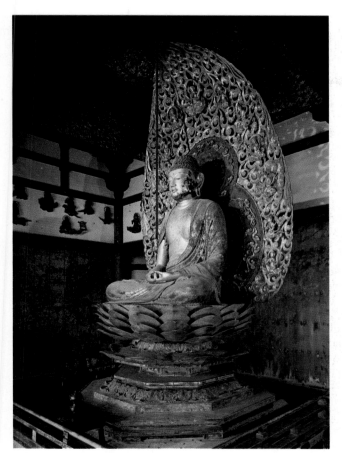

11-11. Jocho. *Amida Buddha*, Byodo-in. Heian period, c. 1053. Gold leaf and lacquer on wood, height 9'8" (2.95 m)

serenity and compassion of the Buddha who welcomes the souls of all believers to his paradise (fig. 11-11). When reflected in the water of the pond before it, the Amida image seems to shimmer in its private mountain retreat. The figure was not carved from a single block of wood like earlier sculpture but from several blocks in Jocho's new **joined-wood** method of construction. This technique allowed sculptors to create larger but lighter por-

---

TECHNIQUE

JOINED-WOOD SCULPTURE

Wood is a temperamental medium, as sculptors who work with it quickly learn. Cut from a living, sap-filled tree, it takes many years to dry thoroughly. The outside dries first, then the inside gradually yields its moisture. As the core dries, however, the resulting shifts in tension can open up gaping cracks. A large statue carved from a single solid block thus runs the risk of splitting as it ages—especially if it has been painted or lacquered, which interferes with the wood's natural "breathing."

One strategy adopted by Japanese sculptors to prevent cracking was to split a completed statue into several pieces, hollow them out, then fit them back together.

A more effective method was the **joined-wood** technique. Here the design for a statue was divided into sections, each of which was carved from a separate block. These sections were then hollowed out and assembled. By using multiple blocks, sculptors could produce larger images than they could from any single block. Moreover, statue sections could be created by teams of carvers, some of whom became specialists in certain parts, such as hands or crossed legs or lotus thrones. Through this cooperative approach, large statues could be produced with great efficiency to meet a growing demand.

WRITING, LANGUAGE, AND CULTURE

Chinese culture enjoyed great prestige in East Asia. Written Chinese served as an international language of scholarship and cultivation, much as Latin did in medieval Europe. Educated Koreans, for example, wrote almost exclusively in Chinese until the fifteenth century. In Japan, Chinese continued to be used for certain kinds of writing, such as philosophical and legal texts, into the nineteenth century.

When it came to writing their own language, the Japanese initially borrowed Chinese characters, or kanji. Differences between the Chinese and Japanese languages made this system extremely unwieldy, so during the ninth century two syllabaries, or kana, were developed from simplified Chinese characters. (A syllabary is a system in which each symbol stands for a syllable.) Katakana, now generally used for foreign words, consists of mostly angular symbols, while the more frequently used hiragana has graceful, cursive symbols.

Japanese written in kana was known as "women's hand," possibly because prestigious scholarly writing still emphasized Chinese, which women were rarely taught. Yet despite the respect for Chinese, Japan had an ancient and highly valued poetic tradition of its own, and women as well as men were praised as poets from earliest times. So while women rarely became scholars, they were often authors. During the Heian period kana were used to create a large body of literature, written either by women or sometimes for women by men.

A charming poem originated in Heian times to teach the new writing system. In two stanzas of four lines each, it uses almost all of the syllable sounds of spoken Japanese and thus almost every kana symbol. It was memorized as we would recite our ABCs. The first stanza translates as:

Although flowers glow with color
They are quickly fallen,
And who in this world of ours
Is free from change?

(Translation by Earl Miner)

Like Chinese, Japanese is written in columns from top to bottom and across the page from right to left. (Following this logic, Chinese and Japanese narrative paintings also read from right to left.) Below is the stanza written three ways. At the right, it appears in katakana glossed with the original phonetic value of each symbol. (Modern pronunciation has shifted slightly.) In the center, the stanza appears in flowing hiragana. To the left is the mixture of kanji and kana that eventually became standard. This alternating rhythm of simple kana symbols and more complex Chinese characters gives a special flavor to Japanese calligraphy.

色は匂へど
散りぬるを
我世誰ぞ
常ならむ

kanji and kana

いろはにほへと
ちりぬるを
わかよたれそ
つねならむ

hiragana

イロハニホヘト
チリヌルヲ
ワカヨタレソ
ツネナラム

I-ro-ha-ni-ho-he-to
Chi-ri-nu-ru-wo
Wa-ka-yo-ta-re-so
Tsu-ne-na-ra-mu

katakana

During the later Heian period, the finest tanka were gathered in anthologies. The poems in one famous early anthology, the *Thirty-Six Immortal Poets*, are still known to educated Japanese today. This anthology was produced in sets of albums called the *Ishiyama-gire*. These albums consist of tanka written elegantly on high-quality papers decorated with painting, **block printing**, scattered gold and silver, and sometimes paper **collage**. The page shown here reproduces two tanka by the courtier Ki no Tsurayuki (fig. 11-12). Both poems express sadness for the loss of a lover, the first lamenting:

Until yesterday
I could meet her,
But today she is gone—
Like clouds over the mountain
She has been wafted away.

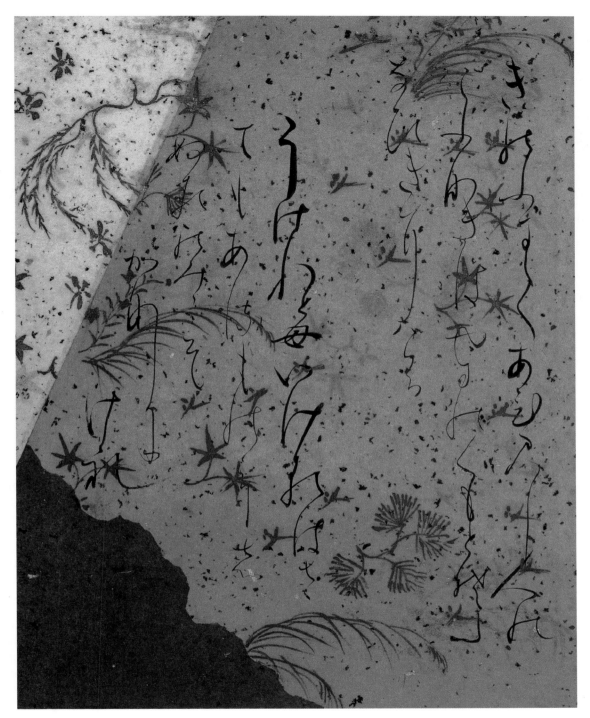

11-12. Album leaf from the *Ishiyama-gire*. Heian period, early 12th century. Ink with gold and silver on decorated and collaged paper, 8 x 6³/₈" (20.3 x 16.1 cm). Freer Gallery of Art, Smithsonian Institution, Washington, D.C.

The spiky, flowing calligraphy and the patterning of the papers, the rich use of gold, and the suggestions of natural imagery match the elegance of the poetry, epitomizing courtly Japanese taste.

Although writing in Japanese, such as in the *Ishiyama-gire*, was considered "women's hand," it is not known how much of the calligraphy of the time was actually written by women. It is sure, however, that women were a vital force in Heian society. Although the place of women in Japanese society was to decline in later periods, they contributed greatly to the art at the Heian court.

Secular Painting

Women were noted for both their poetry and their prose, including diaries, mythical tales, and courtly romances. *The Tale of Genji*, transposing the life-style of the Heian court into fiction in the first known novel, was written at

11-13. Scene from *The Tale of Genji*. Heian period, 12th century. Handscroll, ink and colors on paper, 8⅝ x 18⅞" (21.9 x 47.9 cm). Tokugawa Art Museum, Nagoya

Twenty chapters from *The Tale of Genji* have come down to us in illustrated scrolls such as this one. Scholars assume, however, that the entire novel of fifty-four chapters must have been written out and illustrated—a truly monumental project. Each scroll seems to have been produced by a team of artists. One was the calligrapher, most likely a member of the nobility. Another was the master painter, who outlined two or three illustrations per chapter in fine brushstrokes and indicated the color scheme. Next, colorists went to work, applying layer after layer of color to build up patterns and textures. After they had finished, the master painter returned to reinforce outlines and apply the finishing touches, among them the details of the faces.

the beginning of the eleventh century by Lady Murasaki. It was written in Japanese at a time when men still wrote prose primarily in Chinese, and it remains one of Japan's—and the world's—great novels. Underlying the story of the love affairs of Prince Genji and his companions is the Japanese conception of fleeting pleasures and ultimate sadness in life, an echo of the Buddhist view of the vanity of earthly pleasures.

One of the earliest extant secular paintings from Japan is a series of scenes from *The Tale of Genji*, painted in the twelfth century by unknown artists in "women's hand" painting style. This style was characterized by delicate lines, strong if sometimes muted colors, and asymmetrical compositions usually viewed from above through invisible, "blown-away" roofs. The Genji paintings have a refined, subtle emotional impact. They generally show court figures in architectural settings with the frequent addition of natural elements, such as sections of gardens, that help to represent the mood of the scene. Thus a blossoming cherry tree appears in a scene of happiness, while unkempt weeds appear in a depiction of loneliness. Such correspondence between nature and human emotion is an enduring feature of Japanese poetry and art.

The figures in *The Tale of Genji* paintings do not show their emotions directly on their faces, which are simply rendered with the fewest possible lines. Instead, their feelings are conveyed by colors, poses, and the total composition of the scenes. One evocative scene portrays a seemingly happy Prince Genji holding a baby boy borne

by his wife, Nyosan (fig. 11-13). In fact, the baby was fathered by another court noble. Since Genji himself has not been faithful to Nyosan, who appears in profile below him, he cannot complain; meanwhile the true father of the child has died, unable to acknowledge his only son. The irony is even greater because Genji himself is the illegitimate son of an emperor. Thus what should be a joyful scene has undercurrents that lend it a sense of irony and sorrow.

One might expect a painting of such an emotional scene to focus on the people involved. Instead, they are rendered in rather small size, and the scene is dominated by a screen that effectively squeezes Genji and his wife into a corner. This composition deliberately represents how their positions in courtly society have forced them into this unfortunate situation. In typical Heian style Genji expresses his emotion by murmuring a poem:

How will he respond,
The pine growing on the mountain peak,
When he is asked who planted the seed?

The Tale of Genji scroll represents courtly life as interpreted through refined sensibilities and the "women's hand" style of painting. Heian painters also cultivated a contrasting "men's hand" style. Characterized by strong ink play and lively brushwork, it most often depicts subjects outside the court. One of the masterpieces of this style is *Frolicking Animals*, a set of scrolls satirizing the life of many different levels of society. Painted entirely in ink, the scrolls are attributed to Toba Sojo, the abbot of a

11-14. Attributed to Toba Sojo. Detail of *Frolicking Animals*. Heian period, 12th century. Handscroll, ink on paper, height 12" (30.5 cm). Kozan-ji, Kyoto

11-15. Detail of *Night Attack on the Sanjo Palace*. Kamakura period, late 13th century. Handscroll, ink and colors on paper, height 16¼" (41.3 cm). Museum of Fine Arts, Boston

Fenollosa-Weld Collection

The battles between the Minamoto and Taira clans were fought primarily by mounted and armored warriors, who used both bows and arrows and the finest swords. In the year 1060, some 500 rebels opposed to the retired emperor Go-Shirakawa carried out a daring raid on the Sanjo Palace. In a surprise attack in the middle of the night, they abducted the emperor. The scene was one of great carnage, much of it caused by the burning of the wooden palace. Despite the drama of the scene, this was not the decisive moment in the war. The Minamoto rebels would eventually lose more important battles to their Taira enemies. In turn the Taira clan would eventually be destroyed in 1185 by the victorious Minamoto forces, heirs to those who carried out this raid.

Buddhist temple, and they represent the humor of Japanese art to the full.

In one scene, a frog is seated as a buddha upon an altar while a monkey dressed as a monk prays proudly to him; in other scenes frogs, donkeys, foxes, and rabbits are shown playing, swimming, and wrestling, with one frog boasting of his prowess when he flings a rabbit to the ground (fig. 11-14). Playful and irreverent though it may be, the quality of the painting is remarkable. Each line is brisk and lively, and there are no strokes of the brush other than those needed to depict each scene. Unlike the Genji scroll, there is no text to *Frolicking Animals*, and we must make our own interpretations of the people and events being satirized. Nevertheless, the visual humor is so lively and succinct that we can recognize not only the Japanese of the twelfth century, but perhaps also ourselves.

KAMAKURA PERIOD

The courtiers of the Heian era became so engrossed in their own refinement that they neglected their responsibilities for governing the country. Clans of warriors—samurai—from outside the capital grew increasingly strong. Drawn into the factional conflicts of the imperial court, these samurai leaders soon became the real powers in Japan.

The two most powerful warrior clans were the Minamoto and the Taira, whose battles for domination became famous not only in medieval Japanese history but also in literature and art. One of the great painted handscrolls depicting these battles is *Night Attack on the Sanjo Palace* (fig. 11-15). Painted perhaps a hundred years after the actual event, the scroll conveys a sense of eyewitness reporting even though the anonymous artist

ARMS AND ARMOR

Battles such as the one depicted in *Night Attack on the Sanjo Palace* (see fig. 11-15) were fought largely by archers on horseback. Samurai archers charged the enemy at full gallop and loosed their arrows just before they wheeled away. The scroll clearly shows their distinctive bow, with its asymmetrically placed handgrip. The lower portion of the bow is shorter than the upper so it can clear the horse's neck. The samurai wear a long, curved sword at the waist.

By the tenth century, Japanese swordsmiths had perfected techniques for crafting their legendarily sharp swords. Sword makers face a fundamental difficulty: steel hard enough to hold a razor-sharp edge is brittle and breaks easily, but steel tough enough to withstand rough use is too soft to hold a keen edge. The Japanese ingeniously forged a blade from up to four strengths of steel, cradling a hard cutting edge in a softer, tougher support.

Samurai armor, illustrated here, was made of overlapping iron and lacquered leather scales, punched with holes and laced together with leather thongs and brightly colored silk braids. The principal piece wrapped around the chest, left side, and back. Padded shoulder straps hooked it back to front. A separate piece of armor was tied to the body to protect the right side. The upper legs

helmet

detail of scales

body armor

were protected by a skirt of four panels attached to the body armor, while two large rectangular panels tied on with cords guarded the arms. The helmet was made of iron plates riveted together. From it hung a neckguard flared sharply outward to protect the face from arrows shot at close range as the samurai wheeled away from an attack.

had to imagine the scene from verbal (and at best semi-factual) descriptions. The style of the painting includes some of the brisk and lively linework of *Frolicking Animals* and also traces of the more refined brushwork, use of color, and bird's-eye viewpoint of *The Tale of Genji* scroll. The main element, however, is the savage depiction of warfare (see "Arms and Armor," above). Unlike the Genji scroll, *Night Attack* is full of action: flames sweep the palace, horses charge, warriors behead their enemies, court ladies try to hide, and a sense of energy and violence is conveyed with great sweep and power. The era of poetic refinement was now over in Japan, and the new world of the samurai began to dominate the secular arts.

The Kamakura era (1185–1392) began when Minamoto Yoritomo (1147–1199) defeated his Taira rivals and assumed power as shogun (general-in-chief). In order to resist the softening effects of courtly life in Kyoto, he established his military capital in Kamakura. While

paying respects to the emperor, Yoritomo kept both military and political power for himself. He thus began a tradition of rule by shogun that lasted in various forms until 1868.

Pure Land Buddhist Art

During the early Kamakura period, Pure Land Buddhism remained the most influential form of religion. As noted earlier, it had been spread throughout the country by traveling monks who taught the chant *Namu Amida Butsu*. One of these monks, Kuya (903–972), encouraged people to chant by going through the countryside and singing such simple ditties as:

> I've heard it said that
> Paradise is very far,
> But anyone who tries
> Can surely get there.

11-16. Kosho. *Kuya Preaching*. Kamakura period, before 1207. Painted wood, height 46¼" (117.5 cm). Rokuhara Mitsu-ji, Kyoto

Even by chanting
The name of Amida only once,
A person cannot fail
To reach the Lotus Land.

Kuya was depicted in sculpture by Kosho in the early thirteenth century. A son of the more famous sculptor Unkei, Kosho was a master in the new **naturalistic** style that evolved at this time. Just as the *Night Attack* revealed the political turbulence of the period through its vivid colors and forceful style, Kamakura era portraiture also saw a new emphasis on **realism**, including the use of crystal eyes in sculpture for the first time. Perhaps the warriors had a taste for realism, for many sculptors and painters of the Kamakura period became expert in depicting faces, forms, and drapery with great attention to naturalistic detail. Kosho took on the more difficult task of representing in three dimensions not only the person of the famous monk Kuya but also his chant.

Kosho's solution to putting words into sculptural form was simple but brilliant (fig. 11-16). He carved six small buddhas emerging from Kuya's mouth, one for each of the six syllables *Na-mu-A-mi-da-Buts(u)* (the final *u* is not articulated). Believers would have understood that these six small buddhas embodied the Pure Land chant. The traveling clothes, the small gong, the staff topped by deer horns, and especially the sweetly intense expression of Kuya give this sculpture a radiant sense of faith.

Pure Land Buddhism taught that even one sincere invocation of the sacred chant could lead the most wicked sinner to the Western Paradise. Paintings called *raigo* (literally "welcoming approach") were created depicting the Amida Buddha, accompanied by bodhisattvas, coming down to earth to welcome the soul of the dying believer. Golden cords were often attached to these paintings, which were taken to the homes of the dying. A person near death held onto these cords, hoping that Amida would escort the soul directly to paradise.

11-17. *Descent of the Amida Trinity, raigo* triptych. Kamakura period, late 13th century. Ink and colors with cut gold on silk; each scroll 54 x 19¾" (137.2 x 50.2 cm). The Art Institute of Chicago
Kate S. Buckingham Collection, 1929.855–1929.857

Raigo paintings are quite different in style from the complex mandalas and fierce guardian deities of Esoteric Buddhism. Like Jocho's sculpture of Amida at the Byodo-in, they radiate warmth and compassion. One magnificent *raigo*, a set of three paintings, portrays Amida Buddha descending to earth with two bodhisattvas to welcome the soul of a dying believer (fig. 11-17). They have been portrayed not only with gold paint but also with slivers of **gold leaf** cut in elaborate patterning to suggest the radiance of their draperies. The sparkle of the gold over the figures is heightened by the darkening of the silk behind them, so that the deities seem to come forth from the surface of the painting. In the flickering light of oil lamps and torches, *raigo* paintings would have glistened and gleamed in magical splendor in a temple or a dying person's home.

In every form of Buddhism paintings and sculpture became vitally important elements in religious teaching and belief. In their own time they were not considered works of art but rather visible manifestations of belief.

The Introduction of Zen

Toward the latter part of the Kamakura period still another type of Buddhism appeared, the last major form to reach Japan. This was Zen. In some ways, Zen resembles the original teachings of the historical Buddha in stressing that individuals must reach their own enlightenment through meditation, without the help of deities or magical chants. It was very different from both Esoteric and Pure Land Buddhism, and the time was ripe in Japan for a new approach to age-old Buddhist truths.

Zen had already been highly developed in China for some time, but it had been slow to reach Japan because of the severing of relations between the two countries during the Heian period. During the Kamakura era, however, relations with China were reestablished. Zen was brought to Japan by both visiting Chinese and returning Japanese monks. It appealed to the self-disciplined spirit of the warriors, who were not satisfied with the older forms of Buddhism connected with the Japanese court.

Zen temples were usually built in the mountains rather than in larger cities. An abbot named Kao at an early Zen temple was a pioneer in the kind of rough and simple ink painting that so directly expresses the Zen spirit. We can see this style in a remarkable ink portrait of a monk sewing his robe (fig. 11-18). Bearing the seals of Kao, it has the blunt style, strong sense of focus, and visual intensity of the finest Zen paintings. The almost humorous compression of the monk's face, coupled with the position of the darker robe, focuses our attention on his eyes, which then lead us out to his hand pulling the needle. We are drawn into the activity of the painting rather than merely sitting back and enjoying it as a work of art. This sense of intense activity within daily life, involving the viewer directly with the painter and the subject, is a feature of the best Zen figure paintings.

Buddhist prelates of other sects undoubtedly had assistants to take care of such mundane tasks as repairing a robe, but in Zen Buddhism each monk, no matter how advanced, is expected to do all tasks for himself. This principle extends to the entire monastery. There is no need to depend on contributions from the court or from wealthy believers. Zen monks grow and cook their own food, clean their temples, and are held as responsible for their lives as for their enlightenment. This spirit of self-reliance appealed especially to samurai. As a result, toward the end of the fourteenth century Zen began to dominate many aspects of Japanese culture.

EMPERORS AND WARRIORS

Japan is famous for its imperial system, but for most of its history emperors were under the political control of regents, powerful ministers, or shoguns. It could be argued that the imperial system survived because of this division of power. While the emperors always maintained their social and cultural authority, the fact that they did not rule politically allowed them to remain personally sacrosanct. Occasionally, however, an emperor decided to attempt to hold true power himself. One of these ambitious sovereigns was Go-Daigo (1288–1339), who managed to overthrow the Kamakura shogunate in 1333 and assume full power. His loyalist movement could not control events, however, and by 1392 power had reverted to the shogun. Control of government by the military was reaffirmed, and it was to last in various forms for 500 more years. As the Kamakura era ended, the seeds of the future were planted: warrior control and Zen aesthetics had become established as the leading forces in Japanese life and art.

11-18. Attributed to Kao. *Monk Sewing*. Kamakura period, early 14th century. Ink on paper, 32⅞ x 13¾" (83.5 x 35.4 cm). The Cleveland Museum of Art John L. Severance Fund, 62.163

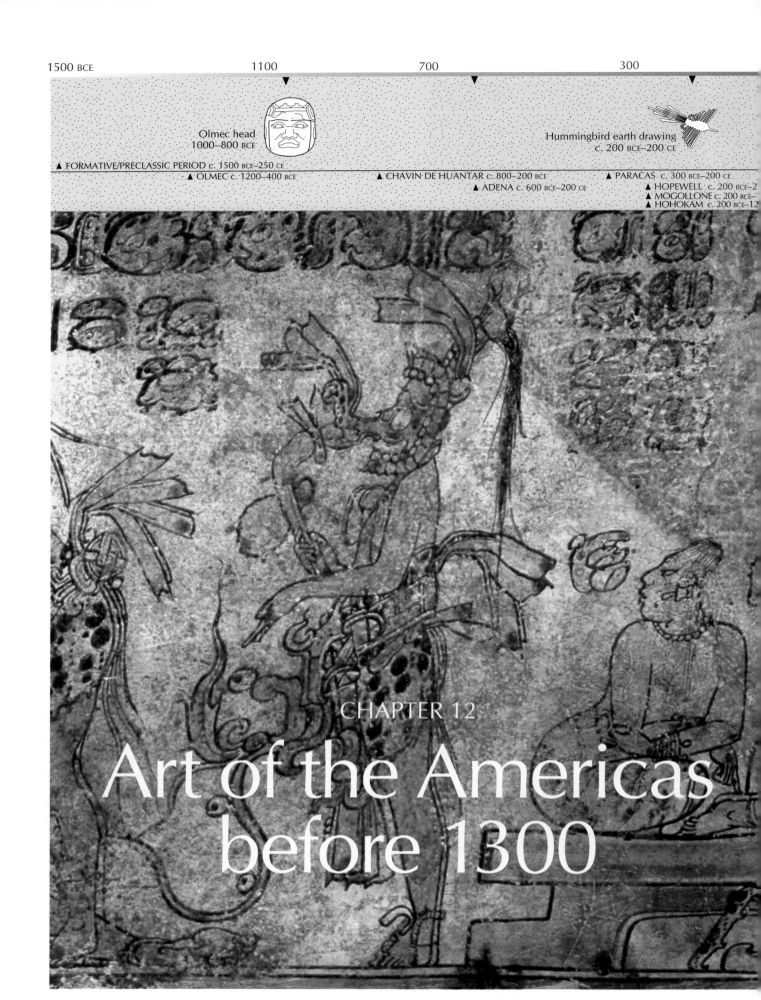

1500 BCE | 1100 | 700 | 300

Olmec head
1000–800 BCE

Hummingbird earth drawing
c. 200 BCE–200 CE

▲ FORMATIVE/PRECLASSIC PERIOD c. 1500 BCE–250 CE
▲ OLMEC c. 1200–400 BCE
▲ CHAVÍN DE HUANTAR c. 800–200 BCE
▲ ADENA c. 600 BCE–200 CE
▲ PARACAS c. 300 BCE–200 CE
▲ HOPEWELL c. 200 BCE–2
▲ MOGOLLONE c. 200 BCE–
▲ HOHOKAM c. 200 BCE–12

CHAPTER 12

Art of the Americas before 1300

Pyramid of the Sun
350–650

Chacmool
9th–13th century

Shaman with
Drum and Snake
c. 1000

Great Serpent Mound
c. 1070 CE

Anasazi seed jar
1100–1300

▲ CLASSIC PERIOD c. 250–900   ▲ POSTCLASSIC PERIOD c. 900–1300

▲ MOCHE c. 200–700   ▲ DIQUIS c. 700–1500

▲ MAYA c. 250–1500   ▲ ANASAZI c. 750–1230

▲ NAZCA c. 100 BCE–700 CE   ▲ TEOTIHUACAN c. 350–650   ▲ MISSISSIPPIAN c. 800–1500

12-1.   Great Serpent Mound, Adams County, Ohio. c. 1070 CE. Length approx. 1,400' (426.7 m)

When the boldest of the white settlers in North America pushed beyond the Appalachian Mountains, they literally walked into a mystery. They found themselves facing, and in some cases climbing over, strange mounds of earth, large and small, that clearly had been created by human hands—a great many hands. The mounds took various forms. Some were shaped like birds and other animals. One, in present-day Ohio, a writhing earthen snake 1,254 feet long and 20 feet wide, meandered along the crest of a ridge overlooking a stream, with its head at the highest point of the ridge (fig. 12-1). The mounds were most concentrated near the Mississippi and Ohio rivers, but at least a few were found throughout the very wide area from the Great Lakes to the Gulf Coast.

The eighteenth-century settlers began to dig around in the mounds—sometimes to sate curiosity, sometimes to seek treasure, sometimes simply to plant their crops. What they found further puzzled them. Some mounds covered piles of refuse from permanent agricultural villages where none had been known to exist. Others were burial sites where human skeletons had been interred with carved artifacts unlike any seen before, sometimes made from materials not native to the area. Theories abounded about the creators of these mounds—including speculations that they had been survivors from the lost island of Atlantis or one of the lost tribes of Israel. Before he became president, Thomas Jefferson had excavated a burial mound in Virginia and had come close to the truth: that these monumental earthworks, in fact, were 800-year-old creations of the earliest peoples to settle the New World.

THE NEW WORLD

During the last Ice Age, which began about 2.5 million years ago, glaciers periodically trapped enough of the world's water to lower the level of the oceans and expose land between Asia and North America. At its greatest extent, this land bridge was a vast, rolling plain a thousand miles wide, where grasses, sagebrush, sedge, and groves of scrub willow provided food and shelter for animals and birds.

Although most areas of present-day Alaska and Canada were covered by glaciers during the Ice Age, a narrow, ice-free corridor provided access to the south. Sometime before about 12,000 years ago, perhaps as early as 20,000 to 30,000 years ago, Paleolithic hunter-gatherers emerged through this corridor and began to spread out into two vast, uninhabited continents. Between 10,000 and 12,000 years ago, bands of hunters whose tool kits included sophisticated fluted-stone spearheads traveled across most of North America. The earliest uncontested evidence puts humans at the southern end of South America by 11,000 years ago. Although contact between Siberia and Alaska continued after the ice had retreated and rising oceans had flooded the Bering Strait, the peoples of the Western Hemisphere were essentially cut off from the peoples of Africa and Eurasia until they were overrun by European conquerors beginning in the late fifteenth century CE.

In this isolation New World peoples experienced many of the same transformations that followed the end of the Paleolithic era elsewhere. In many regions they developed an agricultural way of life, based on the cultivation of corn, beans, and squash. Other plants first domesticated in the New World included potatoes, tobacco, cacao (chocolate), tomatoes, and avocados. New World peoples also domesticated many animals: turkeys, guinea pigs, llamas (and their cousins, the alpacas, guanacos, and vicuñas), and, as did the peoples of the Old World, dogs.

As elsewhere, the shift to agriculture in the Americas was accompanied by population growth and, in some places, the rise of hierarchical societies, the appearance of ceremonial centers and towns with monumental architecture, and the development of elaborate artistic traditions. New World cities such as Teotihuacan in the Valley of Mexico rivaled those of the Old World in size and splendor. New World civilizations produced sophisticated ceramic wares, although they did not develop the potter's wheel or the wheel in general, perhaps because they lacked beasts of burden like horses and oxen for exploiting its potential. The peoples of Mesoamerica—the region that extends from central Mexico to northern Central America—developed writing, a complex and accurate calendar, and a sophisticated system of mathematics. Central and South American peoples developed an advanced metallurgy and produced exquisite gold, silver, and copper jewelry. The smiths of the Andes began to produce metal weapons and agricultural implements in the first millennium CE, but Native Americans in general made tools and weapons from such other materials as bone, ivory, stone, wood, and, where it was available, obsidian, a volcanic glass capable of holding a cutting edge as fine as surgical steel. Native Americans were skilled in basketry, and in the Andes, beginning about 2000 BCE, they developed an enduring tradition of weaving that produced some of the world's finest textiles (see "Andean Textiles," page 458).

Later civilizations such as the Aztec, Inca, and Pueblo of the North American Southwest are perhaps more familiar today, but before 1300 CE extraordinary artistic traditions already flourished in many regions in the Americas. This chapter explores the accomplishments of some of the cultures in five of those regions—Mesoamerica, Central America, the central Andes of South America, the southeastern woodlands and great river valleys of North America, and the North American Southwest.

MESO-AMERICA

Ancient Mesoamerica encompasses the area from north of the Valley of Mexico (the location of Mexico City) to modern Belize, Honduras, and western Nicaragua in Central America. The region is one of great contrasts, ranging from tropical rain forest to semiarid mountains. Reflecting this physical diversity, the civilizations that arose in Mesoamerica varied, but they were linked by trade and displayed an overall cultural unity. Among their common features are a complex calendrical system based on interlocking 260-day and 365-day cycles, a

---

THE COSMIC BALL GAME

The ritual ball game was one of the defining characteristics of Mesoamerican society. Played in some version throughout the region at the time of the Spanish conquest, this game had its origins deep in antiquity, dating at least to Olmec times. The ball game was generally played on a long, rectangular court with a large, solid, heavy rubber ball. Using their elbows, knees, or hips—but not their hands—heavily padded players directed the ball toward a goal or marker. The rules, the size and shape of the court, the number of players on a team, and the nature of the goal varied. The largest surviving ball court, at Chichen Itza, was about the size of a modern football field. The goals of the Chichen Itza court were large stone rings set in the walls of the court about 25 feet above the field.

The game had profound religious and political significance and was a common subject of Mesoamerican art. Players, complete with equipment, appear as figurines and on stone votive sculpture; the game and its attendant rituals were represented in relief sculpture. The movement of the ball represented celestial bodies—the sun, moon, or stars—held aloft and directed by the skill of the players. The ball game was also associated with warfare. Captive warriors might have been made to play the game, and players were often sacrificed.

1100 BCE
1500 BCE   1300 CE

PARALLELS

Years	Period/Culture Peak	Americas	World
Before 10,000 BCE		Paleolithic hunter-gatherers migrate to New World	**Before 10,000 BCE** Ice Age in Europe
c. 1500 BCE–250 CE	**Formative/Preclassic period in Mesoamerica**		**c. 1500 BCE–250 CE** Development of metallurgy (Near East); Great Pyramids at Giza (Egypt); development of writing (China, India); Minoan, Mycenaean cultures (Greece); black-figure and red-figure vase painting (Greece); birth of Siddhartha Gautama, founder of Buddhism (Nepal); Parthenon (Greece); Great Stupa at Sanchi (India); crucifixion of Jesus (Jerusalem); Pantheon (Italy)
	Olmec (Mesoamerica; c. 1200–400 BCE)	San Lorenzo; La Venta; ritual ball games; colossal heads; earliest writing and calendars; early Maya	
	Chavin de Huantar (Andes; Early Horizon period, c. 800–200 BCE)	Innovation in ceramics, metallurgy, textiles	
	Adena (Ohio; c. 600 BCE–200 CE)	Mound building	
	Paracas (Peru; c. 300 BCE–200 CE)	Weaving; embroidery	
	Hokokam (Arizona; c. 200 BCE–1200 CE)	Canals	
	Hopewell (Illinois, Ohio; c. 200 BCE–200 CE)	Mound building; carved jewelry; stone pipes	
	Mogollon (New Mexico, Arizona; c. 200 BCE–1250 CE)	Pit houses	
c. 250–900 CE	**Classic period in Mesoamerica**		**c. 250–900 CE** *Haniwa* figures (Japan); earliest surviving Hindu temples (India); Hagia Sophia (Turkey); birth of Muhammad, founder of Islam (Arabia); Muslim conquests of Arabia, Persia, Egypt, Syria, Palestine, India, North Africa; first block-print text (China)
	Nazca (Peru; c. 100 BCE–700 CE)	Weaving; polychrome pottery; colossal geoglyphs	
	Moche (Peru; c. 200–700 CE)	Sipan; Moche; Pyramid of the Sun	
	Maya (Mesoamerica; c. 250–900 CE)	Tikal; Palenque; hieroglyphic writing; calendar; codex-style painting	
	Teotihuacan (Mesoamerica; c. 350–650 CE)	Temple of the Feathered Serpent; Pyramids of the Sun and the Moon	
c. 900–1500 CE	**Postclassic period in Mesoamerica**	Maya center at Chichen Itza; Castillo	**c. 900–1500 CE** First Viking colony in Greenland; Lady Murasaki's *Tale of Genji* (Japan); the Crusades (Europe); Jenghiz Khan rules Mongols (Central Asia)
	Diquis (Costa Rica; c. 700–1500 CE)	Lost-wax casting; goldwork	
	Anasazi (Four Corners, American southwest; c. 750–1230 CE)	Multistory "apartments"; Pueblo Bonita	
	Mississippian (Illinois; c. 800–1500 CE)	Earthenwork palaces; temples	

12-2.   Great Pyramid and ball court, La Venta, Mexico. Olmec culture, c. 900–600 BCE. Pyramid
height approx. 100' (30 m)

ritual ball game (see "The Cosmic Ball Game," page 445), and aspects of the construction of monumental ceremonial centers. Mesoamerican society was sharply divided into elite and commoner classes.

The transition to farming began in Mesoamerica between 7000 and 6000 BCE, and by 3000 to 2000 BCE settled villages were widespread. Archeologists traditionally have divided the region's subsequent history into three broad periods: Formative or Preclassic (1500 BCE–250 CE), Classic (250–900 CE), and Postclassic (900–1500 CE). This chronology derives primarily from the archeology of the Maya—the people of Guatemala and the Yucatan peninsula. The Classic period brackets the time during which the Maya erected dated stone monuments. The term reflects the view of early Mayanists that it was a kind of golden age, the equivalent of the Classical period in ancient Greece. Although this view is no longer current and the periods are only roughly applicable to other parts of Mesoamerica, the terminology has endured.

The Olmec

The first major Mesoamerican civilization, the Olmec, emerged during the Formative period along the Gulf of Mexico, in the swampy coastal jungles of the modern Mexican states of Veracruz and Tabasco. In dense vegetation along slow, meandering rivers, the Olmec cleared farmland, drained fields, and raised earth mounds on which they constructed religious and political centers. These centers probably housed an elite group of ruler-priests supported by a larger population of farmers who lived in villages of pole-and-thatch houses. The presence at Olmec sites of goods like obsidian, iron ore, and jade that are not found in the Gulf region but come from throughout Mesoamerica indicates that the Olmec participated in extensive long-distance trade.

The earliest Olmec center, at San Lorenzo, flourished from about 1200 to 900 BCE and was abandoned by 400 BCE. The archeological findings here include a possible ball court, an architectural feature of other major Olmec sites. Another center, at La Venta, rose to prominence after San Lorenzo declined, thriving from about 900 to 400 BCE. La Venta was built on high ground between rivers. Its most prominent feature, an earth mound known as the Great Pyramid, still rises to a height of about 100 feet (fig. 12-2). This scalloped mound may have been intended to resemble a volcanic mountain, but its present form may simply be the result of erosion after thousands of years of the region's heavy rains. The Great Pyramid stands at the south end of a large, open court, possibly used as a playing field, arranged on a north-south axis and defined by long, low mounds. An elaborate drainage system of stone troughs may have been used as part of a ritual honoring a water deity. Many of the physical features of La Venta—including the symmetrical arrangement of earth mounds, platforms, and central open spaces along an axis that was probably determined by astronomical observations—are characteristic of later monumental and ceremonial architecture throughout Mesoamerica. Found buried within the site were carved jade, serpentine stone, and granite artifacts.

Among Olmec carvings, the most pervasive images are jaguars and so-called were-jaguars, creatures that combine human and feline features. These images suggest that Olmec religion may have involved a belief in jaguar deities that could assume human form, as well as shaman figures who could assume animal (jaguar) form and mediate between humans and the spirit world. There is also sculpture showing a woman and a jaguar in close association, suggesting an origin myth involving the union of a human with a feline deity.

In addition to the smaller works in jade and serpentine, the Olmec produced an abundance of monumental basalt sculpture, including colossal heads, altars, and seated figures. The huge basalt blocks for the large works of sculpture were quarried at distant sites and transported to San Lorenzo, La Venta, and other centers. The colossal heads, ranging in height from 5 to 12 feet and weighing from 5 to more than 20 tons, are probably the best-known Olmec sculpture today (fig. 12-3). The heads represent adult males wearing close-fitting caps with chin straps and large, round earplugs. The fleshy faces have almond-shaped eyes, flat broad noses, thick protruding lips, a slight frown, and down-turned mouths. Each face is different, suggesting that they may represent specific individuals. Most scholars now consider them to be portraits of rulers. Nine heads were found at San Lorenzo; all had been mutilated and buried about 900 BCE, about the time the site went into decline. Seventy-seven basalt monuments were found at La Venta, including four heads, which faced each other across the ceremonial core of the site.

The colossal heads and the subjects depicted on other monumental sculpture suggest that the Olmec elite, like their counterparts in later Mesoamerican civilizations, particularly the Maya, were preoccupied with the commemoration of rulers and historic events. This preoccupation was probably an important factor in the development of writing and calendrical systems, which first appeared around 600 to 500 BCE in areas with strong Olmec influence. By 200 CE forests and swamps were reclaiming Olmec sites, but Olmec civilization had spread widely throughout Mesoamerica and was to have an enduring influence on its successors. As the Olmec centers of the Gulf Coast faded, the great Classic period centers at Teotihuacan in the Valley of Mexico, at Monte Alban in the Valley of Oaxaca, and in the Maya region were beginning their ascendancy.

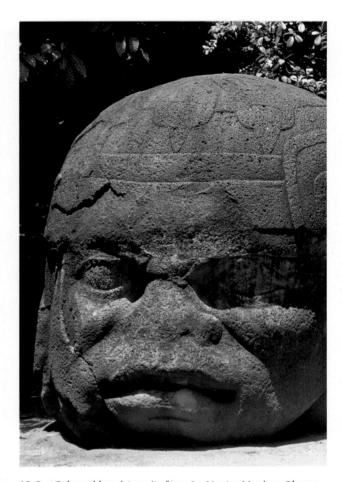

12-3. Colossal head (no. 4), from La Venta, Mexico. Olmec culture, c. 900–500 BCE. Basalt, height 7'5" (2.26 m). La Venta Park, Villahermosa, Tabasco, Mexico

The naturalistic colossal heads found at La Venta and San Lorenzo are sculpture in the round that measure about 8 feet in diameter. They are carved from basalt boulders that were transported to the Gulf Coast from the Tuxtla Mountains, more than 60 miles inland.

Teotihuacan

Teotihuacan is located some 30 miles northeast of present-day Mexico City. Early in the first millennium CE it began a period of rapid growth, and by 200 it had emerged as a significant center of commerce and manufacturing, the first large city-state in the Americas. One reason for its wealth was its control of a source of high-quality obsidian. Goods made at Teotihuacan, including obsidian tools and pottery, were distributed widely throughout Mesoamerica in exchange for luxury items such as the brilliant green feathers of the quetzal bird, used for priestly headdresses, and the spotted fur of the jaguar, used for ceremonial garments. The city's farmers terraced hillsides and drained swamps, and on fertile, reclaimed land they grew the common Mesoamerican staple foods, including corn, squash, and beans. From the fruit of the spiky-leafed maguey plant they fermented pulque, a mildly alcoholic brew still consumed today.

At its height, between 350 and 650 CE, Teotihuacan covered nearly 9 square miles and had a population of some 200,000, making it the largest city in the Americas

12-4. Ceremonial center of the city of Teotihuacan, Mexico. Teotihuacan culture, 350–650 CE

The Pyramid of the Moon is at the lower right, the Pyramid of the Sun at the middle left, and the Ciudadela and the Temple of the Feathered Serpent at the upper left.

12-5. Plan of the ceremonial center of Teotihuacan

and one of the largest in the world at that time (figs. 12-4, 12-5). Whether through conquest or trade—archeologists are not certain which—it exerted far-reaching influence. The site of Kaminaljuyu in the highlands of Guatemala, for example, shows evidence of close contact with Teotihuacan. The people of Teotihuacan worshiped many gods that were recognizably antecedent to gods worshiped by later Mesoamerican people, including the Aztec, who dominated central Mexico at the time of the Spanish conquest. Among these are the Rain God (possibly also the god of war and sacrifice), known to the Aztec as Tlaloc, and the Feathered Serpent, known to the Maya as Kukulcan and to the Aztec as Quetzalcoatl.

Sometime in the middle of the eighth century disaster struck Teotihuacan: the ceremonial center burned, and the city went into a permanent decline. Nevertheless, its influence continued as other centers throughout northern Mesoamerica borrowed and transformed its art and imagery over the next several centuries. The site was never entirely abandoned, however, because it remained a legendary pilgrimage center until the time of the Spanish conquest in the early sixteenth century. The Aztec revered the site, believing it to be the place where the gods created the sun and the moon. Its name, Teotihuacan, is an Aztec word meaning "The City (gathering place) of the Gods." Its principal monuments include the Pyramid of the Sun and the Pyramid of the Moon.

The so-called Avenue of the Dead, the heart of the city, is a broad thoroughfare laid out on a north-south axis and extending for more than 3 miles. Another major thoroughfare intersects it at right angles, establishing a grid to which the rest of the city strictly conforms. Much of the ceremonial center, in a pattern typical of Mesoamerica, is characterized by the symmetrical arrangement of structures around open courts or plazas. The Pyramid of the Sun flanks the Avenue of the Dead to the east. It is built over a four-chambered cave with a spring

that may have been the original focus of worship at the site and the source of its prestige. The largest of Teotihuacan's architectural monuments, the Pyramid of the Sun is more than 210 feet high and measures about 720 feet on each side at its base. It rises in a series of sloping steps to a flat platform, where a two-room temple once stood. A monumental stone stairway led from level to level up the side of the pyramid to the temple platform. The exterior was faced with stone and **stucco** and painted. The Pyramid of the Moon, not quite as large as the Pyramid of the Sun, stands at the north end of the Avenue of the Dead, facing a large plaza flanked by smaller, symmetrically placed platforms.

In the heart of the city, at the intersection of the Avenue of the Dead and the main east-west thoroughfare, is the Ciudadela, a vast sunken plaza surrounded by temple platforms. One of the city's principal religious and political centers, the Ciudadela could accommodate an assembly of more than 60,000 people. Its focal point was the Temple of the Feathered Serpent, or Quetzalcoatl. This structure exhibits the **talud-tablero** construction that is a hallmark of the Teotihuacan architectural style. The sloping base, or *talud*, of each platform supports a vertical *tablero*, or **entablature**, which is surrounded by a frame and often filled with sculptural decoration. The Temple of the Feathered Serpent was enlarged several times, and typical of Mesoamerican practice, each enlargement completely enclosed the previous structure, like the concentric layers of an onion.

12-6. Temple of the
Feathered
Serpent, the
Ciudadela,
Teotihuacan,
Mexico.
Teotihuacan
culture,
c. 350 CE (?)

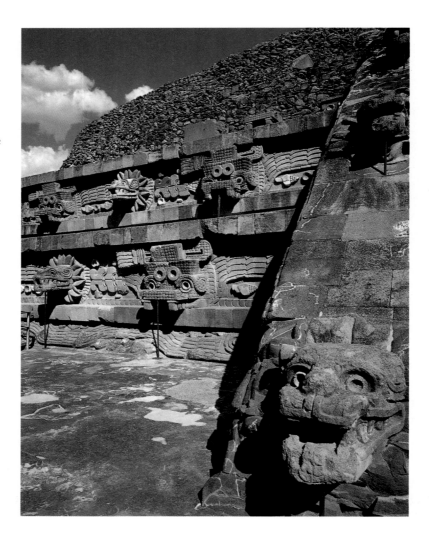

Archeological excavations of earlier-phase *tableros* and a stairway balustrade have revealed painted reliefs of the Feathered Serpent, the goggle-eyed Rain God (or Fire God, according to some), and aquatic shells and snails (fig. 12-6). Their flat, angular, abstract style is typical of Teotihuacan art and is a marked contrast to the three-dimensional, curvilinear style of Olmec art. The Rain God has a squarish, stylized head with protruding lips, huge round eyes originally inlaid with obsidian and surrounded by colored circles, and large, circular earspools. The fanged serpent heads, perhaps composites of snakes and other creatures, emerge from an aureole of stylized feathers. It is tempting to read cosmic imagery into the sculpture. The Rain God and the Feathered Serpent may represent alternating wet and dry seasons, may be symbols of regeneration and cyclical renewal, or may have some other meaning that has been lost.

The residential sections of Teotihuacan adhered to the grid established in the city's center. The large palaces of the elite, with as many as forty-five rooms and seven patios, stood nearest the ceremonial center. Artisans, foreign traders, and peasants lived farther away, in less luxurious compounds. The palaces and more humble homes alike were rectangular, one-story structures with high walls, thatched roofs, and suites of rooms arranged symmetrically around open courts. Walls were plastered and, in the homes of the elite, covered with paintings.

Teotihuacan's artists worked in a true **fresco** technique, applying pigments directly on damp lime plaster. Their flat, abstract-style drawing is assured, and their use of color is subtle—one work may include five shades of red with touches of ocher, green, and blue. A detached fragment of a wall painting, now in The Cleveland Museum of Art, depicts a bloodletting ritual in which an elaborately dressed man enriches and revitalizes the earth with his own blood (fig. 12-7). The man's Feathered Serpent headdress, decorated with precious quetzal feathers, indicates his high rank. He stands between rectangular plots of earth planted with bloody maguey spines and scatters seeds or drops of blood from his right hand, as indicated by the panel with conventionalized symbols for blood, seeds, and flowers. The **speech scroll** emerging from his open mouth symbolizes his ritual chant. The visual weight accorded the headdress and speech scroll suggests that the man's priestly office and chanted words are essential elements of the ceremony. Above the figure is a two-headed, spotted serpent holding two birds in its angular coils. Such bloodletting rituals were not limited to Teotihuacan but were widespread in Mesoamerica.

12-7. *Maguey Bloodletting Ritual*, fragment of a fresco from Teotihuacan, Mexico. Teotihuacan culture, 600–750 CE. Pigment on lime plaster, 32¼ x 45¼" (82 x 116.1 cm). The Cleveland Museum of Art

Purchase from the J. H. Wade Fund (63.252)

The maguey plant supplied the people of Teotihuacan with food; fiber for making clothing, rope, and paper; and the sacramental drink pulque. As this painting indicates, priestly officials used it in rituals of self-sacrifice to draw their own blood.

The Maya

The Maya homeland in southern Mesoamerica includes Guatemala, the Yucatan peninsula, Belize, and the eastern part of Honduras and El Salvador. The remarkable civilization created there endured to the time of the Spanish conquest and is still reflected in the culture of the Maya's present-day descendants. The ancient Maya are noted for a number of achievements. They developed ways to produce high agricultural yields in the seemingly inhospitable tropical rain forest of the Yucatan. In densely populated cities they built imposing pyramids, temples, palaces, and administrative structures. They developed the most advanced hieroglyphic writing in Mesoamerica and the most sophisticated version of the Mesoamerican calendrical system (see "Maya Record Keeping," page 452). With these tools they documented the accomplishments of their rulers in monumental commemorative **stelae**, in books, on ceramic vessels, and on wall paintings. (Scholars have determined the relationship between the Maya calendar and the European calendar, making it possible to date Maya artifacts with a precision unknown elsewhere in the Americas.) They studied astronomy and the natural cycles of plants and animals and developed the mathematical concepts of zero and place value before they were known in Europe.

An increasingly detailed picture of the Maya has been emerging from recent archeological research and advances in deciphering their writing. That picture shows a society divided into competing centers, each with a hereditary ruler and an elite class of nobles and priests supported by a far larger class of farmer-commoners. Rulers established their legitimacy, maintained links with their divine ancestors, and sustained the gods through elaborate rituals, including ball games, bloodletting ceremonies, and human sacrifice. These rituals occurred in the pyramids, temples, and plazas that dominated Maya cities. Rulers commemorated such events and their military exploits on carved stelae. A complex pantheon of deities, many with several manifestations, presided over the Maya universe.

Olmec influence was widespread in the Maya area during the middle Preclassic period (1000–300 BCE). The earliest distinctively Maya centers emerged during the late Preclassic period (300 BCE–250 CE), and Maya civilization reached its peak in the southern lowlands of the Yucatan peninsula during the Classic period (250–900 CE). Probably due to increased warfare and growing pressure on agricultural resources, the sites in the southern lowlands were abandoned at the end of the Classic period. The focus of Maya civilization then shifted to the northern Yucatan during the Postclassic period (900–1500 CE).

MAYA RECORD KEEPING

Since the rediscovery of the Classic period Maya sites in the nineteenth century, scholars have puzzled over the meaning of the hieroglyphic writing that abounds in Maya artwork. They soon realized that many of the glyphs were numeric notations in a complex calendrical system. By the early twentieth century the calendrical system had been interpreted and approximately correlated with the European calendar. The Maya calendar counts time from a starting date some 5,000 years ago, now securely established as August 13, 3114 BCE. This system, known as the long count, incorporates the short-count system, based on interlocking 260-day and 365-day cycles, of other Mesoamerican societies. The long count is unique to the Classic period Maya.

The meaning of the noncalendric inscriptions remained obscure until the late 1950s. Before that time many prominent Mayanists argued that the inscriptions dealt with astronomical and astrological observations, not historical events. This interpretation was in accord with the prevailing view that the Classic period Maya were a peaceful people ruled by a theocracy of learned priests. Since the late 1950s scholars have made enormous progress in deciphering Maya writing. The results of their work, combined with the results of archeological research, have overturned the earlier view of Maya society and Maya writing. The inscriptions on Maya architecture and the many stone stelae erected at Maya sites are, it turns out, almost entirely devoted to historic events in the lives of Maya rulers and the Maya elite. They record the dates of royal marriages, births of heirs, alliances between cities, and great military victories, tying them to astronomical events and propitious periods in the Maya calendar.

Maya writing, like the Maya calendar, is the most advanced in ancient Mesoamerica. About 800 glyphs have been identified, equivalent to the number in ancient Egyptian writing at some periods. The system combines logographs—symbols representing entire words—and symbols representing syllables in the Maya language.

12-8. North Acropolis (right) and Temple I, called the Temple of the Giant Jaguar (tomb of Au Cacau), Tikal, Guatemala. Maya culture. North Acropolis, 5th century CE; Temple I, c. 700 CE

Tikal has been the focus of an extended program of research directed by archeologists from the University of Pennsylvania in cooperation with the Guatemalan government. This research is part of an explosive growth in Maya studies that has enormously enriched our understanding of Maya culture and history.

Classic Period Architecture at Tikal and Palenque.
The monumental buildings of Maya cities were masterful examples of the use of architecture for public display and propaganda. Seen from outside and afar, they would have impressed the common people with the power and authority of the elite and the gods they served.

Tikal, in what is now northern Guatemala, was the largest Classic period Maya city, with a population of as many as 70,000 at its height. Like other Maya cities—and unlike Teotihuacan, with its rigid grid—Tikal conformed to the uneven terrain of the rain forest. Plazas, pyramid-temples, ball courts, and other structures stood on high ground connected by elevated roads, or causeways. One major causeway, 80 feet wide, led from the center of the city to outlying residential areas.

Figure 12-8 shows part of the ceremonial core of Tikal. The structure on the right, known as the North Acropolis, follows a north-south axis and dates to the early Classic period. It contained many royal tombs and covers earlier structures that date to the origin of the city, about 500 BCE. The tall pyramid in the center is known as Temple I or the Temple of the Giant Jaguar. It covers the tomb of Au Cacau (Lord Chocolate, 682–c. 727), who began an ambitious expansion of Tikal after a period in the sixth and early seventh century CE when there was little new construction at this or other major Maya sites. Under Au Cacau and his successors, Tikal's influence grew, with evidence of contacts that extended from highland Mexico to Costa Rica.

Temple I faces a companion pyramid, Temple II, across a large plaza. These two structures changed the orientation of the ceremonial center from north-south to east-west. The new plaza provided a monumental entrance to the North Acropolis, and the two new pyramids framed the ancestral core of the city, visually linking old and new.

From Au Cacau's tomb in the limestone bedrock, Temple I rises above the forest canopy to a height of more than 140 feet. It has nine layers, probably reflecting the belief, current among the Aztec and the Maya at the time of the Spanish conquest, that the underworld had nine levels. Priests climbed the steep stone staircase on the exterior to the temple on top, which consists of two long, parallel rooms covered with a steep roof supported by **corbeled vaults**. It is typical of Maya enclosed stone structures, which resemble the kind of pole-and-thatch

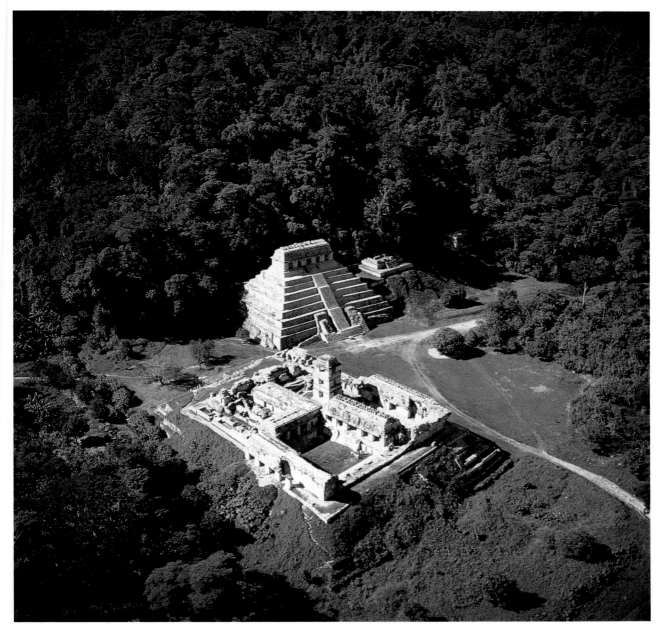

12-9.   Palace (foreground) and Temple of the Inscriptions (tomb-pyramid of Lord Pacal), Palenque, Mexico. Maya culture, 7th century CE

houses the Maya still build in parts of the Yucatan today. The only entrance to the temple was on the long side, facing the plaza and the commemorative stelae erected there. The crest that rises over the roof of the temple, known as a **roof comb**, was originally covered with brightly painted sculpture.

Palenque, located in the Mexican state of Chiapas, rose to prominence in the late Classic period. Hieroglyphic inscriptions record the beginning of its royal dynasty in 431 CE, but the city had only limited regional importance until the ascension of a powerful ruler, Lord Pacal (Maya for "shield"), who ruled from 615 to 683 CE. He and the son who succeeded him commissioned most of the structures visible at Palenque today. As at Tikal, major buildings are grouped on high ground. A northern complex has five temples, two nearby adjacent temples, and a ball court. A central group includes the so-called Palace, the Temple of the Inscriptions, and two other temples (fig. 12-9). A third group of temples lies to the southeast.

The palace in the central group—a series of buildings on two levels around three open courts, all on a raised terrace—may have been an administrative rather than a residential complex. The Temple of the Inscriptions next to it is a pyramid that rises to a height of about 75 feet. Like Temple I at Tikal, it has nine levels. The shrine on the summit consisted of a portico with five entrances and a three-part, vaulted inner chamber surmounted by a tall roof comb. Its facade still retains much of its stucco sculpture. The inscriptions that give the building its name were carved on the back wall of the portico and the central inner chamber.

12-10. Sarcophagus lid, in the tomb of Lord Pacal, Temple of the Inscriptions, Palenque, Mexico. Maya culture. c. 683 ce. Limestone, approx. 12'6" x 7' (3.8 x 2.14 m)

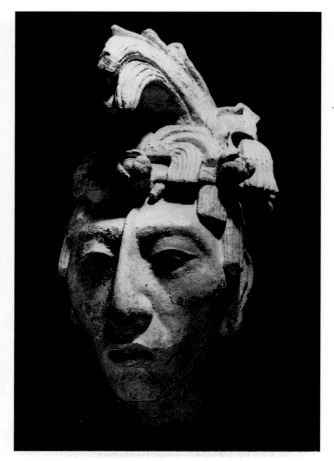

12-11. Portrait of Lord Pacal, from his tomb, Temple of the Inscriptions. Mid-7th century ce. Stucco, height 16⁷⁄₈" (43 cm). Museo Nacional de Antropología, Mexico City

This portrait of the youthful Lord Pacal may have been placed in his tomb as an offering. Possibly it formed part of the original exterior decoration of the Temple of the Inscriptions.

In 1952 an archeologist studying the structure of the Temple of the Inscriptions discovered a corbel-vaulted stairway beneath the summit shrine. This stairway descended almost 80 feet to a small subterranean chamber that contained the undisturbed tomb of Lord Pacal himself, and in it were some remarkable examples of Classic sculpture.

Classic Period Sculpture. Lord Pacal lay in a monolithic sarcophagus with a lid carved in low relief that showed him balanced between the spirit world and the earth (fig. 12-10). With knees bent, feet twisted, and face, hands, and torso upraised, he lies on the head of a creature that represents the setting sun. Together they are falling into the jaws of the underworld. The image above him, which ends in the profile head of a god and a fantastic bird, represents the sacred tree of the Maya. Its roots are in the earth, its trunk is in the world, and its branches support the celestial bird in the heavens. The message is one of death and rebirth. Lord Pacal, like the setting sun, will rise again to join the gods after falling into the underworld. Lord Pacal's ancestors, carved on

the side of his sarcophagus, witness his death and **apotheosis**. They wear elaborate headdresses and are shown only from the waist up, as though emerging from the earth. Among them are Lord Pacal's parents, Lady White Quetzal and Lord Yellow Jaguar-Parrot, supporting the contention of some scholars that both maternal and paternal lines transmitted royal power among the Maya.

Elite men and women, rather than gods, were the usual subjects of Maya sculpture, and most show rulers dressed as warriors performing religious rituals in elaborate costumes and headdresses. The Maya favored low-relief carving with sharp outlines on flat stone surfaces, but they also excelled at three-dimensional clay and stucco sculpture. A stucco portrait of Lord Pacal found with his sarcophagus shows him as a young man wearing a diadem of jade and flowers (fig. 12-11). His features—sloping forehead and elongated skull (babies had their heads bound to produce this shape), large curved nose (enhanced by an ornamental bridge, perhaps of latex), full lips, and open mouth—are characteristic of the Maya ideal of beauty. Traces of pigment indicate that this portrait, like much Maya sculpture, was colorfully painted.

12-12. Cylindrical vessel (composite photograph in the form of a roll-out). Maya culture, 600–900 CE. Painted ceramic; diameter 6½" (16.6 cm); height 8⅜" (21.5 cm). The Art Museum, Princeton University, New Jersey

The clay vessel was first covered by a creamy white slip and then painted in light brown washes and dark brown or black lines. The painter may have used turkey feathers to apply the pigments.

Classic Period Painting. Maya painting survives on ceramics and a few large murals. Most illustrated books have perished except for a few postconquest examples with astronomical and divinatory information. Scribes and vase painters were often members of the ruling elite and perhaps included members of the royal family not in the direct line of succession. Vases painted in the so-called **codex style**, referring to books of folded paper made from the maguey plant, often show a fluid line and elegance similar to that of the manuscripts.

A late Classic cylindrical vase in the codex style (fig. 12-12) may illustrate an episode from a legend recounted in the Book of Popol Vuh, a compendium of Maya myths written in Spanish in the sixteenth century by a Maya noble. The protagonists of this legend, the mythical Hero Twins, defeat the Lords of Xibalba, the Maya underworld, and overcome death. The vessel shows one of the Lords of Xibalba, an aged-looking being known to archeologists as God L, sitting inside a temple on a raised platform. Five female deities attend him. The god ties a wrist cuff on the attendant kneeling to his left. Another attendant, seated outside the temple, looks over her shoulder at a scene in which two men sacrifice a bound victim. A rabbit in the foreground writes in a manuscript, reminding us of the Maya obsession with historical records, as well as of the many books now lost. The two men may be the Hero Twins and the bound victim a bystander they sacrificed and then brought back to life in order to gain the confidence of the Xibalban lords. The inscriptions on the vessel have not been entirely translated. They include a calendar reference to the Death God and to Venus, the evening star, which the Maya associated with war and sacrifice.

12-13. Castillo, with Chacmool in foreground, Chichen Itza, Yucatan, Mexico. Maya culture, 9th–13th century

Postclassic Art. A northern Maya group called the Itza rose to prominence when the focus of Maya civilization shifted northward in the Postclassic period. Their principal center, Chichen Itza, which means "at the mouth of the well of the Itza," grew from a village located near a sacred well. The city flourished from the ninth to the thirteenth century CE, eventually covering about 6 square miles. It shares many features with the site of Tula in central Mexico, but archeologists are uncertain what relationship the two centers had to each other.

One of Chichen Itza's most conspicuous structures is a massive pyramid in the center of a large plaza (fig. 12-13). Embellished with figures of the Feathered Serpent, this structure is known today as the Castillo (Spanish for "castle"). A stairway on each side leads to a square, blocky temple on its summit. At the spring and fall equinoxes, the rising sun casts an undulating, serpentlike shadow on the stairway balustrades. Like earlier Maya pyramids, the Castillo has nine levels, but many other features of Chichen Itza are markedly different from earlier sites. The Castillo, for example, is lower and broader than the stepped pyramids of Tikal and Palenque, and Chichen Itza's buildings have wider rooms. Another prominent feature not found at earlier sites is the use of pillars and columns. Chichen Itza has broad, open galleries surrounding courtyards and inventive columns in the form of inverted, descending serpents. Brilliantly colored relief sculpture covered the buildings of Chichen Itza, and paintings of feathered serpents, jaguars, coyotes, eagles, and composite mythological creatures adorned its interior rooms. The surviving works show narrative scenes that emphasize the prowess of warriors and the skill of ritual ball players.

Sculpture at Chichen Itza, including the serpent columns and the half-reclining figures known as **Chacmools** (see fig. 12-13), has the sturdy forms, proportions, and angularity of architecture. It lacks the curving forms and subtlety of Classic Maya sculpture. The Chacmools probably represent fallen warriors and were used to receive sacrificial offerings. They once typified pre-Columbian sculpture for many Westerners.

After Chichen Itza's decline, Mayapan, on the north coast of the Yucatan, became the principal Maya center. But by the time the Spanish arrived, Mayapan, too, had declined. The Maya people and much of their culture would survive the conquest despite the imposition of Hispanic customs and beliefs. They continue to speak their own languages, to venerate traditional sacred places, and to follow traditional ways.

CENTRAL AMERICA

Unlike their neighbors in Mesoamerica, who lived in complex hierarchical societies, the people of Central America generally lived in extended family groups led by chiefs. A notable example of these small chiefdoms was the Diquis culture, which developed in present-day Costa Rica from about 700 CE to about 1500.

The Diquis occupied fortified villages without monumental architecture or sculpture and seem to have engaged in constant warfare with one another. They nevertheless produced fine featherwork, ceramics, textiles, and gold objects. (The name Costa Rica, which means "rich coast" in Spanish, probably reflects the value the Spaniards placed on the gold.)

Metallurgy and the use of gold and copper-gold alloys were widespread in Central America. The technique of **lost-wax casting** probably first appeared in present-day Colombia between 500 and 300 BCE. From there it spread north to the Diquis. The small, exquisite pendant shown in figure 12-14 illustrates the sophisticated design and technical facility of Diquis goldwork. The pendant depicts a male figure wearing bracelets, anklets, and a belt with a snake-headed penis sheath. He plays a drum while holding the tail of a snake in his teeth and its head in his left hand. The wavy forms with ser-

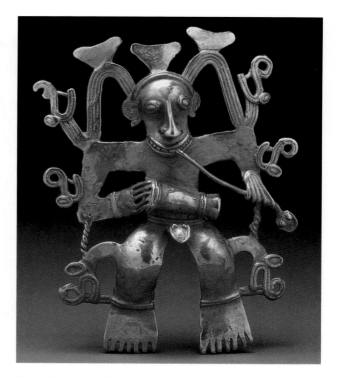

12-14. *Shaman with Drum and Snake*, from Costa Rica. Diquis culture, c. 1000 CE. Gold, 4¼ x 3¼"(10.8 x 8.2 cm). Museos del Banco Central de Costa Rica, San José, Costa Rica

pent heads emerging from his scalp suggest an elaborate headdress, and the creatures emerging from his legs suggest some kind of reptile costume. The inverted triangles on the headdress probably represent birds' tails.

In Diquis mythology serpents and crocodiles inhabited a lower world, humans and birds a higher one. Their art depicts animals and insects as fierce and dangerous. Perhaps the man in the pendant is a shaman transforming himself into a composite serpent-bird or performing a ritual snake dance surrounded by serpents or crocodiles. The scrolls on the sides of his head may represent the shaman's power to hear and understand the speech of animals. Whatever its specific meaning, the pendant evokes a ritual of mediation between earthly and cosmic powers involving music, dance, and costume.

Whether gold figures of this kind were protective amulets or signs of high status, they were certainly more than personal adornment. Shamans and warriors wore gold to inspire fear, perhaps because gold was thought to capture the energy and power of the sun. This energy was also thought to allow shamans to leave their bodies and travel into cosmic realms.

SOUTH AMERICA: THE CENTRAL ANDES

Like Mesoamerica, the central Andes of South America—primarily present-day Peru and Bolivia—saw the development of complex hierarchical societies with rich and varied artistic traditions. The area is one of dramatic contrasts. The narrow coastal plain, bordered by the Pacific Ocean on the west and the abruptly soaring Andes on the east, is one of the driest deserts in the world. Life here depends on the rich marine

12-15. Mantle with bird impersonators, from the Paracas peninsula south coast, Peru. Paracas culture, c. 50–100 CE. Plain weave with stem-stitch embroidery, approx. 40" x 7'11" (101 cm x 2.41 m). Museum of Fine Arts, Boston

Denman Waldo Ross Collection

The stylized figures display the remarkable Paracas sense of color and pattern. The all-directional pattern is also characteristic of Paracas art.

resources of the Pacific and the rivers that descend from the Andes, forming a series of valley oases from south to north. The Andes themselves are a region of lofty snow-capped peaks, high grasslands, steep slopes, and deep, fertile river valleys. The high grasslands are home to the Andean camelids—llamas, alpacas, vicuñas, and guanacos—that have served for thousands of years as beasts of burden and a source of wool and meat. The lush eastern slopes of the Andes descend to the tropical rain forest of the Amazon basin.

The earliest evidence of monumental architecture in Peru dates to the third millennium BCE, contemporary with the earliest pyramids in Egypt. On the coast, sites with ceremonial mounds and plazas were located near the sea. The inhabitants of these centers depended on marine and agricultural resources, farming the floodplains of nearby coastal rivers. Their chief crops were cotton, used to make fishing nets, and gourds, used for floats. Early centers in the highlands consisted of multi-roomed stone-walled structures with sunken central fire pits that served to burn ritual offerings.

In the second millennium BCE, herding and agriculture became prevalent in the highlands. On the coast, people became increasingly dependent on agriculture. They began to build canal irrigation systems, greatly expanding their food supply. Settlements were moved inland, and large, U-shaped ceremonial complexes with circular sunken plazas were built. These complexes were oriented toward the mountains, the direction of the rising sun and the source of the water that nourished their crops. The shift to irrigation agriculture also corresponded to the spread of pottery and ceramic technology in Peru.

Between about 800 and 200 BCE an art style associated with the northern highland site of Chavin de Huantar spread through much of the Andes. In Andean chronology, this era is known as the Early Horizon, the first of three so-called Horizon periods marked by the widespread influence of a single style.

The Chavin site was located on a major trade route between the coast and the Amazon basin, and Chavin art features images of many tropical forest animals. The political and social forces behind the spread of the Chavin style are not known. Many archeologists suspect that they involved an influential religious cult. In any event, the period was one of artistic and technical innovation in ceramics, metallurgy, and textiles. These innovations found continued expression in the textiles of the Paracas culture on the south coast of Peru, the art of the subsequent Nazca culture there, and the ceramics and metalwork of the Moche culture on the north coast.

The Paracas and Nazca Cultures

The Paracas culture of the south coast flourished from about 300 BCE to 200 CE, overlapping with the Chavin period. It is best known for its stunning textiles, which were found in cemeteries wrapped in many layers around the dead. Some bodies were wrapped in as many as fifty pieces of cloth.

Weaving is of great antiquity in the central Andes and continues to be among the most prized arts in the region (see "Andean Textiles," page 458). Fine textiles were a source of prestige and wealth, and the production of textiles was an important factor in the domestication of both cotton and llamas. Andean peoples developed a simple, portable **backstrap loom** in which the **warp** (lengthwise thread) was looped and stretched between two poles. One pole was tied to a stationary object and the other to a strap circling the waist of the weaver. The weaver controlled the tension of the warp threads by leaning back and forth while threading a **bobbin**, or shuttle, through the warp to create the **weft** (crosswise thread).

The designs on Paracas textiles include repeated **embroidered** (needlework) figures of warriors, dancers, and composite creatures such as bird-people (fig. 12-15). Embroiderers used tiny overlapping stitches to create

ANDEAN TEXTILES

The creation of ancient Andean textiles, among the most technically complex cloths ever made, consumed a major portion of their societies' resources. Dyers, weavers, and **embroiderers** used nearly every textile technique known, some of them unique inventions of these cultures, and the production of a single textile might involve a dozen processes requiring highly skilled workers. A tunic would have taken approximately 500 hours of work. Some of the most elaborate textiles were woven, unwoven, and rewoven to achieve special effects that were prized for their labor-intensiveness and difficulty of manufacture as well as their beauty. The most finely woven pieces contain a staggering 500 threads per square inch. Because of their complexity, deciphering how these textiles were made can be a challenge, and scholars rely on contemporary Andean weavers—inheritors of this tradition—for guidance. Then, as now, textile production was primarily in the hands of women.

Cotton was grown in Peru by 3000 BCE and was the most widely used plant fiber. The earliest Peruvian textiles were made without looms, and twining, knotting, wrapping, braiding, and looping continued to be used even after looms were invented in the early second millennium BCE. **Tapestry**-weaving (see below) was the main cloth-making technique for the next thousand or so years, followed by the introduction of embroidery on camelid fibers (llama, alpaca, or vicuña hair), the Andean equivalent of wool. (Embroidery on camelid fiber is seen in the Paracas mantle in figure 12-15.) From about 400 BCE on, animal fibers—superior in warmth and dye absorption—largely replaced cotton in the mountains, where cotton was hard to cultivate.

In tapestry, a technique especially suited to representational textiles, an undyed cotton **warp** was frequently combined with a vividly colored camelid-fiber **weft** that completely covered it. Each colored section was woven as an independent unit (see illustration). Since the shuttle was not passed across the entire width of the fabric in one motion, as in other kinds of weaving, tapestry allowed greater pictorial freedom but was quite time-consuming.

Fabrics were colored with dyes made from plants and a few animals. The deep blue of the Paracas mantle, for instance, was probably derived from the indigo plant. Dyeing technology, too, was an advanced art form in the ancient Andes, with some textiles containing dozens of colors.

Textiles were of enormous importance in Andean life, serving significant functions in both private and public events. Specialized fabrics were developed for everything from ritual burial shrouds and shamans' costumes to rope bridges and knotted record-keeping devices. Clothing indicated ethnic group and social status and was customized for certain functions, the most rarefied being royal ceremonial garments made for specific occasions and worn only once.

Detail of tapestry-weave mantle, from Peru. c. 700–1100 CE. Wool and cotton. The Cleveland Museum of Art
Gift of William R. Carlisle, 56.84

Diagram of toothed tapestry-weaving technique, one of many sophisticated methods used in Andean textiles

colorful, curvilinear patterns, sometimes using as many as twenty-two different colors within a single figure. The effect of the clashing and contrasting colors and tumbling figures is dazzling.

The Nazca culture, which dominated the south coast of Peru from about 100 BCE to 700 CE, overlapped the Paracas culture. Nazca artisans continued to weave fine fabrics, but they also produced multicolored pottery with painted and modeled images reminiscent of those on Paracas textiles.

The Nazca are probably best known for their colossal earthworks, or **geoglyphs**, which dwarf even the most ambitious twentieth-century environmental sculpture. On great stretches of desert they literally drew in the earth. By removing a layer of dark gravel, they exposed the lighter underlying soil, then edged the resulting lines

12-16. Earth drawing of a hummingbird, Nazca Plain, southwest Peru. Nazca culture, c. 200 BCE–200 CE. Length approx. 450' (138 m); wingspan approx. 200' (60.5 m)

with stones. In this way they created gigantic images—including a hummingbird, a killer whale, a monkey, a spider, a duck, and other birds—similar to those with which they decorated their pottery. They also made abstract patterns and groups of straight, parallel lines that extend for up to 12 miles. The beak of the hummingbird in figure 12-16 consists of two parallel lines, each 120 feet long. The purpose of these geoglyphs is not known.

The Moche Culture

The Moche culture dominated the north coast of Peru from the Piura Valley to the Huarmey Valley—a distance of some 370 miles—between about 200 and 700 CE. Moche lords ruled each valley in this region from a ceremonial-administrative center. The largest of these, in the Moche Valley (from which the culture takes its name), contained the so-called Pyramids of the Sun and the Moon. Both pyramids were built entirely of **adobe** bricks. The Pyramid of the Sun, the largest ancient structure in South America, was originally a cross-shaped structure 1,122 feet long by 522 feet wide that rose in a series of terraces to a height of 59 feet. This site had been thought to be the capital of the entire Moche realm, but evidence is accumulating that the Moche were not so centralized.

The Moche were exceptional potters and metalsmiths. They developed ceramic molds, which allowed them to mass-produce some forms. Vessels were made in the shape of naturalistically modeled human beings, animals, and architectural structures. They also created realistic portrait vessels and recorded mythological narratives and ritual scenes in intricate fine-line painting. Similar scenes were painted on the walls of temples and administrative buildings. Moche smiths, the most sophisticated in the central Andes, developed several innovative alloys.

12-17. *Moche Lord with a Feline*, from Moche Valley, Peru. Moche culture, c. 100 BCE–500 CE. Painted ceramic, height 7½" (19 cm). Art Institute of Chicago
Buckingham Fund, 1955–2281

Behind the figure is the distinctive stirrup-shaped handle and spout. Vessels of this kind, used in Moche rituals, were also treasured as special luxury items and were buried in large quantities with individuals of high status.

The ceramic vessel in figure 12-17 shows a Moche lord sitting in a structure associated with high office. He wears an elaborate headdress and large earspools and strokes a cat or perhaps a jaguar cub. The so-called

12-18. Earspool, from Sipan, Peru. Moche culture, c. 300 CE. Gold, turquoise, quartz, and shell, diameter approx. 5" (12.7 cm). Bruning Archeological Museum, Lambayeque, Peru

12-19. Beaver effigy platform pipe, from Bedford Mound, Pike County, Illinois. Hopewell culture, c. 100–200 CE. Pipestone, pearl, and bone, length 4½" (11.4 cm). Gilcrease Museum, Tulsa, Oklahoma

Pipes made by the Hopewell culture may have been used for smoking hallucinatory plants, perhaps during rituals involving the animal carved on the pipe bowl.

stirrup, or **U**-shaped, spout appears on many high-quality Moche vessels. Paintings indicate that vessels of this type were used in Moche rituals.

A central theme in Moche iconography is the sacrifice ceremony, in which prisoners captured in battle are sacrificed and several elaborately dressed figures drink their blood. Archeologists have labeled the principal figure in the ceremony as the Warrior Priest and other important figures as the Bird Priest and the Priestess. The recent discovery of a number of spectacularly rich Moche tombs indicates that the sacrifice ceremony was an actual Moche ritual and that Moche lords assumed the roles of the principal figures. The occupant of a tomb at the site of Sipan in the Lambayeque Valley was buried with the regalia of the Warrior Priest. In a tomb at the site of San José de Moro in the Jequetepeque Valley, an occupant was buried with the regalia of the Priestess.

Among the riches accompanying the Warrior Priest at Sipan was a pair of exquisite gold-and-turquoise earspools, each of which depicts three Moche warriors (fig. 12-18). The central figure is made of beaten gold and turquoise. He and his companions are adorned with tiny gold-and-turquoise earspools. They wear spectacular gold-and-turquoise headdresses topped with delicate sheets of gold that resemble the crescent-shaped knives used in sacrifices. The crests, like feathered fans of gold, would have swayed in the breeze as the wearer moved. The central figure has a crescent-shaped nose ornament and carries a gold club and shield. A necklace of owl's-head beads strung with gold thread hangs around his shoulders. Many of his anatomical features have been rendered in painstaking detail.

NORTH AMERICA

Compared to the densely inhabited agricultural regions of Mesoamerica and South America, most of North America remained sparsely populated until the arrival of European conquerors in the fifteenth century. People lived primarily by hunting, fishing, and gathering edible plants. In the Southeast, in the lands drained by the Mississippi and Missouri river system, a more settled way of life began to emerge, and by around 1000 BCE—in Louisiana as early as 2800 BCE, according to some anthropologists—nomadic hunting and gathering had given way to more settled communities. People cultivated squash, sunflowers, and other plants to supplement their diet of game, fish, and berries. People in the American Southwest began to adopt a sedentary, agricultural life toward the end of the first millennium BCE.

The Mound Builders

Sometime before 1000 BCE, people living in the Mississippi River Valley began building monumental earthworks and burying their leaders with valuable grave goods. The earliest of these earthworks, at Poverty Point in Louisiana, dates to about 1300 BCE. One of the most impressive is the Great Serpent Mound in present-day Adams County, Ohio (see fig. 12-1). Its date is unknown, but it is located near a burial mound of the Adena culture (600 BCE–200 CE). There have been many interpretations of the writhing snake form, especially the "head" at the highest point, which some see as opening its jaws to swallow a huge egg formed by a heap of stones.

12-20. Reconstruction of central Cahokia, East St. Louis, Illinois. Mississippian culture, c. 1150 CE. Earth mounds and wooden structures; east-west length approx. 3 miles (4.5 km), north-south length approx. 2¼ miles (3.6 km); base of great mound, 1,037 x 790' (316 x 241 m), height approx. 100' (30 m). Painting by William R. Iseminger

The people of the Mississippi and Ohio valleys traded widely with other regions. For example, burials of the Adena culture and another mound-building culture, the Hopewell (centered in the Illinois and Ohio valleys, 200 BCE–200 CE), contained jewelry made with copper from Michigan's upper peninsula and silhouettes cut in sheets of mica from the Appalachian Mountains. The Hopewell people also made pipes of fine-grain pipestone carved with realistic representations of forest animals and birds, sometimes with inlaid eyes and teeth of fresh-water pearls and bone. The Hopewell exchanged this pipestone and a flintlike stone used for tool-making for turtle shells and sharks' teeth from Florida. Hopewell pipes and pipestone have been found from Lake Superior to the Gulf of Mexico.

In a combination of realism and aesthetic simplification that is exceptionally sophisticated, a beaver crouching on a platform forms the bowl of a pipe found in Illinois (fig. 12-19). As in a modern pipe, the bowl—a hole in the beaver's back—could be filled with dried leaves (the Hopewell may not have grown tobacco), the leaves lighted, and smoke drawn through the hole in the stem. A second way that these pipes were used was to blow smoke inhaled from another vessel through the pipe to envelop the animal carved on it.

The people of the Mississippian culture (800–1500 CE) continued the mound-building tradition of the earlier southeastern cultures. Cahokia, 16 miles northeast of St. Louis near the juncture of the Illinois, Missouri, and Mis-

12-21. Cahokia

sissippi rivers (now East St. Louis, Illinois), was an urban center that at its height had a population of between 10,000 and 20,000 people, with another 10,000 in the surrounding countryside (figs. 12-20, 12-21). The site's most prominent feature is an enormous earth mound covering 15 acres. The location of the mound and the axis of the ceremonial center it dominated were established during the early part of the city's occupation (c. 900–1050 CE), but most construction occurred later, between about 1050 and 1250. A **stockade**, or fence, of upright wooden posts—a sign of increasing warfare—surrounded the

12-22. Pueblo Bonito, Chaco Canyon, New Mexico. Anasazi culture, c. 900–1250 CE

250-acre core. Within this barrier the principal mound rose in four stages to a height of about 100 feet. On its summit was a small, conical platform that supported a wood fence and a rectangular temple or house. Smaller rectangular and conical mounds in front of the principal mound surrounded a large, roughly rectangular plaza. In all, the walled enclosure contained more than 500 mounds, platforms, wooden enclosures, and houses. The various earthworks functioned as tombs and as bases for palaces and temples. A conical burial mound, for example, was located next to a platform that may have been used for sacrifices.

Postholes indicate that wooden **henges** were a feature of Cahokia. The largest, with a diameter of about 420 feet, had forty-eight posts and was oriented to the cardinal points. Sight lines between a forty-ninth post set east of the center of the enclosure and points on the perimeter enabled native astronomers to determine solstices and equinoxes.

The American Southwest

Three farming cultures emerged in the arid southwestern region of what is now the United States beginning around 200 BCE. The Mogollon culture, located in the mountains of west-central New Mexico and east-central Arizona, flourished from circa 200 BCE to about 1250 CE. The Hohokam culture, centered in central and southern Arizona, emerged around 200 BCE and endured until after

about 1200 CE. The Hohokam built large-scale irrigation systems with canals that were deep and narrow to reduce evaporation and lined with clay to reduce seepage. The Hohokam shared a number of customs with their Mesoamerican neighbors to the south, including the ritual ball game.

The third southwestern culture, the Anasazi (Navajo word meaning "the ancient ones"), emerged in the Four Corners region, where Colorado, Utah, Arizona, and New Mexico meet. The Anasazi, who adopted the irrigation technology of the Hohokam, turned to an agricultural, village way of life somewhat later than the other two groups. Around 750 CE they began building elaborate, multistoried, apartmentlike structures with many rooms for specialized purposes, including communal food storage. The Spaniards called these communities pueblos, or "towns." The descendants of the Anasazi, including the Hopi and Zuni, still occupy similar communities in the Four Corners area.

The largest known ancient Anasazi center is Pueblo Bonito in Chaco Canyon, which was built in stages between the tenth and mid-thirteenth centuries CE (fig. 12-22). In its final form this remarkable, **D**-shaped structure had hundreds of rooms and rose four stories high. Its outer perimeter wall was 1,300 feet long. The sandstone masonry walls on the ground floor were 4 feet thick, and trunks of ponderosa pines were used for roof beams. As new rooms were added over time, older rooms lost access to natural light. Amazingly, all aspects

12-23. Seed jar. Anasazi culture, 1100–1300 CE. Earthenware and black and white pigment, diameter 14½" (36.9 cm). The St. Louis Art Museum, St. Louis, Missouri
Purchase: Funds given by the Children's Art Festival 175:1981

of construction—including quarrying, timber cutting, and transport—were done without draft animals, wheeled vehicles, or metal tools.

Securing a steady food supply in the arid Southwest must have been a constant concern for the people of Chaco Canyon. At Pueblo Bonito the number of rooms far exceeds the evidence of human habitation, and many rooms were almost certainly devoted to food storage. Pueblo Bonito also has more than thirty **kivas**, which were centers of community ritual among pueblo dwellers. The presence of so many of them at Pueblo Bonito—including two that are more than 60 feet in diameter—attests to the importance of ritual at this site. The top of these circular, underground rooms became part of the floor of the communal plaza. Interlocking pine logs formed a shallow, domelike roof with a hole in the center through which only men would have entered. A pit in the floor directly under the entrance hole symbolized the place where the Anasazi ancestors had emerged from the earth in the mythic "first times." Here men performed important rituals and instructed youths in their adult ritual and social responsibilities.

Pueblo Bonito stood at the center of a network of wide, straight roads, in some places with curbs and paving. Almost invisible today, the roads were discovered and studied through aerial photography. The major roads run north and south in perfectly straight lines. The builders made no effort to avoid topographic obstacles;

when they encountered cliffs, they ran stairs up them. These characteristics suggest that the roads served as processional ways rather than practical thoroughfares.

Probably as a result of a climate change that made the Southwest increasingly arid, the population of Chaco Canyon declined during the twelfth century, and building at Pueblo Bonito ceased around 1230.

Women were the potters in Anasazi society. In the eleventh century they perfected a functional, aesthetically pleasing, coil-built earthenware, or low-fired ceramic. This ceramic tradition continues today among the Pueblo peoples of the Southwest. One type of vessel, a wide-mouthed seed jar with a globular body and holes near the rim (fig. 12-23), would have been suspended from roof poles, by thongs attached to the holes, out of reach of voracious rodents. The example shown here is decorated with black-and-white checkerboard and zigzag patterns. The patterns conform to the body of the jar, and in spite of their angularity, they enhance its curved shape. The intricate play of dark and light, positive and negative, suggests lightning flashing over a grid of irrigated fields.

Throughout the Americas for the next several hundred years, artistic traditions would continue to emerge, develop, and be transformed as the indigenous peoples of various regions interacted. The sudden incursions of Europeans, beginning in the late fifteenth century, would have dramatic and lasting impact on these civilizations and their art.

2500 BCE   1800   1200   600

Saharan rock wall painting
c. 2500–1500

Nok head
c. 500 BCE–200 CE

▲ SAHARAN ROCK ART c. 8000–500

NOK
c. 500 BCE–20

CHAPTER 13

Art of Ancient Africa

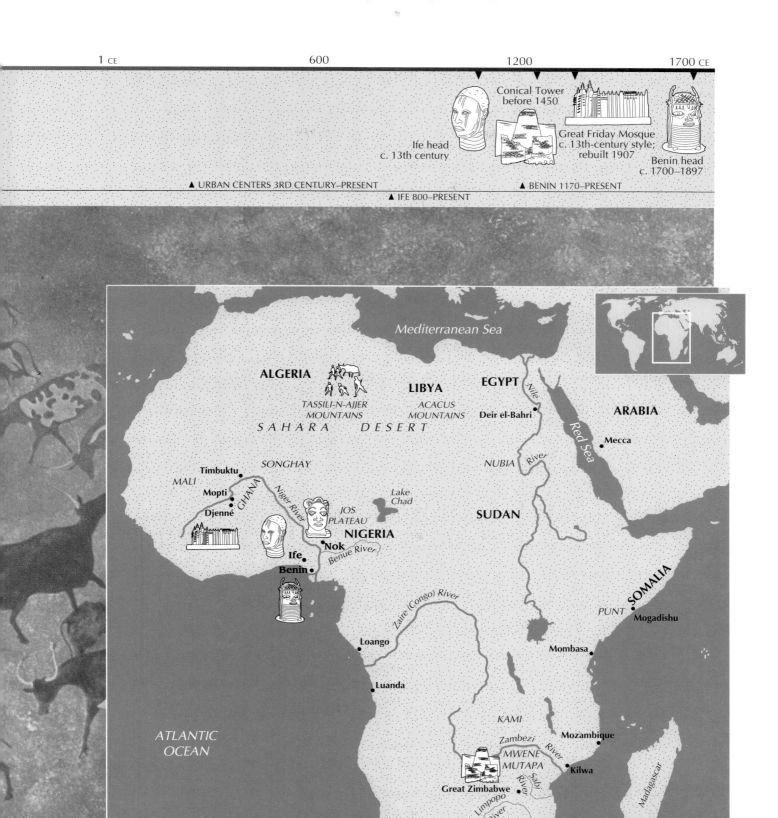

1 CE   600   1200   1700 CE

Conical Tower
before 1450

Ife head
c. 13th century

Great Friday Mosque
c. 13th-century style;
rebuilt 1907

Benin head
c. 1700–1897

▲ URBAN CENTERS 3RD CENTURY–PRESENT   ▲ BENIN 1170–PRESENT

▲ IFE 800–PRESENT

Mediterranean Sea

ALGERIA

LIBYA

EGYPT

ARABIA

TASSILI-N-AJJER
MOUNTAINS

ACACUS
MOUNTAINS

Deir el-Bahri

Nile

S A H A R A   D E S E R T

Mecca

Red Sea

SONGHAY

Timbuktu

NUBIA

River

MALI

Mopti

GHANA

Djenné

Niger River

JOS
PLATEAU

Lake
Chad

SUDAN

NIGERIA

Nok

Ife

Benue River

Benin

Zaïre (Congo) River

PUNT

SOMALIA

Mogadishu

Loango

Mombasa

Luanda

ATLANTIC
OCEAN

KAMI

Mozambique

Zambezi

River

MWENE
MUTAPA

Kilwa

Great Zimbabwe

Sabi

River

Madagascar

Limpopo

River

INDIAN
OCEAN

0   800 miles

0   800 kilometers

descended [the Nile] with three hundred asses laden with incense, ebony, grain, panthers, ivory, and every good product." Thus the Egyptian envoy Harkhuf described his return from Nubia, the Black African land to the south of Egypt, in 2300 BCE. Some eight centuries after Harkhuf's journey, the Egyptian queen Hatshepsut, drawn by such treasures, ordered an expedition to the land of Punt, an African kingdom on the northern coast of present-day Somalia. So important was this kind of contact that portraits of the king and queen of Punt appear in Hatshepsut's funerary temple at Deir el-Bahri.

THE LURE OF ANCIENT AFRICA

The riches of Africa attracted merchants and envoys in ancient times, and through trade the continent was in contact with the rest of the world. Egyptian relations, such as Hatshepsut's with African kingdoms to the south, continued through the Hellenistic era and beyond. To the west, dozens of settlements were founded along the Mediterranean coast of North Africa between 1000 and 300 BCE by Phoenicians and Greeks so that they could extend trade routes across the Sahara to the peoples of Lake Chad and the bend of the Niger River. When the Romans took control of North Africa, they continued this lucrative trans-Saharan trade. In the seventh and eighth centuries CE, the expanding empire of Islam swept across North Africa, and thereafter Islamic merchants were regular visitors to Bilad al-Sudan, the Land of the Blacks. Islamic scholars chronicled the great West African empires of Ghana, Mali, and Songhay, and West African gold financed the flowering of Islamic culture.

East Africa, meanwhile, had been drawn since at least the beginning of the Common Era into the maritime trade that ringed the Indian Ocean and extended east to Indonesia and the South China Sea. Arab, Indian, and Persian ships plied the coastline. A new language, Swahili, evolved from centuries of contact between Arabic-speaking merchants and Bantu-speaking Africans, and great port cities such as Mozambique, Kilwa, Mombasa, and Mogadishu arose.

In the fifteenth century, European ships ventured into the Atlantic Ocean and down the coast of Africa. After being cut off for centuries because of hostile relations with Islam, Europeans were only then rediscovering the continent at first hand. What they found often astonished them. "Dear King My Brother," wrote a fifteenth-century Portuguese king to his new trading partner, the king of Benin in West Africa. The Portuguese king's respect was well founded—Benin was vastly more powerful and more wealthy than the small European country that had just stumbled upon it.

European presence, benign and respectful at first, became over the centuries increasingly aggressive and territorial, culminating with the imposition of colonial rule over the entire continent during the late nineteenth century. European colonization was a watershed for Africa, dividing its long history of relatively independent development and forcing its entry into a world not of its own making.

As we saw in Chapter 3, Africa was home to one of the world's earliest great civilizations, that of ancient Egypt, and as we saw in Chapter 8, Egypt and the rest of North Africa contributed prominently to the development of Islamic art and culture. This chapter examines the artistic legacy of the rest of ancient Africa, beginning with the early peoples of the Sahara, then turning to other early civilizations.

SAHARAN ROCK ART

Like the Paleolithic inhabitants of Europe, early Africans painted and inscribed an abundance of images on the walls of the caves and rock shelters in which they sought refuge. Rock art has been found all over Africa, in sites ranging from small, isolated shelters to great, cavernous formations. The mountains of the central Sahara—principally the Tassili-n-Ajjer range in the south of present-day Algeria and the Acacus Mountains in present-day Libya—have especially fascinating examples of rock art. The images there span a period of thousands of years, recording not only the artistic and cultural development of the peoples who lived in the region, but also the transformation of the Sahara from the fertile grassland it once was to the vast desert we know today.

The earliest images of Saharan rock art are thought to date from at least 8000 BCE, during the transition into a geological period known as the Makalian Wet Phase. At that time the Sahara was a great grassy plain, perhaps much like the game-park areas of modern East Africa. Vivid images of hippopotamus, elephant, giraffe, antelope, and other animals incised into rock surfaces testify to the abundant wildlife that roamed the region. Like the cave paintings in Altamira and Lascaux (Chapter 1), these images may have been intended as magic to ensure plentiful game or a successful hunt, or they may have been symbolic of other life-enhancing activities, such as healing or rainmaking.

By 4000 BCE the climate had become more arid, and hunting had given way to herding as the primary life-sustaining activity of the Sahara's inhabitants. Among the most beautiful and complex examples of Saharan rock art created in this period are scenes of sheep, goats, and cattle and of the daily lives of the people who tended them. One such scene, *The Herders' Village,* was found at Tassili-n-Ajjer and probably dates from late in the herding period, about 2500–1500 BCE (fig. 13-1). Men and women are gathered in front of their round, thatched houses, the men tending the cattle, the

Years	Center	Africa	World
c. 8000–500 BCE	Sahara	Rock art; herding; settled agriculture; Great Pyramids at Giza; Sahara becoming desert; horse introduced; camel introduced; ironworking	**c. 8000–500 BCE** Bronze Age in Europe; plants and animals domesticated (Near East, Southeast Asia, the Americas); development of metallurgy (Near East); development of writing (Near East, China, India); Olmec civilization (Mesoamerica); birth of Laozi, founder of Daoism (China); birth of Siddhartha Gautama, founder of Buddhism (Nepal); Confucius (China)
c. 500 BCE–200 CE	Nok	First known sculpture; terracotta figures	**c. 500 BCE–1000 CE** Parthenon (Greece); crucifixion of Jesus (Jerusalem); Colosseum (Italy); Pantheon (Italy); first Gupta dynasty (India); earliest surviving Hindu temples (India); Hagia Sophia (Turkey); birth of Muhammad, founder of Islam (Arabia); Muslim conquests
c. 200–present	Djenné	Great Friday Mosque	
c. 800 CE–present	Ife	Terra-cotta sculpture; bronze sculpture	
c. 1000 CE–1500 CE	Great Zimbabwe	Stone structures; carvings	**c. 1000–1700 CE** Separation of Eastern and Western Christian Churches; the Crusades; Spanish Inquisition; beginning of Renaissance in Europe; Aztec civilization (Mexico); end of Byzantine Empire; Columbus's voyages; the Reformation; first English colony in North America
c. 1170 CE–present	Benin	Memorial sculpture; trade with Portuguese; Early, Middle, Late periods	

2500 BCE 1700 CE

13-1. *Cattle Gathered next to a Group of Huts*, detail of *The Herders' Village*, rock-wall painting, Tassili-n-Ajjer, Algeria. c. 2500–1500 BCE. Watercolor facsimile painted by students of Henri Lhote. Musée de l'Homme, Paris

THE MYTH OF "PRIMITIVE" ART

The word *primitive* has often been used by Western art historians to lump together the art of Africa, the Pacific islands, and North, South, and Central America before the arrival of Columbus. The label implies, among other things, that all these areas are in some way similar cultures that produced similar art for similar reasons.

The term itself means "early," and its very use implies that these civilizations are frozen at an early stage of development, rather than that their cultures have developed along different paths than those of Europe. In the past, the criteria used for assigning the label *primitive* to a people included so-called Stone Age technology, absence of written histories, and failure to build "great" cities. Yet the accomplishments of the peoples of Africa, to take just one example, strongly belie this categorization: Africans south of the Sahara have smelted and forged iron since at least 500 BCE, as the evidence of the Nok culture in northern Nigeria makes quite clear, and Africans in many areas have long smelted high-quality steel for weapons and tools. Many African peoples have recorded their histories in Arabic since at least the tenth century. And the first European visitors to western Africa expressed their admiration for the political, economic, and social sophistication of such urban centers as Benin, Luanda, and Mbanza Kongo.

Why, then, have labels like *primitive* persisted? Many historical attitudes were formed by Christian missionaries, who long described the people among whom they worked as "heathen," "barbaric," "ignorant," "tribal," "primitive," and other terms rooted in racism and colonialism. As these usages were perpetuated, they were extended to the creations of the cultures, and *primitive art* became the dominant label for the cultural products of these peoples. If the illogical notion that technological development equals quality of art were in fact valid, then the art of twentieth-century Japan, for example, would be considered greater than the art of fifteenth-century Italy.

women preparing a meal and caring for children. A large herd of cattle, many of them tethered to a long rope, has been driven in from pasture. The cattle shown are quite varied. Some are mottled, others are white, red, or black. Some have short, thick horns, while others have graceful, lyre-shaped horns. The overlapping forms and the confident placement of near figures low and distant figures high in the picture create a sense of depth and distance.

By 2500–2000 BCE the Sahara had dried considerably and the great game had gone, but other animals were introduced that appear in the rock art. The horse was brought from Egypt by about 1500 BCE and is seen regularly in rock art over the ensuing millennia. The fifth-century BCE Greek historian Herodotus described a chariot-driving people called the Garamante, whose kingdom corresponded roughly to present-day Libya, and rock-art images of horse-drawn chariots bear out his account. Around 600 BCE the camel was introduced into the region from the east, and images of camels have been painted on and incised into the rock from then to now.

The desiccation of the Sahara coincides with the rise of Egyptian civilization along the Nile Valley to the east. Similarities have been noted between Egyptian and Saharan motifs, among them images of rams with what appear to be disks between their horns. These similarities have been viewed as evidence of Egyptian influence on the less-developed regions of the Sahara. Yet in light of the great age of Saharan rock art, it seems just as plausible that influence flowed the other way, carried by people who had migrated into the Nile Valley in search of arable land and pasture when the grasslands of the Sahara dried up. This migration, by greatly expanding the population of the valley, may also have contributed to the tensions that resulted in the emergence of complex forms of social organization there.

SUB-SAHARAN CIVILIZATIONS

Saharan peoples presumably migrated southward as well, into the Sudan, the broad belt of grassland that stretches across Africa south of the Sahara desert, bringing with them knowledge of settled agriculture and animal husbandry. The earliest evidence for settled agriculture in the Sudan dates from about 3000 BCE. Toward the middle of the first millennium BCE, at the same time that iron technology was being developed elsewhere in Africa, knowledge of ironworking spread across the Sudan, enabling its inhabitants to create more efficient weapons and farming tools. In the wake of these developments, larger and more complex societies emerged, especially in the fertile basins of Lake Chad in the central Sudan and the Niger and Senegal rivers to the west.

Nok Culture

Some of the earliest evidence of iron technology in sub-Saharan Africa comes from the so-called Nok culture, which arose in the western Sudan, in present-day Nigeria, as early as 500 BCE. The Nok people were farmers who grew grain and oil-bearing seeds, but they were also smelters with the technology for refining ore. Slag and the remains of furnaces have been discovered, along with clay nozzles from the bellows used to fan the fires. The Nok people created the earliest known sculpture of sub-Saharan Africa, producing accomplished **terra-cotta** figures of human and animal subjects between about 500 BCE and 200 CE.

Nok sculpture was discovered in modern times by tin miners digging in the alluvial deposits on the Jos plateau north of the confluence of the Niger and Benue rivers. Presumably, floods from centuries past had removed the

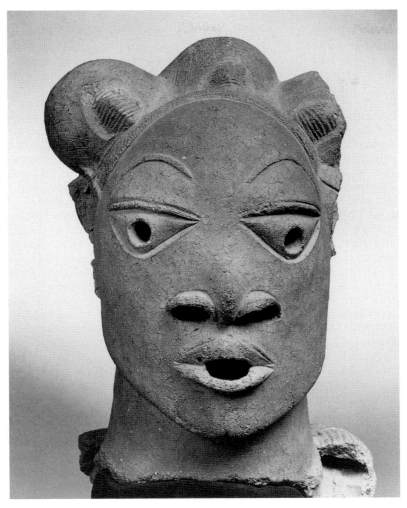

13-2.   Head. Nok culture, c. 500 BCE–200 CE. Terra-cotta, height 14³/₁₆" (36 cm). National Museum, Lagos, Nigeria

figures from their original contexts, dragged and rolled them along, then redeposited them. This rough treatment had scratched and broken many, often leaving only the heads from what must have been complete human figures. Following archeological convention, scholars gave the name of a nearby village, Nok, to the culture that created these works. Nok-style sculpture has since been found in numerous sites over a wide area.

The Nok head shown here (fig. 13-2), slightly larger than lifesize, originally formed part of a complete figure. The triangular or **D**-shaped eyes are characteristic of Nok style and appear also on sculpture of animals. Holes in the pupils, nostrils, and mouth allowed air to pass freely as the figure was fired. Each of the large buns of its elaborate hairstyle is pierced with a hole that may have held ornamental feathers. Other Nok figures boast large quantities of beads and other prestige ornaments. Nok sculpture may represent ordinary people dressed up for a special occasion, or it may portray people of high status, providing evidence of social stratification in this early farming culture. At the very least, the sculpture provides evidence of considerable technical accomplishment. The skill and artistry it reflects have led many

scholars to speculate that Nok culture was built on the achievements of an earlier culture still to be discovered.

Ife

Following the disappearance of the Nok culture, the region of present-day Nigeria remained a vigorous cultural and artistic center. The **naturalistic** sculpture created by the artists of the city of Ife, which arose in the southern, forested part of that region by about 800 CE, are among the most remarkable in art history (see "Who Made African Art?," page 470).

Ife was, and remains, the sacred city of the Yoruba people. Yoruba myth tells how at Ife the gods descended from heaven on iron chains to create the world. A tradition of naturalistic sculpture began there about 1050 CE and flourished for some four centuries. Although the line of Ife kings, or *onis*, continues unbroken from that time to the present, the knowledge of how these works were used has been lost. When archeologists showed the sculpture to members of the contemporary *oni's* court, however, they identified symbols of kingship on sculpture that had been worn within living memory, indicating that the figures represent rulers.

WHO MADE AFRICAN ART?

Today many art museums boast extensive collections of African art. Yet on label after label, a standard piece of information is missing. Where are the artists' names? Who made this art?

Until quite recently, the role of the artist in many African societies was greatly misunderstood, and the answer would have been, "It doesn't matter—the question is irrelevant." Artists working in Africa used to be commonly portrayed as obedient craftsworkers. Bound to the style and iconography dictated to them by village elders, they carved by rote the same images again and again; their work was said to be anonymous and interchangeable.

Over the past several decades, however, these misconceptions have begun to crumble. One of the first non-Africans to understand that African art, as much as European art, was the work of identifiable artists was the Belgian art historian Frans Olbrechts. During the 1930s, while assembling a group of objects from present-day Zaire for an exhibition, Olbrechts noticed that as many as ten figures had been carved in a very distinctive style. A look at the labels revealed that two of the statues had been collected in the same town, Buli, in eastern Zaire. As a scholar of Western art history, Olbrechts was familiar with the practice of identifying individual styles and, when names were not available, assigning the artist an identity such as the Master of Frankfurt or the Master of the Saint Catherine Legend. Accordingly, he named the unknown African artist the Master of Buli.

In the years since Olbrechts's exhibition, eleven more works have been identified as coming either directly from the hand of the Master of Buli or from his workshop. Interestingly, although the town of Buli is in an area populated predominantly by the Luba people, the style of the objects is closer to that of the Hemba people, who live just to the east. It may be that the Master of Buli was a Hemba artist working for Luba clients or for a large clientele spread across southeastern Zaire.

In the late 1970s, an object in the style of the Master of Buli was discovered in the Hemba area. Its owners identified the artist as Ngongo ya Chintu, of Kateba village, a short distance away. Kateba villagers in turn remembered Ngongo ya Chintu as an artist of great skill. His reputation had spread throughout southeastern Zaire, and he had attracted clients from a large area. Clearly, then, African artists did not work anonymously. So why have their names not been preserved?

One reason has to do with some African systems of patronage. As was the case in many lands, artists in many African countries created their works in response to specific commissions rather than to express a personal message. Art might be commissioned by an individual, a family, an organization, or an entire community, and negotiations between patrons and artists over the details of a commission were often protracted. Once the work had been created, however, the name of the artist was not necessarily made public. Instead, the work was generally associated with the names of its owners or commissioners.

Another reason is that early collectors simply failed to ask. During the late nineteenth and early twentieth centuries, when many Western collections of African art were being formed, Westerners generally did not believe that Africans shared their sense of the uniqueness and importance of the individual. Thus the explorers, colonial officers, and missionaries who filled the storerooms of European museums rarely asked who had made or owned the objects they were acquiring. Nor did they always distinguish carefully what part of Africa a work came from. In European eyes Africa was a single country .

As the story of Ngongo ya Chintu indicates, however, Africans are fully aware of the names of their artists. Inspired by Olbrechts's example, art historians and anthropologists have since identified numerous African artists and compiled catalogs of their work. In the case of the Yoruba people of present-day Nigeria, for example, we now know of such artists as Agbonbiofe of the Adeshina family of Efon-Alaye (d. 1945), Obembe Alaye of Efon-Alaye (1869–1939), Maku of Erin (d. 1928), and many others.

Certainly we will never know the names of the vast majority of African artists of the past, just as we do not know the names of the sculptors responsible for the sculpture portraits of late Rome or the monumental reliefs of the Hindu temples of South Asia. As elsewhere, the greatest artists in Africa were famous and sought after, while the others labored honorably at their art.

A lifesize brass head (fig. 13-3) shows the extraordinary artistry of ancient Ife. The modeling of the flesh is supremely sensitive, especially the subtle transitions around the nose and mouth. The lips are full and delicate, and the eyes are strikingly similar in shape to those of some modern Yoruba. The face is covered with thin, parallel **scarification** patterns (decorations made by scarring) in a style that was still occasionally seen on Nigerians until recently.

Holes along the scalp apparently permitted hair or perhaps a beaded veil to be attached. Large holes around the base of the neck may have allowed the head itself to be attached to a wooden mannequin for display during memorial services for a deceased *oni*. The mannequin was probably dressed in the *oni's* robes and his crown was probably attached to the head by means of the holes along the hairline.

The artists of ancient Ife also worked in terra-cotta. Unlike their brass counterparts, terra-cotta heads are not fitted for attachments. They were probably placed in shrines devoted to the memory of each dead king. Two of the most famous Ife sculptures were not found by archeologists but had been preserved through the centuries in the *oni's* palace. One, a terra-cotta head, is said to represent Lajuwa, a court retainer who usurped the throne by intrigue and impersonation (fig. 13-4). The other, a lifesize copper mask, is said to represent Obalufon, the ruler who introduced bronze casting.

13-3. Head of a king, from Ife. c. 13th century CE. Brass, height 11⁷/₁₆" (29 cm). Museum of Ife Antiquities, Ife, Nigeria

The naturalism of Ife sculpture contradicted everything Europeans thought they knew about African art. The German scholar who "discovered" Ife sculpture in 1910 suggested that it had been created not by Africans but by survivors from the legendary lost island of Atlantis. Later scholars speculated that influence from ancient Greece or Renaissance Europe must have reached Ife. Scientific dating methods, however, finally put such misleading comparisons and prejudices to rest. When naturalism flowered in Ife, the ancient Mediterranean world was long gone and the European Renaissance still to come. In addition, the proportions of the few known full figures are characteristically African, with the head comprising as much as one quarter of the total height. These proportions probably reflect a belief in the head's importance as the abode of the spirit and the focus of individual identity.

Scholars continue to debate whether the Ife heads are true portraits. Their striking anatomical individuality strongly suggests that they are. The heads, however, all seem to represent men of the same age and seem to embody a similar concept of physical perfection, suggesting that they are **idealized** images. In the recent past, Africans have not produced naturalistic portraits, fearing that they could house malevolent spirits that would harm the soul of the subject. If the Ife heads are portraits, then perhaps the institution of kingship and the need to revere royal ancestors were strong enough to overcome such concerns.

Benin

Ife was probably the artistic parent of the great city-state of Benin, which arose some 150 miles to the southeast. According to oral histories, the earliest kings of Benin belonged to the Ogiso, or Skyking, dynasty. After a long period of misrule, however, the people of Benin asked the *oni* of Ife for a new ruler. The *oni* sent Prince Oranmiyan, who founded a new dynasty in 1170 CE. Some two centuries later, the fourth king, or *oba,* of Benin decided to start a tradition of memorial sculpture like that of Ife, and he sent to Ife for a master metal caster named

13-4. Head said to represent the Usurper Lajuwa, from Ife. c. 1200–1300 CE. Terra-cotta, height 12¹⁵/₁₆" (32.8 cm). Museum of Ife Antiquities, Ife, Nigeria

13-5. Memorial head, from Benin. c. 1400–1550 CE (Early Period). Brass, height 9³⁄₈" (23.4 cm). The Metropolitan Museum of Art, New York

The Michael C. Rockefeller Memorial Collection, Bequest of Nelson A. Rockefeller, 1979 (1979.206.86)

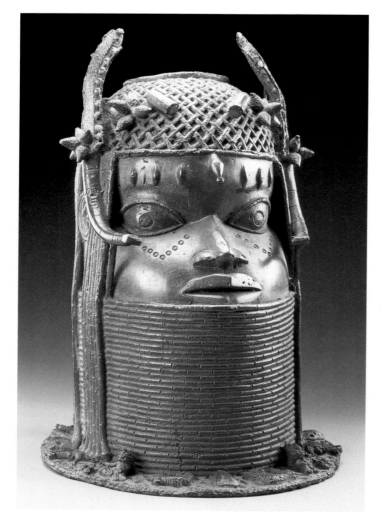

Iguegha. The tradition of casting memorial heads for the shrines of royal ancestors endures among the successors of Oranmiyan to this day.

Benin came into contact with Portugal in the late fifteenth century. The two kingdoms established cordial relations and carried on an active trade, at first in ivory and other forest products but eventually in slaves. Benin flourished until 1897, when, in reprisal for the massacre of a party of trade negotiators, British troops sacked and burned the royal palace, sending the *oba* into an exile from which he did not return until 1914. The palace was later rebuilt, and the present-day *oba* continues the dynasty started by Oranmiyan.

The British invaders discovered shrines to deceased *obas* filled with brass heads, bells, and figures. They also found wooden rattles and enormous ivory tusks carved with images of kings, court attendants, and sixteenth-century Portuguese soldiers. The British appropriated the treasure as war booty, making no effort to note which head came from which shrine. As a result, they destroyed evidence that would have helped establish the relative age of the heads and determine a chronology for the evolution of Benin style. Nevertheless, scholars have managed to piece together a chronology from other evidence.

Benin brass heads range from small, thinly cast, and naturalistic to large, thickly cast, and highly stylized. The heads that were being made at the time of the British invasion are of the latter variety, as are those still being cast today. Many scholars have concluded that the smallest, most naturalistic heads were created during a so-called Early Period (1400–1550 CE), when Benin artists were still heavily influenced by Ife (fig. 13-5). Heads grew increasingly stylized during the Middle Period (1550–1700 CE). Heads from the ensuing Late Period (1700–1897 CE) are very large and heavy, with angular, stylized features and an elaborate beaded crown (fig. 13-6). A similar crown is still worn by the present-day *oba*.

All of the heads include representations of coral-bead necklaces, which have formed part of the royal costume from earliest times to the present day. Small and few in number on Early Period heads, they increase in number until they conceal the chin during the Middle Period. During the Late Period, the necklaces form a tall, cylindrical mass that greatly increases the weight of the sculpture. Broad, horizontal flanges, or projecting edges, bearing small images cast in low relief ring the base of the Late Period statues, adding still more weight. The increase in size and weight of Benin memorial heads over time may reflect the growing power and wealth flowing to the *oba* from Benin's expanding trade with Europe.

The art of Benin is a royal art, for only the *oba* could commission works in brass. Artisans who served the court lived in a separate quarter of the city and were organized into guilds. Among the most remarkable visual records of court life are the hundreds of brass plaques, each about 2 feet square, that once decorated

13-6. Head of an *oba* (king), from Benin. c. 1700–1897 CE (Late Period). Brass, height 17¼" (45 cm). Museum für Völkerkunde, Vienna/Musée Dapper, Paris

13-7. *General and Officers,* from Benin. c. 1550–1650 CE (Middle Period). Brass, height 21" (53.5 cm). National Museum, Lagos, Nigeria

The general wears an elaborate, appliqué apron depicting the head of a leopard, and the flanking officers wear leopard pelts. Leopards were symbols of royalty in Benin. Live leopards were kept at the royal palace, where they were looked after by a special keeper. Water pitchers in the form of leopards were cast in bronze and placed on altars dedicated to ancestors. An engraving from a European travel book of the sixteenth century depicts a procession of courtiers in Benin led by a pair of magnificent leopards.

the walls and columns of the royal palace. Produced during the Middle Period, the plaques are modeled in relief, sometimes in such high relief that the figures are almost freestanding. An exceptionally detailed plaque (fig. 13-7) shows a general in elaborate military dress holding a spear in one hand and a ceremonial sword in the other. Flanking the general, two officers, whose helmets indicate their rank, brandish spears and shields. Smaller figures appear between the three principal figures, one carrying a sword, another sounding a horn. Above the tip of the general's sword is a small figure of a Portuguese soldier.

Obas also commissioned important works in ivory. One example is a beautiful ornamental mask (fig. 13-8)

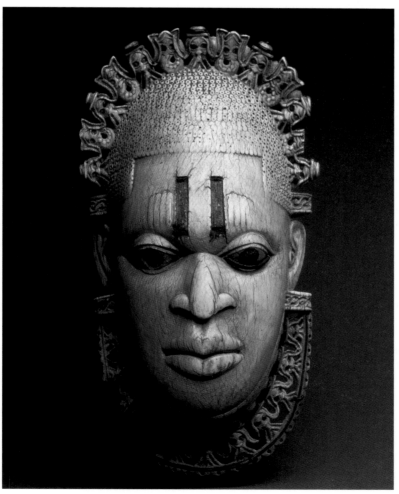

13-8. Mask representing an *iyoba*, from Benin. c. 1550 CE. Ivory, iron, and copper, height 9 3/8" (23.4 cm). The Metropolitan Museum of Art, New York

The Michael C. Rockefeller Memorial Collection, Gift of Nelson A. Rockefeller, 1972 (1978.412.323)

that represents an *iyoba,* or queen mother. The woman who had borne the previous *oba's* first male child (and thus the mother of the current *oba*), the *iyoba* ranked as the senior female member of the court. This mask may represent Idia, the first and best-known *iyoba.* Idia was the mother of Esigie, who ruled as *oba* from 1504 to 1550 CE. She is particularly remembered for raising an army and using her magical powers to help her son defeat his enemies.

The mask was carved as a belt or hip ornament and was probably worn at the *oba's* waist. Its pupils were originally inlaid with iron, as were the scarification patterns on the forehead. The necklace represents heads of Portuguese soldiers with beards and flowing hair. Like Idia, the Portuguese helped Esigie expand his kingdom. In the crown, more Portuguese heads alternate with figures of mudfish, which in Benin iconography symbolized Olokun, the Lord of the Great Waters. Mudfish live on the riverbank, mediating between water and land, just as the *oba,* who is viewed as semidivine, mediates between the human world and the supernatural world of Olokun.

URBAN CENTERS

Ife and Benin were but two of the many cities that arose in ancient Africa. The first European visitors to the West African coast at the end of the fifteenth century were impressed not only by Benin, but also by the cities of Loango and Luanda near the mouth of the Zaire River. Exploring the East African coastline, European ships happened on cosmopolitan cities that had been busily carrying on long-distance trade across the Indian Ocean and as far away as China and Indonesia for hundreds of years.

Important centers also arose in the interior, especially across the central and western Sudan. There cities and the states that developed around them grew wealthy from the trans-Saharan trade that had linked West Africa to the Mediterranean from at least the first millennium BCE. Indeed, the routes across the desert were probably as old as the desert itself. Among the most significant goods exchanged in this trade were salt from the north and gold from West Africa. Such fabled cities as Mopti, Timbuktu, and Djenné were great centers of commerce, where merchants from all over West Africa met caravans arriving from the Mediterranean.

Djenné

In 1655, the Islamic writer al-Sadi wrote this description of Djenné:

> This city is large, flourishing, and prosperous; it is rich, blessed, and favoured by the Almighty. . . . Jenne [Djenné] is one of the great markets of the Muslim world. There one meets the salt merchants from the mines of Teghaza and merchants carrying gold from the mines of Bitou. . . . Because of this blessed city, caravans flock to Timbuktu from all points of the horizon. . . . The area around Jenne is fertile and well populated; with numerous markets held there on all the

days of the week. It is certain that it contains 7,077 villages very near to one another.

> (Translated by Graham Connah in Connah, page 97)

By the time al-Sadi wrote his account, Djenné, in present-day Mali, already had a long history. Archeologists have determined that the city was established by the third century CE and that by the middle of the ninth century it had become a major urban center. By the ninth century also, Islam was becoming an economic and religious force in West Africa, having incorporated North Africa and the northern terminals of the trans-Saharan trade routes into the Islamic empire. Much of what we know about African history from this time on is based on the accounts of Islamic scholars, geographers, and travelers.

When Koi Konboro, the twenty-sixth king of Djenné, converted to Islam in the thirteenth century, he transformed his palace into the first of three successive **mosques** in the city. Like the two that followed, the first mosque was built of **adobe** brick, a sun-dried mixture of clay and straw. With its great surrounding wall and tall towers, it was said to have been more beautiful and more lavishly decorated than the Kaaba, the central shrine of Islam, at Mecca. The mosque eventually attracted the attention of austere Muslim rulers, who objected to its sumptuous furnishings. Among these was the early-nineteenth-century ruler Sekou Amadou, who had it razed and a far more humble structure erected on a new site. This second mosque was in turn replaced by the current grand mosque, constructed between 1906 and 1907 on the ancient site and in the style of the original. The reconstruction was supervised by the architect Ismaila Traoré, the head of the Djenné guild of masons.

The mosque's eastern, or "marketplace," facade boasts three tall towers (fig. 13-9). The finials, or crowning ornaments, at the top of each tower bear ostrich eggs, symbols of fertility and purity. The facade and sides of the mosque are distinguished by tall, narrow, engaged columns, which act as buttresses. These columns are characteristic of West African mosque architecture, and their cumulative rhythmic effect is one of great verticality and grandeur. The most unusual feature of West African mosques are the **torons**, wooden beams projecting from the walls. *Torons* provide permanent supports for the scaffolding erected each year so that the exterior of the mosque can be replastered.

Great Zimbabwe

Several thousand miles from Djenné, in southeastern Africa, an extensive trade network developed along the Zambezi, Limpopo, and Sabi rivers. Its purpose was to funnel gold, ivory, and exotic skins to the coastal trading towns that had been built by Arabs and Swahili-speaking Africans. There, the gold and ivory were exchanged for prestige goods, including porcelain, beads, and other manufactured items. Between 1000 and 1500 CE, this trade was largely controlled from a site that was called Great Zimbabwe.

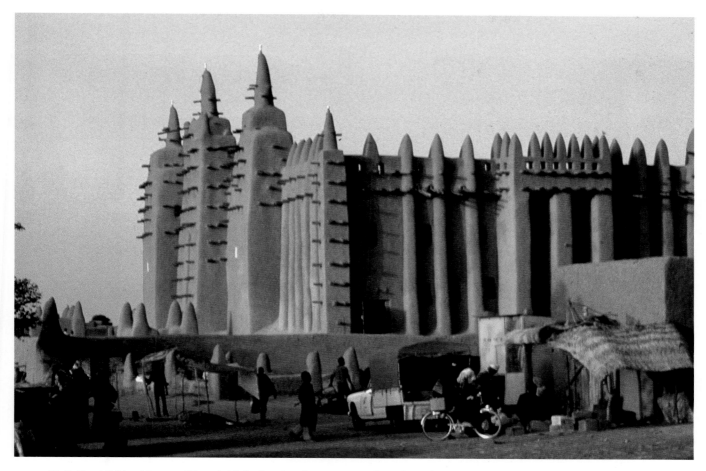

13-9. Great Friday Mosque, Djenné, Mali, showing the eastern and northern facades. Rebuilding of 1907, in the style of 13th-century original

The plan of the mosque is quite irregular. Instead of a rectangle, the building forms a parallelogram. Inside, nine long rows of heavy adobe columns some 33 feet tall run along the north-south axis, supporting a flat ceiling of palm logs. A pointed arch links each column to the next in its row, thereby forming nine east-west archways facing the mihrab, the niche that indicates the direction of Mecca. The mosque is augmented by an open courtyard for prayer on the west side, which is enclosed by a great double wall only slightly lower than the walls of the mosque itself.

The word *zimbabwe* derives from the Shona term for "venerated houses" or "houses of stone." Scholars agree that the stone buildings at Great Zimbabwe were constructed by ancestors of the present-day Shona people, who still live in the region. The earliest construction at the site took advantage of the enormous boulders abundant in the vicinity. Masons incorporated the boulders and used the uniform granite blocks that split naturally from them to build a series of tall enclosing walls high on a hilltop. Each enclosure defined a family's living or ritual space and housed dwellings made of adobe with conical, thatched roofs.

The largest building complex at Great Zimbabwe is located in a broad valley below the hilltop enclosures.

Known as Imba Huru, the Big House, the complex is ringed by a masonry wall more than 800 feet long, 32 feet tall, and 17 feet thick at the base. The buildings at Great Zimbabwe were built without mortar; for stability the walls are **battered**, or built so that they slope inward toward the top. Inside the great outer wall are numerous smaller stone enclosures and adobe foundations.

The complex seems to have evolved with very little planning. Additions and extensions were begun as labor and materials were available and need dictated. Over the centuries, the builders grew more skillful, and the later additions are distinguished by **dressed stones**, or smoothly finished stones, laid in fine, even, level courses. One of these later additions is a fascinating structure

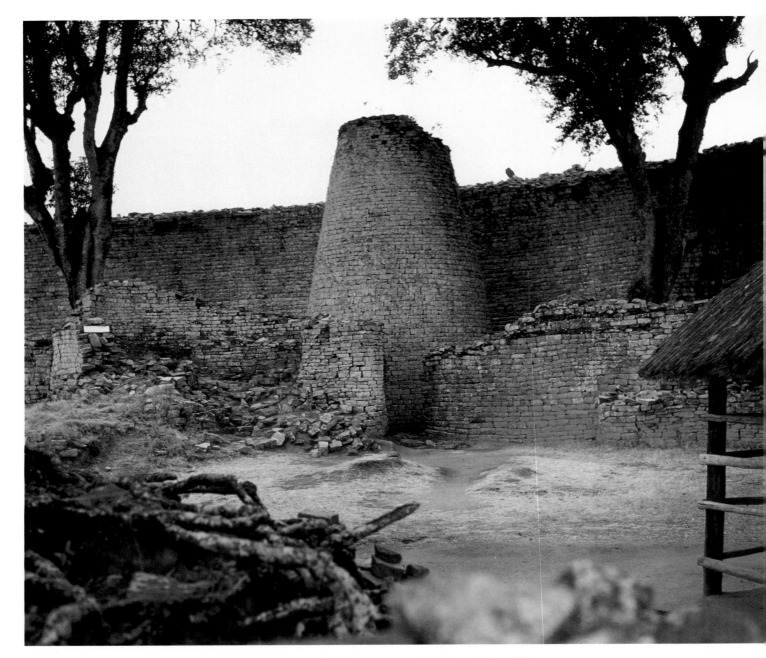

13-10. Conical Tower, Great Zimbabwe. Before 1450 CE

known simply as the Conical Tower (fig. 13-10). Some 18 feet in diameter and 30 feet tall, the tower was originally capped with three courses of ornamental stonework. It may have represented the good harvest and prosperity believed to result from allegiance to the ruler of Great Zimbabwe, for it resembles a present-day Shona granary built large.

Among the many interesting finds at Great Zimbabwe are a series of carved soapstone birds (fig. 13-11). The carvings, which originally crowned tall **monoliths**, seem to depict birds of prey, perhaps eagles. They may, however, represent mythical creatures, for the species cannot be identified. Traditional Shona beliefs include an eagle called *shiri ye denga*, or "bird of heaven," who brings

13-11. Bird, top part of a monolith, from Great Zimbabwe. c. 1200–1400 CE. Soapstone, height 14½" (36.8 cm). Great Zimbabwe Site Museum, Zimbabwe

lightning, a metaphor for communication between the heavens and earth. These soapstone birds may have represented such messengers from the spirit world, or they may have served as symbols of royalty, expressing the king's power to mediate between his subjects and the supernatural world of spirits.

Although some of the enclosures at Great Zimbabwe were built on hilltops, there is no evidence that they were constructed as fortresses. There are neither openings for weapons to be thrust through nor battlements for warriors to stand on. Instead, the walls and structures seem intended to reflect the wealth and power of the city's rulers. The Big House was probably a royal residence, or palace complex, and other structures housed members of the ruler's family and court. The complex formed the nucleus of a city that radiated for almost a mile in all directions. It is estimated that at the height of its power in the fourteenth century, Great Zimbabwe and its surrounding city housed a population of more than 10,000 people. A large cache of goods containing items of such far-flung origin as Portuguese medallions, Persian pottery, and Chinese porcelain testify to the extent of its trade. Yet beginning in the mid-fifteenth century Great Zimbabwe was gradually abandoned. Its power and control of the lucrative southeast African trade network passed to the Mwene Mutapa and Kami empires only a short distance away.

During the twentieth century, the sculpture of traditional African societies—wood carvings of astonishing formal inventiveness and power—have found admirers the world over, becoming virtually synonymous with "African art." Admiration for these art forms was evident in earlier periods as well. In the mid-seventeenth century, for example, a German merchant named Christopher Weickman collected a Yoruba divination board, textiles from the Kongo, and swords with nubbly ray-skin sheaths from the Akan, all of which are now housed in a museum in Ulm, Germany. Wood decays rapidly, however, and little of African wood sculpture remains from before the nineteenth century. As a result, much of ancient Africa's artistic heritage has probably been as irretrievably lost as have, for example, the great monuments of wooden architecture of dynastic China. Yet the beauty of ancient African creations in such durable materials as terracotta, stone, and bronze bears eloquent witness to the skill of ancient African artists and the splendor of the civilizations in which they worked.

South Cross
Ahenny
8th century

▲ CAROLINGIAN
PERIOD 750–90

▲ CHRISTIAN SPAIN 500–
▲ BRITAIN/IRELAND 500–

CHAPTER 14

Early Medieval Art in Europe

lace Chapel
Charlemagne
792–805

Viking burial
ship c. 825

Bird and Serpent,
from a Spanish
manuscript 975

Adam and Eve,
from the Hildesheim
doors 1015

▲ OTTONIAN PERIOD 900–1000

▲ SCANDINAVIAN VIKING 800–1100

ATLANTIC
OCEAN

Urnes

NORWAY

SWEDEN

Oseberg

Larbro Saint
Hammers
GOTLAND

SCOTLAND
IONA

LINDISFARNE

North
Sea

Baltic
Sea

RUSSIA

IRELAND   Kells
Ahenny
Durrow

DENMARK

ENGLAND
WALES   EAST
ANGLIA Sutton HOLLAND
Hoo

Meschede

Hildesheim

KENT   BELGIUM
English Channel   Centula
NORMANDY
BRITTANY

Cologne
Aachen
Reims   GERMANY

FRANCE

AUSTRIA

Reichenau
Lake
Constance

Black
Sea

Liébana
ASTURIAS
LEÓN   Burgos

Ravenna

Tábara

ITALY
Rome

Constantinople

SPAIN

Córdoba

Mediterranean Sea

0   500 Miles

0   500 Kilometers

14-1. Burial ship, from Oseberg, Norway. c. 800. Wood, length 75'6" (23 m). Viking-skiphuset, Universitets Oldsaksamling, Oslo, Norway

This vessel, propelled by both sail and oars, was designed not for ocean voyages but for travel in the relatively calm waters of fjords, narrow coastal inlets. The shelter at the center of this ship was used as the burial chamber for two women. A cart and four sleds, all made of wood with beautifully carved decorations, were stored on board. Fourteen horses, an ox, and three dogs had been sacrificed to accompany the women into the grave. It is also quite possible that one of the women was a willing sacrificial victim for the other, since Viking society believed that a courageous and honorable death was a guarantee of reward in the afterlife.

As a flotilla of 2,000 Viking ships approached Constantinople early in the tenth century, so the story goes, the intimidated Byzantines stretched an enormous chain across the strait to stop them. The remarkable mariners from Scandinavia had sailed eastward across the Baltic Sea and down rivers to the Black Sea. The chain they encountered was no more an obstacle to them than waterfalls and other impassable places on the rivers they had navigated, and they got around it the same way: they lifted their ships from the water, put them on rollers made of tree trunks, and rolled them around the barrier. The Byzantine emperor was so cowed by their ingenuity and aggressiveness that he paid the Vikings a huge tribute, established a trade treaty with them, and hired some of these "ax-bearing barbarians" as an elite guard for the imperial palace.

These Viking ships crossed land to find treasure, but another ship—a 75-foot-long vessel discovered in Oseberg, Norway, and dated about 800—served as the burial site for two women on a journey to eternity (fig. 14-1). The Vikings saw their ships as sleek sea serpents, and the prow and stern of the Oseberg ship rise and coil like a serpent's tail. These suggestive spirals may have been meant to terrify enemies and to protect against evil forces. Although the burial chamber was long ago looted of jewelry and precious objects, the ship itself and the remaining artifacts attest to the wealth and prominence of the ship's owner and have provided insight into the culture of Scandinavia in the Early Middle Ages.

THE MIDDLE AGES

The roughly 1,000 years of European history between the collapse of the Western Roman Empire in the fifth century and the Renaissance in the fifteenth are known as the Middle Ages, or the medieval period. These terms reflect the view of early historians that this was a dark "middle" age of ignorance, decline, and barbarism between two golden ages. Although this view no longer prevails—the Middle Ages are now known to have been a period of great richness, complexity, and innovation that gave birth to modern Europe—the terms have endured. Art historians commonly divide the Middle Ages into three periods: Early medieval (ending in the tenth century), Romanesque (eleventh and twelfth centuries), and Gothic (extending from the mid-twelfth century into the fifteenth). The terms *Romanesque* and *Gothic* refer to distinctive artistic styles that were prevalent during the periods that bear their names. Chapters 7 ("Early Christian, Jewish, and Byzantine Art") and 8 ("Islamic Art") have already touched on some aspects of early medieval art. This chapter covers the art of the Early Middle Ages in western and northern Europe—Scandinavia, Britain, Ireland, Christian Spain, France, and Germany—from the sixth century to the eleventh century. Chapter 15 covers Romanesque art, and Chapter 16 discusses Gothic art.

As Roman authority crumbled at the outset of the Middle Ages, it was replaced by strong local leaders—including the leaders of the various Germanic and other barbarian groups that had invaded or been drawn into the empire over the centuries—and by the Church, which was centered in Rome and retained the hierarchical administrative structure of the empire. The breakdown of central power, the fusion of Germanic and Roman culture, and the unifying influence of Christianity produced distinctive new political, social, and cultural forms. In a process that led ultimately to a type of social organization known as feudalism, relationships of patronage and dependence between the powerful—nobles and church officials—and the less powerful became increasingly important. A pattern of mutual support developed between secular leaders and the Church, with secular leaders defending the claims of the Church and the Church validating their rule. The Church emerged as a repository of learning, and church officials and the nobility became the principal patrons of the arts. The focus of their patronage was the Church itself, its buildings and liturgical equipment, including altars, altar vessels, crosses, candlesticks, **reliquaries** (containers for holy relics), vestments, portrayals of Christian figures and stories, and copies of sacred texts.

As Christianity continued to spread north beyond the borders of the empire, northern artistic traditions similarly worked their way south. Out of a tangled web of themes and styles from north and south, east and west, pagan and Christian, urban and rural, brilliant new artistic styles were born.

SCANDINAVIA

Scandinavia, which encompasses the modern countries of Denmark, Norway, and Sweden, was never part of the Roman Empire. In the fifth century CE it was a land of small kingdoms and independent agricultural communities. Most of its inhabitants spoke variants of a language called Norse and shared a rich mythology with other Germanic peoples. Among other deities, they worshiped Odin, chief of the gods, who protected the courageous in battle and rewarded the fallen by allowing them entrance into Valhalla, the great hall where heroic souls were received.

Sometime in the late eighth century seafaring bands of Scandinavians known as Vikings (*Viken* originally meant "people from the coves" but eventually came to be synonymous with "raiders" or "pirates") began descending on the rest of Europe. Setting off in flotillas of as many as 350 ships, they explored, plundered, traded, and colonized over a vast area. Intermittently looting and destroying coastal and inland river communities, they were an unsettling presence in Europe for nearly 300 years. Frequently, their targets were isolated, but wealthy, Christian monasteries. Among the earliest recorded Viking attacks were two devastating raids: one in 793, on the religious community on Lindisfarne, an island off the northeast coast of Britain, and another, in 794, at Iona, off the west coast. Vikings explored the north Atlantic, settling in Iceland about 870 and Greenland by 1000. They established a short-lived outpost in North America after 1000. They also raided and settled in Ireland, England, Scotland, and France. In the early tenth century, the rulers of France bought off Scandinavian raiders (the Normans, or North men) with a large grant of land that became the duchy of Normandy. Some Viking groups also sailed down rivers to the Black Sea and Constantinople, while others established settlements around Novgorod, which ultimately became the northern state of Rusland, or Russia.

The Danish king Harold Bluetooth brought Christianity to Scandinavia in the middle of the tenth century. In Norway, Olaf Haraldsson, later canonized Saint Olaf (died 1030), is credited with converting his people. Olaf accepted Christianity in Rouen, France while on a Viking expedition. During the eleventh century the new religion spread through the rest of the Scandinavian peninsula. By the beginning of the twelfth century, kings supported by Christian bishops had broken the power of regional rulers. With these developments and the rise of powerful monarchies in England and France, Viking raids and the Viking era came to an end.

During the first millennium BCE, trade, warfare, and migration brought a variety of jewelry, coins, textiles, and other portable objects into northern Europe. Scandinavian artists, who had exhibited a fondness for abstract patterning from early prehistoric times, incorporated the solar disks, spirals, and stylized animals on these objects into their already rich artistic vocabulary (see fig. 1-27). Beginning about 300 CE, Roman influences were noticeable in Scandinavia. By the fifth century CE, the so-called animal style displayed an impressive array of serpents and four-legged beasts, and squat human forms. Certain underlying principles govern works in this complex style: they are generally symmetrically composed, and they

PARALLELS

Years	European Cultural Centers	Europe	World
c. 800–1100	Scandinavian Viking	Viking expeditions in northern Europe; colonies in Russia, Iceland, Greenland, North America; Christianization	**500–1000** Rise of Hinduism (India); Hagia Sophia (Turkey); birth of Muhammad, founder of Islam (Arabia); Muslim conquests of Arabia, Persia, Egypt, Syria, Palestine; Buddhism in Japan; a plague kills half of European population; Tang dynasty (China); Koran (Arabia); first block-print text (China); bronze casting in South America; *Diamond Sutra* (China)
c. 500–present	Britain/Ireland	Celtic culture; Anglo-Saxon culture; *Beowulf*; Hiberno-Saxon Style; *Book of Kells*	
c. 500–present	Christian Spain	Visigoth presence; monumental architecture; Islam conquests; Mozarabic style; *Commentary on the Apocalypse*	
c. 750–900	Carolingian period	Rule of Charlemagne; strengthening of Roman Empire; Caroline minuscule script; *Utrecht Psalter*	
c. 900–1000	Ottonian period	Otto I creates Holy Roman Empire; *Liuthar Gospels*	

depict animals in their entirety from a variety of perspectives—in profile, from above, and sometimes with their ribs and spinal columns exposed as if they had been X-rayed.

The Gummersmark brooch (fig. 14-2), a large silver-gilt pin, probably one of a pair, was used to fasten a cloak around the wearer's shoulders. It is worked in an intricate animal style design. Dating from the sixth century CE and made in Denmark, this elegant ornament consists of a large, rectangular headplate and a medallionlike, open-work footplate connected by an arched central element which acts as a spring to help hold the pin on the garment. Its abstract, geometric motifs include spirals, narrow bands, bird heads, human figures, dogs, and dragons. The artist created a glittering surface by faceting in a technique called chip carving. Earlier, Romans had developed chip carving as a cheap, fast way of decorating molded hardware for military uniforms. The northern artists who adopted the technique carefully crafted each item by hand, turning a process intended for fast production into an art form of great refinement.

The Vikings erected large memorial stones both at home and abroad. Those covered mostly with inscriptions are called **rune stones**; those with figural decoration are called **picture stones**. Runes are letters of an early Germanic alphabet that was probably derived from ancient italic (Italian) alphabets. Traces of pigments suggest that these memorial stones were originally painted in bright colors. Picture stones from Gotland, an island off the east coast of Sweden, share a common design

14-2. Gummersmark brooch, Denmark. 6th century. Silver gilt, height 5¾" (14.6 cm). Nationalmuseet, Copenhagen

The faceted surface of this pin seems to seethe with abstract human, animal, and grotesque forms such as the eye-and-beak motif that frames the headplate, the man compressed between dragons just below the bridge element, and the pair of crouching dogs with spiraling tongues that forms the tip of the footplate.

crew sailing over foamy waves. In Viking iconography, ships symbolize the dead warrior's passage to Valhalla. Viking chiefs were sometimes cremated in a ship in the belief that this hastened their ascent to Valhalla.

The other registers show scenes of battle and scenes from Norse mythology, including rituals associated with the cult of Odin. The third register down, just above a horizontal band of interlace, depicts the ritual hanging of a willing victim in sacrifice to Odin, who among many other titles was known as "the god to the hanged." Directly in front of the hanged man is a burial mound, called the hall of Odin, and above it are symbols of Odin, the eagle and the triple knot.

In the Viking-era burial ship discovered in Oseberg (see fig. 14-1), two women, one young and one old, were laid out in the cabin on separate beds with comforters, blankets, and pillows. The cabin also contained empty chests that no doubt once held precious goods, as well as two looms, perhaps an indication of the craft of one or both women. The cabin walls had been covered with tapestries, fragments of which survived. Among the ship's artifacts are some of the few surviving examples of Scandinavian wood carving, a craft known to have been practiced with skill and imagination throughout the region. The bands of carved low relief running along the ship's bow and stern feature a type of design called **animal interlace**, in which the bodies of animals and birds are elongated into interwoven serpentine ribbons.

Images of strange beasts adorned all sorts of Viking belongings—jewelry, houses, tent poles, beds, wagons, sleds—and later even churches. Found in the cabin of the Oseberg ship were several wooden animal-head posts about 3 feet long with handles, the purpose of which is unknown (fig. 14-4). Although each is unique in style and design, all represent similar long-necked, grotesque, dog- or catlike creatures with bulging eyes, short muzzles, snarling mouths, and large teeth. These ferocious creatures are encrusted with a writhing mass of delicately carved beasts that clutch at each other with small, claw-like hands (fig. 14-5). This type of animal interlace, known as "gripping beasts," is a hallmark of Viking ornament. The beasts are organized into roughly circular, interlocking groups surrounded by decorated bands. The faceted cutting emphasizes the flicker of light over the densely carved surfaces.

The penchant for carved relief decorations seen on the Oseberg ship endured in the decoration of Scandinavia's earliest churches. The facades of these structures often teem with intricate animal interlace. A church at Urnes, Norway, entirely rebuilt in the twelfth century, still has some remnants of the original eleventh-century carving (fig. 14-6). Although it did not originate with this church, the style of these carvings is known as "Urnes." The animal interlace in the Urnes style is composed of serpentine creatures snapping at each other, a transformation of the vicious little gripping beasts of the Oseberg headpost and the interlace pattern of the Oseberg ship's bow and stern. The satin-smooth carving of rounded surfaces, the contrast of thick and very thin elements, and the organization of the interlace into harmoniously balanced figure-8 patterns are characteristic of the Urnes

14-3. Memorial stone, Larbro Saint Hammers, Gotland, Sweden. 8th century

Much of what we know about Viking beliefs comes from later writings, especially the *Prose Edda*, compiled in the early thirteenth century by a wealthy Icelandic farmer-poet, Snorri Sturluson (1178–1241), as a guide to Norse religion and a manual for writing poetry. Among the stories he recounts is that of Gudrun and her brothers, Gunnar and Hogni, which may be the subject of the scene in the register just above the large ship on this stone. According to this legend, Gudrun was engaged to King Atli, who was interested in her only for the treasures her brothers had hidden. The scene on the stone—which shows men with raised swords on each side of a horse trampling a fallen victim and a woman with a sword boldly confronting the horse—may illustrate Gudrun and her brothers in battle against Atli. The brothers were captured in this battle and horribly murdered. Gudrun then made peace with Atli and married him, but she later avenged her family's honor by serving him the hearts and blood of their children at a feast, following which she and a nephew killed Atli and burned his castle.

and a common theme—heroic death in battle and the journey of the dead warriors to Valhalla. An eighth-century stone from Larbro Saint Hammers on Gotland has a characteristic "mushroom" shape (fig. 14-3). The scenes are organized into horizontal registers and surrounded by a band of **ribbon interlace**, a complex pattern of woven and knotted lines that may derive from similar border ornamentation in ancient Greek and Roman mosaics. In northern art such popular patterns probably were not merely decorative but carried some symbolic significance. The bottom panel shows a large Viking ship with a broad sail, intricate rigging, and a full

14-4. Post, from the Oseberg burial ship (fig. 14-1). c. 825. Wood, length approx. 36" (92.3 cm). Vikingskiphuset, Universitets Oldsaksamling, Oslo, Norway

style. The effect is one of aesthetic and technical control rather than wild disarray. Works such as the Urnes doorway panels suggest the persistence of Scandinavia's mythological tradition into the Early Christian period and demonstrate its enriching influence on the vocabulary of Christian art.

14-5. Detail of the Oseberg burial-ship post (fig. 14-4)

14-6. Doorway panels, Parish Church, Urnes, Norway. c. 1050–70. Carved wood

14-7. Purse cover, from the Sutton Hoo burial ship, Suffolk, England. c. 615–30. Cloisonné plaques of gold, garnet and checked millefiore enamel, length 8" (20.3 cm). The British Museum, London.

Only the decorations on this purse cover are original. The lid itself, of a light tan ivory or bone, deteriorated and disappeared centuries ago, and the white backing is a modern replacement. The purse was designed to hang at the waist. A leather pouch held thirty-seven coins, struck in France, the latest dated in the early 630s.

BRITAIN AND IRELAND

When Roman armies first ventured into Britain in 55–54 BCE, it was a well-populated, thriving agricultural land of numerous small communities with close trading links to nearby regions of the European continent. Like the inhabitants of Ireland and much of Roman Gaul (modern France), the Britons were Celtic. (Welsh, Breton—the language of Brittany, in France—and the variants of Gaelic spoken in Ireland and Scotland are all Celtic languages.) Following the Roman subjugation of the island in 43 CE, its fortunes rose and fell with those of the empire. Roman Britain experienced a final period of wealth and productivity from about 296 to about 370. Christianity flourished during this period and spread to Ireland, which was never under Roman control.

The Roman army abandoned Britain in 406 to help defend Gaul against various Germanic peoples pushing into the empire across the Rhine, leaving behind a power vacuum. The historical record for the subsequent period is sketchy, but it appears that civil disturbances erupted, the economy faltered, and large towns lost their commercial function and declined. Powerful Romanized British leaders took control of different areas, vying for dominance with the help of mercenary soldiers from the continent. These mercenaries—Angles, Saxons, and Jutes—soon began to operate independently, settling largely in the southeast part of Britain and gradually extending their control northwest across the island. Over the next 200 years the people under their control adopted Germanic speech and customs, and this fusion of Romanized British and Germanic cultures produced a new Anglo-Saxon culture. By the beginning of the seventh century, several large kingdoms had emerged in Britain, and the arts, which had suffered a serious decline, made a brilliant recovery. Celtic, Roman, and Germanic influences all contributed to vigorous new styles and techniques, especially in metalworking.

Anglo-Saxon literature is filled with references to splendid and costly jewelry and military equipment decorated with gold and silver. Leaders apparently gave such objects to their followers and friends, but few examples survive. The Anglo-Saxon epic *Beowulf*, composed perhaps as early as the seventh century, describes its hero's burial with a hoard of treasure in a mound grave near the sea. Such a grave, located near the North Sea coast in East Anglia at a site called Sutton Hoo (*hoo* means "hill"), was discovered in 1938. As at Oseberg, the grave's occupant had been buried in a ship. His body had disintegrated and no inscriptions record his name.

The treasures buried with him confirm that he was, in any case, a wealthy and powerful man. His burial ship was 86 feet long and shaped much like the Oseberg vessel. In it were weapons, armor, other equipment for the afterlife, and many luxury items, including a large purse filled with coins. Although the leather of the pouch and the bone or ivory of the lid have disintergrated, the gold and garnet fittings and decorations survive (fig. 14-4). The gold frame is set with cloisonne garnets and blue checkered millefiore enamels. The ornaments, in the same materials, consist of truncated pyramids in purely geometrical patterns. Between them four animals with interlacing legs and jaws reinforce the essential symmetry of the design. Below, large, curved-beaked birds attack ducks. Flanking the birds are images of men

THE MEDIEVAL SCRIPTORIUM

Today books are made with the aid of computer software that can lay out pages, set type, and insert and prepare illustrations. Modern presses can produce hundreds of thousands of identical copies in full color. In Europe in the Middle Ages, however, before the invention there of printing from movable type in the mid-1400s, books were made by hand, one at a time, with ink, pen, brush, and paint. Each one was an important, time-consuming, and expensive undertaking.

Medieval books were usually made by monks and nuns in a workshop called a **scriptorium** (plural scriptoria), which was usually within a monastery or a convent. As the demand for books increased, lay professionals joined the work, and great

rulers set up palace workshops supervised by well-known scholars. Books were written on animal skin—either **vellum**, which was fine and soft, or **parchment**, which was heavier and shinier. (Paper did not come into common use in Europe until the early 1400s.) The *Book of Kells* (see fig. 14-9) required the skins of more than 150 calves, a great treasure considering the value of livestock at the time. The skins were cleaned, stripped of hair, and scraped to create a smooth surface that would absorb metallic inks and water-based paints, which themselves required time and experience to prepare. Many pigments—particularly blues and greens—had to be imported and were as costly as semiprecious stones. In early manuscripts, bright yellow was used to suggest gold, but later manu-

scripts were decorated with real **gold leaf** or gold paint.

Sometimes work on a book was divided between a scribe, who copied the text, and one or more artists, who did the illustrations, large initials, and other decorations. More often in the Early Middle Ages, scribe and artist were one. Although most books were produced anonymously, scribes and illustrators began to sign their work and provide a little background information on a page called the **colophon** (see fig. 14-13). One scribe even took the opportunity to warn the reader: "O reader, turn the leaves gently, and keep your fingers away from the letters, for, as the hailstorm ruins the harvest of the land, so does the injurious reader destroy the book and the writing" (cited in Dodwell, page 247).

spread-eagled between two standing beasts. The theme of a human attacked by or controlling a pair of animals is widespread in ancient Near Eastern art and in the Roman world, but this variation of the theme is a Swedish design. The rich blend of motifs in this work heralds the complex Hiberno-Saxon style that flourished in England and Ireland during the seventh and eighth centuries (Hibernia was the Roman name for Ireland).

Although the Anglo-Saxons who settled in Britain were pagans, Christianity endured through the fifth and sixth centuries in southwestern England and in Wales, Scotland, and Ireland. Monasteries began to appear in these regions in the late fifth century. Some were located in inaccessible places, isolating the monks in them from the outside world. In many others, however, monks interacted with local Christian communities. The priests in the Christian communities spoke Celtic languages and had some familiarity with Latin. Cut off from Rome, they developed their own liturgical practices, church calendar, and distinctive artistic traditions. Before the Roman Church reestablished contact with Britain at the end of the sixth century, Irish Christians had founded influential missions in Scotland and northern England. In 597 Pope Gregory the Great (590–604), beginning a vigorous campaign of conversion in England, dispatched a mission from Rome to King Ethelbert of Kent, who had a Frankish Christian wife. The head of this mission, the monk Augustine (d. 604), became the archbishop of Canterbury in 601 and soon established several other bishoprics. The Roman Christian authorities and the Irish monasteries, although allied in the effort to Christianize England, came into conflict over their divergent practices. The Roman Church wanted to bring British Christianity under its authority and eventually triumphed in liturgical and calendrical matters. Local traditions, however, continued to dominate both secular and religious art.

Rich and impressive copies of biblical scripture, especially the Gospels, were among the most prominent expressions of artistic creativity throughout Europe in the Early Middle Ages. Gospel books rested on the altar of every church and quickly became venerated objects as well as the source of liturgical readings. They were produced in local workshops called scriptoria (see "The Medieval Scriptorium," above). Scriptoria became major centers of learning and played a critical role in the diffusion of artistic styles and themes.

Irish monks produced many large, elaborately decorated Gospels, among them the *Gospel Book of Durrow*, dating to about 675. This manuscript is named for Durrow, in Ireland, where it was kept in the late medieval period, but no one knows exactly where it was made. A likely possibility is the monastery founded on the island of Iona off the northwest coast of Scotland by the Irish abbot Columba in the sixth century. The format and text of the book reflect a knowledge of Roman Christian prototypes, but its decoration is practically an encyclopedia of local design motifs, many of them adopted from metalwork. Each of the four books of the Gospel is preceded by a page of pure ornament, followed by a page with the symbol of the Evangelist and then with a decorated letter to begin the text. In the Book of Durrow, the lion, normally the symbol of Saint Mark, introduces the Gospel of Saint John (fig. 14-8). Following an early Christian tradition, the artist applied a very old convention and reversed the lion and eagle, using the lion for John and the eagle for Mark. The lion is a ferocious beast with sharp claws, jagged teeth, curling tail, and wild eye (fig. 14-8). The stylization of the body is based on Pictish (Scottish) stone carving, rather then on a flesh and blood creature. Its eye, tail, and paws and the stylized muscles around hip and shoulder joints are painted yellow to suggest gold. Its head is decorated with a uniform stippled

14-8. Page with *Lion*, Book of John, *Gospel Book of Durrow*, probably made at Iona, Scotland. c. 675. Ink and tempera on parchment, 9⅝ x 5¹¹/₁₆" (24.5 x 14.5 cm). The Board of Trinity College, Dublin, MS 57 (A.4.5), fol. 191v

14-9. *Chi Rho Iota* page, Book of Matthew, *Book of Kells*, probably made at Iona, Scotland. Late 8th or early 9th century. Tempera on vellum, 13 x 9½" (33 x 25 cm). The Board of Trinity College, Dublin, MS 58 (A.1.6.), fol. 34v

The Greek letters *chi rho iota* (*XPI*, or *chri*) form the abbreviation for *Christi*, the first word in the Latin sentence *Christi autem generatio,* meaning: "Now this is how the birth of Jesus Christ came about" (Matthew 1:18). The word *autem* appears as another Latin abbreviation resembling an *h*, which is followed by *generatio* written out. The text continues on the next page. Medieval scribes had to learn a long list of standard abbreviations for Latin words, which were used like modern shorthand to save time and space in transcribing long documents or copying texts. Scribes in the courts of popes and secular rulers were even given the official title of "abbreviator."

pattern, and the surface of its body is covered with diamond patterns similar to those found in enamelwork. The two types of ribbon interlace on the wide border—a dotted pattern on the vertical bands and shifting bright green, red, and yellow on the horizontal bands—also suggest metallic decoration.

The *Book of Kells*, which an eleventh-century observer described as "the chief relic [religious object] of the Western world," is one of the most beautiful, original, and inventive of the surviving Hiberno-Saxon gospel books. It was probably made at the monastery on Iona in the late eighth century and brought to the monastery at Kells, in Ireland, in the late ninth century.

In the twelfth century a priest named Gerald of Wales, describing a Hiberno-Saxon gospel book very much like the *Book of Kells*, wrote: "Fine craftsmanship is all about you, but you might not notice it. Look more keenly at it,

and you will penetrate to the very shrine of art. You will make out intricacies, so delicate and subtle, so exact and compact, so full of knots and links, with colors so fresh and vivid, that you might say that all this was the work of an angel, and not of a man" (cited in Henderson, page 195). A close look at perhaps the most celebrated page in the *Book of Kells*—the one from the Book of Matthew (1:18–25) that begins the account of Jesus' birth—reveals what he means (fig. 14-9). The Greek letters *chi, rho,* and *iota,* the abbreviation for *Christi,* dominate the page. They are set within an irregularly shaped form that resembles a metal brooch. At first glance, the page seems completely abstract. The lines rippling out from the arms of the *chi* may suggest water, perhaps a reference to the mystery of Christ's conception and birth or to the four rivers that were thought to flow from heaven, bringing health to the Church. For those who would "look keenly,"

14-10. South Cross, Ahenny, County Tipperary, Ireland.
8th century

however, there is more. Hidden in the dense thicket of spirals and interlaces are human and animal forms. The curve of the *rho* in the center of the page, for example, ends in the head of a youth with red hair, perhaps representing Christ, the heart of the world, from whom flow the "rivers" of health. Three angels, perhaps representing heaven or air, hold the left edge of the *chi*. Below them, just to the right of the long stroke of the *chi* is a pair of crouching cats defending the Christian wafer (the host, or body, of Christ) from evil mice. Nearby an otter catches a salmon. Such images are not just ornamental, but form a subtle commentary on the text. Even the monastery cats join in the fight against the devil.

Like manuscript **illumination**, the monumental stone crosses erected in Ireland in the eighth century also reflect the influence of metalwork designs and motifs. The origin of these crosses is obscure, but they began to appear throughout the British Isles at roughly the same time. In the Irish "high crosses," so called because of their size, a circle encloses the arms of the cross. The South Cross of Ahenny, County Tipperary, is an especially well-preserved example of this type (fig. 14-10). It seems to have been deliberately modeled on metal ceremonial or **reliquary** crosses, that is, containers of holy relics in the form of a cross. It is outlined with **gadrooning** (notched, convex molding) and covered with spirals and interlace. The large **bosses** (buttonlike projections), which form a cross within the cross, resemble the jewels that were similarly placed on metal crosses.

CHRISTIAN SPAIN

As Roman control of western Europe deteriorated in the fourth and fifth centuries, a Germanic group known as the Visigoths, converts to Arian Christianity (Chapter 7), migrated across Gaul and into Spain. By the sixth century the Visigoths had established themselves as an aristocratic elite over the indigenous Spanish-Roman population, which probably outnumbered them by about 40 to 1. Although the Visigoths adopted Latin for writing and had switched to orthodox Christianity by the seventh century, they were never fully assimilated into Spanish society. Visigothic metalworkers, following the same late-Roman–Germanic tradition they shared with their counterparts in the north, created magnificent cloisonné jewelry similar in style and technique to the Sutton Hoo purse lid (see fig. 14-7).

The few sixth- and seventh-century churches surviving in Spain are among the best-preserved examples of monumental architecture in western Europe from this period. Santa Maria de Quintanilla de las Viñas, located about 150 miles north of Toledo, was built in the late seventh century. This **basilica-plan** church (modeled on the Roman basilica; see "Elements of Architecture," page 298) originally had a nave and two aisles, which no longer exist. The aisles opened through narrow doorways into the **choir**, the area reserved for the clergy, which extended the full width of the church. The narrow doorways suggest that the choir acted more as a barrier than as a connection between the congregation and the priests celebrating the Eucharist in the square sanctuary apse. This marked partitioning of the nave from the choir and sanctuary, found in other Spanish churches of the same period, may reflect a change in liturgical practice in which the congregation was barred from approaching the altar to receive Communion.

A **horseshoe arch** frames the entrance to the apse at Santa Maria at Quintanilla de las Viñas (fig. 14-11), refuting the popular belief that Islamic architects introduced this form in the eighth century (see the discussion of the Great Mosque of Córdoba in Chapter 8 and figure 8-6). The base of the arch juts inward slightly into the apse entrance, and the freestanding columns and large **impost blocks** likewise restrict it. The themes of the crisp bands of carving on the arch and impost blocks are found frequently in Early Christian art. On the impost blocks is Christ Triumphant between Angels. On the arch is a scrolling vine, the loops of which encircle birds and bunches of grapes, symbolic of the Eucharist (fig. 14-12). Like the carved decoration on the roughly contemporary South Cross at Ahenny, the style of these low-relief decorations is reminiscent of metalwork. A grooved border like the setting of a brooch contains the images on the arch, and the little lines that punctuate the border and scrollwork suggest fine threads of metal banding.

The Islamic conquest of Spain in 711 ended Visigothic rule. With some exceptions, Christians and Jews who did not convert to Islam but acknowledged the authority of the new rulers and paid the taxes required of non-Muslims were left free to follow their own religious practices. Christians in the Arab territories were called Mozarabs

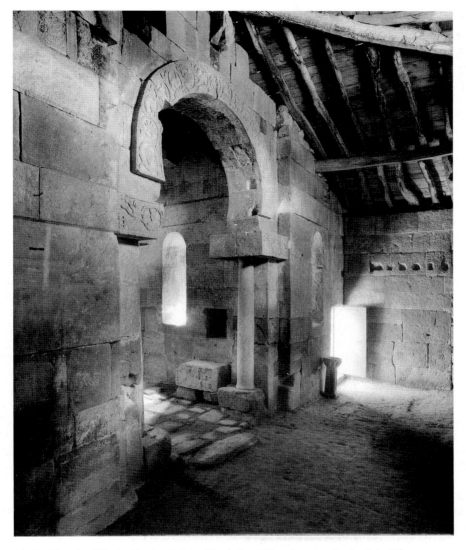

14-11. Church of Santa Maria, Quintanilla de las Viñas, Burgos, Spain. Late 7th century. View from the choir into the apse

(from the Arabic *mustarib,* meaning "would-be Arab"). The conquest resulted in a rich exchange of artistic influences between the Islamic and Christian communities. Christian artists adapted many features of Islamic style to their traditional themes, creating a unique, colorful new style known as Mozarabic. When Mozarabic artists migrated to the monasteries of northern Spain, which reverted to Christian rule not long after the initial Islamic invasion, they took this style with them, and it is known there as transported Mozarabic.

In northern Spain, the antagonisms among Muslims, orthodox Christians, and the followers of various heretical Christian cults provided fertile material for religious

14-12. *Grapes, Vines, and Birds,* carving on the triumphal arch, Church of Santa Maria, Quintanilla de las Viñas

commentaries. One of the most influential of these was the *Commentary on the Apocalypse* compiled in the eighth century by Beatus, abbot of the Monastery of San Martín at Liébana, in the north Spanish kingdom of Asturias. The commentary is an analysis of the visions set down in the Apocalypse (also called the Book of Revelation), which is filled with vivid descriptions of the final, fiery triumph of Christ. Beatus's work is an impassioned justification of orthodox beliefs. It thus had enduring appeal for northern Christians in their long struggle against the Muslim rulers of the rest of Spain, and it was widely read, copied, and illustrated. Two copies from the late tenth century, illustrated in the Mozarabic style, were produced under the direction of the scribe-painter Emeterius, a monk in the workshop of the Monastery of San Salvador at Tábara in the kingdom of León.

The first of these commentaries was completed in 970 by Emeterius and a scribe-painter named Senior, who identified themselves in the manuscript. Artists were beginning to emerge from anonymity throughout Europe at this time. Mozarabic scribes often signed their work, sometimes showed themselves occupied with pen and brush, and occasionally offered the reader spontaneous comments and opinions (see "The Medieval Scriptorium," page 486). On the **colophon**, the page of a manuscript or book that identifies its producers, is a picture of the five-story tower of the Tábara Monastery and the two-story scriptorium attached to it, the earliest known depiction of a medieval scriptorium (fig. 14-13). The tower, with horseshoe-arched windows, and the workshop have been rendered in a two-dimensional cross section that reveals many details of the interior and exterior simultaneously. In the scriptorium, Emeterius on the right and Senior on the left, identified by inscriptions over their heads, are at work at the same small table. A helper in the next room cuts sheets of **parchment** or **vellum** for book pages. A monk standing inside (or perhaps outside) the ground floor of the tower pulls the ropes to the bell in the turret on the right. Three other men climb ladders between the floors, apparently on their way to the balconies on the top level. Brightly glazed tiles in geometric patterns, a common feature of Islamic architecture, cover what could be the tower's interior or exterior wall.

The other Beatus Commentary was produced five years later for a named patron, Abbot Dominicus. The colophon identifies Senior as the scribe for this project. Emeterius and a woman named Ende, who signed herself "painter and servant of God," shared the task of illustration. A full-page painting from this book shows an eaglelike bird with a luxurious tail grasping a glittering snake in its beak (fig. 14-14). With abstract shapes and cloisons of bright color recalling Visigothic metalwork, the image illustrates a metaphorical description in Beatus of the triumph of Christ over Satan. A bird with a powerful beak and beautiful plumage (Christ) covers itself with mud to trick the snake (Satan). Just when the snake decides the bird is harmless, the creature swiftly attacks and kills it. "So Christ in his Incarnation clothed himself in the impurity of our [human] flesh that through

14-13. Emeterius and Senior. Colophon page, *Commentary on the Apocalypse* by Beatus and *Commentary on Daniel* by Jerome, made for the Monastery of San Salvador at Tábara, León, Spain. Completed July 27, 970. Tempera on parchment, 14¼ x 10⅛" (36.2 x 25.8 cm). Archivo Histórico Nacional, Madrid, MS 1079B (formerly 1240)

In medieval manuscripts the colophon was used to provide specific information about the production of a book. In addition to identifying himself and Senior on this colophon, Emeterius also praised his teacher, "Magius, priest and monk, the worthy master painter," who had begun the manuscript prior to his death in 968. Emeterius also took the opportunity to comment on the profession of bookmaking: "Thou lofty tower of Tábara made of stone! There, over thy first roof, Emeterius sat for three months bowed down and racked in every limb by the copying. He finished the book on July 27th in the year 1008 [970, by modern dating] at the eighth hour" (cited in Dodwell, page 247).

a pious trick he might fool the evil deceiver. . . .[W]ith the word of his mouth [he] slew the venomous killer, the devil" (from the Beatus Commentary, cited in Williams, page 95). Symbolic stories, or **allegories**, such as this were popular among artists, writers, and theologians in the Middle Ages. Because allegories translate abstract ideas into concrete events and images, their implications are accessible to almost anyone of any level of education.

14-14. Emeterius and Ende, with the scribe Senior. Page with *Battle of the Bird and the Serpent, Commentary on the Apocalypse* by Beatus and *Commentary on Daniel* by Jerome, made for Abbot Dominicus, probably at the Monastery of San Salvador at Tábara, León, Spain. Completed July 6, 975. Tempera on parchment, 15¾ x 10¼" (40 x 26 cm). Cathedral Library, Gerona, Spain, MS 7[11], fol. 18v

THE CAROLINGIAN PERIOD

A new empire emerged in continental Europe during the second half of the eighth century that was forged by a dynasty known as Carolingian, after its greatest member, Charlemagne, or Charles the Great (*Carolus* is Latin for "Charles"). The Carolingians were Franks, a Germanic people who had settled in northern Gaul by the end of the fifth century. Under Charlemagne (ruled 768–814) the Carolingian realm reached its greatest extent, encompassing western Germany, France, a bit of Spain, and the Low Countries (modern Belgium and Holland). Charlemagne imposed Christianity, sometimes brutally, throughout this territory and promoted church reform. In 800 Pope Leo III (795–816), in a ceremony in the Church of Saint Peter in Rome, granted Charlemagne the title of emperor, declaring him to be the rightful successor to the first Christian Roman emperor, Constantine. This event reinforced Charlemagne's authority over his diverse realm and strengthened the bonds between the papacy and secular government in the West.

Charlemagne sought to restore the Roman Empire as a Christian state and to revive the arts. He placed great emphasis on education, gathering around him the finest scholars of the time, and his court became the leading intellectual center of western Europe. His architects, painters, and sculptors turned to Rome and Ravenna for inspiration, but what they created was not a simple copy of the Imperial Christian style.

Architecture

Charlemagne's biographer, Einhard, reported that the ruler, "beyond all sacred and venerable places . . . loved

14-15. Abbey Church of Saint Riquier, Monastery of Centula, France, dedicated 799. Engraving dated 1612, after an 11th-century drawing. Bibliothèque Nationale, Paris

the church of the holy apostle Peter at Rome." Not surprisingly, Charlemagne's architects turned to Saint Peter's, a basilica-plan church with a long nave and side aisles ending in a projecting apse (see fig. 7-11), as a model for his own churches. These churches, however, included purely northern features and were not simply imitations of Roman Christian structures. Among these northern features was a multistory **narthex**, or vestibule, flanked by attached stair towers. Because church entrances traditionally faced west, this type of narthex is called a **westwork**.

The Abbey Church of Saint Riquier at the Monastery of Centula in northern France was an example of the Carolingian reworking of the Roman basilica-plan church. Built when Angilbert, a Frankish scholar at Charlemagne's court, was abbot at Centula, it was completed about 799. No longer standing, it is known today from archeological evidence and an engraved copy after a lost eleventh-century drawing of the abbey (fig. 14-15). A triangular enclosure linking the church and two independent chapels may have served as a **cloister** for the abbey's more than 300 monks. Cloisters are porticoed courtyards, sometimes with gardens linking the church with the buildings for the monastic community. The small, barnlike building at the right in the drawing was a

chapel dedicated to Saint Benedict. The more elaborate structure at the lower left, a basilica with a rotunda ringed with chapels was dedicated to the Virgin and the twelve Apostles. The interior would have had an altar of the Virgin in the center, an **ambulatory** passageway around it, and altars for each of the apostles against the perimeter walls.

The Church of Saint Riquier followed a basic basilica plan, but it also included two features that gave equal weight to both ends of the nave: a multistory westwork with flanking stair towers to the left and, to the right, a similar structure over the **transept**, the part of the church that crosses the nave at the sanctuary end. A square choir space beyond the **crossing**, the intersection of the nave and transept, lengthened the sanctuary space. The towers, soaring from cylindrical bases through three arcaded levels to cross-topped spires, would have been the most striking feature of the building. They were apparently made of timber, which posed fewer problems for tall construction than masonry. This vertical emphasis was a northern contribution to Christian architecture.

Charlemagne, who enjoyed hunting and swimming, was drawn to the forests and natural hot springs of Aachen (Aix-la-Chapelle in French), in the northern part of his empire. He built a palace complex there and installed his court in it about 794, making it his capital. The complex included administrative offices and royal workshops for making books and luxury items. Directly across from the royal audience hall on the north-south axis of the complex stood the Palace Chapel (fig. 14-16). This structure functioned as Charlemagne's private chapel, the church of his imperial court, a **martyrium** for certain precious relics of saints, and, after the emperor's death, the imperial **mausoleum**. To satisfy all these needs, the emperor's architects created a large, central-plan building similar to that of the Church of San Vitale in Ravenna (see fig. 7-29), adding a square projecting entrance facade with a tall, cylindrical tower on each side. The chapel originally had a very large, walled forecourt where crowds could assemble. Spiral stairs in the twin towers led to a throne room on the second level that opened onto the chapel **rotunda**, allowing the emperor to participate in the Mass. Relics were housed above the throne room on the third level.

The central core of the chapel is an octagon that rises to a **clerestory** above the **gallery** level (fig. 14-17). An ambulatory aisle surrounds this central core to form a sixteen-sided outer wall. The gallery also opens on the central space through arched openings supported by two tiers of Corinthian columns. Compared to San Vitale, where the central space seems to flow outward from the dome into semidomes and the exedra, the Aachen chapel has a clarity created by flat walls and geometric forms. The columns and grilles on the gallery level lie flush with the opening overlooking the central area, screening it from the space beyond. The effect is to create a powerful vertical visual pull from the floor of the central area to the top of the vault. Unlike San Vitale, which is covered by a smooth, round dome, the vault over the Palace Chapel rises from its octagonal base in eight curving masonry

14-16. Reconstruction drawing of the Palace Chapel of Charlemagne, Aachen (Aix-la-Chapelle), Germany. 792–805

14-17. Palace Chapel of Charlemagne

Although this sturdily constructed chapel retains its original design and appearance, much of its decoration either has been restored or dates from later periods. The Gothic-style chapel seen through the center arches on the ground floor replaced the eighth-century sanctuary apse. The enormous "crown of light" suspended over the central space was presented to the church by Emperor Frederick Barbarossa in 1168. Extensive renovations took place both in the nineteenth century, when the chapel was reconsecrated as the Cathedral of Aachen, and in the twentieth century, after it was damaged in World War II.

over the Palace Chapel rises from its octagonal base in eight curving masonry segments. The clear division of the structure into parts and the vertical emphasis are both hallmarks of the new style that developed under Charlemagne.

Monastic communities had grown numerous by the Early Middle Ages and had spread across Europe. In the early sixth century, Benedict of Nursia (c. 480–543) wrote his *Rule for Monasteries,* a set of guidelines for monastic life. Benedictine monasticism quickly became dominant, displacing earlier forms, including the Irish monasticism that had developed in the British Isles. In the early ninth century, Abbot Haito of Reichenau developed a general plan for the construction of monasteries for his colleague Abbot Gozbert of the Benedictine Abbey of Saint Gall near Lake Constance (in modern Switzerland). The Saint Gall

14-18. Plan of the Abbey of Saint Gall (redrawn). c. 817. Original in red ink on parchment, 28 x 44⅛" (71.1 x 112.1 cm). Stiftsbibliothek, St. Gallen, Switzerland, Cod. Sang. 1092

14-19. Model after the Saint Gall monastery plan (fig. 14-18), constructed by Walter Horn and Ernst Born, 1965

plan (fig. 14-18), originally drawn on five pieces of parchment sewn together, combines Benedictine guidelines with later ideas developed at Church councils. Figure 14-19 shows a model based on the original plan.

This extremely functional plan was widely adopted and can still be seen in many Benedictine monasteries. It reserved a central place for a basilica-plan church with apses at both ends and a transept crossing the nave at the eastern end. These apses would have housed separate chapels and displays of relics. Together with the adjacent cloister and **refectory** (dining hall), the church was the heart of the monastery's communal life. Monks entered it from the cloister or by stairs directly from their quarters. Members of the lay community that inevitably developed outside the walls of a large monastery used the main entryway. In the surrounding buildings, monks pursued their individual tasks. Scribes and painters, for example, spent much of their day in the scriptorium studying and copying books, and teachers staffed the monastery's schools and library. Benedictine monasteries generally had two schools, one inside the monastery proper for young monks and novices (those hoping to take vows and become brothers), and another outside for educating the sons of the local nobility.

Benedict insisted that monks extend hospitality to all visitors, and the large building in the upper left of the plan may be a hostel, or inn, for housing them. A porter would have looked after visitors, supplying them from the food produced by the monks. The plan also included a hospice for the poor and an infirmary. A monastery of this size had most of the features of a small town and would have indirectly or directly affected many hundreds of people. Essentially self-supporting, it would have had livestock, barns, agricultural equipment, a bakery and brewery, kitchen gardens (farm fields lay outside the walls), and even a cemetery. It would also have drawn on the support of extensive and widely scattered estates elsewhere.

Books

Books played a central role in the efforts of Carolingian rulers to promote learning, propagate Christianity, and standardize Church law and practice. As a result, much of the artistic energy of the period found an outlet in the empire's great northern scriptoria. One of the main tasks of these centers was to produce authoritative copies of key religious texts, free of the errors that tired, distracted, or confused scribes had introduced over the generations. The scrupulously edited versions of ancient texts that emerged are among the lasting achievements of the Carolingian period. The Anglo-Saxon scholar Alcuin of York, whom Charlemagne called to his court, spent the last eight years of his life producing a corrected copy of the Latin Vulgate Bible. His revision served as the standard text of the Bible for the rest of the Carolingian and subsequent medieval periods.

Carolingian scribes also developed a new, legible script to replace the confusing and hard-to-read scripts used since Roman times. Known as **Caroline minuscule**, it featured consistent separation of words and large capital letters for the opening of important sections. It is similar to many modern printed alphabets and is quite legible to modern readers.

One of the first surviving manuscripts in the new script, produced at Charlemagne's court between 781 and 783, was a collection of readings from the Gospels compiled by the Frankish scribe Godescalc and known as the *Godescalc Gospel Lectionary* or *Godescalc Evangelistary*. This richly illustrated and sumptuously made book (it has gold and silver letters and purple-dyed vellum pages) has a full-page portrait of the evangelist at the beginning of each Gospel section. The style of these illustrations suggests that Charlemagne's artists were familiar with the illusionistic painting style of imperial Rome as it had been preserved in Byzantine manuscripts.

In his portrait Mark is in the act of writing at a lectern tilted up to display his work (fig. 14-20). He appears to be attending closely to the small haloed lion in the upper left corner, the source of his inspiration and the iconographic symbol by which he is known. The artist has modeled the form of his arms, hips, and knees beneath his garment and rendered the bench and lectern to give a hint of three-dimensional space despite the otherwise flat background. Mark's round-shouldered posture and

14-20. Page with *Mark the Evangelist*, Book of Mark, *Godescalc Evangelistary.*
781–83. Ink and colors on vellum. Bibliothèque Nationale, Paris,
MS lat. 1203, fol. 16

sandaled feet, solidly planted on a platform decorated with a classical spiraling-vine motif, contribute an additional naturalistic touch. Stylized plants set the scene out of doors, a convention seen also in an Early Christian mosaic (see fig. 7-14). Probably commissioned to commemorate the baptism of two of Charlemagne's sons in Rome, the *Godescalc Evangelistary* remained at the court for several decades, providing a model for a later series of famous, luxuriously decorated gospel books.

Louis the Pious, Charlemagne's son and only successor, appointed his childhood friend Ebbo as archbishop of Reims, and Ebbo established that northeastern French town as another brilliant center of bookmaking. A portrait of Matthew from a gospel book made for Ebbo, begun after 816 at the Abbey of Hautevillers near Reims, illustrates the unique style that emerged there (fig. 14-21). Although there are some similarities between this painting and the evangelist portraits in books produced at Charlemagne's court (fig. 14-20), the differences

are striking. The figure of Matthew vibrates with intensity, and the landscape in the background threatens to run off the page, contained only by the painted border. Even the acanthus-leaf trim in the frame seems blown by a violent wind. The rapid, calligraphic style focuses attention less on the physical appearance of the evangelist than on his inner, spiritual excitement as he hastens to transcribe the Word of God coming to him from the distant angel (Matthew's symbol) in the upper right corner. His head and neck jut awkwardly out of hunched shoulders, and his left hand clumsily grasps the book and inkhorn. His twisted brow and prominent eyebrows, represented by long, diagonal slashes, lend his gaze an intense, theatrical quality. As if to echo the saint's turbulent emotions, the desk, bench, and footstool tilt every which way and the top of the desk seems about to detach itself from the pedestal.

The most famous of all Carolingian manuscripts, the *Utrecht Psalter*, dating probably between 825 and 850,

14-21. Page with *Matthew the Evangelist*, Book of Matthew, *Ebbo Gospels*. c. 816–40. Ink and colors on vellum, 10¼ x 8¾" (26 x 22.2 cm). Bibliothèque Municipale, Epernay, France, MS 1, fol.18v

was also a product of the Reims workshop (fig. 14-22). This volume contains the Old Testament Book of Psalms illustrated with ink drawings that reflect the same linear vitality as the paintings in the Ebbo gospel book. The Psalms are difficult to represent because they do not tell a straightforward story. The *Utrecht Psalter* solves this problem by combining images derived from the core ideas of each Psalm into a single scene. The drawing in figure 14-22 illustrates Psalm 112.

1 Happy are those who fear the Lord,
   who greatly delight in God's commands.
2 Their descendants shall be mighty in the land,
   a generation upright and blessed.
3 Wealth and riches shall be in their homes;
   their prosperity shall endure forever.
4 They shine through the darkness, a light for the
   upright; they are gracious, merciful, and just.
5 All goes well for those gracious in lending,
   who conduct their affairs with justice.
6 They shall never be shaken;
   the just shall be remembered forever.
7 They shall not fear an ill report;
   their hearts are steadfast, trusting the Lord.
8 Their hearts are tranquil, without fear,
   till at last they look down on their foes.

14-22. Page with the end of Psalm 111 and Psalm 112, with an illustration for Psalm 112 (CXI in the Vulgate Bible), *Utrecht Psalter*. c. 825–50. Ink on vellum or parchment, 13 x 9⅞" (33 x 25 cm). Bibliotheek der Rijksuniversiteit, Utrecht, the Netherlands, MS script. ecol. 484, fol. 73v

14-23. *Crucifixion with Angels and Mourning Figures,* outer cover, *Lindau Gospels.* c. 870–80. Gold, pearls, and gems, 13¾ x 10⅜" (36.9 x 26.7 cm). The Pierpont Morgan Library, New York, MS 1

9 Lavishly they give to the poor;
   their prosperity shall endure forever;
   their horn shall be exalted in honor.
10 The wicked shall be angry to see this;
   they will gnash their teeth and waste away;
   the desires of the wicked come to nothing.

The hand of God is shown emerging from the clouds above the church on the right to bless "those who fear the Lord" (verse 1). The substantial stone buildings with tiled roofs represent their enduring prosperity (verse 3). The numerous hanging lamps in the buildings represent the "light for the upright" shining "through the darkness" (verse 4). A couple dispenses alms to the poor in the doorway of the central building, a deer's head with antlers ("their horn," verse 9, a symbol of vitality and honor) mounted on the roof above them. The people in the foreground, engaged in business, are "gracious in lending" and "conduct their affairs with justice" (verse 5). Such high moral conduct naturally draws "foes," represented here by armed soldiers in the buildings on the left (verse 8). But the wicked, rounded up and tossed into a pit by the devil, "gnash their teeth and waste away" (verse 10). Illustrations like this convey the characteristically close association between text and image in Carolingian art.

The magnificent illustrated manuscripts of the medieval period represented an enormous investment in time, talent, and materials, so it is not surprising that they were often protected with equally magnificent covers. But because these covers were themselves made of valuable materials—ivory, enamelwork, precious metals, and jewels—they were frequently reused or broken up. The elaborate book cover of gold and jewels shown in figure 14-23 was probably made between 870 and 880 at one of the workshops of Charles the Bald (ruled 840–877),

14-24. Church of Saint Cyriakus, Gernrode, Germany. Begun 961 and consecrated 973. The apse seen here replaced the original westwork entrance in the late 12th century.

14-25. Plan of the Church of Saint Cyriakus (after Broadley)

who inherited the portion of Charlemagne's empire that corresponds roughly to modern France after the death of his father, Louis the Pious. It is not known what book it was made for, but sometime before the sixteenth century it became the cover of a Carolingian manuscript known as the *Lindau Gospels*, which was prepared at the Monastery of Saint Gall in the late ninth century.

The cross and the Crucifixion were common themes for medieval book covers. The Crucifixion scene on the front cover of the *Lindau Gospels* is made of gold with figures in **repoussé** relief surrounded by heavily jeweled frames. Angels hover above the arms of the cross. Over Jesus' head, hiding their faces, are figures representing the sun and moon. The graceful, expressive poses of the mourners who float below the arms of the cross reflect the style of the *Utrecht Psalter* illustrations. Jesus has been modeled in a rounded, naturalistic style suggesting classical influence, but his stiff posture and stylized drapery counter the emotional expressiveness of the other figures. He stands straight and wide-eyed with outstretched arms, announcing his triumph over death and welcoming believers into the faith.

THE OTTONIAN PERIOD

The Carolingian Empire broke up when it was divided among the heirs of Louis the Pious. In the tenth century, control of the eastern portion of the empire, which corresponded roughly to modern Germany and Austria, passed to a dynasty of Saxon rulers known as the Ottonians, after its three principal figures, Otto I (ruled 936–973), Otto II (ruled 973–983), and Otto III (ruled 983–1002). Otto I, who took control of Italy in 951, was crowned emperor by the pope in 962, and thereafter he and his successors dominated the papacy and appointments to other high Church offices. This union of Germany and Italy under a German ruler came to be known as the Holy Roman Empire. Modern geographical names are used for convenience. No such country as Germany or Italy existed before the nineteenth century.

Architecture

The Ottonian rulers, in keeping with their imperial status, sought to replicate the splendors of Christian Roman architecture within their realm. The German court in

14-26. Nave, Church of Saint Cyriakus

Rome gave northern architects access to Roman designs, which they reinterpreted in light of their own local materials and time-tested techniques to create a new Ottonian style. Some of their finest churches were also strongly inspired by Carolingian structures like the Abbey Church of Saint Riquier (see fig. 14-15).

One of the best-preserved Ottonian buildings is the Church of Saint Cyriakus at Gernrode (fig. 14-24). A German noble named Gero founded the convent of Saint Cyriakus and commissioned the church in 961. Following the Ottonian policy of appointing relatives and close associates to important church offices, he made his widowed daughter-in-law the convent's first abbess. A basilica-plan structure, Saint Cyriakus originally had a westwork, which was replaced by a second apse in the twelfth century (fig. 14-25). The elevated floor of the choir and sanctuary apse at the east end covers a vaulted space known as a **crypt**. Two entrances on the south provided access between the church and the convent's cloister and dormitories. The towers and other vertical features that dominate the east and west ends of the church are reminiscent of similar features at Saint Riquier's, although not so dramatic as the towers that soared over that church. Windows, arcades, and **blind arcades** break the severity of the church's exterior.

The interior of Saint Cyriakus (fig. 14-26) has three levels: an arcade separating the nave from the side aisles, a gallery with groups of three arched openings, and a clerestory. A **triumphal arch** opening defines the end of the nave, and the flat ceiling is made of wood. Most of these features were also characteristic of Constantinian basilica-plan churches (see fig. 7-12). The alternation of columns and rectangular piers in Saint Cyriakus, how-

14-27. *Otto I Presenting Magdeburg Cathedral to Christ*, one of a series of nineteen ivory plaques, known as the *Magdeburg Ivories*. German or North Italian. c. 962–973. Ivory plaque, 5 x 4½" (12.7 x 11.4 cm). The Metropolitan Museum of Art, New York
Bequest of George Blumenthal, 1941 (41.100.157)

During the reign of Otto I, Magdeburg was on the edge of a buffer zone between the Ottonian Empire and the pagan Slavs. In the 960s, Otto established a religious center there from which the Slavs could be converted. One of the important saints of Magdeburg was Maurice, a Roman Christian commander of African troops who is said to have suffered martyrdom in the third century for refusing to worship in pagan rites. In later times, he was often represented as a dark-skinned African (see fig. 16-58). The warrior saint appears here presenting both Otto and Magdeburg Cathedral to Christ.

ever, creates a different rhythmic effect than the uniform arcading of such earlier churches, which pulled the viewer's gaze forward. Saint Cyriakus is likewise marked by vertical shifts in visual rhythm, with two pairs of arches between piers on the nave level surmounted by three pairs of arches on the gallery level, surmounted in turn by three windows in the clerestory. This seemingly simple architectural aesthetic, with its rhythmic alternation of heavy and light supports and its balancing of rectangular and round forms and horizontal and vertical movement, was to inspire architects for the next 300 years, finding full expression in the Romanesque period.

Sculpture

Carved ivory panels for book covers and diptychs were among the products of both Carolingian and Ottonian bookmaking workshops. An Ottonian plaque that shows Otto I presenting a model of the Magdeburg Cathedral to Christ may once have been part of the decoration of an altar or pulpit in the cathedral, which was dedicated in 968 (fig. 14-27). Otto is the diminutive figure holding the

14.28. (opposite) Doors of Bishop Bernward, Cathedral (Abbey Church of Saint Michael), Hildesheim, Germany. 1015. Bronze, height 16'6" (5 m)

The design of these magnificent doors anticipated by nearly a century the great sculptural programs that would decorate the exteriors of European churches in the Romanesque period. Bishop Bernward, who was both a scholar and a talented artist, is thought to have been intimately involved in planning the iconography of the scenes.

14-29. *The Temptation* (left) and *The Crucifixion* (right), detail of the Doors of Bishop Bernward

cathedral on the left. Christ is seated on a wreath, which may represent the heavens, and his feet rest on an arc that may represent the earth. Christ and Otto are surrounded by a crowd of witnesses. Saint Peter, patron of churches, faces Otto, and Saint Maurice, an important saint in Magdeburg, wraps his arm protectively around him. The action takes place on a very shallow stage. The heavy dignity and intense concentration of the figures are characteristic of the Ottonian court style.

In the eleventh century, Ottonian artists in northern Europe, drawing on Roman, Byzantine, and Carolingian models, created a new tradition of large sculpture in wood and bronze that would have a significant influence on later medieval art. An important patron of these sculptural works was Bishop Bernward of Hildesheim, who was himself an artist. His biographer, the monk Thangmar, described Bernward as a skillful goldsmith who closely supervised the artisans working for him. A pair of bronze doors made under his direction for his Abbey Church of Saint Michael represented the most ambitious and complex bronze-casting project since antiquity (fig. 14-28). The bishop had lived for a while in Rome as tutor for Otto III and may have been inspired by the carved wooden doors of the fifth-century Church of Santa Sabina located near Otto's palace there.

The inscription in the band running across the center of the doors states: "In the year of our lord 1015 Bishop Bernward installed the doors." They stand more than 16 feet tall and are decorated with Old Testament scenes on the left and New Testament scenes on the right. The Old Testament history begins in the upper left-hand panel with the Creation and continues downward to Adam and Eve's expulsion from Paradise, depicting their difficult and sorrowful life on earth, and ends with the terrible sin of brother murdering brother, the story of Cain and Abel. The New Testament follows, beginning with the Annunciation, at the lower right, and reading upward through the early life of Christ and his mother, Mary, through the Crucifixion to the Resurrection, symbolized by the Marys at the tomb and the meeting of Christ and Mary Magdalene in the garden. The Old Testament prefigured the New, and the scenes are paired across the doors to make the relationship clear. For example, the third panel down shows on the left the temptation of Adam and Eve in the Garden of Eden, believed to be the source of human sin, suffering, and death (fig. 14-29). This is paired on the right with the crucifixion of Jesus, whose sacrifice and suffering redeemed humankind, atoned for Adam and Eve's Original Sin, and brought the promise of eternal life.

The doors' rectangular panels recall the framed miniatures in Carolingian gospel books, and the style of the scenes within them is reminiscent of illustrations in works like the *Utrecht Psalter*. Small, extremely active figures populate nearly empty backgrounds. Architectural elements and features of the landscape are depicted in very low relief, forming little more than a shadowy stage for the actors in each scene. The figures stand out prominently, sculpted in varying degrees of relief, with their heads fully modeled in three dimensions. The result is lively and visually stimulating.

Another treasure of Ottonian sculpture is the *Gero Crucifix*, one of the few large works of carved wood to

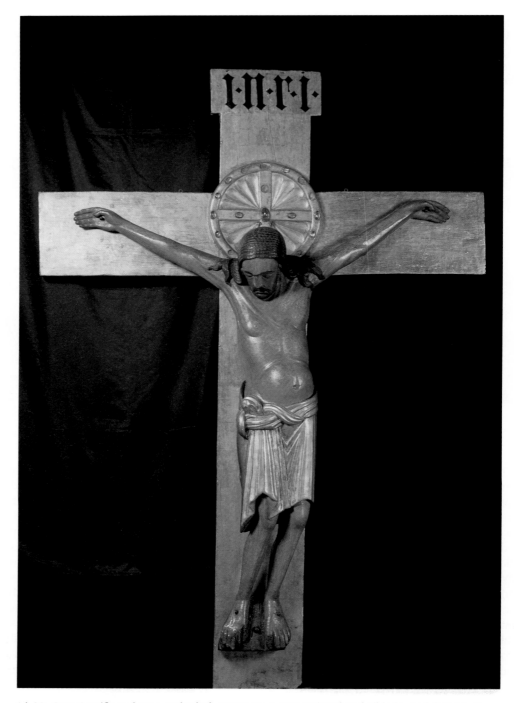

14-30. *Gero Crucifix*, Cologne Cathedral, Germany. c. 970. Painted and gilded wood, height of figure 6'2" (1.87 m)

This lifesize sculpture is both a crucifix to be suspended over an altar and a special kind of reliquary. A cavity in the back of the head was made to hold a piece of the host, or communion bread, already consecrated by the priest. Consequently, the figure not only represents the body of the dying Jesus but also contains within it the "body of Christ" obtained through the Eucharist.

survive from that period (fig. 14-30). It was commissioned by Gero, archbishop of Cologne (969–976), in northwest Germany, and was presented about 970 to his cathedral. (This is a different Gero from the patron of Saint Cyriakus at Gernrode.) The body of Jesus is more than 6 feet tall and made of painted and gilded oak. The focus here, following Byzantine models, is on Jesus' suffering. He is shown as a tortured martyr, not, as on the cover of the *Lindau Gospels* (see fig. 14-23), a triumphant hero. The intent is to inspire pity and awe in the viewer. Jesus' broken body, near death, sags on the cross and his head falls forward, eyes closed. The fall of his golden drapery heightens the impact of his drawn face, emaciated arms and legs, sagging torso, and limp, bloodied hands. In this image of

14-31. Page with *Otto III Enthroned*, *Liuthar Gospels* (*Aachen Gospels*).
c. 1000. Ink and colors on vellum, 10⁷/₈ x 8¹/₂" (27.9 x 21.8 cm).
Cathedral Treasury, Aachen

distilled anguish, the miracle and triumph of Resurrection seem distant indeed.

Books

Great variation in style and approach is characteristic of book illustration in the Ottonian period. Artists worked for different patrons in widely scattered centers, using different models or sources of inspiration. The *Liuthar* (or *Aachen*) *Gospels*, made for Otto III around 1000, is the work of the so-called Liuthar School, named for the scribe or patron responsible for the book. The center of this school was probably a monastic scriptorium in the vicinity of Reichenau or Trier. The dedication page of the *Liuthar Gospels* (fig. 14-31) is as much a work of imperial propaganda as the ancient Roman *Gemma Augustea* (see fig. 6-32). It establishes the divine underpinnings of Otto's authority and depicts him as a near-divine being himself. He is shown enthroned in heaven, surrounded by a **mandorla** and symbols representing the evangelists. The hand of God descends from above to place a

crown on his head. Otto's arms are extended in an all-embracing gesture, and he holds the orb of the world surmounted by a cross in his right hand. His throne, in a symbol of his worldly dominion, rests on the crouching Tellus, the personification of earth. In what may be a reference to the dedication on the facing page—"With this book, Otto Augustus, may God invest thy heart"—the evangelists represented by their symbols hold a white banner across the emperor's breast, dividing body, below, from soul (heart and head) above.

On each side of Otto is an emperor bowing his crowned head toward him. These may represent his Ottonian predecessors or subordinate rulers acknowledging his sovereignty. The bannered lances they hold may allude to the Ottonians' most precious relic, the Holy Lance, believed to be the one with which the Roman soldier Longinus pierced Jesus' side. In the lower register, two warriors face two bishops, symbolizing the union of secular and religious power under the emperor.

A second Gospels made for Otto III by the Liuthar School at about the same time as the *Liuthar Gospels*

14-32. Page with *Christ Washing the Feet of His Disciples, Gospels of Otto III.*
c. 1000. Staatsbibliothek, Munich

The washing of the disciples' feet, as told in John 13, was both a human gesture of hospitality, love, and humility and a symbolic transfer of spiritual power from Jesus to his "vicars," who would remain on earth after his departure to continue his work. At the time this manuscript was made, both the Byzantine emperor and the Roman pope practiced the ritual of foot-washing once a year following the model provided by Jesus: "If I, therefore, the master and teacher, have washed your feet, you ought to wash one another's feet" (13:14). The pope still carries out this ritual, washing the feet of twelve priests on every Maundy Thursday, the day before Good Friday.

contains a full-page illustration of an episode recounted in Chapter 13 of the Gospel according to John (fig. 14-32). Jesus, in one of his acts on the night before his crucifixion, gathered his disciples together to wash their feet. Peter, feeling unworthy, at first protests. The painting shows Jesus in the center, larger than the other figures, extending an elongated arm and hand in blessing toward the elderly apostle. Peter, his foot in a basin of water, reaches toward Jesus with similarly elongated arms. A disciple on the far right unbinds his sandals, and another, next to him, carries a basin of water. Eight other disciples look on from the left. The story is one of humility and mutual service, but the artist has transformed it into a symbolic representation of the all-powerful Christ of the Resurrection. The scene takes place outdoors in front of a gold curtain hung between green marble columns. Behind this barrier is a church, emphasizing an inherent message of the scene, the conferral of Jesus' blessing and authority on the apostles, his vicars on earth after his death.

The illustration on the presentation page of a Gospels made for Hitda (d. 1041), the abbess of the convent

14-33. Presentation page with Abbess Hitda and Saint Walpurga, *Hitda Gospels*. Early 11th century. Ink and colors on vellum, 11³⁄₈ x 5⁵⁄₈" (29 x 14.2 cm). Hessische Landes- und Hochschul-Bibliothek, Darmstadt, Germany

at Meschede, near Cologne, also in the early eleventh century, shows the abbess offering her book to Walpurga, her convent's patron saint (fig. 14-33). The simple contours of the stately figures give them a monumental quality. The artist has arranged the architectural lines of the convent in the background to frame the figures and draw attention to their transaction. The size of the convent underscores the abbess's position of authority. The foreground setting—a rocky, uneven strip of landscape—is meant to be understood as holy ground, separated from the rest of the world by the huge arch-shaped aura

that silhouettes Saint Walpurga. The calm atmosphere conveys a sense of spirituality and contained but deeply felt emotion.

These final manuscript paintings in a sense summarize the high intellectual and artistic qualities of Ottonian art as well as its great variety. Ottonian artists, drawing inspiration from the past—as reflected in the art of Christian Rome—created a monumental style for a Christian, German-Roman empire, the Holy Roman Empire. From such groundwork during the early medieval period emerged the arts of European Romanesque culture.

Speyer
Cathedral
c. 1030–
early 1100s

Cathedral
complex Pisa
begun 1063

Bayeux Tapestry
c. 1066–77

Sainte–Foy
late 10th–11th century

CHAPTER 15

Romanesque Art

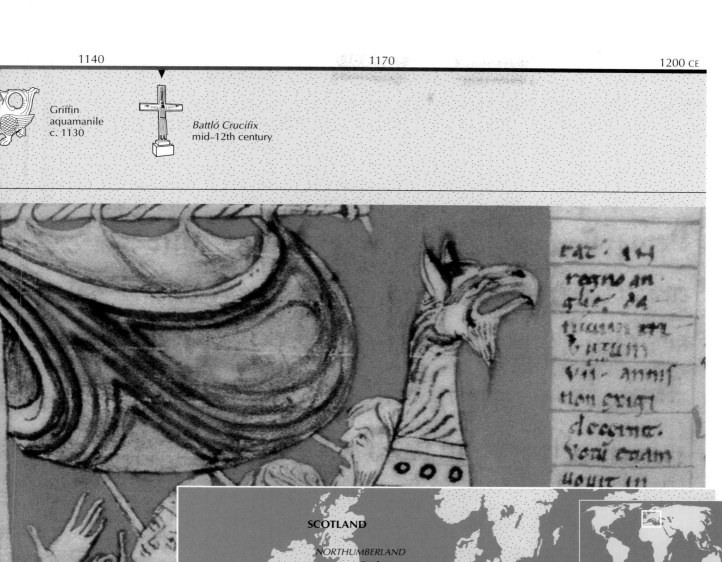

Griffin
aquamanile
c. 1130

Battló Crucifix
mid–12th century

SCOTLAND

NORTHUMBERLAND

IRELAND   • Durham

ENGLAND

Worcester •
WALES
ATLANTIC   Winchester •
OCEAN   HOLLAND

BELGIUM   GERMANY
                                • SAXONY
                          Helmarshausen •
          • Paris

Saint-Savin   Augsburg •
POITOU   FRANCE Vézelay   SWABIA
    Limoges •   Autun • Cîteaux
              Cluny • Clairvaux
              BURGUNDY
Santiago   LOMBARDY
de Compostela   Saint-   AUVERGNE   • Milan   Venice
    León   Sever • Le Puy   EMILIA Modena
  Silos Conques   Genoa •
Puente-la-Reina Moissac   Florence
              TOULOUSE   Pisa TUSCANY
PORTUGAL   ARAGON CATALONIA   ITALY
CASTILE   Rome •
  Toledo • Tahull

SPAIN   SICILY

                        Mediterranean Sea

ATLANTIC OCEAN

RUSSIA

ENGLAND HOLLAND
London •
KENT • Canterbury

NORMANDY   BELGIUM   GERMANY
                          • Liège
Bayeux •   Reims •   Bingen •
      Paris •   LORRAINE • Trier
ÎLE-DE-FRANCE
Chartres •   • Speyer

Loire River
Meuse River
Rhine River
Garonne River

0   500 Miles
0   500 Kilometers

15-1. Reliquary statue of Saint Foy, made in the Auvergne region, France, for the Abbey Church of Sainte-Foy, Conques, Rouergue, France. Late 10th–11th century. Gold repoussé and gemstones over wood core (incorporating a Roman helmet and Roman cameos; later additions 12th–19th centuries), height 33½" (85 cm). Cathedral Treasury, Conques, France

According to legend, Saint Foy was a child martyr, burned to death in 303 for refusing to make sacrifices to pagan gods. The symbolic as well as visual focus of the reliquary, which contains the saint's cranium behind a Roman helmet, is its oversized crowned head. The statue originally stood on an altar in the sanctuary of the church, separated from pilgrims in the ambulatory by a screen. The reliquary and other treasures were discovered inside a wall of the church during restoration in the 1860s. The monks had hidden them there for safekeeping, probably shortly before the abbey was burned by Protestants in 1568. This accident of survival helps us to imagine the original splendor of Romanesque churches.

D uring the late Middle Ages, people in western Europe once again began to travel in large numbers as traders, soldiers, and Christians on pilgrimages. Pilgrims throughout history have journeyed to holy sites—the ancient Greeks to Delphi, early Christians to Jerusalem and to Rome, Muslims to Mecca—but in the eleventh century, pilgrimages to the holy places of Christendom dramatically increased, despite the great financial and physical hardships they entailed (see "The Pilgrim's Journey," page 513).

As difficult and dangerous as these journeys were, there were also rewards along the route even before the pilgrims reached their destination. They were often entertained by itinerant minstrels singing poems of epic heroes, perhaps to attract travelers to the sites where legendary figures were supposed to have been buried. One of the most celebrated epics to have come down through the centuries is *La Chanson de Roland (The Song of Roland)*, composed about 1100 and telling of the heroic death of one of Charlemagne's knights, Roland, who perished defending the Franks from the Moors. The climax of the story is set in the Pyrenees mountains in northwest Spain on the very road taken by pilgrims to the tomb of the apostle Saint James (Santiago) in Santiago de Compostela.

Crowds of pilgrims traveling to the major shrines stopped along the way to venerate relics of local saints. Remains of bodies and items said to have come in contact with a holy person were encased in richly decorated containers called **reliquaries**. The pilgrams left donations and offerings with the churches and monasteries that housed the relics. These relics were widely believed to have miraculous powers, and the demand for them was so great that as early as the seventh century the bodies of saints were divided up and moved from place to place. As a result of the attraction of prestigious relics, monasteries sometimes competed for them. The Benedictine Abbey Church of Sainte-Foy at Conques in south-central France, for instance, drew pilgrims from far and wide to view the skull of the child saint in its famous jewel-encrusted golden reliquary (fig. 15-1). A monk from Conques had stolen her bones from another abbey in the ninth century, and by 883 Saint Foy was the patron of Conques.

To accommodate the faithful and instruct them in Church doctrine, many monasteries on the major pilgrimage routes built large new churches and filled them with sumptuous altars, crosses, and reliquaries. Sculpture and paintings on the walls illustrated important religious stories and doctrines and served to instruct as well as fascinate the faithful. These awe-inspiring works of art and architecture, like most of what has come down to us from the Romanesque period, had a Christian purpose. One monk wrote that by decorating the church "well and gracefully" the artist showed "the beholders something of the likeness of the paradise of God" (Theophilus, page 79).

ROMANESQUE CULTURE

Romanesque means "in the Roman manner," and the term applies specifically to a medieval European style. The word was coined in the early nineteenth century to describe European church architecture of the eleventh and twelfth centuries, which displayed the solid masonry walls, rounded arches, and masonry vaults characteristic of Roman imperial buildings. Soon the term was applied to all the arts of the period from roughly the mid-eleventh to the late-twelfth century, even though the art reflects influences from many sources, including Byzantine, Islamic, and early medieval Europe, as well as Roman art.

During the eleventh and twelfth centuries western Europe was divided into many small territories. The nations we know today did not exist. At the beginning of the eleventh century, Europe was still divided into many small political and economic units ruled by powerful families. The southern part of the region had closer linguistic and cultural ties to northern Spain, and the king of France truly ruled only a small area around Paris. The duke of Normandy (a former Viking region on the northwest coast) and the duke of Burgundy paid the king only token homage. By the end of the twelfth century, however, the French monarchy centered in the Île-de-France around Paris was beginning to emerge as the core of a national state. After the Norman conquest of Anglo-Saxon Britain in 1066, England, too, became a nation. In

Germany and northern Italy, in contrast, the power of local rulers and towns ultimately prevailed against the attempts of the monarchs of the Holy Roman Empire to impose a central authority, and these regions remained politically fragmented until the nineteenth century. Sicily and southern Italy, previously in the hands of Byzantine and Islamic rulers, fell under the control of the Norman adventurers. This political fragmentation led to the many distinctive regional styles that characterize Romanesque art.

An increase in trade during the eleventh and twelfth centuries, promoted the growth of towns, cities, and an urban class of merchants and artisans. Europe remained, however, a predominately agricultural society, with land being the primary source of wealth and power. In many regions the feudal system that had developed in the Early Middle Ages governed social and political relations. In this system, a lord, a landowning aristocrat, granted some of his property to a vassal, offering the vassal protection and receiving in return the vassal's allegiance and promise of military service as an armed knight. Vassals, in turn, could become lords, granting part of their holdings to their own vassals.

The economic foundation for this political structure was the manor, an agricultural estate in which peasants worked in exchange for a place to live, food, military protection, and other services from the lord. Feudal estates, community-based and almost entirely self-sufficient, became hereditary over time. Economic and political power thus came to be distributed through a network of largely inherited but constantly shifting allegiances and obligations that defined relations among lords, vassals, and peasants. Women generally had a subordinate position in this hierarchical, military social system. When necessary, however, aristocratic women took responsibility for managing estates in their male relatives' frequent absences on military missions or pilgrimages. They could also achieve positions of authority and influence as the heads of religious communities. Among peasants and artisans, women and men often worked side by side.

In the Early Middle Ages the Church and state had forged an often fruitful alliance. Christian rulers helped assure the spread of Christianity throughout Europe and supported monastic communities and Church leaders, who were often their relatives, with grants of land. The Church, in return, provided rulers with crucial social and spiritual support, and it supplied them with educated officials. As a result secular and religious authority became tightly intertwined. In the eleventh century the papacy sought to make the Church independent of lay authority, and so sparked a conflict with secular rulers known as the Investiture Controversy over the right to "invest" Church officials with the symbols of office.

In the eleventh and twelfth centuries, Christian Europe, previously on the defense against the expanding forces of Islam, became the aggressor. In Spain the armies of the Christian north were increasingly successful against the Islamic south. In 1095 Pope Urban II, responding to a request for help from the Byzantine emperor, called for a Crusade to retake Jerusalem and the Holy Land. This First Crusade succeeded in establishing a short-lived Christian state in Palestine. Although subsequent Crusades were, for the most part, military failures, the crusading movement as a whole had far-reaching cultural and economic consequences. The West's direct encounters with the more sophisticated material culture of the Islamic world and the Byzantine Empire created a demand for goods from the East. This in turn helped stimulate trade, and with it the rise of an increasingly urban society.

Western scholars rediscovered many classical Greek and Roman texts that had been preserved for centuries in Islamic Spain and the eastern Mediterranean. The combination of intellectual ferment and increased financial resources enabled the arts to flourish. The first universities were established at Bologna (eleventh century) and Paris, Oxford, and Cambridge (twelfth century). This renewed intellectual and artistic activity has been called the twelfth-century "renaissance," a cultural "rebirth." Monastic communities continued to be powerful and influential in Romanesque Europe, as they had been in the Early Middle Ages. Some monks and nuns were highly regarded for their religious devotion, for their learning, as well as for the valuable services they provided, including taking care of the sick and destitute, housing travelers, and educating the laity in monastic schools. Because monasteries were major landholders, they were part of the feudal power structure. The children of aristocratic families who joined religious orders also helped forge links between monastic communities and the ruling elite. As life in Benedictine communities grew increasingly comfortable, reform movements arose within the order itself. The first of these reform movements originated in the abbey of Cluny, founded in 910 in present-day east-central France.

FRANCE AND NORTHERN SPAIN

For most of the Romanesque period, power in France was divided among the nobility, the Church, and the kings of the Capetian dynasty, the successors to the Carolingians. Royal power was negligible in the eleventh century, but Burgundy was stronger than the Île-de-France, the region around Paris. Beginning in the twelfth century, the Capetians began to consolidate their authority in the Île-de-France.

The Iberian peninsula (present-day Spain and Portugal) remained divided between Muslim rulers in the south and Christian rulers in the north. The power of the Christian rulers was growing, however. Their long struggle with the Muslims had heightened their religious fervor, and they joined forces to extend their territory gradually to the south throughout the eleventh and twelfth centuries. The Christians in 1085 reconquered the Muslim capital and stronghold Toledo, a center of Islamic and Jewish culture in Castile. Toledo had been an oasis of concord between Christians, Muslims, and Jews until the early twelfth century; its scholars played an important role in the transmission of classical writings to the rest of Europe, contributing to the cultural renaissance of the twelfth century.

Architecture

The eleventh and twelfth centuries were a period of great building activity in Europe. Castles, churches, and monasteries arose everywhere. As one eleventh-century monk noted, "Each people of Christendom rivaled with the other, to see which should worship in the finest buildings. The world shook herself, clothed everywhere in a white garment of churches" (Radulphus Glaber, cited in Holt, *A Documentary History of Art*, I, page 18). That labor and funds should have been committed on such a scale to monumental stone architecture at the same time as the Crusades and in a period of frequent domestic warfare seems extraordinary today. The buildings that still stand, despite the ravages of weather, vandalism, neglect, and war, testify to the power of religious faith and local pride.

In one sense, Romanesque churches were the result of master builders solving the problems associated with each individual project: its site, its purpose, the building materials and work force available, the builders' own knowledge and experience, and the wishes of the patrons providing the funding. The process was slow, often requiring several different masters and teams of masons over the years. The churches nevertheless exhibit an overall unity and coherence, in which each element is part of a geometrically organized, harmonious whole.

Like the Carolingian churches, the basic form of the Romanesque church derives from earlier churches inspired by Early Christian basilicas. Romanesque builders made several key structural advances and changes in this form. Stone masonry vaulting replaced wooden roofs, increasing the protection from fire and improving the acoustics for music. The addition of ribs—curved and usually projecting stone members—as structual elements to both barrel vaults and **groin vaults** permitted builders more flexibility in laying out interior space (see "Elements of Architecture," page 552). Masonry **buttresses** reinforced walls at critical points. The introduction of an **ambulatory** (walkway) around the apse allowed worshipers to reach additional, radiating chapels and to view relics displayed there. Builders of Romanesque churchs emphasized the symbolic importance of towers, especially over the crossing and the west facade (the entrance to the church and, by extension the gateway to paradise). This new form arose along the pilgrimage

PARALLELS

Europe	1050–1125	1125–1200
France/northern Spain	Strong aristocracy, divided political power; Capetian dynasty; illuminations of Beatus *Commentary*; Church of Santiago de Compostela; Christians capture Toledo from Muslims; Cluny III; Cistercian order founded; *La Chanson de Roland*; Church of Saint-Savin-sur-Gartempe; Church of Saint-Pierre, Moissac; elaborate sculptured portals, the San Clemente Master	Increasingly strong monarchy; University of Paris founded; Virgin Mary as Throne of Wisdom images
Britain and Normandy	Norman Conquest of England; William the Conqueror crowned; Durham Cathedral; *Bayeux Tapestry*; *Domesday Book*; Oxford University founded	*Winchester Psalter; Worcester Chronicle*
Germany/Meuse Valley	Salian dynasty; Investiture Controversy; Speyer Cathedral; Saxon metalwork	Aquamaniles introduced from East; Hildegard of Bingen's *Liber Scivias*
Italy	Baptistry of San Giovanni; Pisa Cathedral; Normans control Sicily and southern Italy the Cluniac; Gregory VII elected pope; Rome sacked by Normans; first narrative portal sculpture; Church of San Clemente rebuilt	Church of San Marco, Venice
World	Separation of Eastern and Western Christian Churches; Seljuk Turks capture Baghdad; Christian Crusaders take Jerusalem; Song dynasty (China); Great Zimbabwe civilization (Africa); mound-building cultures (North America)	Omar Khayyam's *Rubaiyat* (Persia); Muslim conquests in India; Kamakura period (Japan); Jenghiz Khan rules Mongols; Benin civilization (Africa)

15-2. Abbey Church of Sainte-Foy, Conques, Rouergue, France. Mid-11th–12th century. Western towers rebuilt in the 19th century; crossing tower rib-vaulted in the 14th century, restored in the 19th century. View from the northeast

The contrast of nave and transepts, as well as the apse and lower ambulatory, are clearly seen in this exterior view, which supports a French scholar's characterization of Romanesque architecture as "additive."

routes to Santiago de Compostela. One surviving example of such a pilgrimage church, the Benedictine Abbey Church of Sainte-Foy, perches on a remote hillside at Conques in south-central France (fig. 15-2). As already noted, the church was renowned for its golden reliquary with the remains of a child saint (see fig. 15-1).

Construction of a new, larger church at Conques to accommodate the influx of pilgrims began in the mid-eleventh century and continued into the next century. The original **cruciform** (cross-shaped) plan with a wide, projecting transept was typical of Romanesque pilgrimage churches (fig. 15-3). At the west a **portal**—large doorway—opens directly into the broad nave. The facades of the largest churches have three doors, the central leading into the nave and the flanking doors into the side aisles. The elongated **sanctuary** encompasses the **choir** and the **apse**, with its surrounding **ambulatory** and ring of chapels.

The building is made of local sandstone that has weathered to a golden color (fig. 15-4). Light enters indirectly through windows in the outer walls of the aisles and upper-level **galleries**. The galleries replace the

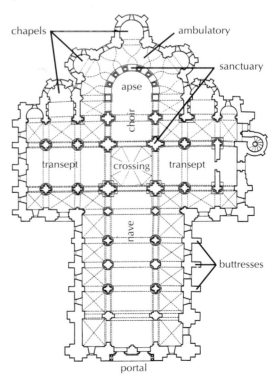

15-3. Plan of Abbey Church of Sainte-Foy

clerestory along the side aisles and overlook the nave. Ribbed barrel vaults cover the nave, groin vaulting spans the side aisles, and half-barrel vaulting called **quadrant vaulting**, the arc of which is one quarter of a circle, covers the galleries. The vaults over the galleries help strengthen the building by carrying the outward thrust of the nave vaults to the outer walls and buttresses.

The solid masonry piers that support the nave arcade have attached half columns on all four sides. This type of support, known as a **compound pier**, gives sculptural form to the interior and was a major contribution of Romanesque builders to architectural structure and aesthetics. Compound piers helped organize the architectural space by marking off the individual square, vaulted bays. Conques' square crossing is lit by an open, octagonal **lantern** tower resting on **squinches**. Light streaming in from the lantern and apse windows acted as a beacon, directing the worshipers' attention forward. During the Middle Ages the laity stood in the nave, separated from the priests and monks who celebrated the Mass in the choir.

Pilgrims arrived at Conques weary after many long days of difficult, perilous travel through dense woods and

THE PILGRIM'S JOURNEY

The eleventh and twelfth centuries in Western Europe saw an explosive growth in the popularity of religious pilgrimages. The rough roads that led to the most popular destinations—the Constantinian churches of Rome and the Cathedral of Santiago de Compostela (Saint James at Compostela) in the northwest corner of Spain—were often crowded with travelers, who had to contend at times with bandits, and dishonest innkeepers and merchants. Pilgrims also set out for the Church of the Holy Sepulchre in Jerusalem. Journeys could last a year or more.

The stars of the Milky Way, it was said, marked the way to Santiago de Compostela (see fig. 17). Still, a guidebook helped, and in the twelfth century the priest Aymery Picaud wrote one for pilgrims on their way to the great shrine through what is now France. In Picaud's time, four main pilgrimage routes crossed France, merging into a single road in Spain at Puente-la-Reina and leading on from there through Burgos and León to Compostela. Conveniently spaced monasteries and churches offered food and lodging. Roads and bridges were maintained by a guild of bridge builders and guarded by the Knights of Santiago.

Picaud described the best-traveled routes and most important shrines to visit. Chartres, for example, housed the tunic that the Virgin was said to have worn when she gave birth to Jesus. At Vézelay were the bones of Saint Mary Magdalen, and at Conques, those of Saint Foy, an early local martyr (see fig. 15-1). Churches associated with miraculous cures—Autun, for example, which claimed to house the bones of Saint Lazarus, raised by Jesus from the dead—were filled with the sick and injured praying to be healed. Like travel guides today, Picaud's book also provided shopping tips, advice on local customs, comments on food and the safety of drinking water, and pocket dictionaries of useful words in the languages the pilgrim would encounter en route. His warnings about the people who prey on travelers seem all too relevant today.

"Das ist der Rom Weg," late map of pilgrimage routes to Rome from Denmark. c. 1500. Woodcut, 15¾ x 11¼" (40 x 28.5 cm). The British Library, London

mountains, probably thankful that they had been protected by the saint against bandits on the way. They no doubt paused in front of the west entrance to study its portal sculpture, a notable feature of Romanesque pilgrimage churches. Portal sculpture communicated the core doctrines of the Church to those who came to read its messages. At Conques, the Last Judgment in the **tympanum** (the **lunette** over the doorway) marked the passage from the secular world into the sacred world within the church. Inside, the walls resounded with the music of the plainchant, also called Gregorian chant after Pope Gregory I (590–604). The Benedictines spent eight-and-a-half to ten hours a day in religious services. Today they still spend two-and-a-half to three hours.

A different Romanesque architecture could be found at the Benedictine Abbey Church of Cluny in Burgundy, founded in 910 as a reformed monastery. Cluny had a special independent status, its abbot answering directly to the pope in Rome rather than to the local bishop and feudal lord. This unique freedom, jealously safeguarded by a series of long-lived and astute abbots, enabled Cluny to become influential and prosperous in the eleventh and early twelfth centuries. Cluniac reform spread to other monasteries within Burgundy and beyond, to the rest of France, Italy, and Germany. Cluny attracted the patronage of successive rulers, as well as the favor of the pope in Rome. By the second half of the eleventh century there were some 300 monks in the abbey at Cluny alone. Cluny founded more than 200 priories (religious houses) in other locations—many along pilgrimage routes—and many more houses were loosely affiliated with it. At the height of its power 1,450 houses answered to the strong central administration of the abbot of Cluny.

Cluniac monks and nuns dedicated themselves to the scholarly and artistic interests of their order. Most important was the celebration of the eight Hours of the Divine Office, including prayers, scripture readings, psalms and hymns, and the Mass, the symbolic rite of the Last Supper, celebrated after the third hour (terce). They depended for support on the labor of laymen and laywomen who had not taken vows. Cluny's extensive land holdings, coupled with gifts of money and treasure, made it wealthy. Cluny and its affiliates were among the major patrons of art in Western Europe.

The great Hugh de Semur, abbot of Cluny for sixty years (1049–1109), began a new church at Cluny in 1088 with the help of financing from King Alfonso VI of León and Castile in northern Spain (ruled 1065–1109). Known to art historians as Cluny III (because it was the third building at the site), it was the largest and most spectacular church in all Europe when it was completed in 1130. Used as a stone quarry in the early 1800s after the French Revolution, the monastery is known today through the work of archeologists (fig. 15-5). Richly carved, painted, and furnished, it was described by a contemporary observer as fit for angels. Music and art were densely interwoven in Cluniac life, shaped by the Cluniac conception of the house of God. The proportions of Cluny III were based on harmonic relationships discussed in ancient Greek musical theory and mathematics. The

15-5. Reconstruction drawing of the Abbey Church (Cluny III), Cluny, Burgundy, France. 1088–1130. View from the east (after Conant)

The magnificence of this church and the Cluniac power it represented made it a particular target of anti-Church violence. It was nearly destroyed after the French Revolution when the owner sold its stones as building material. Only the southeast transept and its tower survive.

towering barrel-vaulted ceiling—more than 100 feet high in a space more than 500 feet long from end to end—enhanced the sound of the monks' chants. Sculpture, too, picked up the musical theme: carvings on two surviving column capitals depict personifications of the eight modes of the plainchant. The hallmarks of Cluniac churches were functional design, skillful masonry technique, and the assimilation of elements from Roman and early medieval architecture and sculpture. Individual Cluniac monasteries, however, were free to follow regional traditions and styles; consequently Cluny III was widely influential, though not copied exactly.

Several new religious orders devoted to an austere spirituality arose in the late eleventh and early twelfth centuries. Among these were the Cistercians, another reform group within the Benedictine order. The Cistercians turned away from Cluny's elaborate liturgical practices and emphasis on the arts to a simpler monastic life. The order was founded in the late eleventh century at Cîteaux (*Cistercium* in Latin, hence the order's name), also in Burgundy. Led by the commanding figure of Abbot Bernard of Clairvaux (abbacy, 1115–1154), the Cistercians thrived on strict mental and physical discipline. These virtues enabled them to settle and reclaim vast tracts of wilderness. In time, their enterprises stretched from present-day Russia to Ireland, and by the end of the

Middle Ages there were approximately 1,500 Cistercian abbeys, half of which were for women. Although their very success eventually undermined their austerity, they were able for a long time to sustain a way of life devoted to prayer and intellectual pursuits combined with shared manual labor. Like the Cluniacs, however, they depended on the assistance of laypersons.

Early Cistercian architecture reflects the ideals of the order. The Abbey Church of Notre-Dame at Fontenay, begun in 1139, is the oldest surviving Cistercian structure in Burgundy. The abbey has a simple geometric plan (fig. 15-6). The church has a long nave with rectangular chapels in the square-ended transept arms, and a shallow choir with a straight end wall. Lay brothers entered through the west doorway, monks from the attached cloister or upstairs dormitory. Situated far from the distractions of the secular world, the building made few concessions to the popular taste for architectural adornment, either outside or in. In other ways, however, Fontenay and other Cistercian monasteries fully reflect the architectural developments of their time in their masonry, vaulting, and proportions.

The Cistercians relied on harmonious proportions and fine stonework, not elaborate surface decoration, to achieve beauty in their architecture (fig. 15-7). A feature of Fontenay often found in Cistercian architecture is the

15-6. Plan of the Abbey of Notre-Dame, Fontenay, Burgundy, France. 1139–47

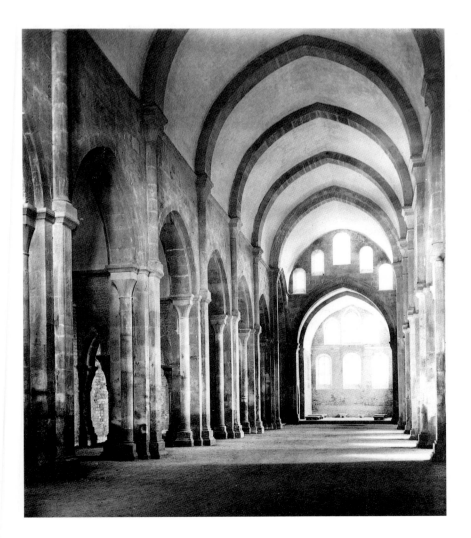

15-7. Nave, Abbey Church of Notre-Dame, Fontenay. 1139–47

The pointed arch began to be used in northwestern Europe in the Romanesque period. Its origin may have been in Islamic building in southern Europe. Pointed arches are structurally more stable than round ones, directing more weight down into the floor instead of outward to the walls, and they can span greater distances at greater heights without collapsing. Visually, pointed arches draw the eye inward and upward, an effect that directs thoughts toward heaven.

15-8. *Doubting Thomas*, pier in the cloister of the Abbey of Santo Domingo de Silos, Castile, Spain. c. 1100

use of pointed ribbed vaults over the nave and pointed arches in the nave arcade and side-aisle bays. Furnishings included little else than altars and candles. The large windows in the end wall, rather than a clerestory, provided light. The triple windows reminded the monks of the Trinity.

This simple architecture spread from the Cistercian homeland in Burgundy to become an international style. From Scotland and Germany to Spain and Italy, Cistercian designs and building techniques varied only slightly. The masonry vaults and harmonious proportions were to be influential in the development of the Gothic style later in the Middle Ages.

Architectural Sculpture

Like Cluny and unlike the severe churches of the Cistercians, many Romanesque churches have a remarkable variety of painting and sculpture. Christ Enthroned in Majesty in heaven may be illustrated, as well as stories of

Jesus among the people, or images of the lives and the miracles of the saints. The Virgin Mary gains importance in the paintings, and the prophets, kings, and queens of the Old Testament prefigure (symbolically foretell) events in the New Testament. Contemporary bishops, abbots, other noble patrons, and even ordinary folk are represented. A profusion of monsters, animals, plants, geometric ornament, allegorical figures such as Lust and Greed, and depictions of real and imagined buildings surround the major works of sculpture. The Elect rejoice in heaven with the angels; the Damned suffer in hell, tormented by demons. Biblical and historical tales come alive, along with scenes of everyday life. All these events seem to take place in a contemporary medieval setting.

Superb reliefs embellish the corner piers in the cloister of the Abbey of Santo Domingo de Silos in the kingdom of Castile. One of these illustrates the story, recounted in the Gospel of John (Chapter 20), in which Christ, appearing to his apostles after the Crucifixion, permits Thomas to touch his wounds to convince the

ELEMENTS OF ARCHITECTURE

The Romanesque Church Portal

The doorways of major Romanesque churches are often grand sculpted **portals**. Wood or metal doors are surrounded by elaborate stone sculpture arranged in zones to fit the architectural elements. The most important imagery is in the semicircular **tympanum** directly over the door lintel.

Archivolts—curved moldings formed by the **voussoirs** of which the arch is constructed—frame the tympanum. **Spandrels** are the flat areas at the outside upper corners of the tympanum area. On both sides of the doors are **jambs** carved in the form of jamb columns, typically decorated with figures, called jamb figures. **Pedestals** sometimes form the bases of jamb columns. The receding jambs form a shallow porch leading into the church.

spandrel
archivolts
voussoir
tympanum
jamb figure
jamb column
colonnette
jamb pedestal

Romanesque church portal

doubting apostle of his Resurrection (fig. 15-8). The organization of the composition is expert. Christ is shown larger than his disciples and placed off-center in the left foreground. His outstretched right arm forms a strong diagonal that bisects the space between his haloed head and that of Thomas in the lower left. Thomas's outstretched arm, reaching toward Christ's side, forms an opposing diagonal parallel to the slope between their heads, leading the eye back to Christ's face. The massed presence of the other apostles, bearing witness to the miracle, gives visual weight to the scene through the rhythmic repetition of form. The effect parallels the way the repetition of the nave bays in a Romanesque church culminates in the apse, its symbolic core.

Miniature buildings and musicians crown the arch that forms a canopy over the apostles' heads in the Silos pier relief. The sculptors used these lively images from medieval life to frame the biblical story, just as medieval preachers used elements of daily life in their sermons to provide a context for biblical messages. The art and lit-

erature of the period frequently combined "official" and "popular" themes in this way.

Carved portals are among the most significant innovations of Romanesque art. These complex works, which combine biblical narrative, legends, folklore, history, and Christian symbolism, represent the first attempt at large-scale architectural sculpture since the end of the Roman Empire. By the early twelfth century, sculpture depicting Christ in Majesty (the Second Coming), the Last Judgment, and the final triumph of good over evil at the Apocalypse could be seen on the portals of churches in northern Spain, southern France, and Burgundy. The churches of Conques and Cluny had carved portals; so did the Churches of Saint-Pierre in Moissac in southern France, the Cathedral of Saint-Lazare at Autun, the Churches of Sainte-Madeleine at Vézelay in Burgundy, and Sainte-Foy at Conques. (We will look at Moissac and Autun as typical examples.)

The Cluniac priory of Saint-Pierre at Moissac was a major pilgrimage stop on the route to Santiago de

15-9. South portal and porch, Priory Church of Saint-Pierre, Moissac, Toulouse, France. c. 1115–30

15-10. *Christ in Majesty*, tympanum of the south portal, Priory Church of Saint-Pierre. Width approx. 18' 6" (5.68 m)

Compostela. The original shrine at the site was reputed to have existed in the Carolingian period. After joining the congregation of Cluny in 1047, the monastery prospered from the donations of pilgrims and the local nobility, as well as from its control of shipping on the nearby Garonne River.

Moissac's monks launched an ambitious building campaign, and much of the sculpture from the cloister (c. 1100) and the church (1115–1130) has survived. The church was completed during the tenure of Abbot Roger (1115–1131), who commissioned the sculpture on the south portal and porch (fig. 15-9). This sculpture represented a genuine departure from earlier works in both the quantity and quality of the carving. The sculpture covers the **tympanum** (the **lunette** over the doorway), the **archivolts** (the curved rows of **voussoirs** outlining the tympanum), and the lintel, doorposts, and porch walls (see "Elements of Architecture," page 517). The stones still bear traces of the original paint.

The sculpture of Christ in Majesty dominates the huge tympanum (fig. 15-10). The scene combines images from the description of the Second Coming of Christ in Chapters 4 and 5 of the Apocalypse with others derived from Old Testament prophecies, all filtered through the early twelfth century's view of Scripture. A gigantic Christ, like an awe-inspiring Byzantine Pantokrator (see fig. 7-47), stares down at the viewer as he blesses and points to the book "sealed with seven seals" (Revelation 5:1). He is enclosed by a **mandorla**, and a cruciform halo rings his head. Four winged creatures symbolizing the evangelists—Matthew the Man (upper left), Mark the Lion (lower left), Luke the Ox (lower right), and John the Eagle (upper right)—frame Christ on either side, each holding a scroll or book representing his Gospel. Two elongated seraphim (angels who view God) stand one on either side of the central group, each holding a scroll. A band beneath Christ's feet and another passing behind his throne represent the waves of the "sea of glass like crystal" (Revelation 4:6). These define three registers in which sit twenty-four elders with "gold crowns on their heads" in varied poses, each holding either a harp or a gold bowl of incense (Revelation 4:4 and 5:8). According to the medieval view, the elders were the kings and prophets of the Old Testament and, by extension, the ancestors and precursors of Christ.

The figures in the tympanum relief reflect a hierarchy of scale and location. Christ, the largest figure, sits at the top center, the spiritual heart of the scene, surrounded by smaller figures of the evangelists and angels. The elders, farthest from Christ, are roughly one-third his size. Despite this formality and the limitations forced on them by the tympanum's shape, the sculptors created a sense of action by turning and twisting the gesturing figures, shifting their poses off-center, and avoiding rigid symmetry or mirror images. Nonfigural motifs above and below Christ, too, skirt the central vertical axis, contributing to the dynamic play across the tympanum's surface. The sculptors carved the tympanum from twenty-eight stone blocks of different sizes. The elders were carved one or two per block, whereas the figures of the central group

15-11. *Lions and Prophet Jeremiah (?)*, trumeau of the south portal, Priory Church of Saint-Pierre

In a letter to fellow cleric William of Saint Thierry, Bernard of Clairvaux, leader of the Cistercian order, objected to what he felt was excessive architectural decoration of Cluniac churches and cloisters. "So many and so marvellous are the varieties of diverse shapes on every hand," he wrote, "that we are more tempted to read in the marble than in our books, and to spend the whole day in wondering at these things rather than in meditating the law of God. For God's sake, if men are not ashamed of these follies, why at least do they not shrink from the expense?" (cited in Davis-Weyer, page 170).

covered one or more blocks as needed. Paint would originally have disguised the join lines. The crowns and incense bowls—described as made of gold in Revelation—may have been gilded. Foliate and geometric ornament covers every surface. Monstrous heads in the lower corners of the tympanum spew ribbon scrolls that run up its periphery. Similar creatures, akin to the beasts seen in the Scandinavian **animal style** of the Early Middle Ages (see fig. 14-5), appear at each end of the lintel, their tongues growing into ropes encircling a line of eight acanthus **rosettes**. A similar combination of animals, interlace, and rosettes can be found in Islamic art. Heraldic beasts and rosettes appeared together on Byzantine and Islamic textiles. Processions of naturalistically

15-12. Gislebertus. *Last Judgment*, tympanum of the west portal, Cathedral of Saint-Lazare, Autun, Burgundy, France. c. 1120–35

15-13. Gislebertus. *Weighing of Souls*, detail of *Last Judgment*

depicted rats and rabbits climb the piers on either side of the doors (fig. 15-11). Halos, crowns, and Christ's throne in the tympanum are adorned with stylized foliage.

Two side **jambs** and a central pier—known as a **trumeau**—support the weight of the lintel and tympanum. Moissac's jambs and trumeau have scalloped profiles (see fig. 15-9). Saint Peter (holding his attribute, the key to the gates of heaven) is carved in high relief on the left jamb, the Old Testament prophet Isaiah on the right jamb. Saint Paul is carved on the left side of the trumeau, and another Old Testament prophet, usually identified as Jeremiah, is on the right. On the front face of the trumeau are pairs of lions crossing each other in **X** patterns. The tall, thin prophet in figure 15-11 twists toward the viewer with his legs crossed. The sculptors placed him skillfully within the constraints of the scalloped trumeau, his head, pelvis, knees and feet falling on the pointed cusps of the curved forms. On the front of the trumeau the lions' bodies also fit the cusps of the scalloped frame. Between each pair of lions are more rosettes. Such decorative scalloping resembles Islamic art. The sculpture at Moissac was created shortly after the First Crusade and Europe's resulting encounter with the Islamic art and architecture of the Holy Land. The lord of the Moissac region was a leader of the Crusade, and his followers presumably brought Eastern art objects and ideas home with them.

A very different pictorial style is seen in Burgundy. On the west portal of the Cathedral of Saint-Lazare at Autun

15-14. *The Magi Asleep*, capital from the nave, Cathedral of Saint-Lazare. c. 1120–32. Musée Lapidaire, Autun

(fig. 15-12), Christ has returned to judge the cowering, naked human souls at his feet. The Damned writhe in torment at his right, while the saved enjoy serene bliss at the left (the right hand of Christ). Christ dominates the composition as he did at Moissac. The surrounding figures are thinner and taller than those at Moissac and are arranged in less regular compartmentalized tiers. The overall effect is less consciously balanced than the pattern-filled composition at Moissac. The stylized figures, stretched out and bent at sharp angles, are powerfully expressive, successfully conveying the terrifying urgency of the moment as they swarm around the magisterially detached Christ figure. Delicate weblike engraving on the robes may have derived from metalwork or manuscript illumination.

Angels trumpet the call to the Day of Judgment at the far left and right of the middle register. Angels also help the departed souls to rise from their tombs and line up to await judgment. In the bottom register two men at the left carry walking staffs and satchels bearing the cross and a scallop-shell badge, attributes identifying them as pilgrims to Jerusalem and Santiago de Compostela. A pair of giant, pincerlike hands descends at the far right to scoop up a soul (fig. 15-13). Above and to the left of these hands, in a scene reminiscent of Egyptian Books of the Dead (see fig. 3-44), the archangel Michael oversees the weighing of souls on the scale of good and evil. In the early decades of the twelfth century, Church doctrine came increasingly to stress the role of the Virgin Mary and the saints as intercessors who could plead for mercy on behalf of repentant sinners. The tympanum at Autun shows angels also acting as intercessors. The archangel Michael shelters some souls in the folds of his robe and may be jiggling the scales a bit. Another angel boosts a saved soul into heaven, bypassing the gate and Saint Peter. By far the most riveting players in the drama are the grotesquely decomposed, screaming demons grabbing at terrified souls and trying to cheat by pushing down souls and yanking the scales to favor evil.

A lengthy inscription in the band beneath Christ's feet identifies the Autun tympanum as the work of Gisle-bertus. This same sculptor may also have been responsible for a representation of the Magi asleep (fig. 15-14), one of the many capitals that illustrate the Bible and the lives of the saints in the nave at Autun. The ingenious compression of instructive narrative scenes into the geometric confines of column capitals was an important Romanesque contribution to architectural decoration. The underlying form was usually that of the flaring **Corinthian** capital. Sculptors used **undercutting**, a technique known since ancient times, to sharpen contours and convey depth.

The Magi Asleep is one of a series of capitals depicting events surrounding the birth of Jesus. Medieval tradition identified the three Magi, or wise men—whom the Gospels say brought gold, frankincense, and myrrh to the newborn Jesus—as the kings Caspar, Melchior, and Balthasar. Caspar, the oldest, is shown bearded here; Melchior has a moustache; and Balthasar, the youngest, is clean shaven. Later, he is often shown as a black African. The Magi, following heavenly signs, traveled from afar to acknowledge Jesus as King of the Jews. The position of the capital in the nave of the church suggests that it was meant to remind worshipers that they were embarking on a metaphorically parallel journey to find Christ. The slumbering Magi, wearing their identifying crowns, share a bed and blanket. An angel has arrived to hurry them on their way, awakening Balthasar and pointing to the Star of Bethlehem that will guide them. The sculptor's use of two vantage points simultaneously—the Magi and the head of their bed viewed from above, the angel and the foot of the bed seen from the side—communicates the key elements of the story with wonderful economy and clarity.

Independent Sculpture

Reliquaries, altar frontals, crucifixes, devotional images, and other sculpture once filled medieval churches. One form of devotional image that became increasingly popular during the later Romanesque period was that of the

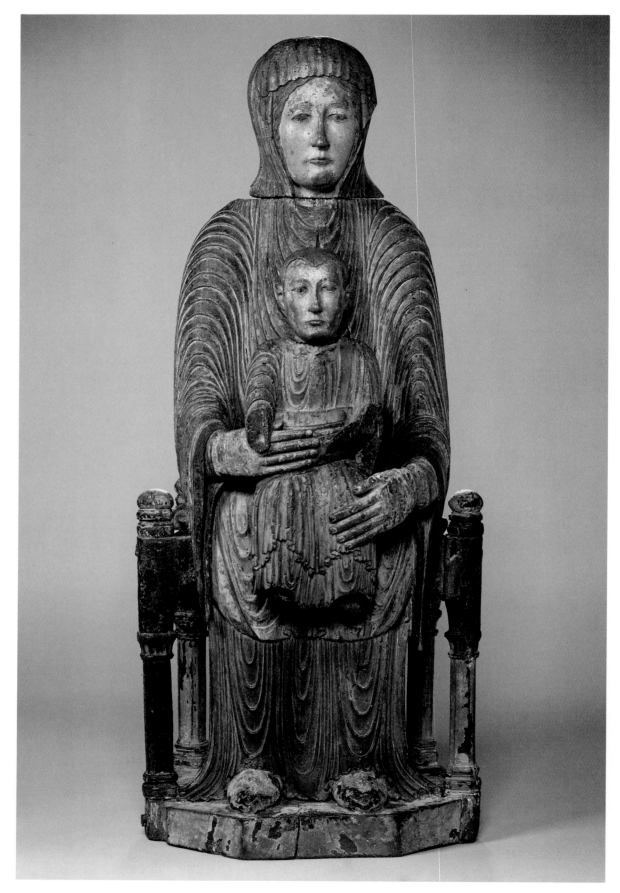

15-15. *Virgin and Child*, from the Auvergne region, France. c. 1150–1200. Oak with polychromy, height 31" (78.7 cm). The Metropolitan Museum of Art, New York

Gift of J. Pierpont Morgan, 1916 (16.32.194)

Virgin Mary holding the Christ Child on her lap, a type known as the Throne of Wisdom. A well-preserved example in painted wood dates from the second half of the twelfth century (fig. 15-15). Such images were a specialty of the Auvergne region of France, but are found throughout Europe. Mother and Child are frontally erect, as rigid as they are regal. Mary is seated on a thronelike bench symbolizing the lion throne of the Old Testament king and symbol of wisdom, Solomon. She supports Jesus with both hands. The small but adult Jesus holds a book—the Word of God—in his left hand and raises his (now missing) right hand in blessing. To the medieval believer, Christ represented the priesthood; Mary, the Church; Christ, humankind and God; Mary, his throne. Mary as earthly mother and God-bearer (Theotokos) gives Jesus his human nature and forms a throne on which he sits in majesty. In Christ, the Wisdom of God has become human; in the medieval scholar's language, he is the Logo Incarnate. As a fourteenth-century churchman wrote, "The throne of the true Solomon is the Most Blessed Virgin Mary, in which sat Jesus Christ, the true Wisdom." (trans: Forsyth, p. 27.)

Earlier in the Middle Ages, small, individual works of art were generally made of costly materials for royal or aristocratic patrons. In the twelfth century, however, when abbeys and local parish churches of more limited means began commissioning hundreds of statues, painted wood became an increasingly common medium. These lightweight devotional images were frequently carried in processions from place to place both inside and outside the churches. A statue of the Virgin and Child, like the one shown here, could also have played an important role in the liturgical drama performed at the Feast of the Epiphany, which in the Western Church celebrates the arrival of the Magi to pay homage to the baby Jesus. Participants representing the Magi would act out their journey by searching through the church until they came to the statue. (Some scholars see this as perhaps the earliest western European drama.)

The Crucifixion continued to be a primary devotional theme in the Romanesque period. The image of Jesus in the mid-twelfth-century *Batlló Crucifix* from Catalonia (fig. 15-16) derives from Byzantine sources and is quite different from the nearly nude, tortured Jesus of the Ottonian-period *Gero Crucifix* (see fig. 14-30). Jesus' bowed head, downturned mouth, and heavy-lidded eyes convey a sense of deep sadness or contemplation; however, he still wears royal robes that emphasize his kingship (see *Rabbula Gospels*, pages 320, 321). He wears a long, medallion-patterned tunic with **pseudo-kufic** inscriptions—designs meant to resemble Arabic script—on the hem. The garment reflects how valuable silk brocades from Islamic Spain were in Europe at this time. They were widely used as **cloths of honor** to designate royal and sacred places, appearing, for example, behind rulers' thrones, or as altar coverings and backdrops. Many wooden crucifixes have survived from the Romanesque period. They were displayed over church altars and, like other devotional statues, were carried in processions.

15-16. *Batlló Crucifix*, from the Olot region, Catalonia, Spain. Mid-12th century. Wood with polychromy, height approx. 36" (91 cm). Museu Nacional d'Art de Catalunya, Barcelona

This crucifix was modeled on a famous medieval sculpture called the *Volto Santo* (Holy Face) that had supposedly been brought from Palestine to Italy in the eighth century. Legend had it that this image had been made by Nicodemus, who helped Joseph of Arimathea bury Jesus. Many replicas of the *Volto Santo* still exist.

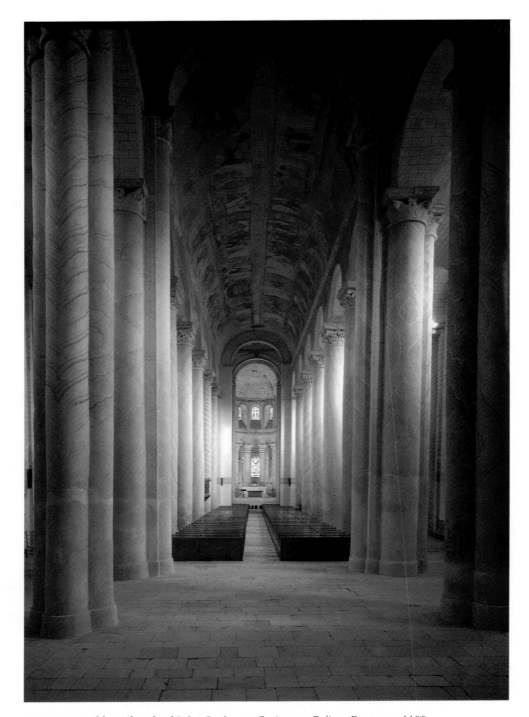

15-17. Nave, Abbey Church of Saint-Savin-sur-Gartempe, Poitou, France. c. 1100

The columns of Saint-Savin, painted to resemble veined marble, support an arcade and barrel vault without intermediate galleries or clerestory windows.

Wall Painting

Throughout Europe paintings on church walls glowed in flickering candlelight amid clouds of incense. Wall painting was subject to the same influences as the other visual arts: The painters were inspired by models available to them locally. Some must have seen examples of Byzantine art. Others had Carolingian or even Early Christian models. During the Romanesque period, painted decoration largely replaced mosaics on the walls of churches. This change occurred, at least partly, because growing demand, due to more churches, led to the use of less expensive materials and techniques.

One of the most extensive programs of Romanesque wall painting is at the Benedictine abbey church of Saint-Savin-sur-Gartempe in the Poitou region of western France. The tunnel-like barrel vault running the length of the nave and choir provides a surface ideally suited to

15-18. *Tower of Babel*, detail of painted nave vaulting, Abbey Church of Saint-Savin-sur-Gartempe

painted decoration (fig. 15-17). The narthex, **crypt**, and chapels were also painted. Old Testament scenes can be seen in the nave; New Testament scenes and scenes from the lives of two local saints, Savin and Cyprian, appear in the transept, ambulatory, and chapels. The paintings were all done about 1100. The painters may have used manuscripts as their primary inspiration. They did not use the wet-plaster **fresco** technique favored in Italy for its long-lasting colors, but they did moisten the walls before painting, which allowed some absorption of pigments into the plaster, making them more permanent than paint applied to a dry surface. Consequently, the colors of the vault have a soft, powdery effect in contrast to the richer, more brilliant colors of Byzantine-inspired painting. Several artists or teams of artists worked in different parts of Saint-Savin. While the vault suggests the energy of Carolingian artists, like those working for Archbishop Ebbo, and the narrative drama of the Ottonian Hildesheim doors, the lives of the saints were painted by artists working under Byzantine inspiration.

The painters of the nave vault seem to have immediately followed the masons and used the same scaffolding. Perhaps this intimate involvement with the building process accounts for the vividness with which they portrayed the biblical story of the Tower of Babel (fig. 15-18). According to the account in Genesis (11:1–9), God punished the prideful people who tried to build a tower to heaven by scattering them and making their languages mutually unintelligible. The tower in the painting is a medieval-looking structure, reflecting the practice of depicting legendary events in contemporary settings. Workers haul heavy stone blocks to the tower, lifting them to masons on the top with a hoist. The giant Nimrod, on the far right, simply hands the blocks up. God confronts the people on the far left. He is shown in a twisting pose like that of the prophet on the trumeau at Moissac (see fig. 15-11). The scene's dramatic action,

large figures, strong outlines, broad areas of color, and simplified modeling all help make it intelligible to a viewer looking up at it in dim light from far below.

Many Romanesque wall paintings survived in churches in the isolated mountain valleys of the Catalonian Pyrenees in northern Spain. The paintings have been detached from the walls and placed in museums for security. Among these are the paintings from the Church of San Clemente in Tahull. A magnificently expressive Christ in Majesty fills the curve of the semidome of the apse (fig. 15-19). Christ's powerful presence recalls the contemporary sculpture at Moissac and Autun (see figs. 15-9, 15-12, 15-13) and the tympanum sculptors may have been inspired by monumental paintings. The San Clemente Christ illustrates a Romanesque transformation of the Byzantine depiction of Christ Pantokrator, ruler and judge of the world. The iconography is traditional. Christ sits within a mandoria; the symbols alpha and omega are on each side of his head. He holds the open Gospel inscribed *"ego sum lux mundi"* (I am the light of the world. John 8:12). Four angels, each grasping an evangelist symbol, float at his sides. At Christ's feet are six apostles, of whom Bartholomew and John are visible here, and the Virgin Mary holding a bowl. Flanking them are columns with stylized capitals and wavy lines indicating marble shafts. The mosaiclike intensity of the colors was created by building up many thin coats of paint, a technique called **glazing**.

The San Clemente Master as the otherwise anonymous Tahul painter is known, was one of the finest Spanish painters of the Romasque period. The elongated oval faces, large staring eyes, and long noses, as well as the placement of figures against flat colored bands and the use of heavy outlining, reflect Mozarabic influence (Chapter 14). The Western artists, however, have adapted the Byzantine style to their own taste for geometric simplicity of form. Faces and figures are strictly

15-19. *Christ in Majesty*, detail of apse painting from the Church of San Clemente, Tahull, Lérida, Spain. c. 1123. Museu Nacional d'Art de Catalunya, Barcelona

15-20. Stephanus Garsia. Page with *Flood*, *Commentary on the Apocalypse*, by Beatus of Liébana, made for the Abbey of Saint-Sever, Gascony, France. 1028–72. Ink and tempera on vellum, 14½ x 11" (36.5 x 28 cm). Bibliothèque Nationale, Paris, MS lat. 8678, fol. 85r

frontal and symmetrical. Modeling from light to dark is accomplished through repeated colored lines of varying width in three shades—dark, medium, and light. Details of faces, hair, hands, and muscles are turned into elegant patterns.

Books

As today, illustrated books played a key role in the transmission of artistic styles and other cultural information from one region to another. Like other arts, the output of books increased dramatically in the eleventh and twelfth centuries, despite the labor and materials required to make them. Monastic **scriptoria** continued to be the centers of production, where monks copied books in the monastic libraries (see "The Medieval Scriptorium," page

486). These monastic scriptoria, sometimes also employed lay artisans who might be itinerant, moving from place to place. Most books had religious subject matter, including scholarly commentaries, lives of saints, collections of letters, and even histories. Liturgical works were often large and lavish; other works were more modest, their embellishment confined to the initial letter of each section of text.

During the Romanesque period, scribes in northern Spain and France continued to copy and illustrate the *Commentary on the Apocalypse* written by Beatus of Liébana in the eighth century. They evoke the dramatic terror of the Apocalypse in a stark, two-dimensional, intensely colored, and emotional style that was introduced by Mozarabic monks in the tenth century (see fig. 14-13). The page shown here (fig. 15-20) is from a copy

quod dſ ſuſcepto̅ e̅ e̅· Dſ e̅i erat
uerbu̅ unigenituſ; gignere co
a̅tuſ; Sed ut mediato̅ daretur
nob· p̅ineffabile̅ g̅ra̅m uerbum
caro factu̅m e̅· & habitau̅ innobiſ·
b LECTIO OCTAVA·
    Hec loquutuſ ſu̅ uob· ut
      gaudiu̅ meu̅ inuob ſit·
  & gaudium u̅r̅m impleatur;
Hoc e̅ p̅ceptu̅ meu̅ ut diligatiſ in
uice· ſicut dilexi uoſ· Audiſtiſ ca
riſſimi d̅n̅m dicente̅ diſcipuliſ ſu
iſ; Hec loquutuſ ſu̅ uob· ut gau
diu̅ meu̅ inuob ſit· & gaudiu̅ u̅r̅m
impleatur; Quod e̅ gaudiu̅ x̅p̅i
innob· niſi quod dignat̅ gaudere
de nob· & qd e̅ gaudiu̅ n̅r̅m qd
dicit implendu̅· niſi c̅u̅ habere con
ſortiu̅· Hoc e̅ p̅t qd beato petro dixe
rat· ſi n̅ lauero te nonhabebiſ par
te̅ meu̅; Gaudiu̅ g̅ eiuſ innobiſ·
g̅ra e̅ qua̅ p̅ſtitit nob· ipſa e̅ itaq;
gaudiu̅ n̅r̅m; Sed de hac ille eti
am ex eternitate gaudebat·
quando noſ elegit ante mundi
conſtitutione̅; Nec recte poſſu
muſ dicere· quod gaudium eiuſ
plenu̅ non erat; Non enim dſ in
p̅fecte aliquando gaudebat·
ſed illud eiuſ gaudiu̅ innob non
erat· quia, nec noſ in quib; e̅ poſ
ſit iam eramuſ· nec quando e̅ ce
pimuſ cu̅ illo e̅ cepimuſ; In ipſo
aut ſemp erat· qui noſ ſuoſ futu
roſ certiſſima ſui p̅ſcientia̅ ueri
tate gaudebat; EVG· Hoc eſt
p̅ceptu̅ meu̅· REd· IN N̅T̅ APtoſ·

eu̅ euangliu̅ legeretur· d̅n̅m di
cente· Si diligitiſ me· mandata mea
ſeruate; Et ego rogabo patrem
meu̅· & aliu̅ paraclitu̅ dabit
uob· ut maneat uobcu̅ in eternu̅·

VDI
VI
MVS
FRATRES

15-21. Page with *Pentecost*, *Cluny Lectionary*. Early 12th century. Ink and tempera on vellum, 9 x 5" (23 x 12.5 cm). Bibliothèque Nationale, Paris, MS lat. 2246, fol. 79v

of the *Commentary* illuminated by a monk named Stephanus Garsia in the middle of the eleventh century for the Abbey of Saint-Sever in Gascony (southern France). It illustrates the ravages of the final flood. Corpses are scattered helter-skelter, broken and awry. A black bird pecks at an eyeball of the man lying on the upper right, compounding the horror. Intense colors— yellow, purple, red, and green—resonate with anguished force across the boldly banded field. The preoccupation with the Apocalypse may reflect the ongoing struggle between Christians and Muslims for control of Spain. In any case, Beatus manuscripts remained a regional phenomenon, although they were influential far beyond the Pyrenees.

An illuminated **lectionary** (fig. 15-21) made for the wealthy monastery of Cluny in the early 1100s seems calm and dignified compared to the Saint-Sever Apocalypse. Lectionaries contained biblical excerpts arranged according to the Church calendar for reading during Mass. This page contains the beginning of the eighth reading (*lectio octava*). The framed scene illustrates the beginning of the second chapter of the Acts of the Apostles, which recounts how "tongues as of fire" from the Holy Spirit descended on each of the apostles while they were assembled for Pentecost, and they began to speak "in tongues." Christ appears at the top of the picture, and glowing red rays—tongues of fire—stream from the gold banner draped over him to the heads of the Twelve Apostles below. Just under the picture is a beautifully interlaced *A*, the first letter of the word *audivimus* ("we have been hearing"). The subject—an unusual one for medieval art—may have been chosen as a symbolic reminder of Cluny's direct tie to the papacy. The picture may suggest that just as the apostles received miraculous powers from Christ, so Cluny derived its power directly from the pope, the heir to the apostle Peter. The image of Christ, like the Tahull *Christ in Majesty* (see fig. 15-19), is a reinterpretation of the Byzantine Pantokrator type. The faces of the figures have been delicately rendered with green and red highlighting. The drapery seems to fall over fleshy limbs. The illuminator deliberately de-emphasized the drama of the supernatural event described in the text, conveying instead the psychological bond among the figures.

Despite their ascetic teachings and austere architecture, the Cistercians produced many elaborately illustrated books. A symbolic image known as the Tree of Jesse appears on a page from a copy of *Saint Jerome's Commentary on Isaiah* made in the scriptorium of the Cistercian mother house at Cîteaux about 1125 (fig. 15-22). Jesse was the father of King David, who was an ancestor of Mary and, through her, of Jesus. The Cistercians were particularly devoted to the Virgin and are credited with popularizing the Tree of Jesse as a device for showing her position as the last link in the genealogy connecting Jesus Christ to the house of David. In the manuscript illustration, *The Tree of Jesse* depicts Jesse asleep, a small tree trunk growing from his body. A monumental Mary, standing on the forking branches of the tree, dwarfs the sleeping patriarch. The Christ Child sits on her right arm, which is swathed in her veil. Following late Byzantine and Romanesque convention, he is portrayed as a miniature adult with his right hand raised in blessing. His cheek presses against Mary's, a display of affection similar to that shown in Byzantine icons like the *Virgin of Vladimir* (see fig. 7-60). Mary holds a flowering sprig from the tree, a symbol for Christ. The building held by the angel on the left refers to Mary as the Christian Church, and the crown held by the angel on the right refers to her as Queen of Heaven. The dove above her halo represents the Holy Spirit. The linear depiction of drapery in **V**-shaped folds and the jeweled hems of Mary's robes reflect Byzantine influence and her elevated status. The subdued colors are in keeping with Cistercian restraint.

15-22. Page with *The Tree of Jesse, Explanatio in Isaiam* (*Saint Jerome's Commentary on Isaiah*), from the Abbey, Cîteaux, Burgundy, France. c. 1125. Ink and tempera on vellum, 15 x 4¾" (38 x 12 cm). Bibliothèque Municipale, Dijon, France, MS 129, fol. 4v

The Tree of Jesse, a pictorial representation of the genealogy of Jesus, was used to illustrate the Church's doctrine that Christ was both human and divine. The growing importance of devotion to Mary as the mother of God led to an emphasis on her place in this illustrious royal line.

15-24. Plan of Durham Castle

In Norman times, the bishops of Durham lived in a three-story residence. An exterior staircase led from the courtyard (inner bailey) to a single undivided, multipurpose room on the middle floor occupied by the bishop and his principal servants (Constable's Hall and the Tunstall's Gallery in the plan). Other people occupied humbler wood structures within the castle complex or outside its walls in the village that served it. The structures at the left date from Gothic times.

15-23. Castle-monastery-cathedral complex, Durham, Northumberland, England. c. 1075–1100s, plus later alterations and additions

Since 1837, the castle has housed the University of Durham (now joined with the University of Newcastle). The castle was added to and rebuilt over the centuries. The Norman portion extends to the left of the keep. The castle and cathedral share a parklike green. South of the cathedral (lower in the photograph), the cloister with chapterhouse, dormitory (now a library), and kitchens are clearly visible. Houses of the old city cluster around the buildings as they would have in earlier days. Trees, however, would not have been allowed to grow near the approaches to this fortified outpost against the Scots.

BRITAIN AND NORMANDY

In the early tenth century a band of Norse raiders seized a peninsula in northwest France that came to be known as Normandy. In 911 their leader, Rollo, gained recognition as duke of the region from the weak Carolingian king. Within little more than a century, Rollo's successors had transformed Normandy into one of Europe's most powerful feudal domains. The Norman dukes were astute and skillful administrators. They formed a close alliance with the Church, supporting it with grants of land and gaining in return the allegiance of abbots and bishops, many of whom also served as vassals of the duke. In 1066 Duke William II of Normandy (1035–1087) invaded England and, as William I ("the Conqueror"), became that country's new king. Norman nobles replaced the Anglo-Saxon nobility, and England became politically and culturally allied to northern France.

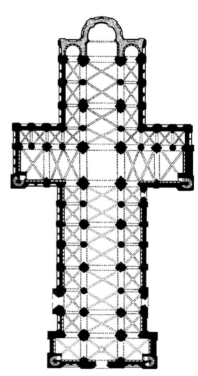

15-25. Plan of Durham Cathedral. 1093–1133

Architecture

Strategically located on England's northern frontier with Scotland, Durham grew after the Norman Conquest into a great fortified complex with a castle, a monastery, and a cathedral (fig. 15-23). (Durham had the relics of Saint Cuthbert, the revered seventh-century bishop of Lindisfarne.) The Norman bishops of Durham also held secular titles, powers, and responsibilities as vassals of the king.

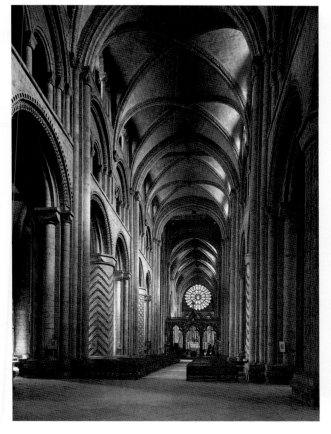

15-26. Nave of Durham Cathedral. 1087–1133. Original apses replaced by a Gothic choir, 1242–c. 1280. View from the west

15-27. Church of Saint-Étienne, Caen, Normandy, France. Begun 1064; facade late 11th century; spires 13th century

Durham Castle is an excellent example of a Norman fortress (fig. 15-24). The only way in and out was over a drawbridge, which was controlled from a gatehouse. Beyond the gatehouse was the **bailey**, or courtyard. In times of danger, the castle's defenders took refuge in the **keep** (*donjon* in French), the massive tower to the east of the bailey. The keep stood atop a steep mound. Other buildings, including the great hall in which the bishops conducted their business, extended along the northern rampart overlooking a sheer cliff. The Norman chapel, located between the great hall and the keep, was built about 1075 and may have been the first stone structure in the compound. Medieval fortresses were often surrounded by a defensive water-filled ditch known as a **moat**. At Durham, the Wear River acted as a natural moat, looping around the high, rocky outcrop on which the complex was built.

Durham Cathedral (figs. 15-23 and 15-25) and its adjoining monastery were built to the south of the castle. The cathedral, begun in 1087 and vaulted beginning in 1093, is one of the most impressive medieval churches. Like most buildings that have been in continuous use, it has been altered several times. The visible parts of the towers, for example, are Gothic with eighteenth-century modifications. The cathedral's decor is as ambitious as its scale (fig. 15-26). Enormous compound piers alternating with robust columns support the nave arcade. The columns are carved with **chevrons**, spiral fluting, and dia-

mond patterns, and some have scalloped, cushion-shaped capitals. The arcades have round moldings and chevron ornaments. All this ornamentation was originally painted.

Above the cathedral's massive walls rise ribbed vaults. While most builders were still using timber roofs, the masons at Durham developed a new system of vaulting. The typical Romanesque ribbed groin vault (best seen in Milan, fig. 15-42) used round arches that produced separate domed-up spatial units. To create a more unified interior space, the Durham builders divided each bay with two pairs of crisscrossing ribs and so kept the crown of the vault at almost the same height as the keystone of the transverse arches. In the transept they also experimented with rectangular rather than square bays. Between 1093 and 1133, when the project was essentially complete, they developed a system of vaulting that was carried to the Norman homeland in France, was perfected in churches such as Saint-Étienne at Caen, then was adopted by French masons in the Gothic period (see "Elements of Architecture," page 552).

Saint-Étienne at Caen (fig. 15-27) was begun nearly a generation before Durham Cathedral, but work continued there through the century (the timber roof was not replaced by a stone vault until 1120). William the Conqueror had founded the monastery and had begun construction of its church by the time of his conquest of England. William's queen, Matilda, had already established an abbey for women in Caen. In spite of the

15-28. John of Worcester. Page with *Dream of Henry I*, *Worcester Chronicle*, Worcester, England, c.1140. Ink and tempera on vellum, each page 12¾ x 9⅜" (32.5 x 23.7 cm). Corpus Christi College, Oxford

One of the most significant achievements of Henry's father, William the Conqueror, was a comprehensive census of English property owners, the *Domesday Book*. Compiled into two huge volumes, this document was used to assess taxes and settle property disputes. After Henry, too, increased taxes and encountered protests, a series of visions and a life-threatening storm at sea made him promise a seven-year delay in implementing higher taxes.

devastation of Normandy in World War II, the two churches survived, their western towers still dominating the skyline. Soaring height was a Norman architectural goal, continuing the tradition of towers and verticality begun by Carolingian builders (see fig. 14-24). The west facade of Saint-Étienne was constructed at the end of the eleventh century, probably about 1096–1100. Wall buttresses divide the facade into three vertical sections, and small **stringcourses**, unbroken cornicelike moldings, at each window level suggest the three stories of the building's interior. Consequently, the design of the facade reflects the plan and elevation of the church itself, an idea that would be adopted by Gothic builders. Norman builders, with their brilliant technical innovations and sophisticated designs, in fact prepared the way for the architectural feats seen in Gothic cathedrals of the twelfth and thirteenth centuries.

Books

The great Anglo-Saxon tradition of book illumination, which declined for a time in the wake of the Norman Conquest, revived after about 1130. The *Worcester Chronicle* is the earliest known illustrated English history. This record of contemporary events by a monk named John was an addition to a work called *The Chronicle of England*, written by Florence, another monk. The pages shown here concern King Henry I (ruled 1100–1135), the second of William the Conqueror's sons to sit on the English throne (fig. 15-28). The text relates a series of dreams the king had on consecutive nights in 1130 in which his subjects demanded tax relief. The illustrations depict the dreams with energetic directness. On the first night, angry farmers confront the sleeping king; on the second, armed knights; and on the third, monks, abbots, and bishops. In the fourth illustration, the king is in a storm at sea and saves himself by promising God to lower taxes for a period of seven years. The *Worcester Chronicle* assured its readers that this story came from a reliable source, the royal physician Grimbald, who appears in the margins next to most scenes.

More characteristic of Romanesque illumination are illustrated psalters. The so-called *Hellmouth* page from a psalter written in Latin and Norman French is one of the masterpieces of English Romanesque art (fig. 15-29). The psalter was produced at a renowned Anglo-Saxon monastic scriptorium in Winchester. The vigorous narrative style for which the scriptorium was famous had its roots in the style of the ninth-century workshop at Reims that produced the *Utrecht Psalter* (see fig. 14-22). The page depicts the gaping jaws of hell, a traditional Anglo-Saxon

15-29. Page with *Hellmouth*, *Winchester Psalter*, Winchester, England. c. 1150. Ink and tempera on vellum, 12³/₄ x 9¹/₈" (32.5 x 23 cm). The British Library, London

There are fascinating parallels between Hellmouth images and the liturgical dramas—known in England as mystery plays—that were performed throughout Europe from the tenth through the sixteenth century. Depictions of the Hellmouth in Romanesque English art were based on the large and expensive stage props used for the hell scenes in mystery plays. Carpenters made the infernal beast's head out of wood, papier-mâché, fabric, and glitter and placed it over a trapdoor on stage. The wide jaws of the most ambitious Hellmouths, operated by winches and cables, opened and closed on the actors. Smoke, flames, foul smells, and loud noises came from within, to the delight of the audience. Hell scenes, with their often scatological humor, were by far the most popular parts of the plays. Performances are still given today.

subject, one that inspired poetry and drama as well as the vivid descriptions of the terrors and torments of hell with which the clergy enlivened their sermons.

The inscription at the top of the page reads: "Here is hell and the angels who are locking the doors." The ornamental frame that fills the page represents the door to hell. An angel on the left turns the key to the door in the keyhole of the big red doorplate. The frenzy of the Last Judgment, as depicted on the tympanum at Autun (see fig. 15-12), has subsided. Inside the door the last of the damned are crammed into the mouth of hell, the wide-open jaw of a grotesque double-headed monster. Sharp-beaked birds and fire-breathing dragons sprout from the monster's mane. Hairy, horned demons torment the lost souls, who tumble around in a dark void. Among them are kings and queens with golden crowns and monks with shaved heads, a daring reminder to the clergy of the vulnerability of their own souls.

The *Bayeux Tapestry*

1100

1050 CE   1200 CE

The best-known work of Norman art is undoubtedly the *Bayeux Tapestry* (fig. 15-30). This narrative wall hanging, 230 feet long and 20 inches high, documents events surrounding the Norman Conquest of England in 1066. Despite its name, the work is **embroidery**, not tapestry. It was embroidered in eight colors of wool on eight lengths of undyed linen that were then stitched together (see "Embroidery Techniques," below). It was made for William the Conqueror's half brother Odo, who was bishop of Bayeux in Normandy and earl of Kent in southern England. Odo commissioned it for his Bayeux Cathedral, and it may have been completed in 1077, in time for the cathedral's consecration. According to an inventory made in 1476, it was "hung round the nave of the church on the Feast of relics" (Rud, page 9). Scholars disagree as to where it was made. Some argue for the famous embroidery workshops of Canterbury, in Kent, and others for Bayeux itself. A Norman probably directed the telling of the story and either an illuminator from a scriptorium or a specialist from an embroidery workshop provided drawings. Recent research suggests that the embroiderers were women.

The *Bayeux Tapestry* is a major political document, celebrating William's victory, validating his claim to the English throne, and promoting Odo's interests as a powerful leader himself. Today it is also a treasury of information about Norman and Anglo-Saxon society and technology, with depictions of everything from farming

TECHNIQUE

EMBROIDERY TECHNIQUES

The embroiderers of the *Bayeux Tapestry* probably followed drawings provided by a Norman, perhaps even an eyewitness to some of the events. The style of the embroidery, however, is Anglo-Saxon, and the embroiderers were probably women. They worked in tightly twisted wool, dyed in eight colors with dyes made from plants and minerals. Only two stitches were used. The quick, overlapping, linear stem stitch produced a slightly jagged outline. The more time-consuming laid-and-couched work used to form blocks of color required three steps. The embroiderer first "laid" a series of long, parallel covering stitches, anchored them with a second layer of regularly spaced crosswise stitches, and finally tacked everything down with tiny "couching" stitches. Some of the tapestry's laid-and-couched work was done in contrasting colors for particular effects. Skin and other light-toned areas were represented by the bare linen ground.

Laid-and-couched work and stem-stitch techniques are clearly visible in this detail of figure 15-30. Stem stitching outlines all the solid areas, is used to draw the facial features, and forms the letters of the inscription.

stem stitching

crosswise stitches

laid threads

couching stitches

15-30. *Bishop Odo Blessing the Feast*, section 47–48 of the *Bayeux Tapestry*, Norman–Anglo-Saxon embroidery from Canterbury, Kent, England, or Bayeux, Normandy, France. c. 1066–82. Linen with wool, height 20" (50.8 cm). Centre Guillaume le Conquérant, Bayeux, France

The top and bottom registers of the *Bayeux Tapestry* contain a variety of subjects separated by diagonal bars. These include heraldic beasts, stylized plants, and figures spilling over from the action in the central register, as well as a knight killing a tethered bear, a pair of naked lovers, and a farmer plowing. Such peripheral imagery was an English specialty throughout the Middle Ages. The sheer number of images in the *Bayeux Tapestry* is staggering: there are some 50 surviving scenes containing 623 human figures, 202 horses, 55 dogs, 505 other creatures, 37 buildings, 41 ships and boats, 49 trees, and nearly 2,000 inch-high letters.

implements to table manners to warfare. The *Bayeux Tapestry* shows broadly gesturing actors on a narrow stage with the clarity and directness of English manuscript illustration. It is laid out in three registers. In the middle register, the central narrative, explained by Latin inscriptions, unfolds in a continuous scroll from left to right. Secondary subjects and decorative motifs adorn the top and bottom registers.

The section illustrated here shows Odo and William, feasting on the eve of battle. Attendants provide roasted birds on skewers, placing them on a makeshift table of the knights' shields laid over trestles. The diners, summoned by the blowing of a horn, gather at a curved table laden with food and drink. Bishop Odo—seated at the center, head and shoulders above William to his right—blesses the meal while others eat. The kneeling servant in the middle proffers a basin and towel so that the diners may wash their hands. The man on Odo's left points impatiently to the next event, a council of war between William (now the central and tallest figure), Odo, and a third man labeled "Rotbert," probably Robert of Mortain, another of William's half brothers. These men held power after the conquest.

GERMANY AND THE MEUSE VALLEY

In the early eleventh century a new dynasty, the Salians, replaced the Ottonians on the throne of the Holy Roman Empire. The third Salian emperor, Henry IV (ruled 1056–1106), became embroiled in the dramatic conflict with the papacy known as the Investiture Controversy. This dispute involved the right of lay rulers to "invest" high-ranking clergy with the symbols of their spiritual offices. In 1075 Pope Gregory VII (papacy, 1073–1085) declared that only the pope and his bishops could appoint bishops, abbots, and other important clergy. The clergy now depended on the pope, not the emperor. Many German nobles sided with the pope; some nobles, with the emperor. The conflict unleashed by the Investiture Controversy divided Germany into many small competing states. The efforts of Holy Roman emperors of the late twelfth and early thirteenth centuries to reimpose imperial authority failed, and Germany remained divided until the late nineteenth century.

Religious and political problems sapped energy and wasted financial resources. Nevertheless, building and the other arts continued. Carolingian and Ottonian cultural traditions persisted in the German lands during the eleventh and twelfth centuries. Ties with the northern Italian region of Lombardy also remained strong and provided another source of artistic influence.

Architecture

The imperial cathedral at Speyer in the Rhine region of southwest Germany was a colossal structure that rivaled Cluny in size and magnificence. The Romanesque cathedral building was constructed on the foundations of an Ottonian imperial church between 1082 and 1106, during the reign of Henry IV. The emperor was fresh from recent successes against the papacy and a German rival, King Rudolf of Swabia, and the monumental rebuilding project was a testament to his power.

A seventeenth-century drawing shows the Romanesque cathedral, which more-recent construction has

15-31. Imperial cathedral (Speyer II), Speyer, Germany. 1030–early 1100s. Ink drawing by Wenzel Hollar, c. 1620. Graphische Sammlung Albertina, Vienna

15-32. Nave, Speyer Cathedral. 1082–1100s; 19th-century alterations. Colored engraving by Carl Mayer, after a painting by J. M. Bayrer, 1855

15-33. Tomb cover with effigy of Rudolf of Swabia; from Saxony, Germany. After 1080. Bronze with niello, approx. 6'5½" x 2'2½" (1.97 x .68 m). Cathedral, Merseburg, Germany

obscured (fig. 15-31). The east and west ends of the church, like its Ottonian predecessor, had nearly equal visual weight, emphasized by clusters of vertical elements. Tall stair towers rose at each side of the narthex and the apse, and octagonal lantern domes marked the crossing and the center narthex bay. Speyer's unusually wide nave, about 45 feet, is balanced by the great height of the groin-vaulted bays, which soar more than 100 feet overhead (fig. 15-32). Massive compound piers mark each nave bay and support the transverse ribs of the high vault. Lighter, simpler piers mark the aisle bays where two smaller bays cover the distance. This rhythmic alternation of heavy and light piers, first suggested for aesthetic reasons in Ottonian architecture, such as in Saint Cyriakus at Gernrode (see fig. 14-24), is regularized in Speyer and became an important design element in

15-34. Roger of Helmarshausen. Portable altar of Saints Kilian and Liborius, from the Abbey, Helmars-hausen, Saxony, Germany. c. 1100, with later additions. Silver with niello and gemstones, 6½ x 13⅝ x 8⅜" (16.5 x 34.5 x 21 cm). Erzbischöfliches Diözesanmuseum und Domschatz-kammer, Paderborn, Germany

Roger, a monk, was also paid for a gold cross and another altar. Some scholars identify him with "Theophilus," the pseudonym used by a monk who wrote an artist's handbook, *On Diverse Arts*, about 1100. The book gives detailed instructions for painting, glassmaking, and goldsmithing. In contrast to Abbot Bernard of Clairvaux, "Theophilus" assured artists that "God delights in em-bellishments" and that artists worked "under the direction and authority of the Holy Spirit." He wrote, "most beloved son, you should not doubt but should believe in full faith that the Spirit of God has filled your heart when you have embellished His house with such great beauty and variety of workmanship. . . . Set a limit with pious consideration on what the work is to be, and for whom, as well as on the time, the amount, and the quality of work, and, lest the vice of greed or cupidity should steal in, on the amount of the recompense (Theophilus, page 43). The last admonishment is a worldly reminder about fair pricing.

Romanesque architecture. The ribbed groin vaults also relieve the stress on the side walls of the building so that windows can be larger. The result is both a physical and a psychological lightening of the building.

Metalwork

For centuries, three centers in western Germany supplied much of the best metalwork for aristocratic and ecclesi-astical patrons throughout Europe: Saxony, the Meuse valley region (in modern Belgium), and the lower Rhine valley. The metalworkers in these areas drew on a variety of stylistic sources, including the work of contemporary Byzantine and Italian artists, as well as classical prece-dents as reinterpreted by their Carolingian forebears.

In the late eleventh century, Saxon metalworkers, already known for their large-scale bronze casting, began making bronze **tomb effigies**, or portraits of the deceased. Thus began a tradition of funerary art that spread throughout Europe and persisted for hundreds

of years. The oldest known bronze tomb effigy is that of King Rudolf of Swabia (fig. 15-33), who sided with the pope against Henry IV during the Investiture Contro-versy. The effigy, made soon after Rudolf's death in bat-tle in 1080, is the work of an artist originally from the Rhine region. Nearly lifesize, it has fine linear detailing in **niello**, an incised design filled with a black alloy. The king's head has been modeled in higher relief than his body. The spurs on his oversized feet identify him as a heroic warrior. In his hands he holds the scepter and orb, emblems of kingship.

Most work of the time is anonymous, but according to the account books of the Abbey of Helmarshausen in Saxony, an artist named Roger was paid on August 15, 1100, for a portable altar dedicated to Saints Kilian and Liborius. Preserved in the treasury of the cathedral there, the foot-long, chestlike altar (one of two extant examples attributed to this artist) was made of silver with gem-stones and niello (fig. 15-34). It rests on three-dimen-sionally modeled animal feet. On one end, in high relief,

15-35. Griffin aquamanile, from Mosan, near Liège, Belgium. c. 1130. Gilt bronze, silver, and niello, height 7¼" (18.5 cm). Victoria and Albert Museum, London

15-36. Page of facsimile with *Hildegard's Vision, Liber Scivias*. c. 1150–1200. Original manuscript lost during World War II

The text that accompanies this picture of Hildegard of Bingen reads: "In the year 1141 of the incarnation of Jesus Christ the Son of God, when I was forty-two years and seven months of age, a fiery light, flashing intensely, came from the open vault of heaven and poured through my whole brain. . . . And suddenly I could understand what such books as the psalter, the gospel and the other catholic volumes of the Old and New Testament actually set forth" (*Scivias*, I, 1).

are two standing saints flanking Christ in Majesty, enthroned on the arc of the heavens. On the front are five apostles, each posed somewhat differently, executed in two-dimensional engraving and niello. Saint Peter sits in the center, holding his key, with two other apostles on each side of him. Roger adapted Byzantine figural conventions to his personal style, and he gave his subjects a sense of life despite their formal setting. He was clearly familiar with classical art, but his geometric treatment of natural forms, his use of decorative surface patterning, and the linear clarity of his composition are departures from the classical aesthetic.

Metalworkers in the Meuse Valley excelled in a very different style, perhaps the most distinctive of all Romanesque regional styles. They were well known for sumptuous small pieces, such as the gilt bronze **aquamanile** shown here, which was made about 1130 (fig. 15-35). Aquamaniles (from the Latin *aqua*, "water," and *manus*, "hand") were introduced into western Europe from the Islamic East, probably by returning Crusaders. In their homelands, Muslims used aquamaniles for rinsing their hands at meals. In the West, they found their way to church altars, where priests purified themselves by pouring water over their hands. This griffin aquamanile recalls its Islamic prototypes (see fig. 8-18). In its liturgical context, however, the hybrid beast known as a griffin symbolized the dual nature of Christ: divine (half eagle) and human (half lion). Black niello sets off the gleaming gold and silver, and the circular handle echoes the curved forms of the rest of the vessel.

Books

The great Carolingian and Ottoman manuscript tradition continued in the Romanesque period. A painting on an opening page from the earliest illustrated copy of the *Liber Scivias* by Hildegard of Bingen (1098–1179) is as notable for the text it illustrates as for its artistic merit (fig. 15-36). Born into an aristocratic German family, Hildegard transcended the barriers that limited most medieval women, and she became one of the towering figures of her age. Like many women of her class, she entered a convent as a child. Developing into a scholar and a capable administrator, Hildegard began serving as leader of the convent in 1136. In about 1147 she founded a new convent near Bingen. Since childhood she had been subject to what she interpreted as divine visions, and in her forties, with the assistance of the

15-37. Page with initial *Q*, in a psalter from a nunnery in Augsburg(?), Swabia, Germany. Late 12th century. Tempera on vellum. Walters Art Gallery, Baltimore, W. 26, fol. 64

monk Volmar, she began to record them. Her book, *Scivias* (from the Latin *scite vias lucis,* "know the ways of the light"), records her visions. In addition to *Scivias,* Hildegard wrote treatises on a variety of subjects, including medicine and natural science. Emerging as a major figure in the intellectual life of her time, she corresponded with emperors, popes, and the Cistercian Abbot Bernard of Clairvaux.

The opening page of this copy of *Scivias* shows Hildegard receiving a flash of divine insight, represented by the tongues of flame encircling her head. She records the vision on a tablet while Volmar, her scribe, waits in the wings. Stylistic affinities suggest to some art historians that this copy of *Scivias* was made at the scriptorium of the monastery of Saint Matthias in Trier, whose abbot was a friend of Hildegard. Others suggest it was made at Bingen under the direction of Hildegard herself.

In the Romanesque period, as earlier in the Middle Ages, women were involved in the production of books as authors, scribes, painters, and patrons (see fig. 14-14). A woman named Claricia may have worked on the decoration of a late-twelfth-century psalter probably from Augsburg, the Swabian capital. On a page from this psalter, a blithely swinging woman forms the tail of the initial *Q* (fig. 15-37). Her uncovered, flying braids and fashionably long-sleeved dress suggest that she was a young, unmarried layperson. A nun or married woman would be dressed modestly, with her head covered. Written on each side of her head is the name Claricia, suggesting that this may be a self-portrait. Recently scholars have questioned this interpretation and have suggested that Clarissa personifies the gossip described in the text.

ITALY

The eleventh and twelfth centuries were a period of significant change on the Italian peninsula. The north, deeply embroiled in the conflict between the papacy and the German emperors, experienced both economic growth and increasing political fragmentation. Toward the end of the eleventh century, towns such as Pisa and Genoa became self-governing municipal corporations known as communes, and by the middle of the twelfth century the major cities and towns of northern and central Italy were independent civic entities, feuding with one another incessantly in a pattern that continued for the next several hundred years. Port cities like Pisa, Genoa, and Venice maintained a thriving Mediterranean trade and also profited from their role in transporting Crusaders and pilgrims to the Holy Land. The great bishops of these urban centers played a leading role as patrons of the arts in the building and furnishing of their cathedrals. In Sicily and southern Italy in the late eleventh century, as Norman adventurers took control and displaced Islamic and Byzantine rulers, a distinctively northern influence appeared. Throughout Italy, moreover, artists looked to the still-standing ruins of imperial Rome. All these influences shaped the character of the Italian Romanesque.

Architecture

Pisa, on the west coast of Tuscany, was a great maritime power from the ninth through the thirteenth century. An expansionist republic, it competed with Muslim centers for control of trade in the western Mediterranean. In 1063 Pisa won a decisive victory over Muslim forces, and the jubilant city soon began constructing an imposing new cathedral dedicated to the Virgin Mary (fig. 15-38). The cathedral complex eventually included the cathedral itself; a **campanile**, or freestanding bell tower, a feature of Italian church architecture since the sixth century (now known for obvious reasons as the Leaning Tower); a baptistry; and the Campo Santo, a walled burial ground. The cathedral, designed by the master builder Busketos, was not completed until the late thirteenth century. Its plan is an adaptation on a grand scale of the cruciform basilica. It has a long nave with double side aisles crossed by a projecting transept each with aisles and an apse like the nave and main sanctuary. Three portals open on the nave and side aisles, and a clerestory rises above the side aisles and second-story galleries. A dome covers the crossing. Pilasters, blind arcades, and narrow galleries adorn the five-story, pale-marble facade. An Islamic bronze griffin sat atop the building from about 1100 until 1828 (see fig. 8-18).

15-38. Cathedral complex, Pisa, Tuscany, Italy. Cathedral begun 1063; baptistry begun 1153; campanile begun 1174; Campo Santo dates from 13th century

When finished in 1350, the "Leaning Tower of Pisa" stood 179 feet high. It had begun to tilt while it was still under construction, and today it leans about 13 feet off the perpendicular. In the latest effort to keep it from toppling, engineers filled the base with tons of lead.

15-39. Nave, Pisa Cathedral. 1063–1100s

The nave arcade on the interior of the cathedral (fig. 15-39), has evenly spaced Corinthian-style columns and a flat, coffered timber ceiling reminiscent of Early Christian basilical churches. The rhythmically progressing arches, a stringcourse, and the plain walls of the clerestory reinforce the horizontal movement. In the gallery arcade,

intermediate columns between piers support two-part openings. Contrasting bands of dark green marble decorate the arches and piers.

The tradition of erecting separate bell towers and round or octagonal baptistries continued in Italy. The Pisa Baptistry was begun in 1153. The arcading and galleries on the lower levels of its exterior match those on the cathedral. The ornate upper levels are in a later, Gothic style. The present exterior dome is also later. The campanile was begun in 1174 by the master Bonanno Pisano. Built on inadequate foundations, it began to lean almost immediately. The cylindrical tower is encased in tier upon tier of marble arcades. This creative reuse of an ancient, classical theme is characteristic of Italian Romanesque art; artists and architects seem always to have been conscious of their Roman past, whether in the marble columns of Pisa or the monumental brickwork of Lombardy in northern Italy.

In Lombardy, the city of Milan had been the capital of the Western Roman Empire for a brief period in the fourth century, and the city's first bishop, Ambrose (d. 397), was one of the "fathers" of the Christian Church. In 1080, construction began on a new Church of Sant'Ambrogio (Saint Ambrose), replacing an often-renovated ninth-century church (figs. 15-40, 15-41). The builders reused much of the earlier structure, including the freestanding tenth-century "monks' tower" (shown at the right in figure 15-40). Lombard Romanesque architecture depended for its austere dignity on harmonious proportions and the restrained use of exterior motifs derived from architectural forms. The exterior of Sant'Ambrogio is decorated

15-40. Church of Sant'Ambrogio, Milan, Lombardy, Italy.
c. 1080–early 12th century. Restored after World War II

15-41. Plan of Church of Sant'Ambrogio

vertically with strip buttresses and horizontally with arched **corbel tables** (appearing as a scallop motif at a distance). The elements can be seen most clearly on the twelfth-century north tower (at the left in figure 15-40). The atrium, narthex, and semi-independent towers reflect the influence of Early Christian architecture still standing in Milan. Five huge arches, which correspond to the nave and side aisles, follow the roofline of the gabled, or pitch-roofed, second-story gallery and give it a dramatic appearance. Many churches in northern Italy adopted this type of gabled facade. The simple architectural decoration of strip buttresses and arched corbel tables was carried to Germany, Normandy, and elsewhere by Lombard clerics and masons.

Following an earthquake in 1117, masons rebuilt the church using a technically advanced system of four-part rib vaulting (fig. 15-42). Compound piers support three domed-up ribbed groin vaults over the nave, and smaller intermediate piers support the ribbed groin vaulting over the side-aisle bays. In addition to the vaulting system, the builders took other steps to assure the stability of the church. Sant'Ambrogio has a nave that was wider than that of Cluny III (with which it was roughly contemporary), but, at 60 feet, only a little more than half as high. Vaulted galleries buttress the nave, and there are windows only in the outer walls.

15-42. Nave, Church of Sant'Ambrogio. Vaulting after 1117

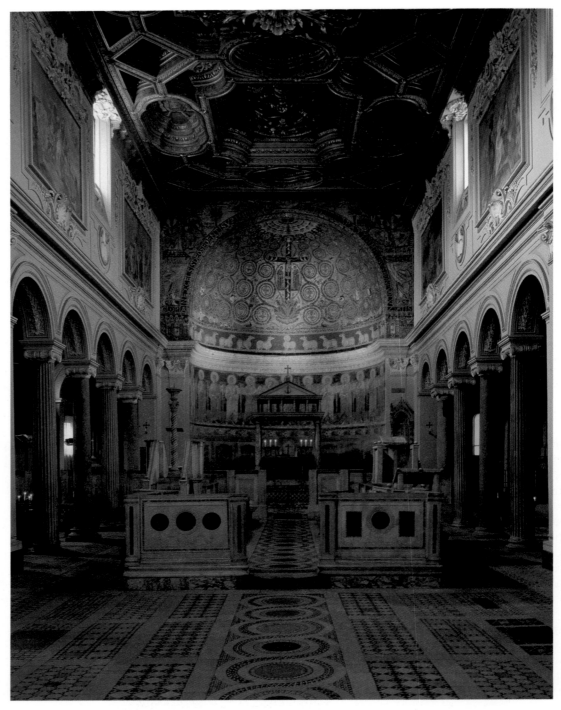

15-43. Nave, Church of San Clemente, Rome c. 1120–30

Ninth-century choir screens were reused from the earlier church. Upper wall and ceiling decoration are eighteenth century. San Clemente contains one of the earliest surviving collections of church furniture: choir stalls, pulpit, lecturn, candlestick, and also the twelfth-century inlaid floor pavement.

During the Investiture Controversy, Pope Gregory VII called on the Norman rulers of southern Italy for help when the forces of Emperor Henry IV threatened Rome in 1084. These erstwhile allies, however, looted and burned the city. Among the architectural victims was the eleventh-century Church of San Clemente. The Benedictines rebuilt the church between 1120 and 1130 as part of a program to restore Rome to its ancient splendor. The new church, built on top of the remains of both a fourth-century basilica and the eleventh-century church, reflects a conscious effort to reclaim the artistic and spiritual legacy of the early Church (fig. 15-43). However, a number of features mark it as a Romanesque structure. A characteristic of early basilica churches, for example, was a strong horizontal movement down the nave to the sanctuary. In the new San Clemente, the rhythmic alternation of rectangular piers and Ionic columns interrupts this horizontal flow. In a configura-

15-44. Wiligelmus. *Creation and Fall*, on the west facade, Modena Cathedral, Emilia, Italy. 1106–20. Height approx. 3' (92 cm)

tion that came to be called the Benedictine plan, the nave and the side aisles each end in a semicircular apse. The different sizes of the apses, caused by the difference in the widths of the nave and the narrower side aisles, creates a stepped outline. The apse of the church followed the outline of the apse of the older structure beneath and was too small to accommodate all the participants in the liturgy of the time. As a result, the choir, defined by the low barrier in the foreground of figure 15-43, was extended into the nave.

Mosaic was a rarely used medium in twelfth-century Europe because it required expensive materials and specialized artisans. The apse of San Clemente, however, is richly decorated with colored marble inlay and a gold mosaic apse semidome, another reflection of its builders' desire to recapture the past. The subject matter—a crucified Jesus, with his mother and Saint John placed against a vine scroll, and sheep representing the apostles and the Lamb of God—and style of the mosaics are likewise archaic. As in other Italian churches of the period, inlaid geometric patterns in marble embellish the floors of San Clemente. They are known as Cosmati work, from the family who perfected it. Ninth-century panels with relief sculptures, saved from the earlier church, formed the wall separating the choir from the nave. A **baldachin** (baldacchino), or canopy of honor symbolizing the Holy Sepulchre, covers the main altar in the apse.

Architectural Sculpture

The spirit of ancient Rome also seems to pervade the sculpture of Romanesque Italy. Horizontal bands of relief on the west facade of the Modena Cathedral, in north-central Italy, are among the earliest narrative portal sculpture in Italy (c. 1106–1120). Wiligelmus, the sculptor, must have seen the sculpture of ancient sarcophagi

and may also have looked at Ottonian carving. He took his subjects from the Old Testament Book of Genesis and included events from the Creation to the Flood. The panel in figure 15-44 shows the Creation and the Fall of Adam and Eve. On the far left is a half-length Christ framed by a mandorla supported by two angels. The scene to the right shows God bringing Adam to life. Next, he brings forth Eve from Adam's side. On the right, Adam and Eve cover their genitals in shame as they greedily eat the fruit of the forbidden tree, around which the serpent twists.

Wiligelmus's deft carving and undercutting give these low-relief figures a strong three-dimensionality. While most Romanesque sculpture seems controlled by a strong frame or architectural setting, Wiligelmus used the arcade to establish a stagelike setting. Rocks and a tree add to the impression that figures interact with stage props. Wiligelmus's figures, although not particularly graceful, have a sense of life and personality and effectively convey the emotional depth of the narrative. Bright paint, now almost all lost, must have increased the impact of the sculpture.

An inscription on one of the panels reads: "Among sculptors, your work shines forth, Wiligelmo [Wiligelmus]." This self-confidence turned out to be justified. Wiligelmus's influence can be traced throughout Italy and as far away as the cathedral of Lincoln in England. Wiligelmus, Roger, Gislebertus, and many anonymous women and men of the eleventh and twelfth centuries created a new art that—although based on the Bible and the lives of the saints—focused on human beings, their stories, and their beliefs. The artists worked on a monumental scale in painting, sculpture, and even embroidery, and their art moved from the cloister to the public walls of churches. While they emphasized the spiritual and intellectual concerns of the Christian Church, they also began to observe and record what they saw around them. In so doing they laid the groundwork for the art of the Gothic period.

Salisbury Cathedral
1220–58

Palma Cathedral
begun 1306

Cathedral of Notre-Dame,
Chartres c. 1134–1220

Giotto
Virgin and Child Enthroned
1310

CHAPTER 16

Gothic Art

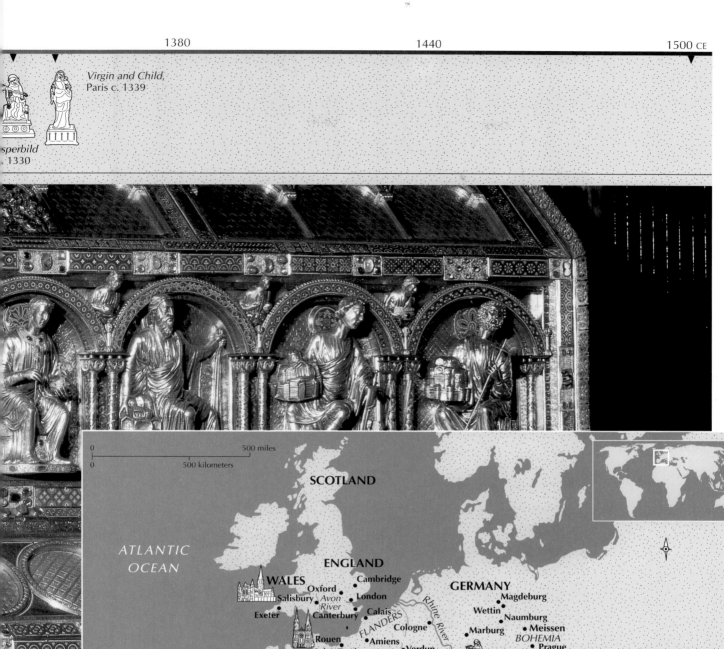

Virgin and Child,
Paris c. 1339

sperbild
1330

0   500 miles

0   500 kilometers

SCOTLAND

ATLANTIC
OCEAN

ENGLAND

WALES
Cambridge
Oxford
London
Salisbury   *Avon River*
Exeter   Canterbury   Calais

GERMANY
Magdeburg
Wettin
Naumburg
Marburg   Meissen
BOHEMIA
Prague

FLANDERS
Cologne
Rouen
Amiens   Verdun
Saint-Denis   Reims
Paris   *Meuse River*
ÎLE-DE-FRANCE   Strasbourg
Chartres
MAINE   Bourges
ANJOU
TOURAINE   *BURGUNDY*
Poitiers

CZECH REPUBLIC

Rhine River

AQUITAINE

FRANCE

LEÓN
CASTILE

ARAGÓN

Avignon

SPAIN

CATALONIA
Barcelona

Córdoba

Palma
Mallorca

Seville

Padua
VENETIA   Venice
TUSCANY   Bologna
Pisa   Florence
Siena
UMBRIA
Assisi
Rome   **ITALY**
APULIA

Mediterranean Sea

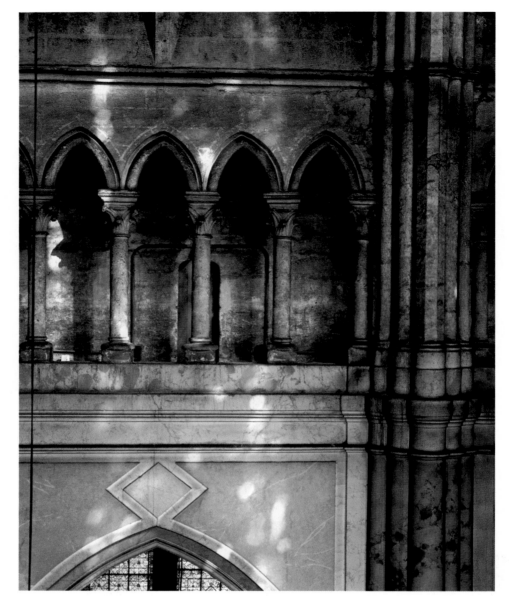

16-1. Triforium wall of the nave, Chartres Cathedral, Île-de-France, France. c. 1200–60

T he twelfth-century Abbot Suger of Saint-Denis was, according to
his biographer Willelmus, "small of body and family, constrained
by twofold smallness, [but] he refused, in his smallness, to be a
small man" (cited in Panofsky, page 33). He was educated at the monastery of Saint-Denis, near Paris, and rose from modest origins to become a
powerful adviser to kings—even regent when the king was on crusade.
And he built what many consider the first Gothic structure in Europe.

After Suger was elected abbot of Saint-Denis, he was determined to
rebuild its church, where the relics of the patron saint were housed
and the kings of the Franks had been buried since the seventh century.
Suger saw Saint-Denis as the preeminent church in France, a church that
embodied the history of the royal dynasty, and he waged a successful
campaign to gain both royal and popular support for his rebuilding plans.
The current building, he pointed out, had become inadequate. With a

touch of exaggeration, he claimed that the crowds of worshipers had become so great that women were being crushed and monks sometimes had to flee with their relics by jumping through windows.

In carrying out his duties, the abbot had traveled widely—in France, the Rhineland, and Italy, including four trips to Rome. As he began his plans for the church, he was familiar with the latest architecture and sculpture of Romanesque Europe. He also turned for inspiration to the authority of Church writings, including treatises erroneously attributed to a first-century follower of Saint Paul named Dionysius, who identified radiant light with divinity. Through the centuries Dionysius had become confused with Saint Denis, so Suger not unreasonably adapted his concept of divine luminosity into the redesign of the church dedicated to Saint Denis. Accordingly, when Suger began work on the choir after completing a magnificent Norman-inspired facade and narthex, he created "a circular string of chapels" so that the whole church "would shine with the wonderful and uninterrupted light of most luminous windows, pervading the interior beauty" (cited in Panofsky, page 101). Although Abbot Suger died before he was able to finish rebuilding Saint-Denis, his presence remained: this cleric of modest origins had himself portrayed in a sculpture at Christ's feet in the central portal, in a mosaic in the chapel, and in a stained-glass window in the apse. Suger is remembered not for these representations, however, but for his inspired departure from traditional architecture in order to achieve radiant light. It was this innovation that introduced the concept of large stained-glass windows, such as those that bathe the inside walls of Chartres Cathedral with sublime washes of color (fig. 16-1).

THE GOTHIC STYLE

In the middle of the twelfth century, when builders throughout Europe worked in the Romanesque style, a distinctive new architecture known today as Gothic emerged in the Île-de-France, the domain of French kings around Paris. The appearance of the new style and building technique there coincided with the emergence of the monarchy as a powerful centralizing force in France. The Gothic style prevailed in western European art from about 1150 to 1400, though it lingered for another century in some regions—the spire of the north tower of Chartres Cathedral, for example, was finished between 1507 and 1513, a period during which Michelangelo was creating Renaissance masterpieces in Florence and Rome. The term Gothic was introduced in the sixteenth century by the Italian artist and historian Giorgio Vasari. Vasari, who esteemed Michelangelo above all others, disparagingly attributed the style to the Goths, Germanic northerners who had destroyed the classical civilization of the Roman Empire that he and his contemporaries so admired. In its own day the Gothic style was simply called modern style or the French style. As it spread from the Île-de-France, it gradually displaced Romanesque forms but took on regional characteristics inspired by those forms. England developed a distinctive national style, which also influenced architectural design in continental Europe. The Gothic style was slow to take hold in Germany but ultimately endured there well into the sixteenth century. Italy proved more resistant to French Gothic elements, and by 1400, Italian artists and builders there sought a return to classical traditions. In the late fourteenth century, the various regional styles of Europe coalesced into what is known as the International Gothic style.

Gothic architecture's elegant, soaring interiors, the light, colors, and sense of transparency produced by great expanses of stained glass, and its linear qualities became more pronounced over time. The style was adapted to all types of structures—including town halls, meeting houses, market buildings, residences, and Jewish synagogues, as well as churches and palaces—and its influence extended beyond architecture and architectural sculpture to other mediums.

The people of western Europe experienced both great achievements and great turmoil during the Gothic period. In the twelfth and thirteenth centuries Europe was enjoying a period of vigor and growth. Town life stimulated intellectual life, and urban universities and cathedral schools supplanted rural monastic schools as centers of learning. The first European university, at Bologna, Italy, was founded in the eleventh century, and

PARALLELS

Europe	1140–1275	1275–1400
France	Saint-Denis; Gothic style emerges; Louis VII; Eleanor of Aquitaine; Notre-Dame de Paris designed; Chartres Cathedral; troubadour songs; University of Paris founded; Amiens Cathedral; Reims Cathedral; Thomas Aquinas; Villard d'Honnecourt's sketchbook; the Sainte-Chapelle; book arts flourish	Papacy in Avignon; Duke Philip the Bold of Burgundy; King Charles V; courtly love themes in literature and art
England	Henry II and Eleanor of Aquitaine found Plantagenet dynasty; Canterbury Cathedral; Cambridge and Oxford universities founded; King John signs Magna Carta; Salisbury Cathedral; Decorated style; Henry III and barons feud	*Windmill Psalter*; opus anglicanum; Hundred Years' War with France begins; first English translation of the Bible; Chaucer's *Canterbury Tales*
Spain	King Alfonso X; Christian reconquest of Muslim Spain continues	Palma Cathedral (Mallorca)
Germany	Nicholas of Verdun; hall churches develop; Holy Roman Emperor Frederick II	Gothic synagogue built in Prague (Bohemia); *Andachtsbilder*
Italy	Pisa Campanile; Saint Francis; Franciscan order founded; Padua University founded; Nicola Pisano; Giovanni Pisano; Cimabue's *Crucifix*	Giotto's frescoes; Duccio's *Maestà*; Dante's *Divine Comedy*; Boccaccio's *Decameron*; Florence Cathedral; "Great Schism" in Western Christian Church; Renaissance style emerges
World	Second to Ninth Crusades; Benin civilization (Africa); Muslim conquest of India; Kamakura period (Japan); Aztec conquer Toltec (South America); Mississippian pottery (North America); Marco Polo in China; Jenghiz Khan invades China; Kublai Khan rules Mongols	Wu Chen's landscapes (China); Black Death ravages Europe; Ming dynasty (China); Tamerlane's conquests in Asia; Golden Pavilion (Japan)

important universities in Paris, Cambridge, and Oxford soon followed. The Gothic period also saw the flowering of distinctive art forms among the nobility—poetry and music in particular—centered on the concept of courtly love (see "Courtly Love," opposite).

Although Europe remained overwhelmingly rural during the Gothic period, towns gained increasing prominence. Nearly all the major cities in western Europe today were sizable urban centers by the late twelfth century. As towns grew, they became increasingly important centers of artistic patronage. The production and sale of goods in many towns was controlled by guilds. Artisans of all types, from bakers to painters, and merchants formed these associations to advance their professional interests. Medieval guilds also played an important social role, safeguarding members' political interests, organizing religious celebrations, and looking after members and their families in times of trouble.

A town's walls enclosed streets, wells, market squares, shops, churches, and schools. Homes ranged from humble wood-and-thatch structures to imposing stone town houses. Although wooden dwellings crowded together made fire an ever-present danger and hygiene was rudimentary at best, towns fostered an energetic civic life and a strong communal identity, reinforced by public projects and ceremonies. An idealized portrait of the town of Siena in the mid-fourteenth century conveys some of the richness and energy of late-medieval civic life (fig. 16-2).

Urban cathedrals, the seats of the ruling bishops, superseded rural monasteries as centers of religious patronage throughout western Europe during the Gothic period. So many of these monumental testaments to the power of the Church were erected between 1150 and 1400 that this period is also known as the great age of cathedral building. Cathedral precincts functioned almost as towns within towns. The great churches dominated their surroundings and were central fixtures of urban life. Their grandeur inspired love and admiration; their great expense and the intrusive power of their bishops inspired resentment and fear. The twelfth century witnessed a growth of intense religiosity among the laity,

COURTLY LOVE

The ideal of courtly love arose in southern France in the early twelfth century during the cultural renaissance that followed the First Crusade. It involved the passionate devotion of lover and loved one. The relationship was almost always illicit—the woman the wife of another, often a lord or patron—and its consummation was usually impossible. This movement transformed the social habits of western Europe's courts and has had an enduring influence on modern ideas of love. Images of gallant knights serving refined ladies, who bestowed tokens of affection on their chosen suitors or cruelly withheld their love on a whim, captured the popular imagination.

The literature of courtly love was initially spread by the musician-poets known as troubadours, some of them professionals, some of them amateur nobles, and at least twenty of them women. They sang of love's joys and heartbreaks in daringly personalized terms, extolling the ennobling effects of the lovers' selfless devotion. From this tradition came the famous romance of Tristam and Ysolt (Tristan and Isolde), so well known that it was the decorative motif on a hair comb from the fifteenth century, seen at the right.

Chrétien de Troyes, a French poet writing in the late twelfth century, tells of the love of the knight Lancelot for Guinevere, the wife of King Arthur. The literature of courtly love marked a major shift from the usually negative way in which women had previously been portrayed as sinful daughters of Eve. The following example, a stylized lovers' debate (the woman speaks first), is an example of courtly love poetry of southern France.

> Friend, because of you I'm
>   filled
> with grievous sorrow and
>   despair,
> but I doubt you feel a trace
> of my affliction.
> Why did you become a lover,
> since you leave the suffering
>   to me?
> Why don't we split it evenly?
>
> Lady, such is love's nature
> when it links two friends
>   together,
> that whatever grief or joy they
>   have
> each feels according to his way.
> The way I see it, and I don't
> exaggerate, all the worst pain's
> been on my end of the game.
>
> Friend, I know well enough
>   how skilled
> you are in amorous affairs,
> and I find you rather changed
> from the chivalrous knight you
>   used to be.
> I might as well be clear,
> for your mind seems quite dis-
>   tracted:
> do you still find me attractive?
>
> Lady, may sparrow-hawk not
>   ride my wrist,
> nor siren fly beside
> me on the chase, if ever
> since you gave me perfect joy

> I possessed another woman;
> I don't lie: out of envy
> evil men insult my name.
>
>   (Attributed to the Countess
>   of Dia and Raimbaut
>   d'Orange, late twelfth
>   century; cited in Bogin,
>   pages 147, 149)

The tradition of courtly love had a lasting influence on the development of Western literature. In Italy the Florentine poet Dante Alighieri (1265–1321) incorporated the form into his great work, *La Divina Commedia* (*The Divine Comedy*, c. 1310–1320), in which his idealized woman, Beatrice, guides him through paradise.

Comb, carved with *The Meeting of Tristam and Ysolt*, from eastern France or Switzerland. Early 15th century. Wood coated with gesso and paint, height 7³/₄ x 7⁵/₈" (19.7 x 19.5 cm). Museum of Fine Arts, Boston
H. E. Bolles Fund

16-2. Ambrogio Lorenzetti. Detail of fresco *Allegory of Good Government in the City*, in the Sala della Pace, Palazzo Pubblico, Siena. 1338–39

particularly in Italy and France. The same devotional intensity gave rise in the early thirteenth century to two new religious orders, the Franciscans and the Dominicans, both of which went out into the world to preach and minister to those in need, rather than confining themselves in monasteries.

The Crusades continued throughout the thirteenth century. In 1204, soldiers of the Fourth Crusade who had set out to conquer Egypt from the Muslims instead seized Constantinople—capital of the Byzantine Empire and the center of the Eastern Christian Church—and the city remained under Western control until 1261. The Crusades and the trade that followed from them brought western Europeans into contact with the Byzantine and Islamic worlds, and through them many literary works of classical antiquity, particularly those of Aristotle. These works posed a problem for medieval scholars because they promoted rational inquiry rather than faith as the path to truth, and their conclusions did not always fit comfortably with Church doctrine. In the thirteenth century, Thomas Aquinas finally brought together faith and reason—the old belief and the new logic—in Scholastic philosophy, which has endured as a basis of Catholic thought to this day.

The all-embracing intellectual systems of the Scholastic thinkers had a profound influence on the arts. The sculptural programs in many cathedrals are as encyclopedic as the *Speculum Maius* (Greater Mirror) of Vincent de Beauvais, a thirteenth-century Parisian Dominican. He organized his eighty-volume encyclopedia to include categories of the Natural World, Doctrine, History, and Morality. Gothic master builders, like the Scholastics, saw divine order in geometric relationships and expressed these relationships in sculpture and architecture. Unlike their Romanesque predecessors, who used stylization and distortion to achieve emotional impact, thirteenth-century sculptors created more naturalistic forms that reflect the idealism and reasoned analysis of Scholastic thought. Gothic religious imagery became all-encompassing, and like Romanesque imagery its purpose was to instruct and convince the viewer. Its effects, however, are more varied and subtle. In the Gothic cathedral it incorporates a wide range of subjects drawn from the natural world. Scholastic logic intermingles with the mysticism of light and color to create for the worshiper the direct, emotional, ecstatic experience of the church as the embodiment of God's house, filled with divine light.

In all these achievements lay potential disaster. By the middle of the fourteenth century much of Europe was in crisis. Prosperity had fostered population growth, which by about 1300 began to exceed food production, and thereafter famines became increasingly common. Peasant revolts began as worsening conditions frustrated rising expectations. In 1337 a prolonged conflict known as the Hundred Years' War (1337–1453) erupted between France and England, devastating much of France. In the middle of the fourteenth century a lethal plague swept northward from Sicily, wiping out as much as 40 percent of Europe's population (see "The Black Death," page 606). By depleting the labor force, however, the plague gave surviving peasants increased leverage over their landlords and increased the wages of artisans. The Church, too, experienced great strain during the fourteenth century. In 1309 the papal court moved from Rome to Avignon, in southeastern France, where it remained until 1377. From 1378 to 1417, in what is known as the Great Schism, the papacy split, with two contending popes, one in Avignon and one in Rome, claiming legitimacy.

FRANCE

The birth and initial flowering of the Gothic style took place in France against the backdrop of the growing power of the French monarchy. Louis VI (ruled 1108–1137) and Louis VII (ruled 1137–1180) consolidated royal authority over the Île-de-France and began to exert control over powerful nobles in other regions. Before succeeding to the throne,

Louis VII had married Eleanor (1122–1204), heir to the region of Aquitaine (southwestern France), the largest and most prosperous feudal domain in western Europe. Eleanor of Aquitaine was one of the great figures of her age. She accompanied Louis on the Second Crusade (1147–1149), but the marriage was later annulled by papal decree. Taking her wealthy province with her, Eleanor then married Henry Plantagenet—the duke of Normandy, count of Anjou, Maine, and Touraine, and soon-to-be King Henry II of England. Their marriage created further dynastic entanglements. Henry and Eleanor together controlled more French territory than the French king, although he was technically their feudal overlord. The resulting tangle of conflicting claims was responsible for centuries of friction between England and France that culminated in the Hundred Years' War.

Eleanor was estranged from Henry in 1170 and plotted with her sons and her former husband, Louis VII, to overthrow him. When these schemes failed, Henry kept her confined for more than a decade. After his death in 1189, the dowager queen Eleanor presided over her court in Poitiers, Aquitaine, while her sons Richard the Lion-Hearted and then John were kings of England and a daughter was queen of Castile in Spain. Poitiers gained renown for its patronage of high culture and the literature of courtly love (see "Courtly Love," page 549). A woman of great courage and stamina, Eleanor had ten children, including two daughters with Louis and five sons and three daughters with Henry. She remained a formidable figure in European politics into her eighties.

The successors to Louis VII continued the consolidation of royal authority and nation building, increasing their domains and privileges at the expense of aristocrats and the Church.

Architecture and Its Decoration

The political events of the twelfth and thirteenth centuries were accompanied by a burst of church-building. It has been estimated that during the Middle Ages several million tons of stone were quarried to build some 80 cathedrals, 500 large churches, and tens of thousands of parish churches, and that within 100 years some 2,700 churches were built in the Île-de-France region alone. This staggering undertaking drew on the wealth generated by the area's agricultural products—particularly wheat and wine—and the commerce and industry of its town dwellers. Stone was but one of the expenses. In some instances, as at Chartres, the clergy already owned the quarry; in others, they bought it. Transporting the stone was sometimes a greater expense than the stone itself. Whenever possible, heavy construction material was transported by water on barges, and sometimes canals were built for this purpose. (Stone from France was often shipped by barge to England for this same reason.) When transport by land was necessary, the shortest possible route was taken, and new types of harnesses for coupling draft horses were developed. The ingenious machines created for lifting heavy materials were well documented in drawings of the time, as was scaffolding—including some suspended from above rather than resting on the ground—and spiral staircases built within the masonry. This explosion of cathedral building began at a historic abbey church on the outskirts of Paris.

Abbey Church of Saint-Denis. The Benedictine monastery of Saint-Denis, a few miles north of central Paris, had great symbolic significance for the French monarchy. It housed the tombs of French kings, regalia of the French Crown, and the relics of Saint Denis, the patron saint of France, who, according to tradition, had been the first bishop of Paris. In the 1130s, under the inspiration of Abbot Suger, construction began on the new abbey church, which is arguably Europe's first Gothic structure. Suger (c. 1081–1151) was a trusted adviser to both Louis VI and Louis VII, and he governed France as regent when Louis VII and Eleanor of Aquitaine led the crusade.

Suger described his administration of the abbey and the building of the Abbey Church of Saint-Denis in three books. His love of magnificent architecture and art brought him into conflict with the Cistercian leader, Abbot Bernard of Clairvaux (Chapter 15). As a widely traveled cleric, Suger knew all the latest developments in church building, and his design combines elements from many sources. Because the Île-de-France had great Carolingian buildings and little monumental Romanesque architecture, Suger brought in masons and sculptors from other regions. Saint-Denis became a center of artistic interchange. Unfortunately for art historians today, Suger did not record the names of the masters he employed, nor information about them and the techniques they used. The abbot took an active part in the building. He found the huge trees and stone needed by the workers on the abbey's own lands. To generate income for the rebuilding, he instituted economic reforms, receiving substantial annual payments from the town's inhabitants and establishing free villages on abbey estates to attract peasants. For additional funds, he turned to the royal coffers and even to fellow clerics.

The first part of the new structure to be completed was the west facade and narthex (1135–1140). Here Suger's masons combined Norman facade design like that at Caen (see fig. 15-27) and rib-vaulted structure like that at Durham (see fig. 15-26) with the richly sculptured portals of Burgundy. The east end represented an even more stunning change. The choir was completed in three years and three months (1140–1144), timing that Abbot Suger found auspicious. The plan of the choir (*chevet* in French) resembled that of a Romanesque pilgrimage church, with a semicircular sanctuary surrounded by an ambulatory from which radiated seven chapels of uniform size (figs. 15-3, 16-3). All the architectural elements of the choir—rib groin vaults springing from round piers, pointed arches, wall buttresses to relieve stress on the walls, and window openings—had already appeared in Romanesque buildings. The dramatic achievement of Suger's master mason was to combine these features into a fully integrated architectural whole that emphasized the open, flowing space. Sanctuary, ambulatory,

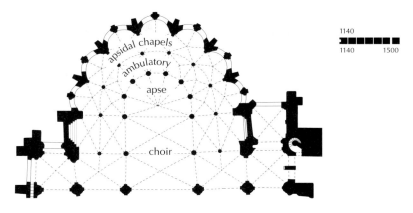

16-3. Plan of the sanctuary, Abbey Church of Saint-Denis, Saint-Denis, Île-de-France, France. 1140–44

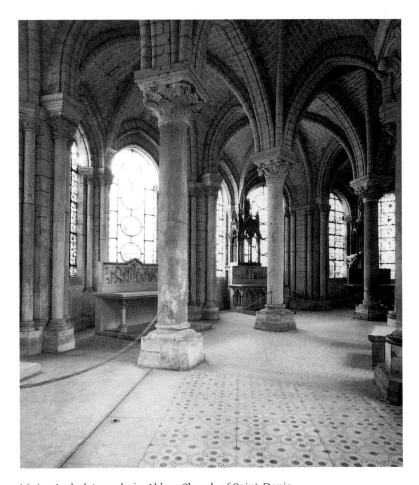

16-4. Ambulatory choir, Abbey Church of Saint-Denis

and chapels opened into one another; walls of stained glass replaced masonry, permitting the light to permeate the interior with color (fig. 16-4). To accomplish this effect, the masons relied on the systematic use of advanced vaulting techniques, the culmination of half a century of experiment and innovation (fig. 16-5; see "Elements of Architecture," page 552).

ELEMENTS OF ARCHITECTURE
Rib Vaulting

Rib vaulting was one of the chief technical contributions of Romanesque and Gothic builders. Rib vaults are a form of **groin vault** (see page 226) in which the ridges (groins) formed by the intersecting vaults may rest on and be covered by curved moldings called ribs. These ribs were usually structural as well as decorative, and they strengthened the joins and helped channel the vaults' thrusts outward and downward. The ribs were constructed first and supported the scaffolding of the vault. Ribs developed over time into an intricate masonry "skeleton" filled with an increasingly light-weight "skin," the web of the vault, or webbing. Sophisticated variations on the basic rib vault created the soaring interiors for which Gothic churches are famous.

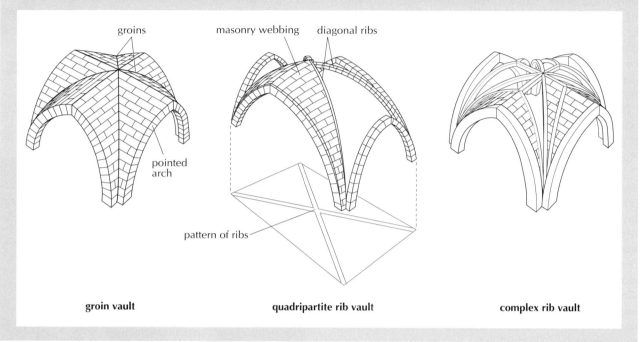

groins   masonry webbing   diagonal ribs

pointed arch

pattern of ribs

groin vault   **quadripartite rib vault**   **complex rib vault**

The apse of Saint-Denis represented the emergence of a new architectural aesthetic based on line and light. Citing early Christian writings, Suger saw light and color as a means of illuminating the soul and uniting it with God, a belief he shared with medieval mystics such as Hildegard of Bingen (Chapter 15). For him, the colored lights of gemstones and stained-glass windows and the glint of golden church furnishings at Saint-Denis transformed the material world into the splendor of paradise.

Louis VII and Eleanor of Aquitaine attended the consecration of the new choir on June 14, 1144. Shortly thereafter the impending Second Crusade became the primary recipient of royal resources, leaving Suger without funds to replace the old nave and transept at Saint-Denis. The abbot died in 1151, and his church remained unfinished for another century. (Saint-Denis suffered extensive damage during the French Revolution in the late eighteenth century. Its current condition is the result of nineteenth- and twentieth-century restorations and cleaning.)

The Abbey Church of Saint-Denis became the prototype for a new architecture of space and light based on a highly adaptable skeletal framework constructed from buttressed perimeter walls and an interior vaulting system of pointed-arch masonry ribs. It initiated a period of competitive experimentation in the Île-de-France and surrounding regions that resulted in ever larger churches enclosing increasingly taller interior spaces walled with ever greater expanses of colored glass (see "Notre-Dame of Paris," page 564). These great churches, with their

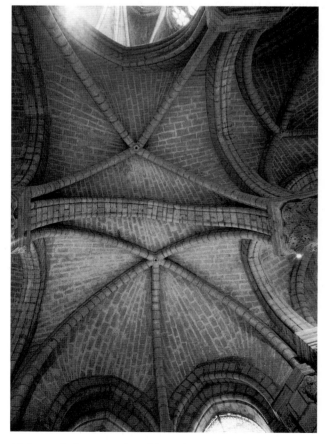

16-5. Ambulatory vaults, Abbey Church of Saint-Denis

16-6. Cathedral of Notre-Dame, Chartres, Île-de-France, France. c. 1194–60; west facade begun c. 1134; north spire 1507–13. View from the southeast

Chartres was the site of a pre-Christian virgin-goddess cult and one of the oldest and most important Christian shrines in France. Its main treasure was a long piece of linen believed to have been worn by Mary—a gift from the Byzantine empress to Charlemagne, donated to the cathedral by King Charles the Bald in 876—that was on display with other relics in a huge basement crypt. The healing powers attributed to this relic and its association with Mary made Chartres a major pilgrimage destination as the cult of the Virgin grew.

unabashed decorative richness, were part of Abbot Suger's legacy to France.

Chartres Cathedral. The great Cathedral of Notre-Dame (Our Lady, the Virgin Mary) dominates the town of Chartres, southwest of Paris (fig. 16-6). For many people, Chartres Cathedral is a near-perfect embodiment of spirit in stone and glass. Constructed in several stages beginning in the mid-twelfth century and extending into the mid-thirteenth, the cathedral reflects the transition from Early to High Gothic. A fire in 1134 that damaged the western facade of an earlier cathedral on the site prompted the building of a new facade, influenced by the Early Gothic style at Saint-Denis. After another fire in 1194 destroyed most of the rest of the original structure, a papal representative convinced reluctant local church officials to undertake a massive rebuilding project. A new cathedral was built between approximately 1194 and 1260.

To erect such an enormous building required vast resources—money, raw materials, and skilled labor. Contrary to common perceptions about "the great age of cathedral building," medieval people did not always support these ambitious undertakings with devout and selfless zeal. Both nobles and ordinary people often opposed the building of cathedrals because of the burden of new taxes. Nevertheless, cathedral officials pledged all or part of their incomes for three to five years. The church's relics were sent on tour as far away as England to solicit contributions. As the new structure rose higher during the 1220s, the work grew more costly and funds dwindled. When the bishop and canons (cathedral clergy) tried to make up the deficit by raising feudal and commercial taxes, they were driven into exile for four years. The economic privileges claimed by the Church for the cathedral sparked intermittent riots by townspeople and the local nobility throughout the thirteenth century. Despite these

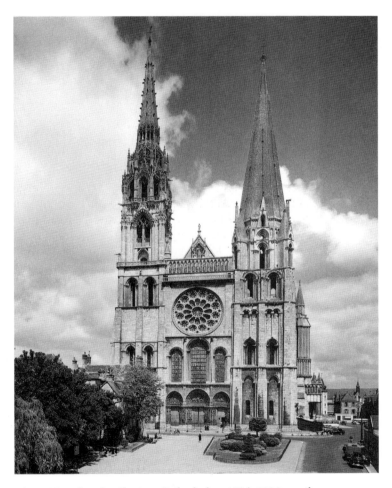

16-7. West facade, Chartres Cathedral. c. 1134–1220; south tower c. 1160; north tower 1507–13

tensions, the new cathedral emerged as a work of remarkable balance and harmony, inspiring even to nonbelievers.

From a distance the most striking features of the west facade are its prominent round **rose window** and two towers, (fig. 16-7). The spire on the north tower (left) was added in the early sixteenth century; the spire on the

16-8. Royal Portal, west facade, Chartres Cathedral. c. 1145–55

16-9. *Prophets and Ancestors of Christ*, right side, central
portal, Royal Portal, Chartres Cathedral. c. 1145–55

south tower dates from the twelfth century. On closer
inspection the facade's three doorways—the so-called
Royal Portal—capture the attention with their sculpture
(fig. 16-8). Christ Enthroned in Royal Majesty dominates
the central tympanum. Flanking the doorways are monumental **column statues**, a form that originated at Saint-
Denis. These column statues depict nineteen of the
twenty-two original Old Testament figures who were
seen as precursors of Christ (fig. 16-9). In other biblical
references the builders of Gothic cathedrals identified
themselves symbolically with Solomon, the builder of
the first Temple in Jerusalem, and the depiction of Old
Testament kings and queens evokes the close ties between the Church and the French royal house. Because
of this relationship, still potent after 600 years, most such
figures at other churches were smashed during the
French Revolution.

Earlier sculptors had achieved dramatic, dynamic
effects by compressing, elongating, and bending figures
to fit them into an architectural framework. At Chartres,
in contrast, the sculptors sought to pose their high-relief
figures naturally and comfortably in their architectural
settings. The erect, frontal column statues, with their
elongated proportions and vertical drapery, echo the
cylindrical shafts from which they emerge. Their heads
are finely rendered with idealized features.

Calm and order prevail in the imagery of the Royal
Portal, in contrast to the somewhat more crowded

16-10. *Saint Stephen* (right, c. 1210–20) and *Saint Theodore* (left, c. 1230–35), left side, left portal, south transept entrance, Chartres Cathedral

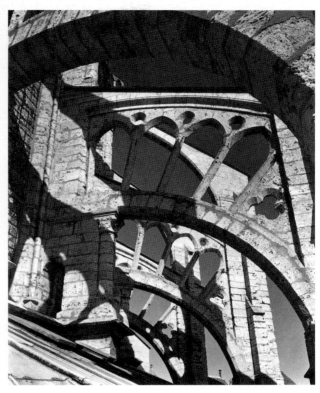

16-11. Flying buttresses, Chartres Cathedral. c. 1200–20

imagery at many Romanesque churches, such as those at Moissac (see fig. 15-9) and Autun (see fig. 15-12). Christ in the central tympanum of the Royal Portal appears imposing but more benign and less terrifying than in earlier representations. The Twelve Apostles in the lintel below him and the twenty-four elders in the archivolts above him have been arranged in a hierarchy of size and location, with little narrative interaction between them. Even in narrative scenes, calm prevails, as in the Ascension of Christ in the tympanum of the left doorway and the enthroned Virgin and Child in the tympanum of the right doorway.

Column statues became standard elements of Gothic church decoration, developing from shaftlike reliefs to fully three-dimensional figures that appear to interact with one another as well as with approaching worshipers. A comparison of the column statues of the Royal Portal with those of the later north and south transept portals illustrates this transition. Figure 16-10 shows two column statues from the south transept portal. *Saint Stephen*, on the right, was made between 1210 and 1220; *Saint Theodore*, on the left, between 1230 and 1235. More lifelike than their predecessors, they seem to stand on projecting bases with carved brackets. The bases reinforce the illusion that the figures are free of the architecture to which they are attached. In another change, the dense geometric patterning and stylized foliage around the earlier statues have given way to plain stone.

Saint Stephen, still somewhat cylindrical, is more naturally proportioned than the earlier figures on the west facade. The sculptor has also created a variety of textures to differentiate cloth, embroidery, flesh, and other features. The later *Saint Theodore* reflects its sculptor's attempt to depict a convincingly "alive" figure. The saint is dressed as a contemporary crusader and stands, purposeful but contemplative, with his feet firmly planted and his hips thrust to the side (a pose often called the Gothic **S**-curve). The meticulous detailing of his expressive face and the textures of his chain mail and surcoat help create a strong sense of physical presence.

Many nearby churches built by local masons about the same time as Chartres Cathedral reflect an earlier style and are relatively dark and squat. Unlike them, Chartres was the work of artisans from areas north and northeast of the town who were accomplished practitioners of the Gothic style. In the new cathedral they brought together the hallmark Gothic structural devices for the first time: the pointed arch, ribbed groin vaulting, the **flying buttress**, and the **triforium**, now designed as a mid-level passageway (see "Elements of Architecture," page 558). The flying buttress, a gracefully arched, skeletal exterior support, counters the outward thrust of the vaulting over the nave and aisles (fig. 16-11). The Gothic triforium (which was a flat wall in the basilica church or a gallery in Byzantine and Romanesque architecture) overlooks the nave through an arcaded screen

16-12. Nave, Chartres Cathedral. c. 1200–20

that contributes to the visual unity of the interior (fig. 16-12). Building on the concept pioneered at Saint-Denis of an elegant masonry shell enclosing a large open space, the masons at Chartres erected a structure with one of the widest naves in Europe and vaults that soar 118 feet above the floor. The enlarged sanctuary, another feature derived from Saint-Denis, occupies one-third of the building (fig. 16-13). Stained glass covers nearly half the clerestory surfaces. The large and luminous clerestory is filled by pairs of tall, arched windows called **lancets** surmounted by circular windows, or **oculi**. Whereas at a Romanesque pilgrimage church like Sainte-Foy (see fig. 15-4) the worshiper's gaze is drawn forward toward the apse, at Chartres it is drawn upward—to the clerestory windows and the soaring vaults overhead—as well as forward. Relatively little interior architectural decoration interrupts the visual rhythm of shafts and arches. Four-part vaulting has superseded more complex

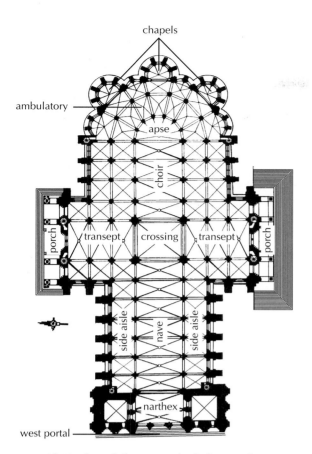

16-13. Plan of Chartres Cathedral. c. 1194–1220

16-14. *Tree of Jesse,* west facade, Chartres Cathedral.
c. 1150–70. Stained glass

systems such as that at Durham Cathedral (see fig. 15-26), and the alternating bays typical of Romanesque naves such as that at Speyer Cathedral (see fig. 15-32) have been eliminated.

At Chartres, architectural engineering went hand in hand with numerical symbolism. An equilateral triangle established the three points of the outer edges of the buttresses and the keystone of the vault in the nave. The addition of the Trinity (three) to the material world, four (the four directions, the four winds, the four seasons, the four rivers of paradise), forms the recurring number seven, the seven liberal arts, the seven gifts of the Holy Spirit. The Virgin, Notre-Dame, to whom the church is dedicated, is enthroned with Christ, who is surrounded by the Liberal Arts in the tympanum and voussoirs of the west portal. The imagery of Chartres, which stresses themes involving Mary and the Old Testament precursors of Christ, as well as the saints coming after the Incarnation, encompasses the entire program of Scholastic thought.

Chartres is unique among French Gothic buildings in that most of its stained-glass windows have survived. The light from these windows changes constantly as sunlight varies with the time of day, the seasons, and the movement of clouds. Stained glass is an expensive and difficult medium, but its effect on the senses and emotions makes the effort worthwhile (see "Stained-Glass Windows," page 559). Chartres was famous for its glass-making workshops, which by 1260 had installed about 22,000 square feet of stained glass in 176 windows. Most of the glass dates between about 1210 and 1250, but a few earlier panels, from around 1150 to 1170, were pre-

served in the west facade. The iconography of the windows echoes that of the portal sculpture.

Among the twelfth-century works in the west wall of the cathedral is the *Tree of Jesse* window (fig. 16-14). The monumental treatment of this Marian subject (relating to Mary), much more complex than its depiction in an early-twelfth-century Cistercian manuscript (see fig. 15-22), was apparently inspired by a similar window at Saint-Denis. The body of Jesse lies at the base of the tree, and in the branches above him appear, first, four kings of Judaea, Christ's royal ancestors, then the Virgin Mary, and finally Christ himself. Seven doves, the seven gifts of the Holy Spirit, encircle Christ, and fourteen prophets stand in the half-moons flanking the tree.

The glass in the *Tree of Jesse* is set within a rectilinear iron armature (visible as silhouetted black lines). In a

ELEMENTS OF ARCHITECTURE

The Gothic Church

Most large Gothic churches in western Europe were built on the **Latin–cross plan**, with a projecting **transept** marking the transition from **nave** to **sanctuary**. The main entrance **portal** was generally on the west, the **choir** and **apse** on the east. A **narthex** led to the nave and **side aisles**. An **ambulatory** with radiating chapels circled the apse and facilitated the movement of worshipers through the church. Above the nave were a **triforium** passageway and windowed **clerestory**. Narthex, side aisles, ambulatory, and nave usually had **rib vaults** in the Gothic period. Church walls were decorated inside and out with **arcades** of round and pointed arches, engaged **columns** and **colonnettes**, and horizontal moldings called **stringcourses**. The roof was supported by a wooden framework. A spire or **crossing** tower above the junction of the transept and nave was usually planned, though often never finished. The **apsidal chapels** ringing the apse were often visible on the exterior, as were the **buttress piers** and **flying buttresses** that countered the outward thrusts of the interior vaults. **Portal** facades were customarily marked by high, flanking towers or **gabled** porches ornamented with **pinnacles** and **finials**. Architectural sculpture covered each portal's **tympanum**, **archivolts**, and **jambs**. A magnificent stained-glass **rose window** typically formed the centerpiece of the portal facades. Stained glass filled the tall, pointed **lancets**.

Chartres Cathedral

TECHNIQUE

STAINED-GLASS WINDOWS

The basic technique for making colored glass has been known since the days of ancient Egypt. It involves the addition of metallic oxides—cobalt for blue, manganese for red and purple—to a basic formula of sand and ash or lime that is fused at high temperature. Such "stained" glass was used on a small scale in church windows during the Early Christian period and in Carolingian and Ottonian churches. Colored glass sometimes adorned Romanesque churches, but the art form reached a height of sophistication and popularity in the cathedrals and churches of the Gothic era.

Making a stained-glass image was a complex and costly process. A designer first drew a composition on a wood panel the same size as the opening of the window to be filled, noting the colors of each of the elements in it. Glass blowers produced sheets of colored glass, and then artisans cut individual pieces from these large sheets and laid them out on the wood template. Painters then added details with enamel emulsion, and the glass was reheated to fuse the enamel. Finally, the pieces were assembled and joined together with narrow lead strips, called **cames**. The assembled pieces were set into iron frames that had been preformed to fit the window opening.

The demand for stained-glass windows stimulated technical experimentation to achieve new colors and greater purity and transparency. The colors of Romanesque glass—mainly reds and blues with touches of dark green, brown, and orange yellow—were so deep that it was nearly opaque. The Cistercians adorned their churches with **grisaille** windows, painting foliage and crosses onto a gray glass. Early uncolored glass was full of impurities, but Gothic artisans developed a clearer material onto which they could draw elaborate narrative scenes. Many new colors were discovered accidentally, such as a sunny yellow produced by the addition of silver oxide. Flashing, in which a layer of one color was fused to a layer of another color, produced an almost infinite range of colors. Blue and yellow, for example, could be combined to make green. In the same way, clear glass could be fused to layers of colored glass in varying thicknesses to produce a range of hues from light to dark. The deep colors of early Gothic stained-glass windows give them a saturated and mysterious brilliance. The richness of some of these colors, particularly blue, has never been surpassed. Pale colors and large areas of grisaille glass became increasingly popular from the mid-thirteenth century on, making the windows of later Gothic churches bright and clear by comparison.

16-15. *Charlemagne Window*, ambulatory apse, Chartres Cathedral. c. 1210–36. Stained glass

This window depicts scenes from the *Song of Roland*, an epic based on events during the reign of Charlemagne; it acquired its final form sometime around 1100. The hero, Roland, was killed fighting Muslims in the Pyrenees Mountains, which lie between France and Spain. Roland is portrayed as an ideal feudal knight, devoted to his lord, his fellow knights, and his faith.

16-16. *Furrier's Shop*, detail of *Charlemagne Window*, Chartres Cathedral

This close-up shows how stained-glass artisans handled form and color. The figures have been reduced to simple shapes and their gestures kept broad to convey meaning from afar. The glass surfaces, however, are painted with fine lines that are invisible from the cathedral's floor. Forms stand out against a lustrous blue ground accented with red. Glowing clear glass serves as white, and violet-pink, green, and yellow complete the palette.

later work, the *Charlemagne Window*, the glass is set within an interlocking framework of medallions so that colored glass and **cames**, the lead strips that join the pieces of glass, work together to make the window imagery more decorative (fig. 16-15). The medallions contain narrative scenes, each surrounded by a field of stylized flowers, leaves, and geometric patterns. At the base of the *Charlemagne Window* is a scene of a customer buying a cloak in a furrier's shop (fig. 16-16). The furrier

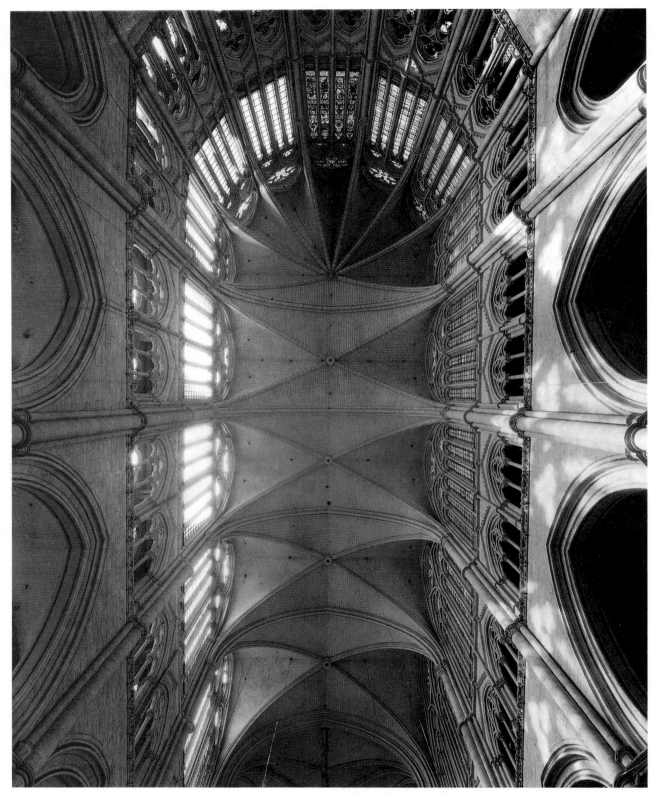

16-17. Vaults, sanctuary, Cathedral of Notre-Dame at Amiens, Île-de-France, France. 1270–88
The light entering the windows at the left illuminates the walls at the right.

displays a large cloak made of small pelts (perhaps rabbit or squirrel) taken from the chest at the right. The potential buyer has removed one glove and reaches out, perhaps to feel the fur, perhaps to bargain. This scene is one of several at Chartres showing various tradespeople at work. Others include bakers, wheelwrights, weavers, goldsmiths, and carpenters. Similar scenes appear in other Gothic churches. They were once thought to have reflected pious donations by local guilds, but recent scholarship suggests that this was not so. The merchants and artisans of Chartres had apparently not yet been permitted to form guilds in the early thirteenth century, and they contributed to the new cathedral only through the taxes assessed on them by Church officials. The vignettes of tradespeople might thus be a form of Church propaganda, images of an ideal world in which the Church was the center of society and the focus of everyone's work.

Amiens and Reims Cathedrals.

As it continued to evolve, Gothic taste favored increasingly sculptural, ornate facades and intricate window tracery. Builders across northern France refined the geometry of church plans and elevations and found ways to engineer ever stronger masonry skeletons with ever larger expanses of stained glass.

The Cathedral of Notre-Dame at Amiens, an important trading and textile-manufacturing center north of Paris, burned in 1218, and as at Chartres, church officials devoted their resources to making its replacement as splendid as possible. Their funding came mainly from the cathedral's rural estates and from important trade fairs. Construction began in 1220 and continued for some seventy years. The result is the supreme architectural statement of elegant Gothic verticality. The nave, only 48 feet wide, soars upward 144 feet. Not only is the nave exceptionally tall, its narrow proportions create an exaggerated sense of height (figs. 16-17, 16-19).

A labyrinth, now destroyed, recorded the names of the master builders at Amiens on the inlaid floor of the nave (see "Master Builders," page 563). This practice honored the mythical Greek hero Daedalus, master builder of the first labyrinth at the palace of King Minos in Crete. The labyrinth identifies Robert de Luzarches (d. 1236) as the builder who established the overall design for the Amiens Cathedral. He was succeeded by Thomas de Cormont, who was followed by his son Renaud. The lower portions of the church were probably substantially complete by around 1240.

The plan of the cathedral of Amiens derived from that of Chartres, with some simple but critical adjustments (fig. 16-18). The narthex was eliminated, while the transept and sanctuary were expanded and the crossing brought forward. The result is a plan that is balanced east and west around the crossing. The elevation of the nave is similarly balanced and compact (fig. 16-19). Chapels of the same size and shape enhance the clarity and regularity of the design. Tracery and **colonnettes** (small columns) unite the triforium and the clerestory, which makes up nearly half the height of the nave. Evenly spaced piers with engaged half columns topped by

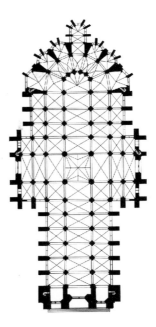

16-18. Robert de Luzarches, Thomas de Cormont, and Renaud de Cormont. Plan of Amiens Cathedral. 1220–88

16-19. Nave, Amiens Cathedral. 1220–88

foliage capitals support the arcades. An ornate floral stringcourse below the triforium level and a simpler one below the clerestory both run uninterrupted across the otherwise plain wall surfaces and colonnettes, providing a horizontal counterpoint. The vaulting and the light-filled choir date to the second phase of construction,

16-20. West facade, Amiens Cathedral. Begun c. 1220

16-21. *Virtues and Vices,* central portal, west entrance,
Amiens Cathedral. c. 1220–35

Quatrefoils appeared here as a framing device for the
first time and soon became one of the most widespread decorative motifs in Gothic art. In the top row
are the Virtues, personified as seated figures. Each
holds a shield with an animal on it that symbolizes a
particular virtue: the lion for Courage, the cow for
Patience, and the lamb for Meekness. Below the Virtues are figures that represent the Vices that correspond to each of the Virtues: a knight dropping his
sword and turning to run when a rabbit pops up
(Cowardice); a woman on the verge of plunging a
sword through a man (Discord); and a woman
delivering a swift kick to her servant (Impatience or
Injustice).

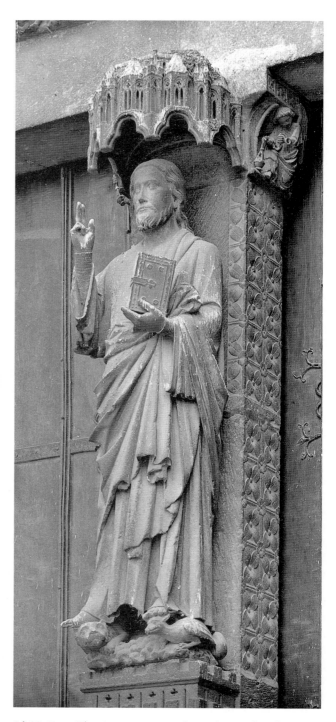

16-22. *Beau Dieu,* trumeau, central portal, west facade,
Amiens Cathedral. c. 1220–35

directed by Thomas de Cormont. The choir is illuminated by large windows subdivided by tracery into slender
lancets crowned by **trefoils** (three-lobed designs) and
circular windows.

The west front of Amiens reflects several stages of
construction (fig. 16-20). The lower levels, designed by
Robert de Luzarches, are the earliest, dating to between
1220 and about 1240, but building continued over the
centuries. The towers date to the fourteenth and fifteenth
centuries, and the tracery in the rose window is also late.
Consequently, the facade has a somewhat disjointed
appearance, and all its elements do not correspond to the

interior spaces behind them. Design begins to become detached from structural logic, an indication of the loosening of the traditional ties between architectural planning and the actual building process. This trend led to the elevation of architectural design—as opposed to structural engineering and construction—to a high status by the fifteenth century.

The sculptural program of the west portals of Amiens presents an almost overwhelming array of images in registers. The sculpture was produced rapidly by a large workshop in only about fifteen years (1220–c. 1235), making it stylistically more uniform than that of the cathedrals of Chartres or Reims. In the mid-thirteenth century Amiens-trained sculptors carried their style to other parts of Europe, especially Castile (Spain) and Italy.

Worshipers approaching the main entrance encountered figures of apostles and saints lined up along the door jambs and projecting buttresses, as were seen at Chartres. At Amiens something new captures the attention. On the base below the figures, at eye level, are **quatrefoils** (four-lobed medallions) containing relief sculpture illustrating Good and Evil in daily life (fig. 16-21), the seasons and labors of the months, the lives of the saints, and biblical stories. High above, in the tympanum

and archivolts of the central portal, the history of humanity ends in the Last Judgment. The left portal sculpture illustrates the life of Saint Firmin, an early bishop of Amiens and the town's patron saint; and those on the right portal are dedicated to Mary and her coronation as Queen of Heaven.

A sculpture of Christ as the *Beau Dieu* (noble, or beautiful, God), the kindly teacher-priest bestowing his blessing on the faithful (fig. 16-22), forms the **trumeau** of the central portal. This exceptionally fine sculpture may have been the work of the master of the Amiens workshop himself. The broad contours of the heavy drapery wrapped around Christ's right hip and bunched over his left arm lead the eye up to the gospel-book he holds and past it to his face, which is that of a young king. He stands on a lion and a dragonlike creature called a basilisk, which symbolizes his kingship and his triumph over evil and death. With its clear, solid forms, elegantly cascading robes, and interplay of close observation with idealization, the *Beau Dieu* embodies the Amiens style and the Gothic spirit.

In the Church hierarchy, the bishop of Amiens was subordinate to the archbishop of Reims. Politically the archbishop also had great power, for the French kings

---

MASTER BUILDERS "At the beginning of the fifth year [of the rebuilding of England's Canterbury Cathedral], suddenly by the collapse of beams beneath his feet, [master William of Sens] fell to the ground amid a shower of falling masonry and timber from . . . fifty feet or more. . . . On the master craftsman alone fell the wrath of God—or the machinations of the Devil" (Brother Gervase, Canterbury, twelfth century, cited in Andrews, page 20).

Master masons, "masters of the works," oversaw all aspects of church construction in the Middle Ages, from design and structural engineering to decoration. The job presented a formidable logistical challenge, especially at the great cathedral sites. The master mason at Chartres coordinated the work of roughly 400 people who were scattered, with their equipment and supplies, at many locations, from distant stone quarries to high scaffolding. This workforce set in place some 200 blocks a day. Master masons gained in prestige during the thirteenth century as they increasingly differentiated themselves from the laborers working under them. In the words of Nicolas de Biard, a thirteenth-century Dominican preacher,

"The master masons, holding measuring rod and gloves in their hands, say to others: 'Cut here,' and they do not work; nevertheless they receive the greater fees" (cited in Frisch, page 55). By the standards of their time they were well read; they traveled widely. They knew both aristocrats and high church officials, and they earned as much as knights. From the thirteenth century on, in what was then an exceptional honor, masters were buried, along with patrons and bishops, in the cathedrals they built. The tomb sculpture of a master mason named Hugues Libergier in the Reims Cathedral portrays him, attended by angels, as a well-dressed figure with his tools and a model of the cathedral. The names of more than 3,000 master masons are known today. In some cases their names were prominently inscribed in the labyrinths on cathedral floors.

The illustration here shows a master—right-angle and compass in hand—conferring with his royal patron while workers carve a capital, hoist stones with a winch, cut a block, level a course of masonry using a plumb, and lay dressed stones in place. Masters and their crews moved constantly from site to site, and several masters contributed to a single

building. A master's training was rigorous but not standardized, so close study of subtle differences in construction techniques can reveal the hand of specific individuals. Fewer than 100 master builders are estimated to have been responsible for all the major architectural projects in the Île-de-France during the century-long building boom there, some of them working on parts of as many as forty churches. Funding shortages and technical delays, such as the need to let mortar harden for three to six months, made construction sporadic.

Page with *King Henry III Supervising the Works*, copy of an illustration from a 13th-century English manuscript; original in The British Library, London

NOTRE-DAME OF PARIS

Think of Gothic architecture. Chances are, the image that springs to mind is the Cathedral of Notre-Dame of Paris. Just as this structure rivals the Eiffel Tower as the symbol of Paris itself, Notre-Dame is the vision of what a Gothic cathedral should look like. In fact, the Notre-Dame we see today began as an early Gothic building that bridged the period between Abbot Suger's rebuilding of the Abbey Church of Saint-Denis and the thirteenth-century Chartres Cathedral. On this site—a small island in the Seine River called the Île de la Cité, where the Parisii people who gave the city its name first settled — Pope Alexander III set the building cornerstone in 1163. Construction was far enough along for the altar to be consecrated twenty years later.

The nave, rising to 115 feet, dates to 1180–1200, the west facade to 1200–1250. By this time, massive walls and buttresses and six-part vaults, adopted from Norman Romanesque architecture, must have seemed very old-fashioned. All the portals have figural sculpture. Tympana on the west facade and the north portal are dedicated to Mary, Notre-Dame. After 1225 new masters modernized the building by reworking the clerestory into the large double lancet and rose windows we see today. Notre-Dame had the first true flying buttresses, although those seen at the right of the photograph, rising dramatically to support the high vault of the choir, result from later Gothic remodeling. (The 290-foot spire over the crossing is the work of the nineteenth-century architect Eugène-Emmanuel Viollet-le-Duc.)

Following centuries of use as a Christian church, French Revolutionaries defamed monuments associated with deposed French nobility, transforming the cathedral temporarily into a secular Temple of Reason from 1793 to 1795. Soon thereafter Notre-Dame returned to Christian use and Napoleon crowned himself emperor at its altar in 1804. In our century the liberation of Paris from the Nazis in August 1944 was celebrated in Notre-Dame. Today, boats filled with tourists circle the Île de la Cité and drift under the Pont Neuf and other bridges, past the flower market, secluded squares, and tree-lined courtyards, to approach the beautiful cathedral. Notre-Dame so resonates with life and history that it has become more than a house of worship and work of art; it is part of the shared culture of humankind.

Cathedral of Notre-Dame, Paris. Begun 1163. View from the south

were crowned in his cathedral, though they were buried at Saint-Denis. Reims, like Saint-Denis, had been a cultural and educational center since Carolingian times. As at Chartres and Amiens, the community at Reims, led by the clerics responsible for the building, began to erect a new cathedral after a fire destroyed an earlier church. And as at Chartres, the expense of the project sparked local opposition, with revolts in the 1230s twice driving the archbishop and canons into exile. Construction of the cathedrals of Chartres, Amiens, and Reims overlapped, and the artisans at each site borrowed ideas from and influenced each other.

Many believe the Cathedral of Notre-Dame at Reims to be the most beautiful of all Gothic cathedrals, sur-

16-23. West facade, Cathedral of Notre-Dame at Reims, Île-de-France, France. 1230s–1260; towers mid-15th century

The cathedral was restored in the sixteenth century and again in the nineteenth and twentieth centuries. During World War I it withstood bombardment by some 3,000 shells, an eloquent testimony to the skills of its builders. It was recently cleaned.

passing even Chartres. Its cornerstone was laid in 1211 and work continued on it throughout the century. Its master builders, their names recorded in the cathedral labyrinth, were Jean d'Orbais, Jean le Loup, Gaucher de Reims, and Bernard de Soissons.

The magnificent west facade at Reims was built from 1255 through 1260 (fig. 16-23). Its massive gabled portals project forward, rising higher than those at Amiens. Their soaring peaks, the center one reaching to the center of the rose window, help to unify the facade. Large windows fill the portal tympana, displacing the sculpture usually found there. The deep porches are encrusted with sculpture that reflects changes in plan, iconography, and sculpture workshops. In a departure from tradition, Mar-

ian rather than Christ-centered imagery prevails in the central portal, a reflection of the growing popularity of Mary's cult. The enormous rose window, the focal point of the facade, fills the entire clerestory level. The towers were later additions, as was the row of carved figures that runs from the base of one tower to the other above the rose window. This "gallery of kings" is the only strictly horizontal element of the facade. Its subject matter is appropriate for a coronation church.

Different workshops and individuals worked at Reims over a period of several decades. Further complicating matters, a number of sculpture have been moved from their original locations, creating sometimes abrupt stylistic shifts. A group of four figures on the right jamb of

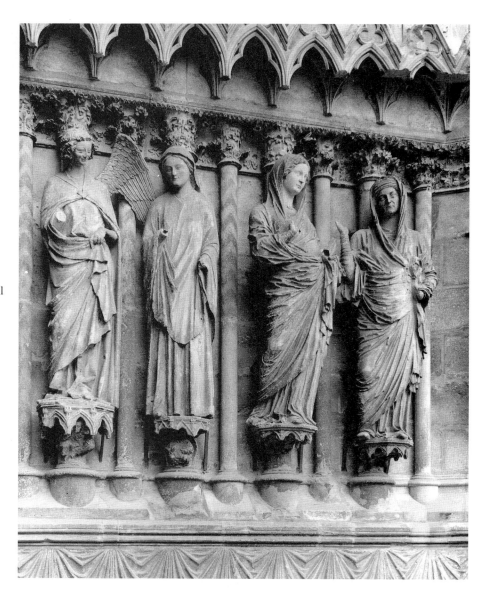

16-24. *Annunciation* (left pair: Mary c. 1245, angel c. 1255) and *Visitation* (right pair: c. 1230), right side, central portal, west facade, Reims Cathedral

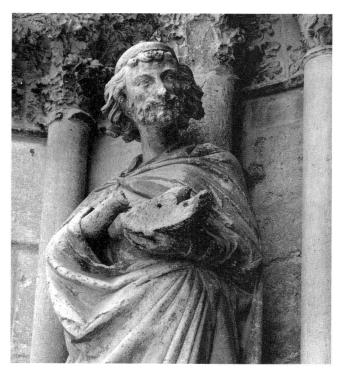

the central portal of the western front illustrates three of the Reims styles (fig. 16-24). The pair on the right is the work of the "Classical Shop," which was active beginning about 1230–1235, during the early years of construction at Reims. The subject of the pair is the Visitation, in which Mary (left), pregnant with Jesus, visits her older cousin, Elizabeth (right), who is pregnant with John the Baptist. The sculptors drew on classical sources, to which they had perhaps been exposed indirectly through earlier Mosan metalwork (see fig. 16-56) or directly in the form of local examples of ancient works (Reims had been an

16-25. *Saint Joseph*, left side, central portal, west facade, Reims Cathedral. c. 1255

On the column behind Joseph's head can be seen a "crescent moon" and four lines. These masons' marks, called setting marks, were used to position a piece of sculpture during installation. A crescent mark indicates the left side of the central doorway, and four lines indicate the fourth in a series. The work site for such an enormous project would have been filled with dressed and undressed stone blocks, sculptors carving slabs in various stages of completion, and work crews hauling and hoisting the finished pieces into place.

16-26. *Last Judgment* (tympanum), *Christ* (trumeau), *Apostles* (jambs), portal, north transept, Reims Cathedral. c. 1230

important Roman center). The heavy figures have the same solidity seen in Roman portrayals of noblewomen, and Mary's full face, gently waving hair, and heavy mantle recall imperial portrait statuary. The contrast between the features of the young Mary and the older Elizabeth is also reminiscent of the contrast between two Flavian portrait heads, one of a young woman and the other of a middle-aged woman (see figs. 6-43 and 6-44). The Reims sculptors used deftly modeled drapery not only to provide volumetric substance that stresses the theme of pregnancy but also to create a stance in which a weight shift with one bent knee allows the figures to seem to turn toward each other. The new freedom, movement, and sense of relationship implied in the sculpture inspired later Gothic artists toward ever greater realism.

The pair on the left of figure 16-24 illustrates the Annunciation; the archangel Gabriel (left) announces to Mary (right) that she will bear Jesus. The Mary in this pair, quiet and graceful, with a slender body, restrained gestures, and refined features, contrasts markedly with the bold tangibility of the Visitation Mary to the right. The drapery style and certain other details resemble those of Amiens, suggesting that those who made this pair—and much of the sculpture of the west entrance as well—may also have worked at Amiens.

The figure of the angel Gabriel illustrates yet a third style, the work of a sculptor known today as the Joseph Master or the Master of the Smiling Angels. This artist created tall, gracefully swaying figures that suggest the fashionable refinement associated with the Parisian court in the 1250s (see fig. 16-36). The facial features of Gabriel—and of Saint Joseph, on the opposite side of the doorway (fig. 16-25)—are typical; small, almost triangular head with a broad brow and pointed chin has short, wavy hair; long, puffy, almond-shaped eyes under arching brows; a well-shaped nose; and thin lips curving into a slight smile. Voluminous drapery arranged in elegant folds adds to the impression of aristocratic grace. These engaging figures were imitated from Paris to Prague, and their elegance and refinement became a guiding force in later Gothic sculpture and painting.

The north transept portal sculpture show more variety. A figure of Christ stands on the trumeau with his apostles on the jambs beside him (fig. 16-26). In the

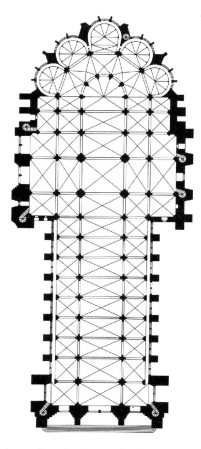

16-27. Plan of Reims Cathedral. 1211–60

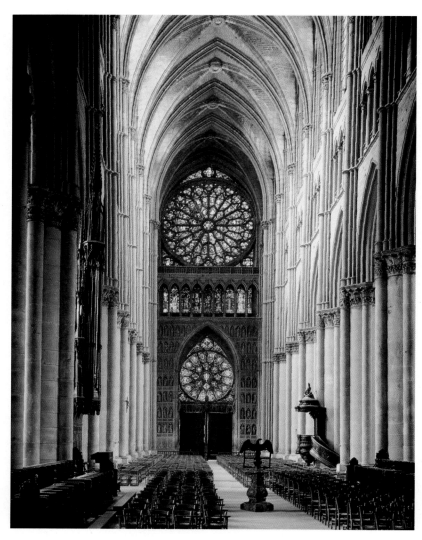

16-28. Nave, Reims Cathedral. 1211–60

tympanum, he appears again as judge in the Last Judgment. How different is this depiction of the Last Judgment from the Romanesque sculpture of Autun (see fig. 15-12). A hierarchy of scale still prevails, but Christ now seems less remote, less isolated from the figures around him. His bare, naturalistically rendered limbs emphasize his three-dimensional, physical presence. His mother and Saint John, as intercessors kneeling at his throne, indicate that he is an approachable, just judge. Humans, angels, and demons at Autun form an interlace of terror, but here at Reims they move in horizontal registers. Deep carving creates the impression of figures acting on a stage. Most of the figures at Autun are shown in profile view; those at Reims are shown from a variety of viewpoints, including some from the back, seated on the sarcophagi from which they arise to face judgment.

The architectural plan of Reims (fig. 16-27), like that of Amiens, was adapted from Chartres. The nave is longer in proportion to the choir, so the building lacks the perfect balance of Amiens. The three-part elevation and ribbed vault are familiar, too (fig. 16-28). The carvings on the capitals in the nave are notable for their variety, nat-

uralism, and quality. Unlike the idealized foliage of Amiens, the Reims carvings depict recognizable plants and figures. The remarkable sculpture and stained glass of the west wall complement the clerestory and choir. A great rose window in the clerestory, a row of lancets at the triforium level, and windows over the portals replace the stone of wall and tympana. Visually the wall "dissolves" in colored light. This great expanse of glass was made possible by **bar tracery**, a technique perfected at Reims, in which thin stone strips, called **mullions**, form a lacy matrix for the glass, replacing the older practice in which glass was inserted directly into window openings. Reims's wall of glass is anchored visually by a masonry screen around the doorway. Here ranks of carved Old Testament prophets and ancestors serve as moral guides for the newly crowned monarchs who faced them after coronation ceremonies.

The Sainte-Chapelle in Paris. In 1243 construction began on a new palace chapel to house Louis IX's prized collection of relics from Christ's Passion. The Sainte-Chapelle was finished in 1248, and soon thereafter Louis

16-29. Interior, upper chapel, the Sainte-Chapelle, Paris. 1243–48

Louis IX avidly collected relics of the Passion, some of which became available in the aftermath of the Crusaders' sack of Constantinople. Those that Louis acquired were supposedly the crown of thorns that had been placed on Jesus' head before the Crucifixion, a bit of the metal lance tip that pierced his side, the vinegar-soaked sponge offered to wet his lips, a nail used in the Crucifixion, and a fragment of the True Cross. The king is depicted in the Sainte-Chapelle's stained glass walking out barefoot to demonstrate his piety and humility when his treasures arrived in Paris.

departed for Egypt on the Seventh Crusade. This exquisite structure epitomizes a new Gothic style known as Rayonnant ("radiant" or "radiating" in French) because of its radiating bar tracery, like that at Reims, or Court style because of its association with Paris and the royal court. The hallmarks of the style include daring engineering, the proliferation of bar tracery, exquisite sculptural and painted detailing, and vast expanses of stained glass.

Originally part of the king's palace and administrative complex, the Sainte-Chapelle is located in the center of Paris. Intended to house precious relics, it resembles a giant reliquary itself, one made of stone and glass instead of gold and gems. It was built in two stories, with a ground-level chapel accessible from a courtyard and a private upper chapel entered from the royal residence. The ground-level chapel has narrow side aisles, but the upper level is a single room with a western porch and a rounded east wall. Climbing up the narrow spiral stairs from the lower to the upper level is like emerging into a kaleidoscopic jewel box (fig. 16-29). The ratio of glass to stone is higher here than in any other Gothic structure, for the walls have been reduced to clusters of slender painted colonnettes framing tall windows filled with brilliant color. Bar tracery in the windows is echoed in the blind arcading and tracery of the **dado**, the decoration on the lower walls at floor level. The dado's surfaces are richly patterned in red, blue, and gilt so that stone and glass seem to merge in the multicol-ored light. Painted statues of the Twelve Apostles stand between window sections, linking the dado and the stained glass. The windows contain narrative and symbolic scenes. Those in the curve of the sanctuary behind the altar and relics, for example, illustrate the Nativity and Passion of Christ, the Tree of Jesse, and the life of Saint John the Baptist. The story of Louis's acquisition of his relics is told in one of the bays, and the Last Judgment appeared in the original rose window on the west.

Later Gothic Architecture. Beginning in the late thirteenth century France began to suffer from overpopulation and economic decline, followed in the fourteenth century by the devastation of the Hundred Years' War and the plague (see "The Black Death," page 607). Large-scale construction gradually ceased, ending the great age of cathedral building. The Gothic style continued to

16-30. West facade, Church of Saint-Maclou, Rouen,
Normandy, France. 1436–1521

develop, however, in smaller churches, municipal and commercial buildings, and private residences. Many of these later buildings were covered with elaborate decoration in the new Flamboyant ("flaming" in French) style, named for the repeated flamelike patterns of its tracery. Flamboyant may have reflected an English architectural style known as Decorated (see fig. 16-42). New window tracery was added to many earlier churches in this period, as at Amiens (see fig. 16-20), and a Flamboyant north spire, built between 1507 and 1513, was even added to the west facade of Chartres (see fig. 16-7).

In the new style, decoration sometimes seems divorced from structure. Load-bearing walls and buttresses often have stone overlays, and traceried pinnacles, gables, and **S**-curve moldings combined with a profusion of geometric and natural ornament to dizzying effect. According to one architectural historian, the style reflects "an almost pathological dread of clarity. Ambiguity is endlessly pursued, and whereas all the elements were once integrated logically and lucidly, they are now dissolved in the shimmering air" (James, page 137).

The facade of the Church of Saint-Maclou in Rouen, begun in 1436, is an outstanding example of the new style (fig. 16-30). The projecting porch bends at the sides to enfold the facade of the church, disguising it behind a screen of openwork tracery. Sunlight on the flame-shaped openings and **crockets**—the small knoblike ornaments in the form of plants that line the steep gables and slender buttresses—casts flickering, changing shadows across the busy, intentionally complex surface.

16-31. Main facade, house of Jacques Coeur, Bourges,
France. 1443–51

Illuminated manuscripts, such as that of Christine de Pisan (see fig. 20), give some indication of the interior richness of a palace or town house owned by a wealthy family. The architecture was often painted and the walls were hung with rich and colorful tapestries. Furnishings were also covered with tapestry and embroideries. Glass windows might be enriched with stained-glass inserts illustrating coats of arms.

Secular architecture and arts flourished. The house of merchant Jacques Coeur in Bourges, in central France, built at great expense between 1443 and 1451, reflects the popularity of the Flamboyant style for secular architecture (fig. 16-31). The main facade hides a rambling structure with many rooms of varying sizes on different levels—all

16-32. *Virgin and Child*, from the Abbey Church of Saint-Denis. c. 1339. Silver gilt and enamel, height 27⅛" (69 cm). Musée du Louvre, Paris

arranged around an open courtyard. The highest roof section covers a private chapel, and the octagonal tower, with its Flamboyant filigree crown, lights a staircase. Flamboyant detailing—the large arched window over the main entrance, the cornice balustrades and window panels, and the gable crockets—punctuates the front of the house. Among the carved decorations are puns on the patron's surname, Coeur ("heart" in French), and half-length portraits of Jacques Coeur and his wife lean from niches in the main facade to watch approaching visitors.

Independent Sculpture

Gothic sculptors found a lucrative new outlet for their work in the growing demand among wealthy patrons for small religious statues intended for homes and personal chapels or as donations to favorite churches. Busy urban workshops produced large quantities of statuettes and reliefs in wood, ivory, and precious metals, often decorated with enamel and gemstones. Much of this art was related to the cult of the Virgin Mary.

An excellent example of such works, among the treasures of the Abbey Church of Saint-Denis, is a silver-gilt image, slightly over 2 feet tall, of a standing Virgin and Child (fig. 16-32). An inscription on the base bears the date 1339 and the name of Queen Jeanne d'Evreux, wife of Charles IV of France (ruled 1322–1328). The Virgin holds her son in her left arm, her weight on her left leg, creating the graceful **S**-curve pose that was a stylistic signature of the period. Fluid drapery with the consistency of heavy silk covers her body. She holds a scepter topped with a large enameled and jeweled fleur-de-lis,

16-33. Lid of a jewelry casket, called *Attack on the Castle of Love*, from Paris. c. 1330–50. Ivory casket with iron mounts, panel 4¹/₂ x 9¹¹/₁₆" (11.5 x 24.6 cm). Walters Art Gallery, Baltimore

the heraldic symbol of French royalty, and she originally had a crown on her head. The scepter served as a reliquary for hairs said to be from Mary's head. Despite this figure's clear association with royalty, Mary's simple clothing and sweet, youthful face anticipate a type of imagery that emerged in the later fourteenth and fifteenth centuries in northern France, Flanders, and Germany: the ideally beautiful mother. The Christ Child, clutching an apple in one hand and reaching with the other to touch his mother's lips, is more babylike in his proportions and gestures than in earlier depictions. Still, prophets and scenes of Christ's Passion in enamel cover the statue's simple rectangular base, a reminder of the suffering to come.

In addition to devotional or moralizing subjects, there was also a strong market for objects with secular subjects taken from popular literature. Themes drawn from the realm of courtly love (see "Courtly Love," page 549) decorated women's jewelry boxes, combs, and mirror cases. A casket for jewelry made in a Paris workshop around 1330–1350 provides a delightful example of such a work (fig. 16-33). Its ivory panels depict scenes of love, including vignettes from the King Arthur legend. The central sections of the lid shown here depict a tournament. Such mock battles, designed to keep knights fit for war, had become one of the chief royal and aristocratic entertainments of the day. In the scene on the lid, women of the court, accompanied by their hunting falcons, watch with great interest as two jousting knights, visors down and lances set, charge to the blare of trumpets played by young boys. In the scene on the left, ardent knights assault the Castle of Love, firing roses from crossbows and a catapult. Love, in the form of a winged boy, aids the women defenders, aiming a giant "Cupid's arrow" at the attackers. The action concludes in the scene on the right,

where the tournament's victor and his lady-love meet in a playful joust of their own.

Book Arts

France gained renown in the thirteenth and fourteenth centuries not only for its new architectural style but also for its book arts. These works ranged from practical manuals for artisans to elaborate devotional works illustrated with exquisite miniatures.

Lodge books were an important tool of the master mason and his workshop, or lodge. Compiled by heads of workshops, lodge books provided visual instruction and inspiration for apprentices and assistants. Since the drawings received hard use, few have survived. One of the most famous architect's collections is the early-thirteenth-century sketchbook of Villard de Honnecourt, a well-traveled master mason who recorded a variety of images and architectural techniques. A section labeled "help in drawing figures according to the lessons taught by the art of geometry" (fig. 16-34) illustrates the use of geometric shapes to form images and how to copy and enlarge images by superimposing geometric shapes over them as guides.

The production of high-quality manuscripts flourished in Paris during the reign of Louis IX, whose royal library was renowned. Queen Blanche of Castile, Louis's mother and granddaughter of Eleanor of Aquitaine, served as regent of France (1226–1234) until he came of age. She and the teenage king appear on the dedication page (fig. 16-35) of a Moralized Bible—one in which selected passages of the Old and New Testaments are paired to give an allegorical, or moralized, interpretation. The royal pair sit against a solid gold background under trilobed arches. Below them a scholar-monk dictates to

16-34. Villard de Honnecourt. Page from a sketchbook, with geometric figures and ornaments, from Paris. 1220–35. Ink on vellum, 9¼ x 6" (23.5 x 15.2 cm). Bibliothèque Nationale, Paris

a scribe. The ornate thrones of Louis and his mother and the buildings arranged atop the arches suggest that the figures are inside a royal palace, and in fact it would not have been unusual for the queen to have housed scholar, scribe, and illuminator while they were executing her commission during her regency. Interestingly, only the slightly oversized heads of the queen and king preserve a sense of hierarchical scale. The scribe, in the lower right, is working on a page with a column of roundels for illustrations. This format of manuscript illustration—used on the pages that follow the Bible's dedication page—derives from stained-glass lancets, with their columns of images in medallions (see fig. 16-29). The illuminators also show their debt to stained glass in their use of glowing red and blue and reflective gold surfaces.

The *Psalter of Saint Louis* (the king was canonized in 1297) defines the Court style in manuscript illumination. The book, containing seventy-eight full-page illuminations, was created for Louis IX's private devotions sometime between 1253 and 1270. The illustrations fall at the

16-35. Page with *Louis IX and Queen Blanche of Castile*, Moralized Bible, from Paris. 1226–34. Ink, tempera, and gold leaf on vellum, 15 x 10½" (38 x 26.6 cm). The Pierpont Morgan Library, New York

M.240, f.8

Thin sheets of gold leaf were painstakingly attached to the vellum and then polished to a high sheen with a tool called a burnisher. Gold was applied to paintings before pigments.

back of the book, preceded by Psalms and other readings unrelated to them. Intricate scrolled borders and a background of Rayonnant architectural features modeled on the Sainte-Chapelle frame the narratives. Figures are rendered in an elongated, linear style. One page (fig. 16-36) illustrates two scenes from the Old Testament story of Abraham, Sarah, and the Three Strangers (Genesis 18). On the left, Abraham greets God, who has appeared to him as three strangers, and invites him to rest. On the right, he offers the men a meal that his wife, Sarah, standing in the doorway of their tent on the far right, has prepared. God says that Sarah will soon bear a child, and she laughs because she and Abraham are old. But God replies, "Is anything too marvelous for the Lord to do?" (18:14). She later gives birth to Isaac, whose name comes from the Hebrew word for "laughter." Christians in the Middle Ages viewed the three strangers in this story as symbols of the Trinity and believed that God's promise to Sarah was a precursor of the Annunciation to Mary.

The architectural background in this painting establishes a narrow stage space in which the story unfolds. Wavy clouds float within the arches under the gables. The imaginatively rendered oak tree establishes the location of the story and separates the two scenes. The gesture of the central haloed figure in the scene on the right and Sarah's presence in the doorway of the tent indicate that we are viewing the moment of divine promise. This new spatial sense, as well as the depiction of oak leaves and acorns, reflects a tentative move toward the representation of the natural world that will gain momentum in the following centuries.

Beginning in the late thirteenth century, more and more laypersons were literate. Private prayer books became popular among those who could afford them. Because such books contained special prayers to be recited at the eight canonical "hours" between morning and night, these books came to be called Books of Hours. The material in them was excerpted from a larger liturgical book called a breviary, which contained all the canonical offices (Psalms, readings, and prayers) used by priests in celebrating Mass. Books of Hours were most commonly devoted to the Virgin, but they could be personalized for particular patrons with prayers to other saints, a calendar of saints' feast days and other Church events, and perhaps other offices, such as that said for the dead. During the fourteenth century a richly decorated Book of Hours, like jewelry, would have been among a noble person's most important portable possessions.

A tiny, exquisite Book of Hours given by Charles IV to his queen, Jeanne d'Evreux, shortly after their marriage in 1325 is the work of an illuminator named Jean Pucelle (fig. 16-37). Instead of the intense colors used by earlier illuminators, Pucelle worked in a technique called **grisaille**—monochromatic painting in shades of gray with faint touches of color (see also "Stained-Glass Windows," page 559)—that emphasized his accomplished drawing. The book combines two narrative cycles. One, the Hours of the Virgin, juxtaposes scenes from the Infancy and Passion of Christ, a form known as the Joys and Sorrows of the Virgin. The other is a collection of scenes from the

16-36. Page with *Abraham, Sarah, and the Three Strangers, Psalter of Saint Louis,* from Paris. 1253–70. Ink, tempera, and gold leaf on vellum, 5 x 3½" (13.6 x 8.7 cm). Bibliothèque Nationale, Paris

The Court style had enormous influence throughout northern Europe, spread by illuminators who flocked to Paris from other regions. There they joined workshops affiliated with the Confrérie de Saint-Jean (Guild of Saint John), supervised by university officials who controlled the production and distribution of manuscripts.

life of Saint Louis (King Louis IX), whose new cult was understandably popular at court. In the pages shown here the "Joy" of the *Annunciation* on the right is paired with the "Sorrow" of the *Betrayal and Arrest of Christ* on the left. Queen Jeanne appears in the initial below the *Annunciation,* kneeling before a lectern and reading from her Book of Hours. This inclusion of the patron in prayer within a scene, a practice that continued in monumental painting and sculpture in the fifteenth century, conveyed the idea that the scenes were "visions" inspired by meditation rather than records of historical events. In this particular case, the young queen would presumably have identified with Mary's joy at Gabriel's message.

In the *Annunciation* Mary is shown receiving the archangel Gabriel in her Gothic style home as rejoicing angels look on from windows under the eaves. The group of romping children at the bottom of the page (known as the *bas-de-page* in French) at first glance seems to echo the joy of the angels. Scholars have determined, however, that the children are playing "froggy in the middle," a game in which one child was tagged by the others (a

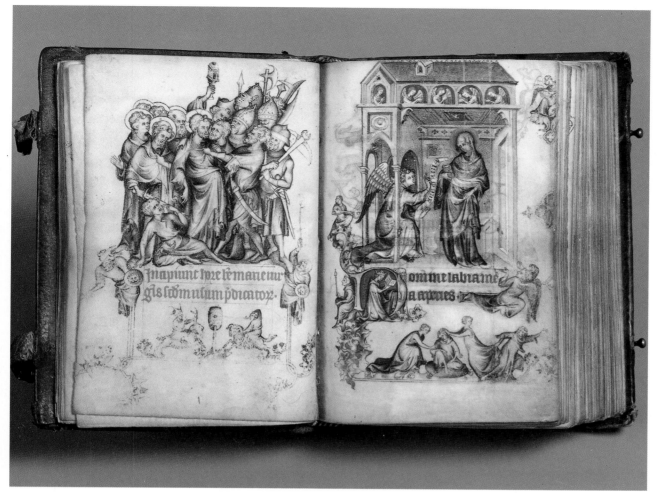

16-37. Jean Pucelle. Pages with *Betrayal and Arrest of Christ*, folio 15v. (left) and *Annunciation*, folio 16r. (right), *Petites Heures of Jeanne d'Evreux*, from Paris. c. 1325–28. Grisaille and color on vellum, each page 3½ x 2¼" (8.2 cm x 5.6 cm). The Metropolitan Museum of Art, New York

The Cloisters Collection, 1954 (54.1.2)

This book was precious to the queen, who mentioned it in her will; she named its illuminator, an unusual tribute.

symbolic reference to the Mocking of Christ). The game thus evokes a darker mood, foreshadowing Jesus' death even as his life is beginning. In the Betrayal scene on the left page, the disciple Judas Iscariot embraces Jesus, thus identifying him to the soldiers who have come to seize him and setting in motion the events that lead to the Crucifixion. Peter, on the left, realizing the danger, draws his sword to defend Jesus and slices off the ear of one of the soldiers. The *bas-de-page* on this side shows "knights" riding goats and jousting at a barrel stuck on a pole, a spoof of military training that is perhaps a comment on the valor of the soldiers assaulting Jesus.

Pucelle's work represents a sophisticated synthesis of French, English, and Italian painting traditions. From English illuminators he borrowed the merging of Christian narrative with allegory, the use of foliate borders filled with real and grotesque creatures (instead of the standard French vine scrolls), and his lively *bas-de-page* illustrations. His presentation of space, with figures placed within coherent architectural settings, apparently reflects his firsthand knowledge of developments in painting in Siena, Italy (for a slightly later example see

fig. 16-73). Pucelle also adapted to manuscript illumination the Parisian Court style in sculpture, with its softly modeled, voluminous draperies gathered around tall, elegantly curved figures with curly hair and broad foreheads. For instance, Jesus on the left page in figure 16-37 and Mary on the right stand in the swaying, **S**-curve pose typical of Court style works in other mediums, such as the Virgin and Child from Saint-Denis (see fig. 16-32). Similarly, the earnest face of the Annunciation archangel resembles that of the smiling Annunciation archangel at Reims (see fig. 16-24).

The thirteenth and fourteenth centuries saw the growing use of book margins for fresh and unusual images. Often drawn by illustrators who specialized in this kind of work, marginal imagery was a world of its own, interacting in unexpected ways with the main images and text, and often deliberately obscure or ambiguous. Visual puns on the main image or text abound. There are also humorous corrections of scribes' errors, pictures of hybrid monsters, erotic and scatological scenes, and charming depictions of ordinary activities and folklore that may or may not have functioned as

16-38. Page with *Fox Seizing a Rooster, Petites Heures of Jeanne d'Evreux.* The Metropolitan Museum of Art, New York
The Cloisters Collection, 1954 (54.1.2 f. 46)

"The Fox," according to a medieval bestiary, "never runs straight but goes on his way with tortuous windings. He is a fraudulent and ingenious animal. When he is hungry and nothing turns up for him to devour, he rolls himself in red mud so that he looks as if he were stained with blood. Then he throws himself on the ground and holds his breath. The birds, seeing that he is not breathing, think he is dead and come down to sit on him. As you can guess, he grabs them and gobbles them up. The Devil has this same nature" (cited in Schrader, page 24). Bestiaries, an English specialty, were popular compilations of animal lore that were sometimes, as here, made into Christian moral tales. Some of these fables or their characterizations survive in twentieth-century folklore, such as this familiar view of the fox as a cunning trickster.

ironic commentaries on what was going on elsewhere on the page. In addition to the *bas-de-page* scenes, the *Petites Heures of Jeanne d'Evreux* contains other minute but vivid marginalia, such as a fox capturing a rooster (fig. 16-38).

ENGLAND

The Plantagenet dynasty, founded by Henry II and Eleanor of Aquitaine in 1154, ruled England until 1485. Under Plantagenet rule, the thirteenth century was marked by conflicts between the Crown and England's feudal barons over their respective rights and the king's demands for funds. In 1215 King John, under compulsion from powerful barons, set his seal to the draft of the Magna Carta (Latin for "Great Charter"), which laid out feudal rights and dues and became an important document in the eventual development of British common law. The thirteenth century also saw the annexation of the western territory of Wales and the settlement of long-standing border disputes with Scotland. In the mid-fourteenth century the Black Death ravaged England as it did the rest of Europe. During the Hundred Years' War (1337–1453), English kings claimed the French throne and by 1429 controlled most of France, but after a number of reversals they were driven from all their holdings in France except Calais.

Late medieval England was characterized by rural villages and bustling market towns, all dominated by the great city of London. England's two universities, Oxford and Cambridge, were both founded by the thirteenth century. The Gothic period was marked by a reassertion of English cultural identity following the imposition of Norman French culture in 1066. A rich store of Middle English literature survives, including the brilliant social commentary of the *Canterbury Tales,* by Geoffrey Chaucer (c. 1342–1400). Many of the Plantagenet kings, especially Henry III, were great patrons of the arts.

Church Architecture

Gothic architecture in England was strongly influenced by Cistercian and Norman Romanesque architecture as well as by French master builders like William of Sens, who directed the rebuilding of Canterbury Cathedral between 1174 and 1178 (see "Master Builders," page 563). English cathedral builders were less concerned with height than their French counterparts, and they constructed long, broad naves, Romanesque-type galleries, and clerestory-level passageways. Walls retained a Romanesque solidity.

Salisbury Cathedral, because it was built in a relatively short period of time, has a consistency of style that makes it an ideal representative of English Gothic architecture (fig. 16-39). The cathedral was begun in 1220 and nearly finished by 1258, an unusually short period for such an undertaking. The west facade was completed by 1265. The huge crossing tower and its 400-foot spire are fourteenth-century additions, as are the flying buttresses that were added to stabilize the tower. Typically English is the parklike setting (the cathedral close) and attached cloister and chapter house for the cathedral clergy. The thirteenth-century structure hugged the earth, more akin to Fontenay, built more than a century earlier, than to the contemporary Amiens Cathedral in France.

In contrast to French cathedral facades, which suggest the entrance to paradise with their mighty towers flanking deep portals, English facades like the one at Salisbury suggest the jeweled wall of paradise itself. The small flanking towers of the west front project beyond the side walls and buttresses, giving the facade an increased width that was underscored by tier upon tier of blind tracery and arcaded niches. Lancet windows grouped in twos, threes, and fives introduce an element of vertical counterpoint.

Typical of English cathedrals, Salisbury has double projecting transepts, a square apse, and a spacious sanctuary (fig. 16-40). The interior reflects enduring Norman traditions, with its heavy walls and tall nave arcade surmounted by a short gallery and a clerestory with simple lancet windows (fig. 16-41). The emphasis on horizontal movement of the arcades, unbroken by colonnettes in the unusually restrained nave, directs worshipers' attention forward to the altar, rather than upward into the vaults. Reminiscent of Romanesque interiors is the use of color in the stonework: the shafts supporting the four-part rib vaults are made of a darker stone that contrasts with the lighter stone of the rest of the interior. The stonework was originally painted and gilded as well as carved.

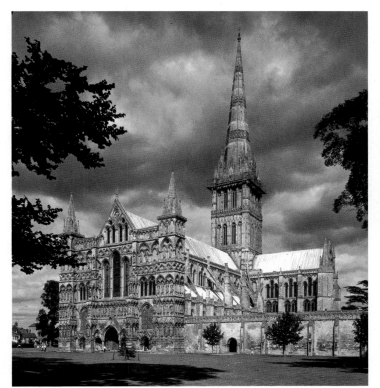

16-39. West facade, Salisbury Cathedral, Salisbury, Wiltshire, England. 1220–58; west facade 1265; spire c. 1320–30

The original cathedral had been built within the hilltop castle complex of a Norman lord. In 1217 Bishop Richard Poore petitioned the pope to relocate the church, claiming the wind howled so loudly there that the clergy could not hear themselves say Mass. A more pressing concern was probably his desire to escape the lord's control; Pope Innocent III (papacy 1198–1216) had only recently lifted a six-year ban on church services throughout England and Wales after King John (ruled 1199–1216) agreed to acknowledge the Church's sovereignty. The town of Salisbury (from the Saxon *Searisbyrig,* meaning "Caesar's burg," or town) was laid out, by the bishop himself, after the cathedral was under way. Material carted down from the old church was used in the cathedral, along with dark, fossil-silted Purbeck stone from quarries in southern England and stone from Caen. The building was abandoned and vandalized during the Protestant Reformation in England initiated by King Henry VIII (ruled 1509– 1547). In the eighteenth century the English architect James Wyatt, called the Destroyer, subjected it to radical renovations, during which the remaining stained glass and figure sculpture were removed or rearranged. Similar campaigns to refurbish medieval churches were common at the time. The motives of the restorers were complex and their results far from our late-twentieth-century notions of historical authenticity. The French architect Eugène-Emmanuel Viollet-le-Duc, the best known of these restorers, redefined the appearance of many of France's greatest twelfth- and thirteenth-century churches in the nineteenth century.

16-40. Plan of Salisbury Cathedral

16-41. Nave, Salisbury Cathedral

16-42. Sanctuary, Exeter Cathedral, Exeter, Devon, England. c. 1270–1366

The Gothiic choir stalls and bishop's throne illustrate the skill of the English woodcarvers and carpenters. Exeter has some of the finest still-surviving medieval furniture.

16-43. William Orchard. First Quadrangle, Magdalen College, Oxford, Oxfordshire, England. c. 1475–1500

Surviving account books reveal how much Orchard was paid for his work. For each of twenty-two cloister windows and buttresses, for example, he received 48 shillings 4 pence. In an early indication of intercollegiate rivalry, the windows were praised for being "as good as those of All Souls or better." As a final reward, the officials of Magdalen gave Orchard a lifetime lease on some college-owned land for an annual rent of one red rose, to be paid on the Feast of Saint John the Baptist.

Just as the Rayonnant style was emerging in France at mid-century, English designers were developing a new Gothic style of their own that has come to be known as the Decorated style (a nineteenth-century term). This change in taste has been credited to King Henry III's ambition to surpass his brother-in-law, Louis IX of France, as a royal patron of the arts.

A splendid example of this new style outside London is Exeter Cathedral, in southwest England. After the Norman Conquest in 1066, a Norman church replaced an earlier structure, and it, in turn, was rebuilt beginning about 1270. When the cathedral was redesigned and vaulted in the first half of the fourteenth century, its interior was turned into a dazzling stone forest of arch moldings and vault ribs (fig. 16-42). From diamond-shaped piers (partly hidden by Gothic choir stalls in the illustration), covered with colonnettes, rise massed moldings that make the arcade seem to ripple. Bundled colonnettes spring from ornate **corbels** between the arches to support conical clusters of thirteen ribs that meet at the summit of the vault, a modest 69 feet above the floor. The basic structure here is the four-part vault with intersecting cross-ribs, but the designer added purely decorative ribs, called **tiercerons**, between the supporting ribs to create a richer linear pattern. Elaborately carved knobs known as **bosses** punctuate the intersections where ribs meet. Large clerestory lancets with bar-tracery mullions illuminate the 300-foot-long nave. Unpolished gray marble shafts, yellow sandstone arches, and a white French stone used in the upper walls add color to the many-rayed space.

Secular Architecture

Although Gothic architectural style is most studied in cathedrals and other church buildings, it also is seen in such secular structures as castles, which during the turbulent Middle Ages were necessary fortress-residences. Castles evolved during the Romanesque and Gothic periods from enclosed and fortified strongholds to elaborate defended residential complexes from which aristocrats ruled their domains. Usually sited on a promontory or similar defensive height, British castles had many elements in common with continental ones (see "Elements of Architecture," opposite).

The final period of English Gothic architecture produced the Perpendicular style, another nineteenth-century term, derived from its characteristic tall, rectilinear decorative elements. The style originated in court-sponsored projects in London at the end of the thirteenth century and was close to the earlier French Rayonnant style in its emphasis on verticality and large areas of glass. As London-trained architects took commissions for work elsewhere, the style spread. Easily adapted by provincial stonemasons, the Perpendicular style appeared across England in parish churches, houses, civic buildings, and the halls, libraries, and residential colleges being added to English universities.

Magdalen College at Oxford (pronounced "maudlin" from the Middle English spelling, *Maudeleyne*) is the late-

ELEMENTS OF ARCHITECTURE

The Gothic Castle

A typical Gothic castle was a defensible, enclosed combination of fortifications and living quarters for the lord and his family and those defending them. It was built on raised ground and sometimes included a **moat** (ditch), filled with water and crossed by a bridge; **ramparts** (heavy walls), which were freestanding or built against earth embankments; **parapets**, into which towers were set; a **keep**, or **donjon**, a tower that was the most secure place within the compound; and a great hall that was where the rulers and their closest associates lived. The **bailey**, a large open courtyard in the center, contained wooden structures such as living quarters and stables, as well as a stone chapel. The castle complex was defended by a wooden **stockade**, or fence, outside the moat; inside the stockade lay **lists**, areas where knightly combats were staged. The main entrance was approached by a wide **bridge**, which passed through moat gateways called **barbicans**, ending in a **drawbridge** and then an iron **portcullis**, a grating set into the doorway. Elsewhere, small doors called **posterns** provided secret access for the castle's inhabitants. Ramparts and walls were topped by stone **battlements** designed to screen defenders standing on **parapet walks** while allowing them to repel attacks through notched **crenellations**. There were covered parapet walks, as well as miniature towers called **turrets**, along the more secure perimeter walls of the castle.

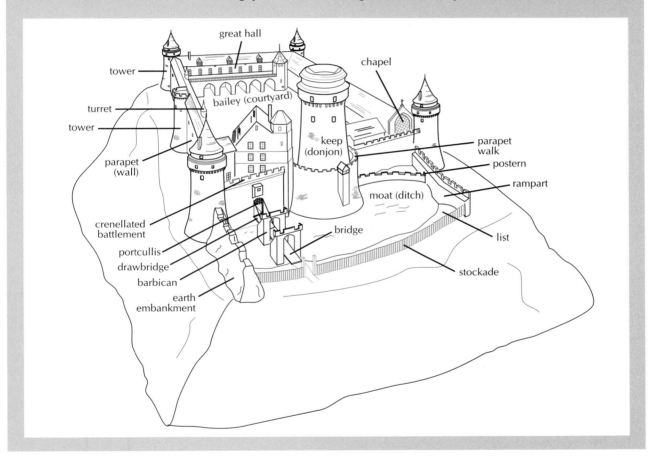

fifteenth-century work (c. 1475–1500) of a local mason, William Orchard. Laid out in an orderly way around a quadrangular courtyard similar to a monastic cloister, it has been called the ideal college, a sober and dignified setting for a life of the mind (fig. 16-43). The facades of the structures on the quadrangle exhibit a Perpendicular grid design, with the vertical lines of the arcade piers and the pinnacles rising from them intersecting the horizontal lines of the projecting stringcourses on the wall buttresses. The **crenellated** roofline—a purely decorative reference to castle battlements—completes the "perpendicular" theme.

Window and arcade openings are either rectangular or nearly so. Orchard's college is a grander version of a fortified aristocratic manor house, with a monumental gatehouse at the right and a great hall and chapel combined in the wing at the left. The turreted, crenellated tower and gatehouse serve no protective purpose but act instead as symbols of collegiate authority. The living quarters for students were built behind and above the covered walkways. A typical college apartment, or "set," accommodated four students in small individual bedrooms arranged around a common living and study room.

16-44. Page with *Psalm 1 (Beatus Vir)*, *Windmill Psalter*, from London. c. 1270–80. Ink pigments and gold on vellum, each page 12¾ x 8¾" (32.3 x 22.2 cm). The Pierpont Morgan Library, New York
M.102, f. lv-2

Book Arts

In France book production had become centralized in the professional **scriptoria** of Paris, and its main patrons were the universities and the court. In thirteenth-century England, by contrast, the traditional centers of production—far-flung rural monasteries that had produced such twelfth-century work as the beautiful *Winchester Psalter* (see fig. 15-29)—continued to dominate the book arts. Toward the close of the thirteenth century, however, secular workshops became increasingly active, reflecting a demand for books from newly literate landowners, townspeople, and students. These people read books, both in English and Latin, for entertainment and general knowledge as well as for prayer. The fourteenth century was a golden age of manuscript production in England, as the thirteenth century had been in France. Among the delights of English Gothic manuscripts are their imaginative marginalia (pictures in margins of pages).

The dazzling artistry and delight in ambiguities that had marked earlier Anglo-Saxon manuscript illumination reappeared in the *Windmill Psalter* (c. 1270–1290), so-called because of a windmill in the initials beginning Psalm 1 (fig. 16-44). The Psalm begins with the words *"Beatus vir qui non abiit"* ("Happy those who do not follow the counsel [of the wicked]," Psalm 1:1). A *B*, the first letter of the Psalm, fills the left page, and an *E*, the second letter, occupies the top of the right page. The rest of the opening words appear on a banner carried by an angel at the bottom of the *E*. The *B* outlines a densely interlaced Tree of Jesse. The *E* is formed from large tendrils that escape from delicate background vegetation to support characters in the story of the Judgment of Solomon. The story, seen as a prefiguration of the Last Judgment, relates how two women (at the right) claiming the same baby came before King Solomon (on the crossbar) to settle their dispute. He ordered a guard to slice the baby in half with his sword and give each woman her share. This trick exposed the real mother, who hastened to give up her claim in order to save the baby's life.

Charming images appear among the pages' foliage, many of them visual puns on the text. For example, a large windmill at the top of the initial *E* illustrates the statement in the Psalm that the wicked would not survive the Judgment but would be "like chaff driven by the wind" (Psalm 1:4). Imagery such as this would have stimulated contemplation of the inner meanings of the text's familiar messages.

Opus Anglicanum

At least since the time of the Norman invasion and the *Bayeux Tapestry* (see fig. 15-30), the English were famous for their embroidery. From the thirteenth through the six-

16-45. *Life of the Virgin*
(Chichester-Consta-
ble chasuble back,
from a set of vest-
ments embroidered
in opus anglicanum),
from southern
England. 1330–50.
Red velvet with silk
and metallic thread;
length 5'6" (164 cm),
width 30" (76 cm).
The Metropolitan
Museum of Art,
New York
Fletcher Fund, 1927
(2.7 162.1)

teenth centuries the pictorial needlework in colored silk and gold thread of English embroiderers, both men and women, gained such renown that it came to be referred to by the Latin term *opus anglicanum* (English work). The pope in Rome, for instance, had more than 100 pieces of this luxurious textile art. The names of several prominent embroiderers are known, such as Mabel of Bury Saint Edmunds, who worked for Henry III, but few can be connected to specific works.

Opus anglicanum was employed for banners, court dress, and other secular uses, as well as for the liturgical vestments worn by the clergy during Mass. A mid-four-teenth-century vestment known as the Chichester-Constable chasuble (fig. 16-45) is embroidered with scenes from the Life of the Virgin—the Annunciation, the Adoration of the Magi, and the Coronation of the Virgin—arranged in three registers on its back. Cusped, crock-eted **S**-shape arches, twisting branches sprouting oak leaves, seed-pearl acorns, and animal faces define each register. The star and crescent moon in the Coronation of the Virgin scene, heraldic emblems of the royal family, suggest that the chasuble may have been made under the patronage of Edward III. The embroidery was done in split stitch with fine gradations of colored silk form-ing the images as subtly as painting (fig. 16-46). Where

16-46. Detail, *Angel of the Annunciation*, Chichester-Constable chasuble

gold threads were laid and couched, the effect is like the burnished gold-leaf backgrounds of manuscript illuminations. During the celebration of the Mass, garments of opus anglicanum would have glinted in the candlelight amid the other treasures of the altar. So heavy did such gold and bejeweled garments become, however, that their wearers often needed help to move.

SPAIN

The Christian reconquest of Muslim Spain gained momentum in the thirteenth century under Alfonso X "the Wise" (ruled 1252–1284), king of the newly unified northern realm of León and Castile. In the east, the union of Aragón with Catalonia created a prosperous realm that benefited from expanding Mediterranean trade. Christian rulers were initially tolerant of the Muslim and Jewish populations that came under their control, but in the late fifteenth century, this tolerance gave way to a drive toward religious conformity. When Spain was united under Christian rule in 1492, Jews were expelled and soon afterward Muslims were forced to convert. Like other areas of Europe, Spain was ravaged by rebellion, war, and plague in the fourteenth century.

From the twelfth century on, the art of Christian Spain reflects the growing influence of foreign styles, particularly those of France and Italy. Patrons often brought in master masons, sculptors, and painters from these regions to direct or execute important projects. The new influences, adapted by local artisans, combined with local traditions to create a recognizably Spanish Gothic style.

Architecture

While most of the great thirteenth-century churches of Castile and Leon were inspired by French Gothic architecture and some even had French masons working on their structure and sculpture, Catalonia and the Balearic Islands developed their own distinctive Catalan Gothic style. Mallorca, a major center of Mediterranean trade, had been captured from the Muslims in 1229 by James I of Aragón (ruled 1213–1276), who converted Palma's mosque into a church. His son initiated the construction of a new cathedral in 1306. The structure has an imposing, fortresslike exterior dominated by closely packed wall buttresses at the continuous line of chapels along the outer aisles. The tall nave, supported by flying buttresses (every third buttress on the exterior), soars to the amazing height of 143 feet; the side aisle vaults rise to more than 94 feet. These tall side aisles, combined with slender polygonal piers in the nave arcade, create a unified interior space. Large windows in the clerestory and both east and western nave walls flood the interior with light.

Book Arts

King Alfonso X of Castile was known as a patron of the arts who maintained a brilliant court of poets, scholars, artists, and musicians during the mid-thirteenth century. He promoted the use of local vernacular languages instead of Latin in his realm for everything from religious

16-47. Cathedral of Palma, Mallorca, Balearic Islands, Spain. Begun 1306. View from the south

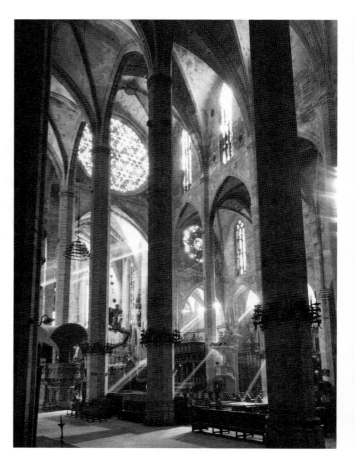

16-48. Nave and side aisle, Palma Cathedral

literature and history to legal codes and translations of important Arabic scientific texts. He was a poet and musician himself, compiling and setting to music a collection of poems, some of them his own, devoted to the Virgin Mary. An illustration from this manuscript, the *Cantigas de Santa María* (*Songs of Saint Mary*), shows Alfonso as poet-musician above one of his own songs (fig. 16-49). Like Queen Blanche and King Louis in the French Court style Moralized Bible seen earlier (see fig. 16-35), Alfonso is shown seated in a Gothic building. He holds a copy of his poetry, which he presents to admiring courtiers.

Painted Altarpieces

The large-scale paintings on or just behind church altars, called **altarpieces**, began to appear in the thirteenth century and came into use throughout Europe thereafter. While manuscript illumination and stained glass, and to some extent the fiber arts of embroidery and tapestry, remained the most important forms of two-dimensional art, in the thirteenth century altarpieces, murals, and smaller paintings on wood panels became increasingly important. Professional painters worked for both individual and institutional patrons. Many were members of painting dynasties that lasted for generations, and some had wide-ranging responsibilities at court.

ALTARS AND ALTARPIECES The altar in a Christian church symbolizes both the table of the Last Supper and the tombs of Christ and the saints. Traditionally the altar is covered with a cloth, and it is usually set with candles and a cross. The reliquary of a patron saint, such as Saint Foy (see fig. 15-1), might be placed on the altar, but it might also be under or even inside the altar. Altarpieces placed behind or at the back of the altar table, the **mensa**, as well as altar frontals (**antependia**) in front of the altar tables, provide the celebrants and worshipers with images of the saints and scenes from their lives and martyrdoms. These painted, carved, or embroidered images were created to help focus meditations and prayers, but unlike Byzantine icons (see fig. 7-61) they were not intended to be conduits for prayers to saints.

The earliest altarpieces were low, fixed panels, but by the Gothic period they became increasingly large and elaborate architectonic structures filled with images and protected by movable wings that functioned like shutters. Eventually, in Spain, they grew to the full height of the building. Many altarpieces had a firm base, called a **predella**, which was also covered with images. The most common type of arrangement was the **triptych**, a central panel flanked by side panels, or wings. Polyptychs such as Duccio's *Maestà* (see fig. 16-71) consisted of many panels in a stationary frame. Wings of altarpieces were painted on both front and back because the altarpieces were kept closed most of the time and were opened on holy days to reveal special imagery.

Altar and triptych altarpiece

16-50. Luis Borrassá. *Virgin and Saint George*, altarpiece in Church of San Francisco, Villafranca del Panadés, Barcelona. c. 1399. Tempera on wood

The contract for another of Borrassá's altarpieces, dated 1402, specifies its subject matter in detail as well as its dimensions and shape. The contract requires the use of high-quality materials and calls for delivery in six months, with payment at specified stages upon inspection of work in progress. It holds the painter responsible for all stages of production "according to what is customary in other beautiful [altarpieces]" (cited in Binski, page 52).

One of the major figures in late medieval Spanish painting was Luis Borrassá (1360–1426). From a Catalán family of painters, he worked for the court of Aragón early in his career, probably in the style favored by the French-born queen. Sometime during the 1380s he set up a workshop in the Catalán capital of Barcelona. Among the altarpieces attributed to him is the *Virgin and Saint George* made for the Church of San Francisco at Villafranca del Panadés (fig. 16-50). This work is a distinctively Spanish-type altarpiece called a **retablo**, which consists of an enormous wooden framework—taking up the whole wall behind an altar—that is filled with either painted or carved narrative scenes. The depiction of space and the lively narrative scenes in the panels of the *Virgin and Saint George* reflect the influence of the painting style that had developed in Tuscany, in northern Italy, but the realistic details, elegant drawing, and rich colors are characteristically Catalán. Borrassá's synthesis of foreign artistic influences reflects the development of the courtly International Gothic style that emerged in much of Europe about the beginning of the fourteenth century.

The panel depicting the *Education of the Virgin* (fig. 16-51) shows Mary among a group of fourteenth-century Spanish girls presenting their embroidery for a teacher's approval. All except Mary have produced the assigned floral design. Mary instead has stitched the enclosed garden of Paradise where five golden-winged angels flutter around the Fountain of Life. Embroidery is such an important art that even the child Mary has learned to do it.

16-51. Luis Borrassá. *Education of the Virgin,* detail from *Virgin and Saint George* altarpiece

16-52. Church of Saint Elizabeth, Marburg, Germany. 1233–83

GERMANY AND THE HOLY ROMAN EMPIRE

In contrast to England and France, which were becoming strong national states, by the middle of the thirteenth century Germany had developed into a decentralized conglomeration of independent principalities, bishoprics, and "free" commercial cities The Holy Roman Empire, weakened by prolonged struggle with the papacy and with German princes, had ceased to be a significant power. Holy Roman emperors were now elected by German princes and had only nominal authority over them. Each emperor ruled from his chosen capital. Charles IV (ruled 1355–1378), for example, who was also king of Bohemia, ruled from the Bohemian city of Prague, which he helped develop into a great city. As patrons, the emperors stimulated the arts, promoting local traditions as well as the spread of the French Court style and the International Gothic style that followed it.

Architecture

A new type of church, the **hall church**, developed in thirteenth-century Germany in response to the increasing importance of sermons within church services. The hall church featured a nave and side aisles with vaults of the same height, creating a spacious and open interior that could accommodate the large crowds drawn by charismatic preachers. The flexible design of these "great halls" was also widely adopted for civic and residential buildings.

The Church of Saint Elizabeth at Marburg, near Cologne in Germany, built between 1233 and 1283, was popular as a pilgrimage site and as a funerary chapel for

16-53. Nave, Church of Saint Elizabeth

the local nobility (fig. 16-52). The earliest example of a hall church, Saint Elizabeth has a beautiful simplicity and purity of line. Light from two stories of tall windows fills the interior, unimpeded by nave arcades, galleries, or triforia (fig. 16-53). The exterior has a similar verticality and geometric clarity.

The Gothic style was also adopted for Jewish religious structures. The oldest functioning synagogue in Europe, Prague's Altneuschul (Old-New Synagogue), was probably built in the late thirteenth or fourteenth century (fig. 16-54). One of two principal synagogues serving the Jews of Prague, it reflects the geometric clarity and regularity of Gothic architecture and demonstrates the adaptability of the Gothic hall-church design for non-Christian use (fig. 16-55). Like a hall church, the vaults of the synagogue are all the same height. Unlike a church, with its nave and side aisles, the Altneuschul has two aisles with three bays each. The bays have four-part vaulting with a decorative fifth rib.

Because of sporadic repression, Jewish communities in the cities of northern Europe tended to be small throughout the Middle Ages. Towns often imposed restrictions on the building of synagogues, requiring, for example, that they be lower than churches. Since local guilds controlled the building trades in most towns, Christian workers usually worked on Jewish construction projects.

The medieval synagogue was both a place of prayer and a communal center of learning and inspiration where men gathered to read and discuss the Torah. The synagogue had two focal points, the *aron*, or shrine for the Torah scrolls, and a raised reading platform called the *bimah*. Worshipers faced the *aron*, which was located on the east wall, in the direction of Jerusalem. The *bimah* stood in the center of the hall. The Gothic-arched *aron* of the Altneuschul can be seen in figure 16-54, partially obscured by an openwork partition around the *bimah*, which straddled the two center bays. The synagogue's single entrance was placed off-center in a corner bay at the west end. Candles along the walls and in overhead chandeliers supplemented natural light from twelve large windows. The interior was also originally adorned with murals (the large, richly decorated Torah case shown on the *bimah* table was made later). Men worshiped and studied in the principal space; women were sequestered in annexes.

Sculpture

Nicholas of Verdun, a pivotal figure in the development of early Gothic sculpture, influenced both French and German art through his work well into the thirteenth century. Born along the Meuse River between Flanders and Germany, he was heir to the great Mosan metalworking tradition (see fig. 15-35). Nicholas worked for a number of important German patrons, including the archbishop of Cologne, for whom he created a magnificent reliquary (c. 1190–c.1205–1210) to hold what were believed to be relics of the Three Magi (fig. 16-56). Called the *Shrine of the Three Kings*, the reliquary resembles a basilica, a traditional reliquary form that evolved to reflect changes in church architecture. It is made of gilded bronze and silver with gemstones and dark blue enamel that accentuate its architectonic details. Mosan classicism reached new heights in this work. Figures are fully and naturalistically modeled in gold **repoussé**. The Magi and Virgin are on the front, and figures of prophets and the apostles

16-54. Interior, Altneuschul, Prague, Bohemia (Czech Republic). c. late 13th century; later additions and alterations. Engraving from *Das Historisches Prag in 25 Stahlstichen*, 1864

16-55. Plan of Altneuschul

16-56. Nicholas of Verdun and workshop. *Shrine of the Three Kings*. c. 1190–c. 1205–10. Silver and bronze with enamel and gemstones, 5'8" x 6' x 3'8" (1.73 x 1.83 x 1.12 m). Cathedral Treasury, Cologne, Germany

fill the niches in the two levels of round-arched arcading on the sides. The work combines robust, expressively mobile sculptural forms with a jeweler's exquisite ornamental detailing to create an opulent, monumental setting for its precious contents.

The sculpture in the facade of Strasbourg Cathedral has a homogeneous classicizing style that reflects the influence of Nicholas of Verdun and shares features with the work produced by the "Classical Shop" at Reims (see fig. 16-24). The works on the Strasbourg facade have an emotional expressiveness, however, that is characteristic of much German medieval sculpture. A relief depicting the death and assumption of Mary, a subject known as the Dormition (Sleep) of the Virgin, fills the tympanum of the south transept portal (fig. 16-57). Mary lies on her deathbed, but Christ has received her soul, the doll-like figure in his arms, and will carry it directly to heaven, where she will be enthroned next to him. The scene is filled with dynamically expressive figures with large heads and short bodies clothed in fluid drapery that envelops their rounded limbs. Deeply undercut, the large figures stand out dramatically in the crowded scene, their grief vividly rendered.

There was a powerful naturalistic current in German Gothic sculpture, and some works—among them a famous statue from Magdeburg Cathedral of Saint Maurice, produced about 1240–1250—may have been based

16-57. *Dormition of the Virgin*, south transept portal tympanum, Strasbourg Cathedral, Strasbourg, France. c. 1230

This sculpture is among the works traditionally attributed to a woman named Sabina, long believed to have been the daughter of the facade's designer. She is now known to have been a patron, not a sculptor. There is no evidence of women masons in medieval Europe, although a number of prominent patrons were women.

16-58. *Saint Maurice*, Magdeburg Cathedral, Magdeburg, Germany. c. 1240–50.
Dark sandstone with traces of polychromy

on living models instead of idealized types (fig. 16-58). Magdeburg Cathedral, in north-central Germany, had been built on the site of an earlier church dedicated to Saint Maurice, and his relics were preserved there. Maurice, the leader of a group of Egyptian Christians in the Roman army in Gaul, was martyred together with his troops in 286 for refusing to fight against Christian peasants. The crusading knights of the Middle Ages viewed him and other warrior-saints, such as Saint Theodore (see fig. 16-10), as models of the crusading spirit. And like Saint George, he was a favorite saint of

military aristocrats. Because he came from Egypt, Maurice was commonly portrayed with black African features. Dressed in a full suit of chain mail covered by a sleeveless coat of leather, Saint Maurice represents another ideal of warrior/manhood.

An exceptional sculptor worked for the bishop of Wettin, Dietrich II, on the decoration of a new chapel-sanctuary built at the west end of the Naumburg Cathedral about 1245–1260. Dietrich, a member of the ruling family of Naumburg, had lifesize statues of twelve ancestors who were patrons of the church placed on pedestals

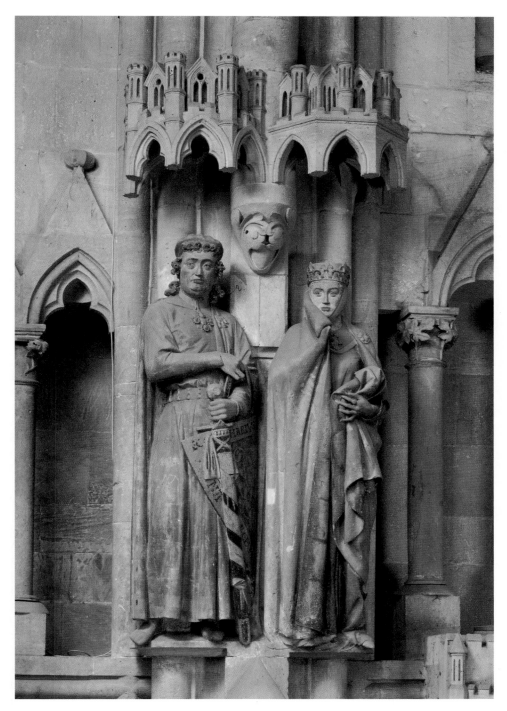

16-59. *Ekkehard and Uta*, west chapel sanctuary, Naumburg Cathedral, Naumburg, Germany. c. 1245–60. Stone, originally polychromed, approx. 6'2" (1.88 m)

around the chapel in perpetual attendance at Mass. Among them are representations of Ekkehard of Meissen and his Polish-born wife, Uta (fig. 16-59). Although long dead when these statues were carved, they seem extraordinarily lifelike and individualized. Ekkehard appears as a proud warrior and no-nonsense administrator, while Uta, coolly elegant, artfully draws her cloak to her cheek. Traces of pigment indicate that the figures were originally painted.

The ordeals of the fourteenth century—famines, wars, and plagues—helped inspire a mystical religiosity that emphasized both ecstatic joy and extreme suffering. The joys and sorrows of Mary, from almost cloying sweetness in Nativity depictions to the excruciatingly graphic physical suffering in portrayals of the Crucifixion and the Lamentation, became important themes. Devotional images, known as *Andachtsbilder* in Germany, inspired the worshiper to contemplate Jesus' first and last hours, especially during evening prayers, vespers. Through such religious exercises, worshipers hoped to achieve understanding of the divine and union with God. In the famous example shown here

16-60. *Vesperbild*, from Middle Rhine region, Germany.
c. 1330. Wood, height 34½" (88.4 cm). Landes-
museum, Bonn

(fig. 16-60), blood gushes from the wounds of an emaciated Christ in hideous rosettes. The Virgin's face conveys the intensity of her ordeal, mingling horror, shock,
pity, and grief. Such images had a profound impact on
later art, both within Germany and beyond.

ITALY The thirteenth century was a period of political division and economic expansion for the
Italian peninsula and its neighboring islands. With the
death of Holy Roman Emperor Frederick II (ruled 1220–
1250), Germany and the empire ceased to be an important factor in Italian politics and culture, and France and
Spain began to vie for control of Sicily and southern Italy.
The prolonged conflict between the papacy and the
empire had created two factions in Italian politics: the
pro-papacy Guelphs and the pro-imperial Ghibellines.
Northern Italy was dominated by several independent
and wealthy city-states controlled by a few powerful families. These cities were subject to chronic internal factional strife and conflict with one another.

In the wake of its conflict with the Holy Roman
Empire, the papacy had emerged as a significant international force. But its temporal success weakened its
spiritual authority and brought it into conflict with the
growing power of the kings of France and England. In
1309, after the election of a French pope, the papal court
moved from Rome to Avignon in southern France. During the Great Schism of 1378 to 1417, there were two
rival lines of popes, one in Rome and one in Avignon.

Great wealth and a growing individualism promoted
arts patronage in northern Italy. It is here that artisans
begin to emerge as artists in the modern sense, both in
their own eyes and the eyes of patrons. Although their
methods and working conditions remained largely
unchanged from before, artisans in Italy belonged to
powerful urban guilds and contracted freely with wealthy
townspeople and nobles and with civic and religious
bodies. Their ambitious, self-aware art reflects their economic and social freedom.

Architecture

Italian Gothic architecture developed from earlier Italian
Romanesque architecture in a way that only marginally
reflects the influence of the French Gothic style. In the
late thirteenth century, however, a new facade was
erected to the Cathedral of Our Lady in Siena, Tuscany,
that incorporated elements of the French style (fig.
16-61). This facade, constructed between 1284 and 1299,
was the work of Giovanni Pisano (active c. 1265–1314),
who may have trained or worked in France. (Giovanni
Pisano was the son of the sculptor Nicola Pisano, who is
discussed later in the chapter.) The new facade transformed the appearance of the cathedral. Although, in the
French manner, it includes three portals and a rose window, it lacks the complex narrative sculptural programs
typical of French Gothic facades. Giovanni limited his
sculpture to architectural decorations like those in the
portal tympana and to the huge, freestanding statues at
the level of the gables and stair towers. Such freestanding statues were to become a standard feature of the
Italian Gothic. As in other Italian churches, the decorative focus is on the doors themselves and, inside, on
furnishings such as pulpits, tomb monuments, and baptismal fonts. The cathedral's two-tone marble banding,
a hallmark of Tuscan churches, was also characteristic
of Italian Gothic churches.

Siena's northern neighbor and rival, Florence, erected
a colossal cathedral (duomo) in the fourteenth century
that dwarfs Siena's (fig. 16-62). The building has a long
and complex history. The original plan, by Arnolfo di
Cambio, was approved in 1294, but political unrest
brought construction to a halt until 1357. Several modifications of the design were made, and Florence Cathedral assumed much of its present appearance between
1357 and 1378. The west facade was rebuilt again in
the sixteenth century. Its veneer of white and green
marble coordinates with that of the nearby Baptistry of
San Giovanni.

16-61. Giovanni Pisano. West facade, Cathedral of Our Lady, Siena. 1284–99; facade above gable peaks 1369–77; original sculpture removed for preservation

16-62. Arnolfo di Cambio, Francesco Talenti, Andrea Orcagna, and others. Florence Cathedral, Florence. Begun 1296; redesigned 1357 and 1366; drum and dome 1420–36; campanile by Giotto, Andrea Pisano, and Francesco Talenti, c.1334–50

The Romanesque Baptistry of San Giovanni stands in front of the *duomo*. In the distance, near the Arno River, is the church of Santa Croce.

16-63. Arnolfo di Cambio, Francesco Talenti, Andrea Orcagna, and others. Nave, Florence Cathedral. 1357–78

16-64. Arnolfo di Cambio, Francesco Talenti, Andrea Orcagna, and others. Plan of Florence Cathedral. 1357–78

The spacious, square-bayed nave on the interior of the cathedral (fig. 16-63) is approximately as tall as the nave at Amiens (see fig. 16-19) but is three times as wide, giving it a radically different appearance. Here well-proportioned form is more important than light. The tall nave arcade, harkening back to single-storied imperial Christian designs, has a short clerestory with a single oculus in each bay and no triforium. The regular procession of four-part ribbed vaults springing from composite piers, however, clearly reflects northern Gothic influence. When the vaults began to crack under their own weight in 1366, unsightly iron tie bars had to be installed to hold them together. Builders in northern Europe solved this problem with exterior buttressing.

Sculptors and painters rather than trained masons were often responsible for designing Italian architecture, and as the plan of Florence Cathedral reflects, they tended to be more concerned with pure design than engineering (fig. 16-64). The long nave ends in an octagonal domed crossing, as wide as the nave and side aisles, from which the apse and transept arms extend. In basic architectural terms, this is a central-plan church grafted onto a basilica-plan church. It symbolically conjoins and separates the Dome of Heaven over the crossing, where the main altar is located, and the worldly realm of the congregation in the nave. The great ribbed dome, so fundamental to this abstract conception, was structurally unrealizable when it was planned in 1365. Not until 1420 did Filippo Brunelleschi solve the engineering problems involved in constructing it.

Sculpture

In the first half of the thirteenth century, Holy Roman Emperor Frederick II fostered a classical revival at his court in southern Italy that is often compared to Charle-

magne's renaissance in the early ninth century. The revival created a trend toward greater naturalism in Italian Gothic sculpture that parallels a similar trend in the north. A leading early exemplar of the trend was Nicola Pisano (active c. 1258–1278), father of Giovanni, who came from the southern town of Apulia, where imperial patronage was strong. An inscription on a freestanding marble pulpit (fig. 16-65) in the Pisa Baptistry (see fig. 15-38) identifies it as Nicola's earliest work in northern Italy. The inscription reads: "In the year 1260 Nicola Pisano carved this noble work. May so gifted a hand be praised as it deserves." The six-sided structure is open on one side for a stairway. It is supported by columns topped with leafy Corinthian capitals and standing figures flanking Gothic trefoil arches. A center column stands on a high base carved with crouching figures and domestic animals. Every second outer column rests on the back of a shaggy-maned lion guarding its prey. The format, style, and technique of Roman sarcophagus reliefs—readily accessible in the burial ground near the cathedral—may have inspired the carving on the pulpit's upper panels. The panels illustrate New Testament subjects, each treated as an independent composition unrelated to the others.

The Nativity cycle panel (fig. 16-66) illustrates three scenes—the Annunciation, the Nativity, and the Adoration—within a shallow space. The reclining Virgin dominates the middle of the composition. In the foreground, midwives wash the infant Jesus as Joseph looks on. In the upper left is the Annunciation, with the archangel Gabriel and the Virgin. The scene in the upper right combines the Adoration with the Annunciation to the Shepherds. The composition leads the eye from group to group back to the focal point in the center, the reclining and regally detached Mother of God. The sculptural treatment of the deeply cut, full-bodied forms is quite classical, as are

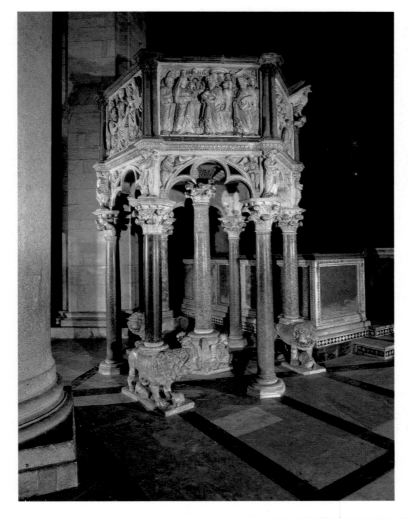

16-65. Nicola Pisano. Pulpit, Baptistry, Pisa. 1260. Marble

16-66. Nicola Pisano. *Nativity*, detail of pulpit, Baptistry, Pisa. 33½ x 44½" (85 x 113 cm)

16-67. Giovanni Pisano. *Nativity*, detail of pulpit, Pisa Cathedral, Pisa. 1302–10. Marble, 34³/₈ x 43" (87.2 x 109.2 cm)

their heavy, placid faces; the congested layout and the use of hierarchical scale are not.

Nicola's son Giovanni, the designer of the facade of the Siena Cathedral (see fig. 16-61), assisted his father in his later projects and emerged as a versatile artist in his own right near the end of the thirteenth century. Between 1302 and 1310, Giovanni created a pulpit for Pisa Cathedral that is similar to his father's in conception and general approach but is significantly different in style and execution. Giovanni's graceful, animated Nativity figures inhabit an uptilted, deeply carved space (fig. 16-67). In place of Nicola's impassive Roman matron, Giovanni depicts a slender young Virgin, sheltered by a shell-like niche, gazing delightedly at her baby. Below her, a midwife who doubted the virgin birth has her withered hand restored by dipping it into the baby Jesus' bathwater.

16-68. Andrea Pisano. *Life of John the Baptist*, south doors, Baptistry of San Giovanni, Florence. 1330–36. Gilded bronze

Angelic onlookers in the upper left have replaced the Annunciation. Sheep, shepherds, and announcing angels spiral up from the right, actively communicating and engaging in their surroundings. Dynamic where Nicola's was static, the scene pulses with energy.

Another Italian sculptor named Pisano (unrelated to Giovanni and Nicola), Andrea Pisano (active c. 1320s–1348), in 1330 was awarded the prestigious commission

16-69. Andrea Pisano. *Burial of John the Baptist*, detail of south doors, Baptistry of San Giovanni, Florence. 9³/₄ x 17" (24.7 x 43 cm)

The death of Saint John the Baptist, described in the Gospel of Mark, has been a popular subject in art since the late Middle Ages. According to Mark's account, the ruler of Judaea, Herod Antipas, at his wife's urging, reluctantly had the preacher-saint arrested after John criticized their marriage. At a banquet, Herod's stepdaughter Salome danced so seductively that he offered to grant her any request. Prompted by her mother, she asked for the saint's head on a platter, and Herod complied. Following John's death, his disciples "came and took his body and laid it in a tomb" (Mark 6:29).

16-70. Coppo di Marcovaldo. *Crucifix*, from Tuscany, Italy. c. 1250–1300. Tempera and gold on wood, 9'7³/₈" x 8'1¹/₄" (2.93 x 2.47 m). Pinacoteca, San Gimignano, Italy

for a pair of gilded bronze doors for the Florentine Baptistry of San Giovanni. Completed within six years, the doors are decorated with twenty-eight scenes from the life of John the Baptist (San Giovanni) set in quatrefoils (fig. 16-68). Surrounding the quatrefoils are lush vine scrolls filled with flowers, fruits, and birds, cast in bronze and applied to the doorway's lintel and jambs. Within the quatrefoils are scenes with figures in the monumental classicizing style then current in Florentine painting. In the *Burial of John the Baptist* (fig. 16-69), the placement and modeling of the figures creates a remarkable illusion of three-dimensionality. The saint's body has been lowered into a sarcophagus by two heavily robed men in the foreground, who are assisted by three others nearly hidden on the far side. The bearded man praying at the right, the monkish figure holding a large candle at the left, and the pinnacled and crocketed trefoil gables of the architectonic **baldachin** provide a vertical balance to the horizontal composition.

Painting

Wall painting, common elsewhere in Europe became a preeminent art form in Italy. Painting on wood panels also surged in popularity (see "Cennini on Panel Painting," page 596). Altarpieces were commissioned not just for the main altars of cathedrals but for secondary altars, parish churches, and private chapels as well. This growing demand reflected the new sources of patronage created by Italy's burgeoning urban society. Art proclaimed a patron's status as much as it did his or her piety.

The capture of Constantinople by Crusaders in 1204 brought an influx of Byzantine art and artists to Italy, influencing Italian painters of the thirteenth and fourteenth centuries to varying degrees. This influence appears strongly in the emotionalism of a large wooden crucifix attributed to the Florentine painter Coppo di Marcovaldo and dated about 1250–1300 (fig. 16-70).

TECHNIQUE

CENNINI ON PANEL PAINTING

Cennino Cennini's *Il Libro dell' Arte* (*The Handbook of the Crafts*), a compendium of early-fifteenth-century Florentine artistic techniques, includes step-by-step instructions for making panel paintings. The wood for these paintings, he specified, should be fine-grained, free of blemishes, and thoroughly seasoned by slow drying. The first step in preparing a panel for painting was to cover its surface with clean white linen strips soaked in a **gesso** made from gypsum, a task best done on a dry, windy day. Gesso provides a ground, or surface, on which to paint. Cennini specified that at least nine layers should be applied, with a minimum of two-and-a-half days' drying time between layers, depending on the weather. The gessoed surface should then be burnished until it resembled ivory. The artist could now sketch the composition of the work with charcoal made from burned willow twigs. At this point, advised the author, "When you have finished drawing your figure, especially if it is in a very valuable [altarpiece], so that you are counting on profit and reputation from it, leave it alone for a few days, going back to it now and then to look it over and improve it wherever it still needs something . . . (and bear in mind that you may copy and examine things done by other good masters; that it is no shame to you)" (cited in Thompson, page 75). The final version of the design should be inked in with a fine squirrel-hair brush, and the charcoal brushed off with a feather. Gold leaf was to be affixed on a humid day over a reddish clay ground called bole, the tissue-thin sheets carefully glued down with a mixture of fine powdered clay and egg white, and burnished with a gemstone or the tooth of a carnivorous animal. Punched and incised patterning was to be added later.

Italian painters at this time worked in a type of paint known as **tempera**, powdered pigments mixed most often with egg yolk, a little water, and an occasional touch of glue. Apprentices were kept busy grinding and mixing paints according to their masters' recipes, setting them out for more senior painters in wooden bowls or shell dishes.

Cennini specified a detailed and highly formulaic painting process. Faces, for example, were always to be done last, with flesh tones applied over two coats of a light greenish pigment and highlighted with touches of red and white. The finished painting was to be given a layer of varnish to protect it and enhance its colors. Reflecting the increasing specialization that developed in the thirteenth century, Cennini assumed that an elaborate frame would have been produced by someone else according to the painter's specifications and brought fully assembled to the studio.

Cennini claimed that panel painting was a gentleman's job, but given its laborious complexity, that was wishful thinking. The claim does, however, reflect the rising social status of painters.

16-71. Duccio di Buoninsegna. *Virgin and Child in Majesty (Maestà)*, main panel of *Maestà Altarpiece*, from Siena Cathedral. 1308–11. Tempera and gold on wood, 7' x 13'6¼" (2.13 x 4.12 m). Museo dell'Opera del Duomo, Siena

"On the day that it was carried to the [cathedral] the shops were shut, and the bishop conducted a great and devout company of priests and friars in solemn procession, accompanied by . . . all the officers of the commune, and all the people, and one after another the worthiest with lighted candles in their hands took places near the picture, and behind came the women and children with great devotion. And they accompanied the said picture up to the [cathedral], making the procession around the Campo [square], as is the custom, all the bells ringing joyously, out of reverence for so noble a picture as is this" (Holt, page 69).

Instead of the *Christus triumphans* type common in earlier Italo-Byzantine painting, Coppo has represented the *Christus patiens*, or suffering Christ, with closed eyes and bleeding, slumped body (see fig. 14-30). The six scenes at the sides of Christ's body tell the Passion story. Such historiated crucifixes were mounted on the **rood screens** (partitions) that hid sanctuary rituals from worshipers (see fig. 16-79). Some were painted on the back, too, suggesting that they were carried in religious processions.

The two most important schools of Italian Gothic painting emerged in Siena and Florence, rivals in this as in everything else. Siena's foremost painter was Duccio di Buoninsegna (active 1278–1318), whose synthesis of Byzantine and northern Gothic influences transformed the tradition in which he worked. Duccio and his studio painted the grand *Maestà* (Majesty) *Altarpiece* for the main altar of the Siena Cathedral—dedicated, like the town itself, to the Virgin—between 1308 and 1311. Creating this altarpiece was an arduous undertaking. The work was large—the central panel alone was 7 by 13 feet—and it had to be painted on both sides because the main altar stood in the center of the sanctuary (fig. 16-71).

Because the *Maestà* was broken up in the eighteenth century, the power and beauty of Duccio's original work must be imagined today from its scattered parts (fig. 16-72). The main scene, depicting the *Virgin and Child in Majesty*, was once accompanied above and below by narrative scenes from the Life of the Virgin and the Infancy of Christ. On the back were scenes from the Life and Passion of Christ. The brilliant palette and ornate **punchwork**–tooled designs in gold leaf are characteristically Sienese. Duccio has combined a softened Italo-Byzantine figure style with the linear grace and the easy relationship between figures and their settings characteristic of the northern High Gothic style. This subtle blending of northern and southern elements can be seen in the haloed ranks around Mary's architectonic throne (which represents both the Church and its specific embodiment, the Siena Cathedral). The central, most holy figures retain an iconic Byzantine solemnity and immobility, but those adoring them reflect a more naturalistic, courtly style which became the hallmark of the Sienese school for years to come.

Simone Martini, a practitioner (active 1315–1344) of the style pioneered by Duccio, may have been among Duccio's assistants on the *Maestà*. One of Martini's outstanding works, an altarpiece depicting the Annunciation (fig. 16-73), was painted in 1333 for the Siena Cathedral. This exquisite work, with its lavish punchwork, reflects a love of ornamental detail. The elegant figures, robed in fluttering draperies and silhouetted against a flat gold ground, seem weightless. Reflecting the Marian literature of his day, the painter has focused on the psychological impact of the Annunciation on a young and very human Mary. Gabriel has just appeared, his plaid-lined cloak swirling about him as he kneels in front of the Virgin. The words of his salutation—"Hail, favored one! The Lord is with you"—run from his mouth to her ear. Interrupted while reading the Bible in her room, Mary recoils in shock

16-72. Diagram, front side of *Maestà Altarpiece*. Panels seen in figure 16-71 are shaded.

Duccio's *Maestà Altarpiece* was removed from the cathedral's main altar in 1505. In 1771 the altarpiece was cut up to make it salable. Over the years, sections were dispersed, appearing later at auctions or in museums and private collections. The value of the panels remaining in Siena was finally recognized, and they were placed in the cathedral museum there in 1878.

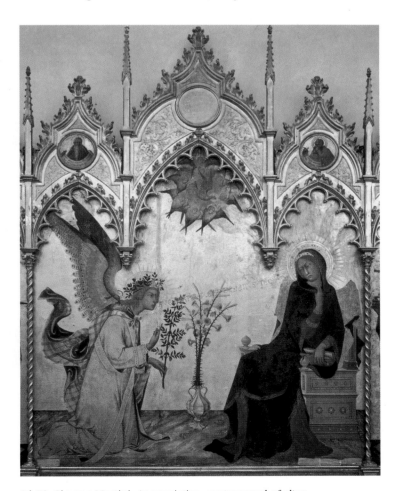

16-73. Simone Martini. *Annunciation*, center panel of altarpiece from Siena Cathedral. 1333. Tempera and gold on wood; 19th-century frame, 10' x 8' 9" (3.05 x 2.67 m). Galleria degli Uffizi, Florence. Side panels with standing prophets by Lippo Memmi not shown

16-74. Pietro Lorenzetti. *Birth of the Virgin*, from Siena Cathedral. 1342. Tempera and gold on wood; frame partially replaced, 6'1½" x 5'11½" (1.88 x 1.82 m). Museo dell'Opera del Duomo, Siena

TECHNIQUE

BUON FRESCO

Buon ("true") *fresco* ("fresh") wall painting on wet plaster was an Italian specialty, derived from Byzantine techniques and distinguished from *fresco secco* ("dry" fresco). The two methods were commonly used together in Italy.

The advantage of *buon fresco* was its durability. A chemical reaction occurred as the painted plaster dried that bonded the pigments into the wall surface. *Fresco secco*, in contrast, tended to flake off over time. The chief disadvantage of *buon fresco* was that it had to be done quickly and in sections. The painter plastered and painted only as much as could be completed in a day. Each section was thus known as a *giornata*, or day's work. The size of a *giornata* varied according to the complexity of the painting within it. The Virgin's face, for instance, could occupy an entire day, whereas large areas of sky could be painted quite rapidly. A wall to be frescoed was first prepared with a rough, thick undercoat of plaster. When this was dry, assistants copied the artist's composition onto it with sticks of charcoal, and he made any necessary adjustments. These drawings, known as **sinopia**, were often beautifully executed. Painting proceeded in irregularly shaped sections conforming to the contours of major figures and objects, with painters working from the top down so that drips fell on unfinished portions. Assistants covered one section at a time with a fresh, thin coat of very fine plaster over the sinopia, and when this was "set" but not dry, pigments mixed with water were painted on. Blue areas, as well as details, were usually painted afterward in tempera using the *fresco secco* method.

---

and fear from this gorgeous apparition. Only essential elements occupy the emotionally charged space. In addition to the two figures, these include Gabriel's olive-branch crown and scepter (emblems of triumph and peace), Mary's thronelike seat (an allusion to her future status as Queen of Heaven), the vase of white lilies (a symbol of her purity), and the dove of the Holy Spirit surrounded by cherubim. Mary's face harks back to Byzantine conventions, but the stylized elegance of her body, seen in the deft curve of her recoiling form, the folds of her rich robe, and her upraised right hand, are characteristic of the Italian Gothic court style. Soon after finishing the *Annunciation*, Simone Martini was summoned to southern France to head a workshop at the papal court in Avignon (he had worked earlier for the French king of Sicily and Naples). His Sienese reformulation of the French Gothic style contributed to the development of the International Gothic style at the turn of the century.

The Lorenzetti brothers, Pietro (active c. 1306–1345) and Ambrogio (active c. 1319–1347), worked in a more robust style that dominated Sienese painting during the second quarter of the fourteenth century. One of Pietro's outstanding works was a **triptych**, the *Birth of the Virgin* (fig. 16-74), painted in 1342 for one of the cathedral's secondary altars. In striking contrast to the *Annunciation*, Pietro's ample figures people a well-furnished scene. The only supernatural elements here are the gold halos identifying the baby Mary and her parents, Anna and Joachim. The painter has attempted to create the illusion of an interior space seen through the "windows" of a triple-arched frame. The center and right windows open into a single room, and the left window opens into an antechamber. Although the figures and the architecture are on different scales, Pietro has conveyed a convincing sense of space through an intuitive system of perspective. The lines of floor tiles, the chest, and the plaid bed-cover, for example, appear to converge as they recede. Thematically, the Virgin's birth is depicted as a forerunner of Jesus, with elements that echo those of Nativity scenes: the mother reclines on a bed, midwives bathe the newborn, the elderly father sits off to one side, and three people bearing gifts appear at the right. The gift bearers are local women with simple offerings of bread and wine (an allusion to the Eucharist) instead of kings bearing treasures. Anna wears the royal color purple, and gold-starred vaulting forms a heavenly canopy.

A few years earlier, in 1338, the Siena city council commissioned Pietro's brother Ambrogio to paint in fresco (see *"Buon Fresco,"* above) a room called the Sala della Pace (Chamber of Peace) in the Palazzo Pubblico (city hall). The allegorical theme chosen for the walls was the contrast between the effects of good and bad government on people's lives (fig. 16-75; see also fig. 16-2, a detail of the same work). For the *Allegory of Good Government in the City*, and in tribute to his patrons, Ambrogio created an idealized but recognizable portrait of Siena and its immediate environs. The cathedral dome and the distinctive striped **campanile** are visible in the upper left-hand corner (compare fig. 16-61). The statue of the wolf suckling Romulus and Remus, the legendary founders of Rome, perched above the portal of the gateway identifies it as Siena's Porta Romana. An allegory of Security as a woman clad only in a wisp of transparent drapery hovers outside the gate, a scroll in one hand and a miniature gallows complete with a hanged man in the other. The scroll bids those entering the city to come in peace, and the gallows is a reminder of the consequences of not doing so.

Ambrogio's achievement in this fresco was twofold. First, he maintained an overall visual coherence despite the shifts in vantage point and scale that help keep all parts of the flowing composition intelligible. Second, he created

16-75. Ambrogio Lorenzetti. *Allegory of Good Government
in the City* and *Allegory of Good Government in
the Country*, frescoes in the Sala della Pace, Palazzo
Pubblico, Siena. 1338–39

a feeling of natural scale in the relationship between figures and environment. From the women dancing to a tambourine outside a shoemaker's shop (see fig. 16-2) to the
contented peasants tending fertile fields and lush vineyards (fig. 16-76), the work conveys a powerful vision of an
orderly society, of peace and plenty at this particular time
and place. Sadly, famine, poverty, and disease overcame
Siena just a few years after this work was completed.

In Florence, the transformation of the Italo-Byzantine
style began somewhat earlier than in Siena. Duccio's Florentine counterpart was an older painter named Cenni di
Pepi (active c. 1272–1302), better known by his nickname,
Cimabue. He is believed to have painted the *Virgin and*

16-76. Ambrogio Lorenzetti. Detail of *Allegory of Good
Government in the Country*

16-77. Cimabue. *Virgin and Child Enthroned*, from the Church of
Santa Trinità, Florence. c. 1280. Tempera and gold on wood,
12'7½" x 7'4" (3.9 x 2.2 m). Galleria degli Uffizi, Florence

Child Enthroned (fig. 16-77) in about 1280 for the main
altar of the Church of Santa Trinità (Holy Trinity) in Florence. At more than 11½ feet high, this enormous panel
painting seems to have set a precedent for monumental
altarpieces. In it, Cimabue follows the Byzantine iconography of the Virgin Pointing the Way. The Virgin sits surrounded by saints, angels, and Old Testament prophets.
She holds the infant Jesus in her lap and points to him as
the path to salvation.

Cimabue employed Byzantine formulas in determining the proportions of his figures, the placement of their
features, and even the tilts of their haloed heads. Mary's

huge throne, painted to resemble gilded bronze with
inset enamels and gems, provides an architectural
framework for the figures. To render her drapery and that
of the infant Jesus, Cimabue used the Italo-Byzantine
technique of highlighting drapery with thin lines of gold
to indicate divinity, as in Mary's blue cloak. The vantage
point suspends the viewer in space in front of the image,
simultaneously looking down on the projecting elements
of the throne and Mary's lap while looking straight on at
the prophets at the base of the throne and the splendid
angels at each side. These interesting spatial ambiguities, as well as subtle asymmetries throughout the com-

16-78. Giotto di Bondone. *Virgin and Child Enthroned*, from the Church of the Ognissanti, Florence. c. 1310. Tempera and gold on wood, 10'8" x 6'8¼" (3.53 x 2.05 m). Galleria degli Uffizi, Florence

position, the Virgin's thoughtful, engaging gaze, and the well-observed faces of the old men are all departures from tradition that enliven the picture. Cimabue's concern for spatial volumes, solid forms, and warmly naturalistic human figures contributed to the course of later Italian painting.

According to the sixteenth-century Renaissance chronicler Vasari, Cimabue discovered a talented shepherd boy, Giotto di Bondone, and taught him how to paint. Then, "Giotto obscured the fame of Cimabue, as a great light outshines a lesser." Vasari also credited Giotto (active c. 1300–1337) with "setting art upon the path

that may be called the true one[, for he] learned to draw accurately from life and thus put an end to the crude Greek [i.e., Italo-Byzantine] manner" (cited in Barroughs, page 97). The painter and commentator Cennino Cennini (c. 1370–1440), writing in the late fourteenth century, was struck by the accessibility and modernity of Giotto's art, which, though it retained traces of the "Greek manner," was moving toward the depiction of a humanized world anchored in three-dimensional form.

Compared to Cimabue's *Virgin and Child Enthroned*, Giotto's 1310 painting of the same subject (fig. 16-78) for the Church of the Ognissanti (All Saints) in Florence,

16-79. Saint Francis Master. *Miracle of the Crib of Greccio*, fresco in Upper Church of San Francesco, Assisi, Umbria, Italy. c. 1295–1301/30

Saint Francis, born Giovanni Bernadone (c. 1181–1226), was the educated son of a rich cloth merchant. After an early career as a soldier, he dedicated himself to God. Embracing poverty, he lived as a wandering preacher. The Franciscan order began after he and his followers gained the recognition of the pope. Contemporaries described him as an innocent eccentric. Two years before his death he experienced the stigmata, wounds in his hands and feet like those of the crucified Christ.

This panel, on a lower nave wall, survived the disastrous earthquake of September 26, 1997.

while retaining certain of Cimabue's conventions, exhibits a groundbreaking spatial consistency and sculptural solidity. The central and largely symmetrical composition, the rendering of the angels' wings, and Mary's Byzantine facial type all reflect Cimabue's influence. Gone, however, are her modestly inclined head and delicate gold-lined drapery. This colossal and mountain-like Mary seems to burst forth from her slender Gothic baldachin. Giotto has imbued the picture with an unprecedented physical immediacy, despite his retention of hierarchical scale, the formal, enthroned image type, and a flat-gold ground. By rendering the play of light and shadow across their substantial forms, he has created the sense that his figures are fully three-dimensional beings inhabiting real space.

Giotto may have collaborated on murals at the prestigious Church of San Francesco in Assisi, the home of Saint Francis, the founder of the new Franciscan order, which was gaining followers throughout western Europe. Saint Francis's message of simple, humble devotion, direct experience of God, and love for all his creatures had a powerful impact on thirteenth-century Italian literature and art. The Church of San Francesco, the Franciscans' mother church, was consecrated by the pope in 1253, and the Franciscans commissioned many works to adorn it. Among those who worked there were Simone Martini, Pietro Lorenzetti, and Cimabue.

The *Life of Saint Francis*, in the upper church at San Francesco, was apparently among the last of the fresco cycles to be completed there. Scholars differ on whether they were painted by the young Giotto as early as 1295–1301 or by his followers as late as 1330; many have adopted the neutral designation of the artist as the Saint Francis Master. One scene, the *Miracle of the Crib at Greccio* (fig. 16-79), shows Saint Francis making the first crèche, a Christmas tableau representing the birth of Jesus, according to legend, in the church at Greccio. The artist of this scene has made great strides in depicting a convincing space with freely moving solid figures. The fresco documents the way the sanctuary of an early Franciscan church looked and the observances that took place within it. A large wooden historiated crucifix similar to the one by Coppo di Marcovaldo (see fig. 16-70) has been suspended from a stand on top of the rood screen. It has been reinforced by cross-bracing on the back and tilted forward to hover over worshipers in the nave. A high pulpit with candlesticks at its corners rises over the screen at the left. Other small but telling touches include a seasonal liturgical calendar posted on the lectern, foliage swags decorating a Gothic baldachin, and the singing monks. Saint Francis, in the foreground, reverently places a statue of the Holy Infant in a plain, boxlike crib next to representations of various animals that might have been present at his birth. Richly dressed people—presumably patrons of the church—stand at the left, while Franciscan nuns, apparently excluded from the sanctuary, look on through an opening in the screen.

Giotto's masterpiece is the frescoed interior of another church, the Arena Chapel in Padua (fig. 16-80), painted about 1305. While working at the Church of

16-80. Giotto di Bondone. *Last Judgment* and frescoes on west wall of Arena Chapel, Padua. 1305–6

THE BLACK DEATH

In the early 1340s rumors began to circulate in Europe of a deadly plague spreading by land and sea from Asia. By 1348 the plague had reached Constantinople, Italy, and France; by the next winter it had struck the British Isles; and by 1350 it had swept across Germany, Poland, and Scandinavia. Successive waves struck again in 1362, 1374, 1383, 1389, and 1400, and new outbreaks continued sporadically for the next 300 years, culminating in England's Great Plague of 1665. As much as half the urban population of Florence and Siena died in the summer of 1348, including many promising artists. England was similarly hard hit.

The plague, known as the Black Death, took two forms, both of which killed rapidly. The bubonic form was spread by fleas from rats, the pneumonic form through the air from the lungs of infected victims. To people of the time, ignorant of its causes and powerless to prevent it, the Black Death was a catastrophe. The fourteenth-century Italian writer Giovanni Boccaccio described how "the calamity had instilled such terror in the hearts of men and women that . . . fathers and mothers shunned their children, neither visiting them nor helping them" (cited in Herlihy, page 355). In their panic, some people turned to escapist pleasure seeking, others to religious fanaticism. Many, seeking a scapegoat, turned against Jews, who were massacred in several cities.

Francesco Traini. *Triumph of Death*, detail of a fresco in the Campo Santo, Pisa. 1325-50

Saint Anthony in Padua, Giotto was approached by a local merchant to decorate a new family chapel. The chapel, named for a nearby ancient Roman arena, is a simple, barrel-vaulted room. Giotto covered the entrance wall with a scene of the Last Judgment. He subdivided the side walls with a dado of allegorical grisaille paintings of the Virtues and Vices, from which rise vertical bands containing quatrefoil portrait medallions. The medallions are set within a framework painted to resemble marble inlay and carved relief. The central band of medallions spans the vault, crossing a brilliant lapis-blue, star-spangled sky in which large portrait disks float like glowing moons. Set into this framework are rectangular narrative scenes juxtaposing the life of the Virgin with that of Jesus. Both the individual scenes and the overall program display Giotto's genius for distilling a complex narrative into a coherent visual experience. Among Giotto's achievements was his ability to model form with color. He rendered his bulky figures as pure color masses, painting the deepest shadows with the most intense hues and highlighting shapes with lighter shades mixed with white. These sculpturally modeled figures enabled Giotto to convey a sense of depth in landscape settings without relying on the traditional convention of an architectural framework, although he did make use of that convention.

In the moving *Lamentation* (fig. 16-81), in the lowest register of the Arena Chapel, Giotto focused the composition for maximum emotional effect off-center on the faces of Mary and the dead Jesus. A great downward-swooping ridge—its barrenness emphasized by a single dry tree, a medieval symbol of death—carries the psychological weight of the scene to its expressive core. Mourning angels hovering overhead mirror the anguish of Jesus' followers. The stricken Virgin communes with her dead son with mute intensity, while John the Evangelist flings his arms back in convulsive despair and other figures hunch over the corpse. Instead of symbolic sorrow, Giotto conveys real human suffering, drawing the viewer into the circle of personal grief. The direct, emotional appeal of his art, as well as its deliberate plainness, embodies Franciscan values.

While Sienese painting was a key contributor to the development of the International Gothic style, Florentine painting in the style originated by Giotto and kept alive by his pupils and their followers was fundamental to the development of Italian Renaissance art over the next two centuries. Before these movements, however, came the disastrous last sixty years of the fourteenth century, in which the world of the Italian city-states—which had seemed so full of promise in Ambrogio Lorenzetti's *Good Government* frescoes—was transformed into a world of

16-81. Giotto di Bondone. *The Lamentation*. 1305–6. Fresco in the Arena Chapel

1500

16-82. Francesco Traini. *Triumph of Death*, fresco in Campo Santo, Pisa. Mid-14th century
The fresco was damaged by American shells during World War II and has been detached from the wall to preserve it.

uncertainty, and desolation by epidemics of the plague.

The horror and the terror of impending death are vividly depicted in the *Triumph of Death* (fig. 16-82). This much-copied fresco was painted by a Pisan named Francesco Traini (active c. 1321–1363) in the Campo Santo, the funerary structure on the grounds of Pisa Cathedral. It shows the encounter between the Three Living (aristocrats leading a hunt) and the Three Dead (corpses in varying stages of decomposition), a grim theme popular in plague-wracked Europe in the mid-fourteenth century. A crowned woman in the center of the leading group of riders recoils at the sight of her dead counterpart, the crowned man in the middle coffin. One of her courtiers covers his nose, gagging at the smell, while his wild-eyed horse cranes its neck forward. The animal's neck and the diagonal, Giottoesque cliff above lead the eye inexorably to the bloated, worm-riddled body in the top coffin. A stern old man unrolls a scroll, symbolically delivering the message of the scene: neither youth nor beauty, wealth nor power, but only piety like that of the hermits on the cliff above provides protection from the wrath of God. It was as if the self-confident hunting party in *Lorenzetti's Allegory of Good Government in the Country* fresco had set forth in sunshine only to return in shadow.

Yet as dark as it must have seemed to the men and women living through those times, beneath the surface profound, unstoppable changes were underway. In a relatively short moment of history, the European Middle Ages gave way to what is known as the Renaissance.

ENDANGERED TREASURES

Throughout the world, human acts threaten works of art and architecture, and this is not a recent problem. Egyptian tombs were plundered many hundreds of years ago. They were also vandalized then—and that is still going on. And today objects of cultural and artistic value are being "poached" from official and unofficial excavation sites, then sold illegally. In industrialized regions of the world, emissions from cars, trucks, buses, and factories damage and, in a true sense, destroy works of art and architecture on which corrosive rain falls. For art, however, war is by far the most destructive of all human enterprises. Virtually countless numbers of churches, synagogues, mosques, temples, and shrines have been burned, bombed, and stripped of decoration in the name of winning a war. So much has been lost and is absolutely irrecoverable.

Ironically, individuals are sometimes moved to deface works of art. More capriciously, nature itself does much damage. Floods, hurricanes, tornadoes, avalanches, mudslides, and earthquakes: All damage and destroy priceless treasures. One of the richest repositories of Italian Gothic and Early Renaissance wall painting, the thirteenth-century Basilica of Saint Francis of Assisi (the small Umbrian town where the saint was born and where he founded the Franciscan order), nearly shook to pieces the morning of September 27, 1997. A strong earthquake caused the vaulting to collapse in two places, sending priceless frescoes attributed to the "first modern artist," Giotto di Bondone (c. 1267–1337), to shatter and plunge to the stone floor.

Lost are two sections of ceiling vaults: one above the entrance to the upper basilica (there is an older lower basilica beneath it) and the other at the crossing, right over the altar, which was also demolished. Also destroyed are four of eight painted archivolts above the entrance door.

When this kind of disaster happens, the whole world seems to respond. Volunteers immediately established organizations to raise money to restore the frescoes, with the hope and intention of paying the decades-long costs of repairing and strengthening the basilica, reassembling the paintings from millions of tiny pieces, and finally reinstalling the restored treasures.

Basilica of St. Francis of Assisi, Assisi, Italy. Completed 1236, with painting of walls and vaulting begun about 1275

Looking from the transept toward the main entrance door (a view of less than half of the entire length of the upper basilica nave), this is how the basilica looked just before the earthquake struck. The man who made this picture, photographer Ghigo Roli, had just finished recording every painted surface of the interior when the "thunder" of first earthquake "explodes into the basilica, lifting it up and dropping it, shaking it throughout. . . . I wanted to cry," he later wrote (Bonsanti and Ghigo, page 16).

This diagram of the entrance end of the upper basilica nave shows areas of ruin. Of the eight archivolt panels in the pointed arch above the entrance door, four collapsed: *Saints Francis and Clare, Saints Anthony of Padua and Benedict, Saints Victorinus and Rufinus*, and *Saints Peter Martyr and Dominic*. All are attributed to Giotto and his assistants and date to about 1275. Above the archivolts, *St. Matthew*, one section of the so-called Vault of the Evangelists, also collapsed. It was painted by the great Italo-Byzantine artist Cimabue (Cenni di Pepi, active 1272–1302).

destroyed section of vault

destroyed archivolts

Caught by a television camera during the quake, the vaulting and archivolts above the entrance plunge to the floor, killing four people. The camera operator eventually emerged, covered with the fine dust of the shattered brickwork and plaster, as a "white, dumbfounded phantom."

1400 1420 1440

Limbourg Brothers
Detail of seated woman,
February. 1413–16

Brunelleschi
Dome of Florence Cathedral
1417–36

Donatello
David
After 1428

Van Eyck
Portrait of Giovanni Arnolfini (?)
and His Wife, Giovanna Cenami (?)
1434

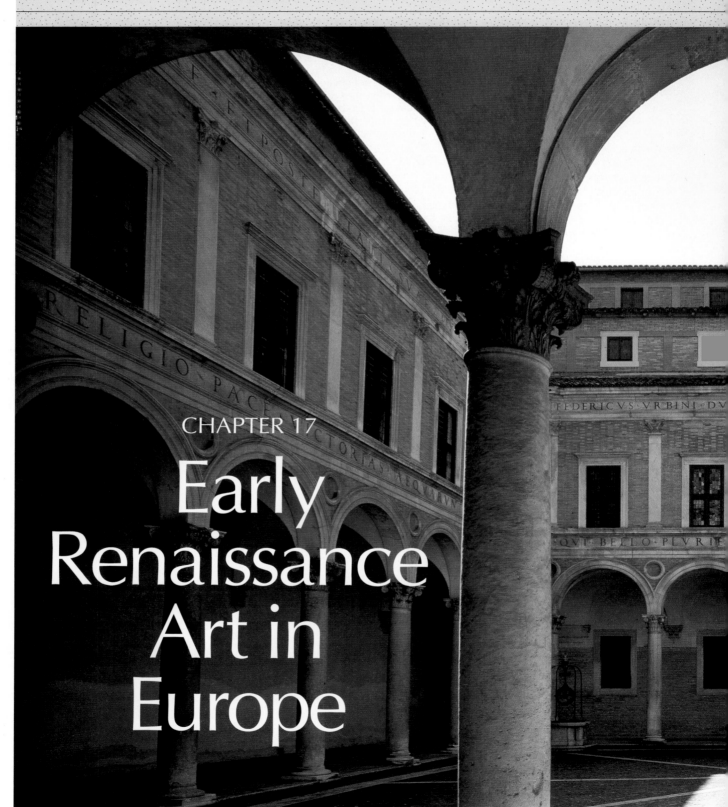

CHAPTER 17

Early Renaissance Art in Europe

ouquet
*tienne Chevalier
nd Saint Stephen*
1450

Alberti
Facade
Church of Sant'Andrea
Designed 1470

Verrocchio
Equestrian monument of
Bartolommeo Colleoni
c. 1481–96

Perugino
*Delivery of the Keys
to Saint Peter*
1482

17-1. Jan and Hubert van Eyck. *Ghent Altarpiece* (open), Cathedral of Saint-Bavo, Ghent, Flanders (Belgium). 1432. Oil on panel, 11'5³/4" x 15'1¹/2" (3.5 x 4.6 m)

T he townspeople of Ghent were awaiting Philip the Good of Burgundy when he entered the Flemish city on a special day in 1458. As he rode past resplendent banners, he encountered a remarkable scene: Among the jostling crowds were small groups of people standing absolutely frozen, like statues. To welcome him they had become *tableaux vivants* ("living pictures") dressed in costume and posed to re-create scenes from their town's most celebrated work of art, Jan and Hubert van Eyck's *Ghent Altarpiece* (fig. 17-1).

This remarkable centerpiece of worship, completed twenty-six years earlier, shows an enthroned figure of God, seated between the Virgin Mary and John the Baptist and flanked by angel musicians. Below is a depiction of the Communion of Saints, based on the passage in the Book of Revelation that describes the Lamb of God receiving the veneration of a multitude of believers (Revelation 14:1). Many of the church fathers, prophets, martyrs, and other saints pictured here were staged that day to greet Philip.

The fascination with this complex and beautiful altarpiece, reflected so early in the *tableaux vivants,* perhaps accounts for its survival through more than five centuries. During political turmoil in the sixteenth century, the panels were twice removed from their frames and hidden in a church tower. Over later centuries, panels were separated and taken to various locations to protect them—in 1894, while in the royal collection in Berlin, the six smallest panels were split through the middle so that both painted sides could be displayed at the same time. After World War I, the altarpiece was reassembled at Ghent, but a thief made off with two panels in 1934. (One, at the far left, was never recovered but was replaced by a faithful copy.) During World War II, the altarpiece panels were moved from town to town for safekeeping. Finally, in 1950–1951, the whole *Ghent Altarpiece*, one of the most studied and respected works of the early Renaissance in Europe, was reconstituted in Ghent.

THE EMERGENCE OF THE RENAISSANCE

In Europe, many developments that had begun in the late Middle Ages reached maturity in the fifteenth century (see "The Middle Ages: Where the Renaissance Began," page 617). Basic to these changes was the economic growth in the late fourteenth century that gave rise to a prosperous middle class in the Netherlands (which then included present-day Belgium), France, and Italy. Unlike the hereditary aristocracy that had dominated society during the Middle Ages, these merchants and bankers had attained their place in the world through personal achievement. In the early fifteenth century, this newly rich middle class supported scholarship, literature, and the arts. Their generous patronage resulted in the explosion of learning and creativity known as the Renaissance. Although artists and patrons shared middle-class values, their absorption in classical thought and art, as well as an intense interest in the natural world, emerged at different times in different regions. This chapter considers the origin and development of the Renaissance, first in northern Europe, then in Italy during the fifteenth century, and Chapter 18 will consider its evolution during the sixteenth century.

HUMANISM AND THE RENAISSANCE

Humanism and *Renaissance* are two words most associated with the fifteenth century in western Europe, but neither is favored by scholars today. Nevertheless, these words continue in our popular vocabulary as conveniences, and they are appropriate as long as we remember that *Renaissance* is a term that should not be given privileged status.

In its traditional usage, *humanism*, a nineteenth-century term, is used narrowly for the revival of classical learning and literature. More generally, the term is used for the liberal arts—grammar, rhetoric, poetry, history, and moral philosophy—in fourteenth- and fifteenth-century Italy. Humanism espouses a worldview that is focused on human beings; an education that perfects individuals through the study of past models of civic and personal virtue; a value system that emphasizes personal effort and responsibility; and a physically or intellectually active life that is directed at a common good as well as individual nobility. To this end, Greek and Latin had to be mastered so that classical literature—history, biography, poetry, letters, orations—could be studied.

Petrarch, the great humanist and poet laureate of fourteenth-century Rome, looked back at the preceding thousand years and saw only "dark ages" extending from the collapse of the Roman Empire to his own time. In Petrarch's view, history fell into three distinct periods: The ancient classical world was a time of high human achievement. It was followed by a decline during the Middle Ages, or "dark ages." The third period was the modern world—his own era—a revival, a rebirth, a renaissance, when at last humanity began to emerge from an intellectual and cultural torpor and scholars again appreciated the achievements of the ancients.

For all our differences, we still live in Petrarch's modern period—a time when human beings, their deeds, and their beliefs have primary importance. But today, we view the past differently. Unlike fourteenth-century scholars, we understand history as a gradual unfolding of events, changing over time. We can see now that the modern worldview that emerged during the fourteenth century was based on continuity and change.

For Petrarch and his contemporaries in Italy, the defining element in the new age was an appreciation of Greek and Roman writers that set them apart from medieval scholars. But today, we see more continuity than disjunction: In fact, throughout the Middle Ages, classical texts had been pivotal for scholars—from the monks in Charlemagne's eighth-century monasteries, who preserved them, to the students who mastered them in the universities that arose in the twelfth and thirteen centuries in Italy, France, and England. Especially important to the Renaissance was the conjunction of faith and reason that was addressed by scholasticism in the twelfth century and was explicated by Thomas Aquinas in the *Summa theologica* of 1267–1273. The same scholasticism underlay such literary works as the *Divine Comedy* of Dante—who with literary figures like Petrarch and Boccaccio and the artists Cimabue (active c. 1272–1302), Duccio (active 1278–1318), and Giotto fueled the great cultural explosion of fourteenth-century Italy. Clearly, then, the modern worldview espoused by Petrarch was the

17-2. Giotto di Bondone. Frescoes, Arena Chapel, Padua. View toward the east wall, 1305–6

product of intellectual, artistic, and spiritual continuity that had existed through the Middle Ages.

In literature Petrarch was a towering figure of change, a poet whose love lyrics were written not in Latin but in vernacular. A similar role was played in painting by the Florentine Giotto di Bondone (1266/7–1337), who created a classically inspired figurative vernacular style that appeared at a turning point in the history of art. Essentially a Gothic artist trained in the Italo-Byzantine style, Giotto introduced heightened human actions and

17-3. Giotto di Bondone. *Marriage at Cana, Raising of Lazarus, Resurrection* and *Noli Me Tangere,* and *Lamentation* (clockwise), frescoes on north wall of Arena Chapel, Padua. 1305–6

emotions by painting massive figures, modeled by a natural and consistent light and acting in a shallow yet clearly defined space.

One of art's great storytellers, Giotto made biblical events and theological implications immediately understandable to the new patrons of art in northern Italy—merchants and bankers like Enrico Scrovegni of Padua, who commissioned Giotto to decorate a chapel dedicated in 1305 to the Virgin of Charity and the Virgin of the Annunciation (fig. 17-2). On the entrance wall, Giotto painted Scrovegni presenting the chapel to the Virgin. Christ sits as judge above the Virgin, who leads the saved toward the enthroned apostles and ranks of angels. The torments of hell fill the lower wall to the viewer's right.

Both Giotto's narrative skills and his awareness of the medieval tradition of **typology**—in which earlier events presage later ones—are apparent in the paintings on the side walls of the chapel (fig. 17-3). The life of the Virgin Mary begins the series. Events in the life and ministry of Jesus circle the chapel in the middle **register**, while scenes of the Passion (the arrest, trial, and Crucifixion of Jesus) fill the lowest register. Thus, the first miracle, when Jesus changes water to wine during the

wedding feast at Cana (recalling that his blood will become the wine of the **Eucharist**, Communion), is followed by the raising of Lazarus (a reference to his own Resurrection). Below, the Lamentation over the body of Jesus by those closest to him leads to the Resurrection, indicated by angels at the empty tomb and his appearance to Mary Magdalen in the Noli Me Tangere ("Do not touch me"). Although the settings are reduced to the minimum, the juxtaposition of dead and live trees becomes a telling detail of death and resurrection.

A consistent pictorial space assumes the viewer to be standing in the center of the chapel. Giotto—very aware of people and their reactions—used only a few large figures and essential props in settings that never distract by their intricate detail. The scenes are reminiscent of the *tableaux vivants* that were played out in the piazza and chapel in Padua, as they would be in Ghent 150 years later, when Philip the Good arrived. The paintings also introduced artistic elements that would mark the Renaissance.

Outside Italy, a pervasive interest in the natural world manifested in the detailed observation and recording of nature. Artists depicted birds, plants, and animals

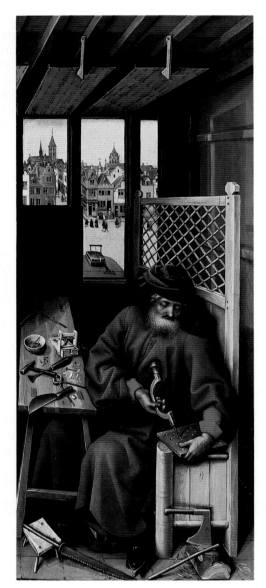

17-4.   Robert Campin. *Joseph in His Carpentry Shop,* right
wing of the *Mérode Altarpiece (Triptych of the Annunciation).* c. 1425–28. Oil on panel, approx. 25³/₈ x 10⅞"
(64.5 x 27.6 cm). The Metropolitan Museum of Art,
New York

The Cloisters Collection, 1956 (56.70)

with breathtaking accuracy. They observed that the sky
is more colorful straight above than at the horizon, and
they painted it that way. They described trees, shrubs,
and even blades of grass with botanical precision.
Enlarging on developments begun in the fourteenth century, such as Giotto's figures, artists emphasized **volumetric** rendering, modeling the volume of forms with
light and shadow.

Along with the desire for accurate depiction came a
new interest in particular personalities. Fifteenth-century
portraits have astonishingly lifelike individuality, combining careful—sometimes even unflattering—description with an uncanny sense of vitality. In a number of
religious paintings, even the saints and angels seem to
be portraits. Indeed, individual personalities were important in every sphere. More names of artists were recorded

during the fifteenth century, for example, than in the
entire span from the beginning of the Common Era to the
year 1400. A similar observation might be made in nearly every other field.

One reason for this new emphasis on individuality
was the humanist interest not only in antiquity but also
in people: While humanists sought the physical as well
as the literary record of the ancient world—assembling
libraries, collecting sculpture and fragments of architecture, and beginning archeological investigations of
ancient Rome—what lay behind this activity was their
desire to fully understand an imagined golden age of
human life and thus to achieve personal freedom and
dignity for laypersons and clergy alike. Their aim was to
live a rich, noble, and productive life within the framework of Christianity. Needless to say, the humanist ideal
was seldom achieved and was usually short-lived. Nevertheless, this humanist spirit extended education to the
laity, investigated the natural world, and subjected philosophical and theological positions to logical scrutiny.
Therefore, it was possible to integrate many diverse cultures—beginning with the classical and medieval—into a
rich and diverse melange. This same spirit constantly
invented new ways to extend humans' intellectual and
physical reach. From the fifteenth-century printing press
to computers, from improved ships and navigational
equipment to rocket science and space stations, from the
Copernican view of the sun to the exploration of Mars,
such achievements stand in a direct line of succession
from Petrarch to the present day.

The rise of humanism did not signify a decline in the
importance of Christian belief. In fact, an intense Christian spirituality continued to inspire and pervade most
European art through the fifteenth century and long after.
But despite the enormous importance of Christian faith,
the established Western Church was plagued with problems in the fifteenth century. Its hierarchy was being bit-
terly criticized for a number of its practices, including its
perceived indifference to the needs of common people.
These strains within the Western Church exemplified the
skepticism of the Renaissance mind. In the next century,
they would give birth to the Protestant Reformation.

While wealthy and sophisticated men in the highest
ranks of the clergy—bishops, cardinals, and the pope
himself—and the royal and aristocratic courts continued
to play major roles in the support of the arts, increasingly the urban lay public sought to express personal and
civic pride in secular architecture, sculptured monuments, paintings directed toward the community, as well
as town houses, fine furnishings, and portraits of family
members. The practical, commonsense values of the
merchants formed a solid underpinning for humanist
theories and enthusiasms.

Two ideal cities, as seen through contemporary eyes,
can sharpen the fifteenth-century view as it emerged in
northern and southern Europe. In Robert Campin's
Mérode Altarpiece (see fig. 17-9), windows in Joseph's
carpentry shop open onto a view of a prosperous Flemish city (fig. 17-4). Tall, well-kept houses crowd around
churches, whose towers dominate the skyline. People

THE MIDDLE AGES: WHERE THE RENAISSANCE BEGAN

The Middle Ages, or medieval period, spans approximately 1,000 years in Europe, from the fifth to the fifteenth century. Far from being the "dark ages" described by the fourteenth-century poet Petrarch, these centuries were filled with brilliant achievements in the arts, philosophy, and theology. During this period, too, the economic and political structures arose that made possible the formation of the nation-states of western Europe.

Medieval society grew after the collapse of the Western Roman Empire in 476, and the empire's vast road and water-supply networks, grandiose buildings, and places of learning declined. Today, we see that the Roman Empire did not really "fall"—as its demise has so often been described—but rather began to evolve during an earlier time, influenced by people outside the "classical" Mediterranean world who were part of the empire but who had different life-styles, goals, and religious beliefs.

The Middle Ages was a period of rapid change, marked by the spread of Christianity under the authority of the pope, the bishop of Rome. Christian clergy were almost the only people during this time who maintained the skills of reading and writing and undertook scholarly endeavors. The Church, as a result, had much influence on the arts.

As the migrating peoples of Europe settled down, they established kingdoms. For a time in the eighth and ninth centuries, Charlemagne, an astute and powerful ruler, united much of what are now France, Germany, Belgium, the Netherlands, and northern Italy into the Carolingian Empire, but his heirs soon divided the empire into separate kingdoms. From about 800 to 1000, Viking invaders from Scandinavia raided parts of Europe. Out of a conglomeration of mainly Germanic and northern Italian states and principalities arose a weak and often divided Holy Roman Empire in the late 900s, ruled by a series of emperors crowned by the pope.

In response to almost constant local warfare, people turned to local political, economic, and social structures for security. A new medieval way of life—combining vestiges of the old Roman Empire with Germanic traditions—expanded throughout Europe, especially after the tenth century. Powerful rulers, in order to obtain a trained local fighting force, promised tracts of land (called fiefs) to vassals, who in turn promised loyalty and military assistance to their lords. In time, wealthy vassals controlled enough land to offer some of it to their own vassals. Vassals and subvassals often attempted to make their fiefs hereditary, which gave rise to a complex legal and economic system of rights, obligations, and dependency known as feudalism.

Most people in agricultural medieval society lived a bleak life as serfs bound to the land, laboring in return for promises of protection, a share of the crops, and economic support from their lord. Manors, or huge estates, were almost self-sufficient units, since people could no longer depend upon the long-distance trade opportunities or large cities of an empire to provide them with goods, services, or courts of law. Life for most people was short, with the events of birth, marriage, and death marked by Christian religious ceremonies conducted by the local clergy.

Beginning in the early 600s, the new religion of Islam spread from Arabia westward across North Africa and then northward into Europe. From about 800 until final victory in 1492, Christian kings fought wars to reconquer the Iberian peninsula (modern Spain and Portugal) from the Muslims. Beginning in 1096, Christian kings also led or sent military expeditions known as the Crusades from Europe into the Middle East to reclaim the Holy Land from Muslim Arabs.

On medieval Europe's southeastern borders, the Byzantine Empire (the eastern part of the former Roman Empire) flourished with a complex blend of ancient Greek, Roman, Christian, and Middle Eastern traditions. The Byzantine Empire lasted until 1453, when its capital, Constantinople, fell to the Muslim Ottoman Turks. In 1054 the Christian Church had split into two parts, the Roman Catholic Church in western Europe, and the Eastern Orthodox Church in the Byzantine Empire, but the Crusades again brought the West into contact with the East and stimulated the flow of new ideas and new wealth from trade.

During the 1100s and 1200s, this new wealth was channeled by taxes into huge building programs, making possible the soaring Gothic cathedrals with their brilliant stained-glass windows. These structures in growing towns gave work to architects, artists, stonemasons, sculptors, carpenters, craftsworkers, and merchants. Within new town-centered universities, students prepared for service in the Church or the government.

During the last few hundred years of the Middle Ages, the feudal system declined. In 1348 a bubonic plague, called the Black Death, struck Europe and killed more than 40 percent of the people. Growing royal power in England, France, and Spain meant a decline in the power of local nobles, who were further weakened by the Hundred Years' War (1337–1453) between England and France. Monarchs used their increased tax revenues to pay for standing armies rather than depend upon the doubtful loyalty of knights and the lessened security of castles. Medieval society was also weakened by disputes within the Church; at times in the 1300s there were two rival popes.

With the revival of urban life, merchants and craftsworkers demanded a greater say in political decisions. In the Italian city-states, in particular, wealthy merchants and rulers supported the renewed interest in ancient Greek and Roman texts, which inspired people to study language, poetry, history, and moral philosophy emphasizing harmony and balance in nature and the importance of individual achievement—ideas soon reflected in works of art and scholarship. After the mid-fifteenth century, printing with movable type made the spread of new knowledge faster and easier. By then the Middle Ages had blossomed into the Renaissance.

17-5. Anonymous. *Ideal City with a Fountain and Statues of the Virtues.* c. 1500. Oil on panel, 30¹/₂" x 7'1⁵/₈" (7.74 x 2.17 m).
Walters Art Gallery, Baltimore

gather in the open market square, walk up a major thoroughfare, and enter the shops, whose open doors and windows suggest security as well as commercial activity. The tall, narrow buildings recall the picturesque look of a medieval town; and the painter, for all his detailed realism, represents the architecture and people as an intuitive visual record.

Compare the ideal Italian city depicted by an anonymous north Italian painter in figure 17-5. Walking through this balanced and harmonious piazza would feel quite different from dropping in on one of the Flemish shops. The Italian cityscape—with its classical references and precise linear perspective (see "Renaissance Perspective Systems," page 650)—invites us, instead, to contemplate the look and clarity of a well-ordered civic life. Cubical palaces flank a vast square closed off by three buildings that recall the Roman Colosseum, Constantine's triumphal arch, and the Florentine Baptistry. In the center of the piazza, a woman draws water from a splendid community well, evidence of the ruler's (or town council's) generosity in providing fresh water for the citizens.

These images of two ideal cities present us with different but congenial aspects of fifteenth-century life and art: the observable reality and bustle of human activity viewed from an artisan's workshop, its spaces created through an intuitive atmosphere, and the orderly city controlled by a benevolent government depicted in a logical, intellectual construct of linear perspective. Yet, one has a warm picturesqueness, while the other suggests a cool, balanced, unachievable ideal. To explore how these two images were forged, let's begin in the powerful courts of French royalty, whose patronage supported and in fact spread the early Renaissance style in northern Europe.

FRENCH COURT ART AT THE TURN OF THE CENTURY

In the late Middle Ages, French kings, with their capital in Paris, began to emerge as the powerful rulers of a national state. Nevertheless, in the fourteenth and fifteenth centuries, their royal authority was constrained by the dukes and other nobles who controlled large territories outside the Paris region. Some of these nobles were even powerful enough to pursue their own policies independently of the king. Many of the great dukes were members of the royal family, however, and their interests often coincided with those of the king. One strong unifying factor was the threat of a common enemy: England, whose kings held large territories in western France and repeatedly invaded France between 1337 and 1453 in a series of conflicts known as the Hundred Years' War.

While the French king was holding court in Paris, the most powerful of the dukes continued to maintain courts in their own capitals. Through much of the fourteenth century, these centers were arbiters of taste for most of Europe. From the last decades of the fourteenth century up to the 1420s, French court patronage was especially influential in northern Europe. The French king and his relatives the dukes of Anjou, Berry, and Burgundy employed not only local artists but also gifted painters and sculptors from the Low Countries (present-day Belgium, Luxembourg, and the Netherlands). At the same time, many Dutch and Flemish artists migrated to France to work. In the south of France, a truly international style emerged at the papal court at Avignon. Of major importance in the creation and spread of the new

PARALLELS

Europe	1400–1450	1450–1500
France	Claus Sluter; Limbourg brothers; Joan of Arc burned at the stake	End of Hundred Years' War with England; René of Anjou; Mary of Burgundy Painter
Flanders	Robert Campin; Jan van Eyck; Rogier van der Weyden; Petrus Christus	Hugo van der Goes; Dirck Bouts; Hans Memling; Hunt of the Unicorn tapestry; first printed book in English by William Caxton (Bruges)
Spain and Portugal	Beginning of European exploration of West Africa's coast	Nuño Gonçalvez; Isabella and Ferdinand unite Spanish peninsula; Diego de la Cruz; beginning of Europe's Atlantic slave trade; Columbus's voyages; Vasco da Gama discovers sea route to India
Germany	Holy Roman Empire; Konrad Witz	Gutenberg's Bible; E. S.'s engravings; Martin Schongauer
Italy	Nanni di Banco; Council of Constance restores papacy to Rome; Kingdom of Naples and Sicily and Papal States begin to dominate politically; Filippo Brunelleschi; Gentile da Fabriano; Masaccio; Fra Angelico; Michelozzo di Bartolommeo; Medici academy for classical learning; Andrea del Castagno	Jacopo Bellini; Leon Battista Alberti; Piero della Francesca; Donatello; Lorenzo de' Medici rules Florence; Antonio del Pollaiuolo; Andrea Mantegna; Andrea del Verrocchio; Domenico del Ghirlandaio; Sandro Botticelli; Perugino, restoration of Sistine Chapel begins; Gentile Bellini; Savonarola preaches against worldliness; Giovanni Bellini
World	Ming dynasty (China); Muromachi period (Japan); Inka Empire established (South America); Montezuma rules Aztec Empire (Central America); Ottoman Turks defeat Crusaders; *The Arabian Nights* collected (Egypt)	Ottoman Turks conquer Constantinople; War of the Roses (England); Mosque of Qait Bey (Egypt); Ivan the Great rules Russia; John Cabot (England) reaches North America; Spanish Inquisition; world population less than 500 million

International Gothic style was the construction and decoration of a monastery and funeral chapel at Champmol near Dijon, Burgundy (see pages 621–622).

The International Gothic style, the prevailing manner of the late fourteenth century, is characterized by gracefully posed figures, sweet facial expressions, and naturalistic details, including carefully rendered costumes and textile patterns, presented in a palette of bright and pastel colors with liberal touches of gold. The International Gothic style was so universally appealing that patrons throughout Europe continued to commission such works well into the fifteenth century, even as Renaissance ideals spread into France. One place the influence of this style was seen was in manuscripts illustrated for French patrons.

Manuscript Illumination

The French nobility were avid collectors of illustrated manuscripts, and in the late fourteenth century the workshops of Paris produced outstanding manuscripts for them. Religious texts were in great demand, as were sec-

ular writings such as herbals (encyclopedias of plants), health manuals, and works of history and literature, both ancient and contemporary.

The painters of Flanders, Holland, and other regions in the Netherlands were increasingly influential in France at the beginning of the fifteenth century. Their fascination with creating an illusion of reality began to have an impact on **illumination**, the illustration of books in color, many of which were decorated by women artists (see "Women Artists in the Late Middle Ages and the Renaissance," page 620). The most famous Netherlandish illuminators of the time were three brothers—Paul, Herman, and Jean—commonly known as the Limbourg brothers. In the fifteenth century, people generally did not have family names but were instead known by their first names, often followed by a reference to their place of origin or parentage. The name used by the three Limbourg brothers, for example, refers to their home region. (Similarly, Jan van Eyck means "Jan from [the town of] Eyck." This chapter uses the forms of artists' names as they most commonly appear in contemporary documents.)

The Limbourg brothers are first recorded as appren-

WOMEN ARTISTS IN THE LATE MIDDLE AGES AND THE RENAISSANCE

Medieval and Renaissance women artists typically learned their trade from members of their families, because formal apprenticeships were not open to them. Noblewomen, who were often educated in convents, learned to draw and paint, skills considered part of the education of a woman of rank. Convents also trained women artists—some of them members of the order, others unaffiliated. One of the earliest examples of a signed work by a woman painter is a tenth-century manuscript of the Apocalypse, illustrated by a woman named Ende, who describes herself as "painteress and helper of God." Particularly remarkable is a twelfth-century collection of sermons decorated by a nun named Guda, who not only signed her work but also included a self-portrait, one of the earliest in Western art.

Jeanne de Montbaston and her husband, Richart, worked together as book illuminators under the auspices of the University of Paris in the fourteenth century. After Richart's death, Jeanne continued the workshop and, following the custom of the time, was sworn in as a *libraire* (publisher) by the university in 1353. In the fifteenth century, women could be admitted to the guilds in some cities, including the Flemish towns of Ghent, Bruges, and Antwerp, and by the 1480s one-quarter of the painters' guild of Bruges was female.

Particularly talented women were given commissions of the highest order. Bourgot, the daughter of the miniaturist Jean le Noir, illuminated books for a number of noble patrons, including Charles V of France and Jean, Duke of Berry. Christine de Pisan (1365–c. 1430), a well-known writer patronized by Philip the Bold of Burgundy and Queen Isabeau of France, described the work of an illuminator named Anastaise, "who is so learned and skillful in painting manuscript borders and miniature backgrounds that one cannot find an artisan . . . who can surpass her . . . nor whose work is more highly esteemed" (*Le Livre de la Cité des Dames*, I.41.4, translated by Earl J. Richards).

Here the anonymous illuminator of a French edition of a book by the Italian author Boccaccio entitled *Concerning Famous Women*, presented to Philip the Bold in 1403, shows Thamyris, an artist of antiquity, at work in her studio. She is depicted in a contemporary fifteenth-century room, painting an image of the Virgin and Child. At the right, an assistant grinds and mixes the colors Thamyris will need to complete her painting. The uptilted ground plane, the minute details of the setting, and the bright colors and patterns exemplify the International Gothic style of illumination favored by the French courts at the beginning of the fifteenth century.

Page with Thamyris, from Giovanni Boccaccio's *De Claris Mulieribus (Concerning Famous Women)*. 1402. Ink and tempera on vellum. Bibliothèque Nationale, Paris

tice goldsmiths in Paris about 1390. About 1404 they entered the service of the duke of Berry, for whom they produced their major work, the so-called *Très Riches Heures* (*Very Sumptuous Hours*), between 1413 and 1416. For the calendar section of this Book of Hours—a selection of prayers and readings keyed to Church rituals—the Limbourgs created full-page paintings to introduce each month, with subjects alternating between peasant labors and aristocratic pleasures.

Like most European artists of the time, the Limbourgs showed the laboring classes in a light acceptable to aristocrats—that is, happily working for their benefit. But the Limbourgs also showed peasants enjoying their own pleasures. Haymakers on the *August* page shed their clothes to take a swim in a stream, and *September* grape pickers pause to savor the sweet fruit they are gathering. In the *February* page (fig. 17-6), farm people relax cozily before a blazing fire. Although many country people at this time lived in hovels, this farm looks comfortable and well maintained, with timber-framed buildings, a row of

beehives, a sheepfold, and tidy woven wattle fences. In the distance are a small village and church.

Most remarkably, the artists convey the feeling of cold winter weather: the breath of the bundled-up worker turning to steam as he blows on his hands, the leaden sky and bare trees, the soft snow covering the landscape, and the comforting smoke curling from the farmhouse chimney. The painting clearly shows several International Gothic conventions: the high placement of the horizon line, the point at which the earth and the sky appear to meet, and the cutaway view of the house showing both interior and exterior. The muted palette is sparked with touches of yellowish orange, blue, and a patch of bright red on the man's turban at the lower left. The integration of human and animal figures and architecture into the landscape has been accomplished within the prevailing Gothic style, but on a more believable scale, with a landscape receding continuously from foreground to middle ground to background. The only nonrealistic element is the elaborate calendar device, with the chariot of the sun and the zodiac symbols.

17-6. Paul, Herman, and Jean Limbourg. Page with *February, Très Riches Heures.*
1413–16. Musée Condé, Chantilly, France

The provenance, or ownership history, of this Book of Hours was unbroken
up to 1530, when it passed at the death of Margaret of Austria, the regent of
the Netherlandish provinces, to Jean Ruffaut, treasurer of the Holy Roman
Empire. After that it dropped out of sight until around 1850, when a French
duke purchased it from an Italian collection. The duke identified its original
owner as Jean, Duke of Berry, from the portrait on the *January* page of the
book's calendar. Not until 1881, however, was the manuscript matched by
art historian Léopold Delisle with an item in Jean's accounts, described as an
incomplete but "very sumptuous hours [*très riches heures*] made by Paul and
his brothers, very richly historiated and illuminated."

Painting and Sculpture for the Chartreuse de Champmol

One of the most lavish projects of Philip the Bold, the
duke of Burgundy (ruled 1363–1404) and son of the
French king, was a Carthusian monastery, or *chartreuse*
("charterhouse," in English). He founded it in 1385 at
Champmol, near his capital at Dijon, and its church was
intended to house his family's tombs. A Carthusian
monastery was particularly expensive because the

Carthusian order is in effect a brotherhood of hermits—
unlike most monks, Carthusians did not provide for
themselves by farming or other physical work but were
dedicated to prayer and solitary meditation. Thus,
although the brothers were free to pray at all hours for
the souls of Philip and his family, they needed continuing
financial support.

Philip commissioned the Flemish sculptor Jean de
Marville (active 1366–1389) to direct the sculptural decoration of the monastery. At Jean's death in 1389, he was

17-7. Claus Sluter. Well of Moses, Chartreuse de Champmol, Dijon, France. 1395–1406. Limestone, height of figures 5'8" (1.69 m)

succeeded by his assistant Claus Sluter (documented from 1379; d. 1405/6), from Haarlem, in Holland. Although much of this splendid complex was destroyed 400 years later during the French Revolution, the quality of Sluter's work can still be seen on the Well of Moses, a monumental sculptured well at the center of the main cloister (fig. 17-7). Begun in 1395, the sculpture was unfinished at Sluter's death. Originally a pier rose from the water to support a large freestanding Crucifixion, with figures of the Virgin Mary, Mary Magdalen, and John the Evangelist. Forming a pedestal for the Crucifixion group are life-size stone figures of Old Testament prophets and heroes who either foretold the coming of Christ or were in some sense his precursors: Moses (the ancient Hebrew prophet and lawgiver), David (king of Israel and an ancestor of Jesus), and the prophets Jeremiah, Zechariah, Daniel, and Isaiah.

Sluter depicted the Old Testament figures as physically and psychologically distinct individuals. Moses' sad old eyes blaze out from a memorable face entirely covered with a fine web of wrinkles. Even his horns—traditionally given to him because of a mistranslation in the Latin Bible—are wrinkled. A mane of curling hair and a beard cascade over his heavy shoulders and chest, and an enormous cloak envelops his body. Beside him stands David, in the voluminous robes of a medieval king, the

personification of nobility. The drapery, with its deep folds creating dark pockets of shadow, is an innovation of Sluter's. While its heavy sculptural masses conceal the body beneath, its strong highlights and shadows visually define the body's volumes. With these vigorous, imposing, and highly individualized figures, Sluter transcended the limits of the International Gothic style and introduced a new Renaissance manner to northern sculpture.

Between 1394 and 1399, the duke also ordered a large altarpiece for the Chartreuse de Champmol. This was a **triptych**, a work in three panels, hinged together side by side so that the two side panels, or **wings**, fold over the central one (for an example of a carved altarpiece in a church, see fig. 17-23). Jacques de Baerze, a wood carver, executed the central panel with the Crucifixion in carved reliefs—figures or objects carved from the surrounding plane. Melchior Broederlam painted the exteriors of the two protective wings, illustrating scenes from the Infancy of Christ (fig. 17-8). The events take place in both architectural and landscape settings that fill the panels. In International Gothic fashion, both interior and exterior of the building are shown, and the floors are tilted up to give clear views of the action. The landscapes have been arranged to lead the eye up from the foreground and into the distance along a rising ground plane. Despite the imaginative architecture, fantasy mountains, miniature trees, and solid gold sky, the artist has created a sense of light and air around solid figures.

On the left wing, in the *Annunciation,* under the benign eyes of God the archangel Gabriel greets Mary with the news of her impending motherhood. A door leads into the dark interior of the tall pink rotunda meant to represent the Temple of Jerusalem, a symbol of the Old Law, where, according to legend, Mary was an attendant prior to her marriage to Joseph. A tiny enclosed garden and a pot of lilies are symbols of Mary's virginity. In the *Visitation,* just outside the temple walls, the now-pregnant Mary greets her older cousin Elizabeth, who is also pregnant and will soon give birth to John the Baptist. On the right wing, in the *Presentation in the Temple,* Mary and Joseph have brought the newborn Jesus to the temple for the Jewish purification rite, where the priest Simeon takes him in his arms to bless him (Luke 2:25–32). At the far right, the Holy Family flees into Egypt to escape King Herod's order to kill all Jewish male infants. The family travels along treacherous terrain similar to that in the *Visitation* scene. Much of the detail comes not from the New Testament accounts but from other legendary writings. Reflecting a new humanizing element creeping into art, Joseph drinks from a flask and carries the family belongings over his shoulder. The statue of a pagan god breaks and tumbles from its pedestal as the Christ Child approaches, visible at the upper right.

FLEMISH ART

The southern Netherlands, known as Flanders (today's Belgium and northeastern France), became the leading center of painting outside Italy in the fifteenth century. Flanders, with its major seaport at Bruges, was the commercial power of northern Europe, rivaled in southern

17-8. Melchior Broederlam. *Annunciation and Visitation* (left); *Presentation in the Temple and Flight into Egypt* (right), wings of an altarpiece for Chartreuse de Champmol. 1394–99. Oil on panel, 5'5³/4" x 4'1¹/4" (1.67 x 1.251 m). Musée des Beaux-Arts, Dijon

Europe only by the Italian city-states of Florence and Venice. The chief sources of Flemish wealth were the wool trade and the manufacture of fine fabrics. Most professionals belonged to a powerful local guild—an association of people engaged in the same business or craft. Guilds oversaw nearly every aspect of their members' lives, and high-ranking guild members served on town councils and helped run city governments.

Artists might work independently in their own studios without the sponsorship of an influential patron, but they had to belong to a local guild. Experienced artists who moved from one city to another usually had to work as assistants in a local workshop until they met the requirements for guild membership. Different kinds of artists belonged to different guilds. Painters, for example, joined the Guild of Saint Luke, the guild of the physicians and pharmacists, because painters used the same techniques of grinding and mixing raw ingredients for their pigments and varnishes that physicians and pharmacists used to prepare salves and potions.

Civic groups, town councils, and wealthy merchants were important art patrons in the Netherlands, where the cities were self-governing, largely independent of the landed nobility. The diversity of clientele encouraged artists to experiment with new types of images—with outstanding results. Throughout most of the fifteenth century, the art and artists of the Netherlands were considered the best in Europe. The new Flemish style of painting was so admired in other countries that artists came from abroad to see the paintings of the major Flem-

ish artists and eventually tried to emulate them. The dukes of Burgundy expanded their empire throughout nearly the entire Netherlands, and they provided stability for the arts to flourish there, as well as spreading the influence of Flemish arts throughout Europe. Only at the end of the fifteenth century did a general preference for the Netherlandish painting style give way to a taste for the new styles of art and architecture developing in Italy.

First-Generation Panel Painters

In the fourteenth century, artists painted on wood **panels** (see "Painting on Panel," page 624), designed tapestries and stained glass, and illuminated manuscripts. By the fifteenth century, panel painting had become the leading medium. The Flemish style originated in manuscript illumination of the late fourteenth century, when artists began to create full-page scenes set off with frames that functioned as windows looking into rooms or out onto landscapes with distant horizons. The panel paintings of the early fifteenth century developed logically from these works.

The most outstanding exponents of the new Flemish style were Robert Campin (documented from 1406; d. 1444), Jan van Eyck (c. 1370/90–1441), and Rogier van der Weyden (c. 1399–1464). Scholars have been able to piece together sketchy biographies for these artists from contracts, court records, account books, and references to their work by contemporaries. Reasonable attributions of a number of paintings have been made to each

TECHNIQUE

PAINTING ON PANEL

Painting pictures on wood has an ancient history, and wood panels were particularly favored by European painters and their patrons in the fifteenth century for works ranging from enormous altarpieces to small portraits. First the wood surface was prepared to make it smooth and nonabsorbent. After being sanded, the panel was coated—in Italy with gesso, a fine solution of plaster, and in northern Europe with a solution of chalk. These coatings soaked in and closed the pores of the wood. Fine linen was often glued down over the whole surface or over the joining lines on large panels made of two or more pieces of wood. The cloth was then also coated with gesso or chalk.

Once the surface was ready, the artist could paint on it with either a water-soluble color, called tempera, or oil paint. Italian artists favored tempera, using it almost exclusively for panel painting until the end of the fifteenth century. Northern European artists preferred the oil technique that Flemish painters so skillfully exploited at the beginning of the century. In some cases, wood panels were first painted with oil, then given fine detailing with tempera, a technique especially popular for small portraits.

Tempera had to be applied in a very precise manner, because it dried almost as quickly as it was laid down. Shading had to be done with careful overlying strokes in tones ranging from white and gray to dark brown and black. Because tempera is opaque—light striking its surface does not penetrate to lower layers of color and reflect back—the resulting surface was matte, or dull, and had to be varnished to give it a sheen. Oil paint, on the other hand, took much longer to dry, and while it was still wet, errors could simply be wiped away with a cloth. Oil could also be made translucent by applying it in very thin layers, called glazes. Light striking a surface built up of glazes penetrates to the lower layers and is reflected back, creating the appearance of glowing from within. In both tempera and oil the desired result in the fifteenth century was a smooth surface that betrayed no brushstrokes and somewhat resembled enamel.

of them, but written evidence is limited. Signatures are rarely found on fifteenth-century paintings, in part because artists customarily signed the frames, which usually have been lost.

Only recently has stylistic analysis convinced most art historians that Robert Campin was the artist formerly known as the Master of Flémalle, named for a pair of panel paintings once thought to have come from the Abbey of Flémalle. Campin's paintings reflect the Netherlandish taste for lively narrative and a bold volumetric treatment of figures reminiscent of the sculptural style of Claus Sluter. About 1425–1428, Campin painted an altarpiece now known as the *Mérode Altarpiece* from the name of modern owners. Slightly over 2 feet tall and about 4 feet wide with the wings open, it probably was made for a small private chapel or altar (fig. 17-9). Campin portrayed the Annunciation inside a Flemish home and integrated common religious symbols into this contemporary setting. The lilies in the **majolica** (glazed earthenware) pitcher on the table, for example, which symbolize Mary's virginity, were a traditional element of Annunciation imagery (see fig. 17-8). The white towel and hanging waterpot in the niche symbolize Mary's purity and her role as the vessel for the Incarnation of Christ. These accouterments of a middle-class home now have a religiously sanctioned status. Such objects are often referred to as "hidden" symbols because they are treated as a normal part of the scene, but their religious meanings would have been widely understood by contemporary people.

Unfortunately, the precise meanings are not always clear today. The central panel may simply portray Gabriel telling Mary that she will be the Mother of Christ. Another interpretation suggests that the painting shows the moment immediately following Mary's acceptance of her destiny. A rush of wind riffles the book pages and snuffs the candle as a tiny figure of Christ carrying a cross descends on a ray of light. Having accepted the miracle of the Incarnation (God assuming human form), Mary reads her Bible while sitting humbly on the footrest of the long bench as a symbol of her submission to God's will. But another interpretation of the scene suggests that it represents the moment just prior to the Annunciation. In this view, Mary is not yet aware of Gabriel's presence, and the rushing wind is the result of the angel's rapid entry into the room, where he appears before her half kneeling and raising his hand in salutation.

The complex treatment of light in the *Mérode Altarpiece* was an innovation of the Flemish painters. The strongest illumination comes from an unseen source at the upper left in front of the **picture plane**, as if the sun entered through a miraculously transparent wall that allows the viewer to observe the scene. In addition, a few rays enter the round window at the left as the vehicle for the Christ Child's descent. More light comes from the window at the rear of the room, and areas of reflected light can also be detected.

Campin maintained the spatial conventions typical of the International Gothic style; the abrupt recession of the bench toward the back of the room, the sharply uplifted floor and tabletop, and the disproportionate relationship between the figures and the architectural space create an inescapable impression of instability. In an otherwise intense effort to mirror the real world, this treatment of space may be a conscious remnant of medieval style, serving the symbolic purpose of visually detaching the religious realm from the world of the viewers. Unlike figures by such International Gothic painters as the Limbourg brothers (see fig. 17-6), the Virgin and Gabriel are massive rather than slender, and their abundant draperies increase the impression of their material weight.

Although in the biblical account Joseph and Mary

17-9. Robert Campin. *Mérode Altarpiece (Triptych of the Annunciation)* (open). c. 1425–28. Oil on panel, center 25¼ x 24⅞"
(64.1 x 63.2 cm); each wing approx. 25⅜ x 10⅞" (64.5 x 27.6 cm). The Metropolitan Museum of Art, New York
The Cloisters Collection, 1956 (56.70)

were not married at the time of the Annunciation, this house clearly belongs to Joseph, shown in his carpentry shop on the right. A prosperous Flemish city can be seen through the shop window, with people going about their business unaware of the drama taking place inside the carpenter's home. One clue indicates that this is not an everyday scene: The shop, displaying carpentry wares—mousetraps, in this case—should be on the ground floor, but its window opens from the second floor. The significance of the mousetraps would have been recognized by knowledgeable people in the fifteenth century as Saint Augustine's reference to Christ as the bait in a trap set by God to catch Satan. Joseph is drilling holes in a small board that may be a drainboard for wine making, symbolizing the central rite of the Church, the Eucharist.

Joseph's house opens onto a garden planted with a red-rose bush, which alludes to the Virgin and also to the Passion. It has been suggested that the man standing behind the open entrance gate, clutching his hat in one hand and a document in the other, may be a self-portrait of the artist. Alternatively, the figure may represent an Old Testament prophet, because rich costumes like his often denoted high-ranking Jews of the Bible. Kneeling in front of the open door to the house are the donors of the altarpiece. They appear to observe the Annunciation through the door, but their gazes seem unfocused. The garden where they kneel is unrelated spatially to the chamber where the Annunciation takes place, suggesting that the scene is a vision induced by their prayers. Such a presentation, often used by Flemish artists, allowed the donors of a religious work to appear in the same space and time—and often on the same scale—as the figures of the saints represented.

Campin's contemporary Jan van Eyck was a trusted official in the court of the duke of Burgundy as well as a painter. Nothing is known of Jan's youth or training, but he was born sometime between 1370 and 1390 in Maaseik, on the Maas (Meuse) River, now in Belgium on the present-day border between Belgium and the Netherlands. He was from a family of artists, including two brothers, Lambert and Hubert, and a sister, Margareta, whom sixteenth-century Flemish writers still remembered with praise. The earliest references to Jan are in 1422 in The Hague, where he was probably involved in the renovation of a castle. He was appointed painter to Philip the Good, the duke of Burgundy, in Bruges on May 19, 1425. His appointment papers state that he had been hired because of his skillfulness in the art of painting, that the duke had heard about Jan's talent from people in his service, and that the duke himself recognized those qualities in Jan van Eyck. The special friendship that developed between the duke and his painter is a matter of record.

Although there are a number of contemporary accounts of Jan's activities, the only reference to specific artworks is to two portraits of Princess Isabella of Portugal, which he painted in that country in 1429 and sent back to Philip in Flanders. Philip and Isabella were married in 1430. The duke alluded to Jan's remarkable technical skills in a letter of 1434–1435, saying that he could find no other painters equal to his taste or so excellent in art and science. Part of the secret of Jan's "science" was his technique of painting with oil glazes on wood panel. So brilliant were the results of his experiments that Jan has been mistakenly credited with being the inventor of **oil painting**. Actually, the medium had been

17-10. Jan van Eyck. *Ghent Altarpiece* (closed), Cathedral of Saint-Bavo, Ghent, Flanders (Belgium).
1432. Oil on panel, 11'5¾" x 7'6¾" (3.5 x 2.3 m)

known for several centuries, and medieval painters had used oil paint to decorate stone, metal, and occasionally plaster walls.

For his paintings on wood panel, Jan built up the images in transparent oil layers, a procedure called **glazing**. His technique permitted a precise, objective description of what he saw, with tiny, carefully applied brushstrokes so well blended that they are only visible at very close range. Other northern European artists of the period worked in the oil medium, although oil and **tempera** were still combined in some paintings, and tempera was used for painting on canvas (see "Painting on Panel," page 624).

Jan's earliest known work, the *Ghent Altarpiece,* was completed in 1432 for a wealthy official of Ghent and his wife. The complexities of this altarpiece can be challenging intellectually and emotionally. The wing exteriors (fig. 17-10) present an Annunciation scene, with Gabriel and the Virgin on opposite sides of a room looking out onto a city. In the panels above are ancient sibyls and Old Testament prophets who foretold the coming of Christ. Below, the donors are portrayed beside statues of the church's patron saints, John the Baptist and John the Evangelist.

The brilliantly painted interior of the altarpiece, which was only opened at Easter (see fig. 17-1), presents the adoration of the Lamb of God. Above are an enthroned

17-11. Jan van Eyck. *Adam* and *Eve,* details of the open *Ghent Altarpiece* (see fig. 17-1)

17-12. Jan van Eyck. *Man in a Red Turban.* 1433. Oil on panel, 10¹/₄ x 7¹/₂" (26 x 19.1 cm). The National Gallery, London

figure of God, the Virgin Mary, John the Baptist, and angel musicians. The jewels and embroidery, meticulously re-created gem by gem and stitch by stitch, are superb examples of Jan's characteristic technique. In almost shocking contrast to the richly clothed angels, Adam and Eve, after the Fall, cover their nakedness (fig. 17-11). Eve holds the forbidden fruit. Above their heads, painted as if carved in stone, their son Cain kills his brother Abel, thus committing the first murder. This act is the terrible consequence of the first couple's disobedience to God, a sin that can be redeemed only by the sacrifice of Christ.

Below these figures and above the fountain of life, the Lamb of God stands on the altar, his blood flowing into a chalice, and directly below, all saints move through a para-disial landscape toward the Lamb. Jan's technique is firmly grounded in the terrestrial world despite his visionary subject. The meadow and woods, painted leaf by leaf and petal by petal, and the distant city have been rendered from a careful observation of nature. Jan noted, for example, that the farther away colors are from a viewer, the more muted they seem. He thus painted the more distant objects with a grayish or bluish cast and the sky paler toward the horizon, an effect called **atmospheric perspective** (see "Renaissance Perspective Systems," page 650).

Jan also painted an Annunciation in which he returned to the convention followed by Broederlam rather than Campin and showed the angelic salutation occurring in a church (see Introduction, fig. 5). The image is as loaded with hidden meanings as is Campin's in spite of its more aristocratic setting.

The *Man in a Red Turban* of 1433 (fig. 17-12) is widely believed to be Jan's self-portrait, partly because of the strong sense of personality it projects, partly because the frame, signed and dated by him, also bears his personal motto, *Als ich chan* ("The best that I am capable of doing"). This motto, derived from classical sources, is a telling illustration of the humanist spirit of the age and the confident expression of an artist who knows his capabilities and is proud to display them.

If the *Man in a Red Turban* is, indeed, the face of Jan van Eyck, it shows us his physical appearance as if seen in an enlarging mirror—every wrinkle and scar, the stubble of a day's growth of beard on the chin and cheeks, and the tiny reflections of light from a studio window in the pupils of the eyes. The outward gaze of the subject is new in portraiture, and it suggests the subject's increased

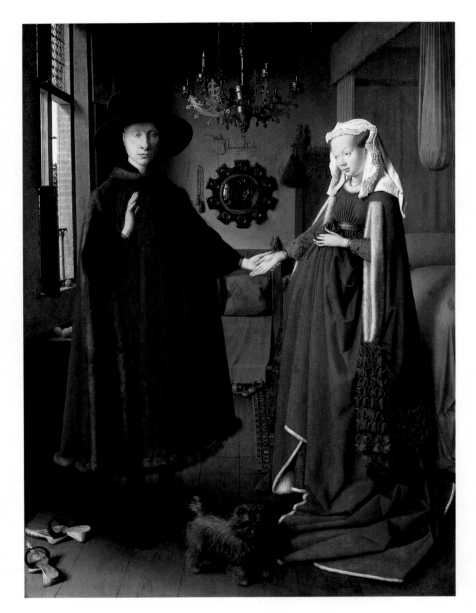

17-13. Jan van Eyck. *Portrait of Giovanni Arnolfini (?) and His Wife, Giovanna Cenami (?)*. 1434. Oil on panel, 33 x 22¹/₂" (83.8 x 57.2 cm). The National Gallery, London

Odd though it may seem today, the fact that Jan chose a bedroom as the setting for such an official occasion is quite in keeping with the fashion of his time, although it is somewhat unlikely that this event actually took place. A beautifully furnished room containing a large bed hung with rich draperies was a source of pride for its owners, and the bedroom was symbolic of marital happiness and pleasure. According to a later inventory description of this painting, the original frame (now lost) was inscribed with a quotation from Ovid, a Roman poet known for his celebration of romantic love.

sense of pride as he seems to catch the viewer's eye.

Jan's best-known painting today is an elaborate portrait of a couple, traditionally identified as Giovanni Arnolfini and his wife, Giovanna Cenami (fig. 17-13). This fascinating work has been, and continues to be, subject to a number of interpretations, most of which suggest that it represents a wedding or betrothal. One remarkable detail is the artist's inscription below the mirror on the back wall: *Johannes de eyck fuit hic 1434* ("Jan van Eyck was here, 1434"). Normally, a work of art in fifteenth-century Flanders would have been signed "Jan van Eyck made this." The wording here specifically refers to a witness to a legal

document, and indeed, two witnesses to the scene are reflected in the mirror, a man in a red turban—perhaps the artist—and one other. The man in the portrait, identified by early sources as a member of an Italian merchant family living in Flanders, the Arnolfini, holds the right hand of the woman in his left and raises his right to swear to the truth of his statements before the two onlookers. The fact that such a scene is shown in a domestic setting, apparently the couple's bedroom, is intriguing.

In the fifteenth century, a marriage was rarely celebrated with a religious ceremony. The couple signed a legal contract before two witnesses, after which the

17-14. Rogier van der Weyden. *Deposition*, from an altarpiece commissioned by the Crossbowmen's Guild, Louvain, Brabant, Belgium. c. 1435. Oil on panel, 7'2⅝" x 8'7⅛" (2.2 x 2.62 m). Museo del Prado, Madrid

bride's dowry might be paid and gifts exchanged. If the painting indeed documents a wedding, the room where the couple stands is a nuptial chamber, whose furnishings were often gifts from the groom to the bride. Recently, however, it has been suggested that, instead of a wedding, the painting might be a pictorial "power of attorney," by which the husband states that his wife may act on his behalf in his absence.

Whatever the painting represents, the artist has juxtaposed the secular and the religious in a work that seems to have several levels of meaning. On the man's side of the painting, the room opens to the outdoors, the external world in which men function, while the woman is silhouetted against the domestic interior, with its allusions to the roles of wife and mother. The couple is surrounded by emblems of wealth, piety, and married life. The convex mirror reflecting the entire room and its occupants is a luxury object described in many inventories of the time, but it may also symbolize the all-seeing eye of God, before whom the man swears his oath. The **roundels** decorating its frame depict the Passion of Christ, a reminder of Christian redemption.

Many other details have religious significance, suggesting the piety of the couple: the crystal prayer beads on the wall; the image of Saint Margaret, protector of women in childbirth, carved on the top of a high-backed chair next to the bed; and the single burning candle in the chandelier, which may be a symbol of Christ's presence. But the candle can also represent a nuptial taper or a sign that a legal event is being recorded. The fruits shown at the left, seemingly placed there to ripen in the sun, may allude to fertility in a marriage and also to the Fall of Adam and Eve and the Garden of Eden. The small dog may simply be a pet, but its rare breed—affenpinscher—suggests wealth and serves also as a symbol of fidelity.

One of the most mysterious of the major early Flemish artists is Rogier van der Weyden. Although his biography has been pieced together from documentary sources, not a single existing work of art bears his name or has an entirely undisputed connection with him. He was thought at one time to be identical with the Master of Flémalle, but evidence now suggests that he studied under Robert Campin, which would explain the similarities in their painting styles. Even his relationship with Campin is not altogether certain, however. At the peak of his career, Rogier maintained a large workshop in Brussels, to which apprentices and shop assistants came from as far away as Italy to learn his style of painting. He died in 1464.

To establish the thematic and stylistic characteristics for Rogier's art, scholars have turned to a painting of the Deposition, the central panel of an altarpiece that once had wings painted with the Four Evangelists—Matthew, Mark, Luke, and John—and Christ's Resurrection (fig. 17-14). The altarpiece was commissioned by the Louvain

17-15. Rogier van der Weyden. *Last Judgment Altarpiece* (open). After 1443. Oil on panel, open 7'4 5/8" x 17'11" (2.25 x 5.46 m). Musée de l'Hôtel-Dieu, Beaune, France

Crossbowmen's Guild sometime before 1443, the date of the earliest known copy after it by another artist.

The Deposition was a popular theme in the fifteenth century because of its dramatic, personally engaging character. Like a *tableau vivant*, the act of removing Jesus' body from the Cross is set on a shallow stage closed off by a wood backdrop that has been **gilded**, or covered with a thin overlay of gold. The solid, three-dimensional figures seem to press forward toward the viewer's space, forcing the viewer to identify with the grief of Jesus' friends, who tenderly and sorrowfully remove his body from the Cross for burial. Here Jesus' suffering and death are made palpably real by the portraitlike faces and elements of contemporary dress in the friends, as well as the lifesize corpse at the center of the composition. Rogier has arranged this figure in a graceful curve, echoed by the form of the fainting Virgin, thereby increasing the viewer's emotional identification with both the Son and the Mother. The artist's compassionate sensibility is especially evident in the gestures of John the Evangelist, who supports the Virgin at the left, and Jesus' friend Mary Magdalen, who wrings her hands in anguish at the right.

Many scholars see Rogier's emotionalism as a tie with the Gothic past, but it can also be interpreted as an example of fifteenth-century humanistic sensibility in its concern for individual expressions of emotion. Although united by their sorrow, the mourning figures react in personal ways.

Rogier's choice of color and pattern balances and enhances his composition. For example, the complexity of the gold brocade worn by Joseph of Arimathea, who offered his new tomb for the burial, and the contorted pose and vivid dress of Mary Magdalen increase the visual impact of the right side of the panel and counter the larger number of figures at the left. The palette of subtle, slightly muted colors is sparked with red and white accents to focus the viewer's attention on the main subject. The whites of the winding cloth and the tunic of the youth on the ladder set off Jesus' pale body, as the white headdress and neck shawl emphasize the ashen face of Mary.

Rogier painted his largest and most elaborate work, the altarpiece of the *Last Judgment,* for a hospital in Beaune founded by the chancellor of the duke of Burgundy (fig. 17-15). Whether Rogier painted this altarpiece before or after he made a trip to Rome for the Jubilee of 1450 is debated by scholars. He would have already known the Last Judgments so common in medieval churches, but he could also have been inspired by the paintings and mosaics in Rome. The tall, straight figure of the archangel Michael, dressed in a white robe and priest's cope, or cloak, dominates the center of the wide **polyptych** (multiple-panel work) as he weighs souls under the direct order of Christ, who sits on the arc of a giant rainbow above him. The Virgin Mary and John the Baptist kneel at either end of the rainbow. Behind them on each side, six apostles, then a king, a queen, and a pope witness the scene. The solid gold background serves, as it did in medieval art, to signify events in the heavenly realm or in a time remote from that of the viewer.

The bodily resurrection takes place on a narrow, barren strip of earth that runs across the bottom of all but the outer panels. Men and women climb out of their tombs, turning in different directions as they react to the call to Judgment. The scale of justice held by Michael tips in an unexpected direction; instead of Good weighing more than Bad, the Saved Soul has become pure spirit and rises, while the Damned one sinks, weighed down by unrepented sins. The Damned throw themselves into the flaming pit of hell; those moving to the left—notably far less numerous—are greeted by the archangel Gabriel at the shining Gate of Heaven, depicted as Gothic architecture.

In his portraiture, Rogier balanced a Flemish love of detailed individuality with a flattering **idealization** of the features of men and women. In *Portrait of a Lady,* dated about 1460, Rogier transformed an ordinary young woman into a vision of exquisite but remote beauty (fig. 17-16). Her long, almond-shape eyes, regular features, and smooth translucent skin characterize women in portraits attributed to Rogier. He popularized the half-length pose that includes the woman's high waistline and clasped hands, which he used for images of the Virgin and Child that often formed **diptychs** (two-panel works) with small portraits of this type. The woman is pious and

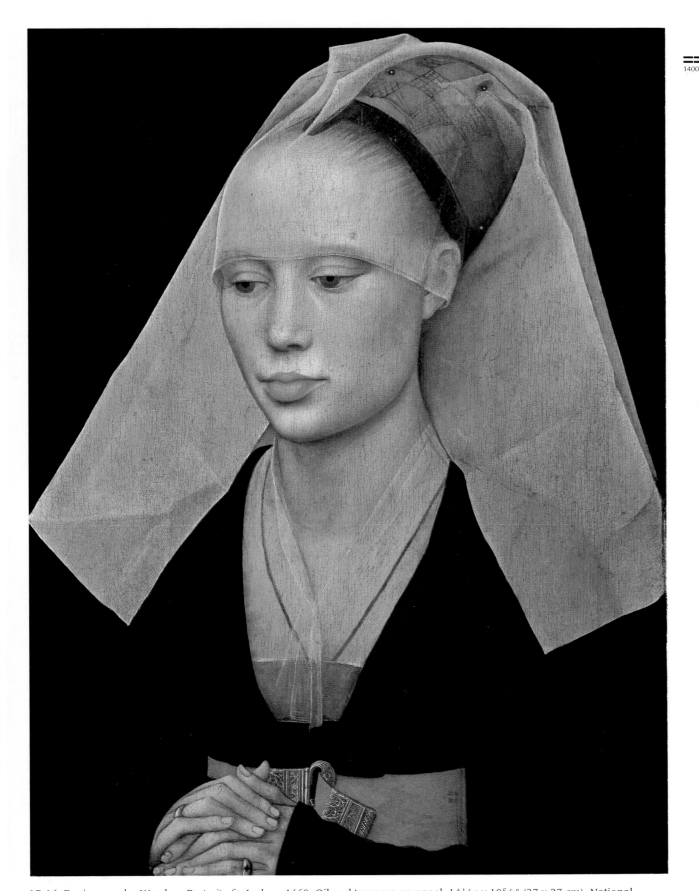

17-16. Rogier van der Weyden. *Portrait of a Lady.* c. 1460. Oil and tempera on panel, 14¹/₁₆ x 10⁵/₈" (37 x 27 cm). National Gallery of Art, Washington, D.C.

Andrew W. Mellon Collection

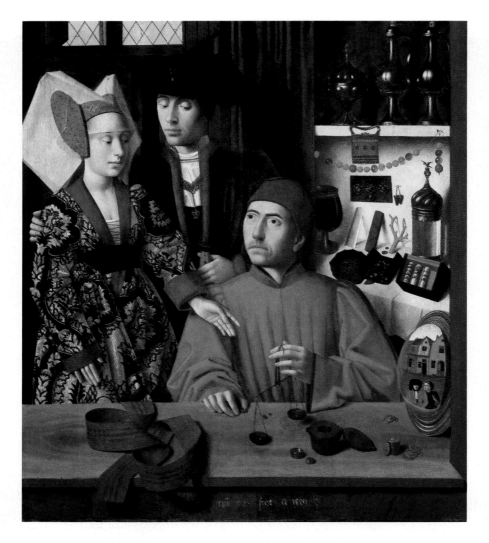

17-17. Petrus Christus. *Saint Eloy (Eligius) in His Shop.* 1449. Oil on oak panel, 38⅝ x 33½" (98 x 85 cm). The Metropolitan Museum of Art, New York
Robert Lehman Collection, 1975 (1975.1.110)

humble, wealthy but proper and modest. The portrait expresses the complex and often contradictory attitudes of the new middle-class patrons of the arts, who balanced pride in their achievements with appropriate modesty.

Second-Generation Panel Painters

The extraordinary achievements of Robert Campin, Jan van Eyck, and Rogier van der Weyden attracted many followers. The work of this second generation of Flemish painters was simpler, more direct, and easier to understand than that of their predecessors. Nevertheless, these artists produced high-quality work of great emotional power, and they were in large part responsible for the rapid spread of the Flemish style through Europe.

One of the most interesting of these second-generation painters was Petrus Christus (documented from 1444; d. c.1475). Nothing is known of his early life before he became a citizen of Bruges in 1444. Although many paintings attributed to him resemble the work of Jan van Eyck, he probably did not know that painter personally, because Jan died three years before Christus arrived in Bruges. In fact, his work seems as much influenced by Rogier van der Weyden as by Jan. Christus may also have spent time in Italy, where a "Piero from Bruges" was active in the ducal court of Milan in 1457.

In 1449 Christus painted *Saint Eloy (Eligius) in His Shop* (fig. 17-17). Eloy, a seventh-century ecclesiastic and a goldsmith and mintmaster for the French court, according to legend, used his wealth to ransom Christian captives. He became the patron saint of metalworkers. Here he weighs a jeweled ring to determine its price, as a handsome couple looks on. Among the objects on the shelf behind him are a number of similar rings. This may be a specific betrothal or wedding portrait, or the couple may be idealized figures personifying marital love.

As in Jan's *Portrait of Giovanni Arnolfini(?) and His Wife, Giovanna Cenami(?)* (see fig. 17-13), a convex mirror extends the viewer's field of vision, in this instance to the street outside, where two men appear. One holds a falcon. All the figures are dressed stylishly, for the court of Burgundy set the fashions for much of Europe. Whether or not the reflected image has symbolic meaning, the mirror had a practical value in allowing the goldsmith to note the approach of a potential customer. The emphasis on everyday details is so strong that the presence of the saint becomes a justification for a secular subject. By the sixteenth century, artists could create clearly secular pictures showing businesspeople in their shops.

An outstanding Haarlem painter who moved south to Flanders, Dirck Bouts (documented from 1457; d. 1475), became the official painter of the city of Louvain in 1468. His mature style shows a strong debt to Jan van Eyck and, especially, Rogier van der Weyden, but not at the expense of his

17-18. Dirck Bouts. *Wrongful Execution of the Count* (left), and companion piece, *Justice of Otto III* (right). 1470–75. Oil on panel, each 12'11" x 6'7½"(3.9 x 2 m). Musées Royaux des Beaux-Arts de Belgique, Brussels, Belgium

own clear-cut individuality. Bouts was an excellent story-teller, a master of direct narration rather than complex symbolism. His best-known works today are two remaining panels (fig. 17-18) from a set of four on the subject of justice. Such paintings were often commissioned for display in municipal buildings, and the town council of Louvain had ordered this set from Bouts for the city hall. The subject of the panels was a fictional twelfth-century story about a real-life Holy Roman emperor. In a continuous narrative in the left panel, *Wrongful Execution of the Count*, the empress falsely accuses a count of a sexual impropriety. Otto III tries and convicts the count, who is put to death by beheading. In the right panel, *Justice of Otto III,* the widowed countess successfully endures a trial by ordeal to prove her husband's innocence. She kneels unscathed before the repentant emperor, holding her husband's head on her right arm and a red-hot iron bar in her left hand. In the far distance, the evil empress is executed by burning at the stake.

Dirck Bouts's work is especially notable for its spacious outdoor settings. Carefully adjusting the scale of his figures to the landscape and architecture, the artist created an illusion of space that recedes continuously and gradually from the picture plane back to the far horizon. For this effect, he employed devices such as walk-ways, walls, and winding roads along which characters in the scene are placed. Bouts's figures are extraordinarily tall and slender and have little or no facial expression. Because Bouts is credited as the inventor of a type of official group portrait in which individuals are integrated into a narrative scene with fictional or religious characters, the Louvain justice panels, with their distinctly individualized protagonists, may have been a vehicle for a group portrait of the town council.

By far the most successful of the second-generation Flemish-school painters was Hans Memling. Memling combines the intellectual depth and virtuoso rendering of his predecessors, but with a delicacy of feeling and exquisite grace. Memling was born in one of the German states about 1430–1435. He may have worked in Rogier van der Weyden's Brussels workshop in the 1460s, for Rogier's style remained the dominant influence on his art. Soon after this master's death in 1464, Memling moved to Bruges, where he worked until his death in 1494. Memling had an international clientele, and his style was widely emulated both at home and abroad.

Among the works securely assigned to Memling is a large wooden **reliquary**, a container for the sacred relics of Saint Ursula, in the form of a Gothic chapel (fig. 17-19). It

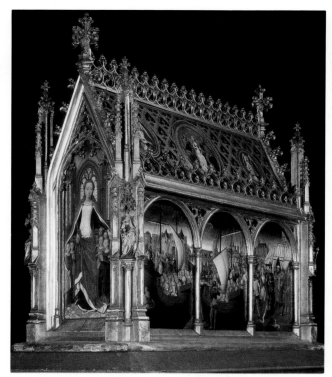

17-19. Hans Memling. Saint Ursula reliquary. 1489. Painted and gilded oak, 34 x 36 x 13" (86.4 x 91.4 x 33 cm). Memling Museum, Hospital of Saint John, Bruges, Belgium

The reliquary was commissioned presumably by the two women dressed in white habits and black hoods worn by hospital sisters and depicted on the end of the reliquary not visible here. One hypothesis is that they are Jossine van Dudzeele and Anna van den Moortele, two administrators of the hospital, where the church-shaped chest has remained continuously for more than five centuries. The story of fourth-century Saint Ursula, murdered by Huns in Cologne after she returned from a visit to Rome, is told on the six side panels. Shown from the left: the pope bidding Ursula good-bye at the port of Rome; the murder of her female companions in Cologne harbor; and Ursula's own death. On the "roof" are roundels with musician angels flanking the Coronation of the Virgin. At the corners are carved saints, and on the end is Saint Ursula in the doorway of the "church," sheltering her followers under her mantle. In early stories, Ursula was accompanied on her trip by ten maidens. By the tenth century, however, she had become the leader of 11,000 women martyrs.

17-20. Hans Memling. *Martyrdom of Saint Ursula,* detail of the Saint Ursula reliquary. Panel 13¾ x 10" (35 x 25.3 cm)

The Gothic cathedral of Cologne, under construction, looms in the background of the *Martyrdom of Saint Ursula* panel. Memling created this deep space as a foil for his idealized female martyr, a calm aristocratic figure amid active men at arms. The surface pattern and intricately arranged folds of the drapery draw our attention to her.

Hugo van der Goes (c. 1440–1482) unites the intellectualism of Jan van Eyck and the emotionalism of Rogier van Weyden in an entirely new style. Hugo's major work was an exceptionally large altarpiece, more than 8 feet tall, commissioned by an Italian living in Bruges, Tommaso Portinari, who managed the Medici bank there (fig. 17-21). Painted in Flanders, probably between 1474 and 1476, the large triptych was transported to Italy and installed in 1483 in the Portinari family chapel in the Church of Saint Egidio, in Florence. Tommaso, his wife, Maria Baroncelli, and their three eldest children are portrayed kneeling in prayer on the wings. With pointing gestures, their patron saints present them. On the left wing, looming larger than life behind Tommaso and his son Antonio, are their name saints, Thomas and Anthony. The younger son, Pigello, born in 1474, was apparently added after the original composition was set and has no patron saint. On the right wing, Maria and her daughter Margherita are presented by Saints Mary Magdalen and Margaret. The theme of the altarpiece is the Nativity of Christ, with the central panel representing the Adoration of the newborn Child by Mary and Joseph, a host of angels, and the shepherds who have rushed in from the fields. In the middle ground of the wings are scenes that precede the Adoration in the central panel. Winding their

was made in 1489 for the Hospital of Saint John in Bruges, now a museum of Memling's works. The painting illustrates the story of Saint Ursula's martyrdom. According to legend, Ursula, the daughter of the Christian king of Brittany, in France, was betrothed to a pagan English prince. She requested a three-year delay in the marriage to travel with 11,000 virgin attendants to Rome, during which time her husband-to-be was to convert to Christianity. On the trip home, the women stopped in Cologne, which had been taken over by Attila the Hun and his nomadic warriors from Central Asia. They murdered her companions, and, when Ursula rejected an offer of marriage, they killed her as well, with an arrow through the heart (fig. 17-20). Although the events supposedly took place in the fourth century, Memling has set them in contemporary Cologne:

17-21. Hugo van der Goes. *Portinari Altarpiece* (open). c. 1474–76. Tempera and oil on panel, center 8'3¹/₂" x 10'
(2.53 x 3.01 m); wings each 8'3¹/₂" x 4'7¹/₂" (2.53 x 1.41 m). Galleria degli Uffizi, Florence

17-22. Hugo van der Goes. Albarelo, detail of the center panel, *Portinari Altarpiece*

Even a little flower has a meaning. Three red carnations, which may refer to the Trinity of Father (God), Son (Jesus), and Holy Ghost, as well as seven blue columbines symbolizing the Virgin's future sorrows. Scattered on the ground are violets, symbolizing humility. The majolica *albarelo* holds a red lily (for the Blood of Christ) and three irises—white for purity and purple for Christ's royal ancestry. The iris, or "little sword," also refers to Simeon's prophetic words to Mary at the Presentation in the Temple: "And you yourself a sword will pierce so that the thoughts of many hearts may be revealed" (Luke 2:35).

way through the winter landscape are two groups headed for Bethlehem, Jesus' birthplace. On the left wing, Mary and Joseph travel to their native city to take part in a census

ordered by the Roman ruler over the region. Near term in her pregnancy, Mary has dismounted from her donkey and staggers before it, supported by Joseph. On the right wing, a servant of the Three Magi, who are coming to honor the awaited Savior, is asking directions from a poor man. The continuous landscape across the wings and central panel is the finest evocation of cold, barren winter since the Limbourg brothers' *February* (see fig. 17-6).

Although the brilliant palette and meticulous accuracy recall Jan van Eyck, and the intense but controlled feelings suggest the emotional content of Rogier van der Weyden's works, the composition and interpretation of the altarpiece are entirely Hugo's. The monumental figures of Joseph, Mary, and the shepherds dominating the central panel are the same size as the patron saints on the wings; the Portinari family and the angels are small in comparison. Hugo uses color as well as the gestures and gazes of the figures to focus our eyes on the center panel, where the mystery of the Incarnation takes place. Instead of lying swaddled in a manger or in his mother's arms, the Child rests naked and vulnerable on the barren ground with rays of light emanating from his body. The source of this image was the visionary writing of the Swedish mystic Bridget (declared a saint in 1391), composed about 1360–1370, which specifically mentions Mary kneeling to adore the Child immediately after giving birth.

Hugo's complex symbolism recalls Jan's *Ghent Altarpiece*. The setting of the central scene refers both to Jesus' birth and to his royal ancestry. Supporting the stable, where the traditional ox and ass observe the event, is a large Roman column, against which Mary was believed to have leaned during the birth. In the background, the ancient palace of King David is identified by his symbol, the harp, over the door, which may itself be a reference to the name Portinari ("gatekeepers"). The inscription above the harp has been interpreted to mean: "Here Christ was born of the Virgin Mary."

The foreground still life of ceramic pharmacy jar *(albarelo)* and glass, flowers, and wheat has multiple meanings (fig. 17-22). The glass vessel symbolizes the

17-23. Mary of Burgundy Painter. Page with *Mary at Her Devotions,* in *Hours of Mary of Burgundy.* Before 1482. 7¹/₂ x 5¹/₄" (19.1 x 13.3 cm). Österreichische National-bibliothek, Vienna

It [Flemish painting] will appeal to women, especially to the very old and the very young, and also to monks and nuns and to certain noblemen who have no sense of true harmony. In Flanders they paint, with a view to deceiving sensual vision, such things as may cheer you and of which you cannot speak ill, as for example saints and prophets. They paint stuffs and masonry, the green grass of the fields, the shadow of trees, and rivers and bridges, which they call landscapes, with many figures on this side and many figures on that. And all this, though it pleases some persons, is done without reason or art, without symmetry or proportion, without skillful selection or boldness, and, finally, without substance or vigor. Nevertheless there are countries where they paint worse than in Flanders. And I do not speak so ill of Flemish painting because it is all bad but because it attempts to do so many things well (each one of which would suffice for greatness) that it does none well. (Reported by Francisco de Hollanda in Klein and Zerner, page 34)

Manuscript Illumination

The rise in popularity of panel painting in the fifteenth century did not diminish the production of richly illustrated books for wealthy patrons (see Introduction, fig. 20). Not surprisingly, developments in manuscript illumination were similar to those in panel painting, although in miniature. Each scene was a tiny image of the world rendered in microscopic detail. Complexity of composition and ornateness of decoration were commonplace, with the framed image surrounded by a fantasy of vines, flowers, insects, animals, shellfish, or other objects painted as if seen under a magnifying glass. Ghent and Bruges were major centers of this exquisite art, and one of the finest practitioners was an anonymous artist known as the Mary of Burgundy Painter from a Book of Hours traditionally thought to have been made for Mary—the daughter and only heir of Charles the Bold, the duke of Burgundy—who married Maximilian of Austria (see page 639). The manuscript dates to sometime prior to Mary's early death, in 1482 (fig. 17-23).

In the Book of Hours frontispiece, the painter has attained a new complexity in treating pictorial space; we look not only through the "window" of the illustration's frame but through another window in the wall of the room depicted in the painting. The young Mary of Burgundy appears twice: once seated in the foreground, reading from her Book of Hours; and again in the background, in a vision inspired by her reading, kneeling with attendants before the Virgin and Child in a church. On the window ledge is an exquisite still life—a rosary, carnations, and a glass vase holding purple irises. The artist has skillfully executed the filmy veil covering Mary's hat, the transparent glass vase, and the bull's-eye panes of the window, circular panes whose center "lump" was formed by the glassblower's pipe. The spatial recession leads the eye into the far reaches of the church interior, past the Virgin and the gilded altarpiece in the sanctuary

entry of the Christ Child into the Virgin's womb without destroying her virginity, the way light passes through glass without breaking it. The *albarelo* is decorated with vines and grapes, alluding to the wine of Communion at the Eucharist, which represents the Blood of Christ. The wheat sheaf refers both to the location of the event at Bethlehem, which in Hebrew means "house of bread," and to the Host, or bread, at Communion, which represents the Body of Christ.

The central panel illustrates more than a historical Nativity scene; it is also an enactment of the Eucharist, the central rite of Christian worship. The angels wear attire appropriate to various roles at a High Mass—but the chief celebrant is missing, and it has been suggested that he is the Infant Christ himself. The exact moment in the liturgy may be indicated by the words *Sanctus, Sanctus, Sanctus* ("Holy, Holy, Holy") embroidered on the edge of the angel's vestment at the right, which are the first lines of a hymn that immediately precedes the Consecration of the Host. Hugo's artistic vision goes far beyond this formal religious symbolism. For example, the shepherds, who stand in unaffected awe before the miraculous event, are among the most sympathetically rendered images of common people to be found in the art of this period. The portraits of the children are among the most sensitive studies of children's features.

Hugo's altarpiece had a profound impact on Florentine painters. Ghirlandaio admired and emulated it; Michelangelo detested it and spoke scathingly:

17-24. Cope, from the Treasury of the Golden Fleece. Flemish, mid-15th century. Cloth with gold and colored silk embroidery, 5'4⁹/₁₆" x 10'9⁵/₁₆" (1.64 x 3.3 m). Kunsthistorisches Museum, Vienna

The Order of the Golden Fleece was an honorary fraternity founded by Duke Philip the Good of Burgundy in 1430 with twenty-three knights chosen for their moral character and bravery. Religious services were an integral part of the meetings of the order, and opulent liturgical and clerical objects were created for the purpose. The insignia of the order were a gold ram skin hung as a pendant from the Collar of the Golden Fleece, given to each knight. These insignia were the property of the order and had to be returned at the death of a member. The gold ram referred to the Greek legend of Jason, who went off on his ship *Argo* to search for the Golden Fleece, the wool of a magical ram that had been sacrificed to Zeus.

to two people conversing in the far distance at the left. In the "painting" within an illumination in a book only 5 by 7 inches in size, reality and vision have been rendered equally tangible, as if captured by a Jan van Eyck or a Robert Campin on a large panel.

The Fiber Arts: Embroidery and Tapestries

The importance of textiles in the fifteenth century cannot be overemphasized. Flemish artists of the period produced outstanding designs for tapestries, embroidery, and needlepoint. These designs exhibit many of the same concerns with the bulk of figures, the illusion of three-dimensional space, and naturalistic details that are seen in Flemish paintings.

A remarkable example is a sumptuous embroidered cope, or ceremonial cloak, now in the Treasury of the Golden Fleece in Vienna (fig. 17-24). The surface of this vestment is divided into compartments, with the standing figure of a saint in each one. At the top of the cloak's back, as if presiding over the standing saints, is an enthroned figure of Christ, flanked by scholar-saints in their studies. The designer of this outstanding piece of needlework was clearly familiar with contemporary Flemish painting, and the embroiderers were able to copy the preliminary drawings with great precision. The particular stitch used here consists of double gold threads tacked down with unevenly spaced colored silk threads to create an iridescent effect. (To view the full effect of a cope, see the angels at the right in the center panel of *Portinari Altarpiece,* fig. 17-21.)

In the fifteenth and sixteenth centuries, Flemish tapestry making was considered the best in Europe. There were major weaving centers at Brussels, Tournai, and Arras where intricately designed wall hangings were made on order for royal and aristocratic patrons, important church officials, and even town councils. Among the most common subjects were foliage and flower patterns, scenes from the lives of the saints, and themes from classical mythology and history. Tapestries provided both insulation and luxurious decoration for the stone walls of castles, churches, and municipal buildings. Often they were woven for specific places or for festive occasions such as weddings, coronations, and other public events. Many were given as diplomatic gifts, and the wealth of individuals can often be judged from the number of tapestries listed in their household inventories. Some of the finest surviving weavings were originally in royal chambers. In one early-fifteenth-century painting, tapestries can be seen hanging on the walls in the private rooms where the French queen Isabeau of Bavaria accepts a bound manuscript from the author Christine de Pizan (see Introduction, fig. 20). More sumptuous textiles covered the queen's bed and were sewn into robes for her and the ladies-in-waiting who are gathered with her.

One of the best-known tapestry suites (now in a museum in the United States) is the Hunt of the Unicorn, whose original five surviving pieces may have been made for Anne of Brittany, the young widow of the French king Charles VIII, to celebrate her marriage to Louis XII of France on January 8, 1499. The first and seventh pieces, *Start of the Hunt* and *Unicorn in Captivity,* were added later. Unfortunately, following the French Revolution all wall

17-25. *Unicorn at the Fountain,* from the Hunt of the Unicorn tapestry series. c. 1498–1500. Wool, silk, and metal thread (13–21 warp threads per inch), 12'1" x 12'5" (3.68 x 3.78 m). The Metropolitan Museum of Art, New York

Gift of John D. Rockefeller, the Cloisters Collection (37.80.2)

The price of a tapestry depended on the materials used. Rarely was a fine, commissioned series woven only with wool; instead, tapestry producers enhanced it to varying degrees with silk, silver, and gold threads. The richest kind of tapestry was one made entirely of silk and gold. Because the silver and gold threads used silk wrapped with real metal, people later burned many tapestries in order to retrieve the precious materials. As a result of this practice, few French royal tapestries survived the French Revolution. Many existing works show obvious signs, however, that the metallic threads were painstakingly pulled out in order to preserve the tapestries.

hangings with royal insignia were ordered destroyed or the identifying marks cut off, as happened with this set. The unicorn, a mythological horselike animal with cloven hooves, a goat's beard, and a single long twisted horn, appears in stories from ancient India, the Near East, and Greece. The creature was said to be supernaturally swift and, in medieval belief, could only be captured by a young virgin, to whom it came willingly. Thus, it became a symbol of the Incarnation, with Christ as the unicorn captured by the Virgin Mary, and also a metaphor for romantic love, suitable as a subject for wedding tapestries.

Each of the tapestry pieces exhibits a number of figures in a dense field with trees, flowers, and a distant view of a castle, as in the *Unicorn at the Fountain* (fig. 17-25). The letters *A* and *E*, hanging by a cord from the fountain, may be a reference to the first and last letters of Anne's name or the first and last letters of her motto, *À ma vie* ("By my life," a kind of pledge). The workshop that produced the Unicorn series is not known, although Brussels is a likely possibility. The unusually fine condition of the piece allows us to appreciate its rich coloration and the subtlety in modeling the faces, creating tonal variations in the animals' fur, and depicting reflections in the water.

Because of its religious connotations, the unicorn was an important animal in the medieval **bestiary**, an encyclopedia of real and imaginary animals, giving information of both moral and practical value. For example, the unicorn's horn (if ever found) was thought to be an antidote to poison. Thus, the unicorn is shown dipping its horn into the fountain's waters to purify them. Other woodland creatures included here have symbolic meanings as well. For example, lions, ancient symbols of power, represent valor, faith, courage, and mercy; the stag is a symbol of Christian resurrection and a protector against poisonous serpents and evil in general; and the gentle, intelligent leopard was said to breathe perfume. Not surprisingly, the rabbits symbolize fertility and the dogs fidelity. The pair of pheasants is an emblem of human love and marriage, and the goldfinch is another symbol of fertility. Only the ducks swimming away seem to have no known message.

The plants, flowers, and trees in the tapestry, identifiable from their botanically correct depictions, reinforce the theme of protective and curative powers. Each has both religious and secular meanings, but the theme of marriage, in particular, is referred to by the presence of such plants as the strawberry, a common symbol of sexual love; the periwinkle, a cure for spiteful feelings and jealousy; the pomegranate, for fertility; and the pansy, for remembrance. The trees include oak for fidelity, beech for nobility, holly for protection against evil, hawthorn for the power of love, and orange for fertility. The parklike setting with its prominent fountain is rooted in a biblical love poem, the Song of Songs (4:12, 13, 15–16): "You are an enclosed garden, my sister, my bride, an enclosed garden, a fountain sealed. You are a park that puts forth pomegranates, with all choice fruits. . . . You are a garden fountain, a well of water flowing fresh from Lebanon. Let my lover come to his garden and eat its choice fruits."

THE SPREAD OF FLEMISH ART IN EUROPE

Just as Flanders was the northern center of fifteenth-century commerce, attracting the newly wealthy merchants and bankers, so too was it the artistic hub to and from which art and patronage flowed. Flemish art—its complex and provocative symbolism, its realism and atmospheric space, its brilliant colors and sensuous textures—delighted wealthy patrons and well-educated courtiers outside Flanders, just as it did the affluent guild members and clergy of Bruges and Brussels. At first, Flemish artists were imported to foreign courts, then many artists came from outside Flanders to study there. Soon, Flemish manuscripts, tapestries, altarpieces, and portraits began to appear in palaces and chapels throughout Europe. Local artists learned Flemish oil painting techniques and emulated the Flemish style, until by the later years of the fifteenth century, distinctive regional variations of Flemish art could be found throughout Europe, from the Atlantic Ocean to the Danube.

17-26. Diego de la Cruz(?). *Visitation,* panel from an altarpiece, Valladolid, Spain. 15th century. Oil on panel, 60 x 36⅞" (152.8 x 93.7 cm). Collection of the University of Arizona Museum of Art, Tucson
Gift of Samuel H. Kress Foundation (61.13.22)

Hispano-Flemish Art of Spain and Portugal

Spanish and Portuguese painters quickly absorbed the new Flemish style to such an extent that the term *Hispano-Flemish* is applied to their works of the second half of the fifteenth century. Not only were Flemish paintings brought to Spain, but Spanish artists went north to study the Flemish style and technique firsthand. Queen Isabella of Castile preferred Flemish painting above all other styles. Her marriage to Ferdinand of Aragon in 1469 and their conquest of Granada from the Muslims in 1492 effectively united the peninsula in what would later become modern Spain. By 1496, when their daughter Joanna married Philip, son and heir of Mary of Burgundy and Maximilian of Austria, the Flemish manner had replaced the earlier Spanish styles.

The marriage of Joanna and Philip was commemorated in an altarpiece, painted probably by Diego de la Cruz, the panels of which are now scattered, many to American collections. The strong impact of Flemish art is unmistakable in this painter's work, as in a panel depicting the Visitation (fig. 17-26). Elizabeth and Mary embrace in front of the castlelike home of Elizabeth and

17-27. Nuño Gonçalvez. *Saint Vincent with the Portuguese Royal Family,* panel from the *Altarpiece of Saint Vincent.* c. 1471–81. Oil on panel, 6'9¾" x 4'2⅝" (2.07 x 1.28 m). Museu Nacional de Arte Antiga, Lisbon

been carved, may have been created to commemorate a Portuguese crusade against the Muslims in Morocco undertaken in 1471 under Vincent's standard. In one of the two largest panels (fig. 17-27), Vincent, magnificent in red and gold vestments, stands in a tightly packed group of people, with members of the royal family at the front and courtiers forming a solid block across the rear. With the exception of the idealized features of the saint, all are portraits: At the right, King Alfonso V kneels before Vincent, while his young son and his deceased uncle, Henry the Navigator, look on. Alfonso and his son rest their hands on their swords; Henry's hands are tented in prayer. At the left, Alfonso's wife and mother hold rosaries. The appearance of Vincent is clearly a vision, brought on by the intense prayer of the individuals around him.

French Art

During the fifteenth century, France was divided into feudal holdings that in theory were under royal rule. Many, however, were held by dukes who were richer and more powerful than the king himself. Throughout much of the century, there were repeated struggles for power. When Charles VI died in 1422, the throne was claimed for the nine-month-old Henry VI of England through his mother, the French princess. The infant king's uncle, the duke of Bedford, then assumed control of the French royal territories as regent, with the support of the duke of Burgundy. The exile of the late French king Charles VI's son, Charles VII, inspired Joan of Arc to lead a crusade to return him to the French throne. Although Joan was captured, condemned on trumped-up charges, and burned at the stake in 1431, the revitalized French forces captured Paris in 1436, and by 1453 the English had finally been driven out. In 1461 Louis XI succeeded his father, Charles VII, on the throne and began a single-minded extension of royal power. He and his successors firmly established the power and wealth of the monarchy, and under their rule the French royal court again became a major source of patronage for the arts.

An outstanding court artist of the period, Jean Fouquet (c. 1420–c. 1481), was born in Tours and may have trained in Paris as an illuminator. He probably traveled to Italy in about 1445, but by about 1450, he was back in Tours, a renowned painter with commissions that included portraits of Charles VII, the royal family, and courtiers, as well as illustrations for manuscripts and designs for tombs. Fouquet's paintings exhibit his familiarity with contemporary Italian architectural decoration, but he was also strongly influenced by Flemish painting.

Among the court officials painted by Fouquet is Étienne Chevalier, the treasurer of France under Charles VII, for whom he painted a diptych showing Chevalier on the left and the Virgin and Child on the right panel (fig. 17-28). According to an inscription, the painting was made to fulfill a vow made by Chevalier to the king's much-loved and respected mistress, Agnès Sorel, who died in 1450. Sorel, whom contemporaries described as a highly

her husband, Zechariah, a Temple priest. Zechariah is reading on the porch in the background, his dog nearby, while two cleaning women on the upstairs gallery are hard at work with mops and ladders, getting everything tidy for the arrival of a guest. The lush garden setting is filled with accurately portrayed plants and flowers, symbolizing Mary's virginity, purity, and humility, as well as foretelling the Passion of Christ, her yet-unborn son. Many plants depicted have medicinal uses, known from herbals of the time, suggesting that Elizabeth's son, John the Baptist, and Mary's son, Jesus, were born to heal the ills of humanity.

Nuño Gonçalvez, a major artist connected with the court of Portugal, also had clearly assimilated much from the Flemish style. His intensity of detail, monumental figures, and rich colors reflect the influence of Jan van Eyck, and Gonçalvez was especially renowned for his portraiture, closer to Dirck Bouts's and Hans Memling's than to Jan's, and for his virtuoso rendering of costumes and draperies. Gonçalvez's only securely attributed works are six panels from a large polyptych made for the Convent of Saint Vincent de Fora in Lisbon between 1471 and 1481. The altarpiece, whose central scene may have

17-28. Jean Fouquet. *Étienne Chevalier and Saint Stephen,* left wing of the *Melun Diptych.* c. 1450. Oil on panel, 36½ x 33½"
(92.7 x 85.5 cm). Staatliche Museen zu Berlin, Preussischer Kulturbesitz, Gemäldegalerie. *Virgin and Child,* right wing of
the *Melun Diptych.* c. 1451. Oil on panel, 36⅝ x 33½" (94.5 x 85.5 cm). Koninklijk Museum voor Shone Kunsten,
Antwerp, Belgium

moral, extremely pious woman, was probably the model for the Virgin, with her features taken from her death mask, which is still preserved.

Chevalier, who kneels in prayer with clasped hands and a meditative gaze, wears a *houppelande,* the voluminous costume of the time. Fouquet has followed the Flemish manner in depicting the courtier's ruddy features as carefully as the reflection in a mirror, and its accuracy is confirmed by other known portraits. Chevalier is presented to the Virgin by his name saint, Stephen (Étienne, in French), whose features are also distinctive enough to have been a portrait. According to legend and biblical accounts, Stephen, a deacon in the early Christian Church in Jerusalem, was the first Christian martyr, stoned to death for his "blasphemous" defense of his beliefs. Here the saint wears liturgical, or ritual, vestments and carries a large stone on a closed Gospel, a volume with the first four books of the New Testament. A trickle of blood can be seen on his tonsure, the shaved head adopted as a sign of humility by male members of some religious orders. The two figures are shown in a large hall decorated with marble paneling and classical **pilasters,** upright strips of wall masonry made to resemble

columns, that have been gilded. Fouquet has arranged the figures in an unusual spatial setting, with the diagonal lines of the wall and uptilted tile floor receding toward an unseen focal point at the right. Despite his debt to Flemish realism and his nod to Italian architectural forms and to linear perspective, Fouquet's somewhat austere style is uniquely his own.

The brother-in-law of Charles VII, René, the duke of Anjou, was a major figure in French culture of the fifteenth century, both as a patron and as a gifted writer. Among René's noted books is a romantic allegory, *Livre du Cuer d'Amours Espris* (*Book of the Heart Captured by Love*), completed in 1457. One of the earliest illustrated copies, completed about 1465, was created by a painter of original talents, probably at René's court. The René Painter exhibits a special ability to render difficult effects of illumination, as seen in the opening illustration, *René Gives His Heart to Desire* (fig. 17-29). The night scene—rare and relatively new in painting—is set in the bedroom of the king, who is unable to sleep and is tormented by desire. The allegory begins with the king's heart being taken by Love (Amour) and given to Desire, who sets off to find the perfect object for the king's affections. In spite

17-29. René Painter. Page with *René Gives His Heart to Desire,* in René of Anjou's *Livre du Cuer d'Amours Espris.* c. 1457–65. Tempera on vellum, 11³/₈ x 8¹/₈" (28.9 x 20.6 cm). Österreichische Nationalbibliothek, Vienna

It was not customary to keep records of works made by official court artists, who were paid yearly salaries or pensions rather than by the piece. At one time, René of Anjou was believed to have been not only a writer but also a painter who illustrated his own books. His accounts show, however, that during the time this manuscript was produced, the duke had in his employ an illuminator named Berthélemy van Eyck, perhaps a younger relation of Jan van Eyck. No clue is given to what Berthélemy painted during his twenty-five years in the duke's employ, but he worked under the close eye of his patron. An inventory of 1471–1472 records the fact that his workroom was just off René's own study.

of the dim light, every detail of the chamber is clear, from the crisp white linens and velvet hangings on the beds to the Oriental rugs and patterned wall design to a fifteenth-century nightlight—a candle burning under a wooden stand.

German Art

In the Holy Roman Empire, a loose confederation of primarily Germanic states that lasted until the early nineteenth century, two major stylistic strains of art existed simultaneously during the first half of the fifteenth century. One continued the International Gothic style with increased prettiness, softness, and sweetness of expression. The other was an intense investigation and detailed description of the physical world. The major exponent of the latter style was Konrad Witz (documented from 1434; d. 1446). Witz, a native of what is now southern Germany, like many artists, was drawn to Basel (in modern Switzerland), where the numerous church officials were

17-30. Konrad Witz. *Miraculous Draft of Fish,* from an altarpiece from the Cathedral of Saint Peter, Geneva, Switzerland. 1444. Oil on panel, 4'3" x 5'1" (1.29 x 1.55 m). Musée d'Art et d'Histoire, Geneva

a rich source of patronage. His career ended with his early death, probably from the plague. Witz's last large commission was an altarpiece dedicated to Saint Peter for the Cathedral of Saint Peter in Geneva, the wings of which he signed and dated in 1444. In the *Miraculous Draft of Fish* (fig. 17-30), a scene from the life of Saint Peter, the Flemish influence can be perceived in the handling of drapery and in details of what ultimately engages our attention: the landscape setting. The painter has created an identifiable topographical portrayal of Lake Geneva, with its dark mountain rising on the far shore behind Jesus and the surrounding Alps shining in the distance. Witz records every nuance of light and water—the rippling surface, the reflections of boats, figures, and buildings, even the lake bottom. Peter's body and legs, visible through the water, are distorted by the refraction. The floating clouds above create shifting light and dark passages over the water. Witz, perhaps for the first time in European art, recorded nature in a way that approached a modern photograph.

THE ITALIAN RENAISSANCE IN FLORENCE

By the end of the Middle Ages, the most important Italian cultural centers were north of Rome at Florence, Pisa, Milan, Venice, and the smaller duchies of Mantua, Ferrara, and Urbino. Much of the power and art patronage was in the hands of wealthy families: the Medici in Florence, the Visconti and Sforza in Milan, the Gonzaga in Mantua, the Este in Ferrara, and the Montefeltro in Urbino. Cities grew in wealth and independence as people moved to them from the countryside in unprecedented numbers, and commerce became increasingly important. In some of the Italian states a noble lineage was no longer necessary for—nor did it guarantee—political and economic success. Now money conferred status, and a shrewd business or political leader could become very powerful.

Patronage of the arts was an important public activity with political overtones. As one Florentine merchant, Giovanni Rucellai, succinctly noted, he supported the arts "because they serve the glory of God, the honour of the city, and the commemoration of myself" (cited in Baxandall, page 2; see fig. 17-36).

The Medici of Florence were leaders in intellectual and artistic patronage, as they were in business practice. Cosimo de' Medici the Elder (1389–1464) founded an academy devoted to the study of the classics, especially the works of Plato and his followers, the Neoplatonists. Neoplatonism is characterized by a sharp opposition between the spiritual (the ideal or Idea) and the carnal (Matter) that can be overcome by severe discipline and denial of the world of the senses. Writers, philosophers, and musicians dominated the Medici Neoplatonic circle. Few architects, sculptors, or painters were included, however, for although some artists had studied Latin or Greek, most had learned their craft in apprenticeships and thus were still considered little more than manual laborers. Nevertheless, interest in the ancient world rapidly spread beyond the Medici circle to artists and craftspeople, who

sought to reflect the new interests of their patrons in their work. Gradually, artists began to see themselves as more than artisans, and society recognized their best works as achievements of a very high order.

Artists, like humanist scholars, looked to Classical antiquity for inspiration. Because few examples of ancient Roman painting were known in the fifteenth century, Renaissance painters looked to Roman sculpture and literature for inspiration. Despite this interest in antiquity, fifteenth-century Italian painting and sculpture continued to be predominantly religious. Secular works were rare until the second half of the century, and even these were chiefly portraits. Allegorical and mythological themes also appeared in the latter decades as patrons began to collect art for their personal enjoyment. The male nude became an acceptable subject, mainly through the study of Classical figures as models for idealized Renaissance sculpture. Other than representations of Eve or an occasional allegorical or mythological figure, female nudes were rare until the end of the century.

Like their Flemish counterparts, Italian painters and sculptors moved gradually toward a greater precision in rendering the illusion of physical reality. They did so in a more analytical way than the Flemings had, with the goal of achieving anatomically correct but idealized figures—perfected, generic types—set within a rationally, rather than intuitively, defined space. Just as Italian architects applied abstract, mathematically derived design principles to their plans and elevations, painters and relief sculptors developed a rational system of linear perspective to achieve the illusion of continuously receding space (see "Renaissance Perspective Systems," page 650).

Architecture

Travelers from across the Alps in the mid-fifteenth century found Florence very different in appearance from the northern cities. Instead of church spires piercing the sky, the Florentine skyline was dominated, as it still is today, by the enormous mass of the cathedral dome rising above low houses, smaller churches, and the blocklike palaces of the wealthy, all of which had minimal exterior decoration.

The major civic project of the early years of the fifteenth century was the still-unfinished cathedral, begun in the late thirteenth century and continued intermittently during the fourteenth century. As early as 1367, its architects had envisioned a very tall dome to span the huge interior space, but they lacked the engineering know-how to construct it. When interest in completing the cathedral was revived around 1407, the technical solution was proposed by a young sculptor-turned-architect, Filippo Brunelleschi (1377–1446). Brunelleschi's intended career as a sculptor had ended with his failure to win a competition in 1402 to design new bronze doors for the Baptistry. Brunelleschi declined a role as assistant on that project and traveled to Rome, probably with his sculptor friend Donatello, where he studied ancient Roman sculpture and architecture.

Brunelleschi, whose father had been involved in the original plans for the dome in 1367, advised constructing first a tall **drum**, or cylindrical base. The drum was

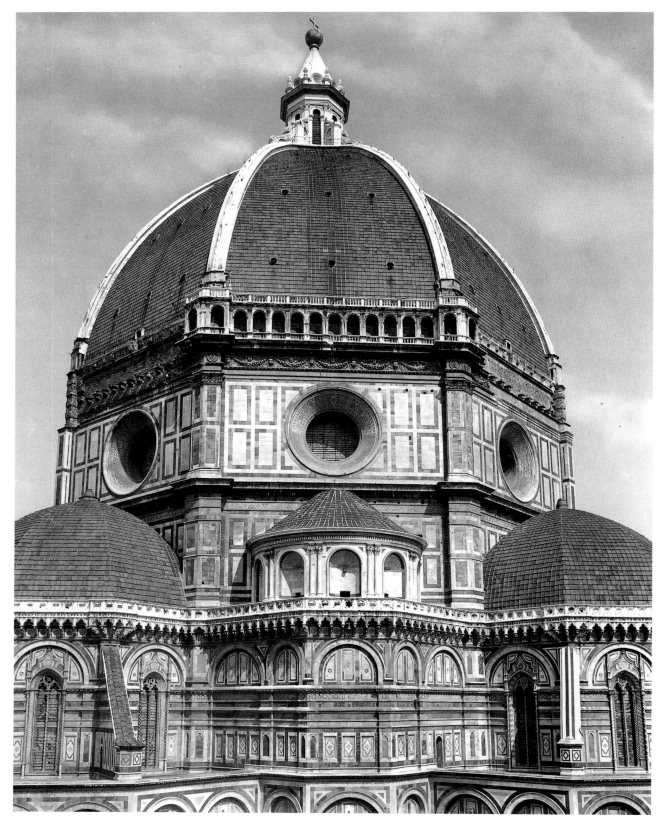

17-31. Filippo Brunelleschi. Dome of Florence Cathedral. 1417–36; lantern completed 1471

The cathedral dome was a source of immense local pride from the moment of its completion. Renaissance architect and theorist Leon Battista Alberti described it as rising "above the skies, large enough to cover all the peoples of Tuscany with its shadow" (cited in Goldwater and Treves, page 33). While Brunelleschi maintained the Gothic pointed-arch profile of the dome established in the fourteenth century, he devised an advanced construction technique that was more efficient, less costly, and safer than earlier systems. An arcaded gallery he planned to install at the top of the tall drum was never built, however. In 1507 Baccio d'Agnolo won a competition to design the gallery, using supports installed on the drum nearly a century earlier. The first of the eight sections, seen here, was completed in 1515.

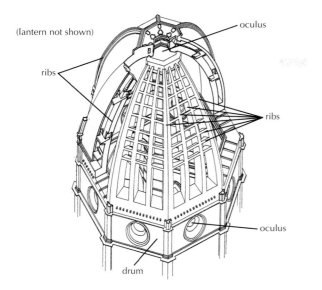

17-32. Cutaway drawing of Brunelleschi's dome, Florence Cathedral. (Drawing by P. Sanpaolesi)

17-33. Filippo Brunelleschi. Plan of the Church of San Lorenzo, Florence. c. 1421–46; plan includes later additions and modifications

17-34. Filippo Brunelleschi. Nave, Church of San Lorenzo

finished in 1410, and in 1417 Brunelleschi was commissioned to design the dome itself (fig. 17-31). Work began in 1420 and was completed by 1471. A revolutionary feat of engineering, the dome is a double shell of masonry that combines Gothic and Renaissance elements. Gothic construction is based on the pointed **arch**, using stone shafts, or **ribs**, to support the **vault**, or ceiling. The octagonal outer shell is essentially a structure of this type, supported on ribs and in a pointed-arch profile; however, like Roman domes, it is cut at the top with an **oculus** (opening) and is surmounted by a **lantern**, a crowning structure made up of Roman architectural forms. The dome's 138-foot diameter would have necessitated the use of **centering**, temporary wooden construction supports that were costly and even dangerous. Therefore, Brunelleschi devised machinery to hoist building materials as needed and invented an ingenious system by which each portion of the structure reinforced the next one as the dome was built up **course**, or layer, by course. The reinforcing elements were vertical marble ribs and horizontal sandstone rings connected with iron rods, with the whole supported by oak staves and beams tying rib to rib (fig. 17-32). The inner and outer shells were also tied together internally by a system of arches. When completed, this self-buttressed unit required no external support to keep it standing.

The cathedral dome was a triumph of engineering and construction technique for Brunelleschi, who was a pioneer in Renaissance architectural design. Other commissions came quickly after the cathedral-dome project, and Brunelleschi's innovative designs were well received by Florentine patrons. From about 1421 to his death in 1446, Brunelleschi was involved in two projects for the Medici parish Church of San Lorenzo. First, the architect designed a **sacristy** (a room where ritual attire and vessels are kept) as a chapel and mausoleum for the Medici. Completed in 1428, it today is called the Old Sacristy to distinguish it from one built in the sixteenth century. Brunelleschi was then commissioned to rebuild the church itself, replacing the eleventh-century **basilica**. The precise history of this second project is obscured by interruptions in the construction and later alterations. Brunelleschi may have conceived the plans for the new church at the same time as he designed the sacristy in 1421 or perhaps as late as about 1425, after new foundations had been laid for the transept and sanctuary.

San Lorenzo has the plan of an early Christian basilica (fig. 17-33). A long **nave**, flanked by single side aisles opening into shallow side chapels, is intersected by a short **transept**. Beyond the square **crossing**, a square sanctuary is flanked by small chapels opening off the transept. Projecting from the eastern transept is Brunelleschi's sacristy.

San Lorenzo is unusual in its mathematical regularity and symmetry. Brunelleschi based his plan on a square, traditionally medieval, module—a basic unit of measure that could be multiplied or divided and applied to every element of the design. The result was a series of clear, rational interior spaces in harmony with each other. Brunelleschi's modular system was also carried through in the proportions of the church's interior elevation (fig. 17-34). Ornamental details, all in a classical

17-35. Michelozzo di Bartolommeo. Palazzo Medici-Riccardi, Florence. Begun 1444

Cosimo de' Medici the Elder's decision to build a new town palace was not just to provide more living space for his family. He also incorporated into the plans offices and storage rooms for conducting his business affairs. For the palace site, he chose the Via de' Gori at the corner of the Via Larga, the widest city street at that time. Despite his practical reasons for constructing a large residence and the fact that he chose simplicity and austerity over grandiosity in the exterior design, his detractors had a field day. As one exaggerated: "[Cosimo] has begun a palace which throws even the Colosseum at Rome into the shade."

style, were carved in *pietra serena,* a grayish stone that became synonymous with Brunelleschi's interiors. Below the plain **clerestory** (upper-story wall of windows) with its unobtrusive openings, the arches of the nave are carried on tall, slender **Corinthian** columns made even taller by the insertion of a favored Brunelleschian device, an **impost block** between the column **capital** and the springing of the round arches. The arcade is repeated in the outer walls of the side aisles in the arched openings to the chapels surmounted by arched **lunettes.** Flattened architectural forms in *pietra serena* articulate the wall surfaces, and each **bay** is covered by its own shallow vault. The square crossing is covered by a hemispherical dome, the nave and transept by flat ceilings.

San Lorenzo was an experimental building combining old and new elements, but Brunelleschi's rational approach, unique sense of order, and innovative incorporation of Classical motifs were inspirations to later Renaissance architects, many of whom learned from his work firsthand by completing his unfinished projects.

Brunelleschi's role in the Medici palace (now known as the Palazzo Medici-Riccardi) in Florence, begun in 1444, is unclear. According to the sixteenth-century painter, architect, and biographer Giorgio Vasari, Brunelleschi's model for the palazzo (palace) was rejected as too grand by Cosimo de' Medici the Elder, who later hired Michelozzo di Bartolommeo (1396–1474), whom most scholars have accepted as the designer of the building. In any case, the palace established a tradition for Italian town houses that, with interesting variations, remained the norm for a century (fig. 17-35). The plain exterior was in keeping with political and religious thinking in Florence, which was strongly influenced by Christian ideals of poverty and charity. Like many other European cities, Florence had sumptuary laws, which forbid ostentatious displays of wealth—but they were often ignored. Under Florentine law, for example, private homes were limited to a dozen rooms; Cosimo, however, acquired and demolished twenty small houses to provide the site for his new residence.

Huge in scale (each story is more than 20 feet high), with fine proportions and details, the building was constructed around a central courtyard surrounded by a **loggia,** or covered gallery. On one side, the ground floor originally opened through large, round arches onto the

17-36. Leon Battista Alberti. Palazzo Rucellai, Florence. 1455–70

street. These arches were walled up in the sixteenth century and given windows designed by Michelangelo. The facade of large, **rusticated** stone blocks—that is, with their outer faces left rough, typical of Florentine townhouse exteriors—was derived from fortifications. On the palace facade, the stories are clearly set off from each other by the change in the stone surfaces from very rough at the ground level to almost smooth on the third. The Medici palace inaugurated a new monumentality and regularity of plan in residential urban architecture.

The relationship of the facade to the body of the building behind it was a continuing challenge for Italian Renaissance architects. Early in his architectural career, Leon Battista Alberti (1404–1472), a humanist turned architect, devised a facade—begun in 1455 but never finished—to be the unifying front for a planned merger of eight adjacent houses in Florence acquired by Giovanni Rucellai (fig. 17-36). Alberti's design, influenced in its basic approach by the Palazzo Medici, was a simple rectangular front suggesting a coherent, cubical three-story building capped with an overhanging **cornice**, a heavy, projecting horizontal molding at the top of the wall. The double windows under round arches were a feature of Michelozzo's Palazzo Medici, but other aspects of the facade were entirely new. Inspired by the ancient Colosseum in Rome, Alberti articulated the surface of the lightly rusticated wall with a horizontal-vertical pattern of pilasters and **architraves** that superimposed the Classical orders: Doric on the ground floor, Ionic on the second, and Corinthian on the third (see "Elements of Architecture," page 686). The Palazzo Rucellai provided a visual lesson for local architects in the use of classical elements and mathematical proportions, and Alberti's enthusiasm for classicism and his architectural projects in other cities were catalysts for the spread of the Renaissance movement. Later, Alberti worked in Mantua and other north Italian cities (see page 686).

Sculpture

In the early fifteenth century, the two most important sculptural commissions in Florence were the new bronze doors for the Florence Cathedral Baptistry and the exterior decoration of the Church of Orsanmichele. Orsanmichele, once an open-arcaded market, was both the municipal granary and a shrine for the local guilds. After its ground floor was walled up near the end of the fourteenth century, each of the twelve niches on the outside of the building was assigned to a guild, which was to commission a large figure of its patron saint or saints for the niche.

Nanni di Banco (c. 1385–1421), son of a sculptor in the Florence Cathedral workshop, produced statues for three of Orsanmichele's niches in his short but brilliant career. The *Four Crowned Martyrs* was commissioned about 1410–1413 by the stone carvers and woodworkers' guild, to which Nanni himself belonged (fig. 17-37). These martyrs, according to legend, were third-century Christian sculptors executed for refusing to make an image of a Roman god. Although the architectural setting resembles a small-scale Gothic chapel, Nanni's figures—

17-37. Nanni di Banco. *Four Crowned Martyrs.* c. 1410–13. Marble, height of figures 6' (1.83 m). Orsanmichele, Florence

with their solid bodies, heavy, form-revealing togas, and stylized hair and beards—nevertheless have the appearance of ancient Roman sculpture. Standing in a semicircle with forward feet and drapery protruding beyond the floor of the niche, the saints convey a sense of realism. They appear to be four individuals talking together. In the relief panels below, showing the four sculptors at work, the forms have a similar solid vigor. Both figures and objects have been deeply undercut to cast shadows and enhance the illusion of three-dimensionality.

In 1402, a competition was held to determine who would provide bronze relief panels for a new set of doors for the north side of the Florence Baptistry of San Giovanni.

17-38. Lorenzo Ghiberti. Gates of Paradise (East Doors), Baptistry of San Giovanni, Florence. 1425–52. Gilt bronze, height 15' (4.57 m). Museo dell'Opera del Duomo, Florence

The door panels contain ten Old Testament scenes from the Creation to the reign of Solomon. The upper left panel depicts the Creation, Temptation, and Expulsion of Adam and Eve from Eden. The murder of Abel by his brother Cain follows in the upper right panel, succeeded in the same order by the Flood and the drunkenness of Noah, Abraham sacrificing Isaac, the story of Jacob and Esau (see fig. 17-39), Joseph sold into slavery by his brothers, Moses receiving the Tablets of the Law, Joshua and the fall of Jericho, David and Goliath, and finally Solomon and the Queen of Sheba. Ghiberti, whose bust portrait appears at the lower right corner of *Jacob and Esau,* wrote in his *Commentaries* (c. 1450–55): "I strove to imitate nature as clearly as I could, and with all the perspective I could produce, to have excellent compositions with many figures."

The commission was awarded to Lorenzo Ghiberti (1381?–1455), a young artist trained as a painter, at the very beginning of his career. His panels were such a success that in 1425 he was awarded the commission for another set of doors for the east side of the Baptistry. Those doors, installed in 1452, were reportedly said by Michelangelo to be worthy of being the Gates of Paradise (fig. 17-38). Overall gilding unifies the ten large, square reliefs. Several panels were organized by a system of linear perspective, approximating the one described by

17-39. Lorenzo Ghiberti. *Jacob and Esau,* panel of the East Doors, Baptistry of San Giovanni. 1425–52. Gilt bronze, 31¼ x 31¼" (79.4 x 79.4 cm). Museo dell'-Opera del Duomo, Florence

17-40. Donatello. *Feast of Herod,* panel of baptismal font, Siena Cathedral Baptistry. c. 1425. Gilt bronze, 23½ x 23½" (59.7 x 59.7 cm)

Alberti in his 1435 treatise on painting (see "Renaissance Perspective Systems," page 650).

One panel (fig. 17-39) illustrates the Old Testament story of the twin brothers Jacob and Esau, whose mother tricked their father, Isaac, into giving his special blessing to Jacob, the younger son, instead of to the rightful firstborn, Esau (Genesis 27). The incidents in the story, including the birth of the twins, take place in different parts of the same overall setting, as if they were one coherent event rather than a sequence of events. Space is organized by a series of arches leading the eye into the distance. Foreground figures, including the scene of blessing at the right, are grouped in the lower third of the panel in an uncrowded relationship with the background architecture, while the other figures decrease gradually in size, suggesting deep space. In the panel, the tall building, which suggests a Roman palace, illustrates the emerging antiquarian tone in Florentine art that would come to full flower in the second half of the fifteenth century. Such details as the conversational groupings of people, dogs sniffing the ground, and Esau climbing the hill with his bow provide immediacy.

The great genius of early Italian Renaissance sculpture was Donatello (Donato di Niccolò Bardi, c. 1386–1466), one of the most influential figures of the century in Italy. During his long and vigorous career, he pursued the goals of the emerging Renaissance movement in Florence but did not adhere rigidly to preconceived notions. Because he executed each commission as if it were a new experiment in expression, his sculpture is like an encyclopedia of types of work, with nearly every piece breaking new ground.

One of Donatello's innovations was a remarkably pictorial approach to relief sculpture. He developed a technique for creating the impression of very deep space by combining the new linear perspective with the ancient Roman technique of varying heights of relief—high relief for foreground figures and very low relief, sometimes approaching engraving, for the background. The *Feast of Herod* (fig. 17-40), a gilded bronze panel made for the baptismal font in the Siena Cathedral Baptistry about 1425, illustrates this technique. As in the relief sculpted below Nanni's *Four Crowned Martyrs* (see fig. 17-37), the contours of the foreground figures have been undercut to emphasize their mass, while figures beyond the foreground are in progressively lower relief. The lines of the brickwork and many other architectural features are incised rather than carved. Anticipating Ghiberti's *Jacob and Esau* relief (see fig. 17-39), Donatello used classical architecture to establish a space implied by one-point linear perspective, yet he avoided the artificiality of precise geometric perspective by handling some peripheral areas more intuitively. The result is a spatial setting in relief sculpture as believable as any illusionistic painting.

In illustrating the biblical story of Salome's dance before her stepfather, Herod Antipas, and her morbid request to be rewarded with the head of John the Baptist on a platter (Mark 6:21–28), Donatello showed Herod's palace as a series of three receding chambers separated from each other by low walls and high, round arches. Although he established a **vanishing point**, the central point where the lines of the architecture converge, he placed the focus of action and emotion—the presentation of the severed head of John the Baptist—in the left foreground, leaving the central axis of the composition empty. As a result, the eye is led past horrified spectators and disinterested musicians to the prison where the beheading has previously taken place to the scene in

RENAISSANCE PERSPECTIVE SYSTEMS

The increasingly human-centered world of the Renaissance was reflected in how artists depicted space. In the fourteenth century, fresco painters such as the Lorenzetti brothers and Giotto in Italy and northern manuscript illuminators such as Jean Pucelle pioneered the rendering of figures and objects within coherent settings that created the illusion of three-dimensional space. They used intuitive perspective to approximate the appearance of things growing smaller and narrowing in the distance (see fig. 17-8).

The humanists' scientific study of the natural world and their belief that "man is the measure of all things" led to the invention of a mathematical system based on proportions of a human male body to enable artists to represent the visible world in a convincingly illusionistic way. This system—known variously as mathematical, linear, or Renaissance perspective—was first demonstrated by the architect Filippo Brunelleschi about 1420. In 1436 Leon Battista Alberti codified mathematical perspective in his treatise *Della Pittura* (*On Painting*), making a standardized, somewhat simplified method available to a larger number of draftspeople, painters, and relief sculptors.

For Alberti, the picture's surface was a flat plane that intersected the viewer's field of vision, which he saw as cone- or pyramid-shaped, at right angles. In Alberti's highly artificial system, a one-eyed viewer was to stand at a prescribed distance from a work, dead center, and remain there. From this fixed vantage point everything appeared to recede into the distance at the same rate, shaped by imaginary lines called orthogonals that met at a single vanishing point, often on the horizon. Orthogonals distort objects by foreshortening them, replicating the optical illusion that things grow smaller and closer together as they get farther away from us. Despite its limitations, mathematical perspective has the advantage of making the viewer feel a direct, almost physical connection to the pictorial space, which seems like an extension of real space. It creates a compelling, even exaggerated sense of depth.

Early Renaissance artists following Alberti's system relied on a number of mechanical methods. Many constructed devices with peepholes through which they sighted the figure or object to be represented. They used mathematical formulas that enabled them to translate three-dimensional forms onto the picture plane, which they overlaid with a grid to provide reference points. One artist, Paolo Uccello (1397–1475), was said to be so obsessed with linear perspective that he talked about it in his sleep until his wife accused him of having a mistress named Perspective. As Italian artists became more comfortable with mathematical perspective in the course of the fifteenth century, they came to rely less on peepholes and formulas and to be less fascinated with linear forms (such as tiled floors and buildings) that had been a hallmark of early Renaissance style. Many artists adopted multiple vanishing points, which gave their work a more relaxed, less tunnel-like feeling.

Meanwhile, in the north, artists such as Jan van Eyck continued to refine intuitive perspective, coupling it with atmospheric, or aerial, perspective. This technique—applied to the landscape scenes that were a northern specialty—was based on the observation that because of haze in the atmosphere, distant elements appear less distinct and become blue-gray, and that the sky becomes paler as it nears the horizon. Among southern artists, Leonardo da Vinci made extensive use of atmospheric perspective, while in the north, the German artist Albrecht Dürer adopted the Italian system of mathematical perspective toward the end of the fifteenth century.

Benozzo Gozzoli. *Saint Augustine Teaching in Rome*. 15th century

which John's head is being carried forward. Donatello demonstrated the fifteenth-century artists' new interest in the individual as he recorded the different reactions to the appalling trophy.

Donatello stands out from all the other artists, for throughout his lifetime he constantly explored human emotions and expressions, the formal problems inherent in representing his visions and insights, and the technical problems posed by various media, from bronze and marble to polychromed wood. In bronze sculpture, he achieved several "firsts"—the first lifesize male nude since antiquity and the first lifesize bronze equestrian portrait since classical Rome.

The sculpture of *David* (fig. 17-41) has been the subject of continuous inquiry and speculation, since nothing is known about the circumstances of its creation. It is first

17-41. Donatello. *David*. After 1428. Bronze, height 5'2¼" (1.58 m). Museo Nazionale del Bargello, Florence

17-42. Donatello. Equestrian monument of Erasmo da Narni (*Gattamelata*), Piazza del Santo, Padua. 1443–53. Bronze, height approx. 12'2" (3.71 m)

recorded in 1469 in the courtyard of the Medici palace, where it stood on a base engraved with an inscription extolling Florentine heroism and virtue. This inscription supports the suggestion that it celebrated the triumph of the Florentines over the Milanese in 1428. Although the statue clearly draws on the Classical tradition of heroic nudity, this sensuous, adolescent boy in jaunty hat and boots has long piqued interest in the meaning of its conception. In one interpretation, the boy's angular pose, his underdeveloped torso, and the sensation of his wavering between childish interests and adult responsibility heighten his heroism in taking on the giant and outwitting him. With Goliath's severed head now under his feet, David seems to have lost interest in warfare and to be retreating into his dreams.

In 1443, Donatello was called to Padua to execute an equestrian statue commemorating the Venetian general Erasmo da Narni (fig. 17-42), nicknamed Gattamelata

("Honeyed Cat," a reference to his mother, Melania Gattelli). Donatello's sources for this statue were two surviving Roman bronze equestrian portraits, one (now lost) in the north Italian city of Pavia, the other of the emperor Marcus Aurelius, which the sculptor certainly saw and probably sketched during his youthful stay in Rome. Donatello's monument, installed on a high base in front of the Church of Sant'Antonio, was the first large-scale bronze equestrian portrait since antiquity. Viewed from a distance, this man-animal juggernaut seems capable of thrusting forward at the first threat. Seen from up close, however, the man's sunken cheeks, sagging jaw, ropey neck, and stern but sad expression suggest a warrior now grown old and tired from the constant need for military vigilance and rapid response. Such expressionism was a recurring theme in Donatello's portrayals.

During the decade that he remained in Padua, Donatello executed other commissions for the Church of

17-44. Andrea del Verrocchio. Equestrian monument of Bartolommeo Colleoni, Campo Santi Giovanni e Paolo, Venice. c. 1481–96. Bronze, height approx. 13' (4 m)

17-43. Donatello. *Mary Magdalen*. c. 1455. Polychromy and gilt on wood, height 6'2" (1.88 m). Museo dell'Opera del Duomo, Florence

Sant'Antonio, including a bronze crucifix and reliefs for the high altar. His presence in the city introduced Renaissance ideas to northeastern Italy and gave rise to a new Paduan school of painting and sculpture.

As Donatello's career drew to a close, his style underwent a profound change, becoming more emotionally expressive. His *Mary Magdalen* of about 1455 shows the saint known for her physical beauty as an emaciated, vacant-eyed hermit clothed by her own hair (fig. 17-43). Few can look at this figure without a wrenching reaction to the physical deterioration of aging and years of self-denial. Nothing is left for her but an ecstatic vision of the hereafter. Despite Donatello's total rejection of Classical form in this figure, the powerfully felt force of the Magdalen's personality makes this a masterpiece of Renaissance imagery.

The expressionism of Donatello's late work inspired some artists to add psychological intensity even in public monuments. In the early 1480s, the Florentine painter and sculptor Andrea del Verrocchio (1435–1488) was commissioned to produce an equestrian memorial to another Venetian general, Bartolommeo Colleoni (d. 1475), this time in Venice itself (fig. 17-44). In contrast to the tragic overtones communicated by Donatello's *Gattamelata,* the impression conveyed by the tense forms of Verrocchio's equestrian monument is one of vitality and brutal energy. The general's determination is clearly expressed in his clenched jaw and staring eyes. The taut muscles of the horse, fiercely erect posture of the rider, and complex interaction of the two make this image of will and domination a singularly compelling monument.

Another form of monument, continuing a medieval tradition, was the portrait tomb. The laudatory tombs by such artists as Desiderio da Settignano (c. 1430–1464), who executed the funerary monument for Carlo Marsuppini (fig. 17-45), extol humanist rather than early Christian values. A noted humanist and chancellor of Florence, Marsuppini wanted his tomb to match in format and decoration that of humanist Leonardo Bruni, also in the Church of Santa Croce. The triumphal arch, Corinthian

17-45. Desiderio da Settignano. Tomb of Carlo Marsuppini, Church of Santa Croce, Florence. c. 1454–64. White and colored marble, 20' x 11'9" (6.1 x 3.6 m)

17-46. Luca della Robbia. *Madonna and Child with Lilies,* Orsanmichele, Florence. c. 1455–60. Enameled terracotta, tondo diameter approx. 6' (1.83 m)

pilasters, classical moldings, marble panels, and carved foliate designs recall the Bruni tomb and, along with the graceful hanging garlands, echo antique motifs. Desiderio's work is distinguished by its tall, elegant proportions and soft modeling. Marsuppini reclines as if napping on a couch atop an elegant sarcophagus with curved sides and spiraling foliate relief decoration. Desiderio's special talent for portraying children can be seen in the charming awkwardness of the young boys standing in front of the flanking pilasters.

To supply the ever-increasing demand for architectural sculpture, artists turned to nontraditional materials such as **terra-cotta**. Luca della Robbia (1399/1400–1482), although an accomplished sculptor in marble, specialized in glazed ceramic reliefs for architectural decoration. His workshop made molds so that a particularly popular work could be replicated many times. Luca favored a limited palette of clear blues, greens, and pale yellows with a great deal of white, as seen in his *Madonna and Child with Lilies* of about 1455–1460, at Orsan-

michele (fig. 17-46). The elegant and lyrical della Robbia style was continued by Luca's nephew Andrea and his children long after Luca's death.

Painting

Italian patrons generally commissioned murals and large altarpieces for their local churches and smaller panel paintings for their private chapels. Home decoration with panel paintings was uncommon until the latter part of the fifteenth century. Artists experienced in **fresco**, mural painting on wet plaster, were in great demand and traveled widely to execute wall and ceiling decorations. Italian panel painters showed little interest in oil painting, continuing to use **tempera** even for their largest works until the last decades of the century, when Venetians began to use the oil medium for major panel paintings.

The new Renaissance style in painting—with its solid, volumetric forms, perspectively defined space, and references to classical antiquity—did not immediately

17-47. Gentile da Fabriano. *Adoration of the Magi*, altarpiece from the Sacristy of the Church of Santa Trinità, Florence. 1423. Oil on panel, 9'10" x 9'3" (3 x 2.85 m). Galleria degli Uffizi, Florence

displace the International Gothic. One of the important painters who retained International Gothic elements in their styles was Gentile da Fabriano (c. 1385–1427), who in 1423 completed the *Adoration of the Magi* (fig. 17-47), a large altarpiece for the Sacristy of the Church of Santa Trinità in Florence. Among the International Gothic elements are the steeply rising ground plane, graceful figural poses, brightly colored costumes and textile patterns, glinting gold accents, and naturalistic rendering of the details of the setting. But Gentile's landscape, with its endless procession of people winding from the far distance toward Bethlehem to worship the Christ Child, is broadly related to the near-contemporary *Ghent Altarpiece* (see fig. 17-1), with its crowds of saints and the Lamb of God. Gentile's painting was done for the wealthy Strozzi family and celebrates the riches of the Magi (and the patrons) as well as their piety.

The most innovative of the early Italian Renaissance painters was Maso di Ser Giovanni di Mone Cassai (1401–1429?), nicknamed Masaccio ("big ugly Tom"). In his short career of less than a decade, he established a new direction in Florentine painting, much as Giotto had a century earlier. The exact chronology of his works is uncertain, and his fresco of the Trinity in the Church of Santa Maria Novella in Florence has been dated as early as 1425 and as late as 1428 (fig. 17-48). The *Trinity* was meant to give the illusion of a stone funerary monument and altar table set below a deep **aedicula** (framed niche) in the wall. The praying donors in front of the pilasters are probably Domenico Lenzi and his wife, whose tombstone lay in front of the painting. The red robes of the male donor at the left signify that he was a member of the governing council of Florence.

Masaccio created the unusual **trompe l'oeil** ("fool-the-eye") effect of looking up into a barrel-vaulted niche through precisely rendered linear perspective. The eye level of an adult viewer determined the horizon line on which the vanishing point was centered, just above the

17-48. Masaccio. *Trinity with the Virgin, Saint John the Evangelist, and Donors*, fresco in the Church of Santa Maria Novella, Florence. c. 1425(?). 21' x 10'5" (6.4 x 3.2 m)

17-49. Interior of the Brancacci Chapel, Church of Santa Maria del Carmine, Florence, with frescoes by Masaccio and Masolino (1424–27) and Filippino Lippi (c. 1482–84)

base of the cross. The painting demonstrates Masaccio's intimate knowledge of both Brunelleschi's perspective experiments and his architectural style (see fig. 17-34, side aisle). The painted architecture is an unusual combination of Classical orders; on the wall surface Corinthian pilasters support a plain architrave below a cornice, while inside the niche Ionic columns support arches on all four sides (see "Elements of Architecture," page 686). The Trinity is represented by Jesus on the Cross, with the dove of the Holy Spirit poised in downward flight between his tilted halo and the head of God the Father, who stands behind the Cross on a high platform apparently supported on the rear columns. The "source" of the consistent illumination modeling the figures with light and shadow lies in front of the picture, casting reflections on the **coffers**, or sunken panels, of the ceiling. As in many scenes of the Crucifixion, Jesus is flanked by the Virgin Mary and John the Evangelist, who contemplate the scene. Mary gazes calmly out at us, her raised hand presenting the Trinity. Below, in an open sarcophagus, is a skeleton, a grim reminder that death awaits us all and that our only hope is redemption and life in the hereafter through Christian belief. The inscription above the skeleton reads: "I was once that which you are, and what I am you also will be."

Masaccio's brief career reached its height in his collaboration with a painter known as Masolino (c. 1400–1440/47) on the fresco decoration of the Brancacci Chapel in the Church of Santa Maria del Carmine in Florence (fig. 17-49). The project was ill-fated: The painters never finished their work—Masolino left in 1425 for Hungary, and Masaccio left for Rome in 1427—and the patron, Brancacci, was exiled in 1435. Eventually, another Florentine painter, Filippino Lippi, finished the painting in the 1480s. The chapel was originally dedicated to Saint Peter, and most frescoes illustrate events in his life. Masaccio's most innovative painting is the *Tribute Money* (fig. 17-50), completed about 1427, rendered in a continuous narrative of three scenes within one setting. The painting illustrates an incident in which a collector of the Jewish temple taxes (tribute money) demands payment from Peter, shown in the central group with Jesus and the other disciples (Matthew 17:24–27). Although Jesus opposes the tax, he instructs Peter to "go to the sea, drop in a hook, and take the first fish that comes up," which Peter does at the far left. In the fish's mouth is a coin worth twice the tax demanded, which Peter gives to the tax collector at the far right. The tribute story was particularly significant for Florentines because in 1427, to raise money for defense against military aggression, the city

17-50. Masaccio. *Tribute Money*, fresco in the Brancacci Chapel. c. 1427. 8'1" x 19'7" (2.3 x 6 m)

Much valuable new information about the Brancacci Chapel frescoes was discovered during the course of a cleaning and restoration carried out between 1981 and 1991. Art historians now have a more accurate picture of how the frescoes were done and in what sequence, as well as which artist did what. One interesting discovery was that all of the figures in the *Tribute Money,* except those of the temple tax collector, originally had gold-leaf halos, several of which had flaked off. Rather than silhouette the heads against flat gold circles in the medieval manner, Masaccio conceived of the halo as a gold disk hovering in space above each head and subjected it to perspective foreshortening depending on the position of the figure.

enacted a graduated tax, based on the ability to pay.

The *Tribute Money* is remarkable for its integration of figures, architecture, and landscape into a consistent whole. The group of Jesus and his disciples forms a clear central focus, from which the landscape seems to recede naturally into the far distance. To create this illusion, Masaccio used linear perspective in the depiction of the house, which he reinforced by diminishing the sizes of the barren trees and reducing Peter's size at the left. The lines of the house converge on the head of Jesus. A second vanishing point determines the steps and stone rail at the right. A recent cleaning of the fresco revealed that Masaccio also used atmospheric perspective in the distant landscape, where mountains fade from grayish green to grayish white and the houses and trees on their slopes are loosely sketched.

Masaccio modeled the foreground figures with strong highlights and cast their long shadows on the ground toward the left, implying a light source at the far right, as if the scene were lit by the actual window in the rear wall of the Brancacci Chapel. Not only does the lighting give the forms sculptural definition, but the colors vary in tone according to the strength of the illumination. Masaccio used a wide range of hues—pale pink, mauve, gold, seafoam, apple green, peach—and a sophisticated color technique in which Andrew's green robe is shaded with red instead of darker green. Another discovery after the cleaning was that—allowing for the difference in mediums between rapidly applied water-based colors in

fresco versus slow-drying oil—the wealth of linear detail is much closer to that of Masaccio's northern European contemporaries than previously thought. In contrast to Jan van Eyck's figure style, however, Masaccio's exhibits an intimate knowledge of Roman sculpture.

Stylistic innovations take time to be fully accepted, and Masaccio's genius for depicting weight and volume, consistent lighting, and spatial integration was best appreciated by a later generation. Many important sixteenth-century Italian artists, including Michelangelo, studied and sketched from Masaccio's Brancacci Chapel frescoes. In the meantime, painting in Florence after Masaccio's death developed along lines somewhat different from that of the *Tribute Money,* as other artists experimented in their own ways with the illusion of a believably receding space.

Fra Angelico ("The Angelic Brother"), born Guido di Pietro (c. 1395–c. 1455), was known to his peers as Fra Giovanni da Fiesole and earned his nickname through his unusually pious nature. He is documented as a painter in Florence during the period 1417–1418 and took his vows as a Dominican monk in nearby Fiesole sometime between 1418 and about 1421. He continued to be a very active painter. One of his most extensive projects was the decoration of the Dominican Monastery of San Marco in Florence between 1435 and 1445. Fra Angelico went to work at the Vatican in Rome in 1445, and the frescoes at San Marco were completed by his assistants several years later.

1480
1400   1500

17-51. Fra Angelico. *Annunciation*, fresco in Cell No. 3, Monastery of San Marco, Florence. c. 1441–45. Image 6'1½" x 5'2" (1.87 x 1.57 m)

If an early legend is true, then Fra Angelico's humility lost him the opportunity to become a saint. He had left the completion of the San Marco frescoes to his assistants in 1445 to answer Pope Eugene IV's summons to Rome. The pope was looking for a new archbishop of Florence at the time, and the current vicar of San Marco, Antonino Pierozzi, was finally appointed to the post in January 1446. When Pierozzi was proposed for canonization in the early sixteenth century, several individuals testified that Pope Eugene's first choice for archbishop had been Fra Angelico, who declined it and suggested his Dominican brother Antonino.

Among the frescoes attributed entirely to Angelico by most scholars is the *Annunciation* in a monk's cell off the east corridor of the upper floor of the monastery (fig. 17-51). Nearly everything about the painting is in keeping with its location. The arched frame echoes the curvature of the cell wall, and the plain white interior of the illusionistic space appears almost to be a nichelike extension of the cell's space. Although the bottom edge of the painting is above normal eye level, the effect is that of looking through a window onto a scene taking place in a cloister portico. In the painting, the ceiling is supported by the wall on one side and by slender Ionic columns on the other. The artist used minimal perspective indications: the edge of the porch, the base of the first column, the lines of the bench, and the angles where the ceiling planes come together. Gabriel and Mary are sim-

plified figures enhanced with plain but glowing draperies whose folds are noticeably affected by gravity. The natural light falls from the left to model the forms, but a supernatural radiance lights Gabriel's hands and face, which ought to be in shadow, and creates a spotlight effect on the back wall. The scene is a vision within a vision; Saint Dominic appears at the left in prayer, giving rise to the vision of the Annunciation, while the whole may be seen as a vision of the resident monk.

Andrea del Castagno (c. 1417/19–1457) worked for a time in Venice before returning to Florence to execute his best-known work, *Last Supper,* painted in 1447 at the Monastery of Sant'Apollonia (fig. 17-52). Extending 32 feet across the end wall of the dining room and rising 15 feet high, the fresco gives the illusion of a raised alcove where Jesus and his disciples are eating their meal along with the monks. Rather than the humble "upper room" where the biblical event took place, the setting resembles a royal audience hall with sumptuous marble panels and inlays. The trompe l'oeil effect is aided by the creation of a focal point on the head and shoulders of the sleeping young disciple John. Some of the lines of the architecture converge here, while others merely come close; a few converge elsewhere. Thus, Andrea appears to have

TECHNIQUE
SINOPIA

Because fresco painting was done on wet plaster, which dries quickly, artists worked in sections to which fresh plaster was applied each day. So that fresco painters could keep their whole composition in mind as they painted, they prepared an underdrawing, or sinopia, of the entire work, which they referred to as they worked on each day's section. The sinopia itself often was a beautiful work, but for all its apparent freedom it was based on a carefully prepared drawing. Most sinopie were, in fact, tracings or from full-scale **cartoons**. Nevertheless, artists frequently reworked each day's sinopia with a stylus on the wet plaster, adjusting elements to ensure that the overall effect was achieved.

Originally, the underdrawings were done using a red pigment known as sinopia after the Black Sea town where it was first processed, and from the mid-thirteenth to the mid-fifteenth century, the term *sinopia* was used to denote these underdrawings.

Andrea del Castagno. Detail of sinopia for *Resurrection* fresco, Refectory, Monastery of Sant'Apollonia, Florence. 1447.

The section seen here is recognizable in the upper section of figure 17-52, around the right window.

17-52. Andrea del Castagno. *Last Supper*, fresco in the Refectory, Monastery of Sant'Apollonia, Florence. 1447. Approx. 15' x 32' (4.6 x 9.8 m)

Above the *Last Supper*, which has been restored, is the unrestored *Resurrection*.

adjusted many of the perspectival elements intuitively to create a more believable spatial representation. The focus on the figure of John, traditionally the "disciple whom Jesus loved" (John 20:2), rather than on Jesus himself, may have been intended to enable the monks in this austere order, whose members rarely had contact with the outside world, to identify themselves with the saint.

Above the *Last Supper* and completely ignoring the illusion of a room cut into the wall, Castagno painted the Entombment and Resurrection of Christ. An unfortunate accident, when these paintings were damaged by water and had to be removed from the wall, has provided a fascinating insight into the working methods of a mural painter. The **sinopia**, or sketch made on the wall before painters begin work, was recovered in the process of restoring the murals. By comparing the drawings and the final paintings, even in their damaged state one can see the careful preparation that was necessary before the frescoes were begun—as well as the amount of freedom given the painter to change and improve, to improvise and refine, his original concept (see "Sinopia," page 658).

The most important Florentine painting workshop of the later fifteenth century was that of the painter known as Domenico del Ghirlandaio ("Garland Maker"), a nickname adopted by his father, a goldsmith noted for his floral designs. A specialist in narrative cycles, Ghirlandaio (1449–1494) incorporated the innovations of his predecessors into a visual language of great descriptive immediacy. He was familiar with examples of Flemish painting, seen in Florence after about 1450, which had considerable impact on his style, especially in portraiture. Instead of the more typical Italian full-profile format (see fig. 17-65), he adopted the three-quarter view and more relaxed pose of early-fifteenth-century Flemish painters, as in his portrait of a

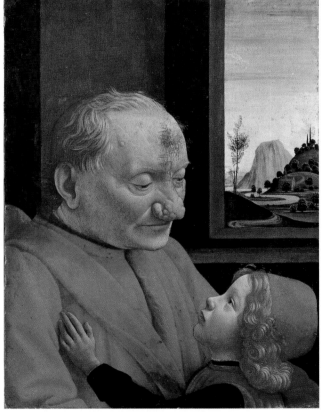

17-53. Domenico del Ghirlandaio. *A Man with His Grandchild.* c. 1480–90. Panel, 24³⁄₈ x 18¹⁄₈" (62 x 46.1 cm). Musée du Louvre, Paris

man and his grandchild of about 1480–1490 (fig. 17-53). Ghirlandaio painted this unknown man posthumously, using a deathbed sketch. Such an objective portrayal—

17-54. Sandro Botticelli. *Primavera*. c. 1482. Panel, 6'8" x 10'4" (2.03 x 3.15 m). Galleria degli Uffizi, Florence

the man's nose is malformed as a result of the condition called rhinophyma—was a special talent of Ghirlandaio's, recalling northern European portraiture. Ghirlandaio's careful study of humankind led him to represent the little boy with equal fidelity and consequently to paint one of the earliest images of childhood. He no longer represents the boy as a miniature adult, but captures the beauty and innocence of youth as well as a tender moment of understanding and trust between the two people. Ghirlandaio's pragmatic naturalism contrasts with the classical idealism of his contemporary Botticelli.

Sandro Botticelli (1445–1510) learned both painting and sculpture from Pollaiuolo and Verrocchio. Like most artists in the second half of the fifteenth century, he mastered the art of drawing and painting sculptural figures that were modeled by light from a consistent source and were placed in a setting rendered with strict linear perspective. An outstanding portraitist, he often included recognizable contemporary figures among the saints and angels in religious paintings. He worked in Florence, then in Rome, where the pope called many painters to decorate the walls of the Sistine Chapel (see page 698).

In 1481, after returning from Rome, Botticelli entered a new phase of his career. Like other artists in the circle of the Medici academy and working for patrons steeped in classical scholarship, Botticelli took more than a philosophy of beauty from their humanistic speculation—he looked to examples of ancient art in the collections of his patrons. For the Medici, Botticelli produced secular paintings of mythological subjects inspired by such ancient works and by contemporary Neoplatonic thought, includ-

ing *Primavera*, or *Spring* (fig. 17-54), and *Birth of Venus* (see fig. 17-55). Silhouetted and framed by an arching view through the trees at the center of *Primavera* is Venus, the goddess of love. She is flanked on the right by Flora, a Roman goddess of flowers and fertility, and on the left by the Three Graces. Her son, Cupid, hovers above, playfully aiming an arrow at the Graces. At the far right is the wind god, Zephyr, in pursuit of the nymph Chloris, his breath causing her to sprout flowers from her mouth. At the far left, the messenger god, Mercury, uses his characteristic snake-wrapped wand, the caduceus, to dispel a patch of gray clouds drifting in Venus's direction. Although this painting reflects Botticelli's characteristically charming ambiance, graceful poses, and linear contours, the overall appearance of *Primavera* recalls Flemish tapestries, which were popular in Italy at the time. The decorative quality of the painting is deceptive, however, for it is a highly complex allegory, interweaving Neoplatonic ideas with esoteric references to classical sources.

Neoplatonic philosophers and poets conceived of Venus as having two natures, one terrestrial and the other celestial. The first ruled over earthly, human love and the second over universal love, making her a classical equivalent of the Virgin Mary. *Primavera* was painted at the time of a Medici wedding, so it may have been intended as a painting on the nuptial theme of love and fertility in marriage. Venus, clothed in contemporary costume and wearing a marriage wreath on her head, here represents her terrestrial nature, governing marital love. She stands in a grove of orange trees weighted down with lush fruit, suggesting human fertility; the orange, called *mala medica*,

660 EARLY RENAISSANCE ART IN EUROPE

17-55. Sandro Botticelli. *The Birth of Venus.* c. 1484–86. Panel, 5'8⅞" x 9'1⅞" (1.8 x 2.8 m). Galleria degli Uffizi, Florence

or "medicinal apple," became a symbol of the Medici, whose name means "doctors." Cupid embodies romantic desire, and as practiced in central Italy in ancient times, the goddess Flora's festival had definite sexual overtones.

Several years later, some of the same mythological figures appear again in Botticelli's *The Birth of Venus* (fig. 17-55), whose central image is based on an antique statue of Venus in the Medici collection, a type known as the modest Venus. The classical goddess of love and beauty, born of sea foam, floats ashore on a scallop shell, gracefully arranging her hands and hair to hide—or enhance—her sexuality. Blown by the wind, Zephyr (and his love, the nymph Chloris), and welcomed by a devotee with a garment embroidered with flowers, Venus arrives at her earthly home. This painting, too, inspired debate about the meaning of the "two Venuses"—one sacred, one profane—and the circumstances of Botticelli's commission are uncertain.

Botticelli's later career was affected by a profound spiritual crisis. While Botticelli was creating his mythologies, a Dominican monk, Fra Girolamo Savonarola, had begun to preach impassioned sermons denouncing the worldliness of Florence. Many Florentines reacted with orgies of self-recrimination, and processions of weeping penitents wound through the streets. In the 1490s, Botticelli, too, fell into a state of religious fervor. In a dramatic gesture of repentance, he burned many of his earlier paintings and began to produce highly emotional, religious pictures. An intense religiosity pervades Botticelli's later painting.

In 1500, at a time when many people feared that the end of the world was imminent, Botticelli painted the *Mystic Nativity* (fig. 17-56), his only signed and dated

17-56. Sandro Botticelli. *Mystical Nativity.* 1500. Panel, 42 x 29½" (106.7 x 74.9 cm). The National Gallery, London

painting. Botticelli's Nativity takes place in a rocky, forested landscape whose cave-stable follows the tradition of the Eastern Orthodox (Byzantine) Church, while the timber shed in front recalls the Western iconographical tradition. In the center of the painting, the Virgin Mary kneels in adoration of the Christ Child, who lies on the earth, as recorded in the vision of Saint Bridget, a fourteenth-century mystic (see also Hugo van der Goes's *Portinari Altarpiece*, fig. 17-21, which would have been a well-known precedent). Joseph crouches and hides his face, while the ox and the ass bow their heads to the Holy Child. The shepherds at the right and the Magi at the left also kneel before the Holy Family. A circle of singing angels holding golden crowns and laurel branches flies jubilantly above the central scene. Tiny devils, vanquished by the coming of Christ, try to escape from the bottom of the picture.

The most unusual element of the painting is the frieze of wrestling figures below the Holy Family. The men are ancient classical philosophers, who ceremonially struggle with angels. Each of the three pairs holds an olive branch and a scroll, as do the angels circling above, whose scrolls are inscribed with the words: "Glory to God in the Highest; peace on earth to men of good will." In fifteenth-century Florence, Palm Sunday was called Olive Sunday, the festival of Christ the King; and olive branches, symbols of peace, rather than palms were carried in processions. The inscription at the top of the painting reads (in Greek): "I Alessandro made this picture at the conclusion of . . . [a millennium and a half], according to the 11th chapter of Saint John in the second woe of the Apocalypse, during the loosing of the devil for three and a half years, then he will be bound in the 12th chapter and we shall see [missing word] as in this picture." The references are to the Book of Revelation, chapter 11, which describes woes to come, and Revelation 12, which includes the vision of a woman crowned with stars and clothed by the sun, taken by Christians as a prophesy of the Virgin Mary, and the description of the defeat of Satan. Thus, in this painting Christ has come to save humankind in spite of the troubled times Botticelli saw all around him in Italy. Savonarola had been burned at the stake only two years before Botticelli painted this picture. By the end of his own life, Botticelli gave up painting altogether.

THE ITALIAN RENAISSANCE OUTSIDE FLORENCE

In the second half of the fifteenth century, the Renaissance began to expand from Florence to the rest of Italy, giving birth to a number of local styles. Renaissance ideas were often spread by artists who had trained or worked in Florence and who then traveled to other cities to work, either temporarily or permanently—including Donatello (Padua, Siena), Alberti (Mantua, Rimini, and Rome), Piero della Francesca (Urbino, Ferrara, Rome), Uccello (Venice, Urbino, Padua), Giuliano da Sangallo (Rome), and Botticelli (Rome). Northern Italy embraced the new Renaissance styles swiftly, with the ducal courts

17-57. Leon Battista Alberti. Plan of the Church of Sant'Andrea, Mantua. Designed 1470

at Mantua and Urbino taking the lead. The Republic of Venice and the city of Padua, which Venice had controlled since 1404, also emerged as innovative art centers in the last quarter of the century.

Architecture

The spread of Renaissance architecture outside Florence was due in significant part to Leon Battista Alberti, who traveled widely and expounded his views to potential patrons. In 1470 the ruler of Mantua commissioned Alberti to enlarge the small Church of Sant'Andrea, which housed a sacred relic believed to be the actual blood of Jesus. To satisfy his patron's desire for a sizable building to handle crowds coming to see the relic, Alberti proposed to build an "Etruscan temple." Work began on the new church in 1472, but Alberti died that summer. Construction went forward slowly, at first according to his original plan, but it was finally completed only at the end of the eighteenth century. Thus, it is not always clear which elements belong to Alberti's original design.

The **Latin-cross plan** (fig. 17-57)—a nave more than 55 feet wide intersected by a transept of equal width; a square, domed crossing; and a rectangular sanctuary on axis with the nave—is certainly in keeping with Alberti's ideas. Alberti was responsible, too, for the barrel-vaulted chapels the same height as the nave and the low chapel niches carved out of the huge piers supporting the barrel vault of the nave. His dome, however, would not have been perforated and would not have been raised on a drum, as this one finally was.

17-58. Leon Battista Alberti. Facade, Church of Sant'Andrea

Alberti's design for the facade of Sant'Andrea (fig. 17-58) fuses a classical temple front and triumphal arch, but the facade now has a clear volume of its own, which sets it off visually from the building behind. Two sets of colossal Corinthian pilasters articulate the porch face. Those flanking the barrel-vaulted triumphal-arch entrance are two stories high, whereas the others, raised on pedestals, run through three stories to support the entablature and pediment of the temple form. The arch itself has lateral barrel-vaulted spaces opening through two-story arches on the left and right.

Neither the simplicity of the plan nor the complexity of the facade hints at the grandeur of Sant'Andrea's interior (fig. 17-59). Its immense barrel-vaulted nave extended on each side by tall chapels was inspired by the monumental interiors of such ancient ruins as the Basilica of Maxentius and Constantine in the Roman Forum. In this clear reference to Roman imperial art put to fully Christian use, Alberti created a building of such colossal scale, spatial unity, and successful expression of Christian humanist ideals that it affected architectural design for centuries.

17-59. Leon Battista Alberti. Nave, Church of Sant'Andrea

17-60. Giuliano da Sangallo. Plan of the Church of Santa Maria delle Carceri, Prato. Before 1485

17-61. Giuliano da Sangallo. Interior view of dome, Church of Santa Maria delle Carceri. 1485–92

17-62. Giuliano da Sangallo. Church of Santa Maria delle Carceri

A fifteenth-century Florentine architect whose work influenced developments in the sixteenth century was Giuliano da Sangallo (c. 1443–1516). From 1464 to 1472, he worked in Rome, where he produced a number of meticulous drawings after the city's ancient monuments, many of which are now lost and are known today only from his work. Back in Florence, he became a favorite of Lorenzo the Magnificent, a great humanist and patron of the arts. In 1484 a child had claimed that a painting of the Virgin on the wall of the town prison had come to life, and plans were soon made to remove the image and preserve it in a votive church (a church built as a special offering to a saint), to be named Santa Maria delle Carceri (Saint Mary of the Prisons). Soon after completing a country villa for Lorenzo, Giuliano submitted a model for the structure that would become this new church, to be built in Prato, near Florence, and he began work in 1485.

Although the need to accommodate processions and the gathering of congregations made the long nave of a basilica almost a necessity for local churches, the votive church became a natural subject for Renaissance experimentation with the central plan. The existing tradition of **central-plan churches** extended back to the Early Christian **martyrium** (a round shrine to a martyred saint) and perhaps ultimately to the Classical **tholos**, or round temple. Alberti in his treatise on architecture had spoken of the central plan as an ideal, derived from the humanist belief that the circle was a symbol of divine perfection and that both the circle inscribed in a square and the cross inscribed in a circle were symbols of the cosmos. Thus, Giuliano's Church of Santa Maria delle Carceri, built on a Greek-cross plan, is one of the finest early Renaissance examples of humanist symbolism in architectural design (fig. 17-60). It is also the first Renaissance church with a true central plan; Brunelleschi's earlier experiment in the Old Sacristy of San Lorenzo, for example, was for an attached structure, and Alberti's Greek-cross plan was never actually built. Drawing on his knowledge of Brunelleschi's works, Giuliano created a

17-63. Luciano Laurana. Courtyard, Ducal Palace, Urbino. 1465–79

square, dome-covered central space extended in each direction by arms whose length was one-half the width of the central space. The arms are covered by barrel vaults extended from the round arches supporting the dome. Giuliano raised his dome on a short, round drum that increased the amount of natural light entering the church. He also articulated the interior walls and the twelve-ribbed dome and drum with **pietra serena** (fig. 17-61). The exterior of the dome is capped with a conical roof and a tall lantern in Brunelleschian fashion.

The exterior of the church is a marvel of Renaissance clarity and order (fig. 17-62). To understand the designer's intention one has but to look at the buildings represented in a painting by Piero della Francesca in Arezzo (see fig. 17-64). Giuliano's ground-floor system of slim Doric pilasters clustered at the corners is repeated in the Ionic order on the shorter upper level, as if the entablature of a small temple had been surmounted with a second, smaller one. The church was entirely finished in 1494 except for installation of the fine green- and white-marble veneer

above the first story. In the 1880s, one section of the upper level was veneered; however, the philosophy of twentieth-century conservation requires that the rest of the building be left in rough stone, as it is today.

The court of Urbino was an outstanding artistic center under the patronage of Federico da Montefeltro, who actively sought out the finest artists of the day to come to Urbino. In 1468, after failing to find a Tuscan to take over the construction of a new ducal palace *(palazzo ducale)* begun about 1450, Federico hired one of the assistants already involved in the project, Luciano Laurana, to direct the work. Among Laurana's major contributions were his closing the courtyard with a fourth wing and redesigning the courtyard facades (fig. 17-63). The result is a superbly rational solution to the problems of courtyard elevation design. The ground-level portico on each side has arches supported by columns; the corner angles are bridged with piers having engaged columns on the arcade sides and pilasters facing the courtyard. This arrangement avoided the awkward visual effect of two

17-64. Piero della Francesca. *Discovery and Testing of the True Cross*, fresco in the Church of San Francesco, Arezzo. 1454–58. 11'8³/₈" x 6'4" (3.56 x 1.93 m)

According to legend, Helena, mother of the first Christian Roman emperor, Constantine, went to Jerusalem in the early fourth century and discovered the "True Cross" on which Jesus was crucified. She was aided by a young Jerusalem Jew named Judas in finding Christ's Cross, whose location had been handed down in his family during the 270 years since the Crucifixion. After being thrown into a well and starved, he led Helena and her companions to the hill of Golgotha (Calvary), where they tore down a temple to Venus and excavated the crosses of Jesus and the two thieves executed with him (at the left). Judas also helped test the crosses. The "true" one was identified when its touch brought back to life a recently deceased man being carried to his tomb (at the right).

arches springing from a single column and gave the corner a greater sense of stability. The **Composite** capital (Corinthian with added Ionic **volutes**) was used, perhaps for the first time, on the ground level. Corinthian pilasters flank the windows in the story above, forming divisions that repeat the bays of the portico. (The two short upper stories were added later.) The plain architrave faces were engraved with inscriptions identifying Federico and lauding his many humanistic virtues. Not visible in the illustration is an innovative feature that became standard in palace courtyard design: the monumental staircase from the courtyard to the main floor.

Painting

One of the finest artists Federico da Montefeltro brought to his court in Urbino was Piero della Francesca (c. 1406/ 12–1492). Piero had worked in Florence in the 1430s before settling down in his native Borgo San Sepolcro, a Tuscan hill town under papal control, and was well acquainted with current thinking in art and art theory—including Brunelleschi's system of spatial illusion and linear perspective, Masaccio's powerful modeling of forms and atmospheric perspective, and especially Alberti's theoretical treatises. Piero was one of the few practicing artists who wrote about his own theories. Not surprisingly, in his treatise on perspective he emphasized

geometry and the volumetric construction of forms and spaces—so apparent in his own work—to an unprecedented degree.

Piero received important commissions that required him to stay in various cities for long periods of time. From about 1454 to 1458, he was in Arezzo, where he decorated the sanctuary of the Church of San Francesco with a cycle of frescoes illustrating the Legend of the True Cross. The finding and testing of the Cross are illustrated in a single fresco (fig. 17-64).

Piero's analytical modeling and perspectival projection resulted in a highly believable illusion of space around his monumental figures. He reduced his figures to cylindrical and ovoid shapes and painted the clothing and other details of the setting with muted colors. The **foreshortening** of figures and objects—shortening the lines of forms seen head-on in order to align them with the overall perspectival system—such as the cross at the right, and the anatomical accuracy of the revived youth's nude figure are particularly remarkable. Unlike many of his contemporaries, however, Piero gave his figures no expression of human emotion.

Of special note in Piero's composition is the inclusion of Classical architecture, which converts ancient Jerusalem into a Renaissance city: Behind the crowd at the right stands an elegant building whose facade reflects Alberti's principles and recommendations for

17-65. Piero della Francesca. *Battista Sforza* (left) and *Federico da Montefeltro* (right). 1472–73. Oil on panel, each 18¹/₂ x 13" (47 x 33 cm). Galleria degli Uffizi, Florence

ideal architecture—an even number of vertical elements, an odd number of openings, and decoration with panels of veined marble framed in plain marble or stone.

Piero's commissions took him later to the court of Federico da Montefeltro at Urbino, for whom he painted a pair of pendant, or companion, portraits in 1472–1473 of Federico and his recently deceased wife, Battista Sforza (fig. 17-65). In the traditional Italian fashion, the figures are portrayed in strict profile, as remote from the viewer as icons. The profile format also allowed for an accurate recording of Federico's likeness without emphasizing two disfiguring scars—the loss of his right eye and the bridge of his nose—from a sword blow. His good left eye is shown, and the angular profile of his nose seems like a distinctive familial trait. Typically, Piero emphasized the underlying geometry of the forms, rendering the figures with an absolute stillness. Dressed in the most elegant fashion, Battista and Federico are silhouetted against a distant view recalling the hilly landscape around Urbino. The portraits may have been hinged as a diptych, since the landscape appears to be nearly continuous across the two panels. The influence of Flemish art is strong in the careful observation of Battista's jewels and in the well-observed atmospheric perspective. Piero has also used another northern European device in the harbor view near the center of Federico's panel: The water narrows into a river and leads the eye into the distant landscape.

Farther north, in Padua, Andrea Mantegna (1431–1506) became one of the most influential fifteenth-century painters born and working outside Florence. Mantegna entered the painters' guild at the age of fifteen. The greatest influence on the young artist was the sculptor Donatello, who arrived in Padua in 1443 for a decade of work there. In his early twenties when Donatello left, Mantegna had fully absorbed the sculptor's Florentine linear-perspective system, which he pushed to its limits with experiments in radical perspective views and the foreshortening of figures. In 1459 Mantegna went to work for Ludovico Gonzaga, the ruler of Mantua, and he continued to work for the Gonzaga family for the rest of his life except for trips to Florence and Pisa in the 1460s and to Rome in 1488–1490. In Mantua the artist became a member of the humanist circle, whose interests in classical literature and archeology he shared. He often signed his name using Greek letters.

Mantegna's mature style is characterized by the virtuosity of his use of perspective, his skillful integration of figures into their settings, and his love of individualization and naturalistic details. This style is exemplified in the frescoes of the Camera Picta ("Painted Room") of Gonzaga's ducal palace, a tower chamber with a lake view, which Mantegna decorated between 1465 and 1474. On the domed ceiling, the artist painted a tour de force of radical perspective called *di sotto in sù* ("seen

17-66. Andrea Mantegna. Frescoes in the Camera Picta, Ducal Palace, Mantua. 1465–74

from directly below"), which began a long-lasting tradition of illusionistic ceiling painting (fig. 17-66). The room appears to be open to a cloud-filled sky through a large oculus in a simulated marble- and mosaic-covered vault. On each side of a precariously balanced planter, three young women and an exotically turbaned African man peer over a marble **balustrade** into the room below. A

fourth young woman in a veil looks dreamily upward. Joined by a large peacock, several **putti** play around the balustrade.

On two adjacent walls, Mantegna created a continuous narrative illustrating aristocratic family life as well as a fascinating moment in Church history (fig. 17-67). Above the fireplace, which is incorporated into the paint-

17-67. (left) Andrea Mantegna. *Gonzaga Family*, wall of the Camera Picta

17-68. (below) Pietro Perugino. *Delivery of the Keys to Saint Peter*, fresco in the Sistine Chapel, Vatican, Rome. 1482. 11'5½" x 18'8½" (3.48 x 5.70 m)

Modern eyes accustomed to gigantic parking lots would not find a large open space in the middle of a city extraordinary, but in the fifteenth century this great piazza was purely the product of artistic imagination. A real piazza this size would have been very impractical. In summer sun or winter wind and rain, such spaces would have been extremely unpleasant for a pedestrian population, but, more important, no city could afford such extravagant use of valuable land within its walls.

ed scene, he produced a group portrait of Ludovico, his wife, Barbara von Hohenzollern, some of their children, and a few courtiers. Ludovico, seated at the far left, has just read a letter announcing the imminent arrival from Rome of their son Francesco, who had gone there to be made a cardinal at the age of thirteen; the young cardinal's arrival is shown on the adjoining wall. Mantegna painted recognizable portraits of the Gonzaga family and rendered the costumes and architectural setting with customary realism, but the glimpse of landscape behind the curtain and the wall is not of the flat plain around Mantua; low, rocky hills are suggested instead.

The establishment of Rome as a Renaissance center of the arts was greatly aided by Pope Sixtus IV's decision

to call to the city the best artists he could find to decorate the walls of his newly built Sistine Chapel. In the early fifteenth century, a schism in the Western Church ended, and the papacy was firmly reestablished in Rome. This event had precipitated the need to restore not only the Vatican but also the whole city as a center worthy of the papal court. Among those who went to Rome was Pietro Vannucci, called Perugino (c. 1445–1523), from near the town of Perugia in Umbria. Perugino had been working in Florence since 1472 and left there in 1481 to travel to Rome to work on the Sistine wall frescoes. His contribution, *Delivery of the Keys to Saint Peter* (fig. 17-68), portrayed the event that provided biblical support for the supremacy of papal authority, Christ's giving the keys to

17-69. Gentile Bellini, *Procession of the Relic of the True Cross before the Church of San Marco.* 1496. Oil on canvas, 10'7" x 14' (3.23 x 4.27 m). Galleria dell'Accademia, Venice

the kingdom of heaven to the apostle Peter (Matthew 16:19), who became the first bishop of Rome.

Delivery of the Keys is a remarkable work in carefully studied linear perspective that reveals much about Renaissance ideas and ideals. In a light-filled piazza whose banded paving stones provide a geometric grid for perspectival recession, the figures stand like chess pieces on the squares, scaled to size according to their distance from the picture plane and modeled by a consistent light source from the upper left. Horizontally, the composition is divided between the lower frieze of massive figures and the band of widely spaced buildings above. Vertically, it is divided by the open space at the center between Christ and Peter and by the symmetrical architectural forms on each side of this central axis. The carefully calibrated scene is softened by the subdued colors, the distant idealized landscape and cloudy skies, and the variety of the figures' positions.

Perugino's painting is, among other things, a representation of Alberti's ideal city, described in his treatise on architecture as having a "temple" (that is, a church) at the very center of a great open space raised on a dais and separate from any other buildings that might obstruct its view. His ideal church had a central plan, illustrated here as a domed octagon.

In the last quarter of the fifteenth century, Venice—once a center of Byzantine art—emerged as a major artistic center of Renaissance painting. From the late 1470s on, the domes of the Church of San Marco dominated the city center, and the rich colors of its glowing mosaics captured painters' imaginations. Venetian painters embraced the oil medium for both panel and canvas painting. The most important Venetian artists of this period were two brothers, Gentile (c. 1429–1507) and Giovanni (c. 1430–1516) Bellini, whose father, Jacopo (active c. 1423–1470), was a central figure in Venetian art. Jacopo, who had worked for

a short time in Florence, was a theorist who produced books of drawings in which he experimented with linear perspective. Andrea Mantegna was also part of this circle, for he had married Jacopo's daughter in 1453.

Gentile Bellini celebrated the daily life of the city in large, lively narratives, such as the *Procession of the Relic of the True Cross before the Church of San Marco* (fig. 17-69). Gentile, painting in 1496, depicted an event more than fifty years earlier: In 1444, during a procession in which a relic of the True Cross was carried through Venice's Piazza San Marco, a miraculous healing occurred, which was attributed to the relic. This accurately detailed cityscape is an early example of the topographical views that would one day be bought by wealthy tourists as souvenirs of their travels.

For almost sixty years, Giovanni Bellini's virtuosity as an artist amazed and attracted patrons. *Virgin and Child Enthroned with Saints Francis, John the Baptist, Job, Dominic, Sebastian, and Louis of Toulouse* (fig. 17-70), painted about 1478 for the Ospedale of San Giobbe (Saint Job), exhibits a dramatic perspectival view up into a vaulted apse. Certainly Giovanni knew his father's perspective drawings well, and he may also have been influenced by his brother-in-law Mantegna's early experiments in radical foreshortening and the use of a low vanishing point. In Giovanni's painting, the vanishing point for the rapidly converging lines of the architecture lies at the center, on the feet of the lute-playing angel. Also, the pose of Saint Sebastian, his body pierced by arrows, at the right recalls a famous *Saint Sebastian* by Mantegna. Giovanni has placed his figures in a Classical architectural interior with a coffered barrel vault, reminiscent of Masaccio's *Trinity* (see fig. 17-48). The gold mosaic, with its identifying inscription and stylized **seraphim**, recalls the art of the Byzantine Empire in the eastern Mediterranean and the long tradition of Byzantine-

17-70. Giovanni Bellini. *Virgin and Child Enthroned with Saints Francis, John the Baptist, Job, Dominic, Sebastian, and Louis of Toulouse*, from the chapel for the Ospedale of San Giobbe, Venice. c. 1478. Panel, 15'4" x 8'4" (4.67 x 2.54 m). Galleria dell'Accademia, Venice

Art historians have given a special name, *sacra conversazione* ("holy conversation"), to this type of composition showing saints, angels, and sometimes even the painting's donors in the same pictorial space with the enthroned Virgin and Child. Despite the name, no conversation or other interaction between the figures takes place in a literal sense. Instead, the individuals portrayed are joined in a mystical and eternal communion occurring outside of time, in which the viewer is invited to share.

inspired painting and mosaics produced in Venice.

Giovanni Bellini demonstrates the intense investigation and recording of nature associated with the early Renaissance. His work matured into a grand, simplified, idealized style during the early years of the sixteenth century. His early painting of *Saint Francis in Ecstasy* (fig. 17-71), painted in the 1470s, illustrates his mastery of an almost Flemish realism. The saint stands in communion with nature, bathed in early morning sunlight, his hands

17-71. Giovanni Bellini. *Saint Francis in Ecstasy*. 1470s. Oil and tempera on panel, 49 x 55⅞" (125 x142 cm). The Frick Collection, New York
Copyright the Frick Collection, New York

outspread showing the **stigmata** (the miraculous wounds of Christ appearing in the saint's own body). Francis had moved to a cave in the barren wilderness in his search for communion with God, but in this landscape, the fields blossom and flocks of animals graze. The grape arbor over his desk and the leafy tree toward which he directs his gaze add to an atmosphere of sylvan delight. True to fifteenth-century religious art, however, Bellini unites Old and New Testament themes to associate Francis with Moses and Christ: The tree symbolizes the burning bush, and the stream, the miraculous spring brought forth by Moses; the grape vine and the stigmata symbolize Christ's sacrifice. The crane and donkey represent the monastic virtue of patience. Both the detailed realism and luminous colors of the painting and the symbolic elements suggest Flemish art. The golden light suffusing the painting, however, is associated with Venice, a city of mist, reflections, and above all, color.

Giovanni's career covered nearly all of the second half of the fifteenth century, but many of his greatest paintings were produced in the sixteenth, before his death in 1516. Although his work is often discussed with that of Leonardo da Vinci in the sixteenth century, it seems fitting to end our consideration of the first phase of Renaissance painting in Italy with Giovanni Bellini as an important and influential bridge to the future.

OBJECTS OF DELIGHT AND ERUDITION

Italian craft artists were inspired by the new Renaissance ideas. As the creators of luxury goods for an educated clientele, they came into direct contact with humanistic ideas and the increased interest in classical antiquity. Particularly in the domain of home furnishings and interior decorations, the field was open for ambitious experiments in new subjects, treatments, and techniques.

Perfect objects for painted decoration were *cassoni* (singular, *cassone,* "chest") used for storing linens, fabrics, and clothing, which were often presented to couples at the time of their marriage. Few such chests survive intact today, often because the painted sections were cut out and sold as individual pictures by art dealers. Although religious subjects are found, especially on chests to store church linens and vestments, the *cassone* painters preferred mythological and historical subjects, allegorical or symbolic inventions, and occasionally scenes of everyday life. An extremely elegant *cassone* by an unknown artist, possibly made as a bride's chest about 1460 in Florence, is painted on both the front panel and the inner side of the lid (fig. 17-72). The reclining male nude on the lid, which may have some symbolic meaning, perhaps as a fertility image, has an immediacy and sensuality suggesting a study from a live model. The front panel, framed by carved Corinthian pilasters and columns, is a panoramic view of a city filled with figures. Although the subject comes from the legendary history of Rome, the setting and costumes are of the fifteenth century.

17-72. Florentine School. *Cassone.* c. 1460. Length 6'8⁷/₁₀" (2.05 m). Statens Museum for Kunst, Copenhagen

The development of linear perspective was a strong inducement for the creation of trompe l'oeil effects in painting, but the designers of **intarsia** (wood inlay) carried it to its ultimate expression. During the reconstruction of the palace at Urbino, Federico da Montefeltro commissioned the intarsia decoration of the walls of his *studiolo,* a room for his private collection of fine books and art objects (fig. 17-73). The trompe l'oeil design gave the small room illusionistic pilasters, carved cupboards with latticed doors, niches with statues, paintings, and built-in tables. A large window looks out onto an elegant marble loggia with a distant view of the countryside

17-73. *Studiolo* of Federico da Montefeltro, Ducal Palace, Urbino. 1470s. Intarsia, height 7'3" (2.21 m)

17-74. Antonio del Pollaiuolo. *Hercules and Antaeus*. c. 1475. Bronze, height with base 18" (45.7 cm). Museo Nazionale del Bargello, Florence

Among the many courageous acts by which Hercules gained immortality was the killing of the evil Antaeus in a wrestling match by lifting him off the earth, which was the source of the giant's great physical power. Hercules had been attacked by Antaeus, the son of the earth goddess Ge (or Gaia), on his search for a garden that produced pure gold apples. Stealing the apples was one of the Twelve Labors assigned to Hercules by King Eurystheus, who promised to let the hero marry his daughter when all were completed. When the king went back on his word, Hercules killed him, too.

17-75. Antico (Pier Jacopo Alari Bonacolsi). *Hercules and the Hydra*. 1495–98. Gilt bronze, diameter 12¼" (29 cm). Museo Nationale del Bargello, Florence

through its arches; and the shelves, cupboards, and tables are filled with all manner of fascinating things—scientific instruments, books, even the duke's armor hanging like a suit in a closet. All of this scene was inlaid in wood on flat surfaces with scrupulously applied linear perspective and foreshortening. On the walls above were paintings by Italian, Spanish, and Flemish artists.

The intarsia of the *studiolo* shows fictive cabinets filled with wonderful objects. The creation of small works of art—such as bronzes—to inspire the mind and delight the eye came into being in the fifteenth century. The enthusiasm of European collectors in the latter part of the fifteenth century for small bronzes contributed to the spread of classical taste. Antonio del Pollaiuolo (c. 1432–1498), multitalented and ambitious, was trained as a goldsmith and embroiderer but came to the Medici court about 1460 as a painter. His sculptures were mostly small bronzes, such as his *Hercules and Antaeus* of about 1475 (fig. 17-74). This study of complex interlock-

ing figures has an explosive energy that can best be appreciated by viewing the sculpture from every angle. Statuettes of religious subjects were still popular, but humanist art patrons began to collect bronzes of Greek and Roman subjects like this one. Many sculptors, especially those trained as goldsmiths, began to cast small copies after well-known Classical sculpture. Some artists executed their own designs *all'antica* ("in the antique style") as well. Although there were outright forgeries of antiquities at this time, works in the antique manner made by such sculptors as Pier Jacopo Alari Bonacolsi (c. 1460–1528) were intended simply to appeal to a cultivated humanist taste. Bonacolsi, who worked in Mantua, was so admired for such sculpture that he was nicknamed "Antico."

On a large bronze relief medallion more than a foot in diameter produced about 1495–1498, Antico represented *Hercules and the Hydra* (fig. 17-75), which shows the hero killing a multiheaded water serpent. Using the skills he had learned as a goldsmith, Antico often enriched his bronzes by gilding or inlaying details in gold and silver. A typical piece, like the one shown here, exhibits satin-smooth, glowing flesh contrasting with fine, realistic details and areas of glittering texture. This mythological scene is enlivened with naturalistic touches, such as the gnarled tree trunk, the carefully observed quiver and bow, and the exquisitely rendered scales of the hydra.

European Printmaking and Book Printing

Printmaking emerged in Europe with the availability of locally manufactured paper at the end of the fourteenth century. Paper had been made in China as early as the second century CE, and small amounts were imported into Europe from the eighth century on. The first European paper was made in the twelfth century, but until the four-teenth century paper was rare and expensive. By the turn of the fifteenth century, however, commercial paper mills in nearly every European country were turning out large supplies that made it fairly inexpensive to use paper for printing. Designs carved in relief on woodblocks had long been used to print on cloth, but the printing of images and texts on paper and the production of books in multiple copies of a single **edition**, or version, rather than copying each book by hand, began in the fifteenth century. Soon both handwritten and printed books were illustrated with printed images. Printed books and single-sheet printed images were sometimes painted with **watercolor**.

The Single-Sheet Print. Single-sheet woodcuts and engravings were made in large quantities in the early decades of the fifteenth century (see "Woodcuts and Engravings on Metal," page 675). In the beginning, woodcuts were often made by woodworkers with no training in drawing, but very quickly artists began to draw images for them to cut from the block. Engravings, on the other hand, seem to have developed from the metalworking techniques of goldsmiths and armorers. When paper became relatively plentiful around 1400, these artisans began to take impressions of the designs they were engraving on metal by rubbing the lines with lampblack and pressing paper over them.

Simply executed woodcut devotional images be-came popular early in the century, and they were sold as souvenirs to pilgrims at holy sites. Images for private devotion were also engraved, and in the hands of an experienced goldsmith they were often highly detailed, such as the *Virgin and Child in a Garden with Saints Mar-garet and Catherine* of about 1461 (fig. 17-76), by Master E. S., an artist known only from the engravings that carry these initials. More than 300 engravings by Master E. S. still exist, ranging in subject from grotesque alphabets to elaborate, symbolic representations of the Virgin. The artist worked in southern Germany, Switzerland, and eastern France from about 1450 to the late 1460s, pro-ducing extremely complex works. His style recalls that of Robert Campin, using a delicate line and fine **cross-hatched** shading to model forms. This charming scene in an enclosed garden, symbolic of virginity, could almost be that of a queen and her ladies-in-waiting watching over a playing child while listening to lute and harp music. But the figures are the Virgin Mary, the Christ Child, and Saints Margaret with her leashed dragon and Catherine with her wheel.

Not all prints were made for religious purposes, or even for sale. Some artists seem to have made them as personal studies, in the manner of drawings, or for use in their shops as models. The Florentine goldsmith and

17-76. Master E. S. *Virgin and Child in a Garden with Saints Margaret and Catherine* (or *Large Enclosed Garden*). c. 1461. Engraving, plate 8⅝ x 6⅜" (21.9 x 16.2 cm). Bibliothèque Nationale, Paris

17-77. Antonio del Pollaiuolo. *Battle of the Nudes.* c. 1465–70. Engraving, 15⅛ x 23¼" (38.3 x 59 cm). Cincinnati Art Museum, Ohio
Bequest of Herbert Greer French. 1943.118

sculptor Antonio del Pollaiuolo may have intended his only known—but highly influential—print, *Battle of the Nudes,* an engraving done about 1465 to 1470, as a study in composition involving the human figure in action (fig. 17-77). The naked men fighting each other ferociously against a tapestrylike background of foliage seem to have been drawn from a single model in a variety of poses, many of which were taken from classical sources. Like the artist's *Hercules and Antaeus* (see fig. 17-74),

TECHNIQUE

WOODCUTS AND ENGRAVINGS ON METAL

Woodcuts are made by drawing on the smooth surface of a block of wood that has a fine grain, such as fruitwood, then cutting away all the areas around the lines with a sharp tool called a gouge, leaving the lines in **high relief**. When the block's surface is inked and a piece of paper pressed down hard on it, the ink on the relief areas is transferred to the paper to create a reverse image. The linear effects can be varied by using thicker and thinner lines, and shading can be achieved by making the lines closer or farther apart. Other techniques—such as punching, cross-hatching, and flicking out short strokes with the gouge—also create pictorial interest. In the fifteenth century, the images were generally left in black and white or painted by hand, although a few artists experimented with adding colors during the inking of the block and using more than one block with one or two colors printed over the black-and-white image.

Engraving on metal requires a technique called **intaglio**, in which the lines are cut into the plate with tools called gravers or **burins**, while the surface remains flat. The engraver carefully scrapes any metal piled up beside the line, then burnishes any scratches left on the plate to give a clean, sharp image. Ink is applied over the whole plate and forced down into the lines, after which the surface of the plate is carefully wiped clean. The ink in the lines prints onto a sheet of paper pressed hard against the metal plate.

Both woodblocks and metal plates could be used repeatedly to make nearly identical images. If the lines of the block or plate wore down, the artists could repair them. Printing large numbers of identical prints of a single version, called an **edition**, was usually a team effort in a busy workshop. One artist would make the drawing. Sometimes it was made directly on the block or plate with ink, in reverse of its printed direction, sometimes on paper to be transferred in reverse onto the plate or block by another person, who then cut the lines. Others would ink and print the images. Prints often were inscribed with the names and occupations (usually given in Latin, and frequently abbreviated) of those who carried out these various tasks. The following are some of the most common inscriptions (Hind, volume 2, page 26):

Sculpsit (sculp., sc.), sculptor: engraved or cut, engraver or cutter
Incidit (incid., inc.), incisor: engraved or cut, engraver or cutter
Fecit (fec., f.): literally "made"; engraved or cut, engraver or cutter
Excudit (excud., exc.): printed, or published
Impressit (imp.): printed
Pinxit (pinx.), pictor: painted, painter
Delineavit (delin.), delineator: drew, draftsperson
Invenit (inv.), inventor: designed, designer

In the illustration of books, the plates or blocks would be reused to print later editions and even adapted for use in other books. A set of blocks or plates for illustrations was a valuable commodity often sold by one workshop to another. Early in publishing, there were no copyright laws, and many entrepreneurs simply had their workers copy book illustrations onto woodblocks and cut them for their own publications.

woodcut

engraving

much of the engraving's fascination lies in how it depicts muscles of the male body reacting under tension.

The German Martin Schongauer, who learned engraving from his goldsmith father, was an immensely skillful printmaker who excelled in drawing and the difficult technique of shading from deep blacks to faintest grays. One of his best-known prints today is the *Temptation of Saint Anthony,* engraved about 1480 to 1490 (fig. 17-78). Schongauer illustrated the original biblical meaning of temptation, expressed in the Latin word *tentatio,* as a physical assault rather than a subtle inducement. Wildly acrobatic, slithery, spiky demons lift Anthony up off the ground to torment and terrify him in midair. The engraver intensified the horror of the moment by condensing the action into a swirling vortex of figures beating, scratching, poking, tugging, and no doubt shrieking at the stoical saint, who remains impervious to all by reason of his faith.

17-78. Martin Schongauer. *Temptation of Saint Anthony*. c. 1480–90. Engraving, 12¼ x 9" (31.1 x 22.9 cm). The Metropolitan Museum of Art, New York
Rogers Fund, 1920 (20.5.2)

The Illustrated Book. The explosion of learning in Europe in the fifteenth century precipitated experiments in faster and cheaper ways of producing books than by hand-copying them. The earliest printed books were **block books,** for which each page of text, with or without illustrations, was cut in relief on a single block of wood.

Movable-type printing, in which individual letters could be locked together, inked, and printed onto paper by a mechanical press, was first achieved in the workshop of Johann Gutenberg in Mainz, Germany. More than forty copies of Gutenberg's Bible, printed in 1456, still exist. With the invention of this fast way to make identical books, the

Canterbury Tales, published in 1484, Caxton added woodblock illustrations by an unknown artist. The assembled pilgrims, whose individual stories make up the *Tales,* appear in the Prologue seated around a table, ready to dine (fig. 17-79). Although technically simple, this woodcut and its companions are effective, original compositions.

Another famous early book was *Hypnerotomachia Poliphili* (*The Love-Dream Struggle of Poliphilo*). This charming romantic allegory tells of the search of Poliphilo through exotic places for his lost love, Polia—much in the manner of René of Anjou's *Livre du Cuer d'Amours Espris* (see fig. 17-29). The book, written in the 1460s or 1470s by Fra Francesco Colonna, was published in 1499 by the noted Venetian printer Aldo Manuzio (Aldus Manutius). Many historians of book printing consider Aldo's *Hypnerotomachia* to be the most beautiful book ever produced, from the standpoint of type and page design. The woodcut illustrations in the *Hypnerotomachia,* such as the *Garden of Love* (fig. 17-80), incorporate linear perspective and pseudoclassical structures that would influence future architects.

Although woodcuts, constantly refined and increasingly complex, would remain a popular medium of book illustration for centuries to come, methods for illustrating books with engravings soon emerged. The potential of these new techniques for printing illustrated books in Europe at the end of the 1400s held great promise for the spread of knowledge and ideas in the following century. The new empirical frame of mind that characterized the fifteenth century gave rise in the sixteenth century to an explosion of inquiry and new ways of looking at the world.

7-79. Page with *Pilgrims at Table,* Prologue to *Canterbury Tales,* by Geoffrey Chaucer, published by William Caxton, London, 1484 (second edition; first with illustrations). Woodcut, 4¹/₁₆ x 4⁷/₈" (10.2 x 12 cm). The Pierpont Morgan Library, New York
PML 693

Chaucer (c. 1342–1400) included in his *Tales* two extremely complex and engaging women, Dorigen and Alice, the Wife of Bath. Dorigen appeared in the Franklin's Tale as a good woman who refused to accept society's advice that she kill herself if her virtue were threatened. Alice, on the other hand, was one of the thirty people who joined her host in making a pilgrimage to the shrine of Saint Thomas à Becket, each one telling a story to entertain the others along the way. Some critics see the Wife of Bath as an example for good women to avoid, but Chaucer put words in the lively Alice's mouth that are well understood by many women today.

intellectual and spiritual life of Europe—and with it the arts—changed forever. As early as 1465, two German printers were working in Italy, and by the 1470s there were presses in France, Flanders, Holland, and Spain.

England got its first printing press in 1481 as the result of a second career launched by a former English cloth merchant, William Caxton (active 1441–1491?). Caxton lived for thirty years in Bruges, where he came in contact with the humanist community, as well as local book-printing ventures. In his spare time, he translated into English Raoul le Fevre's *Histories of Troy,* which became the first book printed in that language. In 1476 Caxton moved back to London, where he established the first English publishing house. He printed eighty books in the next fourteen years, including works by the fourteenth-century English author Geoffrey Chaucer. In the second edition of Chaucer's

17-80. Page with *Garden of Love, Hypnerotomachia Poliphili,* by Fra Francesco Colonna, published by Aldo Manuzio (Aldus Manutius), Venice, 1499. Woodcut, image 5¹/₈ x 5¹/₈" (13.5 x 13.5 cm). The Pierpont Morgan Library, New York
PML 373

1500   1520   1540

1500
Leonardo
The Last
Supper
1495–98

Michelangelo
David
1501–4

Bramante
Tempietto
1502

Bosch
Detail,
Garden of
Delights
1500–5

Grünewald
Crucifixion, from
Isenheim Altarpiece
c. 1510–15

Pontormo
Entombment
1525–28

Clouet
Francis I
1525–30

Holbein the Younger
Henry VIII
1540

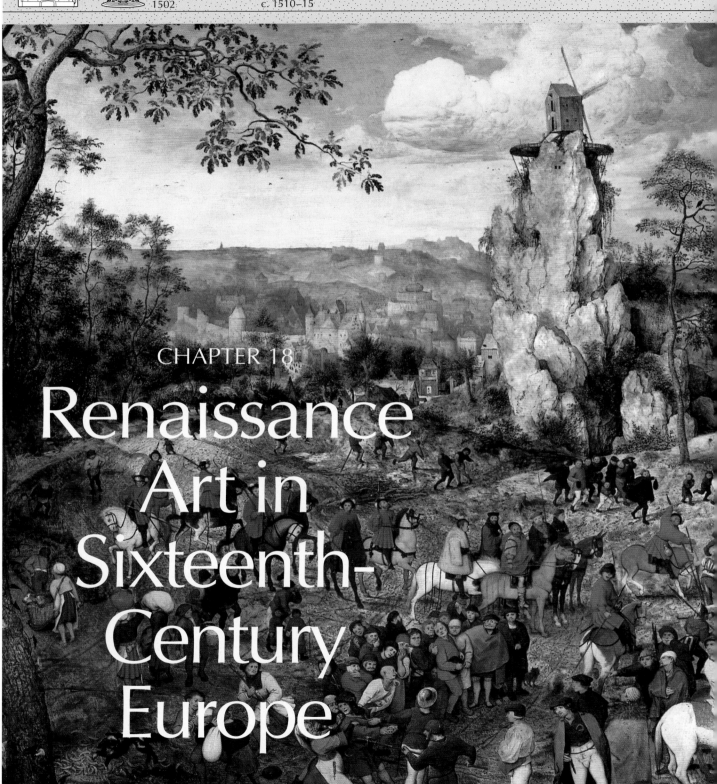

CHAPTER 18

Renaissance Art in Sixteenth-Century Europe

Palladio
San Giorgio Maggiore
1566

El Greco
View of Toledo
1609

Map

IRELAND

Nottingham

ENGLAND
London

THE NETHERLANDS
Rotterdam · Utrecht · **GERMANY** · **POLAND**
Bruges · 's Hertogenbosch · Wittenberg
Antwerp

FLANDERS
Brussels · Halle · *SAXONY* · Cracow
BELGIUM
Maubeuge

Paris · Mainz · Würzburg · Nuremberg
Worms · Rothenburg ob der Tauber
Fontainebleau · Regensburg
Chambord · *ALSACE* · Strasbourg · *BAVARIA*
Isenheim · Augsburg · Munich · Vienna · Danube
Chenonceaux · Basel · **AUSTRIA**

FRANCE · *BURGUNDY* · **SWITZERLAND**
ALPS

Milan · Lake Como · *VENETO* · Venice
Florence · *TUSCANY*
PAPAL STATES
Rome · *UMBRIA* · **ITALY**

PORTUGAL · *CASTILE* · *ARAGON*
Madrid
Toledo
SPAIN

Mediterranean Sea
San Giorgio

Inset (Italy)
Lake Como · Trent
Milan · Maser · Vicenza · *VENETO*
Verona · Padua · Venice
Cremona · Mantua
Parma · Vignola · Ravenna
Carrara · Bologna
Vinci · Florence · Urbino
Siena · *TUSCANY* · Caprese
Perugia · *PAPAL STATES*
Caprarola · *UMBRIA* · **ITALY**
Rome

ATLANTIC OCEAN

0   300 miles
0   300 kilometers

18-1.   Veronese. *Feast in the House of Levi*, from the Monastery of Santi Giovanni e Paolo, Venice. 1573. Oil on canvas, 18'3" x 42' (5.56 x 12.8 m). Galleria dell'Accademia, Venice

Jesus among his disciples at the Last Supper was a popular image during the sixteenth century. So it was not unusual when, in 1573, the highly esteemed painter Veronese revealed an enormous canvas that seemed at first glance to depict this scene—Jesus, indeed, is in the center of the painting, with his followers (fig. 18-1). But the church officials of Venice were shocked and offended—some by Veronese's grandiose portrayal of the subject in the midst of splendor and pageantry, others by the impiety of placing near Jesus a host of extremely unsavory characters. They were so disapproving, in fact, that Veronese was called before the Inquisition to explain his reasons for including such extraneous details as a man picking his teeth, scruffy dogs, a parrot, and foreign soldiers. The subject originally may have been intended to be the Last Supper—the Inquisitors certainly thought so, although Veronese claimed it depicted the Feast in the House of Simon, a small dinner shortly before Jesus' final entry into Jerusalem. Veronese boldly justified his actions by saying: "We painters take the same license the poets and the jesters take. . . . I paint pictures as I see fit and as well as my talent permits" (from the record of the inquiry, cited in Holt, volume 2, pages 68, 69). This statement was a quite unheard-of stance at that time, and his defense fell on unsympathetic ears. He was told to change the painting.

Accordingly, Veronese changed the picture's *title* so that it referred to another banquet, given by the tax collector Levi, whom Jesus had called to follow him. Thus, the "buffoons, drunkards . . . and similar vulgarities" (cited in Holt, volume 2, page 68) remained, and Veronese noted his new source—Luke, Chapter 5—on the balustrade. In that Gospel, one reads that "Levi gave a great banquet for him [Jesus] in his house, and a large crowd of tax collectors and others were at table with them" (Luke 5:29). In changing the declared subject of the painting, Veronese also had modest revenge on the Inquisitors: when Jesus was criticized for associating with such people, he replied, "I have not come to call the righteous to repentance but sinners" (Luke 5:32).

The Inquisitors who under the direction of the Church were scrutinizing works of art for heretical or profane suggestions, the painter who brashly defended his art, the very size and medium and style of the painting itself—all were products of the extraordinarily rich, inspiring, and unpredictable sixteenth century.

EUROPE IN THE SIXTEENTH CENTURY

The sixteenth century in Europe was an age of ferment—social, intellectual, religious, and geographic— that transformed European culture. The humanism of the fourteenth and fifteenth centuries, with its medieval roots and its often uncritical acceptance of the authority of classical texts, slowly gave way to a new spirit of discovery that led Europeans to investigate the natural world around them and to explore lands previously unknown to them. Travel became more common, and new ideas spread through the publication in translation of ancient and contemporary texts. An explosion in the number of books printed both broadened the horizons of educated Europeans and enabled more people to learn to read. Much more than in earlier centuries, artists and their work became mobile, and artistic styles became less regional and more "international."

At the start of the sixteenth century, England, France, and Portugal were national states under strong monarchs. With the succession to the throne of the Habsburg Charles V in 1519, the Habsburg (Holy Roman) Empire became the strongest power in Europe, with vast territories in the Americas as well. Central Europe (Germany) was divided into dozens of free cities and territories ruled by nobles and princes. But even states as powerful as Saxony and Bavaria acknowledged the overlordship of the Habsburg Holy Roman emperors. Italy, also divided into many small states, was a diplomatic and military battlefield where Spain, France, Venice, and the papacy warred against each other in shifting alliances for much of the century. The popes themselves behaved like secular princes, using diplomacy and military force to regain control over the Papal States in central Italy and in some cases even to establish their families as hereditary rulers. The popes' incessant demands for money to finance these campaigns aggravated the religious dissent that had long been developing, especially north of the Alps, and contributed greatly to the rise of Protestantism.

The political maneuvering of Pope Clement VII (papacy 1523–1534) led to a clash with the Holy Roman Emperor Charles V, based in Germany. As a result, in May 1527 the imperial army attacked Rome, beginning a six-month orgy of killing, looting, and burning. The Sack of Rome, as it is called, damaged irreparably the humanistic confidence of the Renaissance, and many artists simply left Rome for good.

The Effects of the Reformation on Art

There had been many dissident movements in the history of the Church. Some had led to great controversy and outright war, but the unity and authority of the Church had always prevailed—until the sixteenth century. Then, reformers (giving this movement the name *Reformation*) not only challenged Church teaching on specific beliefs and religious practices but also denied the very basis of the pope's authority. These reformers—called Protestants because they "protested" against the practices and beliefs of the Catholic Church—succeeded in permanently breaking away from Rome. One factor in their success was the support of powerful rulers in Germany and Scandinavia who saw the Protestant movement as a way of enhancing their own wealth and power. Another was the widespread use of the printing press to make the Bible and other Christian writings available to laypeople, many of whom now could read. Improved communications allowed scholars throughout Europe to debate religious matters and to influence many people who were already dissatisfied with the Church. Two of the most important reformers in the early sixteenth century were themselves Catholic priests and trained theologians, Desiderius Erasmus of Rotterdam (1466?–1536) in Holland and Martin Luther (1483–1546) in Germany. The wide circulation of Luther's writings—especially his German translation of the Bible and his works maintaining that salvation comes through faith alone—eventually led to the establishment of a Protestant church in Germany and Scandinavia.

By the end of the sixteenth century, some form of Protestantism prevailed throughout northern Europe. By the 1560s only Italy, Spain, Ireland, Poland, and Portugal were still entirely Catholic, although France reaffirmed its allegiance to the Roman Catholic Church in the late 1570s after decades of religious civil war. Southern Germany, the Rhineland, Austria, and Hungary also remained predominantly Catholic.

One tragic consequence of the Reformation was the destruction of religious art. In some areas, Protestant zealots smashed sculpture and stained-glass windows and destroyed or whitewashed religious paintings to rid the churches of what they considered to be idolatrous images. With the sudden loss of patronage for religious art in the newly Protestant countries, many artists turned to portraiture and other secular subjects, including

PARALLELS

Europe	1500–1550	1550–1600
Italy	Michelangelo's *David*; Bramante's Tempietto; Pope Julius II; Leonardo's *Mona Lisa*; *Laocoön and His Sons* discovered; rebuilding of Saint Peter's; Giorgione's *Tempest*; Michelangelo's Sistine frescoes; Raphael's *School of Athens*; Pope Leo X; Mannerism emerges; Pope Clement VII; Sack of Rome; Machiavelli's *The Prince*; Michelangelo's *Last Judgment*; Pope Paul III; Titian's *Isabella d'Este*; Bronzino's *Ugolino Martelli*; Council of Trent begins; Ignatius Loyola founds Jesuit order; Inquisition established; Michelangelo takes over rebuilding of Saint Peter's	Vasari's *Lives* of artists; Palladio's San Giorgio and Villa Rotonda; Pope Pius IV; Pope Gregory XIII; Veronese's *Feast in the House of Levi*; Pope Sixtus V; first completely sung opera
France	King Francis I; Château of Chenonceaux; Clouet's *Francis I*; Fontainebleau begun; Reformation in France; Lescot's Cour Carré	Montaigne's *Essays*; reaffirms allegiance to Catholic Church
Netherlands	Bosch's *Garden of Earthly Delights*	Brueghel the Elder's *Return of the Hunters*; Dutch war of independence and establishment of Dutch Republic
Germany	University of Wittenberg founded; Dürer's *Adam and Eve*; Grünewald's *Isenheim Altarpiece*; Luther's "95 Theses" launches Reformation in Germany; landscape painting develops; Holy Roman Emperor Charles V; Dürer's *Four Apostles*	University of Würzberg founded; Holy Roman Emperor Ferdinand I
England	King Henry VIII; More's *Utopia*; England breaks with Rome; Holbein the Younger's *Henry VIII*; King Edward VI	Queen Mary restores Catholicism briefly; Queen Elizabeth I; Drake circumnavigates world; Smythson's Hardwick; Raleigh explores present-day North Carolina and Virginia; Marlowe's *Tamburlaine the Great*; England destroys the Spanish Armada; Shakespeare's early plays; Spenser's *Faerie Queene*; Bacon's *Essays*
Spain	The Inquisition continues; Columbus's final voyages to Americas; Ponce de León claims Florida; Cortés conquers Mexico; Magellan circumnavigates world; Pizarro conquers Inkas	Philip II is king of Spain and ruler of Netherlands, Americas, Milan, Burgundy, and Naples and Sicily; Herrera's El Escorial; El Greco's *Burial of Count Orgaz*
World	Ming dynasty (China); first African slaves in the West Indies; Montezuma II rules Aztec empire (Mexico); Copernicus (Poland) states that Earth revolves around the Sun; Ottomans take Cairo; Europeans expelled from China; Mughal dynasty founded in India; Portuguese reach Japan; Csar Ivan the Terrible (Russia)	Sultan Suleyman I (Turkey); Akbar the Great (India); Oda Nobunaga rules Japan from Kyoto; first kabuki company, established by a woman (Japan); Hideyoshi unifies Japan; Csar Boris Godunov (Russia)

moralizing depiction of human folly and weaknesses, much as reformers such as Erasmus had done in writing. The popularity of these themes stimulated a free market for which artists created works of their own invention that were sold through dealers or by word of mouth.

To counter the Protestant Reformation, the Roman Catholic hierarchy during the Council of Trent (1545–1563) formulated a program that included guidelines for religious art. Traditional images of Christ and the saints would continue to be venerated in churches, but they were to be scrutinized carefully for heresy, profanity, or any other quality that might justify Protestant criticism. Moreover, bishops and priests were to educate laypeople not to view images as having any intrinsic power. Although these rules limited what could be expressed in Christian art and led to the destruction of some works, over time they encouraged artistic creation. Art became a powerful weapon of propaganda, especially in the hands of the Society of Jesus, one of the new religious orders that arose. Confirmed by Pope Paul III in 1540, the Jesuits spread worldwide from Il Gesù (see fig. 18-9), their mother church in Rome, to lead the Counter-Reformation movement within the Catholic Church.

The Changing Status of Artists

Sixteenth-century artists left a considerable record of their activities in diaries, notebooks, and letters. In addition, contemporary writers reported on everything from artists' physical appearances to their personal reputations. Giorgio Vasari's famous *Lives of the Most Excellent Italian Architects, Painters, and Sculptors*—the first art history book—appeared in 1550. As valuable as this work is, scholars approach with caution some of Vasari's strong views—for example, he extolled the work of his fellow Florentines but denigrated the earlier Gothic style, and his ideal art was graceful, elegant, classically inspired, and technically finished.

Clearly, sixteenth-century patrons valued artists highly and rewarded them well, not only with generous commissions but even by elevating some to courtiers and respected colleagues. In the Protestant countries, painters and sculptors became entrepreneurs who ran businesses on the side. The sale of prints by or based on the works of popular artists was a means by which reputations and styles became widely known, and a few artists of stature became international celebrities. With their new fame and independence, the most successful artists could decide which commissions to accept, reject, or leave unfinished—even if the patron was a pope or an emperor.

During this period, theorists increasingly came to regard the conception of a painting, sculpture, or work of architecture as a liberal—rather than a manual—art that thus required artists to be educated in the classics and mathematics as well as having technical training. The artist, it was recognized, could express as much through painted, sculptural, and architectural forms as the poet could with words or the musician through melody. The belief that artists were divinely inspired creative genius-

es became a widespread myth—one that is still with us today. Some historians have suggested that the new status of artists in the sixteenth century worked against the participation of women in the visual arts, because it was then believed that genius was reserved for men. Furthermore, one could not achieve international status without traveling extensively and relocating often in order to follow commissions. Still, women artists were active in Europe despite numerous obstacles to their entering any profession.

ITALIAN ART

By the beginning of the sixteenth century, Renaissance humanism and the Italian Renaissance style could be found throughout the rest of Europe, spread especially through the patronage of foreign courts. The brief phase of Italian art from the 1490s to the Sack of Rome in 1527—characterized by self-confident humanism, admiration of classical forms, and a dominating sense of stability and order—was once called the High Renaissance. Later, many outstanding younger artists trained in Florence and northern Italy worked not only in other Italian cities but also in Spain, France, Germany, and the Netherlands. They interpreted Renaissance forms in their own ways, developing a number of local and personal styles that characterize the Late Renaissance, generally referring to the period after 1530.

Architecture in Rome and the Vatican

As the ruling families of Florence and Milan were beset by political turmoil, Rome became the most active artistic and intellectual center in Italy, with popes and noble Roman families as the most generous patrons. The election of Pope Julius II in 1503 began a resurgence of the power of the papacy. During the ten years of his reign, he fought wars and formed alliances to consolidate his power. But he also enlisted the artists Bramante, Raphael, and Michelangelo to carry out his vision of revitalizing Rome and the Vatican, the pope's residence, as the center of a new Christian art based on classical forms and principles.

Inspired by the achievements of fifteenth-century pioneers and the monuments of antiquity, Renaissance architects working in Rome developed ideals comparable to those of contemporary painters and sculptors. The first-century Roman architect and engineer Vitruvius's ten-volume work on classical architecture (see "The Vitruvian Man," page 692) continued to be an important source for sixteenth-century Italian architects such as

GREAT PAPAL PATRONS OF THE SIXTEENTH CENTURY

Julius II (della Rovere)	papacy 1503–1513
Leo X (Medici)	papacy 1513–1521
Clement VII (Medici)	papacy 1523–1534
Paul III (Farnese)	papacy 1534–1549

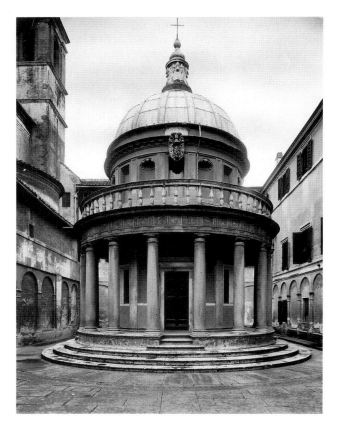

18-2.   Donato Bramante. Tempietto, Church of San Pietro in Montorio, Rome. 1502

Vignola, discussed below. Although religious architecture was a major source of commissions, some of the best opportunities for innovation were urban palaces and large country villas.

Donato Bramante.   Born near Urbino and trained as a painter, Donato Bramante (1444–1514) turned to architectural design early in his career. About 1481, he became attached to the Sforza court in Milan, where he would have known Leonardo da Vinci. In 1499, Bramante settled in Rome, but work came slowly. The architect was nearing sixty when Queen Isabella and King Ferdinand of Spain commissioned him to design a small shrine over the spot in Rome where the apostle Peter was believed to have been crucified (fig. 18-2). The tall **drum**, or circular wall, supporting a hemispheric dome (no longer original), and the centralized plan of his Tempietto ("little temple") recall early Christian shrines built over martyrs' relics, as well as the remains of a small circular, **tholos**-form temple in Rome. Only 15 feet in diameter, Bramante's nearly perfect Renaissance interpretation of the principles of Vitruvius and Alberti has a stepped base and a Doric **peristyle**, or continuous row of columns. (Vitruvius had advised that the Doric order be used for temples to gods of particularly forceful character.) Especially notable is the sculptural effect of the building's exterior, with its deep wall niches creating contrasts of light and shadow, its Doric frieze of carved papal emblems, and its elegant **balustrade**.

Shortly after Julius II's election as pope in 1503, he commissioned Bramante to renovate the Vatican Palace, and in 1506 Julius appointed him chief architect of a project to replace Saint Peter's Basilica in the Vatican, the site of Peter's tomb. Construction had barely begun when Julius died in 1513; Bramante himself died in 1514 without leaving a comprehensive plan. Raphael replaced Bramante as papal architect with responsibility for building Saint Peter's, but after a series of popes and architects and various revisions, the new Saint Peter's was still far from completion when Michelangelo took over the project in 1546 (see "Saint Peter's Basilica," page 688).

Michelangelo.   The Tuscan Michelangelo studied and worked as a sculptor and painter in Florence long before the popes called him to Rome. (For more detailed discussion of Michelangelo's early years, see page 697.) After Michelangelo settled in Rome in 1534, a rich and worldly Roman noble was elected as Pope Paul III (papacy 1534–1549). He surprised his electors by his vigorous pursuit of reform within the Church. He also began renovation of several important sites in Rome and the upgrading of papal properties. Among the projects in which he involved Michelangelo was remodeling the Campidoglio (Capitol), a public square atop the Capitoline Hill, once the citadel of Republican Rome. The buildings covering the irregular site had fallen into disrepair, and the pope saw its renovation as a symbol of both his spiritual and his secular power.

Scholars still debate Michelangelo's role in the Capitoline project, although some have connected the granting of Roman citizenship to him in 1537 with his taking charge of the work. Preserved accounts mention the artist by name only twice: In 1539, he advised reshaping the base for the ancient Roman statue of Marcus Aurelius; in 1563, payment was made "to execute the orders of master Michelangelo Buonarroti in the building of the Campidoglio." Michelangelo's comprehensive plan for what is surely among the most beautiful urban-renewal projects of all time was documented in contemporary prints (fig. 18-3), which the Piazza del Campidoglio today closely resembles even though it was not finished until the seventeenth century, and Michelangelo's exquisite star design in the pavement was not installed until the twentieth century.

In 1537, the city council (the Conservatori) allotted funds to renovate the Palazzo dei Conservatori (fig. 18-4), which contained its offices and meeting rooms. Although only three bays of the new facade were finished by the time of Michelangelo's death in 1564, his repeating vertical elements were continued on the Conservatori facade and on the so-called Palazzo Nuovo facing it across the piazza (see fig. 18-3). The framework of the facade is formed by colossal **Composite order** pilasters raised on tall pedestals and supporting a wide architrave below the heavy cornice. Each ground-level bay opens into the deep portico through Ionic columns supporting their own architraves. On the main level above, although a wide central window was added later, the original design called for identical bays, each with a narrow central

ELEMENTS OF ARCHITECTURE
The Renaissance Palace Facade

By the middle of the fifteenth century, more artists had become students of the past, and a few humanists had ventured into the field of art theory and design. Leon Battista Alberti (1404–1472), a humanist-turned-architect, wrote about his classical theories on art before he ever designed a building. Alberti's various writings present the first coherent exposition of early Italian Renaissance aesthetic theory, including the Italian mathematical perspective system credited to Brunelleschi and ideal proportions of the human body derived from classical art. With Alberti began the gradual change in the status of the architect from a hands-on builder—and thus a manual laborer—to an intellectual expected to know philosophy, history, and the classics as well as mathematics and engineering.

Wealthy and noble families in Renaissance Italy built magnificent city palaces. More than just being large and luxurious private homes, these palaces were designed (often by the best architects of the time) to look imposing and even intimidating. The **facade**, or front face of a building, offers broad clues to what lies behind the facade: a huge central door suggests power; rough, **rusticated** stonework hints of strength and the fortifications of a castle; precious marbles or carvings connote wealth; a **cartouche**, perhaps with a family coat of arms, is an emphatic identity symbol.

Most Renaissance palaces used architectural elements derived from ancient Greek and Roman buildings—**columns** and **pilasters** in the Doric, Ionic, and/or Corinthian orders, decorated **entablatures**, and other such pieces—in a style known as **classicism**. The example illustrated here, the Palazzo Farnese in Rome, was built for the Farneses, one of whom, Cardinal Alessandro Farnese, became Pope Paul III in 1534.

Designed by Sangallo the Younger, Michelangelo, and Giacomo della Porta, this immense building stands at the head of and dominates a broad open public square, or **piazza**. The palace's three stories are clearly defined by two horizontal bands of stonework, or **stringcourses**. A many-layered **cornice** sits on the facade like a weighty crown. The **moldings**, cornice, and entablatures are decorated with classical **motifs** and with the lilies that form the Farnese family coat of arms.

The massive central door is emphasized by elaborate rusticated stonework (as are the building's corners, where the shaped stones are known as **quoins**), and is surmounted by a balcony suitable for ceremonial appearances, over which is set the cartouche with the Farnese arms. Windows are treated differently on each story: on the ground floor, the twelve windows sit on **brackets**, and the window heads are topped with **architraves**. The story directly above is known in Italy as the *piano nobile*, or first floor (Americans would call it the second floor), which contains the grandest rooms. Its twelve windows are decorated with alternating triangular and arched **pediments**, supported by pairs of **engaged half columns** in the Corinthian order. The second floor (or American third floor) has thirteen windows, all with triangular pediments whose supporting Ionic half columns are set on brackets echoing those under the windows on the ground floor.

Renaissance city palaces, in general, were oriented inward, away from the noisy streets. Many contained open courtyards (see fig. 17-63). Classical elements prevailed here, too. The courtyard of the Palazzo Farnese has a **loggia** fronted by an **arcade** at the ground level. Its Classical engaged columns and pilasters present all the usual parts: **pedestal**, **base**, **shaft**, and **capital**. The progression of orders from the lowest to the highest story mirrors the appearance of the orders in ancient Greece: Doric, Ionic, and Corinthian.

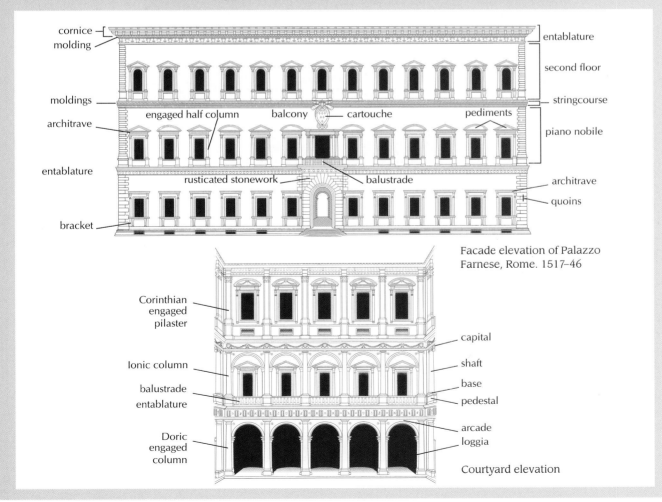

Facade elevation of Palazzo Farnese, Rome. 1517–46

Courtyard elevation

18-3.
Étienne Dupérac. *Piazza del Campidoglio, Rome*, engraving after design of Michelangelo. 1569. Gabinetto Nazionale delle Stampe, Rome

Flanking the entrance to the piazza are the so-called *Dioscuri*, two ancient Roman statues moved to the Capitol by Paul III, along with the bronze *Marcus Aurelius*, an imperial Roman equestrian statue, which was installed at the center of the slightly sunken ovoid fronting the buildings. At the back of the square is the Palazzo Senatorio, whose double-ramp grand staircase is thought to have been designed by Michelangelo. At the right is the Palazzo dei Conservatori, with a new facade designed by Michelangelo, and facing it, the Palazzo Nuovo, which was built in the seventeenth century to match the Conservatori. Today, air pollution so threatens the monuments that some have been brought indoors.

18-4. Michelangelo. Facade of the Palazzo dei Conservatori, Piazza del Campidoglio, Rome. c. 1563

window and a balcony flanked by **engaged columns** supporting **segmental pediments**. The horizontal orientation of the building is emphasized by the plain architrave below the balustrade of the roof and is then picked up below in the broken architrave above the portico.

When Paul III appointed Michelangelo architect of the new Saint Peter's in 1546, Michelangelo was well aware of the efforts of its architects—from Bramante to Raphael to Antonio da Sangallo the Younger—since the laying of the cornerstone, in 1506. Paul III clearly expected to complete the now-forty-year-old project, and the seventy-one-year-old sculptor, confident of his architectural expertise, demanded the right to deal directly with the pope, rather than through a committee of construction deputies. Michelangelo further shocked the deputies—but not the pope—by tearing down or cancel-

ing parts of Sangallo's design and returning to the central plan, long associated with Christian martyria. Seventeenth-century additions and renovations dramatically changed the original plan of the church and the appearance of its interior, but Michelangelo's Saint Peter's (fig. 18-5) can still be seen in the contrasting forms of the flat and angled walls and the three **hemicycles** (semicircular structures), whose colossal pilasters, **blind windows** (having no openings), and niches form the sanctuary of the church. The level above the heavy entablature was later given windows of a different shape. How Michelangelo would have built the great dome is not known; most scholars believe that he would have made it hemispherical. The dome that was erected by Giacomo della Porta in 1588–1590 retains Michelangelo's basic design: a segmented dome with regularly spaced openings, resting on

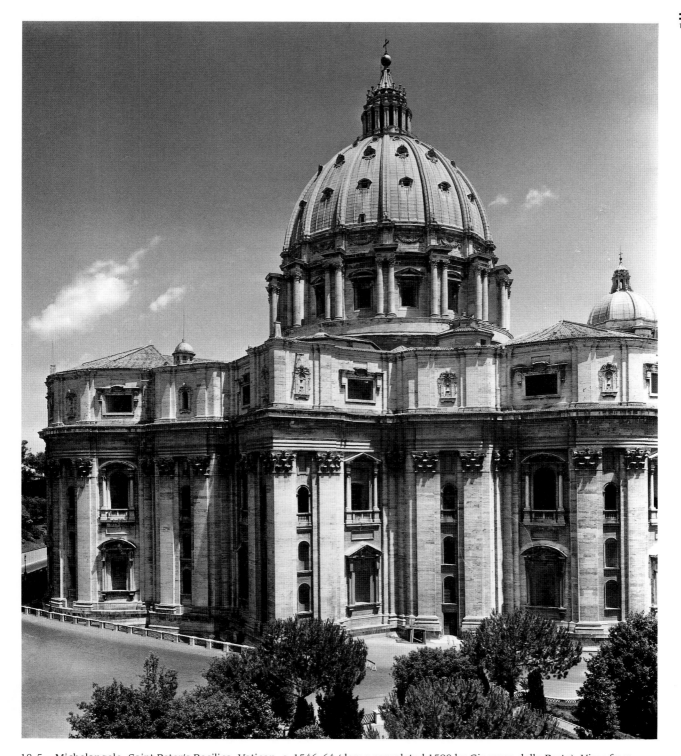

18-5. Michelangelo. Saint Peter's Basilica, Vatican. c. 1546–64 (dome completed 1590 by Giacomo della Porta). View from the southwest

a high drum with pedimented windows between paired columns, and surmounted by a tall lantern reminiscent of Bramante's Tempietto. Della Porta's major changes were raising the dome height, narrowing its segmental bands, and changing the shape of its openings.

Sixteenth-century Rome became more than a city of churches and public monuments, and Michelangelo's work as an architect was not limited to public commissions. Wealthy families, many of whom had connections with the pope or the cardinals—the "princes of the Church"—commissioned architects to design residences to enhance their prestige (see "The Renaissance Palace Facade," page 685). Pope Paul III, while still Cardinal Alessandro Farnese, for example, set Sangallo the Younger

SAINT PETER'S BASILICA

The history of Saint Peter's in Rome is an interesting case of the effects of individual and institutional conceits on the practical congregational needs of a major religious monument. The original church was built in the fourth century CE by Constantine, the first Christian Roman emperor, to mark the grave of the apostle Peter, the first bishop of Rome and therefore the first pope. Because this site was considered one of the holiest in the world, Constantine's architect had to build a monumental structure both to house Saint Peter's tomb and to accommodate the large crowds of pilgrims who came to visit it. To provide a platform for the church, a huge terrace was cut into the side of the Vatican Hill, in the midst of a cemetery across the Tiber River from the city. Here Constantine's architect erected a **basilica**, a type of Roman building used for law courts, markets, and other public gatherings. Like most basilicas, Saint Peter's had a long central chamber, or **nave**, with flanking side aisles set off by **colonnades**, and an **apse**, or large niche-like recess, set into the wall opposite the main door. To allow large numbers of visitors to approach the shrine a new feature was added: a **transept**, or long rectangular area at right angles to the nave. The rest of the church was, in effect, a covered cemetery, carpeted with the tombs of believers who wanted to be buried near the grave of the apostle. In front of the church was a walled forecourt, or **atrium**. When it was built, Constantine's basilica, as befitted an imperial commission, was one of the largest buildings in the world (interior length 368 feet; width 190 feet), and for more than a thousand years it was the most important pilgrim shrine in Europe.

In 1506, Pope Julius II (papacy 1503–1513) made the astonishing decision to demolish the Constantinian basilica, which had fallen into disrepair, and to replace it with a new building. That anyone, even a pope, had the nerve to pull down such a venerated building is an indication of the extraordinary sense of assurance of the age—and of Julius himself. To design and build the new church, the pope appointed Donato Bramante, who had only a few years earlier designed the Tempietto, a small, round, domed shrine at the site of Saint Peter's martyrdom (see fig. 18-2). Bramante envisioned the new Saint Peter's as a grander version of the Tempietto: a central-plan building, in this case a Greek cross (one with four arms of equal length) crowned by an enormous dome. This design was intended to continue the ancient Roman tradition of domed temples and round martyria, which had been revived by Filippo Brunelleschi in Florence Cathedral (see fig. 17-31). In Renaissance thinking, the central plan and dome also symbolized the perfection of God.

The deaths of both pope and architect in 1513–1514 put a temporary halt to the project. Successive plans by the painter Raphael, the architect Antonio da Sangallo, and others changed the Greek cross to a Latin cross (one with three shorter arms and one long one) in order to provide the church with a full-length nave. However, when Michelangelo was appointed architect in 1546, he returned to the Greek-cross plan. Michelangelo simplified Bramante's design to create a single, unified space covered with a hemispherical dome. The dome was finally completed some years after Michelangelo's death by the Baroque architect Giacomo della Porta, who retained Michelangelo's basic design but gave the dome a taller and slimmer profile.

By the early seventeenth century the needs of the basilica had changed. During the Counter-Reformation, the Church emphasized congregational worship, so more space was needed for people and processions. Moreover, it was felt that the new church should more closely resemble Old Saint Peter's and should extend over roughly the same area, including the ground covered by the atrium. In 1606, therefore, more than a hundred years after Julius II had initiated the project, Pope Paul V commissioned the architect Carlo Maderno to change Michelangelo's Greek-cross plan to a Latin-cross plan. Maderno extended the nave to its final length of slightly over 636 feet and added a Baroque facade (see fig. 18-10), thus completing Saint Peter's as it is today. Later in the seventeenth century, the sculptor and architect Gianlorenzo Bernini monumentalized the square in front of the basilica by surrounding it with a great colonnade (see fig. 19-6).

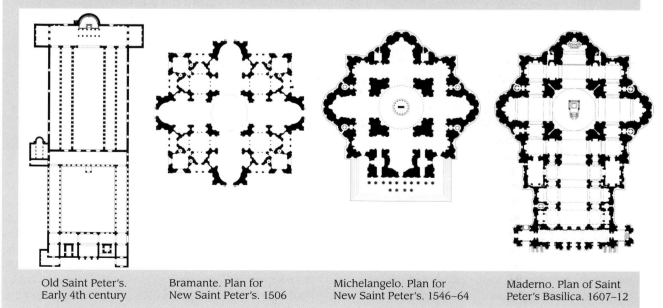

Old Saint Peter's. Early 4th century

Bramante. Plan for New Saint Peter's. 1506

Michelangelo. Plan for New Saint Peter's. 1546–64

Maderno. Plan of Saint Peter's Basilica. 1607–12

the task of building the largest, finest palace in Rome. When Sangallo died in 1546, the pope turned work on the Palazzo Farnese over to Michelangelo (fig. 18-6).

Vignola. Michelangelo designed the most prestigious buildings of sixteenth-century Rome, but he alone could not satisfy the demand for architects. One young artist who helped meet that need was Giacomo Barozzi (1507–1573), known as Vignola after his native town. He worked in Rome in the late 1530s surveying ancient Roman monuments and providing illustrations for an edition of Vitruvius, then worked from 1541 to 1543 in France with Francesco Primaticcio at the Château of Fontainebleau. After Vignola returned, he secured the patronage of the Farnese family, for whom he designed and supervised the building of the Villa Farnese at Caprarola from 1559 until his death.

At Caprarola, Vignola used the fortress built there by Antonio da Sangallo the Younger as a foundation (podium) for his five-sided building. Unlike medieval castle builders, who had taken advantage of the natural contours of the land in their defenses, Renaissance architects imposed geometric forms on the land. Recently developed artillery made the high walls of medieval castles easy targets, so Renaissance engineers built horizontal rather than vertical structures against long-distance firepower. Wide bastions at the outer points of such fortresses provided firing platforms for the defenders' cannons.

Vignola's building rises in three stories around a circular courtyard (fig. 18-7). He decorated the external faces with an arrangement of circles, ovals, and rectangles, just as he had advised in his book *The Rule of the Five Orders of Architecture*, published in 1562. The building was vaulted throughout, and the interior was lighted with evenly spaced windows. The courtyard appears to have only two stories, but a third story of small service rooms is screened by an open, balustraded terrace (fig. 18-8). The first and second stories are ringed with galleries, and like the Palazzo Medici-Riccardi in Florence (see fig. 17-35) the ground level is rusticated. On the second level, Ionic half columns form a triumphal-arch motif, and rectangular niches topped with blind arches echo the arched niches of the first-floor arcade. Behind the palace, formal gardens extended beyond the **moat** (see "The Italian Renaissance Secret Garden," page 690).

Vignola profited from the Counter-Reformation program of church building. The new emphasis on individual emotional participation and on sermons and music required churches with wide naves and unobstructed views rather than the processional interiors of medieval and earlier Renaissance churches. The Spanish noble Ignatius Loyola, founder of the Jesuit order, was determined to build its mother church in Rome, but he did not live to see it finished. Although the cornerstone was laid in 1540, the Jesuits had to raise funds for the large new Church of Il Gesù, so the building was not begun until 1568. Cardinal Alessandro Farnese (Paul III's grandson) became the patron of Il Gesù and selected as architect Vignola, whose work on the family palace and book he

18-6. Antonio da Sangallo the Younger and Michelangelo. Palazzo Farnese, Rome. 1517–50

18-7. Vignola. Villa Farnese, Caprarola. 1559–73. Courtyard view

18-8. G. D. Falda. Cutaway view of the Villa Farnese, engraving from the *Cours d'Architecture* by A. C. Vaviler, published by Nicolas Langois, Paris, 1691. Bibliothèque Nationale, Paris

knew. After Vignola died in 1573, Giacomo della Porta finished the dome and facade.

Il Gesù was admirably suited for its purpose. Vignola designed a wide, barrel-vaulted nave, shallow connected side chapels but not aisles, short transepts that did not extend beyond the line of the outer walls, and a

THE ITALIAN RENAISSANCE SECRET GARDEN

A special feature of Italian Renaissance palaces and villas was the secret garden, a hidden retreat created expressly for the enjoyment of its owners. Secret gardens became very popular in the hot Italian climate as places for intimate conversation and private contemplation, enhanced by the sound of water, the aromas and visual beauty of flowers and boxwood, and often amusing sculpture. Amid clipped hedges and fountains, the nobility could enjoy moments of privacy away from the prying eyes and idle gossip of their courtiers.

Italian architects were great designers of gardens. Alberti, for example, wrote that gardens should have walls as "Defense against Malice," but that they should also be on hillsides to catch the breezes and provide views of the countryside. With classical Renaissance taste, he recommended that plantings be in circles and squares and trees be planted in straight lines. Vignola, one of the greatest of all garden designers, combined formal gardens having fountains and geometric planting with mazes, cascades of water, woods, grottoes, and secret gardens. The grottoes were artificial caves complete with pools, cascades of water, slimy artificial moss, and statues. One of Vignola's most ingenious ideas was a fountain constructed as a stone banquet table, with water running through a trough in the center to cool bottles of wine.

18-9.   Plan and section of the Church of Il Gesù, Rome. Begun on Giacomo da Vignola's design in 1568; completed by Giacomo della Porta c. 1575–84

single huge apse and dome over the crossing (fig. 18-9). The building fit compactly into the city block—now an easier task for the architect since churches no longer had to be oriented east-west. The facade design emphasized the central portal with classical pilasters, engaged columns and pediments, and volutes scrolling out to hide the buttresses of the central vault and to link the tall central section with the lower sides (fig. 18-10). As finally built by Giacomo della Porta, the facade design, in its verticality and centrality, would have significant influence on church design well into the next century (see "Baroque and Rococo Church Facades," page 753). The

facade abandoned the early Renaissance Albertian modular grid of classical pilasters and entablatures for a two-story design of paired colossal orders that reflected and tied together the two stories of the nave elevation. Each of these stories was further subdivided by moldings, niches, and windows. The entrance of the church, with its central portal and tall window, became the focus of the composition. Pediments at every level break into the level above, leading the eye upward to the cartouches with coats of arms. Both Cardinal Farnese, the patron, and the Jesuits (whose arms entail the monogram of Christ, *IHS*) are commemorated here on the facade.

Three Great Renaissance Artists

Florence had been considered the cradle of the Italian Renaissance since Vasari called it so. The frescoes in the Brancacci Chapel (see fig. 17-49), for example, inspired young artists, who came to study Masaccio's solid, monumental figures and eloquent facial features, poses, and gestures. The young Michelangelo's sketches of the chapel frescoes clearly show the importance of Masaccio on his developing style.

At the turn of the sixteenth century, two important changes took place in Italian painting: The use of **tempera** gave way to the more flexible oil technique, and commissions from private sources increased. Many wealthy patrons in Italy and other European countries became avid collectors of paintings, as well as of small bronzes, coins, minerals and fossils from the natural world, and antiquities.

Leonardo da Vinci. Born in the Tuscan village of Vinci, Leonardo da Vinci (1452–1519) was twelve or thirteen when his family moved to Florence. He was apprenticed in the shop of the painter and sculptor Verrocchio until about 1476. After a few years on his own, Leonardo traveled to Milan in 1482 or 1483 to work for the Sforza court. In fact, Leonardo spent much of his time in Milan on military and civil engineering projects, including an urban-renewal plan for the city.

At Duke Ludovico Sforza's request, Leonardo painted one of the defining monuments of Renaissance art, *The Last Supper* (fig. 18-11), in the dining hall of the

18-11. (below) Leonardo. *The Last Supper*, wall painting in the Refectory, Monastery of Santa Maria delle Grazie, Milan, Italy. 1495–98. Tempera and oil on plaster, 15'2" x 28'10" (4.6 x 8.8 m)

Instead of painting in fresco, Leonardo devised an experimental technique for this mural. Hoping to achieve the freedom and flexibility of painting on panel, he worked directly on dry intonaco—a thin layer of smooth plaster—with an oil tempera paint, whose formula is unknown. The result was disastrous. Within a short time, the painting began to deteriorate, and by the middle of the sixteenth century its figures could be seen only with difficulty. In the seventeenth century, the monks saw no harm in cutting a doorway through the lower center of the composition. Since then the work has barely survived, despite many attempts to halt its deterioration and restore its original appearance. The painting narrowly escaped complete destruction in World War II, when the refectory was bombed to rubble around its heavily sandbagged wall. The most recent restoration began in 1979.

18-10. Vignola and della Porta. Facade of the Church of Il Gesù

THE VITRUVIAN MAN

Artists throughout history have turned to geometric shapes and mathematical proportions to seek the ideal representation of the human form. Leonardo da Vinci, and before him Vitruvius, equated the ideal man with both circle and square. Ancient Egyptian artists laid out square cards as aids. Medieval artists adapted a variety of figures, from triangles to pentagrams. The Byzantines used circles swung from the bridge of the nose to create face, head, and halo and then used 3s to determine the length of the torso (three faces) and the height of the figure (nine face lengths).

The first-century BCE Roman architect and engineer Marcus Vitruvius Pollio, in his ten-volume *De Architectura* (*On Architecture*), wrote:

"For if a man be placed flat on his back, with his hands and feet extended, and a pair of compasses centered at his navel, the fingers and toes of his two hands and feet will touch the circumference of a circle described therefrom. And just as the human body yields a circular outline, so too a square figure may be found from it. For if we measure the distance from the soles of the feet to the top of the head, and then apply that measure to the outstretched arms, the breadth will be found to be the same as the height" (Book III, Chapter 1, Section 2). Vitruvius determined that the body should be eight heads high. Leonardo added his own observations in the reversed writing he always used for his notebooks when he created his well-known diagram for the ideal male figure, called the *Vitruvian Man*.

Leonardo da Vinci. *Vitruvian Man.* c. 1490. Ink, approx. 13 1/2 x 9 5/8" (34.3 x 24.5 cm). Galleria dell'Accademia, Venice

18-12. Leonardo. *Virgin and Saint Anne with the Christ Child and the Young John the Baptist.* c. 1500–01. Charcoal heightened with white on brown paper, 54 7/8 x 39 7/8" (139 x 101 cm). The National Gallery, London

Monastery of Santa Maria delle Grazie in Milan between 1495 and 1498. The **one-point perspective** is defined by a **coffered** ceiling and four pairs of tapestries hanging on the walls. Its stagelike space recedes from a long table, placed parallel to the **picture plane**, to three windows on the back wall. Seated behind and at the two ends of this table are Jesus and his disciples. Jesus' outstretched arms form a pyramid at the center, and the disciples are grouped in threes on each side. On one level, the scene is a narrative, capturing the moment when Jesus has told his companions that one of them will betray him. They react with shock, disbelief, and horror. Judas, clutching his money bag in the shadows to the left of Jesus, has recoiled so suddenly that he has upset the salt dish, a bad omen. On the narrative level, the picture offers a study of human emotions, with the disciples modeled on real people Leonardo knew. He is said to have found his Judas, for example, in the thieves' quarter of Milan.

On another level, *The Last Supper* is presented as a symbolic evocation of Christ's coming sacrifice for the salvation of humankind and the institution of the ritual of the Mass. Breaking with traditional representations of the subject, such as the one by Andrea del Castagno (see fig. 17-52), Leonardo placed the traitor Judas in the first triad to the left of Jesus, along with the young John the Evangelist and the elderly Peter, rather than isolating him on the opposite side of the table. Judas, Peter, and John were each to play essential roles in Jesus' mission: Judas, to set in motion the events leading to Jesus' sacrifice; Peter, to lead the Church after Jesus' death; and John, the visionary, to foretell the Second Coming and the Last Judgment in the Apocalypse. By arranging the disciples and architectural elements into four groups of three, Leonardo incorporated a medieval tradition of numerical symbolism. He eliminated another symbolic element, the

18-13. Leonardo. *Mona Lisa*. c. 1503–6. Oil on panel,
30 1/4 x 21" (76.8 x 53.3 cm). Musée du Louvre, Paris

halo, substituting the natural light from a triple window framing Jesus' head.

The pervasive sense of timelessness is reinforced by the painting's careful geometry, the convergence of its perspective lines, and the stability of its pyramidal forms. The calm of Jesus' demeanor in the midst of the general commotion also contributes to this effect. These qualities of stability, calm, and a sense of timeless order, coupled with the already established Renaissance forms modeled after those of classical sculpture, characterize the art of the Renaissance at the beginning of the sixteenth century.

Leonardo left Milan in 1498 for Florence. The next year, his patron Ludovico was defeated by the French, but Leonardo cared little for politics and worked for the French as willingly as for the Milanese. He devoted much of his time to science and engineering as well as to his studies of the natural world. In his drawings of human figures he sought not only the details of anatomy but also the geometric basis of perfect proportions (see "The Vitruvian Man," page 692).

In about 1500, Leonardo produced a large drawing of the *Virgin and Saint Anne with the Christ Child and the Young John the Baptist* (fig. 18-12). This work was once thought to be a full-scale model, called a **cartoon**, for a major painting. But no known painting can be associated with it, so scholars today believe it to be a finished work—perhaps one of the drawings artists often made as gifts in the sixteenth century. Mary sits on the knee of her mother, Anne, and turns to the right to hold the Christ Child, who strains away from her to reach toward his cousin, the young John the Baptist. Leonardo created the illusion of high relief by modeling the figures with strongly contrasted light and shadow, called **chiaroscuro** (Italian for "light-dark"). Carefully placed highlights create a circular movement rather than a central focus, which retains the individual importance of each figure while also making each of them an integral part of the whole. This effect is emphasized by the complex interaction of the exquisitely tender facial expressions, particularly those of Saint Anne and the Virgin.

Between about 1503 and 1506, Leonardo painted his renowned *Mona Lisa* (fig. 18-13), which he kept with him for the rest of his life. The subject may have been twenty-four-year-old Lisa Gherardini del Giocondo, the wife of a prominent merchant in Florence. Remarkably for the time, the young woman is portrayed without any jewelry, not even a ring. The solid pyramidal form of her half-length figure is silhouetted against distant mountains, whose desolate grandeur reinforces the mysterious atmosphere of the painting. Mona Lisa's facial expression has been called enigmatic because her gentle smile is not accompanied by the warmth one would expect to see in her eyes. The contemporary fashion for plucked eyebrows and a shaved hairline to increase the height of the forehead adds to her arresting appearance. Perhaps most unsettling is the bold and slightly flirtatious way her gaze has shifted toward the right to look straight out at the viewer. The implied challenge of her direct stare, combined with her apparent serenity and inner strength, has made the *Mona Lisa* one of the best-known works in the history of art.

A fiercely debated topic in Renaissance Italy was the question of the superiority of painting or sculpture. Leonardo insisted on the supremacy of painting as the best and most complete means of creating an illusion of the natural world while Michelangelo argued for sculpture. Yet Leonardo considered color to be secondary to the depiction of sculptural volume, which he achieved through his virtuosity in highlighting and shading. He also unified his compositions by covering them with a thin, lightly tinted varnish, which resulted in a smoky overall haze called **sfumato**. Because early evening light is likely to produce a similar effect naturally, he considered dusk the finest time of day and recommended that painters set up their studios in a courtyard with black walls and a linen sheet stretched overhead to reproduce twilight.

Leonardo's fame as an artist is based on only a few known works. Unlike his humanist contemporaries, he was not particularly interested in classical literature or archeology. Instead, his great passions were mathematics and the natural world, and he compiled volumes of detailed drawings and notes on anatomy, botany, geology, meteorology, architectural design, and mechanics. Although he lived for a time in the Vatican at the invitation of Pope Leo X, there is no evidence that he produced any art during his stay. In 1517, he accepted Francis I's invitation to resettle in France as an adviser on architecture. He lived there until his death in 1519.

Raphael. In 1504, Raphael (Raffaello Santi, 1483–1520) arrived in Florence from his native Urbino. Raphael had studied in Perugia with the leading artist of that city, Perugino (see fig. 17-68). Raphael quickly became successful in Florence, especially for paintings of the Virgin and Child, such as *The Small Cowper Madonna* (named for a modern owner) of about 1505 (fig. 18-14). Already a superb painter technically, Raphael must have studied the work of Leonardo to achieve the simple grandeur of these monumental shapes, idealized faces, figure-enhancing draperies, and rich colors. The forms are modeled solidly but softly by clear, even lighting that pervades the outdoor setting. Raphael painted at least seventeen Madonnas, several portraits, and a number of other works in the three or four years he spent in Florence, but his greatest achievements were to come in the dozen years he spent in Rome.

Raphael left Florence in about 1508 for Rome, where Pope Julius II put him to work almost immediately decorating the papal apartments. In the library, Raphael painted the four branches of knowledge as conceived in the sixteenth century: Religion (the *Disputà*), Philosophy (the *School of Athens*), Poetry (*Parnassus*, home of the Muses), and Law (the *Cardinal Virtues under Justice*). The shape of the walls and vault determined the composition of the paintings—the circle of clouds and interlocking mandorla of Christ in the *Disputà* or the receding arches and vaults in the *School of Athens*. For all their serene idealism, the figures break classical conventions in their twisting **contrapposto** poses and movement into and out of the frame. In the *Disputà*, theologians and Church officials discuss the meaning of the Eucharist (fig. 18-15). Above them, the three persons of the Trinity, flanked by the apostles, fill the upper half of the painting. (This depiction of Christ with Mary and John the Baptist resembles a Byzantine grouping known as the **Deësis**.) The Host, silhouetted against the sky, rests on the altar, where Julius's name is in the embroidered interlace.

Raphael's most outstanding achievement in the papal rooms (*stanze*, singular *stanza*) was the *School of Athens* (fig. 18-16), painted about 1510–1511, which seems to summarize the ideals of the Renaissance papacy in its grand conception of harmoniously arranged forms and rational space, as well as the calm dignity of its figures. Indeed, the learned Julius II may not have actually devised the subjects painted but certainly approved them.

Viewed through a trompe l'oeil arch, Plato and Aristotle, leaders of Greek philosophy, are silhouetted against the sky, the natural world, and command our attention. At the left, Plato holds his book *Timaeus*—in which creation is seen in terms of geometry, and humanity encompasses and explains the universe—and gestures upward to the heavens as the ultimate source of his philosophy. Aristotle, with his outstretched hand palm down, seems to emphasize the importance of gathering empirical knowledge from observing the material world. Looking down from niches in the walls are Apollo, the god of sunlight, rationality, poetry, and music, and Minerva, the goddess of wisdom. Around Plato and Aristotle are mathematicians, naturalists, astronomers, geographers, and

18-14. Raphael. *The Small Cowper Madonna*. c. 1505. Oil on panel, 23³/₈ x 17³/₈" (59.5 x 44.1 cm). National Gallery of Art, Washington, D.C.
Widener Collection

18-15. (opposite, top) Raphael. *Disputà,* fresco in the Stanza della Segnatura, Vatican, Rome. 1510–11. 19 x 27' (5.79 x 8.24 m)

18-16. (opposite, bottom) Raphael. *School of Athens*, fresco in the Stanza della Segnatura, Vatican, Rome. 1510–11. 19 x 27' (5.79 x 8.24 m)

Raphael gave many of the figures in his imaginary gathering of philosophers the features of his friends and colleagues. Plato, standing immediately to the left of the central axis and pointing to the sky, was said to have been modeled after Leonardo da Vinci; Euclid, shown inscribing a slate with a compass at the lower right, was a portrait of Raphael's friend the architect Donato Bramante. Michelangelo, who was at work on the Sistine ceiling only steps away from the *stanza* where Raphael was painting his fresco, is shown as the solitary figure at the lower left center, leaning on a block of marble and sketching, in a pose reminiscent of the figures of sibyls and prophets on his great ceiling. Raphael's own features are represented on the second figure from the front group at the far right, as the face of a young man listening to a discourse by the astronomer Ptolemy.

other philosophers debating and demonstrating their theories to onlookers. The scene, flooded with a clear, even light from a single source, takes place in an immense barrel-vaulted interior possibly inspired by the new design for Saint Peter's, then being rebuilt by Bramante. The

grandeur of the building is matched by the monumental dignity of the philosophers themselves, each of whom has a distinct physical and intellectual presence. Despite the variety and energy of the poses and gestures, these striking individuals are organized into a dynamic unity by the sweeping arcs of the composition.

Raphael continued to work for Julius II's successor, Leo X (papacy 1513–1521), as director of all archeological and architectural projects in Rome. Raphael's portrait of Leo X (fig. 18-17) depicts the pope as a great collector of books, and indeed, Leo was already planning a new Medici library in Florence (see fig. 18-48). Leo's driving ambition was the advancement of the Medici family, and Raphael's painting is, in effect, a dynastic group portrait. Facing the pope at the left is his cousin Giulio, Cardinal de' Medici; behind him stands Luigi de' Rossi, another relative he had made cardinal. Dressed in splendid brocades and enthroned in a velvet chair, the pope looks up from a richly illuminated fourteenth-century manuscript he has been examining with a magnifying glass. Raphael lovingly depicted the contrasting textures and surfaces in the picture, including the visual distortion caused by the magnifying glass on the book page. In this telling detail, as in the reflection of the window and in Raphael's self-portrait, which are in the polished brass knob on the pope's chair, Raphael acknowledges his debt—despite great stylistic differences—to the fifteenth-century Flemish artist Jan van Eyck and his followers (Chapter 17).

18-17. Raphael. *Leo X with Cardinals Giulio de' Medici and Luigi de' Rossi*. c. 1518. Oil on panel, 5'5⅝"x 3'10⅞" (1.54 x 1.19 m). Galleria degli Uffizi, Florence

18-18. Shop of Pieter van Aelst, Brussels, after Raphael's cartoon. *Miraculous Draft of Fishes*, from the Acts of the Apostles series; lower border, two incidents from the life of Giovanni de' Medici, later Pope Leo X. Woven 1517, installed 1519 in the Sistine Chapel. Wool and silk with silver-gilt threads, 15'11⅚" x 14'5⅚" (4.90 x 4.41 m). Musei Vaticani, Pinacoteca, Rome

Raphael's Acts of the Apostles cartoons were used as the models for several sets of tapestries woven in the van Aelst shop, including one for Francis I of France. In 1630, the Flemish painter Peter Paul Rubens discovered seven of the ten original cartoons in the home of a van Aelst heir and convinced his patron, Charles I of England, to buy them. Still part of the royal collection today, they are exhibited at the Victoria and Albert Museum in London. After being dispersed following the Sack of Rome in 1527, later returned, and dispersed again during the Napoleonic wars, the original Sistine tapestries were purchased by a private collector in 1808 and returned to the Vatican as a gift that year. They are now displayed in the Raphael room of the Vatican Painting Gallery.

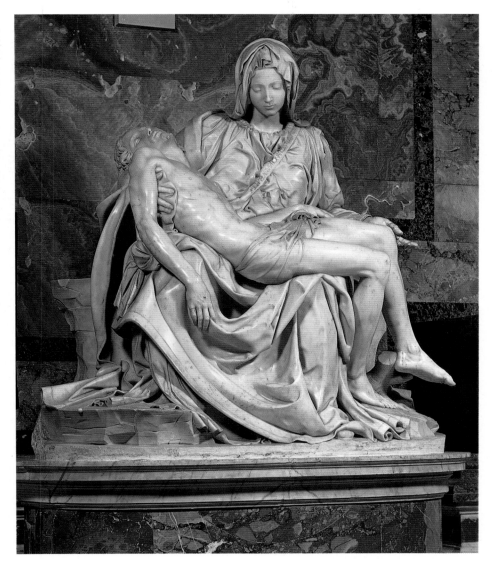

18-19. Michelangelo. *Pietà*, from Old Saint Peter's. c. 1500. Marble, height 5'8¹/₂" (1.74 m). Saint Peter's, Vatican, Rome

At about the same time, Raphael painted cartoons of themes from the Acts of the Apostles for tapestries to cover the **dado** (lower wall) below the fifteenth-century wall paintings of the Sistine Chapel. The first tapestry in the series was the *Miraculous Draft of Fishes,* combined with Christ's calling of his apostles (fig. 18-18). Tapestries, which were extremely expensive, were produced in workshops of France and Flanders for Italian patrons from charcoal cartoons that the artists had painted over with glue-based hues for the weavers to match. Today, the Sistine Chapel dado is painted with trompe l'oeil draperies (see fig. 18-21), and the papal tapestries are used only occasionally.

Raphael died after a brief illness in 1520, at the age of thirty-seven. After a state funeral, he was buried in the ancient Roman Pantheon, originally a classical temple to the gods of Rome, then a Christian church dedicated to the Virgin Mary. His unfinished painting of the *Transfiguration of Christ* was placed over his tomb.

Michelangelo. Michelangelo Buonarroti (1475–1564) was born in the Tuscan town of Caprese and grew up in

Florence. At thirteen, he was apprenticed to the painter Domenico del Ghirlandaio, in whose workshop he learned the rudiments of fresco painting and studied drawings of classical monuments. After approximately a year, Michelangelo joined the household of Lorenzo the Magnificent, where he came into contact with the Neoplatonic philosophers and studied sculpture with Bertoldo di Giovanni, a pupil of Donatello. Bertoldo's sculptures were primarily in bronze, and Michelangelo later claimed that he had taught himself to carve marble by studying the Medici collection of classical statues.

After Lorenzo died in 1492, Michelangelo traveled to Venice and Bologna, then returned to Florence, where he fell under the spell of the charismatic preacher Fra Girolamo Savonarola. The preacher's execution for heresy in 1498 had a traumatic effect on Michelangelo, who said in his old age that he could still hear the sound of Savonarola's voice.

Michelangelo's major early work was a *Pietà* of about 1500, commissioned by a French cardinal and installed as a tomb monument in Old Saint Peter's in the Vatican (fig. 18-19). **Pietàs**—works in which the Virgin is

1500 ■■■■■■
1500   1600

18-20. Michelangelo. *David*. 1501–4. Marble, height 13'5"
(4.09 m). Galleria dell'Accademia, Florence

Michelangelo's most famous sculpture was cut from
an 18-foot-tall marble block already partially carved
by another sculptor during the 1460s. After studying
the block carefully and deciding that it could be
salvaged, Michelangelo made a small model in wax,
then sketched the contours of the figure as they
would appear from the front on one face of the marble. Then, according to his friend and biographer
Vasari, he chiseled in from the drawn-on surface, as
if making a figure in very high relief. The completed
statue took four days to move on tree-trunk rollers
down the narrow streets of Florence from Michelangelo's workshop to its location outside the Palazzo
Vecchio. In 1837, the statue was replaced by a copy
to scale and moved into the museum of the Florence
Academy.

supporting and mourning the dead Jesus—had long been
popular in northern Europe but were rare in Italian art at
the time. Michelangelo traveled to the marble quarries at
Carrara in central Italy to select the block from which to
make this large work, a practice he was to follow for
nearly all of his sculpture. His choice of the stone was
important, for Michelangelo envisioned the statue as
already existing within the marble and needing only to be

"set free" from it. He later wrote in his Sonnet 15 (1536–
1547): "The greatest artist has no conception which a single block of marble does not potentially contain within
its mass, but only a hand obedient to the mind can penetrate to this image."

Michelangelo's *Pietà* is a very young Virgin of heroic
stature holding the lifeless, smaller body of her grown
son. The seeming inconsistencies of age and size are
countered, however, by the sweetness of expression, the
finely finished surfaces, and the softly modeled forms.
Michelangelo's compelling vision of beauty is meant to be
seen up close from directly in front of the statue and on
the statue's own level, so that the viewer can look into
Jesus' face. The twenty-five-year-old artist is said to have
sneaked into the church at night to sign the finished
sculpture, to answer the many questions about its creator.

In 1501, Michelangelo accepted a commission for a
statue of the biblical David (fig. 18-20) to be placed high
atop a buttress of the Florence Cathedral. When it was
finished in 1504, the *David* was so admired that the
Florentine city council placed it in the square next to the
seat of Florence's government. Although Michelangelo's
David embodies the athletic ideal of antiquity in its mus-
cularity, the emotional power of its facial expression and
concentrated gaze is entirely new. Unlike Donatello's
bronze *David* (see fig. 17-41), this is not a triumphant
hero with the head of the giant Goliath under his feet.
Instead, slingshot over his shoulder and a rock in his right
hand, Michelangelo's David frowns and stares into
space, seemingly preparing himself psychologically for
the danger ahead. Here the male nude implies, as it had
in classical antiquity, heroic or even divine qualities. No
match for his opponent in experience, weaponry, or
physical strength, David represents the power of right
over might—a perfect emblematic figure for the Florentines, who twice drove out the powerful Medici and instituted short-lived republics in the early sixteenth century.

Julius II saw Michelangelo as his equal in personal
strength and dedication and thus as an ideal collaborator in the artistic aggrandizement of the papacy. Despite
Michelangelo's contractual commitment to the Florence
Cathedral for statues of the apostles, in 1505 Julius
arranged for him to come to Rome. The sculptor's first
undertaking was the pope's tomb, but this commission
was set aside in 1506 when Julius ordered Michelangelo
to redecorate the ceiling of the Sistine Chapel (fig. 18-21).

Julius's initial mandate for the ceiling was trompe
l'oeil "stucco" coffers to replace the original blue, star-
spangled ceiling. Later he wanted the Twelve Apostles
seated on thrones to be painted in the triangular **spandrels**, the walls between the **lunettes** framing the windows. When Michelangelo objected to the limitations of
Julius's plan, the pope told him to paint whatever he liked
on the ceiling. This he presumably did, although a commission of this importance probably involved supervision from the pope and an adviser in theology. Whatever
their source, the frescoes are a pictorial declaration of
papal authority, derived from the Bible.

First, the artist painted an illusionistic, marblelike
architectural framework on the vault of the chapel

1500   1600

18-21. Interior, Sistine Chapel, Vatican, Rome. Built 1475–81

Named after its builder, Pope Sixtus (Sisto) IV, the chapel is slightly over 130 feet long and about 43½ feet wide, approximately the same measurements recorded in the Old Testament for the Temple of Solomon. The floor mosaic was recut from the colored stones used in the floor of an earlier papal chapel. The plain walls were painted in fresco between 1481 and 1483 with scenes from the life of Moses and the life of Christ by Perugino, Botticelli, Ghirlandaio, and others. Below these are trompe l'oeil painted draperies, where Raphael's tapestries illustrating the Acts of the Apostles once hung (see fig. 18-18). Michelangelo's famous ceiling frescoes begin with the lunette scenes above the windows (see fig. 18-22). On the end above the altar is his *Last Judgment* (see fig. 18-25).

RENAISSANCE ART IN SIXTEENTH-CENTURY EUROPE   *699*

18-22. Michelangelo. Sistine ceiling. Top to bottom: *Expulsion* (center); *Creation of Eve* with *Ezekiel* (left) and *Cumaean Sibyl* (right); *Creation of Adam*; *God Gathering the Waters* with *Persian Sibyl* (left) and *Daniel* (right); and *God Creating the Sun, Moon, and Planets*. Frescoes on the ceiling, Sistine Chapel. 1508–12

(fig. 18-22). Running completely around the ceiling is a painted **cornice**, with prominent projections supported by short pilasters sculpted with the figures of nude baby boys, called **putti**. Set among these projections are figures of a number of Old Testament prophets and Classical sibyls (female prophets) who were believed to have foretold Jesus Christ's birth. Seated in various poses on the cornice projections are heroic figures of nude young men, called *ignudi* (singular, *ignudo*), holding sashes attached to large gold medallions. Rising behind the *ignudi*, shallow bands of stone span the center of the ceiling and divide it into compartments depicting scenes of the Creation, the Fall, and the Flood from Genesis. The narrative sequence begins over the altar and ends near the chapel entrance. God's earliest acts of creation are therefore closest to the altar, the Creation of Eve at the center of the ceiling, followed by the imperfect actions of humanity: the Temptation, the Fall, the Expulsion from Paradise, and God's eventual destruction of all people except Noah and his family by the Flood. The sides of the triangular spandrels, which contain paintings of the ancestors of Jesus, support mirror-image nudes in reclining and seated poses. At the apex of each spandrel-triangle is a *bucranium*, or ox skull, a **motif** (a repeated figure in a design) that appears in ancient Roman paintings and reliefs.

According to discoveries during the most recent restoration (see "The Sistine Ceiling Restoration," page 701), Michelangelo worked on the ceiling in two main stages, beginning in the late summer or fall of 1508 and moving from the chapel's entrance toward the altar, in reverse of the narrative sequence. The first half of the ceiling up to the Creation of Eve was unveiled in August 1511, and the second half in October 1512. Perhaps the most familiar scene is the Creation of Adam. Here Michelangelo depicts the moment when God charges the languorous Adam with the spark of life. As if to echo the biblical text, Adam's heroic body and pose mirror those of God, in whose image he has been created. Directly below Adam is an *ignudo* grasping a bundle of oak leaves and giant acorns, which refer to Pope Julius's family name (della Rovere, or "of the oak"), and possibly also to a passage in the Old Testament prophecy of Isaiah (61:3), "They will be called oaks of justice, planted by the Lord to show his glory."

Michelangelo's first papal sculpture commission, the tomb of Julius II, was to plague him and his patrons for forty years. In 1505, he presented his first designs to the pope for a large freestanding rectangular structure with the pope's sarcophagus and more than forty statues and reliefs in marble and bronze. But after a year of preliminary work on the tomb, Michelangelo angrily left for Florence the day

THE SISTINE CEILING RESTORATION

The cleaning of the frescoes on the walls of the Sistine Chapel, done in the 1960s and 1970s, was so successful that in 1980 a single lunette from Michelangelo's ceiling decoration was cleaned as a test. Underneath layers of soot and dust was found color so brilliant and so different from the long-accepted dusky appearance of the ceiling that conservators summoned their courage and proposed a major restoration. In early 1981, a plan was set to begin cleaning the entire ceiling. The work was completed in the winter of 1989, and the *Last Judgment* over the altar was completed in the spring of 1994.

Although the restorers proceeded with great caution and frequently consulted with other experts in the field, the cleaning created a serious controversy. The greatest fear was that the work was moving ahead too rapidly for absolute safety. There was also great concern that the ceiling's final appearance might not resemble its original state. Some scholars, convinced that Michelangelo had re-

Michelangelo. *Libyan Sibyl*, Sistine Chapel, Vatican, Rome. 1511–12. On the left, the fresco before cleaning; on the right, as it appears today

worked the surface of the fresco after it had dried to soften and tone down the colors, feared that cleaning would remove these finishing touches. Nevertheless, the breathtaking colors of the Sistine ceiling fresco that the cleaning revealed forced scholars to almost completely revise their under-

standing of the art of Michelangelo and the development of sixteenth-century Italian painting. We will never know for certain if some subtleties were lost in the cleaning, and only time will tell if this restoration has prolonged the life of Michelangelo's great work.

---

before the laying of the cornerstone for the new Saint Peter's; he later explained that Julius had halted the tomb project to divert the money to building the church. After Julius died in 1513, his heirs offered the sculptor a new contract and a larger payment for a more elaborate tomb. At this time, between 1513 and 1515, Michelangelo created *Moses* (fig. 18-23), the only sculpture from the original

18-23. Michelangelo. *Moses*, Tomb of Julius II. c. 1513–15. Marble, height 7'8½" (2.35 m). Church of San Pietro in Vincoli, Rome

Princes of the Church, like their secular counterparts, often arranged for their burial and funerary monuments themselves, knowing that their heirs might have other priorities. Although Pope Julius II's immediate survivors ordered an even larger and more costly tomb than Julius himself had commissioned from Michelangelo, during the three decades following his death the projected size and opulence of the monument steadily diminished. In the end, the pope was buried not in Saint Peter's in the Vatican, as he had wished, but elsewhere, and a few salvaged statues and reliefs were mounted with some new pieces by Michelangelo's assistants in a commemorative monument against a wall of the della Rovere family church. In this final setting, the pope's small reclining image was greatly overshadowed by the only statue there made for the original tomb, Michelangelo's superb figure of *Moses*.

18-24. Michelangelo. Tomb of Giuliano de' Medici. 1519–34. Marble, height 22'9" x 15'3" (6.94 x 4.65 m). Medici Chapel (New Sacristy), Church of San Lorenzo, Florence

design to be incorporated into the final, much-reduced monument to Julius II. No longer an actual tomb—Julius was buried elsewhere—the monument was installed in 1545, after decades of wrangling, in the Church of San Pietro in Vincoli, Rome. In the original design, the *Moses* would have been one of four seated figures subordinate to several groups, including the pope supported by angels atop a sarcophagus, a Madonna and Child flanked by saints. In the final configuration, however, the eloquent figure of Moses becomes the focus of the monument and an allegorical representative of the long-dead pope.

Upon the election of Giovanni de' Medici as Pope Leo X, Michelangelo was made chief architect for a facade for the Medici family Church of San Lorenzo in Florence. But in 1519, after about three years of preliminary construction, Leo and his cousin Cardinal Giulio de' Medici (later Pope Clement VII) ordered Michelangelo to work instead on a new Medici Chapel inside the church for the tombs of their fathers, Lorenzo the Magnificent and Giuliano, and two younger dukes, also named Lorenzo and Giuliano. The fathers' tombs were never built, but the unfinished tombs for the younger relatives were placed on opposite side walls of this so-called New

Sacristy, an innovative variation on the Old Sacristy by Filippo Brunelleschi at the other end of the transept (see fig. 17-33). Construction went forward slowly at San Lorenzo, where a library was also being built. Leo's death in 1521 and ongoing political struggles in Florence interrupted the work. In 1534, detested by the new duke of Florence and fearing for his life, Michelangelo returned to Rome, where he lived for the rest of his life. By 1559, others completed the New Sacristy and the library stair (see fig. 18-48).

Each of the two monuments in the New Sacristy consists of an idealized portrait of the deceased seated in a niche above a pseudoclassical sarcophagus and turned to face the family's ancestral tomb (fig. 18-24). Balanced precariously on the sarcophagus tops are male and female figures representing the Times of Day. Their positions would not seem so unsettling had reclining figures of river gods been installed below them, as originally planned, to complete the encircling effect. The Medici are shown in armor, which may designate them as "Christian soldiers." Here, Giuliano, Duke of Nemours, represents the Active Life. His sarcophagus figures are allegories of Night and Day, according to Michelangelo's notes: "Day

18-25. Michelangelo. *Last Judgment*, detail of fresco in the Sistine Chapel. 1536–41, cleaning finished in 1994

and Night speak, and say: We with our swift course have brought the Duke Giuliano to death." Night is accompanied by her symbols: a star and crescent moon on her tiara; poppies, which induce sleep; and an owl under the arch of her leg. The huge mask at her back may allude to Death, since Sleep and Death were said to be the children of Night. According to Vasari, Michelangelo left a small piece of marble for the figure of a mouse, which, like Time, nibbles away at earthly things, but it was never carved. Also never carved were the allegorical figures for the empty niches that flank the tombs. The walls of the sacristy are articulated with Brunelleschian *pietra serena* pilasters and architraves in the Corinthian order.

The figures of the dukes are finely finished, but the Times of Day are notable for their contrasting patches of rough and polished marble, a characteristic of the artist's mature work that some Michelangelo specialists call his *nonfinito* ("unfinished") quality, suggesting that he had begun to view his artistic creations as symbols of human imperfection (also see fig. 18-26). Indeed, Michelangelo's poetry often expressed his belief that humans could achieve perfection only in death.

A quarter of a century after finishing the ceiling, Michelangelo again went to work in the Sistine Chapel. He had complained of feeling old for years, but he accepted the important and demanding task of painting the *Last Judgment* on the 48-by-44-foot end wall above the chapel altar (fig. 18-25). Abandoning the clearly organized medieval conceptions of the Last Judgment, in which the Saved are neatly separated from the Lost, Michelangelo painted a writhing swarm of rising and falling humanity (see fig. 18-21). At the left, the dead are dragged from their

18-26. Michelangelo. *Pietà* (known as the *Rondanini Pietà*). 1555–64. Marble, height 5'3³⁄₈" (1.61 m). Castello Sforzesco, Milan

Shortly before his death in 1564, Michelangelo resumed work on this sculpture group, which he had begun some years earlier. He cut down the massive figure of Jesus, merging the figure's now elongated form with that of the Virgin, who seems to carry her dead son upward toward heaven.

graves and pushed up into a vortex of figures around Christ, who wields his arm like a sword of justice. The shrinking Virgin represents a change from Gothic tradition, where she sat enthroned beside, and equal in size to, her Son. Despite the efforts of several saints to save them at the last minute, the rejected souls are plunged toward hell on the right, leaving the Elect and still-unjudged in a dazed, almost uncomprehending state. To the right of Christ's feet is Saint Bartholomew, who in legend was martyred by being skinned alive, holding his flayed skin, the face of which is painted with Michelangelo's own distorted features. On the lowest level of the mural is the gaping, fiery Hellmouth, toward which Charon propels his craft on the River Styx, which encircles the underworld.

From the beginning, the painting was criticized for its nudity, and bits of drapery were added.

The *Last Judgment,* painted between 1536 and 1541, was the first major commission of Pope Paul III (Alessandro Farnese), who in grappling with the effects of the Protestant Reformation would also be seeking judgment when he convened the Council of Trent in 1545. In the spirit of its original conception, the painting was interpreted as a grim and constant reminder to the celebrants of the Mass—the pope and his cardinals—that ultimately they will be judged for their deeds. However, the brilliant colors revealed by recent cleaning seem to contradict the grim message.

Michelangelo was an intense man who alternated between periods of depression and frenzied activity. He was difficult and often arrogant, yet he was devoted to his friends and helpful to young artists. He believed that his art was divinely inspired; later in life, he became deeply absorbed in religion and dedicated himself chiefly to religious works.

Michelangelo's last days before his death in 1564 were occupied by an unfinished composition now known, from the name of a modern owner, as the *Rondanini Pietà* (fig. 18-26). The *Rondanini Pietà* is the final artistic expression of a lonely, disillusioned, and physically debilitated man who struggled to end his life as he had lived it—working with his mind and his hands. In his youth, the stone had released the *Pietà* in Saint Peter's as a perfect, exquisitely finished work (see fig. 18-19), but this block resisted his best efforts to shape it. The ongoing struggle between artist and medium is nowhere more apparent than in this moving example of Michelangelo's *nonfinito* creations. In his late work, Michelangelo subverted Renaissance ideals and denied his own youthful idealism—and inspired new forms mirroring the tensions in Europe during the second half of the sixteenth century.

Painting and Sculpture in Northern Italy

Correggio in Parma. In his brief but prolific career, Correggio (Antonio Allegri, c. 1489/99–1534) produced most of his work for patrons in Parma and Mantua in north-central Italy. Correggio's great work, *Assumption of the Virgin* (fig. 18-27), a fresco painted about 1520–1524 in the dome of the Cathedral of Parma, distantly recalls the ceiling by Andrea Mantegna in the Gonzaga ducal palace (see fig. 17-66). Leonardo clearly influenced Correggio's use of softly modeled forms, spotlighting effects of illumination, and a slightly hazy overall appearance. Correggio also assimilated elements from Raphael's work in developing his highly personal style, which inspired artists for the next three centuries. In the *Assumption,* the architecture of the dome seems to dissolve, and the viewer is drawn up into the swirling vortex of heavenly beings accompanying the Virgin. The sensuous flesh and clinging draperies of individual figures are drawn with great attention. This, combined with their warm colors, tends to obscure the subject, which is the miraculous transporting of the Virgin directly to

18-27. Correggio. *Assumption of the Virgin*, fresco in main dome interior, Parma Cathedral, Parma, Italy. c. 1520–24. Diameter of base of dome 35'10" x 37'11" (10.93 x 11.56 m)

heaven at the moment of her death. The viewer's strongest impression is of a powerful, spiraling upward motion, as if the artist hoped to convey the spiritual essence of the Assumption. Illusionistic painting directly derived from this work would become a hallmark of ceiling decoration in the following century.

Leone Leoni in Milan. Born near Lake Como in northern Italy, Leone Leoni (1509–1590) traveled widely,

working on commissions in Venice, Padua, Brussels, and Madrid, where his son Pompeo, also a sculptor, was born. By 1542, Leone had settled in Milan, where he produced major works in bronze, many for patrons in other cities or abroad. He worked in Milan for a brother of Pope Pius IV and later became a favorite of Emperor Charles V and his son Philip II of Spain. Elevated to the nobility, the artist became rich from his sculpture, architectural designs, and goldsmith work.

18-28. Leone Leoni. *Charles V Triumphing over Fury*.
1549–55. Bronze, height to top of head 5'8" (1.74 m).
Museo del Prado, Madrid

One of Leone's most dramatic works is the lifesize bronze *Charles V Triumphing over Fury* (fig. 18-28), cast for the emperor between 1549 and 1555. Here Leone created a Herculean image wearing armor that was cast separately and can be removed to reveal a heroic nude. Although the face is recognizably a portrait of the emperor, the features have been idealized to convey an impression of regal strength, experience, and wisdom.

Commissions from the Habsburgs were so numerous that Leone and his son Pompeo could do little more than design and supervise their execution. Pompeo also acted as his father's agent at various courts and ultimately moved permanently to Spain (see page 000).

Painting in Venice

In the sixteenth century, Venice remained an important economic and political center, and its prosperous governors and merchants patronized local artists enthusiastically. Venetian painters, beginning with the Bellini family in the late fifteenth century (see figs. 17-69, 17-70, 17-71), developed a distinctive style and technique in which they used the oil medium for painting on both wood panel and canvas (see "Painting on Canvas," below). Oil paint was particularly suited to the brilliant color and lighting effects of Venice's four major sixteenth-century painters: Giorgione, Titian, Veronese, and Tintoretto.

Giorgione and Titian. The career of Giorgione (Giorgio da Castelfranco, c. 1477–1510) was brief, and most scholars accept only four or five paintings as entirely by his hand. Nevertheless, his importance to Venetian painting is critical. His early life and training are undocumented, but his work suggests that he studied with Giovanni Bellini. There is also a hint of inspiration from Leonardo da Vinci's subtle lighting system and mysterious, intensely observed landscapes.

TECHNIQUE
PAINTING ON CANVAS

Although few good examples survive, canvas paintings—chiefly in **tempera** on linen—were common in the late fifteenth century. From contracts and payment accounts, most of these paintings appear to have been decorations for private homes. Many may have served as inexpensive substitutes for tapestries, but records show that small, framed pictures of various subjects were also common. There are also instances of copies made on canvas of religious works for the patrons who had commissioned the originals for a church. Canvas paintings were clearly considered less important and less expensive than frescoes until the Venetians began to exploit the technique of painting with oils on canvas in the late fifteenth century.

A recent scientific study of Titian's paintings reveals that he ground his pigments much finer than earlier panel painters had. The complicated process by which he produced many of his works began with a charcoal drawing on the prime coat of lead white that was used to seal the pores and smooth the surface of the rather coarse Venetian canvas. The artist then built up the forms with fine glazes of color laid on with brushes, sometimes in as many as ten to fifteen layers. Because patrons customarily paid for paintings according to the painting's size and how richly the paint was applied, thinly painted works may reflect the patron's finances rather than the artist's choice of technique.

The use of large canvas paintings instead of frescoes for wall decoration developed in Venice, then spread elsewhere. Painting on canvas allowed greater flexibility to artists, who could complete the work in their studios and then carry the rolls of canvas to the location where they were to be installed. Because oils dried slowly, errors could be corrected and changes made easily during the work. Thus, the flexibility of the canvas support, coupled with the radiance and depth of oil-suspended color pigments, eventually made oil painting on canvas the almost universally preferred medium.

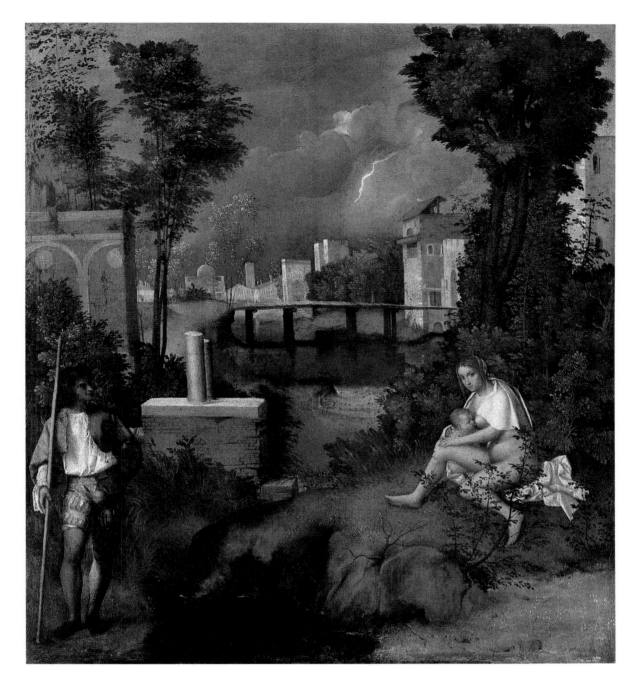

18-29. Giorgione. *The Tempest*. c. 1510. Oil on canvas, 31 x 28³/₄" (79.4 x 73 cm). Galleria dell'Accademia, Venice

Recently, scholars have made many attempts to explain this enigmatic picture—a number of which are so well reasoned that any of them might be a solution to the mystery. However, the subject of the painting, which has so preoccupied twentieth-century art historians, seems not to have particularly intrigued sixteenth-century observers, one of whom described the painting matter-of-factly in 1530 as a small landscape in a storm with a Gypsy woman and a soldier.

Giorgione's most famous work, called today *The Tempest* (fig. 18-29), was painted shortly before his death from the plague in 1510. Simply trying to understand what is happening in the picture piques our interest. At the right, a woman is seated on the ground, nude except for the end of a long white cloth thrown over her shoulders. Her nudity seems maternal rather than erotic as she turns to nurse the baby at her side. Across the dark, rock-edged spring stands a man wearing the costume of a German mercenary soldier. His head is turned toward the woman, but he appears to have paused for a moment before continuing to turn toward the viewer. The spring between them feeds a lake surrounded by substantial houses, and in the far distance a bolt of lightning splits the darkening sky. Indeed, the artist's attention seems focused on the landscape and the unruly elements of nature rather than on the figures.

X rays of the painting show that Giorgione altered his composition while he was still at work on it—the woman on the right was originally balanced by another

18-30. Titian. *Pesaro Madonna*. 1519–26. Oil on canvas, 15'11" x 8'10" (4.85 x 2.69 m).
Pesaro Chapel, Santa Maria Gloriosa dei Frari, Venice

woman on the left—which seems to rule out a specific story as its subject matter. Some scholars have theorized that Giorgione approached his work as many modern-day artists do, by developing subjects in response to personal, private impulses, which he then expressed through his paintings.

Although *The Tempest* may have been painted purely for personal reasons, most of Giorgione's known works were of traditional subjects, produced on commission for clients: portraits, altarpieces, and frescoes to decorate the exterior walls of Venetian buildings. When given the commission in 1507 to paint the exterior of the Fondaco dei Tedeschi, the warehouse and offices of German merchants in Venice, Giorgione hired Titian (Tiziano

Vecelli, c.1478?–1576) as an assistant; from then, the two artists' careers were closely bound together. Everything about Titian's life up to that time is obscure, including his age, which was given at his death in 1576 as 103 (now considered erroneous). He supposedly began an apprenticeship as a mosaicist, then studied painting under Gentile and Giovanni Bellini. His first documented work, the Fondaco frescoes, completed in 1508, has been destroyed except for a fragment of a Giorgionesque female nude preserved in the Accademia museum of Venice. Whatever Titian's work was like before that time, he had completely absorbed Giorgione's style by the time Giorgione died two years later and Titian completed his work. Titian was made official painter to the Republic of Venice when Giovanni Bellini died in 1516.

In 1519, Jacopo Pesaro, commander of a papal fleet that defeated a Turkish force, commissioned Titian to commemorate the victory in a votive altarpiece for his family's church, Santa Maria Gloriosa dei Frari, in Venice. Titian worked on the painting for seven years and changed the concept three times before he finally came up with a revolutionary composition: He created an asymmetrical setting of huge columns on high bases soaring above putti and clouds and right out of the frame (fig. 18-30). After he established this frame, he placed the Virgin and Child on a high throne at one side and arranged saints and the Pesaro family at the side and below on a diagonal axis. The red brocade of Francisco Pesaro's garment and the rich color of the flag set up a second diagonal that crosses the first at Saint Peter. Saint Maurice holds banners with the arms of the pope and the Pesaros, and a cowering Turkish captive reminds the viewer of the Christian victory. Light floods in from above, illuminating not only the faces but also the great columns. Titian was famous for his mastery of light and color even in his own day, but this altarpiece demonstrates that he could also draw and model as solidly as any Florentine. The composition, still perfectly balanced but built on crossing diagonals, presages the art of the seventeenth century.

In 1529 Titian, who was well known outside Venice, began a long professional relationship with Emperor Charles V, who vowed to let no one else paint his portrait. Shortly after being elevated by Charles to noble rank in 1533, Titian was commissioned to paint the portrait of Isabella d'Este (see "Women Patrons of the Arts," below). Isabella was past sixty when Titian portrayed her in 1534–1536 (fig. 18-31), but she asked to appear as she had in her twenties. A true magician of portraiture, Titian was able to satisfy her wish by referring to an early portrait by another artist while also conveying the mature Isabella's strength, self-confidence, and energy.

No photograph can convey the vibrancy of Titian's paint surfaces, which he built up in layers of individual brushstrokes in pure colors, chiefly red, white, yellow, and black. According to a contemporary, Titian could

18-31. Titian. *Isabella d'Este*. 1534–36. Oil on canvas, 40⅛ x 25³/₁₆" (102 x 64.1 cm). Kunsthistorisches Museum, Vienna

make "an excellent figure appear in four brushstrokes." His technique was admirably suited to the creation of female nudes, whose flesh seems to glow with an incandescent light. Paintings of nude reclining women became especially popular in the sophisticated court

WOMEN PATRONS OF THE ARTS In the sixteenth century, many wealthy women, from both the aristocracy and the merchant class, were enthusiastic patrons of the arts. Two English queens, the Tudor half sisters Mary I and Elizabeth I, glorified their combined reigns of half a century with the aid of court artists, as did most sovereigns of the period. The Habsburg princesses Margaret of Austria and Mary of Hungary presided over brilliant humanist courts when they were regents of the Netherlands. But perhaps the Renaissance's greatest woman patron of the arts was the marchesa of Mantua, Isabella d'Este (1474–1539), who gathered painters, musicians, composers, writers, and literary scholars around her. Married to Francesco II Gonzaga at age fifteen, she had great beauty, great wealth, and a brilliant mind that made her a successful diplomat and administrator. A true Renaissance woman, her motto was the epitome of rational thinking—"Neither Hope nor Fear." An avid reader and collector of manuscripts and books, while still in her twenties she sponsored an edition of Virgil. She also collected ancient art and objects, as well as works by contemporary Italian artists such as Botticelli, Mantegna, Perugino, Correggio, and Titian. Her *grotto*, or cave, as she called her study in the Mantuan palace, was a veritable museum for her collections. The walls above the storage and display cabinets were painted in fresco by Mantegna, and the carved-wood ceiling was covered with mottoes and visual references to Isabella's impressive literary interests.

18-32. Titian. *Venus of Urbino.* c. 1538. Oil on canvas, 3'11" x 5'5" (1.19 x 1.65 m). Galleria degli Uffizi, Florence

circles, where the male patrons could enjoy and appreciate the "Venuses" under the cloak of respectable classical mythology. Typical of such paintings is the Venus Titian painted in about 1538 for the duke of Urbino (fig. 18-32). The sensuous quality of this work suggests that Titian was as inspired by flesh-and-blood beauty as by any source from mythology or the history of art. Here, a beautiful Venetian courtesan—whose gestures seem deliberately provocative—stretches languidly on her couch in a spacious palace, white sheets and pillows setting off her glowing flesh and golden hair. A spaniel, symbolic of fidelity, sleeping at her feet and maids assembling her clothing in the background lend a comfortable domestic air. The *Venus of Urbino* has inspired artists as distant in time as Manet (see Chapter 27).

Veronese. The paintings of Paolo Caliari (1528–1588), called Veronese after his hometown of Verona, are nearly synonymous today with the popular image of Venice as a splendid city of pleasure and pageantry sustained by a nominally republican government and great mercan-

tile wealth. His elaborate architectural settings and costumes, still lifes, anecdotal vignettes, and other everyday details unconnected with the main subject proved immensely appealing to Venetian patrons.

Veronese's most famous work is the religious painting of 1573 now called *Feast in the House of Levi* (see fig. 18-1), painted for the Dominican Monastery of Santi Giovanni e Paolo, Venice. At first glance, the true subject of this painting seems to be architecture, with the users of the space secondary to it. The house is represented by an enormous loggia entered through colossal triumphal arches. Beyond the loggia an imaginary city of white marble gleams in the distance. The size of the canvas allowed Veronese to make his figures realistically proportional to the architectural setting without losing their substance. He also maintained visual balance by giving the figures exaggerated, theatrical gestures and poses.

Tintoretto. Another great painter of the Venetian Renaissance, Jacopo Robusti (1518–1594), called Tintoretto ("Little Dyer") because his father was a dyer,

18-33. Tintoretto. *Last Supper*. 1592–94. Oil on canvas, 12' x 18'8" (3.7 x 5.7 m). Church of San Giorgio Maggiore, Venice

Tintoretto, who ran a large workshop, often developed a composition by creating a small-scale model like a miniature stage set, which he populated with wax figures. He then adjusted the positions of the figures and the lighting until he was satisfied with the entire scene. Using a grid of horizontal and vertical threads placed in front of this model, he could easily sketch the composition onto squared paper for his assistants to recopy onto a large canvas. His assistants also primed the canvas, blocking in the areas of dark and light, before the artist himself, now free to concentrate on the most difficult passages, finished the painting. This efficient working method allowed Tintoretto's shop to produce a large number of paintings in all sizes.

worked in a style that developed from, and exaggerated, the techniques of Titian, in whose shop he reportedly apprenticed. Tintoretto's goal, declared on a sign in his studio, was to combine his master's color with the drawing of Michelangelo.

Like Veronese, Tintoretto often received commissions to decorate huge interior spaces, such as the *Last Supper* (fig. 18-33) for the choir of the Church of San Giorgio Maggiore, a building designed by Palladio (see fig. 18-36). The comparison with Leonardo da Vinci's painting almost a century earlier is instructive (see fig. 18-11). Instead of Leonardo's closed and logical space with massive figures reacting in individual ways to Jesus' statement, Tintoretto's viewer observes the room from a corner, with the vanishing point on a high horizon line at the far right side. The table, coffered ceiling, and inlaid floor all seem to plunge dramatically into the distance. The figures, although still large bodies modeled by flowing draperies, turn and move in a continuous serpentine line that unites apostles, servants, and angels. Tintoretto uses two light sources: one real, the other supernatural.

Light streams from the oil lamp flaring dangerously over the near end of the table; angels seem to swirl out from the flame and smoke. A second light emanates from Jesus himself and is repeated in the modest glow of the apostles' halos. The mood of intense spirituality is enhanced by deep colors flashed with bright highlights, as well as elongated figures—treatments that reflect both the Byzantine art of Venice and the Mannerist aesthetic that was beginning to emerge (see page 714). The still life of the table and the **genre** detail of a cat and basket emphasize the reality of the viewers' experience while at the same time the brilliant chiaroscuro and dazzling lights catching forms in near total darkness enhance the convincingly otherworldly atmosphere. The interpretation of the Last Supper also has changed—unlike Leonardo's more secular emphasis on personal betrayal, Tintoretto has returned to the institution of the Eucharist: Jesus offers bread and wine, a model for the priest administering the sacraments at the altar next to the painting.

The speed with which Tintoretto drew and painted was the subject of comment in his own time, and the

18-34. Jacopo Sansovino. Library of San Marco, Piazzas San Marco, Venice. Begun 1536

brilliance and immediacy so admired today were derided as evidence of carelessness. His brilliant slashing brushwork has been fully appreciated only by the gestural painters of the twentieth century. Tintoretto may have seemed to paint so rapidly because in his large workshop he usually provided only the original conception, the beginning drawings, and the final brilliant colors of the finished painting. Tintoretto's workshop included other members of his family—of his eight children, four became artists. His oldest child, Marietta Robusti, worked with him as a portrait painter, and two or perhaps three of his sons also joined the shop. Another daughter, famous for her needlework, became a nun. Marietta, in spite of her fame and many commissions, stayed in her father's shop until she died, at the age of thirty. So skillfully did she capture her father's style and technique that today art historians cannot be certain which paintings are hers.

Architecture in Venice and the Veneto

The Sack of Rome in 1527 benefited other Italian cities when artists fled for their livelihoods, if not for their lives. Venice had long been a vital Renaissance architectural center with its own traditions, but the field was empty when the Florentine sculptor Jacopo Sansovino (1486–1570) arrived there from Rome. As a result, Sansovino became the most important architect of the mid-sixteenth century in Venice. The second half of the century was dominated by Andrea Palladio, a brilliant artist from the Veneto, the mainland region ruled by Venice. Palladio brought new distinction to Venetian Renaissance architecture with his villas, palaces, and churches.

Jacopo Sansovino. Soon after settling in Venice, Sansovino was appointed to renovate the area around the Church of San Marco. In 1536, he created a model for a new library on the south side of the **piazza**, or open square, inspired by such classical structures as the Colosseum in Rome, which featured regular **bays** of superimposed orders. The flexibility of this design, with identical modules that can be repeated indefinitely, is reflected in the history of the Library of San Marco (fig. 18-34). It was opened after the first seven bays were completed at the end of 1546. Then, between 1551 and 1554, seven more bays were added, and in 1589—nearly two decades after the architect's death—more bays were added to provide office space.

Drawing upon his earlier experience as a sculptor, Sansovino enriched the facade with elaborate spandrel figures and a frieze of putti and garlands. The roofline balustrade surmounted at regular intervals by statues elegantly emphasizes the horizontal orientation of the building. The library influenced a young architect from Vicenza, Andrea Palladio, who proclaimed it "the richest and most ornate" building since antiquity.

Palladio. Probably born in Padua, Palladio (Andrea di Pietro, 1508–1580) began his career as a stonecutter. After moving to Vicenza, he was hired by the noble humanist scholar and amateur architect Giangiorgio Trissino, who nicknamed him Palladio, for the Greek goddess of wisdom, Pallas, and the fourth-century Roman writer Palladius. Palladio learned Latin at Trissino's small academy and accompanied his benefactor on three trips to Rome, where he made drawings of Roman monuments. Over the years, he became involved in several publishing ventures, including a guide to Roman antiquities, an illustrated edition of Vitruvius, and books on architecture that for centuries were valuable resources for architectural design.

By 1559, when he settled in Venice, Palladio was one of the foremost architects of Italy. In 1566, he undertook a

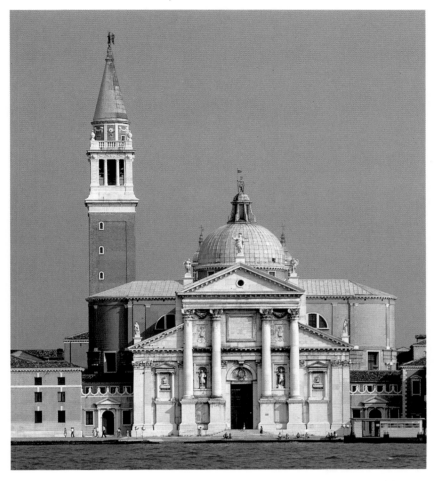

18-35. Palladio. Church of San Giorgio Maggiore, Venice. Begun 1566

major architectural commission: the monastery Church of San Giorgio Maggiore (fig. 18-35). His design for the Renaissance facade to the traditional basilica-plan elevation—a wide lower level fronting the nave and side aisles, surmounted by a narrower front for the nave clerestory—is ingenious. Inspired by Leon Battista Alberti's solution for Sant'Andrea in Mantua (see fig. 17-58), Palladio created the illusion of two temple fronts of different heights and widths, one set inside the other. At the center, colossal columns on high pedestals, or bases, support an entablature and pediment that front the narrower clerestory level of the church. The lower "temple front," which covers the triple-aisle width and slanted side-aisle roofs, consists of pilasters supporting an entablature and pediment running behind the columns of the taller clerestory front. Palladio retained Alberti's motif of the triumphal-arch entrance. Although the facade was not built until after the architect's death, his original design was followed.

The interior of San Giorgio (fig. 18-36) is a fine example of Palladio's harmoniously balanced geometry, expressed here in strong verticals and powerful arcs. The tall engaged columns and shorter pairs of pilasters of the nave arcade echo the two levels of orders on the facade, thus unifying the exterior and interior of the building.

Palladio's diversity can best be seen in numerous villas built early in his career. About 1550, he started his most

18-36. Palladio. Nave, Church of San Giorgio Maggiore

18-37. Palladio. Villa Rotonda (Villa Capra), Vicenza, Venetia, Italy. 1566–69

18-38. Palladio. Plan of the Villa Rotonda. c. 1550?

Palladio was a scholar and an architectural theorist as well as a designer of buildings. His books on architecture provided ideal plans for country estates, using proportions derived from ancient Roman structures. Despite their theoretical bent, his writings were often more practical than earlier treatises. Perhaps his early experience as a stonemason provided him with the knowledge and self-confidence to approach technical problems and discuss them as clearly as he did theories of ideal proportion and uses of the Classical orders. By the eighteenth century, Palladio's *Four Books of Architecture* had become part of the library of most educated people. Thomas Jefferson had one of the first copies in America.

famous villa, just outside Vicenza (fig. 18-37). Although most rural villas were working farms, Palladio designed this one as a retreat for relaxation. To afford views of the countryside, he placed an Ionic order porch on each face of the building, with a wide staircase leading up to it. The main living quarters are on the second level, and the lower level is reserved for the kitchen and other utility rooms. Upon its completion in 1569, the villa was dubbed the Villa Rotonda because it had been inspired by another rotonda (round hall), the Roman Pantheon. After its purchase in 1591 by the Capra family, it became known as the Villa Capra. The villa plan (fig. 18-38) shows the geometric clarity of Palladio's conception: a circle inscribed in a small square inside a larger square, with symmetrical rectangular compartments and identical rectangular projections from each of its faces. The use of a central dome on a domestic building was a daring innovation that effectively secularized the dome. The Villa Rotonda was the first of what was to become a long tradition of domed country houses, particularly in England and the United States.

ITALIAN MANNERISM

The term *Mannerism* comes from the Italian *maniera*, a word used in the sixteenth century to mean charm, grace, or even playfulness and suggesting art concerned with formal beauty for its own sake rather than idealized nature according to Renaissance conventions. In the seventeenth century and later, many critics used the word disparagingly for work they considered superficial, overly ornate, frivolous, or lacking in serious intent. Later, nineteenth-century scholars adopted Mannerism as a convenient category for any sixteenth-century art that did not fit stylistically into the classical Renaissance style.

For this discussion, Mannerism is considered the stylistic movement that emerged at about the same time as the classical Renaissance but had its own aims, rhythms, and sources of influence, which often allowed artistic scope for considerable experimentation and indi-

18-39. Rosso Fiorentino. *Dead Christ with Angels*. 1524–27. Oil on panel, 52¹/₂ x 41" (133.4 x 104.1 cm). Museum of Fine Arts, Boston Charles Potter King Fund

vidual expression. Mannerism, which was stimulated and supported by court patronage, arose in Florence and Rome before 1520—first in painting, then in other mediums—and was spread to other locations when the artists traveled. The major Mannerist artists—Rosso Fiorentino, Pontormo, Parmigianino, Bronzino, Giulio Romano, and Primaticcio—were admirers of and were inspired by the great artists of the earlier generation: Leonardo da Vinci, Raphael, and Michelangelo.

Any attempt to define Mannerism as a single style is futile, but certain characteristics were common: extraordinary virtuosity; sophisticated, elegant compositions; and fearless manipulations or distortions of accepted formal conventions. Artists created irrational spatial effects and figures with elongated proportions, exaggerated poses, and enigmatic gestures and facial expressions. Some artists favored obscure, unsettling, and oftentimes erotic imagery; unusual colors and juxtapositions; and unfathomable secondary scenes. Mannerist sculpture generally exhibited the same characteristics as figural painting, especially in exaggerated body forms and poses. The sculptors also tended to prefer small size, the use of precious metals, and exquisite technical execution. Mannerist architecture involved defiance of the conventional applications of the Classical orders and reversals, rather than structural innovations, of the expected uniformity and rationality of elevation design.

Painting

Mannerism as a style that is clearly differentiated from the classical Renaissance approach began in painting in the second decade of the sixteenth century. In Rome, Raphael had moved in a distinctly Mannerist direction in his final Vatican decorations before his death in 1520, when the first wave of Mannerist painters was already emerging in Florence. Mannerism has been seen as an artistic expression of the unsettled political and religious conditions in Europe and also as an elegant, intriguing art created for sophisticated courtiers. Furthermore, a formal relationship between new painting styles and aesthetic theories began to appear at this time—especially the elevation of "grace" as an ideal.

An early leader of the Mannerist movement was the Florentine painter known as Rosso Fiorentino (1495–1540), who later worked in France on the renovation of the Château of Fontainebleau. Rosso's *Dead Christ with Angels* (fig. 18-39), of 1524–1527, painted while he was working in Rome, exhibits many Mannerist characteristics. The figure of Jesus fills the picture plane and seems to press forward into the viewer's space, its exaggerated **Z** shape providing an odd combination of contortion and almost erotic grace. All traces of the final tortured moments of the Crucifixion have been eliminated. The beautiful candle-bearing angels with curly golden hair and exquisitely colored costumes are a vivid and disturbing contrast to the

18-40. Pontormo. *Entombment*. 1525–28. Oil on panel,
10'3" x 6'4" (3.12 x 1.93 m). Capponi Chapel, Church
of Santa Felicità, Florence

18-41. Parmigianino. *Madonna with the Long Neck*. c. 1535.
Oil on panel, 7'1" x 4'4" (2.16 x 1.32 m). Galleria
degli Uffizi, Florence

enormous corpse, which they effortlessly support on a colorful shroud. Although the scene has been traditionally
identified as a Deposition, it has also been interpreted as
the first moment of Resurrection in the tomb, with Christ's
eyes just beginning to flicker open. Supporting this
hypothesis are the claustrophobic spacelessness of the
painting that seems to deny the material world, the
unmarked flesh of the Savior, whose wounds seem to
have disappeared, and a mood that has no trace of mourning or despair.

Rosso's contemporary Jacopo da Pontormo (1494–
1557), with whom he may have worked in Florence, was
a highly regarded religious painter and a favorite of the
Medici ruling family. Pontormo painted the *Entombment*
(fig. 18-40) in 1525–1528 for the Church of Santa Felicità
in Florence. Like Rosso's painting, its spacial construction
is ambiguous. The rocky ground and cloudy sky give only
the faintest sense of location in space, which is immediately confused by the arrangement of the figures, who are
either levitating or standing on a ring of boulders in the
rocky terrain. Pontormo seems to have chosen a moment

just after Jesus' removal from the Cross, when the youths
who have lowered him have paused to regain their hold.
The emotional atmosphere of the scene is expressed in a
range of facial expressions, odd poses, drastic shifts in
scale, and unusual costumes, but perhaps most poignantly
in the dramatic use of color. The palette is predominantly
blue and pink with accents of olive green, gray, scarlet,
and creamy white. The overall tone of the picture is set by
the color treatment of the crouching youth, whose bright
pink torso is shaded in iridescent, pale gray-green.

When Parmigianino (Francesco Mazzola, 1503– 1540)
arrived in Rome from his native Parma in 1524, the
strongest influence on his work had been Correggio, who
had completed major works in Parma before the younger
artist's departure. While in Rome, Parmigianino met Man-
nerists Rosso Fiorentino and Giulio Romano, and he also
studied Raphael and Michelangelo. His genius was to
assimilate what he saw into his own distinctive style of
Mannerism with none of the nervous, sharply unsettling
qualities of Rosso's or Pontormo's works. After the Sack of
Rome, he moved back to Parma. Dating around 1535 is an

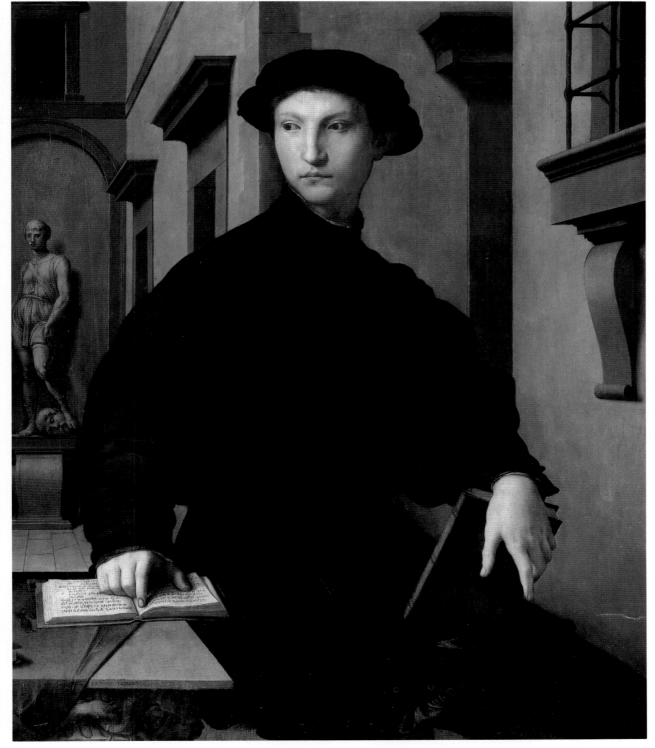

18-42. Bronzino. *Ugolino Martelli*. c. 1535. Oil on panel, 44⅛ x 33½" (112 x 85 cm). Staatliche Museen zu Berlin, Preussischer Kulturbesitz, Gemäldegalerie

unfinished painting known as the *Madonna with the Long Neck* (fig. 18-41). The elongated figure of the Madonna, whose massive legs and lower torso contrast with her narrow shoulders and long neck, resembles the large metal vase inexplicably being carried by the youth at the left. The Madonna's neck also seems to echo the very tall white columns placed, equally mysteriously, in the middle distance. The painting has been interpreted as an abstract conception of beauty in which the female body is compared to the forms of Classical columns and vases. Like Rosso

and Pontormo, Parmigianino presents a common religious image in a manner calculated to unsettle viewers. Are the young people at the left grown-up cherubs or wingless angels? Is the man with the scroll at the right an architect or an Old Testament prophet, perhaps Isaiah, who foretold the birth of Christ? There may be some truth in the explanation given by the theorist Celio Calcagnini (d. 1541): Mannerist taste is admiration for things "that are beautiful just because they are deformed, and thus please by giving displeasure" (cited in Shearman, page 156).

18-43. Sofonisba Anguissola. *Child Bitten by a Crayfish*. c. 1558. Black chalk, 12³⁄₈ x 13³⁄₈" (31.5 x 34 cm). Galleria Nazionale de Capodimonte, Naples

Bronzino (Agnolo Tori, 1503–1572), who may have been nicknamed "Copper-Colored" because of his dark complexion, was born near Florence and became Pontormo's assistant about 1522. He established his own workshop in 1530 but continued to work with Pontormo occasionally on large projects until the older artist's

death. In 1540, Bronzino became court painter to the Medici. Although he was a versatile artist who produced altarpieces, fresco decorations, and tapestry designs over his long career, he is best known today for his portraits in the courtly Mannerist style. *Ugolino Martelli* (fig. 18-42), of about 1535, demonstrates Bronzino's characteristic portrayal of his subjects as intelligent, aloof, elegant, and self-assured. Bronzino's virtuosity in rendering costumes and settings sometimes dominates his compositions, creating a rather cold and formal effect, but the self-contained demeanor of his subjects admirably conveys their personalities, and the wealth and elegance suggested in these portraits were highly prized by his patrons.

Northern Italy, more than any other part of the peninsula, produced a number of gifted woman artists. Sofonisba Anguissola (1528–1625), born into a noble family in Cremona, was unusual in that she was *not* the daughter of an artist. Her father gave all his children a humanistic education and encouraged them to pursue careers in literature, music, and especially painting. He consulted Michelangelo about Anguissola's artistic talents in 1557, asking for a drawing that she might copy and return to be critiqued. Michelangelo not only obliged but also set another task for young Anguissola; she was to send him a drawing of a crying boy. Her sketch of a girl comforting a small boy, wailing because a crayfish is biting his finger (fig. 18-43), so impressed Michelangelo that he gave it as a gift to his closest friend, who later presented it, along

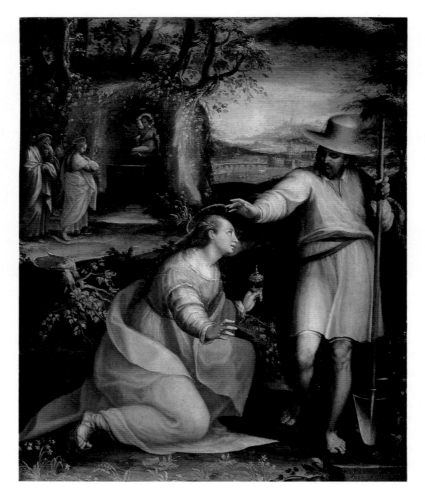

18-44. Lavinia Fontana. *Noli Me Tangere*. 1581. Oil on canvas, 47³⁄₈ x 36⁵⁄₈" (120.3 x 93 cm). Galleria degli Uffizi, Florence

with a drawing by Michelangelo, to Cosimo I de' Medici.

In 1560, Sofonisba accepted the invitation of the queen of Spain to become an official court painter, a post she held for twenty years. In a 1582 Spanish inventory, Sofonisba is described as "an excellent painter of portraits above all the painters of this time"—extraordinary praise in a court that patronized Titian. Unfortunately, most of Sofonisba's Spanish works were lost in a seventeenth-century palace fire.

Another northern Italian, Lavinia Fontana (1552–1614), learned to paint from her father, a Bolognese follower of Raphael. By the 1570s, she was a highly respected painter of narrative as well as of portraits, the more usual field for women artists of the time. Her success was so well rewarded, in fact, that her husband, the painter Gian Paolo Zappi, eventually gave up his own artistic career to care for their large family and help Lavinia with such technical aspects of her work as framing. This situation was not very unusual in Bologna, which boasted some two dozen women painters as well as a number of women scholars who lectured at the university. While still in her twenties, Lavinia painted the *Noli Me Tangere* of 1581 (fig. 18-44), illustrating the biblical story of Christ revealing himself for the first time following his Resurrection to Mary Magdalen (Mark 16:9, John 20:17). The Latin title of the painting means "Don't touch me," Christ's words when she moved to embrace him, explaining that he now existed in a new form somewhere between physical and spiritual. Christ's costume refers to the passage in the Gospel of John, which says that the Magdalen at first mistook Christ for a gardener.

In 1603, Lavinia moved to Rome as an official painter to the papal court. She also soon came to the attention of the Habsburgs, who paid large sums for her work. In 1611, she was honored with a commemorative medal portraying her in a bust as a dignified, elegantly coiffed woman on one side and as an intensely preoccupied artist with rolled-up sleeves and wild, uncombed hair on the other.

Sculpture

Probably the most influential sculptor in Italy in the second half of the sixteenth century was the Flemish artist Jean de Boulogne, better known by his Italian name, Giovanni da Bologna (1529–1608). Born in Flanders, he settled by 1557 in Florence, where both the Medici family and the sizable Netherlandish community there were his patrons. Not only did he influence a later generation of Italian sculptors, but he also spread the Mannerist style to the north through artists who came to study his work.

Although greatly influenced by Michelangelo, Giovanni's distinctive style was generally more concerned with graceful forms and poses, as in his gilded bronze *Astronomy*, or *Venus Urania* (fig. 18-45), of about 1573—the figure's identity suggested by the astronomical device on the base of the **plinth**. Designed with a Classical prototype of Venus in mind, Giovanni's statuette can be seen from any viewpoint. The sculptor twisted Venus's upper torso and arms to the far right and extended her neck in the opposite

18-45. Giovanni da Bologna. *Astronomy,* or *Venus Urania.*
c. 1573. Bronze gilt, height 15¼" (38.8 cm).
Kunsthistorisches Museum, Vienna

direction, so that her chin was over her right shoulder, straining the limits of the human body. The elaborate coiffure of tight ringlets and the detailed textural engraving of the drapery contrast strikingly with the smooth, gleaming flesh of Venus's body. Following common practice for cast-metal sculpture, Giovanni replicated this statuette several times for various patrons.

18-46. Giulio Romano. Palazzo del Tè, Mantua. 1525–32. Courtyard facade

Architecture

Architects, having mastered the Classical style, began to experiment, sometimes rejecting classicism, sometimes playing witty games with Classical features. An important early exponent of architectural Mannerism was Raphael's student Giulio Romano. While Giulio remained attached to the Classical modes, he brought a studied playfulness to his building designs and interior decoration. Giulio's inventive use of traditional forms would inspire later architects.

18-47. Giulio Romano. *Fall of the Giants*, fresco in the Sala dei Giganti, Palazzo del Tè. 1530–32

Giulio Romano. After Raphael's death in 1520, Giulio Romano (c. 1499–1546) completed his unfinished painted works and began the fresco decoration of the last Vatican *stanza*. In 1524, however, he accepted an offer from the ruling Gonzaga family to become their court artist in Mantua, where he spent the rest of his life. He carried out a number of architectural commissions there, but the only well-preserved example is the Palazzo del Tè (fig. 18-46), built on a small nearby island between 1525 and 1532. A country villa rather than a palace, it was used by Federigo Gonzaga for entertaining, which allowed an opportunity for fanciful architectural treatment.

The basic plan is a conventional Renaissance conception: a one-story square building with four wings enclosing a central court. However, the inside face of the east wing, illustrated here, looks more like a fortress than a porticoed Renaissance courtyard (see fig. 18-7). Giulio has used the Doric order, but with typically Mannerist variations. The columns, resting on bases, form with the entablature a projecting screen in front of the rusticated stucco wall. Rather than being evenly spaced, the columns flank a large arched entrance and wall niches of two different sizes. The building's windows are small rectangles that seem to float just under the architrave. Dropped **triglyphs** (three-grooved blocks) on the architrave at the center of each expanse of space between the columns, exaggerated keystones in the arches, and flat arches under pediments make a witty anti-Classical statement, undoubtedly delighting the sophisticated patron and his friends.

In the interior, Giulio created illusions that everyone could quickly appreciate. In the Sala dei Giganti ("Room of the Giants"), he used the entire space—walls, ceiling, and floor—to create the effect that the viewer was in the midst of the mythological battle of the gods and Giants (fig. 18-47). The ceiling depicts the palace of Jupiter floating on a ring of billowing clouds. From its safety, the king of the gods hurls down thunderbolts on the Giants, who are crushed by falling buildings and rocks. The entire room seems to be crashing—a clever comment on Federigo's grandfather's palace, with its illusionistic ceiling painting by Mantegna (see fig. 17-66).

Michelangelo. In addition to the Medici Chapel, Michelangelo worked at San Lorenzo in Florence on the Laurentian Library above the monastery's dormitories, then on a grand staircase to it from a vestibule off the main cloister (fig. 18-48). Michelangelo's staircase—completed in 1559 from a model Michelangelo sent from Rome—was a remarkable Mannerist conception. The spatial proportions are somewhat unsettling: a tall room taken up almost entirely by a staircase cascading like a waterfall—a central flight of large oval steps flanked by narrower flights of rectangular steps that, at the outer edge, form seats with every other step until they join the main flight two-thirds of the way up. Paired columns do not support an entablature but are simply embedded in the walls on the second-floor level; enormous volute brackets, capable of bearing great weight, are merely attached to the wall, supporting nothing. Michelangelo at one point described this project as "a certain stair that comes

18-48. Michelangelo.
Vestibule of the
Laurentian Library,
Monastery of San
Lorenzo, Florence.
1524–33; staircase
completed 1559

18-49. (below). Jean
Clouet. *Francis I*.
1525–30. Oil and
tempera on panel,
37³/₄ x 29¹/₈" (95.9
x 74 cm). Musée du
Louvre, Paris

back to my mind as in a dream," and the strange and powerful effects do indeed suggest a dreamlike imagining brought to physical reality. The Laurentian Library vestibule and stair became an important inspiration for artists in the second half of the sixteenth century, working in the Mannerist style.

THE FRENCH COURT Italy had experienced the military power of French kings since the end of the fifteenth century, and the French kings had experienced the aesthetic power of Italian Renaissance art. The greatest French patron of Italian artists was Francis I (b. 1494; ruled 1515–1547), despite his constant wars against his brother-in-law Holy Roman Emperor Charles V to expand French territory.

Painting

Before the arrival of Italian painters at Francis I's court, the Flemish-born artist Jean Clouet (d. 1540) had found great favor as the king's portraitist. Clouet's origins are obscure, but he was in France as early as 1509, and in 1530 he moved to Paris as principal court painter. Clouet probably painted Francis's official portrait (fig. 18-49)

RENAISSANCE ART IN SIXTEENTH-CENTURY EUROPE   *721*

18-50. Primaticcio. Stucco and wall painting, Chamber of the Duchess of Étampes, Château of Fontainebleau. 1540s

Primaticcio worked on the decoration of Fontainebleau from 1532 until his death in 1570. During that time, he also commissioned and imported a large number of copies and casts made from original Roman sculpture, including the *Apollo Belvedere* in the Vatican gardens, the newly discovered *Laocoön*, and even the relief decoration on the Column of Trajan. These works provided an invaluable visual source for the northern artists employed on the project.

soon after the king's release from imprisonment in Spain by Charles V. His distinctive features have been softened but not completely idealized; the king's thick neck seems at odds with the delicately worked costume of silks, satin, velvet, jewels, and gold embroidery, and his shoulders are broadened by elaborate, puffy sleeves to more than fill the panel, much as parade armor turned scrawny men into giants. In creating such official portraits, artists sketched the subject, then painted a prototype for the official portrait, which, upon approval, was the model for numerous replicas for diplomatic and family purposes.

Architecture and Its Decoration

At the beginning of the sixteenth century, with the enthusiasm of French royalty for things Italian and the widening distribution of Italian books on architecture, the Italian Renaissance style began to appear in French construction. Builders of elegant rural palaces, called **châteaux**, were quick to introduce Italianate decoration on otherwise Gothic buildings, but French architects soon adapted Classical principles of building design as well.

Immediately upon his ascent to the throne in 1515, Francis I showed his desire to "modernize" the French court by acquiring the versatile talents of Leonardo da Vinci, who moved to France in 1516, lived at Cloux, and after he died in 1519 was buried in the château of Amboise in the Loire Valley. But it was not until 1526, after Francis's military defeat by Charles V and a two-year imprisonment in Madrid, that the king began a major renovation of royal properties.

Having chosen as his primary residence the medieval hunting lodge at Fontainebleau, Francis began transforming it into a grand palace. Most of the exterior structure was altered or destroyed by later renovations, but parts of the interior decoration, mainly the work of artists and artisans from Italy, have been preserved and restored. The first artistic director at Fontainebleau, the Mannerist painter Rosso Fiorentino (see fig. 18-39), arrived in 1530. In 1540, he was succeeded by his colleague Francesco Primaticcio (1504–1570), from Mantua, where the latter had worked with Giulio Romano.

Following ancient tradition, the king maintained an official mistress—Anne, the duchess of Étampes, who was in residence at Fontainebleau. Among Primaticcio's

18-51. Pierre Lescot. West wing of the Cour Carré, Palais du Louvre, Paris. Begun 1546

first projects was the redecoration, in the 1540s, of Anne's bedroom (fig. 18-50), which has survived nearly intact. The artist combined the arts of woodworking, stucco relief, and fresco painting in his complex but light-hearted and graceful interior design. The lithe figures of his stucco nymphs, with their long necks and small heads, recall Parmigianino's painting style (see fig. 18-41), and their spiraling postures and bits of clinging drapery are playfully sexual. The wall surface is almost overwhelmed with garlands, mythological figures, and Roman architectural ornament, yet the visual effect is extraordinarily confident and joyous. The first School of Fontainebleau, as this Italian phase of the palace decoration is called, established a tradition of Mannerism in painting and interior design that spread to other centers in France and the Netherlands.

Paris at mid-century saw the birth of a thorough-going classical style. In 1546, the king decided to modernize his medieval Parisian castle, the Louvre. The work began with the replacement of the west wing of the square court, the Cour Carré (fig. 18-51), by the architect Pierre Lescot (c. 1515–1578). Working with the sculptor Jean Goujon (1510–1568), Lescot designed a building incorporating Renaissance ideals of balance and regularity with antique architectural details and a rich sculptural decoration. Turrets with pointed roofs gave way to discreetly rounded segmental arches. Classical pilasters and entablatures replaced Gothic buttresses and string-

18-52. Jean Goujon. *Archimedes and Euclid, with Allegorical Figures*, detail of the sculptural decoration of the west wing of the Cour Carré. 1548–49

courses. And a round-arched arcade on the ground floor, rectangular windows above the balustrade, and its architectural decoration are sumptuously, elegantly French.

Jean Goujon's sculpture, filling the attic story and niches, plays an important role. The elongated figures, with classical heads and form-defining draperies, strike elegant poses within their architectural forms, swirling into decorative surface patterns (fig. 18-52). In the hands of Goujon, the style of the stucco sculpture of Fontainebleau

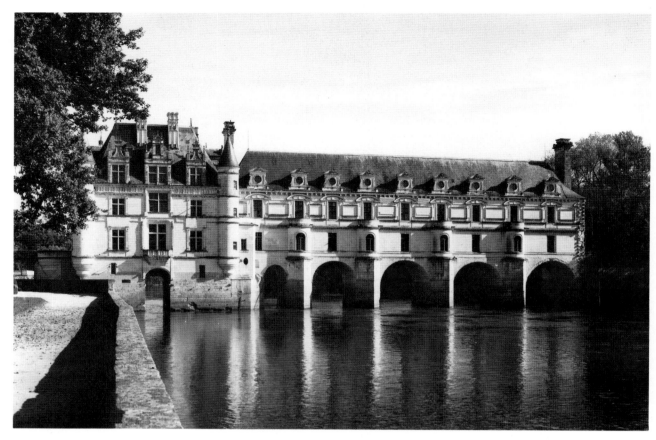

18-53. Château of Chenonceaux. 1515–22, 1556–59, and 1576–81

This château, first acquired by Francis I, was a favorite of his grandson Henry III (ruled 1574–1589). Henry III and his mother, Catherine de' Medici, who had inherited the property, delighted in throwing lavish parties here with costumed young men and women emerging from the woods to greet guests, while singers and musicians entertained from boats on the river. Elaborate extensions of both the building and the gardens were proposed at the end of the century, but they were never carried out.

has been monumentalized and made architectonic.

In rural areas, too, especially in the Loire Valley, builders of elegant châteaux began to add Italianate decoration—pilasters, classical capitals or moldings, swags and putti—and occasionally a symmetrical plan, as at the Château of Chenonceaux. The original residential block (fig. 18-53, at the left), built between 1515 and 1522, used the foundations of a mill built out over the Cher River to create one of the earliest château designs reflecting classical principles of geometric regularity and symmetry. Rooms are arranged on each side of a wide central hall that originally ended in a large window overlooking the river. The château also introduced to French architecture a form of the Italian straight-ramp staircase.

Later, the foremost French Renaissance architect, the Roman-trained Philibert de l'Orme (d. 1570), designed a gallery and bridge extending the rest of the way across the river. The extension, completed about 1581, incorporated contemporary Italianate window treatments, wall moldings, and cornices that harmonized almost perfectly with the forms of the original **turreted** building. Chenonceaux remains today one of the most important—and beautiful—examples of classical influence on French Renaissance architecture.

18-54. Benvenuto Cellini. *Saltcellar of Francis I*. 1539–43. Gold with enamel, 10¼ x 13⅛" (26 x 33.3 cm). Kunsthistorisches Museum, Vienna

18-55. Attributed to Bernard Palissy. Oval plate in "style rustique." 1570–80/90(?). Polychromed tin and glazed earthenware, length 20½" (52 cm). Musée du Louvre, Paris

Craft Arts

Italian craftspeople began to move north after the end of the fifteenth century, and the Fontainebleau treasury includes some of the finest work of the Florentine goldsmith and sculptor Benvenuto Cellini (1500–1571). Cellini worked from just before 1540 to 1545 at Fontainebleau, where he made the famous *Saltcellar of Francis I* (fig. 18-54). A table accessory was transformed into an elegant sculptural ornament by the artist's fanciful imagery and superb execution in gold and enamel. The Roman sea god, Neptune, representing the source of salt, sits next to a tiny boat-shaped container that carries the seasoning, while a personification of the Earth guards the plant-derived pepper, contained in the triumphal arch. The Seasons and the Times of Day on the base refer to both daily meal schedules and festive seasonal celebrations. The two main figures, their poses mirroring each other with one bent and one straight leg, lean away from each other at impossible angles yet are connected and visually balanced by glances and gestures. Their supple, elongated bodies and small heads reflect the Mannerist conventions of Parmigianino and Primaticcio.

Although Italians were prominent at the French court, native French craft artists also attracted royal patronage. Among these was the ceramist Bernard Palissy (c. 1510–c. 1590), called the "Huguenot potter" because of his Protestant faith. In 1563, Palissy was appointed "inventor of rustic figurines" and created in the garden of the Tuileries in Paris a make-believe earthenware grotto, decorated entirely with ceramic rocks, shells, crumbling statues, water creatures, a cat stalking birds, ferns, and garlands of fruits and vegetation—all reportedly made from casts of actual creatures and natural elements. During a period of persecution of Protestants, Palissy was repeatedly arrested; he died in prison around 1590, about the time his

Tuileries grotto was destroyed. He is known today for his distinctive ceramic platters decorated in high relief with plants, flowers, reptiles, water creatures, and insects (fig. 18-55). Existing examples are best called Palissy-style works, however, because their originality is nearly impossible to prove. His designs were copied until the seventeenth century, and pieces in his style are still made today.

NETHER-LANDISH ART A major change in the sixteenth-century Netherlands was the development of stronger, more-affluent art centers, such as Utrecht, in the north. Despite the long struggle for independence from Spain, which led seven northern Protestant provinces to found the United Provinces in 1579 and eventually divided the Netherlands along religious lines, people nevertheless found the resources to patronize artists. Some of these artists capitalized on styles of the late fifteenth century, while others found models in earlier Flemish painters. A few artists—perhaps the best known today—were such individualists that they defy categorization.

Although the Roman Catholic Church continued to commission works of art, religious controversies in the Netherlands led artists to seek private patrons. A market existed for small paintings of secular subjects that were both decorative and interesting conversation pieces for homes. Certain subjects were so popular later in the century that some artists became specialists, rapidly producing variations on a particular theme, with the help of assistants.

In addition to painting, textile arts flourished in the Netherlands during the sixteenth and seventeenth centuries. Antwerp and Brussels were both centers of tapestry weaving and received such commissions as the Sistine Chapel tapestries, for which Raphael provided the cartoons (see fig. 18-18).

18-56. Hieronymus Bosch. *Garden of Earthly Delights*. c. 1505–15. Oil on panel, center panel 7'2½" x 6'4¾" (2.20 x 1.95 m); each wing 7'2½" x 3'2" (2.20 x 0.97 m). Museo del Prado, Madrid

The triptych format that the artist chose may be an understated irony. Before the Reformation, the altarpiece had been synonymous with religious imagery in northern Europe, but this work was commissioned by an aristocrat for his Brussels town house. As a secular work, the *Garden of Earthly Delights* may well have inspired lively discussion and even ribald comment, much as it does today in its museum setting. In addition to painting, textile arts flourished in the Netherlands during the sixteenth and seventeenth centuries. Antwerp and Brussels were both centers of tapestry weaving and received such commissions as the Sistine Chapel tapestries, for which Raphael provided the cartoons (see fig. 18-18). Despite—or perhaps because of—its bizarre subject matter, the triptych was copied in 1566 to make tapestry versions, one for a cardinal (now in El Escorial, Madrid) and another for Francis I. At least one painted copy was made as well. Bosch's original triptych was acquired during the revolt of the Netherlands and sent in 1568 to Spain, where it entered the collection of Philip II.

Hieronymus Bosch. With the work of Hieronymus Bosch (c. 1450–1516), we enter a world of fantastic imagination associated with medieval art. A superb colorist and technical virtuoso, Bosch spent his career in the town whose name he adopted, 's Hertogenbosch, near the German border. Bosch's religious devotion is certain, and his range of subjects shows that he was well educated; a man of many talents, he was also a hydraulic engineer who designed fountains and civic waterworks.

Challenging and unsettling paintings such as Bosch's triptych *Garden of Earthly Delights* (fig. 18-56) have led modern critics to label him scholar, mystic, and social critic. There are many different interpretations of the *Garden,* but a few broad conclusions can be drawn. The subject of the overall work is Sin—that is, the Christian belief in human beings' natural state of sinfulness and their inability to save themselves from its consequences. Because only the Damned are shown in the Judgment scene on the right, the work seems to caution that Damnation is the natural outcome of a life lived in ignorance and folly, that people ensure their damnation through their self-centered pursuit of pleasures of the flesh—the sins of gluttony, lust, avarice, sloth.

The Marriage of Adam and Eve, at the left, is brought about by Christ but is watched by the owl of perverted wisdom. Appearing repeatedly, the owl symbolizes both wisdom and folly, which was as important as Sin to the

18-57. Hieronymus Bosch. Detail of the center panel, *Garden of Earthly Delights*

northern humanists, who believed in the power of education: People would choose the right way if they knew it. Here the owl is in a fantastic plant in a lake from which vicious creatures creep out into the world. Bosch seems obsessed with hybrid forms, unnatural unions in the world. In the central panel, the earth teems with revelers, monstrous birds, and fruits symbolic of fertility and sexual abandon. In hell, the sensual pleasures—eating, drinking,

18-58. Pieter Brueghel the Elder. *Carrying of the Cross*. 1564. Oil on panel, 4'³/₄"x 5'7" (1.23 x 1.70 m). Kunsthistorisches Museum, Vienna

music, and dancing—are turned into elements of torture in a dark world of fire and ice. At the right, for example, a central creature with stump legs watches his own stomach filled with lost souls in a tavern on the road to hell.

One interesting interpretation of the central panel proposes that it is a parable on human salvation in which the practice of alchemy—the process that sought to turn common metals into gold—parallels Christ's power to convert human dross into spiritual gold. In this theory, the bizarre fountain at the center of the lake in the middle distance (fig. 18-57) can be seen as an alchemical "marrying chamber" complete with the glass vessels for collecting the vapors of distillation.

This central pool is also the setting where the power of seductive woman—a relatively new theme in the arts—is presented: Women frolic alluringly in the pool while men dance and ride madly, trying to attract them. In this strange garden, men are slaves to beauty.

One critic wrote about 1600 that the triptych was known as *The Strawberry Plant* because it resembled the "vanity and glory and the passing taste of strawberries or the strawberry plant and its pleasant odor that is hardly remembered once it has passed." Luscious fruits with sexual symbolism—strawberries, cherries, grapes, and pomegranates—appear everywhere in the *Garden*, serving as food, as shelter, and even as a boat. Therefore, the subject of Sin is reinforced by the suggestion that life is as fleeting and insubstantial as the taste of a strawberry.

Pieter Brueghel the Elder. So popular did the works of Hieronymus Bosch remain after his death that, nearly half a century later, the young painter Pieter Brueghel (c. 1525–1569) began his career by imitating Bosch's work. Fortunately, Brueghel's talents went far beyond those of an ordinary copyist. Nothing is known of his early training, but shortly after entering the Antwerp Guild in 1551, he spent time in Bologna and Rome, where he studied Michelangelo's Sistine ceiling and other works in the Vatican.

Brueghel maintained a shop in Antwerp from 1554 until 1563, then moved to Brussels. His style and subjects found great favor with local scholars, merchants, and bankers, who appreciated the beautifully painted, artfully composed works that also reflected contemporary social, political, and religious conditions. Brueghel visited country fairs to sketch the farmers and townspeople who became the focus of his paintings, whether religious or secular. He depicted characters not as unique individuals but as well-observed types whose universality makes them familiar even today. Nevertheless, Brueghel presented Flemish farmers so vividly and sympathetically while also exposing their faults that the middle-class artist earned the nickname "Peasant" Brueghel.

Although Brueghel is not, strictly speaking, a Mannerist, he adopted Mannerist tricks of composition. The main subject of his pictures is often deliberately hidden or disguised by being placed in the distance or amid a teeming crowd of figures, as in the *Carrying of the Cross* (fig. 18-58)

18-59. Pieter Brueghel the Elder. *Return of the Hunters*. 1565. Oil on panel, 3'10¹/₂" x 5'3³/₄" (1.18 x 1.61 m). Kunsthistorisches Museum, Vienna

of 1564. At first glance, the large figures—Saint John and the three Marys—near the picture plane at the lower right seem to be the subject, but they are in fact secondary to the main event: Jesus carrying his Cross to Golgotha. To find Jesus, the viewer must visually enter the painting and search for the principal action, while being constantly distracted by smaller dramas going on among the crowd milling about the large open field or surging around the dire events central to the painting.

Brueghel's panoramic scene is carefully composed to guide our eye in swirling, circular orbits that expand, contract, and intersect. Part of this movement is accomplished by carefully placed bright-red patches, the coats of guards trying to control the crowd. The figure of Jesus is finally discovered at the center of the painting. Far in the distance, on a hill caught by a beam of light in the darkening sky, people already gather early to get a good place in the circle around the spot where the crosses will be set up—perhaps illustrating Brueghel's cynical view of crowd psychology. The landscape recedes skillfully and apparently naturally toward the distant horizon, except for the tall rock outcropping near the center with a wooden windmill on top. The exaggerated shape of the rock is a convention of sixteenth-century northern European landscapes, but the enigmatic windmill suggests the ambiguities of Italian Mannerism.

Brueghel was one of the great landscape painters of all time. His ability to depict nature in all seasons, and in all moods, shines forth in his **cycles**—series of paintings on a single allegorical subject such as the Five Senses or the Seasons, frequently commissioned as decorations for elegant Netherlandish homes. Brueghel's *Return of the Hunters* (fig. 18-59) of 1565 is one of a cycle of six panels, each representing two months of the year. In this November–December scene, Brueghel has captured the atmosphere of the damp, cold winter, with its early nightfall, in the same way that his compatriots the Limbourgs did 150 years earlier in the *February* calendar illustration

for the duke of Berry (see fig. 17-6). In contrast to much Renaissance and Mannerist art, the *Hunters* appears neutral and realistic. The viewer seems to hover with the birds slightly above the ground, looking down first on the busy foreground scene, then across the valley to the snow-covered village and frozen ponds. The main subjects of the painting, the hunters, have their backs turned and do not reveal their feelings as they slog through the snow, trailed by their dogs. They pass an inn, at the left, where a worker moves a table to receive the pig others are singeing in a fire before butchering it. But this is clearly not an accidental image but a slice of everyday life faithfully reproduced with the carefully calculated composition. The sharp diagonals, both on the picture plane and as lines receding into space, are countered by the pointed gables and roofs at the lower right as well as by the jagged mountain peaks linking the valley and the skyline along the right edge. Their rhythms are deliberately slowed and stabilized by a balance of vertical tree trunks and horizontal rectangles of water frozen-over in the distance.

As a depiction of Flemish history, this scene represents a relative calm before the storm. Two years after it was painted, the anguished struggle of the northern provinces for independence from Spain began. Pieter the Elder died young in 1569, leaving two children, Pieter the Younger and Jan, both of whom became successful painters in the next century.

An artist who continued the tradition of painting "Everyman" going about his daily affairs—enlivened with elements of the "power of women" theme—was Marinus van Reymerswaele (c. 1493–after 1567). His well-regarded shop in Antwerp mainly produced secular panel paintings featuring a universally despised class—moneylenders and tax collectors. The *Banker and His Wife* (fig. 18-60), painted in 1538, is almost a caricature of the goldsmith-saint Eloy by Petrus Christus (see fig. 17-17). Now the banker greedily counts coins, avidly watched

18-60. Marinus van Reymerswaele. *Banker and His Wife*. 1538. Oil on panel, 33³/₄ x 45⁷/₈" (85.7 x 116.5 cm). Museo Nazionale del Bargello, Florence

over by his young wife, whose thin, clawlike fingers turn the pages of the account book. Virtuoso painting technique has been applied to a less-than-worthy theme, but more than mere illustration was intended. The painting recalls the biblical parable of the extravagant Prodigal Son, the folly of ill-matched lovers, and the sins caused by love of money rather than the practice of true charity.

Caterina van Hemessen (1528–1587) of Antwerp developed an illustrious international reputation. She had learned to paint from her father, the Flemish Mannerist Jan Sanders van Hemessen, with whom she collaborated on large commissions, but her quiet realism and skilled rendering had roots in Renaissance Romanism—stylistic tendencies brought back to the Netherlands by painters who had visited Italy. To maintain the focus on the foreground subject, Caterina painted the portrait backgrounds in an even dark color, on which she identified her subject and the subject's age, and signed and dated the work. In her *Self-Portrait* (fig. 18-61), the inscription reads: "I Caterina van Hemessen painted myself in 1548. Her age 20." In delineating her own features, Caterina presented a serious young person without personal vanity yet seemingly already self-assured about her artistic abilities. During her early career, spent in Antwerp, she became a favored court artist to Mary of Hungary, regent of the Netherlands and sister of Emperor Charles V, for whom she painted not only portraits but also religious works. In 1554, Caterina married the organist of Antwerp Cathedral, and they accompanied Mary to Spain after she ceased to be regent in 1556. Unfortunately, Caterina's Spanish works have not survived or have been attributed to others.

18-61. Caterina van Hemessen. *Self-Portrait*. 1548. Oil on panel, 12¹/₄ x 9¹/₄" (31.1 x 23.5 cm). Öffentliche Kunstsammlung, Basel, Switzerland

The panel on the easel already has its frame. Catherine holds a small palette and brushes and steadies her right hand with a mauhlstick, an essential tool for an artist doing fine detailed work.

18-62. Matthias Grünewald. *Isenheim Altarpiece*, closed, from the Community of Saint Anthony, Isenheim, Alsace, France. Center panels: *Crucifixion*; predella: *Lamentation*; side panels: Saints Sebastian and Anthony Abbot. c. 1510–15. Oil on panel, center panels 9'9¹/₂" x 10'9" (2.97 x 3.28 m), each wing 8'2¹/₂" x 3'¹/₂" (2.49 x 0.93 m), predella 2'5¹/₂" x 11'2" (0.75 x 3.4 m). Musée d'Unterlinden, Colmar, France

GERMANY AND THE HOLY ROMAN EMPIRE

Through carefully calculated dynastic marriages and some good luck, the Habsburg Holy Roman Emperor Charles V (ruled 1519–1556), also known as Charles I of Spain, ruled over lands from the North Sea to the Mediterranean. Charles was a Roman Catholic throughout his life, but he was forced to accommodate the German Protestant Reformation. Tired of the strain of government and prematurely aged, he abdicated in 1556 and retired to a monastery, where he died two years later. After his death, Habsburg domains were divided. His son, Philip II, became the king of Spain, the Netherlands, and the Americas, as well as ruler of Milan, Burgundy, and the Kingdom of Naples and Sicily. Charles's brother Ferdinand I succeeded him as Holy Roman Emperor. The Habsburg dynasty lasted into the twentieth century.

From the last decades of the fifteenth century up to the 1520s, the arts flourished in Austria, Germany, and the German-speaking regions of Switzerland and Alsace. After that, religious upheavals and **iconoclastic** (image-smashing) purges of religious images began to take a toll. The political situation in Germany helped the reformers—Germany was so politically fragmented that individual rulers and localities had virtually local autonomy on questions of religious practice. Religious strife

was intimately bound up with social and political problems, and some artists found their careers at an end because of their sympathies for rebels and reformers. Others left their homes to seek patronage abroad because of their support for the Roman Catholic Church.

Painting and Printmaking

German art during the first decades of the sixteenth century was dominated by two very different artists, Matthias Gothardt, known as Matthias Grünewald (c. 1480–1528), and Albrecht Dürer (1471–1528). Grünewald's unique style expressed the continuing currents of medieval German mysticism and emotionalism, while Dürer's intense observation of the natural world represented the scientific Renaissance interest in empirical observation, perspective, and a reasoned canon of human proportions. Both artists sympathized with religious reforms, which affected their later lives, and their deaths in 1528 occurred just as the Protestant Reformation gained political power in Germany. Their successors were forced to make drastic efforts to survive in the radically different German market.

Matthias Grünewald. As an artist in the court of the archbishop of Mainz, Grünewald worked as an architect and hydraulic engineer as well as a painter. The work for

18-63. Matthias Grünewald. *Isenheim Altarpiece*, first opening. Left to right: *Annunciation, Virgin and Child with Angels, Resurrection.* c. 1510–15. Oil on panel, center panel 9'9¹/₂" x 10'9" (2.97 x 3.28 m), each wing 8'2¹/₂" x 3'1¹/₂" (2.49 x 0.93 m)

which Grünewald is best known today, the *Isenheim Altarpiece* (figs. 18-62, 18-63), created around 1510–1515, illustrates the same intensity of religious feeling that motivated reformers like Martin Luther. It was created for the Abbey of Saint Anthony in Isenheim, whose hospital specialized in the care of patients with skin diseases, including the plague and leprosy. The altarpiece commemorates a major saint—the fourth-century Egyptian Anthony the Hermit—and was thought to be able to heal those who looked upon it. In fact, viewing the altarpiece was part of the medical care given to patients. The altarpiece is no longer mounted in its original frame, but it is nevertheless monumentally impressive in size and complexity.

The collaboration of painters and sculptors was still as close in northern Europe in the sixteenth century as it had been in the Middle Ages, and the main inner section of the altarpiece is a carved wooden shrine with sculpture (see fig. 18-64) by Nicolas Hagenau of Strasbourg, finished about 1505. The sculpture makes the surrounding paintings come alive, and the painted wings protect the precious carvings. Grünewald painted one set of fixed wings and two sets of movable ones, plus one set of small wings for the **predella**, or supporting platform, so that the altarpiece could be exhibited in different configurations depending upon the Church calendar.

On weekdays, when the altarpiece was closed, viewers saw a shocking image of the Crucifixion in a darkened landscape, a Lamentation below it on the predella, and

lifesize figures of Saints Sebastian and Anthony Abbot standing on trompe l'oeil pedestals on the fixed wings (fig. 18-62). Grünewald represented in the most horrific details the tortured body of Jesus, covered with gashes from being beaten and pierced by the thorns used to form a crown for his head. His ashen-colored body, open mouth, and blue lips indicate that he is dead; in fact, he already appears to be decaying, an effect enhanced by the palette of putrescent green, yellow, and purplish red. A ghostlike Virgin Mary has collapsed in the arms of an emaciated John the Evangelist, and Mary Magdalen has fallen in anguish to her knees; her clasped hands with outstretched fingers seem to echo Jesus' straining, cramping fingers in rigor mortis. At the right, John the Baptist points at Jesus and repeats his prophecy, "He shall increase." The Baptist and the lamb holding a cross and bleeding from its breast into a golden chalice allude to the Christian rites of Baptism and the Eucharist and to Christ as the Lamb of God. In the predella below, Jesus' bereaved mother and friends prepare his body for burial, a scene that must have been familiar in the hospital. On the fixed wings, the martyred Saint Sebastian and the hermit Saint Anthony, saints associated with the plague, intercede for the sick and the dying.

In contrast, the altarpiece when first opened displays Christian events of great joy—the Annunciation, the Nativity, and the Resurrection—expressed in vivid reds and golds accented with high-keyed pink, lemon, and white (fig. 18-63). Unlike the awful darkness of the

18-64. Nicolas Hagenau. *Saint Anthony Enthroned between Saints Augustine and Jerome*, shrine of the *Isenheim Altarpiece*. c. 1505

Crucifixion, the inner scenes are illuminated with clear natural daylight, phosphorescent auras and halos, and the glitter of stars in a night sky. Fully aware of contemporary Renaissance formal achievements, Grünewald created the illusion of three-dimensional space and volumetric figures, and he abstracted, simplified, and idealized the forms. Unlike Italian Renaissance painters, his aim was to strike the heart rather than the mind and to evoke sympathy rather than to create an intellectual ideal. Underlying this deliberate attempt to arouse an emotional response in the viewer is a complex, religious symbolism, undoubtedly the result of close collaboration with his monastic patrons.

The Annunciation on the left wing illustrates a special liturgy called the Golden Mass, which celebrated the divine motherhood of the Virgin and included a staged reenactment of the angel's visit to her. There were also readings from the story of the Annunciation (Luke 1:26–38) and the Old Testament prophecy of the Savior's birth (Isaiah 7:14–15), which is inscribed in Latin on the pages of the Virgin's open book. The event takes place as reenacted in the Mass.

The central panels show the heavenly and earthly realms joined in one space. In a variation on the northern visionary tradition, the new Mother adores her miraculous Child while envisioning her own future as the Queen of Heaven amid angels and cherubs. Grünewald illustrated a range of ethnic types in the heavenly realm, as well as three distinct types of angels seen in the foreground—young, mature, and a feathered hybrid with a birdlike crest on its human head. Perhaps this was

18-65. Albrecht Dürer. *Wehlsch Pirg* (*Italian Mountain*). c. 1495. Watercolor and gouache, 8¼ x 12¼" (21 x 31.1 cm). Ashmolean Museum, Oxford

intended to emphasize the global dominion of the Church, whose missionary efforts were expanding as a result of European exploration. The panel is also filled with symbolic and narrative imagery related to the Annunciation. For example, the Virgin and Child are surrounded by Marian symbols: the enclosed garden, the white towel on the tub, and the clear glass cruet behind it, which signify Mary's virginity; the waterpot next to the tub, which alludes both to purity and to childbirth; and the fig tree at the left, suggesting the Virgin Birth, since figs were thought to bear fruit without pollination. The bush of red roses at the right alludes not only to Mary but also to the Passion of Jesus, thus recalling the Crucifixion on the outer wings and providing a transition to the Resurrection on the right wing. There, the shock of Christ's explosive emergence from his stone sarcophagus tumbles the guards about, and his new state of being—no longer material but not yet entirely spiritual—is vibrantly evident in his dissolving, translucent figure.

The third opening of the altar wings, revealing the sculpture (fig. 18-64), was reserved for the special festivals of Saint Anthony, who has the place of honor in the sculpture and is flanked by the scholarly saints Augustine and Jerome. The donor, Jean d'Orlier, and two other men are offering gifts. The figures of the saints, painted in lifelike colors, are clothed in gold; the secular figures are fully polychromed. In the predella below, Jesus and the apostles bless the altar, Host, and assembled patients in the hospital. The wings in this third open altarpiece are painted with the temptation of Saint Anthony by horrible demons and the meeting of Saint Anthony with the hermit Saint Paul in a fantastic forested wasteland.

Grünewald's artistic career was damaged by his personal identification with and active support of the peasants, who, because of economic and religious oppression, rose up against their feudal overlords in the Peasants' War in 1525. Afterward, he left Mainz and spent his last years in Halle, whose ruler was the chief protector of Martin Luther and a longtime patron of Grünewald's contemporary Albrecht Dürer.

Albrecht Dürer.   Much is known about the life, personality, and thinking of Albrecht Dürer. Studious, analytical,

18-66. Albrecht Dürer. *Four Horsemen of the Apocalypse*, from *The Apocalypse*. 1497–98. Woodcut, 15¹⁄₂ x 11¹⁄₈" (39.4 x 28.3 cm). The Metropolitan Museum of Art, New York
Gift of Junius S. Morgan, 1919 (19.73.209)

18-67. Albrecht Dürer. *Adam and Eve*. 1504. Engraving, 9⁷⁄₈ x 7⁵⁄₈" (25.1 x 19.4 cm). Philadelphia Museum of Art
Purchased: Lisa Nora Elkins Fund

observant, and meticulous—but as self-absorbed and difficult as Michelangelo—Dürer was one of eighteen children of a Nuremberg goldsmith. Nuremberg at that time was a free imperial city with strong business, trade, and publishing interests. The city had an active group of humanists and internationally renowned artists and artisans who exported many works, especially large altarpieces. After an apprenticeship in painting, stained-glass design, and especially the making of woodcuts, in the spring of 1490 Dürer began traveling in order to extend his education and gain experience as an artist. Dürer worked until early 1494 in Basel, Switzerland, providing drawings for woodcut illustrations for books published there.

Not long after his marriage in 1494, Dürer traveled to Italy to seek patrons among the large, rich community of German merchants then living in Venice. Dürer documented his travels in fresh, freely executed watercolors of the alpine landscape, such as the *Wehlsch Pirg (Italian Mountain)*, probably painted in 1495 (fig. 18-65). The artist's interest in landscape and the effects of atmosphere is clear from the tonal variations of the blues and greens in the distant, moisture-laden air. He paints the mountains in a curious reversal of **atmospheric perspective**: The distant mountain looms menacing and dark.

Back in Nuremberg, the young artist had difficulty selling his work. To bolster his income, Dürer began to publish his own prints, and ultimately it was these prints, not his paintings, that made his fortune. His first major publication was the Book of Revelation, or Apocalypse, which appeared simultaneously in German and Latin editions in 1497–1498 and consisted of a woodcut title page and fourteen full-page illustrations with the text printed on the back of each. The best known of the woodcuts is the *Four Horsemen of the Apocalypse* (fig. 18-66), based on figures in Revelation 6:1–8: a crowned rider armed with a bow, on a white horse (Conquest); a rider with a sword, on a red horse (War); a rider with a set of scales, on a black horse (Plague and Famine); and a rider on a sickly pale horse (Death).

Dürer probably did not cut his own woodblocks but rather employed a skilled carver who followed his drawings faithfully. Dürer's dynamic figures show affinities with *The Temptation of Saint Anthony* (see fig. 17-78) by Martin Schongauer, whom he admired, and he adapted for woodcut Schongauer's technique for shading on the engraved plate, using a complex pattern of lines that model the forms with highlights against the tonal ground. Dürer's fifteenth-century training is evident in his meticulous attention to detail, decorative cloud and drapery patterns, and the foreground filled with large, active figures.

Perhaps as early as the summer of 1494, Dürer had begun to experiment with engravings, cutting the plates himself with artistry equal to Schongauer's. His growing interest in Italian art and theoretical investigations is reflected in his 1504 engraving *Adam and Eve* (fig. 18-67),

18-68. Albrecht Dürer. *Melencolia I.* 1514. Engraving, 9³/₈ x 6⁵/₈" (23.8 x 16.8 cm). National Gallery of Art, Washington, D.C.

which represents his first documented use of a canon of ideal human proportions. His nudes were based on Roman copies of Greek gods, probably seen as prints or small sculpture in the antique manner that had become so popular among European collectors by 1500. As idealized as the human figures may be, the flora and fauna are recorded with typically northern European microscopic detail. Dürer embedded the landscape with symbolic content related to the medieval theory that after Adam and Eve disobeyed God, they and their descendants became vulnerable to imbalances in body fluids that altered human temperament: An excess of black bile from the liver produced melancholy, despair, and greed; yellow bile caused anger, pride, and impatience; phlegm in the lungs resulted in a lack of emotion, lethargy, and disinterest; and an excess of blood made a person unusually optimistic but also compulsively interested in pleasures of the flesh.

18-69. Albrecht Dürer. *Four Apostles*, 1526. Oil on panel, each panel 7'1/2" x 2'6" (2.15 x 0.76 m). Alte Pinakothek, Munich

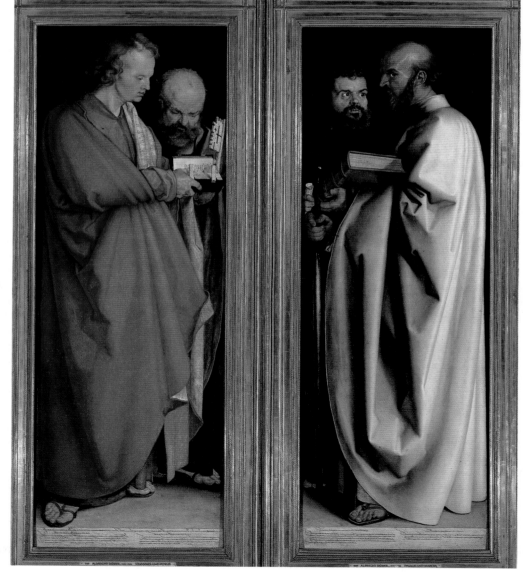

These four human temperaments, or personalities, are symbolized here by the melancholy elk, the choleric cat, the phlegmatic ox, and the sensual rabbit. The mouse is a symbol of Satan, whose earthly power, already manifest in the Garden of Eden, was capable of bringing perfect human beings to a life of woe through their own bad choices. The parrot may symbolize false wisdom, since it speaks but can only repeat mindlessly what is said to it. Dürer's pride in his engraving can be seen in the prominence of his signature—a placard bearing his full name and date hung on a branch of the Tree of Life.

Dürer's familiarity with Italian art was greatly enhanced by a second, more leisurely trip over the Alps in 1505–1506. Thereafter, he seems to have resolved to reform the art of his own country by publishing theoretical writings and manuals that discussed Renaissance problems of perspective, ideal human proportions, and the techniques of painting. Between 1513 and 1515, Dürer created what are known today as his master prints—three engravings that are in many ways an engraver's showpiece, demonstrating his skill at implying color, texture, and space by black line alone. The three prints represent the active and contemplative Christian life (*Knight, Death and the Devil* and *Saint Jerome in His Study*) and the frustrated creativity of the secular life, *Melencolia I* (fig. 18-68).

Melencolia I seems to reflect the self-doubt that beset Dürer after he returned from Italy, caught up in the spirit of the Italian Renaissance, with its humanist ideals of the artist as a divinely inspired creator. Here Dürer created a superhuman figure caught in mental turmoil and brooding listlessly, surrounded by tools and symbols of the arts and humanities, while a bat, inscribed "Melencolia I," flits through the night. The melancholic person was thought to live under the influence of black bile—the bodily fluid associated with things dry and cold, the earth, evening, autumn and age, and the vices of greed and despair—and Dürer's melancholic figure's pose can be seen as that of one in deep thought as well as of sloth, weariness, and despair. In this engraving, Dürer seems to brood on the futility of art and the fleeting nature of human life.

Dürer admired the writings of Martin Luther and had hoped to engrave a portrait of him, as he had other important Reformation thinkers. In 1526, the artist openly professed his belief in Lutheranism in a pair of inscribed panels commonly referred to as the *Four Apostles* (fig. 18-69). The paintings show the apostles John, Peter, Paul, and Mark the Evangelist in an arrangement possibly intended to create an acceptable Protestant imagery. On the left panel, the elderly Peter, the first pope, seems to hold up his key but shrink behind the young John, Luther's favorite evangelist. On the right panel, Mark is nearly hidden behind Paul, whose teachings and epistles were greatly admired by the Protestants. Dürer presented the panels to the city of Nuremberg, which had already adopted Lutheranism as its official religion. Long inscriptions below the figures (not legible here) warn the viewer not to be led astray by "false prophets" but to heed the words of the New Testament. Also included are excerpts from the letters of Peter, John, and Paul and the Gospel

18-70. Hans Baldung Grien. *Stupefied Groom*. 1544. Woodcut, image 13¹⁵/₁₆ x 7⁷/₈" (35.4 x 19.8 cm). Staatliche Museen zu Berlin, Preussischer Kulturbesitz, Kupferstichkabinett

of Mark from Luther's German translation of the New Testament.

Luther, an avowed pacifist, never supported the destruction of religious art, and Dürer's gift to Lutheran Nuremberg was surely meant to demonstrate that a Protestant art was possible. Earlier, the artist had written: "For a Christian would no more be led to superstition by a picture or effigy than an honest man to commit murder because he carries a weapon by his side. He must indeed be an unthinking man who would worship picture, wood, or stone. A picture therefore brings more good than harm, when it is honourably, artistically, and well made" (cited in Snyder, page 347).

Hans Baldung Grien, Lucas Cranach the Elder, and Albrecht Altdorfer. Dürer's most successful pupil and lifelong friend, Hans Baldung (c. 1484–1545) received the nickname "Grien," possibly from his habit of wearing green clothing while an apprentice from about 1503 to 1509. Baldung Grien, from a highly educated German family, spent most of his adult life in Strasbourg. Having specialized at first in religious altarpieces and stained glass, the artist adapted to the advent of Protestantism in

18-71. Lucas Cranach the Elder. *Martin Luther as Junker Jörg.* c. 1521. Oil on panel, 20½ x 13⅝" (52.1 x 34.6 cm). Kunstmuseum, Weimar, Germany

Strasbourg in the late 1520s by painting portraits, classical subjects, and small Madonnas for private clients. He also benefited from the sale of his woodcuts, including the enigmatic *Stupefied Groom* (fig. 18-70), made in 1544, the year before his death. The scene shows a sturdy cavalry horse looking back at a groom, who is lying unconscious (or dead) on a barn floor as an old woman with a firebrand looks on from the window. The woman seems to have frightened the horse, which reacted by kicking the groom, who was currying him. Or has she laid a spell on the man, using the evil-looking horse as her creature? What is the meaning of the forked pitchfork? Or the unicorn on the shield? Baldung Grien's earlier prints included images of witches, as well as of wild horses symbolizing the basic human instincts, so this picture could have been intended as a moral lesson on the power of evil. The preliminary study for the print shows an even more radically foreshortened male figure and no grooming equipment, so the perspective study may have been the focus around which the artist then built his picture.

Another of Dürer's friends, Lucas Cranach the Elder (1472–1553), had moved his workshop to Wittenberg in 1504, after a number of years in Vienna. In addition to the humanist milieu of its university, Wittenberg offered the patronage of the Saxon court. Appointed court painter in 1505, Cranach created all manner of works, including woodcuts, altarpieces, and many portraits. Cranach was

Martin Luther's favorite painter, and one of the most interesting among Cranach's roughly fifty portraits of Luther is *Martin Luther as Junker Jörg* (fig. 18-71). It was painted after the reformer's excommunication by Pope Leo X in early 1521—and after rulers of the German states met in Worms and declared Luther's ideas heresy and Luther himself an outlaw to be captured and handed over to Emperor Charles V. Smuggled out of Worms by Saxon agents, Luther returned to Wittenberg wearing a black beard and moustache, disguised as a knight named Jörg, or George. As Cranach's religious commissions dwindled, his later work tended to be portraits, hunting scenes, and mythological subjects.

Landscape, with or without figures, was an important new category of imagery after the Reformation. Among the most accomplished German landscape painters of the period was Albrecht Altdorfer (c. 1480–1538), who specialized in portraying the Danube River Valley. He probably received his early training in Bavaria from his painter father, then became a citizen in 1505 of the city of Regensburg, located in the Danube River Valley, where he remained for the rest of his life. In addition to civic construction projects, Altdorfer executed many paintings, often combining religious and historical subjects in magnificent landscapes. The artist's varied talents are barely hinted at by the single work illustrated here, his *Danube Landscape* of about 1525 (fig. 18-72), a fine example of pure landscape painting without a narrative subject or human figures, unusual for the time. A small work on vellum laid down on a wood panel, the *Landscape* seems to be a minutely detailed view of the natural terrain, but a close inspection reveals an inescapable picturesqueness—far more poetic and mysterious than Dürer's scientifically observed views of nature—in the low mountains, gigantic lacy pines, neatly contoured shrubberies, and fairyland castle with red-roofed towers at the end of a winding path. The eerily glowing yellow-white horizon below roiling gray and blue clouds in a sky that takes up more than half the composition suggests otherworldly scenes.

Hans Holbein the Younger. A talent for portrait painting was important for nearly all German artists from the 1520s, but Hans Holbein the Younger eventually owed his entire livelihood to it. Born in Augsburg in 1497 (d. 1543), the son of a painter of altarpieces, Holbein worked for a time in Basel, Switzerland, traveled to Italy in 1518–1519, then returned to Switzerland. He received portrait and religious commissions but also capitalized on the growing popularity of fresco decorations for house facades. After the humanist scholar Erasmus of Rotterdam settled in Basel in 1521, Holbein became his portraitist and close friend. The Protestant religion spread to Basel in 1522, and by 1526 religious problems there had greatly escalated. Holbein left with letters of introduction from Erasmus to humanist friends in Antwerp and London, where he received lucrative portrait commissions before returning home in 1528.

Although Holbein had officially become a Protestant by 1532, harassment from the reformers sent him once

18-72. Albrecht Altdorfer. *Danube Landscape*. c. 1525. Oil on panel, 12 x 8³/₄" (30.5 x 22.2 cm). Alte Pinako-thek, Munich

18-73. Hans Holbein the Younger. *Artist's Wife and Children*. 1528/29. Tempera on paper on limewood, 30⅛ x 25¼" (76.5 x 64.1 cm). Öffentliche Kunstsammlung, Basel, Switzerland

again, with letters from Erasmus, to England. Before leaving Basel, however, he painted a portrait of his wife and two children (fig. 18-73), perhaps meant to be paired with a self-portrait placed on the right. The pyramidal composition and monumental figures of *Artist's Wife and Children* immediately recall a Raphael Madonna and Child (see fig. 18-14), but the power of Holbein's work lies in the unidealized, beloved features of his subjects. His wife is already suffering from the eye disease that would eventually blind her, and the children seem on the verge of tears as they look out to the right, perhaps at a painting of their father. Distilled in this work is the sense of hopelessness that prompted the artist to leave his family again. He had every intention of returning to Basel from England, as he had earlier, but Holbein died of the plague in London in 1543, while serving Henry VIII as court painter (see fig. 18-77).

Sculpture

Fifteenth-century German sculpture was closely related to that of France and Flanders, but sixteenth-century sculpture gradually but persistently began to show the influence of the Italian Renaissance and Mannerist styles. Although German sculptors worked in every medium, they produced some of their finest and most original work during this period in limewood. Generally these wood images had been gilded and painted until Tilman Riemenschneider (active 1483–1531) introduced a natural wood finish.

Riemenschneider, after about 1500, ran the largest workshop in Würzburg, which included specialists in every medium of sculpture; he also was politically active in the city's government. Riemenschneider attracted patrons from other cities, and in 1501 he signed a contract for one of his major creations, the *Altarpiece of the Holy Blood*, for the Sankt Jakobskirche (Church of Saint James) in Rothenburg ob der Tauber, where a relic said to be a drop of Jesus' blood was preserved. The construction was to be nearly 30 feet high and made entirely of limewood. A specialist in wood shrines had begun work on the frame in 1499, and Riemenschneider later provided the figures. The relative value of their contribu-

18-74. Tilman Riemenschneider. *Last Supper*, center of the *Altarpiece of the Holy Blood*,
Sankt Jakobskirche, Rothenburg ob der Tauber, Germany. c. 1499–1505.
Limewood, height of tallest figure 39" (99.1 cm); height of altar 29'6" (9 m)

tions can be judged from the fact that the frame carver received fifty florins and Riemenschneider sixty.

The main scene of the altarpiece is the *Last Supper* (fig. 18-74). Like his Italian contemporary Leonardo da Vinci (see fig. 18-11), Riemenschneider depicted the moment of Jesus' revelation that one of his followers would betray him. Unlike Leonardo, Riemenschneider composed his group with Jesus off-center at the left and his disciples packed around him. Judas, at the center, looks stricken as he holds the money bag to which he will soon add the thirty pieces of silver he received for his betrayal. As the event is described in John 13:21–30, the apostles look puzzled by the news that a traitor is among them, and Jesus extends a morsel of food to Judas, signifying that he is the one destined to set in motion the events leading to Jesus' death. The youngest apostle, John, is asleep with his head on the table, following a medieval tradition derived from John 13:23, where "one of his disciples, the one whom Jesus loved," is described as "reclining at Jesus' side." One of the figures in front points down toward the predella, where the Crucifixion is depicted.

Riemenschneider's style is characterized by large heads, prominent features, and elaborate hair treatments with thick wavy locks and deeply drilled curls. The muscles, tendons, and raised veins of the hands and feet are especially lifelike, as are the sharp cheekbones, sagging jowls, baggy eyes, and slim figures of Jesus and his followers. Rather than creating individual portrayals, Riemenschneider simply repeated a limited number of types—Riemenschneider's studio workers copied figures and even different modes of drapery rendering either from drawings or from other carved examples. Here, the deeply hollowed folds and active patterning of the drapery create strong highlights and dark shadows that unify the figural composition and the intricate carving of the framework. The scene is set in a three-dimensional space with actual benches for the figures to rest on and windows at the rear glazed with real bull's-eye glass. Natural light from the church's windows actually illuminates the scene, with effects constantly changing with the time of day and weather. Despite his enormous production of religious images for churches, Riemenschneider's

18-75. Veit Stoss. *Annunciation and Virgin of the Rosary*,
1517–18. Limewood, 12'2" x 10'6" (3.71 x 3.20 m).
Church of Saint Lawrence, Nuremberg

18-76. Peter Flötner. Apollo Fountain. 1532. Bronze,
height without base 30" (76.2 cm). Germanisches
Nationalmuseum, Nuremberg

career ended when his support of the 1525 Peasants' War led to a fine and imprisonment just six years before his death.

Veit Stoss (c. 1438–1533) of Nuremberg spent his career from 1477 to 1496 mainly in Cracow, Poland, where he became wealthy from his sculpture and architectural commissions, as well as from financial investments. After returning to Nuremberg, he began to specialize in limewood sculpture, probably because established artists already dominated commissions in other mediums. Unlike Riemenschneider, he ran a small operation whose output was characterized by an easily recognizable, personal style expressing an obvious taste for German realism. Stoss's unpainted limewood works show a special appreciation for the wood itself, which he exploited for its inherent colorations, grain patterns, and range of surface finishes.

Stoss carved the *Annunciation and Virgin of the Rosary* (fig. 18-75), one of the loveliest images in German art, for the choir of the Church of Saint Lawrence in Nuremberg in 1517–1518. The Annunciation to Mary takes place within a wreath of roses punctuated by disks carved with scenes of her "Joys." At the top of the rosary are additional disks with her Dormition and Coronation. Mary and Saint Michael are adored and supported by angels. Their dignified figures are encased in elaborate crinkled and fluttering drapery that seems to blend with the delicate angels and to cause the entire apparition to float in the upper reaches of the choir. The sculpture continues the expressive, mystical tradition in German art, where the recitation of the rosary had become an important symbol of personal devotions.

Among the earliest German sculptors to embrace the Italian Renaissance movement was Peter Flötner (1486/95–1546). A Swiss native, Flötner became a Nuremberg citizen in 1523, on the eve of the disruptions that made his career a concentrated struggle for survival. Stylistic changes in his work just before the creation of his cast-bronze Apollo Fountain (fig. 18-76) suggest that he had studied Italian engravings or traveled to Italy about 1530. His use of mythological subjects, such as this idealized sun god–archer, signifies a perfect transition from religious patronage—the main source of earlier commissions—to secular and civic markets. He filled gaps between large commissions by producing small sculptural works for home decoration, designs for goldsmiths, and popular prints.

18-77. Hans Holbein the Younger. *Henry VIII*. c. 1540. Oil on panel, 32¹/₂ x 29¹/₂" (82.6 x 75 cm). Galleria Nazionale d'Arte Antica, Rome

Holbein used the English king's great size to advantage for this official portrait, enhancing Henry's majestic figure with embroidered cloth, fur, and jewelry to create one of the most imposing images of power in the history of art.

ENGLAND AND THE ENGLISH COURT

England, in contrast to continental Europe, was economically and politically stable enough to nourish bountiful and sustained support for the arts during the Tudor dynasty in the sixteenth century. Henry VIII (ruled 1509–1547) was known for his love of music (he was a composer of considerable accomplishment himself), but he also competed with the elegant courts of Francis I and Charles V in the visual arts. Although direct contacts with Italy became difficult after Henry's break with the Roman Catholic Church in 1534, the Tudors so favored Netherlandish, German, and French artists that a vigorous English school of painters did not emerge until the eighteenth century. English architects fared better, developing their own style, which incorporated classical features but was generally independent of direct Italian influence. Nevertheless, the first architectural manual in English, published in 1563, was written by John Shute, who had spent time in Italy. Also available were stylebooks and treatises by Flemish, French, and German architects, as well as a number of books on architectural design by the Italian architect Sebastiano Serlio.

Court Painters

A remarkable record of the appearance of the Tudor monarchs survives in portraiture. Hans Holbein the Younger, who had worked for the humanist circle around Thomas More during his first visit to London from 1526 to 1528, was appointed court painter to Henry VIII about four years after he returned to England in 1532. One of Holbein's official portraits of Henry at age forty-nine (fig. 18-77), according to the inscription on the dark background, was painted about 1540, although the dress and appearance of the king had already been established in an earlier prototype based on sketches of the king's features. Henry, who envied Francis I and attempted to outdo him in every way, imitated French fashions and even copied the French king's style of beard. Henry's huge frame—he was well over 6 feet tall and had a 54-inch waist in his maturity—is covered by the latest style of dress: a short puffed-sleeve cloak of heavy brocade trimmed in dark fur; a narrow, stiff white collar fastened at the front; and a doublet, encrusted with gemstones and gold braid, that was slit to expose his silk shirt.

Holbein was not the highest-paid painter in Henry

18-78. Attributed to Levina Bening Teerling. *Elizabeth I as a Princess*. c. 1551. Oil on oak panel, 42³/₄ x 32¹/₄" (108.5 x 81.8 cm). The Royal Collection, Windsor Castle, Windsor, England

VIII's court. That status belonged to a Flemish woman named Levina Bening Teerling, who worked in England for thirty years. The disappearance of her work is an art-historical mystery. At Henry's invitation to become "King's Paintrix," she arrived in London in 1545 from Bruges, accompanied by her husband. She maintained her court appointment until her death around 1576 in the reign of Elizabeth I. Because Levina was the granddaughter and daughter of Flemish manuscript illuminators, she is assumed to have painted mainly miniature portraits or scenes on vellum and ivory. One lifesize portrait frequently attributed to her—but by no means securely—depicts Elizabeth Tudor as a young princess (fig. 18-78). Elizabeth's pearled headcap, an adaptation of the so-called

French hood popularized by her mother, Anne Boleyn, is set back to expose the hair around her face, while the rest of the hood falls on her shoulders at the back. Her brocaded outer dress, worn over a rigid hoop, is split to expose an underskirt of cut velvet. Although her features are softened by youth and no doubt are idealized as well, her long, high-bridged nose and the unusual fullness below her small lower lip give her a distinctive appearance. The prominently displayed books were no doubt included to signify Elizabeth's well-known love of learning.

About the time Elizabeth sat for this portrait, in 1551, her half brother, the Protestant Edward VI, was king, and her half sister, Mary Tudor, was next in line for the throne. But Mary was a Catholic, and Edward and his

18-79. Anthonis Mor. *Mary Tudor*. 1554. Panel, 42⁷/₈ x 33" (108.9 x 83.8 cm). Museo del Prado, Madrid

After Mary Tudor's accession to the English throne, the Scottish Protestant Reformation leader John Knox, royal chaplain under her brother, Edward VI, fled into exile in Switzerland. In 1558, he published *The First Blast of the Trumpet against the Monstrous Regiment of Women*, expressing his view that it was against God's law for a woman to hold supreme political power. The English, however, had little problem with female rule, and public objections to it were rare, perhaps because of a strongly held belief in hereditary descent. Queen Mary I came to be known in history, however, as "Bloody Mary" for her zealous attempt to reestablish the Roman Catholic Church in England. During her reign of less than five years, 280 heretics were burned at the stake, compared with 81 during the long reign of her father, Henry VIII, and only 4 in the more than forty-four years that her half sister Elizabeth I was on the throne.

advisers were Protestants. Therefore, at Edward's death in 1553, the regent tried to proclaim Edward's cousin Jane Grey successor to the throne. The thirty-seven-year-old Mary, every bit as iron-willed and ferocious as her father, Henry VIII, called for the people's support. Within two weeks, she gained the throne. Queen Mary quickly reinstated Catholic practice, and in July 1554 she married the future King Philip II of Spain.

Her marriage portrait (fig. 18-79) is by the internationally renowned painter Anthonis Mor (1512/25–1575), who came to London in 1554 to paint Mary and Philip, perhaps as a member of Philip's retinue. Mor worked for the Habsburg aristocracy and royalty—primarily in Brussels, Augsburg, Rome, Madrid, and Lisbon, though he consid-

18-80. Nicholas Hilliard. *George Clifford, 3rd Earl of Cumberland (1558–1605)*. c. 1585–89. Watercolor on vellum on card, oval 2³/₄ x 2³/₁₆" (7.1 x 5.8 cm). The Nelson-Atkins Museum of Art, Kansas City, Missouri
Gift of Mr. and Mrs. John W. Starr through the Starr Foundation. F58-60/188

ered Utrecht home. Mary I is shown with strong, unrefined features and a bold, self-assertive look. She holds a pink Tudor rose, which symbolizes that the Tudors were the heirs of two earlier English dynasties—the houses of York, whose symbol was the white rose, and of Lancaster, whose symbol was the red rose. Mor's skill at portraying the textures of elegant materials is balanced by his ability to use a dynamic pose and engaging expression to portray a real, even if somewhat idealized, human being.

In five years, Mary died and the Protestant princess Elizabeth assumed the throne. So effective was Elizabeth's rule (1558–1603) that the last decades of the sixteenth century are called the Elizabethan age. In 1570, while Levina Teerling was still active at Elizabeth's court, Nicholas Hilliard (1547–1619) arrived in London from southwest England to pursue a career as a jeweler, goldsmith, and painter of miniatures. Hilliard never received a court appointment but worked instead on commission, creating miniature portraits of the queen and court notables, including George Clifford, third earl of Cumberland (fig. 18-80). This former admiral was a regular participant in

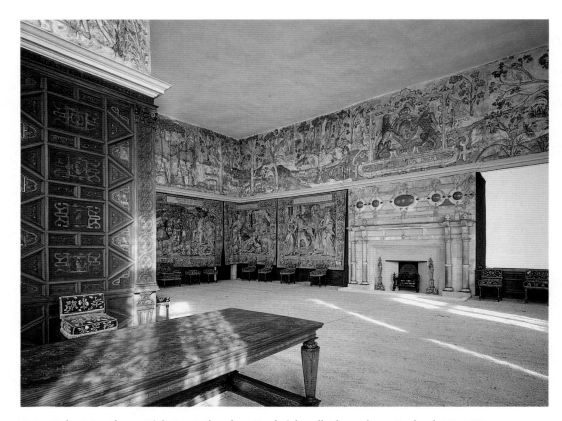

18–81. Robert Smythson. High Great Chamber, Hardwick Hall, Shrewsbury, England. 1591–97

Elizabeth, Countess of Shrewsbury, who commissioned Smythson, participated actively in the design of her houses. (For example, she embellished the roofline with her initials, *ES*, in letters 4 feet tall.) This room was designed to accommodate sixteenth-century Brussels tapestries telling the story of Ulysses, which she had bought in 1587. Other decorations shown include plaster by Abraham Smith on mythological themes, seventeenth-century Farhingale chairs, and rush matting.

WHAT THE QUEEN'S CHAMPION WORE AT THE TILTS

The medieval tradition of tilting competitions at English festivals and public celebrations continued during Renaissance times. Perhaps the most famous of these, the Accession Day Tilts, were held annually to celebrate the anniversary of Elizabeth I's coronation. The gentlemen of the court, dressed in armor made especially for the occasion, rode their horses from opposite directions, trying to strike each other with long lances. Each pair of competitors galloped past each other six times, and the judges rated their performances the way boxers are given points today. Breaking of a competitor's lance was comparable to a knockout.

The elegant armor worn by George Clifford, third earl of Cumberland, at the Accession Day Tilts has been preserved in a nearly complete state in the collection of the Metropolitan Museum of Art in New York.

In honor of the queen, the armor's surface was decorated with engraved Tudor roses and capital *E*s back to back. As the Queen's Champion from 1590 on, Clifford also wore her jeweled glove attached to his helmet as he met all comers in the courtyard of Whitehall Palace in London.

Made by Jacob Halder in the royal armories at Greenwich, the 60-pound suit of armor is recorded in the sixteenth-century *Almain Armourers Album* along with its "exchange pieces." These allowed the owner to vary his appearance by changing mitts, side pieces, or leg protectors, and also provided backup pieces if one piece was damaged.

Armor of George Clifford, 3rd Earl of Cumberland, made in the royal workshop at Greenwich, England. c. 1580–85. Steel and gold, height 5'9½" (1.77 m). The Metropolitan Museum of Art, New York

Munsey Fund, 1932 (32.130.6)

the tilts (jousts) and festivals celebrating the anniversary of Elizabeth I's ascent to the throne. In Hilliard's miniature, Cumberland wears a richly engraved and gold-inlaid suit of armor, forged for his first appearance, in 1583, at the tilts (see "What the Queen's Champion Wore at the Tilts," page 744). Hilliard had a special talent for giving his male subjects an appropriate air of courtly jauntiness and depicting them in extravagant costumes and hairstyles without making them appear foolish. Cumberland, a man of about thirty with a stylish beard, moustache, and curled hair, is humanized by his direct gaze and unconcealed receding hairline. Cumberland's motto, "I bear lightning and water," is inscribed on a stormy sky, with a lightning bolt in the form of a **caduceus** (the symbolic staff with two entwined snakes), one of his emblems.

Architecture

In the years after his 1534 break with the Roman Catholic Church, Henry VIII, as the newly declared head of the Church of England, dissolved the monastic communities in England, seized their land, and sold or gave it to favored courtiers. Many properties were bought by speculators who divided and resold them. To increase support for the Tudor dynasty, Henry and his successors created a new nobility by granting titles to rich landowners and officials. To display their wealth and status, many of these newly created aristocrats embarked on extensive building projects after about 1550. They built lavish country residences, which sometimes surpassed the French châteaux in size and grandeur.

One of the grandest of all these Elizabethan houses was Hardwick Hall, the home of Elizabeth, Countess of Shrewsbury, known as Bess of Hardwick. The redoubtable countess employed Robert Smythson (c. 1535–1614), the first English Renaissance professional architect, to build Hardwick between 1591 and 1597, when she was in her seventies.

At this time, Elizabethan architecture still reflected the late Gothic Perpendicular style, with its emphasis on severe walls and broad expanses of glass, but designers modernized the forms by replacing medieval ornament with classical details learned from architectural handbooks and pattern books. But Smythson's—and Bess's—plan for Hardwick was new. The medieval great hall became a two-story entrance hall, placed at right angles to the entrance so that other buildings could be arranged symmetrically around it—a nod to classical balance. A sequence of rooms leads to the Long Gallery and High Great Chamber (fig. 18-81), where the owners received guests, entertained, and sometimes dined.

SPAIN AND THE SPANISH COURT

Philip II, the only son of Charles V and Isabella of Portugal, preferred Spain as his permanent residence and Madrid as his capital. From an early age, Philip was a serious art collector: For more than half a century, he patronized and supported artists in Spain and abroad. During his long reign (1556–1598), the zenith of

18-82. Juan Bautista de Toledo and Juan de Herrera. El Escorial, Madrid. 1563–84. 625 x 520' (191 x 160 m). Detail from an anonymous 18th-century painting

Spanish power, Spain halted the advance of Islam in the Mediterranean and secured control of most of the Americas. Despite enormous effort and wealth, however, Philip could not suppress the revolt of the northern Netherlands, and his navy, the famous Spanish Armada, was destroyed by the English in 1588.

Architecture

Philip built El Escorial (fig. 18-82), the great monastery-palace complex outside Madrid, partly to comply with his father's direction to construct a "pantheon" in which all Spanish kings might be buried and partly to house his court and government. The basic plan was a collaboration between Philip and Juan Bautista de Toledo, Michelangelo's supervisor at Saint Peter's from 1546 to 1548, summoned from Italy in 1559. Juan Bautista's design reflected his indoctrination with Bramantean classical principles in Rome, but the king himself dictated its severity, and El Escorial's grandeur comes from its great size, excellent masonry, and fine proportions. The complex includes not only the royal residence but also the Royal Monastery of San Lorenzo and a church whose crypt served as the royal burial chamber. From Juan Bautista's death in 1567 until 1569, an Italian architect directed the project. In 1572, Juan Bautista's original assistant, Juan de Herrera, was appointed architect and immediately changed the design, adding second stories on all wings and breaking the horizontality of the main facade with a central frontispiece that resembled superimposed temple fronts. Before beginning the church, Philip solicited the advice of Italian architects—including Vignola and Palladio—and the final design was a composite of ideas that Philip approved and Herrera carried

18-83. Pompeo Leoni. *Philip II and His Family*, Church of San Lorenzo, El Escorial, Madrid. 1591–98. Bronze and enamel, lifesize

out. Although not a replica of any Italian design, the building embodies Italian classicism in its geometric clarity and symmetry and the use of superimposed orders on the temple-front facade.

Sculpture

Philip's conservative tastes in architecture were countered by his commissions and purchase of lavish paintings and sculpture to glorify his reign and adorn the interior of El Escorial. He provided so much work for the Leoni, the Milanese family of sculptors discussed earlier, that Pompeo Leoni (c. 1533–1608) finally moved to Madrid. Among his works are lifesize bronze portrait statues of Philip II and his family, placed inside the church as funerary and dynastic monuments (fig. 18-83). The group kneels, facing the main altar, in a gallery just above the private chapel where the family actually worshiped. Directly opposite is a similar family group around Charles V. Shown with Philip are his wives Maria of Portugal, Elizabeth of Valois, and Anna of Austria, as well as his son by Maria, Don Carlos. Mary Tudor is conspicuously not among them, possibly because Philip's armada had been destroyed by her half sister and successor, Elizabeth I.

Painting

The most famous painter in Spain in the last quarter of the sixteenth century was the Greek painter Domenikos Theotokopoulos (1541–1614), who arrived in 1577 after working for ten years in Italy. El Greco ("The Greek"), as

he is called, was trained as an **icon** painter in the Byzantine manner in his native Crete, then under Venetian rule. In about 1566, he went to Venice and entered Titian's shop, but he must also have closely studied the paintings of Tintoretto and Veronese. From about 1570 to 1577, he worked in Rome, apparently without finding sufficient patronage. Probably encouraged by Spanish Church officials he met in Rome, El Greco immigrated to Toledo, where he soon was given major commissions. He apparently hoped for a court appointment, but Philip II disliked the one large painting he had commissioned from the artist for El Escorial and never gave him work again. Toledo was an important cultural center, and El Greco soon joined the circle of humanist scholars who dominated its intellectual life.

An intense religious revival was under way in Spain, expressed in the impassioned preaching of Ignatius Loyola (c. 1491–1556), the founder of the Society of Jesus, or Jesuit order, as well as in the poetry of the Spanish mystics. El Greco's style—rooted in Byzantine religious art but strongly reflecting Venetian love of rich color and loose brushwork—was the ideal vehicle to express in paint the intense spirituality of the two great Spanish mystics, Teresa of Ávila (1515–1582) and her follower John of the Cross (1542–1591).

In 1586, El Greco was commissioned by the Orgaz family to paint a large canvas illustrating a legend from the fourteenth century, the *Burial of Count Orgaz* (fig. 18-84). The count had been a great benefactor of the Church, and at his funeral Saints Augustine and Stephen were said to have appeared and lowered his body into his tomb as his soul simultaneously was seen ascending to heaven. In El Greco's painting, the miraculous burial takes place slightly off-center in the foreground, while Orgaz's tiny ghostly soul is lifted by an angel along the central axis through the heavenly hosts toward the enthroned Christ at the apex of the canvas. Depicting the legend also allowed El Greco to paint a group portrait of the local aristocracy and religious notables, who fill up the space around the burial scene. El Greco placed his eight-year-old son at the lower left next to Saint Stephen and signed the painting on the boy's white kerchief. El Greco may have put his own features on the man just above the saint's head, the only one who looks straight out at the viewer.

In composing the painting, El Greco used a Mannerist device reminiscent of Rosso and Pontormo, filling up the pictorial field with figures and eliminating specific reference to the spatial setting (see figs. 18-39, 18-40). Yet he has distinguished between heaven and earth by creating a separate light source above in the figure of Christ, who sheds an otherworldly luminescence quite unlike the natural light below. The two realms are connected, however, by the descent of the light from heaven to strike the priestly figure in the white vestment at the lower right.

Late in his life, El Greco commemorated Toledo in *View of Toledo* (fig. 18-85), a topographical cityscape transformed into a mystical illusion by a stormy sky and a narrowly restricted palette of greens and grays. This

18-84. El Greco. *Burial of Count Orgaz*, Church of Santo Tomé, Toledo, Spain. 1586. Oil on canvas, 16' x 11'10" (4.88 x 3.61 m)

conception is very different from Altdorfer's peaceful, idealized *Danube Landscape* of nearly a century earlier (see fig. 18-72). If any precedent comes to mind, it is the lightning-rent sky and prestorm atmosphere in Giorgione's *The Tempest* (see fig. 18-29). In El Greco's painting, the geography and architecture of Toledo seem to have been overridden by the artist's desire to convey his emotional response to the city, his adopted home.

Classical antiquity remained fascinating to artists and patrons, but drama and intense emotions came to be expected of both artist and viewer. A new style was needed to reflect new beliefs and aspirations as the drive to discover all that could be learned about nature and the world continued and intensified, and the emotionalism and dramatic light effects of El Greco's work would be echoed by painters in the seventeenth century in Europe.

18-85. El Greco. *View of Toledo*. 1612. Oil on canvas, 47³/₄ x 42³/₄" (121 x 109 cm). The Metropolitan Museum of Art, New York

The H. O. Havemeyer Collection. Bequest of Mrs. H. O. Havemeyer, 1929 (29.100.6)

1575 CE   1625

Velázquez
Water Carrier
of Seville
c. 1619

Whitehall
Banqueting House
1619–22

Van Dyck
Charles I at the Hunt
1635

Leyster
Self-Portrait
1635

Saint Peter's Square
1656–57

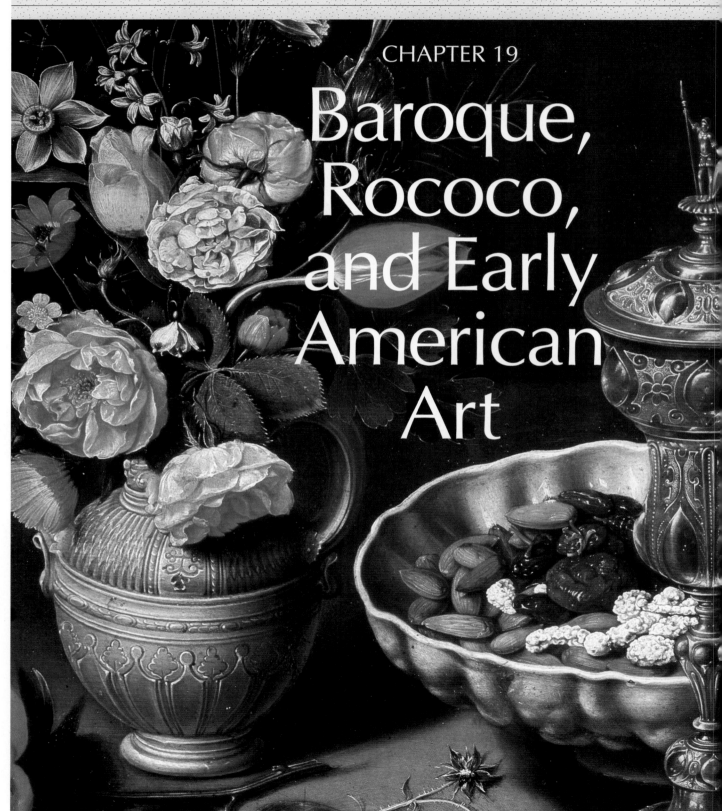

CHAPTER 19

Baroque, Rococo, and Early American Art

Parson Capen House
1683

Rigaud
Louis XIV
1701

Asam
*Angel Kneeling
in Adoration*
1732

Fragonard
The Meeting
1771–73

0   250 miles
0   250 kilometers

SCOTLAND

ENGLAND

HOLLAND

DUTCH
REPUBLIC

Groningen
Leiden
Haarlem
The Hague   Amsterdam
Delft   Utrecht
Rotterdam
Dordrecht
Middelharnis
Antwerp

Berlin

PRUSSIA

GERMANY

Woodstock

London

Düsseldorf

FLANDERS

Brussels

Staffelstein

Würzburg

Osterhofen

NORTH
AMERICA

Topsfield
Boston
Newport
New
York

ARIZONA

Tucson

Beauvais

Versailles   Paris
Sèvres

MAAS RIVER

RHINELAND

Rhine River

Danube River

BAVARIA
Munich

Melk

Vienna

Seine
River

Loire
River

AUSTRIA

ATLANTIC OCEAN

FRANCE

SWITZERLAND

Caravaggio

Parma

Venice

Genoa

Bologna

Florence

PORTUGAL

Ávila
Madrid

SPAIN

VALENCIA

Port'Ercole

Rome

Tiber River

ITALY

Naples

Seville

Mediterranean Sea

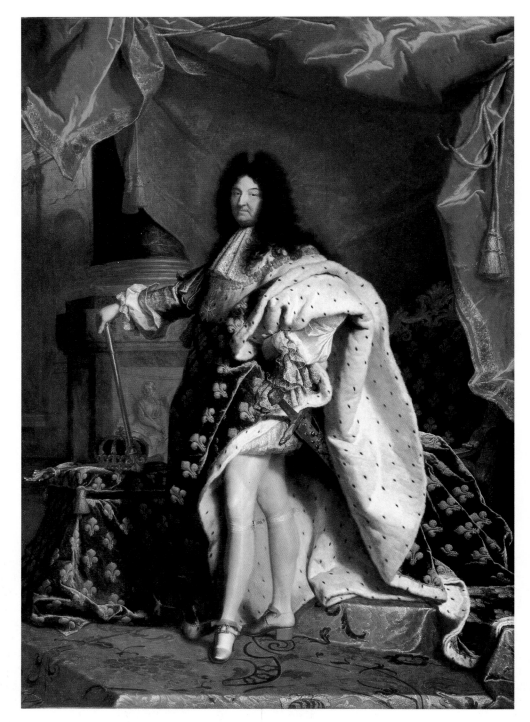

19-1.   Hyacinthe Rigaud. *Louis XIV.* 1701. Oil on canvas, 9'2" x 7'10³/₄" (2.79 x 2.4 m). Musée du Louvre, Paris

I n Hyacinthe Rigaud's 1701 portrait of Louis XIV (fig. 19-1), the richly costumed monarch known as le Roi Soleil ("the Sun King") is presented to
us by an unseen hand that pulls aside a huge billowing curtain. Showing
off his elegant legs, of which he was quite proud, the sixty-three-year-old
French monarch poses in an elaborate robe of state, decorated with gold
fleurs-de-lis and white ermine, and he wears the red-heeled built-up

shoes he had invented to compensate for his shortness. At first glance, the face under the huge wig seems almost incidental to the overall grandeur. Yet the directness of Louis XIV's gaze makes him movingly human despite the pompous pose and the distracting magnificence that surrounds him. Rigaud's genius in portraiture was always to capture a good likeness while idealizing his subjects' less attractive features and giving minute attention to the virtuoso rendering of textures and materials of the costume and setting.

Rigaud had a workshop that produced between thirty and forty such portraits a year. From his meticulous business records, we know the cost of his materials, the salaries of his employees, and the prices he charged. His portraits, for example, varied in price according to whether the entire figure was painted from life or Rigaud merely added a portrait head to a stock figure placed in a composition he had designed but his workshop had executed.

Rigaud's long career spanned a time of great change in Western art. Not only did new manners of representation emerge, but where art had once been under the patronage of the Church and the aristocracy, a kind of broad-based commercialism arose that was reflected not only by Rigaud's "mass-produced" portraits but also by the thousands of still-life painters producing works for the many households that could now afford them. These artistic changes of the seventeenth and eighteenth centuries, the Baroque period, took place in a cultural context in which individuals and organizations were grappling with the effects of religious upheaval, economic growth, political turbulence, and a dramatic explosion of scientific knowledge.

THE BAROQUE PERIOD

By the seventeenth century, Protestantism was already established firmly and irrevocably in much of northern Europe. The permanent division within Europe between Roman Catholicism and Protestantism had a critical effect on European art. In response to the Protestant Reformation of the early sixteenth century, the Roman Catholic Church had embarked in the 1550s on a program of renewal known as the Counter-Reformation. As part of the program, the Church used art to encourage piety among the faithful and to persuade those it regarded as heretics to return to the fold. Counter-Reformation art was intended to be both doctrinally correct and visually and emotionally appealing so that it could influence the largest possible audience. Both the Catholic Church and the Catholic nobility supported ambitious building and decoration projects to achieve these ends.

There was also a variety of civic projects—buildings, sculpture, and paintings—undertaken to support numerous political positions throughout Europe, and private patrons continued to commission works of art. Economic growth in most European countries helped create a large, affluent middle class eager to build and furnish fine houses and even palaces. By the late seventeenth century,

Colonial America, both North and South, was also prospering and had eager buyers for art of every type and quality. The art produced in the American colonies was closely related to, although generally distinct from, that of Europe. In both Europe and America, building projects ranged from enormous churches and palaces to stage sets for plays and ballets, while painting and sculpture varied from large religious works and history paintings to portraits, still lifes, and **genre**, or scenes of everyday life. At the same time, scientific advances forced Europeans to question how they viewed the world. Of great importance was the growing understanding that Earth was not the center of the universe but was a planet revolving around the Sun. In the eighteenth century, scientific literature became so abundant that the period has been called the Age of Enlightenment.

Within this cultural climate, Baroque and Rococo art arose and thrived. The word *baroque* has come to mean both a style with specific formal characteristics and a period in the history of art lasting from the end of the sixteenth century through the seventeenth century. Baroque, as a formal style, is characterized by open compositions in which elements are placed or move diagonally in space. A loose, free technique using rich colors and dramatic contrasts of light and dark produces what one critic called an "absolute unity" of form. Many of these formal characteristics can be seen in other non-classical styles. The term *rococo* was coined by critics who combined the Portuguese word *barroco* and the French word *rocaille* (the artificial shell or rock ornament popular for gardens) to describe the refined, fanciful, and often playful style that became fashionable in France at the end of the seventeenth century and spread throughout Europe in the eighteenth century.

Seventeenth-century art was, above all, **naturalistic**. So admired was the quality of visual verisimilitude that many painters and sculptors aimed to reproduce nature without any improvements—certainly without the idealization of classical and Renaissance styles. The English leader Oliver Cromwell supposedly demanded that his portrait be painted "warts and all." This desire for realism was inspired in part by the growing interest in the natural sciences: Biological sciences added to the artists' knowledge of human and animal anatomy and botany; physics and astronomy changed their concept of space and light. The new understanding of the relationship of Earth and the Sun reaffirmed the expressive power of light, not as an abstract emanation of the divine, as in the Middle Ages, but as a natural phenomenon to be treated with realism and drama.

Artists achieved spectacular technical virtuosity in every medium. Painters manipulated their mediums from the thinnest **glazes** to heavy **impasto**, taking pleasure in the very quality of the material. The leading artists organized their studios into veritable picture factories, without an apparent diminution of quality, for their delight in technical skill permeated their studios and artisan workshops. Artists were admired for the originality of a concept or design, and their shops produced paintings on demand—including copy after copy of popular themes or portraits. The respect for the "original," or first edition, is a modern concept; at that time, an image might be painted in several versions and more than once, but the appreciation for and importance of the work were in no way lessened as long as it was finely crafted.

The role of the viewer changed: An observer's strong personal involvement in artwork was increasingly expected. Earlier, Renaissance painters and patrons had been fascinated with the visual possibilities of perspective, but even such displays as Mantegna's ceiling fresco at Mantua (see fig. 17-66) remained an intellectual conceit. Seventeenth-century masters, on the other hand, treated viewers as participants in the art, and the space of the work included the world beyond the frame. In one example, Gianlorenzo Bernini's David hurls a rock at the giant Goliath, who seems to be standing behind the viewer (see fig. 19-7). In another, Diego Velázquez, in one of the finest imaginary spaces of all, paints himself—painting his subject—reflected in a mirror that just misses the image of the viewer (see fig. 19-34).

Spectators were expected to be emotionally as well as intellectually involved in art. In Catholic countries, representations of horrifying scenes of martyrdom or the passionate spiritual life of a mystic in religious ecstasy inspired a renewed faith. In Protestant countries, images

GREAT PAPAL PATRONS OF THE SEVENTEENTH CENTURY

Paul V (Borghese)	papacy	1605–1621
Urban VIII (Barberini)	papacy	1623–1644
Innocent X (Pamphili)	papacy	1644–1655
Alexander VII (Chigi)	papacy	1655–1667

of civic parades and city views inspired pride in accomplishment. Viewers participated in art like audiences in a theater—vicariously but completely—as the work of art reached out physically and emotionally to draw viewers into its orbit. The seventeenth-century French critic Roger de Piles described this exchange when he wrote: "True painting . . . calls to us; and has so powerful an effect, that we cannot help coming near it, as if it had something to tell us" (quoted in Puttfarken, page 55)

ROME AND THE VATICAN The patronage of the papal court and the Roman nobility dominated much of Italian art from the late sixteenth to the late seventeenth century. Major architectural projects were undertaken in Rome during this period, both to glorify the Church and to improve the city. Pope Sixtus V (papacy 1585–1590) had begun the renewal by cutting long, straight avenues between important churches and public squares, replacing some of Rome's crooked medieval streets. Sixtus also began to renovate the Vatican and its library, completed the dome of Saint Peter's Basilica (Chapter 18), built splendid palaces, and reopened one of the ancient aqueducts to stabilize the city's water supply. Several of Sixtus V's successors, especially Urban VIII (papacy 1623–1644), were also vigorous patrons of art and architecture.

Architecture

A major program of the Counter-Reformation was to embellish the Church with splendid architecture, some of which was so extravagant that the Vatican treasury was nearly bankrupted. In contrast to the Renaissance ideal of the **central-plan church**, Counter-Reformation thinking called for churches with long, wide **naves** to accommodate large congregations and the processional entry of the clergy at the Mass. In the sixteenth century, the decoration of new churches was generally modest, even austere, but seventeenth- and eighteenth-century taste favored opulent and spectacular visual effects to heighten the spiritual involvement of worshipers.

Saint Peter's Basilica in the Vatican. Half a century after Michelangelo had returned Saint Peter's Basilica to Bramante's original vision of a central-plan building, Pope Paul V (papacy 1605–1621) commissioned Carlo Maderno (1556–1629) to provide the church with a longer nave and a new facade (see fig. 19-3). The construction was begun in 1607, and everything but the facade bell towers was

ELEMENTS OF ARCHITECTURE

Baroque and Rococo Church Facades

The two facades featured here demonstrate the shift of taste in architecture—from classicistic to expressionistic—between the beginning of the Baroque and the end of the Rococo. At one end of the spectrum is Giacomo da Vignola and Giacomo della Porta's Roman Baroque facade for Il Gesù (see fig. 18-10), of about 1575–1584, which, like Renaissance and Mannerist buildings, is still firmly grounded in the clean articulation and vocabulary of classical architecture. At the other end is Pedro de Ribera's portal for the Hospicio de San Fernando (see fig.19-28), now a municipal museum in Madrid, which was designed about 150 years later, in 1722. Ribera's portal is Rococo taken to extremes, in which there is nearly a meltdown of heavily encrusted, highly elaborated ornament in the **Churrigueresque** style.

Il Gesù's facade employs the colossal order and at the same time uses huge volutes to hide and aid the transition from the wide lower stories to the narrower upper level. Verticality is also stressed by the large double pediment that rises from the wide entablature and pushes into the transition zone between stories; by the repetition of triangular pedimental forms (above the aedicula window and in the crowning gable); by the rising effect of the volutes; and most obviously by the massing of upward-moving forms at the center of the facade. Cartouches, cornices, and niches provide concave and convex rhythms across the middle zone.

The sandstone portal ensemble of the Hospicio is as much like a painting as architecture gets, and although the architect used classical elements (among them cornices, brackets, pedestals, volutes, finials, swags, and niches) and organized them symmetrically, the parts run together in a wild profusion of theatrical hollows and projections, large forms (such as the broken pediment at the roofline), and small details.

Giacomo da Vignola and Giacomo della Porta. Facade elevation of the Church of Il Gesù, Rome. c. 1575–84

Pedro de Ribera. Portal of the Hospicio de San Fernando, Madrid. 1722

Europe and North America	1575–1675	1675–1775
Italy	Il Gesù; Pope Sixtus V; Farnese ceiling; Gianlorenzo Bernini; first completely sung opera; Francesco Borromini; Caravaggio's *Entombment*; Maderno's facade of Saint Peter's; Galileo constructs and improves telescope and is tried by Inquisition; Stradivari's first violin; Reni's *Aurora*; Pope Urban VIII	Vivaldi's *Four Seasons*; Pope Clement XIV bans Jesuits
France	King Henri IV; Nicolas Poussin; Claude Lorrain; King Louis XIII (Marie de' Medici as regent); French Royal Academy founded; Descartes's *Principles of Philosophy*; wars with Spain end; King Louis XIV; Molière's *Le Misanthrope*; Louvre facade begun; enlargement of Versailles begun	Jean-Antoine Watteau; François Boucher; Honoré Fragonard; chinoiserie design; Voltaire's *Candide*; Clodion's Rococo sculpture
Spain	Annexes Portugal; Jusepe de Ribera; Francisco de Zurbarán; Diego Velázquez; King Philip IV; expulsion of Muslims; Cervantes's *Don Quijote*	King Philip V; War of Spanish Succession; Churrigueresque style emerges
Flanders	Spanish Habsburg rule; Peter Paul Rubens	
Netherlands	Frans Hals; Dutch Republic proclaims independence; Rembrandt van Rijn; Judith Leyster; landscape painting emerges; Jan Vermeer; genre painting emerges; Leeuwenhoek uses microscope	
England	Drake circumnavigates globe; Mary, Queen of Scots, executed; defeat of the Spanish Armada; Marlowe's *Dr. Faustus*; Spenser's *Faerie Queene*; Bacon's *Essays*; Shakespeare's *Macbeth*; King James Bible; Donne's *Holy Sonnets*; Jones introduces Palladianism; First English Civil War; Parliament restores monarchy; plague kills 75,000 people in London; Great Fire in London; Milton's *Paradise Lost*	Wren rebuilds Saint Paul's Cathedral; Newton's *Principia*; Locke's *Essay Concerning Human Understanding*; union of England and Scotland as Great Britain; Swift's *Gulliver's Travels*; Handel's *Messiah*; British Museum founded; Watts develops steam engine; Cook's Pacific voyages
Germany/Austria	University of Würzburg founded; Thirty Years' War begins and spreads throughout Europe	Bach's *Brandenburg* Concerti; Asam's Rococo sculpture; Tiepolo's Residenz frescoes; Mozart's first symphony; Turks besiege Vienna
North America	Raleigh colonizes Roanoke Island (N.C.); first French settlement in Nova Scotia; English settlement of Jamestown (Va.); timber architecture in Northeast and Spanish-style mission design in Southwest; first enslaved Africans arrive in Virginia; Pilgrims at Plymouth Rock; Harvard University founded; European settlers wage wars with Native Americans	Pueblo peoples rise up against Spanish; French Huguenots arrive in North America; witchcraft trials in Salem (Mass.); John Singleton Copley; Palladian-style architecture; Seven Years War; Boston Tea Party; First Continental Congress issues Declaration of Rights and Grievances; Second Continental Congress names George Washington commander in chief
World	Hideyoshi unites Japan; first printing in Peru; Christians banned in Japan; Portugal explores East Africa; Tsar Boris Godunov (Russia); Japanese capital moved to Edo (Tokyo); Taj Mahal (India); Qing dynasty (China)	Peter the Great (Russia); Moscow University founded; Afghanistan conquers Persia; Hermitage Museum founded (Russia); Catherine the Great (Russia)

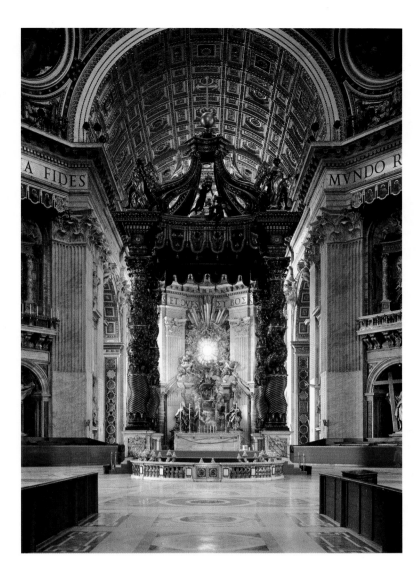

19-2. Gianlorenzo Bernini. *Baldacchino.* 1624–33. Gilt bronze, height approx. 100' (30.48 m). Chair of Peter. 1657–66. Gilt bronze, marble, stucco, and glass. Pier decorations. 1627–41. Gilt bronze and marble. Crossing, Saint Peter's Basilca, Vatican, Rome

completed by 1615. In essence, Maderno took the concept of the Gesù facade (see fig. 18-10 and "Baroque and Rococo Church Facades," page 753) and enhanced its scale to befit the most important church of the Catholic world. Saint Peter's facade, like Il Gesù's, is "stepped out" in three planes: from the corners to the doorways flanking the central entrance area, then the entrance area, then the central doorway itself (see "Saint Peter's Basilica," page 688). Similarly, the colossal orders connecting the first and second stories are flat pilasters at the corners but are fully round columns where they flank the doorways. These columns support a continuous **entablature** that also steps out—following the columns—as it moves toward the central door, which is surmounted by a triangular pediment. Similar to the Gesù facade, the pediment provides a vertical thrust, as does the superimposition of pilasters on the relatively narrow attic story above the entablature.

When Maderno died in 1629, he was succeeded as Vatican architect by his collaborator of five years, Gianlorenzo Bernini (1598–1680). Bernini was born in Naples, but his family had moved to Rome about 1605. Taught by

his father, Gianlorenzo was already a proficient marble sculptor by the age of eight. Part of his training involved sketching the Vatican collection of ancient sculpture, such as *Laocoön and His Sons* (see Introduction, fig. 9), as well as the many examples of Renaissance painting in the papal palace. Throughout his life, Bernini admired antique art and considered himself a classicist, but today we consider his art a breakthrough that takes us from the Renaissance into the Baroque style.

When Urban VIII was elected pope in 1623, he unhesitatingly gave the young Bernini the demanding task of designing an enormous bronze **baldachin**, or canopy, for the high altar of Saint Peter's. The resulting *Baldacchino* (fig. 19-2), completed in 1633, stands almost 100 feet high and exemplifies the Baroque artists' desire to combine architecture and sculpture—and sometimes painting as well—so that works no longer fit into a single category or medium. The twisted columns symbolize the union of Old and New Testaments—the vine of the Eucharist climbing the columns of the Temple of Solomon. The fanciful **Composite capitals**, combining elements of both the Ionic

19-3.   Gianlorenzo Bernini. Saint Peter's Basilica and Square, Vatican, Rome. Carlo
Moderno, facade 1607–15; Bernini, square designed c. 1656–57

Perhaps only a Baroque artist of Bernini's talents could have unified the many artistic
periods and styles that come together in Saint Peter's Basilica. The visitor today
does not see a piecing together of parts made by different builders at different times,
starting with Bramante's original design for the building in the sixteenth century, but
rather encounters a triumphal unity of all the parts in one coherent whole.

and the Corinthian orders, support an entablature with a
crowning element topped with an orb (a sphere representing the universe) and a cross (symbolizing the reign of
Christ). Figures of angels and **putti** decorate the entablature, which is hung with tasseled panels in imitation of a
cloth canopy. These symbolic elements, both architectural
and sculptural, not only mark the site of the tomb of Saint
Peter but also serve as a monument to Urban VIII and his
family, the Barberini, whose emblems—including honey-
bees and suns on the tasseled panels, and laurel leaves on
the climbing vines—are prominently displayed.

Between 1627 and 1641, Bernini and several other
sculptors, again combining architecture and sculpture,
rebuilt Bramante's crossing piers as giant **reliquaries**.
Statues of Saints Helena, Veronica, Andrew, and Longinus stand in niches below alcoves containing their relics,
to the left and right of the *Baldacchino*. Visible through
the *Baldacchino*'s columns in the apse of the church is
another reliquary, the gilded stone, bronze, and stucco
shrine made by Bernini between 1657 and 1666 for the
ancient wooden throne thought to have been used by
Saint Peter as the first bishop of Rome. The Chair of Peter

symbolized the direct descent of Christian authority from
Peter to the current pope, a belief rejected by Protestants
and therefore deliberately emphasized in Counter-
Reformation Catholicism. The chair is carried by four
theologians and is lifted farther by a surge of gilded
clouds moving upward toward the Holy Spirit in the
form of a dove adored by angels. Gilt bronze rays around
a stained-glass panel depicting a dove are lit from a window. The light penetrating the church from this window
and reflected back by the gilding creates a dazzling
effect—the sort that twentieth-century artists achieve by
resorting to electric spotlights.

At approximately the same time that he was at work
on the Chair of Peter, Bernini designed and supervised
the building of a colonnade to form a huge double **piazza** before the entrance to Saint Peter's (fig. 19-3). The
space of the open square that he had to work with was
irregular, and an Egyptian **obelisk**—a four-sided, tapered
shaft ending in a pyramid—as well as one fountain
already in place there had to be incorporated into the
overall plan. Bernini's remarkable design frames the
square with two enormous curved **porticoes**, or cov-

ered walkways, supported by Doric columns 650 feet across the long axis. These are connected to two straight porticoes that lead up a slight incline to the two ends of the church facade. Bernini spoke of his conception as representing the "motherly arms of the Church," reaching out to the world. He intended to build a third section of the colonnade closing the side of the square facing the church so that pilgrims, after crossing the Tiber River bridge and passing through narrow streets, would suddenly emerge into the enormous open space before the church. Encountered this way, the great church, colonnade, and square with its towering obelisk and monumental fountains would have been an awe-inspiring vision.

The Church of San Carlo alle Quattro Fontane.
When young Francesco Borromini (1599–1667), a nephew of the architect Carlo Maderno, arrived in Rome in 1619 from northern Italy, he entered his uncle's workshop. Later, he worked under Bernini's supervision on the decoration of Saint Peter's, and some details of the *Baldacchino* are now attributed to him.

In 1634, Borromini received his first independent commission: to design the Church of San Carlo alle Quattro Fontane (Saint Charles at the Four Fountains). From 1638 to 1641 he planned and constructed the body of this small church, although he was not given the commission for its facade until 1665. Unfinished at Borromini's death in 1667, the church was, nevertheless, completed according to his design.

San Carlo stands on a narrow tract with one corner cut off to make room for one of the four fountains that give the church its name. To fit this site, Borromini created an elongated interior space with undulating walls, set into the irregular shell of the building (fig. 19-4). The powerful sweep of the curves of these walls creates an unexpected feeling of movement, as if the walls were actually heaving in and out. Robust pairs of columns support a massive entablature, over which an oval dome seems to float as light as air. The **coffers** (inset panels in geometric shapes) filling the interior of the dome form an eccentric honeycomb of crosses, elongated hexagons, and octagons (fig. 19-5). These coffers decrease sharply in size as they approach the **apex**, or highest point, so that the dome appears to be inflating. Such devices make a visitor to the church feel as if it were a living, breathing organism.

It is difficult today to appreciate how audacious Borromini's design for this small church was. In it he abandoned the modular system of planning taken for granted by every architect since Brunelleschi (see figs. 17-33, 17-34) and worked instead from an overriding geometric scheme. Moreover, his treatment of the architectural elements as if they were malleable was unprecedented. Borromini's contemporaries understood immediately what an extraordinary innovation the church represented; the monks who had commissioned it received requests for plans from visitors from all over Europe. Although Borromini's invention had little influence on the architecture of classically minded Rome, it was widely imitated in northern Italy and beyond the Alps.

19-4. Francesco Borromini. Plan of the Church of San Carlo alle Quattro Fontane, Rome. Begun 1638

chapel · stair in tower · entrance · church cloister

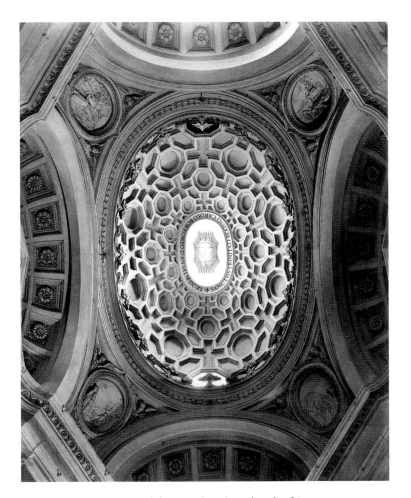

19-5. Francesco Borromini. Dome interior, Church of San Carlo alle Quattro Fontane. Begun 1638

19-6. Francesco Borromini. Facade, Church of San Carlo alle Quattro Fontane. 1665–67

Borromini's design for the facade of the same church (fig. 19-6), done more than two decades later, was as innovative as his plan for its interior had been. He turned the building's front into an undulating, sculpture-filled screen punctuated with large columns and deep niches, which create dramatic effects of light and shadow. Borromini also gave his facade a strong vertical thrust in the center by placing over the tall doorway a statue-filled niche, then a windowed niche covered with a pointed canopy, then a giant **cartouche** (an oval or circular decorative element) held up by angels carved in such high relief that they appear to hover in front of the wall. The entire facade is crowned with a **balustrade**, or railing held up by decorative posts and the sharply pointed frame of the cartouche at the center. Like the interior of the church, Borromini's facade had little effect on the work of Roman architects, but it, too, was enthusiastically imitated in northern Italy and especially in northern and eastern Europe.

Bernini's Sculpture

Gianlorenzo Bernini first became famous as a sculptor, and he continued to work as a sculptor throughout his career, for both the papacy and private clients. His *David* (fig. 19-7), made for the nephew of Pope Paul V in 1623, introduced a new type of three-dimensional composition that intrudes forcefully on the viewer's space. Inspired by Annibale Carracci's athletic figures on the Farnese ceiling, such as a Giant preparing to heave a boulder (see fig. 19-12, far end), Bernini's *David* bends at the waist and twists far to one side, ready to launch the lethal rock. Unlike Michelangelo's cool and self-confident youth (see fig. 18-20), this more mature David, with his lean, sinewy body, is all tension and determination, a frame of mind emphasized by his ferocious expression, tightly clenched mouth, and straining muscles. Bernini's energetic, twisting figure includes the surrounding space as part of the composition by implying the presence of an unseen adversary somewhere behind the viewer. Thus, the viewer becomes part of the action that is taking place at that very moment. This immediacy and the inclusion of the viewer in the work of art become an important new direction for art.

Bernini also created a new form of portrait sculpture. According to one of his biographers, it was Bernini's custom to follow his subjects' daily rounds, sketching them in various activities, trying to capture their personality as

19-7. Gianlorenzo Bernini. *David*. 1623. Marble, height 5'7"
(1.7 m). Galleria Borghese, Rome

19-8. Gianlorenzo Bernini. *Costanza Bonarelli*. c. 1635.
Marble, height 28³⁄₈" (72 cm). Museo Nazionale del
Bargello, Florence

well as appearance. His remarkable marble portraits do, indeed, seem to transcend their medium—not only in representing flesh, hair, and clothing in a lifelike way but also in catching a moment in time, communicating great immediacy and naturalness. One of Bernini's most striking portraits of this type was a bust of Costanza Bonarelli (fig. 19-8), the wife of one of his shop assistants, who was both his model and his lover. Produced about 1635, it is a superb example of Baroque naturalism. Costanza appears unaware of the sculptor. Her open collar, slightly turned head, disheveled hair, and parted lips all contribute to the effect of spontaneity.

Even after Bernini's appointment as Vatican architect in 1629, his organization of a large workshop enabled him to accept outside commissions. Beginning in 1642, he worked on designs for the decoration of the funerary chapel of Cardinal Federigo Cornaro in Carlo Maderno's Church of Santa Maria della Vittoria (fig. 19-9), dedicated to Saint Teresa of Ávila. From 1642 to 1652, Bernini covered the walls with colored marble panels, crowned with a projecting **cornice** supported with marble pilasters. Above the cornice on the back wall, the curved ceiling surrounding the window appears to dissolve into a painted vision of clouds and angels. Kneeling on what appear to

19-9. Gianlorenzo Bernini. Cornaro Chapel, Church of
Santa Maria della Vittoria, Rome. 1642–52

19-10. Gianlorenzo Bernini. *Saint Teresa of Ávila in Ecstasy.* 1645–52. Marble, height of the group 11'6" (3.5 m).
Cornaro Chapel, Church of Santa Maria della Vittoria

be balconies on both sides are portrait statues of Federigo, his deceased father, and six cardinals of the Cornaro family. Unlike the bronze portrait statues of the Spanish royal family in the Escorial (see fig. 18-84), Bernini's figures are informally posed and naturalistically portrayed. Two are reading from their prayer books; others converse; and one leans out from his seat, apparently to look at someone entering the chapel.

Framed by columns in a huge oval niche above the altar, Bernini's marble group *Saint Teresa of Ávila in Ecstasy* (fig. 19-10), created between 1645 and 1652, represents a vision described by the saint, in which an angel pierced Teresa's body repeatedly with an arrow, transporting her to a state of religious ecstasy, a sense of oneness with God. The saint and the angel, who seem to float upward on moisture-laden clouds, are cut from a heavy mass of

19-11. Gianlorenzo Bernini. Four Rivers Fountain. 1648–51. Travertine and marble. Piazza Navona, Rome. Church of Sant'Agnese by Borromini, behind the fountain

solid marble supported on a hidden pedestal and by metal bars sunk deep into the chapel wall. Bernini's skill at capturing the movements and emotions of these figures is matched by his virtuosity in simulating different textures and colors in the pure white medium of marble; the angel's gauzy, clinging draperies seem silken in contrast with Teresa's heavy woolen robe, the habit of her order. Yet Bernini effectively used the configuration of the garment's folds to convey the swooning, sensuous body beneath, even though only Teresa's face, hands, and bare feet are actually visible. The descending rays of light are of gilt bronze illuminated from above by a hidden window. Bernini's complex, theatrical interplay of the various levels of illusion in the chapel, which invites the beholder to identify with Teresa's emotion, was imitated by sculptors throughout Europe.

Bernini was at his most ingenious in his fountain designs, such as that of the Four Rivers Fountain for Rome's Piazza Navona (fig. 19-11), a popular site for festivals and celebrations. The fountain was commissioned by Pope Innocent X (papacy 1644–1655), whose family had built a palace on the piazza. Bernini, who had been publicly disgraced in 1646 when a bell tower he had begun for Saint Peter's threatened to collapse, was not invited to compete for the fountain's design. The contest was won by Francesco Borromini, who originated the

Four Rivers theme and brought in the water supply for the fountain in 1647. With the collusion of a papal relative, however, the pope saw Bernini's design. Pope Innocent X was so impressed that Bernini took over work on the fountain the next year. Executed in marble and **travertine**, a porous stone that is less costly and more easily worked than marble, the fountain was completed in 1651. In the center is a rocky hill covered with animals and vegetation, from which flow the four great rivers of the world, each representing a continent: the Ganges (Asia, facing out); the Nile (Africa, right); the Danube (Europe, left); and the Rio de la Plata (the Americas, not visible in this view). The central rock formation supports an Egyptian obelisk topped by a dove, the emblem of the pope's family. The installation of the obelisk—which weighs many tons—over the hidden collecting pool that feeds the rivers was a technical marvel that did much to reverse Bernini's disgrace over the bell-tower incident.

Illusionistic Ceiling Painting

Baroque ceiling decoration went far beyond Andrea Mantegna's early Renaissance painting in the Gonzaga ducal palace at Mantua (see fig. 17-66) or even Michelangelo's Sistine ceiling (see fig. 18-22). Many Baroque ceiling projects were done entirely in **trompe l'oeil** painting,

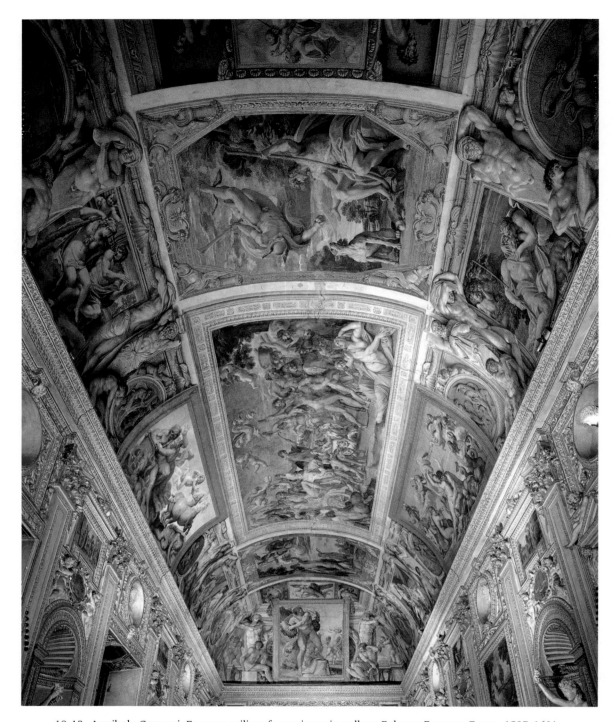

19-12. Annibale Carracci. Farnese ceiling, fresco in main gallery, Palazzo Farnese, Rome. 1597–1601

and some were complex constructions combining architecture, painting, and stucco sculpture. These grand illusionistic projects were carried out on the domes and vaults of churches, civic buildings, palaces, and villas.

The major monument of early Baroque classicism was a ceiling painted for the Farnese family in the last years of the sixteenth century. In 1597, to celebrate the wedding of Duke Ranuccio Farnese of Parma, the family decided to redecorate the **galleria** (great hall) of their immense Roman palace. The commission was given to Annibale Carracci (1560–1609), a noted painter and the

cofounder of an art academy in Bologna with his cousin, Ludovico. Annibale was assisted by his brother Agostino (1557–1602), who also worked briefly in Rome. The Farnese ceiling (fig. 19-12) is an exuberant tribute to earthly love, expressed in mythological scenes. Its primary image, set in the center of the vault, is *The Triumph of Bacchus and Ariadne*, a joyous procession celebrating the wine god Bacchus's love for Ariadne, a woman whom he rescued after her lover, Theseus, abandoned her. Carracci's illusionistic ceiling is a trompe l'oeil assemblage of framed paintings, stone sculpture, bronze medallions,

19-13. Guido Reni. *Aurora*, ceiling fresco in Casino Rospigliosi, Rome. 1613–14

and **ignudi** (nude youths) in an architectural framework, inspired by Michelangelo's Sistine ceiling. The figure types, true to their source, are heroic and muscular and are drawn with precise anatomical accuracy. But instead of Michelangelo's cool illumination and intellectual detachment, the Farnese ceiling glows with a warm light that recalls the work of the Venetian painters Titian and Veronese and seems buoyant with optimism. The ceiling was highly admired and became famous almost immediately. The Farnese family, proud of the gallery, were generous in allowing young artists to sketch the figures there, so that Carracci's classicistic masterpiece influenced Italian art well into the following century.

The most important Italian Baroque classicist after Annibale Carracci was the Bolognese artist Guido Reni (1575–1642), who briefly studied at the Carracci academy in 1595. At the academy, students were expected to study the art of the past—that is, Renaissance painting and antique classical sculpture—as well as nature. The Bolognese painters placed a high value on drawing, complex figure compositions, narrative skills, and technical expertise in both **oil** and **fresco** painting. Shortly after 1600, Reni made his first trip to Rome, where he worked intermittently before returning to Bologna in 1614. In 1613–1614, he decorated the ceiling of a garden house at a palace in Rome with his most famous work, *Aurora* (fig. 19-13). The fresco emulates the illusionistic framed mythological scenes on the Farnese ceiling, although Reni made no effort to relate his painting's space to that of the room. Indeed, *Aurora* appears to be a

framed oil painting incongruously attached to the ceiling. The composition itself, however, is Baroque classicism at its most lyrical. Apollo is shown driving the sun chariot, escorted by Cupid and the Seasons and led by the flying figure of Aurora, goddess of the dawn. The measured, processional staging and idealized forms seem to have been derived from an antique relief, and the precise drawing owes much to Annibale Carracci. But the graceful figures, the harmonious rhythms of gesture and drapery, and the intense color are all Reni's own.

Pietro Berrettini (1596–1669), called Pietro da Cortona after his hometown, carried the development of the Baroque ceiling in another direction altogether. Trained in Florence, the young artist was commissioned in the early 1630s by the Barberini family of Pope Urban VIII to decorate the ceiling of the audience hall of their Roman palace. Pietro's great fresco there, *Triumph of the Barberini* (fig. 19-14), became a model for a succession of Baroque illusionistic ceilings throughout Europe. Its subject is an elaborate **allegory**, or symbolic representation, of the virtues of the papal family. Just below the center of the vault, seated at the top of a pyramid of clouds and figures personifying Time and the Fates, Divine Providence gestures toward three giant bees surrounded by a huge laurel wreath (both Barberini emblems) carried by Faith, Hope, and Charity. Immortality offers a crown of stars, while other symbolic figures present the crossed keys and the triple-tiered crown of the papacy. Around these figures are scenes of Roman gods and goddesses, who demonstrate the pope's virtues by triumphing over the vices.

19-14. Pietro da Cortona. *Triumph of the Barberini*, ceiling fresco in the Gran Salone, Palazzo Barberini, Rome. 1633–39

Pietro, like Annibale Carracci, framed his mythological scenes with painted architecture, but in contrast to Annibale's neat separations and careful framing, Pietro partly concealed his setting with an overlay of shells, masks, garlands, and figures, which unifies the vast illusionistic space. Instead of Annibale's warm, nearly even light, Pietro's sporadic illumination, with its bursts of brilliance alternating with deep shadows, fuses the ceiling into a dense but unified whole.

Perhaps the ultimate illusionistic Baroque ceiling is *Triumph of the Name of Jesus* (fig. 19-15), which fills the vault of Il Gesù (see fig. 18-10). Originally, in the 1560s, Giacomo da Vignola had designed an austere interior for Il Gesù; but when the church was renovated a century later, the Jesuits commissioned a religious allegory to cover the plain ceiling of the nave. The fresco was painted between 1676 and 1679 by Giovanni Battista Gaulli (1639–1709), also called Baciccia. Gaulli, who came to Rome from Genoa in 1657, had worked in his youth for Bernini, from whom he absorbed a taste for drama and for multimedia effects. The elderly Bernini, who worshiped daily at Il Gesù, may well have offered his personal advice to his former assistant, and Gaulli was certainly familiar with other illusionistic paintings in Rome as well, including Pietro da Cortona's Barberini ceiling.

Gaulli's astonishing creation went beyond anything that had preceded it in unifying architecture, sculpture, and painting. Every element is dedicated to the illusion that clouds and angels have floated down through an opening in the church's vault into the upper reaches of the nave. The figures are projected as if seen from below, and the whole composition is focused off-center on the golden aura around the letters *IHS*, the monogram of Jesus and the insignia of the Jesuits. The subject is, in fact, a Last Judgment, with the Elect rising joyfully toward the name of God and the Damned plummeting through the ceiling toward the nave floor. The sweeping inclusion in the work of the space of the nave, the powerful and exciting appeal to the viewer's emotions, and the nearly total unity of visual effect have never been surpassed.

Painting on Canvas

In painting, the Baroque classicism exemplified by Carracci's Farnese ceiling and Guido Reni's *Aurora* was the logical development of mature Renaissance styles with roots in classical antiquity. This style was also popular for altarpieces and other painting on canvas. Il Guercino ("The Little Squinter," Giovanni Francesco Barbieri, 1591–1666) painted *Saint Luke Displaying a Painting of the Virgin* (see Introduction, fig. 14) for the high altar of the Franciscan church in Reggio nell'Emilia, near Bologna. In keeping with the desire for greater naturalism and relevance in religious art, Luke's symbol as an evangelist, the ox, has become a paperweight; and the painting of the Virgin and Child on Luke's easel copies a Byzantine icon believed by the Bolognese to have been painted by Luke himself. Although Protestants ridiculed the idea that paintings by Luke existed, Catholics staunchly defended their authenticity. Guercino's painting, then, is both an homage to the patron saint

19-15. Giovanni Battista Gaulli. *Triumph of the Name of Jesus,* ceiling fresco with stucco figures in the vault of the Church of Il Gesù, Rome. 1676–79

19-16. Caravaggio. *Calling of Matthew*, in the Contarelli Chapel, Church of San Luigi dei Francesci, Rome. c. 1599–1602. Oil on canvas, 11'1" x 11'5" (3.4 x 3.5 m)

of painters and a defense of the miracle-working Madonna di San Luca in his hometown. The classical architecture and idealized figures typify Bolognese **academic** art.

A more naturalistic tendency was introduced by Carracci's younger contemporary Michelangelo Merisi (1573–1610), known as Caravaggio after his birthplace in northern Italy, who arrived in Rome in 1593. At first, Caravaggio painted for a small circle of sophisticated Roman patrons. His subjects from this period include still lifes and low-life scenes featuring fortune-tellers, cardsharps, and street urchins dressed as musicians or mythological figures. The figures in these pictures tend to be large, brightly lit, and set close to the picture plane. Most of his commissions after 1600 were religious, and reactions to them were mixed. On occasion, his powerful, sometimes brutal, naturalism was rejected by patrons as unsuitable to the subject's dignity.

Caravaggio's approach has been likened to the preaching of Filippo Neri, later canonized as Saint Philip Neri (1515–1595), a priest and noted mystic of the Counter-Reformation who founded a Roman religious group called the Congregation of the Oratory. Philip Neri, called the Apostle of Rome, focused his missionary efforts on the people there, for whom he strove to make Christian history and doctrine understandable and meaningful. Caravaggio, too, interpreted his religious subjects directly and dramatically, combining intensely observed forms, poses, and expressions with strong effects of light and color. In the technique known as **tenebrism**, forms emerge from a dark background into a strong light that often falls from a single source outside the painting; the effect is that of a modern spotlight.

One of Caravaggio's earliest religious commissions, the *Calling of Matthew* (fig. 19-16), was painted around 1599–1602 for the private chapel of the Cointrel family (Contarelli in Italian) in the French community's church in Rome. The painting depicts Jesus calling the Roman tax collector Matthew to join his apostles (Matthew 9:9–13).

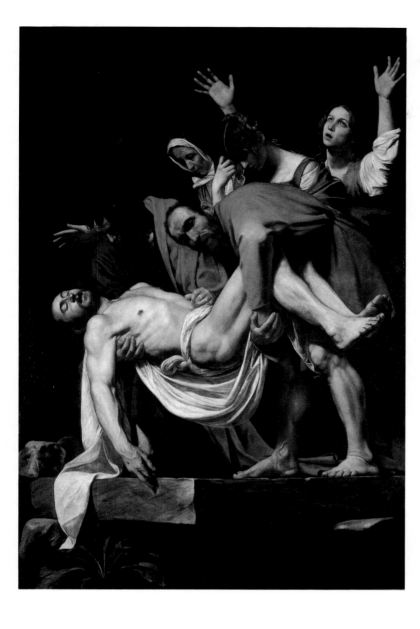

19-17. Caravaggio. *Entombment*, painted for the Vittrice Chapel, Church of Santa Maria in Vallicella, Rome. c. 1603. Oil on canvas, 9'10 1/8" x 6'7 15/16" (3 x 2.03 m). Musei Vaticani, Pinacoteca, Rome

The *Entombment* was one of many paintings confiscated from Rome's churches and taken to Paris during the French occupation by Napoleon's troops in 1798 and 1808–1814. It was one of the few to be returned after 1815 through the negotiations of Pius VII and his agents, who were assisted greatly by the Neoclassical sculptor Antonio Canova, a favorite of Napoleon's. The decision was made not to return the works to their original churches and chapels but rather to assemble them in a gallery where the general public could enjoy them. Today, Caravaggio's painting is one of the most important in the collections of the Vatican Museums.

Matthew sits at a table, counting out gold coins for a boy at the left, surrounded by overdressed young men in plumed hats, velvet doublets, and satin shirts. Nearly hidden behind another figure at the right, the gaunt-faced Jesus points dramatically at Matthew, a gesture that is repeated by the tax collector's surprised response of pointing to himself. An intense raking light enters the painting from a high, unseen source at the right and spotlights the faces of the men. For all of his naturalism, Caravaggio also used antique and Renaissance sources. Jesus' outstretched arm, for example, recalls God's gesture giving life to Adam in Michelangelo's *Creation of Adam* on the Sistine ceiling (see fig. 18-22), now restated as Jesus' command to Matthew to enter a new life as his disciple.

The emotional power of Baroque naturalism combined with a solemn, classical monumentality is embodied in Caravaggio's *Entombment* (fig. 19-17), painted in about 1603 for a chapel in Santa Maria in Vallicella, the church of Philip Neri's Congregation of the Oratory. With almost physical force, the size and immediacy of this painting strike the viewer, whose perspective is from within the burial pit into which Jesus' lifeless body is to be lowered. The figures form a large off-center triangle, within which angular elements are repeated: the projecting edge of the stone slab; Jesus' bent legs; the akimbo arm, bunched coat, and knock-kneed stance of the man on the right; and even the spaces between the spread fingers of the raised hands. The Virgin and Mary Magdalen barely intrude on the scene, which, through the careful placing of the light, focuses on the dead Jesus, the sturdy-legged laborer supporting his body at the right, and the young Saint John at the triangle's apex.

Despite the great esteem in which Caravaggio was held as an artist, his violent temper repeatedly got him into trouble. During the last decade of his life, he was frequently arrested, generally for minor offenses: throwing a plate of artichokes at a waiter, carrying arms illegally, or street brawling. In 1606, however, he killed a man in a

19-18. Atemisia Gentileschi. *Judith and Maidservant with the Head of Holofernes*. 1625. Oil on canvas, 6'1½" x 4'7" (1.84 x 1.41 m). The Detroit Institute of Arts
Gift of Leslie H. Green

fight over a tennis match and had to flee Rome. He went first to Naples, then to Malta, finding work in both places. The Knights of Malta awarded him the cross of their religious and military order in July 1608, but in October he was imprisoned for insulting one of their number, and he had to flee again. The aggrieved knight's agents tracked him to Naples in the spring of 1610 and severely wounded him; the artist recovered and fled north to Port'Ercole, where he died of a fever on July 18, 1610, at age thirty-six. Although his life was plagued by violence and cut short, Caravaggio's naturalism and tenebrist lighting influenced nearly every important European artist of the seventeenth century.

One of Caravaggio's most successful Italian followers was Artemisia Gentileschi (1593–c.1653), whose international reputation helped spread the style of Caravaggio outside Rome. Born in Rome, Artemisia first studied and worked under her father, himself a follower of Caravaggio. In 1616, she moved to Florence, where she worked for the grand duke of Tuscany and was elected, at the age of twenty-three, to the Florentine Academy of Design. As a resident of Florence and member of the academy, Artemisia was well aware of the city's identification with the Jewish hero David and heroine Judith (both subjects of sculpture by Donatello). In one of several versions of Judith triumphant over the Assyrian general Holofernes (fig. 19-18), Artemisia's brilliant use of Baroque naturalism and tenebrist effects dramatically shows Judith still holding the bloody sword and hiding the candle's light as her maid stuffs the general's head into a sack.

19-19. Artemisia Gentileschi. *La Pittura*, a self-portrait. 1630. Oil on canvas, 38 x 29" (96.5 x 73.7 cm). The Royal Collection, Windsor Castle, Windsor, England

QUARREL OF THE ANCIENTS AND THE MODERNS
When the French Royal Academy of Painting and Sculpture was established in 1648, its academicians considered ancient art the absolute standard by which to judge contemporary work. After the reorganization of the Academy in 1663 under Jean-Baptiste Colbert, students at the Academy school were instructed chiefly by drawing casts of Roman sculpture. They attended compulsory lectures on classical art theory.

In the 1680s, however, younger members of the Academy began to rebel against this rigid program. Charles Perrault, brother of architect Claude Perrault, who helped design the east facade of the Louvre, published two tracts in which he argued that artists of his own century had made great advances on the ancients, even surpassing them in some respects. Modern artists, for example, could draw on new styles and utilize linear perspective, which was unknown to the Greeks and Romans. The result was a series of papers and debates, which came to be known as the Quarrel of the Ancients and the Moderns.

Parallel to this quarrel ran another, which debated the value of color versus drawing in painting. The Academy's position was that in painting, drawing was superior to color because drawing appealed to the mind, while color appealed to the senses. Many younger members of the Academy, however, had come to admire the vivid colors of Titian, Veronese, and Rubens. Their position was that the principal aim of painting is to deceive the eye and that color achieves this deception more convincingly than drawing.

The defenders of the Academy position were called *poussinistes* in honor of the artist Nicolas Poussin (who by this time had been dead for six years), because his work was thought to embody perfectly the classical principles of subject and design. The partisans of color were called *rubénistes*, because of their admiration for the color of Rubens. Since these disputes attacked the most cherished academic orthodoxies, the fact that they happened at all caused the Academy's authority to be eroded, and by the end of the century the views of the *rubénistes* came to be generally accepted.

The portraitist and critic Roger de Piles (1635–1709), though not a member of the Academy, took a lively interest in the debate and published his views in a series of pamphlets in which he defended the primacy of color and particularly praised the work of Rubens. In *The Principles of Painting*, de Piles evaluated the most important painters on a scale of 0 to 20 in what he considered the Four Principal Parts of Painting: composition, drawing, color, and expression. He gave no score higher than 18, for no mortal artist could achieve "sovereign perfection," that is, 20 (cited in Holt, volume 2, pages 183–87). Looking at the ratings can give us a good picture of how much criteria have changed since de Piles: Few people today would rank Michelangelo below Primaticcio or give Rembrandt and Caravaggio a 6 in drawing.

The Best-Known Painters	Composition	Drawing	Color	Expression
Albrecht Dürer	8	10	10	8
Giovanni Bellini	4	6	14	0
Annibale Carracci	15	17	13	13
Leonardo	15	16	4	14
Michelangelo	8	17	4	8
Caravaggio	6	6	16	0
Parmigianino	10	15	6	6
Veronese	15	10	16	3
Poussin	15	17	6	15
Primaticcio	15	14	7	10
Raphael	17	18	12	18
Rembrandt	15	6	17	12
Rubens	18	13	17	17
Titian	12	15	18	6
Van Dyck	15	10	17	13

Throughout her life, Artemisia painted images of heroic and abused women—Judith, Susanna, Bathsheba, Esther—and she also became a famous portrait painter. In 1638, Artemisia went to England to assist her ill father, who was working for King Charles I, then she eventually settled in Naples. In 1630, Artemisia painted *La Pittura*, an allegorical self-portrait (fig. 19-19). The image of a woman with palette and brushes, richly dressed, and wearing a gold necklace with a mask pendant comes from a popular sourcebook for such images, the *Iconologia* by Cesare Ripa, which maintains that the mask imitates the human face, as painting imitates nature. The gold chain symbolizes "the continuity and interlocking nature of painting, each man learning from his master and continuing his master's achievements in the next generation" (cited in E. Maser, no. 197). Thus, Artemisia's self-portrait not only commemorates her profession but also pays tribute to her father.

FRENCH BAROQUE
The early seventeenth century was a difficult period in France, marked by almost continuous foreign and civil wars. The assassination of King Henri IV in 1610 left France in the hands of the queen, Marie de' Medici (regency 1610–1624), as regent for her nine-year-old son, Louis XIII

(ruled 1610–1643). When Louis came of age, the brilliant and unscrupulous Cardinal Richelieu became chief minister and set about increasing the power of the Crown at the expense of the French nobility. The death of Louis XIII again left France with a child king, the five-year-old Louis XIV (ruled 1643–1715). His mother, Anne of Austria, became regent, with the assistance of another powerful minister, Cardinal Mazarin. At Mazarin's death in 1661, Louis XIV (see fig. 19-1) began his long personal reign, assisted by yet another able minister, Jean-Baptiste Colbert.

An absolute monarch whose reign was the longest in European history, Louis XIV expanded royal art patronage, making the French court the envy of every ruler in Europe. In 1635, Cardinal Richelieu founded the French Royal Academy to compile a definitive dictionary and grammar of the French language. In 1648, the Royal Academy of Painting and Sculpture was founded, which, as reorganized by Colbert in 1663, maintained strict control over the arts (see "Quarrel of the Ancients and the Moderns," page 769). Although it was not the first European arts academy, none before it had exerted such dictatorial authority—an authority that lasted in France until the late nineteenth century. Membership in the Academy assured an artist of royal and civic commissions and financial success, but many talented artists did well outside it.

Palace Architecture and Its Decoration

French architecture developed along classical lines in the second half of the seventeenth century under the influence of François Mansart (1598–1666) and Louis Le Vau (1612–1670). When the Royal Academy of Architecture was founded in 1671, its members developed guidelines for architectural design based on the belief that mathematics was the true basis of beauty. Their chief sources for ideal models were the books of Vitruvius (see "The Vitruvian Man," page 692), Vignola (see figs. 18-10, 18-7), and Palladio (see fig. 18-37).

In 1668, Louis XIV began to enlarge the small château built by Louis XIII at nearby Versailles, where he eventually moved his entire court. The designers of the palace and garden complex at Versailles (fig. 19-20) were Le Vau, Charles Le Brun (1619–1690), and André Le Nôtre (1613–1700), who planned the gardens. For both political and sentimental reasons, the old Versailles château was left standing, and the new building went up around it. This project consisted of two phases: the first additions by Le Vau, begun in 1668; and an enlargement completed after Le Vau's death by his successor, Jules Hardouin-Mansart (1646–1708), from 1670 to 1685.

In the hands of Le Nôtre, the terrain around the palace became an extraordinary work of art and a visual delight for its inhabitants. The garden designer's neatly contained stretches of lawn and broad, straight vistas seemed to stretch to the horizon, while the formal gardens at the rear of the palace (see the center part of fig. 19-20) became an exercise in precise geometry. Broad intersecting paths separate reflecting pools and planting beds, called embroidered **parterres** for their colorful flower patterns. The entire layout, which includes a mock grotto (cave) and a theater, is accented by fountains, stone sculpture, and trimmed shrubs and small trees. From these gardens, a series of terraces descends to controlled, shaped, wooded areas and the mile-long Grand Canal. Classically harmonious and restful in their symmetrical, geometric design, the Versailles gardens are Baroque in their vast size and extension into the surrounding coun-

BAROQUE GARDEN DESIGN Garden designers had to unify diverse elements—buildings, pools, monuments, plantings, natural land formations—into a coherent whole. A wealthy patron might order a garden that extended over many acres. Thoughtful designers like Le Nôtre succeeded so well in ordering the vast expanses of palace gardens and park at Versailles that his plan, using broad straight avenues radiating from a series of round focal points, inspired urban designers as well as landscape architects. An urban planner had to consider the means by which people would get from home to places of work or recreation. Pierre-Charles L'Enfant, in his plan for Washington, D.C., of 1791, integrated the French radiating avenue design with the ancient city grid plan for housing blocks. The grand avenues of Wash-

Earliest printed version of L'Enfant's plan for the city of Washington (published in *Universal Asylum and Columbian Magazine*, Philadelphia, March 1792).

ington, linking the U.S. Capitol to the Washington Monument and beyond, as well as all the avenues of the states passing through traffic circle after circle, bring some of the grandeur of Louis XIV's aristocratic Versailles into the United States capital.

19-20. Louis Le Vau and Jules Hardouin-Mansart. Palais de Versailles, Versailles, France. Gardens by André Le Nôtre. 1668–85

19-21. Louis Le Vau and Jules Hardouin-Mansart. Central block of the garden face, Palais de Versailles

tryside (see "Baroque Garden Design," page 770).

Le Vau's successor, Hardouin-Mansart, was responsible for the addition of the long lateral wings and the renovation of Le Vau's central block on the garden side to match these wings (fig. 19-21). The three-story elevation has a lightly **rusticated** ground floor, a main floor lined with enormous arched windows separated by Ionic pilasters, an attic level whose rectangular windows are also flanked by pilasters, and a flat, terraced roof. The overall design is a sensitive balance of horizontals and verticals relieved by a restrained overlay of regularly spaced projecting blocks with open, colonnaded porches.

19-22. Jules Hardouin-Mansart and Charles Le Brun. Hall of Mirrors, Palais de Versailles. Begun 1678

In the seventeenth century, mirrors and clear window glass were enormously expensive. To furnish the Hall of Mirrors, hundreds of glass panels of manageable size had to be assembled into the proper shape and attached with "glazing bars," which became part of the decorative pattern of the vast room.

In his renovation of Le Vau's original garden facade in the center block, Hardouin-Mansart enclosed the previously open gallery on the main level, which is about 240 feet long. Architectural symmetry was achieved by lining the interior wall opposite the windows with Venetian glass mirrors—extremely expensive in the seventeenth century—the same size and shape as the arched windows, thus creating the famed Hall of Mirrors (fig. 19-22). The mirrors reflect the natural light from the windows and give the impression of an even larger space. In a tribute to Carracci's Farnese ceiling (see fig. 19-12), Le Brun decorated the vaulted ceiling with paintings glorifying the

reign of Louis XIV. In 1642, Le Brun had studied in Italy, where he came under the influence of the classical style of his compatriot Nicolas Poussin, discussed later in this chapter. Stylistically, Le Brun tempered the more exuberant Baroque ceiling decorations he had seen in Rome with Poussin's classicism to create spectacular decorations. The underlying theme for the design and decoration of the palace was the glorification of the king as Apollo the Sun God, with whom Louis was identified as the Sun King. Louis XIV thought of the duties of kingship, including its pageantry, as a solemn performance, so it was most appropriate that Rigaud's portrait of him shows him

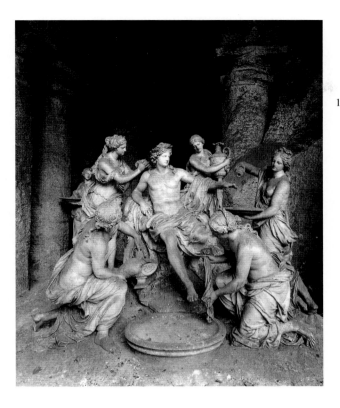

19-23. François Girardon.
*Apollo Attended by the
Nymphs of Thetis,*
from the Grotto of Thetis,
Palais de Versailles,
Versailles, France.
c. 1666–72. Marble,
lifesize. Original setting
destroyed in 1684; re-
installed in a different
configuration in 1778

presented on a raised, stagelike platform, with a theatrical curtain (see fig. 19-1). Versailles was the splendid
stage on which this grandiose drama was played.

Sculpture

In the seventeenth century, French taste in sculpture
tended to favor classicizing works, whose inspiration was
drawn from antiquity and from the Italian Renaissance. A
highly favored sculptor in this classical style, François
Girardon (1628–1715), had studied the monuments of
classical antiquity in Rome in the 1640s. He had worked
with Le Vau and Le Brun earlier and now contributed to
the decoration of Versailles. In keeping with the palace's
repeated identification of Louis XIV with Apollo, he created the group *Apollo Attended by the Nymphs of Thetis* (fig.
19-23), executed in about 1666–1672, to be displayed in
a classical arched niche in the Grotto of Thetis, named
after a sea nymph beloved by the Sun god. The original
grotto was destroyed in 1684 and was replaced by the
present cavelike setting in 1778. The visitor looks into
Thetis's undersea grotto and sees Apollo resting after his
day's journey across the heavens while nymphs wash his
tired body. All these idealized figures are based on Classical prototypes; the hair and features in particular reflect
Roman sculpture.

Painting

French seventeenth-century painting was much affected
by what was happening in Italian art. The lingering Mannerism of the sixteenth century gave way as early as the
1620s to Baroque classicism and **Caravaggism**—the use
of strong **chiaroscuro** and raking light, and the placement
of large-scale figures in the foreground. These Italianate
styles found royal favor, and native French artists also
established successful personal styles. The painters
Claude Gellée (called Claude Lorrain, or simply Claude,
1600–1682) and Nicolas Poussin (1594–1665) worked for
French patrons and significantly influenced other French
artists, although they both pursued their careers in Italy.
Claude and Poussin were classicists in that neither
recorded nature as he found it but instead organized natural elements and figures into idealized compositions.
Both were influenced by Annibale Carracci and somewhat
by Venetian painting, yet each evolved an unmistakable
personal style that conveyed an entirely different mood
from that of their sources and from each other. In the second half of the seventeenth century, the French Academy
took Poussin's paintings and notes on painting as a final
authority. Thereafter, whether as a model to be followed
or one to be reacted against, Poussin influenced French art.

Claude went to Rome in 1613 and studied with a specialist in harbor paintings, which inspired his later enthusiasm for that subject. He dedicated himself to painting
landscapes and harbor views with small figures that activated the space and provided a narrative subject. He was
fascinated with light, and his works are often studies of
the effect of the rising or the setting sun on colors and the
atmosphere. His working method included making many
sketches from nature, which he later referred to while
composing in his studio. A favorite and much imitated
device was to place one or two large objects in the foreground—a tree, building, or hill—past which the viewer's
eye enters the scene and proceeds, often by zigzag paths,
into the distance.

19-24. Claude Lorrain. *Landscape with Merchants.* c. 1630. Oil on canvas, 38¼ x 56½" (97.2 x 143.6 cm). National Gallery of Art, Washington, D.C.
Samuel H. Kress Collection

In his *Landscape with Merchants* (fig. 19-24), of about 1630, Claude presents an idyllic scene in which elegant men proffer handsome goods to passersby as the sun rises on a serene world. Past the framing device of huge trees in the left and busy foreground, the eye moves unimpeded into the open middle ground over gleaming water to arrive at a mill and waterwheel, then on to a hill-top tower illuminated by the rising sun. Along the shore is a walled city, luminous in the early morning haze. Pale blue mountains provide a final closure in the far distance.

Poussin, like Claude, was an important history painter and also created landscapes with small figures, but his effect is different. His *Landscape with Saint John on Patmos* (fig. 19-25), from 1640, is the epitome of the orderly, arranged classical landscape. Poussin created a consistent perspective progression from the picture plane back into the distance through a clearly defined foreground, middle ground, and background. These zones are marked by alternating sunlight and shade, as well as by their architectural elements. Huge, tumbled classical ruins fill the foreground overshadowing the saint, who concentrates on his writing of the Book of Revelation. In the middle distance are a ruined temple and an obelisk, and the round building in the distant city is Hadrian's Tomb, which Poussin knew from Rome. Precisely placed trees, hills, mountains, water, and even clouds take on a solidity of form that seems almost as structural as architecture. The reclining saint and the eagle, his symbol, seem almost incidental to this perfect

landscape. The triumph of the rational mind takes on moral overtones. The subject of Poussin's painting is in effect the balance and order of nature rather than the story of Saint John the Evangelist.

One of Caravaggio's most important followers in France, Georges de La Tour (1593–1652), received major royal and ducal commissions and became court painter to King Louis XIII in 1639. La Tour may have traveled to Italy in 1614–1616, and in the 1620s he almost certainly visited the Netherlands, where Caravaggio's style was being enthusiastically emulated. Like Caravaggio, Georges de La Tour filled the foreground of his canvases with monumental figures; but in his work, Caravaggio's detailed naturalism has given way to a simplified setting and a light source within the picture so intense that it often seems to be the real subject of the painting. In his painting *The Repentant Magdalen* (fig. 19-26), the light emanates from a candle. The hand acts as a device to establish a foreground plane, and the compression of the figure within the pictorial space leads to a sense of intimacy. The light is the unifying element of the painting. Hidden as it is behind a human skull, it is the essential conveyor of mood, a meditation on human frailty and vanity.

A strange sense of foreboding and enigmatic meaning pervades the paintings of the Le Nain brothers, Antoine (c. 1588–1648), Louis (c. 1593–1648), and Mathieu (1607–1677). Although the brothers were working in Paris by about 1630, little else is known about their lives and careers. Because they collaborated closely with each

19-25. Nicolas Poussin. *Landscape with Saint John on Patmos*. 1640. Oil on canvas, 40 x 53¹/₂"(101.8 x 136.3 cm). The Art Institute of Chicago
A. A. Munger Collection, 1930.500

19-26. (right) Georges de La Tour. *The Repentant Magdalen*. c. 1640. Oil on canvas, 44¹/₂ x 36¹/₂" (113 x 92.7 cm). National Gallery of Art, Washington, D.C.
Alisa Mellon Bruce Fund

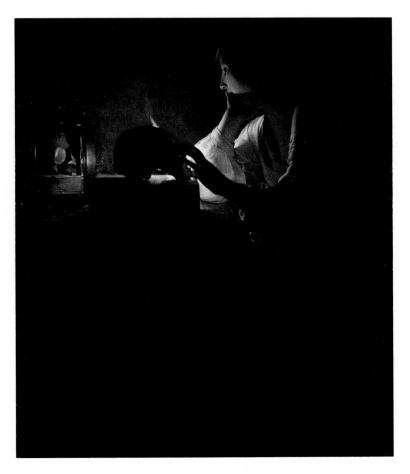

19-27. Antoine Le Nain. *The Village Piper*. 1642. Oil on copper, 8³/₈ x 11¹/₂" (21.3 x 29.2 cm). The Detroit Institute of Arts
City of Detroit Purchase

other, art historians have only recently begun to distinguish their individual styles. They did produce a few history paintings, but their specialty was **genre**. *The Village Piper* (fig. 19-27), of 1642, by Antoine Le Nain, is typical of the brothers' work. Peasant children gather around the figure of a musician. The simple homespun garments and undefined setting turn the painting into a study in neutral colors and rough textures, with soft young faces that contrast with the old man, who seems lost in his music.

Hyacinthe Rigaud (1659–1743), trained by his painter-father, won the Royal Academy's prestigious Prix de Rome in 1682, which would have paid his expenses for study at the Academy's villa in Rome. Rigaud, however, rejected the prize and opened his own Paris studio. After painting a portrait of Louis XIV's brother in 1688, he became a favorite of the king himself. One of his best-known portraits—one representing the height of royal propaganda—is the one of the Sun King painted in 1701, with which we opened the chapter (see fig. 19-1). Although he was well known and popular—and quite influential to later French portraitists—Rigaud was far removed from both the classicizing and the Caravaggesque influences at work on the other French artists.

SPANISH BAROQUE

Spain's Habsburg kings in the seventeenth century—Philip III, Philip IV, and Charles II—saw the decline of the Spanish empire. Agriculture, industry, and trade all suffered, and there were repeated local rebellions, culminating in 1640, when Portugal reestablished its independence. The Spanish Habsburg kings controlled the Kingdom of Naples (all of southern Italy), a rich Catholic province, and the Netherlands, a hotbed of political unrest after the Reformation that became a battlefield. Spain gave up any attempt to hold the north and allowed the once thriving southern Flemish cities to stagnate. Thus, Amsterdam grew into one of the wealthiest cities of Europe, while the once powerful Antwerp declined. The Dutch Republic became an increasingly serious threat to Spanish trade and colonial possessions. Furthermore, what had seemed an endless flow of gold and silver from the Americas diminished, as precious-metal production in Bolivia and Mexico lessened. Despite the decline of the Habsburgs' Spanish empire, seventeenth-century writers and artists produced much of what is considered the greatest Spanish literature and art, and the century is often called the Spanish Golden Age.

Architecture

Turning away from the severity displayed in the sixteenth-century monastery-palace the Escorial (see fig. 18-82), Spanish architects again embraced the lavish decoration that had characterized their art since the fourteenth century. The profusion of ornament typical of later Moorish and Gothic architecture in Spain swept back into fashion in the work of a family of architects and sculptors named Churriguera. The style, known as **Churrigueresque**, found its most exuberant expression in the work of eighteenth-century architects such as Pedro de Ribera (c. 1681–1742) and in the architecture of colonial Mexico and Peru. Ribera's 1722 facade for the Hospicio de San Fernando is typical (see "Baroque and Rococo Church Facades," page 753). The street facade is a severe brick structure with an extraordinarily exuberant sculptured

19-28. Pedro de Ribera. Portal of the Hospicio de San Fernando, Madrid. 1722

portal (fig. 19-28). Like a huge altarpiece, the portal soars upward, the roofline in segmental (semicircular) and triangular pediments and breaking through in a dramatic broken pediment. The structural forms of classical architecture are transformed into projecting and receding layers overlaid with foliage. Carved curtains loop back as if to reveal the doorway, and more drapery surrounds the central niche with figure of the hospital's patron saint, Ferdinand. This florid style was carried by the conquistadores to the Americas, where it forms the basis of a splendid colonial architecture (see fig. 19-85).

Painting

The primary influence on Spanish painting in the fifteenth century had been the art of Flanders, and in the sixteenth, it had been the art of Florence and Rome. Seventeenth-century Spanish painting was characterized by an ecstatic religiosity combined with intense realism whose surface details emerge from the deep shadows of tenebrism—as it was profoundly influenced by Caravaggio's powerful art. This influence is not surprising, since the Kingdom of Naples was in fact ruled by Spanish monarchs, and contact between Naples and the Iberian peninsula was strong and productive. First to Rome, then to Naples, came the young Spanish painter Jusepe Ribera (1591–1652) and there he remained, also known as Lo Spagnoletto ("the Little Spaniard"). Ribera combined the classical and Caravaggesque styles he had learned in Rome, and after he settled in Naples in 1620,

19-29. Jusepe de Ribera. *The Holy Family with Saint Anne and Saint Catherine of Alexandria.* 1648. Oil on canvas, 82¹/₂" x 60³/₄" (2.1 x 1.54 m). Metropolitan Museum of Art, New York
Samuel D. Lee Fund, 1934 (34.73)

19-30. Francisco de Zurbarán. *Saint Serapion.* 1628. Oil on canvas, 47¹/₂ x 40³/₄" (120.7 x 103.5 cm). Wadsworth Atheneum, Hartford, Connecticut
Ella Gallup Sumner and Mary Catlin Sumner Collection

he created a new Neapolitan—and eventually Spanish— style: Ribera provided a link between Caravaggio in Italy and two major painters in Spain, Zurbarán and Velázquez.

In his painting of the Holy Family (fig. 19-29), Ribera for his central figures adopted the Renaissance use of primary colors—red, blue, and yellow—and idealized faces and figures, but also highlighted them with dramatic tenebrism and framed them with intensely realistic aged faces and still lifes of roses, fruit, and a breadbasket. Here Ribera emphasizes family values not only in the tender mother-child relationship and the lovely, adoring Saint Catherine, but also in the framing background figures— the Virgin's own mother, Saint Anne, who offers a rose to the Christ Child (its thorns hinting at the crown of thorns to come), and Mary's husband, Joseph, whose commanding presence rises protectively over the young mother and child. During the seventeenth century, under Counter-Reformation influence, Saint Joseph assumed a new role as strong head of household and was extolled as a masculine role model. Saint Catherine's ecstatic vision of her mystical marriage to Christ, like the ecstasy of Saint Teresa (see fig. 19-10), also reinforces the importance of personal religious experience and intuitive knowledge.

Francisco de Zurbarán (1598–1664) is closely associated with the monastic orders for whom he executed his major commissions. Little is known of his early years before 1625, but he was greatly influenced by the Caravaggesque taste prevalent in Seville. From it he evolved his own distinctive style, incorporating a Spanish taste for abstract design, as in his 1628 *Saint Serapion* (fig. 19-30). Serapion was a member of the thirteenth-century Mercedarians, a Spanish order founded to rescue the Christian prisoners of the Spanish Moors. The work portrays his martyrdom after he had allowed himself to be exchanged for Christian captives. The dead man's pallor, his rough hands, and the coarse ropes emerge from the off-white of his creased Mercedarian habit, its folds carefully arranged in a pattern of highlights and varying depths of shadow. The only colors are the red and gold of the insignia. The effect of this composition, almost timeless in its stillness, is that of a tragic still life.

Late in the sixteenth century, Spanish artists developed a significant interest in paintings of artfully arranged objects rendered with intense attention to detail. Juan Sánchez Cotán (1561–1627) was one of the earliest painters of these pure still lifes in Spain. His *Still Life with*

Quince, Cabbage, Melon, and Cucumber (fig. 19-31), of about 1602, is a prime example of the characteristic Spanish trompe l'oeil rendering of an artificially composed still life. Sánchez Cotán's composition plays off the irregular, curved shapes of the fruits and vegetables against the angular geometry of the setting. His precisely ordered subjects, suspended from strings in a long arc from the upper left to the lower right, are set in a strong light against an impenetrable dark background. This highly artificial arrangement exemplifies a Spanish fascination with spatial ambiguity; it is not clear whether the seemingly airless space is a wall niche or a window ledge, or why these objects have been arranged in this way.

Diego Rodríguez de Silva y Velázquez (1599–1660), the greatest painter to emerge from the Caravaggesque school of Seville and one of the most acclaimed painters of all time, entered Seville's painters' guild in 1617. Like Ribera, he was influenced at the beginning of his career by Caravaggesque tenebrism and naturalism. During his early years, he painted figural works set in taverns, markets, or kitchens, showing still lifes of various foods and kitchen utensils. Velázquez was devoted to studying and sketching from life, and the model for the superb *Water Carrier of Seville* (fig. 19-32), of about 1619, was a well-

19-31. Juan Sánchez Cotán. *Still Life with Quince, Cabbage, Melon, and Cucumber.* c. 1602. Oil on canvas, 27¹⁄₈ x 33¹⁄₄" (68.8 x 84.4 cm). San Diego Museum of Art
Gift of Anne R. and Amy Putnam

19-32. Diego Velázquez. *Water Carrier of Seville.* c. 1619. Oil on canvas, 41¹⁄₂ x 31¹⁄₂" (105.3 x 80 cm). Wellington Museum, London

In the oppressively hot climate of Seville, Spain, where this painting was made, water vendors walked the streets selling their cool liquid from large clay jars like the one in the foreground. In this scene, the clarity and purity of the water are proudly attested to by its seller, who offers the customer a sample poured into a glass goblet. The jug contents were usually sweetened by the addition of a piece of fresh fruit or a sprinkle of aromatic herbs.

19-33. Diego Velázquez. *The Surrender at Breda (The Lances)*. Before April 1635. Oil on canvas, 10'⅞" x 12'½"
(3.07 x 3.67 m). Museo del Prado, Madrid

known Sevillian water seller. Like Sánchez Cotán, Velázquez arranged the elements of his paintings with almost mathematical rigor. The objects and figures allow the artist to exhibit his virtuosity in rendering sculptural volumes and contrasting textures illuminated by dramatic natural light, which reacts to the surfaces: reflecting off the **glazed** waterpot at the left and the matte-, or dull-, finished jug in the foreground; being absorbed by the rough wool and dense velvet of the costumes; and reflecting, being refracted, and passing through the clear glass of and the waterdrops on the jug's skin.

In 1623, Velázquez moved to Madrid, where he became court painter to young King Philip IV (ruled 1621–1665), a comfortable position that he maintained until his death in 1660. The artist's style evolved subtly but significantly over his long career. The Flemish painter Peter Paul Rubens, during a 1628–1629 diplomatic visit to the Spanish court, convinced the king that Velázquez should visit Italy, which Velázquez did in 1629–1631 and again in 1649–1651, thus being exposed to Italian painting of that time.

In the great history painting *The Surrender at Breda* (fig. 19-33), Velázquez treats the theme of triumph and conquest in an entirely new way, unlike the traditional gloating military propaganda. Years earlier, in 1625, the duke of Alba, the Spanish governor, had defeated the Dutch at Breda. In Velázquez's imagination, the opposing armies stand on a hilltop overlooking a vast valley where the city of Breda burns and soldiers are still deployed. The Dutch commander hands over the keys of Breda to the victorious Spanish commander. The entire exchange seems extraordinarily gracious; the painting represents a courtly ideal of gentlemanly conduct. The victors stand at attention, holding their densely packed lances upright—giving the painting the popular name *The Lances*—while the defeated Dutch, a motley group, stand out of order, with pikes and banners drooping.

In *The Lances*, Velázquez displays his ability to arrange a large number of figures into an effective narrative composition. Portraitlike faces, meaningful gestures, and brilliant control of color and texture convince us of the reality of the scene. The landscape painting is almost startling. Across the huge canvas, Velázquez paints an entirely imaginary Netherlands in greens and blues worked with flowing, liquid brushstrokes. The silvery light forms a background for dramatically silhouetted figures and weapons. Velázquez reveals a breadth and intensity unsurpassed in his century that would inspire modern artists from Manet to Picasso.

Although complex compositions were characteristic of many Velázquez paintings, perhaps his most striking and enigmatic work is the enormous multiple portrait, nearly 10½ feet tall and 9 feet wide, known as *Las*

19-34. Diego
Velázquez.
*Las Meninas
(The Maids of
Honor)*. 1656.
Oil on canvas,
10'5" x 9'1/2"
(3.18 x 2.76 m).
Museo del
Prado, Madrid

19-35. Diego Velázquez. Detail of *Las Meninas (The Maids of Honor)*

Meninas (The Maids of Honor) (fig. 19-34). Painted in 1656, near the end of the artist's life, this painting continues to reveal its creator's complex conception. Like Caravaggio's *Entombment* (see fig. 19-17), it draws the viewer directly into its action, for the viewer is standing, apparently, in the space occupied by King Philip and his queen, whose reflections can be seen in the large mirror on the back wall. The central focus, however, is on the couple's five-year-old daughter, the Infanta (Princess) Margarita, surrounded by her attendants, most of whom are identifiable portraits.

A cleaning of *Las Meninas* in 1984 revealed much about Velázquez's methods. He used a minimum of underdrawing, building up his forms with layers of loosely applied paint and finishing off the surfaces with dashing highlights in white, lemon yellow, and pale orange. Velázquez tried to depict the optical properties of light rather than using it to model volumes in the classical manner. While his technique captures the appearance of light on surfaces, at close inspection his forms dissolve into a maze of individual strokes of paint (fig. 19-35).

There has been no consensus on exactly what Velázquez depicted in this monumental painting. Yet, it does not matter whether the painting is meant to show the king and queen while the others look on or to capture the royal pair stepping into the artist's studio just as he is tak-

19-36. Peter Paul Rubens. *The Raising of the Cross*, painted for the Church of Saint Walpurga, Antwerp, Belgium. 1609–10. Oil on canvas, center panel 15'1⅞" x 11'1½" (4.62 x 3.39 m); each wing 15'1⅞" x 4'11"(4.62 x 1.52 m). Cathedral of Our Lady, Antwerp

ing a break from painting the princess. Throughout his life, Velázquez had sought acclaim for himself and for his art. *Las Meninas* seems to have been a personal statement in its own day, not a true court portrait. Dressed as a courtier, the Order of Santiago on his chest, and the keys of the palace in his sash, Velázquez proclaims the dignity and importance of painting as one of the liberal arts.

FLEMISH BAROQUE After a period of relative autonomy from 1598 to 1621 under a Habsburg regent, Flanders returned to direct Spanish rule and remained predominantly Catholic. Antwerp, the capital city and major arts center, gradually recovered from the turmoil of the sixteenth century, and artists of great talent flourished there, establishing international reputations that brought them important commissions from foreign patrons. During the seventeenth century, however, the port silted up and, as in Bruges a century earlier, trade fell off until finally the city was financially destroyed.

Peter Paul Rubens (1577–1640), whose painting has become synonymous with Flemish Baroque, was born in Germany, where his father, a Protestant, had fled from his native Antwerp to escape religious persecution. In 1587, after her husband's death, Rubens's mother and her children returned to Antwerp and to Catholicism. After a youth spent in poverty, Rubens decided in his late teens to become an artist. He was accepted into the Antwerp painters' guild at age twenty-one, a testament to his energy, intelligence, and determination.

In 1600, Rubens left for Italy, taking with him a pupil, whose father may have paid for the trip. While he was in Venice, his work came to the attention of an agent for the duke of Mantua, and Rubens was offered a court post. His activities on behalf of the duke over the next eight years did much to prepare him for the rest of his long and successful career. Other than designs for court entertainments and occasional portraits, the duke never acquired a single original work of art by Rubens. Instead, he had him copy famous paintings in collections all over Italy to add to the ducal collection.

Rubens visited every major Italian city, went to Madrid as the duke's emissary, and spent two extended periods in Rome, where he studied the great works of Roman antiquity and the Italian Renaissance. While in Italy, Rubens studied the work of two contemporaries, Caravaggio and Annibale Carracci. Hearing of Caravaggio's death in 1610, Rubens encouraged the duke of Mantua to buy the artist's painting *Death of the Virgin,* which had been rejected by the patron because of the shocking realism of its portrayal of the Virgin's dead body. Later, Rubens arranged the purchase of a Caravaggio painting by an Antwerp church.

In 1608, Rubens returned to Antwerp, where he accepted employment from the Habsburg governors of Flanders, and shortly afterward, he married. Rubens's first major commission in Antwerp was a large canvas **triptych** for the main altar of the Church of Saint Walpurga, *The Raising of the Cross* (fig. 19-36), painted in 1609–1610. Unlike earlier triptychs, where the side panels contained

19-37. Peter Paul Rubens. *Henri IV Receiving the Portrait of Marie de' Medici*. 1621–25. Oil on canvas, 12'11⅛" x 9'8⅛" (3.94 x 2.95 m). Musée du Louvre, Paris

related but independent images, the wings here extend the action of the central scene and surrounding landscape across the vertical framing. At the center, Herculean figures strain to haul upright the wooden cross with Jesus already stretched upon it. At the left, the followers of Jesus join in mourning, and at the right, indifferent soldiers supervise the execution. Culminating in this work are all the drama and intense emotion of Caravaggio and the virtuoso technique of Annibale Carracci, transformed and reinterpreted according to Rubens's own unique ideal of thematic and formal unity. The heroic nude figures, dramatic lighting effects, dynamic diagonal composition, and intense emotions show his debt to Italian art, but the rich colors and surface realism, with minute attention given to varied textures and forms, belong to his native Flemish tradition.

Rubens had created a powerful, expressive visual

language that was as appropriate for the secular rulers who engaged him as it was for the Catholic Church. Moreover, his intelligence, courtly manners, and personal charm made him a valuable and trusted courtier to his royal patrons, who included Philip IV of Spain, Queen-Regent Marie de' Medici of France, and Charles I of England. In 1630, while Rubens was in England on a peace mission, Charles I knighted him and commissioned him to decorate the ceiling of the new royal Banqueting House at Whitehall Palace, London (see fig. 19-60). He painted the deification of James I and the Stuart dynasty.

In 1621, Marie de' Medici, regent for her young son, Louis XIII, asked Rubens to paint the story of her life, to glorify her role in ruling France and also to commemorate the founding of the new Bourbon royal dynasty. In twenty-four paintings, Rubens portrayed Marie's life and

19-38. Peter Paul Rubens. *Landscape with Rainbow.* c. 1635. Oil on panel, 4'5³/₄" x 7'9¹/₈" (1.36 x 2.36 m). Wallace Collection, London

19-39. Anthony Van Dyck. *Charles I at the Hunt.* 1635. Oil on canvas, 8'11" x 6'11" (2.75 x 2.14 m). Musée du Louvre, Paris

political career as one continuous triumph overseen by the gods. In fact, Marie and her husband, Henri, appear as Roman gods themselves.

In the painting depicting the royal engagement (fig. 19-37), Henri IV falls in love at once with Marie's portrait, shown to him by Cupid and Hymen, the god of marriage, while the supreme Roman god, Jupiter, and his wife, Juno, look down from the clouds. Henri, wearing his steel breastplate and silhouetted against a landscape in which the smoke of a battle lingers in the distance, is encouraged by a personification of France to abandon war for love, as putti play with the rest of his armor. The sustained visual excitement of these enormous canvases makes them not only important works of art but also political propaganda of the highest order.

For all the grandeur of his commissioned paintings, Rubens was a sensitive, innovative painter, as the works he created for his own pleasure clearly demonstrate. One of his greatest joys was his country home, Château de Steen, a working farm with gardens, fields, woods, and streams. Steen furnished subjects for several pastoral paintings, such as *Landscape with Rainbow* (fig. 19-38), of about 1635. The atmosphere after a storm is nearly palpable, with the sun breaking through clouds and the air still moisture laden, as farmworkers resume their labors. These magnificent landscapes had a significant impact on later painting.

Château de Steen was in no sense a "retirement home," and Rubens continued to produce large commissions for clients all over Europe. He employed dozens of assistants, many of whom were, or became, important painters in their own right. Using workshop assistants was standard practice for a major artist, but Rubens was particularly methodical, training or hiring specialists in costumes, still lifes, landscapes, portraiture, and animal painting who together could complete a work from Rubens's detailed sketches.

One of Rubens's collaborators, Anthony Van Dyck (1599–1641), had an illustrious independent career, mainly as a portraitist. Son of an Antwerp silk merchant, he was listed as a pupil of the dean of Antwerp's Guild of Saint Luke at age ten. He had his own studio and roster of pupils at age sixteen but was not made a member of the guild until 1618, the year after he began his association with Rubens as a painter of heads. The necessity for blending his work seamlessly with that of Rubens enhanced Van Dyck's technical

skill. His artistic character was expressed in the elegance and aristocratic refinement of his own work. After a trip to the English court of James I (ruled Great Britain 1603–1625) in 1620, Van Dyck traveled to Italy and worked as a portrait painter to the nobility for seven years before returning to Antwerp. In 1632, he returned to England as the court painter to Charles I, by whom he was knighted and given a studio, a summer home, and a large salary.

Van Dyck's many portraits of the royal family provide a sympathetic record of their features, especially those of King Charles. In *Charles I at the Hunt* (fig. 19-39), of 1635,

19-40. Clara Peeters. *Still Life with Flowers, Goblet, Dried Fruit, and Pretzels.* 1611. Oil on panel, 19³/₄ x 25¹/₄" (50.2 x 64.1 cm). Museo del Prado, Madrid

Like many breakfast pieces, this painting features a pile of pretzels among the elegant tablewares. The word *pretzel*, which comes from the Latin *pretiola*, meaning "small reward," was given to this salty, twisted bread because it was invented by southern German monks to reward children who had learned their prayers. The twisted shape represented the crossed arms of a child praying. Following a long-established Netherlandish tradition, the artist included a portrait of herself in a reflection on the covered goblet at the center and again in the multiple reflections on the pewter pitcher in the right background.

Van Dyck was able, by clever manipulation of the setting, to portray the king truthfully and yet as a quietly imposing figure. Dressed casually for the hunt and standing on a bluff overlooking a distant view, Charles is shown as being taller than his pages and even than his horse, since its head is down and its heavy body is partly off the canvas. The viewer's gaze is diverted from the king's delicate and rather short frame to his pleasant features, framed by his jauntily cocked cavalier's hat. As if in decorous homage, the tree branches bow gracefully toward him, echoing the circular lines of the hat.

A contemporary of Van Dyck in Antwerp who was not associated with Rubens, Clara Peeters (1594–after 1657), an early still-life specialist, was a prodigy whose career seems to have begun before she was fourteen. She married in Antwerp and was a guild member there, but she may have previously spent time in Holland. Of some fifty paintings now attributed to her, many are of the type called **breakfast pieces**, showing a table set for a meal of bread and fruit. As in her *Still Life with Flowers, Goblet, Dried Fruit, and Pretzels* (fig. 19-40), of 1611, Peeters arranged rich tableware and food against neutral, almost black backgrounds, the better to emphasize the fall of light over the contrasting surface textures. The luxurious goblet and bowl contrast with the simple pewterware, as do the flowers with the pretzels. The pretzels, piled high on the pewter tray, are a particularly interesting Baroque element, with their complex multiple curves.

DUTCH BAROQUE

Led by William of Orange, the Dutch northern provinces of Habsburg Flanders successfully broke with Spain in 1568 and joined together. Although the king of Spain had considered the Dutch to be heretical rebels, by 1648 the United Dutch Republic joined Spain, the Vatican, the Holy Roman Empire, and France on equal footing in peace negotiations. Unlike the ruling families in Catholic Europe, however, the House of Orange was not notable for its patronage of the arts.

The Hague was the capital city and the preferred residence of the ruling princes of the House of Orange, but Amsterdam was the true center of power, because of its sea trade and the enterprise of its merchants, who made the city an international commercial center. Royal patronage of the arts improved significantly under Prince Frederick Henry (ruled 1625–1647), and Dutch artists found many other eager patrons among the prosperous middle class in Amsterdam, Leiden, Haarlem, Delft, and Utrecht.

Painting and Prints

The art popular in the seventeenth-century Netherlands shows that the Dutch delighted in depictions of themselves and their country's landscape, cities, and domestic life, not to mention beautiful and interesting objects. In addition, the Dutch, a well-educated people, were fascinated by history, mythology, the Bible, new scientific discoveries, commercial expansion abroad, and colonial exploration (see "Science and the Changing World View," page 785). Many paintings show a continuation of the tradition of Netherlandish art, established in the time of Robert Campin and Jan van Eyck (Chapter 17), in which common objects carried underlying symbolic or moralizing meanings.

Portraits. Dutch Baroque portraiture took many forms, ranging from single portraits in sparsely furnished settings to allegorical depictions of people in elaborate costumes with appropriate symbols. Although the accurate portrayal of settings, costumes, and facial features was the most important gauge of a portrait's success, Dutch painters consistently went beyond pure description to idealize their subjects and to convey a sense of their personalities. Group portraiture that documented the membership of corporate organizations was a Dutch specialty. These large canvases, filled with numerous individuals who shared the cost of the commission, challenged painters to present a coherent, interesting composition that, nevertheless, gave equal attention to each individual portrait.

Frans Hals (c. 1581/85–1666), the leading painter of Haarlem, studied with the Flemish Mannerist Karel van Mander, but little is certain about Hals's work before 1616. He had by then developed a style grounded in the Netherlandish love of realism and inspired by the Caravaggesque style, yet it was far from slavish to either one. Like Velázquez, he tried to re-create the optical

19-41. Frans Hals. *Catharina Hooft and Her Nurse.* c. 1620.
Oil on canvas, 33³/₄ x 25¹/₂" (85.7 x 64.8 cm).
Staatliche Museen zu Berlin, Preussischer Kulturbesitz,
Gëmaldegalerie

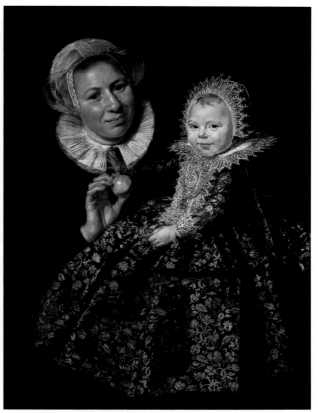

effects of light on the shapes and textures of objects. He
painted boldly, with slashing strokes and angular patches
of paint that coalesce; when seen at a distance, all the
colors merge into solid forms over which a flickering
light seems to move. In Hals's hands, this seemingly
effortless technique suggests a boundless joy of life.

In his unusual painting *Catharina Hooft and Her Nurse*
(fig. 19-41), of about 1620, he captured the vitality of an
instantaneous gesture and a fleeting moment in time.
While the portrait records for posterity the great pride of the
parents in their child and their wealth, it is much more than
a study of rich fabrics, laces, and expensive toys (a golden
rattle). Hals depicts the heartwarming delight of the child,
who seems to be acknowledging the viewer as a loving
family member while her doting nurse tries to distract her
with an apple.

In contrast to this intimate individual portrait are
Hals's official group portraits, such as his *Officers of the*

SCIENCE AND THE CHANGING WORLDVIEW

During the seventeenth and eighteenth centuries, investigations of the natural world begun during the Renaissance changed the way people—including artists—saw the world. Some of the new discoveries brought a sense of the grand scale of the universe without, while others focused more precisely on the complexity of the world within. As frames of reference expanded and contracted, artists found new ways to mirror these changing perspectives in their own works.

Francis Bacon (1561–1626) in England and René Descartes (1596–1650) in France established a new scientific method of studying the world by insisting on scrupulous objectivity and logical reasoning. Bacon proposed that facts be established by observation and tested by controlled experiments. Descartes argued for the deductive method of reasoning, in which a conclusion was arrived at logically from basic premises, the most fundamental of which was "I think, therefore I am." Descartes even used logic to prove the existence of God. Seventeenth-century scientists continued to believe that God had created matter, the basis of all things, and that their discoveries simply amplified human understanding of Creation, and this added to God's glory. Church authorities, however, often disagreed.

In 1543, the Polish scholar Nicolaus Copernicus (1473–1543) published *On the Revolutions of the Heavenly Spheres*, which contradicted the long-held view that Earth is the center of the universe (the Ptolemaic theory) by arguing instead that Earth and other planets revolve around the Sun. The Church viewed the Copernican theory as a challenge to its doctrines and put *On the Revolutions of the Heavenly Spheres* on its Index of Prohibited Books in 1616. At the beginning of the seventeenth century, Johannes Kepler (1571–1630), the court mathematician and astronomer to Holy Roman Emperor Rudolf II, demonstrated that the planets revolve around the Sun in elliptical orbits. Kepler noted a number of interrelated dynamic geometric patterns in the universe, the overall design of which he believed was an expression of divine order.

Galileo Galilei (1564–1642), an astronomer, mathematician, and physicist, was the first to develop a new invention, the telescope, as a tool for observing the heavens. His findings provided further confirmation of the Copernican theory, and after the teaching of that theory was prohibited by the Church, Galileo was tried for heresy by the Inquisition. Under duress, he publicly rejected his views, although at the end of his trial, according to legend, he muttered, "Nevertheless it [Earth] does move." As the first person to see the craters of the moon through a telescope, Galileo began the exploration of space that would culminate in the first human steps on the moon in 1969.

The new seventeenth-century science turned to the study of the very small as well as to the vast reaches of space. Here the new technology included the microscope, developed by the Dutch lens maker and amateur scientist Anton van Leeuwenhoek (1632–1723). Although embroiderers, textile inspectors, manuscript illuminators, and painters already used magnifying glasses in their work, Leeuwenhoek perfected grinding techniques and increased the power of his lenses far beyond what was required for these uses. Ultimately, he was able to study the inner workings of plants and animals and even see microorganisms. Early scientists learned to draw or depended on artists to draw the images revealed by the microscope for further study and publication. Not until the discovery of photography in the nineteenth century could scientists communicate their discoveries without an artist's help.

19-42. Frans Hals. *Officers of the Haarlem Militia Company of Saint Adrian.* c. 1627. Oil on canvas, 6' x 8'8" (1.83 x 2.67 m). Frans Halsmuseum, Haarlem

Hals painted at least six group portraits of civic-guard organizations, including two for the Company of Saint Adrian. The company, made up of several guard units, was charged with the military protection of Haarlem whenever it was needed. Officers came from the upper middle class and held their commissions for three years, whereas the ordinary guards were tradespeople and craftworkers. Each company was organized like a guild under the patronage of a saint. When the men were not on war alert, the company functioned as a fraternal order, holding archery competitions, taking part in city processions, and maintaining an altar in the local church. (See also fig. 19-44.)

Haarlem Militia Company of Saint Adrian (fig. 19-42), of about 1627. Less imaginative artists had arranged their sitters in neat rows to depict every face clearly. Instead, Hals's dynamic composition turned the group portrait into a lively social event, even while maintaining a strong underlying geometry of diagonal lines—gestures, banners, and sashes—balanced by the stabilizing perpendiculars of table, window, tall wineglass, and striped banner. The black suits and hats make the white ruffs and sashes of pink, orange, blue, and green even more brilliant.

The most successful of Hals's contemporaries to adopt his almost boisterous early manner was Judith Leyster (c. 1609–1660). In fact, one painting long praised as one of Hals's finest works was recently discovered to be by Leyster when a cleaning revealed her distinctive signature, the monogram *JL* with a star, in reference to her surname, Leysterre ("Pole Star"), which her family took from the name of their Haarlem brewery.

Although almost nothing is known of her early years, in 1628–1629 she was with her family in Utrecht, where she very likely encountered artists who had traveled to Italy and fallen under the spell of Caravaggio. Leyster's work shows clear echoes of her exposure to these

Utrecht painters who had enthusiastically adopted the Italian master's naturalism, the dramatic tenebrist lighting effects, the large figures pressed into the foreground plane, and, especially, the theatrically presented everyday or low-life themes. In 1631, Leyster signed as a witness at the baptism in Haarlem of one of Frans Hals's children, which has led to the probably incorrect conclusion that she was Hals's pupil. Leyster may have worked in his shop, however, since she entered Haarlem's Guild of Saint Luke only in 1633. Membership allowed her to take pupils into her studio, and her competitive relationship with Frans Hals around that time is made clear by the complaint she lodged against him in 1635 for luring away one of her apprentices.

Leyster is known primarily for her informal scenes of daily life, which often carry an underlying moralistic theme. In her lively *Self-Portrait* of 1635 (fig. 19-43), the artist has paused momentarily in her work to look back, as if the viewer has just entered the room. Her elegant dress and the fine chair in which she sits are symbols of her success as an artist whose popularity was based on the very type of painting under way on her easel. Her subject, a man playing a violin, may be a visual pun on the

19-43. Judith Leyster. *Self-Portrait.* 1635. Oil on canvas, 29½ x 25¾" (74.9 x 65.4 cm). National Gallery of Art, Washington, D.C.
Widener Collection

painter with palette and brush. So that the viewer would immediately see the difference between her painted portrait and the painted painting, she varied her technique, executing the image on her easel more loosely. The narrow range of colors sensitively dispersed in the composition and the warm spotlighting are typical of Leyster's mature style.

Rembrandt van Rijn (1606–1669) was the most important painter working in Amsterdam in the seventeenth century and is now revered as one of the great artists of all time. Rembrandt was one of nine children born in Leiden to a miller and his wife. Rembrandt was sent to the University of Leiden in 1620 at age fourteen, but within a few months he dropped out to study painting. From 1621 to about 1624, he was apprenticed to a Leiden artist, then worked briefly in Amsterdam. He returned to Leiden in 1625 as a painter of religious pic-

tures. In 1631 or 1632, he returned to Amsterdam and broadened his repertoire to include mythological paintings, landscapes, and figure studies, but his primary source of income was portraiture. His work quickly attracted the interest of the secretary to Prince Frederick Henry, whose favorite artist was Peter Paul Rubens. Knowing this, Rembrandt studied Rubens's work and incorporated some of his compositional ideas in a series of paintings for the prince on the subject of the Passion of Christ (c. 1632–c. 1640).

Prolific and popular with Amsterdam clientele, Rembrandt ran a busy studio producing works that sold for high prices. His large workshop and the many pupils who imitated his manner have made it difficult for scholars to define his body of work, and many paintings formerly attributed to him have recently been assigned to other artists. Rembrandt's mature work reflected his new

19-44. Rembrandt van Rijn. *Captain Frans Banning Cocq Mustering His Company (The Night Watch).* 1642. Oil on canvas (cut down from the original size), 11'11" x 14'4" (3.63 x 4.37 m). Rijksmuseum, Amsterdam

environment, his study of science and nature, and the broadening of his artistic vocabulary by the study of Italian Renaissance art, chiefly from engraved copies. In 1639, he purchased a large house, which he filled with art and an enormous supply of studio props, such as costumes, weapons, and stuffed animals.

In 1642, Rembrandt was one of several artists commissioned by a wealthy civic-guard company to create large group portraits of its members for its new meeting hall. The result, *Captain Frans Banning Cocq Mustering His Company* (fig. 19-44), is considered one of Rembrandt's finest works. Because of the dense layer of grime and darkened varnish on it and its dark background architecture, this painting was once thought to be a night scene and was therefore called *The Night Watch.* After recent cleaning and restoration, it now exhibits a natural golden light that sets afire the palette of rich colors—browns, blues, olive green, orange, and red—around a central core of lemon yellow in the costume of a lieutenant. To

the dramatic group composition, showing a company forming for a parade in an Amsterdam street, Rembrandt added several colorful but seemingly unnecessary figures. While the officers stride purposefully forward, the rest of the men and several mischievous children mill about. The young girl at the left, carrying a chicken and wearing a money pouch, and the boy firing a blank rifle at the lieutenant's fancy plumed hat are so unusual that attempts have been made to find symbolic or ironic meaning in them. From the earliest days of his career, however, Rembrandt was devoted to sketching people he encountered in the streets. These figures may simply add lively touches of interesting local color to heighten the excitement of the scene.

Rembrandt was second only to Albrecht Dürer (Chapter 18) in his enthusiasm for printmaking as an important art form with its own aesthetic qualities and expressiveness. His interest focused on **etching**, a relatively minor medium at the time, in which the picture is

TECHNIQUE

ETCHING AND DRYPOINT

Etching with acid on metal was used to decorate armor and other metal wares before it became a printmaking medium. The earliest etchings were made in Germany in the early 1500s, and even Albrecht Dürer experimented with the technique briefly by etching a few plates. These early etchings were made on iron, which tended to produce a ragged, fuzzy line. When printmakers began to work on copper with slow-acting acids, they produced a cleaner, more reliable image. Rembrandt was the first artist to popularize etching as a major form of artistic expression.

In the etching process, a plate, or metal sheet, is coated on both sides with an acid-resistant varnish that dries hard without being brittle. Then, instead of laboriously cutting the lines of the desired image directly into the plate, the artist draws through the varnish with a sharp needle to expose the metal. The plate is then covered with acid, which eats into the metal exposed by the drawn lines. By controlling the time the acid stays on different parts of the plate, the artist can make fine, shallow lines or heavy, deep ones. The varnish covering the plate is removed before an impression is taken. If a change needs to be made, the lines can be "erased" with a sharp metal scraper. Finally, accidental scratches are eliminated by burnishing (polishing). Not surprisingly, a complex image with a wide range of tones requires many steps.

Another technique for registering images on a metal plate is called **drypoint**. A sharp needle is used to scratch lines in the metal, but there are two major differences in technique between the process of engraving and that of drypoint (see "Woodcuts and Engravings on Metal," page 000). The engraving tool, or **burin**, is held straight and throws up equal amounts of metal, called burr, on both sides of the line, but the drypoint needle is held at a slight slant and throws up most of the burr on one side. Also, in engraving the metal burr is scraped off and the plate polished to yield a clean, sharp groove to hold the ink for printing. In drypoint, the burr is left in place, and it, rather than the groove, holds the ink. Thus, under magnification, drypoint lines are white, with ink on both sides, but their rich black appearance when printed is impossible to achieve with engraving or etching. Unfortunately, drypoint burr is fragile, and only a few prints—a dozen or fewer—can be made before it flattens and loses its character. Rembrandt's earliest prints were pure etchings, but later he enriched his prints with drypoint to achieve greater tonal richness.

Like engraving, etching and drypoint use a printing technique called **intaglio**. After the desired image has been etched or scratched into the metal printing surface, printing ink is applied over the whole plate and forced down into the lines; then the surface of the plate is carefully wiped clean. Just as in the engraving process, the ink in the lines prints onto a sheet of paper pressed firmly against the metal plate.

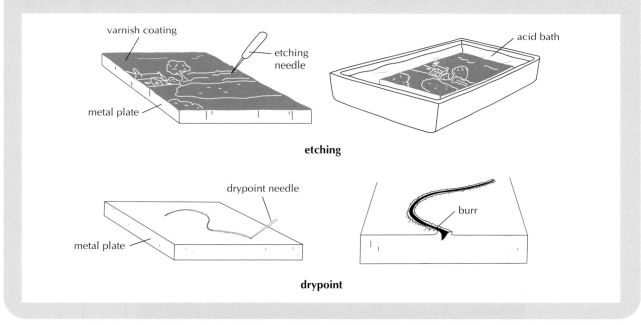

etching

drypoint

created with acid on metal plates. His earliest line etchings date from 1627. About a decade later, he began to experiment with additions in the **drypoint** technique, in which the artist uses a sharp needle to scratch shallow lines in a plate (see "Etching and Drypoint," above). Because etching and drypoint allow the artist to work directly on the plate, the style of the finished print has the relatively free and spontaneous character of a drawing. Rembrandt's commitment to the full exploitation of the medium is indicated by the fact that he alone carried the creative process through from the preparation of the plate to its inking and printing, and he constantly experimented with the technique, with methods of inking, and with papers for printing.

Rembrandt experienced a deepening religiousness that was based on his personal study of the Bible and perhaps also on his association with the pacifist Mennonite sect, whose spirit pervades Rembrandt's treatment of

19-45. Rembrandt van Rijn. *Three Crosses* (first state). 1663.
Drypoint and burin. The Metropolitan Museum of Art,
New York
Gift of Felix M. Warburg and his Family, 1941

19-46. Rembrandt van Rijn. *Three Crosses.* (fourth state).
1663. Drypoint and burin. The Metropolitan Museum
of Art, New York
Gift of Felix M. Warburg and his Family, 1941

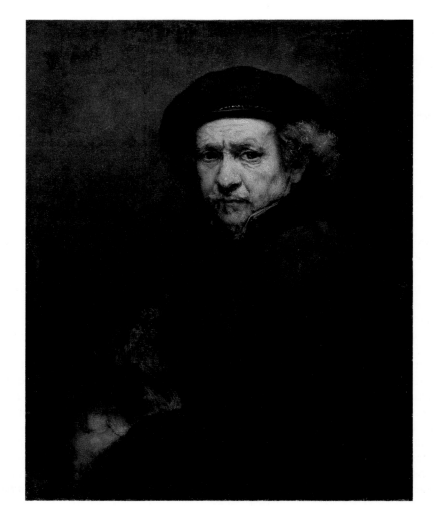

19-47. Rembrandt van
Rijn. *Self-
Portrait.* 1659.
Oil on canvas,
33¼ x 26"
(84 x 66 cm).
National
Gallery of Art,
Washington,
D.C.
Andrew W.
Mellon Collection

19-48. Rembrandt van Rijn. *The Jewish Bride.* c. 1665. Oil on canvas, 3'11³/4" x 5'5¹/2" (1.21 x 1.65 m). Rijksmuseum, Amsterdam

religious themes, from gentle quietism to soul-searching to belief in ultimate forgiveness. These expressions can be studied in a series of prints, *The Three Crosses*, that comes down to us in four states. Rembrandt tried to capture the moment described in the Gospels when darkness covered the earth and Jesus cried out, "Father, into thy hands I commend my spirit." In the first state (fig. 19-45), the centurion kneels in front of the cross while other terrified people run from the scene. The Virgin Mary and John share the light flooding down from heaven. By the fourth state (fig. 19-46), Rembrandt has completely reworked and reinterpreted the theme. A mass of vertical lines, like the rigid body of Jesus, fills the space and virtually eliminates the former image. Even Mary and Jesus' friends disappear. Instead, a horseman holding a lance—who may represent the repentant Pilate—faces Jesus. Compared with the first state, the composition is more compact, the individual elements are simplified, and the emotions are intensified. In each version, the shattered hill of Golgotha fills the lower space. The first state is a detailed rendering of the scene in realistic terms, but realism in Rembrandt's late works becomes realism of the spirit of inner meaning, not of surface details. The fourth state is a reduction of the event to its essence. The composition revolves in an oval of half light around the base of the cross, and the viewer's attention is drawn to the confronted but noncommunicative figures of Jesus and his repentant tormentor. In *The Three Crosses*, Rembrandt defined the mystery of Christianity in Christ's sacrifice, presented in realistic terms but as something beyond rational explanation. The eternal battles of dark and light, doom and salvation, evil and good—all seem to be waged anew.

Rembrandt remained a popular artist and teacher, but he was continually plagued by financial problems. He painted ever more brilliantly in a unique manner that distilled a lifetime of study and contemplation of life and human personalities. His sensitivity to the human condition is perhaps nowhere more powerfully expressed than in a *Self-Portrait* of 1659 (fig. 19-47). Among his other late achievements is *The Jewish Bride* (fig. 19-48), of about 1665. This wedding portrait of the Jewish poet Don Miguel de Barrios and his wife, Abigael de Pina, was probably meant to refer to the marriage of Isaac and Rebecca or some other loving biblical couple. Over the twenty years since the execution of *Captain Frans Banning Cocq Mustering His Company*, the artist's facility with brush and paint had not weakened, and the monumental figures emerge from the same type of dark architectural background, perhaps a garden wall and portico, with the warm light suffusing the scene and setting the reds and golds of their costumes aglow. In comparison with Jan

19-49. Aelbert Cuyp. *Maas at Dordrecht.* c. 1660. Oil on canvas, 3'9¼" x 5'7" (1.15 x 1.70 m). National Gallery of Art, Washington, D.C.
Andrew W. Mellon Collection

van Eyck's emotionally neutral *Portrait of Giovanni Arnolfini (?) and His Wife, Giovanna Cenami (?)* of the early fifteenth century (see fig. 17-13), where the meaning of the picture relied heavily on its symbolic setting, the significance of *The Jewish Bride* is emotional, conveyed by loving expressions and gestures, such as the groom tenderly touching his bride's breast, an ancient symbol of fertility.

Landscapes and Seascapes. The Dutch loved the landscapes and vast skies of their own country, but those who painted them were not slaves to nature as they found it. The artists were never afraid to remake a scene by rearranging, adding, or subtracting to give their compositions formal organization or a desired mood. Starting in the 1620s, view painters generally adhered to a convention in which little color was used beyond browns, grays, and beiges. After 1650, they tended to be more individualistic in their styles, but nearly all brought a broader range of colors into play. One continuing **motif** was the emphasis on cloud-filled expanses of sky dominating a relatively narrow horizontal band of earth below.

From a family of artists, Aelbert Cuyp (1620–1691) of Dordrecht specialized early in his career in view painting.

Cuyp first worked in the older, nearly monochromatic convention for recording the Dutch countryside and waterways. About 1645, his style evolved to include a wider range of colors, while also moving toward more idealized scenes drenched with a warm golden light, such as his *Maas at Dordrecht* (fig. 19-49), painted about 1660. This dramatic change has been attributed to Cuyp's contact with Utrecht painters who were influenced by contemporary landscape painting in Italy, especially the works of the French expatriate Claude Lorrain (see fig. 19-24). However, unlike the Italian and French artists who preferred religious, historical, or other narrative themes expressed through the figures inhabiting the landscape, Cuyp and other Dutch painters tended to represent nature for its own sake, even as they idealized it. The wide, deep harbor of the Maas River at Dordrecht was always filled with cargo ships and military vessels. A contemporary record mentions a fleet of ships with some 30,000 men in the harbor in 1646. If there is any symbolic meaning in Cuyp's seascape, it might express the pride in Dordrecht's contribution to the Dutch Republic's prosperity, independence, and peaceful life.

19-50. Jacob van Ruisdael. *The Jewish Cemetery*. 1655–60. Oil on canvas, 4'6" x 6'2½" (1.42 x 1.89 m). The Detroit Institute of Arts
Gift of Julius H. Haass in memory of his brother Dr. Ernest W. Haass

The Haarlem landscape specialist Jacob van Ruisdael (1628/29–1682) was especially adept at both the invention of dramatic compositions and the projection of moods in his canvases. His *The Jewish Cemetery* (fig. 19-50), of 1655–1660, is a thought-provoking view of silent tombs, crumbling ruins, and stormy landscape, with a rainbow set against dark, scudding clouds. Ruisdael was greatly concerned with spiritual meanings of the landscape, which he expressed in his choice of such environmental factors as the time of day, the weather, the appearance of the sky, or the abstract patterning of sun and shade. Here the tombs, ruins, and fallen and blasted trees suggest an allegory of transience. The somewhat melancholy mood is mitigated by the rainbow, a traditional symbol of renewal.

Ruisdael's popularity drew many pupils to his workshop, the most successful of whom was Meindert Hobbema (1638–1709), who studied with him from 1657 to 1660. Although there are many similarities to Ruisdael's style in Hobbema's earlier paintings, his mature work moved away from the melancholy and dramatic moods of his master. Hobbema's love of the peaceful, orderly beauty of the civilized Dutch countryside is exemplified by one of his best-known paintings, *Avenue at Middelharnis* (fig. 19-51). In contrast with the broad horizontal orientation of many Dutch landscapes, Hobbema's composition draws the viewer into the picture and down the rutted, sandy road toward the distant village of Middelharnis as convincingly and compellingly as if the artist were a student of Italian Renaissance perspective.

Genre Painting. Dutch genre paintings of contemporary life were categorized in their own time by such descriptive titles as the "merry company," "garden party," and "picture with little figures." But scholars have noted that many of these works contain symbolic objects that suggest underlying meanings. Many of these messages seem to be admonitory, warning against alcoholism, gambling, or sexual promiscuity. The artists probably meant for their works to be understood on more than one level, a long tradition in Netherlandish painting. Where religious symbolism had dominated earlier works, Baroque artists painted chiefly for private patrons, who

19-51. Meindert Hobbema. *Avenue at Middelharnis.* 1689. Oil on canvas, 40³/₄ x 55¹/₂" (104 x 141 cm). The National Gallery, London

The power of nature is challenged by a people who have captured their land not from a human rival but from the sea itself. They are constantly aware of the mighty forces of wind and water ever ready to reclaim it.

seem to have wanted paintings to be instructive as well as beautiful. Recent scholarship has found clues to the meaning of Dutch genre paintings in the emblem books that were popular at the time. These books were illustrated catalogues of allegorical or symbolic images, each one generally accompanied by a moralizing verse. Although emblem books tell a great deal about the meanings of Dutch genre painting, they can be confusing. In an emblem book published in 1618, one of the best-known compilers of emblems gave different common meanings for each image, depending upon whether the approach was moralizing, religious, or "romantic."

Before Gerard Ter Borch (1617–1681) began to specialize in genre pictures about 1650, he was highly regarded for his battle scenes and portraits. He was renowned for his exquisite rendition of lace, velvet, and especially satin, a skill well demonstrated in a work traditionally known as *The Suitor's Visit* (fig. 19-52), painted about 1658. It shows a well-dressed man bowing gracefully to an elegant woman in a sumptuously furnished room in which another woman plays the lute. The painting appears to represent a prosperous gentleman paying a call on a lady of equal social status, possibly to propose

marriage. The dog in the painting and the musician seem to be simply part of the scene. We are already familiar with the dog as a symbol of fidelity, and stringed instruments were said to symbolize, through their tuning, the harmony of souls and thus, possibly, a loving relationship. However, Ter Borch's scene has also been interpreted as showing a guest arriving at a luxurious brothel. Supporting this view is the woman's low-cut neckline, which would have been considered improperly revealing for most social occasions in the seventeenth-century Netherlands. Moreover, the dog symbolizes sexual appetite as well as fidelity, and lute playing in the Netherlands was almost always associated with erotic activity.

The genre paintings of Jan Steen (1626–1679), whose larger brushstrokes contrast with the meticulous treatment of Ter Borch, used scenes of everyday life to portray moral tales, illustrate proverbs and folk sayings, or make puns to amuse the spectator. Steen was influenced early in his career by Frans Hals, and his work in turn influenced a **school**, or circle of artists working in a related style, of Dutch artists who emulated his style and subjects. To support his family, Steen worked in a brewery for several years, and from 1670 until his death he kept a

19-52. Gerard Ter Borch. *The Suitor's Visit.* c. 1658. Oil on canvas, 32¹/₂ x 29⁵/₈" (83 x 75 cm). National Gallery of Art, Washington, D.C.
Andrew W. Mellon Collection

tavern in Leiden. He probably found the inspiration for scenes and models in everyday life surrounding him.

Jan Steen's paintings of children are especially remarkable, for he captured not only their childish physiques but also their fleeting moods and expressions. His ability to capture such transitory dispositions was well expressed in his painting *The Drawing Lesson* (see Introduction, fig. 15). Here, a youthful apprentice observes the master artist correct an example of drawing—a skill widely believed to be the foundation of art—but we cannot be certain whether the drawing is the youth's or that of the well-dressed young woman.

Perhaps the greatest of the Dutch genre painters was Jan (Johannes) Vermeer (1632–1675) of Delft. An innkeeper and art dealer who painted only for local patrons, Vermeer entered the Delft artists' guild in 1653. Meticulous in his technique, with a unique compositional approach and painting style, Vermeer produced only a small number of works. They are frequently enigmatic scenes of women in their homes, alone or with a servant, who are occupied with some cultivated activity, such as writing, reading letters, or playing a musical instrument. Vermeer also produced history paintings, views of Delft, and pictures of men

and women together in the manner of Gerard Ter Borch, whom he knew.

Of the fewer than forty canvases securely attributed to Vermeer, most are of a similar type—quiet, low-key in color, and asymmetrical but strongly geometric in organization. Vermeer achieved his effects through a consistent architectonic construction of space in which every object adds to the clarity and balance of the composition. An even light from a window often gives solidity to the figures and objects in a room. All emotion is subdued, as Vermeer evokes the stillness of meditation. Even the brushwork is so controlled that it becomes invisible, except when he paints reflected light as tiny droplets of color.

In *Woman Holding a Balance* (fig. 19-53), perfect balance creates a monumental composition and a moment of supreme stillness and quiet. The woman contemplates the balance and so calls our attention to the act of weighing and judging. Her hand and the scale are central, but directly over her, on the wall of the room, hangs a large painting of the Last Judgment. Thus, Vermeer's painting becomes a metaphor for eternal judgment. The woman's moment of quiet introspection before she touches gold or pearls also recalls the *vanitas* theme of the transience

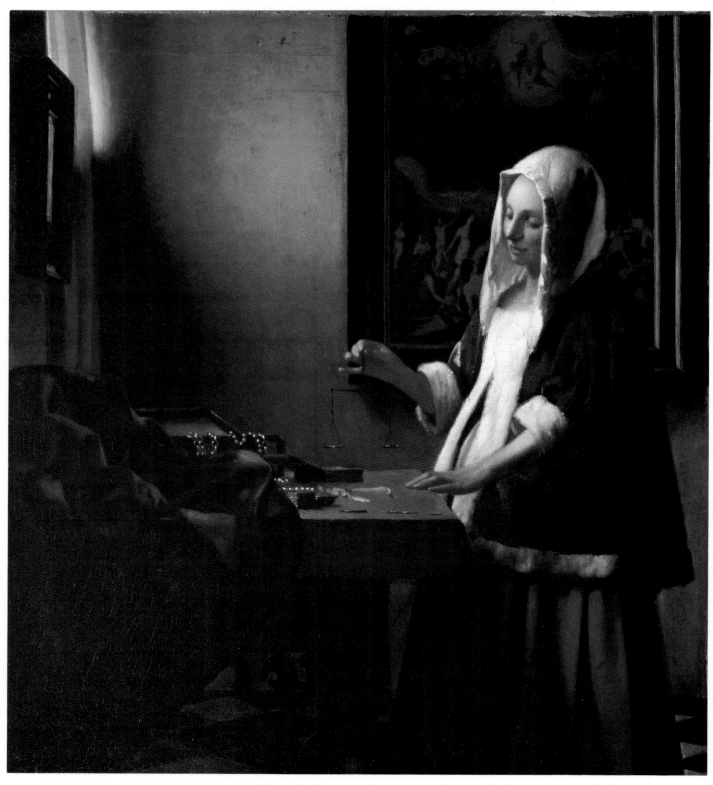

19-53. Jan Vermeer. *Woman Holding a Balance*. c. 1664. Oil on canvas, 16³/₄ x 15" (42.5 x 38.1 cm). National Gallery of Art, Washington, D.C.
Widener Collection, 1942

19-54. Jan Vermeer. *View of Delft.* c. 1662. Oil on canvas, 38½ x 46¼" (97.8 x 117.5 cm). Mauritshuis, The Hague
The Johan Maurits van Nassau Foundation

of life, allowing the painter to comment on the ephemeral quality of material things.

Vermeer's *View of Delft* (fig. 19-54) is no simple cityscape. Although Vermeer convinces the viewer of its authenticity, he does not paint a photographic reproduction of the scene; he moves buildings around to suit his ideal composition. As he does with paintings of interior scenes, he endows the city with a timeless stability created by the careful placement of the buildings, the quiet atmosphere, and the clear, even light. Vermeer may have experimented with the mechanical device known as **camera obscura** (see Chapter 27), not as a method of reproducing the image but as another tool in the visual analysis of the landscape. The optical distortions and the

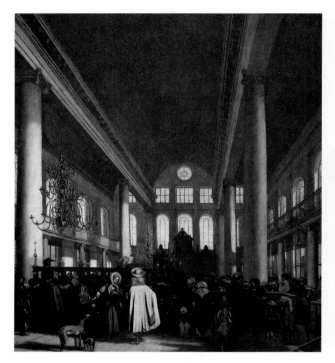

19-55. Emanuel de Witte. *Portuguese Synagogue, Amsterdam.* 1680. Oil on canvas, 43¹/₂ x 39" (110.5 x 99.1 cm). Rijksmuseum, Amsterdam.

Architect Daniel Stalpaert built the synagogue in 1670–75.

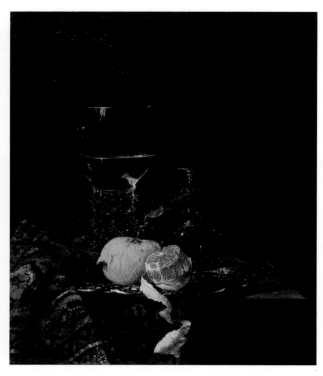

19-56. Willem Kalf. *Still Life with Lemon Peel.* 1659. Oil on canvas, 20 x 17" (50.8 x 43.1 cm). Stichting Vrienden van het Mauritshuis, The Hague

"beading" of highlights evident in this painting would have been enhanced by the camera obscura. This beading technique creates the illusion of brilliant light but does not dissolve the underlying form.

A type of genre picture that achieved great popularity in the Baroque period was the **architectural interior**. These interior views seem to have been painted for their own special beauty, just as exterior views of the land, cities, and harbors were. The Rotterdam portrait and history painter Emanuel de Witte (c. 1617–1692) specialized in this type of work after moving to Delft in 1640 and after settling permanently in Amsterdam in 1652. Although many of his interiors were composites of features from several locations combined in one idealized architectural view, de Witte also painted faithful portraits of actual buildings. One of these is his *Portuguese Synagogue, Amsterdam* (fig. 19-55), of 1680. The synagogue is shown here as a rectangular hall divided into one wide central aisle with narrow side aisles, each covered with a wooden barrel vault resting on lintels supported by columns. De Witte's shift of the viewpoint slightly to one side has created an interesting spatial composition, and strong contrasts of light and shade add dramatic movement to the simple interior. The caped figure in the foreground and the dogs provide a sense of scale for the architecture and add human interest.

Today, the painting is interesting both as a record of seventeenth-century synagogue architecture and as an evidence of Dutch religious tolerance in an age when Jews were often persecuted. Ousted from Spain and Portugal in the late fifteenth and early sixteenth centuries,

many Jews had settled first in Flanders and then in the Netherlands. The Sephardic (Spanish) and Portuguese Jews in Amsterdam enjoyed religious and personal freedom, and their synagogue was considered one of the outstanding sights of the city.

Still Lifes and Flower Pieces. The term **still life** for paintings of artfully arranged objects on a table comes from the Dutch *stilleven,* a word coined about 1650. The Dutch were so proud of their artists' still-life paintings that they presented one to the French queen Marie de' Medici when she made a state visit to Amsterdam. As with genre pictures, still-life paintings often carried allegorical or moralizing connotations. A common type was the *vanitas,* whose elements reminded viewers of the transience of life, material possessions, and even art.

Still-life paintings consisting predominantly of cut-flower arrangements are often referred to as **flower pieces**. Significant advances were made in botany during the Baroque period through the application of orderly scientific methods, and objective observation was greatly improved by the invention of the microscope in 1674 (see "Science and the Changing Worldview," page 785). The Dutch Republic was also a major importer, grower, and exporter of exotic flowers, especially tulips, which appear in nearly every flower piece in dozens of exquisite variations.

Willem Kalf (1619–1693) of Rotterdam, an excellent painter of breakfast pieces, specialized in rich and exotic table settings. This kind of painting was popular in the second half of the seventeenth century, and Kalf helped supply the thriving art market (see "The Dutch Art Market," above). In his *Still Life with Lemon Peel* (fig. 19-56), of 1659, Kalf depicts the surface textures of Chinese porcelain, gold, silver, brass, crystal, and an Oriental rug, which Dutch owners generally used to cover fine wood furniture. The half-peeled lemon—an expensive fruit in the Netherlands at the time—with its peel spiraling down implies that the unseen diner suddenly left the table. Thus, the "interrupted-meal" still life has been interpreted as a *vanitas* reminding the viewer that Death can come in the midst of pleasure. Citrus fruits also had sexual implications, and a half-peeled lemon often appears in depictions of houses of prostitution. No matter what the painting connotes, one gets great pleasure from admiring the artist's virtuosity in rendering the subtle contrasts among the lemon's opaque, oily rind, its soft white pith, and the taut, transparent skin of the interior of the fruit.

Before the invention of photography, scientific investigations relied entirely on drawn and painted illustrations, and researchers hired artists to accompany them on field trips. Anna Maria Sibylla Merian (1647–1717) was unusual in making noteworthy contributions as both researcher and artist. German by birth and Dutch by training, Merian was once described by a Dutch contemporary as a painter of flowers, fruit, birds, worms, flies, mosquitoes, spiders, "and other filth." At the time, it was believed that insects emerged spontaneously from the soil, but Merian's research on the life cycles of insects proved otherwise, findings she published in 1679 and 1683 as *The Wonderful Transformation of Caterpillars and (Their) Singular Plant Nourishment.* In

19-57. Anna Maria Sibylla Merian. Plate 9 from *Dissertation in Insect Generations and Metamorphosis in Surinam.* 1719. Hand-colored engraving, 18⅞ x 13" (47.9 x 33 cm). National Museum of Women in the Arts, Washington, D.C.
Gift of Wallace and Wilhelmina Holladay

1699, Amsterdam subsidized Merian's research on plants and insects in the Dutch colony of Surinam in South America, whose results were published as *Dissertation in Insect Generations and Metamorphosis in Surinam,* illustrated with sixty large plates engraved after her watercolors (fig. 19-57). Each plate is scientifically

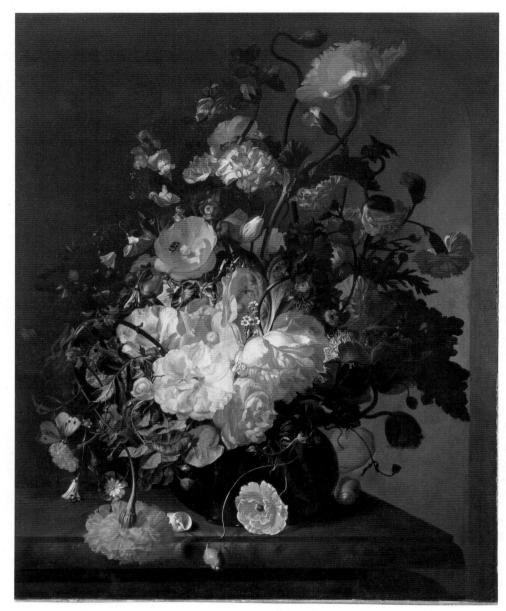

19-58. Rachel Ruysch. *Flower Still Life*. After 1700. Oil on canvas, 30 x 24" (76.2 x 61 cm). The Toledo Museum of Art, Ohio
Purchased with funds from the Libbey Endowment. Gift of Edward Drummond Libbey

Flower painting was a much-admired specialty in the seventeenth-century Netherlands. Such paintings were almost never straightforward depictions of actual fresh flowers. Instead, artists made color sketches of fresh examples of each type of flower and studied scientifically accurate color illustrations in botanical publications. Using their sketches and notebooks, in the studio they could compose bouquets of perfect specimens of a variety of flowers that could never be found blooming at the same time. In fifteenth-century painting, flowers carried religious symbolism, especially in conjunction with images of the Virgin Mary. Baroque flower paintings were less specifically symbolic, but the short life of blooming flowers was a poignant reminder of the fleeting nature of beauty and human life.

James I and his successor, Charles I, were fond of dance-dramas called masques, an important form of performance in early Baroque England. Inspired by Italian theatrical entertainments, the English masque combined theater, music, and dance in a spectacle in which professional actors, courtiers, and even members of the royal family participated. The event was more than extravagant entertainment, however; the dramas also glorified the monarchy. The entertainment began with an antimasque in which actors described a world torn by dissension and vice. Then, to the accompaniment of theatrical effects designed to amaze the spectators, richly costumed lords and ladies of the court appeared in the heavens to vanquish Evil. A dance sequence followed, symbolizing the restoration of peace and prosperity.

Inigo Jones, the court architect, was frequently called on to produce awe-inspiring special effects—storms at sea, blazing hells, dazzling heavens, and other wonders. To meet these demands, Jones revolutionized English stage design. He abandoned the Shakespearean theater, where viewers sat on the stage with the actors, and devised a **proscenium arch** that divided the audience from the stage action. He then created a bilevel stage with an upper area, where celestial visions could take place, and a main lower area, which was equipped with sliding shutters to permit rapid set changes. Jones achieved remarkable effects of deep space using linear perspective to decorate the shutters and the back cloth. His stagecraft is known today from the many working drawings he made, such as the design shown here, which he made for the last scene in court poet Thomas Carew's *Coelum Britannicum*, performed in 1634. This masque, which glorified the union of England and Scotland under James I and Charles I, ended with the appearance in clouds over the royal palace of personifications of Religion, Truth, Wisdom, Concord, Reputation, and Government.

Inigo Jones. *A Garden and a Princely Villa*, sketch for set design for *Coelum Britannicum*, by Thomas Carew. Performed February 18, 1634. Pen and brown ink with green distemper wash, 17$\frac{1}{5}$ x 22$\frac{1}{4}$" (43.7 x 56.5 cm). Devonshire Collection, Chatsworth, England

precise, accurate, and informative, presenting insects in various stages of development along with the plants they live on.

The Dutch tradition of flower painting peaked in the long career of Rachel Ruysch (1664–1750) of Amsterdam. Her flower pieces were highly prized for their sensitive, free-form arrangements and their unusual and beautiful color harmonies. During her seventy-year career, spanning the two Baroque centuries, she became one of the most sought-after and highest-paid still-life painters in Europe. In her *Flower Still Life* (fig. 19-58), painted after 1700, Ruysch placed the container at the center of the canvas's width, then created an asymmetrical floral arrangement of pale oranges, pinks, and yellows rising from lower left to top right of the picture, offset by the strong diagonal of the tabletop. To further balance the painting, she placed highlighted blossoms and leaves against the dark left half of the canvas and silhouetted them against the light wall area on the right. Ruysch often emphasized the beauty of curving flower stems and enlivened her compositions with interesting additions,

such as casually placed pieces of fruit or insects, in this case a large gray moth (lower left) and two snail shells.

ENGLISH BAROQUE

England and Scotland came under the same rule in 1603 with the ascent of James VI of Scotland to the English throne as James I (ruled 1603–1625). James increased the royal patronage of British artists, especially in literature and architecture. William Shakespeare's *Macbeth*, featuring the king's legendary ancestor Banquo, was written in tribute to the new royal family and performed at court in December 1606. James's son Charles I (ruled 1625–1649) was also an important collector and patron of painting.

Unfortunately, religious and political tensions resulted in civil wars beginning in 1642 that cost Charles his throne and his life in 1649. Much of the rest of the Baroque period in England was politically uneasy, with a succession of republican and monarchical rulers, ending with the first three Hanoverian kings, George I, II, and III, the last of whom ruled until 1802.

19-59. Inigo Jones. Banqueting House, Whitehall Palace, London. 1619–22

19-60. Inigo Jones. Interior, Banqueting House, Whitehall Palace. Ceiling paintings by Peter Paul Rubens. 1630–35

19-61. Christopher Wren. Saint Paul's Cathedral, London. 1675–1709

19-62. Plan of Saint Paul's Cathedral

Architecture

In the early seventeenth century, the architect Inigo Jones (1573–1652) introduced into England Renaissance classicism, an architectural design based on the style of the Renaissance architect Andrea Palladio (Chapter 18). Jones had studied Palladio's work in Venice, and Jones's copy of Palladio's *Four Books of Architecture* has been preserved, filled with notes in his hand. Jones was appointed surveyor-general in 1615 and was commissioned to design the Queen's House in Greenwich and the Banqueting House for the royal palace of Whitehall.

The Whitehall Banqueting House (fig. 19-59), built in 1619–1622 to replace an earlier one destroyed by fire, was used for court ceremonies and entertainments such as popular masques (see "The English Court Masque," page 801). The west front shown here, consisting of two upper stories with superimposed Ionic and Composite orders raised over a plain basement level, exemplifies the understated elegance of Jones's interpretation of Palladian design. On the two upper stories, **pilasters** flank the end **bays** (vertical divisions), and engaged columns provide a subtle emphasis to the three bays at the center. These vertical elements are repeated in the **balustrade** along the roofline. A rhythmic effect was created in varying window treatments from triangular and segmental (semicircular) pediments on the first level to cornices with volute (scroll-form) brackets on the second. The sculpted garlands just below the roofline add an unexpected decorative touch, as does the use of a different-

color stone—pale golden, light brown, and white—for each story (no longer visible after the building was refaced in uniformly white Portland stone).

Despite the two stories presented on the exterior, the interior of the Whitehall Banqueting House (fig. 19-60) is actually one large hall with a balcony on the upper level and antechambers at each end. (The entrance is on the short side.) Ionic pilasters suggest a colonnade but do not impinge on the ideal, double-cube space, which measures 55 by 110 feet by 55 feet high. In 1630, Charles I commissioned Peter Paul Rubens to decorate the ceiling. Jones had divided the flat ceiling into nine compartments, for which Rubens painted canvases glorifying the reign of James I. Installed in 1635, the paintings show a series of royal triumphs ending with the king carried to heaven in clouds of glory. So proud was Charles of the result that, rather than allow the smoke of candles and torches to harm the ceiling decoration, he moved the evening entertainments to an adjacent pavilion.

English architecture after 1660 was dominated by Christopher Wren (1632–1723), who built more than fifty Baroque churches. Wren began his professional career in 1659 as a professor of astronomy; architecture was a sideline until 1665, when he traveled to France to further his education. While there, he met with French architects and with Bernini, who was in Paris to consult on his designs for the Louvre. Wren returned to England with architectural books, engravings, and a greatly increased admiration for French classical Baroque design. In 1669, he was made surveyor-general, the position once held by Inigo Jones; in 1673, he was knighted.

After the Great Fire of 1666 demolished central London, Wren was continuously involved in its rebuilding for the rest of the century and beyond. His major project was the rebuilding of Saint Paul's Cathedral (fig. 19-61), carried out from 1675 to 1709, after attempts to salvage the burned-out medieval church failed. Like Saint Peter's Basilica in the Vatican, Saint Paul's has a long nave, short transepts with semicircular ends, and a domed crossing. Like Brunelleschi's dome for the Florence Cathedral, Wren's dome for Saint Paul's has an interior masonry vault with an **oculus** and an exterior sheathing of lead-covered wood (fig. 19-62). As in the two Italian churches,

19-63. John Vanbrugh. Blenheim Palace, Woodstock, Oxfordshire, England. 1705–21

state rooms

service
wing

stables

19-64. John Vanbrugh. Plan of Blenheim Palace

the dome of Saint Paul's is crowned by a tall **lantern**, to which a brick cone rises from the inner oculus to admit light to the interior. The dome itself is plainly derived from Bramante's Tempietto in Rome (see fig. 18-2). On the main west front of Saint Paul's (see fig. 19-61), two stages of paired Corinthian columns support a carved pediment. The deep-set porches and the columned pavilions atop the towers create dramatic areas of light and shadow. The huge size of the cathedral and its triumphant verticality, complexity of form, and chiaroscuro effects make it a major monument of the English Baroque. Wren recognized the importance of the building. On the simple marble slab that forms his tomb in the crypt of the cathedral, he had engraved: "If you want to see his memorial, look around you."

John Vanbrugh (1664–1726), like Wren, came late to architecture. His heavy, angular style was utterly unlike Wren's, but it was well suited to buildings intended to express power and domination, in which Vanbrugh specialized. Perhaps his most important achievement was Blenheim Palace (fig. 19-63), built from 1705 to 1721. Blenheim's enormous size and symmetrical plan (fig. 19-64), with double wings reaching out to encompass the surrounding terrain, was strongly influenced by Versailles (see fig. 19-20). Instead of the refinement of detail to be found there, however, Blenheim's classical

forms, including the temple-front exterior entrance, are large and rugged. They are also combined with the expansive glazed windows characteristic of English palace design since the sixteenth century. The angular exterior, with its towering statues and pinnacles, casts shadows across the central block, creating a dramatic chiaroscuro effect.

GERMAN AND AUSTRIAN BAROQUE

In the seventeenth and eighteenth centuries, the Habsburg emperors ruled their vast territories from Vienna, but the rest of German-speaking Europe remained divided by politics and religion into small principalities. Individual rulers decided on the religion of their territory, with Catholicism prevailing in southern and western Germany, including Bavaria and the Rhineland, and in Austria, while the north was Lutheran. Because of the devastating effects of the seventeenth-century religious wars, the Baroque style did not flourish in Germany and Austria until the eighteenth century, and then primarily under the patronage of Catholic prince-bishops.

Eighteenth-century church architecture in Catholic Germany looked to Italian Baroque developments, which were then added to German medieval forms, such as the **westwork**, a tall west front, and bell towers. With these

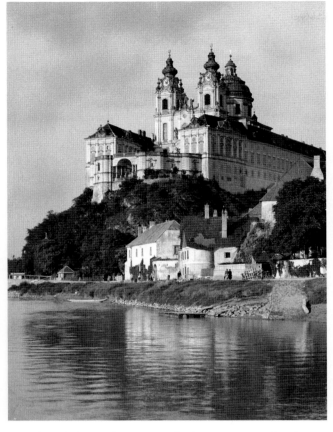

19-65. Jakob Prandtauer. Benedictine Monastery Church, Melk, Austria. 1702–36

19-66. Interior, Benedictine Monastery Church, Melk, Austria. Completed after 1738, after designs of Prandtauer, Antonio Beduzzi, and Joseph Munggenast

elements, German Baroque architects gave their churches an especially strong vertical emphasis. Important secular projects were also undertaken, as princes throughout Germany began building smaller versions of Louis XIV's palace and garden complex at Versailles.

One of the most imposing Baroque buildings is the Benedictine Monastery Church at Melk, built high on a promontory above the Danube River in Austria (fig. 19-65). The architect, Jakob Prandtauer (1660–1726), oversaw its construction from 1702 to 1736 on a site where there had been a Benedictine monastery since the eleventh century. Seen from the river, the monastery appears to be a huge twin-towered church. But the complex also includes two long (1,050 feet) parallel wings flanking the church, one of which contains the monastery's library. The wings are joined at the basement level by a section with a curving facade that descends from the cliff, forming a terrace overlooking the river in front of the church. Large windows and open galleries take advantage of the river view, while colossal pilasters and high bulbous-domed towers stress the verticality of the building by extending the vertical elements to a considerable height. The Melk monastery, as an ancient foundation enjoying imperial patronage, was expected to provide lodging for traveling princes and other dignitaries. Its grand and palacelike appearance—

especially the interior (fig. 19-66)—was appropriate to this function.

THE ROCOCO STYLE

The Rococo style is characterized by pastel colors, delicately curving forms, dainty figures, and a light-hearted mood. It represents a lighter, more specialized phase of Baroque. The Rococo manner may be seen partly as a reaction at all levels of society, even among kings and bishops, against the "grand manner" of art identified with the formality and rigidity of seventeenth-century court life. The movement began in French architectural decoration at the end of Louis XIV's reign (d. 1715) and quickly spread across Europe. The duke of Orléans, regent for the boy-king Louis XV (ruled 1715–1774), made his home in Paris, and the rest of the court—delighted to escape Versailles—also moved there and built elegant town houses (in French, hôtels). The layout, furniture, and decor were designed for these smaller rooms, which became the settings for intimate and fashionable intellectual gatherings and entertainments, called salons, that were hosted by accomplished, educated women of the upper class whose names are still known today—Mesdames de Staël, de La Fayette, de Sévigné, and du Châtelet, among others. The Salon de la Princesse in the Hôtel de Soubise

19-67. Germain Boffrand. Salon de la Princesse, Hôtel de Soubise, Paris. Begun 1732

19-68. Johann Balthasar Neumann. Kaisersaal (Imperial Hall), Residenz, Würzburg, Bavaria, Germany. 1719–44. Fresco by Giovanni Battista Tiepolo. 1751–52

19-69. Giovanni Battista Tiepolo. *The Marriage of the Emperor Frederick and Beatrice of Burgundy,* fresco in the Kaisersaal (Imperial Hall), Residenz. 1751–52

in Paris (fig. 19-67), designed by Germain Boffrand (1667–1754) beginning in 1732, is typical of the delicacy and lightness seen in French Rococo *hôtel* design of the 1730s. Interior designs for palaces and churches built on traditional Baroque plans were also animated by the Rococo spirit, especially in Germany and Austria. In occasional small-scale buildings, the Rococo style was also successfully applied to architectural planning.

Typical Rococo elements in architectural decoration were **arabesques**, **S** shapes, **C** shapes, reverse-**C** shapes, **volutes**, and naturalistic plant forms. The glitter of silver or gold against expanses of white or pastel color, the visual confusion of mirror reflections, delicate ornament in sculpted stucco, carved wood panels called *boiseries*, and inlaid wood designs on furniture and floors were all part of the new look. In residential settings, pictorial themes were often taken from classical love stories, and sculpted ornaments were rarely devoid of putti, cupids, and clouds.

Architecture and Its Decoration in Germany and Austria

A major architectural project influenced by the new Rococo style was the Residenz, a splendid palace created for the prince-bishop of Würzburg from 1719 to 1744 by Johann Balthasar Neumann (1687–1753). The oval Kaiser-

saal, or Imperial Hall (fig. 19-68), illustrates Neumann's great triumph in planning and decoration. Although the clarity of the plan, the size and proportions of the marble columns, and the large windows recall the Hall of Mirrors at Versailles (see fig. 19-22), the decoration of the Kaisersaal, with its white-and-gold color scheme and its profusion of delicately curved forms, embodies the Rococo spirit. Here one can see the earliest development of Neumann's aesthetic of interior design that culminated in his final project, the Church of the Vierzehnheiligen (see fig. 19-70).

Neumann's collaborator on the Residenz was a brilliant Venetian painter, Giovanni Battista Tiepolo (1696–1770), who began to work there in 1750. Venice in the early eighteenth century had surpassed Rome as an artistic center, and Tiepolo was acclaimed internationally for his confident and optimistic expression of the illusionistic fresco painting pioneered by sixteenth-century Venetians such as Veronese. Tiepolo's work in the Kaisersaal—three scenes glorifying the twelfth-century crusader-emperor Frederick Barbarossa, who had been a patron of the bishop of Würzburg—is a superb example of his architectural painting. *The Marriage of the Emperor Frederick and Beatrice of Burgundy* (fig. 19-69) is presented as if it were theater, with painted and gilded stucco curtains drawn back to reveal the sumptuous costumes and splendid setting of an imperial wedding. Like

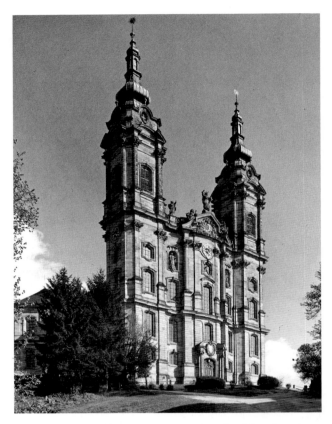

19-70. Johann Balthasar Neumann. Church of the Vierzehnheiligen, near Staffelstein, Germany. 1743–72

In the center of the nave of the Church of Vierzehnheiligen (Fourteen Auxiliary Saints), an elaborate
shrine was built over the spot where, in the fifteenth
century, a shepherd had visions of the Christ Child
surrounded by saints. The saints came to be known
as the Holy Helpers because they assisted people in
need.

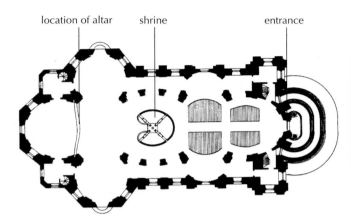

19-71. Johann Balthasar Neumann. Plan of the Church of the
Vierzehnheiligen. c. 1743

19-72. Johann Balthasar Neumann. Interior, Church of the
Vierzehnheiligen. 1743–72

Veronese's grand conceptions (see fig. 18-1), Tiepolo's
spectacle is populated with an assortment of character
types, presented in dazzling light and sun-drenched colors with the assured hand of a virtuoso. Against the opulence of their surroundings, these heroic figures behave
with the utmost decorum and, the artist suggests, nobility of purpose.

Rococo decoration in Germany was as often religious as secular. One of the many opulent Rococo church
interiors still to be seen in Germany and Austria is that of
the Church of the Vierzehnheiligen (Fourteen Auxiliary
Saints) near Staffelstein (fig. 19-70), which was begun by
Neumann in 1743 but was not completed until 1772, long
after his death. The grand Baroque facade gives little hint
of the overall plan (fig. 19-71), which is based on six
interpenetrating oval spaces of varying sizes around a
dominant domed ovoid center. The plan, in fact, recalls
Borromini's design of the Church of San Carlo alle Quattro Fontane (see fig. 19-4). On the interior of the nave (fig.
19-72), the Rococo love of undulating surfaces and overlays of decoration creates a visionary world where flat
wall surfaces scarcely exist. Instead, the viewer is surrounded by clusters of pilasters and engaged columns
interspersed with two levels of arched openings to the

19-73. Egid Quirin Asam. *Angel Kneeling in Adoration*, part of a tabernacle on the main altar, Convent Church, Osterhofen, Germany. c. 1732. Limewood with gilding and silver leaf, height 6'6" (2 m)

side aisles and large clerestory windows illuminating the gold and white of the interior. The foliage of the fanciful capitals is repeated here and there in arabesques, wreaths, and the ornamented frames of the irregular panels that line the vault. What Neumann had begun in the Kaisersaal at Würzburg was brought to full fruition here in the ebullient sense of spiritual uplift achieved by the complete integration of architecture and decoration.

Many sculptors as well as painters found employment in church decoration. White and gold and polychromed wood and plaster created the sumptuous effects of the monastery at Melk and Vierzehnheiligen. Among the Bavarian artists of southern Germany, Egid Quirin Asam (1692–1750) was one of the best. He went to Rome in 1712 with his father, a fresco painter, and his brother, Cosmas Damian (1686–1739). There, they studied Bernini's works and the illusionistic ceilings of Annibale Carracci and others. Back in Bavaria, the brothers often collaborated on interior decoration in the Italian Baroque manner, to which they soon added lighter, more fantastic elements in the French Rococo style. Cosmas specialized in fresco painting and Egid in stone, wood, and stucco sculpture. The Rococo spirit is clearly evident in Egid's *Angel Kneeling in Adoration* (fig. 19-73), a detail of a tabernacle made about 1732 for the main altar of a church in Osterhofen for which Cosmas provided the altarpiece. Carved of limewood and covered with silver leaf and gilding, the over-lifesize figure appears to have landed in a half-kneeling position on a large bracket swinging a censer. Bernini's angel in the Cornaro Chapel (see fig. 19-9) was the inspiration for Asam's figure, but the Bavarian artist has taken the liveliness of pose to an extreme, and the drapery, instead of revealing the underlying forms, swirls about in an independent decorative pattern.

19-74. Clodion. *The Invention of the Balloon.* 1784. Terracotta model for a monument, height 43½" (110.5 cm). The Metropolitan Museum of Art, New York
Rogers Fund and Frederick R. Harris Gift, 1944 (44.21a b)

Clodion had a long career as a sculptor in the exuberant, Rococo manner seen in this work commemorating the 1783 invention of the hot-air balloon. During the austere revolutionary period of the First Republic (1792–1795), he became one of the few Rococo artists to adopt successfully the more acceptable Neoclassical manner (Chapter 26). In 1806, he was commissioned by Napoleon to provide the relief sculpture for two Paris monuments, the Vendôme Column and the Carrousel Arch near the Louvre.

Sculpture and Painting in France

In the last quarter of the eighteenth century, French art generally moved away from Rococo style and toward the classicizing styles that would end in Neoclassicism. But one sculptor who clung to Rococo up to the threshold of the French Revolution in 1789 was Claude Michel, known as Clodion (1738–1814). His major output consisted of playful, erotic tabletop sculpture, mainly in uncolored **terra-cotta**. Typical of Clodion's Rococo designs is the terra-cotta model he submitted to win a 1784 royal commission for a large monument to the invention of the hot-air balloon (fig. 19-74). Although

19-75. Jean-Antoine Watteau. *The Departure from Cythera.* 1717. Oil on canvas, 4'3" x 6'4½" (1.3 x 1.9 m). Musée du Louvre, Paris

Is this fanciful outing ending or about to begin? The French title *Pèlerinage à l'île de Cythère* has been translated as both *Pilgrimage to* and *Pilgrimage on the Isle of Cythera*, since it has never been determined whether or not the bucolic setting represents the mythical island of Venus. Watteau's objective appears to be not to tell a story but to induce the poignant and wistful evocation of love.

Clodion's enchanting piece may today seem inappropriate to commemorate a technological achievement, hot-air balloons then were elaborately decorated with painted Rococo scenes, gold braid, and tassels. Clodion's balloon, decorated with bands of classical ornament, rises from a columnar launching pad in billowing clouds of smoke, assisted at the left by a puffing wind god with butterfly wings and heralded at the right by a trumpeting Victory. A few putti are stoking the fire basket that provided the hot air on which the balloon ascended as a host of others gathers reeds for fuel and flies up toward them.

As for painting, Jean-Antoine Watteau (1684–1721), a Flemish artist living in Paris, epitomizes the French Rococo style. He created a new type of painting when he submitted his official examination painting, *The Departure from Cythera* (fig. 19-75), for admission to membership in the Royal Academy of Painting and Sculpture in 1717. The academicians accepted the painting in a new category, the ***fête galante,*** or elegant outdoor entertainment. *The Departure from Cythera* depicts a dreamworld in which beautifully dressed couples, abetted by putti, take leave of the mythical island of love. The verdant

landscape would never soil the characters' exquisite satins and velvets, nor would a summer shower ever threaten them. This kind of idyllic vision, with its overtones of wistful melancholy, had a powerful attraction in early-eighteenth-century Paris and soon charmed the rest of Europe.

Tragically, Watteau died from tuberculosis when still in his thirties. During his final illness, while staying with the art dealer Edme-François Gersaint, he painted a signboard for Gersaint's shop (fig. 19-76). The dealer later wrote, implausibly, that Watteau had completed the painting in about a week, working only in the mornings because of his failing health. When the sign was installed, it was greeted with almost universal admiration, and Gersaint sold it shortly afterward.

The painting shows an art gallery filled with paintings from the Venetian and Netherlandish schools that Watteau admired. Indeed, the glowing satins and silks of the women's gowns are an homage to artists like Gerard Ter Borch (see fig. 19-52). In certain respects, the composition restages an established Dutch Baroque image, the **cabinet piece**, a portrait of a connoisseur's private

19-76. Jean-Antoine Watteau. *The Signboard of Gersaint*. c. 1721. Oil on canvas, 5'4" x 10'1" (1.62 x 3.06 m). Stiftung Preussische Schlössen und Gärten Berlin-Brandenburg, Schloss Charlottenburg

One of the most beautiful signboards ever created, Watteau's painting was designed to be placed under the canopy of Au Grand Monarque ("At the Sign of the Great King"), an art gallery in Paris belonging to the artist's friend and dealer, Edme-François Gersaint. Gersaint, one of the most successful dealers in eighteenth-century France, introduced the English idea of selling paintings by catalogue. These systematic listings of works for sale gave the name of the artist and the title, medium, and dimensions of each work of art. The shop depicted on the signboard is not Gersaint's, the layout of which is known from contemporary documents, but an ideal gallery visited by elegant and cultivated patrons. The sign was so admired that Gersaint sold it only fifteen days after it was installed. Later it was cut in half down the middle and each piece framed separately, which resulted in the loss of some canvas along the sides of each section.

collection (see Introduction, fig. 21). The visitors to the gallery are elegant ladies and gentlemen, at ease in these surroundings and apparently knowledgeable about paintings. Thus, they create an atmosphere of aristocratic sophistication. At the left, a woman in shimmering pink satin steps across the threshold. Ignoring her companion's outstretched hand, she is distracted by the two porters packing. While one holds a mirror, the other carefully lowers into the wooden case a portrait of Louis XIV, which may be a reference to the name of Gersaint's shop, Au Grand Monarque ("At the Sign of the Great King"). It also suggests the passage of time, for Louis had died in 1715. A number of other elements in the work also gently suggest transience. On the right, the clock positioned directly over the king's portrait, surmounted by an allegorical figure of Fame and sheltering a pair of lovers, is a traditional **memento mori**, a reminder of mortality. The figures on it suggest that both love and fame are subject to the depredations of time. Well-established *vanitas* emblems are the straw (in the foreground), so easily destroyed, and the young woman gazing into the mirror (set next to a vanity case on the counter), for mirrors and

images of young women looking at their reflections were time-honored symbols of the fragility of human life. Watteau, dying, certainly knew how ephemeral life is, and no artist ever expressed the fleeting nature of human happiness with greater subtlety.

Pastel, a new medium for finished works of art, soon became popular among Rococo artists and their patrons. Working with pastel chalks—made of chalk as a base, pulverized pigment, and weak gum water as a binder—allowed for a rapid, sketchlike technique in color, to capture fleeting impressions and moods. One of the most admired practitioners was the Venetian artist Rosalba Carriera (1675–1757), a former miniaturist and pattern-maker for lace, whose pastels earned her an honorary membership in Rome's Academy of Saint Luke in 1705. Watteau already knew and admired her work, for he had written to her in 1719 asking for a sample of it. In return, she had sent a letter whose envelope she decorated with a sketch of the goddess Juno with a peacock. When Carriera arrived in Paris in 1720, Watteau was in London, but the two met after his return, and in the final months before his death in 1721, she did his portrait in pastel

19-77. Rosalba Carriera. *Jean-Antoine Watteau*. 1721. Pastel on paper, 14⁷/₁₆ x 9¹/₁₆" (36.6 x 23 cm). Städelsches Kunstinstitut, Graphische Sammlung, Frankfurt

19-78. François Boucher. *Le Déjeuner* (*Luncheon*). 1739. Oil on canvas, 32¹/₈ x 25³/₄" (81.5 x 65.5 cm). Musée du Louvre, Paris

(fig. 19-77). Having been made a member of the Royal Academy of Painting and Sculpture in 1720, Carriera is credited with introducing French artists to the pastel medium for portraiture, so admirably suited to Rococo style and taste. She returned to Italy in 1721 and enjoyed an illustrious career until failing eyesight made it impossible for her to work.

The artist most closely associated today with Parisian Rococo painting is François Boucher (1703–1770), who never met Watteau. In 1721, Boucher, the son of a minor painter, entered the workshop of an engraver to support himself as he attempted to win favor at the Academy. The young man's skill drew the attention of a devotee of Watteau, who hired Boucher to reproduce Watteau's paintings in his collection, an event that firmly established the direction of Boucher's career.

After studying at the French Academy in Rome from 1727 to 1731, Boucher settled in Paris and became an academician. Soon his life and career were intimately bound up with two women: The first was his artistically talented wife, Marie-Jeanne Buseau, who was a frequent model as well as a studio assistant to her husband. The other was Louis XV's mistress, Madame de Pompadour, who became his major patron and supporter. Pompadour was an amateur artist herself and took lessons from Boucher in printmaking. After Boucher received his first royal commission in 1735, he worked almost continuously to decorate the royal residences at Versailles and Fontainebleau. In 1755, he was made chief inspector at the Gobelins Tapestry Manufactory, and he provided designs to it and to the Sèvres porcelain and Beauvais tapestry manufactories, all of which produced furnishings for the king.

Boucher became First Painter to the King in 1765. Among his many duties, Boucher produced paintings and cartoons of all descriptions, princely decorative schemes, portraits, and scenes of daily life, such as his 1739 painting *Le Déjeuner* (*The Luncheon*, fig. 19-78). Here a mother with her two young children and the children's nurse gather for refreshments as an attentive male serves from a fine silver pot. A distant echo of Dutch family-life pictures, *Le Déjeuner* is a catalog of contemporary French middle-class life in its depiction of the costumes, the Rococo *boiseries*, candle sconces, console, and parquet floor. Even the doll and pull toy the little girl has brought to the room provide interesting details for the modern viewer.

When the mother of young Jean-Honoré Fragonard (1732– 1806) brought her son to Boucher's studio around 1747– 1748, the busy court artist recommended that the boy first study the basics of painting with his contemporary and friend, Jean-Siméon Chardin (see page 932). Within a few months, Fragonard returned with some small paintings done on his own, and Boucher gladly welcomed him as an apprentice-assistant at no charge to his family. Boucher encouraged the boy to enter the competition for the Prix de Rome, which Fragonard won in 1752. Fragonard returned to Paris in 1761, but not until 1765 was he finally accepted into the Royal Academy. Fragonard began catering to the tastes of an aristocratic

19-79. Jean-Honoré Fragonard. *The Meeting*, from The Loves of the Shepherds. 1771–73. Oil on canvas, 10'5¹/₄" x 7'⁵/₈" (3.18 x 2.15 m). The Frick Collection, New York

clientele, and by 1770 he began to fill the vacuum left by Boucher's death as a decorator of interiors.

Fragonard produced fourteen canvases commissioned around 1771 by Madame du Barry, Louis XV's last mistress, to decorate her château. These marvelously free and seemingly spontaneous visions of lovers explode in color and luxuriant vegetation. *The Meeting* (fig. 19-79) shows a secret encounter between a young man and his sweetheart, who looks back anxiously over her shoulder to be sure she has not been followed and

19-80. After a cartoon by François Boucher. *La Foire Chinoise (The Chinese Fair).* Designed 1743; woven 1743–75 at Beauvais, France. Tapestry of wool and silk, approx. 11'11" x 18'2" (3.63 x 5.54 m). The Minneapolis Institute of Arts
The William Hood Dunwoody Fund

clutches the letter that arranged the tryst. The rapid brushwork that distinguishes Fragonard's technique is at its freest and most lavish here. However, Madame du Barry rejected the paintings and commissioned another set in the fashionable Neoclassical style. Her view of Fragonard's manner as passé showed that the Rococo world was, indeed, ending. Fragonard's erotic Rococo style became outmoded, and his last years were spent living on a small pension and the generosity of his highly successful pupil Marguerite Gérard (1761–1837), who was his wife's younger sister.

Rococo Decorative Arts

In the eighteenth century, all media succumbed to the enchantment of Rococo. Royal factories in every country adopted the lively, elegant style in everything from chairs and tables to tapestries, **porcelain**, and silverware. Not only classical art but also the exotic art of the Far East inspired artists—for example, Chinese motifs, known as **chinoiseries**, became a decorative fantasy in *La Foire Chinoise* (*The Chinese Fair*), the tapestry from a six-piece suite done from designs by Boucher (fig. 19-80). Ten sets of the suite were woven between 1743 and 1775, most of them for the king. The artist used his imagination freely to invent a scene in a country he had never visited and probably knew little about beyond the imported Chinese porcelains. Boucher's goal was to create a mood of liveliness and exotic charm rather than an authentic depiction of China.

French chinoiserie design also influenced goldsmiths such as Elizabeth Godfrey (c. 1700–c. 1758), one of several outstanding women craft artists working in London at the time. The daughter of an immigrant French Protestant silversmith and married twice to goldsmiths, Elizabeth first registered her personal mark, used to identify works from her shop, at the death of her first husband in 1731. During her subsequent marriage to Benjamin Godfrey, she apparently worked under his mark, but at his death in 1741 she again registered her own. About this time, Elizabeth responded to the new wave of French taste in England by creating Rococo designs, such as her tea caddies of 1755 (fig. 19-81). The caddies were made to hold a choice of black or green tea, but their shapes have been disguised with curves, spiral scrolls, swags, volutes, and convex side panels containing enchanting little chinoiseries that depict the planting and gathering of tea. Even the jar openings and lids arch up from their concave sides, and the lid knobs are formed by exotic birds.

Europeans, especially Germans, had created their own version of hard-paste, or true, porcelain, of the type imported from China (see "The Secret of Porcelain," page 843). But many wares continued to be made in imitation of Chinese porcelain using soft paste, a cheaper clay mix containing ground glass, which can be fired at lower temperatures. A major production center of soft paste in France was the Royal Porcelain Factory at Sèvres, whose name today is synonymous with fine porcelain. Typical of its elegant creations for the court and other patrons

19-81. Elizabeth Godfrey. Tea caddies, from London. 1755. Silver, height approx. 5½" (14 cm). National Museum of Women in the Arts, Washington, D.C.

Silver Collection assembled by Nancy Valentine, purchased with funds donated by Mr. and Mrs. Oliver Grace and family

Godfrey created her intricate Rococo designs by the repoussé technique, a manner of embossing metal by delicately beating it over forms with small mallets from inside the container. Although made in London, the style of these pieces was derived from French Rococo designs of the type called **chinoiserie**. This term refers to fanciful Chinese-inspired figures and settings used as decorations on porcelains, furniture, silver vessels, and even large tapestries.

able to afford such luxury items is a soft-paste potpourri jar in the shape of a boat (fig. 19-82), dated 1758, which is displayed on a base created for it. This rare technical masterpiece of sculpting and enamel painting is also a prime illustration of Rococo taste. In a typical blend of realistic detail and sheer fantasy, the boat has gilded rope rigging and a rope ladder leading to the crow's nest at the top of the mast, which is wrapped in a fine silken length of cloth embroidered with the royal fleurs-de-lis. The portholes are actually open to the interior to allow the odor of the potpourri (aromatic herbs, rose petals, cinnamon bark, and the like) to escape. In emulation of Chinese vase decoration, the side of the boat is painted with birds and blossoms.

NORTH AMERICA BEFORE 1776

In the seventeenth and eighteenth centuries, the art of North America reflected the tastes of the European countries that ruled the colonies, especially England and Spain. Not surprisingly, much of the colonial art was done by immigrant artists, and styles often lagged behind the European mainstream. Colonial life was still hard in the 1600s, and few could afford to think of fine houses and art collections; the Puritans wanted only the simplest functional buildings for homes and churches. By the eighteenth century, the colonists had become more affluent and had developed pride in their possessions, although they remained conservative. Easier and more frequent travel between the continents contributed to the spread of European styles. Architecture responded more quickly than sculpture, painting, and craft arts in the development of native styles. Unfortunately but understandably, native artists of outstanding talent often found it advantageous to resettle in Europe.

Architecture

Architecture in the British North American colonies can be divided generally into two types: derivations of European provincial timber construction with medieval roots, and the Palladian classical style that arrived from England about the middle of the eighteenth century. In the Southwest, Spanish styles dominated the building of mission-church complexes.

Wood, so easily obtained in the Northeast, was used to create the same kinds of houses and churches then being built in rural England, Holland, or France, depending on the colonists' home provinces. In seventeenth-century New England, for example, many buildings reflected the adaptation of contemporary English country buildings so appropriate to the severe North American winters—**half-timber construction** with steep roofs, massive central fireplaces and chimneys, overhanging

19-82. Potpourri jar, from Sèvres Royal Porcelain Factory, France. 1758. Soft-paste porcelain with polychrome and gold decoration, vase without base 14¾ x 13¾ x 6⅞" (37.5 x 34.6 x 17.5 cm). The Frick Collection, New York

19-83. Parson Capen House, Topsfield, Massachusetts. 1683

19-84. Peter Harrison. Redwood Library, Newport, Rhode Island. 1749

19-85. Mission San Xavier del Bac, near Tucson, Arizona. 1784–97. Arizona Historial Society, Tucson (Ash #41446)

upper stories, and small windows with tiny panes of glass. Following a time-honored tradition, walls consisted of wooden timber frames filled with **wattle and daub** (woven branches packed with clay), or brick in more expensive homes. Instead of leaving this half-timber construction exposed, as was common in Europe, colonists usually weatherproofed it with horizontal plank siding, called **clapboard**. One of the few well-preserved examples is the Parson Capen House in Topsfield, Massachusetts (fig. 19-83), built in 1683. The earliest homes generally consisted of a single "great room" and fireplace, but the Capen House has two stories, each with two

rooms flanking the central fireplace and chimney. The main fireplace was the center of domestic life, where all the cooking was done and the firelight provided illumination for reading and sewing.

The Palladian style, introduced into England by Inigo Jones in the seventeenth century (see fig. 19-59), continued to be popular in England and came to the British North American colonies in the mid-eighteenth century. One of the earliest examples, the work of English-born architect Peter Harrison (1716–1775), is the Redwood Library (fig. 19-84), built in Newport, Rhode Island, in 1749. The fusion of the temple front with a colossal Doric order and a lower

19-86. *Mrs. Freake and Baby Mary.* c. 1674. Oil on canvas, 42¼ x 36¼" (108 x 92.1 cm). Worcester Museum of Art, Worcester, Massachusetts
Gift of Mr. and Mrs. Albert W. Rice

facade with a triangular pediment is not only typically Palladian (see fig. 18-35); it is, in fact, a faithful replica of a design by Palladio in his *Fourth Book of Architecture.* The elegant simplicity of this particular design made it a favorite of English architects for small pleasure buildings on the grounds of estates. The double temple front, used by Palladio for churches, is perfectly suited to a library.

Spanish colonial builders quite naturally tried to replicate the architecture of their homeland. In the Spanish colonial Southwest, the builders of one of the finest examples of mission architecture, San Xavier del Bac near Tucson, Arizona (fig. 19-85), looked to Spain for its inspiration. The foundations were begun by the Jesuit priest Eusebio Kino in 1700, using stone quarried locally by Native Americans of the Pima nation. The desert site had already been laid out with irrigation ditches, and Father Kino wrote in his reports that there would be running water in every room and workshop of the new mission, but the building never proceeded. Instead, Kino's vision was realized by the Spanish Franciscan missionary and master builder Juan Bautista Velderrain (d. 1790), who came to the mission in 1776. Velderrain in his letters spoke of his labors for God and the king of Spain—at that time Charles III, who established royal control over Spanish churches and ousted the Jesuit order from Spain. Thus, Father Kino's Jesuit mission site had been turned over to the Franciscans in 1768.

The huge church, 99 feet long with a domed crossing and flanking bell towers, was unusual for the area in being built of brick and mortar rather than **adobe**, made of earth and straw. The basic structure was finished by the time of

Velderrain's death, in 1790, and the exterior decoration was completed by 1797 under the supervision of his successor. It is generally accepted that the Spanish artists executing the elaborate exterior, as well as the fine interior paintings and sculpture, were from central Mexico. Nearly thirty artists were living there in 1795. Although the San Xavier facade is far from a copy, the focus on the central entrance area, created by a combination of Spanish Churrigueresque decoration and sinuous Rococo lines and spirals, is clearly in the tradition of the earlier eighteenth-century work of Pedro de Ribera in Madrid (see fig. 19-28). The mission was dedicated to Saint Francis Xavier, whose statue once stood at the apex of the portal decoration. In the niches are statues of four female saints tentatively identified as Lucy, Cecilia, Barbara, and Catherine of Siena. Hidden in the sculpted mass is one humorous element: a cat confronting a mouse, which inspired a local Pima saying: "When the cat catches the mouse, the end of the world will come" (cited in Chinn and McCarty, page 12). (Spanish colonial art is discussed in more detail in Chapter 23.)

Painting

Painting and sculpture had to wait for more settled and affluent times in the colonies. For a long time, carved or engraved tombstones were the only sculpture. Painting, too, was considered necessary only as a family record, not as vanity, and portraits done by itinerant "face painters," called **limners**, have a charm and sincerity that appeal to the modern eye. The anonymous painter of *Mrs. Freake and Baby Mary* (fig. 19-86), dated

19-87. John Smibert. *Dean George Berkeley and His Family (The Bermuda Group)*. 1729. Oil on canvas, 5'9½" x 7'9" (1.77 x 2.4 m). Yale University Art Gallery, New Haven, Connecticut
Gift of Isaac Lathrop of Plymouth, Massachusetts

about 1674, seems to have known Dutch portraiture, probably through engraved copies that were imported and sold in the colonies. Even though its painter was clearly self-taught and lacked skills in illusionistic, three-dimensional composition, the spirit of the Freake portrait has much in common with Frans Hals's *Catharina Hooft and Her Nurse* (see fig. 19-41), especially in the care given to minute details of costuming and the focus on large figures in the foreground space. Maternal pride in an infant and hope for her future are universals that seem to apply to little Mary as well as to Catharina, even though their worlds were far apart.

As patronage for portrait paintings grew with the wealth of the colonies, a few traditionally trained European artists immigrated to satisfy the market. Probably the first such artist of stature to arrive was John Smibert (1688–1751), a Scot who had studied in London and spent considerable time in Italy. He came to the colonies in 1728 with one of his patrons, George Berkeley, to be the art professor at the college Berkeley was planning to found in Bermuda. In 1729, while Berkeley and his entourage were in Newport, Rhode Island, to complete their arrangements for the project, Smibert took the opportunity to paint a group portrait, *Dean George Berkeley and His Family,* commonly called *The Bermuda Group* (fig. 19-87). Berkeley, at the right, dictates to a richly dressed man at the table, while Berkeley's wife and child and another couple listen, and Smibert himself appears at the far left.

Smibert's debt to Flemish painting, which was still favored in the English court at the time, is obvious in the balanced but asymmetrical arrangement of figures and the great attention paid to representing textures of the costumes and the pattern of the Oriental rug on the table. The men's features are individualized likenesses, but the women's are idealized according to a convention of female beauty current in English portraiture—ovoid heads with large, plain features, columnlike necks, and tastefully exposed bosoms. The Bermuda project never went forward, and Smibert settled in Boston, working as a portrait painter, art-supply dealer, and printseller. The native Boston artists imitated his rich foreground settings against distant landscape views, his asymmetrical composition, and, especially, his conventions for female beauty.

Among Smibert's friends was Peter Pelham, an English immigrant painter-engraver, who married a Boston widow with a tobacco shop in 1748. Pelham's stepson John Singleton Copley (1738–1815) grew up to be America's first native artist of genius. Copley's sources of inspiration were meager—Smibert's followers and his stepfather's engravings—but his work was already drawing attention when he was fifteen. Young Copley's canny instincts for survival in the colonial art world included an intuitive understanding of the psychology of his middle-class Puritan clientele. They valued not only his excellent technique, which equaled that of European artists, but

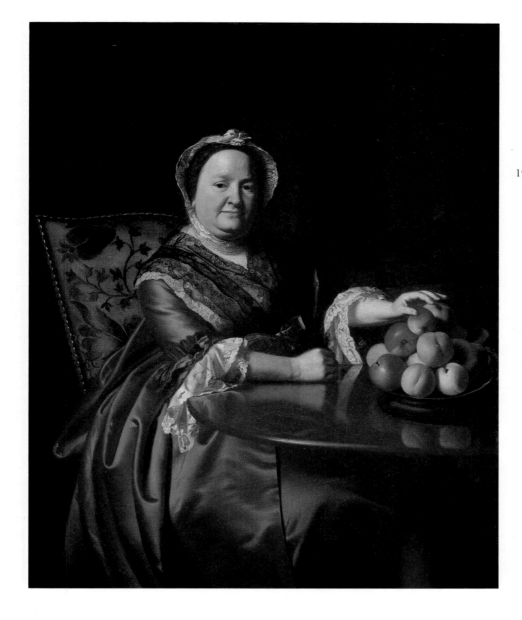

19-88. John Singleton Copley. *Mrs. Ezekiel Goldthwait (Elizabeth Lewis)*. 1771. Oil on canvas, 50³/₈ x 40¹/₄" (128 x 102.2 cm). Museum of Fine Arts, Boston
Bequest of John T. Bowen in memory of Eliza M. Bowen, 1941

also his ability to dignify them while recording their features with unflinching realism.

An example of his mature Boston style is *Mrs. Ezekiel Goldthwait (Elizabeth Lewis)* (fig. 19-88), painted in 1771. Elizabeth Goldthwait was well known for her fine home and gracious dinner parties, but she was also a successful agriculturist whose orchards must have supplied the lush fruits she caresses, as if offering one to the viewer. She is shown in a lace-trimmed silk dress, surrounded by such luxuries as a damask-covered chair and mirror-polished mahogany table. Despite her obvious prosperity, Mrs. Goldthwait's open, amiable features, strong thick wrists, and large capable hands show a lack of vanity and a commitment to hard work that seem to personify the spirit of Puritan New England.

Copley's talents so outdistanced those of his colonial contemporaries that the artist aspired to a larger reputation. In 1766, he had sent a portrait of his half brother, *Boy with a Squirrel,* to an exhibition in London. The critical response was rewarding, and a colonial expatriate from Philadelphia encouraged Copley to study in Europe. At that time, he was kept from following the advice by family ties. But in 1773, revolutionary struggles hit close to home. Colonists dressed as Native Americans boarded a ship carrying tea and threw the cargo into Boston Harbor to protest the British East India Company's monopoly and the tax imposed on tea by the government—an event known as the Boston Tea Party. Copley was divided between two circles: his affluent in-laws and clients who were pro-British, and his radical friends including Paul Revere, John Hancock, and Samuel Adams. Reluctant to take sides, Copley sailed in June 1774 for Europe, where he visited London and Paris, then Italy. While there, he received word of the increasingly dangerous atmosphere in the colonies and urged his family to flee to England. Except for his widowed mother, all were reunited in London in 1775, the eve of the American Revolution. Copley spent the rest of his life in London. We will follow his career in England in Chapter 26.

CHAPTER 20

Art of India after 1100

Taj Mahal
c. 1632–48

Gandhi Bhavan
1959–61

0   300 miles
0   300 kilometers

AFGHANISTAN

TIBET

PAKISTAN

Kangra

Chandigarh

Indus River

PUNJAB
HILLS

Delhi

New Delhi

Yamuna River

Ganges River

HIMALAYA MOUNTAINS

Brahmaputra

NEPAL

BHUTAN

Agra

RAJASTHAN

Karachi

Patna

BIHAR

BANGLA-
DESH

Calcutta

GUJARAT

INDIA

DECCAN

Bombay

*Arabian
Sea*

Vijayanagar

*Bay of
Bengal*

Madras

*TAMIL
NADU*

Madurai

SRI LANKA

INDIAN OCEAN

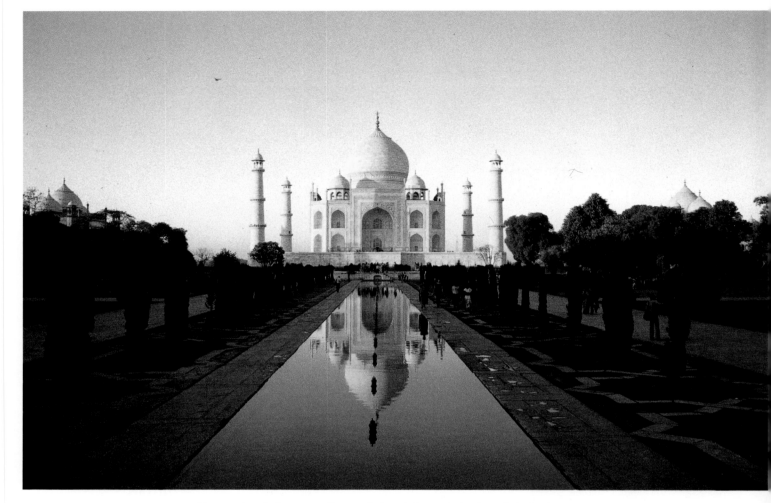

20-1. Taj Mahal, Agra, India. Mughal period, Mughal, reign of Shah Jahan, c. 1632–48

Visitors catch their breath. Ethereal, weightless, the building barely seems to touch the ground. Its reflection shimmers in the pools of the garden meant to evoke a vision of paradise as described in the Koran, the holy book of Islam. Its facades are delicately inlaid with inscriptions and arabesques in semiprecious stones—carnelian, agate, coral, turquoise, garnet, lapis, and jasper. Above, its luminous, white-marble dome reflects each shift in light, flushing rose at dawn, dissolving in its own brilliance in the noonday sun.

One of the most celebrated buildings in the world, the Taj Mahal (fig. 20-1) was built in the seventeenth century by the Mughal ruler Shah Jahan as a mausoleum for his favorite wife, Mumtaz-i-Mahal, who died in childbirth. A dynasty of Central Asian origin, the Mughals were the most successful of the many Islamic groups that established themselves in India beginning in the tenth century. Under their patronage, Persian and Central Asian influences mingled with older traditions of the South Asian subcontinent, adding yet another dimension to the already ancient and complex artistic heritage of India.

LATE MEDIEVAL PERIOD

By 1100 India was already among the world's oldest civilizations (see "Foundations of Indian Culture," below). The art that survives from its earlier periods is almost exclusively sacred, most of it inspired by the three principal religions: Hinduism, Buddhism, and Jainism. At the start of the Late Medieval period, which extends roughly from 1100 to 1526, these three religions continued as the principal focus for Indian art, even as invaders from the northwest began to establish the new religious culture of Islam.

Buddhist Art

After many centuries of prominence, Buddhism had been in decline as a cultural force in India since the seventh century. By the Late Medieval period, the principal Buddhist centers were concentrated in the northeast, in the kingdom ruled by the Pala dynasty. There, in great monastic universities that attracted monks from as far away as China, Korea, and Japan, was cultivated a form of Buddhism known as tantric (Vajrayana) Mahayana. The

practices of tantric Buddhism, which included techniques for visualizing deities, encouraged the development of **iconographic** images such as the gilt bronze sculpture of the **bodhisattva** Avalokiteshvara in figure 20-2. Bodhisattvas are beings who are well advanced on the path to buddhahood (enlightenment), the goal of Mahayana Buddhists, and who have vowed out of compassion to help others achieve enlightenment. Avalokiteshvara, the bodhisattva of greatest compassion, whose vow is to forgo buddhahood until all others become buddhas, became the most popular of these saintly beings in India and in East Asia.

Characteristic of bodhisattvas, he is distinguished in art by his princely garments, unlike a buddha, who wears a monk's robes. Avalokiteshvara is specifically recognized by the lotus flower he holds and by the presence in his crown of his "parent" buddha, in this case Amitabha, buddha of the Western Pure Land. Other marks of Avalokiteshvara's extraordinary status are the third eye (symbolizing the ability to see in miraculous ways) and the wheel on his palm (signifying the ability to teach the Buddhist truth).

FOUNDATIONS OF INDIAN CULTURE

The earliest civilization on the Indian subcontinent flourished toward the end of the third millennium BCE along the Indus River in present-day Pakistan. Remains of its expertly engineered brick cities have been uncovered, together with works of art that intriguingly suggest spiritual practices and reveal artistic traits known in later Indian culture.

The abrupt demise of the Indus Valley civilization during the mid-second millennium BCE coincides with (and may be related to) the arrival from the northwest of a seminomadic warrior people known as the Indo-European Aryans. Over the next millennium they were influential in formulating the new civilization that gradually emerged. The most important Aryan contributions to this new civilization included the Sanskrit language and the sacred texts called the Vedas. The evolution of Vedic thought under the influence of indigenous Indian beliefs culminated in the Upanishads, whose mystical, philosophical texts took shape sometime after 800 BCE.

The Upanishads teach that the material world is illusory; only Brahman, the universal soul, is real and eternal. We—that is, our individual souls—are trapped in this illusion in a relentless cycle of birth, death, and rebirth. The ultimate goal of religious life is to liberate ourselves from this cycle and to unite our individual soul with Brahman.

Buddhism and Jainism are two of the many religious communities that developed in the climate of Upanishadic thought. Buddhism is based on the teachings of Shakyamuni Buddha, who lived in central India about 500 BCE; Jainism was shaped about the same time around the followers of the spiritual leader Mahavira. Both religions acknowledged the cyclical nature of existence and taught a means of liberation from it, but they rejected the authority, rituals, and social strictures of Vedic religion. Whereas the Vedic religion was in the hands of a hereditary priestly class, Buddhist and Jain communities welcomed all members of society, a fact that gave them great appeal. The Vedic tradition eventually evolved into the many sects collectively known as Hinduism.

Politically, India has generally been a mosaic of regional dynastic kingdoms, but from time to time, empires emerged that unified large parts of the subcontinent. The first was the Maurya dynasty (c. 322–185 BCE), whose great king Ashoka patronized Buddhism. From this time Buddhist doctrines spread widely and its artistic traditions were established.

In the first century CE the Kushans, a Central Asian people, created an empire extending from present-day Afghanistan down into central India. Buddhism prospered under Kanishka, the most powerful Kushan king, and spread into Central Asia and to East Asia. At this time, under the evolving thought of Mahayana Buddhism, traditions first evolved for depicting the image of the Buddha in art.

Later, under the Gupta dynasty (c. 320–500 CE) in central India, Buddhist art and culture reached their high point. However, Gupta monarchs also patronized the Hindu religion, which from this time grew to become the dominant Indian religious tradition, with its emphasis on the great gods Vishnu (the Creator), Shiva (the Destroyer), and the Goddess—all with multiple forms.

During the long Medieval period, which lasted from about 650 to 1526 CE, numerous regional dynasties prevailed, some quite powerful and long-lasting. During the early part of this period, to roughly 1100, Buddhism continued to decline as a cultural force, while artistic achievement under Hinduism soared. Hindu temples, in particular, developed monumental and complex forms that were rich in symbolism and ritual function, with each region of India producing its own variation.

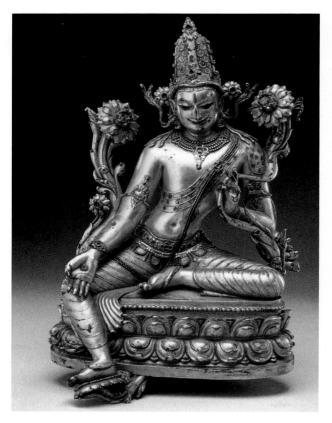

20-2. *The Bodhisattva Avalokiteshvara*, from Kurkihar, Bihar, Central India. Pala dynasty. Late Medieval period, 12th century. Gilt-bronze, height 10" (25.5 cm). Patna Museum, Patna

20-3. Detail of a leaf with *The Birth of Mahavira*, from the *Kalpa Sutra*. Late Medieval period, western Indian school (probably Gujarat), c. 1375–1400. Gouache on paper, 3⅜ x 3" (8.5 x 7.6 cm). Prince of Wales Museum, Bombay

Avalokiteshvara is shown here in the posture of relaxed ease known as the royal pose. One leg angles down; the other is drawn up onto the lotus seat, itself considered an emblem of spiritual purity. His body bends gracefully, if a bit stiffly, to one side. The chest scarf and lower garment cling to his body, fully revealing its shape. Delicate floral patterns enliven the textiles, and closely set parallel folds provide a wiry, linear tension that contrasts with the hard but silken surfaces of the body. Linear energy continues in the sweep of the tightly pleated hem emerging from under the right thigh, the sinuous lotus stalks on each side, and the fluttering ribbons of the elaborate crown. A profusion of details and varied textures creates an ornate effect—the lavish jewelry, the looped hair piled high and cascading over the shoulders, the ripe blossoms, the rich layers of the lotus seat. Though still friendly and human, the image has become rather formalized. The features of the face, where we instinctively look for a human echo, are treated quite abstractly, and despite its reassuring smile, the statue's expression remains somewhat remote. Through richness of ornament and tension of line, this style expresses the heightened power of a perfected being.

With the fall of the Pala dynasty to Turkic invaders in 1199, the last centers of Buddhism in northern India collapsed, and the monks dispersed, mainly into Nepal and Tibet. From that time, Tibet has remained the principal stronghold of Tantric Buddhist practice and its arts.

The artistic style perfected under the Palas, however, became an influential international style throughout East and Southeast Asia.

Jain Art

The Jain religion traces its roots to a spiritual leader called Mahavira (d. 526 BCE), whom it regards as the final in a series of twenty-four saviors known as pathfinders, or *tirthankaras*. Devotees seek through purification to become worthy of rebirth in the heaven of the pathfinders, a zone of pure existence at the zenith of the universe. Jain monks live a life of austerity, and even laypersons avoid killing any living creature.

As Islamic, or Muslim, territorial control over northern India expanded, non-Islamic religions resorted to more private forms of artistic expression, such as illustrating their sacred texts, rather than public activities, such as building temples. In these circumstances, the Jains of western India, primarily in the region of Gujarat, created many stunningly illustrated manuscripts, such as this *Kalpa Sutra*, which explicates the lives of the pathfinders (fig. 20-3). Produced during the late fourteenth century, it is one of the first Jain manuscripts on paper rather than palm leaf, which had previously been used.

With great economy, the illustration, inserted between blocks of Sanskrit text, depicts the birth of Mahavira. He is shown cradled in his mother's arms as she reclines in her

1250
1100　2000

Years	Period	India	World
c. 1100–1526	Late Medieval period	Hinduism, Buddhism, Jainism coexist; Pala dynasty in northeast; Buddhist monastic universities in northeast; Turkic invaders defeat Pala dynasty; Buddhism in India declines; Vijayanagar Hindu kingdom in South India resists Islamic forces; Nayaks' Hindu temple complexes	c. 1100–1600 Mound-building cultures (North America); Oxford and Cambridge (England) and the University of Paris (France) founded; Kamakura period (Japan); Magna Carta (England); Hundred Years' War between England and France; Black Death in Europe; Ming dynasty (China); Great Schism in Roman Catholic Church (Italy, France); Columbus's voyages (Spain); Protestant Reformation
c. 1526–18th century	Mughal period	Babur first Mughal emperor; Rajput kingdoms and schools; *Gita Govinda*; Emperor Akbar; imperial Mughal school workshops; *Hamza-nama*; Emperor Jahangir; Emperor Shah Jahan; Taj Mahal; Mughal Empire unified; British East India Company; Kangra school	c. 1600–1800 First permanent English colony in North America; Thirty Years' War in Europe; union of England and Scotland as Great Britain; James Watt develops steam engine (Scotland); Declaration of Independence (United States); French Revolution; Napoleon's conquests (France)
c. 18th century–present	Modern period	British Empire includes India; New Delhi made capital city; India achieves independence	c. 1800–c. 1950 Simón Bolívar founds independent Venezuela (South America); Monroe Doctrine (United States); Mexico becomes a republic; Canada united; Italy united; Civil War (United States); Sino-Japanese War; Spanish-American War; Wright brothers make first flight (United States); Einstein's theory of relativity (Germany); World War I; Russian Revolution; League of Nations; Spain becomes a republic; World War II; United Nations established; People's Republic of China founded

bed under a canopy connoting royalty, attended by three ladies-in-waiting. Decorative pavilions and a shrine with peacocks on the roof suggest a luxurious palace setting. Everything appears two-dimensional against the brilliant red or blue ground. Vibrant colors and crisp outlines impart an energy to the painting that suggests the arrival of the divine in the mundane world. Transparent garments with variegated designs reveal the swelling curves of the figures, whose alert postures and gestures convey a sense of the importance and excitement of the event. Strangely exaggerated features, such as the protruding eyes, contribute to the air of the extraordinary. With its angles and tense curves, the drawing is closely linked to the aesthetics of Sanskrit calligraphy, and the effect is as if the words themselves had suddenly flared into color and image.

Hindu Art

During the Early Medieval period Hinduism had become the dominant religious tradition of India. With the increasing popularity of Hindu sects came the rapid development of Hindu temples. Spurred by the ambitious building programs of wealthy rulers, well-formulated regional styles had evolved by about 1000 CE. The most spectacular structures of the era were monumental, with a complexity and grandeur of proportion unequaled even in later Indian art.

During the Late Medieval period this emphasis on monumental individual temples gave way to the building of vast **temple complexes** and more moderately scaled yet more richly ornamented individual temples. These

20-4. Outer *gopura* of the Minakshi-Sundareshvara Temple, Madurai, Tamil Nadu, South India. Nayak dynasty. Late Medieval period, mostly 13th to mid-17th centuries

developments took place largely in the south of India, for temple building in the north virtually ceased with the consolidation of Islamic rule there from the beginning of the thirteenth century. The mightiest of the southern Hindu kingdoms was Vijayanagar (c. 1350–1565), whose rulers successfully countered the southward progress of Islamic forces for more than 200 years. Viewing themselves as defenders and preservers of Hindu faith and culture, Vijayanagar kings lavished donations on sacred shrines. Under the patronage of the Vijayanagar and their successors, the Nayaks, the principal monuments of later Hindu architecture were created.

The enormous temple complex at Madurai, one of the capitals of the Nayaks, is an example of this late, fervent expression of Hindu faith. Founded around the thirteenth century, it is dedicated to the goddess Minakshi (the local name for Parvati, the consort of the god Shiva) and to Sundareshvara (the local name for Shiva himself). The temple complex stands in the center of the city and is the focus of Madurai life. At its heart are the two oldest shrines, one to Minakshi and the other to Sundareshvara. Successive additions over the centuries gradually expanded the complex around these small shrines and came to dominate the visual landscape of the city. The most dramatic features of this and similar "temple cities" of the south were the thousand-pillar halls, large ritual-bathing pools, and especially entrance gateways, called **gopuras**, which tower above the temple site and the surrounding city like modern skyscrapers (fig. 20-4).

Gopuras proliferated as a temple city grew, necessitating new and bigger enclosing walls, and thus new gateways. Successive rulers, often seeking to outdo their predecessors, donated taller and taller *gopuras*. As a result, temple cities often have their tallest structures at the periphery rather than for the central temples, which are sometimes totally overwhelmed. The temple complex at Madurai has eleven *gopuras*, the largest well over 100 feet tall.

Formally, the *gopura* has its roots in the **vimana**, the pyramidal tower characteristic of the seventh-century southern temple style. As the *gopura* evolved, it took on the graceful concave silhouette shown here. The exterior is embellished with thousands of sculpted figures, evoking a teeming world of gods and goddesses. Inside, stairs lead to the top for an extraordinary view.

MUGHAL PERIOD

Islam first touched the South Asian subcontinent in the eighth century, when Arab armies captured a small territory near the Indus River. Later, beginning around 1000, Turkic factions from Central Asia, relatively recent converts to Islam, began military campaigns into North India, at first purely for plunder, then seeking territorial control. From 1206, various Turkic dynasties ruled portions of the subcontinent from the northern city of Delhi. These sultanates, as they are known, constructed forts, mausoleums, monuments, and **mosques**. Although these early dynasties left their mark, it was the Mughal dynasty that made the most inspired and lasting contribution to the art of India.

The Mughals, too, came from Central Asia. Babur (ruled 1494–1530), the first Mughal emperor, empha-

TECHNIQUE

INDIAN PAINTING ON PAPER

Before the fourteenth century most painting in India had been made on walls or palm leaves. With the introduction of paper, techniques were adapted from Persia, and over the ensuing centuries Indian artists produced jewel-toned paintings of surpassing beauty on paper.

Painters usually began their training early. As young apprentices, they learned to make brushes and grind pigments. Brushes were made from the curved hairs of a squirrel's tail, arranged to taper from a thick base to a single hair at the tip. Paint came from mineral and vegetable pigments, ground to a paste with water, then bound with a solution of gum from the acacia plant. Blue was made from lapis lazuli, pale green from malachite. Paper, too, was made by hand. Fibers of cotton and jute were crushed to a pulp, poured onto a woven mat, dried, and then burnished with a smooth piece of agate, often to a glossy finish.

Artists frequently worked from a collection of sketches belonging to a master painter's **atelier**. Sometimes sketches were pricked with small, closely spaced holes and wet color daubed over the holes to transfer the drawing to a blank sheet beneath. The dots were connected into outlines, and the painting began. First, the painter applied a thin **wash** of a chalk-based white, which sealed the surface of the paper while allowing the underlying sketch to show through. Next, outlines were filled with thick washes of brilliant, opaque, unmodulated color. When the colors were dry, the painting was laid face down on a smooth marble surface and burnished with a rounded agate stone, rubbing first up and down, then side to side. The indirect pressure against the marble polished the pigments to a high luster. Then outlines, details, and modeling—depending on the style—were added with a fine brush.

Sometimes certain details were purposely left for last, such as the eyes, which were said to bring the painting to life. Along more practical lines, gold and raised details were applied when the painting was nearly finished. Gold paint, made from pulverized, 24-karat **gold leaf** bound with acacia gum, was applied with a brush and burnished to a high shine. Raised details such as the pearls of a necklace were made with thick, white chalk-based paint, with each pearl a single droplet hardened into a tiny raised mound.

1100   1550   2000

sized his Turkic heritage, though he had equally impressive Mongol ancestry. After some initial conquests in Central Asia, he amassed an empire stretching from Afghanistan to Delhi, which he conquered in 1526. Akbar (ruled 1556–1605), the third ruler, extended Mughal control over most of North India, and under Akbar and his two successors, Jahangir and Shah Jahan, northern India was generally unified as the Mughal Empire by 1658.

Mughal Painting

Probably no one had more control over the solidification of the Mughal Empire and the creation of Mughal art than the emperor Akbar. A dynamic, humane, and just leader, Akbar was an avid enthusiast of religious discourse and the arts, especially painting. He created an imperial **atelier** (workshop) of painters, which he placed under the direction of two artists from the Persian court. Learning from these two masters, the Indian painters of the atelier soon transformed Persian styles into the more vigorous, naturalistic styles that mark the Mughal school (see "Indian Painting on Paper," above).

One of the most famous and extraordinary works produced in Akbar's atelier is an illustrated manuscript of the *Hamza-nama*, a Persian classic about the adventures of Hamza, uncle of the Prophet Muhammad. Painted on cotton cloth, each illustration is more than 2½ feet high. The entire project gathered 1,400 illustrations into twelve volumes and took fifteen years to complete.

One illustration shows Hamza's spies scaling a fortress wall and surprising some men as they sleep (fig. 20-5). One man climbs a rope; another has already beheaded a figure in yellow and lifts his head aloft—realistic details are never avoided in paintings from the Mughal atelier. The receding lines of the architecture,

20-5. Page with *Hamza's Spies Scale the Fortress*, from the *Hamza-nama*, North India. Mughal period, Mughal, reign of Akbar, c. 1567–82. Gouache on cotton, 30 x 24" (76 x 61 cm). Museum of Applied Arts, Vienna

20-6.   Abul Hasan and Manohar. Page with *Jahangir in Darbar*, from the *Jahangir-nama*, North India. Mughal period, Mughal, reign of Jahangir, c. 1620. Gouache on paper, 13⅝ x 7⅝" (34.5 x 19.5 cm). Museum of Fine Arts, Boston
Frances Bartlett Donation of 1912 and Picture Fund

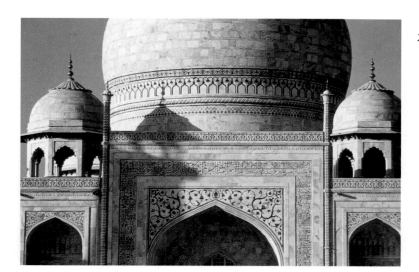

20-7. Taj Mahal, Agra, India. Mughal period, Mughal, reign of Shah Jahan, c. 1632–48

Inside, the Taj Mahal evokes the *hasht behisht*, or "eight paradises," a plan named for the eight small chambers that ring the interior—one at each corner and one behind each iwan. In two stories (for a total of sixteen chambers), the rooms ring the octagonal central area, which rises the full two stories to a domed ceiling that is lower than the outer dome. In this central chamber, surrounded by a finely carved octagonal openwork marble screen, are the exquisite inlaid cenotaphs of Shah Jahan and his wife, whose actual tombs lie in the crypt below.

viewed from a slightly elevated vantage point, provide a reasonably three-dimensional setting. Yet the sense of depth is boldly undercut by the richly variegated geometric patterns of the tilework, which are painted as though they had been set flat on the page. Contrasting with the flat geometric patterns are the large human figures, whose rounded forms and softened contours create a convincing sense of volume. The energy exuded by the figures is also characteristic of painting under Akbar—even the sleepers seem active. This robust, naturalistic figure style is quite different from the linear style seen earlier in Jain manuscripts (see fig. 20-3) and even from the Persian styles that inspired Mughal paintings.

Nearly as prominent as the architectural setting with its vivid human adventure is the sensuous landscape in the foreground, where monkeys, foxes, and birds inhabit a grove of trees that shimmer and glow against the darkened background like precious gems. The treatment of the gold-edged leaves at first calls to mind the patterned geometry of tilework, yet a closer look reveals a skillful naturalism born of careful observation. Each tree species is carefully distinguished—by the way its trunk grows, the way its branches twist, the shape and veining of its leaves, the silhouette of its overall form. Pink and blue rocks with lumpy, softly outlined forms add still further interest to this painting, whose every inch is full of intriguing elements.

Painting from the reign of Jahangir (ruled 1605–1627) presents a different tone. Like his father, Jahangir admired painting and, if anything, paid even more attention to his atelier. Indeed, he boasted that he could recognize the hand of each of his artists even in collaborative paintings, which were common. Unlike Akbar, however, Jahangir preferred the courtly life to the adventurous one, and paintings produced for him reflect his subdued and refined tastes and his admiration for realistic detail.

One such painting is *Jahangir in Darbar* (fig. 20-6). The work, probably part of a series on Jahangir's reign, shows the emperor holding an audience, or *darbar*, at court. Jahangir himself is depicted at top center, seated on a balcony under a bright red canopy. Members of his court, including his son, the future emperor Shah Jahan,

stand somewhat stiffly to each side. The audience, too, is divided along the central axis, with figures lined up in profile or three-quarter view. In the foreground, an elephant and a horse complete the symmetrical format.

Jahangir insisted on fidelity in portraiture, including his own in old age. The figures in the audience are a medley of portraits, possibly taken from albums meticulously kept by the court artists. Some represent people known to have died before Jahangir's reign, so the painting may represent a symbolic gathering rather than an actual event. Standing out amid the bright array of garments is the black robe of a Jesuit priest from Europe. Both Akbar and Jahangir were known for their interest in things foreign, and many foreigners flocked to the courts of these open-minded rulers. The scene is formal, the composition static, and the treatment generally two-dimensional. Nevertheless, the sensitively rendered portraits and the fresh colors, with their varied range of pastel tones, provide the aura of a keenly observed, exquisite ideal reality that marks the finest paintings of Jahangir's time.

Mughal Architecture

Mughal architects were heir to a 300-year-old tradition of Islamic building in India. The Delhi sultans who preceded them had great forts housing government and court buildings. They also introduced two fundamental Islamic structures, the mosque and the tomb, along with construction based on the arch and the dome. (Indian architecture had been based primarily on **post-and-lintel construction**.) In turn, they drew freely on Indian architecture, borrowing both decorative and structural elements to create a variety of hybrid styles. They especially benefited from the centuries-old Indian virtuosity in stone carving and masonry. The Mughals followed in this tradition, synthesizing Indian, Persian, and Central Asian elements for their forts, palaces, mosques, tombs, and **cenotaphs** (tombs or monuments to someone whose remains are actually somewhere else). Mughal architectural style culminated in the most famous of all Indian Islamic structures, the Taj Mahal (figs. 20-1 and 20-7).

20-8. Page with *Krishna and the Gopis*, from the *Gita Govinda*, Rajasthan, India. Mughal period, Rajput, c. 1525–50. Gouache on paper, 4⁷/₈ x 7¹/₂" (12.3 x 19 cm). Prince of Wales Museum, Bombay

The lyrical poem *Gita Govinda*, by the poet-saint Jayadeva, was probably written in eastern India during the latter half of the twelfth century. The episode illustrated here occurs early in the relation of Radha and Krishna, which in the poem is a metaphor for the connection between humans and god. The poem traces the progress of their love through separation, reconciliation, and fulfillment. Intensely sensuous imagery characterizes the entire poem, as in the final song, when Krishna welcomes Radha to his bed (Narayana is the name of Vishnu in his role as cosmic creator):

Leave lotus footprints on my bed of tender shoots, loving Radha!
Let my place be ravaged by your tender feet!
  Narayana is faithful now. Love me Radhika!

I stroke your feet with my lotus hand—you have come far.
Set your golden anklet on my bed like the sun.
  Narayana is faithful now. Love me Radhika!

Consent to my love. Let elixir pour from your face!
To end our separation I bare my chest of the silk that bars your breast.
  Narayana is faithful now. Love me Radhika!

(Translated by Barbara Stoller Miller)

The Taj Mahal is sited on the bank of the Yamuna River at Agra, in northern India. Built between 1632 and 1648, it was commissioned as a **mausoleum** for his wife by the emperor Shah Jahan (ruled 1628–1658), who is believed to have taken a major part in overseeing its design and construction.

Visually, the Taj Mahal never fails to impress (see fig. 20-1). As visitors enter through a monumental, hall-like gate, the tomb looms before them across a spacious garden set with long reflecting pools. Measuring some 1,000 by 1,900 feet, the garden is unobtrusively divided into quadrants planted with trees and flowers and framed by broad walkways and stone inlaid in geometric patterns. In Shah Jahan's time, fruit trees and cypresses—symbolic of life and death, respectively—lined the walkways, and fountains played in the shallow pools. One can imagine the melodies of court musicians that wafted through the garden. Truly, the senses were beguiled in this earthly evocation of paradise.

Set toward the rear of the garden, the tomb is flanked by two smaller structures not visible here, one a mosque and the other, its mirror image, a resting hall. They share a broad base with the tomb and serve visually as stabilizing elements. Like the entrance hall, they are made mostly of red sandstone, rendering even more startling the full glory of the tomb's white marble. The tomb is raised higher than these structures on its own marble platform. At each corner of the platform, a **minaret**, or slender tower, defines the surrounding space. The minarets' three levels correspond to those of the tomb, creating a bond between them. Crowning each minaret is a *chattri*, or pavilion. Traditional embellishments of Indian palaces, *chattris* quickly passed into the vocabulary of Indian Islamic architecture, where they appear prominently. Minarets occur in architecture throughout the Islamic world; from their heights, the faithful are called to prayer.

A lucid geometric symmetry pervades the tomb. It is basically square, but its **chamfered**, or sliced-off, corners create a subtle octagon. Measured to the base of the **finial** (the spire at the top), the tomb is almost exactly as tall as it is wide. Each facade is identical, with a central **iwan** flanked by two stories of smaller iwans. (A typical feature of eastern Islamic architecture, an iwan is a vaulted opening with an arched portal.) By creating voids in the facades, these iwans contribute markedly to the building's sense of weightlessness. On the roof, four octagonal *chattris*, one at each corner, create a visual transition to the lofty, bulbous dome, the crowning element that lends special power to this structure. Framed but not obscured by the *chattris*, the dome rises more gracefully and is lifted higher by its **drum** than in earlier Mughal tombs, allowing the swelling curves and lyrical lines of its beautifully proportioned, surprisingly large form to emerge with perfect clarity.

The pristine surfaces of the Taj Mahal are embellished with utmost subtlety. The sides of the platform are carved in relief with a **blind arcade** motif, and carved relief panels of flowers adorn the base of the building. The portals are framed with verses from the Koran inlaid in black marble, while the **spandrels** are decorated with floral arabesques inlaid in colored semiprecious stones, a technique known by its Italian name, *pietra dura*. Not strong enough to detract from the overall purity of the white marble, the embellishments enliven the surfaces of this impressive yet delicate masterpiece.

Rajput Painting

Outside of the Mughal strongholds at Delhi and Agra, much of northern India was governed regionally by local Hindu princes, descendants of the so-called Rajput warrior clans, whom the Mughals allowed to keep their lands in return for allegiance. Like the Mughals, Rajput princes frequently supported painters at their courts, and in these

settings, free from Mughal influence, a variety of strong, indigenous Indian painting styles were perpetuated.

The Hindu devotional movement known as bhakti, which had done much to spread the faith in the south from around the seventh century, experienced a revival in the north beginning in the Late Medieval period. As it had earlier in the south, bhakti inspired an outpouring of poetic literature, this time devoted especially to Krishna, the popular human incarnation of the god Vishnu. Most renowned is the *Gita Govinda*, a cycle of rhapsodic poems about the love between God and humans expressed metaphorically through the love between the young Krishna and the cowherd Radha.

The illustration here is from a manuscript of the *Gita Govinda* produced in the region of Rajasthan about 1525–1550 (fig. 20-8). The blue god Krishna sits in dalliance with a group of cowherd women. Standing with her maid and consumed with love for Krishna, Radha peers through the trees, overcome by jealousy. Her feelings are indicated by the cool blue color behind her, while the crimson red behind the Krishna grouping suggests passion. The curving stalks and bold patterns of the flowering vines and trees express not only the exuberance of springtime, when the story unfolds, but also the heightened emotional tensions of the scene. Birds, trees, and flowers are brilliant as fireworks against the black, hilly landscape edged in an undulating white line. As in the Jain manuscript earlier (see fig. 20-3), all the figures are of a single type, with plump faces in profile and oversized eyes. Yet the resilient line of the drawing gives them life, and the variety of textile patterns provides some individuality. The intensity and resolute flatness of the scene seem to thrust all of its energy outward, irrevocably engaging the viewer in the drama.

Quite a different mood pervades *Hour of Cowdust*, a work from the Kangra school in the Punjab Hills, foothills of the Himalaya north of Delhi (fig. 20-9). Painted around 1790, some 250 years later than the previous work, it shows the influence of Mughal naturalism on the later schools of Indian painting. The theme is again Krishna. Wearing his peacock crown, garland of flowers, and yellow garment—all traditional iconography of Krishna-Vishnu—he returns to the village with his fellow cowherds and their cattle. All eyes are upon him as he plays his flute, said to enchant all who heard it. Women with water jugs on their heads turn to look; others lean from windows to watch and call out to him. We are drawn into this charming village scene by the diagonal movements of the cows as they surge through the gate and into the courtyard beyond. Pastel houses and walls create a sense of space, and in the distance we glimpse other villagers going about their work or peacefully sitting in their houses. A rim of dark trees softens the horizon, and an atmospheric sky completes the aura of enchanted naturalism. Again, all the figures are similar in type, this time with a perfection of proportion and a gentle, lyrical movement that complements the idealism of the setting. The scene embodies the sublime purity and grace of the divine, which as in so much Indian art is evoked into our human world to coexist with us as one.

20-9.　*Hour of Cowdust*, from Punjab Hills, India. Mughal period, Rajput, Kangra school, c. 1790. Gouache on paper,　10³/₄ x 8¹/₂"
(27.2 x 21.5 cm). Museum of Fine Arts, Boston
Denman W. Ross Collection

20-10. B. P. Mathur and Pierre Jeanneret. Gandhi Bhavan, Punjab University, Chandigarh, North India. Modern period, 1959–61

MODERN PERIOD

By the time *Hour of Cowdust* was painted, India's regional princes had reasserted themselves, and the vast Mughal Empire had shrunk to a small area around Delhi. At the same time, a new power, Britain, was making itself felt, inaugurating a markedly different period in Indian history. First under the mercantile interests of the British East India Company in the seventeenth century, and then under the direct control of the British government as a part of the British Empire in the eighteenth, India was brought forcefully into contact with the West and its culture.

The political concerns of the British Empire extended even to the arts, especially architecture. Over the course of the nineteenth century, the great cities of India, such as Calcutta, Madras, and Bombay, took on a European aspect as British architects built in the revivalist styles favored in England (Chapter 26). During the late nineteenth and early twentieth centuries, architects made an effort to incorporate Indian, usually Mughal, elements into their work. But the results were superficial or overly fantastic and consisted largely of adding ornamental forms such as *chattris* to fundamentally European buildings. The most telling imperial gesture came in the 1920s with the construction of a new, Western-style capital city at New Delhi.

At the same time that the British were experimenting with Indian aesthetics, Indian artists were infusing into their own work Western styles and techniques. One example of this new synthesis is the Gandhi Bhavan at Punjab University in Chandigarh, in North India (fig. 20-10). Used for both lectures and prayer, the hall was designed in the late 1950s by Indian architect B. P. Mathur in collaboration with Pierre Jeanneret, cousin of the French modernist architect Le Corbusier (Chapter 29), whose version of the International Style had been influential in India. The Gandhi Bhavan's three-part, pinwheel plan, abstract sculptural qualities, and fluid use of planes reflect the modern vision of the International Style. Yet other factors speak directly to India's heritage. The merging of sharp, brusque angles with lyrical curves recalls the linear tensions of the ancient Sanskrit alphabet. The pools surrounding the building evoke Mughal tombs, some of which were similarly laid out on terraces surrounded by water, as well as the ritual-bathing pools of Hindu temples. Yet the abstract style is free of specific religious associations.

The irregular stone structure, its smooth surfaces punctuated by only a few apertures, shimmers in the bright Indian sunlight like an apparition of pure form in our ordinary world. Caught between sky, earth, and water, it fittingly evokes the pulsating qualities of a world seen as imbued with divine essence, the world that has always been at the heart of Indian art.

1280 CE   1400   1500   1600

Ni Zan
The Rongxi Studio
1372

Ming porcelain flask
c. 1425–35

▲ YUAN DYNASTY 1280–1368   ▲ MING DYNASTY 1368–1644

CHAPTER 21

Chinese Art
after 1280

1700

1800

1900

1980 CE

Shitao
Landscape
c. 1700

Wu Guanzhong
Pine Spirit
1984

QING DYNASTY 1644–1911

MODERN PERIOD
1911–PRESENT

MONGOLIA

XINJIANG

MANCHURIA

GOBI DESERT

GREAT WALL

GREAT WALL

Beijing

HEBEI

KOREA

SHANXI

Jinan

SHANDONG

Yellow Sea

CHINA

JAPAN

GANSU

Yellow River

HENAN

JIANGSU

Xi'an (Chang'an)

SHAANXI

*HUANG
MOUNTAINS*

TIBET

QINLING
MOUNTAINS

Suzhou

Shanghai

Yangzi River

Hangzhou

*Hangzhou
Bay*

HIMALAYA MOUNTAINS

Jingdezhen

ZHEJIANG

Changsha

JIANGXI

MYANMAR

HUNAN

Taipei

Xi River

Guangzhou
(Canton)

TAIWAN

VIETNAM

Hong Kong

*South China
Sea*

LAOS

0   500 miles
0   500 kilometers

21-1. Garden of the Cessation of Official Life, Suzhou, Jiangsu. Ming dynasty, early 16th century

E arly in the sixteenth century, an official in Beijing, frustrated after serving in the capital for many years without promotion, returned to his home near Shanghai. Taking an ancient poem, "The Song of Leisurely Living," for his model, he began to build a garden. He called his retreat the Garden of the Cessation of Official Life (fig. 21-1) to indicate that he had exchanged his career as a bureaucrat for a life of leisure. By leisure, he meant that he could now dedicate himself to calligraphy, poetry, and painting, the three arts dear to scholars in China.

The scholar class of imperial China was a phenomenon unique in the world, the product of an examination system designed to recruit the finest minds in the country for government service. First instituted during the Tang dynasty (618–907), the civil service examinations were excruciatingly difficult, but for the tiny percentage that passed at the highest level, the rewards were prestige, position, power, and wealth. During the Song dynasty (960–1279) the examinations were expanded and regularized, and more than half of all government positions came to be filled by scholars.

Steeped in the classic texts of philosophy, literature, and history, China's scholars—known as literati—shared a common bond in education and outlook. Their lives typically moved between the philosophical poles of Confucianism and Daoism (see "Foundations of Chinese Culture," opposite). Following the former, they became officials to fulfill their obligation to the world; pulled by the latter, they retreated from society in order to come to terms with nature and the universe: to create a garden, to write poetry, to paint.

Under a series of remarkably cultivated emperors, the literati reached the height of their influence during the Song dynasty. Their world was about to change dramatically, however, with lasting results for Chinese art.

FOUNDATIONS OF CHINESE CULTURE

Chinese culture is distinguished by its long and continuous development. Between 7000 and 2000 BCE a variety of Neolithic cultures flourished across China. Through long interaction these cultures became increasingly similar, and they eventually gave rise to the three Bronze Age dynastic states with which Chinese history traditionally begins: the legendary Xia, the Shang (c. 1700–1100 BCE), and the Zhou (1100–221 BCE).

The Shang developed a culture of splendor and violence. Society was stratified, and the ruling group maintained its authority in part by claiming power as shamans, intermediaries between the human and spirit worlds. Shamanistic practices are responsible for the earliest known examples of Chinese writing—bones inscribed with questions to and answers from the spirit world. Under the Zhou a feudal society developed, with nobles related to the king ruling over numerous small states. During the latter part of the Zhou dynasty, states began to vie for supremacy through intrigue and increasingly ruthless warfare. The collapse of social order inspired China's first philosophers, who largely concerned themselves with the pragmatic question of how to bring about a stable society.

In 221 BCE rulers of the state of Qin triumphed over the remaining states, unifying China as an empire for the first time. The Qin created the mechanisms of China's centralized bureaucracy, but their rule was harsh and the dynasty was quickly overthrown. During the ensuing Han dynasty (206 BCE–220 CE), China at last knew peace and prosperity. Confucianism was made the official state ideology, in the process assuming the form and force of a religion. Developed from the thought of Confucius (551–479 BCE), one of the many philosophers of the Zhou, Confucianism is an ethical system for the management of society based on establishing correct relationships among people. Providing a counterweight was Daoism, which also came into its own during the Han dynasty. Based on the thought of Laozi, a possibly legendary contemporary of Confucius, and the philosopher Zhuangzi (369–286 BCE), Daoism is a kind of nature mysticism that seeks to harmonize the individual with the Dao, or Way, of the Universe. Confucianism and Daoism have remained central to Chinese thought—the one addressing the public realm of duty and conformity, the other the private world of individualism and creativity.

Following the collapse of the Han dynasty, China experienced a long period of disunity (220–589 CE). Invaders from the north and west established numerous kingdoms and dynasties, while a series of six precarious Chinese dynasties held sway in the south. Buddhism, which had begun to filter over trade routes from India during the Han dynasty, now spread widely. The period also witnessed the economic and cultural development of the south (all previous dynasties had ruled from the north).

China was reunited under the Sui dynasty (589–618 CE), which quickly overreached itself and fell to the Tang (618–907 CE), one of the most successful dynasties in Chinese history. Strong and confident, Tang China fascinated and, in turn, was fascinated by the cultures around it. Caravans streamed across Central Asia to the capital, Chang'an, then the largest city in the world. Japan and Korea sent thousands of students to study Chinese culture, and Buddhism reached the height of its influence before a period of persecution signaled the start of its decline.

The mood of the Song dynasty (960–1279 CE) was quite different. The martial vigor of the Tang gave way to a culture of increasing refinement and sophistication, and Tang openness to foreign influences was replaced by a conscious cultivation of China's own traditions. In art, landscape painting emerged as the most esteemed genre, capable of expressing both philosophical and personal concerns. With the fall of the north to invaders in 1126, the Song court set up a new capital in the south, which became the cultural and economic center of the country.

THE MONGOL INVASIONS

At the beginning of the thirteenth century the Mongols, a nomadic people from the steppelands north of China, began to amass an empire. Led at first by Jenghiz Khan (c. 1162–1227), then by his sons and grandsons, they swept westward into central Europe and overran Islamic lands from Central Asia through present-day Iraq. To the east, they quickly captured northern China, and in 1279, led by Kublai Khan, they conquered southern China as well. Grandson of the mighty Jenghiz, Kublai proclaimed himself emperor of China and founder of the Yuan dynasty (1280–1368).

The Mongol invasions were traumatic, and their effect on China was long lasting. During the Song dynasty, China had grown increasingly reflective. Rejecting foreign ideas and influences, intellectuals focused on defining the qualities that constituted true "Chineseness." They drew a clear distinction between their own people, whom they characterized as gentle, erudite, and sophisticated, and the "barbarians" outside China's borders, whom they believed to be crude, wild, and uncultured. Now, faced with the reality of barbarian occupation, China's inward gaze intensified in spiritual resistance. For centuries to come, long after the Mongols had gone, leading scholars continued to seek intellectually more challenging, philosophically more profound, and artistically more subtle expressions of all that could be identified as authentically Chinese.

YUAN DYNASTY

The Mongols established their capital in the northern city now known as Beijing. The cultural centers of China, however, remained the great cities of the south, where the Song court had been located for the previous 150 years. Combined with the tensions of Yuan rule, this separation of China's political and cultural centers created a new situation in the arts.

Years	Period	China	World
1280–1368	**Yuan dynasty**	Kublai Khan, emperor of China, founds Yuan dynasty; Marco Polo in China; Zhao Mengfu's *Autumn Colors on the Qiao and Hua Mountains*	**1280–1400** Book arts flourish in France and England; Gothic style emerges (France); Aztec Empire (Mexico); Hundred Years' War between England and France; Black Death in Europe; Great Schism in Christian Church; Golden Pavilion (Japan)
1368–1644	**Ming dynasty**	Ni Zan's *The Rongxi Studio;* Black Death kills 30 percent of Chinese population; Forbidden City rebuilt; Garden of the Cessation of Official Life; Shen Zhou's *Poet on a Mountain Top*; Dong Qichang's *The Qingbian Mountains*	**1400–1700** Chaucer's *Canterbury Tales* (England); Van Eyck's *Ghent Altarpiece* (Flanders); Inka Empire (South America); Ghiberti's *Gates of Paradise* (Italy); Gutenberg's Bible (Germany); Columbus's voyages (Spain); Michelangelo's *David*; Leonardo's *Mona Lisa*; Michelangelo's Sistine Ceiling (Italy); Protestant Reformation in Europe; Mughal period (India); Baroque style in Europe; Peter Paul Rubens (Flanders); Hideyoshi unites Japan; Rembrandt van Rijn (Netherlands); English colonize North America; Age of Enlightenment begins in Europe
1644–1911	**Qing dynasty**	Individualist painters; Wang Hui's *A Thousand Peaks and Myriad Ravines*; Shitao's *Landscape*; Sino-Japanese War	**1700–1900** Union of England and Scotland as Great Britain; John Singleton Copley (North America); Declaration of Independence (North America); French Revolution; Romanticism and Neoclassicism arise; Mexico becomes a republic; Realism arises in Europe; Marx and Engels's *Communist Manifesto*; Darwin's *Origin of Species*; Italy united; Civil War (United States); Dominion of Canada formed; Impressionism and Post-Impressionism arise
1911–present	**Modern period**	First republic established by Sun Yat-Sen (Sun Yixian); People's Republic of China (Communist) established; Wu Guanzhong's *Pine Spirit*	**1900–1950** Fauve painters emerge (France); German Expressionist movement arises; Cubism (France); World War I; Civil War (Russia); League of Nations founded; World War II; United Nations established

Throughout most of Chinese history, the imperial court had set the tone for artistic taste; artisans attached to the court produced architecture, paintings, gardens, and objects of jade, lacquer, ceramic, and silk especially for imperial use. Over the centuries, painters and calligraphers gradually moved higher up the social scale, for these "arts of the brush" were often practiced as well by scholars and even emperors, whose high status reflected positively on whatever interested them. With the establishment of an imperial painting academy during the Song dynasty, painters finally achieved a status equal to that of court officials. For the literati, painting came to be grouped with **calligraphy** and poetry as the trio of accomplishments suited to members of the cultural elite.

21-2. Zhao Mengfu. Section of *Autumn Colors on the Qiao and Hua Mountains.* Yuan dynasty, 1296. Handscroll, ink and color on paper, 11¼ x 36¾" (28.6 x 93.3 cm). National Palace Museum, Taipei, Taiwan

But while the literati elevated the status of painting by virtue of practicing it, they also began to develop their own ideas of what painting should be. Not having to earn an income from their art, they cultivated an amateur ideal in which personal expression counted for more than "mere" professional skill. They created for themselves a status as artists totally separate from and superior to professional painters, whose art they felt was inherently compromised, since it was done to please others, and impure, since it was tainted by money.

The conditions of Yuan rule now encouraged a clear distinction between court taste, ministered to by professional artists and artisans, and literati taste. The Yuan continued the imperial role as patron of the arts, commissioning buildings, murals, gardens, paintings, and decorative arts. Western visitors such as the Italian Marco Polo were impressed by the magnificence of the Yuan court (see "Marco Polo," above). But scholars, profoundly alienated from the new government, took no notice of these accomplishments, and thus nothing was written about them. Nor did Yuan rulers have much use for scholars, especially those from the south. The civil service examinations were abolished, and the highest government positions were bestowed, instead, on Mongols and their foreign allies. Scholars now tended to turn inward, to search for solutions of their own and to try to express themselves in personal and symbolic terms.

Typical of this trend is Zhao Mengfu (1254–1322), a descendant of the imperial line of Song. Unlike many scholars of his time, he eventually chose to serve the Yuan government and was made a high official. A painter, calligrapher, and poet, all of the first rank, Zhao was especially known for his carefully rendered paintings of horses. But he also cultivated another manner, most famous in his landmark painting, *Autumn Colors on the Qiao and Hua Mountains* (fig. 21-2).

Zhao painted this work for a friend whose ancestors came from Jinan, the present-day capital of Shandong province, and the painting supposedly depicts the landscape there. Yet the mountains and trees are not painted in the accomplished naturalism of Zhao's own time but rather in the archaic yet oddly elegant manner of the earlier Tang dynasty. The Tang dynasty was a great era in Chinese history, when the country was both militarily strong and culturally vibrant. Through his painting Zhao evoked a feeling of nostalgia, not only for his friend's distant homeland but also for China's past.

This educated taste for the "spirit of the antiquity" became an important aspect of **literati painting** in later periods. Also typical of literati taste are the unassuming brushwork, the subtle colors sparingly used (many literati paintings forgo color altogether), the use of landscape to convey personal meaning, and even the intended audience—a close friend. The literati did not paint for

TECHNIQUE

FORMATS OF CHINESE PAINTING

Aside from the large wall paintings that typically decorated palaces, temples, and tombs, most Chinese paintings were done in ink and water-based colors on silk or paper. Finished works were generally mounted on silk as a **handscroll**, a **hanging scroll**, or an **album**.

An album comprises a set of paintings of identical size mounted in an accordion-fold book. (A single painting from an album is called an **album leaf**.) The paintings in an album are usually related in subject, such as various views of a famous site or a series of scenes glimpsed on one trip.

Album-size paintings might also be mounted as a handscroll, a horizontal format generally about 12 inches high and anywhere from a few feet to dozens of feet long. More typically, however, a handscroll would be a single continuous painting. Handscrolls were not meant to be displayed all at once, the way they are commonly presented today in museums. Rather, they were unrolled only occasionally, to be savored in much the same spirit as we might put a favorite film in the VCR. Placing the scroll on a flat surface such as a table, a viewer would unroll it a foot or two at a time, moving gradually through the entire scroll from right to left, lingering over favorite details. The scroll was then rolled up and returned to its box until the next viewing.

Like handscrolls, hanging scrolls were not displayed permanently but were taken out for a limited time—a day, a week, a season. Unlike a handscroll, however, the painting on a hanging scroll was viewed as a whole, unrolled and put up on a wall, with the roller at the lower end acting as a weight to help the scroll hang flat. Although some hanging scrolls are quite large, they are still fundamentally intimate works, not intended for display in a public place.

Creating a scroll was a time-consuming and exacting process. The painting was first backed with paper to strengthen it. Next, strips of paper-backed silk were pasted to the top, bottom, and sides, framing the painting on all four sides. Additional silk pieces were added to extend the scroll horizontally or vertically, depending on the format. The assembled scroll was then backed again with paper and fitted with a half-round dowel, or wooden rod, at the top (of a hanging scroll) or right end (of a handscroll), with ribbons for hanging and tying, and with a wooden roller at the other end. Hanging scrolls were often fashioned from several patterns of silk, and a variety of piecing formats were developed and codified. On a handscroll, a painting was generally preceded by a panel giving the work's title and often followed by a long panel bearing **colophons**—inscriptions such as poems in praise of the work or comments by its owners over the centuries.

colophon panel   title panel

handscroll

label

front   back

hanging scroll

public display but for each other. They favored small formats such as **handscrolls**, **hanging scrolls**, or **album leaves** (book pages), which could easily be taken to show to friends or to share at small gatherings (see "Formats of Chinese Painting," above).

Of the considerable number of Yuan painters who took up Zhao's ideas, several became models for later generations. One such was Ni Zan (1308–1374), whose most famous surviving painting is *The Rongxi Studio* (fig. 21-3). Done entirely in ink, the painting depicts the lake region in Ni's home district. Mountains, rocks, trees, and a pavilion are sketched with a minimum of detail using a dry brush technique—a technique in which the brush is not fully loaded with ink but rather about to run out, so that white paper "breathes" through the ragged strokes. The result is a painting with a light touch and a sense of simplicity and purity. Literati styles were believed to reflect the painter's personality. Ni's spare, dry style became associated with a noble spirit, and many later painters adopted it or paid homage to it.

Ni Zan was one of those eccentrics whose behavior has become legendary in the history of Chinese art. In his early years he was one of the richest men in the region, the owner of a large estate. His pride and his aloofness from daily affairs often got him into trouble with the authorities. His cleanliness was notorious. In addition to washing himself several times daily, he also ordered his servants to wash the trees in his garden and to clean the furniture after his guests had left. He was said to be so unworldly that late in life he gave away most of his possessions and lived as a hermit in a boat, wandering on rivers and lakes.

Whether these stories are true or not, they were important elements of Ni's legacy to later painters, for Ni's life as well as his art served as a model. The painting of the literati was bound up with certain views about what constituted an appropriate life. The ideal, as embodied by Ni Zan and others, was of a brilliantly gifted scholar whose spirit was too fine-tuned for the "dusty world" of government service and who thus preferred to live as a recluse, or as one who had retired after having become frustrated by a brief stint as an official.

MING DYNASTY

The founder of the next dynasty, the Ming (1368–1644), came from a family of poor uneducated peasants. As he rose through the ranks in the army, he enlisted the help of scholars to gain power and solidify his following. Once he had driven the Mongols from Beijing and firmly established himself as emperor, however, he grew to distrust intellectuals. His rule was despotic, even ruthless. Throughout the nearly 300 years of Ming rule, most emperors shared his attitude, so although the civil service examinations were reinstated, scholars remained alienated from the government they were trained to serve.

21-3. Ni Zan. *The Rongxi Studio.* Yuan dynasty, 1372. Hanging scroll, ink on paper, height 29³⁄₈" (74.6 cm). National Palace Museum, Taipei, Taiwan

The idea that a painting is not done to capture a likeness or to satisfy others but is executed freely and carelessly for the artist's own amusement is at the heart of the literati aesthetic. Ni Zan once wrote this comment on a painting: "What I call painting does not exceed the joy of careless sketching with a brush. I do not seek formal likeness but do it simply for my own amusement. Recently I was rambling about and came to a town. The people asked for my pictures, but wanted them exactly according to their own desires and to represent a specific occasion. [When I could not satisfy them,] they went away insulting, scolding, and cursing in every possible way. What a shame! But how can one scold a eunuch for not growing a beard?" (cited in Bush and Shih, page 266).

Court and Professional Painting

The contrast between the luxurious world of the court and the austere ideals of the literati continued through the Ming dynasty. A typical example of Ming court taste is *Hundreds of Birds Admiring the Peacocks*, a large painting on silk by Yin Hong, an artist active during the late fifteenth and early sixteenth centuries (fig. 21-4). A pupil of some well-known courtiers, Yin most probably served in the court at Beijing. The painting is an example of the birds-and-flowers **genre**, which had been popular with artists of the Song academy. Here the subject takes on symbolic meaning, with the homage of the birds to the peacocks representing the homage of court officials to

21-4. Yin Hong. *Hundreds of Birds Admiring the Peacocks*. Ming dynasty, c. late 15th–early 16th centuries. Hanging scroll, ink and color on silk, 7'10½" x 6'5" (2.4 x 1.96 m). The Cleveland Museum of Art

Purchase from the J. H. Wade Fund, 74.31

the emperor. The decorative style goes back to Song academy models as well, although the large format and multiplication of details are traits of the Ming.

The preeminent professional painter in the Ming period was Qiu Ying (1494–1552), who lived in Suzhou, a prosperous southern city. He inspired generations of imitators with exceptional works, such as a long handscroll known as *Spring Dawn in the Han Palace* (fig. 21-5). The painting is based on Tang dynasty depictions of women in the court of the Han dynasty (206 BCE–220 CE). While in the service of a well-known collector, Qiu Ying had the opportunity to study many Tang paintings, whose artists usually concentrated on the figures, leaving out the background entirely. Qiu's graceful and elegant figures—

although modeled after those in Tang works—are portrayed in a setting of palace buildings, engaging in such pastimes as chess, music, calligraphy, and painting. With its antique subject matter, refined technique, and flawless taste in color and composition, *Spring Dawn in the Han Palace* brought professional painting to a new high point.

Gardens and Decorative Arts

Qiu Ying painted to satisfy his patrons in Suzhou. The cities of the south were becoming wealthy, and newly rich merchants collected paintings, antiques, and art objects. The court, too, was prosperous and patronized the arts on a lavish scale. In such a setting, the decorative arts thrived.

21-5. Qiu Ying. Section of *Spring Dawn in the Han Palace*. Ming dynasty, first half of the 16th century. Handscroll, ink and color on silk, 1' x 18'13⁄16" (0.30 x 5.7 m). National Palace Museum, Taipei, Taiwan

21-6. Porcelain flask with decoration in blue underglaze. Ming dynasty, c. 1425–35. Palace Museum, Beijing

Dragons have featured prominently in Chinese folklore from earliest times—Neolithic examples have been found painted on pottery and carved in jade. In Bronze Age China, dragons came to be associated with powerful and sudden manifestations of nature, such as wind, thunder, and lightning. Bronze Age shamans appealed to dragons to learn the weather. At the same time, dragons also became associated with superior beings such as virtuous rulers and sages. With the emergence of China's first firmly established empire during the Han dynasty, the dragon was appropriated as an imperial symbol, and it remained so throughout Chinese history. Dragon sightings were duly recorded and considered auspicious. Yet even the Son of Heaven could not monopolize the dragon. During the Tang and Song dynasties the practice arose of painting pictures of dragons to pray for rain, and for Chan (Zen) Buddhists, the dragon was a symbol of sudden enlightenment.

Like the Song dynasty before it, the Ming has become famous the world over for its exquisite ceramics, especially **porcelain** (see "The Secret of Porcelain," below). The imperial **kilns** in Jingdezhen, in Jiangxi province, became the most renowned center for porcelain not only in all of China but eventually in all the world. Particularly noteworthy are the blue-and-white wares produced during the ten-year reign of the ruler known as the Xuande emperor (ruled 1425–1435), such as the flask in figure 21-6. The subtle shape, the refined yet vigorous decoration of dragons writhing in the sea, and the flawless **glazing** embody the high achievement of Ming artisans.

Chinese furniture, made mainly for domestic use, reached the height of its development in the sixteenth

THE SECRET OF PORCELAIN Marco Polo, it is said, was the one who named a new type of ceramic he found in China. Its translucent purity reminded him of the smooth whiteness of the cowry shell, *porcellana* in Italian. **Porcelain** is made from kaolin, an extremely refined white clay, and petuntse, a variety of the rock-mineral feldspar. When properly combined and fired at a sufficiently high temperature, the two materials fuse into a glasslike, translucent ceramic that is far stronger than it looks.

Porcelaneous stoneware, fired at lower temperatures, was known in China by the seventh century, but true porcelain emerged during the Song dynasty. To create blue-and-white porcelain such as the flask in figure 21-6, blue pigment was made from cobalt oxide, finely ground and mixed with water. The decoration was painted directly onto the unfired porcelain vessel, then a layer of white glaze was applied over it. (In this technique, known as **underglaze**, the decoration is painted beneath the glaze.) After firing, the piece emerged from the kiln with a clear blue design set sharply against a snowy white background.

Entranced with the exquisite properties of porcelain, European potters tried for centuries to duplicate it. The technique was finally discovered in 1708 by Johann Friedrich Böttger in Dresden, Germany, who tried—but failed—to keep it a secret.

and seventeenth centuries. Characteristic of Chinese furniture, the chair in figure 21-7 is constructed without the use of glue or nails. Instead, pieces fit together based on the principle of the **mortise-and-tenon joint**, in which a projecting element (tenon) on one piece fits snugly into a cavity (mortise) on another. Each piece of the chair is carved, as opposed to being bent or twisted, and the joints are crafted with great precision. The patterns of the wood grain provide subtle interest unmarred by any painting or other embellishment. The style, like that of Chinese architecture, is one of simplicity, clarity, symmetry, and balance. The effect is formal and dignified but natural and simple—virtues central to the Chinese view of proper human conduct as well.

The art of landscape gardening also reached a high point during the Ming dynasty, as many literati surrounded their homes with gardens. The most famous gardens were created in the southern cities of the Yangzi River (Chang Jiang) delta, especially Suzhou. The largest surviving garden of the era is the Garden of the Cessation of Official Life, with which this chapter opened (see fig. 21-1). Although modified and reconstructed many times through the centuries, it still reflects many of the basic ideas of the original Ming owner. About a third of the 3-acre garden is devoted to water through artificially created brooks and ponds. The landscape is dotted with pavilions, kiosks, libraries, studios, and corridors. Many of the buildings have poetic names, such as Rain Listening Pavilion and Covered Bridge of Small Flying Rainbow.

21-7. Armchair. Ming dynasty, l6th–17th century. Huanghuali wood (rosewood), 39³⁄₈ x 27¹⁄₄ x 20" (100 x 69.2 x 50.8 cm). The Nelson-Atkins Museum of Art, Kansas City, Missouri
Purchase, Nelson Trust (46-78/1)

21-8. The Forbidden City, now the Palace Museum, Beijing. Mostly Ming dynasty. View from the southwest

GEOMANCY, COSMOLOGY, AND CHINESE ARCHITECTURE

Geomancy is a form of divination that looks for signs in the topography of the earth. In China it has been known from ancient times as *feng shui*, or "wind and water." Still practiced today, *feng shui* assesses *qi*, the primal energy that is believed to flow through creation, to determine whether a site is suitably auspicious for building. *Feng shui* also advises on improving a site's *qi* through landscaping, planting, creating waterways, and building temples and pagodas.

One important task of *feng shui* in the past was selecting auspicious sites for imperial tombs. These were traditionally set in a landscape of hills and winding paths, protected from harmful spiritual forces by a hill to the rear and a winding waterway crossed by arched bridges in front. *Feng shui* was also called on to find and enhance sites for homes, towns, and, especially, imperial cities. The Forbidden City, for example, is "protected" by a hill outside the north wall and a bow-shaped watercourse just inside the entrance.

The layout of imperial buildings was as important as their site and reflected ancient principles of cosmology—ideas about the structure and workings of the universe. Since the Zhou dynasty (1100–221 BCE) the emperor had ruled as the Son of Heaven. If he was worthy and right-acting, it was believed, then all would go well in nature and the cosmos. But if he was not, cosmic signs, natural disasters, and human rebellions would make it clear that Heaven had withdrawn his

dynasty's mandate to rule—traditional histories explained the downfall of a dynasty in just these terms.

Architecture played a major role in expressing this link between imperial and cosmic order. As early as Zhou times, cities were oriented on a north-south axis and built as a collection of enclosures surrounded by a defensive wall. The first imperial city of which we have any substantial knowledge, however, is Chang'an, the capital of the Tang (Tang dynasty, 618–907 CE). Chang'an was a walled city laid out on a rectangular grid measuring 5 miles by 6 miles. At the north end was an imperial enclosure. The palace within faced south, symbolic of the emperor looking out over his city and, by extension, his realm. This orientation was already traditional by Tang times. Chinese rulers—and Chinese buildings—had always turned their backs to the north, from

whence came evil spirits. Confucius even framed his admiration for one early Zhou ruler by saying that all he needed to do to govern was to assume a respectful position and face south, so attuned was he to Heaven's way.

A complex of government buildings stood in front of the imperial compound, and from them a 500-foot-wide avenue led to the city's principal southern gate. The city streets ran north-south and east-west. Each of the resulting 108 blocks was like a miniature city, with its own interior streets, surrounding walls, and gates that were locked at night. Two large markets to the east and west were open at specified hours. Such was the prestige of China during the Tang dynasty that the Japanese modeled their imperial capitals at Nara (built in 710 CE) and Heian (Kyoto, built in 794 CE) on Chang'an, though without the surrounding walls.

Chang'an, China

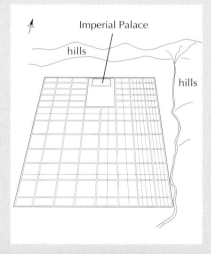

Heian (Kyoto), Japan

Architecture and City Planning

Centuries of warfare and destruction have left very few Chinese architectural monuments intact. The most important remaining example of traditional Chinese architecture is the Forbidden City, the imperial palace compound in Beijing, whose principal buildings were constructed during the Ming dynasty (fig. 21-8).

The basic plan of Beijing was the work of the Mongols, who laid out their capital city according to traditional Chinese principles. City planning began in China in the early seventh century with Chang'an (present-day Xi'an), the capital of the Sui and Tang emperors (see "Geomancy, Cosmology, and Chinese Architecture," above). The walled city of Chang'an was laid out on a rectangular grid, with even-

ly spaced streets that ran north-south and east-west. At the northern end stood a walled imperial complex.

Beijing, too, was developed as a walled, rectangular city with streets laid out in a grid. The palace enclosure occupied the center of the northern part of the city, which was reserved for the Mongols. Chinese lived in the southern third of the city. Later Ming and Qing emperors preserved this division, with officials living in the northern or Inner City, and commoners living in the southern or Outer City. Under the third Ming emperor, Yongle (ruled 1402–1424), the Forbidden City was rebuilt as we see it today.

The approach to the Forbidden City was impressive, and it was meant to be. Visitors entered through the Meridian Gate, a monumental **U**-shaped gate (at the right in fig. 21-8). Inside the Meridian Gate a broad courtyard is crossed

21-9. Shen Zhou. *Poet on a Mountain Top*, leaf from an album of landscapes; painting mounted as part of a handscroll, Ming dynasty, c. 1500. Ink and color on paper, 15¼ x 23¾" (38.1 x 60.2 cm). The Nelson-Atkins Museum of Art, Kansas City, Missouri

Purchase, Nelson Trust (46-51/2)

The poem at the upper left reads:

> White clouds like a belt encircle the mountain's waist
> A stone ledge flying in space and the far thin road.
> I lean alone on my bramble staff and gazing contented into space
> Wish the sounding torrent would answer to your flute.

> (Translated by Richard Edwards, cited in *Eight Dynasties of Chinese Paintings*, page 185)

The style of the calligraphy, like the style of the painting, is informal, relaxed, and straightforward—qualities that were believed to reflect the artist's character and personality.

by a bow-shaped waterway that is spanned by five arched marble bridges. At the opposite end of the courtyard is the Gate of Supreme Harmony, opening onto an even larger courtyard that houses three ceremonial halls raised on a broad platform. First is the Hall of Supreme Harmony, where, on the most important state occasions, the emperor was seated on his throne, facing south. Beyond is the smaller Hall of Central Harmony, then the Hall of Protecting Harmony. Behind these vast ceremonial spaces, still on the central axis, is the inner court, again with a progression of three buildings, this time more intimate in scale. In its balance and symmetry the plan of the Forbidden City reflects ancient Chinese beliefs about the harmony of the universe, and it emphasizes the emperor's role as the Son of Heaven, whose duty was to maintain the cosmic order from his throne in the middle of the world.

Literati Painting

In the south, especially in the district of Suzhou, literati painting remained the dominant trend. One of the major literati figures from the Ming period is Shen Zhou (1427–1509), who had no desire to enter government service but spent most of his life in Suzhou. He studied the Yuan painters avidly and tried to recapture their spirit in such works as *Poet on a Mountain Top* (fig. 21-9). Although the style of the painting recalls the freedom and simplicity of Ni Zan (see fig. 21-3), the motif of a poet surveying the landscape from a mountain plateau is Shen's creation.

In earlier landscape paintings, human figures were typically shown dwarfed by the grandeur of nature. Travelers might be seen scuttling along a narrow path by a stream, while overhead towered mountains whose peaks conversed with the clouds and whose heights were inaccessible. Here, the poet has climbed the mountain and dominates the landscape. Even the clouds are beneath him. Before his gaze, a poem hangs in the air, as though he were projecting his thoughts. The painting reflects Ming philosophy, which held that the mind, not the physical world, was the basis for reality. With its perfect synthesis of poetry, calligraphy, and painting, and its harmony of mind and landscape, *Poet on a Mountain Top* represents the very essence of literati painting.

The ideas underlying literati painting found their

most influential expression in the writings of Dong Qichang (1555–1636). A high official in the late Ming dynasty, Dong Qichang embodied the literati tradition as poet, calligrapher, and painter. He developed a view of Chinese art history that divided painters into two opposing schools, northern and southern. The names have nothing to do with geography—a painter from the south might well be classed as northern—but reflect a parallel Dong drew to the northern and southern schools of Chan (Zen) Buddhism in China. The southern school of Chan, founded by the eccentric monk Huineng (638–713), was unorthodox, radical, and innovative; the northern school was traditional and conservative. Similarly, Dong's two schools of painters represented progressive and conservative traditions. In Dong's view the conservative northern school was dominated by professional painters whose academic, often decorative style emphasized technical skill. In contrast, the progressive southern school preferred ink to color and free brushwork to meticulous detail. Its painters aimed for poetry and personal expression. In promoting this theory, Dong gave his unlimited sanction to literati painting, which he positioned as the culmination of the southern school, and he fundamentally influenced the way the Chinese viewed their own tradition.

Dong Qichang summarized his views on the proper training for literati painters in the famous statement "Read ten thousand books and walk ten thousand miles." By this he meant that one must first study the works of the great masters, then follow "heaven and earth," the world of nature. These studies prepared the way for a transformation to self-expression through brush and ink, the goal of literati painting. Dong's views rested on an awareness that a painting of scenery and the actual scenery are two very different things. The excellence of a painting does not lie in its degree of resemblance to reality—that gap can never be bridged—but in its expressive power. The expressive language of painting is inherently abstract and lies in its nature as a construction of brushstrokes. For example, in a painting of a rock, the rock itself is not expressive; rather, the brushstrokes that add up to "rock" are expressive.

With such thinking Dong brought painting close to the realm of calligraphy, which had long been considered the highest form of artistic expression in China. More than a thousand years before Dong's time, a body of critical terms and theories had evolved to discuss calligraphy in light of the formal and expressive properties of brushwork and composition. Dong introduced some of these terms—ideas such as opening and closing, rising and falling, and void and solid—to the criticism of painting.

Dong's theories are fully embodied in his painting *The Qingbian Mountains* (fig. 21-10). According to Dong's

21-10. Dong Qichang. *The Qingbian Mountains.* Ming dynasty, 1617. Hanging scroll, ink on paper, 21'8" x 7'4³⁄₈" (6.72 x 2.25 m). The Cleveland Museum of Art
Leonard C. Hanna, Jr., Bequest, 80.10

own inscription, the painting was based on a work by the tenth-century artist Dong Yuan. Dong Qichang's style, however, is quite different from the masters he admired. Although there is some indication of foreground, middle ground, and distant mountains, the space is ambiguous, as if all the elements were compressed to the surface of the picture. With this flattening of space, the trees, rocks, and mountains become more readily legible in a second way, as semiabstract forms made of brushstrokes.

Six trees diagonally arranged on a boulder define the extreme foreground and announce themes that the rest of the painting repeats, varies, and develops. The tree on the left, with its outstretched branches and full foliage, is echoed first in the shape of another tree just across the river and again in a tree farther up and toward the left. The tallest tree of the foreground grouping anticipates the high peak that towers in the distance almost directly above it. The forms of the smaller foreground trees, especially the one with dark leaves, are repeated in numerous variations across the painting. At the same time, the simple and ordinary-looking boulder in the foreground is transformed in the conglomeration of rocks, ridges, hills, and mountains above. This double reading, both abstract and representational, parallels the work's double nature as a painting of a landscape and an interpretation of a traditional landscape painting.

The influence of Dong Qichang on the development of Chinese painting of later periods cannot be overstated. Indeed, nearly all Chinese painters since the early seventeenth century have reflected his ideas in one way or another.

QING DYNASTY

In 1644, when the armies of the Manchu people to the northeast of China marched into Beijing, many Chinese reacted as though the world had come to an end. However, the situation turned out to be quite different from the Mongol invasions three centuries earlier. The Manchu had already adopted many Chinese customs and institutions before their conquest. After gaining control of all of China, they showed great respect for Chinese tradition. In art, all the major trends of the late Ming dynasty continued almost without interruption into the Manchu, or Qing, dynasty (1644–1911).

Orthodox Painting

Literati painting was by now established as the dominant tradition; it had become orthodox. Scholars followed Dong Qichang's recommendation and based their approach on the study of past masters, and they painted large numbers of works in the manner of Song and Yuan artists as a way of expressing their learning, technique, and taste.

The grand, symphonic composition *A Thousand Peaks and Myriad Ravines* (fig. 21-11), painted by Wang Hui (1632–1717) in 1693, exemplifies all the basic elements of Chinese landscape painting: mountains, rivers, waterfalls, trees, rocks, temples, pavilions, houses, bridges, boats, wandering scholars, fishers—the familiar and much loved cast of actors from a tradition now many centuries old. At the upper right corner, the artist has written:

Moss and weeds cover the rocks and mist hovers
over the water.
The sound of dripping water is heard in front of the
temple gate.
Through a thousand peaks and myriad ravines the
spring flows,
And brings the flying flowers into the sacred caves.

In the fourth month of the year 1693, in a hotel in the capital, I painted this based on a Tang dynasty poem in the manner of [the painters] Dong [Yuan] and Ju [ran].

(Translated by Chu-tsing Li)

This inscription shares Wang Hui's complex thoughts as he painted this work. In his mind were both the lines of the Tang dynasty poet Li Cheng, which offered the subject, and the paintings of the tenth-century masters Dong Yuan and Juran, which inspired his style. The temple the poem asks us to imagine is nestled on the right bank in the middle distance, but the painting shows us the scene from afar, as when a film camera pulls slowly away from some small human drama until its actors can barely be distinguished from the great flow of nature. Giving viewers the experience of dissolving their individual identity in the cosmic flow had been a goal of Chinese landscape painting since its first era of greatness during the Song dynasty.

All the Qing emperors of the late seventeenth and eighteenth centuries were painters themselves. They collected literati painting, and their conservative taste was shaped mainly by artists such as Wang Hui. Thus literati painting became an academic style and ended up within the court after all.

Individualists

In the long run, the Manchu conquest was not a great shock for China as a whole. But its first few decades were both traumatic and dangerous for those who were loyal—or worse, related—to the Ming. Some committed suicide, while others sought refuge in monasteries or wandered the countryside. Among them were several painters who expressed their anger, defiance, frustration, and melancholy in their art. They took Dong Qichang's idea of painting as an expression of the artist's personal feelings very seriously and cultivated highly original styles. These painters have become known as the individualists.

One of the individualists was Shitao (1642–1707), a descendant of the first Ming emperor who took refuge in Buddhist temples when the dynasty fell. In his later life he brought his painting to the brink of abstraction in such

21-11. Wang Hui. *A Thousand Peaks and Myriad Ravines*. Qing dynasty, 1693. Hanging scroll, ink on paper, 8'2¹/₂" x 3'4¹/₂" (2.54 x 1.03 m). National Palace Museum, Taipei, Taiwan

21-12. Shitao. *Landscape*, leaf from an album of landscapes. Qing dynasty, c. 1700. Ink and color on paper, 9¹/₂ x 11" (24.1 x 28 cm)
Collection C. C. Wang family

21-13. Wu Guanzhong. *Pine Spirit*. 1984. Ink and color on paper, 2'3⁵/₈" x 5'3¹/₂" (0.70 x 1.40 m). Spencer Museum of Art, University of Kansas, Lawrence
Gift of the E. Rhodes and Leonard B. Carpenter Foundation

works as *Landscape* (fig. 21-12). A monk sits in a small hut, looking out onto mountains that seem to be in turmoil. Dots, used for centuries to indicate vegetation on rocks, here seem to have taken on a life of their own. The rocks also seem alive—about to swallow up the monk and his hut. Throughout his life Shitao continued to identify himself with the fallen Ming, and he felt that his secure world had turned to chaos with the Manchu conquest.

THE MODERN PERIOD In the mid- and late nineteenth century China was shaken from centuries of complacency by a series of crushing military defeats by Western powers and Japan. Only then did the government finally realize that these new rivals were not like the Mongols of the thirteenth century. China was no longer at the center of the world, a civilized country surrounded by "barbarians." Spiritual resistance was no longer enough to solve the problems brought on by change. New ideas from Japan and the West began to filter in, and the demand arose for political and cultural reforms. In 1911 the Qing dynasty was overthrown, ending 2,000 years of imperial rule, and China was reconceived as a republic.

During the first decades of the twentieth century Chinese artists traveled to Japan and Europe to study Western art. Returning to China, many sought to introduce the ideas and techniques they had learned and explored ways to synthesize the Chinese and the Western traditions. After the establishment of the present-day Communist government in 1949, individual artistic freedom was curtailed as the arts were pressed into the service of the state and its vision of a new social order. After 1979, however, cultural attitudes began to relax, and Chinese painters again pursued their own paths.

One artist who emerged during the 1980s as a leader in Chinese painting is Wu Guanzhong (b. 1919). Combining his French artistic training and Chinese background, Wu Guanzhong has developed a semiabstract style to depict scenes from the Chinese landscape. His usual method is to make preliminary sketches on site, then, back in his studio, to develop them into free interpretations based on his feeling and vision. An example of his work, *Pine Spirit*, depicts a scene in the Huang (Yellow) Mountains (fig. 21-13). The technique, with its sweeping gestures of paint, is clearly linked to Abstract Expressionism, an influential Western movement of the post–World War II years (Chapter 29); yet the painting also claims a place in the long tradition of Chinese landscape as exemplified by such masters as Shitao.

Like all aspects of Chinese society, Chinese art has felt the strong impact of Western influence, and the question remains whether Chinese artists will absorb Western ideas without losing their traditional identity. Interestingly, landscape remains the most popular subject, as it has been for more than a thousand years. Using the techniques and methods of the West, China's painters still seek spiritual communion with nature through their art as a means to come to terms with human life and the world.

1400 CE   1500   1600

Sesshu
Winter Landscape
c. 1470s

Himeji Castle
1601–9

MOMOYAMA PERIOD
▲ MUROMACHI PERIOD 1392–1568   ▲ 1568–1603   ▲ EDO PERIOD 1603–1853

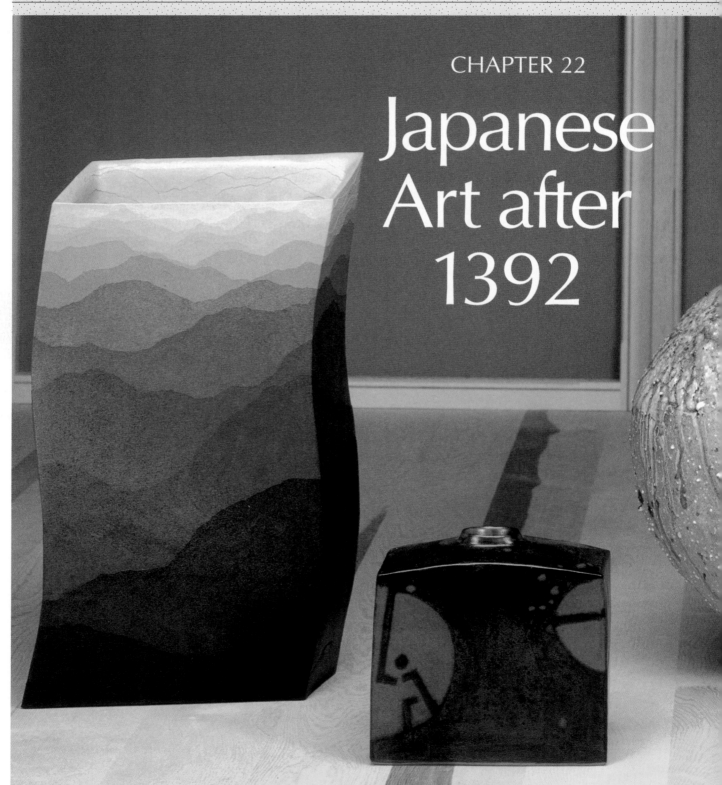

CHAPTER 22

Japanese Art after 1392

Hakuin
Bodhidharma Meditating
18th century

Fujii
Untitled '90
1990

▲ MEIJI AND MODERN PERIODS 1853–PRESENT

CHINA

Hokkaido

Sea of
Japan

JAPAN

Sendai

Matsushima
Islands

Honshu

Tokyo (Edo)

Kamakura

Mount Fuji

Kyoto (Heian)   Onjoji

Osaka   Nara

KOREA

Hyogo

Shikoku

Kyushu

Nagasaki

PACIFIC
OCEAN

0   200 miles
0   200 kilometers

22-1. Katsushika Hokusai. *The Great Wave.* Edo period, c. 1831. Polychrome woodblock print on paper, 9⅞ x 14⅝"
(25 x 37.1 cm). Honolulu Academy of Arts, Honolulu, Hawaii
James A. Michener Collection (HAA 13, 695)

T he great wave rears up like a dragon with claws of foam, ready to
crash down on the figures huddled in the boat below. Exactly at the
point of imminent disaster, but far in the distance, rises Japan's
most sacred peak, Mount Fuji, whose slopes, we suddenly realize, swing
up like waves and whose snowy crown is like foam—comparisons the
artist makes clear in the wave nearest us, caught just at the moment of
greatest resemblance.

If one were forced to choose a single work of art to represent Japan,
at least in the world's eye, it would have to be this woodblock print, popularly known as *The Great Wave*, by Katsushika Hokusai (fig. 22-1). Taken
from his series called *Thirty-Six Views of Fuji*, it has inspired countless imitations and witty parodies, yet its forceful composition remains ever fresh.

Today, Japanese prints are collected avidly around the world, but in
their own day they were barely considered art. Produced by the hundreds
for ordinary people to buy, they were the fleeting souvenirs of their era,
one of the most fascinating in Japanese history. Not until the twentieth
century would the West experience anything like the pluralistic cultural
atmosphere, where so many diverse groups participate in and contribute
to a common culture, as the one that produced *The Great Wave*.

MUROMACHI PERIOD

By the year 1392 Japanese art had already developed a long and rich history (see "Foundations of Japanese Culture," below). Beginning with prehistoric pottery and tomb art, then expanding through cultural influences from China and Korea, Japanese visual expression reached high levels of sophistication in both religious and secular arts. Very early in the tradition, elements of a particularly Japanese aesthetic made themselves felt. These characteristics include a love of natural materials, a taste for asymmetry, a sense of humor, and a tolerance for qualities that may seem paradoxical or contradictory—characteristics that continued to distinguish Japanese art, appearing and reappearing in ever changing guises.

Toward the end of the twelfth century the political and cultural dominance of the emperor and his court gave way to rule by warriors, or samurai, under the leadership of the shogun, the general-in-chief. In 1392 the Ashikaga family gained control of the shogunate and moved their headquarters to the Muromachi district in Kyoto. They reunited northern and southern Japan and retained their grasp on the office for more than 150 years. The Muromachi period after the reunion (1392–1568) is also known as the Ashikaga era.

The Muromachi period is especially marked by the ascendance of Zen Buddhism, whose austere ideals particularly appealed to the highly disciplined samurai. While Pure Land Buddhism, which had spread widely during the latter part of the Heian period (794–1185), remained popular, Zen, patronized by the samurai, became the dominant cultural force in Japan.

1400   2000

FOUNDATIONS OF JAPANESE CULTURE

With the end of the last Ice Age roughly 15,000 years ago, rising sea levels submerged the lowlands connecting Japan to the Asian landmass, creating the chain of islands we know today as Japan. Not long afterward, early Paleolithic cultures gave way to a Neolithic culture known as Jomon (12,000–300 BCE), after its characteristic cord-marked pottery. During the Jomon period, a notably sophisticated hunter-gatherer culture developed. Agriculture supplemented hunting and gathering by around 5000 BCE, and rice cultivation began some 4,000 years later.

A fully settled agricultural society emerged during the Yayoi period (300 BCE–300 CE), accompanied by hierarchical social organization and more-centralized forms of government. As people learned to manufacture bronze and iron, use of those metals became widespread. Yayoi architecture, with its unpainted wood and thatched roofs, already reveals the Japanese affinity for natural materials and clean lines, and the style of Yayoi granaries in particular persisted in the design of shrines in later centuries. The trend toward centralization continued during the Kofun period (300–552 CE), an era characterized by the construction of large royal tombs following Korean practice. Veneration of leaders grew into the beginnings of the imperial system that has lasted to the present day.

The Asuka era (552–646 CE) began with a century of profound change as elements of Chinese civilization flooded into Japan, initially through the intermediary of Korea. The three most significant Chinese contributions to the developing Japanese culture were Buddhism (with its attendant art and architecture), a system of writing, and the structures of a centralized bureaucracy. The earliest extant Buddhist temple compound in Japan—the oldest currently existing wooden building in the world—dates from this period.

The arrival of Buddhism also prompted some formalization of Shinto, the loose collection of indigenous Japanese beliefs and practices. Shinto is a shamanistic religion that emphasizes ceremonial purification. Its rituals include the invocation and appeasement of spirits, including those of the recent dead. Many Shinto deities are thought to inhabit various aspects of nature, such as particularly magnificent trees, rocks, and waterfalls, and living creatures such as deer. Shinto and Buddhism have in common an intense awareness of transience, and as their goals are complementary—purification in the case of Shinto, enlightment in the case of Buddhism—they have generally existed comfortably alongside each other to the present day.

The Nara period (646–794 CE) takes its name from Japan's first permanently established imperial capital. During this time the founding works of Japanese literature were compiled, among them an important collection of poetry called the *Manyoshu*. Buddhism advanced to become the most important force in Japanese culture. Its influence at court grew so great as to become worrisome, and in 794 the emperor moved the capital from Nara to Heian-kyo (present-day Kyoto), far from powerful monasteries.

During the Heian period (794–1185), an extremely refined court culture thrived, embodied today in an exquisite legacy of poetry, calligraphy, and painting. An efficient method for writing the Japanese language was developed, and with it a woman at the court wrote the world's first novel, *The Tale of Genji*. Esoteric Buddhism, as hierarchical and intricate as the aristocratic world of the court, became popular.

The end of the Heian period was marked by civil warfare as regional warrior (samurai) clans were drawn into the factional conflicts at court. Pure Land Buddhism, with its simple message of salvation, offered consolation to many in these troubled times. In 1185 the Minamoto clan defeated their arch rivals, the Taira, and their leader, Minamoto Yoritomo, assumed the position of shogun (general-in-chief). While paying respects to the emperor, Minamoto Yoritomo kept actual military and political power to himself, setting up his own capital in Kamakura. The Kamakura era (1185–1392) began a tradition of rule by shogun that lasted in various forms until 1868.

Years	Period	Japan	World
1392–1568	Muromachi	Ashikaga shogunate; capital in Muromachi district, Kyoto; ascendance of Zen Buddhism; Ikkyu's calligraphy; ink painting flourishes under Shubun, Bunsei, and Sesshu; Ryoan-ji garden; Kano school founded	**1400–1550** Black Death kills 30 percent of Chinese population; Chaucer's *Canterbury Tales* (England); Forbidden City rebuilt (China); Jan van Eyck's *Ghent Altarpiece* (Flanders); Inka Empire (South America); Ghiberti's *Gates of Paradise* (Italy); Gutenberg's Bible (Germany); Columbus's voyages (Spain); Spanish Inquisition; Michelangelo's *David*, Sistine Ceiling (Italy); Leonardo's *Mona Lisa* (Italy); Protestant Reformation in Europe; Spanish conquest of Aztec Empire (Mexico)
1568–1603	Momoyama	Oda Nobunaga shogunate; Westerners arrive; tea ceremony perfected by Sen no Rikyu; Kano school thrives; Toyotomi Hideyoshi shogunate; Himeji Castle	**1550–1600** Mughal period (India); William Shakespeare born (England); Baroque style emerges in Europe; Peter Paul Rubens (Flanders)
1603–1868	Edo	Tokugawa shogunate; period of isolation from foreigners; samurai officials; neo-Confucianism arises; Tawaraya Sotatsu and Rimpa school; Zen Buddhism revival; Maruyama-Shijo school; ukiyo-e; Nanga, or Southern, school; kabuki prints; Hokusai's *Thirty-Six Views of Fuji*; Hiroshige's *Fifty-Three Stations of the Tokaido* isolationism ends; capital at Edo (Tokyo)	**1600–1850** Rembrandt van Rijn (Netherlands); English colonize North America; Qing dynasty (China); Age of Enlightenment in Europe; Union of England and Scotland as Great Britain; James Watt develops steam engine; Declaration of Independence (United States); French Revolution; Romanticism and Neoclassicism arise in Europe; Mexico becomes a republic; Realism arises
1868–present	Meiji and Modern	Meiji Restoration of emperor; blending of foreign and native styles and traditions in art	**1850–present** Italy united; Civil War (United States); Dominion of Canada formed; Impressionism and Post-Impressionism arise; Sino-Japanese War; Chinese republic established by Sun Yat-Sen; World War I; Civil War (Russia); League of Nations; World War II; United Nations established; People's Republic of China; breakup of Soviet Union

Ink Painting

Several forms of visual art flourished during the Muromachi period, but **ink painting**—monochrome painting in black ink and its diluted grays—reigned supreme. Muromachi ink painting was heavily influenced by the aesthetics of Zen, yet it also marked a shift away from the earlier Zen painting tradition. As Zen moved from an "outsider" sect to the chosen sect of the ruling group, the fierce intensity of earlier masters gave way to a more subtle and refined approach. And whereas earlier Zen

artists had concentrated on rough-hewn depictions of Zen figures such as monks and teachers, now Chinese-style landscapes became the most important theme.

The monk-artist Shubun (active 1414–1463) is regarded as the first great master of the ink landscape. Unfortunately, no works survive that can be proven to be his. Two landscapes by Shubun's pupil Bunsei (active c. 1450–1460) have survived, however. In the one shown here (fig. 22-2), the foreground reveals a spit of rocky land with an overlapping series of motifs—a spiky pine tree, a craggy rock, a poet seated in a hermitage, and a

22-2. Bunsei. *Landscape.* Muromachi period, mid-15th century. Hanging scroll, ink and light colors on paper, 28¾ x 13" (73.2 x 33 cm). Museum of Fine Arts, Boston
Special Chinese and Japanese Fund

brushwood fence holding back a small garden of trees and bamboo. In the middleground is space—emptiness, the void.

We are expected to "read" the empty paper as representing water, for subtle tones of gray ink suggest the presence of a few people fishing from their boats near the distant shore. The two parts of the painting seem to echo each other across a vast expanse, just as nature echoes the human spirit in Japanese art. The painting illustrates well the pure, lonely, and ultimately serene spirit of the Zen-influenced poetic landscape tradition.

Ink painting took on a different spirit at the turn of the sixteenth century. By then, temples were asked for so many paintings that they formed **ateliers** staffed by monks who specialized in art rather than religious ritual

22-3. Sesshu. *Winter Landscape.* Muromachi period, c. 1470s. Ink on paper, 18¼ x 11½" (46.3 x 29.3 cm). Tokyo National Museum

or teaching. Some painters even found they could survive on their own as professional artists. Nevertheless, many of the leading masters remained monks, at least in name, including the most famous of them all, Sesshu (1420–1506). Although he lived his entire life as a monk, Sesshu devoted himself primarily to painting. Like Bunsei, he learned from the tradition of Shubun, but he also had the opportunity to visit China in 1467. Sesshu traveled extensively there, viewing the scenery, stopping at Zen monasteries, and seeing whatever Chinese paintings he could. He does not seem to have had access to works by contemporary **literati** masters such as Shen Zhou (see fig. 21-9) but saw instead the works of professional painters. Sesshu later claimed that he learned nothing from Chinese artists, but only from the mountains and rivers he had seen. When Sesshu returned from China, he found his homeland rent by the Onin Wars, which devastated the capital of Kyoto. Japan was to be torn apart by further civil warfare for the next hundred years. The refined art patronized by a secure society in peacetime was no longer possible. Instead, the violent new spirit of the times sounded its disturbing note, even in the peaceful world of landscape painting.

This new spirit is evident in Sesshu's *Winter Landscape,* which makes full use of the forceful style that he developed (fig. 22-3). A cliff descending from the mist seems to cut the composition in half. Sharp, jagged brushstrokes delineate a series of rocky hills, where a

22-4. Ikkyu. *Calligraphy Pair,* from Daitoku-ji, Kyoto. Muromachi period, c. mid-15th century. Ink on paper, each 10'2⅞" x 1'4½" (3.12 x 0.42 m)

lone figure makes his way to a Zen monastery. Instead of a gradual recession into space, flat overlapping planes seem to slice the composition into crystalline facets. The white of the paper is left to indicate snow, while the sky is suggested by tones of gray. The few trees cling desperately to the rocky land, and the harsh chill of winter is boldly expressed.

A third important artist of the Muromachi period was a monk named Ikkyu (1394–1481). A genuine eccentric and one of the most famous Zen masters in Japanese history, Ikkyu derided the Zen of his day, writing, "The temples are rich but Zen is declining, there are only false teachers, no true teachers." Ikkyu recognized that success was distorting the spirit of Zen. Originally, Zen had been a form of counterculture for those who were not

22-5. Stone and gravel garden, Ryoan-ji, Kyoto. Muromachi period, c. 1480

The American composer John Cage once exclaimed that every stone at Ryoan-ji was in just the right place. He then said, "and every other place would also be just right." His remark is thoroughly Zen in spirit. There are many ways to experience Ryoan-ji. For example, we can imagine the rocks as having different visual "pulls" that relate them to one another. Yet there is also enough space between them to give each one a sense of self-sufficiency and permanence.

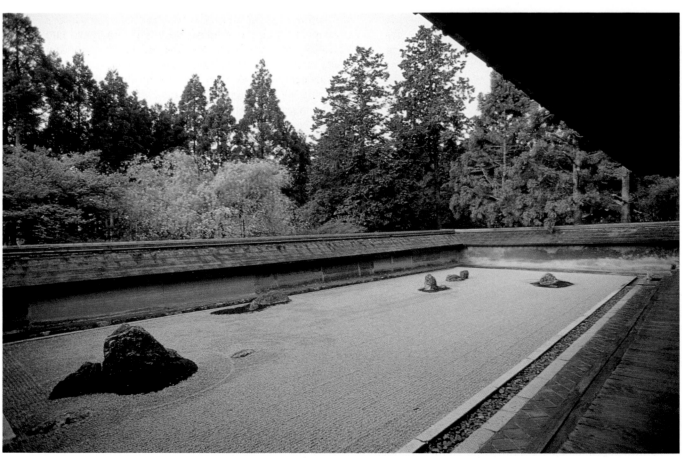

satisfied with prevailing ways. Now, however, Zen monks acted as government advisers, teachers, and even leaders of merchant missions to China. Although true Zen masters were able to withstand all outside pressures, many monks became involved with political matters, with factional disputes among the temples, or with their reputations as poets or artists. Ikkyu did not hesitate to mock what he regarded as "false Zen." He even paraded through the streets with a wooden sword, claiming that his sword would be as much use to a samurai as false Zen to a monk.

Ikkyu was very involved in the arts, although he treated them with extreme freedom. His calligraphy, which is especially admired, has a spirit of spontaneity. To write out the classic Buddhist couplet "Abjure evil, practice only the good," he created this pair of single-line scrolls (fig. 22-4). At the top of each scroll, Ikkyu began with standard script, in which each stroke of a character is separate and distinct. As he moved down the columns he grew more excited and wrote in increasingly cursive script, until finally his frenzied brush did not leave the paper at all. This calligraphy displays the intensity that is the hallmark of Zen.

Ryoan-ji

One of the most renowned Zen creations in Japan is the "dry garden" at the temple of Ryoan-ji in Kyoto (fig. 22-5). There is a record of a famous cherry tree at this spot, so the completely severe nature of the garden may have come about some time after its original founding in the late fifteenth century. Nevertheless, today the garden is celebrated for its serene sense of space and emptiness. Fifteen rocks are set in a long rectangle of raked white gravel. Temple verandas border the garden on the north and east sides, while clay-and-tile walls define the south and west. Only a part of the larger grounds of Ryoan-ji, the garden has provoked so much interest and curiosity that there have been numerous attempts to "explain" it. Some people see the rocks as land and the gravel as sea. Others imagine animal forms in certain of the rock groupings. However, perhaps it is best to see the rocks and gravel as . . . rocks and gravel. The asymmetrical balance in the placement of the rocks and the austere beauty of the raked gravel have led many people to meditation.

The Muromachi period is the only time when an entire culture was strongly influenced by Zen, and the results were mixed. On one hand, works such as Ryoan-ji were created that continue to inspire people to the present day. On the other, the very success of Zen led to a certain secularization and professionalization that masters such as Ikkyu found intolerable.

MOMOYAMA PERIOD

The civil wars sweeping Japan laid bare the basic flaw in the Ashikaga system, which was that samurai were primarily loyal to their own feudal lord, or daimyo, rather than to the central government. Battles between feudal clans grew more frequent, and it became clear that only a daimyo powerful and bold enough to unite the entire country could control Japan. As the Muromachi period drew to a close, three leaders emerged who would change the course of Japanese history.

The first of these leaders was Oda Nobunaga (1534–1582), who marched his army into Kyoto in 1568, signaling the end of the Ashikaga family as a major force in Japanese politics. A ruthless warrior, Nobunaga went so far as to destroy a Buddhist monastery because the monks refused to join his forces. Yet he was also a patron of the most rarefied and refined arts. Assassinated in the midst of one of his military campaigns, Nobunaga was succeeded by the military commander Toyotomi Hideyoshi (1536/37–1598), who soon gained complete power in Japan. He, too, patronized the arts when not leading his army, and he considered culture a vital adjunct to his rule. Hideyoshi, however, was overly ambitious. He believed that he could conquer both Korea and China, and he wasted much of his resources on two ill-fated invasions. A stable government finally emerged in 1600 with the triumph of a third leader, Tokugawa Ieyasu (1543–1616), who established his shogunate in 1603. But despite its turbulence, the era of Nobunaga and Hideyoshi, known as the Momoyama period (1568–1603), was one of the most creative eras in Japanese history.

Architecture

Today the very word *Momoyama* conjures up images of bold warriors, luxurious palaces, screens shimmering with **gold leaf**, and magnificent ceramics. The Momoyama period was also the era when Europeans first made an impact in Japan. A few Portuguese explorers had arrived at the end of the Muromachi era in 1543, and traders and missionaries were quick to follow. It was only with the rise of Nobunaga, however, that Westerners were able to extend their activities beyond the ports of Kyushu, Japan's southernmost island. Nobunaga welcomed foreign traders, who brought him various products, the most important of which were firearms.

European muskets and cannons soon changed the nature of Japanese warfare and even influenced Japanese art. In response to the new weapons, monumental fortified castles were built in the late sixteenth century. Some were eventually lost to warfare or torn down by victorious enemies, and others have been extensively altered over the years. One of the most beautiful of the surviving castles is Himeji, not far from the city of Osaka (fig. 22-6). Rising high on a hill above the plains, Himeji has been given the name White Heron. To reach the upper fortress, visitors must follow angular paths beneath steep walls, climbing from one area to the next past stone ramparts and through narrow fortified gates, all the while feeling as though lost in a maze, with no sense of direction or progress. At the main building, a further climb up a series of narrow ladders leads to the uppermost chamber. There, the foot-sore visitor is rewarded with a stunning 360-degree view of the surrounding countryside. The sense of power is overwhelming.

22-6.   Himeji Castle, Hyogo, near Osaka. Muromachi period, 1601–9

Decorative Painting

Castles such as Himeji were sumptuously decorated, offering artists unprecedented opportunities to work on a grand scale. Large murals on **fusuma**—paper-covered sliding doors—were particular features of Momoyama design, as were folding screens with gold-leaf backgrounds, whose glistening surfaces not only conveyed light within the castle rooms but also vividly demonstrated the wealth of the warrior leaders. Temples, too, commissioned large-scale paintings for their rebuilding projects after the devastation of the civil wars.

The Momoyama period produced a number of artists who were equally adept at decorative golden screens and broadly brushed fusuma paintings. Daitoku-ji, a celebrated Zen monastery in Kyoto, has a number of subtemples that are virtual treasure troves of Japanese art. One, the Juko-in, possesses fusuma by Kano Eitoku (1543–1590), one of the most brilliant painters from the Kano school, a professional school of artists that was patronized by government leaders for several centuries. Founded in the Muromachi period, the Kano school combined training in the ink-painting tradition with new skills in decorative subjects and styles. The illustration here shows two of the three walls of fusuma panels painted when the artist was in his mid-twenties (fig. 22-7). To the left, the subject is the familiar Kano school theme of cranes and pines, both symbols of long life; to

the right is a great gnarled plum tree, symbol of spring. The trees are so massive they seem to extend far beyond the panels. An island rounding both walls of the far corner provides a focus for the outreaching trees. Ingeniously, it belongs to both compositions at the same time, thus uniting them into a single organic whole. Eitoku's vigorous use of brush and ink, his powerfully jagged outlines, and his dramatic compositions all hark back to the style of Sesshu, but the bold new sense of scale in his works is a leading characteristic of the Momoyama period.

Tea

Japanese art is never one-sided. Along with castles, golden screens, and massive fusuma paintings there was an equal interest during the Momoyama period in the quiet, the restrained, and the natural. This was expressed primarily through the tea ceremony.

"Tea ceremony" is an unsatisfactory way to express *cha no yu*, the Japanese ritual drinking of tea, but there is no counterpart in Western culture, so this phrase has come into common use. Tea itself had been introduced to Japan from the Asian continent hundreds of years earlier. At first tea was molded into cakes and boiled. However, the advent of Zen in the late Kamakura period (1185–1392) brought to Japan a different way of preparing tea, with the leaves crushed into powder and then whisked in bowls with hot water. Tea was used by Zen

22-7. Kano Eitoku. Fusuma depicting pine and cranes (left) and plum tree (right), from the central room of the Juko-in, Daitoku-ji, Kyoto. Momoyama period, c. 1563–73. Ink and gold on paper, height 5'9¹⁄₈" (1.76 m)

monks as a slight stimulant to aid meditation, and it also was considered a form of medicine.

The most famous tea master in Japanese history was Sen no Rikyu (1521–1591). He conceived of the tea ceremony as an intimate gathering in which a very few people would enter a small rustic room, drink tea carefully prepared in front of them by their host, and quietly discuss the tea utensils or a Zen scroll hanging on the wall. He did a great deal to establish the aesthetic of modesty, refinement, and rusticity that permitted the tearoom to serve as a respite from the busy and sometimes violent world outside. A traditional tearoom is quite small and simple. It is made of natural materials such as bamboo and wood, with mud walls, paper windows, and a floor covered with **tatami** mats—mats of woven straw. One tearoom that preserves Rikyu's design is named Tai-an (fig. 22-8). Originally built in 1582, it is distinguished by its tiny door (guests must crawl to enter) and its alcove, or **tokonoma**, where a Zen scroll or a simple flower arrangement may be displayed. At first glance, the room seems symmetrical. But the disposition of the tatami mats does not match the spacing of the *tokonoma*, providing a subtle undercurrent of irregularity. A longer look reveals a blend of simple elegance and rusticity. The walls seem scratched and worn with age, but the tatami are replaced frequently to keep them clean and fresh. The mood is quiet; the light is muted and diffused through three small paper windows. Above all, there is

22-8. Sen no Rikyu. Tai-an tearoom, Myoki-an Temple, Kyoto. Momoyama period, 1582

a sense of spatial clarity. All nonessentials have been eliminated, so there is nothing to distract from focused attention. The tearoom aesthetic became an important element in Japanese culture, influencing secular architecture through its simple and evocative form (see "Elements of Architecture," page 862).

ELEMENTS OF ARCHITECTURE
Shoin Design

Of the many expressions of Japanese taste that reached great refinement in the Momoyama period, *shoin* architecture has had perhaps the most enduring influence. *Shoin* are upper-class residences that combine a number of traditional features in more-or-less standard ways, always asymmetically. These features are wide verandas; wood posts as framing and defining decorative elements; woven straw **tatami** mats as floor and ceiling covering; several shallow alcoves for prescribed purposes; **fusuma** (sliding doors) as fields for painting or textured surfaces; and **shoji** screens—translucent, rice-paper–covered wood frames. The *shoin* illustrated here was built in 1601 as a guest hall, called Kojo-in, at the great Onjo-ji monastery. Tatami, shoji, alcoves, and asymmetry are still seen in Japanese interiors today.

In the original *shoin*, one of the alcoves would contain a hanging scroll, an arrangement of flowers, or a large painted screen. Seated in front of that alcove, called **tokonoma**, the owner of the house would receive guests, who could contemplate the object above the head of their host. Another alcove contained staggered shelves, often for writing instruments. A writing space fitted with a low writing desk was on the veranda side of a room, with shoji that could open to the outside.

The architectural harmony of *shoin,* like virtually all Japanese buildings, was based on the mathematics of proportions and on the proportionate disposition of basic units, or modules. The modules were the **bay**, reckoned as the distance from the center of one post to the center of another, and the tatami. Room area in Japan is still expressed in terms of the number of tatami mats, so that, for example, a room is described as a seven-mat room. Although varying slightly from region to region, the size of a single tatami is about 3 feet by 6 feet.

Guest Hall, Kojo-in, Onjo-ji monastery, Shiga prefecture. Momoyama period, 1601

EDO PERIOD

Three years after Tokugawa Ieyasu gained control of Japan, he proclaimed himself shogun. His family's control of the shogunate was to last for over 250 years, a span of time known as the Edo period (1603–1868) or the Tokugawa era.

Under the rule of the Tokugawa family, peace and prosperity came to Japan at the price of an increasingly rigid and often repressive form of government. The problem of potentially rebellious daimyo was solved by ordering all feudal lords to spend either half of each year or every other year in the new capital of Edo (present-day Tokyo), where their wives and children were sometimes required to live permanently. Zen Buddhism was sup-

planted as the prevailing intellectual force by a form of neo-Confucianism, a philosophy formulated in Song dynasty China that emphasized loyalty to the state. More drastically, Japan was soon closed off from the rest of the world by its suspicious government. Japanese were forbidden to travel abroad, and with the exception of small Chinese and Dutch trading communities on an island off the southern port of Nagasaki, foreigners were not permitted in Japan.

Edo society was officially divided into four classes. Samurai officials constituted the highest class, followed by farmers, artisans, and finally merchants. As time went on, however, merchants began to control the money sup-

22-9. Hon'ami Koetsu. Teabowl, called *Mount Fuji*. Edo period, early 17th century. Raku ware, height 3³/₈" (8.5 cm). Sakai Collection, Tokyo

A specialized vocabulary grew up to allow connoisseurs to discuss the subtle aesthetics of tea. A favorite term was *sabi*, which summoned up the particular beauty to be found in stillness or even deprivation. *Sabi* was borrowed from the critical vocabulary of poetry, where it was first established as a positive ideal by the early-thirteenth-century poet Fujiwara Shunzei. Other virtues were *wabi*, conveying a sense of great loneliness or a humble (and admirable) shabbiness, and *shibui*, meaning plain and astringent.

ply, and in Japan's increasingly mercantile economy they soon reached a high, if unofficial, position. Reading and writing became widespread at all levels of society. Many segments of the population—samurai, merchants, intellectuals, and even townspeople—were now able to patronize artists, and a pluralistic cultural atmosphere developed unlike anything Japan had experienced before.

Tea

The rebuilding of temples continued during the first decades of the Edo period, and for this purpose government officials, monks, and wealthy merchants needed to cooperate. The tea ceremony was one way that people of different classes could come together for intimate conversations. Every utensil connected with tea, including the waterpot, the kettle, the bamboo spoon, the whisk, the tea caddy, and, above all, the teabowl came to be appreciated for their aesthetic qualities, and many works of art were created for use in *cha no yu*.

The age-old Japanese admiration for the natural and the asymmetrical found full expression in tea ceramics. Korean bowls made by humble farmers for their rice were suddenly considered the epitome of refined taste. Tea masters even went so far as to advise rural potters in Japan to create imperfect shapes. But not every misshapen bowl would be admired. An extremely subtle sense of beauty developed that took into consideration such factors as how well a teabowl fit into the hands, how subtly the shape and texture of the bowl appealed

to the eye, and who had previously used and admired it. For this purpose, the inscribed box became almost as important as the ceramic that fit within it, and if a bowl had been given a name by a leading tea master, it was especially treasured by later generations.

One of the finest teabowls extant is named *Mount Fuji* after Japan's most sacred peak (fig. 22-9). (Mount Fuji itself is depicted in figure 22-1.) An example of **raku** ware—a hand-built, low-fired ceramic developed especially for use in the tea ceremony—the bowl was crafted by Hon'ami Koetsu (1558–1637), a leading cultural figure of the early Edo period. Koetsu was most famous as a calligrapher, but he was also a painter, **lacquer** designer, poet, landscape gardener, connoisseur of swords, and potter. With its small foot, straight sides, slightly irregular shape, and crackled texture, this bowl exemplifies tea taste. In its rough exterior we seem to sense directly the two elements of earth and fire that create pottery. Merely looking at it suggests the feeling one would get from holding it, warm with tea, cupped in one's hands.

Rimpa School

One of Koetsu's friends was the painter Tawaraya Sotatsu (active c. 1600–1640), with whom he collaborated on several magnificent handscrolls. Sotatsu is considered the first great painter of the Rimpa school, a grouping of artists with similar tastes rather than a formal school such as the Kano school. Rimpa masters excelled in decorative designs of strong expressive force, and they frequently worked in several mediums.

Sotatsu painted some of the finest golden screens that have survived. The splendid pair here depict the celebrated islands of Matsushima near the northern city of Sendai (fig. 22-10). Working in a boldly decorative style, the artist has created asymmetrical and almost abstract patterns of waves, pines, and island forms. On the screen to the right, mountainous islands echo the swing and sweep of the waves, with stylized gold clouds in the upper left. The screen on the left continues the gold clouds until they become a sand spit from which twisted pines grow. Their branches seem to lean toward a strange island in the lower left, composed of an organic, amoebalike form in gold surrounded by mottled ink. This mottled effect was a specialty of Rimpa school painters.

As one of the "three famous beautiful views of Japan," Matsushima was often depicted in art. Most painters, however, emphasized the large number of pine-covered islands that make the area famous. Sotatsu's genius was to simplify and dramatize the scene, as though the viewer were passing the islands in a boat on the roiling waters. Strong, basic mineral colors dominate, and the sparkling two-dimensional richness of the gold leaf contrasts dramatically with the three-dimensional movement of the waves.

The second great master of the Rimpa school was Ogata Korin (1658–1716). Korin copied many designs after Sotatsu in homage to the master, but he also originated many remarkable works of his own, including colorful golden screens, monochrome scrolls, and paintings

22-10. Tawaraya Sotatsu. Pair of six-panel screens, known as the Matsushima screens. Edo period, 17th century. Ink, mineral colors, and gold leaf on paper; each screen 4'9⁷/₈" x 11'8¹/₂" (1.52 x 3.56 m). Freer Gallery of Art, Smithsonian Institution, Washington, D.C. (06.231; 06.232)

The six-panel screen format was a triumph of scale and practicality. Each panel consisted of a light wood frame surrounding a latticework interior covered with several layers of paper. Over this foundation was pasted a high-quality paper, silk, or gold-leaf ground, ready to be painted by the finest artists. Held together with ingenious paper hinges, a screen could be folded for preservation or transportation, resulting in a mural-size painting light enough to be carried by a single person, ready to be displayed as needed.

in glaze on his brother Kenzan's pottery. He also designed some highly prized works in lacquer (see "Lacquer," below). One famous example (fig. 22-11) is a writing box, a lidded container designed to hold tools and materials for calligraphy (see "Inside a Writing Box," opposite). Korin's design for this black lacquer box sets a motif of irises and a plank bridge in a dramatic combination of mother-of-pearl, silver, lead, and gold lacquer. For Japanese viewers the decoration immediately recalls a famous passage from the tenth-century *Tales of Ise*, a classic of Japanese literature. A nobleman poet, having left his wife in the capital, pauses at a place called Eight

TECHNIQUE

LACQUER

Lacquer is derived in Asia from the sap of the lacquer tree, *Rhus verniciflua*. The tree is indigenous to China, where examples of lacquerware have been found dating back to the Neolithic period. Knowledge of lacquer spread early to Korea and Japan, and the tree came to be grown commercially throughout East Asia.

Gathered by tapping into a tree and letting the sap flow into a container, in much the same way as maple syrup, lacquer is then strained to remove impurities and heated to evaporate excess moisture. The thickened sap can be colored with vegetable or mineral dyes and lasts for several years if carefully stored. Applied in thin coats to a surface such as wood or leather, lacquer hardens into a smooth, glasslike, protective coating that is waterproof, heat and acid resistant, and airtight. Lacquer's practical qualities made it ideal for storage containers and vessels for food and drink. In Japan the leather scales of samurai armor were coated in lacquer, as were leather saddles. In China, Korea, and Japan the decorative potential of lacquer was brought to exquisite perfection in the manufacture of expensive luxury items.

The creation of a piece of lacquer is a painstaking process that can take a sequence of specialized crafts-workers several years. First, the item is fashioned of wood and sanded to a flawlessly smooth finish. Next, layers of lacquer are built up. In order to dry properly, lacquer must be applied in extremely thin coats. (If the lacquer is applied too thickly, the lacquer's exterior surface dries first, forming an airtight seal that prevents the lacquer below from ever drying.) Optimal temperature and humidity are also essential to drying, and craftsworkers quickly learned to control them artificially. Up to 30 coats of lacquer, each dried and polished before the next is brushed on, are required to build up a substantial layer.

Many techniques were developed for decorating lacquer. Particularly in China, lacquer was often applied to a thickness of up to 300 coats, then elaborately carved in low relief—dishes, containers, and even pieces of furniture were executed in carved lacquer. In Japan and Korea, **inlay** with mother-of-pearl and precious metals was brought to a high point of refinement. Japanese artisans also perfected a variety of methods known collectively as *maki-e* ("sprinkled design") that embedded flaked or powdered gold or silver in a still-damp coat of lacquer—somewhat like a very sophisticated version of the technique of decorating with glitter on glue.

Bridges, where a river branches into eight streams, each covered with a plank bridge. Irises are in full bloom, and his traveling companions urge the poet to write a *tanka*—a five-line, thirty-one-syllable poem—beginning each line with a syllable from the word *ka·ki·tsu·ba·ta* ("iris"). The poet responds (substituting *ha* for *ba*):

> **Ka**ragoromo
> **kit**sutsu narenishi
> **tsu**ma shi areba
> **ha**rubaru kinuru
> **ta**bi o shi zo omou.

> When I remember
> my wife, fond and familiar
> as my courtly robe,
> I feel how far and distant
> my travels have taken me.

(Translated by Stephen Addiss)

22-11. Ogata Korin. Lacquer box for writing implements. Edo period, late 17th–early 18th century. Lacquer, lead, silver, and mother-of-pearl, 5⁵/₈ x 10³/₄ x 7³/₄" (14.2 x 27.4 x 19.7 cm). Tokyo National Museum

INSIDE A WRITING BOX

The interior of the writing box shown in figure 22-11 is fitted with compartments for holding an ink stick, an ink stone, brushes, an eye-dropper, and paper—tools and materials not only for writing but also for **ink painting**.

Ink sticks are made by burning wood or oil inside a container. Soot deposited by the smoke is collected, bound into a paste with resin, heated for several hours, kneaded and pounded, then pressed into small stick-shaped or cake-shaped molds to harden. Molds are often carved to produce an ink stick (or ink cake) decorated in low relief. The tools of writing and painting are also beautiful objects in their own right.

Fresh ink is made for each writing or painting session by grinding the hard, dry ink stick in water against a fine-grained stone. A typical ink stone has a shallow well at one end sloping up to a grinding surface at the other. The artist fills the well with water, transferring it from a waterpot. The ink stick, held vertically, is dipped into the well to pick up a small amount of water, then is rubbed in a circular motion firmly on the grinding surface. The process is repeated until enough ink has been prepared. Grinding ink is viewed as a meditative task, time for collecting one's thoughts and concentrating on the painting or calligraphy ahead.

Brushes are made from animal hairs set in simple bamboo or hollow-reed handles. Brushes taper to a fine point that responds with great sensitivity to any shift in pressure. Although great painters and calligraphers eventually develop their own styles of holding and using the brush, all begin by learning the basic position for writing. The brush is held vertically, grasped firmly between the thumb and first two fingers, with the fourth and fifth fingers often resting against the handle for more subtle control.

well

ink stone

ink stick

brushes

The poem brought tears to all their eyes, and the scene became so famous that any painting of a group of irises, with or without a plank bridge, immediately calls it to mind.

Nanga School

Rimpa artists such as Sotatsu and Korin are considered quintessentially Japanese in spirit, both in the expressive power of their art and in their use of poetic themes from Japan's past. Other painters, however, responded to the new Confucian atmosphere by taking up some of the ideas of the literati painters of China. These painters are grouped together as the Nanga, or Southern, school. Nanga was not a school in the sense of a professional workshop or a family tradition. Rather, it took its name from the Southern school of amateur artists described by the Chinese literati theorist Dong Qichang (Chapter 21). Educated in the Confucian mold, Nanga masters were individuals and often individualists, creating their own variations of literati painting from unique blendings of Chinese models, Japanese aesthetics, and personal brushwork. They were often experts at calligraphy and poetry as well as painting, but one, Uragami Gyokudo (1745–1820), was even more famous as a musician, an expert on a seven-string Chinese zither called the *qin*. Most instruments are played for entertainment or ceremonial purposes, but the *qin* has so deep and soft a sound that it is played only for oneself or a close friend. Its music becomes a kind of meditation, and for Gyokudo it opened a way to commune with nature and his own inner spirit.

Gyokudo was a hereditary samurai official, but midway through his life he resigned from his position and spent seventeen years wandering through Japan, absorbing the beauty of its scenery, writing poems, playing music, and beginning to paint. During his later years Gyokudo produced many of the strongest and most individualistic paintings in Japanese history, although they were not appreciated by people during his lifetime. *Geese Aslant in the High Wind* is a leaf from an album Gyokudo painted in 1817, three years before his death (fig. 22-12). The creative power in this painting is remarkable. The wind seems to have the force of a hurricane, sweeping the tree branches and the geese into swirls of action. The greatest force comes from within the land itself, which mushrooms out and bursts forth in peaks and plateaus as though an inner volcano were erupting.

The style of the painting derives from the Chinese literati tradition, with layers of calligraphic brushwork building up the forms of mountains, trees, and the solitary human habitation. But the inner vision is unique to Gyokudo. In his artistic world, humans do not control nature but can exult in its power and grandeur. Gyokudo's art may have been too strong for most people in his own day, but in our violent century he has come to be appreciated as a great artist.

Zen

Deprived of the support of the government and samurai officials, Zen initially went into something of a decline

22-12. Uragami Gyokudo. *Geese Aslant in the High Wind.* Edo period, 1817. Ink and light colors on paper, 12³/₁₆ x 9⁷/₈" (31 x 25 cm). Takemoto Collection, Aichi

during the Edo period. In the early eighteenth century, however, it was revived by a monk named Hakuin Ekaku (1685–1769), born in a small village not far from Mount Fuji, who resolved to become a monk after hearing a fire-and-brimstone sermon in his youth. For years he traveled around Japan seeking out the strictest Zen teachers. After a series of enlightenment experiences, he eventually became an important teacher himself.

In his later years Hakuin turned more and more to painting and calligraphy as forms of Zen expression and teaching. Since the government no longer sponsored Zen, Hakuin reached out to ordinary people, and many of his paintings portray everyday subjects that would be easily understood by farmers and merchants. The paintings from his sixties have great charm and humor, and by his eighties he was creating works of astonishing force. Hakuin's favorite subject was Bodhidharma, the semilegendary Indian monk who had begun the Zen tradition in China (fig. 22-13). Here he has portrayed the wide-eyed Bodhidharma during his nine years of meditation in front of a temple wall in China. Intensity, concentration, and spiritual depth are conveyed by broad and forceful brushstrokes. The inscription is the ultimate Zen message, attributed to Bodhidharma himself: "Pointing directly to the human heart, see your own nature and become Buddha."

Hakuin's pupils followed his lead in communicating their vision through brushwork. The Zen figure once again became the primary subject of Zen painting, and the painters were again Zen masters rather than primarily artists.

22-14. Nagasawa Rosetsu. *Bull and Puppy.* Edo period,
   18th century. One of a pair of six-panel screens, ink
   and gold wash on paper, 5'7¼" x 12'3" (1.70 x 3.75 m).
   Los Angeles County Museum of Art
   Joe and Etsuko Price Collection

Maruyama-Shijo School

Zen paintings were given away to all those who wished
them, including poor farmers as well as artisans, merchants, and merchants, and samurai. Many merchants, however, were
more concerned with displaying their increasing wealth
than with spiritual matters, and their aspirations fueled a
steady demand for golden screens and other decorative
works of art. One school that arose to satisfy this demand
was the Maruyama-Shijo school, formed in Kyoto by
Maruyama Okyo (1733–1795). Okyo had studied Western-style "perspective pictures" in his youth, and he was
able in his mature works to incorporate shading and perspective into a decorative style, creating a sense of volume that was new to East Asian painting. Okyo's new
style proved very popular in Kyoto, and it soon spread to
Osaka and Edo (present-day Tokyo) as well. The subjects
of Maruyama-Shijo painting were seldom difficult to
understand. Instead of legendary Chinese themes, Maruyama-Shijo painters portrayed the birds, animals, hills,
trees, farmers, and townsfolk of Japan. Although highly
educated people might make a point of preferring Nanga
painting, Maruyama-Shijo works were perfectly suited to
the taste of the emerging upper middle class.

The leading pupil of Okyo was Nagasawa Rosetsu
(1754–1799), a painter of great natural talent who added
his own boldness and humor to the Maruyama-Shijo tradition. Rosetsu delighted in surprising his viewers with
odd juxtapositions and unusual compositions. One of his
finest works is a pair of screens, the left depicting a bull
and a puppy (fig. 22-14). The bull is so immense that it
fills almost the entire six panels of the screen and still
cannot be contained at the top, left, and bottom. The
puppy, white against the dark gray of the bull, helps to
emphasize the huge size of the bull by its own smallness.
The puppy's relaxed and informal pose, looking happily
right out at the viewer, gives this powerful painting a
humorous touch that increases its charm.

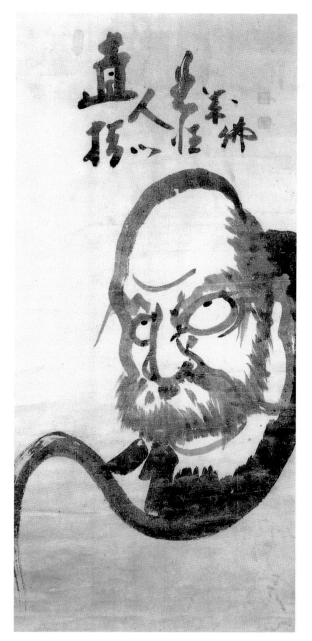

22-13. Hakuin Ekaku. *Bodhidharma Meditating.* Edo period,
   18th century. Ink on paper, 49½ x 21¾" (125.7 x
   55.3 cm). On extended loan to the Spencer Museum
   of Art, University of Kansas, Lawrence

Hakuin had his first enlightenment experience while
meditating upon the koan (mysterious Zen riddle)
about *mu.* One day a monk asked a Chinese Zen master, "Does a dog have the buddha nature?" Although
Buddhist doctrine teaches that all living beings have
buddha nature, the master answered, "*Mu,*" meaning
"has not" or "nothingness." The riddle of this answer
became a problem that Zen masters gave their students as a focus for meditation. With no logical
answer possible, monks were forced to go beyond the
rational mind and penetrate more deeply into
their own being. Hakuin, after months of meditation,
reached a point where he felt "as though frozen
in a sheet of ice." He then happened to hear the sound
of the temple bell, and "it was as though the sheet
of ice had been smashed." Later, as a teacher, Hakuin
invented a koan of his own that has since become
famous: "What is the sound of one hand clapping?"

TECHNIQUE

JAPANESE WOODBLOCK PRINTS

Ukiyo-e ("pictures of the floating world" as these **woodblock prints** are called in Japanese) represent the combined expertise of three people: the artist, the carver, and the printer. Coordinating and funding the endeavor was a publisher, who commissioned the project and distributed the prints to stores or itinerant peddlers, who would sell them.

The artist supplied the master drawing for the print, executing its outlines with brush and ink on tissue-thin paper. Colors might be indicated, but more often they were understood or decided on later. The drawing was passed on to the carver, who pasted it facedown on a hardwood block, preferably cherry wood, so that the outlines showed through the paper in reverse. A light coating of oil might be brushed on to make the paper more transparent, allowing the drawing to stand out with maximum clarity. The carver then cut around the lines of the drawing with a sharp knife, always working in the same direction as the original brushstrokes. The rest of the block was chiseled away, leaving the outlines standing in relief. This block, which reproduced the master drawing, was called the **key block**. If the print was to be **polychrome**, having multiple colors, prints made from the key block were in turn pasted facedown on blocks that would be used as guides for the carver of the color blocks. Each color generally required a separate block, although both sides of a block might be used for economy.

Once the blocks were completed, the printer took over. Paper for printing was covered lightly with animal glue (gelatin). A few hours before printing, the paper was lightly moistened so that it would take ink and color well. Water-based ink or color was brushed over the block, and the paper placed on top and rubbed with a smooth, padded device called a *baren*, until the design was completely transferred. The key block was printed first, then the colors one by one. To ensure that the colors printed exactly within the outlines, each block was carved with two small marks called **registration marks**, in exactly the same place in the margins, outside of the image area—an **L** in one corner, and a straight line in another. By aligning the paper with these marks before letting it fall over the block, the printer ensured that the colors would be placed correctly. One of the most characteristic effects of later Japanese prints is a grading of color from dark to pale. This was achieved by wiping some of the color from the block before printing, or by moistening the block and then applying the color gradually with an unevenly loaded brush—a brush loaded on one side with full-strength color and on the other with diluted color.

An early 20th-century woodblock showing two women cutting and inking blocks

In earlier centuries, when works of art were created largely under aristocratic or religious patronage, Rosetsu's painting might have seemed too mundane. In the Edo period, however, the taste for art had spread so widely through the populace that no single group of patrons could control the cultural climate. Everyday subjects like farm animals were painted as often as Zen subjects or symbolic themes from China. In the hands of a master such as Rosetsu, plebeian subject matter could become simultaneously delightful and monumental, equally pleasing to viewers with or without much education or artistic background.

Ukiyo-e: Pictures of the Floating World

Not only did newly wealthy merchants patronize painters in the middle and later Edo period, but even artisans and tradespeople could purchase works of art. Especially in the new capital of Edo, bustling with commerce and cultural activities, people savored the delights of their peaceful society. Buddhism had long preached that pleasures were fleeting; the cherry tree, which blossoms so briefly, became the symbol for the transience of earthly beauty and joy. Commoners in the Edo period did not dispute this transience, but they took a new attitude: Let's enjoy it to the full as long as it lasts. Thus the Buddhist phrase *ukiyo* ("floating world") became positive rather than negative.

There was no world more transient than that of the pleasure quarters, set up in specified areas of every major city. Here were found restaurants, bathhouses, and brothels. The heroes of the day were no longer famous samurai or aristocratic poets. Instead, swashbuckling actors and beautiful courtesans were admired. These paragons of pleasure soon became immortalized in paintings, and because paintings were often too expensive for common people, in **woodblock prints** known as **ukiyo-e**, "pictures of the floating world" (see "Japanese Woodblock Prints," above).

At first prints were made in black and white, then colored by hand when the public so desired. The first artist to design prints to be printed in many colors was Suzuki Harunobu (1724–1770). His exquisite portrayals of feminine beauty quickly became so popular that soon every artist was designing multicolored *nishiki-e* ("brocade pictures").

22-15. Suzuki Harunobu. *Geisha as Daruma Crossing the Sea.* Edo period, mid-18th century. Color woodcut, 10⁷/₈ x 8¹/₄" (27.6 x 21 cm). Philadelphia Museum of Art

Gift of Mrs. Emile Geyelin, in memory of Anne Hampton Barnes

One print that displays Harunobu's charm and wit is *Geisha as Daruma Crossing the Sea* (fig. 22-15). Harunobu has portrayed a young woman in a red cloak crossing the water on a reed, a clear reference to one of the legends about Bodhidharma, known in Japan as Daruma. To see a young woman peering ahead to the other shore, rather than a grizzled Zen master staring off into space, must have greatly amused the Japanese populace. There was also another layer of meaning in this image because geishas, or courtesans, were sometimes compared to Buddhist teachers or deities in their ability to bring ecstasy, akin to enlightenment, to humans. Harunobu's print suggests these meanings, but it also succeeds simply as a portrait of a beautiful woman, with the gently curving lines of drapery suggesting the delicate feminine form beneath.

The second great subject of ukiyo-e were the actors of the new form of popular theater known as kabuki. Because women had been banned from the stage after a series of scandalous incidents, male actors took both male and female roles. Much as people today buy posters of their favorite sports, music, or movie stars, so, too, in the Edo period people clamored for images of their feminine and masculine ideals.

During the nineteenth century, landscape joined courtesans and actors as a major theme—not the idealized landscape of China, but the actual sights of Japan. The two great masters of landscape prints were Utagawa Hiroshige (1797–1858) and Katsushika Hokusai (1760–1849). Hiroshige's *Fifty-Three Stations of the Tokaido* and Hokusai's *Thirty-Six Views of Fuji* became the most successful sets of graphic art the world has yet known. The blocks were printed and printed again until they were worn out. They were then recarved, and still more copies were printed. This process continued for decades, and thousands of prints from the two series are still extant.

The Great Wave (see fig. 22-1) is the most famous of the scenes from *Thirty-Six Views of Fuji.* Hokusai was already in his seventies, with a fifty-year career behind him, when he designed this image. Such was his modesty that he felt that his Fuji series was only the beginning of his creativity, and he wrote that if he could live until he was 100, he would finally learn how to become an artist.

When seen in Europe and America, these and other Japanese prints were immediately acclaimed, and they strongly influenced late-nineteenth- and early-twentieth-century Western art (Chapter 28). *Japonisme*, or "japonism," became the vogue, and Hokusai and Hiroshige became as famous in the West as in Japan. Indeed, their art was taken more seriously in the West; the first book on Hokusai was published in France, and it has been estimated that by the early twentieth century more than 90 percent of Japanese prints had been sold to Western collectors. Only within the past fifty years have Japanese museums and connoisseurs fully realized the stature of this "plebeian" form of art.

THE MEIJI AND MODERN PERIODS

Pressure from the West for entry into Japan mounted dramatically in the mid-nineteenth century, and in 1853 the policy of national seclusion was ended. Resulting tensions precipitated the downfall of the Tokugawa shogunate, however, and in 1868 the emperor was formally restored to power, an event known as the Meiji Restoration. The court moved from Kyoto to Edo, which was renamed Tokyo, meaning "Eastern Capital."

The Meiji period marked a major change for Japan. After its long isolation Japan was deluged by the influx of the West. Western education, governmental systems, clothing, medicine, industrialization, and technology were all adopted rapidly into Japanese culture. Teachers of sculpture and oil painting were imported from Italy, while adventurous Japanese artists traveled to Europe and America to study.

Japan has always been a country where people have been eager to be up-to-date while at the same time preserving the heritage of the past. Even in the hasty scrambling to become a modern industrialized country, Japan did not lose its sense of tradition, and traditional arts continued to be created even in the days of the strongest Western influence. In modern Japan, artists still choose whether to work in an East Asian style, a Western style, or some combination of the two. Just as Japanese art in earlier periods had both Chinese style and native traditions, so Japanese art of the twentieth century has both Western and native aspects.

Perhaps the most lively contemporary art is ceramics. Japan remains a country where there is widespread appreciation for pottery. Many people still practice the traditional arts of the tea ceremony and flower arranging, both of which require ceramic vessels, and most people would like to own at least one fine ceramic piece. In this atmosphere many potters can earn a comfortable living by making art ceramics, an opportunity that does not occur in other countries. Some ceramists continue to create raku teabowls and other traditional wares, while others experiment with new styles and new techniques. Figure 22-16 shows the work of four contemporary potters, from left to right, Miyashita Zenji (b. 1939), Morino Hiroaki (b. 1934), Tsujimura Shiro (b. 1947), and Ito Sekisui (b. 1941).

Miyashita Zenji, who lives in Kyoto, spends a great deal of time on each piece. He creates the initial form by constructing an undulating shape out of pieces of cardboard, then builds up the surface with clay of many different colors, using torn paper to create irregular shapes. When fired, the varied colors of the clay seem to form a landscape, with layers of mountains leading up to the sky. Miyashita's work is modern in shape, yet also traditional in its evocation of nature.

Morino Hiroaki's works are often abstract and sculptural, without any functional use. He has also made vases, however, and they showcase his ability to create designs in glaze that are wonderfully quirky and playful. His favorite colors of red and black bring out the asymmetrical strength of his compositions, the products of a lively individual artistic personality.

22-16. From left: Miyashita Zenji, Morino Hiroaki, Tsujimura Shiro, Ito Sekisui. Four ceramic vessels. Modern period, after 1970. Spencer Museum of Art, University of Kansas, Lawrence

Gift of the Friends of the Art Museum/Helen Foresman Spencer Art Acquisition Fund

Tsujimura Shiro lives in the mountains outside Nara and makes pottery in personal variations on traditional shapes. He values the rough texture of country clay and the natural ash glaze that occurs with wood firing, and he creates jars, vases, bowls, and cups with rough exteriors covered by rivulets of flowing green glaze that are often truly spectacular. Tsujimura's pieces are always functional, and part of their beauty comes from their suitability for holding food, flowers, or tea.

Ito Sekisui represents the fifth generation of a family of potters. Sekisui demonstrates the Japanese love of natural materials by presenting the essential nature of fired clay in his works. The shapes of his bowls and pots are beautifully balanced with simple clean lines; no ornament detracts from their fluent geometric purity. The warm tan, orange, and reddish colors of the clay reveal themselves in irregularly flowing and changing tones created by allowing different levels of oxygen into the kiln when firing.

These four artists represent the high level of contemporary ceramics in Japan, which is supported by a broad spectrum of educated and enthusiastic collectors and admirers. There is also strong public interest in contemporary painting, prints, calligraphy, textiles, lacquer, architecture, and sculpture.

One of the most adventurous and original sculptors currently working is Chuichi Fujii. Born into a family of sculptors in wood, Fujii found himself as a young artist more interested in the new materials of plastic, steel, and glass. However, in his mid-thirties he took stock of his progress and decided to begin again, this time with wood. At first he carved and cut into the wood, but he soon realized that he wanted to allow the material to express its own natural spirit, so he devised an ingenious new technique that preserved the individuality of each

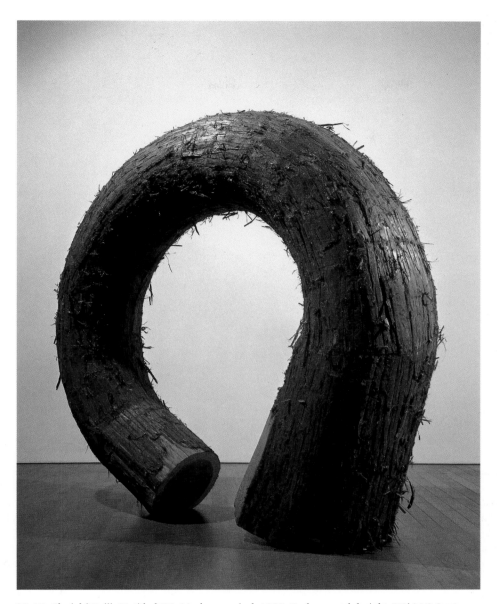

22-17. Chuichi Fujii. *Untitled '90.* Modern period, 1990. Cedar wood, height 7'5½" (2.3 m).
Hara Museum of Contemporary Art, Tokyo

log while making of it something new. As Fujii explains it, he first studies the log in order to come to terms with its basic shape and to decide how far he can "push to the limit the log's balancing point with the floor" (Howard N. Fox, *A Primal Spirit: Ten Contemporary Japanese Sculptors.* Exh. cat., Los Angeles County Museum of Art, 1990, page 63). Next, he inserts hooks into the log and runs wires between them. Every day he tightens the wires, over a period of months gradually pulling the log into a new shape. When he has bent the log tree trunk to the shape he envisioned, Fujii makes a final cut and sees whether his sculpture will stand. If he has miscalculated, he discards the work and begins again.

Here, Fujii has created a circle, one of the most basic forms in nature but never before seen in such a thick tree trunk (fig. 22-17). The work strongly suggests the *enso,* the circle that Zen monks painted to express the universe, the all, the void, the moon—and even a tea cake. Yet Fujii

does not try to proclaim his links with Japanese culture. He says that while his works may seem to have some connections with traditional Japanese arts, he is not conscious of them. He acknowledges, however, that people carry their own cultures inside them, and he claims that all Japanese have had "the experience of sensing with their skin the fragrance of a tree. Without saying it, the Japanese understand that a tree has warmth; I believe it breathes air, it cries" (Fox, page 63).

Fujii's sculpture testifies to the depth of an artistic tradition that has continued to produce visually exciting works for 14,000 years. He has achieved something entirely new, yet his work also embodies the love of asymmetry, respect for natural materials, and dramatic simplicity encountered throughout the history of Japanese art. Whatever the future of art in Japan, these principles will undoubtedly continue to lead to new combinations of tradition and creativity.

1300   1400   1500   1600

The Moon Goddess,
Coyolxauhqui
Aztec
15th century

Silver llama statue
Inka
15th century

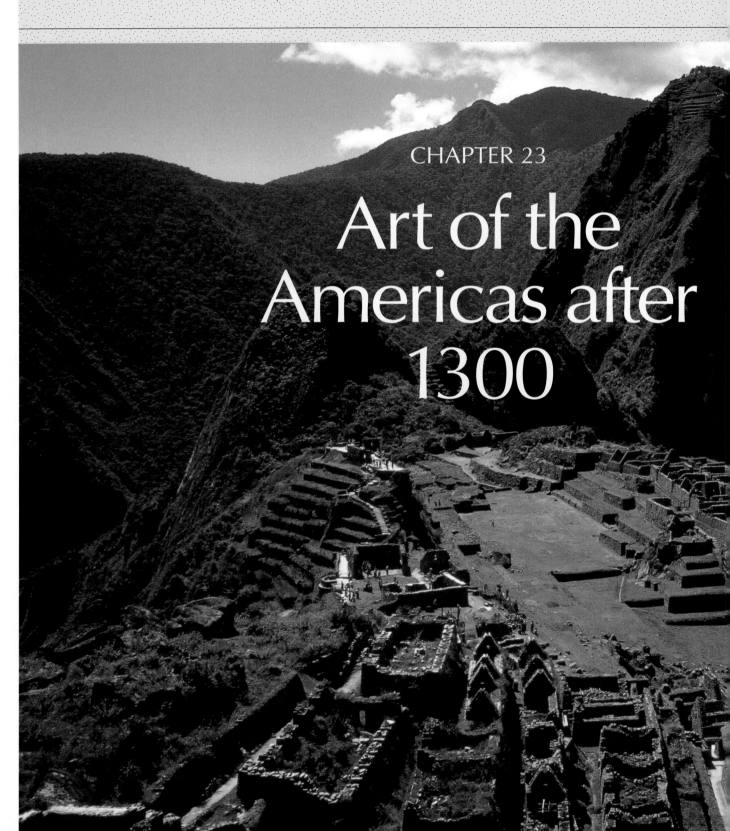

CHAPTER 23

Art of the Americas after 1300

1700
1800
1900
2000

Taos Pueblo
Tewa
c. 1700

Hide painting
Mandan
1797–1805

Partition screen
Tlingit
c. 1840

Martinez
Blackware jar
c. 1942

Bering Strait

NORTH

AMERICA

Hudson
Bay

Queen
Charlotte
Islands

NORTHWEST COAST

ROCKY MOUNTAINS

GREAT PLAINS

Mississippi River

Missouri River

EASTERN
WOODLANDS

*PACIFIC
OCEAN*

Danger Cave

Santa Fe

UNITED STATES

SOUTHWEST

*ATLANTIC
OCEAN*

MEXICO

Gulf of
Mexico

Mexico City

THE
YUCATAN

CUBA

AZTEC EMPIRE

GUATEMALA

NEW MEXICO

Santa Clara
Pueblo

San Ildefonso
Pueblo

Taos Pueblo

Santa Fe

*VALLEY OF
MEXICO*

Tula

Teotihuacan

Mexico City
(Tenochtitlan)

Lake
Texcoco

Malinalco

MEXICO

Quito

ECUADOR

Amazon River

SOUTH

AMERICA

INKA

Urubamba River

PERU

Wari

Machu Picchu

Cuzco

Saqsawaman

ANDES MOUNTAINS

Lake Titicaca

BOLIVIA

EMPIRE

*PACIFIC
OCEAN*

Santiago

CHILE **ARGENTINA**

0   1000 miles
0   1000 kilometers

TIERRA DEL FUEGO

23-1. A view of the world, detail from *Codex Fejervary-Mayer*. Aztec or Mixtec, c. 1400–1521. Paint on animal hide, each page 6⅞ x 6⅞" (17.5 x 17.5 cm), total length 13'3" (4.04 m). The National Museums and Galleries on Merseyside, Liverpool, England

E arly in November 1519, the army of the Spanish conquistador Hernán Cortés beheld for the first time the great Aztec capital of Tenochtitlan. The shimmering city, which seemed to be floating on the water, was built on islands in the middle of Lake Texcoco in the Valley of Mexico, linked by broad causeways to the mainland. One of Cortés's companions later recalled the wonder the Spanish felt at that moment: "When we saw so many cities and villages built on the water and other great towns and that straight and level causeway going towards [Tenochtitlan], we were amazed . . . on account of the great towers and [temples] and buildings rising from the water, and all built of masonry. And some of our soldiers even asked whether the things that we saw were not a dream" (cited in Berdan, page 1).

The startling mirage that Cortés's soldiers saw was indeed real, a city of stone built on islands—a city that held many treasures and many mysteries. Much of the period before the conquistadores' arrival still remains enigmatic, but a rare manuscript that survived the Spanish Conquest depicts the preconquest worldview of peoples of Mexico at that time, though it is uncertain whether the manuscript originated with the Aztec or their rivals the Mixtec. At the center of the image here is the ancient fire god Xiuhtecutli (fig. 23-1). Radiating from him are the four directions—each associated with a specific color—as well as a deity and a tree with a bird in its branches. In each corner, to the right of a **U**-shaped band, is an attribute of the god Tezcatlipoca, an omnipotent, primal deity, the "smoking mirror" who could see everything—in the upper right a head, in the upper left an arm, in the lower left a foot, and in the lower right bones. Streams of blood flow from these attributes to the fire god in the center. Such images are filled with important, symbolically coded information—even the dots refer to the number of days in one aspect of the Mesoamerican calendar—and they were integral parts of the culture of the Americas.

INDIGENOUS AMERICAN ART

When the first European explorers and conquerors arrived, the Western Hemisphere was already inhabited from the Arctic Circle to Tierra del Fuego by peoples with long and complex histories and rich and varied cultural traditions (see "Foundations of Civilization in the Americas," below). This chapter focuses on the arts of the indigenous peoples of Mesoamerica, Andean South America, and North America just prior to and in the wake of their encounter with an expansionist Europe.

Although art was central to their lives, the peoples of the Americas set aside no special objects as "works of art." For them, everything had a function. Some objects were essentially utilitarian and others had ritual uses and symbolic associations, but people drew no distinctions between art and other aspects of material culture or between the fine arts and the decorative arts. Understanding Native American art thus requires an understanding of the cultural context in which it was made, a context that in many cases has been lost to time or to the disruptions of the European conquest. Fortunately, art history and archeology have recently contributed to the recovery of at least some of that lost context.

MEXICO AND SOUTH AMERICA

Two great empires—the Aztec in Mexico and the Inka in South America—rose to prominence in the fifteenth century at about the same time that European adventurers began to explore the oceans in search of new trade routes to Asia. In the encounter that followed, the Aztec and Inka Empires were destroyed.

FOUNDATIONS OF CIVILIZATION IN THE AMERICAS

Humans first entered the Western Hemisphere sometime between 12,000 and 30,000 years ago by way of a land bridge in the Bering region that connected Asia and North America during the last Ice Age. By 11,000 years ago they had spread over both North and South America. In many regions they developed a settled, agricultural way of life. In Mesoamerica, in the Andean region of South America, and for a time in what is now the southeastern United States, they developed hierarchical, urban societies with monumental architecture and elaborate artistic traditions.

Mesoamerica extends from north of the Valley of Mexico into Central America. The civilizations that arose there shared a number of features, including writing, a complex calendrical system, a ritual ball game, and several deities and religious beliefs. Their religious practices included blood and human sacrifice. The earliest Mesoamerican civilization, that of the Olmec, flourished between 1200 and 400 BCE. Maya civilization arose around the beginning of the Common Era in southern Mesoamerica and endured until the Spanish Conquest. Its initial focus, during the Classic period (250–900 CE), was in the southern Yucatan but then shifted to the northern Yucatan. The Classic period Maya developed Mesoamerica's most sophisticated writing and calendrical systems. The Valley of Mexico was dominated during the Classic period by the city of Teotihuacan, which exerted widespread influence throughout Mesoamerica. The Toltec established a state north of the Valley of Mexico that endured from about 1000 to 1200. The Aztec Empire emerged in the Valley of Mexico beginning in the thirteenth and fourteenth centuries. By the end of the fifteenth century the Inka Empire controlled the entire Andean region from north of Quito in modern Ecuador to Santiago in modern Chile.

In North America the people of what is now the southeastern United States adopted a settled way of life by around the end of the second millennium BCE and began building monumental earthworks as early as 1300 BCE. The people of the American Southwest developed a settled, agricultural way of life during the first millennium CE. By around 750 CE the Anasazi—the forebears of the modern Pueblo peoples—began building multistoried, apartmentlike structures with many specialized rooms.

PARALLELS

Years	Americas Cultural Centers	Americas	World
c. 1300–1525	Aztec Empire	Capital of Tenochtitlan founded; empire expands through alliances, marriages, conquest; conquered by the Spanish under Cortés	**1300–1500** Hundred Years' War between England and France; Black Death in Europe; Ming dynasty (China); Great Schism in Christian Church; Gutenberg's Bible; Columbus's voyages (Spain); Spanish Inquisition
c. 1300–1537	Inka Empire	Capital of Cuzco flourishes; strong government and religious hierarchy; empire expands to length of 2,600 miles; government control of agriculture; public-works, military, and agricultural production mandatory; extensive roads and storehouses; assassination of Atahualpa and conquest by the Spanish under Pizarro	**1500–1700** Michelangelo's *David* (Italy); Leonardo's *Mona Lisa* (Italy); Michelangelo's Sistine Ceiling (Italy); Protestant Reformation in Europe; Mughal period (India); William Shakespeare born (England); Baroque style emerges in Europe; Peter Paul Rubens (Flanders); Hideyoshi unites Japan; Rembrandt van Rijn (Netherlands); Qing dynasty (China)
c. 1300–	Eastern Woodlands	Hunting and agricultural communities; birch-bark canoes; pottery; Iroquois confederation; quillwork; beadwork; English settle Jamestown, Va.; French settle Quebec, Canada; trading; European encroachment on Native American lands; Indian Removal Act; Trail of Tears	**1700–1800** Union of England and Scotland as Great Britain; British Museum founded; James Watt develops steam engine (Scotland); French Revolution; Age of Enlightenment in Europe
c. 1300–	Great Plains	Groups in permanent villages pursue agriculture while nomadic groups hunt buffalo; tepees; hunting groups increase after Spanish introduce horses; Spanish introduce firearms; Prairie style incorporates elements from Eastern Woodlands	
c. 1300–	Northwest Coast	Extended family groups living in communal timber dwellings; fishing; dugout canoes; wood carving, weaving, and basketry; arrival of European fur traders	
c. 1300–	Southwest	Pueblo dwellers cultivate crops; Navajos establish semisedentary agricultural and herding groups; weaving, painting, sand painting; Spanish settle Sante Fe; Pueblo peoples rise up against Spanish	

23-2. *The Founding of Tenochtitlan*, page from *Codex Mendoza*. Aztec, 16th century. Ink and color on paper, 8⁷/₁₆ x 12⁶/₁₆" (21.5 x 31.5 cm). The Bodleian Library, Oxford
MS. Arch Selden. A.1.fol. 2r

The Aztec Empire

The people who lived in the remarkable city that Cortés found were then rulers of much of Mexico. Their rise to such power had been recent and swift. Only 400 years earlier, according to their own legends, they had been a nomadic people living on the shores of the mythological Lake Aztlan somewhere to the northwest of the Valley of Mexico, where present-day Mexico City is located. They called themselves the Mexica, hence the name *Mexico*. The term *Aztec* derives from Aztlan.

At the urging of their patron god, Huitzilopochtli, the Aztec began a long migration away from Lake Aztlan, arriving in the Valley of Mexico in the thirteenth century. Driven from place to place, they eventually ended up in the marshes on the edge of Lake Texcoco. There they settled on an island where they had seen an eagle perching on a prickly pear cactus *(tenochtli)*, a sign that Huitzilopochtli told them would mark the end of their wandering. They called the place Tenochtitlan. The city, like Venice, grew on a collection of islands linked by canals.

Through a series of alliances and royal marriages, the Aztec gradually rose to prominence, emerging less than a century before the arrival of Cortés as the head of a powerful alliance and the dominant power in the valley. Only then did they begin the aggressive expansion

that brought them tribute from all over Central Mexico and transformed Tenochtitlan into the glittering capital that so impressed the invading Spanish.

Aztec society was divided into roughly three classes: an elite of rulers and nobles, a middle class of professional merchants and luxury artisans, and a lower class of farmers and laborers. The luxury artisans were known as *Toltecca,* reflecting Aztec admiration for the earlier Toltec civilization, which had fallen in the thirteenth century. Commoners and elite alike received rigorous military training.

Aztec religion was based on a complex pantheon that combined the Aztec deities with more ancient ones that had long been worshiped in Central Mexico. According to Aztec belief, the gods had created the current universe at the ancient city of Teotihuacan. Its continued existence depended on human actions, including rituals of bloodletting and human sacrifice. The end of each round of fifty-two years in the Mesoamerican calendar was a particularly dangerous time, requiring a special fire-lighting ritual. Sacrificial victims sustained the sun god in his daily course through the sky. Huitzilopochtli, son of the earth mother Coatlicue and the Aztec patron deity associated with the sun and warfare, also required sacrificial victims so that he could, in a regular repetition of the events surrounding his birth, drive the stars and the moon from the sky at the beginning of each day. The stars were his half brothers, and the moon, Coyolxauhqui, was his half sister. When Coatlicue conceived Huitzilopochtli by inserting a ball of feathers into her chest as she was sweeping, his jealous siblings conspired to kill her. When they attacked, Huitzilopochtli emerged from her body fully grown and armed, drove off his brothers, and destroyed his half sister, Coyolxauhqui.

Most Aztec books were destroyed in the wake of the Spanish Conquest, but the work of Aztec scribes appears in several documents created for Spanish administrators after the conquest. The first page of the *Codex Mendoza*, prepared for the Spanish viceroy in the sixteenth century, can be interpreted as an idealized representation of both the city of Tenochtitlan and its sacred ceremonial precinct (fig. 23-2). An eagle perched on a prickly pear cactus—the symbol of the city—fills the center of the page. Waterways divide the city into four quarters, which are further subdivided into wards, as represented by the seated figures. The victorious warriors at the bottom of the page represent Aztec conquests.

The focal point of the sacred precinct—probably symbolized in figure 23-2 by the temple or house at the top of the page—was the Great Pyramid, a 130-foot-high stepped double pyramid with dual temples on top, one of which was dedicated to Huitzilopochtli and the other to Tlaloc, the god of rain and fertility. Two steep staircases led up the west face of this structure from the plaza in front of it. Sacrificial victims climbed these stairs to the Temple of Huitzilopochtli at the summit, where several priests threw them over a stone and another quickly cut open their chests and pulled out their still-throbbing hearts. Their bodies were then rolled down the stairs and dismembered. Thousands of severed heads were said to have been kept

23-3.　Rock-cut sanctuary, Malinalco, Mexico. Aztec,
15th century; modern thatched roof

23-4.　*The Moon Goddess, Coyolxauhqui.* Aztec, 15th century.
Stone, diameter 11'6" (3.5 m)

This disk was discovered accidentally in 1978 by workers
from a utility company who were excavating at a street
corner in central Mexico City.

on a skull rack in the plaza, represented in figure 23-2 by
the rack with a single skull to the right of the eagle. During the winter rainy season the sun rose behind the Temple of Tlaloc, and during the dry season it rose behind the
Temple of Huitzilopochtli. The double temple thus united
two natural forces, sun and rain, or fire and water. During
the spring and autumn equinoxes, the sun rose between
the two temples, illuminating the Temple of Quetzalcoatl,
the feathered serpent, an ancient creator god associated
with the calendar, civilization, and the arts.

Like other Mesoamerican peoples, the Aztec intended their temples to resemble mountains. They also
carved shrines and temples directly into the mountains
surrounding the Valley of Mexico. A steep flight of stairs
leads up to one such temple carved into the side of a
mountain at Malinalco (fig. 23-3). The formidable entrance, which resembles the open mouth of the earth
monster, leads into a circular room (the thatched roof is
modern). If the temple itself is a mountain, surely this
space is a symbolic cave, the womb of the earth. A pit for
blood sacrifices opens into the heart of the mountain.
Stylized eagle and jaguar skins carved into a semicircular bench around the interior are symbols of two Aztec
military orders, suggesting that members of those orders
performed rites here.

Sculpture of serpents and serpent heads on the Great
Pyramid in Tenochtitlan associated it with the "Hill of the
Serpent," where Huitzilopochtli slew the moon goddess
Coyolxauhqui. A huge circular relief of the dismembered
goddess once lay at the foot of the temple stairs, as if the
enraged and triumphant Huitzilopochtli had cast her there
like a sacrificial victim (fig. 23-4). Her torso is in the center, surrounded by her head and limbs. A rope around her
waist is attached to a skull. She has bells on her cheeks

23-5.　*The Mother Goddess, Coatlicue.* Aztec, 15th century.
Stone, height 8'6" (2.65 m). Museo Nacional de
Antropología, Mexico City

and balls of down in her hair. She wears a magnificent headdress and has distinctive ear ornaments composed of disks, rectangles, and triangles. The sculpture is two-dimensional in concept with a deeply cut background.

The Spanish built their own capital, Mexico City, over the ruins of Tenochtitlan and built a cathedral on the site of Tenochtitlan's sacred precinct. An imposing statue of Coatlicue, mother of Huitzilopochtli, was found near the cathedral during excavations there in the late eighteenth century (fig. 23-5). One of the conquistadores described seeing such a statue covered with blood inside the Temple of Huitzilopochtli, where it would have stood high above the vanquished Coyolxauhqui. Coatlicue means "she of the serpent skirt," and this broad-shouldered figure with clawed hands and feet has a skirt of twisted snakes. A pair of serpents, symbols of gushing blood, rise from her neck to form her head. Their eyes are her eyes; their fangs, her tusks. The writhing serpents of her skirt also form her body. Around her stump of a neck hangs a necklace of sacrificial offerings—hands, hearts, and a dangling skull. Despite the surface intricacy, the sculpture's simple, bold, and blocky forms create a single visual whole. The colors with which it was originally painted would have heightened its dramatic impact.

The Inka Empire

At the beginning of the sixteenth century the Inka Empire was one of the largest states in the world, rivaling China in size. It extended more than 2,600 miles along western South America, encompassing most of modern Peru, Ecuador, Bolivia, and northern Chile and reaching into modern Argentina. Like the Aztec Empire, its rise had been recent and swift.

The Inka called their empire the Land of the Four Quarters. At its center was their capital, Cuzco, "the navel of the world," located high in the Andes Mountains. The initial history of the Inka people is obscure. The Cuzco region had been under the control of the earlier Wari Empire, and the Inka state was probably one of many small competing kingdoms that emerged in the highlands in the wake of the Wari collapse. In the fifteenth century the Inkas began suddenly and rapidly to expand, and they subdued most of their vast domain—through conquest, alliance, and intimidation—by 1500. To hold their linguistically and ethnically diverse empire together, the Inka relied on an overarching state religion, a hierarchical bureaucracy, and various forms of labor taxation, in which the payment was a set amount of time spent performing tasks for the state. Agricultural lands were divided into three categories: those for the gods, which supported priests and religious authorities; those for the ruler and the state; and those for the local population itself. As part of their labor tax, people were required to work the lands of the gods and the state for part of each year. In return the state provided them with gifts through their local leaders and sponsored lavish ritual entertainments. Men served periodically on public-works projects—building roads and terracing hillsides, for example—and in the army. The Inka also moved about

23-6. Walls of the Temple of the Sun, below the Church of Santo Domingo, Cuzco, Peru. Inka, 15th century

The curving lower wall formed part of the Inka Temple of the Sun, also known as the Golden Enclosure or Court of Gold.

whole subject communities to best exploit the resources of their empire. Ranks of storehouses at Inka administrative centers assured the state's ability to feed its armies and supply the people working for it. No Andean civilization ever developed writing, but the Inka kept detailed accounts on knotted and colored cords.

To move their armies around and speed transport and communication within their empire, the Inka built nearly 15,000 miles of roads. These varied from 50-foot-wide thoroughfares to 3-foot-wide paths. In common with other Native American civilizations, the Inka had no wheeled vehicles. Travelers went on foot, and llamas were used as pack animals. Stairways helped travelers negotiate steep mountain slopes, and rope suspension bridges allowed them to cross river gorges. The main road on the Pacific coast, a desert region, had walls to protect it from blowing sand. All along the roads, the Inkas built administrative centers, storehouses, and roadside lodgings. These lodgings—more than a thousand have been found—were spaced a day's journey apart. A relay system of waiting runners could carry messages between Cuzco and the farthest reaches of the empire in about a week.

Cuzco, a capital of great splendor and magnificence, was home to the Inka, as the ruler of the Inka Empire was called, and the extended ruling group. The city, which may have been laid out to resemble a giant puma, was a showcase of the finest Inka masonry, some of which can still be seen in the modern city. The walls of its most magnificent structure, the Temple of the Sun, served as the foundation for the Spanish colonial Church of Santo Domingo (fig. 23-6). Within the Temple of the Sun was a room adorned

ELEMENTS OF ARCHITECTURE

Inka Masonry

Working with the simplest of tools—mainly heavy stone hammers—and using no mortar, Inka builders created stonework of great refinement and durability: roads and bridges that linked the entire empire, built-up terraces for growing crops, and structures both simple and elaborate. At Machu Picchu (fig. 23-7), all buildings and terraces within its 3-square-mile extent were made of granite, the hard stone occurring at the site. Commoners' houses and some walls were constructed of irregular stones that were carefully fitted together. Some walls and certain domestic and religious structures were erected using squared-off, smooth-surfaced stones laid in even rows. At a few Inka sites, the stones were boulder-size: up to 27 feet tall.

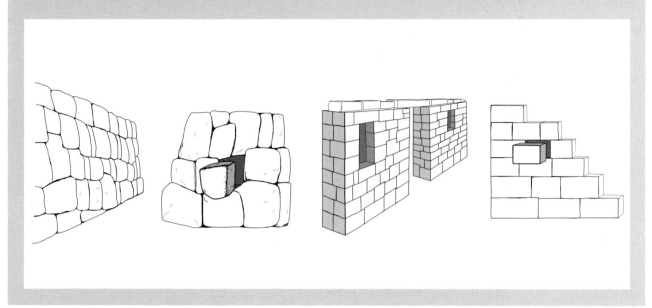

with gold dedicated to the sun and another adorned with silver dedicated to the moon.

Inka masonry has survived earthquakes that have destroyed or seriously damaged later structures. Fine Inka masonry consisted of either rectangular blocks, as in figure 23-6, or irregular polygonal blocks. Both were ground so that adjoining blocks fit tightly together without mortar (see "Elements of Architecture," above). The blocks might be slightly **beveled** so that the stones had a pillowed form and each block retained its identity, or they might, as in figure 23-6, be smoothed into a continuous flowing surface in which the individual blocks form part of a seamless whole. Inka structures had gabled, thatched roofs. Doors, windows, and niches were trapezoid shaped, narrower at the top than the bottom. The effort expended on building by the Inka was prodigious. The temple fortress of Saqsawaman in Cuzco, for example, was reputed to have occupied 30,000 workers for many decades.

Machu Picchu, one of the most spectacular archeological sites in the world, provides an excellent example of Inka architectural planning (fig. 23-7). At 9,000 feet above sea level, it straddles a ridge between two high peaks in the eastern slopes of the Andes and looks down on the Urubamba River. Stone buildings occupy terraces around central plazas, and narrow agricultural terraces descend into the valley. The site lies near the eastern limits of the empire, suggesting that it may have been a frontier outpost. Its temples and carved sacred stones suggest that it also had an important religious function.

The production of fine textiles is of ancient origin in the Andes, and textiles were one of the primary forms of wealth for the Inka. One kind of labor taxation was to require the manufacture of fibers and cloth, and textiles as well as agricultural products filled Inka storehouses. Cloth was a fitting offering for the gods, so fine garments were draped around golden statues, and entire images were constructed of cloth. Garments also carried important symbolic messages. Their patterns and designs were not simply decorative but indicated, among other things, a person's ethnic identity and social rank. Each square in the tunic shown in figure 23-8 represents a miniature tunic, but the meaning of the individual patterns is not yet completely understood. The four-part motifs may refer to the Land of the Four Quarters. The checkerboard pattern designated military officers and royal escorts. The meaning of the diagonal key motif is not known, but it is often found on tunics with horizontal border stripes.

The Spanish who conquered the Inka Empire were far more interested in the Inka's vast quantities of gold and silver objects than in cloth. Whatever they could find, they melted down to enrich themselves and the royal coffers of Spain. The Inka, in contrast, valued gold and silver not as precious metals in themselves but because they saw in them symbols of the sun and the moon. They are said to have called gold the "sweat of the sun" and silver the "tears of the moon." Some small figures, buried as offerings, escaped the conquerors' treasure hunt. The small llama shown in figure 23-9 was found near Lake Titicaca.

23-7. Machu Picchu, Peru. Inka, 15th–16th centuries

23-8. Tunic, from Peru. Inka, c. 1500. Wool and cotton, 35⅞ x 30" (91 x 76.5 cm). Dumbarton Oaks Research Library and Collections, Washington, D.C.

Textile patterns and colors were standardized, like European heraldry or the uniforms of today's sports teams, to convey information at a glance.

23-9. Llama, from Bolivia or Peru, found near Lake Titicaca, Bolivia. Inka, 15th century. Cast silver with gold and cinnabar, 9 x 8½ x 1¾" (22.9 x 21.6 x 4.4 cm). American Museum of Natural History, New York
Trans. #5003

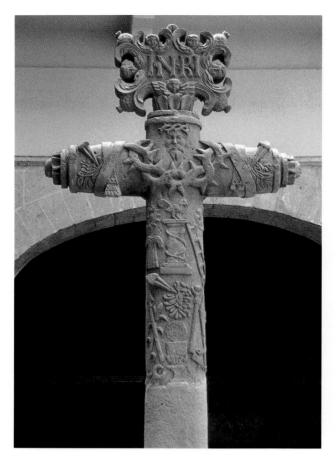

23-10. Atrial cross, from Mexico. Before 1556. Stone, height 11'3" (3.45 m). Chapel of the Indians, Basilica of Guadalupe, Mexico City

The llama had a special connection with the sun, with rain, and with fertility. In Cuzco a llama was sacrificed to the sun every morning and evening. A white llama was kept in the capital as the symbol of the Inka. Dressed in a red tunic and wearing gold jewelry, this llama passed through the streets during April celebrations. According to Spanish commentators, these processions included lifesize gold and silver images of llamas, people, and gods.

The Aftermath of the Spanish Conquest

Hernán Cortés arrived off the coast of Mexico from the Spanish colony in Cuba in 1519. Within two years, after forging alliances with the Aztec's enemies, he had succeeded in taking Tenochtitlan. Over the next several years Spanish forces subdued much of the rest of Mexico and established it as a colony of Spain. In 1532 Francisco Pizarro, following Cortés's example, led an expedition to the land of the Inka. Hearing that the Inka ruler Atahualpa, freshly victorious in the war of succession that followed the death of his father, was progressing south from the city of Quito to Cuzco, Pizarro pressed inland to intercept him. He and his men seized Atahualpa, held him for a huge ransom in gold, then treacherously strangled him. They marched on Cuzco and seized it in 1533. The conquest was followed by a period of disorder,

with Inka rebellions and struggles among the conquistadores themselves, that did not end until about 1550. In both Mexico and Peru the Native American populations declined sharply after the conquest because of the exploitative policies of the conquerors and the ravages of diseases they imported, like smallpox, against which the indigenous people had no immunity.

In the wake of the conquest, Roman Catholicism spread throughout Spanish America, and local beliefs and practices were suppressed. Native American temples were torn down, and churches erected in their place. The work of conversion in the sixteenth century fell to the Franciscan, Dominican, and Augustinian religious orders. Several missionaries were so appalled by the conquerors' treatment of the people they called Indians that they petitioned the Spanish king to improve their condition.

In the course of Native Americans' conversion to Roman Catholicism, their symbolism was to some extent absorbed into Christian symbolism. This process can be seen in the huge early colonial **atrial crosses**, so called because they were located in church atriums, where large numbers of converts gathered for education in their new faith. Early chroniclers wrote that the crosses were decorated with flowers and that children gathered around them for instruction. Missionaries recruited Native American sculptors to carve these crosses. One sixteenth-century atrial cross, now in the Basilica of Guadalupe in Mexico City, suggests pre-Hispanic sculpture in its stark form and rich surface symbols, even though the individual images were probably copied from illustrated books brought by the missionaries (fig. 23-10). The work is made from two large blocks of stone that are entirely covered with low-relief images known as the Arms of Christ, the "weapons" Christ used to defeat the devil. Jesus' Crown of Thorns hangs like a necklace around the cross bar, and with the Holy Shroud, which also wraps the arms, it frames the image of the Holy Face (the cloth with which Veronica wiped Jesus' face). Blood gushes forth where huge nails pierce the ends of the cross. Symbols of regeneration, such as winged **cherub** heads and pomegranates, surround the inscription at the top of the cross.

The cross itself suggests an ancient Mesoamerican symbol, the World Tree or Tree of Life, and the image of blood sacrifice resonates with indigenous beliefs. Like the statue of Coatlicue (see fig. 23-5), the cross is composed of many individual elements that seem compressed to form a shape other than their own. The dense low relief combines into a single massive form. Traditional Christian imagery in a simplified form is clearly visible in the work, although it may not yet have had much meaning or emotional resonance for the artists who put it there.

In 1531 Native American converts gained their own patron saint when the Virgin Mary appeared as a Native American to a Native American named Juan Diego. She is said to have asked that a church be built on a hill where the Aztec mother goddess had once been worshiped. As evidence of this vision, Juan Diego brought flowers that the Virgin had caused to bloom, wrapped in a cloak, to the archbishop. When he opened his bundle, the cloak bore the image of a dark-skinned Virgin Mary, standing on the moon and clothed with the sun, an image known as the Woman of Revelations. The site of the vision was renamed Guadalupe, after Our Lady of Guadalupe in Spain, and became a venerated pilgrimage center. In 1754 the pope declared the Virgin of Guadalupe to be the patron of the Americas.

NORTH AMERICA

The Europeans who settled America north of Mexico were drawn not by gold and silver but by land. As colonists settled what was to become the United States and Canada, claiming land for their towns, farms, and plantations, they dispossessed the people already living there. European explorers and settlers had little interest in Native American arts. Much of it was small, portable, fragile, and impermanent; its symbolic language was misunderstood; and until recently its aesthetic quality was unappreciated.

Eastern Woodlands and the Great Plains

When European settlement began, forests covered eastern North America from Hudson Bay to the Gulf of Mexico and from the Atlantic coast to the Mississippi River and Missouri River watersheds. Between this Eastern Woodlands region and the Rocky Mountains to the west lay an area of prairie grasslands now known as the Great Plains.

The Native American peoples of the Eastern Woodlands supported themselves by a combination of hunting and agriculture. They lived in villages and cultivated corn, squash, and beans. They used flexible and waterproof birch bark to construct their homes and to make the extremely functional river and lake craft known as the canoe. After the arrival of the Europeans, they exchanged furs for such useful items as metal kettles and needles, cloth, and beads. In the sixteenth century one Eastern Woodlands group, the Iroquois, formed a sophisticated and powerful confederation of Native American nations in the Northeast that played a prominent military and political role until after the American Revolution.

Before the coming of the Europeans, two differing ways of life developed on the Great Plains, one nomadic—dependent for food, clothing, and shelter on the region's great migrating herds of buffalo—and the other sedentary and agricultural. The introduction of the horse to the prairies by Spanish explorers in the late seventeenth century transformed Plains life. Horses—and, later, firearms—made buffalo hunting vastly more efficient than before and attracted more people to the nomadic way of life.

As European settlers on the eastern seaboard began to turn forests into farms, they put increasing pressure on the Eastern Woodlands peoples, depriving them of their lands and forcing them westward. This steady encroachment reached a climax when the U.S. Congress passed the Indian Removal Act of 1830, which forced many eastern groups to resettle west of the Mississippi River. Just one of the consequences of this law was the infamous 1838–1839 "Trail of Tears," the forced march of the Cherokee to Oklahoma from their towns and farms in

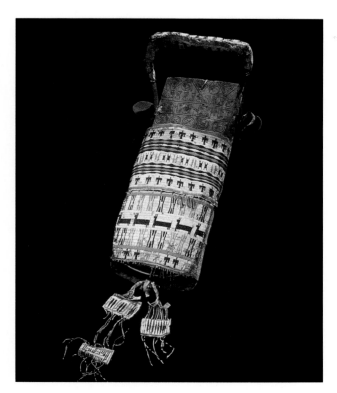

23-11. Baby carrier, from the Upper Missouri River area. Eastern Sioux, 19th century. Board, buckskin, porcupine quill, length 31" (78.8 cm). Smithsonian Institution Libraries, Washington, D.C.

Georgia. The resulting interaction of Eastern Woodlands artists with one another and with Plains artists led to the emergence of the Prairie style among numerous groups.

One distinctively Eastern Woodlands medium that found its way into the Plains was **quillwork** embroidery. Quillwork involved soaking porcupine and bird quills to soften them, dyeing them, and then working them into rectilinear, ornamental surface patterns on deerskin clothing and on birch-bark artifacts like baskets and boxes. A Sioux legend recounts how a mythical ancestor, Doublewoman ("double" because she was both beautiful and ugly, benign and dangerous), appeared to a woman in a dream and taught her the art of quillwork. As this legend suggests, quillwork was a woman's art form. The Sioux baby carrier shown in figure 23-11 is richly decorated with symbols of protection and well-being, including bands of antelopes in profile and thunderbirds with their heads turned and tails outspread. The thunderbird was an especially beneficent symbol, thought to be capable of protecting against both human and supernatural adversaries.

Another medium associated with the Eastern Woodlands groups that was adopted by the Plains peoples was **beadwork**. Eastern Woodlands peoples had long made wampum, belts of cylindrical purple and white beads made from clam shells or the center spirals of conch shells. The Iroquois and Delaware used wampum to keep records and exchanged it to conclude treaties. Decorative beadwork, on the other hand, did not become commonplace until after the European contact. It initially

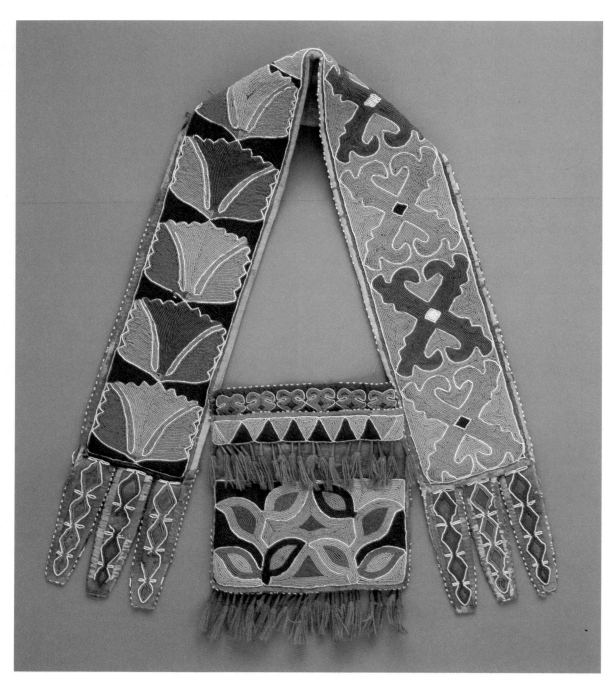

23-12. Shoulder bag, from Kansas. Delaware, c. 1860. Wool fabric, cotton fabric and thread, silk ribbon, and glass beads, 23 x 7¾" (58.5 x 19.8 cm). The Detroit Institute of Arts

Founders Society Purchase (81.216)

mimicked the patterns and colors of quillwork and in the nineteenth century began to replace quillwork in some places. In the late eighteenth century Native American artists began to acquire European colored glass beads, and in the nineteenth century they favored tiny seed beads from Venice and Bohemia. In a process known as **reintegration**, they began to adapt European needlework techniques and patterns and the design of European garments into their own work. Some of the functional aspects of those garments were transformed into purely decorative motifs; a pocket, for example, would be replaced by an area of beadwork in the *form* of a pocket.

An example of beadwork is the shoulder bag from Kansas, made around 1860 by a Delaware woman, shown in figure 23-12. In contrast to the rectilinear patterns of quillwork, the bag is covered with curvilinear plant motifs. White lines outline brilliant pink and blue leaf-shaped forms, heightening the intensity of the colors, and colors alternate within repeated patterns that have no consistent foreground or background.

The nomadic Plains peoples developed a light, portable dwelling known as a **tepee** (fig. 23-13), which was well designed to withstand the wind, dust, and rain of the prairies. The framework of a tepee consisted of a

23-13. Blackfoot women raising a tepee. Photographed c. 1900. Montana Historical Society, Helena

stable frame of three or four long poles, filled out with about twenty additional poles, in a roughly egg-shaped plan. The framework was covered with hides (or, later, with canvas) to form an almost conical structure that leaned slightly in the direction of the prevailing west wind. The hides were specially prepared to make them flexible and waterproof. A typical tepee required about eighteen hides, the largest about thirty-eight hides. The opening at the top served as a smoke hole for the central hearth. The flap-covered door and smoke hole usually faced east, away from the wind. An inner lining covered the lower part of the walls and the perimeter of the floor to protect the occupants from drafts. When packed to be dragged by a horse, the tepee served as a platform for transporting other possessions as well. When the Blackfeet gathered in the summer for their ceremonial Sun Dance, they formed their hundreds of tepees into a circle a mile in circumference. The Sioux encamped in two half circles—one for the sky people and one for the earth people—divided along an east-west axis.

Tepees were the property and responsibility of women, who raised them at new encampments and lowered them when the group moved on. Blackfeet women could set up their huge tepees in less than an hour. Women painted, embroidered, quilled, and beaded tepee linings, backrests, clothing, and equipment. The patterns with which tepees were decorated, as well as their proportions and colors, varied from Native American nation to nation. In general, the bottom was covered with a group's traditional motifs and the center section with personal images.

Plains men recorded their exploits in symbolic and narrative form in paintings on tepee linings and covers and on buffalo-hide robes. The earliest known painted buffalo-hide robe illustrates a battle fought in 1797 between the Mandan of North Dakota and their allies against the Sioux (fig. 23-14). The painter, trying to capture the full extent of a conflict in which five nations took part, shows a party of warriors in twenty-two separate episodes. Their leader appears with a pipe and wears an elaborate eagle-feather headdress. The party is armed with bows and arrows, lances, clubs, and flintlock rifles. The lively stick figures of the warriors have rectangular torsos and tiny round heads. Details of equipment and emblems of rank—headdresses, sashes, shields, feathered

23-14. Battle-scene hide painting, from North Dakota. Mandan, 1797–1805. Tanned buffalo hide, dyed porcupine quills, and black, red, green, yellow, and brown pigment, 7'10" x 8'6" (2.44 x 2.65 m). Peabody Museum of Archaeology, Harvard University, Cambridge, Massachusetts (99-12-10/53121)

This robe, collected by Meriwether Lewis and William Clark on their 1803–1806 expedition into western lands acquired by the United States in the Louisiana Purchase, is the earliest documented example of Plains painting. The robe was one of a number of Native American artworks that Lewis and Clark sent to President Thomas Jefferson. Jefferson displayed the robe in the entrance hall of his home at Monticello, Virginia.

23-15. Edward S. Curtis. Hamatsa dancers, Kwakiutl, Canada. Photographed 1914

The photographer Edward S. Curtis (1868–1952) devoted thirty years to documenting the lives of Native Americans. This photograph shows participants in a film he made about the Kwakiutl. For the film, his Native American informant and assistant, Richard Hunt, borrowed family heirlooms and commissioned many new pieces from the finest Kwakiutl artists. Most of the pieces are now in museum collections. The photograph shows carved and painted posts, masked dancers (including those representing cannibal birds), a chief at the left (holding a speaker's staff and wearing a cedar neck ring), and spectators at the right.

lances, powder horns for the rifles—are accurately depicted. Horses are shown in profile with stick legs and C-shaped hooves. Some have clipped manes, others have flowing manes. The figures stand out against the light-colored, almost white background of the buffalo hide. Lines were pressed into the hide, and black, red, green, yellow, and brown pigments added. A strip of colored porcupine quills runs down the spine. The robe would have been worn draped over the shoulders of the powerful warrior whose deeds it commemorates. As he moved, the painted horses and warriors would have come alive, transforming him into a living representation of his exploits.

The Northwest Coast

From southern Alaska to northern California, the Pacific coast of North America is a region of unusually abundant resources. Its many rivers fill each year with salmon returning to spawn. Harvested and dried, the fish could sustain large populations throughout the year. The peoples of the Northwest Coast—among them the Tlingit, the Haida, and the Kwakiutl—exploited this abundance to develop a complex and distinctive way of life in which the arts played a central role.

Northwest Coast peoples lived in extended family groups in large, elaborately decorated communal houses made of massive timbers and thick planks. Family groups claimed descent from a mythic animal or animal-human ancestor. Social rank within and between related families was based on genealogical closeness to the mythic ancestor. Chiefs, who were in the most direct line of descent from the ancestor, administered a family's spiritual and material resources. Chiefs validated their status and garnered prestige for themselves and their families by holding ritual feasts in which they gave valuable gifts to the invited guests. Shamans, who were sometimes also chiefs, mediated between the human and spirit worlds. A family derived its name and the right to use certain animals and spirits as totemic emblems, or crests, from its mythic ancestor. These emblems appeared prominently in Northwest Coast art, notably in carved house crests and the tall, freestanding poles erected to memorialize dead chiefs.

23-16. Grizzly bear house-partition screen, from the house of Chief Shakes of Wrangell, Canada. Tlingit, c. 1840. Cedar, native paint, and human hair, 15 x 8' (4.57 x 2.74 m). Denver Art Museum

The participants who danced in Northwest Coast ceremonies wore elaborate costumes and striking carved wooden masks. Among the most elaborate masks were those used by the Kwakiutl in their Winter Dance for initiating new members into the shamanistic Hamatsa society (fig. 23-15). The dance reenacted the taming of Hamatsa, a people-eating spirit, and his three attendant bird spirits. Magnificent carved and painted masks transformed the dancers into Hamatsa and the bird attendants, who searched for victims to eat. Strings allowed the dancers to manipulate the masks so that the beaks opened and snapped shut with spectacular effect.

23-17. Chilkat blanket. Tlingit, before 1928. Mountain-goat wool and shredded cedar bark, 4'7 1/8" x 5'3 3/4" (1.40 x 1.62 m). American Museum of Natural History, New York

Trans. #3804

Carved and painted house-partition screens separated a chief's quarters from the rest of a communal house. The screen shown in figure 23-16 came from the house of Chief Shakes of Wrangell (d. 1916), whose family crest was the bear. The image of a rearing grizzly painted on the screen is itself made up of smaller bears and bear heads that appear in its ears, eyes, nostrils, joints, paws, and body. The images within the image enrich the monumental symmetrical design. The oval door opening is a symbolic vagina; passing through it reenacts the birth of the family from its ancestral spirit.

Blankets and other textiles produced by the Chilkat Tlingit had great prestige throughout the Northwest Coast (fig. 23-17). Chilkat men created the patterns, which they drew on boards, and women did the weaving. The blankets are made from shredded cedar bark wrapped with mountain-goat wool. The weavers did not use looms; instead, they hung **warp** threads from a rod and twisted colored threads back and forth through them to make the pattern. The ends of the warp formed the fringe at the bottom of the blanket.

The small face in the center of the blanket shown here represents the body of a stylized creature, perhaps a sea bear or a standing eagle. On top of the body are the creature's large eyes; below it and to the sides are its legs and claws. Characteristic of Northwest painting and weaving, the images are composed of two basic elements: the **ovoid**, a slightly bent rectangle with rounded corners, and the **formline**, a continuous, shape-defining line. Here, subtly swelling black formlines define structures with gentle curves, ovoids, and rectangular **C** shapes. When the blanket was worn, its two-dimensional forms would have become three-dimensional, with the dramatic central figure curving over the wearer's back and the more intricate side panels crossing over his shoulders and chest.

The contemporary Canadian Haida artist Bill Reid (b. 1920) has sought to sustain and revitalize the traditions of Northwest Coast art in his work. Trained as a wood carver, painter, and jeweler, Reid revived the art of carving dugout canoes and totem poles in the Haida homeland of Haida Gwaii—"Islands of the People"—known on maps today as the Queen Charlotte Islands. Late in life he began to create large-scale sculpture in bronze. With their black patina, these works recall traditional Haida carvings in argillite, a shiny black stone. One of them,

23-18. Bill Reid. *The Spirit of Haida Gwaii.* Haida, 1991. Bronze, approx. 13 x 20' (4 x 6 m). Canadian Embassy, Washington, D.C.

The Spirit of Haida Gwaii, now stands outside the Canadian Embassy in Washington, D.C. (fig. 23-18). This sculpture, which Reid views as a metaphor for modern Canada's multicultural society, depicts a collection of figures from the natural and mythic worlds struggling to paddle forward in a canoe. The dominant figure in the center is a shaman in a spruce-root basket hat and Chilkat blanket holding a speaker's pole, a staff that gives him the right to speak with authority. In the prow, the place reserved for the chief in a war canoe, is the Bear. The Bear faces backward rather than forward, however, and is bitten by the Eagle, with formline-patterned wings. The Eagle, in turn, is bitten by the Seawolf. The Eagle and

the Seawolf, together with the man behind them, nevertheless continue paddling. In the stern, steering the canoe, is the Raven, the trickster in Haida mythology. The Raven is assisted by Mousewoman, the traditional guide and escort of humans in the spirit realms. On the other side, not visible here, are the Bear mother and her twins, the Beaver, and the Dogfish Woman. According to Reid, the work represents a "mythological and environmental lifeboat," where "the entire family of living things . . . whatever their differences, . . . are paddling together in one boat, headed in one direction."

The Southwest

The Native American peoples of the southwestern United States include, among others, the Pueblo (village-dwelling) groups and the Navajo. The Pueblo groups are heirs to the ancient Anasazi and Hohokam cultures, which developed a settled, agricultural way of life around the beginning of the Common Era. The Anasazi built the many large, multistoried, apartmentlike villages and cliff dwellings whose ruins are found throughout northern Arizona and New Mexico. The Navajo, who moved into the region more recently—in about the eleventh century or later—developed a semisedentary way of life based on agriculture and, after the introduction of sheep by the Spanish, sheepherding. Both groups have succeeded in maintaining many of their traditions despite first Spanish and then Anglo-American encroachments. Their arts reflect the adaptation of traditional forms to new technologies, new mediums, and the influences of the dominant American culture that surrounds them. Such adaptations are seen among various groups and in all mediums (see "Basketry," below).

TECHNIQUE

BASKETRY

Basketry involves weaving reeds, grasses, and other materials to form containers. In North America the earliest evidence of basketwork, found in Danger Cave, Utah, dates to as early as 8400 BCE. Over the subsequent centuries Native American women, notably in California and the Southwest, developed basketry into an art form that combined utility with great beauty.

There are three principal basket-making techniques: **coiling, twining,** and **plaiting**. Coiling involves sewing together a spiraling foundation of rods with some other material. Twining involves sewing together a vertical **warp** of rods. Plaiting involves weaving strips over and under each other.

The coiled basket shown here was made by the Pomo of California. According to Pomo legend, the earth was dark until their ancestral hero stole the sun and brought it to earth in a basket. He hung the basket first just over the horizon, but, dissatisfied with the light it gave, he kept suspending it in different places across the dome of the sky. He repeats this process every day, which is why the sun moves across the sky from east to west. In the Pomo basket the structure of coiled willow and bracken fern root produces a spiral surface into which the artist worked sparkling pieces of clamshell, trade

beads, and the soft tufts of woodpecker and quail feathers. The underlying basket, the glittering shells, and the soft, moving feathers make this an exquisite container. Such baskets were treasured possessions, cremated with their owners at death.

Wedding basket. Pomo, c. 1877. Willow, bracken fern root, clamshell, trade beads, woodpecker and quail feathers, height 5½" (14 cm), diameter 12" (36.5 cm). Philbrook Museum of Art, Tulsa, Oklahoma
Clark Field Collection

23-19. Laura Gilpin. Taos Pueblo, Tewa, Taos, New Mexico. Photographed 1947. Amon Carter Museum, Forth Worth, Texas

Laura Gilpin Collection (neg. # 2528.1)

The Pueblos. Some Pueblo villages today, like those of their Anasazi forebears, consist of multistoried, apartmentlike dwellings of considerable architectural interest. One of these, Taos Pueblo, shown here in a mid-twentieth-century photograph, is located in north-central New Mexico (fig. 23-19). The northernmost of the surviving Pueblo communities, Taos once served as a trading center between Plains and Pueblo peoples. It burned in 1690 but was rebuilt about 1700 and has often been modified since. Its great "houses," multifamily dwellings, stand on either side of Taos Creek, rising in a stepped fashion to form a series of roof terraces. The houses border a plaza that opens toward the neighboring mountains. The plaza and roof terraces are centers of communal life and ceremony.

Pottery traditionally was a woman's art among Pueblo

peoples, whose wares were made by **coiling** and other handbuilding techniques, then fired at low temperature in wood bonfires. One of the best-known twentieth-century Pueblo potters is Maria Montoya Martinez (1887–1980) of San Ildefonso Pueblo. Inspired by prehistoric **blackware** pottery that was unearthed at nearby archeological excavations, she and her husband, Julian Martinez (1885–1943), developed a distinctive new ware decorated with **matte** (nongloss) black forms on a lustrous black background (fig. 23-20). The Martinezes achieved the ware's black color through creating an oxygen-poor atmosphere by smothering vessels with horse manure and wood ash near the end of a firing. They achieved the lustrous surface areas by polishing the matte areas with a fine shale paste that they discovered in 1918. Their decorative patterns were inspired by both traditional Pueblo imagery and the then-fashionable Euro-American Art Deco style.

In the 1930s Anglo-American art teachers and dealers worked with Native Americans of the Southwest to create a distinctive "Indian" style in several mediums—including jewelry, pottery, weaving, and painting—that would appeal to tourists and collectors. A leader in this effort was Dorothy Dunn, who taught painting in the Santa Fe Indian School, a government high school, from 1932 to 1937. Dunn inspired her students to create a painting style that combined the outline drawing and flat colors of folk art, the decorative qualities of Art Deco, and "Indian" subject matter. The success of the style made painting a viable occupation for young Native American artists.

Pablita Velarde (b. 1918), a 1936 graduate of Dorothy Dunn's school, was only a teenager when one of her paintings was selected for exhibition at the Chicago

23-20. Maria Montoya Martinez and Julian Martinez. Blackware storage jar, from San Ildefonso Pueblo, New Mexico. Hopi, c. 1942. Ceramic, height 18³/₄" (47.6 cm), diameter 22¹/₂" (57.1 cm). Museum of Indian Arts and Culture/ Laboratory of Anthropology, Museum of New Mexico, Santa Fe

23-21. Pablita Velarde. *Koshares of Taos*, from Santa Clara Pueblo, New Mexico. 1946–47. Watercolor, 13⅞ x 22⅜" (35.3 x 56.9 cm). Philbrook Museum of Art, Tulsa, Oklahoma

23-22. Hosteen Klah. *Whirling Log Ceremony*, sand-painting tapestry by Mrs. Sam Manuelito. Navajo, c. 1925. Wool, 5'5" x 5'10" (1.69 x 1.82 m). Heard Museum, Phoenix, Arizona

World's Fair in 1933. Velarde, from the Santa Clara Pueblo in New Mexico, began to document Pueblo ways of life as her work matured. *Koshares of Taos* (fig. 23-21) illustrates a moment during a ceremony celebrating the winter solstice when koshares, or clowns, have taken over the plaza from the kachinas—the supernatural counterparts of animals, natural phenomena like clouds, and geological features like mountains—who are central to traditional Pueblo religion. Kachinas become manifest in the human dancers who impersonate them during the winter solstice ceremony, as well as in the small figures known as kachina dolls that are given to children. Velarde's painting combines bold, flat colors and a simplified decorative line with European perspective to produce a kind of Art Deco abstraction.

The Navajos. Navajo women are renowned for their skill as weavers. According to Navajo mythology, the universe itself is a kind of weaving, spun by Spider Woman out of sacred cosmic materials. Spider Woman taught the art of weaving to Changing Woman (a mother earth figure who constantly changes through the seasons), who in turn taught it to Navajo women. The earliest Navajo blankets have simple horizontal stripes, like those of their Pueblo neighbors, and are limited to the white, black, and brown colors of natural sheep's wool. Over time, the weavers developed finer techniques and introduced more intricate patterns. In the mid-nineteenth century they began unraveling the fibers from commercially manufactured and dyed blankets and reusing them in their own work. By 1870–1890 they were weaving spectacular blankets that were valued as prestige items among the Plains peoples as well as Euro-American collectors.

Another traditional Navajo art, sand painting, is the exclusive province of men. Sand paintings are made to the accompaniment of chants by shaman-singers in the course of healing and blessing ceremonies and have great sacred significance (see "Navajo Night Chant," above). The paintings depict mythic heroes and events; as ritual art they follow prescribed rules and patterns that ensure their power. To make them, the singer dribbles pulverized colored stones, pollen, flowers, and other natural colors over a hide or sand ground. The rituals are intended to restore harmony to the world. The paintings are not meant for public display and are destroyed by nightfall of the day on which they are made.

23-23. Jaune Quick-to-See Smith. *Trade (Gifts for Trading Land with White People)*. Salish-Cree-Shoshone, 1992. Oil and collage on canvas, 5' x 14'2" (1.56 x 4.42 m). Chrysler Museum, Norfolk, Virginia

Courtesy Steinbaum Krauss Collection, New York City

In 1919 a respected shaman-singer named Hosteen Klah began to incorporate sand-painting images into weavings, breaking with the traditional prohibition against making them permanent. Many Navajos took offense at Klah both for recording the sacred images and for doing so in a woman's art form, but the works were ultimately accepted because of his great skill and prestige. Klah's *Whirling Log Ceremony* sand-painting, shown here in a tapestry (fig. 23-22), depicts a part of the Navajo creation myth in which the Holy People divide the world into four parts, create the Earth Surface People (humans), and bring forth corn, beans, squash, and tobacco, the four sacred plants. The Holy People surround the image, and a male-female pair of humans stands in each of the four quarters defined by the central cross. The guardian figure of Rainbow Maiden encloses the scene on three sides. The open side represents the east. Like all Navajo artists, Hosteen Klah hoped that the excellence of the work would make it pleasing to the spirits. Recently, singers have started making permanent sand paintings on boards for sale, but they always introduce slight errors in them to render them ceremonially harmless.

CONTEMPORARY NATIVE AMERICAN ART

Many Native American artists today are seeking to move beyond the occasionally self-conscious revival of traditional forms to a broader art that acknowledges and mediates among the complex cultural forces shaping their lives. One exemplar of this trend is Jaune Quick-to-See Smith (b. 1940), who was raised on Flatrock Reservation in Montana and traces her descent to the Salish of the Northwest Coast, the Shoshone of southern California,

and the Cree, a northern woodlands and plateau people. Quick-to-See Smith described the multiple influences on her work this way: "Inhabited landscape is the continuous theme in my work. Pictogram forms from Europe, the Amur, the Americas; color from beadwork, parfleches, the landscape; paint application from Cobra art, New York expressionism, primitive art; composition from Kandinsky, Klee, or Byzantine art provide some of the sources for my work. Study of the wild horse ranges, western plants and animals, and ancient sites feed my imagination and dreams. This is how I reach out and strike new horizons while I reach back and forge my past" (*Women of Sweetgrass*, page 97).

During the United States' quincentennial celebration of Columbus's arrival in the Americas—in her words, the beginning of "the age of tourism"—Quick-to-See Smith created paintings and collages of great formal beauty that also confronted viewers with their own, perhaps unwitting, stereotypes (fig. 23-23). In *Trade (Gifts for Trading Land with White People)*, a stately canoe floats over a richly colored and textured field, which on closer inspection proves to be a dense collage of newspaper clippings from local Native American newspapers. Wide swatches and rivulets of red, yellow, green, and white cascade over the newspaper collage. On a chain above the painting is a collection of both Native American cultural artifacts—tomahawks, beaded belts, feather headdresses—and American sports memorabilia for teams with names like the Atlanta Braves, the Washington Redskins, and the Cleveland Indians that many Native Americans find offensive. Surely, the painting suggests, Native Americans could trade these goods to retrieve their lost lands, just as European settlers traded trinkets with Native Americans to acquire the lands in the first place.

Mimis and Kangaroo
Aborigine
16,000–7000 BCE

Pottery fragment
Lapita
1200–1100 BCE

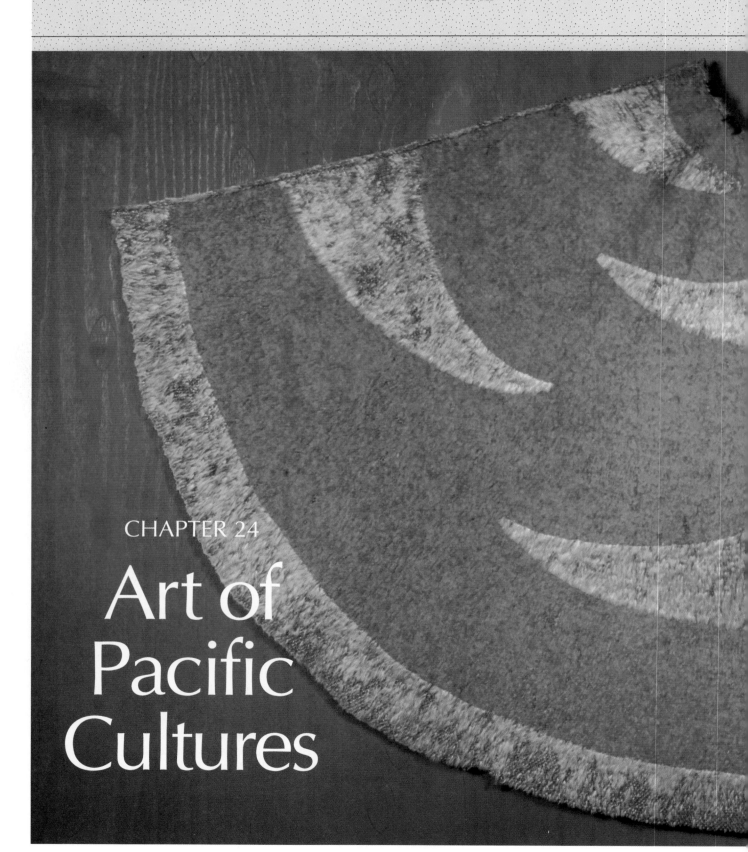

CHAPTER 24

Art of Pacific Cultures

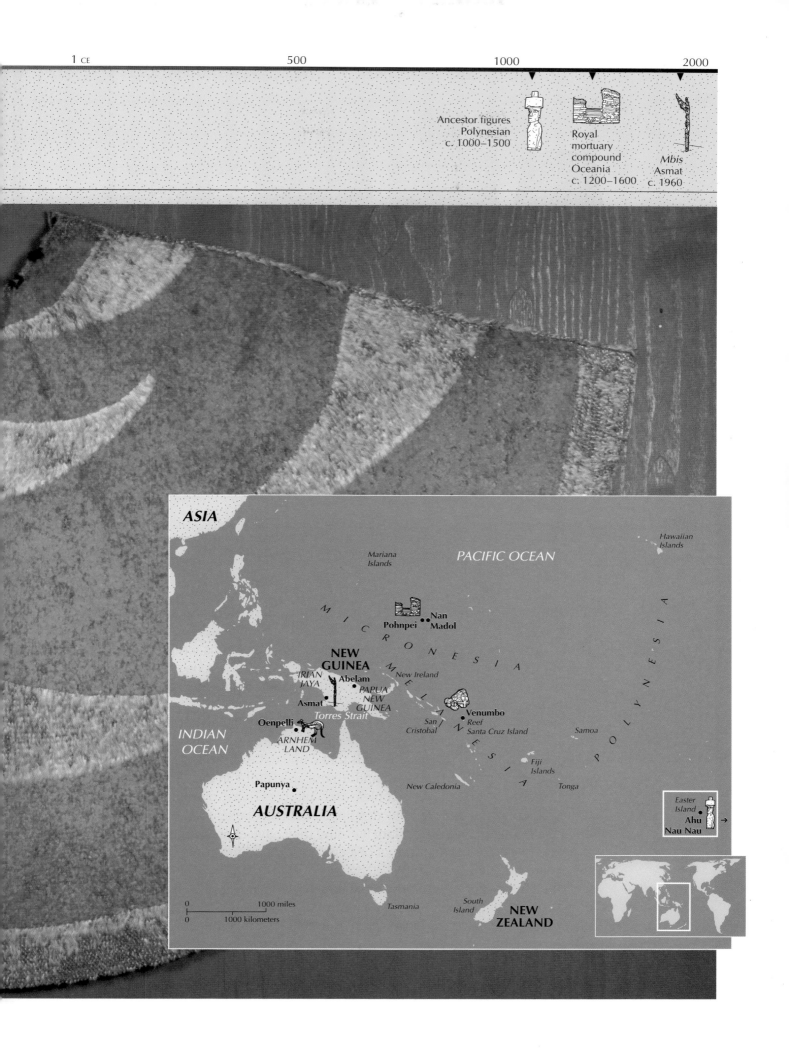

Ancestor figures
Polynesian
c. 1000–1500

Royal
mortuary
compound
Oceania
c. 1200–1600

Mbis
Asmat
c. 1960

ASIA

PACIFIC OCEAN

Hawaiian
Islands

Mariana
Islands

M
I
C
R
O
N
E
S
I
A

Pohnpei Nan
         Madol

NEW
GUINEA

IRIAN
JAYA   Abelam
               PAPUA
Asmat   NEW
           GUINEA

New Ireland

M
E
L
A
N
E
S
I
A

Venumbo
      Reef
San   Santa Cruz Island
Cristobal

Samoa

P
O
L
Y
N
E
S
I
A

Torres Strait

Oenpelli

ARNHEM
LAND

INDIAN
OCEAN

Fiji
Islands

New Caledonia   Tonga

Papunya

AUSTRALIA

Easter
Island

Ahu
Nau Nau

0   1000 miles
0   1000 kilometers

Tasmania

South
Island

NEW
ZEALAND

24-1.   Ancestor figures (*moai*)? Ahu Nau Nau, Easter Island, Polynesia. c. 1000–1500, restored 1978. Volcanic stone (tufa), average height approx. 36' (11 m)

In an effort to preserve the culture and landscape of Easter Island, the Chilean government has made its archeological sites into a national park. Some of the huge stone figures have been re-erected and restored with their coral and stone eyes and their red tufa topknots in place. Some of the topknots are as tall as 9 feet.

In the middle of the Great Ocean, in a region where no one ever passes, there is a mysterious and isolated island; there is no land in the vicinity and, for more than eight hundred leagues in all directions, empty and moving vastness surrounds it. It is planted with tall, monstrous statues, the work of some now-vanished race, and its past remains an enigma" (Pierre Loti, *L'Île de Pâques*, 1872).

The early travelers who successfully reached the islands that lie in the Pacific Ocean found far more than the mysterious, "monstrous" statues of Easter Island (fig. 24-1). Those islands that came to be described as simple paradises by romantic European and American visitors, in fact, support widely differing ecosystems, peoples, and cultures. There, over many thousands of years, people have developed complex belief systems that have encouraged a rich, visionary life. And they have expressed their beliefs in concrete form—in ritual objects, masks, and the enrichment of their material environment.

Nineteenth-century explorers who sought that vastness using the earliest maps of the region, about a hundred years old, found only an uncertain location for the unknown "continent" that mapmakers believed extended to the South Pole. For them, as for us, maps helped to create a view of the world and establish their place in it. European medieval maps, for example, placed Jerusalem in the center, while later cartographers focused on Rome. Westerners are so accustomed to thinking of a world grid originating at an observatory in Greenwich, England, or to imagining a map with the United States as the center of the world that other images are almost inconceivable. From a Northern Hemisphere point of view the great landmasses of Australia, New Guinea, and New Zealand become lands "down under," sliding off under the globe, remote from "our" world. But a simple shift of viewpoint—or a map in which the vast Pacific Ocean forms the center of a composition—suddenly marginalizes the Americas, and Europe disappears altogether.

THE PEOPLING OF THE PACIFIC

On a map with the Pacific Ocean as its center, only the peripheries of the great landmasses of Asia and the Americas appear. This immense, watery region consists of four cultural-geographic areas: Australia, Melanesia, Micronesia, and Polynesia. *Australia* includes the island continent as well as the island of Tasmania to the southeast. *Melanesia* (a term meaning "black islands," a reference to the dark skin color of its inhabitants) includes New Guinea and the string of islands that extends eastward from it as far as Fiji and New Caledonia. *Micronesia* ("small islands"), to the north of Melanesia, is a region of small islands, including the Marianas. *Polynesia* ("many islands") is scattered over a huge, triangular region defined by New Zealand in the south, Easter Island in the east, and the Hawaiian Islands to the north. The last region on earth to be inhabited by humans, Polynesia covers some 7.7 million square miles, of which fewer than 130,000 square miles are dry land—and most of that is New Zealand. Melanesia and Micronesia are also known as Near Oceania, and Polynesia as Far Oceania.

Australia, Tasmania, and New Guinea formed a single continent during the last Ice Age, which began some 2.5 million years ago. Some 50,000 years ago, when the sea level was about 330 feet lower than it is today, people had moved into this continent from Southeast Asia, making at least part of the journey over open water. Some 27,000 years ago they were settled on the large islands north and east of New Guinea as far as San Cristóbal, but they ventured no farther for another 25,000 years. By about 4000 BCE—possibly as early as 7000 BCE—the people of Melanesia were raising pigs and cultivating taro, a plant with edible rootstocks. As the glaciers melted, the sea level rose, flooding low-lying coastal land. By around 4000 BCE a 70-mile-wide waterway, now called the Torres Strait, separated New Guinea from Australia, whose people retained a hunting and gathering way of life into the twentieth century.

The settling of the rest of the islands of Melanesia and the westernmost islands of Polynesia—Samoa and Tonga—coincided with the spread of the seafaring Lapita culture, named for a site in New Caledonia, after about 1500 BCE. The Lapita people were farmers and fisherfolk who lived in often large coastal villages, probably cultivated taro and yams, and produced a distinctive style of pottery. They were skilled shipbuilders and navigators and engaged in interisland trade. Over time the Lapita culture lost its widespread cohesion and evolved into various local forms. Polynesian culture apparently emerged in the eastern Lapita region on the islands of Tonga and Samoa. Around the beginning of the first millennium CE, daring Polynesian seafarers, probably in double-hulled sailing canoes, began settling the scattered islands of Far Oceania and eastern Micronesia. Voyaging over open water, sometimes for thousands of miles, they reached Hawaii and Easter Island after about 500 CE and settled New Zealand by about 800/900–1200 CE.

In this vast and diverse region the arts of the Pacific display enormous variety and are generally closely linked to a community's ritual and religious life. In this context the visual arts were often just one strand in a rich weave that also included music, dance, and oral literature.

AUSTRALIA

The aboriginal inhabitants of Australia, or Aborigines, were nomadic hunter-gatherers closely attuned to the varied environments in which they lived until European settlers disrupted their way of life. The Aborigines had a complex social organization and a rich mythology that was vividly represented in the arts. As early as 18,000 years ago they were painting images on rocks and caves in western Arnhem Land, which is on the northern coast of Australia. One such painting contains a later image superimposed on an earlier one (fig. 24-2). The earlier painting is of skinny,

24-2. *Mimis and Kangaroo,* prehistoric rock art, Oenpelli, Arnhem Land, Australia. Older painting 16,000–7000 BCE. Red and yellow ocher and white pipe clay

PARALLELS

Years	Pacific Cultures	World
c. 50,000–20,000 BCE	People from Southeast Asia migrate to Australia, New Guinea, and nearby islands	Paleolithic hunter-gatherers migrate to New World; *Woman from Willendorf* (Austria)
c. 16,000–1500 BCE	*Mimis* cave paintings in Australia; x-ray style painting in Australia; plants and pigs domesticated	Lascaux cave paintings (France); first pottery vessels (Japan); plants and animals domesticated (Near East, Southeast Asia, Americas); metallurgy (Near East); first writing (Sumer, China, India); Great Pyramids at Giza (Egypt); Stonehenge (England)
c. 1500 BCE–c. 500 CE	Lapita culture spreads through Melanesia	Olmec civilization (Mexico); Rome's legendary founding (Italy); birth of Siddhartha Gautama, founder of Buddhism (Nepal); crucifixion of Jesus (Jerusalem); Maya civilization (Central America)
c. 500–1500 CE	Hawaii and Easter Island settled; Easter Island *moai* figures; Polynesian seafarers settle Far Oceania; monumental structures at Nan Madol in Micronesia	Birth of Muhammad, founder of Islam (Arabia); first Viking colony in Greenland; Marco Polo in China; Ottoman Empire (Asia Minor); Aztec Empire (Mexico); Black Death in Europe; Ming dynasty (China); Great Schism in Christian Church; Inka Empire (South America); Renaissance begins in Europe; Gutenberg's Bible (Germany); Columbus's voyages (Spain)
c. 1500–1900 CE	Captain James Cook explores New Zealand, Australia, and Easter Island; first British settlement in Australia; quilting introduced in Hawaii; Australia becomes British dependency; Peruvian slave hunters decimate Easter Island population	Protestant Reformation in Europe; Mughal period (India); Hideyoshi unites Japan; English colonize North America; Qing dynasty (China); union of England and Scotland as Great Britain; Declaration of Independence (United States); French Revolution; Mexico becomes a republic; Italy is united; Darwin's *Origin of Species*; Civil War (United States); Dominion of Canada is formed
c. 1900 CE–present	Abelam *tamberan* houses in Papua New Guinea; Asmat *mbis* sculpture in Irian Jaya; *malanggan* ceremonies in New Ireland; Confederation of Australia	World War I; World War II; United Nations established; People's Republic of China founded; breakup of the Soviet Union

sticklike humans that the Aborigines call *mimis* (ancestral spirits). Superimposed over the *mimis* is a kangaroo rendered in the distinctive **x-ray style**, in which the artist drew important bones and internal organs—including the spinal column, other bones, the heart, and the stomach—over the silhouetted form of the animal. In the picture shown here, all four of the kangaroo's legs have been drawn, and the ears have been placed symmetrically on top of its head. In some images both eyes appear in the head, which is shown in profile. The x-ray style was still prevalent in western Arnhem Land when European settlers arrived in the nineteenth century.

Bark paintings from northeastern Arnhem Land are entirely filled with elaborate narrative compositions in delicate striping and **cross-hatching**. The Aborigines do not reveal the full meaning of these works to outsiders, but in general they depict origin myths from the Dream Time, when, according to their beliefs, the world and its inhabitants were created. The paintings and the rituals associated with them provide a way to restore contact with the Dream Time. The myths and rituals also explain the origin of important features of the landscape, of climatic phenomena like the monsoon season, and of aboriginal social groupings: In the beginning, the world was

24-3. Mawalan Marika. *The Wawalag Sisters and the Rainbow Serpent.* 1959. Ochers on eucalyptus bark, 18¾ x 10⅛" (48 x 26 cm). Collection, Art Gallery of Western Australia, Perth

The sisters dance outside their home in an attempt to escape the Rainbow Serpent's wrath. The serpent slithers out of his hole at the bottom of the bark. It has already devoured a human and a fish.

flat, but animals and the ancestral beings shaped it into mountains, sand hills, creeks, and water holes. Animals became the totemic ancestors of human groups, and the places associated with them became sacred sites. In one origin myth depicted in a bark painting by Mawalan Marika (1908–1967), the first humans, the Wawalag Sisters (seen at the top of figure 24-3), walked about with their digging sticks, singing, dancing, naming things, and populating the land with their children. But they offended the Rainbow Serpent, a symbol of the monsoon rains that bring both fertility and destruction. The serpent swallowed the sisters and designated the place where their descendants were to perform the Wawalag rituals.

Aboriginal artists have continued to work in time-honored and ritually sanctioned ways, and their explana-

24-4. Fragments of a large Lapita jar, from Venumbo, Reef Santa Cruz Island, Solomon Islands, Melanesia. c. 1200–1100 BCE. Clay, height of human face approx. 1½" (4 cm)

tions of their work provide insight into the meaning of prehistoric images. Paintings in ocher and clay on eucalyptus bark, created in a ritual context, were used to help maintain and transmit cultural traditions from generation to generation. These paintings reduced complex stories and ideas to essentials and served as memory aids that elders could elaborate upon. Aboriginal artists today may paint with **acrylic** paint on canvas instead of with ocher, clay, and charcoal on rock and eucalyptus bark, but their imagery has remained relatively constant.

MELANESIA

Exceptional seafarers spread the Lapita culture throughout the islands of Melanesia beginning around 1500 BCE. They brought with them the plants and animals that colonizers needed for food, thus spreading agricultural practices through the islands. They also carried with them the distinctive ceramics whose remnants today enable us to trace the extent of their travels. Lapita potters, probably women, produced dishes, platters, bowls, and jars. Sometimes they covered their wares with a red **slip**, and they often decorated them with bands of **incised** and stamped geometric patterns—dots, lines, and hatching—heightened with white lime. Most of the decoration was entirely geometric, but some was figurative. The human face that appears on one example (fig. 24-4) is among the earliest representations of a human being in Oceanic art. Over time Lapita pottery evolved into a variety of regional styles in Melanesia, but in western Polynesia, the heartland of Polynesian culture and the easternmost part of the Lapita range, the making of pottery ceased altogether by between 100 and 300 CE.

In Melanesia, as in Australia, the arts were intimately involved with belief and provided a means for communicating with supernatural forces. Rituals and ritual arts were primarily the province of men, who devoted a great

24-5. Detail of *tamberan* house, Sepik River, Papua New Guinea, New Guinea. Abelam, 20th century. Carved and painted wood, with ocher pigments on clay ground

deal of time to both. In some societies most of the adult male population were able to make ritual objects. Although barred from ritual arts, women gained prestige for themselves and their families through their skill in the production of other kinds of goods. To be effective, ritual objects had to be well made, but they were often allowed to deteriorate after they had served their ceremonial function.

Papua New Guinea

New Guinea, the largest island in Melanesia (and at 1,500 miles long and 1,000 miles wide, the second largest island in the world), is today divided between two countries. The eastern half of the island is part of the present-day nation of Papua New Guinea; the western half is Irian Jaya, a province of present-day Indonesia. Located near the equator and with mountains that rise to 16,000 feet, the island's diverse environments range from tropical rain forest to grasslands to snow-covered peaks.

The Abelam, who live in the foothills of the mountains on the north side of Papua New Guinea, raise pigs and cultivate yams, taro, bananas, and sago palms. In traditional Abelam society, people live in extended families or clans in hamlets. A hamlet includes sleeping houses, cooking houses, storehouses for yams, a central space for rituals, and a special men's ceremonial struc-

ture called a *tamberan* house. Wealth among the Abelam is measured in pigs, but men gain status from participation in a yam cult that has a central place in Abelam society and in the **iconography** of its art and architecture. The yams that are the focus of this cult—some of which reach an extraordinary 12 feet in length—are associated with clan ancestors and the potency of their growers. Village leaders renew their relationship with the forces of nature that yams represent during the Long Yam Festival, which is held at harvest time and involves processions, masked figures, singing, and the ritual exchange of the finest yams.

Tamberan houses, which play a central role in these rituals, shelter *tamberans,* images and objects associated with the yam cult and with clan identity, keeping them hidden from women and uninitiated boys. Men gather in these structures to organize rituals, to conduct community business, and, in the past, to plan raids. The prestige of a hamlet is linked to the quality of its *tamberan* house and the size of its yams. Constructed on a frame of poles and rafters and roofed with split cane and thatch, *tamberan* houses have been as much as 280 feet long and more than 40 feet wide. The ridgepole is set at an angle, making one end higher than the other, and the roof extends forward in an overhanging peak that is braced by a carved pole (fig. 24-5). The entrance facade is thus a large, in-folded triangular form, elaborately painted and

24-6. Asmat ancestral spirit poles (*mbis*), Faretsj River, Irian Jaya, Indonesia, New Guinea. c. 1960. Wood, paint, palm leaves, and fiber, height approx. 18' (5.48 m). The Metropolitan Museum of Art, New York

The Michael C. Rockefeller Memorial Collection, Gift of Nelson A. Rockefeller and Mrs. Mary C. Rockefeller, 1965 (1978.412. 1248-50)

(fig. 24-6). The poles are known as *mbis*, and the rituals surrounding them, intended to reestablish the balance between life and death, are known as *mbis* ceremonies. After *mbis* ceremonies, the poles are abandoned and allowed to deteriorate.

Mbis house the souls of the recent dead and stand in front of the village men's house, where the souls can observe the rituals. In the past, once the poles had been carved, villagers would organize a headhunting expedition so that they could place an enemy head in a cavity at the base of each pole. The abstract shapes of the spaces for enemy heads represent the roots of the banyan tree. Above the base are figures representing tribal ancestors supporting figures of the recent dead. The bent pose of the figures associates them with the praying mantis, one symbol of headhunting; another symbol of headhunting is birds breaking open nuts. The large, lacy phalluses emerging from the figures at the top of the poles symbolize male fertility, and the surface decoration suggests tattoos and scarification (patterned scars), common body ornamentation in Melanesia.

New Ireland

The people of the central part of the island of New Ireland, which is one of the large easternmost islands of the nation of Papua New Guinea, are known for their *malanggan* ceremonies, elaborate funerary rituals for which they make striking painted carvings and masks. *Malanggans* involve an entire community as well as its neighbors and serve to validate social relations and property claims.

Because preparations are costly and time consuming, *malanggans* are often delayed for several months or even years after a death and might commemorate more than one person. Although preparations are hidden from women and children, everyone participates in the actual ceremonies. Arrangements begin with the selection of trees to be used for the *malanggan* carvings. In a ceremony marked by a feast of taro and pork, the logs are cut, transported, and ritually pierced. Once the carvings are finished, they are dried in the communal men's house, polished, and then displayed in a *malanggan* house in the village *malanggan* enclosure. Here the figures are painted and eyes made of sea snail shell are inserted. The works displayed in a *malanggan* house include figures on poles and freestanding sculpture representing ancestors and the honored dead, as well as masks and ritual dance equipment. They are accorded great respect for the duration of the ceremony, then allowed to decay.

Another ritual, the *tatanua* dance, assures male power, and men avoid contact with women for six weeks beforehand. *Tatanua* masks, worn for the dance, represent

carved. A lintel with carved heads representing ancestors divides the triangular facade into two parts. The lower section is covered by woven rattan panels. The upper section, fully two-thirds of the facade's height, is covered with detachable panels that are painted in red, ocher, white, and black with the faces of a clan's ancestral spirits. The Abelam believe the paint itself has magical qualities. The effectiveness of the images depends in part on accurate reproduction, and master painters direct the work of younger initiates. Regular, ritual repainting revitalizes the images and ensures their continued potency. Every stage in the construction of a *tamberan* house is accompanied by ceremonies, which are held in the early morning while women and uninitiated boys are still asleep. The completion of a house is celebrated with elaborate fertility rituals and an all-night dance. Women participate in these inaugural ceremonies and are allowed to enter the new house, which is afterward ritually cleansed and closed to them.

Irian Jaya

The Asmat, who live in the grasslands on the southwest coast of Irian Jaya, were known in the past as warriors and headhunters. They believe that a mythic hero carved their ancestors from trees, and to honor the dead they erect memorial poles covered with elaborate sculpture

24-7.   Dancers wearing *tatanua* masks, Pinikindu Village, central New Ireland, Papua New Guinea, New Guinea. 1979. Masks: wood, vegetable fibers, trade cloth, and pigments, approx. 17 x 13" (43 x 33 cm)

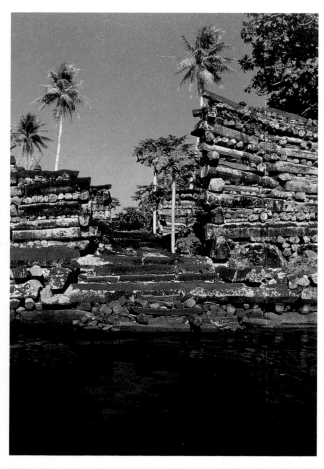

24-8.   Royal mortuary compound, Nan Madol, Pohnpei, Federated States of Micronesia. c.1200/1300–c.1500/1600. Basalt blocks, wall height up to 25' (7.62 m)

the spirits of the dead (fig. 24-7). The helmetlike masks are carved and painted with simple, repetitive motifs such as ladders, zigzags, and stylized feathers. The paint is applied in a ritually specified order: first lime white for magic spells; then red ocher to recall the spirits of those who died violently; then black from charcoal or burned nuts, a symbol of warfare; and finally yellow and blue from vegetable materials. The magnificent crest of plant fiber is a different color on the right and the left sides, perhaps a reflection of a lost hairstyle in which the hair was cut short and left naturally black on one side and dyed yellow and allowed to grow long on the other. The contrasting sides of the masks allow dancers to present a different appearance by turning from side to side. A good performance of the *tatanua* dance is considered a demonstration of strength, while a mistake can bring laughter and humiliation.

MICRONESIA

Over the centuries the people of Oceania erected monumental stone architecture and carvings in a number of places. In some cases, in Polynesia for example, widely scattered structures share enough characteristics to suggest that they spring from a common origin. Others

appear to be unique. The site of Nan Madol, on the southeast coast of Pohnpei in Micronesia, is the largest and one of the most remarkable stone complexes in Oceania. Together with a similar, smaller complex on another island nearby, it is also apparently without precedent.

Pohnpei, where today the Federated States of Micronesia's capital city of Palikir is located, is a mountainous tropical island with cliffs of prismatic basalt. By the thirteenth century CE the island's inhabitants were evidently living in a hierarchical society ruled by a powerful chief with the resources to harness sufficient labor for a monumental undertaking. Nan Madol, which covers some 170 acres, consists of 92 small artificial islands set within a network of canals. Most of the islands are oriented northeast-southwest, receiving the benefit of the cooling prevailing winds. Seawalls and breakwaters 15 feet high and 35 feet thick protect Nan Madol from the ocean. Openings in the breakwaters allowed canoes access to the ocean and allowed seawater to flow in and out with the tides and regularly to flush clean the canals. The islands and structures of Nan Madol are built of prismatic basalt "logs" stacked in alternating **courses** (rows or layers). Through ingenious technology the logs were split from their source by alternately heating the base of a basalt cliff with fire and dousing it with water. Nan Madol at one time was home to as many as 1,000 people, but it was deserted by the time Europeans discovered it in the nineteenth century.

The royal mortuary compound, which once dominated the southeast side of Nan Madol (fig. 24-8), has walls rising in subtle upward and outward curves to a height of 25 feet. To achieve the sweeping, rising lines, the builders increased the number of stones in the **header** courses (the courses with the ends of the stones laid toward the face of the wall) relative to the **stretcher** courses (the courses with the lengths of the stones laid parallel to the face of the wall) as they came to the corners and entryways. The plan of the structure consists simply of rectangles within rectangles: outer walls, interior walls, and a tomb in the center. Visitors arriving at the entrance on the west side and disembarking on the landing there would have stepped up from level to level as they passed through two sets of enclosing walls to an inner courtyard and a small, cubical tomb.

POLYNESIA

The settlers of the far-flung islands of Polynesia quickly developed distinctive cultural traditions but also retained linguistic and cultural affinities that reflect their common origin. Traditional Polynesian society was generally far more stratified than Melanesian society, and Polynesian art objects served as important indicators of rank and status. Reflecting this function, they tended to be more permanent than art objects in Melanesia, and they often were handed down as heirlooms from generation to generation. European colonization had a profoundly disruptive effect on society and art in Polynesia, as elsewhere in Oceania. Ironically, a major factor contributing to that impact was the very high regard these outsiders felt for the art they found. The result was that European artists and collectors admired Polynesian art and purchased it avidly, but in so doing they totally altered the context in which much of it was produced (see "Paul Gauguin on Oceanic Art," above).

Easter Island

Easter Island, the most remote and isolated island in Polynesia, is also the site of Polynesia's most impressive sculpture. Stone temples, or *marae,* with stone altar platforms, or *ahu,* are common and are found throughout Polynesia. Most of the *ahu* are built near the coast, parallel to the shore. About 900 CE, Easter Islanders began to erect huge stone figures on *ahu,* perhaps as memorials to dead chiefs. Nearly 1,000 of the figures, called *moai,* have been found, including some unfinished in the quarries where they were being made. Carved from tufa, a yellowish brown volcanic stone, most are about 36 feet tall, but one unfinished figure measures almost 70 feet. In 1978 several figures were restored to their original condition, with red tufa topknots on their heads and white coral eyes with stone pupils (see fig. 24-1). The heads have deep-set eyes under a prominent browridge; a long, concave, pointed nose; a small mouth with pursed lips; and an angular chin. The extremely elongated earlobes have parallel engraved lines that suggest ear ornaments. The figures have schematically indicated breastbones and pectorals, small arms with hands pressed close to the sides, but no legs.

Easter Islanders stopped erecting *moai* around 1500 and apparently entered a period of warfare among themselves, possibly because overpopulation was straining the island's available resources. Most of the *moai* were knocked down and destroyed during this period. The island's indigenous population, which may at one time have consisted of as many as 10,000 people, was nearly eradicated in the nineteenth century by Peruvian slave traders, who lured inhabitants to the beaches with trading goods, then captured and exported about 1,000 of them. Missionaries secured the freedom of the approximately 100 who survived diseases in Peru, but only 15 lived through the trip home. The smallpox and tuberculosis they brought with them precipitated an epidemic that left only about 600 inhabitants alive on Easter Island.

24-9.   War club, from Marquesas Islands, Polynesia. Early
19th century. Ironwood, length approx. 5' (1.52 m).
Peabody Essex Museum, Salem, Massachusetts

24-10. Skirt originally belonging to Queen Kamamalu,
Hawaii. 1823–24. Paper mulberry (wauke) bark,
stamped patterns, 12'3" x 5'6" (3.77 x 1.7 m). Bishop
Museum, Honolulu

Gift of Evangeline Priscilla Starbuck, 1927 (C.209)

Marquesas Islands

Warfare was common in Polynesia and involved hand-
to-hand combat. Warriors dressed to intimidate and to
convey their rank and status, so weapons, shields, and
regalia tended to be especially splendid creations. A
5-foot-long ironwood war club from the Marquesas
Islands (fig. 24-9) is lavishly decorated, with a Janus-like
double face at the end. More faces appear within these
faces. The high arching eyebrows frame sunburst eyes
whose pupils are tiny faces. Other patterns seem inspired
by human eyes and noses. The overlay of low relief and
engraved patterns suggests tattooing, a highly developed
art in Polynesia (see fig. 24-12).

Hawaiian Islands

Until about 1200 CE the Hawaiian Islands remained in
contact with other parts of Polynesia, but thereafter they
were isolated until the English explorer Captain James
Cook landed there in 1778. Hawaiian society, divided into
several independent chiefdoms, was rigidly stratified. By
1810 one ruler, Kamehameha I (c. 1758–1819), had consolidated the islands into a unified kingdom. The influence of United States missionaries and economic

interests increased during the nineteenth century, and
Hawaii's traditional religion and culture declined. The
United States annexed Hawaii in 1898, and the territory
became a state in 1959.

Decorated bark cloth and featherwork, found elsewhere in Polynesia, were highly developed in Hawaii. Bark
cloth, commonly known as **tapa** (*kapa* in Hawaii), is made
by pounding together moist strips of the inner bark of certain trees, particularly the mulberry tree. The clothmakers,
usually women, used mallets with incised patterns that left
impressions in the cloth. Like a watermark in paper, these
impressions can be seen when the cloth is held up to the
light. Fine bark cloth was dyed and decorated in red or
black with repeated geometric patterns laboriously made
with tiny bamboo stamps. One favorite design consists of
parallel rows of **chevrons** printed close together in sets or
spaced in rows. The cloth could also be worked into a kind
of **appliqué**, in which a layer of cutout patterns, usually in
red, was beaten onto a light-colored backing sheet. The
traditional Hawaiian women's dress consisted of a sheet
of bark cloth worn wrapped around the body either below
or above the breasts. The example shown here (fig. 24-10)
belonged to Queen Kamamalu. Such garments were
highly prized and were considered to be an appropriate
diplomatic gift. The queen took bark-cloth garments with

24-11. Feather cloak, known as the Kearny Cloak, Hawaii. c. 1843. Red, yellow, and black feathers, olona cordage, and netting, length 55¾" (143 cm). Bishop Museum, Honolulu

Hawaiian chiefs wore feather cloaks into battle, making them prized war trophies as well as highly regarded diplomatic gifts. King Kamehameha III (ruled 1824–1854) presented this cloak to Commodore Lawrence Kearny, commander of the U.S. frigate *Constellation*.

her when she and King Kamehameha II made a state visit to London in 1823.

The Hawaiians prized featherwork even more highly than fine bark cloth. Feather cloaks, helmets, capes, blankets, and garlands (leis) conveyed special status and prestige, and only wealthy chiefs could command the resources to make them. Tall feather pompons (*kahili*) mounted on long slender sticks symbolized royalty. And the images of the gods that Hawaiian warriors carried into battle were made of light, basketlike structures covered with feathers. Feather garments, made following strict ritual guidelines, consisted of bundles of feathers tied in overlapping rows to a foundation of plant-fiber netting. Yellow feathers, which came from the Hawaiian honey eater bird, were extremely valuable because one bird produced only seven or eight suitable feathers. Some 80,000 to 90,000 honey eaters were used to make King Kamehameha I's full-length royal cloak. Lesser men had to be satisfied with short capes. Cloaks and capes hung funnel-like from the wearer's shoulders, creating a sensuously textured and colored abstract design. The typical cloak was red (the color of the gods) with a yellow border and sometimes a narrow decorative neckband. The symmetrically arranged geometric decoration in the example shown here (fig. 24-11) falls on the wearer's front and back; the paired crescents on the edge join when the garment is closed to match the forms on the back. Captain Cook, impressed by the "beauty and magnificence" of Hawaiian featherwork, compared it to "the thickest and richest velvet" (*Voyage*, 1784, volume 2, page 206; volume 3, page 136).

New Zealand

New Zealand was the last part of Polynesia to be settled. The first inhabitants had arrived by about the tenth century, and their descendants, the Maori, numbered in the hundreds of thousands by the time of European contact in the seventeenth and eighteenth centuries. Captain Cook, before he landed in Hawaii, led a British scientific

ART AND SCIENCE: THE FIRST VOYAGE OF CAPTAIN COOK The ship *Endeavour*, under the command of Captain James Cook, a skilled geographer and navigator, sailed from Plymouth, England, in August 1768 on a scientific expedition to the Pacific Ocean. On board—in addition to a research team of astronomers, botanists, and other scientists—were two artists, Sydney Parkinson (1745?–1771), a young Scottish botanical drafter, and Alexander Buchan, a painter of landscape and portraits. At that time drawings and paintings served science the way photographs and documentary films and videotapes do today, recording, as Cook wrote, "a better idea . . . than can be expressed by word . . ." (*Journal*, 1773).

The *Endeavour* sailed west to Brazil, then south around South America's Cape Horn, and westward across the Pacific Ocean to Tahiti, where Buchan died. The ship went on to explore New Zealand, Tasmania, Australia, and the Great Barrier Reef before returning to England in July 1771, by sailing westward and around Africa's southern tip, the Cape of Good Hope.

Parkinson, frequently working with decaying specimens in cramped quarters on rough seas or plagued by insects, completed more than 1,300 drawings and paintings. His watercolors of plants are especially outstanding. Although he could not replace Buchan as a portrait painter, he did make a few sketches and wash drawings of people, among them drawings of the Maori that provide valuable evidence of their traditional way of life (see fig. 24-12). He died on the return journey, on January 21, 1771. In addition to fulfilling his duties as expedition artist, Parkinson, like the other expedition members, had kept a journal, which was later published.

24-12. Sydney Parkinson. *Portrait of a Maori*. 1769. Wash drawing, 15½ x 11⅝" (39.37 x 29.46 cm), later engraved and published as plate XVI in Parkinson's *Journal*, 1773. The British Library, London
Add MS 23920 f.55

expedition to the Pacific that explored the coast of New Zealand in 1769. Sydney Parkinson (1745?–1771), an artist on the expedition, documented aspects of Maori life and art at the time (see "Art and Science: The First Voyage of Captain Cook," page 903). An unsigned drawing by Parkinson (fig. 24-12) shows a Maori with facial tattoos (*moko*) wearing a headdress with feathers, a comb, and a hei-tiki (a carved pendant of a human figure).

Combs similar to the one in the drawing can still be found in New Zealand. The long ear pendant is probably made of greenstone, a form of jade found on New Zealand's South Island that varies in color from off-white to very dark green. The Maori considered greenstone to have supernatural powers. The hei-tiki hanging on a cord around the man's neck would have been among his most precious possessions. Such tiki figures, which represented legendary heroes or ancestor figures, gained power from their association with powerful people. The tiki in this illustration has an almost embryonic appearance, with its large tilted head, huge eyes, and seated posture. Some tiki had large eyes of inlaid shell.

The art of tattoo was widespread and ancient in Oceania; bone tattoo chisels have even been found in Lapita sites. Maori men generally had tattoos on the face and on the lower body between the waist and the knees. Women were tattooed around the mouth and on the chin. The typical design of facial tattoos, like the striking one shown here, consisted of broad, curving parallel lines from nose to chin and over the eyebrows to the ears. Small spiral patterns adorned the cheeks and nose. Additional spirals or other patterns were added on the forehead and chin and in front of the ears. A formal, bilateral symmetry controlled the design. Maori men considered their *moko* designs to be so personal that they sometimes signed documents with them. Ancestor carvings in Maori meetinghouses also have distinctive *moko*. According to Maori mythology, tattooing, as well as weaving and carving, was brought to them from the underworld, the realm of the Goddess of Childbirth. *Moko* might thus have a birth-death symbolism that links the living with their ancestors.

The Maori are especially known for their wood carving, which is characterized by a combination of massive underlying forms with delicate surface ornament. This art form found expression in small works like the hei-tiki in Parkinson's drawing as well as in the sculpture that adorned storehouses and meetinghouses in Maori hilltop villages. The meetinghouse in particular became a focal point of local tradition under the influence of one built in 1842–1843 by Raharuhi Rukupo as a memorial to his brother (fig. 24-13). Rukupo, who was an artist, diplomat, warrior, priest, and early convert to Christianity, built the house with a team of eighteen wood carvers. Although they used European metal tools, they worked in the technique and style of traditional carving with stone tools. They finished the carved wood by rubbing it with a combination of red clay and shark-liver oil to produce a rich, brownish red color.

The whole structure symbolizes the sky father. The ridgepole is his backbone, the rafters are his ribs, and the slanting **bargeboards**—the boards attached to the projecting end of the **gable**—are his outstretched enfolding arms. His head and face are carved at the peak of the roof. The curvilinear patterns on the rafters were made with a silhouetting technique. Artists first painted the rafters white, then outlined the patterns, and finally painted the background red or black, leaving the patterns in white. Characteristically Maori is the *koru* pattern, a curling stalk with a bulb at the end that is said to resemble the young tree fern.

Relief figures of ancestors—Raharuhi Rukupo included a portrait of himself among them—cover the support poles, wall planks, and the lower ends of the rafters. The ancestors, in effect, support the house. They were thought to take an active interest in community affairs and to participate in the discussions held in the meetinghouse. Like the hei-tiki in figure 24-12, the figures have large heads. Flattened to fit within the building planks and covered all over with spirals, parallel and hatched lines, and tattoo patterns, they face the viewer head on with glittering eyes of blue-green inlaid shell. Their tongues stick out in defiance from their grimacing mouths, and they squat in the posture of the war dance.

Lattice panels made by women fill the spaces between the wall planks. Because ritual prohibitions, or taboos, prevented women from entering the meetinghouse, they worked from the outside and wove the panels from the back. They created the black, white, and

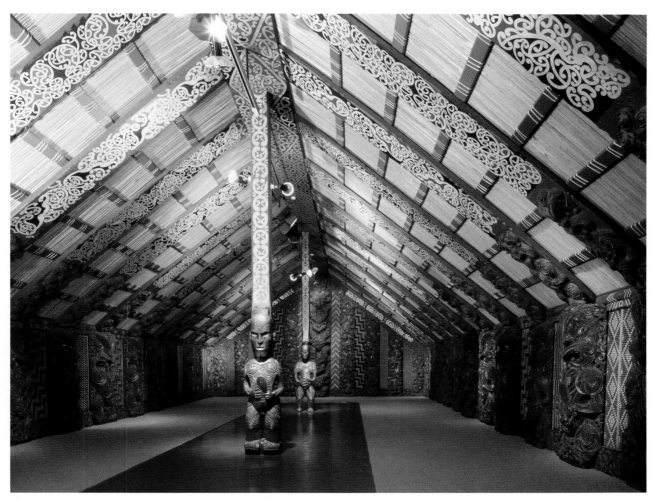

24-13. Raharuhi Rukupo, master carver. Te-Hau-ki-Turanga (Maori meetinghouse), from Manutuke Poverty Bay, New Zealand. 1842–43, restored in 1935. Wood, shell, grass, flax, and pigments. The Museum of New Zealand Te Papa Tongarewa, Wellington, New Zealand

Neg. B18358

orange patterns from grass, flax, and flat slats. Each pattern has a symbolic meaning: Chevrons represent the teeth of the monster Taniwha, steps represent the stairs of Heaven climbed by the hero-god Tawhaki, and diamonds represent the flounder.

Considered a national treasure by the Maori, this meetinghouse was restored in 1935 by Maori artists from remote areas still working in traditional methods, and moved to the Museum of New Zealand.

RECENT ART IN OCEANIA Many contemporary artists in Oceania, in a process anthropologists call **reintegration**, have responded to the impact of European culture by adapting traditional themes and subjects to new mediums and techniques. The work of a Hawaiian quilt maker and an Australian aboriginal painter provide two examples of the striking and challenging results of this process.

Missionaries introduced fabric patchwork and quilting to the Hawaiian Islands in 1820, and Hawaiian women were soon making distinctive, multilayered stitched quilts. Over time, as cloth became increasingly available, the new arts replaced bark cloth in prestige, and today they are held in high esteem. Quilts are brought out for display and given as gifts to mark holidays and rites of passage such as weddings, anniversaries, and funerals. They are also important gifts for establishing bonds between individuals and communities.

Royal Symbols, by Deborah (Kepola) U. Kakalia, is a luxurious quilt with a two-color pattern reminiscent of bark-cloth design (fig. 24-14). It combines heraldic imagery from both Polynesian and European sources to communicate the artist's proud sense of cultural identity. The crowns, the rectangular feather standards (*kahili*) in the corners, and the boldly contrasting red and yellow colors—derived from traditional featherwork—are symbols of the Hawaiian monarchy, even though the crowns have been adapted from those worn by European royalty. The *kahili* are ancient Hawaiian symbols of authority and rule, and the eight arches arranged in a cross in the center symbolize the uniting of Hawaii's eight inhabited islands into a single Christian kingdom. The quilt's design, construction, and strong color contrasts are typically Hawaiian. The artist created the design the way children create paper snowflakes, by folding a piece of red fabric into eight triangular layers, cutting out the pattern,

24-l4.   Deborah (Kepola) U. Kakalia. *Royal Symbols*. 1978. Quilt (*tifaifai*) of cotton fabric and batting, appliqué, and contour quilting, 6'6¼" x 6'4½" (1.98 x 1.96 m). Joyce D. Hammond Collection

and then unfolding it. The red fabric was then sewn onto a yellow background with a technique known as contour stitching, in which the quilter follows the outlines of the design layer with parallel rows of tiny stitches. This technique, while effectively securing the layers of fabric and batting together, also creates a pattern that quilters liken to breaking waves.

In Australia, Aborigine artists have adopted canvas and acrylic paint for rendering imagery traditionally associated with more ephemeral mediums like bark, sand, and body painting. Under the influence of an art teacher named Geoff Bardon, who introduced them to the new mediums, a group of Aborigines expert in **sand painting**—an ancient ritual art form that involves creating large colored designs on the ground—formed an art cooperative in 1971 in Papunya, in central Australia. Their success in transforming their transient, ritual form into a salable commodity encouraged community elders to allow others, including women, to try their hand at painting, which soon became an economic mainstay for many aboriginal groups in the region.

Sand paintings consist of red and yellow ochers, seeds, and feathers arranged on the earth in dots and other symbolic patterns that convey tribal lore to young initiates. Clifford Possum Tjapaltjarri, a founder of the Papunya cooperative who gained an international reputa-

tion after an exhibition of his paintings in 1988, works with his canvases on the floor, using traditional patterns and colors, as well as touches of blue. The superimposed layers of concentric circles and undulating lines and dots in a painting like *Man's Love Story* (fig. 24-15) create an effect of shifting colors and lights. The painting seems entirely abstract, but it actually conveys a complex narrative involving two mythical ancestors. One of these men came to Papunya in search of honey ants; the white **U** shape on the left represents him seated in front of a water hole with an ants' nest, represented by the concentric circles. His digging stick lies to his right, and white sugary leaves lie to his left. The straight white "journey line" represents his trek from the west. The second man, represented by the brown-and-white **U**-shape form, came from the east, leaving footprints, and sat down by another water hole nearby. He began to spin a hair string (a string made from human hair) on a spindle (the form leaning toward the upper right of the painting) but was distracted by thoughts of the woman he loved, who belonged to a kinship group into which he could not marry. When she approached, he let his hair string blow away (represented by the brown flecks below him) and lost all his work. Four women (the dotted **U** shapes) from the group into which he could marry came with their digging sticks and sat around the two men. Rich symbolism fills other areas of

24-15. Clifford Possum Tjapaltjarri. *Man's Love Story*. 1978. Papunya, Northern Territory, Australia. Synthetic polymer paint on canvas, 6'11¾" x 8'4¼" (2.15 x 2.57 m). Art Gallery of South Australia, Adelaide
Visual Arts Board of the Australia Council Contemporary Art Purchase Grant, 1980

the painting: The white footprints are those of another ancestral figure following a woman, and the wavy line at the top is the path of yet another ancestor. The black, dotted oval area indicates the site where young men were taught this story. The long horizontal bars are mirages. The wiggly shapes represent caterpillars, and the dots represent seeds, both forms of food.

The point of view of this work may be that of someone looking up from beneath the surface of the earth rather than down from above. Possum first painted the landscape features and the impressions left on the earth by the figures—their tracks, direction lines, and the **U**-shaped marks they left when sitting. Then, working carefully, dot by dot, he captured the vast expanse and

shimmering light of the arid landscape. The painting's resemblance to modern Western painting styles like Abstract Expressionism, **gestural** painting, or Color Field painting (Chapter 29) is accidental. Possum's work remains deeply embedded in the mythic, narrative traditions of his people. Although few artifacts remain from prehistoric times on the Pacific islands, throughout recorded history artists such as Possum have worked with remarkable robustness, freshness, and continuity. They have consistently created arts that express the deepest meanings of their culture despite the incursions of peoples from the Americas and from Europe, who were, at about the same time, "discovering" the classic arts of another continent, Africa.

Bwami mask
Lega
early 20th century

Spirit spouse
Baule
early 20th century

Kanaga mask
Dogon
early 20th century

Ekpo mask
Anang Ibibio
late 1930s

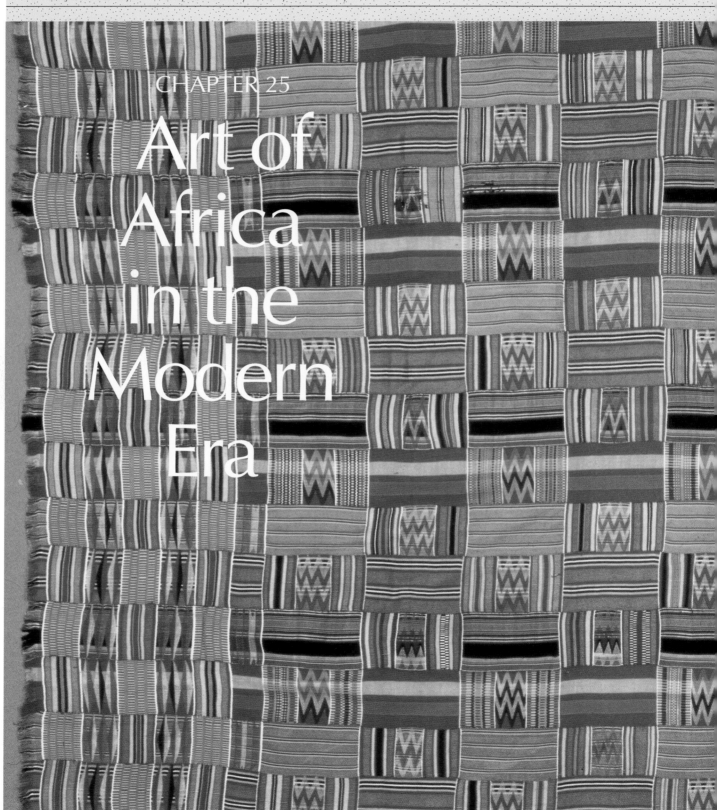

CHAPTER 25

Art of Africa in the Modern Era

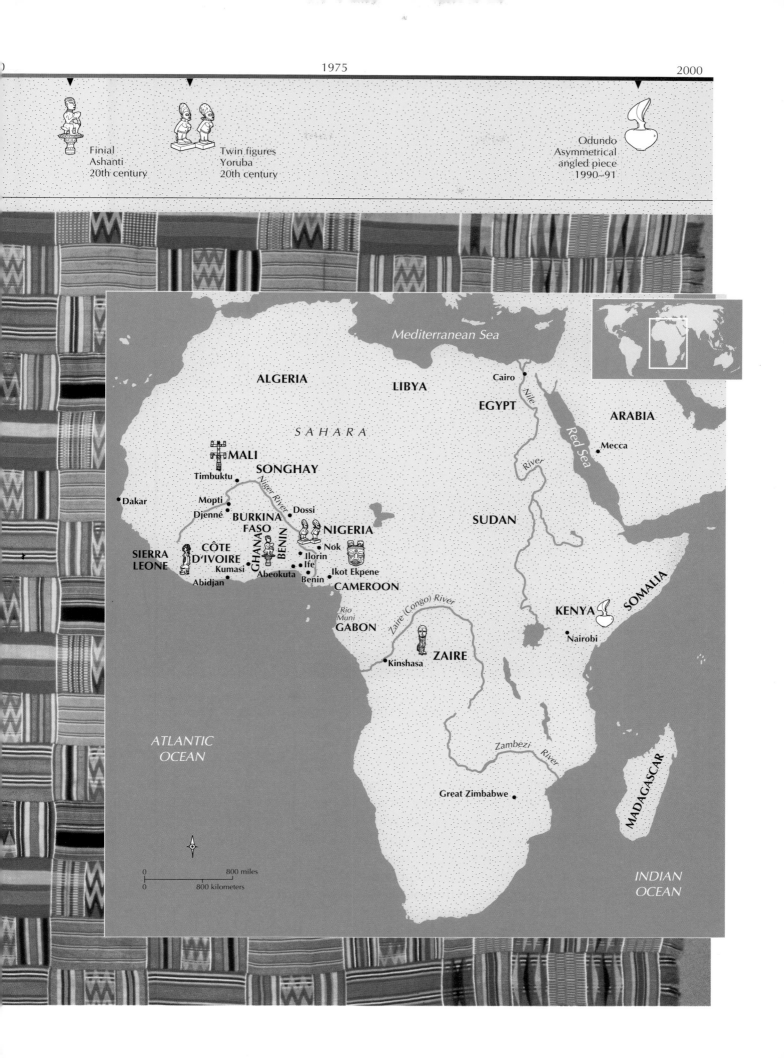

1975   2000

Finial
Ashanti
20th century

Twin figures
Yoruba
20th century

Odundo
Asymmetrical
angled piece
1990–91

Mediterranean Sea

ALGERIA

LIBYA

EGYPT

Cairo

Nile

Red Sea

ARABIA

Mecca

SAHARA

MALI

Timbuktu

SONGHAY

Dakar

Mopti

Djenné

Niger River

Dossi

BURKINA
FASO

NIGERIA

SUDAN

SIERRA
LEONE

CÔTE
D'IVOIRE

GHANA

BENIN

Nok

Kumasi

Ilorin
Ife

Ikot Ekpene

Abidjan

Abeokuta

Benin

CAMEROON

Rio
Muni

GABON

Zaïre (Congo) River

KENYA

SOMALIA

Nairobi

Kinshasa

ZAIRE

ATLANTIC
OCEAN

Zambezi River

Great Zimbabwe

MADAGASCAR

INDIAN
OCEAN

0   800 miles
0   800 kilometers

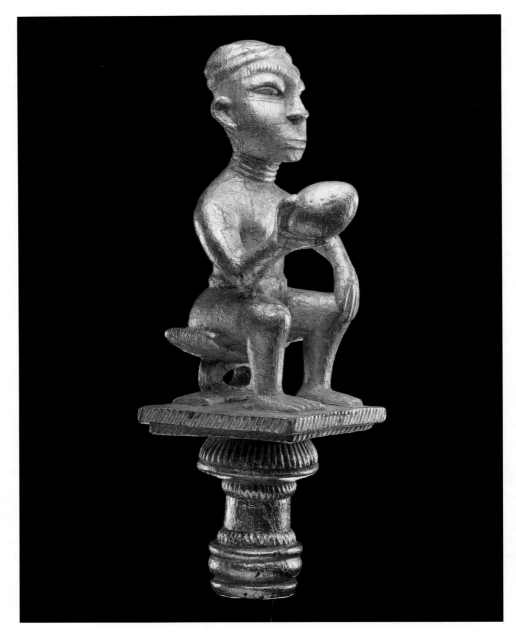

25-1.   Finial of a spokesperson's staff (*okyeame poma*), from Ghana. Ashanti culture, 20th century. Wood and gold, height 11¼" (28.57 cm). Musée Barbier-Mueller, Geneva

Political power is like an egg, says an Ashanti proverb. Grasp it too tightly and it will shatter in your hand; hold it too loosely and it will slip from your fingers. Whenever the *okyeame*, or spokesperson, for one twentieth-century Ashanti ruler was conferring with that ruler or communicating the ruler's words to others, he held before their eyes a staff with this symbolic caution on the use and abuse of power prominently displayed on the gold-leaf–covered **finial** (fig. 25-1).

If we are to attempt to understand African art such as this staff on its own terms, we must first restore it to life. As with the art of so many periods and societies, we must take it out of the glass cases of the museums where we usually encounter it and imagine the artwork playing its vital role in a human community.

TRADITIONAL AND CONTEMPORARY AFRICA

The second largest continent in the world, Africa is a land of enormous diversity. Geographically, it ranges from enormous deserts to tropical rain forest, from flat grasslands to spectacular mountains and dramatic rift valleys. Human diversity in Africa is equally impressive. More than 1,000 languages have been identified, grouped by scholars into five major linguistic families. Various languages represent unique cultures, with their own history, customs, and art forms.

Before the nineteenth century, the most important outside influence in Africa had been the religious culture of Islam, which spread gradually and largely peacefully through much of West Africa and along the East African coast (see "Foundations of African Cultures," below). The modern era, in contrast, begins with the European exploration and subsequent colonization of the African continent, developments that brought traditional African societies into sudden and traumatic contact with the "modern" world that Europe had largely created.

European ships first visited sub-Saharan Africa in the fifteenth century. For the next several hundred years, however, European contact with Africa was almost entirely limited to coastal areas, where trade, including the tragic slave trade, was carried out. During the nineteenth century, as the slave trade was gradually eliminated, European explorers began to investigate the unmapped African interior. They were soon followed by Christian missionaries, whose reports greatly fueled popular interest in the continent. Drawn by the potential wealth of Africa's natural resources, European governments began to seek territorial concessions from African rulers. Diplomacy soon gave way to force, and toward the end of the century, competition among rival powers fueled the so-called scramble for Africa, when European governments raced to lay claim to whatever portion of the continent they were powerful

FOUNDATIONS OF AFRICAN CULTURES

Africa was the site of one of the great civilizations of the ancient world, that of Egypt, which arose along the fertile banks of the Nile River over the course of the fourth millennium BCE and lasted for some 3,000 years. Egypt's rise coincided with the emergence of the Sahara, the largest desert in the world, from the formerly lush grasslands of northern Africa. Some of the oldest known African art, images inscribed and painted in the mountains of the central Sahara beginning around 8000 BCE, bears witness to this gradual transformation as well as to the lives of the pastoral peoples who once lived in the region.

As the grassland dried, its populations most likely migrated in search of pasture and arable land. Many probably made their way to the Sudan, the broad band of savanna south of the Sahara. During the sixth century BCE, knowledge of iron smelting spread across the Sudan, enabling larger and more complex societies to emerge. One such society was the iron-working Nok culture, which arose in present-day Nigeria around 500 BCE and lasted until about 200 CE. **Terra-cotta** figures created by Nok artists are the earliest known sculpture from sub-Saharan Africa.

Farther south in present-day Nigeria, a remarkable culture developed in the city of Ife, which rose to prominence around 800 CE. There, from roughly 1000 to 1400, a tradition of naturalistic sculpture in bronze and terra-cotta flourished, focused on exquisitely modeled memorial heads—possibly actual portraits—of rulers. Ife was, and remains, the sacred city of the Yoruba people, two of whose modern-era sculpture are included in this chapter (figs. 25-3 and 25-10). According to legend, Ife artists brought the techniques of bronze casting to the kingdom of Benin to the southeast. From 1400 through the nineteenth century Benin artists in the service of the court created numerous works in bronze, at first in the naturalistic style of Ife, then becoming increasingly stylized and elaborate.

With the Arab conquest of North Africa during the seventh and eighth centuries, Islamic travelers and merchants became regular visitors to the Sudan. Largely through their writings, we know of the powerful West African empires of Ghana, Mali, and Songhay, which flourished successively from the fourth through the sixteenth centuries along the great bend in the Niger River. All three empires grew wealthy by controlling the flow of African gold and forest products into the lucrative trans-Sahara trade. During their time, such fabled West African cities as Mopti, Djenné, and Timbuktu arose, serving not only as commercial hubs but also as prominent centers of Islam, which became an important cultural force in Africa.

Peoples along the coast of East Africa, meanwhile, had participated since before the Common Era in a maritime trade network that ringed the Indian Ocean and extended east to the islands of Indonesia. Over the course of time, trading settlements arose along the coastline, peopled by Arab, Persian, and Indian merchants as well as Africans. By the thirteenth century these settlements had become important cities, and a new language, Swahili, had developed from the longtime mingling of Arabic with local African languages. Peoples of the interior organized extensive trade networks to funnel goods to these ports, and large-scale political formations grew up around the control of the interior trade. From 1000 to 1500 many of these interior routes were controlled by the Shona people from a site called Great Zimbabwe. The extensive stone ruins of the palace compound there once stood in the center of this city of some 10,000 at its height. With the decline of Great Zimbabwe, control of the southeastern trade network passed to the Mwene Mutapa and Kami empires a short distance to the north.

Numerous cities and kingdoms, often of great wealth and opulence, greeted the astonished eyes of the first European visitors to Africa at the end of the fifteenth century.

PARALLELS

Years	Africa	World
1880–1912	European colonization of all of continent except Ethiopia creates boundaries unrelated to cultural and language groups	Sino-Japanese War; Alfred Nobel's prizes for peace, science, and literature established (Sweden); Spanish-American War; Russo-Japanese War; Albert Einstein's special theory of relativity
1950–1975	European powers begin granting independence to territories in Africa; Egypt becomes republic; Organization of African Unity founded; first successful human heart transplant; severe drought spreads south of the Sahara	Korean War begins; French defeated at Dien Bien Phu (Vietnam); Federal Republic of West Germany established; European Common Market established; first human orbits the earth (Soviet Union); first astronauts land on the moon (United States)
1975–present	Political and social upheaval spreads throughout continent; Namibia gains independence; apartheid in South Africa legally dismantled; AIDS and famine resulting from droughts take heavy tolls	Nuclear nonproliferation treaty signed by fifteen nations; Muslim leaders take control of Iran; Soviet Union invades Afghanistan; Indira Gandhi assassinated (India); discovery of AIDS virus reported (United States, France); first Islamic woman prime minister elected (Pakistan); breakup of Soviet Union

enough to take. By 1914 virtually all of Africa had fallen under colonial rule.

In the years following World War I, nationalistic movements arose across Africa. Their leaders generally did not advocate a return to earlier forms of political organization but rather demanded the transformation of colonial divisions into Western-style nation-states governed by Africans. From 1945 through the mid-1970s one colony after another gained its independence, and the present-day map of modern African nations took shape.

Change has been brought about by contact between one people and another since the beginning of time. And art in Africa has both affected and been affected by such contacts. During the early twentieth century the art of traditional African societies played a pivotal role in revitalizing the Western tradition. The formal inventiveness and expressive power of African sculpture were sources of inspiration for European artists trying to rethink strategies of representation. Many contemporary African artists, especially those from major urban centers, have come of age in the postcolonial culture that mingles European and African elements. Drawing easily on the influences from many cultures, both African and non-African, today's artists have established a firm place in the lively international art scene along with their European, American, and Asian counterparts, and their work is shown as readily in Paris, Tokyo, and Los Angeles as it is in the African cities of Abidjan, Kinshasa, and Dakar.

Many traditional societies persist, both within and across contemporary political borders. From the time of the first European explorations and continuing through the colonial era, quantities of art from traditional African societies were shipped back to Western museums. At first these were not art museums but museums of natural history or ethnography, where the works were exhibited as curious artifacts of "primitive" cultures. Toward the end of the nineteenth century, however, profound changes in Western thinking about art gradually led more and more people to appreciate the inherent **aesthetic** qualities of traditional African "artifacts" and finally to embrace them fully as art. Art museums began to collect African art more seriously and methodically, both in Africa and in the West. Together with the living arts of traditional peoples today, these collections afford us a rich sampling of African art in the modern era.

Traditional African art plays a vital role in the spiritual and social life of the community. It is used to express Africans' ideas about their relation to their world and as a tool to help them survive in a difficult and unpredictable environment. This chapter explores African art in light of how it addresses some of the fundamental concerns of human existence. Because African art must be considered within its cultural and social contexts, in this chapter we look at works of art within various broad contexts rather than by geographical region or time frame.

CHILDREN AND THE CONTINUITY OF LIFE

Among the most fundamental of human concerns is the continuation of life from one generation to the next. In traditional societies children are especially important, for not only do they represent the future of the family and the community, but they are also a form of "social security," guaranteeing that parents will have someone to care for them when they are old.

25-2. Doll (*biiga*), from Burkina Faso. Mossi culture, mid-20th century. Wood, height 11¼" (28.57 cm). Collection Thomas G. B. Wheelock

In the often harsh and unpredictable climates of Africa, human life can be fragile. In some areas half of all infants die before the age of five, and the average life expectancy may be as low as forty years. In these areas women may bear many children in hopes that a few will survive into adulthood, and failure to have children is a disaster for a wife, her husband, and her husband's lineage. It is very unusual for a man to be blamed as the cause of infertility, so women who have had difficulty bearing children appeal with special offerings or prayers, often involving the use of art.

The Mossi people of Burkina Faso, in West Africa, carve a small wooden figure called *biiga*, or "child," as a plaything for little girls (fig. 25-2). The girls feed and

25-3. Twin figures (*ere ibeji*), from Nigeria. Yoruba culture, 20th century. Wood, height 7⅞" (20 cm). The University of Iowa Museum of Art, Iowa City

The Stanley Collection

As with other African sculpture, patterns of use result in particular signs of wear. The facial features of *ere ibeji* are often worn down or even obliterated by repeated feedings and washings. Camwood powder applied as a cosmetic builds to a thick crust in areas that are rarely handled. Even the blue indigo dye regularly applied to the hair eventually builds to a thin layer.

bathe the figures and change their clothes, just as they see their mothers caring for younger siblings. At this level the figures are no more than simple dolls. Like many children's dolls around the world, they show ideals of mature beauty, including elaborate hairstyles, lovely clothing, and developed breasts. The *biiga* shown here wears its hair just as little Mossi girls do, with a long lock projecting over the face. (A married woman, in contrast, wears her lock in back.)

Other aspects of the doll, however, reveal a more complex meaning. The elongated breasts recall the practice of stretching by massaging to encourage lactation, and they mark the doll as the mother of many children. The scars that radiate from the navel mimic those applied to Mossi women following the birth of their first child. Thus, although the doll is called a child, it actually represents the ideal Mossi woman, one who has achieved the goal of providing children to continue her husband's lineage.

Mossi girls do not outgrow their dolls as one would a childhood plaything. When a young woman marries, she brings the doll with her to her husband's home to serve as an aid to fertility. If she has difficulty in bearing her first child, she carries the doll on her back just as she would a baby. When she gives birth, the doll is placed on a new, clean mat just before the infant is placed there, and when she nurses, she places the doll against her breast for a moment before the newborn receives nourishment.

In all societies everywhere, the death of a child is a traumatic event. Many African peoples believe that a dead child continues its life in a spirit world. The parents' care and affection may reach it there, often through the medium of art. The Yoruba people of Nigeria have one of the highest rates of twin births in the world. The birth of twins is a joyful occasion, yet it is troubling as well, for twins are more delicate than single babies, and one or both may well die. When a Yoruba twin dies, the parents consult a diviner, a specialist in ritual and spiritual practices, who may tell them that an image of a twin, or *ere ibeji*, must be carved (fig. 25-3).

The mother cares for the "birth" of this image by sending the artist food while the figure is being carved. When the image is finished, she brings the artist gifts. Then, carrying the figure as she would a living child, she dances home accompanied by the singing of neighborhood women. She places the figure in a shrine in her bedroom and lavishes care upon it, feeding it, dressing it with beautiful textiles and jewelry, anointing it with cosmetic oils. The Yoruba believe that the spirit of a dead twin thus honored may bring its parents wealth and good luck.

The figures here represent female twins. They may be the work of the Yoruba artist Akiode, who died in 1936. Akiode belonged to the school of Esubiyi, an artist who worked in the Itoko quarter of the city of Abeokuta in southwestern Nigeria. Like most objects that Africans produce to encourage the birth and growth of children, the figures emphasize health and well-being. They have beautiful, glossy surfaces, rings of fat as evidence that they are well fed, and the marks of mature adulthood that will one day be achieved. They represent hope for the future, for survival, and for prosperity.

INITIATION

Eventually, an adolescent must leave behind the world of children and take his or her place in the adult world. In contemporary Western societies, initiation into the adult world is extended over several years and punctuated by numerous rites, such as graduating from high school, being confirmed in a religion, earning a driver's license, and reaching the age of majority. All of these steps involve acquiring the spiritual and worldly knowledge Western society deems necessary and accepting the corresponding responsibilities. In other societies, initiation is more concentrated, and the acquisition of knowledge may be supplemented by physical tests and trials of endurance to prove that the candidate is equal to the hardships of adult life.

The Bwa people of central Burkina Faso initiate young men and women into adulthood following the onset of puberty. The initiates are first separated from younger playmates by being "kidnapped" by older relatives, though their disappearance is explained in the community by saying that they have been devoured by wild beasts. The initiates are stripped of their clothing and made to sleep on the ground without blankets. Isolated from the community, they are taught about the world of nature spirits and about the wooden masks that represent them.

The initiates have watched these masks in performance every month for their entire lives. Now, for the first time, they learn that the masks are made of wood and are worn by their older brothers and cousins. They learn of the spirit each mask represents, and they memorize the story of each spirit's encounter with the founding ancestors of the clan. They learn how to construct costumes from hemp to be worn with the masks, and they learn the songs and instruments that accompany the masks in performance. Only the boys wear each mask in turn and learn the dance steps that express the character and personality it represents. Returning to the community, the initiates display their new knowledge in a public ceremony. Each boy performs with one of the masks, while the girls sing the accompanying songs. At the end of the mask ceremony the young men and young women rejoin their families as adults, ready to marry, to start farms, and to begin families of their own.

25-4. Two masks in performance, from Dossi, Burkina Faso. Bwa culture, 1984. Wood, mineral pigments, and fiber, height approx. 7' (2.13 m)

The Bwa have been making and using such masks since well before Burkina Faso achieved its independence in 1960. We might assume their use is centuries old, but in this case, the masks are a comparatively recent innovation. The elders of the Bwa family who own these masks state that they, like all Bwa, once followed the cult of the spirit of Do, who is represented by masks made of leaves. In the last quarter of the nineteenth century the Bwa were the targets of slave raiders from the north and east. Their response to this new danger was to acquire wooden masks from their neighbors, for such masks seemed a more effective and powerful way of communicating with spirits who could help them. Thus, faced with a new form of adversity, the Bwa sought a new tradition to cope with it.

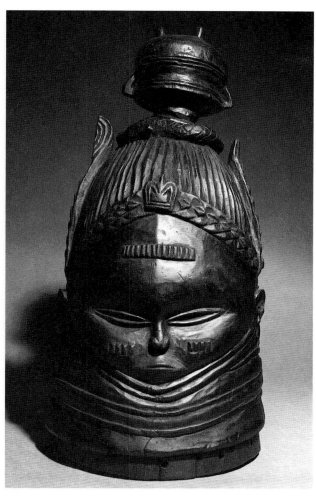

25-5. *Nowo* mask, from Sierra Leone. Mende culture, 20th century. Wood, height 18⅞" (48 cm). The Baltimore Museum of Art

Most Bwa masks depict spirits that have taken an animal form, such as crocodile, hyena, hawk, or serpent. Others represent spirits in human form. Among the most spectacular masks, however, are those crowned with a tall, narrow plank (fig. 25-4), which are entirely **abstract** and represent spirits that have taken neither human nor animal form. The graphic patterns that cover these masks are easily recognized by the initiated. The white crescent at the top represents the quarter moon, under which the initiation is held. The white triangles below represent bull roarers—sacred sound makers that are swung around the head on a long cord to re-create spirit voices. The large central **X** represents the scar that every initiated Bwa wears as a mark of devotion. The horizontal zigzags at the bottom represent the path of ancestors and symbolize adherence to ancestral ways. That the path is difficult to follow is clearly conveyed. The curving red hook that projects in front of the face is said to represent the beak of the hornbill, a bird associated with the supernatural world and believed to be an intermediary between the living and the dead. Through abstract patterns, the mask conveys a message about the proper moral conduct of life with all the symbolic clarity and immediacy of a traffic signal.

Among the Mende people of Sierra Leone, in West Africa, the initiation of young girls into adulthood is organized by a society of older women called Sande. The initiation culminates with a ritual bath in a river, after which the girls return to the village to meet their future husbands. At the ceremony the Sande women wear black gloves and stockings, black costumes of shredded raffia fibers that cover the entire body, and black masks called *nowo* (fig. 25-5).

With its high and glossy forehead, plaited hairstyle decorated with combs, and creases of abundance around the neck, the mask represents the Mende ideal of female beauty. The meanings of the mask are complex. One scholar has shown that the entire mask can be compared to the chrysalis of a certain African butterfly, with the creases in particular representing the segments of the chrysalis. Thus, the young woman entering adulthood is like a beautiful butterfly emerging from its ugly chrysalis. The comparison extends even further, for just as the butterfly feeds on the toxic sap of the milkweed to make itself poisonous to predatory birds, so the medicine of Sande is believed to protect the young women from danger. The creases may also refer to concentric waves radiating outward as the mask emerges from calm waters to appear among humankind, just as the initiates rise from the river to take their place as members of the adult community.

A ceremony of initiation may accompany the achievement of other types of membership as well. Among the Lega people, who live in the dense forests between the headwaters of the Zaire River and the great lakes of East Africa, the political system is based on a voluntary association called *bwami*, which comprises six levels or grades. Some 80 percent of all male Lega belong to *bwami*, and all aspire to the highest grade. Women can belong to *bwami* as well, although not at a higher grade than their husbands.

Promotion from one grade of *bwami* to the next takes many years. It is based not only on a candidate's character but also on his or her ability to pay the initiation fees, which increase dramatically with each grade. No candidate for any level of *bwami* can pay the fees alone, but all must depend on the help of relatives to provide the necessary cowrie shells, goats, wild game, palm oil, clothing, and trade goods. Candidates who are in conflict with their relatives will never be successful in securing such guarantees and thus will never achieve their highest goals. The ambitions of the Lega to move from one level of *bwami* to the next encourage a harmonious and well-ordered community, for all must stay on good terms if they are to advance. The association promotes a lifelong growth in moral character and an ever-deepening understanding of the relationship of the individual to the community.

Bwami initiations are held in the plaza at the center of the community in the presence of all members. Dances and songs are performed, and the values and ideals of the appropriate grade are explained through proverbs and sayings. These standards are illustrated by natural or crafted objects, which are presented to the initiate as signs of membership. At the highest two levels of *bwami*, such objects include masks and sculpted figures.

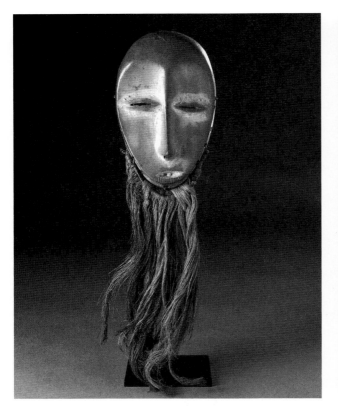

25-6. *Bwami* mask, from Zaire. Lega culture, early 20th century. Wood and kaolin, height 7⁵/₈" (19.3 cm). The University of Iowa Museum of Art, Iowa City
The Stanley Collection

The mask in figure 25-6 is associated with *yananio*, the second highest grade of *bwami*. Typical of Lega masks, the head is fashioned as an oval into which is carved a concave, heart-shaped face with narrow, raised features. The masks are often colored white with clay and fitted with a beard made of hemp fibers. Too small to cover the face, they are displayed in other ways—held in the palm of a hand, for example, or attached to a thigh. Each means of display recalls a different value or saying, so that one mask may convey a variety of meanings. For example, held by the beard and slung over the shoulder, this mask represents "courage," for it reminds the Lega of a disastrous retreat from an enemy village during which many Lega men were slain from behind.

THE SPIRIT WORLD

Why does one child fall ill and die while its twin remains healthy? Why does one year bring rain and a bountiful crop, while the next brings drought and famine? All people everywhere confront such fundamental and troubling questions. For traditional African societies the answers are often felt to lie in the workings of spirits. Spirits are believed to inhabit the fields that produce crops, the river that provides fish, the forest that is home to game, the land that must be cleared in order to build a new village. A family, too, includes spirits—those of its ancestors as well as those of children yet unborn. In the blessing or curse of these myriad surrounding spirits lies the difference between success and failure in life.

25-7. Spirit figure (*boteba*), from Burkina Faso. Lobi culture, 19th century. Wood, height 30¹¹/₁₆" (78 cm). Collection Kerchache, Paris

To communicate with these all-important spirits, African societies usually rely on a specialist in ritual—the person known elsewhere in the world as priest, minister, rabbi, pastor, imam, or shaman. Whatever his or her title, the ritual specialist serves as an essential link between the supernatural and human worlds, opening the lines of communication through such techniques as prayer, sacrifice, offerings, magic, and divination. Each African people has its own name for this specialist, but for simplicity we can refer to them all as diviners. Art often plays an important role in dealings with the spirit world, for art can make the invisible visible, giving identity and personality to what is abstract and intangible.

To the Lobi people of Burkina Faso, the spirits of nature are known as *thila* (singular, *thil*), and they are believed to control every aspect of life. Indeed, their power is so pervasive that they may be considered the true rulers of the community. Lobi houses may be widely scattered

1900
1900   2000

over miles of dry West African savanna. These houses are considered a community when they acknowledge the same *thil* and agree to regulate their society by its rules, called *zoser*. Such rules bear comparison to those binding many religious communities around the world and may include a prohibition against killing or eating the meat of a certain animal, sleeping on a certain type of mat, or wearing a certain pattern or cloth. Totally averse to any form of kingship or centralized authority, the Lobi have no other system of rule but *zoser*.

Thila are normally believed to be invisible. When adversity strikes, however, the Lobi may consult a diviner, who may prescribe the carving of a wooden figure called a *boteba* (fig. 25-7). A *boteba* gives a *thil* physical form. More than simply a carving, a *boteba* is thought of as a living being who can see, move, and communicate with other *boteba* and with its owner. The owner of a *boteba* can thus address the spirit it gives form to directly, seeking its protection or aid.

Each *thil* has a particular skill that its representative *boteba* conveys through pose or expression. A *boteba* carved with an expression of terrible anger, for example, represents a *thil* whose skill is to frighten off evil forces. The *boteba* in figure 25-7 is carved in the characteristic Lobi pose of mourning, with its hands clasped tightly behind its back and its head turned to one side. This *boteba* mourns so that its owner may not be saddened by misfortune. Like a spiritual decoy, it takes on the burden of grief that might otherwise have come to the owner. Shrines may hold dozens of *boteba* figures, each one contributing its own unique skill to the family or community.

Among the most potent images of power in African art are the *nkisi*, or spirit, figures made by the Kongo and Songye peoples of Zaire. The best known of these are the large wooden *nkonde*, which bristle with nails, pins, blades, and other sharp objects (fig. 25-8). A *nkisi nkonde* begins its life as a simple, unadorned wooden figure that may be purchased from a carver at a market or commissioned by a diviner on behalf of a client who has encountered some adversity or who faces some important turning point in his or her life. Drawing on vast knowledge, the diviner prescribes certain magical/medicinal ingredients, called *bilongo*, that will help the client's problem. These *bilongo* are added to the figure, either mixed with white clay and plastered directly onto the body or suspended in a packet from the neck or waist.

The *bilongo* transform the *nkonde* into a living being with frightful powers, ready to attack the forces of evil on behalf of a human client. *Bilongo* ingredients are drawn from plants, animals, and minerals, and may include human hair, nail clippings, and other materials. Each ingredient has a specific role. Some bring the figure to life by embodying the spirit of an ancestor or a soul trapped by a malevolent power. Others endow the figure with specific powers or focus the powers in a particular direction, often through metaphor. For example, the Kongo admire the quickness and agility of a particular species of mouse. Tufts of this mouse's hair included in the *bilongo* act as a metaphor for quickness, ensuring that the *nkisi nkonde* will act rapidly when its powers are activated.

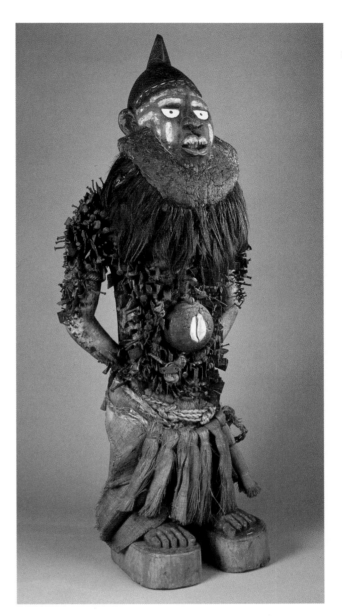

25-8. Power figure (*nkisi nkonde*), from Zaire. Kongo culture, 19th century. Wood, nails, pins, blades, and other materials, height 44" (111.7 cm). The Field Museum, Chicago
Acquisition A109979 c

Nkisi nkonde provide a dramatic example of the ways in which African sculpture are transformed by use. When first carved, the figure is "neutral," with no particular significance or use. Magical materials applied by a diviner transform the figure into a powerful being, at the same time modifying its form. Each client who activates that power further modifies the statue. While the object is empowered, nails may also be removed as part of a healing or oath-taking process. And when the figure's particular powers are no longer needed, the additions may all be stripped away to be replaced with different magical materials that give the same figure a new function. The result is that many hands play a role in creating the work of art we see in a museum. The person we are likely to label as the "artist" is only the initial creator. Many others modify the work, and in their hands the figure becomes a visual document of the history of the conflicts and afflictions that have threatened the community.

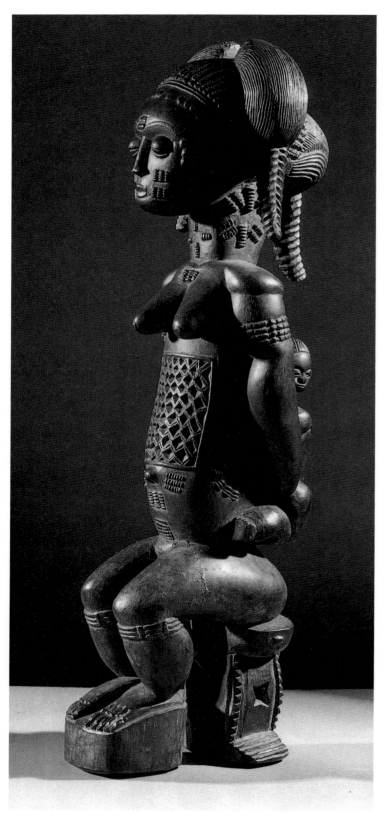

25-9. Spirit spouse (*blolo bla*), from Côte d'Ivoire. Baule culture, early 20th century. Wood, height 17⅛" (43.5 cm). University Museum, University of Pennsylvania, Philadelphia

To activate the powers, clients drive in a nail or other pointed object to get the *nkonde's* attention and prick it into action. A *nkisi nkonde* may serve many private and public functions. Two warring villages might agree to end their conflict by swearing an oath of peace in the presence of the *nkonde* and then driving a nail into it to seal the agreement. Two merchants might agree to a partnership by driving two small nails into the figure side by side and then make their pact binding by wrapping the nails together with a stout cord. Someone accused of a crime might swear his innocence and drive in a nail, asking the *nkonde* to destroy him if he lied. A mother might invoke the power of the *nkonde* to heal her sick children. The objects driven into the *nkonde* may also operate metaphorically. For example, the Kongo use a broad blade called a *baaku* to cut into palm trees, releasing sap that will eventually be fermented into palm wine. The word *baaku* derives from the word *baaka*, which means both "extract" and "destroy." Thus tiny replicas of *baaku* driven into the *nkonde* are believed to destroy those who use evil power.

The word *nkonde* shares a stem with *konda*, meaning "to hunt," for the figure is quick to hunt down a client's enemies and destroy them. The *nkonde* here stands in a pose called *pakalala*, a stance of alertness like that of a wrestler challenging an opponent in the ring. Other *nkonde* figures hold a knife or spear in an upraised hand, ready to strike or attack.

Some African peoples conceive of the spirit world as a parallel realm in which spirits may have families, attend markets, live in villages, and possess personalities complete with faults and virtues. The Baule people in Côte d'Ivoire believe that each of us lived in the spirit world before we were born. While there, we had a spirit spouse, whom we left behind when we entered this life. A person who has difficulty assuming his or her gender-specific role as an adult Baule—a man who has not married or achieved his expected status in life, for example, or a woman who has not borne children—may dream of his or her spirit spouse.

For such a person, the diviner may prescribe the carving of an image of the spirit spouse (fig. 25-9). A man has a female figure (*blolo bla*) carved; a woman has a male figure (*blolo bian*) carved. The figures display the most admired and desirable marks of beauty so that the spirit spouses may be encouraged to enter and inhabit them. Spirit spouse figures are broadly naturalistic, with swelling, fully rounded musculature and careful attention to details of hairstyle, jewelry, and scarification patterns. They may be carved standing in a quiet, dignified pose or seated on a traditional throne. The throne contributes to the status of the figure and thus acts as an added incentive for the spirit to take up residence there. The owner keeps the figure in his or her room, dressing it in beautiful textiles and jewelry, washing it, anointing it with oil, feeding it, and caressing it. The Baule hope that by caring for and pleasing their spirit spouse a balance may be restored that will free their human life to unfold smoothly.

While nature spirits are often portrayed in African art, major deities are generally considered to be far sought him out to ask him to restore order on earth, they found him sitting beneath a palm tree. Olodumare refused to return, although he did consent to give humanity some tools of divination so that they could learn his will indirectly.

The Yoruba have a sizable pantheon of lesser gods, or *orisha*, who serve as intermediaries between Olodumare and his creation. One that is commonly represented in art is Eshu, also called Elegba, the messenger of the gods. Eshu is a trickster, a capricious and mischievous god who loves nothing better than to throw a wrench into the works just when everything is going well. The Yoruba acknowledge that all humans may slip up disastrously (and hilariously) just when it is most important not to, and thus all must recognize and pay tribute to Eshu.

Eshu is associated with two eternal sources of human conflict, sex and money, and is usually portrayed with a long hairstyle, because the Yoruba consider long hair to represent excess libidinous energy and unrestrained sexuality. Figures of Eshu are usually adorned with long strands of cowrie shells, a traditional African currency. Shrines to Eshu are erected wherever there is the potential for encounters that lead to conflict, especially at crossroads, in markets, or in front of banks. Eshu's followers hope that their offerings will persuade the god to spare them the pitfalls he places in front of others.

Eshu is intriguingly ambivalent and may be represented as male or female, as a young prankster or a wise old man. The dance staff here beautifully embodies the dual nature of Eshu (fig. 25-10). To the left he is depicted as a boy blowing loud noises on a whistle just to annoy his elders—a gleefully antisocial act of defiance. To the right he is shown as a wise old man, with wrinkles and a beard. The two faces are joined at the hair, which is drawn up into a long phallic knot. The heads crown a dance wand meant to be carried in performance by priests and followers of Eshu, whose bodies the god is believed to enter during worship.

LEADERSHIP

As in societies throughout the world, art in Africa is also used to identify those who hold power, to validate their right to kingship or their authority as representatives of the family or community and to communicate the rules for moral behavior that must be obeyed by all members of the society.

The gold-and-wood spokesperson's staff with which this chapter opened is an example of the art of leadership (see fig. 25-1). It belongs to the culture of the Ashanti peoples of Ghana, in West Africa, and was probably carved in the 1960s or 1970s by Kojo Bonsu. The son of Osei Bonsu, a famous carver who died in 1977, Kojo Bonsu lives in the Ashanti city of Kumasi and continues to carve prolifically. Gold was a major source of power for the Ashanti, who traded it first via intermediaries across the Sahara to the Mediterranean world, then later directly to Europeans on the West African coast. Along with other peoples of the region, the Ashanti have used gold for jewelry as well as for objects reserved for the use of rulers, such as the staff.

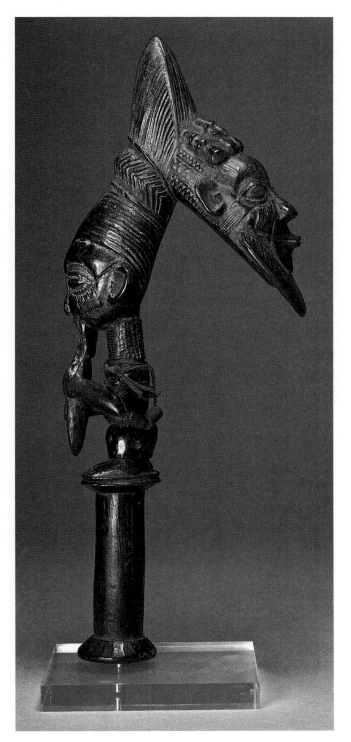

25-10. Dance staff depicting Eshu, from Nigeria. Yoruba culture, 20th century. Wood, height 17" (43.2 cm). The University of Iowa Museum of Art, Iowa City
The Stanley Collection

removed from the everyday lives of humans and are thus rarely depicted. Such is the case with Olodumare, also known as Olorun, the creator god of the Yoruba people of southwestern Nigeria. According to Yoruba myth, Olodumare withdrew from the earth when he was insulted by one of his eight children. When the children later

25-11. *Kente* cloth, from Ghana. Ashanti culture, 20th century. Silk, 6'10⁹/₁₆" x 4'3⁹/₁₆" (2.09 x 1.30 m). National Museum of African Art and National Museum of Natural History, Washington, D.C.
Purchased with funds provided by the Smithsonian Collections Acquisition Program, 1983–85, EJ 10583

The Ashanti are also renowned for the beauty of their woven textiles, called **kente** (fig. 25-11). Ashanti weavers work on small, light, horizontal looms that produce long, narrow strips of cloth. They begin by laying out the long **warp** threads in a brightly colored pattern. Today the threads are likely to be rayon. Formerly, however, they were silk, which the Ashanti produced by unraveling Chinese cloth obtained through European trade. **Weft** threads are woven through the warp to produce complex patterns, including double weaves in which the front and back of the cloth display different patterns. The long strips produced by the loom are then cut to size and sewn together to form large rectangles of finished *kente* cloth.

The *kente* cloth here began with a warp pattern that alternates red, green, and yellow. The pattern is known as *oyokoman ogya da mu*, meaning "there is a fire between two factions of the Oyoko clan," and refers to the civil war that followed the death of the Ashanti king Osai Tutu in about 1730. Traditionally, only the king of the Ashanti was allowed to wear this pattern. Other complex patterns were reserved for the royal family or members of the court. Commoners who dared to wear a restricted pattern were severely punished. In present-day Ghana the wearing of *kente* and other traditional textiles has

25-12. Portrait figure (*ndop*) of Shyaam a-Mbul a-Ngwoong, from Zaire. Kuba culture, mid-17th century. Wood, height 21³/₈" (54.5 cm). Museum of Mankind, London ing mancala, a game he is said to have introduced to the Kuba. Icons of other kings include an anvil for a king who was a skilled blacksmith, a slave girl for a king who married beneath his rank, and a rooster for a twentieth-century king who was exceptionally vigilant.

Kuba *ndop* figures also feature carved representations of royal regalia, including a wide belt of cowrie shells crossing the torso. Below the cowries is a braided belt that can never be untied, symbolizing the ability of the wearer to keep the secrets of the kingdom. Cowrie-shell bands worn on the biceps are called *mabiim*. Commoners are allowed to wear two bands; the royal family wear nine. The brass rings depicted on the forearms may be worn only by the king and his mother. The ornaments over each shoulder are made of cloth-covered cane. They represent hippopotamus teeth, and they reflect the prestige that accrues to a hunter of that large animal. Finally, all of the Kuba king figures wear a distinctive cap with a projecting bill. The bill reminds the Kuba of the story of a dispute that arose between the sons of their creator god in which members of one faction identified themselves by wearing the blade of a hoe balanced on their heads.

Not all African peoples centralized power in a single ruler. Most of the peoples of southeastern Nigeria, for example, depended on a council of male elders or on a men's voluntary association to provide order in the life of the community. The Anang Ibibio people of Nigeria were formerly ruled by a men's society called Ekpo. Ekpo expressed its power in part through art, especially large, dark, purposely frightening masks (fig. 25-13). In most rituals involving masks, it is "the mask," not the person wearing it, who takes the action. Such masks were worn by the younger members of the society when they were sent out to punish transgressors. Accompanied by assistants bearing torches, the mask would emerge from the Ekpo meetinghouse at night and proceed directly to the guilty person's house, where a punishment of beating or even execution might be meted out. The identity of the executioner was concealed by the mask, which identified him as an impersonal representative of Ekpo in much the same way that a uniform makes it clear that a police officer represents the authority of the state.

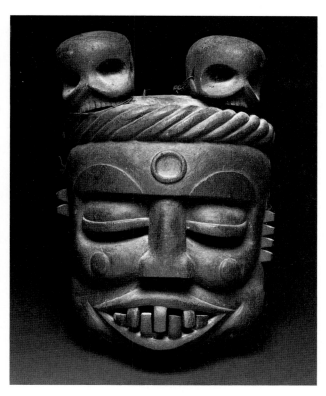

25-13. Ekpo mask, from Nigeria. Anang Ibibio culture, late 1930s. Wood, height 23⅝" (60 cm). Musée Barbier-Mueller, Geneva

This mask embodies many characteristics the Ibibio find repulsive or frightening, such as swollen features, matte black skin, and large, uneven teeth. The pair of skulls atop the head are potent death imagery. The circular scar on the forehead and the ropelike headband indicate membership in the diviner's cult, *idiong*, whose members were particularly feared for their supernatural power. The mask is in the style of the Otoro clan from the Ikot Abia Osom area near the city of Ikot Ekpene.

been encouraged, and patterns are no longer restricted to a particular person or group.

The Kuba people of central Zaire have produced elaborate and sophisticated political art since at least the seventeenth century. Kuba kings were memorialized by portrait sculpture called *ndop* (fig. 25-12). While the king was alive, his *ndop* was believed to house his double, a counterpart of his soul. After his death the portrait was believed to embody his spirit, which was felt to have power over the fertility both of the land and of his subjects. Together, the twenty-two known *ndop* span almost 400 years of Kuba history.

Kuba sculptors did not try to capture a physical likeness of each king. Indeed, several of the portraits seem interchangeable. Rather, each king is identified by an icon, called *ibol*, carved as part of the dais on which he is seated. The *ibol* refers to a skill for which the king was noted or an important event that took place during his lifetime. The *ndop* in figure 25-12 portrays the seventeenth-century king Shyaam a-Mbul a-Ngwoong, founder of the Kuba kingdom. Carved on the front of his dais is a board for play-

DEATH AND ANCESTORS

In the traditional African view, death is not an end but a transition—the leaving behind of one phase of life and the beginning of another. Just as ceremonies marked the initiation of young men and women into the community of adults, so they mark the initiation of the newly dead into the community of spirits. Like the rites of initiation into adulthood, death begins with a separation from the community, in this case the community of the living. A period of isolation and trial follows, during which the newly dead spirit may, for example, journey to the land of ancestors. Finally, the deceased is reintegrated into a community, this time the community of ancestral spirits. The memory of the deceased may be preserved among the living, and his or her spirit may be

25-14. *Kanaga* mask, from Mali. Dogon culture, early 20th century. Wood, height 45¼" (115 cm). Musée Barbier-Mueller, Geneva

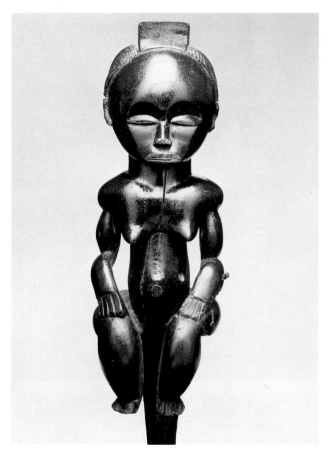

25-15. Reliquary guardian (*nlo byeri*), from Gabon. Fang culture, 19th century. Wood, height 16⅞" (43 cm). Musée Dapper, Paris

appealed to for intercession on their behalf with nature spirits or to prevent the spirits of the dead from using their powers to harm.

Among the Dogon people of Mali, in West Africa, the period of mourning following the death of an elder is brought to an end by a ceremony called *dama*, meaning "forbidden" or "dangerous." During *dama*, masks perform in the public square to the sound of gunfire to drive the soul of the deceased from the village. Among the most common masks is the *kanaga*, whose rectangular face supports a superstructure of planks that depict a crocodile or lizard with splayed legs (fig. 25-14).

If the deceased was a man, men from the community later engage in a mock battle on the roof of his home and participate in ritual hunts; if the deceased was a woman, the women of the community smash her cooking vessels on the threshold of her home. These portions of *dama* are reminders of human activities the deceased will no longer engage in. An elaborate *dama* commissioned by a wealthy

family may last as long as six days and include the performance of as many as 100 masks. Because a *dama* is so costly, it may be performed for several deceased elders, both male and female, at the same time.

The Fang people, who live near the Atlantic coast from southern Cameroon through Rio Muni and into northern Gabon, follow an ancestral religion in which the long bones and skulls of ancestors who have performed great deeds are collected after burial and placed together in a cylindrical bark container called *nsekh o byeri*. Deeds thus honored include killing an elephant, being the first to trade with Europeans, bearing an especially large number of children, or founding a particular lineage or community. On top of the container the Fang place a wooden figure called *nlo byeri*, which represents the ancestors and guards their relics from malevolent spirit forces (fig. 25-15). *Nlo byeri* are carved in a naturalistic style, with carefully arranged hairstyles, fully rounded torsos, and heavily muscled legs and arms. Frequent applications of cleansing and purifying palm oil produce a rich, glossy black surface.

The strong symmetry of the statue is especially notable. The layout of Fang villages is also symmetrical, with pairs of houses facing each other across a single long street. At each end of the street is a large public meetinghouse. The Fang immigrated into the area they now occupy during the early nineteenth century. The

25-16. Ancestor screen (*duen fobara*), from Abonnema village, Nigeria. Kalabari group, Ijo culture, 19th century. The Minneapolis Institute of Arts

experience was disruptive and disorienting, and Fang culture thus emphasizes the necessity of imposing order on a disorderly world. Many civilizations have recognized the power of symmetry to express permanence and stability (see, for example, the Forbidden City in Beijing, China, fig. 21-8).

Internally, the Fang strive to achieve a balance between the opposing forces of chaos and order, male and female, pure and impure, powerful and weak. They value an attitude of quiet composure, of reflection and tranquillity. These qualities are embodied in the powerful symmetry of the *nlo byeri* here, which communicates the calm and wisdom of the ancestor while also instilling awe and fear in those not initiated into the Fang religion.

Among the most complex funerary art in Africa are the memorial ancestral screens made during the nineteenth century by the Ijo people of southeast Nigeria (fig. 25-16). The Ijo live on the Atlantic coast, and with their great canoes formerly mediated the trade between European ships anchored offshore and communities in the interior of Nigeria. During that time groups of Ijo men organized themselves into economic associations called

canoe houses, and the heads of canoe houses had much power and status in the community. When the head of a canoe house died, a screen such as the one in figure 25-16 was made in his memory. The Ijo call these screens *duen fobara*, meaning "foreheads of the dead." (The forehead were believed to be the seat of power and the source of success.) The screens are made of wood and cane that were joined, nailed, bound, and pegged together. The assembly technique is unusual, because most African sculpture is carved from a single piece of wood.

Although each screen commemorates a specific individual, the central figure was not intended as a physical likeness. Instead, as is common in Africa, identity was communicated through attributes of status, such as masks, weapons, or headdresses that the deceased had the right to wear or display. The central figure of the example here wears a hat that distinguishes him as a member of an important men's society called *peri*. He is flanked by assistants, followers, or supporters of the canoe house, who are portrayed on a smaller scale. All three figures originally held weapons or other symbols of aggressiveness and status. Other extant screens include

25-17. Spirit mask in performance, from Côte d'Ivoire. Guro culture, early 1980s. Polychrome wood, height approx. 18" (45.72 cm)

smaller heads attached to the top of the frame, perhaps wearing masks that the deceased had commissioned, and representations of the severed heads of defeated enemies at the feet of the figures.

Memorial screens were placed in the ancestral altars of the canoe house, where they provided a dwelling for the spirit of the dead, who was believed to continue to participate in the affairs of the house after his death, ensuring its success in trade and war.

CONTEMPORARY ART

The photograph in this chapter of the Bwa masks in performance (see fig. 25-4) was taken in 1984. Even as you read this chapter, new costumes are being made for this year's performance, in which the same two masks will participate. Many traditional communities continue their art in contemporary Africa. But these communities do not live as if in a museum, re-creating the forms of the past as though nothing had changed. As new experiences pose new challenges or offer new opportunities, art changes with them.

Perhaps the most obvious change in traditional African art has been in the adaptation of modern materials to traditional forms. The Guro people of Côte d'Ivoire, for example, continue to commission delicate masks dressed with costly textiles and other materials. But now they paint them with oil-based enamel paints, endowing the traditional form with a new range and brilliance of color (fig. 25-17). The Guro have also added inscriptions in French and depictions of contemporary figures to sculptural forms that have persisted since before the colonial period. Other peoples have similarly made use of European textiles, plastics, metal, and even Christmas tree ornaments to enhance the visual impact of their art. Some Yoruba have used photographs and even brightly colored imported plastic children's dolls in place of the traditional *ere ibeji*, the images of twins shown in figure 25-3.

Throughout the colonial period and especially during the years following World War II, Europeans established schools in Africa to train talented artists in the mediums and techniques of European art. In the postcolonial era numerous African artists have studied in Europe and the United States, and many have become known internationally through exhibits in galleries and museums.

One such artist is Ouattara (b. 1957), represented here by *Nok Culture* (fig. 25-18). Ouattara's background exemplifies the fertile cross-cultural influences that shape the outlook of contemporary urban Africans. Born in Côte d'Ivoire, he received both formal French schooling and traditional African spiritual schooling. His father practiced both Western-style surgery and traditional African heal-

25-18. Ouattara. *Nok Culture*. 1993. Acrylic and mixed mediums on wood, 9'8¹/₂" x 6'7³/₄" (2.96 x 2.03 m). Collection of the artist ing. At nineteen Ouattara moved to Paris to absorb at first-hand the modern art of Europe. He currently lives and works in New York, Paris, and Abidjan. In paintings such as *Nok Culture*, Ouattara draws on his entire experience, synthesizing Western and African influences.

Nok Culture is dense with allusions to Africa's artistic and spiritual heritage. Its name refers to a culture that thrived in Nigeria from about 500 BCE to 200 CE and whose naturalistic **terra-cotta** sculpture are the earliest known figurative art from sub-Saharan Africa. Here, thickly applied paint has built up a surface reminiscent of the painted adobe walls of rural architecture. Tonalities of earth browns, black, and white appear frequently in traditional African art, especially in textiles. The conical horns at the upper corners evoke the ancestral shrines common in rural communities as well as the buttresses of West African adobe mosques. The **motif** of concentric circles at the center of the composition looks much like the traditional bull-roarer sound maker used to summon spirits. Suspended in a window that opens into the painting is a lesson board of the type used by Muslim students in Koranic schools. On the board appear Arabic writing, graphic patterns from African initiation rituals, and symbols from the Christian, ancient Egyptian, and mystical Hebrew traditions—a vivid if cryptic evocation of the many spiritual currents that run together in Africa.

Another art that has brought contemporary African artists to international attention is ceramics. Traditionally, most African pottery has been made by women. In some West African societies, potters were married to blacksmiths, both husband and wife making products that take raw ingredients from the earth and transform them by fire. These couples lived apart from the community both physically and socially, respected for their skills yet feared for the intimate contact they had with the powers of earth and fire.

Today, making pottery has enabled many women from traditional communities to attain a measure of economic independence. In Nigeria it is not uncommon to see large trucks stopped at a potters' village, loading up pots to be transported to distant markets. The women do not usually share their pottery income with the male head of the family but keep it to buy food for themselves and their children. In one large pottery community in Ilorin, a northern city of the Yoruba people in Nigeria, women have subcontracted the dreary and physically demanding tasks of gathering raw clay and fuel to local men so that they can concentrate on forming their wares, for which there is a great demand. In this way they control much of the local economy.

Nourished by this long tradition, some women have achieved broader recognition as artists. One is Magdalene Odundo (b. 1950), whose work displays the flawless surfaces of traditional Kenyan pottery (fig. 25-19). Indeed, she forms her pots using the same coiling technique that her Kenyan relatives use. Like Ouattara,

Odundo draws her inspiration from a tremendous variety of sources, both African and non-African. In the workshops she presents at colleges and art schools she shows hundreds of slides of pottery. She begins with images of Kenyan potters and pottery, then quickly moves on to pottery from the Middle East, China and Japan, and ancient North and South America. Odundo works in England, teaches in Europe and the United States, and shows her art through a well-known international dealer. Yet the power of traditional African forms is abundantly evident in the elegant pot illustrated here.

The painter Ouattara probably speaks for most contemporary artists around the world when he says, "[M]y vision is not based only on a country or a continent, it's beyond geography or what you see on a map, it's much more than that. Even though I localize it to make it understood better, it's wider than that. It refers to the cosmos" (cited in McEvilley, page 81). In his emphasis on the inherent spirituality of art, Ouattara voices what is most enduring about the African tradition.

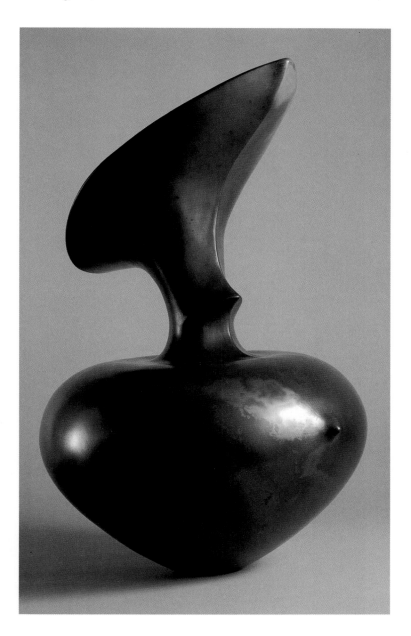

25-19. Magdalene Odundo. *Asymmetrical Angled Piece*. 1991.
   Reduced red clay, height 17" (43.18 cm). Collection of
   Werner Muensterberger

1725   1755   1785

Boyle
Chiswick House
1724–29

Pigalle
Portrait of Diderot
1777

Fuseli
*The
Nightmare*
1781

David
*Oath of
the Horatii*
1784–85

Langhans
Brandenburg
Gate
1788–91

CHAPTER 26

Neoclassicism and Romanticism in Europe and the United States

Goya
Third of May, 1808
1814–15

Ingres
Large Odalisque
1814

Barye
*Python Crushing
an African Horse*
1845

Bingham
*Fur Traders Descending
the Missouri*
c. 1845

26-1. William Hackwood, for Josiah Wedgwood. *"Am I Not a Man and a Brother?"* 1787. Black and white jasperware, 1³/₈ x 1³/₈" (3.5 x 3.5 cm). Trustees of the Wedgwood Museum, Barlaston, Staffordshire, England

F or several hundred years the name *Wedgwood* has been synonymous with exquisitely made English ceramics. Josiah Wedgwood at age nine had begun to work in his family's pottery business, and through sheer inventiveness and superlative taste he transformed ceramics from a minor industry to an important art. He became the maker of "the queen's wares" and created a dinner service for Catherine the Great of Russia.

But there was another side to this man who established a village for those he employed and cared deeply about every aspect of their living conditions. Wedgwood was also very active in the organized international effort to halt the African slave trade and abolish slavery. To publicize the abolitionist cause, he asked the sculptor William Hackwood to design an emblem for the British Committee to Abolish the Slave Trade, formed in 1787. The compelling image created by Hackwood was a small medallion of black and white jasperware, cut like a cameo in the likeness of an African man kneeling in chains, with the legend "Am I Not a Man and a Brother?" (fig. 26–1). Wedgwood sent copies of the medallion to Benjamin Franklin, the president of the Philadelphia Abolition Society, and to others in the abolitionist movement. Later, those active in the women's suffrage movement in the United States adapted the image by representing a woman in chains with the motto "Am I Not a Woman and a Sister?"

A work of fine art as explicitly political as this was highly unusual in the eighteenth century. But it was not unique, for there were artists in both Europe and America who responded to the tumultuous social and political changes with works of art that were both powerful and courageous.

THE ENLIGHTENMENT AND ITS REVOLUTIONS

The eighteenth century represents a great divide in Western history. When the century opened, the West was still semifeudal, both economically and politically. Wealth and power were centered in the hands of an aristocratic elite who owned or controlled the land worked by the largest and poorest class, the farmers. In between was a small "middle class," composed of doctors, lawyers, shopkeepers, artisans, and merchants—most of whom depended for their livelihood on the patronage of the rich. Only those involved in overseas trade operated outside the agrarian system, but even they aspired to membership in the landed aristocracy.

By the end of the century, the situation had changed dramatically. A new source of wealth—industrial manufacture—had been developed, and although this economy was still in its infancy, social visionaries could already see that the future would belong to large industrial communities or centers and to the burgeoning class of technicians, managers, and other professionals who would run them. Such observers expected industry not only to expand the middle class but also to provide a better material existence for all classes. These economic changes were fueled by a genuine concern for the general betterment of all humanity, a concern that extended beyond the purely economic. What became known as the Industrial Revolution was complemented by an equally revolutionary change in politics that conceived of all men (women and minorities were included by some thinkers) as deserving of equal rights and opportunities. The American Revolution of 1776 and the French Revolution of 1789 were the earliest results of this dramatic change in thinking.

The developments in politics and economics were themselves manifestations of a larger, single revolution in human thought: the Enlightenment, a radically new synthesis of ideas concerning humanity, reason, nature, and God. The Enlightenment was the culmination of developments begun when Renaissance humanists revived the Greek and Roman insistence that the powers of the human mind can discern the ordered regularity in nature. This humanism bred the new science and mathematics of Galileo, René Descartes, Francis Bacon, and Isaac Newton. Most importantly, Newton's success in capturing in a few mathematic equations the laws that govern the motions of the planets gave impetus to the growing faith in humanity's capacity to understand the workings of all the various elements of our world.

While such ideas were undermining the traditional Christian notion of a God-driven universe, Reformation thinkers were also disputing the monolithic authority of the Roman Catholic Church, thereby making their contribution to the origins of the Enlightenment. For Martin Luther, as for Descartes, the way to truth lay in the application of human reason: Received authority, whether from the ancients or from the pope, should be subject to the probings of independent minds.

What distinguished the Enlightenment proper from its roots was the way that late-seventeenth- and early-eighteenth-century thinkers began to synthesize these elements into a generally optimistic view that humanity and its institutions could be reformed if not perfected. Bernard de Fontenelle, a French popularizer of the new scientific discoveries of the seventeenth century, writing in 1702, anticipated "a century which will become more enlightened day by day, so that all previous centuries will be lost in darkness by comparison." At the end of the seventeenth and beginning of the eighteenth century, such hopes were expressed by a handful of thinkers, including John Locke, David Hume, the Baron de Montesquieu, G. W. Leibniz, and Voltaire. After 1740, such voices increased in both numbers and power, so that by the last quarter of the century their views dominated the discourse

not only in the arts and sciences but also in every sphere of intellectual life, including that of the European courts. The most prominent and influential of these thinkers, called philosophes (to distinguish their practical concerns from the purely academic ones of philosophers), included Jean-Jacques Rousseau, Denis Diderot, Thomas Jefferson, Benjamin Franklin, and Immanuel Kant.

These philosophes and their growing numbers of influential supporters did not agree on all matters. They quarreled, at times violently, about how to achieve specific reforms and about fundamental questions such as the natures of humanity and divinity. What emerged from these debates was a general worldview that for the sake of convenience and clarity can be summarized around a few key issues. Perhaps the matter that most unified these thinkers was the question of the purpose of humanity. Rejecting conventional notions that men and women were here to serve God or the ruling class, they insisted that humans were born to serve themselves, to pursue their own happiness and fulfillment. The purpose of the State, they agreed, was to facilitate this pursuit. The question of how it could best do so was a more contested one, however, partly because of differences of opinion on the basic goodness of humanity. Despite the pessimism of some and the reservations of others, Enlightenment thinkers were generally optimistic that men and women, when set free from their political and religious shackles, could be expected to act both rationally and morally. Thus, in pursuing their own happiness, they would promote the happiness of others.

Nature, like humanity, was generally seen as both rational and good. The natural world, whether a pure mechanism or a product of a beneficent deity, was amenable to human understanding and, therefore, control. Once the laws governing the natural and human realms were determined, they could be harnessed for our greater happiness. Thus, the industrial and political revolutions that marked the end of the century could not be separated.

This optimism about humanity's future was rejected by few intellectuals in the period before the French Revolution of 1789, but the events set in motion by that revolution—the Reign of Terror, the ascendancy of Emperor Napoleon, and the European wars that followed—created the first crisis of Enlightenment ideals. This crisis, like the Enlightenment itself, is clearly visible in the art of the period.

Although various types of Baroque and Rococo art survived into the late eighteenth century, two general modes characterize the years from roughly 1750 to 1850: Neoclassicism and Romanticism. Neither type is simple or monolithic. In essence, Neoclassicism (neo means "new") presents classical subject matter, mythological or historical, in a style derived from classical Greek and Roman sources. Some of Neoclassicism was conceived to please the senses, and some to teach moral lessons. In its didactic manifestations—usually **history paintings**—Neoclassicism was one of the chief vehicles for Enlightenment hopes. Because many artists combined Neoclassical elements with an appeal to the emotions—which is the essence of Romanticism—the line between the two artistic modes is not always clear. Romanticism

■■■■■ ■
1725   1850

Culture Center	1725–1800	1800–1875
France	Grand Manner emerges; Jean-Jacques Rousseau's *Émile* and *Du Contrat social*; David's *Oath of the Horatii*; Vigée-Lebrun's portraits of Marie Antoinette; French Revolution; David's *Death of Marat*; Napoleon is First Consul; Neo-classicism in France at peak	Napoleon I of First Empire; Ingres's *Large Odalisque*; Romanticism emerges; royal restoration of Louis XVIII; Géricault's *Raft of the "Méduse"*; Charles X; Revolution of 1830; Louis Philippe; Rude's *La Marseillaise*; Napoleon III of Second Empire
Rome	Excavations of Pompeii and Hercula-neum; Winckelmann distinguishes Greek and Roman styles in painting and sculpture; Antonio Canova; Neoclassi-cism emerges	
Britain	Lord Burlington promotes Neoclassical architecture; Hogarth's *Marriage à la Mode*; British landscape and genre paintings increase; British Empire in India; history paintings gain popularity; James Watt develops steam engine; Joshua Reynolds's Grand Manner por-traits; Copley exhibits at London Society of Artists; George III charters Royal Academy of Art; Angelica Kauffmann and Mary Moser named to Royal Academy; Josiah Wedgwood perfects jasperware; Copley's history paintings; Britain recognizes American inde-pendence; Gainsborough's portraits; Romantic literary movement	United Kingdom of Great Britain and Ireland established; Constable's *White Horse*; Houses of Parliament redesigned; Turner's *Fighting "Téméraire"*
Germany	King Frederick William II of Prussia; Langhans's Brandenburg Gate; Mozart's *Don Giovanni*	Beethoven's *Ninth Symphony*; Marx and Engels's *Communist Manifesto*
Spain	King Charles III; King Charles IV	Goya's *Third of May 1808*; King Joseph Bona-parte; King Ferdinand installed by British
United States	Georgian style; Boston Tea Party; Decla-ration of Independence; Federal style; George Washington president	Thomas Jefferson president; Latrobe initiates Greek Revival style; Louisiana Purchase from France doubles U.S. territory; Audubon's *Birds of America*; Cole's *The Oxbow*; Texas annexed; Oregon acquired; California gold rush; Stowe's *Uncle Tom's Cabin*; South Carolina secedes; Civil War begins; Abraham Lincoln assassinated; first transcontinental railroad
World	Qing dynasty continues (China); Cather-ine the Great (Russia); Hermitage Muse-um founded (Russia)	Mexico becomes a republic; South African Republic established; Crimean War between Turkey and its allies versus Russia; Italy is united; Dominion of Canada is formed

26-2. William Hogarth. *The Marriage Contract,* from Marriage à la Mode. 1743–45. Oil on canvas, 28 x 36" (71.7 x 92.3 cm).
The National Gallery, London

was less a style than an approach centered in the strong subjective feelings of the artist. Romanticism, too, could be used for various purposes. In the late eighteenth century, its uses ranged from public entertainment to the purely private, but in the years after the French Revolution it became the chief vehicle for the critique of Enlightenment optimism.

During the final three decades of this period, there was a resurgence of the kind of naturalistic landscape and genre painting popular during the Baroque era, especially in the North. This Romantic Naturalism (an apparent contradiction in terms meant to identify a kind of naturalism popular in the Romantic era) was itself partly a reaction to the industrial forces that survived the crisis of the Enlightenment and were beginning to assert themselves as the dominant realities of modern life.

SURVIVING ART FORMS Although the late eighteenth century witnessed the emergence of Neoclassicism and Romanticism, other approaches were nevertheless evident in the art of the period. While many artists embraced these two major new art forms, others continued to prefer the more traditional approaches that had dominated before about 1750. Even within the boundary of tradition, however, certain changes in attitude, style, and subject matter can be detected.

British and French Moral Genre

One of the art forms that survived from the Baroque era into the eighteenth century was moral **genre** painting. Although generally inspired by the examples of the Dutch masters, the leading exponents of this type of painting in the mid- and late eighteenth century produced works that were less ambiguous with regard to their didactic messages and more inspired by civic than by religious concerns.

This new kind of moral genre first appeared in Britain as a belated consequence of the discontinuation of government censorship in 1695. What followed was a flowering of British literary satire, directed at a variety of political and social targets. The first painter inspired by the work of these pioneering novelists and essayists was William Hogarth (1697–1764). Trained as a portrait painter, Hogarth felt art should participate in the improvement of society. About 1730, he began illustrating moralizing tales of his own invention in sequences of four to six paintings, which he then produced in sets of prints, both to maximize his profits and to influence as many people as possible.

Between 1743 and 1745, Hogarth produced the Marriage á la Mode suite, whose subject was inspired by Joseph Addison's 1712 essay in the *Spectator* promoting the concept of marriage based on love. The opening scene, *The Marriage Contract* (fig. 26-2), shows the gout-

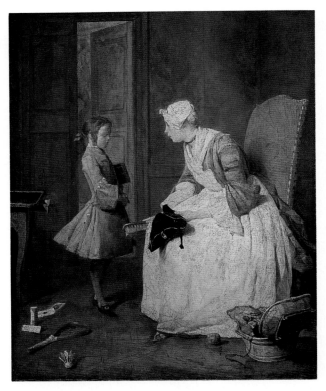

26-3. Jean-Baptiste-Siméon Chardin. *The Governess.* 1739. Oil on canvas, 18¹/₈ x 14³/₄" (46 x 37.5 cm). National Gallery of Canada, Ottawa

ridden Lord Squanderfield arranging the marriage of his son to the daughter of a wealthy merchant. The merchant gains entry for his family into the aristocracy, while the lord gets the money he needs to complete his Palladian house, which is visible out the window. The loveless couple who will be sacrificed to their fathers' deal sit on the couch. While the young Squanderfield stares admiringly at himself in the mirror, his unhappy fiancée is already being wooed by lawyer Silvertongue, who suggestively sharpens his pen. The next five scenes show the progressively disastrous results of such a union, culminating in the killing of Silvertongue by the young lord and the subsequent suicide of his wife.

Stylistically, Hogarth's works combine the additive approach of seventeenth-century Dutch genre painters with the nervous elegance of the Rococo. Hogarth wanted to please and entertain his audience as much as educate them. His work became so popular that in 1745 he was able to give up social portraiture, which he considered a deplorable form of vanity.

The leading French moral genre painter early in the century was Jean-Baptiste-Siméon Chardin (1699–1779), whose work shows the persistence of the seventeenth-century Dutch manner in France. A painter whose output was limited essentially to still lifes and quiet domestic scenes, Chardin tended to work on a small scale, meticulously and slowly. His still lifes consisted of a few simple objects that were to be enjoyed for their subtle differences of shape and texture, not for any virtuoso

26-4. Jean-Baptiste Greuze. *The Drunken Cobbler.* Late 1770s. Oil on canvas, 29⁵/₈ x 36³/₈" (75.2 x 92.4 cm). Portland Art Museum, Portland, Oregon
Gift of Marion Bowles Hollis

In 1769, Greuze submitted a classical history painting to the Salon and requested the French Academy to change his official status from Genre Painter to the higher rank of History Painter. The work and request were refused. Greuze was so angry that he boycotted the Salon in the future, preferring to show his works privately.

performance, complexity of composition, or moralizing content. But in the 1730s, Chardin began to create moral genre works as he focused on simple, mildly touching scenes of everyday middle-class life, such as *The Governess* (fig. 26-3). He was one of the first European artists to treat the lives of women and children with sympathy and to honor the dignity of women's work in his portrayals of young mothers, governesses, and kitchen maids. Ironically, these simple domestic scenes appealed to aristocrats and even to royalty, who bought so many of them that Chardin was kept busy simply making copies of his popular compositions.

Chardin's work was praised by Denis Diderot, a leading Enlightenment figure whom many consider the father of modern art criticism. Diderot's most notable contribution was editing the *Encyclopédie* (1751–1765), a seventeen-volume compendium of knowledge and opinion to which many of the major Enlightenment thinkers contributed. In 1759, Diderot began to write reviews of the official Salon for a periodic newsletter for wealthy subscribers. Diderot believed that it was art's proper function to "inspire virtue and purify manners." He therefore praised artists such as Chardin and criticized the adherents of the Rococo.

Diderot's highest praise went to Jean-Baptiste Greuze (1725–1805)—which is hardly surprising, because Greuze's major source of inspiration came from the kind of *drame bourgeois* ("middle-class drama") that Diderot had inaugurated in France in 1757. In addition to comedy and tragedy, Diderot felt there should be a "middle tragedy" that taught useful lessons to the public with clear, simple stories of ordinary life. Greuze's paintings, such as *The Drunken Cobbler* (fig. 26-4), of the late 1770s, became the visual counterparts of that new theatrical form, which later became known as melodrama. On a shallow, stagelike space and under a dramatic spotlight, a drunken father returns home to his angry wife and hungry children. The gestures of the children make it clear that he has spent the family's grocery money on drink. In other paintings, Greuze offered similar lessons in how not to behave to wives and to children.

British and French Portraiture

While the burgeoning middle classes in France and England were embracing the work of Greuze and Hogarth, their upper-class contemporaries continued to commission flattering portraits. The leading portrait painter in late-eighteenth-century England was probably Joshua Reynolds (1723–1792), the inaugural president of the Royal Academy (established in 1768). His *Fifteen Discourses to the Royal Academy* (1769–1790) set out his theories on art: Artists should follow the rules derived from studying the great masters of the past, especially those who worked in the classical tradition; art should generalize to create the universal rather than the particular; and the highest kind of art is history painting.

Because British patrons preferred portraits of themselves to scenes of classical history, Reynolds attempted to elevate portraiture to the level of history painting by

26-5. Joshua Reynolds. *Lady Sarah Bunbury Sacrificing to the Graces.* 1765. Oil on canvas, 7'10" x 5' (2.42 x 1.53 m). The Art Institute of Chicago

Mr. and Mrs. W. W. Kimball Collection, 1922. 4468

Lady Bunbury was one of the great beauties of her era. A few years before this painting was done, she had turned down a request of marriage from King George III.

giving it a historical or mythological veneer. A good example of this type of portraiture, a form of Baroque classicism that Reynolds called the **Grand Manner**, is *Lady Sarah Bunbury Sacrificing to the Graces* (fig. 26-5). Dressed in a classical costume, Bunbury plays the part of a Roman priestess making a sacrifice to the personifications of female Beauty, the Three Graces. The figure is further aggrandized through the use of the monumental classical arcade behind her, the emphatic classical **contrapposto** of her pose, and the larger-than-life scale of the work. Such works were intended for the grand stairways of aristocratic residences.

A number of British patrons, however, remained committed to the kind of portraiture Van Dyck had brought to England in the 1620s, which had featured more informal poses against natural vistas. Thomas Gainsborough (1727–1788) achieved great success with this mode when he moved to Bath in 1759 to cater to the

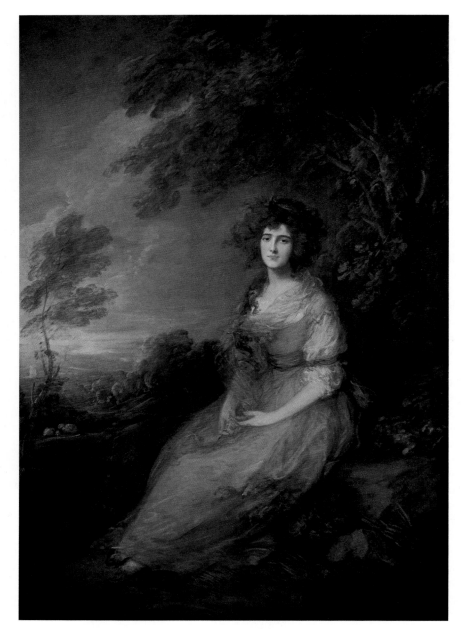

26-6. Thomas Gainsborough. *Portrait of Mrs. Richard Brinsley Sheridan.* 1785–87. Oil on canvas, 7'2¹/₂" x 5'¹/₂" (2.2 x 1.54 m). National Gallery of Art, Washington, D.C.
Andrew W. Mellon Collection

rich and fashionable people who had recently begun to go there in great numbers. A good example of his mature style is the *Portrait of Mrs. Richard Brinsley Sheridan* (fig. 26-6), which shows the professional singer and wife of a celebrated playwright seated informally outdoors. The sloping view into the distance and the use of a tree to frame the sitter's head seem to have been borrowed straight from Van Dyck (see fig. 19-39). But Gainsborough modernized the formula not simply through his lighter, Rococo palette and feathery brushwork but also by integrating the woman into the landscape, thus identifying her with it. The effect is especially noticeable in the way her windblown hair matches the tree foliage

overhead. The work thereby manifests one of the new values of the Enlightenment: the emphasis on nature and the natural as the sources of goodness and beauty.

French portrait painting before the Revolution of 1789 may be characterized as a modified form of the Rococo. Elegant informality continued to be featured, but new themes were introduced, figures tended to be larger and more robust, and compositional arrangements were more stable. Many leading portraitists were women. The most famous was Marie-Louise-Élisabeth Vigée-Lebrun (1755–1842), who in 1779 became painter to Queen Marie Antoinette. In 1787, she presented the queen with her children (fig. 26-7) in conformity with the

26-7. Marie-Louise-Élisabeth Vigée-Lebrun. *Portrait of Marie Antoinette with Her Children*. 1787. Oil on canvas, 9'¼" x 7'⅝" (2.75 x 2.15 m). Musée National du Château de Versailles

As the favorite painter to the queen, Vigée-Lebrun escaped from Paris with her daughter on the eve of the Revolution of 1789 and fled to Rome. After a very successful self-exile working in Italy, Austria, Russia, and England, the artist finally resettled in Paris in 1804 at the invitation of Napoleon I and again became popular with Parisian art patrons. Over her long career, she painted around 800 portraits in a vibrant style that changed very little over the decades.

Enlightenment theme of the good mother (see "Jean-Jacques Rousseau on Educating Children," below). The portrait of the queen as a kindly, stabilizing presence for her offspring was meant to counter her public image as immoral, extravagant, and selfish. The princess leans affectionately against her mother, proof of the queen's natural goodness. In a further attempt to gain the viewer's sympathy, the little dauphin—the eldest son and heir to a throne he would never ascend—points to the empty cradle of a recently deceased sibling. The image also alluded to the well-known allegory of Abundance, suggesting the peace and prosperity of society under the king's rule.

In 1783, Vigée-Lebrun was elected to one of the four places in the French Academy available to women (see "Women and the Academies in the Eighteenth Century," page 937). Also elected that year was Adélaide Labille-Guiard (1749–1803) who in 1790, successfully petitioned to end the restriction on women. Labille-Guiard's commitment to enlarging the number of women painters in

JEAN-JACQUES ROUSSEAU ON EDU-CATING CHILDREN	

JEAN-JACQUES ROUSSEAU ON EDUCATING CHILDREN

Although he never married and he placed his own children in orphanages, the French-Swiss philosopher Jean-Jacques Rousseau (1712–1778) formulated a behavioral program of childhood education that affected all French schools after the Revolution of 1789. His essay on education, *Émile, ou Traité de l'éducation* (*Emile, or Regarding Education*), was written at the same time as his well-known political tract *Du Contrat social (Of the Social Contract)*, in which he argued that all people were equal and inherently good and that rulers held their positions only by the consent of the people they governed. *Émile*, which contained a preliminary outline restating the theory of the social contract, was published in Paris in May 1762. Believing that children were inherently good until society corrupted them and broke their naturally independent, inquisitive spirits, Rousseau advised mothers to breast-feed their babies themselves, dress them in loose clothing with no bonnet, wash them in unheated water, give them freedom to crawl about, and never rock them, which Rousseau considered harmful. As boys grew, they were to be taught to value nature, human liberty, and personal valor and virtue. This environment would inevitably produce a citizen committed to political freedom and civic duty. Girls were to be educated only as needed for their futures as wives and mothers. Once married, women were to stay at home, out of the public eye, caring for their households and children, which Rousseau saw as "the manner of living that nature and reason prescribe for the sex" (Richard and Richard, pages 457–458). *Du Contrat social* became the basis for the French Constitution, and *Émile* turned it into a manual for the country's public education programs.

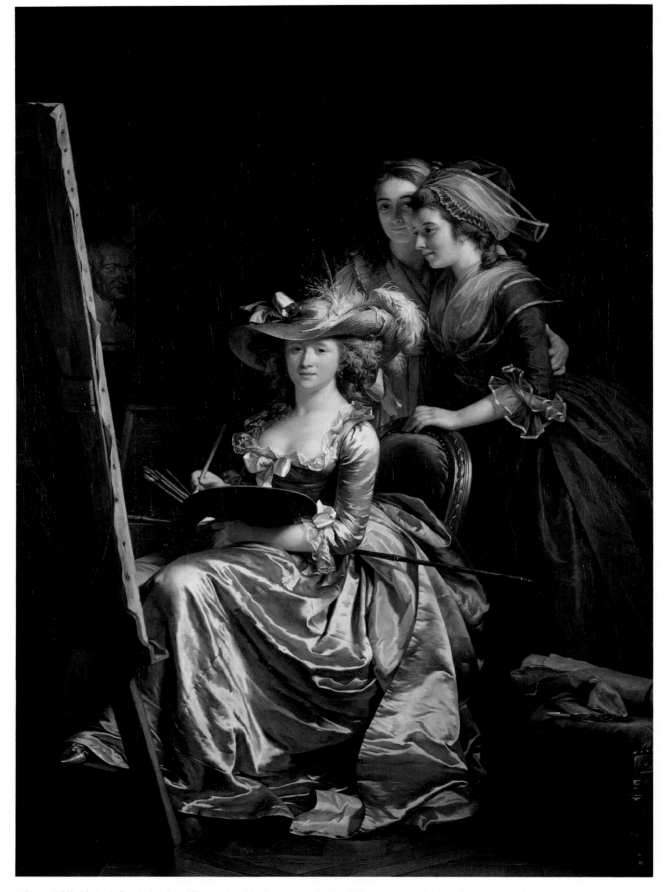

26-8.   Adélaide Labille-Guiard. *Self-Portrait with Two Pupils*. 1785. Oil on canvas, 6'11" x 4'11½" (2.11 x 1.51 m).
The Metropolitan Museum of Art, New York
Gift of Julia A. Berwind, 1953

France is evident in the self-portrait with two pupils (fig. 26-8) that she submitted to the Salon of 1785. The monumental image of the artist at her easel was also meant to answer the sexist rumors that her paintings and those by Vigée-Lebrun had actually been painted by men. In a witty role reversal, the only male in her work is *her* muse—her father, whose bust is behind her. The self-portrait also flatters the painter's conventional feminine charms in a manner generally consistent with the Rococo tradition. A comparison of Labille-Guiard with similar images of women by artists such as Fragonard (see fig. 19-79) reveals the more monumental female type Labille-Guiard favored, in keeping with her conception of women as important contributors to national life, which is a Neoclassical impulse. The solid pyramidal arrangement of the three women adds to the effect.

In sculpture, too, the first signs of the new Enlightenment values were evident in the art of those still working in the basic Rococo idiom. The leading sculptor in France during the middle of the century was Jean-Baptiste Pigalle (1714–1785), who received commissions from the most prestigious clients, including Madame de Pompadour (see Chapter 19). In 1777, he produced a portrait **bust** of the art critic and editor of the *Encyclopédie*, Denis Diderot (fig. 26-9). The casual dress and pose are typically Rococo, although charm has here been sacrificed for intelligence. The thoughtful, far-away look in Diderot's face suggests he may be contemplating the better future he and his fellow philosophes imagined for

26-9. Jean-Baptiste Pigalle. *Portrait of Diderot.* 1777. Bronze, height 16¹/₂" (42 cm). Museé du Louvre, Paris

WOMEN AND THE ACADEMIES IN THE EIGHTEENTH CENTURY   Although only a few women were elected to the European academies of art before the eighteenth century, their inclusion amounted to little more than honorary recognition of their achievements.

In France, Louis XIV had proclaimed in the founding address of the Royal Academy that its intention was to reward all worthy artists, "without regard to the difference of sex," but this resolve was not put into practice. Only seven women were awarded the title of Academician between 1648 and 1706, the year the Royal Academy declared itself closed to women. Nevertheless, by 1770 four women had been admitted to the Academy, and the men became worried that women members would become "too numerous." To ensure the minority status of women members, they declared four women members to be the limit for any one time, noting, however, that the Academy was not obliged to maintain that

number. Young women were not admitted to the Academy school or allowed to compete for Academy prizes, both of which were nearly indispensable for professional success.

Women fared even worse at London's Royal Academy. After the Swiss painters Mary Moser and Angelica Kauffmann were named as founding members in 1768, no other women were elected until 1922, and then only as associates. Johann Zoffany's 1771–1772 portrait of the London academicians shows the men grouped around a nude male model in a studio, along with the Academy's study collection of Classical statues and plaster copies. Propriety disallowed the presence of women in this setting, so Zoffany painted their portraits inconspicuously on the wall. In more formal portraits of the Academy, however, the two women were included.

Johann Zoffany. *Academicians of the Royal Academy.* 1771–72. Oil on canvas, 47¹/₂ x 59¹/₂" (120.6 x 151.2 cm). The Royal Collection, Windsor Castle, New Windsor, England

26-10. Giovanni Paolo Panini. *View of the Piazza del Popolo, Rome.* 1741. Oil on canvas, 38 x 52³/4" (96.6 x 134 cm). Nelson-Atkins Museum of Art, Kansas City, Missouri

Purchase: Acquired Through the Generosity of an Anonymous Donor (F79-3)

Piazza (meaning "public square") del Popolo was named for the church of Sta. Maria del Popolo, not visible in the painting because Panini must have drawn this panoramic cityscape from one of its upper stories. The obelisk was erected in 1589, the twin churches in the 1660s. Three important thoroughfares feed into the square from the south—visible to the left, between, and to the right of the churches: via (often translated "way") Babuino, Corso, and Ripetta.

humanity. Finally, the greater naturalism in Pigalle's handling of Diderot's aging face nicely underscores the sitter's own commitment to truth.

NEOCLASSICISM

By the 1780s, the new Enlightenment ideals in France and elsewhere had found a congenial stylistic vehicle in the revival of classicism that became known as Neoclassicism. The new interest in democracy and responsible citizenship, in particular, was thought to call for classical treatment, not only because Athens was the home of democracy but also because contemporary writing on such themes often looked backed to the examples of well-known Greek and Roman thinkers like Plato and Plutarch.

Neoclassicism also had a less political, more decorative side. In short, a number of Neoclassicists were more committed to aesthetic beauty than to political truths. Nevertheless, both camps looked to Rome as the great repository of classicism. In order to understand the origins of Neoclassicism, then, it is necessary to look at the institution of the Grand Tour, which made Rome the artistic capital of the Western world in the eighteenth century.

The Art of the Grand Tour

From the late 1600s until well into the nineteenth century, the education of a young northern European or American gentleman (and increasingly, gentlewoman) was completed on the Grand Tour, a prolonged visit to the major cultural sites of southern Europe, especially Italy. Accompanied by a tutor and an entourage of servants, the young man or woman began in Paris before moving on to a number of well-preserved Roman buildings and monuments in southern France. The focus of the Grand Tour was Italy, repository of the classical and the Renaissance pasts. There, the principal points of interest were Venice, Florence, Naples, and Rome.

In the first decades of the seventeenth century, these tourists, especially the British, spent their money on

1750
1725 1850

26-11. Giovanni Battista Piranesi. *The Arch of Drusus.* 1748. Etching, $14^{7}/_{16}$ x $28^{3}/_{4}$" (37 x 73 cm). Published in *Le Antichità Romane* (later retitled *Arch Trionfali*), Rome, 1748. The Pierpont Morgan Library, New York PML 12601

Piranesi's children carried on his publishing business after his death. Encouraged by Napoleon's officials, his sons Francesco and Piero moved the operation in 1799 to Paris, where between 1800 and 1807 they made and sold restrikes (posthumous impressions) of all of their father's etchings. Later Piranesi's plates were purchased by the Royal Printing House in Rome and reprinted again.

vedute (Italian for "views"; singular *veduta*), city views that they collected largely as fond reminders of their time in Italy. These paintings were of two types. In one, known as *capriccio* ("fanciful"), artists mixed actual features, especially ruins, into imaginatively pleasing compositions. The second, and by far the more popular type, were naturalistic renderings of well-known tourist attractions—panoramic views that were meticulously detailed, topographically accurate, and populated with a host of contemporary figures engaged in typical activities. The Venetian artist Giovanni Antonio Canal, called Canaletto (1697–1768), became so popular among British clients for his scenes that his dealer arranged for him to work from 1746 to 1755 in England, where he painted topographic views of London and the surrounding countryside, giving impetus to a school of English **landscape painting**.

The most successful of the Roman *vedute* painters was Giovanni Paolo Panini (c. 1692–1765). Like Canaletto, he specialized in documentary vistas. His *View of the Piazza del Popolo, Rome* (fig. 26-10), from 1741, is representative of his work. In order to give the viewer a complete inventory of the square and of the neighboring parts of the city, Panini chose a **bird's-eye view**. The artist's desire for completeness is also evident in the abundance of the work's different figures and elements, including priests, beggars, gentlemen, and elegant carriages. The painting's original owner was meant to take pleasure in examining this microcosm of the life he had known in this agreeable city.

A very different kind of effect was generated by the Roman views of Giovanni Battista Piranesi (1720–1778). Trained in Venice as an architect, Piranesi went to Rome in 1740. After studying etching, he began in 1743 to pro-duce portfolios of prints, and in 1761 he established his own publishing house. Piranesi is best known for his views of ancient Roman ruins, such as *The Arch of Drusus* (fig. 26-11), published in 1748 in a portfolio of etchings called *Le Antichità Romane (Roman Antiquities)*. Such works are fine examples of the new taste for the **picturesque**, which contemporary British theorists defined as a landscape (actual or depicted) with an aesthetically pleasing irregularity in its shapes, composition, and lighting. But in other respects, Piranesi's views are early manifestations of Romanticism. These ruins are emotionally compelling reminders of the passage of time and of its sobering implications: All human achievements, even the great events memorialized in such triumphal arches, eventually come to ruin. The individual human, like those shown in the etching, is ultimately small and insignificant in relation to history and its cycles of birth and death.

Piranesi's and his patrons' interest in Roman ruins and in their tragic implications was fueled by the discoveries made at Herculaneum and Pompeii shortly before midcentury. These prosperous Roman towns near Naples were buried in 79 CE by the sudden eruption of Mount Vesuvius. In 1738, archeologists began to uncover the evidence of this catastrophe at Herculaneum, and ten years later the remains of Pompeii were first unearthed. The extraordinary archeological discoveries made at these two sites, published in numerous illustrated books, excited interest in classical art and artifacts.

The new vogue for collecting and appreciating classical art is evident in the work of Rome's leading portrait painter of the era, Pompeo Batoni (1708–1787). The majority of his clientele were foreign visitors like the

26-12. Pompeo Batoni. *Portrait of Count Razoumowsky.* 1766. Oil on canvas, 9'9¹/₂" x 6'5" (2.99 x 2.07 m). Collection Count Razoumowsky, Vienna

restored by artisans working in the cardinal's employ.

Albani's credentials as the foremost expert on classical art were solidified when he hired as his secretary and librarian Johann Joachim Winckelmann, the leading theoretician of Neoclassicism. The Prussia-born Winckelmann had become an advocate of classical art while working in Dresden, where the French Rococo style he deplored was fashionable. In 1755, he published a pamphlet, *Thoughts on the Imitation of Greek Works in Painting and Sculpture*, in which he attacked the Rococo as decadent and argued that only by imitating Greek art could modern artists become great again. Winckelmann imagined that the temperate climate and natural ways of the Greeks had perfected their bodies and made their artists more sensitive to certain general ideas of what constitutes true and lasting beauty. Shortly after publishing this pamphlet, Winckelmann moved to Rome, where in 1758 he went to work for Albani. In 1764, he published the second of his widely influential treatises, *The History of Ancient Art*, which many consider the beginning of modern art history.

Winckelmann's closest friend and colleague in Rome was a fellow German, Anton Raphael Mengs (1728–1779). Largely as a result of their friendship, Winckelmann's employer, Cardinal Albani, commissioned Mengs to do a painting for the ceiling of the great gallery in his new villa. The *Parnassus* ceiling (fig. 26-13), from 1761, is usually considered the first true Neoclassical painting. The scene takes place on Mount Parnassus in central Greece, which the ancients believed to be sacred to Apollo (the god of poetry, music, and the arts) and the nine Muses (female personifications of artistic inspiration). At the center of the composition is Apollo, holding a lyre and a laurel branch, symbol of immortality. Next to him, resting on a Doric column, is Mnemosyne, the mother of the Muses, who are shown practicing the various arts. Inspired by relief sculpture he had studied at Herculaneum, Mengs arranged the figures in a generally symmetrical, pyramidal grouping parallel to the picture plane. Winckelmann, not surprisingly, praised the work for achieving the "noble simplicity and calm grandeur" that he had found in Greek originals.

The aesthetic ideals of the Albani-Winckelmann circle soon affected contemporary Roman sculptors, who remained committed to this paradigm for the next 100 years. The leading Neoclassical sculptor of the late eighteenth and early nineteenth centuries was Antonio Canova (1757–1822). Born near Venice into a family of stonemasons, Canova in 1781 settled in Rome, where under the guidance of the British painter Gavin Hamilton he adopted the Neoclassical style and quickly became the most sought-after European sculptor of the period.

Canova specialized in two types of work: grand public monuments for Europe's leaders and erotic mythological subjects, like *Cupid and Psyche* (fig. 26-14), for the pleasure of private collectors. *Cupid and Psyche* illustrates the love story of Cupid, Venus's son, and Psyche, a beautiful mortal who had aroused the goddess's jealousy. Venus casts Psyche into a deathlike sleep; moved by Cupid's grief and love for her, the sky god Jupiter (the

Russian Count Razoumowsky (fig. 26-12), president of the St. Petersburg Academy of Science, men who wished to see themselves (and to be seen by others) as cultivated, refined gentlemen. The elegant pose, the richly embroidered costume sparkling with the decorations of his rank, as well as the column and the drapery, all mark this as a late Baroque portrait. What is new here are the accessories to which the count appreciatively gestures: some of the classical sculpture in the papal collection. The work identifies the count as a member of the new group of connoisseurs championing classical art as the one true and timeless style. Ironically, this belief would soon make Batoni's Baroque portraits seem badly dated.

Neoclassicism in Rome

A notable leader of the classical revival was Cardinal Allesandro Albani, who amassed a huge collection of antique sculpture, **sarcophagi**, **intaglios**, **cameos**, and vases. In 1760–1761, he built a villa just outside Rome to house and display his holdings. The Villa Albani became one of the most important spots on the Grand Tour. The villa was more than a museum, however; it was also a kind of shop, where many of the items he sold to satisfy the growing craze for antiquities were faked or heavily

26-13. Anton Raphael Mengs. *Parnassus*, ceiling fresco in the Villa Albani, Rome. 1761

26-14. Antonio Canova. *Cupid and Psyche*. 1787–93. Marble, 5'1" x 5'8¹/₅" (1.55 x 1.73 m). Musée de Louvre, Paris

Roman name for Zeus) takes pity on the pair and gives Psyche immortality. In this version of the theme (he did six), Canova chose the most emotional and tender moment in the story, when Cupid revives the lifeless Psyche with a kiss. Here Canova combined a Romantic interest in emotion with a more typically Neoclassical appeal to the combined senses of sight and touch. Because the lovers gently caress one another, the viewer is invited to run his or her fingers over the graceful contours of their cool, languorous limbs.

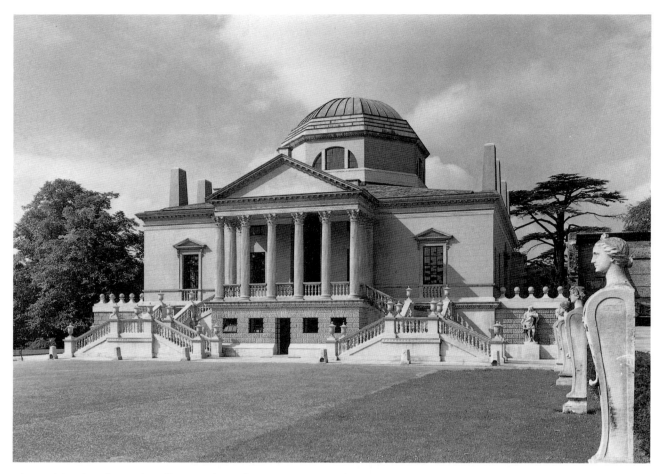

26-15. Richard Boyle, Lord Burlington. Chiswick House, West London, England. 1724–29. Interior decoration (1726–29) and new gardens (1730–40) by William Kent

26-16. Richard Boyle, Lord Burlington. Plan of Chiswick House. 1724

BRITAIN

British tourists and artists in Italy became the leading supporters of Neoclassicism partly because they had been prepared for it by the architectural revival of Renaissance classicism in their homeland earlier in the century.

British Classicism

Just as the Rococo was emerging in France, a group of British professional architects and wealthy amateurs led by the Scot Colin Campbell were taking a stance against what they saw as the immoral extravagance of the Italian Baroque. As a moral corrective, they advocated a return to the austerity and simplicity found in the architecture of Andrea Palladio.

The most famous product of this group was Chiswick House (fig. 26-15), designed in 1724 by its owner, Richard Boyle, the third earl of Burlington (1695–1753). Burlington had visited Italy specifically to study Palladio's architecture, especially his Villa Rotunda (see fig. 18-38), which inspired his plan for Chiswick House. The building plan (fig. 26-16) shares the geometrical symmetry of Palladio's villa, although its central core is octagonal rather than round and there are only two entrances. The main entrance, flanked now by matching staircases, is a Roman temple front, a flattering reference to the building's inhab-

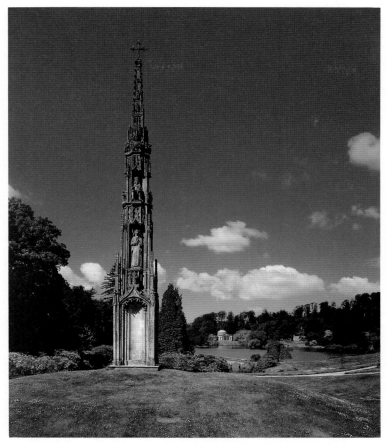

26-17. Henry Flitcroft and Henry Hoare. The Park at Stourhead, Wiltshire, England. Laid out 1743; executed 1744–65, with continuing additions

itant. Chiswick's **elevation** is characteristically Palladian, with a main floor resting on a basement, and tall rectangular windows with triangular **pediments**. The result is a lucid evocation of Palladio's design, whose few but crisp details seem perfectly suited to the refined proportions of the whole. The popularity of the Palladian style among members of Burlington's class during the ensuing decades may be judged by the fact that Hogarth satirized the style in his Marriage à la Mode suite. The architect looking out the window in *The Marriage Contract* (see fig. 26-2) is probably a caricature of Burlington himself.

In Rome, Burlington had persuaded an English expatriate, William Kent (1685–1748), to return to London as his collaborator. Kent designed Chiswick's surprisingly ornate interior as well as the grounds, the latter in a style that became known throughout Europe as the "English landscape garden." Kent's garden, in contrast to the regularity and rigid formality of Baroque gardens (see fig. 19-20), featured winding paths, a lake with a cascade, irregular plantings of shrubs, and other effects imitating the appearance of the natural rural landscape. The English landscape garden was another indication of the growing Enlightenment emphasis on the natural.

Following William Kent's lead, **landscape architecture** flourished in the hands of such designers as Lancelot ("Capability") Brown and Henry Flitcroft. In 1743, the banker Henry Hoare redid the grounds of his estate at Stourhead in Wiltshire (fig. 26-17) with the assistance of Flitcroft, a protégé of Burlington. The resulting gardens at Stourhead carried William Kent's ideas much further. Stourhead is, in effect, an exposition of the picturesque, with orchestrated views dotted with Greek and Roman temples, grottoes, copies of antique statues, and such added delights as a rural cottage, a Chinese bridge, a Gothic spire, and a Turkish tent. In the view illustrated here, a replica of the Pantheon in Rome is just visible across a carefully placed lake. While the nostalgic evocation of an idyllic classical past recalls the work of the seventeenth-century French landscape painter Claude Lorrain, who had found a large market in Britain, the exotic elements here are an early indication of the Romantic taste for the strange and the novel. The garden is therefore an interesting mixture of the Neoclassical and the Romantic.

Another example of the British taste for the classical that helped lay the ground for Neoclassicism was the work of John Wood the Elder (c. 1704–1754), who dreamed of turning into a new Rome his native Bath—a spa town in the west near Wales, originally built by the Romans in the first century. On a large property near the town center, Wood began in 1727 to lay out a public meeting place, sports arena, and gymnasium. Much of his plan was never

26-18. John Wood the Elder and John Wood the Younger. The Circus, Bath, England. 1754–58

carried out, but in 1754 he began building the Circus (fig. 26-18), an elegant housing project that was completed in 1758 by his son, John Wood the Younger (d. 1782). The Circus was a circle of thirty-three town houses, all sharing a single three-story facade modeled on the exterior of the Roman Colosseum, with an attic to house the servants' quarters and steeply pitched roofs and large chimneys as a concession to English winters. The Woods' elegant Circus houses, with their handsome yet modestly scaled classical fronts, were imitated enthusiastically in London and other British and American cities well into the nineteenth century.

Neoclassicism

The most important British contribution to Neoclassicism was a style of interior decoration developed by the Scottish architect Robert Adam (1728–1792). On his Grand Tour in 1754–1758, during which he became a member of Albani's circle of Neoclassicists, Adam largely ignored the civic architecture that had interested British classicists such as Wood and Burlington and focused instead on the

applied ornament of Roman domestic architecture. When he returned to London to set up his architectural firm with his two younger brothers, he brought with him a complete inventory of such decorative motifs, which he then modified in pursuit of a picturesque elegance. His stated aim to "transfuse the beautiful spirit of antiquity with novelty and variety" met with considerable opposition from the Palladian architectural establishment, but it proved ideally suited both to the evolving taste of wealthy clients and to the imperial aspirations of the new king, George III, whose reign began in 1760. In 1761, George appointed Adam Joint Architect of His Majesty's Works.

Adam achieved worldwide fame for his interior renovations, such as those he carried out between 1760 and 1769 for the duke of Northumberland at his country estate, Syon, near London. The opulent colored marbles, gilded relief panels, classical statues, spirals, garlands, **rosettes**, and gilded moldings in the anteroom (fig. 26-19) are luxuriously profuse yet are restrained by the strong geometric order imposed on them and by the plain wall and ceiling surfaces. Adam's preference for bright pastel grounds and small-scale decorative

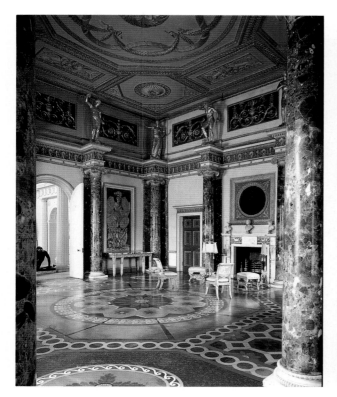

26-19. Robert Adam. Anteroom, Syon House, Middlesex, England. 1760–69

Adam's conviction that it was acceptable to modify details of the Classical orders was generally opposed by the British architectural establishment. As a result of that opposition, Adam was never elected to the Royal Academy.

26-20. Josiah Wedgwood. Vase, made at the Wedgwood Etruria factory, Staffordshire, England. 1786. White jasper body with a mid-blue dip and white relief, height 18" (45.7 cm). Relief of *The Apotheosis of Homer* by John Flaxman, Jr. 1778. Trustees of the Wedgwood Museum, Barlaston, Staffordshire

elements, both inheritances from the Rococo (see fig. 19-68), also helped lighten the effect.

Such interiors were designed partly as the appropriate settings for the art collections of British aristocrats, which included antiquities as well as a range of Neoclassical painting, sculpture, and decorative ware. The most successful producer of Neoclassical decorative art was Josiah Wedgwood (1730–1795). In 1768, near Newcastle, he opened a pottery factory called Etruria after the Etruscan civilization in central Italy believed to have produced the Greek pottery found in its graves. This production-line shop had several divisions, each with its own **kilns** (firing ovens) and workers trained in individual specialties. In 1774–1775, Wedgwood, who had training as a chemist, perfected a fine-grained, unglazed, colored pottery, which he called jasperware (see fig. 26-1). The most popular of his jasperware were those that featured white figures against a blue ground, like that in *The Apotheosis of Homer* (fig. 26-20). The vase was designed by John Flaxman, Jr. (1755–1826), who worked for Wedgwood from 1775 to 1787. Flaxman's scene of Homer being deified was based on a book illustration documenting the classical pottery collection of William Hamilton, a leading collector of antiquities and one of Wedgwood's major patrons. Flaxman's design simplified the original because of the prevailing idealized notion of Greek art and because of the demands of mass production.

Supported in part by Wedgwood (who wanted someone to help supervise the Roman draftspeople he was

26-21. John Flaxman, Jr. *Jupiter and Thetis*. Illustration for *The Iliad of Homer*, engraved by Thomas Piroli. First edition, Rome, 1793.

employing to copy antique friezes), Flaxman stayed in Rome from 1787 until 1794. While there, he devoted himself to sculpture and to illustrating classical literature. His drawings of scenes from Homer's *Odyssey* and *Iliad* were translated into engravings and published in 1793 as picture **folios**, usually with only a short description of the subject. In *Jupiter and Thetis* (fig. 26-21), from Homer's

26-22. Angelica Kauffmann. *Cornelia Pointing to Her Children as Her Treasures*. 1785. Oil on canvas, 40 x 50" (101.6 x 127 cm).
Virginia Museum of Fine Arts, Richmond, Virginia

The Adolph D. and Wilkins C. Williams Fund

In 1767, Kauffmann was briefly married to a man posing as the Swedish Count Frederic de Horn, later exposed as a fraud and a bigamist. She married the Venetian painter Antonio Zucchi in 1781 and returned to Italy, where her career continued to prosper under the patronage of the courts of Naples, Austria, and Russia.

story of the war between the Greeks and the Trojans, the mother of the Greek warrior Achilles is seen using her feminine charms to convince the god Jupiter to help her son. The figures are flattened in the front plane through bodily alignment and also through the utter simplicity of the artist's descriptive style. Modeling has been eliminated in favor of flat, graceful outline. The reductive clarity of Flaxman's graphic style, meant to reinforce Winckelmann's idyllic view of the enviable simplicity and beauty of early Greek life, was highly influential in the spread of Neoclassical taste.

The works of Adam, Wedgwood, and Flaxman were meant simply to be beautiful, to appeal to what the artists and their patrons considered a timeless and universal aesthetic sense. In Britain as elsewhere, another kind of Neoclassicism combined the beautiful with the good in order to teach lessons. The two types are fairly easy to distinguish because mythological subjects tended to be preferred by those interested strictly in beauty while

historical themes usually were favored by those with a moral concern. One of the leading Neoclassical history painters in Britain was Angelica Kauffmann (1741–1807). Born in Switzerland but trained in Italy, she was introduced to Neoclassicism by Winckelmann, whose portrait she painted in 1763. She was invited to England in 1766 by one of her wealthy British clients, and there she became a member of Reynolds's circle. In 1768, Kauffmann was one of two women artists among the founding members of the Royal Academy (see "Women and the Academies in the Eighteenth Century," page 937).

Because of her foreign birth and training, Kauffmann concentrated on the type of history painting that Reynolds advised her to undertake. A good example of her work is *Cornelia Pointing to Her Children as Her Treasures* (fig. 26-22). Like Vigée-Lebrun's *Portrait of Marie Antoinette with Her Children* (see fig. 26-7), this is a "good mother" painting. The work takes place in the second century BCE, during the Republican era of Rome. A

26-23. Benjamin West. *The Death of General Wolfe*. 1770. Oil on canvas, 4'11¹/₂" x 7' (1.51 x 2.14 m). The National Gallery of Canada, Ottawa

Gift of the Duke of Westminster, 1918

The famous Shakespearean actor David Garrick was so moved by this painting that he enacted an impromptu interpretation of the dying Wolfe in front of the work when it was exhibited by the Academy. The mid-eighteenth-century revival of interest in Shakespeare's more dramatic plays, in which Garrick played a leading role, was both a manifestation of and a major factor in the rise of a Romantic taste in Britain.

woman visitor has been showing Cornelia her jewels and then requests to see those of her hostess. In response, Cornelia turns to her two sons and states, *"These* are my jewels!" The lesson in motherhood is made stronger by the fact that under her loving care, the sons, Tiberius and Gaius Grachus, grew up to be political reformers. Although the setting of the work is as severely simple as the message, the effect of the whole is softened by the warm, subdued lighting and by the tranquil grace of the leading characters.

Romantic Painting

Kauffmann's devotion to Neoclassical history painting was at first shared by her American friend Benjamin West (1738–1820), who, after studying in Philadelphia, traveled to Rome in 1759. There he met Winckelmann and became a student of Mengs's (see fig. 26-13). In 1763, West moved permanently to London, where he specialized in Neo-

classical history paintings. In 1768, he became a founding member of the Royal Academy (see "Academies in the Eighteenth and Early Nineteenth Centuries," page 948). Two years later, he shocked Reynolds and his other academic friends with his painting *The Death of General Wolfe* (fig. 26-23) because he chose modern costumes for the event depicted. When Reynolds learned what West was planning to do, he begged him not to continue this aberration of taste. King George III informed West he would not buy a painting with British heroes in modern dress.

The painting shows an important event from the Seven Years War (1756–1763), whose main issue was the struggle between Britain and France for control of various overseas territories, including Canada. The decisive battle for Canada was fought at Quebec City in 1759. Although the British won, their leader, General James Wolfe, died just after receiving word that the French were in retreat. West offers the viewer a highly dramatized account of the event. Instead of showing Wolfe in a tent

ACADEMIES IN THE EIGTEENTH AND EARLY NINETEENTH CENTURIES

The most influential of the foreign academies to be inspired by the Florence Academy of Design was the French Academy, founded in 1648. Established under state control, the French Academy was organized to train students, to serve as a professional organization for its graduates, and to promote their work through exhibitions. These exhibitions, which did not begin on a regular basis until 1737, became known as **Salons** because they were held in the Salon d'Apollon (the Apollo Room) in the Palace of the Louvre. The engraving by Martini included here shows a view of the Salon of 1787.

In recognition of the importance of Rome, the French Academy established a branch there in 1666, where academicians and senior students could study. The model of the French Academy was eventually copied by most Western nations and by a number of provincial centers. Academies were established in Berlin in 1696, Dresden in 1750, London in 1768, Boston in 1780, New York in 1802, and Philadelphia in 1805.

Academic training, which had been established in the sixteenth century to free the artist from the restraints of guild training, became during the late eighteenth and nineteenth centuries the chief obstacle to change and the kind of independent thinking taught by Enlightenment philosophes and first practiced by the Romantics. The academic premise was that the principles of excellence found in the classical masters—both the ancients and their Renaissance followers such as Raphael—could be learned by systematic training of the mind and hand. In addition to learning the kinds of rules found in Reynolds's *Fifteen Discourses to the Royal Academy*, students studied from plaster casts of antique sculpture in order to absorb their lessons. Thus, when the student was finally allowed to work from the live model, he (women were not allowed to work from the nude) was expected to "correct" nature according to the higher conception of human form he had acquired. The student drawing by Edward Valentin illustrated here has been corrected by his teacher, Thomas Couture.

EXPOSITION AU SALON DU LOUVRE EN 1787.

Pietro Antonio Martini. *The Salon of 1787*. 1787. Engraving

Edward V. Valentin, with corrections by Thomas Couture. *Nude Study with Corrections*. 1860. Pencil and charcoal on laid paper, 24¼ x 18¼" (61.6 x 46.4 cm). Valentine Museum, Richmond, Virginia

Artists wishing to work according to their own standards of beauty and relevance increasingly came into conflict with the academies, especially in France. The history of French art from about 1830 to the end of the century is largely that of the struggle between the conservative forces of the Academy and the rebellious innovations of what became known as "the independents." The chief weapon employed by the Academy to keep artists in line was the officially appointed juries for the annual Salons. After 1830, these academic juries systematically rejected work that did not conform to its formal or thematic standards.

26-24. John Singleton Copley. *Watson and the Shark*. 1778. Oil on canvas, 6'1/2" x 7'61/4" (1.84 x 2.29 m). National Gallery of Art, Washington, D.C.
Ferdinand Lammot Belin Fund

surrounded by two or three attendants—as actually occurred—West chose to put him outdoors under a suitably dramatic sky. Beneath the flag that provides the apex of the asymmetrical triangular composition, West placed Wolfe at the center of an intensely concerned group of soldiers. For exotic interest and as an emblem of the natural, West added a Native American. The arrangement of the attendants and the posture of Wolfe were meant to suggest a kind of Lamentation over the dead Christ (see fig. 17-14). Just as Christ died for humanity, Wolfe sacrificed himself for the good of the State.

The work had such an emotional impact on the British public that Reynolds apologized to West, and the king was among four patrons to commission replicas. The work not only helped launch the Romantic movement in Britain but also established the general format for the depiction of contemporary historical events for all European artists in the years around 1800.

One of the first to profit from its lesson was another American, John Singleton Copley (see fig. 19-88). West had seen one of Copley's paintings at an exhibition in London in 1766 and had encouraged him to come to Europe, which Copley at first refused to do. But because of his British sympathies, Copley left Boston just before the War for Independence and settled permanently in London. There he developed a new, more elegant style of portraiture to suit the London market and set his sights on making a name for himself in the more prestigious arena of history painting. Following the success of West's *Death of General Wolfe*, Copley chose to work in a

Romantic vein. His initial and most famous painting of this type is *Watson and the Shark* (fig. 26-24), of 1778, which was a private commission to commemorate the escape of Brook Watson from a shark attack in the Havana Harbor. Although the painting employs a number of Neoclassical devices, including the pyramidal composition and the idealized nude treatment of Watson, it is anything but calm and sedate. Copley has attempted to maximize an emotional response by placing the viewer directly in front of the event at its most dramatic moment. As Watson's rescuers vainly reach for him, the ferocious shark, with teeth bared, moves in for the kill. Only the steady nerve and skill of the harpooner can save him, which, of course, happened. Like West's *Death of General Wolfe*, this painting offers several possible messages or meanings. As an example of style and spirit, it provides insight into the developing Romantic taste for emotional stimulation.

One of the earliest practitioners of a Romantic mode in Britain was Joseph Wright of Derby (1734–1797), who had trained as a portrait painter with Thomas Hudson, Reynolds's teacher. After Wright's Grand Tour of 1773–1775, he returned to the Midlands to paint its local society. Many of those he painted were the self-made entrepreneurs of the first wave of the Industrial Revolution, which was centered there in towns such as Birmingham. Wright was a member of the Lunar Society, a group of industrialists (including Wedgwood), mercantilists, and progressive nobles who met in Derby. As part of the society's attempts to popularize science, Wright painted a series of "enter-

26-25. Joseph Wright. *An Experiment on a Bird in the Air-Pump*. 1768. Oil on canvas, 6 x 8' (1.82 x 2.43 m). The National Gallery, London

26-26. George Stubbs. *Lion Attacking a Horse*. 1770. Oil on canvas, 40⅛ x 50¼" (102 x 128 cm). Yale University Art Gallery, New Haven, Connecticut
Gift of the Yale University Art Gallery Associates

primarily to study the property of gases, it was also widely used to promote the public's interest in science because of its dramatic possibilities. In the experiment shown here, air was pumped out of the large glass bowl until the small creature inside, a bird, collapsed from lack of oxygen; before the animal died, air was reintroduced by a simple mechanism at the top of the bowl. In front of an audience of adults and children, a lecturer is shown on the verge of reintroducing air into the glass receiver. Near the window at right, a boy stands ready to lower a cage when the bird revives. (The moon visible out the window is a reference to the Lunar Society.) By delaying the reintroduction of air, the scientist has created considerable suspense, as the reactions of the two girls indicate. Their father, a voice of reason, attempts to dispel their fears. The dramatic lighting not only underscores the life-and-death issue of the bird's fate but also suggests the fact that science brings light into a world of darkness and ignorance. The lighting adds a religious dimension as well. During the Baroque era, such intimate lighting effects had been used for religious scenes (see fig. 19-26). Here science replaces religion as the great light and hope of humanity. This theme is emphasized through the devout expressions of some of the observers.

taining" scenes of scientific experiments, including *An Experiment on a Bird in the Air-Pump* (fig. 26-25).

The air pump was one of the most innovative scientific developments of the eighteenth century (see "Iron as a Building Material," below). Although it was employed

IRON AS A BUILDING MATERIAL In 1779, Abraham Darby III built a bridge over the Severn River at Coalbrookdale in England. The bridge was a functional structure in the new industrial environment where factories and workers' housing filled the valley. The bridge's importance lies in the fact that it is the first use of structural metal on a large scale. Iron replaced the heavy, hand-cut, stone **voussoirs** used to construct earlier bridges. Five pairs of cast-iron, semicircular arches form a strong, economical hundred-foot span. Technology, the properties of the material, and engineering in large part determine form and often produce an unintended and revolutionary new aesthetic. The light, space, movement, and skeletal structure desired by builders since the twelfth century at last were possible.

26-27. John Henry Fuseli. *The Nightmare.* 1781. Oil on canvas, 39³/₄ x 49¹/₂" (101 x 127 cm). The Detroit Institute of Arts
Gift of Mr. and Mrs. Bert Smokler and Mr. and Mrs. Lawrence A. Fleischmann

Fuseli was not popular with the English critics. One writer said Fuseli's 1780 entry in the London Royal Academy exhibition "ought to be destroyed," and Horace Walpole called another painting in 1785 "shockingly mad, mad, mad, madder than ever." Even after achieving the highest official acknowledgment of his talents, Fuseli was called the Wild Swiss and Painter to the Devil. But the public appreciated his work, and *The Nightmare,* exhibited at the Academy in 1782, was repeated in at least six versions, all of which were sold to commercial engravers for reproduction in prints. One of these prints would one day hang in the office of the Austrian psychoanalyst Sigmund Freud, who believed that dreams were manifestations of the dreamer's repressed desires.

The assumption of Wright's *Experiment on a Bird in the Air-Pump,* and of the Industrial Revolution as a whole, was that nature is a passive and reasonable domain awaiting human understanding and control. But even before the events of the French Revolution of 1789 forced many to see the unreasonable character of humanity, a number of Romantic painters were already sensitive to the violent and hostile forces in nature. For the most part, these reminders were made more in the spirit of public entertainment than serious philosophical debate. Copley's *Watson and the Shark* is one example, as is *Lion Attacking a Horse* (fig. 26-26) by George Stubbs (1724–1806).

Another British painter who supported himself by painting portraits of British aristocrats—and their horses— Stubbs devoted his personal time to the dissection and study of horse anatomy. His studies appeared in *Anatomy of a Horse,* which he published in 1766. In order to augment his income, he produced a series of paintings and etchings of a horse being frightened or attacked by a lion. The first of these appeared in 1762. This violent motif is so uncharacteristic of his mild portraits and objective anatomical studies that it has been suggested that he actually witnessed such an attack during a trip to North Africa. But the theme was probably inspired by an ancient classical sculpture of a lion on the back of a horse, which he saw in Rome during his Grand Tour. The 1770 version shown here is one

of the most Romantic of his series because of the dramatic contrast between light and dark and because of the violent, stormy landscape. Given their place in Stubbs's career, such works seem designed to appeal to and profit from the emerging Romantic taste for high drama.

A more substantive objection to the ideas of the Enlightenment was made in the work of John Henry Fuseli (1741–1825). Born Johann Heinrich Füssli in Zurich, Switzerland, he was raised in an intellectual household where all things French, from the Rococo to the Enlightenment, were opposed. Instead of sensuality and rationality, those who gathered in his father's house celebrated intensity, originality, freedom of expression, and the imaginative power of the irrational. For their models of society and art, they looked to Britain. They were especially inspired by the contemporary emotional trend in British poetry and by the example of Shakespeare, whose dramatic plays were being revived there. It is not surprising that after studying between 1770 and 1778 in Rome—focusing on Michelangelo, not the ancients—Fuseli settled permanently in London and anglicized his name. At first, he supported himself as an illustrator and translator, including works by Shakespeare (into German) and Winckelmann (into English). By the early 1780s, he had begun to make a reputation as a Romantic painter of the irrational and the erotic with works such as *The Nightmare* (fig. 26-27).

26-28. William Blake. *Newton.* c. 1800(?). Color print. Tate Gallery, London

The Nightmare is not a pure fantasy but is inspired by a popular Swiss legend of the Incubus, who was believed to sit on the chest of virgins while they sleep, causing them to have distressing erotic nightmares. The content of this sleeper's dream is suggested by the way the "nightmare," on which the Incubus travels, breaks through the curtains of her room. This was the first of four versions of the theme Fuseli would paint, apparently for his own satisfaction. His motives are perhaps revealed by the portrait on the back of the canvas, which may be that of Anna Landolt. Fuseli had met her in Zurich in the winter of 1778–1779 and had fallen in love with her. After his proposal of marriage was rejected, he returned to London, where he wrote to her that she could not marry another because they had made love in one of his dreams and she therefore belonged to him. The painting may be a kind of illustration of that dream. Fuseli was a very short and unattractive man, not unlike the Incubus.

Fuseli's close friend William Blake (1757–1827), too, was opposed to the Enlightenment emphasis on reason. Blake enrolled briefly at the Royal Academy, where he was subjected to the teachings of Reynolds. The experience convinced him that all rules hinder rather than aid creativity, and he became a lifelong advocate of unfettered imagination. While imagination offered access to the higher realm of the spirit, reason could only provide information about the lower world of matter. Blake's point was explicitly made in *Newton* (fig. 26-28), which shows the father of the Enlightenment metaphorically submerged in the waters of materialism, cramped and looking down instead of up to the heavens, where our attention should be directed. In his hand, Newton holds a compass, a tool of narrow confinement, the very

26-29. Joseph Mallord William Turner. *The Fighting "Téméraire," Tugged to Her Last Berth to Be Broken Up.* 1838. Oil on canvas, 35¼ x 48" (89.5 x 121.9 cm). The National Gallery, London
Reproduced by Courtesy of the Trustees

antithesis of the imagination, which has no limits. In addition to such negative works, Blake illustrated his own poetry, using a free curvilinear style derived from Neoclassicism, which for him suggested the liberating power of the imagination.

Romanticism took a more pessimistic turn in the work of the leading figure of the next generation, Joseph Mallord William Turner (1775–1851). The son of a barber, Turner entered the Royal Academy in 1789. He exhibited his first work two years later. During the 1790s, he belonged to a circle of artists that included Thomas Girtin, who revolutionized the British **watercolor** tradition by rejecting underpainting and topographic accuracy (a standard that Canaletto had helped to establish) in favor of a freer application of paint on semiabsorbent paper and a concern for more generalized atmospheric effects. Shortly after 1800, Turner began to exhibit more ambitious, huge oil paintings that addressed grand natural and historical subjects.

One of Turner's favorite themes was "the course of empire," the inevitable death and decline that comes to all great national extensions, from Rome to Venice to Britain. Intimations of Britain's eventual fate are frequently found in Turner's work, including *The Fighting "Téméraire," Tugged to Her Last Berth to Be Broken Up* (fig. 26-29), of 1838. The *Téméraire*, originally a French vessel, had been the second-ranking British ship in the 1805 Battle of Trafalgar, a great naval victory over the combined fleets of Napoleonic France and Spain. Thirty-three years later, however, the advent of steam-driven paddle ships was making such great sailing ships obsolete. The majestic *Téméraire* is being pulled to her death by one of the new industrial tugboats. Although Turner may have been intending also to comment on the ugliness of the new industrial era, a subject much discussed at the time, primarily he saw the event as emblematic of another controversial topic of the period, the perceived decline of Britain's naval dominance. The blazing sunset in the rear, inspired by a combination of what Turner actually saw and the example of Claude Lorrain's work (see fig. 19-24), is therefore meant not only to record the passing of the great ship but also perhaps of British imperial dominion, which depended on sea supremacy, to foretell the decline.

GOTHIC REVIVAL ARCHITECTURE

The major manifestation of the Romantic spirit in architecture was the Gothic revival that began in Britain in the middle of the eighteenth century and spread to other nations after 1800. The movement was inaugurated by the taste of a single individual, the conservative politician and author Horace Walpole (1717–1797), who shortly before 1750 decided to remodel his house, called Strawberry Hill, in the Gothic manner (fig. 26-30). Gothic renovations were commonly performed in Britain before this date, but only to buildings that dated from the medieval period. Working with a number of friends and architects, Walpole spent nearly thirty years, from 1749 to 1776, transforming his home into a Gothic castle complete with **crenellated battlements**, **tracery** windows, and **turrets**.

26-30. Horace Walpole and others. Strawberry Hill, Twickenham, England. 1749–76

26-31. Horace Walpole, John Chute, and Richard Bentley. Library at Strawberry Hill. After 1754

The interior, too, was totally changed. One of the first rooms Walpole redesigned, with the help of amateurs John Chute and Richard Bentley, was the library (fig. 26-31). Here the three turned for inspiration to illustrations in the antiquarian books that the library would house. For the bookcases, they adapted designs from the old Saint Paul's Cathedral in London that had been destroyed in 1666. Prints of two medieval tombs were used for the chimneypiece. For the ceiling, Walpole incorporated a number of coats of arms of his ancestors—real and imaginary. The reference to fictional relatives offers a clue to Walpole's motives in choosing the medieval style. Walpole meant his house to suggest a castle out of the medievalizing Romantic fiction that he himself was writing. In 1764, he published *The Castle of Otranto*, a highly sensational novel set in the Middle Ages that helped launch the craze for the Gothic novel.

26-32. Charles Barry and Augustus Welby Northmore Pugin. Houses of Parliament, London, England. 1836–60. Royal Commission on the Historical Monuments of England, London

Pugin published two influential books in 1836 and 1841, in which he argued that the Gothic style of Westminster Abbey was the embodiment of true English genius. In his view, the Greek and Roman Classical orders were stone replications of earlier wooden forms and therefore fell short of the true principles of stone construction.

The most famous Gothic Revival buildings in Britain were the Houses of Parliament (fig. 26-32). After Parliament's Westminster Palace burned in 1834, the government opened a competition to design a new building. Entries were required to be in English Gothic not only to be consistent with Westminster Abbey, the thirteenth-century church where the monarchs of England are crowned and many are buried, but also because the British constitutional monarchy dates from the Gothic period. (The Magna Carta, which limited the powers of the king and established certain basic individual rights, was signed in 1215.) For the British, then, the Gothic style has important political connotations.

The commission was given to Charles Barry (1795–1860) and Augustus Welby Northmore Pugin (1812–1852). Barry was responsible for the basic plan of the buildings, while Pugin designed the Gothic decoration. In its basic symmetry, which is meant to suggest the balance of powers inherent in the British system, Barry's plan is classicizing. Pugin, however, was the leading advocate of Gothic architecture in his era. In 1836, he published *Contrasts*, which unfavorably compared the

26-33. Richard Upjohn. Trinity Church, New York City, 1839–46 troubled modern era of materialism and mechanization with the more idyllic Middle Ages, a period of deep spirituality and satisfying handcraft. The widespread popularity of Pugin's ideas led to ten church commissions in 1837–1838. For Pugin, Gothic was not a style but a principle, like classicism. The Gothic, he insisted, embodied two "great rules" of architecture: "first that there should be no features about a building which are not necessary for convenience, construction or propriety; second, that all ornament should consist of enrichment of the essential structure of the building" (from *The True Principles of Pointed or Christian Architecture,* London, 1841).

Although Pugin's principles were widely accepted by architects throughout the English-speaking world, Gothic was usually adopted for churches because of its religious associations. Its origins in Catholic France in the twelfth century led many architects to use it for Roman Catholic churches. But because the High Church of England and its affiliates, the Episcopal churches of Scotland and the United States, adopted Gothic, other architects also employed it, but exclusively for those denominations. The American architect Richard Upjohn (1802–1878), for example, would use the Gothic only for Episcopal commissions. Trinity Church in New York (fig. 26-33), for example, is in the early-fourteenth-century British Gothic style particularly dear to Anglicans and Episcopalians. Every detail is historically accurate, although the vault is plaster.

Nineteenth-century architects had to be able to work in a variety of historical modes, each of which was thought to have appropriate uses, depending on its historical associations. Thus, the **historicist** architect was expected to be able to build in any style and to guide clients in the proper choice of a style—for Congregationalists, for example, Upjohn used Early Christian or Romanesque styles.

FRANCE

During the seventeenth century, the French court had resisted the influence of the Italian Baroque and had opted instead for a classical style. Even during the Rococo period, the French Academy continued to advocate classical principles. As a result of these factors, French artists and architects of the late eighteenth century readily adopted the new classicism coming out of Italy. And because of their deep commitment to Neoclassicism, the French generally rejected the Romanticism arriving from England. Although a few French painters turned to Romanticism early in the nineteenth century, it was not adopted on a large scale until around 1830.

Neoclassical Architecture

French architects of the late eighteenth century generally considered classicism not one of many alternative styles but the single, true style. Such architects and their buildings may be divided into two broad types, what we might call the traditionalists and the radical visionaries.

Representative of the traditionalists are Jacques-Germain Soufflot (1713–1780) and his major accom-

26-34. Jacques-Germain Soufflot. Church of Sainte-Geneviève, Paris. 1755–92

This building, popularly known as the Paris Panthéon, has a strange history. Before it was completed, the revolutionary government in control of Paris confiscated all religious properties to raise desperately needed public funds. Instead of selling Sainte-Geneviève, however, they voted in 1791 to make it the Temple of Fame for the burial of Heroes of Liberty. Under Napoleon I, the building was resanctified as a Catholic church and was again used as such under King Louis Philippe (ruled 1830–1848) and Napoleon III (ruled 1852–1870). Then it was permanently designated a nondenominational lay temple. In 1851, the building was used as a physics laboratory. Here the French physicist Jean-Bernard Foucault suspended his now-famous pendulum on the interior of the high crossing dome and by measuring the path of the pendulum's swing proved his theory that Earth rotated on its axis in a clockwise motion. In 1995, the ashes of Marie Curie, who won the Nobel Prize for Chemistry in 1911, were moved into this "memorial to the great men of France," making her the first woman to be enshrined here for her accomplishments.

plishment, the Church of Sainte-Geneviève (fig. 26-34). In this building, Soufflot attempted to integrate three traditions: the kind of Roman architecture he had seen on his trip to Italy in 1749; French and English Baroque classicism; and the Palladian style being revived at the time in England. The facade, with its huge **portico**, is modeled directly on ancient Roman temples. The dome, on the other hand, was inspired by several seventeenth-century examples, including Wren's Saint Paul's in London (see fig. 19-61). Finally, the radical geometry of its

26-35. Jacques-Germain Soufflot. Plan and section of the Church of Sainte-Geneviève

26-36. Claude-Nicolas Ledoux. Bird's-eye view of the Town of Chaux (never built). Engraving, published 1804

plan (fig. 26-35), a **central-plan** Greek cross, owes as much to Burlington's Chiswick House (see fig. 26-16) as it does to Christian tradition. Soufflot also seems to have been inspired by the plain, undecorated surfaces Burlington used in his home (see fig. 26-15). The result is a building that attempts to maintain and develop the historical continuity of the classical tradition.

In the hands of the visionaries, however, classicism was stripped of its associations with the past and was remade as a vehicle of utopian Enlightenment aspirations—as can be seen in the mature work of Claude-Nicolas Ledoux (1736–1806). Early in his architectural career, Ledoux designed austere Neoclassical residences for the court of Louis XV and his last important mistress, Madame du Barry. During the 1770s and 1780s, inspired by the Enlightenment and supported by the progressive ideas of a number of government ministers, Ledoux turned his attention to town planning.

Ledoux's geometric plan for the city center of Chaux in southeastern France (fig. 26-36), which was never realized, organized a number of large private homes, a school, a church, an army barracks, two public baths, and various businesses around the city's two saltworks factories and their administrative headquarters, which occupy the very center. The different functions of the buildings are impossible to discern because all are in the same style—a stripped-down classicism. The applied decorations that to Ledoux indicated superfluous wealth were eliminated in favor of a more economical and egalitarian style. The plan indicates not only Ledoux's hopes for an orderly, homogenous, and rational future but also

26-37. Étienne-Louis Boullée. Exterior and cross section of the Cenotaph for Isaac Newton (never built). 1784. Ink and wash drawings, 15½ x 25½" (39.4 x 64.8 cm). Bibliothèque Nationale, Paris

his assumption that industry—not the surrounding farms or the peripheral institutions of Church and State—would provide the foundation for that better future.

The Enlightenment desire to understand first principles and to apply them for human betterment also motivated another visionary French architect, Étienne-Louis Boullée (1728–1799). For most of his career, Boullée had designed homes for French aristocrats in a plain, simple brand of Neoclassicism. In 1782, he retired from private practice to devote himself to teaching, writing architectural theory, and designing visionary public buildings. Grandiose projects such as the Cenotaph for Isaac Newton (fig. 26-37) were never meant to be built but rather were intended to illustrate and extend the influence of Boullée's theoretical ideas. By this point, Boullée had decided that copying and adapting classical designs were insufficient; architects needed to go beyond them in the use of the pure, geometric forms of nature. Although his burial monument for the great English scientist who had died in 1727 was inspired by round Roman tombs, which were stepped and planted with trees, Boullée used a formal vocabulary of simple spheres instead of the Classical orders. Appropriately, the monument was meant to suggest a planet set within a series of circular orbits.

Although the project was eminently rational—and was meant to be read as such—its chief function was to appeal to the emotions. Boullée believed that architecture should be "poetic," by which he meant that it should engender feelings appropriate to the building's purpose. Here the desired effect is **sublime**, an awesome, nearly terrifying experience of the infinite described in Edmund Burke's influential essay of 1757, *A Philosophical Enquiry into the Origin of Our Ideas of the Sublime and the Beautiful*. Such an effect would be produced when the spectator enters the cenotaph (tomb) and discovers a monumental space empty except for a small sarcophagus at lower center. The only light would come from small holes in the ceiling, meant to suggest stars in a night sky. Boullée wished the viewer to experience the overwhelming majesty not simply of the universe but also of the Supreme Being who had designed it.

Neoclassical Sculpture

The leading Neoclassical French sculptor was Jean-Antoine Houdon (1741–1828), who had studied with Pigalle (see fig. 26-9). Houdon lived in Italy between 1764 and 1768 after winning the **Prix de Rome**, the competitive five-year scholarship awarded to the top graduating students from the French Academy's art school in both painting and sculpture. Houdon's commitment to Neoclassicism began during his stay in Rome, where he came into contact with some of the leading artists and theorists of the movement.

Houdon, a specialist in portraiture, did busts and full-length views of many important figures of his era, including foreigners. On the basis of his bust of the American ambassador to France, Benjamin Franklin, Houdon was commissioned by the Virginia state legislature to do a portrait of its native son George Washington. Houdon

26-38. Jean-Antoine Houdon. *George Washington*. 1788–92. Marble, height 6'2" (1.9 m). State Capitol, Richmond, Virginia

traveled to the United States in 1785 to make a cast of Washington's features and a bust in plaster. He then executed a lifesize marble figure in Paris (fig. 26-38). For this work, Houdon combined Pigalle's naturalism with the new classicism that many were beginning to identify with republican politics. Although the military leader of the American Revolution of 1776 is dressed in his general's costume (Houdon also used classical dress, or undress, in his works), Washington's serene expression and relaxed contrapposto pose derive from sculpted images of classical athletes. Washington's left hand rests on a fasces, a bundle of rods tied together with an axe face, used in Roman times as a symbol of authority. The thirteen rods bound together are also a reference to the union formed by the original states. Attached to the fasces are a sword of war and a plowshare of peace. Houdon's studio turned out a regular supply of replicas of such works as part of the cult of great men promoted by Enlightenment thinkers as models for all humanity.

Neoclassical Painting

The leading French Neoclassical painter was Jacques-Louis David (1748–1825). David won the Prix de Rome in 1774 and spent the next six years there, assimilating the principles of Neoclassicism. After his return, he produced a series of severely undecorated, anti-Rococo paintings that extolled the antique virtues of stoicism, masculinity, and patriotism.

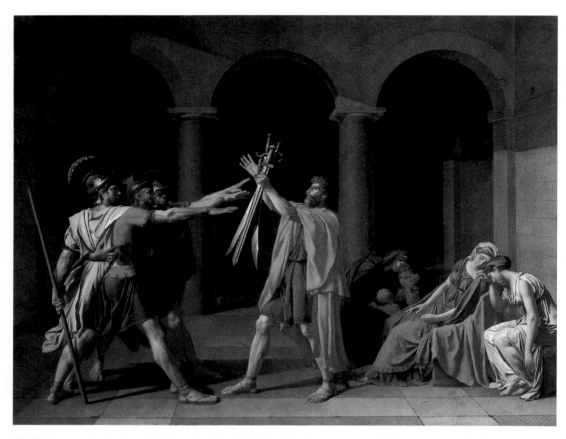

26-39. Jacques-Louis David. *Oath of the Horatii.* 1784–85. Oil on canvas, 10'8¼" x 14' (3.26 x 4.27 m). Musée du Louvre, Paris

26-40. Jacques-Louis David. *Death of Marat.* 1793. Oil on canvas, 5'5" x 4'2½" (1.65 x 1.28 m). Musées Royaux des Beaux-Arts de Belgique, Brussels

In 1793, David was elected as a deputy to the National Convention and was named propaganda minister and director of public festivals. Because he supported Robespierre and the Reign of Terror, he was jailed in 1794. His estranged wife succeeded in winning his early release, an event he memorialized in a painting of 1799 showing a group of women stopping the battle between the Romans and the Sabines.

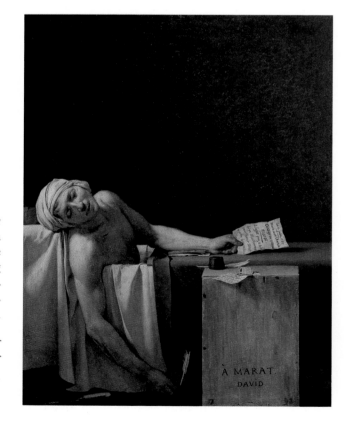

The first and most influential of these was the *Oath of the Horatii* (fig. 26-39), of 1784–1785, which was a royal commission. In general, the work reflects the taste and values of Louis XVI (ruled 1774–1792), who along with his minister of the arts, Count d'Angiviller, was sympathetic to the Enlightenment. Following Diderot's lead, d'Angiviller and the king believed art should improve public morals. Among his first official acts, d'Angiviller banned indecent nudity from the Salon of 1775 and commissioned a series of didactic paintings of French history. David's commission in 1784 was a part of that general program.

David's painting was inspired by Pierre Corneille's seventeenth-century drama *Horace*, although the specific incident David records seems to have been his own invention. The story deals with the early Republican

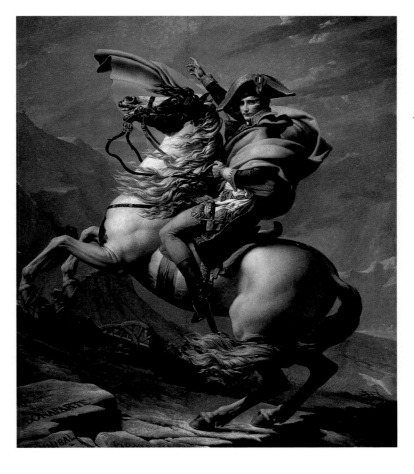

26-41. Jacques-Louis David. *Napoleon Crossing the Saint-Bernard*. 1800–01. Oil on canvas, 8'11" x 7'7" (2.7 x 2.3 m). Musée National du Château de la Malmaison, Rueil-Malmaison

period of Roman history. Rome and Alba, a neighboring city-state, had been at war for some time when it was decided to settle the conflict by a battle to the death between the three best soldiers of each side. The three sons of Horace (the Horatii) were chosen to represent Rome. In David's painting, they are shown with their father, pledging an oath to the State. In contrast to the upright, muscular angularity of the men are a group of limp and weeping women. The women are upset not simply because the Horatii might die but also because the Albans are related to them by marriage. Moreover, one of the Horatii is engaged to Camilla, one of the two Alban sisters at the far right. David meant to contrast what he considered the admirable willingness of the men to sacrifice themselves for the greater good of the State with the inability of the women to rise above their personal, selfish feelings.

David's *Oath* soon became an emblem of the French Revolution of 1789. Its harsh lesson in republican citizenship effectively captured the mood of the new leaders of the French state who came to power in 1793—especially the Jacobins, egalitarian democrats who engaged in terrorist acts, abolished the monarchy, and were responsible for the Reign of Terror in 1793–1794. Under the leadership of Robespierre, the Jacobin-dominated French Assembly ruthlessly executed all opponents, aristocratic or republican, for the greater good of the nation. More than 1,300 men and women died on the guillotine in the final six weeks of their rule.

In 1793, the Jacobins commissioned from David a tribute to one of their slain leaders, Jean-Paul Marat (fig. 26-40), a radical pamphleteer partly responsible for the 1792 riots that had killed hundreds of helpless prisoners. A young woman, Charlotte Corday d'Amont, decided that Marat should pay for his crime. Because Marat suffered from a painful skin ailment, he conducted his official business sitting in a medicinal bath. While Marat was signing a petition Corday had brought in order to gain entry to his office, she stabbed him, then dropped her knife and fled. Instead of handling the event as a Romantic might, David played down the drama and showed us its quiet, still aftermath. Here David combined his reductive Neoclassical style with a Caravaggesque naturalism. Both stylistically and thematically, the *Death of Marat* is, in fact, quite similar to Spanish Baroque religious paintings such as Zurbarán's *Saint Serapion* (see fig. 19-30). The two peaceful martyrs are descriptively convincing and are brought close to the picture plane to make their respective sacrifices tangibly real and accessible for their disciples.

The initial French Republic ended in 1799 when Napoleon Bonaparte, a popular and successful general, was named first consul and the government was reorganized under his absolute rule. David became his unofficial court painter. In the works he did for the ruler who would shortly be crowned emperor, David demonstrated that his commitments to Neoclassicism and republicanism were subsidiary to his patriotism.

One of these paintings is an idealized account of Napoleon leading his troops across the Alps into Italy in 1800 (fig. 26-41). Napoleon, who actually made the crossing on a donkey, is shown calmly astride a rearing,

26-42. Anne-Louis Girodet-Trioson. *Portrait of Jean-Baptiste Belley.* 1797. Oil on canvas, 5'2¹/₂" x 3'8¹/₂" (1.59 x 1.13 m). Musée National du Château de Versailles

excited horse, pointing to the summit and exhorting us to follow him. His windblown cloak, an extension of his arm, suggests that Napoleon directs the winds as well. David further flattered Napoleon by reminding the viewer of the two other great generals from history who had accomplished this difficult feat, Charlemagne and Hannibal. (The names of all three are etched in the rock in the lower left.) Stylistically, the work is Baroque. Instead of the classical pyramid of the *Oath of the Horatii*, David relied on the more dramatic diagonal used, for example, in equestrian portraits by Bernini.

David's Students

David was the leading force in French painting during the revolutionary and Napoleonic eras. Most of the important painters who emerged at this time were his students. The influence of his teachings is evident, for example, in the *Portrait of Jean-Baptiste Belley* (fig. 26-42) by Anne-Louis Girodet-Trioson (1767–1824). Although Girodet also painted mythological subjects in a mode derived from Canova (see fig. 26-14), which annoyed his teacher, this noncommissioned portrait is in keeping with David's early stylistic and thematic principles. Stylistically, the work combines a graceful sculptural pose with the kind of simplicity and descriptive naturalism found in David's *Marat*. The work also has a significant political dimension. Belley was a former slave sent by the colony of Saint-Dominique (now Haiti) as a representative to the French Republican Assembly. In 1794, he led the successful legislative campaign to

abolish slavery in the colonies and grant black people full citizenship. Belley leans casually on a pedestal with the bust of the abbot Guillaume Raynal (d. 1796), the French *philosophe* whose 1770 book condemning slavery had prepared the way for such legislation. Girodet's portrait is therefore more of a tribute to the egalitarian principles Raynal and Belley stood for than it is a conventional portrait meant to flatter a sitter. Unfortunately, in 1801 Napoleon reestablished slavery in the islands.

Most of David's students disappointed him by adapting his austere and didactic Neoclassicism to other ends. Jean-Auguste-Dominique Ingres (1780–1867), for example, turned his principles to the service of conventional masculine taste. Although Ingres fervently desired acceptance as a history painter, his elegant images of classical literature and his uninspired scenes of contemporary history were less successful than his erotically charged portraits of women and female nudes. Ingres's commitment to Raphael's polished conception of beauty (see fig. 18-14) was translated into a style of female portraiture that provided the basis of his successful career. Although he conceived of men as individuals, he portrayed women as variations of a type—beautiful, sensual, and interested in pleasing men.

A representative example of Ingres's female conception is *The Comtesse d'Haussonville* (fig. 26-43), a smooth-skinned young woman in fancy dress posed against a sideboard covered with a number of traditionally feminine items, including flowers and a pair of vases. The cool blues and smooth texture of her dress effectively highlight the warmth and graininess of her exposed skin. Furthermore, the angular folds in her dress play against the long, fluid curves of her arms, neck, and face. The degree to which this provocatively sensual woman is a product of the artist's taste is revealed in a comparison of the final painting with a preliminary sketch (fig. 26-44). In the drawing, her dress is more modest, covering both her arms and neck. Her face is narrower, less fleshy, and its expression is more serious. The erect head and stiff finger add considerably to our sense of her as absorbed in some weighty, substantive matter. In the painting, Ingres not only relaxed her body and softened her facial expression but also added a bow to her hair. What had been a plain, unattractive hairdo consistent with her severe appearance is now calculated to appeal to the men whose calling cards are piled discreetly behind her. The turned corners of these cards indicate that their owners will return another time. The prospect of male company now appears to occupy her thoughts.

The same beautiful and congenial companion appears in Ingres's numerous representations of the **odalisque**, a female slave or concubine in a sultan's harem. During Napoleon's campaigns against the British in North Africa, the French discovered the exotic Near East. Upper-middle-class European men were particularly attracted to the institution of the harem, partly as a reaction against the egalitarian demands of women of their class that had been unleashed by the French Revolution. (Labille-Guiard's petition for female equality in the Academy was symptomatic of these demands.)

26-43. Jean-Auguste-Dominique Ingres. *The Comtesse d'Haussonville*. Dated 1845. Oil on canvas, 51⁷⁄₈ x 36¹⁄₄" (131.8 x 92.1 cm). The Frick Collection, New York

This portrait was painted when the countess was twenty-four years old. A woman of learning, the countess later became a writer of historical romances based on the dramatic lives of Lord Byron, Marguerite de Valois, and the Irish revolutionary Robert Emmet.

26-44. Jean-Auguste-Dominique Ingres. Sketch for *The Comtesse d'Haussonville*. The Frick Collection, New York

26-45. Jean-Auguste-Dominique Ingres. *Large Odalisque*. 1814. Oil on canvas, approx. 35 x 64" (88.9 x 162.5 cm). Musée du Louvre, Paris

Ingres's first treatment, the *Large Odalisque* (fig. 26-45), was painted in Rome in 1814 for a woman, Queen Caroline of Naples, as a pendant to another Ingres nude in her collection (a sleeping woman now lost). The cool gaze this odalisque levels at her master, while turning her naked body away from what we assume is *his* gaze, makes her simultaneously erotic and aloof. The work features the same kinds of linear and textual counterpoint found in his later portrait of *The Comtesse d'Haussonville*. Again, the cool blues are meant to heighten the effect of warm skin while the tight angularity of the sheets nicely accentuates the languid, sensual contours of her form. Ingres repeatedly returned to the odalisque throughout his life. His last version, featuring his new, young wife, was painted at age eighty-two.

Ingres's commitment to fluid line and elegant postures was grounded in his Neoclassical training. Although he was the leading spokesperson of his period for the timeless, universal standards of classical art, his own work not only treated a number of Romantic themes, such as the odalisque, but also did so in a highly personal, almost Mannerist fashion. Here the elongation of the woman's back (she seems to have several extra vertebrae), the widening of her hip, and her tiny, boneless feet are not only anatomically incorrect but also difficult to explain even on purely aesthetic grounds.

Although Ingres sometimes came close to creating Romantic effects, it was another of David's students, Antoine-Jean Gros (1771–1835), who helped launch French Romanticism. Gros's major contribution to the Romantic movement is *Napoleon in the Plague House at Jaffa* (fig. 26-46), a commission from the man crowned

emperor in 1804, the year of its completion. The painting is an idealized account of an actual incident: During Napoleon's campaign against the Turks in 1799, bubonic plague broke out among his troops. Napoleon decided to quiet the fears of the healthy by visiting the sick and dying, who were housed and treated in a converted mosque. The general format of the painting, featuring a shallow stage and a series of arcades behind the main actors, is inspired by David's *Oath of the Horatii* (see fig. 26-39). The general effect is radically different, however, not simply because of the dramatic lighting and the wealth of distracting and emotionally stimulating elements, both exotic and horrific, but also because the main action is meant to incite veneration, not republican virtue. At the center of a small group of soldiers and a doctor, whose various reactions signal aspects of the event, Napoleon calmly reaches toward the sores of one of the victims. The decision to present Napoleon as a Christ-like figure healing the sick with his touch was consciously conceived by Napoleon's art advisers in order to promote an image of him as semidivine and to counteract the unflattering aftermath of the event: Two months later, Napoleon ordered the remaining sick to be poisoned.

Romantic Painting

Much to his later regret, Gros opened the way for other French Romantics, including Théodore Géricault (1791–1824). Géricault began his career painting Napoleonic military themes in a manner inspired by Gros. After a brief stay in 1816–1817 in Rome, where he discovered Michelangelo, Géricault returned to Paris determined to paint a

26-46. Antoine-Jean Gros. *Napoleon in the Plague House at Jaffa.* 1804. Oil on canvas, 17'5" x 23'7" (5.32 x 7.2 m). Musée du Louvre, Paris

26-47. Théodore Géricault. *Raft of the "Méduse."* 1818–19. Oil on canvas, 16'1" x 23'6" (4.9 x 7.16 m). Musée du Louvre, Paris

At the Salon of 1819, this painting was retitled *A Shipwreck Scene*, to avoid the politically inflammatory aspects of the event. Because the monarchy refused to buy the painting, Géricault took it on a two-year tour of England and Ireland, where he exhibited it commercially following the example pioneered by the American Copley in the 1780s. While in England, Géricault did a number of naturalistic lithographs recording London slum life. Géricault produced the first important artistic lithographs, a printmaking technique invented by a music publisher in 1798.

great contemporary history painting. After considering a number of options, he decided to treat the scandalous and sensational shipwreck of the *Méduse* (fig. 26-47). In 1816, the ship of colonists headed for Madagascar ran aground near its destination; its captain was an incompetent aristocrat appointed by the newly restored monarchy for political reasons. Because there were insufficient life-

boats, a raft was hastily built for 149 of the survivors. Too heavy to pull to shore, it was set adrift. When the raft was found thirteen days later, only 15 people remained alive, having survived their last few days on human flesh. Although Géricault considered depicting the cannibalism, he eventually decided to show the moment when the survivors first spotted their rescue ship. The painting of

26-48. Eugène Delacroix. *Scenes from the Massacre at Chios.* 1822–24. Oil on canvas, 13'10" x 11'7"
(4.22 x 3.53 m). Musée du Louvre, Paris

classical nude victims is organized on crossed diagonals. The diagonal beginning in the lower left and extending to the waving figures registers their rising hopes. The diagonal that begins with the dead man in the lower right and extends through the mast and billowing sail, however, directs our attention to a huge wave. Their rescue is not yet assured. The survivors remain tensely caught between salvation and damnation.

Although Géricault's painting registered a criticism of the new monarchy, its larger purpose was to express the artist's pessimistic conviction about the human condition. We are not, Géricault knew from his own experience, the rational heroes of Neoclassical art, in charge of our own fate, but a tiny boat tossed on the stormy seas of life. The metaphor became popular with other disillusioned Romantics of the period.

Eugène Delacroix (1798–1863), who modeled for the victim on the far left of the *Raft*, shared his older colleague's pessimism. He, too, tended to focus on victims and antiheroes. One of the first paintings he exhibited at the Salon was *Scenes from the Massacre at Chios* (fig. 26-48), an event even more terrible than the shipwreck of the *Méduse*. In January 1822, the Greeks began a struggle for independence against the Turks that aroused the sympathies of most Western Europeans. While returning from a naval defeat in April of that year, the Turkish fleet stopped at the peaceful island of Chios and took its revenge. About 20,000 of the 100,000 inhabitants were killed, and the rest were taken into slavery and sold in North Africa.

Delacroix's painting focuses on the exhausted victims, quietly and sadly awaiting their fate. Despite the fighting in the rear and the hint of Turkish brutality evi-

26-49. Eugène Delacroix. *Women of Algiers.* 1834. Oil on canvas, 5'10⁷/₈" x 7'6¹/₈" (1.8 x 2.29 m). Musée du Louvre, Paris

dent on the right, the painting is oddly tranquil and undramatic. As Delacroix himself insisted, the work is "beautiful." The horror of what we know is overcome by the beauty of what we see, an inventory of handsome and beautifully dressed men, women, and children. Even the Turk is visually appealing. Delacroix effectively translated the horrors of life into the beauty of art, a coping strategy also used by other Romantics in this era.

Although Delacroix focused on historical and literary scenes of dramatic conflict, he also did a number of paintings without narrative, including the *Women of Algiers* (fig. 26-49). In 1832, he accompanied the Count de Mornay's diplomatic mission to open relations with Morocco. Delacroix was enthralled with the brilliant color and dignified inhabitants of North Africa. Although he supported the liberal aims of the Revolution of 1830, his visit to Morocco seems to have stirred his more conservative side. His attraction to the country's patriarchal political and social system is evident in the *Women of Algiers*, which he painted from sketches made during a brief visit to a harem. Delacroix presents the three women and their black servant sequestered from men, lounging indolently in tranquil, drug-induced bliss. It is an image of passivity that countered the contemporaneous demands of many Parisian women for property reform, more equitable child-custody laws, and other egalitarian initiatives.

Romantic Sculpture

Because of the strength of the academic tradition in France, Romanticism did not gain general acceptance until after 1830. The July Revolution of that year established a moderate, constitutional monarchy under Louis-Philippe (the so-called July Monarchy, 1830–1848) and with it a new era of middle-class taste. The shift in French popular taste is most evident in sculpture, where a number of practitioners turned away from Neoclassical principles to more dramatic themes and approaches.

Shortly after the monarchy of Louis-Philippe was declared, the king's minister of the interior decided that it would be a useful act of national reconciliation to complete the triumphal arch on the Champs Elysée that Napoleon had begun in 1806. During the Restoration (1814–1830), there had been plans to convert it into a monarchist monument, but nothing came of them. The program designed by Louis-Philippe's minister was meant to appeal to all political factions. François Rude (1784–1855), a former Neoclassicist, received one of the four commissions to decorate the main arcade. He was assigned to commemorate the volunteer army that had halted a Prussian invasion in 1792–1793, which had aimed to restore the rule of Louis XVI. Beneath the violent exhortations of the winged figure of Liberty, the volunteers surge forward, some nude, some in classical

26-50. François Rude. *Departure of the Volunteers of 1792 (The Marseillaise).* 1833–36. Limestone, height approx. 42' (12.8 m). Arc de Triomphe, Place de l'Étoile, Paris

26-51. Antoine-Louis Barye. *Python Crushing an African Horseman.* 1845. Bronze, height 9" (22.8 cm). The Baltimore Museum of Art
George A. Lucas Collection

armor (fig. 26-50). Despite such Neoclassical elements, the effect is Romantic. The crowded, excited grouping so stirred the patriotism of French spectators that it quickly became known as *The Marseillaise*, the name of the French national anthem written in the same year, 1792.

Another popular Romantic sculptor to emerge at the beginning of the July Monarchy was Antoine-Louis Barye (1796–1875), who specialized in the kind of scenes of violent animal combat that Stubbs had introduced in Britain more than a half century earlier (see fig. 26-26). In addition to large works for wealthy patrons, including the king, Barye's studio inaugurated the production of small, relatively inexpensive replicas for the middle-class market such as the 9-by-10-inch *Python Crushing an African Horseman* (fig. 26-51). Such unlikely scenes of exotic violence apparently helped relieve the boredom of ordinary life and may have contributed to the popular view that nature was filled with hostile forces that required human control.

GERMANY

Before unification in 1871, the dominant German state, both politically and culturally, was Prussia. While Neoclassicism tended to dominate its official architecture, Romanticism characterized its art and literature. Prussia's most famous Neoclassical monument is the Brandenburg Gate (fig. 26-52), commissioned by King Frederick William II (ruled 1786–1797) as an entrance to one of the main boulevards of his capital, Berlin. The royal architect Karl Gotthard Langhans (1732–1808) chose as his model the Propylaia, the Doric gateway to the Acropolis in Athens, built in the fifth cen-

tury BCE as an expression of the city's civilized values. The choice was meant to flatter the king's sense of himself as a philosopher-king. In addition to its associations, Langhans and his patron considered the Doric the most masculine of the orders, a quality Langhans enhanced through increased scale and heavier proportions. Langhans's severe Doric style persisted well into the nineteenth century and was a major influence on the formation of Hitler's official architecture for the Third Reich.

The Prussian emphasis on manly virtues was part of the emerging nationalist debate about the essential qualities of the German mentality. German writers and artists hoped to promote the eventual union of the many German states by identifying and cultivating a common set of tendencies and values. Religious piety was considered by many to be particularly German, partly because of the region's medieval heritage and partly in contrast to the rationalism identified with French philosophes. In keeping with the Enlightenment focus on nature, however, German Romantics committed to advancing this national feeling, such as the painter Caspar David Friedrich (1774–1840), felt that God was manifest in the landscape.

Friedrich, who was born on the Baltic coast and trained in a descriptive topographic style brought to Germany by Italian *vedute* painters (see fig. 26-10), believed that art was the ideal mediator between the divinity in nature and the individual. One of his early religious paintings was *Monk by the Sea* (fig. 26-53), which was painted in 1809–1810, during the painful Napoleonic occupation of northern Germany. The work shows a single monk on a desolate beach looking out over the cold Baltic Sea. The figure is shown from the rear in order to make us identify with him and his lonely quest to be at one with the infinite space of the universe. Friedrich makes us experience that sublime space through the tiny scale of the monk and by the absence of framing elements and the opening of the back and sides of his painting. Although our quest for a clear vision of the divine is frustrated by the fog, the morning sun might soon dispel it. The hopeful but uncertain and still gloomy effect Friedrich chose to create here was meant to refer both to the national mood under the occupation and to his own, a result of the recent death of his father.

26-52. Karl Gotthard Langhans. Brandenburg Gate, Berlin. 1788–91

26-53. Caspar David Friedrich. *Monk by the Sea*. 1809–10. Oil on canvas, 43³/₈ x 67¹/₂" (110 x 171.5 cm). Schloss Charlottenberg, Berlin

Friedrich suffered a number of personal tragedies early in his life that even he admitted colored his work. When he was seven, his mother died. The following year, one of his sisters died; five years later, his older brother drowned while saving Caspar, who had fallen through the ice while skating; and another sister died two years later.

SPAIN Neoclassicism had little impact on Spanish art and architecture of the late eighteenth century, despite the presence of Mengs (see fig. 26-13) as court painter to Charles III in the 1770s. Spain produced one major Romantic painter, however: Francisco Goya y Lucientes (1746–1828).

After an early career painting charming Rococo-ish scenes to be used as tapestry designs, Goya moved on to portraiture. In 1786, he was appointed one of the court painters; thirteen years later, he was named Principal Painter to the King. Goya's chief inspiration came not from contemporary European developments but from Velázquez, the great seventeenth-century court painter. Velázquez's influence is openly acknowledged in Goya's *Family of Charles IV* (fig. 26-54), which is based on Velázquez's *Las Meninas* (see fig. 19-34). By placing him-

26-54. Francisco Goya. *Family of Charles IV.* 1800. Oil on canvas, 9'2" x 11' (2.79 x 3.36 m). Museo del Prado, Madrid

self behind the easel on the left, just as Velázquez had done, Goya suggests his desire to emulate his predecessor, a suggestion confirmed in Goya's dazzling paint handling.

Unlike Velázquez's painting, however, Goya's is realistic rather than flattering. This has led to the painting's being seen as a cruel exposé of the royal family as a common, ugly and even inept group of people. Considering Goya's position at the court at the time and of the royal commission, it is difficult to imagine the artist deliberately mocking his most important patron. In fact, Goya made preparatory sketches for the painting, and the family seems to have consented to his rendering of their faces. The viewers who first saw the painting in 1800 would have found it striking not because they believed it to be demeaning, but because its candid representation was refreshingly modern.

Goya belonged to a small but influential circle of Madrid intellectuals that subscribed to the liberal ideals of the French philosophes. Charles III (ruled 1759–1788) had been very sympathetic to their ideas and had inaugurated a number of important reforms, including measures to promote industry, scholarships for study abroad, and the curbing of the power of the Church—especially its Holy Office of the Inquisition. After the chilling events of the early years of the French Revolution, however,

Charles IV reinstituted the Inquisition, stopped most of the French-inspired reforms, and even halted the entry of French books into Spain.

Goya responded to the new situation with *Los Caprichos* (*The Caprices*), which he produced between 1796 and 1798. The meaning of the whole is suggested by the work Goya first intended to use as the **frontispiece** to the folio of eighty etchings, *The Sleep of Reason Produces Monsters* (fig. 26-55). The print shows a personification of Reason having fallen asleep. Behind him are the dark creatures of the night—owls and bats—that are let loose when Reason sleeps. The rest of the etchings enumerate the specific follies of Spanish life that Goya and his circle considered monstrous. The point of the series is didactic, to show Spanish people the errors of their ways, thus reawakening the reason that had guided the policies of Charles III. Although the premise of the series is hopeful, Goya's portrait of human folly and cruelty is very disturbing and suggests he was already beginning to feel a certain despair.

Before his final pessimism took possession of his mind and his work around 1820, Goya made a last effort to awaken Spanish reason in a series of works on war that he produced at the end of the Napoleonic War of 1808–1814. In 1808 Napoleon conquered Spain and placed on its throne his brother Joseph Bonaparte. Many Spanish citi-

26-55. Francisco Goya. *The Sleep of Reason Produces Monsters*, No. 43 from *Los Caprichos* (*The Caprices*). 1796–98. Etching and aquatint, 8¹/₂ x 6" (21.6 x 15.2 cm). Published 1799. The Hispanic Society of America, New York

After printing about 300 sets of this series, Goya offered them for sale in 1799. He withdrew them from sale two days later without explanation. Historians believe that he was probably warned by the Church that if he did not do so he might have to appear before the Inquisition because of his unflattering portrayal of the Church in some of the etchings. In 1803, Goya donated the plates to the Royal Printing Office.

zens, including Goya, welcomed the French because of the liberal reforms they inaugurated, including a new, more liberal constitution. On May 2, 1808, however, a rumor spread in Madrid that the French planned to kill the royal family. The populace rose up, and a day of bloody street fighting ensued. Hundreds of Spanish people were taken to a convent and executed the following morning. The fighting soon spread to the countryside, and for the next six years the Spanish conducted the first guerrilla warfare. After the war, Goya made a series of etchings documenting the atrocities on both sides and a pair of paintings to commemorate the events of May 2 and May 3.

The more famous of the two paintings shows a French firing squad executing helpless Spanish prisoners in the predawn hours of May 3 (fig. 26-56). Like Delacroix's

26-56. Francisco Goya. *Third of May, 1808.* 1814–15. Oil on canvas, 8'9" x 13'4" (2.67 x 4.06 m). Museo del Prado, Madrid

Massacre at Chios (see fig. 26-48), the work focuses on victims and antiheroes. It is not meant to be beautiful, however, but horrible. Goya emphasizes the brutality through the bloody corpses of those just killed. The work is less an indictment of the French than of the faceless and mechanical forces of war itself, blindly killing a representative sampling of humanity, which features a Christ-like figure in white. When asked why he painted such a brutal scene, Goya responded: "To warn men never to do it again." Unfortunately, soon after the Spanish monarchy was restored, it abolished the new constitution and reinstated the Inquisition, which the French had banned. Goya gave up all hope in human progress and retired to his home outside Madrid, where he gave vent to his disillusionment in the "black" paintings he did on its walls.

THE UNITED STATES

American art and architecture of the late eighteenth and early nineteenth centuries were largely dependent on European examples. The one area of major difference was painting. Although a number of American painters wanted to paint in an elevated Neoclassical style, the American public showed little interest in such works. They preferred naturalism, which they considered more democratic because it did not require special knowledge or training to understand.

Neoclassical Architecture and Sculpture

In the period after the War for Independence, called the Federal Period (1783–1830), Neoclassicism dominated American architecture. Despite the recent hostilities with Britain, American domestic architecture remained tied to developments in that country. With regard to interior design, the elegant Neoclassicism that Robert Adam had introduced to British society in the 1760s (see fig. 26-19) became the model for American designers such as John Rawlins and Richard Thorpe. In 1786–1787, they designed the large dining room at George Washington's home, Mount Vernon (fig. 26-57). As Adam himself had

often done, Rawlins and Thorpe set delicate offwhite beadwork against a soft, monochromatic ground. Beneath a simple, classical cornice is the main decorative feature of the room, a Palladian or triumphal-arch window. Its pilasters are decorated with a design of modified Roman lamps. The overall effect is restrained, elegant, and restful.

Thomas Jefferson (1743–1826), principal author of the Declaration of Independence, designed his residence, Monticello, in a style much influenced by British examples. Jefferson was a self-taught architect who in the period before the American Revolution shared the British aristocratic taste for Palladio (see fig. 18-37). His first version of Monticello, built in the 1770s, was based on a design in Palladio's *Four Books on Architecture*.

In 1785, Jefferson went to Paris as the American minister to France. There he discovered an elegant domestic architecture that made his home seem crude and provincial. When he returned in 1793, he completely redesigned Monticello (fig. 26-58) using French doors and tall narrow windows. Attempting to make his home appear to be a single story, in the French manner, he used a balustrade above the unifying cornice to mask the second floor. Despite these French elements and his stated rejection of the British Palladian mode, the building's simplicity and combination of temple front and dome remain closer to Burlington's Chiswick House (see fig. 26-15) than to contemporary French buildings. Compared with Burlington's residence, however, Jefferson's is less pretentious as a result of its humbler building materials, its closer relation to the ground, and its smaller scale.

Jefferson was less concerned with a building style's historical associations than with its aesthetic appeal. During his first year in Paris, he was asked by the Virginia legislature to produce a design for the new state capitol (fig. 26-59). He chose as his model the Maison Carrée in Nîmes, a Roman temple built in the second century BCE. Jefferson chose the building without regard for its republican associations but simply because he considered it, as he said in a letter to James Madison, "the most beautiful and precious morsel of architecture left us by antiquity" (quoted in Koch and Peden, page 380). In the same letter, he explained that his choice was guided by a desire "to improve the taste of my countrymen, to increase their reputation, to [gain for] them the respect of the world, and procure [for] them its praise."

During his presidency (1801–1809), Jefferson was involved in planning the U.S. Capitol. William Thornton, an amateur architect, had won an open competition to design the Capitol in 1792. His monumental plan featured a large dome over a temple front flanked by two large wings to accommodate the House of Representatives and the Senate. The three-story, balustraded wings, set on a rusticated ground floor, were based on French seventeenth-century models, including Versailles (see fig. 19-21). In 1803, Jefferson hired a British-trained professional, Benjamin Henry Latrobe (1764–1820), to oversee the actual construction. After the building was gutted by the British in the War of 1812, Latrobe repaired the wings, designed a new dome, and built a new stairway entrance on the model of Roman temples (fig. 26-60).

26-57. John Rawlins and Richard Thorpe. Large dining room, Mount Vernon, Fairfax County, Virginia. 1786–87

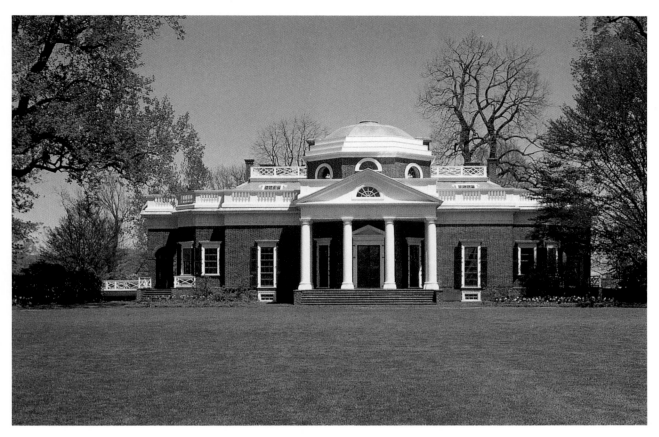

26-58. Thomas Jefferson. Monticello, Charlottesville, Virginia. 1770–84, 1796–1806

26-59. Thomas Jefferson. Virginia State Capitol, Richmond, Virginia. 1785–89

26-60. Benjamin Henry Latrobe. U.S. Capitol, Washington, D.C. c. 1808. Engraving by T. Sutherland, 1825. New York Public Library
I. N. Phelps Stokes Collection

In the interior, Latrobe created a variation on the Corinthian order by substituting indigenous plants, corn (fig. 26-61), and tobacco for the acanthus leaves. Latrobe was determined to find new symbolic forms for the nation within the traditional classical vocabulary. Latrobe resigned as supervisor of public buildings in 1817, and the Capitol reconstruction was completed under Charles Bullfinch. By 1850, the U.S. Congress had grown to 62

senators and 232 representatives, and a major renovation of the Capitol was undertaken that brought the building closer to its present form.

Neoclassicism also provided the dominant vocabulary for American sculpture in this period. After the Revolution, the demand for monumental sculpture in marble and bronze grew significantly in the United States. At first, patrons looked to European Neoclassicists, such as

26-61. Benjamin Henry Latrobe. U.S. Capitol. Corncob capital sculpted by Giuseppe Franzoni, 1809

Canova (see fig. 26-14) and Houdon (see fig. 26-38), but they soon turned to Americans trained abroad. Italy was the wellspring of Neoclassical inspiration in sculpture, as it was in painting, and it was also the source of the materials and skilled workers needed to assist in the execution of large commissions, especially in marble. The first American sculpture students began arriving in Italy around 1825, and by the 1840s they were flocking to the American artists' colonies in Florence and Rome. (After visiting the American sculptors' colony in Rome, Nathaniel Hawthorne made them the protagonists in his novel *The Marble Faun*, published in 1860.)

The most famous American Neoclassicist of his generation was Hiram Powers (1805–1873), who called himself the "Yankee stonecutter." Powers was raised in Cincinnati, Ohio, where as a young man he repaired life-size wax figures for the historical displays at the Western Museum. Encouraged by some of his associates, Powers began formal training with a local sculptor. A Cincinnati art patron then paid Powers's way to Europe to study, and he settled permanently in Florence in 1837.

26-62. Hiram Powers. *The Greek Slave*. 1843. Marble, height 5'5½" (1.68 m). Yale University Art Gallery, New Haven, Connecticut
Olive Louise Dann Fund

In the time-honored tradition, the creation of a large marble statue was rarely carried through from beginning to end by the artist who conceived it. By delegating the more time-consuming processes of execution to specialists, artists were able to accept and carry out more commissions, including replicas of popular works. *The Greek Slave* exists in seven authentic versions produced in Powers's Florence workshop. This statue put Powers in such demand that he was able to charge the then-unheard-of price of $4,000 for each of its six replicas. Unlike many artists, Powers earned a reputation as a hardheaded businessperson; when his patrons did not pay for their portrait busts, he would display them on a shelf in his shop under a large sign saying "Delinquent."

In 1843, Powers created the work that gained him an international reputation, *The Greek Slave* (fig. 26-62). Neoclassical in form, the work's content is Romantic. Inspired by the Greeks' struggle for independence against the Turks and by the accounts of Greek atrocities such as Delacroix recorded in his *Massacre at Chios* (see fig. 26-48), the sculpture portrays a beautiful Greek captive put up for sale in a Turkish slave market. According to Powers's written description, "she stands exposed to the gaze of the people she abhors, and awaits her fate with intense anxiety, tem-

26-63. Thomas Cole. *The Oxbow*. 1836. Oil on canvas, 51¹/₂ x 76" (1.31 x 1.94 m). The Metropolitan Museum of Art, New York
Gift of Mrs. Russell Sage, 1908 (08.228)

pered indeed by the support of her reliance on the goodness of God" (*Nineteenth-Century America: Paintings and Sculpture*, no. 57). The first nude by an American sculptor, the work was banned in Boston. In a pamphlet that eventually accompanied the work—which included approving remarks of London critics and some Cincinnati clergy—Powers explained that it was "not her person but her spirit that stands exposed." The work was privately exhibited in London in 1845 and then in New York the following year, where long lines of people paid 25 cents to view it. It gained international fame when it was exhibited in the American section of the first World Exposition, held in London's Crystal Palace in 1851 (see Chapter 27). Orders for copies poured in, and miniatures in plaster, marble, and china decorated many American mantels.

Romantic Painting

Except for some of the early work of Benjamin West and a handful of other expatriates, America produced little Neoclassical painting. Americans were more interested in the future than in the historical past, especially a classical one. Naturalism was more satisfying to the national taste and more appropriate to its politics and certain of its interests, while Romanticism suited its wild landscapes and the story of their conquest. American painting throughout this period and the later nineteenth century embodies the coexistence of these two traditions.

America's foremost Romantic landscape painter in the first half of the nineteenth century was Thomas Cole (1801–1848), called in his own time the father of American

landscape painting. He emigrated from England at seventeen and by 1820 was working as an itinerant **limner**, or portrait painter, walking through the countryside around New York City with his paints and brushes on his back, finding commissions where he could. On these trips Cole began to sketch and paint the landscape, which quickly became his chief interest, and his views of upstate New York launched what became known as the Hudson River School. Financed with the help of a patron, Cole traveled to Europe from 1829 to 1831. In England, he was impressed with Turner's landscapes (see fig. 26-29). After seeing the ruins of classical antiquity in Italy, he turned to a subject that also preoccupied Turner: the course of empire.

While engaged in the mid-1830s in painting his epic account of the same landscape from its primeval state through its architectural peak under the Roman Empire to its final state of desolation, Cole took occasional breaks to go on sketching trips. One trip resulted in a painting now called *The Oxbow* (fig. 26-63), which Cole made expressly for sale. Cole considered it one of his "view" paintings, which were ordinarily modest in size, but this one is monumental—because it was the only canvas he had on hand. The size effectively suits the theme, however, which is a dramatic view from the top of Mount Holyoke in western Massachusetts across a spectacular oxbow-shape bend in the Connecticut River. To Cole, such ancient geological formations constituted America's "antiquities." Along a great sweeping arc produced by the departing dark clouds and the edge of the mountain, Cole contrasts the two sides of the American landscape, its dense, stormy wilderness and its congenial, pastoral valleys. The fading storm suggests

26-64. John James Audubon. *Common Grackle,* for *The Birds of America.* 1826–39. Watercolor, graphite, and selective glazing, 23⅞ x 18½" (61.22 x 47.44 cm). Collection of the New-York Historical Society, New York City

To create Audubon's *The Birds of America* (1826–1839), his watercolors, like this one of grackles, were copied by the London printmaker Robert Havell using the aquatint process. Broad areas of neutral color were inked on the plates and the rest added by hand on the prints themselves. This bird encyclopedia was Audubon's first successful business venture. The cost to him of the first issue was $100,000, and 2,000 sets were eventually sold at $1,000 each. Between 1840 and 1844, before his health and eyesight began to fail, he supervised the production of *Birds* with reduced-size illustrations.

that the wild will eventually give way to the tame and the civilized. Given Cole's current interest in the course of empire, however, he probably saw this development as merely an early phase of a larger, eventually tragic cycle.

Naturalistic Painting

The civilizing of the American landscape was conducted with the aid of a native brand of naturalistic painting. Before the advent of photography, artists played an important role in the development of knowledge about the natural world. One of America's most celebrated scientific naturalists was John James Audubon (1785–1851), who was born in what is now Haiti and raised in France. In 1803, Audubon was sent to the United States to manage his father's Pennsylvania estate, where he spent most of his time hunting, drawing animals and birds, and collecting ornithological specimens. By 1820, he had embarked on his life's ambition, "to complete a collection of drawings of the Birds of our country, from Nature . . . and to acquire . . . a knowledge of their habitats and residences"

26-65. George Catlin. *Buffalo Bull's Back Fat, Head Chief, Blood Tribe.* 1832. Oil on canvas, 29 x 24" (73.7 x 60.9 cm). National Museum of American Art, Smithsonian Institution, Washington, D.C.

(*Nineteenth-Century America: Paintings and Sculpture*, no. 33). In order to support the publication of his *Birds of America* (completed in 1839), Audubon made paintings after his drawings, which he sold to private collectors. In *Common Grackle* (fig. 26-64), the birds are closely observed and set into their natural habitat, assaulting an ear of corn. The work is the combination of watercolor and drawing that Audubon preferred because of its greater accuracy. Such concerns for conveying information were combined with an effective sense of artistic design—the two grackles are nicely set on opposing diagonals—which raised his work above mere illustration.

Audubon's counterpart in the anthropological field was George Catlin (1796–1872). After a brief law career, Catlin taught himself art and established himself in Philadelphia as a portraitist. Inspired by the eastern visit of a delegation of Native American chiefs, Catlin moved in 1830 to St. Louis, then a frontier city. Over the next six years, he made five extended trips west of the Mississippi to study the life and customs of the Plains peoples. In 1837, he assembled an exhibition, entitled *Gallery of Indians*, which included 200 scenes of Native American village life and hunting forays, 310 portraits of chiefs, and a collection of Native American art and artifacts. The exhibition toured the eastern United States before moving on to London and Paris, where it was better received. Unable during his lifetime to interest the U.S. government in the purchase of his work for a national museum, Catlin's hopes were realized seven years after his death when his life's work was bought for the Smithsonian Institution.

In contrast to the unflattering image of Native Amer-

26-66. George Caleb
Bingham.
*Fur Traders
Descending the
Missouri.*
c. 1845. Oil
on canvas,
29 x 36"
(73.7 x 91.4 cm).
The Metropolitan
Museum of Art,
New York
Morris K. Jesup
Fund, 1933

icans as bloodthirsty barbarians evident in the work of some of his contemporaries, Catlin's portraits, such as *Buffalo Bull's Back Fat, Head Chief, Blood Tribe* (fig. 26-65), are restrained, dignified, and proud. The title is Catlin's translation of this Blackfoot chief's name, which refers to the hump of fat on a male buffalo's back. In a realistic style similar to Audubon's, Catlin described in his notes how the man's deerskin costume was made and decorated. The seams on the sleeves were covered from shoulder to wrist with decorations in porcupine quills and a fringe of black human hair taken from the heads of his enemies. The pipe, made by the chief himself, had a carved red-stone bowl and a long stem wrapped with braided porcupine quills. Used in friendship ceremonies, the pipe suggests the chief's peaceful intentions.

A carefully descriptive style was also employed for the most popular form of American painting during this period, the idyllic scenes of ordinary American life produced by artists such as George Caleb Bingham (1811–1879). Born in Missouri but trained at the Pennsylvania Academy of Fine Arts, Bingham first tried his hand at portrait painting. In 1844, he returned to Missouri and began to record scenes of the life of the traders and boatmen who traveled the Mississippi and its tributaries. In the following year, he began an association with the newly formed American Art-Union in New York. As a way to promote American painters, the union purchased works for a flat fee, then reproduced engraved prints after them to be sold by subscription. A lottery was held for the paintings themselves, which allowed ordinary Americans to own original works of art. *Fur Traders Descending the Missouri* (fig. 26-66) was the first of the works he sold to the union, for $25.

Originally titled *French Trapper and His Halfbreed Son*, the work shows the two trappers with their pet bear cub in

26-67. William Sidney Mount. *Eel Spearing at Setauket.* 1845. Oil on canvas, 28½ x 36" (72.4 x 91.4 cm). New York State Historical Association, Cooperstown, New York

a dugout canoe, gliding peacefully through the early morning stillness. As indicated by the ripples around the tree stump in the foreground, the current beneath the almost glassy surface of the water quietly and effortlessly propels them. Their happy bliss is recorded on the face of the son. Behind them, the still-hidden sun tinges the morning mist a beautiful rosy hue to match the young man's mood. The only ominous note is struck by the mysterious shape of the chained bear, but even this turns out to be a reassuring image of human control of the wild, hostile forces of nature.

At the same time Bingham was painting his idyllic image of life on the frontier, William Sidney Mount (1807–1868) was producing on the eastern seaboard a very similar image of two figures in a boat, *Eel Spearing at Setauket* (fig. 26-67). Mount began his career painting

26-68. John Constable.
The White Horse.
1819. Oil on canvas,
4'3¾" x 6'2⅛"
(1.31 x 1.88 m).
The Frick Collection,
New York

signs in New York. After attending classes at the newly founded National Academy of Design in the mid-1820s, he attempted to paint biblical themes in the Grand Manner. Realizing that he disliked both such subjects and city life, he returned to his birthplace on Long Island and dedicated himself to recording the simple pleasures of its rural life. *Eel Spearing at Setauket* is a nostalgic image inspired by the artist's own childhood, when during the dry summer months he would fish with an old black servant named Hector. Mount and other Americans associated country life with simple, timeless virtues. Here the bonding of the innocent boy and a black woman (reminiscent of the later relationship between Huck Finn and Jim in Mark Twain's 1884 classic) seems to offer an understated lesson in fellowship to a nation struggling with the question of slavery. Like Bingham's *Fur Traders*, Mount's painting is classically organized. Whereas Bingham's is built on series of stabilizing rectangles, Mount's image is organized by the pyramidal structure recommended by the academies. To a nation experiencing an increasing pace of change, such static images seem to have provided a welcome psychological relief.

EUROPEAN "ROMANTIC" NATURALISM

In Europe, as in the United States, naturalistic scenes of rural stability were becoming popular among artists working against the dominant artistic currents. Although the naturalistic tradition that had flowered during the Baroque period never entirely died out during the eighteenth century, it had been reduced to a minor mode. By the second quarter of the nineteenth century, at the height of the Romantic era, a number of European painters turned to the kind of naturalistic landscape practiced by the Dutch. Given the prevailing taste for Romanticism and the dominance of the national academies, such artists were generally treated harshly.

The acknowledged leader in the revival of naturalistic landscape painting was John Constable (1776–1837). The son of a successful miller, Constable claimed that the landscape of his youth in southern England had made him a painter even before he ever picked up a brush. Although he was trained at the Royal Academy—which considered

naturalism an inferior art form—he was most influenced by the British topographic watercolor tradition of the late eighteenth century and by the example of seventeenth-century Dutch landscapists (see fig. 19-51). After moving to London in 1816, he dedicated himself to painting monumental views of the agricultural landscape of his youth.

The White Horse (fig. 26-68), of 1819, is typical of Constable's mature production. The scene, like all his work before the death of his wife in 1829, is a breezy day in late spring or early summer in the Stour Valley. A storm has just passed, and the air is fresh and crisp. (Fuseli said that Constable's landscapes always made him want to reach for his umbrella.) Sunlight glistens off the water and foliage, an effect Constable achieved through tiny dabs of white paint. In the lower left, a farmer and his helpers are ferrying a workhorse across the river. Such elements were never invented by Constable, who insisted that art should not be a product of the imagination but an objective record of things actually seen. Although the contours of the foliage are picturesque, they, too, are copied from a scene that he recorded in a sketch before finishing the painting in his studio. The landscape that Constable presents here and in all his mature work is a pastoral one in which people are harmoniously embedded into nature, like the houses in the middle ground. Constable omitted from his rural idylls any references to either the economic depression or the civil unrest of agrarian workers that was then being experienced in the region.

Whether Constable's art was in part the product of a reaction against the pollution and crowding that attended the industrialization of England is much debated. Whatever the case, there is no doubt that the spread of industrial blight stood behind Constable's growing popularity in Britain. During his lifetime, Constable enjoyed little critical or popular success in his homeland. By the end of the century, however, he had become the most popular artist in Britain. As one critic recently wrote, "His landscape is just what the English feel nostalgic for as they dodge trucks on the bypass amid the billboards and concrete" (Robert Hughes, *Time*, April 25, 1983).

Constable's first critical success was at the Paris Salon of 1824, where one of his landscapes won a gold medal. His example inspired a group of French landscape

26-69. Théodore Rousseau. *Under the Birches, Evening.*
c. 1842–43. Oil on wood panel, 16⅝ x 25⅜" (42.2 x
64.4 cm). The Toledo Museum of Art, Toledo, Ohio
Gift of Arthur J. Sector

Although Rousseau, like the other Barbizon painters, traveled throughout France for their subject matter, his favorite locale was the Fontainebleau Forest, southeast of Paris. When the development of the French railway system after 1850 made tourism affordable and thus popular, Rousseau campaigned for the preservation of the forest against tourism.

painters that emerged in the 1830s and became known as the Barbizon School because a number of them, including Théodore Rousseau (1812–1867), lived in a rural town of that name, not far from Paris. Trained at the Academy, Rousseau turned to landscape around 1830, inspired by the Dutch landscapes he collected, which at the time could be purchased very cheaply. Although Rousseau's first submission to the Salon in 1831 was accepted, his modest canvases of the French countryside were systematically refused between 1836 and 1848 because they were not idealized; they were not peopled with biblical or classical figures, as recommended by the Academy; and because they seemed too sketchy and "unfinished." As a result of this treatment, he became known as *le grand refusé* ("the great refused one").

After the jury turned him down in 1842, the discouraged Rousseau left for a seven-month tour of central France. Rousseau, like the other members of the Barbizon group, did not limit themselves to a favorite geography or season, as did Constable. At the same time, the Barbizon artists generally rejected scenes of agrarian labor. They preferred to show one or two figures traveling through a landscape, enjoying its quiet solitude. While traveling, Rousseau made a sketch for *Under the Birches, Evening* (fig. 26-69), which he finished in his studio during the winter months. Here the figure is a country priest on his horse. Such religious figures were rare in Rousseau's work and should probably not be viewed as evidence of the kind of pantheism one finds in Friedrich, for example (see fig. 26-53). Instead, the painting should be viewed as a record of the autumn splendor with a group of birch trees, whose bright orange arabesque of leaves are contrasted against the cool blues of a darkening sky. The stippled paint surface—which appeared too sketchy for academic jurors—was meant to suggest the changing, flickering light that played across the scene. The painting is more than a simple delight for the eyes, however; like most works by Rousseau and his colleagues, *Under the*

26-70. Christian Købke. *View from Dosseringen near the Sortedam Lake Looking towards Nørrebro.* 1838. Oil on canvas, 20⅞ x 28⅛" (53 x 71.5 cm). Statens Museum for Kunst, Copenhagen, Denmark

Birches invites the spectator to experience the quiet tranquillity of nature. Rousseau's work, like Constable's in Britain, became increasingly popular among Paris collectors as part of their search for relief from the crowding, the air pollution, and the faster, more hectic pace of life.

Naturalistic landscape painting was pursued by a number of artists in other Western European countries during the 1830s and 1840s. For northern European artists, however, such as the Dane Christian Købke (1810–1848), naturalism was neither artistically revolutionary nor socially reactionary, but was a continuing part of the tradition of topographic landscape painting that is reflected in the style, at least, of Friedrich's work (see fig. 26-53). Købke's approach came directly out of that of his teachers at the Royal Academy of Fine Arts in Copenhagen, where he studied from 1822 to 1832.

In 1833, Købke moved to the suburbs of Copenhagen, where he painted scenes of ordinary life, such as *View from Dosseringen near the Sortedam Lake Looking towards Nørrebro* (fig. 26-70). With the crystalline precision typical of the topographic tradition (see fig. 26-10), the artist records an everyday event along the Danish waterways. Beneath the Danish flag that marked its official stops, two women wait for an approaching ferry. The painting has a somewhat magical air because of the combination of pale northern light and the strict geometry of the composition. The simple grid of horizontals and verticals freezes the action and gives the work a timeless air not unlike the effects found in American painting at the same period (see figs. 26-66, 26-67). Whether this was a matter of training, a personal predilection, or a response to social conditions is unclear.

The work of Constable and Rousseau, especially, were early signs of a major shift in European art, which would become dominant in the second half of the nineteenth century. While Neoclassical principles continued to be taught in the national academies of Europe and observed by a number of conservatives, especially sculptors, historical and mythological themes were increasingly eclipsed by the growing fascination with ordinary, everyday subjects, both landscape and genre. Romanticism, on the other hand, was reduced to a minor mode.

CHAPTER 27

Realism to Impressionism in Europe and the United States

Church
Niagara
1857

Nadar. *Portrait of
Charles Baudelaire*
1863

Carpeaux
The Dance
1867–68

Rossetti
La Pia de' Tolomei
1868–69

Monet
Rouen Cathedral
1894

27-1.   Joseph Paxton. Crystal Palace, London. 1850–51. Iron and glass. Lithograph, The Mansell Collection, London

Early in 1850, a British royal commission announced a design competition for a massive temporary edifice to house the London Great Exhibition, which Queen Victoria and her husband, Prince Albert, wanted to open the following year in London's Hyde Park as a tribute to advances in industry and technology. By June, it was evident that none of the 245 entries could possibly be completed in time. Ten days before the commission was to submit its own plan for a domed brick shed—which would also have required additional time—one of the commissioners met Joseph Paxton, a professional gardener who had recently designed a number of impressive greenhouses. Paxton agreed to submit a design, scale drawings, and cost sheets for an exhibition hall that was, in effect, a greatly enlarged greenhouse.

The commissioners, relieved but unenthusiastic, accepted his plan, and the structure was completed in the extraordinarily brief span of just over six months (fig. 27-1). The triple-tiered edifice, dubbed a "crystal palace" by a journalist for a humor magazine, was the largest space ever enclosed up to that time—1,848 feet long, covering more than 18 acres, and providing for almost a million square feet of exhibition space. The central vaulted transept—based on the new railway stations and, like them, meant to echo imperial Roman architecture—rose 108 feet to accommodate a row of elms dear to Prince Albert.

Although everyone agreed that the Crystal Palace was a technological marvel, most architects and critics did not consider it to be legitimate architecture. Some observers, however, were more forward-looking. One visitor called it "a revolution in architecture from which a new style will date." And indeed it was, in fact, an expression of the positivism that would dominate this period.

THE POSITIVIST AGE

The second half of the nineteenth century has been called the positivist age, an age of faith in the positive consequences of what can be achieved through the close observation of the natural and human realms. The term *positivism* was used by the French philosopher Auguste Comte (1798–1857) during the 1830s to describe what he saw as the final stage in the development of philosophy, in which all knowledge would derive from science and scientific methods. One of the founders of sociology, Comte intended to bring to the study of human society the same scientific rigor that was required for fields like physics, biology, astronomy, and chemistry. Comte's faith that science and its objective methods could solve all human problems was not novel; the idea of human progress had been gradually maturing since its first tentative expression by the Enlightenment thinkers of the late eighteenth century. Comte's achievement was to clarify this idea and give it a name. In the second half of the century, the term *positivism* came to be applied widely to any expression of the new emphasis on objectivity.

In the visual arts the positivist spirit is most obvious, perhaps, in the widespread rejection of Romantic subjectivism and imagination in favor of the accurate and apparently objective description of the ordinary, observable world, a change especially evident in painting. Positivist thinking is evident not simply in the growth of naturalism but also in the full range of artistic developments of the period after 1850—from the highly descriptive style of academic art, with its "realistic" figures and elements, to the Impressionist emphasis on the phenomenon of light; and from the development of photography to the application of new technologies in architecture.

PARALLELS

Years	Events
1820–1829	Beethoven's Ninth Symphony (Germany); Niépce makes first positive-image photographs (France); Audubon's *Birds of America* (United States)
1830–1839	Slavery abolished in British Empire; Hokusai's *Hundred Views of Mount Fuji* (Japan); Cole's *The Oxbow* (United States); Houses of Parliament redesigned (England); first daguerreotype made (France)
1840–1849	Talbot publishes first book illustrated with photographs (England); Labrouste's Bibliothèque Sainte-Geneviève (France); Marx and Engels's *Communist Manifesto* (Germany); revolt in Paris establishes French Second Republic; Pre-Raphaelite Brotherhood established in England; Seneca Falls Women's Rights Convention (United States); Courbet's *A Burial at Ornans* (France)
1850–1859	Paxton's Crystal Palace (England); Stowe's *Uncle Tom's Cabin* (United States); Melville's *Moby-Dick* (United States); Napoléon III of Second Empire; South African Republic established; Thoreau's *Walden* (United States); Whitman's *Leaves of Grass* (United States); Millet's *The Gleaners* (France); Flaubert's *Madame Bovary* (France); Darwin's *Origin of Species* (England); Dickens's *A Tale of Two Cities* (England)
1860–1869	Civil War (United States); Italy is united; serfdom abolished in Russia; Hugo's *Les Misérables* (France); Manet's *Le Déjeuner sur l'Herbe* and *Olympia* (France); Tolstoy's *War and Peace* (Russia); Dostoyevsky's *Crime and Punishment* (Russia); Brooklyn Bridge begun (United States); Dominion of Canada is formed; Meiji Restoration of emperor (Japan); revolution in Spain; first transcontinental railroad in United States
1870–1879	Franco-Prussian War; Third Republic in France; first Impressionist art exhibition (France); Tchaikovsky's Piano Concerto No. 1 (Russia); Renoir's *Moulin de la Galette* (France); Alexander Graham Bell patents telephone (United States); William Morris promotes Arts and Crafts Movement (England); Muybridge's motion photography (United States); Edison invents phonograph and electric light (United States)
1880–1889	Major European colonization of Africa begins; Hertz discovers and produces radio waves (Germany); Eastman's box camera (United States)
1890–1899	James's *The Principles of Psychology* (United States); Sino-Japanese War; X rays discovered (Germany); Olympic Games reestablished (Greece); Spanish-American War; aspirin is invented

27-2. John Augustus Roebling and Washington Augustus Roebling. Brooklyn Bridge, New York City. 1867–83

27-3. Henri Labrouste. Reading Room, Bibliothèque Sainte-Geneviève, Paris. 1843–50

TECHNOLOGICAL PROGRESS

The positivist faith that technological progress was the key to human progress spawned a long succession of world's fairs devoted to advances in industry and technology. The first of these fairs, the London Great Exhibition of 1851, introduced new building techniques that ultimately contributed to the temporary abandonment in the twentieth century of **historicism**—the use of historically based styles—in architecture. The revolutionary construction of the Crystal Palace (see fig. 27-1), created for the London Great Exhibition by Joseph Paxton (1801–1865), featured a structural skeleton of cast iron that held iron-framed glass panes measuring 49 by 30 inches, the largest size that could then be mass-produced. Prefabricated wooden ribs and bars supported the panes.

Engineering

Bridge designers had pioneered the use of cast iron as a building material—the first cast-iron bridge had been erected in England in 1776–1779 (see "Iron as a Building Material," page 950)—as well as the use of wrought iron and then steel, the results of new refining processes. The most famous early steel bridge, the Brooklyn Bridge (fig. 27-2), was constructed between 1869 and 1883 to link the burgeoning borough of Manhattan in New York City to the growing city of Brooklyn (which eventually became another borough of New York City). The designer, John Augustus Roebling (1806–1869), a German-born civil engineer, had written his university thesis on the suspension bridge at Bamberg, Germany, one of the first built in Europe. In 1841, ten years after emigrating to the United States, he invented twisted-wire cable, a considerable structural advance over the wrought-iron chains then being used for suspension bridges. In 1867, after designing and supervising the construction of a number of innovative suspension bridges in the eastern United States, Roebling was appointed chief engineer for the long-proposed Brooklyn–Manhattan bridge, whose main span would be the longest in the world at that time. He died in 1869 of

complications from a work-related accident just as construction was to begin, and the project was completed by his engineer son, Washington Augustus Roebling (1837–1926), who had assisted his father in earlier projects.

The bridge roadbed, nearly 6,000 feet long, hangs beneath a web of stabilizing and supporting steel-wire cables (the heaviest of which is 16 inches in diameter) suspended from two massive masonry towers that rise 276 feet above the water. The roadbed and cables are purely functional, with no decorative adornment, but the granite towers feature projecting cornices over pointed-arch roadbed openings. These historicist elements allude both to Gothic cathedrals and to Roman triumphal arches. Rather than military victories, however, Roebling's arches celebrate the triumphs of modern engineers while paying homage to those of their ancient Roman forebears.

Architecture

A less reverent attitude toward technological progress can be seen in the first attempt to incorporate structural iron into architecture proper: the Bibliothèque Sainte-Geneviève (fig. 27-3), a library in Paris designed by Henri Labrouste (1801–1875). Conventionally trained at the École des Beaux-Arts and employed as one of its professors, Labrouste was something of a radical in his desire to reconcile the École's conservative design principles with the technological innovations being developed by industrial engineers. Although reluctant to promote this goal in his teaching, he clearly pursued it in his practice.

Because of the Bibliothèque Sainte-Geneviève's educational function, Labrouste wanted the building to suggest the course of both learning and technology. The window arches on the exterior have panels with the names of 810 important contributors to Western thought from its religious origins to the positivist present, arranged chronologically from Moses to the Swedish chemist Jöns Jakob Berzelius. The exterior's stripped-down Renaissance style reflects the belief that the modern era of learning dates from that period. The move from outside to inside subtly outlines the general evolution of architectural techniques. The exterior of the library features the most ancient of permanent building materials, cut stone, which was then considered the only "noble" construction material—that is, suitable for a serious building. The columns in the entrance hall are solid masonry with cast-iron decorative elements. In the main reading room, however, cast iron plays a structural role. Slender iron columns—cast to resemble the most ornamental Roman **order**, the Corinthian—support two parallel **barrel vaults**. The columns are set on tall concrete pedestals, reminding the attentive viewer that modern construction technology rests on the accomplishments of the Romans, who developed concrete. The design of the delicate floral cast-iron **ribs** in the vaults is borrowed from the Renaissance architectural vocabulary.

Academic architects more typically used iron only as an internal support for conventional materials, as is the case with the Opéra, the Paris opera house (fig. 27-4), designed by Charles Garnier (1825–1898) and built as part of the transformation of Paris begun in the 1850s by Napoleon Bonaparte's nephew, Napoleon III. Elected president of the Second Republic in 1848 and declared emperor in 1852, Napoleon III ruled France until 1870. He inaugurated a controversial program to modernize Paris and promote greater prosperity for its upper and middle classes. The plan, drawn up by Georges-Eugène Haussmann (1809–1891)—who was given the title of baron in 1857 for his administrative work in transforming Paris—included new sewer and water systems, improved railroad lines, parks, and a network of straight, wide boulevards to facilitate business, the flow of traffic, and military action against any threatened insurrections. The Opéra was to be a focal point, located at the intersection of several major boulevards in a chic section of downtown Paris that was full of banks, businesses, and the new department stores for which the city was to become famous.

Garnier was a graduate of the École des Beaux-Arts and one of the architects helping Haussmann realize his plans for Paris. Garnier's design for the Opéra was selected in a competition announced in 1860 for a new building to replace the city's dilapidated opera house. He won the competition despite Empress Eugénie's objection that his proposal resembled no recognizable style. To her charge that it was "neither Louis XIV, nor Louis XV, nor Louis XVI," Garnier retorted, "It is Napoleon III." The massive facade, featuring a row of paired columns above an **arcade**, is essentially a heavily ornamented, Baroque version of the Louvre, an association meant to suggest the continuity of French greatness and to flatter Emperor Napoleon III by comparing him favorably with King Louis XIV. The luxuriant treatment of form, in conjunction with the building's primary function as a place of entertainment, was intended to celebrate the devotion to wealth and pleasure that characterized the Second Empire. The ornate architectural style is also appropriate for the most flamboyant of all musical forms, the opera.

The inside of what some critics called the "temple of pleasure" (fig. 27-5) was even more opulent, with its neo-Baroque sculptural groupings, heavy, gilded decoration,

27-4. Charles Garnier. The Opéra, Paris. 1861–74

27-5. Charles Garnier. Grand staircase, the Opéra

The bronze figures holding the lights on the staircase are by Marcello, the pseudonym of the Duchess Castiglione-Colonna, Adèle d'Affry, as a precaution against the male chauvinism of the contemporary art world.

and lavish mix of expensive, **polychromed** materials. The highlight of the interior was not the spectacle on stage so much as that on the great, sweeping Baroque staircase, where various members of the Paris elite—from old nobility to newly wealthy industrialists—could display themselves, the men in tailcoats accompanying

27-6. Jean-Baptiste Carpeaux. *The Dance*. 1867–68. Plaster, height approx. 23'3¹/₂" (7.1 m). Musée de l'Opéra, Paris

27-7. William-Adolphe Bouguereau. *Nymphs and a Satyr*. 1873. Oil on canvas, 9'3⅜" x 5'10⅞" (2.8 x 1.8 m). Sterling and Francine Clark Art Institute, Williamstown, Massachusetts

women in bustles and long trains. As Garnier himself said, the purpose of the Opéra was to fulfill the most basic of human desires: to hear, to see, and to be seen.

FRENCH ACADEMIC ART

One of the large sculptural groups on the entranceway of the Opéra is *The Dance* (fig. 27-6), by Jean-Baptiste Carpeaux (1827–1875). Carpeaux, who had studied at the École des Beaux-Arts under the Romantic sculptor François Rude (see fig. 26-50), had previously worked in both Romantic and Rococo styles. Dramatic and somber themes, however, were considered inappropriate to the new atmosphere of the capital, and in the years after about 1850 there was a marked decline in Romantic themes in French art and literature. Carpeaux's sculptural subjects, drawn from the eighteenth century, were better suited to the new taste for lighthearted pleasure. In *The Dance* a winged personification of Dance, a slender male carrying a tambourine, leaps up joyfully in the midst of a compact, entwined group of mostly nude female dancers, reflecting the theme of uninhibited Dionysian revelry. The erotic implication of their wild dance is revealed by the presence in the background of a satyr, a mythological creature known for its lascivious appetite.

Many Parisians were upset by the group because Carpeaux had not smoothed and generalized the bodies as Neoclassical sculptors had done (see fig. 26-14). Although the figures are idealized, their anatomically more detailed musculature and bone structure (observe the knees and elbows, for example) make them appear not to be creatures of a higher, better world but to belong, instead, to what we ordinarily call the "real" world. Carpeaux's handling of the body and its parts has therefore been labeled "realistic."

Carpeaux's unwillingness to idealize physical details was symptomatic of a major shift in French academic art in the second half of the nineteenth century. Although the influence of photography on the taste of the period has sometimes been cited as the probable cause of this change, both photography and the new exactitude in academic art were simply manifestations of the increasingly positivist values of the era. These values were particularly evident among the bankers and businesspeople who came to dominate French society and politics in the years after 1830. As patrons, these practical leaders of commerce were generally less interested in art that idealized than in art that brought the ideal down to earth.

The effect of this new taste on academic art is nowhere more evident than in the work of Adolphe-William Bouguereau (1825–1905), who became one of the richest and most powerful painters in France in the late nineteenth century by catering to bourgeois taste. At

27-8. Jean-Léon Gérôme. *Death of Caesar*. 1859. Oil on canvas, 33⁵/₈ x 57¹/₄" (86.2 x 146.8 cm). Walters Art Gallery, Baltimore

Gérôme was one of the leading antagonists of innovative art forms. As a member of the Salon jury during the last four decades of the nineteenth century, he skillfully opposed the acceptance of much of the new art, especially that of the Impressionists, which he considered "the disgrace of French art." In 1884 he fought the installation of the Manet memorial exhibition at the École, and in 1895–1897 he led the fight against the acceptance by the government of Gustave Caillebotte's bequest of Impressionist works.

the beginning of his career, in the middle to late 1850s, Bouguereau specialized in Romantic themes of death and suffering. By the early 1860s, however, he realized that these themes were not compatible with period taste. He later explained: "I soon found that the horrible, the frenzied, the heroic does not pay, and as the public of today prefers Venuses and Cupids and I paint to please the public, it is to Venus and Cupid I chiefly devote myself" (cited in Zafran, page 55).

Bouguereau gave the public not only the subjects it wanted but also the factual detail it loved. In *Nymphs and a Satyr* (fig. 27-7), for example, four young and voluptuous wood nymphs attempt to drag a reluctant satyr into the water. The slight smile on his face and the lack of real struggle on his part suggest that this is good-natured teasing. The painting's power depends less on the subject than on the way Bouguereau was able to make it seem palpable and "real" for the spectator through a heightened depiction of texture and appearance. In order to produce a persuasive satyr Bouguereau made careful anatomical studies of horses' ears and of the hindquarters of goats. Furthermore, Bouguereau makes the scene not only real but accessible. The figure on the right appears to lead both the satyr and the viewer into the scene, so the viewer's world and the world of the painting seem continuous. The viewer is invited to step in and join the figures in their romp.

A positivist taste for descriptive accuracy is also evident in the academic history painting of the period. In *Death of Caesar* (fig. 27-8), for example, Jean-Léon Gérôme (1824–1904) attempted an objective and archeologically correct re-creation of the event. To avoid Romantic emotionalism Gérôme chose to depict not the moment of the assassination but instead the sudden calm that follows as the conspirators rush out to announce their action to the city. Gérôme wanted us to observe a historical event as it might have occurred, not to identify with its protagonists. To this end he combined an impeccably descriptive style with a reporter's concern for the facts. He carefully researched the building where Caesar died, the Theater of Pompey, in order to situate it properly. From historical accounts he learned that the conspirators gave Caesar a petition scroll to distract him, that he knocked over a chair during the assassination, and that he struggled to the base

of the statue of Pompey, which he grasped with his bloodied hands before succumbing. Unlike David, who thought of history in terms of its moral lessons (see fig. 26-39), Gérôme saw it as a set of objective facts. Gérôme, like the middle-class public that supported the arts, was more curious about the way famous events may have looked than about their deeper implications.

French Academic art of the second half of the nineteenth century tended to indulge popular taste. In addition to the erotic and the historically factual, the viewing public also enjoyed the occasional dramatic subject, especially if it had an erotic element. One of the most sensational works of this type was Emmanuel Frémiet's *Gorilla Carrying off a Woman* (fig. 27-9), which was shown at the Salon of 1887. Frémiet (1824–1910), who had succeeded Barye (see fig. 26-51) in 1875 as professor in the natural

27-9. Emmanuel Frémiet. *Gorilla Carrying off a Woman*. 1887. Plaster, lifesize. Musée des Beaux-Arts, Nantes, France

27-10. Gustave Moreau. *Oedipus and the Sphinx*. 1864. Oil on canvas, 6'9¼" x 3'5¼" (2.1 x 1.1 m). The Metropolitan Museum of Art, New York
Bequest of William H. Herriman

history museum of the Paris Zoo, specialized in scenes in which early humans confronted their natural enemies, all of them rendered with anatomical exactitude. Here a Stone Age woman struggles to free herself from a lusty male gorilla, who has picked up a rock to defend himself from her rescuers, but has already been wounded. The spear in his back implies that the drama will end fortunately for the woman.

Early-twentieth-century historians and critics considered nineteenth-century academic art technically proficient but shallow. One academician whose reputation survived the general deprecation was Gustave Moreau (1826–1898). Unlike Bouguereau, Moreau refused to adapt his Romantic interests to popular taste. His early work was influenced by Delacroix, but about 1860 he became preoccupied with a dramatic theme that would also concern many other late-nineteenth- and early-twentieth-century artists and writers: the confrontation between a male hero

and an alluring femme fatale determined to destroy him.

Moreau's first statement of this theme was *Oedipus and the Sphinx* (fig. 27-10), which he produced for the Salon of 1864. The painting's subject, taken from ancient Greek mythology, had been popular among Romantics and other academics. It involves an episode in the tragic life of Oedipus in which he saves the city of Thebes from the tyranny of the Sphinx, a winged creature that was part lion, part woman. The Sphinx required an annual human sacrifice from the city and would leave only when someone correctly answered her riddle: What walks on four legs in the morning, two at noon, and three in the evening? She killed anyone who gave a wrong answer, as was the fate of those whose grisly remains lie in the foreground of Moreau's painting. Oedipus, however, gave the correct answer, which is "human," who crawls in infancy (morning), walks on two legs as an adult (noon), and walks with a stick in old age (evening). Earlier depictions of the story generally showed Oedipus at the decisive moment, giving the answer, but Moreau presented a calm and self-possessed hero determinedly staring down a transfixing woman-animal who looks up into his eyes. Unlike the original myth, which celebrates the victory of human rationality over the irrational forces of nature, Moreau emphasized instead what he saw as a gendered conflict: In his notes Moreau said that the painting pitted moral idealism against sensual desire.

EARLY PHOTOGRAPHY

Another expression of the new, positivist interest in descriptive accuracy—one that had a profound impact on the arts—was the development of photography. Photography as we know it emerged around 1840, but since the late Renaissance, artists and others had been seeking a mechanical method for exactly recording or rendering a scene. One device that emerged for this purpose was the **camera obscura** (Latin for "dark chamber"), which consists of a darkened room or box with a lens on one side. Light passes through the lens, projecting an upside-down image of the outside scene on the opposite wall or side. An artist can trace the image; in the sixteenth century several artists and theoreticians offered practical advice on how to use the camera obscura. By the seventeenth century a small, portable camera obscura, or camera, had become standard equipment for many landscape painters. Photography developed essentially as a way to fix—that is, to make permanent—the images produced by a camera obscura on light-sensitive material.

The first to make a permanent picture by the action of light was Joseph-Nicéphore Niépce (1765–1833), one of the many "gentlemen inventors" in the West in the eighteenth and early nineteenth centuries. In 1816 he and his brother Claude tried unsuccessfully to record camera images on chemically treated surfaces. About twenty years later Niépce resumed experiments to seek a less cumbersome substitute for another recently invented reproductive process, **lithography** (see "Lithography," page 987). After he successfully copied translucent **engravings** by attaching them to pewter plates

TECHNIQUE

LITHOGRAPHY

Aloys Senefelder invented **lithography** in Bavaria, Germany, in 1796 and registered for an exclusive right to the process the following year. Lithography is a planographic process—that is, the printing is done from a flat surface. It was the first wholly new printing process to be introduced since the fifteenth century, when the **intaglio**, or **incising**, process was developed.

Lithography, still popular today, is based on the natural antagonism between oil and water. The artist draws on a flat surface—traditionally, fine-grained stone—with a greasy, crayonlike instrument. The stone's surface is wiped with water, then with an oil-based ink. The ink adheres to the greasy areas but not to the damp ones. A sheet of paper is laid facedown on the inked stone, which is passed through a flatbed press. A scraper applies light pressure from above as the stone and paper pass under it, transferring ink from stone to paper, thus making lith-

ography a direct method of creating a printed image. Francisco Goya, Honoré Daumier, and Henri de Toulouse-Lautrec exploited the medium to great effect.

covered with bitumen, a light-sensitive asphalt used by etchers, Niépce tried this substance in the camera. Using metal and glass plates covered with bitumen, he succeeded around 1826 in making the first positive-image photographs of views from a window of his estate at Gras, France. Only one of his **heliographs** (or "sun drawings") survives (fig. 27-11). This view of the outbuildings on Niépce's estate required an exposure of about eight hours, which explains why sunlight is evident on the inside portions of the taller buildings on both left and right. The image was made permanent, or fixed, simply by cleaning the bitumen from the plate after exposure.

While seeking others' interest in the development of his discovery, Niépce met Louis-Jacques-Mandé Daguerre (1787–1851), a Parisian painter who was also experimenting in creating images for his **diorama** (a popular theater built for the display of huge, dramatically lit, illusionistic paintings on semitransparent fabric). Working with a lens maker, Daguerre had developed an improved camera. In 1829 Daguerre and Niépce formed a partnership. After Niépce's death in 1833, Daguerre continued their research using copper plates coated with iodized silver, long known to be light-sensitive. In 1835 he left one of the plates he had been working on in a cupboard. When he returned several days later, he was amazed to find an image on it. Through a process of elimination, he determined that the vapor of a few drops of spilled mercury from a broken thermometer had produced the effect. Thus Daguerre discovered that an exposure to light of only twenty to thirty minutes would produce a latent image on one of his silvered plates treated with iodine fumes, which could then be made visible through development with mercury vapor. By 1837 he had established a method of fixing the image by bathing the plate in a strong solution of common salt after exposure.

The inventor's first such picture, a **daguerreotype**, was a still life of plaster casts, a wicker-covered bottle, a framed drawing, and a curtain (fig. 27-12). This arrange-

27-11. Joseph Nicéphore Niépce. *View from His Window at Gras*. 1826. Heliograph, 6¹/₂ x 7⁷/₈" (17 x 20 cm). Gernsheim Collection, University of Texas, Austin

27-12. Louis-Jacques-Mandé Daguerre. *The Artist's Studio*. 1837. Daguerreotype, 6¹/₂ x 8¹/₂" (17 x 22 cm). Société Française de Photographie, Paris

ment, reminiscent of a still-life painting convention since, at least, the seventeenth century, indicates Daguerre's intention to emulate not only optical reality but also an artistic tradition. Rather than creating a new expression through his invention, Daguerre simply continued his quest for natural verisimilitude in a different medium.

The 1839 announcement of Daguerre's invention prompted the English scientist William Henry Fox Talbot (1800–1877) to publish the results of his own work on what he later named the **calotype** (from the Greek term for "beautiful image"). Talbot's process, even more than Daguerre's, became the basis of modern photography because, unlike Daguerre's, which produces a single, positive image, Talbot's calotype is a negative image from which an unlimited number of positives can be printed. In his book *The Pencil of Nature* (issued in six parts, 1844–1846), the first books to be illustrated with photographs, Talbot described the evolution of his process from the first experiments in the mid-1830s, when paper impregnated with silver chloride was used. At first, engravings, pieces of lace, and leaves were copied in negative by laying them on chemically treated paper and exposing them to light. By the summer of 1835 he was using this paper in both large and small cameras. Then, in 1840, he discovered, independently of Daguerre, that latent images resulting from exposure to the sun for short periods of time could be developed chemically. Applying the technique he had earlier used with engravings and leaves, he was able to make positive prints from the paper negatives.

One of the calotypes hand-pasted into *The Pencil of Nature* was *The Open Door* (fig. 27-13). The subject, like

27-13. William Henry Fox Talbot. *The Open Door*. 1843. Salt paper print from a calotype negative. Science Museum, London
Fox Talbot Collection

many by Talbot, is rural. As with a number of his contemporaries, he seems to have been distressed by the growing industrialization of Britain. His photograph is a nostalgic evocation of an agrarian way of life that was fast disappearing. The viewer is invited into an old, time-worn cottage in whose doorway Talbot has placed a sturdy broom, the handle carefully positioned to parallel the shadows on the door. This is the kind of traditional, handcrafted broom that mass production was beginning to make obsolete, but the use of photography itself also suggests that something made by mechanical means could have a genuine value, comparable to that of the hand-

TECHNIQUE

HOW PHOTOGRAPHY WORKS

A camera is essentially a lightproof box with a hole, called an aperture, which is usually adjustable in size and which regulates the amount of light that strikes the film. The aperture is covered with a lens, which focuses the image on the film, and a shutter, a kind of door that opens for a controlled amount of time, to regulate the length of time that the film is exposed to light—usually a small fraction of a second. Modern cameras also have a viewer that permits the photographer to see virtually the same image that the film will "see."

Photography is based on the principle that certain substances are sensitive to light and react to light by changing **value**. In modern black-and-white photography, silver halide crystals (silver combined with iodine, chlorine, or other halogens) are suspended in a gelatin base to make an emulsion that coats the film (in early photography, before the invention of plastic, a glass plate was used with a variety of emulsions). The film is then exposed. Light reflected off objects enters the camera and strikes the film. Pale objects reflect more light than do dark ones. The silver in the emulsion collects most densely where it is exposed to the most light, producing a "negative" image on the film. Later, when the film is placed in a chemical bath (developed), the silver deposits turn black, as if tarnishing. The more light the film receives, the denser the black tone created. A positive image is created from the negative in a darkroom; then the film negative is placed over a sheet of paper that, like the film, has been treated to be light-sensitive, and light is directed through the negative onto the paper. Thus, a multiple number of positive prints are able to be made from a single negative.

Color photography works on much the same principle as black-and-white: A light-sensitive emulsion reacts to exposure by changing color. Most color film uses a complicated process based on color theory—the concept that three **primary colors** (red, yellow, and blue) can be combined to make up all the **hues** the eye sees. (Thus, the discovery of color theory that was so important to the Neo-Impressionists was of equal importance to the invention of color photography.) The resulting negative does not reverse black and white values, but "reverses" the primary colors to their **complements**. Originally, this meant that three separate emulsions on the film, each sensitive to a different primary color, had to be developed, using many chemicals, bleaches, and dyes in the darkroom. Later film processes simplified this function. Some color processes are now quite direct and mechanized; others require complex chemistry and much handwork in the darkroom.

27-14. Oscar Rejlander. *The Two Paths of Life*. 1857. Combination albumen print, 16 x 31" (41 x 79.5 cm). George Eastman House, Rochester, New York

made. Talbot's "soliloquy of the broom," as his mother called it, gives evidence of his conviction that photography might offer a creative artistic outlet for those, like himself, without the manual talent to draw or paint.

The final step in the development of early photography was taken in 1851 by Frederick Scott Archer, a British sculptor and photographer, who was one of many in Western Europe trying to find a way to make silver nitrate adhere to glass. The result would be a glass negative, which would be reproducible, like Talbot's, and have the clarity of the daguerreotype. Archer's solution was collodion, a combination of guncotton, ether, and alcohol used in medicinal bandages. He found that a mixture of collodion and silver nitrate, when wet, needed only a few seconds' exposure to light to create an image. Although the wet-collodion process was more cumbersome than earlier techniques, it quickly replaced them because of its greater speed and the sharper tonal subtleties it produced. Moreover, it was universally available because Archer, unlike Daguerre and Talbot, generously refused to patent his invention. Thus the era of modern photography was launched (see "How Photography Works," page 988).

Once a practical photographic process had been invented, the question became how to use it. Those in the sciences agreed on its value for recording data, but artists were less certain how to take advantage of it. For some, like Delacroix, who occasionally worked from photographs instead of a live model, it was a cost-saving convenience. A number of critics argued that it could popularize fine art by making cheap reproductions of famous works available to the masses. For the academic painter Delaroche, however, photography represented a serious threat. Although some artists in the ensuing years may have continued to feel uneasy about photography, it was soon clear that it threatened only one kind of painting: portraiture (see fig. 2, page 17). And even there, it was used mostly as a cheap, democratic substitute for expensive, high-society portraiture that continued undiminished into the twentieth century. The real issue was whether photography, taken on its own terms, could be a new art form.

Among the first photographers to argue for its artistic legitimacy was Oscar Rejlander (1813–1875) of Sweden, who had studied painting and sculpture at the Academy in Rome. In 1841 Rejlander settled in England. He first took up photography in the early 1850s as an aid for painting but was soon attempting to create photographic equivalents of the painted and engraved moral allegories so popular in Britain since the time of Hogarth (see fig. 26-2). In 1857 he produced his most famous work, *The Two Paths of Life* (fig. 27-14), by combining thirty negatives. This allegory of Good and Evil, work and idleness, was loosely based on Raphael's *School of Athens* (see fig. 18-16). At the center an old sage ushers two young men into life. The serene youth on the right turns toward personifications of Religion, Charity, Industry, and other virtues, while his counterpart eagerly responds to the enticements of pleasure. The figures on the left Rejlander described as personifications of "Gambling, Wine, Licentiousness and other Vices, ending in Suicide, Insanity, and Death." In the lower center, with a drapery over her head, is the hopeful figure of "Repentance." Although Queen Victoria purchased a copy of *The Two Paths of Life* for her husband, it was not generally well received as art. One typical response was that "mechanical contrivances" could not produce works of "high art," a criticism that would continue to be raised against photography.

Another pioneer of photography as art was Julia Margaret Cameron (1815–1879), who received her first camera as a gift from her daughters when she was forty-nine. Although she did numerous portraits of her family and of strangers whose faces she found interesting, Cameron's principal subjects were the great men of British arts, letters, and sciences, many of whom had long been family friends.

27-15. Julia Margaret Cameron. *Portrait of Thomas Carlyle*. 1863. Silver print, 10 x 8" (25.4 x 20.3 cm). The Royal Photographic Society, London

27-16. Nadar (Gaspard-Félix Tournachon). *Portrait of Charles Baudelaire*. 1863. Silver print. Caisse Nationale des Monuments Historiques et des Sites, Paris

Although Baudelaire never wrote about the photographic work of his friend Nadar, he was highly critical of the vogue for photography and of its influence on the visual arts. In his Salon review of 1859 he said: "The exclusive taste for the True . . . oppresses and stifles the taste of the Beautiful. . . . In matters of painting and sculpture, the present-day *Credo* of the sophisticated is this: 'I believe in Nature . . . I believe that Art is, and cannot be other than, the exact reproduction of Nature. . . .' A vengeful God has given ear to the prayers of this multitude. Daguerre is his Messiah."

Cameron's work was more personal and less dependent on existing forms than Rejlander's. Like all of Cameron's portraits, that of the famous British historian Thomas Carlyle is slightly out of focus (fig. 27-15). Cameron produced this blurred effect deliberately, consciously rejecting the sharp stylistic precision of popular portrait photography, which she felt accentuated the merely physical attributes and neglected a subject's inner character. By blurring the details she sought to call attention to the light that suffused her subjects—a metaphor for creative genius—and to their thoughtful, often inspired expressions. Carlyle's countenance is so intense that the dramatic lighting of his hair, face, and beard almost seems to emanate from within. In her autobiography Cameron said: "When I have had such men before my camera my whole soul has endeavored to do its duty towards them in recording faithfully the greatness of the inner as well as the features of the outer man." This sense of picturing both what was seen and what was not seen accorded with her larger goals for photography. With regard to her medium Cameron said: "My aspirations are to ennoble Photography and to secure for it the character and uses of High Art by combining the real and ideal." To

this end, she showed her portraits at the major European photographic exhibitions of the period, which were many.

An even more ambitious conception of photography was pursued by the most famous French practitioner of the time, Gaspard-Félix Tournachon, known as Nadar (1820–1910). He began his career as a drama critic. After a variety of other jobs and enthusiasms, including caricatures, he became interested in photography in 1849 as a tool to help him with a project called the Panthéon-Nadar, a series of four lithographs that was to include the faces of all the well-known Parisians of the day. He quickly saw the documentary potential of the photograph and opened a portrait studio in 1853. His thriving studio, which at one point had twenty-six employees, became a meeting place for many of the great intellectuals and artists of the period. The first exhibition of Impressionist art was held there in 1874.

Nadar was a realist in the tradition inaugurated by Daguerre. He embraced photography because of its ability to record people and their surroundings exactly. As part of a heroic effort to produce a comprehensive and factual portrait of his era, in 1858 he took successful aerial photographs of Paris, the first of their kind, from a hot-air balloon. In 1863 he built a balloon called *The Giant* that could carry about fifty passengers and was equipped with a darkroom. At the other extreme he made numerous photographs of the catacombs and sewers of Paris. He also produced a series on typical Parisians. Finally, Nadar attempted to photograph all the leading figures of French culture. As can be seen in his portrait of the poet Charles Baudelaire (fig. 27-16), Nadar eschewed the use of props and avoided formal poses in favor of informal ones determined, like their facial expressions, by the sitters themselves. His goal was not so much an interpretation as a factual record of a sitter's characteristic appearance and demeanor. The drawn expression on Baudelaire's face, for example, tells much about him. The year this photograph was taken, 1863, Baudelaire published "The Painter of Modern Life," a newspaper article in which he called on artists to provide an accurate and insightful portrait of the times. The idea may have come from Nadar, who had been trying to do just that for some time.

FRENCH NATURALISM AND REALISM AND THEIR SPREAD

Although the national academies continued to control both the teaching and the display of art in the second half of the nineteenth century throughout Europe, increasing numbers of artists rejected its precepts in favor of the naturalist credo that art should faithfully record ordinary life. What had been considered a marginal element in landscape painting of the second quarter of the century gradually came to dominate the work of independent-minded landscape and figure painters after 1850. Much of their art was labeled **realism**, a term invented to describe a kind of naturalism with a political or social message. By 1860 the term *realism* had lost its didactic meaning and

had become for most artists and critics simply a synonym for *naturalism* (see "Realist Criticism" page 994).

French Naturalism

The kind of work produced in the 1830s and 1840s by the Barbizon School (see fig. 26-69) became enormously popular with Parisian critics and collectors after 1850, largely because of the radically changed conditions of Parisian life. Between 1831 and 1851 the city's population doubled, and thereafter Haussmann's renovations completed its transformation from a collection of small neighborhoods to a modern, crowded, noisy, and fast-paced metropolis. To those living in this new environment, the image of a peaceful and contented country life began to have increasing appeal.

Another factor in the new acceptance of rural landscapes, especially those featuring farm workers, was the widespread uneasiness over the political and social effects of the Revolution of 1848 and its aftermath. This revolution began in February of that year when Parisian workers overthrew the monarchy and established the Second Republic (1848–1852). Its founders' socialist goals, including collective ownership of means of production and distribution, were abandoned when conservative factions won elections that summer, and fear of further disruptions continued to trouble many. These people found solace in images of the seemingly unchanging and traditional life of the countryside.

One naturalist landscape painter who saw his reputation soar after 1850 was Jean-Baptiste-Camille Corot (1796–1875). Corot had been trained in the 1820s to accept the academic distinction between the heroic landscape—an idealized and carefully finished composite with a subject from the Bible or classical history—and the rural landscape, a direct record of an ordinary country scene. The heroic landscape, because it required learning and imagination as well as technical skill, was considered the nobler of the two. Although Corot produced heroic landscapes for the Salons, like his younger friends the Barbizon painters he found the rural scenes more satisfying. Ironically, just as popular taste was beginning to favor the kind of rural naturalism he had preferred in the period before 1850, Corot moved on to a new kind of landscape painting that mixed naturalistic subject matter with Romantic, poetic effects. A fine example of this is

SCHOOL, FOLLOWER OF, AND OTHER TERMS OF ATTRIBUTION In art history, the word *school* has several meanings. Artists and works that are related by period, **style**, and place are linked by the term *school*, as in "Barbizon School." *School of* is sometimes used for works that are not attributable to a known artist but that show strong stylistic similarities to him or her—for example, "school of Rubens." When a term such as *Sienese school* is used, it means that the work shows traits common in the art from Siena during the period being discussed. *Follower of* most often suggests a second-generation artist working in a variant style of the named artist. *Workshop of* is an attribution appropriate to the centuries when the guild system was in place in Europe and implies that a work was created by an artist or artists trained in the workshop of an established artist. *Attributed to*, like a question mark next to an artist's name, means that there is some uncertainty as to whether the work is by that artist.

27-17. Jean-Baptiste-Camille Corot. *Ville-d'Avray*. 1870. Oil on canvas, 21⅝ x 31½" (54.9 x 80 cm). The Metropolitan Museum of Art, New York

Catharine Lorillard Wolfe Collection, Bequest of Catharine Lorillard Wolfe

Ville-d'Avray (fig. 27-17), which shows a lone peasant woman kneeling at the edge of a pond. Like his earlier production, these paintings were done in the studio on the basis of sketches done at the site. In such late work the silvery palette, the feathery brushwork, the views across water, and the soft, late-afternoon light all combine to create a wistful, dreamy effect that seems to have more to do with the world as fondly remembered than directly confronted. Many of his titles, in fact, included the term *souvenir* (French for "to remember"). Ville-d'Avray, a village that he had often visited and painted since the early 1820s, seemed to hold a certain nostalgic appeal for the artist, which he effectively communicated.

A more objective approach to the French countryside was practiced by Rosa Bonheur (1822–1899), another of the popular painters of the period. Her success in what was then a male domain owed much to the socialist convictions of her parents, who belonged to a radical utopian sect founded by the Comte de Saint-Simon, which believed not only in the equality of women but also in a female Messiah. Of women Bonheur said in her *Reminiscences* (published posthumously in 1910): "I am persuaded that the future belongs to us." Her father, a drawing teacher, provided most of her artistic training.

Bonheur was dedicated to factual depiction of the farm animals she loved. This commitment to rural subjects was partly the result of her aversion to Paris, where she had been raised. To record farm animals accurately, she read zoology books and made detailed studies in the countryside and in slaughterhouses. Because these settings were rugged, she often wore men's clothing, for which she had to get police permission.

Although Bonheur received some critical praise for her animal portraits in the 1840s, her success dates from the Salon of 1848, where she showed eight paintings and won a first-class medal. Shortly after, the government commissioned a work from her, *Plowing in the Nivernais: The Dressing of the Vines* (fig. 27-18). This monumental painting features one of her favorite animals, the ox, engaged in a time-honored rural activity. The powerful beasts, anonymous workers, and fertile soil offer a reassuring image of the continuity of agrarian life. The stately movement of people and animals reflects the kind of carefully balanced compositional schemes taught in the Academy and echoes scenes of processions found in Classical art. The painting's compositional harmony— the shape of the hill is answered by and continued in the general profile of the four white oxen and their handler on the right—as well as its stylistic illusionism, pleasant landscape, and conservative theme were very appealing to the taste of the times, in England and the United States as well as in France. Bonheur became so famous that in 1865 she received France's highest award, membership in the Legion of Honor, becoming the first woman to be awarded its Grand Cross.

The most renowned of the French rural naturalists, Jean-François Millet (1814–1875), actually grew up on a farm. After moving to Paris to study in 1837, he went

27-18. Rosa Bonheur. *Plowing in the Nivernais: The Dressing of the Vines*. 1849. Oil on canvas, 5'9" x 8'8" (1.8 x 2.6 m). Musée d'Orsay, Paris

Bonheur was often compared with Georges Sand, a contemporary woman writer who adopted a male name as well as male dress. Sand devoted several of her novels to the humble life of farmers and peasants. Critics at the time noted that *Plowing in the Nivernais* may have been inspired by a passage in Sand's *The Devil's Pond* (1846) that begins: "But what caught my attention was a truly beautiful sight, a noble subject for a painter. At the far end of the flat ploughland, a handsome young man was driving a magnificent team [of] oxen."

through a difficult period. His teacher, an academician, considered him nearly unteachable, and Millet intensely disliked the city. He stayed on until after the Revolution of 1848, however, becoming a painter of the female nude. The Revolution's preoccupation with ordinary people seems to have led Millet to focus on peasant life, which had been only a marginal concern in his early work, and his support of the Revolution earned him a state commission that allowed him to leave Paris and settle in the village of Barbizon. After moving to Barbizon in 1849, he devoted himself almost exclusively to the difficulties and simple pleasures of rural existence.

Perhaps the most famous of his mature works is *The Gleaners* (fig. 27-19), which shows three women gathering grain at harvesttime. The warm colors and slightly hazy atmosphere are soothing, but the scene is one of extreme poverty. Gleaning, or the gathering of the grains left over after the harvest, was a form of relief offered to the rural poor. It required hours of backbreaking work to gather enough wheat to produce a single loaf of bread. When the painting was shown in 1857, a number of critics thought Millet was attempting to rekindle the sympathies and passions of 1848, especially because he was known to have supported the Revolution, and he was therefore labeled a realist. Yet Millet's intentions were actually quite conservative. An avid reader of the Bible, he saw in such scenes the fate of humanity, condemned since the Expulsion of Adam and Eve from the Garden of Eden to earn its bread by the sweat of its brow. Despite his brief enthusiasm for

27-19. Jean-François Millet. *The Gleaners*. 1857. Oil on canvas, 33 x 44" (83.8 x 111.8 cm). Musée d'Orsay, Paris

the Revolution, Millet was neither a revolutionary nor a reformer but a fatalist who found the peasant's heroic acceptance of the human condition exemplary. To suggest the timeless nature of the scene, Millet generalized, even monumentalized, his figures, making them not specific individuals but representatives of their class. Unlike his contemporaries, Millet avoided the unique and the idiosyncratic by rarely studying from nature. He was also drawn to scenes like that of *The Gleaners* because they evoked an enduring way of life. Millet, who disliked change, purposefully omitted from his paintings any evidence of the technological improvements recently

27-20. Gustave Courbet. *A Burial at Ornans.* 1849. Oil on canvas, 10'3½" x 21'9" (3.1 x 6.6 m). Musée du Louvre, Paris

introduced into French agriculture. He chose instead to emphasize those tools, like the rake and the hoe, that had served humanity from time immemorial. Like Talbot, he was nostalgic for the preindustrial past.

French Realism

Gustave Courbet (1819–1877) was also inspired by the events of 1848 to turn his attention to poor and ordinary people. Trained around 1840 at an independent Paris studio, Courbet had until the Revolution devoted himself primarily to narcissistic images of himself in flattering por-

traits and romantic roles. The street fighting of 1848, however, seems to have radicalized him, as it did some of his close friends. He told one newspaper in 1851 that he was "not only a Socialist but a democrat and a Republican: in a word, a supporter of the whole Revolution." Courbet proclaimed his new political commitment in three large paintings he submitted to the Salon of 1850–1851.

One of these, *A Burial at Ornans* (fig. 27-20), is a monumental 10-by-21-foot canvas showing the funeral of Courbet's grandfather Oudot, who had died in 1847. Conservative critics hated the work for its focus on common people and for its disrespect for compositional stan-

---

REALIST CRITICISM The critical insistence that art should focus not on historical, biblical, or literary themes but on the realities of contemporary life was a major factor in the rise of artistic realism in France around 1848. A French utopian socialist, the Comte de Saint-Simon (1760–1825), was largely responsible for this view. Saint-Simon, like Auguste Comte and Karl Marx after him, believed that the laws of human society could be discovered by science and used to construct what he called the golden age of humanity. Art would contribute significantly to this process, according to Saint-Simon, by preparing the public to accept the changes advocated by the new social scientists. Saint-Simon's *Opinions* (1825) contains a fictional dialogue between such a scientist and an artist in which the artist says: "It is we, artists, who will serve you as avant-garde [vanguard]: the power of the arts is in fact most immediate. . . . When we wish

to spread new ideas among [people], we inscribe them on marble or in canvas."

Saint-Simon's view of art's function was quickly embraced by a number of liberal critics. One of them, Gustave Planche (1808–1857), first applied the word *realism* to art in 1833. For Planche and for others prior to about 1860, *realism* meant a combination of contemporary subjects and socialist intentions. The leading realist critic of the era was probably Théophile Thoré (1807–1869), who during the 1830s and 1840s advised artists to reject as irrelevant to the present the subjects and formulas of the past. He also insisted that art must have a moral dimension.

The ideas of Thoré, Planche, and other realist critics were much discussed by a group of younger critics, artists, poets, and writers who gathered at a Paris beer hall in the years just prior to the Revolution of 1848. Among the regulars were Courbet and the fledgling art and literary critic

known as Champfleury (1821–1889; born Jules-François-Félix Husson). Courbet's first defender, Champfleury later helped the artist to write his so-called Realist Manifesto. When two of Courbet's thirteen submissions were rejected by the jury for the Universal Exposition of 1855, Courbet withdrew and organized a private exhibition for which he and Champfleury wrote a brief catalog introduction. In it Courbet said, "To know in order to be able to create, that was my idea. To be in a position to translate the customs, the ideas, the appearance of my epoch, according to my own estimation; to be not only a painter, but a man as well; in short, to create living art—this is my goal."

In this manifesto Courbet and Champfleury were apparently renouncing the political and moral associations long carried by the term *realism* in favor of the apolitical and individualistic conception that would prevail among the critics and artists of the following generation.

27-21. Honoré Daumier. *The Third-Class Carriage*. c. 1862. Oil on canvas, 25³/₄ x 35¹/₂" (65.4 x 90.2 cm). The National Gallery of Canada, Ottawa

dards: Instead of arranging figures in a conventional pyramid that would indicate a hierarchy of importance, Courbet lined them up in rows across the picture plane—an arrangement he considered more democratic. His political convictions are especially evident in the individual attention and sympathetic treatment he accords the ordinary citizens of Ornans. Courbet's respect and affinity for "the people" is also expressed in the scale of the work—ordinarily reserved for major historical events—and in the way the mourners' genuine sorrow is contrasted with the apparent indifference of the two Church officials dressed in red behind the officiating priest.

On a thematic level, the painting may record the fate of the Revolution of 1848. The July elections that year returned to power a conservative government, which undid the progressive legislation enacted by the revolutionaries. Courbet's grandfather had been involved in the French Revolution of 1789, and the two men to the right of the open grave—dressed not in contemporary but in late-eighteenth-century clothing—are also revolutionaries of Oudot's generation. The gesture of futility offered by the foremost of the pair is indicative that they seem to be burying not simply one of their colleagues but their political hopes as well. As a record of the artist's disappointment, the painting may help us understand why Courbet turned away from sociopolitical subjects soon after this work and dedicated himself to landscape painting.

Partly for convenience, Bonheur, Millet, Courbet, and the other country-life naturalists and realists who emerged in the 1850s are sometimes referred to as the generation of 1848. Because of his sympathy with working-class people, the somewhat older Honoré Daumier (1808–1879) is also grouped with this generation. Unlike Courbet and the others, however, Daumier often depicted urban scenes, as in *The Third-Class Carriage* (fig. 27-21). The painting depicts the interior of one of the large, horse-drawn buses that transported Parisians along Haussmann's new boulevards. Daumier places the viewer in the poor section of the bus, opposite a serene grandmother, her daughter, and her two grandchildren. Although there is a great sense of intimacy and unity among these people (Daumier has arranged them in a pyramid shape), they are physically and mentally

27-22. Honoré Daumier. *This Year, Venuses Again . . . Always Venuses!* No. 2 of the sketches made at the Salon, from *Le Charivari*, May 10, 1864

separated from the upper- and middle-class passengers whose heads appear behind them. This acute depiction of class distinction and urban alienation would become an important topic in art after 1880.

A political liberal like Courbet, Daumier had been greatly affected by the Revolution of 1830. Then a student at the Academy, Daumier began producing anti-monarchist and prorepublican caricatures in leftist journals. He was soon obliged to focus on social and cultural themes rather than strictly political ones, however, because of stringent censorship laws. *This Year, Venuses Again . . . Always Venuses!* (fig. 27-22), for example, humorously contrasts academic standards of ideal female beauty with two quite ordinary women visiting the Salon. One of them turns away from a wall of academic nudes with the comment, "This year, Venuses again . . . always Venuses! As if there really were women built like that!" Such a sentiment may reflect both Daumier's own naturalism in art and the changing taste of the public.

One of the artists who carried the concerns of the realists of 1848 into the later part of the century was the sculptor Aimé-Jules Dalou (1838–1902). Encouraged by Carpeaux, Dalou studied sculpture at the Academy. He enjoyed considerable success in the 1860s for works essentially made for the market. His more personal work emerged in the context of the Commune of 1871, the short-lived socialist government established in Paris after the defeat of the French in the Franco-Prussian War and the abdication of Napoleon III. Like his friend Courbet, Dalou actively supported the Commune. At this time he produced the first of his realist sculptures, a lifesize figure of an embroiderer. When the leaders of the Commune were driven from power, Dalou, like Courbet, was forced

27-23. Aimé-Jules Dalou. *Breton Woman Nursing Her Child*. 1873. Terra-cotta, height 49¾" (126 cm). Victoria and Albert Museum, London

27-24. Wilhelm Leibl. *Three Women in a Village Church*. 1878–81. Oil on canvas, approx. 29 x 25" (73.7 x 63.5 cm). Kunsthalle, Hamburg

About this painting, Leibl wrote to his mother in 1879: "Here in the open country and among those who live close to nature, one can paint naturally. . . . It takes great staying power to bring such a difficult, detailed picture to completion in the circumstances. Most of the time I have literally taken my life in my hands in order to paint it. For up to now the church has been as cold as a grave, so that one's fingers get completely stiff. Sometimes, too, it is so dark that I have the greatest difficulty getting a clear enough view of the part on which I am working. . . . Several peasants came to look at it just lately, and they instinctively folded their hands in front of it. . . . I have always set greater store by the opinion of simple peasants than by that of so-called painters."

into exile. Until the amnesty of 1879–1880 he lived in England, where he specialized in scenes of people engaged in everyday pursuits. Many of these works were later used for **porcelain** figurines issued in large **editions**.

One of Dalou's favorite themes can be seen in *Breton Woman Nursing Her Child* (fig. 27-23). This work delighted the British public when it was exhibited in 1873, possibly because of Dalou's concern for common people and his apparent support for a conservative view then prevalent: Home is a woman's "natural" domain.

Naturalism and Realism outside France

Following the French lead, artists of other Western European nations also embraced naturalism and realism in the period after 1850. Among them was the German painter Wilhelm Leibl (1844–1900). Trained at the Munich Academy, Leibl was a fairly conventional academician until Courbet's visit in 1869 to the Munich International Exhibition, where some of the French artist's paintings were on display. Inspired by Courbet's work, and on his advice, Leibl went to Paris to familiarize himself with its naturalist currents. After Leibl's return to Germany he lived in Munich for several years before moving to rural Bavaria, in southern Germany, where he dedicated himself to peasant subjects.

Leibl's best-known painting is *Three Women in a Village Church* (fig. 27-24), which was based on countless

sittings by villagers he used as models. The work features a young woman, whose fresh beauty stands in sharp contrast to the weathered faces of the women next to her. The contrast is emphasized by the different backgrounds behind the older women and the young woman. The work is more than a reverie on youthful beauty, however. It also extols the conservative customs and values of these peasants. Carrying on the practices of her elders, the young woman manifests the enduring strength of her culture, also embodied in the traditional dress and ardent piety of the three women. Even the elaborately carved pews, which seem to date from the Baroque period, suggest a faithfulness to the past. The scene is rendered with

27-25. Ilya Repin. *Bargehaulers on the Volga*. 1870–73. Oil on canvas, 4'3³/4" x 9'3" (1.3 x 2.81 m). Russian State Museum, St. Petersburg

a minute care that owes more to the examples of Hans Holbein (see figs. 18-73, 18-77) and Jan Vermeer (see fig. 19-53) than to that of Courbet. Leibl thereby demonstrates his own devotion to time-honored artistic standards threatened by innovation and change.

In Russia, too, realism developed in relation to a new concern for the peasantry. In 1861 the czar abolished serfdom, emancipating Russia's peasants from the virtual slavery they had endured on the large estates of the aristocracy. Two years later a group of painters inspired by the emancipation declared allegiance to both the peasant cause and freedom from the St. Petersburg Academy of Art, which had controlled Russian art since 1754. Rejecting what they considered the idealized, "art for art's sake" aesthetics of the Academy, the members of the group dedicated themselves to a socially useful realism. Committed to bringing art to the people in traveling exhibitions, they called themselves the Wanderers. By the late 1870s members of the group, like their counterparts in music and literature, were also becoming active in a broad nationalistic movement to reassert what they considered to be an authentic Russian culture rooted in the traditions of the peasantry. This movement developed in reaction to the Western European customs that had long predominated among the Russian aristocracy. Since the late eighteenth century, for example, French had been spoken at court and among Russia's educated elite.

Ilya Repin (1844–1930), who attended the St. Petersburg Academy and won a scholarship to study in Paris, joined the Wanderers on his return to Russia in 1878. He did a series of works illustrating the social injustices then prevailing in his homeland, the first and most famous of which was *Bargehaulers on the Volga* (fig. 27-25). The painting features a group of wretchedly dressed peasants condemned to the brutal work of pulling ships up the Volga River. In order to heighten our sympathy for these workers, Repin placed a youth in the center of the group, a young man who will soon look as old and tired as his companions unless something is done to rescue him. In this way, the painting is a cry for action.

ART IN THE UNITED STATES

Art in the United States at mid-century, like Russian art after the emancipation of the serfs, was marked by the tension between an academic tradition imported from Western Europe and an unbroken American tradition of realism. In the case of the United States, however, the tension was not recent. The advocates of realism had long considered it distinctively American and democratic; others, in contrast, saw the academic ideal as a link to a higher Western European culture.

Neoclassical Sculpture

In the years immediately before and after the Civil War, sculpture, especially in marble, remained the essential medium for those committed to "high," or European, culture. A new generation of sculptors continued the European Neoclassical tradition established in Rome by Antonio Canova (see fig. 26-14) and brought to the United States in the second quarter of the nineteenth century by artists like Hiram Powers (Chapter 26). Most members of this new generation studied in Rome, including a number of women.

The most important of the Americans in Rome, Harriet Hosmer (1830–1908), had moved there in 1852 after taking anatomy classes at a St. Louis medical school and studying with a Boston sculptor. Among her many works that combine physicality with sentiment in the manner of Canova is *Beatrice Cenci* (fig. 27-26). Beatrice, the daughter of a

27-26. Harriet Hosmer. *Beatrice Cenci*. 1853–55. Marble, 2'4" x 5'2" (0.71 x 1.57 m). The St. Louis Mercantile Library Association, St. Louis, Missouri

27-27. Edmonia Lewis. *Hagar in the Wilderness*. 1875. Marble, 52⅝ x 15¼ x 17" (136.2 x 39.1 x 43.6 cm). National Museum of African Art, Smithsonian Institution, Washington, D.C.

27-28. Erastus Dow Palmer. *The White Captive*. 1857–59. Marble, height 5'6" (1.68 m). The Metropolitan Museum of Art, New York

Gift of Hamilton Fish

Renaissance Roman noble, conspired with her mother and brothers to murder her tyrannical father. At Beatrice's trial, her lawyer said that she had been a victim of incest, but she was nevertheless convicted and beheaded in 1599. Hosmer shows the partially undressed woman asleep the night before her execution, having reconciled herself to her fate through prayer (note the rosary beads in her hand). While her sensuality is evident, Beatrice is depicted not as a femme fatale but a sympathetic figure worthy of admiration.

By the 1860s, Hosmer had become the supportive center of a group of American women sculptors, including Edmonia Lewis (c.1843/45–after 1911). Born in New York State to a Chippewa mother and an African-American father and originally named Wildfire, Lewis was orphaned at four. At thirteen, with the help of abolitionists, she entered Oberlin College, where she took the Christian name Edmonia Lewis. While at Oberlin, she was accused of attempting to poison two classmates. After her acquittal, she moved to Boston, where she became a sculptor. Her highly successful busts and medallions of abolitionist leaders and black Civil War heroes financed her move to Rome in 1867.

In Rome, Lewis continued to dedicate herself to the causes of human freedom, especially those involving women: "I have a strong sympathy for all women who have struggled and suffered," she said (Eisenman, page 183). *Hagar in the Wilderness* (fig. 27-27), for example, tells the story of the Egyptian concubine of the biblical patriarch Abraham, given to him by his childless wife, Sarah, so that he might have a son. When Hagar's son, Ishmael, was in his teens, Sarah gave birth to Isaac and, out of jealousy, demanded that Abraham drive Hagar and her son into the wilderness. When Hagar and Ishmael were dying from thirst, an angel led them to a well and told Hagar that her

son's descendants would be a great nation (Genesis 16: 1-16; 18: 1-21). In Lewis's conception Hagar is shown praying for her rescue, an empty water pitcher at her feet. Because of her African origins, Hagar represented for Lewis the plight and the hope of her entire race.

Not all of the American Neoclassicists studied in Rome or were sensitive to the dilemma of America's minorities. Erastus Dow Palmer (1817–1904), for example, had no formal training. A carpenter from upstate New York, Palmer had begun making small cameo portraits around 1845 and had moved to large-scale marble figures by the early 1850s. He achieved his greatest popular success in 1859, when he exhibited *The White Captive* (fig. 27-28), an obvious remake of Powers's *Greek Slave* (see fig. 26-62) that substitutes as villains Native Americans for Turks. The work, which places a realistic head on a classically idealized body, was displayed alone in a room carefully illuminated by gaslight that warmed the marble to a semblance of flesh. This theatrical presentation, reminiscent more of Daguerre's diorama than of the Paris Salon, was what American public expected and considered as art.

27-29. Frederick Edwin Church. *Niagara*. 1857. Oil on canvas, 3'6½" x 7'6½" (1.1 x 2.30 m). The Corcoran Gallery of Art, Washington, D.C.

Landscape Painting

In contrast to the late Neoclassicism prevalent in sculpture, during the years before the Civil War American landscape painters shifted from the Romantic tradition of Thomas Cole (see fig. 26-63) toward a more factual naturalism. This transition is particularly evident in the work of Frederick Edwin Church (1826–1900), Cole's only student. Like Cole, Church favored the grand spectacles of nature, such as Niagara Falls (fig. 27-29). In its epic aspirations Church's *Niagara* remains Romantic in conception, but its Romanticism is tempered by a scientific eye to detail. The painting's magnificent spectacle, precarious vantage point, and huge scale were designed to generate grand emotions. Its subject also sparked considerable nationalistic pride. Niagara Falls was one of those august places that exemplified to Americans the greatness of their nation. By including a rainbow over the falls, a traditional symbol of divine approval, Church clearly meant to appeal to the public's preconceptions about their national destiny. Drawn to its combination of naturalism, lofty emotion, and nationalism, people flocked to see the painting in New York City in 1857 and, despite a 25-cent fee, on its national tour in 1859. More than 1,100 visitors to the 1857 exhibition ordered colored reproductions of *Niagara*.

One of the visitors, John Frederick Kensett (1816–1872), was a landscape painter with an even more naturalistic approach. Trained as an engraver, Kensett toured and studied in Europe between 1840 and 1847. After his return he traveled in the United States, making detailed records of the beautiful scenery of the Northeast and West. He and a group of his contemporaries—including Fitz Hugh Lane (1804–1865), Martin Johnson Heade (1819–1904), and Worthington Whittredge (1820–1910)—

27-30. John Frederick Kensett. *Beacon Rock, Newport Harbor*. 1857. Oil on canvas, 22½ x 36" (57.2 x 91.4 cm). National Gallery of Art, Washington, D.C.
Gift of Frederick Sturges, Jr.

have come to be known as American Luminists because of the radiant light that suffuses the atmosphere in their landscapes.

Characteristic of Kensett's work in its combination of the documentary with the metaphorical is *Beacon Rock, Newport Harbor* (fig. 27-30). The painting, which shows the entrance to the Rhode Island city's harbor, employs a three-part spatial arrangement that derives ultimately from the seventeenth-century French Baroque painter Claude Lorrain (see fig. 19-24). From a narrow foreground plane, where the viewer stands, the eye moves around a large mass that establishes the middle ground to the elements of the far distance. But whereas Claude and his later imitators composed ideal landscapes to fit this format, Kensett has accommodated the format to the topographical facts. The

27-31. Alexander Gardner. *Confederate Dead Gathered for Burial, Antietam, September 1862.* Albumen silver print. Library of Congress, Washington, D.C.

An 1862 editorial in the *New York Times* on the Antietam photographs commented that Mathew Brady and his assistants "bring home to us the terrible reality . . . of the war. If [they have] not brought bodies and laid them in our door yards . . . [they have] done something very like it."

scene's tranquil noonday light, which looks plainly naturalistic to the twentieth-century eye, must be seen in the context of the mid-nineteenth century's insistence on metaphorical readings of the landscape. Kensett, like his predecessors, seems to have considered light to be evidence of the divine. Unlike his predecessors, however, he shunned the theatrical handling of such metaphors and a preoccupation with their narrative implications. In *Beacon Rock* Kensett makes no claims about the future of the United States. He simply records a single, blessed moment.

Civil War Photography and Sculpture

With hindsight, we know that Kensett's luminous calm was about to be broken by a terrible storm. Four years after he painted *Beacon Rock*, the Civil War erupted. This conflict lasted four bloody years (1861–1865) and cost nearly 620,000 lives, more than all other United States wars combined. It generated intense national and international interest, attracting not only journalists and artists but also practitioners of the new medium of photography. Inspired by the pioneering documentary work of a handful of British war photographers in the middle to late 1850s, more than 300 American and foreign photographers eventually entered the battle zone with passes from the U.S. government.

The first photographer at the front was Mathew B. Brady (1823–1896), who ran large portrait studios in New York City and Washington, D.C. When the war broke out, he used his friendship with the influential government officials whose portraits he had made to gain permission to take a team of photographers and a darkroom wagon to the front, where they endured considerable hardship and danger. After Brady himself was almost killed in an early battle, he left the actual photographing to his twenty assistants. Brady's Photographic Corps amassed more than 7,000 negatives documenting every aspect of the war except the actual fighting, because the cameras were still too slow for action scenes.

27-32. Thomas Ball. *The Emancipation Group.* 1874. Bronze, over lifesize. Lincoln Park, Washington, D.C.

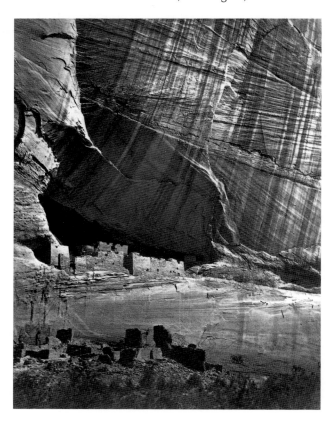

27-33. Timothy H. O'Sullivan. *Ancient Ruins in the Cañon de Chelley, Arizona.* 1873. Albumen print. National Archives, Washington, D.C.

The most memorable images by Brady and his assistants were taken immediately after battles, before the dead could be buried. An example is *Confederate Dead Gathered for Burial, Antietam, September 1862* (fig. 27-31), by Brady's most acclaimed assistant, Alexander Gardner (1821–1882). Lying in a neat, wedge-shaped pile are the corpses of some of the more than 10,000 Confederate soldiers who had fallen in that battle. The grim evidence of carnage in such

27-34. Albert Bierstadt. *The Rocky Mountains, Lander's Peak.* 1863. Oil on canvas, 6'1¼" x 10'3¾" (1.86 x 3 m). The Metropolitan Museum of Art, New York
Rogers Fund

works made a powerful impression on the American public, cutting through the so-called glamour of war.

After the war the nation tried to heal its wounds in a variety of ways. In both North and South, public sculpture was commissioned not only to commemorate the dead and provide an outlet for grief but also to provide satisfactory explanations for the epic sacrifice. One of the most popular subjects in the North was Abraham Lincoln, shown either alone or freeing slaves, as in Thomas Ball's bronze sculpture *The Emancipation Group* (fig. 27-32). Ball (1819–1911), a self-trained sculptor who moved to Italy in 1854, produced this and a number of similarly naturalistic commemorative monuments in his Florence studio. The work shows President Lincoln in contemporary dress, with his 1863 Emancipation Proclamation in one hand, blessing with the other a man who is about to be unshackled and rise a free person. Lincoln was the perfect subject for such explanatory sculpture because his assassination immediately following the war was seen as its final tragedy and epitomizing symbol. For Northerners, at least, his personal sacrifice in the name of a great moral cause personified that of the nation as a whole.

Post–Civil War Photography and Painting

Among the most important factors in the nation's recovery from the war was the massive westward expansion that soon came to preoccupy its citizens. This expansion into the so-called wilderness between the Mississippi River and California—already occupied by Native Americans—was justified as the nation's Manifest Destiny, a term coined in 1845. To help open up territory, the U.S. government sponsored a number of exploratory surveys into the West, and many Civil War photographers, toughened by combat and looking for fresh subjects, accompanied them.

One of those photographers was Timothy H. O'Sullivan (1840–1882), who had trained in Brady's portrait studios and worked for him during the war. As his most famous photograph, *Ancient Ruins in the Cañon de Chelley, Arizona* (fig. 27-33), makes clear, O'Sullivan's landscapes are more a personal expression of awe than they are documentary records. Taken on a government geological survey of the Southwest, this landscape view is virtually without precedent. The 700-foot canyon wall fills the image, giving the viewer no clear vantage point and scant visual relief. The bright, raking sunlight across the rock face reveals little but the cracks and striations formed over countless eons. The image suggests not only the immensity of geological time but also humanity's insignificant place within it. Like the Classical ruins that were a popular theme in European art and poetry, the eleventh-to-fourteenth-century Anasazi ruins suggest the inevitable passing of all civilizations. For O'Sullivan, whose Romantic pessimism was surely fueled by the Civil War, the four puny humans on the left, standing in this majestic yet barren place, would have reinforced the message of human futility and insignificance.

The paintings of Albert Bierstadt (1830–1902) impart a more optimistic view of the Western landscape. Born in Germany and raised in the United States, Bierstadt studied at the Düsseldorf Academy in the mid-1850s. In 1858–1859, just before the Civil War, he accompanied an expedition of U.S. Army engineers, led by Colonel Frederick Lander, mapping an overland route from St. Louis to the Pacific Ocean. Working from his sketches of this pristine territory, especially the Rocky Mountains, he produced a series of paintings that made his fame. The first of these, *The Rocky Mountains, Lander's Peak* (fig. 27-34), sold for $25,000, the highest price an American painting

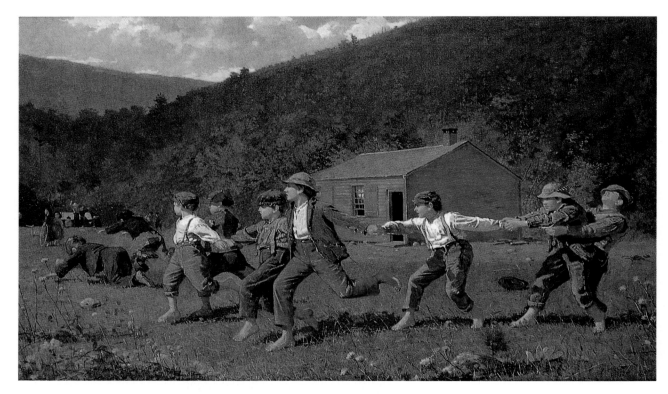

27-35. Winslow Homer. *Snap the Whip*. 1872. Oil on canvas, 22¼ x 36½"(55.9 x 91.4 cm). The Butler Institute of American Art, Youngstown, Ohio

had yet brought—more than forty times what a skilled carpenter or mason then earned per year. The huge canvas, intended for Eastern audiences only slightly familiar with Native Americans and even less familiar with the Rockies, combines a documentary approach to Native American life in the tradition of George Catlin (see fig. 26-65) with an epic, composite landscape in the tradition of Frederick Edwin Church (see fig. 27-29). The painting is more than a geography lesson, however. As in the work of Church and Cole, it conveys an implicit historical narrative. From the Native American encampment in the foreground, with its apparent associations to the Garden of Eden, the eye is drawn into the middle ground by the light on the waterfall, then up to Lander's Peak. To audiences that accepted the concept of a divinely sanctioned Manifest Destiny, the work's spatial progression must have seemed to map out their nation's westward and "upward" course. The painting seems virtually to beckon them into this paradise to displace the Native Americans already inhabiting it.

The myth of America as the new Eden, challenged by the war, also reasserted itself in genre painting and sculpture. One of those who specialized in reassuring scenes of American innocence was the painter Winslow Homer (1836–1910). Homer began his artistic career in 1857 as a freelance illustrator for popular periodicals such as *Harper's Weekly* and *Ballou's Pictorial*. *Harper's* sent him to cover the Civil War in 1862. His quiet scenes of life behind the lines could hardly be more different from the harsh photographs by Gardner and others. In 1866–1867 he spent ten months in France, where the naturalist art he saw may have inspired him to begin painting rural subjects when he returned.

About 1870 Homer began painting scenes based on frequent forays from his New York City home to upstate New York villages. Works like *Snap the Whip* (fig. 27-35), with its depiction of boys playing outside a one-room schoolhouse in the Adirondack Mountains on a glorious day in early fall, evoke the innocence of childhood and the imagined charms of a preindustrial America for an audience that was increasingly urbanized. Homer apparently shared his audience's nostalgia for a more carefree past, and the paintings seem to have reminded him of his own active, outdoor childhood in Cambridge, Massachusetts, then still an almost-rural suburb of Boston. Many of these paintings were reproduced as wood engravings for illustrated books and magazines.

Homer's work was significantly changed by his experiences during 1881–1882 in a tiny English fishing village on the rugged North Sea coast. The strength of character of the people there so inspired him that he turned from idyllic subjects such as *Snap the Whip* to more dramatic and serious themes involving the heroic human struggle against natural adversity. During his stay in England, he was particularly impressed with the breeches buoy, a mechanical apparatus developed by the British to rescue those aboard foundering ships. Homer spent part of the summer of 1883 in Atlantic City, New Jersey, because the lifesaving crew there had imported one of the new devices. He had the crew demonstrate its use while he made sketches, from which he painted *The Life Line* (fig. 27-36) early the following year on the roof of his New York tenement. The painting is a testament not simply to human bravery but to its ingenuity as well.

The human mind is also celebrated in works of the most uncompromising American naturalist of the era,

27-36. Winslow Homer. *The Life Line*. 1884. Oil on canvas, 28³/₄ x 44⁵/₈" (73 x 113.3 cm). Philadelphia Museum of Art
The George W. Elkins Collection

In the early sketches for this work, the man's face was visible. The decision to cover it focuses more attention not only on the victim but also on the true hero, the breeches buoy.

Thomas Eakins (1844–1916). Trained at the Pennsylvania Academy of the Fine Arts, he, too, went to Europe, in 1866, and studied for three years at the French École des Beaux-Arts under Gérôme (see fig. 27-8). Eakins then spent six months in Spain, where he encountered the works of Diego Velázquez and José Ribera, whose profound realism came as a revelation to him. After he returned to Philadelphia in 1870, he specialized in frank portraits and genre scenes whose lack of conventional charm generated little popular interest.

One work did attract attention: *The Gross Clinic* (fig. 27-37) was severely criticized. The painting shows Dr. Samuel Gross performing an operation at the Jefferson

27-37. Thomas Eakins. *The Gross Clinic*. 1875. 8' x 6'5"
(2.44 x 1.98 m). Jefferson Medical College of Thomas Jefferson University, Philadelphia

In 1876 Eakins joined the staff of the Pennsylvania Academy of the Fine Arts, where he taught anatomy and figure drawing. He disapproved of the academic technique of drawing from plaster casts. In an interview in 1879, he said, "At best, they are only imitations, and an imitation of an imitation cannot have so much life as an imitation of nature itself." He added, "The Greeks did not study the antique . . . the draped figures in the Parthenon pediment were modeled from life, undoubtedly." Eakins introduced the study of the nude model, which shocked many in staid Philadelphia society. In 1886 he caused a further scandal when he allowed female students to study from male models. He was given the choice of changing his teaching policy or of resigning. He chose the latter.

Medical College, which commissioned the work. Ranged behind Gross are young medical students, to whom he turns to make a point. The representatives of science—a young medical student, the doctor, and his helpers—are all highlighted. This dramatic use of light, borrowed, like

27-38. Eadweard Muybridge. *Sally Gardner Running at a 1:40 Gait, 19 June, 1878*. 1878. Wet-plate photography. George Eastman House, Rochester

27-39. Thomas Eakins. *The Pole Vaulter*. 1884. Multiple-exposure photograph. The Metropolitan Museum of Art, New York

Gift of Charles Bregler

the theme, from paintings of anatomy lessons by Rembrandt, is not meant to stir emotions but to make a point: Among the darkness of ignorance and fear modern science is the light of knowledge. The light in the center falls not on the doctor's face but on his forehead—on his mind.

Most observers found the work's bluntness offensive, in particular the details of the operation and the blood on the doctor's hand. Refused exhibition space in the art section of the 1876 Philadelphia Centennial, the painting was shown, instead, at the army's hospital display.

Eakins was chosen to paint *The Gross Clinic* because he often attended the doctor's lectures—he included a portrait of himself among the students in the painting—and even wrote a scientific paper on muscles. His interest in anatomy led him in turn to photography, which he used both as an aid for painting and as a tool for studying the body in motion. He made a number of studies with Eadweard Muybridge (1830–1904), a pioneer in motion photography.

Muybridge—who was born in England Edward James Muggeridge but changed his first name to follow the spelling of the Anglo-Saxon king—set up shop as a bookseller in San Francisco in 1855. He began taking landscape photographs in the 1860s and by the end of the decade was employed by the U.S. government for geographic and military surveys. In 1872 railroad owner and former California governor Leland Stanford wanted to prove that a running racehorse has all four feet off the ground at some point in its stride, and he hired Muybridge to establish that proof. John Isaacs, Stanford's engineer, developed a fast new shutter, and after a number of interruptions Muybridge succeeded in 1878 in confirming Stanford's contention (fig. 27-38).

Sally Gardner Running at a 1:40 Gait, 19 June, 1878 was produced by twelve cameras, with shutter speeds, according to Muybridge, of "less than two-thousand part of a second." The cameras, spaced 21 inches apart, were triggered by electric switches attached to thin black threads stretched across the track. In order to maximize the amount of light, the ground was covered with powdered lime and a white screen was set up along the rail, with its linear divisions corresponding to the spacing of

the cameras. When Eakins saw this photograph in 1878, he began a correspondence with Muybridge. Eventually, Eakins himself became interested in photography. He devised a revolving disk that would permit a series of superimposed yet distinguishable images to be taken on one plate. The results are seen in such works as *The Pole Vaulter* (fig. 27-39).

ART IN ENGLAND

In 1848 seven young artists formed the Pre-Raphaelite Brotherhood to counter what they considered the misguided practices of contemporary British art. Instead of the Raphaelesque conventions taught at the Royal Academy, the Pre-Raphaelites advocated the naturalistic approach of certain early Renaissance masters, especially those of northern Europe. They advocated as well a moral approach to art, in keeping with a long tradition in Britain established by Hogarth (see fig. 26-2).

The combination of didacticism and naturalism that characterized the first phase of the movement is best represented in the work of one of its leaders, William Holman Hunt (1827–1910), for whom moral truth and visual accuracy were synonymous. One of the best-known paintings of this academically trained artist is *The Hireling Shepherd* (fig. 27-40). The landscape portions of the composition were painted outdoors, an innovative approach at the time. Space was left for the figures, which were painted in his London studio. The work depicts a paid farmhand neglecting his duties to frolic with a woman, while pretending to discuss a death's-head moth that he holds in his left hand. Meanwhile, some of his employer's sheep are wandering into an adjacent field, where they may die or become sick from eating green corn. Hunt later explained that he meant to satirize pastors who spend time discussing theological questions he deemed to have no value rather than tending to their flock. Still, the painting can also be seen a moral lesson on the perils of temptation. The woman is cast as a latter-day Eve, as she feeds an apple—a symbolic reference to the Fall of humankind from the state of grace—to the lamb on her lap, and distracts the shepherd from his duty.

27-40. William Holman Hunt. *The Hireling Shepherd*. 1851.
Oil on canvas, 30⅛ x 43⅛" (76.4 x 109.5 cm).
Manchester City Art Gallery, England

The other major members of the group, John Everett Millais (1829–1896) and Dante Gabriel Rossetti (1828–1882), were less inclined to this sort of moralizing and by 1852 had broken with Hunt, which led to the dissolution of the group. In 1857 Rossetti, son of an exiled Italian poet, met two young Oxford students, William Morris (1834–1896) and Edward Burne-Jones (1833–1898), while

working on a mural at the university. Their shared interest in the Middle Ages inaugurated the second, unofficial phase of Pre-Raphaelites. Despite Hunt's protests, critics continued to identify Rossetti with the term, which is now more equated with his later work and that of his Oxford friends than with Hunt and the original group.

Morris's wife, Jane Burden, became Rossetti's favorite model. Her particular blend of physical beauty and sad, aloof spirituality perfectly suited Rossetti's vision of the Middle Ages and lent itself to his yearning for the spiritual beauty he found lacking in the present age. After Rossetti and Burden became lovers, sometime in the 1860s, his images of her took on an added biographical dimension. *La Pia de' Tolomei* (fig. 27-41) uses an incident from Dante's *Purgatory* to articulate the artist's own unhappy romantic situation. *La Pia* ("Pious One"), locked up by her husband in a castle, was soon to die. The rosary and prayer book in front of her refer to the piety from which she takes her name. The banner lances of her husband on the ramparts suggest her captivity. The sundial and ravens apparently allude to her impending death. Her continuing love for her husband, who wrote the letters lying under the prayer book, is symbolized by the evergreen ivy behind her. However, the luxuriant fig leaves that surround her,

27-41. Dante Gabriel Rossetti. *La Pia de' Tolomei* 1868–69. Oil on canvas, 41½ x 47½"(105.4 x 119.4 cm). Spencer Museum of Art, University of Kansas, Lawrence

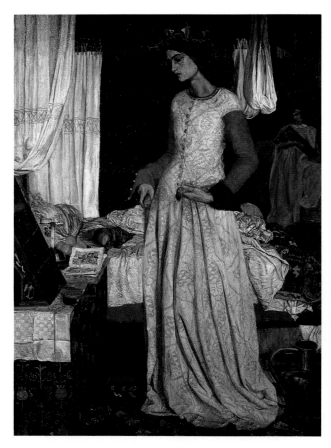

27-42. William Morris. *Queen Guinevere*. 1858. Oil on canvas, 27⁷⁄₈ x 19³⁄₄" (71.8 x 50.2 cm). Tate Gallery, London

27-43. Bedstead, from *The Art Journal Illustrated Catalogue of the Great Exhibition*, London, 1851

27-44. Norman Shaw. Armchair. 1876. Oak with rush seat. Victoria & Albert Museum, London

traditionally associated with lust and the Fall, have no source in Dante's tale. Rossetti personalizes the tale in other ways, showing her fingering her wedding ring, a captive not so much of her husband as of her marriage.

Jane Burden also appears in the only painting ever produced by William Morris, *Queen Guinevere* (fig. 27-42). Ironically, given later events in Morris's and Burden's lives, Guinevere was the unhappy wife of King Arthur, in love with the king's friend and most famous knight of his Round Table, Sir Lancelot. Morris chose the subject not for the story, however, but essentially as an excuse for depicting medieval objects and dress. Morris made the work only at Rossetti's prompting, for he was less interested in painting than in the kinds of handcrafts displayed in *Queen Guinevere*.

Morris's interest in handcrafts developed in the context of a widespread reaction against the gaudy design of industrially produced goods that began with the Crystal Palace exhibition of 1851, like the bed shown here (fig. 27-43). The elaboration of decorative elements at the expense of function and good taste distressed many, including the event's organizers. Prince Albert and his associates sought to improve industrial products through the teaching of better design principles, but a number of critics—led by writer, artist, and art critic John Ruskin— were convinced that industrialism itself was the problem. Morris became the leader of this faction soon after his marriage to Burden in 1859. Unable to find satisfactory furnishings for their new home, Morris, with the help of a number of friends, designed and made them himself. He then founded the decorating firm Morris, Marshall & Faulkner (later changed to Morris & Company) to produce a full range of medieval-inspired objects. Although many of the furnishings offered by Morris & Company were expensive, one-of-a-kind items, others such as the oak armchair designed by Norman Shaw in 1876 (fig. 27-44) were cheap, simple, and basic. They were meant to provide a handcrafted alternative to the vulgar excess characteristic of industrial furniture.

Morris promoted and inspired what became known as the Arts and Crafts Movement. His aim was to benefit not just a wealthy few but society as a whole. As he said in the lectures he began delivering in 1877, "What business have we with art at all unless we can share it?" A socialist, Morris meant to eliminate the machine not only because he found its products ugly but also because of its deadening influence on the worker. With craftwork, he maintained, the laborer gets as much satisfaction as the consumer. Unlike his Pre-Raphaelite friends, who wished to escape into idealizations of the Middle Ages, Morris saw in that era the model for economic and social reform.

Not all of those who participated in the revival of the decorative arts were committed to improving the conditions of modern life. Many, including the American expatriate James Abbott McNeill Whistler (1834–1903), saw in the Arts and Crafts revival simply another way to satisfy an elitist taste for beauty. After failing out of West Point in the early 1850s, Whistler studied art in Paris, where he came under the influence of Courbet. His first important works were **etchings**, which he had learned to make while employed in the U.S. government's Coastal Survey Department in Washington, D.C. One of his early works, *Black Lion Wharf* (fig. 27-45), depicts a naturalistic scene of life along the River Thames. Although inspired by Courbet, Whistler's etching shows little of that artist's interest either in the solid tangibility of things or in the social or human significance of work. Because of its horizontal emphasis and the absence of a strong focal point,

27-45. James Abbott McNeill Whistler. *Black Lion Wharf.* 1859. Etching, 5⁷/₈ x 8⁷/₈" (15 x 22.6 cm). The Metropolitan Museum of Art, New York
Harris Brisbane Dick Fund
A copy of this work can be seen on the wall in his most famous painting, the portrait of his mother.

the eye scans the etching's registers, making a quick survey of its picturesque details before passing on and out of the frame. This approach to composition anticipates the French Impressionists. The work is important, too, because of Whistler's crucial early place in the print revival of the later nineteenth century (see "The Print Revival," below).

Black Lion Wharf was produced soon after Whistler had moved to London early in 1859, partly to separate himself from Courbet and his influence. The new vogue for the arts of Japan helped fuel in him a growing dissatisfaction with naturalism (see "Japonisme," page 1008). Whistler

THE PRINT REVIVAL

During the Romantic period a number of artists, including Théodore Géricault and Eugène Delacroix, had used the new medium of **lithography**, invented in the mid-1790s, to produce fine art prints (see "Lithography," page 987). But as a result of the more prolific use of lithography by newspaper caricaturists such as Honoré Daumier (see fig. 27-22), the medium soon became identified with the popular arts.

Delacroix, Corot, and Millet had also produced the occasional **etching**, an art form at that time employed almost exclusively to produce cheap reproductions of well-known works (see "Etching and Drypoint," page 000). A less-well-known Barbizon artist, Charles-Émile Jacque (1813–1894), who as a student had studied and copied etchings by Rembrandt, was the first to devote himself more fully to the medium. Inspired by the work of Jacque and by the amateur example of his brother-in-law, Francis Seymour Haden, James Abbott McNeill Whistler turned to etching in 1858, just before moving to Britain. Whistler's early work may be said to have inaugurated a great age of etching. The interest it generated convinced an amateur French etcher and printer, Alfred Cadart, to organize the Society of Etchers in 1862. Cadart, who was also a print dealer, conceived the society as a way to bring before the public the kind of innovative work rejected by the Salon jury and to protest the growth and influence of photography. The Romantic poet and critic Théophile Gautier said in his preface to the first volume of etchings Cadart issued:

In these times when photography fascinates the vulgar by the mechanical fidelity of its reproductions, it is needful to assert an artistic tendency in favor of free fancy and picturesque mood. The necessity of reacting against the positivism of the mirrorlike apparatus has made many a painter take to the etcher's needle . . .
(Cited in Leipnik, page 106)

Included in the inaugural volume of etchings were works by forty-eight artists, among them Corot, Charles Daubigny, Édouard Manet, Alphonse Legros (who had introduced Manet to etching in 1861), and C.R. (for Carolus Rex, the king of Sweden). The critical response to Cadart's early annuals was so positive that even the conservative organizers of the Salon decided to dedicate an entire room to etchings at the exhibition of 1866.

Cadart's efforts established a solid foundation for a tradition that eventually included the work of Edgar Degas, Mary Cassatt, and a host of French artists. Cadart also contributed to the spread of etching when he helped form the French Etching Club in New York in 1866.

had been one of the first to collect Japanese art when it became available in curio shops in London and Paris after the 1854 reopening of that nation to the West. The simplified, elegant forms and subtle chromatic harmonies of Japanese art (Chapter 22) had a profound influence on his art in the early 1860s. In 1864 he exhibited three paintings that signaled his new direction. One of them, *Rose and Silver: The Princess from the Land of Porcelain* (see fig. 22, page 26, showing the Peacock Room Whistler later designed to house it), shows a woman posed amid a collection of Asian arts. The work is Whistler's answer to the medieval costume pieces of the Pre-Raphaelites (see fig. 27-41). What Whistler saw in Japanese objects was neither a preferable world nor a way to reform European decorative arts, but rather a model for painting. As the work's main title declares, Whistler attempted to create a formal and coloristic harmony similar to that of the objects displayed in the room. Thus, delicate organic shapes are shown against a rich orchestration of colors featuring silver and rose. By leaving his wet brushmarks visible, Whistler emphasized the paint itself over the depicted subject. In a remark that says more about his own commitments than about those of the Japanese, he later commented: "Japanese art is not merely the incomparable achievement of certain harmonies of color; *it is the negation, the immolation, the annihilation of anything else.*"

Whistler's insistence on art as an antidote to the ugliness of modern life was shared by a number of influential British writers and critics, including Walter Pater (1839–1894) and Oscar Wilde (1854–1900). By the late 1870s this view and its manifestation in artworks like those of Whistler and Rossetti had come to be known as

27-46. Édouard Manet. *Olympia.* 1863. Oil on canvas, 4'3" x 6'2¼" (1.31 x 1.91 m). Musée du Louvre, Paris

JAPONISME In his *Portrait of Émile Zola*, painted in gratitude for the writer's defense of his work, Édouard Manet included a Japanese screen and a portrait of a sumo wrestler by Kuniaki II, a nineteenth-century Japanese printmaker. These items probably say more about Manet's interest in Japanese art than they do about Zola's taste. In particular, the reductive design principle evident in Japanese woodblock prints and their tendency to flatten form probably inspired similar features in some of Manet's early works. On the wall next to the Kuniaki portrait is a print after *Olympia* (see fig. 27-46), which was severely criticized for just these qualities.

Manet's interest in Japanese prints and decorative arts was part of a widespread fascination with Japan and its art that swept across the West in the last half of the nineteenth century. The vogue began shortly after the U.S. Navy forcibly opened Japan to Western trade and diplomacy in 1854. Soon, Japanese lacquers, fans, bronzes, hanging scrolls, kimonos, ceramics, illustrated books, and **ukiyo-e** (prints of the "floating world," the realm of geishas and popular entertainment) were beginning to appear in Western European spe-

cialty shops, art galleries, and even some department stores. French interest in Japan and its arts reached such proportions by 1872 that the art critic Philippe Burty gave it a name: *japonisme*.

Japanese art profoundly influenced Western painting, printmaking, applied arts, and eventually architecture. The tendency toward simplicity, flatness, and the decorative evident in much painting and graphic art in the West between roughly 1860 and 1900 is probably the most characteristic result of that influence. Nevertheless, its impact was extraordinarily diverse. What individual artists took from the Japanese depended on their own interests. Thus, James Abbott McNeill Whistler, for example, found encouragement for his decorative conception of art (see fig. 22, page 26) while Edgar Degas discovered both realistic subjects and interesting compositional arrangements (see fig. 27-52). Those interested in the reform of late-nineteenth-century industrial design, on the other hand, found in Japanese objects both fine craft and a smooth elegance lacking in the West. There were even some, like Vincent van Gogh, who saw in the spare harmony of Japanese art and wares evidence of

an idyllic society, which he considered a model for the West (Chapter 28). Perhaps the most strongly influenced were the new printmakers, like Mary Cassatt, who, lacking a strong tradition of their own, often thought of themselves more as part of the Japanese tradition than the Western.

Édouard Manet. *Portrait of Émile Zola.* c. 1868. Oil on canvas, 57⅛ x 44⅞" (145.3 x 113.8 cm). Musée d'Orsay, Paris

ARTISTIC ALLUSIONS IN MANET'S ART

Manet had in his studio a copy by Henri Fantin-Latour of the *Pastoral Concert*, a work in the Louvre then attributed to Giorgione, now attributed to Titian. It is plain that in painting *Le Déjeuner sur l'Herbe* (see fig. 27-47) he took inspiration from the *Pastoral Concert*, making a modernized reply to its theme of ease in nature.

At the same time, in preparing his composition Manet directly adapted a group of river gods and nymphs from an engraving by Marcantonio Raimondi, based on Raphael's *The Judgment of Paris*—an image that, in turn, looked back to Classical reliefs. Manet's allusion to the engraving was apparently quite clear to some observers at the time; in reviewing the Salon at which the *Déjeuner* was exhibited, the critic Ernest Chesneau specifically noted this borrowing and objected to it.

In making these two references to artworks from the Renaissance, Manet's painting addresses not only the ostensible subject: figures in a landscape. Just as important, it also addresses the history of art and helps define Manet's relationship to it by encouraging the viewer to compare Manet's painting with the works that inspired it. To a viewer who has in mind the traditional perspective and the rounded modeling of forms of the two Renaissance works, the stark lighting of Manet's nude and the flat, cutout quality of his figures become all the more shocking. Thus, by openly referring to these exemplary works of the past, Manet emphasized his own radical innovations.

Titian. *Pastoral Concert* (formerly attributed to Giorgione). c. 1509–10. Oil on canvas, 43¼ x 54⅜" (109.9 x 138.1 cm). Musée du Louvre, Paris

Marcantonio Raimondi. Detail of engraving after Raphael's *The Judgment of Paris*. c. 1520. The Metropolitan Museum of Art, New York
Rogers Fund, 1919

Aestheticism. Aestheticism became so popular in the 1880s that young men and women displayed their devotion to its tenets by carrying peacock feathers.

IMPRESSIONISM

While British artists were moving away from the naturalism advocated by the original Pre-Raphaelite Brotherhood, their French counterparts were pushing the traditions of Courbet, Corot, and the Barbizon painters into new territories. Instead of themes of the working classes and the country, the generation that matured around 1870 was generally devoted to subjects of leisure, the upper middle class, and the city. Although many of these artists specialized in paintings of the country, the point of view they adopted was usually that of a city person there on holiday.

Édouard Manet

The leader of this loosely knit group was Édouard Manet (1832–1883). Born into an upper-middle-class Parisian family, Manet studied in the early 1850s with the painter Thomas Couture (1815–1879), an academician with progressive leanings. Manet often quarreled with Couture and some of the models available to him, however, because he wanted the models to adopt more naturalistic poses and because he thought that during the summer months studies should be done outdoors, under natural light. Manet's naturalist inclinations seem to have been shaped by his friendship with the poet and critic Charles Baudelaire, who in his call for "The Painter of Modern Life" (published in 1863 but written in 1859) had said that if a:

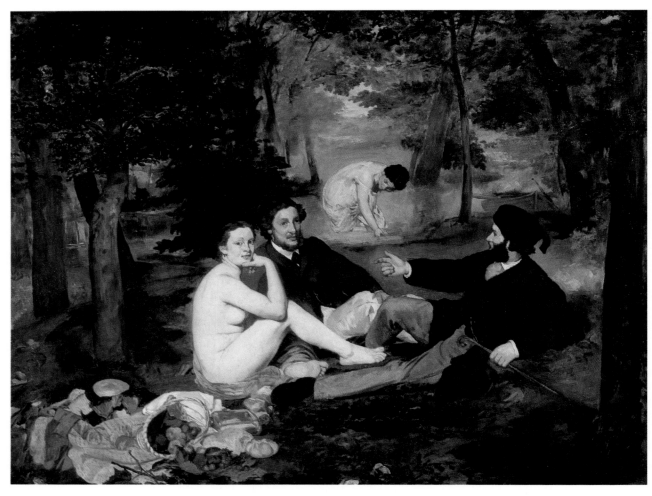

27-47. Édouard Manet. *Le Déjeuner sur l'Herbe (The Luncheon on the Grass)*. 1863. Oil on canvas, 7' x 8'10" (2.13 x 2.64 m). Musée d'Orsay, Paris

feebly imaginative artist has to paint a courtesan of today and takes his "inspiration" . . . from a courtesan by Titian . . . it is only too likely that he will produce a work which is false . . . From the study of a masterpiece of that time and type he will learn nothing of the bearing, the glance, the smile or the living "style" of one of [today's] creatures.

Manet answered his friend's challenge with *Olympia* (fig. 27-46), a common name for prostitutes in the era. The painting is based on Titian's *Venus of Urbino* (see fig. 18-32), which Manet had copied while in Florence in 1856. At first, Manet appears to be paying an homage to the great Venetian painter in terms of the subject matter (the Titian painting was then believed to be the portrait of a Venetian courtesan) and composition. However, Manet in effect made his modern counterpart the very antithesis of the Titian. Whereas Titian's female is curvaceous and softly rounded, Manet's is angular and flattened. Whereas Titian's looks lovingly at the male spectator, Manet's appears coldly indifferent. Our relationship with Olympia is underscored by the reaction of her cat, who—unlike the sleeping dog in the Titian—arches his back at us. Finally, instead of looking up at us, Olympia stares down on us, indicating that she—not we—is in the position of power. In reversing the Titian, Manet subverted the entire tradition of the accommodating female nude.

As part of his Baudelairean program to be "the painter of modern life," Manet also remade another Renaissance masterpiece, Giorgione's *Pastoral Concert* in the Louvre (see "Artistic Allusions in Manet's Art," page 1009). What Manet intended by *Le Déjeuner sur l'Herbe* (fig. 27-47) remains unclear and a matter of considerable debate. One contested theory sees in the work a portrayal of modern alienation, not unlike Daumier's *Third-Class Carriage* (see fig. 27-21). The figures in Manet's painting are distant in both their physical and their psychological relationships. Although the man on the right seems to gesture toward his companions, the other man gazes off absently while the nude turns her attention away from them and to the viewer. Moreover, her gaze makes us conscious of our role as outside observer—as in *Olympia*; we, too, are estranged. Manet's rejection of warm colors for a scheme of cool blues and greens plays an important role, as do his flat, sharply outlined figures, which seem starkly lit because of the near absence of modeling. The figures are not integrated with their natural surroundings, as in the Titian, but seem to stand out sharply against them, as if seated before a painted backdrop.

One historian has argued that Manet may have intended to make a modern version of the popular Renaissance theme of sacred and profane love, a contrast between the higher spiritual love and that of the flesh. Several details in the picture suggest as much. For example, the man on the right makes a curious hand gesture,

27-48. Claude Monet. *Terrasse à Sainte-Adresse*. 1867. Oil on canvas, 38⅝ x 51⅛" (98.1 x 129.9 cm). The Metropolitan Museum of Art, New York

Purchased with special contribution and purchase fund given or bequeathed by friends of the museum, 1967

27-49. Claude Monet. *The Railroad Bridge*. 1874. Oil on canvas, 21¾ x 28⅞" (55.2 x 73.3 cm). Philadelphia Museum of Art

The John G. Johnson Collection

with his thumb pointing to the clothed woman in the stream and his index finger pointing to the nude. Above the woman in the water—itself a symbol of purity—is a bird, traditionally associated with the spirit. In the lower-left corner, next to the nude's discarded garments, is a frog, often an emblem of the flesh. With these hints, perhaps, Manet fulfills Baudelaire's mandate giving us not only "the passing moment" of a contemporary picnic but "all the suggestions of eternity that it contains." It is worth noting in this regard that the "duality of man," which would include the conflict between the sacred and the profane, is one of Baudelaire's central concerns in "The Painter of Modern Life."

Claude Monet

While Manet was attempting to paint modern life without breaking entirely with the great art of the past, most of his slightly younger associates sought a completely fresh and unmediated vision. The leader in this quest was Claude Monet (1840–1926), the son of a grocer. Although Monet studied in the Paris studio of an academician, his real training came at the hands of Barbizon landscape painters such as Charles Daubigny (1817–1878) and a number of lesser-known naturalists associated with them—in particular, Eugène Boudin (1824–1898) and Johan Jongkind (1819–1891), from whom he learned how to transcribe directly his visual sensations of nature. Unlike the Barbizon painters, however, Monet was interested in the landscape in terms of the pleasures, especially visual, that it could provide for the modern city dweller on holiday. *Terrasse à Sainte-Adresse* (fig. 27-48), for example, depicts a busy harbor as seen from the terrace of a fashionable resort hotel. Elegantly dressed members of the *haute bourgeoisie* (upper middle class) are seen enjoying the sights that a bright and beautiful day on the north coast of France can provide—the flags, the boats, the flowers, as well as the clothing of the other guests. The viewer is invited to join these tourists, to relax with them, and to enjoy their particular mode of vision, which is largely unfocused and

unconcerned, one that seeks pleasant retinal stimulation.

Monet's stated aim in his early work was a kind of pure vision. One of the painters he later befriended received this advice in a letter:

"When you go out to paint, try to forget what objects you have before you—a tree, a house, a field, or whatever. Merely think, Here is a little square of blue, here an oblong of pink, here a streak of yellow, and paint it just as it looks to you, the exact color and shape, until it gives your own naive impression of the scene before you."

He [Monet] said he wished he had been born blind and then had suddenly gained his sight so that he could have begun to paint in this way without knowing what the objects were that he saw before him. He held that the first real look at the motif was likely to be the truest and most unprejudiced one (*The American Magazine of Art*, 18 [March 1927]).

Two important ideas are expressed here. One is that a quickly painted oil sketch most accurately records a landscape's general appearance. This view had been a part of academic training since the late eighteenth century, but such sketches were considered merely part of the preparation for a finished work. In essence Monet attempted to raise these traditional "sketch aesthetics" to the same level as a completed painting. As a result, the major criticism at the time was that his paintings were not "finished."

The second idea—that art benefits from a naive vision untainted by intellectual preconceptions—was a part of both the naturalist and the realist traditions, from which his work evolved. Corot and Courbet had expressed a similar desire to regain the unprejudiced vision of the child, but Monet, like his predecessors, could never achieve such a vision. Through the 1870s and 1880s, his quest continued to be colored by the values and tastes of the upper-middle-class tourists he had shown on the terrace of the hotel in Sainte-Adresse and with whom he identified.

27-50. Camille Pissarro. *A Cowherd on the Route du Chou, Pontoise*. 1874. Oil on canvas, 21⅝ x 36¼" (55 x 93 cm). The Metropolitan Museum of Art, New York
Gift of Edna H. Sachs

Monet's early way of looking at the world is especially evident in the works he produced in the 1870s while living in Argenteuil, a flourishing Parisian suburb. Paintings such as *The Railroad Bridge* (fig. 27-49) display Monet's mature style, which combined heightened color and broken brushwork. While the smaller strokes were intended to capture more accurately the shifting surface of natural appearance, the elimination of all dark colors from his palette produced the prettier visual effect and happier mood better suited to his recreational themes. Because of the bright, sunny colors and the emphasis on summertime pleasures, one tends not to notice how often these works feature industrial subjects. Here the sailboat is overshadowed by the modern railway bridge and freight train. The two themes are complementary—two sides of the same socioeconomic coin. Modern industrial progress, as Monet seems to have understood, provided the economic basis for the new leisure pursuits of the burgeoning middle class.

Even though France had suffered a terrible defeat in the Franco-Prussian War of 1870, the early 1870s witnessed an economic boom, which works such as *The Railroad Bridge* seem to record. Industrial production increased by more than 11 percent during the decade, and the earnings of the average French worker rose by 15 percent. In order to share in this new prosperity, Monet revived an idea he and friends had considered in the late 1860s: the formation of an independent society to exhibit and market their art. In 1874 thirty artists exhibited 165 works in Nadar's studio. One of Monet's entries, *Boulevard des Capucines, Paris* (see Introduction, fig. 25), is a view from the studio's window. Hoping to avoid being falsely identified with a single philosophy or movement, they called themselves a Corporation [Société Anonyme]

of Artists, Painters, Sculptors, and Engravers. One critic, however, inspired by Monet's *Impression, Sunrise* (1872), titled his review "Exhibition of Impressionists," and the term *Impressionist* was quickly adopted as a convenient, if not entirely accurate, label for all those who participated in the 1874 show, as well as the seven subsequent exhibitions Monet and his circle organized between 1874 and 1886. These exhibitions inspired other artists to organize their own alternatives to the Salon, a development that by the end of the century ended the stranglehold the French Academy had for centuries enjoyed on the display of art and thus on artistic standards.

Camille Pissarro

The oldest member of the group, Camille Pissarro (1830–1903), began his career under the influence of Corot's naturalism. In 1864 and 1865 Pissarro exhibited at the Salon as a "pupil of Corot," but the two had a falling-out shortly afterward. The dark, Courbet-influenced phase of Pissarro's career soon gave way to an early Impressionist phase in 1870. In that year he and Monet were both living in London, having fled there to escape the Franco-Prussian War. Influenced by John Constable, J. M. W. Turner, and other British landscape painters, they worked closely together, dedicating themselves, as Pissarro later recalled, to "plein air [outdoor], light and fugitive effects." The result, for both painters, was a lightening of color and a loosening of paint handling. After the Franco-Prussian War, Monet and Pissarro returned to France, where they continued to work together on occasion for mutual inspiration.

Pissarro's particular brand of Impressionism had stronger ties to the naturalism of Corot and the Barbizon

27-51. Pierre-Auguste Renoir. *Moulin de la Galette*. 1876. Oil on canvas, 4'3¹/₂" x 5'9" (1.31 x 1.75 m). Musée d'Orsay, Paris

painters than that of his younger colleagues. Reflecting these influences, after his return to France Pissarro settled in Pontoise, a small village not far from Argenteuil but decidedly more agrarian. The works he produced there in the 1870s, such as *A Cowherd on the Route du Chou, Pontoise* (fig. 27-50), are typically Impressionist in their high-keyed color, short brushstrokes, and direct appeal to the eye, but the narrow range of soft greens and blues is closer to Corot than to Monet. An important feature of the painting, the woman with the cow, demonstrates Pissarro's adherence to the previous generation's concept of the landscape as a place where peasants live and work, not simply a vacationer's source of visual pleasure.

Pierre-Auguste Renoir

More typical of the Impressionists in his proclivity for painting scenes of upper-middle-class recreation is Pierre-Auguste Renoir (1841–1919). The son of a tailor, Renoir met Monet at the École des Beaux-Arts after enrolling in 1862. Despite his early predilection for figure painting in a softened, Courbet-like mode, the affable Renoir was encouraged by his more forceful friend Monet to create pleasant, light-filled landscapes, painted outdoors. By the mid-1870s Renoir was combining Monet's style in the rendering of natural light with his own taste for the figure.

Moulin de la Galette (fig. 27-51), for example, features dancers dappled in bright afternoon sunlight. The Moulin de la Galette (the "Pancake Mill"), in the section of Paris called Montmartre, was an old-fashioned Sunday afternoon dance hall, which during good weather made use of its open courtyard. Renoir has glamorized its normally working-class clientele by replacing them with his young artist friends and their models. Frequently seen in Renoir's work of the period, these attractive members of the middle class are shown in attitudes of relaxed congeniality, smiling, dancing, and chatting. The innocence of their flirtations is underscored by the children in the lower left. The lack of tension in their relations is emphasized by the relaxed informality of the composition itself. The painting is knit together not by figural arrangement but by the overall mood, the sunlight falling through the trees, and the way Renoir's soft brushwork weaves his blues and purples through the crowd and across the canvas. This idyllic image of a carefree age of innocence, a kind of paradise, nicely encapsulates Renoir's essential notion of art: "For me a picture should be a pleasant thing, joyful and pretty—yes pretty! There are quite enough unpleasant things in life without the need for us to manufacture more" (cited in Hanson, page 38).

Edgar Degas

The Impressionist whose work most severely tests the legitimacy of the label is Edgar Degas (1834–1917), who preferred to think of himself as a naturalist or a realist. For Degas the two terms were synonymous. The son of a Parisian banker, Degas was closer to Manet than to the

27-52. Edgar Degas. *The Tub* c. 1885–86. Pastel, 27½ x 27½"
(69.9 x 69.9 cm). Hill-Stead Museum, Farmington,
Connecticut

other Impressionists in age and social background. He
entered the École des Beaux-Arts in 1855 but soon
became dissatisfied with its conservatism, so he left to
study on his own. His friendship with Manet, whom he
met in 1862, and with the realist critics in his circle turned
him gradually toward the depiction of contemporary life.
After a period during which he specialized in psychologically probing portraits of friends and relatives, he turned
his attention in the 1870s to a range of Paris amuse-
ments, including the music hall, opera, ballet, circus, and
racetrack. Although a few of these works record the sadder aspects of the times, Degas began to think of art less
as a mirror held up to the world than as a lofty form of
entertainment that employed realistic elements.

Part of Degas's intent was to oppose the clichés of
academic training by revealing certain truths obscured by
them. In Degas's innovative pastel *The Tub* (fig. 27-52), for
example, the bather is off-center and is viewed obliquely
from above because things often appear to us that way,
not centered and stably framed as in great art (see fig. 26-
5). Instead of moving gracefully and effortlessly in accord
with academic standards (see fig. 27-7), Degas's bather
reaches awkwardly, almost uncomfortably, for her soap.
Degas meant such works to be not only naturalistic but
also visually refreshing, a pleasant antidote to the tired
formulas of conventional art and illustration.

Although Degas's works most directly address the
spectator's eye, many also evoke a strong bodily response.
As in *The Tub*, Degas often makes it possible for us to share
in the bodily sensations of his subjects, as they rest, twist,
bend, and stretch. His interest in bodily feeling apparently
led him during the 1870s to begin experimenting in the
more tactile medium of sculpture. After his death about
150 small clay figures of ballerinas, bathers, and horses—
made not for exhibition or sale but for study—were found
in his studio.

Degas exhibited only one piece of sculpture during
his lifetime, a piece in wax of a young dancer, which he

27-53. Edgar Degas. *Young Dancer Fourteen Years Old*.
1880–81. Bronze with gauze tutu and satin hair
ribbon, height 39½" (100.3 cm). The Norton Simon
Museum, Pasadena, California

After Degas's death, a friend recalled that he had said
of his sculpture: "I modeled animals and people in wax
for my own satisfaction, not to take a rest from painting
or drawing, but to give more expression, more spirit,
and more life to my paintings and drawings. . . . And
since, after all, no one will ever see these efforts, no
one should think of speaking about them. . . . After
my death, all that will fall apart by itself." Although
many of the wax originals did fall apart, Degas's heirs
had 22 or more cast in bronze.

showed at the 1881 Impressionist exhibition. The young
girl stands with her arms clasped behind her. She pulls
back her shoulders, stretching her upper chest, while
turning the foot of her extended leg. Because her head is
up and her eyes closed, her mind appears fully preoccupied with the purely physical sensations her complex
pose entails. After his death this work, called *Young
Dancer Fourteen Years Old* (fig. 27-53), was cast in bronze.
The original was done in the hyperrealistic mode now
identified with wax museums: The figure was adorned
with actual slippers, a gauze skirt, and a silk bodice; the
real hair on the head was tied in a cloth ribbon. In the
bronze cast all that remains of this extreme verisimilitude
is the cloth skirt and hair ribbon.

Mary Cassatt

Another artist who showed with the Impressionists was
the American expatriate Mary Cassatt (1845–1926). After
studying at the Pennsylvania Academy of the Fine Arts in

27-54. Mary Cassatt. *Lydia in a Loge, Wearing a Pearl Necklace.* 1879. Oil on canvas, 31⅝ x 23" (80.3 x 58.4 cm). Philadelphia Museum of Art
Bequest of Charlotte Dorrance Wright

27-55. Berthe Morisot. *In the Dining Room.* 1886. Oil on canvas, 24⅛ x 19¾" (61.3 x 50.2 cm). National Gallery of Art, Washington, D.C.
Chester Dale Collection

Philadelphia between 1861 and 1865, Cassatt moved to Paris, where she lived for most of the rest of her life. The realism of the figure paintings she exhibited at the Salons of the early and middle 1870s attracted the attention of Degas, who invited her to participate in the fourth Impressionist exhibition, in 1879. Although she, like Degas, rejected the Impressionist label, her distaste for what she called the tyranny of the Salon jury system made her one of the group's staunchest supporters.

Cassatt focused her work on the world to which she had access: the domestic and social life of well-off women. One of the two paintings she exhibited in 1879 was *Lydia in a Loge, Wearing a Pearl Necklace* (fig. 27-54). The model for the painting was Cassatt's sister, who had recently come to live with her. The painting's bright and luminous color, fluent brushwork, and urban subject were no doubt chosen partly to demonstrate her solidarity with her new associates. (Renoir had exhibited a very similar image of a woman at the opera in 1874.) Reflected in the mirror behind Lydia are other women and men in their boxes, some with opera glasses trained not on the stage but on the crowd around them, scanning it for other elegantly dressed socialites. As Garnier had noted, his new Opéra (see fig. 27-5) was designed partly as an appropriate backdrop for just the kind of display in which Lydia is here engaged. *Lydia in a Loge,* therefore, is an attempt to capture a glamorous aspect of Parisian social life.

Berthe Morisot

Berthe Morisot (1841–1895) also was a prominent French Impressionist artist. Unlike Cassatt, who seems to have decided early on to be a professional, Morisot came to this decision only after a considerable period of painting in the amateur role that was conventional for women at that time (see "The Tradition of the Amateur Artist," page 1016). Morisot and her sister, Edma, studied with a minor drawing teacher in 1857. Admirers of the Barbizon painters, Berthe and Edma then studied with Corot for three years, beginning in 1860. The sisters showed in the five Salons between 1864 and 1868, the year they met Manet. In 1869 Edma married and, following the traditional course, gave up painting to devote herself to domestic duties. Berthe, on the other hand, continued painting after her 1874 marriage to Manet's brother, Eugène. In the same year, she joined the Impressionists, against the advice of Manet, who thought their independent society misguided, and she showed in all but one of their subsequent exhibitions.

Under the influence of Manet and the Impressionists Morisot adopted a looser, more **painterly** style to replace the Corot-influenced style in which she had been working. Like Cassatt, she focused on women and domestic scenes, such as that of *In the Dining Room* (fig. 27-55). Through this subject matter she sought to demonstrate that women had a unique vision, which, she said, was

THE TRADITION OF THE AMATEUR ARTIST

Amateur describes artists—men and women—who draw and paint for their own pleasure (and sometimes because of social expectations), not to make a living from their art. The tradition of the amateur artist is long and honorable; only in our century has the word *amateur* acquired some negative connotations.

Jean-Jacques Rousseau, writing in France at the end of the eighteenth century, was highly influential in prescribing educational goals that fostered amateur artists, especially women (see "Jean-Jacques Rousseau on Educating Children," page 935).

For at least 200 years, as part of their preparation for married life, European women of the upper classes were usually tutored in drawing and water-color—both mediums being portable and needing little equipment. The depiction of family, friends, vignettes of daily life, and scenes from their travels was accepted by both men and women as an effective and virtuous way for women to sharpen and culti-vate sensibilities that would make them "accomplished" women (and, it was assumed, wives and mothers). While in the nineteenth century in particular women were discouraged from having a profession, those who continued to pursue it could do so as amateurs—that is, as artists

who painted or drew or sculpted as a pastime, not as an occupation—and still be considered "respectable" according to the strict social codes of the period.

It is against this backdrop that women such as Rosa Bonheur (see fig. 27-18), Mary Cassatt, and Berthe Morisot (and many others whose works, ignored for so long, have recently begun to be discussed) came forward as professional artists, earn-ing their living from their work. In France and England many women artists, amateur and professional, showed their work in official exhibi-tions. In 1855, for example, 133 works by women were included in the Paris Salon.

"more delicate than that of men." Her brushwork calls attention to the act of painting itself: her touch—although vigorous—is lighter than that of her male col-leagues, and her colors are gentler, with a tendency to pastels. Both the subject and the style of *In the Dining Room* subtly insist that women be taken seriously for

their work. Morisot sought an equality for women that she felt men refused to cede. Late in life she commented: "I don't think there has ever been a man who treated a woman as an equal, and that's all I would have asked, for I know I'm worth as much as they" (cited in Higonnet, page 19).

27-56. Édouard Manet. *A Bar at the Folies-Bergère*. 1881–82. Oil on canvas, 37³/₄ x 51¹/₄" (95.9 x 130 cm). Courtauld Institute Galleries, London
Home House Collection

27-57. Pierre-Auguste Renoir. *Luncheon of the Boating Party*. 1881. Oil on canvas, 4'3" x 5'8" (1.3 x 1.7 m). The Phillips Collection, Washington, D.C.

Later Impressionism

Many Impressionists, including Morisot, continued throughout their careers to work in the manner they developed around 1870. In the years after 1880, however, some began to reconsider their earlier approaches or make important adjustments to them.

Even before what historians now call the crisis of Impressionism, Manet was quietly objecting to its essentially cheerful terms. During the 1860s Manet had engaged in a dialogue with the art of the past, as his *Olympia* (see fig. 27-46) and *Le Déjeuner sur l'Herbe* (see fig. 27-47) attest. After about 1870 he embraced his younger colleagues' brighter palette, and he seems to have adopted as well their more direct approach to modern life. But behind his apparent participation in the Impressionist movement lay a commitment, conscious or not, to use their essentially optimistic interpretation of modern life as the new foil for his more pessimistic one.

The last major painting of Manet's career, *A Bar at the Folies-Bergère* (fig. 27-56), for example, contradicts the happy aura of works such as *Moulin de la Galette* (see fig. 27-51) and *Lydia in a Loge* (see fig. 27-54). In the center of the painting is one of the barmaids at the Folies-Bergère, a large nightclub with a series of bars arranged around a theater that offered vaudevillelike acts. Reflected in the mirror behind the barmaid is part of the elegant crowd, many identifiable as Manet's friends, watching a trapeze act. (The legs of one of the performers can be seen in the upper left.) On the bar itself Manet has placed an assortment of objects, from champagne bottles to tangerines and flowers, that characterize the pleasures for which the place was famous. These items are associated not only with the place but also with the barmaid herself, whose hips, strong neck, and closely combed golden hair are echoed in the champagne bottles. Her demeanor, however, refutes these associations. Manet puts the viewer directly in front of her, in the position of her customer. She neither smiles at this customer, as her male patrons and employers expected her to do, nor gives the slightest hint of recognition. She appears instead to be self-absorbed and downcast. Her reflection and that of her customer in the mirror behind her and to the right, in contrast, tell a different story. There, she leans toward the patron, whose intent gaze she appears to meet; the physical and psychological distance between them has vanished. Exactly what Manet meant to suggest by this juxtaposition has been much debated. One possibility is that he wanted to contrast poignantly the longing for happiness and intimacy within the disappointing reality of ordinary existence.

What many of the Impressionists themselves found objectionable in their earlier art was not its truth value but its lack of permanence. One of the first to reject contemporary urban subjects for something that could compete with the classic art of the past was Renoir. The shift in his work is first signaled in *Luncheon of the Boating Party* (fig. 27-57),

27-58. Pierre-Auguste Renoir. *Bathers*. 1887. Oil on canvas, 3'10³/₈" x 5'7¹/₄" (1.18 x 1.71 m). Philadelphia Museum of Art
Mr. and Mrs. Carroll S. Tyson Collection

the last in a series of works he produced at Chatou on the theme of boating. The village on the Seine just outside Paris had become a favorite site for those Parisians interested in the new vogue for rowing. Here, Renoir depicts a group of rowers, in short sleeves and straw hats (known as boaters), and their friends on the terrace of the popular Restaurant Fournaise, located on the island that divided the Seine at Chatou. The company has gathered on this glorious summer day for refreshments and for the company of other beautiful young men and women. The painting, which again features an assortment of male artist friends and female models, is the suburban equivalent of *Moulin de la Galette* (see fig. 27-51).

Despite the fundamental similarity of conception and the persistent combination of sensual brushwork and lush color, *Luncheon of the Boating Party* differs from earlier works in two fundamental respects. First, the elements, especially the figures, are more solidly and conventionally defined. The arm of the man seated in the foreground, for example, has a descriptive clarity and solidity not seen in Renoir's work since the late 1860s. Second, the composition, too, is more conservative. Beneath the apparent informality is a variation on the traditional pyramidal structure advocated by the academies. A small triangle whose apex is the woman leaning on the rail is set within a larger, somewhat looser one that culminates in the two men in the rear. Thus, instead of a

moment quickly scanned in passing—an impression—Renoir creates a more stable and permanent scene.

The direction signaled by this work was confirmed and further encouraged by Renoir's subsequent visit to Italy in late 1881 and early 1882. In particular, the paintings by Raphael that he saw there made him reconsider his commitment to contemporary themes. Renoir became convinced that, unlike the enduring themes of Renaissance art, his records of modern life were too bound to their time to maintain the interest of future viewers. He therefore began to focus on the nude, a subject more difficult to locate in a particular time and place. The stable, pyramidal grouping of three female *Bathers* (fig. 27-58) was based on a seventeenth-century sculpture by François Girardon at Versailles (see fig. 19-23). This source clearly indicates Renoir's new commitment to the classical tradition of the female nude that originated in the Hellenistic period and was first adopted by French artists during the reign of Louis XIV. The work is perhaps closer to Bouguereau's *Nymphs and a Satyr* (see fig. 27-7) than to *Moulin de la Galette*.

The women are shown from three different views—front, back, and side—a convention that had been established in countless paintings of the Three Graces. Their chiseled contours also reflect a move toward academicism. Only the more loosely brushed landscape, the high-key colors, and the women themselves, who could be

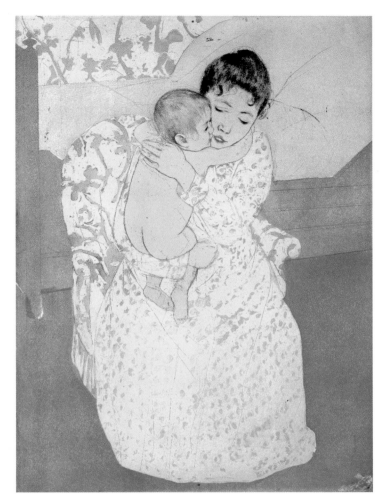

27-59. Mary Cassatt. *Maternal Caress*. 1891. Drypoint, soft-ground etching, and aquatint, 14³/₄ x 10³/₄"(37.5 x 27.3 cm). National Gallery of Art, Washington, D.C.
Rosenwald Collection

contemporary Parisians on the banks of the Seine, prevent the painting from being a wholesale rejection of Impressionism.

Cassatt, too, in the period after 1880 moved toward a firmer handling of form and more classic subjects. The shift is most apparent in her new focus on the theme of mother and child. In *Maternal Caress* (fig. 27-59), for example, one of the many colored prints she produced in her later career, we see her sensitive response to the tradition of the Madonna and Child. Apparently fresh from the bath, the plump infant shares a tender moment with its adoring mother. Their intimacy is underscored by the subtle harmony of apricots and browns. Even the pairing of decorative patterns reinforces the central theme.

These patterns, like the work's simple contours and sharply sloping floor, derive from Japanese prints. Works such as *Maternal Caress* appear to be Cassatt's Western answer to the work of Japanese printmakers such as Utamaro (see fig. 7, page 19) aiming for not only the timeless but also the universal. Like Renoir, Cassatt, too, moved far from her early commitment to depicting only contemporary moments.

Even Monet, who initially appeared immune to the growing crisis of Impressionism, eventually responded to it, first in the choice of some of his themes. During the 1880s he continued to record the transitory appearance of nature's more beautiful sites. In 1890 he appeared to take his brand of Impressionism even further with two series devoted to single themes, one to the haystack and the other to the poplars along a riverbank. Each painting concentrates on the light effects observable at a single instant in time. The two series thus seem to insist that time is but a collection of unique moments with little relation to one another. Monet, however, may have been exploring not only the singular beauty of each isolated moment but also the underlying continuities that link them. The poplar, for example, known as the Tree of Liberty during the French Revolution, had strong and enduring associations in France. The graceful S curves that dominate the paintings, too, have their counterparts in French Rococo art of the eighteenth century, which was then undergoing a revival.

Monet's apparent desire to place Impressionism within the great traditions of French art is most evident

27-60. Claude Monet. *Rouen Cathedral: The Portal (in Sun)*. 1894. Oil on canvas, 39¼ x 26" (99.7 x 66 cm). The Metropolitan Museum of Art, New York
Bequest of Theodore M. Davis

27-61. Claude Monet. *Water Lilies*. c. 1920. Oil on canvas, 6'5½" x 19'7½" (1.99 x 5.99 m). The Museum of Modern Art, New York
Mrs. Simon Guggenheim Fund

in a third series of paintings, devoted to the play of light over the variegated facade of Rouen Cathedral (fig. 27-60). The subject is unusual for Monet. Although he painted it with dazzling colors, the stony surface of the cathedral, unlike a row of poplars, actually has little color. Monet apparently chose the subject for its **iconographic** associations more than its coloristic appeal, for the building symbolizes the continuity of human institutions such as the Church and the enduring presence of the divine. And like the Rococo, the Gothic style of the cathedral originated in France in the Paris region. In effect, *Rouen Cathedral: The Portal (in Sun)* seems to argue that beneath the shimmering, insubstantial veneer of shifting appearances is a complex web of durable and expanding connections. Thus, while Renoir, Cassatt, and others were moving away from Impressionism, Monet was apparently trying to place it in a more enduring, coherent context.

Monet discontinued his preoccupation with nationalistic subjects after the Dreyfus affair of 1906. Dreyfus, a Jewish army officer accused of selling secrets to the Ger-

mans, was apparently charged and convicted largely because of his heritage. The outpouring of racism that the case inspired appalled Monet, who turned for the remainder of his life to the subject of his own extensive gardens at Giverny, especially his lily pond.

By focusing on his gardens, Monet was not emptying his art of meaning but striving after something more elemental, the point where nature and individual sensation coincide. In most of his versions of the lily pond, there is neither a horizon line nor a place for the viewer to stand. Instead of spectators (or tourists) on the edge of a pond, Monet places us in its midst, where we seem to lose ourselves in the fundamental elements of water, sky, and foliage, with the latter two reflected in the pond. The loss of self in nature is especially noticeable in the largest of these canvases, like the one in the Museum of Modern Art in New York (fig. 27-61), which Monet meant to wrap around the spectator, swallowing him or her in the artist's sensations of nature, which are here made timeless, universal.

1880   1890   1900   1910

Rodin
Burghers of Calais
1884–86

van Gogh
The Starry Night
1889

Munch
The Scream
1893

Picasso
*Les Demoiselles
d'Avignon*
1907

Gil
Woolworth Build
1911–

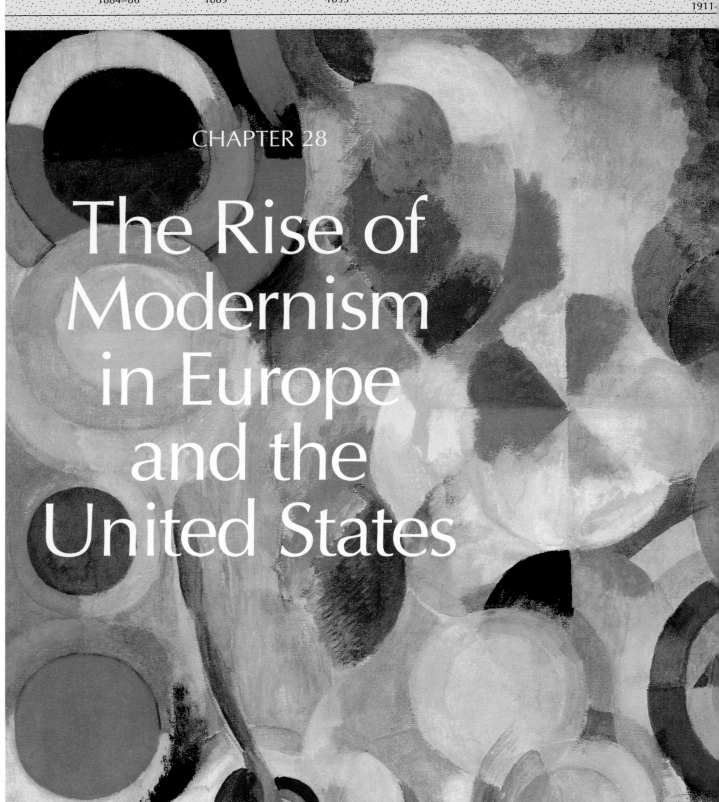

CHAPTER 28

The Rise of Modernism in Europe and the United States

hner
et,
n
3

Boccioni
*Unique Forms of
Continuity in Space*
1913

Malevich
*Suprematist
Painting*
1915

Duchamp
Fountain
1917

Lachaise
*Standing Woman
(Elevation)*
1912–27

Mondrian
*Composition with
Red, Blue, and Yellow*
1930

Miró
Painting
1933

Lange
*Migrant Mother,
Nipomo, California*
1936

28-1. Marcel Duchamp.
Fountain. 1917.
Porcelain plumbing
fixture and enamel
paint, height 24 5/8"
(62.23 cm). Photo-
graph by Alfred
Stieglitz. Philadelphia
Museum of Art
Louise and Walter Arens-
berg Collection

As the American Society of Independent Artists prepared for its first annual exhibition, in 1917, its members were committed to a large, unjuried show. Any artist who paid six dollars could enter a work in its exhibition. But members of the society were stunned—some openly outraged—when a work titled *Fountain*, signed "R. Mutt" and accompanied by the entry fee, turned out to be a urinal mounted in such a way as to be seen from above (fig. 28-1).

In fact, Marcel Duchamp, a founding member of the society and head of the show's hanging committee, had bought the fixture made by the J. L. Mott Iron Works, signed it "R. Mutt," and entered it. Duchamp, who strongly believed that art is a matter of what the head creates, not what the hand makes, submitted *Fountain*, among other reasons, to see just how open the members really were. Because some members of the society considered it gross, offensive, and even indecent, the work was refused. The decision did not surprise Duchamp.

Fountain was more than a cynical vexation, however. In a small journal he helped found, Duchamp published a letter on the Mutt case refuting the immorality charge and wryly noting: "The only works of Art America has given are her plumbing and her bridges." In a more serious vein, he added: "Whether Mr. Mutt with his own hands made the fountain or not has no importance. He CHOSE it. He took an ordinary article of life, placed it so that its useful significance disappeared under the new title and point of view—and created a new thought for that object" (cited in Harrison and Wood, page 248).

Confronted by *Fountain* and other jarringly innovative works, viewers who had previously debated standards for judging the aesthetic quality of works of art found themselves challenged to define the term *art*.

WHAT IS MODERNISM?

The years between 1880 and the outbreak of World War II in 1939 were flooded by a dizzying proliferation of different styles and artistic movements in Western European art and architecture. These various trends, often consciously at odds with one another, are nevertheless traditionally grouped under a common label, *modernism*. Like the word *Romanticism*, the term *modernism* is a disputed one, with neither an authoritative definition nor an entirely agreed-upon time frame. One useful approach is to think of modernism as a set of artistic beliefs that came to dominate thinking between roughly 1880 and 1970. What has distinguished this period, regardless of the name given, is rapid and radical stylistic innovations. Each modernist has reacted differently to the preceding generation, existing canon, even to contemporaneous events and to their colleagues. Some paid homage to and further developed a tradition, while others blatantly rejected and moved away from it. Although architects, like scientists of the time, tended to agree in principle on what constituted the mainstream, modernist artists often disagreed, which is why painting and sculpture of this era are so diverse.

Two broad tendencies can nevertheless be discerned in the visual arts: **formalism**, the aesthetic arrangement of shapes, colors, and forms (the formal elements of art); and **expressionism**, the manipulation of formal or representational elements to convey intense feelings. Formalists—or **abstractionists**, as they are usually called—generally reacted against the confusion of modern life by seeking simpler, more orderly formal arrangements. Expressionists pursued solutions to its tedium, restraint, and superficial materialism by heightening subjective experience. Many artists of each persuasion were convinced that their art would provide more than temporary relief from the ailments of modern life; some believed that their art could actually help solve its basic problems. This conviction that stylistically or conceptually progressive art could be a powerful instrument of social change was the second basic modernist tenet.

Modernism has proved difficult to define because of the lack of consensus among its participants in terms of both artistic and social issues. For example, the most radical and influential stylistic development of the era, the Cubist abstractions of Pablo Picasso and Georges Braque around 1910, was essentially a retreat from the social and personal spheres into that of the purely aesthetic. Although many of the painters and sculptors who followed their lead also supported the notion of art for art's sake, others—especially after World War I—put Cubism's radical stylistic innovations to the task of rebuilding society.

POST-IMPRESSIONIST ART

Although many date the beginnings of modernism to the flattening of form in the work of Manet (see fig. 27-46) or to the stylistic innovations of the early Impressionists (see fig. 27-49), others locate its origins in the work of the Post-Impressionists. Narrowly defined, Post-Impressionism refers to the work of five painters who assimilated much from Impressionism but in the end moved beyond its collective aesthetic principles to develop five different styles: Henri de Toulouse-Lautrec (1864–1901), Paul Cézanne (1839–1906), Georges Seurat (1859–1891), Paul Gauguin (1848–1903), and Vincent van Gogh (1853–1890).

Broadly defined, *Post-Impressionism* refers to the period when these five artists were either active or still influential. Thus, the term encompasses the entire generation of diverse innovators, including sculptors and photographers as well as painters, whose principal work falls between about 1880 and 1910. *Post-Impressionism*, unlike *Impressionism*, does not refer to a collective style but to a time period. The emergence of such a term indicates the increasingly fragmented artistic scene that would come to characterize modern art of the late nineteenth and twentieth centuries.

Auguste Rodin

The most important sculptor of the Post-Impressionist era, as it has been broadly defined, is Auguste Rodin (1840–1917), whose career dates from the mid-1860s but whose work has little in common with that of the five painters of Post-Impressionism narrowly defined. At the beginning of his career, Rodin was rejected three times by the École des Beaux-Arts, and his works were attacked by the academic critics. Yet, his intensely muscular figures in unconventional poses, especially those produced after his 1875 trip to Italy, where he saw the dramatic art of Michelangelo, were increasingly admired by the general public.

Rodin's status as the leading sculptor in France was confirmed in 1884, when he won a competition for *Burghers of Calais* (fig. 28-2), commissioned to commemorate an event from the Hundred Years War. In 1347 King Edward III of England had besieged Calais but offered to spare the city if six leading citizens (or burghers)—dressed only in sackcloth with rope halters and carrying the keys to the city—would surrender themselves to him for execution. Rodin shows the six volunteers marching out to what they assume will be their deaths.

The Calais commissioners were not pleased with Rodin's conception of the work. Instead of calm, idealized heroes, Rodin presented ordinary-looking men in various attitudes of resignation and despair. He expressively lengthened their arms, greatly enlarged their hands and feet, and changed the light fabric he knew they wore into a much heavier one, showing not only how they may have looked but how they must have felt as they forced themselves to take one difficult step after another. Rodin's willingness to alter the human body for expressive purpose was a revolutionary move that opened the way for the more radical innovations of later sculptors.

Nor were the commissioners pleased with Rodin's plan to display the group at close to ground level. Rodin felt that the usual placement of such figures on a high pedestal suggested that only higher, superior humans are capable of heroic action. By placing the figures nearly at

28-2.   Auguste Rodin. *Burghers of Calais.* 1884–86. Bronze, 6'10¹/₂" x 7'11" x 6'6" (2.1 x 2.4 x 2 m). Hirshhorn Museum and Sculpture Garden, Smithsonian Institution, Washington, D.C.

street level, Rodin hoped to convey to viewers that ordinary people, too, are capable of noble acts.

In its focus on great historical events that address human themes, Rodin's work looks back to a long tradition that began with the Greeks. *Burghers of Calais* is thus atypical among the arts produced during the Post-Impressionist era or later. Although the sculptors and painters who followed him absorbed many of Rodin's specific stylistic innovations, their works increasingly responded to contemporary life rather than the past.

Documenting Modern Life

By 1880 the impact of industrialization on the West was becoming clear. Although modern technology had produced new and unheard-of levels of material well-being, it had also created a new set of human problems. Some involved the hardships of industrial working conditions, while others were connected with the growth of massive industrial cities. The separation of these new cities from nature was thought by many to have terrible psychological consequences. When people moved to the urban centers to find work, their old family and community ties were often strained or broken, and they found

themselves surrounded by strangers, feeling alienated and alone.

One common artistic response to these problems was simply to document them, an activity already begun in the preceding era by artists like Honoré Daumier. The Post-Impressionist who identified the most with this current is Henri de Toulouse-Lautrec. Born into an aristocratic family in a small French town, Toulouse-Lautrec had medical problems that drastically stunted his growth and so affected his face that he often drooled. Because of his appearance, he was not welcome in his own family.

In 1882 Toulouse-Lautrec moved permanently to Paris, where he entered the studio of an academic painter. He was soon drawn to the art of the Impressionists, especially that of Edgar Degas. He also discovered Montmartre, a part of Paris devoted to entertainment and inhabited by a large population of social outcasts like himself. From the late 1880s he dedicated himself to documenting this fascinating realm in individual **caricatures**—drawings that exaggerate the characteristic features of a subject for satirical effect—and in naturalistic scenes. He recorded his observations both in the posters for which he became famous (see "Posters and Prints of the 1890s," page 1028) and in paintings.

PARALLELS

Years	Events
1880–1889	Major European colonization of Africa begins; Rodin wins competition for *Burghers of Calais* (France); steel first used in building construction (United States); Neo-Impressionists emerge (France); Seurat's *A Sunday Afternoon on the Island of La Grande Jatte* (France); Richardson's Marshall Field Warehouse (United States); Eastman's box camera (United States); Eiffel Tower (France); Art Nouveau emerges (France);Van Gogh's *The Starry Night* (France)
1890–1899	Riis's *How the Other Half Lives* (United States); Roman School of classicists (France); James's book *The Principles of Psychology* (United States); Sullivan's Wainwright Building (United States); McKim, Mead, and White's Boston Public Library; Horta's Tassel House (Belgium); World's Columbian Exposition in Chicago; Sino-Japanese War; antiacademic Secession movement begins in France; Hunt's Biltmore estate (United States); Olympic Games reestablished (Greece); Spanish-American War; World of Art group forms in St. Petersburg (Russia); Freud's book *The Interpretation of Dreams* (Austria) and advent of psychoanalysis
1900–1909	Stieglitz organizes Photo-Secession group, later known as 291 (United States); Wright brothers' first powered flight (United States); Russo-Japanese War; Fauves named (France); Die Brücke forms (Germany); Golden Fleece group forms in Moscow (Russia); Picasso's *Les Demoiselles d'Avignon* (France); Braque's *Houses at L'Estaque* inspires term *Cubism* (France); Ford's Model T automobile (United States); Ashcan School forms (United States); Braque and Picasso develop Analytic Cubism (France); Futurism emerges (Italy)
1910–1919	Union of South Africa forms; Kandinsky organizes Der Blaue Reiter (Germany); Braque and Picasso evolve Synthetic Cubism (France); Cubo-Futurism emerges (Russia); Balkan Wars; Sun Yat-sen establishes Republic of China; Gilbert's Woolworth Building (United States); Armory Show launches modernism in the United States; World War I; Sant'Elia's *Manifesto of Futurist Architecture* (Italy); Malevich's *Suprematist Painting* (Russia); Wright's Imperial Hotel in Tokyo (Japan); Einstein's general theory of relativity (Germany); Dada movement begins in Switzerland; de Stijl emerges in the Netherlands; Russian Revolution; Purism emerges (France); worldwide influenza epidemic kills 20 million people; Gropius establishes Bauhaus (Germany); League of Nations
1920–1929	Census shows more people living in urban than rural United States; Harlem Renaissance (United States); women citizens granted the right to vote in the United States; Constructivist movement (Russia); Leger's *Three Women* (France); Le Corbusier's design for a Contemporary City of Three Million Inhabitants (France); Eliot's poem *The Waste Land* (England); Joyce's novel *Ulysses* (Ireland); Breton's "Manifesto of Surrealism" (France); Lang's film *Metropolis* (Germany); Rietveld's Schröder House (Netherlands); Hitler publishes *Mein Kampf* (Germany); John Scopes convicted of teaching evolution in public school (United States); Morgan's San Simeon estate (United States); Hemingway's novel *The Sun Also Rises* (United States); Lindbergh makes first solo trans-Atlantic flight (United States); American Scene Painting emerges; Eisenstein's film *October* (Russia); Kellogg-Briand Pact, signed by 62 nations, attempts to end war; Mead's book *The Coming of Age in Samoa* (United States); Rivera's murals for the Mexico City Ministry of Education; dirigible *Graf Zeppelin* circles the globe (Germany); stock-market crash in United States signals worldwide economic depression; Woolf's essay *A Room of One's Own* (England); The Museum of Modern Art founded (United States)
1930–1939	Mondrian's *Composition with Red, Blue, and Yellow* (Netherlands); Regionalist painters emerge (United States); Huxley's novel *Brave New World* (England); Socialist Realism in art instituted by Stalin (Russia); Hitler takes dictatorial power in Germany; Malraux's novel *Man's Fate* (France); Stein's *The Autobiography of Alice B. Toklas* (United States); Lange's *Migrant Mother, Nipomo, California*, photographed for Farm Securities Administration (United States); Roosevelt establishes Federal Arts Project (United States); Mitchell's novel *Gone with the Wind* (United States); Spanish Civil War; American Abstract Artists group forms; Renoir's film *The Grand Illusion* (France); Carlson invents xerography (United States); Nazis launch anti-Jewish campaign throughout Germany; Miller's novel *Tropic of Capricorn* (United States); Steinbeck's novel *Grapes of Wrath* (United States); Kahlo's *Two Fridas* (Mexico); Krasner's *Red, White, Blue, Yellow, Black* (United States); World War II

POSTERS AND PRINTS OF THE 1890S

A second phase in the late-nineteenth-century print renaissance began around 1890 and lasted well into the next decade. Like the first phase (see "The Print Revival," page 1007), it was centered in Paris, but now the medium was **chromolithography**. The artist largely responsible for it was a poster designer, Jules Chéret (1836–1932), who in 1866 opened his own printing business in Paris, where he produced a variety of commercial work, from menus to posters. He specialized in color **lithography**, a technique that he greatly helped to perfect (see "Lithography," page 987). His clever theater and café posters of the late 1860s and 1870s attracted so much attention that in 1880 the critic Joris-Karl Huysmans advised his readers to ignore the paintings and prints at the Salon and to turn, instead, to the "astonishing fantasies of Chéret" that could be found on any street.

In 1884 two histories of the French poster were published. Two years later, Henri Beraldi's *Les Graveurs du XIXe siècle* (*The Print-makers of the Nineteenth Century*) included a section devoted to Chéret's posters. In that year, too, the print dealer Edmond Sagot began listing posters, particularly those by Chéret, among his offerings. Other print dealers soon followed his lead, and by the end of the decade the

poster vogue was in full flower not only in France but throughout the West. Influenced by Japanese prints and Art Nouveau, with its commitment to beautifying the urban environment, a number of talented and ambitious young artists turned their attention to designing them—including Alexandre Steinlen, Eugène Grasset, Alphonse Mucha, Will Bradley, Maxfield Parrish, Ethel Reed, John Sloan, Maurice Prendergast, and the Beggarstaff brothers. The most famous poster artist was Henri de Toulouse-Lautrec, who produced thirty between 1891 and his death in 1901.

One result of the poster phenomenon inaugurated by Chéret was a renewed interest in artistic lithography, especially in color. A number of other famous artists also participated in this development, largely through the urgings of the art dealer Ambroise Vollard. Toulouse-Lautrec's first poster, for example, inspired a greater commitment to the lithographic print. Beginning in 1896 Vollard organized two annual editions of prints similar to those produced two decades earlier by Cadart. In 1896 he published an edition of twenty-four and the following year one containing thirty-two. Vollard's artists included Toulouse-Lautrec, Cézanne, Renoir, Whistler, Gauguin, Pissarro, Bonnard, and Vuillard. Vollard also contributed significantly to the renewed interest in book illustra-

tion, a genre neglected since the days of Édouard Manet. He asked a number of the artists just mentioned, as well as Marc Chagall and Georges Rouault later, to provide original lithographs for books. The best known of the English book illustrators was Aubrey Beardsley, whose work combined influences from Whistler, the second phase of the Pre-Raphaelite movement, and Japanese prints to form a beautifully "unnatural" style.

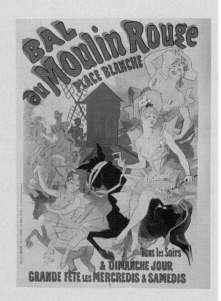

Jules Chéret. *Bal au Moulin Rouge.* 1889. Four-color lithograph, 23½ x 16½" (59.7 x 41.9 cm). Jane Voorhees Zimmerli Art Museum, Rutgers, The State University of New Jersey

At the Moulin de la Galette (fig. 28-3) is a conscious remake of Pierre-Auguste Renoir's earlier painting of the popular dance hall (see fig. 27-51), which Toulouse-Lautrec had recently seen in an exhibition. Clearly, Toulouse-Lautrec wished to contradict the optimistic terms of the earlier work and of Impressionism in general. Whereas Renoir painted idealized, pretty young women and handsome young men, Toulouse-Lautrec depicted the sadder reality of such places. The happy couples in the back of the Toulouse-Lautrec work are only foils for the four lonely, dispirited figures in the front. The diagonal rail, similar to the one found in the Renoir painting, here creates a barrier between the sexes. Moreover, the rail and foreground table separate the viewer from the foreground figures, thus reinforcing the view-

28-3.   Henri de Toulouse-Lautrec. *At the Moulin de la Galette.* 1889. Oil on canvas, 35½ x 39¼" (90.2 x 99.7 cm). The Art Institute of Chicago
Mr. and Mrs. Lewis L. Coburn Memorial Collection

28-4. Eugène Atget. *Magasin, Avenue des Gobelins*. 1925. Albumen-silver print, 9½ x 7" (24.1 x 17.8 cm). The Museum of Modern Art, New York

Abbott-Levy Collection. Partial gift of Shirley C. Burden

er's outside position. With these compositional devices and somber colors, what once was the symbol of urban pleasure has become that of loneliness and alienation.

Another medium, photography, was ideally suited to recording the problems of modern life. One of the most well-known and important photographers of this period is Eugène Atget (1857–1927), an actor who turned to

photography in the early 1890s to earn a living. The Paris business he opened in 1892 specialized in providing artists with photographs on which they would base their compositions. By the end of the 1890s, however, Atget had begun to make two kinds of photographs: documentary images of "old France" and pictures of the new age that threatened it.

A fine example of the latter type is *Magasin, Avenue des Gobelins* (fig. 28-4), which shows the Hôtel des Gobelins—the tapestry workshop established in 1662—reflected in the window of a men's clothing store. The age-old methods of making fabrics by hand are thus contrasted with the modern industrial techniques that produced the cloth in the window. Price labels on the cloth and suits remind us that in factory production, price—not quality—is what matters. The mannequins themselves may well represent Atget's view of modern industrial humanity: anonymous, interchangeable, soulless, and wearing a price tag.

Artistic Alternatives to Modern Life

Magasin, Avenue des Gobelins is less typical of Atget than are his works that fondly record premodern France. These photographs of an older world are countermoves against the encroachment of the new age. In most of his work Atget sought an image of a stable, unchanging world that would provide an escape from the increasingly noisy, unstable world of modernity. *Pontoise, Place du Grand-Martroy* (fig. 28-5), for example, shows the kind of small-town square that had been a center for community life in Renaissance and post-Renaissance Europe. Around the square are the various small, family-run businesses—*boulangerie* ("bakery"), *sabotier* ("wooden-shoe maker"), *pâtisserie* ("pastry shop")—that served community needs long before big department stores began to appear in the late nineteenth century.

28-5. Eugène Atget. *Pontoise, Place du Grand-Martroy*. 1902. Albumen-silver print, 7 x 9⅜" (17.8 x 23.8 cm). The Museum of Modern Art, New York

Abbott-Levy Collection. Partial gift of Shirley C. Burden

Atget's interest in the France of earlier times was part of a larger current in French culture that had begun with the publication of Victor Hugo's medieval tale, *The Hunchback of Nôtre-Dame* (1831). Nostalgia for the premodern era was significantly heightened by Haussmann's renovations of Paris in the 1850s and 1860s (Chapter 27). In the late nineteenth century, local groups throughout the city were organized to preserve what remained of the past, and a number of publications appeared that documented buildings and sites dating from between the Middle Ages and the Revolution of 1789.

28-6.   Pierre-Cécile Puvis de Chavannes. *Summer*. 1889–93. Oil on canvas, applied to wall. Hôtel de Ville, Paris

The square is formally stabilized on two sides by balancing architectural masses and symbolically stabilized by the church at the rear. The church represents both the personal security that belief can provide and a major force for social cohesion. Between the fall of Rome and the advent of the industrial age, Christianity had largely organized the life of Western Europe, but its centrality was now being threatened by science, technology, and commerce. Atget, whether intentionally or not, shows an awareness of that threat.

In this, Atget was not alone. One important countertendency in the modernist era was the search for conservative visual forms that would give psychological relief from the troubling conditions of a rapidly changing and increasingly complicated world. The painter Pierre-Cécile Puvis de Chavannes (1824–1898) was an important early contributor to this tradition. Puvis began his career as a Romantic painter, but partly because his early works were refused by the Paris Salon jury during the 1850s, in 1859 he adopted a **classical** mode. His inspiration came from the so-called Parnassian poets, who were then attempting to escape from the modern present into an idealized antiquity. By the late 1860s municipal buildings had become a major source of commissions for Puvis's large classical murals. Because the great popularity of such works dates from the early 1880s, Puvis, like Rodin, can be grouped with the Post-Impressionists.

A good example of Puvis's canvas murals (he never learned the fresco technique) is *Summer* (fig. 28-6), set, like all his classical views, 2,000 years earlier in an idealized France after the arrival of Greek-Roman civilization. Against a simple agrarian background, a scene of a family bathing suggests both a dignified pace of life and the notion that the larger community was composed of happy family units. To the right of the door, three indolent bathers, meant to resemble classical statuary in color and texture, anchor the scene formally and psychologically. Puvis's lovely park is populated by sculpture; the marblelike figures create a static, timeless quality. The sense of tranquil unreality is further enhanced by the way he has simplified his forms and softly muted his colors.

Puvis's murals contributed to a new wave of antimodernist classicism in French arts and letters around 1900. During the 1890s the literary classicists called themselves l'École Romane ("the Roman School"). The major sculptor of this broad artistic movement was Aristide Maillol (1861–1944), who during the 1880s trained as a painter at the École des Beaux-Arts. Late in the decade he became a member of a group of young artists who greatly admired Puvis's murals. He first adapted Puvis's style to the making of tapestry, but because his eyesight was strained by such work, he turned to creating small sculpted pieces.

Maillol's reputation dates from 1905, when the exhibition of *The Mediterranean* (fig. 28-7) received widespread popular and critical acclaim. The large, relaxed female bather almost seems to have escaped from one of Puvis's murals. The smooth, simplified modeling—so different from the tense, tortured surfaces of Rodin's work—combines with the stable triangular arrangement of the

28-7. Aristide Maillol. *The Mediterranean*. 1902–5. Bronze, height including base 41" (104 cm). The Museum of Modern Art, New York
Gift of Stephen C. Clark

28-8. Constantin Brancusi. *Magic Bird*. 1908–12. White marble, height 22" (55.8 cm), on three-part limestone pedestal, height 5'10" (1.78 m), of which the middle part is the *Double Caryatid* (c. 1908), overall 7'8" x 12³/₄" x 10⁵/₈" (237 x 32 x 27 cm). The Museum of Modern Art, New York
Katherine S. Dreier Bequest

figure to emphasize its psychological calm. As the title indicates, the bather personifies the ideal of the classical Mediterranean world established by Puvis and the Roman School of literature.

The year Maillol exhibited *The Mediterranean*, Constantin Brancusi (1876–1957), who had trained as a sculptor in a Romanian school for arts and crafts, enrolled in the École des Beaux-Arts. Early in 1907 Rodin hired him as an assistant, but Brancusi left after just two months, to avoid being overshadowed by the well-known sculptor. The rough surfaces of Brancusi's first works in France reflect Rodin's influence, but by the end of the decade he had completely rejected Rodin's style for one that emphasized formal and conceptual simplicity. Behind this change stood the ancient Greek philosophy of Plato, who held that all creatures and things are imperfect imitations of perfect models, or Ideas.

Brancusi's quest for the timeless essence of things is most completely expressed in *Magic Bird* (fig. 28-8). The piece is formed of two separate sections. The lower, limestone section has three parts, the middle one showing two rough-hewn figures (one of which has its face buried in the other's shoulder) representing the imperfect world of ordinary human existence. The top section, carved in pure white marble, is a symbol of the higher world of Ideas: the simplified form of a bird in flight.

The bird was apparently inspired by Russian-born composer Igor Stravinsky's 1910 ballet score *The Firebird*, which premiered in Paris. The ballet features a beautiful bird with magical powers that reminded Bran-

cusi of the many Romanian folktales of the *pasarea maiastra*, or magic bird, able to heal the sick and restore sight to the blind. Unlike the magic birds of those tales, which always have dazzling plumage, the beauty of Brancusi's bird is in its utter simplicity. Brancusi tried to eliminate all unnecessary details in his search for the Platonic ideal of "birdness" itself. The bird also represents what many people believe the modern urban mind seeks and needs: the primal simplicity underlying nature. Brancusi's *Magic Bird* may not provide a healing force, but it does offer a satisfying artistic antidote to modern complexity. Because of his radically simplified approach to form, Brancusi is considered by many to be the original modernist sculptor.

Other modernist innovators, including Gustav Klimt (1862–1918), also dedicated their work to providing a satisfying artistic alternative to the perceived deficiencies of modern life. Klimt was a leader in the Austrian Secession, the French-inspired revolt of the 1890s against academic standards in art and architecture. Klimt became the center of the faction dedicated to a richly decorative art and architecture that would offer an escape from the drab, ordinary world.

28-9. Gustav Klimt. *The Kiss*. 1907–8. Oil on canvas, 5'10³/4" x 6' (1.8 x 1.83 m). Österreichische Galerie, Vienna

The Secession was part of a reaction by younger European artists against the conservative society in which they were raised. The generational revolt was also expressed in politics, literature, and the sciences. Sigmund Freud, the founder of psychoanalysis, may be considered part of this larger cultural movement, one of whose major aims was, according to the architect Otto Wagner, "to show modern man his true face."

Between 1907 and 1908 Klimt perfected what is called his golden style, shown in *The Kiss* (fig. 28-9). A man and woman—perhaps Klimt and his mistress—embrace in an aura of golden light. The representational elements here are subservient to the decorative ones. The complex play of the jewellike shapes, colors, and dazzling surface is meant to dominate the human drama of the scene, and there are many incongruities. For example, the position the woman's head—forced uncomfortably against her shoulder—is so improbable that it appears to be detached from her body. And the marked difference between them, not only in terms of their size but also in their nature, is further played out in the forms that decorate their garments—angular shapes dominate those worn by the man, whereas the woman's garment primarily has

rounded forms. What at first appears a single unit is in fact two separate and very distinct beings in a somewhat forced embrace. That they kneel dangerously close to the edge of a precipice further unsettles the initial impression for those willing to look behind the beautiful surface.

Odilon Redon (1840–1916), a French painter and **graphic artist**, developed still another response to the modern world. He considered his visionary works his "revenge on an unhappy world." Examples such as *The Marsh Flower, a Sad and Human Face* (fig. 28-10) are not purely fanciful but express certain of the larger ideas of his era. Growing in a dark, featureless marsh—a scene probably inspired by the landscape of his youth—is a plant whose flower is a sad, lonely face. Specifically, this work exhibits the pessimism that swept France in the

28-10. Odilon Redon. *The Marsh Flower, a Sad and Human Face* (plate 2 from *Homage to Goya*). 1885. Lithograph, 10⁷/₈ x 8" (27.5 x 20.3 cm). The Museum of Modern Art, New York
Abby Aldrich Rockefeller Purchase Fund

28-11. Paul Cézanne. *The Bay from L'Estaque.* 1886. Oil on canvas, 31¹/₂ x 38¹/₂" (80.8 x 98.7 cm). The Art Institute of Chicago
Mr. and Mrs. Martin A. Ryerson Collection

years after the Germans had defeated them in the Franco-Prussian War of 1870–1871. Many felt that France was aging and in decline. Redon's image suggests that nations flower and wilt like plants but also expresses hope for regeneration. That the face glows with a radiant light suggests not only the power of the imagination over the darkness of despair but also Redon's larger hope that his "suggestive art," akin to music, would reverse the French decline and promote "the supreme elevation and expansion of our personal life" (cited in Chipp, page 117).

Redon's art might therefore be said to participate in the broad artistic endeavor actually to change the world. But before examining the work of Seurat and Gauguin, the Post-Impressionists most associated with the idea of art as a social tool, it is essential to turn to Paul Cézanne's, whose stylistic innovations inaugurated the most radical and most characteristic style of modernist art, abstraction.

Paul Cézanne

Cézanne's early work from around 1870 dealt with a number of violently Romantic themes, including murder, in a purposefully dark, crude style. In 1872, under the guidance of Pissarro (see fig. 27-50), he renounced subjectivity—and all that it meant for him personally—for the objective transcription of what he called his "sensations" of nature. In this respect Cézanne was an Impressionist. However, unlike his Impressionist colleagues, he resisted thinking about the landscape in terms of its human uses and his

"sensations" went beyond optical. In what he insisted was his "study" of nature, Cézanne sought also to record its solidity, as we can see in a work such as *The Bay from L'Estaque* (fig. 28-11).

The painting was done in the south of France, the area of his birth, to which he had returned in 1883 to avoid the distractions of the Paris art world. Although the weather is warm and sunny, the effect is not cheerful. The blues of the sky, mountains, and water temper the warm golden colors of the foreground elements, effectively neutralizing their emotional appeal. While one can find a way into an Impressionist's landscape by means of a human being or a road (see fig. 27-50), it is impossible to enter into Cézanne's landscape. Confronted and blocked, the viewer finds himself or herself to be remote and aloof, both physically and emotionally. *The Bay from L'Estaque* can be read as a three-dimensional view into space, with the high vantage point flattening the scene, creating a two-dimensional effect considerably enhanced by the artist's handling of paint. Finally, and perhaps most importantly, the work offers a balance of stable and unstable compositional elements, the most noticeable of which is the tension between the static horizontal of the shoreline at top and the dynamic diagonal of its counterpart below. This contrapuntal effect is especially noticeable in the townscape, where Cézanne has organized the houses, foliage, and land according to a loose grid of horizontal and vertical elements. The effect is not static, however, because of the many irregular contours that are

28-12. Paul Cézanne. *Still Life with Basket of Apples.* 1890–94. Oil on canvas, 24³⁄₈ x 31" (62.5 x 79.5 cm). The Art Institute of Chicago
Helen Birch Bartlett Memorial Collection

28-13. Paul Cézanne. *Mont Sainte-Victoire.* 1904–6. Oil on canvas, 25¹⁄₂ x 32" (65 x 81 cm). Private collection, Pennsylvania

After receiving a considerable inheritance in 1886, Cézanne returned to his hometown, Aix-en-Provence, in the south of France. In 1901–1902 he built a studio in the countryside with a large window facing Mont Sainte-Victoire, to facilitate painting the subject that had increasingly come to preoccupy him.

also introduced. *The Bay from L'Estaque* reveals the artist's "sense" that nature is a harmony of opposites.

At times, especially in Cézanne's still lifes, the effect is less tranquil. In *Still Life with Basket of Apples* (fig. 28-12), for example, an apparently conventional studio arrangement of fruit, biscuits, and wine bottle is, on clos- er examination, on the verge of collapse. The wine bot- tle tips precariously on a tabletop whose two sides do not match. The white cloth—whose dynamic folds add con- siderably to the work's instability—seems both to cover what we must assume to be the table's cracked top and to echo it in its own broad diagonal pleat. Only the folds

28-14. Georges Seurat. *A Sunday Afternoon on the Island of La Grande Jatte.* 1884–86. Oil on canvas, 6'9½" x 10'1¼"
(2.07 x 3.08 m). The Art Institute of Chicago

Helen Birch Bartlett Memorial Collection

Although the painting is highly stylized and carefully composed, it has a strong basis in factual observation. Seurat spent
months visiting the island, making small studies, drawings, and oil paintings of the light and the people he found there. All
of the characters in the final painting, including the woman with the monkey, were based on his observations at the site.

and small tucks in the fabric seem to prevent the apples
from cascading to the floor, inaugurating the general collapse of the rest of the elements. The strained balance in
such studio works suggests that Cézanne is moving
beyond a faithful reproduction of objects in his still lifes;
he is re-creating and reconstructing nature.

The major subject of Cézanne's late period was a
large mountain in the vicinity of his home. Works such as
Mont Sainte-Victoire (fig. 28-13) continued to emphasize
the tensions between warm and cool, two and three
dimensions, and stable and unstable elements. In the
middle section of this work, for example, the solid, rectangular brushstrokes, generally applied horizontally or
vertically, nevertheless form dynamic irregular contours.
What is new here, first, is the play between the permanence of the mountain and the impermanence of foliage
and the atmosphere through which they are seen.
Furthermore, Cézanne is now less concerned with
specifics than with conveying a general effect—that is,
with the deeper truth below or behind appearance.

Picasso, Braque, and others would later view this
move away from descriptive accuracy as evidence of
Cézanne's revolutionary conception of painting as an
aesthetically pleasing arrangement of colored forms on
a canvas support, but that was never Cézanne's intention. Cézanne became the originator of what became
known as abstraction, but he was an abstractionist in the
literal sense of the term: Cézanne *abstracted* what he

considered nature's deepest truth—its essential tension
between stasis and change.

The Avant-Garde

Cézanne's Post-Impressionist colleagues Georges Seurat
and Paul Gauguin were stylistic innovators, but they also
inaugurated a distinctive aspect of modernist art: the
notion of art as a force for social change. The term that
came into general use to describe such art was ***avant-
garde***. Originally a military one meaning "vanguard," it
was used in 1825 by a French socialist to refer to those
artists whose propagandist art would prepare people to
accept the social changes he and his colleagues envisioned (see "Realist Criticism," page 994). The idea of producing a socially revolutionary art had briefly attracted
such artists as Courbet, but the real popularity of this
notion dates from the Post-Impressionist era.

One of the first in his generation apparently to think of
himself in these terms was Georges Seurat, who trained at
the École des Beaux-Arts. After his graduation he devoted
his energies to "correcting" Impressionism, which he
found too intellectually shallow and too improvisational.
In the mid-1880s he gathered around him a circle of young
artists who became known as the Neo-Impressionists. The
work that became the centerpiece of the new movement
and made his reputation was *A Sunday Afternoon on the
Island of La Grande Jatte* (fig. 28-14).

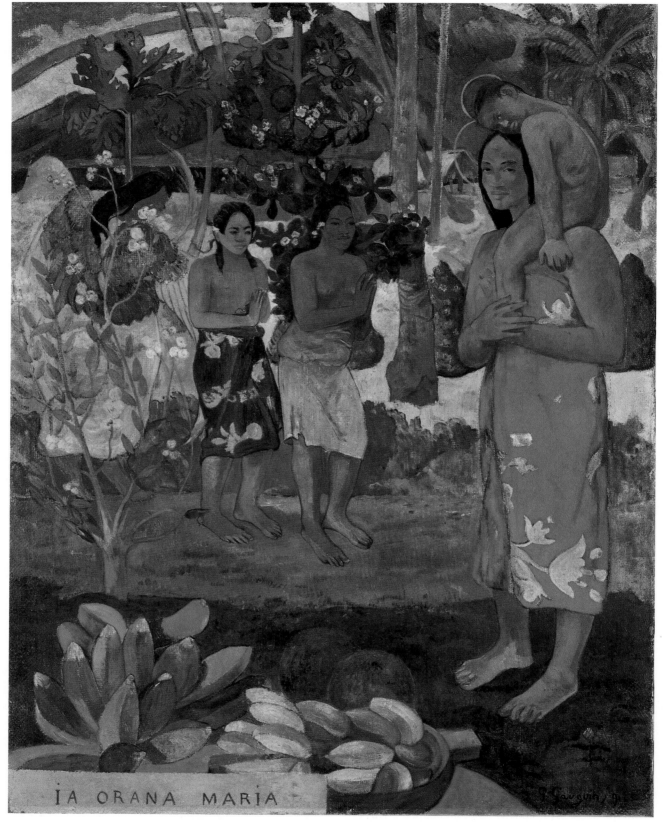

28-15. Paul Gauguin. *Ia Orana Maria* (*We Hail Thee Mary*). c. 1891–92. Oil on canvas, 44³/₄ x 34¹/₂" (113.7 x 87.7 cm). The Metropolitan Museum of Art, New York

Bequest of Samuel A. Lewisohn, 1951

Seurat took a typical Impressionist subject, weekend leisure activities, and gave it an entirely new handling. An avid reader of scientific color theory, he applied his paint in small dots of pure color, known as pointillism, in the belief that when they are "mixed" in the eye—as opposed to being mixed on the palette—the resulting colors would be more luminous. His scientific approach to painting does not work in practice, however, because his dots of color are large

28-16. Vincent van Gogh. *Harvest at La Crau (The Blue Cart)*. 1888. Oil on canvas, 28½ x 36¼" (72.5 x 92 cm). Rijksmuseum Vincent van Gogh, Amsterdam

enough to remain separate to the eye. Other aspects of his rational approach to expression were also problematic. He thought, for example, that upward-moving lines (like the coastline shown here) and warm, bright colors created "happy" paintings. Many viewers, however, find the stiff formality of his figures inconsistent with such a mood, which has led to controversy about the work.

From its first appearance the painting has been subject to a number of conflicting interpretations. Contemporary accounts of the island indicate that on Sundays it was noisy, littered, and chaotic. By painting it the way he did, Seurat may have intended to show how tranquil it should be. Was Seurat merely criticizing the Parisian middle class, or was he trying to establish a social ideal—a model for a more civilized way of life in the modern city? The key to Seurat's ideal, perhaps, is shown in the composure of the central figures, the mother and child who stand as the still point around which the others move. The child, in particular, is a model of self-restraint. She may even represent Seurat's sense of the progress of human evolution, as obliquely suggested by the contrasting presence of the monkey in the right foreground.

Whereas Seurat seems to have felt that people were not civilized enough, the French painter Paul Gauguin held the opposite view. Gauguin led an apparently conventional existence until the age of thirty-seven, when he

quit his job as a Paris stockbroker and left his wife and five children to pursue a full-time painting career. Gauguin so loathed the instinctually restrained and money-oriented modern world that in 1891 he moved to Tahiti, an island in the South Pacific Ocean, in the belief that he could return to what he called Eden.

In Tahiti he wrote an essay arguing that what the modern world needed was Adam and Eve's blissful ignorance before the Temptation. Among the supposedly childlike Tahitians (as he and other Europeans then imagined the people of this French-controlled colony), he thought he could reenter the Garden of Paradise. The first picture he painted there was *Ia Orana Maria (We Hail Thee Mary)* (fig. 28-15). The new Mary, a strong Polynesian woman holding an utterly contented Christ Child, stands in sharp contrast to the crucified Christs and mourning Marys that dominated the Catholicism Gauguin knew and that he himself had sometimes painted in the late 1880s. The warm, rich colors and decorative patterns underscore the message that life in this supposedly uncivilized world is sweet and harmonious. The chief argument, however, is made through the fruit on the table. Like Adam and Eve before the Fall, people here need simply to pick the fruit off the trees. The fruit is put within the viewer's easy reach, as well. As in all of Gauguin's Tahitian works, we, too, are invited to leave a sorry industrial society and enjoy the fruits of Eden.

28-17. Vincent van Gogh. *The Starry Night*. 1889. Oil on canvas, 28³⁄4 x 36¹⁄2" (73 x 93 cm). The Museum of Modern Art, New York

Acquired through the Lillie P. Bliss Bequest

Among the artists in Gauguin's circle before his departure for Tahiti was the Dutch painter Vincent van Gogh. The oldest surviving son of a Protestant minister, van Gogh worked as an art dealer and studied to become a minister himself before he moved in 1880 to Brussels to attend the Academy. In 1886, he moved to Paris, where he was influenced by the work of the Impressionists and Neo-Impressionists and met Gauguin. Van Gogh shared Gauguin's preference for simple, preindustrial life, and they planned to move to the south of France and establish a commune of like-minded artists. In the spring of 1888, van Gogh moved to Arles, where Gauguin was to join him.

The works van Gogh produced in his Arles period, such as *Harvest at La Crau* (*The Blue Cart*, fig. 28-16), were strongly influenced by the Neo-Impressionist interest in **complementary colors**, pairs of colors that optically balance each other, such as blue and orange. But unlike Seurat and his followers, who applied these colors in small dots, van Gogh juxtaposed large color areas, inspired by Japanese prints (see "Japanese Woodblock Prints," page 868). He felt that the combination of Japanese forms and Neo-Impressionist colors effectively expressed the quiet, harmonious life of this rural community.

Works such as *Harvest at La Crau* (*The Blue Cart*) function less to provide an escape from the industrial city than to point the way back to a simpler agrarian life. But around the beginning of 1889, van Gogh's work changed in both style and function. Late in 1888, Gauguin finally arrived in Arles, but constant quarrels led to a violent confrontation in which van Gogh threatened Gauguin with a razor. After Gauguin fled, van Gogh turned the implement on himself and cut off the lobe of his right ear. This incident was the first of a series of psychological crises that led to his eventual suicide in July 1890. Van Gogh's heightened emotional state during the last year and a half of his life was recorded in a series of paintings that contributed significantly to the emergence of the **expressionistic** tradition, in which the intensity of an artist's feelings overrides fidelity to the actual appearance of things.

Expressionism

One of the earliest and most famous examples of Expressionism is *The Starry Night* (fig. 28-17), which van Gogh painted from the window of his cell in a mental

28-18. James Ensor. *The Intrigue*. 1890. Oil on canvas, 35½ x 59" (90.3 x 150 cm). Koninklijk Museum voor Schone Kunsten, Antwerp

asylum. Above the quiet town is a sky pulsating with celestial rhythms and ablaze with exploding stars—clearly a record not of something seen but of what van Gogh felt. One explanation for the intensity of van Gogh's feelings in this case focuses on the then-popular theory that after death people journey to a star, where they continue their lives. Contemplating immortality in a letter, van Gogh wrote: "Just as we take the train to get to Tarascon or Rouen, we take death to reach a star." The idea is given visible form in this painting by the cypress tree, a traditional symbol of both death and eternal life, which dramatically rises to link the terrestrial with the stars. The brightest star is actually Venus, which is associated with love. Is it possible that the picture's extraordinary excitement also expresses van Gogh's euphoric hope of gaining the companionship that had eluded him on earth?

Whether modern artists have faced greater emotional difficulties than those from earlier ages is a matter of conjecture. What cannot be denied is that a great many artists of this period assumed that their chief function as artists was to express their intense feelings to the world. The Belgian painter and printmaker James Ensor (1860– 1949) was such an artist. Except for his four years at the Brussels Academy, Ensor spent his entire life in the coastal resort town of Ostend. Although his sense of isolation was sharpened by the hostile reception to both his early naturalistic and his later expressionistic art, it was apparently formed by his experiences with the ordinary tourists and townspeople of Ostend, as works such as *The Intrigue* (fig. 28-18) clearly attest. The painting shows a crowd of masked revelers celebrating Mardi Gras, one of the main holidays in Ostend. Their grotesque masks are here used to reveal the wearers' true identities, rather than hiding them. Mouths hang open stupidly or smile without warmth. Eyes stare absently into space or focus menacingly on the viewer. The luminous colors oddly increase the sense of caricature, as does the crude handling of form. The rough paint is both expressive and expressionistic: Its lack of subtlety well characterizes the

subjects, while its almost violent application directly records Ensor's feelings toward them.

The Norwegian painter and printmaker Edvard Munch (1863–1944) dealt with problems of a different kind. When he was five, he witnessed his mother's death from tuberculosis, and in 1875 he nearly died of the same disease. Three years later his favorite sister hemorrhaged to death, just as his mother had. As an artist, he was rejected for his frank treatments of death and sex not only by the general public with no particular interest in art but also by progressive artists and critics—the members of the Berlin Secession, who invited him to show his work in 1892, were so shocked by it they closed the exhibition.

Munch's personal and professional anxiety in the aftermath of this rejection found expression in his most famous work, *The Scream* (fig. 28-19). Munch recorded the painting's genesis in his diary: "One evening I was walking along a path; the city was on one side, and the fjord below. I was tired and ill. . . . I sensed a shriek passing through nature. . . . I painted this picture, painted the clouds as actual blood." In the painting itself, however, the figure is on a bridge and the scream emanates from him. Although he vainly attempts to shut out its sound by covering his ears, the scream fills the landscape with clouds of "actual blood." The overwhelming anxiety that sought release in this primal scream was chiefly a dread of death, as the sky and the skull-like head of the figure suggest, but the setting of the picture also reflects Munch's fear of open spaces.

Another painter of intense feelings was the Austrian Egon Schiele (1890–1918). Schiele's father died insane when Egon was fourteen. After a brief period of experimentation with the decorative style of Vienna's most famous artist, Gustav Klimt (see fig. 28-9), Schiele began to do many paintings and drawings of women that had sexual overtones. In 1912 he was jailed briefly for allowing neighborhood children to see some of this work. Even before this traumatic event, Schiele revealed in an extraordinary series of self-portraits a deep ambivalence toward the sexual themes of many of his works. One of these,

28-19. Edvard Munch. *The Scream.* 1893. Tempera and casein on cardboard, 36 x 29" (91.3 x 73.7 cm). Nasjonalgalleriet, Oslo

Self-Portrait Nude (fig. 28-20), presents an image of physical and psychological suffering. The body is emaciated, the sad record of long victimization; the skin is raw, as if flayed. Here, Schiele is the subject and object of his expression.

EXPRESSIONISTIC MOVEMENTS

In the years just before and after 1910 the expressionistic approach pioneered by Ensor, Munch, and van Gogh, in particular, was developed in the work of three artists' groups. The first of these groups to emerge was the Fauves.

The Fauves

In the fall of 1905 a French critic, Louis Vauxcelles, referred to a loosely affiliated group of young painters as *fauves* ("wild beasts"), a term that caught the spirit of the work of the leading members of their circle: André Derain (1880–1954), Maurice de Vlaminck (1876–1958), and Henri Matisse (1869–1954). For some years, these artists had been trying to advance the colorist tradition in modern French painting, which they dated from the work of Eugène Delacroix (see figs. 26-48, 26-49) and which included that of the Impressionists and Neo-Impressionists, such as van Gogh and Gauguin. In *Luxe, Calme, et Volupté* (fig. 28-21) Matisse, who would become the leading figure in the group, had attempted to develop further Seurat's pointillist technique (see fig. 28-14) by enlarging and broadening the individual strokes of pure color. Matisse was thereby attempting to make color operate more expressively than descriptively, a goal that he assumed his predecessors Delacroix, Monet, and Seurat had ultimately been seeking in their art. Rather than a record of something seen, the bold **primary colors** (red, yellow, and blue) are meant to communicate emotions and sensations, as well as deeper meanings.

In the sketch for the painting done in Saint-Tropez in the summer of 1904, only the artist's wife (the dressed woman seated on the left) and son (the small standing figure wrapped in a towel) are evident. Matisse added the

28-20. Egon Schiele. *Self-Portrait Nude*. 1911. Gouache and pencil on paper, 20¼ x 13¾" (51.4 x 35 cm). The Metropolitan Museum of Art, New York
Bequest of Scofield Thayer, 1982 (1984.433.298)

nudes in order to transform his family vacation picture into a Mediterranean pastorale in the tradition of Puvis de Chavannes (see fig. 28-6) and Maillol (see fig. 28-7). The boat was added to underscore the painting's function, which is to transport us to this lovely world. The title of the work, which translates as "luxury, calm, and voluptuousness," comes from the last line of a Baudelaire poem, "The Invitation to a Voyage."

In this phase, Matisse seems to have thought that his primal art would contribute to the revitalization of the French spirit and thus help prepare the way for a return to the golden age pictured in *Luxe, Calme, et Volupté*. For Matisse and his associates Vlaminck and Derain, the key to France's spiritual regeneration was to recover the child's direct approach to the world. The artist most committed to this vision was Vlaminck.

Unlike Derain and Matisse, Vlaminck was self-taught and proud of it. In works like *Landscape near*

28-21. Henri Matisse. *Luxe, Calme, et Volupté*. 1904–5. Oil on canvas, 38½ x 46½" (98.5 x 118 cm). Musée d'Orsay, Paris

28-22. Maurice de Vlaminck. *Landscape near Chatou.* 1906. Oil on canvas, 23 7/8 x 29" (60.6 x 73.7 cm). Stedelijk Museum, Amsterdam

28-23. Henri Matisse. *The Woman with the Hat.* 1905. Oil on canvas, 31 3/4 x 23 1/2" (80.6 x 59.7 cm). San Francisco Museum of Modern Art
Bequest of Elise S. Haas

Chatou (fig. 28-22), he shows even less concern than van Gogh, his major inspiration, with a polished and refined result. The strong colors have been crudely applied with a stiff, broad brush. "I try to paint with my heart and my loins, not bothering about style," he once said.

Vlaminck's influence is evident in the works Matisse produced in 1905, including *The Woman with the Hat* (fig. 28-23). The painting shows his wife, Amélie, who until recently had supported the family with the proceeds from her millinery shop. She looks at the artist with wide, sad eyes, and her mouth is slightly turned down. This highly revealing presentation of feeling and personality is surprising in a painting Matisse considered an exercise in raw, immediate sensation. The work was one of those shown in 1905 that the critic Vauxcelles considered the handiwork of "wild beasts."

Matisse himself very quickly came around to something of this view. In 1908 he published an essay, "Notes of a Painter," in which he rejected his Fauve approach for a more thoughtful and soothing one:

Often when I sit down to work I begin by noting my immediate and superficial color sensations. Some years ago this first result was often enough for me. . . . [But now] I prefer to continue working on it so that later I may recognize it as a work of my mind. There was a time when I never left my paintings hanging on the wall because they reminded me of moments of nervous excitement. . . . Nowadays, I try to put serenity into my pictures and work at them until I feel that I have succeeded.

One of the first of Matisse's post-Fauve works is *The Joy of Life* (fig. 28-24), which he painted in his studio during the winter of 1905–1906. Despite the spontaneous sketch he began with, the finished painting is not a quick response to something seen but a carefully orchestrated

and more fully developed treatment of the bacchanalian theme he had painted the previous winter in *Luxe, Calme, et Volupté.* Here uninhibited, naked revelers dance, make love, commune with nature, or simply stretch out in their idyllic glade by the Mediterranean. The banquet of luscious colors, discovered the previous summer at Collioure in the south of France, are now applied broadly and without any trace of nervous excitement. The brushwork, too, is softer and more careful, subservient to the pure sensuality of the color. The only movement is in the long, flowing curves of the trees and the bodily contours. These undulating rhythms, in combination with the relaxed poses of the two reclining women at the center, establish the "serenity" that Matisse wanted to characterize his work from this point.

In "Notes of a Painter" Matisse explained the purpose of his new emphasis: "What I dream of is an art . . . devoid of troubling or depressing subject matter . . . which might be for every mental worker, be he businessman or writer, like . . . a mental comforter, something like a good armchair in which to rest." Here Matisse signals his new allegiance to the aspect of modernist art that sought relief from the stress of modern life. According to one biographer, Matisse himself was sometimes "madly anxious" and well understood the temporary peace art could provide.

28-24. Henri Matisse. *The Joy of Life*. 1905–6. Oil on canvas. 5'8½" x 7'9¾"(1.74 x 2.38 m). The Barnes Foundation, Merion, Pennsylvania

During an illness in his youth, Matisse was given a box of paints by his mother, a moment that he recalled as fundamental to his later concerns as a painter: "When I started to paint, I felt transported into a kind of paradise. . . . In everyday life, I was usually bored and vexed by the things that people were always telling me I must do. Starting to paint, I felt gloriously free, quiet and alone." The reference to paradise, in particular, suggests that his mature paintings, such as *The Joy of Life*, are not concerned simply with the escapist Western myth of Arcadia but with painting itself as an ideal realm.

Die Brücke

The German counterpart to Fauvism was Die Brücke ("The Bridge"), which formed in the same year the Fauves were named. In 1905 three architecture students at the Dresden Technical College—Karl Schmidt-Rottluff (1884–1976), Erich Heckel (1883–1970), and Ernst Ludwig Kirchner (1880–1938)—decided to take up painting and form a brotherhood. For the next eight years they lived and worked together. Their collective name was taken from a passage in Nietzsche's *Thus Spake Zarathustra* (1883) in which the prophet Zarathustra speaks of contemporary humanity's potential to be the evolutionary "bridge" to a more perfect specimen of the future, the *Ubermensch* ("beyond man," but usually translated as "superman").

In their art, however, the group demonstrated little interest in advancing the evolutionary process. Instead, their paintings, sculpture, and graphics suggest a Gauguinesque yearning to return to imaginary origins. Among their favorite motifs were women living harmoniously in nature, such as depicted in Schmidt-Rottluff's *Three Nudes—Dune Picture from Nidden* (fig. 28-25), which shows three simplified female nudes formally

28-25. Karl Schmidt-Rottluff. *Three Nudes—Dune Picture from Nidden*. 1913. Oil on canvas, 38⅝ x 41¾" (98 x 106 cm). Staatliche Museen zu Berlin, Preussischer Kulturbesitz, Nationalgalerie

28-26. Erich Heckel. *Crouching Woman*. 1912. Painted linden wood, 11⁷⁄₈ x 6³⁄₄ x 3⁷⁄₈" (30 x 17 x 10 cm). Estate of Erich Heckel, Hemmenhofen am Bodensee, Germany

28-27. Ernst Ludwig Kirchner. *Street, Berlin*. 1913. Oil on canvas, 47¹⁄₂ x 35⁷⁄₈" (120.6 x 91 cm). The Museum of Modern Art, New York
Purchase

integrated with their landscape. The style is purposefully simple and direct, in keeping with the painting's evocation of the prehistoric. Instead of the graceful contours of Matisse's erotic nudes in *The Joy of Life*, Schmidt-Rottluff's larger, lumbering subjects have thick, almost angular outlines. Although both artists nostalgically looked back, one looked to the golden age of Greece while the other seemed more interested in Europe's Neolithic past.

The two artists also share a vocabulary of simple, flattened shapes of pure color mostly inspired by the same stylistic sources. Around 1905, when Derain and Vlaminck were discovering African art in Paris's shops and in its natural history museum, their German counterparts were studying African and Oceanic sculpture in their ethnographic museums. This interest led Die Brücke artists to make their own "primitive" sculpture. Heckel's *Crouching Woman* (fig. 28-26) is crudely carved in wood not only to emulate its non-European sources but also to revive what the group considered the more honest methods of German Gothic artists. In turning to

wood they were rejecting the classical tradition of both marble and bronze. What they sought was not refined beauty but earthy strength, as the actions and features of the woman suggest. In this work the medium itself suggests the desire to return to nature that is depicted in Schmidt-Rottluff's *Three Nudes*.

During the summers, Die Brücke artists actually did return to nature. They visited the remotest areas of northern Germany, such as Nidden. But in 1911 they moved to Berlin, perhaps preferring to imagine the simple life rather than live it. Ironically, the images they made of cities, especially Berlin, offer powerful arguments against living there. Kirchner's *Street, Berlin* (fig. 28-27), for example, forcefully demonstrates the isolation that can occur in cities. Although physically close, the well-dressed men and women are psychologically distant. And instead of becoming a larger formal unit, they are presented as a series of independent vertical elements, an accumulation of isolated individuals, not a tight-knit community. The angular, brittle shapes and the sharp contrast of predominantly cool colors formally underscore the message.

What made it possible for modernists like Kirchner to endure such conditions was their collective belief that they lived not in Berlin or Paris or New York but in bohemia, a cultural space uncontaminated by the ordinary conditions of those cities. The term *bohemian* was originally used during the 1830s in Paris to describe cer-

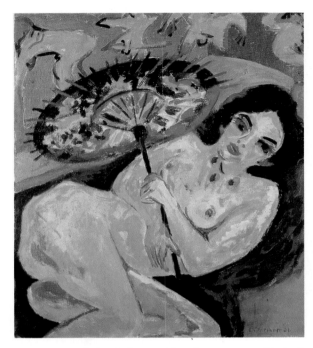

28-28. Ernst Ludwig Kirchner. *Girl under a Japanese Umbrella.*
c. 1909. Oil on canvas, 36¼ x 31½" (92 x 80 cm).
Kunstsammlung Nordrhein-Westfalen, Düsseldorf
Collection Dr. Frederic Bauer Davo

twisting torso intended to suggest an independent creature whose passion challenges that of the artist, just as the painting behind her of naked women in a landscape expresses her vital, "natural" attitude? The umbrella she holds also shows the influence of the Japanese **ukiyo-e** prints then in vogue in Europe, which often featured geishas (see fig. 22-15).

Such images conceive of women in terms of men's desires, and Die Brücke artists restricted women to this role. Although they often depicted themselves and their male friends reading, writing, painting, and playing chess, they almost never showed women engaged in such pursuits. The brotherhood may have been anti-bourgeois in most respects, but its attitudes toward women were utterly traditional.

The women who participated in the modernist enterprise, although tolerated, were rarely treated as equals. One such woman was Paula Modersohn-Becker (1876–1907). In 1896 she enrolled in the Berlin School of Art for Women, where she was allowed to study the female nude and, on occasion, the partially dressed male models. In 1897 Modersohn-Becker moved to Worpswede in northern Germany, one of the many charming and rustic European villages that became famous artists' retreats, where she married Otto Modersohn, a leading painter working in the Barbizon-related style (Chapter 27) identified with the town.

She quickly became dissatisfied with the naturalistic approach to rural life, which she said was not broad enough. Between 1900 and her death in 1907 she made four trips to Paris in order to assimilate the leading developments in Post-Impressionist painting. In particular she found amenable the formal simplicity developed by Gauguin and his circle. Inspired by such examples, she evolved at the end of her life a very personal approach to painting the women of Worpswede, including herself.

Modersohn-Becker's *Self-Portrait with an Amber Necklace* (fig. 28-29), for example, features greatly simplified shapes and crude outlines similar to those used in Schmidt-Rottluff's *Three Nudes—Dune Picture from Nidden* (see fig. 28-25). Avoiding the intense color in that work, however, Modersohn-Becker employed a muted palette of browns and blues. These colors combine with the soft layering of her paint to produce a formal effect similar to the gentle expression on her face. Emphasis is given to the figure's relationship with nature. The artist presented herself against a screen of flowering plants wearing only a necklace. In her large, somewhat awkward hands she tenderly holds the kind of little flower that also decorates her hair. Their shape and color are also echoed in her breasts. Instead of the eroticized object of male design, Modersohn-Becker's woman is a natural being in tune with her surroundings.

Another German who was an important artist of this period is Käthe Schmidt Kollwitz (1867–1945). Raised in a socialist household, she also studied at the Berlin School of Art for Women and at a similar school in Munich. In 1891 she married a doctor who shared her leftist political views, and they settled in a working-class neighborhood of Berlin. Art for her was a political tool,

tain Gypsies (the Romany people, wrongly thought to have originated in Bohemia, a region of central Europe) who lived within a modern urban environment while maintaining a separate cultural identity. The term was then applied to young artists and writers who wanted the advantages of a cultural center without its crass, materialist, "bourgeois" (or middle-class) trappings. They were opposed to the new mass-produced things, like the ready-to-wear suits in Atget's *Magasin, Avenue des Gobelins* (see fig. 28-4), which they considered shoddy and ugly, as well as to what they believed to be the bourgeoisie's appalling lack of interest in the life of the spirit and the mind.

By 1900 these new bohemians in various European centers were committed to resisting both the social fragmentation of the modern city and what they considered the puritanism of bourgeois life. Like Gauguin, many bohemians were attracted to the ideal of so-called primitive culture, imagining in it not only a less alienated society but also a more natural sexuality, free of inhibitions and learned restraints. But unlike Gauguin, who decided to return to what he thought of as a precivilized existence, the artists of Die Brücke attempted to "primitivize" bohemia. Uninhibited sexuality was often featured in one major subject of their art: the life of their studios.

In Kirchner's *Girl under a Japanese Umbrella* (fig. 28-28), for example, the viewer is put in the position of the artist as he gazes at the half-naked model, painted with the bold brushstrokes, crude contours, and intense colors. Were the partially parted lips, flared nostrils, and

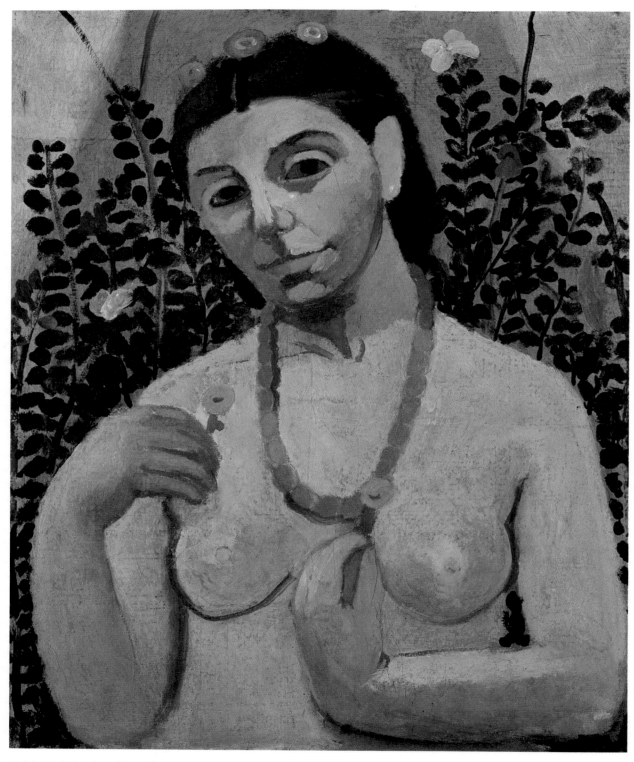

28-29. Paula Modersohn-Becker. *Self-Portrait with an Amber Necklace*. 1906. Oil on canvas, 24 x 19³/₄" (61 x 50 cm). Öffentliche Kunstsammlung, Kunstmuseum, Basel, Switzerland

28-30. Käthe Schmidt Kollwitz. *The Outbreak*, from the Peasants' War. 1903. Etching. Staatliche Museen zu Berlin, Preussischer Kulturbesitz, Kupferstichkabinett

and to reach as many people as possible, she preferred printmaking to other mediums. Although she made a number of effective self-portraits, the main subject of her art is the poor, oppressed worker.

Using a stark graphic style, Kollwitz attempted to win sympathy for working-class people and to inspire them and her viewers to action on their behalf. Between 1902 and 1908 she produced the Peasants' War series, seven etchings that depict events in a rebellion of German peasants in the sixteenth century. In the first completed work of the series, *The Outbreak* (fig. 28-30), Kollwitz shows the peasants' built-up fury from years of mistreatment exploding in mass action against their oppressors. No longer single individuals, the tired and worn figures join in a powerful wedge. To the artist's contemporaries, the work was thus a lesson in the potency of group action. In the front, with her back to us, is Black Anna, the leader of the revolt, who raises her hands to signal the attack. Kollwitz said that she modeled the figure of Anna after herself.

Der Blaue Reiter

The last of the major pre–World War I expressionist groups to come out of the crucible of late-nineteenth-century painting was formed in Munich around the Russian painter Vasily Kandinsky (1866–1944), who was born and raised in Moscow. In 1895 Kandinsky saw a Monet haystack painting whose color so moved him that he decided to give up his law professorship in Moscow and devote himself fully to art. The following year he moved to Munich to study art because of the research being done there on the effects of color and form on the human psyche. During the first decade of the new century he traveled often to Paris and other European centers to familiarize himself with the latest artistic developments. The wealth of expressionist work he encountered convinced him that a new artistic era had begun. The

development of his own style in this period depended not only on the contemporary art he saw but also on the folk and children's art he collected. In 1911 he organized Der Blaue Reiter ("The Blue Rider"), a group of nine artists who shared his interest in the power of color. Der Blaue Reiter was more diverse than the Fauves or Die Brücke, and its name says more about Kandinsky's aims than those of his colleagues.

"Der Reiter" was the popular name for the image of Saint George, mounted and slaying a dragon, that appeared on the Moscow city emblem. According to a long tradition revived around 1900, Moscow would be the new capital of the world during the millennium, the thousand years of Christ's reign on earth that would follow the Apocalypse, as prophesied by Saint John the Divine. Millennial and apocalyptic imagery appears often in Kandinsky's art in the years just prior to World War I. In *Improvisation No. 30 (Warlike Theme)* (fig. 28-31), the firing cannons in the lower right combine with the intense reds, blackened sky, and precariously leaning mountains to suggest a scene from the end of the world. Such paintings, sometimes thought to reflect fear of the coming war, are, in fact, ecstatic visions of the destructive prelude to the Second Coming of Christ. The schematic churches on top of the mountains are based on the churches of the Kremlin, Moscow's central district, and thus symbolize the coming Russian millennium.

Kandinsky never expected his viewers to understand his symbolism, nor did he think they needed to understand it. He intended, instead, to influence them directly through the sheer force of color. As he explained it: "[C]olor directly influences the soul. Color is the keyboard, the eyes are the hammers, the soul is the piano with many strings. The artist is the hand that plays, touching one key or another purposively, to cause vibrations in the soul" (cited in Chipp, pages 154–155). In essence, Kandinsky believed that his "largely unconscious" color improvisations would awaken the spiritual capacity and "urge" of one spectator after another and thus inaugurate "a great spiritual epoch." Kandinsky, then, was "der Reiter" who would prepare the way for the Second Coming.

Der Reiter was blue because Kandinsky and the group's cofounder, Franz Marc (1880–1916), considered blue the color of the male principle of spirituality. Marc, a man of gloomy disposition, was born and trained in Munich. Over the course of his career he moved from naturalism to expressionism, a process that culminated in 1910 when he met Kandinsky and became a member of his circle. Some years earlier Marc had turned to animals as subjects for his work. In *The Large Blue Horses* (fig. 28-32), he shows three horses, each defined by the same colors and shapes, in a tight, homogeneous unit. The fluid neck contours of the two horses in front, echoed in the shape of the third animal, reflect the harmony of their collective existence. With their billowing curves and graceful arabesques, the horses are also shown in perfect harmony with their surroundings. The simple but strong colors reflect their uncomplicated yet intense experience as Marc enviously imagined it.

28-31. Vasily Kandinsky. *Improvisation No. 30 (Warlike Theme)*. 1913. Oil on canvas, 43¼ x 43¼" (109.9 x 109.9 cm). The Art Institute of Chicago

Arthur Jerome Eddy Memorial Collection

The traditional Russian idea that Moscow would be the "third Rome" was central to Kandinsky's art prior to World War I. The first center of Christianity had been Rome itself. The second Rome, according to Russian Orthodox tradition, had been Constantinople, the capital of the Christian world until 1453, when the Muslim Turks conquered it. The third and final Rome would be Moscow, according to the vision of a sixteenth-century monk, whose descriptive letter to the grand prince of Moscow led the prince's successor, Ivan the Terrible, to assume the title *czar*, Russian for "Caesar."

A third major artist associated with Der Blaue Reiter was Paul Klee (1879–1940), who was born near Bern, Switzerland, to a musical family. He married a pianist and until his final illness played the violin for an hour every morning. Although he was included in the second Blaue Reiter exhibition, in 1912, his involvement with the group was never more than tangential. It was not Der Blaue Reiter but a 1914 trip to Tunisia that inspired his interest in the expressive potential of color. "Color and I are one," he wrote in his diary while there.

On his return Klee painted a series of watercolors based on his memories of North Africa, among them *Hammamet with Its Mosque* (fig. 28-33). The play between geometric composition and irregular brushstrokes in this watercolor is reminiscent of Cézanne's work, which Klee had recently seen. The luminous colors and delicate **washes**, or applications of dilute watercolor, result in a gently shimmering effect that is more than a record of something seen under a hot sun. The subtle modulations of red across the bottom, especially, are positively melodic. Klee seems to have wanted to use color the way a musician would use sound, not to describe appearances but to evoke subtle nuances of feel-

28-32. Franz Marc. *The Large Blue Horses.* 1911. Oil on canvas, 3'5³/8" x 5'11¹/4" (1.05 x 1.81 m). Walker Art Center, Minneapolis
Gift of T. B. Walker Collection, Gilbert M. Walter Fund, 1942

ing. The mosque presiding over the picture suggests that color had a spiritual dimension for Klee and thus links his work with Kandinsky's and Marc's. What differentiates it is the absence of any trace of a preconceived intellectual program. Though Klee, too, was a prolific theorist, his art was not meant to illustrate his ideas but rather to explore complicated and difficult-to-verbalize imaginative experiences. The fact that Klee's art usually eludes translation into clear and certain concepts is, for many, the essence of its appeal.

CUBISM

Hammamet with Its Mosque reflects the influence of the most talked-about ism of twentieth-century art, Cubism. The complete flattening of space and the use of independent facets or blocks of color in Klee's painting suggest the influence of the Cubist paintings he had recently seen in Paris. Cubism was the joint invention of two men, Pablo Picasso (1881–1973) and Georges Braque (1882–1963). Their achievement was built upon the foundation of Picasso's early work.

Picasso's Early Art

Picasso was born in Málaga, Spain, where his father taught in the School of Fine Arts. His talent was evident at an early age, and at fifteen he entered the Barcelona Academy. A year later, he was admitted as an advanced student to the Academy in Madrid. Picasso's involvement in the avant-garde began at the end of the 1890s, when he moved back to Barcelona and joined a group of young writers and artists interested in both progressive art and politics. Beginning in 1900 he made frequent extended visits to Paris and moved there in early 1904.

During this time Picasso was drawn to the socially conscious tradition in nineteenth-century French painting

28-33. Paul Klee. *Hammamet with Its Mosque.* 1914. Watercolor and pencil on two sheets of laid paper mounted on cardboard, 8¹/8 x 7⁵/8" (20.6 x 19.7 cm). The Metropolitan Museum of Art, New York
The Berggruen Klee Collection, 1984

that included Honoré Daumier (see fig. 27-22) and Toulouse-Lautrec (see fig. 28-3). In what is known as his Blue Period, he painted the outcasts of Paris in weary poses and a coldly expressive blue. Two factors seem to have been at work

28-34. Pablo Picasso. *Self-Portrait*. 1901. Oil on canvas, 31⁷/₈ x 23⁵/₈" (81 x 60 cm). Musée Picasso, Paris

28-35. Pablo Picasso. *Self-Portrait with Palette*. 1906. Oil on canvas, 36¼ x 28³/₄" (92 x 73 cm). Philadelphia Museum of Art

A. E. Gallatin Collection

in these paintings. The first was Picasso's political sensitivity to those he considered the victims of modern society, which would eventually lead him to join the Communist Party. The second was his own unhappiness, a hint of which appears in his 1901 *Self-Portrait* (fig. 28-34). The painter's sallow complexion and hollow cheeks reveal his familiarity with cold, hunger, and disappointment. Whether his mood colored his perception of the world or merely sharpened his political sensitivity is much debated.

In 1904 Picasso's personal circumstances greatly improved. By the end of the year he had a large circle of supportive friends, and his work had attracted the attention of several important collectors. His works from the end of 1904 and the beginning of 1905, known collectively as the Rose Period because of the introduction of that color into his still predominantly blue palette, show the last vestiges of his earlier despair.

Between early 1905 and the winter of 1906–1907 Picasso's art went through an extraordinary and complex transformation. Wanting to produce art of greater formal and psychological strength, he began to study classical sculpture at the Louvre. Picasso's interest in classical art coincided with a new flowering of the Roman School that followed a Puvis retrospective late in 1904, the exhibition of Maillol's *The Mediterranean* (see fig. 28-7) in 1905, and an Ingres retrospective the same year. Despite his initial attraction to this kind of art, Picasso soon rejected it because of its association with French nationalism. Ever since Louis XIV had resisted the influence of the Italian Baroque in the seventeenth century (Chapter 19), French

critics and historians considered a taste for classical balance to be deeply rooted in the national character. The works of Puvis, Ingres, and Maillol, in line with this tradition, were seen as quintessentially French. In response, the young Picasso began to cultivate his own ethnic identity.

In 1906 the Louvre installed a newly acquired collection of sculpture from the Iberian region (modern Spain and Portugal) that dated to the sixth and fifth centuries BCE. Inspired by these archaic figures, which had been excavated in the province of his birth, Picasso spent the summer of 1906 rediscovering his roots in a small village in the Spanish Pyrenees. The ancient Iberian figures, which he identified with the stoic dignity of the Pyrenean villagers, became the chief influence on his work for the next several years. Another important influence came from Gauguin's "primitive" work, which Picasso also studied at this time. The Gauguin connection allowed Picasso to develop his Spanish identity while simultaneously contributing to a major current in modernist art.

The Iberian influence appears clearly in *Self-Portrait with Palette*, painted in 1906 (fig. 28-35). The frail, sensitive young man of the earlier self-portrait has become strong and self-contained. The simple sculptural modeling of the head lends firmness and certainty to his calm expression. Accentuated by heavy outlines, the powerful upper body and strong right arm, which ends in a fist, add a sense of newfound psychological strength. Picasso pointedly showed himself without a brush in his fist, making a statement as much about himself as a person as about himself as an artist.

28-36. Pablo Picasso. *Les Demoiselles d'Avignon.* 1907. Oil on canvas, 8' x 7'8" (2.43 x 2.33 m). The Museum of Modern Art, New York

Acquired through the Lillie P. Bliss Bequest

Picasso's Iberian period culminated in 1907 in *Les Demoiselles d'Avignon* (fig. 28-36). The painting is Picasso's response to Matisse's *Joy of Life* (see fig. 28-24), exhibited the year before, and to the French classical tradition that stood behind it, which to Picasso was embodied in Ingres's harem paintings exhibited in a 1905 retrospective. Picasso began by substituting the bordello for the harem. The term *demoiselles* is a euphemism for prostitutes, and Avignon refers not to the French town but to a street in the red-light district of Barcelona. In a preliminary study for the painting (fig. 28-37), Picasso had included two men with the five women.

28-37. Pablo Picasso. Study for *Les Demoiselles d'Avignon.*
1907. Pastel on paper, 18¾ x 30" (47.6 x 63.7 cm).
Kunstmuseum, Kupferstichkabinett, Basel, Switzerland

28-38. Georges Braque. *Houses at L'Estaque.* 1908. Oil on canvas, 36¼ x 23⅝" (92 x 60 cm). Kunstmuseum, Bern, Switzerland
Collection Hermann and Magrit Rupf-Stiftung

28-39. D. H. Kahnweiler. Photograph of houses at L'Estaque. 1909

Several studies have suggested that the man on the left holding a book is a student, the seated man a sailor: Picasso may have meant to contrast the contemplative life of the student with the active life of the sailor. His decision to eliminate the men was probably based on a number of considerations. For one, the allegory they suggest detracts from the central issue of sexuality. For another, their confrontation with the women on display makes the viewer a mere onlooker. In the final painting the viewer is a participant: The women now pose for and look directly at the painter and us.

Picasso made a number of other changes. The women in the sketch are conventionally rendered in soft curves, but the only "feminine" curve in the finished painting is the line of the inner arm of the central figure. Elsewhere, there are either sharp curves or angles. Picasso's central pair raise their arms in a conventional gesture of open accessibility, but these actions are contradicted by their hard, piercing gazes and firm mouths. In working out his theme, Picasso completely reversed the conventional male fantasy of easy access to willing women into a hostile confrontation. Even the fruit displayed in the foreground, a traditional symbol of female sexuality, seems hard and dangerous. Picasso flattened the figures and transformed the entire space into a turbulent series of blunt and jagged geometric forms.

Les Demoiselles d'Avignon was also conceived in opposition to Ingres's *Large Odalisque* (see fig. 26-44) and, in fact, to the Western tradition of erotic imagery since the Renaissance. Women, Picasso asserts, are not the gentle and passive creatures men would like them to

be. In remarks to a friend about the African masks he used for the faces of the two *demoiselles* on the right, Picasso spoke of the work's purpose:

> Men had made those masks . . . as a kind of mediation between themselves and the unknown hostile forces that surrounded them, in order to overcome their fear and horror by giving [them] a form and an image. At that moment I realized that . . . painting . . . isn't an aesthetic operation; it's a form of magic designed as a mediator between this . . . hostile world and us, a way of seizing the power by giving form to our terrors as well as our desires (cited in Gilot and Lake, page 266).

When Picasso showed the finished work to his friends, they were horrified. Matisse, for example, accused Picasso of making a joke of modern art and threatened to break off their friendship. Only one artist, Georges Braque, eventually responded positively, and he saw in *Les Demoiselles d'Avignon* a potential that Picasso probably had not fully intended. Picasso had set out to produce a stunningly innovative painting, and he used broken and flattened forms to express his view of women, not consciously to break with the Western pictorial tradition that had been in place since the early-fourteenth-century painter Giotto. However, it was this formal revolution that would put him in control of the Parisian avant-garde, and to which Braque responded and quickly set out, with Picasso's help, to develop.

Analytic Cubism

Georges Braque was born a year after Pablo Picasso, near Le Havre, France, where he trained to become a house decorator like his father and grandfather. In 1900 he moved to Paris to complete his apprenticeship but by 1902 had enrolled in one of the city's private academies. The fledgling painter was so impressed by the Fauves' paintings he saw in 1905 that he joined them, but he soon grew tired of expressionism. The Cézanne retrospective in the fall of 1907 established his future course. He later said that exhibition was "more than an influence, it was an initiation." His interest in altered form and compressed space, kindled by Cézanne, was sharpened by Picasso's *Demoiselles*. Picasso, Braque observed, had flattened space and taken liberties with form much as Cézanne had in his late landscapes (see fig. 28-13).

Picasso's radical painting seems to have emboldened Braque to make his own advances on what he saw as Cézanne's late direction. In *Houses at L'Estaque* (fig. 28-38), painted in 1908 in one of Cézanne's favorite locales (see fig. 28-11), we see the emergence of early Cubism. Inspired by Cézanne's example, Braque has reduced nature's many colors to its essential browns and greens. A comparison of the painting with a photograph of the site taken the following year by Braque's dealer (fig. 28-39) shows that the artist also eliminated architectural detail to emphasize basic geometric forms. The houses have been arranged approximately into a pyramid and reduced to a kind of Platonic "houseness." Those in the distance have been pushed closer to the foreground, so the viewer looks *up* to the canvas more than into it. In short, Braque simplified and reorganized the scene. The painting is less a Cézannesque study of nature than an attempt to translate nature's complexity into an independent, aesthetically satisfying whole; that is, the painting seems not so much a landscape as an arrangement of form and color meant to gratify a classical taste.

Houses at L'Estaque was put on view in Picasso's studio. Matisse said the avant-garde "considered it as something quite new, about which there were many discussions." Matisse explained to the puzzled critic Vauxcelles, who had coined the term *Fauvism*, that Braque made the painting out of "small cubes." When the critic later described the painting in print using that term, the name *Cubism* was born.

Picasso found in Braque's painting the artistic direction he had seemed to lack since the disastrous private showings of *Les Demoiselles d'Avignon*. By the end of 1908 the two artists had begun an intimate working relationship that lasted until Braque went off to war in 1914. During this period Picasso and Braque visited each other's studio almost every evening to see what the other had done during the day. The two were engaged in a difficult quest for a new conception of painting as, first and foremost, an arrangement of form and color on a two-dimensional surface. This arduous journey would require both Picasso's audacity and Braque's sense of purpose.

The move toward abstraction begun in Braque's landscapes in 1908 continued in the series of moderately

28-40. Georges Braque. *Violin and Palette*. 1909–10. Oil on canvas, 36⅛ x 16⅞" (91.8 x 42.9 cm). Solomon R. Guggenheim Museum, New York

scaled still lifes the two artists produced over the next two and a half years. The result of this series is the gradual elimination of space and subject matter. In Braque's *Violin and Palette* (fig. 28-40), the process is well under way. The still-life items are not arranged on a table in **illusionistic** depth but parallel to the picture plane in a shallow space. Using the **passage** technique developed by Cézanne, in which shapes closed on one side are open on another so that they can merge with adjacent shapes, Braque has attempted to knit the various elements together into a single shifting surface of forms and colors.

28-41. Georges Braque. *Fox*. 1912. Drypoint, printed in brown, 21½ x 15" (54.8 x 38 cm). The Museum of Modern Art, New York

Gift of Abby Aldrich Rockefeller

28-42. Pablo Picasso. *Ma Jolie*. 1911–12. Oil on canvas, 39⅜ x 25¾" (100 x 65.4 cm). The Museum of Modern Art, New York

Acquired through the Lillie P. Bliss Bequest

In 1923, Picasso said, "Cubism is no different from any other school of painting. The same principles and the same elements are common to all. The fact that for a long time Cubism has not been understood . . . means nothing. I do not read English, [but] this does not mean that the English language does not exist, and why should I blame anyone . . . but myself if I cannot understand [it]?" (cited in Chipp, page 264).

In some areas of the painting, the right most noticeably, these formal elements have lost not only their natural spatial relations but their identities as well. Where representational motifs remain—the violin, for example—Braque has fragmented them in order to facilitate their integration into the whole.

What Braque was aiming at in the work is indicated by the still-discernible subjects: the palette, sheet music, and violin. In identifying the palette with the musical elements, Braque reveals his and Picasso's new conception of painting. As their close friend the critic and poet Guillaume Apollinaire wrote in 1912, during these years the two were "moving toward an entirely new art which will stand, with respect to painting as envisaged heretofore, as music stands to literature. It will be pure painting, just as music is pure literature" (cited in Chipp, page 222). As the musician arranges sounds to make music, Braque arranged forms and colors to make art. Braque and, to a somewhat lesser extent, Picasso felt that subject matter could sometimes be just as incidental to art as it is to symphonic music.

Braque's and Picasso's paintings of 1909 and 1910 initiated what is known as Analytic Cubism because of the way the artist took objects like the violin in *Violin and Palette* and broke them down into parts as if to analyze

them. The works of 1911 and early 1912 are also grouped under the Analytic label, although they reflect a different approach to the breaking up of forms. Instead of simply fracturing an object, Picasso and Braque picked it apart and rearranged its elements. The process by which they worked is most clearly evident in prints such as Braque's *Fox* (fig. 28-41). Braque began, as they always did, by setting up a still life on a table in the studio. This one included playing cards among the usual bottles and books. Rather than copying these motifs, Braque took from them various shape elements (curves, angles, and lines) and areas of shadow, which he then carefully assembled on the surface of his work in a pyramidal fashion. "The goal," as Braque said, "is not the *reconstitution* of an anecdotal fact, but the *constitution* of a pictorial fact." His concern for a classical balance is also evident in the even distribution of these elements on both sides of the central axis and in the frequent use of **T**-square elements aligned with the paper edge. The "pictorial fact" in *Fox*, as in all the works from this period, is defined not by subject but by the subtle nuance of formal harmonies organized in a classical fashion.

Picasso's *Ma Jolie* (fig. 28-42) was also the product of a careful reworking of a studio motif. Remnants of the subject from which he worked—a woman holding a zither or guitar—are evident throughout the painting, but a search for clues that might allow one to reconstruct that subject would be misguided. The subject provided little more than the raw material for a particular formal arrangement. It is not a painting of a woman, or of a place, or of an event, but simply a painting—or, as Apollinaire said, "pure painting." Again, Picasso has suggested a musical analogy: He has painted in a G clef, and the words at bottom, *Ma Jolie*, were the title of a popular song. These references suggest that the viewer should approach the painting the way one would a musical composition, either by simply enjoying the arrangement of its elements or by analyzing it, but not by asking what it represents.

Throughout the painting, Picasso has maintained a subtle tension between order and disorder. For example, the shifting effect of the surface, a delicately patterned texture of grays and browns, is given regularity through the use of short, horizontal brushstrokes. Similarly, with the linear elements, strict horizontals and verticals dominate, although many irregular curves and angles are also to be found. The combination of horizontal brushwork and right angles firmly establishes a grid that effectively counteracts the surface flux. Moreover, the repetition of certain diagonals and the relative lack of details in the upper left and upper right create a pyramidal shape. Thus, what at first may seem a random assemblage of lines and muted colors turns out to be a well-organized unit. The aesthetic satisfaction of such a work depends on the way chaos seems to resolve itself into order.

Synthetic Cubism

In works like *Ma Jolie*, Picasso and Braque were on the brink of complete **formalism**. Having reached this brink, they retreated, and in the spring of 1912 they began to create works with more clearly discernible subjects. Rather than rendering subjects naturalistically, however, they suggested them. This second major phase of Cubism is known as Synthetic Cubism because of the way the artists created motifs by combining simpler elements, as in a chemical synthesis. Picasso's *Glass and Bottle of Suze* (fig. 28-43), like most of the works he and Braque created from 1912 to 1914, is a **collage**, a work composed of separate elements pasted together. At the center is a combination of newsprint and construction paper cut and assembled to suggest a tray or round table upon which are a glass and a bottle of liquor with an actual label. Around this arrangement, Picasso has pasted larger pieces of newspaper and wallpaper. The elements together evoke not only a place—a bar—but also an activity there: the figure alone with a newspaper, enjoying a quiet drink. The tran-

28-43. Pablo Picasso. *Glass and Bottle of Suze*. 1912. Pasted paper, gouache, and charcoal, 25³/₄ x 19³/₄" (65.4 x 50.2 cm). Washington University Gallery of Art, St. Louis, Missouri
University Purchase, Kende Sale Fund, 1946

quillity of the scene is suggested by the harmony of the browns, grays, and blues and by the classical pyramidal composition of the central elements.

The refuge from daily bustle that both art and quiet bars can provide was a central theme in the Synthetic Cubist works produced by Braque and Picasso. The two artists, however, used different types of newspaper clippings. Braque's clippings deal almost entirely with musical and artistic events. Picasso, signaling a renewed interest in the personal and social themes that had concerned him before his association with Braque, often included references to political events that would soon shatter the peaceful pleasures these works feature.

In *Glass and Bottle of Suze*, for example, the newspaper clippings deal with the First Balkan War of 1912–1913, which contributed to the mounting tensions that resulted in World War I. *Glass and Bottle of Suze* includes graphic descriptions of the war's victims, which are placed upside down in the collage, possibly to suggest a world turned on its head. Also among the clippings is a report of a meeting in France of about 50,000 pacifists from all over Europe hoping to prevent "a general European war." Picasso's collage may record his uneasy response to the political events; or conversely, the clippings may simply document the problems from which bohemian bars and art itself provided a safe, if temporary, refuge.

28-44. Pablo Picasso. *Mandolin and Clarinet.* 1913. Construction of painted wood with pencil marks, 22⁵/₈ x 14¹/₈ x 9" (58 x 36 x 23 cm). Musée Picasso, Paris

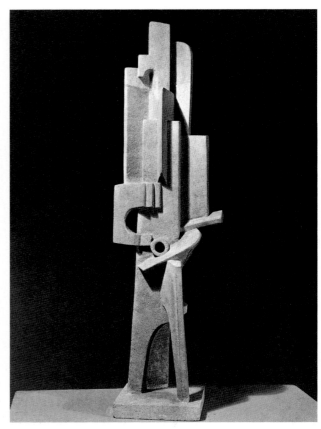

28-45. Jacques Lipchitz. *Man with a Guitar.* 1915. Limestone, 38¹/₄ x 10¹/₂ x 7³/₄" (97.2 x 26.7 x 19.7 cm). The Museum of Modern Art, New York
Mrs. Simon Guggenheim Fund (by exchange)

In addition to collage, Picasso produced a number of Synthetic Cubist sculptures, such as *Mandolin and Clarinet* (fig. 28-44). Composed of wood scraps, the sculpture suggests two musical instruments at right angles to one another. The scrap wood and unfinished surfaces call attention to the everyday world of the workers and craftspeople with whom Picasso and Braque identified themselves at the time. The result is a fascinating integration of the fabricating techniques of the ordinary workplace with the high-art aesthetics of Cubism.

Responses to Cubism

As the various phases of Cubism emerged from the studios of Braque and Picasso, it became clear to the art world that something of great significance was happening. The radical innovations of the new style confused and upset the public and most critics, but the avant-garde saw in them the future of art.

French Responses. Some artists put these innovations into the service of a less radical art, as can be seen in the Cubist-inspired sculpture of Jacques Lipchitz Lithuania (1891–1973). Lipchitz, who came to Paris from Lithuania in 1909, met Picasso in 1913. The influence of both Analytic and Synthetic Cubism can be seen in his work of the period before and during World War I. *Man with a Guitar* (fig. 28-45), for example, is in the Synthetic Cubist mode. Like Picasso in *Mandolin and Clarinet*, Lip-

chitz assembled curvilinear and angular shapes, in this case to approximate a figure holding a guitar. The hole at the center of the work is wittily used to suggest both the sound hole of the guitar and the figure's navel. The piece aims simply to create a pleasant symphony of shifting but ultimately stable forms.

At the other end of the spectrum was the radical painting of Robert Delaunay (1885–1941), who attempted to take a monochromatic, static, and antisocial Analytic Cubism into a new, wholly different direction. By 1904 Delaunay had become a landscape painter, first in the Impressionist mode, then, after 1905, in the Fauvist vein. His insistence on the spirituality of color, which recommended him to Der Blaue Reiter, was first evident in the series of paintings of a Gothic church interior he did in 1909.

Beginning in 1910 he attempted to fuse Fauvist color with Analytic Cubist form in a series of works dedicated to modern technology. One of these, *Homage to Blériot* (fig. 28-46), is a tribute to the French pilot who in 1909 was the first to fly across the English Channel. One of Louis Blériot's early airplanes, somewhat like the Wright brothers used in 1903, is shown in the upper right, just above the Eiffel Tower. The airplane and the Eiffel Tower were powerful symbols of both technological and social progress in this period, and the crossing of the Channel was considered as evidence of a new, unified world without frontiers and national antagonisms. The arrangement of brightly colored circular forms that fills the canvas is more than an expressionistic record of

28-46. Robert Delaunay.
Homage to Blériot.
1914. Tempera
on canvas,
8'2¹/₂" x 8'3"
(2.5 x 2.51 m).
Kunstmuseum,
Basel, Switzerland
Emanuel Hoffman
Foundation

Delaunay's excitement at this prospect. The circular shapes, which suggest both the movement of the propeller on the left and the blazing sun, are meant to evoke as well the great **rose windows** of Gothic cathedrals. By combining images of progressive science with those of divinity, Delaunay meant to suggest that progress is part of God's divine plan. The ecstatic painting is thus a synthesis not only of Fauvist color and Cubist form but also that of conservative religion and modern technology.

Critics labeled Delaunay's art Orphism for its affinities with Orpheus, the legendary Greek poet whose lute playing charmed wild beasts. Delaunay preferred to think of his work in terms of simultaneity, a vague and complicated concept he developed with his wife, the Russian-born artist Sonia Delaunay-Terk (née Sonia Terk, 1885–1979), that centered on a faith in the great unity of opposites.

After marrying Delaunay in 1910, Delaunay-Terk produced paintings very similar to his both in style and in theme. She has received less historical attention than he, partly because she devoted the bulk of her career to the applied arts, fabric and clothing design in particular. Following the birth of their son in 1911, she made him a patchwork quilt, like those produced by Russian peasant women, out of pieces of colored fabric. She soon began designing her own clothes in the "simultaneous" style of the couple's paintings.

In 1915 she began to design costumes for the avant-garde theater and clothes for wealthy women, including movie stars such as Gloria Swanson. In 1920 she established her own fashion house, which, much to the surprise of herself and her bohemian friends, soon became

28-47. Sonia Delaunay-Terk. Clothes and customized Citroën B-12. From *Maison de la Mode*, 1925.

The term *Art Deco* was coined at the 1925 International Exposition of the Decorative Arts in Paris to describe the kind of geometric style evident in many of the works on display, including Delaunay-Terk's clothing and fabric designs.

a flourishing business. She enjoyed her greatest critical success in 1925 at the International Exposition of the Decorative Arts. Organized by the French government to promote the traditional crafts, it became instead a showplace for the new machine age because of exhibitions like Delaunay-Terk's. As part of her pavilion, called *Simultané*, where she exhibited her clothes and fabric, she decorated a Citroën sports car to match one of her coat, dress, and hat ensembles (fig. 28-47). The artist was making a clear statement that her bold geometric designs were an expression of the new automobile age.

Delaunay-Terk chose the Citroën Cabriolet B-12 not simply because it was a sleek, "streamlined" sports car—note the tapering shape of its rear section—but because it was the first vehicle of its type produced cheaply for a mass market. Delaunay-Terk herself had recently brought out a line of inexpensive "ready-to-wear" clothing. Moreover, André Citroën—Europe's Henry Ford—had specifically designed the small three-seater to appeal to the new female market. The fashion model behind the wheel is therefore also an indication of the emergence after World War I of what was called the "new woman," one, like Delaunay-Terk, less tied to home and family and less dependent on men.

Italian Responses. Another of the twentieth century's isms, Futurism, emerged on February 20, 1909, when a controversial Milanese literary magazine editor, Filippo Marinetti, published his "Foundation and Manifesto of Futurism" in a Paris newspaper. An outspoken attack against everything old, dull, "feminine," and safe, Marinetti's **manifesto** promoted the exhilarating "masculine" experiences of warfare and reckless speed (see "The Futurist Manifesto," page 1059). Although the stated aim of Futurism was to free Italy from its past, the deeper purpose was to promote a new taste for heightened experience.

In 1909 a number of artists and poets gathered around Marinetti in Milan to create art forms for a modernized and revitalized Italy. Prominent among the artists was the sculptor and painter Umberto Boccioni (1882–1916). His major sculptural work, *Unique Forms of Continuity in Space* (fig. 28-48), is a powerful nude figure in full stride. The formal vocabulary of exaggerated muscular curves and countercurves was inspired by early Analytic Cubist still lifes and figure studies that he had seen in Paris in 1911. But whereas the Cubists had broken forms to integrate their compositions, here Boccioni dynamically stretches and swells them to express the figure's power and speed. In contrast to the Cubist taste for order and stability, this work revels in movement and change. The figure personifies the new Italian envisioned by the group: a powerful male rushing headlong into the future.

Boccioni's paintings celebrate the modern industrial city. *States of Mind: The Farewells* (fig. 28-49), for example, immerses the viewer in the crowded, exciting chaos of a train station. At the center, with numbers emblazoned on its front, is a powerful steam locomotive. Pulsing across the top of the work is a series of bright curves meant to suggest radio waves emanating from the steel tower in the left rear. Adding to the complexity of the tightly packed surface are the longer, more fluid rhythms that seem to pull a crowd of metallic figures from beneath the tower down and across the work. The figures are actually a single couple shown moving through space and time. Although their simplified, blocky forms were borrowed from Analytic Cubism, their sequential arrangement was inspired by time-lapse photography.

28-48. Umberto Boccioni. *Unique Forms of Continuity in Space.* 1913. Bronze, 43⁷/₈ x 34⁷/₈ x 15³/₄" (111 x 89 x 40 cm). The Museum of Moden Art, New York
Acquired through the Lillie P. Bliss Bequest

Boccioni and the Futurist architect Antonio Sant'Elia (see fig. 28-75) were both killed in World War I. The Futurists had ardently promoted Italian entry into the war on the side of France and England. After the war Marinetti's movement, still committed to nationalism and militarism, supported the rise of fascism under Benito Mussolini, although a number of the original members of the group rejected their radical values.

Boccioni wanted to convey more than a purely physical sense of such a place. He wanted, as well, to evoke the variety of sounds, smells, and emotions that filled the train station and made it the very epitome of the noisy urban existence he and his colleagues so loved.

Time-lapse photography (or chronophotography) provided inspiration for the group's photographer, Anton Giulio Bragaglia (1890–1960), who began his career in the fledgling movie industry of Rome in 1906. He turned to photography in 1910, partly as a result of reading the Futurist manifesto "Futurist Painting: Technical Manifesto." By the following year he had evolved his own brand of photography, which he called Photodynamism. He produced photographs like *Greetings!* (fig. 28-50) by leaving the camera's shutter open while his subjects moved. The polite subject is in keeping with the civilized, less published side of Futurist production. However, Bragaglia also made photographs more consistent with the aggressive values outlined in Marinetti's manifesto, which ultimately helped produce Italian fascism.

28-49. Umberto Boccioni. *States of Mind: The Farewells.* 1911. Oil on canvas, 27⁷/₈ x 37⁷/₈" (70.7 x 96 cm). The Museum of Modern Art, New York

Gift of Nelson A. Rockefeller

THE FUTURIST MANIFESTO On February 20, 1909, the Italian poet and publisher Filippo Tommaso Marinetti, who liked to think of himself as "the caffeine of Europe," published "The Foundation and Manifesto of Futurism" in the French newspaper *Le Figaro*. The manifesto opens with a description of a late-night automobile accident caused by

two cyclists, wavering in front of me like two equally persuasive but contradictory arguments . . . What a nuisance! Auff! . . . I stopped short and—disgusting— was hurled, wheels in the air, into a ditch. . . .

Oh! maternal ditch, almost to the top with muddy water! Fair factory drainage ditch! I avidly savored your nourishing muck. . . . When I got out from under the upturned car—torn, filthy, and stinking—I felt the red-hot iron of joy pass over my heart!

After this preamble, Marinetti declares:

1. We intend to glorify the love of danger . . . the strength of daring. . . .

3. Literature having up to now glorified thoughtful immobility . . . and slumber, we wish to exalt the aggressive movement, the feverish insomnia, running, the perilous leap, the cuff, and the blow.

4. We declare that the splendor of the world has been enriched with a new form of beauty, the beauty of speed. A race-automobile . . . which seems to rush over exploding powder is more beautiful than the *Victory of Samothrace* . . .

7. There is no more beauty except in struggle. No masterpiece without the stamp of aggressiveness . . .

9. We will glorify war—the only true hygiene of the world— militarism, patriotism, the destructive gesture of [the] anarchist, the beautiful Ideas which kill, and the scorn of woman.

10. We will destroy museums, libraries, and fight against moralism, feminism, and all utilitarian cowardice.

11. We will sing the great masses agitated by work, pleasure, or revolt; we will sing the multi-colored and polyphonic surf of revolutions in modern capitals . . .

It is in Italy that we hurl this overthrowing and inflammatory declaration, with which today we found Futurism, for we will free Italy from her numberless museums which cover her with countless cemeteries . . .

To admire an old picture is to pour our sentiment into a funeral urn instead of hurling it forth in violent gushes of action and productiveness . . .

Therefore welcome the kindly incendiarists with the carbon fingers! Here they are! . . . Away and set fire to the bookshelves! . . .

The oldest among us is thirty; we have thus at least ten years in which to accomplish our task. When we are forty, let others— younger and more daring men— throw us into the wastepaper basket like useless manuscripts!

28-50. Anton Giulio Bragaglia. *Greetings!* 1911. From *Foto-dinamismo Futurista*, Rome, 1913

28-51. Natalia Goncharova. *Haycutting*. 1910. Oil on canvas, 38⅝ x 46¼" (98 x 117 cm). Private collection

28-52. Natalia Goncharova. *Aeroplane over Train*. 1913. Oil on canvas, 21⅝ x 32⅞" (55 x 83.5 cm). Kazan-skil Muzej, Russia

Russian Responses. Since the time of Peter the Great (ruled 1682–1725), Russia's ruling classes had turned to Western Europe for cultural models. Throughout the eighteenth and nineteenth centuries, for example, French had been the official language of the Russian court and the educated elite. Until two wealthy young men—Aleksandr Benois (1870–1960) and Serge Diaghilev (1872–1929)—began championing the cutting-edge developments in Western European art in the late nineteenth century, however, these works had been of little interest to Russian artists, writers, and critics. Benois and Diaghilev wanted not just to import Western innovations into Russia but also to make Russia for the first time a center of innovation that would contribute significantly to Western European culture. In 1899 they launched a magazine, *World of Art*, dedicated to international art, literature, and music. In the following year the World of Art group held the first in a series of international art exhibitions, which included works by Degas, Monet, Whistler, and Puvis de Chavannes. Following the group's desire to contribute to Western culture, Diaghilev took an exhibition of contemporary Russian art to Paris in 1906. Three years later he brought the Ballets Russes to the French capital, where it enjoyed enormous success.

The activities of the World of Art group, which was centered in Russia's capital, St. Petersburg, inspired the formation of a similar group in Moscow, the Golden Fleece. In 1906 it launched an art magazine by that name and in 1908 organized a major exhibition of Russian and French art, which included works by Rodin, Maillol, Toulouse-Lautrec, Gauguin, Cézanne, Matisse, Derain, and Braque. This exhibition had a complicated effect on the city's young artists, as is evident in the work of Natalia Goncharova (1881–1962), one of many women in Russia's avant-garde.

By the early 1900s Goncharova had come under the influence of Moscow's pro–Russian (or Slavophile) movement, which opposed the pro–Western European stance in St. Petersburg. She and her friends were convinced that in order to participate in the international avant-garde, they would, ironically, have to return to their own roots. Reflecting these beliefs, the paintings she made around 1905 are based on medieval Russian **icons**. The works that she contributed to the first Golden Fleece exhibition in 1908 created a sensation and launched the Russian Neo-Primitive movement. Goncharova's *Haycutting* (fig. 28-51) is typical of her Neo-Primitive paintings. In it she expresses the Slavophile view that the simple virtues of the provincial peasant represented the best of Russia. Not an idealized depiction meant to delight city people, it is, instead, a tribute to peasant strength in the vein of Jean-François Millet (see fig. 27-19). The crude style, meant to express the quality of peasant life, and the disregard for scale are based on the cheap **woodblock** prints of religious and political scenes (*lubok*) that decorated peasant homes.

Haycutting also seems to support a negative attitude toward the industrialization of Russia. In the face of the recent exodus of peasants to the burgeoning urban centers, this work appears to argue for a traditional way of life. Three years later, however, Goncharova produced *Aeroplane over Train* (fig. 28-52), which suggests a completely changed viewpoint, one now consistent with Futurist values. The work combines two of the leading symbols of technological progress in a style derived from both early Analytic Cubism and Futurism. Blocky Cubist shapes are closely packed in a dynamic Futurist rhythm across a surface also marked by a series of sharp diagonals. Because knowledge of Analytic Cubism and Futurism arrived in Moscow almost simultaneously and because they were superficially similar, artists such as Goncharova tended to link them. Thus, the style that evolved from them in the period 1912–1914 is known as Cubo-Futurism, even though it had less to do with Cubist than with Futurist values.

The brief time between *Haycutting* and *Aeroplane over Train* suggests the considerable confusion that many Russians felt over the questions of rural versus urban, agrarian versus industrial, and Russian versus French. The one issue Goncharova and the Cubo-Futurists were not in doubt about was artistic progress. They embraced Cubism and Futurism out of a commitment to "advance" art. And like Benois and Diaghilev, they were not satisfied simply with keeping up with the new advances; they wanted to contribute to them.

The first Russian to go beyond Cubo-Futurism was Kazimir Malevich (1878–1935). After Goncharova and her husband, the artist Mikhail Larionov (1881–1964), left for Paris in 1915 to work for Diaghilev's Ballets Russes, Malevich emerged as the leading figure in the Moscow avant-garde. By 1913 he was producing his own brand of Cubo-Futurism and his first truly abstract work. According to his later reminiscences, "in the year 1913, in my desperate attempt to free art from the burden of the object, I took refuge in the square form and exhibited a picture which consisted of nothing more than a black square on a white field." Because he did not exhibit such a work until 1915, there is some question about the exact date of his first completely nonrepresentational work. Whatever the case, Malevich exhibited thirty-nine works in this radically new and highly controversial vein at the "Zero Ten" exhibition in St. Petersburg in the winter of 1915–1916. One work, *Suprematist Painting (Eight Red Rectangles)* (fig. 28-53), consists simply of eight red rectangles arranged diagonally on a white painted ground. Here is the move to total abstraction that Picasso and Braque did not make in 1912.

Malevich called this art Suprematism, short for "the supremacy of pure feeling in creative art." Although he sometimes spoke of this feeling in terms of technology ("the sensation of flight . . . of metallic sounds . . . of wireless telegraphy"), a later essay suggests that what motivated these works was "a pure feeling for plastic [that is, formal] values." By eliminating objects and focusing entirely on formal issues, Malevich thought that he was "liberating" the essential beauty of all great art.

While Malevich was launching an art that transcended the events and conditions of the present, his chief competitor for leadership of the Russian avant-garde, Vladimir Tatlin (1885–1953), was somewhat inadvertently opening a very different direction for Russian art, one inspired by Synthetic Cubism. In 1913 Tatlin went to Paris specifically to visit Picasso's studio. What impressed him most was the new Synthetic Cubist sculp-

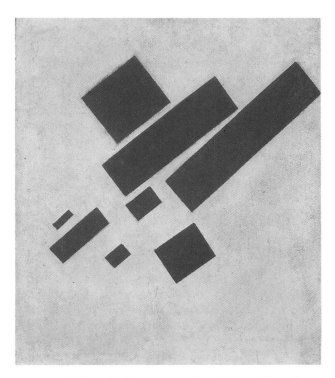

28-53. Kazimir Malevich. *Suprematist Painting (Eight Red Rectangles)*. 1915. Oil on canvas, 22½ x 18⅞" (57 x 48 cm). Stedelijk Museum, Amsterdam

Malevich's Suprematist works, like many abstract paintings, do not reproduce well—their aesthetically appealing subtleties of texture, line, and color are not readily apparent in photographs. Even more than other artworks, they need to be seen firsthand to be fully appreciated.

28-54. Vladimir Tatlin. *Corner Counter-Relief*. 1915. Mixed mediums, 31½ x 59 x 29½" (80 x 150 x 75 cm). Present whereabouts unknown

ture, such as *Mandolin and Clarinet* (see fig. 28-44). After returning to Moscow, Tatlin produced an innovative series of entirely nonrepresentational relief sculpture constructed of various materials, including metal, glass, **stucco**, asphalt, wire, and wood. These Counter-Reliefs, as he called them, were based on the concept of *faktura*, the conviction that each material generates its own precise repertory of forms and colors. Partly because he wanted to place "real materials in real space," and because he thought the usual placement on the wall tended to flatten his reliefs, he began at the "Zero Ten" exhibition of 1915–1916 to suspend them across the upper corners of rooms (fig. 28-54).

The upper corner of a room was also the traditional location for Russian icons. In effect, these Corner Counter-Reliefs were intended to replace the old symbol of Russian faith with one dedicated to the principle of respect for materials. But because his choice of materials increasingly favored the industrial over the natural, these modern icons could also be viewed as incipient expressions of the post–World War I shift away from aestheticism and toward utilitarianism in Russia, a topic to be explored more fully later in this chapter.

ARCHITECTURE BEFORE WORLD WAR I

The history of architecture between 1880 and World War I is a story of the impact of modern conditions and materials on the still-healthy Beaux-Arts **historicist** tradition, a tradition based on the emulation of historical models. Unlike painting and sculpture, where antiacademic forces dominated after 1880, in architecture the search for modern styles occurred somewhat later and met with considerably more resistance. While the figurative art education offered at the École des Beaux-Arts in Paris was rapidly losing importance, its architecture department was becoming the central training ground for the profession in both Europe and the United States.

American Beaux-Arts Architecture

The dean of late-nineteenth-century American architects was Richard Morris Hunt (1827–1895). In 1846 Hunt became the first American to study architecture at the École des Beaux-Arts in Paris. In 1855, determined to raise the standards of American architecture, he opened an office in New York City. Extraordinarily skilled in Beaux-Arts eclecticism, he produced work in every accepted style, including Gothic, French Classicist, and Italian Renaissance. Hunt did much of his work after the American Civil War (1861–1865) for the growing class of wealthy Eastern industrialists and financiers. One of his most impressive works is Biltmore (fig. 28-55), an estate constructed in

Asheville, North Carolina, for George W. Vanderbilt, the youngest son of one of America's richest families.

Vanderbilt conceived the 125,000-acre estate he had assembled as a model farm and forest. With the assistance of Gifford Pinchot, who later established the national park system under President Theodore Roosevelt (in office 1901–1909), he introduced at Biltmore the concept of what he called "selective cutting [of trees] for sustained yield." Surrounding the house are a series of historic gardens designed by Frederick Law Olmsted (1822–1903), the United States' first landscape architect. These include an Italian water garden, a picturesque eighteenth-century English ramble, a walled medieval garden, and, fronting the mansion, a broad esplanade in the manner of those at Versailles (see fig. 19-20). The 225-room house, designed by Hunt, is modeled on a French Renaissance **château**. Its aristocratic pretensions reflect the social ambitions not only of the young Vanderbilt but also of his entire class, which wanted to establish in the United States a hereditary social hierarchy like that of Europe.

While Biltmore was under construction, Hunt participated in another large project with more democratic aims: He was head of the board of architects for the 1893 World's Columbian Exposition in Chicago. For the exposition, organized to commemorate the 400th anniversary of Columbus's arrival in the Americas, the board abandoned the metal-and-glass architecture of earlier world's fairs in favor of the appearance of what it called "permanent buildings—a dream city." (The buildings were actually temporary ones composed of staff, a mixture of plaster and fibrous materials.) To create a sense of unity, they decided to use a single, classical style for all the exposition's buildings. This style, with its associations both to the birth of democracy in ancient Greece and to the imperial power of ancient Rome, reflected United States pride in its democratic institutions and the country's incipient emergence as a world power. Hunt's design for the Administration Building at the end of the Court of Honor (fig. 28-56), like that for most of the buildings, was in the Renaissance classicist mode used by Jefferson and other early American architects for civic buildings (see fig. 26-60). This particular version of the classical was also meant to communicate that the United States was cultivating a new, more democratic renaissance after the Civil War.

The World's Columbian Exposition also provided a model for the new American dream city. The rapidly growing American urban centers of the late nineteenth century were, on the whole, ill-planned, sooty, and overcrowded. The exposition offered reassurance that the city of the future could be clean, timeless, carefully planned, and spacious. One of the most important features of what became known as the City Beautiful movement signaled here was the concern for city parks. Olmsted, who designed the gardens at Biltmore, also contributed to the extensive landscape design of the World's Columbian Exposition. Believing that nature softened many of the harmful effects of modern city life, Olmsted had inaugurated the city park movement in the United States when he designed New York's Central Park in 1857 (fig. 28-57). In order to provide the city with what

28-55. Richard Morris Hunt. Biltmore, George W. Vanderbilt estate, Asheville, North Carolina. 1888–95

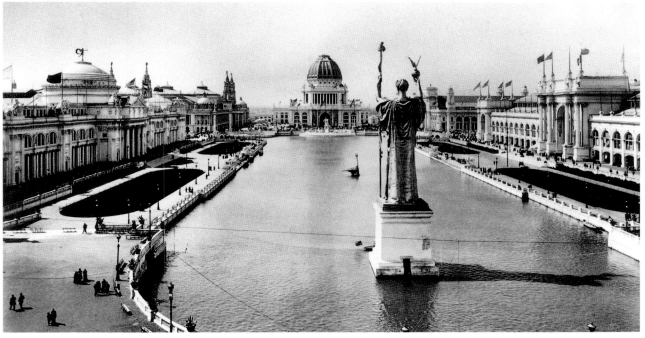

28-56. Richard Morris Hunt. Court of Honor, World's Columbian Exposition, Chicago. 1893

28-57. Frederick Law Olmsted and Calvert Vaux.
Greensward Presentation Sketch No. 5, for Central
Park, New York City, with before and after views.
1858. Oil painting and photograph mounted on board,
28½ x 21" (72.4 x 53.3 cm). The Municipal Archives,
New York

28-58. McKim, Mead, and White. Boston Public Library.
1887–92. View from Copley Square

28-59. McKim, Mead, and White. Boston Public Library.
Ground Plans. 1887–92

he called "a green lung," Olmsted developed a system of
paths, fields, and wooded areas modeled after the informal eighteenth-century English garden (see fig. 26-17).

Many civic buildings of the late nineteenth century
reflect a vision similar to the one that informed the
World's Columbian Exposition: that of the United States
as a site of a democratic renaissance. One such building, the Boston Public Library (figs. 28-58, 28-59), was

28-60. Henry Hobson Richardson. Marshall Field Warehouse, Chicago. 1885–87. Demolished c. 1935

28-61. Louis Sullivan. Wainwright Building, St. Louis, Missouri. 1890–91

designed by the New York architectural firm of Charles Follen McKim (1847–1909), who had studied for three years at the École des Beaux-Arts, William Rutherford Mead (1846–1928), and Stanford White (1853–1906)— then the largest architectural firm in the world. The Boston Public Library has a Renaissance palace–style design that reflects the trustees' request that it be a "palace of the people" (fig. 28-59). On the exterior, **arcaded** windows (set in a row of connected arches) surmount smaller square windows on the street level, much as Alberti had done in his fifteenth-century palaces (see fig. 17-36). And the two-story reading room inside is based on Florentine palace courtyards. Although a group of wealthy families paid for the library, the inscription above the windows states that it was "built by the people and dedicated to the advancement of learning." The building housed the largest circulating library in the world and was intended as a testament to the power of learning.

The second American architect to study at the École des Beaux-Arts was Henry Hobson Richardson (1838–1886). Born in Louisiana and schooled at Harvard, Richardson returned from Paris in 1865. Like Hunt, he worked in a variety of styles, but he became famous for a simplified Romanesque style known as Richardsonian Romanesque. His best-known building is probably the Marshall Field Warehouse in Chicago (fig. 28-60). Although it is reminiscent of Renaissance palaces in form and of Romanesque churches in its heavy stonework and arches, it has no precise historical antecedents. Instead, Richardson took a fresh approach to the design of the utilitarian building. Applied ornament is all but eliminated in favor of the intrinsic appeal of the rough stone

and the subtle harmony between the red sandstone and the darker red granite of the base. The solid corner **piers**, the vertical structural supports, give way to the regular rhythm of the broad arches of the middle floors, which are doubled in the smaller arches above, then doubled again in the square windows of the attic. The integrated mass of the whole is completed in the clean, crisp line of the simple cornice at the top.

Richardson's attempt to break with the historicist tradition may partly be explained in terms of a strong anti–East Coast establishment current among Chicago's businesspeople and architects. Whether or not Richardson intended to appeal to Chicago's businesslike self-image, he certainly did. The plain, sturdy building was a revelation to the young architects of Chicago then engaged in rebuilding the city after the disastrous fire of 1871, which had destroyed the entire downtown. Richardson's building helped them shape their emerging desire to develop a distinctly American architecture.

The American Skyscraper

From a technical standpoint, Richardson's Marshall Field Warehouse represents the end of a short-lived tradition of iron-framed buildings in the United States. Many of the first iron-framed buildings of the mid-nineteenth century also had cast-iron facade elements. These structures were soon found to have a fatal susceptibility to fire; exposed to intense heat, iron will warp, buckle, collapse, or melt altogether. The solution was to encase the internal iron supports in fireproof materials and return to masonry sheathing, which suited Richardson's taste.

The evolution of the skyscraper depended on the development of these essentials: metal beams and girders for the structural-support skeleton; the separation of the building-support structure from the enclosing layer (the cladding); fireproofing materials and measures; elevators; and plumbing, central heating, artificial lighting, and ventilation systems. First-generation skyscrapers, built between about 1880 and 1900, were concentrated in the Midwest, especially Chicago (see figs. 28-60 and 28-61). Second-generation skyscrapers, with more than twenty stories, date from 1895. At first the tall buildings were freestanding towers, sometimes with a base, like the Woolworth Building of 1911–1913 (see fig. 28-63). New York City's Building Zone Resolution of 1916 introduced mandatory setbacks—recessions from the ground-level building line—to ensure light and ventilation of adjacent sites. Built in 1931, the 1,250-foot, setback-form Empire State Building is thoroughly modern in having a streamlined exterior—its cladding is in Art Deco style—that conceals the great complexity of the internal structure and mechanisms that make its height possible. The Empire State Building is still one of the tallest buildings in the world.

The perfection at this time of a technique for making inexpensive steel (a more refined, stronger iron) introduced entirely new possibilities for architecture. Steel was first used for buildings in 1884 by the young architects soon to be grouped under the label of the Chicago School. These architects saw in the stronger, lighter material the answer to both their desire for an independent style and their clients' desire for taller buildings. Interest in tall buildings was essentially economic. By 1880 Chicago was the largest railroad junction in the nation and the hub of the biggest system of inland waterways in the world. Between 1860 and 1880 its population had risen from about 100,000 to more than a million people. The rapidly rising cost of commercial property made

its more efficient use a major consideration for businesspeople. Another technological development that made the tall office building feasible was the passenger elevator, the first of which was installed in 1857. The first electric elevator dates from 1889.

Equipped with steel and with the improved passenger elevators, driven by new economic considerations, and inspired by Richardson's departure from Beaux-Arts historicism, the Chicago School architects produced a new kind of building, the skyscraper, and a new style (see "Elements of Architecture," above). A fine early example of their work, and evidence of its rapid spread throughout the Midwest, is Louis Sullivan's Wainwright Building in St. Louis, Missouri (fig. 28-61). Sullivan (1856–1924),

28-62. Louis Sullivan. Schlesinger and Meyer Department Store (now Carson-Pirie-Scott), Chicago. 1889–1904. Detail of entrance

28-63. Cass Gilbert. Woolworth Building, New York. 1911–13

the creative leader of the firm of Adler and Sullivan, had studied for a year at the Massachusetts Institute of Technology (MIT), home of the United States' first architectural program, and equally briefly at the École des Beaux-Arts, where he seems to have developed his life-long distaste for historicism. After apprenticeships in Philadelphia and in New York with Hunt, he moved to Chicago in 1875, partly because of the building boom there that followed the fire of 1871.

Sullivan may have been against historicism, but he was no revolutionary, as the Wainwright Building attests. Like Richardson's Marshall Field Warehouse, Sullivan's ten-story office building adapts the formal vocabulary of the Beaux-Arts tradition: Its organization into three parts respects the basic compositional rule taught at the French Academy. Although Sullivan claimed to have renounced the classical column, with its base, shaft, and capital, the facade of the Wainwright Building nevertheless conforms to that time-honored model. What is entirely new is the building's vertical emphasis. Unlike Richardson's warehouse, this structure is taller than it is wide; whereas Richardson tried to make his building look shorter by organizing multiple floors into single arcades and by organizing his dominant rhythms horizontally, Sullivan used dominant verticals to emphasize height. The strong corner piers, borrowed from Richardson, rise in clean and uninterrupted lines to the cornice. The smaller piers between the windows, intended to suggest the steel framing beneath them, echo those dominant verticals and reinforce them.

Another aspect of Sullivan's designs that apparently reflects the historicist tradition is his use of architectural ornament. In the Wainwright Building, his characteristic dense vine motif is found on the terra-cotta tiles in the cornice and below the windows. His most famous ornament of this type was the cast-iron tendrils over the entryway of the Schlesinger and Meyer Department Store (now Carson-Pirie-Scott), built in Chicago almost a decade later (fig. 28-62). In contrast to the plain surfaces of the rest of the edifice, this decoration appears an anachronistic carryover from the past, but Sullivan considered this vegetative ornament an expression of the organic principle that dictated the new structure of such buildings. Sullivan believed that architecture, like all aspects of history, is guided by the cyclical natural forces of birth, flowering, decay, and regeneration.

In the period after 1900 New York City assumed leadership in the development of the skyscraper, although clients there rejected the innovative Chicago style for the historicist approach still in favor in the East. The Woolworth Building (fig. 28-63), designed by Cass Gilbert (1859–1934), is representative of this trend. Gilbert studied at MIT for a year before going to work for McKim, Mead, and White in 1880. Three years later, he opened his own office in St. Paul, Minnesota, where he had grown up. He won the prestigious commission to design the Woolworth Building, the headquarters of the giant department-store chain, in 1910. When completed, at 792 feet and 55 floors, the gleaming white structure was the world's tallest office building. The Gothic style of the

28-64. Frank Lloyd Wright. Fallingwater, Mill Run, Pennsylvania. 1937

building, inspired by the great soaring towers of late-medieval churches, resonated as well with the United States' increasing worship of business. Gilbert explained that he wished to make something "spiritual" of what others called his Cathedral of Commerce.

Frank Lloyd Wright

The most celebrated American architect of the Chicago School was Frank Lloyd Wright (1867–1959). His mother, determined that he would be an architect, had hung engravings of cathedrals over his crib. Summers spent working on his uncle's farm in Wisconsin gave him a deep respect for nature, natural materials, and agrarian life. After studying engineering for two years at the University of Wisconsin, Wright apprenticed for a year with a Chicago architect, then spent the next five years with Adler and Sullivan. Wright eventually became their chief drafter, but Sullivan fired him in 1893 for moonlighting. Thus, in the year of the World's Columbian Exposition, Wright opened his own office, specializing in the domestic architecture he had been doing for Sullivan's firm. Seeking better ways to integrate house and site, he turned away from the traditional boxlike design and began by 1900 to create what he called an "organic" architecture that would reflect its surroundings and thus integrate its inhabitants with nature.

Wright's most famous expression of his conviction that buildings ought to be a part of nature—*in* it, not simply on it—is Fallingwater, in rural Pennsylvania (fig. 28-64). The country house was commissioned by Edgar Kaufmann to replace a rudimentary cottage that had long served the family's summer needs. Wright began the project by visiting the site, the main attraction of which was a waterfall that fed into a pool where the family children played and swam. To the Kaufmanns' great surprise, Wright decided to build the house into the cliff over the pool, allowing the waterfall to flow around and under the house. A large boulder on which the family sunbathed was built into the house as the hearthstone of the fireplace. In a dramatic engineering move that experts questioned, Wright cantilevered a series of broad terraces out from the cliffside, echoing the great slabs of rock below. As one engineer recently said, "There is not a city in the United States, even today, where one could obtain a building permit to erect Fallingwater" (Pfeiffer, page 161). The house is further tied to its site through materials. Although the terraces are poured concrete, the wood and stone used elsewhere are either from the site or in harmony with it. Such houses are not simply testaments to the ideal of living in harmony with nature but declarations of warfare on the modern industrial city. When asked what could be done to improve the city, Wright responded: "Tear it down."

28-65. Frank Lloyd Wright. Dining room with original
furniture and ceiling, Wright Home, Oak Park, Illinois.
1889–90

28-66. Julia Morgan. *Drawing for the Oakland YWCA.* 1913.
Pen and ink and watercolor, 11³/₄ x 21" (30 x 53 cm).
Special Collections, California Polytechnic State
University, San Luis Obispo

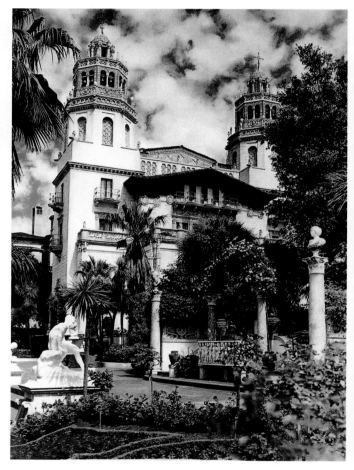

28-67. Julia Morgan. Front entrance, Casa Grande, San Simeon,
California. 1922–26. Special Collections, California Polytechnic State University, San Luis Obispo

Wright also designed the furnishings at Fallingwater.
Unhappy that his early clients had violated the designs of
his homes with eclectic furnishings of their own choosing, he embarked on a comprehensive program to design
everything from lighting units to rugs, wall hangings, and
stained glass. His distinctive style emerged in the renovations he performed on his own home in Oak Park, Illinois,
in 1895. The dining room (fig. 28-65) includes the high
slat-back dining chairs that became a Wright "signature"
piece. He thought that the tall chairs could form a sort of
screen around the family unit, containing, protecting, and
intensifying it. In order to prevent distractions from the
family dinnertime communion, he restricted decorations
in the room. The chief ornament is the ceiling grill, whose
indirect lighting filtered through a series of circular openings he meant to resemble moonlight.

In 1897 Wright helped found the Chicago Arts and
Crafts Society, an outgrowth of the movement begun in
England by William Morris (Chapter 27). But whereas his
English predecessors looked nostalgically back to the
Middle Ages and rejected machine production, Wright
did not. He detested standardization, but he thought the
machine could produce beautiful and affordable objects.

Another architect who participated in the American
Arts and Crafts movement was the Californian Julia Morgan (1872–1957). Morgan received her degree in engineering in 1894 from the University of California at
Berkeley, where she was the only female student. Encouraged by a local architect, she decided to become

one. Although the École des Beaux-Arts did not accept
women, she moved to Paris anyway and in 1896 enrolled
in a private architectural studio. Two years of persistence
paid off, and she was admitted to the École as its first
female student. In 1904 she opened her own office in San
Francisco, and over the course of her career she designed
nearly 800 buildings. By 1927 she had a staff of fourteen
architects, six of them women.

Morgan did much of her early work for friends and for women's organizations. At Mills College for women she designed several buildings in a revival of the increasingly popular Mission Style, first introduced by early Spanish settlers. For the Oakland Young Women's Christian Association (YWCA), however, she used an Italian Renaissance style (fig. 28-66). The YWCA, founded in London in 1855, was one of the many women's organizations intended to address the social problems of the new industrial cities. The YWCA's particular mission was to provide temporary residences and recreational facilities for the young women flocking to cities to take low-paying factory and office jobs. Morgan almost never discussed her work, so it is difficult to know why she and her clients chose a Renaissance–palace style to house poor working women. Certainly the perfect symmetry of her conception suggests that she wanted to provide the short-term residents with an image of stability.

The distinctive feature of Morgan's architecture was the quality and care of its detailing, or finishing elements. In the Oakland YWCA, for example, the terra-cotta decor used around the windows featured California fruits and flowers. The tiles were made in nearby Alameda from Morgan's own handsome designs. The same concern for careful craft is evident in the work she did for her major patron, William Randolph Hearst, shortly after World War I. In 1919 Hearst commissioned her to design a palatial estate on a hilltop in San Simeon, about 200 miles south of San Francisco. Although Hearst mentioned a "Jappo-Swisso bungalow" in his first meeting with her, he eventually decided on the Mission Style for his Casa Grande. The main building (fig. 28-67) of reinforced concrete (see "Space-Spanning Construction Devices," page 32) is a free interpretation of a Spanish Mission church. Above the single doorway and below the pair of wide, sturdy columns typical of such churches, Morgan added a house front to indicate the building's function. Since the Renaissance, the Greek temple had been adapted to domestic architecture, but similar domestic adaptation of the Christian church was rare.

The elaborate decoration on the facade of San Simeon reflects the detailing throughout. The decor and furnishings represent a final manifestation of the Arts and Crafts tradition. Morgan employed a host of stonecutters, experts in ornamental plasters, wood-carvers, iron casters, weavers, tapestry makers, and tile designers. All the craftwork was copied or improvised from historical models.

By the 1920s most young designers, like their architect counterparts, had completely rejected historicism and handcrafts for a modern machine aesthetic. The story of that change begins in Europe in the late nineteenth century.

Art Nouveau

While the Chicago School was looking for an American alternative to the European Beaux-Arts tradition, its European counterparts had been calling for an end to historicism and the invention of an architectural and design style appropriate to the modern age. The search would lead, in the early twentieth century, to the frank acceptance of new industrial materials and techniques—like those that first appeared in buildings such as the Crystal Palace (see fig. 27-1)—as the basis of legitimate architecture. In the interim the Art Nouveau ("New Art") phenomenon of the 1890s in Europe was a brief attempt at something less radical.

Art Nouveau was essentially a Continental development with roots in the English Arts and Crafts Movement. Like that movement, it emerged initially in response to a world's fair, in this case the Paris Universal Exposition of 1889. The centerpiece of the fair was an enormous tower designed by civil engineer Gustave Eiffel (1832–1923), the winner of a competition for the design of a monument that would symbolize French industrial progress. The Eiffel Tower (fig. 28-68), composed of iron latticework, stands on four huge legs reinforced by trussed arches like those Eiffel used for his famous railway bridges. The passenger elevators, themselves an innovation, allowed fairgoers to ascend to the top of what was then, at 984 feet, the tallest structure in the world.

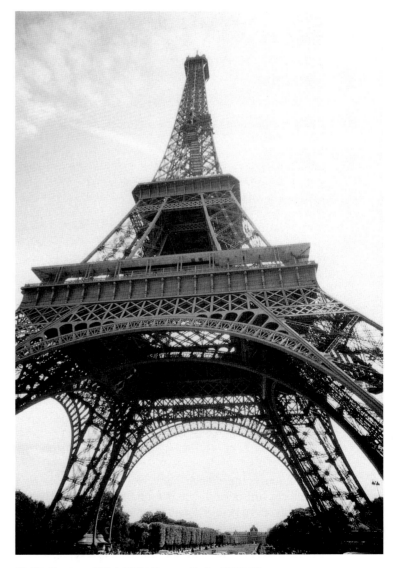

28-68. Gustave Eiffel. Eiffel Tower, Paris. 1887–89

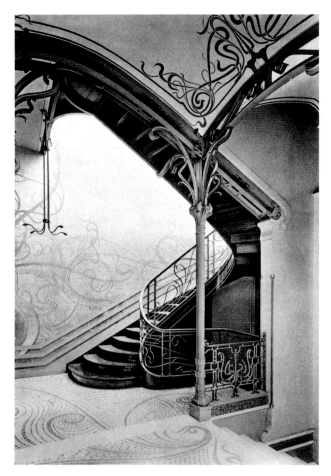

28-69. Victor Horta. Stairway, Tassel House, Brussels. 1892–93

28-70. Hector Guimard. Desk. c. 1899 (remodeled after 1909). Olive wood with ash panels, 28³⁄₄ x 47³⁄₄" (73 x 121 cm). The Museum of Modern Art, New York
Gift of Madame Hector Guimard

Although the French public loved the tower, most architects, artists, and writers found it completely lacking in beauty. Even before it was completed, several dozen of them signed a petition protesting it to the government: "This tower dominating Paris, like a gigantic and black factory chimney, crushing with its barbarous mass Notre-Dame, the Sainte-Chapelle . . . all our monuments

humiliated. . . . And in twenty years we shall see, stretching over the entire city . . . the odious shadow of the odious column built up of riveted iron plates" (cited in Holt, volume 1, page 70). The last part of their protest refers not to the literal shadow of the tower but to its metaphorical one, the negative influence many people anticipated it would have on the future of architecture in Paris.

Art Nouveau, a style that attempted to be modern without the loss of a preindustrial sense of beauty, was one response to this concern, which extended beyond the French borders. Art Nouveau's commitment to the organically beautiful and its emphasis on traditional materials such as stone and wood were in many ways an attempt to forestall what might be called the industrialization of architecture and design. For the practitioners of Art Nouveau, a purely functional structure like the Crystal Palace or a railway bridge was just not beautiful. They appreciated the simplicity of such structures but found their naked engineering lacking in the linear grace long considered the very essence of beauty.

The man who apparently launched the Art Nouveau style of the 1890s was a Belgian, Victor Horta (1861–1947). Horta trained as an architect at the Brussels Academy, then worked in the office of a Neoclassical architect. In 1892 he received his first independent commission, a private residence in Brussels for a Professor Tassel. The result, especially the house's entry hall and staircase (fig. 28-69), was strikingly original. The ironwork, wall decoration, and floor tile were all designed in terms of an intricate series of long, graceful curves. Although Horta's sources are still a matter of debate, he apparently was much impressed with the stylized linear graphics produced by artists of the English Arts and Crafts Movement of the late 1880s, such as the architect and designer Arthur Heygate Mackmurdo (1851–1942) and the painter and illustrator Walter Crane (1845–1915). Horta's concern for integrating the various arts into a more unified whole, like his reliance on a refined decorative line, also derived largely from English reformers.

The application of graceful linear arabesques to all aspects of design, evident in the entry hall of the Tassel House, began a vogue that lasted for more than a decade. During its lifetime the movement had a number of regional names. In Italy it was called *Stile floreale* ("Floral Style") and *Stile Liberty* (after the Liberty department store in London); in Germany, *Jugendstil* ("Youth Style"); in Spain, *Modernismo* (Modernism); in Vienna, *Secessionsstil*, after the secession from the Academy led by Klimt; in Belgium it was called *Paling Style* ("Eel Style"); and in France it had a number of names, including *moderne*. The name eventually accepted in most countries derives from a shop, La Maison de l'Art Nouveau ("The House of the New Art"), which opened in Paris in 1895.

In France it was also sometimes known as *Style Guimard* after its leading French practitioner, Hector Guimard (1867–1942). Like Horta, Guimard was more a designer than an architect in the strictest sense. His major production was in the area of interior design and furnishings. Typical of his work is the desk that he made for himself out of olive wood and ash wood (fig. 28-70). Instead of a static and stable object, Guimard has handcrafted an organic entity that seems to undulate and grow.

Both the organic principle and the concern to unify all areas of life into a beautiful whole relate Art Nouveau to the nearly contemporary work of Frank Lloyd Wright. While Wright wanted to reintegrate humanity with nature in a suburban setting, Art Nouveau designers and architects were content to redecorate the modern city in a style resembling nature—to compensate formally for its gradual disappearance from modern, industrial life.

The Art Nouveau emphasis is also evident in the work of the Catalan architect Antonio Gaudí y Cornet (1852–1926). The son of an ironworker, Gaudí, like Horta, was familiar with the writings of Morris and the graphics of other English Arts and Crafts practitioners. His work paralleled developments in the work of Horta and others but did not depend on them. Almost ten years before Horta's decorative ironwork at the Tassel House, Gaudí had produced similar work in Barcelona for his patron Count Güell.

Gaudí also attempted to introduce the organic principle into the very structure of his buildings. In the Casa Milá apartment house in Barcelona (fig. 28-71), for example, the interior and exterior walls gently undulate like ocean waves. The building has no straight lines. Constructed around a steel frame, it is covered with cut stones hammered to give the surface a look of natural erosion, like beach cliffs. The organic effect is completed by the stylized ironwork, which seems to grow like foliage or seaweed on the balconies. As Wright's architecture was based on his American sensibilities, Gaudí's alternative to both historicism and the threat of industrialism reflected his affinity for Spanish Gothic architecture.

Despite the role the English Arts and Crafts Movement played in the formation of Art Nouveau, the English did not participate in the style. During the 1890s they remained faithful to the styles and principles associated with Morris. One British architect and designer whose work most closely approximates Art Nouveau was the Scot Charles Rennie Mackintosh (1868–1928). In 1891 he and a colleague at his firm, Herbert McNair, met and eventually married two students at the Glasgow School of Art, Margaret Macdonald (1865–1933) and Frances Macdonald (1874–1921), who shared their taste and ideas. The four soon began to collaborate in a variety of decorative projects, including posters, metalwork, glass, and fabrics. Their work, shown at La Maison de l'Art Nouveau in 1896, featured an elegant, elongated line reminiscent of Horta's and Guimard's but used more sparingly and in conjunction with large empty spaces.

The style developed by "The Four," or "Mac's Group," is evident in the Director's Room at the Glasgow School of Art (1897–1909), which was designed largely by Mackintosh but with considerable help from his wife, Margaret Macdonald (fig. 28-72). The Director's Room is the first of the Mackintoshes' innovative "white rooms": The wood paneling, instead of being left naturally dark, is painted white to match the walls. In sharp reaction to both the Victorian and the Arts and Crafts preference for filling the walls with decor, here they are refreshingly clean and spare. The focus is on the wood furniture designed in a simplified medieval

28-71. Antonio Gaudí. Casa Milá apartment building, Barcelona. 1905–7

28-72. Charles Rennie Mackintosh and Margaret Macdonald. Director's Room, Glasgow School of Art. 1897–1909

style and produced by local craftspeople under Mackintosh's supervision. Some of the furniture—particularly the famous high-backed Mackintosh chair with the oval rail seen here—sacrifices utilitarian comfort to beauty. The linear designs used in the metalwork on the cabinet and in the frosted-glass lighting fixtures were inspired by the **interlaces** featured in Celtic manuscripts. The Mackintoshes,

28-73. Adolf Loos. Steiner House, Vienna. 1910

like Wright and Gaudí, were interested in developing not simply a modern style but one based on their own cultures.

Early Modernism

In 1900 the Mackintoshes were invited to design a room for an exhibition in Vienna. The restrained style of the result seems to have encouraged a number of young Viennese architects, already dissatisfied with Art Nouveau, to turn vehemently against it. The most radical of this group was Adolf Loos (1870–1933). Born in Austria-Hungary, Loos studied in Dresden, Germany. He spent three years in the United States and was impressed by the industrial buildings he saw there. In Vienna he began to make a name for himself not with his architecture, of which there is little, but with his writing. In his most famous essay, "Ornament and Crime" (1908), he insisted: "The evolution of culture is synonymous with the removal of ornament from utilitarian objects." For Loos, ornament was a sign of a degenerate culture.

Two years after that essay, Loos designed the Steiner House (fig. 28-73), an impressive building that well illustrates its architect's famous views. The simple stucco construction is devoid of embellishment. Windows are

28-74. Walter Gropius and Adolph Meyer. Fagus Factory, Alfeld-an-der-Leine, Germany. 1911–16

28-75. Antonio Sant'Elia. Central Station project, Milan. 1914. After Banham

"We are no longer the men of the cathedrals, the palaces, the assembly halls," Sant'Elia wrote in the 1914 *Manifesto of Futurist Architecture*, "but of big hotels, railway stations, immense roads, colossal ports, covered markets . . . demolition and rebuilding schemes. We must invent and build the city of the future, dynamic in all its parts . . . and the house of the future must be like an enormous machine."

not arranged decoratively but simply where the needs of the interior call for them. For Loos, an exterior was not to delight the aesthetic sense but simply to provide protection from the elements. The curved roof allows rain and snow to run off but, unlike the traditional steeped roof, creates no wasted space.

The purely functional exteriors of Loos's buildings and his outspoken opposition to ornament qualify him as one of the founders of modernist architecture. Another of its founders is Walter Gropius (1883–1969). After conventional architectural training in Munich and Berlin between 1903 and 1907, Gropius became the chief assistant to Peter Behrens, whose Berlin firm specialized in industrial architecture. In 1910 he opened his own office. His lectures on ways to increase workers' productivity by improving their workplace environment caught the attention of an industrialist, and in 1911 he was commissioned to design the facade for the Fagus Factory (fig. 28-74). This building represents the emergence of modernist architecture from the engineering advances of the nineteenth century. Unlike the Crystal Palace or the Eiffel Tower, it was conceived not to demonstrate those advances or to solve a specific problem but to function as a building. With it Gropius was the first to proclaim that modern architecture should make intelligent and sensitive use of what the engineer can provide.

Inspired partly by Wright, Gropius produced a purely functional building in the tradition of the Crystal Palace. Unlike the buildings of Wright and Behrens, however, the Fagus Factory facade has no elaboration beyond that dictated by its modern construction methods. The slender brick piers along the outer walls mark the building's steel frame, and the narrow bands of brickwork at the top and bottom, like the opaque panels between them, mark floors and ceilings. A **curtain wall**—an exterior wall that bears no weight but simply separates the inside from the outside—hangs over the frame. Large rectangular windows dominate the exterior. The corner piers standard in earlier buildings have been eliminated as unneeded gestures to tradition. The glass both reveals the building's structure and floods the workplace inside with light. This building insists that good engineering is good architecture.

Just prior to World War I, a Futurist architect, Antonio Sant'Elia (1888–1916), conceived a more dynamic, less functional solution to the search for a modern style. Sant'Elia apparently joined the Futurists soon after taking his degree in 1912. Beginning that year, he produced a series of drawings of his vision of the city of the future (fig. 28-75), and in 1914 he published his *Manifesto of Futurist Architecture*, which explains those drawings. His conception of the new city is not based on new technology alone but also on the way it can emphasize the energy of modern life. He wanted to use steel, glass, and reinforced concrete to create an architecture of dynamic appearance. The basic structure of the new city would be the skyscraper, serviced by dramatic exterior glass elevators and connected by open walkways. The stepped-back design of these high-rise buildings, like the soaring towers at their top, is not functional but expressive. The verticals, diagonals, and curves are meant to characterize the essential feature of the new city—rapid movement. Cutting through and beneath the city's architecture would be a network of roads and subways extending in places to seven levels below the ground. Nowhere is there a trace of nature.

Although Sant'Elia's visionary drawings had a profound effect on one strain of architecture after World War I, he did not live to see it. He was among the nearly 10 million young men who died in the war that broke out in 1914.

EUROPEAN ART AND ARCHITECTURE BETWEEN THE WARS

The Great War, as World War I was then known, had a profound effect on Europe's artists and architects. While many responded pessimistically, some sought in the war's ashes the basis for a new, more secure civilization. For those, that basis was to be found in the seemingly timeless culture of the classical tradition.

Postwar Classicism

Perhaps the most unexpected reaction to World War I came from Picasso. After Braque's departure for the front in 1914, Picasso stayed in Paris, where he faced a growing tide of nationalistic criticism against Cubism. Because many of the art dealers who sold Cubist works were German, their collections were confiscated, and Cubism itself was denounced as a manifestation of German "destructive" tendencies. That Spanish and French artists invented it was conveniently ignored in the heated rhetoric aimed at restoring the preeminence of what was considered a spiritually healthy French classicism.

Picasso responded to this climate by adopting a classical style. During the war and for several years after, the man who had earlier spurned a French style, then rejected conventional representation altogether, produced works like *Woman in White* (fig. 28-76). The large, calm, self-contained figure seems to derive directly from ancient Greek sculpture or from Puvis's murals. Even the chalky whites are reminiscent of classical marble and the muted tones Puvis preferred. The Spanish bohemian Picasso of the prewar years gave way to his *haute bourgeois* French counterpart. In 1918 he even married a dancer in Diaghilev's Ballets Russes, Olga Koklova, whose classical beauty reinforced the new stylistic tendency.

The British sculptor Henry Moore (1898–1986) also adopted a form of classicism, but for less self-serving and personal reasons. In his early work from the late 1920s he attempted to reinvigorate the classical tradition with the strength and power of the "primitive" art very much in favor in Britain after the war. His *Reclining Figure*

28-76. Pablo Picasso. *Woman in White* (*Madame Picasso*). 1923. Oil on canvas, 39 x 31½" (99 x 80 cm). The Metropolitan Museum of Art, New York
Rogers Fund

28-77. Henry Moore. *Reclining Figure*. 1929. Brown Hornton stone, 22½ x 33 x 15" (57 x 83.8 x 38 cm). Leeds City Art Gallery, England (fig. 28-77) combines the pose found in certain of the Elgin Marbles (sculpture from the Parthenon, housed in the British Museum) with the blocky formal language of pre-Columbian art. As with the women in Picasso's *Les Demoiselles d'Avignon* (see fig. 28-36), the erotic connotations of the figure's pose are subsumed by her psychological and physical strength. The erect head, based on that of Achilles from the Parthenon **frieze**, suggests intelligence. With its imposing monumentality, Moore's work—almost all of which was made for public display—comforts the modern viewer anxious about the human capacity to endure.

Russian Utilitarian Art Forms

In March 1917 growing Russian dissatisfaction with the war gave revolutionary elements the opportunity to overthrow the czarist monarchy. In October the government was seized by the Bolsheviks ("radical socialists") under Vladimir Lenin, who immediately took Russia out of the war.

Most members of the Russian avant-garde enthusiastically supported the Bolsheviks, who in turn supported them. Vladimir Tatlin's case is fairly representative. In 1919 he was appointed head of the Studio for Volumes, Materials, and Construction at the Petrograd State Free Art Studios (previously the St. Petersburg Academy). As part of his work on the committee to implement Lenin's Plan for Monumental Propaganda, Tatlin devised the Monument to the Third International (fig. 28-78), the 1,300-foot building to house the new Russian congress. Tatlin's visionary plan meant to combine the appearance of avant-garde sculpture with a fully utilitarian building, a new hybrid form as revolutionary as the politics it represented. In Tatlin's model, the steel structural support, a spiraling diagonal, is on the outside of rather than inside the building. Tatlin combined the Eiffel Tower with the formal vocabulary of the Cubo-Futurists to convey the dynamism of the new Soviet state. Inside the steel frame would be four separate spaces: a large cube to house legislative meetings, a smaller pyramid for executive committees, a cylinder for propaganda offices, and a hemisphere at the top, apparently meant for radio equipment. Each of these units would rotate at a different speed, from yearly at the bottom to hourly at the top.

Neither Tatlin nor anyone else had the slightest idea how such a visionary piece of architecture could actually be built. The monument is both an affirmation of faith in what Soviet science could achieve and an object to inspire the genius of the Russian people in that direction. The small model was shown in propaganda parades in 1920 and 1921, and a 130-foot model of iron and glass was later built in Petrograd.

Tatlin's associates in the postrevolutionary period, known as the Constructivists, were committed to the notion that the artist must quit the studio and "go into the factory, where the real body of life is made." In place of those artists now considered "outlaws"—that is, those who were dedicated to pleasing themselves—they envisioned politically committed artists devoted to creating

28-78. Vladimir Tatlin. Model for the Monument to the Third International. 1919–20. Wood, iron, and glass. Destroyed

Karl Marx helped organize the International Working Men's Association, or First International, an uneasy alliance of British trade-union leaders and various continental Communist groups that lasted from 1864 to 1872. By 1889 Socialist parties had gained sufficient strength in a number of European nations to form a loose international association, the Second (or Socialist) International, which came to an end at the onset of World War I, when most Socialist leaders abandoned internationalism for the nationalist interests of the war. The Third (or Communist) International was formed under Vladimir Lenin in March 1919 to promote the spread of communism through what he called permanent revolution.

useful objects and promoting the aims of the collective. One of the founders of the movement, launched in 1921, was Aleksandr Rodchenko (1891–1956). His work in Moscow with Tatlin in about 1917–1919 gradually convinced him that painting and sculpture did not contribute enough to practical needs. In 1921, after exhibiting a **triptych** of red, yellow, and blue canvases that he considered the end of painting, he gave up traditional "high art" mediums (painting and sculpture) to make photographs and to design posters, books, textiles, and theater sets, all of which were intended to promote the ends of the new Soviet society.

In 1925 Rodchenko also designed a model workers' club for the Russian pavilion at the Paris World's Fair

28-79. Aleksandr Rodchenko. View of the Workers' Club, exhibited at the Exposition Internationale des Arts Décoratifs et Industriels Modernes, Paris. 1925. Rodchenko-Stepanova Archive, Moscow

28-80. El Lissitzky. Proun space created for a Berlin art exhibition. 1923, reconstruction 1965. Stedelijk Van Abbemuseum, Eindhoven, the Netherlands

(fig. 28-79). Although Rodchenko said such a club "must be built for amusement and relaxation," the space was essentially a reading room dedicated to the proper training of the Soviet mind. One corner of the room was de-voted to materials on the life and ideas of Lenin, who had died the year before. Even the one recreational element, the chess table in the back beneath Lenin's photograph, sharpens the intellect. The furniture was designed for simplicity of use and ease of construction. It is made of wood because Russian industry was best equipped for mass production in that material. The design of the chairs is not strictly utilitarian, however. The high, straight backs were meant to promote a physical and moral posture of uprightness among the workers.

Not all of the modernists who supported the revolution were willing to give up the traditional high art forms. One of these, El Lissitzky (1890–1941), attempted to fit the formalism of Malevich to the new imperative that art should be useful to the social order. After the revolution, Lissitzky, who had trained as an engineer in Germany, was invited to teach architecture and graphic arts at the Vitebsk School of Fine Arts. There he came under the influence of Malevich, who also taught at the school. By 1919 he was using Malevich's formal vocabulary for propaganda posters and for artworks he called Prouns, an acronym for "Project for the Affirmation of the New." Most are paintings, but a few, like that made for an exhibition in Germany (fig. 28-80), were Proun spaces. Lissitzky, who rejected conventional painting instruments as too personal and imprecise, produced his Prouns with the aid of mechanical instruments. Their engineered look is not merely to celebrate industrial technology but also to encourage precise thinking among the public, to produce, as he suggested in one of his works, a "new man," the new Russian.

As was typical of the general trend in Russian art of the late 1920s, Lissitzky grew disillusioned with the power of formalist art to communicate broadly. By the end of the decade, he, too, had turned to more utilitarian projects—architecture and typography, in particular—and had begun to produce, along with Rodchenko and others, propaganda photographs and **photomontages**, the combination of several photographs into one work. During the 1930s he worked for *USSR in Construction*, a magazine meant to give its foreign readers a positive impression of Soviet society.

The move away from abstraction was led by a group of realists, deeply antagonistic to the avant-garde, who banded together in 1922 to form the Association of Artists of Revolutionary Russia (AKhRR) and promote a clear, representational approach to revolutionary art. The AKhRR looked back to artists such as Repin (see fig. 27-25) and dedicated itself to the depiction of workers, peasants, revolutionary activists, and, in particular, the life and history of the Red Army. After Joseph Stalin succeeded Lenin in 1924, the artists of the AKhRR were more and more often called on to produce images for the state. Their tendency to create huge, overly dramatic canvases on heroic or inspirational themes established the basis for the Socialist Realism instituted by Stalin after he took control of the arts in 1932.

One of the sculptors who worked in this official style was Vera Mukhina (1889–1963), who had studied briefly in Paris before the war. Her most famous work is *Worker and Collective Farm Worker* (fig. 28-81), made for the Soviet Pavilion at the Paris Exposition of 1937. The powerfully built male factory worker and female farm laborer hold aloft their respective tools, a hammer and a sickle,

28-81. Vera Mukhina. *Worker and Collective Farm Worker*, sculpture for the Soviet Pavilion, Paris Exposition. 1937

to mimic their appearance on the Soviet flag. The two figures are shown as equal partners striding purposefully into the future, their determined faces looking forward and upward. The dramatic, windblown drapery and the forward propulsion of their diagonal poses, not unlike the forceful spiraling angles of Tatlin's Monument (see fig. 28-78), enhance the sense of vigorous idealism. The work was not meant for domestic inspiration but to convince an increasingly skeptical international audience of the continuing success of the Soviet system.

Dutch Rationalism

In the Netherlands, the Dutch counterpart to the inspirational formalism of Lissitzky was provided by the de Stijl ("the Style") group, whose leading artist was Piet Mondrian (1872–1944). The turning point in Mondrian's life came in 1911 when he went to Paris and encountered Analytic Cubism. Beginning with works quite similar to Picasso's *Ma Jolie* (see fig. 28-42), he gradually moved from radical abstractions of landscape and architecture to a simple, austere form of geometric art inspired by them. In the Netherlands during World War I, he met Theo van Doesburg, another painter who shared his artistic views, and in 1917 the two started a magazine, *De Stijl*, which became the focal point of a Dutch movement of artists, architects, and designers that lasted until van Doesburg's death in 1931.

28-82. Piet Mondrian. *Composition with Red, Blue, and Yellow.* 1930. Oil on canvas, 20 x 20" (50.3 x 50.3 cm). Private collection

Mondrian so disliked the sight of nature, whose irregularities he held largely accountable for humanity's problems, that when seated at a restaurant table with a view of the outdoors, he would ask to be moved.

The de Stijl movement was grounded in the conviction that there are two kinds of beauty: a sensual or subjective one and a higher, rational or objective—"universal"—kind. In his mature works Mondrian sought the essence of the second kind, eliminating representational elements because of their subjective associations and curves because of their sensual appeal. After about 1920 Mondrian's paintings, such as *Composition with Red, Blue, and Yellow* (fig. 28-82), all employ the same essential formal vocabulary: the three primary hues (red, yellow, and blue), the two primary **values** (white and black), and horizontal and vertical lines. The two linear directions are meant to symbolize the harmony of a series of opposites, including male versus female, individual versus society, and spiritual versus material. For Mondrian the essence of higher beauty was resolved conflict, what he called dynamic equilibrium. Here, as was typical in his work, it was achieved through the precise arrangement of color areas of different weight. The heavier weight of the red threatens to tip the painting to the right, but the placement of the tiny rectangle of yellow at the lower right prevents this imbalance by supporting the red's weight. The ultimate purpose of such paintings is not to provide aesthetic pleasure for a wealthy collector but to demonstrate a universal style with applications beyond the realm of art. Like Art Nouveau, de Stijl wished to redecorate the world. But to Mondrian and his colleagues, nature's example only encourages what they felt were "primitive animal instincts," and they therefore rejected the organic style of Art Nouveau. If, instead of living in a state of nature, we lived

in an environment designed according to the rules of "universal beauty," we too, like our art, would be balanced, our natural instincts "purified." For these reasons, Mondrian hoped to be the world's last artist. He felt that earlier art had provided humanity with something that was lacking in daily life; but if there were beauty in every aspect of our lives, we would have no further need for art.

The major architect and designer of the de Stijl movement was Gerrit Rietveld (1888–1964), whose famous "red and blue" chair is shown here in the bedroom of his most important project, the Schröder House (fig. 28-83) in Utrecht. Inspired partly by both Wright and the Constructivists, Rietveld applied Mondrian's design principle of a dynamic symmetry of rectangular planes of color to the entire house and its built-in furnishings. Some of the compositional planes on the interior were sliding partitions designed to allow modifications in the spaces used for sleeping, working, and entertaining. These innovative wall partitions were actually the idea of the owner, Truus Schröder, who worked with Rietveld on the design of this and several later projects. A wealthy woman, Schröder wanted her austere home to suggest the rejection of luxury for simple necessities, sensitively integrated into a beautiful whole.

French Rationalism

Among French artists, the dominant response to the Great War was similar to that of de Stijl. Many saw the war as the inevitable consequence of a culture in which the spirit of competition and individualism had run amok. For them, the solution was what one conservative critic labeled "the return to order," the formation of a more disciplined society along the lines suggested in visual terms by Seurat in *A Sunday Afternoon on the Island of La Grande Jatte* (see fig. 28-14). One expression of this widespread conviction was Purism, whose leading figure was the Swiss-born Charles-Édouard Jeanneret (1887–1965). A largely self-taught architect and designer, Jeanneret moved to Paris in 1917, where he met Amédée Ozenfant (1886–1966). In 1918 they published a book, *After Cubism*, and between 1920 and 1925 they edited a magazine, *L'Esprit nouveau* (*The New Spirit*).

Like the Constructivists and the proponents of de Stijl, the Purists firmly believed in the power of art to change the world. In 1920 Jeanneret, partly to demonstrate his faith in the ability of individuals to remake themselves, renamed himself Le Corbusier. With Ozenfant, Le Corbusier thought of himself as producing a new and improved Cubism that would not only provide aesthetic pleasure but also, by placing viewers in an orderly frame of mind, promote social order in the world.

One of the artists strongly influenced by Purism was Fernand Léger (1881–1955). In the early 1920s he briefly experimented with Purism in a series of still-life and figure paintings that included *Three Women* (fig. 28-84). His

28-83. Gerrit Rietveld. Interior, Schröder House, Utrecht, the Netherlands. 1924

28-84. Fernand Léger. *Three Women*. 1921. Oil on canvas, 6'1/2" x 8'3" (1.84 x 2.52 m). The Museum of Modern Art, New York
Mrs. Simon Guggenheim Fund

28-85. Charles-Édouard Jeanneret (Le Corbusier). Plan for a Contemporary City of Three Million Inhabitants. 1922

In 1925 Le Corbusier devised a similar plan for Paris, convinced that the center of the city needed to be torn down and rebuilt to accommodate automobile traffic. The Parisian street was a "Pack-Donkey's Way," he said: "Imagine all this junk . . . cleared off and carried away and replaced by immense clear crystals of glass, rising to a height of over six hundred feet!"

28-86. Le Corbusier. Villa Savoye, Poissy-sur-Seine, France. 1929–30

answer to the French odalisque tradition, the painting takes Delacroix's *Women of Algiers* (see fig. 26-49) and transforms it according to a Purist ideal of anonymity and order. The women, arranged within a geometric grid, stare out blankly at us. They have identical faces, and their bodies seem assembled from standardized, detachable metal parts. The bright, cheerful colors and patterns suggest a positive vision of an orderly industrial society.

Purism's most important contributions were not in painting or sculpture but in architecture. Although he never gave up painting, from 1922 until his death Le Corbusier concentrated on architecture and urban planning. One of his first mature projects was his conception for a Contemporary City of Three Million Inhabitants (fig. 28-85), a design he exhibited in Paris in 1922. Le Corbusier hated the crowded, noisy, chaotic, and polluted places that cities had become in the late nineteenth century. What he envisioned for the future was a city of uniform style, laid out on a grid, and dominated, like Sant'Elia's (see fig. 28-75), by skyscrapers, with wide traffic arteries that often passed beneath ground level. Le Corbusier's city would be different from Sant'Elia's, however, in two fundamental respects. First, the buildings would be strictly functional, in the manner of Gropius's Fagus Factory (see fig. 28-74). And second, nature would not be neglected. Set between the widely spaced buildings would be large expanses of parkland. The result, Le Corbusier thought, would be a new, clean, and efficient city filled with light, air, and greenery. Le Corbusier's vision had a profound effect on later city planning, especially in the United States.

During the 1920s Le Corbusier also designed a number of houses for private clients, the most famous of which is the Villa Savoye (fig. 28-86). The last of his Purist villas, it culminated a line of thinking that had begun in 1914 with the so-called domino construction system, in which ferroconcrete (concrete reinforced with steel bars) slabs were floated on six freestanding steel posts (placed at the positions of the six dots on a domino playing piece). Over the next decade the architect explored the possibilities of this structure and in 1926 published "The Five Points of a New Architecture." Its main claims were that houses should be elevated above the ground on *pilotis* (freestanding posts), that roofs should be flat for use as terraces, and that exterior and interior walls should be hung to allow for freedom of design (these are known as **curtain walls** to distinguish them from supporting walls) and for the use of "ribbon windows" (windows that run the length of the wall).

Although none of these ideas was particularly new, they were applied by Le Corbusier in a distinctive fashion that combined two apparently opposed formal systems: the classical Doric architecture of ancient Greece and the clear precision of machinery. Such houses could be effectively placed in nature, as here, but they were meant to represent a higher, transcendent synthesis, as their elevation off the ground and pure white coloring suggest. Because of its beautiful play of curves and angles, the Villa Savoye is more than a house; it is a beautiful piece of sculpture.

The Bauhaus

The German counterpart to the total and rational planning envisioned by de Stijl and Le Corbusier was conceived between 1919 and 1933 at the Bauhaus ("House of Building"), the brainchild of Walter Gropius. Gropius, who belonged to several utopian groups, including one in sympathy with the Russian Revolution, admired the spirit of the medieval building guilds—the Bauhütten—that had built the great German cathedrals. He sought to revive that spirit and commit it to the reconciliation of modern art and industry through what he called a cultural synthesis, which would emerge from the combined efforts of architects, artists, and designers. The Bauhaus was formed in 1919, when Gropius convinced the authorities of Weimar, Germany, to allow him to combine the city's schools of art and craft. The Bauhaus moved to Dessau and then to Berlin, where it remained until 1933, when Hitler, who detested the avant-garde, closed it (see "Suppression of the Avant-Garde in Germany," below). Gropius left the school in 1928.

There was no formal architectural curriculum at the Bauhaus. Gropius felt that workshop courses—in construction, metalwork, carpentry, interior design (including mural painting), and furniture making, all of which emphasized the understanding of materials—had to be fully mastered before architecture. For teachers, Gropius hired ordinary craftspeople as well as famous artists, among them Kandinsky and Klee. The goal was the training of a generation of architects dedicated to "a clear, organic architecture, whose inner logic will be radiant and naked, unencumbered by lying facades and trickeries; we want an architecture adapted to our world of machines, radios and fast motor cars, an architecture whose function is clearly recognizable in the relation of its forms" (cited in Bayer, Gropius, and Gropius, page 27).

What Gropius had in mind may be seen in his design for the new Dessau Bauhaus, built in 1925–1926. The building frankly acknowledges the reinforced concrete, steel, and glass of which it is built; Gropius made no attempt to cover or decorate them. The building is not strictly utilitarian, however. The asymmetrical balancing

SUPPRESSION OF THE AVANT-GARDE IN GERMANY During the 1930s in Germany a serious political reaction against **avant-garde** art arose, and eventually a concerted effort was made to suppress it. One of the principal targets was the Bauhaus (see fig. 28-87), the art and design school founded in 1919 by Walter Gropius, where Paul Klee, Vasily Kandinsky, Josef Albers, Ludwig Mies van der Rohe, and many other luminaries taught (see figs. 28-31, 28-33, 29-37). Through much of the 1920s the Bauhaus had been struggling against an increasingly hostile and reactionary political climate. As early as 1924, conservatives had accused the Bauhaus of being not only educationally unsound but also politically subversive. In order to avoid having the school shut down by this opposition, Gropius moved it to Dessau in 1926, at the invitation of Dessau's liberal mayor, but left soon after the relocation. His successors faced increasing political pressure on the school because it was a prime center of modernist practice, and the Bauhaus was again forced to move in 1932, this time to Berlin.

After Adolf Hitler came to power in 1933, the Nazi Party mounted an aggressive campaign against modern art. In his youth Hitler himself had

been a mediocre academic painter, and he had developed an intense hatred of the avant-garde. During the first year of his regime the Bauhaus was forced to close for good. A number of the artists, designers, and architects who had been on its faculty immigrated to the United States, including Albers, Gropius, and Mies van der Rohe.

The Nazis also launched attacks against the German Expressionists, whose often intense depictions of German soldiers defeated in World War I and of the economic depression following the war were considered unpatriotic. Most of all, the treatment of the human form in these works, such as the expressionistic exaggeration of facial features, was deemed offensive. The works of these and other artists were removed from museums, while the artists themselves were subjected to public ridicule and often forbidden to buy canvas or paint.

As a final move against the avant-garde, the Nazi leadership organized in 1937 a notorious exhibition of banned works. The "Degenerate Art" exhibition was intended to erase modernism once and for all from the artistic life of the nation. Seeking to brand all the advanced movements of art as sick and degenerate, it presented modern artworks

as if they were specimens of pathology. As part of the exhibition, the organizers printed derisive slogans and comments to that effect on the gallery walls. The 650 paintings, sculpture, prints, and books confiscated from German public museums were viewed by 2 million people in the four months the exhibition was on view in Munich and by another million during its subsequent three-year tour of German cities.

By the time World War II broke out, the authorities had confiscated countless works from all over the country. Most were publicly burned, though the Nazi officials sold much of the looted art at public auction in Switzerland to obtain foreign currency.

Among the many artists crushed by the Nazi suppression was Ernst Ludwig Kirchner, whose *Street, Berlin* (see fig. 28-27) was included in "Degenerate Art." The state's open animosity was a factor in his suicide in 1938. Other artists, such as John Heartfield, left the country in order to continue their work and to voice their opposition to the Nazis. In his scathing caricatures of Hitler, such as *Have No Fear—He's a Vegetarian* (see fig. 28-93), Heartfield took some of the modernist artistic innovations that Hitler had condemned and used them to mock him.

28-87. Walter Gropius. Bauhaus Building, Dessau, Germany. 1925–26

The typeface visible on the side of the building is sans serif (meaning without serifs). Its stripped-down, modernistic look is compatible with the Bauhaus architectural style and was much favored by graphic designers of the Bauhaus.

28-88. Ludwig Mies van der Rohe. German Pavilion, International Exposition, Barcelona, Spain, 1929

28-89. Ludwig Mies van der Rohe. Interior, German Pavilion

of the large, cubical structural elements is meant to convey the dynamic quality of modern life (fig. 28-87). (If this design principle seems reminiscent of de Stijl, that is because van Doesburg worked briefly at the old Bauhaus in 1922 and influenced the development of Gropius's ideas.) The expressive glass-panel wall that wraps around two sides of the workshop wing of the building recalls the glass wall of the Fagus Factory (see fig. 28-74) and reflects the industrial activities of the workshop. The raised parapet below the workshop windows demonstrates the ability of modern engineering methods to create light, airy spaces unlike the heavy spaces of past styles.

Between 1930 and its closing in 1933 the Bauhaus's director was Ludwig Mies van der Rohe (1886–1969), the leader of the avant-garde architectural school in Berlin after the war. Although Mies wrote little, one of his aphorisms crystallized the views of his modernist colleagues: "Less is more." His great passion was the subtle perfection of structure, proportion, and detail using sumptuous materials such as travertine, richly veined marbles, tinted glass, and bronze.

Mies's abilities and interests are evident in the elegantly simple German Pavilion (fig. 28-88), which he designed for the 1929 World's Fair held in Barcelona. The exhibition was supposed to stress industries, not nations, but when the Germans learned that the French and English were building separate national pavilions, Mies was hurriedly commissioned to erect one for his government. Mies first visited the showrooms of a marble company in Hamburg, where he found a block of onyx. Mies claimed that the dimensions of the pavilion were determined by the size of the block: twice the width of the slab fixed the ceiling height and twice the slab's length set the dimension of the freestanding screen walls that inflected the interior spaces. For its construction, Mies relied on the domino system developed by Le Corbusier: floor and ceiling slabs supported by a system of slender piers for the interior and exterior curtain walls. For its design, Mies used the de Stijl principle of harmonically balanced rectangles; its interior (fig. 28-89) resembles a Mondrian painting (see fig. 28-82).

Mies also designed furniture for the pavilion: a pair of elegantly simple leather-upholstered, stainless-steel chairs for the king and queen of Spain to sit in during their official visit, as well as a number of ottomans for their entourage. Although they were handmade, they were later mass-produced and have become a status symbol in many homes. Often criticized as uncomfortable, the Barcelona Chair was designed for ceremonial, not ordinary, use.

Dada

The emphasis on individuality and irrational instinct evident in the work of artists like Gauguin and many of the Expressionists did not die out entirely after World War I. It endured in the Dada movement, which began with the opening of the Cabaret Voltaire in Zürich on February 5, 1916. The cabaret's founders, German actor and artist Hugo Ball (1886–1927) and his companion, Emmy Hennings, a nightclub singer, had moved to neutral Switzerland when the war broke out. Their cabaret, in the neighborhood where Lenin then lived in exile, was inspired by the bohemian artists' cafés they had known in Berlin and Munich. It immediately attracted a circle of avant-garde writers and artists of various nationalities who shared in Ball's and Hennings's disgust with bourgeois culture, which they blamed for the war. The way

28-90. Hugo Ball reciting the sound poem "Karawane." Photographed at the Cabaret Voltaire, Zürich, 1916

Ball performed one of his sound poems, "Karawane" (fig. 28-90), reflects the spirit of the place. His legs and body encased in blue cardboard tubes, his head surmounted by a white-and-blue "witch-doctor's hat," as he called it, and his shoulders covered with a huge cardboard collar that flapped when he moved his arms, he slowly and solemnly recited the poem, which consisted entirely of nonsensical sounds. As was typical of Dada, this performance involved two separate and distinct aims, one critical and one playful. The first, as Ball said, was to renounce "the language devastated and made impossible by journalism." In other words, by retreating into precivilized sounds, he avoided language, which had been spoiled by the lies and excesses of journalism and advertising. The second aim was simply to amuse by reintroducing the healthy play of children back into what he considered overly restrained adult lives.

By the end of 1916 it was clear to Ball's circle that the group needed a name. *Dada* seems to have been chosen because of its flexibility. In German the term signifies baby talk; in French it means "hobbyhorse"; in Russian, "yes, yes"; and in Romanian, "no, no." The name and therefore the movement could be defined as the individual wished. Early in 1917 one of Ball's colleagues, Tristan Tzara (1896–1963), organized the Galerie Dada. Tzara also edited a magazine, *Dada*, which soon attracted the attention of like-minded men and women in various European capitals.

THE RISE OF MODERNISM IN EUROPE AND THE UNITED STATES *1083*

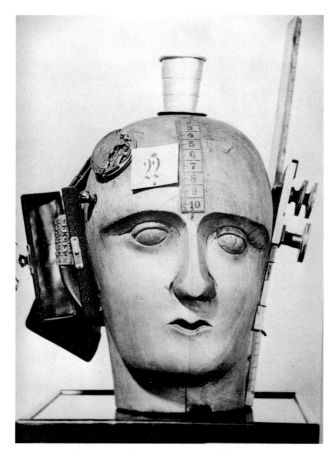

28-91. Raoul Hausmann. *The Spirit of Our Time.* 1921. Assemblage, height 12³/₄" (32 cm). Musée National d'Art Moderne, Centre Georges Pompidou, Paris

28-92. Hannah Höch. *Dada Dance.* 1922. Photomontage, 12⁵/₈ x 9¹/₈" (32 x 23 cm). Collection Arturo Schwartz, Milan

The movement was spread farther when members of Ball's circle returned to their respective homelands after the war. Writer Richard Huelsenbeck brought the Dada movement to Germany, where he helped form the Berlin Dada Club. By early 1919 Huelsenbeck and his associates were organizing Dada evenings featuring nonsense poetry, poems read simultaneously by two or more poets, and other playful events, including a race between a typewriter and a sewing machine. Following the example of some of his Zürich predecessors, Johannes Baader took Dada out of the cabaret into the streets. His most famous "intervention" occurred during the 1919 inauguration of the president of the new German republic, when Baader scattered leaflets from a balcony proclaiming himself President of the World.

One of the distinctive features of Berlin Dada was its sympathies with the newly formed German Communist Party. In 1919 Huelsenbeck and the Austrian painter and photographer Raoul Hausmann (1886–1971) formed a so-called Dadaist Revolutionary Central Council, which published a manifesto, "What Is Dadaism and What Does It Want in Germany?" One of their demands called for "the immediate expropriation of property (socialization) and the communal feeding of all." Such serious demands were undercut, however, by more playful requests.

The coauthor of this manifesto, Hausmann, worked in various mediums, including sculpture. *The Spirit of Our Time* (fig. 28-91) is typical of the Dada artistic approach. The **assemblage** of various objects is not meant to be aesthetically appealing but to satirize contemporary folly. The instruments used for the ears, the clockworks attached to the head, and the measuring tape running down the forehead all refer to the growing popularity in Western Europe of the idea that humans should model themselves on the machine. The dummy's head reminds us that such a notion is dehumanizing.

Another distinctive feature of Berlin Dada was the amount of art it produced, while Dada elsewhere tended to be more literary. Berlin Dada members especially favored the photomontage, and one of the leading figures in this direction was Hannah Höch (1889–1978). From 1916 to 1926 she worked for Berlin's major newspaper in a department that produced brochures on knitting, crocheting, and embroidering. She became romantically involved with Hausmann in 1915 and seems to have been the source of many of his political commitments. Höch, the only woman associated with the Berlin Dada Club, remained a marginal member, apparently because she was a woman. She was admitted to the first Dada exhibition in Berlin in 1920 only

28-93. John Heartfield. *Have No Fear—He's a Vegetarian*. Photomontage in *Regards* no. 121 (153) (Paris), May 7, 1936. Stiftung Archiv der Akademie der Künste, Berlin

because Hausmann threatened to withdraw his works if hers were refused.

Höch's photomontages focus on women's issues. In the aftermath of the war, the status of women improved in Germany as they could vote and new job opportunities opened to them. The subject of the "new woman" was much discussed in the German news media, but Höch's contribution to this discussion was largely critical. In works such as *Dada Dance* (fig. 28-92), she seems to ridicule the way changing fashions establish standards of beauty that women, regardless of their natural appearance, must observe. On the right is an odd composite figure, wearing high-fashion shoes and dress, in a ridiculously elegant pose. The taller figure, with a small, black African head, looks down on her with a pained expression. For Höch, as for many in the modernist era, Africa represented what was natural, so Höch presumably meant to contrast natural elegance with its foolish, overly cultivated counterpart. The work's message is not immediately evident, however, nor is it spelled out clearly by the text, which reads: "The excesses of Hell fell into the cash box for innocent criminal catchers." Whether this statement is meant as an indictment of the fashion business or, in larger terms, of the hellish chaos of contemporary German life is uncertain.

Because the precise meaning of such works is extremely difficult to decipher, their power as social commentary is limited. One of the first to change his approach in recognition of this limitation was John Heartfield (1891–1968). Born Helmut Herzfelde near Berlin, he was drafted in 1914 but after a feigned nervous breakdown was released from the army to work as a letter carrier. He often dumped his mail deliveries in order to encourage dissatisfaction with the war. In protest against the nationalistic war slogan "May God Punish England," Herzfelde anglicized his name to John Heartfield. After the war he joined Berlin Dada but spent most of his time doing election posters and illustrations for Communist newspapers and magazines. Recognizing the primacy of the message, he evolved a clear and simple approach to photomontage that might be called post-Dada.

Typical of his mature work is *Have No Fear—He's a Vegetarian* (fig. 28-93), a version of which appeared in a French magazine in 1936. The work shows Hitler sharpening a knife behind a rooster, the symbol of France. The warning being communicated is ironic, given that the whispering man is Pierre Laval, then the pro-German premier of France. Hitler, at that time rising to power in Germany on a program of nationalism, militarism, and hatred for Jews, would soon occupy France. When the Nazis had gained control of Germany in 1933, Hitler ordered Heartfield's arrest. Heartfield literally jumped out his window to escape and moved to Prague, Czechoslovakia, then to England, where he produced his powerful anti-Hitler photomontages.

Marcel Duchamp

A small group of French and American artists in New York, producing work similar to that of the European Dadaists, also adopted the Dada label. The leading figure in this group was the French artist Marcel Duchamp (1887–1968), who in 1915 left Paris for New York, partly out of disgust with what he called the European "art factory."

Duchamp and his New York group maintained that art should appeal to the mind rather than the senses. A good example of this cerebral approach is Duchamp's *Fountain* (see fig. 28-1), one of the first of Duchamp's **readymades**: ordinary objects transformed into artworks simply through the decision of the artist. The ideas expressed in Duchamp's art are complex and often cynical. Besides those ideas mentioned in the discussion of *Fountain* at the beginning of this chapter is a subtle rejection of the modernist claim that art can change the world. Here, as elsewhere in his art, a useful object is rendered useless by its transformation into art. For Duchamp art making was a challenging form of personal expression and amusement. He thought that his modernist colleagues took it too seriously.

Duchamp's most intellectually challenging work is probably the *Bride Stripped Bare by Her Bachelors, Even* (fig. 28-94), usually called *The Large Glass*. He made his first sketches for the piece in 1913 but did not begin work on it until he arrived in New York. Notes he made while working on it confirm that it is enormously complex in

28-94. Marcel Duchamp. *Bride Stripped Bare by Her Bachelors, Even* (*The Large Glass*). 1915–23. Oil and lead wire on glass, 9'1¹/₄" x 5'¹/₈" (2.77 x 1.76 m). Philadelphia Museum of Art

Bequest of Katherine S. Dreier

conception and operates on several esoteric levels. At the most obvious level it is a pessimistic statement of the insoluble frustrations of male-female relations. The tubular elements encased in glass at the top represent the bride. These release a large romantic sigh that is stimulating to the bachelors below, who are represented by nine different costumes attached to a waterwheel. The wheel resembles and is attached to a chocolate grinder, a reference to a French euphemism for masturbation. A bar separates the males from the female, preventing the fulfillment of their respective sexual desires. Furthermore, male and female are not only separated but fundamentally different. The female is depicted as a gas—the three strips of gauze in her sigh punningly reveal this—while the males are represented as liquids. Duchamp not only contradicts the conventionally optimistic view of male-female relations found in much art but also reverses the conventional power roles of men and women. Unlike what is implied in Kirchner's *Girl under a Japanese Umbrella* (see fig. 28-28), for example, Duchamp places the female in the dominant position, and the males merely react to her.

Surrealism

The second European movement that resisted the rationalist tide of postwar art and architecture, Surrealism, was the creation of a French writer, André Breton (1896–1966), one of the many writers involved in the Paris Dada movement after the war. Breton became dissatisfied with the playful nonsense activities of his colleagues and wished to turn Dada's implicit desire to free human behavior into something more programmatic. In 1924 he published his "Manifesto of Surrealism," outlining his own view of Freud's discovery that the human psyche is a battleground where the rational, civilized forces of the conscious mind struggle against the irrational, instinctual urges of the unconscious. The way to achieve happiness, Breton argued, does not lie in strengthening the repressive forces of reason, as the Purists insisted, but in freeing the individual to express personal desires, as Gauguin and Die Brücke had asserted. Breton and the group around him developed a number of techniques for liberating the individual unconscious, including dream analysis, free association, automatic writing, word games, and hypnotic trances. Their aim was to help people discover the larger reality, or "surreality," that lay beyond the narrow rational notions of what is real.

Among the writers and artists around Breton was the Spanish painter and printmaker Salvador Dalí (1904–1989). In the early 1920s Dalí had trained at the Academy in Madrid, where he quickly mastered the traditional methods of representation. In 1928 he took a taxi from Spain to see Versailles and meet Picasso in Paris. While there, he also met the Surrealists and quickly converted to their cause. For several years Breton considered him the movement's official painter.

Dalí's contribution to Surrealist theory was the "paranoic-critical method," in which the sane man or woman cultivates the ability of the paranoic to misread

28-95. Salvador Dalí. *The Persistence of Memory*.
1931. Oil on canvas, 9¹/₂ x 13" (24.36 x 33.33 cm).
The Museum of Modern Art, New York
Given anonymously. © Demart Pro Arte/Artists Rights Society (ARS), New York

ordinary appearances in order to free himself or herself from the shackles of conventional thought. A good example of this method at work is *The Persistence of Memory* (fig. 28-95), which is set on the Bay of Rosas near his birthplace and based on a childhood memory of a doctor asking to see his tongue. The French words *montrer* ("to show") and *langue* ("tongue"), according to the paranoic-critical method, easily become *montre* ("watch") and *langueur* ("languid"). One of the soft watches drapes over a fetal image of the artist himself, who claimed to have a classic Oedipal love for his mother. The fetus belongs in the mother's womb, where Dalí longed to return. The ants on the hard watch in the foreground are an expression of the anxieties that attended his Oedipal love, namely, the fears of the father's anger. Curiously, Dalí chose a highly realistic style in order to make his irrational world seem more convincing.

The more innovative approach to style adopted by many Surrealists is evident in the work of the other major Spanish painter associated with the Surrealists, Joan Miró (1893–1983). In his early work Miró attempted to reconcile a diversity of French influences with his devotion to his native Catalan landscape. In 1922 he moved to Paris, where he began to produce a fantastic brand of landscape painting, inspired, he later claimed, by the hallucinations brought on by hunger and produced by staring at the cracks in his ceiling. The Surrealist painter André Masson (1896–1987), who lived near Miró, brought his work to the attention of Breton, and he was asked to participate in the first Surrealist exhibition, in 1925, and in subsequent ones. Although Miró showed with the Surrealists, he never shared their theoretical interests.

28-96. Joan Miró. *Painting.* 1933. Oil on canvas, 4'3¹/₄" x 5'3¹/₂" (1.30 x 1.61 m). Wadsworth Atheneum, Hartford, Connecticut

The Ella Gallup Sumner and Mary Catlin Sumner Collection Fund

28-97. Max Ernst. *The Joy of Life.* 1936. Oil on canvas, 28³/₄ x 36¹/₄" (73 x 92 cm). Collection Sir Roland Penrose, London

Typical of his mature work is *Painting* (fig. 28-96), based partly on collages he made using illustrations of machine tools in catalogs. Miró developed these works by freely drawing a series of lines without considering what they might be or become, a technique called **automatism**, which he learned from Surrealists. Next, he consciously reworked the lines into the fantastic animal and vegetable forms that they suggested to his imagination. The result is a charming assortment of delicate flora and fauna that seem to float gracefully and effortlessly across a dry Catalan landscape.

As the work of Miró and Dalí suggests, the artists associated with Breton were generally more concerned with their own needs than with the liberation of others. This was particularly true of one of the most inventive artists in the group, the self-taught painter Max Ernst (1891–1976). Ernst was born near Cologne, Germany, in a family headed by a stern disciplinarian father. Horrified

by World War I, Ernst helped organize a Dada movement in Cologne. In 1922 he moved to Paris and joined the Dada group there. When Paris Dada evolved into Surrealism, he participated in the search for new ways to free his imagination. One of the liberating techniques he developed was **frottage**, the rubbing of a pencil or crayon across a piece of paper placed on a textured surface. Ernst found that these imprints stimulated his imagination. He discovered in them a host of strange creatures and places. A good example of his frottage-inspired work is *The Joy of Life* (fig. 28-97), an ironic remake of Matisse's work by that title (see fig. 28-24). Unlike the radiant paradise of Matisse, Ernst's painting depicts a dense jungle landscape populated by threatening creatures at first difficult to discern.

Breton's quest to free humanity from the tyranny of conscious, practical mental habits was also given a singular expression in the work of the Belgian painter René Magritte (1898–1967). Trained at the Brussels Academy in 1916–1917, he became a member of the city's vanguard literary circle, where the ideas of Dada and eventually Surrealism were discussed and applied. After the unsympathetic critical reception of his earliest Surrealist work, he moved in 1927 to Paris, where he played an active part in Breton's group of artists and writers. In 1930 he returned to Brussels, partly in order to free himself from Breton's emphasis on confessional content.

Magritte's work before 1930 demonstrates two distinct tendencies, one toward the revelation of the psyche and the other toward surprising alterations of ordinary situations, often featuring unusual juxtapositions or changes in scale. It was in this latter mode that Magritte specialized after 1930, largely because he felt that it had a greater potential for public good. *Time Transfixed* (fig. 28-98), for example, features the startling appearance of a locomotive steaming out of an empty fireplace. Some of the work's effect depends on the fact that the two objects are quite explicit symbols of male and female. Magritte himself, however, insisted that his work not be approached in this way, to some extent because he did not wish to be psychoanalyzed via his art, but mostly because he thought that it led viewers away from his conscious intention. His purpose was to discredit ordinary reality and open to view what he called the world's mystery. Psychoanalysis is simply another way to explain things, whereas he, on the contrary, wished to demonstrate the "mystery *that has no meaning.*" Therefore, instead of focusing on the allusive symbolism, Magritte would rather have the viewer simply enjoy the marvelous absurdity of the scene, wondering at the reduction of the locomotive or the enormous enlargement of the room.

A determined enemy of the tired, colorless view of the ordinary, he meant to subvert and defamiliarize the ordinary, showing that it is possible to view the banal objects that populate the immediate existence in fresher, more interesting ways. However, Magritte rarely banished altogether the existential drabness he detested. The dining room in *Time Transfixed* is cold and barren, while the mirror suggests that the rest of the room is even emptier. The prosaic handling of the paint itself con-

28-98. René Magritte. *Time Transfixed*. 1939. Oil on canvas, 57¹/₂ x 38¹/₂" (146 x 97.8 cm). The Art Institute of Chicago
Winterbotham Collection

28-99. Frida Kahlo. *The Two Fridas*. 1939. Oil on canvas. 5'8¹/₂" x 5'8¹/₂"(1.74 x 1.74 m). Museo de Arte Moderno, Instituto Nacional de Bellas Artes, Mexico City

tributes much to a residual sense of the everyday. Magritte was well aware of what he called "my defeatism." In 1943 he wrote: "I have few illusions; the cause is lost in advance. As for me, I do my part, which is to drag a fairly drab existence to its conclusion."

Surrealism, like most of the modernist movements, was essentially a male phenomenon, treating women for the most part merely as sexually desirable creatures who could liberate the male imagination. Beginning with the Surrealist exhibition of 1929, some women were allowed to participate in the movement at its margins. The best known of the women artists associated with Surrealism is Frida Kahlo (1907–1954), born near Mexico City of a German father and a Mexican mother. A nearly fatal trolley accident in 1922 left her crippled and in pain for the rest of her life. While convalescing from the accident, she taught herself to paint. Her work soon brought her into contact with Diego Rivera (see fig. 28-120), one of Mexico's leading artists, whom she later called her "second accident." In 1929, when she was eighteen, they married, but their relationship was always stormy. Although they later remarried, the two were divorced in 1939. While the divorce papers were being processed, she painted *The Two Fridas* (fig. 28-99), a large work that dealt with her personal pain and was intended for an international

Surrealist exhibition in Mexico City in 1940. She once said of her paintings that they were "unimportant, with the same personal subjects that only appeal to myself and nobody else." Here she presents her two ethnic selves: the European one, in a Victorian dress, and the Mexican one, wearing a traditional Mexican peasant skirt and blouse. She told an art historian at the time that the European image was the Frida whom Diego loved and the Mexican one the Frida whom he did not. The two Fridas join hands, and they are intimately connected by the artery running between them. The artery begins at the miniature of Diego as a boy that the Mexican Frida holds, and it ends in the lap of the other Frida, who attempts without success to stem the flow of blood from it.

In 1939 Breton came to Mexico to meet Leon Trotsky, the exiled Russian revolutionary. Rivera arranged for Breton to meet Kahlo at that time, and he was so impressed with her that he wrote the introduction to the catalog of her New York exhibition in 1939 and arranged for her to show in Paris the following year. Although Breton claimed her as a natural Surrealist, she herself said she was not: "I never painted dreams. I painted my own reality." Whether she could have painted it in the imaginative ways that she did without the example of Surrealism is an open question.

28-100. Pablo Picasso. *Guernica*. 1937. Oil on canvas, 11'6" x 25'8" (3.5 x 7.8 m). Museo Nacional Centro de Arte Reina Sofía, Madrid. On permanent loan from the Museo del Prado, Madrid

During World War II, which Picasso spent in Paris, a Nazi officer showed him a reproduction of *Guernica* and asked, "Is that you who did that?" Picasso is said to have replied, "No, it is you."

Picasso and Surrealism

Although Picasso was never a member of the Surrealist group, its radical ideas greatly influenced his production after the mid-1920s. The appearance of Surrealism coincided with Picasso's marital troubles with Olga, and the frustrations and antagonisms he was feeling found release in a series of misogynist fantasies that would not have been possible without the lessons of the Surrealists. Despite the appearance of a new love in Picasso's life in 1927, Marie-Thérèse Walter, such images of women continued to appear in his art into the 1930s.

When the Spanish Civil War erupted in 1936 between the republicans and the fascists, Picasso turned the new Surrealist-inspired language away from his personal life to a condemnation of the fascist leader, General Francisco Franco, and his German supporters. Picasso's most damning indictment of the fascists was *Guernica* (fig. 28-100), which Picasso produced for the Spanish Pavilion at the world's fair in Paris in 1937. Shortly after accepting the commission from the legitimate republican government, Picasso and the world were shocked by the world's first aerial bombing of civilians: German pilots fighting for Franco had bombed and strafed the peaceful Basque town of Guernica, killing hundreds of men, women, and children. Picasso's depiction of this incident is a stark, surrealistic nightmare focusing on the victims. Expressively distorted women, one with her dead child, wail at the carnage. Above a fallen, broken warrior is a screaming horse, symbolizing the suffering republic. To our left is a bull, thought to symbolize either Franco or Spain. An electric light and a woman holding a lantern suggest Picasso's desire to reveal the event in all its horror. The work is in black and white, however, like the newspaper photos that also publicized the atrocity.

AMERICAN ART

American painters and sculptors were slow to assimilate modernism as expressed in European art and architecture. The period between about 1880 and World War I was a time when the United States was consciously defining its "Americanness." Furthermore, many artists in America regarded their work as being modern and thought of their styles as progressive. From the Western European vantage point, however, American art of the time has been viewed as essentially provincial, and, even in America, it had been overshadowed by the interest in American art after World War II. Today, American art of the early twentieth century is increasingly considered a valid modern tradition.

European Influences

The European academic tradition continued to be a strong influence in the United States, partly because of the growing interest of American architects who received the conservative training of the École des Beaux-Arts, as discussed earlier. One of the most important advocates of academic art was the painter and critic Kenyon Cox (1856–1919). Cox studied at the Pennsylvania Academy of the Fine Arts in Philadelphia between 1877 and 1882, then in the Paris studios of several leading academicians, including Gérôme (see fig. 27-8). After his return to the United States, he settled in New York City and specialized in images of classical nudes resting comfortably in idyllic landscapes.

Cox's academic style brought him a number of mural commissions for the Beaux-Arts architecture then in vogue, including in 1890 the two **lunettes** in a long gallery at the new Library of Congress, constructed in a French classical style related to that of the Louvre. The

28-101. Kenyon Cox. *The Arts*, mural in the Library of Congress, Washington, D.C. 1890

style of the two allegories Cox produced—one devoted to the sciences, the other to the arts (fig. 28-101)—was strongly influenced by Puvis de Chavannes, whom he considered the leading artist of the period. He thought, however, that the American public needed a more descriptive approach to the figure and a not-so-subdued color scheme. And unlike the relaxed figures in Puvis's murals and in his own easel pictures, here the symmetrically arranged figures are more monumental, which Cox considered more appropriate to public architecture and better suited to his conservative social message. He believed in a static society, one with as little change as possible. The female figures who personify the various art forms are generically classical and are statically posed and grouped to achieve a sense of timelessness.

The influence of French academicism is also evident in the work of Frederic Remington (1861–1909), still America's most popular chronicler of the old West. In 1880 Remington went to Montana Territory, where he worked briefly as a cowboy, scout, and sheep rancher. After his return to New York he began to produce illustrations of Western life for popular magazines, and he made numerous sketching trips to the West in the ensuing years. His magazine illustrations and paintings became enormously popular and helped shape the romantic conception of the West that eventually found its way into cowboy movies. Despite his claims of being an essentially self-taught, wholly American artist, his descriptive style and his insistence that art should tell a clear, simple story derive from his study of French academic art such as Gérôme's.

28-102. Frederic Remington. *The Bronco Buster*. 1895. Bronze, height 25¼" (64.1 cm). Amon Carter Museum, Fort Worth, Texas

In 1895 Remington extended his work into sculpture with the production of *The Bronco Buster,* which he produced in several editions in the following years (fig. 28-102). These dramatic works, in the tradition of Barye's dramatic bronzes for the popular market (see fig. 26-51),

28-103. Childe Hassam.
Union Square in Spring.
1896. Oil on canvas,
21¹/₂ x 21"
(54.6 x 53.3 cm).
Smith College Museum
of Art, Northampton,
Massachusetts

nicely encapsulate Remington's views of the taming of the "Wild West" by the civilizing forces of white men.

Another European style that American artists adopted after 1880 was Impressionism. During the 1880s, when French artists were reacting against Impressionism, some Americans were still absorbing it. One of these was Childe Hassam (1859–1935), who began his career producing naturalistic paintings of Boston city life. In 1886 he moved to Paris to study at one of the leading private academies. By the time he returned in 1889, he had become an Impressionist. He settled in New York City and specialized in painting pleasant views of the places he lived in and visited. While many, like Remington and Cox, avoided the city, Hassam embraced it and presented it positively, as in *Union Square in Spring* (fig. 28-103), an image of a large, informal park in New York City, where dozens of people are enjoying the fine spring weather. The relaxed, informal brushstrokes add much to our sense of the activities of the place, as do the cheerful, high-key colors.

The African-American painter Henry Ossawa Tanner (1859–1937) also learned from Impressionism. Raised in Philadelphia, Tanner studied under Thomas Eakins at the Pennsylvania Academy of the Fine Arts sporadically between 1879 and 1885. In search of further training and a more hospitable environment for his naturalistic landscape painting, he moved to Paris in 1891. There he assimilated something of the Impressionists' interest in light effects as well as their looser brushwork.

When he returned to Philadelphia in 1893, to recover from typhus, Tanner briefly turned these interests to the depiction of genre subjects featuring African Americans, such as *The Thankful Poor* (fig. 28-104). The light that streams across the wall and over the figures in this painting has less to do with Impressionist concerns than with spiritual connotations of light seen earlier in fifteenth-century Netherlandish painting (see fig. 17-9). Its soft glow and the gentle brushwork that defines it quietly envelop the old man and child, shown offering thanks for their humble lot. The theme of the reverent poor, a popular one in European academic art of the period, was here put to a new use. As Tanner said in his writings, he intended to counter the comic stereotype of African Americans then common in art and literature and to represent, instead, "the serious, and pathetic side of life among them." After his return to Paris in 1894, he gave up such subjects, partly because of a lack of European interest in them and partly as a result of his decision to pursue the goal his minister father imagined for him: to make his art serve religion.

One painter generally thought to have resisted Europe and to have evolved a purely personal style was Albert Pinkham Ryder (1847–1917). During the 1870s Ryder made several brief trips to Europe but never studied there. By the early 1880s he had evolved a distinctive approach to landscapes and seascapes, inspired in part by his love of opera, with its grand, generalized effects and its reliance on classic themes. His interest in these features was also inspired by the European Romantic painting tradition, especially as represented by Delacroix and Turner. Needless to say, the theme and its handling were unusual for the period.

28-104. Henry Ossawa Tanner. *The Thankful Poor.* 1894. Oil on canvas, 35 x 44¼" (88.9 x 112.4 cm). Private collection

A fine example of Ryder's mature work is the biblical *Jonah* (fig. 28-105). Jonah, fleeing from God's command to tell the people of Nineveh of their wickedness, took passage on a ship. When God sent a tempest that threatened to destroy the ship, Jonah's shipmates threw him overboard and he was swallowed by a great fish. But in the end he was saved by the loving God, shown holding the orb, symbol of divine power, who appears in a blaze of redemptive light. Both the subject—being overwhelmed by hostile nature—and its intensified treatment through dynamic curves and sharp contrasts of light and dark are characteristically Romantic. The broad, generalized handling of the violent sea is particularly reminiscent of Turner, whose work Ryder had seen several times in the 1870s.

Realist Styles

By the early 1890s the American author Hamlin Garland was calling for an end to European domination of American art and for the development of a purely American style and subject matter. Perhaps the artist most committed to this cause was Robert Henri (1865–1929). Henri studied between 1886 and 1888 at the Pennsylvania

28-105. Albert Pinkham Ryder. *Jonah.* c. 1885. Oil on canvas, mounted on fiberboard, 27¼ x 34⅜" (69.2 x 87.3 cm). National Museum of American Art, Smithsonian Institution, Washington, D.C.
Gift of John Gellatly

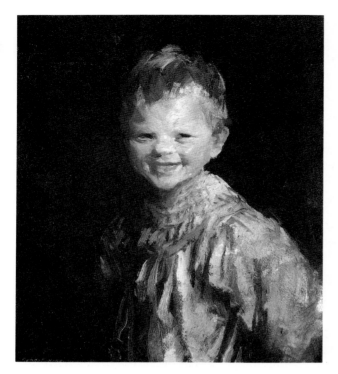

28-106. Robert Henri. *Laughing Child*. 1907. Oil on canvas, 24 x 20" (61 x 50.8 cm). Whitney Museum of American Art, New York

Lawrence H. Bloedel Bequest

28-107. John Sloan. *Backyards, Greenwich Village*. 1914. Oil on canvas, 26 x 32" (66 x 81.3 cm). Whitney Museum of American Art, New York

Purchase

Academy of the Fine Arts, where conventional academic training was tempered by the realist convictions of the director, Thomas Eakins. By 1892 Henri had become the leader of a group of young Philadelphia realists, four of whom were newspaper illustrators: John Sloan (1871–1951), William J. Glackens (1870–1938), Everett Shinn (1876–1953), and George Luks (1867–1933). Henri spoke out against both the academic conventions and the Impressionist style then dominating American art. He advised his unofficial students: "Paint what you see. Paint what is real to you."

Henri nevertheless turned to Europe for models, living in Paris from 1895 to 1900 and studying the great European realists, especially Diego Velázquez, Frans Hals, and Édouard Manet. He particularly admired the rapid brushwork of these artists, which he felt conveyed their fresh and immediate response to their subjects. Henri's own bravura brushwork is evident in *Laughing Child* (fig. 28-106). What mattered to him was not the European roots of this approach but its potential for American art. He felt, somewhat ironically, that by emulating it, American artists could free themselves from European conventions and express "themselves in their own time and in their own land." He also thought that only realism would appeal to the American public and contribute to "the progress of our existence."

Henri's efforts to liberalize the teaching and exhibition standards at New York's National Academy of Design, which had been founded as an American counterpart to the French École des Beaux-Arts, put him at the center of a battle between progressives and conservatives there. When he was not reelected as a member of the Academy's exhibition jury in 1908, he responded by organizing an independent exhibition of eight artists. These artists were often thereafter referred to as The Eight, although they never all exhibited together again.

Five of The Eight were Henri and his earlier colleagues—Sloan, Glackens, Shinn, and Luks—who had moved to New York to be near him. The work of these five formed the core of what was known collectively as the Ashcan School, a name applied largely in response to the work of John Sloan. Sloan briefly attended the Pennsylvania Academy in 1892, then worked as an illustrator for the *Philadelphia Inquirer* newspaper. He moved to New York City in 1903, where he did illustrations for a number of national magazines. Beginning in 1907 he began to devote more time to painting.

Responding to Henri's advice to "paint what is real to you," Sloan painted scenes like *Backyards, Greenwich Village* (fig. 28-107), which depicts the backyard of an apartment in which he and his wife had once lived. Like the laundry in it, the work seems fresh and clean, an effect that depends on both the wet look of the paint and the refreshing blues that dominate it. Balancing those cool tonalities are the warm yellows of the building and fence, which give the work its emotional temperature. Like much of Henri's work, this painting features children. Beneath the laundry, which suggests the presence of caring parents, two warmly dressed children are building a snowman, while an alley cat looks on. The most impor-

28-108. Jacob Riis. *Tenement Interior in Poverty Gap: An English Coal-Heaver's Home*. c. 1889. Museum of the City of New York

The Jacob A. Riis Collection

During the late nineteenth and early twentieth centuries, American social and business life operated under the British sociologist Herbert Spencer's theory of Social Darwinism, which in essence held that only the fittest will survive. Riis saw this theory as merely an excuse for neglecting social problems.

tant figure is the little girl in the window, a stand-in for the artist, who looks out with joy on this ordinary backyard and its simple pleasures.

While Henri and his followers were developing a confident, American brand of realism in painting, a European immigrant, Jacob Riis (1849–1914), was initiating a new and harsher type of realistic documentary photography. The view of American life that emerged from his works was even more blunt and direct than the "objective" view of Henri and Sloan. The difference between these painters and photographers may come from Riis's and his followers' attitude. They did not think of themselves as artists. Their goal was to galvanize public concern for the unfortunate poor. For them photography was a means of bringing about social change, not an art form.

Riis was born in Denmark and learned journalism by helping his father, a schoolteacher, prepare a weekly paper. Riis immigrated to New York City in 1870. Three years later he was hired as a police reporter for the *New York Tribune*. He quickly established himself as a maverick among his colleagues by actually investigating slum life himself rather than merely rewriting police reports. His contact with the poor convinced him that crime, poverty, and ignorance were largely environmental problems that resulted from, rather than caused, harsh slum conditions.

Riis was convinced that if Americans knew the truth about slum life, they would support reforms to provide the poor with better sanitation, housing, education, and jobs. He later recalled: "It was upon my midnight trips

with the . . . police [from the Health Department] that the wish kept cropping up in me . . . [for] some way of putting before the people what I saw there. . . . A drawing might have done it, but it would not have been evidence of the kind I wanted" (cited in Hales, page 169). In 1887 he decided to try the camera. His success was made possible by several technical advances in photography. In the 1870s manufacturers developed a dry-plate process that was much faster and far less clumsy than the wet-plate process still favored by professional photographers for its higher-quality results. Because photographs could now be taken at exposures of one-thirtieth of a second or less, manufacturers began producing cameras for amateurs that could be used either on or off a tripod. To permit interior and nighttime shots, they devised a flash powder. At first Riis employed professional photographers to accompany him into the slums at night, but because they were so often reluctant to go, he soon began taking his own photographs.

His first works, such as *Tenement Interior in Poverty Gap: An English Coal-Heaver's Home* (fig. 28-108), were published in 1890 in his groundbreaking study, *How the Other Half Lives*. All the illustrations were accompanied by texts that described their circumstances in matter-of-fact terms. Riis said he found this family when he visited a house where a woman had been killed by her drunken, abusive husband:

> The family in the picture lived above the rooms where the dead woman lay on a bed of straw, overrun by rats. . . . A patched and shaky stairway led up to their one bare and miserable room. . . . A heap of old rags, in which the baby slept serenely, served as the common sleeping-bunk of father, mother, and children—two bright and pretty girls, singularly out of keeping in their clean, if coarse, dresses, with their surroundings. . . . The mother, a pleasant-faced women, was cheerful, even light-hearted. Her smile seemed the most sadly hopeless of all in the utter wretchedness of the place.

What comes through clearly in the picture itself is the family's attempt to maintain a clean, orderly life despite the rats and the chaotic behavior of their neighbors. The broom behind the older girl implies as much, as does the caring way the father holds his youngest daughter. Despite his matter-of-fact account, Riis is actually advocating that such slum dwellers are decent people who deserve better.

In his successful campaign on behalf of social reform Riis delivered lectures illustrated with slides made from his photographs. Some of the scenes so shocked his audiences that some people are reported to have fainted, while others leapt yelling out of their chairs. In 1893 Riis delivered one of these lectures in Chicago in conjunction with the World's Columbian Exposition. Both he and the architects of the fair were concerned with the condition of the American city, he with its human inhabitants and they with the buildings in which they lived and worked.

Stieglitz and European Modernism

Shortly before Riis discovered the camera's journalistic power, one outspoken opponent of the Henri tradition, Alfred Stieglitz (1864–1946), was developing the camera's aesthetic potential. Stieglitz was born to a wealthy German immigrant family, who sent him to Berlin to study mechanical engineering. Through a course in photochemistry in 1883, he discovered photography and almost immediately, it seems, decided to try to make of it an art form: "I saw that what others were doing was to make hard cold copies of hard cold subjects in hard cold light. I did not see why a photograph should not be a work of art, and I studied to learn to make it one" (cited in Homer, page 13).

His early work, like *Spring Showers* (fig. 28-109), is devoted to atmospheric studies of the city. The sanitation worker behind the tree is not the subject of the image; he is there only to balance the composition. The off-center placement of the tipping tree and the diagonal of the curb, inspired by the example of Japanese prints, would be aesthetically disturbing without the visual weight of his presence. In this case, the sanitation worker functions more like the yellow square in Mondrian's *Composition with Red, Blue, and Yellow* (see fig. 28-82), rather than as a social commentary. The appeal of the work also depends on the contrast between the indefinite forms of the horse-drawn vehicles seen through the drizzle and the sharper forms of the tree and fence in the front. For Stieglitz, the purpose of such a picture was purely aesthetic. He intended it not for public consumption but rather for the few with sufficient education and discernment to appreciate it.

Stieglitz's first vehicle for promoting his conception of photography was the Camera Club of New York. Between 1896 and 1902 he helped organize exhibitions of photographers he believed in, assembled loan shows to national and foreign institutions, and edited and managed *Camera Notes*, the club's quarterly journal. A growing dissatisfaction with Stieglitz's extreme views among the club's conservative rank and file led him to organize the Photo-Secession group in 1902. The following year, he launched the magazine *Camera Works* and two years later opened the Little Galleries of the Photo-Secession on the top floor of 291 Fifth Avenue, which soon became known simply as 291.

Stieglitz's chief ally in these efforts was another American photographer, Edward Steichen (1879–1973), who then lived in Paris. They had decided from the beginning to exhibit modern art as well as photography at 291 in order to help break down what they considered the artificial barrier between the two. Through Steichen's contacts in Paris, the gallery arranged exhibitions unlike any seen before in the United States, including works by Matisse (in 1908 and 1911), Toulouse-Lautrec (1910), Rodin (1908 and 1910), Cézanne (1911), Picasso (1911), Brancusi (1914), and Braque (1915). Thus, in the years around 1910 Stieglitz's gallery became the American focal point not only for the advancement of photographic art but also for the larger cause of European modernism.

28-109. Alfred Stieglitz. *Spring Showers*. 1901. The Art
Institute of Chicago

The event that climaxed Stieglitz's pioneering efforts on behalf of European modernism was the International Exhibition of Modern Art, held in 1913 at the 69th Regiment Armory in Manhattan. It is one of the great ironies of American art that this exhibition, known as the Armory Show, was assembled not by Stieglitz or his colleagues but by one of The Eight, Arthur B. Davies, the only member of Henri's circle to attend events at the 291 gallery. The aim of the exhibition, quite simply, was to demonstrate how outmoded were the views of the

28-110. Max Weber. *Rush Hour, New York.* 1915. Oil on canvas, 36¼ x 30¼" (92 x 76.9 cm). National Gallery of Art, Washington, D.C.
Gift of the Avalon Foundation

National Academy of Design. Unhappily for the Henri group, the Armory Show also demonstrated how out of fashion their realistic approach was.

Of the more than 1,300 works in the show, only about a quarter were by Europeans, but it was to these works that all attention was drawn. Critics claimed that Matisse, Kandinsky, Braque, Duchamp, and Brancusi were the agents of "universal anarchy." Kenyon Cox called them mere "savages." When a selection of works continued on to Chicago, civic leaders there called for a morals commission to investigate the show. Faculty and students at the School of the Art Institute were so enraged they hanged Matisse in effigy.

A number of younger artists, however, responded positively. Although the impact of the Armory Show is sometimes exaggerated, it marks an important turning point. Between the 1913 exhibition and the early 1920s, American art was characterized by a new desire to assimilate the most recent developments from Europe. The issue of realism versus academicism, so critical before 1913, suddenly seemed inconsequential. For the first time in their history, American artists at home began fighting their provincial status.

Indicative of the work produced by Americans in the aftermath of the Armory Show is that of Max Weber (1881–1961). In the new climate established by the exhibition, he produced an American version of Cubo-Futurism, although no one called it that. *Rush Hour, New York* (fig. 28-110), for example, at first seems a fairly typical example of the Futurist embrace of city life. The tightly packed surface of angular and curvilinear elements suggests the noisy, crowded rush hour, but the harmony of soft grays, blues, browns, and greens undercuts that effect considerably and produces an aesthetically pleasing formal symphony as well.

Weber was one of the American artists whom Stieglitz showed at his 291 gallery. Another artist who became a more intimate member of the gallery's circle after the Armory Show was Georgia O'Keeffe (1887–1986). In 1916 one of O'Keeffe's New York friends showed Stieglitz some of her drawings. The friend wrote O'Keeffe that Stieglitz had exclaimed: "At last, a woman on paper!" Without consulting her, Stieglitz included the work in a small group show. The next year she had a one-person exhibition at 291. One critic said that O'Keeffe had "found expression in delicately veiled symbolism for

28-111. Georgia O'Keeffe. *The Lawrence Tree.* 1929. Oil on canvas, 31¹/₁₆ x 39³/₁₆" (79.7 x 100.5 cm). Wadsworth Atheneum, Hartford, Connecticut

Ella Gallup and Mary Catlin Sumner Collection. © 1996 The Georgia O'Keeffe Foundation/Artists Rights Society (ARS), New York

28-112. Gaston Lachaise. *Standing Woman (Elevation).* 1912–27. Bronze, height 5'10" (1.79 m). Albright-Knox Art Gallery, Buffalo, New York

'what every woman knows,' but what women heretofore kept to themselves." This was the beginning of a long line of written criticism that focused on the artist's gender, to which O'Keeffe vehemently objected. She wanted to be considered an artist, not a woman artist.

O'Keeffe and Stieglitz lived together from 1920 and were married in 1924. Although they continued to reside in New York until his death in 1946, O'Keeffe began in 1928 to make yearly visits to New Mexico, where she eventually settled. Her expressive images of the simple grandeur of its landscape, such as *The Lawrence Tree* (fig. 28-111), are her most well-known works. The painting records an experience O'Keeffe had one evening while visiting the writer D. H. Lawrence, who owned a ranch near Taos. Beneath a giant pine, she lay down on a bench to look up at the stars in the sky. With minimal detail, O'Keeffe recorded from memory the essence of that sublime sight.

American sculptors were slower to respond to contemporary developments in Europe than were painters, and none of them produced works in this period comparable to Weber's or O'Keeffe's. The most innovative sculptural work was produced by a Parisian who had moved to the United States, Gaston Lachaise (1882–1935). Lachaise entered the French Academy in 1898. Sometime between 1900 and 1902 he met Isabel Dutaud Nagle, an older married woman from Boston, who redirected the course of his life and his art. In 1906 he moved to Boston, then in 1912 to New York City, to further his career. He dealt with the separation from Isabel by beginning the first of his

monumental images of her, *Standing Woman (Elevation)* (fig. 28-112). The plaster model was shown in 1918, but Lachaise could not afford to cast it in bronze until 1927. The work is in the classical tradition of the strong female nude, and the simplified modeling of form is reminiscent of Maillol's classical nudes (see fig. 28-7). The work is not generic, however, but is a specific tribute to Isabel. Nude photographs of her, now in the Lachaise Foundation, show the same arched back, slender calves and ankles, narrow waist, and proud bearing. What Lachaise exaggerated was her size, for Isabel was only about 5 feet 2 inches tall. The sculpture, almost 6 feet tall, makes her appear larger than life. But Lachaise also succeeded in making her seem quite light by raising her on her toes and by having her gracefully lift her arms. She closes her eyes, suggesting an inwardness that complements and intensifies our sense of her graceful elevation.

American Scene Painting and Photography

The entry of the United States into World War I in 1917 might have further stimulated the new American fascination with contemporary European art. Instead, the

1930
1880 1940

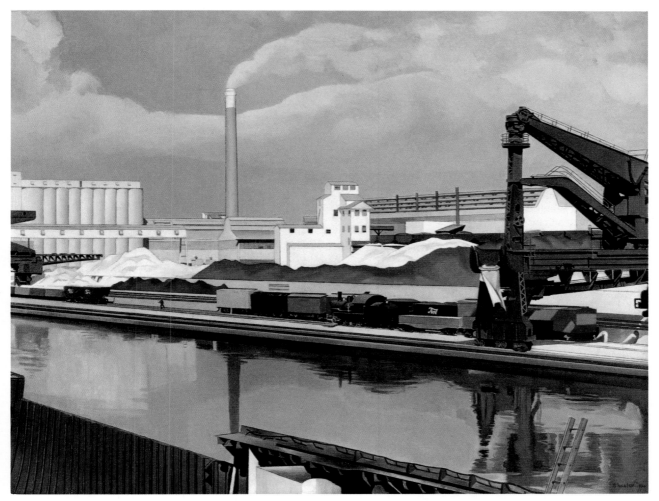

28-113. Charles Sheeler. *American Landscape.* 1930. Oil on canvas, 24 x 31" (61 x 78.7 cm). The Museum of Modern Art, New York
Gift of Abby Aldrich Rockefeller

country entered a period of isolationism that lasted from about 1920 to the bombing of Pearl Harbor in 1941 and had a powerful effect on its artists. A minority continued to look to Europe for direction, but the brief ascendancy of the Stieglitz viewpoint was followed by two decades when convictions more like Henri's prevailed. In the 1920s and 1930s American artists returned to realism, which they used to chronicle American life. The various tendencies of this broad movement in painting are grouped under the term *American Scene Painting.*

The shift back to realism is evident in the work of Charles Sheeler (1883–1965), who attended the Pennsylvania Academy in 1903 after studying for two years at the School of Industrial Art, also in Philadelphia. He apparently objected to the arts-and-crafts orientation but liked industrial design. From early Fauvist still lifes he moved to landscapes inspired by Cézanne and Analytic Cubism. By the early 1920s, however, he had shifted to a highly descriptive realism. This change was partly the result of his growing interest in photography. In 1912 he had opened a photographic business to support himself, and into the 1920s he continued to take commercial assignments, some of which he translated into paintings.

In 1927, for example, he was hired by an advertising firm to take photographs of the new Ford Motor Company plant outside Detroit. In 1930 he used one of these photographs to make *American Landscape* (fig. 28-113), a remarkably faithful transcription of the photograph. Ford, determined to be independent of suppliers, made its own steel on site, so the painting is, among other things, about the transformation of raw materials into industrial goods. The title suggests that Sheeler was responding to the enthusiastic discussion of modern industry that surrounded the opening of the plant. One journalist had commented that "Detroit . . . [should] be considered the mother-city of the new industrial America" (cited in Troyen and Hirschler, page 17). Another saw such factories as the new American churches, the sites of its new faith in a better future. Sheeler's painting seems to confirm this point of view. That he painted the work a year after the great stock-market crash of 1929, which began the Great Depression, suggests that the painting may well be a testament to his continuing faith in American industry and in its fundamental stability.

A small group of American painters that emerged about 1930, known collectively as the Regionalists, also responded to the crisis of the Great Depression but put

THE RISE OF MODERNISM IN EUROPE AND THE UNITED STATES 1099

28-114. John Steuart Curry. *Baptism in Kansas.* 1928. Oil on canvas, 40 x 50" (102.5 x 128 cm). Whitney Museum of American Art, New York Gift of Gertrude Vanderbilt Whitney

Curry painted this work in his Greenwich, Connecticut, studio. He did not revisit the Midwest until the summer of the next year. Between that date and his appointment as artist-in-residence at the College of Agriculture at the University of Wisconsin, he made annual sketching trips to the Midwest for the paintings he produced in his Eastern studio during the winter.

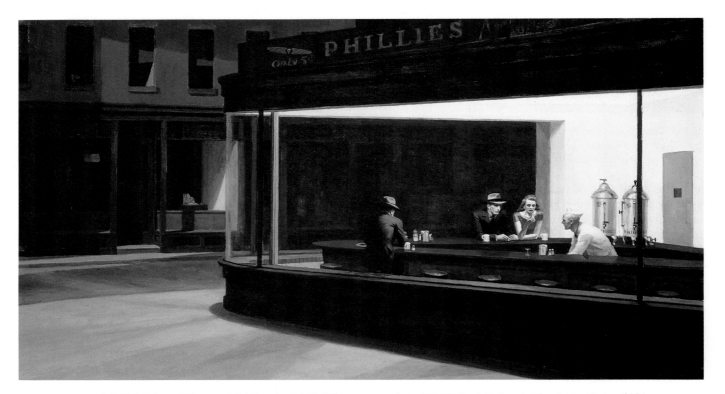

28-115. Edward Hopper. *Nighthawks.* 1942. Oil on canvas, 33 x 60" (83.8 x 152.4 cm). The Art Institute of Chicago

their faith in agriculture. One of these was John Steuart Curry (1897–1946), born on a farm near Dunavant, Kansas. After ten years as a magazine illustrator, he began to specialize in the late 1920s in paintings featuring Kansas farm life. The first and most famous of these is *Baptism in Kansas* (fig. 28-114). The painting, based on a real incident, focuses on a woman being baptized in a farm trough. Arranged in a circle around her is the church community. The solid basis of this larger group is the family, one of whom is featured in the foreground. The painting is characterized by a number of circles, a traditional symbol of unity. That the farm is a holy place

28-116. Isabel Bishop. *Resting*. 1943. Oil on gesso panel, 16 x 17" (40.6 x 43.1 cm). Collection Dr. and Mrs. Howard C. Taylor, Jr., New York

is made clear by the churchlike arrangement of the barn and windmill, as well as the rays of sunshine and the birds, traditionally associated with the divine spirit. The painting thus honors the sanctity of the farm and its stable, conservative way of life.

The 1920 census had demonstrated that, for the first time in history, more Americans were living in urban centers than in rural areas. The work of Curry and two other artists—Grant Wood (1891–1942) and Thomas Hart Benton (1889–1975)—represents one response to that change. These artists insisted that the real solution to the many and growing problems of urban American life, made clear by the Depression, was for the United States to return to its agrarian roots.

The Regionalists' argument received unintentional support from the so-called Urban Realists, who documented life in the American city. One of them, Edward Hopper (1882–1967) had trained with Robert Henri between 1900 and 1906. His work prior to about 1930, which includes many landscapes, is pleasant and unexceptional. After that date, however, he focused on the alienation of modern city life, especially that of New York City, where he lived. Hopper's most famous work is probably *Nighthawks* (fig. 28-115), which shows four people in an all-night diner. The painting seems to have been inspired by Ernest Hemingway's short story "The Killers," about two hired killers who spend several hours before a job waiting in such a diner. The title of Hopper's painting, with its reference to hawks—those who prey on others—seems to suggest this association. But Hopper's image projects none of Hemingway's air of suppressed violence. Instead, it is a study in loneliness and boredom. The anonymous man with his back to us is utterly alone. The couple, too, are just as separate. While the man chats idly with the waiter, the woman examines a book of matches. They seem as cold as the fluorescent light that bathes them and as empty as the streets and stores outside. The viewer, placed on the street, is made to share in their condition. By eliminating the door to the coffee shop, Hopper prevents us from enjoying even the little warmth and shelter it might provide.

Another of the unaffiliated artists grouped under the label *Urban Realist* was Isabel Bishop (1902–1988). Her mother had worked to secure the vote for women in 1920 and had urged Bishop and her sisters toward the independence she had lost when she started her family. Bishop studied illustration at the School of Applied Design for Women in New York. Deciding on a career in painting, she then enrolled at the Art Students League, where she attended lectures by Henri and a course on Cubist painting taught by Weber. Her mentor at the school was another realist, Kenneth Miller, who criticized Picasso and Matisse for celebrating their individual artistic personalities at the expense of commentary on contemporary life. The work of Bishop's new friend Reginald Marsh also reinforced in her the notion that art should address social, not individual, truths.

The social realities she focused on were those of women. Although women figure prominently in the work of her teacher, Bishop's work is unique in its sensitivity to women's strength. In *Resting* (fig. 28-116), for example, she gently undercuts traditional stereotypes by showing a woman supporting a man. The woman's head forms the apex of a stable triangle established by the man's head and the arrangement of her right arm. Her relative strength is also evident in the darker, more sculptural forms used to depict her. His body, in contrast, appears vague and almost vaporous.

An artist not usually grouped with Hopper and Bishop but who perhaps should be is Jacob Lawrence (b. 1917). In 1930 Lawrence moved to Harlem, where he attended neighborhood art classes. Between 1932 and 1934 he studied at the Harlem Art Workshop. There he met Alain Locke, Langston Hughes, and other important thinkers and writers who had contributed to what is known as the Harlem Renaissance of the 1920s.

During World War I thousands of African Americans left the rural South for jobs in Northern defense plants. The Great Migration, as it is known, created racial tensions over housing and employment that in turn fostered a concern for the rights of African Americans. It produced as well a growing concern among African-American

28-117. Jacob Lawrence. *Interior Scene*. 1937. Tempera on paper, 28¹/₂ x 33³/₄" (72.4 x 85.7 cm). Collection Philip J. and Suzanne Schiller

writers and artists with black experience and identity. Alain Locke, educated at Harvard and Oxford and an influential voice in the Harlem Renaissance, encouraged younger black artists and writers to seek their contemporary cultural identity in their African and African-American heritage.

The influence of this advice can be seen in Lawrence's earliest depictions of Harlem. The bright colors and flat areas in *Interior Scene* (fig. 28-117) of 1937, for example, are borrowed from Southern folk art. The cheerful colors and lively patterning lend an almost playful air to what is otherwise a grim scene of a brothel infested with cockroaches and rats. Neighborhood children peek through the window at the women and their disheveled white patrons. Below a **tondo** of the Madonna and Child, a woman tucks her recently earned money into her stocking. The unstable composition and steep perspective suggest a world out of kilter. Lawrence's purposes here are unclear. Is this supposed to be amusing, appalling, or both?

In the final analysis Lawrence's work may occupy a position between the documentary concerns of the Urban Realists and the reformist aims of those artists who specifically used their art to criticize social injustices. Most of these artists, collectively known as the Social Realists, were affiliated with political organizations: with the various Communist groups that sprang up in the United States in the 1920s and 1930s, with labor organizations, and even with the U.S. government under President Franklin D. Roosevelt (in office 1933–1945).

One of the Social Realists associated with the Communists was William Gropper (1897–1977), born to a poor working-class family in New York City. Gropper studied with Henri between 1912 and 1915. He began working as a political cartoonist in 1919, when he was hired by the *New York Tribune*. During the 1920s he contributed biting political caricatures to a number of magazines, including *Vanity Fair* and *New Masses*, a Communist publication launched in 1926. By then he apparently was a convert to communism. In 1927 he visited the Soviet Union with the writers Theodore Dreiser and Sinclair Lewis, and while there he contributed work to the official Communist Party newspaper, *Pravda*. Although he also made paintings, he devoted most of his energy to his drawings and cartoons because they could reach a larger audience.

28-118. William Gropper. *Sweatshop*. c. 1938. Ink, 18 x 15³/4"
(45.7 x 40 cm). Collection Eugene Gropper

Despite state laws enacted in the 1880s and 1890s,
called "anti-sweating" laws, it was not unusual for
people to work ten to twelve hours a day, seven
days a week, in hot, crowded, and unsanitary work-
places. When Gropper made this drawing, effective
labor laws, including minimum-wage legislation,
were still years away.

28-119. Dorothea Lange. *Migrant Mother, Nipomo, California*
February 1936. Gelatin-silver print. Library of
Congress, Washington, D.C.

Sweatshop (fig. 28-118), of about 1938, is typical of
the work he produced for the Communist press. Sweat-
shops—small businesses where people are employed at
low wages, for long hours, and under harsh conditions—
were common in American cities before the strict
enforcement of labor, health, and safety laws and regu-
lations. The destructive physical effect of such working
conditions is clearly evident in the tired and stooped
bodies of the workers shown here. The style is purely
descriptive. "I draw pictures of this world of ours," he
said, "and they're not all pretty." Like Riis, Gropper was
trying to enlist the viewer's sympathy, hoping to translate
it into political action.

The United States government also used art to sell its
political programs during the 1930s and 1940s. President
Roosevelt sought to employ the power and resources of
the federal government to help those in need during the
Depression. Drawing on the tradition inaugurated by Riis,
his newly established Farm Securities Administration
(FSA) began in 1935 to hire photographers to document
the problems of farmers. These photographs, with captions, were supplied free to newspapers and magazines.

Dorothea Lange (1895–1965) played a major role in
the formation of the FSA photography program. After
studying photography in 1917 at Columbia University in
New York City, she opened a studio in San Francisco as a
freelance photographer and portraitist. Distressed by the
Depression, she began photographing the city's poor and
unemployed. After seeing some of these photographs in
1934, Paul S. Taylor, an economics professor at Berkeley,
asked her to collaborate on a report on migrant farm

laborers in California. The report, which helped convince
state officials to build migrant labor camps, was also
influential in the federal government's decision to include
a photographic unit in the FSA. Lange was hired as one of
the first photographers in the unit in 1935.

Perhaps her most famous photograph is *Migrant
Mother, Nipomo, California* (fig. 28-119). The woman in
the picture is Florence Thompson, the thirty-two-year-
old mother of ten children. Two of her children are shown
leaning on her for support. She looks past the viewer
with a preoccupied, worried look. With her knit brow and
her hand on her mouth, she seems to capture the fears of
an entire population of disenfranchised people.

The Roosevelt administration's decision to enlist the
arts on behalf of its social programs had a precedent in
Mexico, where the revolutionary government that took
control in 1921 after a prolonged civil war employed
artists to help forge a national cultural identity. Diego
Rivera (1886–1957), one of the most prominent of these
artists, helped found the modern Mexican mural movement. Rivera, at twenty-one, won a scholarship to
Europe, where he assimilated the work of the modernists
from Cézanne to Picasso and became close friends with
the latter. In 1920 he met David Siqueiros (1896–1974),
another future Mexican muralist, with whom he began to
discuss Mexico's need for a national and revolutionary
art. Rivera was inspired by both the pre-Columbian art
and the great Renaissance frescoes, which he studied in
Italy. When he returned to Mexico in 1921 he began a
series of monumental murals, the first of which were for
Mexican government buildings.

28-120. Diego Rivera. *The Night of the Rich*, mural in the
Ministry of Education, Mexico City. 1923–28

Rivera's second commission was for the courtyard of
the Ministry of Education in Mexico City. Among the
scenes in this mural are *The Night of the Poor* and *The
Night of the Rich*. *The Night of the Poor* shows some peasants sleeping peacefully while others study by lamplight
to educate themselves. *The Night of the Rich* (fig. 28-120),
in contrast, shows wealthy Mexicans and foreigners, the
"debauchers," as Rivera called them, hoarding money
and drinking champagne. One sly-looking man is plying
a woman with the drink, another man has passed out,
while revolutionary soldiers in the background look on
scornfully. The two scenes offer a clear and pointed contrast between the wholesomeness of the poor peasants—the descendants of Mexico's pre-Columbian
civilizations—and the Europeanized decadence of the
wealthy. The simple shapes and outlines, reminiscent of
the art of ancient Maya, reinforce this message.

The Resurgence of Modernism in the 1930s

Although realism dominated American art in the period
between the two world wars, some artists around 1930
showed a renewed interest in the nonrepresentational
styles of European art. One of these was Theodore
Roszak (1907–1981), whose family migrated to Chicago
from Poland when he was two. On a trip to Europe in
1929 he was impressed with the Bauhaus industrial aesthetic, and after his return to New York City in 1931 he
produced a series of constructions in modern industrial
materials. An example is *Airport Structure* (fig. 28-121);
made of copper, aluminum, steel, and brass, the work
resembles a scientific instrument. His celebration of the
beauty and utility of the machine is the nonrepresentational counterpart to Sheeler's homage to American
industry in *American Landscape* (see fig. 28-113).

Roszak later joined the American Abstract Artists, a
group that had banded together in 1937 to promote the
abstract tradition of the European avant-garde. Another
of the approximately forty artists in the group around
1940 was Lee Krasner (1908–1984). An exhibition of
Matisse and Picasso at the Museum of Modern Art in
1929 (the year of its founding) so impressed her and
some of her classmates at New York's conservative
National Academy of Design that, as she put it, they
"staged a revolution" there. When she painted a sketch
in brilliant Fauve colors, her instructor told her to "go
home and take a mental bath." After getting a teaching
certificate, she stopped painting and supported herself as
a waiter. She resumed her studies in 1937 under Hans
Hofmann (1880–1966), a German teacher and painter
who had studied in both Paris and Munich before World
War I and was considered America's living link with the
modernist tradition.

Unlike Hofmann, whose own work from the period
was still tied to representation, Krasner was producing
fully nonrepresentational works such as *Red, White, Blue,
Yellow, Black* (fig. 28-122). This painting, a complicated
arrangement of different shapes and colors, is based on
the Analytic Cubism of Braque and Picasso (see figs. 28-
40, 28-41, 28-42). It threatens to disintegrate into chaos
but is held together by the balancing of colors and the
even distribution of curvilinear and rectangular shapes
across the surface.

The leading critic for the American Abstract Artists,
George L. K. Morris, noted that works such as *Red, White,
Blue, Yellow, Black* allowed one to escape from the problems of life into a world of order, a world where tensions
are resolved. For those Americans tired of the Great
Depression and worried by the growing signs of the coming war in Europe, the pleasures of what they called
"pure" art seemed compelling.

The American Abstract Artists provided an important
training ground for some of the critics and artists, including Krasner, who put the United States in the forefront of
modernism after World War II. Another important factor
in this shift was Roosevelt's Works Progress Administration (WPA), formed in 1935 to help get Americans back to

28-121. Theodore Roszak. *Airport Structure.* 1932. Copper, aluminum, steel, and brass, height 19¹⁄₈" (48.6 cm). Newark Museum, New Jersey
Purchase 1977, The Members Fund

work and remaining in effect until 1943. The most important work-relief agency of the Depression era, the WPA employed more than 6 million workers by that date. Among its initiatives were programs to support the arts, including the Federal Theater Project, the Federal Writers' Project, and the Federal Art Project. Although they involved only about 5 percent of WPA funds and employed only about 38,000 people, these programs had a profound impact on the arts community. The Federal Arts Projects (FAP) paid the then-considerable salary of $26.86 a week (a salesclerk at Woolworth's earned only $10.80), allowing painters and sculptors to devote themselves full-time to art and to think of themselves as professionals in a way few had been able to do before 1935. New York City's painters, in particular, began to develop a group identity, largely because they now had time to meet and discuss art in the bars and coffeehouses of Greenwich Village, the city's answer to the cafés that played such an important role in the art life of Paris. Finally, the FAP gave New York's art community a sense that high culture was important in the United States.

The FAP's monetary support and its professional consequences would prove crucial to the artists later known as the Abstract Expressionists, who would shortly transform New York City into the new art capital of the world.

28-122. Lee Krasner. *Red, White, Blue, Yellow, Black.* 1939. Collage of oil on paper, 19 x 25" (48.5 x 63.5 cm).
Thyssen-Bornemisza Collection, Lugano, Switzerland

Giacometti
City Square
1948

de Kooning
Woman I
1950–52

Johns
Target with Four Faces
1955

Lichtenstein
*Oh, Jeff...I Love You,
Too...But*
1964

Smith
Cubii XIX
1964

Smith
Spiral
1969

CHAPTER 29

Art in the United States and Europe since World War II

1980 1990 2000

Chicago
The Dinner Party
1974–79

Rothenberg
Axes
1976

Serra
Tilted Arc
1981

Clemente
Untitled
1983

Rossi
Town Hall
1986–90

Horn
High Moon
1991

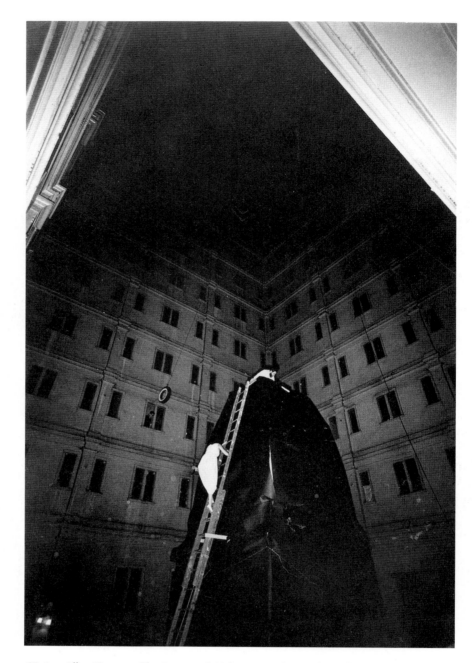

29-1.   Allan Kaprow. *The Courtyard.* 1962. Happening at the Mills Hotel, New York

At an art opening, of a 1962 work by Allan Kaprow called *The Court-yard* (fig. 29-1), the dominant feature of the work was the eruption of tar-paper balls from a volcanic mountain erected in a tenement courtyard. The viewers, who became participants after being given brooms, watched two men build an altar/bed of mattresses on top of the volcano. A young woman, wearing a nightgown and carrying a transistor radio, then climbed to the top of the mountain, where a kind of inverse mountain was lowered over her.

This new kind of art reflected a question and answer raised by musician and philosopher John Cage, who surveyed art and music in 1961 and asked, "Where do we go from here?" His answer: "Towards theater." What emerged were happenings, theatrical events that were, in and of themselves, "objects" of art. Kaprow's works and those of his followers were badly received by the avant-garde New York art critics, because they were considered theater and because spectators enjoyed the happenings so much. One critic even asked the rhetorical question "Is artistic experience about being entertained?" Such questions about what art is and what role it plays in society have marked the richly innovative period following World War II.

THE "MAINSTREAM" CROSSES THE ATLANTIC

When the United States emerged from World War II as the most powerful nation in the world, its new stature was soon reflected in the arts. American artists and architects—especially those living in New York City—assumed a leadership in artistic innovation that by the late 1950s had been acknowledged across the Atlantic, even in Paris. Critics, curators, and art historians, trying to follow art's "mainstream," now focused on New York as the new center of modernism, viewing trends in Europe as secondary. This American dominance endured until around 1970, when the belief that there is such a thing as an identifiable mainstream, or single dominant line of artistic development, began to wane (see "The Idea of the Mainstream," page 1116).

POSTWAR EUROPEAN ART

Despite the shift of critical focus away from Europe, several European artists received worldwide attention following the war. One of these artists was Swiss-born Alberto Giacometti (1901–1966), who in the early 1930s was the leading sculptor in the Surrealist movement. Around 1935 he became dissatisfied with an art of fantasy and returned to working directly from the model. To his own surprise, the figures he made became the antithesis of the classical ideal: small, frail and lumpy, their surfaces rough and crude. Shown alone or in groups, as in *City Square* (fig. 29-2), these anonymous men and women seemed to illustrate the existential philosophy of his close friend Jean-Paul Sartre (1905-1980), who asserted that humans are alone in a meaningless universe. Sartre nevertheless maintained that this situation has a positive potential because it leaves us free to decide our own fate. But Giacometti conveyed only the bleaker side of Sartre's existentialism, a world with small, lonely people wandering aimlessly.

Another of the Europeans who drew international attention was the painter Francis Bacon (1909–1992), born in Dublin but a London resident after 1925. Trained as an interior decorator, Bacon taught himself to paint about 1930 but produced few pictures until the early 1940s, when the onset of World War II crystallized his harsh view of the world. His style draws on the **expressionist** work of Vincent van Gogh (see fig. 28-17) and Edvard Munch (see fig. 28-19), as well as on Picasso's figure paintings. His subject matter comes from a wide variety of sources, including post-Renaissance Western art.

29-2. Alberto Giacometti. *City Square*. 1948. Bronze, 8½ x 25⅜ x 17¼" (21.6 x 64.5 x 43.8 cm). The Museum of Modern Art, New York
Purchase

29-3. Francis Bacon. *Head Surrounded by Sides of Beef*. 1954. Oil on canvas, 50¾ x 48" (129 x 122 cm). The Art Institute of Chicago
Harriott A. Fox Fund

Head Surrounded by Sides of Beef (fig. 29-3), for example, is part of a famous series of paintings inspired by Diego Velázquez's *Pope Innocent X*. Bacon has transformed the solid and imperious pope of the original into an anguished and insubstantial figure howling in a black

29-4. Jean Dubuffet. *Cow with the Subtile Nose.* 1954. Oil on enamel on canvas, 35 x 45¾" (89.7 x 117.3 cm). The Museum of Modern Art, New York
Benjamin Scharps and David Scharps Fund

void. The feeling is reminiscent of Munch's *The Scream*, but unlike Munch's figure on the bridge, Bacon's pope is enclosed in a claustrophobic box that seems to contain his frightful cries. Bacon forces the viewer into that box to share his figure's terror, which the sides of beef behind him, copied from a Rembrandt painting, seem to magnify. (Bacon said that slaughterhouses and meat brought to his mind the Crucifixion of Jesus.) The figure is responding, then, to the realization that humanity is merely mortal flesh.

The French painter Jean Dubuffet (1901–1985) developed a very different but equally distinctive form of expressionism during the war. Dubuffet's paintings were inspired by what he called *art brut* ("raw art")—the work of children and the insane—which he considered "uncontaminated by culture." Like artists as diverse as Paul Gauguin, Maurice de Vlaminck, and the Surrealists, Dubuffet thought that civilization corrupts innate human sensibilities. At times he applied paint mixed with tar, sand, and mud, using his fingers and ordinary kitchen utensils, in a deliberately crude and spontaneous style in imitation of *art brut*. In the early 1950s he began to mix oil paint with new, fast-drying industrial enamels, laying them over a preliminary base of still-wet oils. The result was a texture of fissures and crackles that suggests organic surfaces, like those of *Cow with the Subtile Nose* (fig. 29-4). Dubuffet observed that "the sight of this animal gives me an inexhaustible sense of well-being because of the atmosphere of calm and serenity it seems to generate." What is particularly delightful about this cow is its dazed

expression. The animal seems utterly content and unaware of its own gracelessness. Its entire being seems focused on its "subtile" nose, which appears to twitch just slightly, perhaps at the scent of some grassy morsel.

Dubuffet's celebration of crude, basic forms of self-expression, including **graffiti**, contributed to the emergence of the most distinctive postwar European artistic approach: *art informel* ("formless art"), which was sometimes called Lyrical Abstraction or *tachisme* (a *tache* being a spot or stain). *Art informel* was promoted by the exhibitions and writings of the French critic Michel Tapié, who opposed advocates of geometric formalism as the proper response to the horrors of World War II. He insisted that Dada and the two world wars had discredited all notions of humanity as reasonable, thus creating a *tabula rasa* ("clean slate") for society to invent a new and more authentic concept of our species. Relying heavily on Sartre's ideas about human potential, Tapié encouraged artists to contribute to this rebuilding process by returning to the origins of human expression in the simple, honest mark.

One of the many artists who participated in this broad and multifaceted movement was the Spanish painter Antoni Tàpies (b. 1923), who moved to Paris in 1950. Tàpies was sympathetic to the ideas being expounded by Tapié not only because of his interest in the signs and symbols found in the work of Paul Klee and Joan Miró (see fig. 28-96) but also because of his fascination with "the graffiti of the street . . . a whole world of protest—repressed, clandestine but full of life"

PARALLELS

Years	Events
1940–1949	Modernist period in architecture emerges (United States); New York School arises (United States); Camus's novel *The Stranger* (France); Sartre's book *Being and Nothingness* (France); Jews rise up against Nazis in Warsaw Ghetto (Poland); Pollock pioneers action painting (United States); United States drops first atomic bomb, on Hiroshima, Japan; World War II ends; first digital computer (United States); United Nations first meets; Orwell's novel *1984* (England); (Communist) People's Republic of China established
1950–1959	*Art informel* sweeps Western Europe; President Truman sends first U.S. military advisers to Vietnam; Rothko and Newman pioneer Color Field painting (United States); color television introduced in United States; Salinger's novel *The Catcher in the Rye* (United States); Frankenthaler's *Mountains and Sea* (United States); Independent Group produces British Pop art (England); de Kooning's *Woman I* (United States); Gutai Bijutsu Kyokai formed by Jiro Yoshihara (Japan); Mies van der Rohe's Seagram Building designed (United States); U.S. Supreme Court bans racial segregation in public schools; Satyajit Ray's film *Pather Panchali* (India); Martin Luther King, Jr., leads Montgomery, Ala., bus-desegregation strike, sparking civil rights movement in the United States; Ingmar Bergman's film *The Seventh Seal* (Sweden); Elvis Presley's first recordings released (United States); first Earth-orbiting satellite (Soviet Union); Jewish Museum's "New York School: The Second Generation" exhibition (United States); Kerouac's novel *On the Road* (United States); Kaprow's first happening (United States); Minimalist art emerges (United States); The Museum of Modern Art's "The New American Painting" exhibition (United States); the Beatles are formed (England); Museum of Modern Art's "New Images of Man" exhibition (United States); Resnais's film *Hiroshima, Mon Amour* (France); Wright's Guggenheim Museum opens (United States)
1960–1969	Berlin Wall built (Germany); Heinlein's novel *Stranger in a Strange Land* (United States); Cage's book *Silence* (United States); Friedan's book *The Feminine Mystique* (United States); The Museum of Modern Art's "The Art of Assemblage" exhibition (United States); Peace Corps founded in United States; Carson's book *Silent Spring* (United States); Maciunas launches the Fluxus movement (Germany); Solzhenitsyn's novel *One Day in the Life of Ivan Denisovich* (Soviet Union); Warhol's *Marilyn Diptych* (United States); assassination of President Kennedy (United States); escalation of Vietnam War; Civil Rights Act of 1964 (United States); Lichtenstein's *Oh, Jeff . . .* (United States); *Autobiography of Malcolm X* (United States); National Endowment for the Arts established (United States); Capote's "nonfiction novel" *In Cold Blood* (United States); Masters and Johnson's book *Human Sexual Response* (United States); National Organization for Women founded in the United States; assassination of Martin Luther King, Jr. (United States); student unrest in Europe and the United States; site-specific earthworks emerge (United States); first astronauts on moon (United States); riot at Stonewall Inn in New York City begins gay liberation movement (United States); Woodstock popular music festival attended by 400,000 (United States)
1970–1979	Fiftieth anniversary of women's vote spurs feminist art movement (United States); Angelou's autobiographical novel *I Know Why the Caged Bird Sings* (United States); postmodernist architecture and art arise (United States); Super Realism and Post-Conceptual art emerge (United States); Allen Ginsberg's book *The Fall of America* (United States); last U.S. forces leave Vietnam; Watergate scandal forces President Nixon to resign (United States); Chicago's *The Dinner Party* (United States); first personal computer (United States); Haley's novel *Roots* (United States); New Museum's "Bad Painting" and Whitney Museum's "New Image Painting" exhibitions (United States)
1980–1989	Neo-Expressionism emerges in Europe and the United States; Neo-Conceptualism arises (United States); graffiti art movement launched by "Times Square Show" (United States); discovery of AIDS virus reported (France, United States); Morrison's novel *Beloved* (United States); Communist governments in Eastern Europe collapse; Berlin Wall dismantled (Germany)
1990–present	Unification of Germany; Cincinnati Contemporary Arts Center wins *Mapplethorpe* case (United States); breakup of Soviet Union; Persian Gulf War; apartheid in South Africa legally dismantled; civil wars expand between Bosnians and Serbs and continue in central Africa; cloning of first adult mammal (Scotland); Gehry's Guggenheim Museum Bilbao opens (Spain)

29-5. Antoni Tàpies. *White with Graphism*. 1957. Mixed media on canvas, 6'3⅞ x 5'8¾" (1.93 x 1.75 m). Washington University Gallery of Art, St. Louis, Missouri

Gift of Mr. and Mrs. Richard Weil, 1963

(Penrose, page 59). Beginning in the 1950s in works such as *White with Graphism* (fig. 29-5), he attempted to recover that primordial language. Here the white plaster surface with its crudely drawn and incised marks re-creates the look as well as the actual materials of the city walls that inspired his work in this vein. In these paintings Tàpies did not mean to communicate a particular message but to record the fundamental human urge to self-expression.

In 1953 Tàpies visited New York, where he was pleased to discover that the group of Americans known as the Abstract Expressionists were producing a very similar kind of "formless" art.

ABSTRACT EXPRESSIONISM

The rise of fascism in Europe and the outbreak of World War II led a number of leading European artists and writers to move to the United States. By 1940, for example, André Breton, Salvador Dalí, Fernand Léger, Piet Mondrian, and Max Ernst were all living in New York. Although many of these émigrés kept to themselves, their very presence provoked fruitful discussions among American abstract artists, who were most deeply affected by the ideas of the Surrealists. The main result of this new American fascination with Surrealism was the emergence of Abstract Expressionism, a term that designates a wide variety of work—not all of it **abstract** or **expressionistic**—produced in New York between 1940 and roughly 1960. Abstract Expressionism is also known as the art of the New York School, a more neutral label many art historians prefer.

The Formative Phase

The artists who would become known as Abstract Expressionists found inspiration in Cubist formalism and Surrealist **automatism**, two very different strands of modernism. From the Cubists they learned certain pictorial devices and a standard of aesthetic quality. From the Surrealists they gained a commitment to examining the unconscious and the techniques for doing so. But whereas the European Surrealists had derived their notion of the unconscious from Sigmund Freud, many of the Americans subscribed to the thinking of Swiss psychoanalyst Carl Jung (1875–1961). His theory of the "collective unconscious" holds that beneath one's private memories is a storehouse of feelings and symbolic associations common to all humans. Abstract Expressionists, dissatisfied with what they considered the provincialism of American art in the 1930s, sought the universal themes within themselves.

One of the first artists to bring these various influences together was Arshile Gorky (1904–1948). Gorky was born in Turkish Armenia, and his mother died of starvation during Turkey's brutal repression and eviction of its Armenian population. He emigrated in 1920 and moved to New York in 1925. In the 1930s his work went through a succession of styles that followed the evolution of modernism from Cézanne to Picasso to Miró. Three factors converge in his mature work of the 1940s: his intense childhood memories of Armenia, which provided his primary subject matter; his growing interest in Surrealism, first sparked by a major exhibition, "Dada, Surrealism, Fantastic Art," presented in 1936 at The

29-6. Arshile Gorky. *Garden in Sochi*. c. 1943. Oil on canvas, 31 x 39" (78.7 x 99.1 cm). The Museum of Modern Art, New York
Acquired through the Lillie P. Bliss Bequest
Because of his commitment to Surrealism and to Ingres's linear elegance, Gorky was known as "the Ingres of the Unconscious."

Museum of Modern Art in New York; and the many discussions of Jungian ideas he had with colleagues.

These factors came together in 1940 with Gorky's *Garden in Sochi* (fig. 29-6) and other paintings in the series of the same title. Although the title refers to his father's garden in Armenia, the paintings, rather than illustrating the family's home, are meant to evoke its larger meaning. The fluid, organic shapes and sprouting forms—derived from Miró (see fig. 28-96)—suggest the vital forces of life itself. With these seemingly unpremeditated, automatist-generated forms and colors, Gorky meant to put himself and his viewers in touch not only with his own past but also with a universal, unconscious identification with the earth that dates to humanity's prehistoric, preanalytic past. Despite their improvisational appearance, Gorky's paintings were not completely spontaneous but were the result of a process that involved preparatory drawings. He wanted the paintings to touch his viewers deeply, but he also wanted them to be formally beautiful, like the drawings of Ingres (see fig. 26-44) and Matisse.

Jackson Pollock (1912–1956), the most famous of the Jung-influenced Abstract Expressionists, rejected much of the European tradition of aesthetic refinement—what he referred to as "French cooking"—for cruder, rougher formal values identified with the Wyoming frontier country of his birth. In the context of World War II Pollock's rugged Americanism was much appreciated by New York critics. Pollock had come to New York in the early 1930s and studied with the Regionalist painter Thomas Hart Benton (1889–1975). Self-destructive and alcoholic, Pollock was introduced to Jung's ideas in 1939, when his family sent him to a Jungian therapist. Pollock was reluctant to talk about his problems, so the therapist tried to engage him through his art, analyzing in terms of Jungian symbolism the drawings Pollock brought in each week.

Although the therapy had little apparent effect on Pollock's personal problems, it greatly affected his work, giving him a new vocabulary of signs and symbols and a belief in the therapeutic role of the artist in society. Jung maintained that the artist whose images tapped into "primordial" human consciousness would have a positive

29-7. Jackson Pollock. *Male and Female.* 1942. Oil on canvas, 6'1¼" x 4'1" (1.86 x 1.24 m). Philadelphia Museum of Art

Gift of Mr. and Mrs. Gates Lloyd

The reds and yellows used here, like the diamond shapes featured at center, were inspired by Southwestern Native American art. Native Americans, like other so-called "primitive" peoples, were believed to have had more direct access to the collective unconscious and were thus much studied by Surrealists and early members of the New York School, including Pollock and his psychiatrist.

psychological effect on viewers, even if they did not understand the representations. In paintings such as *Male and Female* (fig. 29-7), which attempt to give new psychological and formal dimensions to a standard Picasso subject from the late 1920s and 1930s—two figures facing one another—Pollock apparently sought to put this belief into practice. The surface of the painting is covered with a variety of signs and symbols Pollock ostensibly retrieved from his unconscious. Beneath this veneer is a firm compositional structure of strong vertical elements flanking a central rectangle—evidence, according to Pollock's therapist, of the healthy, stable adult psyche. In such a psyche, male and female elements are also integrated. We find such elements equally balanced not only throughout the painting but also within the forms that suggest the two facing figures. The female on the left, identifiable by her bright eyes and lashes as well as her red breasts, has as many firm, angular elements as the male on the right has delicate curves.

The painting and the two figures within it represent not only the union of Jung's anima (the female principle in the male) and animus (the male principle in the female) but also that of Pollock and his lover, Lee Krasner (see fig. 28-122). The two had recently remet and begun an intense relationship that would result in their marriage in 1945.

Action Painting

In the second phase of Abstract Expressionism, which dates from the late 1940s, two different approaches to expression emerged—one based on fields of color and the other on active paint handling. The second approach, known as action painting, or **gesturalism**, first inspired the label *Abstract Expressionism*. The term *action painting* was coined by art critic Harold Rosenberg (1906–1978) in his 1952 essay "The American Action Painters," in which he claimed:

> At a certain moment the canvas began to appear to one American painter after another as an arena in which to act—rather than a space in which to reproduce, redesign, analyze, or "express" an object, actual or imagined. What was to go on the canvas was not a picture but an event.

Although he did not mention them by name, Rosenberg was referring primarily to Pollock and to Pollock's chief rival for leadership of the New York School, Willem de Kooning (1904–1997).

Pollock began to replace painted symbols with freely applied paint as the central element of his work during the mid-1940s. After moving in 1945 to The Springs, a small, rural community on Long Island, New York, he created a number of rhythmic, dynamic paintings devoted to nature themes. The largest of these works were done on the floor of his upstairs studio because the room was too small to accommodate an easel.

Pollock found this working method congenial, and when he moved his studio into a renovated barn in the fall of 1946, he continued to place his canvases on the floor and to work on his knees over and around them. Sometime in the winter of 1946–1947, he also began to employ enamel house paints along with conventional oils, dripping them onto his canvases with sticks and brushes, using a variety of fluid arm and wrist movements (fig. 29-8). As a student in 1936, he had experimented with this approach as well as with industrial paints in the studio of the visiting Mexican muralist David Siqueiros. He had no doubt been reminded of those experiments by the 1946 exhibition of small drip paintings of a self-taught painter, Janet Sobel (1894–1968), which he had seen in the company of his chief artistic adviser, the critic Clement Greenberg (1909–1994).

Greenberg's view that the mainstream of modern art (see "The Idea of the Mainstream," page 1116) was flowing away from representation and easel painting toward abstraction and large-scale murals may have also influenced Pollock's formal evolution at this time, but his shift in working method was grounded in his own continuing interests in both automatism and nature. The result over the next four years was a series of graceful linear abstractions such as *Autumn Rhythm* (*Number 30*) (fig. 29-9).

Soon after he began the drip paintings, Pollock wrote: "On the floor I am more at ease. . . . [T]his way I can . . . literally be *in* the painting. . . . When I am in the painting I am not aware of what I am doing. . . . [T]here is pure harmony" (cited in Chipp, page 546). His remarks suggest that one of the deepest pleasures of the new technique for Pollock was the sense it provided him of being fully absorbed in action, which eliminated the anxiety of self-consciousness—the existential sense of estrangement between oneself and the world. Even when the painting is shifted from the floor to the wall, the spectator can vicariously participate in this experience, without knowing about how Pollock painted, because of the mesmerizing way the delicate skeins of paint effortlessly loop over and under one another in a pattern without beginning or end.

In response to Pollock's claim that he found painting "pure harmony," Willem de Kooning insisted, "Art never seems to make me peaceful or pure." De Kooning emigrated from the Netherlands to the United States in 1926, and during the 1930s he shared a studio with his close friend Arshile Gorky. Although de Kooning adopted some of Gorky's formal language, he resisted the shift to Jungian Surrealism. For him it was more important to record accurately and honestly his sense of the world around him, which was never simple or certain. "I work out of doubt," he once remarked. During the course of the 1940s his nervous uncertainty was expressed in the agitated and sometimes frantic way he handled paint itself.

29-8. Hans Namuth. Photograph of Jackson Pollock painting, The Springs, New York. 1950

In the summer and fall of 1950, Namuth made dozens of still photographs and one film of Pollock at work. Pollock apparently agreed to the sessions partly because he understood that they would help promote his growing fame.

29-9. Jackson Pollock. *Autumn Rhythm* (*Number 30*). 1950. Oil on canvas, 8'9" x 17'3" (2.66 x 5.25 m). The Metropolitan Museum of Art, New York
George A. Hearn Fund

THE IDEA OF THE MAINSTREAM

One of the central convictions cherished by modernist artists, critics, and historians has been the existence of an artistic mainstream, the notion that some artworks are more important than others—not by virtue of their aesthetic quality but because they participate in the progressive unfolding of some larger historical purpose. According to this view, the overall evolutionary pattern was what conferred value, and any art that did not fit within it, regardless of how appealing, could be for the most part ignored.

Ultimately, such thinking depended on two long-standing Western ideas about historical change. The first was the ancient Greek belief that history records the steady advance, or progress, of human learning and accomplishment. The second was the Judeo-Christian faith that humanity is passing through successive stages that will inevitably bring it to a final state of perfection on earth, the restoration of Eden in the millennium. The specifically modern notion of the mainstream arose from the way the Enlightenment German philosopher Georg Wilhelm Friedrich Hegel (1770–1831) reformulated these old ideas about progress. In his "Lectures on the Philosophy of History" (first published in 1834, after his death), Hegel argued that history is the gradual manifestation of divinity over time. It is, in other words, the process by which the divine reveals itself to us. As one modern writer succinctly put it, history is thus "the autobiography of God." The important men and women who seem to shape events are actually the vehicles by which the divine "Spirit" unfolds itself.

Hegel's conception of history as the record of large, impersonal forces struggling toward some transcendent end had a profound effect on the following generations of Western European philosophers, historians, and social theorists. In France his ideas were assimilated and developed by the socialists responsible for the concept of the artistic **avant-garde**, a notion of artistic advance central to the rise of modernism.

In the period after World War II the critical discussion of what constituted the modernist mainstream, which had remained largely unstated earlier, was encouraged and shaped by the critical writings of Clement Greenberg (1909–1994), whose thinking was grounded in a Hegelian concept of the development of art since about 1860. In essence, Greenberg argued that modern art since Édouard Manet (Chapter 27) involved the progressive disappearance of both pictorial space and figuration because art itself—whatever the artists may have thought they were doing—was supposedly undergoing its own "process of self-purification" in reaction to a deteriorating civilization. Although Greenberg's conception of the mainstream was rejected by members of the art world during the Abstract Expressionist era, it was embraced by a powerful group of American critics and historians, the so-called Greenbergians, who began to express themselves around 1960.

In the ensuing decades, belief in the concept of the mainstream gradually eroded, partly because of the narrow way it had been conceived by Greenberg and his followers. Because it omitted so much of the history of recent art, observers quite simply began to question whether there had, in fact, ever been a single, dominant mainstream at all. The extraordinary proliferation of art styles and trends in the period after the 1960s greatly contributed to those doubts. Finally, and perhaps most important, these doubts were compounded by the general decline of faith in the very concept of historical progress. Few historians today would disagree with the assessment of the art critic Thomas McEvilley: "History no longer seems to have any shape, nor does it seem any longer to be going any place in particular." Thus, the concept of the mainstream has been relegated to the status of another of modernism's myths.

De Kooning shocked the New York art world in the early 1950s by returning to a figurative focus with a series of paintings of women. The paintings were also shocking because of the brutal way he depicted his subjects. The images in the paintings in this series dramatically veered away from the conventionally pretty women common in American advertising. What emerged is not the elegant companion of Madison Avenue fantasy but a powerful adversary, more dangerous than alluring. The first of the series, *Woman I* (fig. 29-10), took him almost two years (1950–1952) to paint. His wife, the artist Elaine de Kooning (1918–1989), said that he painted it, scraped it, and repainted it at least several dozen times. Only the soft pastel colors and luscious paint surface give any hint of de Kooning's original sources, and these qualities are nearly lost in the furious slashing of the paint. Critics repeatedly questioned de Kooning's feelings toward women. "Women irritate me sometimes," he said. "I painted that irritation in the Woman series." But he also added: "I was painting the woman in me."

De Kooning, like Gorky, was committed to the highest level of **aesthetic** achievement. As one of his friends claimed, for de Kooning being a painter "meant meeting full-force the professional standard set by the great Western painters old and new." Although paintings such as *Woman I* may appear blunt, they represent a carefully orchestrated buildup of interwoven strokes and planes of color based largely on the example of Analytic Cubism (see figs. 28-40, 28-41, 28-42). "Liquefied Cubism" is the way one art historian described them. The real roots of de Kooning's work, however, lie in the Venetian tradition of artists such as Titian (see figs. 18-31, 18-32), Rubens (see fig. 19-37), and their heirs, who superbly transformed flesh into paint.

Color Field Painting

During the 1950s de Kooning dominated the avant-garde in New York. Among the handful of modernist painters who resisted his influence were Mark Rothko (1903–1970) and Barnett Newman (1905–1970). By 1950 these two had evolved individual styles that relied on large rectangles of color to evoke transcendent emotional states. Because of the formal and emotional similarities of their work, they were soon referred to collectively as Color

29-10. Willem de Kooning. *Woman I.* 1950–52. Oil on canvas, 6'3⁷/₈" x 4'10" (1.93 x 1.47 m). The Museum of Modern Art, New York

Purchase

Dissatisfied with the results of his extended work on this painting, de Kooning left it outside his studio, where Meyer Schapiro, a Columbia University art historian and supporter of the New York School, found it when he came to visit. He admired the work and convinced de Kooning that it was worth keeping and exhibiting.

Field painters. The third painter usually included in this grouping is the San Francisco–based Clyfford Still (1904–1980), who developed his style outside of New York and earlier than his two colleagues and whose example greatly influenced Rothko's turn to Color Field.

Rothko discovered Still's work in the summer of 1947, when the two taught together at the California School of Fine Arts in San Francisco. By the end of the summer Rothko was producing a soft-edge version of Still's work, freely painted color abstractions lacking any clear organizational structure. By 1948 he was beginning to organize his colors into rectangular units. And by 1950 he had evolved his mature format, which typically involved two to four soft-edge rectangular blocks of color hovering one above another against a monochrome ground.

In works such as *Homage to Matisse* (fig. 29-11), Rothko consciously sought a profound harmony between the two divergent human tendencies that German philosopher Friedrich Nietzsche (1844–1900) called the Dionysian and the Apollonian. The rich color represents the emotional, instinctual, or Dionysian (after the Greek god of wine, the harvest, and inspiration) element,

whereas the simple compositional structure is its rational, disciplined, or Apollonian (after the Greek god of light, music, and truth) counterpart. In his paintings Rothko pursued transforming this fundamental human duality into a consonant and deeply satisfying unity. The title of *Homage to Matisse*, with its reference to the great colorist and creator of such harmonious works as *The Joy of Life* (see fig. 28-24), reflects this goal.

Unlike Matisse, however, Rothko could never fully surrender himself to the harmonic ideal. He was convinced of Nietzsche's contention, which he reread many times, that the modern individual was "tragically divided." Thus, the surfaces of Rothko's paintings are never completely unified but remain a collection of separate and distinct parts. What gives this fragmentation its particular force is that these elements offer an abstraction of the human form. In *Homage to Matisse*, as elsewhere, the three blocks approximate the human division of head, torso, and legs. The vertical paintings, usually somewhat larger than life, therefore present the viewer with a kind of mirror image of the divided self. Thus the dark tonalities that Rothko increasingly featured in his work emphasize the tragic implications of

1970
1940   2000

29-11. Mark Rothko. *Homage to Matisse.* 1953. Oil on canvas, 8'10" x 4'3" (2.69 x 1.3 m). Collection the Edward R. Broida Trust

29-12. Barnett Newman. *Broken Obelisk*. 1963–67. Steel, height 25'1" (7.6 m). The Rothko Chapel, Houston

When John de Menil purchased his version of *Broken Obelisk* to be placed in the fountain outside the Rothko Chapel, he dedicated the work to the memory of Martin Luther King, Jr., who had been assassinated in 1968.

this division. The best of his mature paintings maintain a tension between the harmony they seem to seek and the fragmentation they regretfully acknowledge.

Sculpture

Rothko's colleague Barnett Newman also wished to communicate the tragedy of modern humanity's lonely condition. Although Newman was essentially a painter—specializing in what could be described as abstract versions of Friedrich's *Monk by the Sea* (see fig. 26-53)—he also made several sculptures, the largest and most impressive of which is *Broken Obelisk* (fig. 29-12). Balanced precariously atop a black steel pyramid is the upper section of an obelisk that seems to have toppled from its own base. From his reading Newman learned that the Egyptian pyramid was not simply a funerary monument but was also the "Place of Ascent," the point from which the dead king rises and sails his astral boat up to the heavens, where he will spend eternity assisting the god Ra in the task of moving the sun through its daily journey. The obelisk, he read, was also a symbol of life and renewal. Tipped with polished gold, it caught the first light of dawn, announcing that the sun had once again emerged from the underworld. Although the broken obelisk and its black coloring are meant to suggest the catastrophe of the modern age, when magic and religious belief have been supplanted by a shallow materialism, the work is ultimately hopeful because the top of the obelisk has been miraculously caught on the pyra-

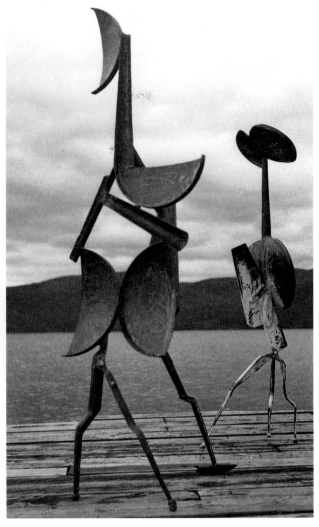

29-13. David Smith. *Tank Totem IV* (left). 1953. Steel, 7'8½" x 3'7½" x 2'5" (2.34 x 1.10 x 0.73 m). Albright-Knox Gallery, Buffalo, New York. *Tank Totem III* (right). 1953. Steel, 7'9" x 2'5" x 2'6½" (2.36 x 0.73 x 0.77 m). Private collection

mid's point of ascent, thus redirecting its energy back toward the sun. Newman hoped that such work would somehow help inspire a modern renewal of life.

The major American sculptor of the New York School was David Smith (1906–1965). Born in Indiana, Smith learned metalworking when, at nineteen, he worked as a riveter in the Studebaker automobile plant in South Bend. Concentrating initially on painting, he turned to sculpture in 1933 after seeing a reproduction of a welded metal sculpture by Picasso and Julio González (1876–1942). Smith's early sculpture is diverse, ranging from social commentary to a three-dimensional version of automatist drawing.

During the 1950s he produced his Tank Totem series, a group of works that seems to look back to the sculpture of Picasso and González. The title of the series combines a reference to army tanks with the concept of a totem, an animal or plant that serves as an emblem for a clan. As a totem for himself, the tank may reflect Smith's belligerent streak as well as his experience as a welder helping to produce tanks during World War II. *Tank Totem III* and *Tank Totem IV* (fig. 29-13), like others in the series,

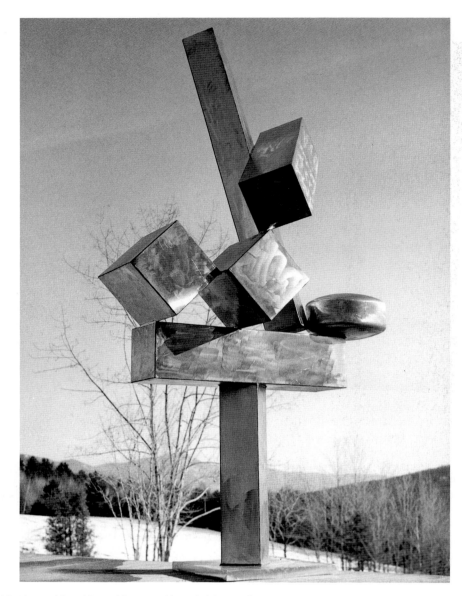

29-14. David Smith. *Cubi XIX*. 1964. Stainless steel, 9'5³/₈" x 1'9³/₄" x 1'8" (2.88 x 0.55 x 0.51 m).
Tate Gallery, London

seem more amusing than dangerous, however. The warriors they portray, armed with shields and swords, strut proudly across a landscape that they mean to conquer or defend, apparently unaware of how frail and foolish they appear.

During the last five years of his life, Smith turned from human and organic themes to formalism. The shift was inspired largely by the artist's discovery of stainless steel. Smith explored both its relative lightness and the beauty of its polished surfaces in the Cubii series, monumental combinations of geometric units inspired by and offering homage to Cubism, the painting style that helped give birth to formalism. Like the Analytic Cubist works of Braque and Picasso (see figs. 28-40, 28-41, 28-42), *Cubi XIX* (fig. 29-14) presents a finely tuned balance of elements that threaten to collapse at the slightest provocation. The viewer's aesthetic pleasure depends on this tension and on the dynamic curvilinear patterns formed by the play of light over the burnished surfaces. The works were meant to be seen outdoors in nature, not only because of the gleaming sunlight but also because of the way natural shapes and materials complement the inorganic ones of his work.

Another member of the loosely affiliated New York School whose work relied on Cubism was Louise Nevelson (1899–1988). Born Louise Berliawsky in Russia, she emigrated to the United States when she was five. In 1920 she married Charles Nevelson, a business executive. In 1931 she studied in Munich with Hans Hofmann, who introduced her to the formal language of Cubism. She turned to sculpture around 1940, working first in a mode reminiscent of Henry Moore (see fig. 28-77) before discovering her talent for evoking ancient ruins, monuments, and royal personages through **assemblage**, the putting together of disparate elements to construct a work of art.

By 1950 Nevelson was prowling downtown Manhattan streets for her materials—the discarded packing boxes into which she would carefully and sensitively arrange, as in an Analytic Cubist painting, chair legs, broom handles, cabinet doors, spindles, and other wooden refuse. She painted her assemblages a **matte** black, both to obscure the identity of the individual elements and to formally integrate them. She also found black

29-15. Louise Nevelson. *Sky Cathedral*. 1958. Assemblage of wood construction, painted black, 11'3½" x 10'1¼" x 18" (3.44 m x 3.05 m x 45.7 cm). The Museum of Modern Art, New York

more mysterious. After stacking several of these boxes together against a studio wall, Nevelson realized that the resulting accumulation made a more powerful effect than the individual units. One of her first wall assemblages was *Sky Cathedral* (fig. 29-15). What she particularly liked about the new monumental schema was the way it could transform an ordinary space into another, higher realm—just as the prosaic elements she worked with had themselves been alchemically changed into something finer. In order to complete this process and add a further poetic dimension, Nevelson first displayed *Sky Cathedral* bathed in soft blue light, like moonlight.

Women in the New York School

Nevelson found it difficult to gain acceptance—in part because her Cubist-inspired work seemed passé to many artists and critics but also because she was a woman. The New York art world of the 1940s and 1950s was still a man's domain. Another of the women who suffered in this prejudicial climate was Lee Krasner, an early member of the American Abstract Artists (see fig. 28-122). When Krasner began living with Pollock (see fig. 29-7) in 1942 she virtually stopped painting in order to devote herself to the conventional role of a supporting wife.

29-16. Lee Krasner. *The Seasons*. 1957. Oil on canvas, 7'8³/4" x 16'11³/4" (2.36 x 5.18 m). Whitney Museum of American Art, New York

Purchased with Funds from Frances and Sydney Lewis (by exchange), the Mrs. Percy Uris Purchase Fund and the Painting and Sculptural Committee

After the couple moved to Long Island in 1945 she set up a small studio in a guest bedroom while Pollock remade the barn into his studio. In these cramped quarters in the late 1940s she produced her Little Image series—small, tight, gestural paintings, many of which were produced on scraps of canvas left over from her husband's monumental works (see fig. 29-9).

After Pollock's death in an automobile crash in 1956 Krasner took over his studio. During the next year and a half she produced a dazzling group of monumental gestural paintings, known as the Earth Green series, which marked her emergence from her husband's shadow. Instead of the constrained marks of the Little Image series, works such as *The Seasons* (fig. 29-16) are painted in bold sweeping curves that express not only her new sense of freedom but also her identification with the forces of nature suggested by the bursting, rounded forms and springlike colors.

Because of her late critical success Krasner is sometimes wrongly grouped with the second-generation Abstract Expressionists, those artists who joined the movement during the 1950s. Among the second generation were a number of women, including Joan Mitchell (1926–1992), Grace Hartigan (b. 1922), and Helen Frankenthaler (b. 1928). Frankenthaler, like Pollock, worked on the floor, drawn to what she described as Pollock's "dancelike use of arms and legs." She produced a huge canvas, *Mountains and Sea* (fig. 29-17), in this way, working from watercolor sketches she had made in Nova Scotia. Instead of using thick, full-bodied paint, as Pollock did, Frankenthaler thinned her oils and applied them in **washes** that soaked into the raw canvas, producing an effect that somewhat resembles watercolor. Clement Greenberg, who had introduced her to Pollock, saw in Frankenthaler's stylistic innovation a possible direction for avant-garde painting as a whole. That recognition played an important part in what happened after the so-called crisis of Abstract Expressionism at the end of the 1950s.

ALTERNATIVE DEVELOPMENTS FOLLOWING ABSTRACT EXPRESSIONISM

In 1958–1959 The Museum of Modern Art organized an exhibition of first-generation Abstract Expressionist work, "The New American Painting," which traveled to eight European capitals before its New York showing. But just at the moment when The Museum of Modern Art and many Europeans were finally acknowledging Abstract Expressionism as "the vanguard of the world," as one Spanish

29-17. Helen Frankenthaler. *Mountains and Sea*. 1952. Oil on canvas, 7'2³/4" x 9'8¹/4" (2.2 x 2.98 m). Collection of the artist on extended loan to the National Gallery of Art, Washington, D.C.

29-18. Richard Diebenkorn. *Girl on a Terrace*. 1956. Oil on canvas, 6'4" x 5'6" (1.93 x 1.68 m). Neuberger Museum of Art, State University of New York at Purchase
Gift of Roy N. Neuberger

29-19. George Segal. *The Diner*. 1964–66. Plaster, wood, chrome, Formica, Masonite, fluorescent tubes, 8'6" x 9' x 7'3" (2.6 x 2.7 x 2.2 m). Walker Art Center, Minneapolis
Gift of the T. B. Walker Foundation

critic called it, there were growing suspicions in the New York art world about the group's right to such a title. The major cause of such doubt was the fact that Abstract Expressionism was no longer, in fact, new. Critic Harold Rosenberg, who disagreed with this emerging critical consensus, nevertheless summed it up succinctly in a published article: "Today it is felt that a new art mode is long overdue, if for no other reason than that the present avant-garde has been with us for fifteen years. . . . No innovating style can survive that long without losing its radical nerve and turning into an Academy." Thus by the end of the 1950s New York critics were dismissing second-generation Abstract Expressionists as "method actors" who faked genuine subjectivity and were accusing members of the first generation, such as de Kooning, of faltering. Amid the growing critical conviction that Abstract Expressionism had lost its innovative edge, attention turned to the question of what would succeed it as the next mainstream development. A number of options quickly emerged.

Return to the Figure

The alternative with the least chance of success was figuration, because the history of modernist art was to a great extent the story of turning away from representation and the human figure and moving toward increasing abstraction. Although many American artists in the 1940s and 1950s had continued to work in a representational mode, their reputations had suffered for it, which deterred others from following their path. The crisis of Abstract Expressionism now freed many of those artists to follow their long-frustrated inclination to paint the figure.

An artist who had returned to figural subjects even before the crisis of Abstract Expressionism, and not without consequences, was Richard Diebenkorn (1922–

1993). After World War II he taught at the California School of Fine Arts, where he came under the influence of his colleagues Still and Rothko, although by 1950 his style was closer to the action painting of de Kooning. About 1954 he resumed working from the model and became a central figure among a group of figurative painters in the San Francisco area that included David Park (1911–1960) and Elmer Bischoff (1916–1991), who held that abstraction lacked sufficient contact with the real world. Many of Diebenkorn's former admirers saw his "defection" not as an act of courage but as a caving in to "provincial" West Coast taste.

Diebenkorn's figure paintings, such as *Girl on a Terrace* (fig. 29-18), reflect the influence of both action painting and Color Field painting. The loose, expressionistic handling of the paint comes from de Kooning, while the large blocks of color and the emphasis on a single figure derive from the work of Rothko. Diebenkorn, however, shared none of Rothko's existential concerns. The woman in the painting may be alone, but the details of her setting and the way she holds one arm behind the other suggest that she is contentedly so. The painting's compositional and coloristic harmony conveys a sense of what the subject is seeing and feeling and, like the paintings of Matisse, elevates her air of tranquillity to a higher, aesthetic plane.

Another artist who participated in the figural revival about 1960 was the sculptor George Segal (b. 1924). As a painter in the early and mid-1950s, he was included among the second generation of Abstract Expressionists. By the late 1950s, however, he had grown tired of the modernist emphasis on flatness, which led him in 1958 to begin experimenting with sculpture. He constructed figures with supports of wood scraps and chicken wire, over which he modeled human forms in plaster. He was comfortable with these cheap materials, he said, because he had used them on the chicken farm he had owned since 1949. In 1961 he discovered that by making casts of live models with plaster-soaked bandages he could get more satisfying results. As in *The Diner* (fig. 29-19), Segal liked to place his white, bandaged figures in realistic, three-dimensional settings. Drained of color and thus emotion, the lonely figure reminds one of those in Hopper's work (see fig. 28-115).

Happenings

Segal's realistic environmental sculpture was largely inspired by the ideas of his friend Allan Kaprow (b. 1927), who, in turn, had been influenced by the ideas of the philosopher and musician John Cage (1912–1992). During the late 1950s Cage taught courses for artists and musicians at the New School for Social Research, in which he argued that art and music should be "an affirmation of life—not an attempt to bring order out of chaos nor to suggest improvements in creation . . . [but] a way of waking up to the very life we're living, which is so excellent once one gets one's mind and one's desires out of its way and lets it act of its own accord." Kaprow incorporated Cage's ideas, including the notion that art should move toward theater, into an influential essay he published in 1958, "The Legacy of Jackson Pollock," his response to the emerging crisis of Abstract Expressionism. In it he argued that Pollock left avant-garde artists with two options: to continue working in Pollock's style or to give up making paintings altogether and develop the ritualistic aspects of Pollock's act of painting. In a willful leap of logic, he concluded that Pollock "left us at the point where we must become preoccupied with . . . the space and objects of our everyday life . . . chairs, food, electric and neon lights, smoke, water, old socks, a dog, movies . . . or a billboard selling Draino [sic]." For modernists this was a shocking statement, for these were precisely the ordinary things they aspired to transcend.

Kaprow's **happenings**—the first of which was held on Segal's chicken farm in 1958—were not so much an embrace of the everyday as an attempt to reestablish meaningful communal rituals. His 1962 happening *The Courtyard* (see fig. 29-1) was not an ordinary event but a revival of some sacrificial ceremony. It was less a Cagean acceptance of ordinary life than a Gauguinesque expression of nostalgia for what modern urban dwellers have lost.

In 1959 Kaprow learned of a Japanese group—the Gutai Bijutsu Kyokai (Concrete Art Association)—that had been producing **performance art** similar to what he was advocating. Gutai had been formed in Osaka in 1954 by Jiro Yoshihara (1905–1972), a leading prewar Japanese abstractionist, in an effort to revitalize Japanese art. Inspired by the rich heritage of the Japanese Dada movement that had helped stimulate the arts in Japan following World War I and by European Dada, Gutai organized a series of outdoor installations, theatrical events, and dramatic displays of art making. At the second Gutai Exhibition, in 1956, for example, Shozo Shimamoto (b. 1928), dressed in protective clothing and eyewear, produced *Hurling Colors* (fig. 29-20) by smashing bottles of paint on a canvas laid on the floor. The event was meant to be more exhilarating than violent. Thus Gutai was apparently pushing Pollock's drip technique (see fig. 29-9) into new and innovative territory some two years

29-20. Shozo Shimamoto. *Hurling Colors.* 1956. Happening

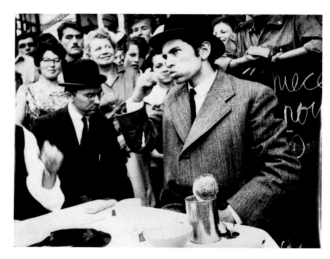

29-21. Ben Vautier brushing his teeth after eating Flux Mystery Food at the "Fluxus Festival of Total Art and Comportment," Nice, France. July 1963

before Kaprow advocated doing so. Despite the lack of critical attention given to happenings produced by members of Kaprow's circle, the artists themselves perceived their actions as part of a truly international movement that extended beyond New York City.

In 1960 one participant in the burgeoning happenings movement, George Maciunas (1931–1978), was led by his interest in avant-garde art and music, especially that of Cage, to open the AG Gallery, which specialized in happenings with a musical component. In 1962, temporarily living in what was then West Germany, Maciunas launched the Fluxus movement with a series of happenings, including *Après John Cage*, and the publication of an art magazine. The main thrust of the movement, he said, was to counter the traditional "separation of art and life," to "promote living art . . . to be grasped by all peoples, not only critics, dilettantes, and professionals."

Fluxus quickly attracted many young artists in Germany and France, among them Ben Vautier (b. 1935), a self-trained artist working in Nice, France. In 1963 he, Maciunas, and others organized the "Fluxus Festival of Total Art and Comportment" in Nice. One of Vautier's contributions to this festival was a work dedicated to the "de-elevation" of art: He ate what he called Flux Mystery Food—canned food from which the labels had been removed—and then brushed his teeth (fig. 29-21). By

29-22. Yves Klein. *Anthropométries of the Blue Period.*
1960. Performance at the Galerie Internationale d'Art
Contemporain, Paris

calling these objects and activities "art," he simultaneously raised the everyday to the level of art and lowered art to the status of an ordinary event, thereby eliminating the distinction between the two. The ultimate goal was less to criticize the transcendent purposes of modernist art than it was to enliven daily life and its stale routines. In this respect Fluxus represented a continuation of the playful side of the earlier Dada movement (Chapter 28). Maciunas, in fact, titled his inaugural lecture on Fluxus "Neo-Dada in the United States." In the fall of 1963 Maciunas returned to New York, which became the new headquarters of his expanding Fluxus movement.

Assemblage

A third alternative was assemblage, the kinds of works created by Louise Nevelson (see fig. 29-15). In 1961 The Museum of Modern Art organized "The Art of Assemblage," whose exhibition catalog argued that assemblage "has indeed provided an effective outlet for artists of a generation weaned on abstract expressionism but unwilling to mannerize Pollock, de Kooning, or other masters who they admire." In other words, assemblage was the work of artists brought up on Abstract Expressionism who sought to move beyond its tired formulas into new and unexplored terrain. Avant-garde critics were not convinced, however: partly because so much of the work looked not like a new development but like a Dada revival; partly because it was mostly sculpture, at a time when painting took pride of place; and partly because almost none of it seemed to "transcend" the ordinary materials from which it was composed.

The European artists in the exhibition were all associated with the Paris-based movement called *nouveau réalisme* ("new realism"), whose best-known figure was Yves Klein (1928–1962). In the mid-1950s he began making transcendent monochrome paintings of various hues, and in 1957 he turned to blue alone, which he considered the most spiritual color. The purpose of these blue paintings, he said, was to imbue the viewer with spirituality. Klein's desire to spiritualize humanity—to bring about what he called a "blue revolution"—was evident in his 1960 *Anthropométries of the Blue Period* (fig. 29-22). For

29-23. Jean Tinguely. *Homage to New York.* 1960. Self-destroying sculpture in the garden of The Museum of Modern Art, New York

this event Klein invited about a hundred members of the Paris art world to watch him direct nude female models covered in blue paint to press themselves against large sheets of paper. This attempt to spiritualize flesh was accompanied by Klein's *Symphonie monoton*—twenty minutes of a slow progression of single notes followed by twenty minutes of silence—which he considered to be the aural equivalent of the color blue. *Anthropométries of the Blue Period* was Klein's only performance piece, although he had been moving toward that form in the late 1950s in the openings to some of his shows. At one of them, for example, he served blue cocktails.

More representative of both *nouveau réalisme* and assemblage were the sculptures of the Swiss-born Jean Tinguely (1925–1991). After producing abstract paintings, constructions of various materials, and a few edible sculptures made of grass, Tinguely moved to Paris in 1951 and gave up painting for kinetic sculpture, or sculpture made of moving parts. He called his awkward and purposely unreliable motor-driven work *métamécaniques* (meaning "beyond the machine," later shortened to *méta-matics*). They were the very antithesis of perfectly calibrated industrial machines. Tinguely, an anarchist, wanted to free the machine, to let it play. "Art hasn't been fun for a long time," he said. Like the creations of his Dada forebears, Tinguely's work was implicitly critical of an overly restrained and practical bourgeois mentality.

Tinguely's most famous work is probably *Homage to New York* (fig. 29-23), which he designed for a special

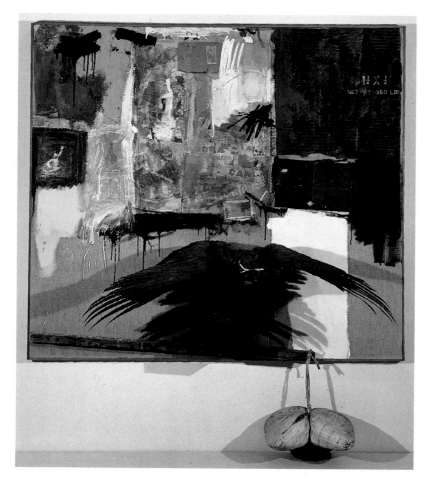

29-24. Robert Rauschenberg. *Canyon.* 1959. Combine painting: oil, pencil, paper, metal, photograph, fabric, wood on canvas, plus buttons, mirror, stuffed eagle, pillow tied with cord, and paint tube, 6'1" x 5'6" x 2'3/4" (1.85 x 1.68 x 0.63 m). Collection Mr. and Mrs. Michael Sonnabend, on infinite loan at the Baltimore Museum of Art

Avant-garde critics were not bothered by the fact that much of Rauschenberg's and the other assemblers' materials were drawn from popular culture. Many of the early-twentieth-century collagists, including Picasso and Braque, had worked with similar materials. However, critics such as Hilton Kramer (at the *New York Times*) and Thomas Hess (at *ArtNews*) pointed out that whereas earlier artists had aesthetically coordinated such elements, transforming the crude materials of life into the finer ones of art, Rauschenberg and his associates left them in their raw, "unpurified" condition. In this view, therefore, such works as this one were not art at all.

one-day exhibition in the sculpture garden of The Museum of Modern Art in New York City. The work was assembled from yards of metal tubing, several dozen bicycle and baby-carriage wheels, a washing-machine drum, an upright piano, a radio, several electric fans, a noisy old Addressograph machine, a bassinet, numerous small motors, two motor-driven devices that produced abstract paintings by the yard, several bottles of chemical stinks, and various noisemakers—all of which was painted white and topped by an inflated orange meteorological balloon. The machine was designed to destroy itself when activated. On the evening of March 17, 1960, before a distinguished group of guests, including Governor Nelson A. Rockefeller of New York, the work was plugged in. As smoke poured out of the machinery and covered the crowd, parts of the contraption broke free and scuttled off in various directions, sometimes frightening the onlookers. A device meant to douse the burning piano—which kept playing only three notes—failed to work, and firefighters had to be called in. They extinguished the blaze and finished the work's destruction to boos from the crowd, who, except for the museum officials present, had been delighted by the spectacle.

Like Tinguely, Robert Rauschenberg (b. 1925), one of two major American artists included in "The Art of Assemblage," was intrigued by the intersection of art and technology, but he rejected the antagonism to ordinary culture that had characterized the avant-garde. Rauschenberg went to Black Mountain College in North Carolina in 1948 and discovered there a congenial mentor in John Cage. Under Cage's influence Rauschenberg evolved a

distinctive style by chaotically mixing painted and found elements in assemblages he called combines. *Canyon* (fig. 29-24), for example, features an assortment of old family photographs (the boy with the upraised arm is Rauschenberg), public imagery (the Statue of Liberty, which echoes the boy's pose), fragments of political posters (in the middle), and various objects salvaged from trash (the flattened steel drum at upper right) or donated by friends (the stuffed eagle). The rich disorder challenges the viewer to make sense of it. In fact, Rauschenberg meant his work to be open to various readings, so he assembled material that each viewer might interpret differently. One could, for example, see the Statue of Liberty in *Canyon* as a symbolic invitation to interpret the work freely. Or perhaps, covered as it is with paint applied in the manner of action painting, it symbolizes that distinctively American style. Following Cage's ideas, Rauschenberg created a work of art that was to some extent beyond his control—a work of **iconographic** as well as formal disarray. Rauschenberg cheerfully accepted the chaos and unpredictability of modern urban experience and tried to find artistic metaphors for it. "I only consider myself successful," he said, "when I do something that resembles the lack of order I sense."

The other major American included in the assemblage exhibition was Rauschenberg's close friend Jasper Johns (b. 1930). In 1954, while working in a bookstore and producing art part-time, Johns had met Rauschenberg, who encouraged him to pursue art more seriously. Unlike Rauschenberg's works, Johns's are controlled, emotionally cool, and highly cerebral. Inspired by the

29-25. Jasper Johns. *Target with Four Faces.* 1955. Assemblage: encaustic on newspaper and cloth over canvas, surmounted by four tinted plaster faces in wood box with hinged front, overall, with box open, 33⅝ x 26 x 3" (85.3 x 66 x 7.6 cm). The Museum of Modern Art, New York

Gift of Mr. and Mrs. Robert C. Scull

example of Marcel Duchamp (see figs. 28-1, 28-92), Johns produced conceptually puzzling works that seemed to bear on issues raised in contemporary art. Art critics and art historians, for example, had praised the evenly dispersed, "nonhierarchical" or "all-over" quality of so much Abstract Expressionist painting, particularly Pollock's (see fig. 29-9). The target in *Target with Four Faces* (fig. 29-25), an emphatically hierarchical, organized image, can be seen as a reference—more of repudiation than affirmation—to this discourse. The image also raises thorny questions about the difference between representation and abstraction. The target, although arguably a representation, is flat, whereas representational art is usually identified with three-dimensional space. The target therefore occupies a troubling middle ground between the two kinds of painting then struggling for dominance in American art.

Johns's works are more than a simple reaction to the emotional and autobiographical dimensions of Abstract Expressionism. They also had a psychological dimension for Johns, providing him with a way literally to cover certain personal anxieties and fears, some of which can be vaguely discerned in the collage materials partially buried beneath the thick **encaustic** paint. Here, for example, the outline of a lone man in a trench coat is discernible in the lower left. Johns's sense of loneliness and emptiness is perhaps also evident in the faces at the top of the work, which have been cut off at eye level, a move that both depersonalizes them and prevents them from connecting with the viewer. Moreover, the faces are as blank and neutral as the target below. One historian has recently suggested that there may also have been a private reference to the fact that, as a homosexual in the homophobic climate of postwar New York, Johns felt like a target.

The work of Johns had a powerful effect on a number of artists who matured around 1960. His cool,

29-26. 1955 Cadillac
convertible

impersonal work contributed to the Minimalist aesthetic, while his interest in Duchamp helped elevate that artist to a place of importance previously occupied by Picasso. Finally, Johns's conceptually intriguing use of subjects from ordinary life, a feature also evident in the work of Rauschenberg, helped open the way for the most controversial development to emerge after Abstract Expressionism, Pop art.

Pop Art

In 1961–1962 several exhibitions in New York City featured art that drew on **popular culture** for style and subject matter. Because of its popular sources (comic books, advertisements, movies, television), this emerging movement came to be called Pop art. Many critics were alarmed by the movement, uncertain whether Pop art was embracing or parodying popular culture and fearful that it threatened the survival of both modernist art and high culture—meaning a civilization's most sophisticated, not its most representative, products.

Such fears were not entirely unfounded. Pop artists' open acknowledgment of the powerfully compelling realm of commercial culture contributed significantly to the eclipse, about 1970, of traditional modernism and thus, some argue, the very notion of "standards" that kept high culture safely insulated from low. This is not to say that all Pop artists embraced popular culture. Even the first post–World War II artists to turn to it for their inspiration, the British Pop group, reveal a somewhat ambivalent attitude toward their sources.

British Pop was the product of the Independent Group (IG), formed in 1952 by a few members of the Institute of Contemporary Art (ICA) in London who resisted the institute's commitment to modernist art, design, and architecture. The IG's most prominent figures were the artists Richard Hamilton (b. 1922) and Eduardo Paolozzi (b. 1924), the architecture critic Reyner Banham (1922–1988), the art critic Lawrence Alloway (1926–1990), and the writer John McHale. At their first meeting Paolozzi showed slides of American ads, whose utopian vision of a future of contented people with ample leisure time to enjoy cheap and plentiful material goods was very appealing to those living under the austerity of postwar Britain. In their publications the group argued against the modernist search for "classic" and "timeless" styles in industrial design, advocating instead those that would appeal to popular taste, thereby stimulating not only production but engineering research, both of which would help raise the general standard of living.

For their model, members of the IG looked to American industry—especially to automobile makers like General Motors—whose products such as the 1955 Cadillac (fig. 29-26) were designed to satisfy consumer demand, not elitist notions of beauty. The combination of grand scale, sleek lines, rocketlike tail fins, and an almost Baroque application of expensive chrome was carefully designed to cater to the fantasies of the newly affluent postwar American male, who wished to dissociate himself from the austerity, poverty, and practicality of the prewar period so obviously embodied in the Ford Model T and its heirs.

One member of the IG, the artist Richard Hamilton, was perhaps the first to create work based entirely on advertising sources. His $he (fig. 29-27), for example, includes a "cornucopia refrigerator" from an RCA Whirlpool ad, a pop-up toaster and a vacuum cleaner from General Electric appliance ads, and a stylized image of Vikky Dougan, a model who specialized in ads for backless dresses and bathing suits. Hamilton said he meant to counter the artistic image of women as timeless beings with the more down-to-earth picture of them presented in advertising. The evocative, somewhat mysterious result, however, seems closer to traditional art than it does to the clear, simple, and straightforward imagery of the advertisements on which it draws. In short, one of the primary imperatives of modern advertising—clarity of message—has here been sacrificed to those of avant-garde art: individuality and provocative invention.

American Pop artists, such as Roy Lichtenstein (1923–1997), were the first to accept the look as well as the subjects of popular culture. In 1961, while teaching at

29-27. Richard Hamilton. $he. 1958–61. Oil, cellulose, collage on panel, 24 x 16" (61 x 40.6 cm). Tate Gallery, London

29-28. Roy Lichtenstein. Oh, Jeff . . . I Love You, Too . . . But . . . 1964. Oil on Magma on canvas, 4 x 4' (1.22 x 1.22 m). Private collection

Rutgers University with Allan Kaprow, who encouraged him, Lichtenstein began producing paintings whose imagery and style—featuring heavy outlines and the **Benday dots** used to add tone in printing—were drawn from cartoons and advertisements.

The most famous of these early works, such as *Oh, Jeff . . . I Love You, Too . . . But . . .* (fig. 29-28), were based on romance comics. When asked about his comic-book sources in 1963, Lichtenstein said that he turned to them for formal reasons. Although many assume that he merely copied from the comics, in fact he made numerous subtle yet important formal adjustments that tightened, clarified, and strengthened the final image. The cartoonist, he said, "intends to depict and I intend to unify." Nevertheless, the paintings retain a sense of the cartoon plots they draw on. *Oh, Jeff*, for example, compresses into a single frame the generic romance-comic story line, in which two people fall in love, face some sort of crisis, or "but," that temporarily threatens their relationship, and then live happily ever after. Lichtenstein reminds the grown-up viewer, however, that this plot is only an adolescent fiction; real-life relationships like his own marriage, then in the process of dissolving, end, as here, with the "but."

Another of the Pop artists who sought to mask his personal concerns behind the impersonal veneer of American popular imagery was Andy Warhol (1928?–1987). A successful commercial illustrator in New York City during the 1950s, Warhol grew envious of Rauschenberg's and Johns's emerging "star" status and decided in 1960 to pursue a career as an artist along the general lines suggested by their work. His decision to focus on popular culture was more than a careerist move, howev-

er; it also allowed him to celebrate the middle-class social and material values he had absorbed growing up amid the hardships of the Great Depression.

A number of these values may be discerned in the *Marilyn Diptych* (fig. 29-29), even in its industrial mode of production. The painting, produced in Warhol's studio called The Factory, is one of the first in which Warhol turned from conventional modes of hand painting to the assembly-line technique of silk-screening photo-images onto canvas. The method was faster and quicker and thus more profitable, and Warhol could also produce many versions of the subject—all of which he considered good business. The subject of the work is also telling. Like so many Americans Warhol was fascinated by American movie stars such as Marilyn Monroe. The strip of pictures in this work suggests the sequential images of film, the medium that made Monroe famous. The face Warhol portrays, taken from a publicity photograph, is not that of Monroe the person but of Monroe the star, since Warhol was interested in her public mask, not in her personality or character. He borrowed the **diptych** format from the Byzantine **icons** of Christian saints he saw at the Greek Orthodox church services he attended every Sunday. By symbolically treating the famous actress as a saint, Warhol shed light on his own fascination with fame. Not only does fame bring wealth and transform the ordinary into the beautiful (Warhol was dissatisfied with his own looks), it also confers, like holiness for a saint, a kind of immortality.

Warhol attempted to keep his personal motives from showing through too clearly in his works, however, and preferred to leave their meaning open to the viewers'

29-29. Andy Warhol. *Marilyn Diptych*. 1962. Oil, acrylic, and silk screen on enamel on canvas, 6'8⅞" x 4'9"
(2.05 x 1.44 m). Tate Gallery, London

Warhol assumed that all Pop artists shared his affirmative view of ordinary culture. In his account of the beginnings of the Pop movement, he wrote: "The Pop artists did images that anybody walking down Broadway could
recognize in a split second—comics, picnic tables, men's trousers, celebrities, shower curtains, refrigerators,
Coke bottles—all the great modern things that the Abstract Expressionists tried so hard not to notice at all."

interpretation. The success of the Marilyn series, in
particular, has depended in great measure on viewers'
ability to reflect onto Warhol's images their own feelings
and ideas about the tragedy of her life.

Swedish-born Claes Oldenburg (b. 1929) took both a
more critical and a more humorous attitude toward his
popular subjects than did his colleagues Warhol and
Lichtenstein. Oldenburg's objections to the increasingly
impersonal and sanitized nature of Western life are evident in his crude, sloppy plaster versions of ordinary
American foods and products, which were meant to render more "human" what he called the "hostile objects" of
commerce. Oldenburg's humor—a fundamental part of
his project to reanimate a dull, lifeless culture—is most
evident in such large-scale public projects as his Lipstick
Monument for his alma mater, Yale University (fig. 29-
30). The work situates a giant lipstick cartridge on a tank
base as a reference to the "militant" feminism that had
recently succeeded in gaining women admission to
Yale's formerly all-male undergraduate programs. The
work also wittily combines male and female sexual references in the lipstick, which could be inflated and
deflated. The Yale administration, in front of whose
offices the work was placed, did not appreciate its irreverent humor and had it removed.

29-30. Claes Oldenburg. *Lipstick (Ascending) on Caterpillar
Tracks*. 1969–74. Installed at Beinecke Plaza, Yale Uni-
versity, New Haven, Connecticut. Yale University Art
Gallery

Gift of Colossal Keepsake Corporation

PATRONAGE AND COMMERCE

Art museums, both public and private, are relatively new, distinctly Western institutions. Museums evolved in the eighteenth century out of the tradition of private collecting. They continued to flourish under the lasting influence of the Enlightenment, which placed a high value on public education. In the twentieth century, museums emerged as major buyers of art and occasional patrons of living artists, sharing with private collectors the roles once played by religious institutions and aristocratic courts.

Major patrons must have money, and patterns of patronage shift according to where money is. For about a hundred years, from the mid-nineteenth to the mid-twentieth century, families of wealth, education, and social privilege were the primary supporters of the arts. Indeed, art patronage could secure or increase social standing. Such families gave heavily to establish and fund museums. Their generosity in lending or giving works of art is often noted on museum labels and in captions for illustrations of works of art in books, including this one. Donor information is a major aspect of a work's **provenance** and for that reason alone merits such notice.

The late 1940s and 1950s were a transition period for art buying in the United States. It is often argued that several critics, notably Clement Greenberg and Harold Rosenberg, had a profound influence on the work of the New York School artists. The truth is, these critics and their opinions carried enormous weight with some museum curators and with collectors who were not paying high prices for the painting and sculptures they added to their collections.

Sometime in the 1960s, as the United States consolidated its position as the wealthiest country in the world, patterns and intentions of art buying and art making began to change. Museums were built where none had been before, especially in the thriving Sun Belt of the United States. People with newly made fortunes, banks, and commercial corporations began to acquire art as investments. Prices rose. Critics began to accuse some contemporary artists of pandering to this new class of patrons.

By the 1980s the art market was booming. In the five years between 1982 and 1987, prices for major Impressionist paintings rose 400 per-cent. The art market went global, with Japanese and Latin American investors putting in some of the highest bids ever offered for "blue chip" Impressionist paintings. A painting by Jasper Johns, a living artist, that might have fetched a quarter of a million dollars in the early 1970s commanded $17 million in the late 1980s. Most museums simply could not compete as buyers in this market. But they did benefit from loans and gifts from collectors, who could reduce their taxes by such largesse. Ironically, artists now began to protest the commercialization of art.

With the advent of the sober 1990s, the "commodification" of art suddenly cooled. Some works offered at auction failed to reach their minimum prices. Many corporations started divesting themselves of their art collections. The private collectors who sold their once overpriced artworks to raise cash rarely recovered what they had paid. Museums were again able to purchase works of art, at least modestly. The trend in the 1980s, then, proved to have been an exception for the art market. For those people who buy art because they love it, not because they plan to sell it for profit, that the inflated market was so short-lived was a relief.

Minimalist Tendencies

Three related styles that emerged in quick succession in the wake of Abstract Expressionism—post-painterly abstraction; Hard Edge, or Minimalist, art; and Conceptualism—shared a commitment to reducing art to its essentials.

Most avant-garde critics, curators, and art historians, following the lead of Clement Greenberg, considered post-painterly abstraction to be the legitimate heir to Abstract Expressionism. Greenberg coined the term *post-painterly* to describe the style that he believed had evolved naturally from the "painterly," or gestural, abstraction of the New York School. He also helped cultivate the style, guiding and promoting some practitioners and praising their efforts as the only "authentically new episode in the evolution of contemporary art."

In 1953 Greenberg introduced Morris Louis (1912–1962), a painter from Washington, D.C., then working in a late Cubist style, to the work of Helen Frankenthaler (see fig. 29-17). Impressed with Frankenthaler's stain technique and apparently convinced by Greenberg's ideas on the evolution of modernism and the historical inevitability of pure formalism (see "The Idea of the Mainstream," page 1116), Louis stepped "beyond" Abstract Expressionism by eliminating all extra-artistic meanings from his work. In paintings such as *Saraband* (fig. 29-31) he purged not only the figural and thematic references found in the

29-31. Morris Louis. *Saraband*. 1959. Acrylic resin on canvas, 8'5¹⁄₈" x 12'5" (2.57 x 3.78 m). Solomon R. Guggenheim Museum, New York

work of Frankenthaler but also the subjective, emotional connotations found in that of Pollock, de Kooning, Rothko, and Newman. Here, color does not represent emotion; it is simply color. Red is red, not passion. The painting is simply a painting, not a representation of something beyond art. The luscious rainbow of colors in *Saraband*—which he created by tipping the canvas to allow the thinned oils to flow according to their inherent properties—offers pure delight to the senses.

While studying painting at Princeton University in the late 1950s, Stella and an undergraduate English major, Michael Fried, often went to New York City to hear Clement Greenberg lecture on the course of modern art. Fried went on to become the leading Greenbergian critic of the 1960s. He primarily wrote for *Artforum*, the most influential art journal of the period. *"Die Fahne Hoch"* is one of the names for the "Horst Wessel Lied," a German folksong that was virtually an anthem for the German army in World War II. It translates as "the banner raised aloft."

Another artist motivated by Greenberg to purge art of its "inessentials" was Frank Stella (b. 1936). In his early Black series stripe paintings such as *"Die Fahne Hoch"* (fig. 29-32), inspired in part by Johns's apparently neutral patterns (see fig. 29-25), he eliminated the conventional notion of individual sensibility: He featured black, for example, not because it appealed to his taste or expressed his mood but because it signifies the absence of color pigment, its denial. The rectangular design elements derive from the shape of the canvas itself. "Depicted shape," the artist claimed, was logically determined by the "literal shape" of the canvas support. Even the 3-inch widths of the stripes were determined by the physical object: The canvas stretchers are 3 inches deep. What Stella achieved was a group of artworks whose features refer not to the artist or the outside world but to the physical aspects of the art object itself. The individual paintings are therefore hermetically sealed from everything beyond their edges except other paintings of the series. In that sense they are "pure."

Stella's interests were shared by the sculptor Donald Judd (1928–1994). Convinced along with Greenberg and others that Abstract Expressionism had deteriorated into a set of techniques for faking both the subjective and the transcendent, Judd began around 1960 to search for an art free of falsehood. By the early 1960s he had decided that sculpture offered a better medium than painting for creating literal, matter-of-fact art. Rather than *depicting* shapes, as Stella did—which Judd thought still smacked of illusionism and therefore fakery—he would create *actual* shapes. In search of a greater simplicity and clarity, he soon evolved a formal vocabulary featuring identical rectangular units arranged in rows and constructed of industrial materials, especially anodized aluminum and Plexiglas. *Untitled* (fig. 29-33) is a typical example of his mature work.

Judd liked industrial materials because they had the crisp "certainty" he sought, were more impersonal than organic materials, and were imbued with their own color, thus minimizing his need to choose a color for them. His later boxes, like those in *Untitled*, are always open, to avoid any uncertainty about what might be inside. He arranged them in rows—the simplest, most impersonal way to integrate them—and avoided sets of two or three because of their potential to be read as representative of something other than a row of boxes. Judd

29-33. Donald Judd. *Untitled*. 1969. Anodized aluminum and blue Plexiglas, each 3'11½" x 4'11⅞" x 4'11⅞" (1.2 x 1.5 x 1.5 m); overall 3'11½" x 4'11⅞" x 23'8½" (1.2 x 1.5 x 7.2 m). The St. Louis Art Museum, St. Louis, Missouri

Purchase funds given by the Shoenberg Foundation, Inc.

29-35. Joseph Kosuth. *One and Three Chairs*. 1965. Wood folding chair, photograph of chair, and photographic enlargement of dictionary definition of chair; chair, 32⅜ x 14⅞ x 20⅞" (82.2 x 37.8 x 53.0 cm); photo panel, 36 x 24⅛" (91.4 x 61.3 cm); text panel 24⅛ x 24½" (61.3 x 62.2 cm). The Museum of Modern Art, New York

Larry Aldrich Foundation Fund

29-34. Eva Hesse. *Hang-Up*. 1965–66. Acrylic on cloth over wood and steel, 6' x 7' x 6'6" (1.8 x 2.1 x 2 m). The Art Institute of Chicago

Through prior gift of Arthur Keating and Mr. and Mrs. Edward Morris, 1988

provided the viewer with a set of clear, self-contained facts, from which the viewer detects the contrast between the work's conceptual clarity and the messy complexity of the real world.

The one important exception to the Minimalist urge to avoid self-expression is the work of Eva Hesse (1936–1970). After graduating from the Yale School of Art in 1959 she painted self-portraits, and in 1964 she began to pro-

duce abstract sculpture that used the vocabulary of Minimalism for that same purpose. In that sense, Hesse was one of the first artists to move beyond the austerity of Minimalism. Instead of sleek surface, her work shows the actual process of art making, which included such malleable techniques as sewing, lacing, and bandaging. In her mature work, like *Hang-Up* (fig. 29-34), contradictions abound—the self-contained and the protruding, the regular and the organic, order and chaos. The tragic absurdity in Hesse's art may reflect the inner conflict within the artist, who died young: "Art and life," she commented, "are very connected and my whole life has been absurd."

While Hesse was moving Minimalism into new territory, a group of New York artists who came to be known as Conceptualists was pushing Minimalism to its logical extreme by eliminating the object itself. Although these artists always produced something physical, it was often no more than a set of directions or a documentary photograph. Part of this shift away from the aesthetic object toward the pure idea was inspired by the growing reputation of Marcel Duchamp and his assertion that art should be a mental, not a physical, activity. Deemphasizing the art object also kept art from becoming simply another luxury product, a concern raised by the booming business for contemporary art that developed as a result of the rising prices of Abstract Expressionist works and the growing popularity of Pop art among collectors (see "Patronage and Commerce," page 1131). Without an object, there would be nothing to sell. Therefore, art would remain safe from bourgeois materialism.

The Conceptual art of the 1960s, unlike the intellectually complex art of Duchamp, aimed for a simplicity and clarity similar to that found in the works of Stella and Judd. For example, Joseph Kosuth's *One and Three Chairs* (fig. 29-35) clearly articulates the fact that the word *chair* can refer to a concept, a representation, or an actual item.

FROM MODERNISM TO POST-MODERNISM

The 1960s was a watershed period in the history of modern art. Little of the earlier modernist faith in the transformative power of art is evident in the works produced during the decade. Although the Minimalists continued to believe that the history of art had a coherent, progressive shape and that art represented a pure realm outside ordinary "bourgeois" culture, the purity, honesty, and clarity of their art were not meant to change the world but to retreat from it. To the next generation, by contrast, the concepts of artistic purity and the mainstream seemed naive. In fact, the entire generation that grew to maturity around 1970 shared little faith in either purity or progress that marked earlier generations. Precisely how and why this loss of faith happened are matters of debate, but among the contributing factors were a widespread sense of disillusionment that followed in the wake of the political protests and social reform movements of the 1960s and the growing awareness that the material improvements brought by industrial technology had a high environmental cost. In short, the utopian optimism that had characterized the beginning of the modernist era and had survived both world wars gave way to a growing uncertainty about the future and about art's power to influence it.

The decline of modernism in the various arts was neither uniform nor sudden. Its gradual erosion occurred over a long period and was the result of many individual transformations. The many approaches to art that have emerged from the ruins of modernism are designated by the catchall term *postmodernism*.

Architecture

As in painting and sculpture, modernism endured in architecture until about 1970. The stripped-down, rationalist style pioneered by Walter Gropius (see figs. 28-73, 28-86) and Le Corbusier (see fig. 28-85) dominated new urban construction in much of the world after World War II and came to be known as the International Style. Many of the most famous examples of International Style architecture were built in the United States by German architects associated with the Bauhaus, who during the Nazi era had been offered prestigious positions in American schools. Gropius, for example, was hired in 1937 by Harvard, where he eventually headed the architecture department. In the same year Mies van der Rohe, who had designed the Barcelona Pavilion (see fig. 28-88), was named director of the Armour Institute in Chicago, which later became the Illinois Institute of Technology.

Whether designing schools, apartments, or office buildings like the Seagram Building in New York City (fig. 29-36), Mies used the same simple, rectilinear industrial vocabulary. The differences among his buildings are to be found in their details. Because he had a large budget for the Seagram Building, for instance, he used custom-made bronze (instead of standardized steel) beams on the exterior, an example of his love of elegant materials.

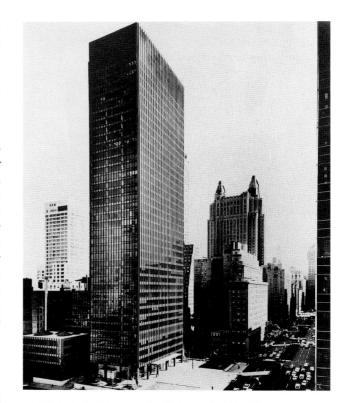

29-36. Ludwig Mies van der Rohe and Philip Johnson. Seagram Building, New York City. 1954–58

Mies would have preferred to leave the steel structural supports visible, but building codes required him to encase them in concrete. The ornamental beams on the outside thus stand in for the functional beams inside, much as the shapes in a Stella painting refer to the structural frame that holds the canvas. The tall, narrow windows emphasize the verticality of the thirty-eight-story building, helping it compete for attention with surrounding skyscrapers. The building is set back from the street and rises quickly and impressively off pilotis (see fig. 28-86) from a sunlit plaza with reflecting pools, fountains, and, originally, beech trees (the city air killed them).

The dark glass and bronze were meant to give the Seagram Company a discreet and dignified image. The building's clean lines and crisp design seemed, in fact, to epitomize the efficiency, standardization, and impersonality that had become synonymous with the modern corporation itself—which, in part, is why this particular style dominated corporate architecture after World War II. Such buildings were also cheaper to build. For Mies, however, the goal was to find a suitable architectural style not only for American businesses but also for modern humanity. He believed that the industrial preoccupation with streamlined efficiency was the dominant value of the entire age and that the only legitimate architecture was one that expressed this modern **zeitgeist** ("spirit of the age").

While business leaders, in particular, were embracing the International Style, a number of critics both inside and outside the architectural profession were growing increasingly hostile to it, not least because it had become so identified with the prevailing corporate zeitgeist. These critics called for an architecture that would provide the starved modern sensibility with the spiritual nourishment it so badly needed.

Among the first architects to offer a radical alternative to the International Style was one of its originators, Le Corbusier. Although he never entirely rejected his original vision of the rational, uniform city of the future (see fig. 28-85), he did come to recognize its deficiencies. In the early 1950s he shocked the architectural profession with his radically antimodernist design for Notre-Dame-du-Haut (fig. 29-37), a pilgrimage church on a hill above Ronchamp, France. Instead of thin curtain walls, the church has thick, rough, masonry walls faced with whitewashed Gunite (sprayed concrete). The darker concrete roof is finished in a contrasting striated pattern. The upward lift of the roof recalls the vertical emphasis of medieval church architecture and responds to the winds that sweep across the hill. The building's organic, gently swelling curves, reminiscent of Henry Moore's sculpture, were inspired, Corbusier said, by a crab shell. Notre-Dame-du-Haut's identification of the natural with the spiritual harks back to the premodern ideas of the Romantics. Its dark, cavelike interior recalls the far earlier association of the natural with the divine that dates to humanity's prehistoric origins.

Louis I. Kahn (1901–1974) developed a less radical antimodernist architecture. Trained in conventional Beaux-Arts methods at the University of Pennsylvania in the early 1920s, he did not fully develop his own theories until he encountered the architecture of ancient Egypt, Greece, and Rome during a year spent at the American Academy of Rome in 1950–1951. What struck him about this architecture was the way it translated clearly conceived functions into boldly simple structures. He returned to the United States committed to finding a modern equivalent of those early Mediterranean styles. Rejecting the modernist preoccupation with a single, uniform style, he sought to tailor the form of each building to its intended use. He viewed a building as a living organism and maintained that like an organism, its form should efficiently integrate its functioning parts.

For the Salk Institute of Biological Studies on the shores of the Pacific Ocean in La Jolla, California, Kahn designed a large laboratory building and two rows of student and faculty housing on a severe courtyard leading to the sea (fig. 29-38). The modular housing units, whose regularity is both punctuated and relieved by the abrupt diagonal juts in the facades, are formed with concrete slabs, which he preferred to thinner industrial materials because of the assertive way they defined space. The windows and balconies are simple geometric cuts in the walls, although the harsh contrast of solid and void is somewhat softened by the wood around the facade openings. Kahn, who asked himself what institutional housing "wanted" to look like, seems to have decided that it should look as if it housed a community of equals. Although Kahn based his ideas on what he viewed as the simple functionalism of ancient architecture, his spare design for the Salk Institute's housing seems consistent with the Minimalism of contemporary painting and sculpture.

29-37. Le Corbusier. Notre-Dame-du-Haut, Ronchamp, France. 1950–55

29-38. Louis I. Kahn. Salk Institute of Biological Studies, La Jolla, California. 1959–65

Postmodern Architecture. Although the historically informed antimodernism of Le Corbusier and Kahn contributed to the decline of modernism, it was the willingness of Robert Venturi (b. 1925) and his associates to turn to vernacular (meaning popular, common, or ordinary) sources that marks the emergence of postmodern architecture. Parodying Mies van der Rohe's famous aphorism "Less is more," Venturi claimed "Less is a bore" in his 1966 pioneering publication, *Complexity and Contradiction in Architecture*. The problem with Mies and the other modernists, he argued, was their impractical unwillingness to accept the modern city for what it is: a complex, contradictory, and heterogeneous collection of "high" and "low" architectural forms. Taking these ideas further in 1972 in *Learning from Las Vegas*, he and his colleagues suggested that rather than turning their backs in disdain at ordinary commercial buildings, architects

29-39. Venturi, Rauch & Scott Brown. Venturi House, Chestnut Hill, Pennsylvania. 1962

29-40. Venturi, Rauch & Scott Brown. Plan for Venturi House

should get in "the habit of looking nonjudgmentally" at them. "Main Street is almost all right," they observed. Just as "we look backward at history and tradition to go forward; we can also look downward to go upward."

While writing *Complexity and Contradiction in Architecture* Venturi designed with his partners John Rauch (b. 1930) and Denise Scott Brown (b. 1930)—who was also his wife—a house for his mother (fig. 29-39), which illustrated many of his new ideas. The building is both simple and complex. The shape of the facade returns to the archetypal "house" shape—evident in children's drawings—that modernists had rejected (see fig. 28-86). Its vocabulary of triangles, squares, and circles is also elementary, although they are arranged in a complex and faulty asymmetry that skews the restful harmonies of modernist design (see fig. 28-82). The most disruptive element on the facade is the deep cleavage over the door, which opens to reveal a mysterious upper wall (which turns out to be a penthouse) and chimney top. On the inside, too, complexity and contradiction reign (fig. 29-40). The irregular floor plan, especially evident in the odd stairway leading to the second floor, is further complicated by the unusual ceilings, some of which are partially cut by a barrel vault.

The Vanna Venturi House also makes reference to a number of other buildings, from Michelangelo's Porta Pia in Rome to a nearby house designed by Venturi's mentor, Louis Kahn. Although these allusions to architectural history were lost on the general public, they provided many architects, including Philip Johnson (b. 1906), with a path out of modernism. Johnson's major contribution

29-41. Philip Johnson and John Burgee. Pencil drawing made in 1977 for AT&T Headquarters, New York. 1978–83

After collaborating on the Seagram Building (see fig. 29-36) with Mies, who had long been his architectural idol, Johnson grew tired of the limited modernist vocabulary. During the 1960s he experimented with a number of alternatives, especially a weighty, monumental style that looked back to nineteenth-century Neoclassicism. At the end of the 1970s he became fascinated with the new possibilities opened by Venturi's postmodernism, which he found "absolutely delightful."

to postmodernism is the AT&T Headquarters in New York City (fig. 29-41), an elegant, granite-clad building whose thirty-six oversize floors reach the height of an ordinary sixty-story building. The AT&T Headquarters makes gestures of accommodation to its surroundings. Its smooth, uncluttered surfaces match those of its International Style neighbors, while the classically symmetrical window groupings between vertical piers echo those in more conservative Manhattan skyscrapers of the early to middle 1900s. What critics focused on, however, was the building's resemblance to a type of eighteenth-century furniture, the Chippendale highboy, a chest of drawers with a long-legged base. The piers at the base of the building resemble a giant highboy's spindly legs, the body of the building its cabinet drawers, and the top its scrolled "bonnet" ornament. Johnson seems to have intended a pun on the terms *highboy* and *high-rise*. In addition, the round notch at the top of the building and the arched entryway at the base recall the coin slot and coin return on old pay telephones. Many critics were not amused by Johnson's effort to add a touch of humor to high architecture. His purpose, however, was less to poke fun at his client or his profession than to create an architecture that would amuse the public and at the same time, like a fine piece of furniture, meet its deeper aesthetic needs with a formal, decorative elegance.

While Johnson was making buildings look like old furniture, many postmodernist designers, including the architect Michael Graves (b. 1924), were making furniture that looked like or incorporated old architectural elements. His Oculus and Finestra chairs (fig. 29-42), for example, feature classical window designs popular in the Renaissance. The **oculus** (Latin for "eye") was a round window type often used by Palladio (see fig. 18-35) and others. *Finestra* is a play on the Latin word for "window," *fenestra*. The simple contours of these elegant, square-backed chairs derive from Neoclassical furniture. Graves eliminated the detailing of the originals, however, in line with modernist taste, which is why such designs are often referred to as Neo-Modern. Graves, like Johnson and Venturi, does not revive the styles of the past as did the nineteenth-century historicists; he reworks them to accord with contemporary taste, much as Robert Adam, for example, had done (see fig. 26-19).

One of the earliest manifestations of the decorative, playful use of historical forms that became identified with postmodern architecture was in the Centre National d'Art et de Culture Georges Pompidou (fig. 29-43) in Paris, designed by Renzo Piano (b. 1937) of Italy and Richard Rogers (b. 1933) of England. The building, which utilizes a modernist vocabulary, appears to have been whimsically turned inside out and then cheerfully painted. The coloring is not random, however. Red designates elevators, blue designates the air-conditioning ducts, green the water pipes, and yellow the electrical units. The external placement of these service structures increases the flexibility of the interior space. The arrangement also makes a historical reference to the origins of functional architecture in Paris, evoking both the glass-and-iron sheds that once stood in the historical market area adjacent to it and the most famous of the exposed-metal structures that gave birth to modernist architecture, the Eiffel Tower (see fig. 28-68).

Unlike Piano and Rogers, whose high-tech architecture lightheartedly revisits the technological basis of modernism, the Italian Aldo Rossi (b. 1931) has attempted to salvage modernism's rationalist and reductive tendencies. His approach to architecture, known as neo-rationalism, is based on a return to certain premodernist building archetypes (**typologies**)—such as the church, the house, and the factory—stripped of all elaboration and ornamentation and reduced to their geometric essentials, much as in the designs of Neoclassicists like Claude-Nicolas Ledoux and Étienne-Louis Boullée (see figs. 26-31, 26-32). His goal has been to achieve both historical continuity and universal timelessness. To enrich the emotional impact of these rationally conceived typologies, Rossi believed that architects should use them in mysterious and evocative ways.

The Town Hall Rossi built in Borgoricco, Italy (fig. 29-44), near Venice, illustrates these concepts. Because Borgoricco is in Italy's industrial belt, he based the central forms of the building on an industrial, rather than a civic,

1990
1940   2000

29-42. Michael Graves. Oculus and Finestra chairs. Manufactured by Atelier International. Beachwood with ebony veneer, 34 5/16 x 23 3/16 x 22" (87 x 59 x 56 cm)

29-43. Renzo Piano and Richard Rogers. Centre National d'Art et de Culture Georges Pompidou, Paris. 1971–77

29-44. Aldo Rossi. Town Hall, Borgoricco, Italy. 1986–90
Courtesy Aldo Rossi

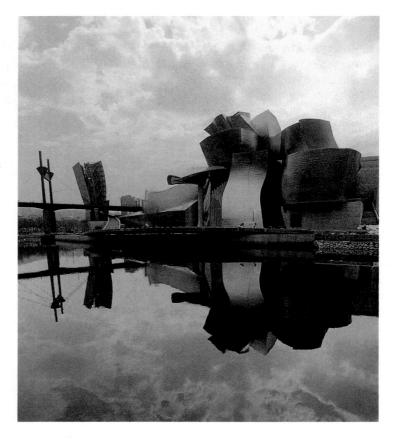

29-45. Frank O. Gehry. Guggenheim Museum Bilbao, Spain. 1997

Philip Johnson, the dean of American architects (see fig. 29-41), called the Guggenheim Museum Bilbao "the greatest building of our century."

typology. The large windows, metal roof, and smokestack are based on nineteenth- and early-twentieth-century factory designs (see fig. 28-74), whereas the temple fronts on the flanking wings, which evoke the building's civic function, are done in a style typical of the aristocratic Palladian housing in the surrounding countryside. The result is a provocative and unexpected marriage of local forms and other European architectural types. The blending succeeds because of the way Rossi played the warm brick against the cool concrete in both the flanking and the central elements and because of the way he reduced the whole to strict geometric forms. This simple geometry and the building's rigorous symmetry give it a stable, timeless air.

One of the most dramatic buildings inspired by architecture of the past is the new Guggenheim Museum Bilbao (fig. 29-45), designed by Frank O. Gehry (b. 1929). Although Gehry had made a reputation during the late 1970s and 1980s for his inventive approach to vernacular forms and cheap materials, his guiding concern was to reconcile the client's needs with his own interest in sculptural form. The commission for the Guggenheim Museum Bilbao provided him with an extraordinary opportunity to realize that goal.

In 1991 Basque officials came to the Guggenheim Museum in New York with an idea for a new museum: The Guggenheim would run it and lend it art from its collection while Basque tax money would build it and pay for its operation. The Guggenheim accepted the offer partly because its museum, designed by Frank Lloyd Wright, could display only part of its collection and none of the largest works. Three architectural firms were invited to submit designs, and Gehry's sprawling, organic plan

29-46. Henri Cartier-Bresson. *The Berlin Wall.* 1963

After World War II, Germany and its capital, Berlin, were both divided into separate zones controlled by the four wartime allies. Those parts of Germany controlled by Britain, France, and the United States became West Germany, while those under Soviet control became the East German Communist state. Most of divided Berlin, though located in East Germany, became part of West Germany, a kind of remote outpost.

was chosen. Like Wright's Guggenheim, which inspired it, Gehry's building resembles, from most vantage points, a living organism, some gigantic metallic flower growing along the banks of the river. Gehry covered the building's complex steel skeleton with a thin skin of silvery titanium that shimmers gold or silver depending on the light. From head-on, however, the building resembles a giant ship, a reference to the shipbuilding so important to the economy of the northern Spanish city. The inside features a giant atrium, which both pays homage to Wright's

29-47. Robert Frank. *Trolley, New Orleans*. 1955–56. Gelatin-silver print, 9 x 13" (23 x 33 cm). The Art Institute of Chicago

Photography

Post–World War II photography before about 1970 can be divided into three categories: abstract, fantastic, and photodocumentary. All three shared both a belief in photography's access to a higher truth (whether aesthetic, personal, or social) and a commitment to a formally handsome finished product. By about 1970, however, a major change in photography, as great as that in architecture, became evident. This change was characterized by a shift—best seen in the photodocumentary works—from what might be called high art photography to deliberately bad, low art photography.

One of the leading photographers of the period before 1970 was Henri Cartier-Bresson (b. 1908) of France, who roamed the world as a freelancer from the late 1940s to 1966, providing photographs for Western newspapers and magazines, including *Life*. Cartier-Bresson's goal was to capture what he called "the decisive moment," one that revealed the essence of his subject in a rigorously organized image. He specialized in subjects of general human and historical interest, such as *The Berlin Wall* (fig. 29-46). The wall, a famous symbol of Communist oppression and the Cold War rivalry between the Soviet Union and the nations of the West, was built in 1961 by the Communist government of East Germany to prevent East Berliners from fleeing to the greater free-

famous one in New York and attempts to outdo it in size and effect. In competing with Wright, Gehry meant to provide for the needs of the artists. "Artists want to be in *great* buildings," he claimed.

doms and economic opportunities of the West. Cartier-Bresson's photograph is both symbolically expressive and formally coherent. In it three men, well dressed and apparently prosperous, peer thoughtfully over the wall from the western side at the abandoned buildings on the eastern side. A gray sky lights this scene of hard, cold surfaces, evocative of the harsh political realities that created it. Two street signs on the far right, one of them marking a street interrupted by the wall, balance the figures on the left, closing the composition and directing the viewer's eye back along the row of houses.

The transition away from Cartier-Bresson's kind of aesthetic standards first appears in the work of the Swiss-born American photographer Robert Frank (b. 1924). Frustrated by the pressure and banality of the various news and fashion assignments on which he had been working, Frank packed his family into a used car in 1955 and undertook a yearlong photographic tour of the United States. From more than 28,000 images, he selected 83 for a book published first in France as *Les Américains* in 1958 and a year later in an English-language edition as *The Americans*, with an introduction by the beat writer Jack Kerouac (1922–1969).

The book was poorly received. The photographic community was disturbed by Frank's often haphazard style—by the way some elements were purposefully out of focus, sloppily cropped, and disorganized. Frank, however, was capable of producing classically balanced and sharply focused images, but only when it suited his sense of the truth. The perfect symmetry of *Trolley, New Orleans* (fig. 29-47), for example, ironically underscores the racial prejudice of segregation that it documents.

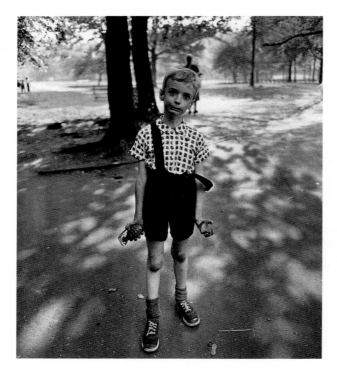

29-48. Diane Arbus. *Child with Toy Hand Grenade, New York.* 1962. Gelatin-silver print, 8¼ x 7¼"(21 x 18.4 cm). The Museum of Modern Art, New York
Purchase

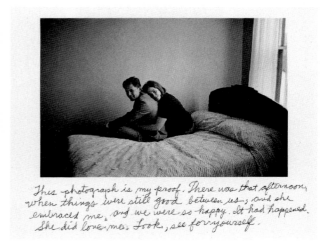

29-49. Duane Michals. *This Photograph Is My Proof.* Gelatin-silver print with text
Courtesy the artist

White passengers sit in the front of the trolley, African Americans in the back. At the same time, the rectangular frames of the trolley windows isolate the individuals looking through them, evoking a sense of urban alienation. Both children and adults stare at the viewer without warmth or recognition.

The harsh view of American life in works such as *Trolley, New Orleans* also upset many people outside the photography profession. What comes through in *The Americans* is a critical, disillusioned portrait of a culture with profound problems that contradicted the contented, self-satisfied view many in the United States had of their country in the 1950s. Frank's questioning perspective pales in comparison to the stark portrait of American people presented during the next decade by Diane Arbus (1923–1971). In her complete preoccupation with subject matter, Arbus, even more than Frank, rejected the concept of the elegant photograph, discarding the niceties of conventional art photography (fig. 29-48). She developed this approach partly in reaction to her experience as a fashion photographer during the 1950s—she and her husband, Allan Arbus, had been *Seventeen* magazine's favorite cover photographers—but mostly because she did not want formal concerns to distract viewers from her compelling, often disturbing subjects.

Among the postmodernist heirs to the tradition of Frank and Arbus, perhaps the most radical was Duane Michals (b. 1932). An art director at *Dance Magazine* and *Time*, Michals became increasingly dissatisfied with photography's inability to deal with the inner life. Inspired by the Surrealist paintings of René Magritte (see fig. 28-98),

whom he came to know quite well, Michals began at the end of the 1960s to fabricate photographic sequences, often accompanied by written narratives. Although those series inspired by his Zen Buddhist convictions are optimistic, most treat themes of human limitation and disappointment. In some cases Michals tells the story in a single frame, as in *This Photograph Is My Proof* (fig. 29-49). Meant to resemble a snapshot in a personal photo album, the work purports to record a young man's attempt to cope with unrequited love. Convinced by the conventional notion that photographs do not lie, the man in the photo tries to persuade himself, and the viewer, that the woman hugging him once really did love him. This picture—a record of a single moment in a bleak little room—is his best and only proof. Michals's deliberate use of amateurish-looking photographs with scratchy writing on them underscores his banal stories and completes the shift from high art photography to the era of so-called bad photography.

Post-Minimalist Tendencies

Michals's rough counterpart in painting was Philip Guston (1913–1980), who had intended to be a cartoonist. Guston's paintings and drawings of the 1930s focused on themes of social injustice, particularly those involving the Ku Klux Klan. After World War II he gave up the figure and evolved a refined, somewhat hesitant gestural style that earned him recognition as a leading member of the New York School. His increasing dissatisfaction with what he came to see as the narrow limitations of

29-50. Philip Guston. *Ladder*. 1978. Oil on canvas, 5'10" x 9' (1.78 x 2.74 m). Collection the Edward R. Broida Trust

29-51. Susan Rothenberg. *Axes*. 1976. Synthetic polymer paint and gesso on canvas, 5'4⅝" x 8'8⅞" (1.64 x 2.66 m). The Museum of Modern Art, New York
Purchased with the aid of funds from the National Endowment for the Arts

Abstract Expressionism, however, reached crisis proportions in the late 1960s, and he returned to figurative work. He later said, "I got sick and tired of all that purity. I wanted to tell stories."

The stories he tells in his late paintings deal with his own shortcomings. Often, as in *Ladder* (fig. 29-50), he represents himself simply by his large, clumsy feet. Here he attempts to climb a ladder to reach a goal on the horizon, a setting sun that is actually the forehead and hair of his wife, Musa. The contrast between her exalted status and his awkward attempt to reach her is more than a confession; it also seems to be a gentle exhortation to the viewer to strive for some higher goal, even if it is unattainable.

Guston's paint handling—"confessionally" crude, coarse, ungainly, and so unlike his elegantly executed work of the 1930s—had far-reaching influence. In 1978, works by artists who could be considered his heirs were shown in two New York exhibitions, "Bad Painting" at the New Museum and "New Image Painting" at the Whitney Museum of American Art. Susan Rothenberg (b. 1945), among those in the Whitney show, developed, like Guston, a self-referential imagery. One day in 1973, she doodled a horse's profile on a small piece of unstretched canvas and something clicked. The horse became her alter ego—a way, perhaps, of dealing with the self while maintaining a distance from the subject. The humanization of horse—or vice versa—is suggested in some 1974 Polaroids she took of a friend on all fours, which resulted in a series of paintings titled *Mary*.

Rothenberg's horses may at first seem somewhat ungainly. For example, because of its off-center placement in the picture frame, the horse in *Axes* (fig. 29-51) appears to be stumbling. The two straight lines, one dividing the picture frame and the other dividing the horse, are the axes of the painting's title. If these axes (and the parts of the horse they align) were reoriented to be parallel to the vertical axis, the animal would be upright, in midstride. The painting's "awkward" aspects are countered by the rich, appealing buildup of painting strokes and the low-key harmony of its creams and blacks—derived, like its simple forms, from the Minimalist aesthetic of the 1960s.

Another, very different kind of painting, which also had ties to Minimalism, developed around 1970 and came to public attention in 1972 in an exhibition called "Sharp Focus Realism" at the Sidney Janis Gallery in New York City. Instead of being personal, deliberately rough, and painterly, works of this kind, known by the label *Super Realist*, are impersonal, technically impressive, and so carefully descriptive that they are often mistaken for color photographs.

One of the leading figures in the Super Realist movement was American painter Richard Estes (b. 1936). Inspired by the urban photographs of Eugène Atget and the paintings of Philip Pearlstein (b. 1924), Estes had developed his mature style by the late 1960s. He was particularly intrigued by Atget's images of reflections in shop windows, like *Magasin, Avenue des Gobelins* (see

29-52. Richard Estes. *Prescriptions Filled* (*Municipal Building*). 1983. Oil on canvas, 3 x 6'
(0.91 x 1.83 m). Private collection

29-53. Audrey Flack. *Marilyn* (*Vanitas*). 1977. Oil over
acrylic on canvas, 8 x 8' (2.4 x 2.4 m). Collection of
the University of Arizona Museum of Art, Tucson
Purchase Edward J. Gallagher, Jr., Memorial Fund

fig. 28-4). During the 1970s and early 1980s he produced a series of paintings on the theme, including *Prescriptions Filled* (*Municipal Building*) (fig. 29-52). Seeking to objectify his scenes, Estes always eliminated people when he transcribed his source photographs to canvas, which emphasized his interest in the aesthetic pleasures of refined compositional arrangements. The window reflection in *Prescriptions Filled*, for example, allows Estes to create a nearly perfect symmetry. The picture's formal tension comes from the subtle differences between the two halves, especially at the very center of the painting, the point between the lamppost and the edge of the glass window.

Estes was also drawn to reflections because they are in some ways visually more stimulating than the solid reality they mirror. The reflection in *Prescriptions Filled* is more engaging than the scene reflected, just as the painting as a whole is more rewarding to look at than the original live scene would have been. Estes thus used the language of realism against realism. Instead of celebrating or condemning something in the world, his cool, static, and closed paintings reinforce the flatness and emptiness of urban life. With Estes's meticulous images, there is no need for accusation; the image is self-indicting.

Much less typical of Super Realist painting in the 1970s is the work of Audrey Flack (b. 1931). In the late 1960s Flack projected a slide image directly onto a canvas in order to copy it and became fascinated with the brilliant colors she observed. Using an airbrush (a mechanical device often used in photo retouching that produces a fine spray of paint), she began to create paintings with colors of an even greater lushness that appealed to her for their emotional effect. During the 1970s she employed these methods to create a series of still lifes inspired by seventeenth-century **vanitas** paintings, a genre dominated by symbols of the transitory nature of life and its pleasures (Chapter 19). Many of these paintings, including *Marilyn* (*Vanitas*) (fig. 29-53), feature imagery that relates specifically to women. The many *vanitas* reminders of time—watch, calendar, hourglass, and candle—are contrasted with conventional and popular objects of another kind of "vanity"—mirror, jewelry, cosmetics—in what can be seen as a powerful comment on the human quest for love and beauty. The text in the book at the back of the painting, decorated by a traditional symbol of love, the rose, poignantly recounts the story of Marylin Monroe, who could feel loved and satisfied only when she was made up and told she was pretty. Her lips rouged, Marilyn's face beams triumphantly from the book. Among the beautiful fruits with which Marilyn is identified is an opened peach, a traditional symbol of female sexuality. The peach pit, however, is a reminder that at her core was a hard, tough center.

Near the middle of the painting is an old photograph, probably of Flack and her brother as children. This detail is not simply another reminder of the passage of time but

29-54. Duane Hanson. *The Shoppers*. 1976. Cast vinyl, polychromed in oil with accessories, lifesize. Collection
the Nerman Family

29-55. Hans Haacke. *Shapolsky et al. Manhattan Real Estate
Holdings, a Real-Time Social System, as of May 1, 1971*.
Photograph by the artist

a signal of Flack's identification with the film star's struggle against it. The drop of bright red paint at the tip of the
artists's paintbrush hovering magically above the open
book is apparently meant to suggest that such paintings
are invested with the artist's own lifeblood.

Another of the Super Realists who wished to communicate inspirational messages was the movement's
major sculptor, Duane Hanson (1925–1996). His earliest
works, which dealt with large social issues such as war,
poverty, and racism, were highly dramatic, but about
1970 he turned to more mundane subjects. As he said of
this change, "You can't always scream and holler, you
have to once in a while whisper, and sometimes that
whisper is more powerful than all the screaming and hol-
lering." After about 1970, Hanson held an unflattering
mirror up to American society, both its work and its
leisure pursuits. One of his favorite themes was the
American obsession with shopping. *The Shoppers*, for
example (fig. 29-54), shows two garishly dressed con-
sumers carrying bags with their recent purchases. The
material goods that are supposed to make them happy
clearly do not. The communicative power of this work
depends greatly on the fact that the figures are not only
lifesize but also lifelike. Every detail is convincing. For
example, Hanson used real hair and clothing (one arm is
detachable to allow for the garments' removal and laun-
dering). Gallerygoers often mistake them for real people,
apologizing when they brush against them.

Hanson's critique of American culture carried a
strain of the modernist reform impulse into the postmodernist era. Most didactic art in the period after 1970

was less ambitious but more political. These qualities are
evident in the work of German-born Hans Haacke (b.
1936), one of a number of artists working in the early
1970s who employed the Conceptual vocabulary of the
preceding decade for decidedly anti-Minimalist purposes.
Because their work otherwise shares little with the
earlier Conceptualists, they are referred to as Post-
Conceptualists.

Haacke came to the United States to teach in 1960. By
the end of the decade he was producing art that featured
simple natural processes. (In one piece, for example, he
planted grass in a gallery.) The turning point in his career
came in 1968, after the assassination of Martin Luther
King, Jr. "Nothing," he wrote in a letter, "but really absolutely nothing is changed by whatever type of painting or
sculpture or happening you produce on the level where it
counts, the political level" (cited in Burnham, page 130).
Despite these misgivings, by 1970 Haacke was making
politically conscious art, although with modest aims and
expectations. Rather than change the world, he hoped
merely to educate a sizable number of people about specific wrongs, many of them involving the art world itself.

One of his first socially conscious pieces was *Shapolsky et al. Manhattan Real Estate Holdings, a Real-Time
Social System, as of May 1, 1971* (fig. 29-55). The work
documented the buildings, some of them slum apartments, owned by a trustee of the Guggenheim Museum,
where an exhibition of Haacke's work was scheduled to
open. When the museum's director learned of the nature
of the work, he claimed that it wasn't art and canceled
the exhibition.

29-56. Michael Heizer. *Double Negative*. 1969–70. 240,000-ton displacement, 1,500 x 50 x 30' (457.2 x 15.2 x 9.1 m). Museum of Contemporary Art, Los Angeles
Gift of Virginia Dwan. Photograph courtesy the artist

29-57. Nancy Holt. *Stone Enclosure: Rock Rings*. 1977–78. Brown Mountain stone, height 10' (3 m), outer ring diameter 40' (12.2 m), inner ring 20' (6.1 m). Western Washington University, Bellingham
Funding from the Virginia Wright Fund, the National Endowment for the Arts, Washington State Arts Commission, Western Washington University Art Fund, and the artist's contributions

Earthworks

As Post-Conceptualism was emerging, a number of sculptors, responding to the New York art scene in general and to the Minimalist retreat from the world in particular, sought to take art back to nature and out of the marketplace. Because they often used raw materials found at the location, their pieces are known as **earthworks**. They pioneered a new category of art making, called **site-specific sculpture**, works designed for a particular location, usually outdoors.

One of the leaders of the earthworks movement was Michael Heizer (b. 1944), the son of a specialist in Native American archeology. Disgusted by the growing emphasis on art as an investment, he spent the summer of 1968 in the Nevada desert, where, among other things, he dynamited huge boulders out of mountainsides and moved them to holes he had dug for them miles away. What Heizer liked about these works was that they could not easily be bought and sold, and they required a considerable commitment of time from viewers who wanted to see them. Recalling the ancient Native American art and architecture to which he had been exposed since childhood, they also seemed to him vaguely religious, suggesting mysterious rites and drawing attention to the sublime qualities of nature.

In 1969–1970 he returned to the Nevada desert and produced his most famous work, *Double Negative* (fig. 29-56). Using a simple Minimalist formal vocabulary, he made two gigantic cuts—the larger of which is longer than the Empire State Building is tall—in a canyon wall. To fully understand the work, the viewer needs to walk into the deep channels and experience their awe-inspiring scale. The work's title refers not only to the two cuts in the earth but also to the double zero on the roulette wheels of Las Vegas, 80 miles away. Heizer, who actually liked to gamble, meant to establish a sharp con-

trast between the raucous artificiality of Las Vegas and the unspoiled simplicity of nature. Heizer's implied criticism of the vulgarity of American culture and his search for a pure, transcendent artistic alternative, so reminiscent of Barnett Newman's work, are more modernist than postmodernist.

Another earthworks artist to carry similar modernist concerns into the postmodernist era is Nancy Holt (b. 1938). Since visiting the Nevada desert in 1968 with Heizer and her husband, Robert Smithson (1938–1973), Holt has specialized in making intimate spaces for viewing the tranquil, sublime beauties of the natural world, especially the sky. In 1977–1978 she built *Stone Enclosure: Rock Rings* (fig. 29-57) on the campus of Western Washington University, in Bellingham. The work consists of two concentric 10-foot-high stone rings, the outer one about 40 feet in diameter. Four aligned doorways suggestive of processional entryways give access to the interior of the rings. Strong, secure, and snug, the interior provides a number of impressive vistas—into the woods, across the campus, or into the heavens. On a clear night the contrast between the small, confined, earthbound space and the infinitely expanding sky is particularly stirring. Sublime, too, is the play between the present and the distant histories of early humans that the work evokes. *Stone Enclosure: Rock Rings* is meant to remind the viewer of a variety of prehistoric and historic forms, from the Neolithic Stonehenge to the Roman Colosseum. As Holt says, "I'm interested in conjuring up a sense of time that is longer than the built-in obsolescence we have all around us."

Holt's husband, Robert Smithson, also wanted to impress the spectator with the vastness of time, but his expression of it was less reassuring than Holt's and not at all modernist. In his mature work he sought to illustrate what he called the "ongoing dialectic" in nature between constructive forces—those that build and shape

29-58. Robert Smithson. *Spiral Jetty.* 1969–70. Black rock, salt crystal, and earth spiral, length 1,500' (457.2 m). Great Salt Lake, Utah

29-59. Christo and Jeanne-Claude. *Running Fence.* 1972–76. Nylon fence, height 18' (5.5 m), length 24½ miles (40 km). Sonoma and Marin Counties in northern California

form—and destructive forces—those that destroy it. *Spiral Jetty* (fig. 29-58), a 1,500-foot spiraling stone and earth platform extending into the Great Salt Lake in Utah, reflects these ideas. Smithson chose the lake because it brought to mind both the origins of life in the salty waters of the primordial ocean and the end of life. One of the few organisms that lives in the otherwise dead lake is a bacterium that gives it a red tinge, vaguely suggestive of blood. Smithson also liked the way the abandoned oil rigs that dot the lake's shores suggested both prehistoric dinosaurs and some vanished civilization. He used the spiral because it is the most fundamental shape in nature, appearing, for example, in galaxies, seashells, DNA molecules, and even salt crystals. Finally, Smithson chose the spiral because, unlike modernist squares, circles, and straight lines, it is a "dialectical" shape, one that opens and closes, curls and uncurls endlessly. More than any other shape, it suggested to him the perpetual "coming and going of things."

The work of two environmental artists, Christo and Jeanne-Claude—both born on June 13, 1935—reflects, in the view of many, a postmodern sense of social mission. Born and trained in Bulgaria, Christo Javacheff (who uses only his first name) emigrated to Paris in 1958, where he met Jeanne-Claude de Guillebon, the *nouveaux réalistes,* and some of the Fluxus artists. His interest in "wrapping" things soon became an obsession, and by the time the pair moved to New York City in 1964, Christo had been "wrapping" progressively larger and larger items. In 1968 Christo and Jeanne-Claude "wrapped" the Kunsthalle, a museum in Berne, Switzerland, and in 1969 one million square feet of the Australian coastline.

Their best-known work, *Running Fence* (fig. 29-59), consisted of a 24½-mile-long, 18-foot-high nylon fence that crossed two counties in northern California and extended into the Pacific Ocean. Although ranchers in South Africa and Mexico had offered them land for *Running Fence,* the artists chose to locate it in Sonoma and Marin Counties because of the beautiful rolling hills there. Their choice was based on pure aesthetics, since

Running Fence was meant to call attention to the beautiful contours of the land and, as they put it, "describe the wind." This concern with aesthetics is common to all their work, in which they reveal the "joy and beauty" of various sites. At the same time, the conflict and collaboration between the artists and various social groups have incidentally opened the workings of the political system to greater scrutiny. For example, Christo and Jeanne-Claude spent forty-two months countering the resistance of county commissioners and social and environmental organizations before *Running Fence* could be created. Meanwhile, the project brought people together to forge a community drawn from groups as diverse as college students, ranchers, lawyers, and artists. In a way, their fence broke down the social barriers that existed among those people.

Feminist Art

An even more ambitious attempt to break down old barriers was initiated by feminist artists. During the 1970s, women finally began to achieve increased recognition in the American art world. The watershed event was the march in 1970 commemorating the fiftieth anniversary of the Nineteenth Amendment to the Constitution, by which women gained the vote. The anniversary gave women an opportunity to assess their progress in various fields since 1920, and they were disappointed by what they found. A survey of women in art, for example, revealed that although they constituted half of the nation's practicing artists, only 18 percent of commercial New York galleries carried works of women. Of the 151 artists in the 1969 Whitney Annual, one of the country's most prominent exhibitions of the work of living artists, only 8 were women. The next year, the ad hoc Group, a number of women critics and artists disappointed by the lukewarm response of the Whitney's director to their concerns, organized a protest at the opening of the 1970 Annual. To focus more attention on women in the arts, feminist artists began organizing women's cooperative galleries. While feminist

29-60. Alice Neel. *Linda Nochlin and Daisy*. 1973. Oil on canvas, 55½ x 44" (141 x 112 cm). Collection of the artist

Neel received solid academic training at the Philadelphia School of Design for Women in the 1920s. Reflecting a series of life crises, including the death in infancy of one of her children and the abduction of another by the child's father, Neel's early work featured distorted, expressionistic images of children. Her style softened after she moved to New York in 1932 and began to specialize in frank and revealing images of the people she knew. She became, as she said, "a collector of souls."

The revival of figurative art in the early 1960s first brought her to the attention of the New York art world, although her penetrating portraits were considered far too subjective for the prevailing aesthetic. Her subjects now included well-known critics, curators, artists, and even an art historian, Linda Nochlin (fig. 29-60). Nochlin, then teaching at Vassar College, had recently inaugurated what would quickly become known as feminist art history with two pioneering efforts. In 1971 she published an essay, "Why Have There Been No Great Women Artists?" The following year she organized a session at the annual College Art Association conference (the professional organization of artists and art historians), entitled "Eroticism and the Image of Woman in Nineteenth-Century Art," which addressed the issue of sexism in art. Neel presents Nochlin as a warm, thoughtful woman, affectionately holding her daughter, a representative of all those other daughters whose future prospects Nochlin was devoted to enlarging.

art historians wrote about women artists and the issues raised by their work in textbooks and journals, feminist curators and critics promoted the work of both emerging women artists and long-neglected ones, such as Alice Neel (1900–1984), who had her first major one-artist show at age seventy-four.

The feminist art movement of the 1970s was a widespread and multifaceted phenomenon nourished by an assortment of common concerns with celebrating and improving the lives of women, especially artists. The category, like so many that historians employ to organize the diverse materials of history, is very flexible and at times simply a matter of emphasis. Audrey Flack, for

29-61. Judy Chicago. *The Dinner Party*. 1974–79. White tile floor inscribed in gold with 999 women's names; triangular table with painted porcelain, sculpted porcelain plates, and needlework, each side 48' (14.6 m). Detail shows two of the place settings
Courtesy the artist

29-62. Miriam Schapiro. *Heartfelt*. 1979. Acrylic and fabric on canvas, 5'10" x 3'4" (1.8 x 1 m). Collection the Norton Neuman Family

Courtesy Steinbaum Krauss Gallery, New York

equality. Each individual place setting has a runner, designed in a style historically appropriate to the woman it represents, and a large ceramic plate. The stitchery, needlepoint, and china painting are all traditional women's art forms that Chicago wished to raise to the status granted to painting and sculpture. Most of the plates feature shapes based on female genitalia because, Chicago says, "that is all [the women at the table] had in common. . . . They were from different periods, classes, ethnicities, geographies, experiences, but what kept them within the same confined historical space" was the fact that they were women (cited in Broude and Garrard, page 71).

Of the various art movements of the 1970s, feminist art most displayed the old modernist optimism about art's capacity to contribute meaningfully to a better future. The function of Chicago's tribute to women and women's traditional art forms, for example, was not simply to improve women's place in history and their sense of themselves but, as she said, "to change the world."

Feminists were outspoken critics, however, of the increasingly restrictive modernist concept of mainstream art and its virtual exclusion of women (see "The Idea of the Mainstream," page 1116). The major champion of a specifically feminine aesthetic was Chicago's partner at CalArts, Miriam Schapiro. During the late 1950s and 1960s Schapiro had made explicitly female versions of the dominant modernist styles. At the end of the 1960s, for example, she was painting reductive, hard-edge abstractions of the female form: large **X** shapes with openings in their center.

Typical of Schapiro's mature work is *Heartfelt* (fig. 29-62), one of a type of construction she called femmage (from *female* and **collage**). Made with painted fabrics, these works celebrate traditional women's craftwork. *Heartfelt* is shaped like a house because that was where most women worked and because their domestic art forms were part of a larger concern with the care of others, which Schapiro associated with the idea of home. The patterns of *Heartfelt* suggest the curtains, shelf papers, wallpapers, quilts, rugs, and other decorative forms women make or use in their domestic spaces. The title and heart shape at the center evoke an essential feature of female sensibility according to Shapiro and her circle: their greater capacity for feeling. Both the formal and the emotional richness of *Heartfelt* were meant to counter the Minimalist aesthetic of the 1960s, which Schapiro and other feminists considered typically male.

Many feminists accepted and celebrated the notion that women have a deeper identification with nature than do men, a belief evident in a number of artworks from the 1970s, including those by Cuban-born Ana Mendieta (1948–1985). By 1972 Mendieta had rejected painting for performance and body art, which she documented through photography, film, and video. Inspired by the customs of Santería, an Afro-Caribbean religion emphasizing immersion in nature, she produced a series of ritualistic performances on film and about 200 earth and body works, called Silhouettes, which she recorded

example, belongs among the feminists if one focuses on the content of much of her work but with the Super Realists if one emphasizes her style (see fig. 29-53).

While events on the East Coast focused on gaining more attention for women artists, on the West Coast two feminist artists and teachers, Judy Chicago (b. 1939) and Miriam Schapiro (b. 1923), established in 1971 at the new California Institute of the Arts (CalArts) the Feminist Art Program, dedicated to training women artists.

Born Judy Cohen in the city whose name she took in 1970, Chicago was originally a Minimalist sculptor, but at the end of the 1960s she began to use female sexual imagery to expose the sexism of the male-dominated art world. Her most famous piece is *The Dinner Party* (fig. 29-61). The finished work, the combined labor of hundreds of women and several men, records the names of 999 notable women and pays special homage to 39 historic and legendary women—from Egyptian Queen Hatshepsut to Georgia O'Keeffe. Each side of the triangular table has thirteen settings, because thirteen is the number of witches in a coven and the number of men at the Last Supper. The triangular shape is a symbol for woman and during the French Revolution was an emblem of

29-63. Ana Mendieta. Untitled work from the Tree of Life series. 1977. Color photograph, 20 x 13¼"
(50.8 x 33.7 cm)

Courtesy Galerie Lelong, New York. © The Estate of Ana Mendieta

29-64. David Salle. *We'll Shake the Bag.* 1980. Acrylic on canvas, 5 x 7' (1.52 x 2.13 m). Collection Ellen and Ellis Kern

Courtesy Gagosian Gallery

in color photographs. Some were done in Mexico, and others, like the Tree of Life series (fig. 29-63), were set in Iowa, where she had moved in 1961, after the Cuban Revolution. In Tree of Life, Mendieta stands covered with mud, her arms upraised like a prehistoric goddess, appearing at one with nature, her "maternal source."

POST-MODERNISM

Much of the art being made by the end of the 1970s was widely considered to be *postmodern.* Although there has been virtually no universal agreement on just what this term means, it involves rejection of the concept of the mainstream and a recognition of artistic **pluralism**, the acceptance of a variety of artistic intentions and styles. A number of critics have resisted using the label *postmodern*, insisting that pluralism applies to modernism as well and has been a characteristic of art since at least the Post-Impressionist era. Others, in response, argue that the art world's attitude toward pluralism has changed. Where critics and artists previously searched for what they considered a historically inevitable mainstream in the midst of pluralistic variety, many now accept pluralism for what it probably always was, a manifestation of our culturally heterogeneous age.

Those who resist the label *postmodern* also point to the continued use of the term *avant-garde* to describe the most recent developments in art. But whereas *avant-garde* formerly indicated a significant newness, it now lacks that connotation. Indeed, many recent avant-garde styles implicitly acknowledge the exhaustion of the old modernist faith in innovation—and in what it implied about the "progressive" course of history—by reviving older styles. For this reason, the names of a number of recent styles, in both art and architecture, begin with the prefix *neo*, denoting a new and different form of something that already exists.

Neo-Expressionism

A number of shows in leading New York art galleries in 1980 signaled the emergence of the first of the neos, Neo-Expressionism. The renewed interest in expressionism, long thought dead, was inspired partly by the emphasis on personal feeling in feminist art and by the example of Philip Guston. Although six of the nineteen artists discussed in an early assessment of Neo-Expressionism in the magazine *Art in America* (December 1982–January 1983) were women, some of them, like Rothenberg, never fit comfortably under the label *Neo-Expressionist.* Other women were soon dropped from the category when critics decided, perhaps somewhat prematurely, that the style was a male phenomenon, reasserting masculine values and viewpoints.

David Salle (b. 1952) has been considered typical of Neo-Expressionism, even though only some aspects of his work are truly expressionistic. Salle studied at CalArts with the Post-Conceptual photographer John Baldessari (b. 1931) and then worked at various jobs, including layout work for a pornographic magazine. Salle combines in his work a variety of source imagery, which he projects onto his canvases and copies. In *We'll Shake the Bag* (fig. 29-64), for example, Salle took the the outlines from an old photograph of boys trying to hold apples in their mouths at a Halloween party and painted them over a scene from a movie. Although the relationship between the two images is not entirely clear, the placement of elements suggests that the woman in bed, now somewhat sad and distant from the man she has just been intimate with, is contemplating more innocent times. In relation to this contrast of innocence and postinnocence, the apples remind one of the temptation of Adam and Eve and of its consequences, the Fall of humanity. While few of Salle's works tell such a clear story, their fragmented parts, poor drafting, and impure, dissonant colors all seem to give evidence of the modern, post-Edenic state.

Once a roommate of Salle at CalArts, Eric Fischl (b. 1948) took a more critical view of the flawed present. Impressed by the emotional and personal content of recent feminist art, in 1976 he invented the Fishers, an archetypal Canadian seafaring family, around whom he built a body of related paintings. The Fishers were an apparent surrogate for the less idyllic Fischl family in which he had grown up in suburban Long Island, New York. Although many of his paintings about American suburban life had connections with his own, what Fischl set out to create about 1980 was a portrait of a class.

Many of his early paintings involve the middle-class pursuit of pleasure. Some, like *A Visit To/A Visit From/The Island* (fig. 29-65), feature an American family on vacation in the tropics. Signaling their desire to "return to nature" à la Gauguin, a mother and her children are naked on an island beach. Although the woman relaxes on a foam mattress, the scene is crowded, nervously painted, and, judging by the motorboat, noisy. The daughter, who stands idly by, seems bored. The unsuccessful "escape" to the tropics is contrasted with the consequences of a more literal attempt at escape shown in the right panel. Here islanders on a stormy beach react to the sight of their dead comrades (one of whose legs seems almost to extend from the sunbathing woman in the left panel), apparently drowned in a desperate bid to flee the island. Exactly what is going on is uncertain, however. Fischl's intention is not to tell a story with a clear conclusion but to force viewers to confront for themselves his ambiguous and morally troubling images.

29-66. Francesco Clemente. Untitled. 1983. Oil on canvas, 6'6" x 7'9" (1.98 x 2.36 m). Collection Thomas Ammann Fine Art, Zürich

The Resurgence of European Art

In the early 1980s the work of a number of European artists, much of it stylistically consistent with the Neo-Expressionism then coming into vogue in the United States, gained widespread critical recognition. The Italian artist Francesco Clemente (b. 1952), for example, searching for an alternative to what he considered the overintellectualization of Italian art and criticism, developed a largely anti-intellectual and amoral form of Neo-Expressionism. Sensual experience and bodily functions became central elements of Clemente's art after he spent 1977 living in Madras, India. His basic premise is stated in an untitled painting (fig. 29-66) that is a kind of self-portrait. In each opening of the subject's head is another head, suggesting that we are what we see, hear, smell, and taste. The work is crudely painted, reflecting a deliberate lack of effort—particularly intellectual effort—and

29-67. Anselm Kiefer. *Heath of the Brandenburg March.* 1984. Oil, acrylic, and shellac on burlap, 3'10½" x 8'4" (1.18 x 2.54 m). Stedelijk Van Abbemuseum, Eindhoven, the Netherlands

testifying to Clemente's pursuit of basic sensation. The problem with ordinary thought, Clemente felt, is that it takes us beyond direct experience to meaning. "Keep on the surface," he advises, "don't look for meaning." Thus, Clemente, like Salle, does not struggle to change, transcend, or even understand the world around him. He tries simply to experience and accept it.

American interest in contemporary European artists increased in 1981, when German art was shown in galleries all over New York City. One of the most fascinating of these German artists was Anselm Kiefer (b. 1945). Born in the final weeks of World War II—in what Germans who wished to erase it from collective memory called Year Zero—Kiefer has long sought to come to grips with his country's Nazi past. In 1969 he produced a book of photographs showing himself offering the Nazi salute in various European sites that had been occupied by Germans during the war. Interpreted by many as a rightwing celebration of Hitler's conquests, the book raised a storm of controversy.

In the early 1970s Kiefer turned to painting but continued his efforts to get other Germans to confront their country's troubled history, "in order," he said, "to understand the madness." The burned and barren landscape in *Heath* (fig. 29-67) evokes the ravages of war that the Brandenburg area, near Berlin, has frequently experienced, most recently in World War II. The road that lures us into the landscape, a standard device in nineteenth-century landscape paintings, here invites us into the history of this region. Like those of his American counterpart Fischl, Kiefer's works compel viewers to come to grips with troubling historical and social realities.

Kiefer's unofficial mentor, Joseph Beuys (1921–1986), helped shape Kiefer's sense of art's social mission. Beuys was one of several older German artists whose reputations in the United States rose dramatically with the resurgent interest in European art. A fighter pilot during World War II, Beuys was shot down over the Soviet Union in 1943 and was saved by nomadic Tatars. Apparently in an effort to assuage the guilt and anxiety with which his war experiences left him, Beuys elaborated his rescue by the Tatars into a personal mythology of rebirth, which became central to his art. After joining Fluxus in 1962 he began producing performance art based on an exaggerated account of this experience in which he insisted not only that the Tatars had saved him—by wrapping him in fat and animal-hair felt—but that their leader had made him an honorary member of their community.

For his 1974 *Coyote: I Like America and America Likes Me* (fig. 29-68), Beuys landed in New York, was wrapped in felt, and was taken by ambulance to a Manhattan gallery, part of which was cordoned off with industrial chain-link fencing. Inside was a live coyote, a symbol of the American wilderness threatened with extinction by modern industrial society. For seven days Beuys and the coyote lived together. Beuys, wrapped in a felt tent from which a shepherd's crook protruded, silently followed the animal around, sometimes mimicking it. Beuys saw felt, in which the Tatars had supposedly wrapped him, as a regenerative natural material, one capable of healing the sick. The crook is the Tatar shaman's symbol. The artist was thus presenting himself as the shaman, come to help save the wildlife of the United States and in this way heal a sick nation. The artist's arrival in an ambulance suggested that he, too, was threatened and needed healing. In effect, the work showed two endangered species healing each other through their mutual communion. The work celebrates the power of empathy to save a world threatened, according to Beuys, by cutthroat economic and political competition.

Another long-neglected European whose reputation rose sharply in the 1980s was Lucian Freud (b. 1922). The grandson of Sigmund Freud, Lucian was born in Berlin and moved with his family to England in 1933. Inspired

29-68. Joseph Beuys. *Coyote: I Like America and America Likes Me.* 1974. Weeklong action staged in the René Block Gallery, New York
Courtesy Ronald Feldman Fine Arts, New York

29-69. Lucian Freud. *Naked Portrait with Reflection.* 1980. Oil on canvas, 35½ x 35½" (90.3 x 90.3 cm). Private collection

by the work of his friend Francis Bacon (see fig. 29-3), he gradually loosened his style, beginning around 1960. Although expressionistic elements appear in his late work, he remained a realist. Freud took his subjects from a group of acquaintances. In his later work he usually portrayed them nude, as in *Naked Portrait with Reflection* (fig. 29-69). Although the woman lies in a characteristically erotic pose, she seems more tired than relaxed or alluring—an impression reinforced by the condition of the couch and Freud's choice of colors. Her flesh is heavy and sad and echoes her weary expression. The painting conveys a sense of the irrevocable processes of age and the body's inevitable decay. Lushly painted, it seems to suggest from a distance that art can provide some consolation for the sadness of life. Up close, however, the coarsely caked paint on the woman's face is a frank reminder of human mortality.

A number of the Europeans suddenly accorded attention in North America were women, including the Polish sculptor Magdalena Abakanowicz (b. 1930). Raised on a 5,000-acre estate outside Warsaw, Abakanowicz saw her mother's arm shot off by the Nazis and her father reduced to running a newsstand in Warsaw under the Communists. In order to study at art school, she was forced to hide her aristocratic background. In the late 1960s she began producing large woven reliefs that soon gave way to figural pieces that challenged the conventional distinctions between craft and sculpture.

Typical of her work is *Backs* (fig. 29-70), eighty headless, limbless, genderless, and hollow-front impressions made on a single mold over a five-year period. The anonymous figures appear to be both resigned and worshiping. Abakanowicz hopes they will convey more than the capacity of humans to endure difficult situations, such as the ones she and other Poles faced under the Germans and the communists. "People ask me," she says, "is this the concentration camp in Auschwitz or is

29-70. Magdalena Abakanowicz. *Backs.* 1976–80. Burlap and resin, each piece approximately 25¾ x 21¾ x 23¾" (65.4 x 55.3 x 60.3 cm). Installed near Calgary, Canada, 1982. Collection of Museum of Modern Art, Pusan, South Korea

it a religious ceremony in Peru . . . and I answer all these questions, 'yes,' because it is . . . about existence in general" (cited in Wheeler, page 322). When shown in nature, as here, the figures appear to grow out of and form a part of it, a result of their organic shapes as well as their materials: coarse, brown, resin-impregnated burlap and twine meant to resemble soil and roots. As a child on the family estate she had developed a deep faith in nature as a spiritual resource. Ultimately, then, *Backs* is a testament to the forces that sustained her through the difficulties of her life and early career.

29-71. Keith Haring. *Art in Transit.* 1982
Courtesy Estate of Keith Haring

During the 1970s the East Village section of New York City was colonized by young artists and art students such as Haring, particularly those from the School of Visual Arts, in search of low-cost housing and gallery space. In addition to alternative galleries and performance-art spaces, a host of nightclubs catering to this clientele sprang up in the area. The art produced by these young artists, often inspired by street graffiti, was frequently used to decorate these nightclubs.

29-72. Jean-Michel Basquiat. *Flexible.* 1984. Acrylic and oilstick on wood, 7'4" x 6'3" (2.59 x 1.9 m)
Courtesy Robert Miller Gallery, New York

Graffiti Art

Another formerly marginal arena that caught the attention of the New York art world about 1980 was street art, or **graffiti** art. The movement took shape following an exhibition called the "Times Square Show," held in an old massage parlor in 1980.

One of the artists to emerge from the "Times Square Show" was Keith Haring (1958–1990), who had been invited to participate on the basis of his graffiti-inspired paintings on black photographic backdrop paper. In 1981 Haring took his art into New York City subway stations. On the black panels used to block out obsolete advertising, he began to make cheerful chalk drawings, like *Art in Transit* (fig. 29-71), of a memorable cast of characters in a distinctive linear style. Haring said he was committed to an art "open to everybody" that would "break down this supposed barrier between low art and high art." His work includes a personalized symbolism, however, that many found puzzling. When asked what a particular figure meant, he answered, "That's your part; I only do the drawings." The figure shown here is the harried commuter, whose head is sometimes a clock but in this example is a radiant heart, a sign of love and perhaps, as one critic observed, of "the unifying force that courses through all beings and things."

Jean-Michel Basquiat (1960–1988) developed a more political brand of graffiti art. Basquiat, originally a street artist whose graffiti featured witty philosophical texts, was invited to paint a large wall for the "Times Square Show." His success encouraged him to begin painting professionally. To give his work a less sophisticated look and to demonstrate his allegiance with naive artists of the Caribbean, he often painted on crudely constructed canvases and surfaces made from wooden slats, as in *Flexible* (fig. 29-72). Although he was untrained and wanted to make "paintings that look as if they were made by a child," he was a sophisticated artist. He carefully studied the Abstract Expressionists, Picasso's late paintings, and the works of Dubuffet (see fig. 29-4), among others.

Like much of his work, *Flexible* features an African American male, perhaps the artist, with angry eyes and mouth. On his head he wears a combination crown and crown of thorns, a symbol Basquiat used to convey a sense of both superiority and suffering. The figure's flexible arms, which give the work its title, may suggest the social flexibility required of people, like the artist, who must live within both their own minority culture and the dominant culture of the larger society. As in paintings in the so-called **x-ray** style of the Australian Aborigines (see fig. 24-2), Basquiat shows the figure's internal organs, perhaps suggesting that beneath the skin we all share a common humanity.

Neo-Conceptualism

An analytic and often cynical style emerged in the mid-1980s that seemed to be a reaction to both the emotionalism of Neo-Expressionism and the populism of graffiti

29-73. Mark Tansey. *Triumph of the New York School.* 1984. Oil on canvas, 6'2" x 10' (1.88 x 3.05 m). Whitney Museum of American Art, New York

Promised gift of Robert M. Kaye

Tansey is the son of art historians. Inspired by the deconstructive critical method of Jacques Derrida, he set out around 1980, as he said, to "problematize and destabilize" some of the leading dogmas in the discourse of contemporary art. He made his monochromatic paintings to resemble photographs because of that medium's reputation for unvarnished truthfulness.

art. Known as Neo-Conceptualism, it reflected the influence of the difficult and usually skeptical ideas on literature, philosophy, and society of a group of French intellectuals—among them Roland Barthes (1915–1980), Jacques Derrida (b. 1930), Jean Baudrillard (b. 1929), and Michel Foucault (1926–1984)—who had become popular among American intellectuals in the late 1970s.

One Neo-Conceptualist, the representational painter Mark Tansey (b. 1949), evolved a working technique by the mid-1980s that involved photocopying elements from his growing picture file and then collaging these pieces into various configurations that allowed him to explore a subject slowly and methodically. Characteristic of his work is *Triumph of the New York School* (fig. 29-73), a brownish monochrome painting that resembles the kind of photographic reproduction that used to appear in Sunday newspapers. The title refers to the received wisdom in art history that the New York School wrested control of art's mainstream from the Paris School after World War II. Tansey's painting, playing on the word *triumph*, depicts the event as a military victory formally recognized by the combatants on both sides—the French on the left in the uniforms of World War I, the Americans on the right in the uniforms of World War II—with the sign-ing of a document of surrender. All the soldiers are identifiable artists and writers. Signing the surrender document for the French, for example, is the Surrealist leader André Breton. Behind him, dressed in fur, is Picasso. The American soldier at the table is Clement Greenberg, smoking a cigarette behind him Jackson Pollock. The work is rich with ironies and subtle references. That Greenberg's "triumph" should be recorded in a backward-looking illusionistic style is but one. In addition to providing a series of tantalizing intellectual treats for the sophisticated viewer, the work's main purpose, following the ideas of the French intellectuals, is to unsettle conventional notions about history and truth. The juxtaposition of soldiers from World War I surrendering to those from World War II is absurd, as is the metaphorical comparison between art and warfare. And in another irony, the photographylike image of an impossible event calls into question the documentary reliability of that medium.

The work of Louise Lawler (b. 1947) also undertakes a thought-provoking investigation into artistic issues. About 1980 she began to document how specific presentations of art objects—from public museums to private homes to exhibition catalogs—reveal the way art is actually used and, thus, how it is conceived. Her photograph

29-74. Louise Lawler. *Pollock and Tureen*. 1984. Cibachrome, 28 x 39" (71 x 99 cm)
Courtesy Metro Pictures, New York

29-75. Peter Halley. *Yellow Cell with Conduits*. 1985. Acrylic and Day-Glo on canvas, 5'4" x 5'4" (1.63 x 1.63 m)
Courtesy the artist

Pollock and Tureen (fig. 29-74), for example, was taken in a private home. It shows a detail of one of Pollock's drip paintings hanging above a sideboard with an antique soup tureen tastefully flanked by two vintage casserole dishes. The classical format and the subtle harmonies between the linear rhythms in the Pollock and those on the tureen's surface and in its shape might suggest that Lawler meant simply to make an aesthetically pleasing photograph. However, her intention was in fact to show how the treatment of this famous painting as a decorative object within a setting of other decorative objects alters the vital meaning that it had for Pollock. The irony here, which Lawler fully appreciates, is that her lovely photograph contributes to this subversion of the painting's meaning. Lawler does not mean to criticize the collectors so much as simply to open to analysis—and its pleasure—the way art objects take on meaning in context.

An equally nonjudgmental social commentary can be found in the work of Peter Halley (b. 1953), which reflects the influence of the French social critics Jean Baudrillard and Michel Foucault. Baudrillard has argued that movies, television, and advertising have made ours the age of the "simulacrum," the substitution of images that simulate reality. These images, moreover, often seem "hyperreal," or more real than the world they purport to reflect. The television stereotype of the average American family, for example, has replaced the social reality of family life, and advertising employs supersaturated colors to make products seem hyperreal.

Halley realized that the fluorescent **Day-Glo** colors he had been using in his work were themselves signs of this new social phenomenon. Moreover, he also began to question the Minimalist assertion that abstract forms are referentially neutral; for example, the stripes in a Stella painting from the mid-1960s could as easily be interpreted as a metaphor for the interstate highway system as an exercise in pure form. By the beginning of the 1980s Halley was making abstract paintings with forms intended to be read as meaningful signs of the contemporary cultural phenomena described by Baudrillard and Foucault.

In *Yellow Cell with Conduits* (fig. 29-75), one of his so-called Neo-Geo (or new geometry) paintings, he applied hyperreal colors to the kind of simulated stucco used in suburban housing. This false stucco surface is itself, therefore, a sign of the new domination of the simulacrum. The large central square, or cell, represents both the home and the brain (which is composed of cells). The rectangular forms that connect with it thus refer on one level to plumbing and electrical circuitry, and on another to information reaching the brain. With the latter idea, the lower piping represents information reaching the brain from the subconscious and the upper piping represents information coming to it through conscious processes. Finally, the central cell has yet another meaning, that of jail, or imprisonment, a reference to Foucault's claim that modern bureaucratic political regimes imprison the individual. The central square has therefore three referents: home, brain cell, and prison cell. Halley's intent in works like *Yellow Cell with Conduits* is not to protest troubling social phenomena but to find an interesting way to illustrate them. The work of all the Neo-Conceptualists has been called "endgame" art, a reference to the moves in a chess game when loss is inevitable.

One of the most famous endgame moves was made by Sherrie Levine (b. 1947), who is known for work in which she "appropriates," or borrows, images from art history (see "Appropriation," page 1155). In 1981 she began to attack the predominantly male Neo-Expressionist movement and its ideas about originality and individuality by making photographic copies of famous twentieth-century originals. As she explained, "I felt

29-76. Sherrie Levine. *Untitled (After Aleksandr Rodchenko: 11)*. 1987. Black-and-white photograph, 20 x 16" (50.8 x 40.6 cm)
Courtesy Marian Goodman Gallery, New York

angry at being excluded. As a woman, I felt there was not room for me. The whole art system was geared to celebrating . . . male desire." Her endgame response was to copy only the work of male artists.

Untitled (After Aleksandr Rodchenko: 11) (fig. 29-76) is not an homage to the Russian Constructivist (see fig. 28-78) but a critique of certain ideas associated with him and with modernism. Levine's work is inspired by the deconstructionism of Jacques Derrida, in which he unravels, or "deconstructs," prevailing cultural assumptions, or "myths," by revealing them to contain self-conflicting messages. By appropriating images of men associated with originality and innovation—the viewpoint of Rodchenko's photography, for example, was considered wholly innovative—Levine intended to deconstruct those concepts and suggest that all art and thought are derivative.

Later Feminism

Because of the feminist content of much of her work, Levine may also be grouped with a second generation of feminists. These artists, who emerged in the 1980s, tended to believe in the idea that differences between the sexes are not intrinsic but fabricated, or "socially constructed," primarily by media images and other cultural forces, to suit the needs of those in power. According to this view, young people, particularly women, learn how to behave

APPROPRIATION During the late 1970s and 1980s, **appropriation**, or the representation of a preexisting image as one's own, became a popular technique among postmodernists in both the United States and Western Europe. The borrowing of figures or compositions has been an essential technique throughout the history of art, but the emphasis had always been on changing or personalizing the source. A copy or reproduction was not considered a legitimate work of art until Marcel Duchamp changed the rules with his **"ready-mades"** (see fig. 28-1). His insistence that the quality of an artwork depends not on formal invention but on the ideas that stand behind it established the theoretical basis for the recent popularity of the technique. Duchamp's own type of appropriations first inspired the Pop artists Andy Warhol and Roy Lichtenstein, whose reuse of imagery from popular culture, high art, ordinary commerce, and the tabloids, in turn, helped point the way for the artists of the 1970s and 1980s.

Unfortunately, perhaps, critics and historians now use the term *appropriation* to describe the activities of two distinct groups. To the first belong artists such as John Baldessari and his student David Salle (see fig. 29-64), who combine and shape their borrowings in personal ways. These artists, along with earlier ones such as Robert Rauschenberg (see fig. 29-24), might be called "collage appropriators." "Straight appropriators," on the other hand, are those, such as Richard Prince, Mike Bidlo, and Sherrie Levine, who simply repaint or rephotograph imagery from commerce or the history of art and present it as their own.

The work of the latter is grounded not only in the Duchampian tradition but also in the recent ideas of the French literary critics known collectively as the Post-Structuralists. Of particular importance was their critique of certain basic and unexamined assumptions about art. In "Death of the Author" (1968), for example, Roland Barthes argued that the meaning of a work of art depends not on what the author meant (which Derrida and others argued was neither certain nor entirely recoverable) but on what the reader understands. Furthermore, Barthes questioned the modernist notion of originality, of the author as a creator of an entirely new meaning. The author, Barthes argued, merely recycles meanings from other sources, saying that a "text is a tissue of quotations drawn from the innumerable centers of culture" (cited in Fineberg, page 454). The work of Prince, Bidlo, and Levine seemed almost to illustrate such ideas.

The "straight appropriators" soon ran into a legal problem. Levine's first high-art reproductions were rephotographs of Edward Weston originals. When lawyers for the Weston estate threatened to sue her for infringement of copyright, she moved to the work Walker Evans produced during the 1930s for the Works Progress Administration, which has no copyright. Others faced with the possibility of legal action, especially from owners of commercial trademarks, have taken the same cautious route. What remains to be settled, then, is whether commercial copyright protections, when applied to art, constitute an infringement of freedom of speech.

29-77. Barbara Kruger. *We Won't Play Nature to Your Culture.* 1983. Photostat, red painted frame, 6'1" x 4'1" (1.85 x 1.24 m)

Courtesy Mary Boone Gallery, New York

During the 1970s Kruger had participated in the fiber-arts movement inaugurated by Miriam Schapiro. One of her wall hangings was included in the 1973 Whitney Biennial.

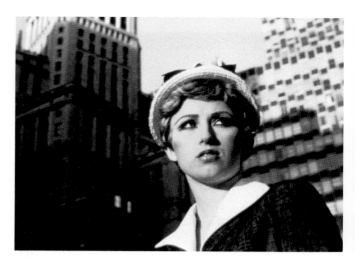

29-78. Cindy Sherman. *Untitled Film Still.* 1978. Black-and-white photograph, 8 x 10" (20.3 x 25.4 cm)

Courtesy Metro Pictures, New York

from the role models they see heralded in magazines, movies, and other sources of cultural coercion. A major task of feminism and feminist art should, therefore, be to resist the power of these forces.

Barbara Kruger (b. 1945) is an important representative of this generation. Drawing on her experience as a designer and photo editor for women's magazines, by the end of the 1970s she began creating works that combined glossy high-contrast images, usually borrowed from advertisements, and bold, easily readable, catchy texts. The purpose of such work was to undermine the media with its own devices, "to break myths," as she put it, "not to create them."

Although she has said of her work that it can be effective in questioning sexual representations, at times she seems to express a sense of futility as well. In *We Won't Play Nature to Your Culture* (fig. 29-77), for example, the voice is strong and defiant but the text is weak. The work states that women will no longer accept the dichotomy—forced on them by men—between men as producers of culture and women as products of nature, but the woman lies passively on her back and is symbolically blinded by the leaves over her eyes.

One of the most written about of the later feminists is Cindy Sherman (b. 1954). After moving from Buffalo to New York City in 1977, she began working on a series of black-and-white photographs that simulate stills from B-grade movies of the 1940s and 1950s. Each photograph from the series, which numbered about seventy-five, shows a single female figure, always Sherman in some guise. In *Untitled Film Still* (fig. 29-78) she is dressed as a perplexed young innocent apparently recently arrived in a big city, its buildings looming threateningly behind her. The image suggests a host of films in which some such character is overwhelmed by dangerous forces, perhaps to be destroyed, or perhaps to be rescued by some male hero. In the context of feminist film criticism's emphasis on the negative impact of movie "representations" that showed women as helpless creatures who need a man to care for them, it appeared that Sherman intended to re-create such roles as part of a critical, deconstructive agenda. Sherman lent this interpretation support when she said she was "making fun of these role models of women from my childhood" (cited in Marks, page 359). Such works were also a pure form of play, however, one that she had loved as a child and continued to engage in as an adolescent. And finally, the roles she played in her first film stills may be a response to her own experience in the big city.

Art and the Public

The issue of the relationship between art and the community at large, long a central concern of the modern period, took on a new prominence in the 1990s and seems destined to shape emerging styles and trends. As artists take advantage of such new mediums as video (see "Video Art," page 1157), they nevertheless continue their search for a set of artistic principles to replace the old modernist ones. At the same time, their search—and their community's response to it—is resulting in many sensational controversies involving public funding, censorship, and individual rights.

One of the most consistent public artists is Jenny Holzer (b. 1950), whose work is often grouped with that of the later feminists. In the mid-1970s Holzer took a course in the history of contemporary art at the Whitney Museum of American Art in New York City. The reading, much of it by the poststructuralists who influenced the Neo-Conceptualists, seemed to her "important and profound." She then set out to try "to translate these things into a language that was accessible. The result was the *Truisms*." For two years, 1977 and 1978, she rephrased the ideas from her reading as one-liners suited to the reading habits of Americans raised on advertising messages. She compiled these statements in alphabetical lists, had them printed, and plastered them all over her neighborhood. With an accumulation of remarks reflecting a variety of viewpoints and voices, such as "Any Surplus Is Immoral" and "Morality Is for Little People," she hoped to "instill some sense of tolerance in the onlookers or the reader."

Since her first posters, Holzer has moved progressively into mediums that would allow her to address even wider audiences. She turned to some of advertising's more technical tools, including electronic signage, to reach more than the proportionally small number of people who

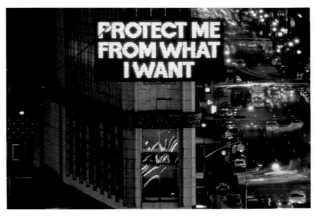

29-79. Jenny Holzer. *Protect Me from What I Want*, excerpt from Survival series. 1985–86. Spectacolor board, Times Square, New York
Courtesy Barbara Gladstone Gallery, New York

go to galleries and museums. Moreover, she preferred to use popular media devices already in place. In her Survival series (fig. 29-79), for example, she used the Spectacolor board in New York City's Times Square to flash a series of short, provocative messages, now in her own words. The one illustrated here, *Protect Me from What I Want*, is a ref-

VIDEO ART Among the many new mediums of art making created by the technology revolution in the late twentieth century, the video monitor is one of the most provocative. The video form, like film, uses a variety of approaches and styles, from raw documentary material to scripted theatrical performance, from animation to pure abstraction. As in film, time is an element of the medium, and video art may consist of images only seconds long or may be a full-length feature. A key difference is that for the video artist the monitor is itself a visible part of the artwork.

Video art may use sophisticated computer programs or a simple handheld video camera. It may include only still images or a running narrative. Originally an inexpensive alternative to film, video has its own distinctive visual qualities, often including washed-out or intense color; unlikely juxtapositions of images and scenes; jerky, staccato camera motions; rough cutting; and a sense of spontaneity and immediacy, as in home movies. The essential technical distinction between video and film is that video is based on an electronic transmission of images, while film is a sequence of translucent images, using projected light and motion.

Because video has developed in a period in which many artists are self-consciously avant-garde, video artists pay particular attention to the relationship between the imagery of popular culture (commercial television, newscasts, advertising) and the traditional arts of painting and sculpture. Video art may be distinguished from other kinds of video (a television show, for example) by its special concern with the visual values of the screen images and its critical, often ironic view of the mass-media television culture to which it refers. Video art is often political in content, and like some experimental dance and theater, it links the performing arts with the visual arts.

Video art sometimes uses monitors inserted as elements within larger sculptures or structures, such as Nam June Paik's 1995 *Electronic Superhighway*. It may be austere and minimal, such as Bruce Nauman's ethereal self-portraits, or quite ornate, as in Paik's colorful, rapidly flickering multiple patterns, which are often computer-generated or manipulated. Installations may be accompanied by sound, music, or a voice-over, and some are interactive, including cameras that permit the viewer to enter the artwork by

appearing on screen. Peter Greenaway and Tom Phillip's collaborations produce painterly collages. Feminist artist Adrian Piper makes harsh, raw, talking heads. Some video art shows the stylized theatricality of performance art, as in the work of Matthew Barney. Alan Rath's richly humorous composite creatures have eyes and noses made from tiny, odd-shaped video screens.

Nam June Paik. *Electronic Superhighway*. 1995. Installation: multiple television monitors, laser disk images, and neon, 15 x 32' (4.57 x 9.75 m). Holly Solomon Gallery, New York
Courtesy Holly Solomon Gallery, New York

erence to the way advertising generates a desire in people for products and services they may not need.

Another socially minded artist who prefers to work outside the museums and galleries is David Hammons (b. 1943). Hammons is an outspoken critic of the gallery system, viewing it as one that encourages and rewards work that is "so watered down that the bourgeoisie can consume it." Art today, he insists, is "like Novocaine. It used to wake you up but now it puts you to sleep." Only street art, uncontaminated by commerce, he maintains, can still serve the old function.

Although Hammons sometimes addresses a broader audience, for the most part his work has been aimed at specific segments of the African-American community. His best-known work is probably *Higher Goals* (fig. 29-80), several versions of which were made between 1982 and 1986. The one shown here, temporarily set up in a Brooklyn park, has backboards and baskets set on telephone poles—a reference to communication—that rise 40 feet into the air. The poles are decorated with bottle caps, a substitute for the cowrie shells used not only in African design but also in some African cultures as money. Although the series may appear to honor the game, Hammons said it is "antibasketball sculpture." "Basketball has become a problem in the black community because kids aren't getting an education. . . . It means you should have higher goals in life than basketball."

As a result of these and many other similar examples, some of them from Europe, the international art world in the 1980s witnessed a growing commitment to the notion that art is most effective as a social tool when it avoids an institutional setting, moves to a specific community, and addresses locally important issues in straightforward language. In other words, like environmental earthworks, socially conscious art seems to function best when it is site-specific.

Following this principle, a European television company collaborated with a regional arts association to commission a series of works for economically and politically troubled places. One of Britain's leading young sculptors, Antony Gormley (b. 1950), was assigned to make a piece for a site overlooking the religiously divided city of Derry in Northern Ireland, a region torn by civil warfare in which Protestants generally support continued union with the United Kingdom and Catholics generally oppose it. From a cast of his own body Gormley made a double image in iron of two figures with arms outstretched, facing away from each other but joined back-to-back (fig. 29-81). With its obvious reference to Jesus on the Cross, the work is a pointed reminder of the countless casualties on both sides—Catholic and Protestant, Irish and British—and a plea to find in shared grief a basis for reconciliation and unity. Within days of installation, the piece was vandalized with political graffiti and a burned tire was hung around its neck, a demonstration that the work had at least been taken seriously.

In the late 1980s Europeans also pioneered a new kind of site-specific art exhibition, temporary pieces by several artists set up throughout a particular community, all dealing with a single relevant political or historical

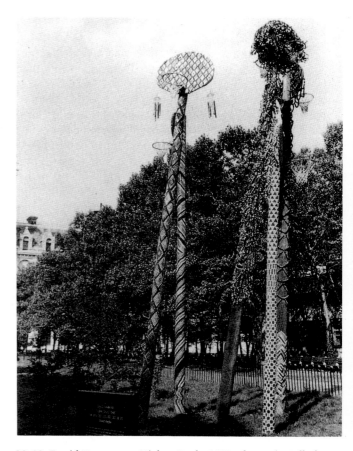

29-80. David Hammons. *Higher Goals*. 1982, shown installed in Brooklyn, New York, 1986. Five poles of mixed mediums, including basketball hoops and bottle caps, maximum height of tallest pole 35' (10.6m)

Hammons likes to allow local conditions and issues to dictate the subjects and to some degree the appearance of his public sculpture. In preparation for a given piece, he goes out onto the streets to discover the local concerns. He admits that in order "to let the community speak, I have to give up my ego."

issue. In 1991 the directors of the Spoleto Festival U.S.A., in Charleston, South Carolina, decided to emulate this European precedent with an event called "Places with a Past." The event's curator invited eighteen artists, including Gormley and Hammons, to find sites in the city for temporary works that would provide an "intimate and meaningful exchange" with the citizens of Charleston on issues from its history.

Because Charleston had been a center for the slave trade in the South and was the place where the Civil War began, Ann Hamilton (b. 1956) originally planned to deal with the issue of slavery in her work for "Places with a Past." When she found an abandoned automobile repair shop on Pinkney Street, however, she decided to treat an aspect of American life ordinarily overlooked by most historians. The street was named for Eliza Lucas Pinkney, who in 1744 introduced the cultivation of indigo to the American colonies. Indigo produces a blue dye used for, among other things, blue-collar work clothes. Hamilton thus decided to use the garage—a blue-collar workplace—for a piece she called *Indigo Blue* (fig. 29-82), the focal point of the piece being a pile of about 48,000 neatly folded work pants and shirts. However, *Indigo Blue* is more a tribute to the women who washed, ironed, and

29-81. Antony Gormley. *Derry Sculpture*. 1987. Cast iron, 6'5⅛" x 6'4" x 1'9¼" (1.96 x 1.93 x 0.54 m)
Courtesy the artist

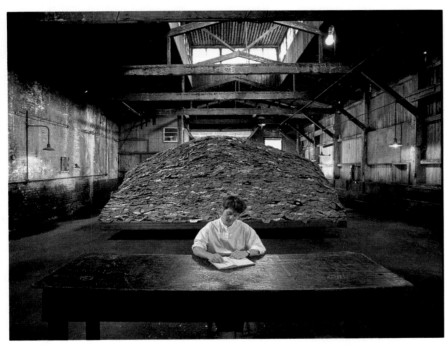

29-82. Ann Hamilton. *Indigo Blue*. 1991. Installation for "Places with a Past," Spoleto Festival U.S.A., Charleston, South Carolina

folded such clothes than to the men who worked in them. The piece is meant to show respect for the labor involved in laundry. In fact, Hamilton and a few women helpers, including her mother, did all the folding and piling. In front of the great mound of shirts and pants sat a woman erasing the contents of old history books—creating page space, Hamilton claimed, for the ordinary, working-class people usually omitted from conventional histories.

The many references and meanings in Hamilton's work perhaps escaped most viewers, though its impressive visual force and moral integrity may have affected many at some level. This piece illustrates a central problem faced by artists trying to communicate to a large public: To what extent should the artist be willing to compromise artistic vision for clear communication?

"Places with a Past" was funded partly through a $200,000 grant from the National Endowment for the Arts (NEA), an agency of the federal government established in 1965 to help support writers, dancers, artists, and the organizations that make their work available to the American public, as well as to fund community art-education programs. In the spring of 1989, the NEA came under fire from members of Congress who threatened to curtail or eliminate the agency's funding because they were offended by the works of a few artists who had received direct or indirect funds from the NEA. Since then, the threat to the NEA and other arts agencies has grown, amplified by those who believe the government has no business spending tax dollars on the arts.

One of the principals who figured in this controversy was Karen Finley (b. 1956), a performance artist. Her work is raw, uninhibited, and, while it often conveys a powerful message, certainly not suited to everyone's taste. In *We Keep Our Victims Ready* (fig. 29-83), she

29-83. Karen Finley. *We Keep Our Victims Ready*. Performance at The Kitchen, New York, 1990

In an interview published in 1991 Finley said: "I was really upset when the NEA tried to censure my work as 'obscene,' because I think my work is extremely moral. I'm trying to speak out about sexual violence and how hateful that is, and make it understandable. Yet many times I'm just viewed as 'hysterical'—as a sexual deviant who's 'out of her mind.'"

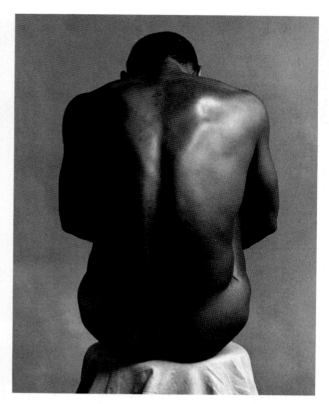

29-84. Robert Mapplethorpe. *Ajitto (Back)*. 1981. Gelatin-silver print, 16 x 20" (40.6 x 50.8 cm). The Robert Mapplethorpe Foundation, New York

denounces the mistreatment of women, the homeless, and people with AIDS by alternately howling, moaning, chanting, crying, and screaming. In another performance that has particularly incensed opponents of NEA and public funding of the arts, she covers her body with chocolate syrup to make a point about the way society perceives women.

An artist whose work was at the core of the controversy over public funding was photographer Robert Mapplethorpe (1946–1989), who was openly gay. Most of the 150 photographs in his 1989–1990 touring retrospective exhibition (funded in part by an NEA grant to the show's organizing institution) consisted of classic studies of nudes and flowers. *Ajitto (Back)* (fig. 29-84), for example, is a fairly conventional investigation of the subtle formal nuances of the human body. Some of the pho-

29-85. Richard Serra. *Tilted Arc*. 1981. Hot-rolled steel, length 120' (36.58 m). Formerly, Federal Plaza, Foley Square, New York; removed in 1989

In his 1989 article on the destruction of the work, Serra pointed out that during a three-day hearing in 1985, some 122 people spoke in favor of retaining the sculpture and only 58 spoke for removal. Moreover, the new petition for removal presented at the hearing had 3,791 signatures, which represented fewer than a quarter of the approximately 12,000 employees in the federal buildings at the site. Also, a petition with 3,763 signatures was presented against removal. He argued that the general perception that the majority of the public wanted its removal was simply untrue, a useful exaggeration for those who simply did not like the work.

29-86. Maya Ying Lin. *Vietnam Veterans Memorial*. 1982. Black granite, length 500' (152 m). The Mall, Washington, D.C.

tographs, however, showed homoerotic subjects and explicit sex acts. Fears of protests by some members of Congress caused the Corcoran Gallery in Washington, D.C., to cancel its plans to mount the show in 1989. The Contemporary Arts Center in Cincinnati, however, presented it in 1990, putting the controversial works in their own room with a clearly printed advisement. Cincinnati officials nevertheless charged the museum and its director with obscenity and put them on trial. The jury was not convinced that the photographs "lack[ed] serious literary, artistic, political, or scientific value"—one of the criteria for obscenity set by the Supreme Court in a 1973 decision—and acquitted the museum and its director. The jury had decided, as one juror commented, "we may not have liked the pictures" but they were art. "We learned," he added, "that art doesn't have to be pretty."

Tilted Arc (fig. 29-85), the Minimalist sculpture by Richard Serra (b. 1939), figured in a different controversy involving art and the public. In this case the issue was the artist's right to control what happens to a work commissioned or purchased for that public. *Tilted Arc*, a steel wall 12 feet high and 120 feet long that tilted 1 foot off its vertical axis, was commissioned for the plaza of a government building complex in New York City on the recommendation of an artists' panel appointed by the NEA. Typical of Serra's work, it was strong, simple, tough, and given its tilt, quite threatening. Some employees in the building found the work objectionable. Calling it an "ugly rusted steel wall" that "rendered useless" their "once beautiful plaza," they petitioned to have it removed. The

government agreed to do so, but Serra went to court to preserve his work. He eventually lost his case, and the sculpture was removed in 1989.

The *Vietnam Veterans Memorial* (fig. 29-86), now widely admired as a fitting and moving testament to the Americans who died in that conflict, was also a subject of public controversy when it was first proposed. In its request for proposals for the design of the monument, the Vietnam Veterans Memorial Fund—composed primarily of veterans themselves—stipulated that the memorial be without political or military content, that it be reflective in character, that it harmonize with its surroundings, and that it include the names of the more than 58,000 dead and missing. In 1981 they awarded the commission to Maya Ying Lin (b. 1960), then an undergraduate in the architecture department at Yale University. Her Minimalist-inspired design called for two 200-foot-long walls (later expanded to almost 250 feet) of polished black granite, to be set into a gradual rise in Constitution Gardens on the Mall in Washington, D.C., meeting at a 136-degree angle at the point where the walls and slope would be at their full 10-foot height. The names of the dead, arranged chronologically in the order in which they died, were to be incised in the stone, with only the dates of the first and last deaths, 1959 and 1975, to be recorded.

While construction was under way, several veterans groups—who had provided much of the approximately $8 million for the project and who had originally supported the Lin proposal—asked that a realistic 8-foot sculpture of three soldiers on patrol be added toward the

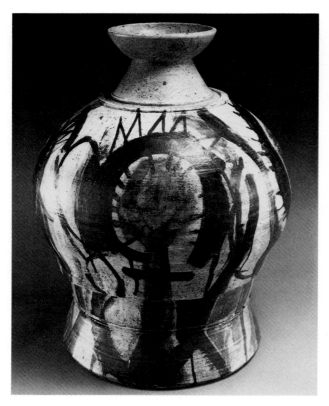

29-87. Peter Voulkos. *Covered Jar*. c. 1956. 25½ x 18½"
(64.8 x 47.0 cm). Everson Museum of Art, Syracuse,
New York
Museum Purchase

apex of the memorial and that a 50-foot flagpole be raised some distance behind. The veterans felt that in this way the survivors, too, would be honored at the site. After much negotiation between the concerned parties, a compromise was worked out whereby the additions would be made farther from the Lin design, at one entrance to the memorial grounds.

Lin's design for the memorial has turned out to be one of the most compelling monuments in the United States, largely because it creates an understated encounter between the living, reflected in the mirrorlike polished granite, and the dead, whose names are etched in its black, inorganic permanence. Quiet and solemn, the work allows visitors the opportunity for individual contemplation. Adding significantly to the memorial's intrinsic power are the many individual mementos, from flowers to items of personal clothing, that have been left below the names of loved ones by friends and relatives.

Art and Craft

Since the Renaissance, Western artists, critics, and art historians have generally maintained a distinction between the so-called high or fine arts—painting, sculpture, and architecture—and the so-called minor arts—such as printmaking, the decorative arts, pottery, and folk art. In recent years, however, the notion that one medium is intrinsically superior to another, like the idea of the mainstream, has come under scrutiny.

Peter Voulkos (b. 1924) is one of many artists who have helped overcome long-standing hierarchical distinctions between art and craft. (Another is glass artist Dale Chihuly; see fig. 13, page 22.) Voulkos was trained as a potter at the California College of Arts and Crafts. His career changed direction when he came under the influence of the gestural painters he met on a visit to New York City in 1953. Inspired by their example, as well as by Picasso's ceramic works, he advocated to his students at the Otis Art Institute in Los Angeles that they freely adapt long-established ceramic traditions to self-expressive ends.

What historians refer to as "the clay revolution," the break from European and Asian traditions, may be said to have begun with a series of ceramic jars Voulkos produced in the mid-1950s. Although some, like the one shown here (fig. 29-87), simply added gesturalist paint and unconscious symbols to the body of a standard vessel type, others rejected tradition entirely for a more revolutionary sculptural approach to the medium. By the late 1950s Voulkos had completely moved away from the pot form and was making monumental, free-form sculptural works.

In 1959 Voulkos left Otis to teach at the University of California at Berkeley, where Robert Arneson (1930–1992), then a conventional potter, became his unofficial student. Under Voulkos's influence Arneson also began experimenting with a more innovative approach to his medium. In 1961, while demonstrating pottery techniques at the California State Fair, he made a sturdy bottle of about quart size, carefully sealed it with a clay bottle cap, and stamped it "No Return." This piece, which provoked the irritation of local critics, was simply the beginning of a series of increasingly uninhibited works that included his John series of toilets—reminiscent of Marcel Duchamp's *Fountain* (see fig. 28-1)—impertinent remakes of famous paintings, and portraits of political figures.

Portrait of George (fig. 29-88) depicts the former San Francisco mayor George Moscone, who with the first openly gay city supervisor, Harvey Milk, was assassinated in 1978 by Dan White, a former city supervisor. Commissioned for San Francisco's new Moscone Center, Arneson's work was considered too irreverent for public display, placed in storage, and later sold to a private collector. The column that supports Moscone's smiling face is adorned with graffitilike writing that gives details of his education and career and the facts surrounding his assassination. The Hostess Twinkies wrapper near the base refers to what has come to be known as the Twinkies defense, the claim that White killed Moscone and Milk while temporarily insane from eating too much junk food. The defense was successful enough that White was sentenced to only eight years in prison.

While the controversy over his portrait of Moscone was raging in San Francisco, another involving Arneson was brewing in New York City as a result of an innovative event at the Whitney Museum: an exhibit of six West Coast ceramists, including Voulkos and Arneson. The first exhibition of its kind in a major New York museum, it appeared to signal the art world's acceptance of ceramics as a legitimate medium for high art.

29-88. Robert Arneson. *Portrait of George*. 1981. Glazed ceramic, height 8' (2.44 m). Collection Foster Gold-strom

Courtesy Estate of Robert Arneson

29-89. Viola Frey. *Woman in Blue and Yellow II*. 1983. Ceramic, 8'8" x 2'2½" x 1'5" (2.64 x 0.67 x 0.43 m)

Courtesy Rena Bransten Gallery, San Francisco

The show was criticized, however, because it included no women. In response, the Whitney organized an exhibition of the work of Viola Frey (b. 1933), another San Francisco Bay Area ceramist. Inspired by Pop art and Arneson's iconoclasm, in the 1960s Frey began to make large-scale works based on the cheap ceramic figurines found in variety stores and flea markets, which reminded her of her childhood. "I decided," she said, "to make them big—take them out of the crib and off the coffee tables, make them myths of childhood." The culmination of this process was the series of 7- to 10-foot figures of women and men that she produced in the late 1970s and 1980s.

The men in this series often appear angry and disapproving, the women either reassuring or fearful. The startled woman in *Woman in Blue and Yellow II* (fig. 29-89), for example, raises her hands protectively. The scale—which

makes adults, including the artist, feel like children—and the 1940s-style clothing suggest that the artist has represented figures and events from her own childhood. By presenting these generalized but often dark events in the beguiling guise of figurines, Frey demonstrates what she sees as the function of figurines: "to make acceptable those things [we find] unacceptable."

The sculptural works of Voulkos, Arneson, and Frey helped ceramics gain acceptance as a high-art medium, leaving intact the distinction between sculpture as art and pottery as craft. The hierarchy of materials had been challenged, but the hierarchy of the arts was still secure. During the 1970s and 1980s, however, a number of critics began to ask why a ceramic pot should not be considered as valuable as a ceramic sculpture. Many of these critics, such as John Perreault, came to question the dogmas of their art-historical training as a result of their

29-91. Romare Bearden. *Quilting Time*. 1985. Paper on board, 19³/₈ x 28¹/₂" (49.2 x 72.4 cm). Founders Society, The Detroit Institute of Arts
Purchased with funds from the Detroit Edison Company

29-90. Lucy M. Lewis. *Black on White Jar with Lightning Pattern*. c. 1970–80. Earthenware, height 5" (12.7 cm), diameter 4" (10.1 cm)
Courtesy Adobe Gallery, Albuquerque, New Mexico
The Lewis heritage is being maintained, in particular, in the work of two of her sons, Ivan and Andrew, and three of her daughters, Emma, Dolores, and Belle.

experience with the new importance given certain craft forms by 1970s feminists (see figs. 29-61, 29-62).

Although critics and historians such as Perreault are still in the minority, they seem to be getting a hearing, partly because of the high quality of the artwork they have attempted to bring to public notice. One of the craft artists who received considerable attention in the 1990s is Pueblo potter Lucy M. Lewis (c. 1900–1992). A member of the Acoma Pueblo people, Lewis grew up near Albuquerque, New Mexico, and learned to make pottery in the traditional manner from her great-aunt. Acoma pottery is based on that of the Anasazi people (Chapter 23), believed to be their ancestors. The Anasazi explored with great ingenuity and finesse a basic format of black paint on a white·ground. The early potters who inherited this tradition quickly transformed it into a less austere and more polychromatic one, adding a greater repertoire of figures to the largely geometric patterns of the Anasazi. Although much of Lewis's work, especially when she was young, was in the traditional orange, brown, and black bird-and-flower patterns, she also revived the austere geometric style of her earlier ancestors, as in *Black on White Jar with Lightning Pattern* (fig. 29-90). The "fine-line decoration" here is Lewis's own invention, inspired

by ancient shards but not a copy of them, seeking personal solutions within the confines of tradition.

Continuity versus Change

The growing interest in works by artists such as Lewis has been fed by a number of extra-aesthetic factors: the fear that traditional methods are fast disappearing; the conviction that art should be an affordable part of daily life, not a luxury item set apart in a gallery or museum; and, not least of all, the psychological appeal that traditional art forms have in an era of rapid, uncertain change. Lewis's pottery, for example, presents a reassuring image of uninterrupted continuity.

The longing for continuity also helps explain the recent interest in the nostalgic **collages** of the African-American artist Romare Bearden (1914–1988). Bearden's professional career went through a number of distinct stages. During the 1930s, while living in Harlem, he participated in the Social Realist movement (see Chapter 28) with biting socially conscious cartoons, some of which dealt with race issues. After the war he produced a series of semiabstract figure paintings devoted to religious subjects before succumbing to the gesturalism that swept up so many North American painters in the 1950s. In the early 1960s Bearden began to experiment with collage, while he was involved in the civil rights movement. But rather than focusing on social injustices, as he had in the 1930s, he began to explore his own pleasant memories of life growing up in rural North Carolina.

Using images cut from popular magazines, Bearden spent the remainder of his life creating delightful representations of a fast-disappearing way of life: slow-paced, communal, and close to nature. *Quilting Time* (fig. 29-91), for example, shows an extended family sitting out of doors on a beautiful, moonlit night, socializing, playing music, and making quilts. The style of the work itself—which features bright, cheerful patterns—pays tribute to both the folk-art tradition of quilting and to the work of other African Americans such as Jacob Lawrence (see fig. 28-117), an artist whom Bearden had known in Harlem in the 1930s.

Part of the success Bearden finally enjoyed at the end of his life depended on the growing influence of **multiculturalism**, the recognition that American culture is a heterogeneous mix of ethnic, racial, sexual, and socioeconomic subcultures. In the domain of the arts, multiculturalism has meant a growing concern to include people of color among those who are exhibited and discussed. The critical interest in artists such as James Hampton (see fig. 11, page 21) and Luis Jimenez (see fig. 16, page 23) is also part of this integrative phenomenon.

Another African American whose work reflects both multiculturalism and the growing taste for an organic type of continuity is the sculptor Martin Puryear (b. 1941). While in the Peace Corps in Sierra Leone on the west coast of Africa, Puryear studied the traditional, preindustrial woodworking methods of local carpenters and artisans. In 1966 he moved to Stockholm, Sweden, to learn the techniques of Scandinavian cabinetmakers. Two years later he began graduate studies in sculpture at Yale, where he encountered the work of a number of visiting Minimalist sculptors, including Serra (see fig. 29-85). By the middle of the 1970s he had combined these formative influences into a distinctive personal style reminiscent, in its organic simplicity, of Constantin Brancusi (see fig. 28-8).

Typical of Puryear's work is *Lever No. 3* (fig. 29-92). The work does not represent anything in particular but is meant to evoke a number of related subjects, including an animal with a long neck, a plant, and even the prow of a ship. Whatever the particular association one prefers, the beauty of the piece lies in its swelling organic curve and its completion in the perfection of a circle. Although the work's organic simplicity recalls Brancusi's sculpture, Puryear does not begin with a particular theme in mind but discovers his final product in the process of making. On the subject of his work, Puryear said: "I think all my work has an element of escape . . . The materials tend to be natural; I don't have a lot of feeling for materials that are highly processed and industrialized. But I am a city person, and perhaps because I am, an urge for the country comes out" (cited in *The Chicago Tribune*, February 1, 1987).

Ironically, the new taste for rounded, organic shapes may also be seen in the kind of industrial products that Puryear scorns. Recent automobile design, for example, was revolutionized by the appearance of the 1986 Ford Taurus (fig. 29-93). When Jack Telnack took over the design department at Ford in 1980 American cars were still boxy and inefficient. Although engineers knew that at 55 miles per hour more than 60 percent of the fuel is consumed simply to plow through air molecules, no serious attempts had been made to accommodate this fact. More importantly for Ford, it was losing money in the automobile market. Its big squared-off automobiles, heirs to those of the 1950s (see fig. 29-26), held little appeal to younger American buyers. Desperate to reverse its fortunes, Ford gambled on a radically aero-

29-92. Martin Puryear. *Lever No. 3*. 1989. Wood, carved and painted, 84½ x 162 x 13" (215 x 412 x 33 cm). National Gallery of Art, Washington, D.C.
Gift of the Collectors Committee

29-93. Ford Taurus, first model year. 1986

dynamic design for its new Taurus. Known as "the car that saved Ford," the Taurus's immense popularity depended less on its fuel efficiency than on its rounded sculptural form, its organic lines.

Another contemporary artist who would rather work within and deepen the artistic traditions of the past than break with them is the painter Brice Marden (b. 1938). A 1963 graduate of the Yale School of Art, he became an important Minimalist, specializing in one-color paintings, usually gray. From these monochromes he moved on in

29-94. Brice Marden. *Cold Mountain 3*. 1988–91. Oil on linen, 9 x 12' (2.74 x 3.66 m). Collection John and Frances Bowes, San Francisco
Courtesy Mary Boone Gallery, New York

the 1970s to paintings with a subtle dialogue between blocks of subdued color. Increasingly interested in Asian art and philosophy, in the mid-1980s Marden started making calligraphic drawings using twigs of ailanthus wood, known to the Chinese as the tree of heaven. From these drawings came a series of large paintings (fig. 29-94) dedicated to Cold Mountain, an eighth-century Chinese poet who quit the imperial court, retired to a mountain community of Buddhist monks, and wrote short, simple, and beautifully penned verses declaring his independence from the material "world of dust." Marden's allegiance to that philosophical stance is demonstrated in his painting style, which combines the delicate nuances and slower rhythms of classic Chinese calligraphy with the monumental scale and looser tracery of Pollock. Marden thus aligns himself with the modernist view of art as a transcendent and spiritually nourishing form of expression. Like those of Puryear and Lewis, his work suggests that innovation need not come at the cost of either disruption or interruption.

The continuing vitality of the contrary view—that avant-garde art should be shockingly new and different—can be seen in the work of the itinerant German artist

Rebecca Horn (b. 1944). Raised in post–World War II Berlin, Horn now divides her time between Hamburg and New York City. In 1968, after a near-fatal asphyxiation from polyester resin fumes, she turned from conventional sculpture to mysterious and ritualistic performances focused on the human body. These works gave way in the late 1970s to a dual focus on fictional films and kinetic installations such as *High Moon* (fig. 29-95), which apparently refers to the concluding shoot-out in the classic Western film *High Noon*. The machines in these installations are human substitutes, or "Melancholic actors," as Horn called them in an interview. Of *High Moon*, Horn said: "In it, two Winchester rifles hanging at about the height of a person's heart move in the gallery space. First, they focus on the people coming into the gallery. Then, they move until they face each other. Finally, they shoot red liquid [fed by tubes from two glass funnels]. I've always wanted to make two rival guns shoot each other with bullets that melt, like a kiss of death." The result is a bloody-looking pool that spills out onto the gallery floor, making it look like a crime scene. Even Horn isn't sure what the work means. "There is never a story per se," she admits. "I simply allow the consequences of whatever the machine

29-95. Rebecca Horn. *High Moon.* 1991. Installation: two Winchester rifles, two glass funnels, motor, metal, water, and dye, dimensions variable
Courtesy Marian Goodman Gallery, New York

is doing to meet with the particular reality or mood each person brings to it." Whatever interpretation one chooses, *High Moon*'s subtle interweaving of contrasting elements—male and female, human and machine, danger and pleasure, life and death—is unsettling.

The contrast between the soothing art of Puryear and Marden and the challenging art of Horn is hardly new. Since the Renaissance, at least, the history of art has involved this debate over the function of art. Some artists have sought to comfort us, others to unsettle us. Both of these positions demonstrate the continuing relevance of art to our lives. The case for art and the artist was eloquently made at a congressional subcommittee

hearing by Robert Motherwell (1915–1991), a major New York School painter:

Most people ignorantly suppose that artists are the decorators of our human existence, the esthetes to whom the cultivated may turn when the real business of the day is done. But actually what an artist is, is a person skilled in expressing human feeling. . . . Far from being merely decorative, the artist's awareness . . . is one . . . of the few guardians of the inherent sanity and equilibrium of the human spirit that we have.

Glossary

abacus The flat, usually square slab forming the top of a **capital**, directly under the **entablature**.

absolute dating A method of assigning a precise historical date to ancient periods and objects based on known and recorded events in the region as well as technically extracted physical evidence (such as carbon-14 disintegration). *See also* **radiometric dating**, **relative dating**.

abstract, abstraction Any art that does not represent observable aspects of nature or transforms visible **forms** into a pattern resembling the orignal model. Also: the formal qualities of this process.

academy, academician An academy is an institutional group established for the training of artists. Most academies date from the Renaissance and after; they were particularly powerful state-run institutions in the seventeenth and eighteenth centuries. In general, academies replaced **guilds** as the venue where students learned the craft of art and were also provided with a complete education, including art theory and artistic rules. The academies helped artists be seen as trained specialists, rather than craftspeople, and promoted the change in the social status of the artist. An academician is an official academy-trained artist, whose work conforms to the accepted **style** of the day.

acanthus A plant whose foliage inspires a leaflike architectural ornamentation used in the **Corinthian** and **Composite orders**.

acropolis The **citadel** of an ancient Greek city, located at its highest point and consisting of temples, a **treasury**, and sometimes a royal palace. The most famous is the Acropolis in Athens, where the ruins of the Parthenon can be found.

acrylic A fast-drying synthetic paint popular since the 1950s.

adobe Sun-baked blocks made of clay mixed with straw. Also: the buildings made with this material.

adyton The innermost **sanctuary** of a Greek temple. If a temple with an **oracle**, the place where the **oracles** were delivered. More generally, a very private space or room.

aedicula (aediculae) A type of decorative architectural frame, usually found around a **niche**, door, or window. An aedicula is made up of a **pediment** and **entablature** supported by **columns** or **pilasters**.

aesthetics The philosophic theories relating to the concept of beauty in art and, by extension, to the history of art appreciation and taste.

agora An open space in a Greek town used as a central gathering place or market. In Roman times, called a **forum**.

album A book consisting of blank pages (leaves) on which typically an artist may sketch, draw, or paint.

album leaves *See* **album**.

alignment In prehistoric architecture, an arrangement of **menhirs** in straight rows.

allegory The representation in a work of art of an abstract concept or idea using specific objects or human figures.

altar A tablelike structure where religious rites are performed. In Christian churches, the **altar** is the site of the rite of the **Eucharist**.

altarpiece A painted or carved panel or **winged** structure placed at the back of or behind an **altar**. Contains religious imagery, often specific to the place of worship for which it was made.

amalaka In Hindu architecture, the circular or square-shaped element on top of a **shikhara**, often crowned with a **finial**, symbolizing the cosmos.

ambulatory The passage walkway around the **apse** in a basilican church or around the central space in a centrally planned building.

amphiprostyle Term describing a building, usually a temple, with **porticoes** at each end but without **columns** along the other two sides.

amphora An ancient Greek jar for storing oil or wine, with an egg-shaped body and two curved handles.

Andachtsbild (Andachtsbilder) Literally "devotional image," a painting or sculpture that depicts themes of Christian grief and suffering, such as the **pietà**, intended to encourage meditation.

aniconic A term describing a representation without images of human figures, often found in Islamic cultures.

animal interlace Decoration made up of interwoven animal or serpent **forms**, often found in Celtic and northern European art of the medieval period.

animal style A type of imagery popular in Europe and western Asia during the ancient and medieval periods, characterized by **linear**, animallike **forms** arranged in intricate patterns or combats.

ankh A **hieroglyph** signifying life, used by ancient Egyptians.

anta (antae) A rectangular **pier** or **pilaster** found at the ends of the framing walls of a recessed **portico**.

antependium (antependia) The front panel of a **mensa** or **altar** table.

anticlassical A term designating any image, idea, or **style** that opposes the **classical** norm.

apex A peak or top point.

apotheosis Deification of an individual. In painting, often shown as an ascent to Heaven, borne by angels or **putti**.

appliqué A piece of any material applied as decoration on another.

apprentice A student artist or craftsperson in training. In a system of artistic training established under the **guilds** and still in use today, master artists took on apprentices (who usually lived with the master's family) for several years. The apprentice was taught every aspect of the artist's craft, and he or she participated in the master's workshop or **atelier**.

appropriation Term used to describe an artist's practice of borrowing from another source for a new work of art. While in previous centuries artists often copied one another's figures, **motifs**, or **compositions**, in modern times the sources for appropriation extend from material culture to works of art.

apse, apsidal A large semicircular or polygonal (and usually **vaulted**) **niche** protruding from the end wall of a building. In the Christian church, it contains the **altar**. Apsidal is an adjective describing the condition of having such a semicircular or polygonal space.

aquamanile A vessel used for washing hands, whether during the celebration of the Catholic Mass or before eating at a secular table. An aquamanile is often formed in the shape of a human figure or a grotesque animal.

aquatint A type of **intaglio** printmaking developed in the eighteenth century that produces an area of even **tone** without laborious **cross-hatching**. Basically similar in technique to an **etching**, the aquatint is made through use of a porous resin coating of a metal plate, which when immersed in acid allows an even, allover biting of the plate. When printed, the end result has a granular, textural effect.

aqueduct A trough to carry flowing water, if necessary, supported by **arches**. Under the Romans, built over long distances at a gradually decreasing incline.

arabesque A type of **linear** surface decoration based on foliage and calligraphic **forms**, usually characterized by flowing lines and swirling shapes.

arcade A series of **arches**, carried by **columns** or **piers** and supporting a common wall or **lintel**. In a blind arcade, the **arches** and supports are engaged (attached to the background wall) and have a decorative function.

arch In architecture, a curved structural element that spans an open space. Built from wedge-shaped stone blocks called **voussoirs**, which, when placed together and held at the top by a trapezoidal **keystone**, form an effective weight-bearing unit. Requires **buttresses** for support at either side to contain outward thrust of structure. Found in a variety of shapes and sizes, depending upon **style** of period. **Corbel arch**: arch or **vault** formed by **courses** of stones, each of which projects beyond the lower **course** until the space is enclosed; usually finished with a **capstone**. **Horseshoe arch**: an arch with a rounded horseshoe shape; the standard arch **form** in western Islamic architecture. **Ogival arch**: a pointed arch created by **S** curves. **Relieving arch**: an arch built into a heavy wall just above a **post-and-lintel** structure (such as a gate, door, or window) to help support the wall above. Relieves some of the weight on the **lintel** by transferring the load to the side walls.

Archaic smile The curved lips of an ancient Greek statue, usually interpreted as a half-smile.

architectonic Resembling or relating to the spatial or structural aspects of architecture.

architectural interior A subject in **genre painting** particularly popular in Holland in the seventeenth century, depicting the interiors of churches and other important civic buildings, usually with small figures going about ordinary activities.

architrave The bottom layer of an **entablature**, beneath the **frieze** and the **cornice**.

ashlar *See* **dressed stone**.

assemblage An artwork created by gathering and manipulating found objects and other three-dimensional items. The technique of assemblage was especially popular in the first half of the twentieth century.

astragal A thin convex decorative **molding**, often found on **Classical entablatures**, and usually decorated with a continuous row of beadlike circles.

atelier The studio or workshop of a master artist or craftsperson, usually consisting of junior associates and **apprentices**.

atmospheric perspective *See* **perspective**.

atrial cross The cross placed in the **atrium** of a church. In Colonial America, used to mark a gathering and teaching place. Atrial crosses were often carved by native sculptors in local **styles**.

atrium An unroofed interior coutyard or room in a Roman house, sometimes having a pool or garden. Also: the open courtyard in front of a Christian church, or an entrance area in modern architecture.

attached column *See* **column**.

attic story The top story of a building. In **classical** architecture, the level above the **entablature**, often decorated or carrying an inscription.

attribute The symbolic object or objects that identify a particular deity, saint, or personification in art.

automatism A technique whereby the usual intellectual control of the artist over his or her brush or pencil is foregone. The artist's aim is to allow the subconscious to create the artwork without rational interference. Also called automatic writing, automatism was developed by the Surrealists in the 1910s, and it was influential for later movements such as Abstract Expressionism.

avant-garde A term derived from the French military word meaning "before the group," or "vanguard." Avant-garde denotes those artists or concepts of a strikingly new, experimental, or radical nature for the time.

axial Term used to describe a **plan** or design that is based on a symmetrical, **linear** arrangement of elements.

axis mundi A concept of an axis of the world, which denotes important sacred sites and provides a link between the human and celestial realms. For example, in Buddhist art, the axis mundi can be marked by **monumental** freestanding decorated **pillars**.

background Within the depicted space of an artwork, the area of the image at the greatest distance from the **picture plane**.

backstrap loom A type of loom common among the indigenous peoples of Asia and the Americas in which the **warp** threads are wound between two bars, one attached to an object such as a pole or tree and the other to the weaver's waist. Also called a body-tensioned loom.

bailey The outermost walled courtyard of castle fortifications. Usually the first line of defense, the bailey was bounded on the outer side by a defensive wall such as a palisade.

baldachin A canopy (whether suspended from the ceiling, projecting from a wall, or supported by **columns**) placed over an honorific or sacred space such as a throne or church **altar**.

balustrade A series of short circular posts (called balusters), with a rail on top. Sometimes balusters are replaced by decorated panels or ironwork under the rail.

baptismal font A large open vessel, usually made of stone, containing water for the Christian ritual of baptism.

baptistry A building used for the Christian ritual of baptism. It is usually separate from the main church and often octagonal or circular in shape.

barbican A defensive structure located at the gate to a city or castle, attached to the exterior wall. A barbican is usually heavily fortified.

bargeboard A wooden board, often carved in a decorative manner, affixed to the sloping sides of a roof **gable** to conceal or protect the end of the roof timbers.

barrel vault *See* **vault.**

bar tracery *See* **tracery**.

base A slab of masonry supporting a statue or the **shaft** of a **column** (also called a **plinth**).

basilica A large rectangular building. Often built with a **clerestory** and side aisles separated from the center **nave** by **colonnades**. Used in Roman times as centers for administration or justice and later adapted to Christian church use. A basilica-plan structure incorporates the essential elements of this plan.

basilica plan *See* **basilica**.

bas-relief *See* **relief sculpture.**

battered A building technique used in the construction of stone walls. For stability, a battered wall is built with a distinct inward slope at the top.

battlement The uppermost, fortified sections of a building or **parapet**, used for military purposes, usually including **crenellated** walls and other defensive structures.

bay One unit of a construction system of a building. Bays divide the space of a building into regular spatial units marked by elements such as **columns**, **piers**, **buttresses**, windows, or **vaults**.

beadwork Any decorative element created with beads. Also: a type of **molding** made from convex circles, often found in **classical** architecture and decoration.

beehive tomb A **corbel vaulted** tomb, conical in shape like a beehive, and covered by an earthen mound.

Benday dots In modern printing and typesetting, the individual dots which, together with many others, make up lettering and images. Often machine- or computer-generated, the dots are very small and closely spaced to give the effect of density and richness of **tone**.

bestiary A book of moralizing tales about real and imaginary animals especially popular during the Middle Ages in western Europe.

bevel, beveling A cut made at any angle except a right angle. Also: the technique of cutting at a slant, which creates shadows. Used in architecture, carpentry, printmaking, metalwork, and sculpture.

bi A jade disk with a hole in the center used in China for the ritual worship of the sky. Also: a badge indicating noble rank.

bird's-eye view Painting, drawing, or print that incorporates high-level **perspective**.

black-figure A decorative **style** of ancient Greek pottery in which black figures are painted on a red clay background.

blackware An ancient ceramic technique that produced pottery with a primarily black surface. As rediscovered and adapted by Maria Montoya Martinez, a Native American potter in the United States, blackware exhibits alternating **matte** and glossy patterns on the black surfaces of the objects.

blind arcade *See* **arcade**.

blind window The outlining elements of a window applied to a solid wall, often to help create symmetry on a **facade**, but without the actual window opening.

block book A book printed from carved wooden blocks. Block books were superseded by the invention, about 1450, of printing from movable type. *See also* **movable-type printing**, **woodblock print**.

block printing A printed image, such as a **woodcut** or wood **engraving**, made from a carved wooden block.

bobbin A cylindrical reel around which a material such as yarn or thread is wound when spinning, sewing, or weaving.

bodhisattva A deity that is far advanced in the long process of transforming itself into a buddha. While seeking enlightenment or emancipation from this world (nirvana), bodhisattvas help others attain this same liberation.

boiserie Wood paneling or wainscotting, usually applied to seventeenth- and eighteenth-century French interiors, where it was often decorated with painting and **relief carving**.

boss A decorative knoblike element. Bosses can be found in many places, such as at the intersection of a Gothic ceiling or **vault** rib (and, similarly, at the end of a **molding**). Also: buttonlike projections in medieval decorations and metalwork.

bracket, bracketing An architectural element that projects from a wall, and that often helps support a horizontal part of a building, such as beams or the eaves of a roof.

breakfast piece A painting depicting a **still life** of plates and food. The breakfast piece was popular in Dutch seventeenth-century painting and may have had a *vanitas* significance.

broken pediment *See* **pediment**.

bronze A metal made from copper alloy, usually mixed with tin. Also: any sculpture or object made from this substance.

bulwark A raised promontory built for purposes of defense.

buon fresco *See* **fresco**.

burin A metal instrument used in the making of **engravings** to cut lines into the metal plate. The sharp end of the burin is trimmed to give a diamond-shaped cutting point, while the other end is finished with a wooden handle that fits into the engraver's palm.

bust A portrait sculpture depicting only the head and shoulders of the subject.

buttress, buttressing A type of architectural support. Usually consists of massive masonry with a wide base built against an exterior wall to brace the wall and strengthen the **vaults**. Acts by transferring the weight of the building from a higher point to the ground. Flying buttress: An **arch** built on the exterior of a building that transfers the thrust of the roof vaults at important stress points through the wall to a detached buttress **pier** leading to the wall buttress.

cabinet piece A term often applied to seventeenth-century Dutch art, meaning a small-scale painting executed with a luscious surface and finest detail. The cabinet piece carries the associations of a precious object meant for close scrutiny and leisured appreciation.

caduceus In Classical mythology, the staff carried by the god Hermes. It possessed various powers, including the guarantee of safe passage by any messenger. The caduceus is shaped like a wand with two wings at the top and snakes intertwined around the **shaft**. Also: the modern symbol of medicine.

cairn A pile of stones or earth and stones that served both as a prehistoric burial site and as a marker of underground tombs.

calligraph A **form** of writing with pictures, as in the Chinese language.

calligraphy The art of highly ornamental handwriting.

calotype The first photographic process utilizing negatives and paper positives. It was invented by William Henry Fox Talbot in the late 1830s.

calyx krater *See* **krater.**

came (cames) A lead strip used in the making of leaded or **stained**-**glass** windows. Cames have an indented vertical groove on the sides into which the separate pieces of glass are fitted to hold the design together.

cameo Gemstone, clay, glass, or shell having layers of color, carved in **low relief** to create an image and ground of diffent colors.

camera obscura An early cameralike device used in the Renaissance and later for capturing images of nature. Made from a dark box (or room) with a hole in one side (sometimes fitted with a lens), the camera obscura operates when bright light shines through the hole, casting an upside-down image of an object outside onto the inside wall of the box. This image then can be traced.

campanile The campanile, from the Italian word meaning "bell tower," is usually a freestanding structure.

canon of proportions A set of ideal mathematical ratios in art, especially sculpture, originally applied by the Egyptians and later the ancient Greeks to measure the various parts of the human body in relation to each other.

capital The sculpted block which tops a **column.** According to the conventions of the **orders,** capitals include different decorative elements. *See* **order.** Also: a historiated capital in Medieval art is a capital displaying a narrative.

capriccio A painting or print of a fantastic, imaginary landscape, usually with architecture.

capstone The final, topmost stone in a **corbel arch** or **vault,** which joins the sides and completes the structure.

Caravaggism A **style** of painting based on the example of the Italian seventeenth-century painter Michelangelo da Caravaggio and popular throughout Europe around 1600–1620. Caravaggist painters are marked by, among other elements, the use of **realism,** strong **chiaroscuro,** and lower-class types for subjects.

caricature An artwork that exaggerates a person's features or individual peculiarities, usually with humorous or satirical intent.

Caroline minuscule The clear and legible script developed in Carolingian times.

cartoon A full-scale drawing used to transfer the outline of a design onto a surface (such as a wall, canvas, or panel) to be painted.

cartouche A frame for a **hieroglyphic** inscription formed by a rope design surrounding an oval space. Used to signify a sacred or honored name. Also: in architecture, a decorative device or plaque, usually with plain center and rolled or sculpted edges, used for inscriptions or epitaphs.

caryatid A sculpture of a draped female figure acting as a **column** that supports an **entablature.**

catacomb An underground cemetery; also called a **hypogeum.** Urns and busts of the dead were placed in **niches** along the tunnels, which crisscrossed the area under an existing cemetery and often incorporated rooms (cubiculae) and several different levels.

cella The principal interior structure at the center of a Greek or Roman temple within which the cult statue was usually housed. Also called the **naos.**

cenotaph A funerary monument commemorating an individual or group buried elsewhere.

centaur In Greek mythology, a creature with the head, arms, and torso of a man and the legs and hind quarters of a horse.

centering A temporary structure which supports the **vault, arch,** or **dome** during construction until the mortar is fully dried and the **arch** is self-sustaining.

central-plan building Any structure designed with a primary central space surrounded by symmetrical areas on each side. For example, **Greek-cross plan** (equal armed cross).

Chacmool In Mayan sculpture, a half-reclining figure, often **monumental** in scale and carved in a blocky **style.** Probably representing offering bearers. Chacmools can be found at Chichen Itza.

chaitya A type of Buddhist temple found in India. Built in the **form** of a hall or basilica, a chaitya hall is highly decorated with sculpture, and usually carved from a cave or natural rock location. It houses the sacred shrine or **stupa** for worship.

chamfer The slanted surface produced when an angle is trimmed or beveled, common in building and metalwork.

château (châteaux) The country house or castle of a French aristocrat. Usually built on a grand scale, châteaux are luxurious homes intended for an elegant lifestyle (although many do incorporate defensive fortifications such as **moats** and towers).

chattri (chattra) A decorative pavilion with an umbrella-shaped **dome** common in Indian architecture.

cherub (cherubim) The second highest order of angels (*see* **seraph**). Popularly, an idealized small child, usually depicted naked and with wings.

chevet The easternmost end of an oriented church, including the **crossing** (such as the **apse, ambulatory,** and radiating apsidal chapels).

chevron A decorative **motif** made up of repeated inverted Vs.

chiaroscuro An Italian word designating the relative contrast of dark and light in a painting, drawing, or print. Artists use chiaroscuro to create spatial depth and **volumetric forms** through slight gradations in the intensity of light and shadow.

chinoiserie The imitation of Chinese art and **style** common in the eighteenth century, and related to the lighthearted art of the Rococo period.

chip carving A type of decorative incision on wood, usually made with a knife or chisel, characterized by small **geometric** patterns and often found on furniture.

chiton A thin sleeveless garment, fastened at waist and shoulders, worn by men and women in ancient Greece.

choir The section of a church, usually between the **crossing** and the **apse,** where the clergy officiate.

chromolithography A type of **lithographic** process utilizing color. A new stone is made for each color, and all are printed onto the same piece of paper to create a single, colorful lithographic image.

chronophotography In the mid-nineteenth century, the development of the camera to the point where quick shutter speeds allowed the freezing of motion, enabling photographers to use multiple-exposure photographs to analyze movement. Chronophotographs, such as those by Eadward Muybridge, showed the subject against a black background performing a particular action, each frame depicting a different moment in the movement.

churrigeresque A showy, **painterly style** of Baroque architecture and ornament seen in Spain, Portugal, and Latin America, named after the Spanish architect José Benito de Churriguera (1665–1725).

ciborium An honorific pavilion erected in Christian churches to mark places of particularly sacred significance, such as an **altar.** The ciborium usually consists of a domed roof supported by **columns,** all highly decorated. Also: the receptacle for the **Eucharist** in the Catholic Mass. *See* baldachin.

circus An oval arena built by ancient Romans and usually enclosed by raised seats for spectators.

citadel An area of a fortress or defended city placed in a high, commanding spot.

clapboard Horizontal planks used as protective siding for buildings, particularly houses in North America.

Classical A term referring to the art and architecture of the ancient Greeks and Romans.

classical, classicism Any aspect of later art or architecture reminiscent of the rules, canons, and examples of the art of ancient Greece and Rome. Also: in general, any art aspiring to the qualities of restraint, balance, and rational **order** exemplified by the ancients.

Classical orders See **order.**

clerestory The topmost zone of a wall with windows (especially of a church or temple), when it extends above any abutting aisles or secondary roofs. Provides direct light into the central interior space.

cloison *See* **cloisonné.**

cloisonné A technique in **enameled** decoration of metal involving metal wire (**filigree**) that is affixed to the surface in a design. The resulting areas (cloisons) are filled with decorative enamel.

cloister An open space, part of a monastery or church, surrounded by an arcaded or **colonnaded** walkway, often having a fountain and garden, and dedicated to non-liturgical activities and the secular life of the religious. Members of a cloistered order do not interact with outsiders.

cloth of honor A piece of fabric, usually rich and highly decorated, hung behind a person of great rank on ceremonial occasions. Signifying the exalted status of the space before it, cloths of honor can be found behind thrones as well as **altars**, or behind representations of holy figures.

codex (codices) A book, or a group of **manuscript** pages, held together by stitching or other binding on one side.

codex style A **style** of vase painting derived from the fluid and elegant script of **manuscripts**.

coffer A recessed decorative panel that, with many other similar ones, is used to decorate ceilings or **vaults**. The use of coffers is called coffering.

coiling A technique in basketry. Coiled baskets are made from a spiraling structure to which another material is sewn.

collage A technique in which cutout paper forms (often painted or printed) are pasted onto another surface in a **composition**. Also: an image created using this technique.

colonnade A sequence or row of **columns**, supporting a straight **lintel** (as in a **porch** or **portico**) or a series of **arches** (an arcade).

colonnette A small **column**like vertical element, usually found attached to a **pier**. Colonnettes are decorative features, and they can reach into the **vaulted** sections of the building, contributing to the vertical effect of a Gothic cathedral.

colophon The data placed at the end of a book, especially a late medieval **manuscript**, listing the book's author, publisher, illuminator, and other information related to its production.

colossal order *See* **order**.

column An architectural element used for support and/or decoration. Consists of a rounded vertical **shaft** placed on a block (base) topped by a larger, usually decorative block (**capital**). Usually built in accordance with the rules of one of the architectural **orders**. Although usually freestanding, **columns** can be attached to a background wall (**engaged**).

column statue A carved **column**, depicting usually a religious person but also **allegorical** or mythological themes.

complementary color The primary and secondary colors across from each other on the color wheel (red and green, blue and orange, yellow and purple). When juxtaposed, the intensity of both colors increase.

Composite order *See* **order**.

composition The arrangement of elements in an artwork.

compound pier Typically found in a Romanesque or Gothic church, a compound pier is a **pier** or large **column** with multiple **shafts**, **pilasters**, or **colonnettes** attached to it on one or all sides.

conch A semicircular recess, such as an apse or **niche**, with a half-dome **vault**.

concrete A building material invented by the Romans, which is easily poured or molded when wet, and hardens into a particularly strong and durable stonelike substance. Made primarily from lime, sand, cement, and rubble mixed with water.

cone mosaic An early type of surface decoration created by pressing colored cones of baked clay into prepared wet plaster; associated with Sumerian architecture.

cong A square or octagonal tube made of jade with a cylindrical hole in the center. A symbol of the earth, it was used for ritual worship and astronomical observations in ancient China.

connoisseurship A term derived from the French word connoisseur, meaning "an expert," and signifying the practice of art history based primarily on formal, visual, and stylistic analysis. A connoisseur studies the **style** and technique of an object to deduce its relative quality and possible maker. This is done through visual association with other, similar objects and styles the connoisseur has seen in his or her study. *See also* **contextualism, formalism**.

content When discussing a work of art, the term can include all of the following: its subject matter; the ideas contained in the work; the artist's intention; and even its meaning for the beholder.

contextualism A methodological approach in art history which focuses on the cultural background of an art object. Unlike **connoisseurship**, contextualism utilizes the literature, history, economics, and social developments (among others) of a period, as well as the object itself, to explain the meaning of an artwork. *See also* **connoisseurship**.

contrapposto A way of representing the human body so that its weight appears to be borne on one leg. Contrapposto first appears in sculpture from the ancient Greece, when sculptors adopted a great degree of **naturalism** in their works.

corbel, corbeling Early roofing and **arching** technique in which each **course** of stone projects inward and slightly beyond the previous layer (a corbel) until the uppermost cobels meet. Results in a high, narrowly pointed **arch** or **vault**. A corbel table is a table supported underneath by corbels.

corbel arch *See* **arch**.

corbel vault *See* **vault**.

Corinthian order *See* **order**.

cornice The uppermost section of a **Classical entablature**. More generally, any horizontally projecting element of a building, usually found at the top of a wall or a **pedestal**. A raking cornice is formed by the junction of two slanted cornices, most often found in **pediments**.

course A horizontal layer of stone used in building.

cove A concave **molding** or area of ceiling where a wall and ceiling converge. A cove ceiling incorporates such moldings on all sides.

cove ceiling *See* **cove**.

crenellation A pattern of open notches built into the top **parapets** and battlements of many fortified buildings for the purposes of defense.

crocket A leaflike decorative element found in Gothic architecture, often on **pinnacles** and

gables. A crocket is shaped like an open leaf that gently curves outward, its edges curling up.

cromlech In prehistoric architecture, a circular arrangement of **menhirs**.

cross vault *See* **vault**.

cross-hatching A technique primarily used in printmaking and drawing, in which a set of parallel lines (hatching) is drawn across a previous set, but from a differing (usually right) angle. Cross-hatching gives a great density of **tone**, and allows the artist to create the illusion of shadows efficiently.

crossing The part of a cross-shaped church where the **nave** and the **transept** meet, often marked on the exterior by a tower or **dome**.

cruciform A term describing anything that is cross-shaped, as in the cruciform **plan** of a church.

crypt The **vaulted** underground space beneath the floor of a church, usually under the sanctuary which may contain tombs and relics.

cubiculum (cubicula) A private chamber for burial in the **catacombs**. The **sarcophagi** of the affluent were housed there in **arched** wall **niches**.

cuneiform writing An early form of writing with wedge-shaped marks; impressed into wet clay with a **stylus**, primarily by ancient Mesopotamians.

curtain wall A wall in a building that does not support any of the weight of the structure. Also: the freestanding outer wall of a castle, usually encircling the inner **bailey** and **keep**.

cycle A series of paintings, **frescoes**, or **tapestries** depicting a single story or theme intended to be displayed together.

cyclopean construction A prehistoric method of building, utilizing megalithic blocks of roughhewn stone. Any large-scale, **monumental** building project that impresses by sheer size. Named after one-eyed giants of legendary strength from Greek myths.

cylinder seal A small cylindrical stone decorated with **incised** patterns. When rolled across soft clay or wax, a raised pattern or design (relief) is made, which served in Mesopotamian and Indus Valley cultures as an identifying signature.

dado (dadoes) The lower part of a wall, differentiated in some way (by a **molding** or different color) from the upper section. Also: the part of a **pedestal** between the base and the **cornice**, usually constructed of plain stone without decoration.

daguerrotype An early photographic process invented and marketed in 1839 by Louis-Jacques Mondé Daguerre. The first practically possible photographic system, a daguerrotype was a positive print made on a light-sensitized copperplate.

Day-Glo A trademark name for fluorescent painted materials.

Deesis In Byzantine art, the representation of Christ flanked by the Virgin Mary and Saint John the Baptist.

demotic writing An informal script developed by the ancient Greeks in about the eighth century BCE, and used exclusively for nonsacred texts.

dentil Small, toothlike blocks arranged in a continuous band to decorate a **Classical entablature**.

diorama A large painting made to create an environment, giving the viewer an impression of being at the site depicted. Usually hung on several walls of a room and specially lit, the diorama was a popular attraction in the nineteenth century, and was sometimes exhibited with sculpted figures.

dipteral A term that describes a building with a double **peristyle**, that is, surrounded by two rows of **columns**.

diptych Two panels of equal size (usually decorated with paintings or reliefs) hinged together.

dogu Small human figurines made in Japan during the Jomon period. Shaped from clay with exaggerated expressions and in contorted poses, dogu were probably used in religious rituals.

dolmen A prehistoric structure made up of two or more large (often upright) stones supporting a large, flat, horizontal slab or slabs (called **capstones**).

dome A **round vault**, usually over a circular space. Consists of the supporting vertical wall (**drum**), from which the **vault** springs, and a curved masonry **vault** of shapes and cross sections that can vary from hemispherical to bulbous to **ovoidal**. May be crowned by an open space (**oculus**) and/or an exterior **lantern**. When a dome is built over a square space, an intermediate element is required to make the transition to a circular drum. There are two types: A dome on **pendentives** (spherical triangles) incorporates **arch**ed, sloping intermediate sections of wall that carry the weight and thrust of the dome to heavily **buttressed** supporting **piers**. A dome on **squinches** uses an **arch** built into the wall (squinch) in the upper corners of the space to carry the weight of the dome across the corners of the square space below.

donjon See **keep**.

Doric order See **order**.

dormer A vertical window built into a sloping roof. A dormer window has its own roof and side walls that adjoin the body of the roof proper.

dressed stone A highly finished, precisely cut block of stone. When laid with others in even **courses**, dressed stone creates a uniform face with fine joints. Most often used as a facing on the visible exterior of a building, especially as a **veneer** for the **facade**. Also called ashlar.

drillwork The technique of using a drill for the creation of certain effects in sculpture.

drum The wall that supports a **dome**. Also: a segment of the circular **shaft** of a **column**.

drypoint An **intaglio** printmaking process by which a metal (usually copper) plate is directly inscribed by means of a pointed instrument (**stylus**). The resulting design of scratched lines is inked, wiped, and printed. Also: the print made by this process.

earthworks Artwork and/or sculpture, usually on a large scale, created by manipulating the natural environment. Also: the earth walls of a fort.

easel painting Any painting of small to intermediate size that can be executed on an artist's easel.

echinus A cushionlike circular element found below the **abacus** of a **Doric capital**. Also: a similarly shaped **molding** (usually with **egg-and-dart motifs**) underneath the **volutes** of an Ionic **capital**.

edition A single printing of a book or print. An edition can be of differing numbers but includes only what is printed at a particular moment, usually pulled from the same press by the same publisher.

egg-and-dart A decorative **molding** made up of an alternating pattern of round (egg) and downward-pointing, tapered (dart) elements.

elevation The arrangement, proportions, and details of any vertical side or face of a building. Also: an architectural drawing showing an exterior or interior wall of a building. A building's main elevation is usually its **facade**.

emblema (emblemata) In a **mosaic**, the elaborate central **motif** on a floor, usually a self-contained unit done in a more refined manner, with smaller **tesserae** of both marble and semi-precious stones. Also: an object or action represented in painting, prints, and drawings as a symbol for an idea, action, or other subject (as in an **allegory**). Emblemata are commonly associated with seventeenth-century Dutch art.

emblem book A collection of individual symbolic images, often concerning a single theme, and published with texts or verse. These books were sometimes used by artists as a source of inspiration. They were especially popular as literature in the Netherlands and England during the sixteenth and seventeenth centuries.

embossing See **repoussé**.

embroidery The technique in needlework of decorating fabric by stitching designs and figures of colored threads of fine material (such as silk) into another material (such as cotton, wool, leather, or paper). Also: the material produced by this technique.

emotionalism Any aspect of art that appeals overtly to sentimentality, melodrama, excitement, or other strong emotion.

enamel A technique in which powdered glass is applied to a metal surface in a decorative design. After firing, the glass forms an opaque or transparent substance that is fixed to the metal background. Also: an object created with enamel technique.

encaustic A type of painting technique utilizing pigments mixed with a **medium** of hot wax. Encaustic paintings were typically made in ancient times, particularly in Egypt, Greece, and Rome.

engaged column See **column**.

engraving An **intaglio** printmaking process of inscribing an image, design, or letters onto a metal or wood surface from which a print is made. An engraving is usually drawn with a sharp implement (burin) directly onto the surface of the plate. Also: the print made from this process.

entablature In the **Classical orders**, the horizontal elements above the **columns** and **capitals**. The entablature consists of, from top to bottom, a **cornice**, **frieze**, and **architrave**.

entasis A slight bulge built into the **shaft** of a Greek **column**. The optical illusion of entasis makes the **column** appear from afar to be straight.

etching An **intaglio** printmaking process, in which a metal plate is coated with acid-resistant resin and then inscribed with a **stylus** in a design, revealing the plate below. The plate is then immersed in acid, and the design of exposed metal is eaten away by the acid. The resin is removed, leaving the design etched permanently into the metal and the plate ready to be inked, wiped, and printed.

Eucharist The central rite of the Christian church, from the Greek word "thanksgiving." Also known as the Mass or Holy Communion, it is based on the Last Supper. According to traditional Catholic Christian belief, consecrecrated bread and wine become the body and blood of Christ; in Protestant belief, bread and wine symbolize body and blood.

exedra (exedrae) In architecture, a semicircular **niche**. On a small scale, often used as decoration, whereas larger exedrae can form interior spaces (such as an **apse**).

expressionism, expressionistic Terms describing a work of art in which **forms** are created primarily to evoke subjective emotions rather than to portray objective reality.

extrados The upper, curving surface of a **vault** or **arch**. See also **intrados**.

facade The face or front wall of a building.

faience A **glazing** technique for ceramic vessels, utilizing a glass paste that, upon firing, acquires a lustrous shine and smooth texture.

faktura An idea current among Russian Constructivist artists and other Russian artists of the early twentieth century that referred to the inherent **forms** and colors suitable to different materials. Used primarily in their mixed-**medium** constructions of a **nonrepresentational** type, faktura focused the artists' attention on the manner in which different materials create a variety of effects.

fang ding A square or rectangular bronze vessel with four legs. The *fang ding* was used for ritual offerings in ancient China during the Shang dynasty.

fête galante A subject in painting depicting well-dressed people at leisure in a park or country setting. It is most often associated with eighteenth-century French Rococo painting and the work of Antoine Watteau.

filigree Delicate, lacelike ornamental work of interwined wire.

finial A knoblike architectural decoration usually found at the top point of a spire, **pinnacle**, canopy, or **gable**. Also found on furniture.

flower piece Any painting with flowers as the primary subject. **Still lifes** of flowers became particularly popular in the seventeenth century in the Netherlands and Flanders.

fluting In architecture, evenly spaced parallel vertical grooves **incised** on **shafts** of **columns** or columnar elements (such as **pilasters**).

flying buttress See **buttress**.

folio A large sheet of paper, which, when folded and cut, becomes four separate or **parchment** pages in a book. Also: a page or leaf in a **manuscript** or book; more generally, any large book.

foreground Within the depicted space of an artwork, the area that is closest to the **picture plane**.

foreshortening The illusion created on a flat painted or drawn surface in which figures and objects appear to recede or project sharply into space. Often accomplished according to the rules of **perspective**.

form In speaking of a work of art or architecture, the term refers to purely visual components: line, color, shape, texture, mass, spatial qualities, and **composition**—all of which are called formal elements.

formal elements *See* **form**.

formalism, formalist An approach to the understanding, appreciation, and valuation of art based almost solely on considerations of **form**. This approach tends to regard an artwork as independent of its time and place of making.

formline In Native American works of art, a line that defines a space or **form**.

forum The central square of a Roman town, often used as a market or gathering area for the citizens. Site of most community temples and administrative buildings.

freestanding column *See* **column**.

fresco A painting technique in which water-based pigments are applied to a surface of wet plaster (called *buon fresco*). *Fresco secco* is created by painting on dried plaster. **Murals** made by both these techniques are called frescoes.

fresco secco *See* **fresco**.

frieze The middle element layer of an **entablature**, between the **architrave** and the **cornice**. Usually decorated with sculpture, painting, or **moldings**. Also: any continuous flat band with **relief sculpture** or painted decorations.

fritware A type of pottery made from a mix of white clay, quartz, and other chemicals that, when fired, produces a highly brittle substance.

frontispiece An illustration opposite or preceding the title page of a book. Also: the primary **facade** or main entrance bay of a building.

frottage A design produced by laying a piece of paper over a relief or **incised** pattern and rubbing with charcoal or other soft **medium**.

fusuma Sliding doors covered with paper, used in an East Asian house. Fusuma are often highly decorated with paintings and colored backgrounds.

gable The triangular wall space found on the end wall of a building between the two sides of a pitched roof. Also: a triangular decorative panel that has a gablelike shape.

gadrooning A form of decoration on architecture and in metalwork; characterized by sequential convex **moldings** that curve around a circular surface.

galleria In church architecture, the story found above the side aisles of a church, usually open to and overlooking the **nave**. Also: in secular architecture, a long room, usually above the ground floor in a private house or a public building, used for entertaining, exhibiting pictures or promenading. In English, gallery.

garbhagriha From the Sanskrit word meaning "womb chamber," a small room or shrine in a Hindu temple containing a holy image.

genre A type or category of artistic form, subject, technique, **style**, or **medium**. *See also* **genre painting**.

genre painting A term used to loosely categorize paintings depicting scenes of everyday life, including (among others) domestic interiors, merry companies, inn scenes, and street scenes.

geoglyphs Earthen designs on a colossal scale, often created in a landscape as if to be seen from an aerial viewpoint.

geometric A term describing Greek art, especially pottery, from about 1100 to 600 bce and characterized by patterns of rectangles, squares, and other **abstract** shapes. Also: any **style** or art using primarily these shapes.

gesso A thick **medium** usually made from glue, gypsum, and/or chalk and often forming the ground, or priming layer, of a canvas. A gesso ground gives a smooth surface for painting and seals the absorbency of the canvas.

gesturalism The motivation behind painting and drawing in which the brushwork or line visibly records the artist's physical gesture at the moment the paint was applied or the lines laid down. Associated especially with expressive **styles**, such as European Baroque, Zen painting, and Abstract Expressionism.

gilding The application of paper-thin **gold leaf** to an object made from another **medium** (for example, a sculpture or painting). Usually used as a decorative finishing detail.

giornata Adopted from the Italian term meaning "a day's work," a giornata is the section of a **fresco** plastered and painted in a single day.

glaze *See* **glazing**.

glazing In ceramics, a method of treating earthenwares with an outermost layer of vitreous liquid (glaze) that, upon firing, renders a waterproof and decorative surface. In painting, a technique particularly used with oil **mediums** in which a transparent layer of paint (glaze) is laid over another, usually lighter, painted or glazed area.

gloss A type of clay **slip** used in ceramics by ancient Greeks and Romans that, when fired, imparts a colorful sheen to the surface.

gold leaf Paper-thin sheets of hammered gold that are used in **gilding**. In some cases (such as Byzantine **icons**), also used as a ground for paintings.

golden section A **linear** measurement said to be of ideal proportions, supposedly discovered by the ancient Greeks. When the measurement is divided into two, the smaller part is the same proportion to the larger as the larger is to the whole.

Good Shepherd A man carrying a sheep or with a sheep at his side. In **Classical** art, the god Hermes; in Christian art, Jesus Christ (an image inspired by the Old Testament 23rd Psalm or the New Testament parable of the Good Shepherd).

gopura The towering gateway to an Indian Hindu **temple complex**. A temple complex can have several different gopuras.

gouache A type of opaque watercolor that has a distinctive, chalky effect.

graffiti Imposed on public structures by anonymous persons, graffiti usually consists of drawings and/or text of an obscene, political, or violent nature, and can be found in all periods and all **mediums**.

Grand Manner A grand and elevated **style** of painting popular in the Neoclassical period of the eighteenth century. An artist working in the Grand Manner looked to the ancients and to the Renaissance for inspiration; for portraits as well as **history painting**, the artist would adopt the poses, **compositions**, and attitudes of Renaissance and antique models.

granulation A technique for decorating gold in which tiny balls of the precious metal are fused to the main surface in a pattern.

graphic arts A term referring to those branches of the arts that utilize paper as primary support. The graphic arts, whether drawn, typeset, or printed, often have a heavy emphasis on **linear** means of expression.

graphic design A concern in the visual arts for shape, line, and two-dimensional patterning, often especially apparent in works including typography and lettering.

Greek-cross plan *See* **central-plan building**.

Greek-key pattern *See* **meander**.

grid A system of regularly spaced horizontally and vertically crossed lines that gives regularity to an architectural **plan**. Also: in painting, a grid enables designs to be enlarged or transferred easily.

griffin A creature with the head, wings, and claws of an eagle and the body and hind legs of a lion.

grisaille A painting executed primarily in various **tones** of gray.

groin vault *See* **vault**.

groundline The solid baseline that indicates the ground plane of an image on which the figure stands. In ancient representations, such as those of the Egyptian, the figures and the objects are placed on the groundline without reference to their actual spatial relationships.

grout A soft cement placed between the **tesserae** of a **mosaic** to hold the design together. Also used in tiling.

guild An association of craftspeople. The medievalguild had great political power, as it controlled the selling and marketing of its members' products, and it provided economic protection, political solidarity, and training in the craft to its members. An artists' guild was usually dedicated to Saint Luke, the patron saint of artists.

half-barrel vault *See* **vault**.

half-timber construction A method of building, particularly in heavily timbered northern European areas, for vernacular structures. Beginning with a timber framework built in the post-and-lintel manner, the builder constructed walls between the timbers with bricks, mud, or wattle. The exterior could then be faced with plaster or other material.

hall church A church (typified by those in the Gothic style in Germany), with a **nave** and aisles that are all the same height, giving the impression of a large, open hall.

halos An outdoor pavement used by ancient Greeks for ceremonial dancing.

handscroll A long, narrow, horizontal painting or text (or combination thereof) common in Chinese and Japanese art, and of a size intended for individual use. A handscroll is stored wrapped tightly around a wooden pin and is unrolled for viewing or reading.

hanging scroll In Chinese and Japanese art, a vertically oriented painting or text mounted within sections of silk. At the top is a semicircular rod; at the bottom is a round dowel. Hanging scrolls are kept rolled and tied except for special occasions, when they are hung for display, contemplation, or commemoration.

haniwa Pottery figures that were placed on top of Japanese tombs or burial mounds.

happening A type of art form incorporating performance, theater, and visual images developed in the 1960s. A happening was organized without a specific narrative or intent; with audience participation, the event proceeded according to chance and individual improvisation.

header In building, a brick laid so that its end, rather than its side, faces out.

heliograph A type of early photograph created by the exposure to sunlight of a plate coated with light-sensitive asphalt.

hemicycle A semicircular interior space or structure.

henge A circular area enclosed by stones or wood posts set up by Neolithic peoples. It is usually bounded by a ditch and raised embankment.

herm A statue that has the head and torso of a human, but the lower part of which is a plain, tapering **pillar** of rectangular shape. Used primarily for architectural decoration.

hieratic In painting and sculpture, when the concern to communicate spiritual values results in a formalized, grand **style** for representing rulers, or sacred or priestly figures. Can also be seen in the use of different scales for holy figures and those of the everyday world.

hieratic scale The larger the figure, the greater the importance.

hieroglyphic Picture writing signs rendered in the form of pictorial symbols, utilized primarily for sacred names and ceremonial inscriptions (**cartouches**) by the ancient Egyptians.

high relief *See* **relief sculpture**.

himation In ancient Greece, a garment wrapped around the body, with a rectangular piece of cloth thrown over the shoulder. Worn by both men and women.

historicism A nineteenth-century consciousness of and attention to the newly available and accurate knowledge of the past, made accessible by historical research, textual study, and archeology.

history painting The term used to denote those paintings that include figures in any kind of historical, mythological, or biblical narrative. Considered since the Renaissance (until the twentieth century) as the noblest form of art, history paintings generally convey a high moral or intellectual idea, and often painted in a grand pictorial **style**.

hollow-casting *See* **lost-wax casting**.

horizon line A horizontal "line" formed by the actual or implied meeting point of earth and sky. In **linear perspective**, the **vanishing point** or points are located on this line.

horseshoe arch *See* **arch**.

house-church In early Christian times, any small and relatively secret church located in a private home.

house-synagogue A Jewish place of worship located in a private home.

hue Pure color. The saturation or intensity of the hue depends on the purity of the color. Its **value** depends on its lightness or darkness.

hydria A large ancient Greek and Roman jar with three handles (horizontal ones at both sides and one vertical at the back), used for storing water.

hypogeum (hypogea) *See* **catacomb**.

hypostyle hall Marked by numerous rows of tall, closely spaced **columns**. In ancient Egyptian architecture, a large interior room of a **temple complex** preceding the **sanctuary**.

icon A painted, **low relief** or **mosaic** image representing a sacred figure or event in the Byzantine, and later the Orthodox, church. Icons were venerated by the faithful who believed them to have miraculous powers.

iconoclasm The banning or destruction of **icons** and religious art. Iconoclasm in eighth and ninth century Byzantium and sixteenth and seventeenth century Protestant territories arose from differing beliefs about the power, meaning, function and purpose of imagery in religion.

iconography In the visual arts, the study of the **subject matter** of a representation and its meaning.

iconology The study of the significance and interpretation of the **subject matter** of art. Iconology often incorporates contextual evidence regarding traditions of representation of specific subjects to aid in understanding.

iconostasis The wall or screen in an Early Christian, Byzantine or Greek Orthodox church between the **sanctuary** (where the Mass is performed) and the body of the church (where the congregation assembles). The iconostasis was usually hung with **icons**.

idealization A process in art through which artists strive to make their forms and figures attain perfection, based on pervading cultural values or their own mental image of what the ideal is.

ideograph A **motif** or written character that expresses an idea or symbolizes an action in the world. It is distinct from a **pictograph**, which symbolizes or represents an actual object, person, or thing. Egyptian hieroglyphs and Chinese calligraphs are examples of writing which consist of both ideographs and pictographs.

illumination A painting on paper or **parchment** used as illustration and/or decoration for **manuscripts** or **albums**. Usually done in rich colors, often supplemented by gold and other precious materials. The illustrators are referred to as illuminators. Also: the technique of decorating manuscripts with such paintings.

illusionism, illusionistic An appearance of reality in art created by the use of certain pictorial means, such as **perspective** and **foreshortening**. Also: the quality of having this type of appearance.

impost, impost block A block, serving to concentrate the weight above, imposed between the **capital** of a **column** and the springing of an **arch** above.

impression Any single printing of an **intaglio** print (**engraving, drypoint** or **etching**). Each and every impression of a print is by nature different, given the possibilities for variation inherent in the printing process, which requires the plate to be inked and wiped between every impression.

in antis Term used to describe the position of **columns** set between two walls, as in a **portico** or a **cella**.

incising A technique in which a design or inscription is cut into a hard surface with a sharp instrument.

ink painting A **style** of painting developed in China using only monochrome colors, usually black ink with gray washes. Ink painting was often used by artists of the **literati painting** tradition and is connected with Zen Buddhism.

inlay A decorative process in which pieces of one material are set into the surface of an object fashioned from a different material.

intaglio Term used for a technique in which the design is carved out of the surface of an object, such an engraved seal stone. In the **graphic arts**, intaglio includes **engraving**, **etching**, and **drypoint**—all processes in which ink transfers to paper from **incised**, ink-filled lines cut into a metal plate.

intarsia The decoration of wood surfaces with **inlaid** designs created of contrasting materials such as metal, shell, and ivory.

interlace A type of **linear** decoration particularly popular in early medieval art, in which ribbon-like bands are **illusionistically** depicted as if woven under and over one another.

intrados The curving inside surface of an **arch** or **vault**. *See also* **extrados**.

intuitive perspective *See* **perspective**.

Ionic order *See* **order**.

isometric projection A building diagram that represents graphically the parts of a building. Isometric projections have all planes of the building parallel to two established vertical and horizontal axes. The vertical axis is true, while the horizontal is drawn at an angle to show the effect of recession. All dimensions in an isometric drawing are proportionally correct. *See also* **plan**, **section**.

iwan A large, **vaulted** chamber in a **mosque** with a **monumental arched** opening on one side.

jamb In architecture, the vertical element found in pairs on both sides of an opening in a wall, such as a door or window.

japonisme A **style** in French and American nineteenth-century art that was highly influenced by Japanese art, especially prints.

joined-wood sculpture A method of constructing large-scale wooden sculpture developed in Japan. The entire work is constructed from smaller hollow blocks, each individually carved, and assembled when complete. The joined-wood technique allowed the production of larger sculpture, as the multiple joints alleviate the problems of drying and cracking found with sculpture carved from a single block.

ka The name given by ancient Egyptians to the human life force, or spirit.

kantharos A type of Greek vase or goblet with two large handles and a wide mouth.

keep The most heavily fortified defensive structure in a castle, a tower located at the heart of the castle complex.

kente A woven cloth made by the Ashanti peoples of Africa. *Kente* cloth is woven in long, narrow pieces in complex and colorful patterns, which are then sewn together.

key block A key block is the master block in the production of a colored **woodcut**, which requires different blocks for each color. The key block is a flat piece of wood with the entire design carved or drawn on its surface. From this, other blocks with partial drawings are made for printing the areas of different colors.

keystone The topmost **voussoir** at the center of an **arch**, usually the last block to be placed. The pressure of this block holds the arch together. Often of a larger size and/or highly decorated.

kiln An oven designed to produce enough heat for the baking, or firing, of clay.

kiva Structure in a Native American pueblo used for community gatherings and rituals.

kondo The main hall inside a Japanese Buddhist temple where the images of Buddha are housed.

kore An archaic Greek statue of a young woman.

kouros An archaic Greek statue of a young man or boy.

krater An ancient Greek vessel for mixing wine and water, with many subtypes that each have a distinctive shape. **Calyx krater**: a bell-shaped vessel with handles near the base that resemble a flower calyx. **Volute krater**: a type of krater with handles shaped like scrolls.

kylix A shallow Greek vessel or cup, used for drinking, with a wide mouth and small handles near the rim.

lacquer A type of hard, glossy surface varnish used on objects in East Asian cultures. Lacquer can be layered and manipulated or combined with pigments and other materials for various decorative effects.

lakshana Term used to designate the thirty-two marks of the Buddha. These characteristics of the historical Buddha have come to be part of the **iconography** of the Buddha in general. The *lakshana* include, among others, the Buddha's golden body, his long arms, the wheel impressed on his palms and the soles of his feet, and his elongated earlobes.

lancet A tall narrow window crowned by a sharply pointed **arch**, typically found in Gothic architecture.

landscape architecture Any design for an outdoor space.

landscape painting A painting in which a natural outdoor scene or vista is the primary subject.

lantern A cylindrical **turret**like structure situated on top of a **dome**, with windows that allow light into the space below.

Latin-cross plan A cross-shaped building plan, incorporating one longer arm (**nave**) and three arms of equal length.

lectionary An ecclesiastical book containing readings from Christian Scripture. It is the book from which the officiant reads to the congregation during holy services.

lekythos A slim Greek oil vase with one handle and a narrow mouth.

limner The name used to denote an artist, particularly a portrait painter, in England during the sixteenth and seventeenth centuries and in New England during the eighteenth and nineteenth centuries.

linear, linearity A descriptive term indicating an emphasis on line, as opposed to mass or color, in art.

linear perspective *See* **perspective**.

lingam shrine A place of worship centered on an object or representation in the form of a phallus (the lingam), which symbolizes the power of the Hindu god Shiva.

lintel A horizontal element of any material carried by two or more vertical supports to form an opening.

list An open section of the grounds of a fortified building or castle, usually in the bailey, that was set aside for knightly combat.

literary illustration An image or artwork with a subject or **content** drawn from a literary source.

literati *See* **literati painting**.

literati painting A **style** of painting that reflects the taste of the educated class of East Asian intellectuals and scholars. Aspects include an appreciation for the antique, smaller scale, and an intimate connection between maker and audience.

lithograph A print made from a design drawn on a flat stone block with greasy crayon. Ink is applied to the stone, and when printed, adheres only to the open areas of the design. *See also* **chromolithography**.

loculus (loculi) A **niche** in a tomb or **catacomb** in which a **sarcophagus** was placed.

loggia Italian term for a covered open-air gallery. Often used as a corridor between buildings or around a courtyard, loggia usually have arcades or **colonnades** and an upper story.

lost-wax casting A method of casting metal, such as bronze, by a process in which a wax mold is covered with clay and plaster, then fired, melting the wax and leaving a hollow **form**. Molten metal is then poured into the hollow space and slowly cooled. When the hardened clay and plaster exterior shell is removed, a solid metal form remains to be smoothed and polished.

low relief *See* **relief sculpture**.

lozenge A decorative **motif** in the shape of a diamond.

lunette A semicircular wall area, framed by an **arch** over a door or window. Can be either plain or decorated.

lusterware A type of ceramic pottery decorated with **glazes**.

madrasa An Islamic institution of higher learning, where teaching is focused on theology, law, and the sciences.

maenad In ancient Greece, a female devotee of the wine god Dionysos who participated in orgiastic rituals. She is often depicted with swirling drapery. (Also called a Bacchante, after Bacchus, the Roman name of Dionysos.)

majolica Pottery painted with a tin **glaze** that, when fired, gives a lustrous and colorful surface.

maki-e In Japanese art, the effect achieved by sprinkling gold or silver powder on successive layers of **lacquer** before each layer dries.

mandala An image of the cosmos represented by an arrangement of circular or concentric **geometric** shapes containing diagrams or images. Used for meditation and contemplation, mandalas are most often found in Buddhist places of worship.

mandapa In a Hindu temple, an open hall dedicated to ritual worship.

mandorla An almond-shaped area in which a sacred figure, such as Christ, is represented.

manifesto A written declaration of an individual or group's ideas, purposes, and intentions.

manuscript A handwritten book or document.

maqsura A separate enclosure in a Muslim **mosque** near the **mihrab**, designated for dignitaries.

martyrium (martyria) In Christian architecture, a church, chapel, or shrine built over the grave of a martyr or the site of a great miracle.

mastaba A flat-topped, one-story building with slanted walls. Invented by the ancient Egyptians to mark a part of underground tombs.

mathematical perspective *See* **perspective**.

matte A surface that is smooth but without shine or luster.

mausoleum A **monumental** building used as a tomb. Named after the tomb of Mausolos erected at Halikarnassos around 350 BCE

meander A type of two-dimensional ornament made up of continuous **geometric motifs** and often used as a decorative border. Also called Greek-key pattern.

medallion In architecture, any round ornament or decoration. Also: a large medal.

medium (mediums, media) In general, the material from which any given object is made. In painting, the liquid substance in which pigments are suspended.

megaron The main hall of a Mycenaean palace or grand house. Usually of a rectangular shape and sometimes subdivided into two unequal spaces by **columns**.

memento mori From Latin terms meaning "reminder of death." An object, such as a skull or extinguished candle, typically found in a *vanitas* image, symbolizing the transience of life.

menhir A megalithic stone block, placed by prehistoric peoples in an upright position.

menorah A Jewish lamp, usually in the form of a candelabrum, divided into seven or nine branches; the nine-branched menorah is used during the celebration of Hanukkah. Representations of the seven-branched menorah, once used in the Temple of Jerusalem, became in general a symbol of Judaism.

mensa The blocklike table serving as the **altar** in a Christian church.

metope The rectangular spaces, sometimes decorated but often plain, between the triglyphs of a **Doric frieze**.

mezzanine Any intermediate story of a building inserted between two stories of regular size.

middle ground Within the depicted space of an artwork, the area that takes up the middle distance of the image. *See also* **foreground**.

mihrab A recess or **niche** that distinguishes the wall oriented toward Mecca (**qibla**) in a **mosque**.

minaret A tall slender tower on the exterior of a **mosque** from which believers are called to prayer.

minbar A high platform or pulpit in an Islamic **mosque**.

miniature A small-scale painting. Miniatures have a variety of uses, from illustrations within **albums** or **manuscripts** to intimate portraits.

mirador In Spanish and Islamic palace architecture, a room with windows and sometimes balconies on three sides overlooking gardens and courtyards.

mithuna The amorous male and female couples in Buddhist sculpture, usually found at the entrance to a sacred building. The *mithuna* symbolize the harmony and fertility of life.

moat A large ditch or canal dug around a castle or fortress for military defense. When filled with water, the moat protects the walls of the building from direct attack.

modeling In painting, the process of creating the illusion of three-dimensionality on a two-dimensional surface by use of light and **shade**. In sculpture, the process of molding a three-dimensional form out of a malleable substance.

module A segment or portion of a repeated design.

molding A shaped or sculpted strip with varying contours and patterns. Used as decoration on architecture, furniture, frames, and other objects.

monolith A single stone, often very large. Monoliths may be set up as focal points for rituals or to define a ritual space.

Monophysitism The Christian doctrine stating that Jesus Christ has only one nature, both divine and human. Declared a heresy in the fifth century.

monoprint A single print pulled from a hard surface (such as a blank plate or stone) that has been prepared with a painted design. Each print is an individual artwork, as the original design is a transient one, lost in the printing process.

monumental A term used to designate a project or object that, whatever its physical size, gives an impression of grandeur and excellence.

mortise-and-tenon joint A method of joining two elements. A projecting pin (tenon) on one element fits snugly into a hole designed for it (mortise) on the other. Such joints are very strong and flexible.

mosaic Images formed by small colored stone or glass pieces (**tesserae**), affixed to a hard, stable surface.

mosque An edifice used for communal Muslim worship.

motif Any recurring element of a design or **composition**. Also: a recurring theme or subject in artwork, often referring to those that can be easily separated from the whole for the purposes of copying or study.

movable-type printing A method of printing text in which the individual letters, cast on small pieces of metal (die), are assembled into words on a mechanical press. When each **edition** was complete, the type could be reused for the next project. Movable-type printing, invented around 1450, revolutionized the printing industry in Europe and allowed the large-scale dissemination of affordable books.

mudra A symbolic hand gesture in Indian art. The many different mudras each denote certain behaviors, actions, or feelings.

mullion A slender vertical element or **colonnette** that divides a window into subsidiary sections.

multiculturalism Recognition of all cultures and ethnicities in a society or civilization.

multiple-point perspective *See* **perspective**.

muqarna The **geometric** patterning used in Islamic architecture to smooth the transition between decorative flat and rounded surfaces; usually found on the **vault** of a **dome**.

mural A large painting or decoration, done either directly on the wall or separately and affixed to it.

naos In ancient art, *See* **cella**. In a Byzantine church, the **nave** and **sanctuary**.

narthex The rectangular vestibule at the main (usually western) entrance of a church. In Early Christian architecture, it can also be an entrance **porch** with **columns** on the outside of a church.

naturalism, naturalistic A **style** of depiction in which the physical appearance of the rendered image in nature is the primary inspiration. A naturalistic work appears to resemble visible nature.

nave The rectangular central aisle of a basilica, two or three stories high and flanked by aisles.

necking The **molding** at the top of the **shaft** of the **column**.

necropolis A large cemetery or burial area.

negative space Empty or open space within or bounding a painting, sculpture, or architectural design. Negative space emphasizes the overall **form** of the work.

niche A hollow or recess in a wall or other solid architectural element. Niches can be of varying size and shape, and may be intended for many different uses, from display of objects to housing of a tomb.

niello An **inlay** technique in which a black sulphur alloy is rubbed into fine lines engraved into a metal (usually gold or silver). The alloy becomes fused with the surrounded metal when heated, and provides contrasting detail.

nishiki-e A multicolored and ornate Japanese print.

nocturne A night scene in painting, usually lit by artifical illumination.

nonrepresentational A term describing any artwork of an **abstract** nature. Nonrepresentational art does not attempt to reproduce the appearance of the natural world.

obelisk A tall stone **shaft** of four-sided rectangular shape, hewn from a single block, that tapers at the top and is completed by a **pyramidion**. Erected by the ancient Egyptians in ceremonial spaces (such as entrances to **temple complexes**). Today used as commemorative monuments and sun symbols.

oblique perspective *See* **perspective**.

oculus (oculi) In architecture, a circular opening. Oculi are usually found either as windows or at the apex of a **dome**. When at the top of a **dome**, an oculus is either open to the sky or covered by a decorative exterior **lantern**.

odalisque A subject in painting of a reclining female nude, usually shown among the accoutrements of an exotic, haremlike environment.

ogival arch *See* **arch**.

oil painting Any painting executed with the pigments floating in a **medium** of oil. Oil paint has particular properties that allow for greater ease of working (among others, a slow drying time, which allows for corrections, and a great range of relative opaqueness of paint layers, which permits a high degree of detail and luminescence). It was adopted on a wide scale in Europe after about 1450.

oil sketch An **oil painting**, usually on a small scale, intended as a preliminary stage for the production of a larger work. Oil sketches are often very **painterly** in technique.

oinoche A Greek wine jug with a round mouth and a curved handle.

olpe Any Greek vase or jug without a spout.

one-point perspective *See* **perspective**.

openwork Decoration, such as **tracery**, with open spaces incorporated into the pattern. Also: a needlework technique in which some of the fabric support is left visible within the design.

oracle A person, usually a priest or priestess, who acts as a conduit for divine information. Also: the information itself or the place at which this information is communicated.

orant The representation, usually in ancient or Early Christian art, of a standing figure praying with outstretched arms.

order A system of proportions in **Classical** architecture. **Doric**: the **column shaft** of the Doric order can be **fluted** or smooth-surfaced and has no **base**. The Doric **capital** consists of an undecorated **echinus** and **abacus**. The Doric **entablature** has a plain **architrave**, a **frieze** with **metopes** and **triglyphs**, and a simple **cornice**. **Tuscan**: a variation of Doric characterized by a smooth-surfaced column shaft with a base, a plain architrave, and an undecorated frieze. **Ionic**: the column of the Ionic order has a base, a fluted shaft and a capital decorated with **volutes**. The Ionic entablature consists of an architrave of two panels and **moldings**, a frieze usually containing sculpted **relief** ornament, and a cornice with **dentils**. **Corinthian**: the most ornate of the orders, the Corinthian includes a base, a fluted column shaft with a capital elaborately decorated with **acanthus** leaf carvings. Its entablature consists of an architrave decorated with moldings, a frieze often containing sculptured reliefs, and a cornice with dentils. **Composite**: a combination of the Ionic and the Corinthian orders. The capital combines acanthus leaves with volute scrolls. A **colossal** order is any of the above built on a large scale, rising through several stories in height and often raised from the ground by a **pedestal**.

orthogonal Any line running back into the represented space of a picture perpendicular to the imagined **picture plane**. In **linear perspective**, all orthogonals converge at a single **vanishing point** in the picture and are the basis for a **grid** that maps out the internal space of the image. An orthogonal **plan** is any plan for a building or city that is based exclusively on right angles, such as the grid plan of many modern cities.

orthogonal plan *See* **orthogonal**.

ovoid An adjective describing a rounded oval object or shape. Also: a characteristic **form** in

Native American art, consisting of a rectangle with bent sides and rounded corners.

pagoda An East Asian temple in the **form** of a tower built with successively smaller, repeated stories. Each story is usually marked by an elaborate projecting roof.

painterly A **style** of painting, that emphasizes the techniques and surface effects of brushwork (also light and **shade**).

palace complex A group of buildings used for living and governing by a particular ruler, usually located in a fortress or **citadel**.

palette A handheld support used by artists for the storage and mixing of paint during the process of painting. Also: the choice of a range of colors made by an artist in a particular work, or typical of his or her **style**.

Palladian An adjective describing a style of architecture, or an architectural detail, reminiscent of the classicizing work of the sixteenth-century Italian architect Andrea Palladio.

palmette A fan-shaped ornament with radiating leaves.

panel painting Any painting executed on a wood support. The wood is usually planed to provide a smooth surface. A panel can consist of several boards joined together.

papyrus A native Egyptian riverine plant from the stems of which ancient Egyptians produced an early form of paper. The papyrus plant was a popular decorative element in Egyptian architecture.

parapet A low wall at the edge of a balcony, bridge, roof, or other place from which there is a steep drop, built for the safety of onlookers. A parapet walk is the passageway, usually open, immediately behind the uppermost exterior wall or battlement of a fortified building.

parapet walk *See* **parapet**.

parchment A writing surface made from treated skins of animals and used during antiquity and the Middle Ages.

Paris Salon The annual display of art by French artists in Paris during the eighteenth and nineteenth centuries. Established in the seventeenth century as a venue to show the work of members of the French **Academy**, the Salon and its judges established the accepted official **style** of the time.

parterre An ornamental, highly regimented flower bed. Parterres became a crucial element of the ornate gardens of seventeenth-century palaces and châteaux.

passage In painting, passage refers to any particular area within a work, often those where **painterly** brushwork or color changes exist. Also: a term used to describe Paul Cézanne's technique of blending adjacent shapes.

passage grave A prehistoric tomb under a cairn, reached by a long, narrow, slab-lined access passageway or passageways.

pastel Dry pigment, chalk, and gum in stick or crayon form.

pedestal A platform or base supporting a sculpture or other monument. Also: the block found below the base of a **Classical column** (or **colonnade**), serving to raise the entire element off the ground.

pediment A triangular **gable** found over major architectural elements such as **Classical** Greek **porticoes**, windows, or doors. Formed by an **entablature** and the ends of a sloping roof or a **raking cornice**. A similar architectural element is often used decoratively above a door or window, sometimes with a curved upper **molding**. A broken pediment is a variation on the traditional pediment, with an open space at the center of the topmost angle and/or the horizontal **cornice**. Often filled with a decorative element, such as a **cartouche**.

pendentive The concave triangular section of a wall that forms the transition between a square or polygonal space and the circular base of a **dome**.

pendentive dome *See* **dome**.

peplos A loose outer garment worn by women of ancient Greece. Belted below the bust or at the hips.

performance art An artwork based on a live, sometimes theatrical performance by the artist.

peripteral A term used to describe any building (or room) that is surrounded by a single row of **columns**. When such columns are engaged instead of freestanding, called pseudo-peripteral.

peristyle A surrounding **colonnade** in Greek architecture. A peristyle building is surrounded on the exterior by a colonnade. Also: a peristyle court is an open colonnaded courtyard, often having a pool and garden.

perspective A system for representing three-dimensional space on a flat surface. **Atmospheric perspective**: A method of rendering the effect of spatial distance on a two-dimensional plane by subtle variations in color and clarity of representation. **One-point** and **multiple-point perspective** (also called **linear**, scientific, or **mathematical perspective**): A method of creating the illusion of three-dimensional space on a two-dimensional surface by delineating a **horizon line** and multiple **orthogonal** lines. These recede to meet at one or more points on the horizon (called **vanishing points**), giving the appearance of spatial depth. Called scientific or mathematical because its use requires some knowledge of geometry and mathematics, as well as optics. **Intuitive perspective**: A method of representing three-dimensional space on a two-dimensional surface by the use of **formal elements** that act to give the impression of recession. This impression, however, is achieved by visual instinct, not by the use of an overall system or program (usually involving scientific principles or mathematics) for depicting the appearance of spatial depth. **Oblique perspective**: An intuitive spatial system used in painting, in which a building or room is placed with one corner in the **picture plane**, and the other parts of the structure all recede to an imaginary vanishing point on its other side. Oblique perspective is not a comprehensive, mathematical system. **Reverse perspective**: A Byzantine perspective theory in which the orthogonals or rays of sight do not converge on a vanishing point in the picture, but are thought to originate in the viewer's eye in front of the picture. Thus, in reverse perspective the image is constructed with orthogonals that diverge, giving a slightly tipped aspect to objects.

photomontage A photographic work created from many smaller photographs arranged (and often overlapping) in a **composition**.

piazza The Italian word for an open city square.

pictograph A highly stylized depiction serving as a symbol for a person or object. Also: a type of writing utilizing such symbols.

picture plane The theoretical spatial plane corresponding with the actual surface of a painting (usually vertical).

picture stone A stone used in medieval northern Europe as a commemorative monument, which is carved or inscribed with representations of human figures or symbolic **forms**.

picturesque A term describing the taste for the familiar, the pleasant, and the pretty, popular in the eighteenth and nineteenth centuries in Europe. When contrasted with the **sublime**, the picturesque stood for all that was ordinary but pleasant.

piece-mold casting A casting technique in which the mold consists of several sections that are connected during the pouring of molten metal, usually bronze. After the cast form has hardened, the pieces of the mold are then disassembled, leaving the completed object. Because it is made in pieces, the mold can be reused.

pier A masonry support made up of many stones, or rubble and **concrete** (in contrast to a **column shaft** which is formed a single stone or a series of drums), often square or rectangular in **plan**, and capable of carrying very heavy architectural loads. *See also* **compound pier**.

pietà A devotional subject in Christian religious art. After the Crucifixion the body of Jesus was laid across the lap of his grieving mother, Mary. When others are present the subject is called the Lamentation.

pietra dura (pietre dure) A type of **mosaic** made in relief from semiprecious stones. Popular among the Florentine nobility of the seventeenth century, pietre dure often depicted ornamental designs such as flowers or fruit.

pietra serena The gray Tuscan limestone used in Florence.

pilaster An **engaged columnar** element that is rectangular in format and used for decoration in architecture.

pillar In architecture, any large, freestanding vertical element. Usually functions as an important weight-bearing unit in buildings.

pinnacle In Gothic architecture, a steep pyramid decorating the top of another element such as a **buttress**.

plaiting In basketry, the technique of weaving strips of fabric or other flexible substances under and over each other.

plan A graphic convention for representing the arrangement of the parts of a building.

plasticity The three-dimensional quality of an object, or the degree to which any object can be modeled, shaped, or altered.

plinth The slablike base or **pedestal** of a **column**, statue, wall, building, or piece of furniture.

pluralism A social structure or goal that allows members of diverse ethnic, racial, or other groups to exist within the society while continuing to practice the customs of their own divergent cultures. Also: an adjective describing the state of having many valid contemporary **styles** available at the same time to artists.

podium A raised platform that acts as the foundation for a building. Most often used for Etruscan, Greek, and Roman temples.

polychromy The multicolored painted decoration applied to any part of a building, sculpture, or piece of furniture.

polyptych An **altarpiece** constructed from multiple panels, sometimes with hinges to allow for movable **wings**.

popular culture The elements of society that are recognized by the general public. Popular culture has the associations of something cheap, fleeting, and accessible to all.

porcelain A type of extremely hard and fine ceramic made from a mixture of kaolin and other minerals. Porcelain is fired at a very high heat, and the final product has a translucent surface.

porch The covered entrance on the exterior of a building. With a row of **columns** or **colonnade**, also called a **portico**.

portal A grand entrance, door, or gate, usually to an important public building, and often decorated with sculpture.

portcullis A fortified gate, constructed to move vertically and often made of metal bars, used for the defense of a city or castle.

portico In architecture, a projecting roof or **porch** supported by **columns**, often marking an entrance.

post-and-lintel construction An architectural system of construction with two or more vertical elements (posts) supporting a horizontal element (**lintel**).

postern A side entrance to a fortified city or castle, usually on a much smaller scale than the main gates.

potsherd A broken piece of ceramic **ware**.

predella The lower zone, or base, of an **altarpiece**, decorated with painting or sculpture related to the main iconographic theme of the altarpiece.

primary colors Blue, red, and yellow, the three colors from which all others are derived.

Prix de Rome A prestigious scholarship offered by the French **Academy** at the time of the establishment of its Roman branch in 1666. The scholarship allowed the winner of the prize to study in Rome for four years at the expense of the state. Originally intended only for painters and sculptors, the prize was later expanded to include printmakers, architects, and musicians.

pronaos The enclosed vestibule of a Greek or Roman temple, found in front of the **cella** and marked by a row of **columns** at the entrance.

propylon (propylaia) A large, often elaborate gateway to a temple or other important building.

proscenium The stage of an ancient Greek or Roman theater. In modern theater, the area of the stage in front of the curtain. Also: the framing **arch** which separates a stage from the audience.

prostyle A term used to describe a **Classical** temple with a **colonnade** placed across the entrance.

provenance The history of ownership of a work of art from the time of its creation to the present.

pseudo-kufic Designs intended to resemble the script of the Arabic language.

pseudo-peripteral See **peripteral**.

punchwork Decorative designs that are stamped onto a surface, such as metal or leather, using a punch (a handheld metal implement).

putto (putti) A divine creature in the **form** of a plump, naked little boy, often with wings. In **classical** art, called a cupid or **cherub** (secular).

pylon A massive gateway formed by a pair of tapering walls of oblong shape. Erected by ancient Egyptians to mark the entrance to a **temple complex**.

pyramidion A pyramid-shaped block set as the finishing element atop an **obelisk**.

qibla The **mosque** wall oriented toward Mecca that includes the **mihrab**.

quadrant vault See **vault**.

quatrefoil A four-lobed decorative pattern common in Gothic art and architecture.

quillwork A Native American decorative craft technique. The quills of porcupines and bird feathers are dyed, woven together in patterns, and attached to fabric, birch bark, or other material.

quincunx A building in which five equal domed bays are arranged within a square, with a central unit and four corner units. (Note: When the central unit has similar units extending from each side, the **form** becomes a Greek cross).

quoin A stone, often extra large or decorated for emphasis, forming the corner of two walls.

radiometric dating A method of dating prehistoric works of art made from organic materials, based on the rate of degeneration of radiocarbons in these materials. See also **relative dating**, **absolute dating**.

raigo A painted image that depicts the Amida Buddha and other Buddhist deities guiding the soul of a dying worshiper to paradise.

raking cornice See **cornice**.

raku A type of ceramic pottery made by hand, coated with a thick, dark **glaze**, and fired at a low heat. The resulting vessels are irregularly shaped and glazed, and are highly prized. Raku **ware** is used in the Japanese tea ceremony.

rampart The raised walls or embankments used as primary protection in the fortification of a city or castle. Ramparts may be of different heights or thicknesses, and are usually surmounted by a **parapet**.

readymade An object from popular or material culture presented without further manipulation as an artwork by the artist.

realism A term first used in Europe around 1850 to designate a kind of **naturalism** with a social or political message, which soon lost its didactic import and became synonymous with naturalism.

recto The right-hand page in the opening of a book or **manuscript**. Also: the principal or front side of a leaf of paper, as in the case of a drawing.

red-figure A **style** of ancient Greek vase painting made in the sixth and fifth century BCE. Characterized by red clay-colored figures on a black background.

refectory The dining hall for monks or nuns in a monastery or convent.

register A device used in systems of spatial definition. In painting, a register indicates the use of differing groundlines to differentiate layers of space within an image. In sculpture, the placement of self-contained bands of reliefs in a vertical arrangement. In printmaking, the marks at the edges used to align the print correctly on the page, especially in multiple-block color printing.

reintegration The process of adaptation and transformation of European techniques and **styles** by artists in colonial areas.

relative dating A method of dating ancient artifacts by their relation to other objects, not to a historical moment. See also **radiometric dating**, **absolute dating**.

relief sculpture A sculpted image or design whose flat background surface is carved away to a certain depth, setting off the figure. Called high or low (bas) depending upon the extent of projection of the image from the background. Called sunken relief when the image is modeled below the original surface of the background, which is not cut away.

relieving arch See **arch**.

reliquary A container, often made of precious materials, used as a repository for sacred relics.

replica A very close copy of a painting or sculpture, sometimes done by the same artist who created the original.

repoussé A technique by which metal reliefs are created. Thin sheets of metal are gently hammered from the back to create a protruding image. More elaborate reliefs are created with wooden **forms** against which the metal sheets are pressed.

representational Any art that attempts to depict an aspect of the external, natural world in a visually understandable way.

reredos A decorated wall behind the **altar** of a church.

retablo The screen placed behind an **altar**. Often built on a large scale, with multiple painted panels and successive stories is a **form** of **altarpiece**. Retablos are most commonly found in Spain or in Spanish-influenced areas such as Latin America.

reverse perspective See **perspective**.

revetment A covering of cut stone, fine brick, or other solid facing material over a wall built of coarser materials. Also: surface covering used to reinforce a retaining wall, such as an embankment.

revivalism The practice of using older **styles** and modes of expression in a conscious manner. Revivalism does not usually entail the same academic and historical interest as **historicism**.

rhyton A vessel in the shape of a figure or an animal, used for drinking or pouring liquids on special occasions.

ribbon interlace A **linear** decoration made up of interwoven bands, often found in Celtic and northern European art of the medieval period.

rib vault See **vault**.

ridge rib A rib running the length of the **vault**.

ring wall Any wall surrounding a building, town, or fortification, intended to separate and protect the enclosed area.

rock-cut tomb Ancient Egyptian multichambered burial site, hewn from solid rock and often hidden.

rood screen In a church, a screen that separates the public **nave** from the private and sacred area of the **choir**. The screen supports a rood (sculpted crucifix).

roof comb In a Mayan building, a masonry wall along the apex of a roof that is built above the level of the roof proper. Roof combs support the highly decorated false **facades** that rise above the height of the building at the front.

rosette A round or oval ornament resembling a rose.

rose window A round window, often filled with **stained glass**, with **tracery** patterns in the form of wheel spokes. Large, elaborate, and finely crafted, rose windows are usually a central element of the **facade** of French Gothic cathedrals.

rotulus (rotuli) A scroll or **manuscripts** rolled in a tubular **form**.

rotunda Any building (or part thereof) constructed in a circular (or sometimes polygonal) shape, usually producing a large open space crowned by a **dome**.

roundel Any element with a circular format, often placed as a decoration on the exterior of architecture.

round vault *See* **vault**.

rune stone A stone used in early medieval northern Europe as a commemorative monument, which is carved or inscribed with ancient German or Scandinavian writing, runes.

running spirals A decorative **motif** based on the shape formed by a line making a continuous spiral.

rustication In building, the rough, irregular, and unfinished effect deliberately given to the exterior facing of a stone edifice. Rusticated stones are often large and used for decorative emphasis around doors or windows, or across the entire lower floors of a building, probably deriving from fortifications.

sacristy In a Christian church, the room in which the priest's robes and the sacred vessels are housed. Sacristies are usually located close to the **sanctuary** and often have a place for ritual washing as well as a private door to the exterior.

sahn The central courtyard of a Muslim **mosque**.

sanctuary In Greek architecture, a sacred or holy enclosure used for worship consisting of one or more temples and an **altar**. Also: the space around the altar in a church, usually at the east end (also called the chancel or presbytery).

sand painting Ephemeral religious designs created with different colored sands by Native Americans of North America, Australian Aborigines, and other peoples in Japan and Tibet.

sanghati The robe worn by a Buddhist monk. Draped over the left shoulder, the robe is made from a single piece of cloth wrapped around the body.

sarcophagus (sarcophagi) A rectangular stone coffin. Often decorated with **relief sculpture**.

scarification Ornamental marks, scars, or scratches made on the human body.

school of artists An art historical term describing a group of artists, usually working at the same time and sharing similar **styles**, influences, and ideals. The artists in a particular school may not necessarily be directly associated with one another, unlike in a workshop or atelier.

scientific perspective *See* **perspective**.

scriptorium (scriptoria) A room in a monastery for writing or copying **manuscripts**.

scroll painting A painting executed on a rolled support. Rollers at either end permit the horizontal scroll to be unrolled as it is studied or the vertical scroll to be hung for contemplation or decoration.

sculpture in the round Three-dimensional sculpture that is carved free of any attaching background or block.

section A method of representing the three-dimensional arrangement of a building in a graphic manner. A section is produced when an imaginary vertical plane intersects with a building, laying bare all the elements that make up the structure at that point. Also: a view of an element of object as if sliced through.

segmental pediment A **pediment** formed when the upper **cornice** is a shallow arc.

sepia An ink **medium** often used in drawing that has an extremely rich, dark **tone** of brownish color.

seraph (seraphim) An angel of the highest rank in the Christian hierarchy.

serdab In Egyptian tombs, the small room in which the **ka** statue was placed.

sesto The curve of an **arch**.

sfumato In painting, the effect of haze in an image. Resembling the color of the atmosphere at dusk, sfumato gives a smoky effect.

shade Any area of an artwork that is shown through various technical means to be in shadow. Also: the technique of making such an effect.

shaft The main vertical section of a **column** between the **capital** and the base, usually circular in cross **section**.

shater A type of roof or **dome** used in Russia and the Near East with a steep pitch and tentlike shape.

shikhara In the architecture of northern India, a conical (or pyramidal) spire found atop a Hindu temple and often crowned with an **amalaka**.

shoin The architecture of the aristocracy and upper classes in Japan, built in traditional asymmetrical fashion and incorporating the traditional elements of residences, such as the *tokonoma* and **shoji** screens.

shoji A standing Japanese screen covered in translucent rice paper and used in interiors.

sinopia The preparatory design or underdrawing of a **fresco**. Also: a reddish chalklike earth pigment.

site-specific sculpture A sculpture commissioned and designed for a particular spot. Most site-specific sculpture requires the location for which it was designed in order to be complete.

slip A mixture of clay and water applied to a ceramic object as a final decorative coat. Also: a solution that binds different parts of a vessel together, such as the handle and the main body.

spandrel The area of wall adjoining the exterior curve of an **arch** between its springing and the **keystone**, or the area between two arches, as in an **arcade**.

speech scroll A scroll painted with words indicating the speech or song of a depicted figure.

squinch An **arch** or **lintel** built over the upper corners of a square space, allowing a circular or polygonal **dome** to be more securely set above the walls.

stadium In ancient Greece, race track with tiers of seats for spectators.

stained glass A decorative process in glassmaking by which glass is given a color (whether intrinsic in the material or painted onto the surface). Stained glass is most often used in windows, for which small pieces of differently colored glass are precisely cut and assembled into a design, held together by **cames**.

stela (stelae) A stone slab placed vertically and decorated with inscriptions or reliefs. Used as a grave marker or memorial.

stigmata Marks resembling the wounds of Christ; said to appear on the bodies of certain holy persons.

still life A type of painting that has as its subject inanimate objects (such as food, dishes, fruit, or flowers).

stoa In Greek architecture, a **portico** or promenade with long rows of **columns** used as a meeting place.

stockade A defensive fencelike wood fortification built around a village, house, or other enclosed area.

stretcher The wooden framework on which an artist's canvas is attached, usually with tacks, nails, or staples. Also: a reinforcing horizontal brace between the legs of a piece of furniture, such as a chair. Also: in building, a brick laid so that its longer edge is parallel to the wall.

stringcourse A continuous horizontal band, such as a **molding**, decorating the face of a wall.

stucco A mixture of lime, sand, and other ingredients into a material that can be easily molded or modeled. When dry, produces a very durable surface used for covering walls or for architectural sculpture and decoration.

stupa In Buddhist architecture, a bell-shaped or pyramidal religious monument, made of piled earth or stone, and containing sacred relics.

style A particular manner, form, or character of representation, construction, or expression typical of an individual artist or of a certain school or period.

stylization A manner of representation that conforms to an intellectual or artistic idea rather than to **naturalistic** appearances.

stylobate In **Classical** architecture, the stone foundation on which a temple **colonnade** stands.

stylus An instrument with a pointed end (used for writing and printmaking), which makes a delicate line or scratch. Also: a special writing tool for **cuneiform writing** with one pointed end and one triangular wedge end.

subject matter *See* **content**.

sublime A concept, thing, or state of exceptional and awe-inspiring beauty and moral or intellectual expression. The sublime was a goal to which many nineteenth-century artists aspired in their artworks.

sunken relief *See* **relief sculpture**.

swag A decorative device in architecture or interior ornament (and in paintings), in which a loosely hanging garland is made to look as if constructed of flowers or gathered cloth.

syncretism In religion or philosophy, the union of different ideas or principles.

talud-tablero A design characteristic of Mayan architecture at Teotihuacan in which a sloping talud at the base of a building supports a wall-like tablero, where ornamental painting and sculpture are usually placed.

taotie A mask with a dragon or animal-like face common as a decorative **motif** in Chinese art.

tapa A cloth made in Polynesia by pounding the bark of a tree, such as the paper mulberry. It is also known as bark cloth.

tapestry Pictorial or decorative weaving meant to be hung on a wall or placed on furniture.

tatami Mats of woven straw used in Japanese houses as a floor covering.

temenos A sacred enclosure. In **classical** architecture, includes temples, treasuries, **altar**s and other buildings and spaces for ritual activities.

tempera A painting **medium** made by blending egg yolks with water, pigments, and occasionally other materials, such as glue. The technique was often used during the fourteenth and fifteenth centuries to paint **frescoes** and **panel paintings**.

temple complex A group of buildings dedicated to a religious purpose, usually located close to one another in a **sanctuary**.

tenebrism A term signifying the prevalent use of dark areas in a painting. A tenebrist **style**, such as **Caravaggism**, uses strong **chiaroscuro** and artificially illuminated areas to create a dramatic contrast of light and dark.

tepee A dwelling constructed from hides stretched on a structure of poles set at the base in a circle and leaning against one another at the top. Tepees were typically found among the nomadic Native Americans of the North American plains.

terminal Any element of sculpture or architecture that functions as decorative closure. Terminals are usually placed in pairs at either end of an object (such as furniture) or **facade** (as on a building) to help frame the **composition**.

terra-cotta A **medium** made from clay fired over a low heat and usually left unglazed. Also: the orange-brown color typical of this medium.

tessera (tesserae) The small piece of stone, glass, or other object that is pieced together with many others to create a **mosaic**.

tholos A small, round building. Sometimes built underground, as in a Mycenaean tomb.

tierceron In **vault** construction, a secondary rib that arcs from a springing point to the rib that runs lengthwise through the **vault**, called the **ridge rib**.

tint The dominant color in an object, image, or pigment.

tokonoma A **niche** for the display of an art object (such as a scroll or flower arrangement) in a Japanese tearoom.

tomb effigy A sculpted portraitlike image on a tomb or **sarcophagus** that represents a deceased individual.

tondo A painting or relief of circular shape.

tone The overall degree of brightness or darkness in an artwork. Also: saturation, intensity, or **value** of color and its effect.

torana In Indian architecture, an ornamented gateway **arch** in a temple, usually leading to the **stupa**.

torii The ceremonial entrance gate to a Shinto temple.

toron In West African **mosque** architecture, the wooden beams that project from the walls. Torons are used as support for the scaffolding erected annually for the replastering of the building.

torque A neckpiece, especially favored by the Celts, fashioned as a twisted metal collar.

tracery The thin stone or wooden bars in a Gothic window, screen, or panel, which create an elaborate decorative matrix or pattern.

transept The arm of a **cruciform** church, perpendicular to the **nave**. The point where the nave and transept cross is called the **crossing**. Beyond the crossing lies the **sanctuary**, whether **apse**, **choir**, or **chevet**.

travertine A mineral building material similar to limestone, typically found in central Italy.

treasury A building or room, for keeping holy (and often highly valuable) objects.

trefoil An ornamental design made up of three rounded lobes placed adjacent to one another.

triforium The element of the interior **elevation** of a church, found directly below the **clerestory** and consisting of a series of **arched** openings. The triforium can be made up of openings from a passageway or gallery, or can be a purely decorative device built into the wall.

triglyph Rectangular blocks between the **metopes** of a **Doric frieze**. Identified by the three carved vertical grooves, which approximate the appearance of the ends of wooden beams.

triptych An artwork made up of three panels. The panels are often hinged together so the side segments (**wings**) fold over the central area.

triumph In Roman times, a celebration of a particular military victory, usually granted to the commanding general upon his return to Rome. Also: in later times, any depiction of a victory.

triumphal arch A freestanding, massive stone gateway with a large central **arch**, built as urban ornament and/or to celebrate military victories (as by the Romans).

trompe l'oeil A manner of representation in which the appearance of natural space and objects is re-created with the express intention of fooling the eye of the viewer, who may be convinced that the subject actually exists as three-dimensional reality.

trophy Captured military objects such as armor

and weapons that Romans displayed in an upheld pole or tree to celebrate victory. Also: a similar grouping that recalls the Roman custom of displaying the looted armor of a defeated opponent.

trumeau A **column**, **pier**, or post found at the center of a large **portal** or doorway, supporting the **lintel**.

tugra The calligraphic imperial monograms used in Ottoman courts.

tunnel vault *See* **vault**.

turret A tall and slender tower.

Tuscan order *See* **order**.

twining A basketry technique in which short rods are sewn together vertically. The panels are then joined together to form a vessel.

tympanum In **Classical** architecture, the vertical panel of the **pediment**. In medieval and later architecture, the area over a door enclosed by an **arch** and a **lintel**, often decorated with sculpture or **mosaic**.

typology The study of symbolic types of representation in art history, especially of Old Testament events of the Bible as they prefigure those of the New Testament.

ukiyo-e A Japanese term for a type of popular art that was favored from the sixteenth century, particularly in the **form** of color **woodblock prints**. Ukiyo-e prints often depicted the world of the common people in Japan, such as courtesans and actors, as well as landscapes and myths.

undercutting A technique in sculpture by which a **form** is carved to project outward, then under. Undercutting gives a highly three-dimensional effect with deep shadows behind the form.

underglaze Color or decoration applied to a ceramic piece before **glazing**.

urna In Buddhist art, the curl of hair on the forehead that is a characteristic mark of a Buddha. The urna is a symbol of divine wisdom.

ushnisha In Asian art, a round turban or tiara symbolizing royalty and, when worn by a Buddha, enlightenment.

value The darkness or lightness of a color (**hue**).

vanishing point In a **perspective** system, the point on the **horizon line** at which **orthogonals** meet. A complex system can have multiple vanishing points.

vanitas An image, especially popular in Europe during the seventeenth century, in which all the objects symbolize the transience of life. *Vanitas* paintings are usually of **still lifes** or **genre** subjects.

vault An **arched** masonry structure covering that spans an interior space. In different shapes, called by different names. **Barrel or tunnel vault**: a continuous semicircular vault. **Corbel vault**: a vault made by the technique of **corbeling**. **Groin or cross vault**: a vault created by the intersection of two barrel vaults of equal size. **Rib vault**: a rib vault is found when the joining of curved sides of a groin vault is demarcated by a raised rib. **Quadrant or half-barrel vault**: a vault with two diagonally crossed ribs, which creates four side compartments of equal size and shape.

veduta (vedute) A term derived from the Italian

word for a vista, or view. Paintings, drawings or prints often of expansive city scenes or of harbors.

vellum A fine animal skin prepared for writing and painting. *See* **parchment**.

veneer In architecture, the exterior facing of a building, often in decorative patterns of fine stone or brick. In decorative arts, a thin exterior layer for decoration laid over wooden objects or furniture. Made of fine materials such as rare wood, ivory, metal, and semiprecious stones.

verism A **style** in which artists concern themselves with capturing the exterior likeness of an object or person, usually by rendering its visible details in a finely executed, meticulous manner.

verso The (reverse) left-hand page of the opening of a book or **manuscript**. Also: the subordinate or back side of a leaf of paper, as in the case of drawings.

vignette A small **motif** or scene that has no established border.

vihara From the Sanskrit term meaning "for wanderers." A vihara is, in general, a Buddhist monastery in India. It also signifies the monks' cells and gathering places in such a monastery.

vimana The main element of a Southern Indian Hindu temple, usually in the shape of a pyramidal or tapering tower raised on a **plinth**.

volumetric A term indicating the concern for rendering the impression of three-dimensional volumes in painting, usually achieved through **modeling** and the manipulation of light and shadow (**chiaroscuro**).

volute A spiral scroll, most often decoration on an **Ionic capital**.

volute krater *See* **krater**.

votive figure An image created as a devotional offering to a god or other deity.

voussoirs The oblong, wedge-shaped stone blocks used to build an **arch**. The topmost voussoir is called a **keystone**.

wall painting *See* **mural**.

ware A general term designating the different techniques by which pottery is produced and decorated. Different wares utilize different procedures to achieve different decorative results. *See also* **black-figure**, **red-figure**, and **white-ground**.

warp The vertical threads in a weaver's loom. Warp threads make up a fixed framework that provides the structure for the entire piece of cloth, and are thus often thicker than weft threads. *See also* **weft**.

wash A diluted watercolor. Often washes are applied to drawings or prints to add **tone** or touches of color.

watercolor A type of painting using water-soluble pigments that are floated in a water **medium** to make a transparent paint. The technique of watercolor is most suited to a paper support.

wattle and daub A wall construction method combining upright branches, woven with twigs (wattles) and plastered or filled with clay or mud (daub).

weft The horizontal threads in a woven piece of cloth. Weft threads are woven at right angles to and through the **warp** threads to make up the bulk of the decorative pattern. In carpets, the weft is often completely covered or formed by the rows of trimmed knots that form the carpet's soft surface.

westwork The **monumental**, west-facing entrance section of a Carolingian, Ottonian, or Romanesque church. The exterior consists of multiple stories between two towers; the interior includes an entrance vestibule, a chapel, and a series of galleries overlooking the **nave**.

white-ground A type of ancient Greek pottery **ware** in which the background color of the object is painted with a type of **slip** that turns white in the firing process. Figures and details were added by painting on or **incising** into this slip. White-ground wares were popular in the High **Classical** period as funerary objects.

wing A side panel of a **triptych** or **polyptych** (usually found in pairs), which was hinged to fold over the central panel. Wings often held the depiction of the donors and/or subsidiary scenes relating to the central image.

woodblock print A print made from a block of wood that is carved in relief or **incised**.

woodcut A type of print made by carving a design into a wooden block. The ink is applied to the plate with a roller. As the ink remains only on the raised areas between the carved-away lines, these carved-away areas and lines provide the white areas of the print. Also: the process by which the woodcut is made.

x-ray style In aboriginal art, a manner of representation in which the artist depicts a figure or animal by illustrating its outline as well as essential internal organs and bones.

yaksha, yakshi The male (yaksha) and female (yakshi) nature spirits that act as agents of the Hindu gods. Their sculpted images are often found on Hindu temples and other sacred places, particularly at the entrances.

zeitgeist From the German word for "spirit of the time," the term means cultural and intellectual aspects of a time period that pervade human experience and are expressed in all creative and social endeavors.

ziggurat In Mesopotamia, a man-made mountain; a tall stepped tower of earthen materials, often supporting a shrine.

Bibliography

Susan Craig

This bibliography is composed of books in English that are appropriate "further reading" titles. Most items on this list are available in good libraries, whether college, university, or public institutions. There are three classifications of listings: general surveys and art history reference tools, including journals; surveys of large periods (ancient art in the Western tradition, European medieval art, European Renaissance through eighteenth-century art, modern art in the West, Asian art, and African and Oceanic art and art of the Americas); and books for individual Chapters 1 through 29. Sources of quotations cited in short form in the text will also be found in this bibliography.

General Art History Surveys and Reference Tools

Adams, Laurie. *A History of Western Art.* Madison: Brown and Benchmark, 1994.
Bazin, Germain. *A Concise History of World Sculpture.* London: David & Charles, 1981.
Brownston, David M., and Ilene Franck. *Timelines of the Arts and Literature.* New York: HarperCollins, 1994.
Bull, Stephen. *An Historical Guide to Arms and Armor.* Ed. Tony North. New York: Facts on File, 1991.
Chadwick, Whitney. *Women, Art, and Society.* New York: Thames and Hudson, 1990.
Cole, Bruce, and Adelheid Gealt. *Art of the Western World: From Ancient Greece to Post-Modernism.* New York: Summit, 1989.
Crofton, Ian, comp. *A Dictionary of Art Quotations.* New York: Schirmer, 1989.
Crouch, Dora P. *A History of Architecture: Stonehenge to Sky-scrapers.* New York: McGraw-Hill, 1985.
Dictionary of Art, The. 34 vols. New York: Grove's Dictionaries, 1996.
Encyclopedia of World Art. 16 vols. New York: McGraw-Hill, 1972–83.
Fleming, John, Hugh Honour, and Nikolaus Pevsner. *The Penguin Dictionary of Architecture.* 4th ed. New York: Penguin, 1991.
Fletcher, Banister. *Sir Banister Fletcher's A History of Architecture.* 19th ed. Ed. John Musgrove. London: Butterworths, 1987.
Gardner, Helen. *Gardner's Art through the Ages.* 9th ed. Ed. Horst de la Croix, Richard G. Tansey, and Diana Kirkpatrick. San Diego: Harcourt Brace College, 1991.
Hall, James. *Dictionary of Subjects and Symbols in Art.* Rev. ed. New York: Harper & Row, 1979.
Hartt, Frederick. *Art: A History of Painting, Sculpture, Architecture.* 4th ed. New York: Abrams, 1993.
Heller, Nancy G. *Women Artists: An Illustrated History.* New York: Abbeville, 1987.
Holt, Elizabeth Gilmore, ed. *A Documentary History of Art.* 3 vols. New Haven: Yale Univ. Press, 1986.
Honour, Hugh. *The Visual Arts: A History.* 3rd ed. New York: Abrams, 1991.
Janson, H. W. *History of Art.* 5th ed. Rev. and exp. Anthony F. Janson. New York: Abrams, 1995.
Jervis, Simon. *The Penguin Dictionary of Design and Designers.* London: Lane, 1984.
Jones, Lois Swan. *Art Information: Research Methods and Resources.* 3rd ed. Dubuque: Kendall/Hunt, 1990.
Kostof, Spiro. *A History of Architecture: Settings and Rituals.* New York: Oxford Univ. Press, 1985.
Kurtz, Bruce D. *Visual Imagination: An Introduction to Art.* Englewood Cliffs, N.J.: Prentice-Hall, 1987.
Lindemann, Gottfried. *Prints and Drawings: A Pictorial History.* Trans. Gerald Onn. Oxford: Phaidon, 1976.
Mair, Roslin. *Key Dates in Art History: From 600 BC to the Present.* Oxford: Phaidon, 1979.
Mayor, A. Hyatt. *Prints and People: A Social History of Printed Pictures.* New York: Metropolitan Museum of Art, 1971.
McConkey, Wilfred J. *Klee as in Clay: A Pronunciation Guide.* Lantham, Md.: Univ. Press of America, 1985.
Myers, Bernard, ed. *McGraw-Hill Dictionary of Art.* 5 vols. New York: McGraw-Hill, 1969.
Rothberg, Robert I., and Theodore K. Rabb, eds. *Art and History: Images and Their Meaning.* Cambridge: Cambridge Univ. Press, 1988.
Stangos, Nikos. *The Thames and Hudson Dictionary of Art and Artists.* Rev ed. World of Art. New York: Thames and Hudson, 1994.
Steer, John, and Antony White. *Atlas of Western Art History: Artists, Sites and Movements from Ancient Greece to the Modern Age.* New York: Facts on File, 1994.
Thacker, Christopher. *The History of Gardens.* Berkeley: Univ. of California Press, 1979.
Trachtenberg, Marvin, and Isabelle Hyman. *Architecture, from Prehistory to Post-Modernism: The Western Tradition.* New York: Abrams, 1986.
Tufts, Eleanor. *Our Hidden Heritage: Five Centuries of Women Artists.* New York: Paddington, 1974.
Wilkins, David G., Bernard Schultz, and Katheryn M. Linduff. *Art Past/Art Present.* 2nd ed. New York: Abrams, 1994.
The World Atlas of Architecture. Boston: Hall, 1984.

Art History Journals: A Selected List

African Arts. Quarterly. Los Angeles, Calif.
American Art. Quarterly. Washington, D.C.
American Journal of Archaeology. Quarterly. Boston, Mass.
Antiquity. Quarterly. Oxford
Apollo. Monthly. London
Architectural History. Annually. London
Archives of American Art Journal. Quarterly. Washington, D.C.
Archives of Asian Art. Annually. New York
Ars Orientalis. Ann Arbor, Mich.
Art Bulletin. Quarterly. New York
Artforum. Monthly. New York
Art History. Quarterly. Oxford
Art in America. Monthly. New York
Art Journal. Quarterly. New York
Art News. Monthly. New York
Arts and the Islamic World. Annually. London
Asian Art and Culture. Triannually. New York
Burlington Magazine. Monthly. London
Flash Art. Bimonthly. New York
Gesta. Semiannually. New York
History of Photography. Quarterly. London
Journal of Egyptian Archaeology. Quarterly. London
Journal of Hellenic Studies. Annually. London
Journal of Roman Archaeology. Annually. Ann Arbor, Mich.
Journal of the Society of Architectural Historians. Quarterly. Philadelphia
Journal of the Warburg and Courtauld Institutes. Annually. London
Marg. Quarterly. Bombay, India
Oriental Art. Quarterly. Richmond, Surrey, England
Oxford Art Journal. Semiannually. Oxford
Simiolus. Quarterly. Apeldoorn, Netherlands
Textile History. Semiannually, London
Woman's Art Journal. Semiannually, Laverock, Penn.

Ancient Art in the Western Tradition, General

Adam, Robert. *Classical Architecture: A Comprehensive Handbook to the Tradition of Classical Style.* New York: Abrams, 1991.
Amiet, Pierre. *Art in the Ancient World: A Handbook of Styles and Forms.* New York: Rizzoli, 1981.
Becatti, Giovanni. *The Art of Ancient Greece and Rome, from the Rise of Greece to the Fall of Rome.* New York: Abrams, 1967.
Ehrich, Robert W., ed. *Chronologies in Old World Archaeology.* 3rd ed. Chicago: Univ. of Chicago Press, 1992.
Groenewegen-Frankfort, H. A., and Bernard Ashmole. *Art of the Ancient World: Painting, Pottery, Sculpture, Architecture from Egypt, Mesopotamia, Crete, Greece, and Rome.* Library of Art History. Englewood Cliffs, N.J.: Prentice-Hall, 1972.
Huyghe, René. *Larousse Encyclopedia of Prehistoric and Ancient Art.* Art and Mankind. New York: Prometheus, 1966.
Laing, Lloyd Robert, and Jennifer Laing. *Ancient Art: The Challenge to Modern Thought.* Dublin: Irish Academic, 1993.
Lloyd, Seton, and Hans Wolfgang Muller. *Ancient Architecture.* New York: Rizzoli, 1986.
Oliphant, Margaret. *The Atlas of the Ancient World: Charting the Great Civilizations of the Past.* New York: Simon & Schuster, 1992.
Powell, Ann. *Origins of Western Art.* London: Thames and Hudson, 1973.
Saggs, H. W. F. *Civilization before Greece and Rome.* New Haven: Yale Univ. Press, 1989.
Scranton, Robert L. *Aesthetic Aspects of Ancient Art.* Chicago: Univ. of Chicago Press, 1964.
Smith, William Stevenson. *Interconnections in the Ancient Near East: A Study of the Relationships between the Arts of Egypt, the Aegean, and Western Asia.* New Haven: Yale Univ. Press, 1965.
Stillwell, Richard, ed. *Princeton Encyclopedia of Classsical Sites.* Princeton: Princeton Univ. Press, 1976.

European Medieval Art, General

Calkins, Robert C. *Monuments of Medieval Art.* New York: Dutton, 1979.
Duby, Georges. *Sculpture: The Great Art of the Middle Ages from the Fifth to the Fifteenth Century.* New York: Skira/Rizzoli, 1990.
Hurlimann, Martin, and Jean Bony. *French Cathedrals.* Boston: Houghton Mifflin, 1951.
Kenyon, John. *Medieval Fortifications.* Leicester: Leicester Univ. Press, 1990.
Labarge, Margaret Wade. *A Small Sound of the Trumpet: Women in Medieval Life.* London: Hamilton, 1990.
Larousse Encyclopedia of Byzantine and Medieval Art. London: Hamlyn, 1963.
Mâle, Emile. *Religious Art in France: The Late Middle Ages: A Study of Medieval Iconography and Its Sources.* Princeton: Princeton Univ. Press, 1986.

Murphey, Cecil B., comp. *Dictionary of Biblical Literacy.* Nashville: Oliver-Nelson, 1989.
Snyder, James. *Medieval Art: Painting-Sculpture-Architecture, 4th–14th Century.* New York: Abrams, 1989.
Stoddard, Whitney. *Art and Architecture in Medieval France: Medieval Architecture, Sculpture, Stained Glass, Manuscripts. The Art of the Church Treasuries.* New York: Harper & Row, 1972.
Stokstad, Marilyn. *Medieval Art.* New York: Harper & Row, 1986.
Zarnecki, George. *The Art of the Medieval World: Architecture, Sculpture, Painting, the Sacred Arts.* New York: Abrams, 1975.

European Renaissance through Eighteenth-Century Art, General

Art and Politics in Late Medieval and Early Renaissance Italy, 1250–1500. South Bend, Ind.: Univ. of Notre Dame Press, 1990.
Black, C. F., et al. *Cultural Atlas of the Renaissance.* New York: Prentice Hall, 1993.
Blunt, Anthony. *Art and Architecture in France, 1500 to 1700.* Pelican History of Art. Harmondsworth, Eng.: Penguin, 1957.
Circa 1492: Art in the Age of Exploration. Washington, D.C.: National Gallery of Art, 1991.
Cole, Bruce. *Italian Art, 1250–1550: The Relation of Renaissance Art to Life and Society.* New York: Harper & Row, 1987.
Cuttler, Charles D. *Northern Painting from Pucelle to Bruegel: Fourteenth, Fifteenth and Sixteenth Centuries.* New York: Holt, Rinehart and Winston, 1973.
Evers, Hans Gerhard. *The Modern Age: Historicism and Functionalism.* Art of the World. London: Methuen, 1970.
Hartt, Frederick. *History of Italian Renaissance Art: Painting, Sculpture, Architecture.* 3rd ed. New York: Abrams, 1987.
Heydenreich, Ludwig Heinrich. *Architecture in Italy, 1400 to 1600.* Pelican History of Art. Harmondsworth, Eng.: Penguin, 1966.
Huizinga, Johan. *Waning of the Middle Ages: A Study of the Forms of Life, Thought, and Art in France and the Netherlands in the XIVth and XVth Centuries.* Garden City, N.Y.: Doubleday, 1954.
Husband, Timothy. *Wild Man: Medieval Myth and Symbolism.* New York: Metropolitan Museum of Art, 1980.
Huyghe, René. *Larousse Encyclopedia of Renaissance and Baroque Art.* Art and Mankind. New York: Prometheus, 1964.
Kubler, George, and Martin Soria. *Art and Architecture in Spain and Portugal and Their American Dominions, 1500–1800.* Pelican History of Art. Harmondsworth, Eng.: Penguin, 1959.
Levey, Michael. *Early Renaissance.* Harmondsworth, Eng.: Penguin, 1967.
Murray, Peter. *Renaissance Architecture.* History of World Architecture. Milan: Electa, 1985.
———, and Linda Murray. *The Art of the Renaissance.* World of Art. London: Thames and Hudson, 1963.
Stechow, Wolfgang. *Northern Renaissance, 1400–1600: Sources and Documents.* Englewood Cliffs, N.J.: Prentice-Hall, 1966.
Waterhouse, Ellis K. *Painting in Britain: 1530 to 1790.* 4th ed. Pelican History of Art. Harmondsworth, Eng.: Penguin, 1978.
Whinney, Margaret Dickens. *Sculpture in Britain: 1530–1830.* 2nd ed. Rev. by John Physick. Pelican History of Art. London: Penguin, 1988.

Modern Art in the West, General

Arnason, H. H. *History of Modern Art: Painting, Sculpture, Architecture, Photography.* 3rd ed. rev. New York: Abrams, 1986.
Bearden, Romare. *A History of African American Artists: From 1792 to the Present.* New York: Pantheon, 1993.
Brown, Milton W. *American Art: Painting, Sculpture, Architecture, Decorative Arts, Photography.* New York: Abrams, 1979.
Canaday, John. *Mainstreams of Modern Art.* 2nd ed. New York: Holt, Rinehart and Winston, 1981.
Chipp, Herschel Browning. *Theories of Modern Art: A Source Book by Artists and Critics.* California Studies in the History of Art. Berkeley: Univ. of California Press, 1984.
Craven, Wayne. *American Art: History and Culture.* New York: Abrams, 1994.
Eitner, Lorenz. *An Outline of Nineteenth Century European Painting: From David to Cezanne.* 2 vols. New York: Harper & Row, 1987.
Ferebee, Ann. *A History of Design from the Victorian Era to the Present.* New York: Van Nostrand Reinhold, 1980.
Ferrier, Jean Louis, ed. *Art of Our Century: The Chronicle of Western Art, 1900 to the Present.* New York: Prentice Hall, 1989.
Frampton, Kenneth. *Modern Architecture: A Critical History.* World of Art. New York: Oxford Univ. Press, 1980.
Hamilton, George Heard. *19th and 20th Century Art: Painting, Sculpture and Architecture.* Library of Art History. New York: Abrams, 1972.

Hammacher, A. M. *Modern Sculpture: Tradition and Innovation.* Enlg. ed. New York: Abrams, 1988.

Handlin, David P. *American Architecture.* World of Art. London: Thames and Hudson, 1985.

Harris, Ann Sutherland, and Linda Nochlin. *Women Artists: 1550–1950.* Los Angeles: Los Angeles County Museum of Art, 1976.

Harrison, Charles, and Paul Wood, eds. *Art in Theory, 1900–1990: An Anthology of Changing Ideas.* Cambridge: Blackwell, 1992.

Hitchcock, Henry Russell. *Architecture: Nineteenth and Twentieth Centuries.* 4th ed. Pelican History of Art. Harmondsworth, Eng.: Penguin, 1977.

Hunter, Sam, and John Jacobus. *American Art of the 20th Century: Painting, Sculpture, Architecture.* New York: Abrams, 1973.

———. *Modern Art: Painting, Sculpture, Architecture.* 3rd ed. New York: Abrams, 1992.

Jeffrey, Ian. *Photography: A Concise History.* London: Thames and Hudson, 1981.

Lynton, Norbert. *The Story of Modern Art.* 2nd ed. Oxford: Phaidon, 1989.

McCoubrey, John W. *American Art, 1700–1960: Sources and Documents.* Englewood Cliffs, N.J.: Prentice-Hall, 1965.

Newhall, Beaumont. *The History of Photography: From 1839 to the Present.* Rev. ed. New York: Museum of Modern Art, 1982.

Pevsner, Nikolaus, Sir. *The Sources of Modern Architecture and Design.* World of Art. New York: Oxford Univ. Press, 1968.

Read, Herbert. *A Concise History of Modern Painting.* London: Thames and Hudson, 1974.

———. *A Concise History of Modern Sculpture.* World of Art. New York: Praeger, 1964.

Rosenblum, Naomi. *A World History of Photography.* Rev. ed. New York: Abbeville, 1989.

Rosenblum, Robert. *19th Century Art.* New York: Abrams, 1984.

Schapiro, Meyer. *Modern Art: 19th and 20th Century Art.* New York: Braziller, 1978.

Selz, Peter. *Art in Our Times: A Pictorial History 1890–1980.* New York: Abrams, 1981.

Sparke, Penny. *Introduction of Design and Culture in the Twentieth Century.* New York: Harper & Row, 1986.

Stangos, Nikos, ed. *Concepts of Modern Art.* 3rd ed. World of Art. New York: Thames and Hudson, 1994.

Tafuri, Manfredo. *Modern Architecture.* 2 vols. History of World Architecture. New York: Electa/Rizzoli, 1986.

Tuchman, Maurice. *The Spiritual in Art: Abstract Painting 1890–1985.* Los Angeles: Los Angeles County Museum of Art, 1986.

Weaver, Mike, ed. *The Art of Photography, 1939–1989.* London: Royal Academy of Arts, 1989.

Wilmerding, John. *American Art.* Pelican History of Art. Harmondsworth, Eng.: Penguin, 1976.

Asian Art, General

Akiyama, Terukazu. *Japanese Painting.* Treasures of Asia. Geneva: Skira, 1961.

Arts of China. 3 vols. Tokyo: Kodansha International, 1968–70.

Blunden, Caroline, and Mark Elvin. *Cultural Atlas of China.* New York: Facts on File, 1983.

Bussagli, Mario. *Oriental Architecture.* 2 vols. History of World Architecture. New York: Electa/Rizzoli, 1989.

Chang, Leon Long-Yien, and Peter Miller. *Four Thousand Years of Chinese Calligraphy.* Chicago: Univ. of Chicago Press, 1990.

Collcutt, Martin, Marius Jansen, and Isao Kumakura. *Cultural Atlas of Japan.* New York: Facts on File, 1988.

Craven, Roy C. *Indian Art: A Concise History.* World of Art. New York: Thames and Hudson, 1985.

Fisher, Robert E. *Buddhist Art and Architecture.* World of Art. New York: Thames and Hudson, 1993.

Frankfort, Henri. *Art and Architecture of the Ancient Orient.* 4th ed. Pelican History of Art. Harmondsworth, Eng.: Penguin, 1970.

Goetz, Hermann. *The Art of India: Five Thousand Years of Indian Art.* 2nd ed. Art of the World. New York: Crown, 1964.

Harle, James C. *Art and Architecture of the Indian Subcontinent.* Pelican History of Art. Harmondsworth, Eng.: Penguin, 1987.

Lee, Sherman E. *A History of Far Eastern Art.* 4th ed. New York: Abrams, 1982.

Loehr, Max. *The Great Painters of China.* New York: Harper & Row, 1980.

Martynov, Anatolii Ivanovich. *Ancient Art of Northern Asia.* Urbana: Univ. of Illinois Press, 1991.

Mason, Penelope. *History of Japanese Art.* New York: Abrams, 1993.

Medley, Margaret. *Chinese Potter: A Practical History of Chinese Ceramics.* 3rd ed. Oxford: Phaidon, 1989.

Michell, George. *The Penguin Guide to the Monuments of India.* 2 vols. New York: Viking, 1989.

Mikami, Tsugio. *Art of Japanese Ceramics.* Trans. Ann Herring. Heibonsha Survey of Japanese Art, vol. 29. New York: Weatherhill, 1972.

Nakata, Yujiro. *Art of Japanese Calligraphy.* Trans. Alan Woodhull. Heibonsha Survey of Japanese Art, vol. 27. New York: Weatherhill, 1973.

Paine, Robert Treat, and Alexander Soper. *Art and Architecture of Japan.* 3rd ed. Pelican History of Art. Harmondsworth, Eng.: Penguin, 1981.

Rowland, Benjamin. *Art and Architecture of India: Buddhist, Hindu, Jain.* Pelican History of Art. Harmondsworth, Eng.: Penguin, 1977.

Seckel, Dietrich. *Art of Buddhism.* Art of the World. New York: Crown, 1964.

Sickman, Lawrence, and Alexander Soper. *Art and Architecture of China.* Pelican History of Art. Harmondsworth, Eng.: Penguin, 1971.

Speiser, Werner. *The Art of China: Spirit and Society.* Art of the World. New York: Crown, 1961.

Stanley-Baker, Joan. *Japanese Art.* World of Art. New York: Thames and Hudson, 1984.

Stutley, Margaret. *Harper's Dictionary of Hinduism: Its Mythology, Folklore, Philosophy, Literature and History.* New York: Harper & Row, 1977.

Tregear, Mary. *Chinese Art.* World of Art. New York: Oxford Univ. Press, 1980.

Vainker, S. J. *Chinese Pottery and Porcelain: From Prehistory to the Present.* London: British Museum, 1991.

Varley, H. Paul. *Japanese Culture.* 3rd ed. Honolulu: Univ. of Hawaii Press, 1984.

Yoshikawa, Itsuji. *Major Themes in Japanese Art.* Trans. Armins Nikovskis. Heibonsha Survey of Japanese Art, vol. 1. New York: Weatherhill, 1976.

African and Oceanic Art and Art of the Americas, General

Anderson, Richard L. *Art in Small-Scale Societies.* 2nd ed. Englewood Cliffs, N.J.: Prentice Hall, 1989.

Berlo, Janet Catherine, and Lee Ann Wilson. *Arts of Africa, Oceania, and the Americas: Selected Readings.* Englewood Cliffs, N.J.: Prentice Hall, 1993.

Blocker, H. Gene. *The Aesthetics of Primitive Art.* Lantham, Md.: Univ. Press of America, 1994.

Coote, Jeremy, and Anthony Shelton, eds. *Anthropology, Art, and Aesthetics.* New York: Oxford Univ. Press, 1992.

D'Azevedao, Warren L. *The Traditional Artist in African Societies.* Bloomington: Indiana Univ. Press, 1989.

Drewal, Henry, and John Pemberton III. *Yoruba: Nine Centuries of African Art and Thought.* New York: Center for African Art, 1989.

Guidoni, Enrico. *Primitive Architecture.* Trans. Robert Eric Wolf. History of World Architecture. New York: Rizzoli, 1987.

Leiris, Michel, and Jacqueline Delange. *African Art.* Arts of Mankind. London: Thames and Hudson, 1968.

Leuzinger, Elsy. *Africa: The Art of the Negro Peoples.* 2nd ed. Art of the World. New York: Crown, 1967.

Mbiti, John S. *African Religions and Philosophy.* 2nd ed. Oxford: Heinemann, 1990.

Mexico: Splendors of Thirty Centuries. New York: Metropolitan Museum of Art, 1990.

Murray, Jocelyn, ed. *Cultural Atlas of Africa.* New York: Facts on File, 1981.

Price, Sally. *Primitive Art in Civilized Places.* Chicago: Univ. of Chicago Press, 1989.

Willett, Frank. *African Art: An Introduction.* Rev ed. World of Art. New York: Thames and Hudson, 1993.

Chapter 1 Prehistory and Prehistoric Art in Europe

Anati, Emmanuel. *Camonica Valley: A Depiction of Village Life in the Alps from Neolithic Times to the Birth of Christ, as Revealed by Thousands of Newly Found Rock Carvings.* Trans. Linda Asher. New York: Knopf, 1961.

Bandi, Hans-Georg, et al. *Art of the Stone Age: Forty Thousand Years of Rock Art.* 2nd ed. Trans. Ann E. Keep. Art of the World. London: Methuen, 1970.

Beltrán Martinez, Antonio. *Rock Art of the Spanish Levant.* Trans. Margaret Brown. Cambridge: Cambridge Univ. Press, 1982.

Castleden, Rodney. *The Making of Stonehenge.* London: Routledge, 1993.

Chippindale, Christopher. *Stonehenge Complete.* New York: Thames and Hudson, 1994.

Freeman, Leslie G. *Altamira Revisited and Other Essays on Early Art.* Chicago: Institute for Prehistoric Investigation, 1987.

Gowlett, John A. J. *Ascent to Civilization: The Archaeology of Early Humans.* 2nd ed. New York: McGraw-Hill, 1993.

Graziosi, Paolo. *Paleolithic Art.* New York: McGraw-Hill, 1960.

Leroi-Gourhan, André. *The Dawn of European Art: An Introduction to Paleolithic Cave Painting.* Trans. Sara Champion. Cambridge: Cambridge Univ. Press, 1982.

———. *Treasures of Prehistoric Art.* New York: Abrams, 1967.

Lewin, Roger. *The Origins of Modern Humans.* New York: Scientific American Library, 1993.

Lhote, Henri. *The Search for the Tassili Frescoes: The Story of the Prehistoric Rock-Paintings of the Sahara.* 2nd ed. Trans. Alan Houghton Brodrick. London: Hutchinson, 1973.

Marshack, Alexander. *The Roots of Civilization: The Cognitive Beginnings of Man's First Art, Symbol, and Notation.* New York: McGraw-Hill, 1971.

Moscati, Sabatino, ed. *The Phoenicians.* New York: Abbeville, 1988.

O'Kelly, Michael J. *Newgrange: Archaeology, Art, and Legend.* New Aspects of Antiquity. London: Thames and Hudson, 1982.

Powell, T. G. E. *Prehistoric Art.* World of Art. New York: Oxford Univ. Press, 1966.

Price, T. Douglas, and Gray M. Feinman. *Images of the Past.* Mountain View, Calif.: Mayfield, 1993.

Renfrew, Colin, ed. *The Megalithic Monuments of Western Europe.* London: Thames and Hudson, 1983.

Ruspoli, Mario. *The Cave of Lascaux: The Final Photographs.* New York: Abrams, 1987.

Sandars, N. K. *Prehistoric Art in Europe.* 2nd ed. Pelican History of Art. Harmondsworth, Eng.: Penguin, 1985.

Sieveking, Ann. *The Cave Artists.* Ancient People and Places, vol. 93. London: Thames and Hudson, 1979.

Soffer, Olga. *The Upper Paleolithic of the Central Russian Plain.* Studies in Archaeology. Orlando, Fla.: Academic, 1985.

Torbrugge, Walter. *Prehistoric European Art.* Trans. Norbert Guterman. Panorama of World Art. New York: Abrams, 1968.

Ucko, Peter J., and Andree Rosenfeld. *Paleolithic Cave Art.* New York: McGraw-Hill, 1967.

Chapter 2 Art of the Ancient Near East

Akurgal, Ekrem. *The Art of the Hittites.* Trans. Constance McNab. New York: Abrams, 1962.

Amiet, Pierre. *Art of the Ancient Near East.* Trans. John Shepley and Claude Choquet. New York: Abrams, 1980.

Baring, Anne, and Jules Cashford. *The Myth of the Goddess: Evolution of an Image.* London: Viking Arkana, 1991.

Bottero, Jean. *Mesopotamia: Writing, Reasoning, and the Gods.* Trans. Zainab Bahrani and Marc Van De Mieroop. Chicago: Univ. of Chicago Press, 1992.

Collon, Dominque. *First Impressions: Cylinder Seals in the Ancient Near East.* Chicago: Univ. of Chicago Press, 1987.

Ferrier, R. W., ed. *Arts of Persia.* New Haven: Yale Univ. Press, 1989.

Ghirshman, Roman. *The Arts of Ancient Iran from Its Origins to the Time of Alexander the Great.* Trans. Stuart Gilbert and James Emmons. Arts of Mankind. New York: Golden, 1964.

Giedion, Sigfried. *The Eternal Present: A Contribution on Constancy and Change.* 2 vols. New York: Pantheon, 1962–64.

Harper, Prudence, Joan Arz, and Françoise Tallon, eds. *The Royal City of Susa: Ancient Near Eastern Treasures in the Louvre.* New York: Metropolitan Museum of Art, 1992.

Kramer, Samual Noah. *History Begins at Sumer: Thirty-Nine Firsts in Man's Recorded History.* 3rd rev. ed. Philadelphia: Univ. of Pennsylvania Press, 1981.

———. *The Sumerians, Their History, Culture, and Character.* Chicago: Univ. of Chicago Press, 1963.

Lloyd, Seton. *Ancient Turkey: A Traveller's History of Anatolia.* Berkeley: Univ. of California Press, 1989.

Mellaart, James. *The Earliest Civilization of the Near East.* London: Thames and Hudson, 1965.

Oppenheim, A. Leo. *Ancient Mesopotamia: Portrait of a Dead Civilization.* Rev. ed. completed by Erica Reiner. Chicago: Univ. of Chicago Press, 1977.

Parrot, André. *The Arts of Assyria.* Trans. Stuart Gilbert and James Emmons. Arts of Mankind. New York: Golden, 1961.

———. *Sumer: The Dawn of Art.* Trans. Stuart Gilbert and James Emmons. Arts of Mankind. New York: Golden, 1961.

Porada, Edith. *The Art of Ancient Iran: Pre-Islamic Cultures.* Art of the World. New York: Crown, 1965.

Roaf, Michael. *Cultural Atlas of Mesopotamia and the Ancient Near East.* New York: Facts on File, 1990.

Roux, Georges. *Ancient Iraq.* 3rd ed. London: Penguin, 1992.

Russell, John Malcolm. *Sennacherib's Palace without Rival at Nineveh.* Chicago: Univ. of Chicago Press, 1991.

Saggs, H. W. F. *Everyday Life in Babylonia and Assyria.* New York: Dorset, 1987.

———. *Civilization before Greece and Rome.* New Haven: Yale Univ. Press, 1989.

Wolkstein, Dianne, and Samuel Noah Kramer. *Inanna: Queen of Heaven and Earth.* New York: Harper & Row, 1983.

Woolley, Leonard. *The Art of the Middle East including Persia, Mesopotamia and Palestine.* Trans. Ann E. Keep. Art of the World. New York: Crown, 1961.

Chapter 3 Art of Ancient Egypt

Aldred, Cyril. *Akenaten and Nefertiti.* New York: Brooklyn Museum, 1973.

———. *Egyptian Art in the Days of the Pharaohs, 3100–320 B.C.* World of Art. London: Thames and Hudson, 1980.

Andrews, Carol. *Ancient Egyptian Jewelry.* New York: Abrams, 1991.

Baines, John, and Jaromir Málek. *Atlas of Ancient Egypt.* New York: Facts on File, 1980.

Bierbrier, Morris. *Tomb-Builders of the Pharaohs.* London: British Museum, 1982.

Breasted, James Henry. *A History of Egypt from the Earliest Times to the Persian Conquest.* New York: Scribner's, 1909.

Brier, Bob. *Egyptian Mummies.* New York: Morrow, 1994.

David, A. Rosalie. *The Pyramid Builders of Ancient Egypt: A Modern Investigation of Pharaoh's Workforce.* London: Routledge, 1986.

Edwards, I. E. S. *The Pyramids of Egypt*. Rev. ed. Harmondsworth, Eng.: Penguin, 1985.

The Egyptian Book of the Dead: The Book of Going Forth by Day: Being the Papyrus of Ani (Royal Scribe of the Divine Offerings). Trans. Raymond O. Faulkner. San Francisco: Chronicle, 1994.

Grimal, Nicolas. *A History of Ancient Egypt*. Trans. Ian Hall. Oxford: Blackwell, 1992.

James, T. G. H. *Egyptian Painting*. London: British Museum, 1985.

———, and W. V. Davies. *Egyptian Sculpture*. Cambridge: Harvard Univ. Press, 1983.

Kozloff, Arielle P., and Betsy M. Bryan. *Egypt's Dazzling Sun: Amenhotep III and His World*. Cleveland: Cleveland Museum of Art, 1992.

Manniche, Lise. *City of the Dead: Thebes in Egypt*. Chicago: Univ. of Chicago Press, 1987.

Martin, Geoffrey Thorndike. *The Hidden Tombs of Memphis: New Discoveries from the Time of Tutankhamun and Ramesses the Great*. London: Thames and Hudson, 1991.

Montet, Pierre. *Everyday Life in Egypt in the Days of Ramesses the Great*. Trans. A. R. Maxwell-Hysop and Margaret S. Drower. Philadelphia: Univ. of Pennsylvania Press, 1981.

Pemberton, Delia. *Ancient Egypt*. Architectural Guides for Travelers. San Francisco: Chronicle, 1992.

Reeves, C. N. *The Complete Tutankhamun: The King, the Tomb, the Royal Treasure*. London: Thames and Hudson, 1990.

Russmann, Edna R. *Egyptian Sculpture: Cairo and Luxor*. Austin: Univ. of Texas Press, 1989.

Smith, W. Stevenson. *The Art and Architecture of Ancient Egypt*. Rev. ed. Pelican History of Art. Harmondsworth, Eng.: Penguin, 1981.

Strouhal, Eugen. *Life of the Ancient Egyptians*. Norman: Univ. of Oklahoma Press, 1992.

Treasures of Tutankhamun. New York: Ballantine, 1976.

Wilkinson, Charles K. *Egyptian Wall Paintings: The Metropolitan Museum of Art's Collection of Facsimiles*. New York: Metropolitan Museum of Art, 1983.

Winstone, H. V. F. *Howard Carter and the Discovery of the Tomb of Tutankhamun*. London: Constable, 1991.

Woldering, Irmgard. *The Art of Egypt: The Time of the Pharaohs*. Trans. Ann E. Keep. Art of the World. New York: Crown, 1963.

Chapter 4 Aegean Art

Barber, R. L. N. *The Cyclades in the Bronze Age*. Iowa City: Univ. of Iowa Press, 1987.

Castleden, Rodney. *The Knossos Labyrinth: A New View of the "Palace of Minos" at Knossos*. London: Routledge, 1990.

Demargne, Pierre. *The Birth of Greek Art*. Trans. Stuart Gilbert and James Emmons. Arts of Mankind. New York: Golden, 1964.

Doumas, Christos. *The Wall-Paintings of Thera*. Trans. Alex Doumas. Athens: Thera Foundation, 1992.

Fitton, J. Lesley. *Cycladic Art*. Cambridge: Harvard Univ. Press, 1990.

Higgins, Reynold. *Minoan and Mycenean Art*. Rev. ed. World of Art. New York: Oxford Univ. Press, 1981.

Immerwahr, Sara Anderson. *Aegean Painting in the Bronze Age*. University Park: Pennsylvania State Univ. Press, 1990.

Marinatos, Nanno. *Art and Religion in Thera: Reconstructing a Bronze Age Society*. Athens: Mathioulakis, 1984.

Marinatos, Spyridon, and Max Hirmer. *Crete and Mycenae*. New York: Abrams, 1960.

Matz, Friedrich. *The Art of Crete and Early Greece: Prelude to Greek Art*. Trans. Ann E. Keep. Art of the World. New York: Crown, 1962.

Morgan, Lyvia. *The Miniature Wall Paintings of Thera: A Study in Aegean Culture and Iconography*. Cambridge: Cambridge Univ. Press, 1988.

Pellegrino, Charles R. *Unearthing Atlantis: An Archaeological Survey*. New York: Random House, 1991.

Chapter 5 Art of Ancient Greece

Akurgal, Ekrem. *The Art of Greece: Its Origins in the Mediterranean and Near East*. Trans. Wayne Dynes. Art of the World. New York: Crown, 1968.

Andrewes, Antony. *The Greeks: History of Human Society*. New York: Knopf, 1967.

Arafat, K. W. *Classical Zeus: A Study in Art and Literature*. Oxford: Clarendon, 1990.

Arias, Paolo. *A History of 1000 Years of Greek Vase Painting*. New York: Abrams, 1962.

Ashmole, Bernard. *Architect and Sculptor in Classical Greece*. Wrightsman Lectures. New York: New York Univ. Press, 1972.

Avery, Catherine, ed. *The New Century Handbook of Greek Mythology and Legend*. New York: Appleton-Century Crofts, 1972.

Berve, Helmut, and Gottfried Gruben. *Greek Temples, Theatres, and Shrines*. New York: Abrams, 1963.

Biers, William. *The Archaeology of Greece: An Introduction*. Rev. ed. Ithaca: Cornell Univ. Press, 1987.

Blumel, Carl. *Greek Sculptors at Work*. 2nd ed. Trans. Lydia Holland. London: Phaidon, 1969.

Boardman, John. *Greek Art*. Rev. ed. World of Art. New York: Oxford Univ. Press, 1973.

———. *Greek Sculpture: The Archaic Period: A Handbook*. World of Art. New York: Oxford Univ. Press, 1978.

———. *Greek Sculpture: The Classical Period: A Handbook*. London: Thames and Hudson, 1985.

———. *Oxford History of the Classical World*. Oxford: Oxford Univ. Press, 1986.

———. *The Parthenon and Its Sculptures*. Austin: Univ. of Texas Press, 1985.

Branigan, Keith, and Michael Vickers. *Hellas: The Civilizations of Ancient Greece*. New York: McGraw-Hill, 1980.

Camp, John M. *The Athenian Agora: Excavations in the Heart of Classical Athens*. New York: Thames and Hudson, 1986.

Carpenter, Thomas H. *Art and Myth in Ancient Greece: A Handbook*. World of Art. London: Thames and Hudson, 1991.

Charbonneaux, Jean, Robert Martin, and François Villard. *Archaic Greek Art (620–480 B.C.)*. Trans. James Emmons and Robert Allen. Arts of Mankind. New York: Braziller, 1971.

———. *Classical Greek Art (480–330 B.C.)*. Trans. James Emmons. Arts of Mankind. New York: Braziller, 1972.

———. *Hellenistic Art (330–50 B.C.)*. Trans. Peter Green. Arts of Mankind. New York: Braziller, 1973.

Chitham, Robert. *The Classical Orders of Architecture*. New York: Rizzoli, 1985.

Finley, Moses. *The Ancient Greeks: An Introduction to Their Life and Thought*. New York: Viking, 1963.

Francis, E. D. *Image and Idea in Fifth-Century Greece: Art and Literature after the Persian Wars*. London: Routledge, 1990.

Havelock, Christine Mitchell. *Hellenistic Art: The Art of the Classical World from the Death of Alexander the Great to the Battle of Actium*. 2nd ed. New York: Norton, 1981.

Homann-Wedeking, Ernst. *The Art of Archaic Greece*. Trans. J. R. Foster. Art of the World. New York: Crown, 1968.

Hood, Sinclair. *Arts in Prehistoric Greece*. Pelican History of Art. Harmondsworth, Eng.: Penguin, 1978.

Hopper, Robert John. *The Acropolis*. London: Weidenfeld and Nicolson, 1971.

Hurwit, Jeffrey M. *The Art and Culture of Early Greece 1100–480 B.C.* Ithaca: Cornell Univ. Press, 1985.

Jenkins, Ian. *The Parthenon Frieze*. Austin: Univ. of Texas Press, 1994.

Kagan, Donald. *The Outbreak of the Peloponnesian War*. Ithaca: Cornell Univ. Press, 1969.

Lawrence, A. W. *Greek Architecture*. 4th ed. Pelican History of Art. Harmondsworth, Eng.: Penguin, 1983.

Lullies, Reinhart, and Max Hirmer. *Greek Sculpture*. Rev. ed. Trans. Michael Bullock. New York: Abrams, 1957.

Martin, Roland. *Greek Architecture: Architecture of Crete, Greece, and the Greek World*. History of World Architecture. New York: Electa/Rizzoli, 1988.

Morg, Catherine. *Athletes and Oracles: The Transformation of Olympia and Delphi in the Eighth Century B.C.* Cambridge: Cambridge Univ. Press, 1990.

Onians, John. *Art and Thought in the Hellenistic Age: The Greek World View 350–50 B.C.* London: Thames and Hudson, 1979.

Papaioannou, Kostas. *The Art of Greece*. Trans. I. Mark Paris. New York: Abrams, 1989.

Pedley, John Griffiths. *Greek Art and Archaeology*. New York: Abrams, 1993.

Pollitt, J. J. *Art in the Hellenistic Age*. Cambridge: Cambridge Univ. Press, 1986.

———. *The Art of Ancient Greece: Sources and Documents*. Cambridge: Cambridge Univ. Press, 1990.

Ridgway, Brunilde Sismondo. *Fifth Century Styles in Greek Sculpture*. Princeton: Princeton Univ. Press, 1981.

———. *Hellenistic Sculpture I: The Styles of ca. 331–200 B.C.* Wisconsin Studies in Classics. Madison: Univ. of Wisconsin Press, 1990.

Robertson, Martin. *Greek Painting: The Great Centuries of Painting*. Geneva: Skira, 1959.

Roes, Anna. *Greek Geometric Art: Its Symbolism and Its Origin*. London: Oxford Univ. Press, 1933.

Schefold, Karl. *Classical Greece*. Trans. J. R. Foster. Art of the World. London: Methuen, 1967.

Schmidt, Evamaria. *The Great Altar of Pergamon*. Trans. Lena Jack. Leipzig: VEB Edition Leipzig, 1962.

Scully, Vincent. *The Earth, the Temple, and the Gods: Greek Sacred Architecture*. Rev. ed. New Haven: Yale Univ. Press, 1979.

Smith, R. R. R. *Hellenistic Sculpture: A Handbook*. World of Art. New York: Thames and Hudson, 1991.

Stewart, Andrew F. *Greek Sculpture: An Exploration*. 2 vols. New Haven: Yale Univ. Press, 1990.

———. *Skopas of Paros*. Park Ridge: Noyes, 1977.

Webster, T. B. L. *The Art of Greece: The Age of Hellenism*. Art of the World. New York: Crown, 1966.

Whitley, A. James M. *Style and Society in Dark Age Greece: The Changing Face of a Pre-literate Society, 1100–700 B.C.* New Studies in Archaeology. Cambridge: Cambridge Univ. Press, 1991.

Chapter 6 Etruscan Art and Roman Art

Andreae, Bernard. *The Art of Rome*. Trans. Robert Erich Wolf. New York: Abrams, 1977.

Aries, Philippe, and Georges Duby, eds. *A History of Private Life*. Vol. 1: *From Pagan Rome to Byzantium*. Trans. Arthur Goldhammer. Cambridge, Mass.: Belknap, 1987.

Balsdon, J. P. V. D. *Roman Women: Their History and Habits*. London: Bodley Head, 1962.

Bianchi Bandinelli, Ranuccio. *Rome: The Centre of Power: Roman Art to A.D. 200*. Trans. Peter Green. Arts of Mankind. London: Thames and Hudson, 1970.

———. *Rome: The Late Empire: Roman Art A.D. 200–400*. Trans. Peter Green. Arts of Mankind. New York: Braziller, 1971.

Bloch, Raymond. *Etruscan Art*. Greenwich, Conn.: New York Graphic Society, 1965.

Boardman, John. *Oxford History of the Classical World*. Oxford: Oxford Univ. Press, 1986.

Boethius, Axel, and J. B. Ward-Perkins. *Etruscan and Early Roman Architecture*. 2nd ed. Pelican History of Art. Harmondsworth, Eng.: Penguin, 1978.

Breeze, David John. *Hadrian's Wall*. London: Allen Lane, 1976.

Brendel, Otto J. *Etruscan Art*. Pelican History of Art. Harmondsworth, Eng.: Penguin, 1978.

Brilliant, Richard. *Roman Art from the Republic to Constantine*. London: Phaidon, 1974.

Brown, Peter. *The World of Late Antiquity: A.D. 150–750*. New York: Norton, 1989.

Buranelli, Francesco. *The Etruscans: Legacy of a Lost Civilization from the Vatican Museums*. Memphis: Lithograph, 1992.

Christ, Karl. *The Romans: An Introduction to Their History and Civilisation*. Berkeley: Univ. of California Press, 1984.

Cornell, Tim, and John Matthews. *Atlas of the Roman World*. New York: Facts on File, 1982.

Guilland, Jacqueline, and Maurice Guilland. *Frescoes in the Time of Pompeii*. New York: Potter, 1990.

Heintze, Helga von. *Roman Art*. New York: Universe, 1990.

Henig, Martin, ed. *A Handbook of Roman Art: A Comprehensive Survey of All the Arts of the Roman World*. Ithaca: Cornell Univ. Press, 1983.

Kahler, Heinz. *The Art of Rome and Her Empire*. Trans. J. R. Foster. Art of the World. New York: Crown, 1963.

Ling, Roger. *Roman Painting*. Cambridge: Cambridge Univ. Press, 1991.

L'Orange, Hans Peter. *The Roman Empire: Art Forms and Civic Life*. New York: Rizzoli, 1985.

MacDonald, William L. *The Architecture of the Roman Empire: An Introductory Study*. Rev. ed. 2 vols. Yale Publications in the History of Art. New Haven: Yale Univ. Press, 1982.

———. *The Pantheon: Design, Meaning, and Progeny*. Cambridge: Harvard Univ. Press, 1976.

Maiuri, Amedeo. *Roman Painting: The Great Centuries of Painting*. Trans. Stuart Gilbert. Geneva: Skira, 1953.

Mansuelli, G. A. *The Art of Etruria and Early Rome*. Art of the World. New York: Crown, 1965.

Pollitt, J. J. *The Art of Rome, c. 753 B.C.–337 A.D.: Sources and Documents*. Englewood Cliffs, N.J.: Prentice-Hall, 1966.

Quennell, Peter. *The Colosseum*. New York: Newsweek, 1971.

Ramage, Nancy H., and Andrew Ramage. *Roman Art: Romulus to Constantine*. New York: Abrams, 1991.

Rediscovering Pompeii. Rome: L'Erma di Bretschneider, 1990.

Sprenger, Maja, and Bartolini, Gilda. *The Etruscans: Their History, Art, and Architecture*. New York: Abrams, 1983.

Strong, Donald. *Roman Art*. 2nd ed. Pelican History of Art. Harmondsworth, Eng.: Penguin, 1988.

Ward-Perkins, J. B. *Roman Architecture*. History of World Architecture. New York: Electa/Rizzoli, 1988.

Wheeler, Robert Eric Mortimer, Sir. *Roman Art and Architecture*. World of Art. New York: Oxford Univ. Press, 1964.

Wilkinson, L. P. *The Roman Experience*. New York: Knopf, 1974.

Chapter 7 Early Christian, Jewish, and Byzantine Art

Age of Spirituality: Late Antique and Early Christian Art, Third to Seventh Century. New York: Metropolitan Museum of Art, 1979.

Beckwith, John. *The Art of Constantinople: An Introduction to Byzantine Art 330–1453*. 2nd ed. London: Phaidon, 1968.

———. *Early Christian and Byzantine Art*. 2nd ed. Pelican History of Art. Harmondsworth, Eng.: Penguin, 1979.

Boyd, Susan A. *Byzantine Art*. Chicago: Univ. of Chicago Press, 1979.

Buckton, David, ed. *The Treasury of San Marco, Venice*. Milan: Olivetti, 1985.

Carr, Annemarie Weyl. *Byzantine Illumination, 1150–1250: The Study of a Provincial Tradition*. Chicago: Univ. of Chicago Press, 1987.

Christe, Yves. *Art of the Christian World, A.D. 200–1500: A Handbook of Styles and Forms*. New York: Rizzoli, 1982.

Cutler, Anthony. *The Hand of the Master: Craftsmanship, Ivory, and Society in Byzantium (9th–11th Centuries)*. Princeton: Princeton Univ. Press, 1994.

Demus, Otto. *Byzantine Art and the West*. Wrightsman Lectures. New York: New York Univ. Press, 1970.

———. *Byzantine Mosaic Decoration: Aspects of Monumental Art in Byzantium*. New Rochelle: Caratzas, 1976.

———. *The Church of San Marco in Venice: History, Architecture, Sculpture*. Washington, D.C.: Dumbarton Oaks, 1960.

Ferguson, George Wells. *Signs and Symbols in Christian Art*. New York: Oxford Univ. Press, 1967.

Gough, Michael. *Origins of Christian Art*. World of Art. London: Thames and Hudson, 1973.

Grabar, André. *The Art of the Byzantine Empire: Byzantine Art in the Middle Ages*. Trans. Betty Forster. Art of the World. New York: Crown, 1966.

———. *Early Christian Art: From the Rise of Christianity to the Death of Theodosius*. Trans. Stuart Gilbert and James Emmons. Arts of Mankind. New York: Odyssey, 1969.

——. *The Golden Age of Justinian from the Death of Theodosius to the Rise of Islam*. Trans. Stuart Gilbert and James Emmons. New York: Odyssey, 1967.

Hubert, Jean, Jean Porcher, and W. F. Volbach. *Europe of the Invasions*. Trans. Stuart Gilbert and James Emmons. Arts of Mankind. New York: Braziller, 1969.

Kitzinger, Ernst. *Byzantine Art in the Making: Main Lines of Stylistic Development in Mediterranean Art, 3rd–7th Century*. Cambridge: Harvard Univ. Press, 1977.

Krautheimer, Richard. *Early Christian and Byzantine Architecture*. 4th ed. Pelican History of Art. Harmondsworth, Eng: Penguin, 1986.

Lane Fox, Robin. *Pagans and Christians*. Harmondsworth, Eng.: Viking, 1986.

Mainstone, R. J. *Hagia Sophia: Architecture, Structure and Liturgy of Justinian's Great Church*. London: Thames and Hudson, 1988.

Mango, Cyril. *Art of the Byzantine Empire, 312–1453: Sources and Documents*. Englewood Cliffs, N.J.: Prentice-Hall, 1972.

——. *Byzantine Architecture*. History of World Architecture. New York: Rizzoli, 1985.

Manicelli, Fabrizio. *Catacombs and Basilicas: The Early Christians in Rome*. Florence: Scala, 1981.

Mathew, Gervase. *Byzantine Aesthetics*. London: J. Murray, 1963.

Milburn, R. L. P. *Early Christian Art and Architecture*. Berkeley: Univ. of California Press, 1988.

Oakshott, Walter Fraser. *The Mosaics of Rome: From the Third to the Fourteenth Centuries*. London: Thames and Hudson, 1967.

Rice, David Talbot. *Art of the Byzantine Era*. New York: Praeger, 1963.

——. *Byzantine Art*. Harmondsworth, Eng.: Penguin, 1968.

Schapiro, Meyer. *Late Antique, Early Christian, and Mediaeval Art*. New York: Braziller, 1979.

Simson, Otto Georg von. *Sacred Fortress: Byzantine Art and Statecraft in Ravenna*. Chicago: Univ. of Chicago Press, 1948.

Snyder, James. *Medieval Art: Painting, Sculpture, Architecture, 4th–14th Century*. Englewood Cliffs, N.J.: Prentice-Hall, 1989.

Stevenson, James. *The Catacombs: Rediscovered Monuments of Early Christianity*. Ancient Peoples and Places. London: Thames and Hudson, 1978.

Weitzmann, Kurt. *Late Antique and Early Christian Book Illumination*. New York: Braziller, 1977.

——. *Place of Book Illumination in Byzantine Art*. Princeton: Art Museum, Princeton Univ., 1975.

Wharton, Annabel Jane. *Art of Empire: Painting and Architecture of the Byzantine Periphery: A Comparative Study of Four Provinces*. University Park: Pennsylvania State Univ. Press, 1988.

Chapter 8 Islamic Art

Akurgal, Ekrem, ed. *The Art and Architecture of Turkey*. New York: Rizzoli, 1980.

Al-Faruqi, Ismail R, and Lois Lamya'al Faruqi. *Cultural Atlas of Islam*. New York: Macmillan, 1986.

Aslanapa, Oktay. *Turkish Art and Architecture*. London: Faber, 1971.

Atasoy, Nurhan. *Splendors of the Ottoman Sultans*. Ed. and Trans. Tulay Artan. Memphis, Tenn.: Lithograph, 1992.

Atil, Esin. *The Age of Sultan Suleyman the Magnificent*. Washington, D.C.: National Gallery of Art, 1987.

——. *Art of the Arab World*. Washington, D.C.: Smithsonian Institution, 1975.

——. *Islamic Art and Patronage: Treasures from Kuwait*. New York: Rizzoli, 1990.

——. *Renaissance of Islam: Art of the Mamluks*. Washington, D.C.: Smithsonian Institution, 1981.

Blair, Sheila S., and Jonathan M. Brown. *The Art and Architecture of Islam 1250–1800*. New Haven: Yale Univ. Press, 1994.

Brend, Barbara. *Islamic Art*. Cambridge: Harvard Univ. Press, 1991.

Dodds, Jerrilynn D., ed. *Al-Andalus: The Art of Islamic Spain*. New York: Metropolitan Museum of Art, 1992.

Ettinghausen, Richard, and Oleg Grabar. *The Art and Architecture of Islam: 650–1250*. Pelican History of Art. Harmondsworth, Eng.: Penguin, 1987.

Falk, Toby, ed. *Treasures of Islam*. London: Sotheby's, 1985.

Ferrier, R. W., ed. *Arts of Persia*. New Haven: Yale Univ. Press, 1989.

Frishman, Martin, and Hasan-Uddin Khan. *The Mosque: History, Architectural Development and Regional Diversity*. London: Thames and Hudson, 1994.

Glasse, Cyril. *The Concise Encyclopedia of Islam*. San Francisco: Harper & Row, 1989.

Grabar, Oleg. *The Alhambra*. Cambridge: Harvard Univ. Press, 1978.

——. *The Formation of Islamic Art*. Rev. ed. New Haven: Yale Univ. Press, 1987.

——. *The Great Mosque of Isfahan*. New York: New York Univ. Press, 1990.

——. *The Mediation of Ornament*. A. W. Mellon Lectures in the Fine Arts. Princeton: Princeton Univ. Press, 1992.

Grube, Ernest J. *Architecture of the Islamic World: Its History and Social Meaning*. Ed. George Mitchell. New York: Morrow, 1978.

Hoag, John D. *Islamic Architecture*. History of World Architecture. New York: Abrams, 1977.

Jones, Dalu, and George Mitchell, eds. *The Arts of Islam*. London: Arts Council of Great Britain, 1976.

Khatibi, Abdelkebir, and Mohammed Sijelmassi. *The Splendour of Islamic Calligraphy*. New York: Rizzoli, 1977.

The Koran. Rev. ed. Trans. N. J. Dawood. London: Penguin, 1993.

Lentz, Thomas W., and Glenn D. Lowry. *Timur and the Princely Vision: Persian Art and Culture in the Fifteenth Century*. Los Angeles: Los Angeles County Museum of Art, 1989.

Papadopoulo, Alexandre. *Islam and Muslim Art*. Trans. Robert Erich Wolf. New York: Abrams, 1979.

Petsopoulos, Yanni, ed. *Tulips, Arabesques and Turbans: Decorative Arts from the Ottoman Empire*. New York: Abbeville, 1982.

Raby, Julian, ed. *The Art of Syria and the Jazira, 1100–1250*. Oxford Studies in Islamic Art. Oxford: Oxford Univ. Press, 1985.

Rice, David Talbot. *Islamic Art*. World of Art. New York: Thames and Hudson, 1965.

Schimmel, Annemarie. *Calligraphy and Islamic Culture*. New York: New York Univ. Press, 1983.

Sharma, Arvind, ed. *Our Religions*. San Francisco: HarperSanFrancisco, 1993.

Ward, R. M. *Islamic Metalwork*. New York: Thames and Hudson, 1993.

Welch, Anthony. *Calligraphy in the Arts of the Muslim World*. Austin: Univ. of Texas Press, 1979.

Chapter 9 Art of India before 1100

Berkson, Carmel. *Elephanta: The Cave of Shiva*. Princeton: Princeton Univ. Press, 1983.

Chandra, Pramod. *The Sculpture of India, 3000 B.C.–1300 A.D.* Washington, D.C.: National Gallery of Art, 1985.

Coomaraswamy, Ananda K. *Yaksas: Essays in the Water Cosmology*. Rev. ed. Ed. Paul Schroeder. New York: Oxford Univ. Press, 1993.

Czuma, Stanislaw J. *Kushan Sculpture: Images from Early India*. Cleveland: Cleveland Museum of Art, 1985.

De Bary, William, ed. *Sources of Indian Tradition*. New York: Columbia Univ. Press, 1958.

Dehejia, Vidya. *Art of the Imperial Cholas*. New York: Columbia Univ. Press, 1990.

——. *Early Buddhist Rock Temples*. Ithaca: Cornell Univ. Press, 1972.

Dessai, Vishakha N., and Darielle Mason. *Gods, Guardians, and Lovers: Temple Sculptures from North India, A.D. 700–1200*. New York: Asia Society Galleries, 1993.

Dimmitt, Cornelia. *Classical Hindu Mythology*. Philadelphia: Temple Univ. Press, 1978.

Eck, Diana L. *Darsan: Seeing the Divine Image in India*. 2nd rev. ed. Chambersburg, Penn.: Anima, 1985.

Errington, Elizabeth, and Joe Cribb, eds. *The Crossroads of Asia: Transformation in Image and Symbol in the Art of Ancient Afghanistan and Pakistan*. Cambridge, Eng.: Ancient India and Iran Trust, 1992.

Goswamy, B. N. *An Early Document of Indian Art: The Citralak-sa-na of Nagnajit*. New Delhi: Manohar Book Service, 1976.

Harle, James C. *Art and Architecture of the Indian Subcontinent*. Pelican History of Art. Harmondsworth, Eng.: Penguin, 1987.

——. *Gupta Sculpture*. Oxford: Clarendon, 1974.

Huntington, Susan L. *Art of Ancient India*. New York: Weatherhill, 1985.

——. *Leaves from the Bodhi Tree: The Art of Pala India (8th–12th Centuries) and Its International Legacy*. Dayton: Dayton Art Institute, 1990.

Hutt, Michael. *Nepal: A Guide to the Art and Architecture of the Kathmandu Valley*. Boston: Shambala, 1995.

Johnston, E. H. *Buddhacharita, or Acts of the Buddha*. 2nd ed. New Delhi: Oriental Books Reprint, 1972.

Knox, Robert. *Amaravati: Buddhist Sculpture from the Great Stupa*. London: British Museum, 1992.

Kramrisch, Stella. *The Art of Nepal*. New York: Abrams, 1964.

——. *The Hindu Temple*. 2 vols. Calcutta: Univ. of Calcutta, 1946.

——. *Presence of Siva*. Princeton: Princeton Univ. Press, 1981.

——. *Vichnudharmottara, Part III: A Treatise on Indian Painting and Image-Making*. 2nd rev. ed. Calcutta: Calcutta Univ. Press, 1928.

Meister, Michael, ed. *Discourses on Siva: On the Nature of Religious Imagery*. Philadelphia: Univ. of Pennsylvania Press, 1984.

O'Flaherty, Wendy. *Hindu Myths*. Harmondsworth, Eng.: Penguin, 1975.

Pal, Pratapaditya, ed. *Aspects of Indian Art*. Leiden: Brill, 1972.

——. *The Ideal Image: The Gupta Sculptural Tradition and Its Influence*. New York: Asia Society, 1978.

Peterson, Indira Vishnvanathan. *Poems to Shiva: The Hymns of the Tamil Saints*. Princeton: Princeton Univ. Press, 1989.

Possehl, Gregory, ed. *Ancient Cities of the Indus*. Durham: Carolina Academic, 1979.

——. *Harappan Civilization: A Recent Perspective*. 2nd ed. New Delhi: American Institute of Indian Studies, 1993.

Poster, Amy G. *From Indian Earth: 4,000 Years of Terracotta Art*. Brooklyn: Brooklyn Museum, 1986.

Rosenfeld, John M. *The Dynastic Arts of the Kushans*. California

Studies in the History of Art. Berkeley: Univ. of California Press, 1967.

Shearer, Alistair. *Upanishads*. New York: Harper & Row, 1978.

Singh, Madanjeet. *The Cave Paintings of Ajanta*. London: Thames and Hudson, 1965.

Skelton, Robert, and Mark Francis. *Arts of Bengal: The Heritage of Bangladesh and Eastern India*. London: Whitechapel Gallery, 1979.

Smith, Bardwell L., ed. *Essays in Gupta Culture*. Delhi: Motilal Banarsidass, 1983.

Thapar, Romila. *Asoka and the Decline of the Mauryas*. 2nd ed. Delhi: Oxford, 1973.

——. *History of India*. Harmondsworth, Eng.: Penguin, 1972.

Weiner, Sheila L. *Ajanta: Its Place in Buddhist Art*. Berkeley: Univ. of California Press, 1977.

Williams, Joanna G. *Art of Gupta India, Empire and Province*. Princeton: Princeton Univ. Press, 1982.

Zimmer, Heinrich Robert. *Myths and Symbols in Indian Art and Civilization*. ed. Joseph Campbell. Bollingen Series. New York: Pantheon, 1946.

Chapter 10 Chinese Art before 1280

Ackerman, Phyllis. *Ritual Bronzes of Ancient China*. New York: Dryden, 1945.

The Art Treasures of Dunhuang. Hong Kong: Joint, 1981.

Arts of China. 3 vols. Tokyo: Kodansha International, 1968–70.

Barnhart, Richard. *Along the Border of Heaven: Sung and Yuan Painting from the C. C. Wang Family Collection*. New York: Metropolitan Museum of Art, 1983.

Billeter, Jean François. *The Chinese Art of Writing*. New York: Skira/Rizzoli, 1990.

Blunden, Caroline, and Mark Elvin. *Cultural Atlas of China*. New York: Facts on File, 1983.

Cahill, James. *Art of Southern Sung China*. New York: Asia Society, 1962.

——. *Chinese Painting*. Treasures of Asia. Geneva: Skira, 1960.

——. *Index of Early Chinese Painters and Paintings: T'ang, Sung, and Yuan*. Berkeley: Univ. of California Press, 1980.

Cleary, Thomas, trans. *The Essential Tao: An Initiation into the Heart of Taoism through the Authentic Tao Te Ching and the Inner Teachings of Chuang Tzu*. San Francisco: HarperSanFrancisco, 1991.

De Silva, Anil. *The Art of Chinese Landscape Painting: In the Caves of Tun-huang*. Art of the World. New York: Crown, 1967.

Fong, Wen, ed. *Beyond Representation: Chinese Painting and Calligraphy, 8th–14th Century*. Princeton Monographs in Art and Archaeology. New York: Metropolitan Museum of Art, 1992.

——. *The Great Bronze Age of China: An Exhibition from the People's Republic of China*. New York: Metropolitan Museum of Art, 1980.

Fong, Wen, and Marilyn Fu. *Sung and Yuan Paintings*. New York: New York Graphic Society, 1973.

Gridley, Marilyn Leidig. *Chinese Buddhist Sculpture under the Liao: Free Standing Works in Situ and Selected Examples from Public Collections*. New Delhi: International Academy of Indian Culture, 1993.

Ho, Wai-kam, et al. *Eight Dynasties of Chinese Painting: The Collections of the Nelson Gallery-Atkins Museum, Kansas City, and the Cleveland Museum of Art*. Cleveland: Cleveland Museum of Art, 1980.

Juliano, Annette L. *Art of the Six Dynasties: Centuries of Change and Innovation*. New York: China House Gallery, 1975.

Lawton, Thomas. *Chinese Art of the Warring States Period: Change and Continuity, 480–222 B.C.* Washington, D.C.: Freer Gallery of Art, Smithsonian Institution, 1982.

——. *Chinese Figure Painting*. Washington, D.C.: Smithsonian Institution, 1973.

Lim, Lucy. *Stories from China's Past: Han Dynasty Pictorial Tomb Reliefs and Archaeological Objects from Sichuan Province, People's Republic of China*. San Francisco: Chinese Culture Foundation, 1987.

Medley, Margaret. *Chinese Potter: A Practical History of Chinese Ceramics*. 3rd ed. Oxford: Phaidon, 1976.

Munakata, Kiyohiko. *Sacred Mountains in Chinese Art*. Champaign: Krannert Art Museum, Univ. of Illinois, 1991.

Paludan, Ann. *Chinese Spirit Road: The Classical Tradition of Stone Tomb Sculpture*. New Haven: Yale Univ. Press, 1991.

——. *Chinese Tomb Figurines*. Hong Kong: Oxford Univ. Press, 1994.

Powers, Martin J. *Art and Political Expression in Early China*. New Haven: Yale Univ. Press, 1991.

Rawson, Jessica. *Ancient China: Art and Archaeology*. London: British Museum, 1980.

Sickman, Lawrence, and Alexander Soper. *Art and Architecture of China*. Pelican History of Art. Harmondsworth, Eng.: Penguin, 1971.

Speiser, Werner. *The Art of China: Spirit and Society*. Art of the World. New York: Crown, 1961.

Tregear, Mary. *Chinese Art*. World of Art. New York: Oxford Univ. Press, 1980.

Vainker, S. J. *Chinese Pottery and Porcelain: From Prehistory to the Present*. London: British Museum, 1991.

Watson, William. *Art of Dynastic China*. New York: Abrams, 1981.

Weidner, Marsha, ed. *Latter Days of the Law: Images of Chinese*

Buddhism, 850–1850. Lawrence: Spencer Museum of Art, Univ. of Kansas, 1994.

Whitfield, Roderick, and Anne Farrer. *Caves of the Thousand Buddhas: Chinese Art from the Silk Route.* London: British Museum, 1990.

Chapter 11   Japanese Art before 1392

Bethe, Monica. *Bugaku Masks.* Japanese Arts Library, vol. 5. New York: Kodansha International, 1978.

Egami, Namio. *The Beginnings of Japanese Art.* Trans. John Bester. Heibonsha Survey of Japanese Art, vol. 2. New York: Weatherhill, 1973.

Elisseeff, Danielle, and Vadime Elisseeff. *Art of Japan.* Trans. I. Mark Paris. New York: Abrams, 1985.

Fujioka, Ryoichi. *Shino and Oribe Ceramics.* Trans. Samuel Crowell Morse. Japanese Arts Library, vol. 1. New York: Kodansha International, 1977.

Fukuyama, Toshio. *Heian Temples: Byodo-in and Chuson-ji.* Trans. Ronald K. Jones. Heibonsha Survey of Japanese Art, vol. 9. New York: Weatherhill, 1976.

Hashimoto, Fumio, ed. *Architecture in the Shoin Style: Japanese Feudal Residences.* Trans. and adapted by H. Mack Horton. Japanese Arts Library, vol. 10. New York: Kodansha International, 1981.

Hayashi, Ryoichi. *Silk Road and the Shoso-in.* Trans. Robert Ricketts. Heibonsha Survey of Japanese Art, vol. 6. New York: Weatherhill, 1975.

Ienaga, Saburo. *Japanese Art: A Cultural Appreciation.* Trans. Richard L. Gage. Heibonsha Survey of Japanese Art, vol. 30. New York: Weatherhill, 1979.

———. *Painting in the Yamato Style.* Trans. John M. Shields. Heibonsha Survey of Japanese Art, vol. 10. New York: Weatherhill, 1973.

Ishida, Hisatoyo. *Esoteric Buddhist Painting.* Trans. and adapted by E. Dale Saunders. Japanese Arts Library, vol. 15. New York: Kodansha International, 1987.

Itoh, Teiji. *Traditional Domestic Architecture of Japan.* Trans. Richard L. Gage. Heibonsha Survey of Japanese Art, vol. 21. New York: Weatherhill, 1972.

Kidder, J. Edward. *Early Buddhist Japan.* Ancient People and Places. New York: Praeger, 1972.

———. *Early Japanese Art: The Great Tombs and Treasures.* Princeton: Van Nostrand, 1964.

———. *Japanese Temples: Sculpture, Paintings, Gardens, and Architecture.* London: Thames and Hudson, 1964.

———. *Prehistoric Japanese Arts: Jomon Pottery.* Tokyo: Kodansha International, 1968.

Kobayashi, Takeshi. *Nara Buddhist Art: Todai-ji.* Trans. and adapted by Richard L. Gage. Heibonsha Survey of Japanese Art, vol. 5. New York: Weatherhill, 1975.

Kurata, Bunsaku. *Horyu-ji, Temple of the Exalted Law: Early Buddhist Art from Japan.* New York: Japan Society, 1981.

Miki, Fumio. *Haniwa.* Trans. and adapted by Gino Lee Barnes. Arts of Japan, 8. New York: Weatherhill, 1974.

Miner, Earl, Hiroko Odagiri, and Robert E. Morrell. *The Princeton Companion to Classical Japanese Literature.* Princeton: Princeton Univ. Press, 1985.

Mino, Yutaka. *The Great Eastern Temple: Treasures of Japanese Buddhist Art from Todai-ji.* Chicago: Art Institute of Chicago, 1986.

Mizuno, Seiichi. *Asuka Buddhist Art: Horyuji.* Trans. Richard L. Gage. Heibonsha Survey of Japanese Art, vol. 4. New York: Weatherhill, 1974.

Mori, Hisashi. *Japanese Portrait Sculpture.* Trans. Widayati Roesijadi. Japanese Arts Library, vol. 2. New York: Kodansha International, 1977.

———. *Sculpture of the Kamakura Period.* Trans. Katherine Eickman. Heibonsha Survey of Japanese Art, vol. 11. New York: Weatherhill, 1974.

Murase, Miyeko. *Iconography of the Tale of Genji: Genji Monogatari Ekotoba.* New York: Weatherhill, 1983.

Nakagawa, Sensaku. *Kutani Ware.* Trans. and adapted by John Bester. Japanese Arts Library, vol. 7. New York: Kodansha International, 1979.

Nishiwara, Kyotaro, and Emily J. Sano. *The Great Age of Japanese Buddhist Sculpture,* A.D. *60–1300.* Fort Worth, Tex.: Kimbell Art Museum, 1982.

Okazaki, Joji. *Pure Land Buddhist Painting.* Trans. Elizabeth ten Grutenhuis. Japanese Arts Library, vol. 4. New York: Kodansha International, 1977.

Okudaira, Hideo. *Narrative Picture Scrolls.* Trans. Elizabeth ten Grutenhuis. Arts of Japan, 5. New York: Weatherhill, 1973.

Ooka, Minoru. *Temples of Nara and Their Art.* Trans. Dennis Lishka. Heibonsha Survey of Japanese Art, vol. 7. New York: Weatherhill, 1973.

Pearson, Richard J. *Ancient Japan.* Washington, D.C.: Sackler Gallery, 1992.

Rosenfield, John M., Fumiko E. Cranston, and Edwin A. Cranston. *The Courtly Tradition in Japanese Art and Literature: Selections from the Hofer and Hyde Collections.* Cambridge: Fogg Art Museum, Harvard Univ., 1973.

———. *Japanese Arts of the Heian Period: 794–1185.* New York: Asia Society, 1967.

Sato, Kanzan. *Japanese Sword.* Trans. and adapted by Joe Earle. Japanese Arts Library, vol. 12. New York: Kodansha International, 1983.

Sawa, Takaaki. *Art in Japanese Esoteric Buddhism.* Trans.

Richard L. Gage. Heibonsha Survey of Japanese Art, vol. 8. New York: Weatherhill, 1972.

Soper, Alexander Coburn. *Evolution of Buddhist Architecture in Japan.* Princeton Monographs in Art and Archaeology, no. 22. New York: Hacker Art, 1978.

Sugiyama, Jiro. *Classic Buddhist Sculpture: The Tempyo Period.* Trans. and adapted by Samuel Crowell Morse. Japanese Arts Library, vol. 11. New York: Kodansha International, 1982.

Suzuki, Kakichi. *Early Buddhist Architecture in Japan.* Trans. and adapted by Mary Neighbor Parent and Nancy Shatzman Steinhardt. Japanese Arts Library, vol. 9. New York: Kodansha International, 1980.

Swann, Peter. *The Art of Japan: From the Jomon to the Tokugawa Period.* Art of the World. New York: Crown, 1966.

Tanaka, Ichimatsu. *Japanese Ink Painting: Shubun to Sesshu.* Trans. Bruce Darling. Heibonsha Survey of Japanese Art, vol. 12. New York: Weatherhill, 1972.

Varley, H. Paul. *Japanese Culture.* 3rd ed. Honolulu: Univ. of Hawaii Press, 1984.

Watanabe, Yasutada. *Shinto Art: Ise and Izumo Shrines.* Trans. Robert Ricketts. Heibonsha Survey of Japanese Art, vol. 3. New York: Weatherhill, 1974.

Yamane, Yuzo. *Momoyama Genre Painting.* Trans. John M. Shields. Heibonsha Survey of Japanese Art, vol. 17. New York: Weatherhill, 1973.

Yonezawa, Yoshiho, and Chu Yoshizawa. *Japanese Painting in the Literati Style.* Trans. and adapted by Betty Iverson Monroe. Heibonsha Survey of Japanese Art, vol. 23. New York: Weatherhill, 1974.

Chapter 12   Art of the Americas before 1300

Abel-Vidor, Suzanne. *Between Continents/Between Seas: Precolumbian Art of Costa Rica.* New York: Abrams, 1981.

Abrams, Elliot Marc. *How the Maya Built Their World: Energetics and Ancient Architecture.* Austin: Univ. of Texas Press, 1994.

Alcina Franch, José. *Pre-Columbian Art.* Trans. I. Mark Paris. New York: Abrams, 1983.

Anton, Ferdinand. *Art of the Maya.* Trans. Mary Whitall. London: Thames and Hudson, 1970.

Berlo, Janet Catherine, ed. *Art, Ideology, and the City of Teotihuacan: A Symposium at Dumbarton Oaks.* Washington, D.C.: Dumbarton Oaks, 1992.

Berrin, Kathleen, ed. *Feathered Serpents and Flowering Trees: Reconstructing the Murals of Teotihuacan.* San Francisco: Fine Arts Museums of San Francisco, 1988.

———, and Esther Pasztory. *Teotihuacan: Art from the City of the Gods.* New York: Thames and Hudson, 1993.

Brody, J. J. *The Anasazi: Ancient Indian People of the American Southwest.* New York: Rizzoli, 1990.

———. *Anasazi and Pueblo Painting.* Albuquerque: Univ. of New Mexico Press, 1991.

Clewlow, C. William. *Colossal Heads of the Olmec Culture.* Contributions of the Univ. of California Archaeological Research Facility. Berkeley: Archaeological Research Facility, Univ. of California, 1967.

Coe, Michael D. *The Jacquar's Children: Pre-Classical Central Mexico.* New York: Museum of Primitive Art, 1965.

Coe, Ralph T. *Sacred Circles: Two Thousand Years of North American Indian Art.* London: Arts Council of Great Britain, 1976.

Donnan, Christopher B. *Ceramics of Ancient Peru.* Los Angeles: Fowler Museum of Cultural History, Univ. of California, 1992.

———. *Moche Art of Peru: Pre-Columbian Symbolic Communication.* Rev. ed. Los Angeles: Museum of Cultural History, Univ. of California, 1978.

Fash, William Leonard. *Scribes, Warriors, and Kings: The City of Copan and the Ancient Maya.* London: Thames and Hudson, 1991.

Fewkes, Jesse Walter. *The Mimbres: Art and Archaeology.* Albuquerque: Avanyu, 1989.

Fitzhugh, William, and Aron Crowell, eds. *Crossroads of Continents: Cultures of Siberia and Alaska.* Washington, D.C.: Smithsonian Institution, 1988.

Frazier, Kendrick. *People of Chaco: A Canyon and Its Culture.* New York: Norton, 1986.

Herreman, Frank. *Power of the Sun: The Gold of Colombia.* Antwerp: City of Antwerp, 1993.

Heyden, Doris, and Paul Gendrop. *Pre-Columbian Architecture of Mesoamerica.* Trans. Judith Stanton. History of World Architecture. New York: Electa/Rizzoli, 1988.

Korp, Maureen. *The Sacred Geography of the American Mound Builders.* Native American Studies. Lewiston, N.Y.: Mellen, 1990.

Kubler, George. *The Art and Architecture of Ancient America: The Mexican, Maya, and Andean Peoples.* 2nd ed. Pelican History of Art. Harmondsworth, Eng.: Penguin, 1975.

———. *Esthetic Recognition of Ancient Amerindian Art.* Yale Publications in the History of Art. New Haven: Yale Univ. Press, 1991.

Miller, Arthur G. *The Mural Painting of Teotihuacan.* Washington, D.C.: Dumbarton Oaks, 1973.

Miller, Mary Ellen. *The Art of Mesoamerica: From Olmec to Aztec.* World of Art. New York: Thames and Hudson, 1986.

———, and Karl Taube. *The Gods and Symbols of Ancient Mexico and the Maya: An Illustrated Dictionary of*

Mesoamerican Religion. New York: Thames and Hudson, 1993.

Moseley, Michael. *The Incas and Their Ancestors: The Archaeology of Peru.* London: Thames and Hudson, 1992.

Pang, Hildegard Delgado. *Pre-Columbian Art: Investigations and Insights.* Norman: Univ. of Oklahoma Press, 1992.

Paul, Anne. *Paracas Art and Architecture: Object and Context in South Coastal Peru.* Iowa City: Univ. of Iowa Press, 1991.

Schele, Linda, and David Freidel. *A Forest of Kings: The Untold Story of the Ancient Maya.* New York: Morrow, 1990.

Schele, Linda, and Mary Ellen Miller. *The Blood of Kings: Dynasty and Ritual in Maya Art.* New York: Braziller, 1986.

Stone-Miller, Rebecca. *To Weave for the Sun: Andean Textiles in the Museum of Fine Arts, Boston.* Boston: Museum of Fine Arts, 1992.

Townsend, Richard, ed. *The Ancient Americas: Art from Sacred Landscapes.* Chicago: Art Institute of Chicago, 1992.

———. *The Aztecs.* Ancient Peoples and Places. London: Thames and Hudson, 1992.

Wuthenau, Alexander von. *The Art of Terracotta Pottery in Pre-Columbian Central and South America.* Art of the World. New York: Crown, 1970.

Chapter 13   Art of Ancient Africa

Bassani, Ezio, and William Fagg. *Africa and the Renaissance: Art in Ivory.* New York: Center for African Art, 1988.

Ben-Amos, Paula. *The Art of Benin.* London: Thames and Hudson, 1980.

———, and Arnold Rubin. *The Art of Power, the Power of Art: Studies in Benin Iconography.* Monograph Series, no. 19. Los Angeles: Museum of Cultural History, Univ. of California, 1983.

Cole, Herbert M. *Igbo Arts: Community and Cosmos.* Los Angeles: Museum of Cultural History, Univ. of California, 1984.

Connah, Graham. *African Civilizations: Precolonial Cities and States in Africa: An Archaeological Perspective.* Cambridge: Cambridge Univ. Press, 1987.

Eyo, Ekpo, and Frank Willett. *Treasures of Ancient Nigeria.* Ed. Rollyn O. Kirchbaum. New York: Knopf, 1980.

Ezra, Kate. *Royal Art of Benin: The Perls Collection in the Metropolitan Museum of Art.* New York: Metropolitan Museum of Art, 1992.

Fagg, Bernard. *Nok Terracottas.* Lagos: Ethnographica, 1977.

Garlake, Peter S. *Great Zimbabwe.* London: Thames and Hudson, 1973.

———. *The Painted Caves: An Introduction to the Prehistoric Art of Zimbabwe.* Harare: Modus, 1987.

Huffman, Thomas N. *Symbols in Stone: Unravelling the Mystery of Great Zimbabwe.* Johannesburg: Witwatersrand Univ. Press, 1987.

Lhote, Henri. *The Search for the Tassili Frescoes: The Story of the Prehistoric Rock-Paintings of the Sahara.* 2nd ed. Trans. Alan Houghton Brodrick. London: Hutchinson, 1973.

Shaw, Thurstan. *Unearthing Igbo-Ukwu: Archaeological Discoveries in Eastern Nigeria.* New York: Oxford Univ. Press, 1977.

Willcox, A. R. *The Rock Art of Africa.* London: Croon Helm, 1984.

Willett, Frank. *Ife in the History of West African Sculpture.* New York: McGraw-Hill, 1967.

Chapter 14   Early Medieval Art in Europe

Alexander, J. J. G. *Medieval Illuminators and Their Methods of Work.* New Haven: Yale Univ. Press, 1992.

Backes, Magnus, and Regine Dolling. *Art of the Dark Ages.* Trans. Francisca Garvie. Panorama of World Art. New York: Abrams, 1971.

Backhouse, Janet, D. H. Turner, and Leslie Webster. *The Golden Age of Anglo-Saxon Art, 966–1066.* Bloomington: Indiana Univ. Press, 1984.

Beckwith, John. *Early Medieval Art: Carolingian, Ottonian, Romanesque.* World of Art. New York: Oxford Univ. Press, 1974.

Calkins, Robert G. *Illuminated Books of the Medieval Ages.* Ithaca: Cornell Univ. Press, 1983.

Cirrker, Blanche, ed. *The Book of Kells: Selected Plates in Full Color.* New York: Dover, 1982.

Conant, Kenneth John. *Carolingian and Romanesque Architecture, 800–1200.* 3rd ed. Pelican History of Art. Harmondsworth, Eng.: Penguin, 1973.

Davis-Weyer, Caecilia. *Early Medieval Art, 300–1150: Sources and Documents.* Englewood Cliffs, N.J.: Prentice-Hall, 1971.

Dodds, Jerrilynn D. *Architecture and Ideology in Early Medieval Spain.* University Park: Pennsylvania State Univ. Press, 1990.

Dodwell, C. R. *The Pictorial Arts of the West, 800–1200.* Pelican History of Art. New Haven: Yale Univ. Press, 1993.

Evans, Angela Care. *The Sutton Hoo Ship Burial.* London: British Museum, 1986.

Fernie, E. C. *The Architecture of the Anglo-Saxons.* London: Batsford, 1983.

Henderson, George. *Early Medieval.* Style and Civilization. Harmondsworth, Eng.: Penguin, 1972.

———. *From Durrow to Kells: The Insular Gospel-Books, 650–800.* London: Thames and Hudson, 1987.

Horn, Walter W., and Ernest Born. *Plan of Saint Gall: A Study of the Architecture and Economy of and Life in a Paradigmatic*

Carolingian Monastery. 3 vols. California Studies in the History of Art. Berkeley: Univ. of California Press, 1979.

Hubert, Jean, Jean Porcher, and W. F. Volbach. *Carolingian Renaissance.* Arts of Mankind. New York: Braziller, 1970.

Laing, Lloyd. *Art of the Celts.* World of Art. New York: Thames and Hudson, 1992.

Lasko, Peter. *Ars Sacra, 800–1200.* Pelican History of Art. Harmondsworth, Eng.: Penguin, 1972.

Mayr-Harting, Henry. *Ottonian Book Illumination: An Historical Study.* 2 vols. New York: Oxford Univ. Press, 1991.

Megaw, Ruth, and Vincent Megaw. *Celtic Art: From Its Beginnings to the Book of Kells.* New York: Thames and Hudson, 1989.

New American Bible. New York: Catholic, 1992.

Nordenfalk, Carl Adam Johan. *Early Medieval Book Illumination.* New York: Rizzoli, 1988.

Palol, Pedro de, and Max Hirmer. *Early Medieval Art in Spain.* Trans. Alisa Jaffa. London: Thames and Hudson, 1967.

Richardson, Hilary, and John Scarry. *An Introduction to Irish High Crosses.* Dublin: Mercier, 1990.

Treasures of Irish Art, 1500 B.C. to 1500 A.D.: From the Collections of the National Museum of Ireland, Royal Irish Academy, Trinity College, Dublin. New York: Metropolitan Museum of Art, 1977.

Verzone, Paola. *The Art of Europe: The Dark Ages from Theodoric to Charlemagne.* Art of the World. New York: Crown, 1968.

Williams, John. *Early Spanish Manuscript Illumination.* New York: Braziller, 1977.

Wilson, David M. *Anglo-Saxon Art: From the Seventh Century to the Norman Conquest.* London: Thames and Hudson, 1984.

———, and Ole Klindt-Jensen. *Viking Art.* 2nd ed. Minneapolis: Univ. of Minnesota Press, 1980.

Chapter 15 Romanesque Art

Armi, C. Edson. *Masons and Sculptors in Romanesque Burgundy: The New Aesthetics of Cluny III.* 2 vols. University Park: Pennsylvania State Univ. Press, 1983.

Busch, Harald, and Bernd Lohse. *Romanesque Sculpture.* London: Batsford, 1962.

Cahn, Walter. *Romanesque Bible Illumination.* Ithaca: Cornell Univ. Press, 1982.

Evans, Joan. *Cluniac Art of the Romanesque Period.* Cambridge: Cambridge Univ. Press, 1950.

Focillon, Henri. *The Art of the West in the Middle Ages.* 2 vols. Ed. Jean Bony. Trans. Donald King. London: Phaidon, 1963.

Forsyth, Ilene H. *The Throne of Wisdom: Wood Sculptures of the Madonna in Romanesque France.* Princeton: Princeton Univ. Press, 1972.

Gantner, Joseph, and Marvel Pobe. *Romanesque Art in France.* London: Thames and Hudson, 1956.

Grape, Wolfgang. *The Bayeux Tapestry: Monument to a Norman Triumph.* New York: Prestel, 1994.

Hearn, M. F. *Romanesque Sculpture: The Revival of Monumental Stone Sculptures in the Eleventh and Twelfth Centuries.* Ithaca: Cornell Univ. Press, 1981.

Holt, Elizabeth Gilmore. *A Documentary History of Art.* 3 vols. Princeton: Princeton Univ. Press, 1982.

Jacobs, Michael. *Northern Spain: The Road to Santiago de Compostela.* Architectural Guides for Travelers. San Francisco: Chronicle, 1991.

Kennedy, Hugh. *Crusader Castles.* Cambridge: Cambridge Univ. Press, 1994.

Kubach, Hans Erich. *Romanesque Architecture.* History of World Architecture. New York: Electa/Rizzoli, 1988.

Kuhnel, Biana. *Crusader Art of the Twelfth Century: A Geographical, and Historical, or an Art Historical Notion?* Berlin: Gebr. Mann, 1994.

Kunstler, Gustav. *Romanesque Art in Europe.* Greenwich, Conn.: New York Graphic Society, 1969.

Little, Bryan D. G. *Architecture in Norman Britain.* London: Batsford, 1985.

Mâle, Emile. *Religious Art in France, the Twelfth Century: A Study of the Origins of Medieval Iconography.* Bollingen Series. Princeton: Princeton Univ. Press, 1978.

Nebosine, George A. *Journey into Romanesque: A Traveller's Guide to Romanesque Monuments in Europe.* Ed. Robyn Cooper. London: Weidenfeld and Nicolson, 1969.

Norton, Christopher, and David Park. *Cistercian Art and Architecture in the British Isles.* Cambridge: Cambridge Univ. Press, 1986.

Radding, Charles M., and William W. Clark. *Medieval Architecture, Medieval Learning: Builders and Masters in the Age of Romanesque and Gothic.* New Haven: Yale Univ. Press, 1992.

Rollason, David, Margaret Harvey, and Michael Prestwich, eds. *Anglo-Norman Durham: 1093–1193.* Rochester, N.Y.: Boydell, 1994.

Schapiro, Meyer. *Romanesque Art.* New York: Braziller, 1977.

———. *The Romanesque Sculpture of Moissac.* New York: Braziller, 1985.

Swarzenski, Hanns. *Monuments of Romanesque Art: The Art of Church Treasures of North-Western Europe.* 2nd ed. Chicago: Univ. of Chicago Press, 1967.

Tate, Robert Brian, and Marcus Tate. *The Pilgrim Route to Santiago.* Oxford: Phaidon, 1987.

Theophilus. *On Divers Arts: The Treatise of Theophilus.* Trans. John G. Hawthorne and Cyril Stanley Smith. Chicago: Univ. of Chicago Press, 1963.

Wilson, David M. *The Bayeux Tapestry: The Complete Tapestry in Color.* New York: Random House, 1985.

The Year 1200. 2 vols. New York: Metropolitan Museum of Art, 1970.

Zarnecki, George. *Romanesque Art.* New York: Universe, 1971.

———, Janet Holt, and Tristam Holland. *English Romanesque Art, 1066–1200.* London: Weidenfeld and Nicolson, 1984.

Chapter 16 Gothic Art

Alexander, Jonathan, and Paul Binski, eds. *Age of Chivalry: Art in Plantagenet England, 1200–1400.* London: Royal Academy of Arts, 1987.

Andrews, Francis B. *The Mediaeval Builder and His Methods.* New York: Barnes & Noble, 1993.

Armi, C. Edson. *The "Headmaster" of Chartres and the Origins of "Gothic" Sculpture.* University Park: Pennsylvania State Univ. Press, 1994.

Aubert, Marcel. *The Art of the High Gothic Era.* Rev. ed. Art of the World. New York: Greystone, 1966.

Binski, Paul. *Medieval Craftsmen: Painters.* London: British Museum, 1991.

Bogin, Magda. *Gothic Cathedrals of France and Their Treasures.* London: Kaye, 1959.

———. *The Women Troubadours.* New York: Norton, 1980.

Bony, Jean. *French Gothic Architecture of the 12th and 13th Centuries.* California Studies in the History of Art. Berkeley: Univ. of California Press, 1983.

Borsook, Eve, and Fiorella Superbi Gioffredi. *Italian Altarpieces, 1250–1550: Function and Design.* Oxford: Clarendon, 1994.

Bottineau, Yves. *Notre-Dame de Paris and the Sainte Chapelle.* Trans. Lovett F. Edwards. London: Allen, 1967.

Branner, Robert. *Manuscript Painting in Paris during the Reign of Saint Louis: A Study of Styles.* California Studies in the History of Art. Berkeley: Univ. of California Press, 1977.

Chiellini, Monica. *Cimabue.* Trans. Lisa Pelletti. Florence: Scala, 1988.

Coe, Brian. *Stained Glass in England, 1150–1550.* London: Allen, 1981.

Cole, Bruce. *Giotto and Florentine Painting, 1280–1375.* New York: Harper & Row, 1975.

Crosby, Sumner McKnight. *The Royal Abbey of Saint-Denis from Its Beginnings to the Death of Suger, 475–1151.* Yale Publications in the History of Art. New Haven: Yale Univ. Press, 1987.

Erlande-Brandenburg, Alain. *Gothic Art.* Trans. I. Mark Paris. New York: Abrams, 1989.

Favier, Jean. *The World of Chartres.* Trans. Francisca Garvie. New York: Abrams, 1990.

Franklin, J. W. *Cathedrals of Italy.* London: Batsford, 1958.

Frisch, Teresa G. *Gothic Art, 1140–c. 1450: Sources and Documents.* Englewood Cliffs, N.J.: Prentice-Hall, 1971.

Grodecki, Louis. *Gothic Architecture.* Trans. I. Mark Paris. History of World Architecture. New York: Electa/Rizzoli, 1985.

———, and Catherine Brisac. *Gothic Stained Glass, 1200–1300.* Ithaca: Cornell Univ. Press, 1985.

Herlihy, David. *Medieval Households.* Cambridge: Harvard Univ. Press, 1985.

Jantzen, Hans. *High Gothic: The Classic Cathedrals of Chartres, Reims, Amiens.* Trans. James Palmes. New York: Pantheon, 1962.

Katzenellenbogen, Adolf. *The Sculptural Programs of Chartres Cathedral: Christ, Mary, Ecclesia.* New York: Norton, 1964.

Mâle, Emile. *Chartres.* Trans. Sarah Wilson. New York: Harper & Row, 1983.

———. *Religious Art in France, the Thirteenth Century: A Study of Medieval Iconography and Its Sources.* Princeton: Princeton Univ. Press, 1984.

Martindale, Andrew. *Gothic Art.* World of Art. London: Thames and Hudson, 1967.

McIntyre, Anthony. *Medieval Tuscany and Umbria.* Architectural Guides for Travellers. San Francisco: Chronicle, 1992.

Moskowitz, Anita Fiderer. *The Sculpture of Andrea and Nino Pisano.* Cambridge: Cambridge Univ. Press, 1986.

Panofsky, Erwin. *Abbot Suger on the Abbey Church of St.-Denis and Its Art Treasures.* 2nd ed. Ed. Gerda Panofsky-Soergel. Princeton: Princeton Univ. Press, 1979.

———. *Gothic Architecture and Scholasticism.* Latrobe, Penn.: Archabbey, 1951.

Pevsner, Nikolaus, and Priscilla Metcalf. *The Cathedrals of England.* 2 vols. Harmondsworth, Eng.: Viking, 1985.

Pope-Hennessy, John. *Italian Gothic Sculpture.* 3rd ed. Oxford: Phaidon, 1986.

Sauerlander, Willibald. *Gothic Sculpture in France, 1140–1270.* Trans. Janet Sandheimer. London: Thames and Hudson, 1972.

Simson, Otto Georg von. *The Gothic Cathedral: Origins of Gothic Architecture and the Medieval Concept of Order.* 3rd ed. Bollingen Series. Princeton: Princeton Univ. Press, 1988.

Smart, Alastair. *The Dawn of Italian Painting, 1250–1400.* Ithaca: Cornell Univ. Press, 1978.

White, John. *Art and Architecture in Italy, 1250 to 1400.* 3rd ed. Pelican History of Art. Harmondsworth, Eng.: Penguin, 1993.

———. *Duccio: Tuscan Art and the Medieval Workshop.* New York: Thames and Hudson, 1979.

Wieck, Roger S. *Time Sanctified: The Book of Hours in Medieval Art and Life.* New York: Braziller, 1988.

Wilson, Christopher. *The Gothic Cathedral: The Architecture of the Great Church, 1130–1530.* New York: Thames and Hudson, 1990.

Chapter 17 Early Renaissance Art in Europe

Ainsworth, Maryan Wynn. *Petrus Christus: Renaissance Master of Bruges.* New York: Metropolitan Museum of Art, 1994.

Baxandall, Michael. *Painting and Experience in Fifteenth-Century Italy: A Primer in the Social History of Pictorial Style.* Oxford: Clarendon, 1972.

Blum, Shirley. *Early Netherlandish Triptychs: A Study in Patronage.* California Studies in the History of Art. Berkeley: Univ. of California Press, 1969.

Borsi, Franco. *Leon Battista Alberti: The Complete Works.* New York: Electa/Rizzoli, 1989.

———, and Stefano Borsi. *Paolo Uccello.* Trans. Elfreda Powell. New York: Abrams, 1994.

Campbell, Lorne. *Renaissance Portraits: European Portrait-Painting in the 14th, 15th, and 16th Centuries.* New Haven: Yale Univ. Press, 1990.

Chastel, André. *The Flowering of the Italian Renaissance.* Trans. Jonathan Griffin. Arts of Mankind. New York: Odyssey, 1965.

———. *Studios and Styles of the Italian Renaissance.* Trans. Jonathan Griffin. Arts of Mankind. New York: Odyssey, 1966.

Christianity and the Renaissance: Image and Religious Imagination in the Quattrocento. Syracuse. N.Y.: Syracuse Univ. Press, 1990.

Christiansen, Keith. *Andrea Mantegna: Padua and Mantua.* New York: Braziller, 1994.

———, Laurence B. Kanter, and Carl Brandon Strehlke. *Painting in Renaissance Siena, 1420–1500.* New York: Metropolitan Museum of Art, 1988.

Cole, Bruce. *Masaccio and the Art of Early Renaissance Florence.* Bloomington: Indiana Univ. Press, 1980.

Davies, Martin. *Rogier van der Weyden: An Essay, with a Critical Catalogue of Paintings Assigned to Him and to Robert Campin.* London: Phaidon, 1972.

de Pisan, Christine. *Le Livre de la Cité des Dames (The Book of the City of Ladies).* Trans. Earl J. Richards. New York: Persea, 1982.

Dhanens, Elisabeth. *Van Eyck: The Ghent Altarpiece.* New York: Viking, 1973.

Flanders in the Fifteenth Century: Art and Civilization. Detroit: Detroit Institute of Arts, 1960.

Freeman, Margaret B. *The Unicorn Tapestries.* New York: Metropolitan Museum of Art, 1976.

Gilbert, Creighton, ed. *Italian Art, 1400–1500: Sources and Documents.* Evanston: Northwestern Univ. Press, 1992.

Goffen, Rona. *Giovanni Bellini.* New Haven: Yale Univ. Press, 1989.

Goldwater, Robert, and Marco Treves. *Artists on Art: From the XIV to the XX Century.* New York: Random House, 1945.

Hind, Arthur M. *An Introduction to a History of Woodcut.* New York: Dover, 1963.

Joannides, Paul. *Masaccio and Masolino: A Complete Catalogue.* London: Phaidon, 1993.

Krautheimer, Richard. *Ghiberti's Bronze Doors.* Princeton: Princeton Univ. Press, 1971.

Lane, Barbara G. *The Altar and the Altarpiece: Sacramental Themes in Early Netherlandish Painting.* New York: Harper & Row, 1984.

Lightbown, Ronald. *Piero della Francesca.* New York: Abbeville, 1992.

———. *Sandro Botticelli: Life and Work.* New ed. New York: Abbeville, 1989.

Lloyd, Christopher. *Fra Angelica.* Rev. ed. London: Phaidon, 1992.

Meiss, Millard. *French Painting in the Time of Jean de Berry: The Limbourgs and Their Contemporaries.* New York: Braziller, 1974.

Muller, Theodor. *Sculpture in the Netherlands, Germany, France, and Spain: 1400–1500.* Trans. Elaine and William Robson Scott. Pelican History of Art. Harmondsworth, Eng.: Penguin, 1966.

Pacht, Otto. *Van Eyck and the Founders of Early Netherlandish Painting.* Ed. Maria Schmidt-Dengler. Trans. David Britt. London: Miller, 1994.

Panofsky, Erwin. *Early Netherlandish Painting: Its Origins and Character.* 2 vols. Cambridge: Harvard Univ. Press, 1966.

Plummer, John. *The Last Flowering: French Painting in Manuscripts, 1420–1530, from American Collections.* New York: Pierpont Morgan Library, 1982.

Pope-Hennessy, Sir John. *Donatello: Sculptor.* New York: Abbeville, 1993.

Saalman, Howard. *Filippo Brunelleschi: The Buildings.* University Park: Pennsylvania State Univ. Press, 1993.

Seymour, Charles. *Sculpture in Italy, 1400–1500.* Pelican History of Art. Harmondsworth, Eng.: Penguin, 1966.

Snyder, James. *Northern Renaissance Art: Painting, Sculpture, the Graphic Arts from 1350 to 1575.* New York: Abrams, 1985.

Vos, Dirk de. *Hans Memling: The Complete Works.* Ghent: Ludion, 1994.

Chapter 18 Renaissance Art in Sixteenth-Century Europe

Ackerman, James S. *The Architecture of Michelangelo.* Rev ed. Studies in Architecture. London: Zwemmer, 1966.

Baldini, Umberto. *The Sculpture of Michelangelo.* Trans. Clare Coope. New York: Rizzoli, 1982.

Baxandall, Michael. *The Limewood Sculptors of Renaissance Germany.* New Haven: Yale Univ. Press, 1980.

Beck, James H. *Raphael.* New York: Abrams, 1994.

Bier, Justus. *Tilman Riemenschneider, His Life and Work.* Lexington: Univ. of Kentucky Press, 1989.

Blankert, A. *Vermeer of Delft.* Oxford: Phaidon, 1978.

Blunt, Anthony. *Art and Architecture in France: 1500–1700.* 4th ed. Pelican History of Art. Harmondsworth, Eng.: Penguin, 1981.

Bosquet, Jacques. *Mannerism: The Painting and Style of the Late Renaissance.* Trans. Simon Watson Taylor. New York: Braziller, 1964.

Boucher, Brude. *Andrea Palladio: The Architect in His Time.* New York: Abbeville, 1994.

Bronstein, Leo. *El Greco (Domenicos Theotocopoulos).* New York: Abrams, 1990.

Brown, Jonathan. *The Golden Age of Painting in Spain.* New Haven: Yale Univ. Press, 1991.

Bruschi, Arnaldo. *Bramante.* London: Thames and Hudson, 1977.

Chastel, André. *The Age of Humanism: Europe, 1480–1530.* Trans. Katherine M. Delavenay and E. M. Gwyer. London: Thames and Hudson, 1963.

Ettlinger, Leopold D., and Helen S. Ettlinger. *Raphael.* Oxford: Phaidon, 1987.

Farmer, John David. *The Virtuoso Craftsman: Northern European Design in the Sixteenth Century.* Worcester, Mass.: Worcester Art Museum, 1969.

Foote, Timothy. *The World of Bruegel, c. 1525–1569.* New York: Time-Life, 1968.

Freedberg, S. J. *Painting in Italy, 1500 to 1600.* 3rd ed. Pelican History of Art. New Haven: Yale Univ. Press, 1993.

Gibson, Walter. *Hieronymus Bosch.* World of Art. New York: Oxford Univ. Press, 1973.

Goldschneider, Ludwig. *Leonardo da Vinci: Life and Work, Paintings and Drawings.* 7th ed. London: Phaidon, 1964.

Hartt, Frederick. *Michelangelo.* New York: Abrams, 1984.

Hayum, André. *The Isenheim Altarpiece: God's Medicine and the Painter's Vision.* Princeton Essays on the Arts. Princeton: Princeton Univ. Press, 1989.

Heydenreich, Ludwig H. *Leonardo—"The Last Supper."* Art in Context. London: Allen Lane, 1974.

Hollingsworth, Mary. *Patronage in Renaissance Italy: From 1400 to the Early Sixteenth Century.* London: Murray, 1994.

Howard, Deborah. *Jacopo Sansovino: Architecture and Patronage in Renaissance Venice.* New Haven: Yale Univ. Press, 1975.

Huse, Norbert, and Wolfgang Wolters. *Art of Renaissance Venice: Architecture, Sculpture and Painting, 1460–1590.* Trans. Edmund Jephcott. Chicago: Univ. of Chicago Press, 1994.

Jones, Roger, and Nicholas Penny. *Raphael.* New Haven: Yale Univ. Press, 1983.

Klein, Robert, and Henri Zerner. *Italian Art, 1500–1600: Sources and Documents.* Englewood Cliffs, N.J.: Prentice-Hall, 1966.

Kubler, George. *Building the Escorial.* Princeton: Princeton Univ. Press, 1982.

Landau, David, and Peter Parshall. *The Renaissance Print: 1470–1550.* New Haven: Yale Univ. Press, 1994.

Langdon, Helen. *Holbein.* 2nd ed. London: Phaidon, 1993.

Lazzaro, Claudia. *The Italian Renaissance Garden: From the Conventions of Planting, Design, and Ornament to the Grand Gardens of Sixteenth-Century Central Italy.* New Haven: Yale Univ. Press, 1990.

Lieberman, Ralph. *Renaissance Architecture in Venice, 1450–1540.* New York: Abbeville, 1982.

Linfert, Carl. *Hieronymus Bosch.* Masters of Art. New York: Abrams, 1989.

Martineau, Jane, and Charles Hope. *The Genius of Venice, 1500–1600.* New York: Abrams, 1984.

McCorquodale, Charles. *Bronzino.* New York: Harper & Row, 1981.

McMullen, Roy. *Mona Lisa: The Picture and the Myth.* Boston: Houghton Mifflin, 1975.

Murray, Linda. *The High Renaissance.* World of Art. New York: Praeger, 1967.

———. *Late Renaissance and Mannerism.* World of Art. London: Thames and Hudson, 1967.

———. *Michelangelo.* World of Art. New York: Oxford Univ. Press, 1980.

Olson, Roberta J. M. *Italian Renaissance Sculpture.* World of Art. New York: Thames and Hudson, 1992.

Osten, Gert von der, and Horst Vey. *Painting and Sculpture in Germany and the Netherlands, 1500–1600.* Pelican History of Art. Harmondsworth, Eng.: Penguin, 1969.

Perlingieri, Ilya Sandra. *Sofonisba Anguissola: The First Great Woman Artist of the Renaissance.* New York: Rizzoli, 1992.

Pietrangeli, Carlo, et al. *The Sistine Chapel: The Art, the History, and the Restoration.* New York: Harmony, 1986.

Pignatti, Terisio. *Giorgione.* New York: Phaidon, 1971.

Pope-Hennessy, Sir John. *Cellini.* New York: Abbeville, 1985.

———. *Italian High Renaissance and Baroque Sculpture.* 3rd ed. Oxford: Phaidon, 1986.

———. *Italian Renaissance Sculpture.* 3rd ed. Oxford: Phaidon, 1986.

Rearick, William R. *The Art of Paolo Veronese, 1528–1588.* Washington, D.C.: National Gallery of Art, 1988.

Rosand, David. *Painting in Cinquecento Venice: Titian, Veronese, Tintoretto.* New Haven: Yale Univ. Press, 1982.

Russell, Francis. *The World of Dürer, 1471–1528.* New York: Time-Life, 1967.

Settis, Salvatore. *Giorgione's Tempest: Interpreting the Hidden Subject.* Trans. Ellen Bianchini. Chicago: Univ. of Chicago Press, 1990.

Shearman, John. *Mannerism.* Harmondsworth, Eng.: Penguin, 1967.

Smith, Jeffrey Chipps. *Nuremberg, a Renaissance City, 1500–1618.* Austin: Huntington Art Gallery, Univ. of Texas, 1983.

Stechow, Wolfgang. *Pieter Bruegel the Elder.* Masters of Art. New York: Abrams, 1990.

Strong, Roy C. *Artists of the Tudor Court: The Portrait Miniature Rediscovered, 1520–1620.* London: Victoria and Albert Museum, 1983.

Summerson, John. *Architecture in Britain: 1530 to 1830.* 7th ed. Pelican History of Art. Harmondsworth, Eng.: Penguin, 1983.

Tavernor, Robert. *Palladio and Palladianism.* World of Art. New York: Thames and Hudson, 1991.

Valcanover, Francesco. *Tintoretto.* Trans. Robert Erich Wolf. Library of Great Painters. New York: Abrams, 1985.

Vasari, Giorgio. *The Lives of the Artists.* Trans. Julia Conaway Bondanella and Peter Bondanella. New York: Oxford Univ. Press, 1991.

Verheyen, Egon. *The Paintings in the Studiolo of Isabella d'Este at Mantua.* Monographs on Archaeology and Fine Arts. New York: New York Univ. Press, 1971.

Vitruvius Pollio. *Vitruvius: The Ten Books on Architecture.* Trans. Morris Hicky Morgan. New York: Dover, 1960.

Whiting, Roger. *Leonardo: A Portrait of the Renaissance Man.* London: Barrie and Jenkins, 1992.

Chapter 19 Baroque, Rococo, and Early American Art

Ackley, Clifford S. *Printmaking in the Age of Rembrandt.* Boston: Museum of Fine Arts, 1981.

The Age of Caravaggio. New York: Metropolitan Museum of Art, 1985.

Bazin, Germain. *Baroque and Rococo.* Trans. Jonathan Griffin. World of Art. New York: Praeger, 1964.

Berger, Robert W. *The Palace of the Sun: The Louvre of Louis XIV.* University Park: Pennsylvania State Univ. Press, 1993.

———. *Versailles: The Chateau of Louis XIV.* Monographs on the Fine Arts. University Park: Pennsylvania State Univ. Press, 1985.

Blunt, Anthony, et al. *Baroque and Rococo Architecture and Decoration.* New York: Harper & Row, 1982.

Boucher, François. *François Boucher, 1703–1770.* New York: Metropolitan Museum of Art, 1986.

Brown, Christopher. *Scenes of Everyday Life: Dutch Genre Painting of the Seventeenth Century.* London: Faber & Faber, 1984.

Brown, Dale. *The World of Velázquez, 1599–1660.* New York: Time-Life, 1969.

Brown, Jonathan. *The Golden Age of Painting in Spain.* New Haven: Yale Univ. Press, 1991.

———. *Velázquez, Painter and Courtier.* New Haven: Yale Univ. Press, 1986.

Domingues Ortiz, Antonio, Alfonso E. Perez Sanchez, and Julian Gallego. *Velázquez.* New York: Metropolitan Museum of Art, 1989.

Enggass, Robert, and Jonathan Brown. *Italy and Spain 1600–1750: Sources and Documents.* Englewood Cliffs, N.J.: Prentice-Hall, 1970.

Frankenstein, Alfred Victor. *The World of Copley, 1738–1815.* New York: Time-Life, 1970.

Fuchs, R. H. *Dutch Painting.* World of Art. New York: Oxford Univ. Press, 1978.

Gerson, Horst, and E. H. ter Kuile. *Art and Architecture in Belgium, 1600–1800.* Pelican History of Art. Baltimore: Penguin, 1960.

———. *Rembrandt Paintings.* Trans. Heinz Norden. Ed. Gary Schwartz. New York: Reynal, 1968.

Grasselli, Margaret Morgan, and Pierre Rosenberg. *Watteau, 1684–1721.* Washington, D.C.: National Gallery of Art, 1984.

Grimm, Claus. *Frans Hals—The Complete Work.* Trans. Jurgen Riehle. New York: Abrams, 1990.

Haak, Bob. *The Golden Age: Dutch Painters of the Seventeenth Century.* Trans. and ed. Elizabeth Willems-Treeman. New York: Abrams, 1984.

Held, Julius Samuel, and Donald Posner. *17th and 18th Century Art: Baroque Painting, Sculpture, Architecture.* Library of Art History. New York: Abrams, 1971.

Hempel, Eberhard. *Baroque Art and Architecture in Central Europe: Germany, Austria, Switzerland, Hungary, Czechoslovakia, Poland. Painting and Sculpture: 17th and 18th Centuries. Architecture: 16th to 18th Centuries.* Trans. Elisabeth Hempel and Marguerite Kay. Pelican History of Art. Harmondsworth, Eng.: Penguin, 1965.

Jacobson, Dawn. *Chinoiserie.* London: Phaidon, 1993.

Kalnein, Wend, and Michael Levey. *Art and Architecture of the Eighteenth Century in France.* Pelican History of Art. Harmondsworth, Eng.: Penguin, 1972.

Köning, Hans. *The World of Vermeer, 1632–1675.* New York: Time-Life, 1967.

Lagerlof, Margaretha Rossholm. *Ideal Landscape: Annibale Caracci, Nicolas Poussin, and Claude Lorrain.* New Haven: Yale Univ. Press, 1990.

Martin, John Rupert. "The Baroque from the Viewpoint of the Art Historian." *Journal of Aesthetics and Art Criticism* 15(2): 164–70.

Moir, Alfred. *Anthony Van Dyck.* New York: Abrams, 1994.

———. *Caravaggio.* Library of Great Painters. New York: Abrams, 1982.

Montagu, Jennifer. *Roman Baroque Sculpture: The Industry of Art.* New Haven: Yale Univ. Press, 1989.

Norberg-Schulz, Christian. *Baroque Architecture.* History of World Architecture. New York: Rizzoli, 1986.

———. *Late Baroque and Rococo Architecture.* History of World Architecture. New York: Rizzoli, 1985.

Rosenberg, Jakob, Seymour Slive, and E. H. ter Kuile. *Dutch Art and Architecture, 1600 to 1800.* 3rd ed. Pelican History of Art. Harmondsworth, Eng.: Penguin, 1977.

Rosenberg, Pierre. *Chardin, 1699–1779.* Trans. Emilie P. Kadish and Ursula Korneitchouk. Ed. Sally W. Goodfellow. Cleveland: Cleveland Museum of Art, 1979.

———. *Fragonard.* New York: Metropolitan Museum of Art, 1988.

Russell, H. Diane. *Claude Lorrain, 1600–1682.* Washington, D.C.: National Gallery of Art, 1982.

Schwartz, Gary. *Rembrandt, His Life, His Paintings.* New York: Penguin, 1991.

Scribner, Charles, III. *Gianlorenzo Bernini.* Masters of Art. New York: Abrams, 1991.

———. *Peter Paul Rubens.* Masters of Art. New York: Abrams, 1989.

Slive, Seymour, et al. *Frans Hals.* London: Royal Academy of Arts, 1989.

Stechow, Wolfgang. *Dutch Landscape Painting of the Seventeenth Century.* 3rd ed. Oxford: Phaidon, 1981.

Summerson, John. *Architecture of the Eighteenth Century.* World of Art. New York: Thames and Hudson, 1986.

———. *Inigo Jones.* Harmondsworth, Eng.: Penguin, 1966.

Sutton, Peter. *The Age of Rubens.* Boston: Museum of Fine Arts, 1993.

Wallace, Robert. *The World of Bernini, 1598–1680.* New York: Time-Life, 1970.

Temple, R. C., ed. *The Travels of Peter Mundy in Europe and Asia, 1608–1667.* London: n.p., 1925.

Wedgwood, C. V. *The World of Rubens, 1577–1640.* New York: Time-Life, 1967.

Welu, James A., and Pieter Biesboer, eds. *Judith Leyster: A Dutch Master and Her World.* New York: Yale Univ. Press, 1993.

Wheelock, Arthur K., Jr. *Jan Vermeer.* New York: Abrams, 1988.

———, Susan J. Barnes, and Julius S. Held. *Anthony Van Dyck.* Washington, D.C.: National Gallery of Art, 1990.

White, Christopher. *Peter Paul Rubens: Man & Artist.* New Haven: Yale Univ. Press, 1987.

———. *Rembrandt.* World of Art. London: Thames and Hudson, 1984.

Wittkower, Rudolf. *Art and Architecture in Italy, 1600 to 1750.* 3rd ed. Pelican History of Art. Harmondsworth, Eng.: Penguin, 1982.

Chapter 20 Art of India after 1100

Asher, Catherine B. *Architecture of Mughal India.* New York: Cambridge Univ. Press, 1992.

Beach, Milo Cleveland. *Grand Mogul: Imperial Painting in India, 1600–1660.* Williamstown: Sterling and Francine Clark Art Institute, 1978.

———. *Imperial Image, Paintings for the Mughal Court.* Washington, D.C.: Freer Gallery of Art, Smithsonian Institution, 1981.

———. *Mughal and Rajput Painting.* New York: Cambridge Univ. Press, 1992.

Blurton, T. Richard. *Hindu Art.* Cambridge: Harvard Univ. Press, 1993.

Davies, Philip. *Splendours of the Raj: British Architecture in India, 1660 to 1947.* London: Murray, 1985.

Desai, Vishakha N. *Life at Court: Art for India's Rulers, 16th–19th Centuries.* Boston: Museum of Fine Arts, 1985.

Losty, Jeremiah P. *The Art of the Book in India.* London: British Library, 1982.

Miller, Barbara Stoller. *Love Song of the Dark Lord: Jayadeva's Gitagovinda.* New York: Columbia Univ. Press, 1977.

Mitchell, George. *The Royal Palaces of India.* London: Thames and Hudson, 1994.

Nou, Jean-Louis. *Taj Mahal.* Text by Amina Okada and M. C. Joshi. New York: Abbeville, 1993.

Pal, Pratapaditya. *Court Paintings of India, 16th–19th Centuries.* New York: Navin Kumar, 1983.

———, et al. *Romance of the Taj Mahal.* Los Angeles: Los Angeles County Museum of Art, 1989.

Tillotson, G. H. R. *Mughal India.* Architectural Guides for Travelers. San Francisco: Chronicle, 1990.

———. *The Tradition of Indian Architecture: Continuity, Controversy and Change since 1850.* New Haven: Yale Univ. Press, 1989.

Welch, Stuart Cary. *The Emperors' Album: Images of Mughal India*. New York: Metropolitan Museum of Art, 1987.

———. *India: Art and Culture 1300–1900*. New York: Metropolitan Museum of Art, 1985.

Chapter 21 Chinese Art after 1280

Andrews, Julia Frances. *Painters and Politics in the People's Republic of China, 1949–1979*. Berkeley: Univ. of California Press, 1994.

Barnhart, Richard M. *Painters of the Great Ming: The Imperial Court and the Zhe School*. Dallas: Dallas Museum of Art, 1993.

———. *Peach Blossom Spring: Gardens and Flowers in Chinese Painting*. New York: Metropolitan Museum of Art, 1983.

———, et al. *The Jade Studio: Masterpieces of Ming and Qing Painting and Calligraphy from the Wong Nan-p'ing Collection*. New Haven: Yale Univ. Art Gallery, 1994.

Beurdeley, Michael. *Chinese Furniture*. Trans. Katherine Watson. Tokyo: Kodansha International, 1979.

Billeter, Jean François. *The Chinese Art of Writing*. New York: Skira/Rizzoli, 1990.

Bush, Susan, and Hsui-yen Shih, eds. *Early Chinese Texts on Painting*. Cambridge: Harvard Univ. Press, 1985.

Cahill, James. *The Compelling Image: Nature and Style in Seventeenth-Century Chinese Painting*. Charles Norton Lectures 1978–79. Cambridge: Harvard Univ. Press, 1982.

———. *The Distant Mountains: Chinese Painting in the Late Ming Dynasty, 1580–1644*. New York: Weatherhill, 1982.

———. *Hills beyond a River: Chinese Painting of the Y'uan Dynasty, 1279–1368*. New York: Weatherhill, 1976.

———. *Parting at the Shore: Chinese Painting of the Early and Middle Ming Dynasty, 1368–1580*. New York: Weatherhill, 1978.

Chan, Charis. *Imperial China*. Architectural Guides for Travelers. San Francisco: Chronicle, 1992.

Fontein, Jan, and Money Hickman. *Zen Painting and Calligraphy: An Exhibition of Works of Art Lent by Temples, Private Collectors, and Public and Private Museums in Japan*. Boston: Museum of Fine Arts, 1971.

Ho, Wai-Kam, ed. *The Century of Tung Ch'i-Chiang*. 2 vols. Kansas City: Nelson-Atkins Museum of Art, 1992.

In Pursuit of the Dragon: Traditions and Transitions in Ming Ceramics: An Exhibition from the Idemitsu Museum of Arts. Seattle: Seattle Art Museum, 1988.

Jenyns, Soame. *Later Chinese Porcelain: The Ch'ing Dynasty, 1644–1912*. 4th ed. London: Faber & Faber, 1971.

Keswick, Maggie. *The Chinese Garden: History, Art and Architecture*. New York: Rizzoli, 1978.

Knapp, Ronald G. *China's Vernacular Architecture: House Form and Culture*. Honolulu: Univ. of Hawaii Press, 1989.

Lee, Sherman, and Wai-Kam Ho. *Chinese Art under the Mongols: The Y'uan Dynasty, 1279–1368*. Cleveland: Cleveland Museum of Art, 1968.

Li, Chu-tsing. *The Autumn Colors on the Ch'iao and Hua Mountains: A Landscape by Chao Meng-fu*. Artibus Asiae, supplementum 21. Ascona: Artibus Asiae, 1965.

Lim, Lucy. *Contemporary Chinese Painting: An Exhibition from the People's Republic of China*. San Francisco: Chinese Culture Foundation of San Francisco, 1983.

———, ed. *Wu Guanzhong: A Contemporary Chinese Artist*. San Francisco: Chinese Culture Foundation, 1989.

Liu, Laurence G. *Chinese Architecture*. New York: Rizzoli, 1989.

Ng, So Kam. *Brushstrokes: Styles and Techniques of Chinese Painting*. San Francisco: Asian Art Museum of San Francisco, 1993.

Polo, Marco. *The Travels of Marco Polo*. Trans. Teresa Waugh and Maria Bellonci. New York: Facts on File, 1984.

Shih-t'ao. *Returning Home: Tao-chi's Album of Landscapes and Flowers*. Commentary by Wen Fong. New York: Braziller, 1976.

Sullivan, Michael. *Symbols of Eternity: The Art of Landscape Painting in China*. Stanford: Stanford Univ. Press, 1979.

Tregear, Mary. *Chinese Art*. World of Art. New York: Oxford Univ. Press, 1980.

Tsu, Frances Ya-sing. *Landscape Design in Chinese Gardens*. New York: McGraw-Hill, 1988.

Vainker, S. J. *Chinese Pottery and Porcelain: From Prehistory to the Present*. London: British Museum, 1991.

Walters, Derek. *Feng Shui: The Chinese Art of Designing a Harmonious Environment*. New York: Simon & Schuster, 1988.

Yu Zhuoyun, comp. *Palaces of the Forbidden City*. Trans. Ng Mau-Sang, Chan Sinwai, and Puwen Lee. New York: Viking, 1984.

Chapter 22 Japanese Art after 1392

Addiss, Stephen. *The Art of Zen: Painting and Calligraphy by Japanese Monks, 1600–1925*. New York: Abrams, 1989.

———. *Zenga and Nanga: Paintings by Japanese Monks and Scholars, Selections from the Kurt and Millie Gitter Collection*. New Orleans: New Orleans Museum of Art, 1976.

Baekeland, Frederick, and Robert Moes. *Modern Japanese Ceramics in American Collections*. New York: Japan Society, 1993.

Doi, Tsugiyoshi. *Momoyama Decorative Painting*. Trans. Edna B. Crawford. Heibonsha Survey of Japanese Art, vol. 14. New York: Weatherhill, 1977.

Forrer, Matthi. *Hokusai*. New York: Rizzoli, 1988.

Hayakawa, Masao. *The Garden Art of Japan*. Trans. Richard L. Gage. Heibonsha Survey of Japanese Art, vol. 28. New York: Weatherhill, 1973.

Hayashiya, Tatsusaburo, Masao Nakamura, and Seizo Hayashiya. *Japanese Arts and the Tea Ceremony*. Trans. and adapted by Joseph P. Macadam. Heibonsha Survey of Japanese Art, vol. 15. New York: Weatherhill, 1974.

Hinago, Motoo. *Japanese Castles*. Trans. and adapted by William H. Coaldrake. Japanese Arts Library, vol. 14. New York: Kodansha International, 1986.

Hirai, Kiyoshi. *Feudal Architecture of Japan*. Trans. Hiroaki Sato and Jeannine Ciliotta. Heibonsha Survey of Japanese Art, vol. 13. New York: Weatherhill, 1973.

Hosono, Masanobu. *Nagasaki Prints and Early Copperplates*. Trans. and adapted by Lloyd R. Craighill. Japanese Arts Library, vol. 6. New York: Kodansha International, 1978.

Leach, Bernard. *Kenzan and His Tradition: The Lives and Times of Koetsu, Sotatsu, Korin and Kenzan*. London: Faber, 1966.

Kanazawa, Hiroshi. *Japanese Ink Painting: Early Zen Masterpieces*. Trans. and adapted by Barbara Ford. Japanese Arts Library, vol. 8. New York: Kodansha International, 1979.

Kawahara, Masahiko. *The Ceramic Art of Ogata Kenzan*. Trans. and adapted by Richard L. Wilson. Japanese Arts Library, vol. 13. New York: Kodansha International, 1985.

Kawakita, Michiaki. *Modern Currents in Japanese Art*. Trans. and adapted by Charles S. Terry. Heibonsha Survey of Japanese Art, vol. 24. New York: Weatherhill, 1974.

Meech-Pekarik, Julia. *The World of the Meiji Print: Impressions of a New Civilization*. New York: Weatherhill, 1986.

Merritt, Helen. *Modern Japanese Woodblock Prints: The Early Years*. Honolulu: Univ. of Hawaii Press, 1990.

Michener, James A. *The Floating World*. New York: Random House, 1954.

Mizuo, Hiroshi. *Edo Painting: Sotatsu and Korin*. Trans. John M. Shields. Heibonsha Survey of Japanese Art, vol. 18. New York: Weatherhill, 1972.

Muraoka, Kageo, and Kichiemon Okamura. *Folk Arts and Crafts of Japan*. Trans. Daphne D. Stegmaier. Heibonsha Survey of Japanese Art, vol. 26. New York: Weatherhill, 1973.

Murase, Miyeko. *Emaki, Narrative Scrolls from Japan*. New York: Asia Society, 1983.

———. *Masterpieces of Japanese Screen Painting: The American Collections*. New York: Braziller, 1990.

———. *Tales of Japan: Scrolls and Prints from the New York Public Library*. Oxford: Oxford Univ. Press, 1986.

Noma, Seiroku. *Japanese Costume and Textiles Arts*. Trans. Armins Nikoskis. Heibonsha Survey of Japanese Art, vol. 16. New York: Weatherhill, 1974.

Oka, Isaburo. *Hiroshige: Japan's Great Landscape Artist*. Trans. Stanleigh H. Jones. Tokyo: Kodansha International, 1992.

Okakura, Kakuzo. *The Book of Tea*. Ed. Everett F. Bleiler. New York: Dover, 1964.

Okamoto, Yoshitomo. *The Namban Art of Japan*. Trans. Ronald K. Jones. Heibonsha Survey of Japanese Art, vol. 19. New York: Weatherhill/Heibonsha, 1972.

Okawa, Naomi. *Edo Architecture: Katsura and Nikko*. Trans. Alan Woodhull and Akito Miyamoto. Heibonsha Survey of Japanese Art, vol. 20. New York: Weatherhill, 1975.

Okyo and the Maruyama-Shijo School of Japanese Painting. Trans. Miyeko Murase and Sarah Thompson. St. Louis: St. Louis Art Museum, 1980.

Takahashi, Seiichiro. *Traditional Woodblock Prints of Japan*. Trans. Richard Stanley-Baker. Heibonsha Survey of Japanese Art, vol. 22. New York: Weatherhill, 1972.

Takeda, Tsuneo. *Kano Eitoku*. Trans. Catherine Kaputa. Japanese Arts Library, vol. 3. New York: Kodansha International, 1977.

Takeuchi, Melinda. *Taiga's True Views: The Language of Landscape Painting in Eighteenth-Century Japan*. Stanford: Stanford Univ. Press, 1992.

Terada, Toru. *Japanese Art in World Perspective*. Trans. Thomas Guerin. Heibonsha Survey of Japanese Art, vol. 25. New York: Weatherhill, 1976.

Thompson, Sarah E., and H. D. Harpptunian. *Undercurrents in the Floating World: Censorship and Japanese Prints*. New York: Asia Society Gallery, 1992.

Wilson, Richard L. *The Art of Ogata Kenzan: Persona and Production in Japanese Ceramics*. New York: Weatherhill, 1991.

Yamane, Yuzo. *Momoyama Genre Painting*. Trans. John M. Shields. Heibonsha Survey of Japanese Art, vol. 17. New York: Heibonsha, 1973.

Chapter 23 Art of the Americas after 1300

Archuleta, Margaret, and Rennard Strickland. *Shared Visions: Native American Painters and Sculptors in the Twentieth Century*. Phoenix: Heard Museum, 1991.

Baquedano, Elizabeth. *Aztec Sculpture*. London: British Museum, 1984.

Berdan, Frances F. *The Aztecs of Central Mexico: An Imperial Society*. New York: Holt, 1982.

Bringhurst, Robert. *The Black Canoe: Bill Reid and the Spirit of Haida Gwaii*. Seattle: Univ. of Washington Press, 1991.

Broder, Patricia Janis. *American Indian Painting and Sculpture*. New York: Abbeville, 1981.

Coe, Ralph. *Lost and Found Traditions: Native American Art 1965–1985*. Ed. Irene Gordon. Seattle: Univ. of Washington Press, 1986.

Conn, Richard. *Circles of the World: Traditional Art of the Plains Indians*. Denver: Denver Art Museum, 1982.

Dockstader, Frederick J. *The Way of the Loom: New Traditions in Navajo Weaving*. New York: Hudson Hills, 1987.

Feest, Christian F. *Native Arts of North America*. Updated ed. World of Art. New York: Thames and Hudson, 1992.

Haberland, Wolfgang. *Art of North America*. Rev. ed. Art of the World. New York: Greystone, 1968.

Hawthorn, Audrey. *Art of the Kwakiutl Indians and Other Northwest Coast Tribes*. Vancouver: Univ. of British Columbia Press, 1967.

Hemming, John. *Monuments of the Incas*. Boston: Little, Brown, 1982.

Highwater, Jamake. *The Sweet Grass Lives On: Fifty Contemporary North American Indian Artists*. New York: Lippincott and Crowell, 1980.

Jonaitis, Aldona. *Art of the Northern Tlingit*. Seattle: Univ. of Washington Press, 1986.

———, ed. *Chiefly Feasts: The Enduring Kwakiutl Potlatch*. Seattle: Univ. of Washington Press, 1991.

Kahlenberg, Mary Hunt, and Anthony Berlant. *The Navajo Blanket*. New York: Praeger, 1972.

Levi-Strauss, Claude. *Way of the Masks*. Trans. Sylvia Modelski. Seattle: Univ. of Washington Press, 1982.

MacDonald, George F. *Haida Monumental Art: Villages of the Queen Charlotte Islands*. Vancouver: Univ. of British Columbia Press, 1983.

Maurer, Evan M. *Visions of the People: A Pictorial History of Plains Indian Life*. Minneapolis: Minneapolis Institute of Arts, 1992.

McNair, Peter L., Alan L. Hoover, and Kevin Neary. *Legacy: Tradition and Innovation in Northwest Coast Indian Art*. Vancouver: Douglas and McIntyre, 1984.

Nicholson, H. B., and Eloise Quinones Keber. *Art of Aztec Mexico: Treasures of Tenochtitlan*. Washington, D.C.: National Gallery of Art, 1983.

Parezo, Nancy J. *Navajo Sandpainting: From Religious Act to Commercial Art*. Tucson: Univ. of Arizona Press, 1983.

Pasztory, Esther. *Aztec Art*. New York: Abrams, 1983.

Penney, David. *Art of the American Indian Frontier: The Chandler-Pohrt Collection*. Detroit: Detroit Institute of Arts, 1992.

Peterson, Susan. *The Living Tradition of Maria Martinéz*. Tokyo: Kodansha International, 1977.

Smith, Jaune Quick-to-See, and Harmony Hammond. *Women of Sweetgrass: Cedar and Sage*. New York: American Indian Center, 1984.

Stewart, Hilary. *Totem Poles*. Seattle: Univ. of Washington Press, 1990.

Stierlin, Henri. *Art of the Aztecs and Its Origins*. New York: Rizzoli, 1982.

———. *Art of the Incas and Its Origins*. New York: Rizzoli, 1984.

Trimble, Stephen. *Talking with the Clay: The Art of Pueblo Pottery*. Santa Fe: School of American Research Press, 1987.

Wade, Edwin, and Carol Haralson, eds. *The Arts of the North American Indian: Native Traditions in Evolution*. New York: Hudson Hills, 1986.

Walters, Anna Lee. *Spirit of Native America: Beauty and Mysticism in American Indian Art*. San Francisco: Chronicle, 1989.

Wood, Nancy C. *Taos Pueblo*. New York: Knopf, 1989.

Chapter 24 Art of Pacific Cultures

Allen, Louis A. *Time before Morning: Art and Myth of the Australian Aborigines*. New York: Crowell, 1975.

Barrow, Terrence. *The Art of Tahiti and the Neighbouring Society, Austral and Cook Islands*. New York: Thames and Hudson, 1979.

———. *An Illustrated Guide to Maori Art*. Honolulu: Univ. of Hawaii Press, 1984.

Buhler, Alfred, Terry Barrow, and Charles P. Montford, *The Art of the South Sea Islands, including Australia and New Zealand*. Art of the World. New York: Crown, 1962.

Caruana, Wally. *Aboriginal Art*. World of Art. New York: Thames and Hudson, 1993.

Craig, Robert D. *Dictionary of Polynesian Mythology*. New York: Greenwood, 1989.

Gauguin, Paul. *Intimate Journals*. Trans. Van Wyck Brooks. Bloomington: Indiana Univ. Press, 1958.

Gell, Alfred. *Wrapping in Images: Tattooing in Polynesia*. Oxford Studies in Social and Cultural Anthropology. New York: Oxford Univ. Press, 1993.

Greub, Suzanne, ed. *Art of Northwest New Guinea: From Geelvink Bay, Humboldt Bay, and Lake Sentani*. New York: Rizzoli, 1992.

Guiart, Jean. *The Arts of the South Pacific*. Trans. Anthony Christie. Arts of Mankind. New York: Golden, 1963.

Hammond, Joyce D. *Tifaifai and Quilts of Polynesia*. Honolulu: Univ. of Hawaii Press, 1986.

Hanson, Allan, and Louise Hanson. *Art and Identity in Oceania*. Honolulu: Univ. of Hawaii Press, 1990.

Heyerdahl, Thor. *The Art of Easter Island*. Garden City, N.Y.: Doubleday, 1975.

Jone, Stella M. *Hawaiian Quilts*. Rev. 2nd ed. Honolulu: Daughters of Hawaii, 1973.

Layton, Robert. *Australian Rock Art: A New Synthesis*. New York: Cambridge Univ. Press, 1992.

Leonard, Anne, and John Terrell. *Patterns of Paradise: The Style and Significance of Bark Cloth around the World*. Chicago: Field Museum of Natural History, 1980.

Mead, Sydney Moko, ed. *Te Maori: Maori Art from New Zealand Collections*. New York: Abrams, 1984.

Morphy, Howard. *Ancestral Connections: Art and an Aboriginal System of Knowledge*. Chicago: Univ. of Chicago Press, 1991.

People of the River, People of the Trees: Change and Continuity in Sepik and Asmat Art. St. Paul: Minnesota Museum of Art, 1989.

Rabineau, Phyllis. *Feather Arts: Beauty, Wealth, and Spirit from Five Continents*. Chicago: Field Museum of Natural History, 1979.

Scutt, R. W. B., and Christopher Gotch. *Art, Sex, and Symbol: The Mystery of Tattooing*. 2nd ed. New York: Cornell Univ. Press, 1986.

Serra, Eudaldo, and Alberto Folch. *The Art of Papua and New Guinea*. New York: Rizzoli, 1977.

Sutton, Peter, ed. *Dreamings, the Art of Aboriginal Australia*. New York: Braziller, 1988.

Wardwell, Allen. *Island Ancestors: Oceania Art from the Masco Collection*. Seattle: Univ. of Washington Press, 1994.

Chapter 25 Art of Africa in the Modern Era

Abiodun, Rowland, Henry J. Drewal, and John Pemberton III, eds. *The Yoruba Artist: New Theoretical Perspectives on African Arts*. Washington, D.C.: Smithsonian Institution, 1994.

Adler, Peter, and Nicholas Barnard. *African Majesty: The Textile Art of the Ashanti and Ewe*. New York: Thames and Hudson, 1992.

Astonishment and Power. Washington, D.C.: National Museum of African Art, Smithsonian Institution, 1993.

Barley, Nigel. *Foreheads of the Dead: An Anthropological View of Kalabari Ancestral Screens*. Washington, D.C.: National Museum of African Art, Smithsonian Institution, 1988.

———. *Smashing Pots: Feats of Clay from Africa*. London: British Museum, 1994.

Biebuyck, Daniel P. *Lega Culture: Art, Initiation, and Moral Philosophy among a Central African People*. Berkeley: Univ. of California Press, 1973.

Brincard, Marie-Therese, ed. *The Art of Metal in Africa*. Trans. Evelyn Fischel. New York: African-American Institute, 1984.

Cole, Herbert M., ed. *I Am Not Myself: The Art of African Masquerade*. Los Angeles: Museum of Cultural History, Univ. of California, 1985.

———. *Icons: Ideals and Power in the Art of Africa*. Washington, D.C.: National Museum of African Art, Smithsonian Institution, 1989.

———. *Mbari, Art and Life among the Owerri Igbo*. Bloomington: Indiana Univ. Press, 1982.

Drewal, Henry John. *African Artistry: Technique and Aesthetics in Yoruba Sculpture*. Atlanta: High Museum of Art, 1980.

———, and Margaret Thompson Drewal. *Gelede: Art and Female Power among the Yoruba*. Bloomington: Indiana Univ. Press, 1983.

Fagg, William Buller, and John Pemberton III. *Yoruba Sculpture of West Africa*. Ed. Bryce Holcombe. New York: Knopf, 1982.

Gilfoy, Peggy S. *Patterns of Life: West African Strip-Weaving Traditions*. Washington, D.C.: National Museum of African Art, Smithsonian Institution, 1992.

Glaze, Anita. *Art and Death in a Senufo Village*. Bloomington: Indiana Univ. Press, 1981.

Heathcote, David. *The Arts of the Hausa*. Chicago: Univ. of Chicago Press, 1976.

Kennedy, Jean. *New Currents, Ancient Rivers: Contemporary Artists in a Generation of Change*. Washington, D.C.: Smithsonian Institution, 1992.

Laude, Jean. *African Art of the Dogon: The Myths of the Cliff Dwellers*. Trans. Joachim Neugroschell. New York: Brooklyn Museum, 1973.

Martin, Phyllis, and Patrick O'Meara, eds. *Africa*. 2nd ed. Bloomington: Indiana Univ. Press, 1986.

McEvilley, Thomas. *Fusion: West African Artists at the Venice Biennale*. New York: Museum for African Art, 1993.

McNaughton, Patrick R. *The Mande Blacksmiths: Knowledge, Power and Art in West Africa*. Bloomington: Indiana Univ. Press, 1988.

Neyt, François. *Luba: To the Sources of the Zaire*. Trans. Murray Wyllie. Paris: Editions Dapper, 1994.

Perrois, Louis, and Marta Sierra Delage. *The Art of Equatorial Guinea: The Fang Tribes*. New York: Rizzoli, 1990.

Picon, John, and John Mack. *African Textiles*. New York: Harper & Row, 1989.

Roy, Christopher D. *Art of the Upper Volta Rivers*. Meudon, France: Chaffin, 1987.

Schildkrout, Enid, and Curtis A. Keim. *African Reflections: Art from Northeastern Zaire*. Seattle: Univ. of Washington Press, 1990.

Sieber, Roy. *African Furniture and Household Objects*. Bloomington: Indiana Univ. Press, 1980.

———. *African Textiles and Decorative Arts*. New York: Museum of Modern Art, 1972.

———, and Roslyn Adele Walker. *African Art in the Cycle of Life*. Washington, D.C.: National Museum of African Art, Smithsonian Institution, 1987.

Thompson, Robert Farris, and Joseph Cornet. *The Four Moments of the Sun: Kongo Art in Two Worlds*. Washington, D.C.: National Gallery of Art, 1981.

Vogel, Susan. *Africa Explores: 20th Century African Art*. New York: Center for African Art, 1991.

Chapter 26 Neoclassicism and Romanticism in Europe and the United States

Abrams, Ann Uhry. *The Valiant Hero: Benjamin West and Grand-Style History Painting*. Washington, D.C.: Smithsonian Institution, 1985.

Age of Neoclassicism. London: Arts Council of Great Britain, 1972.

Bindman, David. *William Blake: His Art and Time*. New Haven: Yale Center for British Art, 1982.

Boime, Albert. *Art in an Age of Bonapartism, 1800–1815*. Chicago: Univ. of Chicago Press, 1990.

———. *Art in an Age of Revolution, 1750–1800*. Chicago: Univ. of Chicago Press, 1987.

Braham, Allan. *The Architecture of the French Enlightenment*. Berkeley: Univ. of California Press, 1980.

Brion, Marcel. *Art of the Romantic Era: Romanticism, Classicism, Realism*. World of Art. New York: Praeger, 1966.

Byson, Norman. *Tradition and Desire: From David to Delacroix*. New York: Cambridge Univ. Press, 1984.

Clark, Kenneth. *The Romantic Rebellion: Romantic versus Classic Art*. New York: Harper & Row, 1973.

Cooper, Wendy A. *Classical Taste in America 1800–1840*. Baltimore: Baltimore Museum of Art, 1993.

Eitner, Lorenz. *Neoclassicism and Romanticism, 1750–1850: An Anthology of Sources and Documents*. New York: Harper & Row, 1989.

French Painting 1774–1830: The Age of Revolution. Detroit: Wayne State Univ. Press, 1975.

Harris, Enriqueta. *Goya*. Rev. ed. London: Phaidon, 1994.

Honour, Hugh. *Neo-Classicism*. Harmondsworth, Eng.: Penguin, 1968.

———. *Romanticism*. London: Allen Lane, 1979.

Kroeber, Karl. *British Romantic Art*. Berkeley: Univ. of California Press, 1986.

Lindsay, Jack. *Death of the Hero: French Painting from David to Delacroix*. London: Studio, 1960.

Manners and Morals: Hogarth and British Painting 1700–1760. London: Tate Gallery, 1987.

Mayoux, Jean-Jacques. *English Painting*. Trans. James Emmons. New York: Grove, 1975.

Middleton, Robin, and David Watkin. *Neoclassical and 19th Century Architecture*. 2 vols. History of World Architecture. New York: Electa/Rizzoli, 1987.

Novotny, Fritz. *Painting and Sculpture in Europe, 1780–1880*. Pelican History of Art. Harmondsworth, Eng.: Penguin, 1980.

Paulson, Ronald. *The Art of Hogarth*. London: Phaidon, 1975.

Perez Sanchez, Alfonso E., and Eleanor A. Sayre. *Goya and the Spirit of Enlightenment*. Boston: Museum of Fine Arts, 1989.

Powell, Earl A. *Thomas Cole*. New York: Abrams, 1990.

Prideaux, Tom. *World of Delacroix, 1798–1863*. New York: Time-Life, 1966.

Roberts, Warren E. *Jacques-Louis David, Revolutionary Artist: Art, Politics, and the French Revolution*. Chapel Hill: Univ. of North Carolina Press, 1989.

Rosenblum, Robert. *Jean-Auguste-Dominique Ingres*. Masters of Art. New York: Abrams, 1990.

Rousseau, Jean-Jacques. *Emile*. Ed. F. and P. Richard. New York: French & European, 1962.

Roworth, Wendy Wassyng. *Angelica Kauffman: A Continental Artist in Georgian England*. London: Reaktion, 1992.

Rykwert, Joseph, and Anne Rykwert. *Robert and James Adam: The Men and the Style*. New York: Rizzoli, 1985.

Shapiro, Michael Edward. *George Caleb Bingham*. New York: Abrams, 1993.

Turner, Roger. *Capability Brown and the Eighteenth Century English Landscape*. London: Weidenfeld and Nicolson, 1985.

Vaughan, William. *German Romantic Painting*. New Haven: Yale Univ. Press, 1980.

———. *Romanticism and Art*. World of Art. New York: Thames and Hudson, 1994.

Walker, John. *John Constable*. New York: Abrams, 1991.

Wilton, Andrew. *Turner in His Time*. New York: Abrams, 1987.

Wolf, Bryan Jay. *Romantic-Revision: Culture and Consciousness in Nineteenth-Century American Painting and Literature*. Chicago: Univ. of Chicago Press, 1986

Chapter 27 Realism to Impressionism in Europe and the United States

Adams, Steven. *The Barbizon School and the Origins of Impressionism*. London: Phaidon, 1994.

Art of the July Monarchy: France, 1830 to 1848. Columbia: Univ. of Missouri Press, 1989.

Ashton, Dore. *Rosa Bonheur: A Life and a Legend*. New York: Viking, 1981.

Barger, M. Susan, and William B. White. *The Daguerreotype: Nineteenth-Century Technology and Modern Science*. Washington, D.C.: Smithsonian Institution, 1991.

Baudelaire, Charles. *The Painter of Modern Life, and Other Essays*. Trans. and ed. Jonathan Mayne. London: Phaidon, 1964.

Boime, Albert. *The Academy and French Painting in the Nineteenth Century*. London: Phaidon, 1971.

Cachin, Françoise, Charles S. Moffett, and Michel Melot, eds. *Manet, 1832–1883*. New York: Metropolitan Museum of Art, 1983.

Clark, T. J. *The Absolute Bourgeois: Artists and Politics in France, 1848–1851*. London: Thames and Hudson, 1973.

———. *Image of the People: Gustave Courbet and the 1848 Revolution*. London: Thames and Hudson, 1973.

Clarke, Michael. *Corot and the Art of Landscape*. London: British Museum, 1991.

Cumming, Elizabeth, and Wendy Caplan. *Arts and Crafts Movement*. World of Art. New York: Thames and Hudson, 1991.

Denvir, Bernard. *The Thames and Hudson Encyclopedia of Impressionism*. World of Art. New York: Thames and Hudson, 1990.

Faxon, Alicia Craig. *Dante Gabriel Rossetti*. Oxford: Phaidon, 1989.

Fried, Michael. *Courbet's Realism*. Chicago: Univ. of Chicago Press, 1982.

Gordon, Robert, and Andrew Forge. *Degas*. Trans. Richard Howard. New York: Abrams, 1988.

Harding, James. *Artistes Pompiers: French Academic Art in the 19th Century*. New York: Rizzoli, 1979.

Hargrove, June, ed. *The French Academy: Classicism and Its Antagonists*. Newark: Univ. of Delaware Press, 1990.

Hendricks, Gordon. *Albert Bierstadt: Painter of the American West*. New York: Abrams, 1974.

Higonnet, Anne. *Berthe Morisot's Images of Women*. Cambridge: Harvard Univ. Press, 1992.

Hilton, Timothy. *Pre-Raphaelites*. World of Art. London: Thames and Hudson, 1970.

Homer, William Innes. *Thomas Eakins: His Life and Art*. New York: Abbeville, 1992.

Mathews, Nancy Mowll. *Mary Cassatt*. Library of American Art. New York: Abrams, 1987.

McKean, John. *Crystal Palace: Joseph Paxton and Charles Fox*. Architecture in Detail. London: Phaidon, 1994.

Mead, Christopher Curtis. *Charles Garnier's Paris Opera: Architectural Empathy and the Renaissance of French Classicism*. Cambridge: MIT Press, 1991.

Murphy, Alexandra R. *Jean-François Millet*. Boston: Museum of Fine Arts, 1984.

Needham, Gerald. *19th-Century Realist Art*. New York: Harper & Row, 1988.

Nochlin, Linda. *Impressionism and Post-Impressionism, 1874–1904: Sources and Documents*. Englewood Cliffs, N.J.: Prentice-Hall, 1966.

———. *Realism and Tradition in Art, 1848–1900: Sources and Documents*. Englewood Cliffs, N.J.: Prentice-Hall, 1966.

Pissarro, Joachim. *Camille Pissarro*. New York: Abrams, 1993.

Pool, Phoebe. *Impressionism*. World of Art. New York: Praeger, 1967.

The Pre-Raphaelites. London: Tate Gallery, 1984.

Prideaux, Tom. *The World of Whistler, 1834–1903*. New York: Time-Life, 1970.

Rewald, John. *The History of Impressionism*. 4th rev. ed. New York: Museum of Modern Art, 1973.

Rouart, Denis. *Renoir*. New York: Skira/Rizzoli, 1985.

Schaaf, Larry J. *Out of the Shadows: Herschel, Talbot and the Invention of Photography*. New Haven: Yale Univ. Press, 1992.

Schneider, Pierre. *The World of Manet, 1832–1883*. New York: Time-Life, 1968.

Spate, Virginia. *Claude Monet: Life and Work*. New York: Rizzoli, 1992.

Stansky, Peter. *Redesigning the World: William Morris, the 1880s, and the Arts and Crafts*. Princeton: Princeton Univ. Press, 1985.

Touissaint, Hélène. *Gustave Courbet, 1819–1877*. London: Arts Council of Great Britain, 1978.

Triumph of Realism. Brooklyn: Brooklyn Museum, 1967.

Valkenier, Elizabeth Kridl. *Ilya Repin and the World of Russian Art*. New York: Columbia Univ. Press, 1990.

Wagner, Anne Middleton. *Jean-Baptiste Carpeaux: Sculptor of the Second Empire*. New Haven: Yale Univ. Press, 1986.

Walker, John. *James McNeill Whistler*. Library of American Art. New York: Abrams, 1987.

Weisberg, Gabriel P. *The European Realist Tradition*. Bloomington: Indiana Univ. Press, 1982.

Wilmerding, John, et al. *American Light: The Luminist Movement, 1850–1875: Paintings, Drawings, Photographs*. Washington, D.C.: National Gallery of Art, 1980.

Chapter 28 The Rise of Modernism in Europe and America

Ades, Dawn. *Photomontage*. Rev ed. World of Art. New York: Thames and Hudson, 1986.

Alexandrian, Sarane. *Surrealist Art*. World of Art. London: Thames and Hudson, 1970.

Art into Life: Russian Constructivism, 1914–32. New York: Rizzoli, 1990.

Baigell, Matthew. *The American Scene: American Painting of the 1930's*. New York: Praeger, 1974.

Banham, Reyner. *Theory and Design in the First Machine Age*. 2nd ed. Cambridge: MIT Press, 1980.

Barr, Alfred H., Jr. *Cubism and Abstract Art: Painting, Sculpture, Constructions, Photography, Architecture, Industrial Arts,*

Theatre, Films, Posters, Typography. Cambridge, Mass.: Belknap, 1986.

Barron, Stephanie, ed. *Degenerate Art: The Fate of the Avant-Garde in Nazi Germany*. Los Angeles: Los Angeles County Museum of Art, 1991.

Bayer, Herbert, Walter Gropius, and Ise Gropius. *Bauhaus, 1919–1928*. New York: Museum of Modern Art, 1975.

Brown, Milton. *Story of the Armory Show: The 1913 Exhibition That Changed American Art*. 2nd ed. New York: Abbeville, 1988.

Champigneulle, Bernard. *Rodin*. World of Art. New York: Oxford Univ. Press, 1980.

Cowling, Elizabeth. *Picasso: Sculptor/Painter*. London: Tate Gallery, 1994.

Curtis, James. *Mind's Eye, Mind's Truth: FSA Photography Reconsidered*. Philadelphia: Temple Univ. Press, 1989.

Curtis, William J. R. *Le Corbusier: Idea and Forms*. New York: Rizzoli, 1986.

Dachy, Marc. *The Dada Movement, 1915–1923*. New York: Skira/Rizzoli, 1990.

Davidson, Abraham A. *Early American Modernist Painting, 1910–1935*. New York: Harper & Row, 1981.

Denvir, Bernard. *Post-Impressionism*. World of Art. New York: Thames and Hudson, 1992.

———. *Toulouse-Lautrec*. World of Art. New York: Thames and Hudson, 1991.

Doherty, Robert J., ed. *The Complete Photographic Work of Jacob A. Riis*. New York: Macmillan, 1981.

Dube, Wolf-Dieter. *Expressionism*. Trans. Mary Whittall. World of Art. New York: Praeger, 1973.

Duncan, Alastair. *Art Nouveau*. World of Art. New York: Thames and Hudson, 1994.

Eldredge, Charles C. *Georgia O'Keeffe*. Library of American Art. New York: Abrams, 1991.

Freeman, Judi. *The Fauve Landscape*. Los Angeles: Los Angeles County Museum of Art, 1990.

Fry, Edward. *Cubism*. New York: McGraw-Hill, 1966.

Gay, Peter. *Art and Act: On Causes in History—Manet, Gropius, Mondrian*. New York: Harper & Row, 1976.

Gerdts, William H. *American Impressionism*. New York: Abbeville, 1984.

Glackens, Ira. *William Glackens and the Ashcan Group: The Emergence of Realism in American Art*. New York: Crown, 1957.

Golding, John. *Cubism: A History and an Analysis, 1907–1914*. Cambridge, Mass.: Belknap, 1988.

Gordon, Donald E. *Expressionism: Art and Idea*. New Haven: Yale Univ. Press, 1987.

Gowing, Lawrence. *Matisse*. World of Art. New York: Oxford Univ. Press, 1979.

Gray, Camilla. *Russian Experiment in Art, 1863–1922*. New York: Abrams, 1970.

Hahl-Koch, Jelena. *Kandinsky*. New York: Rizzoli, 1993.

Haiko, Peter, ed. *Architecture of the Early XX Century*. Trans. Gordon Clough. New York: Rizzoli, 1989.

Hamilton, George Heard. *Painting and Sculpture in Europe, 1880–1940*. 2nd ed. Pelican History of Art. Harmondsworth, Eng.: Penguin, 1981.

Harrison, Charles, Francis Frascina, and Gill Perry. *Primitivism, Cubism, Abstraction: The Early Twentieth Century*. New Haven: Yale Univ. Press, 1993.

Herbert, James D. *Fauve Painting: The Making of Cultural Politics*. New Haven: Yale Univ. Press, 1992.

Herrera, Hayden. *Frida Kahlo: The Paintings*. New York: Harper-Collins, 1991.

Hilton, Timothy. *Picasso*. World of Art. New York: Praeger, 1975.

Holt, Elizabeth Gilmore, ed. *The Expanding World of Art, 1874–1902*. New Haven: Yale Univ. Press, 1988.

Homer, William Innes. *Alfred Stieglitz and the American Avant-Garde*. Boston: New York Graphics Society, 1977.

Hulsker, Jan. *The Complete Van Gogh: Paintings, Drawings, Sketches*. New York: Abrams, 1980.

Hulten, Pontus. *Futurism and Futurisms*. New York: Abbeville, 1986.

Jaffe, Hans L. C. *De Stijl, 1917–1931: The Dutch Contribution to Modern Art*. Cambridge, Mass.: Belknap, 1986.

Kuenzli, Rudolf, and Francis M. Naumann. *Marcel Duchamp: Artist of the Century*. Cambridge: MIT Press, 1989.

Lane, John R., and Susan C. Larsen. *Abstract Painting and Sculpture in America 1927–1944*. Pittsburgh: Museum of Art, Carnegie Institute, 1984.

Larkin, David, and Bruce Brooks Pfeiffer. *Frank Lloyd Wright: The Masterworks*. New York: Rizzoli, 1993.

Lloyd, Jill. *German Expressionism: Primitivism and Modernity*. New Haven: Yale Univ. Press, 1991.

McQuillan, Melissa. *Van Gogh*. World of Art. New York: Thames and Hudson, 1989.

Milner, John. *Vladimir Tatlin and the Russian Avant-Garde*. New Haven: Yale Univ. Press, 1983.

Norman, Dorothy. *Alfred Stieglitz, an American Seer*. New York: Aperture, 1990.

O'Gorman, James F. *Three American Architects: Richardson, Sullivan, and Wright, 1865–1915*. Chicago: Univ. of Chicago Press, 1991.

Overy, Paul. *De Stijl*. World of Art. New York: Thames and Hudson, 1991.

Picon, Gaetan. *Surrealists and Surrealism, 1919–1939*. Trans. James Emmons. New York: Rizzoli, 1977.

Post-Impressionism: Cross-Currents in European and American Painting, 1880–1906. Washington, D.C.: National Gallery of Art, 1980.

Rewald, John. *Post-Impressionism: From Van Gogh to Gauguin*. 3rd ed. New York: Museum of Modern Art, 1978.

Rosenblum, Robert. *Cubism and Twentieth-Century Art*. Rev. ed. New York: Abrams, 1984.

Rubin, William, ed. *Pablo Picasso, a Retrospective*. New York: Museum of Modern Art, 1980.

———, comp. *Picasso and Braque: Pioneering Cubism*. New York: Museum of Modern Art, 1989.

Russell, John. *Seurat*. World of Art. London: Thames and Hudson, 1965.

———. *The World of Matisse, 1869–1954*. New York: Time-Life, 1969.

Spate, Virginia. *Orphism: The Evolution of Non-Figurative Painting in Paris, 1910–1914*. Oxford Studies in the History of Art and Architecture. Oxford: Clarendon, 1979.

Stich, Sidra. *Anxious Visions: Surrealist Art*. New York: Abbeville, 1990.

Sutter, Jean, ed. *The Neo-Impressionists*. Greenwich, Conn.: New York Graphic Society, 1970.

Thomson, Belinda. *Gauguin*. World of Art. New York: Thames and Hudson, 1987.

Tisdall, Caroline, and Angelo Bozzolla. *Futurism*. World of Art. New York: Oxford Univ. Press, 1978.

Verdi, Richard. *Cezanne*. World of Art. New York: Thames and Hudson, 1992.

Weiss, Jeffrey S. *The Popular Culture of Modern Art: Picasso, Duchamp, and Avant-Gardism*. New Haven: Yale Univ. Press, 1994.

Whitford, Frank. *Bauhaus*. World of Art. London: Thames and Hudson, 1984.

Wilkin, Karen. *Georges Braque*. New York: Abbeville, 1991.

Zhadova, Larissa A. *Malevich: Suprematism and Revolution in Russian Art*. Trans. Alexander Lieven. London: Thames and Hudson, 1982.

Chapter 29 Art in the United States and Europe since World War II

Alloway, Lawrence. *Roy Lichtenstein*. New York: Abbeville, 1983.

Andersen, Wayne. *American Sculpture in Process, 1930–1970*. Boston: New York Graphic Society, 1975.

Anfam, David. *Abstract Expressionism*. World of Art. New York: Thames and Hudson, 1990.

Ashton, Dore. *American Art since 1945*. New York: Oxford Univ. Press, 1982.

———. *The New York School: A Cultural Reckoning*. Harmondsworth, Eng.: Penguin, 1979.

Atkins, Robert. *Artspeak: A Guide to Contemporary Ideas, Movements, and Buzzwords*. New York: Abbeville, 1990.

Baker, Kenneth. *Minimalism: Art of Circumstance*. New York: Abbeville, 1988.

Battcock, Gregory. *Idea Art: A Critical Anthology*. New York: Dutton, 1973.

———. *Minimal Art: A Critical Anthology*. New York: Dutton, 1968.

———, and Robert Nickas. *The Art of Performance: A Critical Anthology*. New York: Dutton, 1984.

Beardsley, John. *Earthworks and Beyond: Contemporary Art in the Landscape*. New York: Abbeville, 1984.

Berger, Maurice. *Labyrinths: Robert Morris, Minimalism, and the 1960s*. New York: Harper & Row, 1989.

Blake, Peter. *No Place Like Utopia: Modern Architecture and the Company We Kept*. New York: Knopf, 1993.

Bolton, Richard, ed. *Culture Wars: Documents from the Recent Controversies in the Arts*. New York: New, 1992.

Bourdon, David. *Warhol*. New York: Abrams, 1989.

Broude, Norma, and Mary D. Garrard. *The Power of Feminist Art: The American Movement of the 1970s, History and Impact*. New York: Abrams, 1994.

Castleman, Riva, ed. *Art of the Forties*. New York: Museum of Modern Art, 1991.

Cernuschi, Claude. *Jackson Pollock: Meaning and Significance*. New York: Icon Editions, 1992.

Chase, Linda. *Hyperrealism*. New York: Rizzoli, 1975.

Collins, Michael, and Andreas Papadakis. *Post-Modern Design*. New York: Rizzoli, 1989.

Deutsche, Rosalyn, et al. *Hans Haacke, Unfinished Business*. Ed. Brian Wallis. Cambridge: MIT Press, 1986.

Dormer, Peter. *Design since 1945*. World of Art. New York: Thames and Hudson, 1993.

Endgame: Reference and Simulation in Recent Painting and Sculpture. Boston: Institute of Contemporary Art, 1986.

Ferguson, Russell, ed. *Discourses: Conversations in Postmodern Art and Culture*. Documentary Sources in Contemporary Art. Cambridge: MIT Press, 1990.

Goldberg, Rose Lee. *Performance Art: From Futurism to the Present*. Rev. ed. New York: Abrams, 1988.

Green, Jonathan. *American Photography: A Critical History since 1945 to the Present*. New York: Abrams, 1984.

Greenough, Sarah, and Philip Brookman. *Robert Frank*. Washington, D.C.: National Gallery of Art, 1994.

Grundberg, Andy. *Photography and Art: Interactions since 1945*. New York: Abbeville, 1987.

Hays, K. Michael, and Carol Burns, eds. *Thinking the Present: Recent American Architecture*. New York: Princeton Architectural, 1990.

Henri, Adrian. *Total Art: Environments, Happenings, and Performance*. World of Art. New York: Oxford Univ. Press, 1974.

Hertz, Richard. *Theories of Contemporary Art*. 2nd ed. Englewood Cliffs, N.J.: Prentice Hall, 1993.

Hobbs, Robert Carleton, and Gail Levin. *Abstract Expressionism: The Formative Years*. Ithaca: Cornell Univ. Press, 1981

Hoffman, Katherine. *Explorations: The Visual Arts since 1945*. New York: HarperCollins, 1991.

Jencks, Charles. *Architecture Today*. 2nd ed. London: Academy, 1993.

———. *The New Moderns from Late to Neo-Modernism*. New York: Rizzoli, 1990.

———. *Post-Modernism: The New Classicism in Art and Architecture*. New York: Rizzoli, 1987.

———. *What Is Post-Modernism?* 3rd rev. ed. London: Academy Editions, 1989.

Joachimedes, Christos M., Norman Rosenthal, and Nicholas Serota, eds. *New Spirit in Painting*. London: Royal Academy of Arts, 1981.

Johnson, Ellen H., ed. *American Artists on Art from 1940 to 1980*. New York: Harper & Row, 1982.

Kaprow, Allan. *Assemblage, Environments & Happenings*. New York: Abrams, 1965.

Kingsley, April. *The Turning Point: The Abstract Expressionists and the Transformation of American Art*. New York: Simon & Schuster, 1992.

Kramer, Hilton. *The Age of the Avant-Garde: An Art Chronicle of 1956–1972*. New York: Farrar, Straus & Giroux, 1973.

Kuspit, Donald B. *Clement Greenberg, Art Critic*. Madison: Univ. of Wisconsin Press, 1979.

Levick, Melba. *The Big Picture: Murals of Los Angeles*. Boston: Little, Brown, 1988.

Lewis, Samella S. *African American Art and Artists*. Rev. ed. Berkeley: Univ. of California Press, 1994.

Lippard, Lucy. *Pop Art*. World of Art. New York: Praeger, 1966.

Livingstone, Marco. *Pop Art: A Continuing History*. New York: Abrams, 1990.

Lucie-Smith, Edward. *Art in the Eighties*. Oxford: Phaidon, 1990.

———. *Art in the Seventies*. Ithaca: Cornell Univ. Press, 1980.

———. *Art Today: From Abstract Expressionism to Superrealism*. 3rd ed. Oxford: Phaidon, 1989.

———. *Movements in Art since 1945*. Rev. ed. World of Art. London: Thames and Hudson, 1984.

———. *Super Realism*. Oxford: Phaidon, 1979.

Manhart, Marcia, and Tom Manhart, eds. *The Eloquent Object: The Evolution of American Art in Craft Media since 1945*. Tulsa: Philbrook Museum of Art, 1987.

Meisel, Louis K. *Photo-Realism*. New York: Abrams, 1989.

Morgan, Robert C. *Conceptual Art: An American Perspective*. Jefferson, N.C.: McFarland, 1994.

Nash, Steven A. *Arneson and Politics: A Commemorative Exhibition*. San Francisco: Fine Arts Museums of San Francisco, 1993.

Risatti, Howard, ed. *Postmodern Perspectives: Issues in Contemporary Art*. Englewood Cliffs, N.J.: Prentice Hall, 1990.

Rosen, Randy, and Catherine C. Brawer, comps. *Making Their Mark: Women Artists Move into the Mainstream, 1970–85*. New York: Abbeville, 1989.

Russell, John. *Pop Art Redefined*. New York: Praeger, 1969.

Sandler, Irving. *American Art of the 1960's*. New York: Harper & Row, 1988.

———. *The New York School: The Painters and Sculptors of the Fifties*. New York: Harper & Row, 1978.

———. *The Triumph of American Painting: A History of Abstract Expressionism*. New York: Harper & Row, 1976.

Sayre, Henry M. *The Object of Performance: The American Avant-Garde since 1970*. Chicago: Univ. of Chicago Press, 1989.

Shapiro, David, and Cecile Shapiro. *Abstract Expressionism: A Critical Record*. New York: Cambridge Univ. Press, 1990.

Slivka, Rose. *Peter Voulkos: A Dialogue with Clay*. Boston: New York Graphic Society, 1978.

Smith, Paul J., and Edward Lucie-Smith. *Craft Today: Poetry of the Physical*. New York: American Craft Museum, 1986.

Spaeth, David A. *Mies Van Der Rohe*. New York: Rizzoli, 1985.

Stich, Sidra. *Made in USA: An Americanization in Modern Art, the '50s & '60s*. Berkeley: Univ. of California Press, 1987.

Taylor, Paul, ed. *Post-Pop Art*. Cambridge: MIT Press, 1989.

Vaizey, Marina. *Christo*. New York: Rizzoli, 1990.

Waldman, Diane. *Collage, Assemblage, and the Found Object*. New York: Abrams, 1992.

———. *Jenny Holzer*. New York: Abrams, 1989.

———. *Transformations in Sculpture: Four Decades of American and European Art*. New York: Solomon R. Guggenheim Foundation, 1985.

———. *Willem de Kooning*. Library of American Art. New York: Abrams, 1988.

Wallis, Brian, ed. *Art after Modernism: Rethinking Representation*. Documentary Sources in Contemporary Art. New York: New Museum of Contemporary Art, 1984.

Wheeler, Daniel. *Art since Mid-Century: 1945 to the Present*. Englewood Cliffs, N.J.: Prentice Hall, 1991.

Word as Image: American Art, 1960–1990. Milwaukee: Milwaukee Art Museum, 1990.

Website Directory of Museums

This directory is comprised mainly of the museums that holds works of art illustrated in this book. A few additional institutions are also listed. We have made every effort to provide up-to-date addresses, phone numbers, and websites as of the date of printing.

UNITED STATES

ARIZONA

Center for Creative Photography,
University of Arizona, 843 E. University Blvd., Tuscon 85721. (520)621–7968.
www.ccp.arizona.edu

The Heard Museum,
22 E. Monte Vista Rd., Phoenix 85004. (602)252–8840.
hanksville.phast.umass.edu/defs/independent/Heard/Heard.html

Phoenix Art Museum,
1625 N. Central Ave., Phoenix 85004. (602)257–1880.
www.azcentral.com/community/phxart/home.html

CALIFORNIA

Crocker Museum of Art,
216 O St., Sacramento 95814. (916)264–5423.
www.sacti.org/crocker

The Fine Arts Museums of San Francisco: California Palace of the Legion of Honor,
Lincoln Park, near 34th Ave. and Clement St., San Francisco 94121. (415)863–3330;
M. H. de Young Memorial Museum,
Golden Gate Park, San Francisco 94118. (415)221–4811.
www.famsf.org

Frederick S. Wright Art Gallery,
University of California, Los Angeles, 405 Hilgard Ave., Los Angeles 90024. (213)825–1461

Huntington Library, Art Collections, and Botanical Gardens,
1151 Oxford Rd., San Marino 91108. (818)405–2141.
www.huntington.org/ArtDiv/HEHARTHOME.html

The J. Paul Getty Museum,
17985 Pacific Coast Hwy., Malibu 90265. (310)458–2003.
www.getty.edu/museum

Los Angeles County Museum of Art,
5905 Wilshire Blvd., Los Angeles 90036. (213)857–6111.
www.lacma.org

Museum of Contemporary Art, San Diego,
1001 Kettner Blvd., San Diego 92101, 700 Prospect St., La Jolla 92037. (619)454–3541.
www.sddt.com/features/mca/mcainfo.html

The Museum of Contemporary Art, Los Angeles, 250 S. Grand Ave. at California Plaza, Los Angeles 90012. (213)382–6622, 621–2766.
www.MOCA-LA.org

Norton Simon Museum,
411 W. Colorado Blvd., Pasadena 91105. (818)449–6840; 449–3730.
www.citycet.com/CCC/nsmuseum.htm

San Diego Museum of Art,
Balboa Park, 1450 El Prado, San Diego 92101. (619)232–7931.
www.sddt.com/sdma.html

San Francisco Museum of Modern Art,
151 3rd St., San Francisco 94103. (415)357–4000.
www.sfmoma.org/

San Jose Museum of Art,
110 S. Market St., San Jose 95113. (408)294–2787.
www.sjmusart.org

Santa Barbara Museum of Art,
1130 State St., Santa Barbara 93101. (805)963–4364.
www.artdirect.com/sbma/

Stanford University Museum and Art Gallery,
Lomita Dr. & Museum Way, Palo Alto 94305. (415)725–4177.
www-leland.stanford.edu/dept/SUMA/

University Art Museum and Pacific Film Archive,
University of California, 2626 Bancroft Way, Berkeley 94704. (510)642–0808.
www.uampfa.berkeley.edu

COLORADO

Colorado Springs Fine Arts Center,
30 W. Dale St., Colorado Springs 80903. (719)634–5581.
vanbriggle.com/Pikes-Peak/FineArts/

The Denver Art Museum,
100 W. 14th Ave. Pkwy., Denver 80204. (303)640–2793.
www.denverartmuseum.org

Connecticut

Wadsworth Atheneum,
600 Main St., Hartford 06103. (203)278–2670.
www.hartfordct.com/wad.html

Yale Center for British Art,
1080 Chapel St., New Haven 06520. (203)432–2800.
www.yale.edu/ycba

Yale University Art Gallery,
1111 Chapel St. at York, New Haven 06520. (203)432–0600.
www.yale.edu/yups/yuag/index.html

DELAWARE

Delaware Art Museum,
2301 Kentmere Pkwy., Wilmington 19806. (302)571–9590.
www.udel.edu/delart

District of Columbia

The Corcoran Gallery of Art,
500 17th St. NW, 20006. (202)638–1903.
www.corcoran.org

Freer Gallery of Art, Smithsonian Institution,
Jefferson Dr. at 12th St. SW, 20560. (202)357–4880.
www.si.edu/organiza/museums/freer/start.htm

Hirshhorn Museum and Sculpture Garden, Smithsonian Institution, Independence Ave. at 7th St. SW, 20560. (202)357–2700.
www.si.edu/organiza/museums/hirsh/start.htm

National Gallery of Art,
4th St. at Constitution Ave. NW, 20565. (202)737–4215; (202)842–6176 (TDD).
www.nga.gov

National Museum of American Art,
8th and G Sts., 20560; Renwick Gallery, Pennsylvania Ave. at 17th St. NW, 20006. (202)357–2700.
www.nmaa.si.edu

National Museum of Women in the Arts,
1250 New York Ave. NW, 20005, (202) 783–5000.
www.nmwa.org

National Portrait Gallery,
8th and F Sts. NW, 20560. (202)357–2700.
www.npg.si.edu

The Phillips Collection,
1600 21st St. NW, 20009. (202)387–0961

FLORIDA

John and Mable Ringling Museum of Art,
5401 Bay Shore Rd., Sarasota 34243. (813)359–5700.
www.ringling.org

Lowe Art Museum,
University of Miami, 1301 Stanford Dr., Coral Gables 33124. (305)284–3535.
www.flamuseums.org/fam/flamuseums/pages/185.htm

Museum of Fine Arts, Saint Petersburg, Florida,
255 Beach Dr. NE, Saint Petersburg 33701. (813)896–2667.
www.fine-arts.org

GEORGIA

Georgia Museum of Art, University of Georgia,
Jackson St., North Campus, Athens 30602. (706)542–GMOA or 4662

High Museum of Art,
1280 Peachtree St. NE, Atlanta 30309. (404)733–HIGH or 4444.
www.high.org

HAWAII

Honolulu Academy of Arts,
900 S. Beretania St., Honolulu 96814. (808)532–8700; 532–8701.

Illinois

The Art Institute of Chicago,
111 S. Michigan Ave. at Adams St., Chicago 60603. (312)443–3600; 443–3500.
www.artic.edu

Krannert Art Museum, University of Illinois,
500 E. Peabody Dr., Champaign 61820. (217)333–1861.
www.art.uiuc.edu/kam/

Museum of Contemporary Art,
220 E. Chicago Ave., Chicago 60611. (312)280–2660; 280–5161.
www.mcachicago.org

Oriental Institute Museum, The University of Chicago, 1155 E. 58th St., Chicago 60637. (773)702–9521.
www-oi.uchicago.edu/OI/MUS/OI-Museum.html

Terra Museum of American Art,
666 N. Michigan Ave., Chicago 60611. (312)664–3939

INDIANA

Indianapolis Museum of Art,
1200 W. 38th St., Indianapolis 46208. (317)923–1331.
web.ima-art.org/ima

IOWA

Des Moines Art Center,
4700 Grand Ave., Des Moines 50312. (515)277–4405

University of Iowa Museum of Art,
150 N. Riverside Dr., Iowa City 52242. (319)335–1727

KANSAS

Spencer Museum of Art, University of Kansas,
1301 Mississippi St., Lawrence 66045.
(913)864–4710.
www.ukansas.edu/~sma

Wichita Art Museum,
619 Stackman Dr., Wichita, 67203. (316)268–4921.
www.feist.com/~wam

KENTUCKY

J. B. Speed Art Museum,
2035 S. 3rd St., Louisville 40208. (502)636–2920.
www.speedmuseum.org

LOUISIANA

New Orleans Museum of Art,
1 Collins Diboll Circle, City Park, New Orleans
70124. (504)488–2631.
www.noma.org

MAINE

Bowdoin College Museum of Art,
Walker Art Building, Brunswick 04011.
(207)725–3275. www.bowdoin.edu

Portland Museum of Art,
7 Congress Sq., Portland 04101. (207)775–6148.
www.portlandmuseum.org

MARYLAND

The Baltimore Museum of Art,
Art Museum Dr. at North Charles and 31st Sts.,
Baltimore 21218. (410)396–7100.

Walters Art Gallery,
600 N. Charles St., Baltimore 21201.
(410)547–9000; 547–ARTS.
www.thewalters.org

MASSACHUSETTS

Addison Gallery of American Art, Phillips Academy,
Andover 01810. (508)749–4015.
www.andover.edu/addison/home.html

Davis Museum and Cultural Center, Wellesley College,
106 Central St., Wellesley 02181. (617)283–2051.
www.wellesley.edu/DavisMuseum/
davismenu.html

Harvard University Art Museums,
Cambridge 02138. (617)495–9400
www.fas.harvard.edu/~artmuseums/:
Busch-Reisinger Museum, 32 Quincy St.;
Fogg Art Museum, 32 Quincy St.; The Arthur M.
Sackler Museum, 485 Broadway

Isabella Stewart Gardner Museum,
280 The Fenway, Boston 02115. (617)566–1401.
www.boston.com/ gardner

Mead Art Museum, Amherst College,
Amherst 01002. (413)542–2335.
www.amherst.edu/~mead

Mount Holyoke College Art Museum,
South Hadley 01075. (413)538–2245.
www.myholyoke.edu/offices/artmuse/
general.html

Museum of Fine Arts, Boston,
465 Huntington Ave., Boston 02115.
(617)267–9300.
www.mfa.org

Peabody Essex Museum,
East India Sq., Salem 01970. (508)745–1876.
www.pem.org

Rose Art Museum, Brandeis University,
415 South St., Waltham 02254. (617)736–3434.
www.brandeis.edu/rose/index.html

Smith College Museum of Art,
Elm St. at Bedford Terrace, Northampton 01063.
(413)585–2760.
www.smith.edu/artmuseum/

Sterling and Francine Clark Art Institute,
225 South St., Williamstown 01267.
(413)458–9545.
www.clark.williams.edu

Williams College Museum of Art,
Main St., Williamstown 01267. (413)597–2429.
www.williams.edu/WCMA/

Worcester Art Museum,
55 Salisbury St., Worcester 01609.
(508)799–4406.
www.worcesterart.org

MICHIGAN

The Detroit Institute of Arts,
5200 Woodward Ave., Detroit 48202.
(313)833–7900.
www.dia.org

Grand Rapids Art Museum,
155 Division North, Grand Rapids 49503.
(616)459–4677.
www.grandrapids.org/artmuseum/

The University of Michigan Museum of Art,
525 S. State St., Ann Arbor 48109.
(313)764–0395.
www.umich.edu/~umma

MINNESOTA

The Minneapolis Institute of Arts,
2400 3rd Ave. S., Minneapolis 55404.
(612)870–3131; 870–3200.
www.artsMIA.org

Walker Art Center,
Vineland Pl., Minneapolis 55403.
(612)375–7622.
www.walkerart.org

MISSOURRI

The Nelson-Atkins Museum of Art,
4525 Oak St., Kansas City 64111.
(816)561–4000.
www.nelson-atkins.org

The Saint Louis Art Museum,
1 Fine Arts Dr., Forest Park, St. Louis 63110.
(314)721–0072. www.slam.org

NEBRASKA

Joslyn Art Museum,
2200 Dodge St., Omaha 68102. (402)342–3300.
www.joslyn.org

University of Nebraska-Lincoln/Sheldon Memorial Art Gallery and Sculpture Garden,
12th and R Sts., Lincoln 68588. (402)472–2461.
sheldon.unl.edu

NEW HAMPSHIRE

Hood Museum of Art, Dartmouth College,
Wheelock St., Hanover 03755. (603)646–2808.
gopher://gopher.dartmouth.edu/II/HopHood

NEW JERSEY

The Art Museum, Princeton University,
Princeton 08544. (609)258–3788

Jane Zimmerli Art Museum,
Rutgers The State University of New Jersey,
Hamilton and George Sts., New Brunswick
08903 (732)932–7237.
www-rci.rutgers.edu/~zamuseum/

The Montclair Art Museum,
3 S. Mountain Ave. at Bloomfield Ave.,
Montclair 07042. (973)746–5555.
www.montclair-art.com

The Newark Museum,
49 Washington St., Newark 07101.
(973)596–6550

NEW MEXICO

Millicent Rogers Museum,
1504 Millicent Rogers Rd., Taos 87571.
(505)758–2462

NEW YORK

Albright-Knox Art Gallery,
1285 Elmwood Ave., Buffalo 14222.
(716)882–8700.
www.albright-knox.org

American Craft Museum,
40 W. 53rd St., New York 10019. (212)956–3535

The Brooklyn Museum,
200 Eastern Pkwy., Brooklyn 11238.
(718)638–5000.
www.brooklynart.com

The Cloisters,
Fort Tryon Park, New York 10040.
(212)923–3700.
www.metmuseum.org/htmlfile/gallery/
cloister/cloister.html

Cooper-Hewitt National Museum of Design,
Smithsonian Institution, 2 E. 91st St., New York
10128. (212) 860–6868.
www.si.edu/organiza/museums/design/home
/home.htm

Everson Museum of Art of Syracuse and Onondaga County,
401 Harrison St., Syracuse 13202.
(315)474–6064.
www.everson.org

The Frick Collection,
1 E. 70th St., New York 10021. (212)288–0700

George Eastman House/International Museum of Photography and Film,
900 E. Ave., Rochester 14607. (716)271–3361.
www.eastman.org

The Grey Art Gallery and Study Center, New York University Art Collection,
33 Washington Pl., New York 10003.
(212)998–6780.
www.nyu.edu/greyart

Guggenheim Museum SoHo,
575 Broadway, New York 10012. (212)423–3500.
www.guggenheim.org/soho.html

Herbert F. Johnson Museum of Art, Cornell University,
Ithaca 14853. (607)255–6464.
www.museum.cornell.edu

The Hudson River Museum of Westchester,
511 Warburton Ave., Yonkers 10701.
(914)963–4550.
www.hrm.org

International Center of Photography:
1130 5th Ave., New York 10028.
(212)860–1777;
Midtown, 1133 6th Ave., New York 10036.
(212)860–1783.
www.icp.org

The Jewish Museum,
1109 5th Ave., New York, 10128.
(212)423–3200

Memorial Art Gallery of the University of Rochester,
500 University Ave., Rochester, NY 14607.
(716)473–7720.
www.cc.rochester.edu/MAG

The Metropolitan Museum of Art,
5th Ave. at 82nd St., New York 10028.
(212)879–5500. www.metmuseum.org

The Museum of Modern Art,
11 W. 53rd St., New York 10019. (212)708–9400.
www.moma.org

Munson-Williams-Proctor Institute Museum
of Art, 310 Genesee St., Utica 13502.
(315)797–0000

Neuberger Museum of Art, Purchase College,
State University of New York at Purchase,
735 Anderson Hill Rd., Purchase 10577.
(914)251–6133.
www.neuberger.org

The New Museum of Contemporary Art,
583 Broadway, New York 10012. (212)219–1222.
www.newmuseum.org

The Pierpont Morgan Library, 29 E. 36th St.,
New York 10016. (212)685–0008

Solomon R. Guggenheim Museum,
1071 5th Ave., New York 10128. (212)423–3500.
www.guggenheim.org/srgm.html

The Studio Museum in Harlem,
144 W. 125th St., New York 10027.
(212)864–4500.
www.studiomuseuminharlem.org

Storm King Art Center,
Old Pleasant Hill Rd., Mountainville 10953.
(914)534–3115.
www.skac.org

Whitney Museum of American Art,
945 Madison Ave., New York 10021.
(212)570–3676.
www.echonyc.com/~whitney

NORTH CAROLINA

The Ackland Art Museum, University of North
Carolina, Chapel Hill,
Columbia and Franklin Sts., Chapel Hill 27599.
(919)966–5736.
www.unc.edu/depts/ackland/frontpage.htm

Duke Univerisity Museum of Art,
Buchanan Blvd. at Trinity, East Campus,
Durham 27708. (919)684–5135.
www.duke.edu/web/duma/

North Carolina Museum of Art,
2110 Blue Ridge Rd., Raleigh 27607.
(919)839-6262.
www.ncsu.edu/NCMA/

Weatherspoon Art Gallery, University of
North Carolina, Greensboro,
Spring Garden and Tate Sts., Greensboro 27412.
(910)334–5770.
www.uncg.edu/wag/

OHIO

Allen Memorial Art Museum, Oberlin College,
87 N. Main St., Oberlin 44074. (216)775–8665.
www.oberlin.edu/wwwmap/allen_art.html

The Butler Institute of America,
524 Wick Ave., Youngstown 44502.
(216)743–1711.
www.butlerart.com

Cincinnati Art Museum, Eden Park,
Cincinnati 45202. (513)721–5204.
www.cincinnatiartmuseum.org

The Cleveland Museum of Art,
11150 E. Blvd., Cleveland 44106.
(216)421–7340.
www.clemusart.com

The Columbus Museum of Art,
480 E. Broad St., Columbus 43215.
(614)221–6801

Dayton Art Institute,
456 Belmonte Park North, Dayton 45405.
(513)223–5277.

The Taft Museum,
316 Pike St., Cincinnati 45202. (513)241–0343.
www.taftmuseum.org

The Toledo Museum of Art,
2445 Monroe St., Toledo 43620. (419)255–8000;
(800)644–6862.
www.toledomuseum.org

Wexner Center for the Arts, The Ohio State
University,
North High St. at 15th Ave., Columbus 43210.
(614)292–3535.
web.cgrg.ohio-state.edu/Wexner

OKLAHOMA

Gilcrease Museum,
1400 Gilcrease Museum Rd., Tulsa 74127.
(918)596–2700

The Philbrook Museum of Art,
2727 S. Rockford Rd., Tulsa 74114.
(918)749–7941.

OREGON

Portland Art Museum,
1219 SW Park Ave, Portland 97205.
(503)226–2811.
www.pam.org

PENNSYLVANIA

The Andy Warhol Museum,
117 Sandusky St., Pittsburgh 15212.
(412)237–8300.
www.warhol.org/warhol/

Barnes Foundation,
300 North Natch's Ln., Merion Station 19066.
(610)667–0290

Brandywine River Museum, Brandywine
Conservancy,
Rt. 1 at PA Rt. 100, Chadds Ford 19317.
(610)388–2700.
www.brandywinemuseum.org

The Carnegie Museum of Art,
4400 Forbes Ave., Pittsburgh 15213.
(412)622–3131.
www.warhol.org/moa

The Frick Art Museum,
7227 Reynolds St., Pittsburgh 15208.
(412)371–0600

Institute of Contemporary Art, University
of Pennsylvania,
118 S. 36th St., Philadelphia 19104.
(215)898–7108.
www.upen.edu/ica/

Museum of American Art of the Pennsylvania
Academy of the Fine Arts,
118 N. Broad St., Philadelphia 19102.
(215)972–7600.
www.pond.com/~pafa

Philadelphia Museum of Art,
26th St. and Benjamin Franklin Pkwy.,
Philadelphia 19130. (215)763–8100.
www.philamuseum.org

University of Pennsylvania Museum of
Archaeology and Anthropology,
33rd and Spruce Sts., Philadelphia 19104.
(215)898-4000,4001.
www.upenn.edu/museum

RHODE ISLAND

Museum of Art, Rhode Island School of Design,
224 Benefit St., Providence 02903.
(401)454–6500.
www.risd.edu/museum.html

SOUTH CAROLINA

Greenville County Museum of Art,
420 College St., Greenville 29601. (803)271–7570

TENNESSEE

Knoxville Museum of Art,
410 10th Ave., World's Fair Park,
Knoxville 37916. (615)525–6101.
www.esper.com/kma/index.html

Memphis Brooks Museum of Art,
Overton Park, 1934 Poplar, Memphis 38104.
(901)722–3500.
www.memphisguide.com/Brooks.html

Texas

Amon Carter Museum,
3501 Camp Bowie Blvd., Fort Worth 76107.
(817)738–1933.
www.cartermuseum.org

Contemporary Arts Museum,
5216 Montrose Blvd., Houston 77006.
(713)526–0773. www.camh.org

Dallas Museum of Art,
1717 N. Harwood, Dallas 75201. (214)922–1200.
www.unt.edu/dfw/dma/

Kimbell Art Museum,
3333 Camp Bowie Blvd., Fort Worth 76107.
(817)332–8451.
www.kimbellart.org

Marion Koogler McNay Art Museum,
6000 N. New Braunfels Ave., San Antonio 78209.
(210)824–5368

The Menil Collection,
1515 Sul Ross, Houston 77006.
www.menil.org/~menil

Modern Art Museum of Fort Worth,
1309 Montgomery St. at Camp Bowie Blvd.,
Fort Worth 76107. (817)738–9215

The Museum of Fine Arts, Houston,
1001 Bissonnet St., Houston 77005.
(713)639–7300.
mfah.org

Rothko Chapel,
1409 Sul Ross, Houston 77006. (713)524–9839.
www.menil.org/rothko.html

San Antonio Museum of Art,
200 W. Jones St., San Antonio 78215.
(210)978–8100.
www.samuseum.org

VIRGINIA

The Chrysler Museum,
245 W. Olney Rd.,
Norfolk 23510. (804)664–6200.
www.whro.org/cl/cmhh

Hampton University Museum,
Hampton 23668. (757)727–5308.
www.hamptonu.edu/HUMUS/HUMUS.htm

Monticello,
P. O. Box 316, Charlottesville 22902.
(804)984–9822.
www.monticello.org

Virginia Museum of Fine Arts,
2800 Grove Ave., Richmond 23221.
(804)367–0844.
xroads.virginia.edu/~VAM/VMFA

WASHINGTON
Seattle Art Museum,
100 University St., Seattle 98101. (206)625–8900;
654–3100.
www.sam.tripl.org

Tacoma Art Museum,
1123 Pacific Ave., Tacoma 98402. (206)272–4258.
www.tamart.org

WISCONSIN
Milwaukee Art Museum,
750 N. Lincoln Memorial Dr., Milwaukee 53202.
(414)224–3200.
www.mam.org

OUTSIDE THE UNITED STATES

AUSTRIA
Graphische Sammlung Albertina,
A-1010 Wien, Augustinerstrße 1. (0222)534830.
www2.telecom.at/albertina/welcome1.html

Kunsthistoriches Museum,
A-1010 Wien,
Burgring 5. (0222)525240

Österreichische Galerie Belvedere,
1037 Wien, Prinz-Eugen-Str. 27. (01)79570

BELGIUM
Musée Royaux d'Art et d'Histoire,
Parc du Cinquantenaire 10, 1000 Brussels.
(02)7417211

Musées Royaux des Beaux-Arts de Belgique,
9, Rue de Musée, 1000 Brussels.
(02)5139630.
www.fine-art-museum.be

CANADA
Art Gallery of Ontario, 317 Dundas St. W.,
Toronto, Ontario M5T 1G4. (416)977–6648.
www.ago.net

Canadian Center for Archictecture,
1920, rue Baile, Montréal, Quebec H3H 2S6.
(514)939–7000; 939–7026.
cca.qc.ca

Edmonton Art Gallery,
2 Sir Winston Churchhill Sq., Edmonton,
Alberta T5J 2C1. (403)422–6223

Glenbow,
130 9th Ave., Southeast, Calgary,
Alberta T2G 0P3. (403)268–4100.
www.glenbow.org

Montréal Museum of Fine Arts,
1379-80 Sherbrook St. W., Montréal,
Quebec H36 2T9.
(514)285–1600; 285–2000.
www.mmfa.qc.ca

National Gallery of Canada,
380 Sussex Dr., Ottawa, Ontario K1N 9N4.
(800)319–ARTS; (613)990–1985.
national.gallery.ca

Royal Ontario Museum,
100 Queen's Park, Toronto, Ontario M5S 2C6.
(416)586–5551.
www.rom.on.ca

Vancouver Art Gallery,
750 Hornby St., Vancouver,
British Columbia V6Z 2H7.
(604)682–4668.
www.vanartgallery.bc.ca

CZECH REPUBLIC
National Gallery in Prague,
Hradcanské námesti 15, Prague. (02)536867

DENMARK
Louisiana Museum of Modern Art,
GI Strandvej 13, 3050 Humlebæk. 42190719.
www.louisiana.dk

Ny Carlsberg Glyptotek,
Dantes Plads 7, 1556 Copenhagen. 33418141.
www.kulturnet.dk/homes/ncg/

EGYPT
Egyptian Museum,
Cairo University. Midan el Tahrir,
Cairo. (2)760390.
www.idsc.gov.eg/culture/egy_mus.htm

ENGLAND
Ashmolean Museum of Art and Archaeology,
Beaumont St., Oxford 0X1 2PH. (01865)278000.
www.ashmol.ox.ac.uk

Banqueting House, Whitehall,
London SW1 2ER. (0171)8398919

Birmingham Museum and Art Gallery,
Chamberlain Sq., Birmingham B3 3DH.
(0121)2352834

Blenheim Palace,
Woodstock 0X7 1PX. (01993)811325

British Library Exhibition Galleries,
Great Russell St., London WC1B 3DG.
(0171)4127595

British Museum,
Great Russell St., London WC1B 3DG.
(0171)6361555.
www.british-museum.ac.uk

Courtauld Institute Galleries,
Somerset House, Strand, London WC2R ORN.
(0171)8732526

Durham Cathedral,
Durham DH1 3EH. (0191)3844854

The National Gallery,
Trafalgar Sq., London WC2N 5DN. (0171)7472885.
www.nationalgallery.org.uk

Royal Academy of Arts,
Burlington House, Piccadilly, London W1V 0DS.
(0171)4397438.
www.royalacademy.org.uk

Sir John Soane's Museum,
13 Lincoln's Inn Fields, London WC2A 3BP.
(0171)4052107.
www.demon.co.uk/heritage/soanes/

Tate Gallery,
Millbank, London SWIP 4RG. (0171)8878000.
www.tate.org.uk

Victoria and Albert Museum,
Cromwell Rd., South Kensington,
London SW7 2RL. (0171)9388500.
www.vam.ac.uk

Wellington Museum,
Apsley House, 149 Piccadilly, Hyde Park Corner,
London W1V 9FA. (0171)4995676.
www.vam.ac.uk/apsley/

Westminster Abbey,
London SW1P 3PA. (0171) 2225152

FRANCE
Bibliothèque Nationale de France,
58 Rue de Richelieu, Paris 75002. (1)47038126.
www.bnf.fr

Château de Versailles,
Versailles 78000. (1)30847400.
www.chateauversailles.fr

Chauvet cave,
Vallon-Pont-d'Arc.
www.culture.gouv.fr/culture/arcnat/chauvet/
en/gvpda-d.htm

**Galeries Nationales d'Exposition du Grand
Palais,**
Avenue du Général Eisenhower, Paris 75008.
(1)42895410

Musée Auguste Rodin,
77 Rue de Varenne, Paris 75007. (1)47050134.
www.paris.org/Musee/Rodin

Musée Claude Monet,
Rue Claude Monet, Giverny 27620. 32512821.
giverny.org/monet/welcome.htm

Musée des Antiquités Nationales,
Château de Saint-Germaine-en-Laye, Saint-
Germain-en-Laye 78100. (1)34515365

Musée des Beaux-Arts de Lyon,
Palais St. Pierre, 20 Place des Terreaux, 69001
Lyon. 78280766

Musée du Louvre,
34-36 Quai Louvre, Paris 75058. (1)40205009.
www.Louvre.fr

**Musée National d'Art Moderne—Centre
National d'Art et de Culture Georges
Pompidou,**
19 Rue du Renard, Paris 75191. (1)44781233.
www.cnac-gp.fr

**Musée National du Château de
Fontainebleau,**
Fontainebleau 77300. (1)60715070

Musée d'Orsay,
1 Rue de Bellechasse, Paris 75007. (1)40494814.
www.musee-orsay.fr

Musée Picasso,
Hôtel Salé, 5 Rue de Thorigny, Paris 75003.
(1)42712521

Musée d'Unterlinden,
1 Rue des Unterlinden, Colmar 68000. 89201550

GERMANY
**Ägyptisches Museum und Papyrussammlung,
Staatliche Museeun zu Berlin-Preussischer**
Preußischer Kulturbesitz, Schlossstr. 70,
Berlin 14059. (030)32091261.
userpage.hu-berlin.de/~kurtwagn/gendir/
aegy-pap/aegychar.html

**Alte Pinakothek, Bayerische
Staatsgemäldesammlungen,**
Barer Str. 27, Munich 80333.
(089)23805216.

Brücke-Museum,
Bussardsteig 9, Berlin 14195. (030)8312029.
www/dhm.de/museen/bruecke/

Hamburger Kunsthalle,
Glockengießerwall, Hamburg 20095.
(040)24862612.
www.hamburg.de/Behoerden/Museen/kh/

Museum Ludwig,
Bischofsgartenstr. 1, Cologne 50667.
(0221)2212370.
www.museenkoeln.de/ludwig/

Schloss Charlottenburg,
Luisenplatz, Berlin 14059.

Staatliche Kunsthalle,
Hans-Thoma-Str. 2-6, Karlsruhe 76133.
(0721)9263355.
www.rz.uni- karlsruhe.de/Nick/Karlsruhe/

Staatliche Antikensammlungen und
Glyptothek,
Königspl 1–3, Munich 80333. (089)598359

Staatliche Graphische Sammlung,
Meiserstr. 10, Munich 80333. (089)5591490

Gemäldegalerie, Staatliche Museen zu
Berlin-Preussischer Kulturbesitz,
Arnimallee 23-27, Berlin 14195. (030)8301217

Staatsgalerie Stuttgart,
Konrad-Adenauer Str. 30-32, Stuttgart 70182.
(0711) 2124050.

Städelsches Kunstinstitut und Städtische
Galerie,
Schaumainkai 63, Frankfurt 60596. (069)6050980.

GREECE
Acropolis Museum,
2-3 Makriyianni, Athens 117 42. (01)9238724.
www.culture.gr

Archaeological Museum,
Delphi 33054. (0265)82313.

Archaeological Museum,
Iera Odos, 2, Elefsis (Eleusis) 19200.
(01)5546019

National Archaeological Museum,
Od Tosita 1, Athens 10682. (01)8217717.

HUNGARY
Szépmüvészeti Múzeum, Dózsa György út 41,
Budapest 1146. (01)429759.
origo.hnm.hu

IRAN
Iran Bastan Museum,
Khiaban-e Imam Khomeini, Khiaban-e Siume
Tir, Teheran 11364. (021)672061-6

IRAQ
Iraq Museum,
Karkh Museum Sq., Baghdad. 361215

IRELAND
National Gallery of Ireland,
Merrion Sq. West, Dublin 2. (01)6615133.
indigo.ie/~nmi1/museum/index.htm

ITALY
Galleria Borghese,
Piazzale Scipione Borghese 5, Rome 00197.
(06)858577.
www.thais.it/scultura/rgb.htm

Galleria degli Uffizi,
Piazza degli Uffizi , Florence 50122.
(055)2388651/2.
www.uffizi.firenze.it

Galleria dell'Accademia,
Via Ricasoli 60, Florence 50122. (055)214375

Galleria dell'Accademia,
Campo della Carità, Venice 30121. (041)22247

Galleria Nazionale d'Arte Antica,
Via delle Quattro Fontane 13, Rome 00184.
(06)4824184

Musei Capitolini,
Piazza del Campidoglo, Rome 00186.
(06)67102475

Museo Archeologico Nazionale,
Via Museo 19, Naples 80135. (081)440166

Museo Archeologico Nazionale,
Via Aquilia, Paestum 84063. (0828)811023

Museo Archeologico Nazionale du Firenze,
Via della Colonna 38, Florence 50121.
(055)23575

Museo Civico Archeologico,
Via dell'Archiginnasio 2, Bologna 40124.
(051)233849.
www.commune.bologna.it/bologna/Musei/
Archeologico/1

Museo Civico Cristiano,
Via Musei, 81, Brescia 25100. (030)44327

Museo dei Conservatori,
Piazza del Campidoglio, Rome 00186.
(06)67102475

Museo di Antichità Etrusche e Italiche,
Istituto Etruscologia e Antichità Italiche,
Facoltà di Lettere Università di Roma La
Sapienza, Piazzale Aldo Moro, Rome 00185

Museo e Gallerie Nazionale di Capodimonte,
Palazzo di Capodimonte, Naples 80136.
(081)7410801.
capodimonte.selfin.net

Museo Etrusco,
Piazza della Cattedrale, Chiusi Città 53043

Museo Nazionale del Bargello,
Via del Proconsolo 4, Florence 50122.
(055)210801

Museo Nazionale di Villa Giulia,
Piazza di Villa Giulia 9, Rome 00195. (06)350719

Palazzo della Farnesina,
Via della Lungara 230, Rome 00165. (06)651629

Peggy Guggenheim Collection,
Palazzo Venier dei Leoni, 701 Dorsoduro,
Venice 30123. (041)5206288.
www.guggenheim.org/venice.html

Vatican Museums,
Viale Vaticano, Città del Vaticano 00120, Rome.
(06)698833.
www.christusrex.org/www1/vaticano/
0-Musei.html

JORDAN
Jordan Archaeological Museum,
Amman Citadet, P.O.Box 88, Amman. 638795

THE NETHERLANDS
Centraal Museum Utrecht,
Agnietenst. 1, Utrecht 3500 GC.
(030)362362.

Frans Halsmuseum,
Groot Heiligland 62, Haarlem 2001 DJ.
(023)164200.

Kröller-Müller Museum,
Postbus 1, Otterlo 6730 AA. (08382)1241

Museum Boijmans-van Beuningen,
Museumpark 18-20, Rotterdam 3015 CK.
(010)441400.
www.boijmans.rotterdam.nl

Rijksmuseum,
Stadhouderskade 42, Postbus 74888,
Amsterdam 1070 DN. (020)6732121.

Rijksmuseum Vincent van Gogh,
Paulus Potterstr. 7, Postbus 75366,
Amsterdam 1070 AJ. (020)5705200.

Stedelijk Museum of Modern Art,
Paulus Potterstr. 13, Postbus 75082,
Amsterdam 1070 AB. (020)5732911.
art.cwi.nl

NORWAY
Nasjonalgalleriet,
Universitetsgaten 13, Oslo 0033. 22200404.
www.museumsnett.no/nasjonalgalleriet/eng/
ROMANIA
National Museum of Art,
Str. Stirbei Vida, nr. 1–3, Bucharest 70733.
(01)6155193

RUSSIA
Hermitage Museum,
Dworzowaja Nabereshnaja 34-36, Saint Petersburg 191065, (212)9545.
www.hermitage.ru

Pushkin Museum of Fine Arts,
Ul. Volkhonka 12, Moscow. (095)2037412.
www.rosprint.ru/art/museum/pushkin

SCOTLAND
National Gallery of Scotland,
The Mound, Edinburgh EH2 2EL. (0131)5568921.
www.nms.ac.uk

SPAIN
Museo Nacional Centro de Arte Reina Sofía,
Santa Isabel 52, Madrid 28012. (91)4675062

Museo Nacional del Prado,
Paseo del Prado, Madrid 28014. (91)4680950.
museoprado.mcu.es

SWEDEN
Moderna Museet,
Spårvagnshallarna, Box 16382,
Stokholm 103 27. (08)6664250.
www.modernamuseet.se

Nationalmuseum,
S. Blasieholmshamnen, Box 16176,
Stockholm 103 24. (08)6664250.
www.nationalmuseum.se

University Art Gallery, Uppsala University,
Domkyrkoplam 7, Uppsala 752 20. (018)155400

SWITZERLAND
Kunstmuseum Basel und Museum für
Gegenwartskunst, St. Alban-Graben 16,
Basel 4010. (061)2710828.
www.kunstmuseumbasel.ch

Kunstmuseum Bern,
Hodlerstr. 8-12, Bern CH-3000. (031)3110944

Musée d'Art et d'Histoire,
2 Rue Charles Galland, Geneva 1211.
(022)3114340

TURKEY
Archaeological Museum of Istanbul,
Gülhane Sultanahmet, Istanbul 34400.
(520)7742.
www.exploreturkey.com/ist_arch.htm

Index

Kosho, 439; *Kuya Preaching*, 439, *439*
Kosuth, Joseph, *One and Three Chairs*, 1133, *1133*
kouros, 169–72, 179–80, 229
Kouros (Greek statue), 169–70, *169*
Kramer, Hilton, 1126
Krasner, Lee, 1104, 1114, 1121–22; Earth Green series, 1122; Little Image series, 1122; *Red, White, Blue, Yellow, Black*, 1104, *1105*, 1114, 1121; *The Seasons*, 1122, *1122*
krater, 173
Kritias, 197
Kritios Boy, 180–81, *180*, 195
Kroisos (?) (Greek statue), 170, *170*, 171, 181, 229
Kruger, Barbara, 1156; *We Won't Play Nature to Your Culture*, 1156, *1156*
Kuba people (Zaire), 921
Kublai Khan, 419, 837, 839
kufic script, 348, 349, 352, 355, *355*
Kushan period (India), 378–81
Kuya, 438–39
Kuya Preaching, Kosho, 439, *439*
Kwakiutl people, 886
kylix, 177
Kyoto, Japan. *See* Daitoku-ji; Myoki-an Temple; Ryoan-ji

L

La Banditaccia, Etruscan cemetery, Cerveteri, Italy, 229, *229*; sarcophagus from, 230, *230*; Tomb of the Reliefs, 229, *229*
Labille-Guiard, Adélaïde, 935–37; *Self-Portrait with Two Pupils, Mademoiselle Marie Gabrielle Capet and Mademoiselle Carreux de Rosemond*, *936*, 937
Labrouste, Henri, 982; Bibliothèque Sainte-Geneviève, Reading Room, Paris, France, 982–83, *982*
labyrinth, in Gothic cathedrals, 561, 565
Labyrinth, Cretan, 132, 133
Lachaise, Gaston, 1098; *Standing Woman (Elevation)*, 1098, *1098*
Lachaise Foundation, 1098
lacquer, 863, 864
Lacquer box for writing implements, Ogata Korin, 864–66, *865*
Lactantius, 297
Ladder, Philip Guston, 1141, *1141*
Ladies Preparing Newly Woven Silk (detail) (copy of painting by Zhang Xuan), Emperor Huizong, 414, *415*, 417
Lady Sarah Bunbury Sacrificing to the Graces, Joshua Reynolds, 933, *933*, 1014
La Fayette, Madame de, 805
Lagash (modern Telloh, Iraq), 74–76; votive statue of Gudea from, *75*, 76, 77
La Jolla, California. *See* Salk Institute of Biological Studies
Lake Van, Armenia, Church of the Holy Cross, 324, *324*
lakshanas, 378, 427
Lakshmi, 387
lamb (Christian symbol), 294
Lamentation. See Grünewald, Matthias, *Isenheim Altarpiece*
Lamentation, Nerezi (near Skopje), Macedonia, Saint Panteleimon, 328, *328*
Lamentation, Padua, Italy, Arena Chapel, Giotto, 606, *607*
Lamentation (in Christian art), 307
Laming-Emperaire, Annette, 46
La Mouthe cave, Dordogne, France, lamp with ibex design (Paleolithic), 41, 47, *47*
lamps, prehistoric, 41, 47
lancet, 558, *558*
Lander, Frederick, 1001
Landscape (album), Shitao, *850*, 851
Landscape (hanging scroll), Bunsei, 856–57, *857*
Landscape (wall painting), Akrotiri, Thera, Greek island, 141, *142*
landscape architecture, 943
Landscape near Chatou, Maurice de Vlaminck, 1041–42, *1042*
landscape painting: American, 999–1000; Chinese, 407, 416–18, 837, 846, 848–51; Dutch, 792–93; French, 976–77, 991–94, 1011; German, 736; heroic vs. rural, 991; Japanese, 856–58, 869; naturalist, 991–94; Neoclassical and Romantic, 931, 939; Roman, 258
Landscape with Merchants, Claude Lorrain, 774, *774*, 792
Landscape with Rainbow, Peter Paul Rubens, 783, *783*
Landscape with Saint John on Patmos, Nicolas Poussin, 774, *775*
Lane, Fitz Hugh, 999
Lange, Dorothea, 1103; *Migrant Mother, Nipomo, California*, 1103, *1103*

Langhans, Karl Gotthard, 966; Brandenburg Gate, Berlin, Germany, 966, *967*
lantern, 645, 804
lantern tower, 513
Laocoön and His Sons, 722; Hagesandros, Polydoros, and Athanadoros of Rhodes, 20, *21*, 215–16, *215*, 755
Laozi, 404, 837
La Pia de' Tolomei, Dante Gabriel Rossetti, 1005–6, *1005*
Lapita culture, 895, 897
Lapith Fighting a Centaur, Athens, Greece, Acropolis, Parthenon, metopes sculpture, 189, *189*, 190
Larbro Saint Hammers, Gotland, Sweden, pictured stone, 483, *483*
Large Blue Horses, The, Franz Marc, 1047, *1049*
Large Odalisque, Jean-Auguste-Dominique Ingres, 962, *962*
Larionov, Mikhail, 1061
Lascaux, France, cave paintings, 43–45, 135; *Bird-Headed Man with Bison and Rhinoceros*, 44, *45*; Hall of Bulls, 43, *44*; plan, 43, *44*
Last Judgment (fresco), Rome, Italy, Vatican Palace, Sistine Chapel, Michelangelo, 699, 703–4, *703*
Last Judgment (frescoes), Padua, Italy, Arena Chapel, Giotto, 604–7, *605*
Last Judgment (relief), Autun, Burgundy, France, Saint-Lazare Cathedral, Gislebertus, *520*, 521, 525, 533, 555, 568
Last Judgment (relief), Reims, Île-de-France, France, Notre-Dame Cathedral, 567–68, *567*
Last Judgment Altarpiece, Rogier van der Weyden, 630, *630*
Last Supper (in Christian art), 306
Last Supper, Andrea del Castagno, 658–59, *659*, 692
Last Supper, Leonardo da Vinci, 690–93, *691*, 711, 739
Last Supper, Tintoretto, 711, *711*
Last Supper (center piece). *See* Riemenschneider, Tilman, *Altarpiece of the Holy Blood*
Latin-cross plan churches, 298, 558
Latin language, 233
Latium, 233
La Tour, Georges de, 774; *The Repentant Magdalen*, 774, *775*, 959
Latrobe, Benjamin Henry, 970–71; U.S. Capitol. *See under* Thornton, William
Laugerie-Basse, France, *Pregnant Woman and Deer*, engraved antler, 40, *40*
Laughing Child, Robert Henri, 1094, *1094*
Laurana, Luciano, 665–66; Ducal Palace, Urbino, Italy, 665–66, *665*, 685
Laurentian Library. *See* San Lorenzo, Monastery of
La Venta, Mexico, 447–48; colossal head, 448, *448*; pyramid and ball court, 447–48, *447*
Lawler, Louise, 1153–54; *Pollock and Tureen*, 1154, *1154*
Lawrence, D. H., 1098
Lawrence, Jacob, 1101, 1165; *Interior Scene*, 1102, *1102*, 1165
Lawrence, Saint, 303
Lawrence Tree, The, Georgia O'Keeffe, 1098, *1098*
Le Brun, Charles, 770, 773; Palais de Versailles, Hall of Mirrors (*see under* Hardouin-Mansart, Jules)
LeClear, Thomas, 16–17; *Interior with Portraits*, 16, *17*, 19, 23
Le Corbusier (Charles-Édouard Jeanneret), 1079, 1080, 1134, 1135; *After Cubism* (book) (with Amédée Ozenfant), 1079; "The Five Points of Architecture," 1080; Nôtre-Dame-du-Haut, Ronchamp, France, 1081, 1135, *1135*; Plan for a Contemporary City of Three Million Inhabitants, 1080, *1080*, 1134, 1135; Villa Savoye, Poissy-sur-Seine, France, 1080, *1080*, 1134, 1136
lectionaries, 529
Ledoux, Claude-Nicolas, 956–57, 1137; Bird's-eye view of the Town of Chaux, 956–57, *956*
Leeuwenhoek, Anton van, 785
Lefkandi, Euboea, Greece, *Centaur*, *158*, 159
legalism, 402
Lega people (East Africa), 915–16
Léger, Fernand, 1079, 1112; *Three Women*, 1079–80, *1079*
Legros, Alphonse, 1007
Leibl, Wilhelm, 996–97; *Three Women in a Village Church*, 996–97, *996*
Leibniz, G. W., 929
lekythos, 197
Le Mas d'Azil, Ariège, Dordogne, France, spear thrower, ibex-headed (Paleolithic), 47, *47*
Le Nain, Antoine, 774; *The Village Piper*, 775–76, *775*
Le Nain, Louis, 774
Le Nain brothers, 774–75

L'Enfant, Pierre-Charles, 770
Lenin, Vladimir, 1075
Le Nôtre, André, 770
Leo III, Emperor, 322
Leo III, Pope, 491
Leonardo da Vinci, 650, 684, 690–93, 694, 704, 706, 715, 722, 769; *The Last Supper* (wall painting), Milan, Italy, Santa Maria delle Grazie, 690–93, *691*, 711, 739; *Mona Lisa*, 693, *693*; *Virgin and Saint Anne with the Christ Child and the Young John the Baptist*, 692, 693; *Vitruvian Man*, 692, *692*
Leoni, Leone, 705–6, 746; *Charles V Triumphing over Fury*, 706, *706*
Leoni, Pompeo, 706, 746; *Philip II and His Family*, 746, *746*
Leo X, Pope, 696
Leo X with Cardinals Giulio de' Medici and Luigi de' Rossi, Raphael, 696, *696*
Leroi-Gourhan, André, 46
Leroy, Louis, 28
Lescot, Pierre, 723; Palais du Louvre, Cour Carré, 723, *723*
Le Tuc d'Audoubert, France, *Bison* (relief sculpture), 45–46, *45*
Levant, the, Neolithic, 48
Le Vau, Louis, 770, 773
    Palais de Versailles (with Jules Hardouin-Mansart), Versailles, France, 770–73, *771*, 804, 953, 999; East front (with Claude Perrault and Charles Le Brun), 983
Lever No. 3, Martin Puryear, 1165, *1165*
Levine, Sherrie, 1154–55; *Untitled (After Aleksandr Rodchenko: 11)*, 1155, *1155*
Lewis, Edmonia, 998; *Hagar in the Wilderness*, 998, *998*
Lewis, Lucy M., 1164; *Black on White Jar with Lightning Pattern*, 1164, *1164*
Lewis, Meriwether, 885
Lewis, Sinclair, 1102
Leyland, Frederick, 26
Leyster, Judith, 786–87; *Self-Portrait*, 786, *787*
li, 405, 415, 416
Liang Wudi, 409
Liangzhu culture, 399
Libergier, Hughes, 563
Liber Scivias (Romanesque manuscript), *Hildegard's Vision* page from, 538–39, *538*
Library of Congress, Washington, D.C., 1091, *1091*
Libyan Sibyl, Michelangelo, 701, *701*
Lichtenstein, Roy, 1128–29, 1155; *Oh, Jeff . . . I Love You, Too . . . But . . .*, 1129, *1129*
Licinius, 280
Life (magazine), 17–18; first cover, *17*
Life Line, The, Winslow Homer, 1002, *1003*
"Life of the Virgin" (vestments, English), 581–82, *581*; detail, *Angel of the Annunciation*, 581–82, *581*
Lighthouse of Alexandria, 102, 209
lilies (Minoan symbol), 140, 141
Limbourg, Paul, Herman, and Jean, 619–20; *Très Riches Heures* (illuminated manuscript), page *February*, 620, *621*, 624, 635, 728
limner, 817, 973
Lin, Maya Ying, 1161–62; *Vietnam War Memorial*, 1161–62, *1161*
Linda Nochlin and Daisy, Alice Neel, 1146, *1146*
Lindau Gospels (Carolingian manuscript), 498; *Crucifixion with Angels and Mourning Figures* (book cover), 497–98, *497*, 502
Lindisfarne, 481
line, 29
Linear A, 131
Linear B, 131, 147
linear perspective, 30, 618, 672
linear style, 29
lines of force, 29
lingam shrine, 387
lintel, 283, 384
Lintong, Shaanxi, China, mausoleum of Qin emperor, earthenware soldiers from, *396*, 397, 402
Lion, page from *Gospel Book of Durrow* (Hiberno-Saxon manuscript), 486–87, *487*
lion (Christian symbol), 294, 486–87
Lion Attacking a Horse, George Stubbs, *950*, 951, 966
Lion capital (India, Maurya period), 366, 373–74, *373*
Lioness Gate, Mycenae, Greece, 143, *144*
Lion Gate, Hattushash (Hittite), in modern Turkey, 83–84, *83*, 143
Lion-Human (figurine), Hohlenstein-Stadel, Germany, 38–39, *38*, 45

Nazca culture (Peru), 457, 458–59
Nazca lines, 459, *459*
Nazi Party, 1081
ndop (Kuba), 921
Near East: ancient, 60–89; Neolithic period, 63–85
Near Eastern art, ancient: ceramic technology, 57; compared to Minoan, 135, 136; compared to Mycenaean, 143; influence on Aegean, 128; influence on Greek, 161, 202; influence on Judaic, 291; influence on Minoan, 131–32, 137; jewelry, 136–38
Near Oceania. *See* Melanesia; Micronesia
Nebuchadnezzar II, 81, 102
necking, 165, *165*
necropolis, 99
Neel, Alice, 1146; *Linda Nochlin and Daisy*, 1146, *1146*
Nefertiti, 119–22, 140
Nefertiti (Egyptian), 120, *120*
negative space, 29, 160
Nekhbet, 106
Neo-Babylonia, 63, 81–83
neo-Baroque sculpture, 983
Neoclassicism, 929–31, 938–41, 1137; architecture, 955–57, 970–71; Britain, 944–47; France, 955–62; Germany, 966; painting, 957–62; Rome, 940–41; sculpture, 957, 971–73; Spain, 967–70; United States, 970–73, 997–98
Neo-Conceptualism, 1152–55
Neo-Confucianism, 415–16, 862; "School of the Mind," 419
Neo-Expressionism, 1148–49
Neo-Geo, 1154
Neo-Impressionism, 1035, 1038, 1040
Neolithic period, 37; Aegean, 128–29; China, 57, 397–99; Egypt, 93–94; Europe, 47–58; Near East, 63–85
Neo-Modern, 1137
Neon, Bishop, 304
Neoplatonism, 643
Neo-Primitive movement (Russian), 1060
neo-rationalism, 1137
Nepal, 366
Nephthys, 96, 125
Nerezi (near Skopje), Macedonia, Saint Panteleimon church, 328; *Lamentation*, 328, *328*
Neri, Filippo, 766
Nero, 252
Nerva, 259
Netherlandish art, 725–29, 784, 793; *see also* Dutch art; Flemish art
Netherlands, the, 776
Neumann, Johann Balthasar, 807, 808; Church of the Vierzehnheiligen, near Staffelstein, 807, 808–9, *808*; Residenz, Kaisersall (Imperial Hall), Würzburg, Bavaria, Germany, *806*, 807
Nevelson, Louise, 1120–21; *Sky Cathedral*, 1121, *1121*, 1125
New Caledonia, 895
New Delhi, India, 833
Newgrange, Ireland: passage grave, 144; tomb interior, *52*, 53
New Guinea, 895, 898–99
New Ireland, 899–900
Newman, Barnett, 1116, 1119, 1131, 1144; *Broken Obelisk*, 1119, *1119*
New Museum, "Bad Painting" exhibition (1978), 1141
Newport, Rhode Island. *See* Redwood Library
Newton, Isaac, 929
Newton, William Blake, 952–53, *952*
"new woman," 1058, 1085
New York City: as art center, after World War II, 1109; Building Zone Resolution of 1916, 1065; *see also* AT&T Headquarters; Brooklyn Bridge; Central Park; Empire State Building; Seagram Building; Trinity Church; Woolworth Building
New York School, 1112, 1121–22; *see also* Abstract Expressionism
New Zealand, 895, 903–5
Ngongo ya Chintu, 470
Niagara, Frederick Edwin Church, 999, *999*, 1002
Nicaea: First Council of, 290, 304; Second Council of, 322
niche, *753*; muqarnas-filled, *347*
Nicholas of Verdun, 586, 587; *Shrine of the Three Kings* (reliquary), 566, 586–87, *587*
niello, 58, 137, 149, 537
Niépce, Joseph-Nicéphore, 986–87; *View from His Window at Le Gras*, 987, *987*
Nietzsche, Friedrich, 1117; *Thus Spake Zarathustra*, 1043
Night Attack on the Sanjo Palace (scroll), Kamakura period, Japan, 437–38, *437*
Nighthawks, Edward Hopper, *1100*, 1101, 1124

Nightmare, The, John Henry Fuseli, 951–52, *951*
Night of the Rich and the *Poor*. *See* Rivera, Diego, murals
Nike, 156
Nike (Victory), Samothrace, Macedonia, *214*, 215
Nike (Victory) Adjusting Her Sandal (relief sculpture), Athens, Temple of Athena Nike, 193, *194*, 202, 219, 247
Nile River, 93
Nîmes, France, 243; Maison Carrée, *242*, 243; Pont du Gard, 241–43, *241*
Nineveh (modern Kuyunjik, Iraq), 80; *Assurbanipal and His Queen in the Garden*, 80, *80*; sculpted head of a man, 74, *74*
Nishapur, Iran, 348
nishiki-e, 868
Nizami, *Khamsa* (Five Poems), 362
Ni Zan, 840–41; *The Rongxi Studio* (hanging scroll), 840–41, *841*, 846
nkisi (Kongo/Songye), 917–18
nkonde (Kongo/Songye), 917–18
nlo byeri (Fang), 922–23
Nobunaga, Oda, 859
Nochlin, Linda: "Eroticism and the Image of Woman in Nineteenth-Century Art," 1146; "Why Have There Been No Great Women Artists?" (essay), 1146
Nok (Nigeria), 468–69, 911
Nok culture (mixed media), Ouattara, 924–25, *924*
Noli Me Tangere, Lavinia Fontana, *718*, 719
Noli Me Tangere (in Christian art), 307
nonfinito, 703
nonrepresentational (nonobjective) style, 29
Normandy, France, 481; Romanesque period, 530–35
Normans, 327
architecture of, influence on English, 576
conquest of Britain, 509, 530; tapestry depiction of, 534–35
Norse peoples, 481, 483
North Acropolis, Tikal, 452
North America, 460–63
Northern Song dynasty, 415, 416
Northern Wei dynasty, 409
Notre-Dame Cathedral. *See* Amiens; Paris, France; Reims, Île-de-France, France
Notre-Dame-du-Haut, Le Corbusier, 1081, 1135, *1135*
nouveau réalisme, 1125, 1145
nsekh o byeri (Fang), 922
nudes: in Greek sculpture, 169–70, 201–2; idealistic vs. realistic, 984; models, 1003; as traditional subject, 1018
Nude Study with Corrections, Edward V. Valentin, 948
numerical symbolism, Gothic, 557
Nut, 96
Nymphs and a Satyr, Adolphe-William Bouguereau, *984*, 985, 1014, 1018

O

Oakland YWCA (drawing for), Oakland, Calif., Julia Morgan, *1068*, 1069
Oak Park, Ill., Wright Home, *1068*, 1068
Oath of the Horatii, Jacques-Louis David, 958–59, *958*, 962, 985
oba (Benin royalty), 471–74
obelisk, 116, 756
Obembe Alaye (African artist), 470
Oceanic art: iconography of, 898; recent, 905–7; sculpture, 1044
ocher, 38, 39
Octopus Flask, Palaikastro, Crete, 139, *139*
oculus, 226, 264, 310, 556, 645, 803, 1137
Oculus and Finestra chairs, Michael Graves, 1137, *1137*
odalisque, 960
Odo, bishop of Bayeux in Normandy, 534
Odundo, Magdalene, 925; *Asymmetrical Angled Piece*, 925, *925*
Odysseus, 156
Odyssey, 143, 216
Oedipus and the Sphinx, Gustave Moreau, 986, *986*
Officers of the Haarlem Militia Company of Saint Adrian, Frans Hals, 785–86, *786*
ogival arch, 347, *347*, 354
Oh, Jeff . . . I Love You, Too . . . But . . ., Roy Lichtenstein, 1129, *1129*
oil painting, 624, 625–26
oinochoe (wine pitcher), 161
O'Keeffe, Georgia, 22, 1097–98; *The Lawrence Tree*, 1098, *1098*; *Portrait of a Day, First Day*, 22, *22*
Okyo, Maruyama, 867
Olbrechts, Frans, 470

Oldenburg, Claes, 1130; *Lipstick (Ascending) on Caterpillar Tracks*, 1130, *1130*
Old Saint Peter's, Rome, Italy, 297–99, *297*, 492
Old Testament Trinity, The (Three Angels Visiting Abraham) (icon), Rubiyov, Andrey, 335, *335*, 583
Olmec culture, 447–48, 875; influence on Mayan, 451
Olmsted, Frederick Law, 1062–63; Central Park, New York City (with Calvert Vaux), 1062, *1063*
olpe (wide-mouthed pitcher), 161
Olympia, Édouard Manet, 1008, *1008*, 1010, 1017, 1025
Olympia, Greece
Man and Centaur (statuette), 160, *160*
Sanctuary of Hera and Zeus, 153, 155–57, 178
Temple of Hera, 201
Temple of Zeus, pediment sculpture, 178–79, *178*, *179*, 189, 202; *Athena, Herakles, and Atlas*, 178, *179*, 196, 202
Olympian/ic Games, 153, 157, 179
Olympias (artist), 207
Olympos, Mount, 155, 156
omega symbol, 525
One and Three Chairs, Joseph Kosuth, 1133, *1133*
oni (Yoruba royalty), 469–71
Onjo-ji monastery, Shiga prefecture, Japan, Kojo-in, Guest Hall, 862, *862*
Open Door, The, from *The Pencil of Nature* series, Talbot, William Henry Fox, 988–89, *988*
Opéra, Paris, France, Charles Garnier, 983–84, *983*, 1015; *The Dance* (sculpture), Jean-Baptiste Carpeaux, 984, *984*
opet festival (Egypt), 96
opus anglicanum, 580–82
opus incertum, 236, *236*
opus reticulatum, 236, *236*
opus testaceum, 236, *236*
oracle, 157
oracle bones, 400
Orange, France, Roman theater at, *242*, 243
Orange, House of, 784
orant figures, 291, 293, 295
Orchard, William, 578, 579; Magdalen College, Oxford, 578–79, *578*
orders of architecture. *See* classical orders
Orgaz family, 746
Orientalizing period, Greek, 158, 161–62, 174
originality in art, 752
Orléans, duke of (regent), 805
Orphism, 1057
Orsanmichele, Florence, Italy, 647, 653, *653*
Orthodox Church (Eastern), 290, 291, 323–24
Orthodox Church (Eastern), 617
orthogonal, 30, 198
orthogonal plan, 198–99
Oseberg, Norway, burial ship (Viking), 480, *480*, 483; post with animal figures, 483, *484*, 519
Osiris, 95, 96, 124, 125, 235
Osman, 350
Ostia, Italy, Trajan's Harbor, 268–70
Ostrava Petrkovice, Czech Republic, *Woman* (figurine), 39, *39*
Ostrogoths, 302, 313
O'Sullivan, Timothy H., 1001; *Ancient Ruins in the Cañon de Chelley, Arizona*, *1000*, 1001
Otto I, Emperor, 498, 499
Otto I Presenting Magdeburg Cathedral to Christ (plaque), from *Magdeburg Ivories* (German), 499–501, *499*
Otto II, Emperor, 498
Otto III, Emperor, 498, 501, 503
Otto III Enthroned, page from *Liuthar (Aachen) Gospels* (Ottonian manuscript), 503, *503*
Ottoman Empire, 350, 354
Ottoman Turks, 290, 323, 350, 363; art, 345, 363
Ottonian art, 498–505; influence on Romanesque, 535; stained-glass windows, 559
Ouattara, 924–25; *Nok culture*, 924–25, *924*
Outbreak, The, Käthe Schmidt Kollwitz, *1047*
overlapping, 30
Ovid, 259
ovoid elements, 887
ox (Christian symbol), 294
Oxbow, The, Thomas Cole, 973–74, *973*, 999
Oxford, Oxfordshire, England: Magdalen College, 578–79, *578*; Oxford University, 576
Ozenfant, Amédée, 1079

P

Pacal, Lord, 453–54
Pacific peoples, 894–907; art of (*see* Oceanic art)

Vienna, Austria. *See* Steiner House

Vierzehnheiligen, Church of the, near Staffelstein, Germany, Johann Balthasar Neumann, 807, 808–9, *808*

Vietnam War Memorial, Maya Ying Lin, 1161–62, *1161*

viewer, as participant in work of art, 752

View from Dosseringen near the Sortedam Lake Looking toward Nørrebro, Christian Købke, 977, *977*

View from His Window at Le Gras, Joseph-Nicéphore Niépce, 987, *987*

View of Delft, Jan Vermeer, 797, *797*

View of the Piazza del Popolo, Rome, Giovanni Paolo Panini, *938*, 939, 966, 977

View of Toledo, El Greco, 746–47, *747*

Vigée-Lebrun, Marie-Louise-Élisabeth, 934–35; *Portrait of Marie Antoinette with Her Children*, 934–35, *935*, 946

vignette, 320

Vignola, Giacomo da (Giacomo Barozzi), 689–90, 745, 764, 770; Church of Il Gesù (with Giacomo della Porta), Rome, Italy, 683, 688, 690, *690*, *691*, 753, *753*, 755, 764, 770; *The Rule of the Five Orders of Architecture*, 689; Villa Farnese, 689, *689*, 720, 770

vihara, 375, 377

Vijayanagar, Indian kingdom, 826

Vikings, 480, 481, 617; memorial stones of, 482–83; symbols of, 483

Villa Albani, Rome, museum at, 940

Villafranca del Panadé, Barcelona, Spain, San Francisco church, *Virgin and Saint George* (altarpiece), 584, *584*; *Education of the Virgin* from, 584, *585*

Village Piper, The, Antoine Le Nain, 775–76, *775*

villages, Neolithic, 48, 51

Villanovans, 223

Villa of Livia, Primaporta, Italy, *Garden Scene* (wall painting), 240, 251–52, *251*, 292

Villa of the Mysteries, Pompeii, Italy, *Initiation Rites of the Cult of Bacchus (?)* (wall painting, detail), 250–51, *250*, 292

Villard de Honnecourt, sketchbook, page from, 572, *573*

Villa Savoye, Poissy-sur-Seine, France, Le Corbusier, 1080, *1080*, 1134, 1136

Villa Torlonia, Rome, Italy, *Menorahs and Ark of the Covenant*, 291–92, *292*

Ville-d'Avray, Jean-Baptiste-Camille Corot, 992, *992*

vimana, 375, 389, 826

Vindhya Hills, 366

Violet Persian Set with Red Lip Wraps, Dale Chihuly, 22, *22*, 1162

Violin and Palette, Georges Braque, 1053–54, *1053*, 1104, 1116, 1120

Viollet-le-Duc, Eugène-Emmanuel, 564, 577

Virgin and Child (French Romanesque sculpture), 522, *523*

Virgin and Child (sculpture), Saint-Denis, Île-de-France, France, abbey church, 571–72, *571*, 575

Virgin and Child Enthroned: Cimabue (Cenni di Pepi), 602, *602*; Giotto di Bondone, 603–4, *603*

Virgin and Child Enthroned with Saints Francis, John the Baptist, Job, Dominic, Sebastian, and Louis of Toulouse, Giovanni Bellini, 670–71, *671*, 706

Virgin and Child in a Garden with Saints Margaret and Catherine (or *Large Enclosed Garden*), Master E. S., 674, *674*

Virgin and Child in Majesty, Siena Cathedral, *Maestà Altarpiece*, Duccio di Buoninsegna, 583, 596, 597

Virgin and Child with Angels. See Grünewald, Matthias, *Isenheim Altarpiece*

Virgin and Child with Saints and Angels (Christian icon), Mount Sinai, Egypt, Monastery of Saint Catherine, 322, *323*

Virgin and Saint Anne with the Christ Child and the Young John the Baptist, Leonardo da Vinci, 692, *693*

Virgin and Saint George (altarpiece), Villafranca del Panadé, Barcelona, Spain, San Francisco church, Luis Borrassá, 584, *584*; *Education of the Virgin* from, 584, *585*

Virginia State Capitol, Richmond, Va., Thomas Jefferson, 970, *971*

Virgin Mary, 289, 299

Virgin of Compassion, 335

Virgin of Vladimir (Christian icon), *334*, 335, 529

Virtues and Vices (relief), Amiens, Île-de-France, France, Notre-Dame Cathedral, *562*, 563

Visconti family (Milan), 643

Vishnu, 371, 384–86, 389

Vishnu Narayana on the Cosmic Waters (relief), Deogarh, Uttar Pradesh, India, Vishnu Temple, 384–86, *385*, 387

Vishnu Temple, Deogarh, Uttar Pradesh, India, 383–86, *384*, 390; *Vishnu Narayana on the Cosmic Waters* (relief), 384–86, *385*, 387

Visigoths, 345, 488

Visitation, the (in Christian art), 306

Visitation, Broederlam. *See* Broederlam, Melchior, altarpiece

Visitation (panel from altarpiece), Diego de la Cruz (?), 639–40, *639*

Visitation (relief), Reims, Île-de-France, France, Notre-Dame Cathedral, 566–67, *566*, 575, 587

Visit To/A Visit From/The Island, A, Eric Fischl, 1149, *1149*

Vitalis, Saint, 313

Vitruvian Man, Leonardo da Vinci, 692, *692*

Vitruvius, Marcus Pollio, 225, 227, 683–84, 770; *De Architectura (On Architecture)*, 692

Vlaminck, Maurice de, 1040, 1041–42, 1044, 1110; *Landscape near Chatou*, 1041–42, *1042*

Vollard, Ambroise, 1028

Voltaire, 929

Volto Santo sculptures, 523

volume, 29

volumetric rendering, 616

volute, 165, *165*, 173, 254, 666, *753*, 807

volute capital, 167

volute krater, 173

votive figures, 225; Cycladic, 131; Mesoamerica, 445; Mesopotamian, 69–70, 76

Voulkos, Peter, 1162–63; *Covered Jar*, 1162, *1162*

voussoir, 225, 226, 345, 517, *517*, 519, 557, 950

Vuillard, Édouard, 1028

Vulca, 229

Vulgate Bible, 297, 494

W

Wainwright Building, St. Louis, Missouri, Louis Sullivan, *1064*, 1065–66

wall niche, Pompeii, *240*

wall painting: Byzantine, 328–30, 524; Chinese Buddhist, 412; Egyptian, 93–94, 111; Etruscan, 230–31; Greek, 205–8; Islamic, 361–62; Italian Gothic, 595–97; Minoan, 139–42; Roman, 249–52, 256–59; Romanesque, 524–27; *see also* fresco; murals

wall reliefs, Egyptian, 114

Walpole, Horace, 951, 953; *The Castle of Otranto*, 953; Strawberry Hill, Twickenham, England, 953, *953*, 1137

Walter, Marie-Thérèse, 1090

Wanderers, the, 997

Wang Hui, 848; *A Thousand Peaks and Myriad Ravines* (hanging scroll), 848, *849*

Wang Xizhi, 409; calligraphy sample, *408*, 409

War club, Marquesas Islands, Polynesia, 902, *902*

ware, 57, 84, 129

Wari Empire, 879

Warhol, Andy, 1129–30, 1155; *Marilyn Diptych*, 1129, *1130*

Warring States period (China), 401

Warrior Vase, Mycenae, Greece, 149, *149*

warp: basketry, 888; weaving, 359, 457, 458, 887, 920

wash, 827, 1048, 1122

Washington, D.C.: L'Enfant's plan for, 770, *770*; *see also* Library of Congress; United States Capitol

watchtower, 414; China, *414*

Water and Moon Kuan-yin Bodhisattva, The (Chinese painted panels), 27, *27*

Water Carrier of Seville, Diego Velázquez, 778–79, *778*

watercolor, 674, 953

Water Lilies, Claude Monet, 1021, *1021*

Watson and the Shark, John Singleton Copley, 949, *949*

Watteau, Jean-Antoine, 810–12; *The Pilgrimage to Cythera*, 810, *810*, 937; *The Signboard of Gersaint*, 810–11, *811*

wattle and daub, 816

Wawalag Sisters and the Rainbow Serpent, The, Mawalan Marika, 897, *897*

weaving, 887, 920; Americas, 445; Navaho, 890–91; Peruvian, 457–58; warp, 920; *see also* textiles

Weber, Max, 1097; *Rush Hour, New York*, 1097, *1097*

Wedding basket (Native American, Pomo), 888

Wedgwood, Josiah, 928, 945, 946, 949; Vase (with *Apotheosis of Homer* by John Flaxman, Jr.), 945, *945*

wedjat (Egyptian symbol), 94

weft, 359, 457, 458, 920

Wehlsch Pirg (Italian Mountain), Albrecht Dürer, *732*, 733

Weickman, Christopher, 477

Weighing of Souls, Autun, Burgundy, France, Saint-Lazare Cathedral, *Last Judgment* (relief), Gislebertus, *520*, *521*, 525

We Keep Our Victims Ready (performance), Karen Finley, 1159–60, *1160*

Well of Moses, Claus Sluter, 622, *622*

We'll Shake the Bag, David Salle, 1148–49, *1148*, 1155

West, Benjamin, 947–49, 973; *Death of General Wolfe*, 947–49, *947*

West Africa, 474

Western Church. *See* Roman Catholic Church

Western Paradise of Amitabha Buddha (wall painting), Dunhuang, Gansu, China, 412, *412*, 414

Western Pure Land, 372, 410, 412

Western Roman Empire, 290

Weston, Edward, 1155

west portal, 558

westwork, 492, 804

wet-collodion process, 989

We Won't Play Nature to Your Culture, Barbara Kruger, 1156, *1156*

Weyden, Rogier van der, 623, 629–32; *Deposition* (detail of altarpiece), 629–30, *629*, 949; *Last Judgment Altarpiece*, 630, *630*; *Portrait of a Lady*, 630–32, *631*

Whirling Log Ceremony (woven by Mrs. Sam Manuelito) (sand-painting tapestry), Hosteen Klah, 890, *891*

Whistler, James McNeill, 26, 1007–8, 1028, 1060; *Black Lion Wharf*, 1007, *1007*; *Harmony in Blue and Gold* (The Peacock Room), 26, *26*, 1008; *Rose and Silver: The Princess from the Land of Porcelain*, 26, 1008

White, Stanford, 1064

White Captive, The, Erastus Dow Palmer, 998, *998*

white-ground vase painting, 162, 197

Whitehall Palace, Banqueting House, Inigo Jones, *802*, 803, 816; ceiling painting, Peter Paul Rubens, 782, *802*, 803

White Horse, The, John Constable, 976, *976*

White Temple, Uruk (modern Warka, Iraq), 66, *67*

White with Graphism, Antoni Tàpies, 1112, *1112*

Whitney Museum of American Art, "New Image Painting" exhibition (1978), 1141

Whittredge, Worthington, 999

Wild Blackberry, from Dioscorides, Pedanius, *De Materia Medica* (manuscript), *318*, 319–20

Wilde, Oscar, 1008

"Wild Goat Style" (vase painting), 161–62

Wiligelmus, 543; *Creation and Fall* (relief), 543, *543*

Willendorf, Austria, *Woman* (figurine), 39, *39*, 40, 41

William II of Normandy, Duke (William the Conqueror), 530, 531

William of Saint Thierry, 519

William of Sens, 576

Winchester Psalter (English manuscript), Hellmouth page from, 532–33, *533*, 580

Winckelmann, Johann Joachim, 946, 947, 951; *The History of Ancient Art*, 940; *Thoughts on the Imitation of Greek Works in Painting and Sculpture*, 940

Windmill Psalter, page with *Psalm 1 (Beatus Vir)*, 580, *580*

wings, 622

Winter Landscape, Sesshu, 857–58, *857*

Witte, Emanuel de, 798; *Portuguese Synagogue, Amsterdam*, 798, *798*

Witz, Konrad, 642–43; *Miraculous Draft of Fish* (detail of altarpiece), 642, *643*

Wolf of Rome (Etruscan), 231–32, *232*

Woman (figurine), Brassempouy, France, 39–40, *40*

Woman (figurine), Ostrava Petrkovice, Czech Republic, 39, *39*

Woman (figurine), Willendorf, Austria, 39, *39*, 40, 41

Woman and Maid (vase painting), Achilles Painter, style of, 197, *197*

Woman at the Height of Her Beauty, Utamaro, Kitigawa, 19, *19*, 25, 1019

Woman Holding a Balance, Jan Vermeer, 795–97, *796*

Woman I, Willem de Kooning, 1116, *1117*

Woman in Blue and Yellow II, Viola Frey, 1163, *1163*

Woman in White (Madame Picasso), Pablo Picasso, 1074, *1074*

Woman or Goddess with Snakes, Knossos, Crete, 134–35, *134*

Woman Spinning, Susa (modern Shush, Iran), 85, *85*

Woman with the Hat, The, Henri Matisse, 1042, *1042*

Womb World mandala (Buddhist concept), 427, 431

Womb World mandala (Heian period, Japan), 427, 431–32, *431*

women

archeologists, 143

artists: 19th c., 934–36; African, 925; amateur, tradition of, 1015, 1016; in the European academies, 18th c., 937; Greece, 207; in the late Middle Ages and the

Credits

Text Copyrights